Readings for Liberal Education

I   Toward Liberal Education

II   Introduction to Literature

Fourth Edition

Readings for Liberal Education

Edited by Louis G. Locke, Madison College

William M. Gibson, New York University

George Arms, The University of New Mexico

❀◈

Holt, Rinehart and Winston

New York · Chicago
San Francisco · Toronto

September, 1963

Copyright 1948, 1952, © 1957, by Louis G. Locke,
William M. Gibson, and George Arms
Copyright © 1962 by Holt, Rinehart and Winston, Inc.
All Rights Reserved
Library of Congress Catalog Card Number: 62–9804
25301–0912
Printed in the United States of America

Preface

The idea for this book began some years ago when we were thinking and reading and arguing with our colleagues about liberal education in America. Our constant purpose has been to make an anthology that would help college students understand what liberal education can mean to them.

As it seemed to us, the reading provided in most freshman courses went a good way toward realizing this purpose. But the effort was often partial and sometimes fitful. The principal differences between *Readings for Liberal Education* and earlier collections of readings are those of development rather than of radical change. First, this collection points steadily in the direction indicated by its title. Without deviating into models at one time or mere entertainment at another, it seeks systematically to explore the skills and disciplines of our humanistic culture. Second, it makes this exploration by the use of writing chosen for its intrinsic worth. It does not talk down to its readers.

In the first volume, *Toward Liberal Education*, the first three parts are concerned with the skills of a liberal education: learning, reading and writing, and thinking. The four parts that follow these represent the great areas of liberal learning: the arts, science, society, and philosophy and religion. The second volume, *Introduction to Literature*, turns to that discipline which is particularly cherished by teachers of English: literature of the imagination. Plainly we do believe that literature is an efficient means to the self-examined life, and that no small part of its efficiency to this end lies in the unique pleasure which it affords its readers. It is not the keenest of pleasures, as A. E. Housman has said, but it is yet the least perishable, "the least subject to external things, and the play of chance, and the wear of time."

The development of all eight parts of *Readings for Liberal Education* aims at presenting the material to the student with force and meaning. In arranging the parts in their present order, we thus feel that we have provided a sound framework for a course which uses the anthology. Yet we recognize that each school and each teacher may properly wish to rearrange the order of our materials for special needs. As in earlier editions, we have provided teachers with a wide range of material with the expectation that few will want to assign everything, but with confidence that such abundance of readings provides a latitude of choice which gives individuality and richness to the course.

We have chosen writing that bears the stamp of permanent value. This standard has not meant that we stayed in the past. But it has meant the exclusion of superficial journalizing and a disregard for the timeliness of yesterday's newspaper. College students, we believe, not only are capable of hard, solid reading, but are happier when they are expected to do it. Such reading is not dull, as we hope this book demonstrates; for certainly not wisdom alone, but the sweetness and joy of wisdom, determines a classic.

The fourth edition keeps the same approach and the same quality of readings that have characterized the earlier editions. From our own experience, as well as from the advice of many others who have taught the earlier editions, we have learned where to make certain improvements; we have, accordingly, made a number of changes in selections, which we believe will enhance the value of the book.

In revising *Toward Liberal Education* we have again given special attention to the sections on "Reading and Writing" and on "The Arts," since these portions of the book are always of highest importance in any course taught by members of departments of English. Though the most extensive revision appears in these sections, readers will find that new essays have been introduced in every part and that some older essays no longer appear. Although regretting the omission of some of these, we believe we have replaced them with better essays. And we have, consequently, been delighted to introduce new work of high merit, not only in the interest of freshness, but also to work toward a better multivoiced statement of the meaning of liberal education.

Again in this edition of *Toward Liberal Education* we have also provided an alternate table of contents arranged by rhetorical types. And again, the publishers have agreed to make available to teachers who desire it a pamphlet containing questions, together with editorial observations and other teaching suggestions and aids.

The fourth edition of *Introduction to Literature* includes most of the literature that appeared formerly; but many new poems, stories, and plays appear that we hope will both strengthen and enhance the earlier selection. The drama section, in particular, has been improved by the inclusion of Shaw's *Candida* and Lorca's *Blood Wedding* in addition to Sophocles, Ibsen, Cocteau, and O'Neill, who have been retained.

In the poetry section we have again included some non-English poetry, printing both the originals and translations. Though few if any students will be able to read the originals in all the languages, nearly every student will be able to read the original in one language. We hope that such reading will help make evident the need of other languages in world literature and encourage wider language studies by pointing up the close relationship between departments of English and of modern and classical languages.

In representing the poems and short stories nationally and chronologically, we plead guilty to the prejudices of our own time and place; that is, the literature here collected is mostly English and American from the fourteenth century to the present, with considerable weight being given to contemporary writing. To avoid parochialism we have, as already indicated, included a number of non-English authors to remind students that literature is as old as history and that other great continents lie within the realms of gold. "Macavity" and "The Purist" may at least hint that the republic of letters is a true democracy, with plenty of room in it for "the mystery cat" as well as for Oedipus the King.

Many teachers who used the original edition in their classes have generously made their experience and wisdom available to us, and we wish to make full acknowledgment to them. Particularly we should like to thank Professors Morris Bein, Wallace C. Brown, Alan S. Downer, Richard Eastman, J. Stuart Goodman, Hyatt H. Waggoner, Howard A. Wilson, and James L. Wortham; we also appreciate the assistance of Professors Frank Adams, W. P. Albrecht, E. W. Baughman, Samuel N. Bogorad, George C. Booth, Frederick Bracher, C. A. Brown, Edith Buchanan, Irving L. Churchill, Fletcher Collins, Jr., Margaret James Collins, J. Hal Connor, Ethel C. Cox, Norton B. Crowell, Jay L. Curtis, Charles T. Davis, Franklin M. Dickey, Herbert N. Dillard, Grace Donaldson, Signi Falk, Ethel A. Fleming, Martha Fodaski, Morris Freedman, Boris Gamzue, Eleanor J. Gibson, James J. Gibson, L. P. Goggin, Milton A. Goldberg, Robert M. Gorrell, Hans J. Gottlieb, Françoise C. Gourier, David H. Greene, Donald J. Greene, Irwin Griggs, Margaret L. Haley, Geraldine Hammond, Willis D. Jacobs, William R. Keast, Julia Keleher, John Pendy Kirby, Jane Kluckholn, Arthur Kreisman, David G. Kroft, Daniel Kroll, Joseph M. Kuntz, Juanita Kytle, Richard C. R. Lauder, Thomas Leigh, Vernon Lichtenstein, Oliver Link, Edward C. Lueders, Raymond R. MacCurdy, Catherine Mims, Harry T. Moore, Herbert B. Nelson, Mary E. Osborn, T. M. Pearce, Paul Roberts, Macha L. Rosenthal, Ernest Samuels, Bessie R. Sawhill, Katherine Simons, Dane F. Smith, Hugh L. Smith, Jr., F. Smoyer, Helen Swink, E. W. Tedlock, Jr., John R. Thygerson, Margaret Trotter, Hoyt Trowbridge, Herbert S. Turner, Frank W. Wadsworth, Janice Warnke, R. G. Webster, John Weimer, Alfred Westfall, C. V. Wicker, Ruth Wilkins, and Horace Williston.

Especially for their assistance with this edition of *Toward Liberal Education* and *Introduction to Literature* we wish to thank Professors Robert Christin, Notre Dame University; Meta Riley Emberger, University of Louisville; Norman Gregor, Ball State Teachers College; Charles W. Hagelman, Jr., Lamar State College of Technology; Thomas G. McGuire, Los Angeles Valley College; and Jack Teagarden, Centenary College. We are further aware of indebtedness extending back over many years to teachers, students, and acquaintances of the past.

L. G. L.

W. M. G.

G. A.

January, 1962

Contents

Writing

III. THINKING

IV. THE ARTS

The Fine Arts

The Popular Arts

Literature and Criticism

V. SCIENCE

The Nature of Science

The Sciences

Challenges to Science and Technology

VI. SOCIETY

Social Attitudes

Contents   xiii

Problems of the Social Sciences

VII. PHILOSOPHY AND RELIGION

The Good Life

Religion

The Nature of Reality

Can Philosophy Save Civilization?

Toward Liberal Education

". . . Some will then be chosen for higher privilege. The studies which they pursued without order in their early years will now be brought together, and the students will see the relationship of these studies to one another and to truth."

"Yes," he said. "That is the only kind of knowledge which takes lasting root."

PLATO, *The Republic*

I

Learning

The Campus

❀❖❀

JAMES THURBER

University Days[1]

I passed all the other courses that I took at my University, but I could never pass botany. This was because all botany students had to spend several hours a week in a laboratory looking through a microscope at plant cells, and I could never see through a microscope. I never once saw a cell through a microscope. This used to enrage my instructor. He would wander around the laboratory pleased with the progress all the students were making in drawing the involved and, so I am told, interesting structure of flower cells, until he came to me. I would just be standing there. "I can't see anything," I would say. He would begin patiently enough, explaining how anybody can see through a microscope, but he would always end up in a fury, claiming that I could *too* see through a microscope but just pretended that I couldn't. "It takes away from the beauty of flowers anyway," I used to tell him. "We are not concerned with beauty in this course," he would say. "We are concerned solely with what I may call the *mechanics* of flars." "Well," I'd say, "I can't see anything." "Try it just once again," he'd say, and I would put my eye to the microscope and see nothing at all, except now and again, a nebulous milky substance—a phenomenon of maladjustment. You were supposed to see a vivid, restless clockwork of sharply defined plant cells. "I see what looks like a lot of milk," I would tell him. This, he claimed, was the result of my not having adjusted the microscope properly; so he would readjust it for me, or rather, for himself. And I would look again and see milk.

I finally took a deferred pass, as they called it, and waited a year and tried again. (You had to pass one of the biological sciences or you couldn't graduate.) The professor had come back from vacation brown as a berry, bright-eyed, and eager to explain cell-structure again to his classes. "Well," he said to me, cheerily, when we met in the first laboratory hour of the semester, "we're go-

[1] From *My Life and Hard Times* (New York: Harper & Brothers, 1933). Reprinted by permission of the author. Copyright, 1933, James Thurber. Originally published in *The New Yorker* under the title "College Days."

ing to see cells this time, aren't we?" "Yes, sir," I said. Students to right of me and to left of me and in front of me were seeing cells; what's more, they were quietly drawing pictures of them in their notebooks. Of course, I didn't see anything.

"We'll try it," the professor said to me grimly, "with every adjustment of the microscope known to man. As God is my witness, I'll arrange this glass so that you see cells through it or I'll give up teaching. In twenty-two years of botany, I—" He cut off abruptly for he was beginning to quiver all over, like Lionel Barrymore, and he genuinely wished to hold onto his temper: his scenes with me had taken a great deal out of him.

So we tried it with every adjustment of the microscope known to man. With only one of them did I see anything but blackness or the familiar lacteal opacity, and that time I saw, to my pleasure and amazement, a variegated constellation of flecks, specks, and dots. These I hastily drew. The instructor, noting my activity, came back from an adjoining desk, a smile on his lips and his eyebrows high in hope. He looked at my cell drawing. "What's that?" he demanded, with a hint of a squeal in his voice. "That's what I saw," I said. "You didn't, you didn't, you *didn't!*" he screamed, losing control of his temper instantly, and he bent over and squinted into the microscope. His head snapped up. "That's your eye!" he shouted. "You've fixed the lens so that it reflects! You've drawn your eye!"

Another course that I didn't like, but somehow managed to pass, was economics. I went to that class straight from the botany class, which didn't help me any in understanding either subject. I used to get them mixed up. But not as mixed up as another student in my economics class who came there direct from a physics laboratory. He was a tackle on the football team, named Bolenciecwcz. At that time Ohio State University had one of the best football teams in the country, and Bolenciecwcz was one of its outstanding stars. In order to be eligible to play it was necessary for him to keep up in his studies, a very difficult matter, for while he was not dumber than an ox he was not any smarter. Most of his professors were lenient and helped him along. None gave him more hints, in answering questions, or asked him simpler ones than the economics professor, a thin, timid man named Bassum. One day when we were on the subject of transportation and distribution, it came Bolenciecwcz's turn to answer a question. "Name one means of transportation," the professor said to him. No light came into the big tackle's eyes. "Just any means of transportation," said the professor. Bolenciecwcz sat staring at him. "That is," pursued the professor, "any medium, agency, or method of going from one place to another." Bolenciecwcz had the look of a man who is being led into a trap. "You may choose among steam, horse-drawn, or electrically propelled vehicles," said the instructor. "I might suggest the one which we commonly take in making long journeys across land." There was a profound silence in which everybody stirred uneasily, including Bolenciecwcz and Mr. Bassum. Mr. Bassum abruptly broke this silence in an amazing manner. "Choo-choo-choo," he said, in a low voice, and turned instantly scarlet. He glanced appealingly around the room. All of us, of course, shared Mr. Bassum's desire that Bolenciecwcz should stay abreast of the class in economics, for the Illinois game, one of the hardest and most important of the season, was only a week off. "Toot, toot, too-tooooooot!" some student with a deep voice moaned; and we all looked encouragingly at Bolenciecwcz. Somebody else gave a fine imitation of a locomotive letting off steam. Mr. Bassum himself rounded off the little show. "Ding, dong, ding, dong," he said, hopefully. Bolenciecwcz was staring at the floor now, trying to think, his great brow furrowed, his huge hands rubbing together, his face red.

"How did you come to college this year, Mr. Bolenciecwcz?" asked the professor. "*Chuffa* chuffa, *chuffa* chuffa."

"M'father sent me," said the football player.

"What on?" asked Bassum.

"I git an 'lowance," said the tackle, in a low, husky voice, obviously embarrassed.

"No, no," said Bassum. "Name a means of transportation. What did you *ride* here on?"

"Train," said Bolenciecwcz.

"Quite right," said the professor. "Now, Mr. Nugent, will you tell us———"

If I went through anguish in botany and economics—for different reasons— gymnasium work was even worse. I don't even like to think about it. They wouldn't let you play games or join in the exercises with your glasses on and I couldn't see with mine off. I bumped into professors, horizontal bars, agricultural students, and swinging iron rings. Not being able to see, I could take it but I couldn't dish it out. Also, in order to pass gymnasium (and you had to pass it to graduate) you had to learn to swim if you didn't know how. I didn't like the swimming pool, I didn't like swimming and I didn't like the swimming instructor, and after all these years I still don't. I never swam but I passed my gym work anyway, by having another student give my gymnasium number (978) and swim across the pool in my place. He was a quiet, amiable blond youth, number 473, and he would have seen through a microscope for me if we could have got away with it, but we couldn't get away with it. Another thing I didn't like about gymnasium work was that they made you strip the day you registered. It is impossible for me to be happy when I am stripped and being asked a lot of questions. Still, I did better than a lanky agricultural student who was cross-examined just before I was. They asked each student what college he was in—that is, whether Arts, Engineering, Commerce, or Agriculture. "What college are you in?" the instructor snapped at the youth in front of me. "Ohio State University," he said promptly.

It wasn't that agricultural student but it was another a whole lot like him who decided to take up journalism, possibly on the ground that when farming went to hell he could fall back on newspaper work. He didn't realize, of course, that that would be very much like falling back full-length on a kit of carpenter's tools. Haskins didn't seem cut out for journalism, being too embarrassed to talk

to anybody and unable to use a typewriter, but the editor of the college paper
assigned him to the cow barns, the sheep house, the horse pavilion, and the animal husbandry department generally. This was a genuinely big "beat," for it
took up five times as much ground and got ten times as great a legislative appropriation as the College of Liberal Arts. The agricultural student knew animals, but nevertheless his stories were dull and colorlessly written. He took all
afternoon on each of them, because he had to hunt for each letter on the typewriter. Once in a while he had to ask somebody to help him hunt. "C" and "L,"
in particular, were hard letters for him to find. His editor finally got pretty
much annoyed at the farmer-journalist because his pieces were so uninteresting.
"See here, Haskins," he snapped at him one day, "why is it we never have anything hot from you on the horse pavilion? Here we have two hundred head of
horses on this campus—more than any other university in the Western Conference except Purdue—and yet you never get any real low-down on them. Now
shoot over to the horse barns and dig up something lively." Haskins shambled
out and came back in about an hour; he said he had something. "Well, start it
off snappily," said the editor. "Something people will read." Haskins set to work
and in a couple of hours brought a sheet of typewritten paper to the desk; it
was a two-hundred word story about some disease that had broken out among
the horses. Its opening sentence was simple but arresting. It read: "Who has
noticed the sores on the tops of the horses in the animal husbandry building?"

Ohio State was a land grant university and therefore two years of military
drill was compulsory. We drilled with old Springfield rifles and studied the
tactics of the Civil War even though the World War was going on at the
time. At 11 o'clock each morning thousands of freshmen and sophomores used
to deploy over the campus, moodily creeping up on the old chemistry building.
It was good training for the kind of warfare that was waged at Shiloh but it
had no connection with what was going on in Europe. Some people used to
think there was German money behind it, but they didn't dare say so or they
would have been thrown in jail as German spies. It was a period of muddy
thought and marked, I believe, the decline of higher education in the Middle
West.

As a soldier I was never any good at all. Most of the cadets were glumly indifferent soldiers, but I was no good at all. Once General Littlefield, who was
commandant of the cadet corps, popped up in front of me during regimental
drill and snapped, "You are the main trouble with this university!" I think he
meant that my type was the main trouble with the university but he may
have meant me individually. I was mediocre at drill, certainly—that is, until my
senior year. By that time I had drilled longer than anybody else in the Western
Conference, having failed at military at the end of each preceding year so that
I had to do it all over again. I was the only senior still in uniform. The uniform
which, when new, had made me look like an interurban railway conductor, now
that it had become faded and too tight made me look like Bert Williams in his

bell-boy act. This had a definitely bad effect on my morale. Even so, I had become by sheer practise little short of wonderful at squad manoeuvres.

One day General Littlefield picked our company out of the whole regiment and tried to get it mixed up by putting it through one movement after another as fast as we could execute them: squads right, squads left, squads on right into line, squads right about, squads left front into line, etc. In about three minutes one hundred and nine men were marching in one direction and I was marching away from them at an angle of forty degrees, all alone. "Company, halt!" shouted General Littlefield, "That man is the only man who has it right!" I was made a corporal for my achievement.

The next day General Littlefield summoned me to his office. He was swatting flies when I went in. I was silent and he was silent too, for a long time. I don't think he remembered me or why he had sent for me, but he didn't want to admit it. He swatted some more flies, keeping his eyes on them narrowly before he let go with the swatter. "Button up your coat!" he snapped. Looking back on it now I can see that he meant me although he was looking at a fly, but I just stood there. Another fly came to rest on a paper in front of the general and began rubbing its hind legs together. The general lifted the swatter cautiously. I moved restlessly and the fly flew away. "You startled him!" remarked General Littlefield, looking at me severely. I said I was sorry. "That won't help the situation!" snapped the General, with cold military logic. I didn't see what I could do except offer to chase some more flies toward his desk, but I didn't say anything. He stared out the window at the faraway figures of co-eds crossing the campus toward the library. Finally, he told me I could go. So I went. He either didn't know which cadet I was or else he forgot what he wanted to see me about. It may have been that he wished to apologize for having called me the main trouble with the university; or maybe he had decided to compliment me on my brilliant drilling of the day before and then at the last moment decided not to. I don't know. I don't think about it much any more.

NATHANIEL SOUTHGATE SHALER

How Agassiz Taught Shaler[1]

At the time of my succession from the humanities, Agassiz was in Europe; he did not return, I think, until the autumn of 1859. I had, however, picked up several acquaintances among his pupils, learned what they were about, and

[1] From *Autobiography of Nathaniel Southgate Shaler* (Boston: Houghton Mifflin Company, 1907), pp. 93-100, with omissions. Reprinted by permission of Gabriella Shaler Webb.

gained some notion of his methods. After about a month he returned, and I had my first contact with the man who was to have the most influence on my life of any of the teachers to whom I am indebted. I shall never forget even the lesser incidents of this meeting, for this great master by his presence gave an importance to his surroundings, so that the room where you met him and the furniture stayed with the memory of him.

When I first met Louis Agassiz, he was still in the prime of his admirable manhood; though he was then fifty-two years old, and had passed his constructive period, he still had the look of a young man. His face was the most genial and engaging that I had ever seen, and his manner captivated me altogether. But as I had been among men who had a free swing, and for a year among people who seemed to me to be cold and super-rational, hungry as I doubtless was for human sympathy, Agassiz's welcome went to my heart —I was at once his captive. It has been my good chance to see many men of engaging presence and ways, but I have never known his equal. . . .

As my account of Agassiz's quality should rest upon my experiences with him, I shall now go on to tell how and to what effect he trained me.[2] In that day there were no written examinations on any subjects to which candidates for the Lawrence Scientific School had to pass. The professors in charge of the several departments questioned the candidates, and determined their fitness to pursue the course of study they desired to undertake. Few or none who had any semblance of an education were denied admission to Agassiz's laboratory. At that time, the instructors had, in addition to their meagre salaries—his was then $2,500 per annum—the regular fees paid in by the students under his charge. So I was promptly assured that I was admitted. Be it said, however, that he did give me an effective oral examination, which, as he told me, was intended to show whether I could expect to go forward to a degree at the end of four years of study. On this matter of the degree he was obdurate, refusing to recommend some who had been with him for many years, and had succeeded in their special work, giving as reason for his denial that they were "too ignorant."

The examination Agassiz gave me was directed first to find that I knew enough Latin and Greek to make use of those languages; that I could patter a little of them evidently pleased him. He didn't care for those detestable rules for scanning. Then came German and French, which were also approved: I could read both, and spoke the former fairly well. He did not probe me in my weakest place, mathematics, for the good reason that, badly as I was off in that subject, he was in a worse plight. Then asking me concerning my reading, he found that I had read the *Essay on Classification*, and had noted in it the influence of Schelling's views. Most of his questioning related to this field, and the more than fair beginning of our relations then made was due to the fact that I had some enlargement on that side. So, too, he was pleased to find that I had managed a lot of Latin, Greek, and German

[2] At this time Shaler was nineteen years old.

poetry, and had been trained with the sword. He completed this inquiry by requiring that I bring my foils and masks for a bout. In this test he did not fare well, for, though not untrained, he evidently knew more of the *Schläger* than of the rapier. He was heavy-handed, and lacked finesse. This, with my previous experience, led me to the conclusion that I had struck upon a kind of tutor in Cambridge not known in Kentucky.

While Agassiz questioned me carefully as to what I had read and what I had seen, he seemed in this preliminary going over in no wise concerned to find what I knew about fossils, rocks, animals, and plants; he put aside the offerings of my scanty lore. This offended me a bit, as I recall, for the reason that I thought I knew, and for a self-taught lad really did know, a good deal about such matters, especially as to the habits of insects, particularly spiders. It seemed hard to be denied the chance to make my parade; but I afterward saw what this meant—that he did not intend to let me begin my tasks by posing as a naturalist. The beginning was indeed quite different, and, as will be seen, in a manner that quickly evaporated my conceit. It was made and continued in a way I will now recount.

Agassiz's laboratory was then in a rather small two-storied building, looking much like a square dwelling-house, which stood where the College Gymnasium now stands . . . Agassiz had recently moved into it from a shed on the marsh near Brighton bridge, the original tenants, the engineers, having come to riches in the shape of the brick structure now known as the Lawrence Building. In this primitive establishment Agassiz's laboratory, as distinguished from the storerooms where the collections were crammed, occupied one room about thirty feet long and fifteen feet wide—what is now the west room on the lower floor of the edifice. In this place, already packed, I had assigned to me a small pine table with a rusty tin pan upon it. . . .

When I sat me down before my tin pan, Agassiz brought me a small fish, placing it before me with the rather stern requirement that I should study it, but should on no account talk to any one concerning it, nor read anything relating to fishes, until I had his permission so to do. To my inquiry, "What shall I do?" he said in effect: "Find out what you can without damaging the specimen; when I think that you have done the work I will question you." In the course of an hour I thought I had compassed that fish; it was rather an unsavory object, giving forth the stench of old alcohol, then loathsome to me, though in time I came to like it. Many of the scales were loosened so that they fell off. It appeared to me to be a case for a summary report, which I was anxious to make and get on to the next stage of the business. But Agassiz, though always within call, concerned himself no further with me that day, nor the next, nor for a week. At first, this neglect was distressing; but I saw that it was a game, for he was, as I discerned rather than saw, covertly watching me. So I set my wits to work upon the thing, and in the course of a hundred hours or so thought I had done much—a hundred times as much as seemed possible at the start. I got interested in finding out how the scales went in series, their shape, the form and placement of the teeth, etc. Finally, I felt full of the subject, and probably expressed it in my bearing; as for words about it then, there were none from my master except his cheery "Good morning." At length, on the seventh day, came the question, "Well?" and my disgorge of learning to him as he sat on the edge of my table puffing his cigar. At the end of the hour's telling, he swung off and away, saying: "That is not right." Here I began to think that, after all, perhaps the rules for scanning Latin verse were not the worst infliction in the world. Moreover, it was clear that he was playing a game with me to find if I were capable of doing hard, continuous work without the support of a teacher, and this stimulated me to labor. I went at the task anew, discarded my first notes, and in another week of ten hours a day labor I had results which astonished myself and satisfied him. Still there was no trace of praise in words or manner. He signified that it would do by placing before me about a half a peck of bones, telling me to see what I could make of them, with no further directions to guide me. I soon found that they were the skeletons of half a dozen fishes of different species; the jaws told me so much at a first inspection. The task evidently was to fit the separate bones together in their proper order. Two months or more went to this task with no other help than an occasional looking over my grouping with the stereotyped remark: "That is not right." Finally, the task was done, and I was again set upon alcoholic specimens—this time a remarkable lot of specimens representing, perhaps, twenty species of the side-swimmers or Pleuronectidae.

I shall never forget the sense of power in dealing with things which I felt in beginning the more extended work on a group of animals. I had learned the art of comparing objects, which is the basis of the naturalist's work. At this stage I was allowed to read, and to discuss my work with others about me. I did both eagerly, and acquired a considerable knowledge of the literature of ichthyology, becoming especially interested in the system of classification, then most imperfect. I tried to follow Agassiz's scheme of division into the order of ctenoids and ganoids, with the result that I found one of my species of side-swimmers had cycloid scales on one side and ctenoid on the other. This not only shocked my sense of the value of classification in a way that permitted of no full recovery of my original respect for the process, but for a time shook my confidence in my master's knowledge. At the same time I had a malicious pleasure in exhibiting my "find" to him, expecting to repay in part the humiliation which he had evidently tried to inflict on my conceit. To my question as to how the non-descript should be classified he said: "My boy, there are now two of us who know that."

This incident of the fish made an end of my novitiate. After that, with a suddenness of transition which puzzled me, Agassiz became very communicative; we passed indeed into the relation of friends of like age and purpose, and he actually consulted me as to what I should like to take up as a field of study. Finding that I wished to devote myself to geology, he set me to work on the Brachiopoda as the best group of fossils to serve as data in determining the Palaeozoic horizons. So far as his rather limited knowledge of the matter went, he guided me in the field about Cambridge, in my reading, and to acquaintances of his who were concerned with earth structures. I came thus to know Charles T. Jackson, Jules Marcou, and, later, the brothers Rogers, Henry and James. At the same time I kept up the study of zoology, undertaking to make myself acquainted with living organic forms as a basis for a knowledge of fossils.

ROLLO WALTER BROWN

Kittredge of Harvard[1]

There could be no doubt about the matter: George Lyman Kittredge consisted of more than one man. Just how many men were required to constitute him, nobody seemed able to say. But that he was not less than two, everybody who knew him was ready to admit.

The first of these two—the one he was most widely thought of as being— was the "Kitty" of Harvard Hall. Undergraduates with vivid imaginations made sketches of the old building on the point of blowing up, with zigzag electric fragments of Shakespeare shooting from windows and roof, whenever "Kitty" held forth. To many of them for a lifetime the total meaning of Harvard Hall was "Kitty."

The sight of him as he came to the ten-o'clock class was in itself something that had to be recognized as dramatic. In the pleasant autumn or spring, men stood high on the steps or out on the turf in front and watched in the direction of Christ Church to see who could catch the first glimpse of him.

"There he comes!" somebody called, and then everybody who was in a position to see watched him as he hurried breezily along—a graceful, tallish man in very light gray suit and gray fedora hat, with a full square beard at least as white as his suit, who moved with energy, and smoked passionately at a big cigar. Students used to say that he smoked an entire cigar while he walked the short distance along the iron fence of the old burying ground and across the street to Johnston Gate. But as he came through the gate he tossed the remnant of his cigar into the shrubbery with a bit of a flourish, and the students still outside hurried in and scrambled up the long stairway in order to be in their places—as he liked—before he himself entered. If any of them were still on the stairway when he came in at the outer door

[1] From *Harvard Yard in the Golden Age*, by Rollo Walter Brown. Copyright, 1948, by permission of Current Books, Inc., A. A. Wyn, Publisher, New York.

like a gust, they gave way and he pushed up past them, and into the good-sized room and down the aisle to the front, threw his hat on the table in the corner, mounted the two steps to the platform, looked about with a commanding eye, and there was sudden silence and unrestrained expectancy.

"Any questions?" he asked—meaning questions about matters considered at the last meeting of the course. After five minutes of these questions, he was ready to begin.

The play under consideration was *Macbeth*—let us say; and he was ready to take up Act III. Always his method was a meticulously careful examination of every line, every significant word, with a running commentary on problems of drama and theatre. At the end of the year we were supposed to know five plays—sometimes a sixth—so thoroughly that in the final examination we could spot any line or piece of line that he quoted (usually about sixty), tell what came just before and after, tell who said the words and to whom, and be able to comment on whatever was significant in the passage. Then there were somewhat more than six hundred lines of memory passages. And there were books of assigned reading. Even the least wise in the course filled the margins of his copy of the text, and pages of gummed interleaving paper, with notes against an oncoming evil day.

"Now," he said, after he had read and commented upon Banquo's opening speech, and had reminded us once more that *Macbeth* is a swift-moving play, "there are three very important questions on this next page. They are neatly imbedded, yet for the purposes of the play, they stand out in red ink. What are they?"—and he glanced up and down the class list—"Mr. Howard."

Mr. Howard—it might have been Cabot or Flynn or Jones—did not seem to be present.

"Mr. Howard?" "Kitty" repeated, with the slightest trace of irritation in his voice.

When there was still no response he suddenly exploded. "The college office had two ghost men on my list for two or three weeks before I could get them off! Is this Mr. Howard another?"

There was no response.

"Is there anybody in this room who knows anything about this spook Mr. Howard?"

There was not a murmur, seemingly not even a breath, among the hundred or more students.

He slapped the book down on his desk so sharply that some of the men in the front row jumped. "By heavens, this is not to be endured! I asked a perfectly decent question, and I am going to have an answer if I have to take a poll of the entire class!"

A man in the middle of the room hesitantly lifted a hand. "I am Mr. Howard."

"Then why didn't you answer?"

"I was not prepared."

"Kitty" flew into so vast a rage that even the top of his head was ruddy. "Well, couldn't you at least have identified yourself? Stand up, Mr. Howard" —and he made a movement as if to step down off the platform—"so that this class can see who you are. And"—after Mr. Howard had very promptly stood up—"you are to come over to Sever 3 at twelve o'clock and expostulate with me—in the Elizabethan sense."

He picked up the book and in a twinkling went on, quite as if nothing unusual had happened, to point out that the three questions down the page were the ones that Macbeth asked Banquo:

Ride you this afternoon?
Is't far you ride?
Goes Fleance with you?

And then in an engaging smoothness of temper and in flowing brilliance he commented on one passage after another, made compact explanation of linguistic details, reminded us that it was not the words that had become obsolete that made the most trouble for us in understanding Shakespeare, but the words that had not become obsolete, and otherwise rounded out the whole scene until we felt as if we must be knowing the play somewhat as the audience knew it when it was originally produced.

He came to a very brief stage direction. "Note that Shakespeare is usually brief. If Mr. George Bernard Shaw had been writing that stage direction, he would have filled a page, at least."

There was a flutter of mirthfulness. It was the style then to laugh at any mention of this new playwright, as though of course he could not be much.

"Incidentally," he said, as he paced the platform, "there are other differences between William Shakespeare and Mr. Shaw."

There was greater mirthfulness still; and time flowed on harmoniously.

Some professor of economics had great charts and maps on rollers all over the front of the room, and there were two or three long, gracefully sloping pointers at hand. "Kitty" picked up one of these and used it as a stafflike cane as he paced back and forth and commented. He was magnificent. He was an Anglo-Saxon king speaking to his people.

Once in his march as he socked the royal staff down, it came in two where there was a knot in the wood, and he made a somewhat unkingly lurch. A few students snickered very cautiously.

He glowered upon them. "You have a fine sense of humor!" Then without taking his eyes off the humbled faces, he drew his arm back as if he were hurling a javelin, and drove the long remnant of the pointer into the corner of the room. "Now laugh!" he dared them.

When "Kitty" was having a run of bad days, an hour might be highly electric from beginning to end.

One wintry morning when he was late and the legitimate seven minutes of grace had ticked away, somebody called bravely, "All out!" There was

much shuffling of feet and there were echoing cries all over the room,
"Time up!" "Let's go!" But nobody moved. Finally one man arose and marched
defiantly toward the door, to the accompaniment of whoops and cheers.

Soon there was a solid procession pushing out through the doorway. Just
when the Arnolds and Bonbrights from down in front were approaching the
door and the room suddenly looked deserted, somebody called from downstairs: "Here he is!"

There was a mad scramble to get back into the room. But he was moving
faster than any crowd could move. On the long semicircular stairway he
pushed through with his green bookbag and smart gray hat held high, and
let everyone give way in the manner possible. He was in the front of the
room, and had his hat and overcoat and bookbag on the table, and was
mounting the platform all in readiness to begin before the last of the returning students were in their chairs.

He waited for a moment of silence before he spoke—with something of
scorn in his voice. "When I was an undergraduate in this college, by thunder
we never went back for a professor."

Then for an hour he treated us as if we were a bunch of softies. He
commented on words, on lines, on entire speeches with lightning speed. He
assumed vast historical and linguistic knowledge on our part which we did
not possess. He fired questions in every direction. One of these he addressed
to a thirty-eight-year-old graduate student—a professor on leave from a well-
known institution—and gave him such a cross-examination that he never
came back to the course.

And then, just before bell time when even the laziest student in the
course had been stimulated by the charged atmosphere to make notes and
otherwise try to keep up, "Kitty" broke off in the middle of a sentence with
a terrifying shout that was also a roar, slapped his copy of the play down
on the desk, hurried toward the door, nervously pushing his hand back
through his white hair, and disappeared into the hallway.

A moment later he reappeared at the door, bowing a man in with extraordinary graciousness. The man was frightened almost beyond speech.

"I b-beg your pardon," he stammered, "I am not a member of the course;
I am a visitor."

"That does not excuse you from the rules of courtesy. You were disrespectful
to me and to the young gentlemen of the class. Nobody leaves this room
till the bell rings."

By the time he was back at his desk and had found the interrupted sentence in the play, the bell was ringing and he made a gesture of dismissal.
As the men crowded toward the door they somehow felt sheepish, like schoolboys.

It was always a double experience. "Kitty" might suddenly step out of the
Elizabethan world and pounce upon some man and scare him until he was
unable to define the diaphragm—it once happened—and require him to come

to the next meeting "prepared to discuss the diaphragm" as a preliminary to an hour of *King Lear*. No man might feel altogether sure that he would escape. Once "Kitty" read with such a poetic impression of reality that a man who was later to be widely known as a magazine editor sat lost in rapturous enjoyment. Suddenly "Kitty" stopped. "Now what is the commanding word in that passage"—and he picked up the printed class list and let his eye run down over the names—"Mr. . . . Smith?" Mr. Smith had been so rapturously lost that he did not even know where the passage was. A neighbor whispered the number of the line to him and he answered correctly: "Why—'God.'" "Don't you 'Why—God' me!" "Kitty" stormed back at him, and then gave him such a dressing down for using the unnecessary word as he had never known, so that he always had that to carry along with his memory of the perfect reading. On another occasion "Kitty" picked up the class list, started on the *R*'s, became interested in one man's brilliant answers to his rapid-fire cross-examination, and left the rest of the *R*'s dangling in suspense throughout the three remaining months of the year.

Men knew that he was a miracle man, and thought it worth accepting all hazards in order to possess some part of his basic richness of life. They completed the year, grumbled a little about the marks he gave them—there were few A's—and very probably came back the next year to study the alternating group of plays. In that case they had the thorough knowledge of ten or eleven plays, instead of five or six; they knew eleven or twelve hundred lines of good passages by heart; they had vast information about drama and theatre and sources and language and Elizabethan life, and they had interesting fragments of such a store of miscellaneous knowledge and wisdom as they had not supposed until last year could be the possession of any one human being.

That was one of the men in the total George Lyman Kittredge. That part of him could not be brushed aside as if it were not an essential part. It was. But it was the more external part. Many of the men in the course in Shakespeare knew this well enough. They saw that it was their irresponsibility, or laziness, or grotesque ignorance, that touched him off into his tantrums. His disgust and amazement and scorn were release for a sensitive mind—usually in need of sleep—whose everyday high level made it impossible for him not to suffer in the presence of unlimited imperfections. And his graduate students who had never taken the course in Shakespeare found it difficult to believe the wild stories about him. For to them he was a courteous gentleman who begged them to smoke some of his good cigars and know that they were potential scholars about to be admitted to the most honorable company of men on earth.

His courtesy did not prevent him from exercising the dominant mind. When a student explained somewhat fearfully that he had noticed in the dictionary that a certain word was accented on the second syllable, "Kitty" said, as he put the word down on the back of an envelope, "That's wrong; I'll see that that is changed." Through generations of Shakespeare students—and his

place on the board of editors of one dictionary—he caused a shift in preference to the pronunciation of "Elizabethan" with an accented long *e*. But he
could never establish "Shakspere" as a preferred spelling. Sometimes, too, his
overpositiveness came back upon him in ironic ways. He insisted on with-
holding a degree from a man for insufficient acquaintance with the drama
who later became a national figure in play-writing. He once prevented a man
from receiving honors in English with whom ten years later he marched
down the aisle at a university commencement where both received honorary
degrees—the young author and the white-haired professor.

Men who were chiefly concerned with the literature of the eighteenth and
nineteenth centuries very justly felt that he placed heavy emphasis on the early
centuries. But he insisted that the early centuries were of the utmost importance, and that they were full of interest. The age of Chaucer, he contended, was closer to us than the age of Pope. Always there were students
who had looked upon Chaucer as some vague accident back there on the edge
of the pure night of the Dark Ages, and for a time they sat skeptical,
although they assumed that Chaucer was somebody about whom they should
know a little.

But when they listened to Professor Kittredge—or "Mr. Kittredge"—they
saw the age of Chaucer coming to such vividness of view that they had to
admit that it outshone the nearer centuries in brightness. He invited them
to see that

> the spirit of radicalism was abroad in the land. To describe as an era of
> dumb submissiveness the age of Wyclif, and John Huss, and the Great
> Schism, of the Jacquerie in France and Tyler and Ball in England, is to
> read both literature and history with one's eyes shut. . . . It was a scram-
> bling and unquiet time when nobody was at rest but the dead. In a word,
> it was a good age to live in, and so Chaucer found it.[2]

And so they found it—and the heroic world of Beowulf, and the world of
English and Scottish popular ballads, and all the other less familiar worlds
to which he introduced them. Something of his own vividness had gone into
his original exploring, and now something of it went into the revelation of
what he had discovered.

But whatever the area in which he for the moment was occupied, he was
engaged in perhaps the most difficult—and most desperately needed—of all
educational endeavors in the United States; that is, in having pure scholarship
recognized as a source of life for all men. Scholarship is the final high honesty.
Men worked with Professor Kittredge—always the least bit awesomely—and
came to feel how great was the disgrace of a human mind that let itself be
content with anything short of the completest disinterested understanding.

From his fortunate position he all the while was sending out great numbers
of men to important college and university posts. They were such men as

[2] *Chaucer and His Poetry.* 1915. Harvard University Press. By permission.

John M. Manly, of the University of Chicago, one of his earliest students; Walter Morris Hart, of the University of California; John Samuel Kenyon, of Hiram College; Karl Young, of Yale; Carleton Brown, chiefly of Bryn Mawr; John A. Lomax, of the field of American ballads and folk songs; John Livingston Lowes, who came back from Washington University to teach in the Yard for the rest of his active life—and write *The Road to Xanadu.*

At times the objection made its way back to Cambridge that some of his disciples were not important men of this kind, but only "little Kittredges." And sometimes the reports were true. If men are basically small they are sure to adopt the accessible mannerisms of anyone whose superior qualities are out of reach. But Professor Kittredge's distinguished former students constituted a great company. In Texas, in Iowa, in Pennsylvania, in California, men accustomed to the ax-to-grind sort of thinking in what they called the practical world looked upon these honest scholars as an ultimate standard of excellence to be applied in matters of every perplexing sort.

And in Professor Kittredge it was more than honesty; it was high faith in honesty. His former students often traveled a thousand miles—sometimes farther—to have his counsel when they were in doubt. A young professor in a Midwestern college had confided in an older man in one of the chief universities of America about an original project that he had in mind for the next year, and then found that the older man had immediately hurried off a young colleague to work at the idea and be first in the field. Sleepless, the young professor went to consult someone who was wise.

Professor Kittredge sat erect and smoked at a great fragrant cigar and listened in silence until the man was through. Then he said without a moment's hesitation: "Don't let the matter trouble you for one minute. And don't modify your plans—not by as much as a hair. Scurvy business of that kind doesn't work out—in the end. It is not the other man's idea; he is working at it because his chief suggested it to him. He will make little of it. The idea is yours, from the inside of you, and consequently you will be aware of all sorts of possibilities in it that the other man, whoever he is, will never see." And when it turned out precisely so, Professor Kittredge said with a trace of a smile round his eyes and down into his white beard, "We have to count on its being like that."

He gave his complete self to the world of the teacher. He required nothing else. In it he had labor and recreation and profound joy—without end. For forty-eight years (1888-1936) he taught at Harvard. He never took a year of leave, nor a half year. He did not like to have breaks in his work. He did not like to go off to other universities to lecture in term time. He made a number of trips to Europe, but with one exception he made them in the summer-vacation period. England was his great fascination east of the Atlantic. When he was made an honorary fellow of Jesus College, Cambridge, he was delighted and proud. When Oxford wished to confer on him an honorary degree he felt highly honored, of course. But the great joy of work was at home.

In this world of the teacher to which he was devoted, he carried on endless research. When he was confronted by the teacher's much-discussed choice between teaching and research, he said: "Thank you, I'll take both."

In his own explorations the range that he covered was so wide that some persons actually believed that there were at least two persons named G. L. Kittredge writing at the time. He was interested in such matters as Increase Mather's views on smallpox, the ballads of Kentucky, the vocabulary of the Australasians, the history of witchcraft, the history of words for popular reading, cowboy songs, the early Teutonic notions of immortality, the toad in folklore, Chaucer on marriage, the history of religion, and scores of subjects thought of as more strictly within the field of language and literature. And his books ranged from *Chaucer and His Poetry* to *The Old Farmer and His Almanack*—and manuals of grammar and composition for high school.

It was at Barnstable, down on the Cape, that he was able to do much of his own work. For there he had long summer weeks that were little interrupted. If one chanced to be at the house on Hilliard Street in Cambridge just when he was about to go away for the summer, one might well decide that he was leaving for all time, so completely did he seem to be transferring his scholarly effects. Eventually he built a study a little away from the house in Barnstable so that he might work in entire seclusion, with only the cheerful voices of his children and their friends on the tennis court to remind him pleasantly—if he heard them at all—that he was not completely isolated in time and space.

On the Cape, too, he could be elementally refreshed. On the Cape, he was happy to say, he—or his son—had come upon the perfect pessimist, a native who grew chickens. When it was suggested that a few chicks just outside a coop were sturdy youngsters, the native replied, "Yes, but the trouble is, the old hen hatched out six, and by God all of them have died on me but five."

The Cape was heaven for work; yet back in Cambridge in the autumn he carried his own work right along with his teaching—and thereby constantly gave his teaching enrichment. He moved briskly from his classroom to Gore Hall, and very quickly disappeared. Then one came upon him somewhere deep in the stacks, lost to the immediate world over a puzzling text or fat galleys of proofs. The library was nothing musty and dead for him. It was man recorded. When the great new Widener Memorial Library was spoken of as an elephant among the other buildings in the Yard, he asked, "What if it is? You could destroy all the other Harvard buildings to the northward, and with Widener left standing, still have a university."

If days were not long enough, always there were nights. Like Charles Péguy, he considered night as the part of existence that holds everything together that is sacred to man, "wherein he accomplishes his being." But for Professor

Kittredge this was not to be done through sleep; it was to be done through work.

For many years one of his intimate friends walked from Boston to Cambridge on Sunday afternoon, had supper with the Kittredges, and then the two read Greek together till eleven o'clock—as relaxation. But that still left the body of the night ahead. So, too, was it when his "ballad course" met at his house in the evening, and some of the most enthusiastic lingered a little in the big study. It was when his own house had become quiet, and the lights in houses everywhere were beginning to disappear, and the roar of the city had lost its nearness, and the world was otherwise losing the last signs of its daytime confusion, that he knew freedom. In the enveloping quiet he could give himself to work without fear of distraction. If he felt the need of diversion, he could read one more detective story.

When Mrs. Kittredge chanced to know at two or two-thirty or three in the morning that he was still at work, she would slip down and remind him that it was time for him to be getting some sleep. Very obediently he would go off to bed for the rest of the night. In the course of years, Mrs. Kittredge wearied a little of making the trip downstairs and had an electric bell installed with a button by her bed. But he did not like it. In the perfect quiet of night it made him jump. Sometimes nobody reminded him that he ought to be in bed, and he did not think of the matter himself; and when Thomas the chore man slipped into the study at six in the morning to build a new fire, there sat Professor Kittredge peacefully asleep in his comfortable chair before the empty fireplace, with one hand clutching a book on the arm of the chair as firmly as if he were awake. On such a night he did not get to bed at all.

When a vivid man does a sufficient number of things that are unfailingly characteristic, legend begins to attach itself to his name. And when he lives on and on through one college generation after another until men who were in his classes almost a half century before come back to visit their grandsons in the freshman class and find him still teaching with the same old fire, the contributions of legendary instance mount till they constitute a kind of running supplemental biography.

Men argued over the original color of his hair and beard, for he was gray —or white—so early that nobody could quite remember him when he was not gray or white. They liked to speak, too, of the fact tht "Kitty" never bothered with any degree except an A.B. They laughed over the gushing woman who asked in disappointment why he had never taken a Ph.D. and his supposed reply: "Who would have examined me?" Or they repeated the story of the famous woman college president who wished a Harvard man as an instructor in English, but said she could not consider anyone who lacked a Ph.D., and of Charles Townsend Copeland's stentorian reply to her: "Thank God, then we'll not lose Kittredge!"

Legend was helped, too, by the fact that in his highly charged life there was always unpredictable heartening for the less positive, the less courageous. When a frightened young candidate for honors in English had to say in reply to a question: "I'm afraid I can't answer; I have not read all of Wordsworth," Professor Kittredge brought him quickly to life and confidence by replying: "Neither have I! I couldn't be hired to!" When the efficiency experts were rising up everywhere in institutions, and one of them asked Professor Kittredge just how many hours and minutes it took him to prepare one of his "lectures" on Shakespeare, he replied: "I refuse to answer. It's one of my trade secrets." Then he relented and said, "Just a lifetime—can't you see that?" When graduate students in the field of English made their way to Professor K. G. T. Webster's house at Gerry's Landing for a relaxing great dinner and then a joyous session on the third floor in a room that some of the guests thought of as an Anglo-Saxon mead hall, Professor Kittredge was always so full of wit and generosity of spirit that the guests were stirred to believe they could face anything.

So there he was, about to be seventy-five, full of fiery power, and seemingly without a thought that he had already taught ten years past the usual retiring age. He walked energetically through the traffic of Harvard Square and the policeman said bravely but so that Professor Kittredge would be sure not to hear, "Be a little careful there, Santa Claus!" In the Yard the general assumption seemed to be that nobody quite dared to tell him that he must retire.

On his seventy-fifth birthday, when he went to his class at Radcliffe the girls had put seventy-five magnificent crimson roses on his desk.

What was this they had done? Often enough he had scolded them. Sometimes he had walked out on them when they did not come up to his expectations in brilliance. And now they had remembered him in this fashion. They had almost taken an unfair advantage of him—so startling was it all. He told them—and suddenly he was deeply touched—that he found it difficult to express his great appreciation. "If it would help, I'd declare a holiday. And I do hereby declare a holiday." Then quite as suddenly he recovered his usual manner, looked up, and said with a self-defiant kind of smile: "Now if only some of you will tell me how to get them home without looking like a bridegroom!"

At home he admitted modestly to his wife that not every man received that many roses from his girl students on his seventy-fifth birthday. In the afternoon when one of his former students and his wife dropped in to offer best wishes, he was in the happiest of moods. He told them how near he had come to being born on the twenty-ninth of February. He admitted in great joviality that undergraduates had at times led him to make "characteristic remarks" and do "characteristic things," and he drew out of the past a few instances himself. Yes, he supposed he would be giving up teaching sooner or later, for he had in mind finishing that annotated edition of such plays of

Shakespeare as had interested him most, and that would keep him busy for a number of years ahead.

And so it did.

ARTHUR MILLER

University of Michigan[1]

My first affection for the University of Michigan was due, simply, to their accepting me. They had already turned me down twice because my academic record (I had flunked algebra three times in my Brooklyn high school) was so low as to be practically invisible, but the dean reversed himself after two letters in which I wrote that since working for two years—in a warehouse at $15 a week—I had turned into a much more serious fellow. He said he would give me a try, but I had better make some grades. I could not conceive of a dean at Columbia or Harvard doing that.

When I arrived in 1934, at the bottom of the depression, I fell in love with the place, groggy as I was from the bus ride, because I was out of the warehouse at last, and at least formally a part of a beautiful town, the college town of Ann Arbor. I resolved to make good for the dean, and studied so hard my first semester that in the history exam my mind went completely blank and the professor led me out of the class and told me to go to sleep and to come back and take the exam again.

I loved it also because of the surprises. Elmo Hamm, the son of a potato farmer in Upper Michigan, turned out to be as sharp a student as any of the myopic drudges who got the best grades in New York. I loved it because Harmon Remmel, the son of an Arkansas banker, lived in the room next to mine and from him I got a first glimpse of what the South meant to a Southerner, a Southerner who kept five rifles racked on the wall, and two .38's in his valise, and poured himself bullets in a little mold he kept on his desk. (In his sophomore year he disappeared, and I found out he had been unable to bear it any longer once duck-hunting time had rolled around again.)

I loved the idea of being separated from the nation, because the spirit of the nation, like its soil, was being blown by crazy winds. Friends of mine in New York, one of them a *cum laude* from Columbia, were aspiring to the city fireman's exam, but in Ann Arbor I saw that if it came to the worst a man could live on nothing for a long time. I earned $15 a month for feeding a building full of mice—the National Youth Administration footing the bill—and out of it I paid $1.75 a week for my room and squeezed the rest for my Granger

[1] From *Holiday*, XIV (December, 1953), 68 *et passim*. © Copyright by *Holiday*, 1953, © copyright by Arthur Miller, 1956.

tobacco (two packs for thirteen cents), my books, laundry and movies. For my meals I washed dishes in the co-op cafeteria. My eyeglasses were supplied by the Health Service, and my teeth were fixed for the cost of materials. The girls paid for themselves, including the one I married.

I think I sent more students to Michigan than anybody else who ever went there.

It was a great place for anybody who wanted to write. The Hopwood Awards, with prizes ranging from $250 to $1500, were an incentive, but there was something more. The English Department had, and still has, a serious respect for undergraduate writing efforts. Prof. Kenneth Rowe, who teaches playwriting, may not have created a playwright (no teacher ever did), but he surely read what we wrote with the urgency of one who actually had the power to produce the play. I loved the place, too, because it was just big enough to give one the feeling that his relative excellence or mediocrity had real meaning, and yet not so big as to drown one in numbers.

I remember the June of each year when the Hopwood Awards were announced, and the crowds would form to hear the featured speaker—some literary light from the book world—after which the presentations were made. How I hated those speakers for holding up the awards! And those prizes meant more than recognition. In my case at least, they meant the end of mouse-feeding and room-sharing, and the beginning of a serious plan to become a playwright. Avery Hopwood made millions by writing bedroom farces like *Getting Gertie's Garter* and *Up in Mabel's Room*; if my sense of it is correct, never was so much hope created in so many people by so modest an accomplishment. I have never sweated on an opening night the way I did at Hopwood time.

I do not know whether the same thing happened at Harvard or Columbia or Yale, but when I was at Ann Arbor I felt I was at home. It was a little world and it was man-sized. My friends were the sons of die-makers, farmers, ranchers, bankers, lawyers, doctors, clothing workers and unemployed relief recipients. They came from every part of the country and brought all their prejudices and special wisdoms. It was always so wonderful to get up in the morning. There was a lot learned every day. I recall going to hear Kagawa, the Japanese philosopher, and how, suddenly, half the audience stood up and walked out because he had used the word Manchukuo, which is Japanese, for the Chinese province of Manchuria. As I watched the Chinese students excitedly talking outside on the steps of Hill Auditorium, I felt something about the Japanese attack on China that I had not felt before.

It was a time when the fraternities, like the football team, were losing their glamour. Life was too earnest. But I remember glancing with sadness at the photographs of Newman, Oosterbaan and the other gridiron heroes and secretly wishing that the gladiatorial age had not so completely disappeared. Instead, my generation thirsted for another kind of action, and we took great pleasure in the sit-down strikes that burst loose in Flint and Detroit, and we gasped when Roosevelt went over the line with the TVA, and we saw a new world coming every third morning, and some of the old residents thought we had gone stark raving mad.

I tell you true, when I think of the Library I think of the sound of a stump speaker on the lawn outside because so many times I looked up from what I was reading to try to hear what issue they were debating now. The place was full of speeches, meetings and leaflets. It was jumping with Issues.

But political facts of life were not all I learned. I learned that under certain atmospheric conditions you could ice-skate up and down all the streets in Ann Arbor at night. I learned that toward June you could swim in a certain place without a suit on, and that the Arboretum, a tract of land where the botanists studied plants and trees, was also good for anatomical studies, especially in spring under a moon. I had come to school believing that professors were objective repositories of factual knowledge; I found that they were not only fallible but some of them were damn fools, and enough of them seekers and questioners to make talking with them a longlasting memory.

I left Ann Arbor in the spring of 1938 and in two months was on relief. But, whether the measurement was false or not, I felt I had accomplished something there. I knew at least how much I did not know. I had found many friends and had the respect of the ones that mattered to me. It had been a small world, gentler than the real one but tough enough. It was my idea of what a university ought to be.

What is it now? You can see at once, I hope, that my judgment is not objective if only because my memories of the place are sweet, and so many things that formed those memories have been altered. There are buildings now where I remembered lawn and trees. And yet, I told myself as I resented these intrusions, in the Thirties we were all the time calling for these dormitories and they are finally built. In my day bequests were used for erecting less useful things—the carillon tower whose bells woke us up in the morning, the Rackham Building, a grand mausoleum which seemed to have been designed for sitting around in a wide space.

There are certain facts about the University today that can be disposed of right off. In almost every field of study, a student will probably find no better training anywhere than at Michigan. Some say that in Forestry, Medicine, Creative Writing, and many other fields it is really the top. I wouldn't know, I never went to any other school.

The student will need about a thousand dollars a year, which is cheaper than a lot of places. He will get free medical care and hospitalization; he will be able to borrow money from the University if he needs it and may take nearly forever to pay it back; he will use modern laboratories in the sciences and an excellent library in the humanities; as a freshman he will live in new dormitories, and the girls will have to be in bed at ten-thirty; if he flies to school he will land at the Willow Run Airport, the safest in the country, owned now by the University; he will have a radio station and a television station to try his scripts, if he writes, and if he is more literary than that he can try for a Hopwood Award in poetry, drama, the essay and the novel.

He will meet students of many backgrounds. Two thirds will be from Michigan, and a large proportion of those from small towns. About nine hundred will be foreign, including Japanese, Turks, Chinese and Europeans. If he is Negro he will find little discrimination, except in a few Greek-letter fraternities. Most of his classes will be large in the first years, but his teachers have regular visiting hours and with a little push he can get to know them. He will not be permitted to drive a car or to keep liquor in his room.

On many winter mornings he will wake to find great snows, and there will be a serene hush upon the campus and the creaking of branches overhead as he walks to his class. In spring he will glance outside at a blossoming world and resolve to keep his eye away from the girl sitting beside him. By June, the heat of the prairies will threaten to kill him and he will leave just in time.

If he has the talent, he may join the *Michigan Daily* staff, and the *Daily* is as close to a real newspaper as he will find in any school. On its own press, it prints about 7500 copies a day, has the Associated Press wire service and syndicated columnists, and its student staff is paid $12 a month and up. The university athletic plant includes a stadium seating nearly 100,000 people, indoor and outdoor tennis courts, swimming pools, and so on.

If a figure can convey an idea of complexity and size—it costs about $40,000,000 a year to keep the place going. There are now better than 18,000 students and nearly 1200 faculty, and the figures will rise next year and the year after. The school has just bought 347 acres for new buildings. More facts may be had for the asking; but in any case, you couldn't do better for facilities.

Things seem to be getting *done* now. For instance, on the north side of the campus the Phoenix Project is going up, the only thing of its kind in the country. It was conceived by an alumnus in the advertising business who discovered, while traveling through Europe, that we were being accused of using the atom for war only. Returning here, he began a campaign for alumni contributions to create an institute which will accept no Government money, do no war work, and instead of operating in secrecy will attempt to discover and disperse the knowledge of the atom that will, some say, revolutionize human life. Research projects are under way, although the scientists are not yet housed in one building, and already a method has been found by which the dreaded trichina, often found in pork, is destroyed. One of the men in charge of the project told me that the implications of Phoenix will reach into every science, that it has already moved into botany, medicine, dentistry, and eventually will span them all.

There is an enormous growth in all kinds of theater since I was at Michigan. Somewhere, sometime this year on campus, you could have seen *Brigadoon*, Gilbert and Sullivan, a German play, a French play, Aristophanes, Pirandello, *Deep Are the Roots*, *Faust*, *Madame Butterfly*, *Mister Roberts*, and more, all acted by students. A professional theater has done Camus, Bridie, Shakespeare, Saroyan, Yeats, Gertrude Stein, Sophocles, Synge and the Norwegian Krog. A symphony orchestra and a jazz band play student compositions frequently; there is a practically continuous art show going on with both traveling and local exhibitions on view; the best foreign and art films are shown once a week and the joint is jumping with concerts. All this is proof that a considerable number of people in Ann Arbor are looking for more than technology and are eager to feed their souls—a fact sometimes doubted by many in and out of the University.

The increase in students goes far to explain the impression of great activity, of building, of research, the scores of research projects, and of course the great increases in the faculty, especially in the English and Psychology departments. But the changes are also qualitative. As one small sign, the Music School has a few teachers who actually compose. The old idea of the University is not passing away, it is being worked away, it seems; the study of phenomena is giving way to the creation of useful things. *Generation*, the literary magazine, does not merely publish essays on music but new scores, as well as poetry, photographs and stories.

The University has the feel of a practical workshop these days. In my time a great deal of research and thesis writing was carried on by people who were simply hiding from the Depression. When you asked undergraduates what they intended to major in, and what career they meant to follow, you saw an oblong blur float across their eyes. These days nearly everybody seems to be quite sure. I knew graduate students who lived in an abandoned house with no electricity or heat, and never took the boardings off the windows for fear of discovery, and one of them had been around so long he had gone through every course in the Lit school but Roman Band Instruments. The lucky ones got an assistantship at $600 a year and even so looked like they had dropped out of a novel by Dostoevski. Now, in some departments, a man doing his dissertation hooks into a research project and earns $2400 a year and sometimes gets secretarial help in the bargain.

The Psychology Department, for instance, which used to have about a half-dozen members, and was year in year out trying to discover the learning processes of rats put through an enormous maze, now spreads out over a whole floor of offices, and spends tens of thousands investigating mass behavior of *people*, of all things, problems of industrial psychology, and in the words of one troubled researcher, "how to make people do what you want them to while thinking they are doing it because *they* want to."

From the physical, quantitative point of view, it seems to me that if by some magic this University of 1953 had suddenly materialized on a morning in 1935, let's say, we would have decided that the millennium had arrived. The mere fact that every morning the Michigan *Daily* displays two columns of invitations from corporations and Government bureaus to students to apply for positions would have been enough.

The millennium is here, and yet it isn't here. What's wrong, then? I have no proof for this, but I felt it many times in my stay and I'll say it: I did not feel any love around the place. I suspect that I resent the Detroit Modern architecture of the new Administration Building and the new Haven and Mason Halls, and the fluorescent lighting and the gray steel furniture in the teachers' office cubicles. Can steel furniture ever belong to anybody, or can anybody ever belong to steel furniture? Is it all right to need so much administration that you have to put up an office building with nothing but administrators in it? Maybe it's all right, but God, it's not a University, is it? Why not? I don't know why not, it just feels like an insurance company, that's all. And yet, with eighteen to twenty thousand students, I suppose you've got to have it. Somebody's got to count them. But there is no love in it.

There is a certain propriety around the place that I found quite strange. Or was it always that way and I didn't notice? I do not remember teachers lowering their voices when they spoke to you in the corridors, but they do that now. At first I thought it was my imagination, and I asked a few men about it, but they denied that they do it. Still, they are doing it. The place is full of comportment. Maybe I have been around theatrical folk too long but it seemed to me that everybody had turned into engineers—in my day all engineers wore black suits and short, antiseptic haircuts. The curious thing is that now the engineers affect buckskin shoes and dungarees or tan chino work pants.

The lists of help-wanted notices alone would have solved the problem of my generation. And yet in talking with a certain high administrative official, it quickly became evident that the millennium had not yet arrived. I found it hard to believe that this gentleman had been elevated to Administration, because when he was my teacher several hundred years ago he used to drop his coat on the floor sometimes and forget about tying his tie correctly, and his suits were usually rumpled. He just wasn't executive. Now his suits are pressed, and finished worsted not tweed, but the smile is still warm and the eyes crinkle with a great love for humanity. He is very proud of the school, but there is a cloud. There is a cloud over the whole place which is hard to define, and here is part of it. I do not quote him but summarize what he said.

There is less hanging around the lamppost than there used to be. The student now is very young and he has little background. He generally comes with high respect for Michigan's academic standards. The school takes the top half of the in-state students and the top 20 per cent of the out-staters. Fear of the competition is one reason why they absorb themselves in the pursuit of grades. Another is that they do not want to lose their Army deferments. Finally, in the old days a corporation would interview a C student because he might have other valuable qualities, while today the selections are almost statistical— they see the very top of the class and no others. The students know this and are more methodical about grades to the neglect of other interests.

The implication seemed to be that they are more machinelike and perhaps even duller. Or perhaps he meant only that some spirit had departed.

What spirit was he referring to? I think I know. The word University used to imply a place of gentle inquiry, an absorbing waste of time from the money point of view, a place where one "broadened" oneself. And I think he meant that everything is being *defined* now, it is all becoming so purposeful in the narrow sense of the trade school that some of the old separation between University and commerce, University and vocation, University and practicality in the narrow sense, is disappearing.

One symptom of this is the growing and dangerous rivalry with Michigan State College. In my day State was an agricultural college, and the University of Michigan was "The Harvard of the West." Today State is challenging the University for supremacy in all departments, even threatening to rename itself Michigan State *University*. Dr. John A. Hannah, State's vigorous president, has been able to raise enough funds to build a row of impressive dormitories along the main road. The public can see and count the things it is getting for its money. The University cannot compete for the public's appreciation—and support—on the basis of invisible accomplishments like culture and broadening. Consequently, a new and in my time unheard-of slogan is going around the faculty gatherings. Service to the State is the idea. Do things they can *see*. My friend spoke with startlingly serious irritation, real misgivings, about State's victories over Michigan in football. It has come even to that.

As in everything else, therefore, the competition must be carried through on the level of the lowest bidder. Michigan State has always been able to show that where one blade of corn had grown now there were two because of its new insecticides, and the cows were happier for its vaccines. Michigan State went on television, got its own station, so the University decided to win friends and acquire *its* station.

A professor of English was speaking to me in his office. I must note the incongruity of this particular man sitting in this particular office. In my time this man was, how shall I say, dusty. We were all afraid of him because in his classes you either knew your stuff or you didn't. His subject had made him pale and austerely exact. A great poem was a structure that had to be turned and turned until you understood its time, its place, its rhythms and the telling reference in every line. Only a powerful love for the poem itself could have generated his kind of energy in teaching it. He is the kind of man who just does not go with fluorescent lighting and long hallways with little cubicles opening off them, and rivalry toward Michigan State. Or so it seemed long ago.

I asked if he noticed any difference between the present student and school, and the student and school of fifteen years ago. A repressed anger crackled in his eyes.

"It's *all* different. Take the study of literature. Who are its judges? The psychologist is looked to for an analysis of motivations. But even that isn't as bad as looking at a book or a play to discover what kind of Oedipus complex the author had. The sociologists are deferred to as the only men who can really say how typical the situation is in society, and the anthropologist also has a few words handy. Now, I am only an amateur in these disciplines. They are the experts. And what about the literary people? They are becoming experts in their own way. We have what are called The New Critics. The poem to them is a thing in itself. If the diction is exact, the imagery consistent, the writing original and the form consonant with the breadth of the matter, that's the end of it. It is as though the values of humanity—"

The Values. A certain few themes kept coming up wherever I went, and The Values were in the center. The impression gained from certain quarters is that, in 1953, it is thought sufficient to have described a piece of existence, whether it is a book or an isotope. The conflict is being played around certain connected themes. One is The Values. Another is Apathy.

Another English teacher told me: "The student today has no spine. He thinks he is here to receive something that is wrapped up, easily digestible and complete. He is not really working anything *out*."

The *Michigan Daily* keeps bewailing "apathy" among the students. One reason is that it cannot find enough men to man its positions. The Values and Apathy.

I went back to the *Daily* building and looked up the papers of my day, '34 to '38. I was surprised and amused to read that the Michigan student was a lizard, apathetic, uninterested in campus affairs.

So it gets more complicated. The student is apathetic, but the *Daily* thought he was apathetic in 1936. In those days we laughed at research-for-its-own-sake and now people are disturbed because everything has got so practical, provable and dangerously unvague.

A psychology professor told me: "The student *is* different. The back-talk is feeble. They *are* passive. Imagine a graduate student asking me to tell him what his dissertation subject should be. I couldn't believe my ears at first, but it is happening regularly now. And more than that, they expect me to lay out the lines of their research, and when I try not to do it they are astonished. They regard themselves as instruments. It is as though they thought it a waste of time to speculate, to move into unknown territory, which is just what they should be doing."

Another psychologist said: "The most embarrassing question you can ask a researcher is, 'Why are you doing this?' He can tell you its immediate application, but whether it is good or bad to apply it or whether it could be a disastrous power to put in the wrong hands either is not his business or else he is just hoping for the best."

I began to feel after a while that something was chasing everybody here. The Necessity to Keep Doing. A fantastic number of discoveries being made and a gnawing worry about What it is All For. I think the Phoenix Project is one answer, a statement of the University's conscience.

One example of this atmosphere of pursuit is the television question.

A professor of English: "Now we are going on television. Why? Allegedly to spread education among the people. But is that really why? It is not. It is because Michigan State is winning friends and influencing people, so we must. Did you know that they send out calendars reading, 'Come to Michigan State, The Friendly College'? We are now going to be 'friendly'! Can you really teach people on a University level through TV? My subject is hard. It requires that a student work to understand it. Isn't it inevitable that we will have to make it easier and easier, and lower our standards in order to compete? The TV audience is profoundly passive. It is looking for a massage, not a message. And in addition my subject has 'controversial' aspects. Can a teacher maintain the courage to speak his heart in the face of the pressure groups and the mass ignorance they can arouse against him? I don't believe it. We are being asked to become entertainers, and the time will come when a professor will be cast for voice, looks and camera manners. Oh, you can laugh, but it is absolutely in the cards. We are going to have to put ourselves over, we are going to have to sell Michigan. The neon age of education is upon us. And don't confuse this with Democracy. It is the triumph of the Leveler, and the man in charge is an advertising man."

I could go on endlessly because in nearly every conversation these themes kept cropping up. But there are many who deny their validity.

A physicist: "I know they are all beefing about passivity but I don't find it in my field. They are as hep and alive as they ever were. Some of this 'apathy' is really a kind of maturity. Kids don't join things so much now because they are more serious. There is, of course, the problem of values. The atomic boys found that out with a jolt. It is not enough to discover something, one must work on the problem of its use. And you can be sure that a scientist who has the brains to work in nuclear physics is intelligent enough to worry about values. So much so that some people risked a great deal and went to the Government to implore them to understand what the atom implied. Don't think for a minute that we are automatons without conscience. Nothing is farther from the truth."

Another English professor: "I can't tell any great difference between these kids and any peacetime class. I think what some of the others are complaining about is really based on our experience with the veterans who left here about 1948. It's true, they were thrilling people to teach. They were serious but inquisitive, they were after the facts but they knew that a philosophy, a standard of values, was of first importance. But the prewar classes didn't measure up to the veterans either."

I met students in the restaurants, in dormitories, classrooms, hallways, and in the Union, the center for nonfraternity students. If there were no two alike they nevertheless had certain common feelings that came up to the surface very quickly. Michigan means freedom to them. It has nothing to do with academic freedom but a release from home and the neighborhood or town they came from. This is as it always was, but I had forgotten what an adventure it was to leave home. One afternoon I sat with the girls on the veranda of the Martha

Cook dormitory. Martha Cook is brick and ivy, lawns and old trees, and windows you remember as leaded but which are not, mellow wood and an outline of Tudor-out-of-Yale.

The Girl From Massachusetts: "Oh, gosh, yes. I would never dare do at home what I think nothing of doing here. What, exactly? Well, I don't know, but I go out with fellows my parents wouldn't approve of. You couldn't be friendly, really, with a Chinese or a Negro in my town. Not really, you couldn't. You can here."

The Girl From New York (the intellectual): "Well, that's not quite true. It's very complicated."

The Girl From Ohio (who will marry a law student after graduation and settle in Rio, where he will practice): "I think it's enormously freer. It's like, well, it's an explosion, almost. I started in literature, then I went to botany, and now I'm in music." And brother, she was. As they used to say, she was bursting with life, sitting there in blue jeans, her heels tucked against her buttocks, her knees up around her cheeks, and a sunburned face sucking in everything that was said and ever would be said. But the others thought she was hasty in planning to settle outside the country. I was surprised. I had thought they would all be thrilled at the prospect of foreign lands. It took a minute for them to say exactly why they thought her hasty.

"There might be a revolution there," they finally agreed. It would be better to stay home.

Maybe they were just envious. But they weren't apathetic, if that means dull, without thought. The Depression means to them what World War I meant to us; that is, an old-fashioned thing. Time after time I got the same image —"It couldn't happen that way again. The Government wouldn't let it, I don't think." They seem to feel that society is under control; it is so enormous, and it *is* operating, that there is just nothing to think about in that department. They feel there is enormous opportunity for anybody; that men are rewarded pretty much according to their abilities, and time and time again said the same line, "It's up to me."

The famous panty raids that swept the country started at Michigan last year and these girls had witnessed that strange crusade. It seems that some guy was blowing a trumpet in one of the men's dorms and somebody else yelled at him to stop, and the trumpet player dared the other guy to make him stop, but instead of fighting they decided to invade the women's dormitories and steal panties. A crowd gathered, and kept getting bigger all night as one dormitory after another was entered. Martha Cook was among those that "fell." The girls were quite gay about it and told the story as though they kind of wished more of the same would happen now and then.

The story sounded as though it might well have happened at any time, the Thirties included, but to my ear there was nevertheless a strange note in it. It did not sound like a simple sexual outburst. As the girls spoke, I had the feeling that the panty raids were one of those phenomena which are only superficially sexual and were directed more as a challenge to the atmosphere of paternal repression which is, and always was, quite strong at Michigan.

An administrative official arranged a luncheon for me with a dozen or so student leaders. I feared this would be a polite waste of time and it is no reflection on the man to say that they were under wraps in his presence. As they themselves told me later, the paternalism of the administration is not conducive to student expression. It was always a rather heavily administration-dominated school, but in the old days they had a fight for their money. I remember one hell of a racket when Fred Warner Neal, probably the most prolific reporter the paper ever had, resigned from the *Daily*—which gave him a full column on Page 1 to write his resignation—because the administration had forbidden him to write some story or other. And I remember he was reinstated. I remember committees demanding to see the president whenever they didn't like something, and I remember a few times when they won the argument, or half won it.

These dozen, being interested enough to head up the student legislature, the interfraternity council and so on, were the contemporary equivalents of the people who made the noise in my time. While the official was with us they weren't very noisy; it might have been a meeting of young bankers. But he had to leave soon and we were alone and it started coming.

"People are afraid to say anything."

Afraid of what?

"Well, for instance, a lot of people are tired of paying high prices for books. We want a University bookstore, but we know we'll never get one because the bookstores will raise hell and, besides, the Administration won't pay any attention to us."

But you're evidently not afraid to make the demand.

"No, not exactly afraid—"

What do you think would happen if you tried to rally support on campus for a demand like that?

"You mean, like to have a meeting or demonstrate?"

They all looked uncomfortable. Some laughed nervously.

One boy said, "We'd be called communists."

You mean that truly?

"Sure. But the worst thing would be that back home the papers would pick up our names and there might be trouble."

You mean they'd think you'd been turned into Reds here?

"Some people would think so, but it's not exactly being called communists, it's different."

What exactly is it?

"Well, it's that when you went to, let's say, the local plant for a job and if they found out about it they would—well, they wouldn't like you."

Oh.

A girl: "I live in a co-operative house." And really, she blushed. "I'm getting ashamed to mention it because people on campus ask me why do you live with those collectivists? But it's cheaper, and anyway they're not collectivists." They all laughed but they knew that what she was saying was true.

A boy hitherto silent: "I know for a fact that everything you do is being written down and sent to the authorities."

Like what?

"Never mind, I just know it."

I had, the day before, been sitting in the *Daily* building going through the 1934-38 papers. A middle-aged man with eyeglasses and a thick neck took out a file and after a while began noting things down. A reporter came over to me and whispered that this man was a state policeman, and his job was to check up on subversives in the school. The reporter said that he and the others on the paper were always trying to tell the man that the people he was listing were not Reds, but he went right on, in a very affable way, listing anyone who was connected with anything "controversial."

It is necessary to add that at the luncheon, the very broaching of this subject reddened some faces. They were bravely willing to discuss it, and really quite eager to, but if they were not in fear I do not understand anything.

"That's why everybody wants to get into Intelligence."

What's that?

"I'm telling you the facts."

"Oh, go on, they just feel they won't get shot in Intelligence."

"There's a lot of jobs in the Army where you don't get shot. I swear, they all want to get into Intelligence."

So that they can investigate other people?

"No, they don't want to investigate other people, but they feel once they get in there they won't be bothered any more."

Would you like to get into Intelligence?

Laughter. "Sure, I'd take it."

And he blushes. That is, he blushes, but he would take it although he's against it.

There are more evidences of gumshoeing around the campus, but it would be false to picture the place as being in fear of any specific thing. The important fact to me is that the gumshoeing is disliked, sometimes scorned, but accepted as perfectly natural. Sometimes the old liberalism will crop up, however. Not long ago the University prohibited a communist from speaking on campus, and Professor Slosson went to the hall where the man had to make his address, debated with him, and from all accounts slaughtered him.

Compared to my years at Michigan there does seem to be a blanket over the place now. The tone is more subdued, if one measures tone by the amount of discussion, argument and protest openly indulged in. In my day we were more likely to believe that what we thought and did would have an effect upon events, while the present student sees himself separated from the great engine that is manufacturing his and the country's fate.

But it would be inaccurate to think that these boys and girls are inert. I sat in on a graduate seminar in Political Science one afternoon at which five students and a professor were discussing the subtlest relationship between political ideologies over a span of three centuries. It is a long time since I witnessed such complete concentration upon essentials, sharpness of mind, and freedom from cant and sloganeering. In the Thirties such a discussion would have verged on partisanship after an hour, but it never did here, and that is a big change, I think.

They know now that the old easy solutions are suspect, and they are examining rather than exhorting each other. In this sense they are more mature than we were, yet they are also more separated and removed from the idea of action. But action is immensely more complicated than it was and more difficult to conceive—for instance, one of the heaviest loads they bear is the Army draft. In my day we could rally and vote against conscription because it was only a threat, while today there is nothing to be done about it, and it makes futile many of their plans and weakens as well the very idea of controlling their own destinies.

I do not know how things will work out at Michigan any more than the next man does. It may be the faculty men are correct who see a profound shift of values which will make of Michigan a place not unintelligent, not overtly browbeaten, but a school of obedient pragmatists where each individual walks in blinders toward his niche in government or giant corporation, his soul unswept by the hot blasts of new ideas and vast social concepts. The very bigness of Michigan, the size of the investment in it, and the mutual suspicion that is gripping so many people are forces that would help such a process along. And there is a deeper, less-noticed frame of mind which goes even farther to create such an atmosphere, and I think of the faculty man-of-good-will, in this context, who was talking to me about a certain administrator who paid no attention to the students' ideas or complaints or suggestions. "It's a pity," said this faculty man, "that X's public relations are not better." Whether X might in fact have *been* authoritarian and unheeding was evidently beside the point. The fault to remedy was X's inability to put himself over. It is in such remarks and attitudes that one sees the absence of an idealism I clearly remember at Michigan, and in its place a kind of pragmatism that threatens to create a race of salesmen in the tawdry sense of that word.

I cannot promise that it will not end this way—a chromium-plated silence, a highly organized, smoothly running factory for the production of conformism. I only know that in my time it was supposed to be a training ground for leftists or, from the opposite viewpoint, a cave of vigilantism, and it turned out to be neither. I know that when I recently sat with individual students they spoke like seekers, their clean, washed faces as avid for truth as I suppose we were so long ago. I know that they do not think of themselves as a "silent generation" or as a generation at all but simply as "me." I know that in their rooming houses and dormitories the old bull sessions go on into the mornings, but I also know that what so many of them really feel—and here, I think, lies the difference between the generations—they are not saying in public nowadays, if it seems to question that this is the best of all possible worlds. It is simply not done in 1953.

When I stood waiting for the plane at Willow Run I tried to summon up the memory of the other time I had left Ann Arbor, in the fall of 1938. I had had a ride to New York with a young salesman of saddles and riding equipment who had just passed through Ann Arbor. He had been in contact only with the upper echelons of the community—certain high officials, industrialists, a regent or two who owned horses. He had sold a lot of saddles in Ann Arbor. He was leaving with the impression of a fairly ritzy school. For myself, I had not known a single soul in four years who had mounted a horse.

As he started the engine I waved to a girl who was standing in front of the Women's League, a girl that I dared not dream I would ever have money enough, or security of soul enough, to marry. As we drove east, through Toledo, Ashtabula, the red-brick roads through the Ohio farmlands, I tried to tell him what Michigan really was. It was the professor who, with selected members of his class, held séances during which the spirits of Erasmus, Luther and other historical figures were summoned and listened to. It was fraternity boys sitting on the porches of their mansions, singing nostalgic Michigan songs as in a movie, and it was three radicals being expelled. It was, in short, the testing ground for all my prejudices, my beliefs and my ignorance, and it helped to lay out the boundaries of my life. For me it had, above everything else, variety and freedom. It is probably the same today. If it is not, a tragedy is in the making.

DAVID BOROFF

California's Five-College Experiment[1]

To some people, Southern California is a neon world of hamburger stands, screwball religious sects, used-car lots, and starlets. But tucked away amid the strident tastelessness are tidy little communities more reminiscent of New England than of Southern California. Claremont, thirty-five miles east of Los Angeles, is such a town. Snuggled against the magnificent San Gabriel Mountains, it used to be all sagebrush and rattlesnakes and orange groves. The only concession it makes to the region is the restrained Spanish architecture of its pastel houses sparkling in the sunlight.

California—dizzy with growth and the home of the fresh start—has begotten in Claremont a plan to meet the burgeoning needs of higher education. Its

[1] From *Harper's Magazine*, CCXIX (December, 1959), 70-78. This is also a chapter in the author's *Campus U.S.A.* (New York: Harper & Brothers, 1961). Reprinted here by permission of the author.

answer is the Associated Colleges at Claremont, a federation of independent colleges grouping together for common advantages. Typically Californian in its confident facing-up to future growth, Claremont is far from worshiping size for its own sake. It is wedded to a New England ideal of quality—to be attained through small schools—and its work ethos is as unsparing as that of Amherst or Harvard.

The Associated Colleges now number five, and acreage has been earmarked for additional schools. Dr. Robert J. Bernard, who told me the story of the founding of these colleges, a rugged man in his sixties, was named president of Claremont College last July after serving the colleges in various roles since 1925. With a visionary gleam in his eyes and the indomitable energy of a wagon-train leader, Dr. Bernard talks with a robust optimism refreshing in a time of almost universal whimpering in education circles.

"No period in American history has a monopoly on founding," he said vigorously as he pointed out to me acres of sagebrush where new schools will rise. "It's been the thrill of my life to see the birth of new colleges. There is nothing to be undone here; we start from scratch." He recalled that President Lowell of Harvard had said to Dr. James A. Blaisdell, the founder of the Associated Colleges idea: "We can't do it, but you can in California." And in Claremont, with its lush gardens, its broad, calm streets, and the benign sunshine washing over everything, the Earthly Paradise shimmers around the next turn of Highway 66, where only twenty years ago, Okies, sullen with want, went silently past in battered cars.

The Group Plan at Claremont is an arrangement in which a number of colleges share a common campus and certain common facilities—auditorium, library, and health center—and yet maintain their own autonomy. The rationale is that the colleges can remain small and preserve their own peculiar genius. At the same time, the advantages of a university are there at least in germ: the faculties and students can stimulate each other if they like, students can take courses at other schools, and the colleges can do things together they could not do alone, e.g., graduate courses, concert series, etc. (In effect, through their house plans, Harvard and Yale follow this pattern.)

The complex administrative structure has attracted wide interest among professionals; a local joke has it that any student who can explain the modus operandi of the Associated Colleges automatically gets a degree. The federation idea smacks of that hopeful American tendency to make the best of two worlds. But it was the example of Oxford University that inspired the experiment. Claremont is sometimes called the Oxford of the Orange Belt, and, appropriately, Honnold Library has the largest collection of Oxfordiana this side of the Atlantic. Pomona's president, a former Rhodes Scholar, is editor of the American Oxonian.

The first college of the Claremont group was co-educational Pomona, founded in 1887. By 1925, population pressures forced it to decide whether to limit its enrollment or take in a horde of students clamoring at its gates. The answer was the Group Plan. Claremont College and then Scripps College for women were organized first. A men's school was projected, but the depression and the war intervened. Expansion began in earnest in 1947 with Claremont Men's College; and Harvey Mudd College opened its doors for science and engineering in 1957. The capital in this academic federalism is Claremont College, the graduate and co-ordinating school headed by Dr. Bernard. Faculty from all the schools teach its courses; it administers the common facilities, and is charged with bulldozing new colleges into existence.

The Academic Pentagon

The casual onlooker sees a vast barony of academia at Claremont—500 acres, a mile and a half of academic workshop and bedroom and lounge. This astonishing profusion of building and campus caters to the needs of only 2,000 students in all. Someone from the East can contemplate its sheer spaciousness only with envy. (Brooklyn College, for example, ministers to the needs of 20,000 students on a paltry forty-two acres.) The colleges have total resources, private in origin, of over $60 million.

The apologetics for the Group Plan is cheerfully contradictory. Each college has its own board of trustees for its special interests, but a central board of trustee presidents assures central control. Deans become as common as gardeners—and no more awesome. "You see, it's the law of diminishing utilities," a political scientist explained. "When there are so many administrators, no single one can be terribly important. It means that all these wretched deans are put in their place."

Under the Group Plan, students in any one college may take some courses offered in the others, and those available are listed in each catalogue. Pomona, the Big Daddy of the group, sometimes shies away from equality with its offspring. It has its own newspaper and news service and used to dominate in athletics. Since the fall of 1958, there have been two organized athletic programs, with the intention of giving more students a chance to play. The first football game between Pomona and the Claremont Men's and Harvey Mudd joint team was a rousing success this fall.

Claremont effectively refutes the glib idea that college students are the same from coast to coast. Each college has its own personality, and students learn early in the game about prevailing stereotypes from their upper-class sponsors. Even the presidents—all Ph.D.'s with a background of college teaching—show these differences too. Pomona has perhaps the most formal head in Dr. E. Wilson Lyon; while at Scripps, Frederick Hard, gracious and courtly in manner, represents the Southern scholarly tradition. The heads of Claremont Men's College and Harvey Mudd are the new breed of college president—determinedly informal, youthful in manner if not in years. Joe Platt of Harvey Mudd—no one above the age of twenty-one calls him anything else—plays the guitar and sings academic ballads for his students. George Benson at CMC has the engaging air of a branch manager of an insurance company and issues epistles to the unconverted full of brisk common sense. ("Does your talk at the family dinner table turn as often to literature as it does to snow in the mountains, Volkswagens, and the price of beef?")

California youth was recently described as "big, bronzed, and beautiful." To this observer they seemed indistinguishable from college students everywhere, who tend to be well-nourished, cheerful, and only passing fair. Despite high academic standards, life is agreeable for Claremont students. The Pacific Ocean is only an hour away, and so is Palm Springs. Male students, out on a tear, will push on to Las Vegas where one proud covey of CMC men were photographed with strip-tease artist Tempest Storm. But the gaudy glories of Hollywood are remote from the even tenor of life at Claremont. Some years ago when Clark Gable, hurtling by on Route 66, stopped at a student eating place to buy cigarettes, the Scripps girls poured out of their dorms.

Informality is an article of faith with California students, strenuously inculcated in high school. "I'm from California, and we're informal," a young man said to me with what amounted to truculence. Students are prone to drop in casually on their professors and perch on their desks. With a few regional variations, dress at Claremont is that of the collegiate mass-man—the boys in crew-cuts and Ivy League clothes, the girls, short-haired and trim, in sensible college garb or Bermudas. At present, they said, there is a big thing with "go-aheads," Japanese sandals which fall off if one walks backwards.

A kind of domesticated beatness prevails. Jazz has many devotees, and *The Associated*, one of the local newspapers, goes in for a curious argot made up of hipster chatter, local idiom, and adolescent bravado. The report of a recent escapade began: "Herf, the steel baron, and Sheets made it up to watch the sweaty sweethearts of Grace Scripps take off a few tons tumbling. Since it was past pad-time, the portals were padlocked. . . ."

But beatness does not connote any flagging of vital energies. I watched an inter-fraternity track meet. The same boys I had seen sitting in class, loutishly uneasy, displayed a heroic energy on the track field. In a bicycle relay, one husky kid took a spill that would have hospitalized a fullback. He rose up out of a cloud of dust and blood and tried to mount the bicycle. It was twisted hopelessly out of shape by the violence of the fall. Little daunted, he picked the bicycle up, tucked it under his arm, and took off in pursuit of the pack on foot.

Slang is Claremont's *lingua franca*. *Jazzed* means feeling good, while *unjazzed* means depressed. *To mouse* is to neck. The Religious Center is *God's office*, and the area in front of the library is *the park of rest and culture*. A *wimp* is a grind, dismally unathletic. Perhaps the raciest bit of patois is the oft-heard line: "Let's go check the bods in the fishbowl." Translated into more sedate prose it means: "Let's go to the glass-enclosed reference room in Honnold Library and look over the girls." Scripps girls complain that local boys, linguistically stunted, respond to almost anything with, "Were you?" or, "Don't you?" or, "All the time."

The closest thing to a common campus for all the schools is The Wash, forty acres of sagebrush and serpentine dirt road—and, at night, parked cars. It is the unofficial "mousing" and drinking area. "On a busy Saturday night," a wise-guy student remarked, "you need a traffic cop."

Pomona's Ardent Eggheads

Pomona College started in 1887 in the small town of Pomona, then faltered. When a real-estate boom in neighboring Claremont (. . . "the leading town-site on the great Santa Fe route" . . .) fell apart, the Claremont Hotel, small and unfinished, was offered to the struggling school. It is now Sumner Hall.

Pomona was organized as a "Christian college of the New England type" by Congregationalists—the denomination which founded Harvard and worked on west, pulling out when a college was well launched. It has been described as the Swarthmore of the West—or as the best college south of Reed and west of Oberlin. It has a fistful of distinctions: the third Phi Beta Kappa Chapter in the state; the highest percentage of graduates in Who's Who in America in California; second place among colleges in 1945-55 in the winning of Woodrow Wilson Fellowships.

Pomona is a traditional liberal-arts college with 1,000 students and is regarded as the most grimly intellectual of all Claremont's schools. Status, in some measure, is determined by graduate plans (more than 60 per cent do graduate work), and even girls feel pressure to continue. "The real heroes among the students," President Lyon stated, "are those who get the big awards—the National Science, Danforth, and Woodrow Wilson Fellowships." This academic status-seeking has its critics. "You study for grades, not ideas," an articulate girl observed. "Grad schools aren't interested in ideas but in your grades."

Pomona's staff is a good one—so good, in fact, that President Lyon observed: "Between the research grants and the Fulbright Fellowships it's hard to keep our faculty on campus." One industrious statistician came up with the fact that the faculty has studied in, or visited, eighty foreign countries.

Among Pomona's recent innovations are two science buildings that rival any in the nation's liberal-arts colleges, and the student-operated radio station, KSPC, which broadcasts good programs to the whole Los Angeles area.

Pomona is co-ed; its neighbor to the north, Scripps College, is for girls. Pomona boys watch the nervous competition between the two groups of girls with smug pleasure. Folklore has it that Pomona boys date Scrippsies but marry Pomona girls. The standard gag, before students became motorized, was that you dated a Scripps girl because in the tired, stale hours of Sunday morning, all you had to do was roll downhill to get home. The stereotype is that the Scrippsy has a dainty, ladylike quality, while the Pomona girl is ferociously intellectual, barefoot, even disheveled. A Pomona girl said: "We feel like bulls in a china shop at Scripps. We're large and gross. We knock over vases." But I noticed that the Pomona and Scripps girls have one thing in common: the California girl's firm handshake and the tendency to talk first in social contact.

I attended a reception for graduating seniors. It was all conscientious smiles and talk about future plans. Suddenly, a young man revealed a trustee's boast about having finally hired a political science professor who was a Republican. (They are evidently pretty scarce.) There was a nervous titter, and then President Lyon said somewhat magisterially: "The faculty and administration select the faculty—not the trustees."

Later, I attended an inter-fraternity beer party in one of the canyons. We got into a car and snaked up a mountain road. There were hundreds of students in shaggy outdoor garb, many of them kneeling before beer kegs like supplicants before Druidic gods. Great heaps of food were being dispensed. Here and there a couple had climbed up a ridge and sat quietly in the waning sun, the girl with inclined head as she listened to a boy expostulate bitterly about a classroom injustice, a balky term paper, trouble in the fraternity.

There was one scar in this gentle landscape. A few boys from one fraternity had gotten drunk. Two were rolling on the ground near the rim of the cliff pummeling each other. A third was grandiloquently intoning: "Drunkenness and violence . . . that's our fraternity . . . drunkenness and violence." The girl friend of one of these boys turned to me. They were, she explained, really good, warm-hearted boys, with a great joy of life. It was the others—the dour scholars, the grinds—who were destroying them. There was no place at Pomona for them, and this was the only way they could protest. Near us, on the edge of the cliff, the sensitive thugs continued to roll in the dust.

Girls on the Grass

Scripps College (250 students, faculty of 43) is a kind of cloistered Sarah Lawrence—without the social reformism and the commitment to experience that sends Sarah Lawrence girls pell-mell to field work in Puerto Rico and Canada. (Local students call Scripps "The Monastery" or "The Great White Wall.") What it has in common with its suburban New York counterpart is a girlish reverence for great works and a serious involvement in the creative arts. "This is not a Saks-Fifth Avenue kind of school," an administrator remarked. But, in truth, the perfume-laden air of a finishing school does hover faintly over the Scripps campus. This is not to suggest that the girls are empty dolls or vague dilettantes. There are thousands of strenuous hours in the humanities program, and there can be genuine aesthetic fulfillment in a well-wrought urn.

The physical setting is a fantasy of patrician ease—grassy lawns, rows of lemon and orange trees, and even a "cutting garden," brilliantly abloom, so that the girls can snip fresh flowers for their rooms. There are numerous cool, tree-shaded courts with fountains and statuary. A high-school senior, out to case the place, was startled to see a bevy of girls, their feet dangling in a fountain, taking an exam under the auspices of the honor code.

The atmosphere is compounded of quiet decorum (the girls dress for dinner) and academic earnestness. It is a gentle place, so gentle that there are two grades of F—a soft F, which can be redeemed into a D after appropriate academic penance, and a despairing FF, which can only be made up by repeating the course.

The heart of Scripps is the humanities program—three years of double courses for all, comprising two-fifths of the student's work during those years. The first year deals with the ancient world, the second with the Middle Ages and the Renaissance, and the third with the modern era. At the very least, the Scripps girl is likely to know a little about a lot. There is even a fighting chance that she will know a lot about a little. During her second year, the student takes an intensive seminar in a limited area. She also does a research paper, which gives her a chance, a Scripps brochure states, "to know this abbot or that artist . . . to put on the bones of any one of a thousand general statements about the past the flesh of the particular."

In her senior year, each student does a senior thesis or project. An art major did a study of "Ceramics in Medieval England," which itself looked like a medieval manuscript. She used parchment and India ink and wrote in pseudo-medieval calligraphy. (She was aided by a remarkable collection of medieval manuscripts to which students have easy access.) Some girls go in for a relentless integration of fields. A student interested in French *and* drama chose a one-act play by Anouilh, translated and adapted it, prepared the prompt book, and then, like a latterday Renaissance man, directed and produced it.

This bearing down on the humanities means a scanting of other things. A girl who wants a mundane course in calculus or economics has to trot off to Pomona. Such a program also slips easily into extravagances. Exam questions are sometimes amusing leaps of the imagination. One quiz opened with this piquant situation:

"You find yourself in the company of the Canterbury pilgrims who, while riding, are discussing symbolism in art . . ."

Another question was steeped in a deep Spenglerian gloom: "You find yourself in heaven at a congress of historians debating whether or not Western civilization has defeated itself . . ."

The Scrippsies are so imbued with passion for the timeless in literature that they scorn the contemporary (unless it is foreign). Only classics need apply even for informal dorm reading. The college librarian, exhausted by this intellectual mountain climbing, remarked tartly: "I sometimes wish they would join the Book-of-the-Month Club."

Scripps faculty, always first-rate, has been a kind of hatchery for college presidents. Pusey of Harvard, Jordan of Radcliffe, and Hayens at Wilson all taught humanities there. There are no departments ("We meet in the corridors"), but faculty interchange is almost continuous. The humanities people meet regularly for discussion ("I got my liberal education at Scripps," a professor remarked). However, determined to escape the taint of the committee, they call their chairman a "convener." Each professor has his own private staff room—a delicious luxury which helps faculty amiability no end.

Endless consorting with students can, of course, be wearing. At Christmas, a faculty member comes as Santa Claus and has to read student messages in verse—"not quatrains but epics," he said grimly. The college runs a Spanish fiesta and barbecue. Getting into the spirit of things, one dignified classicist came as a Mexican cowboy, his unprepossessing shanks encased in tight pants. In the dressing-room, he encountered another professor, equally outlandish in the garb of an Argentine ranch hand. "You know," he said sheepishly, "I always did say you should read the small print in those damn college contracts."

As in any small family, there is a wry pleasure in local idiosyncrasies. Richard Armour, English professor and highly successful author of light verse and satire, is a push-up specialist. A lecturer who gets around the country, he once startled some genteel club ladies in the midst of a lecture by doing push-ups on the arms of a chair.

There are probably more visiting ceramicists debarking at Scripps than at any school in the country. (A guest potter declared sonorously: "T. S. Eliot says, 'Good prose cannot be written without convictions,' and I should like to add, 'nor good pots made either'.") A girl held up a vase for my approval. "This is a hand-thrown pot right from the artsy-craftsy Scrippsy studio," she said with a twinkle.

I attended a rehearsal of "Jeremiah," a stark modern dance composition. Leotard-clad girls moved resolute and strong-thighed across one of the lawns. The lead dancer was a natural—she had a gorgeous dancer's body and superb control, but with just a faint touch of Hollywood she wore dark sunglasses against the ubiquitous California sun.

In a discreet but stubborn way, Scrippsies want to marry. Some attend for two years, then shift to a university where the number of "eligibles" is larger. This would make of Scripps a kind of junior college—or, even worse, a finishing school. The faculty patiently explains that there is no *natural* break in college after two years.

Adam Smith Revised

Claremont Men's College (370 students and a faculty of 38) is lively and pleasantly brash. Militantly committed to free enterprise and "intelligent conservatism" (the adjective speaks volumes), it is no factory for NAM platitudes. It has an only partly tamed Marxist on its faculty, and academic freedom is untrammeled. CMC is interested in the area where economics and government intersect and has therefore refurbished the archaic term "political economy." The school is designed to train leaders for business and government (and the less government the better!).

President George C. S. Benson argues that the United States has more political science teachers than the rest of the world; yet our political institutions are in sorry shape. He is vexed also by a curious distortion in higher education: by his estimate, political science departments are 90 per cent Democratic in politics, and economics departments run 75 per cent. CMC, therefore, shops around for talented conservatives. "Benson," a professor explained reasonably, "is trying to redress the balance which now favors a soft, conformist liberalism. The school's ideology is a loose one: there is some connection between economic and political freedom; you cannot impair one without peril to the other."

"We're not a business-administration school," Benson said testily. "The Scripps people haven't awakened to that fact yet. We have no professor of salesmanship or advertising. We do *not* belong to the Association of Collegiate Schools of Business. However, we do have economics majors, and we sharpen them up with tool subjects like accounting and statistics."

The quality of the students has picked up since 1947, when CMC began, and most of them currently come from the top quarter of their class. There is some congruence between the students and ethos of the college. Would-be tycoons, future Rotarians—CMC boys are exuberantly extroverted, tireless cheer leaders of fun, and, in their own self-image, mad, bad playboys. "Good dates," said one Scripps girl. "Idiots," said another. They are vociferously phallic, and the section on social life in their last yearbook was introduced by a photo of a handsomely constructed wench, barefoot and crinolined, landing rump-down on the ground.

Benson described them as ". . . free enterprise types." There is a tangy individualism among them. Beards are not unknown among these students of high finance—nor bathing trunks in class. In a meeting I had with a group of students, the only one decorously dressed—in blue suit, white shirt, and tie—was the son of a trade-union official.

Their antics are legendary. *Item:* A Jaguar was found one morning straddling a small pool. *Item:* As a gag, the president of the sophomore class was shipped to Alaska. *Item: The Associated* reported matter-of-factly: "This semester's weenie-bake drew a fair-sized crowd, three police cars, two fire engines, and Dean Alamshah." *Item:* A youthful buccaneer in Honnold Library calmly took an electric shaver out of his attaché case, plugged it in, and began to shave. When he was sent on his way, he announced the date for an even bolder escapade. On the appointed date, before an immense audience, he pulled an electric iron out of his case, removed his pants, and began to iron them with impressive aplomb. (He was wearing bright red shorts.) Police were summoned, and in the ensuing commotion, the boy fled down the back stairs where he stumbled on the officers. "Go right up," he shouted. "There's a crazy guy loose up there who's ironing his pants." The story has a melancholy ending. He was put on conduct probation and became a good, gray citizen—even on Student Council.

CMC's program is rigorous: four years of humanities, senior thesis and comprehensive exam, summer internship in government or industry. However, the grinds of Pomona are so odious to the CMC boys that they would prefer to disguise their intellectual status than be tarred with the image of the *wimp*. "We study in our closets," a CMC wag remarked.

President Benson spoke bluntly about academic standards: "CMC doesn't subsidize students; we attract them. We're now rejecting boys who would have been admitted to Pomona five years ago. We are in the top fifty or sixty colleges in the country admitting men—to judge by the College Board aptitude scores—but of course some students don't pan out."

Benson is admired by his faculty. And a visiting professor from another campus declared after talking with him. "My God! A college president who knows something!"

The danger in a new school is callowness, but CMC's staff consists of seasoned pros. The college has no beginning instructors, and as a result the faculty is more stable and mature than the average. In hiring faculty, CMC behaves with businesslike dispatch. "They made a direct offer fast," a professor recalled. "In other places, there's usually a lot of stalling on both sides."

The college makes a neat distinction between itself and the University of California. CMC's goal is that of the teacher-scholar; at Berkeley, it is the scholar-teacher. It believes that twenty young men well-taught are worth more than a minor research paper. On the other hand, a good teacher is expected to do some research—"solitary confinement at hard labor." But as one man said, "You don't worry about how many pounds you published this year." In any case, CMC has lured faculty away from such modish places as Harvard, Michigan, and Chicago.

Teaching at CMC is often an intellectual brawl. "The students," said Benson, "are basically conservative, but they get unsettled. Even when they're not bright, they give you a fight." Professors tease these paladins of free enterprise with Keynesian economics ("It kind of breaks them up a little"). But the faculty takes mundane pleasure in the success stories among alumni, some of whom are already heads of companies or big-time executives. A Pomona professor boasted about the Ph.D.'s his students would achieve. "But our students will hire them," a CMC teacher snapped.

Slide-Rule Cowboys

The baby-brother of the Associated Colleges is Harvey Mudd College of Science and Engineering. Under way in 1957, it now has 160 students, including a few girls, and a faculty of 27. Last June it held its first commencement exercises for two lonely graduates (transfer students). Designed ultimately for 375 students, the program at Harvey Mudd is geared to the needs of generalists in engineering or science rather than specialists. The college proceeds from the recognition that there is a new social dimension in the enormous power wielded by science. Formerly, the question was: what *can* we do? Today it is: what *should* we do? Accordingly, one-third of the curricular time is devoted to the humanities and the social sciences. (Some students are seduced by the humanities and abandon science.) In graduate school, Harvey Mudd products are likely to be a little ahead in science, a good deal ahead in the humanities, and slightly lagging in engineering.

The academic scrimmage at Harvey Mudd is bruising. Ten per cent of the first class, which was carefully selected, flunked out. The usual explanation is that California high schools, in the fell clutch of Life Adjustment, are too easy. At Harvey Mudd, classes are small, the tone intimate. "They have a distinguished faculty at Caltech," President Joseph Platt remarked, "but who teaches their freshman courses?"

Young as it is, the college has already spawned its student stereotype: precocious, addicted to hi-fi, home chemistry, and studies, unfrenzied socially. They see themselves as "the slide-rule cowboys from the North Campus." In the boy-girl department, they do all right. "Most of the Scrippsies are thinking of marriage," a boy observed, "and an engineer or scientist these days is a gilt-edged security." Moreover, the emphasis on humanities at Harvey Mudd narrows the interest gap between them and the Scripps girls. A professor remarked: "Few are now intimidated by the Scripps girls, traditionally bluestockings, who two years ago, seemed to our students to be intellectual snobs."

There is a good deal of excitement about getting a new college started. For one thing, it's no closet drama; lots of people—particularly the foundations—get in on the act. The faculty was given money to enable them to survey other programs before the college opened, and there was a six-week curriculum conference to which topdrawer educators from all over the country were invited. Two million words were recorded "to perpetuate our inconclusions." An authority on verbiage estimates that the Fund for the Advancement of Education got more words per dollar out of this grant than ever before. Some of these words were an indigestible farrago of pedagogy and engineering:

"Devising a curiculum is itself an engineering problem, involving definition of purpose, boundary conditions, and the optimization of the many possible solutions against an acceptable payoff function."

Far more attractive was a modest diary of the early days kept by Dr. George Wickes of Harvey Mudd's English Department. These are some entries:

September 26, 1957: After Chaplain Rankin had pronounced the benediction, we marched into the sun again, feeling a little solemn and a little gay, and altogether pleased that our college was now properly launched.

October 8: General alarm as Bill Davenport reported that some of our students are discouraged about their studies, a few to the point of being panic-stricken, one even ready to bolt. Probably they suffer only from a routine case of freshman blues, but without upper-classmen to diagnose their ailment, they are understandably demoralized.

December 2: We lost our first student today.

February 4, 1958: With so many nonsmokers on the faculty, Gray has been offering lollipops in lieu of cigars. Too bad the Ford Foundation couldn't see us at faculty seminar this evening, sitting around in a circle sucking lollipops while dreaming up a scheme for the advancement of education.

The Associated Colleges are an upbeat academia. Robustly Californian, Claremont triumphs over problems which harass the rest of the country. The Group Plan adroitly combines the irresistible principle of growth in higher education with individuality. To the paleface Easterner, there is an overpowering impression of energy, money, and will. He hears talk in Claremont of a social-science college for women, another co-ed school, and a school of creative writing. But even in California, amid the fury of planning and building, basic questions about higher education remain finally unresolved. For whom? Toward what end?

RANDALL STEWART

On the Meaning of Vanderbilt[1]

I don't want to be too personal, but I must begin by telling you a little about myself.

I was born in Fayetteville, Lincoln County, Middle Tennessee. I believe no plaque or marker has been put up down there yet, but a student of mine from Fayetteville told me the other day that he's going to look into the matter. I came to Nashville at a tender age, and grew up here, and went to the public schools. I followed the Commodores in the local sports column—written by Grantland Rice. Jumped up and down (I was six) when Vanderbilt beat the Carlisle Indians. (Look that one up in Fred Russell's *Fifty Years of Vanderbilt Football*. Hardly a man is now alive who remembers that famous day and year.) I came to Vanderbilt. I remember the consternation on the campus in the fall of my senior year, on that late dark afternoon in November when word came over the electric telegraph from faraway Knoxville that we had lost to Tennessee. The news was incredible, because it was the first time the Vols had ever beat the Commodores. It was not the last, as is generally known. But really, things had been almost too monotonous before.

After graduation, I knocked about the educational world, in the West (at Oklahoma, at Idaho) and in New England (at Harvard, at Yale) for seventeen years before the homing instinct caught up with me, and I returned to Vanderbilt in 1934 as a Professor of English, My colleagues in the Department were Edwin Mims, Walter Clyde Curry, John Crowe Ransom, and Donald Davidson. I was certainly the insignificant member in that outfit, the dwarf among those giants, but what an honor and thrill to belong to what was undoubtedly

[1] *On the Meaning of Vanderbilt* (Nashville, 1959). An address to the Class of 1961. Reprinted by permission of the author.

(leaving myself out of account) the most distinguished small English department in the country at that time. Three years later, in 1937 (such are the vagaries of youth) I allowed myself to be lured back to New England, this time to Brown, where I stayed grimly on for eighteen years—until 1955, when Chancellor Branscomb invited me back to alma mater, to be Chairman of the English Department. Grateful tears wetted the page of my letter of acceptance.

This thumbnail, rather too sentimental autobiography will prepare you for this frank declaration: I love Vanderbilt. I am proud to be an alumnus of Vanderbilt. Whenever anybody, anywhere in the world, asks me where I went to college, I reply, "Vanderbilt," neither timidly nor defiantly, but plainly, matter-of-factly, without a trace of deprecation or apology, and without a trace of boastfulness either, for boastfulness, the psychologists tell us, springs from a feeling of inferiority.

I like to hear a man praise his college. I heard a man not long ago (he's a thousand miles from here, and he wasn't talking about Vanderbilt) speak disrespectfully of his college. It affected me very much as if he had been speaking disrespectfully of his mother. I thought it was in very poor taste, and it produced in me a strong repugnance. I like not such men, as Shakespeare might say. Such men are dangerous; they are deficient in humanity; they are fit for treason, stratagems, and spoils.

A college is a community, and a community consists of people who are bound together by personal ties. The relation between teacher and student is a personal relation. There must be a mutual interest, a mutual helpfulness. No mechanical device can ever take the place of this personal connection. No TV screen can respond to your responses, or share your joys and sorrows, or chat with you over a coke or coffee in the Commodore Room. To mechanize education, to depersonalize it, is to deprive it of its most precious ingredient. Let us cherish this personal element at all costs. Vanderbilt, fortunately, is not too big for us to know one another, and take an interest in one another. Vanderbilt is not too big for us to be friends.

A student's life is filled with a number of things.

This time of year, we should all go out and cheer for the team. (Oh yes, I'm a fan. I've stood up and cheered for the team year in and year out, in rain, sleet, and snow, in sunshine *and* shadow, in victory *and* defeat, and I intend to keep on as long as God gives me strength.) Some places overemphasize football, but Vanderbilt is not one of those places. We know that there is more to a college than football. We know that a great football team doesn't make a great college. We know that Oklahoma could beat Harvard fifty to nothing any Saturday, yet Harvard is a greater university than Oklahoma. We know all these things, but we still have a perfect right to like football. Our life would lose a lot of color and zest without it.

Activities are good and beneficial, in moderation, but activities alone don't make a college. The student should give serious attention to his studies. He is here to learn, and to think. A good college has an atmosphere of studiousness, and of intellectual inquiry. This is a cooperative effort between students and faculty. The student should read the assignment regularly, in advance of the class meeting, and if the class is small enough to permit the free exchange of ideas, the class ought to be conducted, in part at least, on a discussion basis. The student should feel an obligation to contribute something, to pull his weight in the boat. The unprepared student, who comes to class, childlike, with his empty pail, expecting the professor to fill it, without any effort on the student's part; the student who has a purely passive attitude; the rote-student who memorizes the class notes, and hands them back on the examination without generating a single idea of his own—that student is not getting an education, and a professor who conducts that kind of a course is not doing the job he ought to do.

It is, in fact, more important that a professor ask questions than that he answer them.

Vanderbilt has always stood for the higher literacy, and by the higher literacy I mean the ability to read intelligently and write respectably. Reading intelligently means more than the ability to pronounce the words; it means understanding what is read, understanding the meaning or meanings, reading between the lines, catching the overtones, discovering and uncovering layers of meanings, as in a novel by Faulkner or a play by Shakespeare. And writing respectably means more than so-called "proficiency," matching verbs and nouns, and the like. It means writing with discrimination, with a feeling for words. Words are wonderful instruments, but very tricky, and one has to know what he is about when he uses them. In our Freshman English course, we have both reading and writing. They go together. If a man can't read, he can't write either.

Writing is not the monopoly of the English Department, and the art of writing should be practiced in all courses, in all departments. The increase in the use of the so-called objective tests—where one has to be able to write nothing except his name, and even that isn't absolutely necessary, for he can now put down his number, if he can remember it—is one of the alarming indications of a growing illiteracy in our colleges. The president of a well-known liberal arts college in New England recently told his faculty that it was a serious question as to how much longer they could continue to call themselves a liberal arts college in view of the general prevalence of the objective test. Well, the English Department at Vanderbilt has never given such a test, and never will. And I hope this is true of other departments as well.

Answers should be essay answers. A man who can't write a respectable essay isn't an educated man.

A good college like Vanderbilt has traditions and ideals, and these traditions and ideals bind us together in a community. A community is not a physical agglomeration. It is essentially spiritual, and unless we are bound together by spiritual ties, we are not a community. The great virtue of a college like Vanderbilt—as distinct from the big state universities—is that we are, or can be, a community; we are, or can be, bound together by spiritual ties.

One of the special, distinctive features of life at Vanderbilt is the Honor System, and this has been true as far back as I can remember, which, as you know, is quite a while. I can truthfully say that when I was an undergraduate here, the Honor System was taken very seriously. Infractions were rare indeed, and offenders, more often than not, were speedily expelled. It was generally felt that they didn't belong. But whether expelled or not, an offender lost face, lost social standing, lost popularity. His associates looked askance at him. He felt a silent disapproval, which is the most devastating of all disapprovals.

A college can have an Honor System only if the spirit of the honor system is alive among both students and faculty. The Honor System has nothing to do with rules and regulations, trials and retrials, fines and punishments. It withers in an atmosphere of cynicism and distrust. It flourishes only in a climate of mutual trust and loyalty.

It helps a lot to have been brought up in such an atmosphere. But those who haven't been brought up in it, can have a change of heart if they honestly desire it. It's a contagious thing, this Honor System. Everyone can rise to it, students and faculty, if they want to. But it is not a matter for debate. It is an outward and visible sign of an inward and spiritual grace. It is an act of faith.

I congratulate the members of the class of '61. You are among the more privileged members of society. Special privileges carry with them inescapable obligations. Noblesse oblige: which means, in Biblical language, "For unto whomsoever much is given, of him shall be much required."

Your appreciation of Vanderbilt—even of this required chapel—will grow through the years. Your affection and loyalty will grow. "There are few earthly things," said England's Poet Laureate, John Masefield, "more beautiful than a University. Wherever a University stands, it stands and shines. Wherever a University exists, the free minds of men may still bring wisdom into human affairs."

May we in our life together at Vanderbilt exemplify the truth of these words. May we be a shining example before the world. May we be instrumental in the bringing of wisdom into human affairs.

Education

❖◊

ALAN SIMPSON

The Marks of an Educated Man[1]

Any education that matters is *liberal*. All the saving truths and healing graces that distinguish a good education from a bad one or a full education from a half-empty one are contained in that word. Whatever ups and downs the term "liberal" suffers in the political vocabulary, it soars above all controversy in the educational world. In the blackest pits of pedagogy the squirming victim has only to ask, "What's liberal about this?" to shame his persecutors. In times past a liberal education set off a free man from a slave or a gentle-man from laborers and artisans. It now distinguishes whatever nourishes the mind and spirit from the training which is merely practical or professional or from the trivialities which are no training at all. Such an education involves a combination of knowledge, skills, and standards.

So far as knowledge is concerned, the record is ambiguous. It is sufficiently confused for the fact-filled freak who excels in quiz shows to have passed himself off in some company as an educated man. More respectable is the notion that there are some things which every educated man ought to know; but many highly educated men would cheerfully admit to a vast ignorance, and the framers of curriculums have differed greatly in the knowledge they prescribe. If there have been times when all the students at school or college studied the same things, as if it were obvious that without exposure to a com-mon body of knowledge they would not be educated at all, there have been other times when specialization ran so wild that it might almost seem as if educated men had abandoned the thought of ever talking to each other once their education was completed.

If knowledge is one of our marks, we can hardly be dogmatic about the kind or the amount. A single fertile field tilled with care and imagination can probably develop all the instincts of an educated man. However, if the framer of a curriculum wants to minimize his risks, he can invoke an ancient doctrine which holds that an educated man ought to know a little about everything and a lot about something.

The "little about everything" is best interpreted these days by those who

1 From *Context*, I, No. 1 (Spring, 1961), pp. 4-7. Copyright by Alan Simpson, 1961, and reprinted with his permission.

have given most thought to the sort of general education an informed individual ought to have. More is required than a sampling of the introductory
courses which specialists offer in their own disciplines. Courses are needed in
each of the major divisions of knowledge—the humanities, the natural sciences,
and social sciences—which are organized with the breadth of view and the
imaginative power of competent staffs who understand the needs of interested
amateurs. But, over and above this exciting smattering of knowledge, students
should bite deeply into at least one subject and taste its full flavor. It is not
enough to be dilettantes in everything without striving also to be craftsmen
in something.

If there is some ambiguity about the knowledge an educated man should
have, there is none at all about the skills. The first is simply the training of
the mind in the capacity to think clearly. This has always been the business
of education, but the way it is done varies enormously. Marshalling the notes
of a lecture is one experience; the opportunity to argue with a teacher is
another. Thinking within an accepted tradition is one thing; to challenge the
tradition itself is another. The best results are achieved when the idea of the
examined life is held firmly before the mind and when the examination is
conducted with the zest, rigor, and freedom which really stretches everyone's
capacities.

The vital aid to clear thought is the habit of approaching everything we
hear and everything we are taught to believe with a certain skepticism. The
method of using doubt as an examiner is a familiar one among scholars and
scientists, but it is also the best protection which a citizen has against the
cant and humbug that surround us.

To be able to listen to a phony argument and to see its dishonesty is
surely one of the marks of an educated man. We may not need to be educated
to possess some of this quality. A shrewd peasant was always well enough protected against impostors in the market place, and we have all sorts of businessmen who have made themselves excellent judges of phoniness without the
benefit of a high-school diploma; but this kind of shrewdness goes along with
a great deal of credulity. Outside the limited field within which experience
has taught the peasant or the illiterate businessman his lessons, he is often
hopelessly gullible. The educated man, by contrast, has tried to develop a
critical faculty for general use, and he likes to think that he is fortified
against imposture in all its forms.

It does not matter for our purposes whether the impostor is a deliberate
liar or not. Some are, but the commonest enemies of mankind are the unconscious frauds. Most salesmen under the intoxication of their own exuberance seem to believe in what they say. Most experts whose *expertise* is only a
pretentious sham behave as if they had been solemnly inducted into some
kind of priesthood. Very few demagogues are so cynical as to remain undeceived by their own rhetoric, and some of the worst tyrants in history have
been fatally sincere. We can leave the disentanglement of motives to the

students of fraud and error, but we cannot afford to be taken in by the shams.

We are, of course, surrounded by shams. Until recently the schools were full of them—the notion that education can be had without tears, that puffed rice is a better intellectual diet than oatmeal, that adjustment to the group is more important than knowing where the group is going, and that democracy has made it a sin to separate the sheep from the goats. Mercifully, these are much less evident now than they were before Sputnik startled us into our wits.

In front of the professor are the shams of the learned fraternity. There is the sham science of the social scientist who first invented a speech for fuddling thought and then proceeded to tell us in his lockjawed way what we already knew. There is the sham humanism of the humanist who wonders why civilization that once feasted at his table is repelled by the shredded and desiccated dishes that often lie on it today. There is the sham message of the physical scientist who feels that his mastery of nature has made him an expert in politics and morals, and there are all the other brands of hokum which have furnished material for satire since the first quacks established themselves in the first cloisters.

If this is true of universities with their solemn vows and limited temptations, how much truer is it of the naughty world outside, where the prizes are far more dazzling and the only protection against humbug is the skepticism of the ordinary voter, customer, reader, listener, and viewer? Of course, the follies of human nature are not going to be exorcised by anything that the educator can do, and I am not sure that he would want to exorcise them if he could. There is something irresistibly funny about the old Adam, and life would be duller without his antics. But they ought to be kept within bounds. We are none the better for not recognizing a clown when we see one.

The other basic skill is simply the art of self-expression in speech and on paper. A man is uneducated who has not mastered the elements of clean forcible prose and picked up some relish for style.

It is a curious fact that we style everything in this country—our cars, our homes, our clothes—except our minds. They still chug along like a Model T—rugged, persevering, but far from graceful.

No doubt this appeal for style, like the appeal for clear thinking, can be carried too far. There was once an American who said that the only important thing in life was "to set a chime of words ringing in a few fastidious minds." As far as can be learned, he left this country in a huff to tinkle his little bell in a foreign land. Most of us would think that he lacked a sense of proportion. After all, the political history of this country is full of good judgment expressed in bad prose, and the business history has smashed through to some of its grandest triumphs across acres of broken syntax. But we can discard some of these frontier manners without becoming absurdly precious.

The road ahead bristles with obstacles. There is the reluctance of many people to use one word where they can get away with a half-dozen or a word of one syllable if they can find a longer one. No one has ever told them about the first rule in English composition: every slaughtered syllable is a good deed. The most persuasive teachers of this maxim are undoubtedly the commercial firms that offer a thousand dollars for the completion of a slogan in twenty-five words. They are the only people who are putting a handsome premium on economy of statement.

There is the decay of the habit of memorizing good prose and good poetry in the years when tastes are being formed. It is very difficult to write a bad sentence if the Bible has been a steady companion and very easy to imagine a well-turned phrase if the ear has been tuned on enough poetry.

There is the monstrous proliferation of gobbledy-gook in government, business, and the professions. Take this horrible example of verbal smog.

> It is inherent to motivational phenomena that there is a drive for more gratification than is realistically possible, on any level or in any type of personality organization. Likewise it is inherent to the world of objects that not all potentially desirable opportunities can be realized within a human life span. Therefore, any personality must involve an organization that allocates opportunities for gratifications, that systematizes precedence relative to the limited possibilities. The possibilities of gratification, simultaneously or sequentially, of all need-dispositions are severely limited by the structure of the object system and by the intra-systemic incompatibility of the consequences of gratifying them all.

What this smothered soul is trying to say is simply, "We must pick and choose, because we cannot have everything we want."

Finally, there is the universal employment of the objective test as part of the price which has to be paid for mass education. Nothing but the difficulty of finding enough readers to mark essays can condone a system which reduces a literate student to the ignoble necessity of "blackening the answer space" when he might be giving his mind and pen free play. Though we have managed to get some benefits from these examinations, the simple fact remains that the shapely prose of the Declaration of Independence or the "Gettysburg Address" was never learned under an educational system which employed objective tests. It was mastered by people who took writing seriously, who had good models in front of them, good critics to judge them, and an endless capacity for taking pains. Without that sort of discipline, the arts of self-expression will remain as mutilated as they are now.

The standards which mark an educated man can be expressed in terms of three tests.

The first is a matter of sophistication. Emerson put it nicely when he talked about getting rid of "the nonsense of our wigwams." The wigwam may be an uncultivated home, a suburban conformity, a crass patriotism, or a cramped dogma. Some of this nonsense withers in the classroom. More of it rubs off by simply mixing with people, provided they are drawn from a wide range of backgrounds and exposed within a good college to a civilized tradition. An educated man can be judged by the quality of his prejudices. There is a refined nonsense which survives the raw nonsense which Emerson was talking about.

The second test is a matter of moral values. Though we all know individuals who have contrived to be both highly educated and highly immoral, and though we have all heard of periods in history when the subtlest resources of wit and sophistication were employed to make a mockery of simple values, we do not really believe that a college is doing its job when it is simply multiplying the number of educated scoundrels, hucksters, and triflers.

The health of society depends on simple virtues like honesty, decency, courage, and public spirit. There are forces in human nature which constantly tend to corrupt them, and every age has its own vices. The worst features of ours is probably the obsession with violence. Up to some such time as 1914, it was possible to believe in a kind of moral progress. The quality which distinguished the Victorian from the Elizabethan was a sensitivity to suffering and a revulsion from cruelty which greatly enlarged the idea of human dignity. Since 1914 we have steadily brutalized ourselves. The horrors of modern war, the bestialities of modern political creeds, the uncontrollable vices of modern cities, the favorite themes of modern novelists—all have conspired to degrade us. Some of the corruption is blatant. The authors of the best sellers, after exhausting all the possibilities of sex in its normal and abnormal forms and all the variations of alcoholism and drug addiction, are about to invade the recesses of the hospitals. A clinical study of a hero undergoing the irrigation of his colon is about all there is left to gratify a morbid appetite.

Some of the corruption is insidious. A national columnist recently wrote an article in praise of cockfighting. He had visited a cockfight in the company of Ernest Hemingway. After pointing out that Hemingway had made bullfighting respectable, he proceeded to describe the terrible beauty of fierce indomitable birds trained to kill each other for the excitement of the spectators. Needless to say, there used to be a terrible beauty about Christians defending themselves against lions or about heretics being burned at the stake, and there are still parts of the world where a public execution is regarded as a richly satisfying feast. But for three or four centuries the West taught itself to resist these excitements in the interest of a moral idea.

Educators are needlessly squeamish about their duty to uphold moral values and needlessly perplexed about how to implant them. The corruptions of our times are a sufficient warning that we cannot afford to abandon the duty to the homes and the churches, and the capacity which many institutions have shown to do their duty in a liberal spirit is a sufficient guaranty against bigotry.

Finally, there is the test imposed by the unique challenge of our own times. We are not unique in suffering from moral confusion—these crises are a familiar story—but we are unique in the tremendous acceleration of the rate of social change and in the tremendous risk of a catastrophic end to all our hopes. We cannot afford educated men who have every grace except the gift for survival. An indispensable mark of the modern educated man is the kind of versatile, flexible mind that can deal with new and explosive conditions.

With this reserve, there is little in this profile which has not been familiar for centuries. Unfortunately, the description which once sufficed to suggest its personality has been debased in journalistic currency. The "well-rounded man" has become the organization man, or the man who is so well rounded that he rolls wherever he is pushed. The humanists who invented the idea and preached it for centuries would recoil in contempt from any such notion. They understood the possibilities of the whole man and wanted an educational system which would give the many sides of his nature some chance to develop in harmony. They thought it a good idea to mix the wisdom of the world with the learning of the cloister, to develop the body as well as the mind, to pay a great deal of attention to character, and to neglect no art which could add to the enjoyment of living. It was a spacious idea which offered every hospitality to creative energy. Anyone who is seriously interested in a liberal education must begin by rediscovering it.

JEROME ELLISON

Are We Making a Playground Out of College?[1]

During a sunny day one autumn a colleague of mine was counseling a freshman girl at the University of Georgia. He explained that a certain course could not be taken without prerequisites amounting to about two years' work. "But I won't be here that long," the lass protested. "At the end of this school year I'm getting married."

Just to be nice my friend asked who the lucky man was. "Oh, I've just got here," said the miss, "and haven't met him yet." Out of curiosity, the professor kept tabs. The wedding took place in a burst of orange blossoms just after the close of the next semester, as planned.

This sort of thing is so common in the large, tax-supported coeducational plants that turn out more than half of all our college graduates, that most people assume it's probably all right.

After four years on the inside, as a member of a university faculty, I, for

[1] From *The Saturday Evening Post,* CCXXXVI (March 7, 1959), 19-20 *et passim.* Reprinted by permission of the author.

one, am not at all sure it's all right. It's part of a growing national inclination to push education aside whenever it interferes with love or comfort, money or fun.

In today's world I question whether we can afford it. Communists and free men agree on at least one thing—the abler, better-informed side in this contest is more likely to prevail. Higher education will play an increasingly vital role in the struggle. We water it down, it seems to me, at our own great peril. And watering it down we certainly are.

The boys, I have noticed, go along in the business as readily as the girls. In one of my own courses at Indiana University there enrolled, not long ago, a male predentistry student. He was a sophomore, personable, fairly intelligent, had a car, and was going steady with a girl in his home town, a hundred miles away.

"Man, this is wearing—driving back and forth to Kokomo twice a week!" he said one time when on the carpet about a late assignment. Later, on a like occasion, "Man, this is killing—all these science courses!"

He shortly solved all his problems by marrying the girl, moving into a university-subsidized apartment on campus, and switching from dentistry to recreation—a curriculum which allows one to become a bachelor of science without ever having to study mathematics, language, chemistry, physics, history or science, but only things like volley ball, archery, lacrosse, deep breathing and refereeing.

My quarrel here is not with the change in career, but with the reasons. Our crowded, roaring slums testify to our need for trained recreation people. But this young oaf switched, not because he had discovered a national need, but because he thought recreation would be easier. One has a feeling that when the sun beats hot on the city pavements and the slum kids really need him, he'll be at home in front of the air conditioner.

Frequently, when counseling a bright student, I point out that we live in an age of science, that one of the bases of science is mathematics, and that the educated man of our day should have a little math. The point that math matters is never questioned. "But," I am almost always told, "it's hard!" The student paws through the catalogue again, seeking a course which is easier but probably irrelevant to his total plan.

Similarly, we often cite the need—in a nation that has a mere 6 per cent of earth's people, and must for its survival learn to get on with the other 94 per cent—for language training. Here again, the cry goes up, "Too hard!"

Some students go to extremes to avoid a language. I worked with one lad who planned from the first to be a journalist, and who has now, at last, become one. But the course in journalism required eighteen hours of a foreign tongue. He enrolled in a teacher-training course, which did not require a language for a degree, and took his journalism in electives—"on the side"!

The prevalence of this sort of thing, and the extent to which school authorities play along with it, is something, I here assert, really to be exercised about.

I have seen too much of the power of higher education to widen and ennoble human life to stand by without protest while this vital power is vitiated. It was through a land-grant university that my father worked his way from the rudest of back-country farms into the vastly expanded horizons of a respected profession. A similar school helped me to spend my own life in the kind of work I love. And if I have learned anything from that work—twenty-five years of editing, writing, teaching and publishing—it is that the fate of man depends now more than ever before upon an educated citizenry. Half-educated won't do. Man's survival hangs now upon his wisdom.

In the light of this conclusion, some things about our mass higher education seem basically immoral. I am not here referring to the sexual aspect of morality. An informal consensus of deans seems to be that the standard in this particular is possibly a shade higher than that of the parents of today's students. Of course, young people in and out of college, today as always, get into scrapes through mismanagement of their sex lives. But for sheer bawdy brazenness I have seen nothing to vie with the letter to the Wisconsin student paper which opened: "We who are not virgins smile at the notion that we have lost our self-respect," and went on to expound the "fuller" life. This was written in the 1930's by a girl who may now be a staid grandmother.

The thing that concerns me is an intellectual immorality—the encroachment upon the main business of college of an accumulation of irrelevancies which together make up a "Second Curriculum" that often takes precedence over the first.

The Second Curriculum is that odd mixture of status hunger, voodoo, tradition, lust, stereotyped dissipation, love, solid achievement, and plain good fun sometimes called "college life." It drives a high proportion of our students through college chronically short of sleep, behind in their work, and uncertain of the exact score in any department of life.

To gain some notion of the extent to which the Second Curriculum has taken over, we'll whisk through, in a moment, an ordinary year's calendar at a Big Ten school. First let us set the scene. You start with a broad expanse of tree-studded lawn, perhaps half a mile square, dotted with buildings rendered in several versions of collegiate architecture.

One of these structures is the student union, a rallying point for snacking, dalliance and amusement. From morning until night it resounds to the blare of the jukebox, the clink of coffee cups, the clatter of bowling pins, the click of billiard balls, the slap of playing cards, the gentle creak of lounge chairs and, in the plushier ones, the splash of languid bodies in tepid swimming pools. There's likely to be an informal dance here every Friday and Saturday night. They have a ball—banquet or name-band dance—about every weekend in the ballroom.

Fringing the main campus and sprawling for a mile in every direction are student living quarters—fraternities and rooming houses both stately and squat, trailer camps, huge residence units resembling, according to the architectural mood, medieval castles or modern luxury hotels.

The whole panorama—so well has Joe College sold his old man on the principle that a car is needed for study—is overrun with automobiles. Our big campuses are churning in a traffic turmoil that almost has to be seen to be believed. Some schools—Indiana is one—issue stickers, dubbed "hunting licenses," which permit the student to park on campus if he can find a place. Others, following a method used at Wisconsin, provide parking at some distance from the university and charge a fee, which covers shuttle-bus service to school.

In some of the better-motorized universities, more than half the students have cars. Duke, Fairleigh Dickinson, Johns Hopkins, Houston, Louisiana, Maryland, Nebraska, Oregon State, Syracuse, Texas and Iowa all average— according to a study made at the University of Houston—over half a car, and up to one car, per student. Ohio State's 19,000 students operate 11,640 motor vehicles. The student-to-car ratio at Wisconsin, 15,000-5800; at Purdue, 13,000-5100; at Northwestern, 15,000-2500; at Illinois, 23,000-5000; at Indiana, 11,000-4500; at Michigan State, 19,000-6400. These cars support enterprises —drive-in restaurants, drive-in theaters (known in college jargon as "passion pits"), miniature golf courses, roller-skating rinks, gin mills—many miles from the campus.

More than a fifth of the students are married. This statistic has profoundly affected university life at all levels. For one thing, the housing people have been caught short. The Indiana campus, which is typical, was several hundred units short in married-student housing last fall, while newly completed quarters for single students stood vacant. The big coed plants are building married housing pell-mell, trying to catch up with a growing trend. In eleven state universities with a total enrollment of 160,000, more than 21 per cent of last autumn's students were married. The expected figure for four years hence is one in four.

The large married minority strongly influences the single majority. Most of the girls are striving, sometimes with unladylike eagerness, to get married— the Georgia coed mentioned earlier has her counterparts in every state. The steps to success are going steady, "pinning"—exchange of fraternity badges or other club symbols—formal engagement and marriage. Monthly box scores of pinnings, published by some college papers, are read with sports-page avidity.

Since even the bottom rung of the coed success ladder cannot be mounted unless one is dated, the pressure to date is enormous. The emotional backlash of failure to date is profound, particularly among women students. A Wisconsin coed, writing in the student daily, reports that half the sorority pillows are "wet with tears" of a Saturday night—no dates. I know of one attempted suicide over the business.

The male reacts to the same pressures in a variety of ways. He may affect a cynical Don Juanism of a guarded wariness. Or his own pillow may be wet with tears, or he may simply yield to community pressure and start populating the nursery school the university maintains for married students' children. In any event, both male and female live in daily tension, varying from mild to acute, over some aspect of dating or mating.

It is in this over-all atmosphere that the Second Curriculum is pursued. An important part of it is, of course, the standard, souped-up program of professionalized athletics. Since this phenomenon has been ably dealt with in a number of recent articles, it is enough to note here that a normal season may include eight major basketball games and four football games. Each has its influx of alumni and visitors, its bands and cheering sections, its squads of bench warmers, its round of dances and fights, its frenzy of warm-ups, post-mortems, hospitality and decorations.

For the Homecoming Game, each housing unit prepares elaborate lawn statuary, built of papier-mâché and crepe paper on the colossal scale. These devices, illuminated and sometimes animated by intricate machinery, consume vast ingenuity and time. The control panel for one of the displays at Indiana was hardly less complex than the switchboard of a fair-sized telephone exchange. A recent prize winner was an enormous red bull (Indiana) towing a corn cutter which mowed down cornstalks (Iowa men) and delivered them in bags. There were fifty-one entries in Wisconsin's Homecoming decoration contest. The winner was a gigantic prostrate Indian whose eyes lighted up and moved from side to side, whose head moved on a swivel and whose chest heaved.

Each spring has its special big weekend. Indiana has a fifty-mile bicycle relay race in May. Work on it begins the preceding November, with the appointment of a student committee of 192 persons. The bike teams practice all year. One rider makes weekend trips to Indianapolis, fifty miles away, on his bike, just to keep in shape. The big weekend itself offers a tricycle relay race featuring costumed sorority girls, a golf tournament, social activities at each of the university's fifty fraternities and sororities, two all-campus dances and a home-talent vaudeville show, in addition to the main race.

Every weekend is special for something. Illinois has a Dad's Day Revue, a stunt show, a Hawaiian-hoop contest, the John Street Pajama Race, the burning of a twenty-five-foot statue called Winter's Gloom, and Men's Economic Recovery Campaign Week, during which coeds make dates and pay for them. Ohio State has a Circus Party with real elephants, a Greek Week, a May Week Carnival, a Rose Formal and a Pumpkin Prom.

All-campus dances at Indiana include the Freshman Frolic, the First Fling, the Sophomore Cotillion, the Junior Prom, the Dames Ball, the Military Ball, the Mardi Gras Ball, the Blanket Hop, the Bicycle Bump, the Opening of Formal, the Street Dance, the Wellhouse Waltz and a jitterbug contest. Wisconsin fraternities specialize in costume dances inviting the nearest tolerable approach to nudity—a Mammoth Brawl, simulating cavemen days, a Roman Party in togas, the Cherokee Chugalug in loincloths and the Pajama Party.

Each week has its list of home-talent entertainments and stunts. Our calendar brings us the Jordan River Tug of War, The Watermelon Mess, the Fall Carnival (coeds dressed as underworld characters, running wheels of chance and performing skits for charity), the all-university competitive sing, numerous pep rallies, including the burning in effigy of John Purdue; the Gridiron Banquet, the Football Banquet, the Athletic Banquet, the Turtle Derby, the Greek Week Chariot Race, the Fun Frolic (rides, concessions and a Ferris wheel), a fashion show, a Panhellenic Circus, a Barbecue, a Round-up and a Sports-Car Rally. Wisconsin has all this plus a Man-with-the-Most-Beautiful-Legs Contest, a Yell-like-Hell Contest and the Haresfoot musical show, in which the boys dress up as girls.

In the big coeducational schools an immense amount of time and energy goes into the election of "queens"—a reflection, perhaps, of the statistic that 35 per cent of all college students are females. At Indiana the queen season opens in September with the nomination of two queens from each women's dormitory or sorority to appear at a pep rally, where one of them is designated football queen. Later in the same month, after an all-campus sweepstakes, including preliminaries, semifinals and finals, somebody is crowned sweater queen.

In October and November various queens and sweethearts—a sweetheart of, say, Beta Theta Pi, Sigma Chi or Dodds House, is about the same as a queen— are elevated. With sandwich men, posters, torchlight and sports-car parades, students elect a homecoming queen, a military-ball queen, a queen of the autumn formal, a yearbook queen, a queen of the athletic lettermen, a junior-prom queen, and some others. This year some publication students, seeking a device to promote the sale of the college annual, came up with the idea of electing a *queen* queen. Nobody was eligible who had not previously been a queen of something. Forty-three young women qualified.

Our queen program, my research has revealed, lags somewhat behind Big Ten standards. Ohio State has everything we have plus a pumpkin-prom queen, a rose queen, a Greek Week queen, a May queen, and a boat-race queen. Illinois has a men's-residence-hall queen, a sno-ball queen, a dolphin queen, a Miss Photoflash, a star-and-scroll queen, a Sheequon queen and a plowboy-prom queen.

As with the goose, so with the gander—bachelors and kings are selected from among the male students. The Indiana campus elects a bachelor of the year, Illinois elevates a most-eligible bachelor, Ohio State elects a Greek Week king, Wisconsin honors a campus clown, a dorm duke, a KD king and a Kat's Meow.

Once a year at Indiana there's a protest against the whole silly business in the form of a "most-useless-man" contest. Typical campaign ad: "He's so useless the state has paid his tuition for ten years to keep him out of industry."

One time a few years ago some pranksters, fed up with queens, ran a nanny goat for prom queen. Horrified campus politicians protested that she was not female and therefore not eligible. When her backers produced a veterinarian to attest her femininity, her foes finally got her disqualified on the ground that she had not been in residence on campus the preceding year. Nevertheless, she ran a strong third in the voting.

These diversions are, of course, over and above those amusements which are considered by school authorities to have cultural, educational or recreational value. Every university schedules a dazzling string of road shows for its auditorium. A typical year will bring two Broadway musical comedies, two celebrated violinists, two world-famous symphony orchestras, a renowned opera company, two first-rate ballet companies and an assortment of nationally advertised jazz musicians, pianists, sopranos, bands and lecturers. Besides this, university academic departments, particularly those of music, theater and dance, offer several entertainments and lectures weekly for the diversion of the student.

But come, does not all work and no play make Jack a dull boy? Lest ennui overtake Jack, the typical student union offers a bridge club, an arts-and-crafts club, a chess club, a photo club, a sailing club and a golf club besides bowling, billiards and record concerts. We shall have sound minds in sound bodies—as long as both can stand the strain. The year-round program of intramural sports is open to all students—touch football, softball, badminton, golf, table tennis.

In schools which offer what is considered an adequate Second Curriculum, each college generation is expected to produce its quota of pranks, "outbreaks" and illegal highjinks. Last year, five Ohio State freshmen got drunk in Kentucky, stole a corpse from an undertaking parlor, transported it a hundred miles and placed it in front of the union building on the Columbus campus.

The same year, at Ohio University, Athens, Ohio, police had to use tear gas to break up a riot, over nothing in particular, of 3000 students who invaded the city's business district. The riot started with a few students pelting each other with oranges, and wound up with twenty-eight of them in jail on charges of disorderly conduct, assault and battery, throwing firecrackers, resisting arrest, blocking traffic, and unsafe operation of motor vehicles.

Illinois' contribution to this lore is the celebrated water fight of April, 1958, in which 6000 berserk students opened fire hydrants, routed the local fire department and drenched the dean of students. I am impressed by the fact that the year in which college students in Hungary started an immortal revolution to free their country from tyranny, the big thing on the Indiana campus was a panty raid. On the day in which a local school was bombed and the countdown began for one of our major satellite attempts, a Big Ten student paper carried the headline, LIZ HAMILTON ELECTED HOMECOMING QUEEN.

Fun, yes; love, certainly; marriage in good time, of course. But shall these things be gained out of season, at too dear a price? Some of us are beginning to ask what very little work and an awful lot of play makes Jack.

What should be done? Half a dozen useful suggestions are in circulation and receiving minority support among the faculties of our colleges and universities. All that is needed to place them on the action agenda is a little public outcry.

The first step would be to prohibit automobiles. There would be a pitiable bleating, but all, I am sure, would pronounce the action a benefit. Princeton men do not appear unhappier than most, and their scholarship ranks with the world's best. Yet they are not allowed to operate motor vehicles while attending college.

The next step would be to disband fraternities and sororities. Here, I must confess, my heart skips a beat as I turn in my old badge. I have even shed a quiet tear, for the associations of my college fraternity are deep and dear. But the plain fact is that the system has outlived its usefulness. This fact must be faced, even by sentimental fraternity men like myself. Glenn H. Goodman, of the Ohio State faculty, has let fly at fraternities for "picking top men and isolating them in an atmosphere of football, adolescent discussions, dating and drinking."

I could add other serious charges. Besides providing the prime breeding grounds of the "minimum effort" attitude, fraternities too often breed a tawdry Don Juanism, a callow and provincial snobbishness, the habit of getting drunk and a world view no broader than a dollar bill. Worst of all, they consume quantities of time, effort, money and emotional stress—with their chronic financial troubles, panicked rushing season, and social-alcoholic-political monkeyshines—out of all proportion to the good they offer in terms of fellowship.

My apologies are tendered to chapters which do not deserve such harsh words. But enough of them do, and have deserved them for so long a time that they doom the whole system.

The same apology goes to those students—and I have known quite a number —with the integrity and plain nerve to resist the pressures of the conforming mob, place the Second Curriculum firmly in second place and do a job in college. The fact that a few unusual individuals can win through to an education does not, however, weaken my case—which is that universities have no right to make it almost impossible for students to study.

Several other things might be done to cut down ill-formed attitudes toward scholarship, toward marriage, and toward the relationship between them. Plush university housing should not be offered until the head of the house is at least a senior, usually achieved at the age of twenty-one. This would remove cheap, pleasant, subsidized living—an abnormal condition which the young couple cannot expect to find later on—as a temptation to impulsive teen-age marriage. At the same time it would not obstruct love so deep and true, though young, that it is determined to find a way.

Standards of scholarship are responsive to public expectation. Our state universities face a rising—and, in my thinking, justified—public opinion that education beyond high school is every child's right. Let us, then, offer a two-year university curriculum, crowned with an associate-in-arts degree for those who pass it successfully. Our many junior colleges have set the precedent. Let it be tough, and let it be the same for everybody. Those who wish to go on for the full four years would return to college in a frame of mind to get down to business. A re-entrance examination at the beginning of the junior year should be tough enough to weed out those who are in college mainly for the Second Curriculum.

These are some of the suggestions currently in the air, and there are others —the problem is nationwide. Citing popular pressure for easy, fun-packed college degrees, Richard B. Hovey of Western Maryland College, addressing the College English Association, has come down smartly on the head of the nail.

Hovey has pointed out that a shocking number of college graduates can't even write grammatically or spell correctly, and has asked the reasons. He finds that standards are shot, and that there's not much a teacher can do about it. "An individual teacher cannot suddenly decide to have standards; let him fail half or more of a class, and he will soon be in trouble with his administrators." He finds, moreover, that students understand this and take advantage of it: "Our student knows that unless he is . . . unforgivably negligent, he will get by."

The burden of the Second Curriculum is wryly acknowledged everywhere. To him who may question its baleful effect, I extend the invitation to take my place some morning. Let him face an early class he's knocked his brains out to prepare for. Let him address the blank stares and vacant faces of a roomful of students who knocked their brains out the night before at the Sophomore Twitch, the Winter Willies, the Monumental Maul, the Greek Tweak or, in short, at goofing off.

Now that we're over on the teaching side, what about the teachers? The faculty, as certain current novels suggest, is far from perfect. Entering the academic life from the "outside world," one is disappointed by the banality of conversation at social gatherings, and by attitudes of old-fashioned trade-unionism centering on "tenure," a word which means that after they've kept you on for seven years it's almost impossible for them to fire you. This concern for tenure bends many teachers toward cautious utterance, often blunting the kind of searching, outspoken discourse that might explode into exciting teaching and learning.

Here, though, I'd like to say a word in defense of the kind of repetitious teaching called "time serving." There are certain foundation subjects, often humdrum, that the student simply has to "get." These are the barren places in the terrain of learning which must be crossed to reach the thrilling peaks beyond. The work is a rut, and here the patient Mr. Chips serves well.

For inspiration one looks to the faculty "star," and every faculty has some bright ones. When my own resolve flags, I can look to men like H. J. Muller, our Nobel Prize winner in genetics; Bob Byrnes in history; Bill Wilson in English; Schuyler Otteson in economics and Bill Moore in physiology, and I become refreshed. These men have broken the confines of their own specialties to look at the universe and have found courage to state their views regardless of what special interest may be offended.

In intellectual daring of this order we may hope to find, through education, the glory of the future. And what a future beckons! The purely mechanical side already has been pretty well publicized—the two-day work week, the trips through space, world tours as a standard part of grade-school education, the time when the deserts will bloom and the jungles will be made into gardens.

The new day of the human soul has, however, scarcely been mentioned. Some think the long-sought substitute for war is close to being found—that peaceful means actually exist for converting an enemy into a co-operative and willing friend. In the resulting leisure and plenty, man might begin to develop his potential in art and philosophy. The artist and poet in each of us would find expression. We would stand before the goal of goals for all men—the penetration into the deepest meaning of life itself.

These wonders will not drop into our laps without our effort. Indeed, to avoid a quick catastrophe, we'll have to work as never before. And the kind of work most urgently demanded is work of the mind.

We'll have to *think* our way out of this one. We need tough, seasoned, disciplined thinkers, incorruptible, enormously well informed, skilled in their chosen specialties, but with an appreciation of all specialties—thinkers who cannot be diverted to limited or shoddy goals—and we need a lot of them.

For these reasons, the Second Curriculum must be trimmed. This must be done, not in spite or through outraged morality, but to make room for something wonderfully better.

We who are concerned about Jack and Jacqueline would like to see more, not less, love on the campus. Besides the inevitable and proper love of comfort and fun, of boy for girl, of status and position, of exercise and sport, of family and children, we'd like to see some love of truth and intellectual achievement, of discovery and high adventure, of beauty, harmony, design and great precision, of mankind and its farthest destiny. We would like, in short, to see the First Curriculum come first.

DAVID RIESMAN

Where Is the College Generation Headed?[1]

The conflict of the generations is neither a new nor a particularly American story, but it is perhaps exacerbated by the self-consciousness and the partial segregation of teen-age culture, to such an extent that both old and young

[1] From *The Atlantic Monthly*, CCVII (April, 1961), 39-45. Reprinted by permission of the author.

are exceptionally vulnerable to their mutual criticisms. I do not care to add to the complacency of my agemates who, from their clubs, pulpits, and other rostrums, attack the alleged "softness" of the young, whom they have themselves brought up, while failing to see the difficulties young people face today precisely because the manifest hardships with which earlier Americans coped have been, for millions, attenuated. These hardships cannot be artificially restored, at least for people over twelve; however, I believe that college students are now beginning to find new ways to become active politically, and hence responsible humanly.

It is easy to underestimate the importance of this in America, where students until recently did not play the role in politics that they do in Latin America, Turkey, Korea, or Japan. For, the cadres of the disinherited who once helped power political change in this country are diminished in numbers and even more diminished in leadership, now that nearly every bright, motivated boy gets funneled into college if he wants to go. Thus, our expanding colleges absorb increasingly large fractions of the available idealism and dynamism of our society. And at the same time, as I shall try to show, many students are not attracted by the traditional goals of commercial or professional ambition; the best of them have no love for the status quo. Rejecting careerism, they often choose familism instead. But shaken out of this, either by the open discrimination felt by Negroes or the subtler dissatisfaction with contemporary life felt by whites, they comprise a privileged minority, ignorant of its strength, yet capable of change.

College students today often act as if they believed that work in large organizations, and beyond that, work in general, could not be basically satisfying (or, at times, even honest), but is primarily a way to earn a living, to find a place in the social order, and to meet nice or not-so-nice people. This is a conclusion which is partly projected upon the occupational scene as the result of their experience with the curriculum in college and university, and also as the result of experience with college and university as organizations which are viewed as bureaucratic, monolithic, and unchangeable by many students.

I do not think it is the primary task of education to prepare students for their later occupational roles, or, indeed, any narrowly specialized roles, nor to teach them to enjoy work regardless of its quality and meaning. Rather, the relation of education to later life should be a dialectical and critical one. If, however, one result of going to college is to become alienated from work per se and defeatist about the possibility of altering one's relation to it, then it seems to me one ought to re-examine academic institutions themselves and see whether anything in them, or in one's own attitudes, or in both might be changed.

In the spring of 1955, several hundred interviews were done (at the behest of *Time* magazine) with seniors at twenty colleges throughout the country, most of them colleges of distinction. The seniors were supposed to be reasonably representative, but what this was taken to mean and how it was applied at different colleges and universities varied greatly. A good many student leaders were chosen, a good many bright people, but hardly any women were included (a questionnaire circulated by *Mademoiselle* gave me somewhat comparable data concerning college women). When I first examined the interviews, and now again when I have once more gone over them, I have been struck by what appears to be a not quite conscious ambivalence toward work in large organizations. Nevertheless, the majority are planning to enter large organizations in pursuit of their careers: big corporations, big governments, big law offices, and so on. Only a few seek independence in their work, either in terms of old-fashioned ideals of entrepreneurship or in terms of the desire to become a foreign correspondent, to enter politics, or to follow some other individualistic or exotic calling. (Moreover, hardly anyone expresses resentment against his prospective army service on the ground that the army is a large organization; there is no eagerness for service, but rather resignation to it as one of the givens of life.)

And yet, when these young people are asked about their lives outside of work, a very different picture merges. There, bigness and scale are definitely not valued. Only a tiny fraction want to head for the metropolis, even if their careers might make such a location convenient. They want the suburbs—not later, after some bachelor independence in the big city, but now, on graduation. The great majority either are already married or plan to get married soon (even if there is no special one in mind at the moment); they plan to start having children at once and to begin building a community-centered life in the suburbs. They envisage a two-car, but usually not a two-career, family, in which the prospective wife will be active in the parent-teacher association, with assistance from the husband, and in which both spouses will concern themselves with a manageable bit of real estate in a suburban neighborhood in which they can at once be active and hope to make a difference. It does not occur to them that they might be gifted and energetic enough to make a difference even in a big city. Rather, they want to be able to work through a face-to-face group—the postcollegiate fraternity of the small suburbs.

Correspondingly, the very emphasis on family life, which is one of the striking and, in so many ways, attractive qualities of young people today, is an implicit rejection of large organization. The suburban family, with its garden, its barbecue, its lack of privacy in the open-plan house, is itself a manifesto of decentralization, even though it makes use of centralized services such as television, clinics, chain stores, and *House Beautiful*. The wish to build a nest, even if a somewhat transient one, is a striking feature of the interviews, in contrast with the wish to build a fortune or a career, which might have dominated some comparable interviews a generation earlier.

This pattern—the acceptance of large organizations, combined with tacit and uncrystallized resistance to them—appears not only in the respondents' emphasis on the family but also in what they say about their plans and attitudes toward their future work. I get a sense from the material, and from other comparable data, of a certain withdrawal of emotional adherence from work. To be sure, it has become fashionable to speak of one's work or other activities in deprecatory terms and to adopt a pose of relative indifference to the larger goals of an organization. In an era of political, economic, and cultural salesmanship, such deprecation is a way of guarding against being exploited for ends outside one's self. It is as if one had constantly to conduct psychological warfare against an outside enemy. But, as in any such process, students become to some extent the victims of their own defenses. They come to believe that work cannot really be worth doing for its own sake, whether or not it is done on behalf of a large, impersonal organization. They fear overcommitment to their work even while they are at the workplace. In the course of getting rid of earlier collegiate or rah-rah enthusiasm, these young people have come to feel that work is not worth even their part-time devotion, and perhaps that nothing, except the family, deserves their wholehearted allegiance.

We see the same attitudes, of course, among the junior echelons now engaged in work. One hears them talk of their benevolent company as "a mink-lined rat trap," or speak of "the rat race," or refer to fights over principles as "ruckuses" or "blowups"—if somebody cares, he is said to "blow his top." In a number of business novels, of which *The Man in the Gray Flannel Suit* is representative, it is taken for granted that a sensible fellow, and, indeed, an honest one, will prefer surburban domesticity and a quiet niche to ulcerous competition for large business stakes, despite the view from the top and the interesting climb.

Attitudes such as these are of course an aspect of a general cultural shift, not confined to students and not confined to those who seek employment in large organizations; similar attitudes turn up in some measure even among those who, studiously avoiding such organizations, look for a professional career in which they hope to be their own masters. Scholars, for example, are not immune to distaste for their work, nor are architects or physicians. But, while I do not intend to imply that a life without any boredom is conceivable, except for a very stupid person, still, I think we are witnessing a silent revolution against work on the part of even those relatively privileged groups who have been free to choose their work and to exercise some freedom in the doing of it. This reflects, in part, the fact that much work is meaningless per se, save as a source of income, prestige, and sociability, but it also indicates, as I have already implied, that people too readily accept their work as it comes, without the hope of making it more meaningful.

Not all large organizations are alike, despite the sorts of institutional similarities investigated by sociologists, and, of course, not all positions in them are alike. Many, although their top executives clamor for creativity and independence of mind, largely manage to process these qualities out of "their" people in the lower ranks. Others stockpile talent and expect it to keep as gold keeps at Fort Knox. Still others make products or provide services which are either antisocial or useless. But here and there one finds companies which face real and not contrived problems and apply to them an intelligence which is often remarkably disinterested and, in the best sense of the term, "academic." Young people in search of challenge and development would do well to seek out such relatively productive climates, rather than to assume offhand that these (as is true of so many brand-name products) are all alike except for the advertising and the label. And this search is necessary precisely because many of the motives which impelled work in the older generation have fortunately become attenuated, motives such as money for its own sake, power, and fame—goals, that is, whose emptiness became evident with their attainment. Our industrial and commercial plant no longer "needs" such compulsive attachments to work, which are based not on any genuine creative impulse but on the drying up of other alternatives and on the pressure of extrinsic standards of value.

There is a further issue concerning work in larger organizations where, again, differentiation is required. I refer to the conception that work in organizations requires surrender of independence of judgment, if not of intregrity. When I was in college, there was a prevalent feeling among the more sensitive that this was true only of business and commercial organizations, not of governmental or philanthropic ones, and young men debated whether they would enter Wall Street and make money, or enter government or teaching and be saved. This dichotomy has in large measure vanished, although traces of it do survive among the less cynical. For instance, I have known many graduate students in social psychology who believe that if they teach, they can be honest, but that if they work in market research, they will serve manipulation and corruption and will have no power over their own work. Such judgments oversimplify the ethical dilemmas of any calling and are, in addition, snobbish; one can find hucksterism (often hypocritically veiled) among academic people in search of reputations, grants, and promotions, as well as among market researchers and other businessmen.

Indeed, I am inclined to think that, at present, many observant young people do not need to be persuaded of this; many are actually overpersuaded to the point of believing that every occupation is a racket and that at best some of the racketeers are less pious about it than others. And this, I suspect, is one of the reasons they tend to withdraw emotional allegiance from their work—with the impression that they have no control over it anyway, that all is in the hands of the mysterious men upstairs who run the show. If there is greater wisdom in their belief that all occupations, like all forms of power, are corrupting in some degree, there is also greater resignation, greater passivity and fatalism.

Where are such attitudes learned and confirmed? Even at some of the leading colleges, the more intellectual colleges, the colleges which produce literary magazines, the relation of students to the curriculum has a certain alienated quality, in the sense that the students do not believe they have any control over their own education.

In the last few years I have visited a number of colleges of high quality, colleges which turn out eminent professional men, scholars, and scientists, and I have made it my business to talk with students informally, to read their student newspapers and, where possible, student council reports. At a number of these institutions, the livelier students complain of the educational fare they are getting, of the very little contact the curriculum makes with the problems that are meaningful to them. Sometimes they feel that opportunities for a civilized and intellectual life on campus are wanting—for example, that there are few inviting places to study or to talk, that social pressures in dormitories force any intellectual life out of the group setting, that student publications are either dominated by the school administration or devoted to campus news and trivia, that the bookstore is inadequate, or that the library is geared to meet research needs rather than to attract undergraduate browsers. They often feel that they have no access to the faculty for other than merely routine matters. Sometimes students complain about the prerequisites of a department, which serve its monopolistic aims or protect its mediocre teachers from boy-cott rather than serve any defensible pedagogic aims.

Yet, when I ask such students what they have done about these things, they are surprised at the very thought that they could do anything. They think I am joking when I suggest that, if things came to the worst, they could picket! They think I am wholly unrealistic when I say that many on the faculty might welcome student initiative in revising the curriculum, or that it might be pos-sible to raise modest sums of money among alumni or others to bring visiting lecturers or poets to the campus, or to furnish commodious rooms for interest-group meetings. When I tell them that the Harvard house plan came about in considerable measure because of the report of a student council committee in 1926 which caught the attention of the philanthropist Edward Harkness, they shrug. That must have been a golden era, they say; nothing like that could happen now. Of course, as long as they think that, they will conduct themselves accordingly.

Why is it that students, often so precocious about many things—about each other, about sex, about their families, and occasionally even about national and world affairs—are comparatively inattentive to what concerns them as closely as does their curriculum?

For one thing, it seems to me that students do not want to believe that their activities might make a difference, because, in a way, they profit from their lack of commitment to what they are doing. I do not mean that they are not industrious students; they go through the required motions of working, but they seldom get really involved with the content of their courses. It is here that the better, more conscientious students sabotage their own education and restrict production; true enough, they turn out the credits and the grades, but they do not believe that it really matters in any fundamental sense what they think and feel.

When I have discussed this with students, they have often told me that it doesn't pay to be too interested in anything, because then one is tempted to spend too much time on it, at the expense of that optimal distribution of effort which will produce the best grades—and after all, they do have to get into medical school, keep their scholarship, and "please the old man." Now, I am convinced that grades contaminate education—they are a kind of currency which, like money, gets in the way of students' discovering their intellectual interests—but here, too, the students in their realism are being somewhat unrealistic. They assume, for one thing, that it is hopeless to try to alter the curriculum so that it might penalize them less for serious interest in one topic at the expense of others, or so that there might be more emphasis on reading and discussion and more opportunity for independent thinking. And here, also, the students have a distorted image of what will actually make an impression on their teachers either now or later. On this point, I have some evidence to back me up.

After I had tried in vain for some time to persuade graduate students at Chicago that they could be more independent in their course and thesis work without any heroism, any martyrdom, there was a thesis done by a student which documented my arguments. The student went around to the departments and asked them which students in recent years they had recommended for jobs or advanced training or fellowships and which they had not. Then he interviewed some of these students in various categories of faculty blessing or disapproval, looked at their grades, and so on. He concluded that those students frequently fared best who were not too obedient, who did not get an undiluted, uncomplicated, straight-A record. (The straight-A students, in fact, sometimes slipped away without anyone's noticing.)

The students who were most successful were a bit rebellious, a bit offbeat, though not entirely "goof-offs"; these were the students likely to appeal to a faculty member who had not entirely repressed a rebelliousness of his own that had led him to be a teacher in the first place, a faculty member who was looking for signs of life, even if they gave him a bit of trouble at times. To be sure, such a student had to do well in something to earn this response, but he was often better off to have written a brilliant paper or two than to have divided his time, as an investment banker his money, among a variety of subjects. Those students who were the most self-consciously opportunistic and realistic in allocating their time and emotion were in fact sacrificing themselves unprofitably, suffering not only now, during the studies which they regarded as an anteroom to life, but later on as well.

Now, not all departments at Chicago were alike in this matter; some gave more play to defiance and deviation than others. Moreover, this study encompassed only the social science departments. No doubt departments and institutions differ very much in this respect. But that is just the point I want to emphasize: by concluding prematurely that all organizations are alike, that all demand the same kinds of conformity, students not only surrender the chance to experience an atmosphere that is freer and more conducive to their own development but perpetuate a myth that then controls their passage through jobs in later life. If the University of Chicago or even one's department itself cannot be changed from below, how can one expect to change General Motors, or *Look* magazine, or the big hospitals of San Francisco? And if that is so, then why not settle for the fringe benefits, for a position of moderate respectability and adequate, if not dazzling, salary?

At work here is a characteristic social pattern in which individuals, hesitant to reveal feelings they have scarcely voiced to themselves, are misled about what in effect could be done if they expressed themselves, thereby discovering others who might share their views. (Sociologists refer to this process as "pluralistic ignorance.") Leadership, of course, whether in politics or in other affairs, often serves to help a group change its apparent mood to conform to its actual or potential but repressed views, but leadership also may, and frequently does, serve to continue enforcing the repression. Even in a large organization, radical and what were previously regarded as "impossible" changes come about almost instantaneously once people discover that views they had previously regarded as unacceptable or idiosyncratic are in fact widely shared.

The students know that there are many decisions out of their conceivable control, decisions upon which their lives and fortunes truly depend. But what I am contending is that this truth, this insight, is overgeneralized, and that, being believed, it becomes more and more "true." Not only do we fail to spot those instances in which intervention might change things quite substantially, but we fail to develop the competence and the confidence in ourselves that are necessary to any large endeavor. In that sense, despite our precociousness, we fail to grow up; we remain the children of organization, not the masters of it.

For Americans, there is something paradoxical about this development. Americans in the past have not been overimpressed by mechanical achievements. Workers in a steel mill are not awed by the giant rollers, and we take for granted that we are not awed by any large physical construction made by our hands and brains. Contrary to the prevalent impression abroad that we are slaves to our machines, we are actually relatively uninvolved with them, and we surely do not feel dominated by them. But it seems to be different with the organizational machines. These are as much the product of our thinking and our imagination as any technological feat; yet, as Erich Fromm has said, we worship like idolaters the product we have created, an image not of stone but of other images.

It is a commonplace observation that in organizational life we use arguments to convince others which we think will appeal to them, even though they do not convince us. We try to persuade people to behave justly to Negroes because "discrimination makes the United States look bad in the Cold War," as if that were why we ourselves behaved decently. Or we persuade businessmen to give money to colleges for all sorts of public relations reasons, playing on their fear of radicalism or federal control or whatnot, whereas we ourselves devote our lives to education for quite different reasons. All arguments of this nature have two qualities: they patronize the other person and they perpetuate "pluralistic ignorance." It can be contended that there may be occasions when we must appeal to others as they are, not as we should like them to be; when there is not time for idealism. But, in our realism, we often make mistakes about what others will actually respond to, and we sacrifice the integrity and clarity of our argument to our false image of what will go over. The result: we conclude that one cannot be honest while working for an organization, that one can be honest only when one is at home with one's family in the suburbs.

There is another result as well; namely, that we often end up in doubt as to what we ourselves think. We come to believe what we say to others and thus become "more sincere" in the subjective sense, but at the price of becoming still more confused as to what is actually so: we are the first victims of our own propaganda. No wonder we end up without emotional ties to what we do, for it is no longer we who do it, but some limited part of ourselves, playing a role. Not recognizing that we in some measure have done this to ourselves, we attribute to organizations the power and the primacy we have lost. And then, as I have said, we strike back, not directly, but by a kind of emotional attrition in which we lend to our work willingness without enthusiasm, conscientiousness without creativity.

I am sure that many college students who are not only serious but dedicated know this as well as I do. Such students have managed to make college serve their purposes and have in this way gained some rational confidence that they will be able to do the same in the organizations they will enter later, whether these are universities, business concerns, or the many voluntary organizations through which we Americans carry out much of our communal work. What I have principally sought to do in these remarks is to encourage greater and more differentiated realism than many young people already possess, a realism which does not take for granted the social structures which seem so impressive but which looks for the points of leverage where one's own effort, joined to that of others similarly freed from mythology, might make a difference. In many situations, there is more leeway than students think, and college is a good place to find this out.

Three years later, I have naturally asked myself to what extent the foregoing remarks still strike me as true. I had in 1955 and 1957 paid very brief visits to several of the Southern Negro colleges that have since been in the fore-front of sit-in demonstrations; at that time they seemed to me, as to some of their own faculty members, acquiescent and cautious, preparing students to enter the army uncomplainingly, the "Black Bourgeoisie" unthinkingly. Of course, the students were aware of the struggles over integration, but for them the issues remained somewhat abstract, particularly as many of them had chosen the shelter of a segregated college, as in their prospective occupations—teaching, the ministry, Negro business—many would choose the still segregated occupations.

As so often, appearances were deceptive; some of these students carried out the first sit-ins and refused to become daunted or disorganized when either their own pressured administrations or reactive whites sought to end the picketing and protests; a brave few, in active civil disobedience, have chosen jail rather than bail. Relatively immune to the economic boycotts that can hamstring their parents, and free, too, of the traditional Negro leadership in their communities, they have discovered their organizational powers and talents. This has been bracing and highly educative.

Meanwhile, among white students in the North, sympathetic picketing of the chain stores was rapidly organized, and many campuses had their first taste of political life in twenty years. The young people I have been describing are markedly tolerant; in the 1955 interviews, hardly any exhibited bigotry (at the Southern universities many said that once the old folks are gone, the race problem will die with them). Moreover, tolerance appears to them a virtue that is civic and personal, tied into one's own immediate human reactions and relations; to be tolerant to classmates, one does not have to fight city hall, though one may sometimes have to fight alumni guardians of the more collegiate fraternities.

Furthermore, the simplicity of the race issue, the near lack of rational or civilized defense of segregation and discrimination, allows Northern students to extrapolate public activity on the basis of private decency, without feeling themselves to be involved in "politics" or in ideology. True, the planned picketing has involved these highly individualistic students in more organization and decision making than appeals to most of them; the term "politician" is as much one of contempt on the better campuses as it is generally in American life. Even so, many students have discovered, though less dramatically than the Southern Negro students, that they are capable of action in areas outside the usual complaints about library hours, dormitory food, and parking, and that even such seemingly large outfits as Woolworth's are not invulnerable.

So, too, there have recently been some energetic student actions in the area of curriculum. In the spring of 1958, students at the University of Wisconsin submitted a petition to the administration requesting more challenge and stimulation in their courses and in their educational program generally. During the same period, undergraduates at Chicago mobilized to defend the general education program against attempts to subordinate it to the requirements of the graduate departments. A group of students at Wesleyan last year arranged a series of discussions on education, geared to the problems and opportunities faced by a liberal arts college; apparently the students helped influence curricular change. While, in some instances, students could graduate before realizing that what they did had any impact, others learned from their experiences that institutions are man-made and subject to change.

It is understandably seldom that such sporadic and ad hoc actions have been carried over into political controversies on the national scene. There have been occasional protests against compulsory ROTC, based as much on the unintellectual waste of time of the programs as on any explicit antimilitarist views. The student political party (Slate) at Berkeley was a factor in last year's protest against the Un-American Activities Committee hearings in San Francisco—a brave protest, since many students fear it will go on their records in an FBI dossier. And, increasingly, the issues of peace and disarmament have found a student audience. Students are picketing weekly on Boston Common under the auspices of the Committee for a Sane Nuclear Policy and are encountering, as they did to only a minor degree in picketing the chain stores, violent and jeering attacks as Reds or yellow appeasers. Challenge at Michigan and Yale, Concern at Ohio Wesleyan, Tocsin at Harvard are among the groups that have sprung up to discuss peace and other political questions. Only a very small minority are involved—but then only a small minority were involved in the supposedly activist 1930s. Probably some of these organizations will last only for the college lifetimes of a handful of committed students.

Indeed, the very fact that academic values have triumphed on many campuses puts heavy competition in the way of all extracurricular activity, including politics. I recall one student who recently felt he had to choose between active participation in organizing a student chapter of SANE and writing a senior distinction thesis; he believed that if he did not do the latter, he would not get into graduate school (not an unrealistic fear) and would jeopardize his whole career (in my judgment, a less realistic fear). Perhaps more important, the professors have taught, especially the better students, that all questions are complex, all ideologies suspect, and all larger passions fanatical; the fear of being naïve prevents many young people from feeling confidence in any action or reaction. (Some of these same adults then criticize the students for apathy!) Questions of foreign policy and disarmament *are* complex—in a way that the race question is not—and students have in the past feared to take a position that expert or "classified" knowledge might explode. Once they begin, however, these same academic values lead them to a seriousness illustrated by the Tocsin students, who have organized seminars on technical problems of disarmament and, as the phrase goes, "done their homework" in Kahn, Kissinger, King-Hall, the *Bulletin of the Atomic Scientists,* and so on.

The long-buried idealism of many gifted and sensitive students has come out most strongly, however, in their response to President Kennedy's proposal of a Peace Corps. It is exciting to watch a group of them examining in detail what American students might contribute to secondary education in Nigeria and what qualities of judgment, self-reliance, pertinacity, and technique such students would need to be of real help. I have seen students who seemed, even in their own eyes, cool customers, ready to ride the organizational escalator, discover in themselves unexpected resources of dedication when beckoned by a chance to serve in an underdeveloped country. To be sure, such service appears to many students as quite unpolitical, outside the polemical orbit of American domestic struggles; and one could argue that there are escapist elements in this choice, this interpretation. But one has to start somewhere, and when one is emerging from privatism, the first movements are apt to be tentative.

We must still ask whether there will be any carry-over from these campus stirrings into the attitudes that college graduates take toward their work: will they continue to regard it as mere "bread," needful for existence, but not a locus either for defining the self or changing the world? If one is apathetic about one's work, it is hard to prevent this apathy from spreading to other areas, even to those on which one had originally thought to build one's life: domesticity, the arts, and personal relations. But, conversely, the vitality and sense for relevant accomplishment that students may gain in college should spread to their academic work and thence to their lifework. For, in the more selective colleges at present, as I have already indicated, there is very little left of the collegiate or teen-ager high jinks of the former *jeunesse dorée*; it is in the high schools now that these ersatz values reign. Thus, college is already, not always happily, an aspect of adult life, not simply a playful preparation, and experience there is no longer compartmentalized as a childish thing.

ROBERT M. HUTCHINS

The Meaning and Significance of Academic Freedom[1]

The arguments for academic freedom are the same as those for freedom of speech, and they rest on the same foundation. Here are the familiar words of John Stuart Mill:

> If all mankind minus one were of one opinion, and only one person were of the contrary opinion, mankind would be no more justified in silencing that one person, than he, if he had the power, would be justified in silencing mankind. . . . the peculiar evil of silencing the expression of an opinion is,

[1] From *The Annals of the American Academy of Political and Social Science*, XXX (July, 1955), 72-78. Copyright, 1955, The American Academy of Political and Social Science.

that it is robbing the human race; posterity as well as the existing generation; those who dissent from the opinion, still more than those who hold it. If the opinion is right, they are deprived of the opportunity of exchanging error for truth: if wrong, they lose, what is almost as great a benefit, the clearer perception and livelier impression of truth, produced by its collision with error.

Man is a learning animal. The state is an association the primary aim of which is the virtue and intelligence of the people. Men learn by discussion, through the clash of opinion. The best and most progressive society is that in which expression is freest. Mill said, "There ought to exist the fullest liberty of professing and discussing, as a matter of ethical conviction, any doctrine, however immoral it may be considered." The civilization we seek is the civilization of the dialogue, the civilization of the logos.

In such a society the intelligent man and the good citizen are identical. The educational system does not aim at indoctrination in accepted values but at the improvement of society through the production of the intelligent man and the good citizen. Education necessarily involves the critical examination of conflicting points of view; it cannot flourish in the absence of free inquiry and discussion.

In a democracy what the public needs to know about the teachers in the educational system is that they are competent. The competent teacher knows the subject he is teaching and how to communicate it to his pupils. Unlike the teacher in a totalitarian state, he is not supposed to purvey the prevailing dogma. He is supposed to encourage his students to use their own intelligence and to reach their own conclusions.

The definition of competence does not shift with every wind of prejudice, religious, political, racial, or economic. If competence had been the issue at Brown University during the free silver controversy, the President would not have been asked to resign because of his premature distaste for the Gold Standard. The modern note was struck there. What was requested of the President was "not a renunciation of his views, but a forbearance to promulgate them." And the reason was that these views were "injurious to the pecuniary interests of the University." On the other hand, the standard of competence did protect a professor at the University of Chicago who was a leading critic of Samuel Insull and the other local oligarchs of the time. He was doubtless injurious to the pecuniary interests of the university, but he and it lived through it, and he is today the senior Senator from Illinois.

Wrong Questions

We have been stifling education in this country because we have been asking the wrong questions. If you are asking the right questions, you ask about a subject of discussion whether it is important. You do not forbid students to discuss a subject, like the entry of Red China into the United Nations, on the ground that it is too important. The right question about a subject of research and the methods of investigation is whether competent scholars believe that the subject should be investigated and that this is the way to investigate it. You do not permit the Post Office Department to protect the Johns Hopkins School of Advanced International Studies from *Izvestia* and *Pravda*. The right question about a textbook is whether competent people think it can make a contribution to education. You do not ask whether incompetent people are going to be offended by passages taken out of context. The right question about a research man on unclassified work is whether he is competent to do it. You do not act like the United States Public Health Service and weaken the country by withdrawing contracts from research workers on unstated grounds that can only be grounds of loyalty.

As I have said, the right question about a teacher is whether he is competent. If we had been asking about competence we should have had quite a different atmosphere in the case of teachers who were Communists or ex-Communists, who refused to testify about themselves, or who declined to discuss the political affiliations of others. We have been so busy being sophisticated anti-Communists, detecting the shifts and devices of Communist infiltration, that we have failed to observe that our educational responsibility is to have a good educational system. We do not discharge that responsibility by invading civil liberties, reducing the number of qualified teachers available, eliminating good textbooks, and intimidating the teaching staff. The standard of competence means that there must be some relation between the charges against a teacher and the quality of his teaching. The standard of competence would have protected us against teachers following a party line or conducting propaganda. If a teacher sought to indoctrinate his pupils, which is the only circumstance under which he could be dangerous as a teacher, he would be incompetent, and should be removed as such. The standard of competence would have saved us from the excesses of the silly season, such as the refusal of the University of Washington to let Professor Oppenheimer lecture there on physics, and from the consequences of concentrating on the negative task of preventing one particular unpopular variety of infiltration. If we had used the standard of competence we should have been free to fix our minds on the positive responsibility of building an educational system, and with half the energy we have put into being scared to death we might have built a great one.

Since our guilty conscience tells us that there ought to be some connection between what a man does and the punishment visited upon him, we often try to pretend that this is the rule we are following. The Attorney General of the United States, speaking in New York three weeks ago, said that schools should not be sanctuaries or proving grounds "for subversives shaping the minds of innocent children."

This picture of subversives shaping the minds of innocent children has nothing to do with the case. The teachers who have lost their jobs in the campaign against subversives have not been charged with doing anything to the minds of any children. The case of Goldie Watson here in Philadelphia is typical: testimony about the good she had done the minds of the children in her classes was rejected as impertinent. The only evidence allowed was as to whether she had declined to answer questions about her political affiliations. She had, and she was fired. The same procedure seems to be followed everywhere, even at Harvard. When a professor there is called on the carpet, the issue is whether he is a member of something or other, or whether he has lied or refused to answer questions about such membership. The matter of his competence in his field or what he has done to the innocent minds of the Harvard students is never referred to.

Fear of Ideas

We are getting so afraid of ideas that we are afraid of people who associate with people who are said to have ideas, even if they themselves have not expressed them. The State Curriculum Commission of California is now studying investigators' reports on the authors of twenty-three textbooks. Dr. C. C. Trillingham, Los Angeles County Superintendent of Schools and a member of the commission, said, "If an author is aligned with the Communists, we don't want his textbook, even if there is no Red propaganda in it."

We regard what a man says as irrelevant in determining whether we will listen to him. What a man does in his job is irrelevant in determining whether he should continue in it. This amounts to a decision that people whose ideas or whose associates' ideas we regard as dangerous cannot be permitted to earn a living or make a contribution in any capacity to the well-being of the community. The Supreme Court of California has just taken this logical next step: it has held, in effect, that a Communist can have no contractual rights that the rest of us are bound to respect.

Not long ago at a dinner of the senior members of the faculty of the University of Birmingham in England, I sat across the table from a professor who is a member of the executive committee of the Communist party of Great Britain. The British appear to be getting value out of a scholar whom none of the great American universities could appoint.

Fifth Amendment

One of the more important advances in law and government effected by the struggles of our ancestors is that proclaimed by the Fifth Amendment. Why should the government demand that a man convict himself out of his own mouth instead of requiring prosecution to make the effort to establish the charges that it has brought against him? All the Fifth Amendment means is: prove it. Injury is added to insult if there is no pretence that the questions asked must be relevant or proper. In some public school systems refusal to answer any questions by the Board of Education or any other public body is insubordination; insubordination justifies dismissal.

Surely the issue is whether the questions are legitimate. It cannot be insubordination to refuse to answer illegitimate questions. We have gone very far under the influence of one of the rollicking dicta of Mr. Justice Holmes, that there is no constitutional right to be a policeman; but not so far that public employment can be denied on a ground that has nothing to do with the duties to be performed. If the President were to refuse to employ baldheaded men in the federal establishment, the Supreme Court would find, I believe, that the bald had been deprived of their constitutional rights.

Is It Too Late?

You may say that the issue I am discussing is academic in every sense: there is no use now in talking about the right of Communists, ex-Communists, or persons who decline to answer questions about their political affiliations to teach in the United States. Milton Mayer in his forthcoming book, *They Thought They Were Free,* tells the story of the way history passed Martin Niemoeller by. When the Nazis attacked the Communists, he was a little uneasy, but he was not a Communist, and he did nothing. When they attacked the Socialists, he was uneasy, but he was not a Socialist, and he did nothing. They went after the schools, the press, and the Jews, but he was not directly affected, and he did nothing. Then they attacked the Church. Pastor Niemoeller was a churchman. He tried to do something, but it was too late.

I hope it is not too late to point out where our preoccupation with public relations and our failure of courage and intelligence may take us. The New York *Times* on March 17 and the New York *Herald Tribune* on March 19 published editorials on the question whether teachers who decline to testify about others should be dismissed. The significant thing about the editorials is this: they both, perhaps unconsciously, extend the limits of the prevailing boycott. The *Times* condemns "adherence to Communist doctrine," thus adding theoretical Marxists to those automatically disqualified. The *Herald Tribune* comes out against Communists "or any other brands of subversives," thus opening vast new unmapped areas of investigation, recrimination, and confusion.

Reece Committee

These two newspapers bitterly attacked the Reece committee, appointed in the House to investigate foundations; but they appear to have succumbed to its influence, which is another evidence that if you say something outrageous authoritatively, loudly, and often enough you will eventually find yourself quoted in the most respectable places. The Reece committee includes among the subversives almost anybody who differs with the two members of the committee who constitute the majority. Zechariah Chafee, Jr., said at the University of Oregon last October, "The word 'subversive' has no precise definition in American law. It is as vague as 'heretical' was in the medieval trials which sent men to the stake." Leading the list of Reece committee subversives are those who do not share its philosophical prejudices. The committee condemned a philosophical doctrine, empiricism, and those who hold it as the fountainhead of the subversive tendencies now engulfing the country. If a philosophical position can be treasonable, particularly one as harmless as a preference for fact over theory, and if two politicians can make it treasonable, freedom of thought, discussion, and teaching may not be with us long.

By repetition the Reece committee is obtaining unconscious acceptance of another proposition, which, coupled with the proposition that politicians may declare a doctrine and its adherents subversive, still further imperils freedom of teaching and inquiry. This is the proposition that tax-exempt money is public money and that a tax-exempt institution is therefore subject to a special variety of public surveillance. An extension of this proposition is found in the California statute requiring all claimants of tax exemption to take a nondisloyalty oath. If carried to the logical limits hinted at in the Reece Report, this notion of the public control of private, tax-exempt corporations could deprive the independent educational institutions of this country of their autonomy, that characteristic which has given them their value in the development of the American educational system.

Tax exemption is conferred for the purpose of facilitating the performance of a public task by a private agency. A corporation that carries on education and research to that extent relieves the taxpayers of their obligation to finance such work in state-supported institutions. Tax exemption imposes no duty on colleges and universities except that of conducting teaching and research according to their best judgment of what good teaching and research are. It does not impose the duty of making sure that the teaching and research conform to the views of the majority of a legislative committee.

California Senate Committee on Un-American Activities

Consider what those views might be. Richard E. Combs, Chief Counsel for the California Senate Committee on Un-American Activities, testified two years ago before a subcommittee of the United States Senate. He gave an account of how Communists reorient courses of instruction. He thought it worth while to report that the name of a course at a California university had been changed from public speaking to speech, and the books had been changed from Robert Louis Stevenson, Masefield, and Kipling to John Stuart Mill. The subversive nature of these changes may not be clear to you, but it was clear to Mr. Combs and, from all that appears, to the California committee that employs him and the committee of the United States Senate before which he testified. The appraisal of courses of study or of the performance of teachers is a professional job, not to be undertaken by the naïve and unskilled.

Consider the role of the California Senate Committee on Un-American Activities in the administration of California institutions of higher learning. The committee claims that a chain of security officers on campuses has been welded by its efforts. If its claims are correct—and they have been disputed—professors and students at eleven institutions are being continuously spied upon for the benefit of a legislative committee. The committee has an arrangement whereby it passes on the qualifications of members and prospective members of the faculties from the standpoint of their Americanism. The reason for this is said to be that the colleges and universities are not competent to assess the

Americanism of their teachers, and the committee is. According to the committee at least a hundred members of these faculties have been forced to resign and at least one hundred prospective members have failed of appointment because of the committee's work. It is too bad that the committee has not disclosed the information that led to the interdiction of its victims. One shudders to think that it may have been enough to have been heard quoting John Stuart Mill.

Behind Academic Freedom

But the issue of legal control is not basic. Academic freedom comes and goes because of some conviction about the purpose of education on the part of those who make the decisions in society. The Kaiser gave professors freedom of research because he believed that this was one way to make Germany strong and prosperous. This freedom did not extend to professors who wanted to engage actively in politics on the wrong side, the side of the Social Democratic party. The Kaiser did not set a high value on independent criticism.

In a democratic community the question is what do the people think education is and what do they think it is for? I once asked a former Minister of Education of the Netherlands what would have happened if he had exercised his undoubted legal authority and appointed professors of whom the faculties of the Dutch universities did not approve. He said, "My government would have fallen." He meant that the people of Holland would not tolerate political interference with the universities: they understood the universities well enough to recognize interference when they saw it and felt strongly enough about it to make their wishes effective.

The public officers and businessmen who are the trustees of the provincial universities in the United Kingdom have legal control over them, but would never think of exercising it in any matter affecting education and research. They limit themselves to business. The taxpayers now meet more than half the cost of Oxford and Cambridge, but no Englishman supposes that this entitles the government to exert any influence in their academic affairs.

If the people believe that independent thought and criticism are essential to the progress of society, if they think that universities are centers of such criticism and that the rest of the educational system is intended primarily to prepare the citizen to think for himself, then academic freedom will not be a problem, it will be a fact. Under these circumstances teachers would not be second-class citizens, subject to limitations of expression and behavior that show the public thinks the teacher of today is the nursemaid of yesterday. A teacher would be appointed because he was capable of independent thought and criticism and because he could help the rising generation learn to think for itself. He would be removed only if those who appointed him proved to be mistaken in these matters. The proof of their error would have to be made to persons who could understand the issue—an out-of-hand administrative removal approved by a board of laymen without participation by academic experts is a denial of academic freedom.

Academic Responsibility

The people of this country think that education is a perfectly splendid thing and have not the faintest idea of what it is about. The reason that they are in this condition is that educators have had no time and little inclination to explain. After all, the great desideratum of American education in the last thirty-five years has been money. If you want money, you do not talk about independent thought and criticism; you do not engage in it too obtrusively; you may even suppress it if it becomes too flagrant. To get money you must be popular. "He thinks too much" is a classical reference to an unpopular man. Or as a great industrialist once remarked to a friend of mine, "You are either a Communist or a thinker."

I have no doubt that much of the trouble of recent years about academic freedom has been the result of the cold war and our panic about it. As Professor Chafee has said, "Freedom of speech belongs to a people which is free from fear." But the basic issue is public understanding. If public understanding had been serious and complete, the cold war could not have thrown us off our balance.

I do not deny that many eloquent statements of the purpose of American education have been made. They cannot offset the impression created by the official propaganda of educational institutions, by their fatuous efforts to please everybody, and by their emphasis on the nonintellectual and even anti-intellectual activities associated with education in this country. Freedom of teaching and research will not survive unless the people understand why it should. They will not understand if there is no relation between the freedom that is claimed and the purpose it is supposed to serve. If the teacher of today is the nursemaid of yesterday, he does not need academic freedom—at least the nursemaid never did.

Academic freedom is indispensable to the high calling of the academic profession. If the profession is true to the calling, it will deserve the freedom, and it will get it.

A. E. HOUSMAN

Introductory Lecture[1]

The acquisition of knowledge needs no formal justification: its true sanction is a much simpler affair, and inherent in itself. People are too prone to torment themselves with devising far-fetched reasons: they cannot be content with the simple truth asserted by Aristotle: "all men possess by nature a craving for

[1] From A. E. Housman, *Introductory Lecture, Delivered . . . October 3, 1892* (1937), pp. 26-36. By permission of Cambridge University Press.

knowledge."πάντες ἄνθρωποι τοῦ εἰδέναι ὀρέγονται φύσει. This is no rare endowment scattered sparingly from heaven that falls on a few heads and passes others by: curiosity, the desire to know things as they are, is a craving no less native to the being of man, no less universal through mankind, than the craving for food and drink. And do you suppose that such a desire means nothing? The very definition of the good, says Aristotle again, is that which all desire. Whatever is pleasant is good, unless it can be shewn that in the long run it is harmful, or, in other words, not pleasant but unpleasant. Mr. Spencer himself on another subject speaks thus: "So profound an ignorance is there of the laws of life, that men do not even know that their sensations are their natural guides, and (when not rendered morbid by long continued disobedience) their trustworthy guides." The desire of knowledge does not need, nor could it possibly possess, any higher or more authentic sanction than the happiness which attends its gratification.

Perhaps it will be objected that we see, every day of our lives, plenty of people who exhibit no pleasure in learning and experience no desire to know; people, as Plato agreeably puts it, who wallow in ignorance with the complacency of a brutal hog. We do; and here is the reason. If the cravings of hunger and thirst are denied satisfaction, if a man is kept from food and drink, the man starves to death, and there is an end of him. This is a result which arrests the attention of even the least observant mind; so it is generally recognised that hunger and thirst cannot be neglected with impunity, that a man ought to eat and drink. But if the craving for knowledge is denied satisfaction, the result which follows is not so striking to the eye. The man, worse luck, does not starve to death. He still preserves the aspect and motions of a living human being; so people think that the hunger and thirst for knowledge can be neglected with impunity. And yet, though the man does not die altogether, part of him dies, part of him starves to death: as Plato says, he never attains completeness and health, but walks lame to the end of his life and returns imperfect and good for nothing to the world below.

But the desire of knowledge, stifle it though you may, is none the less originally born with every man; and nature does not implant desires in us for nothing, nor endow us with faculties in vain. "Sure," says Hamlet,

> Sure, He that made us with such large discourse,
> Looking before and after, gave us not
> That capability and godlike reason
> To fust in us unused.

The faculty of learning is ours that we may find in its exercise that delight which arises from the unimpeded activity of any energy in the groove nature meant it to run in. Let a man acquire knowledge not for this or that external and incidental good which may chance to result from it, but for itself; not because it is useful or ornamental, but because it is knowledge, and therefore good for man to acquire. "Brothers," says Ulysses in Dante, when with his old and tardy companions he had left Seville on the right hand and Ceuta on the other, and was come to that narrow pass where Hercules assigned his landmarks to hinder man from venturing farther: "Brothers, who through a hundred thousand dangers have reached the West, deny not, to this brief vigil of your senses that remains, experience of the unpeopled world behind the sunset. Consider of what seed ye are sprung: ye were not formed to live like brutes, but to follow virtue and knowledge." For knowledge resembles virtue in this, and differs in this from other possessions, that it is not merely a means of procuring good, but is good in itself simply: it is not a coin which we pay down to purchase happiness, but has happiness indissolubly bound up with it. Fortitude and continence and honesty are not commended to us on the ground that they conduce, as on the whole they do conduce, to material success, nor yet on the ground that they will be rewarded hereafter: those whose office it is to exhort mankind to virtue are ashamed to degrade the cause they plead by proffering such lures as these. And let us too disdain to take lower ground in commending knowledge: let us insist that the pursuit of knowledge, like the pursuit of righteousness, is part of man's duty to himself, and remember the Scripture where it is written: "He that refuseth instruction despiseth his own soul."

I will not say, as Prof. Tyndall has somewhere said, that all happiness belongs to him who can say from his heart "I covet truth." Entire happiness is not attainable either by this or by any other method. Nay it may be urged on the contrary that the pursuit of truth in some directions is even injurious to happiness, because it compels us to take leave of delusions which were pleasant while they lasted. It may be urged that the light shed on the origin and destiny of man by the pursuit of truth in some directions is not altogether a cheerful light. It may be urged that man stands to-day in the position of one who has been reared from his cradle as the child of a noble race and the heir to great possessions, and who finds at his coming of age that he has been deceived alike as to his origin and his expectations, that he neither springs of the high lineage he fancied, nor will inherit the vast estate he looked for, but must put off his towering pride, and contract his boundless hopes, and begin the world anew from a lower level: and this, it may be urged, comes of pursuing knowledge. But even conceding this, I suppose the answer to be that knowledge, and especially disagreeable knowledge, cannot by any art be totally excluded even from those who do not seek it. Wisdom, said Aeschylus long ago, comes to men whether they will or no. The house of delusions is cheap to build, but draughty to live in, and ready at any instant to fall; and it is surely truer prudence to move our furniture betimes into the open air than to stay indoors until our tenement tumbles about our ears. It is and it must in the long run be better for a man to see things as they are than to be ignorant of them; just as there is less fear of stumbling or of striking against corners in the daylight than in the dark.

Nor again will I pretend that, as Bacon asserts, "the pleasure and delight of knowledge and learning far surpasseth all other in nature." This is too much the language of a salesman crying his own wares. The pleasures of the intellect are notoriously less vivid than either the pleasures of sense or the pleasures of the affections, and therefore, especially in the season of youth, the pursuit of knowledge is likely enough to be neglected and lightly esteemed in comparison with other pursuits offering much stronger immediate attractions. But the pleasure of learning and knowing, though not the keenest, is yet the least perishable of pleasures; the least subject to external things, and the play of chance, and the wear of time. And as a prudent man puts money by to serve as a provision for the material wants of his old age, so too he needs to lay up against the end of his days provision for the intellect. As the years go by, comparative values are found to alter: Time, says Sophocles, takes many things which once were pleasures and brings them nearer to pain. In the day when the strong men shall bow themselves, and desire shall fail, it will be a matter of yet more concern than now, whether one can say "my mind to me a kingdom is"; and whether the windows of the soul look out upon a broad and delightful landscape, or face nothing but a brick wall.

Well then, once we have recognised that knowledge in itself is good for man, we shall need to invent no pretexts for studying this subject or that; we shall import no extraneous considerations of use or ornament to justify us in learning one thing rather than another. If a certain department of knowledge specially attracts a man, let him study that, and study it because it attracts him; and let him not fabricate excuses for that which requires no excuse, but rest assured that the reason why it most attracts him is that it is best for him. The majority of mankind, as is only natural, will be most attracted by those sciences which most nearly concern human life; those sciences which, in Bacon's phrase, are drenched in flesh and blood, or, in the more elegant language of the *Daily Telegraph*, palpitate with actuality. The men who are attracted to the drier and the less palpitating sciences, say logic or pure mathematics or textual criticism, are likely to be fewer in number; but they are not to suppose that the comparative unpopularity of such learning renders it any the less worthy of pursuit. Nay they may if they like console themselves with Bacon's observation that "this same *lumen siccum* doth parch and offend most men's watery and soft natures," and infer, if it pleases them, that their natures are less soft and watery than other men's. But be that as it may, we can all dwell together in unity without crying up our own pursuits or depreciating the pursuits of others on factitious grounds. We are not like the Ottoman sultans of old time, who thought they could never enjoy a moment's security till they had murdered all their brothers. There is no rivalry between the studies of Arts and Laws and Science but the rivalry of fellow-soldiers in striving which can most victoriously achieve the common end of all, to set back the frontier of darkness.

It is the glory of God, says Solomon, to conceal a thing: but the honour of kings is to search out a matter. Kings have long abdicated that province; and we students are come into their inheritance: it is our honour to search out the things which God has concealed. In Germany at Easter time they hide coloured eggs about the house and the garden that the children may amuse themselves in hunting after them and finding them. It is to some such game of hide-and-seek that we are invited by that power which planted in us the desire to find out what is concealed, and stored the universe with hidden things that we might delight ourselves in discovering them. And the pleasure of discovery differs from other pleasures in this, that it is shadowed by no fear of satiety on the one hand or of frustration on the other. Other desires perish in their gratification, but the desire of knowledge never: the eye is not satisfied with seeing nor the ear filled with hearing. Other desires become the occasion of pain through dearth of the material to gratify them, but not the desire of knowledge: the sum of things to be known is inexhaustible, and however long we read we shall never come to the end of our story-book. So long as the mind of man is what it is, it will continue to exult in advancing on the unknown throughout the infinite field of the universe; and the tree of knowledge will remain for ever, as it was in the beginning, a tree to be desired to make one wise.

Reading and Writing

Reading

❀❀❀❀❀❀❀❀❀❀❀❀❀❀❀❀❀❀❀❀❀❀❀❀❀❀❀❀❀❀❀❀

FRANCIS BACON

Of Studies[1]

Studies serve for delight, for ornament, and for ability. Their chief use for delight is in privateness and retiring; for ornament, is in discourse; and for ability, is in the judgment and disposition of business; for expert men can execute, and perhaps judge of particulars, one by one; but the general counsels, and the plots and marshaling of affairs come best from those that are learned. To spend too much time in studies is sloth; to use them too much for ornament is affectation; to make judgment wholly by their rules is the humor of a scholar. They perfect nature, and are perfected by experience; for natural abilities are like natural plants, that need pruning by study; and studies themselves do give forth directions too much at large, except they be bounded in by experience. Crafty men contemn studies, simple men admire them, and wise men use them; for they teach not their own use; but that is a wisdom without them and above them, won by observation. Read not to contradict and confute, nor to believe and take for granted, nor to find talk and discourse, but to weigh and consider. Some books are to be tasted, others to be swallowed, and some few to be chewed and digested; that is, some books are to be read only in parts; others to be read but not curiously, and some few to be read wholly, and with diligence and attention. Some books also may be read by deputy, and extracts made of them by others; but that would be only in the less important arguments and the meaner sort of books; else distilled books are, like common distilled waters, flashy things. Reading maketh a full man; conference a ready man; and writing an exact man. And, therefore, if a man write little, he had need have a great memory; if he confer little, he had need have a present wit; and if he read little, he had need have much cunning, to seem to know that he doth not. Histories make men wise; poets, witty; the mathematics, subtle; natural philosophy, deep; moral, grave; logic and rhetoric, able to contend; *Abeunt studia in mores.*[2] Nay, there is no stand or impediment in the wit but

---

1 From *The Essayes or Counsels, Civill and Morall* (enlarged ed., London, 1625), No. 50. The text has been somewhat modernized.
2 Studies form manners.

may be wrought out by fit studies; like as diseases of the body may have appropriate exercises. Bowling is good for the stone and reins, shooting for the lungs and breast, gentle walking for the stomach, riding for the head and the like. So if a man's wit be wandering, let him study the mathematics; for in demonstrations, if his wit be called away never so little, he must begin again. If his wit be not apt to distinguish or find differences, let him study the schoolmen; for they are *cymini sectores*.[3] If he be not apt to beat over matters, and to call up one thing to prove and illustrate another, let him study the lawyers' cases; so every defect of the mind may have a special receipt.

HAROLD TAYLOR

The Private World of the Man with a Book[1]

The temptation of the educator is to explain and describe, to organize a body of knowledge for the student, leaving the student with nothing to do. I have never been able to understand why educators do this so often, especially where books are concerned. Much of the time they force their students to read the wrong books at the wrong time, and insist that they read them in the wrong way. That is, they lecture to the students about what is in the books, reduce the content to a series of points that can be remembered, and, if there are discussions, arrange them to deal with the points.

Schools and colleges thus empty books of their true meaning, and addict their students to habits of thought that often last for the rest of their lives. Everything must be reduced to a summary, ideas are topic sentences, to read is to prepare for a distant test. This is why so many people do not know how to read. They have been taught to turn books into abstractions.

This goes against everything we know about what it means to read a book in real life, life, that is to say, which is uncorrupted by educational purpose. There is only one way to read a book, to give yourself up to it, alone, without instruction as to what you should be finding in it, without the necessity of making it into a series of points, but enjoying it, coming to know in personal terms what is in the mind of the writer. Only after that should there be discussion, criticism, comment by the educators. Otherwise education becomes too much like another kind of real life, the kind in which nobody reads the book, everyone reads the reviews, and everyone talks as if he knew the book.

The difficulty is that something happens to educators, and to other people, when they think or talk about education. They draw themselves to their full height and make large statements. They seem not to think that what applies to human experience in general may also apply to experience in schools and

[3] Dividers of cuminseed, i.e. hairsplitters.

[1] From *Saturday Review*, XLIV (January 7, 1961), 17-19. Reprinted by permission of the author and of *Saturday Review*.

colleges. They assume that there is something peculiar about education which demands that unless a book is read out of a sense of duty, as a piece of "material" to be "covered," in order for the reader to become "educated," it is not serving the cause of education.

Yet most of the most important experiences that truly educate cannot be aranged ahead of time with any precision. All the educator can do is to surround the student with a rich variety of intellectual and personal experience chosen with a view to quickening his mind and emotions into action. The ends are achieved by indirect means—something said in private conversation one day in the street, a remark by a teacher in the middle of a discussion, a book picked up in someone's room. When George Saintsbury was once asked how to interest the young in good literature, he replied, "Leave books around."

I grew up in a city that was culturally sterile, in a college whose curriculum lacked intellectual vitality. There were no little magazines, no experimental theatres, no dance groups, no philosophical movements, no strong views held, no centers of new effort. Those of us who were happy to know about Auden, Spender, MacNeice, Isherwood, Malraux, Faulkner, Hemingway, Melville, James, Dostoevsky, Tolstoy, Dewey, or Marx were quite rare, and we pursued our illicit reading without benefit of curriculum or librarians.

We read and talked in our rooms, in the newspaper office, in drugstores, and found the writers who meant most to us in little bookstores and reading rooms, where one person speaks of a book to another, where the books have been left around. In this way we learned what it was like to become so involved with an idea that sleep was impossible, or, to put it more broadly, to possess an intellectual life of our own. We did the educational things required of us, because that was what the educators wanted. We did them well, won prizes for them. But our real lives were elsewhere.

From that day to this I have never been able to understand why educators do not seize upon this truth and make it the center of their educational plans, make one life of the double lives which students lead. The heart of education, where books are concerned, is to get the student alone with a book, in a right state of mind.

Students are made to read more than they can ever enjoy, too little of too many things, in a way calculated to destroy personal involvement with the writer. The brighter the student, the more he is asked to read, until he develops prodigious skill in reading quickly and cleverly, for purposes of taking examinations and talking in discussions. Students are always reading to deadlines, in order to return books to the library, in order to answer questions and prove only that they have covered the ground. The educational system thus becomes a barrier to the creation by the student of a body of knowledge of his own.

True learning is not a matter of the formal organization of knowledge of books. It is a series of personal experiences. The written word makes public a state of mind; it transfers from private to public expression a set of ideas and facts that might otherwise remain unknown. For the writer, it is more than communication. It is the revelation, to oneself as writer, of things that have been hidden, now forced into expression.

On the other side, the side of the reader, it is the revelation of one person to another, a personal communication in an impersonal world. The reader in his true role is a private person, learning what another private person has to tell him. He may be seated in a library with a thousand others, but his way of knowing is by taking to himself the writer whose book he is reading. The teacher exists to get his students ready to read for and by themselves.

I would mark down as one of the physical barriers to the free flow of knowledge in the university and the American community, the absence of a sufficient number of intimate little bookshops and reading rooms where the librarian or the owner who loves books and knows what is in them has assembled a spread of inviting titles to capture the affection and involvement of the reader who comes as a welcome guest.

We will not have the atmosphere for learning or the true content of learning until we have teachers who themselves haunt the bookshops and who think of librarians as friends and companions in the pursuit of ideas rather than as clerks and custodians of book collections. Nor will we have the atmosphere for learning in our colleges and in our libraries unless we have librarians who work directly with teachers and students because they want to, and because they too are involved in the intellectual life of their own time.

My plea is for the restoration of the personal element in modern life and in modern education at a time when everything is pushing us into collective states of mind, when intellectuals huddle together in committees that issue reports in anonymous prose, when so many people are willing to strip themselves of their personal qualities in order to become clusters of approved characteristics.

It is a time when everybody talks and nobody listens. Instead, people exchange statements which each thinks will raise himself in the estimate of the other. Had we in the United States in recent months been listening to intelligent private persons in Cuba, Japan, Korea, Turkey, and elsewhere in Asian countries, we would have known that their best thinking and their deepest motivations were not of a kind that could respond to the policies which our government had designed for them and so innocently applied.

Most communications to the world by governments are calculated efforts at raising the level of impersonality and at concealment of the reality with which they are concerned. This habit of concealment in public speech has crept into private discourse and is seen, for example, in the loss of the old-fashioned habit of writing personal letters which are so honestly personal that they are not intended for eventual publication.

At another level, it has meant no longer asking our students for private essays each week which can give their teachers an understanding of who the student is and what are his honest thoughts, what are his weaknesses and inadequacies, what are his strengths, his needs, his hopes. Instead we seek for ways in which he can provide answers to questions he would never dream of asking, answers that merely reflect the demands we make upon him for information on topics of our choosing.

In the United States we justify our impersonality and lack of sensitivity to students by referring to the growing size of the student body, the excess of numbers of students who thus cannot be dealt with in personal ways, and we turn to technology for more devices to do the teaching for us. This is surely sensible where mechanical tasks, like keeping records, can be done mechanically, where films and television can bring the immediacy of the outside world into the school and college, or in cases where information is to be conveyed quickly and effectively.

But as far as the deeper aims of education are concerned, the problem is not how to distribute more information to larger numbers of students. That, as we have seen, is fairly easy to solve. You put more students into the same classes and pump the material in.

The question is: What intellectual, personal, and moral qualities are we developing in our students? What are they learning to care about? What are they doing with their lives?

It is as if we were deliberately turning back from the real problems, and keeping ourselves busy while we hope they will go away. We are asking not to know our students by what they say in writing or in speech, but to know whether or not they possess correct information as revealed in mechanical tests that can be graded like eggs, by nonhuman means.

What has happened is that many of the concepts of an American public-relations culture and the mass media have been transferred from the realm of business and industry into education, and the university has been organized not as a place where student talent is nurtured but as a bureaucracy for the dissemination of information. It has its own organization man, its own managerial class, its own habits of the market place by which the man with the largest amount of published academic prose commands the highest salary and receives the ultimate reward of the university—not to have to teach. With the combination of speeded-up sabbaticals, foundation grants, and continuous leaves of absence, the criterion of highest prestige for the university scholar will soon be that he is excused even from residence at the university and will be paid simply for the privilege of listing his name in the faculty roster. In the meantime, there are students.

We must teach these students and citizens the necessity of withdrawal into their own thoughts as a preparation for independent thinking and independent action. They must learn to feel their own emotions, not those that are considered culturally appropriate by the educational authorities or politically correct by their government. This is why the question of what books should be in the curriculum is one that should be decided, not by committees, but by teachers who themselves can enter into the experience of the young and feel with them the impulses of their own time, by teachers who know the responses the young are making to their own society.

Each generation has its own truth, its own private world, its own way of knowing, and we who are educators would be wise to listen to them for the knowledge they can bring. The young have the supreme advantage of not having been here before; they are not yet settled, they have almost no history and they can consider the world freshly (that is, they can and do when they talk to each other), and they test and retest the ideas that are old and known and reputable. They reject some, they revive and re-create others.

The comradeship of the young both sustains them in their own image of themselves and gives them the emotional sustenance they need for the independence of their lives. They live apart from us, they hold themselves back, and from the untouchable center of their personal lives they look distantly at our existence and our knowledge as items possessed by beings on a different planet. They are not what they seem to the professor who merely looks at the faces before him. He cannot be certain even of their attention, since they have learned how to occupy a classroom and look attentive while they take their minds elsewhere. He cannot be sure of their respect, since they have learned how to be quiet and how to act respectfully. The silence of the present generation has been in many ways deceptive, and it is false to assume that the silence has meant either consent or lack of creative and critical thought. They have played the system but have not been convinced of its claim to be believed in.

They are not to be presented with the familiar lists of the Great Books with an air of authority vested in the educators and the curriculum-makers. The students must be asked to determine for themselves which books are great, which ideas are viable, which values are compelling. To do otherwise is to use the familiar brand-name approach as a form of intellectual propaganda, like saluting the flag or bowing to royalty. It is to take the young through an educational tour of the museums of literature, to inspire a dutiful and pious attitude to authors rather than an attitude of expectancy and involvement.

If our aim is to create a vivid sense of awareness of the joy in learning and the satisfaction of intellectual mastery, we must trust the student to come away from his experience with the authors we ask him to read with ideas and convictions of his own. From the point of view of the student, every idea is inert until it comes alive in his consciousness. But first he must learn to read in personal terms, to invest himself in the reading, to bring something of his own to the book. If the books in his education are ill-chosen, or chosen chiefly on the basis of scholarly correctness, the student can bring almost nothing of himself to the enterprise, because what the author is saying corresponds to nothing in his lived experience. In order to learn how to expand that experience in imagination, to make links to the past and to cultures alien to his own, he must first learn how to come close to books and ideas themselves, he must have an experience with the immediacy of ideas. This involves a different way of choosing books for his education, and usually a sequence different from conventional chronology or historical periods.

If he reads, for example, in order to be able to tell an eighteenth-century rationalist from a nineteenth-century romantic, he may very well not be able to tell more than this, nor be able to enter into the experience of the writer whose work he is studying. Or he may simply be able to say to himself that he has read the best representatives of all the great periods in cultural history.

Whenever we take a writer out of his natural element, that is, treat him as other than a human being who is writing what he knows, we run the risk of destroying his value to the reader by making him represent a category of thought to which he has been assigned after the fact, usually after his death. In graduate schools, this unnatural treatment of writers leads to the continual preoccupation with tracing influences, classifying authors into categories, and otherwise drawing attention away from the writer himself. The writer must be allowed to stand on his own feet. Indeed, his greatness is established by the fact that he continues to stand on his own feet from generation to generation, and that he is perpetually rediscovered for himself and for what he has to say.

The student who is being educated is in fact discovering his own self and learning how to relate it to other selves. At its best, education is a series of private conversations in which all sham, pretense, and intellectual hypocrisy or name-dropping is stripped away and the student is free to respond with honesty to the intellectual and personal situation in which he finds himself. This is why it is so important to keep the student's situation as free of educational formalities as possible, to insist upon some version of the tutorial system, to resist all effort to build an impersonal administrative machine in place of a fascinating intellectual community, to assure that the student and the teacher are known to each other and that the student may thus benefit by the fact that his individuality is known, recognized, and respected.

For it is finally in the individual response of one person to another—whether through books or in person—that the heart of the matter rests.

IRWIN EDMAN

Unrequired Reading[1]

The title of this essay may strike you as a typographical error. You may be saying to yourself that the writer really means required reading, and the phrase conjures up for you, I suspect, lists distributed on the first days of college

[1] *Saturday Review*, XXXIII (November 4, 1950), 9-10, 36-38. Copyright, The Saturday Review Associates. Reprinted by permission of the author and the publisher.

courses: Volume One of this distinguished scholar's work on the Byzantine empire in the fourth century, that brochure on the economic interpretation of the Constitution, this pundit's principles of economics, that pedant's source book.

Or, perhaps, still under the apprehension that I mean required reading, you are reminded of what by now is one of the more maddening insolences of criticism, or at any rate of book reviewing. "This," says Mr. Notability, "is a *must* book." This in the atomic age is compulsory reading. In a world of anxiety this uneasy novel is not to be passed by.

I beg of you to forget such obligations and responsibilities. To this day you have to forget that you *had* to read "Macbeth" in order to begin to remember how perturbingly moving a play it is. Hardly anyone would reread Burke's "Speech on Conciliation" if he recalled how he had to make an abstract of it in high school. For one forgets the delight in the obligation, the eloquence in the remembered pressure. In one way or another even the nonprofessional reader reads from some felt or alleged obligation, some illusion of responsibility. He reads to know or to be in the know, to acquire a mature mind, to insure peace of soul, to understand what to do when the bomb drops, or when peace breaks out. We read because we feel we must know what's what, who is who, why is why. We read because in some way it seems compulsory to know Gide and Proust and Kafka and Sartre, because existentialism is being talked about, first in the small worlds of the little reviews, and then in the larger domains of the gossip columns, the digests, the library forums at the women's clubs.

In the sociology of our culture reading has, in so far as it has at all survived television and the comic strip, survived as a form of obligation. The student, the publisher, the editor, the scholar, even those, including the ladies who feel only the obligation to be *au courant, à la page,* or knowledgeable, read, for the most part, because they have to or think they have to. Not that anyone in any of these groups has necessarily actually read all that the mandarins of literate society expect or enjoin. At college even the most industrious or conforming of us did not do, as we used to put it, all the assigned reading, despite the ominous final examinations as reasons for doing so.

Nor as adults do we read all the books we are supposed to read. We compromise by reading with care the leading book reviews. For purposes of dinner-party conversation the latter method is not without its virtues. One's mind is not cluttered up with the actual details, one's imagination is not haunted by the actual flavor of the book, and one has a good lead and a good authority on what one is supposed to say and think. This obligation to read fashionable current works, to know this year's Hemingway and next year's Toynbee, to know —or to know about—cybernetics, all this makes it almost impossible even for those who have no professional commitments and concerns with books to retain the quality and status of amateurs and to read books for pleasure, to peruse a volume for pure enjoyment, to read not for food but for love.

The inability, including that of lack of time, to read for pleasure, is perhaps especially to be noticed among those whose professional concern *is* with books.

The student, the scholar, the teacher, the editor, the publisher all have to do a good deal of reading for special purposes, in special areas, for special reasons. Even when a student enjoys his required reading in a course he still has in mind, if only half consciously, his responsibilities to a teacher and to an examination. An advanced scholar may enjoy a new monograph in his own field, but he cannot read it simply as a delighted dilettante. The chances are that if it is by a rival scholar his delight would in any case not be unqualified. Even, or particularly, if it is good he may not like it. The brochure is an instrument in his work and also a challenge to his own hypotheses and standards of criticism. He is alerted for errors, inconsistencies, and exaggerations. Even if it is good he cannot read it merely as a pastime. And to the specialist there is usually no time to read books outside the specialty.

The editor and the publisher are in much the same dilemma, even the most imaginative editor, and the type of publisher—not, I am told, too current—who likes books even when he doesn't like authors. He may, like Maxwell Perkins, be adventurously alert for new talent. He may be solicitously on the lookout for genius, but in reading a manuscript he has to read with the hunter's eye, the collector's zeal, rather than with the freedom of pleasure.

And yet somehow reading for the love of it persists, both among those who have to deal with books all the time and among those who read largely to keep up with the Joneses intellectually or earnestly to know the best that is being said and thought in the contemporary world or because they feel they have fallen into a rut of illiteracy, what with the demands of their children, canasta, and television. The man or woman who has to read professionally steals time, sometimes late at night, to recover the youthful and delicious pleasure of reading for its own sake. He has just read a novel of lust and pillage in the Deep South, or of neurosis in Newtown, Conn. His eyes are tired and his mind dulled. And suddenly on his shelves he sees a volume of George Borrow, and he is off selling Bibles in Spain, meeting a liberal mayor in a provincial town, who releases him from arrest because he comes from the land of the great Jeremy Bentham. He picks up Jane Austen and is in the Grand Pump Room at Bath.

To what books does one turn, what pleasures does one rediscover when one is too tired or too indolent or too rebellious to read what one must? I remember as a college student being somewhat shocked to learn that Woodrow Wilson—and, what to me at the time was worse, John Dewey—turned for relaxation to detective stories. Since that time so many eminent persons, including my own valued colleagues, have turned to detective stories, too (and written treatises on their hobby), that I have ceased to be shocked, although I have not arrived at being converted. The detective stories that are simply puzzles seem to me weariness compounded, or those tricked out with a whimsy of culture, pure drivel. There are other avenues of literature to turn to more liberating and enchanting.

The curious fact is that quite difficult books are a relaxation and a pleasure, and complex tomes a delight when one has no immediate responsibility whatever for them. I discovered this very early as have thousands of those who began their reading young. For me the insight came in a branch library of the New York Public Library, where a librarian, Miss Lawrence by name, seeing me somewhat nearsightedly exploring the shelves, came to help me. "Are you looking for anything special?" she asked. Somewhat ashamed, I said that I was not. I was wandering in what to me was a fresh and wonderful wilderness. But I began to discover that there it was a well-organized forest, in which trees of the same family stood beside each other and which some forester had labeled with mystical numbers that indicated relationship. It was naturally the Eight Hundreds that I first wandered among. Even in a small branch library in 1910 New York there were a surprising number of books classified under literature. Close by were the biographies, and the number of novels and lives-and-times I read while I was in my early teens is astonishing to myself now that I look back on it. It is the endlessness of the number of books that both appealed to me and appalled me. At the same age when one has a good appetite physically in a parallel way one is stimulated by quantity in print, and frightened that one may cease to be before one has read everything. I think that was one of the things that impressed me about the novels of William de Morgan and Arnold Bennett, not to add Dickens and Thackeray. These were wonderful vast realms to enter into, to lose one's self in. It was here, too, that one discovered quite by accident, as Henry Adams said he discovered Beethoven by accident in a German beer garden, volumes of history and biography often simply by their title.

It is difficult to know what is so attractive about the title "The Rise of the Dutch Republic" or why it should fascinate a fourteen-year-old boy. "The Oregon Trail" was another matter; any American boy would have his mind stirred by any glance at a page of that stunning work of imaginative history. Next to quantity and variety was the joy of discovering things that because I had heard no one mention them came to me with the force of discovery. I think Hamlin Garland was for me a genuine find. I don't know that I had ever heard anyone refer to him and suddenly I came across a dusty brown book about dusty country. It was called "Main-Travelled Roads," and it gave me a sense of the Middle West more profound, accurate, and touching, I think, than I was to get from "Main Street" years later. Was it (I am quite certain it was) in the same library that I came across "Looking Backward"? It made me a Socialist at the age of fifteen and gave me my first boy's dream of Utopia. But, best of all, I discovered the books in the One Hundreds: philosophy, which dealt with first and last things (there was actually H. G. Wells's book by that title), and psychology, with its books on the working of the human mind. To this day I can never pass a branch library without a thrill of memory. This is where I learnt to read for pleasure and where I discovered the lineaments of nature and life.

I continued to learn thus in college, too, for it is in wandering around the shelves and later among the stacks that one acquires the sense that at almost

any random number of library classification one may run across something unexpected in the way of beauty and truth. For the pleasure in reading is far from
being that simply of nibbling literary hors d'oeuvres. De Quincey divided books
into those of knowledge and those of power, power over our hearts and imagination. But there are books of knowledge that have that power. There happened to be published in this country just at the time I was a freshman the
series of volumes written mostly by Britons called the Home University Library.
The little yellow volumes contained small masterpieces of exposition of important things, presented without either dullness or pomposity. Bertrand Russell's "Problems of Philosophy," Whitehead's "Introduction to Mathematics,"
Marett's "Anthropology"—all opened up vistas of unexplored possibility for
me, and from H. N. Brailsford's "Shelley, Godwin, and Their Circle" I got
more of a sense of the romantic movement in English poetry than from the
more pretentious works of scholarship I was asked to read. Not that the book
was better than those, but it was small, modest, intimate, and I had found it
for myself. On the reading lists were always books that were merely suggested,
and those seemed ever so much more inviting than those that were commanded. Conybeare's "Myth, Magic, and Morals"—I don't know whether it
was as good as it then seemed—but I am sure Fustel de Coulanges's "The
Ancient City" was.

As it turned out Fate or accident brought me into a life of professional dealing with books. I read them as a professional student of philosophy, I review
them as a professional reviewer, occasionally I read them in manuscript to tell
publishers with an intended mixture of shrewdness and academic responsibility
whether they are worth publishing for themselves or for profit or for both. But
all that reading I do not think really counts, not as entertainment, not as education. It is the unrequired reading one steals time for that is the reader's lifeblood.

The great thing about a book is having it in one's home like a medicine or
an analgesic, a stimulus or a soporific when the drugstores are all closed. Late at
night one's private library is like a medicine chest. One cannot tell what one
will be in the mood for or what one's spirit will most urgently crave. Or if the
analogy seems too medicinal, perhaps the refrigerator or the cookie jar will do.
Who knows when suddenly, late at night when libraries and bookstores are
tight shut, there will come into one's head the sudden passionate need to reread some Dickens? Or, if the truth be told, to read some of him for the first
time? Somewhere one day, in a critic I greatly respected, I found a paran-
thetic clause which said, " 'Our Mutual Friend,' which is, of course, Dickens's
masterpiece." I bridled a little at the "of course." I tried to think back to the
book itself and to my discomfiture I realized I had never read it. That night I
was happy that a year ago I had purchased a set of Dickens in big, clear type on
a spacious page. After about fifty pages I began to see the plausibility of the
easy dogmatism of my critical friend.

Again there may pop into one's head a passage which had bemused one

many years ago, like the opening chapter on the London fog in "Bleak House"
or the death of the Bishop's wife in Trollope's "Last Chronicles of Barset," that
definitive portrait of a dominating woman in whose death scene, at once ironic
and pathetic, one may find one of the places where it is impossible to condescend to Trollope. There are any number of books I should, I think, never
have read had I not prudently bought them against the time I should have the
time to read them, the letters of Edward Fitzgerald, for example, or those
of Lady Mary Wortley Montagu or Kilvert's Diary, the journal of that gifted
and obscure provincial English cleric whose tender and acute notes on life
and nature, and on his life and nature, came to light only a few years ago. And
there are works born to be read perennially like the essays of Emerson, the
sermons of Donne.

Raiding the icebox is not half so much fun as raiding one's shelves, and
sometimes one is surprised to find what books one has bought or received
through the kind (or calculated thoughtfulness) of some publisher heaven
knows when. When on earth and where did one pick up Henry James's "Notes
of a Son and Brother" with its emotions recollected from boyhood of New
York of a century ago? One recalls perhaps where one found "A Little Tour
in France." There is the familiar paper-covered Tauchnitz edition of prewar
memory found in a little bookshop at Nimes, along with other apparatus, like
guide-books for English-speaking tourists visiting the magical landscape of
Provence for the first time.

And that by a natural association leads me to consider the reading one has
done, not only unrequiredly but unexpectedly largely because of the distribu-
tive enterprise of American publishers. The twenty-five-cent, now more likely
the thirty-five-cent, book and the Modern Library found in small stationery
shops or drugstores in remote prairie towns—what a boon these are to the
traveler, how much they provide pleasure and enlightenment for hours that
would otherwise be fretfully or dully passed in airports or railway stations
waiting for delayed planes or trains. Often it is true that one can go through a
whole sheaf of reprints to find nothing save "Blood on the Moon" or "Thun-
derbird on the Trail," but, especially lately, the foraging is better. Sometimes,
because the choices worth consideration are few, one is happily constrained to
light upon something that is not exactly in the mood one had been looking
for but establishes another mood and opens another realm of gold or truth.
What I was hoping for one day, marooned for hours in Great Falls, Montana,
was a novel, say, by Virginia Woolf. What I found was George Gamow's "Life
and Death of the Sun," a book calculated to give one a more stable sense of
proportion, even of orientation on the Korean or any other crisis than could
the most comprehensive picture weekly or the most thorough review of the
week. These reprint series afford wonderful chances, at odd moments and at
minimal expense, to take a look—often at the outset a prejudiced look—at
books that have had an undignified popularity, and to discover that even if it
isn't true in the phrase of a once-famous advertising slogan that such popularity

must be deserved, at least there are reasons popularity is attained, reasons not altogether of high-pressure publicity.

I have written for the most part as if unrequired meant necessarily scattered or relatively trivial reading. There must be earnest souls among my readers who feel that it ought to be said that reading even for pleasure includes the pleasures of knowledge and of thought as well as those of imagination and of fancy. It does. I have been stressing the interest of the general or the common reader. But the general reader is with respect to specific fields always in some mild respect a specialist, even if only in the matter of taste; when Samuel Johnson used the term common reader he meant it as a compliment, and the common reader is often uncommonly serious in his literary pleasures. There are books of knowledge that give twin delights: first that of pleasure in exposition lucidly and persuasively done, and the larger joy of vision of the world—a wider and a more exact vision of the universe around us or some crucial, timely, or timeless aspect of it. There are volumes of the gravest history, the most severe speculative philosophy, poetry, the most concentrated and reflective, so long as they are read not because one feels one must fill in this gap in one's knowledge of medieval history or that hole in one's knowledge of the byways of metaphysics or that era or school of poetry. It is clear that the line between reading and study is not a sharp one. But there is a distinction. One does not just *read* Spinoza's "Ethics" (it is a work demanding the severest concentration) but also one does not always read late at night or when one is quite tired. It is possible to read for fun when one is full of energy and health, on a summer day at a mountain altitude, and on vacation, and it is at such times that such intellectually muscular exercise is a true pleasure. In music there are *divertimenti*, serenades, and bagatelles which are enjoyed simply for their delicious minor selves. In music, too, there are requiem masses, sonatas, and symphonies, and there are the late quartets of Beethoven that at least one serious writer has held to disclose whole other worlds or aspects of *our* whole world not expressible in any other way. Most of this article I have been discussing the *divertimenti* of literature. But there is no essential reason why the most demanding and profound of books should not provide along with the tension of effort the pleasures that one may, I think, without professional bias call philosophical.

The analogy with music is not merely fanciful. In music, too, especially when one is only half and dreamily listening or listening with the unthinking ear, it is in smaller incidental works that one may most acutely be aware of the delicacies of counterpoint and rhythms, of melody, color, and orchestration. But in listening to works on a scale grander both in size and in reference one is not listening simply to the surface of sounds but to the meaning and structure of a world, perhaps, as Schopenhauer thought, of *the* world. It is in the printed word and by way of it that these wider and more comprehensive delights, that the joys of contemplative insight as well as the athletic virtuosities of thought may be experienced. For centuries men have climbed mountains for the sheer arduous enterprising pleasure of it, as well as for the ultimate rewarding view. There are books the very reading of which by slow, ascending, total comprehension constitutes stringent but genuine joy. But to take Spinoza's "Ethics" again as an example. Through the careful mastery of it it comes to be enjoyable; the final joy is the achieved vision, the perspective opened upon the eternally glowing serenity that such a perspective yields.

I do not mean to imply that serious works in philosophy are always hard reading though they may demand, even to enjoy them as writing, intense and wakeful alertness. There is a spurious superstition, fortified I fear by the practice of many American scholars, that profound books must be difficult, that serious works must be written with awkward want of grace. It is true that nobody reads Aristotle's "Metaphysics" for its prose style nor, for that matter, works by John Dewey. But there is a long and splendid tradition in philosophy of books at once serious as to matter, distinguished and beguiling as to style; one has but to remember David Hume and Bishop Berkeley. There are in all conscience ultimate ambiguities about life and nature, but even the difficulties of understanding the world can be clearly stated, and it was Aristotle himself who suggested that to know anything was to be able to state it.

It therefore turns out that there are occasions in our reading when the joys of unrequired reading are matched by the profit of wisdom. Books read for pleasure turn out to be liberators of imagination, transmitters of insight, disclosures of life seen steadily and whole; books written out of the most serious concerns of existence turn out to be entrancing literature. There is an aftermath of Puritanism, of moral asceticism among us that makes us suspicious of reading done for the spontaneity or the devil of it. Especially in times of crisis (crisis now seems to have become the normal weather of the world) reading for fun seems to have the immorality of a holiday at the wrong time, an escape from things that urgently need doing. Such spare time as we have we are frequently asked to turn to useful reading. We must find out more about civil defense, about soil erosion, about the welfare or, as its opponents think, the illfare of the state. We need to be briefed at once concerning the history and culture of Korea. We have to know all about Indo-China, and now. Doubtless we do, if only to become armchair strategists.

But at the risk of being thrown to the Congressional Committees as a saboteur I would like to plead not only the intrinsic enjoyments but the timely social usefulness of unrequired reading. As we are often reminded (even at the wrong moment) there is slave labor in Russia. We need to beware lest, out of hysterical fear, we make standard among ourselves the habit of a slave labor of the mind. The freedom of joy, including the freedom to enjoy reading, the liberty for play of imagination, for roving over the whole domain of time and space and humanity—these will help keep freedom alive among us politically. It is not slaves who will be concerned about freedom, and it is only free minds that will keep the values of civilization fresh and growing among us. One of those values is the unrequired adventuring among books, the lifeblood of our civilization.

HENRY DAVID THOREAU

Reading[1]

With a little more deliberation in the choice of their pursuits, all men would perhaps become essentially students and observers, for certainly their nature and destiny are interesting to all alike. In accumulating property for ourselves or our posterity, in founding a family or a state, or acquiring fame even, we are mortal; but in dealing with truth we are immortal, and need fear no change nor accident. The oldest Egyptian or Hindoo philosopher raised a corner of the veil from the statue of the divinity; and still the trembling robe remains raised, and I gaze upon as fresh a glory as he did, since it was I in him that was then so bold, and it is he in me that now reviews the vision. No dust has settled on that robe; no time has elapsed since that divinity was revealed. That time which we really improve, or which is improbable, is neither past, present, nor future.

My residence was more favorable, not only to thought, but to serious reading, than a university; and though I was beyond the range of the ordinary circulating library, I had more than ever come within the influence of those books which circulate round the world, whose sentences were first written on bark, and are now merely copied from time to time onto linen paper. Says the poet Mîr Camar Uddîn Mast, "Being seated, to run through the region of the spiritual world; I have had this advantage in books. To be intoxicated by a single glass of wine; I have experienced this pleasure when I have drunk the liquor of the esoteric doctrines." I kept Homer's Iliad on my table through the summer, though I looked at his page only now and then. Incessant labor with my hands, at first, for I had my house to finish and my beans to hoe at the same time, made more study impossible. Yet I sustained myself by the prospect of such reading in future. I read one or two shallow books of travel in the intervals of my work, till that employment made me ashamed of myself, and I asked where it was then that I lived.

The student may read Homer or Æschylus in the Greek without danger of dissipation or luxuriousness, for it implies that he in some measure emulate their heroes, and consecrate morning hours to their pages. The heroic books, even if printed in the character of our mother tongue, will always be in a lan-

[1] From *Walden*, ed. by Norman Holmes Pearson, "Rinehart Editions" (New York: Holt, Rinehart and Winston, Inc., 1948), pp. 81-90. First printed in 1854.

guage dead to degenerate times; and we must laboriously seek the meaning of each word and line, conjecturing a larger sense than common use permits out of what wisdom and valor and generosity we have. The modern cheap and fertile press, with all its translations, has done little to bring us nearer to the heroic writers of antiquity. They seem as solitary, and the letter in which they are printed as rare and curious, as ever. It is worth the expense of youthful days and costly hours, if you learn only some words of an ancient language, which are raised out of the trivialness of the street, to be perpetual suggestions and provocations. It is not in vain that the farmer remembers and repeats the few Latin words which he has heard. Men sometimes speak as if the study of the classics would at length make way for more modern and practical studies; but the adventurous student will always study classics, in whatever language they may be written and however ancient they may be. For what are the classics but the noblest recorded thoughts of man? They are the only oracles which are not decayed, and there are such answers to the most modern inquiry in them as Delphi and Dodona never gave. We might as well omit to study Nature because she is old. To read well, that is, to read true books in a true spirit, is a noble exercise, and one that will task the reader more than any exercise which the customs of the day esteem. It requires a training such as the athletes underwent, the steady intention almost of the whole life to this object. Books must be read as deliberately and reservedly as they were written. It is not enough even to be able to speak the language of that nation by which they were written, for there is a memorable interval between the spoken and the written language, the language heard and the language read. The one is commonly transitory, a sound, a tongue, a dialect merely, almost brutish, and we learn it unconsciously, like the brutes, of our mothers. The other is the maturity and experience of that; if that is our mother tongue, this is our father tongue, a reserved and select expression, too significant to be heard by the ear, which we must be born again in order to speak. The crowds of men who merely *spoke* the Greek and Latin tongues in the Middle Ages were not entitled by the accident of birth to *read* the works of genius written in those languages; for these were not written in that Greek or Latin which they knew, but in the select language of literature. They had not learned the nobler dialects of Greece and Rome, but the very materials on which they were written were waste paper to them, and they prized instead a cheap contemporary literature. But when the several nations of Europe had acquired distinct though rude written languages of their own, sufficient for the purposes of their rising literatures, then first learning revived, and scholars were enabled to discern from that remoteness the treasures of antiquity. What the Roman and Grecian multitude could not *hear*, after the lapse of ages a few scholars *read*, and a few scholars only are still reading it.

However much we may admire the orator's occasional bursts of eloquence, the noblest written words are commonly as far behind or above the fleeting spoken language as the firmament with its stars is behind the clouds. *There* are

the stars, and they who can may read them. The astronomers forever comment on and observe them. They are not exhalations like our daily colloquies
and vaporous breath. What is called eloquence in the forum is commonly
found to be rhetoric in the study. The orator yields to the inspiration of a
transient occasion, and speaks to the mob before him, to those who can *hear*
him; but the writer, whose more equable life is his occasion, and who would
be distracted by the event and the crowd which inspire the orator, speaks to the
intellect and heart of mankind, to all in any age who can *understand* him.

No wonder that Alexander carried the Iliad with him on his expeditions in
a precious casket. A written word is the choicest of relics. It is something at
once more intimate with us and more universal than any other work of art. It
is the work of art nearest to life itself. It may be translated into every language,
and not only be read but actually breathed from all human lips;—not be represented on canvas or in marble only, but be carved out of the breath of life
itself. The symbol of an ancient man's thought becomes a modern man's
speech. Two thousand summers have imparted to the monuments of Grecian
literature, as to her marbles, only a maturer golden and autumnal tint, for they
have carried their own serene and celestial atmosphere into all lands to protect
them against the corrosion of time. Books are the treasured wealth of the
world and the fit inheritance of generations and nations. Books, the oldest and
the best, stand naturally and rightfully on the shelves of every cottage. They
have no cause of their own to plead, but while they enlighten and sustain the
reader his common sense will not refuse them. Their authors are a natural and
irresistible aristocracy in every society, and, more than kings or emperors, exert
an influence on mankind. When the illiterate and perhaps scornful trader has
earned by enterprise and industry his coveted leisure and independence, and is
admitted to the circles of wealth and fashion, he turns inevitably at last to
those still higher but yet inaccessible circles of intellect and genius, and is
sensible only of the imperfection of his culture and the vanity and insufficiency
of all his riches, and further proves his good sense by the pains which he takes
to secure for his children that intellectual culture whose want he so keenly
feels; and thus it is that he becomes the founder of a family.

Those who have not learned to read the ancient classics in the language in
which they were written must have a very imperfect knowledge of the history
of the human race; for it is remarkable that no transcript of them has ever been
made into any modern tongue, unless our civilization itself may be regarded
as such a transcript. Homer has never yet been printed in English, nor Æschylus, nor Virgil even,—works as refined, as solidly done, and as beautiful almost
as the morning itself; for later writers, say what we will of their genius, have
rarely, if ever, equalled the elaborate beauty and finish and the lifelong and
heroic literary labors of the ancients. They only talk of forgetting them who
never knew them. It will be soon enough to forget them when we have the
learning and the genius which will enable us to attend to and appreciate them.
That age will be rich indeed when those relics which we call Classics, and the

still older and more than classic but even less known Scriptures of the nations, shall have still further accumulated, when the Vaticans shall be filled with Vedas and Zendavestas and Bibles, with Homers and Dantes and Shakespeares, and all the centuries to come shall have successively deposited their trophies in the forum of the world. By such a pile we may hope to scale heaven at last.

The works of the great poets have never yet been read by mankind, for only great poets can read them. They have only been read as the multitude read the stars, at most astrologically, not astronomically. Most men have learned to read to serve a paltry convenience, as they have learned to cipher in order to keep accounts and not be cheated in trade; but of reading as a noble intellectual exercise they know little or nothing; yet this only is reading, in a high sense, not that which lulls us as a luxury and suffers the nobler faculties to sleep the while, but what we have to stand on tip-toe to read and devote our most alert and wakeful hours to.

I think that having learned our letters we should read the best that is in literature, and not be forever repeating our a-b-abs, and words of one syllable, in the fourth or fifth classes, sitting on the lowest and foremost form all our lives. Most men are satisfied if they read or hear read, and perchance have been convicted by the wisdom of one good book, the Bible, and for the rest of their lives vegetate and dissipate their faculties in what is called easy reading. There is a work in several volumes in our Circulating Library entitled "Little Reading," which I thought referred to a town of that name which I had not been to. There are those who, like cormorants and ostriches, can digest all sorts of this, even after the fullest dinner of meats and vegetables, for they suffer nothing to be wasted. If others are the machines to provide this provender, they are the machines to read it. They read the nine thousandth tale about Zebulon and Sophronia, and how they loved as none had ever loved before, and neither did the course of their true love run smooth,—at any rate, how it did run and stumble, and get up again and go on! how some poor unfortunate got up on to a steeple, who had better never have gone up as far as the belfry; and then having needlessly got him up there, the happy novelist rings the bell for all the world to come together and hear, O dear! how he did get down again! For my part, I think that they had better metamorphose all such aspiring heroes of universal noveldom into man weather-cocks, as they used to put heroes among the constellations, and let them swing round there till they are rusty, and not come down at all to bother honest men with their pranks. The next time the novelist rings the bell I will not stir though the meeting-house burn down. "The Skip of the Tip-Toe-Hop, a Romance of the Middle Ages, by the celebrated author of 'Tittle-Tol-Tan,' to appear in monthly parts; a great rush; don't all come together." All this they read with saucer eyes, and erect and primitive curiosity, and with unwearied gizzard, whose corrugations even yet need no sharpening, just as some little four-year-old bencher his two-cent gilt-covered edition of Cinderella,—without any improvement, that I can see, in the pronunciation, or accent, or emphasis, or any more skill in extracting or in-

serting the moral. The result is dulness of sight, stagnation of the vital circula-
tions, and a general deliquium and sloughing off of all the intellectual faculties.
This sort of gingerbread is baked daily and more sedulously than pure wheat
or rye-and-Indian in almost every oven, and finds a surer market.

The best books are not read even by those who are called good readers. What
does our Concord culture amount to? There is in this town, with a very few
exceptions, no taste for the best or for very good books even in English literature, whose words all can read and spell. Even the college-bred and so-called
liberally educated men here and elsewhere have really little or no acquaintance
with the English classics; and as for the recorded wisdom of mankind, the ancient classics and Bibles, which are accessible to all who will know of them,
there are the feeblest efforts anywhere made to become acquainted with them.
I know a woodchopper, of middle age, who takes a French paper, not for news
as he says, for he is above that, but to "keep himself in practice," he being a
Canadian by birth; and when I ask him what he considers the best thing he
can do in this world, he says, beside this, to keep up and add to his English. This
is about as much as the college-bred generally do or aspire to do, and they
take an English paper for the purpose. One who has just come from reading
perhaps one of the best English books will find how many with whom he can
converse about it? Or suppose he comes from reading a Greek or Latin classic
in the original, whose praises are familiar even to the so-called illiterate; he will
find nobody at all to speak to, but must keep silence about it. Indeed, there is
hardly the professor in our colleges, who, if he has mastered the difficulties of
the language, has proportionally mastered the difficulties of the wit and poetry
of a Greek poet, and has any sympathy to impart to the alert and heroic reader;
and as for the sacred Scriptures, or Bibles of mankind, who in this town can
tell me even their titles? Most men do not know that any nation but the
Hebrews have had a scripture. A man, any man, will go considerably out of
his way to pick up a silver dollar; but here are golden words, which the wisest
men of antiquity have uttered, and whose worth the wise of every succeeding age have assured us of;—and yet we learn to read only as far as Easy Reading, the primers and class-books, and when we leave school, the "Little Reading," and story-books, which are for boys and beginners; and our reading, our
conversation and thinking, are all on a very low level, worthy only of pygmies
and manikins.

I aspire to be acquainted with wiser men than this our Concord soil has produced, whose names are hardly known here. Or shall I hear the name of Plato
and never read his book? As if Plato were my townsman and I never saw him,
—my next neighbor and I never heard him speak or attended to the wisdom of
his words. But how actually is it? His Dialogues, which contain what was immortal in him, lie on the next shelf, and yet I never read them. We are underbred and low-lived and illiterate; and in this respect I confess I do not make
any very broad distinction between the illiterateness of my townsman who cannot read at all and the illiterateness of him who has learned to read only what

is for children and feeble intellects. We should be as good as the worthies of antiquity, but partly by first knowing how good they were. We are a race of tit-men, and soar but little higher in our intellectual flights than the columns of the daily paper.

It is not all books that are as dull as their readers. There are probably words addressed to our condition exactly, which, if we could really hear and understand, would be more salutary than the morning of the spring to our lives and possibly put a new aspect on the face of things for us. How many a man has dated a new era in his life from the reading of a book! The book exists for us, perchance, which will explain our miracles and reveal new ones. The at present unutterable things we may find somewhere uttered. These same questions that disturb and puzzle and confound us have in their turn occurred to all the wise men; not one has been omitted; and each has answered them, according to his ability, by his words and his life. Moreover, with wisdom we shall learn liberality. The solitary hired man on a farm in the outskirts of Concord, who has had his second birth and peculiar religious experience, and is driven as he believes into silent gravity and exclusiveness by his faith, may think it is not true; but Zoroaster, thousands of years ago, travelled the same road and had the same experience; but he, being wise, knew it to be universal, and treated his neighbors accordingly, and is even said to have invented and established worship among men. Let him humbly commune with Zoroaster then, and through the liberalizing influence of all the worthies, with Jesus Christ himself, and let "our church" go by the board.

We boast that we belong to the Nineteenth Century and are making the most rapid strides of any nation. But consider how little this village does for its own culture. I do not wish to flatter my townsmen, nor to be flattered by them, for that will not advance either of us. We need to be provoked,—goaded like oxen, as we are, into a trot. We have a comparatively decent system of common schools, schools for infants only; but excepting the half-starved Lyceum in the winter, and latterly the puny beginning of a library suggested by the State, no school for ourselves. We spend more on almost any article of bodily aliment or ailment than on our mental aliment. It is time that we had uncommon schools, that we did not leave off our education when we begin to be men and women. It is time that villages were universities, and their elder inhabitants the fellows of universities, with leisure—if they are, indeed, so well off—to pursue liberal studies the rest of their lives. Shall the world be confined to one Paris or one Oxford forever? Cannot students be boarded here and get a liberal education under the skies of Concord? Can we not hire some Abélard to lecture to us? Alas! what with foddering the cattle and tending the store, we are kept from school too long, and our education is sadly neglected. In this country, the village should in some respect take the place of the nobleman of Europe. It should be the patron of the fine arts. It is rich enough. It wants only the magnanimity and refinement. It can spend money enough on such things as farmers and traders value, but it is thought Utopian to propose spending money for things which more intelligent men know to be of far more worth. This town has spent seventeen thousand dollars on a town-house, thank fortune or politics, but probably it will not spend so much on living wit, the true meat to put into that shell, in a hundred years. The one hundred and twenty-five dollars annually subscribed for a Lyceum in the winter is better spent than any other equal sum raised in the town. If we live in the Nineteenth Century, why should we not enjoy the advantages which the Nineteenth Century offers? Why should our life be in any respect provincial? If we will read newspapers, why not skip the gossip of Boston and take the best newspaper in the world at once?—not be sucking the pap of "neutral family" papers, or browsing "Olive-Branches" here in New England. Let the reports of all the learned societies come to us, and we will see if they know anything. Why should we leave it to Harper & Brothers and Redding Co. to select our reading? As the nobleman of cultivated tastes surrounds himself with whatever conduces to his culture,—genius—learning—wit—books—paintings—statuary—music— philosophical instruments, and the like; so let the village do,—not stop short at a pedagogue, a parson, a sexton, a parish library, and three selectmen, because our Pilgrim forefathers got through a cold winter once on a bleak rock with these. To act collectively is according to the spirit of our institutions; and I am confident that, as our circumstances are more flourishing, our means are greater than the nobleman's. New England can hire all the wise men in the world to come and teach her, and board them round the while, and not be provincial at all. That is the *uncommon* school we want. Instead of noblemen, let us have noble villages of men. If it is necessary, omit one bridge over the river, go round a little there, and throw one arch at least over the darker gulf of ignorance which surrounds us.

LEONARD Q. ROSS

Mr. K*a*p*l*a*n and Shakespeare[1]

It was Miss Higby's idea in the first place. She had suggested to Mr. Parkhill that the students came to her class unaware of the *finer* side of English, of its beauty and, as she put it, "the glorious heritage of our literature." She suggested that perhaps poetry might be worked into the exercises of Mr. Parkhill's class. The beginner's grade had, after all, been subjected to almost a year of English and might be presumed to have achieved some linguistic sophistication. Poetry would make the students conscious of precise enunciation; it would

1 From *The Education of Hyman Kaplan*, by Leonard Q. Ross, pp. 129-140. Copyright, 1937, by Harcourt, Brace & World, Inc. Originally published in *The New Yorker*.

make them read with greater care and an ear for sounds. Miss Higby, who had once begun a master's thesis on Coventry Patmore, *loved* poetry. And, it should be said in all justice, she argued her cause with considerable logic. Poetry *would* be excellent for the enunciation of the students, thought Mr. Parkhill.

So it was that when he faced the class the following Tuesday night, Mr. Parkhill had a volume of Shakespeare on his desk, and an eager, almost an expectant, look in his eye. The love that Miss Higby bore for poetry in general was as nothing compared to the love that Mr. Parkhill bore for Shakespeare in particular. To Mr. Parkhill, poetry meant Shakespeare. Many years ago he had played Polonius in his senior class play.

"Tonight, class," said Mr. Parkhill, "I am going to try an experiment."

The class looked up dutifully. They had come to regard Mr. Parkhill's pedagogical innovations as part of the natural order.

"I am going to introduce you to poetry—great poetry. You see—" Mr. Parkhill delivered a modest lecture on the beauty of poetry, its expression of the loftier thoughts of men, its economy of statement. He hoped it would be a relief from spelling and composition exercises to use poetry as the subject matter of the regular Recitation and Speech period. "I shall write a passage on the board and read it for you. Then, for Recitation and Speech, you will give short addresses, using the passage as the general topic, telling us what it has brought to your minds, what thoughts and ideas."

The class seemed quite pleased by the announcement. Miss Mitnick blushed happily. (This blush was different from most of Miss Mitnick's blushes; there was aspiration and idealism in it.) Mr. Norman Bloom sighed with a businesslike air: you could tell that for him poetry was merely another assignment, like a speech on "What I Like to Eat Best" or a composition on "A Day at a Picnic." Mrs. Moskowitz, to whom any public performance was unpleasant, tried to look enthusiastic, without much success. And Mr. Hyman Kaplan, the heroic smile on his face as indelibly as ever, looked at Mr. Parkhill with admiration and whispered to himself: "Poyetry! Now is poyetry! My! Mus' be progriss ve makink awreddy!"

"The passage will be from Shakespeare," Mr. Parkhill announced, opening the volume.

An excited buzz ran through the class as the magic of that name fell upon them.

"Imachine!" murmured Mr. Kaplan. "Jakesbeer!"

"*Shake*speare, Mr. Kaplan!"

Mr. Parkhill took a piece of chalk and, with care and evident love, wrote the following passage on the board in large, clear letters:

> Tomorrow, and tomorrow, and tomorrow
> Creeps in this petty pace from day to day,
> To the last syllable of recorded time;

And all our yesterdays have lighted fools
The way to dusty death. Out, out, brief candle!
Life's but a walking shadow, a poor player
That struts and frets his hour upon the stage,
And then is heard no more; it is a tale
Told by an idiot, full of sound and fury,
Signifying nothing.

A reverent hush filled the classroom, as eyes gazed with wonder on this passage from the Bard. Mr. Parkhill was pleased at this.

"I shall read the passage first," he said. "Listen carefully to my enunciation—and—er—let Shakespeare's thoughts sink into your minds."

Mr. Parkhill read: " 'Tomorrow, and tomorrow, and tomorrow . . .' " Mr. Parkhill read very well and this night, as if some special fire burned in him, he read with rare eloquence. "Out, out, brief candle!" In Miss Mitnick's eyes there was inspiration and wonder. "Life's but a walking shadow . . ." Mrs. Moskowitz sat with a heavy frown, indicating cerebration. "It is a tale told by an idiot . . ." Mr. Kaplan's smile had taken on something luminous; but his eyes were closed: it was not clear whether Mr. Kaplan had surrendered to the spell of the Immortal Bard or to that of Morpheus.

"I shall—er—read the passage again," said Mr. Parkhill, clearing his throat vociferously until he saw Mr. Kaplan's eyes open. " 'Tomorrow, and tomorrow, and tomorrow. . . .' "

When Mr. Parkhill had read the passage for the second time, he said: "That should be quite clear now. Are there any questions?"

There were a few questions. Mr. Scymzak wanted to know whether "frets" was "a little kind excitement." Miss Schneiderman asked about "struts." Mr. Kaplan wasn't sure about "cripps." Mr. Parkhill explained the words carefully, and several illustrative uses of each word. "No more questions? Well, I shall allow a few minutes for you all to—er—think over the meaning of the passage. Then we shall begin Recitation and Speech."

Mr. Kaplan promptly closed his eyes again, his smile beatific. The students sank into that revery miscalled thought, searching their souls for the symbols evoked by Shakespeare's immortal words.

"Miss Caravello, will you begin?" asked Mr. Parkhill at last.

Miss Caravello went to the front of the room. "Da poem isa gooda," she said slowly. "Itsa have—"

"It *has.*"

"It hasa beautiful wordsa. Itsa lak Dante, Italian poet—"

"Ha!" cried Mr. Kaplan scornfully. "Shaksbeer you metchink mit Tante? *Shaksbeer?* Mein Gott!"

It was obvious that Mr. Kaplan had identified himself with Shakespeare and would tolerate no disparagement of his *alter ego.*

"Miss Caravello is merely expressing her own ideas," said Mr. Parkhill pacifically. (Actually, he felt completely sympathetic to Mr. Kaplan's point of view.)

"Hau Kay," agreed Mr. Kaplan, with a generous wave of the hand. "But to me is no comparink a high-cless man like Shaksbeer mit a Tante, dat's all."

Miss Caravello, her poise shattered, said a few more words and sat down.

Mrs. Yampolsky's contribution was brief. "This is full deep meanings," she said, her eyes on the floor. "Is hard for a person not so good in English to unnistand. But I like."

" 'Like!' " cried Mr. Kaplan with a fine impatience. " 'Like?' Batter love, Yampolsky. Mit Shaksbeer mus' be love!"

Mr. Parkhill had to suggest that Mr. Kaplan control his aesthetic passions. He did understand how Mr. Kaplan felt, however, and sensed a new bond between them. Mrs. Yampolsky staggered through several more nervous comments and retired.

Mr. Bloom was next. He gave a long declamation, ending: "So is passimistic ideas in the poem, and I am optimist. Life should be happy—so we should remember this is only a poem. Maybe is Shakespeare too passimistic."

"You wronk, Bloom!" cried Mr. Kaplan with prompt indignation. "Shaksbeer is passimist because is de life passimist also!"

Mr. Parkhill, impressed by this philosophical stroke, realized that Mr. Kaplan, afire with the glory of the Swan of Avon, could not be suppressed. Mr. Kaplan was the kind of man who brooked no criticism of his gods. The only solution was to call on Mr. Kaplan for his recitation at once. Mr. Parkhill was, indeed, curious about what fresh thoughts Mr. Kaplan would utter after his passionate defences of the Bard. When Mr. Parkhill had corrected certain parts of Mr. Bloom's speech, emphasizing Mr. Bloom's failure to use the indefinite article, he said: "Mr. Kaplan, will you speak next?"

Mr. Kaplan's face broke into a glow; his smile was like a rainbow. "Soitinly," he said, walking to the front of the room. Never had he seemed so dignified, so eager, so conscious of a great destiny.

"Er—Mr. Kaplan," added Mr. Parkhill, suddenly aware of the possibilities which the situation (Kaplan on Shakespeare) involved: "Speak carefully."

"Spacially careful vill I be," Mr. Kaplan reassured him. He cleared his throat, adjusted his tie, and began: "Ladies an' gantleman, you hoid all kinds minninks abot dis piece poyetry, an'—"

"Poetry."

"—abot dis piece poetry. But to me is a difference minnink altogadder. Ve mus' tink abot Julius Scissor an' how he falt!"

Mr. Parkhill moved nervously, puzzled.

"In dese exact voids is Julius Scissor sayink—"

"Er—Mr. Kaplan," said Mr. Parkhill once he grasped the full import of Mr. Kaplan's error. "The passage is from 'Macbeth.' "

Mr. Kaplan looked at Mr. Parkhill with injured surprise. "Not fromm 'Julius Scissor'?" There was pain in his voice.

"No. And it's—er—'Julius *Cae*sar.'"

Mr. Kaplan waited until the last echo of the name had permeated his soul. "Podden me, Mr. Pockheel. Isn't '*seezor*' vat you cottink somting op mit?"

"That," said Mr. Parkhill quickly, "is 'scissor.' You have used 'Caesar' for 'scissor' and 'scissor' for 'Caesar.'"

Mr. Kaplan nodded, marveling at his own virtuosity.

"But go on with your speech, please." Mr. Parkhill, to tell the truth, felt a little guilty that he had not announced at the very beginning that the passage was from "Macbeth." "Tell us *why* you thought the lines were from 'Julius Caesar.'"

"Vell," said Mr. Kaplan to the class, his smile assuming its normal serenity. "I vas positif, becawss I can *see* de whole ting." He paused, debating how to explain this cryptic remark. Then his eyes filled with a strange enchantment. "I see de whole scinn. It's in a tant, on de night bafore dey makink Julius de Kink fromm Rome. So he is axcited an' ken't slip. He is layink in bed, tinking: 'Tomorrow an' tomorrow an' tomorrow. How slow dey movink! Almost cripps! Soch a pity de pace!'"

Before Mr. Parkhill could explain that "petty pace" did not mean "Soch a pity de pace!" Mr. Kaplan had soared on.

"De days go slow, fromm day to day, like leetle tsyllables on phonograph racords fromm time."

Anxiety and bewilderment invaded Mr. Parkhill's eyes.

"'An' vat abot yestidday?' tinks Julius Scissor. Ha! 'All our yestiddays are only makink a good light for fools to die in de dost!'"

"'Dusty death' doesn't mean—" There was no interrupting Mr. Kaplan.

"An' Julius Scissor is so tired, an' he vants to fallink aslip. So he hollers, mit fillink, 'Go ot! Go ot! Short candle!' So it goes ot."

Mr. Kaplan's voice dropped to a whisper. "But he ken't slip. Now is bodderink him de idea fromm life. 'Vat is de life altogadder?' tinks Julius Scissor. An' he gives ensver, de pot I like de bast. 'Life is like a bum actor, strottink an' hollerink arond de stage for only vun hour bafore he's kicked ot. Life is a tale told by idjots, dat's all, full of fonny sonds an' phooey!'"

Mr. Parkhill could be silent no longer. "'Full of sound and fury!'" he cried desperately. But inspiration, like an irresistible force, swept Mr. Kaplan on.

"'Life is monkey business! It don' minn a ting. It signifies nottink!' An' den Julius Scissor closes his ice fest—" Mr. Kaplan demonstrated the Consul's exact ocular process in closing his "ice"—"an' falls dad!"

The class was hushed as Mr. Kaplan stopped. In the silence, a tribute to the fertility of Mr. Kaplan's imagination and the power of his oratory, Mr. Kaplan went to his seat. But just before he sat down, as if adding a postscript, he sighed: "Dat vas mine idea. But ufcawss is all wronk, becawss Mr. Pockheel said de voids ain't abot Julius Scissor altogadder. It's all abot an Irishman by de name Macbat."

Then Mr. Kaplan sat down.

It was some time before Mr. Parkhill could bring himself to criticize Mr. Kaplan's pronunciation, enunciation, diction, grammar, idiom, and sentence structure. For Mr. Parkhill discovered that he could not easily return to the world of reality. He was still trying to tear himself away from that tent outside Rome, where "Julius Scissor," cursed with insomnia, had thought of time and life—and philosophized himself to a strange and sudden death.

Mr. Parkhill was distinctly annoyed with Miss Higby.

Writing

F. L. LUCAS

What Is Style?[1]

When it was suggested to Walt Whitman that one of his works should be bound in vellum, he was outraged—"Pshaw!" he snorted, "—hangings, curtains, finger bowls, chinaware, Matthew Arnold!" And he might have been equally irritated by talk of style; for he boasted of "my barbaric yawp"—he would *not* be literary; his readers should touch not a book but a man. Yet Whitman took the pains to rewrite *Leaves of Grass* four times, and his style is unmistakable. Samuel Butler maintained that writers who bothered about their style became unreadable but he bothered about his own. "Style" has got a bad name by growing associated with precious and superior persons who, like Oscar Wilde, spend a morning putting in a comma, and the afternoon (so he said) taking it out again. But such abuse of "style" is misuse of English. For the word means merely "a way of expressing oneself, in language, manner, or appearance"; or, secondly, "a *good* way of so expressing oneself"—as when one says, "Her behavior never lacked style."

Now there is no crime in expressing oneself (though to try to *im*press oneself on others easily grows revolting or ridiculous). Indeed one cannot help expressing oneself, unless one passes one's life in a cupboard. Even the most rigid Communist, or Organization-man, is compelled by Nature to have a unique voice, unique fingerprints, unique handwriting. Even the signatures of the letters on your breakfast table may reveal more than their writers guess. There are blustering signatures that swish across the page like cornstalks bowed before a tempest. There are cryptic signatures, like a scrabble of lightning across

[1] From *Holiday*, XXVII (March, 1960), 11 *et passim*. Reprinted by permission of the author.

a cloud, suggesting that behind is a lofty divinity whom all must know, or an aloof divinity whom none is worthy to know (though, as this might be highly inconvenient, a docile typist sometimes interprets the mystery in a bracket underneath). There are impetuous squiggles implying that the author is a sort of strenuous Sputnik streaking round the globe every eighty minutes. There are florid signatures, all curlicues and danglements and flamboyance, like the youthful Disraeli (though these seem rather out of fashion). There are humble, humdrum signatures. And there are also, sometimes, signatures that are courteously clear, yet mindful of a certain simple grace and artistic economy —in short, of style.

Since, then, not one of us can put pen to paper, or even open his mouth, without giving something of himself away to shrewd observers, it seems mere common sense to give the matter a little thought. Yet it does not seem very common. Ladies may take infinite pains about having style in their clothes, but many of us remain curiously indifferent about having it in our words. How many women would dream of polishing not only their nails but also their tongues? They may play freely on that perilous little organ, but they cannot often be bothered to tune it. And how many men think of improving their talk as well as their golf handicap?

No doubt strong silent men, speaking only in gruff monosyllables, may despise "mere words." No doubt the world does suffer from an endemic plague of verbal dysentery. But that, precisely, is bad style. And consider the amazing power of mere words. Adolf Hitler was a bad artist, bad statesman, bad general, and bad man. But largely because he could tune his rant, with psychological nicety, to the exact wave length of his audiences and make millions quarrelsome-drunk all at the same time by his command of windy nonsense, skilled statesmen, soldiers, scientists were blown away like chaff, and he came near to rule the world. If Sir Winston Churchill had been a mere speechifier, we might well have lost the war; yet his speeches did quite a lot to win it.

No man was less of a literary aesthete than Benjamin Franklin; yet this tallow-chandler's son, who changed world history, regarded as "a principal means of my advancement" that pungent style which he acquired partly by working in youth over old *Spectators*; but mainly by being Benjamin Franklin. The squinting demagogue, John Wilkes, as ugly as his many sins, had yet a tongue so winning that he asked only half an hour's start (to counteract his face) against any rival for a woman's favor. "Vote for you!" growled a surly elector in his constituency. "I'd sooner vote for the devil!" "But in case your friend should not stand . . . ?" Cleopatra, that ensnarer of world conquerors, owed less to the shape of her nose than to the charm of her tongue. Shakespeare himself has often poor plots and thin ideas; even his mastery of character has been questioned; what does remain unchallenged is his verbal magic. Men are often taken, like rabbits, by the ears. And though the tongue has no bones, it can sometimes break millions of them.

"But," the reader may grumble, "I am neither Hitler, Cleopatra, nor Shakespeare. What is all this to me?" Yet we all talk—often too much; we all have to write letters—often too many. We live not by bread alone but also by words. And not always with remarkable efficiency. Strikes, lawsuits, divorces, all sorts of public nuisance and private misery, often come just from the gaggling incompetence with which we express ourselves. Americans and British get at cross-purposes because they use the same words with different meanings. Men have been hanged on a comma in a statute. And in the valley of Balaclava a mere verbal ambiguity, about *which* guns were to be captured, sent the whole Light Brigade to futile annihilation.

Words can be more powerful, and more treacherous, than we sometimes suspect; communication more difficult than we may think. We are all serving life sentences of solitary confinement within our own bodies; like prisoners, we have, as it were, to tap in awkward code to our fellow men in their neighboring cells. Further, when A and B converse, there take part in their dialogue not two characters, as they suppose, but six. For there is A's real self—call it A_1; there is also A's picture of himself—A_2; there is also B's picture of A—A_3. And there are three corresponding personalities of B. With six characters involved even in a simple tête-à-tête, no wonder we fall into muddles and misunderstandings.

Perhaps, then, there are five main reasons for trying to gain some mastery of language:

We have no other way of understanding, informing, misinforming, or persuading one another.

Even alone, we think mainly in words; if our language is muddy, so will our thinking be.

By our handling of words we are often revealed and judged. "Has he written anything?" said Napoleon of a candidate for an appointment. "Let me see his *style*."

Without a feeling for language one remains half-blind and deaf to literature.

Our mother tongue is bettered or worsened by the way each generation uses it. Languages evolve like species. They can degenerate; just as oysters and barnacles have lost their heads. Compare ancient Greek with modern. A heavy responsibility, though often forgotten.

Why and how did I become interested in style? The main answer, I suppose, is that I was born that way. Then I was, till ten, an only child running loose in a house packed with books, and in a world (thank goodness) still undistracted by radio and television. So at three I groaned to my mother, "Oh, I *wish* I could read," and at four I read. Now travel among books is the best travel of all, and the easiest, and the cheapest. (Not that I belittle ordinary travel—which I regard as one of the three main pleasures in life.) One learns to write by reading good books, as one learns to talk by hearing good talkers. And if I have learned anything of writing, it is largely from writers like Montaigne, Dorothy Osborne, Horace Walpole, Johnson, Goldsmith, Montesquieu, Voltaire, Flaubert and

Anatole France. Again, I was reared on Greek and Latin, and one can learn much from translating Homer or the Greek Anthology, Horace or Tacitus, if one is thrilled by the originals and tries, however vainly, to recapture some of that thrill in English.

But at Rugby I could *not* write English essays. I believe it stupid to torment boys to write on topics that they know and care nothing about. I used to rush to the school library and cram the subject, like a python swallowing rabbits; then, still replete as a postprandial python, I would tie myself in clumsy knots to embrace those accursed themes. Bacon was wise in saying that reading makes a full man; talking, a ready one; writing, an exact one. But writing from an empty head is futile anguish.

At Cambridge, my head having grown a little fuller, I suddenly found I *could* write—not with enjoyment (it is always tearing oneself in pieces)—but fairly fluently. Then came the War of 1914-18; and though soldiers have other things than pens to handle, they learn painfully to be clear and brief. Then the late Sir Desmond MacCarthy invited me to review for the *New Statesman*; it was a useful apprenticeship, and he was delightful to work for. But I think it was well after a few years to stop; reviewers remain essential, but there are too many books one *cannot* praise, and only the pugnacious enjoy amassing enemies. By then I was an ink-addict—not because writing is much pleasure, but because not to write is pain; just as some smokers do not so much enjoy tobacco as suffer without it. The positive happiness of writing comes, I think, from work when done—decently, one hopes, and not without use—and from the letters of readers which help to reassure, or delude, one that so it is.

But one of my most vivid lessons came, I think, from service in a war department during the Second War. Then, if the matter one sent out was too wordy, the communication channels might choke; yet if it was not absolutely clear, the results might be serious. So I emerged, after six years of it, with more passion than ever for clarity and brevity, more loathing than ever for the obscure and the verbose.

For forty years at Cambridge I have tried to teach young men to write well, and have come to think it impossible. To write really well is a gift inborn; those who have it teach themselves; one can only try to help and hasten the process. After all, the uneducated sometimes express themselves far better than their "betters." In language, as in life, it is possible to be perfectly correct—and yet perfectly tedious, or odious. The illiterate last letter of the doomed Vanzetti was more moving than most professional orators; 18th Century ladies, who should have been spanked for their spelling, could yet write far better letters than most professors of English; and the talk of Synge's Irish peasants seems to me vastly more vivid than the later style of Henry James. Yet Synge averred that his characters owed far less of their eloquence to what he invented for them than to what he had overheard in the cottages of Wicklow and Kerry:

"*Christy.* 'It's little you'll think if my love's a poacher's, or an earl's itself, when you'll feel my two hands stretched around you, and I squeezing kisses on your puckered lips, till I'd feel a kind of pity for the Lord God is all ages sitting lonesome in His golden chair.'

"*Pegeen.* 'That'll be right fun, Christy Mahon, and any girl would walk her heart out before she'd meet a young man was your like for eloquence, or talk at all.' "

Well she might! It's not like that they talk in universities—more's the pity.

But though one cannot teach people to write well, one can sometimes teach them to write rather better. One can give a certain number of hints, which often seem boringly obvious—only experience shows they are not.

One can say: Beware of pronouns—they are devils. Look at even Addison, describing the type of pedant who chatters of style without having any: "Upon enquiry I found my learned friend had dined that day with Mr. Swan, the famous punster; and desiring *him* to give me some account of Mr. Swan's conversation, *he* told me that *he* generally talked in the Paronomasia, that *he* sometimes gave in to the Plocé, but that in *his* humble opinion *he* shone most in the Antanaclasis." What a sluttish muddle of *he* and *him* and *his!* It all needs rewording. Far better repeat a noun, or a name, than puzzle the reader, even for a moment, with ambiguous pronouns. Thou shalt not puzzle thy reader.

Or one can say: Avoid jingles. The B.B.C. news bulletins seem compiled by earless persons, capable of crying round the globe: "The enemy is re*port*ed to have seized this im*port*ant *port*, and reinforcements are hurrying up in sup*port*." Any fool, once told, can hear such things to be insupportable.

Or one can say: Be sparing with relative clauses. Don't string them together like sausages, or jam them inside one another like Chinese boxes or the receptacles of Buddhas' tooth. Or one can say: Don't flaunt jargon, like Addison's Mr. Swan, or the type of modern critic who gurgles more technical terms in a page than Johnson used in all his *Lives* or Sainte-Beuve in thirty volumes. But dozens of such snippety precepts, though they may sometimes save people from writing badly, will help them little toward writing well. Are there no general rules of a more positive kind, and of more positive use?

Perhaps. There *are* certain basic principles which seem to me observed by many authors I admire, which I think have served me and which may serve others. I am not talking of geniuses, who are a law to themselves (and do not always write a very good style, either); nor of poetry, which has different laws from prose; nor of poetic prose, like Sir Thomas Browne's or DeQuincey's, which is often more akin to poetry; but of the plain prose of ordinary books and documents, letters and talk.

The writer should respect truth and himself; therefore honesty. He should respect his readers; therefore courtesy. These are two of the cornerstones of style. Confucius saw it, twenty-five centuries ago: "The Master said, The gentleman is courteous, but not pliable: common men are pliable, but not courteous."

First, honesty. In literature, as in life, one of the fundamentals is to find, and be, one's true self. One's true self may indeed be unpleasant (though one can try to better it); but a false self, sooner or later, becomes disgusting—just as a nice plain woman, painted to the eyebrows, can become horrid. In writing, in the long run, pretense does not work. As the police put it, anything you say may be used as evidence against you. If handwriting reveals character, writing reveals it still more. You cannot fool *all* your judges *all* the time.

Most style is not honest enough. Easy to say, but hard to practice. A writer may take to long words, as young men to beards—to impress. But long words, like long beards, are often the badge of charlatans. Or a writer may cultivate the obscure, to seem profound. But even carefully muddied puddles are soon fathomed. Or he may cultivate eccentricity, to seem original. But really original people do not have to think about being original—they can no more help it than they can help breathing. They do not need to dye their hair green. The fame of Meredith, Wilde or Bernard Shaw might now shine brighter, had they struggled less to be brilliant; whereas Johnson remains great, not merely because his gifts were formidable but also because, with all his prejudice and passion, he fought no less passionately to "clear his mind of cant."

Secondly, courtesy—respect for the reader. From this follow several other basic principles of style. Clarity is one. For it is boorish to make your reader rack his brains to understand. One should aim at being impossible to misunderstand—though men's capacity for misunderstanding approaches infinity. Hence Molière and Po Chu-i tried their work on their cooks; and Swift his on his menservants—"which, if they did not comprehend, he would alter and amend, until they understood it perfectly." Our bureaucrats and pundits, unfortunately, are less considerate.

Brevity is another basic principle. For it is boorish, also, to waste your reader's time. People who would not dream of stealing a penny of one's money turn not a hair at stealing hours of one's life. But that does not make them less exasperating. Therefore there is no excuse for the sort of writer who takes as long as a marching army corps to pass a given point. Besides, brevity is often more effective; the half can say more than the whole, and to imply things may strike far deeper than to state them at length. And because one is particularly apt to waste words on preambles before coming to the substance, there was sense in the Scots professor who always asked his pupils—"Did ye remember to tear up that fir-r-st page?"

Here are some instances that would only lose by lengthening:

It is useless to go to bed to save the light, if the result is twins. (Chinese proverb.)

My barn is burnt down—

Nothing hides the moon. (Complete Japanese poem.)

Je me regrette. (Dying words of the gay Vicomtesse d'Houdetot.)

I have seen their backs before. (Wellington, when French marshals turned their backs on him at a reception.)

Continue until the tanks stop, then get out and walk. (Patton to the Twelfth Corps, halted for fuel supplies at St. Dizier, 8/30/44.)

Or there is the most laconic diplomatic note on record: when Philip of Macedon wrote to the Spartans that, if he came within their borders, he would leave not one stone of their city, they wrote back the one word—"If."

Clarity comes before even brevity. But it is a fallacy that wordiness is necessarily clearer. Metternich when he thought something he had written was obscure would simply go through it crossing out everything irrelevant. What remained, he found, often became clear. Wellington, asked to recommend three names for the post of Commander-in-Chief, India, took a piece of paper and wrote three times—"Napier." Pages could not have been clearer—or as forcible. On the other hand the lectures, and the sentences, of Coleridge became at times bewildering because his mind was often "wiggle-waggle"; just as he could not even walk straight on a path.

But clarity and brevity, though a good beginning, are only a beginning. By themselves, they may remain bare and bleak. When Calvin Coolidge, asked by his wife what the preacher had preached on, replied "Sin," and, asked what the preacher had said, replied, "He was against it," he was brief enough. But one hardly envies Mrs. Coolidge.

An attractive style requires, of course, all kinds of further gifts—such as variety, good humor, good sense, vitality, imagination. Variety means avoiding monotony of rhythm, of language, of mood. One needs to vary one's sentence length (this present article has too many short sentences; but so vast a subject grows here as cramped as a djin in a bottle); to amplify one's vocabulary; to diversify one's tone. There are books that petrify one throughout, with the rigidly pompous solemnity of an owl perched on a leafless tree. But ceaseless facetiousness can be as bad; or perpetual irony. Even the smile of Voltaire can seem at times a fixed grin, a disagreeable wrinkle. Constant peevishness is far worse, as often in Swift; even on the stage too much irritable dialogue may irritate an audience, without its knowing why.

Still more are vitality, energy, imagination gifts that must be inborn before they can be cultivated. But under the head of imagination two common devices may be mentioned that have been the making of many a style—metaphor and simile. Why such magic power should reside in simply saying, or implying, that A is like B remains a little mysterious. But even our unconscious seems to love symbols; again, language often tends to lose itself in clouds of vaporous abstraction, and simile or metaphor can bring it back to concrete solidity; and, again, such imagery can gild the gray flats of prose with sudden sun-glints of poetry.

If a foreigner may for a moment be impertinent, I admire the native gift of Americans for imagery as much as I wince at their fondness for slang. (Slang seems to me a kind of linguistic fungus; as poisonous, and as short-lived, as toad-stools.) When Matthew Arnold lectured in the United States, he was likened by one newspaper to "an elderly macaw pecking at a trellis of grapes"; he observed, very justly, "How lively journalistic fancy is among the Americans!" General Grant, again, unable to hear him, remarked: "Well, wife, we've paid to see the British lion, but as we can't hear him roar, we'd better go home." By simile and metaphor, these two quotations bring before us the slightly pompous, fastidious, inaudible Arnold as no direct description could have done.

Or consider how language comes alive in the Chinese saying that lending to the feckless is "like pelting a stray dog with dumplings," or in the Arab proverb: "They came to shoe the pasha's horse, and the beetle stretched forth his leg"; in the Greek phrase for a perilous cape—"stepmother of ships"; or the Hebrew adage that "as the climbing up a sandy way is to the feet of the aged, so is a wife full of words to a quiet man"; in Shakespeare's phrase for a little England lost in the world's vastness—"in a great Poole, a Swan's-nest"; or Fuller's libel on tall men—"Ofttimes such who are built four stories high are observed to have little in their cockloft"; in Chateaubriand's "I go yawning my life"; or in Jules Renard's portrait of a cat, "well buttoned in her fur." Or, to take a modern instance, there is Churchill on dealings with Russia: "Trying to maintain good relations with a Communist is like wooing a crocodile. You do not know whether to tickle it under the chin or beat it over the head. When it opens its mouth, you cannot tell whether it is trying to smile or preparing to eat you up." What a miracle human speech can be, and how dull is most that one hears! Would one hold one's hearers, it is far less help, I suspect, to read manuals on style than to cultivate one's own imagination and imagery.

I will end with two remarks by two wise old women of the civilized 18th Century.

The first is from the blind Mme. du Deffand (the friend of Horace Walpole) to that Mlle. de Lespinasse with whom, alas, she was to quarrel so unwisely: "You must make up your mind, my queen, to live with me in the greatest truth and sincerity. You will be charming so long as you let yourself be natural, and remain without pretension and without artifice." The second is from Mme. de Charrière, the Zélide whom Boswell had once loved at Utrecht in vain, to a Swiss girl friend: "Lucinde, my clever Lucinde, while you wait for the Romeos to arrive, you have nothing better to do than become perfect. Have ideas that are clear, and expressions that are simple." ("Ayez des idées nettes et des expressions simples.") More than half the bad writing in the world, I believe, comes from neglecting those two very simple pieces of advice.

In many ways, no doubt, our world grows more and more complex; sputniks cannot be simple; yet how many of our complexities remain futile, how many of our artificialities false. Simplicity too can be subtle—as the straight lines of a Greek temple, like the Parthenon at Athens, are delicately curved, in order to look straighter still.

MORTON W. BLOOMFIELD

The Problem of Fact and Value
in the Teaching of English [1]

The increase of accurate knowledge about the history of the English language and of linguistic processes in general during the last hundred years has begun only recently to have its impact upon the teaching of English, and especially of grammar, in the schools. Greater and more accurate knowledge is bound to affect the attitudes toward and the aims of any academic subject as well as its content. It is therefore proper to consider just what changes are called for in the teaching of English on the basis of our enlarged knowledge.

Some linguists in America during the last two decades have become exercised over the traditional prescriptionist attitude toward grammar which has long been one of the chief factors contributing to the conviction held by a vast majority of Americans that the "rules" of grammar are laws, in the same sense as the regularities of nature were laws in nineteenth-century eyes, or moral imperatives on a level with the Ten Commandments. Some, in disgust, have been led to the extreme of suggesting that "anything goes," that one should leave one's language alone, and that all teaching of English should be confined to a description of the state of the language or to its history. Very recently, in American cultural and literary journals, there have been disputes between these ardent linguists and those who favor some kind of prescriptionist approach. At the same time, one hears over and over again, in the teaching and other professions, the wail that young people do not know how to read and write their own language.

Embedded in these disputes and complaints is a philosophic problem of the first magnitude of which many participants do not seem to be aware—the relation of fact to value. In the background are tacit assumptions about this relationship which, if they cannot be simply solved, should at least be thrust into the light. The purpose of this article is to point up some of these basic issues in their bearing on the teaching of English in the schools.

The problem of what to teach to youngsters in English is first of all a question of value not of fact. As Professor Northrop has written: "The characteristic of a problem of value . . . is that, in part at least, it raises a question concerning what ought to be, rather than what is, the case." [2] The question of the relation of fact to value is an exceedingly complex one. That facts have some bearing on value is clear. What man ought to do is at least limited by what he

[1] From *College English*, XV (October, 1953), 33-37. Reprinted by permission of the author and of the Editors of *College English*.
[2] *The Logic of the Sciences and the Humanities* (New York, 1947), p. 20.

is; the values set up or discovered cannot violate his nature. On the other hand, the mere presence of certain facts does not make them valuable. Possibly more than 50 per cent of humanity desire to steal, at least on occasion, but this "fact" does not mean that stealing is a value. When Hegel wrote that whatever is is right, what he meant was that everything has a reason, that is, is capable of rational explanation. He did not necessarily approve of whatever is. Some social scientists and linguists, however, follow Hegel's dictum to the letter.

The problem of value impinges on the science of linguistics on various levels, but it is not my intention here to discuss the general philosophical issues involved but to limit myself to their bearing on the subject of teaching English. There is, for example, the problem of value involved in the very subject matter of the science. The question of what language is must be answered, implicitly or explicitly, before the subject matter of linguistics can be properly delimited and understood. This involves general values, but they shall not be my concern here.[3] I shall start with the assumption—not completely agreed upon—that we know what language is and what its facts are.

In relation to the teaching of English the question of what ought to be taught about the language to students cannot be completely answered by a knowledge of the facts of the language (or by linguists as linguists), because, first, value questions are never completely answered by the facts and, second, facts and values from areas other than language must be taken into consideration. Furthermore, the aim of education is not a linguistic question.

In order to decide what ought to be taught in elementary English classes, we not only have to find out what are the facts of language but what are the facts of society and man, problems which are difficult and which involve from the very beginning value questions. We are concerned with what we want to do for a child; with the desirability of advocating norms in the speaking and writing of English and with educational aims generally. Everyone who argues what ought to be taught in English classes—even those who believe that nothing should be recommended—has made certain value judgments as to the nature of man, society, and education and as to what a command of language means. Ultimately, the question which we must basically consider in dealing with the teaching of English is what kind of men we want to make of our students. This cannot be solved by a knowledge of the history of the English language.

The general picture of man behind the pure descriptionist's recommendation is a completely passive one. Having discovered that language is always changing and that past attempts to fix it have failed,[4] he concludes that language should be left alone. It will change anyway; usage determines correctness; all will work

[3] For my views on this subject see "Some Problems of Method in Linguistics," *Studium Generale*, V (August, 1952), 437-43.
[4] Not always true, incidentally, in the short range. The schoolmarm reintroduced the $[\eta]$ sound at the end of the present participles in formal and informal levels of English usage. In the long run, however, the generalization is true, although the long run may be very long.

out well. This argument is on the level of another: All men must die eventually; therefore, when you are sick, do not go to the doctor.

But man is not a purely passive creature of circumstance. Circumstances help to make him, but he also makes circumstances. He is limited by historical, biological, and psychological forces, but within these limits he can do a great deal —with language as with other instruments and structures. The picture of the purely passive man acted upon by forces over which he has no control is not only untrue but dangerous—and an out-of-date picture of the human personality to boot.

The key to the whole problem as regards English is the doctrine of usage. We must recognize today that usage is sovereign in the long run; but man determines usage, whether consciously or unconsciously, and the long run can make a lot of difference. In the long run we will all be dead, but this need not lead us to commit suicide.

Is there any value in the relative stability which grammatical norms can give a language? The question cannot be answered from the history of language alone. Other factors must be considered. The eighteenth century had a genuine point when it foolishly tried to "ascertain" the language. It did not realize how impossible it was because of its lack of knowledge, but it did know how useful a relative stability could be in making for clarity, exactitude, and an understanding of the past. To slow down the rate of language change—putting the eighteenth-century desire into modern terms—is a desirable goal.

What are the reasons for teaching some kind of prescriptionist grammar on a formal and informal level in the schools? Why must we decide that this is a value? I do not necessarily approve of the present methods of teaching grammar, nor do I think that old-fashioned drill and rules are the most satisfactory method, but I do think some choice on the side of prescription must be made. Why?

1. *Social utility.*—It is a fact that society as a whole, however mistaken, believes that there is a correct grammar and will judge our students by it. Ultimately this attitude may be changed but certainly not in the foreseeable future. The honest teacher is as responsible for teaching the static in language as he is for teaching the dynamic. His task is neither to hinder nor to hurry change— but to teach realities. A certain amount of standardization in practice is also useful and valuable.

2. *Aid in understanding the past.*—The quicker language changes the sooner the literature and documents of the past become unreadable to the majority of the American people. With the precarious situation of the humanities in America, those who believe in the spiritual value of the humanities must not labor to make them even more difficult and strange to our students.

3. *Aesthetics.*—The beauty and value of the literature of the past and present are lost to those who speak only vulgate English (the language of the majority). Vulgate English has an advantage over the other levels only in vigor, when vigor is appropriate, as in the obscene, but in almost every other sense—

in subtlety, sonorousness, ambiguity, cleverness, breadth—it is deficient. A person who cannot recognize the superior beauty of "Forever wilt thou love and she be fair" to "I ain't got no dough" is not fit to be teaching English.

4. *Intellectual breadth.*—Speakers limited to vulgate cannot discuss a variety of ideas because they do not have the vocabulary and grasp of linguistic structure for ideas beyond those of a most primitive type. It is most improbable that one who speaks and has command only of vulgate English could write a book on leaving one's language alone. A whole range of ideas is inaccessible to him. He cannot even talk about his talking vulgate in vulgate.

For these reasons, most of which are independent of the facts of linguistics, we can defend some form of study of formal and informal English (the language of the educated) on some kind of prescriptionist level.

The problem facing the teacher and supervisors of English is similar to that facing the teacher of civics. To the political scientist qua scientist, all political constitutions are of equal importance, all come down to the level of facts and per se no fact is more important than any other fact. To him as scientist the political constitution of Tibet—if there is one—is as important as that of the U.S.A. But in the schools and universities we emphasize the constitution of the U.S.A. and ignore, for all practical purposes, the constitution of Tibet. For teaching purposes a value judgment is made on grounds other than those provided by the facts of political science. On utilitarian grounds we recognize that the student is an American who will presumably become an adult citizen of America and will exercise his democratic rights here. A knowledge of his government is most desirable. Also, on philosophical grounds, we assume that intrinsically the American Constitution is a more profound and more satisfactory constitution than that of Tibet. But, as a science, political science says nothing of this at all. Similarly, as a science, linguistics cannot favor formal and informal English (or for that matter Bantu) to vulgate English. All linguistic facts are per se of equal importance or of equal unimportance. But on other grounds we can and must choose our values and say that we can justifiedly teach a type of prescriptive grammar and emphasize formal and informal English in the schools. Majorities in language matters are not necessarily decisive. For five hundred years at least the contraction "ain't" has been used by, I'm sure, a majority of English-speaking people, but it still is not used in formal and higher informal discourse. The fact that a majority of the people may be dishonest does not mean that we should teach dishonesty in the schools, though we may, of course, be concerned to understand the ways in which dishonesty originates or to describe dishonesty so that it can be recognized.

But, the question arises, what good then is a knowledge of linguistics and an awareness of the doctrine of usage? Is the great increase in linguistic knowledge of no value or use in teaching English? I think it is of great value, though in a different way from that in which many regard it.

The facts of language set a limit to our application of values. In a negative sense they make us aware of where prescription dare not tread. They make us more open-minded, more willing to accept divided usage, more willing to give up unimportant battles (as, e.g., over "contact" as a noun). They contribute to the peace of mind of the teacher and thereby to that of the pupil. If the teacher recognizes that the "rules" of grammar are not heaven-sent, he can with more equanimity discuss with his students the problems involved. He will be more apt to avoid mechanical drill and avoid the *odium grammaticum.* He can make grammar and language study more pleasant and exciting by giving a sense of the past to his drive toward the present and future. He can create a sense of the excitement of linguistic awareness and language study. And, above all, he can keep the prescriptions down to a minimum, stress usage as the final arbiter, and concentrate on style, which is certainly even more important than grammar.

Some of the new work in structural linguistics may be of practical value in actually teaching the structure of present-day English. We are not necessarily tied to the traditional grammatical analysis of English which is largely based on that of Latin and Greek. In fact, the categories laid down in a recent work by Charles Fries[5] may prove to be more useful in teaching English. We are not necessarily committed to the traditional approach. But the problem of value is still with us, no matter what system we may adopt. It is never solved merely by reference to the internal facts of a subject. More is needed, and the teacher or supervisor must face the problem if he is to be successful in his task.

ARCHIBALD   A.   HILL

Prescriptivism and
Linguistics in English Teaching[1]

In a recent article in *College English*[2] Morton W. Bloomfield presents a cogent, informed, and admirably good-natured account of the problem involved in teaching English to native speakers of the language, now that linguistic scientists

---

[5] *The Structure of English: An Introduction to the Construction of English Sentences* (1952).

I myself am not convinced that this work, which considers English almost completely in oral terms, which is based on behavioristic psychology, which plays down the basic characteristic of language—meaning—and which introduces categories as complicated and probably as inconsistent as the present system is really what we need. The book, however, has opened new perspectives in the practical analysis of our language and is an important contribution to its understanding. However, some kind of prescriptionist commitment such as I am advocating here is not tied to any particular type of language analysis—even the traditional one.

[1] From *College English*, XV (April, 1954), 395-399. Reprinted by permission of the author and of the Editors of *College English*.
[2] October, 1953.

(a notably prickly group of men) have begun to question many traditional attitudes and even to deny vehemently, not always wisely but sometimes certainly with good evidence, some of the things we all learned in the classroom as gospel truth. Professor Bloomfield comes to the conclusion that what is taught in an English class must be some form of wise and moderate prescriptivism, checked by the limits of fact as established by linguistics. The reason for his position is that the teaching of English involves questions of value, which characteristically are not settled merely by the accumulation of facts.

It is probably natural that Bloomfield, as a man primarily interested in the discipline of English, though aware of linguistics, should lean in the direction of value, just as it is natural that a linguist, even though he be a practicing teacher of English, should lean in the direction of fact. I do not wish to question Bloomfield's central thesis or to add fuel to an already unfortunate blaze. Rather it seems to me possible, if a linguist states some modifications of what Bloomfield seems to believe the linguists' position to be, that the area of mutual understanding may be increased, with benefit to all.

Bloomfield defends prescriptivism first because it has social utility. That is, the public judges, and will continue to judge, our students by the language they use. Therefore, he says, the honest teacher must neither hinder nor hurry change but teach realities; an unwise liberalism will expose students to censure. With this position the majority of responsible linguists would agree. We are to blame for not having made ourselves clear on the point, though my own experience in the failure of serious attempts at explanation leads me to believe that perhaps not all the blame lies with the linguists. No intelligent linguist would think of denying that the use of a given linguistic form will have inevitable social consequences for the user—the position that language patterns are a part of larger patterns of social behavior and that each reacts on the other is central to linguistics. In my own classes, as an example of social consequences from language use, I often tell a story told me by an old Charlestonian. She had brought a beau home for family inspection, and her father was proudly displaying his collection of art. "Now this," he said, "is called 'The Broken Pitcher.'"

"Yes," said the young man, "I see the corner's damaged." The suitor was never invited to the house again. The form "pitcher" cannot be ugly in itself—we use it as a perfectly good word. Nor can the confusion of two words, as the result of natural tendencies of change, be a very heinous sin. Millions probably confuse them, just as even more millions confuse *affect* and *effect*. The point, however, is not that it would be easy to defend the young man's misunderstanding. It is rather that the consequences of it were very real for him and presumably unpleasant. The nonlinguist often argues violently that there is something inherently wrong, ugly, or illogical in such a form as "pitcher" and equates any denial of the inherent "wrongness" of the form with a denial of the social consequences of using it.

The linguist maintains merely that in itself a form, say *golpet*, is as good as another form, say *thaltep*; the difference between them is merely one of attitudes, not of inherent qualities. I have chosen nonsense illustrations deliberately, in an effort to find forms to which the reader has not already learned to respond with conditioned attitudes of value. It seems to me that a linguist is performing a service in attempting to separate such conditioned value reactions from the inherent qualities of the stimulus and that we have a right to complain when our attempts to do so are received as further illustrations of the blindness of men who are supposed to believe that "anything goes."

Bloomfield's second reason for teaching a prescriptive grammar and usage is that it is an aid in understanding the past. Again a linguist cannot quarrel, at least with the aim. Yet it is to be doubted whether prescriptive grammar is always conservative. For instance, one of Bloomfield's examples of vulgate (the language of the majority) which he would rightly resist in classroom use is "I ain't got no dough." Two of the three objectionable forms in this sentence, *ain't* and the double negative, are older than the prescriptivist objection to them and are therefore more in line with past usage than are the modern condemnations. A linguist would hope to accomplish Bloomfield's aim of understanding past language structures not by reliance on prescriptivism but by knowing the structures of the present, with adequate recognition of the fact that different forms and structures are in use in the English-speaking community, in different places, on different social levels, and for different purposes. With such a background a student would, we hope, be ready to deal with the language of the past not as a primitive jargon less perfect than his own speech but as a structure to be respected and understood—a structure different from others, as all language structures are, and, by virtue of difference, capable of artistic effects as good as any open to Hemingway or Housman.

Bloomfield's third and fourth reasons for rejecting vulgate in favor of a prescriptive norm are that vulgate is deficient in all artistic qualities except vigor and is likewise deficient in intellectual breadth and depth. The two statements are closely related and should be discussed together. In a measure, a linguist can agree. If we listen to talk heard on street corners or in grocery stores, it is true that we hear little that is memorable for beauty or intellectual penetration. Language use is an art, and all can agree that great practitioners of any art are few in number. Similarly it is a truism that intellectual leaders are anything but numerous—otherwise they would not be leaders. Yet many linguists would feel that, when Bloomfield says that vulgate is deficient in beauty and intellectual qualities, he is confusing the language with its use. We can agree with him heartily that good models of language use should be given to our students, but we would maintain that the nature of an instrument is different from its employment.

Language structure, with which linguists are primarily concerned, remains relatively constant, and in all important ways is shared by all members of the community, both those who use the language well and those who use it ill. For instance, though it is not universally agreed to by all linguists, many would now say that English has four degrees of stress. If so, this is an example of an important structural feature shared by normal English contemporary speech on all levels and in all localities. Even if we grant that such structural characteristics can only be created by the habitual usage of the community and are further changed only as these habits change, the striking fact about such structural features is how slowly and how little they change. If English has four stresses, it has acquired the fourth at some time since the Norman Conquest; otherwise the stress system has apparently remained unchanged for approximately two thousand years. If there should be only three significant stresses in Modern English, there has been no change at all. If such structural features can remain so little changed in the face of all the social upheavals and linguistic rivalries of two millenniums, it would seem that we should not worry too much over such details as where a student stresses a word like *justifiable*. At most the choice can affect the student and this particular word; the system of stress distinctions will remain the same. It should be emphasized that structure in language is something more, and more important, than a collection of items. A change in the number or type of stress distinctions would be vastly more important (for good or ill) than the introduction or the loss of vocabulary items. I am aware for instance, that confusion of *distinterested* and *uninterested* destroys a useful vocabulary item and one which I would have been glad to see preserved, even though nowadays I cannot talk of "disinterested judges" for fear of being misunderstood. But, though vocabulary items can be lost, others can be gained, and somehow we manage to carry on our necessary business with the vocabulary we have at any one time. Therefore, it seems to me that we need not fear that the whole of our language will be damaged by those who would say "bored, disinterested judges." For the individual and the community, structure is a broad, pervasive pattern, already determined, and capable of very little change. As such it is relatively neutral and colorless. Indeed, in large measure, it is something which escapes the user's conscious attention. The use he makes of his structure and the items within it is something different. Language use is important to the individual; he is highly conscious of it and rightly seeks advice and help in improving it.

For the reasons which I have tried to outline, when Bloomfield goes on to say that to accept the use made of our language by the majority would be to destroy the beauties of the language itself, I think it is necessary to disagree. He is here assuming that poor use is essentially the same thing as poor structure. I should rather say that the use of language is an area in which value judgments must indeed be made, and is an area in which English teachers should increase both their vigilance and their research, but that structure is different and is not subject to the same kind of criticism we would bring to bear in order to evaluate a paragraph by Winston Churchill or a sonnet by Shelley. Bloomfield goes so far as to say that one who does not recognize the beauty of "Forever wilt thou love and she be fair" is unfit to teach English. But the example belongs to art and is beautiful because it is a part of a literary work the totality of whose beauty we all admire. It is difficult to argue that the forms contained in the line—considered either as separate items or as a special dialect—are in themselves any better or more beautiful than the forms of vulgate. For instance, if *wilt* is more beautiful than *will*, does that lead us to the conclusion that the sequence *-lt* is beautiful, so that *kilt* is better than *killed*? Or if a dialect employing a distinction between singular and plural in second-person pronouns is better and more logical than one which does not, are we to defend the metropolitan low-class distinction between *you* singular, and *youse* plural? I wish, however, to be as clear as possible and therefore to say as emphatically as I can that I agree that anyone who cannot appreciate the beauty of the Keats poem is unfit to teach English. And I should add further that, if there is any student who has drawn from linguistics the idea that the poem is in a strange and inferior dialect because its vocabulary and forms differ from contemporary everyday usage, he holds a horrifying and absurd conclusion. If linguistics leads to such beliefs, it earns nothing but opposition. May I hope, however, should any student of literature be led into the equally horrifying and absurd idea that the dialect employed by Keats is better than vulgate in all social and even in all artistic situations, that Bloomfield would join me in giving such a fallacious conclusion as vigorous opposition as I am sure he would give the other?

Much the same sort of objection applies to Bloomfield's fear that too much liberalism would destroy intellectual activity. It is usual in our culture to write about intellectual matters in a very formal kind of English, which it is all too easy to identify with the intellectual activity itself. The same thing is true of other cultures, yet elsewhere in the world the disappearance or replacement of a special intellectual language or dialect has not meant the disappearance of intellectual activity. Such replacements have almost always been by the form of language originally regarded as an unintellectual vulgate. Yet, when the replacement takes place, the old vulgate quickly becomes the new intellectual language. For instance, no one would maintain that the body of intellectual writing in the vernacular tongues is inferior to that in Latin or that intellectual vigor has been circumscribed by the disuse of the scholar's language. For once, therefore, I think I am safe in denying one of Bloomfield's theses. If, by vulgate, Bloomfield means the language structure used by the majority, then I should oppose him with this statement: Good style, whether artistic or intellectual, is possible in any language structure. Mark Twain, in *Huckleberry Finn*, employed the vulgate structure of rural America in his day, yet Huck's descriptions of a village funeral and of a backwoods front parlor are among the classics of our literature. It seems to me that as teachers of English, whether with or without linguistic training, we should strive for clarity. If we assume that style and structure need no differentiation, we are in danger of obscuring both.

I have tried to equal Bloomfield's urbanity and his grasp of first things first. I may have failed, but I hope I may permit myself to believe that he as English teacher, I as linguist, might agree that all who teach the native language have a solemn duty in understanding language, its structure, its social implications, and the use, beautiful or otherwise, which men have put it to. Further, since literature is necessarily a part of language, all that a linguist can discover about his subject should not merely limit what the English teacher can say but is of positive though potential value to him in all his work.

GEORGE ORWELL

Politics and the English Language[1]

Most people who bother with the matter at all would admit that the English language is in a bad way, but it is generally assumed that we cannot by conscious action do anything about it. Our civilization is decadent, and our language—so the argument runs—must inevitably share in the general collapse. It follows that any struggle against the abuse of language is a sentimental archaism, like preferring candles to electric light or hansom cabs to aeroplanes. Underneath this lies the half-conscious belief that language is a natural growth and not an instrument which we shape for our own purposes.

Now, it is clear that the decline of a language must ultimately have political and economic causes: it is not due simply to the bad influence of this or that individual writer. But an effect can become a cause, reinforcing the original cause and producing the same effect in an intensified form, and so on indefinitely. A man may take to drink because he feels himself to be a failure, and then fail all the more completely because he drinks. It is rather the same thing that is happening to the English language. It becomes ugly and inaccurate because our thoughts are foolish, but the slovenliness of our language makes it easier for us to have foolish thoughts. The point is that the process is reversible. Modern English, especially written English, is full of bad habits which spread by imitation and which can be avoided if one is willing to take the necessary trouble. If one gets rid of these habits one can think more clearly, and to think clearly is a necessary first step towards political regeneration: so that the fight against bad English is not frivolous and is not the exclusive concern of professional writers. I will come back to this presently, and I hope that by that time the meaning of what I have said here will have become clearer. Meanwhile, here are five specimens of the English language as it is now habitually written.

These five passages have not been picked out because they are especially bad —I could have quoted far worse if I had chosen—but because they illustrate various of the mental vices from which we now suffer. They are a little below the average, but are fairly representative samples. I number them so that I can refer back to them when necessary:

(1) I am not, indeed, sure whether it is not true to say that the Milton who once seemed not unlike a seventeenth-century Shelley had not become, out of an experience ever more bitter in each year, more alien (sic) to the founder of that Jesuit sect which nothing could induce him to tolerate.

Professor Harold Laski (Essay in Freedom of Expression)

(2) Above all, we cannot play ducks and drakes with a native battery of idioms which prescribes such egregious collocations of vocables as the Basic *put up with* for *tolerate* or *put at a loss* for *bewilder*.

Professor Lancelot Hogben (Interglossa)

(3) On the one side we have the free personality; by definition it is not neurotic, for it has neither conflict nor dream. Its desires, such as they are, are transparent, for they are just what institutional approval keeps in the forefront of consciousness; another institutional pattern would alter their number and intensity; there is little in them that is natural, irreducible, or culturally dangerous. But *on the other side*, the social bond itself is nothing but the mutual reflection of these self-secure integrities. Recall the definition of love. Is not this the very picture of a small academic? Where is there a place in this hall of mirrors for either personality or fraternity?

Essay on psychology in Politics (New York)

(4) All the "best people" from the gentlemen's clubs, and all the frantic fascist captains, united in common hatred of Socialism and bestial horror of the rising tide of the mass revolutionary movement, have turned to acts of provocation, to foul incendiarism, to medieval legends of poisoned wells, to legalize their own destruction of proletarian organizations, and rouse the agitated petty-bourgeoisie to chauvinistic fervor on behalf of the fight against the revolutionary way out of the crisis.   Communist pamphlet

(5) If a new spirit *is* to be infused into this old country, there is one thorny and contentious reform which must be tackled, and that is the humanization and galvanization of the B.B.C. Timidity here will bespeak canker and atrophy of the soul. The heart of Britain may be sound and of strong beat, for instance, but the British lion's roar at present is like that of Bottom in Shakespeare's *Midsummer Night's Dream*—as gentle as any sucking dove. A virile new Britain cannot continue indefinitely to be traduced in the eyes, or rather ears, of the world by the effete languors of Langham Place, brazenly masquerading as "standard English." When the Voice of Britain is heard at nine o'clock, better far and infinitely less ludicrous to hear aitches honestly dropped than the present priggish, inflated, inhibited, school-ma'amish arch braying of blameless bashful mewing maidens.

Letter in Tribune

Each of these passages has faults of its own, but quite apart from avoidable ugliness, two qualities are common to all of them. The first is staleness of imagery; the other is lack of precision. The writer either has a meaning and cannot express it, or he inadvertently says something else, or he is almost indifferent as to whether his words mean anything or not. This mixture of vagueness and sheer incompetence is the most marked characteristic of modern English prose, and especially of any kind of political writing. As soon as certain topics are raised, the concrete melts into the abstract and no one seems able to think of turns of speech that are not hackneyed: prose consists less and less of *words* chosen for the sake of their meaning, and more and more of *phrases* tacked together like the sections of a prefabricated hen-house. I list below, with notes and examples, various of the tricks by means of which the work of prose-construction is habitually dodged:

Dying metaphors. A newly-invented metaphor assists thought by evoking a visual image, while on the other hand a metaphor which is technically "dead" (e.g., *iron resolution*) has in effect reverted to being an ordinary word and can generally be used without loss of vividness. But in between these two classes there is a huge dump of worn-out metaphors which have lost all evocative power and are merely used because they save people the trouble of inventing phrases for themselves. Examples are: *Ring the changes on, take up the cudgels for, toe the line, ride roughshod over, stand shoulder to shoulder with, play into the hands of, an axe to grind, grist to the mill, fishing in troubled waters, on the order of the day, Achilles' heel, swan song, hotbed.* Many of these are used without knowledge of their meaning (what is a "rift," for instance?), and incompatible metaphors are frequently mixed, a sure sign that the writer is not interested in what he is saying. Some metaphors now current have been twisted out of their original meaning without those who use them even being aware of the fact. For example, *toe the line* is sometimes written *tow the line*. Another example is *the hammer and the anvil*, now always used with the implication that the anvil gets the worst of it. In real life it is always the anvil that breaks the hammer, never the other way about: a writer who stopped to think what he was saying woud be aware of this, and would avoid perverting the original phrase.

Operators, or verbal false limbs. These save the trouble of picking out appropriate verbs and nouns, and at the same time pad each sentence with extra syllables which give it an appearance of symmetry. Characteristic phrases are: *render inoperative, militate against, prove unacceptable, make contact with, be subjected to, give rise to, give grounds for, have the effect of, play a leading part* (role) *in, make itself felt, take effect, exhibit a tendency to, serve the purpose of, etc., etc.* The keynote is the elimination of simple verbs. Instead of being a single word, such as *break, stop, spoil, mend, kill,* a verb becomes a phrase, made up of a noun or adjective tacked on to some general-purposes verb such as *prove, serve, form, play, render.* In addition, the passive voice is wherever possible used in preference to the active, and noun constructions are used instead of gerunds (*by examination of* instead of *by examining*). The range of verbs is further cut down by means of the *-ize* and *de-* formations, and banal statements are given an appearance of profundity by means of the *not un-* formation. Simple conjunctions and prepositions are replaced by such phrases as *with respect to, having regard to, the fact that, by dint of, in view of, in the interests of, on the hypothesis that*; and the ends of sentences are saved from anti-climax by such resounding commonplaces as *greatly to be desired, cannot be left out of account, a development to be expected in the near future, deserving of serious consideration, brought to a satisfactory conclusion,* and so on and so forth.

Pretentious diction. Words like *phenomenon, element, individual* (as noun), *objective, categorical, effective, virtual, basis, primary, promote, constitute, exhibit, exploit, utilize, eliminate, liquidate,* are used to dress up simple statements and give an air of scientific impartiality to biased judgments. Adjectives like *epoch-making, epic, historic, unforgettable, triumphant, age-old, inevitable, inexorable, veritable,* are used to dignify the sordid processes of international politics, while writing that aims at glorifying war usually takes on an archaic color, its characteristic words being: *realm, throne, chariot, mailed fist, trident, sword, shield, buckler, banner, jackboot, clarion.* Foreign words and expressions such as *cul de sac, ancien régime, deus ex machina, mutatis mutandis, status quo, gleichschaltung, weltanschauung,* are used to give an air of culture and elegance. Except for the useful abbreviations *i.e., e.g.,* and *etc.,* there is no real need for any of the hundreds of foreign phrases now current in English. Bad writers, and especially scientific, political and sociological writers, are nearly always haunted by the notion that Latin or Greek words are grander than Saxon ones, and unnecessary words like *expedite, ameliorate, predict, extraneous, deracinated, clandestine, subaqueous* and hundreds of others constantly gain ground from their Anglo-Saxon opposite numbers.[2] The jargon peculiar to Marxist writing (*hyena, hangman, cannibal, petty bourgeois, these gentry, lackey, flunkey, mad dog, White Guard, etc.*) consists largely of words and phrases translated from Russian, German or French; but the normal way of coining a new word is to use a Latin or Greek root with the appropriate affix and, where necessary, the *-ize* formation. It is often easier to make up words of this kind (*deregionalize, impermissible, extramarital, non-fragmentary* and so forth) than to think up the English words that will cover one's meaning. The result, in general, is an increase in slovenliness and vagueness.

[2] An interesting illustration of this is the way in which the English flower names which were in use till very recently are being ousted by Greek ones, *snap-dragon* becoming *antirrhinum, forget-me-not* becoming *myosotis,* etc. It is hard to see any practical reason for this change of fashion: it is probably due to an instinctive turning-away from the more homely word and a vague feeling that the Greek word is scientific.

Meaningless words. In certain kinds of writing, particularly in art criticism and literary criticism, it is normal to come across long passages which are almost completely lacking in meaning.[3] Words like *romantic, plastic, values, human, dead, sentimental, natural, vitality,* as used in art criticism, are strictly meaningless, in the sense that they not only do not point to any discoverable object, but are hardly even expected to do so by the reader. When one critic writes, "The outstanding feature of Mr. X's work is its living quality," while another writes, "The immediately striking thing about Mr. X's work is its peculiar deadness," the reader accepts this as a simple difference of opinion. If words like *black* and *white* were involved, instead of the jargon words *dead* and *living,* he would see at once that language was being used in an improper way. Many political words are similarly abused. The word *Fascism* has now no meaning except in so far as it signifies "something not desirable." The words *democracy, socialism, freedom, patriotic, realistic, justice,* have each of them several different meanings which cannot be reconciled with one another. In the case of a word like *democracy,* not only is there no agreed definition, but the attempt to make one is resisted from all sides. It is almost universally felt that when we call a country democratic we are praising it: consequently the defenders of every kind of régime claim that it is a democracy, and fear that they might have to stop using the word if it were tied down to any one meaning. Words of this kind are often used in a consciously dishonest way. That is, the person who uses them has his own private definition, but allows his hearer to think he means something quite different. Statements like *Marshal Pétain was a true patriot, The Soviet Press is the freest in the world, The Catholic Church is opposed to persecution,* are almost always made with intent to deceive. Other words used in variable meanings, in most cases more or less dishonestly, are: *class, totalitarian, science, progressive, reactionary, bourgeois, equality.*

Now that I have made this catalogue of swindles and perversions, let me give another example of the kind of writing that they lead to. This time it must of its nature be an imaginary one. I am going to translate a passage of good English into modern English of the worst sort. Here is a well-known verse from *Ecclesiastes:*

I returned, and saw under the sun, that the race is not to the swift, nor the battle to the strong, neither yet bread to the wise, nor yet riches to men of understanding, nor yet favor to men of skill; but time and chance happeneth to them all.

[3] Example: "Comfort's catholicity of perception and image, strangely Whitmanesque in range, almost the exact opposite in aesthetic compulsion, continues to evoke that trembling atmospheric accumulative hinting at a cruel, an inexorably serene timelessness . . . Wrey Gardiner scores by aiming at simple bullseyes with precision. Only they are not so simple, and through this contented sadness runs more than the surface bittersweet of resignation." (*Poetry Quarterly.*)

Here it is in modern English:

> Objective consideration of contemporary phenomena compels the conclusion that success or failure in competitive activities exhibits no tendency to be commensurate with innate capacity, but that a considerable element of the unpredictable must invariably be taken into account.

This is a parody, but not a very gross one. Exhibit (3), above, for instance, contains several patches of the same kind of English. It will be seen that I have not made a full translation. The beginning and ending of the sentence follow the original meaning fairly closely, but in the middle the concrete illustrations—race, battle, bread—dissolve into the vague phrase "success or failure in competitive activities." This had to be so, because no modern writer of the kind I am discussing—no one capable of using phrases like "objective consideration of contemporary phenomena"—would ever tabulate his thoughts in that precise and detailed way. The whole tendency of modern prose is away from concreteness. Now analyze these two sentences a little more closely. The first contains 49 words but only 60 syllables, and all its words are those of everyday life. The second contains 38 words of 90 syllables: 18 of its words are from Latin roots, and one from Greek. The first sentence contains six vivid images, and only one phrase ("time and chance") that could be called vague. The second contains not a single fresh, arresting phrase, and in spite of its 90 syllables it gives only a shortened version of the meaning contained in the first. Yet without a doubt it is the second kind of sentence that is gaining ground in modern English. I do not want to exaggerate. This kind of writing is not yet universal, and outcrops of simplicity will occur here and there in the worst-written page. Still, if you or I were told to write a few lines on the uncertainty of human fortunes, we should probably come much nearer to my imaginary sentence than to the one from *Ecclesiastes*.

As I have tried to show, modern writing at its worst does not consist in picking out words for the sake of their meaning and inventing images in order to make the meaning clearer. It consists in gumming together long strips of words which have already been set in order by someone else, and making the results presentable by sheer humbug. The attraction of this way of writing is that it is easy. It is easier—even quicker, once you have the habit—to say *In my opinion it is a not unjustifiable assumption that* than to say *I think*. If you use ready-made phrases, you not only don't have to hunt about for words; you also don't have to bother with the rhythms of your sentences, since these phrases are generally so arranged as to be more or less euphonious. When you are composing in a hurry—when you are dictating to a stenographer, for instance, or making a public speech—it is natural to fall into a pretentious, Latinized style. Tags like *a consideration which we should do well to bear in mind* or *a conclusion to which all of us would readily assent* will save many a sentence from coming down with a bump. By using stale metaphors, similes and idioms, you save much mental effort at the cost of leaving your meaning vague, not only for your reader but for yourself. This is the significance of mixed metaphors. The sole aim of a metaphor is to call up a visual image. When these images clash—as in *The Fascist octopus has sung its swan song, the jackboot is thrown into the melting pot*—it can be taken as certain that the writer is not seeing a mental image of the objects he is naming; in other words he is not really thinking. Look again at the examples I gave at the beginning of this essay. Professor Laski (1) uses five negatives in 53 words. One of these is superfluous, making nonsense of the whole passage, and in addition there is the slip *alien* for akin, making further nonsense, and several avoidable pieces of clumsiness which increase the general vagueness. Professor Hogben (2) plays ducks and drakes with a battery which is able to write prescriptions, and, while disapproving of the everyday phrase *put up with*, is unwilling to look *egregious* up in the dictionary and see what it means. (3), if one takes an uncharitable attitude towards it, is simply meaningless: probably one could work out its intended meaning by reading the whole of the article in which it occurs. In (4), the writer knows more or less what he wants to say, but an accumulation of stale phrases chokes him like tea leaves blocking a sink. In (5), words and meaning have almost parted company. People who write in this manner usually have a general emotional meaning—they dislike one thing and want to express solidarity with another—but they are not interested in the detail of what they are saying. A scrupulous writer, in every sentence that he writes, will ask himself at least four questions, thus: What am I trying to say? What words will express it? What image or idiom will make it clearer? Is this image fresh enough to have an effect? And he will probably ask himself two more: Could I put it more shortly? Have I said anything that is avoidably ugly? But you are not obliged to go to all this trouble. You can shirk it by simply throwing your mind open and letting the ready-made phrases come crowding in. They will construct your sentences for you—even think your thoughts for you, to a certain extent—and at need they will perform the important service of partially concealing your meaning even from yourself. It is at this point that the special connection between politics and the debasement of language becomes clear.

In our time it is broadly true that political writing is bad writing. Where it is not true, it will generally be found that the writer is some kind of rebel, expressing his private opinions and not a "party line." Orthodoxy, of whatever color, seems to demand a lifeless, imitative style. The political dialects to be found in pamphlets, leading articles, manifestoes, White Papers and the speeches of under-secretaries do, of course, vary from party to party, but they are all alike in that one almost never finds in them a fresh, vivid, home-made turn of speech. When one watches some tired hack on the platform mechanically repeating the familiar phrases—*bestial atrocities, iron heel, bloodstained tyranny, free peoples of the world, stand shoulder to shoulder*—one often has a curious feeling that one is not watching a live human being but some kind of dummy: a feeling which suddenly becomes stronger at moments when the

light catches the speaker's spectacles and turns them into blank discs which
seem to have no eyes behind them. And this is not altogether fanciful. A
speaker who uses that kind of phraseology has gone some distance towards
turning himself into a machine. The appropriate noises are coming out of his
larynx, but his brain is not involved as it would be if he were choosing his
words for himself. If the speech he is making is one that he is accustomed to
make over and over again, he may be almost unconscious of what he is saying,
as one is when one utters the responses in church. And this reduced state
of consciousness, if not indispensable, is at any rate favorable to political conformity.

In our time, political speech and writing are largely the defense of the indefensible. Things like the continuance of British rule in India, the Russian
purges and deportations, the dropping of the atom bombs on Japan, can indeed be defended, but only by arguments which are too brutal for most people
to face, and which do not square with the professed aims of political parties.
Thus political language has to consist largely of euphemism, question-begging
and sheer cloudy vagueness. Defenseless villages are bombarded from the air,
the inhabitants driven out into the countryside, the cattle machine-gunned,
the huts set on fire with incendiary bullets: this is called *pacification*. Millions
of peasants are robbed of their farms and sent trudging along the roads with
no more than they can carry: this is called *transfer of population* or *rectification
of frontiers*. People are imprisoned for years without trial, or shot in the back
of the neck or sent to die of scurvy in Arctic lumber camps: this is called *elimination of unreliable elements*. Such phraseology is needed if one wants to name
things without calling up mental pictures of them. Consider for instance some
comfortable English professor defending Russian totalitarianism. He cannot
say outright, "I believe in killing off your opponents when you can get good results by doing so." Probably, therefore, he will say something like this:

> While freely conceding that the Soviet régime exhibits certain features
> which the humanitarian may be inclined to deplore, we must, I think, agree
> that a certain curtailment of the right to political opposition is an unavoid-
> able concomitant of transitional periods, and that the rigors which the
> Russian people have been called upon to undergo have been amply justified
> in the sphere of concrete achievement.

The inflated style is itself a kind of euphemism. A mass of Latin words falls
upon the facts like soft snow, blurring the outlines and covering up all the
details. The great enemy of clear language is insincerity. When there is a gap
between one's real and one's declared aims, one turns, as it were instinctively,
to long words and exhausted idioms, like a cuttlefish squirting out ink. In our
age there is no such thing as "keeping out of politics." All issues are political
issues, and politics itself is a mass of lies, evasions, folly, hatred and schizo-
phrenia. When the general atmosphere is bad, language must suffer. I should
expect to find—this is a guess which I have not sufficient knowledge to verify

—that the German, Russian and Italian languages have all deteriorated in the last ten or fifteen years as a result of dictatorship.

But if thought corrupts language, language can also corrupt thought. A bad usage can spread by tradition and imitation, even among people who should and do know better. The debased language that I have been discussing is in some ways very convenient. Phrases like *a not unjustifiable assumption, leaves much to be desired, would serve no good purpose, a consideration which we should do well to bear in mind,* are a continuous temptation, a packet of aspirins always at one's elbow. Look back through this essay, and for certain you will find that I have again and again committed the very faults I am protesting against. By this morning's post I have received a pamphlet dealing with conditions in Germany. The author tells me that he "felt impelled" to write it. I open it at random, and here is almost the first sentence that I see: "[The Allies] have an opportunity not only of achieving a radical transformation of Germany's social and political structure in such a way as to avoid a nationalistic reaction in Germany itself, but at the same time of laying the foundations of a cooperative and unified Europe." You see, he "feels impelled" to write—feels, presumably, that he has something new to say—and yet his words, like cavalry horses answering the bugle, group themselves automatically into the familiar dreary pattern. This invasion of one's mind by ready-made phrases (*lay the foundations, achieve a radical transformation*) can only be prevented if one is constantly on guard against them, and every such phrase anesthetizes a portion of one's brain.

I said earlier that the decadence of our language is probably curable. Those who deny this would argue, if they produced an argument at all, that language merely reflects existing social conditions, and that we cannot influence its development by any direct tinkering with words and constructions. So far as the general tone or spirit of a language goes, this may be true, but it is not true in detail. Silly words and expressions have often disappeared, not through any evolutionary process but owing to the conscious action of a minority. Two recent examples were *explore every avenue* and *leave no stone unturned,* which were killed by the jeers of a few journalists. There is a long list of fly-blown metaphors which could similarly be got rid of if enough people would interest themselves in the job; and it should also be possible to laugh the *not un-* formation out of existence,[4] to reduce the amount of Latin and Greek in the average sentence, to drive out foreign phrases and strayed scientific words, and, in general, to make pretentiousness unfashionable. But all these are minor points. The defense of the English language implies more than this, and perhaps it is best to start by saying what it does *not* imply.

To begin with, it has nothing to do with archaism, with the salvaging of obsolete words and turns of speech, or with the setting-up of a "standard

4 One can cure oneself of the *not un-* formation by memorizing this sentence: A *not unblack dog was chasing a not unsmall rabbit across a not ungreen field.*

English" which must never be departed from. On the contrary, it is especially concerned with the scrapping of every word or idiom which has outworn its usefulness. It has nothing to do with correct grammar and syntax, which are of no importance so long as one makes one's meaning clear, or with the avoidance of Americanisms, or with having what is called a "good prose style." On the other hand it is not concerned with fake simplicity and the attempt to make written English colloquial. Nor does it even imply in every case preferring the Saxon word to the Latin one, though it does imply using the fewest and shortest words that will cover one's meaning. What is above all needed is to let the meaning choose the word, and not the other way about. In prose, the worst thing one can do with words is to surrender to them. When you think of a concrete object, you think wordlessly, and then, if you want to describe the thing you have been visualizing, you probably hunt about till you find the exact words that seem to fit it. When you think of something abstract you are more inclined to use words from the start, and unless you make a conscious effort to prevent it, the existing dialect will come rushing in and do the job for you, at the expense of blurring or even changing your meaning. Probably it is better to put off using words as long as possible and get one's meaning as clear as one can through pictures or sensations. Afterwards one can choose—not simply *accept*—the phrases that will best cover the meaning, and then switch round and decide what impressions one's words are likely to make on another person. This last effort of the mind cuts out all stale or mixed images, all prefabricated phrases, needless repetitions, and humbug and vagueness generally. But one can often be in doubt about the effect of a word or a phrase, and one needs rules that one can rely on when instinct fails. I think the following rules will cover most cases:

(i) Never use a metaphor, simile or other figure of speech which you are used to seeing in print.

(ii) Never use a long word where a short one will do.

(iii) If it is possible to cut a word out, always cut it out.

(iv) Never use the passive where you can use the active.

(v) Never use a foreign phrase, a scientific word or a jargon word if you can think of an everyday English equivalent.

(vi) Break any of these rules sooner than say anything barbarous.

These rules sound elementary, and so they are, but they demand a deep change of attitude in anyone who has grown used to writing in the style now fashionable. One could keep all of them and still write bad English, but one could not write the kind of stuff that I quoted in these five specimens at the beginning of this article.

I have not here been considering the literary use of language, but merely language as an instrument for expressing and not for concealing or preventing thought. Stuart Chase and others have come near to claiming that all abstract words are meaningless, and have used this as a pretext for advocating a kind of political quietism. Since you don't know what Facism is, how can you struggle against Fascism? One need not swallow such absurdities as this, but one ought to recognize that the present political chaos is connected with the decay of language, and that one can probably bring about some improvement by starting at the verbal end. If you simplify your English, you are freed from the worst follies of orthodoxy. You cannot speak any of the necessary dialects, and when you make a stupid remark its stupidity will be obvious, even to yourself. Political language—and with variations this is true of all political parties, from Conservatives to Anarchists—is designed to make lies sound truthful and murder respectable, and to give an appearance of solidity to pure wind. One cannot change this all in a moment, but one can at least change one's habits, and from time to time one can even, if one jeers loudly enough, send some worn-out and useless phrase—some *jackboot, Achilles' heel, hotbed, melting pot, acid test, veritable inferno* or other lump of verbal refuse—into the dustbin where it belongs.

OGDEN NASH

Laments for a Dying Language[1]

What's the monster of this week?
"Mystique"—
A noun that in its current arcane use leaves me frigid,
Since it is not to be found in either the O.E.D. or Webster's Unabridgèd.
It is primarily the invention of the mystagogues of esoteric criticism, so it means
       whatever they choose,
But I will give you an example of what I think they think it means, only from
       the domain of a different muse.
I recently heard on the air a song in which the lover states that the loved one is
       his idea
Of a band of angels singing "Ave Maria."
This is not only a metaphor unique,
It is also an example of the songwriter's mystique at its peak.

II

Someone comes up with a linguistic gimmick,
And thousands flock to mimic.

[1] From *The New Yorker*, XXXVI (April 23, 1960), 43. Reprinted by permission of Curtis Brown, Ltd. © 1960 by Ogden Nash.

This noisy age, when big loud bangs give way to bangs louder and bigger still,
And admirals, congressmen, and minor government officials pop off at will,
Gives us two gimmicks that reflect our minds' corrosion:
"Crash program" and "explosion."
See here the population explosion, the freedom explosion, the Broadway and
    off-Broadway incest-theme explosion, the explosion of British secretaries
    in offices of grandiose pretensions,
And there the crash program for defense, for space exploration, for a third
    major league, for nominating the candidates previous to the conventions.
With each successive bang my hopes grow limper
That the world's end will be a simple whimper.

III

In the nice-minded Department of Prunes and Prisms,
It's I for you
And euphemisms.
Hence the phrase I would eagerly jettison:
"Senior citizen."
Let us, then, retranslate
Joel, 2, 28.
To the sociologist squeamish
The words "Your old men shall dream dreams" are less than beamish,
So "Your senior citizens shall dream dreams" it shall henceforth be,
Along with Hemingway's "The Senior Citizen and the Sea."
I, though no Joel, prophesy that someday while the senior citizens are project-
    ing the image of an age-adjusted social group,
The old men will rise up and knock them for a loop.

IV

Those authors I can never love
Who write, "It fit him like a glove."
Though baseballs may be hit, not "hitted,"
The past of "fit" is always "fitted."
The sole exception worth a *haricot*
Is "Joshua fit de battle ob "Jericho."

V

Coin brassy words at will, debase the coinage;
We're in an if-you-cannot-lick-them-join age,
A slovenliness-provides-its-own-excuse age,
Where usage overnight condones misusage.
Farewell, farewell to my beloved language,
Once English, now a vile orangutanguage.

GEOFFREY T. HELLMAN

"Time" Lumbers On[1]

You can't always put your finger on what it is that makes a person attractive. The people in *Time* have long seemed unusually attractive to me, and I have sometimes wondered why this was so, since they are, by and large, the same bunch you find in the papers and in *Newsweek*, where they seem O.K. but not as compelling. I have gone to some pains to analyze the matter by studying *Time* carefully for the past several months, and I think the chief source of their charm is the way their voltage gets stepped up once they get into *Time*. Most of the people in *Time* are men. What steps up men's voltage? Girls. The biggest category on *Time*'s masthead of two hundred and nineteen names is that of its sixty-two girl editorial researchers. I suspect that it's largely the presence of these ladies—especially the ones with the wonderful names, like Bernadine Beerheide, Harriet Ben Ezra, Quinera Sarita King, Danuta Reszke-Birk, Deirdre Mead Ryan, and Yi Ying Sung—that peps up *Time*'s denizens. *Newsweek* has far fewer girls, and their names aren't quite as stimulating. No offense, I hope. Mrs. Reid is the only girl on the *Herald Tribune*'s masthead, and as for the *Times*, it's Arthur Hays Sulzberger, Julius Ochs Adler, Orvil E. Dryfoos, Amory H. Bradford, Francis A. Cox all the way. Confidence-inspiring, but not pulse-quickening.

Be that as it may (and what isn't?), the people in *Time* are possessed of an unusual vigor, which is reflected in their gait, in the pace of their vehicles, and in their conversation. Take President Eisenhower, for example. He rarely walks in *Time*; he strides. "A smiling Dwight Eisenhower . . . strode to the rostrum" in the January 17th *Time*. More recently, in the February 28th issue, he "strode into the Congressional Room of Washington's Statler Hotel." To stride, according to Webster, means "to walk with long steps, esp. in a measured or pompous manner." *Time* is a patriotic magazine, and I have a feeling that when the President strides in its pages he is doing it in a measured rather than a pompous manner. Furthermore, when he writes a letter, he doesn't dictate it lackadaisically and then glue it up in an envelope with a lacklustre lick; he treats it like a fire-cracker, or a twenty-one-gun salute: "Last week Ike fired off a new letter to CAB."

Another February 28th *Time* strider, and a man whose vehicular pace is well calculated to make Quinera and Danuta sit up and take notice, is Colonel Marcos Pérez Jiménez, President of Venezuela. "Stopping the procession," *Time* states, "he strode over to the Mercedes-Benz." Pérez Jiménez is playing ball with us when it comes to oil, and I'm glad to learn that a strider rather

[1] From *The New Yorker*, XXX (April 16, 1955), 34-36. Permission the author.
© 1955 The New Yorker Magazine, Inc.

than a sidler, he. It's good to know, too, that when he gets into a car he doesn't just drive; he snakes, streaks off, swerves along, speeds away, flashes by, hurries dustily on, and coasts. What a delightfully spirited Good Neighbor he is! "In gullied wastelands, the shriek of [his] tires and the stench of scorched rubber filled entire valleys." Can this be? Can one man stink up an entire valley? No matter. The concept is gargantuan; the Colonel is my boy.

Still another *Time* strider, and also a fast man on wheels, is Harlow H. Curtice, president of General Motors. "Into a large, cluttered Detroit studio one day 18 months ago strode a trim, lean man with the suave good looks of an ambassador and the cheery smile of a salesman," *Time* writes. Most people would pick their way in a cluttered studio, but not Curtice. As if striding, and looking as suave as Clare Boothe Luce, weren't enough to make you love the man, *Time* calls him "Red" seven times in one article. (Red is Harlow's nickname, not a crack.) When Red travels, he doesn't drive, or fly, or take a train; he swings. "Curtice swung around the country getting to know his harried dealers." This sounds as though he had a prehensile tail, which I, for one, find attractive, though I suppose it might harry a conventional Cadillac dealer. I don't mean to make a monkey out of Red; according to *Time*, he is closer to a Cadillac than to a marmoset:

> His bright blue eyes sparkle like a newly polished car [*Time* writes], his smile is as broad as a Cadillac grille. His voice is quiet, his manner calm. But under the Curtice hood there throbs a machine with the tireless power of one of his own 260-h.p. engines.

Curtice's voice may be quiet but his conversation is forceful. When he announces an expansion program, he does it "boldly"; his predictions are "right on the button"; "on weekends he likes to drop in on the nearby Buick division, shoot the breeze with anyone from a sweeper to a foreman."

Time gets a little mixed up about Red—he "never seems to be in a hurry," it says, and, two paragraphs later, "Curtice has a hot-rodder's feeling for cars . . . likes to dash around his home town of Flint in a sporty grey-blue Buick Skylark" —but, all in all, the picture of a bold, hooded, throbbing, breeze-shooting, skylarking president is an engaging one.

For a while after reading about Curtice, Eisenhower, and Pérez Jiménez, I had the idea that only presidents strode in *Time*. Not at all. Look at Scotland's Roman Catholic Father Sydney MacEwan, "a white-haired but boyish-looking priest in a knee-length clerical coat [who] strode to the dais in the Waldorf-Astoria's Jade Room." But I regret to state that striders don't always stay boyish-looking; sometimes their strides give out, and they are reduced to walking. "An old man climbed aboard United Air Lines flight 709 in New York . . . to fly to Los Angeles," *Time* writes of General Douglas MacArthur. "His famous stride had become a careful step, his hands looked transparent and his skin like parchment. . . ."

This brings me to another attractive locomotive trait of *Time*'s cast of characters. They don't *get* into vehicles; they *climb* into them, which sounds more manly. They also climb out of them. When MacArthur got to Los Angeles, he "climbed out." John Foster Dulles is forever climbing in and out of planes in *Time*, and President René Coty, of France, "climbed from his bed to confer with pouchy-eyed politicians," while his wife, whose movements also eschew the humdrum, "padded about the palace kitchen . . . serving endless cups of coffee." Did Coty climb *up* from his bed or *down* from it? Up, I guess; those politicians were hanging from the ceiling, and were pouchy-eyed from looking down on their recumbent leader. My favorite *Time* climber is Coty's compatriot Pierre Mendès-France, who "climbed into his black Citroën." This is a real feat, even for a Frenchman who has stunted his growth by drinking milk.

I'm sorry that Mendès-France is out of office, and therefore presumably out, or relatively out, of the pages of *Time*. He will be missed. When he wasn't climbing in *Time*, he was hurrying out or walking briskly, and when he talked, he snapped. "*Eh bien*," he once snapped in *Time*, "I seem to have plenty of friends but few supporters." His downfall is clearly attributable to overexercise. He got so bushed bustling about *Time*'s Foreign News department that he was too exhausted to repair his political fences.

Time's snappers girdle the globe. " 'We are not prepared to accept the proposition that because the Soviet Union and the U.S. are agreed, all problems are solved,' snapped [India's Krishna] Menon," while the Americas abound in snappers:

"It's unanimous!" snapped Congressman William Dawson.

Private Schine snapped: "I have stopped speaking to newspapermen."

Joe [McCarthy] snapped back: "They have been shooting at me, and I've got to get back at them."

"I am here to apply the law and you ask me to break it!" snapped Café Filho [President of Brazil].

Asked by waiting newsmen about his intentions, [Marlon Brando] snapped: "It is not a publicity stunt, and I do intend to marry the girl."

Brando's girl, by the way, burbles, which makes for a nice combination. They can play burble-and-snap:

"I know I am going to start a new life with the help of Marlon, and it will be different from what I have done so far," burbled she.

When the two of them get into a vehicle in *Time*, they hop on and chug off, and when he leaves her, he speeds off.

McCarthy's snaps sometimes cause other Senators to gruff:

But when he heard of McCarthy's statement, Colorado's tough, burly [Edwin C.] Johnson gruffed: "This is the first time I've ever been called a hand-maiden."

McCarthy not only snaps, he also ambles, lumbers, elbows, and careens:

A scowling, puffy-eyed McCarthy . . . lumbered into the hearing room
. . . then he ambled out. . . . McCarthy elbowed his way through the
crowd . . .

Careening about his old stamping grounds in his home town of Appleton,
Wisconsin's Senator Joseph R. McCarthy . . .

McCarthy's closest locomotive parallel is Ernest Hemingway:

Rolling to starboard like an old freighter, Ernest Hemingway lumbered
about his weather-beaten manor. . . .

Not so peppy, perhaps, but a novelty. And when it comes to the girls on *Time*'s
masthead, Hemingway knows what he's doing; he married one of them.

A more athletic note is struck by Governor Craig of Indiana, Admiral Halsey, and Nehru:

Having vaulted into the governor's office in a hurry, George Craig landed
running, has been in a hurry ever since.

After the game . . . Fleet Admiral (ret.) William F. ("Bull") Halsey
. . . bounced around like a midshipman . . .

A slender man with jodhpured legs and a rose-bud in his buttonhole
scooted about the diplomatic conference rooms of London with whispered
propositions on his lips. India's Jawaharlal Nehru wanted to be helpful.

But don't think that Nehru always scoots around whispering in *Time*; sometimes he croaks:

"Since the dawn of history," croaked Nehru throatily . . .

As in the case of McCarthy's snaps, one colorful *Time* vocalization often begets another. Nehru's croaks are followed by conversational chuckles from his
colleagues:

Pudgy Rafi Ahmad Kidwai, 60, Minister of Food and Agriculture . . .
chuckled: "That will make Nehru think twice."

And here's a pounce that flushed a weasel:

His interrogator pounced: "But you did say it! Why?" Weaseled (Alfred)
Hitchcock uneasily: "It depends what press it was."

Before going on to some of the other ways in which the people in *Time*
exercise their vocal cords, let us observe how certain ladies among them move:

Mrs. George Malone . . . flounced from the banquet hall.

One day Oveta Culp Hobby clicked in with a bundle of charts.

Very well. Back to *Time*'s conversationalists. In addition to snapping, snorting, burbling, chuckling, croaking, pouncing, weaseling, and shooting the breeze, they groan, coo, snarl, taunt, thunder, chortle, crack, intone, growl, drawl, sneer, grumble, rumble, blurt, smirk, purr, husk, rasp, bubble, beam, smile, grin, drone, roar amid guffaws, sigh, worry, and spit entire sentences and even paragraphs. I have all the documentation at hand, but suffice it to bellow that Billy Graham and Senator Irving M. Ives thunder; Frank Lloyd Wright chortles; Konrad Adenauer growls; Winston Churchill growls, rumbles, and worries (he is also a snapper); Georgia's Governor Marvin Griffin drawls genially; Montgomery Ward Chairman Sewell Avery smiles "Do you know anyone who has $600 million all wrapped up in a bundle?;" Nat (King) Cole, a singer, husks, while shrugging, "Dialogue is just lyrics that don't rhyme"; and a "disgruntled hotelman" sighs "That is a sight that Pondicherry will not again see."

Adenauer, incidentally, whistle-stops when he takes a train, while Senator Ives, in a Caddy, roars down (without guffaws) to Manhattan. I've found only one man in *Time* who makes a really poor vehicular showing—Senator Wayne Morse:

> One jungle-hot afternoon a weathered Model T lurched down the 1600 block of Pennsylvania Avenue. . . . Out popped Wayne Morse.

Time is a Republican magazine, so perhaps Morse, who reneged on the Republicans, doesn't feel at home in it. He lurches and pops out, instead of roaring and climbing, because he's ill at ease.

Well, I think I'll gruff my analysis to a close, but first I want to point to a character trait that enhances the attractiveness of *Time* people all over the world: dutifulness. They do everything from talking dutifully to marrying dutifully:

> Said Maurine [Neuberger, wife of the Senator from Oregon] dutifully: she will retire from politics to help her husband in Washington.

> [Matyas] Rakosi [former Premier of Hungary] dutifully sent word that he agreed completely with the newest New Course.

> Pérez Jiménez [remember the old strider, dusty hurrier, and stinker-upper?] dutifully put down a dozen or so minor uprisings.

> Queen Elizabeth II's younger sister dutifully attended to the routine chores of visiting royalty.

> On [the Queen Mother's] arrival at the center, bystanding neighborhood ragamoppets applauded her dutifully.

> Crown Prince of Rumania . . . Carol Hohenzollern . . . dutifully married Princess Helen of Greece.

> Dutifully, Faure tried.

Faure, of course, is Mendès-France's successor, and in *Time* he's dutifully trying to get the support of the Socialists for a left-center coalition. He didn't succeed (some ragamoppets grimaced him down), but what can you expect of a man who—so far, at any rate—hasn't stridden, vaulted, bounced, or *entrechatted* his way into a conference room? I never heard of a Frenchman who didn't want to get on the good side, or sides, of sixty-two girls. Faure is warming up. He sighed in the March 28th issue of *Time*, and as of April 4th he is credited with a seven-sentence snap. I hear he's hired a drive-yourself Renault, and that we may hope for a shrieking-tired ricochet any week.

FRANK SULLIVAN

The Cliché Expert Reveals Himself in His True Colors[1]

Q: MR. ARBUTHNOT, would you mind telling us today how you happened to become a cliché expert? Was it easy?

A: Easy! Don't make me laugh, Mr. Crouse. It was an uphill climb. A cliché novitiate is no bed of roses, and if anyone ever tells you it is, do you know how I want you to take his statement?

Q: How?

A: With a grain of salt. I shall tell you about my career, since you insist, and as a special treat, I shall describe it to you entirely in terms of the seesaw cliché.

Q: The seesaw cliché?

A: You'll see what I mean. Before I made my mark as a cliché expert, I had my ups and downs. Sometimes, when everything was at sixes and sevens, it almost seemed as though my dearest ambitions were going to wrack and ruin. I had moments when I was almost tempted to believe that everything was a snare and a delusion. Even my own flesh and blood discouraged me, in spite of the fact that I was their pride and joy . . . You aren't listening, Mr. Crouse.

Q: Yes I am. I just closed my eyes because the light hurt. You were saying that your own kith and kin discouraged you.

A: I didn't say kith and kin, but it doesn't matter. For a considerable period of time it was nip and tuck whether I would sink or swim. If I had not been hale and hearty, and well equipped for a rough-and-tumble struggle, I wouldn't have come through. But I kept at it, hammer and tongs. I gave 'em tit for tat . . . Mr. Crouse, you *are* asleep.

[1] From *A Pearl in Every Oyster* (Boston: Little, Brown and Company, 1938), pp. 284-290. Reprinted by permission of the author.

Q: No, I'm not, Mr. Arbuthnot. You were saying you went after your goal hard and fast.

A: I did. I eschewed wine, woman, and song—

Q: Ah, but wine, woman, and song is not a seesaw cliché, Mr. Arbuthnot.

A: Yes it is, too. Woman is standing in the middle, balancing. I worked morning, noon, and night, and kept to the straight and narrow. The consequence was that in the due course of time—

Q: And tide?

A: Please! In the due course of time things began to come my way by fits and starts, and a little later by leaps and bounds. Now, I'm fine and dandy.

Q: High, wide, and handsome, eh?

A: I wish I had said that, Mr. Crouse.

Q: You—

A: Will, Oscar. Had you there, Mr. Crouse, didn't I, ha ha! When I started I was free, white, and twenty-one. Now I'm fat, fair, and forty, and I venture to predict that no man, without regard to race, creed, or color, is a better master of the cliché than your servant—your *humble* servant—Magnus Arbuthnot. So much for my life story in terms of the seesaw cliché.

Q: It certainly is an interesting story, Mr. Arbuthnot—by and large.

A: Well, in all due modesty, I suppose it is, although sometimes, to tell you the truth, I think there is neither rhyme nor reason to it.

Q: Where were you born, Mr. Arbuthnot?

A: In the altogether.

Q: I see. How?

A: On the impulse of the moment.

Q: And when?

A: In the nick of time.

Q: It is agreeable to find a man so frank about himself, Mr. Arbuthnot.

A: Why not? You asked me a question. You know what kind of question it was?

Q: Impertinent?

A: Oh, my dear man, no.

Q: Personal?

A: Civil. You asked me a civil question. I answered you by telling you the truth. I gave it to you, if I may be permitted to say so, straight from the shoulder. I revealed myself to you in my—

Q: True colors?

A: Ah, someone told you. Rather, someone *went* and told you.

Q: Were you ever in love, Mr. Arbuthnot, or am I out of order in asking that?

A: Not at all. I have had my romances.

Q: How nice.

A: Ah, you wouldn't say so if you knew what kind of romances they were.

Q: What kind were they?

A: Blighted romances, all of 'em. I kept trying to combine single blessed-ness with wedded bliss. It didn't work. I had a sweetheart in every port, and I worshiped the ground they walked on, each and every one of them. This ground amounts to a matter of 18,467 acres, as of my latest blighted romance.

Q: Hm! You must have been quite a pedestrian.

A: Well, those are the figures when the tide was out; only 16,468 acres at the neap. I was land-poor at the end. And you take the advice of a sadder—

Q: And a wiser man.

A: That's what I was going to say. And never trust the weaker sex, or you'll have an awakening. You seem to be so smart, interrupting me all the while, maybe you can tell me what kind of awakening.

Q: Awakening? Awakening? I'm afraid you have me.

A: Rude awakening.

Q: Oh, of course. Now, I don't think your story would be complete, Mr. Arbuthnot, without some statement from you regarding your material circum-stances. Are you well-to-do, or are you—

A: Hard pressed for cash? No, I'm solvent. I'm well paid.

Q: You mean you get a handsome salary?

A: I prefer to call it a princely stipend. You know what kind of coin I'm paid in?

Q: No. What?

A: Coin of the realm. Not that I give a hoot for money. You know how I refer to money?

Q: As the root of all evil?

A: No, but you have a talking point there. I call it lucre—filthy lucre.

Q: On the whole, you seem to have a pretty good time, Mr. Arbuthnot.

A: Oh, I'm not complaining. I'm as snug as a bug in a rug. I'm clear as crystal—when I'm not dull as dishwater. I'm cool as a cucumber, quick as a flash, fresh as a daisy, pleased as Punch, good as my word, regular as clockwork, and I suppose at the end of my declining years, when I'm gathered to my ancestors, I'll be dead as a doornail.

Q: *Eh bien! C'est la vie!*

A: *Mais oui, mon vieux.* I manage. I'm the glass of fashion and the mold of form. I have a finger in every pie, all except this finger. I use it for pointing with scorn. When I go in for malice, it is always malice aforethought. My nods are significant. My offers are standing. I am at cross-purposes and in dire straits. My motives are ulterior, my circles are vicious, my retainers are faithful, and my hopefuls are young. My suspicions are sneaking, my glee is fiendish, my stories are likely. I am drunk.

Q: Drunk?

A: Yes, with power. You know where?

Q: Where?

A: Behind the throne. I am emotional. My mercies are tender, and when I cry, I cry quits. I am lost in thought and up in arms. I am a square shooter with my trusty revolver. My courage is vaunted and my shame is crying, but I don't care—a rap. I have been in the depths of despair, when a watery grave in the briny deep seemed attractive. Eventually I want to marry and settle down, but the woman I marry must be clever.

   Q: Clever?

   A: With the needle.

   Q: Well, I'd certainly call you a man who had led a full life, Mr. Arbuthnot, and a likable chap, too.

   A: Yes, I'm a peach of a fellow. I'm a diamond in the rough, all wool and a yard wide. I'm too funny for words and too full for utterance. I'm a gay dog, and I like to trip the light fantastic and burn the candle at both ends with motley throngs of boon companions. I may be foolish but my folly is at least sheer.

   Q: I think you certainly have run—

   A: I certainly have. The entire gamut of human emotions. I know the facts of life. I'm afraid I've got to go now, Mr. Crouse. I'm due back at my abode. Do you know what kind of abode I live in?

   Q: Humble, Mr. Arbuthnot?

   A: Certainly not. Palatial! Goodbye, my little periwinkle!

GEOFFREY MOORE

American Prose Today[1]

But is there such a thing as an American prose? I refer here to nonfiction, the prose of exposition, the ordinary literary means of communication.

The sophist might answer: Yes, American prose is prose written by Americans. But, we persist: Is it different from English prose, and, if so, how? Or, alternatively: Is there "an American style"? The answer might be that there are a number of American styles and that they owe their nature to the circumstances of American development. Not merely racial, or religious, or social differences, but, as Mr. Wallace Stevens once said, physical ones too, have made the attitude of the people different, and the attitude of a people is reflected in its prose. Add to this the spirit which founded the United States, the early struggles, the theocratic art-banishing society of New England, the early establishment of a unique kind of democracy, the distrust of aristocratic virtues (elegance, propriety, mannered grace, intellect) and the acceptance of brotherhood-become-chumminess, and you have a taste of the brew which might be

[1] From *New World Writing*, Eighth Mentor Selection (New York: New American Library, 1955), pp. 47-70, with omissions. Copyright ©, 1955, by Geoffrey Moore.

expected to make American prose different from British. From the first, the American moved about a lot and so, despite the difference in accent between, say, South Carolina and New Hampshire, usage was sufficiently standard that he could be understood in any part of the country. In England, however, as Mr. Harold Whitehall has pointed out, the inhabitants of, for example, Howden in Yorkshire used to find it very difficult to understand the inhabitants of Dewsbury, forty miles away. And so, largely on the basis of aristocratic speech, Britain developed a *lingua franca*, Received Standard English, the rules of which could be laid down and accepted as gospel. H. W. Fowler could write a *Modern English Usage*, but no American ever either dared to write, or felt the necessity of writing, a *Modern American Usage*. Mr. Horwill, an Englishman, did, of course, produce one, but that was for the aid of the British. However, there seems, by this time, to have developed a generally accepted and, as it were, legitimate body of American usage which can be called Standard without fear of offending Americans' own susceptibilities. At least I take it to be so and, with this in mind, I should like to examine various examples of modern "expositional" American prose in an effort to discover whether they have the "independence and vigour" which, in 1954, *The Times Literary Supplement* found so marked in American creative writing. Although this will involve commenting on usage, I do not propose to single out American usages which are now perfectly acceptable in Britain.

Political Prose

My purpose was to sketch the genesis and set in some crude historical perspective the present troubled world scene, and then to attempt to defrost a tiny segment of the opaque window through which we see others and others see us—and to do it briefly, having listened to many lectures myself!

This is from the foreword to Adlai Stevenson's *Call to Greatness*. Two things are immediately noticeable: first, the modest tone, and, second, the use of an original figure of speech which has been drawn naturally and unaffectedly from American experience. Almost all Americans, except those who live in the extreme Southern states, find it necessary at some time during the winter to "defrost," either manually or by aid of a device built into their cars, a driving window which has been made opaque by frost or frozen snow. The style might be described as "literary" (e.g., "genesis," "present troubled world scene"), yet it gives an impression of ease. It has the ring of sincerity and makes us feel that we can trust a man who is at once so unpretentious and yet so quietly convinced that he can clarify our vision of world affairs.

Having come to the above conclusion about this passage, I was surprised, on re-reading it, to find that it is actually ungrammatical. I say "surprised" since, as a teacher, my eye is, if anything, over-alert to such things. The fault is in the first line, in which, to make grammatical sense, there should be an "of" after "genesis." It gives a very awkward ring to the sentence, however, and the writer, being American, was led to reject it. An Englishman would probably either have put it in or re-worded the sentence. It is, I think, a good example of how even the most educated and highly literate of Americans have, when they feel like it, a cavalier attitude toward the niceties of grammar. I have noticed that in the *non solum, sed etiam* construction, for example, Americans rarely put in the "also."

Historical Prose

(a) As the sectional tension increased, the sense of irrepressible differences, long buried in the national consciousness, began to burst into the clear. The growing pressure on the North had finally persuaded many Northerners that the slavery system embodied a fundamental threat to free society.

(b) August gave way to September, September to October, and the clamor grew increasingly furious. Jackson men paraded the streets in the glare of torches, singing campaign songs, carrying hickory poles, gathering around huge bonfires blazing high into the night.

These two extracts are both from Arthur M. Schlesinger, Jr.'s *The Age of Jackson*. Together they make a point better than one alone, and that point is that the methods and the vocabulary of the journalist have invaded the writing of history. (Cf. *Time*, April 22, 1955, "Warm in the April sunshine, London's upper-crust horseplayers crowded the club enclosure at Kempton Park Race Track. Peeresses in Dior tweeds appraised each other. . . ." etc.) The tone is different. *Time*'s is not merely colourful; it is impertinent. Mr. Schlesinger is not writing sensationally, he is merely trying to "bring the scene to life." Although he is in no sense perverting the facts, he is nonetheless "popularising" history. And since he is not merely a famous historian, but also an academic one, approved of academically, the method is worth remarking on. It is not entirely new. Strachey was, of course, a populariser and, so to pick an example from a number of others, was Philip Guedalla; but the texture of these English writers was finer grained, more glittering. Mr. Schlesinger's style, although it is not bad, is without flair, bouncy yet workaday ("as sectional tension increased," "embodied a fundamental threat"), with an occasional, rather disconcerting vernacular phrase (e.g., "into the clear"). It is the style of a man who has not thought much about language. The four parts of Mr. Schlesinger's first sentence create four different effects. The first gives us the sense of *pulling*, the second of energy contained under *pressure*, like steam in a kettle, the third *buries* this steam kettle, the fourth allows it to "burst into the clear" which seems superficially to fit with the idea of "irrepressible differences," but is vaguely disconcerting until we realize that the stress is on "into the clear," which is a hunting term. There is, in other words, a confusion of different kinds of language. This is for me a most interesting discovery, since I did not pick

Mr. Schlesinger invidiously, but in a spirit of enquiry, knowing him to be one of the most outstanding of the younger American historians.

Critical Prose

(a) Such an art when it pretends to measure life is essentially vicarious; it is a substitute for something that never was—like a tin soldier, or Peter Pan. It has all the flourish of life and every sentimental sincerity. Taken for what it is, it is charming and even instructive. Taken solemnly, as it is meant to be, the distortion by which it exists is too much for it, and it seems a kind of baby-talk.

(b) . . . aesthetic value has been defined as conformity to or expression of a culture. This is the side of formism most prevalent today. A work of art has aesthetic value in proportion as it gives expression to its age. This definition tends to run over into a cultural relativism very congenial to contemporary art historians, and in marked contrast to the universality of aesthetic values emphasized in the first formulation of aesthetic value for formism above as representation of the universal.

(c) There is nothing to do different from what we already do: if poets write poems and readers read them, each as best they can—if they try to live not as soldiers or voters or intellectuals or economic men, but as human beings—they are doing all that can be done. But to expect them (by, say, reciting one-syllable poems over the radio) to bring back that Yesterday in which people stood on chairs to look at Lord Tennyson, is to believe that General Motors can bring back "the tradition of craftsmanship" by giving, as it does, prizes to Boy Scouts for their scale-models of Napoleonic coaches; to believe that the manners of the past can be restored by encouraging country-people to say *Grüss Gott* or *Howdy, stranger* to the tourists they meet along summer lanes.

The first extract is from R. P. Blackmur's essay on the verse of E. E. Cummings in *The Double Agent*; the second is from Stephen C. Pepper's *The Basis of Criticism in the Arts*; and the third from Randall Jarrell's *Poetry and the Age*. The field of criticism in the United States is so rich that I should have preferred to take at least two or three more examples—from Edmund Wilson, say, or Van Wyck Brooks, or the late F. O. Matthiessen. However, these three samples do at least reveal three important aspects of American criticism. The second passage is of the kind which is so often the target for British writers— jargon criticism. I could have quoted more extreme examples (from Kenneth Burke, for instance) for there is a great deal of this kind of thing, particularly in academic or semi-academic writing, of which there is so much more in the United States than anywhere else. I think of it sometimes as a Germanic derivation. "The side of formism," "cultural relativism," and the garbled mumble of the end of the final sentence—this is the antithesis of clarity. Perhaps it is the result of Coleridge's example; he learnt from Germany too. Perhaps it is the overseriousness and earnestness of the American commentator. Perhaps it is a little of the unconscious desire to blind the vulgar with science. Perhaps it is an attempt to order a frighteningly vast world of thought and feeling. Perhaps it is—as Marius Bewley suggested of Kenneth Burke—that these "methodological" critics have developed their jargon and their unreadable style in order to isolate them "against the shock of the work of art itself." But, whatever the reason, the effect is both exasperating and perturbing.

The Blackmur passage, on the other hand, is a good illustration of what we mean when we say that someone's writing "has style." The language is both elegant and precise, the manner judicious but not portentous, flavored by just the right amount of everyday reference ("tin soldier, or Peter Pan" and "baby-talk"). It is the writing of an acute sensibility. We cannot help feeling the force of the conviction behind the sentiments, not only because of what they say but because of the manner of their expression. The language is faintly Jamesian, ("all the flourish of life and every sentimental sincerity"). The final effect is of a man who respects literature too much to make it merely a stamping-ground for pseudo-scientific theories.

Mr. Jarrell, in his conversational ease, his common sense and his liveliness, is representative of the young generation of American critics. He will not allow his individual perception and spirit to be subdued by the acceptances of academic style and theory. His is a style of wit and irony, which can sometimes approach the self-consciously brilliant but is anchored to earth (and this is why it is so effective for most readers) by the essential rightness of the sentiments. The style is more noticeably idiosyncratic than Mr. Blackmur's. It is perceptive, impressionistic, and opinionated. But in the last resort it obtains its effect by laying the cards on the table and saying, as it were, "Now, after all. . . ." Only a man with a wide cultural background and a sureness of judgment based on good taste can afford to do this. Finally, the style achieves a vividness and concreteness by reference to manners and institutions well known in American life.

Letters: Official and Otherwise

(a) Keeping company with these people in their notion is the man who gets a hard-to-understand Government letter. To be sure, he is peeved upon being muddled by a phrase such as "noncompensable evaluation heretofore assigned," but he is seldom really mad.

This is not from a letter but from an American government manual telling officials how to write letters more economically and less pretentiously (*Plain Letters*, published by the U. S. National Archives and Records Service in Washington, March, 1955). The writer, Miss Mona Sheppard, "staff specialist in correspondence management," has fallen, in her desire to avoid officialese and use what she calls, after Franklin K. Lane, "straightaway English," into another kind of jargon, the jargon of chumminess. Perhaps I am morbidly sensitive, but to read this passage chills my spine and raises my hackles. It is full of the kind of matey journalese which is found not only in the newspapers and on the radio but in bank circulars, advertising letters, exhortations from alumni associations, or invitations to Old Home Week with the Elks. My complaint is not with colloquial American, as such, which is extremely effective when used with skill and discrimination, by, say, Thurber, or Robert Benchley, or E. B. White, or the general run of *New Yorker* writers (or funny, in a sad sort of way, when used creatively by, say, Ring Lardner). My complaint is rather with the barbarous tone of this specimen, the absence of feeling for the values of words, the sheer lack of grace. "Keeping company with these people in their notion" is roundabout and ugly. "Hard-to-understand" is an example of the prostitution of English which is increasingly found in British as well as American daily journalism. But if I spend any longer on this passage I shall get mad too.

The language of the model letters which the Manual holds up for approval is not quite so ungraceful as the language of the instructions, but it is frequently inept, equally lacking in any sort of ear for the English language. And since, at this point, I anticipate cries of rage, and, possibly, of misunderstanding, from the direction of Washington, let me say that Style, as I understand it, is at the farthest possible remove from ornament, flourish, or affectation. It is, in Sir Arthur Quiller-Couch's words, "the power to touch with ease, grace, precision, any note in the gamut of human thought or emotion." "But essentially," Sir Arthur goes on, "it resembles good manners. It comes of endeavouring to understand others, of thinking for them rather than for yourself. . . ." (This is a point that the jargon critics could well bear in mind.)

> (b) You make me feel very much at home in Pittsburgh. I like the people I meet there; and I am enthusiastic about the job you are doing. But I would be showing rank favoritism if I were to move to go out there to start off your Institute. I have to catch up with my obligations in other parts of the country. I am, of course, flattered that you asked me to come.

This extract, from a letter held up as a good example for Government letter writers, breathes insincerity through its very heartiness. The punctuation and grammar (the placing of the semicolon and the use of "would" instead of "should") are the work of an imperfectly educated man, and the cliché, "showing rank favoritism," clashes horribly with the self-consciously colloquial "to move to go out there to start off. . . ." This is the literary equivalent of the glad hand, and just as distasteful.

The fact that the best letter in *Plain Letters* is by Abraham Lincoln is ominous. President Lincoln's letter is exact, entirely unaffected, and, through its very simplicity, a noble piece of writing, worthy to be quoted in full. It runs:

WASHINGTON, July 13, 1863

MAJOR GENERAL GRANT. My Dear General: I do not remember that you and I ever met personally. I write this now as a grateful acknowledgement for the almost inestimable service you have done the country. I wish to say a word further. When you first reached the vicinity of Vicksburg, I thought you should do what you finally did—march the troops across the neck, run the batteries with the transports, and thus go below; and I never had any faith, except a general hope that you knew better than I, that the Yazoo Pass expedition and the like could succeed. When you got below and took Port Gibson, Grand Gulf, and vicinity, I thought you should go down the river and join General Banks, and when you turned northward, east of the Big Black, I feared it was a mistake. I now wish to make the personal acknowledgement that you were right and I was wrong.

Yours very truly,

A. Lincoln

There is one last, interesting point about this American government manual. It concerns itself only with letters written by officials to the general public. The British Government publication, *The Complete Plain Words* (1954), written by Sir Ernest Gowers, (who is not a "staff specialist in correspondence management" but merely an educated man) is by comparison "pure," being concerned with the encouragement of good, clear prose in whatever kind of communication. The idea that clear prose ought to be encouraged *because* it establishes better communication, and relations, between the Government and the public, would, I am sure, be abhorrent to Sir Ernest, as it would to any man of principle.

Journalistic Prose

In a democratic country, in which almost everyone can read and in which everyone is supposed to have equal opportunities for education, or for anything else, one might expect to find a "typical" or "representative" American style, in the kind of publication which is read by the majority. According to figures taken from the polls of the Princeton Institute of Public Opinion and Mr. J. K. Wood's *Magazines of the United States*, although only approximately 20 per cent of Americans read books at all, 83 per cent regularly read newspapers and magazines.

1. *Newspapers*

(a) Secretary of Agriculture Ezra Taft Benson has called on western Kansas farmers to begin a day of "prayer and supplication to ask God in heaven to send rain." Well, that's one way of stopping the good Kansas dirt from blowing over to Russia. It's certainly not the best way. The secretary has made a tour; he's impressed. But first and foremost the secretary is a politician, not a conservationist. It will take a little more than politics to keep that western Kansas dirt on the ground.

This passage from a student newspaper editorial seems clear and direct—"conversational," "natural," in fact, yet not altogether or ingenuously so. The tone is cocky. "Secretary of Agriculture Ezra Taft Benson" is borrowed from

Time's style, which was presumably invented to give the impression that every-body's time including *Time's*, was limited. Yet the saving of one three-letter word and two commas is not worth the ungracefulness of the usage. One feels that the writer is breathing down one's neck. A cliché slips in ("first and fore-most"). "Impressed" gives one a feeling of inadequately describing Mr. Ben-son's possible reactions. Noticeable American usages are "called on," which has a Town Meeting ring, and "politician," which in England means someone in politics but in the United States is a bad word.

(b) Reed's number one problem is working capital. So in order to get money for equipment and to meet his payroll until he gets to rolling, he is incorporating the business and plans to sell stock. The telephone switchboard will be installed soon and within the next few weeks he plans to have a grand opening.

This is from an article in the *St. Louis Post-Dispatch*, and is sub-colloquial. It reads like a cross between the vernacular and the language of radio copy-writers—more the latter. Few in conversation talk about their "number one" problem, but writers of "commercials" do. "Meet his payroll" and "get to roll-ing" are examples of those vivid coinages which arise out of a forceful expand-ing society in which the tone of general prose is set by the majority, who have no ear for subtlety of language. They are designed to give an impressionistic pic-ture to people whose range of communication, understanding, and imagination is narrow. This kind of prose does not work through the intelligence but through the emotions. The repetition of "get" and "plan" emphasises the nar-rowness of the vocabulary. Within its limits it is a most effective kind of com-munication, and sufficiently hard-punching to penetrate the dullest mind ca-pable of reading words on a page. It is an example of American pragmatism. It is probably inevitable in a democratic society in which the mass media have superseded the printed page as the chief means of communication. It reflects the speech and the habits of mind of the majority of people and it would be sentimental, ineffectual, and entirely unrealistic (not to say reactionary) for one to regret that this particular form of speech ever invaded prose. But one does.

(c) The Pakistan grain storage contract presents a flagrant case of official negligence and mismanagement. Any monkey business with government contracts can and should be a matter of public concern. So we have this rela-tively small item of grain elevators grown into a national story.

(d) For the present, and with all due consideration of both Soviet aims and motivations, it appears as if the Soviets are prepared to give ground at least in part and at least at one point—Austria. After stalling and sabotaging the Austrian treaty in more than 260 treaty meetings stretching over nearly a decade, they have now reached agreement with Austria on the terms of lib-eration which, barring new Soviet demands, the West is likely to accept.

These two passages are from editorials, the first in the *Kansas City Star* for May 4, 1955, the second from *The New York Times* for May 2, 1955. The most noticeable thing about the first is the way in which it combines an elevated and judicious style with colloquialisms. "Presents a flagrant case" in the first passage consorts oddly with "monkey business." The grave "can and should be a matter of public concern" is immediately followed by the colloquial "So we have this . . . ," as one might say, to a friend, "So we have this fellow (or car, or problem) on our hands." This lack of taste, of consistency of tone, of feeling for what is appropriate in the context may arise from the comparative lack of literary training in American, particularly Middle Western, schools. *The New York Times* passage is a much better piece of writing and much more of a piece. It is much less "literary" than a leader in the London *Times* would be, but more pompous. To some extent, "stalling," which is vivid and vernacular, conflicts with the high editorial style ("all due consideration").

2. *Magazines*

(a) The only comment on the American economy that can be made with perfect assurance is that nobody really understands it. On the whole, this is a good thing. An economy capable of being thoroughly understood would probably prove treacherous. Of course, there are always a few professionals who like to believe that they understand the American economy, and these people turn up at Congressional hearings to explain why the market acts the way it does, but it is quite obvious that they are just groping their way along, the same as everybody else.

This is from the editorial page of *The New Yorker* entitled "Talk of the Town," the nearest thing to the essay one can find in the United States today. It is highly intelligent and professionally polished, yet intimate and engaging in its manner. The man who wrote this passage did have an ear, and he did have taste. The short second sentence picks up an echo both of the New York Yiddish colloquialism "This is a good thing?" and the British (1066 *and All That*) "a Good Thing," and yet is simply effective without these probably unintended connotations. The third sentence is disarming. It is as sensitively balanced as a line of verse. "Treacherous" strikes one as being just the right word; no other will do. It is meaningful, connotative, and funny, yet not fancy. "Of course," "these people," and "the same as everybody else" keep the level down, an important thing in a milieu in which ceremony or over-refinement are quickly smelled out. This kind of prose mirrors the most attractive kind of American personality, that of a man who is polite but not deferential, droll, easy in manner, and responsive.

(b) Barsov went. At his own request, the U.S. authorities flew him to Linz. "Are you sure you want to go back?" they asked him at the end. He was.

The Soviets had a propaganda bonanza in Barsov; they pointed to him as an example of what happens to those who desert the Soviets and trust the West.

This quotation from an article in the *Reader's Digest* is an example of "bright" snappy journalism. The clipped style ("Barsov went," "He was.") probably owes something to the Walter Winchell manner of radio reporting. The American slang word "bonanza" (a rich strike) is a good choice since it adds, like a raccoon's tail to a streamlined car, a human touch to prose which is in danger of becoming cold through its professional terseness. This prose is tailored for "modern people" who, after a day in the office or the factory, believe that the best way to relax is by not mentally taxing themselves. It has, therefore, a "cat on the mat" simplicity and clarity, otherwise a number of readers (who knows how many?) would consider themselves too tired even to try to grasp its import. This kind of prose must also have a reasonable quota of direct speech and be sharply paragraphed, for unrelieved indirect speech and normal paragraphing would be too dull and difficult to lure the fickle attention of the new kind of reader. Such devices are, of course, used in other publications too, both inside and outside the United States. In Britain, for example, the *Daily Express*, which is much influenced by the fashions of the United States, is an extreme example of bright journalism. . . .

> (c) The speaker rustled his notes, clinked a pocketful of keys and stared at the ceiling while he fumbled for words. Then his wife's voice cut through the jangle: "Put your keys down, honey." Meekly, irascible Columnist West-brook Pegler obeyed. For once the foaming temper was in check. Mellow with memory, onetime Sportswriter Pegler had turned out for the Tucson, Ariz. Press Club dinner, greeting the new baseball season.
>
> Peg. . . .

This passage is, of course, from *Time* (April 11, 1955). The formula is familiar and highly successful: first, the dramatic opening, the deliberate holding back of the name. Who can this Milquetoast be? To our surprise, it is none other than irascible Columnist Westbrook Pegler, who, having been introduced in a cloud of unknowing, soon becomes, in the democratic fashion, our friend, "Peg." This richly staged introduction, as designing as an advertiser's banquet, achieves its purpose admirably, again within the imaginative scope and vocabulary of the lowest common denominator of readers, although the level is, one suspects, rather higher than that of the *Reader's Digest*. It is the most lavish example so far of the presentation of factual material in an emotional way. It was prophesied by Tocqueville as a concomitant of the Age of Democracy. Everyone can read, but few can or want to read properly. Even to say "properly" is suspect in this time of the triumph of the mindless. Must democracy inevitably lead to the relaxing of standards and pandering to increasingly jaded palates? It is a nice question. The "average reader" cannot be expected to use his brain because he wants "relaxation" after his day's work, or because he has no time to spare, or because he wasn't taught properly in High School. So the writers of *Time* labour (and they probably have some fun doing it, too) to present him with ever more brightly written and attractively presented material. If they did not, their public would go off and read *Newsweek*, no doubt.

Advertising Prose

(a) Yes, only Viceroy has this filter composed of 20,000 tiny filter traps. You cannot obtain the same filtering action in *any other cigarette*. . . . That's why more college men and women smoke Viceroys than any other filter cigarette. . . .

This passage, taken from an advertisement by the makers of Viceroy cigarettes in a student newspaper, is typical of nationwide current advertising technique for cigarettes, and of the kind of prose used in such advertisements.

The copywriters have apparently now reached their nadir, for they are using the same formula in print as on the radio. Perhaps this is significant in terms of the relationship of speech to literature in the United States, but I doubt it. The method is one of insidious hammering, as if with a little rubber hammer which the torturer wields tirelessly, so that, in the end, one's whole body is in tune with the nagging rhythmic blows. Four (at least four) things are constant: first, the meaningless and tiresome "yes," worn like a charm to scare away the advertising man's bogey (lack of smoothness, lack of a "friendly" yet authoritative, selling ring); second, the appeal to "science"; third, the "You cannot . . . in *any other cigarette*" (which varies in some cases to "No other cigarette made . . ." etc.); and fourth, the repetition on the same, though slightly modulated note ("That's why . . . than any other filter smoke"). Writers on the traditional ballad tell us that their anonymous authors used the device of "incremental repetition" in order that a rhythmic, memorable pattern might be retained in the minds of an audience which lived in an oral tradition. Here is incremental repetition today, serving other ends in another society.

Why Swelter? Just a Twist of the Wrist Changes
Hot Misery . . . to Cool Comfort!
Live and Work in G-E "Comfort-Conditioned Air"!

Simply dial out swelter wtih this great new General Electric Room Air Conditioner! You can sleep dry and cool tonight in G-E "Comfort-Conditioned Air"—air that's always cool, dry and filtered to reduce dust, dirt and pollen.

Why Not Call on Your General Electric Dealer Now?

The most noticeable thing about this passage, which is taken from an advertisement in *Life*, is its colourful and highly sensory use of language. This, coupled with the exclamatory style, creates an effect of pseudo-momentousness. Nothing more, possibly, in the way of emotive effect, could have been crammed into the headline. The advertising copywriters are, as I believe Mr. Hayakawa once pointed out, the folk-poets of modern commercial civilization. They know all the tricks of language that a poet or a short story writer knows, but they put them to the service, not of art, but of commercial persuasion. As Tocqueville said, "Democracy not only infuses a taste for letters among the trading classes, but introduces a trading spirit into literature." The writer of this copy ("Just a Twist of the Wrist") had an ear for the fundamental rhythms of the English language, a language which naturally and easily falls into patterns of rhyme, alliteration and onomatopoeia. These are patterns which can be found as easily in literature as in ordinary speech, from "A faire felde ful of folke / Fonde I there bytwene," of William Langland to "The breezes blew, the white foam flew, / The furrow follow'd free" of Coleridge, from Cockney rhyming slang to the "What's cookin', good-lookin' " of the American high school boy.

"Dial it out" is another example of verbal ingenuity devoted to the end of persuading. The effect is concentrated and dramatic. One can see oneself just dialling away "swelter," (i.e. the state of sweltering) by that "twist of the wrist." The use of "swelter" here, incidentally, is an interesting illustration of the extreme grammatical flexibility of the English language in communicating sensations, and also of the streamlining tendency of American English.

Another interesting invention is "Comfort-Conditioned Air." Perhaps the copywriter, like Fleming with his moulds, made the discovery by sheer accident. At any rate, it seems to be a reversal of the familiar "Air-Conditioned Comfort." And the wonder of it is that it means something. The poet, fiddling with words, struck rich ore (a bonanza). The effect of it was so heady that when he came to compose the whole line he made the very air, now "cool, dry and filtered," the property of General Electric. What kind of air have you there, Mr. Jones? I have G.E. Comfort-Conditioned Air in here, Mr. Smith.

One last point calls for mention and that is the use of "great," which, second to "beautiful," seems to be the most overworked word in the English language. If this air-conditioner is "great," what then was the invention of the aeroplane or the propounding of the Theory of Relativity?

I trust that my own tone, in commenting on these examples, has not at times seemed like that of the Reverend John Witherspoon. The Reverend John was mild in comparison with later British commentators who were apt to report on the misuse of language in the United States with shouts of glee, thus arousing the animosity and eventually the triumphant counter-cries of H. L. Mencken. A pre-Revolutionary (immigrant) American, the Reverend John hoped for a specifically American style, to be watched over by some "center of learning and politeness." In the meantime he thought it his duty to point out the various misuses of the English language in America, which he listed under the headings of: (1) Americanisms, (2) vulgarisms in England and America, (3) vulgarisms in America alone, (4) local phrases or terms, (5) common blunders arising from ignorance, (6) cant phrases, (7) personal blunders, and (8) technical terms introduced into the language.

On subjects like America and Prose one's mind cannot be made a blank. One has impressions, and my impression, before examining the samples I have chosen, was that in spite of some obvious examples of excessive rhetoric, of ineptness in handling words, of crudeness, of a peculiarly American kind of inflation, American prose as a whole had more naturalness than the English and at its best a transparent sincerity and simplicity worthy of American ideals. I did not, however, choose my quotations to prove this point. I threw my net as wide as I could, examined the pieces as objectively as possible, and relied on my findings to provide me with some conclusions which might or might not prove what I had previously accepted.

I find, on the whole, that my preconceptions are borne out only in so far as the best topical commentary, the best political writing, the best criticism and, above all, the best humorous writing is concerned. Elsewhere, there are great variations. Of course, the reader might object that he could have chosen a whole set of other samples which would alter the emphasis, or alternatively, that the quotations were far too short for judgment. This might be true, but short of conducting a statistical survey I do not see what else could be done. Perhaps, before our time runs out, one of the great Foundations will have provided funds for such an enterprise. But since language cannot be gauged like physical reactions, and the value of the comments depends on the taste of the investigator, it would be a difficult task. In the meantime, and in the light of my own crude sampling, I offer, diffidently, some general conclusions.

In the first place, it seems to me that American "expositional prose" is much weaker than American creative prose. Only in the case of people of acute sensibility, at the highest level, do we find a kind of prose which, by its tasteful natural diction, its use of figures drawn from American life, and its ease of manner can be held up as an example of the use of English which is both good and distinctively American. The American temperament seems better fitted to explore the creative possibilities of language, and one can find all kinds of examples to support this from the ebullience but relative crudeness of Thomas Wolfe to the fine-grained yet almost overwhelmingly rhetorical "immediacy" of William Faulkner. In the hands of the modern American short story writer, particularly, American prose is both beautiful and exciting to read. Life leaps from the page: sights, colours, smells, all the multifarious aspects of common and uncommon human existence make an impact which British creative prose rarely achieves. But the cultural climate of the United States in the 20th century has apparently not been conducive to the development of a widespread and distinctively American instrument for conveying facts, ideas, and comment at the general level. Feelings and emotions get in the way, for one thing. There is too commonly an inability to express a logical sequence of thought with "ease, grace, precision," what I have called "having no ear" for the English language. One reason for this lies, I am sure, in the deep-seated American feeling that "style" is something ornamental, part of a way of life that is variously called "British" or "aristocratic." It does not matter that the reaction, which is an emotional one, is understandable. What matters is that it is bad for American prose. To quote Sir Arthur Quiller-Couch again:

> The editor of a mining paper in Denver, U.S.A., boldly the other day laid down this law, that niceties of language were mere "frills": all a man needed was "to get there," that is, to say what he wished in his own way. But just here . . . lies the mischief. You will not get there by hammering away on your own untutored impulse. You must first be your own reader, chiselling out the thought definitely for yourself: and, after that, must carve out the intaglio more sharply and neatly, if you would impress its image accurately upon the wax of other men's minds.

But there is another reason, I believe, for the comparative lack of literary ability in all but the exceptional in the United States and this lies in the tendency to "educate for life" and to relegate literature to an inferior place. A questionnaire sent out in 1949 for *Harper's Magazine* by Norman Lewis revealed what Mr. Lewis called a "linguistic liberalism" among those people in the United States who "use the English language as a direct means of earning a livelihood." This meant accepting such expressions as "His work is different *than* mine," "I encountered *less* difficulties than I had expected" (attributed to Mr. Arthur Schlesinger, Jr.), and "The reason I'm worried is *because* I think she's ill." If we substitute "sloppy English" for "linguistic liberalism" we are, I think, nearer the mark. Yet, as against ninety-three American College Professors of English who rejected the first expression there were sixty-two who accepted it as worthy of currency in educated speech. Forty-nine out of the one hundred and fifty-five even accepted the barbarous second example, and the astounding total of eighty-nine out of one hundred and fifty-five the third. This perhaps partly explains why college students' essays are such examples of bad prose. But what is far more perturbing than uneducated usage in educated exposition is the sheer muddle of the language, the lack of an ability, in the college group, to express ideas lucidly and coherently. Yet even those who seem on the page to be semi-literate morons can make good sense when they speak, be ready in comment, even advance ideas. One's conclusion cannot but be that American conditions, educational and otherwise, have militated against clear and graceful literary expression. Yet Abraham Lincoln, that self-educated man, could express himself simply, cogently, and with style. Could he have learnt it had he grown up in America today? Where would he find models? Well, he could find them for one thing in Mr. Stevenson's prose, or in Mr. Oppenheimer's, or Mr. Randall Jarrell's, or Mr. Thurber's. He could read *The New Yorker*, or the *Atlantic*, or *Harper's*. The compilers of college textbooks of exposition certainly seem to strive to put good examples of prose before their readers. One wonders what the 40 per cent of college professors of English who say "His work is different *than* mine" do with them. Point out their queer usage perhaps?

It seems, then, that "independence and vigour," which the United States has in abundance, may produce good novels and stories but does not make a good climate for expositional prose which, unlike creative writing, touches everybody. In fact, the outstanding exceptions which I have noted would be classified by some as outside the mainstream of American culture. It almost seems as if there were, as Disraeli said of 19th century English society, "two nations" in America, but instead of these two nations being the rich and the poor they are the educated and the uneducated, the literate and the semi-literate. One remembers some of Tocqueville's prophecies:

> The most common expedient employed by democratic nations to make an innovation in language consists in giving some unwonted meaning to an expression already in use. This method is very simple, prompt, and convenient; no learning is required to use it aright, and ignorance itself rather facilitates the practice; but that practice is most dangerous to the language.

There will always, I feel, be Americans to whom these practices will be abhorrent. They will uphold the standards of American prose to the end. But to whom will they make their communication, except to each other?

All this raises, no doubt, most interesting questions, some as basic as one could wish for, such as: Does literacy matter? It is true that one can be intelligent without being literate. But Western Civilisation is built upon such principles and traditions as demand literacy. To deny it is to deny Western Civilisation as an idea and to prepare the way for barbarism. Yet some years ago a Californian professor seriously suggested, not merely that the oral might eventually entirely supersede the written communication, but that it was a good thing that it should do so. Perhaps in the end it will be so. Perhaps the triumph of the mass media and the encouragement of "speech" rather than literature in schools has started a tide which cannot be turned. And what, when it is upon them, will the publishers and manufacturers of typewriters do then, poor things? If they are, like the rest of us, still here, that is.

H. L. MENCKEN

The American Language[1]

The first Englishman to notice an Americanism sneered at it aloofly, thus setting a fashion that many of his countrymen have been following ever since. He was one Francis Moore, a ruffian who came out to Georgia with Oglethorpe in 1735, and the word that upset him was *bluff*, in the sense of "a cliff or headland with a broad precipitous face." He did not deign to argue against it; he

[1] From *The Yale Review*, XXV (March, 1936), 538-552, with omissions. Copyright Yale University Press.

simply dismissed it as "barbarous," apparently assuming that all Englishmen of decent instincts would agree with him. For nearly a century they seem to have done so, and *bluff* lingered sadly below the salt. When it was printed at all in Great Britain it was set off by sanitary quotation marks, or accompanied by other hints of deprecation, as *rubberneck*, *hot spot* and *nerts* are accompanied today. But then, in 1830, the eminent Sir Charles Lyell used it shamelessly in the first volume of his monumental "Principles of Geology," and from that day to this it has been a perfectly respectable if somewhat unfamiliar word in England, with a place in every dictionary.

Its history is the history of almost countless other Americanisms. They have been edging their way into English since early colonial times, and, for more than a century past, in constantly increasing volume, but I can't recall one that didn't have to run a gauntlet of opposition in the motherland, at times verging upon the frantic. After the Revolution, that opposition took on the proportions of a holy war. Never an American book came out that the English reviewers did not belabor its vocabulary violently. The brunt of the attack, of course, had to be borne by the poetasters of the era—for example, Joel Barlow, whose "Columbiad" (1807) loosed a really terrifying geyser of abuse. But even the most serious writers got their share—among them, Jefferson, John Marshall, Noah Webster, and John Quincy Adams. Jefferson's crime was that he had invented the verb to *belittle*. It was, one may argue plausibly, a very logical, useful, and perhaps even nifty word, and seventy-five years later the prissy Anthony Trollope was employing it without apology. But when Jefferson ventured to use it in his "Notes on Virginia" (1787) "The London Review" tossed and raged in a manner befitting the discovery of a brace of duelling pistols beneath the cope of the Archbishop of Canterbury, and for several years following its dudgeon was supported virtuously by most of the other reviews. "What an expression!" roared the "London." "It may be an elegant one in Virginia, but for our part, all we can do is to *guess* at its meaning. For shame, Mr. Jefferson! Freely, good sir, will we forgive all your attacks, impotent as they are illiberal, upon our national character: but for the future spare—O spare, we beseech you, our mother-tongue!"

The underscoring of *guess* was a fling in passing at another foul Americanism. It was the belief of most Englishmen then, as it is today, that the use of the verb in the sense of to *suppose* or *assume* originated in this country. It is actually to be found, in that meaning precisely, in "Measure for Measure" and "Henry VI"; nay, in Chaucer, Wycliffe, and Gower. But such historical considerations have never daunted the more ardent preservers of the King's English. When a word acquires an American flavor it becomes anathema to them, even though it may go back to Boadicea. *To advocate* offers an instructive example. It appeared in English in the dark backward and abysm of time, but during the eighteenth century it seems to have dropped out of general use, though Burke used it. Towards the end of the century it came into vogue in this country and soon it made its way back to the land of its birth. It was received with all the honors proper to an invasion of Asiatic cholera. The reviews denounced it as loutish, "Gothic," and against God, and lumped it with *to compromit* and *to happify* as proof that civilization was impossible in America, and would be so forevermore. Even Benjamin Franklin, returning from England in 1789, was alarmed into begging Noah Webster to "reprobate" it, along with *to notice, to progress,* and *to oppose.* There is no record of Noah's reply, but it is most unlikely that he did any reprobating, for when he began to make dictionaries he included all four verbs, and they have been listed in every considerable dictionary published since, whether in this country or in England.

The leader of the heroic struggle to keep Americanisms out of Britain, in its early stages, was the celebrated William Gifford, editor of "The Quarterly Review." Gifford was a killer in general practice, and his savage assaults on Wordsworth, Shelley, and Keats are still unpleasantly remembered. He was the first magazine editor in history to make the trade pay, and when he died in 1828 he left £25,000 and was buried in Westminster Abbey. One of his major specialties was the villainousness of everything American, from politics to table manners and from theology to speechways. Among the allegations that he either made himself or permitted his contributors to make were these: (*a*) that the Americans employed naked colored women to wait upon them at table, (*b*) that they kidnapped Scotsmen, Irishmen, Hollanders, and Welshmen and sold them into slavery, and (*c*) that they were planning to repudiate the English language altogether, and adopt Hebrew in its place. This last charge, as it flew from tongue to tongue, acquired variorum readings. One of them made the new American language an Indian dialect, another made it Greek, and a third was to the effect that the people of Britain would be forced to acquire Greek, thus leaving English to the wicked will of the barbaric Yankees. It all sounds idiotic today, but in 1814 it was taken quite seriously by many Englishmen. Gifford was a tyrannical editor and so vastly enjoyed slashing his contributors' copy that Southey once denounced him as "a butcherly review-gelder." But anything that was against the damyankee passed his eye unscathed, and he piled up accusations in a manner so shameless that "The North American Review" was moved to protest that if the tirade went on it would "turn into bitterness the last drops of good-will towards England that exist in the United States."

In the early Twenties of that century there was some amelioration, and when Gifford retired from the "Quarterly" in 1824, voices that were almost conciliatory began to be heard. They heaped praises on Niagara Falls, found something to commend in Cooper's "Spy," and even had kind words for the speed and luxuriousness of American canalboats. But my most diligent researches have failed to unearth anything complimentary to the American language. It continued to be treated as a grotesque and immoral gibberish, full of uncouth terms and at war with all the canons of English. Every British traveller who came to these shores between the War of 1812 and the Civil War had something to say about the neologisms his ears and eyes encountered on his tour, and nearly all were constrained to deplore them. Captain Basil Hall, who was here in 1827 and 1828, went about in a palpitating daze, confounded and outraged by the signs on American places of business. *Clothing Store* he interpreted after long thought, and *Flour and Feed Store* after prayer and soul-searching, but what on earth was a *Leather and Finding Store*? Captain Thomas Hamilton, who followed five years later, found it impossible to penetrate to "the precise import" of *Dry-Goods Store*, and when he encountered an established offering *Hollow Ware, Spiders, and Fire-Dogs* he gave up in despair.

Hall was not one to take it lying down. He decided to call upon Noah Webster, whose American Dictionary of the English Language had just come out, to find out what the Yankees meant by using the mother tongue so cruelly. Webster shocked him by arguing stoutly that "his countrymen had not only a right to adopt new words, but were obliged to modify the language to suit the novelty of the circumstances, geographical and political, in which they were placed." The great lexicographer "who taught millions to spell but not one to sin" went on to observe judicially that it was "quite impossible to stop the progress of language—it is like the course of the Mississippi, the motion of which, at times, is scarcely perceptible; yet even then it possesses a momentum quite irresistible. Words and expressions will be forced into use in spite of all the exertions of all the writers in the world."

"But surely," persisted Hall, "such innovations are to be deprecated?"

"I don't think that," replied old Noah. "If a word becomes universally current in America, where English is spoken, why should it not take its station in the language?"

"Because," declared Hall with magnificent pertinacity, "there are words enough already."

This heroic dogma is still heard in England, where even native novelties are commonly opposed violently, and not infrequently strangled at birth. There seems to be, in the modern Englishman, very little of that ecstasy in word-making which so prodigiously engrossed his Elizabethan forebears. Shakespeare alone probably put more new words into circulation than all the English writers since Carlyle, and they were much better ones. The ideal over there today is not picturesque and exhilarating utterance, but correct and reassuring utterance, and one of its inevitable fruits is that bow-wow jargon which Sir Arthur Quiller-Couch describes in "On the Art of Writing" as "the medium through which boards of government, county councils, syndicates, committees, commercial firms, express the processes as well as the conclusions of their thought, and so voice the reason of their being." It is, at its worst, at least in accord with what are taken to be the principles of English grammar, and at its best it shows excellent manners and even a kind of mellifluous elegance; indeed, the English, taking one with another, may be said to write much better than we do—at all events by the standards of the schoolmaster. But what they write is seldom animated by anything properly describable as bounce. It lacks novelty, variety, audacity. There is little juice in it. The reader confronted by it is treated politely and lulled pleasantly, but he seldom enjoys the enchantment of surprise. That diligent search for new and racy locutions which occupied so much of the work day of Walt Whitman and William Dean Howells alike, and is practised so assiduously by scores of saucy Andersons and Hemingways, Sandburgs and Saroyans today, is carried on across the ocean by only a few extravagant eccentrics, virtually all of whom—for example, James Joyce and Ezra Pound—are non- and even anti-Englishmen. The hundred-per-cent English writers, save when they stoop to conscious wickedness, seldom depart very far from the jargon of Quiller-Couch. It is by no means a monopoly of the classes he named, nor is it reserved for solemn occasions. I find it also in my favorite English weekly, the "News of the World," which is devoted principally to sports, the theatres, and the more scabrous varieties of crime, and is probably a far better mirror of England than the "Times." When the "News of the World" reports the downfall of a rural dean or a raid on a Mayfair night club, the thing is done in a style so tight and brittle that nothing to match it is discoverable in this country, at least outside the pages of "The Homiletic Review." "When we want to freshen our speech," Mrs. Virginia Woolf was lately saying, "we borrow from American—*poppycock, rambunctious, flip-flop, booster, good mixer*. All the expressive, ugly, vigorous slang which creeps into use among us, first in talk, later in writing, comes from across the Atlantic." . . .

Whenever an Americanism comes publicly into question in England, there are efforts to track down its etymology, and sometimes the theories offered are extremely bizarre. In January, 1935, for example, the London "Morning Post" opened its columns to a furious and fantastic discussion of the verb-phrase, *to get his goat*. I content myself with one of the explanations: "Among the Negroes in Harlem it is the custom for each household to keep a goat to act as general scavenger. Occasionally one man will steal another's goat, and the household débris then accumulates to the general annoyance." The truth is that *to get his goat* seems to be of French origin, and in the form of *prendre sa chèvre* philological genealogists have traced it back to the year 1585. But whatever is strange and upsetting is put down, in England, to the hellish ingenuity of Americans—save, of course, when genuine Americanisms are claimed as really English. This last happens often enough to give what may be called a cockeyed aspect to the perennial pother. In 1934 even the learned Dr. C. T. Onions, one of the editors of the great Oxford Dictionary, succumbed to the madness by offering to find in the dictionary any alleged Americanism that a reporter for the London "Evening News" could name. The reporter began discreetly with *fresh* (in the sense of *saucy*), *to figure* (in the sense of *to believe* or *conclude*), and *to grill* (in the sense of *to question*), and Dr. Onions duly found them all. But when the reporter proceeded to *bunkum*, the learned editor had to forget conveniently that its progenitor was the thoroughly American *buncombe*, when *rake-off* followed he had to admit that the earliest example in the dictionary was from an American work, and when *baloney* and *nerts* were hurled at him he blew up with a bang.

Here, of course, Dr. Onions and his interlocutor ended on the level of slang, but there is no telling where they would be if they could be translated to the year 2036. *Baloney*, like *to belittle*, has the imprimatur of an eminent tribune of the people, and is quite as respectable, philologically speaking, as *buncombe*, *gerrymander*, *pork barrel*, *filibuster*, *carpetbagger*, *gag rule*, or *on the fence*. All these came into American from the argot of politics, and got only frowns from the schoolmarm, but they are all quite sound American today, and most of them have gone into English. As for *nerts*, it seems to be but one more member of an endless dynasty of euphemisms, beginning with *zounds* and coming down to *son-of-a-gun*, *gee*, and *darn*. *Darn*, like *nerts*, is an Americanism, and Dr. Louise Pound has demonstrated that it descends from *eternal*, which first turned into *tarnal* and then lost its tail and borrowed the head of *damn*. I have heard a bishop use it freely in private discourse, with a waggish sprinkling of actual *damns*. *Son-of-a-gun* is now so feeble and harmless that the Italians in America use it as a satirical designation for native Americans, who seem to them to fall far behind the Italian talent for profanity and objurgation. It is, I believe, a just criticism. Some time ago I was engaged by a magazine to do an article on American and English swearwords. After two or three attempts I had to give it up, for I found that neither branch of our ancient Frisian tongue could show anything worthy of serious consideration. The antinomians of England stick to two or three banal obscenities, one of which, *bloody*, is obscene only formally, and we Americans seldom get beyond variations of *hell* and *damn*. A single Neapolitan boatman could swear down the whole population of Anglo-Saxondom.

Bloody is perfectly innocuous in the United States, and it may be innocuous in England also on some near tomorrow—or even more disreputable than it is today. There is no predicting the social career of words. Dr. Leonard Bloomfield says that even "our word *whore*, cognate with the Latin *carus* (dear), must have been at one time a polite substitute for some term now lost." Prophecy fails just as dismally when propriety does not come into question. Shakespeare's numerous attempts to introduce new words, some of them his own inventions and others borrowed from the slang of the Bankside, failed almost as often as they succeeded. He found ready takers for *courtship*, *lonely*, *sportive*, *multitudinous*, *hubbub* and *bump*, but his audiences would have none of *definement*, in the sense of description, or of *citizen* as an adjective, and both seem strange and uncouth to us today, though all the others are as familiar and as decorous as *cat* or *rat*. When John Marston used *strenuous* in 1599 it was attacked by Ben Jonson as barbarous, but a dozen years later it had got into Chapman's Homer, and by 1670 it was being used by Milton. It remained perfectly respectable until 1900, when Theodore Roosevelt announced the Strenuous Life. Both the idea and the term struck the American fancy, and in a little while the latter passed into slang, and was worn so threadbare that all persons of careful speech sickened of it. To this day it carries a faintly ridiculous connotation, and is seldom used seriously. But by 1975 it may be restored to the dignity of *psychopath* or *homoousian.* No one can say yes with any confidence, and no one can say no. "Even the greatest purist," observes Robert Lynd, "does not object to the inclusion of *bogus* in a literary English vocabulary, though a hundred years ago it was an American slang word meaning an apparatus for coining false money. *Carpetbagger* and *bunkum* are other American slang words that have naturalized themselves in English speech, and *mob* is an example of English slang that was once as vulgar as *photo.*" . . .

One finds in current American all the characters and tendencies that marked the rich English of Shakespeare's time—an eager borrowing of neologisms from other languages, a bold and often very ingenious use of metaphor, and a fine disdain of the barricades separating the parts of speech. The making of new words is not carried on only, or even principally, to fill gaps in the vocabulary; indeed, one may well agree with Captain Hall that "there are words enough already." It is carried on because there survives in the American something that seems to have faded out of the Englishman: an innocent joy in word-making for its own sake, a voluptuous delight in the vigor and elasticity of the language. The search for the *mot juste* is an enterprise that is altogether too pedantic for him; he much prefers to solve his problem by non-Euclidian devices. *Hoosegow* was certainly not necessary when it appeared, for we already had a large repertory of synonyms for *jail.* But when the word precipitated itself from the Spanish *juzgado* somewhere along the Rio Grande it won quick currency, and in a little while it was on the march through the country, and soon or late, I suppose, it will produce its inevitable clipped forms, *hoose* and *gow,* and its attendant adjective and verb. *Corral,* which entered by the same route in the Forties of the last century, had hatched a verb before the Civil War, and that verb, according to Webster's New International (1934), now has four separate and distinct meanings. *Bummer,* coming in from the German, is now clipped to *bum,* and is not only noun, verb, and adjective but also adverb. *Buncombe,* borrowed by the English as *bunkum,* has bred *bunco* and *bunk* at home, both of which rove the parts of speech in a loose and easy way, and the last of which has issue in the harsh verb *to debunk,* still under heavy fire in England.

The impact of such lawless novelties upon the more staid English of the motherland is terrific. The more they are denounced as heathen and outlandish, the quicker they get into circulation. Nor do they prosper only on the level of the vulgate, and among careless speakers. There are constant complaints in the English newspapers about their appearance in the parliamentary debates, and even in discourses from the sacred desk, and they begin to show themselves also in *belles-lettres,* despite the English dislike of new ways of writing. Their progress, in fact, is so widespread and so insidious that they often pop up in the diatribes that revile them; the Englishman, conquered at last, can no longer protest against Americanisms without using them. Moreover, they are now supported actively by a definitely pro-American party of writers and scholars, and though it is still small in numbers, at least compared to the patriot band, it shows some distinguished names. The late Robert Bridges, Poet Laureate, was an active member of it, and among its other adherents are Wyndham Lewis, Edward Shanks, Richard Aldington, and Sir John Foster Fraser. Sir William Craigie, perhaps the first living lexicographers, is so greatly interested in the American form of English that he has spent the years since 1925 in a scientific examination of it, and will presently begin the publication of an elaborate dictionary. If only because of the greater weight of the population behind it, it seems destined to usurp the natural leadership of British English, and to determine the general course of the language hereafter. But its chief advantage in this struggle is really not the numerical one, but the fact that its daring experiments and iconoclasms lie in the grand tradition of English, and are signs of its incurable normalcy and abounding vigor.

How far it will move away from the theorizing of grammarians and the policing of schoolmarms remains to be seen. They will make valiant efforts to curb its wayward spirit, but with gradually diminishing success. When, a few years ago, the late Sterling A. Leonard of the University of Wisconsin submitted a long series of their admonitions to a committee of educated Americans, including many philologians, he found that opinion was against them on that high level almost as decidedly as it was on lower ones. His judges favored scores of forms that the school grammars and popular handbooks of usage still condemn. Since then a more direct attack upon the conservative position has been made by Dr. Robert C. Pooley of the same university. He shows that some of the rules laid down with most assurance by pedants have no support in either history or logic, and are constantly violated by writers of unquestionable authority. There have even been rumblings of revolt in the conservative camp. The late George Philip Krapp of Columbia, who was surely anything but a radical, was of the opinion that English would undergo profound changes in the United States, and that many of them would be of such a character that its very grammatical structure would be shaken. Dr. George O. Curme of Northwestern University is another eminent grammarian who warns his colleagues that the rules they cherish have no genuine authority, and must be overhauled from time to time. Once they steel themselves to that sacrifice of their professional dignity, he says, "it will give a thrill to English-speaking students to discover that the English language does not belong to the schoolteacher but belongs to them, and that its future destiny will soon rest entirely in their hands."

Dr. Curme is always careful to think and speak of American as no more than a variation of English. But it must be obvious that, in late years, the tail has begun a vigorous wagging of the dog. "The facts that we ought to realize," says Edward Shanks to his fellow Britons, "and that we ignore when we talk loftily about Americanisms, are that America is making a formidable contribution to the development of our language, and that all our attempts to reject that contribution will in the long run be vain."

III
Thinking

❖❖❖❖❖❖❖❖❖❖❖❖❖❖❖❖❖❖❖❖❖❖❖❖❖❖❖❖❖❖❖❖❖❖❖❖❖❖❖

GILBERT HIGHET

The Unpredictable Intellect[1]

Yet we cannot foresee the stages of this war in which we are all engaged—
the war for the enslavement or liberation of the mind of humanity. The movement of the human intellect is impossible to prophesy: difficult even to record
and analyze. Whether we shall ever be able to write a systematic history of
thought, explaining the laws that govern its growth and movement, I know not;
but at present those who have studied the migration of ideas find it far beyond
their powers. Historians such as Sorokin and Toynbee and anthropologists
such as Kroeber and Linton have found it hard enough to describe the manifold, the illimitably various stimuli that awaken the sleeping reason and the
multiple channels through which thought flows from one mind to another, from
one region to another. So far, scholars have been able to establish only the
broadest and vaguest rules to assist us in understanding these processes. They
are wonders. They are mysteries.

It is difficult, for instance, to see why a single nation should be able in one
century to produce a thousand inventors, philosophers, poets, and statesmen,
and then, within a few generations, become speechless and apparently thoughtless. Why should one country seethe with intellectual energy as long as it is
poor and danger-ridden, only to fall into indolent stupor when it gets wealth
and security, while its neighbor, long silent during centuries of poverty and humiliation, finds its voice only after acquiring power and riches? How is it that,
within the same country at different times, scientists are now admired and now
neglected, poets are sometimes blessed as benefactors and sometimes despised
as eccentrics? We know well how often two men, or two groups in different
parts of the world, will make the same discovery or think similar thoughts without knowing each other; and that is strange; but it is stranger still to roam
through the history of genius, and watch, and see how often mighty minds have

[1] From *Man's Unconquerable Mind* (New York: Columbia University Press,
1954), pp. 29-45. Copyright, 1954, Columbia University Press.

appeared in lonely lands and savage tribes and eras full of repression and of hateful violence.

Lonely Genius

Sometimes, climbing among the western mountains, one crosses a long wind-lashed and snow-beaten shoulder of harsh broken rocks; and in a tiny hollow halfway across it, see, there is a tuft of bright flowers. Sometimes, from higher up, one looks down into a barren canyon, whose stony walls echo with the dull roar of the torrent below and with the crash of crumbling slabs and pinnacles above: there is not a patch of green, not a visible handful of nourishing earth; but halfway down those precipitous walls, raising its gallant head and spreading its hopeful arms, there grows a pine tree rooted in an invisible notch, and the birds flicker around it.

No less delightful and wonderful is it to read the history of some bloody epoch, crusted with murder and torture, resounding with dull groans, choked hymns, and shouts of senseless violence, and in the midst of it to meet a serene and gracious mind, studying nature and making poetry; or to discover, among lazy bourgeois or glum earthbound peasants, a powerful intellect grappling with abstractions of number, producing unique inventions, or building a systematic interpretation of the universe.

Such was the Buddha. Such was Sequoyah, the Cherokee Indian who, alone, created a written language for his people. Such was the greatest philosopher of the Dark Ages, Johannes Scotus Eriugena—John the Celt from Ireland, as he emphatically called himself—who, almost alone in western Europe at that time, contrived to learn Greek, and created a vast philosophical vision of the spiritual world such as no thinker today could equal. Such was Gregor Mendel, the quiet monk who worked and thought patiently in his garden until he had discovered some of the fundamental laws of heredity. And such were many artists who lived obscurely and whose personalities are all but forgotten, but who made masterpieces of beauty. We may know the name of Aleijadinho, that pathetic figure who became the finest sculptor of Latin America; but the carvers of Chartres are known only by their work, and we cannot even guess the race of the artist who made the exquisite bronze heads from Benin in west Africa.

New Synthesis

Yet even apart from such lonely geniuses there are other surprises in the history of thought, phenomena almost as unexpected and almost as inexplicable. There are men who express the age and the milieu in which they were educated, but who, by the intensity of their imagination, the sweep of their knowledge, and their astounding versatility, rise high above their era and their neighbors, so that they inhabit both time and eternity at once. When we analyze their minds we can identify nearly all the component elements, tracing this to family and that to school and the other to social climate, and yet the compound is far more than the sum of all these elements: richer, intenser, different in quality as a diamond is different from carbon. Shallow thinkers often fail to understand that this qualitative difference occurs again and again in the realm of the intellect. That is what leads some critics to deny that Shakespeare could have written those plays because he was only a middle-class provincial youth who went from a small-town school to become an actor: they expect the real author to be someone calculable, like the university-trained lawyer and statesman Bacon, or a witty and graceful young nobleman with the learning and worldly experience of the Renaissance in his very blood. But they are wrong. They are making the elementary error of believing that, in the world of the mind, two and two make four.

Such people can never have taught. One of the few but great rewards of teaching is to see, not once but again and again, how one boy indistinguishable from the others in an average group, will, stimulated by a single remark of the teacher or excited by exploring a new subject, suddenly begin to change. He grows in wisdom; he throws out original ideas of his own; his very speech and handwriting become more mature; he lives on a new time-scale; he changes so rapidly that he distances all his friends and cannot remember or recognize his twelve-months-younger self. Somehow, some happy chance or providential effort has—what can we say? there are no images to describe the event, which is as mysterious as all vital processes—something has caused the energies of his mind, hitherto dissonant or unused, and the emotions with which he once played, or which played with him, to combine into a new, living, active, creative synthesis. This boy astonishes his friends and his parents: usually not himself, for he feels he is simply learning to use powers which are already his own; and never the teacher, who knows the almost limitless treasures of ability and creativity that every pupil carries about in the locked safe of his mind, and who always hopes and strives to unlock it.

And further, those who believe that forces and results in the field of the intellect are always calculable—those who think Bacon or Oxford ought to have written the Shakespearean dramas because that would be easier to understand —must know very little of the personal history of genius. In a touchingly awkward poem representing the shy self-encouragement of a lonely young man in a far country, John Masefield writes

> I have seen flowers come in stony places;
> And kindness done by men with ugly faces;
> And the gold cup won by the worst horse at the races;
> So I trust, too.

And one certain truth about the great works of the mind—inventions, philosophical systems, poems and plays, pictures and music, scientific discoveries and political institutions—is that many of them were made by men who started life in ordinary, even in unfavorable, situations and then far outsoared their origins.

Isaac Newton was the son of a Lincolnshire farmer: unlike some mathematicians, he was not even bright in boyhood; he was a mediocre student when he went to Cambridge; and then within a few years, the spark descended. Gauss, one of the supreme geniuses of mathematics and electromagnetism, was a village boy like a million others. The founder of modern art-history, Winckelmann, was miserably poor and started as a hack schoolmaster, taking classes all day, sleeping in his schoolhouse, staying awake half the night to teach himself Latin and Greek in preparation for the magnificent career he could only dimly foresee. The by-blow of an Italian gentleman and a country girl was apprenticed to the trade of painting, like many thousands before and after him: but this one was Leonardo da Vinci. Such handicaps hamper but do not crush the growth of the mind: they may even stimulate it. Even the general enemy, ordinariness and routine, cannot always spoil the seed. Loyola, founder of the Jesuits, was a brave ignorant soldier in an age full of stupid men with swords. Luther and Rabelais were monks indistinguishable from myriads of other monks in other lands and times. Socrates was a stonemason in a city crowded with builders. No, the whole history of human thought is as various, as marvelous, as unexpected, and as inexplicable as other mysteries of this universe. Science, with its search for laws, always oversimplifies. But the wise scientist always makes his way through the realm of law into the region of wonder. In a few years he can master the principles of plant and animal life, reproduction, and distribution—and then, for ever thereafter, he remains astounded by the incalculable multiplicity of animal forms, the unthinkable subtlety of plants, knowing that when new varieties are discovered they may contain something as unpredictable as a new divine creation. The complexities of human language, the intricate life of microorganisms, the invisible radiations that fill the universe, the power of mutation in living forms—all these can be faintly or crudely grasped, but never fully understood. One of the truest sayings of the medieval thinkers was OMNIA EXEVNT IN MYSTERIVM, *All things pass into mystery*. We are not intended only to diagnose and calculate, but also to wonder, to admire; to expect the unexpected.

The Mind a Mystery

Yes, the outer world—both visible and invisible—is ultimately a mystery. So too is the other world we inhabit—the inner world, the world of the mind. Not one of us knows what his own mind contains. Not one of us knows what his own mind can do, or will produce.

Some of the busy and complex activity of the mind is permanently hidden. We can scarcely ever see its vaguest outlines, except now and then in dreams or apparently purposeless actions. Priests at confession, psychoanalysts listening and probing, lawyers and judges analyzing acts of cunning and violence, ethnologists examining myths, and critics penetrating poems, yes, all of us when we listen to music, that wordless language of the soul, experience something of that powerful and terrible world, but can never know it fully. It means to hide itself. The pupils of Freud have sometimes made the problem too simple, saying that the inner activity of the mind was a ferment of "immoral" or rejected, censored, and repressed material—a living skeleton chained in our cupboard. But the true picture is far more complex. Much of our hidden life literally cannot be dominated, directly helped or impeded, or ever understood by our reasoning mind. The instincts, memory, invention, imagination—these and other activities lie largely outside the range of consciousness. The reason can observe them at work, occasionally intervene, and with constant and difficult effort learn to influence them; but their origins, their full power, their methods, all remain beyond its scope. Jesus once asked "Which of you, by thinking about it, can add a foot to his height?" But we might also ask ourselves whether any of us can forecast what ideas will be put up by his mind a year from now; a week from now; tomorrow; within the next hour.

We are all cave men. The cave we inhabit is our own mind; and consciousness is like a tiny torch, flickering and flaring, which can at best show us only a few outlines of the cave wall that stands nearest, or reflect a dangerous underground river flowing noiselessly at our feet, so that we start back in horror before we are engulfed; as we explore, we come often on shapes of beauty, glittering stalactites, jewel-encrusted pillars, delicate and trusting animals which befriend and follow us; sometimes we even find relics of an earlier time, a primitive statue with flowers still fresh at its feet, or shapes of beasts painted on the wall with bloody handprints beside them; now and then we stumble over a heap that crackles and mutters and moves, but we turn our light away and hurry on; the path we follow sometimes seems to trace an elaborate pattern, although our little flame shows us only a few lines, converging and then curving off into darkness; often its rays die down, threatening to go out altogether and leave us in the resounding gloom; at least thrice in our journey we must crouch down because the cave roof sinks low above us, so that we can go forward only on our knees; when we emerge, it is into another cavern larger than the last but more awesome, where we hear the beat of unseen wings above our head; there are side openings into which our light shines only faintly, to reveal glowing eyes and fearful teeth far in their recesses; the worst of all our trials is that when we venture to speak, the vast invisible walls and roof distort our words into formidable echoes, dying away in superhuman whispers or hateful growls; and, after many a year of wandering, when our torch gleams upon a silent pool and we bend over its calm surface, we do not recognize the face that stares up into our anxious and astonished eyes.

The self is hidden. We do not know ourselves, our brothers and sisters, husbands or wives or children. No friend knows his friend.

Yet all this mystery holds greatness as well as darkness. The cavern is dim, somber, unexplored; but it contains treasures. Every human brain is filled with unused power. Out of all the billions of men and women who have lived, only a few hundred thousand have been able to employ so much of that power as to change the world. The rest have been dutiful or lazy, good or bad, sensuous or self-denying, thrifty or wasteful, cowardly or brave. Those few hundred thousand, perhaps only a score of thousands in all, are the minds that have made our world. Scientists, strategists, industrialists, aesthetes, explorers, inventors, organizers, authors, musicians, philosophers, doctors and teachers, lawyers and statesmen, several thousand in each class, these are the minds who have given the rest of mankind incalculable benefits, or done it immeasurable damage. They are responsible for much of human history.

Consider the world, apart from mankind. It is either static or else changing in a gradual and apparently automatic rhythm. The planet swings around the sun, steadily slowing down. The tides flow back and forward with the retreating and returning moon. Weather wears the rocks, the sea eats at the shores, the polar ice advances and recedes. The air and land and water are filled with living things—but they scarcely ever change, or if they do, it is over vast spaces of time. Ferns grow and fish swim and micro-organisms vibrate in our world just as they did long before men walked upon the earth; the industrious ants continue with their routine of self-preservation and self-perpetuation as they did when the dinosaurs ruled. But man, in his brief history, has transformed both the world and himself. His specific quality is purposeful change through thought. He is most truly alive when he thinks.

There are only three secular explanations of history. One is that it is made by groups of people acting together. The second is that historical change is produced by blind impersonal "forces." The third is that it is decided and led by powerful individuals. Of course all these theories are true to some extent; and none is true exclusively. Climatic shifts and epidemic diseases move or destroy populations. Social, economic, religious, aesthetic patterns are worked out by successive generations; vast migrations occur without a single leader. Heroes and villains and geniuses preach, rebel, invent, govern. Yet in man's more recent history many of the most powerful and vital changes have been initiated by strong individuals. Not all of these were thinkers. Some were driven by passions of love or hatred or violence or pride. But the work of the thinking man has been more lasting.

Since it is all a mystery, we can never tell how great thinkers emerge. There are very few rules for producing them. They do not grow like trees; they cannot be bred like selected animals. People are not born thoughtless or thoughtful. Probably the surest way to grow up stupid is to be part of a large static population doing manual labor and living just on the level of subsistence; and the next best is to be born in a nice family with inherited wealth, brought up in an assured social position, and sent to a quiet and correct school. The young ploughboy and the young marquis are both in a mental prison, one following the furrow, the other set in his comfortable rut.

Training the Thinker

No, we can never tell how great minds arise, and it is very hard to tell how to detect and encourage them when they do appear. But we do know two methods of feeding them as they grow.

One is to give them constant challenge and stimulus. Put problems before them. Make things difficult for them. They need to think. Produce things for them to think about and question their thinking at every stage. They are inventive and original. Propose experiments to them. Tell them to discover what is hidden.

The second method is to bring them into contact with other eminent minds. It is not enough, not nearly enough, for a clever boy or girl to meet his fellows and his teachers and his parents. He (or she) must meet men and women of real and undeniable distinction. That is, he must meet the immortals. That brilliant and pessimistic scoundrel Plato died just over 2,300 years ago, but through his books he is still talking and thinking and leading others to think; and there is no better way, none, for a young man to start thinking about any kind of philosophical problem—human conduct, political action, logical analysis, metaphysics, aesthetics—than by reading Plato and trying to answer his arguments, detect his sophisms, resist his skillful persuasions, and become both his pupil and his critic. No one can learn to write music better than by studying *The Well-tempered Clavier* of Bach and the symphonies of Beethoven. A young composer who does so will not, if he is any good, write music like Bach and Beethoven. He will write music more like the music that he wanted to write. A man may become a routine diplomat by following the rule book and solving every problem as it comes up, but if he is to grow into a statesman he must read his Machiavelli and consider the lives of Bismarck and Lincoln and Disraeli. The best way toward greatness is to mix with the great.

Challenge and experiment; association with immortal minds: these are the two sure ways of rearing intelligent men and women. And these two opportunities for greatness are, or ought to be, provided by schools and colleges and universities. "But," you will ask, "do schools exist only to train geniuses?" No, but they do not exist only to train the average and to neglect or benumb the talented. They exist to make the best of both. One of the heaviest responsibilities in education is to do justice to exceptional minds, remembering that they may emerge in any place, at any time, and in any body—even a clumsy and misshapen frame may hold a brilliant mind. It must be a strange experience to teach in a little country school, the same subjects year after year to the same families, and then to find a gifted young engineer or a born dramatist among one's pupils. Disconcerting. Difficult. Difficult to know how to encourage without patronizing; difficult not to be a little jealous. Yet the history of knowledge is filled with true stories of teachers who recognized outstanding gifts in a pupil and gave him all he needed to set him on his way to eminence: touching and encouraging, these tales. Such is the story of the Spanish peasant boy who was drawing with charcoal on a plank when a teacher saw him, started training him, and helped to make the artist Goya. Such is the tale of the thin sensitive undersized London schoolboy whose schoolmaster's son gave him the run of his private library: it was among those shelves and as a result of that kindness that the youngster wrote a poem called "On First Looking into Chapman's Homer." Behind almost every great man there stands either a good parent or a good teacher.

Education in America and in the other countries of the West is an inspiriting achievement: all those light, healthy schools, those myriad colleges, so many youngsters having a fine time and not working too hard. Yet it has a couple of weaknesses. One is that education has become almost too easy to get. It is accepted like a supply of pure water: no one expects to get much stimulus or nourishment from it, but it is used to keep the tissues well filled and the outer surface clean. The other is that it does not often carry over into mature life. The average American would rather be driving a car along a crowded highway than reading a book and thinking. The average Frenchman would rather be drinking an extra bottle of wine than watching a play by Racine. The average Britisher would rather fill up a football-pool form than listen to Elgar's *Enigma*. Why this should be so, I cannot tell. It must be something wrong with education. Probably it is the cult of the average: the idea that schools exist in order to make everyone pretty much the same, and that happiness consists in sharing a group life, sweet, humming, undifferentiated, and crowded like bees in a hive.

Schools do exist for the average. They also exist to serve the distinguished. America was built both by a multitude of common men and women and also by a few eccentrics, heroes, and giants, those whom Stephen Spender exalts when he writes

> I think continually of those who were truly great.
> Who, from the womb, remembered the soul's history
> Through corridors of light where the hours are suns
> Endless and singing. Whose lovely ambition
> Was that their lips, still touched with fire,
> Should tell of the spirit clothed from head to foot in song.
>
> .   .   .
>
> Born of the sun they travelled a short while towards the sun
> And left the vivid air signed with their honour.

The life of every teacher is partly dedicated to discovering and encouraging those few powerful minds who will influence our future, and the secret of education is never to forget the possibility of greatness.

We owe them reverence, the great minds of the past and present and future. It is inspiring and delightful even to scan their names. One shines on another, receiving light in return. It is like looking at the stars, when the eye travels from the Bear to Orion, from Aldebaran to Sirius and Vega, from glory to glory.

When we think of the most majestic mind of the Middle Ages, of Dante, our thought soon travels to his master and companion Vergil, who guided him through Hell and Purgatory until he attained the vision of the beloved; from Dante to the prose counterpart of his poem, the *Summa* of St. Thomas Aquinas; and back from St. Thomas to his master Aristotle. If we read an essay by

Francis Bacon, we soon remember the earlier, kinder essayist Montaigne; and then, recalling that Bacon was a scientific thinker, we turn to Descartes, and from him to a kindred mind, Leibnitz, and so from greatness to greatness. Descartes and Newton both interpreted the universe: from Newton it is inevitable to travel back to Kepler and Brahe, forward to Laplace. Sometimes, again, great minds recall each other because, although they were strangers and worked in different media, they saw similar aspects of the universe. It is difficult to play certain fugues by Bach (such as the E flat minor in Book II, full of cold harmonies, meditative rhythms, and somber melancholy) without thinking of the wise old men with unsmiling wrinkled faces and deep eyes, who watch us from the shadows of Rembrandt's last pictures. It is difficult to look at Dürer's mystical etchings without thinking of Goethe's *Faust*.

Such men were not—as shallow historians try to tell us—creatures of their time and place. Often they were eccentrics who ignored or preceded their epoch; nearly always they were largely self-made; by giving their age a voice and by teaching it, they helped to form it, to dominate it. To read the life of even one such thinker is to renew one's faith in humanity, one's sense of duty to the world. To move freely among the captain minds of any one great age— say the seventeenth century, or the century that produced Cicero, Lucretius, Vergil, Horace, and Livy, or the nineteenth century—is to be perpetually astounded at the depth unplumbable, the infinite variety of the human mind, and to repeat the words of the Greek tragedian:

> Wonders are many, but none,
> none is more wondrous than man.

JOHN KENNETH GALBRAITH

The Businessman As Philosopher[1]

The American businessman is a notable figure in our time, and it is rather surprising that so little self-conscious consideration has been given to his attitudes and beliefs. The ideas of any other group of like prominence in the political and economic life of the United States, or any of the other Western democracies, would almost certainly have been the subject of deep interest and endless discussion. No doubt this neglect of the businessman is in part the ancient snobbery of intellectuals—an aspect of the notion that all bourgeois thoughts are stereotyped, without content, and hence not worth talk-

[1] From *Perspectives USA*, No. 13. (Autumn, 1955), 57-69. Copyright 1955 by Intercultural Publications Inc. Reprinted by permission of Intercultural Publications Inc.

ing about. In part the neglect may be a tribute to the very eminence of the businessman in American life—he is accorded an oracular role which places his ideas above discussion. Certainly, there is one type of tycoon, who, when he opens his mouth, expects to hear no bark of dogs. However, it seems likely that the principal explanation is a much simpler one. The American businessman's beliefs are so familiar that they are taken almost completely for granted. They are not universally accepted, just as the articles of faith of the Baptist Church are not universally accepted. But, for the same reason, they are not debated.

The religious simile is an enticing one, for there is also a certain ritualistic aspect to the usual exposition of the American business creed. The occasions, which have something of the standing of folk rites in our life, are the luncheon talk and the convention address. Scores of times each week and thousands of times during the course of any year, business orators articulate—normally for an audience of other businessmen—their attitudes toward the political, economic, and moral problems of the time, or of all time. The speaker ordinarily makes clear that his are the beliefs only of a "plain businessman." This disavowal is not, however, received as an apology; rather it is taken as it is meant, as a claim to straightforward and uncomplicated thought. All business expression sets a great store by the presumed ability to proceed promptly to the heart of a problem. Proof is often deemed implicit in blunt, emphatic statement. Much is also ascribed to the speaker's personal experience. The conventional statement of business belief also normally calls for an active and even an aggressive posture toward the beliefs enunciated. The speaker who has descried a tendency for people to rely excessively on the government is expected to call for a crusade by his audience for increased self-reliance. The audience, for its part, recognizes the ritualistic nature of this call and does not, in fact, feel called upon to do anything. Indeed, while the custom of such rites requires a respectful show of attention and vigorous applause, it does not impose any obligation to listen to what is said. Politicians alone excepted, businessmen have probably outdistanced all other Americans in their immunity to oratory.

As there is an element of ritual in the voicing of business beliefs, so there is, inevitably, in the beliefs that are voiced. This is a matter of considerable importance, and to overlook it is to do serious injustice to business intelligence and perspicacity. Whatever the diversity of belief among businessmen, it is almost certainly greater than among those who speak for businessmen. The individual businessman is also much more flexible in his views and much more pragmatic in his judgments than his spokesmen. A careful distinction must be made, therefore, between formal or ritualistic beliefs of business and those which actually govern private business behavior. However, the ritualistic or formal beliefs are not unimportant. They have an important bearing on a very wide variety of public attitudes and policies.

The two words which are by far the most important in the formal beliefs of American business are competition and individualism. These are held both to explain the success and to provide the moral justification for American capitalism. (The term capitalism, incidentally, is not popular in the American business lexicon. Perhaps because it is reminiscent of Marxian categories and jargon, it is widely regarded as having a semantically unhealthy tone.) Competition in the business creed, and in accordance with the presuppositions of classical economics from which it is derived, is the great regulatory mechanism of the economy. It keeps the producer from exploiting his customers by overcharging them, or his workers and suppliers by underpaying them. Since competition regulates economic relations and insures that no one suffers any enduring damage, it is unnecessary for the state or any other higher agency to intervene. Accordingly, competition provides the framework and the opportunity for individualism. Because of competition we are permitted to have a society wherein the individual is allowed to work out his destiny with a minimum of social assistance or restraint. The notion that competition regulates individual relationships with great reliability—"competition will take care of matters"—is firmly imbedded in the formal business faith.

However, in this creed competition is much more than the classical regulatory apparatus. It also motivates nearly all progress and, indeed, nearly all change. Man is stagnant or retrograde except as his energies are pitted against another's. The engine for advance is a relentless contest in which the weak, the incompetent, and, above all, the unimaginative are extruded from the economy, while the strong and vigorous and the aggressive draw refreshment from the struggle. To competition, thus, we owe the extraordinary vigor of the American economy. One measure of the importance ascribed to competition is the near unanimity with which American business spokesmen ascribed Europe's postwar economic weakness to its absence. Few European entrepreneurs can have escaped a lecture on the point: "Frankly, the trouble with you fellows is you have forgotten how to compete."

Competition in the American business faith is functional, though it has moral overtones—"a good man isn't afraid of a little competition." The case of individualism is almost precisely the reverse. Individualism is essentially a moral concept, although it has utilitarian aspects. The individualism of the formal business creed holds that man has a deep moral right to be free from overt direction, guidance, and restraint in economic life. It follows that the independent businessman is in some sense superior to, say, the salaried public official or the salaried employee. Because he assumes responsibility, makes decisions, and shoulders risk, he is a stronger and more virile man—as well as a more useful one. It follows that any measure which inhibits or restrains, or, for that matter, removes responsibility from this independent entrepreneur is subversive of individualist values.

At this point, the faith in individualism becomes co-ordinate with suspicion of, and resistance to, government intervention. In the American business creed few things are viewed with more suspicion than government intervention in the economy. Nothing more frequently receives the condemnation of those who articulate the creed than meddling, intrusive, paternalistic, unnecessary, or wasteful economic activities of the state, and in many business circles there is rarely a reference to any other kind of state action. This is not a matter of party or politics. While Republicans are regarded as less inimical in this respect than Democrats, the interventionist tendencies of the state are assumed to have a dynamic all of their own. Tentacles will always be reaching out to any surviving area of economic freedom. The individualist who strikes at these tentacles is not only the custodian of the freedom of economic decision, but, by many spokesmen, he is identified with the whole system of human liberty.

Such is the formal avowal on competition and individualism. The actual behavior of the American businessman, however, suggests the existence of conflicting attitudes which, if less brave than those just outlined, are also a good deal more practical. It is doubtful if the United States or any other country could survive a rigorous application of the doctrines just mentioned, and it is certain that no business firm could. Happily the businessman does not hesitate to adjust his behavior to the facts of life.

Thus, competition has always meant a vigorous rivalry to offer the most for the lowest prices. Competition, in other words, has meant price competition. It has also meant freedom to enter a given line of business and tolerable ease in doing so. Adam Smith and his followers would not only have insisted on the importance of these attributes of competition, but they would have said that this is precisely what competition is.

In the characteristic American industry, the ones that best typify American industrial structure, there are ordinarily a small number of large firms. Vigorous price competition, or price cutting, when indulged in by such firms, is dangerous and, if carried to extremes, disastrous. By a consent so tacit that its existence often goes unrecognized, such uninhibited price competition is avoided. Vigorous commercial rivalry continues—this must be stressed—but it takes the less dangerous forms of improving the product, providing new and novel appurtenances or services, or using more, or more ingenious, advertising.

In smaller-scale industries, retailing and agriculture in particular, price competition is even officially deplored. The legal restraints of the Robinson-Patman Act (a federal statute) and the Fair Trade Laws of the several states have been developed to prevent it. While competition is central to the formal creed, there is no business disposition to be martyrs to the faith. Nor is it evident, for that matter, that such martyrdom would be always in the public interest.

Similarly, there is little disposition among businessmen to worry about the substantial abridgment of freedom of entry into the modern industry. The capital requirements for effective operation in such established industries as automobile, steel, aluminum, tobacco, rubber, copper, or chemical production are immense. As a result, the *dramatis personæ* of the characteristic American industry changes little from year to year. New entrants, when they do appear, are often under the sponsorship of large firms in other industries. All this is accepted by most businessmen as a matter of course. It is only as one leaves the domain of big business for the far less characteristic world of small enterprises—coal mining, agriculture, trade—that one finds freedom of entry at all approaching the classical sense.

Thus competition, in the American business faith, is no rigorous, classical ideal toward which, however painfully, the economy must be made to conform. There is a singular—and no doubt quite sensible—unwillingness to die in its name.

The concept of a rigorous individualism is also subject to practical compromise, and this is achieved with no greater difficulty. As noted, the most characteristic feature of the American economic landscape is the giant corporation—between a third and a half of all manufactured output is provided by a comparative handful (fewer than two hundred) of these mammoth firms. This means that the typical American businessman is exceptionally subject to the restraints of organization and authority of the large firm. All of his active life is lived in a hierarchy which, if less formal than that of a military organization, is no less insistent in its demands for team play and discipline. All, including the infinitesimal few who emerge at the top, are subject to the restraints which are imposed by any great organization on all who comprise it, commanders and commanded alike.

As a result, there are few people who more rigorously eschew the mannerisms and behavior of the uninhibited individualist than the American businessman. The individualist relies on himself; the businessman succeeds by his capacity to work with others. The individualist is indifferent to, where he is not contemptuous of, authority; the good businessman has a highly developed sense of the larger corporate personality of which he is a part and of his own implicit subordination to its needs and ends.

Beyond this, there are few men more considerate of the pride and sensibilities of others, more tolerant of unavoidable inadequacy, or more wary of impulsive or arbitrary action than the modern business executive. He is, in short, the creature of modern business administration in all its modern vastness and intricacy of human association. No one could be more hopelessly miscast in such a *milieu* than the swashbuckling individualist idealized by the formal creed.

The emphasis on individualism undoubtedly owes something to the relatively undramatic character of modern business achievement. At its best, the modern business corporation is an efficient, intelligently administered bureaucracy. In the absence of color and glamour, it is tempting to devise some. Accordingly, just as the present-day officer in a mechanized division likes to identify himself with the cavalryman of old, so the modern administrator reaches for the mantle of the merchant adventurer or the free-booting industrialist. For many, and perhaps most, businessmen, the conformity imposed by life in a large corporation is not especially painful—indeed, for few of us is the restraint imposed by voluntary association of this sort either irksome or, in fact, noticeable. (The government service has regularly attracted men of independent disposition who have not found the conformity it requires especially burdensome.) As a result, the illusion of individualism is sustained with much more ease than might be supposed even in the modern large corporation.

Everyday behavior does not diverge so radically from the formal creed on all matters as it does on competition and individualism. A deep partiality to technological innovation and progress and a profound belief in social conservatism are commonplaces with those who articulate the business creed. These attitudes are substantially reflected in the actual behavior of most American businessmen.

The virtues of technological innovation in American business philosophy are nearly absolute. One could argue persuasively that not all of the inventions adopted in the last hundred years have been to the common benefit. A generation ago in New York, cigar-makers made cigars by hand while a hired reader delighted and enlightened them from the world of literature. The machine that destroyed these scholars should never have been invented. However, the case against technical progress is one that few businessmen—for that matter, few Americans—care to make. The case for change is assumed. The technical progressiveness of our economy is, indeed, its most frequently iterated justification. The American businessman rarely meets in convention without being reminded that his "is the most dynamic, the most progressive economy in the world."

As noted, this attitude is deeply reflected in individual belief and behavior. There is a clear presumption in most business firms in favor of the man who advocates something new and against the man who argues for the comfortable familiarity of the present products or processes. Corporate managements can more easily defend the absence of profits than the absence of progress. There are few crimes in which an American businessman would be more reluctant to be caught than in an effort to suppress a patent or otherwise defer the adoption and use of some invention.

However, a considerable suspicion of social innovation is the counterpart of this deference to technical change. To be sure the American businessman, though decidedly conservative in his attitudes toward social change, is not quite as conservative as his spokesmen. The National Association of Manufacturers, a leading articulant of the formal creed, has a nearly unbroken record of initial opposition to unions and collective bargaining, progressive taxation, social insurance, and other social welfare legislation. It has become, to many Americans, something of a symbol of resistance to social experiment. There have been recurrent indications that this is regretted by many business members of the NAM.

Also, while the American businessman is clearly disposed to look upon any particular innovation with distaste, he is also likely to approve it once it has become a matter of experience. A generation ago most businessmen regarded unions as a misfortune to be resisted where they could not be destroyed. Now the great majority of American businessmen admit of the inevitability and even urge the desirability of unions. The social welfare and regulatory legislation of the New Deal was once deeply disliked by businessmen, and it led to the now nearly complete identification of American businessmen with the Republican Party. (In 1948, a country-wide poll of business executives conducted by *Fortune* magazine showed 96 per cent of those responding as favoring the Republican candidate for President.) Now this social legislation is approved by most businessmen. It has been accepted by the business members of the Eisenhower Administration, some of whom, without doubt, were originally inspired to active participation in politics by the seeming threat of these very measures.

Further, in the American business tradition there has always been a minority of businessmen who have had a strong humanitarian interest in social reform or who have identified long-run conservatism with short-run radicalism. These men have viewed unions as a highly desirable redress of weak bargaining position and, thus, as a conservative solvent of social tensions. Social insurance has been viewed in a similar light. They have believed that capitalism would best secure its future by providing some promise of employment to willing workers. Business reformers in this tradition—Edward A. Filene, the Boston merchant, James Couzens, the one-time partner of Henry Ford, Henry S. Dennison, the Framingham paper manufacturer, and others—anticipated in their thinking most of the social innovations of the New Deal. In more recent times another business group, centering on the Committee for Economic Development, has strongly affirmed the need for a strong government policy on behalf of high and stable economic performance. As noted, in the formal business creed there are few more dubious concepts.

While the businessmen who have taken a sympathetic view of social innovation have been extraordinarily important in American social history, they have been, it must be emphasized, a minority. Nor is this surprising. The common consequence of all forms of social innovation is some subtraction from the income or, more commonly, the power and prestige of the businessman. This is what unions, regulatory legislation, most social welfare measures, even policies designed to insure a high level of employment and output all threaten. (A commitment to full employment policies means at a minimum that the state replaces the businessman as the symbol of leadership in the economy.)

Social innovation, moreover, involves an increased role for government, which, as noted, has its own uniquely repugnant implications. Finally, social innovation is a constant source of uneasiness. In the formal business view, capitalism does not, oddly enough, have an especially rugged constitution. On the contrary, it is regarded as a delicate flower, highly susceptible to blight by ill-considered or unwise legislation. Predictions that a particular bill, policy, or institutional trend (i.e., the development of the closed shop) will destroy the economy are made almost daily. Given this supposed fragility, the resistance to social innovation follows almost automatically. Any step might be the fatal one. It is hardly surprising that the American businessman is a conservative in social philosophy. And he is.

The final and in some respects the most complex of the tenets of the business faith concerns the much-controverted question of materialism. In the nineteenth and early twentieth century, the American entrepreneur was supposed by most Europeans to have a peculiarly forthright interest in making money and in enjoying, or at least accumulating and displaying, the things money could buy. The belief that the United States in general, and the American businessman in particular, is still strongly materialistic is by no means dead.

In the formal creed of the American businessman, however, materialism is a fighting word. Nothing more strongly stigmatizes communism than a reference to its Godless materialism. In the litany of the luncheon address there is a heavy emphasis on the "other things in life," which means things other than making money. Not, perhaps, since the ancient Israelites have a people been so regularly reminded as Americans that those who lose touch with spiritual values are surely doomed.

This is the formal creed, and it is by no means without influence. The modern business concern is strongly disposed to make service and not earnings the asserted goal of its existence. Profits are rarely defended as something to which investors have a right and never as something which they will enjoy spending. Rather they are an index of the quality of the service that the company is rendering and the assurance that it will continue in business to render service in the future. No businessman boasts of his salary or income if these are large. To do so is to confess a materialistic scale of values which is completely abhorrent. (The return from a particular business coup may be cited, but only to signify the intellectual ingenuity or enterprise that was manifested.) It is unthinkable that an American businessman would appeal for lower taxes, a higher tariff, or relief from some government regulation on the ground that he wanted to make more money. The plea must be based on the benefit (e.g., the income, employment, or investment) that will accrue to the community and to the country and in relation to which the businessman is only an interested bystander. Even labor leaders are now likely to avoid arguments that have materialist overtones. It is not that their members need more money to buy television sets. Rather, the increased purchases of television sets resulting from a wage increase will be good for the country.

The need to avoid any suggestion of materialist motivation has had a marked effect on the businessman's way of life and work. In the nineteenth century and in the early decades of the twentieth, the American entrepreneur was joyously proud of his wealth, and he made this evident in the magnificence of his house, stables, and wife. Now, while comfort and even a measure of elegance are permissible, ostentation in living arrangements, except as it nourishes some interesting personality trait or eccentricity or as it is disguised as serious economic activity, is rigorously excluded. (It is far better to spend money on cattle than on race horses; the businessman's dairy barn may be a show place, but not his country home.) As he climbs the corporate ladder, the modern businessman must devote an increasing proportion of his time to educational, charitable, or other civic enterprise or—a recent development—to service in Washington.

The variety and vitality of voluntary activity in the United States owe much to the support and leadership of businessmen. Indeed, there is no other country, Canada perhaps excepted, where community leadership is assumed in the same measure by businessmen. In most communities, the businessman who avoids civic tasks—who confines himself to running his enterprise and making money—risks being stigmatized a poor citizen.

However, once again a too literal acceptance of the formal creed would lead to an unjust and erroneous view of the beliefs that actually govern behavior. To accept at face value the businessman's disavowal of material goals and his insistence on service as the criterion of business performance would be to make him the ultimate arbiter and custodian of the public welfare. It would mean that the businessman decided what to produce, at what price, and with what returns to his investors, his workers, and himself in accordance with his own interpretation of the social good. In such an economy, there would be no standards and no internal order except the businessman's personal interpretation of that social good. Capitalism assumed that, in the course of a more or less singleminded pursuit of profits, the businessman automatically served the public. Here, instead, we have a world of big brothers in business suits.

However, his disavowal notwithstanding, the American businessman almost certainly retains an intelligent and reassuring preoccupation with making money. He disavows materialism but, happily, he does not forswear it. It is noticeable that most of the actions which businessmen cite as showing their concern for service and the public good are also consistent with favorable business earnings. No one ever suggests that Service requires selling at a loss. Tax policies that are advocated by business in the public interest are, as a matter of common observation, normally those which offer the most relief to the corporate rates or in the higher brackets of the personal income tax. Thus it can still be assumed that the motivations of the businessman are more those of a profit-maker than a welfare administrator. Even the public service activities of the man who has reached the top of the corporate hierarchy may make it possible for the firm to be guided by younger, more imaginative, and more efficient administrators. A loan of talent to Washington is often consistent with better management and higher profits in Pittsburgh.

Equally important, the high material standard of living of the American people is something which the American business philosophy views with complete approval. The businessman does not measure his own success by the number of his bathrooms, but he unhesitatingly applies this test to the community at large. As a principal custodian of the nation's material well-being, it would be a misfortune were the businessman to lose confidence in his primary goal, which is to make money by making goods. Living by these standards, both he and the country have lived well. As a social service rather than a profit-making enterprise, there is no particular reason to think American business would be a success. However, the danger of this development, the formal creed to the contrary, seems not too grave.

Two things emerge from this view of the American business philosophy. There is obviously a considerable difference between the beliefs which render regular work-a-day service and those which, in effect, are used as Sunday garb. Many of the latter beliefs, it is clear, are not especially useful or practical. Indeed, as noted, the economy would not survive their rigorous application. They call for a kind of competition which could not be tolerated in the modern industrial market, for an individualism which would reduce modern corporate administration to anarchy, for a resistance to social innovation which could be a prime source of social tension, and, finally, for a disavowal of material aims which, if carried to extremes, would deny the very rationale of business itself.

However, it is equally evident that, where it is inconvenient or impractical, the American businessman has a notable capacity either to accommodate his philosophy to the facts of life or to forget it entirely. This is a point of widespread importance. Like all men of sincerity, the American businessman has been a frequent evangelist for his beliefs. Ordinarily, however, it is the formal creed which has been the subject of his evangelism. He has far less frequently explained that he rarely allows this creed to keep him from acting as practical circumstances require.

C. NORTHCOTE PARKINSON

Injelititis, or Palsied Paralysis[1]

We find everywhere a type of organization (administrative, commercial, or academic) in which the higher officials are plodding and dull, those less senior are active only in intrigue against each other, and the junior men are frustrated or frivolous. Little is being attempted. Nothing is being achieved. And in contemplating this sorry picture, we conclude that those in control have done

[1] From *Parkinson's Law and Other Studies in Administration,* C. Northcote Parkinson (Boston: Houghton Mifflin Company, 1957), pp. 78-90. Copyright, 1957, by C. Northcote Parkinson. Reprinted by permission of Houghton Mifflin Company and John Murray, Ltd.

their best, struggled against adversity, and have finally admitted defeat. It now appears from the results of recent investigation, that no such failure need be assumed. In a high percentage of the moribund institutions so far examined the final state of coma is something gained of set purpose and after prolonged effort. It is the result, admittedly, of a disease, but of a disease that is largely self-induced. From the first signs of the condition, the progress of the disease has been encouraged, the causes aggravated, and the symptoms welcomed. It is the disease of induced inferiority, called Injelititis. It is a commoner ailment than is often supposed, and the diagnosis is far easier than the cure.

Our study of this organizational paralysis begins, logically, with a description of the course of the disease from the first signs to the final coma. The second stage of our inquiry concerns symptoms and diagnosis. The third stage should properly include some reference to treatment, but little is known about this. Nor is much likely to be discovered in the immediate future, for the tradition of British medical research is entirely opposed to any emphasis on this part of the subject. British medical specialists are usually quite content to trace the symptoms and define the cause. It is the French, by contrast, who begin by describing the treatment and discuss the diagnosis later, if at all. We feel bound to adhere in this to the British method, which may not help the patient but which is unquestionably more scientific. To travel hopefully is better than to arrive.

The first sign of danger is represented by the appearance in the organization's hierarchy of an individual who combines in himself a high concentration of incompetence and jealousy. Neither quality is significant in itself and most people have a certain proportion of each. But when these two qualities reach a certain concentration—represented at present by the formula I^3J^5—there is a chemical reaction. The two elements fuse, producing a new substance that we have termed "injelitance." The presence of this substance can be safely inferred from the actions of any individual who, having failed to make anything of his own department, tries constantly to interfere with other departments and gain control of the central administration. The specialist who observes this particular mixture of failure and ambition will at once shake his head and murmur, "Primary or idiopathic injelitance." The symptoms, as we shall see, are quite unmistakable.

The next or secondary stage in the progress of the disease is reached when the infected individual gains complete or partial control of the central organization. In many instances this stage is reached without any period of primary infection, the individual having actually entered the organization at that level. The injelitant individual is easily recognizable at this stage from the persistence with which he struggles to eject all those abler than himself, as also from his resistance to the appointment or promotion of anyone who might prove abler in course of time. He dare not say, "Mr. Asterisk is too able," so he says, "Asterisk? Clever perhaps—but is he sound? I incline to prefer Mr. Cypher." He dare not say, "Mr. Asterisk makes me feel small," so he says, "Mr. Cypher appears to me to have the better judgment." Judgment is an interesting word that signifies in this context the opposite of intelligence; it means, in fact, doing what was done last time. So Mr. Cypher is promoted and Mr. Asterisk goes elsewhere. The central administration gradually fills up with people stupider than the chairman, director, or manager. If the head of the organization is second-rate, he will see to it that his immediate staff are all third-rate; and they will, in turn, see to it that their subordinates are fourth-rate. There will soon be an actual competition in stupidity, people pretending to be even more brainless than they are.

The next or tertiary stage in the onset of this disease is reached when there is no spark of intelligence left in the whole organization from top to bottom. This is the state of coma we described in our first paragraph. When that stage has been reached the institution is, for all practical purposes, dead. It may remain in a coma for twenty years. It may quietly disintegrate. It may even, finally, recover. Cases of recovery are rare. It may be thought odd that recovery without treatment should be possible. The process is quite natural, nevertheless, and closely resembles the process by which various living organisms develop a resistance to poisons that are at first encounter fatal. It is as if the whole institution had been sprayed with a DDT solution guaranteed to eliminate all ability found in its way. For a period of years this practice achieves the desired result. Eventually, however, individuals develop an immunity. They conceal their ability under a mask of imbecile good humor. The result is that the operatives assigned to the task of ability-elimination fail (through stupidity) to recognize ability when they see it. An individual of merit penetrates the outer defenses and begins to make his way toward the top. He wanders on, babbling about golf and giggling feebly, losing documents and forgetting names, and looking just like everyone else. Only when he has reached high rank does he suddenly throw off the mask and appear like the demon king among a crowd of pantomime fairies. With shrill screams of dismay the high executives find ability right there in the midst of them. It is too late by then to do anything about it. The damage has been done, the disease is in retreat, and full recovery is possible over the next ten years. But these instances of natural cure are extremely rare. In the more usual course of events, the disease passes through the recognized stages and becomes, as it would seem, incurable.

We have seen what the disease is. It now remains to show by what symptoms its presence can be detected. It is one thing to detail the spread of the infection in an imaginary case, classified from the start. It is quite a different thing to enter a factory, barracks, office, or college and recognize the symptoms at a glance. We all know how an estate agent will wander round a vacant house when acting for the purchaser. It is only a question of time before he throws open a cupboard or kicks a baseboard and exclaims, "Dry rot!" (acting for the vendor, he would lose the key of the cupboard while drawing attention to the view from the window). In the same way a political scientist can recognize the symptoms of Injelititis even in its primary stage. He will pause, sniff, and nod wisely, and it should be obvious at once that he knows. But how does he know? How can he tell that injelitance has set in? If the original source of the infection were present, the diagnosis would be easier, but it is still quite possible when the germ of the disease is on holiday. His influence can be detected in the atmosphere. It can be detected, above all, in certain remarks that will be made by others, as thus: "It would be a mistake for us to attempt too much. We cannot compete with Toprank. Here in Lowgrade we do useful work, meeting the needs of the country. Let us be content with that." Or again, "We do not pretend to be in the first flight. It is absurd the way these people at Much-Striving talk of their work, just as if they were in the Toprank class." Or finally, "Some of our younger men have transferred to Toprank—one or two even to Much-Striving. It is probably their wisest plan. We are quite happy to let them succeed in that way. An exchange of ideas and personnel is a good thing—although, to be sure, the few men we have had from Toprank have been rather disappointing. We can only expect the people they have thrown out. Ah well, we must not grumble. We always avoid friction when we can. And, in our humble way we can claim to be doing a good job."

What do these remarks suggest? They suggest—or, rather, they clearly indicate—that the standard of achievement has been set too low. Only a low standard is desired and one still lower is acceptable. The directives issuing from a second-rate chief and addressed to his third-rate executives speak only of minimum aims and ineffectual means. A higher standard of competence is not desired, for an efficient organization would be beyond the chief's power to control. The motto, "Ever third-rate" has been inscribed over the main entrance in letters of gold. Third-rateness has become a principle of policy. It will be observed, however, that the existence of higher standards is still recognized. There remains at this primary stage a hint of apology, a feeling of uneasiness when Toprank is mentioned. Neither this apology nor unease lasts for long. The second stage of the disease comes on quickly and it is this we must now describe.

The secondary stage is recognized by its chief symptom, which is Smugness. The aims have been set low and have therefore been largely achieved. The target has been set up within ten yards of the firing point and the scoring has therefore been high. The directors have done what they set out to do. This soon fills them with self-satisfaction. They set out to do something and they have done it. They soon forget that it was a small effort to gain a small result. They observe only that they have succeeded—unlike those people at Much-Striving. They become increasingly smug and their smugness reveals itself in remarks such as this: "The chief is a sound man and very clever when you get to know him. He never says much—that is not his way—but he seldom makes a mistake." (These last words can be said with justice of someone who never does anything at all.) Or this: "We rather distrust brilliance here. These clever people can be a dreadful nuisance, upsetting established routine and proposing all sorts of schemes that we have never seen tried. We obtain splendid results by simple common sense and teamwork." And finally this: "Our canteen is something we are really rather proud of. We don't know how the caterer can produce so good a lunch at the price. We are lucky to have him!" This last remark is made as we sit at a table covered with dirty oilcloth, facing an uneatable, nameless mess on a plate and shuddering at the sight and smell of what passes for coffee. In point of fact, the canteen reveals more than the office. Just as for a quick verdict we judge a private house by inspection of the WC (to find whether there is a spare toilet roll), just as we judge a hotel by the state of the cruet, so we judge a larger institution by the appearance of the canteen. If the decoration is in dark brown and pale green; if the curtains are purple (or absent); if there are no flowers in sight; if there is barley in the soup (with or without a dead fly); if the menu is one of hash and mold; and if the executives are still delighted with everything—why, then the institution is in a pretty bad way. For self-satisfaction, in such a case, has reached the point at which those responsible cannot tell the difference between food and filth. This is smugness made absolute.

The tertiary and last stage of the disease is one in which apathy has taken the place of smugness. The executives no longer boast of their efficiency as compared with some other institution. They have forgotten that any other institution exists. They have ceased to eat in the canteen, preferring now to bring sandwiches and scatter their desks with the crumbs. The bulletin boards carry notices about the concert that took place four years ago; Mr. Brown's office has a nameplate saying, "Mr. Smith." Mr. Smith's door is marked, "Mr. Robinson," in faded ink on an adhesive luggage label. The broken windows have been repaired with odd bits of cardboard. The electric light switches give a slight but painful shock when touched. The whitewash is flaking off the ceiling and the paint is blotchy on the walls. The elevator is out of order and the cloakroom tap cannot be turned off. Water from the broken skylight drips wide of the bucket placed to catch it, and from somewhere in the basement comes the wail of a hungry cat. The last stage of the disease has brought the whole organization to the point of collapse. The symptoms of the disease in this acute form are so numerous and evident that a trained investigator can often detect them over the telephone without visiting the place at all. When a weary voice answers "Ullo!" (that most unhelpful of replies), the expert has often heard enough. He shakes his head sadly as he replaces the receiver. "Well on in the tertiary phase," he will mutter to himself, "and almost certainly inoperable." It is too late to attempt any sort of treatment. The institution is practically dead.

We have now described this disease as seen from within and then again from outside. We know now the origin, the progress, and the outcome of the infection, as also the symptoms by which its presence is detected. British medical skill seldom goes beyond that point in its research. Once a disease has been identified, named, described, and accounted for, the British are usually quite satisfied and ready to investigate the next problem that presents itself. If asked about treatment they look surprised and suggest the use of penicillin preceded or followed by the extraction of all the patient's teeth. It becomes clear at once that this is not an aspect of the subject that interests them. Should our attitude be the same? Or should we as political scientists consider what, if anything, can be done about it? It would be premature, no doubt, to discuss any possible treatment in detail, but it might be useful to indicate very generally the lines along which a solution might be attempted. Certain principles, at least, might be laid down. Of such principles, the first would have to be this: a diseased institution cannot reform itself. There are instances, we know, of a disease vanishing without treatment, just as it appeared without warning; but these cases are rare and regarded by the specialist as irregular and undesirable. The cure, whatever its nature, must come from outside. For a patient to remove his own appendix under a local anaesthetic may be physically possible, but the practice is regarded with disfavor and is open to many objections. Other operations lend themselves still less to the patient's own dexterity. The first principle we can safely enunciate is that the patient and the surgeon should not be the same person. When an institution is in an advanced state of disease, the services of a specialist are required and even, in some instances, the services of the greatest living authority: Parkinson himself. The fees payable may be very heavy indeed, but in a case of this sort, expense is clearly no object. It is a matter, after all, of life and death.

The second principle we might lay down is this, that the primary stage of the disease can be treated by a simple injection, that the secondary stage can be cured in some instances by surgery, and that the tertiary stage must be regarded at present as incurable. There was a time when physicians used to babble about bottles and pills, but this is mainly out of date. There was another period when they talked more vaguely about psychology; but that too is out of date, most of the psychoanalysts having since been certified as insane. The present age is one of injections and incisions and it behooves the political scientists to keep in step with the Faculty. Confronted by a case of primary infection, we prepare a syringe automatically and only hesitate as to what, besides water, it should contain. In principle, the injection should contain some active substance—but from which group should it be selected? A kill-or-cure injection would contain a high proportion of Intolerance, but this drug is difficult to procure and sometimes too powerful to use. Intolerance is obtainable from the bloodstream of regimental sergeant majors and is found to comprise two chemical elements, namely: (a) the best is scarcely good enough (GG^{nth}) and (b) there is no excuse for anything (NE^{nth}). Injected into a diseased institution, the intolerant individual has a tonic effect and may cause the organism to turn against the original source of infection. While this treatment may well do good, it is by no means certain that the cure will be permanent. It is doubtful, that is to say, whether the infected substance will be actually expelled from the system. Such information as we have rather leads us to suppose that this treatment is merely palliative in the first instance, the disease remaining latent though inactive. Some authorities believe that repeated injections would result in a complete cure, but others fear that repetition of the treatment would set up a fresh irritation, only slightly less dangerous than the original disease. Intolerance is a drug to be used, therefore, with caution.

There exists a rather milder drug called Ridicule, but its operation is uncertain, its character unstable, and its effects too little known. There is little reason to fear that any damage could result from an injection of ridicule, but neither is it evident that a cure would result. It is generally agreed that the injelitant individual will have developed a thick protective skin, insensitive to ridicule. It may well be that ridicule may tend to isolate the infection, but that is as much as could be expected and more indeed than has been claimed.

We may note, finally, that Castigation, which is easily obtainable, has been tried in cases of this sort and not wholly without effect. Here again, however, there are difficulties. This drug is an immediate stimulus but can produce a result the exact opposite of what the specialist intends. After a momentary spasm of activity, the injelitant individual will often prove more supine than before and just as harmful as a source of infection. If any use can be made of castigation it will almost certainly be as one element in a preparation composed otherwise of intolerance and ridicule, with perhaps other drugs as yet untried. It only remains to point out that this preparation does not as yet exist.

The secondary stage of the disease we believe to be operable. Professional readers will all have heard of the Nuciform Sack and of the work generally associated with the name of Cutler Walpole. The operation first performed by that great surgeon involves, simply, the removal of the infected parts and the simultaneous introduction of new blood drawn from a similar organism. This operation has sometimes succeeded. It is only fair to add that it has also sometimes failed. The shock to the system can be too great. The new blood may be unobtainable and may fail, even when procured, to mingle with the blood previously in circulation. On the other hand, this drastic method offers, beyond question, the best chance of a complete cure.

The tertiary stage presents us with no opportunity to do anything. The institution is for all practical purposes dead. It can be founded afresh but only with a change of name, a change of site, and an entirely different staff. The temptation, for the economically minded, is to transfer some portion of the original staff to the new institution—in the name, for example, of continuity. Such a transfusion would certainly be fatal, and continuity is the very thing to avoid. No portion of the old and diseased foundation can be regarded as free from infection. No staff, no equipment, no tradition must be removed from the original site. Strict quarantine should be followed by complete disinfection. Infected personnel should be dispatched with a warm testimonial to such rival institutions as are regarded with particular hostility. All equipment and files should be destroyed without hesitation. As for the buildings, the best plan is to insure them heavily and then set them alight. Only when the site is a blackened ruin can we feel certain that the germs of the disease are dead.

ROBERT M. HUTCHINS

That Candles May Be Brought[1]

My father came home from India about thirty years ago with the story of a British woman who was plagued to death by the questions of her Indian servant. Finally she said to him, "Why don't you use your common sense?" He replied, "Lady, common sense is the gift of God; I have only a technical education."

In college students learn to think. The question is whether they continue to do so upon graduation. We know that whereas a great deal of thinking is required to get through college, none is necessary to get through life. By definition a moron is a person who cannot think, and one of the benefits conferred upon us by the Industrial Revolution is that it has made it possible for morons to be successful. In 1948, Dr. Ruby Jo Reeves Kennedy, sociologist at the Connecticut College for Women, reported to the American Association on Mental Deficiency that the typical male moron earned as much as $3.50 a week more than the average industrial wage and that the female moron uniformly made more money than the normal industrial worker.

These figures should not surprise us, for it is obvious that the aim of mechanization is to get the operation simplified to the point where only his presence, and very little of that, is demanded of the operator. A capacity to think, and still worse, an insistence on doing so, may in such operations be a positive handicap.

We here begin to discern one of the reasons for the prevailing anti-intellectualism in this country. People who think do not fit in easily. The trouble with thinking is that it leads to criticism. A person who thinks is one who dislikes falsehood. And since it is impossible to dislike it and never say anything about it, it is impossible to think and never say anything controversial.

The unpopularity of thinking has a good deal to do with bringing about the alteration in the aims of educaton that has taken place in the thirty-five years and more that I have been employed by educational institutions. We exhibit a certain shyness now when we talk about those aims, intellectual training and intellectual activity, which were accepted as a matter of course in my youth. The current doctrine is that the aim of education is to adjust the young to the group. Not long ago a young woman at a co-educational college in Oklahoma was asked why she was depressed. She replied, "I come here to be went with and I ain't." The failure of education to perform its proper function in her case justified her disappointment with it.

Thinking is painful, unnecessary, and unpopular. The din of public and private propaganda in which we live, the pressure exerted by the institutions in which we work and have our being, and the tyranny of our neighbor's lifted

[1] From *Recall*, I (November-December, 1959), 5-10. Reprinted by permission of the author.

eyebrow are making thinking next to impossible. Under these circumstances the habit of not thinking, of not caring, or not protesting is the easiest in the world to acquire. The most common statement you can hear today is, "I don't want to get involved."

Thinking proceeds in the effort to raise and answer questions. The Socratic dialogue is the model of civilized society. Certain technical and economic changes have placed the present generation at a disadvantage. The forum and the general store, which used to be the centers of discussion in this country, are being driven out of business by television and the supermarket. There can't be much conversation when you are watching that little screen or pushing your cart down those unending corridors of cans.

Far more serious are the fashions of silence with which we are afflicted. Only the other day the commandants of the Military and Naval Academies thought it dangerous to have their young gentlemen on either side of the question whether Red China should be admitted to the United Nations. Nobody would care to ask today whether our conviction that we need to spend twice or twenty times the amount of money on education that we now devote to it is justified by the quality of education that our children are now receiving or precisely how the quality of education is to be improved by the expenditures proposed. It is now tacitly understood that American education needs nothing but money, that all teachers, all subjects, and all schools and colleges need more money, and it would be rude to ask whether it is absolutely certain that they all deserve it.

If it is possible to ask a question, it may not be possible to get an intelligible answer. The world is hidden from us by the cliché curtain. Just as the question of the actual danger from the Communist Party in America can't be raised because the Party is a treasonable conspiracy, and the question of educational expenditures can't be raised because education is a good thing, so the question of Strontium 90 is disposed of by saying that if leukemia doesn't get us the Russians will, desegregation in the South by saying that everything takes time, inflation by saying that we must reduce Federal expenditures, and the problems of labor organization by referring to the right to work.

According to the law of contradiction, it is impossible to say that the same statement is at the same time in the same respect both true and false. One reason why the Civilization of the Dialogue is so hard to attain is that constant efforts are made to repeal this law. So the great historian of freedom, Lord Acton, had no difficulty in concluding that slavery was necessary to democracy, because, he said, the lower elements in the population would degrade it if they were allowed membership in the political society. According to Acton, slavery is essential if a democratic state is to be free. So, in spite of the fact that Christian love would seem to require that distinctions based on color should never appear in Christian congregations, it has been said that segregation reaches its peak in this country at 11 o'clock on Sunday mornings.

Consider the possibilities in a local wit's report that the cigarette companies are about to embark on a national advertising campaign with the slogan, "Cancer is good for you." The more one ponders this suggestion the more probable it sounds. If the cigarette companies did enter upon this campaign, who can doubt that it would succeed? The genius and the devices at the disposal of private and public propaganda have made smooth the pathway to 1984, where slavery is freedom, war is peace, hate is love, and disease is health. We are so used to violations of the law of contradiction that we are startled when the Supreme Court upholds it and rules in civil liberties cases that the Constitution means what it says.

If thinking is painful, unnecessary, unpopular, and, under present circumstances, next to impossible, why should you do it? Consider what our problems are. They are how to make democracy work, how to survive in the nuclear age, and what to do with ourselves if we do survive.

The first of these questions is how to make democracy work. It is basically the question of how we get the information and intelligence to cope with the totally new economic, social and political situation in which we find ourselves. When it appears likely that $175,000,000 was spent in the last national election, when fewer and fewer voices can be heard through the media of mass communications, when those media are chiefly devoted to mass entertainment, and when the educational system is dedicated largely to adjusting the young to the group, we see that discussion has been replaced by private and public propaganda and that the kind of education we are offering is unlikely to provide a defense against it.

Nor can we suppose that without thought we can survive in the nuclear age. Since we know that the simultaneous explosion of a finite number of bombs can make the world uninhabitable, we must recognize that in two hundred years we have moved from polite wars for limited aims fought without disturbing most of the population to the point where we can all go up in one big megabang. To suppose that we can avoid this fate by preparing to make the bang bigger or by talking about the reduction of one or two kinds of forces in one or two kinds of places is as absurd as it was to imagine that the last wars could be avoided by an armament race or by endless conferences about whether the armor plate permitted on a battleship should be reduced by one-quarter or one-eighth of an inch.

And what shall we do with ourselves if we do survive? We have almost reached the 36-hour week, and as automation and atomic energy are brought into industrial use the proportion of our time that we shall have to devote to earning a living will decline still further. In my lifetime the hours of labor have been cut by a third. We don't know what to do with ourselves now. Some think that there is no limit to the capacity and willingness of people to seek and enjoy entertainment, relaxation, and recreation. I do not believe it. It is more likely that the alternatives presented by modern technology are either that we shall all be killed or we shall all be bored to death.

There are two ways to get through life that the educated person cannot permit himself, and they are to fill the time with aimless, and hence thoughtless activity, or to sink into a vegetable torpor. The reasons why these pastimes fail is that neither one is human. Every human being sooner or later has to feel that there is some meaning to his life. He must have a purpose.

You must think for your own sake, and also for your country's. We can be contented with nothing less for this nation than that it should cherish the best things there are. It seems altogether likely that these are art and education, freedom and justice, courage and compassion—the things the ancients summed up under the three heads of truth, beauty, and goodness. And what are these but the fullest development of man's highest powers in their individual and social aspects?

Let us remember that there have been dark days in the past. There was a famous one in New England in 1780 when the sun scarcely appeared at all. Thousands of people took it for the end of the world. Among them were many in the Connecticut Assembly, in which Colonel Abraham Davenport was sitting. It was proposed that the Assembly adjourn. Colonel Davenport said, "The Day of Judgment is either approaching or it is not. If it is not, there is no cause for adjournment. If it is, I choose to be found doing my duty. I wish therefore that candles may be brought."

SUSANNE K. LANGER

Language and Thought[1]

A symbol is not the same thing as a sign; that is a fact that psychologists and philosophers often overlook. All intelligent animals use signs; so do we. To them as well as to us sounds and smells and motions are signs of food, danger, the presence of other beings, or of rain or storm. Furthermore, some animals not only attend to signs but produce them for the benefit of others. Dogs bark at the door to be let in; rabbits thump to call each other; the cooing of doves and the growl of a wolf defending his kill are unequivocal signs of feelings and intentions to be reckoned with by other creatures.

We use signs just as animals do, though with considerably more elaboration. We stop at red lights and go on green; we answer calls and bells, watch the

[1] From Susanne K. Langer, "The Lord of Creation." Reprinted from the January 1944 issue of *Fortune* Magazine by special permission of the Editors. Copyright, 1944, Time, Inc.

sky for coming storms, read trouble or promise or anger in each other's eyes. That is animal intelligence raised to the human level. Those of us who are dog lovers can probably all tell wonderful stories of how high our dogs have sometimes risen in the scale of clever sign interpretation and sign using.

A sign is anything that announces the existence or the imminence of some event, the presence of a thing or a person, or a change in a state of affairs. There are signs of the weather, signs of danger, signs of future good or evil, signs of what the past has been. In every case a sign is closely bound up with something to be noted or expected in experience. It is always a part of the situation to which it refers, though the reference may be remote in space and time. In so far as we are led to note or expect the signified event we are making correct use of a sign. This is the essence of rational behavior, which animals show in varying degrees. It is entirely realistic, being closely bound up with the actual objective course of history—learned by experience, and cashed in or voided by further experience.

If man had kept to the straight and narrow path of sign using, he would be like the other animals, though perhaps a little brighter. He would not talk, but grunt and gesticulate and point. He would make his wishes known, give warnings, perhaps develop a social system like that of bees and ants, with such a wonderful efficiency of communal enterprise that all men would have plenty to eat, warm apartments—all exactly alike and perfectly convenient—to live in, and everybody could and would sit in the sun or by the fire, as the climate demanded, not talking but just basking, with every want satisfied, most of his life. The young would romp and make love, the old would sleep, the middle-aged would do the routine work almost unconsciously and eat a great deal. But that would be the life of a social, superintelligent, purely sign-using animal.

To us who are human, it does not sound very glorious. We want to go places and do things, own all sorts of gadgets that we do not absolutely need, and when we sit down to take it easy we want to talk. Rights and property, social position, special talents and virtues, and above all our ideas, are what we live for. We have gone off on a tangent that takes us far away from the mere biological cycle that animal generations accomplish; and that is because we can use not only signs but symbols.

A symbol differs from a sign in that it does not announce the presence of the object, the being, condition, or whatnot, which is its meaning, but merely *brings this thing to mind*. It is not a mere "substitute sign" to which we react as though it were the object itself. The fact is that our reaction to hearing a person's name is quite different from our reaction to the person himself. There are certain rare cases where a symbol stands directly for its meaning: in religious experience, for instance, the Host is not only a symbol but a Presence. But symbols in the ordinary sense are not mystic. They are the same sort of thing that ordinary signs are; only they do not call our attention to something necessarily present or to be physically dealt with—they call up merely a conception of the thing they "mean."

The difference between a sign and a symbol is, in brief, that a sign causes us to think or act *in face of* the thing signified, whereas a symbol causes us to think *about* the thing symbolized. Therein lies the great importance of symbolism for human life, its power to make this life so different from any other animal biography that generations of men have found it incredible to suppose that they were of purely zoological origin. A sign is always embedded in reality, in a present that emerges from the actual past and stretches to the future; but a symbol may be divorced from reality altogether. It may refer to what is *not* the case, to a mere idea, a figment, a dream. It serves, therefore, to liberate thought from the immediate stimuli of a physically present world; and that liberation marks the essential difference between human and nonhuman mentality. Animals think, but they think *of* and *at* things; men think primarily *about* things. Words, pictures, and memory images are symbols that may be combined and varied in a thousand ways. The result is a symbolic structure whose meaning is a complex of all their respective meanings, and this kaleidoscope of *ideas* is the typical product of the human brain that we call the "stream of thought."

The process of transforming all direct experience into imagery or into that supreme mode of symbolic expression, language, has so completely taken possession of the human mind that it is not only a special talent but a dominant, organic need. All our sense impressions leave their traces in our memory not only as signs disposing our practical reactions in the future but also as symbols, images representing our *ideas* of things; and the tendency to manipulate ideas, to combine and abstract, mix and extend them by playing with symbols, is man's outstanding characteristic. It seems to be what his brain most naturally and spontaneously does. Therefore his primitive mental function is not judging reality, but *dreaming his desires.*

Dreaming is apparently a basic function of human brains, for it is free and unexhausting like our metabolism, heartbeat, and breath. It is easier to dream than not to dream, as it is easier to breathe than to refrain from breathing. The symbolic character of dreams is fairly well established. Symbol mongering, on this ineffectual, uncritical level, seems to be instinctive, the fulfillment of an elementary need rather than the purposeful exercise of a high and difficult talent.

The special power of man's mind rests on the evolution of this special activity, not on any transcendently high development of animal intelligence. We are not immeasurably higher than other animals; we are different. We have a biological need and with it a biological gift that they do not share.

Because man has not only the ability but the constant need of *conceiving* what has happened to him, what surrounds him, what is demanded of him—in short, of symbolizing nature, himself, and his hopes and fears—he has a constant and crying need of *expression*. What he cannot express, he cannot conceive; what he cannot conceive is chaos, and fills him with terror.

If we bear in mind this all-important craving for expression we get a new picture of man's behavior; for from this trait spring his powers and his weaknesses. The process of symbolic transformation that all our experiences undergo is nothing more nor less than the process of *conception*, which underlies the human faculties of abstraction and imagination.

When we are faced with a strange or difficult situation, we cannot react directly, as other creatures do, with flight, aggression, or any such simple instinctive pattern. Our whole reaction depends on how we manage to conceive the situation—whether we cast it in a definite dramatic form, whether we see it as a disaster, a challenge, a fulfillment of doom, or a fiat of the Divine Will. In words or dreamlike images, in artistic or religious or even in cynical form, we must *construe* the events of life. There is great virtue in the figure of speech, "I can *make* nothing of it," to express a failure to understand something. Thought and memory are processes of *making* the thought content and the memory image; the pattern of our ideas is given by the symbols through which we express them. And in the course of manipulating those symbols we inevitably distort the original experience, as we abstract certain features of it, embroider and reinforce those features with other ideas, until the conception we project on the screen of memory is quite different from anything in our real history.

Conception is a necessary and elementary process; what we do with our conceptions is another story. That is the entire history of human culture—of intelligence and morality, folly and superstition, ritual, language, and the arts—all the phenomena that set man apart from, and above, the rest of the animal kingdom. As the religious mind has to make all human history a drama of sin and salvation in order to define its own moral attitudes, so a scientist wrestles with the mere presentation of "the facts" before he can reason about them. The process of *envisaging* facts, values, hopes, and fears underlies our whole behavior pattern; and this process is reflected in the evolution of an extraordinary phenomenon found always, and only, in human societies—the phenomenon of language.

Language is the highest and most amazing achievement of the symbolistic human mind. The power it bestows is almost inestimable, for without it anything properly called "thought" is impossible. The birth of language is the dawn of humanity. The line between man and beast—between the highest ape and the lowest savage—is the language line. Whether the primitive Neanderthal man was anthropoid or human depends less on his cranial capacity, his upright posture, or even his use of tools and fire, than on one issue we shall probably never be able to settle—whether or not he spoke.

In all physical traits and practical responses, such as skills and visual judgments, we can find a certain continuity between animal and human mentality. Sign using is an ever evolving, ever improving function throughout the whole animal kingdom, from the lowly worm that shrinks into his hole at the sound of an approaching foot, to the dog obeying his master's command, and even to the learned scientist who watches the movements of an index needle.

This continuity of the sign-using talent has led psychologists to the belief that language is evolved from the vocal expressions, grunts and coos and cries, whereby animals vent their feelings or signal their fellows; that man has elaborated this sort of communion to the point where it makes a perfect exchange of ideas possible.

I do not believe that this doctrine of the origin of language is correct. The essence of language is symbolic, not signific; we use it first and most vitally to formulate and hold ideas in our own minds. Conception, not social control, is its first and foremost benefit.

Watch a young child that is just learning to speak play with a toy; he says the name of the object, e.g.: "Horsey! horsey! horsey!" over and over again, looks at the object, moves it, always saying the name to himself or to the world at large. It's quite a time before he talks to anyone in particular; he talks first of all to himself. This is his way of forming and fixing the *conception* of the object in his mind, and around this conception all his knowledge of it grows. *Names* are the essence of language; for the *name* is what abstracts the conception of the horse from the horse itself, and lets the mere idea recur at the speaking of the name. This permits the conception gathered from one horse experience to be exemplified again by another instance of a horse, so that the notion embodied in the name is a general notion..

To this end, the baby uses a word long before he *asks* for the object; when he wants his horsey he is likely to cry and fret, because he is reacting to an actual environment, not forming ideas. He uses the animal language of *signs* for his wants; talking is still a purely symbolic process—its practical value has not really impressed him yet.

Language need not be vocal; it may be purely visual, like written language, or even tactual, like the deaf-mute system of speech; but it *must be denotative*. The sounds, intended or unintended, whereby animals communicate do not constitute a language, because they are signs, not names. They never fall into an organic pattern, a meaningful syntax of even the most rudimentary sort, as all language seems to do with a sort of driving necessity. That is because signs refer to actual situations, in which things have obvious relations to each other that require only to be noted; but symbols refer to ideas, which are not physically there for inspection, so their connections and features have to be represented. This gives all true language a natural tendency toward growth and development, which seems almost like a life of its own. Languages are not invented; they grow with our need for expression.

In contrast, animal "speech" never has a structure. It is merely an emotional response. Apes may greet their ration of yams with a shout of "Nga!" But they do not say "Nga" between meals. If they could *talk about* their yams instead of just saluting them, they would be the most primitive men instead of the most anthropoid of beasts. They would have ideas, and tell each other things true or false, rational or irrational; they would make plans and invent laws and sing their own praises, as men do.

JAMES HARVEY ROBINSON

Four Kinds of Thinking[1]

We do not think enough about thinking, and much of our confusion is the result of current illusions in regard to it. Let us forget for the moment any impressions we may have derived from the philosophers, and see what seems to happen in ourselves. The first thing that we notice is that our thought moves with such incredible rapidity that it is almost impossible to arrest any specimen of it long enough to have a look at it. When we are offered a penny for our thoughts we always find that we have recently had so many things in mind that we can easily make a selection which will not compromise us too nakedly. On inspection we shall find that even if we are not downright ashamed of a great part of our spontaneous thinking it is far too intimate, personal, ignoble or trivial to permit us to reveal more than a small part of it. I believe this must be true of everyone. We do not, of course, know what goes on in other people's heads. They tell us very little and we tell them very little. The spigot of speech, rarely fully opened, could never emit more than driblets of the ever renewed hogshead of thought—*noch grösser wie's Heidelberger Fass.* We find it hard to believe that other people's thoughts are as silly as our own, but they probably are.

We all appear to ourselves to be thinking all the time during our waking hours, and most of us are aware that we go on thinking while we are asleep, even more foolishly than when awake. When uninterrupted by some practical issue we are engaged in what is now known as a *reverie.* This is our spontaneous and favorite kind of thinking. We allow our ideas to take their own course and this course is determined by our hopes and fears, our spontaneous desires, their fulfillment or frustration; by our likes and dislikes, our loves and hates and resentments. There is nothing else anything like so interesting to ourselves as ourselves. All thought that is not more or less laboriously controlled and directed will inevitably circle about the beloved Ego. It is amusing and pathetic to observe this tendency in ourselves and in others. We learn politely and generously to overlook this truth, but if we dare to think of it, it blazes forth like the noontide sun.

The reverie or "free association of ideas" has of late become the subject of scientific research. While investigators are not yet agreed on the results, or at least on the proper interpretation to be given to them, there can be no doubt that our reveries form the chief index to our fundamental character. They are a reflection of our nature as modified by often hidden and forgotten experiences. We need not go into the matter further here, for it is only necessary to observe that the reverie is at all times a potent and in many cases an omnipotent rival to every other kind of thinking. It doubtless influences all our speculations in its persistent tendency to self-magnification and self-justification, which are its chief preoccupations, but it is the last thing to make directly or indirectly for honest increase of knowledge.[2] Philosophers usually talk as if such thinking did not exist or were in some way negligible. This is what makes their speculations so unreal and often worthless.

The reverie, as any of us can see for himself, is frequently broken and interrupted by the necessity of a second kind of thinking. We have to make practical decisions. Shall we write a letter or no? Shall we take the subway or a bus? Shall we have dinner at seven or half-past? Shall we buy U.S. Rubber or a Liberty Bond? Decisions are easily distinguishable from the free flow of the reverie. Sometimes they demand a good deal of careful pondering and the recollection of pertinent facts; often, however, they are made impulsively. They are a more difficult and laborious thing than the reverie, and we resent having to "make up our mind" when we are tired, or absorbed in a congenial reverie. Weighing a decision, it should be noted, does not necessarily add anything to our knowledge, although we may, of course, seek further information before making it.

A third kind of thinking is stimulated when any one questions our belief and opinions. We sometimes find ourselves changing our minds without any resistance or heavy emotion, but if we are told that we are wrong we resent the imputation and harden our hearts. We are incredibly heedless in the formation of our beliefs, but find ourselves filled with an illicit passion for them when anyone proposes to rob us of their companionship. It is obviously not the ideas themselves that are dear to us, but our self-esteem, which is threatened. We are by nature stubbornly pledged to defend our own from attack, whether it be our person, our family, our property, or our opinion. A United States Senator once remarked to a friend of mine that God Almighty could not make him change his mind on our Latin-America policy. We may surrender, but rarely confess ourselves vanquished. In the intellectual world at least peace is without victory.

---

[2] The poet-clergyman, John Donne, who lived in the time of James I, has given a beautifully honest picture of the doings of a saint's mind: "I throw myself down in my chamber and call in and invite God and His angels thither, and when they are there I neglect God and His angels for the noise of a fly, for the rattling of a coach, for the whining of a door. I talk on in the same posture of praying, eyes lifted up, knees bowed down, as though I prayed to God, and if God or His angels should ask me when I thought last of God in that prayer I cannot tell. Sometimes I find that I had forgot what I was about, but when I began to forget it I cannot tell. A memory of yesterday's pleasures, a fear of tomorrow's dangers, a straw under my knee, a noise in mine ear, a light in mine eye, an anything, a nothing, a fancy, a chimera in my brain troubles me in my prayer."—Quoted by Robert Lynd, *The Art of Letters*, pp. 46-47.

Few of us take the pains to study the origin of our cherished convictions; indeed, we have a natural repugnance to so doing. We like to continue to believe what we have been accustomed to accept as true, and the resentment aroused when doubt is cast upon any of our assumptions leads us to seek every manner of excuse for clinging to them. *The result is that most of our so-called reasoning consists in finding arguments for going on believing as we already do.*

I remember years ago attending a public dinner to which the Governor of the state was bidden. The chairman explained that His Excellency could not be present for certain "good" reasons; what the "real" reasons were the presiding officer said he would leave us to conjecture. This distinction between "good" and "real" reasons is one of the most clarifying and essential in the whole realm of thought. We can readily give what seem to us "good" reasons for being a Catholic or a Mason, a Republican or a Democrat, an adherent or opponent of the League of Nations. But the "real" reasons are usually on a quite different plane. Of course the importance of this distinction is popularly, if somewhat obscurely, recognized. The Baptist missionary is ready enough to see that the Buddhist is not such because his doctrines would bear careful inspection, but because he happened to be born in a Buddhist family in Tokio. But it would be treason to his faith to acknowledge that his own partiality for certain doctrines is due to the fact that his mother was a member of the First Baptist church of Oak Ridge. A savage can give all sorts of reasons for his belief that it is dangerous to step on a man's shadow, and a newspaper editor can advance plenty of arguments against the Bolsheviki. But neither of them may realize why he happens to be defending his particular opinion.

The "real" reasons for our beliefs are concealed from ourselves as well as from others. As we grow up we simply adopt the ideas presented to us in regard to such matters as religion, family relations, property, business, our country, and the state. We unconsciously absorb them from our environment. They are persistently whispered in our ear by the group in which we happen to live. Moreover, as Mr. Trotter has pointed out, these judgments, being the product of suggestion and not of reasoning, have the quality of perfect obviousness, so that to question them

> . . . is to the believer to carry skepticism to an insane degree, and will be met by contempt, disapproval, or condemnation, according to the nature of the belief in question. When, therefore, we find ourselves entertaining an opinion about the basis of which there is a quality of feeling which tells us that to inquire into it would be absurd, obviously unnecessary, unprofitable, undesirable, bad form, or wicked, we may know that that opinion is a non-rational one, and probably, therefore, founded upon inadequate evidence.[3]

Opinions, on the other hand, which are the result of experience or of honest reasoning do not have this quality of "primary certitude." I remember when as a youth I heard a group of business men discussing the question of the im-

[3] *Instincts of the Herd*, p. 44.

mortality of the soul, I was outraged by the sentiment of doubt expressed by one of the party. As I look back now I see that I had at the time no interest in the matter, and certainly no least argument to urge in favor of the belief in which I had been reared. But neither my personal indifference to the issue, nor the fact that I had previously given it no attention, served to prevent an angry resentment when I heard *my* ideas questioned.

This spontaneous and loyal support of our preconceptions—this process of finding "good" reasons to justify our routine beliefs—is known to modern psychologists as "rationalizing"—clearly only a new name for a very ancient thing. Our "good" reasons ordinarily have no value in promoting honest enlightenment, because, no matter how solemnly they may be marshaled, they are at bottom the result of personal preference or prejudice, and not of an honest desire to seek or accept new knowledge.

In our reveries we are frequently engaged in self-justification, for we cannot bear to think ourselves wrong, and yet have constant illustrations of our weaknesses and mistakes. So we spend much time finding fault with circumstances and the conduct of others, and shifting on to them with great ingenuity the onus of our own failures and disappointments. *Rationalizing is the self-exculpation which occurs when we feel ourselves, or our group, accused of misapprehension or error.*

The little word *my* is the most important one in all human affairs, and properly to reckon with it is the beginning of wisdom. It has the same force whether it is *my* dinner, *my* dog, and *my* house, or *my* faith, *my* country, and *my* God. We not only resent the imputation that our watch is wrong, or our car shabby, but that our conception of the canals of Mars, of the pronunciation of "Epictetus," of the medicinal value of salicine, or the date of Sargon I, is subject to revision.

Philosophers, scholars, and men of science exhibit a common sensitiveness in all decisions in which their *amour propre* is involved. Thousands of argumentative works have been written to vent a grudge. However stately their reasoning, it may be nothing but rationalizing, stimulated by the most commonplace of all motives. A history of philosophy and theology could be written in terms of grouches, wounded pride, and aversions, and it would be far more instructive than the usual treatments of these themes. Sometimes, under Providence, the lowly impulse of resentment leads to great achievements. Milton wrote his treatise on divorce as a result of his troubles with his seventeen-year-old wife, and when he was accused of being the leading spirit in a new sect, the Divorcers, he wrote his noble *Areopagitica* to prove his right to say what he thought fit, and incidentally to establish the advantage of a free press in the promotion of Truth.

All mankind, high and low, thinks in all the ways which have been described. The reverie goes on all the time not only in the mind of the mill hand and the Broadway flapper, but equally in weighty judges and godly bishops. It has gone on in all the philosophers, scientists, poets, and theologians that have ever lived. Aristotle's most abstruse speculations were doubtless tempered by highly irrelevant reflections. He is reported to have had very thin legs and small eyes, for which he doubtless had to find excuses, and he was wont to indulge in very conspicuous dress and rings and was accustomed to arrange his hair carefully.[4] Diogenes the Cynic exhibited the impudence of a touchy soul. His tub was his distinction. Tennyson in beginning his "Maud" could not forget his chagrin over losing his patrimony years before as the result of an unhappy investment in the Patent Decorative Carving Company. These facts are not recalled here as a gratuitous disparagement of the truly great, but to insure a full realization of the tremendous competition which all really exacting thought has to face, even in the minds of the most highly endowed mortals.

And now the astonishing and perturbing suspicion emerges that perhaps almost all that had passed for social science, political economy, politics, and ethics in the past may be brushed aside by future generations as mainly rationalizing. John Dewey has already reached this conclusion in regard to philosophy.[5] Veblen[6] and other writers have revealed the various unperceived presuppositions of the traditional political economy, and now comes an Italian sociologist, Vilfredo Pareto, who, in his huge treatise on general sociology, devotes hundreds of pages to substantiating a similar thesis affecting all the social sciences.[7] This conclusion may be ranked by students of a hundred years hence as one of the several great discoveries of our age. It is by no means fully worked out, and it is so opposed to nature that it will be very slowly accepted by the great mass of those who consider themselves thoughtful. As a historical student I am personally fully reconciled to this newer view. Indeed, it seems to me inevitable that just as the various sciences of nature were, before the opening of the seventeenth century, largely masses of rationalizations to suit the religious sentiments of the period, so the social sciences have continued even to our own day to be rationalizations of uncritically accepted beliefs and customs.

It will become apparent as we proceed that the fact that an idea is ancient and that it has been widely received is no argument in its favor, but should immediately suggest the necessity of carefully testing it as a probable instance of rationalization.

This brings us to another kind of thought which can fairly easily be distinguished from the three kinds described above. It has not the usual qualities of

---

[4] Diogenes Laertius, book v.

[5] *Reconstruction in Philosophy.*

[6] *The Place of Science in Modern Civilization.*

[7] *Traité de Sociologie Générale, passim.* The author's term *"derivations"* seems to be his precise way of expressing what we have called the "good" reasons, and his *"residus"* correspond to the "real" reasons. He well says, "*L'homme éprouve le besoin de raisonner, et en outre d'étendre un voile sur ses instincts et sur ses sentiments"*—hence, rationalization. (P. 788.) His aim is to reduce sociology to the "real" reasons. (P. 791.)

the reverie, for it does not hover about our personal complacencies and humilia-tions. It is not made up of the homely decisions forced upon us by everyday needs, when we review our little stock of existing information, consult our con-ventional preferences and obligations, and make a choice of action. It is not the defense of our own cherished beliefs and prejudices just because they are our own—mere plausible excuses for remaining of the same mind. On the contrary, it is that peculiar species of thought which leads us to *change* our mind.

It is this kind of thought that has raised man from his pristine, subsavage ignorance and squalor to the degree of knowledge and comfort which he now possesses. On his capacity to continue and greatly extend this kind of thinking depends his chance of groping his way out of the plight in which the most civilized peoples of the world now find themselves. In the past this type of thinking has been called Reason. But so many misapprehensions have grown up around the word that some of us have become suspicious of it. I suggest, there-fore, that we substitute a recent name and speak of "creative thought" rather than of Reason. *For this kind of meditation begets knowledge, and knowledge is really creative inasmuch as it makes things look different from what they seemed before and may indeed work for their reconstruction.*

In certain moods some of us realize that we are observing things or making reflections with a seeming disregard of our personal preoccupations. We are not preening or defending ourselves; we are not faced by the necessity of any prac-tical decision, nor are we apologizing for believing this or that. We are just wondering and looking and mayhap seeing what we never perceived before.

Curiosity is as clear and definite as any of our urges. We wonder what is in a sealed telegram or in a letter in which some one else is absorbed, or what is being said in the telephone booth or in low conversation. This inquisitiveness is vastly stimulated by jealousy, suspicion, or any hint that we ourselves are di-rectly or indirectly involved. But there appears to be a fair amount of per-sonal interest in other people's affairs even when they do not concern us except as a mystery to be unraveled or a tale to be told. The reports of a divorce suit will have "news value" for many weeks. They constitute a story, like a novel or play or moving picture. This is not an example of pure curiosity, however, since we readily identify ourselves with others, and their joys and despair then be-come our own.

We also take note of, or "observe," as Sherlock Holmes says, things which have nothing to do with our personal interests and make no personal appeal either direct or by way of sympathy. This is what Veblen so well calls "idle cu-riosity." And it is usually idle enough. Some of us when we face the line of people opposite us in a subway train impulsively consider them in detail and engage in rapid inferences and form theories in regard to them. On entering a room there are those who will perceive at a glance the degree of preciousness of the rugs, the character of the pictures, and the personality revealed by the books. But there are many, it would seem, who are so absorbed in their personal reverie or in some definite purpose that they have no bright-eyed energy for idle curiosity. The tendency to miscellaneous observation we come by honestly enough, for we note it in many of our animal relatives.

Veblen, however, uses the term "idle curiosity" somewhat ironically, as is his wont. It is idle only to those who fail to realize that it may be a very rare and indispensable thing from which almost all distinguished human achievement proceeds, since it may lead to systematic examination and seeking for things hitherto undiscovered. For research is but diligent search which enjoys the high flavor of primitive hunting. Occasionally and fitfully idle curiosity thus leads to creative thought, which alters and broadens our own views and aspirations and may in turn, under highly favorable circumstances, affect the views and lives of others, even for generations to follow. An example or two will make this unique human process clear.

Galileo was a thoughtful youth and doubtless carried on a rich and varied reverie. He had artistic ability and might have turned out to be a musician or painter. When he had dwelt among the monks at Valambrosa he had been tempted to lead the life of a religious. As a boy he busied himself with toy machines and he inherited a fondness for mathematics. All these facts are of record. We may safely assume also that, along with many other subjects of contemplation, the Pisan maidens found a vivid place in his thoughts.

One day when seventeen years old he wandered into the cathedral of his native town. In the midst of his reverie he looked up at the lamps hanging by long chains from the high ceiling of the church. Then something very difficult to explain occurred. He found himself no longer thinking of the building, worshipers, or the services; of his artistic or religious interests; of his reluctance to become a physician as his father wished. He forgot the question of a career and even the *graziosissime donne*. As he watched the swinging lamps he was suddenly wondering if mayhap their oscillations, whether long or short, did not occupy the same time. Then he tested his hypothesis by counting his pulse, for that was the only timepiece he had with him.

This observation, however remarkable in itself, was not enough to produce a really creative thought. Others may have noticed the same thing and yet nothing came of it. Most of our observations have no assignable results. Galileo may have seen that the warts on a peasant's face formed a perfect isosceles triangle, or he may have noticed with boyish glee that just as the officiating priest was uttering the solemn words, *ecce agnus Dei*, a fly lit on the end of his nose. To be really creative, ideas have to be worked up and then "put over," so that they become a part of man's social heritage. The highly accurate pendulum clock was one of the later results of Galileo's discovery. He himself was led to reconsider and successfully to refute the old notions of falling bodies. It remained for Newton to prove that the moon was falling, and presumably all the heavenly bodies. This quite upset all the consecrated views of the heavens as managed by angelic engineers. The universality of the laws of gravitation stimulated the attempt to seek other and equally important natural laws and cast grave doubts on the miracles in which mankind had hitherto believed. In short, those who dared to include in their thought the discoveries of Galileo and his successors found themselves in a new earth surrounded by new heavens.

On the 28th of October, 1831, two hundred and fifty years after Galileo had noticed the isochronous vibrations of the lamps, creative thought and its currency had so far increased that Faraday was wondering what would happen if he mounted a disk of copper between the poles of a horseshoe magnet. As the disk revolved, an electric current was produced. This would doubtless have seemed the idlest kind of experiment to the stanch business men of the time who, it happened, were just then denouncing the child-labor bills in their anxiety to avail themselves to the full of the results of earlier idle curiosity. But should the dynamos and motors which have come into being as the outcome of Faraday's experiment be stopped this evening, the business man of to-day, agitated over labor troubles, might, as he trudged home past lines of "dead" cars, through dark streets to an unlighted house, engage in a little creative thought of his own and perceive that he and his laborers would have no modern factories and mines to quarrel about if it had not been for the strange, practical effects of the idle curiosity of scientists, inventors, and engineers.

The examples of creative intelligence given above belong to the realm of modern scientific achievement, which furnishes the most striking instances of the effects of scrupulous, objective thinking. But there are, of course, other great realms in which the recording and embodiment of acute observation and insight have wrought themselves into the higher life of man. The great poets and dramatists and our modern story-tellers have found themselves engaged in productive reveries, noting and artistically presenting their discoveries for the delight and instruction of those who have the ability to appreciate them.

The process by which a fresh and original poem or drama comes into being is doubtless analogous to that which originates and elaborates so-called scientific discoveries; but there is clearly a temperamental difference. The genesis and advance of painting, sculpture, and music offer still other problems. We really as yet know shockingly little about these matters, and indeed very few people have the least curiosity about them.[8] Nevertheless, creative intelligence in its various forms and activities is what makes man. Were it not for its slow, painful, and constantly discouraged operations through the ages man would be no more than a species of primate living on seeds, fruit, roots, and uncooked flesh, and wandering naked through the woods and over the plains like a chimpanzee.

The origin and progress and future promotion of civilization are ill under-

[8] Recently a re-examination of creative thought has begun as a result of new knowledge which discredits many of the notions formerly held about "reason." See, for example, *Creative Intelligence*, by a group of American philosophic thinkers; John Dewey, *Essays in Experimental Logic* (both pretty hard books); and Veblen, *The Place of Science in Modern Civilization*. Easier than these and very stimulating are Dewey, *Reconstruction in Philosophy*, and Woodworth, *Dynamic Psychology*.

stood and misconceived. These should be made the chief theme of education, but much hard work is necessary before we can reconstruct our ideas of man and his capacities and free ourselves from innumerable persistent misapprehensions. There have been obstructionists in all times, not merely the lethargic masses, but the moralists, the rationalizing theologians, and most of the philosophers, all busily if unconsciously engaged in ratifying existing ignorance and mistakes and discouraging creative thought. Naturally, those who reassure us seem worthy of honor and respect. Equally naturally, those who puzzle us with disturbing criticisms and invite us to change our ways are objects of suspicion and readily discredited. Our personal discontent does not ordinarily extend to any critical questioning of the general situation in which we find ourselves. In every age the prevailing conditions of civilization have appeared quite natural and inevitable to those who grew up in them. The cow asks no questions as to how it happens to have a dry stall and a supply of hay. The kitten laps its warm milk from a china saucer, without knowing anything about porcelain; the dog nestles in the corner of a divan with no sense of obligation to the inventors of upholstery and the manufacturers of down pillows. So we humans accept our breakfasts, our trains and telephones and orchestras and movies, our national Constitution, our moral code and standards of manners, with the simplicity and innocence of a pet rabbit. We have absolutely inexhaustible capacities for appropriating what others do for us with no thought of a "thank you." We do not feel called upon to make any least contribution to the merry game ourselves. Indeed, we are usually quite unaware that a game is being played at all.

We have now examined the various classes of thinking which we can readily observe in ourselves and which we have plenty of reasons to believe go on, and always have been going on, in our fellowmen. We can sometimes get quite pure and sparkling examples of all four kinds, but commonly they are so confused and intermingled in our reverie as not to be readily distinguishable. The reverie is a reflection of our longings, exultations, and complacencies, our fears, suspicions, and disappointments. We are chiefly engaged in struggling to maintain our self-respect and in asserting that supremacy which we all crave and which seems to us our natural prerogative. It is not strange, but rather quite inevitable, that our beliefs about what is true and false, good and bad, right and wrong, should be mixed up with the reverie and be influenced by the same considerations which determine its character and course. We resent criticisms of our views exactly as we do of anything else connected with ourselves. Our notions of life and its ideals seem to us to be *our own* and as such necessarily true and right, to be defended at all costs.

We very rarely consider, however, the process by which we gained our convictions. If we did so, we could hardly fail to see that there was usually little ground for our confidence in them. Here and there, in this department of knowledge or that, some one of us might make a fair claim to have taken some trouble to get correct ideas of, let us say, the situation in Russia, the sources of our food supply, the origin of the Constitution, the revision of the tariff, the policy of the Holy Roman Apostolic Church, modern business organization, trade unions, birth control, socialism, the League of Nations, the excess-profits tax, preparedness, advertising in its social bearings; but only a very exceptional person would be entitled to opinions on all of even these few matters. And yet most of us have opinions on all these, and on many other questions of equal importance, of which we may know even less. We feel compelled, as self-respecting persons, to take sides when they come up for discussion. We even surprise ourselves by our omniscience. Without taking thought we see in a flash that it is most righteous and expedient to discourage birth control by legislative enactment, or that one who decries intervention in Mexico is clearly wrong, or that big advertising is essential to big business and that big business is the pride of the land. As godlike beings, why should we not rejoice in our omniscience?

It is clear, in any case, that our convictions on important matters are not the result of knowledge or critical thought, nor, it may be added, are they often dictated by supposed self-interest. Most of them are *pure prejudices* in the proper sense of that word. We do not form them ourselves. They are the whispering of "the voice of the herd." We have in the last analysis no responsibility for them and need assume none. They are not really our own ideas, but those of others no more well informed or inspired than ourselves, who have got them in the same careless and humiliating manner as we. It should be our pride to revise our ideas and not to adhere to what passes for respectable opinion, for such opinion can frequently be shown to be not respectable at all. We should, in view of the considerations that have been mentioned, resent our supine credulity. As an English writer has remarked:

> If we feared the entertaining of an unverifiable opinion with the warmth with which we fear using the wrong implement at the dinner table, if the thought of holding a prejudice disgusted us as does a foul disease, then the dangers of man's suggestibility would be turned into advantages.[9]

The purpose of this essay is to set forth briefly the way in which the notions of the herd have been accumulated. This seems to me the best, easiest, and least invidious educational device for cultivating a proper distrust for the older notions on which we still continue to rely.

The "real" reasons, which explain how it is we happen to hold a particular belief, are chiefly historical. Our most important opinions—those, for example, having to do with traditional, religious, and moral convictions, property rights, patriotism, national honor, the state, and indeed all the assumed foundations of society—are, as I have already suggested, rarely the result of reasoned consideration, but of unthinking absorption from the social environment in which we live. Consequently, they have about them a quality of "elemental certitude,"

[9] Trotter, [*Instincts of the Herd*], p. 45. The first part of this little volume is excellent.

and we especially resent doubt or criticism cast upon them. So long, however, as we revere the whisperings of the herd, we are obviously unable to examine them dispassionately and to consider to what extent they are suited to the novel conditions and social exigencies in which we find ourselves to-day.

The "real" reasons for our beliefs, by making clear their origins and history, can do much to dissipate this emotional blockade and rid us of our prejudices and preconceptions. Once this is done and we come critically to examine our traditional beliefs, we may well find some of them sustained by experience and honest reasoning, while others must be revised to meet new conditions and our more extended knowledge. But only after we have undertaken such a critical examination in the light of experience and modern knowledge, freed from any feeling of "primary certitude," can we claim that the "good" are also the "real" reasons for our opinions.

I do not flatter myself that this general show-up of man's thought through the ages will cure myself or others of carelessness in adopting ideas, or of unseemly heat in defending them just because we have adopted them. But if the considerations which I propose to recall are really incorporated into our thinking and are permitted to establish our general outlook on human affairs, they will do much to relieve the imaginary obligation we feel in regard to traditional sentiments and ideals. Few of us are capable of engaging in creative thought, but some of us can at least come to distinguish it from other and inferior kinds of thought and accord to it the esteem that it merits as the greatest treasure of the past and the only hope of the future.

PHILIP WHEELRIGHT

The Limits of Plain Sense[1]

When people stammer together that is thinking. GERTRUDE STEIN

There is no more ironic illusion than to suppose that one has escaped from illusions. So subtly do the real and the illusory interpenetrate that their difference is never finally clear. Mind is by nature a meddler, and there are no self-evident criteria by which to discriminate its insights from its commentaries. Still, the quest for certainty persists. The history of philosophy, save for sceptical interludes, is a record of men's shifting intellectual stratagems by which to secure some firm line of demarcation between truth and error.

In the everyday business of living we do indeed establish convenient rules

[1] From *The Burning Fountain: A Study in the Language of Symbolism* (Bloomington: Indiana University Press, 1954), pp. 30-51, with omissions. Copyright, 1954, Indiana University Press. Reprinted by permission.

of thumb to indicate, for practical convenience, what can be handled and by what laws it may be expected to operate. Such public operables, actual and potential, constitute our physical world; the study of their regularities of operation is empirical science, and the practical exploitation of those regularities is technology. From time to time, but especially in our day, certain theorists, impressed by the science and technology and wishing a short-cut to first principles, advance this study of public operables as the one valid form of cognition, the sole way of escape from illusionistic muddle, and the system of public operables themselves as the only genuine kind of reality. Such postulation generates the philosophy known variously as materialism, naturalism, and positivism. The last name, positivism, being freest of adventitious connotations, is the one I shall mainly employ: it may be defined precisely as the philosophy which identifies "reality" with the public operables which can be scientifically determined (space-time events and their correlations), and "truth" with the system of empirically verified propositions about such operables and their interrelations, together perhaps with propositions established by deduction from mathematical and logical axioms.

Positivism in the twentieth century goes beyond older forms of materialism: not only because of its recognition of revolutionary new scientific developments, but also—what pertains to the theme of this book—by virtue of having worked out a semantic, which is to say a theory of meaning, of its own. Positivism in this guise may be called *semantic positivism*. Whereas a positivist in general is anyone who identifies reality with the system of public operables that constitutes the physical world, and truth with the system of verifiable propositions describing that reality, a semantic positivist takes the yet more drastic step of identifying *meaning* with such terms and propositions as denote such operables. In other words, the semantic positivist starts off with a judgment about *language*. The only language that really means anything, he declares, is language which refers to things, events, and relations in the physical world. If it does not refer to the physical world, it does not refer to anything (for nothing else exists), and is therefore, strictly speaking, meaningless. By this bold stratagem the positivist gains an enviable advantage: instead of having to argue with dissenters he need only declare that the terms in which they formulate their opposition do not conform to the conditions of meaningfulness which he has set up; in short, he dismisses them as talking nonsense.

As a matter of fact, semantic positivism only puts in plainer and more uncompromising form, with a more explicit statement of its postulates, an attitude which is shared by many so-called hard-headed realists—people who are fond of saying, "It all boils down to this"—and which may be called the Dogma of Plain Sense. Such an attitude represents, on its affirmative side, the excellent intention of promoting intelligibility and avoiding confusion. It proceeds from the principle that we ought to be as clear as possible about the meaning of our utterances, and be able to know when we are speaking sense and when we are just vaporizing. With this general aim every candid thinker will agree. The question is, where the line between sense and vaporizing is to be drawn. Semantic positivists have no difficulty in drawing it. Language may, on the one hand, they declare, assert something in the form of a proposition about what is "actually the case"; on the other it may, in the words of Rudolf Carnap, "express the emotions, fancies, images, or wishes of the speaker, and under proper conditions evoke emotions, wishes, or resolutions in the hearer."

It is instructive in this connection to have another look at the much discussed theory once espoused by I. A. Richards. Since Professor Richards is one of the most alert of contemporary thinkers, it might not seem fair to saddle his present reputation with views which he expressed over twenty-five years ago. His more recent writings have shown a tendency to liberalize and soften the hard semantic postulates which he advocated during the 'twenties. Nevertheless the influence of those early books has persisted, and the point of view which they advocate is still very much alive. Inasmuch as that point of view, consistently developed, destroys the very basis of that poetic vision of the world which alone can give human life its transcendental significance, there is as much pertinence now as there ever was in subjecting it to critical scrutiny.

In *The Meaning of Meaning* (written in collaboration with C. K. Ogden), *Principles of Literary Criticism*, and *Science and Poetry* Richards struck virtually the same note of semantic positivism which receives fuller technical development in writers like Carnap:

> A statement may be used for the sake of the *reference*, true or false, which it causes. This is the *scientific* use of language. But it may also be used for the sake of the effects in emotion and attitude produced by the reference it occasions. This is the *emotive* use. The distinction once clearly grasped is simple. We may either use words for the sake of the reference they promote, or we may use them for the sake of the attitudes and emotions which ensue.

The distinction is simple enough, to be sure; indeed, far too over-simple. What follows from so uncompromising an "either-or"? The consequences for poetry and religion had been stated frankly enough in *The Meaning of Meaning* a few years earlier, where it was argued that as poetry and religion do not employ words scientifically, so neither of them employs words referentially— that is to say, neither of them is capable of speaking *about* anything: the one plain test of whether a given use of words is essentially symbolic and referential or essentially emotive being the question, "Is it true or false in the ordinary strict scientific sense?"

The ontological basis of Richards' semantic position became clarified in his article, "Between Truth and Truth," published in 1931. Two years earlier, in *Practical Criticism*, he had pursued more fully the question of communication in literature. From that standpoint he now reformulated his position. A poem, he now declared, describes and communicates something, but what? "Two alternatives, and not more I think, are before us, two main senses of 'describe' and 'communicate.' . . . The first sense is that in which a form of words describes or communicates the state of mind or experience of the speaker; the second is that in which it describes or communicates some state of affairs or fact which the speaker is thinking of or knowing (something in all but one case, that of introspection, *other than* the experience which is his thinking of it or knowing it). . . . To take an extreme instance, when a man says 'I'm damned!' he may be saying that eternal judgment has gone against him or showing that he is surprised or annoyed."

Richards then turns to John Clare's description of the primrose—

> With its crimp and curdled leaf
> And its little brimming eye,

about which, in a previous article, J. Middleton Murry had remarked that it "is surely an accurate description, but accurate with an accuracy unknown to and unachievable by science." Richards complains: Mr. Murry "does not say explicitly whether he takes it as a description of an object (the primrose) or of the experience of seeing one." And he adds: "It seems to me not likely that there will be widespread disagreement with the view that the description applies to the experience of seeing or imagining a primrose rather than to actual primroses."

But how absurd! Surely any observant flower lover, unless constrained by loyalty to a preconceived theory, will disagree. Neither the lexicographer's definition of the primrose as a "plant or flower of the genus Primula" nor a botanist's or biochemist's analysis of it into scientifically discoverable elements and processes can describe the perceived primrose in its full living actuality as adequately as Clare's lines have done. If we are willing to consider such words as "crimp" and "curdled" in their descriptive function (as Richards has done in formulating his complaint against Murry above), then clearly it is not the *experience* of a primrose that is being described (for it is not my experience that is crimp and curdled!) but *the primrose as experienced*.

The trouble is that Professor Richards had fallen here without realizing it into the trap of metaphysics. The defection is particularly noticeable in a footnote to the article just mentioned, where he distinguishes the "sensed or imagined primrose" from the "inferred or constructed common or gardener's primrose" on the ground that the former lacks such scientifically determinable characteristics as weight! The distinction does not stand up under examination. The very same primrose which I see as crimp and curdled I can also pick up and feel as having a trifling bit of weight. Such visual and such kinaesthetic experiences refer to what I naturally and reasonably regard as constituting a single object. So, too, but less directly, do the experiences of looking at the notches of a scale on which the primrose is being weighed. On the basis of this latter type of experience (mine or another's) the primrose is assigned a numerical figure which we call its "objective weight"—bearing some relation no doubt, but not a strictly determinable one, to the kinaesthetic experience of lightness which I feel when I take the flower in my hand. Now the fallacy of the semantic positivist is to reject the "crimp and curdled" kind of experience, and the kinaesthetic kind of experience ("Why, this flower weighs practically nothing!") for the kind of experience which consists in looking at notches on a scale or some other measuring instrument. For the notch on the scale to which the pointer turns can be securely agreed on by everyone who is not blind; and such agreement is unlikely in the case of the other qualities mentioned.

When I say "reject," of course I do not mean that a semantic positivist wants nothing to do with the more colorful and feelingful qualities of things. He may indeed, as Mr. Richards explicitly does, consider them more "valuable" for the larger human purposes than a knowledge of such abstract properties as length and weight. His rejection is not practical but ontological. He asserts that only *abstract objects*, like the scientist's primrose with its numerical length and weight and its chemical properties, have real existence whereas concrete objects, like Clare's primrose with its plenitude of warmly experienced qualities, are not really objects at all. He asserts, therefore, that when a poet or anyone else appears to be speaking about such qualities he is not really speaking *about* anything, but is merely ejaculating the history of his mind, "his feelings and attitudes in the moment of speaking, and conditions of their governance in the future." Naturally I do not deny that poetry does and should express in some degree the poet's feelings, nor that it may and should have for a reader the beneficial and equilibrating effects described in Richards' *Principles of Literary Criticism*. These things have their own kind of importance, but from the standpoint of interpreting what the poem *says* they are strictly secondary and sometimes quite irrelevant. Every science has its proper object; and the object of poetic interpretation, rightly conceived, is the poem under consideration, and not either the poet's supposed feelings or the reader's expected benefits. An adequate study of the meaning of poetry, then—what I shall call *the semantics of poetry*—must first establish unhampering postulates and find a suitable language whereby the nature and reference of poetic utterance can be indicated, without evasion into fields of discourse peripheral and sometimes alien to poetry. . . .

Nor does the problem of poetry stand alone. For the issue which I have been discussing amounts to this: whether there is such a thing as *poetic vision*, or whether the only true vision of things must be ultimately scientific. If you accept the latter alternative—the position of semantic positivism—then the consequences, provided you carry them out vigorously, will be utterly destructive for religion, for metaphysics, and even for ethics as independent disciplines; and that is to say, for the very mainsprings of significant human living. The truth-claims of these three disciplines necessarily transcend the reach of scientific methods of validation; therefore (so the positivist's argument runs) they cannot be validated at all, and so have a merely subjective status. Metaphysics is either preëmpted as an organon of the sciences—a critical instrument by which the methods of the individual sciences may be brought into greater unity with one another—or else is dismissed as presumptuous vaporizing and word-play. Religion and ethics are explained away as mere projections of personal or group emotions; and, when they seem to give any real insight into the nature of reality, they are denounced as shams.

Now ethics is important for everybody; for while there are individuals who think they are able to do without religion, metaphysics, and poetry (I am not now discussing whether they are self-deceived), it is obvious that human life cannot be lived in anything like a human way without some implicit acknowledgment of moral principles. The alternative, as Hobbes has memorably said, is a life "nasty, brutish, and short." Yet as we ponder the assumptions of positivism we are forced to the realization that on the basis which they set up there are no real moral issues. At least one eminent positivist, Alfred Ayer, faces the consequence frankly, and accepts it. An apparent moral statement, such as "You acted wrongly in stealing that money," is really, he maintains, nothing more than the simple factual statement, "You stole that money." The first sentence does not *mean* anything different from the second; it merely "evinces" the speaker's emotional disapproval—as if one had said, "You stole that money" in a peculiar tone of horror.

So extreme a form of positivism as Ayer's is not hard to refute. Two weaknesses are quickly apparent. We might first appeal to the testimony of reflective experience that moral issues do exist. We might argue that deliberations, disputes, and decisions about right and wrong, good and evil, are at least as real a part of human life as any of the sensory and the scientifically determined data on which Ayer bases his position. We might conclude that a philosophy which writes off the evidence of mankind's experience in such a high-handed manner is grossly over-simplified and rather foolishly naïve. But we can also attack Ayer's argument on its home territory. If the ethical element in the sentence, "You did wrong in stealing that money"—i.e., the element which differentiates it from the factual statement, "You stole that money"—were *nothing more than* an expression of horror, it would follow that our judgment of the immorality of the act must increase and diminish in exact ratio to the changes in the feeling-tone of horror. This, however, is obviously not what actually happens. Horror or no horror, we can still raise and consider the moral issue. We can ask, "Is our horror or repugnance in this case *morally justified?*" Ayer would have to take this to mean, "How much horror do I feel at myself for feeling horror?"—which is plainly not what we mean when asking whether the original horror is justified. Ayer's theory of meaning is too black-and-white an affair to be capable of handling the moral dimension of human experience. . . .

My objection to the theory which I have been examining under the general name of "semantic positivism" may now be summed up. It requires, in effect, that the truth of a poem, or of a religious belief, or of a philosophical insight—of anything, in short, which is not a scientific statement of verifiable fact—be judged ultimately by its emotive and conative affects. Hence it may be aptly spoken of as the Affective Theory of poetic, religious, and philosophical truth.

From its standpoint the existence of poetry can be justified only on one or other of two grounds: either on the hedonistic ground that it gives pleasure to those who like it, or on the clinical grounds defended by the earlier Richards and implicit in Morris that it tends to promote a healthier equilibrium of attitudes in the reader and therefore possibly in the society wherein he moves. Even religion can be given no firmer justification than one or the other of these, if the Affective Theory is true. There are, however, two grave flaws in that theory, one in the flower and one in the root. Experientially, the theory does not do justice to the full nature of either poetic or religious experience; and logically, it rests upon an arbitrary (and I believe false) presupposition.

On the first count let it be considered that neither the pleasurable nor the therapeutic effects of poetry or religion are fortuitous. While those of poetry may partly proceed from the direct propulsions of rhythm and imagery upon the physio-psychic organism, they most characteristically involve something more. A poem affects a mature reader as it does partly because it seems to him, notwithstanding its fantasies and pseudo-statements, to be offering a kind of genuine insight and thereby to be revealing, however obscurely and elusively, a kind of truth. In *King Lear*, for example, the language and imagery and character developments and story are inseparable aspects of the total poem and legitimate factors in its appeal. But *King Lear's* principal claim to greatness transcends these components: it is great because in and through such poetic devices it reveals depth-meaning—it adumbrates truths and quasi-truths of high importance about such matters as human nature, old age, false seeming, and self-confrontation through suffering. The depth-meaning of *Lear*—the "poetic truth" to be discovered in the play—is what mainly accounts for and justifies the Fit Reader's full response, an inseparable blending of emotive and intellectual. If the depth-meaning is not at least dimly and subconsciously adumbrated—and perhaps too sharp a focus of it is generally undesirable—the reader's response will hardly be the same. Impoverishment or distortion of the intellectual response will involve some impoverishment or distortion of the emotive. To regard the specifically poetic response as purely emotive, then, is a naïve way of psychologizing.

The shallowness of the positivistic interpretation of religion is even more evident. For in religion the depth-meaning is *all* that matters. If you ignore the depth-meanings of Sophocles or Dante or Shakespeare, something of the nature of poetry still remains in them; and those whose response is limited to story, imagery, and versification may still be responding in a way proper to poetry, though but limitedly so. But if you ignore the depth-meanings of religion, what you have left is not religion at all, but sabbatical play-acting. Prayer and worship can be justified as psychic therapy only if the postulant and worshiper believes that his utterance is somehow heard and somehow responded to. Now it is possible of course—I mean it is *logically* possible—that the religious believer is mistaken, and that his conviction of entering into a responsive relationship with a Power or Powers transcending the human condition is illusory. Whether transcendental existence and men's intercommunication with it are real or illusory is, as Pascal demonstrated, the most important question of all; and it cannot be settled by ruling out all answers but one as "meaningless." An adequate semantic organon should make it possible to formulate *both* theses—the religious and the anti-religious—intelligibly. A semantic theory which denies meaning to any and all specifically religious affirmations thereby prevents us from inquiring and discussing whether particular religious affirmations are true or false. Its denial of their meaning is a disguised way of rejecting their truth—claims *a priori*, and thus of prejudging the question of religious truth wholesale.

The other and more analytic objection to the Affective Theory concerns the presumed dichotomy on which it rests. Two types or modes or uses of discourse are sharply distinguished: typically called the referential and the emotive. Referential statements, as the previous exposition has shown, are postulated or defined to be true insofar as they correspond with, and truly describe, what is actually the case, false insofar as they do the contrary; and it is further postulated that in all instances of a referential satement it is possible to specify the empirical conditions under which it could be verified or disproved. Emotive discourse, on the other hand, is taken as expressing some emotive-conative state of the writer (or speaker) or as aiming to arouse such a state in the reader (or hearer), and therefore as not being intrinsically referential. The unguarded inference from "intrinsically emotive" to "not intrinsically referential" reveals the main logical presupposition of the Affective Theory: that language which is intrinsically the one cannot be intrinsically the other; that the terms "referential" and "emotive" (or their synonyms) constitute a natural dichotomy. This is a presupposition which must now be challenged.

For clarity it should be noted that ordinary "mixed discourse," which semanticists of all schools admit as a familiar possibility, is not what I am speaking about. A cry of "Fire!" for instance simultaneously conveys information—i.e., refers to an actual state of affairs—and expresses and communicates an emotive attitude. But the relation here between the two functions is extrinsic. The test of its extrinsicality is a simple one: the referential meaning can be explicated in propositional non-emotive form without loss. "A fire has broken out in this building," perhaps with some such corollary as "There is danger" or "There is need of immediate action"—this conveys virtually the same information as the original outcry, and indeed conveys it more exactly. In the case of poetic, and more generally of expressive discourse, on the contrary, such prosaic restatement is not possible without essential loss. My thesis is that truly expressive symbolism—in a poem, for example—means, refers, awakens insight, *in and through* the emotions which it engenders, and that so far as the emotion is not aroused the full insight is correspondingly not awakened. Granted that irrelevant emotions may be aroused, still the problem of learning to know and understand a poem is largely also the problem of distinguishing the relevant from the irrelevant—of distinguishing, that is to say, the responses aroused by the whole poem's intrinsic emotivity from the incidental responses aroused by isolated parts and fortuitous associations. In religious insight, too (as distinguished from blind acceptance on the one hand and from theological ratiocination on the other) emotion may play a legitimate role. But it is of utmost importance to distinguish the quality of emotion which reveals some aspect of the Divine from the quality of emotion which obscures and confuses; the clarifying act of self-transcending reverence from the muck and muddle of self-deluding religiosity. In short, I am asserting that poetic and religious emotions, when they are depth-oriented, may have or come to have distinctively ontological bearings of their own. Whether one agrees or disagrees with this thesis, it is not a new or trifling one, and it ought not to be ruled out by the a priori maneuver of setting up a dichotomy that leaves no room for it.

Let us therefore reopen the logical possibilities of the situation by conceiving "referential" and "emotive" not as contraries but as independent variables. The negative of *referential* is not emotive but *non-referential*; the negative of *emotive* is not referential but *non-emotive*. This logical truism enables us to construct a two-dimensional graph in which the vertical axis has "referential" (R) and "non-referential" (non-R) as its poles, the horizontal axis "emotive" (E) and "non-emotive" (non-E).

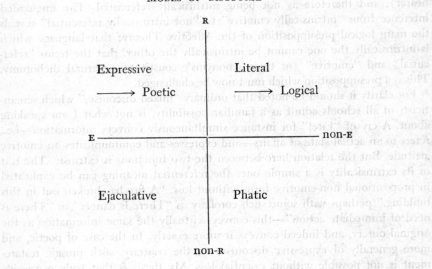

MODES OF DISCOURSE

Four areas are thus established, representing four modes of discourse:

R, non-E: *Literal discourse*: ordinary everyday language in its referential mode. *Logical discourse* is its ideally perfected form.

Non-R, non-E: *Phatic discourse*: "good morning," etc.

Non-R, E: *Ejaculative discourse*: "damn!" etc.—where, as distinguished from phatic discourse, something is really felt. For clarity's sake we must avoid the practice of some semanticists, of applying the word "expressive" in this connection.

R, E: *Expressive discourse:* language which is referential and emotive at once —not by incidental conjunction as in the cry of "Fire!" but in the more organic sense that the referential function, the proper meaning, takes at least some of its essential character from the emotivity of the language, and changes therefore as the emotivity changes. *Poetic discourse* is a species of expressive discourse, in which the main part of the meaning is controlled by the poet's art rather than by social custom and fortuitous association.

What I am proposing, in short, is a sort of Copernican Revolution in semantics. Or perhaps non-Euclidean, or trans-Euclidean, would offer an apter analogy. For whereas Euclidean geometry was once regarded as the be-all and end-all of geometrical truth, modern mathematicians are able to regard a world in which the postulate of parallels holds true, as merely a *limiting case* (perhaps also an actual one) in the universe of possibilities. Analogously, we may regard the semantic positivists as residing too doggedly in a Euclidean-like world. The aim, the instrument, and the presuppositions of logical discourse, as developed by the formal and experimental sciences, they accept without serious question. And my belief is that they are wrong, dead wrong—not of course in the contributions they have made to logical clarity in fields where it suitably belongs, but in their refusal to admit the possibility of other kinds of semantic objectivity—the possibility of meanings other than those which logical language can formulate. Such metalogical meanings are of dominant importance in religion, in poetry and expressive prose literature, in all the arts that "say" anything, and in moral wisdom as distinguished from moral rules; they are present helter-skelter in the vagaries of daily experience; and they even, I suspect, play a bigger role than is usually admitted in science, particularly when it comes to the discovery of fresh hypotheses. Accordingly, what any adequate theory of semantics should include, and what has not yet been systematically attempted so far as I am aware, is an exposition of the basic principles of metalogical signification.

ROBERT GORHAM DAVIS
Logical Fallacies[1]

Undefined Terms

The first requirement for logical discourse is knowing what the words you use actually mean. Words are not like paper money or counters in a game. Except for technical terms in some of the sciences, they do not have a fixed face value. Their meanings are fluid and changing, influenced by many considerations of

[1] From *Handbook for English A* (Cambridge, Mass.: Harvard University, 1941), pp. 58-66. Reprinted by permission of Theodore Morrison and Robert Gorham Davis.

context and reference, circumstance and association. This is just as true of common words such as *fast* as it is of literary terms such as *romantic*. Moreover, if there is to be communication, words must have approximately the same meaning for the reader that they have for the writer. A speech in an unknown language means nothing to the hearer. When an adult speaks to a small child or an expert to a layman, communication may be seriously limited by lack of a mature vocabulary or ignorance of technical terms. Many arguments are meaningless because the speakers are using important words in quite different senses.

Because we learn most words—or guess at them—from the contexts in which we first encounter them, our sense of them is often incomplete or wrong. Readers sometimes visualize the Assyrian who comes down like the wolf on fold as an enormous man dressed in cohorts (some kind of fancy armor, possibly) gleaming in purple and gold. "A rift in the lute" suggests vaguely a cracked mandolin. Failure to ascertain the literal meaning of figurative language is a frequent reason for mixed metaphors. We are surprised to find that the "devil" in "the devil to pay" and "the devil and the deep blue sea" is not Old Nick, but part of a ship. Unless terms mean the same thing to both writer and reader, proper understanding is impossible.

Abstractions

The most serious logical difficulties occur with abstract terms. An abstraction is a word which stands for a quality found in a number of different objects or events from which it has been "abstracted" or taken away. We may, for instance, talk of the "whiteness" of paper or cotton or snow without considering qualities of cold or inflammability or usefulness which these materials happen also to possess. Usually, however, our minds carry over other qualities by association. See, for instance, the chapter called "The Whiteness of the Whale" in *Moby Dick*.

In much theoretic discussion the process of abstraction is carried so far that although vague associations and connotations persist, the original objects or events from which the qualities have been abstracted are lost sight of completely. Instead of thinking of words like *sincerity* and *Americanism* as symbols standing for qualities that have to be abstracted with great care from examples and test cases, we come to think of them as real things in themselves. We assume that Americanism is Americanism just as a bicycle is a bicycle, and that everyone knows what it means. We forget that before the question, "Is Father Coughlin sincere?" can mean anything, we have to agree on the criteria of sincerity.

When we try to define such words and find examples, we discover that almost no one agrees on their meaning. The word *church* may refer to anything from a building on the corner of Spring Street to the whole tradition of institutionalized Christianity. *Germany* may mean a geographical section of Europe, a people, a governing group, a cultural tradition, or a military power. Abstractions such as *freedom, courage, race, beauty, truth, justice, nature, honor, humanism, democracy*, should never be used in a theme unless their meaning is defined or indicated clearly by the context. Freedom for whom? To do what? Under what circumstances? Abstract terms have merely emotional value unless they are strictly defined by asking questions of this kind. The study of a word such as *nature* in a good unabridged dictionary will show that even the dictionary, indispensable though it is, cannot determine for us the sense in which a word is being used in any given instance. Once the student understands the importance of definition, he will no longer be betrayed into fruitless arguments over such questions as whether free verse is "poetry" or whether you can change "human nature."

Name-Calling

It is a common unfairness in controversy to place what the writer dislikes or opposes in a generally odious category. The humanist dismisses what he dislikes by calling it *romantic*; the liberal, by calling it *fascist*; the conservative, by calling it *communistic*. These terms tell the reader nothing. What is *piety* to some will be *bigotry* to others. *Non-Catholics* would rather be called *Protestants* than *heretics*. What is *right-thinking* except a designation for those who agree with the writer? Labor leaders become *outside agitators*; industrial organizations, *forces of reaction*; the Child Labor Amendment, the *youth control bill*; prison reform, *coddling*; progressive education, *fads and frills*. Such terms are intended to block thought by an appeal to prejudice and associative habits. Three steps are necessary before such epithets have real meaning. First, they must be defined; second, it must be shown that the object to which they are applied actually possesses these qualities; third, it must be shown that the possession of such qualities in this particular situation is necessarily undesirable. Unless a person is alert and critical both in choosing and in interpreting words, he may be alienated from ideas with which he would be in sympathy if he had not been frightened by a mere name.

Generalization

Similar to the abuse of abstract terms and epithets is the habit of presenting personal opinions in the guise of universal laws. The student often seems to feel that the broader the terms in which he states an opinion, the more effective he will be. Ordinarily the reverse is true. An enthusiasm for Thomas Wolfe should lead to a specific critical analysis of Wolfe's novels that will enable the writer to explain his enthusiasm to others; it should not be turned into the argument that Wolfe is "the greatest American novelist," particularly if the writer's knowledge of American novelists is somewhat limited. The same questions of *who* and *when* and *why* and under what *circumstances* which are used to check abstract terms should be applied to generalizations. Consider how contradictory proverbial wisdom is when detached from particular circumstances. "Look before you leap," but "he who hesitates is lost."

Superlatives and the words *right* and *wrong*, *true* and *untrue*, *never* and *al-*

ways must be used with caution in matters of opinion. When a student says flatly that X is true, he often is really saying that he or his family or the author of a book he has just been reading, persons of certain tastes and background and experience, *think* that X is true. Unless these people are identified and their reasons for thinking so explained, the assertion is worthless. Because many freshmen are taking survey courses in which they read a single work by an author or see an historical event through the eyes of a single historian whose bias they may not be able to measure, they must guard against this error.

Sampling

Assertions of a general nature are frequently open to question because they are based on insufficient evidence. Some persons are quite ready, after meeting one Armenian or reading one medieval romance, to generalize about Armenians and medieval romances. One ought, of course, to examine objectively as many examples as possible before making a generalization, but the number is less important than the representativeness of the examples chosen. The Literary Digest Presidential Poll, sent to hundreds of thousands of people selected from telephone directories, was far less accurate than the Gallup Poll which questioned far fewer voters, but selected them carefully and proportionately from all different social groups. The "typical" college student, as portrayed by moving pictures and cartoons, is very different from the "representative" college student as determined statistically. We cannot let uncontrolled experience do our sampling for us; instances and examples which impress themselves upon our minds do so usually because they are exceptional. In propaganda and arguments extreme cases are customarily treated as if they were characteristic.

If one is permitted arbitrarily to select some examples and ignore others, it is possible to find convincing evidence for almost any theory, no matter how fantastic. The fact that the mind tends naturally to remember those instances which confirm its opinons imposes a duty upon the writer, unless he wishes to encourage prejudice and superstition, to look carefully for exceptions to all generalizations which he is tempted to make. We forget the premonitions which are not followed by disaster and the times when our hunches failed to select the winner in a race. Patent medicine advertisements print the letters of those who survived their cure, and not of those who died during it. All Americans did not gamble on the stock exchange in the twenties, and all Vermonters are not thin-lipped and shrewd. Of course the search for negative examples can be carried too far. Outside of mathematics or the laboratory, few generalizations can be made airtight, and most are not intended to be. But quibbling is so easy that resort to it is very common, and the knowledge that people can and will quibble over generalizations is another reason for making assertions as limited and explicitly conditional as possible.

False Analogy

Illustration, comparison, analogy are most valuable in making an essay clear and interesting. It must not be supposed, however, that they prove anything or have much argumentative weight. The rule that what is true of one thing in one set of circumstances is not necessarily true of another thing in another set of circumstances seems almost too obvious to need stating. Yet constantly nations and businesses are discussed as if they were human beings with human habits and feelings; human bodies are discussed as if they were machines; the universe, as if it were a clock. It is assumed that what held true for seventeenth century New England or the thirteen Atlantic colonies also holds true for an industrial nation of 130,000,000 people. Carlyle dismissed the arguments for representative democracy by saying that if a captain had to take a vote among his crew every time he wanted to do something, he would never get around Cape Horn. This analogy calmly ignores the distinction between the lawmaking and the executive branches of constitutional democracies. Moreover, voters may be considered much more like the stockholders of a merchant line than its hired sailors. Such arguments introduce assumptions in a metaphorical guise in which they are not readily detected or easily criticized. In place of analysis they attempt to identify their position with some familiar symbol which will evoke a predictable, emotional response in the reader. The revival during the 1932 presidential campaign of Lincoln's remark, "Don't swap horses in the middle of the stream," was not merely a picturesque way of saying keep Hoover in the White House. It made a number of assumptions about the nature of depressions and the function of government. This propagandist technique can be seen most clearly in political cartoons.

Degree

Often differences in degree are more important than differences in kind. By legal and social standards there is more difference between an habitual drunkard and a man who drinks temperately, than between a temperate drinker and a total abstainer. In fact differences of degree produce what are regarded as differences of kind. At known temperatures ice turns to water and water boils. At an indeterminate point affection becomes love and a man who needs a shave becomes a man with a beard. The fact that no men or systems are perfect make rejoinders and counter-accusations very easy if differences in degree are ignored. Newspapers in totalitarian states, answering American accusations of brutality and suppression, refer to lynchings and gangsterism here. Before a disinterested judge could evaluate these mutual accusations, he would have to settle the question of the degree to which violent suppression and lynching are respectively prevalent in the countries under consideration. On the other hand, differences in degree may be merely apparent. Lincoln Steffens pointed out that newspapers can create a "crime wave" any time they wish, simply by emphasizing all the minor assaults and thefts commonly ignored or given an inch or two on a back page. The great reported increases in insanity may be due to the fact that in a more urban and institutionalized society cases of insanity more fequently come to the attention of authorities and hence are recorded in statistics.

Causation

The most common way of deciding that one thing causes another thing is the simple principle: *post hoc, ergo propter hoc,* "After this, therefore because of this." Rome fell after the introduction of Christianity; therefore Christianity was responsible for the fall of Rome. Such reasoning illustrates another kind of faulty generalization. But even if one could find ten cases in which a nation "fell" after the introduction of Christianity, it still would not be at all certain that Christianity caused the fall. Day, it has frequently been pointed out, follows night in every observable instance, and yet night cannot be called the cause of day. Usually a combination of causes produces a result. Sitting in a draught may cause a cold, but only given a certain physical condition in the person sitting there. In such instances one may distinguish between necessary and sufficient conditions. Air is a necessary condition for the maintenance of plant life, but air alone is not sufficient to produce plant life. And often different causes at different times may produce the same result. This relation is known as plurality of causes. If, after sitting in a stuffy theatre on Monday, and then again after eating in a stuffy restaurant on Thursday, a man suffered from headaches, he might say, generalizing, that bad air gave him headaches. But actually the headache on Monday may have been caused by eye-strain and on Thursday by indigestion. To isolate the causative factor it is necessary that all other conditions be precisely the same. Such isolation is possible, except in very simple instances, only in the laboratory or with scientific methods. If a picture falls from the wall every time a truck passes, we can quite certainly say that the truck's passing is the cause. But with anything as complex and conditional as a nation's economy or human character, the determination of cause is not easy or certain. A psychiatrist often sees a patient for an hour daily for a year or more before he feels that he understands his psychosis.

Ordinarily when we speak of cause we mean the proximate or immediate cause. The plants were killed by frost; we had indigestion from eating lobster salad. But any single cause is one in an unbroken series. When a man is murdered, is his death caused by the loss of blood from the wound, or by the firing of the pistol, or by the malice aforethought of the murderer? Was the World War "caused" by the assassination at Sarajevo? Were the Navigation Acts or the ideas of John Locke more important in "causing" the American Revolution? A complete statement of cause would comprise the sum total of the conditions which preceded an event, conditions stretching back indefinitely into the past. Historical events are so interrelated that the isolation of a causative sequence is dependent chiefly on the particular preoccupations of the historian. An economic determinist can "explain" history entirely in terms of economic developments; an idealist, entirely in terms of the development of ideas.

Syllogistic Reasoning

The formal syllogism of the type,

> All men are mortal
> John is a man
> Therefore John is mortal,

is not so highly regarded today as in some earlier periods. It merely fixes an individual as a member of a class, and then assumes that the individual has the given characteristics of the class. Once we have decided who John is, and what "man" and "mortal" mean, and have canvassed all men, including John, to make sure that they are mortal, the conclusion naturally follows. It can be seen that the chief difficulties arise in trying to establish acceptable premises. Faults in the premises are known as "material" fallacies, and are usually more serious than the "formal" fallacies, which are logical defects in drawing a conclusion from the premises. But although directly syllogistic reasoning is not much practiced, buried syllogisms can be found in all argument, and it is often a useful clarification to outline your own or another writer's essay in syllogistic form. The two most frequent defects in the syllogism itself are the undistributed and the ambiguous middle. The middle term is the one that appears in each of the premises and not in the conclusion. In the syllogism,

> All good citizens vote
> John votes
> Therefore John is a good citizen,

the middle term is not "good citizens," but "votes." Even though it were true that all good citizens vote, nothing prevents bad citizens from voting also, and John may be one of the bad citizens. To distribute the middle term "votes" one might say (but only if that is what one meant),

> All voters are good citizens
> John is a voter
> Therefore John is a good citizen.

The ambiguous middle term is even more common. It represents a problem in definition, while the undistributed middle is a problem in generalization. All acts which benefit others are virtuous, losing money at poker benefits others, therefore losing at poker is a virtuous act. Here the middle term "act which benefits others" is obviously used very loosely and ambiguously.

Non-Sequitur

This phrase, meaning "it does not follow," is used to characterize the kind of humor found in pictures in which the Marx Brothers perform. It is an amusing illogicality because it usually expresses, beneath its apparent incongruity, an imaginative, associative, or personal truth. "My ancestors came over on the *Mayflower*; therefore I am naturally opposed to labor unions." It is not logically necessary that those whose ancestors came over on the *Mayflower* should be opposed to unions; but it may happen to be true as a personal fact in a given case. Contemporary psychologists have effectively shown us that there is often such a wide difference between the true and the purported reasons for an attitude that, in rationalizing our behavior, we are often quite unconscious of the motives that actually influence us. A fanatical antivivisectionist, for instance, may have temperamental impulses toward cruelty which he is suppressing and compensating for by a reasoned opposition to any kind of permitted suffering. We may expect, then, to come upon many conclusions which are psychologically interesting in themselves, but have nothing to do with the given premises.

Ignoratio Elenchi

This means, in idiomatic English, "arguing off the point," or ignoring the question at issue. A man trying to show that monarchy is the best form of government for the British Empire may devote most of his attention to the character of George V and the affection his people felt for him. In ordinary conversational argument it is almost impossible for disputants to keep to the point. Constantly turning up are tempting side-issues through which one can discomfit an opponent or force him to irrelevant admissions that seem to weaken his case.

Begging the Question; Arguing in a Circle

The first of these terms means to assume in the premises what you are pretending to prove in the course of your argument. The function of logic is to demonstrate that because one thing or group of things is true, another must be true as a consequence. But in begging the question you simply say in varying language that what is assumed to be true is assumed to be true. An argument which asserts that we shall enjoy immortality because we have souls which are immaterial and indestructible establishes nothing, because the idea of immortality is already contained in the assumption about the soul. It is the premise which needs to be demonstrated, not the conclusion. Arguing in a circle is another form of this fallacy. It proves the premise by the conclusion and the conclusion by the premise. The conscience forbids an act because it is wrong; the act is wrong because the conscience forbids it.

Arguments ad Hominem and ad Populum

It is very difficult for men to be persuaded by reason when their interest or prestige is at stake. If one wishes to preach the significance of physiognomy, it is well to choose a hearer with a high forehead and a determined jaw. The arguments in favor of repealing the protective tariff on corn or wheat in England were more readily entertained by manufacturers than by landowners. The cotton manufacturers in New England who were doing a profitable trade with the South were the last to be moved by descriptions of the evils of slavery. Because interest and desire are so deeply seated in human nature, arguments are frequently mingled with attempts to appeal to emotion, arouse fear, play upon pride, attack the characters of proponents of an opposite view, show that their practice is inconsistent with their principles; all matters which have, strictly speaking, nothing to do with the truth or falsity, the general desirability or undesirability, of some particular measure. If men are desperate enough they will listen to arguments proper only to an insane asylum but which seem to promise them relief.

After reading these suggestions, which are largely negative, the student may feel that any original assertion he can make will probably contain one or several logical faults. This assumption is not true. Even if it were, we know from reading newspapers and magazines that worldly fame is not dimmed by the constant and, one suspects, conscious practice of illogicality. But generalizations are not made only by charlatans and sophists. Intelligent and scrupulous writers also have a great many fresh and provocative observations and conclusions to express and are expressing them influentially. What is intelligence but the ability to see the connection between things, to discern causes, to relate the particular to the general, to define and discriminate and compare? Any man who thinks and feels and observes closely will not want for something to express.

And in his expression a proponent will find that a due regard for logic does not limit but rather increases the force of his argument. When statements are not trite, they are usually controversial. Men arrive at truth dialectically; error is weeded out in the course of discussion, argument, attack, and counter-attack. Not only can a writer who understands logic show the weaknesses of arguments he disagrees with, but also, by anticipating the kind of attack likely to be made on his own ideas, he can so arrange them, properly modified with qualifications and exceptions, that the anticipated attack is made much less effective. Thus, fortunately, we do not have to depend on the spirit of fairness and love of truth to lead men to logic; it has the strong support of argumentative necessity and of the universal desire to make ideas prevail.

FRANCIS BACON

Idols of the Mind[1]

XXXVIII

The idols and false notions which are now in possession of the human under-standing, and have taken deep root therein, not only so beset men's minds that truth can hardly find entrance, but even after entrance obtained, they will again in the very instauration of the sciences meet and trouble us, unless men being forewarned of the danger fortify themselves as far as may be against their assaults.

There are four classes of Idols which beset men's minds. To these for dis-tinction's sake I have assigned names—calling the first class *Idols of the Tribe*; the second, *Idols of the Cave*; the third, *Idols of the Marketplace*; the fourth, *Idols of the Theatre*.

The formation of ideas and axioms by true induction is no doubt the proper remedy to be applied for the keeping off and clearing away of idols. To point them out, however, is of great use; for the doctrine of Idols is to the Interpreta-tion of Nature what the doctrine of the refutation of Sophisms is to common Logic.

XLI

The Idols of the Tribe have their foundation in human nature itself, and in the tribe or race of men. For it is a false assertion that the sense of man is the measure of things. On the contrary, all perceptions as well of the sense as of the mind are according to the measure of the individual and not according to the measure of the universe. And the human understanding is like a false mirror, which, receiving rays irregularly, distorts and discolours the nature of things by mingling its own nature with it.

XLII

The Idols of the Cave are the idols of the individual man. For every one (be-sides the errors common to human nature in general) has a cave or den of his own, which refracts and discolours the light of nature; owing either to

[1] From *The Works of Francis Bacon*, ed. by James Spedding, Robert Ellis, and Douglas Heath (New York: Hurd and Houghon, 1869), VIII, 76-90. The *Novum Organum* was first printed in 1620.

his own proper and peculiar nature; or to his education and conversation with others; or to the reading of books, and the authority of those whom he esteems and admires; or to the differences of impressions, accordingly as they take place in a mind preoccupied and predisposed or in a mind indifferent and settled; or the like: So that the spirit of man (according as it is meted out to different individuals) is in fact a thing variable and full of perturbation, and governed as it were by chance. Whence it was well observed by Heraclitus that men look for sciences in their own lesser worlds, and not in the greater or common world.

XLIII

There are also Idols formed by the intercourse and association of men with each other, which I call Idols of the Marketplace, on account of the commerce and consort of men there. For it is by discourse that men associate; and words are imposed according to the apprehension of the vulgar. And therefore the ill and unfit choice of words wonderfully obstructs the understanding. Nor do the definitions or explanations wherewith in some things learned men are wont to guard and defend themselves, by any means set the matter right. But words plainly force and overrule the understanding, and throw all into confusion, and lead men away into numberless empty controversies and idle fancies.

XLIV

Lastly, there are Idols which have immigrated into men's minds from the various dogmas of philosophies, and also from wrong laws of demonstration. These I call Idols of the Theatre; because in my judgment all the received systems are but so many stage-plays, representing worlds of their own creation after an unreal and scenic fashion. Nor is it only of the systems now in vogue, or only of the ancient sects and philosophies, that I speak; for many more plays of the same kind may yet be composed and in like artificial manner set forth; seeing that errors the most widely different have nevertheless causes for the most part alike. Neither again do I mean this only of entire systems, but also of many principles and axioms in science, which by tradition, credulity, and negligence have come to be received.

But of these several kinds of Idols I must speak more largely and exactly, that the understanding may be duly cautioned.

XLV

The human understanding is of its own nature prone to suppose the existence of more order and regularity in the world than it finds. And though there be many things in nature which are singular and unmatched, yet it devises for them parallels and conjugates and relatives which do not exist. Hence the fiction that all celestial bodies move in perfect circles; spirals and dragons being (except in name) utterly rejected. Hence too the element of Fire with its orb is brought in, to make up the square with the other three which the sense perceives. Hence also the ratio of density of the so-called elements is arbitrarily fixed at ten to one. And so on of other dreams. And these fancies affect not dogmas only, but simple notions also.

XLVI

The human understanding when it has once adopted an opinion (either as being the received opinion or as being agreeable to itself) draws all things else to support and agree with it. And though there be a greater number and weight of instances to be found on the other side, yet these it either neglects and despises, or else by some distinction sets aside and rejects; in order that by this great and pernicious predetermination the authority of its former conclusions may remain inviolate. And therefore it was a good answer that was made by one who when they showed him hanging in a temple a picture of those who had paid their vows as having escaped shipwreck, and would have him say whether he did not now acknowledge the power of the gods——— "Aye," asked he again, "but where are they painted that were drowned after their vows?" And such is the way of all superstition, whether in astrology, dreams, omens, divine judgments, or the like; wherein men, having a delight in such vanities, mark the events where they are fulfilled, but where they fail, though this happen much oftener, neglect and pass them by. But with far more subtlety does this mischief insinuate itself into philosophy and the sciences; in which the first conclusion colours and brings into conformity with itself all that come after, though far sounder and better. Besides, independently of that delight and vanity which I have described, it is the peculiar and perpetual error of the human intellect to be more moved and excited by affirmatives than by negatives; whereas it ought properly to hold itself indifferently disposed towards both alike. Indeed in the establishment of any true axiom, the negative instance is the more forcible of the two.

XLVII

The human understanding is moved by those things most which strike and enter the mind simultaneously and suddenly, and so fill the imagination; and then it feigns and supposes all other things to be somehow, though it cannot see how, similar to those few things by which it is surrounded. But for that going to and fro to remote and heterogeneous instances, by which axioms are tried as in the fire, the intellect is altogether slow and unfit, unless it be forced thereto by severe laws and overruling authority.

XLVIII

The human understanding is unquiet; it cannot stop or rest, and still presses onward, but in vain. Therefore it is that we cannot conceive of any end or limit to the world; but always as of necessity it occurs to us that there is something beyond. Neither again can it be conceived how eternity has flowed down to the present day; for that distinction which is commonly received of infinity in time past and in time to come can by no means hold; for it would thence follow that one infinity is greater than another, and that infinity is wasting away and tending to become finite. The like subtlety arises touching the infinite divisibility of lines, from the same inability of thought to stop. But this inability interferes more mischievously in the discovery of causes; for although the most general principles in nature ought to be held merely positive, as they are discovered, and cannot with truth be referred to a cause; nevertheless the human understanding being unable to rest still seeks something prior in the order of nature. And then it is that in struggling towards that which is further off it falls back upon that which is more nigh at hand; namely, on final causes: which have relation clearly to the nature of man rather than to the nature of the universe; and from this source have strangely defiled philosophy. But he is no less an unskilled and shallow philosopher who seeks causes of that which is most general, than he who in things subordinate and subaltern omits to do so.

XLIX

The human understanding is no dry light, but receives an infusion from the will and affections; whence proceed sciences which may be called "sciences as one would." For what a man had rather were true he more readily believes. Therefore he rejects difficult things from impatience of research; sober things, because they narrow hope; the deeper things of nature, from superstition; the light of experience, from arrogance and pride, lest his mind should seem to be occupied with things mean and transitory; things not commonly believed, out of deference to the opinion of the vulgar. Numberless in short are the ways, and sometimes imperceptible, in which the affections colour and infect the understanding.

L

But by far the greatest hindrance and aberration of the human understanding proceeds from the dullness, incompetency, and deceptions of the senses; in that things which strike the sense outweigh things which do not immediately strike it, though they be more important. Hence it is that speculation commonly ceases where sight ceases; insomuch that of things invisible there is little or no observation. Hence all the working of the spirits inclosed in tangible bodies lies hid and unobserved of men. So also all the more subtle changes of form in the parts of coarser substances (which they commonly call alteration, though it is in truth local motion through exceedingly small spaces) is in like manner unobserved. And yet unless these two things just mentioned be searched out and brought to light, nothing great can be achieved in nature, as far as the production of works is concerned. So again the essential nature of our common air, and of all bodies less dense than air (which are very many), is almost unknown. For the sense by itself is a thing infirm and erring; neither can instruments for enlarging or sharpening the senses do much; but all the truer kind of interpretation of nature is effected by instances and experiments fit and apposite; wherein the sense decides touching the experiment only, and the experiment touching the point in nature and the thing itself.

LI

The human understanding is of its own nature prone to abstractions and gives a substance and reality to things which are fleeting. But to resolve nature into abstractions is less to our purpose than to dissect her into parts; as did the school of Democritus, which went further into nature than the rest. Matter rather than forms should be the object of our attention, its configurations and changes of configuration, and simple action, and law of action or motion; for forms are figments of the human mind, unless you will call those laws of action forms.

LII

Such then are the idols which I call *Idols of the Tribe*; and which take their rise either from the homogeneity of the substance of the human spirit, or from its preoccupation, or from its narrowness, or from its restless motion, or from an infusion of the affections, or from the incompetency of the senses, or from the mode of impression.

LIII

The *Idols of the Cave* take their rise in the peculiar constitution, mental or bodily, of each individual; and also in education, habit, and accident. Of this kind there is a great number and variety; but I will instance those the pointing out of which contains the most important caution, and which have most effect in disturbing the clearness of the understanding.

LIV

Men become attached to certain particular sciences and speculations, either because they fancy themselves the authors and inventors thereof, or because they have bestowed the greatest pains upon them and become most habituated to them. But men of this kind, if they betake themselves to philosophy and contemplations of a general character, distort and colour them in obedience to their former fancies; a thing especially to be noticed in Aristotle, who made his natural philosophy a mere bond-servant to his logic, thereby rendering it contentious and well nigh useless. The race of chemists again out of a few experiments of the furnace have built up a fantastic philosophy, framed with reference to a few things; and Gilbert also, after he had employed himself most laboriously in the study and observation of the loadstone, proceeded at once to construct an entire system in accordance with his favourite subject.

LV

There is one principal and as it were radical distinction between different minds, in respect of philosophy and the sciences; which is this: that some minds are stronger and apter to mark the differences of things, others to mark their resemblances. The steady and acute mind can fix its contemplations and dwell and fasten on the subtlest distinctions: the lofty and discursive mind recognises and puts together the finest and most general resemblances. Both kinds however easily err in excess, by catching the one at gradations, the other at shadows.

LVI

There are found some minds given to an extreme admiration of antiquity, others to an extreme love and appetite for novelty; but few so duly tempered that they can hold the mean, neither carping at what has been well laid down by the ancients, nor despising what is well introduced by the moderns. This however turns to the great injury of the sciences and philosophy; since these affectations of antiquity and novelty are the humours of partisans rather than judgments; and truth is to be sought for not in the felicity of any age, which is an unstable thing, but in the light of nature and experience, which is eternal. These factions therefore must be abjured, and care must be taken that the intellect be not hurried by them into assent.

LVII

Contemplations of nature and of bodies in their simple form break up and distract the understanding, while contemplations of nature and bodies in their composition and configuration overpower and dissolve the understanding: a distinction well seen in the school of Leucippus and Democritus as compared with the other philosophies. For that school is so busied with the particles that it hardly attends to the structure; while the others are so lost in admiration of the structure that they do not penetrate to the simplicity of nature. These kinds of contemplation should therefore be alternated and taken by turns; that so the understanding may be rendered at once penetrating and comprehensive, and the inconveniences above mentioned, with the idols which proceed from them, may be avoided.

LVIII

Let such then be our provision and contemplative prudence for keeping off and dislodging the *Idols of the Cave*, which grow for the most part either out of the predominance of a favourite subject, or out of an excessive tendency to compare or to distinguish, or out of partiality for particular ages, or out of the largeness or minuteness of the objects contemplated. And generally let every student of nature take this as a rule—that whatever his mind seizes and dwells upon with peculiar satisfaction is to be held in suspicion, and that so much the more care is to be taken in dealing with such questions to keep the understanding even and clear.

LIX

But the *Idols of the Marketplace* are the most troublesome of all: idols which have crept into the understanding through the alliances of words and names. For men believe that their reason governs words; but it is also true that words react on the understanding; and this it is that has rendered philosophy and the sciences sophistical and inactive. Now words, being commonly framed and applied according to the capacity of the vulgar, follow those lines of division which are most obvious to the vulgar understanding. And whenever an understanding of greater acuteness or a more diligent observation would alter those lines to suit the true divisions of nature, words stand in the way and resist the change. Whence it comes to pass that the high and formal discussions of learned men end oftentimes in disputes about words and names; with which (according to the use and wisdom of the mathematicians) it would be more prudent to begin, and so by means of definitions reduce them to order. Yet even definitions cannot cure this evil in dealing with natural and material things; since the definitions themselves consist of words, and those words beget others: so that it is necessary to recur to individual instances, and those in due series and order; as I shall say presently when I come to the method and scheme for the formation of notions and axioms.

LX

The idols imposed by words on the understanding are of two kinds. They are either names of things which do not exist (for as there are things left unnamed through lack of observation, so likewise are there names which result from fantastic suppositions and to which nothing in reality corresponds), or they are names of things which exist, but yet confused and ill-defined, and hastily and irregularly derived from realities. Of the former kind are Fortune, the Prime Mover, Planetary Orbits, Element of Fire, and like fictions which owe their origin to false and idle theories. And this class of idols is more easily expelled, because to get rid of them it is only necessary that all theories should be steadily rejected and dismissed as obsolete.

But the other class, which springs out of a faulty and unskilful abstraction, is intricate and deeply rooted. Let us take for example such a word as *humid*; and see how far the several things which the word is used to signify agree with each other; and we shall find the word *humid* to be nothing else than a mark loosely and confusedly applied to denote a variety of actions which will not bear to be reduced to any constant meaning. For it both signifies that which easily spreads itself round any other body; and that which in itself is indeterminate and cannot solidise; and that which readily yields in every direction; and that which easily divides and scatters itself; and that which easily unites and collects itself; and that which readily flows and is put in motion; and that which readily clings to another body and wets it; and that which is easily reduced to a liquid, or being solid easily melts. Accordingly when you come to apply the word—if you take it in one sense, flame is humid; if in another, air is not humid; if in another, fine dust is humid; if in another, glass is humid. So that it is easy to see that the notion is taken by abstraction only from water and common and ordinary liquids, without any due verification.

There are however in words certain degrees of distortion and error. One of the least faulty kinds is that of names of substances, especially of lowest species and well-deduced (for the notion of *chalk* and of *mud* is good, of *earth* bad); a more faulty kind is that of actions, as *to generate, to corrupt, to alter*; the most faulty is of qualities (except such as are the immediate objects of the sense) as *heavy, light, rare, dense,* and the like. Yet in all these cases some notions are of necessity a little better than others, in proportion to the greater variety of subjects that fall within the range of the human sense.

LXI

But the *Idols of the Theatre* are not innate, nor do they steal into the understanding secretly, but are plainly impressed and received into the mind from the play-books of philosophical systems and the perverted rules of demonstration. To attempt refutations in this case would be merely inconsistent with what I have already said: for since we agree neither upon principles nor upon demonstrations there is no place for argument. And this is so far well, inasmuch as it leaves the honour of the ancients untouched. For they are no wise disparaged—the question between them and me being only as to the way. For as the saying is, the lame man who keeps the right road outstrips the runner who takes a wrong one. Nay it is obvious that when a man runs the wrong way, the more active and swift he is the further he will go astray.

But the course I propose for the discovery of sciences is such as leaves but little to the acuteness and strength of wits, but places all wits and understandings nearly on a level. For as in the drawing of a straight line or a perfect circle, much depends on the steadiness and practice of the hand, if it be done by aim of hand only, but if with the aid of rule or compass, little or nothing: so is it exactly with my plan. But though particular confutations would be of no avail, yet touching the sects and general divisions of such systems I must say something; something also touching the external signs which show that they are unsound; and finally something touching the causes of such great infelicity and of such lasting and general agreement in error; that so the access to truth may be made less difficult, and the human understanding may the more willingly submit to its purgation and dismiss its idols.

The Arts

The Fine Arts

✿◈

SUSANNE K. LANGER

The Cultural Importance of the Arts[1]

Every culture develops some kind of art as surely as it develops language. Some primitive cultures have no real mythology or religion, but all have some art—dance, song, design (sometimes only on tools or on the human body). Above all, dances; that seems to be the oldest elaborated art.

The ancient ubiquitous character of art contrasts sharply with the prevalent idea that art is a luxury product of civilization, a cultural frill, a piece of social veneer.

It fits better with the conviction held by most artists, that art is the epitome of human life, the truest record of insight and feeling, and that the strongest military or economic society without art is poor in comparison with the most primitive tribe of savage painters, dancers, or idol-carvers. Wherever a society has really achieved culture (in the ethnological, not the popular sense of social form) it has begotten art, not late in its career, but at the very inception of it.

Art is, indeed, the spearhead of human development, social and individual. The vulgarization of art is the surest symptom of ethnic decline. The growth of a new art or even a great and radically new style always bespeaks a young and vigorous mind, whether collective or single.

What sort of thing is art, that it should play such a leading role in human development? It is not an intellectual pursuit, but is necessary to intellectual life; it is not religion, but grows up with religion, serves it and in large measure determines it (as Herodotus said, "Homer made the gods," and surely the Egyptian deities grew under the chisels of sculptors in strangely solemn forms).

We cannot enter here on a long discussion of what has been claimed as the essence of art, the true nature of art, or its defining function; in a single lecture dealing with one aspect of art, namely its cultural influence, I can

[1] From *Creation and Expression* by Susanne Langer, copyright 1957 by Susanne Langer. Used by permission of Charles Scribner's Sons.

only give you by way of preamble my own definition of art, with categorical brevity. That does not mean that I set up this definition in a categorical spirit, but only that we have no time to debate it, so you are asked to accept it as an assumption underlying these reflections.

Art, in the sense here intended—that is, the generic term subsuming painting, sculpture, architecture, music, dance, literature and drama—may be defined as the practice of creating perceptible forms expressive of human feeling. I say "perceptible" rather than "sensuous" forms because some works of art are given to imagination rather than to the outward senses. A novel, for instance, usually is read silently with the eye, but is not made for vision, as a painting is; and though sound plays a vital part in poetry, words even in poetry are not essentially sonorous structures like music. Dance requires to be seen, but its appeal is to deeper centers of sensation. The difference between dance and mobile sculpture makes this immediately apparent. But all works of art are purely perceptible forms that seem to embody some sort of feeling.

"Feeling" as I am using it here covers much more than it does in the technical vocabulary of psychology, where it denotes only pleasure and pain, or even in the shifting limits of ordinary discourse, where it sometimes means sensation (as when one says a paralyzed limb has no feeling in it), sometimes sensibility (as we speak of hurting someone's feelings), sometimes emotion (e.g., as a situation is said to harrow your feeling, or to evoke tender feeling), or a directed emotional attitude (we say we feel strongly *about* something), or even our general mental or physical condition, feeling well or ill, blue, or a bit above ourselves. As I use the word, in defining art as the creation of perceptible forms expressive of human feeling, it takes in all those meanings; it applies to *everything that may be felt.*

Another word in the definition that might be questioned is "creation." I think it is justified, not pretentious, as perhaps it sounds; but that issue is slightly beside the point here, so let us shelve it. If anyone prefers to speak of the "making" or "construction" of expressive forms that will do here just as well.

What does have to be understood is the meaning of "form," and more particularly "expressive form"; for that involves the very nature of art and therefore the question of its cultural importance.

The word "form" has several current uses; most of them have some relation to the sense in which I am using it here, though a few, such as: "a *form* to be filled in for tax purposes," or "a mere matter of form," are fairly remote, being quite specialized. Since we are speaking of art, it might be good to point out that the meaning of *stylistic patter*—"the sonata form," "the sonnet form"—is not the one I am assuming here. I am using the word in a simpler sense, which it has when you say, on a foggy night, that you see dimly moving forms in the mist; one of them emerges clearly, and is the form of a man. The trees are gigantic forms; the rills of rain trace sinuous forms on the window pane. The rills are not fixed things; they are forms of motion. When you watch gnats weaving in the air, or flocks of birds wheeling overhead, you see dynamic forms—forms made by motion.

It is in this sense of an apparition given to our perception, that a work of art is a form. It may be a permanent form like a building or a vase or a picture, or a transient, dynamic form like a melody or a dance, or even a form given to imagination, like the passage of purely imaginary, apparent events that constitutes a literary work. But it is always a perceptible, self-identical whole; like a natural being, it has a character of organic unity, self-sufficiency, individual reality. And it is thus, as an appearance, that a work of art is good or bad or perhaps only rather poor; as an appearance, not as a comment on things beyond it in the world, nor as a reminder of them.

This, then, is what I mean by "form"; but what is meant by calling such forms "expressive of human feeling"? How do apparitions "express" anything—feeling, or anything else? First of all, let us ask just what is meant here by "express"; what sort of "expression" we are talking about.

Most people believe that music and poetry are expressions of emotion, and will further agree that a picture is a glimpse of reality seen through a temperament. Even a Gothic cathedral is supposed to express the religious emotions of its countless, anonymous builders. Its age makes the process indistinct enough to put it beyond very searching question. But it is harder to imagine how a modern office building or a fine, flung-out overpass across a highway—an architectural work of art, as many of our offices and ramps and bridges are—could be, in any essential way, an expression of its designer's emotion or state of mind. To treat it just like a lyric or an easel picture seems a bit silly.

The incongruity, however, points to a misunderstanding that becomes apparent only when we try to conceive the skyscraper as an emotional exhibition, but that really confuses our judgment of the lyric and the picture as well. It is a misconception of what is meant by "expression" in art.

The word "expression" has two principal meanings: in one sense it means *self*-expression—giving vent to our feelings. In this sense it refers to a *symptom* of what we feel. Self-expression is a spontaneous reaction to a situation, an event, the company we are in, things people say, or what the weather does to us; it bespeaks the physical and mental state we are in and the emotions that stir us. In another sense, however, "expression" means the presentation of an idea, usually by the proper and apt use of words. But a device for the presentation of an idea is what we call a *symbol*, not a symptom. Thus a *word* is a symbol, and so is a meaningful combination of words. A common word, such as "horse," conveys an idea even when no one is exclaiming over the presence of a horse, or offering his kingdom for one—for instance, in the phrase "White Horse Whiskey," or in the dictionary, somewhere between "horror" and "horticulture."

A sentence, which is a special combination of words, expresses the idea of some state of affairs, real or imagined. Sentences are complicated symbols—so complicated, sometimes, that we have to consider them word by word and analyze the way they are put together to understand the meanings they convey. And sometimes the meaning is an idea we never had before, or concerns something we have never seen—a new animal, a foreign place, or what not. Language will formulate new ideas as well as communicate old ones, so that all people know a lot of things that they have merely heard or read about. Symbolic expression, therefore, extends our knowledge beyond the scope of our actual experience.

If an idea is clearly conveyed by means of symbols we say it is *well expressed*. A person may work for a long time to give his statement the best possible form, to find the exact words for what he means to say and to carry his account or his argument most directly from one point to another. But a discourse so worked out is certainly not a spontaneous reaction. Giving expression to an idea is obviously a different thing from giving expression to feelings by laughing, crying, blushing, or quivering. You do not say of a man in a rage that his anger is well expressed; you either try to calm him down, or you rage back at him, but in either case you understand quite well that he is furious. The symptoms just are what they are, there is no critical standard for symptoms. If, on the other hand, the angry man tries to tell you what he is fuming about, he will have to collect himself, curtail his emotional expression, and find words to express his ideas. For to tell a story coherently involves "expression" in quite a different sense: this sort of expression is not "self-expression," but may be called "conceptual expression."

Language, of course, is our prime instrument of conceptual expression. The things we can say are in effect the things we can think. Words are the terms of our thinking as well as the terms in which we present our thoughts, because they present the objects of thought to the thinker himself. Before language communicates ideas, it gives them form, makes them clear, and in fact makes them what they are. Whatever has a name is an object for thought. Without words, sense experience is only a flow of impressions, as subjective as our feelings; words make it objective, and carve it up into *things* and *facts* that we can note, remember, and think about. Language gives outward experience its form, and makes it definite and clear.

There is, however, an important part of reality that is quite inaccessible to the formative influence of language: that is the realm of so-called "inner experience," the life of feeling and emotion. The reason why language is so powerless here is not, as many people suppose, that feeling and emotion are irrational; on the contrary, they seem irrational because language does not help to make them conceivable, and most people cannot conceive anything without the logical scaffolding of words. The unfitness of language to convey subjective experience is a somewhat technical subject, easier for logicians to understand than for artists; but the gist of it is that the form of language does not reflect the natural form of feeling, so we cannot shape any concepts of feeling with the help of ordinary, discursive language. Therefore the words whereby we refer to feeling only name very general kinds of inner experience—excitement, calm, joy, sorrow, love, hate, etc. But there is no language to describe just how one joy differs so radically from another, or what the experience of hate is really like, how it can interplay with feelings usually called love, how it burns and then goes cold in almost the same moment. The real nature of feeling is something language as such—as discursive symbolism—cannot render.

For this reason, the phenomena of feeling and emotion are usually treated by philosophers as irrational. The only pattern discursive thought can find in them is the pattern of outward events that occasion them. There are different degrees of fear, but they are thought of as so many degrees of the same simple feeling.

But human feeling is a fabric, not a vague mass. It has an intricate dynamic pattern, possible combinations and new emergent phenomena. It is a pattern of organically interdependent and interdetermined tensions and resolutions; a pattern of almost infinitely complex activation and cadence. To it belongs the whole gamut of our sensibility, the sense of straining thought, all mental attitude and motor set. Those are the deeper reaches that underlie the surface waves of our emotion, and make human life a *life of feeling* instead of an unconscious metabolic existence interrupted by feelings.

It is, I think, this dynamic pattern that finds its formal expression in the arts. The expressiveness of art is like that of a symbol, not that of an emotional symptom; it is as a formulation of feeling for our conception that a work of art is properly said to be expressive. It may serve somebody's need of self-expression besides; but that is not what makes it good or bad art. In a special sense one may call a work of art a symbol of feeling, for, like a symbol, it formulates our ideas of inward experience, as discourse formulates our ideas of things and facts in the outside world. A work of art differs from a genuine symbol—that is, a symbol in the full and usual sense—in that it does not point beyond itself to something else. The word "symbol" does not originally connote any representative function, or reference to something beyond itself; it means "thrown together"—συμβαλλειν. But in English usage it has come to mean a sign that stands for something else to which it directs our attention. This is something a work of art does not do. Its relation to feeling is a rather special one that we cannot undertake to analyze here; in effect, the feeling it expresses appears to be directly given with it, as the sense of a true metaphor, or the value of a religious myth, is not separable from its expression. We speak of the feeling *of*, or the feeling *in*, a work of art, not the feeling it means. And we speak truly; a work of art presents something like a direct vision of vitality, emotion, subjective reality.

The primary function of art is to objectify feeling so we can contemplate and understand it. It is the formulation of so-called "inward experience," the "inner life," that is impossible to achieve by discursive thought, because its forms are incommensurable with the forms of language and all its derivatives (e.g. mathematics, symbolic logic). Art objectifies the sentience and desire, self-consciousness and world-consciousness, emotions and moods that are generally regarded as irrational because words cannot give us clear ideas of them. But the premise tacitly assumed in such a judgment—namely, that anything language cannot express is formless and irrational—seems to me to be an error. I believe the life of feeling is not irrational; its logical forms are merely very different from the structures of discourse. But they are so much like the dynamic forms of art that art is their natural symbol. Through plastic works, music, fiction, dance, or dramatic forms we can conceive what vitality and emotion feel like.

All this time I have been expounding, word by word, what I mean by the definition of art proposed at the beginning of this lecture: Art is the practice of creating perceptible forms expressive of human feeling. We have dwelt on the exact sense of "form," and "expressive," and "feeling." Form in this context means a configuration, something seen or heard or imaginatively grasped as an entity, an integral whole given to perception like an apparition. Every work of art is a form in this sense. It may be a solid form, or a dynamic form like a whirl or a stream, or it may be a sounding form like a melody, or even the image of events known as a story, that, like dreams or memory, presents its form to imagination alone. "Expression" is here taken to mean articulation, not *self*-expression or venting of one's feeling. And "feeling," finally, is used in the broadest sense, denoting anything that can or could be felt—sensation, emotion, every tension in a sentient organism, from the feeling of vitality itself to the highest development of personal or even transcendent consciousness. The reason why works of art can express the nature of feeling, which language cannot present, is that artistic forms and the forms of feeling, or subjective reality, are logically similar, so that our directly felt life is reflected, symbolically articulated, and objectively presented to our understanding in works of art.

This brings us, at last, to the question of the cultural importance of the arts. Why is it so apt to be the vanguard of cultural advance, as it was in Egypt, in Greece, in Christian Europe (think of Gregorian music and Gothic architecture), in Renaissance Italy—not to speculate about ancient cavemen, whose art is all that we know of them? One thinks of culture as economic increase, social organization, the gradual ascendancy of rational thinking and scientific control of nature over superstitious imagination and magical practices. But art is not practical; it is neither philosophy nor science; it is not religion, morality, nor even social comment (as many drama critics take comedy to be). What does it contribute to culture that could be of major importance?

It merely presents forms—sometimes intangible forms—to imagination. Its direct appeal is to that faculty, or function, that Lord Bacon considered the chief stumbling block in the way of reason, that enlightened writers like Stuart

Chase never tire of condemning as the source of all nonsense and bizarre erroneous beliefs. And so it is; but it is also the source of all insight and true beliefs. Imagination is probably the oldest mental trait that is typically human—
older than discursive reason; it is probably the common source of dream, reason,
religion, and all true general observation. It is this primitive human power—imagination—that engenders the arts and is in turn directly affected by their products.

Somewhere at the animalian starting line of human evolution lie the beginnings of that supreme instrument of the mind, language. We think of it as a
device for communication among the members of a society. But communication
is only one, and perhaps not even the first, of its functions. The first thing it
does is to break up what William James called the "blooming, buzzing confusion" of sense perception into units and groups, events and chains of events—
things and relations, causes and effects. All these patterns are imposed on our experience by language. We think, as we speak, in terms of objects and their
relations.

But the process of breaking up our sense experience in this way, making
reality conceivable, memorable, sometimes even predictable, is a process of
imagination. Primitive conception is imagination. Language and imagination
grow up together in a reciprocal tutelage.

What discursive symbolism—language in its literal use—does for our awareness of things about us and our own relation to them, the arts do for our awareness of subjective reality, feeling and emotion; they give inward experiences form
and thus make them conceivable. The only way we can really envisage vital
movement, the stirring and growth and passage of emotion, and ultimately the
whole direct sense of human life, is in artistic terms. A musical person thinks of
emotions musically. They cannot be discursively talked about above a very
general level. But they may none the less be known—objectively set forth, publicly known—and there is nothing necessarily confused or formless about
emotions.

As soon as the natural forms of subjective experience are abstracted to the
point of symbolic presentation, we can use those forms to *imagine* feeling and
understand its nature. Self-knowledge, insight into all phases of life and mind,
springs from artistic imagination. That is the cognitive value of the arts.

But their influence on human life goes deeper than the intellectual level. As
language actually gives form to our sense-experience, grouping our impressions
around those things which have names, and fitting sensations to the qualities
that have adjectival names, and so on, the arts we live with—our picture books
and stories and the music we hear—actually form our emotive experience.
Every generation has its styles of feeling. One age shudders and blushes and
faints, another swaggers, still another is godlike in a universal indifference. These
styles in actual emotion are not insincere. They are largely unconscious—determined by many social causes, but *shaped* by artists, usually popular artists of the

screen, the juke-box, the shop window and the picture magazine. (That, rather than incitement to crime, is my objection to the comics.) Irwin Edman remarks in one of his books that our emotions are largely Shakespeare's poetry.

This influence of art on life gives us an indication why a period of efflorescence in the arts is apt to lead a cultural advance: it formulates a new way of feeling, and that is the beginning of a cultural age. It suggests another matter for reflection, too: that a wide neglect of artistic education is a neglect in the education of feeling. Most people are so imbued with the idea that feeling is a formless total organic excitement in humans as in animals, that the idea of educating feeling, developing its scope and quality, seems odd to them, if not absurd. It is really, I think, at the very heart of personal education.

There is one other function of the arts that benefits not so much the advance of culture as its stabilization; an influence on individual lives. This function is the converse and complement of the objectification of feeling, the driving force of creation in art: it is the education of vision that we receive in seeing, hearing, reading works of art—the development of the artist's eye, that assimilates ordinary sights (or sounds, motions, or events) to inward vision, and lends expressiveness and emotional import to the world. Wherever art takes a motif from actuality—a flowering branch, a bit of landscape, a historic event or a personal memory, any model or theme from life—it transforms it into a piece of imagination, and imbues its image with artistic vitality. The result is an impregnation of ordinary reality with the significance of created form. This is the *subjectification of nature*, that makes reality itself a symbol of life and feeling.

I cannot say much about this last point because I am just working with the idea myself. One of my students gave it to me, in a criticism of my own theory. But it seems to me to be of great significance.

Let us sum up briefly, then, why the arts, which many people regard as a cultural frill, are actually never a late addition to civilized life, an ornament gracing society like tea ceremonies or etiquette, but are born during the rise and the primitive phases of cultures, and often outrun all other developments in achieving mature character and technical competence. Cultures begin with the development of personal and social and religious feeling. The great instrument of this development is art. For, (1) art makes feeling apparent, objectively given so we may reflect on it and understand it; (2) the practice and familiar knowledge of any art provides forms for actual feeling to take, as language provides forms for sensory experience and factual observation; and (3) art is the education of the senses to see nature in expressive form. Thereby the actual world becomes in some measure symbolic of feeling (without being "anthropomorphized," supposed to *have* feelings) and personally significant.

The arts objectify subjective reality, and subjectify outward experience of nature. Art education is the education of feeling, and a society that neglects it gives itself up to formless emotion. Bad art is corruption of feeling. This is a large factor in the irrationalism which dictators and demagogues exploit.

CLEMENT GREENBERG

The Case for Abstract Art[1]

Many people say that the kind of art our age produces is one of the major symptoms of what's wrong with the age. The disintegration and, finally, the disappearance of recognizable images in painting and sculpture, like the obscurity in advanced literature, are supposed to reflect a disintegration of values in society itself. Some people go further and say that abstract, nonrepresentational art is pathological art, crazy art, and that those who practice it and those who admire and buy it are either sick or silly. The kindest critics are those who say it's all a joke, a hoax, and a fad, and that modernist art in general, or abstract art in particular, will soon pass. This sort of thing is heard or read pretty constantly, but in some years more often than others.

There seems to be a certain rhythm in the advance in popularity of modernist art, and a certain rhythm in the counter-attacks which try to stem it. More or less the same words or arguments are used in all the polemics, but the targets usually change. Once it was the impressionists who were a scandal, next it was Van Gogh and Cézanne, then it was Matisse, then it was cubism and Picasso, after that Mondrian, and now it is Jackson Pollock. The fact that Pollack was an American shows, in a backhanded way, how important American art has lately become.

Some of the same people who attack modernist art in general, or abstract art in particular, happen also to complain that our age has lost those habits of disinterested contemplation, and that capacity for enjoying things as ends in themselves and for their own sake, which former ages are supposed to have cultivated. This idea has been advanced often enough to convert it into a cliché. I hate to give assent to a cliché, for it is almost always an oversimplification, but I have to make an exception in this case. While I strongly doubt that disinterested contemplation was as unalloyed or as popular in ages past as is supposed, I do tend to agree that we could do with more of it in this time, and especially in this country.

I think a poor life is lived by anyone who doesn't regularly take time out to stand and gaze, or sit and listen, or touch, or smell, or brood, without any further end in mind, simply for the satisfaction gotten from that which is gazed at, listened to, touched, smelled or brooded upon. We all know, however, that the climate of Western life, and particularly of American life, is not conducive to this kind of thing; we are all too busy making a living. This is another cliché, of course. And still a third cliché says that we should learn from Oriental

1 From *Adventures of the Mind*, ed. Richard Thruelsen and John Kobler (New York: Vintage Books, 1960), pp. 270-280. Copyright 1958, 1959, The Curtis Publishing Company. Reprinted by permission of Clement Greenberg.

society how to give more of ourselves to the life of the spirit, to contemplation and meditation, and to the appreciation of what is satisfying or beautiful in its own sole right. This last is not only a cliché, but a fallacy, since most Orientals are even more preoccupied than we are with making a living. I hope that I myself am not making a gross and reductive simplification when I say that so much of Oriental contemplative and aesthetic discipline strikes me as a technique for keeping one's eyes averted from ugliness and misery.

Every civilization and every tradition of culture seem to possess capacities for self-cure and self-correction that go into operation automatically, unbidden. If the given tradition goes too far in one direction it will usually try to right itself by going equally far in the opposite one. There is no question but that our Western civilization, especially in its American variant, devotes more mental energy than any other to the production of material things and services; and that, more than any other, it puts stress on interested, purposeful activity in general. This is reflected in our art, which, as has been frequently observed, puts such great emphasis on movement and development and resolution, on beginnings, middles, and endings—that is, on dynamics. Compare Western music with any other kind, or look at Western literature, for that matter, with its relatively great concern with plot and over-all structure and its relatively small concern with tropes and figures and ornamental elaborations; think of how slow-moving Chinese and Japanese poetry is by comparison with ours, and how much it delights in static situations; and how uncertain the narrational logic of non-Western fiction tends to be. Think of how encrusted and convoluted Arabic poetry is by contrast even with our most euphuistic lyrical verse. And as for non-Western music, does it not almost always, and literally, strike us as more monotonous than ours?

Well, how does Western art compensate for, correct, or at least qualify its emphasis on the dynamic—an emphasis that may or may not be excessive? And how does Western life itself compensate for, correct, or at least qualify its obsession with material production and purposeful activity? I shall not here attempt to answer the latter question. But in the realm of art an answer is beginning to emerge of its own accord, and the shape of part of that answer is abstract art.

Abstract decoration is almost universal, and Chinese and Japanese calligraphy is quasi-abstract—abstract to the extent that few occidentals can read the characters of Chinese or Japanese writing. But only in the West, and only in the last fifty years, have such things as abstract pictures and free-standing pieces of abstract sculpture appeared. What makes the big difference between these and abstract decoration is that they are, exactly, pictures and free-standing sculpture—solo works of art meant to be looked at for their own sake and with full attention, and not as the adjuncts, incidental aspects, or settings of things other than themselves. These abstract pictures and pieces of sculpture challenge our capacity for disinterested contemplation in a way that is more concentrated and, I daresay, more conscious than anything else I know of in art. Music is an essentially abstract art, but even at its most rarefied and abstract, and whether it's Bach's or the middle-period Schoenberg's music, it does not offer this challenge in quite the same way or degree. Music tends from a beginning through a middle toward an ending. We wait to see how it "comes out"—which is what we also do with literature. Of course, the *total* experience of literature and music is completely disinterested, but it becomes that only at a further remove. While undergoing the experience we are caught up and expectant as well as detached—disinterested and at the same time interested in a way resembling that in which we are interested in how things turn out in real life. I exaggerate to make my point—aesthetic experience *has* to be disinterested, and when it is genuine it always is, even when bad works of art are involved—but the distinctions I've made and those I've still to make are valid nevertheless.

With representational painting it is something like what it is with literature. This has been said before, many times before, but usually in order to criticize representational painting in what I think is a wrong-headed when not downright silly way. What I mean when I say, in this context, that representational painting is like literature, is that it tends to involve us in the interested as well as the disinterested by presenting us with the images of things that are inconceivable outside time and action. This goes even for landscapes and flower pieces and still lifes. It is not simply that we sometimes tend to confuse the attractiveness of the things represented in a picture with the quality of the picture itself. And it is not only that attractiveness as such has nothing to do with the abiding success of a work of art. What is more fundamental is that the meaning—as distinct from the attractiveness—of what is represented becomes truly inseparable from the representation itself. That Rembrandt confined impasto—thick paint, that is—to his highlights, and that in his later portraits especially these coincide with the ridges of the noses of his subjects is important to the artistic effect of these portraits. And that the effectiveness of the impasto, as impasto—as an abstract element of technique—coincides with its effectiveness as a means of showing just how a nose looks under a certain kind of light is also genuinely important. And that the lifelike delineation of the nose contributes to the evocation of the personality of the individual to whom the nose belongs is likewise important. And the manner and degree of insight into that individual's personality which Rembrandt exhibits in his portrait is important too. None of these factors can be, or ought to be, separated from the legitimate effect of the portrait as a picture pure and simple.

But once we have to do with personalities and lifelikeness we have to do with things from which we cannot keep as secure a distance for the sake of disinterestedness as we can, say, from abstract decoration. As it happens, the whole tendency of our Western painting, up until the later stages of impressionism, was to make distance and detachment on the part of the spectator as insecure as possible. It laid more of a stress than any other tradition on creating a sculpture-like, or photographic, illusion of the third dimension, on thrusting images at the eye with a lifelikeness that brought them as close as possible to their originals. Because of their sculptural vividness, Western paintings tend to be far less quiet, far more agitated and active—in short, far more explicitly dynamic—than most non-Western paintings do. And they involve the spectator to a much greater extent in the practical and actual aspects of the things they depict and represent.

We begin to wonder what we think of the people shown in Rembrandt's portraits, *as* people; whether or not we would like to walk through the terrain shown in a Corot landscape; about the life stories of the burghers we see in a Steen painting; we react in a less than disinterested way to the attractiveness of the models, real or ideal, of the personages in a Renaissance painting. And once we begin to do this we begin to participate in the work of art in a so-to-speak practical way. In itself this participation may not be improper, but it does become so when it begins to shut out all other factors. This it has done and does, all too often. Even though the connoisseurs have usually been able in the long run to prefer the picture of a dwarf by Velasquez to that of a pretty girl by Howard Chandler Christy, the enjoyment of pictorial and sculptural art in our society has tended, on every other level than that of professional connoisseurship, to be excessively "literary," and to center too much on merely technical feats of copying.

But, as I've said, every tradition of culture tends to try to correct one extreme by going to its opposite. And when our Western tradition of painting came up at last with reservations about its forthright naturalism, these quickly took the form of an equally forthright antinaturalism. These reservations started with late impressionism, and have now culminated in abstract art. I don't at all wish to be understood as saying that it all happened because some artist or artists decided it was time to curb the excesses of realistic painting, and that the main historical significance of abstract art lies in its function as an antidote to these. Nor do I wish to be understood as assuming that realistic or naturalistic art inherently needs, or ever needed, such a thing as an antidote. The motivations, conscious and unconscious, of the first modernist artists, and of present modernists as well, were and are quite different. Impressionism itself started as an effort to push naturalism further than ever before. And all through the history of art—not only in recent times—consequences have escaped intentions.

It is on a different, and more impersonal and far more general level of meaning and history that our culture has generated abstract art as an antidote. On that level this seemingly new kind of art has emerged as an epitome of almost everything that disinterested contemplation requires, and as both a challenge and a reproof to a society that exaggerates, not the necessity, but the intrinsic value of purposeful and interested activity. Abstract art comes, on this level, as a relief, an archexample of something that does not have to mean, or be useful for, anything other than itself. And it seems fitting, too, that abstract art should at present flourish most in this country. If American society is indeed given over as no other society has been to purposeful activity and material production, then it is right that it should be reminded, in extreme terms, of the essential nature of disinterested activity.

Abstract art does this in very literal and also in very imaginative ways. First, it does not exhibit the illusion or semblance of things we are already familiar with in real life; it gives us no imaginary space through which to walk with the mind's eye; no imaginary objects to desire or not desire; no imaginary people to like or dislike. We are left alone with shapes and colors. These may or may not remind us of real things; but if they do, they usually do so incidentally or accidentally—on our own responsibility as it were; and the genuine enjoyment of an abstract picture does not ordinarily depend on such resemblances.

Second, pictorial art in its highest definition is static; it tries to overcome movement in space or time. This is not to say that the eye does not wander over a painted surface, and thus travel in both space and time. When a picture presents us with an illusion of real space, there is all the more inducement for the eye to do such wandering. But ideally the whole of a picture should be taken in at a glance; its unity should be immediately evident, and the supreme quality of a picture, the highest measure of its power to move and control the visual imagination, should reside in its unity. And this is something to be grasped only in an indivisible instant of time. No expectancy is involved in the true and pertinent experience of a painting; a picture, I repeat, does not "come out" the way a story, or a poem, or a piece of music does. It's all there at once, like a sudden revelation. This "at-onceness" an abstract picture usually drives home to us with greater singleness and clarity than a representational painting does. And to apprehend this "at-onceness" demands a freedom of mind and untrammeledness of eye that constitute "at-onceness" in their own right. Those who have grown capable of experiencing this know what I mean. You are summoned and gathered into one point in the continuum of duration. The picture does this to you, willy-nilly, regardless of whatever else is on your mind; a mere glance at it creates the attitude required for its appreciation, like a stimulus that elicits an automatic response. You become all attention, which means that you become, for the moment, selfless and in a sense entirely identified with the object of your attention.

The "at-onceness" which a picture or a piece of sculpture enforces on you is not, however, single or isolated. It can be repeated in a succession of instants, in each one remaining an "at-onceness," an instant all by itself. For the cultivated eye, the picture repeats its instantaneous unity like a mouth repeating a single word.

This pinpointing of the attention, this complete liberation and concentration of it, offers what is largely a new experience to most people in our sort of society. And it is, I think, a hunger for this particular kind of experience that helps account for the growing popularity of abstract art in this country: for the way it is taking over in the art schools, the galleries, and the museums.

The fact that fad and fashion are also involved does not invalidate what I say. I know that abstract art of the latest variety—that originating with painters like Pollock and Georges Mathieu—has gotten associated with progressive jazz and its cultists; but what of it? That Wagner's music became associated with German ultranationalism, and that Wagner was Hitler's favorite composer, still doesn't detract from its sheer quality as music. That the present vogue for folk music started, back in the 1930's, among the Communists doesn't make our liking for it any the less genuine, or take anything away from folk music itself. Nor does the fact that so much gibberish gets talked and written about abstract art compromise it, just as the gibberish in which art criticism in general abounds, and abounds increasingly, doesn't compromise art in general.

One point, however, I want to make glaringly clear. Abstract art is not a special kind of art; no hard-and-fast line separates it from representational art; it is only the latest phase in the development of Western art as a whole, and almost every "technical" device of abstract painting is already to be found in the realistic painting that preceded it. Nor is it a superior kind of art. I still know of nothing in abstract painting, aside perhaps from some of the near-abstract cubist works that Picasso, Braque and Léger executed between 1910 and 1914, which matches the highest achievements of the old masters. Abstract painting may be a purer, more quintessential form of pictorial art than the representational kind, but this does not of itself confer quality upon an abstract picture. The ratio of bad abstract painting to good is actually much greater than the ratio of bad to good representational painting. Nonetheless, the very best painting, the major painting, of our age is almost exclusively abstract. Only on the middle and lower levels of quality, on the levels below the first-rate—which is, of course, where most of the art that gets produced places itself—only there is the better painting preponderantly representational.

On the plane of culture in general, the special, unique value of abstract art, I repeat, lies in the high degree of detached contemplativeness that its appreciation requires. Contemplativeness is demanded in greater or lesser degree for the appreciation of every kind of art, but abstract art tends to present this requirement in quintessential form, at its purest, least diluted, most immediate. If abstract art—as does happen nowadays—should chance to be the first kind of pictorial art we learn to appreciate, the chances are that when we go to other kinds of pictorial art—to the old masters, say, and I hope we all do go to the old masters eventually—we shall find ourselves all the better able to enjoy them. That is, we shall be able to experience them with less intrusion of irrelevancies, therefore more fully and more intensely.

The old masters stand or fall, their pictures succeed or fail, on the same ultimate basis as do those of Mondrian or any other abstract artist. The abstract formal unity of a picture by Titian is more important to its quality than what that picture images. To return to what I said about Rembrandt's portraits, the whatness of what is imaged is not unimportant—far from it—and cannot be separated, really, from the formal qualities that result from the way it is imaged. But it is a fact, in my experience, that representational paintings are essentially and most fully appreciated when the identities of what they represent are only secondarily present to our consciousness. Baudelaire said he could grasp the quality of a painting by Delacroix when he was still too far away from it to make out the images it contained, when it was still only a blur of colors. I think it was really on this kind of evidence that critics and connoisseurs, though they were almost always unaware of it, discriminated between the good and the bad in the past. Put to it, they more or less unconsciously dismissed from their minds the connotations of Rubens' nudes when assessing and experiencing the final worth of his art. They may have remained aware of the pinkness as a *nude* pinkness, but it was a pinkness and a nudity devoid of most of their usual associations.

Abstract paintings do not confront us with such problems. Or at least the frequenting of abstract art can train us to relegate them automatically to their proper place; and in doing this we refine our eyes for the appreciation of non-abstract art. That has been my own experience. That it is still relatively rare can be explained perhaps by the fact that most people continue to come to painting through academic art—the kind of art they see in ads and in magazines—and when and if they discover abstract art it comes as such an overwhelming experience that they tend to forget everything produced before. This is to be deplored, but it does not negate the value, actual or potential, of abstract art as an introduction to the fine arts in general, and as an introduction, too, to habits of disinterested contemplation. In this respect, the value of abstract art will, I hope, prove far greater in the future than it has yet. Not only can it confirm instead of subverting tradition; it can teach us, by example, how valuable so much in life can be made without being invested with ulterior meanings. How many people I know who have hung abstract pictures on their walls and found themselves gazing at them endlessly, and then exclaiming, "I don't know what there is in that painting, but I can't take my eyes off it." This kind of bewilderment is salutary. It does us good not to be able to explain, either to ourselves or to others, what we enjoy or love; it expands our capacity for experience.

FRANK JEWETT MATHER, JR.

Botticelli's *Primavera*[1]

In the year 1477, Lorenzo di Pierfrancesco de' Medici having bought a villa at Castello, on the Prato road, commissioned a young Florentine painter, Sandro Botticelli, to paint a decorative panel for his villa. The dimensions,

[1] *Concerning Beauty* (Princeton, N. J.: Princeton University Press, 1935), pp. 70-76. Copyright, 1935, Princeton University Press.

PRIMAVERA

Botticelli

NO. 5, 1950   *Jackson Pollock*

Jackson Pollock: *No. 5, 1950.* New York: The Museum of Modern Art, Gift of Mr. and Mrs.
Walter Bareiss. (Reverse) *Primavera* by permission of David Ashley, Inc.

about seven by ten feet, and the subject, the "Coming of Spring," were pre-scribed. Lorenzo, not to be confused with his cousin and more illustrious namesake, was himself a minor poet and in touch with the great humanist poet Angelo Poliziano. Thus he was a patron of a kind to feel the loveliness of a Tuscan springtime. Botticelli accepted the theme with enthusiasm and cast about for its embodiment.

Instantaneously the general decorative arrangement flashed into Botticelli's mind, for a pattern is already there, waiting for a subject. He has admired the great new engraving of ten fighting men by one of his masters, Antonio Pollaiolo—a fine arabesque of tensely constructed white bodies effectively con-trasting with the formal verticals of a grove in the background. Sometime Sandro meant to use the motive more exquisitely. This is his opportunity. His figures shall show a greater variety in drapery and semi-nudity.

It was perhaps at this stage some humanist friend called Sandro's attention to the beautiful lines in which Lucretius described the coming of spring.

> It ver et Venus, et Veneris praenuntius ante
> Pennatus graditur, zephyri vestigia propter
> Flora quibus mater praespargens ante viai
> Cuncta coloribus egregiis et odoribus opplet.

Spring and Venus move by, and the winged herald of Venus goes before; and close upon the track of the West Wind Flora, their mother, strews flowers ahead, covering all the paths with fairest colors and odors.

A group of five figures begins to order itself in Botticelli's mind; the composi-tion now has found its main theme, but he consciously transforms the pro-cessional order of Lucretius. Spring no longer leads with Venus, but is blown and chased in by Zephyr at the rear of the line. And the trees shall bend as Zephyr passes, admitting his gentle power. As for Zephyr, Poliziano, in the "*Stanze*" is better than Lucretius. He represents Zephyr as lustful and flying behind Flora. Such shall be his relation to Spring. Flora does not follow Zephyr, but treads daintily ahead of him, behind Venus. Cupid's place as herald is above Venus and a little before her, and since he has wings, shall he not fly rather than walk? In its essentials the group at the right-hand side of the panel, the group that carries the meaning, is now established.

The carpet of spring flowers is obvious. Does not Lucretius suggest it? The flowers shall be so truthful that you could pluck them. They will contrast effectively with the formality of the paling of orange trees which he will pick out decoratively and conventionally with gold. But he will not stand on the somewhat monotonous verticalities of Pollaiolo's paling of trees. His paling shall be interspersed with olive branches delicately sharp against the sky. Everything shall be as fine and precise as any goldsmith's work.

So far everything has gone swimmingly. Presumably sketches have been made of the five figures, the group has taken on organization, at least men-tally. Enrichments and refinements have occurred. Out of Spring's lovely mouth roses shall grow; the flowers woven in Flora's frock shall proclaim her function; Venus shall be gravid and heavily draped, for contrast with the semi-nude figures and because spring is the birthday of the year. But now comes an unforeseen difficulty; on the small scale customary at the time, the five figures will never make out a composition for the big, oblong panel. Some filling figures of a congruous kind are indispensable. What figures?

Sandro is reasonably educated, but no scholar. He consults a humanist friend who has the ready answer. Of course Mercury and the Three Graces are the fitting attendants for Venus. Did not Horace, Book I, Ode xxx, when he bid Venus visit the home of his mistress Glycera, summon also the Graces with girdles loosed and Mercury, who withal is a minor cloud-dispeller? Witness *Aeneid*, IV, 245. As for the Graces, Sandro's own fellow Florentine, Leonbattista Alberti, in his treatise *Della Pittura*, which Sandro has doubtless duly read, tells us that their hands should be intertwined, and they themselves clothed in ungirt and transparent veils—quoting Seneca, "implexis inter se manibus, ridentes, solutaque, perlucida veste ornatas." So the humanist counsellor.

Sandro thinks it over. Here are the needed filling figures, and excellent figures for the purpose. Mercury shall be fanning the mists from an orange tree with his caduceus. That will carry the processional rhythm across the picture up to a high finish. He shall then be the terminal figure of the group. But the Graces shall be treading a solemn measure and not smiling. Only the hoyden Spring with the rose in her mouth shall be joyous.

The rest shall be pensive, or like Flora, enigmatically detached, for if spring is the beginning of new life in the world, is it not also the beginning of new death? The flowers and love itself are but for a moment between budding and withering.

Something like this is in Sandro's mind as he sketches the four new figures and considers the organization of the two groups into one. Here the general cadence is clear. The onrush of Zephyr and Spring shall be retarded into the dainty treading of Flora, shall come to a monitory full pause in the heavily clad figure of gravid Venus, shall be resumed in a moderate and more subtle fashion in the dance of the Graces, shall end with the resolutely poised figure of Mercury with his back turned while his hand and magic wand make on high a closing repetend of the right to left motion.

The composition of the picture is now mentally complete. Remains a task of some days to set it down in all its details in a working drawing—a drawing unhappily lost, for which any sensible collector would mortgage his house to the limit. Remained still a task of many months to paint it through on the panel. Rapturous work, work under highest tension, nothing lost of the freshness of the primal vision, much added by way of fit enrichment; fastidiousness in choice of shapes and tints never relaxing, never overasserting itself; a marvel of taste, a miracle of executive prowess.

When it was set in the wall at Castello, Botticelli, unless he was entirely unlike any other painters, relatively lost interest in it. He was now at work

on his nobly tragic "St. Augustine" for Ognissanti in competition with the
formidably popular Ghirlandaio's "St. Jerome," he was already thinking of
great frescoes to be made in Pope Sixtus's new chapel at Rome. Botticelli's
part of the esthetic transaction connected with the "Allegory of Spring" was
completed and well completed. That the transaction should continue was now
the responsibility of others.

The painting is now ready to play its part in the esthetic transaction. Let
me imagine myself before it. First at a distance I perceive the general
design—a very varied processional advance of clothed and lightly draped forms
from right to left across a quite formal paling of orange trees. Here I have
repeated the primal vision of Botticelli as elaborated by trial and error. Of
this trial and error virtually nothing comes to my attention, though I may
note that the four figures on the left are out of the main action, may divine
that they were an afterthought.

On nearer approach I grasp the exquisiteness of the detail without losing
the sense of the whole picture. This detail, the ripe oranges on the trees, the
iris, larkspurs, daisies, wild orchid, wood-strawberry daintily balancing in the
grass tell me that it is early springtime. Herewith comes the meaning of
the figures. Gravid Venus is identified by her winged son. The fantastic figure
with a beflowered frock, and strewing flowers must be Flora. An associational
item confirms and extends the identifications. I have read Herbert Horne's
happy citation of the lines from Lucretius which names all five figures for
me. This literary association is legitimately part of my appreciation, for it
guided Botticelli in creation. Since it was important for him, it is important
for me.

As I identify the main figures I sense their fastidiously distinguished character and the loveliness of the postures, actions and details which represent
and delicately emphasize their functions. What a cadence it is, rising from the
solemn boisterousness of Zephyr, through the adorable awkward twist of escaping Spring, to the mincing elegance of Flora's measured stride, and the full
stop where Venus stands in undulating repose. It is also an undulation in
depth, coming forward with Flora and the Graces at the ends, receding with
Venus at the center. My sense of the whole picture is being constantly
deepened and enriched as I make these explorations of details, and continue
then through the flowery sward, the grove, the group of Mercury and the
Graces. Here in appreciation I am perceiving that infinite delicate elaboration
and richness which arising in Botticelli's imagination commanded his nervous
and fastidious hand. These observations gradually tell me of the language in
which Botticelli's meaning is expressed. While there is a lovely accompaniment of muted color, it is primarily a language of line—line that races,
slows, darts, turns, stops, resumes, always giving assurance of form in implied
motion. My soul has echoed the controlled sweep of Botticelli's hand. The
sense of the pervading wistful, tranquil melancholy that surrounds and almost
denies the high spirits of romping Spring grows deeper as I look.

The experiences which words can only enumerate as successive, have actu-

ally overlapped, interwoven, blended, and have uninterruptedly built up that
psychical volume which is my appreciation of this lively picture, my virtual if
also approximate repetition of what was essential in Botticelli's creative processes—my complete *geniessen*,[2] my partial but sufficient *nachschaffen*.[3]

FRANK LLOYD WRIGHT

Modern Architecture: The Cardboard House[1]

Let us take for text on this, our fourth afternoon, the greatest of all references to simplicity, the inspired admonition: *"Consider the lilies of the
field—they toil not, neither do they spin, yet verily I say unto thee—Solomon in all his glory was not arrayed like one of these."* An inspired saying—
attributed to an humble Architect in ancient times, called Carpenter, who gave
up Architecture nearly two thousand years ago to go to work upon its Source.

And if the text should seem to you too far away from our subject this
afternoon—

"The Cardboard House"

—consider that for that very reason the text has been chosen. The cardboard
house needs an antidote. The antidote is far more important than the house.
As antidote—and as practical example, too, of the working out of an ideal of
organic simplicity that has taken place here on American soil, step by step,
under conditions that are your own—could I do better than to take apart for
your benefit the buildings I have tried to build, to show you how they were,
long ago, dedicated to the Ideal of Organic Simplicity? It seems to me that
while another might do better than that, I certainly could not—for that is,
truest and best, what I know about the Subject. What a man *does, that* he
has.

When, "in the cause of Architecture," in 1893, I first began to build the
houses, sometimes referred to by the thoughtless as "The New School of the
Middle West" (some advertiser's slogan comes along to label everything in
this our busy woman's country), the only way to simplify the awful building
in vogue at the time was to conceive a finer entity—a better building—and
get it built. The buildings standing then were all tall and all tight. Chimneys were lean and taller still, sooty fingers threatening the sky. And beside

[2] Enjoying.

[3] Re-creating.

[1] *Modern Architecture, Being the Kahn Lecture for 1930* (Princeton, N. J.:
Princeton University Press, 1931), pp. 68-80. Copyright, 1931, by Frank Lloyd
Wright. Reprinted by permission of author and the Princeton University Press.

them, sticking up by way of dormers through the cruelly sharp, saw-tooth roofs, were the attics for "help" to swelter in. Dormers were elaborate devices, cunning little buildings complete in themselves, stuck to the main roof slopes to let "help" poke heads out of the attic for air.

Invariably the damp sticky clay of the prairie was dug out for a basement under the whole house, and the rubblestone walls of this dank basement always stuck up above the ground a foot or more and blinked, with half-windows. So the universal "cellar" showed itself as a bank of some kind of masonry running around the whole house, for the house to sit up on—like a chair. The lean, upper house-walls of the usual two floors above this stone or brick basement were wood, set on top of this masonry-chair, clapboarded and painted, or else shingled and stained, preferably shingled and mixed, up and down, all together with mouldings crosswise. These overdressed wood house-walls had, cut in them—or cut out of them, to be precise—big holes for the big cat and little holes for the little cat to get in and out or for ulterior purposes of light and air. The house-walls were be-corniced or bracketed up at the top into the tall, purposely profusely complicated roof, dormers plus. The whole roof, as well as the roof as a whole, was scalloped and ridged and tipped and swanked and gabled to madness before they would allow it to be either shingled or slated. The whole exterior was be-deviled—that is to say, mixed to puzzle-pieces, with corner boards, panel-boards, window-frames, corner-blocks, plinth-blocks, rosettes, fantails, ingenious and jigger work in general. This was the only way they seemed to have, then, of "putting on style." The scroll-saw and turning-lathe were at the moment the honest means of this fashionable mongering by the wood-butcher and to this entirely "moral" end. Unless the householder of the period were poor indeed, usually an ingenious corner-tower on his house eventuated into a candle-snuffer dome, a spire, an inverted rutabaga or radish or onion or—what is your favorite vegetable? Always elaborate bay-windows and fancy porches played "ring around a rosy" on this "imaginative" corner feature. And all this the building of the period could do equally well in brick or stone. It was an impartial society. All material looked pretty much alike in that day.

Simplicity was as far from all this scrap-pile as the pandemonium of the barn-yard is far from music. But it was easy for the Architect. All he had to do was to call: "Boy, take down No. 37, and put a bay-window on it for the lady!"

So—the first thing to do was to get rid of the attic and, therefore, of the dormer and of the useless "heights" below it. And next, get rid of the unwholesome basement, entirely—yes, absolutely—in any house built on the prairie. Instead of lean, brick chimneys, bristling up from steep roofs to hint at "judgment" everywhere, I could see necessity for one only, a broad generous one, or at most, for two, these kept low down on gently sloping roofs or perhaps flat roofs. The big fireplace below, inside, became now a place for a real fire, justified the great size of this chimney outside. A real fireplace at that time was extraordinary. There were then "mantels" instead. A mantel was a marble frame for a few coals, or a piece of wooden furniture with tiles stuck in it and a "grate," the whole set slam up against the wall. The "mantel" was an insult to comfort, but the *integral* fireplace became an important part of the building itself in the houses I was allowed to build out there on the prairie. It refreshed me to see the fire burning deep in the masonry of the house itself.

Taking a human being for my scale, I brought the whole house down in height to fit a normal man; believing in no other scale, I broadened the mass out, all I possibly could, as I brought it down into spaciousness. It has been said that were I three inches taller (I am 5 feet 8½ inches tall), all my houses would have been quite different in proportion. Perhaps.

House-walls were now to be started at the ground on a cement or stone water-table that looked like a low platform under the building, which it usually was, but the house-walls were stopped at the second story window-sill level, to let the rooms above come through in a continuous window-series, under the broad eaves of a gently sloping, overhanging roof. This made enclosing screens out of the lower walls as well as light screens out of the second story walls. Here was true *enclosure of interior space*. A new sense of building, it seems.

The climate, being what it was, a matter of violent extremes of heat and cold, damp and dry, dark and bright, I gave broad protecting roof-shelter to the whole, getting back to the original purpose of the "Cornice." The undersides of the roof projections were flat and light in color to create a glow of reflected light that made the upper rooms not dark, but delightful. The overhangs had double value, shelter and preservation for the walls of the house as well as diffusion of reflected light for the upper story, through the "light screens" that took the place of the walls and were the windows.

At this time, a house to me was obvious primarily as interior space under fine shelter. I liked the sense of *shelter*. I liked the sense of shelter in the "look of the building." I achieved it, I believe. I then went after the variegated bands of material in the old walls to eliminate odds and ends in favor of one material and a single surface from grade to eaves, or grade to second story sill-cope, treated as simple enclosing screens,—or else made a plain screen band around the second story above the window-sills, turned up over on to the ceiling beneath the eaves. This screen band was of the same material as the under side of the eaves themselves, or what architects call the "soffit." The planes of the building parallel to the ground were all stressed, to grip the whole to earth. Sometimes it was possible to make the enclosing wall below this upper band of the second story, from the second story window-sill clear down to the ground, a heavy "wainscot" of fine masonry material resting on the cement or stone platform laid on the foundation. I liked that wainscot to be of masonry material when my clients felt they could afford it.

As a matter of form, too, I liked to see the projecting base, or water-table, set out over the foundation walls themselves—as a substantial preparation for the building. This was managed by setting the studs of the walls to the inside of the foundation walls, instead of to the outside. All door and window tops were now brought into line with each other with only comfortable head-clearance for the average human being. Eliminating the sufferers from the "attic" enabled the roofs to lie low. The house began to associate with the ground and become natural to its prairie site. And would the young man in architecture ever believe that this was all "new" then? Not only new, but destructive heresy—or ridiculous eccentricity. So New that what little prospect I had of ever earning a livelihood by making houses was nearly wrecked. At first, "they" called the houses "dress-reform" houses, because Society was just then excited about that particular "reform." This simplification looked like some kind of "reform" to them. Oh, they called them all sorts of names that cannot be repeated, but "they" never found a better term for the work unless it was "Horizontal Gothic," "Temperance Architecture" (with a sneer), etc., etc. I don't know how I escaped the accusation of another "Renaissance."

What I have just described was all on the *outside* of the house and was there chiefly because of what had happened *inside*. Dwellings of that period were "cut-up," advisedly and completely, with the grim determination that should go with any cutting process. The "interiors" consisted of boxes beside or inside other boxes, called *rooms*. All boxes inside a complicated boxing. Each domestic "function" was properly box to box. I could see little sense in this inhibition, this cellular sequestration that implied ancestors familiar with the cells of penal institutions, except for the privacy of bed-rooms on the upper floor. They were perhaps all right as "sleeping boxes." So I declared the whole lower floor as one room, cutting off the kitchen as a laboratory, putting servants' sleeping and living quarters next to it, semi-detached, on the ground floor, screening various portions in the big room, for certain domestic purposes —like dining or reading, or receiving a formal caller. There were no plans like these in existence at the time and my clients were pushed toward these ideas as helpful to a solution of the vexed servant-problem. Scores of doors disappeared and no end of partition. They liked it, both clients and servants. The house became more free as "space" and more liveable, too. Interior spaciousness began to dawn.

Having got what windows and doors that were left lined up and lowered to convenient human height, the ceilings of the rooms, too, could be brought over on to the walls, by way of the horizontal, broad bands of plaster on the walls above the windows, the plaster colored the same as the room ceilings. This would bring the ceiling-surface down to the very window tops. The ceilings thus expanded, by extending them downward as the wall band above the windows, gave a generous overhead to even small rooms. The sense of the whole was broadened and made plastic, too, by this expedient. The enclosing walls and ceilings were thus made to flow together.

Here entered the important element of Plasticity—indispensable to successful use of the Machine, for true expression of Modernity. The outswinging windows were fought for because the casement window associated the house with out-of-doors—gave free openings, outward. In other words the so-called "casement" was simple and more human. In use and effect, more natural. If it had not existed I should have invented it. It was not used at that time in America, so I lost many clients because I insisted upon it when they wanted the "guillotine" or "double-hung" window then in use. The Guillotine was not simple nor human. It was only expedient. I used it once in the Winslow House—my first house—and rejected it thereafter—forever. Nor at that time did I entirely eliminate the wooden trim. I did make it "plastic," that is, light and continuously flowing instead of the heavy "cut and butt" of the usual carpenter work. No longer did the "trim," so-called, look like carpenter work. The machine could do it perfectly well as I laid it out. It was all after "quiet." This plastic trim, too, with its running "back-hand" enabled poor workmanship to be concealed. It was necessary with the field resources at hand at that time to conceal much. Machinery versus the union had already demoralized the workmen. The Machine resources were so little understood that extensive drawings had to be made merely to show the "mill-man" what to leave off. But the "trim" finally became only a single, flat, narrow, horizontal wood-band running around the room, one at the top of the windows and doors and another next to the floors, both connected with narrow, vertical, thin wood-bands that were used to divide the wall-surfaces of the whole room smoothly and flatly into folded color planes. The trim merely completed the window and door openings in this same plastic sense. When the interior had thus become wholly plastic, instead of structural, a New element, as I have said, had entered Architecture. Strangely enough an element that had not existed in Architectural History before. Not alone in the trim, but in numerous ways too tedious to describe in words, this revolutionary sense of the plastic whole, an instinct with me at first, began to work more and more intelligently and have fascinating, unforeseen consequences. Here was something that began to organize itself. When several houses had been finished and compared with the house of the period, there was very little of that house left standing. Nearly every one had stood the house of the period as long as he could stand it, judging by appreciation of the change. Now all this probably tedious description is intended to indicate directly in bare outline how thus early there *was* an ideal of organic simplicity put to work, with historical consequences, here in your own country. The main motives and indications were (and I enjoyed them all):

First—To reduce the number of necessary parts of the house and the separate rooms to a minimum, and make all come together as enclosed space—so divided that light, air and vista permeated the whole with a sense of unity.

Second—To associate the building as a whole with its site by extension and emphasis of the planes parallel to the ground, but keeping the floors off the best part of the site, thus leaving that better part for use in connection with

the life of the house. Extended level planes were found useful in this connection.

Third—To eliminate the room as a box and the house as another by making
all walls enclosing screens—the ceilings and floors and enclosing screens to
flow into each other as one large enclosure of space, with minor subdivisions
only.

Make all house proportions more liberally human, with less wasted space
in structure, and structure more appropriate to material, and so the whole
more liveable. *Liberal* is the best word. Extended straight lines or stream-
lines were useful in this.

Fourth—To get the unwholesome basement up out of the ground, entirely
above it, as a low pedestal for the living-portion of the home, making the
foundation itself visible as a low masonry platform, on which the building
should stand.

Fifth—To harmonize all necessary openings to "outside" or to "inside" with
good human proportions and make them occur naturally—singly or as a
series in the scheme of the whole building. Usually they appeared as "light-
screens" instead of walls, because all the "Architecture" of the house was
chiefly the way these openings came in such walls as were grouped about the
rooms as enclosing screens. The *room* as such was now the essential architectural expression, and there were to be no holes cut in the walls as holes are
cut in a box, because this was not in keeping with the ideal of "plastic."
Cutting holes was violent.

Sixth—To eliminate combinations of different materials in favor of mono-
material so far as possible; to use no ornament that did not come out of the
nature of materials to make the whole building clearer and more expressive
as a place to live in, and give the conception of the building appropriate revealing emphasis. Geometrical or straight lines were natural to the machinery at work in the building trades then, so the interiors took on this
character naturally.

Seventh—To incorporate all heating, lighting, plumbing so that these systems
became constituent parts of the building itself. These service features became architectural and in this attempt the ideal of an organic architecture
was at work.

Eighth—To incorporate as organic Architecture—so far as possible—furnishings, making them all one with the building and designing them in simple
terms for machine work. Again straight lines and rectilinear forms.

Ninth—Eliminate the Decorator. He was all curves and all efflorescence, if not
all "period."

This was all rational enough so far as the thought of an organic architecture
went. The particular forms this thought took in the feeling of it all could only
be personal. There was nothing whatever at this time to help make them what

they were. All seemed to be the most natural thing in the world and grew up out of the circumstances of the moment. Whatever they may be worth in the long run is all they are worth.

Now *simplicity* being the point in question in this early constructive effort, organic simplicity I soon found to be a matter of true coordination. And Beauty I soon felt to be a matter of the sympathy with which such coordination was affected. Plainness was not necessarily simplicity. Crude furniture of the Roy-croft-Stickley-Mission Style, which came along later, was offensively plain, plain as a barn door—but never was simple in any true sense. Nor, I found, were merely machine-made things in themselves simple. To think "in simple," is to deal in simples, and that means with an eye single to the altogether. This, I believe, is the secret of simplicity. Perhaps we may truly regard nothing at all as simple in itself. I believe that no one thing in itself is ever so, but must achieve simplicity (as an Artist should use the term) as a perfectly realized part of some organic whole. Only as a feature or any part becomes an harmonious element in the harmonious whole does it arrive at the estate of simplicity. Any wild flower is truly simple, but double the same wild flower by cultivation, it ceases to be so. The *scheme* of the original is no longer clear. Clarity of design and perfect significance both are first essentials of the spontaneously born simplicity of the lilies of the field who neither toil nor spin, as contrasted with Solomon who had "toiled and spun"—that is to say, no doubt had put on himself and had put on his temple, properly "composed," everything in the category of good things but the cook-stove.

Five lines where three are enough is stupidity. Nine pounds where three are sufficient is stupidity. But to eliminate expressive words that intensify or vivify meaning in speaking or writing is not simplicity; nor is similar elimination in Architecture simplicity—it, too, may be stupidity. In Architecture, expressive changes of surface, emphasis of line and especially textures of material, may go to make facts eloquent, forms more significant. Elimination, therefore, may be just as meaningless as elaboration, perhaps more often so. I offer any fool, for an example.

To know what to leave out and what to put in, just where and just how— Ah, *that* is to have been educated in knowledge of SIMPLICITY.

As for Objects of Art in the house even in that early day they were the "bête noir" of the new simplicity. If well chosen, well enough in the house, but only if each was properly digested by the whole. Antique or modern sculpture, paintings, pottery, might become objectives in the Architectural scheme and I accepted them, aimed at them, and assimilated them. Such things may take their places as elements in the design of any house. They are then precious things, gracious and good to live with. But it is difficult to do this well. Better, if it may be done, to design all features together. At that time, too, I tried to make my clients see that furniture and furnishings, not built in as integral features of the building, should be designed as attributes of whatever furniture was built in and should be seen as minor parts of the building itself, even if

detached or kept aside to be employed on occasion. But when the building itself was finished, the old furniture the clients already possessed went in with
them to await the time when the interior might be completed. Very few of the
houses were, therefore, anything but painful to me after the clients moved in
and, helplessly, dragged the horrors of the old order along after them.

But I soon found it difficult, anyway, to make some of the furniture in the
"abstract"; that is, to design it as architecture and make it "human" at the same
time—fit for human use. I have been black and blue in some spot, somewhere,
almost all my life from too intimate contacts with my own furniture. Human
beings must group, sit or recline—confound them—and they must dine, but
dining is much easier to manage and always was a great artistic opportunity.
Arrangements for the informality of sitting comfortably, singly or in groups,
where it is desirable or natural to sit, and still to belong in disarray to the
scheme as a whole—that is a matter difficult to accomplish. But it can be done
now, and should be done, because only those attributes of human comfort and
convenience, made to belong in this digested or integrated sense to the architecture of the home as a whole, should be there at all, in Modern Architecture.
For that matter about four-fifths of the contents of nearly every home could be
given away with good effect to that home. But the things given away might go
on to poison some other home. So why not at once destroy undesirable things
. . . make an end of them?

Here then, in foregoing outline, is the gist of America's contribution to
Modern American Architecture as it was already under way in 1893. But the
gospel of elimination is one never preached enough. No matter how much
preached, Simplicity is a spiritual ideal seldom organically reached. Nevertheless, by assuming the virtue by imitation—or by increasing structural make-
shifts to get superficial simplicity—the effects may cultivate a taste that will
demand the reality in course of time, but it may also destroy all hope of the real
thing.

Standing here, with the perspective of long persistent effort in the direction
of an organic Architecture in view, I can again assure you out of this initial experience that Repose is the reward of true simplicity and that organic simplicity
is sure of Repose. Repose is the highest quality in the Art of Architecture,
next to integrity, and a reward for integrity. Simplicity may well be held to
the fore as a spiritual ideal, but when actually achieved, as in the "lilies of the
field," it is something that comes of itself, something spontaneously born out
of the nature of the doing whatever it is that is to be done. Simplicity, too,
is a reward for fine feeling and straight thinking in working a principle, well
in hand, to a consistent end. Solomon knew nothing about it, for he was only
wise. And this, I think, is what Jesus meant by the text we have chosen for
this discourse—"Consider the lilies of the field," as contrasted, for beauty,
with Solomon.

Now, a chair *is* a machine to sit in.

A home *is* a machine to live in.

The human body *is* a machine to be worked by will.

A tree *is* a machine to bear fruit.

A plant *is* a machine to bear flowers and seeds.

And, as I've admitted before somewhere, a heart *is* a suction-pump. Does that idea thrill you?

Trite as it is, it may be as well to think it over because the *least* any of these things may be, *is* just that. All of them are that before they are anything else. And to violate that mechanical requirement in any of them is to finish before anything of higher purpose can happen. To ignore the fact is either sentimentality or the prevalent insanity. Let us acknowledge in this respect, that this matter of mechanics is just as true of the work of Art as it is true of anything else. But, were we to stop with that trite acknowledgment, we should only be living in a low, rudimentary sense. This skeleton rudiment accepted, *understood*, is the first condition of any fruit or flower we may hope to get from ourselves. Let us continue to call this flower and fruit of ourselves, even in this Machine Age, ART. Some Architects, as we may see, now consciously acknowledge this "Machine" rudiment. Some will eventually get to it by circuitous mental labor. Some *are* the thing itself without question and already in need of "treatment." But "Americans" (I prefer to be more specific and say "Usonians") have been educated "blind" to the higher human uses of it all—while actually in sight of this higher human use all the while.

Therefore, now let the declaration that "all is machinery" stand nobly forth for what it is worth. But why not more profoundly declare that "Form follows Function" and let it go at that? Saying, "Form follows Function," is not only deeper, it is clearer, and it goes further in a more comprehensive way to say the thing to be said, because the implication of this saying includes the heart of the whole matter. It may be that Function follows Form, as, or if, you prefer, but it is easier thinking with the first proposition just as it is easier to stand on your feet and nod your head than it would be to stand on your head and nod your feet. Let us not forget that Simplicity of the Universe is very different from the Simplicity of a Machine.

New significance in Architecture implies new materials qualifying form and textures, requires fresh feeling, which will eventually qualify both as "ornament." But "Decoration" must be sent on its way or now be given the meaning that it has lost, if it is to stay. Since "Decoration" became acknowledged as such, and ambitiously set up for itself as Decoration, it has been a make-shift, in the light of this ideal of Organic Architecture. Any House Decoration, as such, is an architectural makeshift, however well it may be done, unless the decoration, so called, is part of the Architect's design in both concept and execution.

Since Architecture in the old sense died and Decoration has had to shift for itself more and more, all so-called Decoration has become *ornamental*, therefore no longer *integral*. There can be no true simplicity in either Architecture or Decoration under any such condition. Let Decoration, therefore, die for

Architecture, and the Decorator become an Architect, but not an "Interior Architect."

Ornament can never be applied to Architecture any more than Architecture should ever be applied to Decoration. All ornament, if not developed within the nature of Architecture and as organic part of such expression, vitiates the whole fabric no matter how clever or beautiful it may be as something in itself.

Yes—for a century or more Decoration has been setting up for itself, and in our prosperous country has come pretty near to doing very well, thank you. I think we may say that it is pretty much all we have now to show as Domestic Architecture, as Domestic Architecture still goes with us at the present time. But we may as well face it. The Interior Decorator thrives with us because we have no Architecture. Any Decorator is the natural enemy of organic simplicity in Architecture. He, persuasive Doctor-of-Appearances that he *must* be when he becomes Architectural substitute, will give you an imitation of anything, even an imitation of imitative simplicity. Just at the moment, May 1930, he is expert in this imitation. France, the born Decorator, is now engaged with "Madame," owing to the good fortune of the French market, in selling us this ready-made or made-to-order simplicity. Yes, Imitation Simplicity is the latest addition to imported "stock." The Decorators of America are now equipped to furnish *especially* this. Observe. And how very charming the suggestions conveyed by these imitations sometimes are!

Would you have again the general principles of the spiritual-ideal of organic simplicity at work in our Culture? If so, then let us reiterate: First, Simplicity is Constitutional Order. And it is worthy of note in this connection that 9 times 9 equals 81 is just as simple as 2 plus 2 equals 4. Nor is the obvious more simple necessarily than the occult. The obvious is obvious simply because it falls within our special horizon, is therefore easier for us to *see*; that is all. Yet all simplicity near or far has a countenance, a visage, that is characteristic. But this countenance is visible only to those who can grasp the whole and enjoy the significance of the minor part, as such, in relation to the whole when in flower. This is for the critics.

This characteristic visage may be simulated—the real complication glossed over, the internal conflict hidden by surface and belied by mass. The internal complication may be and usually is increased to create the semblance of and get credit for—simplicity. This is the Simplicity-lie usually achieved by most of the "surface and mass" architects. This is for the young architect.

Truly ordered simplicity in the hands of the great artist may flower into a bewildering profusion, exquisitely exuberant, and render all more clear than ever. Good William Blake says exuberance is *beauty*, meaning that it is so in this very sense. This is for the Modern Artist with the Machine in his hands. False Simplicity—Simplicity as an affectation, that is Simplicity constructed as a Decorator's outside put upon a complicated, wasteful engineer's or carpenter's "Structure," outside or inside—is not good enough Simplicity. It cannot be simple at all. But that is what passes for Simplicity, now that startling Simplicity-effects are becoming the *fashion*. That kind of Simplicity is *violent*. This is for "Art and Decoration."

Soon we shall want Simplicity inviolate. There is one way to get that Simplicity. My guess is, there is *only* one way really to get it. And that way is, on principle, by way of *Construction* developed as Architecture. That is for us, one and all.

LEWIS MUMFORD

The Imperial Façade[1]

The decade between 1890 and 1900 saw the rise of a new period in American architecture. This period had, it is true, been dimly foreshadowed by the grandiose L'Enfant, but if the superficial forms resembled those of the early republic, and if the precedents of classic architecture again became a guide, the dawning age was neither a revival nor a continuation.

In the meanwhile, fresh influences had entered. The generation of students who had studied in the Ecole des Beaux Arts after the Civil War was ready, at last, to follow the lone trail which Richard H. Hunt had blazed. Richardson's most intimate disciples reacted against the stamp of his personality and sought a more neutral mode of expression, consecrated by established canons of good taste. On top of this, the introduction of steel-cage construction removed the necessity for solid masonry, and placed a premium upon the mask. The stage was set for a new act of the drama.

All these influences shaped the style of our architecture when it arose; but the condition that gave it a substantial base was the rise of a new order in America's economic life. Up to this time, the chief industrial problem had been to improve the processes of mechanical production and to stake out new areas for exploitation. One may compare these economic advances to the separate sorties of an army operating on a wide front: any lone adventurer might take his courage in his hands and exploit an invention, or sink an oil well, if he could find it. By 1890 the frontier had closed; the major resources of the country were under the control of the monopolist; it became more important to consolidate gains than freshly to achieve them. Separate lines of railroads were welded into systems; separate steel plants and oil plants were wrought into trusts; and where monopoly did not rest upon a foundation of natural advantage, the "gentleman's agreement" began its service as a useful substitute. The popular movements which sought to challenge the forces of this new regime—

[1] From *Sticks and Stones* (New York: Boni & Liveright, 1924), pp. 123-151, with minor changes in the text made by the author. Reprinted by permission of the author.

the labor movement, socialism, populism—had neither analyzed the situation with sufficient care nor attracted the adherence of the majority. The defeat of Henry George as a local political candidate was symbolic: by 1888 a humane thinker like Edward Bellamy had already accepted the defeat, had embraced the idea of the trust, and had conceived a comprehensive utopia on the basis of letting the process of monopoly go the limit, so that finally, by a mere yank of the levers, the vast economic organizations of the country would become the "property" of the people.

The drift to the open lands came to a full pause. The land-empire had been conquered, and its overlords were waxing in power and riches: the name "millionaire" became the patent of America's new nobility. With the shift from industry to finance went a shift from the producing towns to the spending towns: architecture came to dwell in the stock exchanges, the banks, the shops, and the clubs of the metropolis; if it sought the countryside at all, it established itself in the villas that were newly laid out on hill and shore in the neighborhood of the great cities. The keys to this period are opulence and magnitude: "money to burn."

These years witnessed what the Roman historian, Ferrero, has called a "véritable recommencement d'histoire." In the new centers of privilege there arose a scale of living and a mode of architecture which, with all its attendant miseries, depletions, and exploitations, recalled the Rome of the first and second centuries after Christ. It is needless to say that vast acres of buildings, factories, shops, homes, were erected which had no relation at all to the imperial regime; for not everyone participated in either the benefits or the depressions that attended the growth of monopoly; but the accent of this period, the dominant note, was an imperial one. While the commonplace building of the time cannot be ignored, it remains, so to say, out of the picture.

Hardly had the process of concentration and consolidation begun before the proper form manifested itself. The occasion for its appearance was the World's Columbia Exposition, opened in 1893. In creating this fair, the enterprise and capacity for organization which the architects of Chicago had applied to the construction of the skyscraper transformed the unkempt wilderness of Jackson Park into the Great White City in the space of two short years. Here the architects of the country, particularly of New York and Chicago, appeared for the first time as a united profession, or, to speak more accurately, as a college. Led by the New Yorkers, who had come more decisively under European influence, they brought to this exposition the combination of skill and taste in all the departments of the work that had, two centuries earlier, created the magnificent formalities of Versailles. There was unity of plan in the grouping of the main buildings about the lagoon; there was unity of tone and color in the gleaming white façades; there was unity of effect in the use of classic orders and classic forms of decoration. Lacking any genuine unity of ideas and purposes—for Root had initially conceived of a variegated oriental setting—the architects of the exposition had achieved the effects of unity by subordinating

their work to an established precedent. They chanted a Roman litany above
the Babel of individual styles. It was a capital triumph of the academic imagination. If these main buildings were architecture, America had never seen so
much of it at one time before. Even that belated Greco-Puritan, Mr. Charles
Eliot Norton, was warm in praise.

It would be foolish to quarrel with the style that was chosen for these exposition buildings, or to deny its propriety. Messrs. McKim, White, Hunt, and
Burnham divined that they were fated to serve Renaissance despots and emperors with more than Roman power, and unerringly they chose the proper
form for their activities. Whereas Rome had cast its spell over the architects
of the early Renaissance because they wished once more to enter into its life,
the life of its sages and poets and artists, it attracted the architects of the White
City because of its external features—because of its stereotyped canons and
rules—because of the relatively small number of choices it offered for a lapse
in taste—because of its skill in conspicuous waste, and because of that very
noncommittal quality in its massive forms which permitted the basilica to
become a church, or the temple to become a modern bank.

Of all the Renaissance architects, their impulses and interests were nearest,
perhaps, to Robert Adam, whose church at West Wycombe could be turned
into a ballroom by the simple act of removing the pews, and permitting the gay
walls and decorations to speak for themselves. Behind the white stiff façade of
the World's Fair buildings was the steel and glass structure of the engineer:
the building spoke one language and the "architecture" another. If the coming
of the skyscraper had turned masonry into veneer, here was a mode of architecture which was little but veneer.

In their place, at the Fair, these classic buildings were all that could be
demanded: Mr. Geoffrey Scott's defense of the Baroque, in The Architecture
of Humanism, applies particularly to its essential manifestations in the Garden
and the Theater—and why not in the Fair? Form and function, ornament and
design, have no inherent relation, one with the other, when the mood of the
architect is merely playful: there is no use in discussing the anatomy of architecture when its only aim is fancy dress. As a mask, as a caprice, the classic
orders are as justifiable as the icing on a birthday cake: they divert the eye without damaging the structure that they conceal. Unfortunately, the architecture
of the Renaissance has a tendency to imitate the haughty queen who advised
the commons to eat cake. Logically, it demands that a Wall Street clerk shall
live like a Lombardy prince, that a factory should be subordinated to esthetic
contemplation; and since these things are impossible, it permits "mere building" to become illiterate and vulgar below the standards of the most debased
vernacular. Correct in proportion, elegant in detail, courteous in relation to each
other, the buildings of the World's Fair were, nevertheless, only the simulacra
of a living architecture: they were the concentrated expression of an age which
sought to produce "values" rather than goods. In comparison with this new
style, the romanticism of the Victorian Age, with its avid respect for the medieval building traditions, was honesty and dignity itself.

The Roman precedent, modified by the work of Louis XIV and Napoleon III, by Le Nôtre and Haussmann, formed the basis not merely for the World's Fair, but for the host of city plans that were produced in the two decades that followed. It seemed for a while as if the architect might take the place of the engineer as city planner, and that the mangled regularity of the engineer's gridiron plan, laid down without respect to topographic advantage or to use, might be definitely supplanted in the remodeled central districts and in the new extensions and suburbs of the American city. The evil of the World's Fair triumph was that it suggested to the civic enthusiast that every city might become a fair: it introduced the notion of the City Beautiful as a sort of municipal cosmetic, and reduced the work of the architect to that of putting a pleasing front upon the scrappy building, upon the monotonous streets and the mean houses, that characterized vast areas in the newer and larger cities.

If the engineer who had devoted himself to sewers and street-plans alone had been superficial, the architectural city planner who centered attention upon parkways alone, grand avenues alone, and squares like the Place de l'Etoile alone, was equally superficial. The civic center and the parkway represented the better and more constructive side of this effort: in Cleveland, in Pittsburgh, in Springfield, Mass., harmonious groups of white buildings raised their heads above the tangle of commercial traffic, and in the restoration of L'Enfant's plan for Washington, the realities of the imperial regime at length caught up with the dreamer born out of his due time. A good many of these plans, however, were pathetically immature. One of the reports for Manhattan, for example, devoted pages and pages to showing the improvement that would follow the demolition of the wall around Central Park—and the importance of clipped trees in the design of grand avenues!

Plainly, the architect did not face with sufficient realism the colossal task with which he was confronted in the renovation of the city. He accepted his improvements too much at the value placed upon them by the leaders of Big Business—as a creator of land-values, as an element in increasing the commercial attractiveness of the city. Did not Mr. Daniel Burnham himself point to the improvements in Periclean Athens, not as the embodiment of Athenian citizenship and religion at its highest point, but as a measure for increasing the attractiveness of the city to visitors from abroad? Cut off from his true function to serve and beautify the community, made an accessory of business itself, like the merest salesman or advertising agent, it is no wonder that the architect speedily lost his leadership; and that the initiative went once again into the hands of the engineer.

The main merit of all these efforts to perpetuate the World's Fair is that they sought to achieve some of the dignity and decisiveness of the formal plan. Their weakness was that they neglected new elements, like the billboard, the skysign, the subway, the tall building, which undermined the effects of the plan even when it was achieved. In their efforts to escape from the welter of misguided commercial enterprise, the advocates of the city beautiful placed too great reliance upon spots of outward order and decency; they took refuge in the paper symmetry of axial avenues and round-points, as one finds them in Haussmann's Paris, and neglected the deeper and more genuine beauties of, let us say, the High Street in Oxford or Chipping Camden, or of many another European town that had achieved completion in its essentials before the nineteenth century.

In short, the advocates of the city beautiful sought a remedy on paper which could be purchased only by a thorough reorganization of the community's life. If all this applies to the better side of the World's Fair, it touches even more emphatically the worse.

The twenty years between 1890 and 1910 saw the complete rehabilitation of the Roman mode, as the very cloak and costume of imperial enterprise. The main effort of architecture was to give an effect of dignity and permanence to the façades of the principal thoroughfares: the public buildings must dominate the compositions, numerous boulevards and avenues must concentrate the traffic at certain points and guide the stranger to the markets and amusements: where possible, as in the Chicago plan, by Messrs. Burnham and Bennett, avenues must be cut through the gridiron pattern of blocks in order to achieve these effects. If this imperial street system is somewhat arbitrary, and if the necessary work of grading, filling, demolishing, and purchasing existing property rights is extremely costly, the end, nevertheless, justifies the means—the architecture impresses and awes a populace that shares vicariously in its glories. Should the effect prove a little too austere and formidable, the monuments will be offset with circuses and hippodromes.

In all this, the World's Fair was a precise and classic example, for it reproduced in miniature the imperial order. When the panic of 1893 kept people away from the exhibitions of art, industry, and culture, sideshows were promptly introduced by the astute organizers. Beyond the serene classic façades, which recalled the elevation of a Marcus Aurelius, sprawled the barkers, the freaks, and the tricksters, whose gaudy booths might have reminded the spectator of the other side of the imperial shield—the gaminism of Petronius Arbiter. The transformation of these white façades into the Gay White Ways came during the next decade; whilst the sideshows achieved a separate existence as "Coney Island." On top of this came the development of the mildly gladiatorial spectacles of football and baseball: at first invented for playful exercises, they became a standard means of exhibition by more or less professional performers. The erection of numerous amphitheaters and arenas, such as the Yale Bowl, the Harvard Stadium, the Lewisohn Stadium, and their counterparts in the West, rounded out the imperial spectacle.

By a happy congruence of forces, the large-scale manufacture of Portland cement, and the reintroduction of the Roman method of concrete construction, came during the same period. Can anyone contemplate this scene and still fancy that imperialism was nothing more than a move for foreign markets and territories of exploitation? On the contrary, it was a tendency that expressed itself in every department of Western civilization, and if it appears most naked, perhaps, in America, that is only because, as in the earlier periods, there was so little here to stand in its way. Mr. Louis Sullivan might well complain, in The Autobiography of an Idea, that imperialism stifled the more creative modes of architecture which might have derived from our fine achievements in science, from our tentative experiments in democracy. It seems inevitable, however, that the dominant fact in our civilization should stamp the most important monuments and buildings with its image. In justice to the great professors of the classic style, Messrs. McKim and Burnham and Carrere and Hastings, one must admit that the age shaped them and chose them and used them for its ends. Their mode of building was almost unescapably determined by the milieu in which they worked.

The change in the social scene which favored an imperial setting was not without its effects upon the industries that supplied the materials for architecture, and upon the processes of building itself. Financial concentration in the stone quarries, for example, was abetted by the creation of a national system of rail transportation, and partly, perhaps, by the elaboration of the mechanical equipment for cutting and trimming stone beyond a point where a small plant could work economically. The result was that during this period numerous small local quarries, which had been called into existence by Richardson's fine eye for color contrasts, were allowed to lapse. Vermont marble and Indiana limestone served better the traditions that had been created in the White City.

The carrying of coals to Newcastle is always a pathetic practice; it remained for the imperial age to make it a subject for boasting. Just as many Connecticut towns whose nearby fields are full of excellent granite boulders, boast a bank or a library of remote marble, so New York City, which has a solid foundation of schist, gneiss, and limestone, can point to only a handful of buildings, notably the College of the City of New York and Mr. Goodhue's Church of the Intercession, in which these excellent local materials were used. The curious result of being able by means of railway transportation to draw upon the ends of the earth for materials has been, not variety, but monotony. Under the imperial order the architect was forced to design structures that were identical in style, treatment, and material, though they were placed thousands of miles apart and differed in every important function. This ignorance of regional resources is not incompatible with grand effects, or even on occasion with decently good architecture. But it does not profit by that fine adaptation to site, that justness of proportion in the size of window and slope of roof, which is an earnest of the architect's mastery of the local situation. Substitute Manila for the military colony of Timgad, or Los Angeles for Alexandria, and it is plain that we have here another aspect of Ferrero's generalization. Even architects whose place of work was nearer to the site of their buildings were, nevertheless, compelled to copy the style of the more successful practitioners in New York and Chicago.

In government, in industry, in architecture, the imperial age was one. The underlying policy of imperialism is to exploit the life and resources of separate regions for the benefit of the holders of privilege in the capital city. Under this rule, all roads lead literally to Rome. While, as the German historian, W. H. Riehl, points out, the provincial highroads served to bring the city out into the countryside, the railroads served to bring the major cities together and to drain the products of rural regions into the metropolis. It was no accident that the great triumphs of American architecture during the imperial period were the railroad stations; particularly the Pennsylvania and the Grand Central in New York, and the Union Station in Washington. Nor is it by mere chance that the Washington and the Pennsylvania stations are the monuments to two architects, McKim and Burnham, who worshiped most whole-heartedly at the imperial shrine. With capital insight, these men established the American Academy at Rome: they recognized their home.

Esthetically considered, it is true, perhaps, that the finest element in the Pennsylvania station is the train hall, where the architect has dealt sincerely with his steel elements and has not permitted himself to cast a fond, retrospective eye upon the Roman baths. When all allowances are made, however, there remains less for criticism in the railway stations and the stadiums—those genuinely Roman bequests—than in any of the other imperial monuments. Indeed, so well does Roman architecture lend itself to the railroad station that one of the prime virtues of such a building, namely ease of circulation, was even communicated to the New York Public Library, where it is nothing but a nuisance, since it both increases the amount of noise and diminishes the amount of space for reading rooms that are already overcrowded.

Here, indeed, is the capital defect of an established and formalized mode: it tends to make the architect think of a new problem in terms of an old solution for a different problem. Mr. Charles McKim, for example, found himself hampered in the competition over the New York Public Library because the demands of the librarian for a convenient and expeditious administration of his business interfered with the full-blown conception which Mr. McKim had in mind. All this happened after years of demonstration in the Boston Library of Messrs. McKim and White's failure to meet the problem squarely; and it apparently was not affected by Mr. McKim's experience with the great Columbia Library, which has ample space for everything except books. In short, the classic style served well enough only when the building to be erected had some direct relation to the needs and interests of the Roman world—the concourse of idlers in the baths or the tiers of spectators in the circuses and hippodromes. When it came face to face with our own day, it had but little to say, and it said that badly, as anyone who will patiently examine the superimposed orders on the American Telegraph Building in New York will discover for himself.

With the transition from republican to imperial Rome, numerous monuments were erected to the Divine Caesar. Within a much shorter time than marked the growth of the imperial tradition in America, a similar edification of patriotic memories took place.

In the restoration of the original plan of Washington, which began in 1901, the axis of the plan was so altered as to make it pass through the Washington Monument; and at the same time the place of the Lincoln Memorial, designed by the late Mr. Henry Bacon, a pupil of Mr. McKim's, was assigned. This was the first of a whole series of temples devoted to the national deities. In the Lincoln Memorial, in the McKinley Memorial at Niles, Ohio, in the Hall of Fame at New York University, and in their prototype, Grant's Tomb, one feels not the living beauty of our American past, but the mortuary air of archaeology. The America that Lincoln was bred in, the homespun and humane and humorous America that he wished to preserve, has nothing in common with the sedulously classic monument that was erected to his memory. Who lives in that shrine, I wonder—Lincoln, or the men who conceived it: the leader who beheld the mournful victory of the Civil War, or the generation that took pleasure in the mean triumph of the Spanish-American exploit, and placed the imperial standard in the Philippines and the Caribbean?

On the plane of private citizenship, a similar movement took place: while before 1890 one can count the tombs in our cemeteries that boast loudly of the owner's earthly possessions and power, from that time onward the miniature temple-mausoleum becomes more and more frequent. In fact, an entire history of architecture could be deduced from our cemeteries; all that has so far been described could be marked in the progress from the simple slab, carved in almost Attic purity with a weeping willow or a cubistic cherub, that characterized the eighteenth century, to the bad lettering and the more awkward headstones of the early nineteenth century; and from this to the introduction of polished granite and iron ornament in the post-Civil War cemetery, down to the mechanically perfect mausoleum, where the corpses are packed like the occupants of a subway train, that some of our more effusively progressive communities boast of today. As we live, so we die: no wonder Shelley described Hell as a place much like London.

The Roman development of New York, Chicago, Washington, and the lesser metropolises, had an important effect upon the homes of the people. Historically, the imperial monument and the slum-tenement go hand in hand. The same process that creates an unearned increment for the landlords who possess favored sites, contributes a generous quota—which might be called the unearned excrement—of depression, overcrowding, and bad living, in the dormitory districts of the city. This had happened in imperial Rome; it had happened again in Paris under Napoleon III, where Haussmann's sweeping reconstructions created new slums in the districts behind the grand avenues, quite as bad, if far less obvious, as those that had been cleared away; and it happened once again in our American cities. Whereas in Rome a certain limit, however, was placed upon the expansion of the city because of the low development of vehicular traffic, the rise of mechanical transportation placed no bounds at all on the American city. If Rome was forced to create huge engineering projects like aqueducts and sewers in order to cleanse the inhabitants and remove the offal of its congested districts, the American city followed the example of the modern Romes like London and Paris by devising man-sewers, in which the mass of plebeians could be daily drained back and forth between their dormitories and their factories.

So far from relieving congestion, these colossal pieces of engineering only made more of it possible: by pouring more feeder lines into the central district of New York, Boston, Chicago, or where you will, rapid transit increased the housing congestion at one end and the business-congestion at the other. As for the primary sewer system devised for the imperial metropolis, it could scarcely even claim, with rapid transit, that it was a valuable commercial in-vestment. The water outlets of New York are so thoroughly polluted that not merely have the shad and the oyster beds vanished from the Hudson River, where both once flourished, but it is a serious question whether the tides can continue to transport their vast load of sewage without a preliminary reduction of its content. Like the extension of the water conduits into the Adirondacks, all these necessary little improvements add to the per capita cost of living in an imperial metropolis, without providing a single benefit that a smaller city with no need for such improvements does not enjoy. In the matter of public parks, for example, the Committee on Congestion in New York, in 1911, cal-culated that the park space needed for the East Side alone, on the scale provided by the city of Hartford, would be greater than the entire area of Manhattan Island. In short, even for its bare utilitarian requirements, the mass-city, as the Germans call it, costs more and gives less than communities which have not had imperial greatness inflicted upon them.

As to the more positive improvements under the imperial regime, history leaves no doubt as to their dubious character, and current observation only rein-forces history's lesson. In discussing the growth of the tenement in Rome after the Great Fire, Friedlander says:

"The motives for piling up storeys were as strong as ever: the site for Caesar's Forum had cost over £875,000 compensation to tenants and ground landlords. Rome had loftier houses than modern capital. A disproportionately large part of the area available for building was monopolized by the few, in consequence of the waste of space in the plethoric architecture of the day, and a very con-siderable portion was swallowed up by the public places, such as the imperial forums, which took up six hectares, as well as by the traffic regulations and extensions of the streets. The transformation and decoration of Rome by the Caesars enhanced the scarcity of housing, as did Napoleon III's improvements in Paris. A further adjutory cause of the increase in the price of dwellings was the habit of speculation in house property (which Crassus had practiced in great style) and the monopoly of the proprietors, in consequence of which houses were let and sublet."

It would be tedious to draw out the parallel: given similar social conditions in America we have not been able to escape the same social results, even down to the fact that the palliatives of private philanthropy flourish here again as they had not flourished anywhere on the same scale since the Roman Empire.

So much for imperial greatness. When an architect like Mr. Edward Bennett can say, as he did in The Significance of the Fine Arts: "House the people densely, if necessary, but conserve great acres for recreation," we need not be in doubt as to who will profit by the density and who will profit, at the other end, by the recreation. It is not merely that the park must be produced to remedy the congestion: it is even more that the congestion must be produced in order to provide for the park. To profit by both the disease and the remedy is one of the masterstrokes of imperialist enterprise. Mr. Daniel Burnham said of the World's Fair, according to Mr. Bennett and Mr. Charles Moore, "that it is what the Romans would have wished to create in permanent form." One may say of our imperial cities that they are what the Romans did create—but whether the form will be permanent or not is a matter we may leave to the sardonic attentions of history.

For my own part, I think we have at last acquired a criterion which will enable us to sum up the architecture of the imperial age, and deal justly with these railroad stations and stadiums, these sewers and circuses, these aqueducts and parkways and grand avenues. Our imperial architecture is an architecture of compensation: it provides grandiloquent stones for people who have been deprived of bread and sunlight and all that keeps man from becoming vile. Behind the monumental façades of our metropolises trudges a landless proletariat, doomed to the servile routine of the factory system; and beyond the great cities lies a countryside whose goods are drained away, whose children are uprooted from the soil on the prospect of easy gain and endless amusements, and whose remaining cultivators are steadily drifting into the ranks of an abject tenantry. This is not a casual observation: it is the translation of the last three census reports into plain English. Can one take the pretensions of this architecture seriously; can one worry about its esthetics or take delight in such forms as Mr. Pope's Temple of the Scottish Rite in Washington, or Mr. Bacon's Lincoln Memorial? Yes, perhaps—if one refuses to look beyond the mask.

Even in some of its proudest buildings, the imperial show wears thin; and one need not peer into the slums beyond in order to realize its defects. The rear of the Metropolitan Museum or the Brooklyn Museum, for example, might be the rear of a row of Bronx tenements or Long Island City factories, so gaunt and barren and hideous is their aspect. If the imperial age was foreshadowed in the World's Fair, it has received its apotheosis in the museum. In contrast to the local museums one still finds occasionally in Europe, which are little more than extensions of the local curio cabinet, the imperial museum is essentially a loot-heap, a comprehensive repository for plunder. The sage Viollet-le-Duc once patly said that he preferred to see his apples hanging on a tree, rather than arranged in rows in the fruit shops; but the animus of the museum is to value the plucked fruit more than the tree that bore it.

Into the museum come the disjecta membra of other lands, other cultures, other civilizations. All that had once been a living faith and practice is here reduced to a separate specimen, pattern, or form. For the museum, the world of art has already been created: the future is restricted to a duplication of the perfected past. This animus is identic with that which made the Romans so skillful in copying Greek statues and so dull in carving their own; a desirable habit of humility were it not for the fact that the works of art in the past could not have been created had our ancestors been so punctual in respect to finished designs. The one thing the museum cannot attempt to do is to supply a soil for living art: all that it can present is a pattern for reproduction. To the extent that an insincere or imitative art is better than no art at all, the Imperial Age marked an advance: to the extent, however, that a living art is a fresh gesture of the spirit, the museum confessed all too plainly that the age had no fresh gestures to make; on that score, it was a failure, and the copying of period furniture and the design of period architecture were the livid proofs of that failure.

The museum is a manifestation of our curiosity, our acquisitiveness, our essentially predatory culture; and these qualities were copiously exhibited in the architecture of imperialism. It would be foolish to reproach the great run of architects for exploiting the characteristics of their age; for even those who in belief and design have remained outside the age—such resolute advocates of a medieval polity as Dr. Ralph Adams Cram—have not been able to divert its currents. In so far as we have learned to care more for empire than for a community of freemen living the good life, more for dominion over palm and pine than for the humane discipline of ourselves, the architect has but enshrined our desires. The opulence, the waste of resources and energies, the perversion of human effort represented in this architecture are but the outcome of our general scheme of working and living. Architecture, like government, is about as good as a community deserves. The shell that we create for ourselves marks our spiritual development as plainly as that of a snail denotes its species. If sometimes architecture becomes frozen music, we have ourselves to thank when it is a pompous blare of meaningless sounds.

BERNARD SHAW

Handel's Messiah and Beethoven's Centenary[1]

Handel's Messiah

Christmas being the season of mirth, music, the great English killjoy, with its intolerable hypocrisies, is gladly put away until it is time to return to work and duty and mental improvement and other unpleasantnesses; consequently

[1] From *Shaw on Music: A Selection from the Music Criticism of Shaw*, by Eric Bentley (New York: Anchor Books, Doubleday & Company, Inc., 1955), pp. 245-252, 83-89. Reprinted by permission of The Public Trustee and The Society of Authors.

my critical machinery has got out of gear somewhat. I might have kept off the rust by attending the regulation Christmas performance of *The Messiah*; but I have long since recognized the impossibility of obtaining justice for that work in a Christian country. Import a choir of heathens, restrained by no considerations of propriety from attacking the choruses with unembarrassed sincerity of dramatic expression, and I would hasten to the performance if only to witness the delight of the public and the discomfiture of the critics. That is, if anything so indecent would be allowed here. We have all had our Handelian training in church, and the perfect churchgoing mood is one of pure abstract reverence. A mood of active intelligence would be scandalous. Thus we get broken in to the custom of singing Handel as if he meant nothing; and as it happens that he meant a great deal, and was tremendously in earnest about it, we know rather less about him in England than they do in the Andaman Islands, since the Andamans are only unconscious of him, whereas we are misconscious. To hear a thousand respectable young English persons jogging through *For He shall purify the sons of Levi* as if every group of semiquavers were a whole bar of four crotchets a capella, or repeating *Let Him deliver Him if He delight in Him* with exactly the same subdued and uncovered air as in *For with His stripes we are healed,* or lumbering along with *Hallelujah* as if it were a superior sort of family coach: all this is ludicrous enough; but when the nation proceeds to brag of these unwieldy choral impostures, these attempts to make the brute force of a thousand throats do what can only be done by artistic insight and skill, then I really lose patience. Why, instead of wasting huge sums on the multitudinous dullness called a Handel Festival does not somebody set up a thoroughly rehearsed and exhaustively studied performance of *The Messiah* in St. James's Hall with a chorus of twenty capable artists? Most of us would be glad to hear the work seriously performed once before we die.

However, if I did not go to *The Messiah*, I ventured on a pantomime, although in London we are unable to produce an endurable pantomime for exactly the same reasons that prevent us from achieving an endurable performance of *The Messiah*. Therefore I did not make the experiment in London. I found myself one evening in Bristol with nothing better to do than to see whether pantomime is really moribund. I am bound to say that it seems to me to be as lively as it was twenty-five years ago. The fairy queen, singing In Old Madrid with reckless irrelevance at the entrance to the cave where Aladdin found the lamp, was listened to with deep respect as an exponent of the higher singing; and in the cave itself The Bogie Man, in about fifty verses, took immensely. A street scene at night, with Chinese lanterns and a willow-pattern landscape, were stage pictures with just the right artistic quality for the occasion; and the absurdity of the whole affair on the dramatic side was amusing enough from an indulgent holiday point of view. There were no processions presenting one silly idea and over again in different colored tights, until a thousand pounds had been wasted in boring the audience to distraction. And— though here I hardly expect to be believed—there was not a single child under ten on the stage. I told Mr. Macready Chute, the manager, that he should come to London to learn from our famous stage-managers here how to spend ten times as much money on a pantomime for one-tenth of the artistic return. I bade him, if he thirsted for metropolitan fame, to take for his triple motto, Expenditure, inanity, vulgarity, and that soon no spectacular piece would be deemed complete without him. With these precepts I left him, assuring him that I felt more than ever what a privilege it was to live in a convenient art-centre like London, where the nearest pantomime is at Bristol, and the nearest opera at Bayreuth.

21 January 1891

The Messiah Again

Fundamentally my view of the Handel Festival is that of a convinced and ardent admirer of Handel. My favorite oratorio is *The Messiah*, with which I have spent many of the hours which others give to Shakespeare, or Scott, or Dickens. But for all this primary bias in favor of Handel, my business is still to be that of the critic, who, invited to pronounce an opinion on the merits of a performance by four thousand executants, must judge these abnormal conditions by their effect on the work as open-mindedly as if there were only four hundred, or forty, or four. And I am bound to add that he who, so judging, delivers a single and unqualified verdict on the Festival, stultifies himself. The very same conditions which make one choral number majestic, imposing, even sublime, make another heavy, mechanical, meaningless. For instance, no host could be too mighty for the Hallelujah Chorus, or See the Conquering Hero. In them every individual chorister knows without study or instruction what he has to do and how he has to feel. The impulse to sing spreads even to the audience; and those who are old hands at choral singing do not always restrain it.

I saw more than one of my neighbors joining in the Hallelujah on the first day; and if my feelings at that moment had permitted me to make a properly controlled artistic effort, I think I should have been no more able to remain silent than Santley was. Under the circumstances, however, I followed the example of Albani, who, knowing that she had to save her voice for *I know that my Redeemer liveth*, kept a vocal score tightly on her mouth the whole time, and looked over it with the expression of a child confronted with some intolerably tempting sweetmeat which it knows it must not touch.

But *The Messiah* is not all Hallelujah. Compare such a moment as I have just described with the experience of listening to the fiercely tumultuous *He trusted in God*, with its alternations of sullen mockery with high-pitched derision, and its savage shouts of *Let Him deliver Him if He delight in Him*, jogging along at about half the proper speed, with an expression of the deepest respect and propriety, as if a large body of the leading citizens, headed by the mayor, were presenting a surpassingly dull address to somebody. There may be, in the way of the proper presentation of such a chorus as this, something of the difficulty which confronted Wagner at the rehearsals of Tannhäuser in Paris in

1861, when he asked the ballet master to make his forces attack the Bacchanal in a bacchanalian way. "I understand perfectly what you mean," said the functionary; "but only to a whole ballet of *premiers sujets* dare I breathe such suggestions."

No doubt Mr. Manns's three thousand five hundred choristers might better his instructions so heartily as to go considerably beyond the utmost licence of art if he told them that unless they sang that chorus like a howling bloodthirsty mob, the utter loneliness of *Thy rebuke hath broken his heart*, and *Behold and see*, must be lost, and with it the whole force of the tragic climax of the oratorio. Besides which, there is the physical difficulty, which only a skilled and powerful orator could fully surmount, of giving instruction of that kind to such a host. But I see no reason why matters should not be vastly improved if Mr. Manns would adopt throughout the bolder policy as to speed which was forced on him after four on Selection day by the silent urgency of the clock, and persisted in to some extent—always with convincing effect—in Israel. Increased speed, however, is not all that is wanted. To get rid completely of the insufferable lumbering which is the curse of English Handelian choral singing, a spirited reform in style is needed.

For instance, Handel, in his vigorous moods, is fond of launching the whole mass of voices into florid passages of great brilliancy and impetuosity. In one of the most splendid choruses in *The Messiah, For He shall purify the sons of Levi*, the syllable "fy" comes out in a single trait consisting of no less than thirty-two semiquavers. That trait should be sung with one impulse from end to end without an instant's hesitation. How is it actually done in England? Just as if the thirty-two semiquavers were eight bars of crotchets taken alla breve in a not very lively tempo. The effect, of course, is to make the chorus so dull that all the reputation of Handel is needed to persuade Englishmen that they ought to enjoy it, whilst Frenchmen go away from our festivals confirmed in their skepticism as to our pet musical classic. When I had been listening for some minutes on Wednesday to the festival choristers trudging with ludicrous gravity through what they called *Tellit Outa Mongthe Hea-ea Then*, I could not help wishing that Santley, who roused them to boundless enthusiasm by his singing of *Why do the nations*, had given them a taste of their own quality by delivering those chains of triplets on the words "rage" and "counsel," as quavers in twelve-eight time in the tempo of the Pastoral Symphony. The celestial *Lift up your heads, O ye gates*, lost half its triumphant exultation from this heaviness of gait.

Again, in the beginning of *For unto us*, the tenors and basses told each other the news in a prosaic, methodical way which made the chorus quite comic until the thundering *Wonderful, Counsellor*, one of Handel's mightiest strokes, was reached; and even here the effect was disappointing, because the chorus, having held nothing in reserve, could make no climax. The orchestra needed at that point about twenty more of the biggest of big drums. Another lost opportunity was the pathetically grand conclusion of *All we like sheep*.

Nothing in the whole work needs to be sung with more intense expression than *But the Lord hath laid on Him the iniquity of us all*. Unless it sounds as if the singers were touched to their very hearts, they had better not sing it at all. On that Monday it came as mechanically as if the four entries of the voices had been produced by drawing four stops in an organ. This was the greater pity, because it must be conceded to our young Handel-sceptics that the preceding musical portraiture of the sheep going astray has no great claims on their reverence.

I am aware that many people who feel the shortcomings of our choral style bear with it under the impression, first, that the English people are naturally too slow and shy in their musical ways, and, second, that bravura vocalization and impetuous speed are not possible or safe with large choruses. To this I reply, first, that the natural fault of the English when they are singing with genuine feeling is not slowness, but rowdiness, as the neighbors of the Salvation Army know; second, that it would undoubtedly be as risky to venture far in the bravura direction with a very small chorus as to attempt the Walküre fire-music or Liszt's Mazeppa in an ordinary theatre orchestra with its little handful of strings. But both these compositions are safe with sixteen first and sixteen second violins, because, though notes are dropped and mistakes made, they are not all made simultaneously, and the result is that at any given instant an overwhelming majority of the violins are right. For the same reason, I do not see why nine hundred basses, even if they were the stiffest and slowest in the world, could not be safely sent at full speed in the bravura style through Handel's easy diatonic semiquaver traits, as safely as our violinists are now sent through Wagner's demisemiquavers.

So much for the compatibility of speed with accuracy. As to safety, I need only appeal to the results achieved by Mr. Manns on Friday, when he got away from *The Messiah*, which is too sentimental for him, to *Israel*, which is far more congenial to his temperament. The only choral number in this which was quite unsatisfactory was *I will exalt Him*; and here the shortcoming was made unavoidable by the peculiar style of the chorus, since it—like *And with His stripes* in *The Messiah*—requires a beauty of execution which would suffice for a mass by Palestrina, and which is out of the question under Handel Festival conditions. The other choruses were spirited and forcible—some of them magnificent. *He gave them hailstones*, *But the waters overwhelmed*, and *The horse and his rider* were tremendous: one felt after them that the festival had justified its existence beyond all cavil.

If these criticisms are to bear any fruit in raising the festival performances of *The Messiah* to a typical artistic perfection—a result which I believe to be quite possible, and certainly well worth striving for—they must be weighed, not by Mr. Manns or the Crystal Palace authorities, but by the local conductors throughout the country, who coach their contingents in the work, and send them up with preconceived ideas as to its execution which Mr. Manns is powerless to change or even greatly to modify. Every contingent trained by a mere organist, to whom *The Messiah* is but a part of the drudgery of his professional routine, is simply a nuisance on the Handel orchestra. And every contingent trained by an artist who ranks the work among his treasures, and part of whose artistic ambition it is to hear at last in England a really adequate performance of it, is, as Judas Maccabeus says, "a thousand men."

1 July 1891

Beethoven's Centenary

A hundred years ago a crusty old bachelor of fifty-seven, so deaf that he could not hear his own music played by a full orchestra, yet still able to hear thunder, shook his fist at the roaring heavens for the last time, and died as he had lived, challenging God and defying the universe. He was Defiance Incarnate: he could not even meet a Grand Duke and his court in the street without jamming his hat tight down on his head and striding through the very middle of them. He had the manners of a disobliging steamroller (most steamrollers are abjectly obliging and conciliatory); and he was rather less particular about his dress than a scarecrow: in fact he was once arrested as a tramp because the police refused to believe that such a tatterdemalion could be a famous composer, much less a temple of the most turbulent spirit that ever found expression in pure sound. It was indeed a mighty spirit; but if I had written the mightiest, which would mean mightier than the spirit of Handel, Beethoven himself would have rebuked me; and what mortal man could pretend to a spirit mightier than Bach's? But that Beethoven's spirit was the most turbulent is beyond all question. The impetuous fury of his strength, which he could quite easily contain and control, but often would not, and the unroariousness of his fun, go beyond anything of the kind to be found in the works of other composers. Greenhorns write of syncopation now as if it were a new way of giving the utmost impetus to a musical measure; but the rowdiest jazz sounds like *The Maiden's Prayer* after Beethoven's third *Leonora* overture; and certainly no negro corobbery that I ever heard could inspire the blackest dancer with such *diable au corps* as the last movement of the *Seventh Symphony*. And no other composer has ever melted his hearers into complete sentimentality by the tender beauty of his music, and then suddenly turned on them and mocked them with derisive trumpet blasts for being such fools. Nobody but Beethoven could govern Beethoven; and when, as happened when the fit was on him, he deliberately refused to govern himself, he was ungovernable.

It was this turbulence, this deliberate disorder, this mockery, this reckless and triumphant disregard of conventional manners, that set Beethoven apart from the musical geniuses of the ceremonious seventeenth and eighteenth centuries. He was a giant wave in that storm of the human spirit which produced the French Revolution. He called no man master. Mozart, his greatest predecessor in his own department, had from his childhood been washed, combed, splendidly dressed, and beautifully behaved in the presence of royal personages and peers. His childish outburst at the Pompadour, "Who is this woman who does not kiss me? The Queen kisses me," would be incredible of Beethoven, who was still an unlicked cub even when he had grown into a very grizzly bear. Mozart had the refinement of convention and society as well as the refinement of nature and of the solitudes of the soul. Mozart and Gluck are refined as the court of Louis XIV was refined: Haydn is refined as the most cultivated country gentlemen of his day were refined: compared to them socially Beethoven was an obstreperous Bohemian: a man of the people. Haydn, so superior to envy that he declared his junior, Mozart, to be the greatest composer that ever lived, could not stand Beethoven: Mozart, more farseeing, listened to his playing, and said "You will hear of him some day"; but the two would never have hit it off together had Mozart lived long enough to try. Beethoven had a moral horror of Mozart, who in *Don Giovanni* had thrown a halo of enchantment round an aristocratic blackguard, and then, with the unscrupulous moral versatility of a born dramatist, turned round to cast a halo of divinity round Sarastro, setting his words to the only music yet written that would not sound out of place in the mouth of God.

Beethoven was no dramatist: moral versatility was to him revolting cynicism. Mozart was still to him the master of masters (this is not an empty eulogistic superlative: it means literally that Mozart is a composer's composer much more than he has ever been a really popular composer); but he was a court flunkey in breeches whilst Beethoven was a Sansculotte; and Haydn also was a flunkey in the old livery: the Revolution stood between them as it stood between the eighteenth and nineteenth centuries. But to Beethoven Mozart was worse than Haydn because he trifled with morality by setting vice to music as magically as virtue. The Puritan who is in every true Sansculotte rose up against him in Beethoven, though Mozart had shewn him all the possibilities of nineteenth-century music. So Beethoven cast back for a hero to Handel, another crusty old bachelor of his own kidney, who despised Mozart's hero Gluck, though the pastoral symphony in *The Messiah* is the nearest thing in music to the scenes in which Gluck, in his Orfeo, opened to us the plains of Heaven.

Thanks to broadcasting, millions of musical novices will hear the music of Beethoven this anniversary year for the first time with their expectations raised to an extraordinary pitch by hundreds of newspaper articles piling up all the conventional eulogies that are applied indiscriminately to all the great composers. And like his contemporaries they will be puzzled by getting from him not merely a music that they did not expect, but often an orchestral hurlyburly that they may not recognize as what they call music at all, though they can appreciate Gluck and Haydn and Mozart quite well. The explanation is simple enough. The music of the eighteenth century is all dance music. A dance is a symmetrical pattern of steps that are pleasant to move to; and its music is a symmetrical pattern of sound that is pleasant to listen to even when you are not dancing to it. Consequently the sound patterns, though they begin by being as simple as chessboards, get lengthened and elaborated and enriched with harmonies until they are more like Persian carpets; and the composers who design these patterns no longer expect people to dance to them. Only a whirling Dervish could dance a Mozart symphony: indeed, I have reduced two young and practised dancers to exhaustion by making them dance a Mozart overture. The very names of the dances are dropped: instead of suites consisting of sarabands, pavanes, gavottes, and jigs, the designs are presented as sonatas and symphonies consisting of sections called simply movements, and labelled according to their speed (in Italian) as allegros, adagios, scherzos, and prestos. But all the time, from Bach's preludes to Mozart's *Jupiter Symphony*, the music makes a symmetrical sound pattern, and gives us the dancer's pleasure always as the form and foundation of the piece.

Music, however, can do more than make beautiful sound patterns. It can express emotion. You can look at a Persian carpet and listen to a Bach prelude with a delicious admiration that goes no further than itself; but you cannot listen to the overture to *Don Giovanni* without being thrown into a complicated mood which prepares you for a tragedy of some terrible doom overshadowing an exquisite but Satanic gaiety. If you listen to the last movement of Mozart's *Jupiter Symphony*, you hear that it is as much a riotous corobbery as the last movement of Beethoven's *Seventh Symphony*: it is an orgy of ranting drumming tow-row-row, made poignant by an opening strain of strange and painful beauty which is woven through the pattern all through. And yet the movement is a masterpiece of pattern designing all the time.

Now what Beethoven did, and what made some of his greatest contemporaries give him up as a madman with lucid intervals of clowning and bad taste, was that he used music altogether as a means of expressing moods, and completely threw over pattern designing as an end in itself. It is true that he used the old patterns all his life with dogged conservatism (another Sansculotte characteristic, by the way); but he imposed on them such an overwhelming charge of human energy and passion, including that highest passion which accompanies thought, and reduces the passion of the physical appetites to mere animalism, that he not only played Old Harry with their symmetry but often made it impossible to notice that there was any pattern at all beneath the storm of emotion. *The Eroica Symphony* begins by a pattern (borrowed from an overture which Mozart wrote when he was a boy), followed by a couple more very pretty patterns; but they are tremendously energized, and in the middle of the movement the patterns are torn up savagely; and Beethoven, from the point of view of the mere pattern musician, goes raving mad, hurling out terrible chords in which all the notes of the scale are sounded simultaneously, just because he feels like that, and wants you to feel like it.

And there you have the whole secret of Beethoven. He could design patterns with the best of them; he could write music whose beauty will last you all your life; he could take the driest sticks of themes and work them up so interestingly that you find something new in them at the hundredth hearing: in short, you can say of him all that you can say of the greatest pattern composers; but his diagnostic, the thing that marks him out from all the others, is his disturbing quality, his power of unsettling us and imposing his giant moods on us. Berlioz was very angry with an old French composer who expressed the discomfort Beethoven gave him by saying *"J'aime la musique qui me berce,"* "I like music that lulls me." Beethoven's is music that wakes you up; and the one mood in which you shrink from it is the mood in which you want to be let alone.

When you understand this you will advance beyond the eighteenth century and the old-fashioned dance band (jazz, by the way, is the old dance band Beethovenized), and understand not only Beethoven's music, but what is deepest in post-Beethoven music as well.

From the Radio Times
18 March 1927

AARON COPLAND

How We Listen[1]

We all listen to music according to our separate capacities. But, for the sake of analysis, the whole listening process may become clearer if we break it up into its component parts, so to speak. In a certain sense we all listen to music on three separate planes. For lack of a better terminology, one might name these: (1) the sensuous plane, (2) the expressive plane, (3) the sheerly musical plane. The only advantage to be gained from mechanically splitting up the listening process into these hypothetical planes is the clearer view to be had of the way in which we listen.

The simplest way of listening to music is to listen for the sheer pleasure of the musical sound itself. That is the sensuous plane. It is the plane on which we hear music without thinking, without considering it in any way. One turns on the radio while doing something else and absent-mindedly bathes in the sound. A kind of brainless but attractive state of mind is engendered by the mere sound appeal of the music.

You may be sitting in a room reading this book. Imagine one note struck on the piano. Immediately that one note is enough to change the atmosphere of the room—proving that the sound element in music is a powerful and mysterious agent, which it would be foolish to deride or belittle.

The surprising thing is that many people who consider themselves qualified music lovers abuse that plane in listening. They go to concerts in order to lose themselves. They use music as a consolation or an escape. They enter an

[1] With permission of the publishers from *What to Listen for in Music*, Revised Edition by Aaron Copland. Copyright © 1957 by the McGraw-Hill Book Company, Inc.

ideal world where one doesn't have to think of the realities of everyday life. Of course they aren't thinking about the music either. Music allows them to leave it, and they go off to a place to dream, dreaming because of and apropos of the music yet never quite listening to it.

Yes, the sound appeal of music is a potent and primitive force, but you must not allow it to usurp a disproportionate share of your interest. The sensuous plane is an important one in music, a very important one, but it does not constitute the whole story.

There is no need to digress further on the sensuous plane. Its appeal to every normal human being is self-evident. There is, however, such a thing as becoming more sensitive to the different kinds of sound stuff as used by various composers. For all composers do not use that sound stuff in the same way. Don't get the idea that the value of music is commensurate with its sensuous appeal or that the loveliest sounding music is made by the greatest composer. If that were so, Ravel would be a greater creator than Beethoven. The point is that the sound element varies with each composer, that his usage of sound forms an integral part of his style and must be taken into account when listening. The reader can see, therefore, that a more conscious approach is valuable even on this primary plane of music listening.

The second plane on which music exists is what I have called the expressive one. Here, immediately, we tread on controversial ground. Composers have a way of shying away from any discussion of music's expressive side. Did not Stravinsky himself proclaim that his music was an "object," a "thing," with a life of its own, and with no other meaning than its own purely musical existence? This intransigent attitude of Stravinsky's may be due to the fact that so many people have tried to read different meanings into so many pieces. Heaven knows it is difficult enough to say precisely what it is that a piece of music means, to say it definitely, to say it finally so that everyone is satisfied with your explanation. But that should not lead one to the other extreme of denying to music the right to be "expressive."

My own belief is that all music has an expressive power, some more and some less, but that all music has a certain meaning behind the notes and that that meaning behind the notes constitutes, after all, what the piece is saying, what the piece is about. This whole problem can be stated quite simply by asking, "Is there a meaning to music?" My answer to that would be, "Yes." And "Can you state in so many words what the meaning is?" My answer to that would be, "No." Therein lies the difficulty.

Simple-minded souls will never be satisfied with the answer to the second of these questions. They always want music to have a meaning, and the more concrete it is the better they like it. The more the music reminds them of a train, a storm, a funeral, or any other familiar conception the more expressive it appears to be to them. This popular idea of music's meaning—stimulated and abetted by the usual run of musical commentator—should be discouraged wherever and whenever it is met. One timid lady once confessed to me that she suspected something seriously lacking in her appreciation of music because of her inability to connect it with anything definite. That is getting the whole thing backward, of course.

Still, the question remains, How close should the intelligent music lover wish to come to pinning a definite meaning to any particular work? No closer than a general concept, I should say. Music expresses, at different moments, serenity or exuberance, regret or triumph, fury or delight. It expresses each of these moods, and many others, in a numberless variety of subtle shadings and differences. It may even express a state of meaning for which there exists no adequate word in any language. In that case, musicians often like to say that it has only a purely musical meaning. They sometimes go farther and say that *all* music has only a purely musical meaning. What they really mean is that no appropriate word can be found to express the music's meaning and that, even if it could, they do not feel the need of finding it.

But whatever the professional musician may hold, most musical novices still search for specific words with which to pin down their musical reactions. That is why they always find Tschaikovsky easier to "understand" than Beethoven. In the first place, it is easier to pin a meaning-word on a Tschaikovsky piece than on a Beethoven one. Much easier. Moreover, with the Russian composer, every time you come back to a piece of his it almost always says the same thing to you, whereas with Beethoven it is often quite difficult to put your finger right on what he is saying. And any musician will tell you that that is why Beethoven is the greater composer. Because music which always says the same thing to you will necessarily soon become dull music, but music whose meaning is slightly different with each hearing has a greater chance of remaining alive.

Listen, if you can, to the forty-eight fugue themes of Bach's *Well Tempered Clavichord*. Listen to each theme, one after another. You will soon realize that each theme mirrors a different world of feeling. You will also soon realize that the more beautiful a theme seems to you the harder it is to find any word that will describe it to your complete satisfaction. Yes, you will certainly know whether it is a gay theme or a sad one. You will be able, in other words, in your own mind, to draw a frame of emotional feeling around your theme. Now study the sad one a little closer. Try to pin down the exact quality of its sadness. Is it pessimistically sad or resignedly sad; is it fatefully sad or smilingly sad?

Let us suppose that you are fortunate and can describe to your own satisfaction in so many words the exact meaning of your chosen theme. There is still no guarantee that anyone else will be satisfied. Nor need they be. The important thing is that each one feel for himself the specific expressive quality of a theme or, similarly, an entire piece of music. And if it is a great work of art, don't expect it to mean exactly the same thing to you each time you return to it.

Themes or pieces need not express only one emotion, of course. Take such a theme as the first main one of the *Ninth Symphony*, for example. It is clearly made up of different elements. It does not say only one thing. Yet anyone hearing it immediately gets a feeling of strength, a feeling of power. It isn't a power that comes simply because the theme is played loudly. It is a power inherent in the theme itself. The extraordinary strength and vigor of the theme results in the listener's receiving an impression that a forceful statement has been made. But one should never try to boil it down to "the fateful hammer of life," etc. That is where the trouble begins. The musician, in his exasperation, says it means nothing but the notes themselves, whereas the nonprofessional is only too anxious to hang on to any explanation that gives him the illusion of getting closer to the music's meaning.

Now, perhaps, the reader will know better what I mean when I say that music does have an expressive meaning but that we cannot say in so many words what that meaning is.

The third plane on which music exists is the sheerly musical plane. Besides the pleasurable sound of music and the expressive feeling that it gives off, music does exist in terms of the notes themselves and of their manipulation. Most listeners are not sufficiently conscious of this third plane. It will be largely the business of this book to make them more aware of music on this plane.

Professional musicians, on the other hand, are, if anything, too conscious of the mere notes themselves. They often fall into the error of becoming so engrossed with their arpeggios and staccatos that they forget the deeper aspects of the music they are performing. But from the layman's standpoint, it is not so much a matter of getting over bad habits on the sheerly musical plane as of increasing one's awareness of what is going on, in so far as the notes are concerned.

When the man in the street listens to the "notes themselves" with any degree of concentration, he is most likely to make some mention of the melody. Either he hears a pretty melody or he does not, and he generally lets it go at that. Rhythm is likely to gain his attention next, particularly if it seems exciting. But harmony and tone color are generally taken for granted, if they are thought of consciously at all. As for music's having a definite form of some kind, that idea seems never to have occurred to him.

It is very important for all of us to become more alive to music on its sheerly musical plane. After all, an actual musical material is being used. The intelligent listener must be prepared to increase his awareness of the musical material and what happens to it. He must hear the melodies, the rhythms, the harmonies, the tone colors in a more conscious fashion. But above all he must, in order to follow the line of the composer's thought, know something of the principles of musical form. Listening to all of these elements is listening on the sheerly musical plane.

Let me repeat that I have split up mechanically the three separate planes on which we listen merely for the sake of greater clarity. Actually, we never listen on one or the other of these planes. What we do is to correlate them—listening in all three ways at the same time. It takes no mental effort, for we do it instinctively.

Perhaps an analogy with what happens to us when we visit the theater will make this instinctive correlation clearer. In the theater, you are aware of the actors and actresses, costumes and sets, sounds and movements. All these give one the sense that the theater is a pleasant place to be in. They constitute the sensuous plane in our theatrical reactions.

The expressive plane in the theater would be derived from the feeling that you get from what is happening on the stage. You are moved to pity, excitement, or gayety. It is this general feeling, generated aside from the particular words being spoken, a certain emotional something which exists on the stage, that is analogous to the expressive quality in music.

The plot and plot development is equivalent to our sheerly musical plane. The playwright creates and develops a character in just the same way that a composer creates and develops a theme. According to the degree of your awareness of the way in which the artist in either field handles his material will you become a more intelligent listener.

It is easy enough to see that the theatergoer never is conscious of any of these elements separately. He is aware of them all at the same time. The same is true of music listening. We simultaneously and without thinking listen on all three planes.

In a sense, the ideal listener is both inside and outside the music at the same moment, judging it and enjoying it, wishing it would go one way and watching it go another—almost like the composer at the moment he composes it; because in order to write his music, the composer must also be inside and outside his music, carried away by it and yet coldly critical of it. A subjective and objective attitude is implied in both creating and listening to music.

What the reader should strive for, then, is a more *active* kind of listening. Whether you listen to Mozart or Duke Ellington, you can deepen your understanding of music only by being a more conscious and aware listener—not someone who is just listening, but someone who is listening *for* something.

ARTHUR KOESTLER

Cultural Snobbery[1]

A friend of mine, whom I shall call Brenda, was given for her birthday by one of her admirers a Picasso line drawing in a simple modern frame. It was an admirable and typical sample of Picasso's "classical" period: a Greek youth

[1] From *The Anchor Review Number One*, ed. Melvin J. Lasky (Garden City, N.Y.: Doubleday Anchor Books, 1955), pp. 3-14. Reprinted by permission of A. D. Peters.

carrying a girl in his arms, the contours of the two figures somehow mixed up and partly indistinguishable like those of Siamese twins with shared limbs, yet adding up to a charming and harmonious total effect. It looked like a lithograph, but it bore no serial number, so Brenda took it to be a reproduction and hung it, somewhat disappointed with the gift, over her staircase. On my next visit, several weeks later, it was hanging over her drawing room mantelpiece. "I see the Picasso reproduction has been promoted," I said. "*Reproduction!*" she cried indignantly. "It turned out it's an *original!* Isn't it lovely? Look at that line along the girl's hip . . . . ," etc.

As a matter of fact, it *was* an original—a shyly understated gift of the mumbling and devoted admirer. But as it was a line drawing consisting of nothing but black contour on white paper, it needed an expert, or at least a good magnifying lens, to decide whether it was an original, a lithograph, or a reproduction. Neither Brenda nor any of her visitors could tell the difference. But they took it for granted, as we all do, that an original deserves a proud display, whereas a reproduction belongs, at best, over the staircase.

I shall now try to analyze, in a pedantic way, the reason for this apparently so natural attitude. The original is of course many times more expensive than a reproduction; but we would indignantly reject the idea of displaying a picture simply because it is expensive; we pretend to be guided in these matters by purely aesthetic considerations. Next, one might surmise that our contempt for reproductions originates in the poor quality and even poorer choice of subjects of the Victorian print. But modern printing techniques have achieved miracles, and some Ganymede reproductions are almost indistinguishable from the original. In the extreme case of the line drawing, we have complete aesthetic equivalence between original and reproduction.

And yet there is something revolting in this equivalence. It even takes a certain courage to admit to oneself that the aesthetic effect of a copy might be indistinguishable from that of the original. We live in an age of stereotyped mass production; and after mass-produced furniture, mass-produced and prefabricated houses, the idea of mass-produced Piero della Francescas is indeed revolting. But then, we have no similar objection to mass-produced gramophone records. Nor to mass-produced books, and yet they too fall into the category of "reproductions." Why then do you prefer, according to your income, a more or less second-rate original picture on the wall to a first-rate reproduction of a masterpiece? Would you rather read a mediocre young poet in manuscript than Shakespeare in a paper-cover edition?

Our argument seems to have become bogged down. Let us find out what Brenda herself has to say to explain her behavior, in a dialogue with the writer:

BRENDA: "I simply can't understand what all this fuss and talk is about. But *of course* my attitude to the drawing has changed since I know that Picasso himself did it. That's nothing to do with snobbery—it's just that I wasn't told before."

K: "Your attitude has changed—but has that thing on the wall changed?"

B: "Of course it hasn't, but now I *see* it differently!"

K: "I would like to understand what it is that determines your attitude to a picture in general."

B: "Its quality, of course."

K: "And what determines its quality?"

B: "Oh, don't be such a pedant. Color, composition, balance, harmony, power, what have you."

K: "So, in looking at a picture, you are guided by purely aesthetic value judgments, depending on the qualities you mentioned?"

B: "Of course I am."

K: "Now, as that picture hasn't changed, and its qualities haven't changed, how can your attitude have changed?"

B: "But I have told you before, you idiot. Of course my attitude to it is now different, since I know it isn't one reproduction in a million, but done by Picasso himself. Can't you see?"

K: "No, I can't; you are contradicting yourself. The rarity of the object, and your knowledge of the manner in which it came into being, do not alter the qualities of that object, and accordingly should not alter your judgment of it, if it were really based on purely aesthetic criteria—as you believe it to be. But it isn't. Your judgment is not based on what you *see*, but on a purely accidental bit of information, which might be right or wrong and is entirely extraneous to the issue."

B: "Wrong? How *dare* you insinuate that my Picasso isn't an original? And how *dare* you say that the question whether he drew it himself is 'extraneous' to the issue?"

And so it will go on indefinitely. Yet Brenda is not stupid; she is merely confused in believing that her attitude to an object of art is determined by purely aesthetic considerations, whereas in fact it is decisively influenced by factors of a quite different order. She is unable to see her picture isolated from the context of her knowledge of its origin. For, in our minds, the question of origin, authorship, or authenticity, *though in itself extraneous to aesthetic value,* is so intimately and indistinguishably fused with our attitude to the object that we find it well-nigh impossible to isolate the two. Thus, Brenda unconsciously projects one scale of values onto a system of quite different values.

Is Brenda, then, a snob? It depends on the definition of snobbery at which we hope to arrive at the end. But as a working hypothesis, I would like to suggest that this process of unconsciously applying to any given field a judgment derived from an alien system of values constitutes the essence of the phenomenon of snobbery. By these standards Brenda would *not* be a snob if she had said: "The reproduction in this case is just as beautiful as the original. But one gives me a greater thrill than the other for reasons which have nothing to do with beauty." She is an unconscious snob because she is unable to distinguish between the two elements of her experience, unable to name the extraneous cause of her biased aesthetic judgment, or to see that it is biased.

I am aware of pedantically laboring an apparently obvious point. But it will become at once less obvious if we turn to a different yet related problem.

In 1948, a German art restorer named Dietrich Fey, engaged in reconstruction work on Lübeck's ancient St. Marien Church, stated that his workmen had discovered traces of old Gothic wall paintings dating back to the thirteenth century, under a coating of chalk on the church walls. The restoration of the paintings was entrusted to Fey's assistant, Lothar Malskat, who finished the job two years later. In 1950, Chancellor Adenauer presided over the ceremonies marking the completion of the restoration work in the presence of art experts from all parts of Europe. Their unanimous opinion, voiced by Chancellor Adenauer, was that the twenty-one thirteenth-century Gothic saints on the church walls were "a valuable treasure and a fabulous discovery of lost masterpieces."

None of the experts on that or any later occasion expressed doubt as to the authenticity of the frescoes. It was Herr Malskat himself who, two years later, disclosed the fraud. He presented himself on his own initiative at Lübeck police headquarters, where he stated that the frescoes were entirely his own work, undertaken by order from his boss, Herr Fey, and asked to be tried for forgery. The leading German art experts, however, stuck to their opinion: the frescoes, they said, were no doubt genuine, and Herr Malskat was merely seeking cheap publicity. An official Board of Investigation was appointed which came to the conclusion that the restoration of the wall paintings was a hoax—but only after Herr Malskat had confessed that he had also manufactured hundreds of Rembrandts, Watteaus, Toulouse-Lautrecs, Picassos, Henri Rousseaus, Corots, Chagalls, Vlamincks, and other masters, and sold them as originals—some of which were actually found by the police in Herr Fey's house. Without this evidence, it is doubtful whether the German experts would ever have admitted having been fooled.

My point is not the fallibility of the experts. Herr Malskat's exploit is merely the most recent of a number of similarly successful hoaxes and forgeries—of which the most fabulous were probably van Megeeren's false Vermeers. The disturbing question which they raise is whether the Lübeck saints are less beautiful, and have ceased to be "a valuable treasure of masterpieces," simply because they had been painted by Herr Malskat and not by somebody else?

There are several answers to this line of argument, but before going into them I want to continue in the part of *advocatus diaboli* by considering an example of a forgery in a different field: Macpherson's *Ossian*. The case is so notorious that the facts need only be briefly mentioned. James Macpherson (1736-96), a Scottish poet and adventurer, alleged that in the course of his wanderings in the Highlands he had discovered some ancient Gaelic manuscripts. Enthusiastic Scottish littérateurs put up a subscription to enable Macpherson to pursue his researches, and in 1761 he published *Fingal, an Ancient Epic Poem in Six Books, together with Several Other Poems composed by*

Ossian, the Son of Fingal. Ossian is the legendary third-century hero and bard of Celtic literature. *Fingal* was soon followed by the publication of a still larger Ossianic epic called *Temora,* and this by a collected edition, *The Works of Ossian.* The authenticity of Macpherson's text was at once questioned in England, particularly by Dr. Johnson (whom Macpherson answered by sending him a challenge to a duel), and to his death Macpherson refused, under various unconvincing pretexts, to publish his alleged Gaelic originals. By the turn of the century the controversy was settled and it was established that, while Macpherson had used fragments of ancient Celtic lore, most of the "Ossianic" texts were of his own making.

Yet here again the question arises whether the poetic quality of the work itself is altered by the fact that it was written not by Ossian, the son of Fingal, but by James Macpherson? The "Ossianic" texts were translated into many languages, and had a considerable influence on the literature and cultural climate of Europe at the late eighteenth and early nineteenth centuries. This is how the *Encyclopedia Britannica* sums up its evaluation of Macpherson:

> The varied sources of his work and its worthlessness as a transcript of actual Celtic poems do not alter the fact that he produced a work of art which . . . did more than any single work to bring about the romantic movement in European, and especially in German, literature. . . . Herder and Goethe . . . were among its profound admirers.

These examples could be continued indefinitely. Antique furniture, Roman statuary, Greek tanagra figures, and Italian madonnas are being forged, copied, counterfeited all the time, and the value we set on them is not determined by aesthetic appreciation and pleasure to the eye, but by the precarious and often uncertain judgment of experts. A mediocre but authenticated picture by a known master is held in higher esteem than an artistically superior work of his unknown pupil or "school"—not only by art dealers guided by "investment," but by all of us, including this writer. Are we, then, all snobs to whom a signature, an expert testimonial, or the postmark of a given period is more important than the intrinsic beauty of the object itself?

I now propose to present the case for the defense. It can be summed up in a single sentence: our appraisal of any work of literature or art is never a unitary act, but the result of two independent and simultaneous processes which tend to distort each other.

When we look at an Egyptian fresco, we do not enjoy the painting at its face value, but by means of an unconscious reattunement of the mind to the values of the period. We know, for instance, that the Egyptians had not discovered the technique of perspective in depth. We know that on certain Egyptian murals the size of the figures is determined by their relative social rank. Similarly, we look at every picture through a double frame: the solid frame which isolates it from its surroundings and creates for it a hole in space, as it were; and the unconscious frame of reference in our minds which creates for it a hole in time and locates it in its period and cultural climate. Every time we think that we are making a purely aesthetic judgment based on pure sensory perception, we are in fact judging relative to this second frame or context or mental field.

Any work of art, or literature, or music, can only be appreciated against the background of its period, and that is what we unconsciously do: when we naïvely believe that we are applying absolute criteria, we are in fact applying relative ones. When we contemplate the false Vermeer the first time believing it to be authentic and the second time knowing that it is a fake, our aesthetic experience will indeed completely change, though the picture has remained the same. For it is now seen in a different frame of reference and therefore, in fact, differently. The same considerations apply to the perpetrator of the fake. He may be able to imitate the technique of the eighteenth-century Flemish School, but he could not spontaneously start painting like Vermeer—because his visual organization is different, his perception of reality is different, and because he cannot, except by an artificial effort, erase from his mind the accumulated experience of everything that happened in painting since Vermeer. And if, by a tour de force, a contemporary artist succeeded in reconditioning his own vision to that of the Flemish eighteenth century or the Italian *quattrocento*, he would have to use mass hypnosis to recondition the vision of his customers in a similar manner.

We can add to our knowledge and experience, but we cannot subtract from it. When Picasso decides to disregard the laws of perspective, that means that he has passed through and beyond a certain technique—unlike the Egyptian painter, who has never acquired it. Evolution is an irreversible process; the culture of a period might apparently point into the same direction as an earlier one, but it does so from a different turn of the spiral. A modern primitive is different from a primitive primitive; contemporary classicism is different from any classical classicism; only the mentally insane are able to amputate part of their past.

And yet when we contemplate works of the past, we must perform just such a process of mental subtraction, by attuning our minds to the climate and experience of the period. In order to appreciate them, we must enter into their spirit, by forgetting our modern experience and all that we have learnt since that Homeric epic or Byzantine mosaic was created. We must descend into the past, making our mind a blank; and as we do so, we unconsciously condescend. We close our eyes to crudities of technique, naïveties of perception, prevailing superstitions, limitations of knowledge, factual errors. We make allowances. A little honest introspection will always reveal the element of condescension contained in our admiration for the classics; and part of our enjoyment when listening to the voices of the past is derived from this half-consciously patronizing attitude—"how clever of them to know that at their age." We feel that we have descended a turn of the spiral; we are looking up in awe and wonder at Dante's dreadful Paradise, but at the same time we seem to be bending down, with a tender, antiquarian stoop.

This legitimate kind of aesthetic double-think degenerates into snobbery at the point where the frame of reference becomes more important than the picture, when the thrill derived from the gesture of bending over the past dominates the aesthetic experience. The result is a widespread confusion of critical judgment—overestimation of the dead and belittlement of the living, indiscriminate reverence for anything that is "classical," "antique," "primitive," or simply old. In its extreme form this tendency prompts people to have their wall brackets and picture frames artificially dirtied to lend them the patina of age; so let us call it the "patina snobbery."

The process that leads to these distortions of judgment is basically the same as outlined before: the projection of one scale of values to a psychologically related but objectively alien field of experience. The essence of snobbery is to assess value according to a wrong type of scale; the snob is always trying to measure beauty with a thermometer or weight with a clock.

The thirteen-year-old daughter of a friend was recently taken to the Greenwich Museum. When she was asked which was the most beautiful thing she had seen in the Museum, she said unhesitatingly: "Nelson's shirt." When asked what was so beautiful about it, she explained: "That shirt with the blood on it was jolly nice. Fancy real blood on a real shirt, which belonged to somebody really historic!"

The child's thrill is obviously derived from the same source as the magic that emanates from Napoleon's inkpot, the lock of hair on the Egyptian mummy's head, the relic of the saint carried in annual procession, the strand of the rope by which a famous murderer was hanged, and from Tolstoi's laundry bill. In the mentality of the primitive, an object which had been in contact with a person is not merely a souvenir: it becomes magically imbued with the substance of that personality and in turn magically emanates something of that substance.

"There is, I am sure, for most of us, a special pleasure in sinking your teeth into a peach produced on the estate of an earl who is related to the Royal Family," a London columnist wrote recently in the *Daily Express*.

Primitive magic survives in the subconscious; the strand of hair carried in the locket, grandmother's wedding dress, the faded fan of the first ball, the regimental badge, all have a half-conscious fetish character. The bobby-soxers who tear shreds off the crooner's garb are the vulgarized twentieth-century version of the worshipers cherishing a splinter from a saint's bone. The value that we set on original manuscripts, on "signed" pieces of furniture, on Dickens' quill and Kepler's telescope, are more dignified manifestations of the same unconscious tendency. It is, as the child said, "jolly nice" to behold a fragment of a marble by Praxiteles—even if it is battered out of human shape, with a leper's nose and broken ears. The contact with the master's hand has imbued it with a magic quality which has lingered on and radiates at us, conveying the same thrill as "the real blood on Nelson's real shirt."

The change in our attitude—and in the art dealer's price—when it is learned that a cracked and blackened piece of canvas is an "authenticated" work by X has nothing to do with beauty, aesthetics, or what have you—it is the working of sympathetic magic in us. (See Brenda and her Picasso drawing.) The inordinate importance that we attribute to the original, the authenticated, in those borderline cases where only the expert could tell the difference, is a derivative from primitive fetishism. And as every honest art dealer will admit, these borderline cases are so frequent as to be almost the rule. Moreover, it was a general practice in the past for the master to let his pupils assist in the execution of larger undertakings. It is not the eye that guides the average museum visitor, but the magic of names and the magic of age. The bedevilment of aesthetic experience by unconscious fetish worship and patina snobbery is so general that it has become a major factor in our attitude to the art of past epochs—an attitude as remote from spontaneous appreciation as the "Emperor's Clothes" fallacy regarding hyper-modern art forms.

The Popular Arts

❀❈❀❈❀❈❀❈❀❈❀❈❀❈❀❈❀❈❀❈❀❈❀❈❀❈❀❈❀❈❀❈❀❈❀❈❀❈

DWIGHT MACDONALD

A Theory of Mass Culture[1]

For about a century, Western culture has really been two cultures: the traditional kind—let us call it "High Culture"—that is chronicled in the textbooks, and a "Mass Culture" manufactured wholesale for the market. In the old art forms, the artisans of Mass Culture have long been at work: in the novel, the line stretches from Eugène Sue to Lloyd C. Douglas; in music, from Offenbach to Tin-Pan Alley; in art from the chromo to Maxfield Parrish and Norman Rockwell; in architecture, from Victorian Gothic to suburban Tudor. Mass Culture has also developed new media of its own, into which the serious artist rarely ventures: radio, the movies, comic books, detective stories, science fiction, television.

It is sometimes called "Popular Culture," [2] but I think "Mass Culture"

[1] From Diogenes (Summer, 1953), No. 3, pp. 1-17, with omissions. Copyright, 1953, by Intercultural Publications, Inc. Reprinted by permission of the author.
[2] As I did myself in "A Theory of Popular Culture" (Politics, February, 1944), parts of which have been used or adapted in the present article.

a more accurate term, since its distinctive mark is that it is solely and directly an article for mass consumption, like chewing gum. A work of High Culture is occasionally popular, after all, though this is increasingly rare. Thus Dickens was even more popular than his contemporary, G. A. Henty, the difference being that he was an artist, communicating his individual vision to other individuals, while Henty was an impersonal manufacturer of an impersonal commodity for the masses.

The Nature of Mass Culture

The historical reasons for the growth of Mass Culture since the early 1800's are well known. Political democracy and popular education broke down the old upper-class monopoly of culture. Business enterprise found a profitable market in the cultural demands of the newly awakened masses, and the advance of technology made possible the cheap production of books, periodicals, pictures, music, and furniture, in sufficient quantities to satisfy this market. Modern technology also created new media such as the movies and television which are specially well adapted to mass manufacture and distribution.

The phenomenon is thus peculiar to modern times and differs radically from what was hitherto known as art or culture. It is true that Mass Culture began as, and to some extent still is, a parasitic, a cancerous growth on High Culture. As Clement Greenberg pointed out in "Avant-Garde and Kitsch" (*Partisan Review*, Fall, 1939): "The precondition of *kitsch* (a German term for 'Mass Culture') is the availability close at hand of a fully matured cultural tradition, whose discoveries, acquisitions, and perfected self-conscious *kitsch* can take advantage of for its own ends." The connection, however, is not that of the leaf and the branch but rather that of the caterpillar and the leaf. *Kitsch* "mines" High Culture the way improvident frontiersmen mine the soil, extracting its riches and putting nothing back. Also, as *kitsch* develops, it begins to draw on its own past, and some of it evolves so far away from High Culture as to appear quite disconnected from it.

It is also true that Mass Culture is to some extent a continuation of the old Folk Art which until the Industrial Revolution was the culture of the common people, but here, too, the differences are more striking than the similarities. Folk Art grew from below. It was a spontaneous, autochthonous expression of the people, shaped by themselves, pretty much without the benefit of High Culture, to suit their own needs. Mass Culture is imposed from above. It is fabricated by technicians hired by businessmen; its audiences are passive consumers, their participation limited to the choice between buying and not buying. The Lords of *kitsch*, in short, exploit the cultural needs of the masses in order to make a profit and/or to maintain their class rule—in Communist countries, only the second purpose obtains. (It is very different to *satisfy* popular tastes, as Robert Burns' poetry did, and to *exploit* them, as Hollywood does.) Folk Art was the people's own institution, their private little garden walled off from the great formal park of their masters' High Culture. But Mass Culture breaks down the wall, integrating the masses into a debased form of High Culture and thus becoming an instrument of political domination. If one had no other data to go on, the nature of Mass Culture would reveal capitalism to be an exploitative class society and not the harmonious commonwealth it is sometimes alleged to be. The same goes even more strongly for Soviet Communism and its special kind of Mass Culture.

Mass Culture: U.S.S.R.

"Everybody" knows that America is a land of Mass Culture, but it is not so generally recognized that so is the Soviet Union. Certainly not by the Communist leaders, one of whom has contemptuously observed that the American people need not fear the peace-loving Soviet state which has absolutely no desire to deprive them of their Coca-Cola and comic books. Yet the fact is that the U.S.S.R. is even more a land of Mass Culture than is the U.S.A. This is less easily recognizable because their Mass Culture is in *form* just the opposite of ours, being one of propaganda and pedagogy rather than of entertainment. None the less, it has the essential quality of Mass, as against High or Folk, Culture: it is manufactured for mass consumption by technicians employed by the ruling class and is not an expression of either the individual artist or the common people themselves. Like our own, it exploits rather than satisfies the cultural needs of the masses, though for political rather than commercial reasons. Its quality is even lower: our Supreme Court building is tasteless and pompous, but not to the lunatic degree of the proposed new Palace of the Soviets—a huge wedding cake of columns mounting up to an eighty-foot statue of Lenin; Soviet movies are so much duller and cruder than our own that even the American comrades shun them; the childish level of *serious* Soviet magazines devoted to matters of art or philosophy has to be read to be believed, and as for the popular press, it is as if Colonel McCormick ran every periodical in America.

Gresham's Law in Culture

The separation of Folk Art and High Culture in fairly watertight compartments corresponded to the sharp line once drawn between the common people and the aristocracy. The eruption of the masses onto the political stage has broken down this compartmentation, with disastrous cultural results. Whereas Folk Art had its own special quality, Mass Culture is at best a vulgarized reflection of High Culture. And whereas High Culture could formerly ignore the mob and seek to please only the *cognoscenti*, it must now compete with Mass Culture or be merged into it.

The problem is acute in the United States and not just because a prolific Mass Culture exists here. If there were a clearly defined cultural *élite*, then the masses could have their *kitsch* and the *élite* could have its High Culture, with everybody happy. But the boundary line is blurred. A statistically significant part of the population, I venture to guess, is chronically confronted with a choice between going to the movies or to a concert, between reading Tolstoy or a detective story, between looking at old masters or at a TV show; i.e., the pattern of their cultural lives is "open" to the point of being porous. Good art competes with *kitsch*, serious ideas compete with commercialized formulae—and the advantage lies all on one side. There seems to be a Gresham's Law in cultural as well as monetary circulation: bad stuff drives out the good, since it is more easily understood and enjoyed. It is this facility of access, which at once sells *kitsch* on a wide market and also prevents it from achieving quality.[3] Clement Greenberg writes that the special aesthetic quality of *kitsch* is that it "predigests art for the spectator and spares him effort, provides him with a shortcut to the pleasures of art that detours what is necessarily difficult in genuine art" because it includes the spectator's reactions in the work of art itself instead of forcing him to make his own responses. Thus "Eddie Guest and the Indian Love Lyrics are more 'poetic' than T. S. Eliot and Shakespeare." And so, too, our "collegiate Gothic" such as the Harkness Quadrangle at Yale is more picturesquely Gothic than Chartres, and a pinup girl smoothly airbrushed by Petty is more sexy than a real naked woman.

When to this ease of consumption is added *kitsch's* ease of production because of its standardized nature, its prolific growth is easy to understand. It threatens High Culture by its sheer pervasiveness, its brutal, overwhelming *quantity*. The upper classes, who begin by using it to make money from the crude tastes of the masses and to dominate them politically, end by finding their own culture attacked and even threatened with destruction by the instrument they have thoughtlessly employed. (The same irony may be observed in modern politics, where most swords seem to have two edges; thus Nazism began as a tool of the big bourgeoisie and the army *Junkers* but ended by using *them* as *its* tools.)

Homogenized Culture

Like nineteenth-century capitalism, Mass Culture is a dynamic, revolutionary force, breaking down the old barriers of class, tradition, taste, and dissolving all cultural distinctions. It mixes and scrambles everything together, producing what might be called homogenized culture, after another

[3] The success of *Reader's Digest* illustrates the law. Here is a magazine that has achieved a fantastic circulation—some fifteen millions, much of which is accounted for by its foreign editions, thus showing that *kitsch* by no means appeals only to Americans—simply by reducing to even lower terms the already superficial formulae of other periodicals. By treating a theme in two pages which they treat in six, the *Digest* becomes "readable" and three times as superficial.

American achievement, the homogenization process that distributes the globules of cream evenly throughout the milk instead of allowing them to float separately on top. It thus destroys all values, since value judgments imply discrimination. Mass Culture is very, very democratic: it absolutely refuses to discriminate against, or between, anything or anybody. All is grist to its mill, and all comes out finely ground indeed.

Consider *Life*, a typical homogenized mass-circulation magazine. It appears on the mahogany library tables of the rich, the glass end-tables of the middle-class and the oilcloth-covered kitchen tables of the poor. Its contents are as thoroughly homogenized as its circulation. The same issue will contain a serious exposition of atomic theory alongside a disquisition on Rita Hayworth's love life; photos of starving Korean children picking garbage from the ruins of Pusan and of sleek models wearing adhesive brassieres; an editorial hailing Bertrand Russell on his eightieth birthday ("A GREAT MIND IS STILL ANNOYING AND ADORNING OUR AGE") across from a full-page photo of a housewife arguing with an umpire at a baseball game ("MOM GETS THUMB"); a cover announcing in the same size type "A NEW FOREIGN POLICY, BY JOHN FOSTER DULLES" and "KERIMA: HER MARATHON KISS IS A MOVIE SENSATION"; nine color pages of Renoirs plus a memoir by his son, followed by a full-page picture of a roller-skating horse. The advertisements, of course, provide even more scope for the editor's homogenizing talents, as when a full-page photo of a ragged Bolivian peon grinningly drunk on coca leaves (which Mr. Luce's conscientious reporters tell us he chews to narcotize his chronic hunger pains) appears opposite an ad of a pretty, smiling, well-dressed American mother with her two pretty, smiling, well-dressed children (a boy and a girl, of course—children are always homogenized in American ads) looking raptly at a clown on a TV set ("RCA VICTOR BRINGS YOU A NEW KIND OF TELEVISION—SUPER SETS WITH 'PICTURE POWER' "). The peon would doubtless find the juxtaposition piquant if he could afford a copy of *Life* which, fortunately for the Good Neighbor Policy, he cannot.

Academicism and Avantgardism

Until about 1930, High Culture tried to defend itself against the encroachments of Mass Culture in two opposite ways: Academicism, or an attempt to compete by imitation; and Avantgardism, or a withdrawal from competition.

Academicism is *kitsch* for the *élite*: spurious High Culture that is outwardly the real thing but actually as much a manufactured article as the cheaper cultural goods produced for the masses. It is recognized at the time for what it is only by the Avantgardists. A generation or two later, its real nature is understood by everyone and it quietly drops into the same oblivion as its franker sister-under-the-skin. Examples are painters such as Bougereau and Rosa Bonheur, critics such as Edmund Clarence Stedman and Edmund Gosse, the Beaux Arts school of architecture, composers such as the late Sir Edward Elgar, poets such as Stephen Phillips, and novelists such as Alphonse Daudet, Arnold Bennett, James Branch Cabell and Somerset Maugham.

The significance of the Avantgarde movement (by which I mean poets such as Rimbaud, novelists such as Joyce, composers such as Stravinsky, and painters such as Picasso) is that it simply refused to compete. Rejecting Academicism—and thus, at a second remove, also Mass Culture—it made a desperate attempt to fence off some area where the serious artist could still function. It created a new compartmentation of culture, on the basis of an intellectual rather than a social *élite*. The attempt was remarkably successful: to it we owe almost everything that is living in the art of the last fifty or so years. In fact, the High Culture of our times is pretty much identical with Avantgardism. The movement came at a time (1890-1930) when bourgeois values were being challenged both culturally and politically. (In this country, the cultural challenge did not come until World War I, so that our Avantgarde flourished only in the twenties.) In the thirties the two streams mingled briefly, after each had spent its real force, under the aegis of the Communists, only to sink together at the end of the decade into the sands of the wasteland we still live in. The rise of Nazism and the revelation in the Moscow Trials of the real nature of the new society in Russia inaugurated the present period, when men cling to the evils they know rather than risk possibly greater ones by pressing forward. Nor has the chronic state of war, hot or cold, that the world has been in since 1939 encouraged rebellion or experiment in either art or politics.

A Merger Has Been Arranged

In this new period, the competitors, as often happens in the business world, are merging. Mass Culture takes on the color of both varieties of the old High Culture, Academic and Avantgarde, while these latter are increasingly watered down with Mass elements. There is slowly emerging a tepid, flaccid Middlebrow Culture that threatens to engulf everything in its spreading ooze. Bauhaus modernism has at last trickled down, in a debased form of course, into our furniture, cafeterias, movie theatres, electric toasters, office buildings, drug stores, and railroad trains. Psychoanalysis is expounded sympathetically and superficially in popular magazines, and the psychoanalyst replaces the eccentric millionaire as the *deus ex machina* in many a movie. T. S. Eliot writes *The Cocktail Party* and it becomes a Broadway hit. (Though in some ways excellent, it is surely inferior to his *Murder in the Cathedral*, which in the unmerged thirties had to depend on WPA to get produced at all.)

The typical creator of *kitsch* today, at least in the old media, is an indeterminate specimen. There are no widely influential critics so completely terrible as, say, the late William Lyon Phelps was. Instead we have such gray creatures as Clifton Fadiman and Henry Seidel Canby. The artless numbers of an Eddie Guest are drowned out by the more sophisticated though equally commonplace strains of Benet's *John Brown's Body*. Maxfield Parrish yields to Rockwell Kent, Arthur Brisbane to Walter Lippman, Theda Bara to Ingrid Bergman. We even have what might be called *l'avantgarde pompier* (or, in American, "phoney Avantgardism"), as in the buildings of Raymond Hood and the later poetry of Archibald MacLeish, as there is also an academic Avantgardism in *belles lettres* so that now the "little" as well as the big magazines have their hack writers.

All this is not a raising of the level of Mass Culture, as might appear at first, but rather a corruption of High Culture. There is nothing more vulgar than sophisticated *kitsch*. Compare Conan Doyle's workmanlike and unpretentious Sherlock Holmes stories with the bogus "intellectuality" of Dorothy M. Sayers, who, like many contemporary detective-story writers, is a novelist *manquée* who ruins her stuff with literary attitudinizing. Or consider the relationship of Hollywood and Broadway. In the twenties, the two were sharply differentiated, movies being produced for the masses of the hinterland, theatre for an upper-class New York audience. The theatre was High Culture, mostly of the Academic variety (Theatre Guild) but with some spark of Avantgarde fire (the "little" or "experimental" theatre movement). The movies were definitely Mass Culture, mostly very bad but with some leaven of Avantgardism (Griffith, Stroheim) and Folk Art (Chaplin and other comedians). With the sound film, Broadway and Hollywood drew closer together. Plays are now produced mainly to sell the movie rights, with many being directly financed by the film companies. The merger has standardized the theatre to such an extent that even the early Theatre Guild seems vital in retrospect, while hardly a trace of the "experimental" theatre is left. And what have the movies gained? They are more sophisticated, the acting is subtler, the sets in better taste. But they too have become standardized: they are never as awful as they often were in the old days, but they are never as good either. They are better entertainment and worse art. The cinema of the twenties occasionally gave us the fresh charm of Folk Art or the imaginative intensity of Avantgardism. The coming of sound, and with it Broadway, degraded the camera to a recording instrument for an alien art form, the spoken play. The silent film had at least the *theoretical possibility*, even within the limits of Mass Culture, of being artistically significant. The sound film, within those limits, does not. . . .

The Problem of the Masses

Conservatives such as Ortega y Gasset and T. S. Eliot argue that since "the revolt of the masses" has led to the horrors of totalitarianism (and of California roadside architecture), the only hope is to rebuild the old class walls and bring the masses once more under aristocratic control. They think of the popular as synonymous with cheap and vulgar. Marxian radicals and liberals, on the other hand, see the masses as intrinsically healthy but as the dupes and victims of cultural exploitation by the Lords of *kitsch*—in the style of Rousseau's "noble savage" idea. If only the masses were offered good stuff instead of *kitsch*, how they would eat it up! How the level of Mass Culture would rise! Both these diagnoses seem to me fallacious: they assume that Mass Culture is (in the conservative view) or could be (in the liberal view) an expression of *people*, like Folk Art, whereas actually it is an expression of *masses*, a very different thing.

There are theoretical reasons why Mass Culture is not and can never be any good. I take it as axiomatic that culture can only be produced by and for human beings. But in so far as people are organized (more strictly, disorganized) as masses, they lose their human identity and quality. For the masses are in historical time what a crowd is in space: a large quantity of people unable to express themselves as human beings because they are related to one another neither as individuals nor as members of communities—indeed, they are not related *to each other* at all, but only to something distant, abstract, nonhuman: a football game or bargain sale in the case of a crowd, a system of industrial production, a party or a State in the case of the masses. The mass man is a solitary atom, uniform with and undifferentiated from thousands and millions of other atoms who go to make up "the lonely crowd," as David Riesman well calls American society. A folk or a people, however, is a community, i.e., a group of individuals linked to each other by common interests, work, traditions, values, and sentiments; something like a family, each of whose members has a special place and function as an individual while at the same time sharing the group's interests (family budget) sentiments (family quarrels), and culture (family jokes). The scale is small enough so that it "makes a difference" what the individual does, a first condition for human—as against mass-existence. He is at once more important as an individual than in mass society and at the same time more closely integrated into the community, his creativity nourished by a rich combination of individualism and communalism. (The great culture-bearing *élites* of the past have been communities of this kind.) In contrast, a mass society, like a crowd, is so undifferentiated and loosely structured that its atoms, in so far as human values go, tend to cohere only along the line of the least common denominator; its morality sinks to that of its most brutal and primitive members, its taste to that of the least sensitive and most ignorant. And in addition to everything else, the scale is simply too big, there are just *too many people*.

Yet this collective monstrosity, "the masses," "the public," is taken as a human norm by the scientific and artistic technicians of our Mass Culture. They at once degraded the public by treating it as an object, to be handled with the lack of ceremony and the objectivity of medical students dissecting a corpse, and at the same time flatter it, pander to its level of taste and ideas by taking these as the criterion of reality (in the case of questionnaire-sociologists and other "social scientists") or of art (in the case of the Lords of *kitsch*). When one hears a questionnaire-sociologist talk about how he will "set up" an investigation, one feels he regards people as a herd of dumb animals, as mere congeries of conditioned reflexes, his calculation being which reflex will be stimulated by which question. At the same time, of necessity, he sees the statistical majority as the great Reality, the secret of life he is trying to find out; like the *kitsch* Lords, he is wholly without values, willing to accept any idiocy if it is held by many people. The aristocrat and the democrat both criticize and argue with popular taste, the one with hostility, the other in friendship, for both attitudes proceed from a set of values. This is less degrading to the masses than the "objective" approach of Hollywood and the questionnaire-sociologists, just as it is less degrading to a man to be shouted at in anger than to be quietly assumed to be part of a machine. But the *plebs* have their dialectical revenge: complete indifference to their human *quality* means complete prostration before their statistical *quantity*, so that a movie magnate who cynically "gives the public what it wants"—i.e., assumes it wants trash— sweats with terror if box-office returns drop 10 per cent.

The Future of High Culture: Dark

The conservative proposal to save culture by restoring the old class lines has a more solid historical base than the Marxian hope for a new democratic, classless culture, for, with the possible (and important) exception of Periclean Athens, all the great cultures of the past were *élite* cultures. Politically, however, it is without meaning in a world dominated by the two great mass nations, U.S.A. and U.S.S.R., and becoming more industrialized, more massified all the time. The only practical thing along those lines would be to revive the *cultural élite* which the Avantgarde created. As I have already noted, the Avantgarde is now dying, partly from internal causes, partly suffocated by the competing Mass Culture, where it is not being absorbed into it. Of course this process has not reached 100 per cent, and doubtless never will unless the country goes either Fascist or Communist. There are still islands above the flood for those determined enough to reach them, and to stay on them: as Faulkner has shown, a writer can even use Hollywood instead of being used by it, if his purpose is firm enough. But the homogenization of High and Mass Culture has gone far and is going farther all the time, and there seems little reason to expect a revival of Avantgardism, that is, of a successful countermovement to Mass Culture. Particularly not in this country, where the blurring of class lines, the absence of a stable cultural tradition, and the greater facilities for manufacturing and marketing *kitsch* all work in the other direction. The result is that our intelligentsia is remarkably small, weak, and disintegrated. One of the odd things about the American cultural scene is how many brainworkers there are and how few intellectuals, defining the former as specialists whose thinking is pretty much confined to their limited "fields" and the latter as persons who take all

culture for their province. Not only are there few intellectuals, but they
don't hang together, they have very little *esprit de corps*, very little sense of
belonging to a community; they are so isolated from each other they don't
even bother to quarrel—there hasn't been a really good fight among them
since the Moscow Trials.

The Future of Mass Culture: Darker

If the conservative proposal to save our culture via the aristocratic Avantgarde seems historically unlikely, what of the democratic-liberal proposal?
Is there a reasonable prospect of raising the level of Mass Culture? In his
recent book, *The Great Audience*, Gilbert Seldes argues there is. He blames
the present sad state of our Mass Culture on the stupidity of the Lords of
kitsch, who underestimate the mental age of the public; the arrogance of
the intellectuals, who make the same mistake and so snobbishly refuse to
work for such mass media as radio, TV and movies; and the passivity of
the public itself, which doesn't insist on better Mass Cultural products. This
diagnosis seems to me superficial in that it blames everything on subjective,
moral factors: stupidity, perversity, failure of will. My own feeling is that,
as in the case of the alleged responsibility of the German (or Russian)
people for the horrors of Nazism (or Soviet Communism), it is unjust to
blame social groups for this result. Human beings have been caught up in
the inexorable workings of a mechanism that forces them, with a pressure
only heroes can resist (and one cannot *demand* that anybody be a hero,
though one can *hope* for it), into its own pattern. I see Mass Culture as a
reciprocating engine, and who is to say, once it has been set in motion,
whether the stroke or the counterstroke is "responsible" for its continued
action?

The Lords of *kitsch* sell culture to the masses. It is a debased, trivial
culture that voids both the deep realities (sex, death, failure, tragedy) and
also the simple, spontaneous pleasures, since the realities would be too real
and the pleasures too *lively* to induce what Mr. Seldes calls "the mood of
consent," i.e., a narcotized acceptance of Mass Culture and of the commodities it sells as a substitute for the unsettling and unpredictable (hence
unsalable) joy, tragedy, wit, change, originality and beauty of real life. The
masses, debauched by several generations of this sort of thing, in turn come
to demand trivial and comfortable cultural products. Which came first, the
chicken or the egg, the mass demand or its satisfaction (and further stimulation) is a question as academic as it is unanswerable. The engine is reciprocating and shows no signs of running down.

Indeed, far from Mass Culture getting better, we will be lucky if it
doesn't get worse. When shall we see another popular humorist like Sholem
Aleichem, whose books are still being translated from the Yiddish and for
whose funeral in 1916 a hundred thousand inhabitants of the Bronx turned
out? Or Finley Peter Dunne, whose Mr. Dooley commented on the American

scene with such wit that Henry Adams was a faithful reader and Henry
James, on his famous return to his native land, wanted to meet only one
American author, Dunne? Since Mass Culture is not an art form but a
manufactured commodity, it tends always downward, toward cheapness—
and so standardization—of production. Thus, T. W. Adorno has noted, in
his brilliant essay "On Popular Music" (*Studies in Philosophy and Social
Science,* New York, No. 1, 1941) that the chorus of every popular song
without exception has the same number of bars, while Mr. Seldes remarks
that Hollywood movies are cut in a uniformly rapid tempo, a shot rarely
being held more than forty-five seconds, which gives them a standardized
effect in contrast to the varied tempo of European film cutting. This sort of
standardization means that what may have begun as something fresh and
original is repeated until it becomes a nerveless routine—*vide* what happened
to Fred Allen as a radio comedian. The only time Mass Culture is good is
at the very beginning, before the "formula" has hardened, before the money
boys and efficiency experts and audience-reaction analysts have moved in.
Then for a while it may have the quality of real Folk Art. But the Folk
artist today lacks the cultural roots and the intellectual toughness (both of
which the Avantgarde artist has relatively more of) to resist for long the
pressures of Mass Culture. His taste can easily be corrupted, his sense of
his own special talent and limitations obscured, as in what happened to
Disney between the gay, inventive early Mickey Mouse and Silly Symphony
cartoons and the vulgar pretentiousness of *Fantasia* and heavy-handed sentimentality of *Snow White,* or to Westbrook Pegler who has regressed from
an excellent sports writer, with a sure sense of form and a mastery of colloquial satire, into the rambling, coarse-grained, garrulous political pundit
of today. Whatever virtues the Folk artist has, and they are many, staying
power is not one of them. And staying power is the essential virtue of one
who would hold his own against the spreading ooze of Mass Culture.

LESLIE A. FIEDLER

The Middle against Both Ends [1]

I am surely one of the few people pretending to intellectual respectability who
can boast that he has read more comic books than attacks on comic books. I
do not mean that I have consulted or studied the comics—I have read them,
often with some pleasure. Nephews and nieces, my own children, and the children of neighbors have brought them to me to share their enjoyment. An old

[1] From *Encounter,* V (1955), 16-23. Copyright, 1955. Reprinted by permission of
the author and the publisher.

lady on a ferry boat in Puget Sound once dropped two in my lap in wordless sympathy; I was wearing, at the time, a sailor's uniform.

I have somewhat more difficulty in getting through the books that attack them. I am put off, to begin with, by inaccuracies of fact. When Mr. Geoffrey Wagner in his *Parade of Pleasure* calls Superboy "Superman's brother" (he is, of course, Superman himself as a child), I am made suspicious. Actually, Mr. Wagner's book is one of the least painful on the subject; confused, to be sure, but quite lively and not in the least smug; though it propounds the preposterous theory that the whole of "popular literature" is a conspiracy on the part of the "plutos" to corrupt an innocent American people. Such easy melodrama can only satisfy someone prepared to believe, as Mr. Wagner apparently does, that the young girls of Harlem are being led astray by the *double-entendres* of blues records!

Mr. Wagner's notions are at least more varied and subtle than Mr. Gershon Legman's, who cries out in his *Love and Death* that it is simply our sexual frustrations which breed a popular literature dedicated to violence. But Mr. Legman's theory explains too much: not only comic books but Hemingway, war, Luce, Faulkner, the status of women—and, I should suppose, Mr. Legman's own shrill hyperboles. At that, Mr. Legman seems more to the point in his search for some deeply underlying cause than Frederic Wertham, in *Seduction of the Innocent*, with his contention that the pulps and comics in themselves are schools for murder. That the undefined aggressiveness of disturbed children can be given a shape by comic books, I do not doubt; and one could make a good case for the contention that such literature standardizes crime woefully or inhibits imagination in violence, but I find it hard to consider so obvious a symptom a prime cause of anything. Perhaps I am a little sensitive on this score, having heard the charge this week that the recent suicide of one of our college freshmen was caused by his having read (in a course of which I am in charge) Goethe, Dostoevsky, and *Death of a Salesman*. Damn it, he *had* read them, and he *did* kill himself!

In none of the books on comics I have looked into, and in none of the reports of ladies' clubs, protests of legislators, or statements of moral indignation by pastors, have I come on any real attempt to understand comic books: to define the form, midway between icon and story; to distinguish the subtypes—animal, adolescent, crime, western, etc.; or even to separate out, from the deadpan varieties, tongue-in-cheek sports like *Pogo*, frank satire like *Mad*, or semi-surrealist variations like *Plastic Man*. It would not take someone with the talents of an Aristotle, but merely with his method, to ask the rewarding questions about this kind of literature that he asked once about an equally popular and bloody genre: what are its causes and its natural form?

A cursory examination would show that the super-hero comic (*Superman, Captain Marvel, Wonder Woman*, etc.) is the final form; it is statistically the most popular with the most avid readers, as well as providing the only new legendary material invented along with the form rather than adapted to it.

Next, one would have to abstract the most general pattern of the myth of the super-hero and deduce its significance: the urban setting, the threatened universal catastrophe, the hero who never uses arms, who returns to weakness and obscurity, who must keep his identity secret, who is impotent, etc. Not until then could one ask with any hope of an answer: what end do the comics serve? Why have they gained an immense body of readers precisely in the past fifteen or twenty years? Why must they be disguised as children's literature though read by men and women of all ages? And having answered these, one could pose the most dangerous question of all: why the constant virulent attacks on the comics, and, indeed, on the whole of popular culture of which they are especially flagrant examples?

Strategically, if not logically, the last question should be asked first. Why the attacks? Such assaults by scientists and laymen are as characteristic of our age as puritanic diatribes against the stage of the Elizabethan Era, and pious protests against novel reading in the later eighteenth century. I suspect that a study of such conventional reactions reveals at least as much about the nature of a period as an examination of the forms to which they respond. The most fascinating and suspicious aspect of the opposition to popular narrative is its unanimity; everyone from the members of the Montana State Legislature to the ladies of the Parent Teachers Association of Boston, Massachusetts, from British M.P.'s to the wilder post-Freudians of two continents agree on this, though they may agree on nothing else. What they have in common is, I am afraid, the sense that they are all, according to their lights, righteous. And their protests represent only one more example (though an unlikely one) of the notorious failure of righteousness in matters involving art.

Just what is it with which vulgar literature is charged by various guardians of morality or sanity? With everything: encouraging crime, destroying literacy, expressing sexual frustration, unleashing sadism, spreading anti-democratic ideas, and, of course, corrupting youth. To understand the grounds of such charges, their justification and their bias, we must understand something of the nature of the subart with which we are dealing.

Perhaps it is most illuminating to begin by saying that it is a peculiarly American phenomenon, an unexpected by-product of an attempt, not only to extend literacy universally, but to delegate taste to majority suffrage. I do not mean, of course, that it is found only in the United States, but that wherever it is found, it comes first from us, and is still to be discovered in fully developed form only among us. Our experience along these lines is, in this sense, a preview for the rest of the world of what must follow the inevitable dissolution of the older aristocratic cultures.

One has only to examine certain Continental imitations of picture magazines like *Look* or *Life* or Disney-inspired cartoon books to be aware at once of the debt to American examples and of the failure of the limitations. For a true "popular literature" demands a more than ordinary slickness, the sort of high finish possible only to a machine-produced commodity in an economy of maximum prosperity. Contemporary popular culture, which is a function of an industrialized society, is distinguished from older folk art by its refusal to be shabby or second-rate in appearance, by a refusal to know its place. It is a product of the same impulse which has made available the sort of ready-made clothing which aims at destroying the possibility of knowing a lady by her dress.

Yet the articles of popular culture are made, not to be treasured, but to be thrown away; a paperback book is like a disposable diaper or a paper milk-container. For all its competent finish, it cannot be preserved on dusty shelves like the calf-bound volumes of another day; indeed, its very mode of existence challenges the concept of a library, private or public. The sort of conspicuous waste once reserved for an élite is now available to anyone; and this is inconceivable without an absurdly high standard of living, just as it is unimaginable without a degree of mechanical efficiency that permits industry to replace nature, and invents—among other disposable synthetics —one for literature.

Just as the production of popular narrative demands industrial conditions most favorably developed in the United States, its distribution requires the peculiar conditions of our market places: the mass or democratized market. Subbooks and subarts are not distributed primarily through the traditional institutions: museums, libraries, and schools, which remain firmly in the hands of those who deplore mass culture. It is in drugstores and supermarkets and airline terminals that this kind of literature mingles without condescension with chocolate bars and soapflakes. We have reached the end of a long process, begun, let us say, with Samuel Richardson, in which the work of art has approached closer and closer to the status of a commodity. Even the comic book is a last descendant of *Pamela*, the final consequence of letting the tastes (or more precisely, the buying power) of a class unpledged to maintaining the traditional genres determine literary success or failure.

Those who cry out now that the work of a Mickey Spillane or *The Adventures of Superman* travesty the novel, forget that the novel was long accused of travestying literature. What seems to offend us most is not the further downgrading of literary standards so much as the fact that the medium, the very notion and shape of a book, is being parodied by the comics. Jazz or the movies, which are also popular urban arts, depending for their distribution and acceptance on developments in technology (for jazz, the phonograph), really upset us much less.

It is the final, though camouflaged, rejection of literacy implicit in these new forms which is the most legitimate source of distress; but all arts so universally consumed have been for illiterates, even stained glass windows and the plays of Shakespeare. What is new in our present situation, and hence especially upsetting, is that this is the first art for *post*literates, i.e., for those who have refused the benefit for which they were presumed to have sighed in their long exclusion. Besides, modern popular narrative is disconcertingly not oral; it will not surrender the benefits of the printing press as a machine, however indifferent it may be to that press as the perpetuator of techniques devised first for pen or quill. Everything that the press can provide—except matter to be really read—is demanded: picture, typography, even in many cases the illusion of reading along with the relaxed pleasure of illiteracy. Yet the new popular forms remain somehow prose narrative or pictographic substitutes for the novel; even the cognate form of the movies is notoriously more like a novel than a play in its handling of time, space and narrative progression.

From the folk literature of the past, which ever since the triumph of the machine we have been trying sentimentally to recapture, popular literature differs in its rejection of the picturesque. Rooted in prose rather than verse, secular rather than religious in origin, defining itself against the city rather than the world of outdoor nature, a by-product of the factory rather than agriculture, present-day popular literature defeats romantic expectations of peasants in their embroidered blouses chanting or plucking balalaikas for the approval of their betters. The haters of our own popular art love to condescend to the folk; and on records or in fashionable night clubs in recent years, we have had entertainers who have earned enviable livings producing commercial imitations of folk songs. But contemporary vulgar culture is brutal and disturbing: the quasi-spontaneous expression of the uprooted and culturally dispossessed inhabitants of anonymous cities, contriving mythologies which reduce to manageable form the threat of science, the horror of un-limited war, the general spread of corruption in a world where the social bases of old loyalties and heroisms have long been destroyed. That such an art is exploited for profit in a commercial society, mass produced by nameless collaborators, standardized and debased, is of secondary importance. It is the patented nightmare of us all, a packaged way of coming to terms with one's environment sold for a dime to all those who have rejected the unasked-for gift of literacy.

Thought of in this light, the comic books with their legends of the eternally threatened metropolis eternally protected by immaculate and modest heroes (who shrink back after each exploit into the image of the crippled newsboy, the impotent and cowardly reporter) are seen as inheritors, for all their superficial differences, of the *inner* impulses of traditional folk art. Their gross drawing, their poverty of language cannot disguise their heritage of aboriginal violence, their exploitation of the ancient conflict of black magic and white. Beneath their journalistic commentary on A-bomb and Communism, they touch archetypal material: those shared figures of our lower minds more like the patterns of dream than fact. In a world where men threaten to dissolve into their most superficial and mechanical techniques, to become their borrowed newspaper platitudes, they remain close to the impulsive, subliminal life. They are our not quite machine-subdued Grimm, though the Black Forest has become, as it must, the City; the Wizard, the Scientist; and Simple Hans, Captain Marvel. In a society which thinks of itself as "scientific"—and of the Marvelous as childish—such a literature must seem primarily children's literature, though, of course, it is read by people of all ages.

We are now in a position to begin to answer the question: what do the righteous really have against comic books? In some parts of the world, simply the fact that they are American is sufficient, and certain homegrown self-contemners follow this line even in the United States. But it is really a minor argument, lent a certain temporary importance by passing political exigencies. To declare oneself against "the Americanization of culture" is meaningless unless one is set resolutely against industrialization and mass education.

More to the point is the attack on mass culture for its betrayal of literacy itself. In a very few cases, this charge is made seriously and with full realization of its import; but most often it amounts to nothing but an accusation of "bad grammar" or "slang" on the part of some school marm to whom the spread of "different than" seems to threaten the future of civilized discourse. What should set us on guard in this case is that it is not the fully literate, the intellectuals and serious writers, who lead the attack, but the insecure semiliterate. In America, there is something a little absurd about the indignant delegation from the Parent Teachers Association (themselves clutching the latest issue of *Life*) crying out in defense of literature. Asked for suggestions, such critics are likely to propose the *Readers' Digest* as required reading in high school—or to urge more comic-book versions of the "classics": emasculated Melville, expurgated Hawthorne, or a child's version of something "uplifting" like "The Fall of the House of Usher." In other countries, corresponding counterparts are not hard to find.

As a matter of fact, this charge is scarcely ever urged with much conviction. It is really the portrayal of crime and horror (and less usually sex) that the enlightened censors deplore. It has been charged against vulgar art that it is sadistic, fetishistic, brutal, full of terror; that it pictures women with exaggeratedly full breasts and rumps, portrays death on the printed page, is often covertly homosexual, etc., etc. About these charges, there are two obvious things to say. First, by and large, they are true. Second, they are also true about much of the most serious art of our time, especially that produced in America.

There is no count of sadism and brutality which could not be equally proved against Hemingway or Faulkner or Paul Bowles—or, for that matter, Edgar Allan Poe. There are certain more literate critics who are victims of their own confusion in this regard, and who will condemn a Class B movie for its images of flagellation or bloodshed only to praise in the next breath

such an orgy of highminded sadism as *Le Salaire de la Peur*. The politics of
the French picture may be preferable, or its photography; but this cannot
redeem the scene in which a mud- and oil-soaked truckdriver crawls from a
pit of sludge to reveal the protruding white bones of a multiple fracture of
the thigh. This is as much horror-pornography as *Scarface* or *Little Caesar*.
You cannot condemn *Superman* for the exploitation of violence, and praise
the existentialist-homosexual-sadist shockers of Paul Bowles. It is possible
to murmur by way of explanation something vague about art or catharsis;
but no one is ready to advocate the suppression of anything merely because
it is aesthetically bad. In this age of conflicting standards, we would all soon
suppress each other.

An occasional Savonarola is, of course, ready to make the total rejection;
and secretly or openly, the run-of-the-mill condemner of mass culture does
condemn, on precisely the same grounds, most contemporary literature of
distinction. Historically, one can make quite a convincing case to prove that
our highest and lowest arts come from a common antibourgeois source. Edgar
Allan Poe, who lived the image of the dandy that has been haunting high art
ever since, also, one remembers, invented the popular detective story; and
there is a direct line from Hemingway to O'Hara to Dashiell Hammett to
Raymond Chandler to Mickey Spillane.

Of both lines of descent from Poe, one can say that they tell a black and
distressing truth (we are creatures of dark impulse in a threatened and guilty
world), and that they challenge the more genteel versions of "good taste."
Behind the opposition to vulgar literature, there is at work the same fear
of the archetypal and the unconscious itself that motivated similar attacks
on Elizabethan drama and on the eighteenth-century novel. We always judge
Gosson a fool in terms of Shakespeare; but this is not the point—he was just
as wrong in his attack on the worst-written, the most outrageously bloody and
bawdy plays of his time. I should hate my argument to be understood as a
defense of what is banal and mechanical and dull (there is, of course, a great
deal!) in mass culture; it is merely a counterattack against those who are aiming through that banality and dullness at what moves all literature of worth.
Anyone at all sensitive to the life of the imagination would surely prefer his
kids to read the coarsest fables of Black and White contending for the City
of Man, rather than have them spell out, "Oh, see, Jane. Funny, funny Jane,"
or read to themselves hygienic accounts of the operation of supermarkets or
manureless farms. Yet most schoolboard members are on the side of mental
hygiene; and it is they who lead the charge against mass culture.

Anyone old enough to have seen, say, *Rain*, is on guard against those who
in the guise of wanting to destroy savagery and ignorance wage war on
spontaneity and richness. But we are likely to think of such possibilities
purely in sexual terms; the new righteous themselves have been touched
lightly by Freud and are firm believers in frankness and "sex education." But

in the very midst of their self-congratulation at their emancipation, they have become victims of a new and ferocious prudery. One who would be ashamed to lecture his masturbating son on the dangers of insanity, is quite prepared (especially if he has been reading Wertham) to predict the electric chair for the young scoundrel caught with a bootlegged comic. Superman is our Sadie Thompson. We live in an age when the child who is exposed to the "facts of life" is protected from "the facts of death." In the United States, for instance, a certain Doctor Spock has produced an enlightened guide to childcare for modern mothers—a paperback book which sold, I would guess, millions of copies. Tell the child all about sex, the good doctor advises, but on the subject of death—hush!

By more "advanced" consultants, the taboo is advanced further toward absurdity: no bloodsoaked Grimm, no terrifying Andersen, no childhood verses about cradles that fall—for fear breeds insecurity; insecurity, aggression; aggression, war. There is even a "happy," that is to say, expurgated, Mother Goose in which the three blind mice have become "kind mice"—and the farmer's wife no longer hacks off their tails, but "cuts them some cheese with a carving knife." Everywhere the fear of fear is endemic, the fear of the very names of fear; those who have most ardently desired to end warfare and personal cruelty in the world around them, and are therefore most frustrated by their persistence, conspire to stamp out violence on the nursery bookshelf. This much they can do anyhow. If they can't hold up the weather, at least they can break the bloody glass.

This same fear of the instinctual and the dark, this denial of death and guilt by the enlightened genteel, motivates their distrust of serious literature, too. Faulkner is snubbed and the comic books are banned, not in the interests of the classics or even of Robert Louis Stevenson, as the attackers claim, but in the name of a literature of the middle ground which finds its fictitious vision of a kindly and congenial world attacked from above and below. I speak now not of the few intellectual converts to the cause of censorship, but of the main body of genteel book-banners, whose idol is Lloyd Douglas or even A. J. Cronin. When a critic such as Mr. Wagner is led to applaud what he sees as a "trend" toward making doctors, lawyers, etc., the heroes of certain magazine stories, he has fallen into the trap of regarding middling fiction as a transmission belt from the vulgar to the high. There is no question, however, of a slow climb from the level of literature which celebrates newspaper reporters, newsboys, radio commentators (who are also super-heroes in tight-fitting uniforms with insignia), through one which centers around prosperous professionals, to the heights of serious literature, whose protagonists are suicides full of incestuous longings, lady lushes with clipped hair, bootleggers, gangsters, and broken-down pugs. To try to state the progression is to reveal its absurdity.

The conception of such a "trend" is nothing more than the standard atti-

tude of a standard kind of literature, the literature of slick-paper ladies' magazines, which prefers the stereotype to the archetype, loves poetic justice, sentimentality, and gentility, and is peopled by characters who bathe frequently,
live in the suburbs, and are professionals. Such literature circles mindlessly
inside the trap of its two themes: unconsummated adultery and the con-
summated pure romance. There can be little doubt about which kind of
persons and which sort of fables best typify our plight, which tell the truth
—or better, a truth—in the language of those to whom they speak.

In the last phrase, there is a rub. The notion that there is more than one
language of art, or rather, that there is something not quite art, which performs art's function for most men in our society, is disquieting enough for
anyone, and completely unacceptable to the sentimental egalitarian, who had
dreamed of universal literacy leading directly to a universal culture. It is here
that we begin to see that there is a politics as well as a pathology involved
in the bourgeois hostility to popular culture. I do not refer only to the explicit
political ideas embodied in the comics or in the literature of the cultural élite;
but certainly each of these arts has a characteristic attitude: populist-authori-
tarian on the one hand and aristocratic-authoritarian on the other.

It is notorious how few of the eminent novelists or poets of our time have
shared the political ideals we would agree are the most noble available to us.
The flirtations of Yeats and Lawrence with fascism, Pound's weird amalgam
of Confucianism, Jeffersonianism, and social credit, the modified Dixiecrat
principles of Faulkner—all make the point with terrible reiteration. Between
the best art and poetry of our age and the critical liberal reader there can be
no bond of shared belief; at best we have the ironic confrontation of the
sceptical mind and the believing imagination. It is this division which has,
I suppose, led us to define more and more narrowly the "aesthetic experience,"
to attempt to isolate a quality of seeing and saying that has a moral value
quite independent of *what* is seen or heard.

> Time that with this strange excuse
> Pardoned Kipling and his views,
> And will pardon Paul Claudel,
> Pardons him for writing well.

But the genteel middling mind which turns to art for entertainment and
uplift, finds this point of view reprehensible; and cries out in rage against
those who give Ezra Pound a prize and who claim that "to permit other considerations than that of poetic achievement to sway the decision would . . .
deny the validity of that objective perception of value on which any civilized
society must rest." We live in the midst of a strange two-front class war: the
readers of the slicks battling the subscribers to the "little reviews" and the
consumers of pulps; the sentimental-egalitarian conscience against the ironical-
aristocratic sensibility on the one hand and the brutal-populist mentality on
the other. The joke, of course, is that it is the "democratic" center which calls

here and now for suppression of its rivals; while the élite advocate a condescending tolerance, and the vulgar ask only to be let alone.

It is disconcerting to find cultural repression flourishing at the point where middling culture meets a kindly, if not vigorously thought-out, liberalism. The sort of right-thinking citizen who subsidizes trips to America for Japanese girls scarred by the Hiroshima bombing, and deplores McCarthy in the public press, also deplores, and would censor, the comics. In one sense, this is fair enough; for beneath the veneer of slogans that "crime doesn't pay" and the superficial praise of law and order, the comics do reflect that dark populist faith which Senator McCarthy has exploited. There is a kind of "black socialism" of the American masses which underlies formal allegiances to one party or another: the sense that there is always a conspiracy at the centers of political and financial power; the notion that the official defenders of the commonwealth are "bought" more often than not; an impatience with moral scruples and a distrust of intelligence, especially in the expert and scientist; a willingness to identify the enemy, the dark projection of everything most feared in the self, on to some journalistically defined political opponent of the moment.

This is not quite the "fascism" it is sometimes called. There is, for instance, no European anti-Semitism involved, despite the conventional hooked nose of the scientist-villain. (The inventors and chief producers of comic books have been, as it happens, Jews.) There is also no adulation of a dictator-figure on the model of Hitler or Stalin; though one of the archetypes of the Deliverer in the comics is called Superman, he is quite unlike the Nietzschean figure—it is the image of Cincinnatus which persists in him, an archetype that has possessed the American imagination since the time of Washington: the leader who enlists for the duration and retires unrewarded to obscurity.

It would be absurd to ask the consumer of such art to admire in the place of images that project his own impotence and longing for civil peace some hero of middling culture—say, the good boy of Arthur Miller's *Death of a Salesman*, who, because he has studied hard in school, has become a lawyer who argues cases before the Supreme Court and has friends who own their own tennis courts. As absurd as to ask the general populace to worship Stephen Dedalus or Captain Ahab! But the high-minded petty-bourgeois cannot understand or forgive the rejection of his own dream, which he considers as nothing less than the final dream of humanity. The very existence of a kind of art depending on allegiances and values other than his challenges an article of his political faith; and when such an art is "popular," that is, more read, more liked, more bought than his own, he feels his *raison d'être*, his basic life-defense, imperilled. The failure of the petty-bourgeoisie to achieve cultural hegemony threatens their dream of a truly classless society; for they believe, with some justification, that such a society can afford only a single culture. And they see, in the persistence of a high art and a low art on either side of their average own, symptoms of the re-emergence of classes in a quarter where no one had troubled to stand guard.

The problem posed by popular culture is finally, then, a problem of class distinction in a democratic society. What is at stake is the refusal of cultural equality by a large part of the population. It is misleading to think of popular culture as the product of a conspiracy of profiteers against the rest of us. This venerable notion of an eternally oppressed and deprived but innocent people is precisely what the rise of mass culture challenges. Much of what upper-class egalitarians dreamed for him, the ordinary man does not want—especially literacy. The situation is bewildering and complex, for the people have not rejected completely the notion of cultural equality; rather, they desire its symbol but not its fact. At the very moment when half of the population of the United States reads no *hard-covered* book in a year, more than half of all high-school graduates are entering universities and colleges; in twenty-five years almost all Americans will at least begin a higher education. It is clear that what is demanded is a B.A. for everyone, with the stipulation that no one be forced to read to get it. And this the colleges, with "objective tests" and "audio-visual aids," are doing their reluctant best to satisfy.

One of the more exasperating aspects of the cultural defeat of the egalitarians is that it followed a seeming victory. For a while (in the Anglo-Saxon world at least) it appeared as if the spread of literacy, the rise of the bourgeoisie, and the emergence of the novel as a reigning form would succeed in destroying both traditional folk art and an aristocratic literature still pledged to epic, ode, and verse tragedy. But the novel itself (in the hands of Lawrence, Proust, Kafka, etc.) soon passed beyond the comprehension of those for whom it was originally contrived; and the retrograde derivations from it—various steps in a retreat toward wordless narrative: digests, pulp fiction, movies, picture magazines—revealed that middling literature was not in fact the legitimate heir of either folk art or high art, much less the successor of both, but a *tertium quid* of uncertain status and value.

The middlebrow reacts with equal fury to an art that baffles his understanding and to one which refuses to aspire to his level. The first reminds him that he has not yet, after all *arrived* (and, indeed, may never make it); the second suggests to him a condition to which he might easily relapse, one perhaps that might have made him happier with less effort (and here exacerbated puritanism is joined to baffled egalitarianism), even suggests what his state may appear like to those a notch above. Since he cannot, on his own terms, explain to himself why anyone should choose any level but the highest (that is, his own), the failure of the vulgar seems to him the product of mere ignorance and laziness—a crime! And the rejection by the advanced artist of his canons strikes him as a finicking excess, a pointless and unforgivable snobbism. Both, that is, suggest the intolerable notion of a hierarchy of taste, a hierarchy of values, the possibility of cultural classes in a democratic state; and before this, puzzled and enraged, he can only call a cop. The fear of the vulgar is the obverse of the fear of excellence, and both are aspects of the fear of difference: symptoms of a drive for conformity on the level of the timid, sentimental, mindless-bodiless genteel.

E. J. KAHN, JR.

Ooff!! (Sob!) Eep!! (Gulp!) Zowie!!![1]

A few years ago, the Boston *Globe*, perhaps hoping to evoke a handsome testimonial to the influence of its editorial page, asked some of its readers who were attending college, and were thus possibly a cut above the intellectual average, to tell why they preferred the *Globe* to its competitors. Ninety per cent of the students said that they favored the *Globe* because it carried "Li'l Abner," a comic strip that is more or less concerned with the diverting antics of a singular tribe of hillbillies native to Dogpatch, a community situated somewhere in the mountains of the southeastern United States. The results of the *Globe's* survey were conveyed, in due course, to Al Capp, the man who draws and writes "Li'l Abner." Capp is a dark, heavy-set, brash, exuberant, witty, rowdy, and inventive man of thirty-eight, who sometimes professes to despise comic strips and might take a firmer stand against them than he does were it not for the fact that they earn him, before taxes, nearly a quarter of a million dollars a year, a sum that he cannot bring himself to despise. His first reaction to the *Globe's* findings, when a friend told him the news, was commendably objective. "This is deplorable," said Capp. "Is the younger generation utterly without taste?" A moment later, partly disengaging his teeth from the hand that so royally feeds him, he added, "Still, think how much more deplorable it would have been if those imbeciles had said they read the *Globe* because of 'Jane Arden.'"

Capp's full name is Alfred Gerald Caplin, but since the summer of 1934, when he introduced "Li'l Abner" to what he has grown fond of describing as a horrified public, he has been using the sawed-off version, being convinced that many readers of comics are apt to become restless and irritable when confronted with polysyllabic words. Last year, at the invitation of the Encyclopædia Britannica, Capp wrote a critical essay about the American comic strip for a four-volume supplement called "Ten Eventful Years." Capp noticed delightedly that he had been identified as "A. Cp.," a signature far outdoing in economy his own effort. He was about to write the Britannica editors a congratulatory note when a learned acquaintance explained that these scholars abbreviate all their

[1] Reprinted by permission from *The New Yorker*, XXIII (November 29, 1947), 45-57. Copyright, 1947, The New Yorker Magazine, Inc.

contributors' names, even those never previously cropped. According to Capp's article, "The comic strip during the decade 1937-1946 became, in terms of the constancy of the devotion of its followers, the most popular U.S. entertainment, surpassing radio and the motion picture." In any terms, the comics are thriving. Every month, nearly forty million comic books are bought and presumably read. Every day, seventy million people, or half the population of the country, are reputed to read, openly or furtively, comic strips in the newspapers. It is difficult to arrive at the exact number of readers of any given strip, since the syndicates that distribute these profitable features are partial to dealing in round, if not downright puffy, figures. The United Feature Syndicate, which transmits Capp's work to a waiting world, computed recently, with exceptional precision, that "Li'l Abner" was printed in 30,189,151 copies of daily newspapers in this country, as well as in a large but indeterminable quantity abroad. Any analysis of such statistics is apt to bring on a headache. In the fall of 1944, for instance, United Feature, then dealing in conventional globular figures, announced that Capp had twenty-seven million readers and that he had acquired them at the rate of seventy-five hundred a day. In the fall of 1945, the syndicate announced that in the preceding twelve months he had picked up 77,923 readers. This amounted to a daily gain for that year of a mere two hundred and thirteen and a half readers, but the syndicate, instead of apologizing for this sudden diminution of converts per day, deftly shifted its ground and let it be known that Capp habitually ensnared new readers at the rate of four and a half a minute. It is agreed by people who ponder such matters that the field is led today by five comic strips—"Blondie," "Dick Tracy," "Joe Palooka," "Little Orphan Annie," and "Li'l Abner," though not necessarily in that order. Each one appears in over twenty-five million copies of newspapers a week, and each copy probably has at least one reader, or, in round figures, each strip has fifty readers per second, day or night, rain or shine, dead or alive.

Partisans of each of the five most illustrious serials, including the men who turn them out, are inclined to think that their own favorite is coincidentally the national favorite. "More Americans give me a piece of their day," Capp recently told a friend, "than anyone else in the country." He is not alone in viewing himself as top dog. The *Illinois State Journal*, published in Springfield, observed last year that "Al Capp, more than any other comic strip artist, has won the complete confidence and genuine affection of the American people. . . . Li'l Abner [has] become an American institution." The Charlotte, North Carolina, *News*, further defining the strip's institutional status, called it "as much a part of the national life as ice cream cones and taxes." These periodicals are among the four hundred and twenty-seven daily and one hundred and seventy-nine Sunday papers in the United States that carry "Li'l Abner." They pay, depending on their size and other factors, from seventy-five cents to six hundred dollars a week for the privilege. Tributes to Capp's eminence have not come only from publications that contentedly serve as the oysters for his pearls. A federal law-enforcement officer in San Antonio once wrote Capp that in the course of his duties he had met up with people suffering from the stings of scorpions, from overdoses of marijuana, and from hydrophobia, but that he had never encountered anybody "who spouted more varied and distorted ideas than you do."

When Capp started "Li'l Abner," comic strips were around forty years old. The early comics were unpretentious illustrated gags; they were comical, or tried to be. By the thirties, according to the Britannica's Mr. Cp., "The clowns had been pushed off the comic page by the misery-vendors, the horror-vendors, the blood-merchants. The hilarious 'Bam!!!' or 'Zowie!!!!' ending of the comic simpleton overcome by the brutality, misunderstanding, avariciousness, or bad temper of his fellow man had been supplanted by the 'Help!! The rattlesnake is strangling me, Mother, dear!!!'—or—'Take dat, you copper—right t'roo de head!!!' type of ending wherein the comic simpleton was supplanted by a pathetic, golden-haired little girl simpleton or a blue-eyed, white-lipped, red-blooded detective simpleton, whose perils never ended—in fact, increased each day in violence and intricacy. . . . The comic strips, with a few die-hard, hard-fighting exceptions, were no longer comic. . . . The word went out from circulation departments that anxiety about the fate of Orphan Annie's dog sold far more papers than did joy over the foolishness of Boob McNutt." Capp is the hardest-fighting exception to the trend he disapproves of. His principal character, a young man named Li'l Abner Yokum, is a simpleton of inimitable foolishness, and practically everybody he meets up with is brutal, misunderstanding, avaricious, or bad-tempered. Abner is a handsome youth with an impressive physique, and he is constantly being troubled by the advances of highly attractive young ladies, but he admits to being in love only with such things as a dressmaker's dummy and a cockroach. Male readers of "Li'l Abner," contemplating this grotesque state of affairs, presumably indulge in a smug, self-satisfied smile, fairly certain that if *they* were ever to be pursued by a host of beautiful women, they would know what to do about it. Capp, working on the popular assumption that people of either sex derive immense satisfaction from laughing at the misadventures of creatures to whom they feel superior, has endowed his characters with such nonsensical traits that it is impossible for the most backward citizen of this country not to consider them inferior to himself. Capp's hillbillies are not all in love with cockroaches, but they are thoroughly individualistic in one way or another. They are uneducated, uninhibited, unsanitary, unconventional, and uncompromising, and it always surprises them that the rest of the world is out of step. By continually enmeshing these rural folk in the complexities of organized society, Capp produces the same kind of laughter aroused, in other fields, by the nonconformist struggles of Charlie Chaplin and Groucho Marx. Capp, an exceptionally worldly fellow, has a low opinion of the present state of organized society, and the fantasies he creates often touch upon current events and are heavily flavored with satire. "It's hard to know just how to sum up Al," a friend of Capp's said recently. "If you rule out the possibility that he is a madman, I guess I would call him an outrageously talented author of terribly funny illustrated topical fairy tales—with social significance."

Capp is perhaps without an equal among contemporary fairy-tale composers in his ability to proceed with engaging plausibility from a ludicrous premise to a preposterous conclusion. "My readers have a hard time," he said a while ago. "They have to learn to accept the incredible as the normal run of things." His readers can be divided into three categories, corresponding to the three levels upon which "Li'l Abner" is constructed. The base level is in the Bam!!!-and-Zowie!!!! tradition, a broad, slapstick foundation of frenzied adventure, such as hair-raising chases, violent fights, and people hanging by their fingertips from the edges of precipitous cliffs. Readers of all ages who like to browse on this level are apt to be quite concerned about the outcome of Capp's elaborate and giddy plots, and those who get a chance always ask him whether Li'l Abner is ever going to marry the heroine of the strip, a handsome but vacuous young lady named Daisy Mae Scragg, whose love for Abner is equaled only by his distaste for her entire sex. Capp is sometimes tolerant of, but always bored with, people who make this inquiry about this foolish young couple, and he refers to them brusquely as "Abner fans." Readers who indicate to him that they are especially pleased with the middle, or socially significant, level of his work, and who ask him when he is going to take another poke at radio commercials or the United States Senate, are, he thinks, much more estimable citizens, and he calls them, approvingly, "disgusting Abner fans." The third level, sometimes of microscopic dimensions, consists of bits of Rabelaisian humor, often so adroitly covered up that, like rare archeological treasures, they are less likely to be spotted by children at play than by people who set out looking for them. These mischievous escapades in print amuse Capp more than anything else about his work, and the thought that few of his readers share this enjoyment with him depresses him. If, however, he were to make these touches more obvious, it is possible that his strip might be banned not only in Boston but in Springfield, Charlotte, and San Antonio as well.

When Capp encounters a reader who enjoys not only the two lower levels but the nuances on Level Three, he confers on the fellow the highest possible token of his esteem, the designation of "slobbering Abner fan." People who have thus been honored realize that the title is a compliment, since "slob" is one of Capp's favorite nouns. "To me, the word 'slob' has a great deal of force and humor," he has said. "It's one of those really choice and charming words." It is not regarded with the same fervor by the United Feature Syndicate, whose editors feel obliged to tone down Capp's material when they detect something that particularly worries them. (A United Feature man was once described by a sympathetic friend as a "quivering Abner fan," and a piece of promotional literature that the syndicate issued a couple of years ago said, with perhaps unconscious wistfulness, "You never know what's coming next when it comes off the pen of the creator of 'Li'l Abner.' ") One of Capp's favorite characters is a

Dogpatch girl called Moonbeam McSwine, whose name indicates her paradoxical nature, since although she is uncommonly good-looking, she detests bathing
and prefers the company of hogs to that of men. Six years ago, Capp had her
say, "Ah is a lazy good-fo'-nothin' slob!" Somebody in the United Feature offices
gave this confessional a scrubbing on its way to the public, and when it finally
appeared in print it read, "Ah is a lazy good-fo'-nothin'!" Capp was distressed
by the disappearance of what to him had been the only really charming word in
the sentence, but he cheered up a few years later when he succeeded in having
Daisy Mae, a girl of profound delicacy, call Moonbeam McSwine a slob.

Capp is not a self-effacing man, but he has stubbornly resisted the temptation
to consider himself, as many of his fellow-citizens do, the world's greatest contemporary comic-strip artist. He feels that he is merely one of the two greatest,
the other being Milton Caniff, the gifted inventor of "Terry and the Pirates"
(now being done by another man) and at present the shepherd of "Steve
Canyon." Capp's estimate seems to be shared by the School of Education of
New York University, which, when it revealed, not long ago, that it planned to
conduct a study of "the cartoon narrative as a medium of communication," said
that Caniff and Capp were the only two cartoon narrators who were slated to
take part in the inquiry. Caniff does not share Capp's shy reluctance to put one
man at the top of the list; Caniff puts Capp there. "Al's the best of us all,"
he said recently. "To me, he is the only really funny man in the funnies business." Capp's professional honors are numerous. For one thing, he was the first
comic-strip creator (a noun used in the business to describe anyone who both
writes and draws a strip) to introduce parodies of other comic strips into his
own. For another, he was the first comic-strip man to effect a profitable tieup,
in his strip, with commercial broadcasting. Last year, he collaborated on a song
about Li'l Abner and, after persuading several important radio vocalists to plug
it, worked them into the plot of his strip. Then, on whatever day they were
scheduled to sing the number, caricatures of them appeared in "Li'l Abner"
and mentioned their broadcasts. Considering that comic strips have to be put
together several weeks before publication and that radio programs are often
torn apart at the last minute, the fact that Capp managed to synchronize events
in the two media was impressive.

Capp has done a great many things other comic-strip artists might well be
afraid to attempt. "The funnies have always avoided the enormous comic gold
mine of sex," he once said. He was not referring to his own strip. When a
song entitled "Six Lessons from Madame La Zonga," which he did not help
compose, was at its height, Capp introduced into "Li'l Abner" an engaging
and romantic character named Adam Lazonga. "He was a perilous experiment,"
Capp wrote to a friend, "because he was the master of how to woo, Dogpatch
style—a kinda wooing the details of which were never very clear to the reader
or to me, but which was superior to all other styles—and because he had won
loving cups in exhibitions of Dogpatch-style wooing the world over. It was a
nervous moment when I let him loose in the nation's family newspapers.

Readers were shocked as it dawned on them what he was famous for doing, but delighted by his courtly and genteel way of doing it, and his dignified attitude toward his work."

Capp has many distinctions besides that of digging pay dirt out of the gold mine of sex. Most comic-strip creators are sedentary folk. Capp is wildly peripatetic. He lives with his wife and their three children on a farm in New Hampshire, has a studio apartment in Boston, and spends from ten days to two weeks of every month relaxing, with indefatigable intensity, in New York. Moreover, he is the only major practitioner of his art involved in two richly rewarding strips. He does the plotting and writes the dialogue for "Abbie an' Slats," which appears in a hundred and thirty daily and eighty Sunday papers in this country. "Abbie" is officially the handiwork of Raeburn Van Buren, who draws it and signs it, but Capp thought up the idea for it eleven years ago, sold it to United Feature, has done all the writing for it ever since, and receives half the net proceeds from it. Neither Capp nor United Feature has ever publicly admitted his connection with "Abbie," perhaps out of consideration for the feelings of comic-strip creators who have barely enough imagination and energy to keep one serial going. Capp enjoys pretending that he has no stake in "Abbie," and when asked by interviewers from high-school papers, as he often is, to name his favorite strip next to "Li'l Abner," he usually pauses, seems to think hard for a moment, and then solemnly plumps for "Abbie an' Slats." In his Britannica article, he modestly mentions "Abner" only once, but he twice praises "Abbie." Just a week ago, Capp established some kind of precedent by reviving, in "Abbie," a character who had been unequivocally killed off several months before. "In comic strips," Capp wrote in a note to his readers that was signed "R.V.B.," "if *you* want it hard enough and if the cartoonist has *nerve* enough, we can get together, remake the make-believe world in which, for a few moments each day, we all meet." Having the continuities of two major comic strips at his mercy, Capp has been able to indulge in a good deal of horseplay. Among the characters who have turned up in "Li'l Abner" are Raeburn Van Huron, an Indian chief, and Bullseye Van Suren, a champion dart-thrower; "Abbie an' Slats" was once given over for several weeks to the story of a conceited, gluttonous, drunken, disorderly, and untalented comic-strip artist named Hal Yapp, the creator of a strip called "Li'l Ebenezer." Yapp worked—at a time when the late George Carlin was managing United Feature —for a syndicate run by George Garlic. Capp often ridicules public figures, and he receives a lot of indignant letters of protest from people who admire his victims. When the Hal Yapp continuity appeared in "Abbie an' Slats," a great many alert Al Capp fans addressed vituperative letters to Raeburn Van Buren, who has since been regarded in the profession as the most stoical member of the human race since Sparta.

Capp's best-known victim is Chester Gould, creator of "Dick Tracy." Three years ago, in "Li'l Abner," Capp unveiled a cartoonist named Lester Gooch, creator of a gory strip entitled "Fearless Fosdick." The title character of this strip-within-a-strip is a detective of immense stupidity and is the idol of Li'l Abner Yokum, whom Capp has described as an individual of average comic-strip-reading mentality. "When Yokum speaks," Capp once wrote in "Li'l Abner," in a further explanation of his hero's mentality, "he speaks for millions of morons." In the lampoons of "Dick Tracy" that Capp has turned out, he has made some sharp observations upon the effect of comics on the American mind. A year and a half ago, Capp began a "Fearless Fosdick" sequence with a letter to Gooch written by Yokum, who was probably speaking not only for millions but for Capp, too. "Yore drawrins cood allus be dependid on to frigten li'l chillun an ole ladys into fitts on account they was so ugly yore drawrins I meen," wrote Abner, the only member of his family, aside from a small pig, who is literate. "Yo has allus bin the leeder of yore profeshun naimly skeerin the liver out of yore fateful reeders. But, laitly, things has changed, Gooch. Lately, *other* comical stripp cree-ay-ters bin cree-ay-tin even *more* horibul cree-ay-shuns then *yo!* Like ladys wif gravel in thar hare, mudd in thar eyes and who smells badd. Natcherly, the Americun public injoys this vurry much, Gooch. The trubble, Gooch, is all *yo* drawrs is horribul *gennulmin!!* Oh, Gooch, don't lett yore galentry hold yo back! Yo kin drawr worse than any of 'em. Go to it, Gooch, whomp up a lady thet is *so* itchy, *so* shakey, *so* smelly, and *so* onbarubbly digustin that once again you will be the king of the funny page."

Shortly thereafter, Capp, who, naturally, aspires to be the king of the funny page himself, took his own advice and whomped up a lady named Lena the Hyena, an inhabitant of a country he called, to show what he thought of it, Lower Slobbovia. Lena had a face so unbearably disgusting that a coal-black shark, happening to glimpse and then to swallow a photograph of it, shrieked, turned white, and sank to the bottom of the sea. Capp did not, however, plan to frighten little children and old ladies into fits by letting them see Lena's face—or so he insists today. He left the space above her neck blank and wrote "Deleted by Editor" across it. Immediately, some of his readers, eager to have the livers scared out of them, wrote to him pleading for a look at the lady's features. Capp then announced, in "Li'l Abner," that only a morbid horror seeker could be interested in the sight. This provoked more letters from confessed morbid horror seekers. Capp, delighted, decided to open a contest for drawings of the worst-looking woman in the world, the winning picture to be used in the strip and the winning artist to receive a prize of five hundred dollars. Three hundred and eighty-one of the newspapers that run "Li'l Abner" joined in, and most of them offered additional awards. Close to a million entries were submitted. On the periphery of the big contest, people all over the country—including a group of adult members of the First Congregational Church of Toledo—banded together to hold elimination contests of their own. A schoolboy who said he owned an authentic likeness of Lena grew rich, by charging his classmates a nickel a peek, before his teacher took it away from him. The annual Homecoming Queen beauty contest of the University of

Colorado was disrupted by a write-in movement for Lena, who did so much better than any of the six attractive live candidates that the president of the university hastily called off the competition. Just before Election Day, a California paper that was participating in the contest asked its readers to send in questions they wished to have answered by prospective office-holders. The paper got a total of thirty political questions and seven thousand drawings of Lena the Hyena.

There has been only the one Lena contest. For the last ten years, however, every November has been brightened by the celebration, on hundreds of campuses and in other arenas, of an as yet unofficial holiday known as Sadie Hawkins Day, which, according to the Birmingham, Alabama, *Post*, a paper that publishes "Li'l Abner," has become "so firmly entrenched as part of the American way of life that it would take an act of Congress to wipe it off the books." In Dogpatch, Sadie Hawkins Day provides unmarried women with an opportunity to obtain husbands by catching the community's eligible men in a foot race. In the rest of the country, the day is a less forthright variation of the leap-year idea. At many academies where it is observed, it is simply an excuse for the temporary reversal of normal social relationships: girls date boys. On some campuses the holiday lasts for a week or more, usually ending with a costume party, for which the guests dress in the fashion of "Li'l Abner" characters, a most scantily clad crew. Every year, Capp is invited to take in a couple of thousand of these parties. Last November, after consenting to look in on eighteen of them, he said to a friend, "Aren't they a wonderful idea? A girl can look charming for nothing!" Halfway through his tour, when he entered an armory where twelve thousand young people, dressed charmingly in rags, had gathered to do him homage, he appeared to have lost some of his enthusiasm. "What have I wrought!" he was heard to mutter. After the eighteenth party, he retired to his studio, sat down, and dashed off a snarling "Li'l Abner" sequence about the kind of people who go to Sadie Hawkins Day parties. Half the girls who attend these functions come dressed as Daisy Mae, and usually they participate in a beauty contest, the winner of which is designated the Daisy Mae of her community. Capp is often invited to serve as a judge. A year ago, he was chief judge and guest of honor at a Sadie Hawkins Day frolic at a large state university. The governor of the state was also present. For several weeks, there had been primary elections to winnow out hundreds of aspiring Daisy Maes. Finally, one chilly night, ten attractive survivors were lined up in a gymnasium for Capp's scrutiny. He is often lax about keeping appointments, and in this instance he was a full hour late. "There were the ten Daisy Maes," he told a friend afterward, "waiting for me, shivering. Usually, when I handle the finals, I spot a couple of standouts right away, either one of whom would be all right to pick. But every now and then it's just no contest. This was one of those cases. One little girl in the line was the loveliest thing I had ever seen. As I was looking them all over, I couldn't help grinning at her. She smiled back. She knew she'd win. Well, there were a lot of photographers hanging around, as always, and I thought I'd be polite and let the governor, who was also hanging around, into the act. I gave him a loving cup and whispered to him, 'The third from the left.' I should have known better than to entrust something like that to a politician. The governor stepped forward and handed the cup to the second from the left, and before I could do anything about it, flash bulbs began popping all over the place and the audience was clapping and cheering. I was stupefied with horror. The poor little third from the left! I couldn't even tell her later about the mistake. It would have created too much of a furor on the campus."

Capp's success in arousing interest in the subject matter of his strip has been thoughtfully noted by many people with axes to grind, and press agents buzz around him as enthusiastically as if he were a syndicated columnist instead of a syndicated cartoonist. When the American Heritage Foundation, sponsor of the Freedom Train, wanted some extra-special publicity for the beginning of its journey, an appeal was made to Capp. He obliged by turning "Li'l Abner," for two weeks, into a dramatization of the Bill of Rights. Some weeks ago, he received a request from Albert Einstein for assistance in disseminating the solemn propaganda of the Emergency Committee of Atomic Scientists. "Will handle in Slobbovia sequence," Capp wrote on the margin of Einstein's letter, and there is no reason to believe that he will not. Capp does not have to be nudged to espouse a cause. Entirely on his own, he has worked up spirited campaigns against, for instance, zoot suits, Southern congressmen, big business, intolerance, and outdoor advertising signs. Once he put Li'l Abner and Daisy Mae in an automobile and sent them off on a sightseeing trip during which, to view the scenery, Abner was compelled to uproot a hundred and fifty obstructive billboards along a ten-mile stretch of otherwise scenic highway. "Gosh!!" said Daisy Mae afterward. "Hain't America a *bootiful* country—it's even more *bootiful* than billboards advertisin' pork, beans, girdles, shoes, cheese, an' crackers!!" Advertising men have tried to dissuade Capp from this particular crusade. "The implications of such an act," the president of the Outdoor Advertising Association of North Carolina wrote him after Abner's prodigious feats of upheaving, "can hardly remain unnoticed by . . . law-abiding citizens of the United States. . . . If, in the immediate future, a wave of vandalism or property destruction of panels occurs typifying your hero's actions, it will not be a difficult matter to place the blame in the proper quarter." The wave never broke, perhaps because most Americans cannot pull up billboards barehanded. Sometimes, when Capp gets mad, he merely threatens people or institutions with notoriety. During the war, he made a short journey in a day coach and didn't care for it. "I'd never seen anything like the stinking, screaming horror of the whole set-up," he said to an acquaintance. "The poor passengers were treated like prisoners of war. I wrote a letter to the president of the railroad saying that I was planning to have some Dogpatchers take that same trip and that I was going to have them insulted and reviled and knocked about like Polish Jews on a German train on the way to a crematorium. 'I'm going to make it like Dante's "Inferno," ' I told him, 'and I want no protest out of you! I hadn't drawn a line of any such sequence and didn't intend to, but that railroad president called me up every half hour for four days, conducted a long investigation, discharged two employees, suspended fourteen others, and undoubtedly hasn't had a good night's sleep since."

Some citizens are as eager to get into Capp's strip as others are to stay out. Four years ago, he started using his space on Christmas Day to extend holiday greetings to his friends. Along Broadway, it is now considered even more desirable to get on Capp's December honors list than to be wished happy birthday by Nick Kenny. "You made me the happiest man in the world," a prominent comedian who got mentioned wired Capp last December 26th. As early as the Fourth of July, Capp begins receiving telegrams from press agents reminding him how friendly he feels towards their clients. "It's getting so that if I leave off anybody who was on the year before, he fires his press agent," Capp says. "Why, a music publisher I know called me up the other day and said, 'Al, if you don't include Dick Haymes the way I promised him, I may lose him entirely as a plugger of my songs.' " Capp likes to live well, and he includes on his Christmas list the names of the managers of whatever hotels and night clubs he expects to be spending a substantial amount of time in. Last year he ended his list with the Hampshire House, where he has never since had any trouble reserving a suite. The year before, he extended seasonal wishes to "Halifax." A friend asked him whether he meant the British Ambassador or the city. "I wasn't sure at the time I put it in," Capp replied, "but I got a nice letter of thanks from both." Throughout the year, Capp is offered small gifts if he will make even a casual mention in "Li'l Abner" of something or somebody with a commercial angle, but he has always refused. Once, he was oddly penalized for giving a free plug. The occasion was the opening in New York, in April, 1944, of a musical comedy, "Allah Be Praised!," whose producer, Alfred Bloomingdale, is a friend of Capp's. The cartoonist regards himself as an astute theatrical critic, especially of musical comedies. He attended several rehearsals of "Allah Be Praised!," was delighted with what he saw, and decided to give the show a helping hand. In the strips to be published during the month after the show opened, he decorated a number of walls and fences with placards saying, "Allah Bloomingdale Presents 'Allah Bloomingdale Be Praised.' " The show folded after twenty performances, by which time Capp's outdoor advertising on its behalf had long since been distributed to his newspapers, so it kept coming out for another ten days. Capp was annoyed that "Allah Be Praised!" closed with such inconvenient celerity, and he immediately began writing the book of a musical comedy of his own, an adaptation of "Li'l Abner," which he is still working on.

Outspoken admirers of Capp's work have hailed him as a writer comparable to Lewis Carroll, Mark Twain, Dickens, and Dostoevski, and as an artist comparable to Hogarth, Daumier, and Low. Capp is embarrassed by such accolades. He prefers to think of himself as a simple, incomparable entertainer who specializes in the art of imaginative storytelling. "Practically any artist is better than I am," he once said. "As an artist, I'm just capable." He had such doubts about his capabilities as a writer that three years after starting "Li'l Abner," he took a short-story course at Harvard. His instructor told him that he was not without promise and gave him a B-minus. Technological improvements in communications have given Capp many advantages over earlier storytellers. Homer, for instance, was unable to make himself heard beyond the range of his voice. Capp, without having to raise his voice, can almost simultaneously tell the story of "Li'l Abner" in five languages, in eighteen countries, including Sweden and Venezuela. For telling a black-and-white Monday-through-Saturday continued story and a four-color Sunday-to-Sunday story, he receives around thirty-five hundred dollars a week. His yarns have become so popular in the thirteen years he has been spinning them that he takes in an additional twelve thousand or so a year from royalties on the sales of comic books, toys, costume jewelry, ladies' blouses, cosmetics, and music that have something to do with his comic strip. On behalf of Cream of Wheat, he does six "Li'l Abner" advertisements a year, for which he gets two thousand dollars apiece. "Abbie an' Slats" is good for another twenty thousand annually. Capp has a couple of assistants who do some of his drawing, but even before he took the course at Harvard he declined all offers of assistance in writing. "Li'l Abner" requires an average of a hundred words a day. A fellow-author, arbitrarily assigning half of Capp's gross income from the syndication of "Abner" to its text, has computed that each word, including "Eep" and "Ooff," brings its author three dollars. Capp is not satisfied with this word rate. Most syndicated comic-strippers receive fifty per cent of the gross. Capp now gets sixty-five per cent and is due to get an increase to seventy in 1949. Nevertheless, he is suing United Feature for fourteen and a half million dollars, which he contends the syndicate has deprived him of, in one way or another, since 1934. This may well be the largest claim ever filed by a single literary man against a corporate patron of the arts. The case is an extremely complex one, and unless it is settled out of court, as it may well be, it could drag on for two or three years, like some comic-strip sequences. In the meantime, Capp and United Feature are still working together, in a tight-lipped way.

The success of any storyteller can be measured at least in part by the extent to which his inventions become idiom. Who can utter the words "wine-dark sea" without recalling Homer? Capp's literary achievements, although they have yet to appear in an anthology of quotations, have become a part of the language. He has persuaded a great many of his fellow-citizens that "gulp" and "sob" are expressions that can be legitimately inserted at any point in any sentence. He is responsible for the fact that "oh, happy day!," "amoozin' but confoozin'," "writ by hand," and "as any fool can plainly see" are now used with merciless persistence by millions of Americans. The current enormous popularity of the adverb "naturally" and its variants "natcherly" and "natch" may well be the result of his devotion to them. His nonchalant approach to grammar, punctuation, and spelling has been a stimulating challenge to teachers of English composition, many of whose pupils have indicated a determination to pattern their prose after Al Capp's rather than Dr. Samuel Johnson's. A high-school junior in Lake Bluff, Illinois, assigned to three weeks of earnest study of "some great poet, author, or other writer who symbolizes American literature," chose Capp. In halls of higher learning, too, Capp is a man to reckon with. A year ago, at the College of William and Mary, a debate was held on the subject "Resolved: That 'Dick Tracy' means more to the American public than 'Li'l Abner.' " Two teams, each made up of an undergraduate and a professor, declaimed their arguments. A jury of three other faculty members unanimously returned a verdict in favor of "Li'l Abner."

Some, though by no means all, educators have come to assume that comic strips are read mostly by children and that it is harmful for young and impressionable minds to be continually exposed to characters like Moonbeam McSwine, whose distaste for soap, except as food, has never visibly impaired her physical well-being. The creators of comics, however, long ago abandoned the notion that their readers are all, or even predominantly, children. In a recent survey of adult readers of a number of metropolitan papers that print "Li'l Abner," seventy per cent of the men and sixty per cent of the women questioned said that they followed the strip. Most of the members of our war-time armed forces were of voting age, and their allegiance to "Li'l Abner" seemed at times second only to the one they had pledged to the flag. When the Paris edition of *Stars & Stripes* was unable, for a brief spell, to publish "Abner," it ran an apologetic note saying, "We admit that no newspaper is much good without 'Li'l Abner,' but you'll have to read the rest of the paper for a few days." When "Li'l Abner" failed to appear for three days running in the Vancouver *Sun*, its editors made a great to-do over its absence, which they treated as a news event. Actually, the *Sun* could have published the strip on the second and third day—a delay in the mails had caused a week's worth of "Abner" to arrive twenty-four hours late—but the editors withheld the strip, on the theory, which proved correct, that the despair and then the relief of their readers would be enormously increased. Like many prominent providers of mass-distributed entertainment in an era notable for the affection consumers of this commodity lavish upon its manufacturers, Capp has a vast supply of fervent admirers who aspire to touch or at least to ogle him, and he enjoys his celebrity. He does not, however, receive all the adulation stored up for him, because, unlike most celebrities, his face is not known to all his fans. Some of them aren't even sure of his name: to them he is only that fellow who does "Li'l Abner." At that, his face and name are perhaps better known than are the faces and names of most comic-strip creators, owing to his repeated use of caricatures of the face and variations of the name in the body of his strip. He has always been fond of devising names such as J. P. Gorganfeller, for a millionaire, and

Southbrook Juggler, for a columnist, and he is particularly happy when he concocts something like Al Capricorn, for an astrologist, or George Cappley, for a late Bostonian. Connoisseurs of "Li'l Abner" are inclined to the belief that Capp has never got a bigger laugh out of anybody's name than he did out of his own in the fall of 1945, when he had one Westbrook P. Buckingham, the wealthy distiller of a soft drink called Burpsi-Booma, discuss the financing of a proposed new elixir, Eleven Urp, with a pair of Indians belonging to the Seegarstor tribe. "I need capital," said Buckingham. "Capital in Washin'ton. No can move um. Too big," said one of the Indians. "Me once scalp paleface name of 'Al Capital,'" remarked the other Indian triumphantly. There is no evidence that Dickens, Twain, Carroll, or Dostoevski ever contrived anything comparable.

Capp is also working on the project of enabling his admirers to recognize him in the flesh. His calling cards, of which he always carries a bountiful supply, bear on them not merely his name but Li'l Abner's easily recognizable features. When Capp travels, it is usually in a brand-new Cadillac convertible coupé, with the words "Al Capp," in a reproduction of the script in which he signs the strip, printed on the door. At present, he has two 1947 Cadillac convertible coupés, both painted in eye-catching colors and both autographed. While he is riding in either of them, his movements are characterized by a refreshing disdain for the traffic regulations devised by a hundred and forty million other people simply to inconvenience him, and also for policemen churlish enough to wish to enforce them. Some of his friends think that he is, in the vulgar phrase, a cop-hater, but he disagrees. Once, though, he depicted Li'l Abner being mauled by five loutish policemen simply for having picked a flower near a "Keep Off the Grass" sign; this assault occurred immediately after the same officers had unconcernedly watched a couple of thugs spend half an hour beating up an old man. Another time, while Abner and his parents were in London, Capp had them severely dress down a bobby for being polite to them, an attitude that, they told him, was, in a policeman, un-American. Capp himself rarely has any trouble with the police. Whenever a cop does wander across the street to argue with him as he sits in his car, the officer is usually disarmed either by the signature on the car door or, if he doesn't notice that, by the illustrated calling card Capp thrusts upon him. Practically all policemen, it seems, are "Li'l Abner" fans and cannot bring themselves, even after seeing Abner's creator execute a double U turn on a crowded parkway, to be Capp-haters. Capp is usually glad that his prominence can save him from difficulties, but there are moments when he wonders whether it might not be nice to be—instead of a widely acclaimed, splendidly motorized funny man—plain Alfred G. Caplin, a travelling salesman, say, in an unsigned Chevrolet. "My God," he once said, "if only you could imagine the sheer, soul-racking horror of knowing that whenever you are introduced to a stranger as the creator of—gulp—'Li'l Abner,' he'll respond by saying not 'How do you do' but 'Ha ha.'"

BARRY ULANOV

What Is Jazz?[1]

In *The American Scene*, Henry James said of American cities, "So there it all is; arrange it as you can. Poor dear bad bold beauty; there must indeed be something about her . . . !" The same thing can be said of American jazz.

On the surface there is disorder and conflict in jazz. No common definition of this music has been reached. It resists dictionary definition, and its musicians splutter nervously and take refuge in the colorful ambiguities of its argot. Nonetheless, its beauty can be probed; its badness can be separated from its boldness. The process is a difficult one, as it is in any art, and in jazz two arts, the composing and the performing arts, are joined together. But if one goes beneath the surface and does not allow the contradictions and the confusions of appearances to put one off, much becomes clear, and the mystery at the center is seen to be the central mystery of all the arts.

The cortex of jazz consists of several layers, alternately hard and soft, complex in structure, and hard to take apart. It is compounded of the history of the music and of the many styles of jazz. At first the history seems disjointed and the styles contradictory. One marks a confounding series of shifts in place and person and style. One finds a music dominated by Negroes in New Orleans, by white musicians in Chicago, by important but apparently unrelated figures in New York. One discovers a disastrous split in jazz inaugurated by the swing era and intensified during the days of bebop and so-called progressive jazz. But then one looks and listens more closely, and order and continuity appear.

Americans have long been wedded to the boom-and-bust cycle, and their culture reflects that dizzying course. Jazz is not like that; it has no cycles; it doesn't spiral. Whether you adopt the approach of the economic historian, the cultural anthropologist, or the aesthetic philosopher, you will not find an easy reflection of a theory in jazz. While much of America—crises and ecstasies and even a moment or two of exaltation—has found its way into jazz, the history of jazz is a curiously even one, chaotic at any instant, but always moving ahead in what is for an art form almost a straight line.

For most of its history, jazz, rejected in its homeland, has had consciously to seek survival, conscientiously to explain and defend its existence. From its early homes, the Ozark hills, the Louisiana bayous, the Carolina cotton fields, the Virginia plantations, through the New Orleans bordellos and barrelhouses to its latter-day efflorescence it has been alternately condemned and misunderstood. Variously banned and bullied and sometimes cheered beyond its merits,

[1] From *A History of Jazz in America* by Barry Ulanov (New York: The Viking Press, Inc., 1954), Chap. 1. Copyright 1952 by Barry Ulanov. Reprinted by permission of The Viking Press, Inc.

jazz has led a lonely life but a full one. It is still with us and looks to be around for quite a while.

No matter what the fortunes of jazz, its nucleus has remained constant, little touched by extravagances of opinion, sympathetic or unsympathetic. The nucleus of jazz—as differentiated from its cortex—contains its nerve center, its source of life, and here are its mystery and meaning. The nucleus of jazz is made up of melody, harmony, and rhythm, the triune qualities of the art of music which, as everybody knows, can be fairly simply defined. In bare definition, melody is any succession of notes, harmony any simultaneity of tones, rhythm the arithmetic measure of notes or tones. In closer examination, melody appears as a vast variety of things, ranging from so simple a tune as "Yankee Doodle" to the complexity of one of Arnold Schoenberg's constructions. In more detailed analysis, harmony shows up as a vertical ordering of a Bach fugue, or a tight structuring based entirely on whole tones in the impressionism of Debussy. But bewildering as the complications of melody and harmony can be, they are easier to analyze and verbalize than rhythm or any of its parts, and rhythm is the most important of the three in jazz.

Before attempting a synoptic definition of jazz as a noun (or discussing the misuse of "jazz" as a verb and "jazzy" as an adjective), and of the various corollary terms that explain the meaning of this music, it might be instructive to examine definitions by musicians themselves. The following definitions were made by jazz musicians in 1935, when their music was undergoing a revival as a result of the then current vogue for the jazz that went by the new name of swing. Benny Goodman was a great success, and jam sessions had become public again. Musicians themselves found it difficult to define "swing," by which of course they merely meant the 1935 version of jazz, which wasn't very different from the 1930 or 1925 music. Let us examine the definitions.

WINGY MANONE: "Feeling an increase in tempo though you're still playing at the same tempo."

MARSHALL STEARNS AND JOHN HAMMOND (jazz authorities) AND BENNY GOODMAN: "A band swings when its collective improvisation is rhythmically integrated."

GENE KRUPA: "Complete and inspired freedom of rhythmic interpretation."

JESS STACY: "Syncopated syncopation."

MORTON KAHN AND PAYSON RE: "Feeling a multitude of subdivisions in each beat and playing or implying the accents that you feel; that is, if the tune is played at the proper tempo, so that when you're playing it, you'll feel it inside."

GLENN MILLER: "Something that you have to feel; a sensation that can be conveyed to others."

FRANKIE FROEBA: "A steady tempo, causing lightness and relaxation and a feeling of floating."

TERRY SHAND: "A synthetic cooperation of two or more instruments helping along or giving feeling to the soloist performing."

OZZIE NELSON: "A vague something that you seem to feel pulsating from a danceable orchestra. To me it is a solidity and compactness of attack by which the rhythm instruments combine with the others to create within the listeners the desire to dance."

CHICK WEBB: "It's like lovin' a gal, and havin' a fight, and then seein' her again."

LOUIS ARMSTRONG: "My idea how a tune should go."

ELLA FITZGERALD: "Why, er—swing is—well, you sort of feel—uh—uh—I don't know—you just swing!"

These musicians were looking for a new set of terms that would catch the beat so basic to jazz; they were stumped for the words to describe the kind of improvisation necessary to jazz.

In the simple, compressed, sometimes too elliptic vocabulary of the jazz musician, one learns a great deal about the music he plays. One learns that "jazz" is a noun, that it is not American popular music (as it has often been thought to be), that the jazz musician is most interested in the rhythmic connotation of the word and in little else. If you tell him that some say the term comes from the phonetic spelling of the abbreviation of a jazz musician named Charles (Charles, Chas., Jass, Jazz), he is not in the least interested. If you tell him that there is a great deal of substance to the claim that the word comes from the French word *jaser*—to pep up, to exhilarate—he may nod his head with a degree of interest but ask you, "What about the beat?" You will learn from the jazz musician that "swing" is no longer a noun, in spite of the fact that it was first so used in the title of a Duke Ellington recording in 1931, "It Don't Mean a Thing if It Ain't Got that Swing," which gives it a kind of ex cathedra endorsement. You will learn that "swing" is a verb, a way of describing the beat, even as Ellington's title for another tune, "Bouncing Buoyancy," is a description of the same beat, even as the term "jump" is, even as "leaps" is, even as the description of jazz as "music that goes" is, even as in the thirties the compliment of "solid" to performer or performance was like "gone," "crazy," "craziest," "the end," and "cool" today. They are descriptions of the beat.

From an examination of jazz musicians' own words, it is possible to glean the subtle, unruly, and almost mystical concept of the jazz spirit, or feeling, or thinking—it is all these things and is so understood by the jazz musician himself. The jazzman has his own way of getting at the center of his music, and thus he formulates his own musical language. Also he converts the musical language into a verbal dialect of his own. In his own set of terms, musical and verbal, he thinks, he feels; he rehearses, he performs; he scores, he improvises; he gets a beat.

To get that elusive beat a jazzman will do anything. Without it, he cannot do anything. With it, he is playing jazz, and that is a large and satisfying enough accomplishment. When a jazzman picks up a familiar tune, banal or too well-known through much repetition, and alters its rhythmic pattern in favor of a steady if sometimes monotonous beat, and varies its melodies and maybe even changes its chords, he is working freely, easily, and with as much spontaneity as he can bring to his music. That freedom, ease, and spontaneity brought him to jazz; within those determining limits he will find a place for himself or get out, or join one of the bands whose frightening parodies of jazz are so often more popular than the real thing. It is by his formal understanding of certain definite values that the jazz musician has conceived, organized, and developed his art. It has been hot; it has become cool. It has jumped and swung; it has sauntered. It has borrowed; it has originated. It has affected a change, a literal transformation; inherited conventions have gradually been restated, reorganized, and ultimately restructured as a new expression. It may be that jazz musicians have simply rediscovered a controlling factor in music, the improvising performer. Without any awareness of what he has done, the jazzman may have gone back to some of the beginnings of music, tapping once more the creative roots which nourished ancient Greek music, the plain chant, the musical baroque and its immediate successors and predecessors. We know that seventeenth- and eighteenth-century composers were improvisers and that when they brought their scores to other musicians they left the interpretation of parts to the discretion of the performers, even as an arranger for a jazz band does today.

But the jazz musician has brought more than procedures, composing conceptions, and improvisation to his music. Techniques have been developed that have broadened the resources and intensified the disciplines of certain instruments far beyond their use in other music. Colors have been added to solo instruments and to various combinations and numbers of instruments that are utterly unlike any others in music. New textures have emerged from a conception of tonality and of pitch that is not original but is entirely fresh in its application. The improvising jazz musician has a different and more responsible and rewarding position from that of his counterparts in earlier art and folk music. The rhythmic base of music has been reinterpreted, making the central pulse at once more primitive than it has been before in Western music, and more sophisticated in its variety.

This, then, is how one might define jazz: it is a new music of a certain distinct rhythmic and melodic character, one that constantly involves improvisation—of a minor sort in adjusting accents and phrases of the tune at hand, of a major sort in creating music extemporaneously, on the spot. In the course of creating jazz, a melody or its underlying chords may be altered. The rhythmic valuations of notes may be lengthened or shortened according to a regular scheme, syncopated or not, or there may be no consistent pattern of rhythmic variations so long as a steady beat remains implicit or explicit. The beat is usually four quarter-notes to the bar, serving as a solid rhythmic base for the improvisation of soloists or groups playing eight or twelve measures, or some multiple or dividend thereof.

These things are the means. The ends are the ends of all art, the expression of the universal and the particular, the specific and the indirect and the intangible. In its short history, jazz has generally been restricted to short forms and it has often been directed toward the ephemeral and the trivial, but so too has it looked toward the lasting perception and the meaningful conclusion. Much of the time jazz musicians have sought and obtained an unashamed aphrodisiac effect; they have also worshiped in their music, variously devout before the one God and the unnamed gods. Like poets and painters, they are of all faiths, their doctrines are many; but they are united in one conviction, that they have found a creative form for themselves, for their time, for their place.

At the opening of the *Gradus ad Parnassum*, the dialogue offered as a study of counterpoint by Johann Josef Fux in 1725, the music master Aloysius warns the student Josef: "You must try to remember whether or not you felt a strong natural inclination to this art even in childhood." The student answers: "Yes, most deeply. Even before I could reason, I was overcome by the force of this strange enthusiasm and I turned all my thoughts and feelings to music. And now the burning desire to understand it possesses me, drives me almost against my will, and day and night lovely melodies seem to sound around me. Therefore I think I no longer have reason to doubt my inclination. Nor do the difficulties of the work discourage me, and I hope that with the help of good health I shall be able to master it." Several jazz musicians have read Fux, even as Haydn and Beethoven did, though perhaps with less immediate application. They have, however, echoed the pupil's "strange enthusiasm"; that, these jazz-men said, was their experience, their "burning desire." Following the "inclination," jazz musicians have not had much of the help of good health; some of them have flaunted their doggedly unreasonable living habits and suffered the personal and public consequences of the habits and of the flaunting. All this their music has reflected, and sometimes it is noisy and grotesque as a result. More often it has a fullness and richness of expression. Slowly, clearly, the music is maturing, and, for it and with it and by it, so are the musicians.

Literature and Criticism

❖❖❖❖❖❖❖❖❖❖❖❖❖❖❖❖❖❖❖❖❖❖❖❖❖❖❖❖❖❖❖❖❖

MATTHEW ARNOLD

Dover Beach

The sea is calm to-night.
The tide is full, the moon lies fair
Upon the straits; on the French coast, the light
Gleams and is gone; the cliffs of England stand,
Glimmering and vast, out in the tranquil bay.
Come to the window, sweet is the night-air!

Only, from the long line of spray
Where the sea meets the moon-blanched land,
Listen! you hear the grating roar
Of pebbles which the waves draw back, and fling,
At their return, up the high strand,
Begin and cease, and then again begin,
With tremulous cadence slow, and bring
The eternal note of sadness in.

Sophocles long ago
Heard it on the Aegean, and it brought
Into his mind the turbid ebb and flow
Of human misery: we
Find also in the sound a thought,
Hearing it by this distant northern sea.

The sea of faith
Was once, too, at the full, and round earth's shore
Lay like the folds of a bright girdle furled.
But now I only hear
Its melancholy, long, withdrawing roar,
Retreating, to the breath
Of the night-wind, down the vast edges drear
And naked shingles of the world.

Ah, love, let us be true
To one another, for the world, which seems
To lie before us like a land of dreams,
So various, so beautiful, so new,
Hath really neither joy, nor love, nor light,
Nor certitude, nor peace, nor help for pain;
And we are here as on a darkling plain
Swept with confused alarms of struggle and flight,
Where ignorant armies clash by night.

THEODORE MORRISON

Dover Beach Revisited: A New Fable for Critics[1]

Early in the year 1939 a certain Professor of Educational Psychology, occupying a well-paid chair at a large endowed university, conceived a plot.
From his desk in the imposing Hall of the Social Sciences where the Research

1 "Dover Beach Revisited: A New Fable for Critics," *Harper's Magazine*, CLXXX
(February, 1940), 235-244. Reprinted by permission of the author.

Institute in Education was housed he had long burned with resentment against teachers of literature, especially against English departments. It seemed to him that the professors of English stood square across the path of his major professional ambition. His great desire in life was to introduce into the study, the teaching, the critical evaluation of literature some of the systematic method, some of the "objective procedure" as he liked to call it, some of the certainty of result which he believed to be characteristic of the physical sciences. "You make such a fetish of science," a colleague once said to him, "why aren't you a chemist?"—a question that annoyed him deeply.

If such a poem as Milton's "Lycidas" has a value—and most English teachers, even to-day, would start with that as a cardinal fact—then that value must be measurable and expressible in terms that do not shift and change from moment to moment and person to person with every subjective whim. They would agree, these teachers of literature, these professors of English, that the value of the poem is in some sense objective; they would never agree to undertake any objective procedure to determine what that value is. They would not clearly define what they meant by achievement in the study of literature, and they bridled and snorted when anyone else attempted to define it. He remembered what had happened when he had once been incautious enough to suggest to a professor of English in his own college that it might be possible to establish norms for the appreciation of Milton. The fellow had simply exploded into a peal of histrionic laughter and then had tried to wither him with an equally histrionic look of incredulity and disgust.

He would like to see what would happen if the teachers of English were forced or lured, by some scheme or other, into a public exposure of their position. It would put them in the light of intellectual charlatanism, nothing less . . . and suddenly Professor Chartly (for so he was nicknamed) began to see his way.

It was a simple plan that popped into his head, simple yet bold and practical. It was a challenge that could not be refused. A strategically placed friend in one of the large educational foundations could be counted on: there would be money for clerical expenses, for travel if need be. He took his pipe from his pocket, filled it, and began to puff exultantly. To-morrow he must broach the scheme to one or two colleagues; to-night, over cheese and beer, would not be too soon. He reached for the telephone.

The plan that he unfolded to his associates that evening aroused considerable skepticism at first, but gradually they succumbed to his enthusiasm. A number of well-known professors of literature at representative colleges up and down the land would be asked to write a critical evaluation of a poem prominent enough to form part of the standard reading in all large English courses. They would be asked to state the criteria on which they based their judgment. When all the answers had been received the whole dossier would be sent to a moderator, a trusted elder statesman of education, known everywhere for his dignity, liberality of intelligence, and long experience. He would be asked to make a preliminary examination of all the documents and to determine from the point of view of a teacher of literature whether they provided any basis for a common understanding. The moderator would then forward all the documents to Professor Chartly, who would make what in his own mind he was frank to call a more scientific analysis. Then the jaws of the trap would be ready to spring.

Once the conspirators had agreed on their plot their first difficulty came in the choice of a poem. Suffice it to say that someone eventually hit on Arnold's "Dover Beach," and the suggestion withstood all attack. "Dover Beach" was universally known, almost universally praised; it was remote enough so that contemporary jealousies and cults were not seriously involved, yet near enough not to call for any special expertness, historical or linguistic, as a prerequisite for judgment; it was generally given credit for skill as a work of art, yet it contained also, in its author's own phrase, a "criticism of life."

Rapidly in the days following the first meeting the representative teachers were chosen and invited to participate in the plan. Professional courtesy seemed to require the inclusion of an Arnold expert. But the one selected excused himself from producing a value judgment of "Dover Beach" on the ground that he was busy investigating a fresh clue to the identity of "Marguerite." He had evidence that the woman in question, after the episode hinted at in the famous poems, had married her deceased sister's husband, thus perhaps affecting Arnold's views on a social question about which he had said a good deal in his prose writings. The expert pointed out that he had been given a half-year's leave of absence and a research grant to pursue the shadow of Marguerite through Europe, wherever it might lead him. If only war did not break out he hoped to complete this research and solve one of the vexing problems that had always confronted Arnold's biographers. His energies would be too much engaged in this special investigation to deal justly with the more general questions raised by Professor Chartly's invitation. But he asked to be kept informed, since the results of the experiment could not fail to be of interest to him.

After a few hitches and delays from other quarters, the scheme was ripe. The requests were mailed out, and the Professor of Educational Psychology sat back in grim confidence to await the outcome.

II

It chanced that the first of the representative teachers who received and answered Professor Chartly's letter was thought of on his own campus as giving off a distinct though not unpleasant odor of the ivory tower. He would have resented the imputation himself. At forty-five Bradley Dewing was handsome in a somewhat speciously virile style, graying at the temples, but still well-knit and active. He prided himself on being able to beat most of his students at tennis; once a year he would play the third or fourth man on the varsity and go down to creditable defeat with some elegiac phrases on the ravages of time. He thought of himself as a man of the world; it was well for his contentment, which was seldom visibly ruffled, that he never heard the class mimic reproducing at a fraternity house or beer parlor his manner of saying: "After all, gentlemen, it is pure poetry that lasts. We must never forget the staying power of pure art." The class mimic never represents the whole of class opinion but he can usually make everyone within earshot laugh.

Professor Dewing could remember clearly what his own teachers had said about "Dover Beach" in the days when he was a freshman in college himself, phrases rounded with distant professional unction: faith and doubt in the Victorian era; disturbing influence of Darwin on religious belief; Browning the optimist; Tennyson coming up with firm faith after a long struggle in the waters of doubt; Matthew Arnold, prophet of skepticism. How would "Dover Beach" stack up now as a poem? Pull Arnold down from the shelf and find out.

Ah, yes, how the familiar phrases came back. The sea is calm, the tide is full, the cliffs of England stand. . . . And then the lines he particularly liked:

> Come to the window, sweet is the night air!
> Only, from the long line of spray
> Where the ebb meets the moon-blanch'd sand,
> Listen! you hear the grating roar
> Of pebbles which the waves draw back, and fling,
> At their return, up the high strand,
> Begin, and cease, and then again begin,
> With tremulous cadence slow . . .

Good poetry, that! No one could mistake it. Onomatopoeia was a relatively cheap effect most of the time. Poe, for instance: "And the silken sad uncertain rustling of each purple curtain." Anyone could put a string of s's together and make them rustle. But these lines in "Dover Beach" were different. The onomatopoeia was involved in the whole scene, and it in turn involved the whole rhythmical movement of the verse, not the mere noise made by the consonants or vowels as such. The pauses—only, listen, draw back, fling, begin, cease—how they infused a subdued melancholy into the moonlit panorama at the same time that they gave it the utmost physical reality by suggesting the endless iteration of the waves! And then the phrase "With tremulous cadence slow" coming as yet one more touch, one "fine excess," when it seemed that every phrase and pause the scene could bear had already been lavished on it: that was Miltonic, Virgilian.

But the rest of the poem?

> The sea of Faith
> Was once, too, at the full, and round earth's shore
> Lay like the folds of a bright girdle furl'd . . .

Of course Arnold had evoked the whole scene only to bring before us this metaphor of faith in its ebb-tide. But that did not save the figure from triteness and from an even more fatal vagueness. Everything in second-rate poetry is compared to the sea: love is as deep, grief as salty, passion as turbulent. The sea may look like a bright girdle sometimes, though Professor Dewing did not think it particularly impressive to say so. And in what sense is *faith* a bright girdle? Is it the function of faith to embrace, to bind, to hold up a petticoat, or what? And what is the faith that Arnold has in mind? The poet evokes no precise concept of it. He throws us the simple, undifferentiated word, unites its loose emotional connotations with those of the sea, and leaves the whole matter there. And the concluding figure of "Dover Beach":

> we are here as on a darkling plain
> Swept with confused alarms of struggle and flight,
> Where ignorant armies clash by night.

Splendid in itself, this memorable image. But the sea had been forgotten now; the darkling plain had displaced the figure from which the whole poem tacitly promised to evolve. It would not have been so if John Donne had been the craftsman. A single bold yet accurate analogy, with constantly developing implications, would have served him for the whole poem.

Thus mused Professor Dewing, the lines of his verdict taking shape in his head. A critic of poetry of course was not at liberty to pass judgment on a poet's thought; he could only judge whether, in treating of the thought or sensibility he had received from his age, the poet had produced a satisfactory work of art. Arnold, Professor Dewing felt, had not been able to escape from the didactic tone or from a certain commonness and vagueness of expression. With deep personal misgivings about his position in a world both socially and spiritually barbarous, he had sought an image for his emotion, and had found it in the sea—a natural phenomenon still obscured by the drapings of conventional beauty and used by all manner of poets to express all manner of feelings. "Dover Beach" would always remain notable, Professor Dewing decided, as an expression of Victorian sensibility. It contained lines of ever memorable poetic skill. But it could not, he felt, be accepted as a uniformly satisfactory example of poetic art.

III

It was occasionally a source of wonder to those about him just why Professor Oliver Twitchell spent so much time and eloquence urging that man's lower nature must be repressed, his animal instincts kept in bounds by the exertion of the higher will. To the casual observer, Professor Twitchell himself did not seem to possess much animal nature. It seemed incredible that a desperate struggle with powerful bestial passions might be going on at any moment within his own slight frame, behind his delicate white face in which the most prominent feature was the octagonal glasses that focused his eyes on the outside world. Professor Twitchell was a good deal given to discipleship but not much to friendship. He had himself been a disciple of the great Irving Babbitt, and he attracted a small number of disciples among his own more earnest students. But no one knew him well. Only one of his colleagues, who took a somewhat sardonic interest in the mysteries of human nature, possessed a possible clue to the origin of his efforts to repress man's lower nature and vindicate his higher. This colleague had wormed his way sufficiently into Oliver Twitchell's confidence to learn about his family, which he did not often mention. Professor Twitchell, it turned out, had come of decidedly unacademic stock. One of his brothers was the chief salesman for a company that made domestic fire-alarm appliances. At a moment's notice he would whip out a sample from his bag or pocket, plug it into the nearest electric outlet, and while the bystanders waited in terrified suspense, would explain that in the dead of night, if the house caught fire, the thing would go off with a whoop loud enough to warn the soundest sleeper. Lined up with his whole string of brothers and sisters, all older than he, all abounding in spirits, Professor Twitchell looked like the runt of the litter. His colleague decided that he must have had a very hard childhood, and that it was not his own animal nature that he needed so constantly to repress, but his family's.

Whatever the reasons, Professor Twitchell felt no reality in the teaching of literature except as he could extract from it definitions and illustrations of man's moral struggle in the world. For him recent history had been a history of intellectual confusion and degradation, and hence of social confusion and degradation. Western thought had fallen into a heresy. It had failed to maintain the fundamental grounds of a true humanism. It had blurred the distinction between man, God, and nature. Under the influence of the sciences, it had set up a monism in which the moral as well as the physical constitution of man was included within nature and the laws of nature. It had, therefore, exalted man as naturally good, and exalted the free expression of all his impulses. What were the results of this heresy? An age, complained Professor Twitchell bitterly, in which young women talked about sexual perversions at the dinner table; an age in which everyone agreed that society was in dissolution and insisted on the privilege of being dissolute; an age without any common standards of value in morals or art; an age, in short, without discipline, without self-restraint in private life or public.

Oliver Twitchell when he received Professor Chartly's envelope sat down with a strong favorable predisposition toward his task. He accepted wholeheartedly Arnold's attitude toward literature: the demand that poetry should be serious, that it should present us with a criticism of life, that it should be measured by standards not merely personal, but in some sense *real*.

"Dover Beach" had become Arnold's best-known poem, admired as his masterpiece. It would surely contain, therefore, a distillation of his attitude. Professor Twitchell pulled down his copy of Arnold and began to read; and as he read he felt himself overtaken by surprised misgiving. The poem began well enough. The allusion to Sophocles, who had heard the sound of the retreating tide by the Ægean centuries ago, admirably prepared the groundwork of high seriousness for a poem which would culminate in a real criticism of human experience. But did the poem so culminate? It was true that the world

> Hath really neither joy, nor love, nor light, . . .
> Nor certitude, nor peace, nor help for pain

if one meant the world as the worldling knows it, the man who conducts his life by unreflective natural impulse. Such a man will soon enough encounter the disappointments of ambition, the instability of all bonds and ties founded on nothing firmer than passion or self-interest. But this incertitude of the world, to a true disciple of culture, should become a means of self-discipline. It should lead him to ask how life may be purified and ennobled, how we may by wisdom and self-restraint oppose to the accidents of the world a true human culture based on the exertion of a higher will. No call to such a positive moral will, Professor Twitchell reluctantly discovered, can be heard in "Dover Beach." Man is an ignorant soldier struggling confusedly in a blind battle. Was this the culminating truth that Arnold the poet had given men in his masterpiece? Professor Twitchell sadly revised his value-judgment of the poem. He could not feel that in his most widely admired performance Arnold had seen life steadily or seen it whole; rather he had seen it only on its worldly side, and seen it under an aspect of terror. "Dover Beach" would always be justly respected for its poetic art, but the famous lines on Sophocles better exemplified the poet as a critic of life.

                                                            IV

As a novelist still referred to in his late thirties as "young" and "promising," Rudolph Mole found himself in a curious relation toward his academic colleagues. He wrote for the public, not for the learned journals; hence he was spared the necessity of becoming a pedant. At the same time the more lucrative fruits of pedantry were denied to him by his quiet exclusion from the guild. Younger men sweating for promotion, living in shabby genteel poverty on yearly appointments, their childless wives mimicking their academic shop-talk in bluestocking phrases, would look up from the stacks of five-by-three cards on which they were constantly accumulating notes and references, and would say to him, "You don't realize how lucky you are, teaching composition. You aren't expected to know anything." Sometimes an older colleague, who had passed through several stages of the mysteries of preferment, would belittle professional scholarship to him with an elaborate show of graciousness and envy. "We are all just pedants," he would say. "You teach the students what they really want and need." Rudolph noticed that the self-confessed pedant went busily on publishing monographs and being promoted, while he himself remained, year by year, the English Department's most eminent poor relation.

He was not embittered. His dealings with students were pleasant and interesting. There was a sense of reality and purpose in trying to elicit from them a better expression of their thoughts, trying to increase their understanding of the literary crafts. He could attack their minds on any front he chose, and he could follow his intellectual hobbies as freely as he liked, without being confined to the artificial boundaries of a professional field of learning.

Freud, for example. When Professor Chartly and his accomplices decided that a teacher of creative writing should be included in their scheme and chose Rudolph Mole for the post, they happened to catch him at the height of his enthusiasm for Freud. Not that he expected to psychoanalyze authors through their works; that, he avowed, was not his purpose. You can't deduce the specific secrets of a man's life, he would cheerfully admit, by trying to fit his works into the text-book patterns of complexes and psychoses. The critic, in any case, is interested only in the man to the extent that he is involved in his work. But everyone agrees, Rudolph maintained, that the man is involved in his work. Some part of the psychic constitution of the author finds expression in every line that he writes. We can't understand the work unless we can understand the psychic traits that have gained expression in it. We may never be able to trace back these traits to their ultimate sources and causes, probably buried deep in the author's childhood. But we need to gain as much light on them as we can, since they appear in the work we are trying to apprehend, and determine its character. This is what criticism has always sought to do. Freud simply brings new light to the old task.

Rudolph was fortunate enough at the outset to pick up at the college bookstore a copy of Mr. Lionel Trilling's recent study of Matthew Arnold. In this volume he found much of his work already done for him. A footnote to Mr. Trilling's text, citing evidence from Professors Tinker and Lowry, made it clear that "Dover Beach" may well have been written in 1850, some seventeen years before it was first published. This, for Rudolph's purposes, was a priceless discovery. It meant that all the traditional talk about the poem was largely null and void. The poem was not a repercussion of the bombshell that Darwin dropped on the religious sensibilities of the Victorians. It was far more deeply personal and individual than that. Perhaps when Arnold published it his own sense of what it expressed or how it would be understood had changed. But clearly the poem came into being as an expression of what Arnold felt to be the particular kind of affection and passion he needed from a woman. It was a love poem, and took its place with utmost naturalness, once the clue had been given, in the group of similar and related poems addressed to "Marguerite." Mr. Trilling summed up in a fine sentence one strain in these poems, and the principal strain in "Dover Beach," when he wrote that for Arnold "fidelity is a word relevant only to those lovers who see the world as a place of sorrow and in their common suffering require the comfort of constancy."

> Ah, love, let us be true
> To one another! for the world . . .
> Hath really neither joy, nor love, nor light . . .

The point was unmistakable. And from the whole group of poems to which "Dover Beach" belonged, a sketch of Arnold as an erotic personality could be derived. The question whether a "real Marguerite" existed was an idle one, for the traits that found expression in the poems were at least "real" enough to produce the poems and to determine their character.

And what an odd spectacle it made, the self-expressed character of Arnold as a lover! The ordinary degree of aggressiveness, the normal joy of conquest and possession, seemed to be wholly absent from him. The love he asked for was essentially a protective love, sisterly or motherly; in its unavoidable ingredient of passion he felt a constant danger, which repelled and unsettled him. He addressed Marguerite as "My sister!" He avowed and deplored his own woman-ish fits of instability:

> I too have wish'd, no woman more,
> This starting, feverish heart, away.

He emphasized his nervous anguish and contrary impulses. He was a "teas'd o'erlabour'd heart," "an aimless unallay'd Desire." He could not break through his fundamental isolation and submerge himself in another human soul, and he believed that all men shared this plight:

> Yes: in the sea of life enisl'd,
> With echoing straits between us thrown,
> Dotting the shoreless watery wild,
> We mortal millions live *alone*.

He never "without remorse" allowed himself

> To haunt the place where passions reign,

yet it was clear that whether he had ever succeeded in giving himself up whole-heartedly to a passion, he had wanted to. There could hardly be a more telltale phrase than "Once-long'd-for storms of love."

In short much more illumination fell on "Dover Beach" from certain other verses of Arnold's than from Darwin and all his commentators:

> Truth—what is truth? Two bleeding hearts
> Wounded by men, by Fortune tried,
> Outwearied with their lonely parts,
> Vow to beat henceforth side by side.
>
> The world to them was stern and drear;
> Their lot was but to weep and moan.
> Ah, let them keep their faith sincere,
> For neither could subsist alone!

Here was the nub. "Dover Beach" grew directly from and repeated the same emotion, but no doubt generalized and enlarged this emotion, sweeping into one intense and far-reaching conviction of insecurity not only Arnold's personal fortunes in love, but the social and religious faith of the world he lived in. That much could be said for the traditional interpretation.

Of course, as Mr. Trilling did not fail to mention, anguished love affairs, harassed by mysterious inner incompatibilities, formed a well-established literary convention. But the fundamental scene of insecurity in "Dover Beach" was too genuine, too often repeated in other works, to be written off altogether to that account. The same sense of insecurity, the same need for some rock of protection, cried out again and again, not merely in Arnold's love poems but in his elegies, reflective pieces, and fragments of epic as well. Whenever Arnold produced a genuine and striking burst of poetry, with the stamp of true self-expression on it, he seemed always to be in the dumps. Everywhere dejection, confusion, weakness, contention of soul. No adequate cause could be found in the events of Arnold's life for such an acute sense of incertitude; it must have been of psychic origin. Only in one line of effort this fundamental insecurity did not hamper, sadden, or depress him, and that was in the free play of his intelligence as a critic of letters and society. Even there, if it did not hamper his efforts, it directed them. Arnold valiantly tried to erect a barrier of culture against the chaos and squalor of society, against the contentiousness of men. What was this barrier but an elaborate protective device?

The origin of the psychic pattern that expressed itself in Arnold's poems could probably never be discovered. No doubt the influence that Arnold's father exercised over his emotions and his thinking, even though Arnold rebelled to the extent at least of casting off his father's religious beliefs, was of great importance. But much more would have to be known to give a definite clue—more than ever could be known. Arnold was secure from any attempt to spy out the heart of his mystery. But if criticism could not discover the cause, it could assess the result, and could do so (thought Rudolph Mole) with greater understanding by an attempt, with up-to-date psychological aid, to delve a little deeper into the essential traits that manifested themselves in that result.

v

In 1917 Reuben Hale, a young instructor in a western college, had lost his job and done time in the penitentiary for speaking against conscription and for organizing pacifist demonstrations. In the twenties he had lost two more academic posts for his sympathies with Soviet Russia and his inability to forget his Marxist principles while teaching literature. His contentious, eager, lovable, exasperating temperament tried the patience of one college administration after another. As he advanced into middle age, and his growing family suffered repeated upheavals, his friends began to fear that his robust quarrels with established order would leave him a penniless outcast at fifty. Then he was invited to take a flattering post at a girls' college known for its liberality of views. The connection proved surprisingly durable; in fact it became Professor Hale's turn to be apprehensive. He began to be morally alarmed at his own security, to fear that the bourgeois system which he had attacked so valiantly had somehow outwitted him and betrayed him into allegiance. When the C.I.O. made its initial drive and seemed to be carrying everything before it, he did his best to unseat himself again by rushing joyfully to the nearest picket lines and getting himself photographed by an alert press. Even this expedient failed, and he reconciled himself, not without wonder, to apparent academic permanence.

On winter afternoons his voice could be heard booming out through the closed door of his study to girls who came to consult him on all manner of subjects, from the merits of Plekhanov as a Marxist critic to their own most personal dilemmas. They called him Ben; he called them Smith, Jones, and Robinson. He never relaxed his cheerful bombardment of the milieu into which they were born, and of the larger social structure which made bourgeois wealth, bourgeois art, morals, and religion possible. But when a sophomore found herself pregnant it was to Professor Hale that she came for advice. Should she have an abortion or go through with it and heroically bear the social stigma? And it was Professor Hale who kept the affair from the Dean's office and the newspapers, sought out the boy, persuaded the young couple that they were desperately in love with each other, and that pending the revolution a respectable marriage would be the most prudent course, not to say the happiest.

James Joyce remarks of one of his characters that she dealt with moral problems as a cleaver deals with meat. Professor Hale's critical methods were comparably simple and direct. Literature, like the other arts, is in form and substance a product of society, and reflects the structure of society. The structure of society is a class structure: it is conditioned by the mode of production of goods, and by the legal conventions of ownership and control by which the ruling class keeps itself in power and endows itself with the necessary freedom to exploit men and materials for profit. A healthy literature, in a society so constituted, can exist only if writers perceive the essential economic problem and ally themselves firmly with the working class.

Anyone could see the trouble with Arnold. His intelligence revealed to him the chaos that disrupted the society about him; the selfishness and brutality of the ruling class; the ugliness of the world which the industrial revolution had created, and which imperialism and "liberalism" were extending. Arnold was at his best in his critical satire of this world and of the ignorance of those who governed it. But his intelligence far outran his will, and his defect of will finally blinded his intelligence. He was too much a child of his class to disown it and fight his way to a workable remedy for social injustice. He caught a true vision of himself and of his times as standing between "two worlds, one dead, one powerless to be born." But he had not courage or stomach enough to lend his own powers to the birth struggle. Had he thrown in his sympathies unreservedly with the working class, and labored for the inescapable revolution, "Dover Beach" would not have ended in pessimism and confusion. It would have ended in a cheerful, strenuous, and hopeful call to action. But Arnold could not divorce himself from the world of polite letters, of education, of culture, into which he had been born. He did his best to purify them, to make them into an instrument for the reform of society. But instinctively he knew that "culture" as he understood the term was not a social force in the world around him. Instinctively he knew that what he loved was doomed to defeat. And so "Dover Beach" ended in a futile plea for protection against the hideousness of the darkling plain and the confused alarms of struggle and flight.

Professor Chartly's envelope brought Reuben Hale his best opportunity since the first C.I.O. picket lines to vindicate his critical and social principles. He plunged into his answer with complete zest.

VI

When Peter Lee Prampton agreed to act as moderator in Professor Chartly's experiment he congratulated himself that this would be his last great academic chore. He had enjoyed his career of scholarship and teaching, no man ever more keenly. But now it was drawing to an end. He was loaded with honors from two continents. The universities of Germany, France, and Britain had first laid their formative hands on his learning and cultivation, then given their most coveted recognition to its fruits. But the honor and the glory seemed a little vague on the June morning when the expressman brought into his library the sizable package of papers which Professor Chartly had boxed and shipped to him. He had kept all his life a certain simplicity of heart. At seventy-four he could still tote a pack with an easy endurance that humiliated men of forty. Now he found himself giving in more and more completely to a lust for trout. Half a century of hastily snatched vacations in Cape Breton or the Scottish Highlands had never allowed him really to fill up that hollow craving to find a wild stream and fish it which would sometimes rise in his throat even in the midst of a lecture.

Well, there would be time left before he died. And meanwhile here was this business of "Dover Beach." Matthew Arnold during one of his American lecture tours had been entertained by neighbors of the Pramptons. Peter Lee Prampton's father had dined with the great man, and had repeated his conversation and imitated his accent at the family table. Peter himself, as a boy of nineteen or so, had gone to hear Arnold lecture. That, he thought with a smile, was probably a good deal more than could be said for any of these poor hacks who had taken Professor Chartly's bait.

At the thought of Arnold he could still hear the carriage wheels grate on the pebbly road as he had driven, fifty odd years ago, to the lecture in town, the prospective Mrs. Prampton beside him. His fishing rod lay under the seat. He chuckled out loud as he remembered how a pound-and-a-half trout had jumped in the pool under the clattering planks of a bridge, and how he had pulled up the horse, jumped out, and tried a cast while Miss Osgood sat scolding in the carriage and shivering in the autumn air. They had been just a little late reaching the lecture, but the trout, wrapped in damp leaves, lay safely beside the road.

It was queer that "Dover Beach" had not come more recently into his mind. Now that he turned his thoughts in that direction the poem was there in its entirety, waiting to be put on again like a coat that one has worn many times with pleasure and accidentally neglected for a while.

The sea of faith was once, too, at the full.

How those old Victorian battles had raged about the Prampton table when he was a boy! How the names of Arnold, Huxley, Darwin, Carlyle, Morris, Ruskin had been pelted back and forth by the excited disputants! *Literature and Dogma, God and the Bible, Culture and Anarchy.* The familiar titles brought an odd image into his mind: the tall figure of his father stretching up to turn on the gas lamps in the evening as the family sat down to dinner; the terrific pop of the pilot light as it exploded into a net of white flame, shaped like a little beehive; the buzz and whine of a jet turned up too high.

> Ah, love, let us be true
> To one another! for the world, which seems
> To lie before us like a land of dreams,
> So various, so beautiful, so new,
> Hath really neither joy, nor love, nor light,
> Nor certitude, nor peace, nor help for pain . . .

Peter Lee Prampton shivered in the warmth of his sunny library, shivered with that flash of perception into the past which sometimes enables a man to see how all that has happened in his life, for good or ill, turned on the narrowest edge of chance. He lived again in the world of dreams that his own youth had spread before him, a world truly various, beautiful, and new; full of promise, adventure, and liberty of choice, based on the opportunities which his father's wealth provided, and holding out the prospect of a smooth advance into a distinguished career. Then, within six months, a lavish demonstration that the world has neither certitude, nor peace, nor help for pain; his mother's death by cancer, his father's financial overthrow and suicide, the ruin of his own smooth hopes and the prospect instead of a long, hampered, and obscure fight toward his perhaps impossible ambition. He lived again through the night hours when he had tramped out with himself the youthful question whether he could hold Miss Osgood to her promise in the face of such reversals. And he did not forget how she took his long-sleepless face between her hands, kissed him, and smiled away his anxiety with unsteady lips. Surely everyone discovers at some time or other that the world is not a place of certitude; surely everyone cries out to some other human being for the fidelity which alone can make it so. What more could be asked of a poet than to take so profound and universal an experience and turn it into lines that could still speak long after he and his age were dead?

The best of it was that no one could miss the human feeling, the cry from the heart, in "Dover Beach"; it spoke so clearly and eloquently, in a language everyone could understand, in a form classically pure and simple. Or did it? Who could tell what any job-lot of academicians might be trusted to see or fail to see? And this assortment in Chartly's package might be a queer kettle of fish! Peter Lee Prampton had lived through the *Yellow Book* days of Art for Art's sake; he had read the muckrakers, and watched the rise of the Marxists and the Freudians. Could "Dover Beach" be condemned as unsympathetic with labor? Could a neurosis or a complex be discovered in it? His heart sank at the sharp sudden conviction that indeed these and worse discoveries about the poem might be seriously advanced. Well, he had always tried to go on the principle that every school of criticism should be free to exercise any sincere claim on men's interest and attention which it could win for itself. When he actually applied himself to the contents of Professor Chartly's bale he would be as charitable as he could, as receptive to light from any quarter as he could bring himself to be.

But the task could wait. He felt the need of a period of adjustment before he could approach it with reasonable equanimity. And in the meanwhile he could indulge himself in some long-needed editorial work on his dry-fly book.

ARISTOTLE

Poetics[1]

TRANSLATED BY INGRAM BYWATER

1

Our subject being Poetry, I propose to speak not only of the art in general but also of its species and their respective capacities; of the structure of plot required for a good poem; of the number and nature of the constituent parts of a poem; and likewise of any other matters in the same line of inquiry. Let us follow the natural order and begin with the primary facts.

Epic poetry and Tragedy, as also Comedy, Dithyrambic poetry, and most flute-playing and lyre-playing, are all, viewed as a whole, modes of imitation. But at the same time they differ from one another in three ways, either by a difference of kind in their means, or by differences in the objects, or in the manner of their imitations.

Just as colour and form are used as means by some, who (whether by art or constant practice) imitate and portray many things by their aid, and the voice is used by others; so also in the above-mentioned group of arts, the means with them as a whole are rhythm, language, and harmony—used, however, either

[1] From Richard McKeon, ed., *The Basic Works of Aristotle* (New York: Random House, 1941), pp. 1455-1487 with omissions.

singly or in certain combinations. A combination of harmony and rhythm alone is the means in flute-playing and lyre-playing, and any other arts there may be of the same description, e.g. imitative piping. Rhythm alone, without harmony, is the means in the dancer's imitations; for even he, by the rhythms of his attitudes, may represent men's characters, as well as what they do and suffer. There is further an art which imitates by language alone, without harmony, in prose or in verse, and if in verse, either in some one or in a plurality of metres. This form of imitation is to this day without a name. We have no common name for a mime of Sophron or Xenarchus and a Socratic Conversation; and we should still be without one even if the imitation in the two instances were in trimeters or elegiacs or some other kind of verse—though it is the way with people to tack on 'poet' to the name of a metre, and talk of elegiac-poets and epic-poets, thinking that they call them poets not by reason of the imitative nature of their work, but indiscriminately by reason of the metre they write in. Even if a theory of medicine or physical philosophy be put forth in a metrical form, it is usual to describe the writer in this way; Homer and Empedocles, however, have really nothing in common apart from their metre; so that, if the one is to be called a poet, the other should be termed a physicist rather than a poet. We should be in the same position also, if the imitation in these instances were in all the metres, like the *Centaur* (a rhapsody in a medley of all metres) of Chaeremon; and Chaeremon one has to recognize as a poet. So much, then, as to these arts. There are, lastly, certain other arts, which combine all the means enumerated, rhythm, melody, and verse, e.g. Dithyrambic and Nomic poetry, Tragedy and Comedy; with this difference, however, that the three kinds of means are in some of them all employed together, and in others brought in separately, one after the other. These elements of difference in the above arts I term the means of their imitation.

Our subject being Poetry, I propose to speak, not only of the art in general,   **2**

The objects the imitator represents are actions, with agents who are necessarily either good men or bad—the diversities of human character being nearly always derivative from this primary distinction, since the line between virtue and vice is one dividing the whole of mankind. It follows, therefore, that the agents represented must be either above our own level of goodness, or beneath it, or just such as we are; in the same way as, with the painters, the personages of Polygnotus are better than we are, those of Pauson worse, and those of Dionysius just like ourselves. It is clear that each of the above-mentioned arts will admit of these differences, and that it will become a separate art by representing objects with this point of difference. Even in dancing, flute-playing, and lyre-playing such diversities are possible; and they are also possible in the nameless art that uses language, prose or verse without harmony, as its means; Homer's personages, for instance, are better than we are; Cleophon's are on our own level; and those of Hegemon of Thasos, the first writer of parodies, and Nicochares, the author of the *Diliad*, are beneath it.

The same is true of the Dithyramb and the Nome: the personages may be presented in them with the difference exemplified in the . . . of . . . and Argas, and in the Cyclopses of Timotheus and Philoxenus. This difference it is that distinguishes Tragedy and Comedy also; the one would make its personages worse, and the other better, than the men of the present day.

3

A third difference in these arts is in the manner in which each kind of object is represented. Given both the same means and the same kind of object for imitation, one may either (1) speak at one moment in narrative and at another in an assumed character, as Homer does; or (2) one may remain the same throughout, without any such change; or (3) the imitators may represent the whole story dramatically, as though they were actually doing the things described.

As we said at the beginning, therefore, the differences in the imitation of these arts come under three heads, their means, their objects, and their manner.

So that as an imitator Sophocles will be on one side akin to Homer, both portraying good men; and on another to Aristophanes, since both present their personages as acting and doing. This in fact, according to some, is the reason for plays being termed dramas, because in a play the personages act the story. Hence too both Tragedy and Comedy are claimed by the Dorians as their discoveries; Comedy by the Megarians—by those in Greece as having arisen when Megara became a democracy, and by the Sicilian Megarians on the ground that the poet Epicharmus was of their country, and a good deal earlier than Chionides and Magnes; even Tragedy also is claimed by certain of the Peloponnesian Dorians. In support of this claim they point to the words 'comedy' and 'drama.' Their word for the outlying hamlets, they say, is *comae*, whereas Athenians call them *demes*—thus assuming that comedians got the name not from their *comoe* or revels, but from their strolling from hamlet to hamlet, lack of appreciation keeping them out of the city. Their word also for 'to act', they say, is *dran*, whereas Athenians use *prattein*.

So much, then, as to the number and nature of the points of difference in the imitation of these arts.

4

It is clear that the general origin of poetry was due to two causes, each of them part of human nature. Imitation is natural to man from childhood, one of his advantages over the lower animals being this, that he is the most imitative creature in the world, and learns at first by imitation. And it is also natural for all to delight in works of imitation. The truth of this second point is shown by experience: though the objects themselves may be painful to see, we delight to view the most realistic representations of them in art, the forms for example of the lowest animals and of dead bodies. The explanation is to be found in a further fact: to be learning something is the greatest of pleasures

not only to the philosopher but also to the rest of mankind, however small
their capacity for it; the reason of the delight in seeing the picture is that one
is at the same time learning—gathering the meaning of things, e.g. that the
man there is so-and-so; for if one has not seen the thing before, one's pleasure
will not be in the picture as an imitation of it, but will be due to the execution or colouring or some similar cause. Imitation, then, being natural to us—
as also the sense of harmony and rhythm, the metres being obviously species
of rhythms—it was through their original aptitude, and by a series of improvements for the most part gradual on their first efforts, that they created poetry
out of their improvisations.

Poetry, however, soon broke up into two kinds according to the differences
of character in the individual poets; for the graver among them would represent noble actions, and those of noble personages; and the meaner sort the actions of the ignoble. The latter class produced invectives at first, just as others
did hymns and panegyrics. We know of no such poem by any of the pre-
Homeric poets, though there were probably many such writers among them;
instances, however, may be found from Homer downwards, e.g. his *Margites*,
and the similar poems of others. In this poetry of invective its natural fitness
brought an iambic metre into use; hence our present term 'iambic', because it
was the metre of their 'iambs' or invectives against one another. The result
was that the old poets became some of them writers of heroic and others of
iambic verse. Homer's position, however, is peculiar: just as he was in the
serious style the poet of poets, standing alone not only through the literary
excellence, but also through the dramatic character of his imitations, so too he
was the first to outline for us the general forms of Comedy by producing not
a dramatic invective, but a dramatic picture of the Ridiculous; his *Margites* in
fact stands in the same relation to our comedies as the *Iliad* and *Odyssey* to
our tragedies. As soon, however, as Tragedy and Comedy appeared in the field,
those naturally drawn to the one line of poetry became writers of comedies instead of iambs, and those naturally drawn to the other, writers of tragedies instead of epics, because these new modes of art were grander and of more esteem than the old.

If it be asked whether Tragedy is now all that it need be in its formative
elements, to consider that, and decide it theoretically and in relation to the
theatres, is a matter for another inquiry.

It certainly began in improvisations—as did also Comedy; the one originating with the authors of the Dithyramb, the other with those of the phallic
songs, which still survive as institutions in many of our cities. And its advance
after that was little by little, through their improving on whatever they
had before them at each stage. It was in fact only after a long series of changes
that the movement of Tragedy stopped on its attaining to its natural form. (1)
The number of actors was first increased to two by Aeschylus, who curtailed
the business of the Chorus, and made the dialogue, or spoken portion, take
the leading part in the play. (2) A third actor and scenery were due to

Sophocles. (3) Tragedy acquired also its magnitude. Discarding short stories and a ludicrous diction, through its passing out of its satyric stage, it assumed, though only at a late point in its progress, a tone of dignity; and its metre changed then from trochaic to iambic. The reason for their original use of the trochaic tetrameter was that their poetry was satyric and more connected with dancing than it now is. As soon, however, as a spoken part came in, nature herself found the appropriate metre. The iambic, we know, is the most speakable of metres, as is shown by the fact that we very often fall into it in conversation, whereas we rarely talk hexameters, and only when we depart from the speaking tone of voice. (4) Another change was a plurality of episodes or acts. As for the remaining matters, the superadded embellishments and the account of their introduction, these must be taken as said, as it would probably be a long piece of work to go through the details.

5

As for Comedy, it is (as has been observed) an imitation of men worse than the average; worse, however, not as regards any and every sort of fault, but only as regards one particular kind, the Ridiculous, which is a species of the Ugly. The Ridiculous may be defined as a mistake or deformity not productive of pain or harm to others; the mask, for instance, that excites laughter, is something ugly and distorted without causing pain.

Though the successive changes in Tragedy and their authors are not unknown, we cannot say the same of Comedy; its early stages passed unnoticed, because it was not as yet taken up in a serious way. It was only at a late point in its progress that a chorus of comedians was officially granted by the archon; they used to be mere volunteers. It had also already certain definite forms at the time when the record of those termed comic poets begins. Who it was who supplied it with masks, or prologues, or a plurality of actors and the like, has remained unknown. The invented Fable, or Plot, however, originated in Sicily with Epicharmus and Phormis; of Athenian poets Crates was the first to drop the Comedy of invective and frame stories of a general and nonpersonal nature, in other words, Fables or Plots.

Epic poetry, then, has been seen to agree with Tragedy to this exent, that of being an imitation of serious subjects in a grand kind of verse. It differs from it, however, (1) in that it is in one kind of verse and in narrative form; and (2) in its length—which is due to its action having no fixed limit of time, whereas Tragedy endeavours to keep as far as possible within a single circuit of the sun, or something near that. This, I say, is another point of difference between them, though at first the practice in this respect was just the same in tragedies as in epic poems. They differ also (3) in their constituents, some being common to both and others peculiar to Tragedy—hence a judge of good and bad in Tragedy is a judge of that in epic poetry also. All the parts of an epic are included in Tragedy; but those of Tragedy are not all of them to be found in the Epic.

6

Reserving hexameter poetry and Comedy for consideration hereafter,[2] let us proceed now to the discussion of Tragedy; before doing so, however, we must gather up the definition resulting from what has been said. A tragedy, then, is the imitation of an action that is serious and also, as having magnitude, complete in itself; in language with pleasurable accessories, each kind brought in separately in the parts of the work; in a dramatic, not in a narrative form; with incidents arousing pity and fear, wherewith to accomplish its catharsis of such emotions. Here by 'language with pleasurable accessories' I mean that with rhythm and harmony or song superadded; and by 'the kinds separately' I mean that some portions are worked out with verse only, and others in turn with song.

I. As they act the stories, it follows that in the first place the Spectacle (or stage-appearance of the actors) must be some part of the whole; and in the second Melody and Diction, these two being the means of their imitation. Here by 'Diction' I mean merely this, the composition of the verses; and by 'Melody', what is too completely understood to require explanation. But further: the subject represented also is an action; and the action involves agents, who must necessarily have their distinctive qualities both of character and thought, since it is from these that we ascribe certain qualities to their actions. There are in the natural order of things, therefore, two causes, Thought and Character, of their actions, and consequently of their success or failure in their lives. Now the action (that which was done) is represented in the play by the Fable or Plot. The Fable, in our present sense of the term, is simply this, the combination of the incidents, or things done in the story; whereas Character is what makes us ascribe certain moral qualities to the agents; and Thought is shown in all they say when proving a particular point or, it may be, enunciating a general truth. There are six parts consequently of every tragedy, as a whole (that is) of such or such quality, viz. a Fable or Plot, Characters, Diction, Thought, Spectacle, and Melody; two of them arising from the means, one from the manner, and three from the objects of the dramatic imitation; and there is nothing else besides these six. Of these, its formative elements, then, not a few of the dramatists have made due use, as every play, one may say, admits of Spectacle, Character, Fable, Diction, Melody, and Thought.

II. The most important of the six is the combination of the incidents of the story. Tragedy is essentially an imitation not of persons but of action and life, of happiness and misery. All human happiness or misery takes the form of action; the end for which we live is a certain kind of activity, not a quality. Character gives us qualities, but it is in our actions—what we do—that we are happy or the reverse. In a play accordingly they do not act in order to portray the Characters; they include the Characters for the sake of the ac-

[2] For hexameter poetry cf. Chap. 23 f.; comedy was treated of in the lost Second Book.

tion. So that it is the action in it, i.e. its Fable or Plot, that is the end and purpose of the tragedy; and the end is everywhere the chief thing. Besides this, a tragedy is impossible without action, but there may be one without Character. The tragedies of most of the moderns are characterless—a defect common among poets of all kinds, and with its counterpart in painting in Zeuxis as compared with Polygnotus; for whereas the latter is strong in character, the work of Zeuxis is devoid of it. And again: one may string together a series of characteristic speeches of the utmost finish as regards Diction and Thought, and yet fail to produce the true tragic effect; but one will have much better success with a tragedy which, however inferior in these respects, has a Plot, a combination of incidents, in it. And again: the most powerful elements of attraction in Tragedy, the Peripeties and Discoveries, are parts of the Plot. A further proof is in the fact that beginners succeed earlier with the Diction and Characters than with the construction of a story; and the same may be said of nearly all the early dramatists. We maintain, therefore, that the first essential, the life and soul, so to speak, of Tragedy is the Plot; and that the Characters come second—compare the parallel in painting, where the most beautiful colours laid on without order will not give one the same pleasure as a simple black-and-white sketch of a portrait. We maintain that Tragedy is primarily an imitation of action, and that it is mainly for the sake of the action that it imitates the personal agents. Third comes the element of Thought, i.e. the power of saying whatever can be said, or what is appropriate to the occasion. This is what, in the speeches in Tragedy, falls under the arts of Politics and Rhetoric; for the older poets make their personages discourse like statesmen, and the modern like rhetoricians. One must not confuse it with Character. Character in a play is that which reveals the moral purpose of the agents, i.e. the sort of thing they seek or avoid, where that is not obvious—hence there is no room for Character in a speech on a purely indifferent subject. Thought, on the other hand, is shown in all they say when proving or disproving some particular point, or enunciating some universal proposition. Fourth among the literary elements is the Diction of the personages, i.e., as before explained, the expression of their thoughts in words, which is practically the same thing with verse as with prose. As for the two remaining parts, the Melody is the greatest of the pleasurable accessories of Tragedy. The Spectacle, though an attraction, is the least artistic of all the parts, and has least to do with the art of poetry. The tragic effect is quite possible without a public performance and actors; and besides, the getting-up of the Spectacle is more a matter for the costumier than the poet.

7

Having thus distinguished the parts, let us now consider the proper construction of the Fable or Plot, as that is at once the first and the most important thing in Tragedy. We have laid it down that a tragedy is an imitation of an action that is complete in itself, as a whole of some magnitude;

for a whole may be of no magnitude to speak of. Now a whole is that which
has beginning, middle, and end. A beginning is that which is not itself necessarily after anything else, and which has naturally something else after it; an
end is that which is naturally after something itself, either as its necessary or
usual consequent, and with nothing else after it; and a middle, that which is
by nature after one thing and has also another after it. A well-constructed
Plot, therefore, cannot either begin or end at any point one likes; beginning
and end in it must be of the forms just described. Again: to be beautiful,
a living creature, and every whole made up of parts, must not only present
a certain order in its arrangement of parts, but also be of a certain definite
magnitude. Beauty is a matter of size and order, and therefore impossible
either (1) in a very minute creature, since our perception becomes indistinct
as it approaches instantaneity; or (2) in a creature of vast size—one, say,
1,000 miles long—as in that case, instead of the object being seen all at
once, the unity and wholeness of it is lost to the beholder.

Just in the same way, then, as a beautiful whole made up of parts, or a
beautiful living creature, must be of some size, but a size to be taken in by
the eye, so a story or Plot must be of some length, but of a length to be
taken in by the memory. As for the limit of its length, so far as that is relative to
public performances and spectators, it does not fall within the theory of poetry.
If they had to perform a hundred tragedies, they would be timed by water-
clocks, as they are said to have been at one period. The limit, however, set
by the actual nature of the thing is this: the longer the story, consistently
with its being comprehensible as a whole, the finer it is by reason of its
magnitude. As a rough general formula, 'a length which allows of the hero
passing by a series of probable or necessary stages from misfortune to happiness, or from happiness to misfortune', may suffice as a limit for the magnitude of the story.

8

The Unity of a Plot does not consist, as some suppose, in its having
one man as its subject. An infinity of things befall that one man, some of
which it is impossible to reduce to unity; and in like manner there are many
actions of one man which cannot be made to form one action. One sees,
therefore, the mistake of all the poets who have written a *Heracleid*, a *Theseid*,
or similar poems; they suppose that, because Heracles was one man, the story
also of Heracles must be one story. Homer, however, evidently understood this
point quite well, whether by art or instinct, just in the same way as he excels the rest in every other respect. In writing an *Odyssey*, he did not make
the poem cover all that ever befell his hero—it befell him, for instance, to
get wounded on Parnassus and also to feign madness at the time of the call
to arms, but the two incidents had no necessary or probable connexion with
one another—instead of doing that, he took as the subject of the *Odyssey*,
as also of the *Iliad*, an action with a Unity of the kind we are describing.

The truth is that, just as in the other imitative arts one imitation is always of one thing, so in poetry the story, as an imitation of action, must represent one action, a complete whole, with its several incidents so closely connected that the transposal or withdrawal of any one of them will disjoin and dislocate the whole. For that which makes no perceptible difference by its presence or absence is no real part of the whole.

9

From what we have said it will be seen that the poet's function is to describe, not the thing that has happened, but a kind of thing that might happen, i.e. what is possible as being probable or necessary. The distinction between historian and poet is not in the one writing prose and the other verse—you might put the work of Herodotus into verse, and it would still be a species of history; it consists really in this, that the one describes the thing that has been, and the other a kind of thing that might be. Hence poetry is something more philosophic and of graver import than history, since its statements are of the nature rather of universals, whereas those of history are singulars. By a universal statement I mean one as to what such or such a kind of man will probably or necessarily say or do—which is the aim of poetry, though it affixes proper names to the characters; by a singular statement, one as to what, say, Alcibiades did or had done to him. In Comedy this has become clear by this time; it is only when their plot is already made up of probable incidents that they give it a basis of proper names, choosing for the purpose any names that may occur to them, instead of writing like the old iambic poets about particular persons. In Tragedy, however, they still adhere to the historic names; and for this reason: what convinces is the possible; now whereas we are not yet sure as to the possibility of that which has not happened, that which has happened is manifestly possible, else it would not have come to pass. Nevertheless even in Tragedy there are some plays with but one or two known names in them, the rest being inventions; and there are some without a single known name, e.g. Agathon's *Antheus*, in which both incidents and names are of the poet's invention; and it is no less delightful on that account. So that one must not aim at a rigid adherence to the traditional stories on which tragedies are based. It would be absurd, in fact, to do so, as even the known stories are only known to a few, though they are a delight none the less to all.

It is evident from the above that the poet must be more the poet of his stories or Plots than of his verses, inasmuch as he is a poet by virtue of the imitative element in his work, and it is actions that he imitates. And if he should come to take a subject from actual history, he is none the less a poet for that; since some historic occurrences may very well be in the probable and possible order of things; and it is in that aspect of them that he is their poet.

Of simple Plots and actions the episodic are the worst. I call a Plot episodic when there is neither probability nor necessity in the sequence of its episodes. Actions of this sort bad poets construct through their own fault, and good ones on account of the players. His work being for public performance, a good poet often stretches out a Plot beyond its capabilities, and is thus obliged to twist the sequence of incident.

Tragedy, however, is an imitation not only of a complete action, but also of incidents arousing pity and fear. Such incidents have the very greatest effect on the mind when they occur unexpectedly and at the same time in consequence of one another; there is more of the marvellous in them than if they happened of themselves or by mere chance. Even matters of chance seem most marvellous if there is an appearance of design as it were in them; as for instance the statue of Mitys at Argos killed the author of Mitys' death by falling down on him when a looker-on at a public spectacle; for incidents like that we think to be not without a meaning. A Plot, therefore, of this sort is necessarily finer than others.

10

Plots are either simple or complex, since the actions they represent are naturally of this twofold description. The action, proceeding in the way defined, as one continuous whole, I call simple, when the change in the hero's fortunes takes place without Peripety or Discovery; and complex, when it involves one or the other, or both. These should each of them arise out of the structure of the Plot itself, so as to be the consequence, necessary or probable, of the antecedents. There is a great difference between a thing happening *propter hoc* and *post hoc*.

11

A Peripety is the change of the kind described from one state of things within the play to its opposite, and that too in the way we are saying, in the probable or necessary sequence of events; as it is for instance in *Oedipus*: here the opposite state of things is produced by the Messenger, who, coming to gladden Oedipus and to remove his fears as to his mother, reveals the secret of his birth. And in *Lynceus*: just as he is being led off for execution, with Danaus at his side to put him to death, the incidents preceding this bring it about that he is saved and Danaus put to death. A Discovery is, as the very word implies, a change from ignorance to knowledge, and thus to either love or hate, in the personages marked for good or evil fortune. The finest form of Discovery is one attended by Peripeties, like that which goes with the Discovery in *Oedipus*. There are no doubt other forms of it; what we have said may happen in a way in reference to inanimate things, even things of a very casual kind; and it is also possible to discover whether some one has done or not done something. But the form most directly connected with the Plot and the action of the piece is the first-mentioned. This, with a Peripety, will arouse either pity or fear—actions of that nature being what

Tragedy is assumed to represent; and it will also serve to bring about the happy or unhappy ending. The Discovery, then, being of persons, it may be that of one party only to the other, the latter being already known; or both the parties may have to discover themselves. Iphigenia, for instance, was discovered to Orestes by sending the letter; and another Discovery was required to reveal him to Iphigenia.

Two parts of the Plot, then, Peripety and Discovery, are on matters of this sort. A third part is Suffering; which we may define as an action of a destructive or painful nature, such as murders on the stage, tortures, woundings, and the like. The other two have been already explained.

12

The parts of Tragedy to be treated as formative elements in the whole were mentioned in a previous Chapter.[3]

From the point of view, however, of its quantity, i.e. the separate sections into which it is divided, a tragedy has the following parts: Prologue, Episode, Exode, and a choral portion, distinguished into Parode and Stasimon; these two are common to all tragedies, whereas songs from the stage and *Commoe* are only found in some. The Prologue is all that precedes the Parode of the chorus; an Episode all that comes in between two whole choral songs; the Exode all that follows after the last choral song. In the choral portion the Parode is the whole first statement of the chorus; a Stasimon, a song of the chorus without anapaests or trochees; a *Commos*, a lamentation sung by chorus and actor in concert. The parts of Tragedy to be used as formative elements in the whole we have already mentioned; the above are its parts from the point of view of its quantity, or the separate sections into which it is divided.

13

The next points after what we have said above will be these: (1) What is the poet to aim at, and what is he to avoid, in constructing his Plots? and (2) What are the conditions on which the tragic effect depends?

We assume that, for the finest form of Tragedy, the Plot must be not simple but complex; and further, that it must imitate actions arousing fear and pity, since that is the distinctive function of this kind of imitation. It follows, therefore, that there are three forms of Plot to be avoided. (1) A good man must not be seen passing from happiness to misery, or (2) a bad man from misery to happiness. The first situation is not fear-inspiring or piteous, but simply odious to us. The second is the most untragic that can be; it has no one of the requisites of Tragedy; it does not appeal either to the human feeling in us, or to our pity, or to our fears. Nor, on the other hand, should (3) an extremely bad man be seen falling from happiness into misery. Such a story may arouse the human feeling in us, but it will not move us to either pity or fear; pity is occasioned by undeserved misfortune, and fear by

[3] Ch. 6.

that of one like ourselves; so that there will be nothing either piteous or
fear-inspiring in the situation. There remains, then, the intermediate kind of
personage, a man not preeminently virtuous and just, whose misfortune, however, is brought upon him not by vice and depravity but by some error of
judgment, of the number of those in the enjoyment of great reputation and
prosperity; e.g. Oedipus, Thyestes, and the men of note of similar families. The
perfect Plot, accordingly, must have a single, and not (as some tell us) a
double issue; the change in the hero's fortunes must be not from misery to
happiness, but on the contrary from happiness to misery; and the cause of it
must lie not in any depravity, but in some great error on his part; the man
himself being either such as we have described, or better, not worse, than that.
Fact also confirms our theory. Though the poets began by accepting any
tragic story that came to hand, in these days the finest tragedies are always
on the story of some few houses, on that of Alcmeon, Oedipus, Orestes,
Meleager, Thyestes, Telephus, or any others that may have been involved, as
either agents or sufferers, in some deed of horror. The theoretically best tragedy, then, has a Plot of this description. The critics, therefore, are wrong who
blame Euripides for taking this line in his tragedies, and giving many of them
an unhappy ending. It is, as we have said, the right line to take. The best
proof is this: on the stage, and in the public performances, such plays, properly
worked out, are seen to be the most truly tragic; and Euripides, even if
his execution be faulty in every other point, is seen to be nevertheless the
most tragic certainly of the dramatists. After this comes the construction of
Plot which some rank first, one with a double story (like the *Odyssey*) and
an opposite issue for the good and the bad personages. It is ranked as first
only through the weakness of the audiences; the poets merely follow their
public, writing as its wishes dictate. But the pleasure here is not that of Tragedy. It belongs rather to Comedy, where the bitterest enemies in the piece
(e.g. Orestes and Aegisthus) walk off good friends at the end, with no slaying
of any one by any one.

14

The tragic fear and pity may be aroused by the Spectacle; but they may
also be aroused by the very structure and incidents of the play—which is
the better way and shows the better poet. The Plot in fact should be so framed
that, even without seeing the things take place, he who simply hears the account of them shall be filled with horror and pity at the incidents; which is
just the effect that the mere recital of the story in *Oedipus* would have on
one. To produce this same effect by means of the Spectacle is less artistic, and
requires extraneous aid. Those, however, who make use of the Spectacle to put
before us that which is merely monstrous and not productive of fear, are
wholly out of touch with Tragedy; and not every kind of pleasure should be
required of a tragedy, but only its own proper pleasure.

The tragic pleasure is that of pity and fear, and the poet has to produce it by a work of imitation; it is clear, therefore, that the causes should be included in the incidents of his story. Let us see, then, what kinds of incident strike one as horrible, or rather as piteous. In a deed of this description the parties must necessarily be either friends, or enemies, or indifferent to one another. Now when enemy does it on enemy, there is nothing to move us to pity either in his doing or in his meditating the deed, except so far as the actual pain of the sufferer is concerned; and the same is true when the parties are indifferent to one another. Whenever the tragic deed, however, is done within the family—when murder or the like is done or meditated by brother on brother, by son on father, by mother on son, or son on mother—these are the situations the poet should seek after. The traditional stories, accordingly, must be kept as they are, e.g. the murder of Clytaemnestra by Orestes and of Eriphyle by Alcmeon. At the same time even with these there is something left to the poet himself; it is for him to devise the right way of treating them. Let us explain more clearly what we mean by 'the right way'. The deed of horror may be done by the doer knowingly and consciously, as in the old poets, and in Medea's murder of her children in Euripides. Or he may do it, but in ignorance of his relationship, and discover that afterwards, as does the Oedipus in Sophocles. Here the deed is outside the play; but it may be within it, like the act of the Alcmeon in Astydamas, or that of the Telegonus in *Ulysses Wounded*. A third possibility is for one meditating some deadly injury to another, in ignorance of his relationship, to make the discovery in time to draw back. These exhaust the possibilities, since the deed must necessarily be either done or not done, and either knowingly or unknowingly.

The worst situation is when the personage is with full knowledge on the point of doing the deed, and leaves it undone. It is odious and also (through the absence of suffering) untragic; hence it is that no one is made to act thus except in some few instances, e.g. Haemon and Creon in *Antigone*. Next after this comes the actual perpetration of the deed meditated. A better situation than that, however, is for the deed to be done in ignorance, and the relationship discovered afterwards, since there is nothing odious in it, and the Discovery will serve to astound us. But the best of all is the last; what we have in *Cresphontes*,[4] for example, where Merope, on the point of slaying her son, recognizes him in time; in *Iphigenia*, where sister and brother are in a like position; and in *Helle*,[5] where the son recognizes his mother, when on the point of giving her up to her enemy.

This will explain why our tragedies are restricted (as we said just now) to such a small number of families. It was accident rather than art that led the poets in quest of subjects to embody this kind of incident in their Plots. They

[4] By Euripides.
[5] Authorship unknown.

are still obliged, accordingly, to have recourse to the families in which such horrors have occurred.

On the construction of the Plot, and the kind of Plot required for Tragedy, enough has now been said.

In the Characters there are four points to aim at. First and foremost, that they shall be good. There will be an element of character in the play, if (as has been observed) what a personage says or does reveals a certain moral purpose; and a good element of character, if the purpose so revealed is good. Such goodness is possible in every type of personage, even in a woman or a slave, though the one is perhaps an inferior, and the other a wholly worthless being. The second point is to make them appropriate. The Character before us may be, say, manly; but it is not appropriate in a female Character to be manly, or clever. The third is to make them like the reality, which is not the same as their being good and appropriate, in our sense of the term. The fourth is to make them consistent and the same throughout; even if inconsistency be part of the man before one for imitation as presenting that form of character, he should still be consistently inconsistent. We have an instance of baseness of character, not required for the story, in the Menelaus in *Orestes*; of the incongruous and unbefitting in the lamentation of Ulysses in *Scylla*,[6] and in the (clever) speech of Melanippe,[7] and of inconsistency in *Iphigenia at Aulis*, where Iphigenia the suppliant is utterly unlike the later Iphigenia. The right thing, however, is in the Characters just as in the incidents of the play to endeavour always after the necessary or the probable; so that whenever such-and-such a personage says or does such-and-such a thing, it shall be the necessary or probable outcome of his character; and whenever this incident follows on that, it shall be either the necessary or the probable consequence of it. From this one sees (to digress for a moment) that the Dénouement also should arise out of the plot itself, and not depend on a stage-artifice, as in *Medea*, or in the story of the (arrested) departure of the Greeks in the *Iliad*. The artifice must be reserved for matters outside the play—for past events beyond human knowledge, or events yet to come, which require to be foretold or announced; since it is the privilege of the Gods to know everything. There should be nothing improbable among the actual incidents. If it be unavoidable, however, it should be outside the tragedy, like the improbability in the *Oedipus* of Sophocles. But to return to the Characters. As Tragedy is an imitation of personages better than the ordinary man, we in our way should follow the example of good portrait-painters, who reproduce the distinctive features of a man, and at the same time, without losing the likeness, make him handsomer than he is. The poet in like manner,

[6] A dithyramb by Timotheus.
[7] (Euripides).

in portraying men quick or slow to anger, or with similar infirmities of character, must know how to represent them as such, and at the same time as good men, as Agathon and Homer have represented Achilles.

All these rules one must keep in mind throughout, and, further, those also for such points of stage-effect as directly depend on the art of the poet, since in these too one may often make mistakes. Enough, however, has been said on the subject in one of our published writings.[8]

16

Discovery in general has been explained already. As for the species of Discovery, the first to be noted is (1) the least artistic form of it, of which the poets make most use through mere lack of invention, Discovery by signs or marks. Of these signs some are congenital, like the 'lance-head which the Earth-born have on them,'[9] or 'stars,' such as Carcinus brings in his Thyestes; others acquired after birth—these latter being either marks on the body, e.g. scars, or external tokens, like necklaces, or (to take another sort of instance) the ark in the *Discovery of Tyro*.[10] Even in these, however, admit of two uses, a better and a worse; the scar of Ulysses is an instance; the Discovery of him through it is made in one way by the nurse[11] and in another by the swineherds.[12] A Discovery using signs as a means of assurance is less artistic, as indeed are all such as imply reflection; whereas one bringing them in all of a sudden, as in the *Bath-story*,[13] is of a better order. Next after these are (2) Discoveries made directly by the poet; which are inartistic for that very reason; e.g. Orestes' Discovery of himself in *Iphigenia*: whereas his sister reveals who she is by the letter,[14] Orestes is made to say himself what the poet rather than the story demands.[15] This, therefore, is not far removed from the first-mentioned fault, since he might have presented certain tokens as well. Another instance is the 'shuttle's voice' in the *Tereus* of Sophocles. (3) A third species is Discovery through memory, from a man's consciousness being awakened by something seen. Thus in *The Cyprioe of Dicaeogenes*, the sight of the picture makes the man burst into tears; and in the *Tale of Alcinous*,[16] hearing the harper Ulysses is reminded of the past and weeps; the Discovery of them being the result. (4) A fourth kind is Discovery through reasoning; e.g. in *The Choephoroe*,[17] 'One like me is here; there is no one like me but Orestes; he, therefore, must be here.' Or that which Polyidus the Sophist suggested for *Iphigenia*; since it was natural for Orestes to reflect: 'My sister was sacrificed, and I am to be sacrificed like her.' Or that in the *Tydeus of*

[8] In the lost dialogue *On Poets*.   [9] Authorship unknown.
[10] By Euripides.   [11] *Od.* xix. 386-475.
[12] *Od.* xxi. 205-25.   [13] *Od.* xix. 392.
[14] *Iph. Taur.* 727 ff.   [15] Ib., 800 ff.
[16] *Od.* viii, 521 ff. (Cf. viii, 83 ff.)   [17] 11. 168-234.

Theodectes: 'I came to find a son, and am to die myself.' Oɪ that in *The Phinidae*: on seeing the place the women inferred their fate, that they were to die there, since they had also been exposed there. (5) There is, too, a composite Discovery arising from bad reasoning on the side of the other party. An instance of it is in *Ulysses the False Messenger*:[18] he said he should know the bow—which he had not seen; but to suppose from that that he would know it again (as though he had once seen it) was bad reasoning. (6) The best of all Discoveries, however, is that arising from the incidents themselves, when the great surprise comes about through a probable incident, like that in the *Oedipus* of Sophocles; and also in Iphigenia;[19] for it was not improbable that she should wish to have a letter taken home. These last are the only Discoveries independent of the artifice of signs and necklaces. Next after them come Discoveries through reasoning.

17

At the time when he is constructing his Plots, and engaged on the Diction in which they are worked out, the poet should remember (1) to put the actual scenes as far as possible before his eyes. In this way, seeing everything with the vividness of an eye-witness as it were, he will devise what is appropriate, and be least likely to overlook incongruities. This is shown by what was censured in Carcinus, the return of Amphiaraus from the sanctuary; it would have passed unnoticed, if it had not been actually seen by the audience; but on the stage his play failed, the incongruity of the incident offending the spectators. (2) As far as may be, too, the poet should even act his story with the very gestures of his personages. Given the same natural qualifications, he who feels the emotions to be described will be the most convincing; distress and danger, for instance, are portrayed most truthfully by one who is feeling them at the moment. Hence it is that poetry demands a man with a special gift for it, or else one with a touch of madness in him; the former can easily assume the required mood, and the latter may be actually beside himself with emotion. (3) His story, again, whether already made or of his own making, he should first simplify and reduce to a universal form, before proceeding to lengthen it out by the insertion of episodes. The following will show how the universal element in *Iphigenia*, for instance, may be viewed: A certain maiden having been offered in sacrifice, and spirited away from her sacrificers into another land, where the custom was to sacrifice all strangers to the Goddess, she was made there the priestess of this rite. Long after that the brother of the priestess happened to come; the fact, however, of the oracle having for a certain reason bidden him go thither, and his object in going, are outside the Plot of the play. On his coming he was arrested, and about to be sacrificed, when he revealed who he was—either as Euripides puts it, or (as suggested by Polyidus) by the not improbable excla-

[18] Authorship unknown.
[19] *Iph. Taur.* 582.

mation, 'So I too am doomed to be sacrificed, as my sister was'; and the disclosure led to his salvation. This done, the next thing, after the proper names have been fixed as a basis for the story, is to work in episodes or accessory incidents. One must mind, however, that the episodes are appropriate, like the fit of madness[20] in Orestes, which led to his arrest, and the purifying,[21] which brought about his salvation. In plays, then, the episodes are short; in epic poetry they serve to lengthen out the poem. The argument of the *Odyssey* is not a long one. A certain man has been abroad many years; Poseidon is ever on the watch for him, and he is all alone. Matters at home too have come to this, that his substance is being wasted and his son's death plotted by suitors to his wife. Then he arrives there himself after his grievous sufferings; reveals himself, and falls on his enemies; and the end is his salvation and their death. This being all that is proper to the *Odyssey*, everything else in it is episode.

18

(4) There is a further point to be borne in mind. Every tragedy is in part Complication and in part Dénouement; the incidents before the opening scene, and often certain also of those within the play, forming the Complication; and the rest the Dénouement. By Complication I mean all from the beginning of the story to the point just before the change in the hero's fortunes; by Dénouement, all from the beginning of the change to the end. In the *Lynceus* of Theodectes, for instance, the Complication includes, together with the presupposed incidents, the seizure of the child and that in turn of the parents; and the Dénouement all from the indictment for the murder to the end. Now it is right, when one speaks of a tragedy as the same or not the same as another, to do so on the ground before all else of their Plot, i.e. as having the same or not the same Complication and Dénouement. Yet there are many dramatists who, after a good Complication, fail in the Dénouement. But it is necessary for both points of construction to be always duly mastered.
(5) There are four distinct species of Tragedy—that being the number of the constituents also that have been mentioned:[22] first, the complex Tragedy, which is all Peripety and Discovery; second, the Tragedy of suffering, e.g. the *Ajaxes* and *Ixions*; third, the Tragedy of character, e.g. *The Phthiotides*[23] and *Peleus*.[24] The fourth constituent is that of "Spectacle," exemplified in *The Phorcides*,[25] in *Prometheus*,[26] and in all plays with the scene laid in the nether world. The poet's aim, then, should be to combine every element of interest, if possible, or else the more important and the major part of them. This is now especially necessary owing to the unfair criticism to which the poet is

[20] *Iph. Taur.* 281 ff.   [21] Ib., 1163 ff.
[22] This does not agree with anything actually said before.
[23] By Sophocles.   [24] Probably Sophocles' *Peleus* is incorrect.
[25] By Aeschylus.   [26] Probably a satyric drama by Aeschylus.

subjected in these days. Just because there have been poets before him strong
in the several species of tragedy, the critics now expect the one man to surpass that which was the strong point of each one of his predecessors. (6) One
should also remember what has been said more than once, and not write
a tragedy on an epic body of incident (i.e. one with a plurality of stories
in it), by attempting to dramatize, for instance, the entire story of the *Iliad*.
In the epic owing to its scale every part is treated at proper length; with a
drama, however, on the same story the result is very disappointing. This is
shown by the fact that all who have dramatized the fall of Ilium in its entirety, and not part by part, like Euripides, of the whole of the Niobe story,
instead of a portion, like Aeschylus, either fail utterly or have but ill success
on the stage; for that and that alone was enough to ruin even a play by
Agathon. Yet in their Peripeties, as also in their simple plots, the poets I mean
show wonderful skill in aiming at the kind of effect they desire—a tragic
situation that arouses the human feeling in one, like the clever villain (e.g.
Sisyphus) deceived, or the brave wrongdoer worsted. This is probable, however, only in Agathon's sense, when he speaks of the probability of even improbabilities coming to pass. (7) The Chorus too should be regarded as one of
the actors; it should be an integral part of the whole, and take a share in
the action—that which it has in Sophocles, rather than in Euripides. With the
later poets, however, the songs in a play of theirs have no more to do with
the Plot of that than of any other tragedy. Hence it is that they are now
singing intercalary pieces, a practice first introduced by Agathon. And yet
what real difference is there between singing such intercalary pieces, and attempting to fit in a speech, or even a whole act, from one play into another?

19

The Plot and Characters having been discussed, it remains to consider the
Diction and Thought. As for the Thought, we may assume what is said of
it in our Art of Rhetoric, as it belongs more properly to that department of
inquiry. The Thought of the personages is shown in everything to be effected by their language—in every effort to prove or disprove, to arouse emotion (pity, fear, anger, and the like), or to maximize or minimize things. It is
clear, also, that their mental procedure must be on the same lines in their
actions likewise, whenever they wish them to arouse pity or horror, or to have
a look of importance or probability. The only difference is that with the act
the impression has to be made without explanation; whereas with the spoken
word it has to be produced by the speaker, and result from his language.
What, indeed, would be the good of the speaker, if things appeared in the
required light even apart from anything he says? . . .

21

. . . Metaphor consists in giving the thing a name that belongs to something else; the transference being either from genus to species, or from species

to genus, or from species to species, or on the grounds of analogy. That from genus to species is exemplified in 'Here stands my ship'; for lying at anchor is the 'standing' of a particular kind of thing. That from species to genus in 'Truly ten thousand good deeds has Ulysses wrought,' where 'ten thousand,' which is a particular large number, is put in place of the generic 'a large number.' That from species to species in 'Drawing the life with the bronze,' and in 'Severing with the enduring bronze'; where the poet uses 'draw' in the sense of 'sever' and 'sever' in that of 'draw,' both words meaning to 'take away' something. That from analogy is possible whenever there are four terms so related that the second (B) is to the first (A), as the fourth (D) to the third (C); for one may then metaphorically put D in lieu of B, and B in lieu of D. Now and then, too, they qualify the metaphor by adding on to it that to which the word it supplants is relative. Thus a cup (B) is in relation to Dionysus (A) what a shield (D) is to Ares (C). The cup accordingly will be metaphorically described as the 'shield of *Dionysus*' (D+A), and the shield as the 'cup *of Ares*' (B+C). Or to take another instance: As old age (D) is to life (C), so is evening (B) to day (A). One will accordingly describe evening (B) as the 'old age *of the day*' (D+A)—or by the Empedoclean equivalent; and old age (D) as the 'evening' or 'sunset *of life*' (B+C). It may be that some of the terms thus related have no special name of their own, but for all that they will be metaphorically described in just the same way. Thus to cast forth seed-corn is called 'sowing'; but to cast forth its flame, as said of the sun, has no special name. This nameless act (B), however, stands in just the same relation to its object, sunlight (A), as sowing (D) to the seed-corn (C). Hence the expression in the poet, 'sowing around a god-created *flame*' (D+A). There is also another form of qualified metaphor. Having given the thing the alien name, one may by a negative addition deny of it one of the attributes naturally associated with its new name. An instance of this would be to call the shield not the 'cup *of Ares*,' as in the former case, but a 'cup *that holds no wine*' . . . .

22

The perfection of Diction is for it to be at once clear and not mean. The clearest indeed is that made up of the ordinary words for things, but it is mean, as is shown by the poetry of Cleophon and Sthenelus. On the other hand the Diction becomes distinguished and non-prosaic by the use of unfamiliar terms, i.e. strange words, metaphors, lengthened forms, and everything that deviates from the ordinary modes of speech.—But a whole statement in such terms will be either a riddle or a barbarism, a riddle, if made up of metaphors, a barbarism, if made up of strange words. . . . It is a great thing, indeed, to make a proper use of these poetical forms, as also of compounds and strange words. But the greatest thing by far is to be a master of metaphor. It is the one thing that cannot be learnt from others; and it is also a sign of genius, since a good metaphor implies an intuitive perception of the similarity in dissimilars. . . .

Let this, then, suffice as an account of Tragedy, the art imitating by means of action on the stage.

23

As for the poetry which merely narrates, or imitates by means of versified language (without action), it is evident that it has several points in common with Tragedy.

I. The construction of its stories should clearly be like that in a drama; they should be based on a single action, one that is a complete whole in itself, with a beginning, middle, and end, so as to enable the work to produce its own proper pleasure with all the organic unity of a living creature. Nor should one suppose that there is anything like them in our usual histories. A history has to deal not with one action, but with one period and all that happened in that to one or more persons, however disconnected the several events may have been. Just as two events may take place at the same time, e.g. the sea-fight off Salamis and the battle with the Carthaginians in Sicily, without converging to the same end, so too of two consecutive events one may sometimes come after the other with no one end as their common issue. Nevertheless most of our epic poets, one may say, ignore the distinction.

Herein, then, to repeat what we have said before, we have a further proof of Homer's marvellous superiority to the rest. He did not attempt to deal with the Trojan war in its entirety, though it was a whole with a definite beginning and end—through a feeling apparently that it was too long a story to be taken in in one view, or if not that, too complicated from the variety of incident in it. As it is, he has singled out one section of the whole; many of the other incidents, however, he brings in as episodes, using the Catalogue of the Ships, for instance, and other episodes to relieve the uniformity of his narrative. As for the other epic poets, they treat of one man, or one period; or else of an action which, although one, has a multiplicity of parts in it. This last is what the authors of the *Cypria*[27] and *Little Iliad* [27] have done. And the result is that, whereas the *Iliad* or *Odyssey* supplies materials for only one, or at most two tragedies, the *Cypria* does that for several and the *Little Iliad* for more than eight: for an *Adjudgment of Arms*, a *Philoctetes*, a *Neoptolemus*, a *Eurypylus*, a *Ulysses as Beggar*, a *Laconian Women*, a *Fall of Ilium*, and a *Departure of the Fleet*; as also a *Sinon*, and a *Women of Troy*.

24

II. Besides this, Epic poetry must divide into the same species as Tragedy; it must be either simple or complex, a story of character or one of suffering. Its parts, too, with the exception of Song and Spectacle, must be the same, as it requires Peripeties, Discoveries, and scenes of suffering just like Tragedy. Lastly, the Thought and Diction in it must be good in their way. All these elements appear in Homer first; and he has made due use of them. His two

27 Authorship unknown.

poems are each examples of construction, the *Iliad* simple and a story of suffering, the *Odyssey* complex (there is Discovery throughout it) and a story of character. And they are more than this, since in Diction and Thought too they surpass all other poems.

There is, however, a difference in the Epic as compared with Tragedy, (1) in its length, and (2) in its metre. (1) As to its length, the limit already suggested will suffice: it must be possible for the beginning and end of the work to be taken in in one view—a condition which will be fulfilled if the poem be shorter than the old epics, and about as long as the series of tragedies offered for one hearing. For the extension of its length epic poetry has a special advantage, of which it makes large use. In a play one cannot represent an action with a number of parts going on simultaneously; one is limited to the part on the stage and connected with the actors. Whereas in epic poetry the narrative form makes it possible for one to describe a number of simultaneous incidents; and these, if germane to the subject, increase the body of the poem. This then is a gain to the Epic, tending to give it grandeur, and also variety of interest and room for episodes of diverse kinds. Uniformity of incident by the satiety it soon creates is apt to ruin tragedies on the stage. (2) As for its metre, the heroic has been assigned it from experience; were any one to attempt a narrative poem in some one, or in several, of the other metres, the incongruity of the thing would be apparent. The heroic in fact is the gravest and weightiest of metres—which is what makes it more tolerant than the rest of strange words and metaphors, that also being a point in which the narrative form of poetry goes beyond all others. The iambic and trochaic, on the other hand, are metres of movement, the one representing that of life and action, the other that of the dance. Still more unnatural would it appear, if one were to write an epic in a medley of metres, as Chaeremon did.[28] Hence it is that no one has ever written a long story in any but heroic verse; nature herself, as we have said, teaches us to select the metre appropriate to such a story.

Homer, admirable as he is in every other respect, is especially so in this, that he alone among epic poets is not unaware of the part to be played by the poet himself in the poem. The poet should say very little *in propria persona*, as he is no imitator when doing that. Whereas the other poets are perpetually coming forward in person, and say but little, and that only here and there, as imitators, Homer after a brief preface brings in forthwith a man, a woman, or some other Character—no one of them characterless, but each with distinctive characteristics.

The marvellous is certainly required in Tragedy. The Epic, however, affords more opening for the improbable, the chief factor in the marvellous, because in it the agents are not visibly before one. The scene of the pursuit of Hector would be ridiculous on the stage—the Greeks halting instead of pur-

[28] *Centaur.*

suing him, and Achilles shaking his head to stop them;[29] but in the poem the absurdity is overlooked. The marvellous, however, is a cause of pleasure, as is shown by the fact that we all tell a story with additions, in the belief that we are doing our hearers a pleasure.

Homer more than any other has taught the rest of us the art of framing lies in the right way. I mean the use of paralogism. Whenever, if A is or happens, a consequent, B, is or happens, men's notion is that, if the B is, the A also is—but that is a false conclusion. Accordingly, if A is untrue, but there is something else, B, that on the assumption of its truth follows as its consequent, the right thing then is to add on the B. Just because we know the truth of the consequent, we are in our own minds led on to the erroneous inference of the truth of the antecedent. Here is an instance, from the *Bath-story* in the *Odyssey*.[30]

A likely impossibility is always preferable to an unconvincing possibility. The story should never be made up of improbable incidents; there should be nothing of the sort in it. If, however, such incidents are unavoidable, they should be outside the piece, like the hero's ignorance in *Oedipus* of the circumstances of Laius' death; not within it, like the report of the Pythian games in *Electra*,[31] or the man's having come to Mysia from Tegea without uttering a word on the way, in *The Mysians*.[32] So that it is ridiculous to say that one's Plot would have been spoilt without them, since it is fundamentally wrong to make up such Plots. If the poet has taken such a Plot, however, and one sees that he might have put it in a more probable form, he is guilty of absurdity as well as a fault of art. Even in the *Odyssey* the improbabilities in the setting-ashore of Ulysses[33] would be clearly intolerable in the hands of an inferior poet. As it is, the poet conceals them, his other excellences veiling their absurdity. Elaborate Diction, however, is required only in places where there is no action, and no Character or Thought to be revealed. Where there is Character or Thought, on the other hand, an over-ornate Diction tends to obscure them.

25

As regards Problems and their Solutions, one may see the number and nature of the assumptions on which they proceed by viewing the matter in the following way. (1) The poet being an imitator just like the painter or other maker of likenesses, he must necessarily in all instances represent things in one or other of three aspects, either as they were or are, or as they are said or thought to be or to have been, or as they ought to be. (2) All this he does in language, with an admixture, it may be, of strange words and metaphors, as also of the various modified forms of words, since the use of these is conceded in poetry. (3) It is to be remembered, too, that there is not the same kind of correctness in poetry as in politics, or indeed any other

[29] *Il.* xxii. 205.   [30] xix. 164-260.   [31] Soph. *El.* 660 ff.
[32] Probably by Aeschylus.   [33] xiii. 116 ff.

art. There is, however, within the limits of poetry itself a possibility of two kinds of error, the one directly, the other only accidentally connected with the art. If the poet meant to describe the thing correctly, and failed through lack of power of expression, his art itself is at fault. But if it was through his having meant to describe it in some incorrect way (e.g. to make the horse in movement have both legs thrown forward) that the technical error (one in a matter of, say, medicine or some other special science), or impossibilities of whatever kind they may be, have got into his description, his error in that case is not in the essentials of the poetic art. These, therefore, must be the premises of the Solutions in answer to the criticisms involved in the Problems.

I. As to the criticisms relating to the poet's art itself. Any impossibilities there may be in his descriptions of things are faults. But from another point of view they are justifiable, if they serve the end of poetry itself—if (to assume what we have said of that end) they make the effect of either that very portion of the work or some other portion more astounding. The Pursuit of Hector is an instance in point. If, however, the poetic end might have been as well or better attained without sacrifice of technical correctness in such matters, the impossibility is not to be justified, since the description should be, if it can, entirely free from error. One may ask, too, whether the error is in a matter directly or only accidentally connected with the poetic art; since it is a lesser error in an artist not to know, for instance, that the hind has no horns, than to produce an unrecognizable picture of one.

II. If the poet's description be criticized as not true to fact, one may urge perhaps that the object ought to be as described—an answer like that of Sophocles, who said that he drew men as they ought to be, and Euripides as they were. If the description, however, be neither true nor of the thing as it ought to be, the answer must be then, that it is in accordance with opinion. The tales about Gods, for instance, may be as wrong as Xenophanes thinks, neither true nor the better thing to say; but they are certainly in accordance with opinion. Of other statements in poetry one may perhaps say, not that they are better than the truth, but that the fact was so at the time; e.g. the description of the arms: 'their spears stood upright, butt-end upon the ground';[34] for that was the usual way of fixing them then, as it is still with the Illyrians. As for the question whether something said or done in a poem is morally right or not, in dealing with that one should consider not only the intrinsic quality of the actual word or deed, but also the person who says or does it, the person to whom he says or does it, the time, the means, and the motive of the agent—whether he does it to attain a greater good, or to avoid a greater evil.

III. . . . Speaking generally, one has to justify (1) the Impossible by reference to the requirements of poetry, or to the better, or to opinion. For the purposes of poetry a convincing impossibility is preferable to an unconvincing

[34] *Il*. x. 152.

possibility; and if men such as Zeuxis depicted be impossible, the answer is that it is better they should be like that, as the artist ought to improve on his model. (2) The Improbable one has to justify either by showing it to be in accordance with opinion, or by urging that at times it is not improbable; for there is a probability of things happening also against probability. (3) The contradictions found in the poet's language one should first test as one does an opponent's confutation in a dialectical argument, so as to see whether he means the same thing, in the same relation, and in the same sense, before admitting that he has contradicted either something he has said himself or what a man of sound sense assumes as true. But there is no possible apology for improbability of Plot or depravity of character, when they are not necessary and no use is made of them, like the improbability in the appearance of Aegeus in *Medea*[35] and the baseness of Menelaus in Orestes.

The objections, then, of critics start with faults of five kinds: the allegation is always that something is either (1) impossible, (2) improbable, (3) corrupting, (4) contradictory, or (5) against technical correctness. The answers to these objections must be sought under one or other of the above-mentioned heads, which are twelve in number.

26

The question may be raised whether the epic or the tragic is the higher form of imitation. It may be argued that, if the less vulgar is the higher, and the less vulgar is always that which addresses the better public, an art addressing any and every one is of a very vulgar order. It is a belief that their public cannot see the meaning, unless they add something themselves, that causes the perpetual movements of the performers—bad flute-players, for instance, rolling about, if quoit-throwing is to be represented, and pulling at the conductor, if Scylla is the subject of the piece. Tragedy, then, is said to be an art of this order—to be in fact just what the later actors were in the eyes of their predecessors; for Mynniscus used to call Callippides 'the ape,' because he thought he so overacted his parts; and a similar view was taken of Pindarus also. All Tragedy, however, is said to stand to the Epic as the newer to the older school of actors. The one, accordingly, is said to address a cultivated audience, which does not need the accompaniment of gesture; the other, an uncultivated one. If, therefore, Tragedy is a vulgar art, it must clearly be lower than the Epic.

The answer to this is twofold. In the first place, one may urge (1) that the censure does not touch the art of the dramatic poet, but only that of his interpreter; for it is quite possible to overdo the gesturing even in an epic recital, as did Sosistratus, and in a singing contest, as did Mnasitheus of Opus. (2) That one should not condemn all movement, unless one means to condemn even the dance, but only that of ignoble people—which is the point of the criticism passed on Callippides and in the present day on others, that their

[35] 1. 663.

women are not like gentlewoman. (3) That Tragedy may produce its effect even without movement or action in just the same way as Epic poetry; for from the mere reading of a play its quality may be seen. So that, if it be superior in all other respects, this element of inferiority is no necessary part of it.

In the second place, one must remember (1) that Tragedy has everything that the Epic has (even the epic metre being admissible), together with a not inconsiderable addition in the shape of the Music (a very real factor in the pleasure of the drama) and the Spectacle. (2) That its reality of presentation is felt in the play as read, as well as in the play as acted. (3) That the tragic imitation requires less space for the attainment of its end; which is a great advantage, since the more concentrated effect is more pleasurable than one with a large admixture of time to dilute it—consider the *Oedipus* of Sophocles, for instance, and the effect of expanding it into the number of lines of the *Iliad*. (4) That there is less unity in the imitation of the epic poets, as is proved by the fact that any one work of theirs supplies matter for several tragedies; the result being that, if they take what is really a single story, it seems curt when briefly told, and thin and waterish when on the scale of length usual with their verse. In saying that there is less unity in an epic, I mean an epic made up of a plurality of actions, in the same way as the *Iliad* and *Odyssey* have many such parts, each one of them in itself of some magnitude; yet the structure of the two Homeric poems is as perfect as can be, and the action in them is as nearly as possible one action. If, then, Tragedy is superior in these respects, and also, besides these, in its poetic effect (since the two forms of poetry should give us, not any or every pleasure, but the very special kind we have mentioned), it is clear that, as attaining the poetic effect better than the Epic, it will be the higher form of art.

So much for Tragedy and Epic poetry—for these two arts in general and their species; the number and nature of their constitutent parts; the causes of success and failure in them; the Objections of the critics, and the Solutions in answer to them.

T. S. E L I O T

On Teaching the Appreciation of Poetry[1]

I hold no diploma, certificate, or other academic document to show that I am qualified to discuss this subject. I have never taught anybody of any age how to enjoy, understand, appreciate poetry, or how to speak it. I have known a great many poets, and innumerable people who wanted to be told that they

[1] From *The Critic*, XVIII (1960). By permission of the editor and Mr. Eliot.

were poets. I have done some teaching, but I have never "taught poetry." My excuse for taking up this subject is of wholly different origin. I know that not only young people in colleges and universities, but secondary school children also, have to study, or at least acquaint themselves with, poems by living poets; and I know that my poems are among those studied, by two kinds of evidence. My play *Murder in the Cathedral* is a set book in some schools: there is an edition of the English text published in Germany with notes in German, and an edition published in Canada with notes in English. The fact that this play, and some of my other poems, are used in schools brings some welcome supplement to my income; and it also brings an increase in my correspondence, which is more or less welcome, though not all the letters get answered. These are letters from the children themselves, or more precisely, the teenagers. They live mostly in Britain, the United States, and Germany, with a sprinkling from the nations of Asia. It is in a spirit of curiosity, therefore, that I approach the subject of the teaching of poetry: I should like to know more about these young people and about their teachers and the methods of teaching.

For some of my young correspondents seem to be misguided. Sometimes I have been assigned to them as a "project," more often they have made the choice themselves—it is not always clear why. (There was one case, that of an Egyptian boy, who wanted to write a thesis about my work, and as none of my work was locally available and as he wanted to read it, asked me to send him all my books. That was very exceptional, however.) Very often the writers ask for information about myself, sometimes in the form of a questionnaire. I remember being asked by one child whether it was true that I only cared to associate with lords and bishops. Sometimes a photograph is asked for. Some young persons seem to want me to provide them with all the material for a potted biography, including mention of my interests, tastes, and ways of amusing myself. Are these children studying poetry, or merely studying poets? Very often they want explanations, either of a whole poem ("what does it mean") or of a particular line or phrase; and the kind of question they ask often suggests that their approach to that poem has been wrong, for they want the wrong kind of explanation, or ask questions which are simply unanswerable. Sometimes, but more rarely, they are avid for literary sources, which would seem to indicate that they have started too early on the road to Xanadu.

The Older Pattern

Now, when I was young, this sort of thing did not happen. I did study English at school, beginning, thank God, with grammar, and going on to "rhetoric"—for which also I am grateful. And we had to read a number of set books of prose and verse—mostly in school editions which made them look peculiarly unappetizing. But we never were made to read any literature which could be called contemporary: Tennyson could hardly be called "contempo-

rary" by the time I had to study some of the *Idylls of the King*. I must admit
that at the turn of the twentieth century there were precious few great poets
about, and still fewer poets whom the authorities would have considered suitable for our perusal. Swinburne would hardly have done in those days; I don't
know whether he has reached the school curriculum today. Yeats was still a
minor poet of the 'Nineties. But even if Trumbull Stickney and George Cabot
Lodge, two poets of whose work I remain ignorant to this day, had been famous instead of merely respectable, I doubt if my school authorities would
have set any of their poetry for us.

No. Not only were we not encouraged to take an interest in the poetry
actually being written, but even had we been, I doubt whether we should have
thought of entering into correspondence with the authors. Some of the juvenile correspondence I receive seems to be instigated by the teachers, but
the greater part does not. Indeed, some of my letters, I suspect, are inspired
by a desire to score off teacher in the hope of getting some statement from
the horse's mouth which will be a direct contradiction of what has been
taught. (I confess that this last type of letter is one which I sometimes take
pleasure in answering—when teacher seems to me to have been wrong.) But
my point is that this pressure upon the poet from young people who have
been compelled to read his work is a modern phenomenon. I don't believe
that Tennyson and Browning, Longfellow and Whittier (to say nothing of
Poe and Whitman, poets whose works we did not study) were embarrassed
by juvenile correspondence choking up their letter boxes. The teaching of the
contemporary literature, the introduction of the young to poetry by living
poets, is something that came about in my time without my being aware of
what was happening. I have had other surprises of this kind. When I returned to give a course of lectures at Harvard in 1932, after seventeen years'
absence from America, I looked out of my window and saw a bird which arrested my attention because it looked like a starling. As a boy I had been an
eager bird-watcher, and I knew most of the resident and migratory birds of
New England, but I knew no bird with that peculiar stumpy tail. On inquiry, I found that it *was* a starling: that bird had arrived and multiplied in
America while I wasn't looking. The starling has come to stay, and so, I
think, has the academic study of the work of living authors.

I do not wish to suggest that I deplore the introduction of the young, as a
part of their education, to the work of living authors—to the work of *some*
living authors. Nor am I suggesting that I think that the methods of teaching
are altogether wrong. All I aim to indicate is that the teaching of contemporary poetry is a difficult task, and that contemporary poetry cannot be taught
by exactly the same methods as are suitable for poetry of the past. And I mean
by "poetry of the past" the poetry of any period as soon as that period
has become a part of history. The teacher who aims at teaching pupils to
appreciate contemporary poetry, to distinguish between the good and the
bad, the genuine and the spurious, the original and the imitative, to enjoy

the best and only the best, needs himself to have both enthusiasm and discrimination. He needs to be as well educated, as scholarly in his knowledge of the literature of the past, as the teacher who confines his tuition to the literature of the past; and he needs independent good taste.

Poetry as History

I am not suggesting that to teach the curriculum as it was taught when I was a boy, we can dispense with enthusiasm and good taste. But that curriculum was limited to authors whose place had been pretty well fixed by the judgment of time. It included a couple of plays of Shakespeare, several of Milton's minor poems, and selections from standard English and American authors down to the latter part of the nineteenth century. These were authors of whose works, it could be assumed, no educated man should be wholly ignorant. And here, as I have already asserted, is the important difference: the poetry of the past is already a part of history. No man can be called educated if ignorant of the history of his own country, or his own race, or his own language: indeed we should know something of the history of civilization, of the struggle of man to raise himself from savagery to the condition of the highest triumphs of the arts and sciences, of religion and morals. And our historical knowledge of any past age is incomplete unless we know something of the literature of that age. To enter imaginatively into the life of men in a past age we need everything we can learn from their literature, and particularly from their poetry, of the way they thought and felt. Thus, the teacher of the literature of the past may find his task to be primarily that of an historian, though he should also be a lover of that literature and have the capacity to communicate his feeling for it to his pupils. But the poetry of the present, the best of which *will become* a part of history, cannot be studied in exactly the same way as the poetry which is already history.

Let me at this point consider first the drawbacks to that school study of the poetry of the past which ignores the fact that poetry is something which *goes on being written*, which is being written now while the pupils are sitting at their desks construing *L'Allegro* or *Il Penseroso*, and that the poet hopes that people will read it for enjoyment. And then let me consider the disadvantages of over-emphasis upon actuality which ignores the fact that much of the poetry written in the same language in the past is as good as, and that some of it is better than, what is being written now.

The great weakness of the method by which I was introduced—academically introduced, I mean—to English poetry was that it did not help me to enjoy it. I think that many people have suffered in the same way from their introduction to the plays of Shakespeare: I took a dislike to *Julius Caesar* which lasted, I am sorry to say, until I saw the film of Marlon Brando and John Gielgud, and a dislike to *The Merchant of Venice* which persists to this day. Perhaps the fact that I had to memorize and declaim, in front of the class,

Antony's oration and Portia's quality of mercy, and that I was a very poor declaimer, may have had something to do with it. But I also disliked *L'Allegro* and *Il Penseroso*. I am thankful that I did not have to study *Lycidas* in the same way. Coleridge's *Ancient Mariner* barely survived. I have no fault to find with our teacher. We had examinations to pass; and it was his business to see that we should be able to answer the questions.

I do not know that there is any better way of studying English literature at that stage; and it may be that a few plays and poems must be sacrificed in order that we may learn that English literature exists, and that an orderly historical acquaintance with it is desirable. We also, I remember, had a history book of English literature to study, and we had to learn something about the great writers of every period from the Age of Shakespeare to the end of the nineteenth century. The knowledge that we acquired served a purpose; and I do not believe it would have served that purpose so well if the emphasis had been on appreciation instead of on an orderly outline of literature and some information about the chief historical reputations. After all, how many boys and girls of thirteen or fourteen can appreciate Shakespeare or Milton? I didn't.

The Discovery of Poetry

I think I have mentioned somewhere among my essays that my first experience of intense excitement from poetry came when I was fourteen, and came, not from anything put in my way by my work at school, but by happening to pick up at home a copy of FitzGerald's *Omar Khayyám*. And, at the risk of repeating myself, I will suggest that it is at or on the approach of puberty that a boy or girl may suddenly discover that poetry is capable of giving a kind of delight hitherto wholly unsuspected. Very likely this illumination will come as the sudden shock of a particular poem: a poem discovered by oneself or presented by an older person or by one's teacher. But it will probably not be one of the poems that one has had to study in a school text supported by notes (and for passing examinations the notes may be more important than the text!). I am not sorry that I was made to study certain things of Shakespeare and Milton in the way I have described. But the discovery of poetry is a different experience altogether, and the discovery may be more important than the poem through which we make the discovery. Our first "discovery" of poetry—say at fourteen or fifteen or sixteen—may be through a poem of which, after our acquaintance is wider and our taste more developed, we cease to think very highly.

There are, in fact, some poems and some poets whose function seems to be to awaken our capacity for enjoyment, to retire later on to a lower (but still, most often, honorable) place. The earlier poems of Byron, for instance; *The Shropshire Lad* of A. E. Housman; the poems of Rupert Brooke. The greatest poets are those whom we have to grow up to and whose work we appreciate more fully as we mature. At sixteen I discovered (by reading a section of our history of English literature which we were *not* required to read) Thomson's *The City of Dreadful Night* and the poems of Ernest Dowson. Each was a new and vivid experience. But *The City of Dreadful Night* or Dowson's *Impenitentia Ultima* would hardly, even today, be considered suitable for academic study at the age I have in mind. It is in fact *necessary* to choose works by the greatest writers for us to study at an age at which we are not yet mature enough to enjoy them.

The Training of Taste

Let me now consider the situation when our emphasis, in teaching children of the same ages, is on enjoyment rather than on information, and upon contemporary poets rather than upon a selection of the great classics. This offers the teacher greater liberty, but prepares for him greater pitfalls. That rough and ready valuation, ordinarily called "the verdict of history," has not yet been passed, and the teacher must follow his own judgment as to what poets, and what poems, he should choose for initiating his pupils into the delights of poetry. There is plenty of contemporary poetry to serve the purpose. But opinion about the relative importance of living poets can vary widely, even among persons of taste, apart from the permanent chasm between those who lean towards what is called "traditional" verse and those who prefer the "experimental." And the successful teacher, who teaches the poetry of his choice with enthusiasm, will be in danger of implanting his own personal tastes in the minds of his pupils, or (what is worse) teaching them to parrot opinions which they are too passive to share. But even if we postulate an ideal teacher of impeccable taste—and I have never known anyone incapable of going wrong at one time or another about living authors, and I include myself in this universal fallibility—that teacher could rouse enthusiasm but could do little to train taste and understanding. For without some knowledge of the poetry of the past and enjoyment of what we know, we cannot really appreciate the poetry of the present.

The dangers of a concentration of interest upon contemporary poetry appears most clearly and painfully when the reader aspires to write poetry himself, or herself. I have never judged a poetry competition, but I have known those who have. One friend who had on one occasion undertaken to read a great number of such contributions was appalled by the evidence of the meagerness of the contestants' knowledge of poetry of the past. Most aspirants had some acquaintance with the poetry of John Donne; a good many had read poems by Blake; and coming down to recent times, they were familiar with the work of Gerard Manley Hopkins and William Butler Yeats. There are would-be poets who write regular verse with, at best, dull metronomic accuracy: modern poetry is unknown to them. There are others who write "free verse" with an ear untrained by the practice of regular verse: they have probably dieted solely on contemporary verse.

Past and Present

It is not, however, for students who aspire to write poetry, but simply with those capable of becoming intelligent and sensitive readers, that I am chiefly concerned. I maintain that no one can go very far in the discerning enjoyment of poetry who is incapable of enjoying any poetry other than that of his own place and time. It is in fact a part of the function of education to help us to escape—not from our own time, for we are all bound by that—but from the intellectual and emotional limitations of our own time. It is a commonplace that we appreciate our home all the more fully and consciously after foreign travel; it is not such a commonplace to assert that we can appreciate the poetry of our own time better for knowing and enjoying the best poetry of previous ages. We understand and appreciate our own language the better for having some command of a foreign language. Those whose knowledge of poetry in the English language extends no further than to the immediate precursors of the poetry of our time, such as Hopkins and Yeats, or whose knowledge of the past is limited to the poetry extolled by some persuasive critic of the day (like myself), are limited in their understanding of the poetry that they do know. If, as I believe, poetry plays an important part in the process of education, then these readers are uneducated.

You may think at this point that I have reached an *impasse*. On the one hand, the historical approach to English and American literature, with obligatory reading, of a selection of classics, seems unlikely to awaken any appetite or curiosity that would lead to independent reading; nor does it present poetry and prose as living arts. On the other hand, the study of contemporary poetry, while it may be an immediate stimulant, may encourage a provincialism of taste—for provincialism in *time* is as deplorable as provincialism in *place*—which is the opposite of educative.

To me it seems that the two ways of approach to poetry should be combined, so that young people might be brought to see literature—and poetry especially—both in its historical aspect and in its actuality as a permanent heritage and as something which is still going on, as a necessary part of knowledge and as something to be enjoyed. Here are involved two different, though related meanings of the word *understanding*. In the teaching of the great literature of the past, *understanding* is primarily what ensues from a knowledge of historical and biographical facts, the conditions under which a masterpiece was written, the peculiarities of idiom and vocabulary which mark it as of a different age from ours, etc. In approaching a contemporary work, a poem by a living poet, our understanding is primarily a matter of insight. I know of one teacher who, without any preliminary explanation, played to her pupils a gramophone record of a poem by a living poet. She played it twice and then told her girls to write down their feelings and impressions, to put in words as well as they could what this poem had meant to them. And I know that for one of her pupils at least—they were girls of fourteen—the impres-

sion that this poem made upon her opened the path to understanding not only
of other poems of the same poet, but to poetry of earlier times, indeed to all
poetry. And the teacher had not told the class that they were to admire this
poem, still less what they were to admire about it; least of all had she given
any hint as to what it was about or what it meant. She had chosen wisely and
with taste, but had left the poem to do its own work.

This incident seems to me to suggest that at that age—from fourteen to
sixteen I should say—when the sensibility begins, if ever, to respond passionately to poetry, the poetry of our own age may be able to make a more immediate impact than that of earlier generations. It is not merely that there are
no difficulties of style and idiom; not merely that there is less oppression by
the mass of critical opinion. There is more than enough of the latter: and may
I suggest in passing that the young should be encouraged to read poetry by
living poets rather than books about contemporary poetry—that they should
know and love certain poetry before they read *about* that poetry. I think that
young people often recognize obscurely that the poet speaking to them is of
their own time and that his sensibility and theirs have something in common.

The Ideal Teacher

I do not believe that the work of living poets should be taught formally.
I do not believe that youngsters should take examinations in it. I think that
the choice of poems to present to a class should represent the taste of the
teacher, not be set by a board. Unless the teacher is a person who reads poetry
for enjoyment, he or she cannot stimulate pupils to enjoy it. Nor should the
young have a great deal of contemporary verse forced upon them; at this
stage we are not concerned to equip young people with a familiarity with the
names of all the living poets of reputation, but with starting them on the way
to enjoying poetry.

I am assuming, of course, that the teacher who introduces them to modern poetry will be the same teacher who takes them through their annotated
textbooks of the classics and who wants them to pass their examination on
these texts with credit. Perhaps I am merely clamouring for the Ideal Teacher.
But don't "educationists" sometimes forget, in their teaching about teaching,
that the one essential for good teaching is the good teacher? The good teacher
then will instruct his or her pupils well in the historical understanding of literature, and at the same time will lead those of them who have the capacity
to see that the literature of the past, about which the educated person must
be informed as a part of history, is also literature to be enjoyed, and that without enjoyment it is meaningless. The good teacher will make pupils aware that
literature is a continuous activity, and that more literature is being made even
while they are busy with that of the past. In introducing the pupils to modern
poetry that the teacher likes, he will be reminding them of the essential part
of enjoyment. For it doesn't matter so much, in my opinion, that the teacher's enthusiasm should be aroused by the very best contemporary poetry—

in other words, the poetry of which I myself approve—as that the enthusiasm should be infectious. The pupils capable of developing good taste will eventually discover for themselves the better poetry, and as for the others it is probably better that they should like the second rate, the unoriginal, than that they should not like any poetry at all.

My Ideal Teacher, accordingly, will teach the prescribed classics of literature as history, as a part of history which every educated person should know something about whether he likes it or not; and then he should lead some of the pupils to enjoyment and the rest at least to the point of recognizing that there are other persons who do enjoy it. And he will introduce the pupils to contemporary poetry by exciting enjoyment: enjoyment first and understanding second. It may be only by reading such poetry to them as an extracurricular activity, or it may be by a reading or a gramophone record, and then asking the class to set down impressions and reactions. I think that such an introduction to poetry is justifiable even for those pupils who never come to show any love for poetry or any intelligent and sensitive appreciation of it. And the pupils who have some aptitude for enjoyment and understanding of what is good in literature (and as this is a question of degree, there can be no clear division between the sheep and the goats) will find that their knowledge of the great poetry which has had the approval of successive generations will sharpen their discrimination and refine their enjoyment of the poetry which is being written in their own time, and their enjoyment of the poetry written in their own time will help them towards enjoyment of the classics of literature. For our own poetry of today and that of our forefathers, the foundations upon which we build and without which our poetry would not be what it is, will eventually be seen as forming one harmonious whole.

ARTHUR MILLER

The Family in Modern Drama[1]

Most people, including the daily theater reviewers, have come to assume that the forms in which plays are written spring either from nowhere or from the temperamental choice of the playwrights. I am not maintaining that the selection of a form is as objective a matter as the choice of let us say a raincoat instead of a linen suit for a walk on a rainy day; on the contrary, most playwrights, including myself, reach rather instinctively for that form, that way of telling a play, which seems inevitably right for the subject at hand. Yet I

[1] From *The Atlantic Monthly*, CXCVII (April, 1956), 36-41. © Copyright by The Atlantic Monthly Company; © copyright by Arthur Miller, 1956.

wonder whether it is all as accidental, as "free" a choice, as it appears to be at a superficial glance. I wonder whether there may not be within the ideas of family on the one hand, and society on the other, primary pressures which govern our notions of the right form for a particular kind of subject matter.

It has gradually come to appear to me over the years that the spectrum of dramatic forms, from Realism over to the Verse Drama, the Expressionistic techniques, and what we call vaguely the Poetic Play, consists of forms which express human relationships of a particular kind, each of them suited to express either a primarily familial relation at one extreme, or a primarily social relation at the other.

When we think of Realism we think of Ibsen—and if we don't we ought to, because in his social plays he not only used the form but pressed it very close to its ultimate limits. What are the main characteristics of this form? We know it by heart, of course, since most of the plays we see are realistic plays. It is written in prose; it makes believe it is taking place independently of an audience which views it through a "fourth wall," the grand objective being to make everything seem true to life in life's most evident and apparent sense. In contrast, think of any play by Aeschylus. You are never under an illusion in his plays that you are watching "life"; you are watching a play, an art work.

Now at the risk of being obvious I must remind you that Realism is a style, an artful convention, and not a piece of reportage. What, after all, is real about having all the furniture in a living room facing the footlights? What is real about people sticking to the same subject for three consecutive hours? Realism is a style, an invention quite as consciously created as Expressionism, Symbolism, or any of the other less familiar forms. In fact, it has held the stage for a shorter period of time than the more poetic forms and styles which dominate the great bulk of the world repertoire, and when it first came into being it was obvious to all as a style, a poet's invention. I say this in order to make clear that Realism is neither more nor less "artistic" than any other form. The only trouble is that it more easily lends itself in our age to hack work, for one thing because more people can write passable prose than verse. In other ages, however, as for instance in the lesser Elizabethan playwrights, hack work could also make of the verse play a pedestrian and uninspired form.

As with any artist, Ibsen was writing not simply to photograph scenes from life. After all, at the time he wrote *A Doll's House* how many Norwegian or European women had slammed the door upon their hypocritical relations with their husbands? Very few. So there was nothing, really, for him to photograph. What he was doing, however, was projecting through his personal interpretation of common events what he saw as their concealed significance for society. In other words, in a perfectly "realistic" way he did not report so much as project or even prophesy a meaning. Put in playwriting terms, he created a symbol on the stage.

We are not ordinarily accustomed to juxtaposing the idea of a symbol with the idea of Realism. The symbolic action, symbolic speech, have come to be reserved in our minds for the more poetic forms. Yet Realism shares equally with all other ways of telling a play this single mission. It must finally arrive at a meaning symbolic of the underlying action it has set forth. The difference lies in its method of creating its symbol as opposed to the way the poetic forms create theirs.

Now, then, the question arises: Why, if Ibsen and several other playwrights could use Realism so well to make plays about modern life, and if in addition the modern American audience is so quickly at home with the form—why should playwrights over the past thirty years be so impatient with it? Why has it been assaulted from every side? Why do so many people turn their backs on it and revere instead any kind of play which is fanciful or poetic? At the same time, why does Realism always seem to be drawing us all back to its arms? We have not yet created in this country a succinct form to take its place. Yet it seems that Realism has become a familiar bore; and by means of cutout sets, revolving stages, musical backgrounds, new and more imaginative lighting schemes, our stage is striving to break up the old living room. However, the perceiving eye knows that many of these allegedly poetic plays are Realism underneath, tricked up to look otherwise. I am criticizing nobody, only stating that the question of form is a deeper one, perhaps, than we have been willing to admit.

As I have indicated, I have come to wonder whether the force or pressure that makes for Realism, that even requires it, is the magnetic force of the family relationship within the play, and the pressure which evokes in a genuine, unforced way the un-realistic modes is the social relationship within the play. In a generalized way we commonly recognize that forms do have some extra-theatrical, common-sense criteria; for instance, one of the prime difficulties in writing modern opera, which after all is lyric drama, is that you cannot rightly sing so many of the common thoughts of common life. A line like "Be sure to take your bath, Gloria," is difficult to musicalize, and impossible to take seriously as a sung concept. But we normally stop short at recognition of the ridiculous in this problem. Clearly, a poetic drama must be built upon a poetic idea, but I wonder if that is the whole problem. It is striking to me, for instance, that Ibsen, the master of Realism, while writing his realistic plays in quite as serious a frame of mind as in his social plays, suddenly burst out of the realistic frame, out of the living room, when he wrote *Peer Gynt*. I think that it is not primarily the living room he left behind, in the sense that this factor had made a poetic play impossible for him, but rather the family context. For Peer Gynt is first of all a man seen alone; equally, he is a man confronting non-familial, openly social relationships and forces.

I warn you not to try to apply this rule too mechanically. A play, like any human relationship, has a predominant quality, but it also contains powerful elements which although secondary may not be overlooked, and may in fact be crucial in the development of that relationship. I offer this concept, therefore, as a possible tool and not as a magic key to the writing or understanding of plays and their forms.

I have used Ibsen as an example because he wrote in several forms; another equally experimental dramatist was O'Neill. It ought to be noted that O'Neill himself described his preoccupation as being not with the relations between man and man, but with those between man and God. What has this remark to do with dramatic form? Everything, I think. It is obvious, to begin with, that Ibsen's mission was to create not merely characters, but a context in which they were formed and functioned as people. That context, heavily and often profoundly delineated, was his society. His very idea of fate, for instance, was the inevitability residing in the conflict between the life force of his characters struggling with the hypocrisies, the strangling and abortive effects of society upon them. Thus, if only to create a climax, Ibsen had to draw society in his plays as a realistic force embodied in money, in social mores, in taboos, and so on, as well as an internal, subjective force within his characters.

O'Neill, however, seems to have been seeking for some fate-making power behind the social force itself. He went to ancient Greece for some definition of that force; he reached toward modern religion and toward many other possible sources of the poetic modes. My point here, however, is that so long as the family and family relations are at the center of his plays his form remains—indeed, it is held prisoner by—Realism. When, however, as for instance in *The Hairy Ape* and *Emperor Jones*, he deals with men out in society, away from the family context, his forms become alien to Realism, more openly and self-consciously symbolic, poetic, and finally heroic.

2

Up to this point I have been avoiding any question of content except that of the family relation as opposed to relations out in the world—social relations. Now I should like to make the bald statement that all plays we call great, let alone those we call serious, are utimately involved with some aspect of a single problem. It is this: How may a man make of the outside world a home? How and in what ways must he struggle, what must he strive to change and overcome within himself and outside himself if he is to find the safety, the surroundings of love, the ease of soul, the sense of identity and honor which, evidently, all men have connected in their memories with the idea of family?

One ought to be suspicious of any attempt to boil down all the great themes to a single sentence, but this one—"How may a man make of the outside world a home?"—does bear watching as a clue to the inner life of the great plays. Its aptness is most evident in the modern repertoire; in fact, where it is not the very principle of the play at hand we do not take the play quite seriously. If, for instance, the struggle in *Death of a Salesman* were simply between father and son for recognition and forgiveness it would diminish in importance. But when it extends itself out of the family circle and into society, it broaches those questions of social status, social honor and recognition, which expand its vision and lift it out of the merely particular toward the fate of the generality of men.

The same is true—although achieved in different ways—of a play like *A Streetcar Named Desire*, which could quite easily have been limited to a study of psychopathology were it not that it is placed clearly within the wider bounds of the question I am discussing. Here Blanche Dubois and the sensitivity she represents has been crushed by her moving out of the shelter of the home and the family into the uncaring, anti-human world outside it. In a word, we begin to partake of the guilt for her destruction, and for Willy's, because the blow struck against them was struck outside the home rather than within it—which is to say that it affects us more because it is a social fact we are witnessing.

The crucial question has an obverse side. If we look at the great plays—at *Hamlet, Oedipus, Lear*—we must be impressed with one fact perhaps above all others. These plays are all examining the concept of loss, of man's deprivation of a once-extant state of bliss unjustly shattered—a bliss, a state of equilibrium, which the hero (and his audience) is attempting to reconstruct or to recreate with new, latter-day life materials. It has been said often that the central theme of the modern repertoire is the alienation of man, but the idea usually halts at the social alienation—he cannot find a satisfying role in society. What I am suggesting here is that while this is true of our plays, the more or less hidden impulse antedating social alienation, the unsaid premise of the very idea of "satisfaction," is the memory of both playwright and audience of an enfolding family and of childhood. It is as though both playwright and audience believed that they had once had an identity, a *being*, somewhere in the past which in the present has lost its completeness, its definitiveness, so that the central force making for pathos in these large and thrusting plays is the paradox which Time bequeaths to us all: we cannot go home again, and the world we live in is an alien place.

One of the forms most clearly in contrast to Realism is Expressionism. I should like now to have a look at its relevancy to the family-social complex.

3

The technical arsenal of Expressionism goes back to Aeschylus. It is a form of play which manifestly seeks to dramatize the conflict of either social, religious, ethical, or moral forces *per se*, and in their own naked roles, rather than to present psychologically realistic human characters in a more or less realistic environment. There is, for instance, no attempt by Aeschylus to create the psychology of a violent "character" in *Prometheus Bound*, or of a powerful one; rather he brings on two figures whose names are Power and Violence, and they behave as the *idea* of Power and the *idea* of Violence ought to behave, according to the laws of Power and Violence. In Germany after the First World War, playwrights sought to dramatize and unveil the social condition of man with similar means. For instance, in *Gas I* and *Gas II* Georg Kaiser placed the figure of man against an image of industrial society but without the slightest attempt to characterize the man except as a representative of one or the other of the social classes vying for control of the machine. There are, of course, numerous other examples of the same kind of elimination of psychological characterization in favor of what one might call the presentation of forces. In *The Great God Brown*, for instance, as well as in *The Hairy Ape*, O'Neill reached toward this very ancient means of dramatization without psychology—without, one might say, behavior as we normally know it. *Everyman* is another work in that long line.

In passing, I must ask you to note that expressionist plays—which is to say plays preoccupied with the open confrontation of moral, ethical, or social forces —seem inevitably to cast a particular kind of shadow. The moment realistic behavior and psychology disappear from the play all the other appurtenances of Realism vanish too. The stage is stripped of knickknacks; instead it reveals symbolic *designs* which function as overt pointers toward the moral to be drawn from the action. We are no longer under quite the illusion of watching through a transparent fourth wall. Instead we are constantly reminded, in effect, that we are watching a theater piece. In short, we are not bidden to lose our consciousness of time and place, the consciousness of ourselves, but are appealed to through our intelligence, our faculties of knowing rather than of feeling.

This difference in the area of appeal is the difference between our familial emotions and our social emotions. The two forms not only spring from different sectors of human experience but end up by appealing to different areas of receptivity within the audience. Nor is this phenomenon confined to the play.

When one is speaking to one's family, for example, one uses a certain level of speech, a certain plain diction perhaps, a tone of voice, an inflection, suited to the intimacy of the occasion. But when one faces an audience of strangers, as a politician does, for instance—and he is the most social of men—it seems right and proper for him to reach for the well-turned phrase, even the poetic word, the aphorism, the metaphor. And his gestures, his stance, his tone of voice, all become larger than life; moreover, his character is not what gives him these prerogatives, but his role. In other words, a confrontation with society permits us, or even enforces upon us, a certain reliance upon ritual. Similarly with the play.

The implications of this natural wedding of form with inner relationships are many, and some of them are complex. It is true to say, I think, that the language of the family is the language of the private life—prose. The language of society, the language of the public life, is verse. According to the degree to which the play partakes of either relationship, it achieves the right to move closer or further away from either pole. I repeat that this "right" is given by some common consent which in turn is based upon our common experience in life.

It is interesting to look at a couple of modern plays from this viewpoint and to see whether critical sense can be made of them. T. S. Eliot's *The Cocktail Party,* for instance, drew from most intelligent auditors a puzzled admiration. In general, one was aware of a struggle going on between the apparencies of the behavior of the people and what evidently was the preoccupation of the playwright. There were a Husband and a Wife whom we were evidently expected to accept in that commonly known relationship, especially since the setting and the mode of speech and much of its diction were perfectly real if inordinately cultivated for a plebeian American audience. Even the theme of the play was, or should have been, of importance to most of us. Here we were faced with the alternative ways of giving meaning to domestic existence, one of them being through the cultivation of self, partly by means of the psychoanalytic ritual; the other and victorious method being the martyrization of the self, not for the sake of another, or as a rebuke to another, as martyrdom is usually indulged in in family life, but for the sake of martyrdom, of the disinterested action whose ultimate model was, according to the author, Jesus Christ. The heroine is celebrated for having been eaten alive by ants while on missionary work among the savages, and the very point is that there was no point—she converted nobody at all. Thus she gained her self by losing self or giving it away. Beyond the Meaningless she found Meaning at last.

To say the least, Eliot is manifestly an apt writer of verse. The inability of this play to achieve a genuine poetic level cannot therefore be laid to the usual cause—the unpoetic nature of the playwright's talent. Indeed, *Murder in the Cathedral* is a genuine poetic play, so he had already proved that he could achieve a wholeness of poetic form. I believe that the puzzlement created by *The Cocktail Party,* the sense of its being drawn in two opposite directions, is the result of the natural unwillingness of our minds to give to the Husband-Wife relation—a family relation—the prerogatives of the poetic mode, especially when the relationship is originally broached, as it is in this play, through any means approaching Realism.

Whether consciously or not, Eliot himself was aware of this dichotomy and wrote, and has said that he wrote, a kind of line which would not seem obtrusively formal and poetic to the listening ear. The injunction to keep it somehow unpoetic was issued by the central family situation, in my opinion. There was no need to mask his poetry at all in *Murder in the Cathedral,* because the situation is social, the conflict of a human being with the world. That earlier play had the unquestioned right to the poetic because it dealt with man as a public figure and could use the public man's style and diction.

4

We recognize now that a play can be poetic without verse, and it is in this middle area that the complexities of tracing the influence of the family and social elements upon the form become more troublesome. *Our Town* by Thornton Wilder is such a play, and it is important not only for itself but because it is the progenitor of many other works.

This is a family play which deals with the traditional family figures, the father, mother, brother, sister. At the same time it uses this particular family as a prism through which is reflected the author's basic idea, his informing principle —which can be stated as the indestructibility, the everlastingness, of the family and the community, its rhythm of life, its rootedness in the essentially safe cosmos despite troubles, wracks, and seemingly disastrous, but essentially temporary, dislocations.

Technically it is not arbitrary in any detail. Instead of a family living room or a house, we are shown a bare stage on which actors set chairs, a table, a ladder to represent a staircase or an upper floor, and so on. A narrator is kept in the foreground as though to remind us that this is not so much "real life" as an abstraction of it—in other words, a stage. It is clearly a poetic rather than a realistic play. What makes it that? Well, let us first imagine what would make it more realistic.

Would a real set make it realistic? Not likely. A real set would only discomfit us by drawing attention to what would then appear to be a slightly unearthly quality about the characterizations. We should probably say, "People don't really act like that." In addition, the characterization of the whole town could not be accomplished with anything like its present vividness if the narrator were removed, as he would have to be from a realistic set, and if the entrances and exits of the environmental people, the townspeople, had to be justified with the usual motives and machinery of Realism.

The preoccupation of the entire play is quite what the title implies—the town, the society, and not primarily this particular family—and every stylistic means used is to the end that the family foreground be kept in its place, merely as a foreground for the larger context behind and around it. In my opinion, it is this larger context, the town and its enlarging, widening significance, that is the bridge to the poetic for this play. Cut out the town and you will cut out the poetry.

The play is worth examining further against the Ibsen form of Realism to which it is inevitably related if only in contrast. Unlike Ibsen, Wilder sees his characters in this play not primarily as personalities, as individuals, but as forces, and he individualizes them only enough to carry the freight, so to speak, of their roles as forces. I do not believe, for instance, that we can think of the brother in this play, or the sister or the mother, as having names other than Brother, Sister, Mother. They are not given that kind of particularity or interior life. They are characterized rather as social factors, in their roles of Brother, Sister, Mother, in Our Town. They are drawn, in other words, as forces to enliven and illuminate the author's symbolic vision and his theme, which is that of the family as a timeless, stable quantity which has not only survived all the turmoil of time but is, in addition, beyond the possibility of genuine destruction.

The play is important to any discussion of form because it has achieved a largeness of meaning and an abstraction of style that created that meaning, while at the same time it has moved its audiences subjectively—it has made them laugh and weep as abstract plays rarely if ever do. But it would seem to contradict my contention here. If it is true that the presentation of the family on the stage inevitably forces Realism upon the play, how did this family play manage to transcend Realism to achieve its symbolistic style?

Every form, every style, pays its price for its special advantages. The price paid by *Our Town* is psychological characterization forfeited in the cause of the symbol. I do not believe, as I have said, that the characters are identifiable in a psychological way, but only as figures in the family and social constellation, and this is not meant in criticism, but as a statement of the limits of this form. I would go further and say that it is not *necessary* for every kind of play to do every kind of thing. But if we are after ultimate reality we must make ultimate demands.

I think that had Wilder drawn his characters with a deeper configuration of detail and with a more remorseless quest for private motive and self-interest, for instance, the story as it stands now would have appeared oversentimental and even sweet. I think that if the play tested its own theme more remorselessly, the world it creates of a timeless family and a rhythm of existence beyond the disturbance of social wracks would not remain unshaken. The fact is that the juvenile delinquent is quite directly traced to the breakup of family life and, indeed, to the break in that ongoing, steady rhythm of community life which the play celebrates as indestructible.

I think, further, that the close contact which the play established with its audience was the result of its coincidence with the deep longing of the audience for such stability, a stability which in daylight out on the street does not truly exist. The great plays pursue the idea of loss and deprivation of an earlier state of bliss which the characters feel compelled to return to or to recreate. I think this play forgoes the loss and suffers thereby in its quest for reality, but that the audience supplies the sense of deprivation in its own life experience as it faces what in effect is an idyl of the past. To me, therefore, the play falls short of a form that will press into reality to the limits of reality, if only because it could not plumb the psychological interior lives of its characters and still keep its present form. It is a triumph in that it does open a way toward the dramatization of the larger truths of existence while using the common materials of life. It is a truly poetic play.

5

Were there space, I should like to go into certain contemporary works with a view to the application in them of the forces of society and family—works by

Clifford Odets, Tennessee Williams, Lillian Hellman, William Saroyan, and others. But I will jump to the final question I have in mind. If there is any truth in the idea of a natural union of the family and Realism as opposed to society and the poetic, what are the reasons for it?

First, let us remind ourselves of an obvious situation, but one which is often overlooked. The man or woman who sits down to write a play, or who enters a theater to watch one, brings with him in each case a common life experience which is not suspended merely because he has turned writer or become part of an audience. We—all of us—have a role anteceding all others: we are first sons, daughters, sisters, brothers. No play can possibly alter this given role.

The concepts of Father, Mother, and so on were received by us unawares before the time we were conscious of ourselves as selves. In contrast, the concepts of Friend, Teacher, Employee, Boss, Colleague, Supervisor, and the many other social relations came to us long after we gained consciousness of ourselves, and are therefore outside ourselves. They are thus in an objective rather than a subjective category. In any case, what we feel is always more "real" to us than what we know, and we feel the family relation while we only know the social one. Thus the former is the very apotheosis of the real and has an inevitability and a foundation indisputably actual, while the social relation is always relatively mutable, accidental, and consequently of a profoundly arbitrary nature to us.

Today the difficulty in creating a form that will unite both elements in a full rather than partial onslaught on reality is the reflection of the deep split between the private life of man and his social life. Nor is this the first time in history that such a separation has occurred. Many critics have remarked upon it, for instance, as a probable reason for the onset of Realism in the later Greek plays, for it is like a rule of society that, as its time of troubles arrives, its citizens revert to a kind of privacy of life that excludes society, as though man at such times would like to banish society from his mind. When this happens, man excludes poetry too.

All of which, while it may provide a solution, or at least indicate the mansion where the solution lives, only serves to point to the ultimate problem more succinctly. Obviously, the playwright cannot create a society, let alone one so unified as to allow him to portray man in art as a monolithic creature. The playwright is not a reporter, but in a serious work of art he cannot set up an image of man's condition so distant from reality as to violate the common sense of what reality is. But a serious work, to say nothing of a tragic one, cannot hope to achieve truly high excellence short of an investigation into the whole gamut of causation of which society is a manifest and crucial part. Thus it is that the common Realism of the past forty or fifty years has been assaulted—because it could not, with ease and beauty, bridge the widening gap between the private life and the social life. Thus it is that the problem was left unsolved by Expressionism, which evaded it by forgoing psychological realism altogether and leaping over to a portrayal of social forces alone. Thus it is that there is now a certain decadence about many of our plays; in the past ten years they have come more and more to dwell solely upon psychology, with little or no attempt to locate and dramatize the social roles and conflicts of their characters. For it is proper to ascribe decay to that which turns its back upon society when, as is obvious to any intelligence, the fate of mankind is social.

6

Finally, I should say that the current quest after the poetic as poetic is fruitless. It is the attempt to make apples without growing trees. It is seeking poetry precisely where poetry is not: in the private life viewed entirely within the bounds of the subjective, the area of sensation, or the bizarre and the erotic. From these areas of the private life have sprung the mood plays, the plotless plays for which there is much admiration as there is much relief when one turns from a problem to a ramble in the woods. I do not ask you to disdain such plays, for they are within the realm of art; I say only that the high work, the tragic work, cannot be forged waywardly, while playing by ear. There is a charm in improvisation, in letting one chord suggest the other and ending when the moment wanes. But the high order of art to which drama is fated will come only when it seeks to account for the total condition of man, and this cannot be improvised.

Whatever is said to describe a mood play, one point must be made: such plays all have in common an air of self-effacement—which is to say that they wish to seem as though they had not only no plot but no writer. They would convince us that they "just happen," that no directing hand has arranged matters—contrary to the Ibsen plays, for instance, or, for that matter, the Shakespearean play or the Greek.

Furthermore, the entire operation is most moody when the characters involved have the least consciousness of their own existence. The mood play is a play in hiding. A true plot is an assertion of meaning. The mood play is not, as it has been mistaken for, a rebellion of any kind against the so-called well-made play, especially when Ibsen is widely held to be a writer of well-made plays. For there is as much subjectivity and inner poetry in *Hedda Gabler*—I daresay a lot more—as in any of these mood plays. What is really repulsive in Ibsen to one kind of contemporary mind is not openly mentioned: it is his persistent search for an organizing principle behind the "moods" of existence and not the absence of mood in his work.

An art form, like a person, can achieve greatness only as it accepts great challenges. Over the past few decades the American theater, in its best moments, has moved courageously and often beautifully into the interior life of man, an area that had most often been neglected in the past. But now, I think, we are in danger of settling for tears, as it were—for any play that "moves" us, quite as though the ultimate criterion of the art were lachrymosity. For myself, I find that there is an increasing reliance upon what pass for realistic, even tough, analytical picturizations of existence, which are really quite sentimental underneath; and the sentiment is getting thicker, I think, and an end in itself. Sentimentalism is perfectly all right, but it is nowhere near a great challenge, and to pursue it, even under the guide of the exotic atmosphere and the celebration of the sensuous, is not going to bring us closer to the fated mission of the drama.

What, after all, is that mission? I may as well end with such a question because it underlies and informs every word I have written. I think of it so: Man has created so many specialized means of unveiling the truth of the world around him and the world within him—the physical sciences, the psychological sciences, the disciplines of economic and historical research and theory. In effect, each of these attacks on the truth is partial. It is within the rightful sphere of the drama—it is, so to speak, its truly just employment and its ultimate design—to embrace the many-sidedness of man. It is as close to being a total art as the race has invented. It can tell, like science, what is—but more, it can tell what ought to be. It can depict, like painting, in designs and portraits, in the colors of the day or night; like the novel it can spread out its arms and tell the story of a life, or a city, in a few hours—but more, it is dynamic, it is always on the move as life is and it is perceived like life through the motions, the gestures, the tones of voice, and the gait and nuance of living people. It is the singer's art and the painter's art and the dancer's art, yet it may hew to fact no less tenaciously than does the economist or the physician. In a word, there lies within the dramatic form the ultimate possibility of raising the truth-consciousness of mankind to a level of such intensity as to transform those who observe it.

The problem, therefore, is not simply an aesthetic one. As people, as a society, we thirst for clues to the past and the future; least of all, perhaps, do we know about the present, about what *is*. It is the present that is always most evasive and slippery, for the present always threatens most directly our defenses against seeing what we are, and it is the present, always the present, to which the dramatic form must apply or it is without interest and a dead thing, and forms do die when they lose their capacity to open up the present. So it is its very nature to bring us closer to ourselves if only it can grow and change with the changing world.

In the deepest sense, I think, to sophisticated and unsophisticated alike, nothing is quite so real to us, so extant, as that which has been made real by art. Nor is this ironical and comic. For the fact is that art is a function of the civilizing act quite as much as is the building of the water supply. American civilization is only recently coming to a conscious awareness of art not as a luxury but as a necessity of life. Without the right dramatic form a genuine onslaught upon the veils that cloak the present is not possible. In the profoundest sense I cannot create that form unless, somewhere in you, there is a wish to know the present and a demand upon me that I give it to you.

For at bottom what is that form? It is the everlastingly sought balance between order and the need of our souls for freedom; the relatedness between our vaguest longings, our inner questions, and private lives and the life of the generality of men which is our society and our world. How may man make for himself a home in that vastness of strangers and how may he transform that vastness into a home? This, as I have repeated, is the question a form must solve anew in every age. This, I may say, is the problem before you too.

ROBERT PENN WARREN

A Lesson Read in American Books[1]

Once upon a time there was a nation, which we shall call X. At the time of which we write this nation stood at a moment of great power and great promise. A few generations earlier it had concluded a long and bloody civil war to achieve unity. More recently, in that unity, it had won a crashing victory over foreign foes. It had undergone, and was undergoing, a social revolution; there was unparalleled prosperity, a relaxing of old sanctions and prejudices, a widening of opportunity for all classes, great rewards for energy and intelligence. Its flag was on strange seas; its power was felt in the world. It was, even, producing a famous literature.

But—and here is the strange thing in that moment of energy and optimism —a large part, the most famous part, of that literature exhibited violence, degradation and despair as part of the human condition: tales of the old time of the civil war, tales of lust and horror, brother pimping for sister, father lusting for daughter, a head of the state doting on a fair youth, an old man's eyes plucked out, another old man killed in his sleep, friendship betrayed, obligations foregone, good men cursing the gods, and the whole scene drenched in blood. Foreigners encountering this literature might well conclude that the Land of X was peopled by degenerates sadly lacking in taste, manners and principle.

This is England, Elizabethan England, that we are talking about, and not the United States in this year of Our Lord and the Great Prosperity. But *mutatis mutandis*, and with proper recognition of the fact that we can scarcely claim a William Shakespeare, only John Fords and John Websters, we can talk about the United States in this connection, and join in conversation with Father Bruckberger, who has lately appeared in these pages, and with the editorial writer of *Life* magazine for Sept. 12.

[1] From *The New York Times Book Review*, December 11, 1955. Reprinted by permission of the author and *The New York Times Book Review*.

These writers are concerned, as we must all be concerned, with America's image in the eyes of the world. "Is it right," asks Father Bruckberger, a sympathetic Frenchman visiting our shores, "that the great *flowering* of the American novel should hamper . . . America's leadership of the free world?" And the editorial writer in *Life*: "Europeans are already prejudiced against America by savage animadversions in their own classics against our 'vulgar' democracy. . . . Small wonder that our own self-depreciation helps them enlarge the evil image. . . ."

These two quotations raise a question, vexed and vexing, a question already old, no doubt, when the Greeks worried about it: how should esthetic value be related to prudential considerations? Presumably some of our literature has esthetic value (Father Bruckberger handsomely calls it a "flowering"), but it confirms some Europeans in their inherited low opinion of America, the country of "the almighty dollar," and of "respect to ordinary artisans," as Stendahl puts it, and the "land of money and selfishness, where souls are cold," as Balzac puts it. What do we do, then, when esthetic value is in conflict, or in apparent conflict, with political values?

Father Bruckberger does not undertake to answer this for us. On the one hand, he says that the "honor" of a literature is that it creates and sustains "a great quarrel within the national consciousness." But on the other hand, he bewails the effect abroad of this very quarrel within our national consciousness. Certainly, he is too informed to attempt to resolve the difficulty along the lines laid down by the editorial writer in *Life*, who, with certain ritualistic reservations, says that because America is now enjoying a boom, our literature should be optimistic, and applauds the current success of *The Man in the Gray Flannel Suit* because, though "flimsy art," it is "at least affirmative."

In fact, the editorial writer of *Life* takes as his golden text a quotation from Sloan Wilson, the author of *The Man in the Gray Flannel Suit*: "The world's treated me awfully well, and I guess it's crept into my work. . . . These are, we forget, pretty good times. Yet too many novelists are still writing as if we were back in the Depression years."

Though I have not yet read *The Man in the Gray Flannel Suit*, I should venture to doubt that the world is going to treat its author quite as well as it has treated Ernest Hemingway, William Faulkner, Theodore Dreiser, Sinclair Lewis, T. S. Eliot, Robert Frost, and quite a few other American writers who never found such a ready equation between bank balance and philosophy. What is really at stake in this is a question of freedom. If the creative act is of any value it is, in its special way, an act of freedom. It is, of course, conditioned by a thousand factors, but study of its conditions—economic, biologic, or whatever—has yet to reveal the secret of how that new intuition, the truly created object whose *newness* is the mark of freedom, comes to be. But Mr. Wilson, and presumably the approving editorial writer in *Life*, would deny this freedom, would, in fact, go even farther than Karl Marx in asserting the economic determinism of literature. If you are not making dough, you will not be a booster. Literature is a reflex of the stock market.

The philosophers of the Age of Conformism grant, however, that criticism was once all right, long back. As the *Life* editorial puts it: "*The Great Gatsby* still speaks eloquently of Prohibition's frauds and deceits, *Main Street* of the high tide of provincial self-satisfaction, *The Grapes of Wrath* with a just anger for the unnecessary humiliations of Depression. . . ." But criticism isn't all right in this day and time, for there is nothing really wrong now to be criticized, and anybody who is critical, who isn't "affirmative," is a fool or knave, a traitor or a sexual deviant, or a failure. May we not, however, in some chill hour between dark and dawn, have the thought that our own age may—just possibly—have its own frauds and deceits, deeper and more ambiguous than those anatomized in *The Great Gatsby*, that though this is not the age of provincial self-satisfaction, it may be the age of national self-righteousness and require a sharper scalpel than even *Main Street*, and that Divine Providence has given no written guarantee that It will not rebuke the smuggery of the Great Boom?

I do not think that the novel has yet been written to anatomize adequately this moment of our history, and I share the distaste of the editorial writer in *Life* for some of the works he alludes to, but the "American novel" which we should call for would not be less, but more, critical than those now current. At the same time I should hope that the literature to come will be more "affirmative," to use the word of the editorial. But the paradox here is that the literature that is most truly and profoundly critical is always the most profoundly affirmative.

In so far as a literature struggles to engage the deep, inner issues of life, the more will that literature be critical—the more, that is, will it engender impatience with the compromises, the ennui, the materialism, the self-deception, the complacency, and the secret, unnamable despairs that mark so much of ordinary life. Such a critical literature is at the same time affirmative because it affirms the will and courage to engage life at fundamental levels: the rock, if struck hard enough, will give forth the living waters.

The editorial writer in *Life* would not, I suppose, find these kinds of affirmation significant. He is concerned with doctrine, more or less explicitly put. But sometimes, even when doctrine is explicitly put, he has not, cannot, or does not, read it. Faulkner, he says, "for all his enormous gifts, can be searched in vain for that quality of redemption, through love and brotherhood, which always shines amid Dostoevsky's horrors." That very redemption, and its cost, is a recurrent theme of Faulkner's work. There is, for example, *The Bear*, with old Ike's vision of man's place in creation: God created man to hold suzerainty over the earth in His name, "not to hold for himself and his descendants' inviolable title forever, generation after generation, to the oblongs and squares of the earth, but to hold the earth mutual and intact in the communal anonymity of brotherhood, and all the fee He asked was pity and humility and sufferance and endurance and the sweat of his face for bread."

But let us go back where we started: the bad political impression which some of our literature presumably gives abroad. What are we to do? If we can't get writers to write the kind of literature we think useful for foreign consumption—if there really isn't such a thing as literature to specification—what then?

The answer is, I think, simple—and appalling. We must trust in our humility, and in our strength.

We must trust in our humility, because only by humility, the recognition that we have not fulfilled our best possibilities, can we hope to fulfill those possibilities. Some day, far-called, our navies may melt away, and on that day we may need the wisdom of ultimate humility. Meanwhile, in our moment of strength we hope that our strength is more than a historical accident, an index of the weakness of others. We hope that it has a moral grounding. But if that hope is to be more than a hope, it must be subjected to the test of conscience, and literature is one of the voices of our national conscience, however faltering and defective that voice may sometimes be. We must rebuke our *hubris*, not out of fear, but from love of a truth that we hope is within us.

We must trust in our strength, because only the strong can afford the luxury of radical self-criticism. Only if we believe in our strength can we take the risks of our full political and cultural development, with all the disintegrative and paradoxical possibilities in that dialectic. We should trust our strength, because America has a secret weapon, if we choose to use it: the weapon of not having a secret. It is the weapon of radical self-criticism—*radical* in the non-political and literal sense of the word. There was an old name for this, a name not often now used in this connection. That name was *democracy*.

So much for ourselves. But what of those poor foreigners who are so readily deceived by our literature? Are they, in the long run, quite so trapped in their prejudice, quite so incapable of the imaginative act, as Father Bruckberger seems to think? If so, why do they find our literature so fascinating, and why do they honor it? Can it be that, in a measure, they find in it a vital image of man, and some comment on his condition? Do they find in it, in the very fact of its existence, some mark of freedom?

I shall tell a story. A little while after the war in Europe I became acquainted with a young Italian who, in the first year of the war, as an officer in the Fascist Army, had deserted and taken to the mountains, to fight on our side. I once asked him what led him to this drastic step. He replied that American novelists had converted him. How, I asked. "Well," he said, "the Fascists used to let us read American fiction because it gave, they thought, a picture of a decadent America. They thought it was good propaganda for fascism to let us read Dreiser, Faulkner, Sinclair Lewis. But you know, it suddenly occurred to me that if democracy could allow that kind of criticism of itself, it must be very strong and good. So I took to the mountains."

LIONEL TRILLING

Manners, Morals, and the Novel[1]

The invitation that was made to me to address you this evening was couched in somewhat uncertain terms. Time, place, and cordiality were perfectly clear, but when it came to the subject our hosts were not able to specify just what they wanted me to talk about. They wanted me to consider literature in its relation to manners—by which, as they relied on me to understand, they did not really mean *manners*. They did not mean, that is, the rules of personal intercourse in our culture; and yet such rules were by no means irrelevant to what they did mean. Nor did they quite mean manners in the sense of *mores*, customs, although, again, these did bear upon the subject they had in mind.

I understood them perfectly, as I would not have understood them had they been more definite. For they were talking about a nearly indefinable subject.

Somewhere below all the explicit statements that a people makes through its art, religion, architecture, legislation, there is a dim mental region of intention of which it is very difficult to become aware. We now and then get a strong sense of its existence when we deal with the past, not by reason of its presence in the past but by reason of its absence. As we read the great formulated monuments of the past, we notice that we are reading them without the accompaniment of something that always goes along with the formulated monuments of the present. The voice of multifarious intention and activity is stilled, all the buzz of implication which always surrounds us in the present, coming to us from what never gets fully stated, coming in the tone of greetings and the tone of quarrels, in slang and humor and popular songs, in the way children play, in the gesture the waiter makes when he puts down the plate, in the nature of the very food we prefer.

Some of the charm of the past consists of the quiet—the great distracting buzz of implication has stopped and we are left only with what has been fully phrased and precisely stated. And part of the melancholy of the past comes from our knowledge that the huge, unrecorded hum of implication was once there and left no trace—we feel that because it is evanescent it is especially human. We feel, too, that the truth of the great preserved monuments of the past does not fully appear without it. From letters and diaries, from the remote, unconscious corners of the great works themselves, we try to guess what the sound of the multifarious implication was and what it meant.

Or when we read the conclusions that are drawn about our own culture by some gifted foreign critic—or by some stupid native one—who is equipped only with a knowledge of our books, when we try in vain to say what is wrong,

[1] From *The Liberal Imagination*, by Lionel Trilling. Copyright, 1948, 1950, by Lionel Trilling. Reprinted by permission of The Viking Press, Inc., New York.

when in despair we say that he has read the books "out of context," then we are aware of the matter I have been asked to speak about tonight.

What I understand by manners, then, is a culture's hum and buzz of implication. I mean the whole evanescent context in which its explicit statements are made. It is that part of a culture which is made up of half-uttered or unuttered or unutterable expressions of value. They are hinted at by small actions, sometimes by the arts of dress or decoration, sometimes by tone, gesture, emphasis, or rhythm, sometimes by the words that are used with a special frequency or a special meaning. They are the things that for good or bad draw the people of a culture together and that separate them from the people of another culture. They make the part of a culture which is not art, or religion, or morals, or politics, and yet it relates to all these highly formulated departments of culture. It is modified by them; it modifies them; it is generated by them; it generates them. In this part of culture assumption rules, which is often so much stronger than reason.

The right way to begin to deal with such a subject is to gather together as much of its detail as we possibly can. Only by doing so will we become fully aware of what the gifted foreign critic or the stupid native one is not aware of, that in any complex culture there is not a single system of manners but a conflicting variety of manners, and that one of the jobs of a culture is the adjustment of this conflict.

But the nature of our present occasion does not permit this accumulation of detail and so I shall instead try to drive toward a generalization and an hypothesis which, however wrong they turn out to be, may at least permit us to circumscribe the subject. I shall try to generalize the subject of American manners by talking about the attitude of Americans toward the subject of manners itself. And since in a complex culture there are, as I say, many different systems of manners and since I cannot talk about them all, I shall select the manners and the attitude toward manners of the literate, reading, responsible middle class of people who are ourselves. I specify that they be reading people because I shall draw my conclusions from the novels they read. The hypothesis I propose is that our attitude toward manners is the expression of a particular conception of reality.

All literature tends to be concerned with the question of reality—I mean quite simply the old opposition between reality and appearance, between what really is and what merely seems. "Don't you see?" is the question we want to shout at Oedipus as he stands before us and before fate in the pride of his rationalism. And at the end of Oedipus Rex he demonstrates in a particularly direct way that he now sees what he did not see before. "Don't you see?" we want to shout again at Lear and Gloucester, the two deceived, self-deceiving fathers: blindness again, resistance to the clear claims of reality, the seduction by mere appearance. The same with Othello—reality is right under your stupid nose, how dare you be such a gull? So with Molière's Orgon—my good man, my honest citizen, merely look at Tartuffe and you will know what's what. So with Milton's Eve—"Woman, watch out! Don't you see—anyone can see—that's a *snake!*"

The problem of reality is central, and in a special way, to the great forefather of the novel, the great book of Cervantes, whose four-hundredth birthday was celebrated in 1947. There are two movements of thought in *Don Quixote*, two different and opposed notions of reality. One is the movement which leads toward saying that the world of ordinary practicality *is* reality in its fullness. It is the reality of the present moment in all its powerful immediacy of hunger, cold, and pain, making the past and the future, and all ideas, of no account. When the conceptual, the ideal, and the fanciful come into conflict with this, bringing their notions of the past and the future, then disaster results. For one thing, the ordinary proper ways of life are upset—the chained prisoners are understood to be good men and are released, the whore is taken for a lady. There is general confusion. As for the ideal, the conceptual, the fanciful, or romantic—whatever you want to call it—it fares even worse: it is shown to be ridiculous.

Thus one movement of the novel. But Cervantes changed horses in midstream and found that he was riding Rosinante. Perhaps at first not quite consciously—although the new view is latent in the old from the very beginning —Cervantes begins to show that the world of tangible reality is not the real reality after all. The real reality is rather the wildly conceiving, the madly fantasying mind of the Don: people change, practical reality changes, when they come into its presence.

In any genre it may happen that the first great example contains the whole potentiality of the genre. It has been said that all philosophy is a footnote to Plato. It can be said that all prose fiction is a variation on the theme of *Don Quixote*. Cervantes sets for the novel the problem of appearance and reality: the shifting and conflict of social classes becomes the field of the problem of knowledge, of how we know and of how reliable our knowledge is, which at that very moment of history is vexing the philosophers and scientists. And the poverty of the Don suggests that the novel is born with the appearance of money as a social element—money, the great solvent of the solid fabric of the old society, the great generator of illusion. Or, which is to say much the same thing, the novel is born in response to snobbery.

Snobbery is not the same thing as pride of class. Pride of class may not please us but we must at least grant that it reflects a social function. A man who exhibited class pride—in the day when it was possible to do so—may have been puffed up about what he *was*, but this ultimately depended on what he *did*. Thus, aristocratic pride was based ultimately on the ability to fight and administer. No pride is without fault, but pride of class may be thought of as today we think of pride of profession, toward which we are likely to be lenient.

Snobbery is pride in status without pride in function. And it is an uneasy pride of status. It always asks, "Do I belong—do I really belong? And does he belong? And if I am observed talking to him, will it make me seem to belong

or not to belong?" It is the peculiar vice not of aristocratic societies which have
their own appropriate vices, but of bourgeois democratic societies. For us the
legendary strongholds of snobbery are the Hollywood studios, where two thousand dollars a week dare not talk to three hundred dollars a week for fear he
be taken for nothing more than fifteen hundred dollars a week. The dominant
emotions of snobbery are uneasiness, self-consciousness, self-defensiveness, the
sense that one is not quite real but can in some way acquire reality.

Money is the medium that, for good or bad, makes for a fluent society. It
does not make for an equal society but for one in which there is a constant
shifting of classes, a frequent change in the personnel of the dominant class.
In a shifting society great emphasis is put on appearance—I am using the word
now in the common meaning, as when people say that "a good appearance is
very important in getting a job." To appear to be established is one of the
ways of becoming established. The old notion of the solid merchant who owns
far more than he shows increasingly gives way to the ideal of signalizing status
by appearance, by showing more than you have: status in a democratic society
is presumed to come not with power but with the tokens of power. Hence the
development of what Tocqueville saw as a mark of democratic culture, what he
called the "hypocrisy of luxury"—instead of the well-made peasant article and
the well-made middle-class article, we have the effort of all articles to appear as
the articles of the very wealthy.

And a shifting society is bound to generate an interest in appearance in the
philosophical sense. When Shakespeare lightly touched on the matter that so
largely preoccupies the novelist—that is, the movement from one class to another—and created Malvolio, he immediately involved the question of social
standing with the problem of appearance and reality. Malvolio's daydreams of
bettering his position present themselves to him as reality, and in revenge his
enemies conspire to convince him that he is literally mad and that the world
is not as he sees it. The predicament of the characters in A Midsummer Night's
Dream and of Christopher Sly seems to imply that the meeting of social extremes and the establishment of a person of low class in the privileges of a
high class always suggested to Shakespeare's mind some radical instability of
the senses and the reason.

The characteristic work of the novel is to record the illusion that snobbery
generates and to try to penetrate to the truth which, as the novel assumes, lies
hidden beneath all the false appearances. Money, snobbery, the ideal of status,
these become in themselves the objects of fantasy, the support of the fantasies
of love, freedom, charm, power, as in Madame Bovary, whose heroine is the
sister, at a three-centuries' remove, of Don Quixote. The greatness of Great
Expectations begins in its title: modern society bases itself on great expectations which, if ever they are realized, are found to exist by reason of a sordid,
hidden reality. The real thing is not the gentility of Pip's life but the hulks
and the murder and the rats and decay in the cellarage of the novel.

An English writer, recognizing the novel's central concern with snobbery, recently cried out half-ironically against it. "Who cares whether Pamela finally exasperates Mr. B. into marriage, whether Mr. Elton is more or less than moderately genteel, whether it is sinful for Pendennis nearly to kiss the porter's daughter, whether young men from Boston can ever be as truly refined as middle-aged women in Paris, whether the District Officer's fiancée ought to see so much of Dr. Aziz, whether Lady Chatterly ought to be made love to by the gamekeeper, even if he was an officer during the war? Who cares?"

The novel, of course, tells us much more about life than this. It tells us about the look and feel of things, how things are done and what things are worth and what they cost and what the odds are. If the English novel in its special concern with class does not, as the same writer says, explore the deeper layers of personality, then the French novel in exploring these layers must start and end in class, and the Russian novel, exploring the ultimate possibilities of spirit, does the same—every situation in Dostoevski, no matter how spiritual, starts with a point of social pride and a certain number of rubles. The great novelists knew that manners indicate the largest intentions of men's souls as well as the smallest and they are perpetually concerned to catch the meaning of every dim implicit hint.

The novel, then, is a perpetual quest for reality, the field of its research being always the social world, the material of its analysis being always manners as the indication of the direction of man's soul. When we understand this we can understand the pride of profession that moved D. H. Lawrence to say, "Being a novelist, I consider myself superior to the saint, the scientist, the philosopher and the poet. The novel is the one bright book of life."

Now the novel as I have described it has never really established itself in America. Not that we have not had very great novels but that the novel in America diverges from its classic intention, which, as I have said, is the investigation of the problem of reality beginning in the social field. The fact is that American writers of genius have not turned their minds to society. Poe and Melville were quite apart from it; the reality they sought was only tangential to society. Hawthorne was acute when he insisted that he did not write novels but romances—he thus expressed his awareness of the lack of social texture in his work. Howells never fulfilled himself because, although he saw the social subject clearly, he would never take it with full seriousness. In America in the nineteenth century, Henry James was alone in knowing that to scale the moral and aesthetic heights in the novel one had to use the ladder of social observation.

There is a famous passage in James's life of Hawthorne in which James enumerates the things which are lacking to give the American novel the thick social texture of the English novel—no state; barely a specific national name; no sovereign; no court; no aristocracy; no church; no clergy; no army; no diplomatic service; no country gentlemen; no palaces; no castles; no manors; no old country houses; no parsonages; no thatched cottages; no ivied ruins; no cathedrals; no great universities; no public schools; no political society; no sporting class—no Epsom, no Ascot! That is, no sufficiency of means for the display of a variety of manners, no opportunity for the novelist to do his job of searching out reality, not enough complication of appearance to make the job interesting. Another great American novelist of very different temperament had said much the same thing some decades before: James Fenimore Cooper found that American manners were too simple and dull to nourish the novelist.

This is cogent but it does not explain the condition of the American novel at the present moment. For life in America has increasingly thickened since the nineteenth century. It has not, to be sure, thickened so much as to permit our undergraduates to understand the characters of Balzac, to understand, that is, life in a crowded country where the competitive pressures are great, forcing intense passions to express themselves fiercely and yet within the limitations set by a strong and complicated tradition of manners. Still, life here has become more complex and more pressing. And even so we do not have the novel that touches significantly on society, on manners. Whatever the virtues of Dreiser may be, he could not report the social fact with the kind of accuracy it needs. Sinclair Lewis is shrewd, but no one, however charmed with him as a social satirist, can believe that he does more than a limited job of social understanding. John Dos Passos sees much, sees it often in the great way of Flaubert, but can never use social fact as more than either backdrop or "condition." Of our novelists today perhaps only William Faulkner deals with society as the field of tragic reality and he has the disadvantage of being limited to a provincial scene.

It would seem that Americans have a kind of resistance to looking closely at society. They appear to believe that to touch accurately on the matter of class, to take full note of snobbery, is somehow to demean themselves. It is as if we felt that one cannot touch pitch without being defiled—which, of course, may possibly be the case. Americans will not deny that we have classes and snobbery, but they seem to hold it to be indelicate to take precise cognizance of these phenomena. Consider that Henry James is, among a large part of our reading public, still held to be at fault for noticing society as much as he did. Consider the conversation that has, for some interesting reason, become a part of our literary folklore. Scott Fitzgerald said to Ernest Hemingway, "The very rich are different from us." Hemingway replied, "Yes, they have more money." I have seen the exchange quoted many times and always with the intention of suggesting that Fitzgerald was infatuated by wealth and had received a salutary rebuke from his democratic friend. But the truth is that after a certain point quantity of money does indeed change into quality of personality: in an important sense the very rich *are* different from us. So are the very powerful, the very gifted, the very poor. Fitzgerald was right, and almost for that remark alone he must surely have been received in Balzac's bosom in the heaven of novelists.

It is of course by no means true that the American reading class has no interest in society. Its interest fails only before society as it used to be represented by the novel. And if we look at the commercially successful serious novels of the last decade, we see that almost all of them have been written from an intense social awareness—it might be said that our present definition of a serious book is one which holds before us some image of society to consider and condemn. What is the situation of the dispossessed Oklahoma farmer and whose fault it is, what situation the Jew finds himself in, what it means to be a Negro, how one gets a bell for Adano, what is the advertising business really like, what it means to be insane and how society takes care of you or fails to do so—these are the matters which are believed to be most fertile for the novelist, and certainly they are the subjects most favored by our reading class.

The public is properly not deceived about the quality of most of these books. If the question of quality is brought up, the answer is likely to be: no, they are not great, they are not imaginative, they are not "literature." But there is an unexpressed addendum: and perhaps they are all the better for not being imaginative, for not being literature—they are not literature, they are reality, and *in a time like this* what we need is reality in large doses.

When, generations from now, the historian of our times undertakes to describe the assumptions of our culture, he will surely discover that the word *reality* is of central importance in his understanding of us. He will observe that for some of our philosophers the meaning of the word was a good deal in doubt, but that for our political writers, for many of our literary critics, and for most of our reading public, the word did not open discussion but, rather, closed it. Reality, as conceived by us, is whatever is external and hard, gross, unpleasant. Involved in its meaning is the idea of power conceived in a particular way. Some time ago I had occasion to remark how, in the critical estimates of Theodore Dreiser, it is always being said that Dreiser has many faults but that it cannot be denied that he has great power. No one ever says "a kind of power." Power is assumed to be always "brute" power, crude, ugly, and undiscriminating, the way an elephant appears to be. It is seldom understood to be the way an elephant actually is, precise and discriminating; or the way electricity is, swift and absolute and scarcely embodied.

The word *reality* is an honorific word and the future historian will naturally try to discover our notion of its pejorative opposite, appearance, mere appearance. He will find it in our feeling about the internal; whenever we detect evidences of style and thought we suspect that reality is being a little betrayed, that "mere subjectivity" is creeping in. There follows from this our feeling about complication, modulation, personal idiosyncrasy, and about social forms, both the great and the small.

Having gone so far, our historian is then likely to discover a puzzling contradiction. For we claim that the great advantage of reality is its hard, bedrock, concrete quality, yet everything we say about it tends toward the abstract and it almost seems that what we want to find in reality is abstraction itself. Thus we believe that one of the unpleasant bedrock facts is social class, but we become extremely impatient if ever we are told that social class is indeed so real that it produces actual differences of personality. The very people who talk most about class and its evils think that Fitzgerald was bedazzled and Hemingway right. Or again, it might be observed that in the degree that we speak in praise of the "individual" we have contrived that our literature should have no individuals in it—no people, that is, who are shaped by our liking for the interesting and memorable and special and precious.

Here, then, is our generalization: that in proportion as we have committed ourselves to our particular idea of reality we have lost our interest in manners. For the novel this is a definitive condition because it is inescapably true that in the novel manners make men. It does not matter in what sense the word manners is taken—it is equally true of the sense which so much interested Proust or of the sense which interested Dickens or, indeed, of the sense which interested Homer. The Duchesse de Guermantes unable to delay departure for the dinner party to receive properly from her friend Swann the news that he is dying but able to delay to change the black slippers her husband objects to; Mr. Pickwick and Sam Weller; Priam and Achilles—they exist by reason of their observed manners.

So true is this, indeed, so creative is the novelist's awareness of manners, that we may say that it is a function of his love. It is some sort of love that Fielding has for Squire Western that allows him to note the great, gross details which bring the insensitive sentient man into existence for us. If that is true, we are forced to certain conclusions about our literature and about the particular definition of reality which has shaped it. The reality we admire tells us that the observation of manners is trivial and even malicious, that there are things much more important for the novel to consider. As a consequence our social sympathies have indeed broadened, but in proportion as they have done so we have lost something of our power of love, for our novels can never create characters who truly exist. We make public demands for love, for we know that broad social feeling should be infused with warmth, and we receive a kind of public product which we try to believe is not cold potatoes. The reviewers of Helen Howe's novel of a few years ago, We Happy Few, thought that its satiric first part, an excellent comment on the manners of a small but significant segment of society, was ill-natured and unsatisfactory, but they approved the second part, which is the record of the heroine's self-accusing effort to come into communication with the great soul of America. Yet it should have been clear that the satire had its source in a kind of affection, in a real community of feeling, and told the truth, while the second part, said to be so "warm," was mere abstraction, one more example of our public idea of ourselves and our national life. John Steinbeck is generally praised both for his reality and his warmheartedness, but in The Wayward Bus the lower-class characters receive a doctrinaire affection in proportion to the suffering and sexuality which define their existence, while the ill-observed middle-class characters are made to submit not only to moral judgment but to the withdrawal of all fellow-feeling, being mocked for their very misfortunes and almost for their susceptibility to death. Only a little thought or even less feeling is required to perceive that the basis of his creation is the coldest response to abstract ideas.

Two novelists of the older sort had a prevision of our present situation. In Henry James's *The Princess Casamassima* there is a scene in which the heroine is told about the existence of a conspiratorial group of revolutionaries pledged to the destruction of all existing society. She has for some time been drawn by a desire for social responsibility; she has wanted to help "the people," she has longed to discover just such a group as she now hears about, and she exclaims in joy, "Then it's real, it's solid!" We are intended to hear the Princess's glad cry with the knowledge that she is a woman who despises herself, "that in the darkest hour of her life she sold herself for a title and a fortune. She regards her doing so as such a terrible piece of frivolity that she can never for the rest of her days be serious enough to make up for it." She seeks out poverty, suffering, sacrifice, and death because she believes that these things alone are real; she comes to believe that art is contemptible; she withdraws her awareness and love from the one person of her acquaintance who most deserves them, and she increasingly scorns whatever suggests variety and modulation, and is more and more dissatisfied with the humanity of the present in her longing for the more perfect humanity of the future. It is one of the great points that the novel makes that with each passionate step that she takes toward what she calls the real, the solid, she in fact moves further away from the life-giving reality.

In E. M. Forster's *The Longest Journey* there is a young man named Stephen Wonham who, although a gentleman born, has been carelessly brought up and has no real notion of the responsibilities of his class. He has a friend, a country laborer, a shepherd, and on two occasions he outrages the feelings of certain intelligent, liberal, democratic people in the book by his treatment of his friend. Once, when the shepherd reneges on a bargain, Stephen quarrels with him and knocks him down; and in the matter of the loan of a few shillings he insists that the money be paid back to the last farthing. The intelligent, liberal, democratic people know that this is not the way to act to the poor. But Stephen cannot think of the shepherd as the poor nor, although he is a country laborer, as an object of research by J. L. and Barbara Hammond; he is rather a reciprocating subject in a relationship of affection—as we say, a friend—and therefore liable to anger and required to pay his debts. But this view is held to be deficient in intelligence, liberalism, and democracy.

In these two incidents we have the premonition of our present cultural and social situation, the passionate self-reproachful addiction to a "strong" reality which must limit its purview to maintain its strength, the replacement by abstraction of natural, direct human feeling. It is worth noting, by the way, how clear is the line by which the two novels descend from *Don Quixote*—how their young heroes come into life with large preconceived ideas and are knocked about in consequence; how both are concerned with the problem of appearance and reality, *The Longest Journey* quite explicitly, *The Princess Casamassima* by indirection; how both evoke the question of the nature of reality by contriving a meeting and conflict of diverse social classes and take scrupulous note of the differences of manners. Both have as their leading characters people who are specifically and passionately concerned with social injustice and both agree in saying that to act against social injustice is right and noble but that to choose to act so does not settle all moral problems but on the contrary generates new ones of an especially difficult sort.

I have elsewhere given the name of moral realism to the perception of the dangers of the moral life itself. Perhaps at no other time has the enterprise of moral realism ever been so much needed, for at no other time have so many people committed themselves to moral righteousness. We have the books that point out the bad conditions, that praise us for taking progressive attitudes. We have no books that raise questions in our minds not only about conditions but about ourselves, that lead us to refine our motives and ask what might lie behind our good impulses.

There is nothing so very terrible in discovering that something does lie behind. Nor does it need a Freud to make the discovery. Here is a publicity release sent out by one of our oldest and most respectable publishing houses. Under the heading "What Makes Books Sell?" it reads, "Blank & Company reports that the current interest in horror stories has attracted a great number of readers to John Dash's novel . . . because of its depiction of Nazi brutality. Critics and readers alike have commented on the stark realism of Dash's handling of the torture scenes in the book. The publishers originally envisaged a woman's market because of the love story, now find men reading the book because of the other angle." This does not suggest a more than usual depravity in the male reader, for "the other angle" has always had a fascination, no doubt a bad one, even for those who would not themselves commit or actually witness an act of torture. I cite the extreme example only to suggest that something may indeed lie behind our sober intelligent interest in moral politics. In this instance the pleasure in the cruelty is protected and licensed by moral indignation. In other instances moral indignation, which has been said to be the favorite emotion of the middle class, may be in itself an exquisite pleasure. To understand this does not invalidate moral indignation but only sets up the conditions on which it ought to be entertained, only says when it is legitimate and when not.

But, the answer comes, however important it may be for moral realism to raise questions in our minds about our motives, is it not at best a matter of secondary importance? Is it not of the first importance that we be given a direct and immediate report on the reality that is daily being brought to dreadful birth? The novels that have done this have effected much practical good, bringing to consciousness the latent feelings of many people, making it harder for them to be unaware or indifferent, creating an atmosphere in which injustice finds it harder to thrive. To speak of moral realism is all very well. But it is an elaborate, even fancy, phrase and it is to be suspected of having the intention of sophisticating the simple reality that is easily to be conceived. Life presses us so hard, time is so short, the suffering of the world is so huge, simple, unendurable —anything that complicates our moral fervor in dealing with reality as we immediately see it and wish to drive headlong upon it must be regarded with some impatience.

True enough: and therefore any defense of what I have called moral realism must be made not in the name of some highflown fineness of feeling but in the name of simple social practicality. And there is indeed a simple social fact to which moral realism has a simple practical relevance, but it is a fact very difficult for us nowadays to perceive. It is that the moral passions are even more willful and imperious and impatient than the self-seeking passions. All history is at one in telling us that their tendency is to be not only liberating but also restrictive.

It is probable that at this time we are about to make great changes in our social system. The world is ripe for such changes and if they are not made in the direction of greater social liberality, the direction forward, they will almost of necessity be made in the direction backward, of a terrible social niggardliness. We all know which of those directions we want. But it is not enough to want it, not even enough to work for it—we must want it and work for it with intelligence. Which means that we must be aware of the dangers which lie in our most generous wishes. Some paradox of our nature leads us, when once we have made our fellow men the objects of our enlightened interest, to go on to make them the objects of our pity, then of our wisdom, ultimately of our coercion. It is to prevent this corruption, the most ironic and tragic that man knows, that we stand in need of the moral realism which is the product of the free play of the moral imagination.

For our time the most effective agent of the moral imagination has been the novel of the last two hundred years. It was never, either aesthetically or morally, a perfect form and its faults and failures can be quickly enumerated. But its greatness and its practical usefulness lay in its unremitting work of involving the reader himself in the moral life, inviting him to put his own motives under examination, suggesting that reality is not as his conventional education has led him to see it. It taught us, as no other genre ever did, the extent of human variety and the value of this variety. It was the literary form to which the emotions of understanding and forgiveness were indigenous, as if by the definition of the form itself. At the moment its impulse does not seem strong, for there never was a time when the virtues of its greatness were so likely to be thought of as weaknesses. Yet there never was a time when its particular activity was so much needed, was of so much practical, political, and social use—so much so that if its impulse does not respond to the need, we shall have reason to be sad not only over a waning form of art but also over our waning freedom.

WILLIAM FAULKNER

Man Will Prevail[1]

*Speech of Acceptance upon the award of the Nobel
Prize for Literature, delivered in Stockholm on
the tenth of December, nineteen hundred fifty.*

I feel that this award was not made to me as a man, but to my work—a life's
work in the agony and sweat of the human spirit, not for glory and least of
all for profit, but to create out of the materials of the human spirit something
which did not exist before. So this award is only mine in trust. It will not be
difficult to find a dedication for the money part of it commensurate with the
purpose and significance of its origin. But I would like to do the same with
the acclaim too, by using this moment as a pinnacle from which I might be
listened to by the young men and women already dedicated to the same anguish
and travail, among whom is already that one who will some day stand here
where I am standing.

Our tragedy today is a general and universal physical fear so long sustained
by now that we can even bear it. There are no longer problems of the spirit.
There is only the question: When will I be blown up? Because of this, the
young man or woman writing today has forgotten the problems of the human
heart in conflict with itself which alone can make good writing because only
that is worth writing about, worth the agony and the sweat.

He must learn them again. He must teach himself that the basest of all
things is to be afraid; and, teaching himself that, forget it forever, leaving no
room in his workshop for anything but the old verities and truths of the heart,
the old universal truths lacking which any story is ephemeral and doomed—
love and honor and pity and pride and compassion and sacrifice. Until he does
so, he labors under a curse. He writes not of love but of lust, of defeats in
which nobody loses anything of value, of victories without hope and, worst of
all, without pity or compassion. His griefs grieve on no universal bones, leaving no scars. He writes not of the heart but of the glands.

Until he relearns these things, he will write as though he stood among and
watched the end of man. I decline to accept the end of man. It is easy enough
to say that man is immortal simply because he will endure: that when the last
ding-dong of doom has clanged and faded from the last worthless rock hanging tideless in the last red and dying evening, that even then there will still
be one more sound: that of his puny inexhaustible voice, still talking. I refuse
to accept this. I believe that man will not merely endure: he will prevail. He
is immortal, not because he alone among creatures has an inexhaustible voice,

[1] Reprinted by courtesy of Random House, Inc.

but because he has a soul, a spirit capable of compassion and sacrifice and endurance. The poet's, the writer's, duty is to write about these things. It is his privilege to help man endure by lifting his heart, by reminding him of the courage and honor and hope and pride and compassion and pity and sacrifice which have been the glory of his past. The poet's voice need not merely be the record of man, it can be one of the props, the pillars to help him endure and prevail.

V

Science

The Nature of Science

⊕◇

JAMES B. CONANT

Concerning Electricity and Combustion[1]

This book is in no sense a presentation of the history of science or of any branch of science. The objective is to indicate how certain principles might be taught by illustrations drawn from the development of science. . . . In this chapter two case histories are presented both drawn from the end of the eighteenth century. The first concerns the discovery of the electric battery, the second concerns the chemical revolution which placed our knowledge of combustion on a sound basis. . . .

The Role of the Accidental Discovery

The layman is frequently confused in regard to the role of the accidental discovery on the one hand and the planned experiment on the other. This is particularly true in connection with the development of new techniques and the evolution of new concepts from experiment. The case history which I recommend for a study of these topics is the work of Galvani and Volta on the electric current. This case history illustrates the fact that an accidental discovery may lead by a series of experiments (which must be well planned) to a new technique or a new concept or both; it also shows that in the exploration of a new phenomenon the experiments may be well planned without any "working hypothesis" as to the nature of the phenomenon, but that shortly an explanation is sure to arise. A new conceptual scheme will be evolved. This may be on a grand scale and have wide applicability, or may be strictly limited to the phenomenon in question. A test of the new concept or group of concepts in either instance will probably lead to new discoveries and the eventual establishment, modification, or overthrow of the conceptual scheme in question.

[1] From James B. Conant, *On Understanding Science: An Historical Approach* (New Haven, Conn.: Yale University Press, 1947), pp. 65-97, with omissions. Reprinted by permission of the publishers.

Galvani's Discoveries

The case history begins with certain observations made by Luigi Galvani, an Italian physician, a professor at Bologna, some time before 1786. This investigator noted the twitching of a frog's leg when the crural nerves were touched by a metallic scalpel in the neighborhood of an electrostatic machine from which sparks were drawn. *He followed up his observation.* At this point in a course on the Tactics and Strategy of Science the instructor would wax eloquent. He would remind the class that time and time again throughout the history of science the consequences of following up or not following up accidental discoveries have been very great. The analogy of a general's taking advantage of an enemy's error or a lucky break, like the capture of the Remagen bridge, could hardly fail to enter the discussion. Pasteur once wrote that "chance favors only the prepared mind." This is excellently illustrated by the case history at hand. The Dutch naturalist, Swammerdam, had previously discovered that if you lay bare the muscle of a frog in much the same way as Galvani did, grasp a tendon in one hand and touch the frog's nerve with a scalpel held in the other hand, a twitching will result. But Swammerdam never followed up his work. Galvani did. In his own words, "I had dissected and prepared a frog . . . and while I was attending to something else, I laid it on a table on which stood an electrical machine at some distance. . . . Now when one of the persons who were present touched accidentally and lightly the inner crural nerves of the frog with the point of a scalpel all the muscles of the legs seemed to contract again and again. . . . Another one who was there, who was helping us in electrical researches, thought that he had noticed that the action was excited when a spark was discharged from the conductor of the machine. Being astonished by this new phenomenon he called my attention to it, who at that time had something else in mind and was deep in thought. Whereupon I was inflamed with an incredible zeal and eagerness to test the same and to bring to light what was concealed in it."

Galvani did not succeed in bringing to light all that was concealed in the new phenomenon. But he proceeded far enough to make the subsequent discoveries inevitable. In a series of well-planned experiments he explored the obvious variables, but without a clear-cut, over-all hypothesis. This is the usual situation when a new phenomenon is encountered by a gifted experimenter. A series of working hypotheses spring to mind, are tested and either discarded or incorporated into a conceptual scheme which gradually develops. For example, Galvani first determined whether or not sparks had to be drawn from the electrical machine in order to occasion twitching. He found "Without fail there occurred lively contractions . . . at the same instant as that in which the spark jumped. . . ."

The nerves and muscles of the frog's leg constituted a sensitive detector of an electric charge. Galvani found that not only must a spark be passing from the electrostatic machine but the metallic blade of the scalpel must be in contact with the hand of the experimenter. In this way a small charge originating from the electrical disturbance, namely the spark, passed down the conducting human body through the scalpel to the nerve. So far the physician was on sound and fruitful ground. There now occurred one of those coincidences which more than once has initially baffled an investigator but eventually led to great advances. The frog's leg could under certain circumstances act not only as a sensitive electrical detector but as a source of electricity as well. When this happened, the electricity self-generated so to speak actuated the detector. One can readily see that the superposition of these two effects could be most bewildering and misleading. This was particularly so since the conditions under which the frog's leg became a source of electricity were totally unconnected with any electrical phenomena then known. The variable was the nature of the metal or I should say metals used. For Galvani discovered and duly recorded that the electrostatic machine could be dispensed with if the leg and the nerve were connected together by two *different* metals. Under these conditions the twitching occurred. (The experiment was usually performed as follows: a curved rod was made to touch simultaneously both a hook passing through the spinal cord of the frog and the "muscles of the leg or the feet.") "Thus, for example," wrote Galvani, "if the whole rod was iron or the hook was iron . . . the contractions either did not occur or were very small. But if one of them was iron and the other brass, or better if it was silver (silver seems to us the best of all the metals for conducting animal electricity) there occur repeated and much greater and more prolonged contractions."

Galvani had discovered the principle of the electric battery without knowing it. His two metals separated by the moist animal tissue were a battery, the frog's leg the detector. Every reader can perform the equivalent of Galvani's experiment himself. A copper coin and a silver one placed above and below the tongue when touched together produce in the tongue a peculiar "taste." A very small electric current flows and our tongue records the fact through a series of interactions of electricity and nerves much in the same way as did Galvani's "prepared" frogs. Not having a suspicion of all this, however, Galvani developed a conceptual scheme (an hypothesis on the grand scale, we might say) to account for all the phenomena in terms of what was then known about electricity which was derived entirely from experiment with electrostatic machines. Having found outside electrical disturbances unnecessary (when he unwittingly used the *right* metallic combination!) the experiments, he says, "cause us to think that possibly the electricity was present in the animal itself." Galvani's following up of an accidental discovery by a series of controlled experiments had led to a recording of the significant facts, but it was to be another Italian who developed the fruitful concept. It was Volta who in the late 1790's, continuing the study of the production of electricity by the contact of two different metals, invented the electric battery as a source of what we now often call Galvanic electricity.

Volta's Invention of the Electric Battery

Alessandro Volta (1745-1827) of Padua had earlier invented a new form of instrument for detecting small charges of electricity. He began by agreeing with Galvani about animal electricity and went about studying it. With his new instrument, a sensitive condensing electrometer, Volta explored various combinations of variables related to Galvani's early experiments and found that the frog could be eliminated in favor of almost any moist material. This discovery might be considered an example of the accidental discovery, but if so it is of a different order from that of Galvani. Explorations with new techniques and tools, if undertaken in a more or less orderly fashion, almost always turn up unexpected facts. In this sense a great majority of new facts of science are accidental discoveries. But the difference between this sort of experience and the example afforded by Galvani's work is obvious. Volta's new discovery amounted, of course, to the invention of the electric battery; for he showed that electricity was produced when two different metals were separated by water containing salt or lye. This was most conveniently done by using moistened paper. In a letter to the President of the Royal Society of London in 1800 Volta wrote "30, 40, 60 or more pieces of copper, or rather of silver, each in contact with a piece of tin, or of zinc, which is much better, and as many layers of water or of some other liquid which is a better conductor than pure water, such as salt-water or lye and so forth, or pieces of pasteboard or of leather, etc. well soaked with these liquids; . . . such an alternative series of these three sorts of conductors always in the same order, constitutes my new instrument; which imitates . . . the effects of Leyden jars. . . ." (see

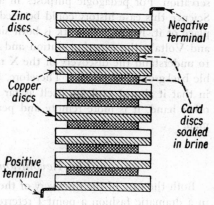

FIG. 1. *One form of Volta's battery or pile.*

Figure 1). This new battery was a source of electricity different from the electrostatic generator already known in 1800; it was the first source of continuous current. The battery produced electricity of low potential but of considerable quantity (low voltage, relatively high amperage); the sparks from a frictional machine are brief spasms of current of high potential but very low amperage.

There was a hot controversy between Galvani's disciples (Galvani died in 1798) and Volta about whether or not there was such a thing as animal electricity, and what caused the twitching of the frog's legs in the first experiments. Volta soon lost interest in the quarrel and devoted his attention to the study of his new battery. Today we have a rather complete and highly satisfactory conceptual scheme in which all the facts about electric batteries find their place. This is not the case, however, with observations about muscles, nerves, and electric currents in animal tissue. In this field one working hypothesis still replaces another and new experiments are still throwing new light on an ancient phenomenon. In a sense, we have not yet finished with Galvani's very first observation, but have finished with Volta's discovery. The original controversy centered on the question, is there animal electricity? This has now become largely a meaningless question, but in attempting to find an answer Volta discovered the electric battery. Such is often the course of scientific history. We end by solving a problem other than the one first at issue.

Another case history which illustrates the role of the accidental discovery, the well-planned experiments by which it may be followed up, the role of the working hypothesis, the development of an hypothesis on the grand scale, and the rapid emergence of both a new technique and a new concept is furnished by a study of the discovery of X rays. The story is familiar to all scientists though perhaps it is not generally known that before Roentgen announced his discovery, several other investigators had noticed the fogging of photographic plates near an electric discharge tube. Roentgen followed up his accidental observation. For pedagogic purposes in a course on the Tactics and Strategy of Science this case history could be used to supplement the one just given or in place of it. Roentgen's work is both simpler and more complex than Galvani's and Volta's; the experimentation and reasoning are more straightforward, but to understand the discovery of the X rays the student should have a considerable background of physics. Therefore, the eighteenth-century example is better in that it almost explains itself as far as technical terms are involved. On the other hand, it is more remote and perhaps less interesting to the average layman.

The Revolutionary Effect of New Techniques

Both the case of the discovery of the electric battery and that of X rays show in a dramatic fashion a point I referred to in the last chapter, namely, that a new technique may have an almost revolutionary effect. With the new electric battery in the beginning of the nineteenth century, Humphry Davy and many others discovered all sorts of new electrochemical and physical phenomena; from them in turn came in rapid succession new techniques and new concepts. Likewise in our own day after the publication of an account of the X-ray tube, new experimental facts came forth in torrents. Tremendous spurts in the progress of the various sciences are almost always connected with the development of a new technique or the sudden emergence of a new concept. It is as though a group of prospectors were hunting in barren ground and suddenly struck a rich vein of ore. All at once everyone works feverishly and the gold begins to flow.

will say that in the case mentioned it is a group of carbon compounds, and
some the products of whose combustion are carbon dioxide, CO_2, and water. I have assumed a knowledge of chemical symbols nat-

Two Further Principles in
the Tactics and Strategy of Science

Let us now turn to the second case history to be considered in this chapter.
It is an example drawn from the history of chemistry in the second half of the
eighteenth century, and, it is only fair to warn the reader, a most complicated
case. Perhaps too much effort is required to master the facts involved to make
this a good example for the layman. But I believe it should be included in the
course I am proposing because in it two important principles in the Tactics and
Strategy of Science are illustrated in a peculiarly striking fashion. These principles are as follows:

First, a useful concept may be a barrier to the acceptance of a better one if
long-intrenched in the minds of scientists.

Second, experimental discoveries must fit the time; facts may be at hand for
years without their significance being realized; the total scientific situation must
be favorable for the acceptance of new views.

The Overthrow of the Phlogiston Theory

The case history which illustrates excellently these two important points
might be entitled "the overthrow of the phlogiston theory" or "Lavoisier's work
on combustion in the 1770's." As indicated by the first phrase the case also
affords a classic example of the mustering of evidence pro and con when two
rival concepts are in collision. This phenomenon though frequent is usually so
transient in the history of science as to be hard to capture for purposes of
historical study. In the investigation of combustion the normal progress of science was, so to speak, delayed; this fact, in a sense, accounts for why a study of
this difficult passage in scientific history is of special significance to those interested in the Tactics and Strategy of Science.

The easiest way to understand the revolution in chemistry associated with
the name of Lavoisier is first to describe the phenomena in question in terms of
modern concepts; then to show how for nearly a hundred years everyone was
thoroughly confused. This pedagogic device would have to be used by the instructor in the course I am suggesting. It involves the dogmatic statement of a
certain amount of popularized physics and chemistry, but I doubt if the presentation would be much more arbitrary in this respect than most freshman
courses. Indeed, some of the material might be said to be common knowledge
today.

Almost every high-school graduate "knows" (I put quotation marks around
the word) that air is primarily a mixture of oxygen gas and nitrogen gas; furthermore, when a candle or a match or a cigarette "burns," heat and light are
being evolved by a chemical reaction involving oxygen. This is called "combustion." If we burn enough material in a closed space, the combustion stops because the oxygen is used up. What burns? Some but not all of the students

will say that in the cases mentioned it is a group of carbon compounds, and some will add that the products of combustion are carbon dioxide, CO_2 and water, H_2O. Anyone who has an elementary knowledge of chemical symbols usually loves to share the information! Suppose you heat molten tin in air at a high temperature for a long time, and the bright metal becomes covered with a scum, obviously not a metal. What has happened? A combination with oxygen —an oxide is formed—the bright boys and girls answer. Correct. Suppose we heat this non-metallic substance, an oxide, with carbon. What would happen? The carbon would combine with the oxygen, giving an oxide of carbon and leaving the metal. This is what happens in making iron from iron ore, the very bright boy tells you.

All very simple and plain. And you can set students to work in high-school laboratories to prove it. Yet it is an historic fact that at the time of the American Revolution not one philosopher or experimentalist out of one hundred could have given you an inkling of this explanation which we now designate as "correct." Instead, they would have talked learnedly of "phlogiston," a name probably totally unfamiliar to all but the chemists who read this book. Nearly a hundred years after Newton, and still everyone was thoroughly bewildered by such a simple matter as combustion! This fact needs to be brought home to all who would understand science and who talk of the "scientific method."

The chemical revolution was practically contemporary with the American Revolution and, of course, just preceded the French Revolution. Lavoisier, the man who singlehanded but building on the work of others made the revolution, lost his head at the hands of the Revolutionary Tribune in 1794 (though he was by no means hostile to the basic aims of the great social and political upheaval). Whether or not he was betrayed by a scientific colleague (Fourcroy) who at least was an ardent supporter of the extreme party then in power, is an intriguing historical question; its study would be a by-product of this case history in which certain students would take great interest. Likewise, the fact that another prominent figure in the final controversy was Priestley, a Unitarian clergyman, who was made an honorary citizen by the French Assembly and then fled to America in the very year of Lavoisier's execution to escape a reactionary English mob, adds zest to the story. There is no lack of material to connect science with society in the late eighteenth century, though the connection I think is more dramatic than significant; at all events, for keeping up students' interest it can hardly be surpassed.

The Classic Experiment on the Role of Oxygen in Combustion

The chemical revolution took place during the years 1772-78. By the later date Lavoisier had made clear to the scientific world the role of oxygen in combustion. His classic experiment, often described in elementary textbooks, was as follows: Mercury heated in common air produces a red material (an oxide we would say, a "calx" to the chemists of the eighteenth century). In a closed space about one fifth of the air disappears. The red material weighs more than the metal from which it was formed. Therefore, something has disappeared from the air and combined with the metal. The red material, the oxide or calx, is next strongly heated in an enclosed space with the sun's rays brought to a focus by a large lens or "burning glass," a gas is evolved and the metal regenerated. The new gas is the "something" which disappeared from the original air, for the amount is the same, and the calx has lost weight in the right amount. The new gas (oxygen) mixed with the residue from the first experiment yields a mixture which is identical with common air. (Figures 2 and 3.)

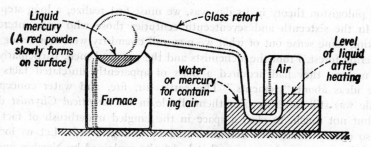

FIG. 2. *Mercury heated in air absorbs oxygen.*

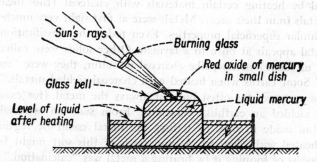

FIG. 3. *Red oxide of mercury heated very hot evolves oxygen.*
(The temperature in this experiment must be very much higher than in the formation of the oxide.)

The experiments are simple, the proof appears to be complete. (Lavoisier, of course, generalized far beyond the case of mercury.) But the new conceptual scheme was by no means accepted at once with great acclaim. Quite the contrary. Lavoisier had to drive home his points with telling arguments. Slowly his French contemporaries were won over, but Priestley and Watt of the steam-engine fame and Cavendish and scores of others continued to cling to the phlogiston theory for a decade. Priestley's case is particularly interesting. This English experimenter had actually provided Lavoisier with an important clue when in 1774 he told him about his preparation of oxygen gas by heating red oxide of mercury. But Priestley died in 1804 without ever being converted to the new doctrine.

Why was there this reluctance to modify ideas in the light of beautifully clear experiments, and why were the men of the eighteenth century so long in getting on the right track? There were two reasons: first, one conceptual scheme—the phlogiston theory—had acquired an almost paralyzing hold on their minds; and second, elucidating the facts necessary to overthrow the theory involved experiments with gases which were then extremely difficult.

The Significance of the Phlogiston Theory

The phlogiston theory in its day was, we must first realize, a long step forward. In the sixteenth and seventeenth centuries those who were interested in making some sense out of what we now call chemistry were wandering in a bewildering forest. From the alchemists and the practical men, particularly the metal makers, they had acquired a mass of apparently unrelated facts and strange ideas about "elements." The earth, air, fire, and water concept of Aristotle was still hovering over them. Boyle in his *Skeptical Chymist* did a little, but not much, to clear a space in the tangled underbrush of fact and fancy so closely interwoven and cemented by strange words. Let us look at some of the common phenomena that had to be explained by Newton and his contemporaries, that is to say, fitted into a conceptual scheme. Metals could be obtained by heating certain materials with charcoal (the ancient art of winning metals from their ores). Metals were at first sight very much the same; they had similar superficial properties. Even today the classification of metal and nonmetal appeals at once to a layman. Other solids were called "earths" (oxides for us today) or else, like charcoal or sulfur, they were "combustible principles." Some earths when heated with charcoal yielded metals. This process could be reversed, for often but not always the metal (for example, tin) on heating yielded an earthlike substance. From such an artificial earthlike substance (an oxide in modern terms) the metal could be regained if the earth was heated with charcoal. A pure earth of this sort might be called a calx, the process of forming it by heating a metal was "calcination."

How were all these facts, inherited from the Middle Ages and before, to be fitted together? By the introduction of a principle called phlogiston, closely related to Aristotle's old element, fire—closely related, yet the relationship was never clear. To those who sought for clarity it seemed evident that there must be some common principle involved in the process of making various metals from their calces and vice versa. Therefore, let us call this something phlogiston, they in effect declared. When phlogiston was added to a calx you had a metal, when you removed it from a metal a calx was formed; phlogiston was in a sense a metalizing principle. Note there is a common-sense assumption more or less implied in this line of reasoning: except for gold, and occasionally a few other metals, calces *not* metals occur in nature. Therefore, these calces were the simpler materials, something must be added to them to make them metals. Since metals were so alike, the "something" was obviously the same in all cases. We shall call it phlogiston, said Becher, and his pupil Stahl in a series of books published in 1703-31.

Here was a key to unlock a maze, and it was immediately accepted. Here was a concept which provided a pattern into which a mass of otherwise unrelated phenomena could be fitted. Substances were rich or poor in phlogiston, this seemed easy to establish. What was phlogiston itself? It probably was never to be seen. Substances rich in phlogiston easily took fire and, indeed, fire was perhaps a manifestation of phlogiston, or worked with it at least. For some, fire was still an element. Charcoal was a phlogiston-rich material and on heating with a metallic calx gave up its phlogiston to the calx, making a metal. By itself charcoal burned, the phlogiston appearing as fire or combined with the air. Sulfur, using the word in its modern sense, was found free in nature; it burned when heated and yielded an acid, vitriolic acid (sulfuric acid in modern terms). Clearly, this sulfur was only vitriolic acid highly "phlogisticated"; the burning set the phlogiston free and yielded the acid.

We can write these changes in diagrammatic form to illustrate how the chemists of the eighteenth century thought:

Calx + phlogiston (from charcoal) ⟶ metal.

Metal heated in air ⟶ calx + phlogiston (to the air).

Charcoal burned yields phlogiston to the air accompanied by fire.

Phlogisticated vitriolic acid (sulfur to us) burns yielding phlogiston

(to the air) + vitriolic acid (sulfuric acid).

There was one very simple flaw in all this argument and the interesting fact is that this flaw was known and talked about for fifty years before the phlogiston theory was even shaken, much less overthrown. This is a beautiful illustration of the principle in the Tactics and Strategy of Science referred to at the beginning of this section, namely, that a scientific discovery must fit the times. As early as 1630 (note the date—before Boyle was born) a Frenchman, Jean Rey, studied the calcination of tin and showed that the calx weighed more than the tin from which it was formed. More than that, he gave an explanation closely in accord with Lavoisier's ideas of 150 years later. For he said, "this increase in weight comes from the air, which in the vessel has been rendered denser, heavier, and in some measure adhesive . . . which air mixes with the calx . . . and becomes attached to its most minute particles. . . ." Boyle confirmed the increase in weight of metals in calcination in 1673 but added no support to Rey's shrewd guess (it was little more) as to the reason. In fact, if anything, he led subsequent investigators down the wrong path. At least in retrospect it seems that if he had followed up only a little more boldly his own experiments, the phlogiston theory might never have been proposed or, if proposed, never accepted seriously. Yet it is all too easy to imagine that even a still greater genius than Boyle could have discovered oxygen and revealed its role in combustion and calcination in the seventeenth century. Too much physics as well as chemistry lay under wraps which were only slowly removed by the labors of many men.

At all events, Boyle put forward the hypothesis that fire, the Aristotelian principle, had passed through the walls of the glass vessel used and combined with the metal, thereby giving it weight. This was, of course, not the same as the phlogiston theory formulated a generation later; in a sense it was the opposite because according to Boyle something was *added* to the metal in calcination, namely, fire. While in the phlogiston theory something, namely, phlogiston, was *removed*. But Boyle's writings did focus attention on the heat and flame (a characteristic of fire and calcination) rather than on the air which had figured in Rey's explanation.

A Scientific Discovery Must Fit the Times

Rey's ideas about the air seem to have been lost in the subsequent 150 years, but not the facts of calcination. That a calx weighed more than the metal was well known throughout the eighteenth century, but this fact was *not* recognized as being fatal to the phlogiston theory. Here is an important point. Does it argue for the stupidity of the experimental philosophers of the day as a few writers once would have us think? Not at all; it merely demonstrates that in complex affairs of science, one is concerned with trying to account for a variety of facts and with welding them into a conceptual scheme; one fact is not by itself sufficient to wreck the scheme. In discussing Galileo's failure and Torricelli's successful interpretation of lift pumps, I referred to the principle that a conceptual scheme is never discarded merely because of a few stubborn facts with which it cannot be reconciled; a concept is either modified or replaced by a better concept, never abandoned with nothing left to take its place.

Not only was it known in 1770 that a calx weighed more than the metal from which it was formed (which means to us that something must have been taken up in its formation), but Boyle himself back in the 1660's showed that air was necessary for fire. John Mayow and Robert Hooke at about the same date had written about burning and the respiration of animals in terms of air being "deprived of its elastic force by the breathing of animals very much in the same way as by the burning of flame." Stephen Hales, fifty years later, spoke the same language. But these men were all ahead of their times. As we reread their papers we see in spite of strange words and ill-defined ideas they had demonstrated that air in which material had been burned or animals had respired would no longer sustain fire or life; furthermore, they showed that there was an actual diminution of the volume of the air in such cases. All of which seems to force the right explanation to our eyes; not so to the chemists of the eighteenth century.

Air which would no longer support combustion had merely become so rich in phlogiston it could take up no more, the "phlogistonists" declared. Indeed, when Priestley discovered how to prepare essentially pure nitrogen, it was quite natural for him to regard it as completely "phlogisticated air," because nitrogen will not support combustion. Likewise, when he discovered how to prepare essentially pure oxygen gas by heating red oxide of mercury, he called it "dephlogisticated air." He found this gas to be like common air, though a candle burned in it more brightly than even in common air. Upon the whole, said Priestley, it may safely be concluded, "that the purest air is that which contains the least phlogiston: that air is impure (by which I mean that it is unfit for respiration, and for the purpose of supporting flame) in proportion as it contains more of that principle." This letter was read to the Royal Society on May 25, 1775. And in the same year in another letter he spoke of his newly discovered oxygen as "[an air] that is five or six times better than common air, for the purposes of respiration, inflammation and, I believe, every other use of common atmospherical air. As I think I have sufficiently proved that the fitness of air for respiration depends on its capacity to receive the *phlogiston* exhaled from the lungs this species of air may not improperly be called, *dephlogisticated air.*"

Experimental Difficulties with Gases

A chemist reading the papers of the phlogistonists clutches his head in despair; he seems to be transported to an Alice-through-the-looking-glass world! But if he is patient and interested he soon recognizes that much of the difficulty stemmed from the experimenters' inability to handle and characterize different gases. This fact illustrates once again the third point of the principles outlined in the last chapter, the difficulty of experimentation. Metals and calxes, inflammable substances like sulfur, charcoal, and phosphorus, the chemists of the eighteenth century could recognize and manipulate since they were solids. Even some liquids like vitriolic acid, water, and mercury were quite definite individuals. But two gases, neither of which would support fire, like nitrogen and carbon dioxide, were often hopelessly confused; or two which burned, like hydrogen and carbon monoxide. Nearly all gases look alike except for the few which are colored. They are compressible and subject to thermal expansion to about the same degree. Their densities, i.e., the weight of a unit volume, differ but that was something not easy to determine in those days. Indeed, in the eighteenth century the distinction between weight and density (i.e., weight per unit volume) even for solids and liquids was often confused. The chemical properties of each gas are characteristic and the way each gas is prepared is different; and it was these differences that finally led to a straightening out of some of the tangled skein.

To understand the difficulties of the chemists of 175 years ago, imagine yourself an elementary student in a laboratory given glass bottles of air, of oxygen, of nitrogen, and one containing air saturated with ether vapor, and asked to tell whether or not all the "airs" or gases in the bottles are identical. The air containing the ether vapor (actually still largely air) will be the only one at first recognized as distinct. A student does not know how to proceed to examine these gases except by looking at them, smelling them, or testing their solubility in water. And from Boyle's day to Priestley's the experimenters were largely in the same predicament. They spoke of different "airs," but hardly

knew whether the differences were real or due to the presence of some impurity. Thus, Priestley, writing in 1777, said:

"Van Helmont and other chymists who succeeded him, were acquainted with
the property of some *vapours* to suffocate, and extinguish flame, and of others
to be ignited. . . . . But they had no idea that the substances (if, indeed they
knew that they were *substances*, and not merely *properties*, and *affections* of
bodies which produced those effects) were capable of being separately exhibited in the form of a *permanently elastic vapour* . . . any more than the
thing that constitutes *smell*. In fact they knew nothing at all of any air besides
common air, and therefore they applied the term to no other substances whatever. . . . ."

The history of the study of gases covers a hundred years from Boyle's day.
A number of important improvements in techniques were made. They were
brought to a focus by Priestley who in 1772 carried out extensive and very
original experiments with "airs." He improved still further several techniques
of handling these airs or gases which enormously simplified the experimental
procedures. Before Priestley's work only three "different airs" were known. In a
few years he had discovered eleven more, including oxygen. Here is another
illustration of the importance of techniques, though here we meet with an evolutionary rather than a revolutionary change.

Though Priestley was the chief figure in extending the knowledge of gases,
his stubborn refusal to accept the consequences of his own discoveries has already been mentioned. It is not necessary in this chapter to discuss either
Priestley or Lavoisier as individuals, though the instructor using the case history of combustion would certainly wish to do so. Nor do I propose to digress
by examining the priority problems involved in the work of these two men and
the Swedish chemist, Scheele, who also discovered oxygen. Such matters fall
within the province of the historian of science. For the purposes of the present
exposition the important questions are: Why did it take the scientists of the
eighteenth century so long to get on the right road? And why were there so
many stubborn travelers on the wrong road after the right one had been discovered?

The Phlogiston Theory,
a Block to a New Concept

It is sometimes said that the experimenters before Lavoisier's day did not
carry out quantitative experiments, that is, they did not use the balance. If
they had, we are told, they would have discovered that combustion involves an
increase in weight and would have rejected the phlogiston theory. This is nonsense. Rey, as I have already explained, long before the beginning of the phlogiston period showed that a calx weighed more than a metal. Quantitative experiments, though, of course, not very accurate ones, were repeatedly made.
Everyone knew that a calx weighed more than the metal from which it was
formed. No straightforward statement of the phlogiston theory could accommodate this fact. Yet the phlogiston theory was so useful that few if any in the

mid-eighteenth century were looking to overthrow it or disprove it. Rather, they were interested in reconciling one inconvenient set of facts with what seemed from their point of view an otherwise admirable conceptual scheme. How they twisted and squirmed to accommodate the quantitative facts of calcination with the phlogiston theory makes an interesting chapter in the history of science. The eighteenth-century accounts are often confusing. Fortunately their many details need not concern the readers of this book, nor except in broad outline need they concern one teaching the principles of the Tactics and Strategy of Science with the aid of the eighteenth-century studies on combustion.

The principle which emerges is one already encountered, namely, that it takes a new conceptual scheme to cause the abandonment of an old one: when only a few facts appear to be irreconcilable with a well established conceptual scheme, the first attempt is *not* to discard the scheme but to find some way out of the difficulty and keep it. Likewise the proponents of new concepts are rarely shaken by a few alleged facts to the contrary. They seek at first to prove them wrong or to circumvent them. Thus Lavoisier persisted with his own new concept in spite of the fact that certain experiments seemed to be completely inexplicable in its terms. It was later found that the interpretation of the experiments was in error. Not so in the case of the calcination of metals: there could be no doubt in the mind of anyone by 1770 that the increase in weight during calcination was real. There was also no doubt that there should be a loss in weight according to the phlogiston theory. Or at best no change in weight if phlogiston were an imponderable substance like fire.

Attempts to Reconstruct the Phlogiston Theory

One attempt to get out of the dilemma of calcination took refuge in a confusion between weight and density (calxes are less dense than metals, but the total weight in the calcination increased). This was soon put right by clear thinking. Another attempt involved assigning a negative weight to phlogiston. This illustrates how desperately men may strive to modify an old idea to make it accord with new experiments. But in this case the modification represented not a step forward but several steps to the rear! What was gained by accommodating the quantitative aspect of calcination was lost by following the consequences of negative weight to a logical conclusion. What manner of substance or principle could phlogiston be that when it was added to another material the total mass or weight diminished? The idea that phlogiston had negative weight strained the credulity, and for the most part this logical extension of the phlogiston theory (logical in one sense, highly illogical in another) was never widely accepted. But before we laugh too hard at the investigators of the eighteenth century, let us remember that before the nineteenth century heat was considered a corporeal substance and the whole concept of the atomic and molecular theory of matter lay over the distant horizon.

To some of the chemical experimenters, the dilemma presented by the quantitative facts of calcination seems to have been accepted as just one of those things which cannot be fitted in. And this attitude is much more common in the history of science than most historians would have you believe. Indeed, it is in a way a necessary attitude at certain stages of development of any concept. The keen-minded scientist, the real genius, is the man who keeps in the forefront of his thoughts these unsolved riddles. He then is ready to relate a new discovery or a new technique to the unsolved problems. He is the pioneer, the revolutionist. And it is this combination of strategy and tactics in the hands of a master which is well worthy of study if one would try to understand science through the historical approach.

Lavoisier's Clue

To recount the history of Lavoisier's development of his new theory, and the way in which the new discoveries of the time were fitted into his scheme would mean the recital of a long story. Such an account would be out of place in this volume, though a considerable portion of it would be involved in a thorough study of the case histories at hand. Let me take a few moments of the reader's time, however, to point out how Lavoisier first seems to have taken the right turn in the road. In a famous note of 1772, he wrote as follows:

"About eight days ago I discovered that sulphur in burning, far from losing weight, on the contrary gains it; . . . it is the same with phosphorus; this increase of weight arises from a prodigious quantity of air that is fixed during the combustion and combines with the vapours.

"This discovery, which I have established by experiments that I regard as decisive, has led me to think that what is observed in the combustion of sulphur and phosphorus may well take place in the case of all substances that gain in weight by combustion and calcination: and I am persuaded that the increase in weight of metallic calces is due to the same cause. . . ."

Here we seem to see the mental process at work to which I referred a few moments ago: the perception that a new fact properly interpreted enables one to explain an old dilemma, an outstanding unsolved problem. In a sense, in this note Lavoisier outlined the whole new chemistry, as he always later claimed. (The note was deposited sealed with the Secretary of the French Academy on November 1, 1772.) To be sure, at first Lavoisier mistook the gas evolved in the reduction of a calx with charcoal (carbon dioxide, the "fixed air" of that day) with the gas absorbed in calcination. The study we can now make of his notebooks as well as his later publications makes it plain that it was not until after Priestley's discovery of oxygen and Lavoisier's repetition of some of Priestley's experiments with the new gas that the nature of the gas absorbed in calcination became clear. It was only then that all the pieces of the puzzle fitted together, with the newly discovered oxygen occupying the central position in the picture. But at the outset Lavoisier recognized that something was absorbed from the air. Unconsciously he was retracing the steps Jean Rey had taken nearly 150 years earlier and which had never been followed up. Rey's almost forgotten book was called to Lavoisier's attention shortly after his first publications of his new theory.

An interesting question that will at once come to the mind of many is the following: why did the study of sulfur and phosphorus lead Lavoisier to the right type of explanation? Why after experiments with those substances did he set out full of confidence on a set of planned experiments along a new line? This is one of those historical riddles which can never be answered, but concerning which it is not entirely profitless to speculate. I suggest that the key word in Lavoisier's note of November 1, 1772, is "prodigious"—"this increase of weight arises from a prodigious quantity of air that is fixed." If this is so, we have again another illustration of how experimental difficulties or the lack of them condition the evolution of new concepts. To determine whether air is absorbed or not during the calcination of a metal is not easy; the process takes a long time, a high temperature, and both the increase in weight and the amount of oxygen absorbed are small. But with phosphorus and sulfur the experiment was relatively easy to perform (the materials burn at once on ignition with a burning glass); furthermore, the effect observed is very large. The reason for this in terms of modern chemistry is that sulfur and phosphorus have low atomic weights of 32 and 31 (oxygen is 16), and in the combustion 1 atom of phosphorus combines with 5 of oxygen; 1 atom of sulfur with 3 of oxygen. The atomic weight of the metals is high, the number of atoms of oxygen combining with them, fewer. Thus 62 weights of phosphorus will yield $62 + (5 \times 16) = 142$ parts of combustion product; while in the case of tin, the atomic weight is 118 and only 2 atoms of oxygen are involved. Thus 118 weights of tin would yield only $118 + (2 \times 16) = 150$ weights of calx or an increase of only about 25 per cent. Note that with phosphorus the increase is more than double. The corresponding differences would be reflected in the volume of oxygen absorbed, and furthermore, since the calcination of tin was a long process at a high temperature in a furnace, no entirely satisfactory way of measuring the volume of air absorbed was at hand in 1770.

Quantitative Measurements and Accidental Errors

As a matter of fact, until Lavoisier was put on the track of the gas prepared by heating mercuric oxide by Priestley, he had a hard time proving that metallic calxes did gain in weight *because* of absorption of something from the air. The method he used was to repeat certain experiments of Boyle with a slight modification. Both the modification and the difficulties are of interest and point an obvious moral to the tale. Boyle had sealed tin in a glass vessel and heated the vessel a long time on a charcoal fire (which he says is a very dangerous operation as the glass may well explode). Boyle then removed the vessel from the fire and after cooling opened the glass, reweighed the vessel and noted the increase in weight. This was one of the many well-known experiments showing that the calx weighed more than the metal. (Boyle, the reader will recall, believed the increase to be due to the fire particles which passed through the glass.) Now, said Lavoisier, where Boyle went wrong was in not weighing the vessel *before* opening it. For if his explanation were right and the fire had passed through the glass and combined with the tin, the increase would have occurred before the air was admitted. While if oxygen were involved, the increase in weight would occur *after* the air was admitted. The results obtained by Lavoisier on repeating this experiment were as expected, but were far from being as striking as those obtained with phosphorus for the reasons just explained. The increase was 10 parts in a total of 4,100 in one experiment and 3 parts in about the same amount in another! We now know that the difficulties of weighing a large glass vessel with a high degree of accuracy are great, due to film moisture and electrical charges. It is, therefore, not surprising that the glass retort, after heating, varied in weight from day to day almost as much as the total gain in weight in one of the two experiments.

These tough facts of experimentation are of great importance. To me, they indicate strongly that even if Boyle had weighed his vessel before and after admitting the air, the uncertainties of his figures would probably have been so great as to confuse him and subsequent investigators. *Important advances in science are based on quantitative measurements only if the measured quantity is large as compared with possible systematic and accidental errors.* The principle of significant figures which plays so large a part in later scientific history is foreshadowed in a crude way by this episode involving the combustion of phosphorus and the calcination of tin. Therefore, in considering the case history at hand the instructor would undoubtedly wish to enlarge at some length on the whole problem of the controlled variable and the role of quantitative measurements.

Lavoisier and Priestley's Stubborn Facts

For students who had some prior knowledge of chemistry, say a good highschool course, the study of the last days of the phlogiston theory might be rewarding. For the controversy between Lavoisier and Priestley not only illustrates with what tenacity an able man may cling to a hopeless position, but also the boldness with which the innovator pushes forward. Even if a few facts appear to be to the contrary, he still pushes his new ideas just as his conservative opponent stoutly maintains his own tenets in spite of contradictory evidence. In such tugs of war which are the commonest experience in science, though usually in highly restricted areas and with limited significance, the innovator is by no means always right. This point needs to be made perfectly clear. Several case histories to this end would be worth recounting. A few dramatic instances would be in order where some bold man put forward a new idea based on alleged facts which turned out to be erroneous or erroneously interpreted.

The record of Lavoisier was the opposite. For the facts he ignored were indeed not facts at all. Priestley's main points against Lavoisier's views were based on a mistaken identification of two different gases. This fact again emphasizes the difficulties of experimentation. Two gases, both inflammable, carbon monoxide and hydrogen, were at that period confused, even by the great experimenters with gases. Assuming their identity Priestley could ask Lavoisier to account for phenomena which were indeed inexplicable according to the new chemistry, but could be accommodated in the phlogiston theory, now being twisted more each day to conform to new discoveries. Not until long after Lavoisier's execution in 1794 was the relationship between the two gases straightened out. Therefore, Lavoisier was never able to respond to the most weighty of Priestley's arguments against his doctrine. He merely ignored the alleged facts, much as Priestley ignored the unexplained gain in weight or calcination. Each undoubtedly believed that some way would be found around the difficulty in question. Lavoisier's hopes, not Priestley's, proved well founded. So proceeds the course of science. Sometimes it turns out that difficulties with a concept or conceptual scheme are wisely ignored, sometimes unwisely. To suppose, with some who write about the "scientific method," that a scientific theory stands or falls on the issue of one experiment is to misunderstand science indeed.

A study of the overthrow of the phlogiston theory is thus seen to be more than a single case history; it is a related series of case histories. The student's knowledge of chemistry or willingness to take time to obtain this knowledge would be the limiting factor on the use of this material. Even without prior study of chemistry, I believe, a profitable excursion into this complicated bit of scientific history could be undertaken. From such an excursion would come a deeper appreciation of the two principles to which I earlier referred in this chapter. Having studied the phlogiston theory no one would fail to realize that old concepts may present barriers to the development of new ones; having traced the course of the history of experiments with gases and calcination, no one could fail to realize that scientific discoveries must fit the times if they are to be fruitful. In addition, other principles of the Tactics and Strategy of Science are constantly recurring throughout the somewhat lengthy story: the influence of new techniques, the difficulties of experimentation, the value of the controlled experiment, the evaluation of new concepts from experiment—all these are to be found illustrated more than once by those who have patience to study a strange and often neglected chapter in the history of science.

ABRAHAM   FLEXNER

The Usefulness of Useless Knowledge[1]

Is it not a curious fact that in a world steeped in irrational hatreds which threaten civilization itself, men and women—old and young—detach themselves wholly or partly from the angry current of daily life to devote themselves

[1] "The Usefulness of Useless Knowledge," Harper's Magazine, CLXXIX (October, 1939), 544-550, with omissions. Reprinted by permission of the author.

to the cultivation of beauty, to the extension of knowledge, to the cure of disease, to the amelioration of suffering, just as though fanatics were not simultaneously engaged in spreading pain, ugliness, and suffering? The world has always been a sorry and confused sort of place—yet poets and artists and scientists have ignored the factors that would, if attended to, paralyze them. From a practical point of view, intellectual and spiritual life is, on the surface, a useless form of activity, in which men indulge because they procure for themselves greater satisfactions than are otherwise obtainable. In this paper I shall concern myself with the question of the extent to which the pursuit of these useless satisfactions proves unexpectedly the source from which undreamed-of utility is derived.

We hear it said with tiresome iteration that ours is a materialistic age, the main concern of which should be the wider distribution of material goods and worldly opportunities. The justified outcry of those who through no fault of their own are deprived of opportunity and a fair share of worldly goods therefore diverts an increasing number of students from the studies which their fathers pursued to the equally important and no less urgent study of social, economic, and governmental problems. I have no quarrel with this tendency. The world in which we live is the only world about which our senses can testify. Unless it is made a better world, a fairer world, millions will continue to go to their graves silent, saddened, and embittered. I have myself spent many years pleading that our schools should become more acutely aware of the world in which their pupils and students are destined to pass their lives. Now I sometimes wonder whether that current has not become too strong and whether there would be sufficient opportunity for a full life if the world were emptied of some of the useless things that give it spiritual significance; in other words, whether our conception of what is useful may not have become too narrow to be adequate to the roaming and capricious possibilities of the human spirit.

We may look at this question from two points of view: the scientific and the humanistic or spiritual. Let us take the scientific first. I recall a conversation which I had some years ago with Mr. George Eastman on the subject of use. Mr. Eastman, a wise and gentle farseeing man, gifted with taste in music and art, had been saying to me that he meant to devote his vast fortune to the promotion of education in useful subjects. I ventured to ask him whom he regarded as the most useful worker in science in the world. He replied instantaneously: "Marconi." I surprised him by saying, "Whatever pleasure we derive from the radio or however wireless and the radio may have added to human life, Marconi's share was practically negligible."

I shall not forget his astonishment on this occasion. He asked me to explain. I replied to him somewhat as follows:

"Mr. Eastman, Marconi was inevitable. The real credit for everything that has been done in the field of wireless belongs, as far as such fundamental credit can be definitely assigned to anyone, to Professor Clerk Maxwell, who in 1865 carried out certain abstruse and remote calculations in the field of magnetism and electricity. Maxwell reproduced his abstract equations in a treatise published in 1873. At the next meeting of the British Association Professor H. J. S. Smith of Oxford declared that 'no mathematician can turn over the pages of these volumes without realizing that they contain a theory which has already added largely to the methods and resources of pure mathematics.' Other discoveries supplemented Maxwell's theoretical work during the next fifteen years. Finally in 1887 and 1888 the scientific problem still remaining— the detection and demonstration of the electromagnetic waves which are the carriers of wireless signals—was solved by Heinrich Hertz, a worker in Helmholtz's laboratory in Berlin. Neither Maxwell nor Hertz had any concern about the utility of their work; no such thought ever entered their minds. They had no practical objective. The inventor in the legal sense was of course Marconi, but what did Marconi invent? Merely the last technical detail, mainly the now obsolete receiving device called coherer, almost universally discarded."

Hertz and Maxwell could invent nothing, but it was their useless theoretical work which was seized upon by a clever technician and which has created new means for communication, utility, and amusement by which men whose merits are relatively slight have obtained fame and earned millions. Who were the useful men? Not Marconi, but Clerk Maxwell and Heinrich Hertz. Hertz and Maxwell were geniuses without thought of use. Marconi was a clever inventor with no thought but use.

The mention of Hertz's name recalled to Mr. Eastman the Hertzian waves, and I suggested that he might ask the physicists of the University of Rochester precisely what Hertz and Maxwell had done; but one thing I said he could be sure of, namely, that they had done their work without thought of use and that throughout the whole history of science most of the really great discoveries which had ultimately proved to be beneficial to mankind had been made by men and women who were driven not by the desire to be useful but merely the desire to satisfy their curiosity.

"Curiosity?" asked Mr. Eastman.

"Yes," I replied, "curiosity, which may or may not eventuate in something useful, is probably the outstanding characteristic of modern thinking. It is not new. It goes back to Galileo, Bacon, and to Sir Isaac Newton, and it must be absolutely unhampered. Institutions of learning should be devoted to the cultivation of curiosity and the less they are deflected by considerations of immediacy of application, the more likely they are to contribute not only to human welfare but to the equally important satisfaction of intellectual interest which may indeed be said to have become the ruling passion of intellectual life in modern times."

II

What is true of Heinrich Hertz working quietly and unnoticed in a corner of Helmholtz's laboratory in the later years of the nineteenth century may be said of scientist and mathematicians the world over for several centuries past.

We live in a world that would be helpless without electricity. Called upon to mention a discovery of the most immediate and far-reaching practical use we might well agree upon electricity. But who made the fundamental discoveries out of which the entire electrical development of more than one hundred years has come?

The answer is interesting. Michael Faraday's father was a blacksmith; Michael himself was apprenticed to a bookbinder. In 1812, when he was already twenty-one years of age, a friend took him to the Royal Institution where he heard Sir Humphry Davy deliver four lectures on chemical subjects. He kept notes and sent a copy of them to Davy. The very next year, 1813, he became an assistant in Davy's laboratory, working on chemical problems. Two years later he accompanied Davy on a trip to the Continent. In 1825, when he was thirty-four years of age, he became Director of the Laboratory of the Royal Institution where he spent fifty-four years of his life.

Faraday's interest soon shifted from chemistry to electricity and magnetism, to which he devoted the rest of his active life. Important but puzzling work in this field had been previously accomplished by Oersted, Ampère, and Wollaston. Faraday cleared away the difficulties which they had left unsolved and by 1841 had succeeded in the task of induction of the electric current. Four years later a second and equally brilliant epoch in his career opened when he discovered the effect of magnetism on polarized light. His earlier discoveries have led to the infinite number of practical applications by means of which electricity has lightened the burdens and increased the opportunities of modern life. His later discoveries have thus far been less prolific of practical results. What difference did this make to Faraday? Not the least. At no period of his unmatched career was he interested in utility. He was absorbed in disentangling the riddles of the universe, at first chemical riddles, in later periods, physical riddles. As far as he cared, the question of utility was never raised. Any suspicion of utility would have restricted his restless curiosity. In the end, utility resulted, but it was never a criterion to which his ceaseless experimentation could be subjected.

In the atmosphere which envelops the world to-day it is perhaps timely to emphasize the fact that the part played by science in making war more destructive and more horrible was an unconscious and unintended by-product of scientific activity. Lord Rayleigh, president of the British Association for the Advancement of Science, in a recent address points out in detail how the folly of man, not the intention of the scientists, is responsible for the destructive use of the agents employed in modern warfare. The innocent study of the chemistry of carbon compounds, which has led to infinite beneficial results, showed that the action of nitric acid on substances like benzene, glycerine, cellulose, etc., resulted not only in the beneficent aniline dye industry but in the creation of nitro-glycerine, which has uses good and bad. Somewhat later Alfred Nobel, turning to the same subject, showed that by mixing nitroglycerine with other substances, solid explosives which could be safely handled could be produced—among others, dynamite. It is to dynamite that we owe our progress in mining, in the making of such railroad tunnels as those which now pierce the Alps and other mountain ranges; but of course dynamite has been abused by politicians and soldiers. Scientists are, however, no more to blame than they are to blame for an earthquake or a flood. The same thing can be said of poison gas. Pliny was killed by breathing sulphur dioxide in the eruption of Vesuvius almost two thousand years ago. Chlorine was not isolated by scientists for warlike purposes, and the same is true of mustard gas. These substances could be limited to beneficent use, but when the airplane was perfected, men whose hearts were poisoned and whose brains were addled perceived that the airplane, an innocent invention, the result of long disinterested and scientific effort, could be made an instrument of destruction, of which no one had ever dreamed and at which no one had ever deliberately aimed.

In the domain of higher mathematics almost innumerable instances can be cited. For example, the most abstruse mathematical work of the eighteenth and nineteenth centuries was the "Non-Euclidian Geometry." Its inventor, Gauss, though recognized by his contemporaries as a distinguished mathematician, did not dare to publish his work on "Non-Euclidian Geometry" for a quarter of a century. As a matter of fact, the theory of relativity itself with all its infinite practical bearings would have been utterly impossible without the work which Gauss did at Göttingen.

Again, what is known now as "group theory" was an abstract and inapplicable mathematical theory. It was developed by men who were curious and whose curiosity and puttering led them into strange paths; but "group theory" is today the basis of the quantum theory of spectroscopy, which is in daily use by people who have no idea as to how it came about. . . .

III

I am pleading for the abolition of the word "use," and for the freeing of the human spirit. To be sure, we shall thus free some harmless cranks. To be sure, we shall thus waste some precious dollars. But what is infinitely more important is that we shall be striking the shackles off the human mind and setting it free for the adventures which in our own day have, on the one hand, taken Hale and Rutherford and Einstein and their peers millions upon millions of miles into the uttermost realms of space and, on the other, loosed the boundless energy imprisoned in the atom. What Rutherford and others like Bohr and Millikan have done out of sheer curiosity in the effort to understand the construction of the atom has released forces which may transform human life; but this ultimate and unforeseen and unpredictable practical result is not offered as a justification for Rutherford or Einstein or Millikan or Bohr or any of their peers. Let them alone. No educational administrator can possibly direct the channels in which these or other men shall work. The waste, I admit again, looks prodigious. It is not really so. All the waste that could be summed up in developing the science of bacteriology is as nothing compared to the advantages which have accrued from the discoveries of Pasteur, Koch, Ehrlich, Theobald Smith, and scores of others—advantages that could never have accrued if the idea of possible use had permeated their minds. These great artists —for such are scientists and bacteriologists—disseminated the spirit which prevailed in laboratories in which they were simply following the line of their own natural curiosity.

I am not criticising institutions like schools of engineering or law in which the usefulness motive necessarily predominates. Not infrequently the tables are turned, and practical difficulties encountered in industry or in laboratories stimulate theoretical inquiries which may or may not solve the problems by which they were suggested, but may also open up new vistas, useless at the moment, but pregnant with future achievements, practical and theoretical.

With the rapid accumulation of "useless" or theoretic knowledge a situation has been created in which it has become increasingly possible to attack practical problems in a scientific spirit. Not only inventors, but "pure" scientists have indulged in this sport. I have mentioned Marconi, an inventor, who, while a benefactor to the human race, as a matter of fact merely "picked other men's brains." Edison belongs to the same category. Pasteur was different. He was a great scientist; but he was not averse to attacking practical problems—such as the condition of French grapevines or the problems of beer-brewing—and not only solving the immediate difficulty, but also wresting from the practical problem some far-reaching theoretic conclusion, "useless" at the moment, but likely in some unforeseen manner to be "useful" later. Ehrlich, fundamentally speculative in his curiosity, turned fiercely upon the problem of syphilis and doggedly pursued it until a solution of immediate practical use—the discovery of salvarsan—was found. The discoveries of insulin by Banting for use in diabetes and of liver extract by Minot and Whipple for use in pernicious anemia belong in the same category; both were made by thoroughly scientific men, who realized that much "useless" knowledge had been piled up by men unconcerned with its practical bearings, but that the time was now ripe to raise practical questions in a scientific manner.

Thus it becomes obvious that one must be wary in attributing scientific discovery wholly to any one person. Almost every discovery has a long and precarious history. Some one finds a bit here, another a bit there. A third step succeeds later and thus onward till a genius pieces the bits together and makes the decisive contribution. Science, like the Mississippi, begins in a tiny rivulet in the distant forest. Gradually other streams swell its volume. And the roaring river that bursts the dikes is formed from countless sources.

I cannot deal with this aspect exhaustively, but I may in passing say this: over a period of one or two hundred years the contributions of professional schools to their respective activities will probably be found to lie, not so much in the training of men who may to-morrow become practical engineers or practical lawyers or practical doctors, but rather in the fact that even in the pursuit of strictly practical aims an enormous amount of apparently useless activity goes on. Out of this useless activity there come discoveries which may well prove of infinitely more importance to the human mind and to the human spirit than the accomplishment of the useful ends for which the schools were founded.

The considerations upon which I have touched emphasize—if emphasis were needed—the overwhelming importance of spiritual and intellectual freedom. I have spoken of experimental science; I have spoken of mathematics; but what I say is equally true of music and art and of every other expression of the untrammeled human spirit. The mere fact that they bring satisfaction to an individual soul bent upon its own purification and elevation is all the justification that they need. And in justifying these without any reference whatsoever, implied or actual, to usefulness we justify colleges, universities, and institutes of research. An institution which sets free successive generations of human souls is amply justified whether or not this graduate or that makes a so-called useful contribution to human knowledge. A poem, a symphony, a painting, a mathematical truth, a new scientific fact, all bear in themselves all the justification that universities, colleges, and institutes of research need or require. . . .

This is not a new idea. It was the idea which animated von Humboldt when, in the hour of Germany's conquest by Napoleon, he conceived and founded the University of Berlin. It is the idea which animated President Gilman in the founding of the Johns Hopkins University, after which every university in this country has sought in greater or less degree to remake itself. It is the idea to which every individual who values his immortal soul will be true whatever the personal consequences to himself.

The Sciences

❀❖❀

ARTHUR STANLEY EDDINGTON

The Evolution of the Physical World[1]

Looking back through the long past we picture the beginning of the world —a primeval chaos which time has fashioned into the universe that we know. Its vastness appalls the mind; space boundless though not infinite, according to the strange doctrine of science. The world was without form and almost void.

[1] From Arthur Stanley Eddington, Science and the Unseen World, 1930, pp. 11-21. Copyright, 1930, by The Macmillan Company. By permission of The Macmillan Company, publishers.

But at the earliest stage we can contemplate the void is sparsely broken by tiny electric particles, the germs of the things that are to be; positive and negative they wander aimlessly in solitude, rarely coming near enough to seek or shun one another. They range everywhere so that all space is filled, and yet so empty that in comparison the most highly exhausted vacuum on earth is a jostling throng. In the beginning was vastness, solitude and the deepest night. Darkness was upon the face of the deep, for as yet there was no light.

The years rolled by, million after million. Slight aggregations occurring casually in one place and another drew to themselves more and more particles. They warred for sovereignty, won and lost their spoil, until the matter was collected round centers of condensation leaving vast empty spaces from which it had ebbed away. Thus gravitation slowly parted the primeval chaos. These first divisions were not the stars but what we should call "island universes" each ultimately to be a system of some thousands of millions of stars. From our own island universe we can discern the other islands as spiral nebulae lying one beyond another as far as the telescope can fathom. The nearest of them is such that light takes 900,000 years to cross the gulf between us. They acquired rotation (we do not yet understand how) which bulged them into flattened form and made them wreathe themselves in spirals. Their forms, diverse, yet with underlying regularity, make a fascinating spectacle for telescopic study.

As it had divided the original chaos, so gravitation subdivided the island universes. First the star clusters, then the stars themselves were separated. And with the stars came light, born of the fiercer turmoil which ensued when the electrical particles were drawn from their solitude into dense throngs. A star is not just a lump of matter casually thrown together in the general confusion; it is of nicely graded size. There is relatively not much more diversity in the masses of new-born stars than in the masses of new-born babies. Aggregations rather greater than our Sun have a strong tendency to subdivide, but when the mass is reduced a little the danger quickly passes and the impulse to subdivision is satisfied. Here it would seem the work of creation might cease. Having carved chaos into stars, the first evolutionary impulse has reached its goal. For many billions of years the stars may continue to shed their light and heat through the world, feeding on their own matter which disappears bit by bit into aetherial waves.

Not infrequently a star, spinning too fast or strained by the radiant heat imprisoned within it, may divide into two nearly equal stars, which remain yoked together as a double star; apart from this no regular plan of further development is known. For what might be called the second day of creation we turn from the general rule to the exceptions. Amid so many myriads there will be a few which by some rare accident have a fate unlike the rest. In the vast expanse of the heavens the traffic is so thin that a star may reasonably count on travelling for the whole of its long life without serious risk of collision. The risk is negligible for any individual star, but ten thousand million stars in our own system and more in the systems beyond afford a wide playground for chance. If the risk is one in a hundred millions some unlucky victims are doomed to play the role of "one." This rare accident must have happened to our Sun—an accident to the Sun, but to us the cause of our being here. A star journeying through space casually overtook the Sun, not indeed colliding with it, but approaching so close as to raise a great tidal wave. By this disturbance jets of matter spurted out of the Sun; being carried round by their angular momentum they did not fall back again but condensed into small globes—the planets.

By this and similar events there appeared here and there in the universe something outside Nature's regular plan, namely a lump of matter small enough and dense enough to be cool. A temperature of ten million degrees or more prevails through the greater part of the interior of a star; it cannot be otherwise so long as matter remains heaped in immense masses. Thus the design of the first stage of evolution seems to have been that matter should ordinarily be endowed with intense heat. Cool matter appears as an afterthought. It is unlikely that the Sun is the only one of the starry host to possess a system of planets, but it is believed that such development is very rare. In these exceptional formations Nature has tried the experiment of finding what strange effects may ensue if matter is released from its usual temperature of millions of degrees and permitted to be cool.

Out of the electric charges dispersed in the primitive chaos ninety-two different kinds of matter—ninety-two chemical elements—have been built. This building is also a work of evolution, but little or nothing is known as to its history. In the matter which we handle daily we find the original bricks fitted together and cannot but infer that somewhere and somewhen a process of matter-building has occurred. At high temperature this diversity of matter remains as it were latent; little of consequence results from it. But in the cool experimental stations of the universe the differences assert themselves. At root the diversity of the ninety-two elements reflects the diversity of the integers from one to ninety-two; because the chemical characteristics of element No. 11 (sodium) arise from the fact that it has the power at low temperatures of gathering round it eleven negative electric particles; those of No. 12 (magnesium) from its power of gathering twelve particles; and so on.

It is tempting to linger over the development out of this fundamental beginning of the wonders studied in chemistry and physics, but we must hurry on. The provision of certain cool planetary globes was the second impulse of evolution, and it has exhausted itself in the formation of inorganic rocks and ores and other materials. We must look to a new exception or abnormality if anything further is to be achieved. We can scarcely call it an accident that among the integers there should happen to be the number 6; but I do not know how otherwise to express the fact that organic life would not have begun if Nature's arithmetic had overlooked the number 6. The general plan of ninety-two elements, each embodying in its structural pattern one of the first ninety-two numbers, contemplates a material world of considerable but limited diversity;

but the element carbon, embodying the number 6, and because of the peculiarity of the number 6, rebels against limits. The carbon atoms love to string themselves in long chains such as those which give toughness to a soap-film. Whilst other atoms organise themselves in twos and threes or it may be in tens, carbon atoms organise themselves in hundreds and thousands. From this potentiality of carbon to form more and more elaborate structures, a third impulse of evolution arises.

I cannot profess to say whether anything more than this prolific structure-building power of carbon is involved in the beginning of life. The story of evolution here passes into the domain of the biological sciences for which I cannot speak, and I am not ready to take sides in the controversy between the Mechanists and the Vitalists. So far as the earth is concerned the history of development of living forms extending over nearly a thousand million years is recorded (though with many breaks) in fossil remains. Looking back over the geological record it would seem that Nature made nearly every possible mistake before she reached her greatest achievement Man—or perhaps some would say her worst mistake of all. At one time she put her trust in armaments and gigantic size. Frozen in the rock is the evidence of her failures to provide a form fitted to endure and dominate—failures which we are only too ready to imitate. At last she tried a being of no great size, almost defenceless, defective in at least one of the more important sense-organs; one gift she bestowed to save him from threatened extinction—a certain stirring, a restlessness, in the organ called the brain.

And so we come to Man.

DONALD CULROSS PEATTIE

Chlorophyll: The Sun Trap[1]

What we love, when on a summer day we step into the coolness of a wood, is that its boughs close up behind us. We are escaped, into another room of life. The wood does not live as we live, restless and running, panting after flesh, and even in sleep tossing with fears. It is aloof from thoughts and instincts; it responds, but only to the sun and wind, the rock and the stream— never, though you shout yourself hoarse, to propaganda, temptation, reproach, or promises. You cannot mount a rock and preach to a tree how it shall attain the kingdom of heaven. It is already closer to it, up there, than you will grow to be. And you cannot make it see the light since in the tree's sense you are blind. You have nothing to bring it, for all the forest is self-sufficient; if you burn it, cut, hack through it with a blade, it angrily repairs the swathe

[1] From *Flowering Earth* by Donald Culross Peattie copyright 1939. G. P. Putnam's Sons.

with thorns and weeds and fierce suckers. Later there are good green leaves again, toiling, adjusting, breathing—forgetting you.

For this green living is the world's primal industry; yet it makes no roar. Waving its banners, it marches across the earth and the ages, without dust around its columns. I do not hold that all of that life is pretty; it is not, in purpose, sprung for us, and moves under no compulsion to please. If ever you fought with thistles, or tried to pull up a cattail's matted root-stocks, you will know how plants cling to their own lives and defy you. The pond-scums gather in the cistern, frothing and buoyed with their own gases; the storm waves fling at your feet upon the beach the limp sea-lettuce wrenched from its submarine hold—reminder that there too, where the light is filtered and refracted, there is life still to intercept and net and by it proliferate. Inland from the shore I look and see the coastal ranges clothed in chaparral—dense shrubbery and scrubbery, close-fisted, intricately branched, suffocating the rash rambler in the noon heat with its pungency. Beyond, on the deserts, under a fierce sky, between the harsh lunar ranges of unweathered rock, life still, somehow, fights its way through the year, with thorn and succulent cell and indomitable root.

Between such embattled life and the Forest of Arden, with its ancient beeches and enchanter's nightshade, there is no great biologic difference. Each lives by the cool and cleanly and most commendable virtue of being green. And though that is not biological language, it is the whole story in two words. So that we ought not to speak of getting at the root of a matter, but of going back to the leaf of things. The orator who knows the way to the country's salvation and does not know that the breath of life he draws was blown into his nostrils by green leaves, had better spare his breath. And before anyone builds a new state upon the industrial proletariat, he will be wisely cautioned to discover that the source of all wealth is the peasantry of grass.

The reason for these assertions—which I do not make for metaphorical effect but maintain quite literally—is that the green leaf pigment, called chlorophyll, is the one link between the sun and life; it is the conduit of perpetual energy to our own frail organisms.

For inert and inorganic elements—water and carbon dioxide of the air, the same that we breathe out as a waste—chlorophyll can synthesize with the energy of sunlight. Every day, every hour of all the ages, as each continent and, equally important, each ocean rolls into sunlight, chlorophyll ceaselessly creates. Not figuratively, but literally, in the grand First Chapter Genesis style. One instant there are a gas and water, as lifeless as the core of earth or the chill of space; and the next they are become living tissue—mortal yet genitive, progenitive, resilient with all the dewy adaptability of flesh, ever changing in order to stabilize some unchanging ideal of form. Life, in short, synthesized, plant-synthesized, light-synthesized. Botanists say photosynthesized. So that the post-Biblical synthesis of life is already a fact. Only when man has done as much, may he call himself the equal of a weed.

Plant life sustains the living world; more precisely, chlorophyll does so, and where, in the vegetable kingdom, there is not chlorophyll or something closely like it, then that plant or cell is a parasite—no better, in vital economy, than a mere animal or man. Blood, bone and sinew, all flesh is grass. Grass to mutton, mutton to wool, wool to the coat on my back—it runs like one of these cumulative nursery rhymes, the wealth and diversity of our material life accumulating from the primal fact of chlorophyll's activity. The roof of my house, the snapping logs upon the hearth, the desk where I write, are my imports from the plant kingdom. But the whole of modern civilization is based upon a whirlwind spending of the plant wealth long ago and very slowly accumulated. For, fundamentally, and away back, coal and oil, gasoline and illuminating gas had green origins too. With the exception of a small amount of water power, a still smaller of wind and tidal mills, the vast machinery of our complex living is driven only by these stores of plant energy.

We, then, the animals, consume those stores in our restless living. Serenely the plants amass them. They turn light's active energy to food, which is potential energy stored for their own benefit. Only if the daisy is browsed by the cow, the maple leaf sucked of its juices by an insect, will that green leaf· become of our kind. So we get the song of a bird at dawn, the speed in the hoofs of the fleeing deer, the noble thought in the philosopher's mind. So Plato's Republic was builded on leeks and cabbages.

Animal life lives always in the red; the favorable balance is written on the other side of life's page, and it is written in chlorophyll. All else obeys the thermodynamic law that energy forever runs down hill, is lost and degraded. In economic language, this is the law of diminishing returns, and it is obeyed by the cooling stars as by man and all the animals. They float down its Lethe stream. Only chlorophyll fights up against the current. It is the stuff in life that rebels at death, that has never surrendered to entropy, final icy stagnation. It is the mere cobweb on which we are all suspended over the abyss.

And what then is this substance which is not itself alive but is made by life and makes life, and is never found apart from life?

I remember the first time I ever held it, in the historic dimness of the old Agassiz laboratories, pure, in my hands. My teacher was an owl-eyed master, with a chuckling sense of humor, who had been trained in the greatest laboratory in Germany, and he believed in doing the great things first. So on the first day of his course he set us to extracting chlorophyll, and I remember that his eyes blinked amusement behind his glasses, because when he told us all to go and collect green leaves and most went all the way to the Yard for grass, I opened the window and stole from a vine upon the wall a handful of Harvard's sacred ivy.

We worked in pairs, and my fellow student was a great-grand-nephew or something of the sort, of Elias Fries, the founder of the study of fungi. Together we boiled the ivy leaves, then thrust them in alcohol. After a while it was the leaves which were colorless while the alcohol had become green. We had to dilute this extract with water, and then we added benzol, because this will take the chlorophyll away from the alcohol which, for its part, very conveniently retains the yellow pigments also found in leaves. This left us with a now yellowish alcohol and, floating on top of it, a thick green benzol; you could simply decant the latter carefully off into a test tube, and there you had chlorophyll extract, opaque, trembling, heavy, a little viscous and oily, and smelling, but much too rankly, like a lawn-mower's blades after a battle with rainy grass.

Then, in a darkened room where beams from a spectroscope escaped in painful darts of light as from the cracks in an old-fashioned magic lantern, we peered at our extracted chlorophyll through prisms. Just as in a crystal chandelier the sunlight is shattered to a rainbow, so in the spectroscope light is spread out in colored bands—a long narrow ribbon, sorting the white light by wave lengths into its elemental parts. And the widths, the presence or the absence, of each cross-band on the ribbon, tell the tale of a chemical element present in the spectrum, much as the bands on a soldier's insignia ribbon show service in Asia, in the tropics, on the border, in what wars. When the astronomer has fixed spectroscope instead of telescope upon a distant star, he reads off the color bands as easily as one soldier reads another's, and will tell you whether sodium or oxygen, helium or iron is present.

Just so our chlorophyll revealed its secrets. The violet and blue end of the spectrum was almost completely blacked out. And that meant that chlorophyll absorbed and used these high-frequency waves. So, too, the red and orange were largely obliterated, over at the right hand side of our tell-tale bar. It was the green that came through clearly. So we call plants green because they use that color least. It is what they reject as fast as it smites the upper cells; it is what they turn back, reflect, flash into our grateful retinas.

It was only routine in a young botanist's training to make an extraction and spectrum analysis of chlorophyll. My student friends over in the chemistry laboratories were more excited than I about it. They were working under Conant, before he became president of Harvard and had to sneak into his old laboratory at night with a key he still keeps. For chlorophyll was Conant's own problem. His diagram of its structure, displayed to me by his students, was closely worked over with symbols and signs, unfolded to something like the dimensions of a blue print of Boulder Dam, and made clear—to anyone who could understand it!—how the atoms are arranged and deployed and linked in such a tremendous molecule as $MgN_4C_{55}H_{72}O_5$.

To Otto and Alfred and Mort every jot and joint in the vast Rube Goldberg machinery of that structural formula had meaning, and more than meaning—the geometrical beauty of the one right, inevitable position for every atom. To me, a botanist's apprentice, a future naturalist, there was just one fact to quicken the pulse. That fact is the close similarity between chlorophyll and hemoglobin, the essence of our blood.

So that you may lay your hand upon the smooth flank of a beech and say, "We be of one blood, brother, thou and I."

The one significant difference in the two structural formulas is this: that the hub of every hemoglobin molecule is one atom of iron, while in chlorophyll it is one atom of magnesium.

Iron is strong and heavy, clamorous when struck, avid of oxygen and capable of corruption. It does not surprise us by its presence in our blood stream. Magnesium is a light, silvery, unresonant metal; its density is only one seventh that of iron, it has half of iron's molecular weight, and melts at half the temperature. It is rustless, ductile and pliant; it burns with a brilliant white light rich in actinic rays, and is widely distributed through the upper soil, but only, save at mineral springs, in dainty quantities. Yet the plant succeeds always in finding that mere trace that it needs, even when a chemist might fail to detect it.

How does the chlorophyll, green old alchemist that it is, transmute the dross of earth into living tissue? Its hand is swifter than the chemist's most sensitive analyses. In theory, the step from water and carbon dioxide to the formation of sugar (the first result readily discerned) must involve several syntheses; yet it goes on in a split hundredth of a second. One sunlight particle or photon strikes the chlorophyll, and instantaneously the terribly tenacious molecule of water, which we break down into its units of hydrogen and oxygen only with difficulty and expense, is torn apart; so too is the carbon dioxide molecule. Building blocks of the three elements, carbon, hydrogen and oxygen, are then whipped at lightning speed into carbonic acid; this is instantly changed over into formic acid—the same that smarts so in our nerve endings when an ant stings us. No sooner formed than formic acid becomes formaldehyde and hydrogen peroxide. This last is poisonous, but a ready enzyme in the plant probably splits it as fast as it is born into harmless water and oxygen, while the formaldehyde is knocked at top speed into a new pattern—and is grape sugar, glucose. And all before you can say Albert Einstein. Indeed, by the time you have said Theophrastus Bombastus Aureolus Paracelsus von Hohenheim, the sugar may have lost a modicum of water—and turned into starch, the first product of photosynthesis that could be detected by the methods of fifty years ago.

At this very instant, with the sun delivering to its child the earth, in the bludgeoning language of mathematics, 215×10^{15} calories per second, photosynthesis is racing along wherever the leaf can reach the light. (All else goes to waste.) True, its efficiency is very low—averaging no better than one per cent, while our machines are delivering up to twenty-five per cent of the fuel they combust. But that which they burn—coal and gas, oils and wood—was made, once, by leaves in ancient geologic times. The store of such energy is strictly finite. Chlorophyll alone is hitched to what is, for earthly purposes, the infinite.

Light, in the latest theory, is not waves in a sea of ether, or a jet from a nozzle; it could be compared rather to machine gun fire, every photo-electric bullet of energy traveling in regular rhythm, at a speed that bridges the astronomical gap in eight minutes. As each bullet hits an electron of chlorophyll it sets it to vibrating, at its own rate, just as one tuning fork, when struck, will cause another to hum in the same pitch. A bullet strikes—and one electron is knocked galley west into a dervish dance like the madness of the atoms in the sun. The energy splits open chlorophyll molecules, recombines their atoms, and lies there, dormant, in foods.

The process seems miraculously adjusted. And yet, like most living processes it is not perfect. The reaction time of chlorophyll is not geared as high as the arrival of the light-bullets. Light comes too fast; plants, which are the very children of light, can get too much of it. Exposure to the sunlight on the Mojave desert is something that not a plant in my garden, no, nor even the wiry brush in the chaparral, could endure. Lids against the light plants do not have; but by torsions of the stalk some leaves may turn their blades edge-on to dazzling radiation, and present them again broadside in failing light. Within others the chlorophyll granules too, bun or pellet-shaped as they are, can roll for a side or frontal exposure toward the light. In others they can crowd to the top of a cell and catch faint rays, or sink or flee to the sides to escape a searing blast. . . .

When I began to write these pages, before breakfast, the little fig tree outside my window was rejoicing in the early morning light. It is a special familiar of my work, a young tree that has never yet borne fruit. It is but a little taller than I, has only two main branches and forty-three twigs, and the brave if not impressive sum of two hundred and sixteen leaves—I have touched every one with a counting finger. Though sparse, they are large, mitten-shaped, richly green with chlorophyll. I compute, by measuring the leaf and counting both sides, that my little tree has a leaf surface of about eighty-four square feet. This sun-trap was at work today long before I.

Those uplifted hand-like leaves caught the first sky light. It was poor for the fig's purpose, but plant work begins from a nocturnal zero. When I came to my desk the sun was full upon those leaves—and it is a wondrous thing how they are disposed so that they do not shade each other. By the blazing California noon, labor in the leaves must have faltered from very excess of light; all the still golden afternoon it went on; now as the sun sets behind a sea fog the little fig slackens peacefully at its task.

Yet in the course of a day it has made sugar for immediate burning and energy release, put by a store of starch for future use; with the addition of nitrogen and other salts brought up in water from the roots it has built proteins too—the very bricks and mortar of the living protoplasm, and the perdurable stuff of permanent tissue. The annual growth ring in the wood of stem and twigs has widened an infinitesimal but a real degree. The fig is one day nearer to its coming of age, to flowering and fruiting. Then, still leafing out each spring, still toiling in the sunlight that I shall not be here to see, it may go on a century and more, growing eccentric, solidifying whimsies, becoming a friend to generations. It will be "the old fig" then. And at last it may give up the very exertion of bearing. It will lean tough elbows in the garden walks, and gardeners yet unborn will scold it and put up with it. But still it will leaf out till it dies.

Dusk is here now. So I switch on the lamp beside my desk. The powerhouse burns its hoarded tons of coal a week, and gives us this instant and most marvelous current. But that light is not new. It was hurled out of the sun two hundred million years ago, and was captured by the leaves of the Carboniferous tree-fern forests, fell with the falling plant, was buried, fossilized, dug up and resurrected. It is the same light. And, in my little fig tree as in the ancient ferns, it is the same unchanging green stuff from age to age, passed without perceptible improvement from evolving plant to plant. What it is and does, so complex upon examination, lies about us tranquil and simple, with the simplicity of a miracle.

WILLIAM HARVEY

Of the Quantity of Blood Passing through the Heart[1]

Thus far I have spoken of the passage of the blood from the veins into the arteries, and of the manner in which it is transmitted and distributed by the action of the heart; points to which some, moved either by the authority of Galen or Columbus, or the reasonings of others, will give in their adhesion. But what remains to be said upon the quantity and source of the blood which thus passes, is of so novel and unheard-of character, that I not only fear injury to myself from the envy of a few, but I tremble lest I have mankind at large for my enemies, so much doth wont and custom, that become as another nature, and doctrine once sown and that hath struck deep root, and respect for antiquity influence all men: Still the die is cast, and my trust is in my love of truth, and the candour that inheres in cultivated minds. And sooth to say, when I surveyed my mass of evidence, whether derived from vivisec-

[1] From William Harvey, *On the Motion of the Heart and Blood in Animals*, Robert Willis trans., revised by Alexander Bowie in *Scientific Papers, Physiology, Medicine, Surgery, Geology* (New York: P. F. Collier & Son Corporation, 1910), p. 382. Reprinted by permission of the publishers.

tions, and my various reflections on them, or from the ventricles of the heart and the vessels that enter into and issue from them, the symmetry and size of these conduits—for nature doing nothing in vain, would never have given them so large a relative size without a purpose—or from the arrangement and intimate structure of the valves in particular, and of the other parts of the heart in general, with many things besides, I frequently and seriously bethought me, and long revolved in my mind, what might be the quantity of blood which was transmitted, in how short a time its passage might be effected, and the like; and not finding it possible that this could be supplied by the juices of the ingested aliment without the veins on the one hand becoming drained, and the arteries on the other getting ruptured through the excessive charge of blood, unless the blood should somehow find its way from the arteries into the veins, and so return to the right side of the heart; I began to think whether there might not be a MOTION, AS IT WERE, IN A CIRCLE. Now this I afterwards found to be true; and I finally saw that the blood, forced by the action of the left ventricle into the arteries, was distributed to the body at large, and its several parts, in the same manner as it is sent through the lungs, impelled by the right ventricle into the pulmonary artery, and that it then passed through the veins and along the vena cava, and so round to the left ventricle in the manner already indicated. Which motion we may be allowed to call circular, in the same way as Aristotle says that the air and the rain emulate the circular motion of the superior bodies; for the moist earth, warmed by the sun, evaporates; the vapours drawn upwards are condensed, and descending in the form of rain, moisten the earth again; and by this arrangement are generations of living things produced; and in like manner too are tempests and meteors engendered by the circular motion, and by the approach and recession of the sun.

And so, in all likelihood, does it come to pass in the body, through the motion of the blood; the various parts are nourished, cherished, quickened by the warmer, more perfect, vaporous, spirituous, and, as I may say, alimentive blood; which, on the contrary, in contact with these parts becomes cooled, coagulated, and, so to speak, effete; whence it returns to its sovereign the heart, as if to its source, or to the inmost home of the body, there to recover its state of excellence or perfection. Here it resumes its due fluidity and receives an infusion of natural heat—powerful, fervid, a kind of treasury of life, and is impregnated with spirits, and it might be said with balsam; and thence it is again dispersed; and all this depends on the motion and action of the heart.

The heart, consequently, is the beginning of life; the sun of the microcosm, even as the sun in his turn might well be designated the heart of the world; for it is the heart by whose virtue and pulse the blood is moved, perfected, made apt to nourish, and is preserved from corruption and coagulation; it is the household divinity which, discharging its function, nourishes, cherishes, quickens the whole body, and is indeed the foundation of life, the source of all action. But of these things we shall speak more opportunely when we come to speculate upon the final cause of this motion of the heart.

Hence, since the veins are the conduits and vessels that transport the blood, they are of two kinds, the cava and the aorta; and this not by reason of there being two sides of the body, as Aristotle has it, but because of the difference of office; nor yet, as is commonly said, in consequence of any diversity of structure, for in many animals, as I have said, the vein does not differ from the artery in the thickness of its tunics, but solely in virtue of their several destinies and uses. A vein and an artery, both styled vein by the ancients, and that not undeservedly, as Galen has remarked, because the one, the artery to wit, is the vessel which carries the blood from the heart to the body at large, the other or vein of the present day bringing it back from the general system to the heart; the former is the conduit from, the latter the channel to, the heart; the latter contains the cruder, effete blood, rendered unfit for nutrition; the former transmits the digested, perfect, peculiarly nutritive fluid.

CLAUDE BERNARD

Carbon Monoxide Poisoning[1]

About 1846, I wished to make experiments on the cause of poisoning with carbon monoxide. I knew that this gas had been described as toxic, but I knew literally nothing about the mechanism of its poisoning; I therefore could not have a preconceived opinion. What, then, was to be done? I must bring to birth an idea by making a fact appear, i.e., make another experiment to see. In fact I poisoned a dog by making him breathe carbon monoxide and after death I at once opened his body. I looked at the state of the organs and fluids. What caught my attention at once was that its blood was scarlet in all the vessels, in the veins as well as the arteries, in the right heart as well as in the left. I repeated the experiment on rabbits, birds and frogs, and everywhere I found the same scarlet coloring of the blood. But I was diverted from continuing this investigation, and I kept this observation a long time unused except for quoting it in my course a propos of the coloring of blood.

In 1856, no one had carried the experimental question further, and in my course at the Collège de France on toxic and medicinal substances, I again took up the study of poisoning by carbon monoxide which I had begun in 1846. I found myself then in a confused situation, for at this time I already knew that poisoning with carbon monoxide makes the blood scarlet in the

1 From Claude Bernard, An Introduction to the Study of Experimental Medicine, translated by Henry Copley Greene (New York: The Macmillan Company, 1927), pp. 159-161. Reprinted by permission of the General Education Board.

whole circulatory system. I had to make hypotheses, and establish a preconceived idea about my first observation, so as to go ahead. Now, reflecting on the fact of scarlet blood, I tried to interpret it by my earlier knowledge as to the cause of the color of blood. Whereupon all the following reflections presented themselves to my mind. The scarlet color, said I, is peculiar to arterial blood and connected with the presence of a large proportion of oxygen, while dark coloring belongs with absence of oxygen and presence of a larger proportion of carbonic acid; so the idea occurred to me that carbon monoxide, by keeping venous blood scarlet, might perhaps have prevented the oxygen from changing into carbonic acid in the capillaries. Yet it seemed hard to understand how that could be the cause of death. But still keeping on with my inner preconceived reasoning, I added: If that is true, blood taken from the veins of animals poisoned with carbon monoxide should be like arterial blood in containing oxygen; we must see if that is the fact.

Following this reasoning, based on interpretation of my observation, I tried an experiment to verify my hypothesis as to the persistence of oxygen in the venous blood. I passed a current of hydrogen through scarlet venous blood taken from an animal poisoned with carbon monoxide, but I could not liberate the oxygen as usual. I tried to do the same with arterial blood; I had no greater success. My preconceived idea was therefore false. But the impossibility of getting oxygen from the blood of a dog poisoned with carbon monoxide was a second observation which suggested a fresh hypothesis. What could have become of the oxygen in the blood? It had not changed with carbonic acid, because I had not set free large quantities of that gas in passing a current of hydrogen through the blood of the poisoned animals. Moreover, that hypothesis was contrary to the color of the blood. I exhausted myself in conjectures about how carbon monoxide could cause the oxygen to disappear from the blood; and as gases displace one another I naturally thought that the carbon monoxide might have displaced the oxygen and driven it out of the blood. To learn this, I decided to vary my experimentation by putting the blood in artificial conditions that would allow me to recover the displaced oxygen. So I studied the action of carbon monoxide on blood experimentally. For this purpose I took a certain amount of arterial blood from a healthy animal; I put this blood on the mercury in an inverted test tube containing carbon monoxide; I then shook the whole thing so as to poison the blood sheltered from contact with the outer air. Then, after an interval, I examined whether the air in the test tube in contact with the poisoned blood had been changed, and I noted that the air thus in contact with the blood had been remarkably enriched with oxygen, while the proportion of carbon monoxide was lessened. Repeated in the same conditions, these experiments taught me that what had occurred was an exchange, volume by volume, between the carbon monoxide and the oxygen of the blood. But the carbon monoxide, in displacing the oxygen that it had expelled from the blood, remained chemically combined in the blood and could no longer be displaced either by oxygen or by other gases. So that death came through death of the molecules of blood, or in other words by stopping their exercises of a physiological property essential to life.

This last example, which I have very briefly described, is complete; it shows from one end to the other, how we proceed with the experimental method and succeed in learning the immediate cause of phenomena. To begin with I knew literally nothing about the mechanism of the phenomenon of poisoning with carbon monoxide. I undertook an experiment to see, i.e., to observe. I made a preliminary observation of a special change in the coloring of blood. I interpreted this observation, and I made an hypothesis which proved false. But the experiment provided me with a second observation about which I reasoned anew, using it as a starting point for making a new hypothesis as to the mechanism, by which the oxygen in the blood was removed. By building up hypotheses, one by one, about the facts as I observed them, I finally succeeded in showing that carbon monoxide replaces oxygen in a molecule of blood, by combining with the substance of the molecule. Experimental analysis, here, has reached its goal. This is one of the cases, rare in physiology, which I am happy to be able to quote. Here the immediate cause of the phenomenon of poisoning is found and is translated into a theory which accounts for all the facts and at the same time includes all the observations and experiments. Formulated as follows, the theory posits the main facts from which all the rest are deduced: Carbon monoxide combines more intimately than oxygen with the hemoglobin in a molecule of blood. It has quite recently been proved that carbon monoxide forms a definite combination with hemoglobin. So that the molecule of blood, as if petrified by the stability of the combination, loses its vital properties. Hence everything is logically deduced: because of its property of more intimate combination, carbon monoxide drives out of the blood the oxygen essential to life; the molecules of blood become inert, and the animal dies, with symptoms of hemorrhage, from true paralysis of the molecules.

Freud. Translated by W. J. H. Sprott.

SIGMUND FREUD
The Anatomy of the Mental Personality[1]

Ladies and Gentlemen—I am sure you all recognise in your dealings, whether with persons or things, the importance of your starting-point. It was the same with psycho-analysis: the course of development through which it has

[1] From *New Introductory Lectures in Psycho-Analysis* by Sigmund Freud, by permission of W. W. Norton & Company, Inc. Copyright 1933 by Sigmund

passed, and the reception which it has met with have not been unaffected by the fact that what it began working upon was the symptom, a thing which is more foreign to the ego than anything else in the mind. The symptom has its origin in the repressed, it is as it were the representative of the repressed in relation to the ego; the repressed is a foreign territory to the ego, an internal foreign territory, just as reality is—you must excuse the unusual expression—an external foreign territory. From the symptom the path of psycho-analysis led to the unconscious, to the life of the instincts, to sexuality, and it was then that psycho-analysis was met by illuminating criticisms to the effect that man is not merely a sexual being but has nobler and higher feelings. It might have been added that, supported by the consciousness of those higher feelings, he often allowed himself the right to think nonsense and to overlook facts.

You know better than that. From the very beginning our view was that men fall ill owing to the conflict between the demands of their instincts and the internal resistance which is set up against them; not for a moment did we forget this resisting, rejecting and repressing factor, which we believed to be furnished with its own special forces, the ego-instincts, and which corresponds to the ego of popular psychology. The difficulty was that, since the progress of all scientific work is necessarily laborious, psycho-analysis could not study every part of the field at once or make a pronouncement on every problem in one breath. At last we had got so far that we could turn our attention from the repressed to the repressing forces, and we came face to face with the ego, which seemed to need so little explanation, with the certain expectation that there, too, we should find things for which we could not have been prepared; but it was not easy to find a first method of approach. That is what I am going to talk to you about to-day.

Before I start, I may tell you that I have a suspicion that my account of the psychology of the ego will affect you differently than the introduction into the psychological underworld that preceded it. Why that should be the case, I cannot say for certain. My original explanation was that you would feel that, whereas hitherto I have been telling you in the main about facts, however strange and odd they might appear, this time you would be listening chiefly to theories, that is to say, speculations. But that is not quite true; when I weighed the matter more carefully I was obliged to conclude that the part played by intellectual manipulation of the facts is not much greater in our ego-psychology than it was in the psychology of the neuroses. Other explanations turned out to be equally untenable, and I now think that the character of the material itself is responsible, and the fact that we are not accustomed to dealing with it. Anyhow I shall not be surprised if you are more hesitant and careful in your judgment than you have been hitherto.

The situation in which we find ourselves at the beginning of our investigation will itself suggest the path we have to follow. We wish to make the ego the object of our study, our own ego. But how can we do that? The ego is the subject *par excellence*, how can it become the object? There is no doubt, however, that it can. The ego can take itself as object, it can treat itself like any other object, observe itself, criticise itself, and do Heaven knows what besides with itself. In such a case one part of the ego stands over against the other. The ego can, then, be split; it splits when it performs many of its functions, at least for the time being. The parts can afterwards join up again. After all that is saying nothing new; perhaps it is only underlining more than usual something that every one knows already. But on the other hand we are familiar with the view that pathology, with its magnification and exaggeration, can make us aware of normal phenomena which we should otherwise have missed. Where pathology displays a breach or a cleft, under normal conditions there may well be a link. If we throw a crystal to the ground, it breaks, but it does not break haphazard; in accordance with the lines of cleavage it falls into fragments, whose limits were already determined by the structure of the crystal, although they were invisible. Psychotics are fissured and splintered structures such as these. We cannot deny them a measure of that awe with which madmen were regarded by the peoples of ancient times. They have turned away from external reality, but for that very reason they know more of internal psychic reality and can tell us much that would otherwise be inaccessible to us. One group of them suffer what we call delusions of observation. They complain to us that they suffer continually, and in their most intimate actions, from the observation of unknown powers or persons, and they have hallucinations in which they hear these persons announcing the results of their observations: "now he is going to say this, now he is dressing himself to go out," and so on. Such observation is not the same thing as persecution, but it is not far removed from it. It implies that these persons distrust the patient, and expect to catch him doing something that is forbidden and for which he will be punished. How would it be if these mad people were right, if we all of us had an observing function in our egos threatening us with punishment, which, in their case, had merely become sharply separated from the ego and had been mistakenly projected into external reality?

I do not know whether it will appeal to you in the same way as it appeals to me. Under the strong impression of this clinical picture, I formed the idea that the separating off of an observing function from the rest of the ego might be a normal feature of the ego's structure; this idea has never left me, and I was driven to investigate the further characteristics and relations of the function which had been separated off in this way. The next step is soon taken. The actual content of the delusion of observation makes it probable that the observation is only a first step towards conviction and punishment, so that we may guess that another activity of this function must be what we call conscience. There is hardly anything that we separate off from our ego so regularly as our conscience and so easily set over against it. I feel a temptation to do something which promises to bring me pleasure, but I refrain from doing it on the ground that "my conscience will not allow it." Or I allow myself to be persuaded by the greatness of the expectation of pleasure into doing something against which the voice of my conscience has protested, and after I have done it my conscience punishes me with painful reproaches, and makes me feel remorse for it. I might say simply that the function which I am beginning to distinguish within the ego is the conscience; but it is more prudent to keep that function as a separate entity and assume that conscience is one of its activities, and that the self-observation which is necessary as a preliminary to the judicial aspect of conscience is another. And since the process of recognizing a thing as a separate entity involves giving it a name of its own, I will henceforward call this function in the ego the "super-ego."

At this point I am quite prepared for you to ask scornfully whether our ego-psychology amounts to no more than taking everyday abstractions literally, magnifying them, and turning them from concepts into things—which would not be of much assistance. My answer to that is, that in ego-psychology it will be difficult to avoid what is already familiar, and that it is more a question of arriving at new ways of looking at things and new groupings of the facts than of making new discoveries. I will not ask you, therefore, to abandon your critical attitude but merely to await further developments. The facts of pathology give our efforts a background for which you will look in vain in popular psychology. I will proceed. No sooner have we got used to the idea of this super-ego, as something which enjoys a certain independence, pursues its own ends, and is independent of the ego as regards the energy at its disposal, than we are faced with a clinical picture which throws into strong relief the severity, and even cruelty, of this function, and the vicissitudes through which its relations with the ego may pass. I refer to the condition of melancholia, or more accurately the melancholic attack, of which you must have heard often enough, even if you are not psychiatrists. In this disease, about whose causes and mechanism we know far too little, the most remarkable characteristic is the way in which the super-ego—you may call it, but in a whisper, the conscience—treats the ego. The melancholiac during periods of health can, like any one else, be more or less severe towards himself; but when he has a melancholic attack, his super-ego becomes over-severe, abuses, humiliates, and ill-treats his unfortunate ego, threatens it with the severest punishments, reproaches it for long forgotten actions which were at the time regarded quite lightly, and behaves as though it had spent the whole interval in amassing complaints and was only waiting for its present increase in strength to bring them forward, and to condemn the ego on their account. The super-ego has the ego at its mercy and applies the most severe moral standards to it; indeed it represents the whole demands of morality, and we see all at once that our moral sense of guilt is the expression of the tension between the ego and the super-ego. It is a very remarkable experience to observe morality, which was ostensibly conferred on us by God and planted deep in our hearts, functioning as a periodical phenomenon. For after a certain number of months the whole moral fuss is at an end, the critical voice of the super-ego is silent, the ego is reinstated. and enjoys once more all the rights of man until the next attack. Indeed in many forms of the malady something exactly the reverse takes place during the intervals; the ego finds itself in an ecstatic state of exaltation, it triumphs, as though the super-ego had lost all its power or had become merged with the ego, and this liberated, maniac ego gives itself up in a really uninhibited fashion, to the satisfaction of all its desires. Happenings rich in unsolved riddles!

You will expect me to do more than give a mere example in support of my statement that we have learnt a great deal about the formation of the super-ego, that is of the origin of conscience. The philosopher Kant once declared that nothing proved to him the greatness of God more convincingly than the starry heavens and the moral conscience within us. The stars are unquestionably superb, but where conscience is concerned God has been guilty of an uneven and careless piece of work, for a great many men have only a limited share of it or scarcely enough to be worth mentioning. This does not mean, however, that we are overlooking the fragment of psychological truth which is contained in the assertion that conscience is of divine origin! but the assertion needs interpretation. Conscience is no doubt something within us, but it has not been there from the beginning. In this sense it is the opposite of sexuality, which is certainly present from the very beginning of life, and is not a thing that only comes in later. But small children are notoriously a-moral. They have no internal inhibitions against their pleasure-seeking impulses. The rôle, which the super-ego undertakes later in life, is at first played by an external power, by parental authority. The influence of the parents dominates the child by granting proofs of affection and by threats of punishment, which, to the child, mean loss of love, and which must also be feared on their own account. This objective anxiety is the forerunner of the later moral anxiety; so long as the former is dominant one need not speak of super-ego or of conscience. It is only later that the secondary situation arises, which we are far too ready to regard as the normal state of affairs; the external restrictions are introjected, so that the super-ego takes the place of the parental function, and thenceforward observes, guides and threatens the ego in just the same way as the parents acted to the child before.

The super-ego, which in this way has taken over the power, the aims and even the methods of the parental function, is, however, not merely the legatee of parental authority, it is actually the heir of its body. It proceeds directly from it, and we shall soon learn in what way this comes about. First, however, we must pause to consider a point in which they differ. The super-ego seems to have made a one-sided selection, and to have chosen only the harshness and severity of the parents, their preventive and punitive functions, while their loving care is not taken up and continued by it. If the parents have really ruled with a rod of iron, we can easily understand the child developing a severe super-ego, but, contrary to our expectations, experience shows that the super-ego may reflect the same relentless harshness even when the up-bringing has been gentle and kind, and avoided threats and punishment as far as possible. We shall return to this contradiction later, when we are dealing with the transmutation of instincts in the formation of the super-ego.

I cannot tell you as much as I could wish about the change from the parental function to the super-ego, partly because that process is so complicated that a description of it does not fit into the framework of a set of introductory lectures such as these, and partly because we ourselves do not feel that we have fully understood it. You will have to be satisfied, therefore, with the following indications. The basis of the process is what we call an identification, that is to say, that one ego becomes like another, one which results in the first ego behaving itself in certain respects in the same way as the second; it imitates it, and as it were takes it into itself. This identification has been not inappropriately compared with the oral cannibalistic incorporation of another person. Identification is a very important kind of relationship with another person, probably the most primitive, and is not to be confused with object-choice. One can express the difference between them in this way: when a boy identifies himself with his father, he wants to *be like* his father; when he makes him the object of his choice, he wants to *have* him, to possess him; in the first case his ego is altered on the model of his father, in the second case that is not necessary. Identification and object-choice are broadly speaking independent of each other; but one can identify oneself with a person, and alter one's ego accordingly, and take the same person as one's sexual object. It is said that this influencing of the ego by the sexual object takes place very often with women, and is characteristic of femininity. With regard to what is by far the most instructive relation between identification and object-choice, I must have given you some information in my previous lectures. It can be as easily observed in children as in adults, in normal as in sick persons. If one has lost a love-object or has had to give it up, one often compensates oneself by identifying oneself with it; one sets it up again inside one's ego, so that in this case object-choice regresses, as it were, to identification.

I am myself not at all satisfied with this account of identification, but it will suffice if you will grant that the establishment of the super-ego can be described as a successful instance of identification with the parental function. The fact which is decisively in favour of this point of view is that this new creation of a superior function within the ego is extremely closely bound up with the fate of the Oedipus complex, so that the super-ego appears as the heir of that emotional tie, which is of such importance for childhood. When the Oedipus complex passes away the child must give up the intense object-cathexes which it has formed towards its parents, and to compensate for this loss of object, its identifications with its parents, which have probably long been present, become greatly intensified. Identifications of this kind, which may be looked on as precipitates of abandoned object-cathexes, will recur often enough in the later life of the child; but it is in keeping with the emotional importance of this first instance of such a transformation that its product should occupy a special position in the ego. Further investigation also reveals that the super-ego does not attain to full strength and development if the overcoming of the Oedipus complex has not been completely successful. During the course of its growth, the super-ego also takes over the influence of those persons who have taken the place of the parents, that is to say of persons who have been concerned in the child's upbringing, and whom it has regarded as ideal models. Normally the super-ego is constantly becoming more and more remote from the original parents, becoming, as it were, more impersonal. Another thing that we must not forget is that the child values its parents differently at different periods of its life. At the time at which the Oedipus complex makes way for the super-ego, they seem to be splendid figures, but later on they lose a good deal of their prestige. Identifications take place with these later editions of the parents as well, and regularly provide important contributions to the formation of character; but these only affect the ego, they have no influence on the super-ego, which has been determined by the earliest parental images.

I hope you will by now feel that in postulating the existence of a super-ego I have been describing a genuine structural entity, and have not been merely personifying an abstraction, such as conscience. We have now to mention another important activity which is to be ascribed to the super-ego. It is also the vehicle of the ego-ideal, by which the ego measures itself, towards which it strives, and whose demands for ever-increasing perfection it is always striving to fulfil. No doubt this ego-ideal is a precipitation of the old idea of the parents, an expression of the admiration which the child felt for the perfection which it at that time ascribed to them. I know you have heard a great deal about the sense of inferiority which is said to distinguish the neurotic subject. It crops up especially in the pages of works that have literary pretensions. A writer who brings in the expression "inferiority-complex" thinks he has satisfied all the demands of psycho-analysis and raised his work on to a higher psychological plane. As a matter of fact the phrase "inferiority-complex" is hardly ever used in psycho-analysis. It does not refer to anything which we regard as simple, let alone elementary. To trace it back to the perception in oneself of some organic disability or other, as the school of so-called Individual Psychologists like to do, seems to us a short-sighted error. The sense of inferiority has a strong erotic basis. The child feels itself inferior when it perceives that it is not loved, and so does the adult as well. The only organ that is really regarded as inferior is the stunted penis—the girl's clitoris. But the major part of the sense of inferiority springs from the relationship of the ego to its super-ego, and, like the sense of guilt, it is an expression of the tension between them. The sense of inferiority and the sense of guilt are exceedingly difficult to distinguish. Perhaps we should do better if we regarded the former as the erotic complement to the sense of moral inferiority. We have paid but little attention to such questions of conceptual differentiation in psycho-analysis.

Seeing that the inferiority-complex has become so popular, I shall venture to treat you to a short digression. A historical personage of our time, who is still living but who for the present has retired into the background, suffers from the mal-development of a limb caused by an injury at birth. A very well-known contemporary writer who has a predilection for writing the biographies of famous persons, has dealt with the life of the man to whom I am referring. Now if one is writing a biography, it is naturally very difficult to suppress the urge for psychological understanding. The author has therefore made an attempt to build up the whole development of his hero's character on the basis of a sense of inferiority, which was caused by his physical defect. While doing this he has overlooked a small but not unimportant fact. It is usual for mothers to whom fate has given a sickly or otherwise defective child to try to compensate for this unfair handicap with an extra amount of love. In the case we are speaking of, the proud mother behaved quite differently; she withdrew her love from the child on account of his disability. When the child grew up into a man of great power, he proved beyond all doubt by his behaviour that he had never forgiven his mother. If you will bear in mind the importance of mother-love for the mental life of the child, you will be able to make the necessary corrections in the inferiority-theory of the biographer.

But let us get back to the super-ego. We have allocated to it the activities of self-observation, conscience, and the holding up of ideals. It follows from our account of its origin that it is based upon an overwhelmingly important biological fact no less than upon a momentous psychological fact, namely the lengthy dependence of the human child on its parents and the Oedipus complex; these two facts, moreover, are closely bound up with each other. For us the super-ego is the representative of all moral restrictions, the advocate of the impulse towards perfection, in short it is as much as we have been able to apprehend psychologically of what people call the "higher" things in human life. Since it itself can be traced back to the influence of parents, teachers, and so on, we shall learn more of its significance if we turn our attention to these sources. In general, parents and similar authorities follow the dictates of their own super-egos in the up-bringing of children. Whatever terms their ego may be on with their super-ego, in the education of the child they are severe and exacting. They have forgotten the difficulties of their own childhood, and are glad to be able to identify themselves fully at last with their own parents, who in their day subjected them to such severe restraints. The result is that the super-ego of the child is not really built up on the model of the parents, but on that of the parents' super-ego; it takes over the same content, it becomes the vehicle of tradition and of all the age-long values which have been handed down in this way from generation to generation. You may easily guess what great help is afforded by the recognition of the super-ego in understanding the social behaviour of man, in grasping the problem of delinquency, for example, and perhaps, too, in providing us with some practical hints upon education. It is probable that the so-called materialistic conceptions of history err in that they underestimate this factor. They brush it aside with the remark that the "ideologies" of mankind are nothing more than resultants of their economic situation at any given moment or superstructures built upon it. That is the truth, but very probably it is not the whole truth. Mankind never lives completely in the present; the ideologies of the super-ego perpetuate the past, the traditions of the race and the people, which yield but slowly to the influence of the present and to new developments, and, so long as they work through the super-ego, play an important part in man's life, quite independently of economic conditions.

In 1921 I tried to apply the distinction between the ego and the super-ego to the study of group psychology. I reached a formula, which ran like this: A psychological group is a collection of individuals, who have introduced the same person into their super-ego, and on the basis of this common factor have identified themselves with one another in their ego. This naturally only holds for groups who have a leader. If we could find more applications of this kind, the hypothesis of the super-ego would lose all its strangeness for us, and we should be entirely relieved of the embarrassment which we cannot help feeling when, used as we are to the atmosphere of the underworld, we make excursions into the more superficial and higher planes of the mental apparatus. Of course we do not for a moment think that the last word on ego-psychology has been spoken with the demarcation of the super-ego. It is rather the beginning of the subject, but in this case it is not only the first step that is difficult.

But now another task awaits us, as it were at the opposite end of the ego. This question is raised by an observation which is made during analytic work, an observation which is, indeed, an old one. As so often happens, it has taken a long time for its true value to be appreciated. As you are aware, the whole of psycho-analytic theory is in fact built up on the perception of the resistance exerted by the patient when we try to make him conscious of his unconscious. The objective indication of resistance is that his associations stop short or wander far away from the theme that is being discussed. He may also become subjectively aware of the resistance by experiencing painful feelings when he approaches the theme. But this last indication may be absent. In such a case we say to the patient that we conclude from his behaviour that he is in a state of resistance, and he replies that he knows nothing about it and is only aware of a difficulty in associating. Experience shows that we were right, but, if so, his resistance too must have been unconscious, just as unconscious as the repressed material which we were trying to bring to the surface. Long ago we should have asked from which part of the mind such an unconscious resistance could operate. The beginner in psycho-analysis will be ready at once with the answer that it must be the resistance of the unconscious. An ambiguous and useless answer! If it means that the resistance operates from the repressed, then we must say: "Certainly not!" To the repressed we must rather ascribe a strong upward-driving force, an impulsion to get through to consciousness. The resistance can only be a manifestation of the ego, which carried through the repression at one time or other and is now endeavouring to keep it up. And that too was our earlier view. Now that we have posited a special function within the ego to represent the demand for restriction and rejection, i.e. the super-ego, we can say that repression is the work of the super-ego,—either that it does its work on its own account or else that the ego does it in obedience to its orders. If now we are faced with the case where the patient under analysis is not conscious of his resistance, then it must be either that the super-ego and the ego can operate unconsciously in quite important situations, or, which would be far more significant, that parts of both ego and super-ego themselves are unconscious. In both cases we should have to take account of the disturbing view that the ego (including the super-ego) does not by any means completely coincide with the conscious, nor the repressed with the unconscious.

Ladies and Gentlemen—I feel I must have a little breathing space, which I expect you will welcome with relief, and before I go on I must make an apology. Here am I giving you a supplement to the introduction to psycho-analysis which I started fifteen years ago, and I am behaving as though you yourselves had been doing nothing but psycho-analysis all that time. I know it is a monstrous supposition, but I am helpless, I have no alternative. The reason is that it is exceedingly difficult to give an insight into psycho-analysis to any one who is not himself a psycho-analyst. I assure you that we do not like to give the effect of being members of a secret society carrying on a secret science. And yet we have been obliged to recognise and state as our considered opinion that no one has a right to say in psycho-analysis unless he has been through certain experiences which he can only have by being analysed himself. When I delivered my lectures to you fifteen years ago I tried to let you off certain speculative parts of our theory, but it is with those very parts that are connected the new discoveries which I am going to speak of to-day.

Now let me return to my theme. With regard to the two alternatives—that the ego and the super-ego may themselves be unconscious, or that they may merely give rise to unconscious effects—we have for good reasons decided in favour of the former. Certainly, large portions of the ego and super-ego can remain unconscious, are, in fact, normally unconscious. That means to say that the individual knows nothing of their contents and that it requires an expenditure of effort to make him conscious of them. It is true, then, that ego and conscious, repressed and unconscious do not coincide. We are forced fundamentally to revise our attitude towards the problem of conscious and unconscious. At first we might be inclined to think very much less of the importance of consciousness as a criterion, since it has proved so untrustworthy. But if we did so, we should be wrong. It is the same with life: it is not worth much, but it is all that we have. Without the light shed by the quality of consciousness we should be lost in the darkness of depth-psychology. Nevertheless we must try to orientate ourselves anew.

What is meant by "conscious," we need not discuss; it is beyond all doubt. The oldest and best meaning of the word "unconscious" is the descriptive one; we call "unconscious" any mental process the existence of which we are obliged to assume—because, for instance, we infer it in some way from its effects—but of which we are not directly aware. We have the same relation to that mental process as we have to a mental process in another person, except that it belongs to ourselves. If we want to be more accurate, we should modify the statement by saying that we call a process "unconscious" when we have to assume that it was active *at a certain time*, although *at that time* we knew nothing about it. This restriction reminds us that most conscious processes are conscious only for a short period; quite soon they become *latent*, though they can easily become conscious again. We could also say that they had become unconscious, if we were certain that they were still something mental when they were in the latent condition. So far we should have learnt nothing, and not even have earned the right to introduce the notion of the unconscious into psychology. But now we come across a new fact which we can already observe in the case of errors. We find that, in order to explain a slip of the tongue, for instance, we are obliged to assume that an intention to say some particular thing had formed itself in the mind of the person who made the slip. We can infer it with certainty from the occurrence of the speech-disturbance, but it was not able to obtain expression; it was, that is to say, unconscious. If we subsequently bring the intention to the speaker's notice, he may recognise it as a familiar one, in which case it was only temporarily unconscious, or he may repudiate it as foreign to him, in which case it was permanently unconscious. Such an observation as this justifies us in also regarding what we have called "latent" as something "unconscious." The consideration of these dynamic relations puts us in a position to distinguish two kinds of unconscious: one which is transformed into conscious material easily and under conditions which frequently arise, and another in the case of which such a transformation is difficult, can only come about with a considerable expenditure of energy, or may never occur at all. In order to avoid any ambiguity as to whether we are referring to the one or the other unconscious, whether we are using the word in the descriptive or dynamic sense, we make use of a legitimate and simple expedient. We call the unconscious which is only latent, and so can easily become conscious, the "preconscious," and keep the name "unconscious" for the other. We have now three terms, "conscious," "preconscious," and "unconscious," to serve our purposes in describing mental phenomena. Once again, from a purely descriptive point of view, the "preconscious" is also unconscious, but we do not give it that name, except when we are speaking loosely, or when we have to defend in general the existence of unconscious processes in mental life.

You will, I hope, grant that so far things are not so bad and that the scheme is a convenient one. That is all very well; unfortunately our psycho-analytic work has compelled us to use the word "unconscious" in yet another, third, sense; and this may very well have given rise to confusion. Psycho-analysis has impressed us very strongly with the new idea that large and important regions of the mind are normally removed from the knowledge of the ego, so that the processes which occur in them must be recognized as unconscious in the true dynamic sense of the term. We have consequently also attributed to the word "unconscious" a topographical or systematic meaning; we have talked of *systems* of the preconscious and of the unconscious, and of a conflict between the ego and the Ucs. system; so that the word "unconscious" has more and more been made to mean a mental province rather than a quality which mental things have. At this point, the discovery, inconvenient at first sight, that parts of the ego and super-ego, too, are unconscious in the dynamic sense, has a facilitating effect and enables us to remove a complication. We evidently have no right to call that region of the mind which is neither ego nor super-ego the Ucs. system, since the character of unconsciousness is not exclusive to it. Very well; we will no longer use the word "unconscious" in the sense of a system, and to what we have hitherto called by that name we will give a better one, which will not give rise to misunderstandings. Borrowing, at G. Groddeck's suggestion, a term used by Nietzsche, we will call it henceforward the "id." This impersonal pronoun seems particularly suited to express the essential character of this province of the mind—the character of being foreign to the ego. Super-ego, ego and id, then, are the three realms, regions or provinces into which we divide the mental apparatus of the individual; and it is their mutual relations with which we shall be concerned in what follows.

But before we go on I must make a short digression. I have no doubt that you are dissatisfied with the fact that the three qualities of the mind in respect to consciousness and the three regions of the mental apparatus do not fall together into three harmonious pairs, and that you feel that the clarity of our conclusions is consequently impaired. My own view is that we ought not to deplore this fact but that we should say to ourselves that we had no right to expect any such neat arrangement. Let me give you an analogy; analogies prove nothing, that is quite true, but they can make one feel more at home. Let us picture a country with a great variety of geographical configurations, hills, plains and chains of lakes, and with mixed nationalities living in it, Germans, Magyars and Slovaks, who, moreover, are engaged upon a number of different occupations. Now the distribution might be such that the Germans lived in the hills and kept cattle, the Magyars on the plains and grew corn and vines, while the Slovaks lived by the lakes and caught fish and plaited reeds. If this distribution were neat and exact it would no doubt give great satisfaction to a President

Wilson; it would also be convenient for giving a geography lesson. It is probable, however, that you would find a less orderly state of affairs if you visited the
region. Germans, Magyars and Slovaks would be living everywhere mixed up
together, and there would be cornfields too in the hills, and cattle would be
kept on the plains as well. One or two things would be as you expected, for
one cannot catch fish on the mountains, and wine does not grow in water. The
picture of the region which you had brought with you might on the whole fit
the facts, but in details you would have to put up with departures from it.

You must not expect me to tell you much that is new about the id, except
its name. It is the obscure inaccessible part of our personality; the little we
know about it we have learnt from the study of dream-work and the formation
of neurotic symptoms, and most of that is of a negative character, and can only
be described as being all that the ego is not. We can come nearer to the id with
images, and call it a chaos, a cauldron of seething excitement. We suppose that
it is somewhere in direct contact with somatic processes, and takes over from
them instinctual needs and gives them mental impression, but we cannot say in
what substratum this contact is made. These instincts fill it with energy, but it
has no organisation and no unified will, only an impulsion to obtain satisfaction
for the instinctual needs, in accordance with the pleasure-principle. The laws
of logic—above all, the law of contradiction—do not hold for processes in the
id. Contradictory impulses exist side by side without neutralising each other or
drawing apart; at most they combine in compromise formations under the overpowering economic pressure towards discharging their energy. There is nothing in the id which can be compared to negation, and we are astonished to find
in it an exception to the philosophers' assertion that space and time are necessary forms of our mental acts. In the id there is nothing corresponding to the
idea of time, no recognition of the passage of time, and (a thing which is very
remarkable and awaits adequate attention in philosophic thought) no alteration of mental processes by the passage of time. Conative impulses which have
never got beyond the id, and even impressions which have been pushed down
into the id by repression, are virtually immortal and are preserved for whole
decades as though they had only recently occurred. They can only be recognised as belonging to the past, deprived of their significance, and robbed of
their charge of energy, after they have been made conscious by the work of
analysis, and no small part of the therapeutic effect of analytic treatment rests
upon this fact.

It is constantly being borne in upon me that we have made far too little use
of our theory of the indubitable fact that the repressed remains unaltered by
the passage of time. This seems to offer us the possibility of an approach to
some really profound truths. But I myself have made no further progress here.

Naturally, the id knows no values, no good and evil, no morality. The economic, or, if you prefer, the quantitative factor, which is so closely bound up
with the pleasure-principle, dominates all its processes. Instinctual cathexes
seeking discharge,—that, in our view, is all that the id contains. It seems, in-

deed, as if the energy of these instinctual impulses is in a different condition from that in which it is found in the other regions of the mind. It must be far more fluid and more capable of being discharged, for otherwise we should not have those displacements and condensations, which are so characteristic of the id and which are so completely independent of the qualities of what is cathected. (In the ego we should call it an idea.) What would one not give to understand these things better? You observe, in any case, that we can attribute to the id other characteristics than that of being unconscious, and you are aware of the possibility that parts of the ego and super-ego are unconscious without possessing the same primitive and irrational quality. As regards a characterisation of the ego, in so far as it is to be distinguished from the id and the super-ego, we shall get on better if we turn our attention to the relation between it and the most superficial portion of the mental apparatus; which we call the Pcpt-cs (perceptual-conscious) system. This system is directed on to the external world, it mediates perceptions of it, and in it is generated, while it is functioning, the phenomenon of consciousness. It is the sense-organ of the whole apparatus, receptive, moreover, not only of excitations from without but also of such as proceed from the interior of the mind. One can hardly go wrong in regarding the ego as that part of the id which had been modified by its proximity to the external world and the influence that the latter has had on it, and which serves the purpose of receiving stimuli and protecting the organism from them, like the cortical layer with which a particle of living substance surrounds itself. This relation to the external world is decisive for the ego. The ego has taken over the task of representing the external world for the id, and so of saving it; for the id, blindly striving to gratify its instincts in complete disregard of the superior strength of outside forces, could not otherwise escape annihilation. In the fulfilment of this function, the ego has to observe the external world and preserve a true picture of it in the memory traces left by its perceptions, and, by means of the reality-test, it has to eliminate any element in this picture of the external world which is a contribution from internal sources of excitation. On behalf of the id, the ego controls the path of access to motility, but it interpolates between desire and action the procrastinating factor of thought, during which it makes use of the residues of experience stored up in memory. In this way it dethrones the pleasure-principle, which exerts undisputed sway over the processes in the id, and substitutes for it the reality-principle, which promises greater security and greater success.

The relation to time, too, which is so hard to describe, is communicated to the ego by the perceptual system; indeed it can hardly be doubted that the mode in which this system works is the source of the idea of time. What, however, especially marks the ego out in contradistinction to the id, is a tendency to synthesise its contents, to bring together and unify its mental processes which is entirely absent from the id. When we come to deal presently with the instincts in mental life, I hope we shall succeed in tracing this fundamental characteristic of the ego to its source. It is this alone that produces that high degree of organisation which the ego needs for its highest achievements. The ego advances from the function of perceiving instincts to that of controlling them, but the latter is only achieved through the mental representative of the instinct becoming subordinated to a larger organisation, and finding its place in a coherent unity. In popular language, we may say that the ego stands for reason and circumspection, while the id stands for the untamed passions.

So far we have allowed ourselves to dwell on the enumeration of the merits and capabilities of the ego; it is time now to look at the other side of the picture. The ego is after all only a part of the id, a part purposively modified by its proximity to the dangers of reality. From a dynamic point of view it is weak; it borrows its energy from the id, and we are not entirely ignorant of the methods—one might almost call them "tricks"—by means of which it draws further amounts of energy from the id. Such a method, for example, is the process of identification, whether the object is retained or given up. The object-cathexes proceed from the instinctual demands of the id. The first business of the ego is to take note of them. But by identifying itself with the object, it recommends itself to the id in the place of the object and seeks to attract the libido of the id on to itself. We have already seen that, in the course of a person's life, the ego takes into itself a large number of such precipitates of former object-cathexes. On the whole the ego has to carry out the intentions of the id; it fulfils its duty if it succeeds in creating the conditions under which these intentions can best be fulfilled. One might compare the relation of the ego to the id with that between a rider and his horse. The horse provides the locomotive energy, and the rider has the prerogative of determining the goal and of guiding the movements of his powerful mount towards it. But all too often in the relations between the ego and the id we find a picture of the less ideal situation in which the rider is obliged to guide his horse in the direction in which it itself wants to go.

The ego has separated itself off from one part of the id by means of repression-resistances. But the barrier of repression does not extend into the id; so that the repressed material merges into the rest of the id.

The proverb tells us that one cannot serve two masters at once. The poor ego has a still harder time of it; it has to serve three harsh masters, and has to do its best to reconcile the claims and demands of all three. These demands are always divergent and often seem quite incompatible; no wonder that the ego so frequently gives way under its task. The three tyrants are the external world, the super-ego and the id. When one watches the efforts of the ego to satisfy them all, or rather, to obey them all simultaneously, one cannot regret having personified the ego, and established it as a separate being. It feels itself hemmed in on three sides and threatened by three kinds of danger, towards which it reacts by developing anxiety when it is too hard pressed. Having originated in the experiences of the perceptual system, it is designed to represent the demands of the external world, but it also wishes to be a loyal servant of the id, to remain upon good terms with the id, to recommend itself to the id as an object, and to draw the id's libido on to itself. In its attempt to mediate between the id and reality, it is often forced to clothe the Ucs. commands of the id with its own Pcs. rationalisations, to gloss over the conflicts between the id and reality, and with diplomatic dishonesty to display a pretended regard for reality, even when the id persists in being stubborn and uncompromising. On the other hand, its every movement is watched by the severe super-ego, which holds up certain norms of behaviour, without regard to any difficulties coming from the id and the external world; and if these norms are not acted up to, it punishes the ego with the feelings of tension which manifest themselves as a sense of inferiority and guilt. In this way, goaded on by the id, hemmed in by the super-ego, and rebuffed by reality, the ego struggles to cope with its economic task of reducing the forces and influences which work in it and upon it to some kind of harmony; and we may well understand how it is that we so often cannot repress the cry: "Life is not easy." When the ego is forced to acknowledge its weakness, it breaks out into anxiety: reality anxiety in face of the external world, normal anxiety in face of the super-ego, and neurotic anxiety in the face of the strength of the passions in the id.

I have represented the structural relations within the mental personality, as I have explained them to you, in a simple diagram, which I here reproduce.

You will observe how the super-ego goes down into the id; as the heir to the Oedipus complex it has, after all, intimate connections with the id. It lies further from the perceptual system than the ego. The id only deals with the external world through the medium of the ego, at least in this diagram. It is certainly still too early to say how far the drawing is correct; in one respect I know it is not. The space taken up by the unconscious id ought to be incomparably greater than that given to the ego or to the preconscious. You must, if you please, correct that in your imagination.

And now, in concluding this certainly rather exhausting and perhaps not very illuminating account, I must add a warning. When you think of this dividing up of the personality into ego, super-ego and id, you must not imagine sharp dividing lines such as are artificially drawn in the field of political geography. We cannot do justice to the characteristics of the mind by means of

linear contours, such as occur in a drawing or in a primitive painting, but we need rather the areas of colour shading off into one another that are to be found in modern pictures. After we have made our separations, we must allow what we have separated to merge again. Do not judge too harshly of a first attempt at picturing a thing so elusive as the human mind. It is very probable that the extent of these differentiations varies very greatly from person to person; it is possible that their function itself may vary, and that they may at times undergo a process of involution. This seems to be particularly true of the most insecure and, from the phylogenetic point of view, the most recent of them, the differentiation between the ego and the super-ego. It is also incontestable that the same thing can come about as a result of mental disease. It can easily be imagined, too, that certain practices of mystics may succeed in upsetting the normal relations between the different regions of the mind, so that, for example, the perceptual system becomes able to grasp relations in the deeper layers of the ego and in the id which would otherwise be inaccessible to it. Whether such a procedure can put one in possession of ultimate truths, from which all good will flow, may be safely doubted. All the same, we must admit that the therapeutic efforts of psycho-analysis have chosen much the same method of approach. For their object is to strengthen the ego, to make it more independent of the super-ego, to widen its field of vision, and so to extend its organisation that it can take over new portions of the id. Where id was, there shall ego be.

It is reclamation work, like the draining of the Zuyder Zee.

HARLOW SHAPLEY

Man's Fourth Adjustment[1]

The scattering of galaxies, the habits of macromolecules, and the astounding abundance of stars are forcing those who ponder such matters to a further adjustment of their concept of the place and functioning of man in the material universe.

In the history of the evolving human mind, with its increasing knowledge of the surrounding world, there must have been a time when the philosophers of the early tribes began to realize that the world was not simply anthropocentric—centered on man himself. The geocentric concept became common doctrine. It accepted a universe centered on the earth. This first adjustment was only mildly deflationary to the human ego, for man appeared to surpass all other living forms.

The second adjustment in the relation of man to the physical universe, that is, the abandonment of the earth-center theory, was not generally acceptable until the sixteenth-century Copernican revolution soundly established the heliocentric concept—the theory of a universe centered on the sun. Man is a stubborn adherent to official dogma. Eventually, however, he accepted the sun as the center not only of the local family of planets, but also of the total sidereal assemblage, and long held that view.

He had slowly given up the earth-center. But why, in spite of increasing evidence, did he then hold so persistently to the heliocentric view? Was it only because of vanity—his feeling, nourished by the unscientific dogmatists, that he is of paramount significance in the world? There were several better reasons for his second delusion. For example, the Milky Way is a great circle, a band of starlight that divides the sky into two nearly equal parts. It is of about

[1] From *The American Scholar*, XXV (Autumn, 1956), 453-457. Copyright by Harlow Shapley, 1956. Reprinted by permission of the author.

the same brightness in all its parts. By implication, therefore, the sun and earth are centrally located. Also, the numbers of stars seemed to the early census-takers to fall off with distance from the sun as though it were central, and such a position for his star among the stellar millions brought to man a dignity of position not at all disagreeable.

The shift from the geocentric to the heliocentric concept doubtless had some philosophical impact in the sixteenth century, but not much. After all, the hot, turbulent, gaseous sun is no place for the delicate biology in which man finds himself at or near the top. Earth-center or sun-center seemed to make little difference to cosmic thinking during the past four centuries. But then, less than forty years ago, came the inescapable need for a third adjustment— one that should have deeply affected and to some extent has disturbed man's thoughts about his place, his career and his cosmic importance.

This shift has dug deeply into man's pride and self-assurance, for it has carried with it the knowledge of the appalling number of galaxies. He could accept rather cheerfully the Darwinian evidence of his animal origin, for that still left him at the summit of all terrestrial organisms. But the abandonment of the heliocentric universe on the authority of the astronomical evidence was certainly deflationary, from the standpoint of man's position in the material world, however flattering it was to the human mind.

The "galactocentric universe" suddenly puts the earth and its life near the edge of one great galaxy in a universe of millions of galaxies. Man becomes peripheral among the billions of stars of his own Milky Way; and, according to the revelations of paleontology and geochemistry, he is recent and apparently ephemeral in the unrolling of cosmic time. And here is a somber or happy thought, whichever mood you prefer. There is no retreat! The inquiring human has passed the point of no return. We cannot restore geocentrism or heliocentrism. The apes, eagles and honeybees may be wholly content to be peripheral ephemerals, and thus miss the great vision that opens before us. For them, egocentrism and lococentrism may suffice; for us, no! And since we cannot go back to the cramped but comfortable past (without sacrificing completely our cultures and civilizations), we go forward and find there is more to the story.

The downgrading of the earth and sun, and the elevation of the galaxies, is not the end of this progress of scientific pilgrims through philosophic fields. The need for a further jolting adjustment now appears—not wholly unexpected by workers in science, nor wholly the result of one or two scientific revelations.

Our new problem concerns the spread of life throughout the universe. As unsolicited spokesmen for all the earthly organisms of land, sea and air, we ask the piquant question: Are we alone?

From among the many measures and thoughts that promote this fourth adjustment of Homo sapiens sapiens in the galaxy of galaxies (the metagalaxy), I select three phenomena as most demanding of our consideration. The first refers to the number of stars, the second to catastrophes of ancient days, and the third to the origin of self-duplicating molecules.

To the ancients, only a few thousand stars were known; to the early telescopes, however, it was a million; and that astounding number has increased spectacularly with every telescopic advance. Finally, with the discovery that the "extragalactic nebulae" are in reality galaxies, each with its hundreds or thousands of millions of stars, and with our inability to "touch metagalactic bottom" with the greatest telescopes, we are led to accept the existence of more than 10^{20} stars in our explorable universe, perhaps many more.

The significance of this discovery, or rather of this uncovering, is that we have at hand—that is, the universe contains—more than one hundred million million million sources of light and warmth for whatever planets accompany these radiant stars.

The second phenomenon, the expanding metagalaxy, bears on the question: Do planets accompany at least some of the stars that pour forth energy suitable for the complex biological activity that we call life?

We now accept the observational evidence for an expanding universe of galaxies. The rapid expansion of the measurable part of the metagalaxy implies an increasingly greater concentration of these cosmic units (galaxies) as we go back in time. A few thousand million years ago, the average density of matter in space was so great that collisions, near encounters, and gravitational disruptions were of necessity frequent. The crust of the earth, radioactively measured, is also a few thousand million years old, and therefore the earth and the other planets of our sun's system were "born" in those days of turbulence. At that time countless millions of other planetary systems must have developed, for our sun is of a very common stellar variety. (Miss Cannon's catalogue of spectra reports forty thousand sun-like stars in our immediate neighborhood.)

Other ways in which planets may form—other than this primitive process of the early days—are recognized. The contraction of protostars out of the hypothetical primeval gas, giving birth on the way to protoplanets, is an evolutionary process now widely favored. It would imply the existence of countless planets.

The head-on-collision theory of planetary origin has also been considered. But the stars are now so widely dispersed that collisions must be exceedingly rare—so very unlikely, in fact, that we might claim uniqueness for our planetary system and for ourselves if planet birth depended only on such procedure. The expanding universe discovery, however, has shown the crowded conditions when our earth was born.

Passing over details, we state the relevant conclusion: *Millions of planetary systems must exist.* Whatever the method of origin, planets may be the common heritage of all stars except those so situated that planetary materials would be swallowed or cast off through gravitational action. In passing we note that astrophysicists have shown that our kinds of chemistry and physics prevail throughout the explorable universe. There is nothing uncommon here or now.

Remembering our 10^{20} stars and the high probability of millions of planets with suitable chemistry, dimensions and distance from their nutrient stars, we are ready for the question: On some of these planets is there actually life; or is that biochemical operation strangely limited to our planet, No. 3 in the family of the sun, which is a run-of-the-mill star located in the outer part of a galaxy that contains a hundred thousand million other stars—and this galaxy but one of millions already on the records?

Is life thus restricted? Of course not. We are not alone. And we can accept life's wide dispersion still more confidently when our third argument is indicated.

To put it briefly: biochemistry and microbiology, with the assistance of geophysics, astronomy and other sciences, have gone so far in bridging the gap between the inanimate and the living that we can no longer doubt but that whenever the physics, chemistry and climates are right on a planet's surface, life will emerge and persist.

This consequence has long been suspected by scientists, but the many researches of the past few years in the field of macromolecules have made it unnecessary any longer to postulate miracles and the supernatural for the origin of life.

The astronomical demonstration of the great number of stars, and therefore the abundance of life opportunities, naturally leads to the belief that countless planets have had long and varied experience with biochemical evolution. Thousands of kinds of terrestrial animals are known to develop neurotic complexes, that is "intelligence." It comes naturally. No higher animal is without it in high degree. Could it be otherwise on another life-bearing planet?

And here we must end with the simple but weighty proposal: There is no reason in the world to believe that our own mental stature has not been excelled by that of sentient beings elsewhere. I am not suggesting, however, that *Homo* is repeated. There are a million variations on the animal theme.

In conclusion, I need not emphasize the possible relevance to philosophy and perhaps to religion of this fourth adjustment in man's view of himself in the material universe.

DAVID M. POTTER

Democracy and Abundance [1]

One of the most widely current phrases of the second World War was the designation of the countries in arms against the axis as the "freedom-loving nations." It was a conveniently vague term for masking the diversity of the cobelligerents, and its essential irony was not at the time apparent, even when it was applied to the Soviet Union. But, apart from its value as an expedient,

[1] From *People of Plenty* (Chicago: The University of Chicago Press, 1954). Chap. V. Copyright 1954 by The University of Chicago.

the phrase undoubtedly gained great vitality from a genuine belief among Americans that the peoples of the world fall into two categories: those who love freedom and those who do not. Implicitly, we understood, of course, that we were the most devoted of all and that, while other countries might prove fickle in their affection, we could pride ourselves upon a record of constant fidelity. It was as if all the world had been presented with a choice between a right principle of government and a wrong one, and we, more than any others, had been unequivocal in choosing the right.

It is not unnatural, of course, for Americans to take this view of their political institutions. Americans have always been especially prone to regard all things as resulting from the free choice of a free will. Probably no people have so little determinism in their philosophy, and as individuals we have regarded our economic status, our matrimonial happiness, and even our eternal salvation as things of our own making. Why should we not then regard our political felicity, likewise, as a virtue which is also virtue's reward?

If this way of explaining ourselves to ourselves had no other result than to nourish our self-esteem, it would hardly be worthy of any special attention, for excessive national pride is in no sense peculiar to the United States. But our conception of democracy as a simple matter of moral choice has caused us to hope falsely that other countries will embrace democracy as we understand it, and to misconstrue badly the reasons for their failure to do so. It has even led us to condemn, quite unjustly, the countries which fail to establish a democracy like our own, as if it were plain obstinacy or even outright iniquity which explains their behavior.[2]

By viewing democracy simply as a question of political morality, we have blinded ourselves to the fact that, in every country, the system of government is a by-product of the general conditions of life, including, of course, the economic conditions, and that democracy, like any other system, is appropriate for countries where these conditions are suited to it and inappropriate for others with unsuitable conditions, or at least that it is vastly more appropriate for some than for others. Viewed in these terms, there is a strong case for believing that democracy is clearly most appropriate for countries which enjoy an economic surplus and least appropriate for countries where there is an economic insufficiency. In short, economic abundance is conducive to political democracy.[3]

[2] "We have believed as a nation that other peoples had only to will our democratic institutions in order to repeat our own career" (Frederick Jackson Turner, The Frontier in American History [New York: Holt, Rinehart and Winston, Inc., 1920], p. 244).
[3] "Political democracy came to the United States as the result of economic democracy. . . . This nation came to be marked by political institutions of a democratic type because it had, still earlier, come to be characterized in its economic life by democratic arrangements and practices" (J. Franklin Jameson, The American Revolution Considered as a Social Movement [Princeton: Princeton University Press, 1926], p. 41).

At first glance this proposition may seem abjectly deterministic and may seem to imply that our democracy, like our climate, is a mere matter of luck, involving no merit. But it does not necessarily mean that we enjoy democracy without achieving it; rather, it means that we have achieved it less by sheer ideological devotion to the democratic principle than by the creation of economic conditions in which democracy will grow. In doing this, we have, of course, enjoyed the advantage of unequaled natural resources, but, as I have already sought to show, abundant physical endowments do not automatically or invariably produce an economic surplus for the area which possesses them. For instance, New England, poorly endowed by nature, became, in the nineteenth century, one of the richest regions of the United States, while the Cotton South, richly endowed, committed itself to a slave-labor system, a one-crop system, and an economy restricted to producing raw materials, which, in the end, left it the poorest part of the nation.

These instances and many others indicate that man may, through cultural processes, use environment well or use it ill; he may make his political system one of the instruments for such use; he may apply democratic devices for the purpose of developing or distributing abundance, and then he may use abundance as a base for the broadening and consolidation of his democracy. Or, to put it another way, he may use an economic surplus for the purpose of furthering a democratic system which will, in turn, enable him to increase further his economic surplus.

But, though this view does not, in a deterministic sense, deny man credit for democratic accomplishments, it does argue that he should distinguish very carefully the things for which credit is claimed. A nation may properly be proud that it has developed the economic means which enable it to afford a full-fledged democracy or that it has utilized democratic practices to create the economic base on which a democracy can be further broadened. But it cannot, with any validity, attribute its democracy to sheer moral and ideological virtue. Shaw stated the point forcibly in his Preface to *John Bull's Other Island*, when he said, "The virtues of the English soil are not less real because they consist of coal and iron, not of metaphysical sources of character. The virtues of Broadbent [the Englishman] are not less real because they are the virtues of the money that coal and iron have produced."

To understand why a democratic system depends upon an economic surplus, one has only to remember what a democracy offers to its citizens and what other regimes offer. All social systems, of course, seek to keep the bulk of their people contented, and all of them make promises of one kind or another in order to do this—some have promised a utopia in the indefinite future; others have offered, instead of real welfare, inexpensive distractions such as the bread and circuses of the Romans or the lotteries of modern Spain and Latin America; still others have attempted to provide real cradle-to-the-grave security. But however much or little a society, or a government acting for the society, may have to allot, it is axiomatic that it must not arouse expectations very much higher than it is able to satisfy. This means that it must not hold out the promise of opportunity unless there is a reasonable prospect of the opportunity's being fulfilled. It must not invite the individual to compete for prizes unless there are a substantial number of awards to be passed out.[4]

In all societies of economic insufficiency, which is the only kind that existed up to about two centuries ago, certain social conditions have been fixed and inevitable. The vast majority of the people were inescapably destined to heavy toil and bare subsistence, and the economic surplus in excess of such bare subsistence was not sufficient to give leisure and abundance to more than a tiny minority. In these circumstances, certainly the society could not afford either the economic or the emotional costs of conducting a great social steeplechase for the purpose of selecting a handful of winners to occupy the few enviable positions.[5] It was much sounder public policy to assign these positions by an arbitrary system of status and at the same time to assign to the great bulk of the people the burdens which most of them were destined to bear regardless of what regime was in power. Under a system of subordination transmitted by heredity, social competition, with its attendant loss of energy through friction, was avoided; the status-bound individual often gained a sense of contentment with his lot and even a dignity within his narrow sphere, and all that he sacrificed for this psychological advantage was a statistically negligible chance for advancement. Moreover, in a relatively static and relatively simple society such at that of Tudor or Stuart England, the problems of government were not very intricate, and the only qualities required in the local ruling class were integrity and a willingness to accept responsibility. These qualities could usually be found and could readily be transmitted even, in a squirearchy of low intellectual attainments, and therefore there was no need to recruit widely for leadership, as a society must do when it requires intelligence, specialized skill, and adaptability in its administration.

A country with inadequate wealth, therefore, could not safely promise its citizens more than security of status—at a low level in the social hierarchy and with a meager living. But this promise is, in its denial of equality, by definition, undemocratic. A democracy, by contrast, setting equality as its goal, must promise opportunity, for the goal of equality becomes a mockery unless there is some means of attaining it. But in promising opportunity, the democracy is constantly arousing expectations which it lacks the current means to fulfil and is

[4] For extended, systematic consideration of the manner in which a society motivates its members to perform the roles necessary to the functioning of the social system see Talcott Parsons, *Essays in Sociological Theory* (New York: The Free Press, 1949), and Robert K. Merton, *Social Theory and Social Structure* (New York: The Free Press, 1949).

[5] "And yet, Burke might have countered, once the masses were fated by the laws of political economy to toil in misery, what else was the idea of equality but a cruel bait to goad mankind into self-destruction" (Karl Polanyi, *The Great Transformation* [New York: Holt, Rinehart and Winston, Inc., 1944], p. 119).

betting on its ability to procure the necessary means by the very act of stimulating people to demand them and go after them. It is constantly educating large numbers of people without waiting to see whether jobs requiring education are available for all of them; it does this in the expectation that the supply will create a demand and that a society constantly rising in the level of its education will constantly generate new posts in which educated people are needed. Also, democracy is forever encouraging individuals to determine their own goals and set their own course toward these goals, even though only a small proportion can attain complete success; the time and effort of many may be wasted in the pursuit, but the advantage to society of having the maximum number of people developing their maximum potentialities of intellect and personality is thought to justify the social cost.

All this is very well and works admirably if the country following these practices has the necessary physical resources and human resourcefulness to raise the standard of living, to create new occupational opportunities, and to find the outlets for the abilities of an ever increasing class of trained men. But it must have this endowment to begin with, or it is certain to suffer intensely from the social waste that results from giving training which cannot be utilized and from the psychological damage that results when a competition has an excess of participants and a paucity of rewards. In short, to succeed as a democracy, a country must enjoy an economic surplus to begin with or must contrive to attain one.[6]

If this is true, it means that the principles of democracy are not universal truths, ignored during centuries of intellectual darkness and brought to light at last in the age of the American Revolution, but rather that democracy is the foremost by far of the many advantages which our economic affluence has bought for us. To say this, of course, is also to say that, when we propose world-wide adoption of democracy, our problem is not merely to inspire a belief in it but to encourage conditions conducive to it. About a year ago an English visitor in America made a comparison between socialism and free-enterprise democracy, which illustrated extremely well, though quite unwittingly, the reliance of democracy upon these conditions.

The comparison was based on a contrast between the ways in which the two systems in question might deal with the departure of a passenger train. Under a thoroughgoing system of socialism, said the description, the seating of all passengers would be directed. Station attendants would supervise the seating of every ticket-holder. They would arbitrarily place together people who did not want to sit together or place individuals in seats with ventilation or sunlight which those individuals particularly disliked. At the scheduled hour of departure, they would delay the train in order to complete the arrangements. Cost

---

[6] John Taylor of Caroline said, "Wealth, like suffrage, must be considerably distributed to sustain a democratick republic; and hence, whatever draws a considerable proportion of either into a few hands will destroy it" (*An Inquiry into the Principles and Policy of the Government of the United States* [Fredericksburg, Va., 1814], pp. 274-75).

of operations would be increased, passengers vexed, and timetables disrupted.

In a democracy of the American kind, said the comparison, those who particularly want good seats come early, while those who do not care come late, quite prepared to accept what is left. Individuals indulge their own preferences and aversions as to sunlight and in the choice of neighbors. They distribute themselves, automatically and to the maximum satisfaction of all concerned, throughout the train, and all this is accomplished without supervision, without expense, and without delay.

Like all analogies, this one probably has its pitfalls; but, without stopping to look for them, can we not observe one major unstated assumption in the description of the democratic train? It is the simple assumption that *there will be enough seats for everyone*; that the average passenger stands a reasonably good chance of finding one that will satisfy him. If the passenger train symbolizes the American economy, this assumption is valid, but for other countries it may or may not be valid, and certainly it is the sufficiency of seats, quite as much as the method of seat-selection, which makes the democratic system work.

Not only has the presence of more than enough seats, more than enough rewards for those who strive, made the maintenance of a democratic system possible in America; it has also given a characteristic tone to American equalitarianism as distinguished from the equalitarianism of the Old World. Essentially, the difference is that Europe has always conceived of redistribution of wealth as necessitating the expropriation of some and the corresponding aggrandizement of others; but America has conceived of it primarily in terms of giving to some without taking from others. Hence, Europe cannot think of altering the relationship between the various levels of society without assuming a class struggle; but America has altered and can alter these relationships without necessarily treating one class as the victim or even, in an ultimate sense, the antagonist of another. The European mind often assumes implicitly that the volume of wealth is fixed; that most of the potential wealth has already been converted into actual wealth; that this actual wealth is already in the hands of owners; and, therefore, that the only way for one person or group to secure more is to wrest it from some other person or group, leaving that person or group with less. The British Labour party, for instance, has, I believe, placed greater emphasis upon the heavy taxation of the wealthy and less upon the increase of productive capacity than an American labor party might have done. The American mind, by contrast, often assumes implicitly that the volume of wealth is dynamic, that much potential wealth still remains to be converted; and that diverse groups—for instance, capital and labor—can take more wealth out of the environment by working together than they can take out of one another by class warfare.

European radical thought is prone to demand that the man of property be stripped of his carriage and his fine clothes; but American radical thought is likely to insist, instead, that the ordinary man is entitled to mass-produced copies, indistinguishable from the originals. Few Americans feel entirely at ease

with the slogan "Soak the rich," but the phrase "Deal me in" springs spontaneously and joyously to American lips.

This American confidence that our abundance will suffice for the attainment
of all the goals of social justice is evident throughout the greater part of our
national history. Even before the American Revolution, squatters who had entered into illegal occupation of land on the Pennsylvania frontier justified their
action by declaring that "it was against the law of God and nature that so much
land should be idle while so many Christians wanted it to labor on to raise
bread." They did not contend, it is worth noticing, that it was wrong in general
for man to want bread. They probably had been taught to regard want as
part of the order of nature; but, where so much land was available, then it was
wrong for men to want. In other words, the availability of an economic surplus
altered the standards of social justice.

It has been altering them ever since. It enabled Dr. Townsend to win a vast
following for the belief that it was wrong for old people to receive less than
thirty dollars every Thursday; it enabled Upton Sinclair to come within an ace
of being elected governor of what is now the second state of the Union, on
a platform that demanded an end of poverty in California. It was this same attitude of mind on which Huey P. Long capitalized in his "share-our-wealth" program—and capitalized to such good effect that he became for a while Franklin
Roosevelt's most dangerous adversary. In his formal argument, Long employed
a simple fallacy: he computed the value of America's wealth, developed and un-
developed, liquid and nonliquid, and then proceeded to treat the total sum as if
it were in the form of cash available for distribution. Granted the validity of
his calculation, the phrase "every man a king" did not seem excessive. But, despite this sophistry, Long was not relying primarily upon the arithmetical
naïveté of the American people; he was relying upon their belief in the inexhaustible plenty of North America and in their own unrestrained right to enjoy this plenty without brain trust or dogma.

Long, Townsend, and Sinclair have provided striking though extreme examples of the American faith in plenty; but it is perhaps more revealing to consider a program which gained the support of a clear majority of all Americans
—namely, the New Deal. For Franklin Roosevelt, too, was an apostle of
abundance and, accordingly, of the view that the one-third who were unfortunate could be cared for without detriment to existing interests. Although hated
in conservative circles as an expropriator and a fomentor of class antagonisms,
Roosevelt in fact attempted to create a real balance between various class interests, such as those of labor and those of management; and this balance was
predicated on an idea which was the very antithesis of the class struggle—the
idea that no one need lose anything: debts were not scaled down, mortgages
were not canceled, imminent bankruptcies which would have paved the way for
nationalization were not permitted to occur. Even "the unscrupulous money-
changers," as Roosevelt called them, were not driven from the temples of
finance. They were simply required to suspend operations for a brief time.

Landlords collected farm benefits; industrialists under the NRA secured indulgence for monopolistic practices that had been under fire from more conservative administrations for forty years; while little businesses were protected by
Thurman Arnold and the TNEC. At the nadir of the Depression, when capitalism was fearfully vulnerable and almost unresisting to attack and when many
doctrinaires would have said that the overthrow of capitalism was the prerequisite to reform, Roosevelt unhesitatingly assumed that the country could afford
to pay capitalism's ransom and to buy reform, too. One of his most irritating
and most successful qualities was his habit of assuming that benefits could be
granted without costs being felt—an assumption rooted in his faith in the potentialities of the American economy.

Going beyond Roosevelt himself, it is interesting to consider the attitude of
the American people as a whole toward the idea of class struggle. Antipathy to
the concept is a well-known American trait, and it is frequently associated with
or attributed to America's faith in the ideal of equality and America's reluctance
to admit that social stratification exists. Certainly this commitment to the ideal
of equality has a deep bearing; but is not our hostility to the class-struggle
concept also linked with our reluctance to entertain the thought that American
wealth has ceased to grow, that we can no longer raise the standard of living
at one point without lowering it somewhere else?

Occasionally, one encounters the statement that Americans believe in leveling up rather than in leveling down. The truth of the assertion is more or less
self-evident, but the basic meaning is less so. Clearly, if one is leveling a fixed
number of items, say, personal incomes, the very process of leveling implies the
reduction of the higher ones. But in order to raise the lower without reducing
the higher, to level *up*, it is necessary to increase the total of all the incomes—
that is, to introduce new factors instead of solving the problem with the factors originally given. And it is by this strategem of refusing to accept the factors given, of drawing on nature's surplus and on technology's tricks, that
America has often dealt with her problems of social reform.

This, in turn, may explain another distinctive feature of the American record,
and that is the relative lack of intellectualism in its reform or radical movements. For instance, by European standards the Populists of the late nineteenth
century, and even more the Progressives of the early twentieth, would have
seemed incredibly muddled, sentimental, and superficial in their thinking. European radicalism almost invariably has had a highly articulated rationale, a fully
developed doctrinal system. European radicals have kept their ideological weapons sharpened to razor edge, so that they are ever ready to follow logic through
the most complex maze or to split the hairs of heresy in disputes over minor
points of doctrine. They do this, in part, I believe, because the social problems
with which they deal are relatively fixed, and disciplined intelligence in the one
means through which they can hope to attain a solution. But the social problems of America were not at all fixed, and their mutability has made logical
solutions unnecessary.

Our practice, indeed, has been to overleap problems—to bypass them—rather than to solve them. For instance, in the 1880's and 1890's there seemed to be three major public problems—the problem of a shrinking bullion supply; the problem of the control of an entire industry by a small group of monopolists, like John D. Rockefeller and his associates in the oil industry; and the problem of regulation of the railroads, which enjoyed a natural monopoly of transportation. Reformers struggled with all three of these problems, and various political solutions were proposed: the adoption of a bimetallic currency to relieve the bullion stringency, the enactment of an anti-trust law to curb Mr. Rockefeller, and the adoption of an Interstate Commerce Act to protect the shipper vis-à-vis the railroads. But in each case technological change interposed to relieve the acuteness of the problem or even to make it obsolete: the discovery of new gold supplies in the Klondike and of new methods of recovering gold reversed the process of shrinkage in the bullion supply; the discovery of the vast new deposits of oil in Texas and elsewhere undermined the dominance of Rockefeller in the oil industry as no legislative prohibition was ever able to do; and the introduction of trucks moving over a network of national highways ended the natural monopoly of transportation by the railroads before Congress ceased the long quest for a legislative solution.

There is a widespread belief in the United States that the basic policy of our government underwent a sudden change about twenty years ago, with the advent of the New Deal. According to this belief, the American Republic had been a thoroughgoing laissez faire state during its first century and a half—a state where government scrupulously refrained from intervention in the economic sphere, and private enterprise alone shaped the country's economic progress. Then, it is supposed, an abrupt reversal of policy took place, and, turning our backs upon the principles that had guided us to our earlier economic triumphs, we embraced a paternalistic program of governmental regulation and control which started us on the road to the welfare state. This view is probably most widely prevalent in conservative circles, but among people who are left of center there is also a widespread belief that government in the nineteenth and early twentieth centuries held aloof from economic problems and that this negative attitude continued until the time of Franklin Roosevelt, who followed a trail blazed by the Progressives and asserted a more constructive function for public authority. In short, left and right are in dispute as to the merit of this change, but they are inclined to agree that a complete change took place.

Without denying that a major transformation occurred, we need to be aware of the strands of continuity, as well as of the shifts and new departures in our history. If we are to appreciate the links with the past, we must recognize that laissez faire was not the unique principle of policy in our eighteenth- and nineteenth-century development but that one of the key principles was certainly the constant endeavor of government to make the economic abundance of the nation accessible to the public. The tactics by which this was done changed as the form of abundance itself changed, but the basic purpose—to keep our population in contact with the sources of wealth—has remained steadily in the ascendant throughout our history.

In the early nineteenth century the major form in which abundance presented itself was the fertility of unsettled land. For a people of whom 90 per cent followed agricultural pursuits, access to abundance meant opportunity to settle the new lands. The government responded by a series of land laws, beginning with the Ordinance of 1785 and extending far past the Homestead Act of 1862, which made land progressively easier for settlers to attain, until at last they could acquire title to 160 acres absolutely free. Over the years, while this was happening, some eminently public spirited men like John Quincy Adams contended for a program that would have conserved the assets of the public domain by distributing it gradually and on a basis that would yield revenue to the Treasury; but all such proposals were defeated, and quick settlement was stimulated even by legislation which encouraged squatters to occupy the land before it had been opened to public entry. Widespread access to wealth was preferred over the public capitalization of a great economic asset.

Relatively early, however, it became clear that access to soil did not mean access to wealth unless it was accompanied by access to market. Fertile soil remained a mere potentiality when its products could not reach the consumer. The market was the source of wealth to which access was needed, and again government responded by providing the internal improvements which would give such access. Sometimes the federal government did this, as, for instance, by the construction of the Cumberland Pike; sometimes the state governments took the initiative, as New York did with the digging of the Erie Canal; and sometimes government did not execute the project itself but encouraged private interests to do so by offering such tangible inducements as direct financial support, use of the public credit, and use of the power of eminent domain. Even in so great a project as the building of the first transcontinental railroad, the government virtually furnished all the funds, and, though the ownership was private, a congressman from New York could truthfully point out that the government in fact had built the railroads.

Later still, the wealth to which access was needed appeared increasingly in forms that could not be handled by the individual acting as a solitary operator. Iron resources, coal resources, petroleum resources, water-power resources, and other physical assets promised to raise the standard of living; but the only means of access to their value was through large-scale concentration of capital and labor. Again, government responded by facilitating the means of access: it made easy the process of concentration by sanctioning the wide use of the practice of incorporation; it assured the new corporations, through judicial interpretation of the Fourteenth Amendment, that they would enjoy the fullest legal security and even advantage; by the tariffs of the Civil War and post-Civil War periods, it guaranteed the corporations control of the American market. In return they did what was expected of them: they converted potential wealth into usable wealth, wastefully, selfishly, and ruthlessly in many cases, but quickly—and results were the primary thing demanded of them.

By the third decade of the twentieth century, the form in which wealth appeared had again altered drastically. No longer did it consist in natural resources of soil or subsoil, requiring to be put into operation. Access to wealth was now dependent upon the continued movement of the production lines rather than upon the throwing open of untapped resources. In these circumstances, the operation of the business cycle, manifesting itself in the great Depression, seemed to block access to wealth as completely as the barriers of physical distance had blocked it a century earlier. In both cases, though the overt circumstances seemed wholly dissimilar, Americans found consolation in the same basic and comforting conviction—that abundance was there, and the problem was not to create it or to get along without it but simply to find how to get at it. And in both cases government responded with steps to provide access. If access depended upon the creation of purchasing power, government under the New Deal was ready to create it by spending, lending, priming the pump, and enacting minimum-wage laws; if it depended upon the capacity of workers to bargain collectively, government was ready to confer that capacity by law; if it depended upon securing industry against some of the hazards of competition, government offered a National Industrial Recovery Act to remove these hazards.

Writers on public questions often assume that in our early history we had a basic commitment to individualism and that we have recently abandoned this traditional principle just for the sake of security. But what we really were committed to was realizing on the potentialities of our unmatched assets and raising our standard of living. Because the standard of living involves comfort and material things, a basic concern with it is commonly regarded as ignoble; yet, as I have already suggested, it is only because we have attained a relatively high standard of living that we can afford to own and operate a democratic system. But, whether noble or not, our commitment to abundance was primary, and individualism was sanctioned as the very best means of fulfilling the possibilities of abundance. When it ceased to be the best means, we modified it with a readiness alarming to people who had supposed that it was the individualism itself which was basic. We did this because a great many people had never regarded it, at bottom, as more than a means to an end. The politics of our democracy was a politics of abundance rather than a politics of individualism,[7] a politics of increasing our wealth quickly rather than of dividing it precisely, a politics which smiled both on those who valued abundance as a means to safeguard freedom and on those who valued freedom as an aid in securing abundance.

In so far as Americans have succeeded in equating abundance and freedom, it becomes something of an abstraction to question which is the means and which is the end. The historical analyst may itch to discover which one is basic and

[7] "Thomas Carlyle once said to an American: 'Ye may boast o' yer dimocracy, or any ither 'cracy, or any kind o' poleetical roobish; but the reason why yer laboring folk are so happy is thot ye have a vost deal o' land for a verra few people'" (Josiah Strong, *Our Country* [1885], p. 153).

which derivative, but the purpose of Americans, generally, will be to make the two coincide in such a way that, as factors, they cannot be isolated. In this sense it may seem somewhat metaphysical to make heavy-handed distinctions between these two ingredients—freedom and abundance—which are to such a great extent fused in American democratic thought.

But, though Americans have caused freedom and abundance to converge, the two are not by nature prone to convergence, and for the world at large they have not been closely linked. Consequently, when America, out of her abundance, preaches the gospel of democracy to countries which see no means of attaining abundance, the message does not carry the meaning which it is meant to convey. No other part of American activity has been so consistently and so completely a failure as our attempt to export democracy. At this point, the duality between abundance and freedom in the American democratic formula ceases to be abstract and becomes painfully concrete, for it is the lack of understanding of what we have to offer the rest of the world that has vitiated our efforts to fulfil a national mission which we undertook with a real dedication and for which we have made real sacrifices. But the discussion of this aspect of the relation between democracy and abundance will involve a consideration of the world relations of the American Republic, and this is so extensive a subject that it must be left for another chapter.

Challenges to Science and Technology

❖❖

C. P. SNOW

The Two Cultures[1]

It is about three years since I made a sketch in print of a problem which had been on my mind for some time.[2] It was a problem I could not avoid just because of the circumstances of my life. The only credentials I had to ruminate on the subject at all came through those circumstances, through nothing more than a set of chances. Anyone with similar experience would have seen much the same things and I think made very much the same comments about them. It just happened to be an unusual experience. By training I was a

[1] From The Two Cultures and the Scientific Revolution by C. P. Snow (New York: Cambridge University Press), pp. 1-22. Reprinted by permission of the publishers.
[2] "The Two Cultures," New Statesman, 6 October 1956.

scientist: by vocation I was a writer. That was all. It was a piece of luck, if you like, that arose through coming from a poor home.

But my personal history isn't the point now. All that I need say is that I came to Cambridge and did a bit of research here at a time of major scientific activity. I was privileged to have a ringside view of one of the most wonderful creative periods in all physics. And it happened through the flukes of war— including meeting W. L. Bragg in the buffet on Kettering station on a very cold morning in 1939, which had a determining influence on my practical life —that I was able, and indeed morally forced, to keep that ringside view ever since. So for thirty years I have had to be in touch with scientists not only out of curiosity, but as part of a working existence. During the same thirty years I was trying to shape the books I wanted to write which in due course took me among writers.

There have been plenty of days when I have spent the working hours with scientists and then gone off at night with some literary colleagues. I mean that literally. I have had, of course, intimate friends among both scientists and writers. It was through living among these groups and much more, I think, through moving regularly from one to the other and back again that I got occupied with the problem of what, long before I put it on paper, I christened to myself as the "two cultures." For constantly I felt I was moving among two groups—comparable in intelligence, identical in race, not grossly different in social origin, earning about the same incomes, who had almost ceased to communicate at all, who in intellectual, moral and psychological climate had so little in common that instead of going from Burlington House or South Kensington to Chelsea, one might have crossed an ocean.

In fact, one had travelled much further than across an ocean—because after a few thousand Atlantic miles, one found Greenwich Village talking precisely the same language as Chelsea, and both having about as much communication with M.I.T. as though the scientists spoke nothing but Tibetan. For this is not just our problem; owing to some of our educational and social idiosyncrasies, it is slightly exaggerated here, owing to another English social peculiarity it is slightly minimised; by and large this is a problem of the entire West.

By this I intend something serious. I am not thinking of the pleasant story of how one of the more convivial Oxford greats dons—I have heard the story attributed to A. L. Smith—came over to Cambridge to dine. The date is perhaps the 1890's. I think it must have been at St. John's, or possibly Trinity. Anyway, Smith was sitting at the right hand of the President—or Vice-Master—and he was a man who liked to include all round him in the conversation, although he was not immediately encouraged by the expressions of his neighbours. He addressed some cheerful Oxonian chit-chat at the one opposite to him, and got a grunt. He then tried the man on his own right hand and got another grunt. Then, rather to his surprise, one looked at the other and said, "Do you know what he's talking about?" "I haven't the least idea." At this, even Smith was getting out of his depth. But the President, acting as a social emollient, put him at his ease, by saying, "Oh, those are mathematicians! We never talk to *them*."

No, I intend something serious. I believe the intellectual life of the whole of western society is increasingly being split into two polar groups. When I say the intellectual life, I mean to include also a large part of our practical life, because I should be the last person to suggest the two can at the deepest level be distinguished. I shall come back to the practical life a little later. Two polar groups: at one pole we have the literary intellectuals, who incidentally while no one was looking took to referring to themselves as "intellectuals" as though there were no others. I remember G. H. Hardy once remarking to me in mild puzzlement, some time in the 1930's: "Have you noticed how the word 'intellectual' is used nowadays? There seems to be a new definition which certainly doesn't include Rutherford or Eddington or Dirac or Adrian or me. It does seem rather odd, don't y' know." [3]

Literary intellectuals at one pole—at the other scientists, and as the most representative, the physical scientists. Between the two a gulf of mutual incomprehension—sometimes (particularly among the young) hostility and dislike, but most of all lack of understanding. They have a curious distorted image of each other. Their attitudes are so different that, even on the level of emotion, they can't find much common ground. Non-scientists tend to think of scientists as brash and boastful. They hear Mr. T. S. Eliot, who just for these illustrations we can take as an archetypal figure, saying about his attempts to revive verse-drama, that we can hope for very little, but that he would feel content if he and his co-workers could prepare the ground for a new Kyd or a new Greene. That is the one, restricted and constrained, with which literary intellectuals are at home: it is the subdued voice of their culture. Then they hear a much louder voice, that of another archetypal figure, Rutherford, trumpeting: "This is the heroic age of science! This is the Elizabethan age!" Many of us heard that, and a good many other statements beside which that was mild; and we weren't left in any doubt whom Rutherford was casting for the role of Shakespeare. What is hard for the literary intellectuals to understand, imaginatively or intellectually, is that he was absolutely right.

And compare "this is the way the world ends, not with a bang but a whimper"—incidentally, one of the least likely scientific prophecies ever made—compare that with Rutherford's famous repartee, "Lucky fellow, Rutherford, always on the crest of the wave." "Well, I made the wave, didn't I?"

The non-scientists have a rooted impression that the scientists are shal-

---

[3] This lecture was delivered to a Cambridge audience, and so I used some points of reference which I did not need to explain. G. H. Hardy, 1877-1947, was one of the most distinguished pure mathematicians of his time, and a picturesque figure in Cambridge both as a young don and on his return in 1931 to the Sadleirian Chair of Mathematics.

lowly optimistic, unaware of man's condition. On the other hand, the scientists believe that the literary intellectuals are totally lacking in foresight, peculiarly unconcerned with their brother man, in a deep sense anti-intellectual, anxious to restrict both art and thought to the existential moment. And so on. Anyone with a mild talent for invective could produce plenty of this kind of subterranean back-chat. On each side there is some of it which is not entirely baseless. It is all destructive. Much of it rests on misinterpretations which are dangerous. I should like to deal with two of the most profound of these now, one on each side.

First, about the scientists' optimism. This is an accusation which has been made so often that it has become a platitude. It has been made by some of the acutest non-scientific minds of the day. But it depends upon a confusion between the individual experience and the social experience, between the individual condition of man and his social condition. Most of the scientists I have known well have felt—just as deeply as the non-scientists I have known well—that the individual condition of each of us is tragic. Each of us is alone: sometimes we escape from solitariness, through love or affection or perhaps creative moments, but those triumphs of life are pools of light we make for ourselves while the edge of the road is black: each of us dies alone. Some scientists I have known have had faith in revealed religion. Perhaps with them the sense of the tragic condition is not so strong. I don't know. With most people of deep feeling, however high-spirited and happy they are, sometimes most with those who are happiest and most high-spirited, it seems to be right in the fibres, part of the weight of life. That is as true of the scientists I have known best as of anyone at all.

But nearly all of them—and this is where the colour of hope genuinely comes in—would see no reason why, just because the individual condition is tragic, so must the social condition be. Each of us is solitary: each of us dies alone: all right, that's a fate against which we can't struggle—but there is plenty in our condition which is not fate, and against which we are less than human unless we do struggle.

Most of our fellow human beings, for instance, are underfed and die before their time. In the crudest terms, *that* is the social condition. There is a moral trap which comes through the insight into man's loneliness: it tempts one to sit back, complacent in one's unique tragedy, and let the others go without a meal.

As a group, the scientists fall into that trap less than others. They are inclined to be impatient to see if something can be done: and inclined to think that it can be done, until it's proved otherwise. That is their real optimism, and it's an optimism that the rest of us badly need.

In reverse, the same spirit, tough and good and determined to fight it out at the side of their brother men, has made scientists regard the other culture's social attitudes as contemptible. That is too facile: some of them are, but they are a temporary phase and not to be taken as representative.

I remember being cross-examined by a scientist of distinction. "Why do most writers take on social opinions which would have been thought distinctly uncivilised and démodé at the time of the Plantagenets? Wasn't that true of most of the famous twentieth-century writers? Yeats, Pound, Wyndham Lewis, nine out of ten of those who have dominated literary sensibility in our time—weren't they not only politically silly, but politically wicked? Didn't the influence of all they represent bring Auschwitz that much nearer?"

I thought at the time, and I still think, that the correct answer was not to defend the indefensible. It was no use saying that Yeats, according to friends whose judgment I trust, was a man of singular magnanimity of character, as well as a great poet. It was no use denying the facts, which are broadly true. The honest answer was that there is, in fact, a connection, which literary persons were culpably slow to see, between some kinds of early twentieth-century art and the most imbecile expressions of anti-social feeling.[4] That was one reason, among many, why some of us turned our backs on the art and tried to hack out a new or different way for ourselves.[5]

But though many of those writers dominated literary sensibility for a generation, that is no longer so, or at least to nothing like the same extent. Literature changes more slowly than science. It hasn't the same automatic corrective, and so its misguided periods are longer. But it is ill-considered of scientists to judge writers on the evidence of the period 1914-50.

Those are two of the misunderstandings between the two cultures. I should say, since I began to talk about them—the two cultures, that is—I have had some criticism. Most of my scientific acquaintances think that there is something in it, and so do most of the practising artists I know. But I have been argued with by non-scientists of strong down-to-earth interests. Their view is that it is an over-simplification, and that if one is going to talk in these terms there ought to be at least three cultures. They argue that, though they are not scientists themselves, they would share a good deal of the scientific feeling. They would have as little use—perhaps, since they knew more about it, even less use—for the recent literary culture as the scientists themselves. J. H. Plumb, Alan Bullock and some of my American sociological friends have said that they vigorously refuse to be corralled in a cultural box with people they wouldn't be seen dead with, or to be regarded as helping to produce a climate which would not permit of social hope.

I respect those arguments. The number 2 is a very dangerous process. Attempts to divide anything into two ought to be regarded with much suspicion.

4 I said a little more about this connection in *The Times Literary Supplement*, "Challenge to the Intellect," 15 August 1958. I hope some day to carry the analysis further.
5 It would be more accurate to say that, for literary reasons, we felt the prevailing literary modes were useless to us. We were, however, reinforced in that feeling when it occurred to us that those prevailing modes went hand in hand with social attitudes either wicked, or absurd, or both.

I have thought a long time about going in for further refinements: but in the end I have decided against. I was searching for something a little more than a dashing metaphor, a good deal less than a cultural map: and for those purposes the two cultures is about right, and subtilising any more would bring more disadvantages than it's worth.

At one pole, the scientific culture really is a culture, not only in an intellectual but also in an anthropological sense. That is, its members need not, and of course often do not, always completely understand each other; biologists more often than not will have a pretty hazy idea of contemporary physics; but there are common attitudes, common standards and patterns of behaviour, common approaches and assumptions. This goes surprisingly wide and deep. It cuts across other mental patterns, such as those of religion or politics or class.

Statistically, I suppose slightly more scientists are in religious terms unbelievers, compared with the rest of the intellectual world—though there are plenty who are religious, and that seems to be increasingly so among the young. Statistically also, slightly more scientists are on the Left in open politics—though again, plenty always have called themselves conservatives, and that also seems to be more common among the young. Compared with the rest of the intellectual world, considerably more scientists in this country and probably in the U.S. come from poor families.[6] Yet, over a whole range of thought and behaviour, none of that matters very much. In their working, and in much of their emotional life, their attitudes are closer to other scientists than to non-scientists who in religion or politics or class have the same labels as themselves. If I were to risk a piece of shorthand, I should say that naturally they had the future in their bones.

They may or may not like it, but they have it. That was as true of the conservatives J. J. Thomson and Lindemann as of the radicals Einstein or Blackett: as true of the Christian A. H. Compton as of the materialist Bernal: of the aristocrats Broglie or Russell as of the proletarian Faraday: of those born rich, like Thomas Merton or Victor Rothschild, as of Rutherford, who was the son of an odd-job handyman. Without thinking about it, they respond alike. That is what a culture means.

At the other pole, the spread of attitudes is wider. It is obvious that between the two, as one moves through intellectual society from the physicists to the literary intellectuals, there are all kinds of tones of feeling on the way. But I believe the pole of total incomprehension of science radiates its influence on all the rest. That total incomprehension gives, much more pervasively than we realise, living in it, an unscientific flavour to the whole "traditional" culture, and that scientific flavour is often, much more than we admit, on the point of turning anti-scientific. The feelings of one pole become the anti-feelings of

[6] An analysis of the school from which Fellows of the Royal Society come tells its own story. The distribution is markedly different from that of, for example, members of the Foreign Service or Queen's Counsel.

the other. If the scientists have the future in their bones, then the traditional culture responds by wishing the future did not exist.[7] It is the traditional culture, to an extent remarkably little diminished by the emergence of the scientific one, which manages the western world.

This polarisation is sheer loss to us all. To us as people, and to our society. It is at the same time practical and intellectual and creative loss, and I repeat that it is false to imagine that those three considerations are clearly separable. But for a moment I want to concentrate on the intellectual loss.

The degree of incomprehension on both sides is the kind of joke which has gone sour. There are about fifty thousand working scientists in the country and about eighty thousand professional engineers or applied scientists. During the war and in the years since, my colleagues and I have had to interview somewhere between thirty to forty thousand of these—that is, about 25 per cent. The number is large enough to give us a fair sample, though of the men we talked to most would still be under forty. We were able to find out a certain amount of what they read and thought about. I confess that even I, who am fond of them and respect them, was a bit shaken. We hadn't quite expected that the links with the traditional culture should be so tenuous, nothing more than a formal touch of the cap.

As one would expect, some of the very best scientists had and have plenty of energy and interest to spare, and we came across several who had read everything that literary people talk about. But that's very rare. Most of the rest, when one tried to probe for what books they had read, would modestly confess, "Well, I've *tried* a bit of Dickens," rather as though Dickens were an extraordinarily esoteric, tangled and dubiously rewarding writer, something like Rainer Maria Rilke. In fact that is exactly how they do regard him: we thought that discovery, that Dickens had been transformed into the type-specimen of literary incomprehensibility, was one of the oddest results of the whole exercise.

But of course, in reading him, in reading almost any writer whom we should value, they are just touching their caps to the traditional culture. They have their own culture, intensive, rigorous, and constantly in action. This culture contains a great deal of argument, usually much more rigorous, and almost always at a higher conceptual level, than literary persons' arguments—even though the scientists do cheerfully use words in senses which literary persons don't recognise, the senses are exact ones, and when they talk about "subjective," "objective," "philosophy" or "progressive," [8] they know what they mean, even though it isn't what one is accustomed to expect.

[7] Compare George Orwell's 1984, which is the strongest possible wish that the future should not exist, with J. D. Bernal's World without War.

[8] *Subjective*, in contemporary technological jargon, means "divided according to subjects." *Objective* means "directed towards an object." *Philosophy* means "general intellectual approach or attitude" (for example, a scientist's "philosophy of guided weapons" might lead him to propose certain kinds of "objective research"). A "progressive" job means one with possibilities of promotion.

Remember, these are very intelligent men. Their culture is in many ways an exacting and admirable one. It doesn't contain much art, with the exception, an important exception, of music. Verbal exchange, insistent argument. Long-playing records. Colour-photography. The ear, to some extent the eye. Books, very little, though perhaps not many would go so far as one hero, who perhaps I should admit was further down the scientific ladder than the people I've been talking about—who when asked what books he read, replied firmly and confidently: "Books? I prefer to use my books as tools." It was very hard not to let the mind wander—what sort of tool would a book make? Perhaps a hammer? A primitive digging instrument?

Of books, though, very little. And of the books which to most literary persons are bread and butter, novels, history, poetry, plays, almost nothing at all. It isn't that they're not interested in the psychological or moral or social life. In the social life, they certainly are, more than most of us. In the moral, they are by and large the soundest group of intellectuals we have; there is a moral component right in the grain of science itself, and almost all scientists form their own judgments of the moral life. In the psychological they have as much interest as most of us, though occasionally I fancy they come to it rather late. It isn't that they lack the interests. It is much more that the whole literature of the traditional culture doesn't seem to them relevant to those interests. They are, of course, dead wrong. As a result, their imaginative understanding is less than it could be. They are self-impoverished.

But what about the other side? They are impoverished too—perhaps more seriously, because they are vainer about it. They still like to pretend that the traditional culture is the whole of "culture," as though the natural order didn't exist. As though the exploration of the natural order was of no interest either in its own value or its consequences. As though the scientific edifice of the physical world was not, in its intellectual depth, complexity and articulation, the most beautiful and wonderful collective work of the mind of man. Yet most non-scientists have no conception of that edifice at all. Even if they want to have it, they can't. It is rather as though, over an immense range of intellectual experience, a whole group was tone-deaf. Except that this tone-deafness doesn't come by nature, but by training, or rather the absence of training.

As with the tone-deaf, they don't know what they miss. They give a pitying chuckle at the news of scientists who have never read a major work of English literature. They dismiss them as ignorant specialists. Yet their own ignorance and their own specialisation is just as startling. A good many times I have been present at gatherings of people who, by the standards of the traditional culture, are thought highly educated and who have with considerable gusto been expressing their incredulity at the illiteracy of scientists. Once or twice I have been provoked and have asked the company how many of them could describe the Second Law of Thermodynamics. The response was cold: it was also negative. Yet I was asking something which is about the scientific equivalent of: *Have you read a work of Shakespeare's?*

I now believe that if I had asked an even simpler question—such as, What do you mean by mass, or acceleration, which is the scientific equivalent of saying, *Can you read?*—not more than one in ten of the highly educated would have felt that I was speaking the same language. So the great edifice of modern physics goes up, and the majority of the cleverest people in the western world have about as much insight into it as their neolithic ancestors would have had.

Just one more of those questions, that my non-scientific friends regard as being in the worst of taste. Cambridge is a university where scientists and non-scientists meet every night at dinner.[9] About two years ago, one of the most astonishing experiments in the whole history of science was brought off. I don't mean the sputnik—that was admirable for quite different reasons, as a feat of organisation and a triumphant use of existing knowledge. No, I mean the experiment at Columbia by Yang and Lee. It is an experiment of the greatest beauty and originality, but the result is so startling that one forgets how beautiful the experiment is. It makes us think again about some of the fundamentals of the physical world. Intuition, common sense—they are neatly stood on their heads. The result is usually known as the contradiction of parity. If there were any serious communication between the two cultures, this experiment would have been talked about at every High Table in Cambridge. Was it? I wasn't here: but I should like to ask the question.

There seems then to be no place where the cultures meet. I am not going to waste time saying that this is a pity. It is much worse than that. Soon I shall come to some practical consequences. But at the heart of thought and creation we are letting some of our best chances go by default. The clashing point of two subjects, two disciplines, two cultures—of two galaxies, so far as that goes—ought to produce creative chances. In the history of mental activity that has been where some of the breakthroughs came. The chances are there now. But they are there, as it were, in a vacuum, because those in the two cultures can't talk to each other. It is bizarre how very little of twentieth-century science has been assimilated into twentieth-century art. Now and then one used to find poets conscientiously using scientific expressions, and getting them wrong—there was a time when "refraction" kept cropping up in verse in a mystifying fashion, and when "polarised light" was used as though writers were under the illusion that it was a specially admirable kind of light.

Of course, that isn't the way that science could be any good to art. It has got to be assimilated along with, and as part and parcel of, the whole of our mental experience, and used as naturally as the rest.

I said earlier that this cultural divide is not just an English phenomenon: it exists all over the western world. But it probably seems at its sharpest in England, for two reasons. One is our fanatical belief in educational specialisation, which is much more deeply ingrained in us than in any country in the world, west or east. The other is our tendency to let our social forms crystallise.

[9] Almost all college High Tables contain Fellows in both scientific and non-scientific subjects.

This tendency appears to get stronger, not weaker, the more we iron out economic inequalities: and this is specially true in education. It means that once anything like a cultural divide gets established, all the social forces operate to make it not less rigid, but more so.

The two cultures were already dangerously separate sixty years ago; but a prime minister like Lord Salisbury could have his own laboratory at Hatfield, and Arthur Balfour had a somewhat more than amateur interest in natural science. John Anderson did some research in organic chemistry in Würzburg before passing first into the Civil Service, and incidentally took a spread of subjects which is now impossible.[10] None of that degree of interchange at the top of the Establishment is likely, or indeed thinkable, now.[11]

In fact, the separation between the scientists and non-scientists is much less bridgeable among the young than it was even thirty years ago. Thirty years ago the cultures had long ceased to speak to each other: but at least they managed a kind of frozen smile across the gulf. Now the politeness has gone, and they just make faces. It is not only that the young scientists now feel that they are part of a culture on the rise while the other is in retreat. It is also, to be brutal, that the young scientists know that with an indifferent degree they'll get a comfortable job, while their contemporaries and counter-parts in English or History will be lucky to earn 60 per cent as much. No young scientist of any talent would feel that he isn't wanted or that his work is ridiculous, as did the hero of Lucky Jim, and in fact, some of the disgruntle-ment of Amis and his associates is the disgruntlement of the under-employed arts graduate.

There is only one way out of all this: it is, of course, by rethinking our education. In this country, for the two reasons I have given, that is more difficult than in any other. Nearly everyone will agree that our school educa-tion is too specialised. But nearly everyone feels that it is outside the will of man to alter it. Other countries are as dissatisfied with their education as we are, but are not so resigned.

The U.S. teach out of proportion more children up to eighteen than we do: they teach them far more widely, but nothing like so rigorously. They know that: they are hoping to take the problem in hand within ten years, though they may not have all that time to spare. The U.S.S.R. also teach out of propor-tion more children than we do: they also teach far more widely than we do (it is an absurd western myth that their school education is specialised) but

[10] He took the examination in 1905.
[11] It is, however, true to say that the compact nature of the managerial layers of English society—the fact that "everyone knows everyone else"—means that scien-tists and non-scientists do in fact know each other as people more easily than in most countries. It is also true that a good many leading politicians and adminis-trators keep up lively intellectual and artistic interests to a much greater extent, so far as I can judge, than is the case in the U.S. These are both among our assets.

much too rigorously.[12] They know that—and they are beating about to get it right. The Scandinavians, in particular the Swedes, who would make a more sensible job of it than any of us, are handicapped by their practical need to devote an inordinate amount of time to foreign languages. But they too are seized of the problem.

Are we? Have we crystallised so far that we are no longer flexible at all?

Talk to schoolmasters, and they say that our intense specialisation, like nothing else on earth, is dictated by the Oxford and Cambridge scholarship examinations. If that is so, one would have thought it not utterly impracticable to change the Oxford and Cambridge scholarship examinations. Yet one would underestimate the national capacity for the intricate defensive to believe that that was easy. All the lessons of our educational history suggest we are only capable of increasing specialisation, not decreasing it.

Somehow we have set ourselves the task of producing a tiny *élite*—far smaller proportionately than in any comparable country—educated in one academic skill. For a hundred and fifty years in Cambridge it was mathematics: then it was mathematics: then it was mathematics or classics: then natural science was allowed in. But still the choice had to be a single one.

It may well be that this process has gone too far to be reversible. I have given reasons why I think it is a disastrous process, for the purpose of a living culture. I am going on to give reasons why I think it is fatal, if we're to perform our practical tasks in the world. But I can think of only one example, in the whole of English educational history, where our pursuit of specialised mental exercises was resisted with success.

It was done here in Cambridge, fifty years ago, when the old order-of-merit in the Mathematical Tripos was abolished. For over a hundred years, the nature of the Tripos had been crystallising. The competition for the top places had got fiercer, and careers hung on them. In most colleges, certainly in my own, if one managed to come out as Senior or Second Wrangler, one was elected a Fellow out of hand. A whole apparatus of coaching had grown up. Men of the quality of Hardy, Littlewood, Russell, Eddington, Jeans, Keynes, went in for two or three years' training for an examination which was intensely competitive and intensely difficult. Most people in Cambridge were very proud of it, with a similar pride to that which almost anyone in England always has for our existing educational institutions, whatever they happen to be. If you study the fly-sheets of the time, you will find the passionate arguments for keeping the examination precisely as it was to all eternity: it was the only way to keep up standards, it was the only fair test of merit, indeed, the only seriously objective test in the world. The argument, in fact, were almost exactly those which are used today with precisely the same passionate sincerity if anyone suggests that the scholarship examinations might conceivably not be immune from change.

[12] I tried to compare American, Soviet and English education in "New Minds for the New World," *New Statesman*, 6 September 1956.

In every respect but one, in fact, the old Mathematical Tripos seemed perfect. The one exception, however, appeared to some to be rather important. It was simply—so the young creative mathematicians, such as Hardy and Littlewood, kept saying—that the training had no intellectual merit at all. They went a little further, and said that the Tripos had killed serious mathematics in England stone dead for a hundred years. Well, even in academic controversy, that took some skirting round, and they got their way. But I have an impression that Cambridge was a good deal more flexible between 1850 and 1914 than it has been in our time. If we had had the old Mathematical Tripos firmly planted among us, should we have ever managed to abolish it?

MORRIS FREEDMAN

Our Know-Nothing Scientists[1]

When I was a boy, one of my most frightening bogeymen was the scientist. I still remember my terror at seeing the Invisible Man pouring liquids from one test tube into another, drinking the mixture, becoming transparent, then launching on a spree of individual and mass murder, throttling policemen, derailing passenger trains. The Invisible Man and Mr. Hyde, who also drank brews that transformed one, took their place alongside Fu Manchu, snarling gang leaders, cowboy bad guys with black Stetsons, sadistic school teachers, Boris Karloff, Bela Lugosi, Lon Chaney. A white coated, bespectacled man mixing liquids in a room filled with glass piping or standing before an instrument board with knobs and dials that controlled crackling giant electric sparks was a sure sign that something depraved would soon be taking place, like the manufacture of a death ray or a monster. It is no wonder that Frankenstein, the scientist, has always been confused in popular thought with the monster he created. Both the scientist and his product are equally terrifying.

It is of course anti-intellectual and lowbrow to continue in a fear of scientists (and their counterparts, the engineers) these days, especially since they have become celebrities like jazz musicians and baseball players. One television panel featured Norbert Wiener, the bearded cybernetics man from M.I.T., alongside Phil Rizzuto, clean-shaven ex-Yankee shortstop. And the scientist has even emerged from his obscure laboratory to participate in high councils of state. "I know many times we bowed out and did not answer the questions which were not technical and scientific," Dr. Oppenheimer was quoted as having remarked about his government experience. "Often we were seduced into answering them." And who but the lowest conformist would

[1] Reprinted from Confessions of a Conformist by Morris Freedman. By permission of W. W. Norton & Company, Inc. Copyright © 1961 by Morris Freedman.

suggest that a scientist could not offer better advice on governmental problems than a mere politician or general?

In recent years, indeed, scientists have been giving the country the benefit of their wisdom on education (Teller), religion (Einstein), politics, military strategy (*Bulletin of the Atomic Scientist* is always running pieces on politics and military strategy). Of course, there is nothing wrong with any citizen expressing himself freely on any subject. But while most of us will not take seriously just anyone who has a theory about nuclear physics, some of us tend to listen reverently to the scientist or engineer, whether he talks on atoms, missiles, public schools, presidential candidates, churches, or our culture in general. My old fear of the scientists is returning as a result, for most technologists I have paid attention to are no more qualified to talk about any subject outside their special field than most of us are about the inside of the atom.

The scientist indeed may be less qualified than the nonscientist to talk outside his field, for his education is likely to have become rigorously narrow. Unless he has had the good fortune to attend an old-fashioned liberal arts college, he will have had the most superficial and hurried contact with the social sciences and humanities. If he has gone to one of the larger colleges of engineering, many of which are now turning out scientists as well as engineers, his contact may well have been nonexistent, for many such schools design special humanities and social-science courses which have been dehydrated of their most vital content. He will not know the facts and concepts of history or sociology or the ideas and values of literature or philosophy. Even if the scientist's undergraduate studies were sufficiently humane and liberal, the world he moves in makes for narrowness and, except in his own discipline, for shallowness. A physical chemist, lamenting his restricted focus, once complained to me in desperation that he can scarcely keep up with the work being done in his particular specialty, let alone in physical chemistry itself; he long ago gave up hope of keeping up with the whole of chemistry. His only reading outside chemistry since his one undergraduate course in humanities was for an inter-disciplinary honors class he was assigned to for one year.

Just what has brought about the transformation of the scientist from an evil figure in a remote, test-tube-cluttered laboratory to a contemporary culture hero at the center of our society? Certainly the publicity press releases attending the atom bomb had much to do with it, but long before Alamogordo and Hiroshima we were beginning to be impressed by the fabulous obscurity of the scientists. "Not even other scientists understand him," used to be the marveling comment about Einstein. Our society does respect learning and expertness, and the more recondite the learning and expertness are, the more they are respected. We simply have to be convinced of the genuine difficulty of the expertness, and the publicity—movies, books, magazine articles, newspaper features, television interviews—about our nuclear scientists has overwhelmingly persuaded us of the incredible complexity of their work.

As our scientists moved into areas that seemed quite mathematically pure—

nuclear physics, for example—and out of the H. G. Wellsian or Aldous Hux-
leyan domains, in which they manipulated human life in one way or another,
it became safe to respect scientists once again. We tend to approach our
scientists with a fond protectiveness, and we are the more protective the more
incomprehensible their findings. In a sense, we hesitate to offend or ignore
them: who can afford to challenge the medicine man, the witch doctor? He
may, after all, have magic on his side. Einstein had every word of his on
politics and religion scrupulously, awesomely recorded, even when some of
what he had to say was plain nonsense. We excuse our scientists from the
normal rules of conduct; after all we cannot expect workers in ivory towers
to behave like persons on the mundane plains below: all sorts of rationalizations, for example, were made to forgive the nuclear physicists for their loose
and casual attitudes on security which were revealed during the atom spy investigations.

Some scientists, carried away by the public reverence of themselves, behave
like culture heroes when they do appear in public, condescending, tolerant,
graciously offering an oracular tidbit, a glimpse of their Olympian camaraderie.
"He's a mean, caustic, and boorish man," Samuel Goudsmidt, co-formulator of
the electron spin theory, remarked about an associate. "I once dined with him
in a restaurant and he hounded the waiter until the poor fellow got so nervous
he dropped his tray, and that made my friend howl with glee. To most people,
he would be *persona non grata*. To me, he is a man who has solved difficult
scientific problems, and in my home, he is welcome." The freemasonry of
science would seem to justify any social behavior; it suggests the society of gods
on Olympus, whimsically toying with men and feuding with each other, but
also frequently aiding one another without regard to any other value but loyalty
to the fraternity.

The peculiar and rare expertness of scientists has always compelled them
to exist in enclaves—like circus performers, or movie actors, or Northwest
loggers, or surgeons—where rules of morality and behavior and even of knowledge are much more familiar and casual, and where one can safely and comfortably indulge oneself in lapses from ordinary requirements of deportment
and evaluation. Scientists frequently present a front suggesting that they are
devoted to more transcendent objectives than mere worldly ones (as when they
resign from Los Alamos or from an aircraft company to join a university
faculty to do "pure" research). With a sloganlike emphasis, some insist on the
purity and remoteness from practicality of all of their research. This endows
the research with the perfection of the abstract. It excludes questions of value
or of guilt. It is a way also of removing themselves from the technological and
manipulatory, the application of their work to the problems of actual human
existence. Scientists pride themselves on being detached, unbiased, objective
in their work, but, as Lionel Trilling has wondered, may not this very compulsion toward objectivity itself be a bias, itself be a way of avoiding an area
of reality?

Even the hobbies of the scientists are arcane. Einstein read Greek tragedy in the original; Oppenheimer knows Sanskrit; Goudsmidt studied Egyptology. Goudsmidt took up the study of scarabs when one of his college instructors complained that all he seemed interested in was the structure of the atom nucleus. The fact that Egyptian scarabs might be almost as obscure as protons and electrons seems not to have occurred to him.

One element in the scientist's current popularity may well be his youthfulness. A number of Nobelists in physics were in their early thirties when they received their awards. It seems to be an understanding among physicists that if a man has not made his great finding before he is thirty-five, he can consider himself washed up—at least in terms of being tapped for the Nobel Prize. A good number of the leading scientists and engineers at present engaged in nuclear and missiles research are in their thirties.

This youthfulness of the scientist, which puts him in the same endearing category with teen-age musical prodigies, chess players, and bonus baseball players, somewhat frightens me. I suspect, too, that, while the general public might be enchanted by the boy scientist, as by the child musician, and wish him well, there is a certain shakiness in the respect paid to him. After all, playing with hydrogen bombs or intercontinental ballistic missiles is not quite the same as playing with a bat and ball or a piano or a chess set. Mixed with the public respect for the boy scientist is an apprehensive hope that he really knows what he is doing.

But what kind of a discipline must the study of physics be if it can be mastered and revolutionized by a man before he is thirty? It must be of the very special order which includes the playing of chess, of musical instruments, and of sports. No doubt great talents or genius is essential to becoming outstanding in any of these fields. The admiration and respect of the ordinary man naturally go out to chess champions, musical performers, home-run hitters, as they do to acrobats, animal trainers, great inventors, ingenious wood-whittlers, and all sorts of persons with unique skills. Without meaning in any way to obscure or denigrate the special nature of scientific study, I submit that any area in which a man can make his greatest achievement so early in his life is not one in which the special capacities that come with maturity—wisdom, ripeness, extensive as well as intensive knowledge, balance, subtlety, breadth of vision, a developed moral sense, a system of values, etc.—are normally employed.

Now I am perfectly happy, delighted, that our country has been able to turn out brilliant young scientists. But my happiness does not prevent me from asking certain questions: how much history do these young men know, how much literature, how much social science, how much philosophy, how are they different from their youthful counterparts in the Soviet Union, or under Nazi Germany? Are they like the British scientists who defected to Russia? Might they ever become like the Nazi engineers and scientists who perverted science to the ends of barbarism? I do not much care whether the boy who leaves high school to pitch for the Milwaukee Braves knows his history or not; or whether Van Cliburn happened to have read Arthur Koestler or George Orwell before he made his trip to Moscow; but I do care whether the chief scientist at one of our rocket-testing stations has a sense of the relation of his work to human history, to human capacity, to human values. Does he really know the difference between an electronic brain and a human one?

The professional and personal alienation from society of the scientist is trivial compared with his political innocence. His naïveté in politics can lead to disaster. The casualness of some atomic scientists toward security before Russia perfected her atom bomb was no doubt a reasoned thing, based on the certainty that Russia would inevitably have the bomb simply by following widely known principles. But for some scientists, at least, the casualness was the result of a simple-mindedness about Communism. Goudsmidt was ready in the midst of the war, while engaged on an American mission connected with the atom bomb, to rush off for a *gemütlich* reunion in Switzerland with an old friend and teacher, Werner Heisenberg, the Nazi counterpart of Oppenheimer. He hoped, he explained to the military man assigned to accompany him, that in the course of the surely warm and excited conversation, he would pick up some scraps to indicate the extent of German exploration of the atom. "And while he's giving you a lead on them, why wouldn't you be giving him a lead on us?" his dry, practical colleague wanted to know, forbidding the rendezvous.

A liberal education hopefully gives a man a meaningful and fixed area from which to view the world, in which to root his values, from which to recognize the complexity and often indeterminate nature of moral and political problems. It does not encourage a whimsical shifting of ground. In the course of a book-length account of Edward Teller's "paternity" of the H-bomb, he is described, at one time, as languishing on the A-bomb (intended for Germany and Japan), then vigorously supporting the development of the H-bomb (during the early days of the cold war with Russia), and, at still another time, disclaiming the need of scientists to be impelled by political considerations at all in offering their advice or their skills. It will be remembered that the decision to develop the H-bomb was in large measure based on political and philosophical considerations, many of these settled by politicians and statesmen. Whether the decision was good or bad is not to the point at present; what is to the point is that no pure scientist using only his pure science could have contributed very much to the ultimate decision.

Von Braun's case is more illuminating. He may be no more responsible, as he claims, for the V-2's being launched against London than Einstein was for the atom bomb. (The parallel eludes me: Einstein's formula, $e = mc^2$, was abstract and had nothing to do with Hiroshima, which was many years away; Von Braun worked not on a principle of physics but on a weapon whose specific function was to kill civilians in London. And even if Einstein had been as active as Von Braun in the development of hardware, there surely was a basic moral difference between helping the Nazis to beat the Allies, and vice versa.) Von Braun takes himself, to judge from the portrait of him in Daniel Lang's book, *The Man in the Thick Lead Suit*, as another figure in the great tradition of dedicated scientists, committed entirely to the pursuit of knowledge, wherever it may take him. Yet we are expected to sympathize with him when we read the record of how the stupid, vulgar, ignorant, boorish Nazi bureaucrats prevented him from concentrating fully on his scientific work—which aimed, ultimately, at the perfection of a revenge rocket to hit New York! The book, V-2, by Von Braun's superior at Peenemunde (the German rocket-testing station), General Walter Dornberger, sustains this particular and astonishing complaint throughout its length, that Hitler interfered with the perfection of the vengeance rocket against civilians, making as its sole gesture toward decency a reference, in the preface, to the peacetime possibilities of rockets.

Goudsmidt's report of his mission with the invasion forces to determine the state of German atomic development provides additional evidence of the moral emptiness of German science. "If only the government had taken the true scientists into its confidence instead of . . . charlatans," the Germans complained to Goudsmidt. Most competent German scientists became anti-Nazi only after they were insultingly rejected by the Nazis. Goudsmidt analyzes Heisenberg's opposition to the Nazis as follows:

> "Although he fought courageously against Nazi excesses and especially Nazi stupidities, his motives were not as noble as one might have hoped from such a great man. He fought the Nazis not because they were bad, but because they were bad for Germany, or at least for German science. His principal concern was that Germany might lose its lead in science, especially physics. That is why he strenuously objected to the exile of German Jewish physicists."

Goudsmidt records the macabre and meaningless thoroughness of the German scientific mind. He described the graphs that were kept of the temperature rise of a man who was frozen nearly to death, then subjected to "rewarming by one woman," "rewarming by two women," and "rewarming by women after coitus."

Goudsmidt quite clearly sees that the ugly failure of German science was not a matter of individual frailty. "It was indeed a serious indictment of the German system of education that it produced men who could, at one time, have done outstanding work in a narrow field of research, and yet proved themselves to be dangerously unbalanced in their judgment and behavior once outside their specialized rut. Such men can hardly be called scholars, or even educated human beings. They have the characteristics of a machine or a super robot, which performs a certain prescribed task absolutely correctly, but blows the fuse if used for some task other than that for which it was built."

One is tempted strongly to forgive the sentiments of persons conditioned by Nazis. Von Braun has now spent more than a decade in the United States. He has even expressed himself as having come to believe that religion is man's answer to his problems of politics. On a recent trip to London, however, Von Braun was asked what he thought of his vengeance rockets that fell on the city. According to the newspapers, he defended himself vigorously and declared, among other things, "My country right or wrong."

Von Braun's philosophy, his orientation in the world, may have less to do with his being brought up under Hitler than with his simply being brought up in the world of science. Mrs. Enrico Fermi, for example, who happens to be Jewish like Goudsmidt, mentions in her amiable reminiscences the nuisance of her Jewishness with a wry hesitancy as being perhaps the chief reason why the Fermis left Italy when Mussolini introduced an Italian version of the Nuremberg laws. Fascism itself, to judge from her record, scarcely bothered the Fermis in its other ideological aspects.

I am glad that Von Braun is on our side rather than on the Russians', and that Fermi came to the United States and did not remain in Italy. But I must wonder, perhaps cynically, how much difference it would have made to Von Braun if the Russians had got to him first, as they did to many of his colleagues, and whether, if Mussolini had not adopted anti-Semitism, the Fermis would really have come to America.

I emphasize that I am frightened by the scientific spirit, not because it could develop intercontinental ballistic missiles, but because it could fret when the high command interfered with allowing the development of a missile to fall on New York. I am not frightened by the spirit which prompts the physician to heal all men, but by the one that prompted the German doctors to experiment on human beings; not by the spirit that will devote itself to increasing food production, but by the one that will turn up a theory, the way Lysenko did, to satisfy ideological needs.

In short, I am not frightened by the objectivity, detachment, respect for truth, selflessness, dedication to method, which we are told over and over again are the marks of the scientist; these I admire and respect and am in awe of. But I am frightened when these characteristics are not grounded in a respect for human history and human value, when these are free-floating, for sale to any bidder who happens to be around, when these characteristics are perverted, in the very name of science, to the services of the depraved and immoral or inhuman; I am terrified when these characteristics are exalted by the scientists themselves or by their sophomoric admirers into supreme values that take precedence over all other values.

I intend no facile paradox when I describe our scientists as "know-nothing." Their knowledge of physics and chemistry and chess and hi-fi and engineering and mathematics, even of Sanskrit and Greek (I am not sure about Egyptology), are attainments not very far superior to the skills of electronic machines. To be sure, machines cannot make complex judgments; they cannot make moral evaluations; they cannot use history and literature; they cannot respond esthetically. But to what serious extent can scientists as a class do these things respectably? There are without question many, many individual scientists as humane and as politically sophisticated as any man of good education, but when they are so they have broken the barriers of their institutional education. Physicians, too, biological as well as physical scientists, and engineers are also likely to be bigoted and illiterate as a direct result of their particular education.

It is no counter argument at all to point to persons in the humanities as also deserving the designation of "know nothing." I am uncomfortably aware of many academic persons in English, languages, history, social science, philosophy; of writers and painters and musicians, who are dense and intolerant about world and national politics, science, history, business, philosophy, popular culture—in short, the full and varied world of mankind. This is no less tragic than the scientists' lack of scope and depth. But at least we cannot blame their education: their ignorance is personal and willful and not the result of social and institutional forces. They have been exposed at some length to the proper influences. It is not, so to speak, inevitable under the circumstances. Nor is it as likely to be fraught with danger. Humanists, enlightened or otherwise, will not be the ones who, like the two military scientists in E. B. White's short story, will be circling the earth in a satellite, able to press the button of Armageddon. Persons in the humanities will never have buttons to press, for better or worse; they are simply not in the business of counting backwards from ten.

Recently, a brilliant young colleague of mine, a mammalogist, and I spent an evening arguing the opposition between the scientist and the humanist. This was the climax of a series of skirmishes that had extended over several years. I was very pleased to engage with him, for, unlike most scientists, he was aware of the conflict and willing to argue the matter, to teach or be taught. Many scientists and engineers are scarcely conscious that there is another view of the universe than their own mechanistic one. Some who are so aware will not deign to enlighten the ignorant, fuzzy-headed humanist; they will not stoop to discussion or argument.

My friend and I joined the issue rather promptly on the subject of sex, with specific reference to Kinsey's work and to Lionel Trilling's critique of the Report in his book *The Liberal Imagination*. We were at loggerheads at once. I defined sex as having to do with relations between human beings; he as having to do with evolution. I think I put it fairly when I say that I, having read Darwin, understood what he meant; but he, not having read, say, Shakespeare or Lawrence or Meredith or the Brontës, insisted that my definition was quite meaningless. He insisted that one could find out nothing useful about the subject from studying novelists, that Kinsey's method, whatever shortcomings there may have been in details, was the only way of ascertaining the nature of any sort of truth.

However much one can discover about the world by pursuing the best scientific method, one can obviously not discover everything. I submit that there is at least an area as large as that staked out by science which can be explored only by the humanists, by the person who, first by education, then perhaps by temperament, knows the world through his senses, instincts, experiences, tastes, intuitions, emotions; all of these appropriately cultivated, appropriately apprehended, appropriately applied. The scientist is usually barred from this area, for he has not only not been introduced to specific portions of it, he has been totally discouraged from acknowledging the possibility that it exists, or, if it does exist, that it has any validity. Whatever latent tendencies he may have had to trust his subjective responses have either been allowed to atrophy for lack of nourishment or have been deliberately destroyed by the constant poison fed into his intellectual system by his training.

My friend was not denying the existence and power of nonscientific forces, the values of emotional and esthetic response, the creativity of imagination and thought; he was denying, as I understood him, their usefulness in determining the nature of man and of the world. The humanist's values, he said, are much too personal, impressionistic, and arbitrary, often a mere matter of taste; they shift constantly, from person to person, place to place, time to time; they are imprecise, ephemeral, without limits or substance. Of course, he is right, and he was accurately describing the nature of man.

The way of the humanist—if I may use the term to include the painter, the musician, the writer, the philosopher—is to use himself, his senses, his mind, his particularly developed artfulness, not only to explore the world, to uncover recognizable but hitherto unapprehended territories, but, far more importantly perhaps, *to make new things*. The humanist's way of recording and creating is certainly not the scientist's. But only through an evil and grotesque distortion of the nature of man, of the sort that is imagined in *Brave New World* and in *1984*, will the scientist ever imagine himself as capable of separating every last component that goes into emotional vitality or creative attainment, and feed these into machines. Only in a society where persons have lost their humanity will machines stimulate sexual awareness or turn out novels.

The education of the physician acutely points up the conflict. The physicist or chemist or geologist may always, after all, argue that his work does not bring him necessarily into contact with human beings. The physician cannot easily make a similar argument, although some medical man will indeed suggest that they do not work on human beings but on a complex walking system in which some mechanism has malfunctioned. I once heard a psychosomatically oriented physician criticize his colleagues for just this sort of response to patients, developed, he indicated, by a medical training which includes a great deal of work on cadavers. "Ask some man with an extreme faith in surgery," he said, "what he would do for a person who is always crying, and he would probably recommend excision of the tear glands."

Medical schools today, of course, emphasize "the whole man," but with the exception of those which prefer a broadly, liberally trained applicant to one who specializes in the usual pre-medical majors (biology or chemistry), most simply pay lip service to the concept. These will offer perhaps one course surveying psychiatry, but it is impossible to make up in one medical-school course the lack of an undergraduate education. It seems to me not at all excessive to expect of doctors that at some time in their career they put in a good deal of time studying the humanities since they will be working on human beings. I would even submit that medical science with all of its magnificent advances has not been fulfilling its whole function, either in research or in treatment, simply because it has failed to approach its problems or its patients to the necessary degree in terms of human values.

To return to my mammalogist friend. He would argue, I am sure, in agreement with many physicians, that all the areas I consider outside the mechanically scientific may one day with greater knowledge be found actually to belong inside. Some types of mental illness, for example, have indeed turned out to be related to purely physical and chemical causes, or, at least, have responded very well to various physical or chemical treatments. Perhaps this is so, although I always think of the prefrontal lobotomy, hailed as a great boon to the mentally ill, which simply changed sick humans into well and permanent zombies. And of tranquilizers, which turn us all into temporary zombies. Like surgery which removes tear ducts, these seem to me evasions of the problem, eminently scientific though they may be.

Perhaps we should suspend our cynicism, accepting that, indeed, all human areas, including the emotions and instincts, will indeed be understood some day as thoroughly and systematically as our purely physiological ones, with no need for intuition or art or imagination in diagnosis or treatment. But resolving the issue of values will still remain outside any pure scientist's capacity or interest: for example, to cite a simple dilemma, is it better to have a well zombie than a sick person? There is no simple answer to this question, certainly, but how often has the medical scientist even asked this question? Does he even know the question exists?

It might appear that I consider that a barrier exists between humanist and scientist, between artist and engineer. Not at all. The study of science, both pure and applied, has always been an integral part of a liberal education, of the humanities. The poet, the painter, the pianist can no more understand what man is, what man has done and thought, without a sense and some knowledge of science and mathematics than the scientist can without reading a sonnet, looking at a painting, listening to a sonata. The tactics and strategy of science, its products, its details of fact and procedure are as liberalizing as the substance of literature and history and philosophy. Even the products of engineering belong to the heart of the humanities: consider bridges and roads and buildings; plants for cracking oils or for producing electricity; dams, automobiles, the dozens of daily things we use. Many critics have justly placed engineered objects alongside more purely created ones, nonfunctional ones, and have been as much enchanted with the operation of the things as with their appearance. The range of the humanities would be unwholesomely constricted if they were ever thought to exclude science, mathematics, or technology.

It would be easy, I think, to make out a utilitarian argument for scientists, engineers, technologists to study the humanities. Such arguments are repeatedly made out for businessmen. The humanities will help you get ahead; you will know what to talk about; you will have interests to occupy your leisure time; you will make better objects; you will make more money; you will understand better what you are doing. Yet the best argument, it seems to me, has nothing to do with usefulness or value in any sense of application to design, business, research, or after-work living. The best argument for knowing something rather than knowing nothing must be one that does not root itself in the practical at all. The best argument for knowledge must ultimately be based on the realization that knowledge is "useless" in many ways we sometimes say it may be used.

The liberal arts, a liberal education, the humanities, if we pause to consider the implication of the words themselves, are designed to make us "free" as "human beings." The more we know about everything and anything, the more we realize how little we know, the more fulfilled we become as human beings, the more ready we are to learn, to grow, to extend the areas of our knowledge.

Precisely because my friend the mammalogist asks questions, is aware of the issue, does not take it as settled, doubts himself and doubts me, he is in the best sense a humanist liberally trained. The fact that he has a tremendous faith in science in no whit detracts from his liberalism or humanism. Scientists who understand and appreciate the humanities are never lesser scientists: they are better ones.

Scientists like Oppenheimer, who seem aware of the limits of their wisdom, do not trouble me. I am afraid of our know-nothing scientists precisely because this group does not seem to know how little it knows. One of the signs of an ignorant man, of course, in all ages has been his incapacity to realize how ignorant he is. To the degree that scientists positively know how much they know, to that degree I fear them. I do not trust the invisible scientist—or Frankenstein, or the practitioners of prefrontal lobotomy, or engineers who forget that bridges and machines are ultimately for people—to make decisions involving mankind, or myself personally, or to attain a place in our society of oracles and elder statesmen. Until their education will ensure their knowing something—most of all the limits of their knowledge—the scientist in our society does indeed bear being feared and watched.

MORRIS BISHOP

The Reading Machine[1]

"I have invented a reading machine," said Professor Entwhistle, a strident energumen whose violent enthusiasms are apt to infect his colleagues with nausea or hot flashes before the eyes.

Every head in the smoking room of the Faculty Club bowed over a magazine, in an attitude of prayer. The prayer was unanswered, as usual.

"It is obvious," said Professor Entwhistle, "that the greatest waste of our civilization is the time spent in reading. We have been able to speed up practically everything to fit the modern tempo—communication, transportation, calculation. But today a man takes just as long to read a book as Dante did, or—"

"Great Caesar!" said the Professor of Amphibology, shutting his magazine with a spank.

"Or great Caesar," continued Professor Entwhistle. "So I have invented a machine. It operates by a simple arrangement of photoelectric cells, which scan a line of type at lightning speed. The operation of the photoelectric cells is synchronized with a mechanical device for turning the pages—rather ingenious. I figure that my machine can read a book of three hundred pages in ten minutes."

"Can it read French?" said the Professor of Bio-Economics, without looking up.

"It can read any language that is printed in Roman type. And by an alteration of the master pattern on which the photoelectric cells operate, it can be fitted to read Russian, or Bulgarian, or any language printed in the Cyrillic alphabet. In fact, it will do more. By simply throwing a switch, you can adapt it to read Hebrew, or Arabic, or any language that is written from right to left instead of from left to right."

"Chinese?" said the Professor of Amphibology, throwing himself into the arena. The others still studied their magazines.

"Not Chinese, as yet," said Professor Entwhistle. "Though by inserting the pages sidewise . . . Yes, I think it could be done."

"Yes, but when you say this contrivance reads, exactly what do you mean? It seems to me—"

"The light waves registered by the photoelectric cells are first converted into sound waves."

"So you can listen in to the reading of the text?"

"Not at all. The sound waves alter so fast that you hear nothing but a continuous hum. If you hear them at all. You can't, in fact, because they are on a wave length inaudible to the human ear."

"Well, it seems to me——"

"Think of the efficiency of the thing!" Professor Entwhistle was really warming up. "Think of the time saved! You assign a student a bibliography of fifty books. He runs them through the machine comfortably in a weekend. And on Monday morning he turns in a certificate from the machine. Everything has been conscientiously read!"

"Yes, but the student won't remember what he has read!"

"He doesn't remember what he reads now."

"Well, you have me there," said the Professor of Amphibology. "I confess you have me there. But it seems to me we would have to pass the machine and fail the student."

"Not at all," said Professor Entwhistle. "An accountant today does not think of doing his work by multiplication and division. Often he is unable to multiply and divide. He confides his problem to a business machine and the machine does his work for him. All the accountant has to know is how to run the machine. That is efficiency."

"Still, it seems to me that what we want to do is to transfer the contents of the book to the student's mind."

"In the mechanized age? My dear fellow! What we want is to train the student to run machines. An airplane pilot doesn't need to know the history of aerodynamics. He needs to know how to run his machine. A lawyer doesn't want to know the development of theories of Roman law. He wants to win cases, if possible by getting the right answers to logical problems. That is largely a mechanical process. It might well be possible to construct a machine. It could begin by solving simple syllogisms, you know—drawing a conclusion from a major premise and a minor premise—"

"Here, let's not get distracted. This reading machine of yours, it must do something, it must make some kind of record. What happens after you get the sound waves?"

"That's the beauty of it," said Professor Entwhistle. "The sound waves are converted into light waves, of a different character from the original light waves, and these are communicated to an automatic typewriter, working at inconceivable speed. This transforms the light impulses into legible typescript, in folders of a hundred pages each. It tosses them out the way a combine tosses out sacked wheat. Thus, everything the machine reads is preserved entire, in durable form. The only thing that remains is to file it somewhere, and for this you would need only the services of a capable filing clerk."

"Or you could read it?" persisted the Professor of Amphibology.

"Why, yes, if you wanted to, you could read it," said Professor Entwhistle.

An indigestible silence hung over the Faculty Club.

"I see where the Athletic Association has bought a pitching machine," said the Assistant Professor of Business Psychology (Retail). "Damn thing throws any curve desired, with a maximum margin of error of three centimetres over the plate. What'll they be thinking of next?"

"A batting machine, obviously," said Professor Entwhistle.

JACQUES BARZUN

The Ivory Lab[1]

I degrade Physics into an implement of culture, and this is my deliberate design.—JOHN TYNDALL, *Fragments of Science*

Most of the excitement about "higher education" in the last three years has been about the teaching of history, languages, and "great books." But the most serious and pressing need in colleges today seems to me to be the teaching of science. It may appear paradoxical that I speak of a "need" which everyone believes to be adequately met, but paradox disappears when the point of view changes. From one point of view, science is taught in every American college; from another point of view, it is taught in none, or very few. Looked at in a certain light, science teaching today is the most efficient, up to date, and worldly-wise. In another light, it is backward, wasteful and "escapist." Let me explain these contrasts.

Fifty or sixty years ago, science was a new academic subject. People mistrusted its power to educate, and many of its proponents seemed as if they could never be educated themselves. The tradition of liberal studies had always included mathematics, because mathematics was supposed to train the mind; but the new physical sciences were first seen as manual arts, messy and expensive, and with no more "discipline" to them than a pair of elastic-sided boots. At the time of the fight for adding science to the curriculum, the defensive position was held by Greek and Latin, which unfortunately adopted a "scorched earth" policy. I mean that they allowed themselves to be invaded by the "scientific spirit" and in trying to compete with it reduced their field to a wasteland of verbal criticism, grammar, and philology. Literature was relegated to a second place and studying the classics came to mean research into the uses of *utor, fruor,* and *fungor.*

Naturally the classics were exterminated, for science could beat them at their own game. A young man trained in science could on graduation get any of a hundred desirable jobs in industry. A young "scientific" classicist could only

1 From *Teacher in America* by Jacques Barzun. Copyright, 1944, 1945, by Jacques Barzun. Reprinted by permission of Little, Brown & Company and the Atlantic Monthly Press.

hope to teach his own subject to a dwindling number of students. That is what invariably comes of trying to put belles-lettres into utilitarian envelopes. As Dean Briggs of Harvard said when the Bachelor of Science degree was established: "It does not guarantee that the holder knows any science, but it does guarantee that he does *not* know any Latin." When the study of classical literature in translation was reintroduced for freshmen at Columbia College a few years ago, the undergraduate department of classics was surprised to find its enrollment in beginning Greek increased 150 per cent: they now had ten students.

But the bitter joke is not on the Classics alone. Having stepped into Greek's vacated place, Science now occupies its position, not with respect to size of enrollment, but with respect to educational attitude. It is now in power and it acts disdainful, holier-than-thou, and prudish. Someone once asked, "What is it that our men of science are guarding like a threatened virginity?" "Oh," was the answer, "they have a Vestal interest in their subject." Considered—somewhat unfairly—in the mass, science teachers may be said to contribute the greatest proportion of backward-looking, anti-intellectual, mechanic-minded members to the faculty. Characteristically, single departments of physical science have in certain institutions tried to set up separate schools, where only their one science would be taught for four years and rewarded with some kind of Bachelor's degree. The intention was to monopolize the student's time, cram him full of "practical" knowledge, and sell him to the highest bidder the moment he had clutched his diploma and redeemed his ten-dollar deposit for apparatus.

Doubtless there is a demand for such prefabricated industrial robots and I see no reason why such schools should not function in a manner useful to the commonwealth—off the campus. But departments that once clamored for admission to university status and have had it for fifty years are unwilling to give up all the *douceurs* of the association. They would still like to profit from the university connection, to color their degree with a faint tincture of liberal teaching—perhaps they would require a year of English and a year of history and economics—and to boast that their own subject, be it chemistry or geology, is also one of the "humanities." They want to eat their cake as many times over as a cow does her cud.

A crowd of evils springs from this ambiguous mood in the present college curriculum. There is an undignified scramble for the student's time, with broad hints on the part of the scientist that the rest of the program is folderol. Repressed antagonisms divide teachers of the humanities (vague, pointless, unpractical subjects—except economics) from teachers of the real stuff represented by science. Moreover, departments of physics and chemistry require mathematical preparation in strict amount and order of time, with the result that all scheduling revolves around their claims. Since most young Americans discover their vocational bent while undergraduates, the wish to qualify for a profession is a powerful lever to make everyone study science for one or two years under these barbaric conditions. The doctor, the engineer, the research man in any science must gobble up as many courses as he can; and the man uninterested in science must "fulfill the requirement." Both are often judged on their science record, in the belief that it unmistakably reveals "real brains" or the lack of them.

The worst of all this is that neither group of students learns much about science but goes to swell the ranks of the two great classes of modern men— the single-track expert and the scientific ignoramus. Could anything more plainly demonstrate the failure of science to become a subject fit for college teaching? What makes a subject fit for the higher curriculum is surely no novelty: it is that it shall enlighten all the corners of the mind and teach its own uses. The humble three R's begin in strict utility and end up in poetry, science, and the search for the Infinite. They can and should therefore be taught indefinitely. Men have known for three thousand years that other matters of knowledge naturally divide themselves into special and general, that both are needful, but that whereas the special *add* to one's powers, the general *enhance the quality* of all of them.

At a recent educational conference, the Dean of a Midwestern university complained humorously that he was always being asked to give credits for impossible subjects—subjects that, he said, deserved to be called *in-credible*. A transfer student, for example, wanted "points" for seven hours of saw filing. Undeniably saw filing is a necessary art, but its merits as a general enhancer of power and personality stop accruing so soon after study is begun that it is not properly a branch of academic learning. The same is true of still more complex matters like shorthand, typewriting, and dress designing. Farther on in the series, it becomes harder to draw the line: stamp collecting is subeducational but numismatics is a province of history.

Fortunately there is no doubt whatever about the place of the sciences: they *are* humanities and they belong in the college curriculum. Accordingly, they should be introduced into it *as humanities*, at the earliest possible moment. How? I have some tentative suggestions to make, but first I want to stress the danger of further delay and of the continuance of our present malpractice.

The worst danger is the creation of a large, powerful, and complacent class of college-trained uneducated men at the very heart of our industrial and political system. We may be too near to judge, but it strikes me that one of the conditions that made possible the present folly in Germany was the split among three groups: the technicians, the citizens, and the irresponsible rabble. This becomes persuasively plain if you consider the professional army caste as a group of unthinking technicians. The rabble together with the technicians can cow the citizenry; the technicians—wedded solely to their workbench—will work for any group that hires; and the rabble, worshiping "science" to the exclusion of less tangible necessaries, are perfectly willing to sacrifice the citizen. They probably think that, if necessary, "science" could manufacture German citizens—out of wolfram.

Such principles will hardly give long life and happiness to a democracy. The only hope for a democratic state is to have more citizens than anything else. Hence technicians must not be allowed to hibernate between experiments, but must become conscious, responsible, politically and morally active men. Otherwise they will find not only that representative government has slipped out of their fingers, but that they have also lost their commanding position. They will be paid slaves in the service of some rabble, high or low. Meanwhile our present stock of citizens must not simply gape at the wonders of science, but must understand enough of its principles to criticize and value the results. As for the rabble, it must be transmuted as fast as it forms, by science and morals both.

All this clearly depends on teaching our easygoing, rather credulous college boys and girls what science is. If they leave college thinking, as they usually do, that science offers a full, accurate, and literal description of man and Nature; if they think scientific research by itself yields final answers to social problems; if they think scientists are the only honest, patient, and careful workers in the world; if they think that Copernicus, Galileo, Newton, Lavoisier, and Faraday were unimaginative plodders like their own instructors; if they think theories spring from facts and that scientific authority at any time is infallible; if they think that the ability to write down symbols and read manometers is fair grounds for superiority and pride, and if they think that science steadily and automatically makes for a better world—then they have wasted their time in the science lecture room; they live in an Ivory Laboratory more isolated than the poet's tower[2] and they are a plain menace to the society they belong to. They are a menace whether they believe all this by virtue of being engaged in scientific work themselves or of being disqualified from it by felt or fancied incapacity.

I return to what might perhaps be done preventively and constructively. To begin with, a change of direction must be imparted to the teaching of science. The fact must be recognized that most students still do not make science their profession.[3] Consequently, for future lay citizens the compulsory science requirement in force nearly everywhere must be justified by a course explicitly designed for them. Such a course must not play at making physicists or biologists, but must explain the principles of the physical sciences in a coherent manner. A "survey" of all the sciences is out of the question. It would be at once superficial and bewildering. But an intelligent introduction to principles can be given. The assumptions that connect and that differentiate the sciences of matter, of living beings, and of logical relation can be taught; the meaning

[2] To judge by results, it would seem that the poet climbs to the top of his tower to look out on the world and write about it. Why cavil at the building material— at once durable and attractive and requiring no upkeep?

[3] Statistics for the Middle West, based on large freshman enrollments, show that 50 percent of those taking Chemistry 1, 60 percent of those taking Geology 1, 73 percent of those taking Physics 1, 75 percent of those taking Biology 1, and 82 percent of those taking Botany 1, never go further into the science.

and the grounds of great unifying theories can be explained, and significant demonstrations and experiments can be shown to and made by the students.

Out of such a course there would surely come a changed attitude on the part of teachers and indeed a change in teaching personnel. At present, side by side with wise men and ripe teachers in the sciences, one finds many highly trained and absolutely uneducated practitioners. One also finds fanatics of the order that Dickens described in Professor Dingo, who, being caught defacing houses with his geological hammer, replied that "he knew of no building save the Temple of Science." Many university scientists openly scorn teaching and use their appointment to boil the pot of individual research. Now a life of research is a worthy one, but no amount of worthy motive justifies false pretenses and fraudulent impersonation—in this case the pretense of imparting knowledge and the impersonation of a teacher.

In the classroom, such men usually are neither civil, nor literate, nor even scientific, for their knowledge of science is purely from inside—a limitation equally bad but more misleading than the limitation of knowing it purely from outside. "What do they know of science who only science know?" They teach it as a set of rules, and speak of the profession as a "game." Drill in manual dexterity they entrust to laboratory assistants, who are only younger editions of themselves, and for whom a good notebook or speed in performing repetitious experiments is the passport to approval. There is seldom any consideration of the students as thinking minds, of the proper allocation of effort among the many interests legitimate at their time of life, nor of the philosophical implications which the words, the history, and the processes of the particular science disclose.

To offset this lamentable state of things, it must be said that two of the professions most concerned with scientific training—engineering and medicine —have lately amended their outlook and made overtures to the humanities. The medical schools have declared that cramming the student with science in college was a poor thing. He had better study other, less "practical," more formative subjects and postpone advanced chemistry and biology until medical school, where they will be taught him again in a fashion better tailored to his needs. This new policy is excellent, but it is not yet sufficiently enforced. The lesser medical schools—and some others—do not trust their own belief in the principle; they still appeal to "practical" views and judge applicants by A's in science.

Similarly, the Society for the Promotion of Engineering Education has passed splendid resolutions approving what they call the "social-humanistic stem"— by which they mean a few branches of non-engineering study; more accurately then, the "social-humanistic faggots." But here again, engineering thought is ahead of the engineer's emotions. When it comes to the test, the student or the program is pushed around to suit engineering subject matter.

If you add to this the important fact that many young Americans choose "engineering" in the belief that this means a career of research in pure science, you may form some notion of the present anarchical mess. The would-be engineer of seventeen finds that what he really wants to work at is pure research in electricity, that is, to be a physicist. He must therefore back water, change his course, and take some new prerequisites. Meanwhile his upbringing as a man and citizen goes by the board. He is caught between two grindstones, each indifferent to the effect of its motion, just as if the boy being put through this mill were not a human being, a student of the university, and a future citizen of the nation. Who is being "practical" now?

Some would probably still maintain that the professional schools in contact with "the world" know best what is the practical view, and that the college is as ever utopian. But there is one curious fact to be added. It is that the scientific professional schools have a way of relaxing their jaws into a smile whenever the market demand for their product decreases: it is a reflex action. They fall in love with the humanities all over again and raise the amount they require for admission, until outside pressure once again lowers the floodgates and the frown succeeds the smile. This self-regulating action is a feat of engineering in itself—or shall I say of doctoring the supply for public consumption?

The question is not whether this is the easy way to go about marketing young men, but whether it is a responsible grown-up way of replenishing the professional class of society. Granted that practice is the test of all schemes and ideals, is this the most practical scheme that American ingenuity can devise? I concede that in the present state of mind of the American public, desire for vocational training takes the lead over anything else. But are the directing members of the university world to follow other people's untutored impulses or to guide and redirect them? We may well ask when we reflect that the first victims of the system are the children of the unthinking public and the public itself. For it is the oldest fallacy about schooling to suppose that it can train a man for "practical" life. Inevitably, while the plan of study is being taught, "practical life" has moved on. "They did it this way three months ago, now they do it this way." No employer who knows anything about men will value a beginner because he knows the ropes of a particular changeable routine. It would be as sensible to require that newcomers know the floor plan of the factory ahead of time.[4]

The corporations employing the largest numbers of engineers and scientific research men are on this matter way ahead of the colleges. One such firm conducted a survey last year to find out where and how its first-rate executives had

---

[4] The S.P.E.E. reports: "From its very nature, engineering education operates under changing conditions which constantly challenge its processes and test its results . . . so as to adapt itself to changing needs." (*Draft of a Report*, etc., November 16, 1939, p. 1.) This is fine and good, but it holds true of every other professional subject and most academic ones. The old belief that only a few schools are in touch with the "real world" is untrue, even if the newer belief should prove true that it is best for the world to have the school conform to every change outside.

been prepared. They came from the most unexpected places—including small liberal arts colleges, the teaching profession, the stage, and the Baptist ministry. It was found that the engineering schools—particularly those sensible ones that make no pretense at intellectual *cachet*—turned out a good average product, but few leaders. The company's own institutes and night courses raised the chance of foremen and district managers—but only up to a point. The survey concluded that what it wanted as material to shape future executives was graduates of liberal arts colleges, trained in history and economics, in philosophy and in good English, and likewise possessed of *an intelligent interest in science and technology*. Gentlemen, the path lies open.

II

My friend Dean Finch, of the Columbia University School of Engineering, might not agree with all I have just said, but I think he would approve of one element in my suggestions which I casually threw in. I mean the utility of history in the teaching of science. He himself is an historian of technology and offers in Columbia College a most valuable course in the subject for the use of "lay" students. What is surprising is that similar courses, accompanied by others in the history of pure science, are not given—indeed required—on every American campus.

The very idea, it must be said, is shrouded in the smoke of battle. When I mention it, some of my scientific colleagues slap me on the back and say "more power to you." They may express doubts about persuading their fellows, or finding good instructors, but they want to see it tried. Moreover they do not feel robbed when in my own teaching of nineteenth-century history I discuss Dalton and Darwin, Liebig and Faraday, Mayer and Clerk Maxwell. Though scientists, these colleagues of mine can see that to complain of general ignorance about the role of science in modern history, and to prevent historians from mentioning it, is to love monopoly above riches.

Others take the view that science has no history because every new achievement supersedes previous ones. The history of science, they feel, is nothing but biographical chitchat about scientists. Or else they admit that it is useful to find out what the Middle Ages thought of natural science, but only in order to point the lesson of freedom from church authority and fight anew the old battle of science against religion.

This angry confusion about the history of science is dense but not impenetrable. Three things may be distinguished. First there is historical research into the beginnings of science—Greek or Arabic or Medieval. This goes on as advanced study and concerns undergraduates only in the form of broad tested conclusions. Then there is the biography of scientists, which is of immense educational importance—whatever laboratory men may say. Biography does not mean recounting Newton's imaginary embroilments with women or Lavoisier's perfectly real ones with public finance. It means finding out from the lives of great scientific creators what they worked at and how their minds functioned. How tiresome it is to hear nothing from our scientic departments but Sunday-school homilies on the gameness of Galileo, the patience of Pasteur, and the carefulness of Madame Curie. And how uninstructive! Any man who accomplishes anything in any field is as patient as he has to be, and even little boys know that glass being breakable, you have to be careful.[5]

What would be far more significant and novel, though true, would be to teach that Copernicus gambled on insufficient evidence; and Kepler was chiefly a horoscope-caster; that Faraday probably believed more wrong theories than any man alive—and turned them to good use in experiment; that Darwin, on his own admission, made awful blunders and admired the art of wriggling out of them; that T. H. Morgan's laboratory was rather messy; that Newton could not see how his own astronomy contradicted the Bible; that scientific men have suppressed and persecuted opponents of their theories, and that the best scientific truth can end in a rigid and mistaken orthodoxy—as happened after Newton and Darwin. The point is that science is made by man, in the light of interests, errors, and hopes, just like poetry, philosophy, and human history itself.

To say this is not to degrade science, as naïve persons might think; it is on the contrary to enhance its achievements by showing that they sprang not from patience on a monument but from genius toiling in the mud. I leave unexplained here all that accrues from studying how we came to use atoms or devise Absolute Zero or to state the Law of Conservation of Energy (including the reasons why energy is a better word than the earlier "force") or what steps led first to the abandonment and then to the later salvaging of Avogadro's hypothesis. A good scientist-historian would exhibit the assumptions and habits which affected scientific opinion at important turning points. He would unite science to other thought by discussing the nature of its evidence at various periods. And he would show the role of the pure imagination in all great scientific work. I know Bacon promised that science would level all the minds of its devotees to average size, and he is right insofar as drilling can make ordinary men into patient, careful laboratory workers. But science has not yet managed to get along without ideas, and these come only from men of special, powerful, and irreducible aptitudes. The chronological study of these men and ideas is the proper subject matter for an undergraduate course in the history of science.[6]

I know the common objection offered to all this—to an historical and a

[5] The self-righteousness of the man of science is universal enough to sustain advertising appeals: "Like the scientist, NEWSWEEK . . . makes it its business to search out truth by continual research, relentless checking and re-checking of the facts." A grim grind!

[6] Some very useful works already exist which exemplify the historical and inductive method of teaching science; among others: Ostwald's *Schule der Chemie* (translated by E. C. Ramsay), Ida Freund's *The Study of Chemical Composition* and *The Experimental Basis of Chemistry*, Norman Campbell's *Physics: The Elements*, and H. T. Pledge's *Science Since 1500*.

synoptic account of scientific principles in place of the "regular" science courses:
it is that the substitutes would be merely talk about science and not science
itself. Grant this for argument's sake. The objectors miss the point if they do not
see that talk about science has a place in the curriculum and that such talk
may be good or bad, quite all right or all quite wrong, exactly like talk about
art. If science is one of the humanities it must be capable of being looked at
and thought about apart from direct doing—at least until we require every
concertgoer to write a symphony before being allowed to take his seat at Car-
negie Hall. Besides, the synoptic course I have in view would include laboratory
work, and it would rest with the scientists themselves whether the students
mastered enough of the operative side of true science to keep them from
irresponsible talk about it. If science teachers think that a year's drudgery in
physics as now given prevents silly notions in those who take it in college, they
are either inobservant or illogical.

Doubtless it is bad logic they suffer from—the usual weakness of scientists
. . . and of the rest of mankind, who generally want to have things both
ways. Take as an example a comment made on the relation of science and
history in the excellent study of Lavoisier by J. A. Cochrane. The author complains that "although Lavoisier was at the time of his death and for at least
fifteen years before it one of the most eminent men in France, the general historian does not think it worth while to make any mention of him. . . . Science
has undoubtedly changed the face of the world, and yet practically the only
credit given to it by the historian is the Industrial Revolution . . . and even
then the facts are not always accurate."

This is very sound criticism, but the scientist at once reasserts his monopoly:
"No doubt the historian, having no qualifications to discuss the progress of
science, feels that he had best leave it severely alone, but he can scarcely claim
to trace the evolution of the modern world if he omits one of the most important factors in that evolution." Which will the author have—treatment
with inevitable errors or leaving the sacred objects "severely alone"? So long
as we act like watchdogs over our little plots, it is obvious that we cannot have
the comprehensive views that all profess to desire. Somebody has to take the
first step—and suffer for his pains.

But it would be unfair if I gave the impression that the opposition to teaching the history of science to college students was universal or came only from
certain scientists. At one great university near New York there was a thriving
enterprise of this sort, popular with students and science departments alike. It
was given by a young man, equally gifted in the humanities and in his chosen
physical science—a budding *uomo universale*, whom fellow scientists were
willing to aid, guide, and correct—if need be—on the remoter details of their
science. After a few years this course built up a tradition, exerted an influence,
reached a kind of perfection in the fulfillment of its aim.

With the war, changes came in staff and direction; the instructor left and
the opposition rallied to abolish the course. It will scarcely be believed when I

say that the prime mover in this *Putsch* was a philosopher. What inspired him, the Absolute only knows. The science course did not teach any philosophy contrary to his own; it only taught the historical fact that great men of science have employed varying philosophical assumptions to gain their ends. It taught, besides, that the several sciences do not look at the world all in the same way and that so far as science has a unified point of view, it is not exclusive of others —the ways, namely, of art, philosophy, religion, and common sense. Lastly, the course imparted a fair amount of matters of fact and showed how wrong was the man who said: "You don't have to teach the history of science to make a man understand that water is H_2O." It is precisely what you have to teach, unless you are willing to barter understanding for mere voodoo formulas.

What more could any philosophy department want? Their students were lucky enough to be taught to think. Is there any other use to make of the four years of college? The world being full of a number of things, it takes practice to think easily about the chief ones. Does philosophy pretend to monopolize cogitation because Descartes said, "Don't doubt I'm thinking!"

The fact is that philosophy has suffered emotionally, like Greek and Latin, from the triumph of science. Philosophy was a minor partner in the defeat of the classics, and that has left it laboring under the same sense of wrong, the same fancied need to be haughty—and even hoity-toity. In the '80s science said: "We bring you the answers. Philosophy will gradually be pushed out as we extend our certainty." Many philosophers agreed and looked for their retirement at the first outrush of some naked Archimedes shouting "Eureka." Other philosophers, courageously holding their ground, fought as critics of science's faulty logic or extreme arrogance, just as a few classicists kept saying, "Poison gas marks a great step forward but have you taken in the meaning of Thucydides's 'Peloponnesian War'?"

The time has now come for the three-cornered duel on the campus to cease. The classics, philosophy, and science are at once overlapping and complementary disciplines. No need even to adjust boundary differences. The students are well able to take care of seeming conflicts, and in truth profit from them, since opposition reinforces attention by heightening the drama of human thought. Science must be taught, and historically, too, or the people will perish. Philosophy likewise must have a voice in all courses throwing light on the history of ideas. It will save philosophy as a subject and save the students from caddishness and provincialism. But philosophy has other obvious collegiate duties. It must read its great masterpieces with the new generation, expound ethical and metaphysical theory, help teach logic, and do liaison work with historians, scientists, and theologians. Once in a while an original philosopher will arise, unsought, in the midst of his colleagues, and the world will know him to its own profit.

The classics, too, must enter the dance. They hold the key to the meaning of our long journey from the cave to—precisely—the laboratory.

VI

Society

Social Attitudes

◈◈◈◈◈◈◈◈◈◈◈◈◈◈◈◈◈◈◈◈◈◈◈◈◈◈◈◈◈◈◈◈◈◈◈

CLYDE KLUCKHOHN

An Anthropologist Looks at the United States[1]

Suppose that archaeologists five hundred years hence were to excavate the ruins of settlements of various sizes in Europe, in America, in Australia, and in other regions. They would properly conclude that American culture was a variant of a culture of world-wide occurrence, distinguished by elaboration of gadgets and especially by the extent to which these were available to all sorts and conditions of men. Careful studies of distribution and diffusion would indicate that the bases of this civilization had been developed in northern Africa, western Asia, and Europe. The shrewd archaeologist would, however, infer that twentieth-century American culture was no longer colonial. He would see that distinctive features in the physical environment of the United States had made themselves perceptible in the warp of the American cultural fabric and that large-scale cultural hybridization and native inventions were continuing to produce a new texture and new patterns in the weft.

Unfortunately, the social anthropologist of 1948 cannot develop this picture much farther and remain in the realm of demonstrated fact. The anthropological study of American communities was initiated in *Middletown* (1928) and *Middletown in Transition* (1937). Since then we have had a series of monographs on *Yankee City*; two books on *Southerntown*; *Plainville, U.S.A.*; brief studies of six different communities by the Department of Agriculture; Margaret Mead's popular book *And Keep Your Powder Dry*; and a score of scattered papers. Very recently Warner and Havighurst have published a study of class structure and education, *Who Shall be Educated?* Walter Goldschmidt has given us *As You Sow*, a report on California agricultural communities; and the publications on a Middle Western town, *Jonesville, U.S.A.*, have begun to appear. Yet contrast this total handful with the countless valuable volumes that have been published on the history, government, geography, and

[1] From *Mirror for Man* (New York: McGraw-Hill Book Company, Inc., 1949), pp. 228-261. Copyright, 1949, McGraw-Hill Book Company, Inc.

economy of the United States. Of this culture in the anthropological sense we know less than of Eskimo culture.

In treating American culture one must resort to an analysis that goes only a shade beyond impressionism. There is the special danger, considering the small quantity of recent field work, of describing American culture more as it has been than as it is. Yet a sketch of characteristic thought patterns, values, and assumptions may help us a little to understand ourselves and thus to understand other peoples better. One can assemble points of agreement in the anthropological studies that have been made, in the testimony of astute European and Asiatic observers, in personal observations. This has been a business civilization—not a military, ecclesiastical, or scholarly one. The brevity of our national history has made for this dominance of the economic as well as for the stress upon the potential as opposed to the actual society. Lacking the inertia of a deeply rooted culture pattern and given the high standard of living, American customs have changed rapidly under the influence of automobiles, radio, and moving pictures. There are many culture traits which are too obvious to require a massing of evidence: love of physical comfort, a cult of bodily cleanliness, finance capitalism. Certain values, such as fair play and tolerance, are generally agreed to but represent modifications of our British heritage rather than anything distinctively American. Rather than cataloguing traits exhaustively, however, this chapter will treat selectively some related traits that appear best to bring out the underlying organization of the culture.

American culture has been called a culture of paradoxes. Nevertheless national advertising and a national moving-picture industry would be impossible were there not certain terms in which one can appeal to the vast majority of this capturable people. Though sectional, economic, and religious differences are highly significant in some respects, there are certain themes that transcend these variations. Some life goals, some basic attitudes tend to be shared by Americans of every region and of all social classes.

To start with the commonplace: even the most bitter critics of the United States have conceded us material generosity. In spite of the romanticism of "public-spirited disinterestedness" most Americans are outgoing and genuinely benevolent. Sometimes, to be sure, American humanitarianism is linked with the missionary spirit—the determination to help others by making the world over on the American model.

Perhaps no huge society has ever had such generalized patterns for laughter. In older civilizations it is commonly the case that jokes are fully understood and appreciated only by class or regional groups. It is true that it is some distance from the sophisticated humor of *The New Yorker* to the slapstick of popular radio programs. But the most widespread formulas reach all Americans. Some of the most characteristic of these are related to the cult of the average man. No one becomes so great that we cannot make fun of him. Humor is an important sanction in American culture. Probably the ridicule of

Hitler did more than all the rational critiques of Nazi ideology to make the man in the street contemptuous of Nazism.

All European travelers are struck by American attitudes toward women. They often note that "Americans spoil their women," or that "America is dominated by petticoats." The truth is more complicated. On the one hand, it is clear that a very large number of American women of privileged economic position are freed by labor-saving devices from much household drudgery—particularly after their few children have entered school. Their abundant leisure goes into women's clubs, community activities, "cultural" organizations, unhealthy devotion to their children, other mildly or seriously neurotic activities. It is also true that many American men are so wrapped up in pursuit of the success goal that they largely abdicate control over their children's upbringing to their wives. The responsibility of American women for moral and cultural questions is tremendous. On the other hand, it is too often forgotten that in 1940, 26 out of every 100 women of working age worked outside the home, that almost every girl who graduates from high school or college has had some job training. We interest women in careers but make it difficult for them to attain a full life in one. In a culture where "prestige" is everything we have felt it necessary to set aside Mother's Day as a symbolic atonement for the lack of recognition ordinarily given to domestic duties.

In Japan a year ago Japanese of many classes complained to me that it was difficult to understand American democracy because Americans seemed to lack an explicit ideology that they could communicate. The Japanese contrasted the Russians who could immediately give a coherent account of their system of beliefs. Various Americans have remarked that what the United States needed more than a good five-cent cigar was a good five-cent ideology. Such explicit ideology as we have derives largely from the political radicalism of the late eighteenth century. We repeat the old words, and some of the ideas are as alive now as then. But much of this doctrine is dated, and a new latent ideology inherent in our actual sentiments and habits is waiting for popular expression.

Particularly since the drastic disillusionment that followed the fine Wilsonian phrases of World War I, Americans have been shy at expressing their deepest convictions and have been verbally cynical about Fourth of July oratory. Yet devotion to the American Way has been none the less passionate. It is significant that aviators in this past war who were under narcotics in the course of psychotherapy would not only talk freely about personal emotional problems but were equally articulate on the ideological reasons for American participation in the war.

The pattern of the implicit American creed seems to embrace the following recurrent elements: faith in the rational, a need for moralistic rationalization, an optimistic conviction that rational effort counts, romantic individualism and the cult of the common man, high valuation of change—which is ordinarily taken to mean "progress," the conscious quest for pleasure.

Mysticism and supernaturalism have been very minor themes in American life. Our glorification of science and our faith in what can be accomplished through education are two striking aspects of our generalized conviction that secular, humanistic effort will improve the world in a series of changes, all or mainly for the better. We further tend to believe that morality and reason must coincide. Fatalism is generally repudiated, and even acceptance seems to be uncongenial—though given lip service in accord with Christian doctrine.

The dominant American political philosophy has been that the common man would think and act rationally. The same premises are apparent in typical attitudes toward parental responsibility. The individual, if "let alone" and not "corrupted by bad company" will be reasonable. If a child does not turn out well, the mother or both parents tend to blame themselves or to explain the failure by "bad blood"—as if action-guided-by-reason could of itself always produce well-adjusted children when the biological inheritance was adequate.

While many Americans are in some senses profoundly irreligious, they still typically find it necessary to provide moral justifications for their personal and national acts. No people moralizes as much as we do. The actual pursuit of power, prestige, and pleasure for their own sakes must be disguised (if public approval is to be obtained) as action for a moral purpose or as later justified by "good works." Conversely, a contemplative life tends to be considered "idleness."

The American mother offers her love to her child on the condition of his fulfilling certain performance standards. No conversational bromides are more characteristically American than "Let's get going"; "Do something"; "Something can be done about it." Although during the thirties there was widespread devaluation of present and future and though pessimism and apathy about the atomic bomb and other international problems are certain strong currents in contemporary national thinking, the dominant American reaction is still—against the perspective of other cultures—that this is a world in which effort triumphs. A recent public opinion study showed that only 32 per cent of Americans were concerned about social security—for themselves.

Countless European observers have been impressed by "enthusiasm" as a typically American quality. During the war military analysts noted repeatedly that the British were better at holding a position but the Americans at taking one. As Margaret Mead has observed, the British cope with a problem; Americans start from scratch and build completely anew.

Americans are not merely optimistic believers that "work counts." Their creed insists that anyone, anywhere in the social structure, can and should "make the effort." Moreover, they like to think of the world as man-controlled. This view about the nature of life is thus intimately linked with that conception of the individual's place in society which may be called "romantic individualism."

In the English-speaking world there are two principal ideologies of individualism. The English variety (which may be tagged with the name of Cobden) is capitalistic in its basic outlook. American individualism has agrarian roots and may be associated with Jefferson. To this day Americans hate "being told what to do." They have always distrusted strong government. The social roles most frequently jibed at in comic strips are those that interfere with the freedom of others: the dog-catcher, the truant officer, the female social climber (Mrs. Jiggs) who forces her husband and family to give up their habitual satisfactions. "My rights" is one of the commonest phrases in the American language. This historically conditioned attitude toward authority is constantly reinforced by child-training patterns. The son must "go farther" than his father, and revolt against the father in adolescence is expected.

However, as de Tocqueville pointed out, Americans are characteristically more interested in equality than in liberty. "I'm as good as the next man," seems at first a contradiction of the American emphasis upon success and individual achievement within a competitive system. It is true that there are relatively few places at the top in a social pyramid—*at any one time*. But the American faith that "there is always another chance" has its basis in the historical facts of social mobility and the fluidity (at least in the past) of our economic structure. "If at first you don't succeed, try, try again." The American also feels that if he himself does not "get a break," he has a prospect for vicarious achievement through his children.

American individualism centers upon the dramatization of the individual. This is reflected in the tendency to personalize achievement, good or bad. Americans prefer to attack men rather than issues. Corporations are personified. Public power projects were advertised as much as a means of beating the Utility Devil as a way of getting better and cheaper service.

The less opportunity the greater the merit of success. "You can't keep a good man down." Conversely, failure is a confession of weakness, and status distinctions and even class lines are rationalized on such grounds as, "he got there by hard work," "it's his own fault that he didn't get on." Such attitudes—and the idealization of the "tough guy" and the "red-blooded American" and the fear of "being a sucker"—derive both from the Puritan ethic and from the American pioneer era. Aggressive activity and rapid mobility were effectual in the rapid development of a new country, and it made sense then that the rewards in money and status should be high.

The worship of success has gone farther than in any known culture, save possibly prewar Japan. This is reflected in countless staple phrases such as "bettering yourself," "getting ahead," and "how are you getting on?" The opposition to Roosevelt's proposal for a taxation program that would limit net income to $25,000, attests to the depth of feeling for slogans like "the sky's the limit." But the striving for money is not simply the pursuit of purposeless materialism. Money is primarily a symbol. The deeper competition is for power and prestige. "Aggressive" is, in American culture, a descriptive adjective of high praise when applied to an individual's personality or character. "You have to be aggressive to be a success." The obvious crudities of aggression are, as Lynd says, explained away by identifying them with the common good.

But there is a defensive note in this aggressiveness which is also sympto-
matic. Competitive aggressiveness against one's fellows is not just playing
a part in a drama. The only way to be safe in American life is to be a
success. Failure to "measure up" is felt as deep personal inadequacy. In a
phrase, the American creed is equality of opportunity, not equality of man.

The cult of the average man might seem to imply disapproval of outstanding
individuals of every sort. Certainly it is true that a great deal of hostility is
directed upward. However, under the influence of the dramatic and success aspects of the "romantic individualism" orientation, the typical attitude toward
leaders may best be described as one of mixed feelings. On the one hand, there
is a tendency to snipe at superior individuals with a view to reducing them to
the level of their fellows. On the other hand, their very success is a dramatic
vindication of the American way of life and an invitation to identification
and emulation.

The cult of the average man means conformity to the standards of the current majority. To de Tocqueville this was "enfeeblement of the individual." A
more recent observer, Fromm, who also looked at the American scene from a
European viewpoint, likewise finds this conformity repressive to self-expression. But he fails to see that the American is not a passive automaton submitting to cultural compulsives like European provincials. The American voluntarily and consciously seeks to be like others of his age and sex—without in
any way becoming an anonymous atom in the social molecule. On the contrary, all the devices of the society are mobilized to glamorize the individual
woman and to dramatize every achievement of men and women that is unusual—but still within the range of approved aspirations of the conforming majority. "Miss America" and "the typical American mother" are widely publicized
each year, but an announced atheist (no matter of what brilliance and accomplishment) cannot be elected President.

American devotion to the underdog must be linked to this attitude. As Lynd
points out, we worship bigness yet we idealize "the little man." "Griping" is a
characteristic American trait, but the griping of American soldiers against the
officer caste system is to be understood in terms of American egalitarian notions and especially of the cult of the average man. The fact that officers and
enlisted men did not have equal access to various facilities for recreation and
transportation enraged what were felt to be the most basic sentiments in the
American code. To some extent this aspect of the cult of the average man
doubtless represents a refuge for those who fail to "rise," a justification for
envy of those who do.

Because of the cult of the average man, superficial intimacy is easy in America. People of every social class can talk on common topics in a way that is
not so easy in Europe where life is based more on repetition of patterns of
early family routines that are differentiated by class. However, American friend-
ships tend to be casual and transitory.

Thanks to our expanding economy and to national folklore created by various historical accidents, the nineteenth-century faith in "progress" became intrenched in the United States as nowhere else. As Lovejoy and Boas have pointed out, America's golden age has been located mainly in the future rather than in the past. To some extent, to be sure, the future has been brought into the present by installment plan buying, the philosophy of "spend, don't save," etc. But the basic underlying notions have been well made explicit by Carl Becker.

> By locating perfection in the future and identifying it with the successive achievements of mankind, the doctrine of progress makes a virtue of novelty and disposes men to welcome change as in itself a sufficient validation of their activities.

Western Europeans and Americans tend to be fundamentally different in their attitudes toward conforming. Americans believe in conforming only to the standards of one's own age group and change-in-time is a strong value; Europeans believe—or have believed—in conforming to a past society and have found security in traditional behavior; yet conformity to contemporary society is only incidental and not a value. There are, to be sure, wide disparities in American hospitality to change. We take pride in material change but are, on the whole, more hostile than contemporary Europeans to changes in our institutions (say the Constitution or the free enterprise system). In some ways the conformity of middle-class Englishmen, for instance, is more rigid than that of Americans—but in other ways it is less so. American attitudes toward change make generational conflicts more serious. These very generational conflicts, however, make certain types of social change possible. As Mead points out, children can be more "successful" than their parents, hence "better."

Americans publicly state that having a good time is an important part of life and admit to craving "something new and exciting." In terms of this ideology we have created Hollywood, our Forest of Arden type of college life, our National Parks, Monuments, and Forests. Leaders of our entertainment industry are the best paid men and women in the United States. In 1947 the American people spent nearly twenty billion dollars for alcoholic beverages, theater and movie tickets, tobacco, cosmetics, and jewelry. We spend as much for moving pictures as for churches, more for beauty shops than for social service. However, because of the Puritan tradition of "work for work's sake," this devotion to recreation and material pleasure is often accompanied by a sense of guilt—another instance of the bipolarity of many features of American culture. The pleasure principle attains its fullest development in American youth culture. Youth is the hero of the American Dream. Most especially, the young girl ready for marriage is the cynosure of American society.

We have borrowed ideas and values from countless sources. If one takes single features, one can match almost every instance in a dozen or more cultures, including the primitive. For example, during the last war many of our soldiers carried magic amulets, such as a miniature wooden pig which was said to have raised fogs, smoothed out a high sea, commuted an execution, or cured assorted cases of illness. But if one looks at the total combination of premises and attitudes one sees a pattern that has its own special flavor, even though this description is too brief to take account of regional, class, ethnic group, and generational variations.

An anthropological snapshot of the American way of life cannot catch all the details, but, with other cultures in the background, it should highlight some meaningful interplay of light and shadow. And the attempt is needed. No amount of knowledge of Russian or Chinese culture will avail in the solution of our international problems unless we know ourselves also. If we can predict our own reactions to a probable next move in the Russian gambit and have some clues as to why we shall react in that manner, the gain to self-control and toward more rational action will be tremendous. Because of our tradition of assimilating immigrants and because of our overweening pride in our own culture it is particularly difficult to get Americans to understand other cultures.

Seen in the perspective of the range of human institutions, the following combination of outstanding features define the American scene: consciousness of diversity of biological and cultural origins; emphasis upon technology and upon wealth; the frontier spirit; relatively strong trust in science and education and relative indifference to religion; unusual personal insecurity; concern over the discrepancy between the theory and the practice of the culture.

"The melting pot" is one of the surest catchwords that has ever been applied to the United States. Probably much of the vitality of American life and the increased stature and other evidences of physical superiority for new generations of Americans must be attributed to the mingling of diverse cultural and biological strains as well as to dietary and environmental factors. The "Ballad for Americans" triumphantly proclaims our manifold origins. Newspapers during the war proudly referred to the fact that Eisenhower was a German name but he was an American, to the fact that another general was an Indian, to the variety of names in American platoons and in American graveyards overseas. The distinguished record of Japanese-Americans in the armed services was used to document the success of the American Way.

Heterogeneity has, in fact, become one of the organizing principles of American culture. Ripley's "Believe it or Not," "Quiz Kids" programs, "Information Please," and other formal and informal educational devices are evidence that Americans value disconnected pieces of information and feel that people must be prepared to live in a world in which generalizations are hard to apply.

If one looks at a culture as a system in which traits mainly received by borrowing are being patterned in response to situational factors and organic needs our American position at present bears a few compelling resemblances to that of Europe in perhaps the twelfth century. It was only then that a quasi-permanent integration had been attained in the European cultural melting pot. Pagan and Christian, Greco-Roman and Germanic culture elements had seethed in troubled opposition during the centuries of the movements of peo ple. Our mass movements stopped only a generation ago with the closing of the frontier. During the tenth and eleventh centuries in Europe forests were cleared and swamps were drained; cities were built in large numbers in Northern Europe, and there came to be some fixity in the distribution and density of population.

Because of the very fact that diversity is an explicit theme of American culture one must be careful not to overemphasize the threats of the admitted contradictions in our way of life. Those who look longingly back to the good old days of a fancied homogeneity in American values forget that the Tories almost equaled the Patriots in number, do not remember the details of the situation that demanded the Federalist papers, neglect the two radically opposed sets of values that led to the War between the States. Actually, we must agree with Frank Tannenbaum that the harmony best suited to a democratic society "is one which comes from many-sided inner tensions, strains, conflicts, and disagreements." Though the stability of a culture depends on how much the conflicts it engenders can be supplied adequate outlets, still the strength of the democratic process is that it not only tolerates but welcomes difference. Democracy is based not upon a single value but upon a subtle and intricate multiple of values. Its strength rests in the balance of social institutions.

Although the definition of an American as a person who is endlessly catching trains is a caricature, the phrase of G. Lowes Dickinson "contemptuous of ideas but amorous of devices" remains uncomfortably correct as a characterization of all save a tiny minority of Americans. And while we indignantly met the Fascist label of "plutocracy!" by pointing to our humanitarian organizations, our numerous foundations dedicated to the spending of untold millions for lofty aims, and the generosity of individual citizens, it remains true that not only are we the wealthiest nation in the world but that money comes closer with us than with any other people to being the universal standard of value.

This is why the level of intellectual ability is very much higher in the Harvard Law School than in the Harvard Graduate School of Arts and Sciences. The ablest undergraduates in Harvard College do not always receive the highest honors. The energies of many are often, realistically enough, consecrated to "making contacts" through "activities," through a sedulous campaign to acquire membership in a "final club." This is not necessarily because they are congenitally uninterested in ideas, but because they have been effectually conditioned by family pressure and by certain schools. They have considerable intuitive insight into the structure of our culture. They know that intellectual endeavor will lead them to little "recognition" and less salary. They know how vital is "success" to security in our society. Brilliant young men voluntarily condemn themselves to lives of cutthroat competition and narrow slavery.

Our economy is a prestige economy to a pathological extent. The wife must buy fur coats and drive an expensive automobile because she too is an item of conspicuous consumption. Even in the supposedly uncommercial halls of learning the awed whisper is heard, "Why, he is a $15,000-a-year professor." The numerical system of grading, an unmistakably American invention, is simply another projection of our conviction that all attainments can be expressed in figures.

Suppose that an intellectual Australian aborigine, who was also a trained anthropologist, were to write a monograph on our culture. He would unequivocally assert that machines and money are close to the heart of our system of symbolic logics. He would point out that the two are linked in a complex system of mutual interdependence. Technology is valued as the very basis of the capitalistic system. Possession of gadgets is esteemed as a mark of success to the extent that persons are judged not by the integrity of their characters or by the originality of their minds but by what they seem to be—so far as that can be measured by the salaries they earn or by the variety and expensiveness of the material goods which they display. "Success" is measured by two automobiles—not by two mistresses as in some cultures.

Could our aboriginal anthropologist introduce some time perspective into his study, he would note that this value system has shown some signs of alteration during the last two decades. However, against the background of all known cultures, American culture would still stand out for its quantitative and materialistic orientations.

Americans love bigness—so far as things and events are concerned. Their constant overstatement appears to others as boasting. Americans love to speak in numbers. They like to "get down to brass tacks" and "want the lowdown." Europeans are usually content to rate students according to categories corresponding to "high honors," "honors," "pass." Only Americans think that the relative standing of students in a course can be measured on a continuous scale from zero to 100. This emphasis on the quantitative must not be too easily taken as proof of a thoroughgoing materialism. But Americans do tend to get very excited about things as opposed to ideas, people, and aesthetic creations. "Virtuous materialism" has tended to be part of the American creed.

Status in the United States is determined more by the number and price of automobiles, air-conditioning units, and the like owned by a family than by the number of their servants or the learning and aesthetic skills of family members. In fact, Americans usually are scared out of being artists. There is reverence only for the man who *does things* in a big way." Most Americans do subscribe to the current Einstein legend, but *Time* has recently pointed out that many did not take this very seriously until they were told that Einstein's "theories" had made the atomic bomb possible. It is significant that Edison is a household name, whereas only the professors have heard of Willard Gibbs.

John Dewey says that American thinking is characterized by a "lust after absolutes." By this he does not, of course, mean a hankering for the "absolutes" of religion and philosophy. He refers to the tendency to think that, because simple questions can be posed, there exist simple answers, which classify ideas and individuals as all black or all white. For this reason "compromise" has an unfavorable connotation in American English. Worship of the external and quantitative leaves little patience for the infinite shadings and variations of direct experience. Doubtless the vastness of the American scene and the impermanence of social place create a need to generalize. Europeans are ordinarily more sensitive to the complexity of situations.

Our phrase "pioneer of industry" is not a haphazard combination of words. The patterns of the American Way were set during that period when the United States was on the skirmish line of civilization. The frontier has been a predominant influence in the shaping of American character and culture, in the molding of American political life and institutions; the frontier is the principal, the recurring theme in the American symphony. Whatever distinction we have as a people, whatever differentiates us from the other branches of Western European civilization we owe in large part to the presence of the frontier—its unappropriated wealth, its dangers and challenges.

Unfortunately, many of the responses which made for survival under those conditions are singularly unsuited to our present situation. To some considerable degree, frontier virtues are the intolerable vices of contemporary America. To extemporize and not to plan "paid off" then. Unhappily, we have tended to see these qualities as absolutes rather than from the perspective of cultural relativity. Aggressive and childish young Mickey Rooney was recently the hero of a population which ought to have grown up. A reactionary comic strip which portrays the triumphs Orphan Annie and Daddy Warbucks attain by stubborn clinging to pioneer attitudes and habits is still the inspirational reading of millions of Americans. Egoistic individualism remains long after the economic place for it has passed.

This same frontier spirit, however, affords the spiritual sources which can swiftly bring about potential reforms. If we Americans are restless, unanchored in our ideas as in our habitations, if also we may boast a certain freedom, a flexibility in our thinking and a vigor and independence in our action, it is in some degree traceable to the constant flux of American life, always westward, always away from old and permanent things. The American tempo has not become a sophisticated dignified one, measured in harmony with the persisting splendor of ancient palaces, and the symmetry of great parks carpeted with lawns such as only centuries of tending could produce. We have not evolved a splendid system of common law out of the crude folk code of the German forest by a millennium of patient and slow change. Our political institutions did not grow deep in the shadow which the *imperium Romanum*, the *pax Romana*, the *instituta Gaii* have always cast over the ideas of the men of Western Europe. We on this continent have not upreared under the goad of a common ecstasy and mighty aspiration a sky-striving shrine for Our Lady of Chartres, nor a great temple for the Three Kings of Cologne. We share, to be sure, in all the achievements of Western Europe because we have a common ancestry in blood and in ideas with the men of Western Europe, but we share more distantly, more and more differently. The common ecstasy of our great-grandfathers went toward the conquest of a vast and magnificent, a sometimes pitiless and terrible land; our grandfathers were born beside covered wagons in mountain passes, on the prairie, on the desert; the Vigilantes administered the laws in many of our early communities. If our whole economic development as a nation was conditioned by the fact that for more than a century there was always free land in the West for the man who had lost his job in the East, it is equally true that this terrible struggle for survival against the Indian and against the land itself begot in our forefathers not a slow, ordered, conventionalized response to a given stimulus but a quick tense reaction to fit each differing need: the temper of American life to this day.

Assembly-line factories and skyscrapers must, in part, be understood in terms of the frontier. Our so rapid development in invention and technique, our gigantic financial and industrial systems—in general, the fact that we adjusted so completely and quickly, albeit so inharmoniously, to the Technical Age is to be traced to the absence of an ancient order of society and the presence of the frontier where we had to adapt ourselves to vastness with decision, speed, and skill. In an old culture there is a belief in the established order, a rooted opposition to change, a constitutional imperviousness to new ideas which would involve radical alteration in the mode of life. The frontier liberated the American spirit. It developed generosity and radiant vitality, together with a restlessness which was both good and ill, but did certainly bring with it a resiliency of mind, fluidity of idea and of society, a willingness for bold experiment.

Mass education, like mass suffrage and mass production, is a leading trait of our code. During the last generation education has supplanted the frontier as a favorite means of social mobility, for we have continued to define success in terms of mobility rather than in terms of stability. Our educational system has recently been built upon a kind of watery intellectualism. We have too often naïvely assumed that, if people were "well informed" and taught to reason in accord with accepted canons of logic, their characters would take care of themselves, and they would automatically acquire the point of view requisite in the citizen of a great society. Meanwhile, the toughening influences of frontier conditions were becoming steadily more dilute. Children of the economically dominant classes were being brought up in relative luxury. Parents failed to condition their offspring to rigorous standards of conduct because they were themselves confused. Actually many educative functions formerly carried out by the family have been surrendered to the school. The existing educational system is hopelessly irresolute on many fronts. It vacillates between training girls to be housewives or career women; it is torn between conditioning children for the theoretically desirable cooperative objectives or to the existing competitive realities. In spite of the terrific demands made upon them, elementary and high-school teachers are underpaid and lack social status. Psychiatrists are agreed that the elimination of social disorganization, as well as of personal disorganization, can be furthered only by more consistent educational practices both in the home and in the school because automatic actions based on the habits of early life are the most stable.

The anthropologist must also characterize our culture as profoundly irreligious. More than half of our people still occasionally go through the forms, and there are rural and ethnic islands in our population where religion is still a vital force. But very few of our leaders are still religious in the sense that they are convinced that prayer or the observance of church codes will affect the course of human events. Public figures participate in public worship and contribute financially to a church for reasons of expediency or because they know that churches represent one of the few elements of stability and continuity in our society. But belief in God's judgments and punishments as a motive for behavior is limited to a decreasing minority. Feelings of *guilt* are common but the sense of *sin* is rare.

The legend of Jesus lives in men's hearts and the Christian ethic is far from dead. As Bridges reminds us: "They who understand not cannot forget, and they who keep not His commandments call Him Master and Lord." But, in the opinion of many acute observers, American Protestantism is vital today primarily as an agency of benign social work. Relatively few Protestants, except in a few sects and in some rural areas, manifest deep religious feeling. The Roman Church certainly retains vigor, and parts of the encyclicals of recent Popes are not the least impressive of utterances upon contemporary life. To more than a few intellectuals of recent years the Catholic Church has appeared as the one firm rock in a sea of chaos and decay. To others it seems that the authoritarian Church, for all the social wisdom she has shown, for all the subtlety of her doctors, has purchased peace of mind in their time for her communicants by identifying ephemeral cultural expedients with immutable human nature. A system of beliefs, profoundly felt, is unquestionably necessary to the suvival of any society, but an increasing number of Americans debate the extent to which the dogmas of any organized Christian Church are compatible with contemporary secular knowledge.

Much of this debate reflects the shallowness of certain aspects of American culture. The alternative of science *or* religion is fictitious once it be granted that the functions of religion are primarily symbolic, expressive, and orientative. Every culture must define its ends as well as perfect its means. The logical and symbolic expressions of the ultimate values of a civilization cannot arise directly from scientific investigation, though it is fair to demand that they should not rest upon premises contrary to known fact or proven theory. A mechanistic, materialistic "science" hardly provides the orientations to the deeper problems of life that are essential for happy individuals and a healthy social order. Nor does a political philosophy such as "democracy." Men need tenets that do not outrage the brain but are meaningful to the viscera and the aesthetic sensibilities. They must be symbolized in rites that gratify the heart, please the ear and eye, fulfill the hunger for drama.

Observers agree on the poverty of American ceremonial life. American ceremonialism is too overwhelmingly that of Shriner conventions and labor rallies. If such national sentiments as we possess are to be maintained at a degree of intensity sufficient to preserve them, they must be given collective expression on suitable occasions. If the conduct of the individual is to be regulated in accord with the needs and purposes of the society, the society's sentiments must be periodically reinforced in the individual by gatherings in which all classes assert in symbolic form: "we are one people." [2]

Mass economic upheaval following upon unprecedented economic growth; lack of attention to the human problems of an industrial civilization; the impersonality of the social organization of cities; the melting pot, transitory geographical residence, social mobility, weakening of religious faith—all of these trends have contributed to make Americans feel unanchored, adrift upon a meaningless voyage. The American family system is in process of settling into a new type of organization and such a phase does not make for psychic ease. Why are Americans a nation of joiners? In part this is a defense mechanism against the excessive fluidity of our social structure. Weary of the tension of continual struggle for social place, people have tried to gain a degree of routinized and recognized fixity by allying themselves with others in voluntary associations.

The smooth working of all societies depends upon individuals not having to think about many of their acts. They can carry out their specialized functions better if much of their behavior is a more or less automatic reaction to a standardized situation in a socially appropriate fashion. A man meets a woman acquaintance on the street. He raises his hat. Such small acts bind a society together by making one's behavior intelligible to one's neighbors and give the participants a sense of security. Because one knows what to do and knows what the other person will do everything seems to be under control. Such patterns likewise release energy for the activities in which the individual is really interested. The trouble in our society is that the cluster of meanings upon which such an expective, repetitive way of behaving must depend is sadly disorganized. The cultural dislocation of emigrant groups, the rapid and disorderly expansion of cities, and many other factors have all contributed to the disorientation of individuals from a cohesive social matrix. Technicians have applied science to industry without either management, unions, or the state making more than feeble attempts at the indispensable compensatory adjustments in social structure.

A disproportionate technological development has given tempo to American life but denied it rhythm. It has provided the constant overstimulation neces-

[2] These statements may seem to imply an exaltation of nationalism or at least an acceptance of its inevitability for all time. Nothing of the sort is intended. I am primarily interested in calling attention to the empirical fact of the connection between means and ends. Also, I believe that certain American sentiments have a value to us and to the world—at least until the millennium of a world society arrives.

sary to throw many of us into a perpetual state of neurotic indecision. The disparity between our ingenuity in solving mechanical as opposed to human problems is a grave question. It would be infantile, of course, to say "away with the machine!" Obviously, it is not machines but our lack of scientific attention to the problems they raise which is evil. It is a legitimate hope that machines may free the majority of humans from drudgery and thus afford an escape from industrial feudalism. Further, as Mumford has urged, machines and the rapid transportation and distribution of goods which they make possible, create an international reciprocity and dependency such as to make the peace and order of nations more nearly a condition which *must* be attained rather than a pious desirability.

In rural areas and small towns, quick and direct response of neighbors can make for great personal security and for other values enriching to life. In cities, however, the economy is so finely organized and specialized that the dependency of one individual upon another, though actually more acute, is not felt in warm personal terms. People miss a network of relationships linking the job, the family, the church and other institutions. They feel the lack of personal appreciation of the products of their labors and of nonutilitarian creativity. Edward Sapir has well contrasted our psychological position with that of the primitive:

> So long as the individual retains a sense of control over the major goods of life, he is able to take his place in the cultural patrimony of his people. Now that the major goods of life have shifted so largely from the realm of immediate to that of remote ends, it becomes a cultural necessity for all who would not be looked upon as disinherited to share in the pursuit of these remoter ends. Nor harmony and depth of life . . . is possible when activity is well-nigh circumscribed by the sphere of immediate ends and when functioning within that sphere is so fragmentary as to have no inherent intelligibility or interest. Here lies the grimmest joke of our present American civilization. The vast majority of us, deprived of any but an insignificant and culturally abortive share in the satisfaction of the immediate wants of mankind, are further deprived of both opportunity and stimulation to share in the production of non-utilitarian values. Part of the time we are dray horses; the rest of the time we are listless consumers of goods which have received no least impress of our personality. In other words, our spiritual selves go hungry, for the most part, pretty much all of the time.

Most thoughtful Americans are concerned about the fact that the theory and the practice of our culture are hopelessly out of line. It is well established that while cultural content often changes rapidly, cultural forms often have extraordinary permanency. Thus it is only the *tradition* of economic independence which truly survives. For all our talk of free enterprise we have created the most vast and crushing monopolies in the world. Although the fable that every boy can become president has been repeatedly scoffed at in recent years, parents and children still act upon the ruling motivation that hard work, training, and aggressiveness can overcome almost all limitations. The result is, of course, countless disgruntled or bitter men and women, for as Veblen has shown, in a capitalistic economy the number of places at the top is disappointingly few. A cramping constriction will be felt by individuals so long as our ideal pattern is proclaimed as equality of opportunity for all. "Freedom" likewise has become fertile of disillusioned cynicism because of increasing realization of the truth of Durkheim's words, "I can be free only to the extent that others are forbidden to profit from their physical, economic, or other superiority to the detriment of my liberty." And much of the exultation in our "high standard of living" is, as Norman Thomas contends, "ludicrously beside the point. What the workers have a right to demand of the machine age is not that it will give them more bathtubs than Henry VIII had for his troublesome domestic establishment; they have a right to ask that machinery will conquer poverty rather than increase insecurity."

A society may indeed be viewed as a structure of expectancies. Neuroses have been produced experimentally in laboratory animals by causing the relation between stimulus and proper response to be irregular and haphazard. It follows that if the expectancies which are generated by the cultural ideology are notably unrealistic, mass frustration and mass neurosis are the inescapable consequences.

The diversity of ethnic origins in our forming nation provided strong psychological reinforcement of the doctrines of human equality which were the gospel of the Age of Enlightenment and of the Romantic Movement. Had not a belief in mystic equality become part of the official ideology of American culture and offered psychological security to non-Anglo-Saxons, these divergent groups might well have remained tight little islands of transplanted Europeans. But the contrast between this legal and political theory and the private theories and practices of too many American citizens (as symbolized in labels like "wops" and "greasers," in Jim Crow laws and lynchings) constitutes one of the severest strains undermining the equilibrium of the American social system. The Negroes and, to only a slightly lesser extent, the Spanish-speaking Americans constitute caste groups—that is, normal intermarriage does not occur between them and the rest of the population. Segregation in housing and discriminatory practices in our armed services stand out as intolerable contradictions in the institutions of a free society.

In the last fifteen years anthropologists have presented evidence that, in contrast to our official beliefs, a class structure has even now considerably crystallized in at least some parts of the United States. Lloyd Warner and his associates distinguish a six-class system: upper-upper, lower-upper, upper-middle, lower-middle, upper-lower, lower-lower. These groupings are not solely economic. In fact, members of the top class ordinarily have less money than those of the lower-upper group. Nor does stratification correspond entirely to occupational lines. Physicians, for example, are found in all of the first four classes.

In Warner's sense a class consists of persons who visit in one another's home, belong to the same social clubs, exchange gifts, and show awareness of themselves as a group set apart from others, and in a subordinate or superior position to others.

Whether the six-class system is generally valid or whether a larger or smaller subdivision better represents the facts in some communities is a factual question that cannot be answered until there have been more studies. The division of labor in a complex society makes some form of class stratification almost inevitable. It just so happens that in American culture recognition of the facts is repugnant to the American creed. Public-opinion polls indicate that 90 per cent of Americans insist that they are "middle class" despite wide variations in income level, occupation, and social habits. One study shows that 70 per cent of low-income groups claim middle-class social position. Warner, however, places 59 per cent of the people in one New England town in the two lower classes.

Under the influence of the depression and of Marxian theories discussion of class in the United States has increased greatly in the past twenty years. When class position is grudgingly recognized, it is often with anger—as something un-American and hence wrong. Some students of American class structure have failed to examine the significance of values—adhered to by almost all Americans—which operate to deny and tear down class divisions. Except possibly in limited areas of the eastern seaboard, the South, and the San Francisco area, the lines are still relatively fluid and everyone hopes to rise. The statement that American culture is dominantly a middle-class culture is something more than an acceptance of popular ideology which glosses over the sometimes ugly facts of differentiation. Hence "class," though a real phenomenon, does not have precisely the sense that it does in Europe. Certainly Americans are increasingly conscious of status, but the ranking of individuals and their immediate families is often still divorced from that of their close relatives. And the place of the whole body of kin in the smaller communities is frequently based primarily on length of residence there. Our society remains in important respects an open society.

Nevertheless the facts indicate that rapid rise through sheer ability and industry is much more difficult than it was a generation or two ago. Status is harder to achieve by one's own initiative and easier to acquire through family connections. In Washington during the war it was noted that considerable communication and power flowed through channels that were not only nonofficial but not those of political or other normal American interest groups. For the first time since the Age of Jackson an upper class appeared to be operating without much reference to regional or political lines. The class problem is also manifesting itself in the schools. Teachers, themselves usually of middle-class position, discriminate against lower-class children. The children sense that they are punished for following the cultural patterns of their parents. If effort and ability are not rewarded, the way to delinquency or stolid escapism is inviting. In short, class typing rather than individual typing has become one American mode of granting or denying recognition to other people.

Americans are at present seeing social change of a vastness difficult to comprehend. Concretely, social change has its origins in the strains and dissatisfactions felt by specific individuals. When personal insecurity is sufficiently intense and sufficiently widespread, new patterns are germinated in the few creative individuals, and there will be willingness to try them out on the part of larger numbers. Such is the present condition of American society. If a society be regarded as a system in equilibrium, it may be said that in the decade following 1918 the prewar equilibrium was precariously reattained. But the depression and World War II appear to have destroyed the old equilibrium beyond repair. At the moment Americans are in the tortures of attempting to reach a new and differently based equilibrium. The devastating appropriateness of the phrase, "the neurotic personality of our time," is both the condition and the result of this circumstance.

The basis of social life is the sensitivity of human beings to the behavior of other human beings. In a complex society the need for correct interpretation and response to the demands of others is especially great. But in American culture the first experiences of the growing child tend so to emphasize prestige (especially economic prestige) needs that the ego requirements of our adults are often too tremendous for them to follow any other pattern. As Horney says, "the striving for prestige as a means of overcoming fears and inner emptiness is certainly culturally prescribed." Such a device, however, like the intemperate devotion to the pleasure principle, is but a feeble palliative. The popular motto, "every man for himself," was less socially dangerous when firm and generally held beliefs in the afterworld provided some check upon rampant individualism.

The frontier code of sturdy individualism needs tempering and modification the more because it is seldom possible of attainment in the present situation. As Sirjamaki says, "The culture posits individualism as a basic social value but places overwhelming burdens upon its realization." In most aspects of social life American demands for conformity are too great. After the passing of the frontier, individualism was expressed mainly in the economic part of the culture. Today the United States is almost the only country in the world in which large numbers of people cling to laissez-faire principles in economics and government. In its extreme form this is utterly unrealistic, a fixation upon a vain phantasm of our past.

Some acceptance of planning and of stability as a value would decrease the envy and strife that go with incessant mobility. In a society where everybody is either going up or going down there is an excessive psychological necessity to cherish the familiar. This exaggerated stress upon conformity plus our business externalism has created what Fromm has recently termed "the personality of the market place" as the most frequent type in our culture. Given the pressures to conformity, personality fulfillment is denied to many, perhaps most, of our citizens.

America's claim to greatness thus far is not through its Whitmans and Melvilles, nor its Woods and Bentons, nor its Michelsons and Comptons. Still less does it consist in its having added to the contemplative or religious treasures of mankind. Emerson, Thoreau, James, and Dewey are distinguished thinkers, but that they are of the stature of many other ancient and modern philosophers is doubtful. Mary Baker Eddy, Joseph Smith, and other leaders of cultist or revivalistic sects represent all that is characteristically American in religion.

Americans have, however, been inventive in more than one sphere. Admirable and useful as are those material inventions which have made "the American standard of living" an international byword, American social inventions are the most distinctive contributions made by the United States to world culture. The cult of the average man is an even more characteristically American invention than the assembly line. Philosophers of many nations had dreamed of a state guided by a skillfully trained but small group of the good and wise. The United States, however, was the first country to dedicate itself to the conception of a society where the lot of the common man would be made easier, where the same opportunities would be available to all, where the lives of all men and women would be enriched and ennobled. This was something new under the sun.

We cannot rest upon the laurels of past achievement. E. H. Carr has bluntly stated the alternatives:

> The impact of the Soviet Union has fallen on a western world where much of the framework of individualism was already in decay, where faith in the self-sufficiency of individual reason had been sapped by the critique of relativism, where the democratic community was in urgent need of reinforcement against the forces of disintegration latent in individualism, and where the technical conditions of production on the one hand, and the social pressures of mass civilization on the other, were already imposing far-reaching measures of collective organization. . . . The fate of the western world will turn on its ability to meet the Soviet challenge by a successful search for new forms of social and economic action in which what is valid in individualist and democratic tradition can be applied to the problems of mass civilization.[3]

All advocates of government by an élite, from Plato to Hitler and Stalin, have ridiculed the competence of average citizens to form rational opinions upon complex issues. There is no doubt that many nineteenth-century utterances absurdly exalted rationality. Yet the best anthropological evidence, as

[3] From E. H. Carr, *The Soviet Impact on the Western World*. Copyright 1947 by The Macmillan Company and used with their permission and that of the author.

Franz Boas pointed out, is that the judgment of the masses is sounder than the judgment of the classes on broad questions of policy where sentiments and values are concerned. This doctrine must not be perverted into a claim for the common man's expertness on technical or artistic matters. Nor does contemporary thought refer to the individual citizen's judgments. Rather, it refers to collective decisions arrived at in group interaction and dealing with "matters of common concern which depend upon estimates of probability." As Carl Friedrich continues:

> This concept of the common man salvages from the onslaught of the irrationalist revolt those elements in the older doctrine which are essential to democratic politics. It seeks a middle ground between the extreme rationalistic ideas of an earlier day and the denial of all rationality by those who were disappointed over its limitations. . . . Enough common men, when confronted with a problem, can be made to see the facts in a given situation to provide a working majority for a reasonable solution, and such majorities will in turn provide enough continuing support for a democratic government to enforce such common judgments concerning matters of common concern.

What is the prospect for American culture? Let one anthropologist, though bearing in mind the principles of his science, speak unashamedly in terms of his own American sentiments. Given our biological and material wealth, given the adaptive genius which is the constructive heritage of our peculiarly American frontier spirit, it will be the fault not of angels but of ourselves if our problems are not in large part resolved. The decisive factor will be the extent to which individual Americans feel a personal responsibility. This, in turn, depends upon an intangible: their total philosophic attitude. James Truslow Adams in *The Epic of America* urges that the meaningful contribution which the United States has made to the totality of human culture is "the American Dream," "a vision of a society in which the lot of the common man will be made easier and his life enriched and ennobled." It was in the ideological field that America made its first and can still make its greatest contribution to the world. In the New World, peopled by robust men and women who had the courage to emigrate and many of whom were impelled by the active vision of a nobler society, Americans enlarged the meaning of freedom and gave it many new expressions.

It is this prospect for American culture which we must cherish and believe in. Nor is there anything in science which indicates that the dreams of man do not influence, nay sometimes determine, his behavior. While choice is most often a flattering illusion, while antecedent and existent hard-sense data usually shape our destinies, there are moments in the careers of nations, as well as in the careers of individuals, when opposing external forces are about equally balanced, and it is then that intangibles like "will" and "belief" throw the scales. Cultures are not altogether self-contained systems which inevitably follow out their own self-determined evolution. Sorokin and other prophets of doom fail to see that one of the factors which determines the next step in the evolution of a system is precisely the dominant attitudes of people. And these are not completely determined by the existent culture. John Dewey has shown us that in "judgments of practice" the hypothesis itself has a crucial influence upon the course of events: "to the extent that it is seized and acted upon, it weights events in its favor."

Even that erstwhile pessimist, Aldous Huxley, has seen that the discoveries of modern psychology have been perverted to bolster a false determinism. If responses can be conditioned, they can by the same token be deconditioned and reconditioned—though neither individuals nor peoples change suddenly and completely. We are now released from the dominantly external and material demands which frontier conditions made upon our society. Intelligent planning can ease the hostile tensions of national anarchy by providing both security and socialized freedom for the individual. Ideals of flourishing freshness that adapt to changed conditions and to what is sound and creative in the distinctive American Way are the only sure antidote for our social ills. Only those ideals will spread and be accepted which correspond to the culturally created emotional needs of the people. Scientific humanism is such an ideal. Rooted in the tradition of Americans to value scientific achievement highly, scientific humanism can actualize the American Dream. As our culture has come from all the world, so must we give back to all the world not that technological materialism which is science cheapened and debased but the scientific attitude woven into the stuff of people's daily lives. This is a vision of humility in the face of the complexity of things, of the joyous pursuit of ideas of which there is no exclusive possession. This is science not as the provider of the agencies of barbarism but science as revealing the order in experience, as heightening the sense of our precarious dependence one upon the other, as the surest and most powerful of internationalizing forces.

Scientific humanism should be the sturdy creed of the future. Despite uncritical worship of invention and technology, the masses are still, in Carlson's expression, "innocent of science, in the sense of the spirit and the method of science as part of their way of life. . . . Science in this sense has as yet hardly touched the common man or his leaders." An effective working majority of our citizens need no longer base their personal security upon expectation of future life or adult dependency upon the projected images of parent-persons. The scientific vision is the vision which Plato saw in the *Symposium*, a security system which is depersonalized but humanized rather than dehumanized. To try to make such a vision real, offers American men and women that common nobility of purpose which is the vitalizing energy of any significant culture. The venture demands a courage analogous to religious faith, a courage undismayed by the failure of any specific experiment, a courage ready to offer the renunciations of waiting long, a courage which recognizes that even negative knowledge means growth, a courage realizing that the general hypotheses underlying the venture will be proved only if diminished anxiety and greater gusto in day-to-day living transform the lives of us all.

CARL   BINGER,   M. D.

The Pressures on College Girls Today[1]

In our culture, women still seem to regard themselves as inferior. Perhaps it is a genuine feeling of their own, or perhaps it is imposed upon them by men. The new freedom has not done away with it—not the vote, nor trousers, nor cigarettes, nor even standards of sexual behavior that are somewhat similar to men's standards. Indeed, all of these indexes of equality with men appear often as an uncertain effort to deny the confusion of roles in which modern society has placed women.

Although the formal college curriculum does not recognize a difference between male and female students, this does not mean that their needs are identical—far from it. I know that to generalize here is risky business and that what I shall say may be only partially true. But it seems obvious enough that as a boy approaches graduation he will have his eye out for a job or a career, and a girl will have hers on marriage. This does not mean that college boys are indifferent to finding a wife or that girls are unconcerned about earning money soon after graduation. The many early collegiate marriages in which young wives today contribute to the family income—if, indeed, they do not pay for most of their husbands' graduate tuition—would belie any such notion.

Whether they are gainfully employed or not, however, or whether or not they have decided to go to graduate school and perhaps prepare themselves for one of the professions—architecture, business, city planning, engineering, medicine, the ministry, law, scientific research, social work, teaching, or others (all are now open to women)—they usually are interested, first and foremost, in finding a mate. They do not shout this from the housetops. They often spend a good deal of their time and energy in trying to conceal it from themselves and from others.

There are exceptions, of course, among them some few dedicated female scholars who put their work ahead of everything else—often, to be sure, at great cost. But this is not true of the run of the mill. For them, marriage is the paramount goal and the presiding wish. Sometimes they are willing to post-

[1] From Carl A. L. Binger, "Emotional Disturbances Among College Women" in *Emotional Problems of the Student*, 1961, by Blaine, G. B., Jr., and McArthur, C. C. Courtesy Appleton-Century-Crofts, Inc. Slightly revised with the consent of the author.

pone it until they have achieved more proximal goals—this degree or that job, for example—but it is pretty constantly in the back of their minds.

In some women's colleges as many as 50 per cent of the senior class continue their formal education in graduate school. Many of these young women prepare themselves for the professions or continue their studies for various motives other than a clear interest in scholarship: to postpone the evil day of going out into the world; to raise their market value in getting jobs; to remain in the relatively protected environment of an institution of learning; to continue to meet interesting people. "People," it should be said, is the current euphemism for men. (One must not call the devil by his name.) We know that the motive behind study may have a determining influence both on the quality of the work and on the enthusiasm with which it is undertaken. When motives are too mixed they may result in confusion, conflict, and dissatisfaction. Graduate work in itself, however, need no longer be a deterrent to marriage. Many young women combine the two ventures with surprising skill and apparent equanimity.

The median age of girls when they marry is now about twenty, and the preoccupation with marriage becomes fairly persistent when this age is past. One can observe this frequently among graduate students. Today a young lady of twenty-one who is still single is apt to think of herself as an old maid. She prefers, however, to see herself as well settled with the man of her choice, or of her dreams, who loves and cherishes her and by whom she will eventually have about four children. Once she has met him, she often appears to care little about how much money they will have, what side of the tracks he was born on, his social or ethnic background, or his religion. Love is what counts, or at least what seems to be love. And she thinks she wants a man whom she can look up to, who has been exposed to at least an equivalent formal education and is perhaps a little better in his studies than she is. This makes her feel more secure.

One hears a great deal about security. It has become the golden calf of today. When one stops to analyze what is meant by it, one soon learns that it has little to do with jobs, with income, or with social status, but is a subjective feeling derived usually from a certain sense of approbation and depending more on self-approbation than on anything else. This is the rock on which many young college women founder. To have the affection and esteem of a young man whom they admire seems to many the safest bulwark against their self-doubt and their feelings of insufficiency. But the young man is often very young, far less ready for a real, rewarding, and growing relationship than is the girl. And so the bulwark often turns out to be but a slender reed, at least from the point of view of her needs.

Naturally enough, this may lead to trouble. The single most frequently encountered emotional disturbance among these young women is depression. Sometimes it is so sweeping that little seems left of the normally functioning personality, and there may then be a real risk of suicide. Fortunately, this is relatively rare. What is common, however, in the college girl is a loss of zest, a feeling of apathy or fatigue, and an apparent need for extra hours of sleep, a very much lowered self-esteem, with sensitivity to other people's opinions and reactions, and, above all, an inability to get work done. To hand in written material on time means somehow to commit oneself, to expose oneself to comment and criticism before which failing spirits falter. Often the printed page seems to lack meaning; attention, concentration, and comprehension are at a low level. Instead, there is brooding, daydreaming, mounting dissatisfaction with self, and a feeling of guilt because of time and opportunities wasted—guilt tinctured with anxiety: "What will happen to me?" "Will my scholarship be renewed?" "I mustn't let my parents down; sending me to college has been a great sacrifice for them." "I can't understand it. At high school I was third in my class of 250 and was President of Student Council." And so it goes.

This phenomenon, in greater or lesser degree, is sufficiently common to be called "normal." I have called it a depression; I do not insist on this as a clinical diagnosis. It has been described by some as an identity crisis, by others as adolescent turmoil. Behind it there are, of course, feelings of inadequacy, self-absorption, worry, and accompanying anxiety. The significant facts are the lowered self-esteem and the diminution in zest, energy, and capacity to function in a creative way. The depression seems to be a kind of declaration of dependence, of helplessness, and a muted cry for help as well. And it occurs at some time and in varying intensity in practically every girl during her career at college.

Now, the student who experiences this need not be severely neurotic, nor are these manifestations necessarily evidence of any profound or abnormal emotional disturbance. They may simply represent—in a freshman, for example— the first response of a sensitive, naïve adolescent to a new, frighteningly complicated, and sophisticated environment. After all, some of these girls are only sixteen or barely seventeen. They may have come from small towns, and they may be the first ones from their high schools to be accepted in one of the major women's colleges. All eyes are on them, and their parents are inordinately proud. The girls feel that they are in heaven at last. But they soon find the atmosphere rarefied and the air heady. They may never before have had to work hard, even in order to lead their classes. They are asked to write a paper not on the character of Silas Marner or on the most interesting experience they had during their summer vacations (in many high schools they are not given any written assignments), but, for example, on "The Relation of Leonardo's Writing to His Painting and to Fifteenth-Century Art in General." After chewing their pencils for a while and twirling a lock of hair, they finally brazen it out and go to the library. Even after they have mastered the indexing system, they are appalled by the number of cards under the heading "Leonardo," and they find nothing whatever on the assigned topic. Perhaps for the first time in their lives they are forced to read actively instead of passively and to do some quiet, hard thinking. This is not only a strange experience but almost akin to physical pain. And so there is a flight into solace: a little chat with the girl in the next room, who may have been to one of those progressive schools where this kind of assignment was familiar enough; or perhaps their neighbor attended a high-powered, exclusive boarding school and has gained so much poise and self-assurance that nothing appears to daunt her.

Or maybe our young freshman is the daughter of a trustee and her mother was the college heroine of her day—not only Phi Beta Kappa, but the belle of the ball as well. This puts additional pressure on the student, who develops an egregious need to make good in spite of the awareness of her own ineptitude.

The reaction of depression is not confined to young freshmen, however, nor is it necessarily related to difficulties associated with study. The student may be in the graduate school, already past the first flush of youth, and perhaps a little *triste* or weary from the steady grind and worried by constant competition with a most gifted, accomplished, and brilliant galaxy of colleagues. At such times there may be a kind of tacit rebellion, an intellectual sit-down strike, so to speak, when the mind seems to refuse to do more work. Any one of the many circumstances can bring this about—impending orals, a thesis due or overdue, an unhappy love relationship, or disquieting news from home. Even conspicuous success can bring on this reaction in some individuals.

Of course, the common-sense attitude would be to quit for a while, to do something else, to have some fun and then come back with renewed vigor. But this seldom occurs to them, partly because they have already lost some resilience and resourcefulness. The thought of absenting themselves from work is far too perilous. Instead, these students prefer to whip the tired horse. They stay up later and get up earlier, and they worry about all the ground they still have to cover. Sometimes fate takes over. They come down with the flu or "a virus," or they develop infectious mononucleosis. This seems a welcome and respectable respite, but it usually leaves them more exhausted than the illness itself could account for, and still unable to work.

Many other devices are automatically resorted to as defensive maneuvers against the underlying depression. Instead of doing extra work, the student may stay in bed in the mornings and sleep until noon, thereby missing her lectures or even hour exams. Her academic plight goes from bad to worse, her depression and feelings of guilt increase, and her self-esteem continues to plummet. She may adopt a kind of cynical, supersophisticated, and supercilious attitude toward the whole academic community and cease to be a functioning part of it.

These, together with the other defenses I shall mention, are maladaptive, in the sense that they are unrealistic and make matters worse rather than better.

Another common defense among young girls has to do with their eating habits. They try to allay their uneasiness and anxiety by eating too much. Some of them will stuff themselves with bread and butter at mealtime; others will fill up on ice cream and candy between meals; still others become night feeders and ransack the kitchen when they should be asleep. This extra feeding, which has little to do with hunger, may be episodic around examination time; it may be a reaction to having been jilted; or, again, it may have become a kind of chronic addiction. Of course, it feeds as well the lowered self-esteem, puts an end to dating, and becomes a new source of discouragement. This phenomenon is seen almost exclusively in girls, seldom in boys.

The relations between college boys and girls are a tender subject, seldom discussed between the generations. The contemporary sexual mores of young people are so different from those which governed their parents' or teachers' lives that a common meeting ground between them scarcely exists. (It is possible that the parents have forgotten some of the details of their own past experiences.) Girls seldom, if ever, discuss their sexual experiences with their parents, and when they do—unless they are facing a crisis—one cannot escape the impression that the parent-child relationship is a little unhealthy. To be sure, girls often come to college with standards handed to them by their mothers and tacitly upheld by their fathers. Letting a boy kiss you good night, for example, is all right, but preferably not on the first date. Here is where conflict often begins. If the girl is standoffish and stiff, the chances are she will not see the boy again. But this is just what she wants to forestall unless he is a "jerk," and so, partly to secure her aim and partly because she is moved and flattered, she accepts his kisses, and soon after, if she has not already learned, she is taught to "kiss back."

From this point on, the boy takes over, unless he himself is very timid. He tries to impose his standards and rationalizations on her. . . . In any case, he is usually as idealistic as she is and not just out for fun or experience, but he is eager to prove himself. Since, by this time, she has been aroused—the more so because the boy is usually serious—and is, as the modern cliché has it, "emotionally involved," she may accede to his wishes, often, to be sure, with serious misgivings and with a feeling of guilt. . . .

The present arrangement in coeducational or quasi-coeducational institutions facilitates these intimacies. Boys and girls are pretty constantly together in the classroom, in the library, at dances, at parties, at rehearsals. They drink their Martinis and gin and tonics together. They light each other's cigarettes. And they study together, often in the boy's room, and sometimes they do more than study. Roommates are an inconvenience but seldom a real hindrance. Much that is unspoken is understood. The girl and boy become each other's property. At a dance they dance together all evening. To pursue another boy's date is to commit the unpardonable act of "bird-dogging." This is not acceptable behavior. Girls, as well, impose their proprietary rights on their dates. Promiscuity is not a manifestation of sexual freedom, but rather a symptom of a disordered personality.

The foregoing description is of one kind of behavior, but of one only. It is difficult to generalize here, and not too satisfactory to try to create stereotypes. None of them is fixed or unvarying. Behavior changes in response to outer impacts and inner needs and to those mores and conventions which the girl brings with her from school.

There are, of course, "popular" girls who have a different date every night and like to keep lots of boys on the string; idealistic girls who want to keep themselves pure for the great love to come; shy, immature girls who do not date; and girls who manage to make themselves so unattractive by overeating or by their slovenly dress that they are seldom approached by boys. The boys themselves are often strikingly immature, adolescent, and dependent, and get much comfort and support from the steady affection of motherly young women.

One gets the impression that the relationship between the sexes is still in an experimental phase, that it is motivated partly by idealism, partly by a spirit of rebellion against parents or others in authority, partly by the desire of young people to find out about themselves, partly by loneliness, partly by a kind of new conventionality and a wish not to miss anything, but above all, for the girls, by the feeling of approbation which the steady attention of one boy gives them. When he does not call up for two days, the girl's world begins to totter. The demands are often unequal and at variance. By the time the girl has said "yes" to herself and has stilled her doubts and her feeling of guilt, the boy may be on the way out of the relationship. This leads to quarreling and a loss of dignity and self-esteem in the girl. She may feel bereft, or "all empty inside." When she is then asked to do a paper on "Iambulos' Sun-state and Its Relation to the Pergamene Revolt under Aristonicos in 133 B.C." or on "Turkish Naval Power in the Sixteenth Century," she may well be dismayed as she stares, with a blank mind, at a blank piece of paper.

It seems to me that educators have at least the responsibility of looking facts in the face. If they relax parietal rules sufficiently to permit girls to go to boys' rooms and remain there until late, then they should realize what the consequences are likely to be. They should realize, too, that these pressures on girls, even the most resilient and well balanced of them, will at times interfere with their work. It is all very well to say that this is part of life and that they must learn to take things in their stride. We seem to forget that life is fuller and moves faster for them than it did for us at their age. They have more "experiences" in a week than most of us had in a year.

Dean Briggs of Harvard used to say that college is a place to make mistakes, but mistakes today are far costlier than they once were. The price of academic failure, or even mediocre performance, may be great. It means that further graduate study is probably barred or that good jobs are not easily come by. The price of mistakes in relations with the opposite sex can be high indeed, sometimes nearly ruinous.

Young girls, one must remember, are vulnerable, sensitive, idealistic, often introspective and emotional, inclined to think ill of themselves and to compare themselves, to their own disadvantage, with men, whose good opinion means so much to them. We should recognize them for what they are, as wonderful young women in their own right, and build up this positive picture.

I have been greatly impressed with their candor and frankness, with their willingness to avow their feelings and to cut through much conventional cant and nonsense. Many of them have a gift for understanding themselves and others and a need to talk out some of their perplexities and to find some ethical and aesthetic pattern for their lives. They are distressed by the formless chaos that surrounds them and sometimes recognize this for what it is, as evil. They know intuitively that the unexamined life is not worth living. They are, of course, concerned with themselves and revel in their own freedom, but they are willing to prepare themselves, emotionally, at least, for the eventual task of child rearing, which they appear to do with so much competence and even joy.

A college which disregards their essential nature is doing only part of its job. If it wants girls to get the best out of their courses of instruction, then provision must be made for some easement and for some time for discussion with intelligent and reasonably mature adults who are not too quick to give advice but are willing to listen. I recall a young girl saying to me once that she could do her work all right, but it didn't leave her time to grow up. Young people need time for this and time to talk and to give expression to some of their perplexities. I realize that we have not found the ideal way to success in this enterprise, that each college will have to follow the plan that fits its own tradition. The problems in exclusively female institutions are not essentially different from those in coeducational ones, since they are both dependent upon pressures and upon the natural vulnerability which the girl brings with her. Everyone concerned with young people must be concerned with this aspect of their development. If not, what passes for education may be only a kind of "intellectual conditioning," without depth of meaning, or hope for the future.

I have no wish to end this article on a negative note, nor to leave the reader with the impression that nothing can be accomplished either by way of preventing these emotional disturbances in young college women or of dealing with them once they have arisen. Exactly the reverse is true. There is probably no segment of the population which appears to be more amenable to treatment than just this group of intelligent, sensitive, idealistic young women with their futures before them.

We have no sure formula to prevent the kind of depression I have described in this article. We do not know how to instill humor where none exists. But we can encourage self-acceptance and a sense of identity; and, unless the student has been too much damaged in childhood by a lack of trust, we can provide an atmosphere, even a rigorously competitive one, in which courage does not too quickly flag.

There is much to be said for confrontation with more mature persons, not

only in the faculty but in the student body, too, where the inclusion of some
older men and women, who are completing unfinished college work, can add
to the meaningfulness of study. And the choice of new members of a faculty
should be made with an eye to their concern for students as well as for their
creative scholarship. When the two are combined, the stage is well set. There
is a salutary effect also in good talk, not only of the bull-session kind, but
talk with sophisticated, critical persons who are concerned with the human
situation. Out of this can come compelling and charismatic ideas, which may
last a lifetime. Nothing we can do for this generation or the next can be
more important than to help these young women toward a clearer image of
themselves. This will give them the self-esteem they need and the vigor to lead
satisfying and creative lives.

PHILIP WYLIE

Common Women[1]

Mom[2] Is the End Product of She

She is Cinderella . . . the shining-haired, the starry-eyed, the ruby-lipped virgo
æternis, of which there is presumably one, and only one, or a one-and-only
for each male, whose dream is fixed upon her deflowerment and subsequent
perpetual possession. This act is a sacrament in all churches and a civil affair
in our society. The collective aspects of marriage are thus largely compressed
into the rituals and social perquisites of one day. Unless some element of
mayhem or intention of divorce subsequently obtrudes, a sort of privacy en-
gulfs the union and all further developments are deemed to be the business
of each separate pair, including the transition of Cinderella into mom, which,
if it occasions any shock, only adds to the huge, invisible burthen every man
carries with him into eternity. It is the weight of this bundle which, incidentally, squeezes out of him the wish for death, his last positive biological resource.

Mom is an American creation. Her elaboration was necessary because she
was launched as Cinderella. Past generations of men have accorded to their
mothers, as a rule, only such honors as they earned by meritorious action in
their individual daily lives. Filial *duty* was recognized by many sorts of civili-

---

1 From *Generation of Vipers*. Copyright 1942, 1954, by Philip Wylie, and reprinted by permission of Holt, Rinehart and Winston, Inc., New York.
2 You are now about to read (or re-read) one of the most renowned (or notorious)
passages in modern English Letters.

This chapter has put the word "momism" indelibly in our language, it has
broken a path through sacred preserves into which all manner of amateur critics

zations and loyalty to it has been highly regarded among most peoples. But I cannot think, offhand, of any civilization except ours in which an entire division of living men has been used, during wartime, or at any time, to spell out the word "mom" on a drill field, or to perform any equivalent act.

The adoration of motherhood has even been made the basis of a religious cult, but the mother so worshiped achieved maternity without change in her virgin status—a distinction worthy of contemplation in itself—and she thus in no way resembled mom.

Hitherto, in fact, man has shown a considerable qui vive to the dangers which arise from momism and freely perceived that his "old wives" were often vixens, dragons, and Xanthippes. Classical literature makes a constant point of it. Shakespeare dwelt on it. Man has also kept before his mind an awareness that, even in the most lambent mother love, there is always a chance some extraneous current will blow up a change, and the thing will become a consuming furnace. The spectacle of the female devouring her young in the firm belief that it is for their own good is too old in man's legends to be overlooked by any but the most flimsily constructed society. . . .

Megaloid momworship has got completely out of hand. Our land, subjectively mapped, would have more silver cords and apron strings crisscrossing it than railroads and telephone wires. Mom is everywhere and everything and damned near everybody, and from her depends all the rest of the U.S. Disguised as good old mom, dear old mom, sweet old mom, your loving mom, and so on, she is the bride at every funeral and the corpse at every wedding. Men live for her and die for her, dote upon her and whisper her name as they pass away, and I believe she has now achieved, in the hierarchy of miscellaneous articles, a spot next to the Bible and the Flag, being reckoned part of both in a way. . . .

_____

(along with the stateliest psychiatrists and the United States Armed Services) have since proceeded, pouring out articles, monographs, bulletins, research reports and shelves of books showing how right I was to speak as I did of a certain, prevalent sub-species of middle-class American woman; and the chapter has typed me apparently forever as a woman hater—indeed, as the all-out, all-time, high-scoring world champion misogynist.

It is this last I regret. The fact that legions of individuals, and finally the Army, followed me in condemnation of that special type of American mother I called "mom" merely affirms my work: the Oedipus complex had become a social fiat and a dominant neurosis in our land. It was past time somebody said so. As a way of life, it is shameful in grownups of both sexes; as a national cult, it is a catastrophe.

But, since I love women more than most men, I believe I love them more deeply and knowingly, and since I respect motherhood whenever and wherever it is worthy of respect, I find it somewhat distressing to be forever tagged as Woman's Nemesis. The fact is that only moms—or incipient moms—could imagine, after a close reading of this very chapter, that I had any other sensation for *real* women

Mom is something new in the world of men. Hitherto, mom has been so busy raising a large family, keeping house, doing the chores, and fabricating everything in every home except the floor and the walls that she was rarely a problem to her family or to her equally busy friends, and never one to herself. Usually, until very recently, mom folded up and died of hard work somewhere in the middle of her life. Old ladies were scarce and those who managed to get old did so by making remarkable inner adjustments and by virtue of a fabulous horniness of body, so that they lent to old age not only dignity but metal.

Nowadays, with nothing to do, and tens of thousands of men . . . to maintain her, every clattering prickamette in the republic survives for an incredible number of years, to stamp and jibber in the midst of man, a noisy neuter by natural default or a scientific gelding sustained by science, all tongue and teat and razzmatazz. The machine has deprived her of social usefulness; time has stripped away her biological possibilities and poured her hide full of liquid soap; and man has sealed his own soul beneath the clamorous cordillera by handing her the checkbook and going to work in the service of her caprices. . . .

Satan, we are told, finds work for idle hands to do. There is no mistaking the accuracy of this proverb. Millions of men have heaped up riches and made a conquest of idleness so as to discover what it is that Satan puts them up to. Not one has failed to find out. But never before has a great nation of brave and dreaming men absent-mindedly created a huge class of idle, middle-aged women. Satan himself has been taxed to dig up enterprises enough for them. But the field is so rich, so profligate, so perfectly to his taste, that his first effort, obviously, has been to make it self-enlarging and self-perpetuating. This he has done by whispering into the ears of girls that the only way they can cushion the shock destined to follow the rude disillusionment over the fact

---

than love. Quite a few thousand ladies perceived that fact and so wrote to me. But millions, who thought they read otherwise—or who never read the text but took rumor of my diatribe as Gospel (in mom's fashion)—have given me a false name.

To such females, womanhood is more sacrosanct by a thousand times than the Virgin Mary to popes—and motherhood, that degree raised to astronomic power. They have eaten the legend about themselves and believe it; they live it; they require fealty of us all.

From them, I received dozens of scurrilous, savage, illiterate, vulgar and obscene epistles, letters which but made my point that much clearer—to me. But I have had hundreds of *times* as many communications from moms who confessed, from the sons and daughters of moms who suddenly saw whence their sickly dependencies came, and from multitudes of the learned, the celebrated, the world's leaders, who said in effect: *Thanks.*

So, for individuals, the message has often been of value. But insofar as its effect on this great nation is concerned (about which possibility people sometimes enquire), my risky effort to sever the psychic umbilicus by which millions of moms holds millions of grown American men and women in diseased serfdom, *achieved nothing.*

that they are not really Cinderella is to institute momworship. Since he had already infested both male and female with the love of worldly goods, a single step accomplished the entire triumph: he taught the gals to teach their men that dowry went the other way, that it was a weekly contribution, and that any male worthy of a Cinderella would have to work like a piston after getting one, so as to be worthy, also, of all the moms in the world. . . .

Mom got herself out of the nursery and the kitchen. She then got out of the house. She did not get out of the church, but, instead, got the stern stuff out of *it*, padded the guild room, and moved in more solidly than ever before. No longer either hesitant or reverent, because there was no cause for either attitude after her purge, she swung the church by the tail as she swung everything else. In a preliminary test of strength, she also got herself the vote and, although politics never interested her (unless she was exceptionally naïve, a hairy foghorn, or a size forty scorpion), the damage she forthwith did to society was so enormous and so rapid that even the best men lost track of things. Mom's first gracious presence at the ballot-box was roughly concomitant with the start toward a new all-time low in political scurviness, hoodlumism, gangsterism, labor strife, monopolistic thuggery, moral degeneration, civic corruption, smuggling, bribery, theft, murder, homosexuality, drunkenness, financial depression, chaos and war. Note that.

The degenerating era, however, marked new highs in the production of junk. Note that, also.

Mom, however, is a great little guy. Pulling pants onto her by these words, let us look at mom.

She is a middle-aged puffin with an eye like a hawk that has just seen a rabbit twitch far below. She is about twenty-five pounds overweight, with no

---

Mom still commands. Mom's more than ever in charge. Hardly five Americans in a hundred know today that mom and her bogus authority have ever been questioned—by me, or by anybody else. The nation can no longer say it contains many great, free, dreaming men. We are deep in the predicted nightmare now and mom sits on its decaying throne—who bore us, who will soon, most likely, wrap civilization in mom's final, tender garment: a shroud.

Today, as the news photos abundantly make plain, mom composes the majority of Senator McCarthy's shock troops—paying blind tribute to a blind authoritarianism like her own. Mom reaches out from her shrieking hordes, cries, "I touched him!" and faints away. The tragic Senator stalks smiling to the podium and leads the litany of panic, the rituals of logic perverted, the induced madness of those the gods have marked for destruction. "McCarthyism," the rule of unreason, is one with momism: a noble end aborted by sick-minded means, a righteous intent—in terrorism fouled and tyranny foundered.

Today, too, there is mom and her mass affaire with Liberace. . . .

Tomorrow, she will shriek around and dote upon some other Hero, as sick, or as fatuous.

Today, while decent men struggle for seats in government with the hope of saving our Republic, mom makes a condition of their election the legalizing of sprint, but sharp heels and a hard backhand which she does not regard as a foul but a womanly defense. In a thousand of her there is not sex appeal enough to budge a hermit ten paces off a rock ledge. She none the less spends several hundred dollars a year on permanents and transformations, pomades, cleansers, rouges, lipsticks, and the like—and fools nobody except herself. If a man kisses her with any earnestness, it is time for mom to feel for her pocketbook, and this occasionally does happen.

She smokes thirty cigarettes a day, chews gum, and consumes tons of bon-bons and petit fours. The shortening in the latter, stripped from pigs, sheep and cattle, shortens mom. She plays bridge with the stupid voracity of a hammerhead shark, which cannot see what it is trying to gobble but never stops snapping its jaws and roiling the waves with its tail. She drinks moderately, which is to say, two or three cocktails before dinner every night and a brandy and a couple of highballs afterward. She doesn't count the two cocktails she takes before lunch when she lunches out, which is every day she can. On Saturday nights, at the club or in the juke joint, she loses count of her drinks and is liable to get a little tiddly, which is to say, shot or blind. But it is her man who worries about where to acquire the money while she worries only about how to spend it, so he has the ulcers and colitis and she has the guts of a bear; she can get pretty stiff before she topples.

Her sports are all spectator sports.

She was graduated from high school or a "finishing" school or even a college in her distant past and made up for the unhappiness of compulsory education by sloughing all that she learned so completely that she could not pass the final examinations of a fifth grader. She reads the fiction in three women's magazines each month and occasionally skims through an article, which usually

---

Bingo. What will she want tomorrow when the world needs saving even more urgently?

We must understand mom before we lose touch with understanding itself.

I showed her as she is—ridiculous, vain, vicious, a little mad. She is her own fault first of all and she is dangerous. But she is also everybody's fault. When we and our culture and our religions agreed to hold woman the inferior sex, cursed, unclean and sinful—we made her mom. And when we agreed upon the American Ideal Woman, the Dream Girl of National Adolescence, the Queen of Bedpan Week, the Pin-up, the Glamour Puss—we insulted woman and disenfranchised millions from love. We thus made mom. The hen-harpy is but the Cinderella chick come home to roost: the taloned, cackling residue of burnt-out puberty in a land that has no use for mature men or women.

Mom is a human calamity. She is also, like every calamity, a cause for sorrow, a reproach, a warning siren and a terrible appeal for amends.

While she exists, she will exploit the little "sacredness" we have given motherhood as a cheap-holy compensation for our degradation of woman: she will remain irresponsible and unreasoning—for what we have believed of her is reckless and untrue. She will act the tyrant—because she is a slave. God pity her—and us all!

angers her so that she gets other moms to skim through it, and then they have a session on the subject over a canister of spiked coffee in order to damn the magazine, the editors, the author, and the silly girls who run about these days. She reads two or three motion-picture fan magazines also, and goes to the movies about two nights a week. If a picture does not coincide precisely with her attitude of the moment, she converses through all of it and so whiles away the time. She does not appear to be lecherous toward the movie photographs as men do, but that is because she is a realist and a little shy on imagination. However, if she gets to Hollywood and encounters the flesh-and-blood article known as a male star, she and her sister moms will run forward in a mob, wearing a joint expression that must make God rue his invention of bisexuality, and tear the man's clothes from his body, yea, verily, down to his B.V.D.'s.

Mom is organization-minded. Organizations, she has happily discovered, are intimidating to all men, not just to mere men. They frighten politicians to sniveling servility and they terrify pastors; they bother bank presidents and they pulverize school boards. Mom has many such organizations, the real purpose of which is to compel an abject compliance of her environs to her personal desires. With these associations and committees she has double parking ignored, for example. With them she drives out of the town and the state, if possible, all young harlots and all proprietors of places where "questionable" young women (though why they are called that—being of all women the least in question) could possibly foregather, not because she competes with such creatures but because she contrasts so unfavorably with them. With her clubs (a solid term!) she causes bus lines to run where they are convenient for her rather than for workers, plants flowers in sordid spots that would do better with sanitation, snaps independent men out of office and replaces them with clammy castrates, throws prodigious fairs and parties for charity and gives the proceeds, usually about eight dollars, to the janitor to buy the committee some beer for its headache on the morning after, and builds clubhouses for the entertainment of soldiers where she succeeds in persuading thousands of them that they are momsick and would rather talk to her than to take Betty into the shrubs. All this, of course, is considered social service, charity, care of the poor, civic reform, patriotism, and self-sacrifice. . . .

Knowing nothing about medicine, art, science, religion, law, sanitation, civics, hygiene, psychology, morals, history, geography, poetry, literature, or any other topic except the all-consuming one of momism, she seldom has any especial interest in *what*, exactly, she is doing as a member of any of these endless organizations, so long as it is *something*. . . .

In churches, the true purpose of organized momhood is to unseat bishops, snatch the frocks off prelates, change rectors just for variety, cross-jet community gossip, take the customary organizational kudos out of the pot each for each, bestow and receive titles, and short-circuit one another.

Mom also has patriotism. If a war comes, this may even turn into a genuine feeling and the departure of her son may be her means to grace in old age. Often, however, the going of her son is only an occasion for more show. She has, in that case, no deep respect for him. What he has permitted her to do to him has rendered him unworthy of consideration—and she has shown him none since puberty. She does not miss him—only his variety—but over that she can weep interminably. . . .

But, peace or war, the moms have another kind of patriotism that, in the department of the human spirit, is identical to commercialized vice, because it captures a good thing and doles it out for the coin of unctuous pride—at the expense of deceased ancestors rather than young female offspring. By becoming a Daughter of this historic war or that, a woman makes herself into a sort of madam who fills the coffers of her ego with the prestige that has accrued to the doings of others. A frantic emptiness of those coffers provides the impulse for the act. There are, of course, other means of filling them, but they are difficult, and mom never does anything that is difficult—either the moving of a piano or the breaking of a nasty habit. . . .

In the matter of her affiliation of herself with the Daughters of some war the Hitler analogue especially holds, because these sororities of the sword often constitute her Party—her shirtism. Ancestor worship, like all other forms of religion, contained an instinctual reason and developed rituals thought to be germane to the reason. People sedulously followed those rituals, which were basically intended to remind them that they, too, were going to be ancestors someday and would have to labor for personal merit in order to be worthy of veneration. But mom's reverence for her bold forebears lacks even a ritualistic significance, and so instructs her in nothing. She is peremptory about historical truth, mandates, custom, fact, and point. She brushes aside the ideals and concepts for which her forebears perished fighting, as if they were the crumbs of melba toast. Instead, she attributes to the noble dead her own immediate and selfish attitudes. She "knows full well what they would have thought and done," and in that whole-cloth trumpery she goes busting on her way.

Thus the long-vanished warriors who liberated this land from one George in order to make another its first president guide mom divinely as she barges along the badgering boulevard of her life, relaying fiats from the grave on birth control, rayon, vitamins, the power trust, and a hundred other items of which the dead had no knowledge. To some degree most people, these days, are guilty of this absurd procedure. There has been more nonsense printed lately detailing what Jefferson would say about matters he never dreamed of than a sensible man can endure. (I do not have any idea, for instance, and I am sure nobody has any idea, what Jefferson would think about the giddy bungle of interstate truck commerce; but people, columnists especially, will tell you.)

Mom, however, does not merely quote Thomas Jefferson on modern topics: she *is* Thomas Jefferson. This removes her twice from sanity. Mom wraps herself in the mantle of every canny man and coward who has drilled with a musket on this continent and reproduced a line that zigzagged down to mom. In that cloak, together with the other miters, rings, scepters, and power symbols which she has swiped, she has become the American pope.

People are feebly aware of this situation and it has been pointed out at one time or another that the phrase "Mother knows best" has practically worn out the staircase to private hell. Most decriers of matriarchy, however, are men of middle age, like me.

Young men whose natures are attuned to a female image with more feelings than mom possesses and different purposes from those of our synthetic arche-type of Cinderella-the-go-getter bounce anxiously away from their first few brutal contacts with modern young women, frightened to find their shining hair is vulcanized, their agate eyes are embedded in cement, and their ruby lips case-hardened into pliers for the bending males like wire. These young men, fresh-startled by learning that She is a chrome-plated afreet, but not able to discern that the condition is mom's unconscious preparation of somebody's sister for a place in the gynecocracy—are, again, presented with a soft and shimmering resting place, the bosom of mom. . . . .

"Her boy," having been "protected" by her love, and carefully, even shud-deringly, shielded from his logical development through his barbaric period, or childhood (so that he has either to become a barbarian as a man or else to spend most of his energy denying the barbarism that howls in his brain— an autonomous remnant of the youth he was forbidden), is cushioned against any major step in his progress toward maturity. Mom steals from the genera-tion of women behind her (which she has, as a still further defense, also sterilized of integrity and courage) that part of her boy's personality which should have become the love of a female contemporary. Mom transmutes it into sentimentality for herself. . . .

As men grow older, they tend to become more like women, and vice versa. Even physically, their characteristics swap; men's voices rise, their breasts grow, and their chins recede; women develop bass voices and mustaches. This is another complementary, or opposite, turn of nature. It is meant to reconcile sexuality and provide a fountainhead of wisdom uncompromised by it, in the persons of those individuals who are hardy enough and lucky enough to sur-vive to old age in a natural environment. But survival, as I have said, no longer depends on any sort of natural selection, excepting a great basic one which our brains are intended to deal with, and which, if allowed to go brainlessly on, will have to reduce our species to savagery in order to get back to a level on which instinct itself can rule effectively. . . .

I have explained how the moms turned Cinderellaism to their advantage and I have explained that women possess some eighty per cent of the nation's money (the crystal form of its energy) and I need only allude, I think, to the statistical reviews which show that the women are the spenders, wherefore the controlling consumers of nearly all we make with our machines. The steel puddler in Pittsburgh may not think of himself as a feminine tool, but he is really only getting a Chevrolet ready for mom to drive through a garden wall. I should round out this picture of America existing for mom with one or two more details, such as annual increase in the depth of padding in vehicles over the past thirty years due to the fact that a fat rump is more easily irritated than a lean one, and the final essential detail of mom's main subjective preoccupation, which is listening to the radio. The radio is mom's soul; a detail, indeed.

It is also a book in itself, and one I would prefer to have my reader write after he has learned a little of the art of catching overtones as a trained ear, such as mine, catches them. But there must be a note on it.

The radio has made sentimentality the twentieth century Plymouth Rock. As a discipline, I have forced myself to sit a whole morning listening to the soap operas, along with twenty million moms who were busy sweeping dust under carpets while planning to drown their progeny in honey or bash in their heads. This filthy and indecent abomination, this ·trash with which, until lately, only moron servant girls could dull their credulous minds in the tawdry privacy of their cubicles, is now the national saga. Team after team of feeble-minded Annies and Davids crawl from the loudspeaker into the front rooms of America. The characters are impossible, their adventures would make a saint spew, their morals are lower than those of ghouls, their habits are uncleanly, their humor is the substance that starts whole races grinding bayonets, they have no manners, no sense, no goals, no worthy ambitions, no hope, no faith, no information, no values related to reality, and no estimate of truth. They merely sob and snicker—as they cheat each other. . . .

The radio is mom's final tool, for it stamps everybody who listens with the matriarchal brand—its superstitions, prejudices, devotional rules, taboos, musts, and all other qualifications needful to its maintenance. Just as Goebbels has revealed what can be done with such a mass-stamping of the public psyche in his nation, so our land is a living representation of the same fact worked out in matriarchal sentimentality, goo, slop, hidden cruelty, and the foreshadow of national death.

That alone is sinister enough, but the process is still more vicious, because it fills in every crack and cranny of mom's time and mind—and pop's also, since he has long ago yielded the dial-privilege to his female; so that a whole nation of people lives in eternal fugue and never has to deal for one second with itself or its own problems. Any interior sign of worry, wonder, speculation, anxiety, apprehension—or even a stirring of an enfeebled will to plan sanely—can be annihilated by an electrical click whereby the populace puts itself in the place, the untenable place—of somebody called Myrt—and never has even to try to *be* itself alone in the presence of this real world.

This is Nirvana at last. It is also entropy. For here the spirit of man, absorbed, disoriented, confused, identified with ten thousand spurious personalities and motives, has utterly lost itself. By this means is man altogether lost. The radio, in very truth, sells soap. We could confine it to music, intelligent discourse, and news—all other uses being dangerous—but mom will not let us. Rather than study herself and her environment with the necessary honesty, she will fight for this poisoned syrup to the last. Rather than take up her democratic responsibility in this mighty and tottering republic, she will bring it crashing down simply to maintain to the final rumble of ruin her personal feudalism. Once, sentimentalism was piece work, or cost the price of a movie or a book; now it is mass produced and not merely free, but almost compulsory.

I give you mom. I give you the destroying mother. I give you her justice— from which we have never removed the eye bandage. I give you the angel— and point to the sword in her hand. I give you death—the hundred million deaths that are muttered under Yggdrasill's ash. I give you Medusa and Stheno and Euryale. I give you the harpies and the witches, and the Fates. I give you the woman in pants, and the new religion: she-popery. I give you Pandora. I give you Proserpine, the Queen of Hell. The five-and-ten-cent-store Lilith, the mother of Cain, the black widow who is poisonous and eats her mate, and I designate at the bottom of your program the grand finale of all the soap operas: the mother of America's Cinderella.

We must face the dynasty of the dames at once, deprive them of our pocketbooks when they waste the substance in them, and take back our dreams which, without the perfidious materialism of mom, were shaping up a new and braver world. We must drive roads to Rio and to Moscow and stop spending all our strength in the manufacture of girdles: it is time that mom's sag became known to the desperate public; we must plunge into our psyches and find out there, each for each, scientifically, about immortality and miracles. To do such deeds, we will have to make the conquest of momism, which grew up from male default.

THORSTEIN VEBLEN

Pecuniary Canons of Taste[1]

The caution has already been repeated more than once, that while the regulating norm of consumption is in large part the requirement of conspicuous waste, it must not be understood that the motive on which the consumer acts in any given case is this principle in its bald, unsophisticated form. Ordinarily his motive is a wish to conform to established usage, to avoid unfavourable notice and comment, to live up to the accepted canons of decency in the kind, amount, and grade of goods consumed, as well as in the decorous em-

[1] From The Theory of the Leisure Class by Thorstein Veblen. Copyright 1899, 1912 by The Macmillan Company. Reprinted by permission of The Viking Press, Inc., New York.

ployment of his time and effort. In the common run of cases this sense of prescriptive usage is present in the motives of the consumer and exerts a direct constraining force, especially as regards consumption carried on under the eyes of observers. But a considerable element of prescriptive expensiveness is observable also in consumption that does not in any appreciable degree become known to outsiders—as, for instance, articles of underclothing, some articles of food, kitchen utensils, and other household apparatus designed for service rather than for evidence. In all such useful articles a close scrutiny will discover certain features which add to the cost and enhance the commercial value of the goods in question, but do not proportionately increase the serviceability of these articles for the material purposes which alone they ostensibly are designed to serve.

Under the selective surveillance of the law of conspicuous waste there grows up a code of accredited canons of consumption, the effect of which is to hold the consumer up to a standard of expensiveness and wastefulness in his consumption of goods and in his employment of time and effort. This growth of prescriptive usage has an immediate effect upon economic life, but it has also an indirect and remoter effect upon conduct in other respects as well. Habits of thought with respect to the expression of life in any given direction unavoidably affect the habitual view of what is good and right in life in other directions also. In the organic complex of habits of thought which make up the substance of an individual's conscious life the economic interest does not lie isolated and distinct from all other interests. Something, for instance, has already been said of its relation to the canons of reputability.

The principle of conspicuous waste guides the formation of habits of thought as to what is honest and reputable in life and in commodities. In so doing, this principle will traverse other norms of conduct which do not primarily have to do with the code of pecuniary honour, but which have, directly or incidentally, an economic significance of some magnitude. So the canon of honorific waste may, immediately or remotely, influence the sense of duty, the sense of beauty, the sense of utility, the sense of devotional or ritualistic fitness, and the scientific sense of truth.

It is scarcely necessary to go into a discussion here of the particular points at which, or the particular manner in which, the canon of honorific expenditure habitually traverses the canons of moral conduct. The matter is one which has received large attention and illustration at the hands of those whose office it is to watch and admonish with respect to any departures from the accepted code of morals. In modern communities, where the dominant economic and legal feature of the community's life is the institution of private property, one of the salient features of the code of morals is the sacredness of property. There needs no insistence or illustration to gain assent to the proposition that the habit of holding private property inviolate is traversed by the other habit of seeking wealth for the sake of the good repute to be gained through its conspicuous consumption. Most offences against property, especially offences of an appreciable magnitude, come under this head. It is also a matter of common notoriety and byword that in offences which result in a large accession of property to the offender he does not ordinarily incur the extreme penalty or the extreme obloquy with which his offence would be visited on the ground of the naïve moral code alone. The thief or swindler who has gained great wealth by his delinquency has a better chance than the small thief of escaping the rigorous penalty of the law; and some good repute accrues to him from his increased wealth and from his spending the irregularly acquired possessions in a seemly manner. A well-bred expenditure of his booty especially appeals with great effect to persons of a cultivated sense of the proprieties, and goes far to mitigate the sense of moral turpitude with which his dereliction is viewed by them. It may be noted also—and it is more immediately to the point—that we are all inclined to condone an offence against property in the case of a man whose motive is the worthy one of providing the means of a "decent" manner of life for his wife and children. If it is added that the wife has been "nurtured in the lap of luxury," that is accepted as an additional extenuating circumstance. That is to say, we are prone to condone such an offence where its aim is the honorific one of enabling the offender's wife to perform for him such an amount of vicarious consumption of time and substance as is demanded by the standard of pecuniary decency. In such a case the habit of approving the accustomed degree of conspicuous waste traverses the habit of deprecating violations of ownership, to the extent even of sometimes leaving the award of praise or blame uncertain. This is peculiarly true where the dereliction involves an appreciable predatory or piratical element.

This topic need scarcely be pursued farther here; but the remark may not be out of place that all that considerable body of morals that clusters about the concept of an inviolable ownership is itself a psychological precipitate of the traditional meritoriousness of wealth. And it should be added that this wealth which is held sacred is valued primarily for the sake of the good repute to be got through its conspicuous consumption. . . .

Obviously, the canon of conspicuous waste is accountable for a great portion of what may be called devout consumption; as, e.g., the consumption of sacred edifices, vestments, and other goods of the same class. Even in those modern cults to whose divinities is imputed a predilection for temples not built with hands, the sacred buildings and the other properties of the cult are constructed and decorated with some view to a reputable degree of wasteful expenditure. And it needs but little either of observation or introspection —and either will serve the turn—to assure us that the expensive splendour of the house of worship has an appreciable uplifting and mellowing effect upon the worshipper's frame of mind. It will serve to enforce the same fact if we reflect upon the sense of abject shamefulness with which any evidence of indigence or squalor about the sacred place affects all beholders. The accessories of any devout observance should be pecuniarily above reproach. This requirement is imperative, whatever latitude may be allowed with regard to these accessories in point of æsthetic or other serviceability.

It may also be in place to notice that in all communities, especially in neighbourhoods where the standard of pecuniary decency for dwellings is not high, the local sanctuary is more ornate, more conspicuously wasteful in its architecture and decoration, than the dwelling-houses of the congregation. This is true of nearly all denominations and cults, whether Christian or Pagan, but it is true in a peculiar degree of the older and maturer cults. At the same time the sanctuary commonly contributes little if anything to the physical comfort of the members. Indeed, the sacred structure not only serves the physical well-being of the members to but a slight extent, as compared with their humbler dwelling-houses; but it is felt by all men that a right and enlightened sense of the true, the beautiful, and the good demands that in all expenditure on the sanctuary anything that might serve the comfort of the worshipper should be conspicuously absent. If any element of comfort is admitted in the fittings of the sanctuary, it should at least be scrupulously screened and masked under an ostensible austerity. In the most reputable latter-day houses of worship, where no expense is spared, the principle of austerity is carried to the length of making the fittings of the place a means of mortifying the flesh, especially in appearance. There are few persons of delicate tastes in the matter of devout consumption to whom this austerely wasteful discomfort does not appeal as intrinsically right and good. Devout consumption is of the nature of vicarious consumption. This canon of devout austerity is based on the pecuniary reputability of conspicuously wasteful consumption, backed by the principle that vicarious consumption should conspicuously not conduce to the comfort of the vicarious consumer.

The sanctuary and its fittings have something of this austerity in all the cults in which the saint or divinity to whom the sanctuary pertains is not conceived to be present and make personal use of the property for the gratification of luxurious tastes imputed to him. The character of the sacred paraphernalia is somewhat different in this respect in those cults where the habits of life imputed to the divinity more nearly approach those of an earthly patriarchal potentate—where he is conceived to make use of these consumable goods in person. In the latter case the sanctuary and its fittings take on more of the fashion given to goods destined for the conspicuous consumption of a temporal master or owner. On the other hand, where the sacred apparatus is simply employed in the divinity's service, that is to say, where it is consumed vicariously on his account by his servants, there the sacred properties take the character suited to goods that are destined for vicarious consumption only. . . .

These canons of reputability have had a similar, but more far-reaching and more specifically determinable, effect upon the popular sense of beauty or serviceability in consumable goods. The requirements of pecuniary decency have, to a very appreciable extent, influenced the sense of beauty and of utility in articles of use or beauty. Articles are to an extent preferred for use on account of their being conspicuously wasteful; they are felt to be serviceable somewhat in proportion as they are wasteful and ill adapted to their ostensible use.

The utility of articles valued for their beauty depends closely upon the expensiveness of the articles. A homely illustration will bring out this dependence. A hand-wrought silver spoon, of a commercial value of some ten to twenty dollars, is not ordinarily more serviceable—in the first sense of the word—than a machine-made spoon of the same material. It may not even be more serviceable than a machine-made spoon of some "base" metal, such as aluminum, the value of which may be no more than some ten to twenty cents. The former of the two utensils is, in fact, commonly a less effective contrivance for its ostensible purpose than the latter. The objection is of course ready to hand that, in taking this view of the matter, one of the chief uses, if not the chief use, of the costlier spoon is ignored; the hand-wrought spoon gratifies our taste, our sense of the beautiful, while that made by machinery out of the base metal has no useful office beyond a brute efficiency. The facts are no doubt as the objection states them, but it will be evident on reflection that the objection is after all more plausible than conclusive. It appears (1) that while the different materials of which the two spoons are made each possesses beauty and serviceability for the purpose for which it is used, the material of the hand-wrought spoon is some one hundred times more valuable than the baser metal, without very greatly excelling the latter in intrinsic beauty of grain or colour, and without being in any appreciable degree superior in point of mechanical serviceability; (2) if a close inspection should show that the supposed hand-wrought spoon were in reality only a very clever imitation of hand-wrought goods, but an imitation so cleverly wrought as to give the same impression of line and surface to any but a minute examination by a trained eye, the utility of the article, including the gratification which the user derives from its contemplation as an object of beauty, would immediately decline by some eighty or ninety per cent, or even more; (3) if the two spoons are, to a fairly close observer, so nearly identical in appearance that the lighter weight of the spurious article alone betrays it, this identity of form and colour will scarcely add to the value of the machine-made spoon, nor appreciably enhance the gratification of the user's "sense of beauty" in contemplating it, so long as the cheaper spoon is not a novelty, and so long as it can be procured at a nominal cost.

The case of the spoons is typical. The superior gratification derived from the use and contemplation of costly and supposedly beautiful products is, commonly, in great measure a gratification of our sense of costliness masquerading under the name of beauty. Our higher appreciation of the superior article is an appreciation of its superior honorific character, much more frequently than it is an unsophisticated appreciation of its beauty. The requirement of conspicuous wastefulness is not commonly present, consciously, in our canons of taste, but it is none the less present as a constraining norm selectively shaping and sustaining our sense of what is beautiful, and guiding our discrimination with respect to what may legitimately be approved as beautiful and what may not.

It is at this point, where the beautiful and the honorific meet and blend, that a discrimination between serviceability and wastefulness is most difficult in any concrete case. It frequently happens that an article which serves the honorific purpose of conspicuous waste is at the same time a beautiful object; and the same application of labour to which it owes its utility for the former purpose may, and often does, go to give beauty of form and colour to the article. The question is further complicated by the fact that many objects, as, for instance, the precious stones and metals and some other materials used for adornment and decoration, owe their utility as items of conspicuous waste to an antecedent utility as objects of beauty. Gold, for instance, has a high degree of sensuous beauty; very many if not most of the highly prized works of art are intrinsically beautiful, though often with material qualifications; the like is true of some stuffs used for clothing, of some landscapes, and of many other things in less degree. Except for this intrinsic beauty which they possess, these objects would scarcely have been coveted as they are, or have become monopolised objects of pride to their possessors and users. But the utility of these things to the possessor is commonly due less to their intrinsic beauty than to the honour which their possession and consumption confers, or to the obloquy which it wards off.

Apart from their serviceability in other respects, these objects are beautiful and have a utility as such; they are valuable on this account if they can be appropriated or monopolised; they are, therefore, coveted as valuable possessions, and their exclusive enjoyment gratifies the possessor's sense of pecuniary superiority at the same time that their contemplation gratifies his sense of beauty. But their beauty, in the naïve sense of the word, is the occasion rather than the ground of their monopolisation or of their commercial value. "Great as is the sensuous beauty of gems, their rarity and price adds an expression of distinction to them, which they would never have if they were cheap." There is, indeed, in the common run of cases under this head, relatively little incentive to the exclusive possession and use of these beautiful things, except on the ground of their honorific character as items of conspicuous waste. Most objects of this general class, with the partial exception of articles of personal adornment, would serve all other purposes than the honorific one equally well, whether owned by the person viewing them or not; and even as regards personal ornaments it is to be added that their chief purpose is to lend éclat to the person of their wearer (or owner) by comparison with other persons who are compelled to do without. The æsthetic serviceability of objects of beauty is not greatly nor universally heightened by possession.

The generalisation for which the discussion so far affords ground is that any valuable object in order to appeal to our sense of beauty must conform to the requirements of beauty and of expensiveness both. But this is not all. Beyond this the canon of expensiveness also affects our tastes in such a way as to inextricably blend the marks of expensiveness, in our appreciation, with the beautiful features of the object, and to subsume the resultant effect under the head of an appreciation of beauty simply. The marks of expensiveness come to be accepted as beautiful features of the expensive articles. They are pleasing as being marks of honorific costliness, and the pleasure which they afford on this score blends with that afforded by the beautiful form and colour of the object; so that we often declare that an article of apparel, for instance, is "perfectly lovely," when pretty much all that an analysis of the æsthetic value of the article would leave ground for is the declaration that it is pecuniarily honorific.

This blending and confusion of the elements of expensiveness and of beauty is, perhaps, best exemplified in articles of dress and of household furniture. The code of reputability in matters of dress decides what shapes, colours, materials, and general effects in human apparel are for the time to be accepted as suitable; and departures from the code are offensive to our taste, supposedly as being departures from æsthetic truth. The approval with which we look upon fashionable attire is by no means to be accounted pure make-believe. We readily, and for the most part with utter sincerity, find those things pleasing that are in vogue. Shaggy dress-stuffs and pronounced colour effects, for instance, offend us at times when the vogue is goods of a high, glossy finish and neutral colours. A fancy bonnet of this year's model unquestionably appeals to our sensibilities to-day much more forcibly than an equally fancy bonnet of the model of last year; although when viewed in the perspective of a quarter of a century, it would, I apprehend, be a matter of the utmost difficulty to award the palm for intrinsic beauty to the one rather than to the other of these structures. So, again, it may be remarked that, considered simply in their physical juxtaposition with the human form, the high gloss of a gentleman's hat or of a patent-leather shoe has no more of intrinsic beauty than a similarly high gloss on a threadbare sleeve; and yet there is no question but that all well-bred people (in the Occidental civilised communities) instinctively and unaffectedly cleave to the one as a phenomenon of great beauty, and eschew the other as offensive to every sense to which it can appeal. It is extremely doubtful if any one could be induced to wear such a contrivance as the high hat of civilised society, except for some urgent reason based on other than æsthetic grounds.

By further habituation to an appreciative perception of the marks of expensiveness in goods, and by habitually identifying beauty with reputability, it comes about that a beautiful article which is not expensive is accounted not beautiful. In this way it has happened, for instance, that some beautiful flowers pass conventionally for offensive weeds; others that can be cultivated with relative ease are accepted and admired by the lower middle class, who can afford no more expensive luxuries of this kind; but these varieties are re-

jected as vulgar by those people who are better able to pay for expensive
flowers and who are educated to a higher schedule of pecuniary beauty in
the florist's products; while still other flowers, of no greater intrinsic beauty
than these, are cultivated at great cost and call out much admiration from
flower-lovers whose tastes have been matured under the critical guidance of a
polite environment. . . .

It is not only with respect to consumable goods—including domestic animals—that the canons of taste have been coloured by the canons of pecuniary
reputability. Something to the like effect is to be said for beauty in persons.
In order to avoid whatever may be matter of controversy, no weight will be
given in this connection to such popular predilection as there may be for the
dignified (leisurely) bearing and portly presence that are by vulgar tradition
associated with opulence in mature men. These traits are in some measure
accepted as elements of personal beauty. But there are certain elements of
feminine beauty, on the other hand, which come in under this head, and
which are of so concrete and specific a character as to admit of itemised appreciation. It is more or less a rule that in communities which are at the stage of
economic development at which women are valued by the upper class for
their service, the ideal of female beauty is a robust, large-limbed woman. The
ground of appreciation is the physique, while the conformation of the face
is of secondary weight only. A well-known instance of this ideal of the early
predatory culture is that of the maidens of the Homeric poems.

This ideal suffers a change in the succeeding development, when, in the
conventional scheme, the office of the high-class wife comes to be a vicarious
leisure simply. The ideal then includes the characteristics which are supposed
to result from or to go with a life of leisure consistently enforced. The ideal
accepted under these circumstances may be gathered from descriptions of
beautiful women by poets and writers of the chivalric times. In the conventional scheme of those days ladies of high degree were conceived to be in
perpetual tutelage, and to be scrupulously exempt from all useful work. The
resulting chivalric or romantic ideal of beauty takes cognizance chiefly of
the face, and dwells on its delicacy, and on the delicacy of the hands and
feet, the slender figure, and especially the slender waist. In the pictured representations of the women of that time, and in modern romantic imitators of
the chivalric thought and feeling, the waist is attenuated to a degree that implies extreme debility. The same ideal is still extant among a considerable
portion of the population of modern industrial communities; but it is to be
said that it has retained its hold most tenaciously in those modern communities
which are least advanced in point of economic and civil development, and
which show the most considerable survivals of status and of predatory institutions. That is to say, the chivalric ideal is best preserved in those existing
communities which are substantially least modern. Survivals of this lackadaisical
or romantic ideal occur freely in the tastes of the well-to-do classes of Continental countries.

In modern communities which have reached the higher levels of industrial development, the upper leisure class has accumulated so great a mass of wealth as to place its women above all imputation of vulgarly productive labour. Here the status of women as vicarious consumers is beginning to lose its place in the affections of the body of the people; and as a consequence the ideal of feminine beauty is beginning to change back again from the infirmly delicate, translucent, and hazardously slender, to a woman of the archaic type that does not disown her hands and feet, nor, indeed, the other gross material facts of her person. In the course of economic development the ideal of beauty among the peoples of the Western culture has shifted from the woman of physical presence to the lady, and it is beginning to shift back again to the woman; and all in obedience to the changing conditions of pecuniary emulation. The exigencies of emulation at one time required lusty slaves; at another time they required a conspicuous performance of vicarious leisure and consequently an obvious disability; but the situation is now beginning to outgrow this last requirement, since, under the higher efficiency of modern industry, leisure in women is possible so far down the scale of reputability that it will no longer serve as a definitive mark of the highest pecuniary grade.

Apart from this general control exercised by the norm of conspicuous waste over the ideal of feminine beauty, there are one or two details which merit specific mention as showing how it may exercise an extreme constraint in detail over men's sense of beauty in women. It has already been noticed that at the stages of economic evolution at which conspicuous leisure is much regarded as a means of good repute, the ideal requires delicate and diminutive hands and feet and a slender waist. These features, together with the other related faults of structure that commonly go with them, go to show that the person so affected is incapable of useful effort and must therefore be supported in idleness by her owner. She is useless and expensive, and she is consequently valuable as evidence of pecuniary strength. It results that at this cultural stage women take thought to alter their persons, so as to conform more nearly to the requirements of the instructed taste of the time; and under the guidance of the canon of pecuniary decency, the men find the resulting artificially induced pathological features attractive. So, for instance, the constricted waist which has had so wide and persistent a vogue in the communities of the Western culture, and so also the deformed foot of the Chinese. Both of these are mutilations of unquestioned repulsiveness to the untrained sense. It requires habituation to become reconciled to them. Yet there is no room to question their attractiveness to men into whose scheme of life they fit as honorific items sanctioned by the requirements of pecuniary reputability. They are items of pecuniary and cultural beauty which have come to do duty as elements of the ideal of womanliness. . . .

. . . Among objects of use the simple and unadorned article is æsthetically the best. But since the pecuniary canon of reputability rejects the inexpensive in articles appropriated to individual consumption, the satisfaction of our craving for beautiful things must be sought by way of compromise. The canons of beauty must be circumvented by some contrivance which will give evidence of a reputably wasteful expenditure, at the same time that it meets the demands of our critical sense of the useful and the beautiful, or at least meets the demand of some habit which has come to do duty in place of that sense. Such an auxiliary sense of taste is the sense of novelty; and this latter is helped out in its surrogateship by the curiosity with which men view ingenious and puzzling contrivances. Hence it comes that most objects alleged to be beautiful, and doing duty as such, show considerable ingenuity of design and are calculated to puzzle the beholder—to bewilder him with irrelevant suggestions and hints of the improbable—at the same time that they give evidence of an expenditure of labour in excess of what would give them their fullest efficiency for their ostensible economic end. . . . .

This process of selective adaptation of designs to the end of conspicuous waste, and the substitution of pecuniary beauty for æsthetic beauty, has been especially effective in the development of architecture. It would be extremely difficult to find a modern civilised residence or public building which can claim anything better than relative inoffensiveness in the eyes of any one who will dissociate the elements of beauty from those of honorific waste. The endless variety of fronts presented by the better class of tenements and apartment houses in our cities is an endless variety of architectural distress and of suggestions of expensive discomfort. Considered as objects of beauty, the dead walls of the sides and back of these structures, left untouched by the hands of the artist, are commonly the best feature of the building. . . .

The position here taken is enforced in a felicitous manner by the place assigned in the economy of consumption to machine products. The point of material difference between machine-made goods and the hand-wrought goods which serve the same purposes is, ordinarily, that the former serve their primary purpose more adequately. They are a more perfect product—show a more perfect adaptation of means to end. This does not save them from disesteem and depreciation, for they fall short under the test of honorific waste. Hand labour is a more wasteful method of production; hence the goods turned out by this method are more serviceable for the purpose of pecuniary reputability; hence the marks of hand labour come to be honorific, and the goods which exhibit these marks take rank as of higher grade than the corresponding machine product. Commonly, if not invariably, the honorific marks of hand labour are certain imperfections and irregularities in the lines of the hand-wrought article, showing where the workman has fallen short in the execution of the design. The ground of the superiority of hand-wrought goods, therefore, is a certain margin of crudeness. This margin must never be so wide as to show bungling workmanship, since that would be evidence of low cost, nor so narrow as to suggest the ideal precision attained only by the machine, for that would be evidence of low cost.

The appreciation of those evidences of honorific crudeness to which hand-wrought goods owe their superior worth and charm in the eyes of well-bred people is a matter of nice discrimination. It requires training and the formation of right habits of thought with respect to what may be called the physiognomy of goods. Machine-made goods of daily use are often admired and preferred precisely on account of their excessive perfection by the vulgar and the underbred who have not given due thought to the punctilios of elegant consumption. The ceremonial inferiority of machine products goes to show that the perfection of skill and workmanship embodied in any costly innovations in the finish of goods is not sufficient of itself to secure them acceptance and permanent favour. The innovation must have the support of the canon of conspicuous waste. Any feature in the physiognomy of goods, however pleasing in itself, and however well it may approve itself to the taste for effective work, will not be tolerated if it proves obnoxious to this norm of pecuniary reputability.

The ceremonial inferiority or uncleanness in consumable goods due to "commonness," or in other words to their slight cost of production, has been taken very seriously by many persons. This objection to machine products is often formulated as an objection to the commonness of such goods. What is common is within the (pecuniary) reach of many people. Its consumption is therefore not honorific, since it does not serve the purpose of a favourable invidious comparison with other consumers. Hence the consumption, or even the sight of such goods, is inseparable from an odious suggestion of the lower levels of human life, and one comes away from their contemplation with a pervading sense of meanness that is extremely distasteful and depressing to a person of sensibility. . . .

The position of machine products in the civilised scheme of consumption serves to point out the nature of the relation which subsists between the canon of conspicuous waste and the code of proprieties in consumption. Neither in matters of art and taste proper, nor as regards the current sense of the serviceability of goods, does this canon act as a principle of innovation or initiative. It does not go into the future as a creative principle which makes innovations and adds new items of consumption and new elements of cost. The principle in question is, in a certain sense, a negative rather than a positive law. It is a regulative rather than a creative principle. It very rarely initiates or originates any usage or custom directly. Its action is selective only. Conspicuous wastefulness does not directly afford ground for variation and growth, but conformity to its requirements is a condition to the survival of such innovations as may be made on other grounds. In whatever way usages and customs and methods of expenditure arise, they are all subject to the selective action of this norm of reputability; and the degree in which they conform to its requirements is a test of their fitness to survive in the competition with other similar usages and customs. Other things being equal, the more obviously wasteful usage or method stands the better chance of survival under this law. The law of conspicuous waste does not account for the origin of variations, but only for the persistence of such forms as are fit to survive under its dominance. It acts to conserve the fit, not to originate the acceptable. Its office is to prove all things and to hold fast that which is good for its purpose.

JOHN DOS PASSOS

The Bitter Drink[1]

Veblen,

a greyfaced shambling man lolling resentful at his desk with his cheek on his hand, in a low sarcastic mumble of intricate phrases subtly paying out the logical inescapable rope of matteroffact for a society to hang itself by,

dissecting out the century with a scalpel so keen, so comical, so exact that the professors and students ninetenths of the time didn't know it was there, and the magnates and the respected windbags and the applauded loudspeakers never knew it was there.

Veblen

asked too many questions, suffered from a constitutional inability to say yes.

Socrates asked questions, drank down the bitter drink one night when the first cock crowed,

but Veblen

drank it in little sips through a long life in the stuffiness of classrooms, the dust of libraries, the staleness of cheap flats such as a poor instructor can afford. He fought the boyg all right, pendantry, routine, timeservers at office desks, trustees, collegepresidents, the plump flunkies of the ruling businessmen, all the good jobs kept by yesmen, never enough money, every broadening hope thwarted. Veblen drank the bitter drink all right.

The Veblens were a family of freeholding farmers.

The freeholders of the narrow Norwegian valleys were a stubborn hardworking people, farmers, dairymen, fishermen, rooted in their fathers' stony fields, in their old timbered farmsteads with carved gables they took their names from, in the upland pastures where they grazed the stock in summer.

During the early nineteenth century the towns grew; Norway filled up with landless men, storekeepers, sheriffs, moneylenders, bailiffs, notaries in black with stiff collars and briefcases full of foreclosures under their arms. Indus-

[1] From John Dos Passos, U.S.A. (Boston: Houghton Mifflin Company, 1936), pp. 93-105. Copyright by John Dos Passos, 1936, 1937.

tries were coming in. The townsmen were beginning to get profits out of the country and to finagle the farmers out of the freedom of their narrow farms.

The meanspirited submitted as tenants, daylaborers; but the strong men went out of the country

as their fathers had gone out of the country centuries before when Harald the Fairhaired and St. Olaf hacked to pieces the liberties of the northern men, who had been each man lord of his own creek, to make Christians and serfs of them,

only in the old days it was Iceland, Greenland, Vineland the northmen had sailed west to; now it was America.

Both Thorstein Veblen's father's people and his mother's people had lost their farmsteads and with them the names that denoted them free men.

Thomas Anderson for a while tried to make his living as a traveling carpenter and cabinetmaker, but in 1847 he and his wife, Kari Thorsteinsdatter, crossed in a whalingship from Bremen and went out to join friends in the Scandihoovian colonies round Milwaukee.

Next year his brother Haldor joined him.

They were hard workers; in another year they had saved up money to preempt a claim on 160 acres of uncleared land in Sheboygan County, Wisconsin; when they'd gotten that land part cleared they sold it and moved to an all-Norway colony in Manitowoc County, near Cato and a place named Valders after the valley they had all come from in the old country;

there in the house Thomas Anderson built with his own tools, the sixth of twelve children, Thorstein Veblen was born.

When Thorstein was eight years old, Thomas Anderson moved west again into the blacksoil prairies of Minnesota that the Sioux and the buffalo had only been driven off from a few years before. In the deed to the new farm Thomas Anderson took back the old farmstead name of Veblen.

He was a solid farmer, builder, a clever carpenter, the first man to import merino sheep and a mechanical reaper and binder; he was a man of standing in the group of Norway people farming the edge of the prairie, who kept their dialects, the manner of life of their narrow Norway valleys, their Lutheran pastors, their homemade clothes and cheese and bread, their suspicion and stubborn dislike of townsmen's ways.

The townspeople were Yankees mostly, smart to make two dollars grow where a dollar grew before, storekeepers, middlemen, speculators, moneylenders, with long heads for politics and mortgages; they despised the Scandihoovian dirtfarmers they lived off, whose daughters did their wives' kitchenwork.

The Norway people believed as their fathers had believed that there were only two callings for an honest man, farming or preaching.

Thorstein grew up a hulking lad with a reputation for laziness and wit.
He hated the irk of everrepeated backbreaking chores round the farm. Reading he was happy. Carpentering he liked or running farmmachinery. The
Lutheran pastors who came to the house noticed that his supple mind slid
easily round the corners of their theology. It was hard to get farmwork out
of him, he had a stinging tongue and was famous for the funny names he
called people; his father decided to make a preacher out of him.

When he was seventeen he was sent for out of the field where he was
working. His bag was already packed. The horses were hitched up. He was
being sent to Carleton Academy in Northfield, to prepare for Carleton College.

As there were several young Veblens to be educated their father built
them a house on a lot near the campus. Their food and clothes were sent to
them from the farm. Cash money was something they never saw.

Thorstein spoke English with an accent. He had a constitutional inability
to say yes. His mind was formed on the Norse sagas and on the matteroffact
sense of his father's farming and the exact needs of carpenterwork and threshingmachines.

He could never take much interest in the theology, sociology, economics
of Carleton College where they were busy trimming down the jagged dogmas
of the old New England bibletaught traders to make stencils to hang on the
walls of commissionmerchants' offices.

Veblen's collegeyears were the years when Darwin's assertions of growth
and becoming were breaking the set molds of the Noah's Ark world,

when Ibsen's women were tearing down the portieres of the Victorian
parlors,

and Marx's mighty machine was rigging the countinghouse's own logic to
destroy the countinghouse.

When Veblen went home to the farm he talked about these things with
his father, following him up and down at his plowing, starting an argument
while they were waiting for a new load for the wheatthresher. Thomas Anderson had seen Norway and America; he had the squarebuilt mind of a carpenter and builder, and an understanding of tools and the treasured elaborated
builtupseasonbyseason knowledge of a careful farmer,

a tough whetstone for the sharpening steel of young Thorstein's wits.

At Carleton College young Veblen was considered a brilliant unsound eccentric; nobody could understand why a boy of such attainments wouldn't
settle down to the business of the day, which was to buttress property and
profits with anything usable in the debris of Christian ethics and eighteenthcentury economics that cluttered the minds of collegeprofessors, and to reinforce the sacred, already shaky edifice with the new strong girderwork of science
Herbert Spencer was throwing up for the benefit of the bosses.

People complained they never knew whether Veblen was joking or serious.

In 1880 Thorstein Veblen started to try to make his living by teaching. A year in an academy at Madison, Wisconsin, wasn't much of a success. Next year he and his brother Andrew started graduate work at Johns Hopkins. Johns Hopkins didn't suit, but boarding in an old Baltimore house with some ruined gentlewomen gave him a disdaining glimpse of an etiquette motheaten now but handed down through the lavish leisure of the slaveowning planters' mansions straight from the merry England of the landlord cavaliers.

(The valley farmers had always been scornful of outlanders' ways.)

He was more at home at Yale where in Noah Porter he found a New England roundhead granite against which his Norway granite rang in clear dissent. He took his Ph.D. there. But there was still some question as to what department of the academic world he could best make a living in.

He read Kant and wrote prize essays. But he couldn't get a job. Try as he could he couldn't get his mouth round the essential yes.

He went back to Minnesota with a certain intolerant knowledge of the amenities of the higher learning. To his slight Norwegian accent he'd added the broad a.

At home he loafed about the farm and tinkered with inventions of new machinery and read and talked theology and philosophy with his father. In the Scandihoovian colonies the price of wheat and the belief in God and St. Olaf were going down together. The farmers of the Northwest were starting their long losing fight against the parasite businessmen who were sucking them dry. There was a mortgage on the farm, interest on debts to pay, always fertilizer, new machines to buy to speed production to pump in a halfcentury the wealth out of the soil laid down in a million years of buffalograss. His brothers kept grumbling about this sardonic loafer who wouldn't earn his keep.

Back home he met again his college sweetheart, Ellen Rolfe, the niece of the president of Carleton College, a girl who had railroadmagnates and money in the family. People in Northfield were shocked when it came out that she was going to marry the drawling pernickety bookish badly dressed young Norwegian ne'erdowell.

Her family hatched a plan to get him a job as economist for the Santa Fe Railroad but at the wrong moment Ellen Rolfe's uncle lost control of the line. The young couple went to live at Stacyville where they did everything but earn a living. They read Latin and Greek and botanized in the woods and along the fences and in the roadside scrub. They boated on the river and Veblen started his translation of the *Laxdælasaga*. They read *Looking Backward* and articles by Henry George. They looked at their world from the outside.

In '91 Veblen got together some money to go to Cornell to do postgraduate work. He turned up there in the office of the head of the economics department wearing a coonskin cap and grey corduroy trousers and said in his low sarcastic drawl, "I am Thorstein Veblen," but it was not until several years later, after he was established at the new University of Chicago that had grown up next to the World's Fair, and had published *The Theory of the Leisure Class*, put on the map by Howells' famous review, that the world of the higher learning knew who Thorstein Veblen was.

Even in Chicago as the brilliant young economist he lived pioneerfashion. (The valleyfarmers had always been scornful of outlanders' ways.) He kept his books in packingcases laid on their sides along the walls. His only extravagances were the Russian cigarettes he smoked and the red sash he sometimes sported. He was a man without smalltalk. When he lectured he put his cheek on his hand and mumbled out his long spiral sentences, reiterative like the eddas. His language was a mixture of mechanics' terms, scientific latinity, slang and Roget's Thesaurus. The other profs couldn't imagine why the girls fell for him so.

The girls fell for him so that Ellen Rolfe kept leaving him. He'd take summer trips abroad without his wife. There was a scandal about a girl on an ocean liner.

Tongues wagged so (Veblen was a man who never explained, who never could get his tongue around the essential yes; the valleyfarmers had always been scornful of the outlanders' ways, and their opinions) that his wife left him and went off to live alone on a timberclaim in Idaho and the president asked for his resignation.

Veblen went out to Idaho to get Ellen Rolfe to go with him to California when he succeeded in getting a job at a better salary at Leland Stanford, but in Palo Alto it was the same story as in Chicago. He suffered from woman trouble and the constitutional inability to say yes and an unnatural tendency to feel with the workingclass instead of with the profittakers. There were the same complaints that his courses were not constructive or attractive to big money bequests and didn't help his students to butter their bread, make Phi Beta Kappa, pick plums off the hierarchies of the academic grove. His wife left him for good. He wrote to a friend: "The president doesn't approve of my domestic arrangements; nor do I."

Talking about it he once said, "What is one to do if the woman moves in on you?"

He went back up to the shack in the Idaho woods.

Friends tried to get him an appointment to make studies in Crete, a chair at the University of Pekin, but always the boyg, routine, businessmen's flunkeys in all the university offices . . . for the questioner the bitter drink.

His friend Davenport got him an appointment at the University of Missouri. At Columbia he lived like a hermit in the basement of the Davenports' house, helped with the work round the place, carpentered himself a table and chairs. He was already a bitter elderly man with a grey face covered with a net of fine wrinkles, a vandyke beard and yellow teeth. Few students could follow his courses. The college authorities were often surprised and somewhat chagrined that when visitors came from Europe it was always Veblen they wanted to meet.

These were the years he did the most of his writing, trying out his ideas on his students, writing slowly at night in violet ink with a pen of his own designing. Whenever he published a book he had to put up a guarantee with the publishers. In *The Theory of Business Enterprise, The Instinct of Workmanship, The Vested Interests and the Common Man,*

    he established a new diagram of a society dominated by monopoly capital, etched in irony

    the sabotage of production by business,

    the sabotage of life by blind need for money profits,

    pointed out the alternatives: a warlike society strangled by the bureaucracies of the monopolies forced by the law of diminishing returns to grind down more and more the common man for profits,

    or a new matteroffact commonsense society dominated by the needs of the men and women who did the work and the incredibly vast possibilities for peace and plenty offered by the progress of technology.

These were the years of Debs's speeches, growing laborunions, the I.W.W. talk about industrial democracy: these years Veblen still held to the hope that the workingclass would take over the machine of production before monopoly had pushed the western nations down into the dark again.

War cut across all that: under the cover of the bunting of Woodrow Wilson's phrases the monopolies cracked down. American democracy was crushed.

The war at least offered Veblen an opportunity to break out of the airless greenhouse of academic life. He was offered a job with the Food Administration, he sent the Navy Department a device for catching submarines by trailing lengths of stout bindingwire. (Meanwhile the government found his books somewhat confusing. The postoffice was forbidding the mails to *Imperial Germany and the Industrial Revolution* while propaganda agencies were sending it out to make people hate the Huns. Educators were denouncing *The Nature of Peace* while Washington experts were clipping phrases out of it to add to the Wilsonian smokescreen.)

For the Food Administration Thorstein Veblen wrote two reports: in one he advocated granting the demands of the I.W.W. as a wartime measure and conciliating the workingclass instead of beating up and jailing all the honest leaders; in the other he pointed out that the Food Administration was a businessman's racket and was not aiming for the most efficient organization of the country as a producing machine. He suggested that, in the interests of the efficient prosecution of the war, the government step into the place of the middleman and furnish necessities to the farmers direct in return for raw materials;

but cutting out business was not at all the Administration's idea of making the world safe for democracy,

so Veblen had to resign from the Food Administration.

He signed the protests against the trial of the hundred and one wobblies in Chicago.

After the armistice he went to New York. In spite of all the oppression of the war years, the air was freshening. In Russia the great storm of revolt had broken, seemed to be sweeping west, in the strong gusts from the new world in the east the warsodden multitudes began to see again. At Versailles allies and enemies, magnates, generals, flunkey politicians were slamming the shutters against the storm, against the new, against hope. It was suddenly clear for a second in the thundering glare what war was about, what peace was about.

In America, in Europe, the old men won. The bankers in their offices took a deep breath, the bediamonded old ladies of the leisure class went back to clipping their coupons in the refined quiet of their safedeposit vaults,

the last puffs of the ozone of revolt went stale

in the whisper of speakeasy arguments.

Veblen wrote for the *Dial*,

lectured at the New School for Social Research.

He still had a hope that the engineers, the technicians, the nonprofiteers whose hands were on the switchboard might take up the fight where the workingclass had failed. He helped form the Technical Alliance. His last hope was the British general strike.

Was there no group of men bold enough to take charge of the magnificent machine before the pigeyed speculators and the yesmen at office desks irrevocably ruined it

and with it the hopes of four hundred years?

No one went to Veblen's lectures at the New School. With every article he wrote in the *Dial* the circulation dropped.

Harding's normalcy, the new era was beginning;

even Veblen made a small killing on the stockmarket.

He was an old man and lonely.

His second wife had gone to a sanitarium suffering from delusions of persecution.

There seemed no place for a masterless man.

Veblen went back out to Palo Alto

to live in his shack in the tawny hills and observe from outside the last grabbing urges of the profit system taking on, as he put it, the systematized delusions of dementia praecox.

There he finished his translation of the *Laxdœlasaga*.

He was an old man. He was much alone. He let the woodrats take what they wanted from his larder. A skunk that hung round the shack was so tame he'd rub up against Veblen's leg like a cat.

He told a friend he'd sometimes hear in the stillness about him the voices of his boyhood talking Norwegian as clear as on the farm in Minnesota where he was raised. His friends found him harder than ever to talk to, harder than ever to interest in anything. He was running down. The last sips of the bitter drink.

He died on August 3, 1929.

Among his papers a penciled note was found:

It is also my wish, in case of death, to be cremated if it can conveniently be done, as expeditiously and inexpensively as may be, without ritual or ceremony of any kind; that my ashes be thrown loose into the sea or into some sizeable stream running into the sea; that no tombstone, slab, epitaph, effigy, tablet, inscription or monument of any name or nature, be set up to my memory or name in any place or at any time; that no obituary, memorial, portrait or biography of me, nor any letters written to or by me be printed or published, or in any way reproduced, copied or circulated;

but his memorial remains
riveted into the language:
the sharp clear prism of his mind.

H. L. MENCKEN

Professor Veblen [1]

Back in the year 1909, being engaged in a bombastic discussion with what was then known as an intellectual Socialist (like the rest of the *intelligentsia*, he succumbed to the first fife-corps of World War I, pulled down the red flag, damned Marx as a German spy, and began whooping for Woodrow Wilson and Otto Kahn), I was greatly belabored and incommoded by his long quotations from a certain Prof. Thorstein Veblen, then quite unknown to me. My antagonist manifestly attached a great deal of importance to these borrowed sagacities, for he often heaved them at me in lengths of a column or two, and urged me to read every word of them. I tried hard enough, but found it impossible going. The more I read them, in fact, the less I could make of them, and

[1] From *A Mencken Chrestomathy* by H. L. Mencken, pp. 265-275. Copyright 1949 by Alfred A. Knopf, Inc. Reprinted from *Prejudices: First Series*, 1919, pp. 59-83. Copyright 1919 by Alfred A. Knopf, Inc. Reprinted by permission of Alfred A. Knopf, Inc.

so in the end, growing impatient and impolite, I denounced this Prof. Veblen as a geyser of pish-posh, refused to waste any more time upon his incomprehensible syllogisms, and applied myself to the other Socialist witnesses in the case, seeking to set fire to their shirts.

That old debate, which took place by mail (for the Socialist lived in levantine luxury on his country estate and I was a wage-slave attached to a city newspaper), was afterward embalmed in a dull book, and got the mild notice of a day. The book, by name, *Men vs. the Man*,[2] is now as completely forgotten as Baxter's *Saint's Rest* or the Constitution of the United States. I myself am perhaps the only man who remembers it at all, and the only thing I can recall of my opponent's argument (beyond the fact that it not only failed to convert me to Marxism, but left me a bitter and incurable scoffer at democracy in all its forms) is his curious respect for the aforesaid Veblen, and his delight in the learned gentleman's long, tortuous and (to me, at least) intolerably flapdoodlish phrases.

There was, indeed, a time when I forgot even this—when my mind was empty of the professor's very name. That was, say, from 1909 or thereabout to the middle of 1917. During those years, having lost all my former interest in Socialism, even as a species of insanity, I ceased to read its literature, and thus lost track of its Great Thinkers. The periodicals that I then gave an eye to, setting aside newspapers, were chiefly the familiar American imitations of the English weeklies of opinion, and in these the dominant Great Thinker was, first, the late Dr. William James, and, after his decease in 1910, Dr. John Dewey. The reign of James, as the illuminated will recall, was long and glorious. For three or four years running he was mentioned in every one of those American *Spectators* and *Saturday Reviews* at least once a week, and often a dozen times. Among the less somber gazettes of the republic, to be sure, there were other heroes: Maeterlinck, Rabindranath Tagore, Judge Ben B. Lindsey, and so on, and still further down the literary and intellectual scale there were yet others: Hall Caine, Brieux and Jack Johnson among them, with paper-bag cookery and the twilight sleep to dispute their popularity. But on the majestic level of the pre-Villard *Nation*, among the white and lavender peaks of professional ratiocination, there was scarcely a serious rival to James. Now and then, perhaps, Jane Addams had a month of vogue, and during one winter there was a rage for Bergson, but taking one day with another James held his own against the field. . . .

Then, of a sudden, Siss! Boom! Ah! Then, overnight, the upspringing of intellectual soviets, the headlong assault upon all the old axioms of pedagogical speculation, the nihilistic dethronement of Prof. Dewey—and rah, rah, rah for Prof. Dr. Thorstein Veblen! Veblen? Could it be——? Aye, it was! My old acquaintance! The *doctor obscurus* of my half-forgotten bout with the so-called intellectual Socialist! The Great Thinker redivivus! Here, indeed, he was again, and in a few months—almost it seemed a few days—he was all over the *Nation*, the *Dial*, the *New Republic* and the rest of them, his books and pam-

[2] New York, 1910. The Socialist was Robert Rives La Monte.

phlets began to pour from the presses, the newspapers reported his every wink and whisper, and everybody who was anybody began gabbling about him. The spectacle, I do not hesitate to say, somewhat disconcerted me and even distressed me. On the one hand, I was sorry to see so learned and interesting a man as Dr. Dewey sent back to the insufferable dungeons of Columbia, there to lecture in imperfect Yiddish to classes of Grand Street Platos. And on the other hand, I shrank supinely from the appalling job, newly rearing itself before me, of reading the whole canon of the singularly laborious and muggy, the incomparably tangled and unintelligible works of Prof. Veblen.

But if a sense of duty tortures a man, it also enables him to achieve prodigies, and so I managed to get through the whole infernal job. I read *The Theory of Business Enterprise* (1904), and then I read *The Instinct of Workmanship* (1914). A hiatus followed; I was racked by a severe neuralgia, with delusions of persecution. On recovering I tackled *Imperial Germany and the Industrial Revolution* (1915). Marasmus for a month, and then *The Nature of Peace and the Terms of Its Perpetuation* (1917). What ensued was never diagnosed; probably it was some low infection of the mesentery or spleen. When it passed off, leaving only an asthmatic cough, I read *The Higher Learning in America* (1918), and then went to Mt. Clemens to drink the Glauber's salts. Eureka! the business was done! It had strained me, but now it was over. Alas, a good part of the agony had been needless. What I found myself aware of, coming to the end, was that practically the whole system of Prof. Veblen was in his first book and his last—that is, in *The Theory of the Leisure Class*, and *The Higher Learning in America*.[3] I pass on the news to literary archeologists. Read these two, and you won't have to read the others. And if even two daunt you, then read the first. Once through it, though you will have missed many a pearl and many a pain, you will have an excellent grasp of the gifted metaphysician's ideas.

For those ideas, in the main, were quite simple, and often anything but revolutionary in essence. What was genuinely remarkable about them was not their novelty, or their complexity, nor even the fact that a professor should harbor them; it was the astoundingly grandiose and rococo manner of their statement, the almost unbelievable tediousness and flatulence of the gifted headmaster's prose, his unprecedented talent for saying nothing in an august and heroic manner. There are tales of an actress of the last generation, probably Sarah Bernhardt, who could put pathos and even terror into a recitation of the multiplication table. Something of the same talent, raised to a high power, was in this Prof. Veblen. If one tunneled under his great moraines and stalagmites of words, dug down into vast kitchen-midden of discordant and raucous polysyllables, blew up the hard, thick shell of his almost theological manner, what one found in his discourse was chiefly a mass of platitudes—the self-evident made horrifying, the obvious in terms of the staggering.

[3] He wrote four books between *The Higher Learning* and his death in 1929, but they were only reboilings of old bones, and attracted no notice.

Marx, I daresay had said a good deal of it long before him, and what Marx overlooked had been said over and over again by his heirs and assigns. But Marx, at this business, labored under a technical handicap; he wrote in German, a language he actually understood. Prof. Veblen submitted himself to no such disadvantage. Though born, I believe, in These States, and resident here all his life, he achieved the effect, perhaps without employing the means, of thinking in some unearthly foreign language—say Swahili, Sumerian or Old Bulgarian —and then painfully clawing his thoughts into a copious but uncertain and book-learned English. The result was a style that affected the higher cerebral centers like a constant roll of subway expresses. The second result was a sort of bewildered numbness of the senses, as before some fabulous and unearthly marvel. And the third result, if I make no mistake, was the celebrity of the professor as a Great Thinker. In brief, he stated his hollow nothings in such high, astounding terms that inevitably arrested and blistered the right-thinking mind. He made them mysterious. He made them shocking. He made them portentous. And so, flinging them at naïve and believing souls, he made them stick and burn.

Consider this specimen—the first paragraph of Chapter XIII of *The Theory of the Leisure Class*:

In an increasing proportion as time goes on, the anthropomorphic cult, with its code of devout observances, suffers a progressive disintegration through the stress of economic exigencies and the decay of the system of status. As this disintegration proceeds, there come to be associated and blended with the devout attitude certain other motives and impulses that are not always of an anthropomorphic origin, nor traceable to the habit of personal subservience. Not all of these subsidiary impulses that blend with the bait of devoutness in the later devotional life are altogether congruous with the devout attitude or with the anthropomorphic apprehension of sequence of phenomena. Their origin being not the same, their action upon the scheme of devout life is also not in the same direction. In many ways they traverse the underlying norm of subservience or vicarious life to which the code of devout observances and the ecclesiastical and sacerdotal institutions are to be traced as their substantial basis. Through the presence of these alien motives the social and industrial regime of status gradually disintegrates, and the canon of personal subservience loses the support derived from an unbroken tradition. Extraneous habits and proclivities encroach upon the field of action occupied by this canon, and it presently comes about that the ecclesiastical and sacerdotal structures are partially converted to other uses, in some measure alien to the purpose of the scheme of devout life as it stood in the days of the most vigorous and characteristic development of the priesthood.

Well, what have we here? What does this appalling salvo of rhetorical artillery signify? What was the sweating professor trying to say? Simply that in the course of time the worship of God is commonly corrupted by other enterprises, and that the church, ceasing to be a mere temple of adoration, becomes the headquarters of these other enterprises. More simply still, that men sometimes vary serving God by serving other men, which means, of course, serving themselves. This bald platitude, which must be obvious to any child who has ever been to a church bazaar, was here tortured, worried and run through rollers until it spread out to 241 words, of which fully 200 were unnecessary. The next paragraph was even worse. In it the master undertook to explain in his peculiar dialect the meaning of "that non-reverent sense of aesthetic congruity with the environment which is left as a residue of the latter-day act of worship after elimination of its anthropomorphic content." Just what did he mean by this "non-reverent sense of aesthetic congruity"? I studied the whole paragraph for three days, halting only for prayer and sleep, and I came to certain conclusions. What I concluded was this: he was trying to say that many people go to church, not because they are afraid of the devil but because they enjoy the music, and like to look at the stained glass, the potted lilies and the rev. pastor. To get this profound and highly original observation upon paper, he wasted, not merely 241, but more than 300 words. To say what might have been said on a postage stamp he took more than a page in his book.

And so it went, alas, alas, in all his other volumes—a cent's worth of information wrapped in a bale of polysyllables. In *The Higher Learning in America* the thing perhaps reached its damndest and worst. It was as if the practise of that incredibly obscure and malodorous style were a relentless disease, a sort of progressive intellectual diabetes, a leprosy of the horse sense. Words were flung upon words until all recollection that there must be a meaning in them, a ground and excuse for them, were lost. One wandered in a labyrinth of nouns, adjectives, verbs, pronouns, adverbs, prepositions, conjunctions and participles, most of them swollen and nearly all of them unable to walk. It was, and is, impossible to imagine worse English, within the limits of intelligible grammar. It was clumsy, affected, opaque, bombastic, windy, empty. It was without grace or distinction and it was often without the most elementary order. The professor got himself enmeshed in his gnarled sentences like a bull trapped by barbed wire, and his efforts to extricate himself were quite as furious and quite as spectacular. He heaved, he leaped, he writhed; at times he seemed to be at the point of yelling for the police. It was a picture to bemuse the vulgar and to give the judicious grief.

Worse, there was nothing at the bottom of all this strident wind-music— the ideas it was designed to set forth were, in the overwhelming main, poor ideas, and often they were ideas that were almost idiotic. The concepts underlying, say, *The Theory of the Leisure Class* were simply Socialism and well water; the concepts underlying *The Higher Learning in America* were so childishly obvious that even the poor drudges who wrote editorials for newspapers often voiced them, and when, now and then, the professor tired of this emission of stale bosh and attempted flights of a more original character, he straightway came tumbling down into absurdity. What the reader then had to struggle with was not only intolerably bad writing, but also loose, flabby, cocksure and preposterous thinking. . . . Again I take refuge in an example. It is from Chapter IV of *The Theory of the Leisure Class*. The problem before the author here had to do with the social convention which, in pre-Prohibition 1899, frowned upon the consumption of alcohol by women—at least to the extent to which men might consume it decorously. Well, then, what was his explanation of this convention? Here, in brief, was his process of reasoning:

1. The leisure class, which is the predatory class of feudal times, reserves all luxuries for itself, and disapproves their use by members of the lower classes, for this use takes away their charm by taking away their exclusive possession.

2. Women are chattels in the possession of the leisure class, and hence subject to the rules made for inferiors. "The patriarchal tradition . . . says that the woman, being a chattel, should consume only what is necessary to her sustenance, except so far as her further consumption contributes to the comfort or the good repute of her master."

3. The consumption of alcohol contributes nothing to the comfort or good repute of the woman's master, but "detracts sensibly from the comfort or pleasure" of her master. Ergo, she is forbidden to drink.

This, I believe, was a fair specimen of the Veblenian ratiocination. Observe it well, for it was typical. That is to say, it started off with a gratuitous and highly dubious assumption, proceeded to an equally dubious deduction, and then ended with a platitude which begged the whole question. What sound reason was there for believing that exclusive possession was the hall-mark of luxury? There was none that I could see. It might be true of a few luxuries, but it was certainly not true of the most familiar ones. Did I enjoy a decent bath because I knew that John Smith could not afford one—or because I delighted in being clean? Did I admire Beethoven's Fifth Symphony because it was incomprehensible to Congressmen and Methodists—or because I genuinely loved music? Did I prefer kissing a pretty girl to kissing a charwoman because even a janitor may kiss a charwoman—or because the pretty girl looked better, smelled better and kissed better?

Confronted by such considerations, it seemed to me that there was little truth left in Prof. Veblen's theory of conspicuous consumption and conspicuous waste—that what remained of it, after it was practically applied a few times, was no more than a wraith of balderdash. What could have been plainer than his failure in the case of the human female? Starting off with a platitude, he ended in absurdity. No one could deny, I was willing to grant, that in a clearly limited sense, women occupied a place in the world—or, more accurately, aspired to a place in the world—that had some resemblance to that of a chattel. Marriage, the goal of their only honest and permanent hopes, invaded their individuality; a married woman (I was thinking, remember, of 1899) became the function of another individuality. Thus the appearance she presented to the world was often the mirror of her husband's egoism. A rich man hung his wife with expensive clothes and jewels for the same reason, among others, that he drove an expensive car: to notify everybody that he could afford it—in brief, to excite the envy of Marxians. But he also did it, let us hope, for another and far more powerful reason, to wit, that he delighted in her, that he loved her—and so wanted to make her gaudy and happy. This reason, to be sure, was rejected by the Marxians of the time, as it is rejected by those of ours, but nevertheless, it continued to appeal very forcibly, and so continues in our own day, to the majority of normal husbands in the nations of the West. The American husband, in particular, dresses his wife like a circus horse, not primarily because he wants to display his wealth upon her person, but because he is a soft and moony fellow and ever ready to yield to her desires, however preposterous. If any conception of her as a chattel were actively in him, even unconsciously, he would be a good deal less her slave. As it is, her vicarious practise of conspicuous waste commonly reaches such a development that her master himself is forced into renunciations—which brought Prof. Dr. Veblen's theory to self-destruction.

His final conclusion was as unsound as his premises. All it came to was a plain begging of the question. Why does a man forbid his wife to drink all the alcohol she can hold? Because, he said, it "detracts sensibly from his comfort or pleasure." In other words, it detracts from his comfort and pleasure because it detracts from his comfort and pleasure. Meanwhile, the real answer is so plain that even a professor should know it. A man forbids his wife to drink too much because, deep in his secret archives, he has records of the behavior of other women who drank too much, and is eager to safeguard his wife's connubial rectitude and his own dignity against what he knows to be certain invasion. In brief, it is a commonplace of observation, familiar to all males beyond the age of twenty-one, that once a woman is drunk the rest is a mere matter of time and place: the girl is already there. A husband, viewing this prospect, perhaps shrinks from having his chattel damaged. But let us be soft enough to think that he may also shrink from seeing humiliation and bitter regret inflicted upon one who is under his protection, and one whose dignity and happiness are precious to him, and one whom he regards with deep and (I surely hope) lasting affection. A man's grandfather is surely not his chattel, even by the terms of the Veblen theory, yet I am sure that no sane man would let the old gentleman go beyond a discreet cocktail or two if a bout of genuine bibbing were certain to be followed by the complete destruction of his dignity, his chastity and (if a Presbyterian) his immortal soul.

One more example of the Veblenian logic and I must pass on. On page 135 of *The Theory of the Leisure Class* he turned his garish and buzzing searchlight upon another problem of the domestic hearth, this time a double one.

First, why do we have lawns around our country houses? Secondly, why don't we use cows to keep them clipped, instead of employing Italians, Croatians and blackamoors? The first question was answered by an appeal to ethnology: we delight in lawns because we are the descendants of "a pastoral people inhabiting a region with a humid climate"—because our dolicho-blond ancestors had flocks, and thus took a keen professional interest in grass. (The Marx motif! The economic interpretation of history in E flat.) But why don't we keep flocks? Why do we renounce cows and hire Jugo-Slavs? Because "to the average popular apprehension a herd of cattle so pointedly suggests thrift and usefulness that their presence . . . would be intolerably cheap." Plowing through a bad book from end to end, I could find nothing sillier than this. Here, indeed, the whole "Theory of conspicuous waste" was exposed for precisely what it was: one per cent platitude and ninety-nine per cent nonsense. Had the genial professor, pondering his great problems, ever taken a walk in the country? And had he, in the course of that walk, ever crossed a pasture inhabited by a cow (*Bos taurus*)? And had he, making that crossing, ever passed astern of the cow herself? And had he, thus passing astern, ever stepped carelessly, and—

DAVID RIESMAN

Character and Society[1]

What is the relation between social character and society? How is it that every society seems to get, more or less, the social character it "needs"? Erik H. Erikson writes, in a study of the social character of the Yurok Indians, that ". . . systems of child training . . . represent unconscious attempts at creating out of human raw material that configuration of attitudes which is (or once was) the optimum under the tribe's particular natural conditions and economic-historic necessities."[2]

From "economic-historic necessities" to "systems of child training" is a long jump. Much of the work of students of social character has been devoted to closing the gap and showing how the satisfaction of the largest "needs" of society is prepared, in some half-mysterious way, by its most intimate practices. Erich Fromm succinctly suggests the line along which this connection between

1 From *The Lonely Crowd* by David Riesman, Nathan Glazer, and Reuel Denney (New York: Doubleday & Company, 1955), pp. 19-48, with omissions. Copyright, 1950, 1953, by Yale University Press. Reprinted by permission of Yale University Press.

2 "Observations on the Yurok: Childhood and World Image," *University of California Publications in American Archaeology and Ethnology*, XXXV (1943), iv.

society and character training may be sought: "In order that any society may function well, its members must acquire the kind of character which makes them *want* to act in the way they *have* to act as members of the society or of a special class within it. They have to *desire* what objectively is *necessary* for them to do. *Outer force* is replaced by *inner compulsion*, and by the particular kind of human energy which is channeled into character traits." [3]

Thus, the link between character and society—certainly not the only one, but one of the most significant, and the one I choose to emphasize in this discussion—is to be found in the way in which society ensures some degree of conformity from the individuals who make it up. In each society, such a mode of ensuring conformity is built into the child, and then either encouraged or frustrated in later adult experience. (No society, it would appear, is quite prescient enough to ensure that the mode of conformity it has inculcated will satisfy those subject to it in every stage of life.) I shall use the term "mode of conformity" interchangeably with the term "social character"—though certainly conformity is not all of social character: "mode of creativity" is as much a part of it. However, while societies and individuals may live well enough— if rather boringly—without creativity, it is not likely that they can live without some mode of conformity—even be it one of rebellion.

My concern . . . is with two revolutions and their relation to the "mode of conformity" or "social character" of Western man since the Middle Ages. The first of these revolutions has in the last four hundred years cut us off pretty decisively from the family- and clan-oriented traditional ways of life in which mankind has existed throughout most of history; this revolution includes the Renaissance, the Reformation, the Counter-Reformation, the Industrial Revolution, and the political revolutions of the seventeenth, eighteenth, and nineteenth centuries. This revolution is, of course, still in process, but in the most advanced countries of the world, and particularly in America, it is giving way to another sort of revolution—a whole range of social developments associated with a shift from an age of production to an age of consumption. . . . The second revolution, which is just beginning, has interested many contemporary observers, including social scientists, philosophers, and journalists. Both description and evaluation are still highly controversial; indeed, many are still preoccupied with the first set of revolutions and have not invented the categories for discussing the second set. In this book I try to sharpen the contrast between, on the one hand, conditions and character in those social strata that are today most seriously affected by the second revolution, and, on the other hand, conditions and character in analogous strata during the earlier revolution; in this perspective, what is briefly said about the traditional and feudal societies which were overturned by the first revolution is in the nature of backdrop for these later shifts.

[3] "Individual and Social Origins of Neurosis," *American Sociological Review,* IX (1944), 380; reprinted in *Personality in Nature, Society and Culture,* edited by Clyde Kluckhohn and Henry Murray (New York, Alfred A. Knopf, 1948).

One of the categories I make use of is taken from demography, the science that deals with birth rates and death rates, with the absolute relative numbers of people in a society, and their distribution by age, sex, and other variables, for I tentatively seek to link certain social and characterological developments, as cause and effect, with certain population shifts in Western society since the Middle Ages.

It seems reasonably well established, despite the absence of reliable figures for earlier centuries, that during this period the curve of population growth in the Western countries has shown an S-shape of a particular type (as other countries are drawn more closely into the net of Western civilization, their populations also show a tendency to develop along the lines of this S-shape curve). The bottom horizontal line of the S represents a situation where the total population does not increase or does so very slowly, for the number of births equals roughly the number of deaths, and both are very high. In societies of this type, a high proportion of the population is young, life expectancy is low, and the turnover of generations is extremely rapid. Such societies are said to be in the phase of "high growth potential"; for should something happen to decrease the very high death rate (greater production of food, new sanitary measures, new knowledge of the causes of disease, and so on), a "population explosion" would result, and the population would increase very rapidly. This in effect is what happened in the West, starting with the seventeenth century. This spurt in population was most marked in Europe, and the countries settled by Europeans, in the nineteenth century. It is represented by the vertical bar of the S. Demographers call this the stage of "transitional growth" because the birth rate soon begins to follow the death rate in its decline. The rate of growth then slows down, and demographers begin to detect in the growing proportion of middle-aged and aged in the population the signs of a third stage, "incipient population decline." Societies in this stage are represented by the top horizontal bar of the S, again indicating, as in the first stage, that total population growth is small—but this time because births and deaths are low.

The S-curve is not a theory of population growth so much as an empirical description of what has happened in the West and in those parts of the world influenced by the West. After the S runs its course, what then? The developments of recent years in the United States and other Western countries do not seem to be susceptible to so simple and elegant a summing up. "Incipient population decline" has not become "population decline" itself, and the birth rate has shown an uncertain tendency to rise again, which most demographers think is temporary.[4]

It would be very surprising if variations in the basic conditions of reproduction, livelihood, and survival chances, that is, in the supply of and demand for

[4] The terminology used here is that of Frank W. Notestein. See his "Population —The Long View," in *Food for the World*, edited by Theodore W. Schultz (University of Chicago Press, 1945).

human beings, with all it implies in change of the spacing of people, the size of markets, the role of children, the society's feeling of vitality or senescence, and many other intangibles, failed to influence character. My thesis is, in fact, that each of these three different phases on the population curve appears to be occupied by a society that enforces conformity and molds social character in a definably different way.

The society of high growth potential develops in its typical members a social character whose conformity is insured by their tendency to follow tradition: these I shall term *tradition-directed* people and the society in which they live *a society dependent on tradition-direction*.

The society of transitional population growth develops in its typical members a social character whose conformity is insured by their tendency to acquire early in life an internalized set of goals. These I shall term *inner-directed* people and the society in which they live *a society dependent on inner-direction*. . . .

Finally, the society of incipient population decline develops in its typical members a social character whose conformity is insured by their tendency to be sensitized to the expectations and preferences of others. These I shall term *other-directed* people and the society in which they live one *dependent on other-direction*. . . .

High Growth Potential: Tradition-Directed Types

The phase of high growth potential characterizes more than half the world's population: India, Egypt, and China (which have already grown immensely in recent generations), most preliterate peoples in Central Africa, parts of Central and South America, in fact most areas of the world relatively untouched by industrialization. Here death rates are so high that if birth rates were not also high the populations would die out.

Regions where the population is in this stage may be either sparsely populated, as are the areas occupied by many primitive tribes and parts of Central and South America; or they may be densely populated, as are India, China, and Egypt. In either case, the society achieves a Malthusian bargain with the limited food supply by killing off, in one way or another, some of the potential surplus of births over deaths—the enormous trap which, in Malthus' view, nature sets for man and which can be peaceably escaped only by prudent cultivation of the soil and prudent uncultivation of the species through the delay of marriage. Without the prevention of childbirth by means of marriage postponement or other contraceptive measures, the population must be limited by taking the life of living beings. And so societies have "invented" cannibalism, induced abortion, organized wars, made human sacrifice, and practiced infanticide (especially female) as means of avoiding periodic famine and epidemics.

Though this settling of accounts with the contradictory impulses of hunger and sex is accompanied often enough by upheaval and distress, these societies in the stage of high growth potential tend to be stable at least in the sense that their social practices, including the "crimes" that keep population down, are institutionalized and patterned. Generation after generation, people are born, are weeded out, and die to make room for others. The net rate of natural increase fluctuates within a broad range, though without showing any long-range tendency, as is true also of societies in the stage of incipient decline. But unlike the latter, the average life expectancy in the former is characteristically low: the population is heavily weighted on the side of the young, and generation replaces generation far more rapidly and less "efficiently" than in the societies of incipient population decline.

In viewing such a society we inevitably associate the relative stability of the man-land ratio, whether high or low, with the tenacity of custom and social structure. However, we must not equate stability of social structure over historical time with psychic stability in the life span of an individual: the latter may subjectively experience much violence and disorganization. In the last analysis, however, he learns to deal with life by adaptation, not by innovation. With certain exceptions conformity is largely given in the "self-evident" social situation. Of course nothing in human life is ever really self-evident; where it so appears it is because perceptions have been narrowed by cultural conditioning. As the precarious relation to the food supply is built into the going culture, it helps create a pattern of conventional conformity which is reflected in many, if not all, societies in the stage of high growth potential. This is what I call tradition-direction.

A Definition of Tradition-Direction

Since the type of social order we have been discussing is relatively unchanging, the conformity of the individual tends to be dictated to a very large degree by power relations among the various age and sex groups, the clans, castes, professions, and so forth—relations which have endured for centuries and are modified but slightly, if at all, by successive generations. The culture controls behavior minutely, and, while the rules are not so complicated that the young cannot learn them during the period of intensive socialization, careful and rigid etiquette governs the fundamentally influential sphere of kin relationships. Moreover, the culture, in addition to its economic tasks, or as part of them, provides ritual, routine, and religion to occupy and to orient everyone. Little energy is directed toward finding new solutions of the age-old problems, let us say, of agricultural technique or "medicine," the problems to which people are acculturated.

It is not to be thought, however, that in these societies, where the activity of the individual member is determined by characterologically grounded obedience to traditions, the individual may not be highly prized and, in many instances, encouraged to develop his capabilities, his initiative, and even, within very narrow time limits, his aspirations. Indeed, the individual in some primitive societies is far more appreciated and respected than in some sectors of modern society. For the individual in a society dependent on tradition-direction has a well-defined functional relationship to other members of the group. If he is not killed off, he "belongs"—he is not "surplus," as the modern unemployed are surplus, nor is he expendable as the unskilled are expendable in modern society. But by very virtue of his "belonging," life goals that are *his* in terms of conscious choice appear to shape his destiny only to a very limited extent, just as only to a limited extent is there any concept of progress for the group.

In societies in which tradition-direction is the dominant mode of insuring conformity, relative stability is preserved in part by the infrequent but highly important process of fitting into institutionalized roles such deviants as there are. In such societies a person who might have become at a later historical stage an innovator or rebel, whose belonging, as such, is marginal and problematic, is drawn instead into roles like those of the shaman or sorcerer. That is, he is drawn into roles that make a socially acceptable contribution, while at the same time they provide the individual with a more or less approved niche. The medieval monastic orders may have served in a similar way to absorb many characterological mutations.

In some of these societies certain individuals are encouraged toward a degree of individuality from childhood, especially if they belong to families of high status. But, since the range of choice, even for high-status people, is minimal, the apparent social need for an individuated type of character is also minimal. It is probably accurate to say that character structure in these societies is very largely "adjusted," in the sense that for most people it appears to be in tune with social institutions. Even the few misfits "fit" to a degree; and only very rarely is one driven out of his social world.

This does not mean, of course, that the people are happy; the society to whose traditions they are adjusted may be a miserable one, ridden with anxiety, sadism, and disease. The point is rather that change, while never completely absent in human affairs, is slowed down as the movement of molecules is slowed down at low temperature; and the social character comes as close as it ever does to looking like the matrix of the social forms themselves.

In western history the Middle Ages can be considered a period in which the majority were tradition-directed. But the term tradition-directed refers to a common element, not only among the people of precapitalist Europe but also among such enormously different types of people as Hindus and Hopi Indians, Zulus and Chinese, North African Arabs anad Balinese. . . .

Transitional Growth: Inner-Directed Types

Except for the West, we know very little about the cumulation of small changes that can eventuate in a breakup of the tradition-directed type of society, leading it to realize its potential for high population growth. As for the West, however, much has been learned about the slow decay of feudalism and the subsequent rise of a type of society in which inner-direction is the dominant mode of insuring conformity.

Critical historians, pushing the Renaissance ever back into the Middle Ages, seem sometimes to deny that any decisive change occurred at all. On the whole, however, it seems that the greatest social and characterological shift of recent centuries did indeed come when men were driven out of the primary ties that bound them to the western medieval version of tradition-directed society. All later shifts, including the shift from inner-direction to other-direction, seem unimportant by comparison, although of course this latter shift is still under way and we cannot tell what it will look like when—if ever—it is complete.

A change in the relatively stable ratio of births to deaths, which characterizes the period of high growth potential, is both the cause and consequence of other profound social changes. In most of the cases known to us a decline takes place in mortality prior to a decline in fertility; hence there is some period in which the population expands rapidly. The drop in death rate occurs as the result of many interacting factors, among them sanitation, improved communications (which permit government to operate over a wider area and also permit easier transport of food to areas of shortage from areas of surplus), the decline, forced or otherwise, of infanticide, cannibalism, and other inbred kinds of violence. Because of improved methods of agriculture the land is able to support more people, and these in turn produce still more people.

Notestein's phrase, "transitional growth," is a mild way of putting it. The "transition" is likely to be violent, disrupting the stabilized paths of existence in societies in which tradition-direction has been the principal mode of insuring conformity. The imbalance of births and deaths puts pressure on the society's customary ways. A new slate of character structures is called for or finds its opportunity in coping with the rapid changes—and the need for still more changes—in the social organization.

A Definition of Inner-Direction

In western history the society that emerged with the Renaissance and Reformation and that is only now vanishing serves to illustrate the type of society in which inner-direction is the principal mode of securing conformity. Such a society is characterized by increased personal mobility, by a rapid accumulation of capital (teamed with devastating technological shifts), and by an almost constant expansion: intensive expansion in the production of goods and people, and extensive expansion in exploration, colonization, and imperialism. The greater choices this society gives—and the greater initiatives it demands in order to cope with its novel problems—are handled by character types who can manage to live socially without strict and self-evident tradition-direction. These are the inner-directed types.

The concept of inner-direction is intended to cover a very wide range of types. Thus, while it is essential for the study of certain problems to differentiate between Protestant and Catholic countries and their character types, between the effects of the Reformation and the effects of the Renaissance, between the puritan ethic of the European north and west and the somewhat more hedonistic ethic of the European east and south, while all these are valid and, for certain purposes, important distinctions, the concentration of this study on the development of modes of conformity permits their neglect. It allows the grouping together of these otherwise distinct developments because they have one thing in common: *the source of direction for the individual is "inner" in the sense that it is implanted early in life by the elders and directed toward generalized but nonetheless inescapably destined goals.*

We can see what this means when we realize that, in societies in which tradition-direction is the dominant mode of insuring conformity, attention is focused on securing external *behavioral* conformity. While behavior is minutely prescribed, individuality of character need not be highly developed to meet prescriptions that are objectified in ritual and etiquette—though to be sure, a social character *capable* of such behavioral attention and obedience is requisite. By contrast, societies in which inner-direction becomes important, though they also are concerned with behavioral conformity, cannot be satisfied with behavioral conformity alone. Too many novel situations are presented, situations which a code cannot encompass in advance. Consequently the problem of personal choice, solved in the earlier period of high growth potential by channeling choice through rigid social organization, in the period of transitional growth is solved by channeling choice through a rigid though highly individualized character.

This rigidity is a complex matter. While any society dependent on inner-direction seems to present people with a wide choice of aims—such as money, possessions, power, knowledge, fame, goodness—these aims are ideologically interrelated, and the selection made by any one individual remains relatively unalterable throughout his life. Moreover, the means to those ends, though not fitted into as tight a social frame of reference as in the society dependent on tradition-direction, are nevertheless limited by the new voluntary associations— for instance, the Quakers, the Masons, the Mechanics' Associations—to which people tie themselves. Indeed, the term "tradition-direction" could be misleading if the reader were to conclude that the force of tradition has no weight for the inner-directed character. On the contrary, he is very considerably bound by traditions: they limit his ends and inhibit his choice of means. The point is rather that a splintering of tradition takes place, connected in part with the increasing division of labor and stratification of society. Even if the individual's choice of tradition is largely determined for him by his family, as it is in most cases, he cannot help becoming aware of the existence of competing traditions —hence of tradition as such. As a result he possesses a somewhat greater degree of flexibility in adapting himself to ever changing requirements and in return requires more from his environment.

As the control of the primary group is loosened—the group that both socializes the young and controls the adult in the earlier era—a new psychological mechanism appropriate to the more open society is "invented": it is what I like to describe as a psychological gyroscope.[5] This instrument, once it is set by the parents and other authorities, keeps the inner-directed person, as we shall see, "on course" even when tradition, as responded to by his character, no longer dictates his moves. The inner-directed person becomes capable of maintaining a delicate balance between the demands made upon him of his life goal and the buffetings of his external environment.

This metaphor of the gyroscope, like any other, must not be taken literally. It would be a mistake to see the inner-directed man as incapable of learning from experience or as insensitive to public opinion in matters of external conformity. He can receive and utilize certain signals from outside, provided that they can be reconciled with the limited maneuverability that his gyroscope permits him. His pilot is not quite automatic.

Huizinga's *The Waning of the Middle Ages* gives a picture of the anguish and turmoil, the conflict of values, out of which the new forms slowly emerged. Already by the late Middle Ages people were forced to live under new conditions of awareness. As their self-consciousness and their individuality developed, they had to make themselves at home in the world in novel ways. They still have to.

Incipient Decline of Population: Other-Directed Types

The problem facing the societies in the stage of transitional growth is that of reaching a point at which resources become plentiful enough or are utilized effectively enough to permit a rapid accumulation of capital. This rapid accumulation has to be achieved even while the social product is being drawn on at an accelerated rate to maintain the rising population and satisfy the consumer demands that go with the way of life that has already been adopted. For most countries, unless capital and techniques can be imported from other countries in still later phases of the population curve, every effort to increase national resources at a rapid rate must actually be at the expense of current standards of living. We have seen this occur in the U.S.S.R., now in the stage of transitional growth. For western Europe this transition was long-drawn-out and painful. For America, Canada, and Australia—at once beneficiaries of European techniques and native resources—the transition was rapid and relatively easy.

The tradition-directed person, as has been said, hardly thinks of himself as an individual. Still less does it occur to him that he might shape his own destiny in terms of personal, lifelong goals or that the destiny of his children might be separate from that of the family group. He is not sufficiently separated psychologically from himself (or, therefore, sufficiently close to himself), his fam-

[5] Since writing the above I have discovered Gardner Murphy's use of the same metaphor in his volume *Personality* (New York, Harper, 1947).

ily, or group to think in these terms. In the phase of transitional growth, however, people of inner-directed character do gain a feeling of control over their own lives and see their children also as individuals with careers to make. At the same time, with the shift out of agriculture and, later, with the end of child labor, children no longer become an unequivocal economic asset. And with the growth of habits of scientific thought, religious and magical views of human fertility—views that in an earlier phase of the population curve made sense for the culture if it was to reproduce itself—give way to "rational," individualistic attitudes. Indeed, just as the rapid accumulation of productive capital requires that people be imbued with the "Protestant ethic" (as Max Weber characterized one manifestation of what is here termed inner-direction), so also the decreased number of progeny requires a profound change in values—a change so deep that, in all probability, it has to be rooted in character structure.

As the birth rate begins to follow the death rate downward, societies move toward the epoch of incipient decline of population. Fewer and fewer people work on the land or in the extractive industries or even in manufacturing. Hours are short. People may have material abundance and leisure besides. They pay for these changes however—here, as always, the solution of old problems gives rise to new ones—by finding themselves in a centralized and bureaucratized society and a world shrunken and agitated by the contact—accelerated by industrialization—of races, nations, and cultures.

The hard enduringness and enterprise of the inner-directed types are somewhat less necessary under these new conditions. Increasingly, *other people* are the problem, not the material environment. And as people mix more widely and become more sensitive to each other, the surviving traditions from the stage of high growth potential—much disrupted, in any case, during the violent spurt of industrialization—become still further attenuated. Gyroscopic control is no longer sufficiently flexible, and a new psychological mechanism is called for.

Furthermore, the "scarcity psychology" of many inner-directed people, which was socially adaptive during the period of heavy capital accumulation that accompanied transitional growth of population, needs to give way to an "abundance psychology" capable of "wasteful" luxury consumption of leisure and of the surplus product. Unless people want to destroy the surplus product in war, which still does require heavy capital equipment, they must learn to enjoy and engage in those services that are expensive in terms of man power but not of capital—poetry and philosophy, for instance.[6] Indeed, in the period of incipient decline, nonproductive consumers, both the increasing number of old people and the diminishing number of as yet untrained young, form a high proportion of the population, and these need both the economic opportunity to be prodigal and the character structure to allow it.

[6] These examples are given by Allan G. B. Fisher, *The Clash of Progress and Security* (London, Macmillan, 1935).

Has this need for still another slate of character types actually been acknowledged to any degree? My observations lead me to believe that in America it has.

A Definition of Other-Direction

The type of character I shall describe as other-directed seems to be emerging in very recent years in the upper middle class of our larger cities: more prominently in New York than in Boston, in Los Angeles than in Spokane, in Cincinnati than in Chillicothe. Yet in some respects this type is strikingly similar to *the* American, whom Tocqueville and other curious and astonished visitors from Europe, even before the Revolution, thought to be a new kind of man. Indeed, travelers' reports on America impress us with their unanimity. The American is said to be shallower, freer with his money, friendlier, more uncertain of himself and his values, more demanding of approval than the European. It all adds up to a pattern which, without stretching matters too far, resembles the kind of character that a number of social scientists have seen as developing in contemporary, highly industrialized, and bureaucratic America: Fromm's "marketer," Mills's "fixer," Arnold Green's "middle class male child." [7]

It is my impression that the middle-class American of today is decisively different from those Americans of Tocqueville's writings who nevertheless strike us as so contemporary, and much of this book will be devoted to discussing these differences. It is also my impression that the conditions I believe to be responsible for other-direction are affecting increasing numbers of people in the metropolitan centers of the advanced industrial countries. My analysis of the other-directed character is thus at once an analysis of the American and of contemporary man. Much of the time I find it hard or impossible to say where one ends and the other begins. Tentatively, I am inclined to think that the other-directed type does find itself most at home in America, due to certain unique elements in American society, such as its recruitment from Europe and its lack of any feudal past. As against this, I am also inclined to put more weight on capitalism, industrialism, and urbanization—these being international tendencies—than on any character-forming peculiarities of the American scene.

Bearing these qualifications in mind, it seems appropriate to treat contemporary metropolitan America as our illustration of a society—so far, perhaps, the only illustration—in which other-direction is the dominant mode of insuring conformity. It would be premature, however, to say that it is already the dominant mode in America as a whole. But since the other-directed types are to be found among the young, in the larger cities, and among the upper income

[7] See Erich Fromm, *Man for Himself*; C. Wright Mills, "The Competitive Personality," *Partisan Review*, XIII (1946), 433; Arnold Green, "The Middle Class Male Child and Neurosis," *American Sociological Review*, XI (1946), 31. See also the work of Jurgen Ruesch, Martin B. Loeb, and co-workers on the "infantile personality."

groups, we may assume that, unless present trends are reversed, the hegemony of other-direction lies not far off.

If we wanted to cast our social character types into social class molds, we could say that inner-direction is the typical character of the "old" middle class—the banker, the tradesman, the small entrepreneur, the technically oriented engineer, etc.—while other-direction is becoming the typical character of the "new" middle class—the bureaucrat, the salaried employee in business, etc. Many of the economic factors associated with the recent growth of the "new" middle class are well known. They have been discussed by James Burnham, Colin Clark, Peter Drucker, and others. There is a decline in the numbers and in the proportion of the working population engaged in production and extraction—agriculture, heavy industry, heavy transport—and an increase in the numbers and the proportion engaged in white-collar work and the service trades. People who are literate, educated, and provided with the necessities of life by an ever more efficient machine industry and agriculture, turn increasingly to the "tertiary" economic realm. The service industries prosper among the people as a whole and no longer only in court circles.

Education, leisure, services, these go together with an increased consumption of words and images from the new mass media of communications. While societies in the phase of transitional growth begin the process of distributing words from urban centers, the flow becomes a torrent in the societies of incipient population decline. This process, while modulated by profound national and class differences, connected with differences in literacy and loquacity, takes place everywhere in the industrialized lands. Increasingly, relations with the outer world and with oneself are mediated by the flow of mass communication. For the other-directed types political events are likewise experienced through a screen of words by which the events are habitually atomized and personalized—or pseudo-personalized. For the inner-directed person who remains still extant in this period the tendency is rather to systematize and moralize this flow of words.

These developments lead, for large numbers of people, to changes in paths to success and to the requirement of more "socialized" behavior both for success and for marital and personal adaptation. Connected with such changes are changes in the family and in child-rearing practices. In the smaller families of urban life, and with the spread of "permissive" child care to ever wider strata of the population, there is a relaxation of older patterns of discipline. Under these newer patterns the peer-group (the group of one's associates of the same age and class) becomes much more important to the child, while the parents make him feel guilty not so much about violation of inner standards as about failure to be popular or otherwise to manage his relations with these other children. Moreover, the pressures of the school and the peer-group are reinforced and continued—in a manner whose inner paradoxes I shall discuss later—by the mass media: movies, radio, comics, and popular culture media generally. Under these conditions types of character emerge that we shall here term other-directed. . . . *What is common to all the other-directed people is that their contemporaries are the source of direction for the individual—either those known to him or those with whom he is indirectly acquainted, through friends and through the mass media. This source is of course "internalized" in the sense that dependence on it for guidance in life is implanted early. The goals toward which the other-directed person strives shift with that guidance: it is only the process of striving itself and the process of paying close attention to the signals from others that remain unaltered throughout life.* This mode of keeping in touch with others permits a close behavioral conformity, not through drill in behavior itself, as in the tradition-directed character, but rather through an exceptional sensitivity to the actions and wishes of others.

Of course, it matters very much who these "others" are: whether they are the individual's immediate circle or a "higher" circle or the anonymous voices of the mass media; whether the individual fears the hostility of chance acquaintances or only of those who "count." But his need for approval and direction from others—and contemporary others rather than ancestors—goes beyond the reasons that lead most people in any era to care very much what others think of them. While all people want and need to be liked by some of the people some of the time, it is only the modern other-directed types who make this their chief source of direction and chief area of sensitivity.[8]

It is perhaps the insatiable force of this psychological need for approval that differentiates people of the metropolitan, American upper middle class, whom we regard as other-directed, from very similar types that have appeared in capital cities and among other classes in previous historical periods, whether in imperial Canton, in eighteenth- and nineteenth-century Europe, or in ancient Athens, Alexandria, or Rome. In all these groups fashion not only ruled as a substitute for morals and customs, but it was a rapidly changing fashion that held sway. It could do so because, although the mass media were in their infancy, the group corresponding to the American upper middle class was comparably small and the elite structure was extremely reverberant. It can be argued, for example, that a copy of *The Spectator* covered its potential readership more thoroughly in the late eighteenth century than *The New Yorker* covers its readership today. In eighteenth- and nineteenth-century English, French, and Russian novels, we find portraits of the sort of people who operated in the upper reaches of bureaucracy and had to be prepared for rapid changes of signals. Stepan Arkadyevitch Oblonsky in *Anna Karenina* is one of the more likable and less opportunistic examples, especially striking because of the way Tolstoy contrasts him with Levin, a moralizing, inner-directed person. At any dinner

[8] This picture of the other-directed person has been stimulated by, and developed from, Erich Fromm's discussion of the "marketing orientation" in *Man for Himself*, pp. 67-82. I have also drawn on my portrait of "The Cash Customer," *Common Sense*, XI (1942), 183.

party Stepan manifests exceptional social skills; his political skills as described in the following quotation are also highly social:

Stepan Arkadyevitch took in and read a liberal newspaper, not an extreme one, but one advocating the views held by the majority. And in spite of the fact that science, art, and politics had no special interest for him, he firmly held those views on all subjects which were held by the majority and by his paper, and he only changed them when the majority changed them—or, more strictly speaking, he did not change them, but they imperceptively changed of themselves within him.

Stepan Arkadyevitch had not chosen his political opinions or his views; these political opinions and views had come to him of themselves, just as he did not choose the shapes of his hats or coats, but simply took those that were being worn. And for him, living in a certain society—owing to the need, ordinarily developed at years of discretion, for some degree of mental activity —to have views was just as indispensable as to have a hat. If there was a reason for his preferring liberal to conservative views, which were held also by many of his circle, it arose not from his considering liberalism more rational, but from its being in closer accord with his manner of life. . . . And so liberalism had become a habit of Stepan Arkadyevitch's, and he liked his newspaper, as he did his cigar after dinner, for the slight fog it diffused in his brain.

Stepan, while his good-natured gregariousness makes him seem like a modern middle-class American, is not fully other-directed. This gregariousness alone, without a certain sensitivity to others as individuals and as a source of direction, is not the identifying trait. Just so, we must differentiate the nineteenth-century American—gregarious and subservient to public opinion though he was found to be by Tocqueville, Bryce, and others—from the other-directed American as he emerges today, an American who in his character is more capable of and more interested in maintaining responsive contact with others both at work and at play. This point needs to be emphasized, since the distinction is easily misunderstood. The inner-directed person, though he often sought and sometimes achieved a relative independence of public opinion and of what the neighbors thought of him, was in most cases very much concerned with his good repute and, at least in America, with "keeping up with the Joneses." These conformities, however, were primarily external, typified in such details as clothes, curtains, and bank credit. For, indeed, the conformities were to a standard, evidence of which was provided by the "best people" in one's milieu. In contrast with this pattern, the other-directed person, though he has his eye very much on the Joneses, aims to keep up with them not so much in external details as in the quality of his inner experience. That is, his great sensitivity keeps him in touch with others on many more levels than the externals of appearance and propriety. Nor does any ideal of independence or of reliance on

God alone modify his desire to look to the others—and the "good guys" as well as the best people—for guidance in what experiences to seek and in how to interpret them.

The Three Types Compared

One way to see the structural differences between the three types is to see the differences in the emotional sanction or control in each type.

The tradition-directed person feels the impact of his culture as a unit, but it is nevertheless mediated through the specific, small number of individuals with whom he is in daily contact. These expect of him not so much that he be a certain type of person but that he behave in the approved way. Consequently the sanction for behavior tends to be the fear of being *shamed*.

The inner-directed person has early incorporated a psychic gyroscope which is set going by his parents and can receive signals later on from other authorities who resemble his parents. He goes through life less independent than he seems, obeying this internal piloting. Getting off course, whether in response to inner impulses or to the fluctuating voices of contemporaries, may lead to the feeling of *guilt*.

Since the direction to be taken in life has been learned in the privacy of the home from a small number of guides and since principles, rather than details of behavior, are internalized, the inner-directed person is capable of great stability. Especially so when it turns out that his fellows have gyroscopes too, spinning at the same speed and set in the same direction. But many inner-directed individuals can remain stable even when the reinforcement of social approval is not available—as in the upright life of the stock Englishman isolated in the tropics.

Contrasted with such a type as this, the other-directed person learns to respond to signals from a far wider circle than is constituted by his parents. The family is no longer a closely knit unit to which he belongs but merely part of a wider social environment to which he early becomes attentive. In these respects the other-directed person resembles the tradition-directed person: both live in a group milieu and lack the inner-directed person's capacity to go it alone. The nature of this group milieu, however, differs radically in the two cases. The other-directed person is cosmopolitan. For him the border between the familiar and the strange—a border clearly marked in the societies depending on tradition-direction—has broken down. As the family continuously absorbs the strange and so reshapes itself, so the strange becomes familiar. While the inner-directed person could be "at home abroad" by virtue of his relative insensitivity to others, the other-directed person is, in a sense, at home everywhere and nowhere, capable of a rapid if sometimes superficial intimacy with and response to everyone.

The tradition-directed person takes his signals from others, but they come in a cultural monotone; he needs no complex receiving equipment to pick them up. The other-directed person must be able to receive signals from far and near; the sources are many, the changes rapid. What can be internalized, then, is not a code of behavior but the elaborate equipment needed to attend to such messages and occasionally to participate in their circulation. As against guilt-and-shame controls, though of course these survive, one prime psychological lever of the other-directed person is a diffuse *anxiety*. This control equipment, instead of being like a gyroscope, is like a radar.[9]

The Case of Athens

Could other civilizations, such as the ancient Hebrew, Greek, and Roman, also be characterized at successive stages in their population-subsistence development as tradition-directed, inner-directed, and other-directed? In all likelihood the tremendous growth of world population since about 1650—and consequently the S-curve of population growth—is unique in the history of mankind and the consequence of an altogether new (industrialized) type of technological, economic, and social organization. Nonetheless, the fact that every society has some form of organization and some "technology," be it the most unscientific ritual, constitutes proof of an effort, more or less successful, to bring down the death rate and improve the standard of living over that of mere animal existence. And an exploratory study of the Athenian empire suggests that there, too, a correlation between population growth and social character of the type we have described for the recent West may be discerned.[10]

What scant evidence we have of the long-term trend of population growth in the empire must be derived from the patient studies of present-day demographers and from the remarks of ancient Greek authors. The Homeric epics depict a volatile society in which the institution of private property had already disrupted the tradition-directed communal organization of tribe, phratry, and clan. Revolutionary improvements in cultivation of the soil, made possible by continued settlement in one place, increased the standard of living and, as a corollary, initiated a phase of population growth that was to continue for several centuries. Private ownership, the development of an exchange economy, and the patrilineal inheritance of property encouraged the concentration of wealth and produced economic and social inequality. A new, three-fold social stratification interpenetrated the traditional organization and not only loosened the hold of the clan upon its members but also encouraged the coalescence of individuals with like economic status from different tribes and phratries. The reform measures taken by Solon and others in succeeding generations also clearly imply that some individuals and families were far more successful than others in achieving the new economic goals of leisure and material wealth.

During the five hundred years after the founding of the Athenian state there seems to have existed an expanding "frontier" economy, based in part

[9] The "radar" metaphor was suggested by Karl Wittfogel.
[10] The following discussion draws on an unpublished monograph by Sheila Spaulding, "Prolegomena to the Study of Athenian Democracy" (Yale Law School Library, 1949).

upon the exploitation of internal resources, made possible by technological improvement and the institution of slavery, and in greater part upon the conquest of other peoples and the incorporation of their wealth into the domestic economy. One might well adduce as indications of inner-direction during this period the changing attitudes toward the family and the upbringing of children; the laws which enhanced the freedom of the individual, for example, the significant reforms which permitted the free alienation of property and the initiation of a criminal prosecution by a "third party"; the multiplication of opportunities for profitable employment in commerce, agriculture, and industry; the drift from country to city; the enthusiasm for exploration and conquest; and the increasing interest in philosophic speculation and science.

By the turn of the fifth century the Athenian empire had reached the zenith of its power; and the Greeks of this period were familiar with the idea of an expanding population. Both Plato and Aristotle advocated a stationary population. Two centuries later we find that the problem has radically shifted and the fear of overpopulation has been replaced by the fear of depopulation. Polybius, writing in the second century, declared that the population of Greece was dying out because of the practice of infanticide. This is undoubtedly an overstatement; infanticide was confined, as contraception tends to be today, largely to the upper and upper middle classes. Nevertheless, it indicates the trend toward artificial limitation of the size of the family and suggests that the population had reached the period not only of incipient but of actual decline. It is as an expanding population begins to reach its peak that we see the rise of social forms that seem to indicate the presence of the other-directed mode of conformity.

For example, the institution of ostracism, introduced as a means of preventing tyranny, became in the fifth century a formidable weapon of public opinion, wielded capriciously as a means of insuring conformity of taste and "cutting down to size" those statesmen, playwrights, and orators of markedly superior ability. In addition, the common people produced a numerous brood of informers "who were constantly accusing the better and most influential men in the State, with a view to subjecting them to the envy of the multitude." In *The Jealousy of the Gods and Criminal Law in Athens* Svend Ranulf has meticulously traced the incidence and development of the "disinterested tendency to inflict punishment" which, based upon a diffuse characterological anxiety, could perhaps be described as the ascendancy of an omnipotent "peer-group."

All this was accompanied by a decline in inner-directed dutifulness toward the political sphere. In spite of the deference shown by many authors to Athenian "democracy" of the fifth century, one is struck by the apathy of the voting population. What had earlier been a hard-won privilege of the lower classes—attendance at the ecclesia or popular assembly—became during the rule of the demos an obligation. Various punitive measures were introduced to insure a quorum; and when these failed, the "right to vote" became a paid service to the state.

Here in the history of the Athenian empire we have an area in which more detailed research and analysis might very profitably be undertaken; obviously, no more has been done in these remarks than to suggest certain problems that would be relevant for such research. Similarly, the problems of Rome during the reign of Augustus suggest the emergence and ascendancy of the other-directed character type as the population reached the phase of incipient decline. The importation of a new poetic language legitimating the importance of subtle states of personal feeling, in the Alexandrian-influenced work of such poets as Catullus, and probably Gallus, may evidence shifts toward other-direction in the dominant classes.

Some Necessary Qualifications

The limitations of language lead me to speak as if I saw societies as always managing to produce the social organization and character types they need in order to survive. Such an assumption, raising the image of a separate body, "society," making certain demands on people and testing out various processes, would introduce an unwarranted teleology into social change. What seems to happen is that by sheer "accident" any of a number of ways of insuring charac-terological conformity may exist in a given society. Those which have been suc-cessful in preserving a coherent society are transmitted as unconsciously as they arose; but, since by their historical success they present themselves for study and investigation, it appears as if some teleological force, serving the interest of society, has introduced the successful—or fairly successful—mode of insuring conformity. Yet we must recognize that societies do disintegrate and die out despite what may appear to be successful methods of insuring character per-petuation. Correspondingly, we must not deny the probability that societies can tolerate, even without disintegration, much more disorganization and even ruin than many people recognize.

We must not overestimate the role of character in the social process. It is not a sufficient explanation, for instance, to say, as some students have said, that the German army held together because "the Germans" had an authoritarian character, since armies of very diverse character type do in fact hold together under given conditions of battle and supply. Nor will it do to assume, as American aptitude-testers sometimes do, that certain jobs can be successfully handled only by a narrowly limited range of character types: that we need "ex-trovert" or "oral" salesmen and administrators, and "introvert" or "anal" chem-ists and accountants. Actually, people of radically different types can adapt themselves to perform, adequately enough, a wide variety of complex tasks. Or, to put the same thing in another way, social institutions can harness a gamut of different motivations, springing from different character types, to perform very much the same kinds of socially demanded jobs. And yet, of course, this is not to say that character is merely a shadowy factor in history, like some Hegelian spirit. Character will affect the style and psychic costs of job per-formances that, in economic or political analysis, look almost identical.

Thus we are forced to take account of the possibility that people may be compelled to behave in one way although their character structure presses them to behave in the opposite way. Society may change more rapidly than character, or vice versa. Indeed, this disparity between socially required behavior and characterologically compatible behavior is one of the great levers of change. Fortunately we know of no society like the one glumly envisaged by Aldous Huxley in *Brave New World*, where the social character types have been completely content in their social roles and where consequently, barring accident, no social change exists.

Finally, it is necessary to point out that social character types are abstractions. They refer back to the living, concrete human being, and in order to arrive at them, as we saw at the beginning of this chapter, it is necessary first to abstract from the real individual his "personality," then to abstract from that his "character," finally to abstract from that the common element that forms "social character."

In fact, the discerning reader may already have realized that in the nature of the case there can be no such thing as a society or a person wholly dependent on tradition-direction, inner-direction, or other-direction: each of these modes of conformity is universal, and the question is always one of the degree to which an individual or a social group places reliance on one or another of the three available mechanisms. Thus, all human beings are inner-directed in the sense that, brought up as they are by people older than themselves, they have acquired and internalized some permanent orientations from them. And, conversely, all human beings are other-directed in the sense that they are oriented to the expectations of their peers and to the "field situation" (Kurt Lewin) or "definition of the situation" (W. I. Thomas) that these peers at any moment help to create.[11]

Since, furthermore, each of us possesses the capacity for each of the three modes of conformity, it is possible that an individual may change, in the course of his life, from greater dependence on one combination of modes to greater dependence on another (though radical shifts of this kind, even when circumstances encourage them, are unlikely). For, unless individuals are completely crazy—and, indeed, they are never *completely* crazy—they both organize the cues in their social environment and attend to those cues. Thus, if a predomi-

---

11 In this connection, it is revealing to compare the conceptions of the socialization process held by Freud and Harry Stack Sullivan. Freud saw the superego as the internalized source of moral life-directions, built in the image of the awesome parents, and transferred thereafter to parent-surrogates such as God, the Leader, Fate. Sullivan does not deny this happens but puts more emphasis on the role of the peer-group—the chum and group of chums who take such a decisive hand in the socialization of the American child. Sullivan's very insistence on the importance of interpersonal relations—which led him to believe, much more than Freud, in the adaptability of men and the possibilities of social peace and harmony—may itself be viewed as a symptom of the shift toward other-direction.

nantly other-directed individual were placed in an environment without peers, he might fall back on other patterns of direction. Similarly, it is clear that no individual, and assuredly no society, ever exists without a heavy reliance on tradition, much as this may appear to be overlaid by swings of fashion.

It is important to emphasize these overlappings of the several types in part because of the value judgments that readers are likely to attach to each type in isolation. Since most of us value independence we are likely to prefer the inner-directed type and overlook two things. First, the gyroscopic mechanism allows the inner-directed person to appear far more independent than he really is: he is no less a conformist to others than the other-directed person, but the voices to which he listens are more distant, of an older generation, their cues internalized in his childhood. Second, as just indicated, this type of conformity is only one, though the predominant, mechanism of the inner-directed type: the latter is not characteristically insensitive to what his peers think of him, and may even be opportunistic in the highest degree. Thus, he need not always react to other people as if they were merely stand-ins for his parents. Rather, the point is that he is somewhat less concerned than the other-directed person with continuously obtaining from contemporaries (or their stand-ins: the mass media) a flow of guidance, expectation, and approbation.

Let me repeat: the types of character and society dealt with in this book are *types*: they do not exist in reality, but are a construction, based on a selection of certain historical problems for investigation. By employing more types, or subtypes, one could take account of more facts (or mayhap, the same facts with less violence!), but my collaborators and I have preferred to work with a minimum of scaffolding; throughout, in seeking to describe by one interrelated set of characteristics both a society and its typical individuals, we have looked for features that connect the two and ignored those aspects of behavior—often striking—which did not seem relevant to our task.

LIONEL TRILLING

Review of Riesman's *The Lonely Crowd*[1]

David Riesman's *The Lonely Crowd* seems to me one of the most important books about America to have been published in recent times. And quite apart from the particularity of its subject, it is one of the most interesting books I have ever read.

This is very large praise, and as I write it I find myself wondering whether

[1] From *A Gathering of Fugitives* by Lionel Trilling (Boston: The Beacon Press, 1956), pp. 107-112. Copyright, 1956, by Lionel Trilling. Reprinted by permission of the Beacon Press and of Martin Secker & Warburg, Limited.

I may not be overstating the case for this sociological study in order to counter-act the antagonisms to the social sciences which I know to be pretty common among people who like literature very much. But I do not think I am saying more than I mean. My opinion was formed before I ever thought of writing about Mr. Riesman's book and I have tested it by more than one reading.

Yet since I have raised the question of the literary suspiciousness of the social sciences, especially sociology, it might be well to take it specifically into account in connection with *The Lonely Crowd.*

One reason for this suspiciousness is that sociology tends to use a kind of language which must arouse antagonism in people who are at all sensitive to language. This is not because the language of sociology is scientific but because it is often pseudo-scientific and jargonistic and has the effect of giving a false value to ideas that are simple and platitudinous. To any such charge *The Lonely Crowd* is certainly not liable. Mr. Riesman uses two terms that some might boggle at—he speaks of people as being "inner-directed" and "other-directed." But I do not know how else he could denominate the two categories of character that are essential to his thought. In general the book is precisely a work of literature in the old comprehensive sense of the word according to which Hume's essays are literature, or Gibbon's history, or Tocqueville's *Democracy in America.*

Another objection is that sociology is likely to be tendentious without admit-ting it is, and that it proceeds on unexamined assumptions while insisting that it is wholly objective. But we can count on Mr. Riesman's objectivity because he admits his subjectivity and the hypothetical nature of his enterprise. He is under no illusion of scientific neutrality. He admires certain human qualities and makes no bones about wanting them to be influential in our national life.

Then it is said, and with justice, that sociology often gives the appearance of denying personal autonomy. What is more, much sociological investigation has for its avowed aim the discovery of how to manipulate human behavior in clandestine ways. But Mr. Riesman's book is as far as it can be from denying the possibility of autonomy without denying the inescapable limits of civilized society. Its whole effort, indeed, is directed toward the affirmation of the possi-bility of autonomy.

People of literary inclinations, I believe, have a natural jealousy of sociology because it seems to be in process of taking over from literature one of litera-ture's most characteristic functions, the investigation and criticism of morals and manners. Yet it is but fair to remark that sociology has preempted only what literature has voluntarily surrendered. Twenty years ago, when the Lynds produced their famous study, *Middletown,* it was possible to say that with all their staff and paraphernalia they had not really told us more about American life than we had learned from a solitary insightful observer, which is what some sociologists call a novelist—they had done no more than confirm *Babbitt* by statistics. Since that time, however, few novelists have added anything genuinely new to our knowledge of American life. But the sociologists have, and Mr. Reisman, writing with a sense of social actuality which Scott Fitzgerald might have envied, does literature a service by suggesting to the novelists that there are new and wonderfully arable social fields for them to till.

The research from which *The Lonely Crowd* developed began as an investigation of the social causes of political attitudes, specifically that of apathy to politics. The book does not consist of conclusions drawn from this research but was written in the course of the still continuing enterprise as the hypothesis on which the research might proceed. In its simplest form this hypothesis consists of the statement that there has been a change in the character of the American people, that where once men whose character was "inner-directed" were dominant in our culture, the tendency is now toward the dominance of men of "other-directed" character. Inner-directed persons are those who internalize adult authority, most notably the ideals and demands of their parents. Other-directed persons are those whose character is formed chiefly by their contemporaries and peers, the formation beginning as soon as they enter social life in play or at school.

Something of the nature of the inner-directed man may be understood from the phrase which, in the nineteenth century, he so often made his motto—"*Ad astra per aspera*," through difficulties to the seemingly unattainable heights. The old tag might also be translated, "To the heights by means of asperity," for a kind of asperity marks the dealings of the inner-directed man with the world, his fellow-men, and himself. The man of business as well as the scientific or artistic genius, or the religious leader, or the philosopher, were all at one in their submission to inner-direction. The belief that energy, self-control, and self-reverence would achieve miracles was held not only by the dullest spirits of the age but also by the noblest. We must think of the Alger books as being the expression not merely of a strenuous philistinism but of a general culture in which strenuousness was valued in all walks of life. There was a connection between the passions of a Bounderby and a Beethoven.

In America, even as far back as Tocqueville's visit, there was always a tendency for inner-direction to be modified by what Tocqueville regarded as an extravagant awareness of the opinion of others. Emerson believed that this tendency constituted a prime threat to the American spirit and he never wearied of warning his countrymen that Self Reliance—his name for inner-direction—was sadly on the wane. Yet in nineteenth century America the "hardness of the material" still called for a large measure of inner-direction— there were still frontiers to be conquered, social forms to be imposed or broken, technology to be established. It was still useful to idealize "faith," the belief that one's personal vision was right no matter how the world mocked it. School children were assiduously taught in their readers that the heroic man was one who followed his gleam, and that society as a whole was likely to be stupid, retrograde, and cowardly, as witness its treatment of Columbus. And in the poem that every child learned, it was right of Columbus, and not arrogant or undemocratic of him, to say, "Sail on! Sail on!" when his men begged him to turn back. To be "misunderstood," to be alone with one's rightness and virtue, was the stuff of the dreams of youth.

But in the early years of the twentieth century—around 1920, Mr. Riesman believes—the inner-directed character began to lose its ascendancy. The hard, resistant materiality of the world no longer supplied the goal and validated the hard, strenuous will of inner-directed people. Children were less impelled to establish the old parental authority within themselves—parents were less certain of how to establish it in their children and of whether it ought to be established at all. It was by no means clear that the old standards applied to the new kind of work. For in the degree that work had less to do with *things*, it had more to do with *people*. In Mr. Riesman's phrase, the interest shifted from the hardness of the material to the softness of the personnel, and the arts of personality, by which one could manipulate one's fellows or win valuable approval from them, because more important to more people than the direct force of the will exerted upon material difficulties. And children increasingly formed their characters according to the demands of their playmates and schoolmates, equipping themselves with a quick, unconscious sensitivity to the judgment of others—they became increasingly other-directed.

The evidence of this new means of character-formation is manifest in every discussion of juvenile or adolescent social behavior, in which it is always taken for granted that parents are virtually helpless before the power of the child-society. And indeed this power is supported and rationalized by the family and the school, which, on theories of normality and adjustment, second the anxious antagonism which the child-society directs upon any show of difference. For the group life of contemporary children achieves its particular kind of democracy by suppressing special interests and abilities (except in athletics) and by prohibiting the display of vanity or ambition. Even before the child is ready for sociability, his life in literature has prepared him for social adjustment and conformity. *Scuffy the Tugboat* instructs him in the dangers of the Columbus principle, while *Tootle the Engine* leads him to believe that he must not fail to be like all the other little engines and never leave the track to stray into green fields, like a horse.

The ideal of behavior which is indigenous to the social life of the modern child is the model and perhaps the mold of the ideal of adults, at least of the middle class. We are coming to be a civilization in which overt ambition, aggression, and competition are at a discount. Not, of course, that the sources of natural aggression are drying up or that people no longer seek prestige. But self-aggrandizement takes new forms as the ideals of other-direction become increasingly compelling. Overt ambition gives way to what Mr. Riesman calls antagonistic co-operation, which implies affability, blandness, a lively sensitivity to the opinion of the group, the suppression of asperity. Social differences must be minimized as far as possible. Wealth must depreciate itself, and must seek to express itself not in symbols of power but in fineness of taste. Food is ordered less for the old-fashioned virtues of substantiality and abundance, than for the new charms of elegance and artistry—but in this limited space it is impossible to follow Mr. Riesman in the fascinating detail of his description of the cultural changes which other-direction is instituting.

The general opinion is not likely to be in accord with Mr. Riesman—the general opinion is that our culture is marked by an especially fierce and open competitiveness, an unmasked aggressiveness, a crude assertiveness. This is the received idea of a great deal of our literature and of our progressive social thought. It is the pious certainty of Europe, constituting, one sometimes feels, the larger part of the European social and political thought of the moment. And Mr. Riesman's students at the University of Chicago tell him that American life resembles the grim, paranoid Dobu culture or the competitive conspicuously-consuming Kwakiutl culture—none ever finds any resemblance to the peaceable, co-operative Pueblo Indians, although *all* of them wish they could.

I am sure that it is Mr. Riesman who is in the right of the matter. My own experience in teaching confirms his, one incident in particular. For some time I had been increasingly aware that my students had no very great admiration for Stendahl's *The Red and the Black,* gave it nothing like the response that it had had from my college generation. Then one day a whole class, almost all its members gifted men, agreed in saying that they were bored by Julien Sorel and didn't like him. Bored by Julien Sorel! But didn't he, I asked, represent their own desires for preeminence, their own natural young ambition? They snubbed me with their answer and fixed between themselves and me the great gulf of the generations: they did not, they said, understand ambition of Julien's self-referring kind; what they wanted was a decent, socially useful co-operative work to do. I felt like an aging Machiavelli among the massed secretariat of the U.N.

Young men of this kind certainly do not represent anything like the full development of the other-directed character which Mr. Riesman describes. It is even possible that their rejection of the extreme inner-direction of Julien Sorel is not so much in favor of other-direction as of the "autonomous" character which Mr. Riesman proposes as the possible optimum of our culture. More likely, however, they represent a compromise between inner-direction and other-direction. As such they make a spectacle which in many ways is very attractive.

But the tendency of other-direction does not stop with the character of these young men. And the consequences of its fuller development are disquieting. Mr Riesman remarks that he has found it almost impossible to make a comparison of the two forms of character-direction without making inner-direction seem the more attractive of the two. I don't agree with Mr. Riesman that the preference is a mere prejudice which we must guard against. Granting all that is to be said against the tendency of inner-direction to cut itself off from what is warm and personal, granting too all that may be said for what other-direction does to refine leisure and consumption, it is still inner-direction that must seem the more fully human, even in its excess. Mr. Riesman himself seems to be saying something of this sort when, in speaking of the autonomous character, he remarks that the inner-directed character more closely resembles it than does the other-directed, and that, indeed, it is easier for inner-directed people to approach actual autonomy.

It is in any case true, on Mr. Riesman's showing, that the political life is far more likely to be healthy in a culture in which inner-direction is dominant. The exacerbated sense of others, of oneself in relation to others, does not, it seems, make for the sense of the polity. On the contrary—other-direction is concomitant with a sense of powerlessness in political matters, and this impotence masks itself in many ways, often as hatred or of contempt for politics. This in turn is easily rationalized into a desire for metapolitics, for a perfect and absolute form of government which shall make impossible the conflict of wills of actual politics.

And the apathy which marks our political life lies as a threat beneath all the life of other-direction. Social approval and the desire for it are not love, nor even friendship, nor even community. The life of leisure, of fun, of narcissism, of right choice among the articles of consumption, of sex as the "last frontier" of adventure, of bland adjustment—this life is at every moment susceptible to the cankering boredom which lies beneath its surface.

This is not, I must make clear, the note on which Mr. Riesman ends. It is one of his decisive intellectual virtues that he has no love for the opiate of pessimism. He is not charmed by apocalyptic visions. It is not the end of a culture that he has undertaken to describe but a moment in its history.

CLINTON ROSSITER

The Legacy of John Adams [1]

The most revealing sign of the present American mood is our universal habit of appealing to tradition. Despite our youth as a nation, or more probably because of it, we have always been fond of rituals and slogans that bind us to the legendary dead. Now, in an age of anxious hesitation, we shout our devotion to the American tradition in every corner and courthouse and classroom throughout the land. Never have we searched more purposefully among our ancestors for deeds that inspire and words that comfort; never have we been so diligent in summoning the past to light up the present.

We have been inspired and comforted but hardly enlightened by our devotion to the great men who shaped our tradition. For many Americans the appeal to Jefferson and Lincoln has become a substitute for thought, for many

[1] From *The Yale Review* No. 4 (June, 1957), 528-550, with omissions. Copyright by *The Yale Review*, 1957. Reprinted by permission of *The Yale Review*.

a refuge from reality; and for all of us it is a weapon that is easy to wield and hard to parry, and therefore a weapon we wield at our peril.

Yet the appeal can be immensely rewarding if tempered with caution and common sense. If we look at our great men with quizzical affection, if we take their measure with honesty as well as piety, if we recognize their blunders even as we delight in their glories, we will find that they have far more to give us than we have hitherto imagined. Indeed, I make bold to say that we have only begun to assess the legacies of deed and word that are ours to enjoy in trust, and that when we have assessed them in good faith, as honorable trustees, we will be prepared as never before to attack our problems confidently in the spirit of liberty.

I should like to make such an assessment of John Adams of Massachusetts, whose legacy to modern America has rested too long in the vaults of indifference and hostility. Adams is rarely admitted, except as an afterthought, to the inmost circle with Washington, Jefferson, Franklin, Hamilton, Marshall, Lincoln, and Lee; and even when admitted he is left standing by himself, shy and perplexing, over to one side. We make a huge mistake in treating John Adams so casually, for in this age of conservatism he has as much to teach us as any American who ever lived.

Certainly he passes all the rigorous tests that a man must pass to be considered the source and symbol of a legacy for modern Americans. He was somebody: a founding father without whose help the founding might have miscarried. He stood for something: the old and tried American virtues of which we can never have enough in public life. He believed in something and found words to express it: a political faith that lies at the core of the American tradition.

Adams himself, in a typically masochistic letter to Benjamin Rush in 1809, predicted neglect if not oblivion for his name and deeds: "Mausoleums, statues, monuments will never be erected to me. . . . Panegyrical romances will never be written, nor flattering orations spoken to transmit me to posterity in brilliant colors."

He had a right to be a little sorry for himself in the first years of his retirement, for no one had labored more devotedly for freedom through all the years from 1765 to 1801, and no one had reaped less public acclaim. Major figure in Boston's resistance to the Stamp Act, "Atlas of Independence" in the Continental Congress, administrator and diplomat of the Revolution, author of the celebrated Massachusetts Constitution of 1779, Vice-President and President of the United States—Adams gave more of himself to the new Republic than did any other man except Washington. Had the Navy, in Jefferson's words, not "always been his hobby horse," had he not practiced the arts of diplomacy in Holland so fruitfully in 1782, had he not appointed John Marshall to be Chief Justice in 1801, the course of American history would have flowed less smoothly to grandeur. Had he followed any other President but Washington, had he come earlier to suspect the perfidy of his closest associates in the Presidency, above all had he been present at the Convention of 1787, the course of his own history would have flowed more directly to fame. But the Adamses have never done things easily, and the first Adams would probably be less surprised than embarrassed to learn that someone is still trying to elevate him to his proper seat in our patriotic heaven.

Two events in Adams's career seem especially pertinent to an assessment of his legacy: the defense in 1770 of Captain Thomas Preston and the eight soldiers of the Twenty-ninth Regiment, who found their place in history by being panicked into perpetrating the Boston Massacre, and the move in 1799 for peace with France in defiance of Alexander Hamilton's dreams of empire. It took rare independence of judgment for a leader of the patriot cause to seek justice for Preston; it took dogged courage for a Federalist President to reopen negotiations with the French Directory. But independence and courage were qualities of which Adams had a double portion, and on these two widely separated occasions he played his favorite role—the unpopular man—with relish and success. Of all his hundreds of deeds and services these, I am certain, are what he would have called "the most splendid diamonds" in his legacy to our America. They show him in his best colors; they bring him very near to a generation faced with much the same kind of dangers and problems. . . .

On other occasions, to be sure, he was led astray by these traits. Certainly he would get higher marks from history if he had been more tactful and flexible in his missions to France during the Revolution, more faithful to his better nature in the sordid drama of the Alien and Sedition Acts. The most fatal blunder of his entire career was an act of omission: the failure, perhaps unavoidable under the circumstances, to name his own chief lieutenants when he was raised to the Presidency in 1797. By taking over in its entirety a Cabinet chosen by Washington and, for the most part, loyal to Hamilton, he doomed his Presidency to disorder and early sorrow. The most disquieting event was a case of plain bad manners: the departure from Washington in the early hours of March 4, 1801. He made up for this offense many times over in his wonderful correspondence with Jefferson over the last fourteen years of their lives, but there will always be something a little mean about that angry, weary exit from Washington.

In the end, his many triumphs and few failures are swallowed up in the paramount fact that he fulfilled the conservative mission with genuine distinction. All our historians have written of "the ebb and flow of American politics," of the providential way in which seasons of progressivism and conservatism have succeeded one another throughout our history. But few have really understood and therefore admitted gracefully the necessity of recurring conservatism. As a result, most of them have failed to estimate properly the immense service of thoughtful conservatives to the cause of liberty and progress. It can be argued that the seasons of conservatism should be short and very occasional; it can even be argued that conservatives should always be in a minority. But it cannot be denied that men like Adams have an essential task to perform, that without their steadying hand the Republic might long ago have foundered on the shoals of innovation.

It is no easy thing, even for an Adams, to be an unwavering conservative. The reasonable man is asked to distrust reason, the kindly man to counsel patience in the face of suffering, the sensitive man to expose himself to the slings of the Jacobins and the arrows of the Tories; and Adams, be it remembered, was a reasonable, kindly, sensitive man. Yet he went upon the conservative mission with considerable enthusiasm, and he could measure his success in the scars on his tough old spirit. For his pains in opposing the innovators of every stripe, for despising Hamilton's vision of Detroit and doubting Jefferson's dreams of Arcady, he became a favorite target of extremists on the right as well as the left. Modern conservatives, still caught in the crossfire, may draw comfort from his stout example.

Adams was, as Lord Howe once said in his presence, a "decided character," a unique bundle of strengths and weaknesses. Indeed, so admirable were his strengths and so deplorable his weaknesses that one is often tempted to think of him as two people. He was, by universal report, a man of immense virtue, and thus especially worthy of contemplation by men who forget that free government is primarily an exercise in practical ethics. I have already touched upon his most compelling qualities, independence and courage, and I would be laboring the obvious to insist that he never ran with the pack and never played the coward.

His other virtues are spread upon the records of the age: old-fashioned integrity, old-fashioned even in his time, for he would have none of the fad for speculation in land and paper; equally old-fashioned simplicity, which led him to yearn amid scenes of splendor for "a frock and trowsers, a hoe and a spade"; industry and frugality, the Yankee formula for freedom, which he applied with a consistency that would have frightened Franklin; and Christian charity, which tempered the harshness of an often intolerant mind with the kindness of an always understanding heart. Perhaps his most remarkable trait was the urge to probe the conduct and motives of John Adams.

A moderate in most things, he often failed to use moderation in these inquests into his own character. He had much too lively a sense of persecution, much too perverse a desire to be misunderstood, much too developed a talent for self-debasement; and this intemperance in judging himself certainly impaired his usefulness as a public servant. Indeed, it is this aspect of his character that makes it difficult to love John Adams. One does not embrace lightly the man who wore the scratchiest hair shirt over the thinnest skin in American history. Adams, of course, would suspect our motives for embracing him at all. If he was hard on others, he was even harder on himself. If other men found him vain, tactless, pompous, and self-righteous, he found himself even more of a prickly pear. When Franklin wrote from France that Adams was "always an honest man, often a wise one, but sometimes, and in some things, absolutely out of his senses," he was saying something that Adams had known about himself for years.

It seems irreverent to pin a label on a man like John Adams, yet I would suggest that he cannot be adequately understood except as a model of genuine conservatism. He responded to conservative urges, he formed conservative habits, he cherished conservative virtues, he lived a conservative life. He was reverent if not always pious, self-disciplined if not always self-contained; and he admired prudence greatly even when he failed to display it. His sense of history, the greatest of teachers, was keen; his devotion to tradition, the essence of wisdom, was respectful; his reliance on an unknowable God was a tribute to his ancestors and to his humility. Finally, his concern for the public interest, sustained by spotless patriotism and expressed in years of ill-rewarded service, was the sign of a true if entirely self-made aristocrat.

The richest portion of Adams's legacy lies in his writings on men and politics. Had he never left Boston to hazard all for independence, he would still be a man for us to mark and cherish, for buried in the massive accretion of sixty years of ceaseless speculation is a genuine treasure: a full-bodied political theory, one of the few ever produced in this country. So rich is this treasure in insight, so impressive in scope, that most historians of the American mind agree that Adams has no master, and no peers except Calhoun, Madison, and Jefferson, among political thinkers on this side of the Atlantic. He loved the study of government—to him "no romance was more entertaining"—and his writings radiate an enthusiasm that must infect even the hostile reader.

The sources of Adams's thought are of special interest, for no other man in that glorious age of learned statesmen ranged farther afield for instruction and inspiration. One need only peek at random in the "Defence of the Constitutions" and watch the long parade of philosophers and historians go slogging by to realize that Adams was a scholar with few equals in his time. Like all his fellows he was essentially an English thinker; unlike most of them he was proud to acknowledge it. He never, in all his rambles through the learning of the ages, cut himself off from Locke, Milton, Sidney, Bolingbroke, and Harrington. He went to school with the ancient writers, especially Aristotle, Cicero, and Polybius. He learned much from Montesquieu and Adam Smith, even more from Hobbes, Hume, and Machiavelli, although from the last three he accepted nothing that might corrupt his ethical approach to the problem of political power. He remained to the end a sound Whig for whom the higher law of Cicero, the constitutionalism of Locke, and the republicanism of Harrington were the sum of political wisdom.

His purpose, too, remained steadfast from the "Dissertation on the Canon and Feudal Law" in 1765 to his last letter to Jefferson sixty years later: to defend intelligently, with learning as well as with reverence, a social and political order that he found, even in his more fanciful moments, the best of all possible worlds. His constant theme was the preservation, not the achievement or even the expansion, of human liberty, and the nature of his thought reflected this high purpose. . . . It can best be described as deeply, bitterly antiideological. A champion at sneering, Adams saved his most truculent sneers for those he labeled the "ideologians," the "prophets of progress" like Condorcet and Turgot who ignored experience out of deference to hope and worshiped pure reason as the essence of wisdom. Theirs was "the wildest philosophy which was ever professed in this world, since the building of Babel." His was the sanest, the product of "facts, observations, and experiments."

The core of Adams's political thought was an austere opinion of the nature of man compounded of skepticism, distrust, pity, and charity. Rejecting alike the dogma of total depravity he had been taught in his youth and the vision of total innocence he had been tempted with in France, Adams found man a wondrous blend of ennobling excellencies and degrading imperfections. The blend was universal: all men, even the thrice-blessed Americans, were bundles of virtue and vice. It was constant: no amount of social progress would ever drive weakness and wickedness from the hearts of men. And it was weighted heavily against innocence: men's virtues were few and largely a product of nurture; their vices were many and largely a product of nature.

Adams had nothing unusual to say about the identity of these virtues and vices. Like most of his learned colleagues in the founding of the Republic, he gave man credit for a social nature, innate dignity, "benevolence and general affections," a desire for freedom, and—the grace that saves man and makes civilization possible—an astounding capacity for education. He was only a little more truculent than his circle in calling attention to the irrationality, selfishness, indolence, and avarice that lurk eternally beneath the veneer of civilized behavior. But he turned out from the familiar path of early American thought— under the guidance, be it noted, of Adam Smith—by insisting that the "passion for distinction" and the "love of power" were the supreme urges in the human spirit. Adams was not the least surprised or distressed by this discovery. To be sure, these two closely related impulses had been the cause of trouble since the world began, but they had also been the cause of freedom and progress. In his opinion, the forces holding the balance in every man's heart between good and evil—the desire to be esteemed and the urge to dominate—were pointed always in both directions. Properly restrained and directed, they might lead to liberty by way of ambition; unrestrained and misdirected, they were sure to lead to tyranny by way of corruption. It was the quest of political science to find ways to harness these urges to virtuous and fruitful ends.

Adams gave some of his best thoughts to the problem of equality, especially in his late letters to John Taylor of Caroline, and there can be no mistaking the nature and implications of his views. For him the blunt fact of inequality among men was no less certain, and no less essential "for the order of society, and the benefit of mankind," than the twin passions for distinction and domination. A life-long member of the school of natural law and natural rights, Adams conceded gratefully the fact of moral equality. All men were created equal; all were equal in the sight of God; all were entitled to be treated as ends and not means. But, as he wrote to Taylor at the height of their celebrated debate:

> To teach that all men are born with equal powers and faculties, to equal influence in society, to equal property and advantages through life, is as gross a fraud, as glaring an imposition on the credulity of the people, as ever was practised by monks, by Druids, by Brahmins, by priests of the immortal Lama, or by the self-styled philosophers of the French revolution. For honour's sake, Mr. Taylor, for truth and virtue's sake, let American philosophers and politicians despise it.

Even his "dearest friend" Abigail had to listen to lectures on this favorite subject:

> By the law of nature, all men are men, and not angels—men, and not lions—men, and not whales—men, and not eagles—that is, they are all of the same species; and this is the most that the equality of nature amounts to. But man differs by nature from man, almost as much as man from beast. The equality of nature is moral and political only, and means that all men are independent. But a physical inequality, an intellectual inequality, of the most serious kind, is established unchangeably by the Author of nature; and society has a right to establish any other inequalities it may judge necessary for its good.

Adams would have insisted that this last comment be interpreted narrowly. What I am sure he meant is this: that sharp inequalities in "strength, stature, activity, courage, hardiness, industry, patience, ingenuity, wealth, knowledge, fame, wit, temperance, constancy, and wisdom" will arise in every society; that the silent workings of prescription will translate these into accepted customs and vested interests; and that as the society matures it may come in time, for the sake of its own stability, to recognize some of these differences legally in terms of titles and privileges. Adams hoped that he himself could live in a society where legal inequalities were held to a minimum, but he was ready to concede that only so much equality could be preserved by law as was "compatible with the people's security against foreign invasion and domestic usurpation." Even in the most harassed societies, however, government had no sterner obligation than to extend the equal protection of the laws to all who owed it allegiance. Adams's belief in moral equality and in the duty of government to protect it swept any weakness for autocracy or slavery right out of his system.

There is a refreshing candor in Adams's opinions of the human race, the more refreshing because, in his peculiar way, he was full of benevolence and wished it well. But in owing men pity and love he also owed them honesty, and he flattered them no more in public than he did in private. It is astounding to think that a man who spoke so openly about "the general frailty and depravity of human nature" could have scored so many successes at the polls in a free country.

Adams was no less concerned with society and its structure than with man and his nature. He had no truck with notions of anarchy and isolation, for he recognized clearly the social nature of man. "Nature," he wrote, "intended men for society."

The good society, in his conservative view, was marked by stability, order, peace, justice, and equity. He was much too realistic, of course, to believe that more than a few societies in all the ages had met even the simplest tests of goodness. Jealousy among men and conflict among classes kept most communities in a state of turmoil or exhaustion. Adams could find no society in history that was free from the afflictions of the class struggle. Nevertheless, he did find in his own beloved New England a working model for a society in which rivalries would be tempered and distinctions put to work for progress. The chief characteristics of his ideal social order were these:

It would be composed of prescriptive groups rather than lonely individuals. The key group, of course, was the family, an institution ordained by God and nature and deserving of every encouragement by constituted authority. . . . But other groups, too, were essential to this order. As he wrote in his diary in 1786:

> Major Langbourne dined with us again. He was lamenting the difference of character between Virginia and New England. I offered to give him a receipt for making a New England in Virginia. He desired it; and I recommended to him . . . the towns, militia, schools, and churches, as the four causes of the growth and defence of New England. The virtues and talents of the people are there formed; their temperance, patience, fortitude, prudence, and justice, as well as their sagacity, knowledge, judgment, taste, skill, ingenuity, dexterity, and industry.

The society would be grounded on a simple agrarian economy. Through all his life Adams remained an essentially agrarian thinker who exulted "in the present state of society and manners in America, with a people living chiefly by agriculture, in small numbers, sprinkled over large tracts of land." Hamilton dreamed of an America filled with factories and hard-packed cities; Adams, no less than Jefferson, dreaded it.

Change would be confined by a popular mistrust of innovation and a dispersion of the power to initiate reforms. Adams himself mistrusted innovation on intellectual as well as temperamental grounds, and he was especially concerned that the inexorable currents of change be channeled cautiously into the stream of genuine progress.

Finally, the society would exhibit a class structure. Adams was never entirely clear or consistent in his theory of social classes. Sometimes he seemed to be thinking of an infinite number of layers, a great chain of being in which every man had his place and every man's place was different. Sometimes he fell back on the easy dichotomy of the few and the many, the aristocrats and the democrats, "the gentlemen and the simplemen." For the most part, however, he had in mind the existence of three main classes. Like his own New England, the good society would be made up of "the better sort," "the middling sort," and "the meaner sort," although the latter would be "mean" by comparison only.

Adams put special trust in the middle class. He saluted it as "that great and excellent portion of society upon whom so much of the liberty and prosperity of nations so greatly depends." He was only slightly less solicitous of the lower class, in which, he knew from experience, men of virtue and steadfast purpose were always to be found. But his real concern was the better sort, and he is rightly known as one of the most trenchant thinkers on aristocracy in all the history of political thought. Out of the vast, uneven bulk of his writings on this subject we may extract these essentials of his system:

There has never yet been a society in which aristocracy was not present in force. In a marginal note in his copy of Mary Wollstonecraft's "French Revolution," Adams exploded with a vehemence that even he, a vehement writer in margins, rarely matched: "And does this foolish woman expect to get rid of an aristocracy? God Almighty has decreed in the creation of human nature an eternal aristocracy among men. The world is, always has been, and ever will be governed by it."

Aristocracy arises from natural inequality among men, and the things of this world in which men are most unequal—"beauty, wealth, birth, genius, and virtue"—are its "five pillars." Adams himself thought most highly of the last two qualities. Hamilton and his friends spoke of "the wise and good and rich," but Adams cut the formula down to "the wise and good." Plutocracy was the one kind of aristocracy for which he had no use, and he looked with anxiety on the steady advance of wealth to the summit of American life.

Aristocracy must be understood largely in terms of influence over social policy. In a famous passage in his dialogue with John Taylor he wrote: "Without searching volumes, Mr. Taylor, I will tell you in a few words what I mean by an aristocrat, and, consequently, what I mean by aristocracy. By an aristocrat, I mean every man who can command or influence TWO VOTES; ONE BESIDES HIS OWN."

Finally, civilization is largely the work of a few men of superior talent and energy, and civilization is therefore committed to the search for genuine aristocrats. If it cannot find them, it must resign itself to decline and destruction.

Yet what happens when the search is successful, when men of merit are found and then elevated to power and influence? The answer, said Adams, who never missed a chance to douse hope with skepticism, is that the aristocrats become one of the chief worries of civilization. Such men have destroyed just as many flourishing cities and states as they have created, and men must learn the hard way that this sword, too, can cut in both directions. In a characteristic passage in a letter to Benjamin Rush, Adams expressed this ambivalent view of aristocracy: "I can never too often repeat that aristocracy is the monster to be chained; yet so chained as not to hurt, for he is a most useful and necessary animal in his place. Nothing can be done without him. . . . Bind aristocracy then with a double cord. Shut him up in a cage, from which however he may be let out to do good but never to do mischief."

Acknowledgment of its status, protection of its property, deference to its judgments, reward for its services—in the good society all these things would be accorded the aristocracy by custom and law, and thus it would be discouraged from doing evil and encouraged to do good. Most important of all, to the well-being of the aristocracy and to the peace of mind of the common people, its political power would be held under tight rein. "In my opinion," Adams wrote, "everything depends on the form of government."

Adams was, at one and the same time, a conservative skeptic who doubted the power of any human agency to set things right and a political scientist who was deeply in love with his subject. In most of his writings love conquered doubt. No first-rate American political thinker ever had more respect for the uses of political authority; no dedicated conservative in any country ever took more delight in studying and practicing the art of governing men. He hated politics, but he loved political science, especially when he could apply theory to fact in his favorite trade of constitution-making.

There should be no mistake about the importance he ascribed to government. It served all the purposes that most men of Adams's time conceded to it: it secured the rights and protected the property of men, guarded them against the violence they might do one another, and acted as symbol of unity and purveyor of equity. But it also served a great many more: it separated men's virtues from their vices by rewarding the former and discouraging the latter; it guided the passions for distinction and domination toward healthy ends; it harnessed the natural aristocracy to the plow of progress; and it promoted the welfare and happiness of the community by taking a strong lead in the areas of morals and education. Adams had no truck with those like Paine who insisted that "government, even in its best state, is but a necessary evil." To the contrary, government was "founded in nature and reason," and "the blessings of society" depended "entirely on the constitutions of government."

In order to understand Adams's own choice of a constitution of government, we must first recall what he said about aristocracy and then hear what he said about democracy. In the proper constitutional balance of these two great forces lay the happiness and prosperity of every land.

Without an aristocracy no nation could exist; without a dedicated aristocracy no nation could flourish. From this position Adams never wandered. Yet he also never wandered—rather, his prejudices and learning were strengthened by experience—from the assumption that aristocrats, too, were men and therefore subject to the vices, passions, and temptations of other men. He agreed unreservedly with Taylor that aristocrats in all ages, with precious few exceptions, had "waged everlasting war against the common rights of men." At the same time, "the nobles have been essential parties in the preservation of liberty, whenever and wherever it has existed." One-half the problem of government was therefore this: to discover constitutional techniques that could restrain without deadening the ambitions of aristocracy.

The other half was to do much the same for the mass of men: to keep them from running roughshod over the rights and property of the aristocrats and to give them every chance to lead useful, law-abiding lives. Adams is usually listed among the all-time critics of democracy, but too many historians have convicted him of heresy without taking into account two major facts; first, he was just as hard on aristocracy as on democracy, for he found no man exempt from the harsh laws of human nature: "My opinion is, and always has been, that absolute power intoxicates alike despots, monarchs, aristocrats, and democrats, and jacobins, and *sans culottes.*"

And second, he defined democracy almost exclusively in constitutional terms —as a form of government in which all authority was centered, undiluted and unchecked, in an assembly of the people or of their immediate representatives. It is, therefore, entirely wrong, a malicious insult to a stout friend of liberty, to quote Adams in derogation of all popular government. It is entirely correct, a compliment for which he would be properly grateful, to quote him as a bitter foe of what his age called "Jacobinism" and ours knows as "people's democracy."

He was, to be sure, a lively critic of the foibles of the mass of men. With tactless pen he recorded the preference of the people for flatterers, knaves, and demagogues in office; their instability and fondness for violence as a solution to their problems; their historic habit of handing over all their fears and troubles to absolute monarchy; their lack of concern for justice and their contempt for learning; and, most prophetically, their peculiar weakness for luxury, for "levity, gaiety, inconstancy, dissipation, intemperance, debauchery, and a dissolution of manners." As to the so-called wisdom of the majority:

> We may appeal to every page of history we have hitherto turned over, for proofs irrefragable, that the people, when they have been unchecked, have been as unjust, tyrannical, brutal, barbarous and cruel as any king or senate possessed of uncontrollable power. The majority has eternally and without one exception usurped over the rights of the minority.

Yet having said all this, Adams made clear that the people had a place, if not the whole place, in any sound system of government.

> Democracy, nevertheless, must not be disgraced; democracy must not be despised. Democracy must be respected; democracy must be honored; democracy must be cherished; democracy must be an essential, an integral part of the sovereignty, and have a control over the whole government, or moral liberty cannot exist, or any other liberty.

It was not simply a question of bribing the people into good behavior by giving them some measure of self-government. No state could afford to ignore the talent and wisdom sprinkled all through the common people.

What, then, was the solution to this two-edged problem? How was the aristocracy to be controlled and the democracy sobered? The answer, in a word— Adams's favorite word—was *balance*. The entire three volumes of the "Defence of the Constitutions," his major work, were devoted to expounding a form of government in which the mass of people were represented in an assembly and the gentry in a senate, and in which the balance between these two participants in sovereign authority was held by executive power. For such government Adams made extravagant claims: it alone could harvest the fruits of aristocracy and control the fires of democracy; it alone could guarantee stability by protecting property; it alone was consistently favorable to liberty, learning, simplicity, merit, and every virtue; it alone rested on the firm ground of reason and nature.

He was especially insistent that the substantial interests of society be represented—and isolated—in a senate.

The rich, the well-born, and the able, acquire an influence among the people that will soon be too much for simple honesty and plain sense, in a house of representatives. The most illustrious of them must, therefore, be separated from the mass, and placed by themselves in a senate; this is, to all honest and useful intents, an ostracism.

On the other side of this balance stood the assembly of the people, grounded firmly on a strict equality of representation:

A constitution in which the people reserve to themselves the absolute control of their purses, one essential branch of the legislature, and the inquest of grievances and state crimes, will always produce patriotism, bravery, simplicity, and science.

And between them, the guardian of the constitution in the image of Bolingbroke's patriot king, stood the executive—strong, independent, watchful, and above all disinterested.

Neither the rich nor the poor can be defended by their respective guardians in the constitution, without an executive power, vested with a negative, equal to either, to hold the balance even between them, and decide when they cannot agree. . . .

If "the essence of free government consists in an effectual control of rivalries," some power had to rise calm and steady above all party and faction. Adams never did make clear just how the head of government, whether hereditary or elective, would be drained of political blood and bile, but he never doubted that such an executive was the pivot of free government. Without it there could be "no government, no security for life, liberty or property." In his correspondence with Taylor and others in his last years, he insisted that the chief fault with the American Presidency was that it "has not influence enough, and is not independent enough." Indeed, in several of his public and private letters he spoke like a John the Baptist for the coming of Andrew Jackson.

What Adams seems to have had in mind most of the time was a balance of forces in society rather than a separation of powers in government. He had a typically conservative feeling for social equilibrium, even if he had a most unconservative confidence in the power of constitutional techniques to preserve it. Although the balance of senate, assembly, and executive was most essential to ordered liberty, the best of constitutions would incorporate subsidiary balances. . . . The most perfect system would be an entire complex of pluralized and balanced authority. In a letter to Taylor in 1814, he took particular delight in discovering eight distinct balances in the Constitution of the United States, ranging from the balance of Senate against House to that of states against nation.

In the end, Adams, like most political scientists, blended the balance of social forces and separation of political powers into one grand system. He put these two related concepts together in a solemn promise to Philip Mazzei in 1787:

> To defend the separation of the legislative, executive, judicial powers from each other, and the division of the legislative into three branches, from the attacks of county committees, riotous assemblies, and uninformed philosophers and statesmen, will be the burden of my song. . . . Such a distribution of power appears to me the *unum necessarium* of liberty, safety, and good order.

So gladly did Adams sing the song of balance over the next forty years that he neglected a number of other themes in political and constitutional theory to which he should also have lent his full voice. Still, we may cite him confidently as a stout friend of republicanism, although the friendship was occasionally strained by his frank admiration for the British Constitution; of civil supremacy, an ancient New England prejudice in which he was strengthened by his suspicions of Hamilton's thirst for military glory; and of the independence of the judiciary, one of the essential balances in the American system. He was, however, strangely silent on the principle of judicial review both before and after "Marbury v. Madison" (1803). He never let his love for Massachusetts and his approval of the federal balance get in the way of a stout conviction that the Union was "the rock of our salvation." He rarely let his hatred of faction and his personal independence blind him to the importance of parties to the workings of government. Although he considered it the duty of every man, and especially every gentleman, to answer the call of public service, he insisted that such service be decently rewarded by the people. . . . "Mankind will never be happy nor their liberties secure," he wrote, "until the people shall lay it down as a fundamental rule to make the support and reward of public offices a matter of justice and not gratitude." The letter containing this remark, which was occasioned by an article in the first Constitution of Pennsylvania that decried "offices of profit," is a minor masterpiece of political realism.

His major masterpiece was the "Defence of the Constitutions"—ponderous, repetitious, full of undigested learning, and five times too long, but a masterpiece nonetheless—and we should end this inquiry into his thoughts on government by restating its major theme: that power unchecked, power centered in one agency, is the open door to tyranny, and that power checked, power dispersed among many agencies, is the strait gate to liberty. His formula for free men and free government was simple: "Power must be opposed to power, force to force, strength to strength, interest to interest, as well as reason to reason, eloquence to eloquence, passion to passion."

Man's place in society and under government was a problem on which Adams, like all genuine conservatives, refused to take a doctrinaire stand. He was an eloquent champion of both the rights of the individual and the needs of the community; he never knowingly tipped the balance too far in either direction. Neither a professional libertarian like Paine nor a case-hardened autocrat like Hamilton, Adams had faith that the marvelous alchemy of nature and reason, aided by the benign influence of a mixed constitution, would work out an adjustment suitable to the condition of each society. In the best of societies the balance would be held, and the rough contacts between man and state made tolerable, by what Burke called the "little platoons." Adams was always a champion of every natural and sensible form of human association—from the family to the militia by way of the congregation.

His thoughts on liberty were characteristically abrasive. A faithful child of Cicero and Locke, a constant friend of "revolution principles," he would admit no doubt of the doctrine of natural, inalienable rights. But he did make a sharp distinction between freedom in the abstract, which all men had as children of God, and freedom in fact, which all men did not have as members of society. "The love of liberty," Samuel Adams wrote to him in 1790, "is interwoven in the soul of man." "So it is," he replied, "according to La Fontaine, in that of a wolf; and I doubt whether it be much more rational, generous, or social, in one than in the other, until in man it is enlightened by experience, reflection, education."

True liberty, that is to say, belonged to those men only who had submitted patiently to the great self-discipline of knowledge. Hardly less important was the self-discipline of virtue. "The happiness of man," he asserted, "as well as his dignity, consists in virtue." Nothing was more fatal to liberty than luxury, avarice, corruption, and wrong-dealing, nothing more propitious than the practice of the old-fashioned virtues, the queen of which, in this conservative's view, was prudence.

Adams, like most men of his age, included property in the definition of liberty. He never stated clearly whether he considered it primarily a natural or social right; the distinction, which several of his correspondents labored pedantically, was to him a matter of indifference. Men had a natural right to mix their labor with the soil and to enjoy the fruits that resulted, but they also had to recognize that their property was largely a "creature of convention, of social laws and artificial order." Without the protection of the community they could not enjoy their property in peace of mind; without its guidance they would probably misuse it. In any case, the need for property was ingrained in the nature of man, and the well-ordered community would recognize property as a right no less essential to happiness than freedom of expression and even freedom of conscience.

In Adams's writings property appeared as something more than a personal right. It was a form of power and carried power with it; it was a breeder of responsibility and thus a support of rational liberty. Most important, it was the basis of stable government, and the makers of constitutions would recognize this stern fact by giving property special representation in one of the legislative branches and by restricting the suffrage to those who held some modest amount. Adams was never entirely comfortable with the doctrine that men with no property at all should be rigidly excluded from political activity. Indeed, he confessed to Madison that it was a "difficult" question. In the end, he was too sound a conservative, too dutiful a child of his age, to divest himself of the inherited opinion that a man should have a visible stake in his community before he had the right to vote at all and the ability to vote well. Yet he also believed, for the sake of order and freedom alike, that the laws should "make the acquisition of land easy to every member of society . . . so that the multitude may be possessed of land estates." His model constitution was the charter of a property-owner's democracy.

The richest portion of Adams's legacy to our America is his political theory. Though his deeds were memorable and his character sterling, on neither of these grounds was he in a class with Washington. In the realm of political ideas, however, he had no master—and I would think no peer—among the founding fathers. As we turn ever more hopefully for comfort and instruction to the men of that golden age of political thought, we must find ourselves ever more deeply in Adams's debt.

The debt of American conservatism is especially large, because Adams is as much the great man of our conservatism as Jefferson is of our progressivism. The men who are most often advanced as challengers to his claim to the summit are Hamilton, Calhoun, Washington, and Lincoln, and no one of them passes the necessary tests so convincingly as Adams. Hamilton was too full of plutocratic schemes for making over America, Calhoun too harshly dedicated to a special interest. Washington and Lincoln, who are, after all, the property of all Americans, simply did not do enough hard thinking and writing on the subject. In reacting instinctively to the "foul abominations" of the French Revolution, Adams proved himself a conservative in temper and taste. In warning against the heresies of unlimited perfectibility, unlimited progress, and unlimited power, he proved himself a conservative in faith. In offering his age an alternative system grounded on realism as well as good will, he created a theory out of his faith—one of the rarest acts in which a conservative can engage.

There are those who cherish Edmund Burke as the intellectual father of American conservatism, but Burke himself, I feel sure, would decline the honor with thanks. No man, he would say, can really speak clearly across the boundaries of national pride and tradition; Americans must look to America for their heroes of principle as well as of action. I would agree vigorously, and I would remind the partisans of Burke of the distinguishing mark of any genuinely conservative system of thought: that it is a defense of a specific established order, that it loses much of its character when detached from its institutional base. The base of Burke's thought was the monarchy, peerage, estates, and Church of old England. The base of Adams's was the town meetings, schools, farms, and churches of New England. His political thought was indelibly American, never more so than when he, like all the giants of his time, invoked the splendid vision of the American mission: "I always consider the settlement of America with reverence and wonder, as the opening of a grand scene and design in Providence for the illumination of the ignorant, and the emancipation of the slavish part of mankind all over the earth."

American progressivism, too, has a debt to Adams, and the debt will grow larger as more and more men of this persuasion retreat to the firm ground of "tough-minded liberalism" already occupied by such as Reinhold Niebuhr and George Kennan. Adams speaks today to all Americans, and his message comes in two parts.

He gives us first a hard-headed statement of the inexorable conditions for preserving democracy in the United States:

Democracy cannot exist apart from the spirit and forms of constitutionalism, for the essence of political liberty is an agreement to govern and be governed through safe, sober, predictable methods.

Democracy cannot exist unless knowledge, virtue, and property are widely diffused among the people; for knowledge is essential to wise decision, virtue to unforced obedience, and property to personal independence and social progress.

The second part of Adams's message strikes a more personal note, a note of warning against the maudlin hope of liberalism and the harsh despair of reaction. The voice of Adams is the voice of true conservatism, pitched at a fuzzy but golden mean in its reading of the prospects for humanity. On one hand: "Cold will still freeze, and fire will never cease to burn; disease and vice will continue to disorder, and death to terrify mankind." On the other: "I am a believer in the probable improvability and improvement, the ameliorability and amelioration in human affairs."

One thing is certain: if we are to inch our way painfully toward a better world, we must do it along the paths staked out by the guides of our past:

Without wishing to damp the ardor of curiosity, or influence the freedom of inquiry, I will hazard a prediction, that, after the most industrious and impartial researches, the longest liver of you all will find no principles, institutions, or systems of education more fit, in general, to be transmitted to your posterity, than those you have received from your ancestors.

The legacy of John Adams is cold water and cold porridge, which will account for both the popularity he does not have and the appeal he should have among Americans of the twentieth century. He pours cold water on hopes that still aspire to earthly salvation; he offers cold porridge to appetites that are much too greedy for our own good and seem only to grow greedier on our present diet of luxury, lust, and power. He would not want to drown or starve us; he would ask only that we aim at the possible rather than the desirable, and that we discipline ourselves against the "avarice" that is still "the most dreadful and alarming enemy America has to oppose." And in closing out the testament of his legacy to our generation, he would say to us as he said to his friend James Madison:

May you live to a greater age than mine, and be able to die with brighter prospects for your species than can fall to the lot of your friend.

                                                                                            JOHN ADAMS

HENRY DAVID THOREAU

On the Duty of Civil Disobedience[1]

I heartily accept the motto—"That government is best which governs least"; and I should like to see it acted up to more rapidly and systematically. Carried out, it finally amounts to this, which also I believe,—"That government is best which governs not at all"; and when men are prepared for it, that will be the kind of government which they will have. Government is at best but an expedient; but most governments are usually, and all governments are sometimes, inexpedient. The objections which have been brought against a standing army, and they are many and weighty, and deserve to prevail, may also at last be brought against a standing government. The standing army is only an arm of the standing government. The government itself, which is only the mode which the people have chosen to execute their will, is equally liable to be abused and perverted before the people can act through it. Witness the present Mexican war, the work of comparatively a few individuals using the standing govern-

1 From Norman Holmes Pearson, ed., Walden and On the Duty of Civil Disobedience, "Rinehart Editions" (New York: Holt, Rinehart and Winston, Inc., 1948), pp. 281-304, with omissions. First printed in 1849.

ment as their tool; for, in the outset, the people would not have consented to this measure.

This American government—what is it but a tradition, though a recent one, endeavoring to transmit itself unimpaired to posterity, but each instant losing some of its integrity? It has not the vitality and force of a single living man; for a single man can bend it to his will. It is a sort of wooden gun to the people themselves. But it is not the less necessary for this; for the people must have some complicated machinery or other, and hear its din, to satisfy that idea of government which they have. Governments show us how successfully men can be imposed on, even impose on themselves, for their own advantage. It is excellent, we must all allow. Yet this government never of itself furthered any enterprise, but by the alacrity with which it got out of its way. *It* does not keep the country free. *It* does not settle the West. *It* does not educate. The character inherent in the American people has done all that has been accomplished; and it would have done somewhat more, if the government had not sometimes got in its way. For government is an expedient by which men would fain succeed in letting one another alone; and, as has been said, when it is most expedient, the governed are most let alone by it. Trade and commerce, if they were not made of India-rubber, would never manage to bounce over the obstacles which legislators are continually putting in their way; and, if one were to judge these men wholly by the effects of their actions and not partly by their intentions, they would deserve to be classed and punished with those mischievous persons who put obstructions on the railroads.

But, to speak practically and as a citizen, unlike those who call themselves no-government men, I ask for, not at once no government, but *at once* a better government. Let every man make known what kind of government would command his respect, and that will be one step toward obtaining it.

After all, the practical reason why, when the power is once in the hands of the people, a majority are permitted, and for a long period continue, to rule is not because they are most likely to be in the right, nor because this seems fairest to the minority, but because they are physically the strongest. But a government in which the majority rule in all cases cannot be based on justice, even as far as men understand it. Can there not be a government in which majorities do not virtually decide right and wrong, but conscience?—in which majorities decide only those questions to which the rule of expediency is applicable? Must the citizen ever for a moment, or in the least degree, resign his conscience to the legislator? Why has every man a conscience, then? I think that we should be men first, and subjects afterward. It is not desirable to cultivate a respect for the law, so much as for the right. The only obligation which I have a right to assume is to do at any time what I think right. It is truly enough said, that a corporation has no conscience; but a corporation of conscientious men is a corporation *with* a conscience. Law never made men a whit more just; and, by means of their respect for it, even the well-disposed are daily made the agents of injustice. A common and natural result of an undue respect for law is, that you may see a file of soldiers, colonel, captain, corporal, privates, powder-monkeys, and all, marching in admirable order over hill and dale to the wars, against their wills, ay, against their common sense and consciences, which makes it very steep marching indeed, and produces a palpitation of the heart. They have no doubt that it is a damnable business in which they are concerned; they are all peaceably inclined. Now, what are they? Men at all? or small movable forts and magazines, at the service of some unscrupulous man in power? Visit the Navy-Yard, and behold a marine, such a man as an American government can make, or such as it can make a man with its black arts,—a mere shadow and reminiscence of humanity, a man laid out alive and standing, and already, as one may say, buried under arms with funeral accompaniments, though it may be,—

> Not a drum was heard, not a funeral note,
> As his corpse to the rampart we hurried;
> Not a soldier discharged his farewell shot
> O'er the grave where our hero we buried.

The mass of men serve the state thus, not as men mainly, but as machines, with their bodies. They are the standing army, and the militia, jailors, constables, posse comitatus, etc. In most cases there is no free exercise whatever of the judgment or of the moral sense; but they put themselves on a level with wood and earth and stones; and wooden men can perhaps be manufactured that will serve the purpose as well. Such command no more respect than men of straw or a lump of dirt. They have the same sort of worth only as horses and dogs. Yet such as these even are commonly esteemed good citizens. Others—as most legislators, politicians, lawyers, ministers, and officeholders—serve the state chiefly with their heads; and, as they rarely make any moral distinctions, they are as likely to serve the Devil, without *intending* it, as God. A very few, as heroes, patriots, martyrs, reformers in the great sense, and *men*, serve the state with their consciences also, and so necessarily resist it for the most part; and they are commonly treated as enemies by it. A wise man will only be useful as a man, and will not submit to be "clay," and "stop a hole to keep the wind away," but leave that office to his dust at least:—

> I am too high-born to be propertied,
> To be a secondary at control,
> Or useful serving-man and instrument
> To any sovereign state throughout the world.

He who gives himself entirely to his fellow-men appears to them useless and selfish; but he who gives himself partially to them is pronounced a benefactor and philanthropist.

How does it become a man to behave toward this American government to-day? I answer, that he cannot without disgrace be associated with it. I cannot for an instant recognize that political organization as *my* government which is the *slave's* government also.

All men recognize the right of revolution; that is, the right to refuse allegiance to, and to resist, the government, when its tyranny or its inefficiency are great and unendurable. But almost all say that such is not the case now. But such was the case, they think, in the Revolution of '75. If one were to tell me that this was a bad government because it taxed certain foreign commodities brought to its ports, it is most probable that I should not make an ado about it, for I can do without them. All machines have their friction; and possibly this does enough good to counterbalance the evil. At any rate, it is a great evil to make a stir about it. But when the friction comes to have its machine, and oppression and robbery are organized, I say, let us not have such a machine any longer. In other words, when a sixth of the population of a nation which has undertaken to be the refuge of liberty are slaves, and a whole country is unjustly overrun and conquered by a foreign army, and subjected to military law, I think that it is not too soon for honest men to rebel and revolutionize. What makes this duty the more urgent is the fact that the country so overrun is not our own, but ours is the invading army. . . .

> A drab of state, a cloth-o'-silver slut,
> To have her train borne up, and her soul trail in the dirt.

Practically speaking, the opponents to a reform in Massachusetts are not a hundred thousand politicians at the South, but a hundred thousand merchants and farmers here, who are more interested in commerce and agriculture than they are in humanity, and are not prepared to do justice to the slave and to Mexico, *cost what it may*. I quarrel not with far-off foes, but with those who, near at home, coöperate with, and do the bidding of, those far away, and without whom the latter would be harmless. We are accustomed to say, that the mass of men are unprepared; but improvement is slow, because the few are not materially wiser or better than the many. It is not so important that many should be as good as you, as that there be some absolute goodness somewhere; for that will leaven the whole lump. There are thousands who are *in opinion* opposed to slavery and to the war, who yet in effect do nothing to put an end to them; who, esteeming themselves children of Washington and Franklin, sit down with their hands in their pockets, and say that they know not what to do, and do nothing; who even postpone the question of freedom to the question of free-trade, and quietly read the prices-current along with the latest advices from Mexico, after dinner, and, it may be, fall asleep over them both. What is the price-current of an honest man and patriot to-day? They hesitate, and they regret, and sometimes they petition; but they do nothing in earnest and with effect. They will wait, well disposed, for others to remedy the evil, that they may no longer have it to regret. At most, they give only a cheap vote, and a feeble countenance and God-speed, to the right, as it goes by them.

There are nine hundred and ninety-nine patrons of virtue to one virtuous man. But it is easier to deal with the real possessor of a thing than with the temporary guardian of it.

All voting is a sort of gaming, like checkers or backgammon, with a slight moral tinge to it, a playing with right and wrong, with moral questions; and betting naturally accompanies it. The character of the voters is not staked. I cast my vote, perchance, as I think right; but I am not vitally concerned that that right should prevail. I am willing to leave it to the majority. Its obligation, therefore, never exceeds that of expediency. Even voting *for the right* is *doing* nothing for it. It is only expressing to men feebly your desire that it should prevail. A wise man will not leave the right to the mercy of chance, nor wish it to prevail through the power of the majority. There is but little virtue in the action of masses of men. When the majority shall at length vote for the abolition of slavery, it will be because they are indifferent to slavery, or because there is but little slavery left to be abolished by their vote. *They* will then be the only slaves. Only *his* vote can hasten the abolition of slavery who asserts his own freedom by his vote.

I hear of a convention to be held at Baltimore, or elsewhere, for the selection of a candidate for the Presidency, made up chiefly of editors, and men who are politicians by profession; but I think, what is it to any independent, intelligent, and respectable man what decision they may come to? Shall we not have the advantage of his wisdom and honesty, nevertheless? Can we not count upon some independent votes? Are there not many individuals in the country who do not attend conventions? But no: I find that the respectable man, so called, has immediately drifted from his position, and despairs of his country, when his country has more reason to despair of him. He forthwith adopts one of the candidates thus selected as the only *available* one, thus proving that he is himself *available* for any purposes of the demagogue. His vote is of no more worth than that of any unprincipled foreigner or hireling native, who may have been bought. O for a man who is a *man*, and, as my neighbor says, has a bone in his back which you cannot pass your hand through! Our statistics are at fault: the population has been returned too large. How many *men* are there to a square thousand miles in this country? Hardly one. Does not America offer any inducement for men to settle here? The American has dwindled into an Odd Fellow,—one who may be known by the development of his organ of gregariousness, and a manifest lack of intellect and cheerful self-reliance; whose first and chief concern, on coming into the world, is to see that the Almshouses are in good repair; and, before yet he has lawfully donned the virile garb, to collect a fund for the support of the widows and orphans that may be; who, in short, ventures to live only by the aid of the Mutual Insurance company, which has promised to bury him decently.

It is not a man's duty, as a matter of course, to devote himself to the eradication of any, even the most enormous wrong; he may still properly have other concerns to engage him; but it is his duty, at least, to wash his hands of it, and, if he gives it no thought longer, not to give it practically his support. If I devote myself to other pursuits and contemplations, I must first see, at least, that I do not pursue them sitting upon another man's shoulders. I must get off him first, that he may pursue his contemplations too. See what gross inconsistency is tolerated. I have heard some of my townsmen say, "I should like to have them order me out to help put down an insurrection of the slaves, or to march to Mexico;—see if I would go"; and yet these very men have each, directly by their allegiance, and so indirectly, at least, by their money, furnished a substitute. The soldier is applauded who refuses to serve in an unjust war by those who do not refuse to sustain the unjust government which makes the war; is applauded by those whose own act and authority he disregards and sets at naught; as if the state were penitent to that degree that it hired one to scourge it while it sinned, but not to that degree that it left off sinning for a moment. Thus, under the name of Order and Civil Government, we are all made at last to pay homage to and support our own meanness. After the first blush of sin comes its indifference; and from immoral it becomes, as it were, unmoral, and not quite unnecessary to that life which we have made.

The broadest and most prevalent error requires the most disinterested virtue to sustain it. The slight reproach to which the virtue of patriotism is commonly liable, the noble are most likely to incur. Those who, while they disapprove of the character and measures of a government, yield to it their allegiance and support are undoubtedly its most conscientious supporters, and so frequently the most serious obstacles to reform. Some are petitioning the state to dissolve the Union, to disregard the requisitions of the President. Why do they not dissolve it themselves—the union between themselves and the state,—and refuse to pay their quota into its treasury? Do not they stand in the same relation to the state that the state does to the Union? And have not the same reasons prevented the state from resisting the Union which have prevented them from resisting the state?

How can a man be satisfied to entertain an opinion merely, and enjoy *it*? Is there any enjoyment in it, if his opinion is that he is aggrieved? If you are cheated out of a single dollar by your neighbor, you do not rest satisfied with knowing that you are cheated, or with saying that you are cheated, or even with petitioning him to pay you your due; but you take effectual steps at once to obtain the full amount, and see that you are never cheated again. Action from principle, the perception and the performance of right, changes things and relations; it is essentially revolutionary, and does not consist wholly with anything which was. It not only divides states and churches, it divides families; ay, it divides the *individual*, separating the diabolical in him from the divine.

Unjust laws exist: shall we be content to obey them, or shall we endeavor to amend them, and obey them until we have succeeded, or shall we transgress them at once? Men generally, under such a government as this, think that they ought to wait until they have persuaded the majority to alter them. They think that, if they should resist, the remedy would be worse than the evil. But it is the fault of the government itself that the remedy *is* worse than the evil. *It* makes it worse. Why is it not more apt to anticipate and provide for reform? Why does it not cherish its wise minority? Why does it cry and resist before it is hurt? Why does it not encourage its citizens to be on the alert to point out its faults, and *do* better than it would have them? Why does it always crucify Christ, and excommunicate Copernicus and Luther, and pronounce Washington and Franklin rebels?

One would think, that a deliberate and practical denial of its authority was the only offense never contemplated by government; else, why has it not assigned its definite, its suitable and proportionate penalty? If a man who has no property refuses but once to earn nine shillings for the state, he is put in prison for a period unlimited by any law that I know, and determined only by the discretion of those who placed him there; but if he should steal ninety times nine shillings from the state, he is soon permitted to go at large again.

If the injustice is part of the necessary friction of the machine of government, let it go, let it go: perchance it will wear smooth,—certainly the machine will wear out. If the injustice has a spring, or a pulley, or a rope, or a crank, exclusively for itself, then perhaps you may consider whether the remedy will not be worse than the evil; but if it is of such a nature that it requires you to be the agent of injustice to another, then, I say, break the law. Let your life be a counter friction to stop the machine. What I have to do is to see, at any rate, that I do not lend myself to the wrong which I condemn.

As for adopting the ways which the state has provided for remedying the evil, I know not of such ways. They take too much time, and a man's life will be gone. I have other affairs to attend to. I came into this world, not chiefly to make this a good place to live in, but to live in it, be it good or bad. A man has not everything to do, but something; and because he cannot do *everything*, it is not necessary that he should do *something* wrong. It is not my business to be petitioning the Governor or the Legislature any more than it is theirs to petition me; and if they should not hear my petition, what should I do then? But in this case the state has provided no way: its very Constitution is the evil. This may seem to be harsh and stubborn and unconciliatory; but it is to treat with the utmost kindness and consideration the only spirit that can appreciate or deserves it. So is all change for the better, like birth and death, which convulse the body.

I do not hesitate to say, that those who call themselves Abolitionists should at once effectually withdraw their support, both in person and property, from the government of Massachusetts and not wait till they constitute a majority of one, before they suffer the right to prevail through them. I think that it is enough if they have God on their side, without waiting for that other one. Moreover, any man more right than his neighbors constitutes a majority of one already.

I meet this American government, or its representative, the state government, directly, and face to face, once a year—no more—in the person of its tax-gatherer; this is the only mode in which a man situated as I am necessarily meets it; and it then says distinctly, Recognize me; and the simplest, most effectual, and, in the present posture of affairs, the indispensablest mode of treating with it on this head, of expressing your little satisfaction with and love for it, is to deny it then. My civil neighbor, the tax-gatherer, is the very man I have to deal with,—for it is, after all, with men and not with parchment that I quarrel,—and he has voluntarily chosen to be an agent of the government. How shall he ever know well what he is and does as an officer of the government, or as a man, until he is obliged to consider whether he shall treat me, his neighbor, for whom he has respect, as a neighbor and well-disposed man, or as a maniac and disturber of the peace, and see if he can get over this obstruction to his neighborliness without a ruder and more impetuous thought or speech corresponding with his action. I know this well, that if one thousand, if one hundred, if ten men whom I could name,—if ten *honest* men only,—ay, if *one* HONEST man, in this State of Massachusetts, *ceasing to hold slaves*, were actually to withdraw from this copartnership, and be locked up in the county jail therefor, it would be the abolition of slavery in America. For it matters not how small the beginning may seem to be: what is once well done is done forever. But we love better to talk about it: that we say is our mission. Reform keeps many scores of newspapers in its service, but not one man. If my esteemed neighbor, the State's ambassador, who will devote his days to the settlement of the question of human rights in the Council Chamber, instead of being threatened with the prisons of Carolina, were to sit down the prisoner of Massachusetts, that State which is so anxious to foist the sin of slavery upon her sister,—though at present she can discover only an act of inhospitality to be the ground of a quarrel with her,—the Legislature would not wholly waive the subject the following winter.

Under a government which imprisons any unjustly, the true place for a just man is also a prison. The proper place to-day, the only place which Massachusetts has provided for her freer and less desponding spirits, is in her prisons, to be put out and locked out of the State by her own act, as they have already put themselves out by their principles. It is there that the fugitive slave, and the Mexican prisoner on parole, and the Indian come to plead the wrongs of his race should find them; on that separate, but more free and honorable ground, where the State places those who are not *with* her, but *against* her,—the only house in a slave State in which a free man can abide with honor. If any think that their influence would be lost there, and their voices no longer afflict the ear of the State, that they would not be as an enemy within its walls, they do not know by how much truth is stronger than error, nor how much more eloquently and effectively he can combat injustice who has experienced a little in his own person. Cast your whole vote, not a strip of paper merely, but your whole influence. A minority is powerless while it conforms to the majority; it is not even a minority then; but it is irresistible when it clogs by its whole weight. If the alternative is to keep all just men in prison, or give up war and slavery, the State will not hesitate which to choose. If a thousand men were not to pay their tax-bills this year, that would not be a violent and bloody measure, as it would be to pay them, and enable the State to commit violence and shed innocent blood. This is, in fact, the definition of a peaceable revolution, if any such is possible. If the tax-gatherer, or any other public officer, asks me, as one has done, "But what shall I do?" my answer is, "If you really wish to do anything, resign your office." When the subject has refused allegiance, and the officer has resigned his office, then the revolution is accomplished. But even suppose blood should flow. Is there not a sort of blood shed when the conscience is wounded? Through this wound a man's real manhood and immortality flow out, and he bleeds to an everlasting death. I see this blood flowing now.

I have contemplated the imprisonment of the offender, rather than the seizure of his goods,—though both will serve the same purpose,—because they who assert the purest right, and consequently are most dangerous to a corrupt State, commonly have not spent much time in accumulating property. To such the State renders comparatively small service, and a slight tax is wont to appear exorbitant, particularly if they are obliged to earn it by special labor with their hands. If there were one who lived wholly without the use of money, the State itself would hesitate to demand it of him. But the rich man —not to make any invidious comparison—is always sold to the institution which makes him rich. Absolutely speaking, the more money, the less virtue; for money comes between a man and his objects, and obtains them for him; and it was certainly no great virtue to obtain it. It puts to rest many questions which he would otherwise be taxed to answer; while the only new question which it puts is the hard but superfluous one, how to spend it. Thus his moral ground is taken from under his feet. The opportunities of living are diminished in proportion as what are called the "means" are increased. The best thing a man can do for his culture when he is rich is to endeavor to carry out those schemes which he entertained when he was poor. Christ answered the Herodians according to their condition. "Show me the tribute-money," said he;—and one took a penny out of his pocket;—if you use money which has the image of Cæsar on it and which he has made current and valuable, that is, *if you are men of the State*, and gladly enjoy the advantages of Cæsar's government, then pay him back some of his own when he demands it. "Render therefore to Cæsar that which is Cæsar's, and to God those things which are God's,"—leaving them no wiser than before as to which was which; for they did not wish to know. . . .

I have paid no poll-tax for six years. I was put into a jail once on this account, for one night; and, as I stood considering the walls of solid stone, two or three feet thick, the door of wood and iron, a foot thick, and the iron grating which strained the light, I could not help being struck with the foolishness of that institution which treated me as if I were mere flesh and blood and bones, to be locked up. I wondered that it should have concluded at length that this was the best use it could put me to, and had never thought to avail itself of my services in some way. I saw that, if there was a wall of stone between me and my townsmen, there was a still more difficult one to climb or break through before they could get to be as free as I was. I did not for a moment feel confined, and the walls seemed a great waste of stone and mortar. I felt as if I alone of all my townsmen had paid my tax. They plainly did not know how to treat me, but behaved like persons who are underbred. In every threat and in every compliment there was a blunder; for they thought that my chief desire was to stand the other side of that stone wall. I could not but smile to see how industriously they locked the door on my meditations, which followed them out again without let or hindrance, and *they* were really all that was dangerous. As they could not reach me, they had resolved to punish my body; just as boys, if they cannot come at some person against whom they have a spite, will abuse his dog. I saw that the State was half-witted, that it was timid as a lone woman with her silver spoons, and that it did not know its friends from its foes, and I lost all my remaining respect for it, and pitied it.

Thus the State never intentionally confronts a man's sense, intellectual or moral, but only his body, his senses. It is not armed with superior wit or honesty, but with superior physical strength. I was not born to be forced. I will breathe after my own fashion. Let us see who is the strongest. What force has a multitude? They only can force me who obey a higher law than I. They force me to become like themselves. I do not hear of *men* being *forced* to live this way or that by masses of men. What sort of life were that to live? When I meet a government which says to me, "Your money or your life," why should I be in haste to give it my money? It may be in a great strait, and not know what to do: I cannot help that. It must help itself; do as I do. It is not worth the while to snivel about it. I am not responsible for the successful working of the machinery of society. I am not the son of the engineer. I perceive that, when an acorn and a chestnut fall side by side, the one does not remain inert to make way for the other, but both obey their own laws, and spring and grow and flourish as best they can, till one, perchance, over-shadows and destroys the other. If a plant cannot live according to its nature, it dies; and so a man. . . .

When I came out of prison,—for some one interfered, and paid that tax,—I did not perceive that great changes had taken place on the common, such as he observed who went in a youth and emerged a tottering and gray-headed man; and yet a change had to my eyes come over the scene,—the town, and State, and country,—greater than any that mere time could effect. I saw yet more distinctly the State in which I lived. I saw to what extent the people among whom I lived could be trusted as good neighbors and friends; that their friendship was for summer weather only; that they did not greatly propose to do right; that they were a distinct race from me by their prejudices and superstitions, as the Chinamen and Malays are; that in their sacrifices to humanity they ran no risks, not even to their property; that after all they were not so noble but they treated the thief as he had treated them, and hoped, by a certain outward observance and a few prayers, and by walking in a particular straight though useless path from time to time, to save their souls. This may be to judge my neighbors harshly; for I believe that many of them are not aware that they have such an institution as the jail in their village.

It was formerly the custom in our village, when a poor debtor came out of jail, for his acquaintances to salute him, looking through their fingers, which were crossed to represent the grating of a jail window. "How do ye do?" My neighbors did not thus salute me, but first looked at me, and then at one another, as if I had returned from a long journey. I was put into jail as I was going to the shoemaker's to get a shoe which was mended. When I was let out the next morning, I proceeded to finish my errand, and, having put on my mended shoe, joined a huckleberry party, who were impatient to put themselves under my conduct; and in half an hour,—for the horse was soon tackled, —was in the midst of a huckleberry field, on one of our highest hills, two miles off, and then the State was nowhere to be seen. . . .

I have never declined paying the highway tax, because I am as desirous of being a good neighbor as I am of being a bad subject; and as for supporting schools, I am doing my part to educate my fellow-countrymen now. It is for no particular item in the tax-bill that I refuse to pay it. I simply wish to refuse allegiance to the State, to withdraw and stand aloof from it effectually. I do not care to trace the course of my dollar, if I could, till it buys a man or a musket to shoot with,—the dollar is innocent,—but I am concerned to trace the effects of my allegiance. In fact, I quietly declare war with the State, after my fashion, though I will still make what use and get what advantage of her I can, as is usual in such cases.

If others pay the tax which is demanded of me, from a sympathy with the State, they do but what they have already done in their own case, or rather they abet injustice to a greater extent than the State requires. If they pay the tax from a mistaken interest in the individual taxed, to save his property, or prevent his going to jail, it is because they have not considered wisely how far they let their private feelings interfere with the public good.

This, then, is my position at present. But one cannot be too much on his guard in such a case, lest his action be biased by obstinacy or an undue regard for the opinions of men. Let him see that he does only what belongs to himself and to the hour.

I think sometimes, Why, this people mean well, they are only ignorant; they would do better if they knew how: why give your neighbors this pain to treat you as they are not inclined to? But I think again, This is no reason why I should do as they do, or permit others to suffer much greater pain of a different kind. Again, I sometimes say to myself, When many millions of men, without heat, without ill will, without personal feeling of any kind, demand of you a few shillings only, without the possibility, such is their constitution, of retracting or altering their present demand, and without the possibility, on your side, of appeal to any other millions, why expose yourself to this overwhelming brute force? You do not resist cold and hunger, the winds and the waves, thus obstinately; you quietly submit to a thousand similar necessities. You do not put your head into the fire. But just in proportion as I regard this as not wholly a brute force, but partly a human force, and consider that I have relations to those millions as to so many millions of men, and not of mere brute or inanimate things, I see that appeal is possible, first and instantaneously, from them to the Maker of them, and, secondly, from them to themselves. But if I put my head deliberately into the fire, there is no appeal to fire or to the Maker of fire, and I have only myself to blame. If I could convince myself that I have any right to be satisfied with men as they are, and to treat them accordingly, and not according, in some respects, to my requisitions and expectations of what they and I ought to be, then, like a good Mussulman and fatalist, I should endeavor to be satisfied with things as they are, and say it is the will of God. And, above all, there is this difference between resisting this and a purely brute or natural force, that I can resist this with some effect; but I cannot expect, like Orpheus, to change the nature of the rocks and trees and beasts.

I do not wish to quarrel with any man or nation. I do not wish to split hairs, to make fine distinctions, or set myself up as better than my neighbors. I seek rather, I may say, even an excuse for conforming to the laws of the land. I am but too ready to conform to them. Indeed, I have reason to suspect myself on this head; and each year, as the tax-gatherer comes round, I find myself disposed to review the acts and position of the general and State governments, and the spirit of the people, to discover a pretext for conformity.

> We must affect our country as our parents,
> And if at any time we alienate
> Our love or industry from doing it honor,
> We must respect effects and teach the soul
> Matter of conscience and religion,
> And not desire of rule or benefit.

I believe that the State will soon be able to take all my work of this sort out of my hands, and then I shall be no better a patriot than my fellow-countrymen. Seen from a lower point of view, the Constitution, with all its faults, is very good; the law and the courts are very respectable; even this State and this American government are, in many respects, very admirable, and rare things, to be thankful for, such as a great many have described them; but seen from a point of view a little higher, they are what I have described them; seen from a higher still, and the highest, who shall say what they are, or that they are worth looking at or thinking of at all?

However, the government does not concern me much, and I shall bestow the fewest possible thoughts on it. It is not many moments that I live under a government, even in this world. If a man is thought-free, fancy-free, imagination-free, that which *is not* never for a long time appearing *to be* to him, unwise rulers or reformers cannot fatally interrupt him.

I know that most men think differently from myself; but those whose lives are by profession devoted to the study of these or kindred subjects content me as little as any. Statesmen and legislators, standing so completely within the institution, never distinctly and nakedly behold it. They speak of moving society, but have no resting-place without it. They may be men of a certain experience and discrimination, and have no doubt invented ingenious and even useful systems, for which we sincerely thank them; but all their wit and usefulness lie within certain not very wide limits. They are wont to forget that the world is not governed by policy and expediency. Webster never goes behind government, and so cannot speak with authority about it. His words are wisdom to those legislators who contemplate no essential reform in the existing government; but for thinkers, and those who legislate for all time, he never once glances at the subject. I know of those whose serene and wise speculations on this theme would soon reveal the limits of his mind's range and hospitality. Yet, compared with the cheap professions of most reformers, and the still cheaper wisdom and eloquence of politicians in general, his are almost the only sensible and valuable words, and we thank Heaven for him. Comparatively, he is always strong, original, and, above all, practical. Still, his quality is not wisdom, but prudence. The lawyer's truth is not Truth, but consistency or a consistent expediency. Truth is always in harmony with herself, and is not concerned chiefly to reveal the justice that may consist with wrong-doing. He well deserves to be called, as he has been called, the Defender of the Constitution. There are really no blows to be given by him but defensive ones. He is not a leader, but a follower. His leaders are the men of '87. "I have never made an effort," he says, "and never propose to make an effort; I have never countenanced an effort, and never mean to countenance an effort, to disturb the arrangement as originally made, by which the various States came into the Union." Still thinking of the sanction which the Constitution gives to slavery, he says, "Because it was a part of the original compact,—let it stand." Notwithstanding his special acuteness and ability, he is unable to take a fact out of its merely political relations, and behold it as it lies absolutely to be disposed of by the intellect,— what, for instance, it behooves a man to do here in America to-day with regard to slavery,—but ventures, or is driven, to make some such desperate answer as the following while professing to speak absolutely, and as a private man,— from which what new and singular code of social duties might be inferred? "The manner," says he, "in which the governments of those States where slavery exists are to regulate it is for their own consideration, under their responsibility to their constituents, to the general laws of propriety, humanity, and justice, and to God. Associations formed elsewhere, springing from a feeling of humanity, or other cause, have nothing whatever to do with it. They have never received any encouragement from me, and they never will."

They who know of no purer sources of truth, who have traced up its stream no higher, stand, and wisely stand, by the Bible and the Constitution, and drink at it there with reverence and humility; but they who behold where it comes trickling into this lake or that pool, gird up their loins once more, and continue their pilgrimage toward its fountainhead.

No man with a genius for legislation has appeared in America. They are rare in the history of the world. There are orators, politicians, and eloquent men, by the thousand; but the speaker has not yet opened his mouth to speak who is capable of settling the much-vexed questions of the day. We love eloquence for its own sake, and not for any truth which it may utter, or any heroism it may inspire. Our legislators have not yet learned the comparative value of free-trade and of freedom, of union, and of rectitude, to a nation. They have no genius or talent for comparatively humble questions of taxation and finance, commerce and manufactures and agriculture. If we were left solely to the wordy wit of legislators in Congress for our guidance, uncorrected by the seasonable experience and the effectual complaints of the people, America would not long retain her rank among the nations. For eighteen hundred years, though perchance I have no right to say it, the New Testament has been written; yet where is the legislator who has wisdom and practical talent enough to avail himself of the light which it sheds on the science of legislation?

The authority of government, even such as I am willing to submit to,—for I will cheerfully obey those who know and can do better than I, and in many things even those who neither know nor can do so well,—is still an impure one: to be strictly just, it must have the sanction and consent of the governed. It can have no pure right over my person and property but what I concede to it. The progress from an absolute to a limited monarchy, from a limited monarchy to a democracy, is a progress toward a true respect for the individual. Even the Chinese philosopher was wise enough to regard the individual as the basis of the empire. Is a democracy, such as we know it, the last improvement possible in government? Is it not possible to take a step further towards recognizing and organizing the rights of man? There will never be a really free and enlightened State until the State comes to recognize the individual as a higher and independent power, from which all its own power and authority are derived, and treats him accordingly. I please myself with imagining a State at last which can afford to be just to all men, and to treat the individual with respect as a neighbor; which even would not think it inconsistent with its own repose if a few were to live aloof from it, not meddling with it, nor embraced by it, who fulfilled all the duties of neighbors and fellow-men. A State which bore this kind of fruit, and suffered it to drop off as fast as it ripened, would prepare the way for a still more perfect and glorious State, which also I have imagined, but not yet anywhere seen.

E. B. WHITE

Walden—1954[1]

In his journal for July 10-12, 1841, Thoreau wrote: "A slight sound at evening lifts me up by the ears, and makes life seem inexpressibly serene and grand. It may be in Uranus, or it may be in the shutter." The book into which he later managed to pack both Uranus and the shutter was published in 1854, and now, a hundred years having gone by, Walden, its serenity and grandeur unimpaired, still lifts us up by the ears, still translates for us that language we are in danger of forgetting, "which all things and events speak without metaphor, which alone is copious and standard."

Walden is an oddity in American letters. It may very well be the oddest of our distinguished oddities. For many it is a great deal too odd, and for many it is a particular bore. I have not found it to be a well-liked book among my acquaintances, although usually spoken of with respect, and one literary critic for whom I have the highest regard can find no reason why anyone gives Walden a second thought. To admire the book is, in fact, something of an embarrassment, for the mass of men have an indistinct notion that its author was a sort of Nature Boy.

I think it is of some advantage to encounter the book at a period in one's life when the normal anxieties and enthusiasms and rebellions of youth closely resemble those of Thoreau in that spring of 1845 when he borrowed an axe, went out to the woods, and began to whack down some trees for timber. Received at such a juncture, the book is like an invitation to life's dance, assuring the troubled recipient that no matter what befalls him in the way of success or failure he will always be welcome at the party—that the music is played for him, too, if he will but listen and move his feet. In effect, that is what the book is—an invitation, unengraved; and it stirs one as a young girl is stirred by her first big party bid. Many think it a sermon; many set it down as an attempt to rearrange society; some think it an exercise in nature-loving; some find it a rather irritating collection of inspirational puffballs by an eccentric show-off. I think it none of these. It still seems to me the best youth's companion yet written by an American, for it carries a solemn warning against the loss of one's valuables, it advances a good argument for traveling light and trying new adventures, it rings with the power of positive adoration, it contains religious feeling without religious images, and it steadfastly refuses to record bad news. Even its pantheistic note is so pure as to be noncorrupting—pure as the flute-

[1] From The Yale Review, XLIV (Autumn, 1954). Copyright, 1954, by Yale University Press. Reprinted by permission.

note blown across the pond on those faraway summer nights. If our colleges and universities were alert, they would present a cheap pocket edition of the book to every senior upon graduating, along with his sheepskin, or instead of it. Even if some senior were to take it literally and start felling trees, there could be worse mishaps: the axe is older than the Dictaphone and it is just as well for a young man to see what kind of chips he leaves before listening to the sound of his own voice. And even if some were to get no farther than the table of contents, they would learn how to name eighteen chapters by the use of only thirty-nine words and would see how sweet are the uses of brevity.

If Thoreau had merely left us an account of a man's life in the woods, or if he had simply retreated to the woods and there recorded his complaints about society, or even if he had contrived to include both records in one essay, Walden would probably not have lived a hundred years. As things turned out, Thoreau, very likely without knowing quite what he was up to, took man's relation to nature and man's dilemma in society and man's capacity for elevating his spirit and he beat all these matters together, in a wild free interval of self-justification and delight, and produced an original omelette from which people can draw nourishment in a hungry day. Walden is one of the first of the vitamin-enriched American dishes. If it were a little less good than it is, or even a little less queer, it would be an abominable book. Even as it is, it will continue to baffle and annoy the literal mind and all those who are unable to stomach its caprices and imbibe its theme. Certainly the plodding economist will continue to have rough going if he hopes to emerge from the book with a clear system of economic thought. Thoreau's assault on the Concord society of the mid-nineteenth century has the quality of a modern Western: he rides into the subject at top speed, shooting in all directions. Many of his shots ricochet and nick him on the rebound, and throughout the melee there is a horrendous cloud of inconsistencies and contradictions, and when the shooting dies down and the air clears, one is impressed chiefly by the courage of the rider and by how splendid it was that somebody should have ridden in there and raised all that ruckus.

When he went to the pond, Thoreau struck an attitude and did so deliberately, but his posturing was not to draw the attention of others to him but rather to draw his own attention more closely to himself. "I learned this at least by my experiment: that if one advances confidently in the direction of his dreams, and endeavors to live the life which he has imagined, he will meet with a success unexpected in common hours." The sentence has the power to resuscitate the youth drowning in his sea of doubt. I recall my exhilaration upon reading it, many years ago, in a time of hesitation and despair. It restored me to health. And now in 1954 when I salute Henry Thoreau on the hundredth birthday of his book, I am merely paying off an old score—or an installment on it.

In his journal for May 3-4, 1838—Boston to Portland—he wrote: "Midnight—head over the boat's side—between sleeping and waking—with glimpses of one or more lights in the vicinity of Cape Ann. Bright moonlight—the effect heightened by seasickness." The entry illuminates the man, as the moon the sea on that night in May. In Thoreau the natural scene was heightened, not depressed, by a disturbance of the stomach, and nausea met its match at last. There was a steadiness in at least one passenger if there was none in the boat. Such steadiness (which in some would be called intoxication) is at the heart of *Walden*—confidence, faith, the discipline of looking always at what is to be seen, undeviating gratitude for the life-everlasting that he found growing in his front yard. "There is nowhere recorded a simple and irrepressible satisfaction with the gift of life, any memorable praise of God." He worked to correct that deficiency. *Walden* is his acknowledgment of the gift of life. It is the testament of a man in a high state of indignation because (it seemed to him) so few ears heard the uninterrupted poem of creation, the morning wind that forever blows. If the man sometimes wrote as though all his readers were male, unmarried, and well-connected, it is because he gave his testimony during the callow years, and, for that matter, never really grew up. To reject the book because of the immaturity of the author and the bugs in the logic is to throw away a bottle of good wine because it contains bits of the cork.

Thoreau said he required of every writer, first and last, a simple and sincere account of his own life. Having delivered himself of this chesty dictum, he proceeded to ignore it. In his books and even in his enormous journal, he withheld or disguised most of the facts from which an understanding of his life could be drawn. *Walden*, subtitled "Life in the Woods," is not a simple and sincere account of a man's life, either in or out of the woods; it is an account of a man's journey into the mind, a toot on the trumpet to alert the neighbors. Thoreau was well aware that no one can alert his neighbors who is not wide awake himself, and he went to the woods (among other reasons) to make sure that he would stay awake during his broadcast. What actually took place during the years 1845-47 is largely unrecorded, and the reader is excluded from the private life of the author, who supplies almost no gossip about himself, a great deal about his neighbors and about the universe.

As for me, I cannot in this short ramble give a simple and sincere account of my own life, but I think Thoreau might find it instructive to know that this memorial essay is being written in a house that, through no intent on my part, is the same size and shape as his own domicile on the pond—about ten by fifteen, tight, plainly finished, and at a little distance from my Concord. The house in which I sit this morning was built to accommodate a boat, not a man, but by long experience I have learned that in most respects it shelters me better than the larger dwelling where my bed is, and which, by design, is a manhouse not a boathouse. Here in the boathouse I am a wilder and, it would appear, a healthier man, by a safe margin. I have a chair, a bench, a table, and I can walk into the water if I tire of the land. My house fronts a cove. Two fishermen have just arrived to spot fish from the air—an osprey and a man in a small yellow plane who works for the fish company. The man, I have noticed, is less well equipped than the hawk, who can dive directly on his fish and carry it away, without telephoning. A mouse and a squirrel share the house with me. The building is, in fact, a multiple dwelling, a semidetached affair. It is because I am semidetached while here that I find it possible to transact this private business with the fewest obstacles.

There is also a woodchuck here, living forty feet away under the wharf. When the wind is right, he can smell my house; and when the wind is contrary, I can smell his. We both use the wharf for sunning, taking turns, each adjusting his schedule to the other's convenience. Thoreau once ate a woodchuck. I think he felt he owed it to his readers, and that it was little enough, considering the indignities they were suffering at his hands and the dressing-down they were taking. (Parts of *Walden* are pure scold.) Or perhaps he ate the woodchuck because he believed every man should acquire strict business habits, and the woodchuck was destroying his market beans. I do not know. Thoreau had a strong experimental streak in him. It is probably no harder to eat a woodchuck than to construct a sentence that lasts a hundred years. At any rate, Thoreau is the only writer I know who prepared himself for his great ordeal by eating a woodchuck; also the only one who got a hangover from drinking too much water. (He was drunk the whole time, though he seldom touched wine or coffee or tea.)

Here in this compact house where I would spend one day as deliberately as Nature if I were not being pressed by *The Yale Review*, and with a woodchuck (as yet uneaten) for neighbor, I can feel the companionship of the occupant of the pondside cabin in Walden woods, a mile from the village, near the Fitchburg right of way. Even my immediate business is no barrier between us: Thoreau occasionally batted out a magazine piece, but was always suspicious of any sort of purposeful work that cut into his time. A man, he said, should take care not to be thrown off the track by every nutshell and mosquito's wing that falls on the rails.

There has been much guessing as to why he went to the pond. To set it down to escapism is, of course, to misconstrue what happened. Henry went forth to battle when he took to the woods, and *Walden* is the report of a man torn by two powerful and opposing drives—the desire to enjoy the world (and not be derailed by a mosquito wing) and the urge to set the world straight. One cannot join these two successfully, but sometimes, in rare cases, something good or even great results from the attempt of the tormented spirit to reconcile them. Henry went forth to battle, and if he set the stage himself, if he fought on his own terms and with his own weapons, it was because it was his nature to do things differently from most men, and to act in a cocky fashion. If the pond and the woods seemed a more plausible site for a house than an intown location, it was because a cowbell made for him a sweeter sound than a churchbell. *Walden*, the book, makes the sound of a cowbell, more than a churchbell, and proves the point, although both sounds are in it, and both remarkably clear and sweet. He simply preferred his churchbell at a little distance.

I think one reason he went to the woods was a perfectly simple and commonplace one—and apparently he thought so, too. "At a certain season of our life," he wrote, "we are accustomed to consider every spot as the possible site of a house." There spoke the young man, a few years out of college, who had not yet broken away from home. He hadn't married, and he had found no job that measured up to his rigid standards of employment, and like any young man, or young animal, he felt uneasy and on the defensive until he had fixed himself a den. Most young men, of course, casting about for a site, are content merely to draw apart from their kinfolks. Thoreau, convinced that the greater part of what his neighbors called good was bad, withdrew from a great deal more than family: he pulled out of everything for a while, to serve everybody right for being so stuffy, and to try his own prejudices on the dog.

The house-hunting sentence above, which starts the Chapter called "Where I Lived, and What I Lived For," is followed by another passage that is worth quoting here because it so beautifully illustrates the offbeat prose that Thoreau was master of, a prose at once strictly disciplined and wildly abandoned. "I have surveyed the country on every side within a dozen miles of where I live," continued this delirious young man. "In imagination I have bought all the farms in succession, for all were to be bought, and I knew their price. I walked over each farmer's premises, tasted his wild apples, discoursed on husbandry with him, took his farm at his price, at any price, mortgaging it to him in my mind; even put a higher price on it—took everything but a deed of it—took his word for his deed, for I dearly love to talk—cultivated it, and him too to some extent, I trust, and withdrew when I had enjoyed it long enough, leaving him to carry it on." A copydesk man could get a double hernia trying to clean up that sentence for the management, but the sentence needs no fixing; for it perfectly captures the meaning of the writer and the quality of the ramble.

"Wherever I sat, there I might live, and the landscape radiated from me accordingly." Thoreau, the home-seeker, sitting on his hummock with the entire State of Massachusetts radiating from him, is to me the most humorous of the New England figures, and *Walden* the most humorous of the books, though its humor is almost continuously subsurface and there is nothing funny anywhere, except a few weak jokes and bad puns that rise to the surface like the perch in the pond that rose to the sound of the maestro's flute. Thoreau tended to write in sentences, a feat not every writer is capable of, and *Walden* is, rhetorically speaking, a collection of certified sentences, some of them, it would now appear, as indestructible as they are errant. The book is distilled from the vast journals, and this accounts for its intensity: he picked out bright particles that pleased his eye, whirled them in the kaleidoscope of his content, and produced the pattern that has endured—the color, the form, the light.

On this its hundredth birthday, Thoreau's *Walden* is pertinent and timely.

In our uneasy season, when all men unconsciously seek a retreat from a world that has got almost completely out of hand, his house in the Concord woods is a haven. In our culture of gadgetry and the multiplicity of convenience, his cry "Simplicity, simplicity, simplicity!" has the insistence of a fire alarm. In the brooding atmosphere of war and the gathering radioactive storm, the innocence and serenity of his summer afternoons are enough to burst the remembering heart, and one gazes back upon that pleasing interlude—its confidence, its purity, its deliberateness—with awe and wonder, as one would look upon the face of a child asleep.

"This small lake was of most value as a neighbor in the intervals of a gentle rain-storm in August, when, both air and water being perfectly still, but the sky overcast, midafternoon had all the serenity of evening, and the wood-thrush sang around, and was heard from shore to shore." Now, in the perpetual overcast in which our days are spent, we hear with extra perception and deep gratitude that song, tying century to century.

I sometimes amuse myself by bringing Henry Thoreau back to life and showing him the sights. I escort him into a phone booth and let him dial Weather. "This is a delicious evening," the girl's voice says, "when the whole body is one sense, and imbibes delight through every pore." I show him the spot in the Pacific where an island used to be, before some magician made it vanish. "We know not where we are," I murmur. "The light which puts out our eyes is darkness to us. Only that day dawns to which we are awake." I thumb through the latest copy of "Vogue" with him. "Of two patterns which differ only by a few threads more or less of a particular color," I read, "the one will be sold readily, the other lie on the shelf, though it frequently happens that, after the lapse of a season, the latter becomes the most fashionable." Together we go outboarding on the Assabet, looking for what we've lost—a hound, a bay horse, a turtledove. I show him a distracted farmer who is trying to repair a hay baler before the thunder shower breaks. "This farmer," I remark, "is endeavoring to solve the problem of a livelihood by a formula more complicated than the problem itself. To get his shoe strings he speculates in herds of cattle."

I take the celebrated author to Twenty-One for lunch, so the waiters may study his shoes. The proprietor welcomes us. "The gross feeder," remarks the proprietor, sweeping the room with his arm, "is a man in the larva stage." After lunch we visit a classroom in one of those schools conducted by big corporations to teach their superannuated executives how to retire from business without serious injury to their health. (The shock to men's systems these days when relieved of the exacting routine of amassing wealth is very great and must be cushioned.) "It is not necessary," says the teacher to his pupils, "that a man should earn his living by the sweat of his brow, unless he sweats easier than I do. We are determined to be starved before we are hungry."

I turn on the radio and let Thoreau hear Winchell beat the red hand

around the clock. "Time is but the stream I go a-fishing in," shouts Mr.
Winchell, rattling his telegraph key. "Hardly a man takes a half hour's nap
after dinner, but when he wakes he holds up his head and asks, 'What's the
news?' If we read of one man robbed, or murdered, or killed by accident, or
one house burned, or one vessel wrecked, or one steamboat blown up, or one
cow run over on the Western Railroad, or one mad dog killed, or one lot of
grasshoppers in the winter—we need never read of another. One is enough."

I doubt that Thoreau would be thrown off balance by the fantastic sights
and sounds of the twentieth century. "The Concord nights," he once wrote,
"are stranger than the Arabian nights." A four-engined air liner would merely
serve to confirm his early views on travel. Everywhere he would observe, in
new shapes and sizes, the old predicaments and follies of men—the desperation, the impediments, the meanness—along with the visible capacity for
elevation of the mind and soul. "This curious world which we inhabit is more
wonderful than it is convenient; more beautiful than it is useful; it is more
to be admired and enjoyed than used." He would see that today ten thousand
engineers are busy making sure that the world shall be convenient if they bust
doing it, and others are determined to increase its usefulness even though
its beauty is lost somewhere along the way.

At any rate, I'd like to stroll about the countryside in Thoreau's company
for a day, observing the modern scene, inspecting today's snowstorm, pointing
out the sights, and offering belated apologies for my sins. Thoreau is unique
among writers in that those who admire him find him uncomfortable to live
with—a regular hairshirt of a man. A little band of dedicated Thoreauvians
would be a sorry sight indeed: fellows who hate compromise and have com-
promised, fellows who love wildness and have lived tamely, and at their side,
censuring them and chiding them, the ghostly figure of this upright man, who
long ago gave corroboration to impulses they perceived were right and issued
warnings against the things they instinctively knew to be their enemies. I
should hate to be called a Thoreauvian, yet I wince every time I walk into the
barn I'm pushing before me, seventy-five feet by forty, and the author of
Walden has served as my conscience through the long stretches of my trivial
days.

Hairshirt or no, he is a better companion than most, and I would not swap
him for a soberer or more reasonable friend even if I could. I can reread his
famous invitation with undiminished excitement. The sad thing is that not
more acceptances have been received, that so many decline for one reason or
another, pleading some previous engagement or ill health. But the invitation
stands. It will beckon as long as this remarkable book stays in print—which will
be as long as there are August afternoons in the intervals of a gentle rainstorm,
as long as there are ears to catch the faint sounds of the orchestra. I find it
agreeable to sit here this morning, in a house of correct proportions, and hear
across a century of time his flute, his frogs, and his seductive summons to the
wildest revels of them all.

PLATO

The Apology of Socrates[1]

Socrates' Defence

What effect my accusers had upon you, Men of Athens, I know not. As for me, they well-nigh made me forget who I was, so telling were their speeches! And yet, so to say, not one atom of truth did they utter. But that which astonished me most among all their fabrications was this, that they said you must be on your guard, and not be deceived by me, as I was a masterly speaker. That they should not be ashamed when they were promptly going to be caught by me in a lie, through the fact, since I shall show myself to be no orator at all, therein methought they reached the very height of their effrontery; unless perchance what they call masterly speaker means the one who tells the truth. If that is what they are saying, then I will admit I am an orator, though not of the sort they describe.

Well then, as I say, these men have uttered nothing, or next to nothing, that is true. From me, however, you shall hear the simple truth. But, by Heaven! fellow citizens, it will not be in language like theirs, decked out with epithets and phrases, nor beautifully ordered; rather you shall hear such utterances as come to me, in any words that offer, for of the justice of what I say I am convinced, and from me you need none of you expect aught else. No, Gentlemen! it would hardly befit a man of my age to come into your presence moulding phrases like a youngster. And nevertheless, my fellow citizens, and above all, I do request and beg of you this thing: if you should hear me pleading my cause with the same expressions I habitually have used in speaking, whether at the market by the counters, where many of you have heard me, or elsewhere, do not for that reason marvel and make a disturbance. The facts stand thus. At the age of seventy years I now for the first time have come up before a tribunal, and so I am an absolute stranger to the language of this place. Let it be as if I really were a foreigner here, since then you surely would excuse me if I used the accent and manner of speech in which I was reared. And so I now make this request of you, a matter of justice as it seems to me, that you let me use my way of speaking; it may be better, it may be worse, but the only thing you have to consider is this, and this is what you have to put your mind on, whether that which I say is right or not. That is the merit of a judge; the merit of a speaker is to tell the truth.

To begin with, fellow citizens, it is right for me to answer the earliest

[1] *Plato on the Trial and Death of Socrates*, Lane Cooper trans. (Ithaca, N. Y.: Cornell University Press, 1941), pp. 49-77. Reprinted by permission of the publishers.

charges falsely brought against me, and my first accusers, and then I must answer the charges and accusers that come later.

Many, in fact, were they who formerly brought charges against me, yes many years ago, and spoke not a word of truth. And them I fear more than I do the group of Anytus, dangerous as these are too. No, Gentlemen, those others are more dangerous, for they have prejudiced the major part of you since your childhood, convincing you of an utterly false charge against me; to wit, 'There is a person, Socrates by name, a "wise man," who speculates about the heavens above, and also searches into everything below the earth, and in argument can make the worse case win.' [2] Those persons who have spread this charge abroad, they, fellow citizens, are my dangerous accusers; for people who listen to them think that men who make the said investigations do not believe in any gods. Add that these accusers are many in number, have brought their charges for a long time now, and, moreover, made them to you when you most readily believed things, when some of you were children or striplings; sheer accusation of an absent person without anybody to defend him. And what is most baffling of all, it is impossible to identify and name them, unless perchance in the case of a certain comic poet. For the rest, for all who through jealousy and malice misled you, and those who, once they were misled, got others to believe the same—with all these it is impossible to deal. There is no means of bringing one of them here to court, or putting a single one to cross-examination. No, in making my defence I am simply forced to fight, as it were, with shadows, and to question with nobody to make reply. Accordingly, I ask you to assume with me that, as I say, my accusers fall into these two classes, one group who are accusing me at present, the other those who of old accused me as aforesaid; and understand that it is these I must reply to first, for it is they whom you heard bringing charges earlier, and far more than this group who now come after.

Well then, fellow citizens, I must now make my defence, and must try to clear away in this brief time that calumny which you have entertained so long. I would that this might come to pass, if so it should be better for both you and me, and if it profits me to plead. But I think the task to be a hard one, and what its nature is I am by no means unaware. Still, let the outcome be as it pleases God; the law must be obeyed, and the defence be made.

Let us, then, go back and look at the original accusation from which the slander arose, the slander that gave Meletus his ground for this indictment he has lodged against me. Let us see. Precisely what did the slanderers say when they slandered? We must read their complaint as if it were a legal accusation: 'Socrates is wicked; overdoes inquiry into what occurs below the earth and in the heavens; in arguing makes the worse case win; and teaches others to do the same as he.' Such is in substance the accusation—what you actually saw in the comedy [the *Clouds*] of Aristophanes, where a man called 'Socrates' is swung about, declaring that he treads the air, and sputtering a deal of other

[2] The proverbial translation is: 'To make the worse appear the better reason.'

nonsense on matters of which I have not one bit of knowledge either great or small. And I do not say so in disparagement of any science such as that, if any one is learned in such matters; I should not wish to be attacked by Meletus upon so grave a charge. But actually, fellow citizens, to me these matters are of absolutely no concern. I call the greater part of you yourselves to witness, and beg all who ever heard me in discussion to tell one another and declare it; many of you are in a position to do this. Declare to one another, therefore, whether any of you ever heard me dealing with such matters either briefly or at length. In that way you will see what all the rest amounts to of what the generality of people say concerning me.

No, there is nothing in it whatsoever. And if you have heard anybody say that I profess to give instruction, and get money in that way, neither is that true; although to my mind it is very fine indeed if any one is able to instruct his fellows, as are Gorgias of Leontini, and Prodicus of Ceos, and Hippias of Elis. Each one of them is able, Gentlemen, to go to city after city and attract young men; youths who might without expense consort with any one they chose among their own fellow citizens, these they persuade to give up that fellowship, to consort with them, to pay them money, and to be grateful to them besides. And indeed there is another man of learning here, from Paros, who, I learned, was staying in the City, for I happened to be calling on a man, Callias son of Hipponicus, who has paid more money to the Sophists than have all the others put together. And so I questioned him, he having, in fact, two sons:

'Callias,' said I, 'if your two sons had been colts or calves, we should have no trouble in finding some one to look after them, who for pay would make them fine and good according to the standard of their kind. We should pick some trainer of horses, say, or farmer. But now that they are human beings, whom have you in mind to put in charge of them? Who is there with a knowledge of their proper quality, the excellence of a human being and a citizen? I fancy you have given thought to this since you have sons. Is there any one,' said I, 'or not?'

'Yes, certainly,' said he.

'Who?' said I. 'Whence comes he? What does he charge for teaching?'

'Socrates,' he said, 'it is Evenus; comes from Paros; charge, five minae.' So I thought Evenus was a lucky man if he really had this art, and would teach it at so reasonable a rate. For myself, I should be very proud and self-conceited if I knew all that. But the truth is, fellow citizens, I have no such knowledge.

Then perhaps some one of you may be inclined to ask: 'But, Socrates, what is the matter with you? What is the origin of these charges that are made against you? Unless you acted very differently from everybody else, surely no such story and repute would have arisen—if you did not do something other than most people do. Tell us what it is, in order to keep us from rushing to our own conclusion about you.'

That, I take it, would be fairly spoken; and I shall try to show you what it is that has given me this name and ill repute. Pray listen. Some of you, perhaps, will take me to be joking, but be assured that I shall tell you the simple truth. The fact is, fellow citizens, that I have got this name through my possession of a certain wisdom. What sort of wisdom is it? A wisdom, doubtless, that appertains to man. With respect to this, perhaps, I actually am wise; whereas those others whom I just now mentioned may possibly be wise with a wisdom more than human, or else I do not know what to say of it; as for me, I certainly do not possess it, and whoever says I do is lying, and seeks to injure me.

And, fellow citizens, do not interrupt me even if I say what seems extravagant, for the statement I shall make is not my own; instead, I shall refer you to a witness whose word can be accepted. Your witness to my wisdom, if I have any, and to its nature, is the god at Delphi. You certainly knew Chaerephon. He was a friend of mine from our youth, and a friend of your popular party as well; he shared in your late exile, and accompanied you on your return. Now you know the temper of Chaerephon, how impulsive he was in everything he undertook. Well so it was when once he went to Delphi, and made bold to ask the oracle this question—and, Gentlemen, please do not make an uproar over what I say; he asked if there was any one more wise than I. Then the Pythian oracle made response that there was no one who was wiser. To this response his brother here will bear you witness, since Chaerephon himself is dead.

Now bear in mind the reason why I tell you this. It is because I am going on to show you whence this calumny of me has sprung; for when I heard about the oracle, I communed within myself: 'What can the god be saying, and what does the riddle mean? Well I know in my own heart that I am without wisdom great or small. What is it that he means, then, in declaring me to be most wise? It cannot be that he is lying; it is not in his nature.' For a long time I continued at a loss as to his meaning, then finally decided, much against my will, to seek it in the following way.

I went to one of those who pass for wise men, feeling sure that there if anywhere I could refute the answer, and explain to the oracle: 'Here is a man that is wiser than I, but you said I was the wisest.' The man I went to see was one of our statesmen; his name I need not mention. Him I thoroughly examined, and from him, as I studied him and conversed with him, I gathered, fellow citizens, this impression. This man appeared to me to seem to be wise to others, and above all to himself, but not to be so. And then I tried to show him that he thought that he was wise, but was not. The result was that I gained his enmity and the enmity as well of many of those who were present. So, as I went away, I reasoned with myself: 'At all events I am wiser than this man is. It is quite possible that neither one of us knows anything fine and good. But this man fancies that he knows when he does not, while I, whereas I do not know, just so I do not fancy that I know. In this small item, then, at least, I seem to be wiser than he, in that I do not fancy that I know what I do not.' Thereafter I went to another man, one of those who passed for wiser than the first, and I got the same impression. Whereupon I gained his enmity as well as that of many more.

Thereafter I went from one man to another, perceiving, with grief and apprehension, that I was getting hated, but it seemed imperative to put the service of the god above all else. In my search for the meaning of the oracle I must go to all who were supposed to have some knowledge. And, fellow citizens, by the Dog, since I have to tell you the truth, here is pretty much what I encountered. The persons with the greatest reputation seemed to me to be the ones who were well-nigh the most deficient, as I made my search in keeping with the god's intent; whereas others of inferior reputation I found to be men superior in regard to their possession of the truth. I needs must tell you all about my wandering course, a veritable round of toils heroic, which I underwent to prove that the oracle was not to be refuted.

After the statesmen, I went to the poets, tragic, dithyrambic, and the rest. There, I thought, my ignorance would be self-evident in comparison with them. So I took those poems of theirs which seemed to me to have been most carefully wrought by them, and asked the authors what they meant, in order that I might at the same time learn from them. Well, Gentlemen, I am ashamed to tell you the truth; and yet it must be done. The fact is, pretty nearly everybody, so to say, who was present could have spoken better than the authors did about the poems they themselves had written. So here again in a short time I learned this about the poets too, that not by wisdom do they make what they compose, but by a gift of nature and an inspiration similar to that of the diviners and the oracles. These also utter many beautiful things, but understand not one of them. And such, I saw, was the experience of the poets. At the same time I perceived that their poetic gift led them to fancy that in all else, too, they were the wisest of mankind, when they were not. So I went away from them as well, believing that I had the same advantage over them as over the statesmen.

To make an end, I went, then, to the artisans. Conscious that I did not, so to say, know anything myself, I was certain I should find that they knew many things and fine. Nor in that was I deceived; they did indeed know things which I did not, and in that they were wiser than I. But, fellow citizens, these excellent workmen seemed to me to have the same defect as the poets. Because they were successful in the practice of their art, each thought himself most wise about all other things of the highest import, and this mistake of theirs beclouded all that wisdom. So I asked myself the question, for the oracle, whether I preferred to be just what I was, neither wise as they were wise nor ignorant as they were ignorant, or to be both wise and ignorant like them. And my response to myself and the oracle was that it paid me to be as I was.

Such, fellow citizens, was the quest which brought me so much enmity, hatreds so utterly harsh and hard to bear, whence sprang so many calumnies, and this name that is given me of being 'wise'; for every time I caught another person in his ignorance, those present fancied that I knew what he did not. But, Gentlemen, in all likelihood it really is the god who is wise, and by that oracle he meant to say that human wisdom is of little worth, or none. And it appears that when he picked out 'Socrates,' he used my name to take me for an example; it was as if he said: 'O race of men, he is the wisest among you, who, like Socrates, knows that in truth his knowledge is worth nothing.' So even now I still go about in my search, and, in keeping with the god's intent, question anybody, citizen or stranger, whom I fancy to be wise. And when it seems to me that he is not, in defence of the god I show that he is not. And this activity has left me without leisure either to take any real part in civic affairs or to care for my own. Instead, I live in infinite poverty through my service to the god.

In addition, the young men who of their own accord are my companions, of the class who have most leisure, sons of the very rich—they listen with joy to the men who are examined; they often imitate me, and in turn attempt to test out others. And thereupon, I take it, they find a great abundance of men who imagine they have some knowledge, and yet know little or nothing. And then these men whom they examine get angry, not at them, but at me, and say there is one Socrates, a perfect blackguard, who corrupts the young. Yet when anybody asks them how he does it, and by teaching what, they have nothing to tell, nor do they know. But in order not to seem quite at a loss, they make the usual attacks that are leveled at philosophers, namely, about 'things occurring in the heavens and below the earth,' 'not believing in the gods,' and 'making the worse case win.' What they do not care to utter, I imagine, is the truth: that they have been shown up in their pretence to knowledge when they actually knew nothing. Accordingly, since they are proud, passionate, and numerous, and organized and effective in speaking about me, they have long since filled your ears with their violent calumnies.

From among them have come Meletus, Anytus, and Lycon to attack me; Meletus aggrieved on behalf of the poets, Anytus on behalf of the artists and the politicians, Lycon on behalf of the rhetoricians. Consequently, as I said at the beginning, I shall be surprised if I succeed, within so short a time, in ridding you of all this swollen mass of calumny.

There, fellow citizens, you have the truth. I hide nothing from you, either great or small, nor do I dissimulate. And yet I know that even by this I stir up hatred, which itself proves that I tell the truth, and that it is precisely this that constitutes the charge against me, and is the cause of it. And whether now or later you investigate the matter, you will find it to be so.

Therewith let me close my defence to you on the charges made against me by my first accusers. As for Meletus, that honest man and good friend of the City, as he styles himself, to him and my more recent foes I will now endeavour to reply.

Here again, since the present charges vary from the former, let us take the actual text of the complaint. It runs, in effect, as follows: 'Socrates,' it declares, 'offends against the law since he corrupts the young, does not believe in the gods the State believes in, and believes in novel deities [spirits, *daimonia*] instead.' Such is the accusation. Let us examine it point by point.

First, it holds that I offend by corrupting the young. But I, fellow citizens, I hold that Meletus offends in that he makes a jest of a serious matter, when he lightly brings men to trial on questions in which he pretends to be deeply interested and concerned, whereas he never took the slightest interest in any of them. That this is so, I will try to prove to you.

Your attention, Meletus! Answer! Do you not attach the utmost importance to the moral improvement of our youth?

[MELETUS.] I do indeed.

Well then, tell the assembly here, who makes the young men better? You obviously know, for it is your special concern. You have discovered, so you state, who it is that corrupts them: I, whom you bring hither and accuse. Come now, tell who the person is who makes them better, and name him to these judges.

See, Meletus, you are silent. Have you nothing to say? Doesn't that seem shameful to you, and proof enough of my assertion that you have had no interest in the matter? But come, friend, say who makes them better?

[MELETUS.] The laws.

No, my good fellow, that is not what I ask. I mean, what man? for, obviously, first of all he will have to know this very thing, the laws.

[MELETUS.] These judges, Socrates.

What say you, Meletus? These judges here are competent to instruct the young, and make them better?

[MELETUS.] Most certainly.

All are able? Or some are, and some are not?

[MELETUS.] All of them!

By Hera, that is welcome news! We have an ample store of men who benefit their kind! What next? What about the audience here, do these too make them better?

[MELETUS.] Yes, they too.

What about the Council?

[MELETUS.] Yes, the Council also.

But, Meletus, what about the men in the Assembly, the members of it, do they corrupt the young, or do they one and all make young men better?

[MELETUS.] Yes, they do it too.

So it seems that every one in Athens except me makes them fine and good, and I alone corrupt them. Is that your meaning?

[MELETUS.] Precisely that.

You detect me in a most unlucky situation. Answer me, though. Does the same thing seem to you to hold for horses too? Do you think all other men make horses better, and only one man ruins them? Or is it just the opposite of this, that some one man, or a very few, the horsemen, can improve them, whereas most people, if they have to deal with horses, and to make use of them, will spoil them? Is that not so, Meletus, both with horses and all other animals? It surely is, whether Anytus and you deny it or admit it. And what wonderful luck it would be for the young people if there were only one who did them harm, and all others did them good! But no, Meletus, you give ample proof that you never cared at all about the young; and your indifference is clearly shown—that you had no interest whatever in the things for which you bring me into court.

Now, Meletus, another question. In the name of Zeus, tell us whether it is better to live with honest citizens or with bad ones. Answer, friend; I ask you nothing difficult. Don't the wicked always do some evil to their neighbours, and the good some good?

[MELETUS.] Certainly.

Well, is there anybody who would rather be harmed than helped by those he lives with? Answer, my friend; the law requires you to do so. Does anybody like to be injured?

[MELETUS.] Certainly not.

Come now. When you bring me into court for corrupting the younger generation and making them worse, do you charge that I do so purposely or without design?

[MELETUS.] Purposely, say I.

What's that, Meletus? Are you at your age so much wiser than I am at mine? And thus, while you know that the wicked always do some injury to their nearest neighbours, and the good some good, I, you think, am come to such a state of ignorance as not to know that if I make some one I live with bad, I run the risk of getting injured by him? So according to you I do myself all this harm on purpose! That, Meletus, you will not get me to believe, nor, I fancy, anybody else in all the world. No, either I do not corrupt them, or if I do corrupt them, it is not by design. So either way you lie. If I ruin them unwittingly, the case is that of an involuntary error which does not legally bring me before this court; the proper thing would be to take me privately, and to instruct and warn me; for obviously when I learn better I shall stop doing what I do unwittingly. But you avoided joining me in order to instruct me; you chose not to do it. You bring me to this court where it is legal to try those who stand in need of punishment, not of learning.

There, fellow citizens, you have evidence enough of what I said, that Meletus has not taken the slightest interest in these matters.

Yet tell us, Meletus: in what way do you say I corrupt the younger men? Or is it not clear from the text of your complaint that you mean I teach them not to believe in the gods the State believes in, but in other new divinities? Isn't that the way you mean I corrupt them by my teaching?

[MELETUS.] Yes, that is just what I assert.

In that case, Meletus, in the name of those very gods we are discussing, explain your meaning still more clearly to these gentlemen here and me, for there is a point I am unable to make out. If you mean that I teach them to believe in the existence of certain gods, then I myself believe that there are gods, and so I am not out and out an atheist, and do not break the law in that respect. Or do you mean that they are not the gods the State believes in, but other gods instead, and is this the point of your complaint, that they are different? Or do you say that I myself do not believe in any gods at all, and that I teach this disbelief to others?

[MELETUS.] Yes, that is what I maintain, that you do not believe in any gods at all.

You amaze me, Meletus. How can you say so? Do you mean that I do not, like other men, regard the sun and moon as gods?

[MELETUS.] By Heaven, Gentlemen of the Jury, he does not; he holds that the sun is a stone, and the moon an earth.

You must think you are accusing Anaxagoras, my dear Meletus. Have you such a poor opinion of these men here, and do you think them so illiterate as not to know that the works of Anaxagoras of Clazomenae are full of these ideas? And so you think that the young men learn these things from me, when on occasion they could buy the books for a drachma at most in the orchestra, and then laugh at Socrates if he pretended that these theories were his—apart from the fact that they are so bizarre! But, by Heaven, is that the way you think of me, that I don't believe in any god whatever?

[MELETUS.] No, by Heaven, not a single one.

Now that, Meletus, is incredible, and something that I take it you do not believe yourself. In my opinion, fellow citizens, this man is an utterly overweening and unbridled person, who has brought this accusation simply out of insolence, intemperance, and youthful rashness. It looks as if he had made up a riddle with which to try me out: 'See whether Socrates, the wise man, will know that I am jesting and self-contradictory, or whether I shall fool him and all the rest who listen'; for to me he clearly contradicts himself in the complaint, where in effect he says: 'Socrates offends by not believing in gods, but by believing in gods.' And that is simply joking.

Examine with me, Gentlemen, my way of showing that he says this. And, Meletus, you answer us. But, Gentlemen, remember the request I made at the outset, and do not interrupt if I pursue the argument in my customary fashion.

Is there any living man, Meletus, who believes that there are human things, but does not believe that there are human beings? Let him answer, Gentlemen, and not make noisy protests beside the point. Does any one believe in horsemanship, and not in horses? Or does any one believe there is an art of piping, but that there are no pipers? No, honorable sir, there isn't any one who does it. If you do not choose to answer, I will speak for you and these others here as well. But give the answer to this. Is there anybody who believes in the doings of spirits [daimonia], but thinks there are no spirits [daimones]?

[MELETUS.] No.

How you oblige me by the grudging answer these gentlemen force you to make! Well then, you admit, I believe and teach that there are doings of spirits, whether recent or of old. At all events I do believe in them according to your statement; you have even sworn to this in your complaint. But if I believe in them, then quite necessarily, I suppose, I must believe in spirits. Isn't it so? It must be. I put you down as in agreement since you make no reply.

Now, must we not consider spirits as either gods or the offspring of gods? Say yes or no.

[MELETUS.] Yes, certainly.

If, then, I think that there are spirits, as you assert, and if the spirits are in some way gods, am I not right in saying that you talk in riddles and are jesting? First you say that I do not believe in gods, and next that I do believe in them inasmuch as I believe in spirits. Or again: if the spirits [daimones] are illegitimate children of the gods, whether by nymphs or other mothers as report will have it, who on earth will ever think that there are children of the gods, but that there are no gods? It would be as queer as to think that mules were the offspring of horses and asses, but that horses and asses did not exist. No, Meletus, there is no way out of it; either you formulated this complaint in order to try us out, or else you could find no real crime with which to charge me. That you could get a living person with the least intelligence to admit that a given man believed in the doings of spirits but not of gods, and that the same man, again, believed in neither spirits, gods, nor heroes, is quite beyond the bounds of possibility.

No, fellow citizens, that I am guiltless with respect to Meletus' indictment seems to me to call for no long defence; rather, let this argument suffice. But what I have said before, that much antagonism has arisen against me in the minds of many, rest assured that it is true. And this it is that will undo me, if I am undone, not Meletus nor Anytus, but the slander of the many, and their malice. Many another man, and good ones, has it undone, and, methinks, it will yet undo. There is no danger that the thing may stop with me.

Perhaps some one will say: 'Well, Socrates, aren't you ashamed that you pursued a course from which you now are in danger of death?' To that it would be right for me to reply: Good sir, it is not well said if you think that a man of any worth at all ought to calculate his chances of living or dying, and not rather look to this alone, when he acts, to see if what he does is right or wrong, and if his are the deeds of a good man or a bad. By your account, the demigods who fell at Troy would be sorry fellows, all of them, and notably the son of Thetis, who so despised all danger in comparison with any disgrace awaiting him, and with what result? When his mother saw him eager to slay Hector, she, the goddess, addressed him, as I recall, approximately thus: "My child, if you avenge the death of your comrade Patroclus by slaying Hector, then you yourself will die. For you the lot of death," she said, "comes straightway after Hector's." But he, on hearing that, made light of death and danger, fearing far more to live a coward and not avenge his loved ones. "Straightway let me die," said he, "once I give the villain his reward, and not continue here, a laughing-stock, beside the hollow ships, a burden to the earth." Do you think that he took heed of death or danger?

That, fellow citizens, is the way things really stand. If any one is stationed where he thinks it is best for him to be, or where his commander has put him, there, as it seems to me, it is his duty to remain, no matter what the risk, heedless of death or any other peril in comparison with disgrace.

It would have been dreadful conduct, fellow citizens, had I acted otherwise. When the leaders you had chosen to command me assigned a post to me at Potidaea, at Amphipolis, and at Delium, in the face of death itself I was as steadfast as any one could be in holding the position where they placed me; and when the god, as I believed and understood, assigned to me as my duty that I should live the life of a philosopher, and examine myself and others, it would have been dreadful had I through fear of death, or of anything else whatever, deserted my post. Dreadful indeed would it be, and verily any one would then be justified in bringing me to trial for not believing in gods, when I had disobeyed the oracle, feared death, and thought that I was wise when I was not.

For, Gentlemen, to be afraid of death is nothing else than thinking that one is wise when one is not, since it means fancying that one knows what one does not. Nobody knows, in fact, what death is, nor whether to man it is not perchance the greatest of all blessings; yet people fear it as if they surely knew it to be the worst of evils. And what is this but the shameful ignorance of supposing that we know what we do not? It is there and in that perhaps that I differ, Gentlemen, from the majority of mankind; and if I might call myself more wise than another, it would be in this, that as I do not know enough about what goes on in Hades, so too I do not think that I know. But doing wrong, and disobeying the person who is better than myself, be it god or man, that I know is base and wicked. Therefore never for the sake of evils which I know to be such will I fear or flee from what for all I know may be a good.

Accordingly, suppose you were now to acquit me, and went against Anytus; he who says that either I ought not to have been summoned hither to begin with, or, once I appeared I must inevitably be put to death; for he tells you that, if I am freed, your sons, who already put in practice what Socrates teaches, will all be utterly ruined. Suppose with reference to that you were to say to me: 'Socrates, at present we shall not give Anytus our assent, but will acquit you, yet upon one condition, namely, that hereafter you shall not pass your time in this investigation nor pursue philosophy; if you are caught doing it again, you die.' Well, as I said, if you were ready to let me go upon these conditions, my reply to you would be:

'Fellow citizens, I respect and love you, but I must obey the god rather than you, and so long as I draw breath, and can pursue philosophy, I will not cease from it nor from exhorting you, and ever pointing out the way to any one of you I meet, saying to him as I have been wont: "Good friend, you are a citizen

of Athens, the greatest of all cities and the most renowned for power and learning, and yet you feel no shame at giving your mind to money so that you may
get as much as possible, and to your reputation and to honor; but for insight,
for the truth, for your soul and how it shall be at its best, you do not care nor
trouble." '

And if any one of you disputes it, and says that he does care, I shall not
forthwith dismiss him and go away, but will question him, and sift him, and
put him to the test; and if he seems to me to have no fund of virtue, while
professing to have it, I shall reproach him with attaching little value to what
has most importance, and taking paltry things for what is larger. So will I do
with young and old, whatever he be that I meet with, foreigner or native, yet
rather with you citizens since you are nearer to me by kin; for this, you may
rest assured, is what the god demands of me. And I think that there never came
to you a greater good in the City than the service I render the god.

All I do is to go about persuading you, both young and old, not to think
first of your bodies or your property, nor to be so mightily concerned about
them as about your souls, how the spirit shall be at its best; it is my task to tell
you that virtue does not spring from wealth, but that wealth and every other
good that comes to men in private life or in public proceed from virtue. If it
is by saying this that I corrupt the young, then this must be injurious; but any
one who holds that I say anything save this says nothing. On that head, fellow
citizens, I may assure you that whether you trust Anytus or not, and whether
you acquit me or do not acquit me, I shall not alter my course, no matter if I
have to die a hundred times.

Now, fellow citizens, do not interrupt, but continue granting my request of
you not to cry out at what I may say, but to listen; I do believe that you will
profit if you listen. I am, in fact, about to tell you certain other things at which
you might possibly protest. Yet please do not. No; for you may rest assured
that if you condemn me to death, I being such a person as I say, you will do
yourselves more harm than you do me. As for me, Meletus will no more hurt
me than will Anytus. It does not lie in his power, for in my belief the eternal
order does not permit a better man to be harmed by a worse. Oh yes! quite
possibly he might kill or banish me, or rob me of my civil rights; and doubtless this man and the next will think that these are major evils. I do not think
them such; no, I think it a far greater evil for a man to do what this man now
is doing, namely trying to get a man condemned to death unjustly.

So, fellow citizens, at present I am far from making my defence upon my
own account, as one might think; I make it for your sake, in order that you may
not, by condemning me, do wrong about the gift of the god to you; for if you
have me put to death, you will not easily find another of the sort, fastened upon
the City by the god, for all the world (if I may use a rather ludicrous comparison) like a gadfly on a great and noble horse that is somewhat sluggish
on account of his size and needs the fly to wake him up. So, it seems to me, the
god has fastened me like that upon the City, to rouse, exhort, and rebuke each

one of you, everywhere besetting you, and never once ceasing all day long. Another one like that, Gentlemen, you will not come by so easily; but if you listen to me, you will take good care of me. You may, however, quite possibly be annoyed, like people awakened from their slumbers, and, striking out at me, may listen readily to Anytus and condemn me to death. Then you would finish out the rest of your life in sleep, unless the god were in mercy to send you some one else to take my place. That it is the deity by whom I, such as I am, have been given to the City you may see from this: it is not like human nature for me to neglect all my own concerns, to put up with a neglected household all these years, and to attend to your affair, ever going to you individually in private, like a father or an elder brother, urging you to care for your moral welfare. And if I got any profit from it all, if these exhortations brought me any pay, there would seem to be some reason in my conduct. As it is, you see for yourselves that my accusers, who, unashamed, have brought so many other charges against me, have yet not had the effrontery to present a witness to allege that I ever took any sort of fee or sought one. Why not? Because, methinks, the witness I present to show that I speak the truth is quite enough—my poverty.

Possibly it may look odd that I should busily go about in private with my counsels, but in public dare not approach the mass of you with counsel for the City. The reason for that is something you have often heard me speak of in many a place; it is that there comes to me a thing divine and spiritual, what Meletus has mockingly referred to in his indictment. From childhood on, this sign has come to me; it is a voice, which, when it comes, always deters me from what I am about to do, but never urges me to act. It is this that fights against my entering political affairs; and the opposition strikes me as being altogether good; for, fellow citizens, you may rest assured that if I, long ago, had tried to take up politics, I should long ago have perished, and been of no service whatever either to you or to myself. And do not be aggrieved at me for telling the truth: there is not a man on earth that is safe if he nobly puts himself in opposition to you or to any other crowd, and strives to stop all sorts of wrong and lawlessness in the State. But if any one is really going to battle for the right, and to be safe for some short time in doing it, he must perforce remain a private citizen; he must not appear in public life.

Of that I will furnish you with telling evidence, not arguments, but what you value, facts. Listen to what happened in my case, and you will see that I am not a man to yield to any one unjustly for fear of death, not even if by my not yielding I were at once to perish. The tale I shall tell you is of the legal sort and uninspiring, but is true.

I never held any public office, fellow citizens, but one: I was a member of the Council. And it happened that our tribe, Antiochis, had the executive function [prytany] at the time you wished to sentence in a body the ten commanders who failed to pick up the survivors of the naval action [at Arginusae]. The procedure was illegal, as after a while you all admitted. But at the time I was the only one of the prytanes who stood out against your doing an illegal act and voted against you; and although the orators were ready to indict me and arrest me, while you urged them on and made an uproar, I thought that I ought to risk all danger on the side of law and justice rather than side with you in an unjust decree for fear of imprisonment or death.

This took place while Athens still was a democracy. But again, when the oligarchy was established, the Thirty had me and four others summoned to the Rotunda, and ordered us to go get Leon of Salamis, and bring him thence to have him put to death; they gave such orders frequently to many other persons in order to involve as many as they could in their crimes. But there again I showed, by deeds, and not by words, that death, if I may speak quite baldly, meant nothing at all to me, while not to do an unjust or an impious act, this meant everything; for that power, however huge its sway, did not terrify me into doing what was wrong. No, when we came out of the Rotunda, the other four went off to Salamis and brought back Leon, and as for me I went to my home. And for that I might well have paid with my life, had the government not promptly fallen. Of these facts many persons will bear witness to you.

Well then, do you think I could have survived through all these years if I had taken part in state affairs, and, acting properly as a good citizen, had fought for justice, making this perforce of paramount importance? Far from it, fellow citizens; nor could any other living man have done it. As for me, all my life long, if ever I did anything in an official way, I showed myself to be that sort of person, and in private just the same; never once did I yield to anyone in any point against the right, not even to one of those whom my slanderers declare to be my pupils.

But I never have been anybody's teacher. If anyone cares to listen to me as I speak and carry on my special function, be he young or old, I never have begrudged it. I am not one who will engage in discussion if he gets money, and if not refuses. No, rich and poor alike I am prepared to question, and whoever will may listen to what I say when I make reply. And for my part, if any of them turns out well or ill, I cannot rightly be held responsible when I never offered to give any one instruction, nor gave it. If any one asserts that he ever learned or heard a thing from me other than what all the others heard as well, rest assured that he who says so does not tell the truth.

Well then, why do certain persons like to spend so much of their time with me? I told you, fellow citizens, what the reason is. The truth of the matter is just what I said: they like to hear the sifting out of those who think that they are wise, but are not. The thing, in fact, is not unpleasant. But for me, as I aver, it is a task enjoined upon me by the deity, through oracles, through dreams, and in every single way that ever a divine injunction was laid upon a man to do a thing. These statements, fellow citizens, are true and are easily proved. Suppose I am at present ruining some of the young people, and already have perverted others; then necessarily, no doubt, a number of them, when they grew older, would have seen that on occasion, when they were young, I gave them evil advice, and would now appear in court to accuse and punish me. Or, if they themselves were unwilling to do it, then some of their relations, fathers, brothers, or others of their kin—if it were true that members of the family had received some injury from me—would now remember it, and have me punished. Certainly there are many of them present whom I see: first Crito here, a man of my own generation and my deme, father of yon Critobulus; next, Lysanias of Sphettus, father of yon Aeschines; add Antiphon here of Kephisia, father of Epigenes. Among others, men whose brothers have attended at the pastime, Nicostratus, son of Theozotides and brother of Theodotus—as for Theodotus, he is dead, and therefore could not plead for me against him; so also Paralus here whose father is Demodocus and whose brother is Theages, Adeimantus son of Ariston whose brother is Plato here, and Aiantodorus, whose brother is yon Apollodorus. And many others I could name to you, of whom Meletus surely ought to have offered somebody as witness in his accusation. If he forgot it then, let him present it now—I yield the point—and let him say if he has any evidence of the sort. But, Gentlemen, you will find the case to be the very opposite of that; will find them all prepared to help me, the ruiner, the man who has done injury to their kin, as Meletus and Anytus aver. The ruined themselves, of course, might have some reason for coming to my aid. But those who are not ruined, men already mature, the relatives of these, what other reason could they have for coming to my aid except the straight and just one, that they know that Meletus is lying, and that I am telling the truth?

There you have it, Gentlemen. That is pretty much what I might have to say in my defence, that with possibly some additions, to the like effect. Perhaps, however, one or another of you will be angry when he recalls his own experience, in some trial he was engaged in of less gravity than this; if he besought and with many tears implored the judges, and, in order to arouse the greatest pity, brought in his children along with others of his kin and many friends; while, as for me, I shall do nothing of the sort, although I am in danger, as I might suppose, to the last degree of peril. Perhaps, then, as he thinks of this, he will bear himself with the less remorse towards me, and, irritated by these very things, will cast his vote in anger. Now if any of you feels so, though for my part I do not impute it—but if anybody feels that way, then it seems to me the proper thing for me to say to him would be: 'Good friend, I too have friends and relatives; in fact, my case is just as Homer says. "I did not spring from either oak or rock," but from mankind, and so I have a family and sons; three sons, my fellow citizens, one a youth, and the other two are little boys.' Nevertheless not one of them will I bring hither imploring you to let me off. And why shall I do nothing of all that? Not, fellow citizens, out of hardihood, nor in disdain of you. And whether I fear death or not is another question; but for my own honor, and yours, and the honor of the entire City, it does not seem proper for me at my age, and with the name I have, to do any of these things. The opinion may be true, or may be false; at all events the view is held that Socrates is somehow different from the mass of men. Well, if those of you who are regarded as distinguished in point of wisdom, or of courage, or of any other quality, behaved like that, it would be shameful. And yet, often enough, I have seen persons of such sort, persons of some reputation, behaving in extraordinary fashion when they were to hear the verdict, as if they thought they must be going to suffer something terrible if they had to die—as if they thought that they would be immortal in case you did not condemn them. To my mind, they brought shame upon the City; anybody from another city would infer that the Athenians who were eminent for their virtue, those whom their fellows selected as their rulers and for other places of distinction, were in no way better than women. These things, fellow citizens, it behoves us not to do if we have any reputation whatsoever; and if we do them, you should not allow it. No; you should make this very thing quite clear, that you will far more readily give your vote against the person who drags in these tearful dramas, and makes the City ridiculous, than against the man who argues quietly.

But apart from the question of propriety, Gentlemen, it does not seem right to me to beg the judge for mercy, or, by doing it, to get away, when one ought rather to enlighten and convince him. He does not take his seat for this, the judge, to render justice as a favor, but to decide on what is just. Indeed he took an oath that he would not favor people according to his notion of them, but that he would give judgment in accordance with the laws. And so we should not get you into the habit of perjuring yourselves, nor should you get into it; neither of us should commit impiety. So do not ask me, fellow citizens, to treat you in a way which I take to be dishonorable, wrong, and impious; above all, by Zeus! when I am under accusation of impiety by this Meletus here present; for obviously, if I swayed you and by begging forced you to act against your oath, I would be teaching you not to believe that there are gods, and by my defence would simply accuse myself of not believing in them. But that be far from me! I do believe in them, my fellow citizens, as none of my accusers does; and to you I commend myself, and to the Deity, to judge concerning me what shall be best at once for me and for you.

After the Vote against Him

If I am not distressed, my fellow citizens, at what has happened in that you voted to convict me, there are many reasons for it, and in particular that the outcome was to me not unexpected. What is to me far more surprising is the actual division of the votes. I thought for my part that the vote would go not by this small majority, but by a large one. As it is, apparently, if only thirty votes had gone the other way, I should have been acquitted. Accordingly, so far as Meletus is concerned, it seems to me I do now stand acquitted, and not only that, but it must be clear to everyone that if Anytus and Lycon had not come hither to accuse me, he would have had to pay one thousand drachmas as a fine for not obtaining a fifth part of the votes.

Meanwhile the man proposes for me the penalty of death. So be it. What penalty, fellow citizens, am I to offer you instead? Evidently what I ought to get? What is it, then? What do I deserve to get or pay? I who, when I had learned a thing, did not lead my life in peace, but neglecting what the many care for—wealth, household matters, military leadership and civic and the other high positions, coalitions, factions that arise in the State—thought myself in fact too good a man to enter into these affairs with safety. I did not enter there where if I came I was not to be of any use either to you or to myself, but going to you one by one in private, I did you, I aver, the greatest service possible. There I went trying to persuade each one of you not to care first for his own possessions before caring for himself and how he might be at his best and wisest, nor to set the affairs of the City above the City itself, and to give attention to all other things in just that way. Being a man of that description, what ought I to get? Something good, my fellow citizens, if the award must truly square with the desert; and the good ought further to be something that fits my case. What, then, befits a poor man, a benefactor, who needs leisure for the office of exhorting you? Nothing is so proper as the maintenance of such a man in the Prytaneum, a reward far more befitting him than for any one of you who may have won a victory at Olympia with a horse or a pair of them or four. He makes you think that you are happy; I cause you to be so. He, moreover, has no need of maintenance; I stand in need of it. And so if I must get what I deserve, there is my proposal: maintenance in the Prytaneum.

Perhaps when I say that to you, you will think that I am talking with the same bravado as about the tears and supplications. It is not, fellow citizens, as you think; no, it is more like this. I am persuaded that I never willingly wronged any man, but I have not persuaded you, since we have had small time to reach an understanding; whereas if the law with you were what it is with others, if a case involving the penalty of death could not be settled in a day, but took a number, I believe I would have won you over. As matters stand, it is not easy in a limited time to refute a mass of slanders.

Persuaded that I do no wrong to any one, I am far from ready to do injustice to myself, and will not say of myself that I merit some evil, and should allot myself that sort of penalty. In fear of what? For fear that otherwise I shall suffer the thing which Meletus proposes, that of which I say I know not whether it is good or evil? Instead of that ought I to choose one of the things that I know for certain to be ills, and penalize myself with that? Imprisonment? Why should I live in prison, a slave to a recurrent board of governors, the Eleven? Or say a fine, and to be jailed until I pay it? But that would be no different for me from what I just now mentioned, since I have no money to pay with. Well, suppose I offered to go into exile. Perhaps you would accept that. But truly, fellow citizens, the love of life must have a powerful hold on me, and make me heedless, if I cannot reason thus: You who are my fellow citizens could not endure my doings and discussions; no, they were too much for you, and so irritating that now you seek to be rid of them. Well, will others bear them easily? Far from it, fellow citizens. And what a fine existence that would be, for a man of my age to go away and live a wanderer and a waif driven from city to city; for well I know that wherever I went the young would listen to me just as they do here. And if I drove them off, they would get the older men's permission, and themselves expel me. And if I did not, their fathers and relations would expel me on the sons' account.

Well, perhaps some one will say: 'Why can't you go away from us, and then keep quiet, Socrates, and live in peace?' But that is the thing that is hardest of all to make some of you see. If I say that this means disobedience to the god, and for that very reason I cannot keep still, you will not believe me, but will think I speak in irony. If, on the other hand, I say it is perhaps the greatest good that can befall a man, daily to argue about virtue, and to discuss the other subjects about which you have heard me debating and examining myself as well as others, if I add that for mankind the unexamined life is not worth living, still less will you believe me when I tell you that. These matters stand, however, Gentlemen, precisely as I say, only it is not easy to convince you. And meanwhile, for my part, I am not in the habit of thinking that I merit ill at all. If I had wealth, I would suggest a sum that I was in a position to pay, for in that case I should do myself no harm. But now the fact is that I haven't, unless you chose to set a fine for me at a rate that I could pay. Perhaps I could pay you a silver mina; so that is what I offer.

But Plato here, my fellow citizens, and Crito, Critobulus, and Apollodorus, bid me offer thirty minæ upon their security. Well then, I offer that; these men will be adequate security to you for the amount.

After He Is Condemned to Death

For no great thrift in time, my fellow citizens, you will have from those who wish to vilify the City the name and blame of having put to death the wise man, Socrates; for they will call me wise, even if I am not, they who would defame you. If only you had waited for a little while, the thing would have occurred for you in the course of nature; for you can see my age, that I am far along in life, and near to death. I say this, not to all of you, but only to those who voted for my death. And to them I have also to say this as well. It may be, Gentlemen, that you think I lost my cause for lack of arguments of the sort with which I might have won you over, if I had thought that I ought to say and do all things in order to escape the verdict. Far from it. I lost for a lack, but not of arguments; it was for lack of impudence and daring, and for not being ready to say to you the sort of thing it would have given you most pleasure to hear—me weeping and wailing, and doing and saying any and every sort of thing that I hold to be unworthy of me, but you are accustomed to hear from the rest. No, I did not then believe that, to avoid a danger, I ought to do anything unseemly in a freeman, nor do I now regret my manner of defence. No, far rather would I choose this manner of defence, and die, than follow that, and live. Whether in a court of justice or in war neither I nor any other man should seek by using every means conceivable to escape from death; for in battle you very often see that if you throw away your weapons and beg those who are pursuing you for mercy, you may get out of dying. Indeed, in every sort of danger there are various ways of winning through, if one is ready to do and say anything whatever. No, Gentlemen, that is not the hard thing, to escape from death; ah no, far harder is it to escape from sin, for sin is swifter than death. And so I, being old and slow, am overtaken by the slower enemy; while my accusers, who are strong and swift, have been caught by the swifter, namely wickedness. And so I now depart, by you condemned to pay the penalty of death; and they, by the truth convicted of a base injustice. And as I abide the payment, so do they. Who knows? Perhaps it had to be so, and I think that things are as they ought to be.

Touching the future, I desire to make for you who voted to condemn me, a prediction; for I am at the point where men foresee the future best—when they are soon to die. Let me tell you then, you men who have condemned me, that after I am gone there will straightway come upon you a chastisement far heavier, by Zeus, than the death you have set for me. You have now done this in the belief that you have freed yourselves from giving any reckoning for your life; but I tell you the result will be the very opposite for you. There will be more inquisitors to sift you, men whom I now hold in check without your knowing it. And they will be more critical as they are younger, and will annoy you more; for if you think that by putting men to death you will prevent the slur from being cast at you that you do not live aright, you are in error. This way of getting freedom is neither very sure nor fine; no, the finest and readiest way is this, not to interfere with other people, but to render oneself as good a man as possible. There is the prophecy I make for you who voted to condemn me. And of them I take my leave.

With those of you who voted to acquit me I should be glad to talk about this thing that has occurred, while the magistrates are busy and it is not time for me to go to the place where I must die. So, Gentlemen, please wait with me as long as that. There is nothing to keep us from talking to each other as long as it is allowed. To you as to friends I wish to explain the real meaning of what has just happened to me.

Justices, for when I call you that I am naming you aright, the thing that has come to me is wonderful.

My customary warning, by the spirit, in previous times has always, up to now, come to me very often to oppose me, even when a matter was quite important, if ever I was going to do something amiss. But to-day, as you yourselves have witnessed, that thing has happened to me which anybody might suppose, and which is considered, to be the uttermost of evils. Yet neither did the sign from god oppose me when I left my house this morning, nor at the point when I ascended here to the tribunal, nor in my speech at anything I was about to say; though often when I have been talking elsewhere it has stopped me in the middle of a speech. But to-day, with reference to the whole procedure, not once did it oppose me in a thing I did or said. What, then, do I take to be the cause of this? No doubt this thing that has happened to me is good, and it cannot be that our supposition is correct when any of us think that death is a misfortune. For me, the proof of this is telling: it cannot be but that the customary sign would have opposed me, if I had not been about to do a thing that was good.

Let us view in another way how ample are the grounds for our hope that death is good. To be dead is one of two things. Either it is a sort of non-existence, and the dead man has no feeling about anything whatever, or else, as people say, the soul experiences a shift and a migration from here into another place. Now if there is no feeling, if death is like a sleep in which one does not even dream, what a wonderful gain it would be! I believe if a man were to take that night in which he slept so deeply that he did not have a single dream, and compared it with the other nights and days of his life; if he had to say, upon reflection, how many days and nights, all told, in his life, he had passed better and more sweetly than that night; I believe that every one, not merely any private citizen, but the Great King himself, would find them easy to count up in comparison with all the others. So if death is a sleep like that, I say it is a gain; for thus all time appears to be no more than a single night. If, on the other hand, death is like a journey from here to another place, and if what they say is true, that everybody who has died is there, then, Justices, what greater good than this could there be? If, on arriving in Hades, one could be freed from those who here pretend that they are Justices, and there find those who by report deal real justice, Minos, Rhadamanthus, Aæcus, and Triptolemus, and all the rest of the demigods who were just in their lives here, what a small thing would that journey seem! Or, again, to be with Orpheus and Musæus, with Hesiod and Homer, what price would not any of you pay for that? I would gladly die repeatedly, if all that is true. To me it would be a wonderful way to pass my time, there where I could meet with Palamedes and with Ajax son of Telamon, and any one else among the ancients who died through an unjust decision. To compare my lot with theirs, methinks, would not be so unpleasant; and most important of all would be to go on sifting people there, as here, and finding out who is wise, and who thinks he is so, but is not. What would not anybody give to examine, Justices, the leader of that mighty expedition against Troy, or else Odysseus, or Sisphus, or a myriad of others one might mention, men and women too? There to talk with them, consort with them, examine them, would be a happiness beyond compare! Surely there, I take it, they do not put a man to death for doing that; for, happy in all else, people are happier there than here in that henceforth they are immortal, at all events if what is said is true.

But, Justices, you also it behoves to have good hope with reference to death, and this one thing you must bear in mind as true, that, living or dead, to a good man there can come no evil, nor are his affairs a matter of indifference to the gods. Nor has my destiny now come about by chance; rather, it is clear to me that it was better for me now to die and to be released from my troubles. That is why the sign did not at any point deter me, and why I am not very bitter at those who voted to condemn me, or at my accusers. It is true they did not have this notion in condemning and accusing me; no, they thought to injure me, and therein they merit blame.

One thing, however, I do beg of them. When my sons grow up, then, Gentlemen, I ask you to punish them, you hurting them the same as I hurt you, if they seem to you to care for money, or aught else, more than they care for virtue. And if they pretend to be somewhat when they are nothing, do you upbraid them as I upbraided you, for not regarding as important what they ought to think so, and for thinking they have worth when they do not. If you do that, I shall have received just treatment from you, and my sons as well.

And now the time has come for our departure, I to die, and you to live. Which of us goes to meet the better lot is hidden from all unless it be known to God.

THUCYDIDES

The Funeral Oration of Pericles[1]

The Setting of the Speech

During the following winter the Athenians, in keeping with a time-honored custom, held a state funeral for those who were the first to fall in this war.[2] The ceremonies are as follows. First the bodies of the deceased lie in state for three days in a special pavilion; during this time the relatives bring whatever offerings they wish. In the procession to the grave cypress-wood coffins are carried on wagons, one for each tribe, and each containing the bodies of the dead from that tribe. One wagon carries an empty bier, fully decked, for the missing, those whose bodies could not be found for burial. Anyone who wishes, citizen or foreigner, may join in the procession, and the women of the family also attend and set up the cry of mourning at the grave.

The burial takes place at the state monument, which stands in the most beautiful suburb of the city. All the war dead of Athens have been buried there except the men of Marathon, whose valor was considered so pre-eminent that their tomb was built on the battlefield itself. After the interment is finished, a man chosen by the citizens, someone of high reputation for intelli-

[1] From Thucydides' *History*, transl. by Gerald F. Else, in *Classics in Translation*, ed. Paul L. MacKendrick and Herbert M. Howe (Madison: The University of Wisconsin Press, 1952), I, 239-243. Copyright, 1952, by the Regents of the University of Wisconsin. Reprinted by permission.

[2] Between Athens and Sparta—The Peloponnesian War, 431-404 B.C.

gence and prominent in the community, pronounces a fitting eulogy over the dead, and the gathering disperses. Such are the state funerals; and the custom was maintained throughout the war whenever there was occasion for it. At this first observance the chosen speaker was Pericles son of Xanthippus. When the proper moment came he stepped forward from the monument onto a high platform constructed so that he could be heard by as many of the throng as possible, and spoke more or less as follows:

Difficulty of the Speaker's Task

"Most of the previous speakers on these occasions have praised the man who added this oration to the ceremonies; they considered it a fine and fitting thing that it should be delivered over our war dead. I on the contrary should think it would be sufficient for men who have shown their bravery in action to have their honors paid them in action also, as in fact you see has been done in this solemn ceremony under the auspices of the state, and that the reputation of so many men should not be made to depend on the chance of a single speaker's eloquence or lack of it. It is difficult, you know, to speak fittingly on a subject in which one can hardly hope to gain credit for telling the truth. The friends of the dead, who know something about the case, may well feel that the speaker falls short of their expectation and their knowledge, while the stranger, out of jealousy at any story that goes beyond his own powers, may suspect him of exaggeration. A man can usually tolerate praise of others only up to the point where he thinks that he could have done the same; anything that exceeds his own capacity arouses his jealousy and therefore his disbelief. However, since this custom was sanctioned by past generations as a fitting one, I too must abide by the law and try to satisfy the expectations and beliefs of each of you so far as I can.

Tribute to the Builders of the Athenian Empire

"I will begin first with our forefathers. It is both right and appropriate on an occasion like this to pay them this tribute of remembrance; for they were the same stock that has dwelt in the land from the beginning, and by their valor, in unbroken succession of generations, handed it down to us a free country. They deserve our praise and admiration, but our own fathers deserve it still more; it was they who added to their inheritance the great empire we now possess and, not without toil, left it to us of this generation. Finally, those of us who are still more or less in the prime of life have given the empire its further expansion and provided our city with all the resources needed to make it completely self-sufficient in war and peace.

The Way of Life That Has Made Athens Great

"The various wars and campaigns through which our conquests were made, the stout resistance that we or our fathers have offered against invasion by Greek or foreign invaders—all that you know and I do not want to dwell on it at length. Instead I will speak first of the way of life that is responsible for our achievements, the form of government and kind of character that have made Athens a great city. I am prefacing all this to my eulogy of the dead because I think it is not only suitable to the occasion but profitable for this whole gathering of citizens and foreigners to hear.

"Our form of government is not modelled on the constitutions of our neighbors; instead of imitating others we are actually an example to them. So far as the name goes we are called a democracy, because the power rests with the majority instead of a few. But though every citizen has equal rights under the law with respect to his private disputes, high standing, and honor in the community depend on a man's merits, his achievement in some pursuit, and no one is debarred by poverty and obscurity of birth from contributing what he can to the well-being of the city. We are a free people not only in our management of public affairs but in our personal tolerance of one another's everyday conduct. We do not get angry at our neighbors for doing as they please, or try to inflict on them the petty marks of disapproval which, though harmless, are so unpleasant to experience. While this spirit of tolerance prevails in our private lives, in our public affairs it is fear more than anything else that keeps us law-abiding, obedient to the magistrates of the moment and to the laws, especially those whose purpose is to help the victims of wrongdoing and those unwritten laws which men by common consent are ashamed to transgress.

"Not only that, but we have provided for our enjoyment a great variety of relaxations from the day's work: games, contests, festivals lasting through the year, and beautiful private homes and furnishings. To see all this around us every day cheers us and drives away fatigue. Also, thanks to the greatness of Athens, the wares of the whole world find their way to us; we are in a position to enjoy the products of the rest of mankind as easily and naturally as we do our own crops from our own land.

"We also hold an advantage over our opponents in our way of preparing for war. Our city is open to everybody; there are no periodical deportations to keep foreigners from learning or observing things that might be of use to an enemy if they were not concealed. We put our trust in our own inborn readiness for action rather than in armaments and military secrets. Their system of training involves the pursuit of courage through laborious discipline, beginning in their youth, while we allow ourselves some relaxation and yet are equally prepared to face any reasonable danger.

"The proof is that the Spartans have not invaded our country with their own forces alone but have brought along all their allies; we manage to attack our neighbors' territory without help and usually win, though fighting on foreign soil and against men who are defending their own homes and possessions. No enemy has ever yet encountered the full strength of our combined forces, since we have the maintenance of our navy to think about as well as the dispatch of armies by land to a number of places at once. If they do engage a small force of ours somewhere and defeat it, they boast that they have repelled us all, and when they are beaten, that they were defeated by us all. Now if we choose relaxation in the face of danger instead of endless drill, and rely on native courage rather than rules and regulations, the advantage is ours twice over: we do not wear ourselves out over future troubles, and when they do come we show as much venturesomeness as those who are forever moiling and toiling. Athens has a claim to men's admiration for all this, and for other things besides.

"We strive for distinction, but with economy, and for intelligence without loss of energy. Thus we use wealth to meet the needs of action, not the craving for display, and think it is no disgrace to admit poverty but a real disgrace not to act to escape it. Again, we combine the conduct of public and private affairs in the same persons and make it possible for others, though absorbed in their work, to gain some insight into politics; for unlike other peoples we judge the man who takes no part in this at all a useless, not just a 'quiet,' person. Hence also we arrive at sound decisions, or at least sound ideas, on policy, because we do not believe that action is spoiled by discussion, but by failure to be informed through debate before the necessary action is taken. In fact this is another point in our superiority: we are usually daring and also unusually disposed to weigh the pros and cons of a proposed undertaking, while with others ignorance brings boldness and second thought brings hesitation. One would not go wrong in saying that the bravest men are those who foresee most clearly the dangerous as well as the pleasurable possibilities and still are not deterred from taking the risk.

"Again, so far as generosity goes we are the opposite of most men: we try to win friends not by accepting kindness but by conferring it. We know that the man who does a favor is the firmer friend: he will keep the debt alive out of good will towards the recipient, while the debtor does not feel it so keenly, knowing that a good turn will be put down as payment on his debt, not as a real favor. Our fearless way of serving others rests on the confidence of freedom rather than on calculations of profit; and in this too we are unique.

"To sum it all up, I say not only that our city as a whole is a model of all Greece, but that, in my opinion, there is no other place where the individual can develop independence and self-reliance so easily, so gracefully, and in so many directions. That all this is not a matter of boastful talk for this occasion, but of plain truth, is proved by the fact of our power, which we acquired because we possessed those qualities. Athens alone, in our time, is greater than her own fame when the test comes; she alone gives the invader no excuse for annoyance at the quality of the foe who handles him so roughly, and her subjects no ground for complaint that their masters do not deserve to rule them.

"Our power is surely not unsubstantiated; we have given weighty proofs of it that will earn us the admiration of our own time and of posterity. We have no need of a Homer to sing our praises, or anyone whose poetic language will please for the moment but whose mere guesses at the facts will be wrecked by the truth. We have assured our own fame by forcing every land and every sea to become a path for our adventuring spirit and by founding memorials of our enmity and favor in every part of the world. That is the kind of city for which these men died, facing battle with the high determination that she should not be taken from them; and it is only fitting that every man who is left should be willing to suffer for her.

The Dead Were Worthy of Such a City

"The reason why I have expatiated on Athens at such length is that I wanted to demonstrate to you how much greater is our stake in this struggle than theirs who do not share our advantages, and also to give force to my eulogy of the dead by citing real evidence. I have almost finished; for the glories of Athens, the theme of my hymn of praise, are the garland she owes to these men and others like them. Few Greeks can show so equal a balance as they between their deeds and what we say about them. I think that their recent death, still fresh in our minds, is both the first evidence and the final confirmation of their worth as men. If some of them fell short in other things, we have every right to put their brave defense of the fatherland in time of war first in the reckoning; the good has erased the bad from our memory, the benefits of their common service outweigh any harm they did in private life. Not one of these men turned soft because he preferred the continual enjoyment of his own wealth; not one was tempted by poverty to put off the danger, hoping that he might still escape it and grow rich. Welcoming vengeance on the enemy as a prize more to be coveted than these, and considering the present danger nobler than any other, they accepted it and chose vengeance for the one part, renunciation for the other. They left to hope the unforeseeable chances of future success, but were men enough to rely on themselves in action, where the issue was already clear; convinced that to fight hard and endure is in itself a better guarantee of survival than surrender, they shrank from the reproach of men's words but stood the brunt of action with their lives, and so passed away in that brief moment in the play of fortune when their glory and not their fear was at its prime.

"If they were brave, then, it was a bravery characteristic of Athenians, and those who are left behind should pray that their resolution towards the enemy may be less hazardous, but determine that it shall be no less valorous, than theirs. Do not weigh the benefits merely in words—an orator could remind you at length of what you know as well as he, reciting all the manifold blessings of a firm defense against the enemy—but fix your eyes on the power of Athens as you see it in action from day to day, make yourselves her lovers, and when you find her a great city remember that men won that greatness for her by their boldness, their ability to grasp what was required of them, and the sense of honor with which they carried it out. Even when one of their ventures failed they would not stoop to injure the city by denying her the best of their manhood, but showered it upon her as their finest offering.

"Through this common gift of their lives they won for themselves individually unfading glory and the most conspicuous of all monuments: not the one in which they lie here but the one in which their fame survives them, to be remembered afresh as each new occasion arises for speech or action. For the real tomb of famous men is the whole earth; they are marked out not merely by the inscription over a grave in their own country but in other lands also by an unwritten memory, recording their spirit more than their actions, which lives on in the minds of men. Emulate them, then, in your own lives; learn from them that the key to happiness is freedom, the key to freedom a stout heart, and do not set a false value on the dangers of war. It is not the unfortunate, those with no hope of anything better, who have most reason to sacrifice their lives freely, but those who face the danger of a change for the worse if they go on living and, if they come to disaster in any undertaking, risk the greatest loss. To a man of any spirit the suffering and humiliation that go with cowardice are more painful to endure than a quick death, coming unnoticed in the full flush of strength and common hopes.

Exhortation to the Bereaved Relatives

"And for the same reason I offer good courage instead of mourning to the parents of these dead, those of them who are present. You know that your lives have seen all kinds of fortune, good and bad, and that the luckiest are those who have been vouchsafed the most glorious end, like these—or grief, like you—whose lives were so measured that their allotment of happiness and of death came to an even balance. I know this will be hard for you to believe; you will be reminded of them again and again when you see others with the happiness that you once enjoyed yourselves. And it is true, we do not grieve at being deprived of blessings we have never tasted, but at losing what we had grown accustomed to.

"But you should bear up in the hope of having more children, those of you who are still of an age to do so. Not only will the new ones help many of you individually to forget those who are gone, but the city will profit doubly, by not being depopulated, and in her security; for a citizen cannot possibly weigh the issue fairly and impartially if he has no children to contribute and so does not share the danger equally.

"As for those of you who are past the prime, set down the longer and happier part of your lives as profit, remember that the rest will be short, and let your sons' glory lighten the burden. Only the craving for honor is ageless, and in a man's declining years it is not profit, as some say, but the sense of being honored that brings real joy.

"Again, for those of you who are sons or brothers of these men I see a great contest in the making; for people always tend to praise those who are gone, and you will find that it takes a supreme effort to be rated, not even equal, but nearly equal to them. Men envy the living because they are competitors; what does not stand in their way they honor freely, with a good will untouched by rivalry.

"Finally, if I must say something about womanly virtue, for those of you who will be widows henceforth, I will sum it all up in one brief exhortation. Great is your good name when you do not fall below the standards of your sex, and when you give men the least occasion to talk about you, whether it be by way of praise or blame.

"Thus, so far as words go, I too have complied with the law and said what I had to say. As for acts, part of the funeral honors have already been paid the dead, and the rest will be paid by the city in public maintenance of their children until they come of age. That is the garland, worth while to the survivors as well as the dead, which she awards for this kind of contest: for the best men serve that state where the best prizes for merit are offered. And now make your lamentations, each for your own relatives, and then depart."

JONATHAN SWIFT

A Modest Proposal[1]

For Preventing the Children of Poor People From Being A Burthen to Their Parents or Country, and for Making Them Beneficial to the Public.

It is a melancholy object to those who walk through this great town, or travel in the country, when they see the streets, the roads, and cabin-doors crowded with beggars of the female sex, followed by three, four, or six children, *all in rags*, and importuning every passenger for an alms. These mothers, instead of being able to work for their honest livelihood, are forced to employ all their time in strolling, to beg sustenance for their helpless infants, who, as they grow up, either turn thieves for want of work, or leave their dear Native Country to fight for the Pretender in Spain, or sell themselves to the Barbadoes.

I think it is agreed by all parties that this prodigious number of children, in the arms, or on the backs, or at the heels of their mothers, and frequently of their fathers, is in the present deplorable state of the kingdom a very great additional grievance; and therefore whoever could find out a fair, cheap, and easy method of making these children sound useful members of the commonwealth would deserve so well of the public as to have his statue set up for a preserver of the nation.

But my intention is very far from being confined to provide only for the children of professed beggars; it is of a much greater extent, and shall take in the whole number of infants at a certain age who are born of parents in effect as little able to support them as those who demand our charity in the streets.

[1] First published in 1729.

As to my own part, having turned my thoughts, for many years, upon this important subject, and maturely weighed the several schemes of other projectors, I have always found them grossly mistaken in their computation. It is true a child, just dropped from its dam, may be supported by her milk for a solar year with little other nourishment, at most not above the value of two shillings, which the mother may certainly get, or the value in scraps, by her lawful occupation of begging, and it is exactly at one year old that I propose to provide for them, in such a manner as, instead of being a charge upon their parents, or the parish, or wanting food and raiment for the rest of their lives, they shall, on the contrary, contribute to the feeding and partly to the clothing of many thousands.

There is likewise another great advantage in my scheme, that it will prevent those voluntary abortions, and that horrid practice of women murdering their bastard children, alas, too frequent among us, sacrificing the poor innocent babes, I doubt, more to avoid the expense than the shame, which would move tears and pity in the most savage and inhuman breast.

The number of souls in this kingdom being usually reckoned one million and a half, of these I calculate there may be about two hundred thousand couple whose wives are breeders, from which number I subtract thirty thousand couple who are able to maintain their own children, although I apprehend there cannot be so many under the present distresses of the kingdom, but this being granted, there will remain an hundred and seventy thousand breeders. I again subtract fifty thousand for those women who miscarry, or whose children die by accident or disease within the year. There only remain an hundred and twenty thousand children of poor parents annually born: The question therefore is, how this number shall be reared, and provided for, which, as I have already said, under the present situation of affairs, is utterly impossible by all the methods hitherto proposed, for we can neither employ them in handicraft, or agriculture; we neither build houses (I mean in the country), nor cultivate land: they can very seldom pick up a livelihood by stealing till they arrive at six years old, except where they are of towardly parts, although I confess they learn the rudiments much earlier, during which time they can however be properly looked upon only as *probationers*, as I have been informed by a principal gentleman in the County of Cavan, who protested to me that he never knew above one or two instances under the age of six, even in a part of the kingdom so renowned for the quickest proficiency in that art.

I am assured by our merchants that a boy or a girl, before twelve years old, is no saleable commodity, and even when they come to this age, they will not yield above three pounds, or three pounds and half-a-crown at most on the Exchange, which cannot turn to account either to the parents of the kingdom, the charge of nutriment and rags having been at least four times that value.

I shall now therefore humbly propose my own thoughts, which I hope will not be liable to the least objection.

I have been assured by a very knowing American of my acquaintance in London, that a young healthy child well nursed is at a year old a most delicious, nourishing, and wholesome food, whether stewed, roasted, baked, or boiled, and I make no doubt that it will equally serve in a fricassee, or a ragout.

I do therefore humbly offer it to public consideration, that of the hundred and twenty thousand children already computed, twenty thousand may be reserved for breed, whereof only one fourth part to be males, which is more than we allow to sheep, black-cattle, or swine, and my reason is that these children are seldom the fruits of marriage, a circumstance not much regarded by our savages, therefore one male will be sufficient to serve four females. That the remaining hundred thousand may at a year old be offered in sale to the persons of quality, and fortune, through the kingdom, always advising the mother to let them suck plentifully in the last month, so as to render them plump, and fat for a good table. A child will make two dishes at an entertainment for friends, and when the family dines alone, the fore or hind quarters will make a reasonable dish, and seasoned with a little pepper or salt will be very good boiled on the fourth day, especially in winter.

I have reckoned upon a medium, that a child just born will weigh 12 pounds, and in a solar year if tolerably nursed increaseth to 28 pounds.

I grant this food will be somewhat dear, and therefore very proper for landlords, who, as they have already devoured most of the parents, seem to have the best title to the children.

Infants' flesh will be in season throughout the year, but more plentiful in March, and a little before and after, for we are told by a grave author, an eminent French physician, that fish being a prolific diet, there are more children born in Roman Catholic countries about nine months after Lent than at any other season; therefore reckoning a year after Lent, the markets will be more glutted than usual, because the number of Popish infants is at least three to one in this kingdom, and therefore it will have one other collateral advantage by lessening the number of Papists among us.

I have already computed the charge of nursing a beggar's child (in which list I reckon all cottagers, labourers, and four-fifths of the farmers) to be about two shillings per annum, rags included, and I believe no gentleman would repine to give ten shillings for the carcass of a good fat child, which, as I have said, will make four dishes of excellent nutritive meat, when he hath only some particular friend or his own family to dine with him. Thus the Squire will learn to be a good landlord, and grow popular among his tenants, the mother will have eight shillings net profit, and be fit for work till she produces another child.

Those who are more thrifty (as I must confess the times require) may flay the carcass; the skin of which, artificially dressed, will make admirable gloves for ladies, and summer boots for fine gentlemen.

As to our City of Dublin, shambles may be appointed for this purpose, in the most convenient parts of it, and butchers we may be assured will not be wanting, although I rather recommend buying the children alive, and dressing them hot from the knife, as we do roasting pigs.

A very worthy person, a true lover of this country, and whose virtues I highly esteem, was lately pleased, in discoursing on this matter, to offer a refinement upon my scheme. He said that many gentlemen of this kingdom, having of late destroyed their deer, he conceived that the want of venison might be well supplied by the bodies of young lads and maidens, not exceeding fourteen years of age, nor under twelve, so great a number of both sexes in every country being now ready to starve, for want of work and service: and these to be disposed of by their parents if alive, or otherwise by their nearest relations. But with due deference to so excellent a friend, and so deserving a patriot, I cannot be altogether in his sentiments; for as to the males, my American acquaintance assured me from frequent experience that their flesh was generally tough and lean, like that of our schoolboys, by continual exercise, and their taste disagreeable, and to fatten them would not answer the charge. Then as to the females, it would, I think with humble submission, be a loss to the public, because they soon would become breeders themselves: And besides, it is not improbable that some scrupulous people might be apt to censure such a practice (although indeed very unjustly) as a little bordering upon cruelty, which, I confess, hath always been with me the strongest objection against any project, however so well intended.

But in order to justify my friend, he confessed that this expedient was put into his head by the famous Psalmanazar, a native of the island Formosa, who came from thence to London, above twenty years ago, and in conversation told my friend that in his country when any young person happened to be put to death, the executioner sold the carcass to persons of quality, as a prime dainty, and that, in his time, the body of a plump girl of fifteen, who was crucified for an attempt to poison the emperor, was sold to his Imperial Majesty's Prime Minister of State, and other great Mandarins of the Court, in joints from the gibbet, at four hundred crowns. Neither indeed can I deny that if the same use were made of several plump young girls in this town, who, without one single groat to their fortunes, cannot stir abroad without a chair, and appear at the playhouse, and assemblies in foreign fineries, which they never will pay for, the kingdom would not be the worse.

Some persons of a desponding spirit are in great concern about that vast number of poor people, who are aged, diseased, or maimed, and I have been desired to employ my thoughts what course may be taken to ease the nation of so grievous an encumbrance. But I am not in the least pain upon that matter, because it is very well known that they are every day dying, and rotting, by cold, and famine, and filth, and vermin, as fast as can be reasonably expected. And as to the younger labourers they are now in almost as hopeful a condition. They cannot get work, and consequently pine away for want of nourishment, to a degree, that if at any time they are accidentally hired to common labour, they have not strength to perform it; and thus the country and themselves are happily delivered from the evils to come.

I have too long digressed, and therefore shall return to my subject. I think the advantages by the proposal which I have made are obvious and many, as well as of the highest importance.

For first, as I have already observed, it would greatly lessen the number of Papists, with whom we are yearly over-run, being the principal breeders of the nation, as well as our most dangerous enemies, and who stay at home on purpose with a design to deliver the kingdom to the Pretender, hoping to take their advantage by the absence of so many good Protestants, who have chosen rather to leave their country than stay at home, and pay tithes against their conscience to an Episcopal curate.

Secondly, the poorer tenants will have something valuable of their own, which by law be made liable to distress, and help to pay their landlord's rent, their corn and cattle being already seized, and *money a thing unknown*.

Thirdly, Whereas the maintenance of an hundred thousand children, from two years old, and upwards, cannot be computed at less than ten shillings a piece *per annum*, the nation's stock will be thereby increased fifty thousand pounds *per annum*, besides the profit of a new dish, introduced to the tables of all gentlemen of fortune in the kingdom, who have any refinement in taste, and the money will circulate among ourselves, the goods being entirely of our own growth and manufacture.

Fourthly, The constant breeders, besides the gain of eight shillings sterling *per annum*, by the sale of their children, will be rid of the charge of maintaining them after the first year.

Fifthly, This food would likewise bring great custom to taverns, where the vintners will certainly be so prudent as to procure the best receipts for dressing it up to perfection, and consequently have their houses frequented by all the fine gentlemen, who justly value themselves upon their knowledge in good eating; and a skillful cook, who understands how to oblige his guests, will contrive to make it as expensive as they please.

Sixthly, This would be a great inducement to marriage, which all wise nations have either encouraged by rewards, or enforced by laws and penalties. It would increase the care and tenderness of mothers toward their children, when they were sure of a settlement for life, to the poor babes, provided in some sort by the public to their annual profit instead of expense. We should see an honest emulation among the married women, which of them could bring the fattest child to the market, men would become as fond of their wives, during the time of their pregnancy, as they are now of their mares in foal, their cows in calf, or sows when they are ready to farrow, nor offer to beat or kick them (as it is too frequent a practice) for fear of a miscarriage.

Many other advantages might be enumerated: For instance, the addition of some thousand carcasses in our exportation of barrelled beef; the propagation of swine's flesh, and improvement in the art of making good bacon, so much wanted among us by the great destruction of pigs, too frequent at our tables, which are no way comparable in taste or magnificence to a well-grown, fat yearling child, which roasted whole will make a considerable figure at a Lord Mayor's feast, or any other public entertainment. But this and many others I omit, being studious of brevity.

Supposing that one thousand families in this city would be constant customers for infants' flesh, besides others who might have it at merry-meetings, particularly weddings and christenings, I compute that Dublin would take off annually about twenty thousand carcasses, and the rest of the kingdom (where probably they will be sold somewhat cheaper) the remaining eighty thousand.

I can think of no one objection that will possibly be raised against this proposal, unless it should be urged that the number of people will be thereby much lessened in the kingdom. This I freely own, and it was indeed one principal design in offering it to the world. I desire the reader will observe, that I calculate my remedy for this one individual *Kingdom of Ireland, and for no other that ever was, is, or, I think, ever can be upon earth.* Therefore let no man talk to me of other expedients: *Of taxing our absentees at five shillings a pound: Of using neither clothes, nor household furniture, except what is of our own growth and manufacture: Of utterly rejecting the materials and instruments that promote foreign luxury: Of curing the expensiveness of pride, vanity, idleness, and gaming in our women: Of introducing a vein of parsimony, prudence, and temperance: Of learning to love our Country, wherein we differ even from* LAPLANDERS, *and the inhabitants of* TOPINAMBOO: *Of quitting our animosities and factions, nor act any longer like the Jews, who were murdering one another at the very moment their city was taken: Of being a little cautious not to sell our country and consciences for nothing: Of teaching landlords to have at least one degree of mercy toward their tenants. Lastly, of putting a spirit of honesty, industry, and skill into our shopkeepers, who, if a resolution could now be taken to buy only our native goods, would immediately unite to cheat and exact upon us in the price, the measure, and the goodness, nor could ever yet be brought to make one fair proposal of just dealing, though often and earnestly invited to it.*

Therefore I repeat, let no man talk to me of these and the like expedients, till he hath at least some glimpse of hope that there will ever be some hearty and sincere attempt to put them in practice.

But as to myself, having been wearied out for many years with offering vain, idle, visionary thoughts, and at length utterly despairing of success, I fortunately fell upon this proposal, which as it is wholly new, so it hath something solid and real, of no expense and little trouble, full in our own power, and whereby we can incur no danger in *disobliging* ENGLAND. For this kind of commodity will not bear exportation, the flesh being too tender a consistence to admit a long continuance in salt, *although perhaps I could name a country which would be glad to eat up our whole nation without it.*

After all I am not so violently bent upon my own opinion as to reject any offer, proposed by wise men, which shall be found equally innocent, cheap, easy, and effectual. But before something of that kind shall be advanced in contradiction to my scheme, and offering a better, I desire the author, or authors, will be pleased maturely to consider two points. First, as things now stand, how they will be able to find food and raiment for an hundred thousand useless mouths and backs. And secondly, there being a round million of creatures in human figure, throughout this kingdom, whose whole subsistence put into a common stock would leave them in debt two millions of pounds sterling; adding those, who are beggars by profession, to the bulk of farmers, cottagers, and labourers with their wives and children, who are beggars in effect. I desire those politicians, who dislike my overture, and may perhaps be so bold to attempt an answer, that they will first ask the parents of these mortals whether they would not at this day think it a great happiness to have been sold for food at a year old, in the manner I prescribe, and thereby have avoided such a perpetual scene of misfortunes as they have since gone through, by the oppression of landlords, the impossibility of paying rent without money or trade, the want of common sustenance, with neither house nor clothes to cover them from the inclemencies of the weather, and the most inevitable prospect of entailing the like, or greater miseries upon their breed for ever.

I profess in the sincerity of my heart that I have not the least personal interest in endeavoring to promote this necessary work, having no other motive than the *public good of my country, by advancing our trade, providing for infants, relieving the poor, and giving some pleasure to the rich.* I have no children by which I can propose to get a single penny; the youngest being nine years old, and my wife past child-bearing.

THOMAS JEFFERSON

Declaration of Independence

The unanimous declaration of the thirteen United States of America, in Congress, July 4, 1776

When, in the course of human events, it becomes necessary for one people to dissolve the political bands which have connected them with another, and to assume among the powers of the earth the separate and equal station to which the laws of nature and of nature's God entitle them, a decent respect to the opinions of mankind requires that they should declare the causes which impel them to the separation.

We hold these truths to be self-evident: That all men are created equal; that they are endowed by their Creator with certain inalienable rights; that among these are life, liberty, and the pursuit of happiness. That, to secure these rights, governments are instituted among men, deriving their just powers from the consent of the governed; that, whenever any form of government becomes destructive of these ends, it is the right of the people to alter or to abolish it, and to institute a new government, laying its foundation on such principles, and organizing its powers in such form, as to them shall seem most likely to effect their safety and happiness. Prudence, indeed, will dictate that governments long established should not be changed for light and transient causes; and accordingly all experience hath shown that mankind are more disposed to suffer, while evils are sufferable, than to right themselves by abolishing the forms to which they are accustomed. But when a long train of abuses and usurpations, pursuing invariably the same object, evinces a design to reduce them under absolute despotism, it is their right, it is their duty, to throw off such government and to provide new guards for their future security. Such has been the patient suffering of these colonies, and such is now the necessity which constrains them to alter their former systems of government. The history of the present king of Great Britain is a history of repeated injuries and usurpations, all having in direct object the establishment of an absolute tyranny over these states. To prove this, let facts be submitted to a candid world.

He has refused his assent to laws the most wholesome and necessary for the public good.

He has forbidden his governors to pass laws of immediate and pressing importance, unless suspended in their operation till his assent should be obtained, and, when so suspended, he has utterly neglected to attend to them.

He has refused to pass other laws for the accommodation of large districts of people, unless those people would relinquish the right of representation in the legislature—a right inestimable to them and formidable to tyrants only.

He has called together legislative bodies, at places unusual, uncomfortable, and distant from the repository of their public records, for the sole purpose of fatiguing them into compliance with his measures.

He has dissolved representative houses repeatedly for opposing with manly firmness his invasions on the rights of the people.

He has refused for a long time after such dissolutions to cause others to be elected; whereby the legislative powers, incapable of annihilation, have returned to the people at large for their exercise: the state remaining, in the meantime, exposed to all the dangers of invasion from without and convulsions within.

He has endeavored to prevent the population of these states; for that purpose obstructing the laws for naturalization of foreigners; refusing to pass others to encourage their migration hither, and raising the conditions of new appropriations of lands.

He has obstructed the administration of justice by refusing his assent to laws for establishing his judiciary powers.

He has made judges dependent on his will alone for the tenure of their offices and the amount and payment of their salaries.

He has erected a multitude of new offices and sent hither swarms of officers to harass our people and eat out their substance.

He has kept among us, in times of peace, standing armies without the consent of our legislatures.

He has affected to render the military independent of and superior to the civil power.

He has combined with others to subject us to a jurisdiction foreign to our constitutions and unacknowledged by our laws, giving his assent to their acts of pretended legislation:

For quartering large bodies of armed troops among us;

For protecting them by a mock trial from punishment for any murders which they should commit on the inhabitants of these states;

For cutting off our trade with all parts of the world;

For imposing taxes on us without our consent;

For depriving us in many cases of the benefits of trial by jury;

For transporting us beyond seas to be tried for pretended offenses;

For abolishing the free system of English laws in a neighboring province, establishing therein an arbitrary government, and enlarging its boundaries so as to render it at once an example and fit instrument for introducing the same absolute rule into these colonies;

For taking away our charters, abolishing our most valuable laws, and altering fundamentally the forms of our government;

For suspending our own legislatures and declaring themselves invested with power to legislate for us in all cases whatsoever.

He has abdicated government here by declaring us out of his protection and waging war against us.

He has plundered our seas, ravaged our coasts, burnt our towns and destroyed the lives of our people.

He is at this time transporting large armies of foreign mercenaries to complete the work of death, desolation, and tyranny already begun, with circumstances of cruelty and perfidy scarcely parallelled in the most barbarous ages and totally unworthy the head of a civilized nation.

He has constrained our fellow citizens taken captive upon the high seas to bear arms against their country, to become the executioners of their friends and brethren, or to fall themselves by their hands.

He has excited domestic insurrection amongst us, and has endeavored to bring on the inhabitants of our frontiers the merciless Indian savages, whose known rule of warfare is an undistinguished destruction of all ages, sexes, and conditions.

In every stage of these oppressions we have petitioned for redress, in the most humble terms; our repeated petitions have been answered only by repeated injury. A prince whose character is thus marked by every act which may define a tyrant is unfit to be the ruler of a free people.

Nor have we been wanting in attention to our British brethren. We have warned them, from time to time, of attempts by their legislature to extend an unwarrantable jurisdiction over us. We have reminded them of the circumstances of our emigration and settlement here. We have appealed to their native justice and magnanimity; and we have conjured them by the ties of our common kindred, to disavow these usurpations, which would inevitably interrupt our connections and correspondence. They, too, have been deaf to the voice of justice and consanguinity. We must, therefore, acquiesce in the necessity which denounces our separation, and hold them, as we hold the rest of mankind, enemies in war; in peace, friends.

We, therefore, the representatives of the United States of America, in general congress assembled, appealing to the Supreme Judge of the World for the rectitude of our intentions, do, in the name and by the authority of the good people of these colonies, solemnly publish and declare that these united colonies are, and of right ought to be, free and independent states; that they are absolved from all allegiance to the British crown, and that all political connection between them and the state of Great Britain is, and ought to be, totally dissolved; and that as free and independent states they have full power to levy war, conclude peace, contract alliances, establish commerce, and to do all other acts and things which independent states may of right do. And for the support of this declaration, with a firm reliance on the protection of Divine Providence, we mutually pledge to each other our lives, our fortunes, and our sacred honor.

THOMAS PAINE

The American Crisis, I[1]

These are the times that try men's souls: The summer soldier and the sunshine patriot will, in this crisis, shrink from the service of his country; but he that stands it NOW, deserves the love and thanks of man and woman. Tyranny, like hell, is not easily conquered; yet we have this consolation with us, that the harder the conflict, the more glorious the triumph. What we obtain too cheap, we esteem too lightly:—'Tis dearness only that gives everything its value. Heaven knows how to put a proper price upon its goods; and it would be strange indeed if so celestial an article as FREEDOM should not be highly rated. Britain, with an army to enforce her tyranny, has declared that she has a right (not only to TAX) but "to BIND us in ALL CASES WHATSOEVER"; and if being bound in that manner is not slavery, then is there not such a thing

1 First published December 19, 1776.

as slavery upon earth. Even the expression is impious; for so unlimited a power can belong only to GOD.

Whether the independence of the continent was declared too soon, or delayed too long, I will not now enter into as an argument; my own simple opinion is, that had it been eight months earlier, it would have been much better. We did not make a proper use of last winter; neither could we, while we were in a dependent state. However, the fault, if it were one, was all our own; we have none to blame but ourselves. But no great deal is lost yet. All that Howe has been doing for this month past is rather a ravage than a conquest, which the spirit of the Jerseys a year ago would have quickly repulsed, and which time and a little resolution will soon recover.

I have as little superstition in me as any man living; but my secret opinion has ever been, and still is, that God Almighty will not give up a people to military destruction, or leave them unsupportedly to perish, who have so earnestly and so repeatedly sought to avoid the calamities of war, by every decent method which wisdom could invent. Neither have I so much of the infidel in me as to suppose that he has relinquished the government of the world, and given us up to the care of devils; and as I do not, I cannot see on what grounds the king of Britain can look up to Heaven for help against us; a common murderer, a highwayman, or a house-breaker, has as good a pretense as he.

'Tis surprising to see how rapidly a panic will sometimes run through a country. All nations and ages have been subject to them: Britain has trembled like an ague at the report of a French fleet of flat-bottomed boats; and in the fourteenth century the whole English army, after ravaging the kingdom of France, was driven back like men petrified with fear; and this brave exploit was performed by a few broken forces collected and headed by a woman, Joan of Arc. Would that heaven might inspire some Jersey maid to spirit up her countrymen, and save her fair fellow sufferers from ravage and ravishment! Yet panics, in some cases, have their uses; they produce as much good as hurt. Their duration is always short; the mind soon grows through them, and acquires a firmer habit than before. But their peculiar advantage is, that they are the touchstones of sincerity and hypocrisy, and bring things and men to light, which might otherwise have lain forever undiscovered. In fact, they have the same effect on secret traitors which an imaginary apparition would have upon a private murderer. They sift out the hidden thoughts of man, and hold them up in public to the world. Many a disguised tory has lately shown his head, that shall penitentially solemnize with curses the day on which Howe arrived upon the Delaware.

As I was with the troops at Fort Lee, and marched with them to the edge of Pennsylvania, I am well acquainted with many circumstances which those who live at a distance know but little or nothing of. Our situation there was exceedingly cramped, the place being a narrow neck of land between the North River and Hackensack. Our force was inconsiderable, being not one-fourth so great as Howe could bring against us. We had no army at hand to have relieved the garrison, had we shut ourselves up and stood on our defence. Our ammunition, light artillery, and the best part of our stores, had been removed, on the apprehension that Howe would endeavor to penetrate the Jerseys, in which case Fort Lee could be of no use to us; for it must occur to every thinking man, whether in the army or not, that these kind of field forts are only for temporary purposes, and last in use no longer than the enemy directs his force against the particular object which such forts are raised to defend. Such was our situation and condition at Fort Lee on the morning of the 20th of November, when an officer arrived with information that the enemy with 200 boats had landed about seven miles above. Major General Green, who commanded the garrison, immediately ordered them under arms, and sent express to General Washington at the town of Hackensack, distant by the way of the ferry, six miles. Our first object was to secure the bridge over the Hackensack, which laid up the river between the enemy and us, about six miles from us, three from them. General Washington arrived in about three-quarters of an hour, and marched at the head of the troops towards the bridge, which place I expected we should have a brush for; however, they did not choose to dispute it with us, and the greatest part of our troops went over the bridge, the rest over the ferry except some which passed at a mill on a small creek between the bridge and the ferry, and made their way through some marshy grounds up to the town of Hackensack, and there passed the river. We brought off as much baggage as the wagons could contain, the rest was lost. The simple object was to bring off the garrison, and march them on till they could be strengthened by the Jersey or Pennsylvania militia, so as to be enabled to make a stand. We staid four days at Newark, collected our outposts with some of the Jersey militia, and marched out twice to meet the enemy on being informed that they were advancing, though our numbers were greatly inferior to theirs. Howe, in my opinion, committed a great error in generalship in not throwing a body of forces off from Staten Island through Amboy, by which means he might have seized all our stores at Brunswick and intercepted our march into Pennsylvania; but if we believe the power of hell to be limited, we must likewise believe that their agents are under some providential control.

I shall not now attempt to give all the particulars of our retreat to the Delaware; suffice it for the present to say that both officers and men, though greatly harassed and fatigued, frequently without rest, covering, or provision, the inevitable consequences of a long retreat, bore it with a manly and martial spirit. All their wishes centered in one; which was, that the country would turn out and help them to drive the enemy back. Voltaire has remarked that King William never appeared to full advantage but in difficulties and in action; the same remark may be made on General Washington, for the character fits him. There is a natural firmness in some minds which cannot be unlocked by trifles, but which, when unlocked, discovers a cabinet of fortitude; and I reckon it among those kinds of public blessings, which we do not immediately see, that GOD hath blessed him with uninterrupted health, and given him a mind that can even flourish upon care.

I shall conclude this paper with some miscellaneous remarks on the state of our affairs; and shall begin with asking the following question, Why is it that the enemy have left the New England provinces, and made these middle ones the seat of war. The answer is easy: New England is not infested with tories, and we are. I have been tender in raising the cry against these men, and used numberless arguments to show them their danger, but it will not do to sacrifice a world either to their folly or their baseness. The period is now arrived in which either they or we must change our sentiments, or one or both must fall. And what is a tory? Good GOD! What is he? I should not be afraid to go with a hundred whigs against a thousand tories, were they to attempt to get into arms. Every tory is a coward; for servile, slavish self-interested fear is the foundation of toryism; and a man under such influence, though he may be cruel, never can be brave.

But, before the line of irrecoverable separation be drawn between us, let us reason the matter together: Your conduct is an invitation to the enemy, yet not one in a thousand of you has heart enough to join him. Howe is as much deceived by you as the American cause is injured by you. He expects you will all take up arms and flock to his standard with muskets on your shoulders. Your opinions are of no use to him unless you support him personally, for 'tis soldiers, and not tories, that he wants.

I once felt all that kind of anger, which a man ought to feel, against the mean principles that are held by the tories: A noted one, who kept a tavern at Amboy, was standing at his door, with as pretty a child in his hand, about eight or nine years old, as I ever saw, and after speaking his mind as freely as he thought was prudent, finished with this unfatherly expression, "Well! Give me peace in my day." Not a man lives on the continent but fully believes that a separation must some time or other finally take place, and a generous parent should have said, "If there must be trouble, let it be in my day, that my child may have peace"; and this single reflection, well applied, is sufficient to awaken every man to duty. Not a place upon earth might be so happy as America. Her situation is remote from all the wrangling world, and she has nothing to do but to trade with them. A man can distinguish himself between temper and principle, and I am as confident as I am that GOD governs the world, that America will never be happy till she gets clear of foreign dominion. Wars, without ceasing, will break out till that period arrives, and the continent must in the end be conqueror; for though the flame of liberty may sometimes cease to shine, the coal can never expire.

America did not, nor does not want force; but she wanted a proper application of that force. Wisdom is not the purchase of a day, and it is no wonder that we should err at the first setting off. From an excess of tenderness, we were unwilling to raise an army, and trusted our cause to the temporary defence of a well-meaning militia. A summer's experience has now taught us better; yet with those troops, while they were collected, we were able to set bounds to the progress of the enemy, and thank God! they are again assembling. I always considered militia as the best troops in the world for a sudden exertion, but they will not do for a long campaign. Howe, it is probable, will make an attempt on this city; should he fail on this side of the Delaware, he is ruined. If he succeeds, our cause is not ruined. He stakes all on his side against a part on ours; admitting he succeeds, the consequences will be, that armies from both ends of the continent will march to assist their suffering friends in the middle states; for he cannot go everywhere, it is impossible. I consider Howe as the greatest enemy the Tories have; he is bringing a war into their country, which, had it not been for him and partly for themselves, they had been clear of. Should he now be expelled, I wish with all the devotion of a Christian, that the names of Whig and Tory may never more be mentioned; but should the Tories give him encouragement to come, or assistance if he come, I as sincerely wish that our next year's arms may expel them from the continent, and the Congress appropriate their possessions to the relief of those who have suffered in well-doing. A single successful battle next year will settle the whole. America could carry on a two years' war by the confiscation of the property of disaffected persons, and be made happy by their expulsion. Say not that this is revenge; call it rather the soft resentment of a suffering people, who, having no object in view but the GOOD of ALL, have staked their OWN ALL upon a seemingly doubtful event. Yet it is folly to argue against determined hardness; eloquence may strike the ear, and the language of sorrow draw forth the tear of compassion, but nothing can reach the heart that is steeled with prejudice.

Quitting this class of men, I turn with the warm ardor of a friend to those who have nobly stood, and are yet determined to stand the matter out: I call not upon a few, but upon all: not on THIS state or THAT state, but on EVERY state: up and help us; lay your shoulders to the wheel; better have too much force than too little, when so great an object is at stake. Let it be told to the future world, that in the depth of winter, when nothing but hope and virtue could survive, that the city and the country, alarmed at one common danger, came forth to meet and to repulse it. Say not that thousands are gone, turn out your tens of thousands; throw not the burden of the day upon Providence, but "shew your faith by your works," that God may bless you. It matters not where you live, or what rank of life you hold, the evil or the blessing will reach you all. The far and the near, the home counties and the back, the rich and the poor, will suffer or rejoice alike. The heart that feels not now is dead; the blood of his children will curse his cowardice who shrinks back at a time when a little might have saved the whole and made them happy. I love the man that can smile in trouble, that can gather strength from distress and grow brave by reflection. 'Tis the business of little minds to shrink; but he whose heart is firm, and whose conscience approves his conduct, will pursue his principles unto death. My own line of reasoning is to myself as straight and clear as a ray of light. Not all the treasures of the world, so far as I believe, could have induced me to support an offensive war, for I think it murder; but if a thief breaks into my house, burns and destroys my property, and kills or threatens to kill me or those that are in it, and to *"bind me in all cases whatsoever"* to his absolute will, am I to suffer it? What signifies it to me whether he who does it is a king or a common man; my countryman or not my countryman; whether it be done by an individual villain, or an army of them? If we reason to the root of things we shall find no difference; neither can any just cause be assigned why we should punish in the one case and pardon in the other. Let them call me rebel and welcome, I feel no concern from it; but I should suffer the misery of devils, were I to make a whore of my soul by swearing allegiance to one whose character is that of a sottish, stupid, stubborn, worthless, brutish man. I conceive likewise a horrid idea in receiving mercy from a being, who at the last day shall be shrieking to the rocks and mountains to cover him, and fleeing with terror from the orphan, the widow, and the slain of America.

There are cases which cannot be overdone by language, and this is one. There are persons, too, who see not the full extent of the evil which threatens them; they solace themselves with hopes that the enemy, if he succeed, will be merciful. It is the madness of folly, to expect mercy from those who have refused to do justice; and even mercy, where conquest is the object, is only a trick of war. The cunning of the fox is as murderous as the violence of the wolf, and we ought to guard equally against both. Howe's first object is, partly by threats and partly by promises, to terrify or seduce the people to deliver up their arms and receive mercy. The ministry recommended the same plan to Gage, and this is what the tories call making their peace, *"a peace which passeth all understanding,"* indeed! A peace which would be the immediate forerunner of a worse ruin than any we have yet thought of. Ye men of Pennsylvania, do reason upon these things! Were the back counties to give up their arms, they would fall an easy prey to the Indians, who are all armed: this perhaps is what some tories would not be sorry for. Were the home counties to deliver up their arms, they would be exposed to the resentment of the back counties, who would then have it in their power to chastise their defection at pleasure. And were any one state to give up its arms, THAT state must be garrisoned by all Howe's army of Britons and Hessians to preserve it from the anger of the rest. Mutual fear is the principal link in the chain of mutual love, and woe be to that state that breaks the compact. Howe is mercifully inviting you to barbarous destruction, and men must be either rogues or fools that will not see it. I dwell not upon the vapors of imagination; I bring reason to your ears, and, in language as plain as ABC, hold up truth to your eyes.

I thank GOD that I fear not. I see no real cause for fear. I know our situation well, and can see the way out of it. While our army was collected, Howe dared not risk a battle; and it is no credit to him that he decamped from the White Plains, and waited a mean opportunity to ravage the defenceless Jerseys; but it is great credit to us, that with a handful of men, we sustained an orderly retreat for near an hundred miles, brought off our ammunition, all our field pieces, the greatest part of our stores, and had four rivers to pass. None can say that our retreat was precipitate; for we were near three weeks in performing it, that the country might have time to come in. Twice we marched back to meet the enemy, and remained out till dark. The sign of fear was not seen in our camp, and had not some of the cowardly and disaffected inhabitants spread false alarms through the country, the Jerseys had never been ravaged. Once more we are again collected and collecting; our new army at both ends of the continent is recruiting fast, and we shall be able to open the next campaign with sixty thousand men, well armed and clothed. This is our situation, and who will may know it. By perseverance and fortitude we have the prospect of a glorious issue; by cowardice and submission, the sad choice of a variety of evils: a ravaged country—a depopulated city—habitations without safety, and slavery without hope—our homes turned into barracks and bawdy-houses for Hessians—and a future race to provide for, whose fathers we shall doubt of. Look on this picture and weep over it! and if there yet remains one thoughtless wretch who believes it not, let him suffer it unlamented.

The Bill of Rights[1]

ARTICLE I

Congress shall make no law respecting an establishment of religion, or prohibiting the free exercise thereof; or abridging the freedom of speech, or of the press; or the right of the people peaceably to assemble, and to petition the government for a redress of grievances.

ARTICLE II

A well regulated militia, being necessary to the security of a free State, the right of the people to keep and bear arms, shall not be infringed.

ARTICLE III

No soldier shall, in time of peace be quartered in any house, without the consent of the owner, nor in time of war, but in a manner to be prescribed by law.

ARTICLE IV

The right of the people to be secure in their persons, houses, papers, and effects, against unreasonable searches and seizures, shall not be violated, and

[1] Passed by Congress, September 25, 1789; ratified by three-fourths of the states, December 15, 1791.

no warrants shall issue, but upon probable cause, supported by oath or affirmation, and particularly describing the place to be searched, and the persons or things to be seized.

ARTICLE V

No person shall be held to answer for a capital, or otherwise infamous crime, unless on a presentment or indictment of a grand jury, except in cases arising in the land or naval forces, or in the militia, when in actual service in time of war or public danger; nor shall any person be subject for the same offense to be twice put in jeopardy of life or limb; nor shall be compelled in any criminal case to be a witness against himself, nor be deprived of life, liberty, or property, without due process of law; nor shall private property be taken for public use without just compensation.

ARTICLE VI

In all criminal prosecutions, the accused shall enjoy the right to a speedy and public trial, by an impartial jury of the State and district wherein the crime shall have been committed, which district shall have been previously ascertained by law, and to be informed of the nature and cause of the accusation; to be confronted with the witnesses against him; to have compulsory process for obtaining witnesses in his favor, and to have the assistance of counsel for his defense.

ARTICLE VII

In suits at common law, where the value in controversy shall exceed twenty dollars, the right of trial by jury shall be preserved, and no fact tried by a jury shall be otherwise reexamined in any court of the United States, than according to the rules of the common law.

ARTICLE VIII

Excessive bail shall not be required, nor excessive fines imposed, nor cruel and unusual punishments inflicted.

ARTICLE IX

The enumeration in the Constitution of certain rights shall not be construed to deny or disparage others retained by the people.

ARTICLE X

The powers not delegated to the United States by the Constitution, nor prohibited by it to the States, are reserved to the States respectively, or to the people.

LEARNED HAND

A Plea for the Freedom of Dissent[1]

What do we mean by "principles of civil liberties and human rights"? We cannot go far in that inquiry until we have achieved some notion of what we mean by Liberty; and that has always proved a hard concept to define. The natural, though naïve, opinion is that it means no more than that each individual shall be allowed to pursue his own desires without let or hindrance; and that, although it is true that this is practically impossible, still it does remain the goal, approach to which measures our success. Why, then, is not a beehive or an anthill a perfect example of a free society? Surely you have been a curious and amused watcher beside one of these.

In and out of their crowded pueblo the denizens pass in great number, each bent upon his own urgent mission, quite oblivious of all the rest except as he must bend his path to avoid them. It is a scene of strenuous, purposeful endeavor in which each appears to be, and no doubt in fact is, accomplishing his own purpose; and yet he is at the same time accomplishing the purpose of the group as a whole. As I have gazed at it, the sentence from the Collect of the Episcopal prayerbook has come to me: "Whose service is perfect freedom."

Why is it, then, that we so positively rebel against the hive and the hill as a specimen of a free society? Why is it that such prototypes of totalitarianisms arouse our deepest hostility? Unhappily it is not because they cannot be realized, or at least because they cannot be approached, for a substantial period. Who can be sure that such appalling forecasts as Aldous Huxley's Brave New World or Orwell's 1984 are not prophetic? Indeed, there have often been near approaches to such an order.

Germany at the end of 1940 was probably not far removed from one, and who of us knows that there are not countless persons today living within the boundaries of Russia and perhaps of China who are not willing partners, accepting as their personal aspirations the official definitions of the good, the true and the beautiful? Indeed, there have been, and still are, in our own United States large and powerful groups who, if we are to judge their purposes by their conduct, see treason in all dissidence and would welcome an era in which all of us should think, feel and live in consonance with duly prescribed patterns.

Human nature is malleable, especially if you can indoctrinate the disciple with indefectible principles before anyone else reaches him. (I fancy that the Janissaries were as fervent Mohammedans as the authentic Turks.) Indeed, we hear from those who are entitled to an opinion that at times the abject con-

1 From The New York Times Magazine (February 6, 1955), pp. 11 ff. Copyright, 1955, by The New York Times. Reprinted by permission.

fessions made in Russia by victims who know that they are already marked for slaughter are not wrung from them by torture or threats against their families. Rather, they come from partisans, so obsessed with the faith that when they are told that the occasion calls for scapegoats and that they have been selected, recognize and assent to the propriety of the demand and cooperate in its satisfaction. It is as though, when the right time comes, the drones agreed to their extinction in the interest of the hive.

Nor need we be surprised that men so often embrace almost any doctrines, if they are proclaimed with a voice of absolute assurance. In a universe that we do not understand, but with which we must in one way or another somehow manage to deal, and aware of the conflicting desires that clamorously beset us, between which we must choose and which we must therefore manage to weigh, we turn in our bewilderment to those who tell us that they have found a path out of the thickets and possess the scales by which to appraise our needs.

Over and over again such prophets succeed in converting us to unquestioning acceptance; there is scarcely a monstrous belief that has not had its day and its passionate adherents, so eager are we for safe footholds in our dubious course. How certain is any one of us that he, too, might not be content to follow any fantastic creed, if he was satisfied that nothing would ever wake him from the dream? And, indeed, if there were nothing to wake him, how should he distinguish its articles from the authentic dictates of verity?

Remember, too, that it is by no means clear that we are happier in the faith we do profess than we should be under the spell of an orthodoxy that was sage against all heresy. Cruel and savage as orthodoxies have always proved to be, the faithful seem able to convince themselves that the heretics, as they continue to crop up, get nothing worse than their due, and to rest with an easy conscience.

In any event, my thesis is that the best answer to such systems is not so much in their immoral quality—immoral though they be—as in the fact that they are inherently unstable because they are at war with our only trustworthy way of living in accord with the facts. For I submit that it is only by trial and error, by insistent scrutiny and by readiness to re-examine presently accredited conclusions that we have risen, so far as in fact we have risen, from our brutish ancestors, and I believe that in our loyalty to these habits lies our only chance, not merely of progress, but even of survival.

They were not indeed a part of our aboriginal endowment: Man, as he emerged, was not prodigally equipped to master the infinite diversity of his environment. Obviously, enough of us did manage to get through; but it has been a statistical survival, for the individual's native powers of adjustment are by no means enough for his personal safety any more than are those of other creatures. The precipitate of our experience is far from absolute verity, and our exasperated resentment at all dissent is a sure index of our doubts. Take, for instance, our constant recourse to the word, "subversive," as a touchstone of impermissible deviation from accepted canons.

All discussion, all debate, all dissidence tends to question and in consequence to upset existing convictions: that is precisely its purpose and its justification. He is, indeed, a "subversive" who disputes those precepts that I most treasure and seeks to persuade me to substitute his own. He may have no shadow of desire to resort to anything but persuasion; he may be of those to whom any forcible sanction of conformity is anathema; yet it remains true that he is trying to bring about my apostasy, and I hate him just in proportion as I fear his success.

Contrast this protective resentment with the assumption that lies at the base of our whole system that the best chance for truth to emerge is a fair field for all ideas. Nothing, I submit, more completely betrays our latent disloyalty to this premise to all that we pretend to believe than the increasingly common resort to this and other question-begging words. Their imprecision comforts us by enabling us to suppress arguments that disturb our complacency and yet to continue to congratulate ourselves on keeping the faith as we have received it from the Founding Fathers.

Heretics have been hateful from the beginning of recorded time; they have been ostracized, exiled, tortured, maimed and butchered; but it has generally proved impossible to smother them, and when it has not, the society that has succeeded has always declined. Façades of authority, however imposing, do not survive after it has appeared that they rest upon the sands of human conjecture and compromise.

And so, if I am to say what are "the principles of civil liberties and human rights," I answer that they lie in habits, customs—conventions, if you will— that tolerate dissent and can live without irrefragable certainties; that are ready to overhaul existing assumptions; that recognize that we never see save through a glass, darkly, and that at long last we shall succeed only so far as we continue to undertake "the intolerable labor of thought"—that most distasteful of all our activities.

If such a habit and such a temper pervade a society, it will not need institutions to protect its "civil liberties and human rights"; so far as they do not, I venture to doubt how far anything else can protect them: whether it be Bills of Rights, or courts that must in the name of interpretation read their meaning into them.

This may seem to you a bleak and cheerless conclusion, too alien to our nature to be practical. "We must live from day to day"—you will say—"to live is to act, and to act is to choose and decide. How can we carry on at all without some principles, some patterns to meet the conflicts in which each day involves us?" Indeed, we cannot, nor am I suggesting that we should try; but I *am* suggesting that it makes a vital difference—*the* vital difference—whether we deem our principles and our patterns to be eternal verities, rather than the best postulates so far attainable.

Was it not Holmes who said: "The highest courage is to stake everything on a premise that you know tomorrow's evidence may disprove"? "Ah"—you will reply—"there's the rub. That may be the highest courage, but how many have it? You are hopelessly wrong if you assume the general prevalence of such a virtue; ordinary men must be given more than conjectures if they are to face grave dangers."

But do you really believe that? Do you not see about you every day and everywhere the precise opposite? Not alone on the battlefield but in the forest, the desert and the plain; in the mountains, at sea, on the playing field, even in the laboratory and the factory—yes (do not laugh), at the card table and the racetrack—men are forever putting it "upon the touch to win or lose it all." Without some smack of uncertainty and danger, to most of us the world would be a tepid, pallid show.

Surely, like me, you have all felt something of this when you have looked on those pathetic attempts to depict in paint or stone the delights of Paradise. I own that the torments of hell never fail to horrify me; not even the glee of the demons in charge is an adequate relief, though the artist has generally been successful in giving a veracious impression of the gusto with which they discharge their duties.

But when I turn to the Congregation of the Blessed, I cannot avoid a sense of anticlimax; strive as I may, the social atmosphere seems a bit forced; and I recall those very irreverent verses of Lowes Dickinson:

> Burning at first no doubt would be worse,
> But time the impression would soften,
> While those who are bored with praising the Lord,
> Would be more bored with praising him often.

By some happy fortuity man is a projector, a designer, a builder, a craftsman; it is among his most dependable joys to impose upon the flux that passes before him some mark of himself, aware though he always must be of the odds against him. His reward is not so much in the work as in its making; not so much in the prize as in the race. We may win when we lose, if we have done what we can; for by so doing we have made real at least some part of that finished product in whose fabrication we are most concerned—ourselves.

And if at the end some friendly critic shall pass by and say, "My friend, how good a job do you really think you have made of it all?" we can answer, "I know as well as you that it is not of high quality, but I did put into it whatever I had, and that was the game I started out to play."

It is still in the lap of the gods whether a society can succeed, based on "civil liberties and human rights," conceived as I have tried to describe them; but of one thing at least we may be sure: the alternatives that have so far appeared have been immeasurably worse, and so, whatever the outcome, I submit to you that we must press along. Borrowing from Epictetus, let us say to ourselves: "Since we are men we will play the part of a Man," and how can I better end than by recalling to you the concluding passage of "Prometheus Unbound"?

> To suffer woes which Hope thinks infinite;
> To forgive wrongs darker than death or night;
> To defy Power, which seems omnipotent
> To love, and bear; to hope till Hope creates
> From its own wreck the thing it contemplates;
> Neither to change, nor falter, nor repent;
> This, like thy glory, Titan, is to be
> Good, great and joyous, beautiful and free;
> This is alone Life, Joy, Empire and Victory.

Problems of the Social Sciences

❦❦❦❦❦❦❦❦❦❦❦❦❦❦❦❦❦❦❦❦❦❦❦❦❦❦❦❦❦❦❦❦❦❦❦❦❦❦

FREDERICK JACKSON TURNER

The Significance of the Frontier in American History[1]

In a recent bulletin of the Superintendent of the Census for 1890 appear these significant words: "Up to and including 1880 the country had a frontier of settlement, but at present the unsettled area has been so broken into by isolated bodies of settlement that there can hardly be said to be a frontier line. In the discussion of its extent, its westward movement, etc., it cannot, therefore, any longer have a place in the census reports." This brief official statement marks the closing of a great historic movement. Up to our own day American history has been in a large degree the history of the colonization of the Great West. The existence of an area of free land, its continuous recession, and the advance of American settlement westward, explain American development.

Behind institutions, behind constitutional forms and modifications, lie the vital forces that call these organs into life and shape them to meet changing conditions. The peculiarity of American institutions is the fact that they have been compelled to adapt themselves to the changes of an expanding people— to the changes involved in crossing a continent, in winning a wilderness, and in developing at each area of this progress out of the primitive economic and political conditions of the frontier into the complexity of city life. Said Cal-

1 From The Frontier in American History (with omissions) by Frederick Jackson Turner. Copyright, 1920, by Frederick J. Turner. Copyright, 1948, by Caroline M. S. Turner. By permission of Holt, Rinehart and Winston, Inc.

houn in 1817, "We are great, and rapidly—I was about to say fearfully—growing!" So saying, he touched the distinguishing feature of American life. All peoples show development; the germ theory of politics has been sufficiently emphasized. In the case of most nations, however, the development has occurred in a limited area; and if the nation has expanded, it has met other growing peoples whom it has conquered. But in the case of the United States we have a different phenomenon. Limiting our attention to the Atlantic coast, we have the familiar phenomenon of the evolution of institutions in a limited area, such as the rise of representative government; the differentiation of simple colonial governments into complex organs; the progress from primitive industrial society, without division of labor, up to manufacturing civilization. But we have in addition to this a recurrence of the process of evolution in each western area reached in the process of expansion. Thus American development has exhibited not merely advance along a single line, but a return to primitive conditions on a continually advancing frontier line, and a new development for that area. American social development has been continually beginning over again on the frontier. This perennial rebirth, this fluidity of American life, this expansion westward with its new opportunities, its continuous touch with the simplicity of primitive society, furnish the forces dominating American character. The true point of view in the history of this nation is not the Atlantic coast, it is the Great West. Even the slavery struggle, which is made so exclusive an object of attention by writers like Professor von Holst, occupies its important place in American history because of its relation to westward expansion.

In this advance, the frontier is the outer edge of the wave—the meeting point between savagery and civilization. Much has been written about the frontier from the point of view of border warfare and the chase, but as a field for the serious study of the economist and the historian it has been neglected. The American frontier is sharply distinguished from the European frontier —a fortified boundary line running through dense populations. The most significant thing about the American frontier is, that it lies at the hither edge of free land. In the census reports it is treated as the margin of that settlement which has a density of two or more to the square mile. The term is an elastic one, and for our purposes does not need sharp definition. We shall consider the whole frontier belt, including the Indian country and the outer margin of the "settled area" of the census reports. This paper will make no attempt to treat the subject exhaustively; its aim is simply to call attention to the frontier as a fertile field for investigation, and to suggest some of the problems which arise in connection with it.

In the settlement of America we have to observe how European life entered the continent, and how America modified and developed that life and reacted on Europe. Our early history is the study of European germs developing in an American environment. Too exclusive attention has been paid by institutional students to the Germanic origins, too little to the American factors. The frontier is the line of most rapid and effective Americanization. The wilderness masters the colonist. It finds him a European in dress, industries, tools, modes of travel, and thought. It takes him from the railroad car and puts him in the birch canoe. It strips off the garments of civilization and arrays him in the hunting shirt and the moccasin. It puts him in the log cabin of the Cherokee and Iroquois and runs an Indian palisade around him. Before long he has gone to planting Indian corn and plowing with a sharp stick; he shouts the war cry and takes the scalp in orthodox Indian fashion. In short, at the frontier the environment is at first too strong for the man. He must accept the conditions which it furnishes, or perish, and so he fits himself into the Indian clearings and follows the Indian trails. Little by little he transforms the wilderness, but the outcome is not the old Europe, not simply the development of Germanic germs, any more than the first phenomenon was a case of reversion to the Germanic mark. The fact is, that here is a new product that is American. At first, the frontier was the Atlantic coast. It was the frontier of Europe in a very real sense. Moving westward, the frontier became more and more American. As successive terminal moraines result from successive glaciations, so each frontier leaves its traces behind it, and when it becomes a settled area the region still partakes of the frontier characteristics. Thus the advance of the frontier has meant a steady movement away from the influence of Europe, a steady growth of independence on American lines. And to study this advance, the men who grew up under these conditions, and the political, economic, and social results of it, is to study the really American part of our history. . . .

The Atlantic frontier was compounded of fisherman, fur-trader, miner, cattle-raiser, and farmer. Excepting the fisherman, each type of industry was on the march toward the West, impelled by an irresistible attraction. Each passed in successive waves across the continent. Stand at Cumberland Gap and watch the procession of civilization, marching single file—the buffalo following the trail to the salt springs, the Indian, the fur-trader and hunter, the cattle-raiser, the pioneer farmer—and the frontier has passed by. Stand at South Pass in the Rockies a century later and see the same procession with wider intervals between. The unequal rate of advance compels us to distinguish the frontier into the trader's frontier, the rancher's frontier, or the miner's frontier, and the farmer's frontier. When the mines and the cow pens were still near the fall line the traders' pack trains were tinkling across the Alleghenies, and the French on the Great Lakes were fortifying their posts, alarmed by the British trader's birch canoe. When the trappers scaled the Rockies, the farmer was still near the mouth of the Missouri.

Why was it that the Indian trader passed so rapidly across the continent? What effects followed from the trader's frontier? The trade was coeval with American discovery. The Norsemen, Vespucius, Verrazani, Hudson, John Smith, all trafficked for furs. The Plymouth pilgrims settled in Indian corn-fields, and their first return cargo was of beaver and lumber. The records of the various New England colonies show how steadily exploration was carried into the wilderness by this trade. What is true for New England is, as would be expected, even plainer for the rest of the colonies. All along the coast from Maine to Georgia the Indian trade opened up the river courses. Steadily the trader passed westward, utilizing the older lines of French trade. The Ohio, the Great Lakes, the Mississippi, the Missouri, and the Platte, the lines of western advance, were ascended by traders. They found the passes in the Rocky Mountains and guided Lewis and Clark, Frémont, and Bidwell. The explanation of the rapidity of this advance is connected with the effects of the trader on the Indian. The trading post left the unarmed tribes at the mercy of those that had purchased fire-arms—a truth which the Iroquois Indians wrote in blood, and so the remote and unvisited tribes gave eager welcome to the trader. "The savages," wrote La Salle, "take better care of us French than of their own children; from us only can they get guns and goods." This accounts for the trader's power and the rapidity of his advance. Thus the disintegrating forces of civilization entered the wilderness. Every river valley and Indian trail became a fissure in Indian society, and so that society became honeycombed. Long before the pioneer farmer appeared on the scene, primitive Indian life had passed away. The farmers met Indians armed with guns. The trading frontier, while steadily undermining Indian power by making the tribes ultimately dependent on the whites, yet, through its sale of guns, gave to the Indian increased power of resistance to the farming frontier. French colonization was dominated by its trading frontier; English colonization by its farming frontier. There was an antagonism between the two frontiers as between the two nations. Said Duquesne to the Iroquois, "Are you ignorant of the difference between the king of England and the king of France? Go see the forts that our king has established and you will see that you can still hunt under their very walls. They have been placed for your advantage in places which you frequent. The English, on the contrary, are no sooner in possession of a place than the game is driven away. The forest falls before them as they advance, and the soil is laid bare so that you can scarce find the wherewithal to erect a shelter for the night."

And yet, in spite of this opposition of the interests of the trader and the farmer, the Indian trade pioneered the way for civilization. The buffalo trail became the Indian trail, and this became the trader's "trace"; the trails widened into roads, and the roads into turnpikes, and these in turn were transformed into railroads. The same origin can be shown for the railroads of the South, the Far West, and the Dominion of Canada. The trading posts reached by these trails were on the sites of Indian villages which had been placed in positions suggested by nature; and these trading posts, situated so as to command the water systems of the country, have grown into such cities as Albany, Pittsburgh, Detroit, Chicago, St. Louis, Council Bluffs, and Kansas City. Thus civilization in America has followed the arteries made by geology, pouring an ever richer tide through them, until at last the slender paths of aboriginal intercourse have been broadened and interwoven into the complex mazes of modern commercial lines; the wilderness has been interpenetrated by lines of civilization growing ever more numerous. It is like the steady growth of a complex nervous system for the originally simple, inert continent. If one would understand why we are to-day one nation, rather than a collection of isolated states, he must study this economic and social consolidation of the country. . . .

The exploitation of the beasts took hunter and trader to the west, the exploitation of the grasses took the rancher west, and the exploitation of the virgin soil of the river valleys and prairies attracted the farmer. Good soils have been the most continuous attraction to the farmer's frontier. The land hunger of the Virginians drew them down the rivers into Carolina, in early colonial days; the search for soils took the Massachusetts men to Pennsylvania and to New York. As the eastern lands were taken up migration flowed across them to the west. Daniel Boone, the great backwoodsman, who combined the occupations of hunter, trader, cattle-raiser, farmer, and surveyor—learning, probably from the traders, of the fertility of the lands of the upper Yadkin, where the traders were wont to rest as they took their way to the Indians, left his Pennsylvania home with his father, and passed down the Great Valley road to that stream. Learning from a trader of the game and rich pastures of Kentucky, he pioneered the way for the farmers to that region. Thence he passed to the frontier of Missouri, where his settlement was long a landmark on the frontier. Here again he helped to open the way for civilization, finding salt licks, and trails, and land. His son was among the earliest trappers in the passes of the Rocky Mountains, and his party are said to have been the first to camp on the present site of Denver. His grandson, Col. A. J. Boone, of Colorado, was a power among the Indians of the Rocky Mountains, and was appointed an agent by the government. Kit Carson's mother was a Boone. Thus this family epitomizes the backwoodsman's advance across the continent. . . .

Omitting those of the pioneer farmers who move from the love of adventure, the advance of the more steady farmer is easy to understand. Obviously the immigrant was attracted by the cheap lands of the frontier, and even the native farmer felt their influence strongly. Year by year the farmers who lived on soil whose returns were diminished by unrotated crops were offered the virgin soil of the frontier at nominal prices. Their growing families demanded more lands, and these were dear. The competition of the unexhausted, cheap, and easily tilled prairie lands compelled the farmer either to go west and continue the exhaustion of the soil on a new frontier, or to adopt intensive culture. Thus the census of 1890 shows, in the Northwest, many counties in which there is an absolute or a relative decrease of population. These States have been sending farmers to advance the frontier on the plains, and have themselves begun to turn to intensive farming and to manufacture. A decade before this, Ohio had shown the same transition stage. Thus the demand for land and the love of wilderness freedom drew the frontier ever onward.

Having now roughly outlined the various kinds of frontiers, and their modes of advance, chiefly from the point of view of the frontier itself, we may next inquire what were the influences on the East and on the New World. . . .

First, we note that the frontier promoted the formation of a composite nationality for the American people. The coast was preponderantly English, but the later tides of continental immigration flowed across to the free lands. This was the case from the early colonial days. The Scotch-Irish and the Palatine Germans, or "Pennsylvania Dutch," furnished the dominant element in the stock of the colonial frontier. With these peoples were also the freed indented servants, or redemptioners, who at the expiration of their time of service passed to the frontier. . . . Very generally these redemptions were of non-English stock. In the crucible of the frontier the immigrants were Americanized, liberated, and fused into a mixed race, English in neither nationality nor characteristics. The process has gone on from the early days to our own. . . .

In another way the advance of the frontier decreased our dependence on England. The coast, particularly of the South, lacked diversified industries, and was dependent on England for the bulk of its supplies. In the South there was even a dependence on the Northern colonies for articles of food. . . . Before long the frontier created a demand for merchants. As it retreated from the coast it became less and less possible for England to bring her supplies directly to the consumer's wharfs, and carry away staple crops, and staple crops began to give way to diversified agriculture for a time. The effect of this phase of the frontier action upon the northern section is perceived when we realize how the advance of the frontier aroused seaboard cities like Boston, New York, and Baltimore, to engage in rivalry for what Washington called "the extensive and valuable trade of a rising empire."

The legislation which most developed the powers of the national government, and played the largest part in its activity, was conditioned on the frontier. Writers have discussed the subjects of tariff, land, and internal improvement, as subsidiary to the slavery question. . . . This is a wrong perspective. The pioneer needed the goods of the coast, and so the grand series of internal improvement and railroad legislation began, with potent nationalizing effects. Over internal improvements occurred great debates, in which grave constitutional questions were discussed. Sectional groupings appear in the votes, profoundly significant for the historian. Loose construction increased as the nation marched westward. But the West was not content with bringing the farm to the factory. Under the lead of Clay—"Harry of the West"—protective tariffs were passed, with the cry of bringing the factory to the farm. The disposition of the public lands was a third important subject of national legislation influenced by the frontier.

The public domain has been a force of profound importance in the nationalization and development of the government. The effects of the struggle of the landed and the landless States, and of the Ordinance of 1787, need no discussion. Administratively the frontier called out some of the highest and most vitalizing activities of the general government. The purchase of Louisiana was perhaps the constitutional turning point in the history of the Republic, inasmuch as it afforded both a new area for national legislation and the occasion of the downfall of the policy of strict construction. But the purchase of Louisiana was called out by frontier needs and demands. As frontier States accrued to the Union the national power grew. In a speech on the dedication of the Calhoun monument Mr. Lamar explained: "In 1789 the States were the creators of the Federal Government; in 1861 the Federal Government was the creator of a large majority of the States."

When we consider the public domain from the point of view of the sale and disposal of the public lands we are again brought face to face with the frontier. The policy of the United States in dealing with its lands is in sharp contrast with the European system of scientific administration. Efforts to make this domain a source of revenue, and to withhold it from emigrants in order that settlement might be compact, were in vain. The jealousy and the fears of the East were powerless in the face of the demands of the frontiersmen. John Quincy Adams was obliged to confess: "My own system of administration, which was to make the national domain the inexhaustible fund for progressive and unceasing internal improvement, has failed." The reason is obvious; a system of administration was not what the West demanded; it wanted land. Adams states the situation as follows: "The slaveholders of the South have bought the cooperation of the western country by the bribe of the western lands, abandoning to the new Western States their own proportion of the public property and aiding them in the design of grasping all the lands into their own hands." . . .

It is safe to say that the legislation with regard to land, tariff, and internal improvements—the American system of the nationalizing Whig party—was conditioned on frontier ideas and needs. But it was not merely in legislative action that the frontier worked against the sectionalism of the coast. The economic and social characteristics of the frontier worked against sectionalism. The men of the frontier had closer resemblances to the Middle region than to either of the other sections. Pennsylvania had been the seed-plot of frontier emigration, and, although she passed on her settlers along the Great Valley into the west of Virginia and the Carolinas, yet the industrial society of these Southern frontiersmen was always more like that of the Middle region than like that of the tide-water portion of the South, which later came to spread its industrial type throughout the South.

The Middle region, entered by New York harbor, was an open door to all Europe. The tide-water part of the South represented typical Englishmen, modified by a warm climate and servile labor, and living in baronial fashion on great plantations; New England stood for a special English movement—Puritanism. The middle region was less English than the other sections. It had a wide mixture of nationalities, a varied society, the mixed town and county system of local government, a varied economic life, many religious sects. In short, it was a region mediating between New England and the South, and the East and the West. It represented that composite nationality which the contemporary United States exhibits, that juxtaposition of non-English groups, occupying a valley or a little settlement, and presenting reflections of the map of Europe in their variety. It was democratic and nonsectional, if not national; "easy, tolerant, and contented"; rooted strongly in material prosperity. It was typical of the modern United States. . . .

It was this nationalizing tendency of the West that transformed the democracy of Jefferson into the national republicanism of Monroe and the democracy of Andrew Jackson. The West of the War of 1812, the West of Clay, and Benton and Harrison, and Andrew Jackson, shut off by the Middle States and the mountains from the coast sections, had a solidarity of its own with national tendencies. On the tide of the Father of Waters, North and South met and mingled into a nation. Interstate migration went steadily on—a process of cross-fertilization of ideas and institutions. The fierce struggle of the sections over slavery on the western frontier does not diminish the truth of this statement; it proves the truth of it. Slavery was a sectional trait that would not down, but in the West it could not remain sectional. It was the greatest of frontiersmen who declared: "I believe this Government cannot endure permanently half slave and half free. It will become all of one thing or all of the other." Nothing works for nationalism like intercourse with the nation. Mobility of population is death to localism, and the western frontier worked irresistibly in unsettling population. The effect reached back from the frontier and affected profoundly the Atlantic coast and even the Old World.

But the most important effect of the frontier has been in the promotion of democracy here and in Europe. As has been indicated, the frontier is productive of individualism. Complex society is precipitated by the wilderness into a kind of primitive organization based on the family. The tendency is antisocial. It produces antipathy to control, and particularly to any direct control. The tax-gatherer is viewed as a representative of oppression. Prof. Osgood, in an able article, has pointed out that the frontier conditions prevalent in the colonies are important factors in the explanation of the American Revolution, where individual liberty was sometimes confused with absence of all effective government. The same conditions aid in explaining the difficulty of instituting a strong government in the period of the confederacy. The frontier individualism has from the beginning promoted democracy.

The frontier States that came into the Union in the first quarter of a century of its existence came in with democratic suffrage provisions, and had reactive effects of the highest importance upon the older States whose peoples were being attracted there. An extension of the franchise became essential. It was western New York that forced an extension of suffrage in the constitutional convention of that State in 1821; and it was western Virginia that compelled the tide-water region to put a more liberal suffrage provision in the constitution framed in 1830, and to give to the frontier region a more nearly proportionate representation with the tide-water aristocracy. The rise of democracy as an effective force in the nation came in with western preponderance under Jackson and William Henry Harrison, and it meant the triumph of the frontier —with all of its good and with all of its evil elements. . . .

So long as free land exists, the opportunity for a competency exists, and economic power secures political power. But the democracy born of free land, strong in selfishness and individualism, intolerant of administrative experience and education, and pressing individual liberty beyond its proper bounds, has its dangers as well as its benefits. Individualism in America has allowed a laxity in regard to governmental affairs which has rendered possible the spoils system and all the manifest evils that follow from the lack of a highly developed civic spirit. . . .

From the conditions of frontier life came intellectual traits of profound importance. The works of travelers along each frontier from colonial days onward describe certain common traits, and these traits have, while softening down, still persisted as survivals in the place of their origin, even when a higher social organization succeeded. The result is that to the frontier the American intellect owes its striking characteristics. That coarseness and strength combined with acuteness and inquisitiveness; that practical, inventive turn of mind, quick to find expedients; that masterful grasp of material things, lacking in the artistic but powerful to effect great ends; that restless, nervous energy; that dominant individualism, working for good and for evil, and withal that buoyancy and exuberance which comes with freedom—these are traits of the frontier, or traits called out elsewhere because of the existence of the frontier. Since the days when the fleet of Columbus sailed into the waters of the New World, America has been another name for opportunity, and the people of the United States have taken their tone from the incessant expansion which has not only been open but has even been forced upon them. He would be a rash prophet who should assert that the expansive character of American life has now entirely ceased. Movement has been its dominant fact, and unless this training has no effect upon a people, the American energy will continually demand a wider field for its exercise. But never again will such gifts of free land offer themselves. For a moment, at the frontier, the bonds of custom are broken and unrestraint is triumphant. There is not *tabula rasa*. The stubborn American environment is there with its imperious summons to accept its conditions; the inherited ways of doing things are also there; and yet, in spite of environment, and in spite of custom, each frontier did indeed furnish a new field of opportunity, a gate of escape from the bondage of the past; and freshness, and confidence, and scorn of older society, impatience of its restraints and its ideas, and indifference to its lessons, have accompanied the frontier. What the Mediterranean sea was to the Greeks, breaking the bond of custom, offering new experiences, calling out new institutions and activities, that, and more, the ever retreating frontier has been to the United States directly, and to the nations of Europe more remotely. And now, four centuries from the discovery of America, at the end of a hundred years of life under the Constitution, the frontier has gone, and with its going has closed the first period of American history.

ARNOLD J. TOYNBEE

Does History Repeat Itself?[1]

Does history repeat itself? In our Western world in the eighteenth and nineteenth centuries, this question used to be debated as an academic exercise. The spell of well-being which our civilization was enjoying at the time had dazzled our grandfathers into the quaint pharisaical notion that they were "not as other men are"; they had come to believe that our Western society was exempt from the possibility of falling into those mistakes and mishaps that have been the ruin of certain other civilizations whose history, from beginning to end, is an open book. To us, in our generation, the old question has rather suddenly taken on a new and very practical significance. We have awakened to the truth (how, one wonders, could we ever have been blind to it?) that Western man and his works are no more invulnerable than the now extinct civilizations of the Aztecs and the Incas, the Sumerians and the Hittites. So today, with some anxiety, we are searching the scriptures of the past to find out whether they contain a lesson that we can decipher. Does history give us any information about our own prospects? And, if it does, what is the burden of it? Does it spell out for us an inexorable doom, which we can merely await with folded hands—resigning ourselves, as best we may, to a fate that we cannot avert or even modify by our own efforts? Or does it inform us, not of certainties, but of probabilities, or bare possibilities, in our own future? The practical difference is vast, for, on this second alternative, so far from being stunned into passivity, we should be roused to action. On this second alternative, the lesson of history would not be like an astrologer's horoscope; it would be like a navigator's chart, which affords the seafarer who has the intelligence to use it a much greater hope of avoiding shipwreck than when he was sailing blind, because it gives him the means, if he has the skill and courage to use them, of steering a course between charted rocks and reefs.

It will be seen that our question needs defining before we plunge into an attempt to answer it. When we ask ourselves "Does history repeat itself?" do we mean no more than "Does history turn out to have repeated itself, on occasions, in the past?" Or are we asking whether history is governed by inviolable laws which have not only taken effect in every past case to which they have applied but are also bound to take effect in every similar situation that may

[1] From *Civilization on Trial* by Arnold J. Toynbee. Copyright 1948 by Oxford University Press, Inc., and reprinted by permission.

arise in the future? On this second interpretation, the word "does" would mean "must"; on the other interpretation it would mean "may." On this issue, the writer of the present article may as well put his cards on the table at once. He is not a determinist in his reading of the riddle of human life. He believes that where there is life there is hope, and that, with God's help, man is master of his own destiny, at least to some extent in some respects.

But as soon as we have taken our stand on this issue between freedom and necessity that is raised by the ambiguous word "does," we find ourselves called upon to define what we mean by the word "history." If we have to limit the field of history to events that are wholly within the control of human wills, then, to be sure, for a non-determinist no difficulty would arise. But do such events ever actually occur in real life? In our personal experience, when we are making a decision, do we not always find ourselves only partly free and partly bound by past events and present facts in our own life and in our social and physical environment? Is not history itself, in the last analysis, a vision of the whole universe on the move in the four-dimensional framework of spacetime? And, in this all-embracing panorama, are there not many events that the most staunch believer in the freedom of the human will would admit, as readily as the most thoroughgoing determinist, to be inexorably recurrent and precisely predictable?

Some events of this undisputedly recurrent predictable order may have little apparent bearing upon human affairs—as, for example, the repetitions of history in nebulae outside the system of the Milky Way. There are, however, some very obvious cyclic movements in physical nature that do affect human affairs in the most intimate fashion—as, for example, the recurrent predictable alternations of day and night and of the seasons of the year. The day-and-night cycle governs all human work; it dictates the schedules of the transportation systems of our cities, sets the times of their rush hours, and weighs on the minds of the commuters whom it shuttles to and fro, twice in every twenty-four hours, between "dormitory" and "workshop." The cycle of the seasons governs human life itself by governing our food supply.

It is true that man, by taking thought, can win a measure of freedom from these physical cycles that is beyond the reach of birds and beasts. Though the individual cannot break the tyranny of the day-and-night cycle by leading a waking life for twenty-four hours in the day, like the legendary Egyptian Pharaoh Mycerinus, human society can achieve Mycerinus' mythical feat collectively by a planned co-operation and a division of labour. Industrial plants can be operated for twenty-four hours in the day by successive shifts of workers, and the labours of workers who work by day can be prepared for and be followed up by the labours of other workers who rest by day and work by night. The tyranny of the seasons, again, has been broken by a Western society that has expanded from the northern temperate zone into the tropics and the southern temperate zone and has devised a technique of refrigeration. Nevertheless, these triumphs of man's mind and will over the tyranny of the two physical cycles of the day and the year are comparatively small gains for human freedom, remarkable though these triumphs are. On the whole, these recurrent predictable events in physical nature remain masters of human life—even at the present level of Western man's technology—and they show their mastery by subduing human affairs, as far as their empire over them extends, to their own recurrent predictable pattern.

But are there, perhaps, human acts, in other fields of action, that are not—or at any rate not so completely—under physical nature's control? Let us examine this question in a familiar concrete case. When, in the last days of April 1865, the horses that, in the first days of that month, had been the cavalry and artillery horses of the Army of Northern Virginia, were being driven behind the plough by the men who, at the beginning of that April, had been General Lee's cavalrymen and artillerymen, those men and horses were once again performing an annually recurrent agricultural operation which they themselves had performed a number of times before in their lives and which predecessors of theirs, in the Old World before Europeans discovered the New World, and in other societies before our Western society's birth, had been performing, year by year, for some five or six thousand years past. The invention of ploughing is coeval with the species of society that we call civilizations, and pre-plough methods of agriculture—likewise governed by the year cycle—were already in use for perhaps an equal length of time before that, during the neolithic dawn by which the sunrise of civilization was heralded. In the spring of 1865, agriculture in the ex-Confederate States of North America was governed by the seasons very rigidly. A few weeks' delay, and the season would have been too late—with the disastrous consequence that the food-producing capacities of those horses and men would have been lost to the community for a whole year longer.

Thus, in the last days of April 1865, the horses and men of the former Army of Northern Virginia were performing a historical act—the spring ploughing —which had repeated itself, by that date, some five or six thousand times at least, and was still repeating itself in 1947. (In that year the writer of this article witnessed the spring ploughing in Kentucky, and noted the farmers' anxiety when, in the middle of that April, their work was interrupted by heavy rainfall.)

But what about the history that General Lee's horses and men were making, not at the end of April, but at the beginning? Is the kind of history that is represented by the last act of the Civil War a kind that repeats itself—as ploughing and commuting repeat themselves owing to their close and obvious dependence on recurrent predictable cycles in physical nature? Are we not confronted here with a kind of human action that is more or less independent of physical cycles and is capable of overriding them? Suppose that General Lee had not found himself constrained to capitulate till June 1865? Or suppose that, General Lee having capitulated when he did, General Grant had not been moved to make his celebrated concession of allowing the Confederate soldiers who had just laid down their arms to take their horses back with them to their farms, notwithstanding the contrary provision in the terms of surrender that had just been agreed upon. Would not either of these hypothetical man-made variations on the actual course of historical events have prevented history from repeating itself in the Southern States in the spring ploughing of 1865?

The province of history that we are considering now is one that used to be treated as the whole field of history before the provinces of economic and social history were opened up. In this old-fashioned field of battles and policies, captains and kings, does history turn out to have repeated itself as it does in fields of human activity that are manifestly governed by cycles in the movement of physical nature? Was the Civil War, for instance, a unique event, or do we find other historical events that display sufficient similarity and affinity to it to warrant us in treating it and them as so many representatives of a class of events in which history has repeated itself at least to some extent? The present writer inclines to this latter view.

The crisis represented in American history by the Civil War was, surely, repeated in a significant sense in the contemporary crisis in German history that is represented by the Bismarckian wars of 1864-71. In both cases an imperfect political union had threatened to dissolve altogether. In both cases, the issue between the dissolution of the union and its effective establishment was decided by war. In both cases, the partisans of effective union won, and, in both, one of the causes of their victory was their technological and industrial superiority over their opponents. In both, finally, the victory of the cause of union was followed by a great industrial expansion which turned both the postbellum United States and the Second German Reich into formidable industrial competitors of Great Britain. And here we have hit upon another repetition of history; for, throughout the century ending about 1870, the industrial revolution in Great Britain might have appeared to be a unique historical event, whereas, since 1870, it has come to appear, in its true light, as simply the earliest instance of an economic transformation which was eventually to occur likewise in a number of other Western countries and in some non-Western countries too. Moreover, if we shift our attention from the economic common feature of industrialization to the political common feature of federal union, we shall see the history of the United States and Germany at this point repeating itself once again in the history of a third country—in this case not Great Britain but Canada, whose constituent provinces entered into their present federation in 1867, two years after the *de facto* re-establishment of the unity of the United States in 1865 and four years before the foundation of the Second German Reich in 1871.

In the formation, in the modern Western world, of a number of federal unions, and in the industrialization of these and other countries, we see history repeating itself in the sense of producing a number of more or less contemporary examples of the same human achievement. The contemporaneity of the different instances is, however, no more than approximate. The industrial revolution occurred as an apparently unique event in Great Britain at least two generations before its occurrence in America, and Germany proved it to be a repetitive phenomenon. The insecurely welded pre-Civil-War United States had existed for "four score and seven years," and the ramshackle post-Napoleonic German Confederation for half a century, before the crucial events of the eighteen-sixties proved that federal union was a repetitive pattern which was to recur not only in Canada but in Australia, South Africa, and Brazil. Contemporaneity is not an essential condition for the repetition of history on the political and cultural plane of human affairs. The historical events that repeat themselves may be strictly contemporary or they may overlap in time or they may be entirely non-contemporaneous with one another.

The picture remains the same when we turn to the consideration of the greatest human institutions and experiences that are known to us: the civilizations in their births and growths, their breakdowns, declines, and falls; the higher religions in their foundation and evolution. Measured by our subjective personal measuring rod of the average span of the memory of a single human being who lives to a normal old age, the time interval that divides our present generation from the date of the emergence of the Sumerian civilization in the fourth millennium B.C. or from the date of the beginning of the Christian era itself seems, no doubt, a very long one. Yet it is infinitesimally small on the objective time scale that has recently been given to us by the discoveries of our geologists and astronomers. Our modern Western physical science tells us that the human race has been in existence on this planet for at least 600,000 and perhaps a million years, life for at least 500 million and perhaps 800 million years, and the planet itself for possibly 2000 million years. On this time scale the last five or six thousand years that have seen the births of civilizations, and the last three or four thousand years that have seen the births of higher religions are periods of such infinitesimal brevity that it would be impossible to show them, drawn to scale, on any chart of the whole history of this planet up to date. On this true time scale, these events of "ancient history" are virtually contemporary with our own lifetime, however remote they may appear to be when viewed through the magnifying lens of the individual human midget's subjective mental vision.

The conclusion seems to be that human history does turn out, on occasions, to have repeated itself up to date in a significant sense even in spheres of human activity in which the human will is at its nearest to being master of the situation and is least under the domination of cycles in physical nature. Must we go on to conclude that, after all, the determinists are right and that what looks like free will is an illusion? In the present writer's opinion, the correct conclusion is just the opposite. As he sees it, this tendency towards repetition, which thus asserts itself in human affairs, is an instance of one of the well-known devices of the creative faculty. The works of creation are apt to occur in bunches: a bunch of representatives of a species, a bunch of species of a genus. And the value of such repetitions is, after all, not difficult to discern. Creation could hardly make any headway at all if each new form of creature were not represented by numerous eggs distributed among numerous baskets. How else could a creator, human or divine, provide himself with sufficient materials for bold and fruitful experiment and with effective means of retrieving inevitable failures? If human history repeats itself, it does so in accordance with the general rhythm of the universe; but the significance of this pattern of repetition lies in the scope that it gives for the work of creation to go forward. In this light, the repetitive element in history reveals itself as an instrument for freedom of creative action, and not as an indication that God and man are the slaves of fate.

What is the bearing of these conclusions about history in general on the particular question of the prospects of our Western civilization? As we observed at the beginning of this paper, the Western world has become rather suddenly very anxious about its own future, and our anxiety is a natural reaction to the formidableness of the situation in which we now find ourselves. Our present situation is formidable indeed. A survey of the historical landscape in the light of our existing knowledge shows that, up to date, history has repeated itself about twenty times in producing human societies of the species to which our Western society belongs, and it also shows that, with the possible exception of our own, all these representatives of the species of society called civilizations are already dead or moribund. Moreover, when we study the histories of these dead and moribund civilizations in detail, and compare them with one another, we find indications of what looks like a recurring pattern in the process of their breakdowns, declines, and falls. We are naturally asking ourselves today whether this particular chapter of history is bound to repeat itself in our case. Is that pattern of decline and fall in store for us in our turn, as a doom for which no civilization can hope to escape? In the writer's opinion, the answer to this question is emphatically in the negative. The effort to create a new manifestation of life—be it a new species of mollusc or a new species of human society—seldom or never succeeds at the first attempt. Creation is not so easy an enterprise as that. It wins its ultimate successes through a process of trial and error; and accordingly the failure of previous experiments, so far from dooming subsequent experiments to fail in their turn in the same way, actually offers them their opportunity of achieving success through the wisdom that can be gained from suffering. Of course a series of previous failures does not guarantee success to the next comer, any more than it condemns him to be a failure in his turn. There is nothing to prevent our Western civilization from following historical precedent, if it chooses, by committing social suicide. But we are not doomed to make history repeat itself; it is open to us, through our own efforts, to give history, in our case, some new and unprecedented turn. As human beings, we are endowed with this freedom of choice, and we cannot shuffle off our responsibility upon the shoulders of God or nature. We must shoulder it ourselves. It is up to us.

What shall we do to be saved? In politics, establish a constitutional co-operative system of world government. In economics, find working compromises (varying according to the practical requirements of different places and times) between free enterprise and socialism. In the life of the spirit, put the secular super-structure back onto religious foundations. Efforts are being made in our Western world today to find our way towards each of these goals. If we had arrived at all three of them, we might fairly feel that we had won our present battle for our civilization's survival. But these are, all of them, ambitious undertakings, and it will call for the hardest work and the highest courage to make any progress at all towards carrying any one of them through to achievement.

Of the three tasks, the religious one is, of course, in the long run by far the most important, but the other two are the more urgent, because, if we were to fail in these in the short run, we might lose forever our opportunity of achieving a spiritual rebirth which cannot just be whistled for at our convenience, but will only come, if it comes at all, at the unhurrying pace at which the deepest tides of spiritual creation flow.

The political task is the most urgent of all. The immediate problem here is a negative one. Faced, as we are, with the prospect that—given our present interdependence and present weapons—the world is now on the eve of being unified politically by one means or another, we have to stave off the disastrous dénouement of unification by force of arms: the familiar method of the forcible imposition of a *Pax Romana* which is probably the line of least resistance for the resolution of the formidable political forces in whose grip our own world finds itself today. Can the United States and the other Western countries manage to co-operate with the Soviet Union through the United Nations? If the United Nations organization could grow into an effective system of world government, that would be much the best solution of our political crux. But we have to reckon with the possibility of this enterprise's failing, and to be ready, should it fail, with an alternative to fall back upon. Could the United Nations split, *de facto*, into two groups without a breach of the peace? And, supposing that the whole face of the planet could be partitioned peacefully into an American and a Russian sphere, could two worlds on one planet live side by side on a footing of "non-violent non-co-operation" for long enough to give a chance for a gradual mitigation of the present differences in their social and ideological climates? The answer to this question would depend on whether, on these terms, we could buy the time needed to carry out our economic task of finding a middle way between free enterprise and socialism.

These riddles may be hard to read, but they do tell us plainly what we most need to know. They tell us that our future largely depends upon ourselves. We are not just at the mercy of an inexorable fate.

E. M. FORSTER

Toward a Definition of Tolerance[1]

Can you define tolerance? I can't, any more than I could define love or faith, or fate, or any other abstraction. My mind slips about, tries a definition, finds it won't quite work, drops it, tries another, and so on. And people whose minds are better than my own seem to be in the same plight here. They propound definitions, they defend them stoutly and philosophically, but sooner or later the definition crumbles under the onslaught of some other philosopher, and the world is left where it was. Well, not quite where it was. Despite the failure, two valuable things have occurred. Firstly, the human mind has been exercising itself, and, my goodness, how desirable that is! It has been trying to discover something, and it has become stronger and more agile in consequence, even though nothing has been discovered. And, secondly, the abstract subjects on which it has exercised itself have gained in prestige. Tolerance is important, no one can deny that, and if it is talked about so that people dispute what it is, or isn't, its importance should be maintained or increased.

Let me therefore set up an Aunt Sally.

Aunt Sallys are not as common in my country as they were, and for all I know they may have never crossed the Atlantic. Certainly I cannot imagine one on the Mayflower. So I had better define, and definition in this case is not so difficult. Aunt Sally is, or was, an elderly doll who was set up on a fairground to be shied at. She was tied to a stick or attached to a hinge. Three shies for a penny at Aunt Sally! Perhaps there was a prize if one hit her; perhaps the pleasure of bashing her face in was in itself sufficient reward. I forget. But she has become a symbol for the tentative definition. Knock her over if you can.

Let me therefore define tolerance as tolerating other people even when they don't tolerate you.

It is an austere definition. No politician would accept it. But if tolerance is to play any practical part in the modern world, if any headway is to be made against fanaticism, if there is to be any easing of the tensions between class and class, race and race, country and country, then tolerance must be more than a pious wish, more than a woolly assertion of goodwill. It must have courage, and it must be prepared to take risks.

At this point someone shies a ball at my Aunt Sally. It hits her. She staggers.

Someone has in effect said: "The modern world is indeed dangerous, and that is exactly why one can't take risks in it. It is so dangerous that tolerance

1 From *The New York Times Magazine* (February 22, 1953), p. 13. Copyright, 1953, by The New York *Times*. Reprinted by permission of the author.

is a luxury, which we can only indulge with those who reciprocate it. I don't like the color of so-and-so's face—it's green and I dislike green faces—still I'll put up with his face if he'll put up with mine. Mine is, of course, blue, the proper color for faces, and if he complains of it, if he threatens it, then my only remedy is to drop a bomb on him before he drops one on me. Tolerance is all very well, but there is such a thing as self-preservation."

Aunt Sally staggers but she does not fall. From her vantage post she can see that the modern world is not only dangerous: it is crowded, it is small and it has been contracted by science. A few hundred years ago she might not have said, "Tolerate other people even when they don't tolerate you." She might have said, "Fight it out, little blue face and little green face, if you want to. There is plenty of room for your quarrel; your muskets don't carry far and even if both of you are killed, civilization will survive." Today she is not so sure. One explosion may destroy us all. Tolerance assumes a new importance in a crowded world. The duty of running a risk has increased.

The heavenly counterpart of tolerance is love. Between the two a great gulf is set. Love is positive; tolerance negative. Love involves passion; tolerance is humdrum and dull. Love may explain the universe; tolerance, through common sense and good temper, tries to avert further disaster from the earth. Yet despite the gulf between, these two abstractions have problems in common. Love, too, has been asked to take risks: "Love your enemies, do good to them that hate you" is a text that has needed a good deal of explanation on the part of theologians. And love, in a pregnant line of W. H. Auden's, has been assigned the role which I have here claimed for tolerance: "We must love one another or die," the line runs. In another poem he tells us that we must love our crooked neighbor with our crooked heart; and how else shall we tolerate him?

Tolerance is not only needed to avoid disaster. It is also needed in peace conditions, if a community is to remain healthy and creative. An intolerant community, exacting the "right point of view" is condemned to monotony, even if the right point of view is a good one. Its citizens would lack curiosity. They would tend to be all alike for the sake of avoiding friction. They would educate their children the same way, eat the same food at the same time, laugh at the same jokes, succumb to the same advertisements, go to the same places in the same planes, and they would denounce as subversive any one who criticized them. Money—and money alone—would distinguish one human being in that community from another and the spiritual tyranny of the income-bracket would triumph.

I would certainly sooner live in a monotonous community than in a world of universal war, but I would sooner be dead than live in either of them. My heart is in the world of today, with its varieties and contrasts, its blue and green faces, and my hope is that, through courageous tolerance, the world of today may be preserved. Risks must be taken. It's difficult. Aunt Sally trembles on her perch as the well-directed missiles hit her. But what's your alternative?

BERTRAND RUSSELL

Co-existence or No
Existence: The Choice Is Ours[1]

The recent changes in the technique of war have produced a situation which is wholly unprecedented. War has existed ever since there were organized states, that is to say for some six thousand years. This ancient institution is now about to end. There are two ways in which the end may come about: the first is the extinction of the human race; the second is an agreement not to fight. I do not know which of these will be chosen.

Neither the general public nor the majority of powerful statesmen have as yet realized that war with modern weapons cannot serve the purposes of any government in the world. It is of the first importance that this should be realized by those who control policy both in the East and in the West. It is generally conceded by those who are in a position to speak with authority that no complete defense against an H-bomb attack is possible. We must, I think, consider it the most likely hypothesis that if a great war broke out tomorrow each side would be successful in attack and unsuccessful in defense. This means that in the first days of such a war all the great centers of population on each side would be obliterated. Those who survived this first disaster would perish slowly or quickly as a result of the fall-out from radioactive cloud. Destruction of life from this cause would not be confined to the belligerent countries. The winds would gradually spread death throughout the world. This, at least, is what is to be feared. It cannot be said that the worst outcome is certain, but it is sufficiently probable to deter any sane man from incurring the risk.

Apart from the totality of destruction, there is another new element in the situation. In old days if you had a military advantage over your enemy, you might hope to win in time. But now, if each side has enough H-bombs to wipe out the other, there is no longer any advantage in having twice as many as your adversary.

Both in the United States and in Great Britain there has been much talk of civil defense. Russian military journals contain talk of the same kind. All such plans, I am convinced, show either ignorance or hypocrisy in those who advocate them. Deep shelters would enable a portion of the population to survive the first explosion, but sooner or later these people would have to emerge from their shelters into a radioactive world.

Although the H-bomb is the center of public attention at the moment, it is

[1] From *The Nation*, CLXXX (June 18, 1955). Copyright 1955 by *The Nation*. Reprinted by permission of the author, of Public Interest, Inc., and of *The Nation*.

only one of the possibilities of destruction which science has put in the hands of irresponsible politicians. Chemical and bacteriological warfare are studied by all powerful states and may have consequences at least as horrifying as those of the H-bomb. There is no visible end to the methods of inflicting death that may be invented. Even if a portion of the human race were to survive a great war now, it cannot be doubted that the next war, if scientific technique survives, would complete what its predecessor had left unfinished.

There is therefore no escape from the choice that lies before us: Shall we renounce war, or shall we bring our species to an end?

Escape from Reality

If men realized that these are the only alternatives, no one can doubt that they would choose peace. But there are various ways in which people escape the realization of unpleasant facts. I have seen statements by Russians and Chinese that a thermonuclear war would of course destroy the rotten capitalistic civilization of the West but would not vitally injure the sturdy Communist nations of the East. I have also seen statements by American authorities claiming that the West would be victorious. Both seemed to me, if genuinely believed, to be mere fantasies of wish-fulfillment and, if not genuinely believed, to be part of the silly game of bluff which great nations have been allowing themselves. I hope that this is beginning to be understood. Recently there have been hopeful signs that neither side is willing to push issues to the point of war. And with every month that passes there is a better chance that statesmen both in the East and in the West will become aware of some of the important facts by which their policy ought to be guided.

Another widespread delusion is that perhaps in a great war H-bombs would not be employed. People point to the fact that gas was not employed in the Second World War. They forget that gas had not proved a decisive weapon even in the First World War and that in the meantime gas-masks had been provided which were a complete protection. Any analogy is therefore entirely misleading.

It is thought by many that the first step forward should be an international agreement not to use H-bombs in the event of war, and this is generally coupled with the suggestion that both sides should destroy their existing stock of these weapons. This suggestion has certain merits but also certain drawbacks. Its chief merit is that if the destruction of existing stocks were honestly carried out, the danger of a sudden attack in the style of Pearl Harbor would be lessened. Against this we must set the fact that no system of inspection can now make sure that bombs are not being manufactured. This is a new fact. At the time of the Baruch proposal it was still possible for an inspectorate to gain control of the raw materials, but this is so no longer. Each side would therefore suspect that the other side was manufacturing bombs surreptitiously, and this might make relations worse than if no agreement had been concluded. What is even more important is that, if war did break out, neither side would consider itself bound by the agreement, and after a certain number of months H-bomb warfare would be in full swing. Only by not making war can the danger be avoided. We must therefore turn our thoughts away from war to the methods by which peace can be made secure.

Peace by Stages

The transition from the cold war to a condition of secure peace cannot be made in a day. But it can be made, and it must be made. It will have to be made by stages. The first stage will consist in persuading all powerful governments of the world that their aims, whatever they may be, cannot be achieved by war. In this first stage, scientists—not only nuclear physicists but also physiologists, geneticists, and bacteriologists—have a very important part to play. Their discoveries have created the dangers, and it is their obvious duty to arouse the public and the governments to a sense of the risks they are running. They may, in performing this duty, be compelled to take action of which their governments disapprove, but loyalty to mankind should be for them the paramount consideration. I am convinced that it is within their power to persuade the governments both of the East and of the West to look to negotiation rather than war for a solution of their problems.

The next stage must be to create temporary machinery to negotiate settlements of all the questions at present causing conflict between East and West. It will be necessary to refer such questions to a body of negotiators in which East and West have equal representation and the balance of power is in the hands of the neutrals. I do not venture to suggest what solution should be reached on any of the vexed questions of the present. I think that a body constituted as I have suggested would avoid gross unfairness to either side, and subject to this condition almost any settlement would be preferable to a continuation of the present state of tension. A very important part of any settlement should of course be a drastic reduction of armaments. It is hardly to be supposed that the very delicate negotiations which will be required can be conducted successfully in the atmosphere of strained hostility that has existed during recent years. Each side will have to abandon perpetual abuse of the other and learn to practice that degree of toleration which after centuries of warfare was at last achieved between Christians and Moslems and between Catholics aand Protestants. We cannot now wait for the slow operation of reason through the discouragements of long indecisive wars. We must learn in advance a manner of thinking and feeling which in the past has been learned slowly and through bitter experience. I will not pretend that this is easy. But if men can be made to realize the dreadful alternative I do not think it will prove impossible.

The Third Step

If the immediate problems that now divide East and West were settled in some such way, we could reach the third stage of progress toward secure peace. The international problems of our day are not the last that will ever arise.

There will be new problems, perhaps dividing the world quite differently from the way in which it is now divided between Communist and anti-Communist blocs. So long as there is not an established international authority capable of enforcing peace, the risk of war will remain, and with every advance in science the risk will become more terrible. The international anarchy resulting from a multitude of states with unrestricted sovereignty must be brought to an end. The international authority which is to end it will have to be federal and endowed with only such powers as are necessary for preserving the peace of the world. The most important of these powers, and also the most difficult to secure, will be an obvious preponderance of armed forces over those of any national state or alliance of states. The anarchic liberty at present enjoyed by sovereign states is dear to most people and will not be surrendered easily, but it will have to be surrendered if the human species is to survive. The process required is a continuation of that which occurred in the fifteenth and sixteenth centuries. Before that time powerful barons in their castles could defy national governments, and there was the same sort of anarchy within a nation as now exists between nations. Gunpowder and artillery put an end to internal anarchy in France, Spain, and England. The hydrogen bomb has the same part to play in ending international anarchy. The loss of liberty, though it may be distasteful, is precisely of the same kind as that which private individuals suffer by being forbidden to commit murder, for after all it is the right to murder which hitherto sovereign states will be asked to surrender.

Legitimate Hopes

I have been speaking of dangers and how to avoid them, but there is another thing which it is just as important to emphasize, for while fears are at present unavoidable, hopes are equally legitimate. If we take the measures needed to end our fears, we shall thereby create a world capable of such well-being as has never been known and scarcely even imagined. Throughout the long ages since civilization began, the bulk of mankind have lived lives of misery and toil and bondage. All the long burden of misery that has darkened the slow progress of mankind has now become unnecessary. If we can learn to tolerate each other and to live in amity, poverty can be abolished everywhere more completely than it is now abolished in the most fortunate nations. Fear can be so much diminished that a new buoyancy and a new joy will brighten the daily lives of all. The work of science, which while war survives is largely evil, will become wholly beneficent. Nothing stands in the way but the darkness of atavistic evil passions. New technical possibilities of well-being exist, but the wisdom to make use of them has hitherto been lacking. Shall we collectively continue to turn our back upon the things that each one of us individually desires? We can make a world of light, or we can banish life from our planet. One or other we must do, and do soon. A great duty rests upon those who realize these alternatives, for it is they who must persuade mankind to make the better choice.

VII

Philosophy and Religion

The Good Life

◈◇◈

ARISTOTLE

Virtue[1]

But it may be asked what we mean by saying that people must become just by doing what is just and temperate by doing what is temperate. For if they do what is just and temperate, they are *ipso facto* proved, it will be said, to be just and temperate in the same way as, if they practise grammar and music, they are proved to be grammarians and musicians.

But is not the answer that the case of the arts is not the same? For a person may do something that is grammatical either by chance or at the suggestion of somebody else; hence he will not be a grammarian unless he not only does what is grammatical but does it in a grammatical manner, i.e. in virtue of the grammatical knowledge which he possesses.

There is another point too of difference between the arts and the virtues. The productions of art have their excellence in themselves. It is enough therefore that, when they are produced, they should be of a certain character. But actions in accordance with virtue are not e.g. justly or temperately performed because they are in themselves just or temperate. It is necessary that the agent at the time of performing them should satisfy certain conditions, i.e. in the first place that he should know what he is doing, secondly that he should deliberately choose to do it and to do it for its own sake, and thirdly that he should do it as an instance of a settled and immutable moral state. If it be a question whether a person possesses any art, these conditions, except indeed the condition of knowledge, are not taken into account; but if it be a question of possessing the virtues, the mere knowledge is of little or no avail, and it is the other conditions, which are the results of frequently performing just and temperate actions, that are not of slight but of absolute importance. Accordingly deeds are said to be just and temperate, when they are such as a just or temperate person would do, and a just and temperate person is not merely one

[1] From *The Nichomachean Ethics of Aristotle*, translated by J. E. C. Weldon (London: Macmillan & Co., Ltd., 1920), Book II, with omissions. Reprinted by permission of Macmillan & Co., Ltd.

who does these deeds but one who does them in the spirit of the just and the temperate.

It may fairly be said then that a just man becomes just by doing what is just and a temperate man becomes temperate by doing what is temperate, and if a man did not so act, he would not have so much as a chance of becoming good. But most people, instead of doing such actions, take refuge in theorizing: they imagine that they are philosophers and that philosophy will make them virtuous; in fact they behave like people who listen attentively to their doctors but never do anything that their doctors tell them. But it is as improbable that a healthy state of the soul will be produced by this kind of philosophizing as that a healthy state of the body will be produced by this kind of medical treatment.

We have next to consider the nature of virtue.

Now, as the qualities of the soul are three, viz. emotions, faculties and moral states, it follows that virtue must be one of the three. By the emotions I mean desire, anger, fear, courage, envy, joy, love, hatred, regret, emulation, pity, in a word whatever is attended by pleasure or pain. I call those faculties in respect of which we are said to be capable of experiencing these emotions, e.g. capable of getting angry or being pained or feeling pity. And I call those moral states in respect of which we are well or ill disposed towards the emotions, ill-disposed e.g. towards the passion of anger, if our anger be too violent or too feeble, and well-disposed, if it be duly moderated, and similarly towards the other emotions.

Now neither the virtues nor the vices are emotions; for we are not called good or evil in respect of our emotions but in respect of our virtues or vices. Again, we are not praised or blamed in respect of our emotions; a person is not praised for being afraid or being angry, nor blamed for being angry in an absolute sense, but only for being angry in a certain way; but we are praised or blamed in respect of our virtues or vices. Again, whereas we are angry or afraid without deliberate purpose, the virtues are in some sense deliberate purposes, or do not exist in the absence of deliberate purpose. It may be added that while we are said to be moved in respect of our emotions, in respect of our virtues or vices we are not said to be moved but to have a certain disposition.

These reasons also prove that the virtues are not faculties. For we are not called either good or bad, nor are we praised or blamed, as having an abstract capacity for emotion. Also while Nature gives us our faculties, it is not Nature that makes us good or bad, but this is a point which we have already discussed. If then the virtues are neither emotions nor faculties, it remains that they must be moral states.

The nature of virtue has been now generically described. But it is not enough to state merely that virtue is a moral state, we must also describe the character of that moral state.

It must be laid down then that every virtue or excellence has the effect of producing a good condition of that of which it is a virtue or excellence, and of enabling it to perform its function well. Thus the excellence of the eye makes the eye good and its function good, as it is by the excellence of the eye that we see well. Similarly, the excellence of the horse makes a horse excellent and good at racing, at carrying its rider and at facing the enemy.

If then this is universally true, the virtue or excellence of man will be such a moral state as makes a man good and able to perform his proper function well. We have already explained how this will be the case, but another way of making it clear will be to study the nature or character of this virtue.

Now in everything, whether it be continuous or discrete,[2] it is possible to take a greater, a smaller, or an equal amount, and this either absolutely or in relation to ourselves, the equal being a mean between excess and deficiency. By the mean in respect of the thing itself, or the absolute mean, I understand that which is equally distinct from both extremes; and this is one and the same thing for everybody. By the mean considered relatively to ourselves I understand that which is neither too much nor too little; but this is not one thing, nor is it the same for everybody. Thus if 10 be too much and 2 too little we take 6 as a mean in respect of the thing itself; for 6 is as much greater than 2 as it is less than 10, and this is a mean in arithmetical proportion. But the mean considered relatively to ourselves must not be ascertained in this way. It does not follow that if 10 pounds *of meat* be too much and 2 be too little for a man to eat, a trainer will order him 6 pounds, as this may itself be too much or too little for the person who is to take it; it will be too little e.g. for Milo,[3] but too much for a beginner in gymnastics. It will be the same with running and wrestling; *the right amount will vary with the individual.* This being so, everybody who understands his business avoids alike excess and deficiency; he seeks and chooses the mean, not the absolute mean, but the mean considered relatively to ourselves.

Every science then performs its function well, if it regards the mean and refers the works which it produces to the mean. This is the reason why it is usually said of successful works that it is impossible to take anything from them or to add anything to them, which implies that excess or deficiency is fatal to excellence but that the mean state ensures it. Good artists too, as we say, have an eye to the mean in their works. But virtue, like Nature herself, is more accurate and better than any art; virtue therefore will aim at the mean; —I speak of moral virtue, as it is moral virtue which is concerned with emotions and actions, and it is these which admit of excess and deficiency and the mean. Thus it is possible to go too far, or not to go far enough, in respect of fear, courage, desire, anger, pity, and pleasure and pain generally, and the excess and the deficiency are alike wrong; but to experience these emotions at the right times and on the right occasions and towards the right persons and

2 In Aristotelian language, as Mr. Peters says, a straight line is a "continuous quantity" but a rouleau of sovereigns a "discrete quantity."
3 The famous Crotoniate wrestler.

for the right causes and in the right manner is the mean or the supreme good, which is characteristic of virtue. Similarly there may be excess, deficiency, or the mean, in regard to actions. But virtue is concerned with emotions and actions, and here excess is an error and deficiency a fault, whereas the mean is successful and laudable, and success and merit are both characteristics of virtue.

It appears then that virtue is a mean state, so far at least as it aims at the mean.

Again, there are many different ways of going wrong; for evil is in its nature infinite, to use the Pythagorean[4] figure, but good is finite. But there is only one possible way of going right. Accordingly the former is easy and the latter difficult; it is easy to miss the mark but difficult to hit it. This again is a reason why excess and deficiency are characteristics of vice and the mean state a characteristic of virtue.

For good is simple, evil manifold.[5]

Virtue then is a state of deliberate moral purpose consisting in a mean that is relative to ourselves, the mean being determined by reason, or as a prudent man would determine it.

It is a mean state *firstly as lying* between two vices, the vice of excess on the one hand, and the vice of deficiency on the other, and secondly because, whereas the vices either fall short of or go beyond what is proper in the emotions and actions, virtue not only discovers but embraces the mean.

Accordingly, virtue, if regarded in its essence or theoretical conception, is a mean state, but, if regarded from the point of view of the highest good, or of excellence, it is an extreme.

But it is not every action or every emotion that admits of a mean state. There are some whose very name implies wickedness, as e.g. malice, shamelessness, and envy, among emotions, or adultery, theft, and murder, among actions. All these, and others like them, are censured as being intrinsically wicked, not merely the excesses or deficiencies of them. It is never possible then to be right in respect of them; they are always sinful. Right or wrong in such actions as adultery does not depend on our committing them with the right person, at the right time or in the right manner; on the contrary it is sinful to do anything of the kind at all. It would be equally wrong then to suppose that there can be a mean state or an excess or deficiency in unjust, cowardly or licentious conduct; for, if it were so, there would be a mean state of an excess or of a deficiency, an excess of an excess and a deficiency of a deficiency. But as in temperance and courage there can be no excess or deficiency because the mean is, in a sense, an extreme, so too in these cases there

[4] The Pythagoreans, starting from the mystical significance of number, took the opposite principles of "the finite" (τὸ πέρασ or τὸ πεπερασμένου) and "the infinite" (τὸ απειρου) to represent good and evil.

[5] A line—perhaps Pythagorean—of unknown authorship.

cannot be a mean or an excess or deficiency, but, however the acts may be done, they are wrong. For it is a general rule that an excess or deficiency does not admit of a mean state, nor a mean state of an excess or deficiency.

But it is not enough to lay down this as a general rule; it is necessary to apply it to particular cases, as in reasonings upon actions, general statements, although they are broader, are less exact than particular statements. For all action refers to particulars, and it is essential that our theories should harmonize with the particular cases to which they apply.

We must take particular virtues then from the catalogue[6] of *virtues*.

In regard to feelings of fear and confidence, courage is a mean state. On the side of excess, he whose fearlessness is excessive has no name, as often happens, but he whose confidence is excessive is foolhardy, while he whose timidity is excessive and whose confidence is deficient is a coward.

In respect of pleasures and pains, although not indeed of all pleasures and pains, and to a less extent in respect of pains than of pleasures, the mean state is temperance, the excess is licentiousness. We never find people who are deficient in regard to pleasures, accordingly such people again have not received a name, but we may call them insensible.

As regards the giving and taking of money, the mean state is liberality, the excess and deficiency are prodigality and illiberality. Here the excess and deficiency take opposite forms; for while the prodigal man is excessive in spending and deficient in taking, the illiberal man is excessive in taking and deficient in spending.

(For the present we are giving only a rough and summary account *of the virtues*, and that is sufficient for our purpose; we will hereafter determine their character more exactly.)

In respect of money there are other dispositions as well. There is the mean state which is magnificence; for the magnificent man, as having to do with large sums of money, differs from the liberal man who has to do only with small sums; and the excess *corresponding to it* is bad taste or vulgarity, the deficiency is meanness. These are different from the excess and deficiency of liberality; what the difference is will be explained hereafter.

In respect of honour and dishonour the mean state is highmindedness, the excess is what is called vanity, the deficiency littlemindedness. Corresponding to liberality, which, as we said, differs from magnificence as having to do *not with great but* with small sums of money, there is a moral state which has to do with petty honour and is related to highmindedness which has to do with great honour; for it is possible to aspire to honour in the right way, or in a way which is excessive or insufficient, and if a person's aspirations are excessive, he is called ambitious, if they are deficient, he is called unambitious, while if they are between the two, he has no name.

Anger, like other emotions, has its excess, its deficiency, and its mean state.

[6] It would seem that a catalogue of virtues (διαγραφή or ὑπογραφή) must have been recognized in the Aristotelian school. Cp. *Eud. Eth.* ii, ch. 3.

It may be said that they have no names, but as we call one who observes the mean gentle, we will call the mean state gentleness. Among the extremes, if a person errs on the side of excess, he may be called passionate and his vice passionateness, if on that of deficiency, he may be called impassive and his deficiency impassivity.

There are also three other mean states with a certain resemblance to each other, and yet with a difference. For while they are all concerned with intercourse in speech and action, they are different in that one of them is concerned with truth in such intercourse, and the others with pleasantness, one with pleasantness in amusement and the other with pleasantness in the various circumstances of life. We must therefore discuss these states in order to make it clear that in all cases it is the mean state which is an object of praise, and the extremes are neither right nor laudable but censurable. It is true that these mean and extreme states are generally nameless, but we must do our best here as elsewhere to give them a name, so that our argument may be clear and easy to follow.

In the matter of truth then, he who observes the mean may be called truthful, and the mean state truthfulness. Pretence, if it takes the form of exaggeration, is boastfulness, and one who is guilty of pretence is a boaster; but if it takes the form of depreciation it is irony, and he who is guilty of it is ironical.

There are also mean states in the emotions and in the expression of the emotions. For although modesty is not a virtue, yet a modest person is praised as if he were virtuous; for here too one person is said to observe the mean and another to exceed it, as e.g. the bashful man who is never anything but modest, whereas a person who has insufficient modesty or no modesty at all is called shameless, and one who observes the mean modest.

Righteous indignation, again, is a mean state between envy and malice. They are all concerned with the pain and pleasure which we feel at the fortunes of our neighbours. A person who is righteously indignant is pained at the prosperity of the undeserving; but the envious person goes further and is pained at anybody's prosperity, and the malicious person is so far from being pained that he actually rejoices *at misfortunes*. . . .

There are then three dispositions, two being vices, viz. one the vice of excess and the other that of deficiency, and one virtue, which is the mean state between them; and they are all in a sense mutually opposed. For the extremes are opposed both to the mean and to each other, and the mean is opposed to the extremes. For as the equal if compared with the less is greater but if compared with the greater is less, so the mean states, whether in the emotions or actions, if compared with the deficiencies, are excessive, but if compared with the excesses are deficient. Thus the courageous man appears foolhardy as compared with the coward, but cowardly as compared with the foolhardy. Similarly, the temperate man appears licentious as compared with the insensible but insensible as compared with the licentious, and the liberal man appears prodigal as compared with the illiberal, but illiberal as compared with the prodigal. The result is that the extremes mutually repel and reject the mean; the coward calls the courageous man foolhardy, but the foolhardy man calls him cowardly, and so on in the other cases.

But while there is this mutual opposition between the extremes and the mean, there is greater opposition between the two extremes than between either extreme and the mean; for they are further removed from each other than from the mean, as the great from the small and the small from the great than both from the equal. Again, while some extremes exhibit more or less similarity to the mean, as foolhardiness to courage and prodigality to liberality, there is the greatest possible dissimilarity between the extremes. But things which are furthest removed from each other are defined to be opposites; hence the further things are removed, the greater is the opposition between them.

It is in some cases the deficiency and in others the excess which is the more opposed to the mean. Thus it is not foolhardiness the excess, but cowardice the deficiency which is the more opposed to courage, nor is it insensibility the deficiency, but licentiousness the excess which is the more opposed to temperance. There are two reasons why this should be so. One lies in the nature of the thing itself; for as one of the two extremes is the nearer and more similar to the mean, it is not this extreme, but its opposite, that we chiefly set against the mean. For instance, as it appears that foolhardiness is more similar and nearer to courage than cowardice, it is cowardice that we chiefly set against courage; for things which are further removed from the mean seem to be more opposite to it. This being one reason which lies in the nature of the thing itself, there is a second which lies in our own nature. It is the things to which we ourselves are naturally more inclined that appear more opposed to the mean. Thus we are ourselves naturally more inclined to pleasures *than to their opposites*, and are more prone therefore to licentiousness than to decorum. Accordingly we speak of those things, in which we are more likely to run to great lengths, as being more opposed to the mean. Hence it follows that licentiousness which is an excess is more opposed to temperance than insensibility.

It has now been sufficiently shown that moral virtue is a mean state, and in what sense it is a mean state; it is a mean state as lying between two vices, a vice of excess on the one side and a vice of deficiency on the other, and as aiming at the mean in the emotions and actions.

The Sermon on the Mount[1]

And seeing the multitudes, he went up into a mountain; and when he was set, his disciples came unto him: and he opened his mouth, and taught them, saying, Blessed are the poor in spirit: for theirs is the kingdom of heaven.

1 From *The Gospel According to Saint Matthew* (King James Version of the Bible), Chapters 5, 6, 7.

Blessed are they that mourn: for they shall be comforted. Blessed are the meek: for they shall inherit the earth. Blessed are they which do hunger and thirst after righteousness: for they shall be filled. Blessed are the merciful: for they shall obtain mercy. Blessed are the pure in heart: for they shall see God. Blessed are the peacemakers: for they shall be called the children of God. Blessed are they which are persecuted for righteousness' sake: for theirs is the kingdom of heaven. Blessed are ye, when men shall revile you, and persecute you, and shall say all manner of evil against you falsely, for my sake. Rejoice, and be exceeding glad: for great is your reward in heaven: for so persecuted they the prophets which were before you.

Ye are the salt of the earth: but if the salt have lost his savour, wherewith shall it be salted? it is thenceforth good for nothing, but to be cast out, and to be trodden under foot of men. Ye are the light of the world. A city that is set on an hill cannot be hid. Neither do men light a candle, and put it under a bushel, but on a candlestick; and it giveth light unto all that are in the house. Let your light so shine before men, that they may see your good works, and glorify your Father which is in heaven. Think not that I am come to destroy the law, or the prophets; I am not come to destroy, but to fulfil. For verily I say unto you, Till heaven and earth pass, one jot or one tittle shall in no wise pass from the law, till all be fulfilled. Whosoever therefore shall break one of these least commandments, and shall teach men so, he shall be called the least in the kingdom of heaven: but whosoever shall do and teach them, the same shall be called great in the kingdom of heaven. For I say unto you, That except your righteousness shall exceed the righteousness of the scribes and Pharisees, ye shall in no case enter into the kingdom of heaven.

Ye have heard that it was said by them of old time, Thou shalt not kill; and whosoever shall kill shall be in danger of the judgment: but I say unto you, That whosoever is angry with his brother without a cause shall be in danger of the judgment: and whosoever shall say to his brother, Raca, shall be in danger of the council: but whosoever shall say, Thou fool, shall be in danger of hell fire. Therefore if thou bring thy gift to the altar, and there rememberest that thy brother hath ought against thee; leave there thy gift before the altar, and go thy way; first be reconciled to thy brother, and then come and offer thy gift. Agree with thine adversary quickly, whiles thou art in the way with him; lest at any time the adversary deliver thee to the judge, and the judge deliver thee to the officer, and thou be cast into prison. Verily I say unto thee, Thou shalt by no means come out thence, till thou hast paid the uttermost farthing.

Ye have heard that it was said by them of old time, Thou shalt not commit adultery; but I say unto you, That whosoever looketh on a woman to lust after her hath committed adultery with her already in his heart. And if thy right eye offend thee, pluck it out, and cast it from thee: for it is profitable for thee that one of thy members should perish, and not that thy whole body should be cast into hell. And if thy right hand offend thee, cut it off, and cast it from thee: for it is profitable for thee that one of thy members should perish, and not that thy whole body should be cast into hell. It hath been said, Whosoever shall put away his wife, let him give her a writing of divorcement: but I say unto you, That whosoever shall put away his wife, saving for the cause of fornication, causeth her to commit adultery: and whosoever shall marry her that is divorced committeth adultery.

Again, ye have heard that it hath been said by them of old time, Thou shalt not forswear thyself, but shalt perform to the Lord thine oaths: but I say unto you, Swear not at all; neither by heaven; for it is God's throne: nor by the earth; for it is his footstool: neither by Jerusalem; for it is the city of the great King. Neither shalt thou swear by thy head, because thou canst not make one hair white or black. But let your communication be, Yea, yea; Nay, nay: for whatsoever is more than these cometh of evil.

Ye have heard that it hath been said, An eye for an eye, and a tooth for a tooth: but I say unto you, That ye resist not evil: but whosoever shall smite thee on thy right cheek, turn to him the other also. And if any man will sue thee at the law, and take away thy coat, let him have thy cloke also. And whosoever shall compel thee to go a mile, go with him twain. Give to him that asketh thee, and from him that would borrow of thee turn not thou away.

Ye have heard that it hath been said, Thou shalt love thy neighbor, and hate thine enemy. But I say unto you, Love your enemies, bless them that curse you, do good to them that hate you, and pray for them which despitefully use you, and persecute you; that ye may be the children of your Father which is in heaven; for he maketh his sun to rise on the evil and on the good, and sendeth rain on the just and on the unjust. For if ye love them which love you, what reward have ye? do not even the publicans the same? And if ye salute your brethren only, what do ye more than others? do not even the publicans so? Be ye therefore perfect, even as your Father which is in heaven is perfect.

Take heed that ye do not your alms before men, to be seen of them: otherwise ye have no reward of your Father which is in heaven. Therefore when thou doest thine alms, do not sound a trumpet before thee, as the hypocrites do in the synagogues and in the streets, that they may have glory of men. Verily I say unto you, They have their reward. But when thou doest alms, let not thy left hand know what thy right hand doeth: that thine alms may be in secret: and thy Father which seeth in secret himself shall reward thee openly. And when thou prayest, thou shalt not be as the hypocrites are: for they love to pray standing in the synagogues and in the corners of the streets, that they may be seen of men. Verily I say unto you, They have their reward. But thou, when thou prayest, enter into thy closet, and when thou hast shut thy door, pray to thy Father, which is in secret; and thy Father which seeth in secret shall reward thee openly. But when ye pray, use not vain repetitions, as the heathen do: for they think that they shall be heard for their much speaking. Be not ye therefore like unto them: for your Father knoweth what things ye have need of, before ye ask him. After this manner therefore pray ye: Our Father which art in heaven, Hallowed be thy name. Thy kingdom come.

Thy will be done in earth, as it is in heaven. Give us this day our daily bread. And forgive us our debts, as we forgive our debtors. And lead us not into temptation, but deliver us from evil: for thine is the kingdom, and the power, and the glory, for ever. Amen. For if ye forgive men their trespasses, your heavenly Father will also forgive you: but if ye forgive not men their trespasses, neither will your Father forgive your trespasses.

Moreover when ye fast, be not, as the hypocrites, of a sad countenance: for they disfigure their faces, that they may appear unto men to fast. Verily I say unto you, They have their reward. But thou, when thou fastest, anoint thine head, and wash thy face; that thou appear not unto men to fast, but unto thy Father which is in secret; and thy Father, which seeth in secret, shall reward thee openly.

Lay up not for yourselves treasures upon earth, where moth and rust doth corrupt, and where thieves break through and steal: but lay up for yourselves treasures in heaven, where neither moth nor rust doth corrupt, and where thieves do not break through nor steal: for where your treasure is, there will your heart be also. The light of the body is the eye: if therefore thine eye be single, thy whole body shall be full of light. But if thine eye be evil, thy whole body shall be full of darkness. If therefore the light that is in thee be darkness, how great is that darkness! No man can serve two masters: for either he will hate the one, and love the other; or else he will hold to the one, and despise the other. Ye cannot serve God and mammon. Therefore I say unto you, Take no thought for your life, what ye shall eat, or what ye shall drink; nor yet for your body, what ye shall put on. Is not the life more than meat, and the body than raiment? Behold the fowls of the air: for they sow not, neither do they reap, nor gather into barns; yet your heavenly Father feedeth them. Are ye not much better than they? Which of you by taking thought can add one cubit unto his stature? And why take ye thought for raiment? Consider the lilies of the field, how they grow; they toil not, neither do they spin: and yet I say unto you, That even Solomon in all his glory was not arrayed like one of these. Wherefore, if God so clothe the grass of the field, which to day is, and to morrow is cast into the oven, shall he not much more clothe you, O ye of little faith? Therefore take no thought, saying, What shall we eat? or, What shall we drink? or, Wherewithal shall we be clothed? (For after all these things do the Gentiles seek:) for your heavenly Father knoweth that ye have need of all these things. But seek ye first the kingdom of God, and his righteousness; and all these things shall be added unto you. Take therefore no thought for the morrow: for the morrow shall take thought for the things of itself. Sufficient unto the day is the evil thereof.

Judge not, that ye be not judged. For with what judgment ye judge, ye shall be judged: and with what measure ye mete, it shall be measured to you again. And why beholdest thou the mote that is in thy brother's eye, but considerest not the beam that is in thine own eye? Or how wilt thou say to thy brother, Let me pull out the mote out of thine eye; and, behold, a beam is in thine own eye? Thou hypocrite, first cast out the beam out of thine own eye; and then shalt thou see clearly to cast out the mote out of thy brother's eye.

Give not that which is holy unto the dogs, neither cast ye your pearls before swine, lest they trample them under their feet, and turn again and rend you. Ask, and it shall be given you; seek and ye shall find; knock, and it shall be opened unto you: for every one that asketh receiveth; and he that seeketh findeth; and to him that knocketh it shall be opened. Or what man is there of you, whom if his son ask bread, will he give him a stone? Or if he ask a fish, will he give him a serpent? If ye then, being evil, know how to give good gifts unto your children, how much more shall your Father which is in heaven give good things to them that ask him? Therefore all things whatsoever ye would that men should do to you, do ye even so to them: for this is the law and the prophets.

Enter ye in at the strait gate: for wide is the gate, and broad is the way, that leadeth to destruction, and many there be which go in thereat: because strait is the gate, and narrow is the way, which leadeth unto life, and few there be that find it. Beware of false prophets, which come to you in sheep's clothing, but inwardly they are ravening wolves. Ye shall know them by their fruits. Do men gather grapes of thorns, or figs of thistles? Even so every good tree bringeth forth good fruit; but a corrupt tree bringeth forth evil fruit. A good tree cannot bring forth evil fruit, neither can a corrupt tree bring forth good fruit. Every tree that bringeth not forth good fruit is hewn down, and cast into the fire. Wherefore by their fruits ye shall know them. Not every one that saith unto me, Lord, Lord, shall enter into the kingdom of heaven; but he that doeth the will of my Father which is in heaven. Many will say to me in that day, Lord, Lord, have we not prophesied in thy name? And in thy name have cast out devils? and in thy name done many wonderful works? And then will I profess unto them, I never knew you: depart from me, ye that work iniquity. Therefore whosoever heareth these sayings of mine, and doeth them, I will liken him unto a wise man, which built his house upon a rock: and the rain descended, and the floods came, and the winds blew, and beat upon that house; and it fell not: for it was founded upon a rock. And every one that heareth these sayings of mine, and doeth them not, shall be likened unto a foolish man, which built his house upon the sand: and the rain descended, and the floods came, and the winds blew, and beat upon that house; and it fell: and great was the fall of it. And it came to pass, when Jesus had ended these sayings, the people were astonished at his doctrine: For he taught them as one having authority, and not as the scribes.

MARCUS AURELIUS

The Stoic Code[1]

Begin the morning by saying to thyself, I shall meet with the busybody, the ungrateful, arrogant, deceitful, envious, unsocial. All these things happen to them by reason of their ignorance of what is good and evil. But I who have seen the nature of the good that it is beautiful, and of the bad that it is ugly, and the nature of him who does wrong, that it is akin to me, not [only] of the same blood or seed, but that it participates in [the same] intelligence and [the same] portion of the divinity, I can neither be injured by any of them, for no one can fix on me what is ugly, nor can I be angry with my kinsman, nor hate him. For we are made for co-operation, like feet, like hands, like eyelids, like the rows of the upper and lower teeth. To act against one another, then, is contrary to nature; and it is action against one another to be vexed and to turn away.

2. Whatever this is that I am, it is a little flesh and breath, and the ruling part. Throw away thy books; no longer distract thyself: it is not allowed; but as if thou wast now dying, despise the flesh; it is blood and bones and a network, a contexture of nerves, veins, and arteries. See the breath also, what kind of a thing it is; air, and not always the same, but every moment sent out and again sucked in. The third, then, is the ruling part; consider thus: Thou art an old man; no longer let this be a slave, no longer be pulled by the strings like a puppet to unsocial movements, no longer be either dissatisfied with thy present lot, or shrink from the future.

3. All that is from the gods is full of providence. That which is from fortune is not separated from nature or without an interweaving and involution with the things which are ordered by providence. From thence all things flow; and there is besides necessity, and that which is for the advantage of the whole universe, of which thou art a part. But that is good for every part of nature which the nature of the whole brings, and what serves to maintain this nature. Now the universe is preserved, as by the changes of the elements so by the changes of things compounded of the elements. Let these principles be enough for thee; let them always be fixed opinions. But cast away the thirst after books, that thou mayest not die murmuring, but cheerfully, truly, and from thy heart thankful to the gods.

4. Remember how long thou hast been putting off these things, and how often thou hast received opportunity from the gods, and yet dost not use it. Thou must now at last perceive of what universe thou art a part, and of what administrator of the universe thy existence is an efflux, and that a limit of time

[1] From *The Thoughts of the Emperor Marcus Aurelius,* translated by George Long (Boston: Little, Brown & Company, 1897), Book II.

is fixed for thee, which if thou dost not use for clearing away the clouds from thy mind, it will go and thou wilt go, and it will never return.

5. Every moment think steadily as a Roman and a man to do what thou hast in hand with perfect and simple dignity, and feeling of affection, and freedom, and justice, and to give thyself relief from all other thoughts. And thou wilt give thyself relief if thou doest every act of thy life as if it were the last, laying aside all carelessness and passionate aversion from the commands of reason, and all hypocrisy, and self-love, and discontent with the portion which has been given to thee. Thou seest how few the things are, the which if a man lays hold of, he is able to live a life which flows in quiet, and is like the existence of the gods; for the gods on their part will require nothing more from him who observes these things.

6. Do wrong to thyself, do wrong to thyself, my soul; but thou wilt no longer have the opportunity of honoring thyself. Every man's life is sufficient. But thine is nearly finished, though thy soul reverences not itself, but places thy felicity in the souls of others.

7. Do the things external which fall upon thee distract thee? Give thyself time to learn something new and good, and cease to be whirled around. But then thou must also avoid being carried about the other way; for those too are triflers who have wearied themselves in life by their activity, and yet have no object to which to direct every movement, and, in a word, all their thoughts.

8. Through not observing what is in the mind of another a man has seldom been seen to be unhappy; but those who do not observe the movements of their own minds must of necessity be unhappy.

9. This thou must always bear in mind, what is the nature of the whole, and what is my nature, and how this is related to that, and what kind of a part it is of what kind of a whole, and that there is no one who hinders thee from always doing and saying the things which are according to the nature of which thou art a part.

10. Theophrastus, in his comparison of bad acts—such a comparison as one would make in accordance with the common notions of mankind—says, like a true philosopher, that the offences which are committed through desire are more blamable than those which are committed through anger. For he who is excited by anger seems to turn away from reason with a certain pain and unconscious contraction; but he who offends through desire, being overpowered by pleasure, seems to be in a manner more intemperate and more womanish in his offences. Rightly, then, and in a way worthy of philosophy, he said that the offence which is committed with pleasure is more blamable than that which is committed with pain; and on the whole the one is more like a person who has been first wronged and through pain is compelled to be angry; but the other is moved by his own impulse to do wrong, being carried towards doing something by desire.

11. Since it is possible that thou mayest depart from life this very moment, regulate every act and thought accordingly. But to go away from among men,

if there are gods, is not a thing to be afraid of, for the gods will not involve thee in evil; but if indeed they do not exist, or if they have no concern about human affairs, what is it to me to live in a universe devoid of gods or devoid of providence? But in truth they do exist, and they do care for human things, and they have put all the means in man's power to enable him not to fall into real evils. And as to the rest, if there was anything evil, they would have provided for this also, that it should be altogether in a man's power not to fall into it. Now that which does not make a man worse, how can it make a man's life worse? But neither through ignorance, nor having the knowledge but not the power to guard against or correct these things, is it possible that the nature of the universe has overlooked them; nor is it possible that it has made so great a mistake, either through want of power or want of skill, that good and evil should happen indiscriminately to the good and the bad. But death certainly, and life, honor and dishonor, pain and pleasure,—all these things equally happen to good men and bad, being things which make us neither better nor worse. Therefore they are neither good nor evil.

12. How quickly all things disappear,—in the universe the bodies themselves, but in time the remembrance of them. What is the nature of all sensible things, and particularly those which attract with the bait of pleasure or terrify by pain, or are noised abroad by vapory fame; how worthless, and contemptible, and sordid, and perishable, and dead they are,—all this it is the part of the intellectual faculty to observe. To observe too who these are whose opinions and voices give reputation; what death is, and the fact that, if a man looks at it in itself, and by the abstractive power of reflection resolves into their parts all the things which present themselves to the imagination in it, he will then consider it to be nothing else than an operation of nature; and if any one is afraid of an operation of nature, he is a child. This, however, is not only an operation of nature, but it is also a thing which conduces to the purposes of nature. To observe too how man comes near to the Deity, and by what part of him, and when this part of man is so disposed.

13. Nothing is more wretched than a man who traverses everything in a round, and pries into the things beneath the earth, as the poet says, and seeks by conjecture what is in the minds of his neighbors, without perceiving that it is sufficient to attend to the daemon within him, and to reverence it sincerely. And reverence of the daemon consists in keeping it pure from passion and thoughtlessness, and dissatisfaction with what comes from gods and men. For the things from the gods merit veneration for their excellence; and the things from men should be dear to us by reason of kinship; and sometimes even, in a manner, they move our pity by reason of men's ignorance of good and bad; this defect being not less than that which deprives us of the power of distinguishing things that are white and black.

14. Though thou shouldest be going to live three thousand years, and as many times ten thousand years, still remember that no man loses any other life than this which he now lives, nor lives any other than this which he now

loses. The longest and shortest are thus brought to the same. For the present is the same to all, though that which perishes is not the same; and so that which is lost appears to be a mere moment. For a man cannot lose either the past or the future: for what a man has not, how can any one take this from him? These two things then thou must bear in mind; the one, that all things from eternity are of like forms and come round in a circle, and that it makes no difference whether a man shall see the same things during a hundred years, or two hundred, or an infinite time; and the second, that the longest liver and he who will die soonest lose just the same. For the present is the only thing of which a man can be deprived, if it is true that this is the only thing which he has, and that a man cannot lose a thing if he has it not.

15. Remember that all is opinion. For what was said by the Cynic Monimus is manifest: and manifest too is the use of what was said, if a man receives what may be got out of it as far as it is true.

16. The soul of man does violence to itself, first of all, when it becomes an abscess, and, as it were, a tumor on the universe, so far as it can. For to be vexed at anything which happens is a separation of ourselves from nature, in some part of which the natures of all other things are contained. In the next place, the soul does violence to itself when it turns away from any man, or even moves towards him with the intention of injuring, such as are the souls of those who are angry. In the third place, the soul does violence to itself when it is overpowered by pleasure or by pain. Fourthly, when it plays a part, and does or says anything insincerely and untruly. Fifthly, when it allows any act of its own and any movement to be without an aim, and does anything thoughtlessly and without considering what it is, it being right that even the smallest things be done with reference to an end; and the end of rational animals is to follow the reason and the law of the most ancient city and polity.

17. Of human life the time is a point, and the substance is in a flux, and the perception dull, and the composition of the whole body subject to putrefaction, and the soul a whirl, and fortune hard to divine, and fame a thing devoid of judgment. And, to say all in a word, everything which belongs to the body is a stream, and what belongs to the soul is a dream and vapor, and life is a warfare and a stranger's sojourn, and after-fame is oblivion. What then is that which is able to conduct a man? One thing, and only one, philosophy. But this consists in keeping the daemon within a man free from violence and unharmed, superior to pains and pleasures, doing nothing without a purpose, nor yet falsely and with hypocrisy, not feeling the need of another man's doing or not doing anything; and besides, accepting all that happens, and all that is allotted, as coming from thence, wherever it is, from whence he himself came; and, finally, waiting for death with a cheerful mind, as being nothing else than a dissolution of the elements of which every living being is compounded. But if there is no harm to the elements themselves in each continually changing into another, why should a man have any apprehension about the change and dissolution of all the elements? For it is according to nature, and nothing is evil which is according to nature.

MICHEL EYQUEM DE MONTAIGNE

The Enjoyment of Living[1]

I am not excessively fond of salads or fruit, with the exception of melons. My father hated every kind of sauce; I like them all. Eating too much makes me uncomfortable; but in respect of its properties I am not yet very certain that any kind of food disagrees with me. Nor have I noticed that I am affected by full or new moons, by autumn or spring.

We are subject to fickle and inexplicable changes. For example, radishes, which I first found to agree with me, afterwards disagreed, and now they agree again. In several things I have found my stomach and palate to vary in the same way: I have changed more than once from white wine to claret, and back again from claret to white wine.

I have a dainty tooth for fish, and the meatless days are my meat-days; my fasts are my feasts. Besides, I believe that it is, as some people say, more easily digested than meat. As it goes against my conscience to eat meat on fish-days, so my taste rebels against mixing meat and fish; the difference seems to me too wide.

From my youth up I have occasionally skipped a meal; either to sharpen my appetite for the next day (for, as Epicurus used to fast and make lean meals in order to accustom his greed to dispense with plenty, I do so, on the contrary, in order to train my greed to take better advantage of plenty and to enjoy it more cheerfully); or I used to fast to keep my strength for the performance of some mental or bodily action; for both my body and mind are made cruelly sluggish by repletion. (And especially do I hate the foolish idea of coupling so healthy and active a goddess with that little pot-bellied, belching god, all swelled up with the fumes of his liquor.) Or again, to cure my ailing digestion; or for want of congenial company; for with that same Epicurus I say that we should not so much look to what we eat as to whom we eat with. And I applaud Chilo, who would not promise to accept Periander's invitation to a feast until he was informed who were the other guests.

To me no dressing is so acceptable, and no sauce so appetizing, as that derived from good company.

I think it is more wholesome to eat more at leisure, and less, and to eat oftener. But I would give hunger and appetite their due; I should take no pleasure in dragging through three or four wretched repasts a day, restricted by doctors' orders. Who will assure me that I can recover at supper-time the good appetite I had this morning? Let us old men especially take the first

[1] From *The Essays of Montaigne*, translated by E. J. Trechmann (London: Oxford University Press, 1927), II, 584-601. Reprinted by permission of the publishers.

opportunity that comes our way. Let us leave the making of dietaries to doctors and almanac-makers.

The best fruit of my health is sensual pleasure; let us seize the first that is present and known. I avoid consistency in these laws of fasting. He who wishes to benefit by a habit, let him avoid continuing it. We become hardened, our powers are dulled by it; six months after your stomach will be so inured to it, that all the advantage you have gained will be to have lost the freedom of doing otherwise except to your prejudice.

I do not cover my legs and thighs more in winter than in summer: simple silk hose. For the relief of my colds I gave way to the habit of keeping my head warmer, and my belly on account of the colic. But in a few days my ailments became accustomed to them and scorned my ordinary precautions: from a cap I advanced to a kerchief, and from a bonnet to a lined hat. The wadding of my doublet is now only ornamental. All that would be of no avail unless I added a hare's skin or a vulture's plumage, with a skull-cap for the head. Continue this gradual progress and you will go a long way. I shall take care not to do so, and would gladly go back to where I began, if I dared.

"Have you developed a new ailment? Is the remedy no longer of any avail? You have grown accustomed to it? Then try another." In this way they ruin their health who allow themselves to be fettered by enforced rules, and superstitiously adhere to them; they need more and more, and after that more again. There is no end.

To suit our occupations, and for pleasure, it is much more convenient to lose one's dinner, as the ancients did, and defer making good cheer till the time of retirement and rest, instead of cutting up the day: that is what I used to do. For health's sake, on the other hand, I have since found by experience that it is better to dine, and that I digest better when awake.

I am not very subject to thirst, whether I am well or ill; in the latter case I very often have a dry mouth, but without thirst, and as a rule I only drink from the desire which comes with eating, and when the meal is well advanced. I drink pretty well for a man of ordinary build; in summer, and with an appetizing repast, I not only exceed the limits of Augustus, who drank only three times and no oftener, but, in order not to violate Democritus' rule, which forbade stopping at four as an unlucky number, I slide on, if need be, to the fifth: about three half-pints. For little glasses are my favourites, and I like to drain them, a thing which others avoid as unbecoming.

As a rule I dilute my wine with half, sometimes a third part of water. And when at home, following an old custom which my father's doctor recommended to him and himself followed, the wine I need is mixed in the buttery, two or three hours before it is served.

It is said that Cranaus, King of the Athenians, first introduced the custom of mixing wine with water; whether beneficially or not has been a matter for debate. I think it more seemly and more wholesome for children not to take wine before they are sixteen or eighteen years of age.

The best mode of life is that which is most usual and common; I think all singularity should be avoided. And I should hate to see a German putting water into his wine as I should to see a Frenchman drinking his pure. General use lays down the law in such things.

I fear a confined atmosphere, and have a mortal dread of smoke (the first repairs I set about in my house were those of the chimneys and the privies which are commonly defective in old buildings, and not to be tolerated); and among the discomforts of war I include the thick clouds of dust in which we are buried in the hot weather for a whole day's march.

My breathing is free and easy, and my colds generally pass off without a cough, and without injury to the lungs.

The rigour of summer is more hostile to me than that of winter; for, besides the discomfort caused by the heat, which is less easily to be remedied than that of cold, and the force of the sunbeams that strike upon my head, my eyes are afflicted by any dazzling light. I cannot even now sit down to dinner opposite a brightly burning fire.

To counteract the whiteness of the paper, when I used to read more than I do now, I laid a piece of glass upon my book, and felt great relief from it. To this moment I am ignorant of the use of spectacles, and can see as far as I ever did, and as any other person. As the day declines my eyes certainly begin to feel a little dim and weak when reading, an exercise that has always tried them, but especially at night-time.

This is a step backwards, but very hardly perceptible. I shall be retiring another step, from the second to the third, from the third to the fourth, so softly that I must needs become really blind before I feel the age and decay of my sight. So cunningly do the Fates unwind our life's thread!

And so I doubt whether my hearing is hesitating on its way to hardness, and you will see that, before I have half lost it, I shall still blame the voices of those who are speaking to me. We must, indeed, put great pleasure on the soul to make it feel how it ebbs away.

My step is quick and firm; and I know not which of the two, my mind or my body, I have had most difficulty in arresting at the same point. The preacher who can hold my attention during a whole sermon is very much my friend. On solemn occasions, when the faces of all are so rigid, and when I have seen ladies keep even their eyes so steady, I could never succeed in keeping some part or other of me from ever wandering; though I may be seated, I am anything but settled.

As the house-slave of Chrysippus the philosopher said of her master that he was only drunk in his legs (for he had the habit of moving them about, in whatever position he was in; and she said it when the others were excited by wine and he felt no effects from it), it might have been said of me too that from my childhood I had madness in my feet, or quicksilver, so restless and fidgety are they, wherever I place them.

It is unmannerly, besides being prejudicial to health and even to one's pleasure, to eat greedily as I do. I often bite my tongue in my haste, and sometimes my fingers. Diogenes, meeting a boy who was eating in that way, gave his tutor a box on the ear. There were people at Rome who taught others to masticate, as well as to walk,[2] gracefully. This habit leaves me no time for talking, which gives so agreeable a relish to the dinner-table, provided that the conversation be in keeping, agreeable, and brief.

There is jealousy and envy between our pleasures; they clash and counteract one another. Alcibiades, a man who understood the art of entertainment, banished even music from his tables, lest it should disturb the pleasure of conversation, for the reason that Plato ascribes to him, "that it is the custom of vulgar men to call singers and instrumentalists to their feasts, for want of good conversation and agreeable entertainment, with which intelligent men know how to regale each other."

Varro makes the following requirements for a banquet:

"A company of persons of handsome presence and pleasing conversation, who must be neither dumb nor loquacious: cleanliness and daintiness in the food and in the chamber; and fine weather." It needs no little skill to provide good entertainment, and it is attended with no little pleasure. Neither great generals nor great philosophers have disdained the knowledge and practice of good eating. My imagination has given three repasts to my memory's keeping, which chanced to be particularly pleasant to me, at different times of my greater prime. For each of the guests brings the principal charm with him, according to the good temper of body and mind in which he appears to be at the time. My present condition excludes me from those pleasures.

I who am but of the earth earthy, dislike that inhuman sapience which would have us despise and hate the care of the body. I think it equally wrong to be out of love with natural pleasures and to be too much in love with them.

Xerxes was a coxcomb who, lapped in all human delights, offered a prize to the man who should invent others; but not much less of a coxcomb is a man who cuts himself off from those that Nature has invented for him. We must neither pursue nor flee them; we must accept them. I accept them a little more generously and graciously, and allow myself more readily to follow the bent of Nature.

We have no need to exaggerate their emptiness; it makes itself sufficiently felt and manifest, thanks to our morbid, kill-joy mind, which disgusts us with them as well as with itself. It treats both itself and all that it takes in, now well, now ill, according to its insatiable, erratic and versatile nature.

> Unless the vessel you would use be sweet,
> 'Twill sour whatever you may pour therein. (HORACE.)

I who boast of embracing so eagerly and particularly all amenities of life, find in them, when I look at them thus closely, little more than wind. But what would you have? We are all wind throughout. And the wind too, more

[2] A *mascher comme à marcher*. Montaigne cannot keep away from his *jeux de mots*.

wisely than we, loves to bluster and shift about, and is content with its own functions, with no desire for stability and solidity, which are none of its properties.

The unmixed pleasures of the imagination, as well as its unmixed pains, are, as some say, greater than all others, as hinted at by Critolaus and his scales.[3] It is not to be wondered at, since she composes them at her own sweet will, and cuts them out of the whole cloth. Of this I see every day notable and perhaps desirable examples. But I, who am of a mixed and coarse grain, cannot so fully bite at this single and so simple object presented by the imagination, but that I let myself go, in all my grossness, after the present pleasures prescribed by human and universal laws, intellectually perceptible and perceptibly intellectual.

The Cyronaic philosophers hold that, like bodily pains, so also bodily pleasures are the more powerful, as being both twofold[4] and more rational.

There are some who with savage stupidity, as Aristotle says, express disgust of pleasures; I know some who do so from ambition. Why do they not also forswear breathing? Why do they not live on their own breath, and refuse the light, because it shines gratis, and costs them neither invention nor strength? Let them try to find sustenance in Mars or Pallas or Mercury, and see what happens, instead of Venus, Ceres, and Bacchus. Are not those the sort of people who will try to square the circle when perched on their wives?

I hate to be told that my spirit should be in the clouds whilst my body is at table. I would have the spirit not nailed down to it, nor sprawling upon it, but attending to it; it should sit at it, and not lie upon it.

Aristippus stood up for the body alone, as if we had no soul; Zeno embraced only the soul, as if we had no body. Both of them mistakenly. They say that Pythagoras followed a philosophy that was all contemplation, Socrates one that was all conduct and action; Plato found the adjustment of it between the two. But they say that to make up a tale. And the true adjustment is found in Socrates, and Plato is much more Socratic than Pythagorean; and it becomes him better.

When I dance, I dance; when I sleep, I sleep. Aye, and when I take a solitary stroll in a beautiful garden, if some part of the time my thoughts dwell on outside events, for some other part I recall them to my walk, to the garden, to the sweetness of the solitude and to myself.

Nature has, with motherly care, observed this rule, that the actions she has laid upon us for our need should give us pleasure; and she invites us to them, not only through our reason but also through our desire. It is wrong to infringe her rules.

When I see both Caesar and Alexander, in the thick of their great labours,

---

[3] "Supposing all the goods of the mind to be put into one scale, and the goods of the body into the other, Critolaus thought the goods of the mind would outweigh the others so far, that they would require the whole earth and sea to equalize the balance."—Cicero, *Tusc. Quaes.*, v. 17.

[4] i.e., both physical and mental.

so fully enjoying natural, and therefore necessary and reasonable pleasures, I do not call it a relaxing of their minds; I call it a stiffening of their minds to subordinate, by strength of spirit, their strenuous occupations and heavy thoughts to the usages of everyday life. Wise they would have been if they could have believed that the latter was their ordinary, the former their extraordinary vocation.

What fools we are! "He has spent his life in idleness," we say; "I have done nothing to-day." What, have you not lived? That is not only the fundamental but the most honourable of your occupations. "If I had been given an opportunity to manage great affairs, I might have shown what I can do." Have you been able to meditate and manage your own life? Then you have performed the greatest work of all. In order to show herself and get to work, Nature has no need of a great destiny; she will show herself equally in all ranks, both behind a curtain and without one.

It is our duty to compose our character, not to compose books, and to win, not battles and provinces, but order and tranquillity for our conduct of life.

Our great and glorious masterpiece is to live to the purpose; all other things, ruling, laying up treasures, building, are at the most but appendicles and adminicles.

I delight in contemplating an army-general, at the foot of a breach he is about to attack, devoting himself entirely and free from cares to his dinner and to this table-talk among his friends. And Brutus, with heaven and earth conspiring against him and Roman liberty, stealing an hour or two from his nightly rounds, to read and epitomize Polybius in all security. It is the part of a little soul, buried under the weight of business, not to be able to get clean away from it, to lay it aside and take it up again:

> Now ye brave hearts that have weathered
> Many a sorer strait with me,
> Chase your cares with wine—to-morrow
> We shall plough the mighty sea! (Horace.)

Whether it be in jest or in earnest that the wine of the Divines[5] and the Sorbonne has become proverbial, like their banquets, I think it reasonable that they should dine more agreeably and cheerfully for having been usefully and seriously employed in the morning teaching their classes. The consciousness of having made good use of the other hours is the right savory sauce for the table.

Thus did the Sages live. And that inimitable straining after virtue which excites our admiration in both of the Catos, that austere turn of mind that is carried to obtrusiveness, has thus tamely and complacently submitted to the laws of human nature, and to Venus and Bacchus; in accordance with the teachings of their school, which require the perfect sage to be as skilled and

[5] *Vin Théologal:* notable good and strong wine; or the best wine, of what kind soever.—Cotgrave.

experienced in the enjoyment of natural pleasures, as in any other of life's duties. A *wise palate should go with a wise judgement* (Cicero).

The power to relax and assume easy manners is highly honourable, I think, and the most becoming trait in a strong and generous soul. Epaminondas never imagined it to be derogatory to the honour of his glorious victories and the perfect purity of his morals to mingle with the dance of the boys in his town, and to sing, play an instrument, and give his whole mind to these recreations.

And among the many admirable actions of Scipio, the grandfather,[6] a man worthy to be reputed of celestial origin, there is none that shows him in such a charming light as to see him strolling along the beach with Laelius, playing the fool like a careless boy, picking up and selecting shells and playing ducks and drakes; and in bad weather amusing and tickling himself with reproducing in written comedies the commonest and most vulgar actions of the people,[7] and, with his thoughts taken up with that wonderful expedition against Hannibal and Africa, visiting the schools in Sicily and attending lectures in Philosophy, thus arming the teeth of the blind envy of his enemies at Rome.

And there is nothing more remarkable in the life of Socrates than that he found time in his old age to learn to dance and play on instruments, and thought it was time well spent.

This same man was once seen standing for a whole day and night in a trance, in the presence of the whole Greek army, his mind caught and carried away by some deep thought. He first, among so many valiant men of the army, ran to the help of Alcibiades, when the latter was overwhelmed by the enemy, covered him with his body and by main force of arms extricated him from the throng. And he first, among all the Athenians, who, like him, were incensed by so shameful a sight, came forward to rescue Theramenes, who was being led to his death by the satellites of the Thirty Tyrants. And, although he was joined by only two other men, all told, only at the instance of Theramenes himself did he desist from this bold undertaking. Although he was run after by a fair lady with whom he was in love, he was known, in spite of pressing need, to observe strict chastity. At the battle of Delium he was seen to pick up and save Xenophon, who had been thrown by his horse. He was always seen to march to war and tread the ice barefoot, to wear the same

---

[6] The original reading of the 1588 edition was "of the younger Scipio (when all is considered, the first of the Romans)." Montaigne seems to have forgotten that it was the younger Scipio who was contemporary with Laelius and Terence.

[7] Montaigne was quite convinced that Scipio and Laelius wrote the comedies of Terence; see Book I, ch. 4. The 1588 edition had this passage, afterwards deleted. "I am exceedingly vexed that the lives of those two great men, Epaminondas and the younger Scipio, by common consent of the world, the one the first of the Greeks, the other the first of the Romans, the finest pair of lives that Plutarch wrote, should have been among the first to be lost."

gown winter and summer, to surpass all his comrades in enduring hardships, and to eat no more at a banquet than at his ordinary. He was seen for twenty-seven years to endure, with unchanged countenance, hunger, poverty, the perverseness of his children, his wife's clawings, and in the end, calumny, tyranny, imprisonment, fetters, and poison.

But if ever he was challenged to a drinking-bout, he accepted as a matter of civility, and of all the army he was the man who came off best. And he never disdained to play at knuckle-bones with the boys or to ride with them on a hobby-horse, and he did it all gracefully; for all actions, says Philosophy, are equally becoming and honourable in a sage. We have material enough, and we should never weary of presenting the picture of this great man as a pattern and ideal of perfection in all things.

There are very few examples of a pure and perfect life, and our education is all wrong when every day we are shown such crazy and defective models, scarce to be commended for any quality, which rather pull us backward; corrupters rather than correctors.

People generally go wrong: it is much easier to go along the side-path, where the boundary serves as a check and guide, than by the broad and open middle way to be guided by art rather than by Nature; but also much less noble and less commendable.

Greatness of soul consists not so much in soaring high and in pressing forward, as in knowing how to adapt and limit oneself. It regards as great all that is sufficient, and shows its distinction in choosing the mean things rather than the eminent.

There is nothing so noble and so right as to play the man well and fitly, nor anything so difficult to learn as how to live this life well and according to Nature; and the most inhuman of our diseases is to despise our being.

Religion

❖◆❖

BERTRAND RUSSELL

A Free Man's Worship[1]

To Dr. Faustus in his study Mephistopheles told the history of the Creation, saying:

"The endless praises of the choirs of angels had begun to grow wearisome;

[1] Reprinted from *Mysticism and Logic*, pp. 46-57, by Bertrand Russell, by permission of W. W. Norton & Company, Inc. Copyright 1929 by the publishers.

for, after all, did he not deserve their praise? Had he not given them endless joy? Would it not be more amusing to obtain undeserved praise, to be worshipped by beings whom he tortured? He smiled inwardly, and resolved that the great drama should be performed.

"For countless ages the hot nebula whirled aimlessly through space. At length it began to take shape, the central mass threw off planets, the planets cooled, boiling seas and burning mountains heaved and tossed, from black masses of cloud hot sheets of rain deluged the barely solid crust. And now the first germ of life grew in the depths of the ocean, and developed rapidly in the fructifying warmth into vast forest trees, huge ferns springing from the damp mould, sea monsters breeding, fighting, devouring, and passing away. And from the monsters, as the play unfolded itself, Man was born, with the power of thought, the knowledge of good and evil, and the cruel thirst for worship. And Man saw that all is passing in this mad, monstrous world, that all is struggling to snatch, at any cost, a few brief moments of life before Death's inexorable decree. And Man said: 'There is a hidden purpose, could we but fathom it, and the purpose is good; for we must reverence something, and in the visible world there is nothing worthy of reverence.' And Man stood aside from the struggle, resolving that God intended harmony to come out of chaos by human efforts. And when he followed the instincts which God had transmitted to him from his ancestry of beasts of prey, he called it Sin, and asked God to forgive him. But he doubted whether he could be justly forgiven, until he invented a divine Plan by which God's wrath was to have been appeased. And seeing the present was bad, he made it yet worse, that thereby the future might be better. And he gave God thanks for the strength that enabled him to forgo even the joys that were possible. And God smiled; and when he saw that Man had become perfect in renunciation and worship, he sent another sun through the sky, which crashed into Man's sun; and all returned again to nebula.

" 'Yes,' he murmured, 'it was a good play; I will have it performed again.' "

Such, in outline, but even more purposeless, more void of meaning is the world which Science presents for our belief. Amid such a world, if anywhere, our ideals henceforward must find a home. That Man is the product of causes which had no prevision of the end they were achieving; that his origin, his growth, his hopes and fears, his loves and his beliefs, are but the outcome of accidental collocations of atoms; that no fire, no heroism, no intensity of thought and feeling, can preserve an individual life beyond the grave; that all the labours of the ages, all the devotion, all the inspiration, all the noonday brightness of human genius, are destined to extinction in the vast death of the solar system, and that the whole temple of Man's achievement must inevitably be buried beneath the débris of a universe in ruins—all these things, if not quite beyond dispute, are yet so nearly certain, that no philosophy which rejects them can hope to stand. Only within the scaffolding of these truths, only on the firm foundation of unyielding despair, can the soul's habitation henceforth be safely built.

How, in such an alien and inhuman world, can so powerless a creature as Man preserve his aspirations untarnished? A strange mystery it is that Nature, omnipotent but blind, in the revolutions of her secular hurryings through the abysses of space, has brought forth at last a child, subject still to her power, but gifted with sight, with knowledge of good and evil, with the capacity of judging all the works of his unthinking Mother. In spite of Death, the mark and seal of the parental control, Man is yet free, during his brief years, to examine, to criticise, to know, and in imagination to create. To him alone, in the world with which he is acquainted, this freedom belongs; and in this lies his superiority to the resistless forces that control his outward life.

The savage, like ourselves, feels the oppression of his impotence before the powers of Nature; but having in himself nothing that he respects more than Power, he is willing to prostrate himself before his gods, without inquiring whether they are worthy of his worship. Pathetic and very terrible is the long history of cruelty and torture, of degradation and human sacrifices endured in the hope of placating the jealous gods: surely, the trembling believer thinks, when what is most precious has been freely given, their lust for blood must be appeased, and more will not be required. The religion of Moloch—as such creeds may be generically called—is in essence the cringing submission of the slave, who dare not, even in his heart, allow the thought that his master deserves no adulation. Since the independence of ideals is not yet acknowledged, Power may be freely worshipped, and receive an unlimited respect, despite its wanton infliction of pain.

But gradually, as morality grows bolder, the claim of the ideal world begins to be felt; and worship, if it is not to cease, must be given to gods of another kind than those created by the savage. Some, though they feel the demands of the ideal, will still consciously reject them, still urging that naked Power is worthy of worship. Such is the attitude inculcated in God's answer to Job out of the whirlwind: the divine power and knowledge are paraded, but of the divine goodness there is no hint. Such also is the attitude of those who, in our own day, base their morality upon the struggle for survival, maintaining that the survivors are necessarily the fittest. But others, not content with an answer so repugnant to the moral sense, will adopt the position which we have become accustomed to regard as specially religious, maintaining that, in some hidden manner, the world of fact is really harmonious with the world of ideals. Thus Man creates God, all-powerful and all-good, the mystic unity of what is and what should be.

But the world of fact, after all, is not good; and, in submitting our judgment to it, there is an element of slavishness from which our thoughts must be purged. For in all things it is well to exalt the dignity of Man, by freeing him as far as possible from the tyranny of non-human Power. When we have realised that Power is largely bad, that Man, with his knowledge of good and evil, is but a helpless atom in a world which has no such knowledge, the choice is again presented to us: Shall we worship Force, or shall we worship Goodness?

Shall our God exist and be evil, or shall he be recognised as the creation of our own conscience?

The answer to this question is very momentous, and affects profoundly our whole morality. The worship of Force, to which Carlyle and Nietzsche and the creed of Militarism have accustomed us, is the result of failure to maintain our own ideals against a hostile universe: it is itself a prostrate submission to evil, a sacrifice of our best to Moloch. If strength indeed is to be respected, let us respect rather the strength of those who refuse that false "recognition of facts" which fails to recognise that facts are often bad. Let us admit that, in the world we know, there are many things that would be better otherwise, and that the ideals to which we do and must adhere are not realised in the realm of matter. Let us preserve our respect for truth, for beauty, for the ideal of perfection which life does not permit us to attain, though none of these things meet with the approval of the unconscious universe. If Power is bad, as it seems to be, let us reject it from our hearts. In this lies Man's true freedom: in determination to worship only the God created by our own love of the good, to respect only the heaven which inspires the insight of our best moments. In action, in desire, we must submit perpetually to the tyranny of outside forces; but in thought, in aspiration, we are free, free from our fellowmen, free from the petty planet on which our bodies impotently crawl, free even, while we live, from the tyranny of death. Let us learn, then, that energy of faith which enables us to live constantly in the vision of the good; and let us descend in action, into the world of fact, with that vision always before us.

When first the opposition of fact and ideal grows fully visible, a spirit of fiery revolt, of fierce hatred of the gods, seems necessary to the assertion of freedom. To defy with Promethean constancy a hostile universe, to keep its evil always in view, always actively hated, to refuse no pain that the malice of Power can invent, appears to be the duty of all who will not bow before the inevitable. But indignation is still a bondage, for it compels our thoughts to be occupied with an evil world; and in the fierceness of desire from which rebellion springs there is a kind of self-assertion which it is necessary for the wise to overcome. Indignation is a submission of our thoughts, but not of our desires; the Stoic freedom in which wisdom consists is found in the submission of our desires, but not of our thoughts. From the submission of our desires springs the virtue of resignation; from the freedom of our thoughts springs the whole world of art and philosophy, and the vision of beauty by which, at last, we half reconquer the reluctant world. But the vision of beauty is possible only to unfettered contemplation, to thoughts not weighted by the load of eager wishes; and thus Freedom comes only to those who no longer ask of life that it shall yield them any of those personal goods that are subject to the mutations of Time.

Although the necessity of renunciation is evidence of the existence of evil, yet Christianity, in preaching it, has shown a wisdom exceeding that of the Promethean philosophy of rebellion. It must be admitted that, of the things

we desire, some, though they prove impossible, are yet real goods; others, however, as ardently longed for, do not form part of a fully purified ideal. The
belief that what must be renounced is bad, though sometimes false, is far less
often false than untamed passion supposes; and the creed of religion, by providing a reason for proving that it is never false, has been the means of
purifying our hopes by the discovery of many austere truths.

But there is in resignation a further good element: even real goods, when
they are unattainable, ought not to be fretfully desired. To every man comes,
sooner or later, the great renunciation. For the young, there is nothing unattainable; a good thing desired with the whole force of a passionate will, and
yet impossible, is to them not credible. Yet, by death, by illness, by poverty, or
by the voice of duty, we must learn, each one of us, that the world was not
made for us, and that, however beautiful may be the things we crave, Fate
may nevertheless forbid them. It is the part of courage, when misfortune comes,
to bear without repining the ruin of our hopes, to turn away our thoughts from
vain regrets. This degree of submission to Power is not only just and right; it
is the very gate of wisdom.

But passive renunciation is not the whole of wisdom; for not by renunciation alone can we build a temple for the worship of our own ideals. Haunting
foreshadowings of the temple appear in the realm of imagination, in music, in
architecture, in the untroubled kingdom of reason, and in the golden sunset
magic of lyrics, where beauty shines and glows, remote from the touch of
sorrow, remote from the fear of change, remote from the failures and dis-
enchantments of the world of fact. In the contemplation of these things the
vision of heaven will shape itself in our hearts, giving at once a touchstone to
judge the world about us, and an inspiration by which to fashion to our needs
whatever is not incapable of serving as a stone in the sacred temple.

Except for those rare spirits that are born without sin, there is a cavern of
darkness to be traversed before that temple can be entered. The gate of the
cavern is despair, and its floor is paved with the gravestones of abandoned
hopes. There Self must die; there the eagerness, the greed of untamed desire
must be slain, for only so can the soul be freed from the empire of Fate. But
out of the cavern the Gate of Renunciation leads again to the daylight of
wisdom, by whose radiance a new insight, a new joy, a new tenderness, shine
forth to gladden the pilgrim's heart.

When, without the bitterness of impotent rebellion, we have learnt both to
resign ourselves to the outward rule of Fate and to recognise that the non-
human world is unworthy of our worship, it becomes possible at last so to
transform and refashion the unconscious universe, so to transmute it in the
crucible of the imagination, that a new image of shining gold replaces the
old idol of clay. In all the multiform facts of the world—in the visual shapes
of trees and mountains and clouds, in the events of the life of Man, even in
the very omnipotence of Death—the insight of creative idealism can find the

reflection of a beauty which its own thoughts first made. In this way mind asserts its subtle mastery over the thoughtless forces of Nature. The more evil the material with which it deals, the more thwarting to untrained desire, the greater is its achievement in inducing the reluctant rock to yield up its hidden treasures, the prouder its victory in compelling the opposing forces to swell the pageant of its triumph. Of all the arts, Tragedy is the proudest, the most triumphant; for it builds its shining citadel in the very centre of the enemy's country, on the very summit of his highest mountain; from its impregnable watch-towers, his camps and arsenals, his columns and forts, are all revealed; within its walls the free life continues, while the legions of Death and Pain and Despair, and all the servile captains of tyrant Fate, afford the burghers of that dauntless city new spectacles of beauty. Happy those sacred ramparts, thrice happy the dwellers on that all-seeing eminence. Honour to those brave warriors who, through countless ages of warfare, have preserved for us the priceless heritage of liberty, and have kept undefiled by sacrilegious invaders the home of the unsubdued.

But the beauty of Tragedy does but make visible a quality which, in more or less obvious shapes, is present always and everywhere in life. In the spectacle of Death, in the endurance of intolerable pain, and in the irrevocableness of a vanished past, there is a sacredness, an overpowering awe, a feeling of the vastness, the depth, the inexhaustible mystery of existence, in which, as by some strange marriage of pain, the sufferer is bound to the world by bonds of sorrow. In these moments of insight, we lose all eagerness of temporary desire, all struggling and striving for petty ends, all care for the little trivial things, that, to a superficial view, make up the common life of day by day; we see, surrounding the narrow raft illumined by the flickering light of human comradeship, the dark ocean on whose rolling waves we toss for a brief hour; from the great night without, a chill blast breaks in upon our refuge; all the loneliness of humanity amid hostile forces is concentrated upon the individual soul, which must struggle alone, with what of courage it can command, against the whole weight of a universe that cares nothing for its hopes and fears. Victory, in this struggle with the powers of darkness, is the true baptism into the glorious company of heroes, the true initiation into the overmastering beauty of human existence. From that awful encounter of the soul with the outer world, renunciation, wisdom, and charity are born; and with their birth a new life begins. To take into the inmost shrine of the soul the irresistible forces whose puppets we seem to be—Death and change, the irrevocableness of the past, and the powerlessness of Man before the blind hurry of the universe from vanity to vanity—to feel these things and know them is to conquer them.

This is the reason why the Past has such magical power. The beauty of its motionless and silent pictures is like the enchanted purity of late autumn, when the leaves, though one breath would make them fall, still glow against the sky in golden glory. The Past does not change or strive; like Duncan, after life's fitful fever it sleeps well; what was eager and grasping, what was petty and transitory, has faded away, the things that were beautiful and eternal shine out of it like stars in the night. Its beauty, to a soul not worthy of it, is unendurable; but to a soul which has conquered Fate it is the key of religion.

The life of Man, viewed outwardly, is but a small thing in comparison with the forces of Nature. The slave is doomed to worship Time and Fate and Death, because they are greater than anything he finds in himself, and because all his thoughts are of things which they devour. But, great as they are, to think of them greatly, to feel their passionless splendour, is greater still. And such thought makes us free men; we no longer bow before the inevitable in Oriental subjection, but we absorb it, and make it a part of ourselves. To abandon the struggle for private happiness, to expel all eagerness of temporary desire, to burn with passion for eternal things—this is emancipation, and this is the free man's worship. And this liberation is effected by a contemplation of Fate; for Fate itself is subdued by the mind which leaves nothing to be purged by the purifying fire of Time.

United with his fellow-men by the strongest of all ties, the tie of a common doom, the free man finds that a new vision is with him always, shedding over every daily task the light of love. The life of Man is a long march through the night, surrounded by invisible foes, tortured by weariness and pain, towards a goal that few can hope to reach, and where none may tarry long. One by one, as they march, our comrades vanish from our sight, seized by the silent orders of omnipotent Death. Very brief is the time in which we can help them, in which their happiness or misery is decided. Be it ours to shed sunshine on their path, to lighten their sorrows by the balm of sympathy, to give them the pure joy of a never-tiring affection, to strengthen failing courage, to instil faith in hours of despair. Let us not weigh in grudging scales their merits and demerits, but let us think only of their need—of the sorrows, the difficulties, perhaps the blindnesses, that make the misery of their lives; let us remember that they are fellow-sufferers in the same darkness, actors in the same tragedy with ourselves. And so, when their day is over, when their good and their evil have become eternal by the immortality of the past, be it ours to feel that, where they suffered, where they failed, no deed of ours was the cause; but wherever a spark of the divine fire kindled in their hearts, we were ready with encouragement, with sympathy, with brave words in which high courage glowed.

Brief and powerless is Man's life; on him and all his race the slow, sure doom falls pitiless and dark. Blind to good and evil, reckless of destruction, omnipotent matter rolls on its relentless way; for Man, condemned to-day to lose his dearest, to-morrow himself to pass through the gate of darkness, it remains only to cherish, ere yet the blow falls, the lofty thoughts that ennoble his little day; disdaining the coward terrors of the slave of Fate, to worship at the shrine that his own hands have built; undismayed by the empire of chance, to preserve a mind free from the wanton tyranny that rules his outward life;

proudly defiant of the irresistible forces that tolerate, for a moment, his knowledge and his condemnation, to sustain alone, a weary but unyielding Atlas, the world that his own ideals have fashioned despite the trampling march of unconscious Power.

The Providence of God[1]

LORD, thou hast been our dwelling place in all generations.

Before the mountains were brought forth, or ever thou hadst formed the earth and the world, even from everlasting to everlasting, thou art God.

Thou turnest man to destruction; and sayest, Return, ye children of men.

For a thousand years in thy sight are but as yesterday when it is past, and as a watch in the night.

Thou carriest them away as with a flood; they are as a sleep: in the morning they are like grass which groweth up.

In the morning it flourisheth, and groweth up; in the evening it is cut down, and withereth.

For we are consumed by thine anger, and by thy wrath are we troubled.

Thou hast set our iniquities before thee, our secret sins in the light of thy countenance.

For all our days are passed away in thy wrath: we spend our years as a tale that is told.

The days of our years are threescore years and ten; and if by any reason of strength they be fourscore years, yet is their strength labour and sorrow; for it is soon cut off, and we fly away.

Who knoweth the power of thine anger? even according to thy fear, so is thy wrath.

So teach us to number our days, that we may apply our hearts unto wisdom.

Return, O LORD, how long? and let it repent thee concerning thy servants.

O satisfy us early with thy mercy; that we may rejoice and be glad all our days.

Make us glad according to the days wherein thou hast afflicted us, and the years wherein we have seen evil.

Let thy work appear unto thy servants, and thy glory unto their children.

And let the beauty of the LORD our GOD be upon us: and establish thou the work of our hands upon us; yea, the work of our hands establish thou it.

He that dwelleth in the secret place of the most High shall abide under the shadow of the Almighty.

I will say of the LORD, He is my refuge and my fortress: my God; in him will I trust.

[1] From *The Book of Psalms* (King James Version of the Bible), Chapters 90, 91.

Surely he shall deliver thee from the snare of the fowler, and from the noisome pestilence.

He shall cover thee with his feathers and under his wings shalt thou trust: his truth shall be thy shield and buckler.

Thou shalt not be afraid for the terror by night; nor for the arrow that flieth by day;

Nor for the pestilence that walketh in darkness; nor for the destruction that wasteth at noonday.

A thousand shall fall at thy side, and ten thousand at thy right hand; but it shall not come nigh thee.

Only with thine eyes shalt thou behold and see the reward of the wicked.

Because thou hast made the LORD, which is my refuge, even the most High, thy habitation;

There shall no evil befall thee, neither shall any plague come nigh thy dwelling.

For he shall give his angels charge over thee, to keep thee in all thy ways.

They shall bear thee up in their hands, lest thou dash thy foot against a stone.

Thou shalt tread upon the lion and adder: the young lion and the dragon shalt thou trample under feet.

Because he hath set his love upon me, therefore will I deliver him: I will set him on high, because he hath known my name.

He shall call upon me, and I will answer him: I will be with him in trouble; I will deliver him, and honour him.

With long life will I satisfy him, and shew him my salvation.

JOHN DONNE

Meditation XVII[1]

Nunc lento sonitu dicunt, morieris[2]

Perchance he for whom this bell tolls may be so ill as that he knows not it tolls for him; and perchance I may think myself so much better than I am as that they who are about me and see my state may have caused it to toll for me, and I know not that. The church is catholic, universal, so are all her actions; all that she does belongs to all. When she baptizes a child, that action con-

---

[1] From *Devotions upon Emergent Occasions* by John Donne (London, 1624).
[2] Now this bell tolling softly says, you must die.

cerns me; for that child is thereby connected to that body which is my head too and ingrafted into that body whereof I am a member. And when she buries a man, that action concerns me. All mankind is of one author, and is one volume; when one man dies, one chapter is not torn out of the book, but translated into a better language; and every chapter must be so translated. God employs several translators; some pieces are translated by age, some by sickness, some by war, some by justice; but God's hand is in every translation, and his hand shall bind up all our scattered leaves again for that library where every book shall lie open to one another. As therefore the bell that rings to a sermon calls not upon the preacher only but upon the congregation to come, so this bell calls us all; but how much more me who am brought so near the door by this sickness! There was a contention as far as a suit—in which piety and dignity, religion and estimation, were mingled—which of the religious orders should ring to prayers first in the morning; and it was determined that they should ring first that rose earliest. If we understand aright the dignity of this bell that tolls for our evening prayer, we would be glad to make it ours by rising early, in that application, that it might be ours as well as his, whose indeed it is. The bell doth toll for him that thinks it doth; and though it intermit again, yet from that minute that that occasion wrought upon him he is united to God. Who casts not up his eye to the sun when it rises? but who takes off his eye for a comet when that breaks out? Who bends not his ear to any bell which upon any occasion rings? but who can remove it from that bell which is passing a piece of himself out of this world? No man is an island entire of itself; every man is a piece of the continent, a part of the main. If a clod be washed away by the sea, Europe is the less, as well as if a promontory were, as well as if a manor or thy friend's or of thine own were. Any man's death diminishes me, because I am involved in mankind, and therefore never send to know for whom the bell tolls; it tolls for thee. Neither can we call this a begging of misery or a borrowing of misery, as though we were not miserable enough of ourselves but must fetch in more from the next house, in taking upon us the misery of our neighbors. Truly it were an excusable covetousness if we did, for affliction is a treasure, and scarce any man hath enough of it. No man hath affliction enough that is not matured and ripened by it and made fit for God by that affliction. If a man carry treasure in bullion or in a wedge of gold and have none coined into current money, his treasure will not defray him as he travels. Tribulation is treasure in the nature of it, but it is not current money in the use of it, except we get nearer and nearer our home, heaven, by it. Another man may be sick too, and sick to death, and this affliction may lie in his bowels as gold in a mine and be of no use to him; but this bell that tells me of his affliction digs out and applies that gold to me, if by this consideration of another's danger I take mine own into contemplation and so secure myself by making my recourse to my God, who is our only security.

JOHN WOOLMAN

In His Will Is Our Peace [1]

Twenty-sixth of eighth month [1772].—Being now at George Crosfield's, in the county of Westmoreland, I feel a concern to commit to writing the following uncommon circumstance.

In a time of sickness, a little more than two years and a half ago, I was brought so near the gates of death that I forgot my name. Being then desirous to know who I was, I saw a mass of matter of a dull gloomy color between the south and the east, and was informed that this mass was human beings in as great misery as they could be, and live, and that I was mixed with them, and that henceforth I might not consider myself as a distinct or separate being. In this state I remained several hours. I then heard a soft melodious voice, more pure and harmonious than any I had heard with my ears before; I believed it was the voice of an angel who spake to the other angels; the words were, "John Woolman is dead." I soon remembered that I was once John Woolman, and being assured that I was alive in the body, I greatly wondered what that heavenly voice could mean. I believed beyond doubting that it was the voice of an holy angel, but as yet it was a mystery to me.

I was then carried in spirit to the mines where poor oppressed people were digging rich treasures for those called Christians, and heard them blaspheme the name of Christ, at which I was grieved, for his name to me was precious. I was then informed that these heathens were told that those who oppressed them were the followers of Christ, and they said among themselves, "If Christ directed them to use us in this sort, then Christ is a cruel tyrant."

All this time the song of the angel remained a mystery; and in the morning, my dear wife and some others coming to my bedside, I asked them if they knew who I was, and they telling me I was John Woolman, thought I was lightheaded, for I told them not what the angel said, nor was I disposed to talk much to anyone, but was very desirous to get so deep that I might understand this mystery.

My tongue was often so dry that I could not speak till I had moved it about and gathered some moisture, and as I lay still for a time I at length felt a Divine power prepare my mouth that I could speak, and I then said, "I am crucified with Christ, nevertheless I live; yet not I, but Christ liveth in me. And the life which I now live in the flesh I live by the faith of the Son of God, who loved me and gave himself for me." Then the mystery was opened and I perceived there was joy in heaven over a sinner who had repented, and that the language "John Woolman is dead," meant no more than the death of my own will. . . .

[1] From the *Journal* of John Woolman. First printed in 1774.

·After this sickness I spake not in public meetings for worship for nearly one year, but my mind was very often in company with the oppressed slaves as I sat in meetings; and though under his dispensation I was shut up from speaking, yet the spring of the gospel ministry was many times livingly opened in me, and the Divine gift operated by abundance of weeping, in feeling the oppression of this people. It being so long since I passed through this dispensation, and the matter remaining fresh and lively in my mind, I believe it safest for me to commit it to writing.

ALFRED NORTH WHITEHEAD

Religion and Science[1]

The difficulty in approaching the question of the relations between Religion and Science is, that its elucidation requires that we have in our minds some clear idea of what we mean by either of the terms, "religion" and "science." Also I wish to speak in the most general way possible, and to keep in the background any comparison of particular creeds, scientific or religious. We have got to understand the type of connection which exists between the two spheres, and then to draw some definite conclusions respecting the existing situation which at present confronts the world.

The *conflict* between religion and science is what naturally occurs to our minds when we think of this subject. It seems as though, during the last half-century, the results of science and the beliefs of religion had come into a position of frank disagreement, from which there can be no escape, except by abandoning either the clear teaching of science, or the clear teaching of religion. This conclusion has been urged by controversialists on either side. Not by all controversialists, of course, but by those trenchant intellects which every controversy calls out into the open.

The distress of sensitive minds, and the zeal for truth, and the sense of the importance of the issues, must command our sincerest sympathy. When we consider what religion is for mankind, and what science is, it is no exaggeration to say that the future course of history depends upon the decision of this generation as to the relations between them. We have here the two strongest general forces (apart from the mere impulse of the various senses) which influence men, and they seem to be set one against the other—the force of our religious intuitions, and the force of our impulse to accurate observation and logical deduction.

[1] From *Science and the Modern World*, by Alfred North Whitehead. Copyright, 1925 by The Macmillan Company, renewed 1953 by Evelyn Whitehead. Used with permission of The Macmillan Company.

A great English statesman once advised his countrymen to use large-scale maps, as a preservative against alarms, panics, and general misunderstanding of the true relations between nations. In the same way in dealing with the clash between permanent elements of human nature, it is well to map our history on a large scale, and to disengage ourselves from our immediate absorption in the present conflicts. When we do this, we immediately discover two great facts. In the first place, there has always been a conflict between religion and science; and in the second place, both religion and science have always been in a state of continual development. In the early days of Christianity, there was a general belief among Christians that the world was coming to an end in the lifetime of people then living. We can make only indirect inferences as to how far this belief was authoritatively proclaimed; but it is certain that it was widely held, and that it formed an impressive part of the popular religious doctrine. The belief proved itself to be mistaken, and the Christian doctrine adjusted itself to the change. Again in the early Church individual theologians very confidently deduced from the Bible opinions concerning the nature of the physical universe. In the year A.D. 535, a monk named Cosmas wrote a book which he entitled, *Christian Topography.* He was a travelled man who had visited India and Ethiopia; and finally he lived in a monastery at Alexandria, which was then a great centre of culture. In this book, basing himself upon the direct meaning of Biblical texts as construed by him in a literal fashion, he denied the existence of the antipodes, and asserted that the world is a flat parallelogram whose length is double its breadth.

In the seventeenth century the doctrine of the motion of the earth was condemned by a Catholic tribunal. A hundred years ago the extension of time demanded by geological science distressed religious people, Protestant and Catholic. And today the doctrine of evolution is an equal stumbling-block. These are only a few instances illustrating a general fact.

But all our ideas will be in a wrong perspective if we think that this recurring perplexity was confined to contradictions between religion and science; and that in these controversies religion was always wrong, and that science was always right. The true facts of the case are very much more complex, and refuse to be summarized in these simple terms.

Theology itself exhibits exactly the same character of gradual development, arising from an aspect of conflict between its own proper ideas. This fact is a commonplace to theologians, but is often obscured in the stress of controversy. I do not wish to overstate my case; so I will confine myself to Roman Catholic writers. In the seventeenth century a learned Jesuit, Father Petavius, showed that the theologians of the first three centuries of Christianity made use of phrases and statements which since the fifth century would be condemned as heretical. Also Cardinal Newman devoted a treatise to the discussion of the development of doctrine. He wrote it before he became a great Roman Catholic ecclesiastic; but throughout his life, it was never retracted and continually reissued.

Science is even more changeable than theology. No man of science could subscribe without qualification to Galileo's beliefs, or to Newton's beliefs, or to all his own scientific beliefs of ten years ago.

In both regions of thought, additions, distinctions, and modifications have been introduced. So that now, even when the same assertion is made today as was made a thousand, or fifteen hundred years ago, it is made subject to limitations or expansions of meaning, which were not contemplated at the earlier epoch. We are told by logicians that a proposition must be either true or false, and that there is no middle term. But in practice, we may know that a proposition expresses an important truth, but that it is subject to limitations and qualifications which at present remain undiscovered. It is a general feature of our knowledge, that we are insistently aware of important truths; and yet that the only formulations of these truths which we are able to make presuppose a general standpoint of conceptions which may have to be modified. I will give you two illustrations, both from science: Galileo said that the earth moves and that the sun is fixed; the Inquisition said that the earth is fixed and the sun moves; and Newtonian astronomers, adopting an absolute theory of space, said that both the sun and the earth move. But now we say that any one of these three statements is equally true, provided that you have fixed your sense of "rest" and "motion" in the way required by the statement adopted. At the date of Galileo's controversy with the Inquisition, Galileo's way of stating the facts was, beyond question, the fruitful procedure for the sake of scientific research. But in itself it was not more true than the formulation of the Inquisition. But at that time the modern concepts of relative motion were in nobody's mind; so that the statements were made in ignorance of the qualifications required for their more perfect truth. Yet this question of the motions of the earth and the sun expresses a real fact in the universe; and all sides had got hold of important truths concerning it. But with the knowledge of those times, the truths appeared to be inconsistent.

Again I will give you another example taken from the state of modern physical science. Since the time of Newton and Huyghens in the seventeenth century there have been two theories as to the physical nature of light. Newton's theory was that a beam of light consists of a stream of very minute particles, or corpuscles, and that we have the sensation of light when these corpuscles strike the retinas of our eyes. Huyghens' theory was that light consists of very minute waves of trembling in an all-pervading ether, and that these waves are travelling along a beam of light. The two theories are contradictory. In the eighteenth century Newton's theory was believed, in the nineteenth century Huyghens' theory was believed. Today there is one large group of phenomena which can be explained only on the wave theory, and another large group which can be explained only on the corpuscular theory. Scientists have to leave it at that, and wait for the future, in the hope of attaining some wider vision which reconciles both.

We should apply these same principles to the questions in which there is a variance between science and religion. We would believe nothing in either sphere of thought which does not appear to us to be certified by solid reasons based upon the critical research either of ourselves or of competent authorities. But granting that we have honestly taken this precaution, a clash between the two on points of detail where they overlap should not lead us hastily to abandon doctrines for which we have solid evidence. It may be that we are more interested in one set of doctrines than in the other. But, if we have any sense of perspective and of the history of thought, we shall wait and refrain from mutual anathemas.

We should wait: but we should not wait passively, or in despair. The clash is a sign that there are wider truths and finer perspectives within which a reconciliation of a deeper religion and a more subtle science will be found.

In one sense, therefore, the conflict between science and religion is a slight matter which has been unduly emphasized. A mere logical contradiction cannot in itself point to more than the necessity of some readjustments, possibly of a very minor character on both sides. Remember the widely different aspects of events which are dealt with in science and in religion respectively. Science is concerned with the general conditions which are observed to regulate physical phenomena; whereas religion is wholly wrapped up in the contemplation of moral and aesthetic values. On the one side there is the law of gravitation, and on the other the contemplation of the beauty of holiness. What one side sees, the other misses; and vice versa.

Consider, for example, the lives of John Wesley and of Saint Francis of Assisi. For physical science you have in these lives merely ordinary examples of the operation of the principles of physiological chemistry, and of the dynamics of nervous reactions: for religion you have lives of the most profound significance in the history of the world. Can you be surprised that, in the absence of a perfect and complete phrasing of the principles of science and of the principles of religion which apply to these specific cases, the accounts of these lives from these divergent standpoints should involve discrepancies? It would be a miracle if it were not so.

It would, however, be missing the point to think that we need not trouble ourselves about the conflict between science and religion. In an intellectual age there can be no active interest which puts aside all hope of a vision of the harmony of truth. To acquiesce in discrepancy is destructive of candour, and of moral cleanliness. It belongs to the self-respect of intellect to pursue every tangle of thought to its final unravelment. If you check that impulse, you will get no religion and no science from an awakened thoughtfulness. The important question is, In what spirit are we going to face the issue? There we come to something absolutely vital.

A clash of doctrines is not a disaster—it is an opportunity. I will explain my meaning by some illustrations from science. The weight of an atom of nitrogen was well known. Also it was an established scientific doctrine that the average weight of such atoms in any considerable mass will be always the same.

Two experimenters, the late Lord Rayleigh and the late Sir William Ramsay, found that if they obtained nitrogen by two different methods, each equally effective for that purpose, they always observed a persistent slight difference between the average weights of the atoms in the two cases. Now I ask you, would it have been rational of these men to have despaired because of this conflict between chemical theory and scientific observation? Suppose that for some reason the chemical doctrine had been highly prized throughout some district as the foundation of its social order:—would it have been wise, would it have been candid, would it have been moral, to forbid the disclosure of the fact that the experiments produced discordant results? Or, on the other hand, should Sir William Ramsay and Lord Rayleigh have proclaimed that chemical theory was now a detected delusion? We see at once that either of these ways would have been a method of facing the issue in an entirely wrong spirit. What Rayleigh and Ramsay did was this: They at once perceived that they had hit upon a line of investigation which would disclose some subtlety of chemical theory that had hitherto eluded observation. The discrepancy was not a disaster: it was an opportunity to increase the sweep of chemical knowledge. You all know the end of the story: finally argon was discovered, a new chemical element which had lurked undetected, mixed with the nitrogen. But the story has a sequel which forms my second illustration. This discovery drew attention to the importance of observing accurately minute differences in chemical substances as obtained by different methods. Further researches of the most careful accuracy were undertaken. Finally another physicist, F. W. Aston, working in the Cavendish Laboratory at Cambridge in England, discovered that even the same element might assume two or more distinct forms, termed *isotopes*, and that the law of the constancy of average atomic weight holds for each of these forms, but as between the different isotopes differs slightly. The research has effected a great stride in the power of chemical theory, far transcending in importance the discovery of argon from which it originated. The moral of these stories lies on the surface, and I will leave to you their application to the case of religion and science.

In formal logic, a contradiction is the signal of a defeat: but in the evolution of real knowledge it marks the first step in progress towards a victory. This is one great reason for the utmost toleration of variety of opinion. Once and forever, this duty of toleration has been summed up in the words, "Let both grow together until the harvest." The failure of Christians to act up to this precept, of the highest authority, is one of the curiosities of religious history. But we have not yet exhausted the discussion of the moral temper required for the pursuit of truth. There are short cuts leading merely to an illusory success. It is easy enough to find a theory, logically harmonious and with important applications in the region of fact, provided that you are content to disregard half your evidence. Every age produces people with clear logical intellects, and with the most praiseworthy grasp of the importance of some sphere of human experience, who have elaborated, or inherited, a scheme of thought which exactly fits those experiences which claim their interest. Such people are apt resolutely to ignore, or to explain away, all evidence which confuses their scheme with contradictory instances. What they cannot fit in is for them nonsense. An unflinching determination to take the whole evidence into account is the only method of preservation against the fluctuating extremes of fashionable opinion. This advice seems so easy, and is in fact so difficult to follow.

One reason for this difficulty is that we cannot think first and act afterwards. From the moment of birth we are immersed in action, and can only fitfully guide it by taking thought. We have, therefore, in various spheres of experience to adopt those ideas which seem to work within those spheres. It is absolutely necessary to trust to ideas which are generally adequate, even though we know that there are subtleties and distinctions beyond our ken. Also apart from the necessities of action, we cannot even keep before our minds the whole evidence except under the guise of doctrines which are incompletely harmonized. We cannot think in terms of an indefinite multiplicity of detail; our evidence can acquire its proper importance only if it comes before us marshalled by general ideas. These ideas we inherit—they form the tradition of our civilization. Such traditional ideas are never static. They are either fading into meaningless formulae, or are gaining power by the new lights thrown by a more delicate apprehension. They are transformed by the urge of critical reason, by the vivid evidence of emotional experience, and by the cold certainties of scientific perception. One fact is certain, you cannot keep them still. No generation can merely reproduce its ancestors. You may preserve the life in a flux of form, or preserve the form amid an ebb of life. But you cannot permanently enclose the same life in the same mold.

The present state of religion among the European races illustrates the statements which I have been making. The phenomena are mixed. There have been reactions and revivals. But on the whole, during many generations, there has been a gradual decay of religious influence in European civilization. Each revival touches a lower peak than its predecessor, and each period of slackness a lower depth. The average curve marks a steady fall in religious tone. In some countries the interest in religion is higher than in others. But in those countries where the interest is relatively high, it still falls as the generations pass. Religion is tending to degenerate into a decent formula wherewith to embellish a comfortable life. A great historical movement on this scale results from the convergence of many causes. I wish to suggest two of them which lie within the scope of this chapter for consideration.

In the first place for over two centuries religion has been on the defensive, and on a weak defensive. The period has been one of unprecedented intellectual progress. In this way a series of novel situations have been produced for thought. Each such occasion has found the religious thinkers unprepared. Something, which has been proclaimed to be vital, has finally, after struggle, distress, and anathema, been modified and otherwise interpreted. The next generation of religious apologists then congratulates the religious world on the deeper insight which has been gained. The result of the continued repetition of this undignified retreat, during many generations, has at last almost entirely destroyed the intellectual authority of religious thinkers. Consider this contrast: when Darwin or Einstein proclaim theories which modify our ideas, it is a triumph for science. We do not go about saying that there is another defeat for science, because its old ideas have been abandoned. We know that another step of scientific insight has been gained.

Religion will not regain its old power until it can face change in the same spirit as does science. Its principles may be eternal, but the expression of those principles requires continual development. This evolution of religion is in the main a disengagement of its own proper ideas from the adventitious notions which have crept into it by reason of the expression of its own ideas in terms of the imaginative picture of the world entertained in previous ages. Such a release of religion from the bonds of imperfect science is all to the good. It stresses its own genuine message. The great point to be kept in mind is that normally an advance in science will show that statements of various religious beliefs require some sort of modification. It may be that they have to be expanded or explained, or indeed entirely restated. If the religion is a sound expression of truth, this modification will only exhibit more adequately the exact point which is of importance. This process is a gain. In so far, therefore, as any religion has any contact with physical facts, it is to be expected that the point of view of those facts must be continually modified as scientific knowledge advances. In this way, the exact relevance of these facts for religious thought will grow more and more clear. The progress of science must result in the unceasing codification of religious thought, to the great advantage of religion.

The religious controversies of the sixteenth and seventeenth centuries put theologians into a most unfortunate state of mind. They were always attacking and defending. They pictured themselves as the garrison of a fort surrounded by hostile forces. All such pictures express half-truths. That is why they are so popular. But they are dangerous. This particular picture fostered a pugnacious party spirit which really expresses an ultimate lack of faith. They dared not modify, because they shirked the task of disengaging their spiritual message from the associations of a particular imagery.

Let me explain myself by an example. In the early medieval times, Heaven was in the sky, and Hell was underground; volcanoes were the jaws of Hell. I do not assert that these beliefs entered into the official formulations: but they did enter into the popular understanding of the general doctrines of Heaven and Hell. These notions were what everyone thought to be implied by the doctrine of the future state. They entered into the explanations of the influential exponents of Christian belief. For example, they occur in the *Dialogues* of Pope Gregory, the Great, a man whose high official position is surpassed only by the magnitude of his services to humanity. I am not saying what we ought to believe about the future state. But whatever be the right doctrine, in this instance the clash between religion and science, which has relegated the earth to the position of a second-rate planet attached to a second-rate sun, has been greatly to the benefit of the spirituality of religion by dispersing these medieval fancies.

Another way of looking at this question of the evolution of religious thought is to note that any verbal form of statement which has been before the world for some time discloses ambiguities; and that often such ambiguities strike at the very heart of the meaning. The effective sense in which a doctrine has been held in the past cannot be determined by the mere logical analysis of verbal statements, made in ignorance of the logical trap. You have to take into account the whole reaction of human nature to the scheme of thought. This reaction is of a mixed character, including elements of emotion derived from our lower natures. It is here that the impersonal criticism of science and of philosophy comes to the aid of religious evolution. Example after example can be given of this motive force in development. For example, the logical difficulties inherent in the doctrine of the moral cleansing of human nature by the power of religion rent Christianity in the days of Pelagius and Augustine— that is to say, at the beginning of the fifth century. Echoes of that controversy still linger in theology.

So far, my point has been this: that religion is the expression of one type of fundamental experiences of mankind: that religious thought develops into an increasing accuracy of expression, disengaged from adventitious imagery: that the interaction between religion and science is one great factor in promoting this development.

I now come to my second reason for the modern fading of interest in religion. This involves the ultimate question which I stated in my opening sentences. We have to know what we mean by religion. The churches, in their presentation of their answers to this query, have put forward aspects of religion which are expressed in terms either suited to the emotional reactions of bygone times or directed to excite modern emotional interests of nonreligious character. What I mean under the first heading is that religious appeal is directed partly to excite that instinctive fear of the wrath of a tyrant which was inbred in the unhappy populations of the arbitrary empires of the ancient world, and in particular to excite that fear of an all-powerful arbitrary tyrant behind the unknown forces of nature. This appeal to the ready instinct of brute fear is losing its force. It lacks any directness of response, because modern science and modern conditions of life have taught us to meet occasions of apprehension by a critical analysis of their causes and conditions. Religion is the reaction of human nature to its search for God. The presentation of God under the aspect of power awakens every modern instinct of critical reaction. This is fatal; for religion collapses unless its main positions command immediacy of assent. In this respect the old phraseology is at variance with the psychology of modern civilizations. This change in psychology is largely due to science, and is one of the chief ways in which the advance of science has weakened the hold of the old religious forms of expression. The non-religious motive which has entered into modern religious thought is the desire for a comfortable organization of modern society. Religion has been presented as valuable for the ordering of life. Its claims have been rested upon its function as a sanction to right conduct. Also the purpose of right conduct quickly degenerates into the formation of pleasing social relations. We have here a subtle degradation of religious ideas, following upon their gradual purification under the influence of keener ethical intuitions. Conduct is a by-product of religion—an inevitable by-product, but not the main point. Every great religious teacher has revolted against the presentation of religions as a mere sanction of rules of conduct. Saint Paul denounced the Law, and Puritan divines spoke of the filthy rags of righteousness. The insistence upon rules of conduct marks the ebb of religious fervor. Above and beyond all things, the religious life is not a research after comfort. I must now state, in all diffidence, what I conceive to be the essential character of the religious spirit.

Religion is the vision of something which stands beyond, behind, and within, the passing flux of immediate things; something which is real, and yet waiting to be realized; something which is a remote possibility, and yet the greatest of present facts; something that gives meaning to all that passes, and yet eludes apprehension; something whose possession is the final good, and yet is beyond all reach; something which is the ultimate ideal, and the hopeless quest.

The immediate reaction of human nature to the religious vision is worship. Religion has emerged into human experience mixed with the crudest fancies of barbaric imagination. Gradually, slowly, steadily the vision recurs in history under nobler form and with clearer expression. It is the one element in human experience which persistently shows an upward trend. It fades and then recurs. But when it renews its force, it recurs with an added richness and purity of content. The fact of the religious vision, and its history of persistent expansion, is our one ground for optimism. Apart from it, human life is a flash of occasional enjoyments lighting up a mass of pain and misery, a bagatelle of transient experience.

The vision claims nothing but worship; and worship is a surrender to the claim of assimilation, urged with the motive force of mutual love. The vision never overrules. It is always there, and it has the power of love presenting the one purpose whose fulfilment is eternal harmony. Such order as we find in nature is never force—it presents itself as the one harmonious adjustment of complex detail. Evil is the brute motive force of fragmentary purpose, disregarding the eternal vision. Evil is overruling, retarding, hurting. The power of God is the worship He inspires. That religion is strong which in its ritual and its modes of thought evokes an apprehension of the commanding vision. The worship of God is not a rule of safety—it is an adventure of the spirit, a flight after the unattainable. The death of religion comes with the repression of the high hope of adventure.

REINHOLD NIEBUHR

Christ vs. Socrates[1]

The discussion in a group of enlightened moderns centered on comparison of the outstanding moral exemplars in world history. Inevitably, as in college days of bygone years, Socrates and Christ were presented as outstanding exemplars of virtue. That was not surprising. In purely moral terms there was little to choose between the "martyrdom" of the two: Socrates drinking the cup of hemlock and Jesus on the Cross. (It is significant that a martyr's death is regarded as the supreme act of goodness in an age which implicitly defines the end of life as "the pursuit of happiness." But perhaps this observation is beside the point.) The point of the discussion was that the champions of Socrates were quite convinced that Christ would have a far better chance with our generation if Christians did not insist on confusing the issue by making absurd claims for His divinity. These claims, it was felt, were unfair and prejudiced His example.

This debate illustrates the profound misunderstanding between a so-called "secular" and idealistic culture and the character of the Christian faith. The idea that Christians are unenlightened people who insist on incredible divinities in human life is very widespread. It obscures the real debate between a "Socratic" and a Christian view of man and the mystery of existence. And this second debate is centered on different issues from the relative merits of Jesus and Socrates as moral exemplars.

We may define as "Socratic" any view which shares Socrates's conviction that men "would do the good if they only knew it." This conviction makes virtue the consequence of reason and naturally assumes that the only prerequisite of good conduct is the right formula and exemplar of good conduct. In contrast to this Socratic view, which has been accepted by most moderns since the Renaissance, and which seemed to have triumphed completely over Christianity in the eighteenth and nineteenth centuries, we can put the simple Pauline confession: "The good that I would do I do not do and the evil that I would not, that I do." According to the Christian interpretation every man is at variance with himself and ultimately with God because there is a "law in his members which wars against the law that is in his mind." The acceptance of the highest ideals of conduct is no guarantee against the force of self-regard, expressed either individually or collectively. Much evil is undoubtedly done in sheer stupidity, but the basic human problem is the constant ex-

[1] From *The Saturday Review*, XXXVII (December 18, 1954). Copyright 1954 by Saturday Review Associates, Inc. Reprinted by permission of the author and of Saturday Review Associates, Inc.

pression of the self's pride, will-to-power, and avarice. Bertrand Russell defines the basic human inclination as the desire for "power and glory." That is probably as good a definition of sin as any.

But what has this analysis of the human situation—which any thoughtful observer must recognize as being more illuminating about man, particularly man in the contemporary setting, than all the Socratic interpretations which try to derive virtue from intelligence—what has this to do with the worship of Christ as a revelation of God?

In answering that question we must recognize that interpretations of the self and of the ultimate mystery of existence are closely related. The conception of the self's freedom to defy the laws of its own existence is part and parcel of the Christian conception of the self's radical freedom, particularly its freedom over its own mind. In short, the self has a mystery which cannot be equated with its reason. The self uses its reason but it is not reason. The self has the freedom to transcend nature and reason to survey all the world's coherences and rational intelligibilities and to inquire after the source and end of the meaning of its existence. This freedom either proves the existentialists right in their insistence that the self has no law but its freedom; or it points to the validity of the Biblical faith that there is a deeper and higher source of meaning than the coherences discovered by science and philosophy. The Biblical faith, in short, does not equate God with cosmic reason any more than it equates the self with its own reason. It declares that the mystery of the divine is related to the mystery of creation, and that creation is not identical with the causal sequences which science can chart. The worship of God is thus in the first instance the worship of "God, the Almighty maker of heaven and earth," the mysterious power transcending the causal sequences and coherences of the world. It must be noted that only on the presupposition of such a God does the self have "headroom" for the unique freedom which gives it a vantage point above natural and rational coherences. This divine source and end of all things is a mystery beyond every rational intelligibility, though it is the capstone of every system of meaning.

Perhaps the reader will impatiently insist that faith in a mysterious creator-God and the knowledge of the radical character of human freedom still leave us far from any knowledge of faith in Christ as the revelation of God. In an effort to draw nearer it may be relevant to observe that the modern "Socratic" culture has not stated the questions for which such a faith is the answer, even if it acknowledged the reality and the "dignity" of human selfhood. It did not do so because it prided itself on the "dignity" of man but never came to terms with the "misery" of man. Briefly, that "misery" is man's inclination to use his freedom not as the instrument of virtue, but as a tool of self-glorification, and consequently as an instrument of social strife and injustice. There has been a strain of uneasy conscience in human life, to which the Babylonian penitential Psalms and the Pyramid texts of Egypt first gave eloquent expression. It expressed itself before and outside of the Biblical faith. It has only been in this post-Christian era of Western civilization that men have tried to obscure the guilt, in which all men are involved, and to pretend that the problem of being "good" could be solved if only men had the proper moral exemplars. Ironically enough, it is this age which has involved us in the collective guilt of possible atomic warfare and has initiated even the "pure" scientists into the problem of guilt, as they found themselves unwittingly becoming the weapon-manufacturers of an atomic age.

Through all ages men have wondered about the divine mystery which hovered over the strange drama of human history and was obviously more than the mystery of creation. They felt that the meaning in the mystery obviously spelled judgment upon evil, but they wondered how mercy and forgiveness were related to the judgment.

It was to these questions that the revelation in Christ offered the definitive answer. The Church was founded on the faith that this revelation was final and definitive. The drama of Christ's life was seen by faith to be more than a drama in history, and therefore Jesus was more than a revered historical martyr. This drama furnished the clue to the ultimate mystery. Through it faith was able to discern that the power of God and the love of God are one; and that the love of God contains both the severity of his justice and the kindness of his mercy to those who contritely acknowledge their sins and cease to pretend that men are virtuous and possess a "dignity" which is not contaminated by the false and idolatrous use they make of their freedom. The Christian doctrine of the "Atonement" asserts that judgment and forgiveness are contradictory, yet two facets of the same divine love. Those who recognize this clue to the mystery will stop pretending they are more righteous than they are; and will, with broken spirit and contrite heart, be enabled to live charitably with their neighbors.

Humility is the basis of charity. This age, which has extolled "humanism" so much, is singularly lacking in the spirit of charity. It is filled with the fury of self-righteousness expressed by the warring political, national, and rationalistic and pious groups. A few intellectuals, having discerned the mystery of selfhood above the level of nature, have found Christian faith incredible and have preferred the mystical way defined by—among others—Aldous Huxley in "The Perennial Philosophy." These intellectuals seem not to have noticed that this alternative does indeed assert a divine, but also a total mystery. It suggests an "eternity" which may purify, but which also annuls, history with all its strange dramas, its joys and its sorrows, its responsibilities, victories, and defeats. It also annuls the meaning of the existence of this strange creature—the human individual.

To assert that the Jesus of history is the Christ, and that "God was in Christ reconciling the world unto Himself," is an affirmation of faith which insists that the variance between man and God cannot be finally overcome by the virtue of man. All human virtue remains ambiguous to the end. It can be overcome only by a "suffering" God who takes the sins of the world upon Himself.

Of course, this faith will seem quite incredible to modern men partly because they have suppressed the internal problems of the human soul for which it is the answer, and partly because they find it difficult to believe that a character and drama in history are lifted into the ultimate dimension as a clue to the very meaning and mystery of existence. They are accustomed to find the ultimate either in some eternal pattern within the flux of the temporal or (in more modern terms) to find the very flux to be the ultimate (Bergson).

Nevertheless, it is not only the modern mind which finds the affirmation that a crucified Saviour is the "very image of God" scandalous. St. Paul gloried in the fact that this faith was a scandal but nevertheless that it was, once accepted, the source of "wisdom and power." In other words, it is incredible in prospect but the source of wisdom in retrospect. It furnishes the clue through which we can make sense out of the seeming nonsense of the historical drama and the drama of our own existence.

When the problems of man are deeply felt men will come to such a faith in any age, no matter how sophisticated it may think itself. Thus, Pascal lived in an age dominated by Cartesian rationalism. He was himself a very great mathematician and scientist. He could not, of course, find peace in the knowledge of "the God of the philosophers," which means the God revealed in the rational or natural structure of things but having no word of judgment and mercy for proud and tortured human souls. We have no Pascal in our own day to match our numerous Cartesian rationalists. But Pascal's experience is undoubtedly analogous to the experience of many who have found their way back to faith in the "God and Father of our Lord Jesus Christ" even under the derision of their peers, who worried about the growing "irrationalism" and piety of a culture which had so recently celebrated its emancipation from every religious belief.

The figure of Christ in Christian faith is not that of a theophany—a miraculous appearance of the divine in history. Even those traditions which insist upon the Virgin Birth as a part of the accreditation of His divinity fully understand that He was "true man." He walked on earth, subject to the necessities of human life, and did not escape either death or the tragedy of martyrdom. But it is not in the first instance as moral exemplar that He is the key figure in Christian faith, though He is defined in the tradition as the "second Adam," who restores the lost innocence of man and defines the *summum bonum* of human life. In brief, that is the sacrificial love which His life incarnated. But when modern Christians sought to interpret Him merely as man, as moral example, in trying to adjust themselves to the prejudices of the age, they succeeded only in reducing the Christian faith to the general moral sentimentality of the age or even in aggravating that sentimentality. This was true because this view of Christ rested upon a false estimate of human nature. According to that view love was a simple possibility of human existence. The

power and persistence of self-regard were obscured. An ancillary consequence
was that Christian thought became as irrelevant to every political problem as
did every other form of modern utopianism.

There is thus a vast difference in seeing in Jesus an exemplar of the nobility of
vicarious suffering, from regarding the whole drama of His life as "the light
that shineth in darkness" as a revelation of the mystery of God's justice and
mercy as it comes to terms with the perpetual rebellion of human ambitions
against the divine will. To regard Him as this key which resolves mystery into
meaning is to look at the whole drama of human existence without either obscuring the tragic factors in man's persistent egotism or in seeking vain
methods of eliminating that egotism by mystical techniques of self-annulment
or dangerous political strategies of suppressing self-interest, the most consistent form of which has generated the horrible tyranny of Communism.
These alternative techniques are defined in Koestler's "The Yogi and the
Commissar."

The Christian answer to the problem is that there are indeterminate possibilities of escaping from the prison-house of self and establishing creative relations with our fellows, both by the shattering of the self-concerned self through
divine judgment and by the operations of "common grace," which is to say, the
erosion of egotism through our affections and responsibilities. But there is no
final possibility of an ultimate redemption of the self from itself. In the end
God must take the sins of human history upon Himself and heal the breach
between man and God. Wherever that is recognized it is possible for sinful
men to lead charitable lives because the fury of their self-righteousness has
been overcome and they know themselves to be "forgiven sinners." The New
Testament is full of admonitions which are well summarized in the Pauline
advice "Be ye kindly affectioned one with another, forgiving each other as God
also in Christ has forgiven you."

It is this sense of humility and contrition which must restore the lost
charity and humaneness of an age which is submerged in all the inhumanities
of self-righteous men who suppose that they can establish a more genuine
"humanity" with enlightenment and moral idealism. Men do not forgive
each other because they are compelled by duty to do so. This kind of charity is
beyond the power of the sense of obligation. It is possible only to those who are
of "broken spirit and contrite heart." In short, the principles by which modern men have sought to do justice to the drama of human existence have been
inadequate to contain either the heights or the depths of the drama or the
complexities of the endless variations of love and self-love in human history.
The "humanitarian" principles have been drawn from either nature or reason.
But man in his freedom is not contained in either nature or mind. He is able
to elaborate an historical drama in which he discerns more or less rational
"causes and effects," but the ultimate dimension and motif of the world transcend every system of rational intelligibility. Life ends in mystery. The issue
between Christianity, with its assertion of a "revelation" which has pierced the

mystery and given it meaning, and classical mysticism is whether the final mystery annuls all historical meanings or whether meaning can feed on mystery on the one hand even as it must be supported by rational intelligibility on the other hand.

A final word must be said about the way Christians enter into this debate on Christ and modern culture. They are certainly justified to call attention to ironic distortions which have overwhelmed the idealism, the humanism, and the utopianism of modern culture and have given new relevance to the Christian interpretation of life. But every lesson thus learned can be obscured if Christians fail to understand that piety as well as "idealism" can be made the servant of human self-esteem, that religion has been as fruitful of fanaticism as of charity in the past and present; that modern culture began with a justified protest against religiously inspired fanaticism; and that the religious life is frequently conventional, bigoted, narrow, and graceless. An adequate view of life from the standpoint of the Christian revelation must be able to appreciate all the virtues which may develop through cultural enlightenment and to know that religion may be the engine of cruelty.

If this is not done Christ ceases to be the mediator of the divine judgment and mercy upon all men and becomes the dubious ally of the pious "righteous" against the "secular humanists." It is certainly revealing about human nature that pious men are as rarely truly charitable as rationalists are "reasonable." This is so because both use their supposed devotion to God or the "truth" as an instrument of the self. True Christians will understand this better than the pure rationalists. But they are not true Christians if they imagine that their understanding of the mysteries of sin is a badge of virtue.

Thus, one writes apologetically of the Christian faith. A humanist and idealist generation is prepared to entertain the "moral ideals" of Jesus if only the Christians will abate their claims of His divinity. But involved in those claims is the whole Biblical view of the character of the human drama and of the self-contradiction in which all men are involved. It has become fashionable among some Christians to assert that the Christian ethic, which even secular humanists cherish, is not possible without "faith in God." We accuse the Communists of being "atheists," and imply that faith in God will somehow guarantee virtue. But these defenses of the faith miss the point. The question is whether the self has encountered at the ultimate reaches of consciousness the God both just and merciful, and whether the self has no illusions about itself on the one hand and no despair about the inner contradictions of the soul. The question in short is whether it has encountered the "God who is revealed in Christ." From that encounter come the "truth and grace" which make it possible to enjoy the beauty of life and to be unafraid of its terrors; to assume responsibilities in the complex tasks of achieving community and justice amidst the claims and counter-claims of men without either seeking the perfect and impossible solution or of being unconscious of the dangers of trying.

One word must be said about the explicit faith which must be summoned for the venture of accepting Christ as the revelation of the mystery of the divine, particularly the mystery of the divine justice and mercy. Every world view, philosophy, or religion rests upon an act of faith. But most faith is implicit rather than explicit. The commitment of faith is obscured by the belief that the view is arrived at not by faith, but by a rational analysis of the coherences of the world. The liberal idea of historical progress and the Marxist idea of an historical dialectic are both faiths; and both faiths have some evidence to support them. But they both depend upon a commitment which selects the evidence by which they are supposedly supported. Whether the faith is implicit or explicit it must ultimately be validated by the evidence, but the commitment tends to select the evidence.

The Christian commitment is more explicit than any of its secular alternatives because it deals with discontinuities rather than continuities, with the human person and with the person of God in their respective freedoms. Personality is imbedded in an order, but it rises in freedom above its organism. The relation between personalities must be by faith and love rather than by reason because persons are discrete, unique, and discontinuous; they cannot be comprehended in a rational form. In terms of Biblical faith the encounter between man and God is analogous to the encounter between persons. Personality, or any other human quality, is ascribed to God with due regard to the inadequacy of analogy. But analogy is necessary to emphasize a freedom in both God and man, above the organism of man and above the order of the world. In this encounter the fact that man has made a false use of his freedom to center life upon and in himself is discovered. Therefore, the encounter is one which produces an uneasy conscience in man. He discerns the divine judgment. The revelation in Christ assures man that there is not only judgment but mercy; that the two are facets of the same holiness and love, though justice and forgiveness stand in provisional contradiction to each other. If the judgment is accepted the forgiveness becomes a reality in a "new" life.

This is the revelation in Christ upon which the Christian church is founded and which is the capstone of a Christian view of life. The relative merits of Jesus and Socrates as exemplars of goodness have little relevance to this assurance. It must of course be accepted by faith. That is to say, there is no rational analysis of the structure of the world which compels anyone to accept the truth about himself and his relation to God. Such acceptance comes not primarily through the mind but through the whole personality. Faith requires repentance and repentance produces faith. In that sense the Christian faith is "existential." The "existing" individual ceases to be an observer of the world and comes to terms with his own situation ultimately. This observation might persuade us to say a qualifying word about Socrates. He is supposed to be the fountain and source of all rational identifications of virtue and reason. But after all it was Socrates who said "Know thyself." By that much the view of Socrates and Christ share a common "existentialism."

It is of course not easy to follow Socrates's advice within a Socratic framework. The problem of self-knowledge is essentially unsolved despite the glories of the psychological sciences. It is unsolved because the human self is a creature, and moreover a rational creature; but also one which possesses this curious yearning for the ultimate. Either the self engages in the abortive enterprise of regarding itself as ultimate (existentialism) or of losing itself, and annulling its contingent existence, in the ultimate (mysticism); or in finding itself in a dialogic relation with the divine. The revelation of Christ has meaning only in the context of such a dialogic relationship. The Christian faith stands or falls by the affirmation that true self-knowledge, in which the self becomes aware of both its dignity and its sinful self-assertion, is the fruit of such a dialogue. The Revelation in Christ is the definitive exposition of the character of the dialogue.

MARTIN BUBER

God and the Spirit of Man [1]

This book discusses the relations between religion and philosophy in the history of the spirit, and deals with the part that philosophy has played in its late period in making God and all absoluteness appear unreal.

If philosophy is here set in contrast to religion, what is meant by religion is not the massive fullness of statements, concepts, and activities that one customarily describes by this name and that men sometimes long for more than for God. Religion is essentially the act of holding fast to God. And that does not mean holding fast to an image that one has made of God, nor even holding fast to the faith in God that one has conceived. It means holding fast to the existing God. The earth would not hold fast to its conception of the sun (if it had one), nor to its connection with it, but to the sun itself.

In contrast to religion so understood, philosophy is here regarded as the process, reaching from the time when reflection first became independent to its more contemporary crisis, the last stage of which is the intellectual letting go of God.

This process begins with man's no longer contenting himself, as did the prephilosophical man, with picturing the living God, to whom one formerly only called—with a call of despair or rapture which occasionally became his first name—as a Something, a thing among things, a being among beings, an It.

---

[1] From *Eclipse of God: Studies in the Relation between Philosophy and Religion* (New York: Harper & Brothers, 1952), Chapter VIII. Copyright, 1952, by Harper & Brothers. Reprinted by permission. "God and the Spirit of Man" is the substance of a lecture delivered by Buber at a number of American universities in 1951.

The beginning of philosophizing means that this Something changes from an object of imagination, wishes, and feelings to one that is conceptually comprehensible, to an object of thought. It does not matter whether this object of thought is called "Speech" (*Logos*), because in all and each one hears it speak, answer, and directly address one; or "the Unlimited" (*Apeiron*), because it has already leapt over every limit that one may try to set for it; or simply "Being," or whatever. If the living quality of the conception of God refuses to enter into this conceptual image, it is tolerated alongside of it, usually in an unprecise form, as in the end identical with it or at least essentially dependent on it. Or it is depreciated as an unsatisfactory surrogate, helpful to men incapable of thought.

In the progress of its philosophizing, the human spirit is ever more inclined to fuse characteristically this conception, of the Absolute as an object of an adequate thought, with itself, the human spirit. In the course of this process, the idea which was at first noetically contemplated finally becomes the potentiality of the spirit itself that thinks it, and it attains on the way of the spirit its actuality. The subject, which appeared to be attached to being in order to perform for it the service of contemplation, asserts that it itself produced and produces being. Until, finally, all that is over against us, everything that accosts us and takes possession of us, all partnership of existence, is dissolved in free-floating subjectivity.

The next step already takes us to the stage familiar to us, the stage that understands itself as the final one and plays with its finality: the human spirit, which adjudges to itself mastery over its work, annihilates conceptually the absoluteness of the absolute. It may yet imagine that it, the spirit, still remains there as bearer of all things and coiner of all values; in truth, it has also destroyed its own absoluteness along with absoluteness in general. The spirit can now no longer exist as an independent essence. There now exists only a product of human individuals called spirit, a product which they contain and secrete like mucus and urine.

In this stage, there first takes place the conceptual letting go of God because only now philosophy cuts off its own hands, the hands with which it was able to grasp and hold him.

But an analogous process takes place on the other side, in the development of religion itself (in the usual broad sense of the word).

From the earliest times, the reality of the relation of faith, man's standing before the face of God, world-happening as dialogue, has been threatened by the impulse to control the power yonder. Instead of understanding events as calls which make demands on one, one wishes oneself to demand without having to hearken. "I have," says man, "power over the powers I conjure." And that continues, with sundry modifications, wherever one celebrates rites without being turned to the Thou and without really meaning its Presence.

The other pseudo-religious counterpart of the relation of faith, not so elementally active as conjuration but acting with the mature power of the intellect, is unveiling. Here one takes the position of raising the veil of the manifest, which divides the revealed from the hidden, and leading forth the divine mysteries. "I am," says man, "acquainted with the unknown, and I make it known." The supposedly divine It that the magician manipulates as the technician his dynamo, the gnostic lays bare—the whole divine apparatus. His heirs are not "theosophies" and their neighbors alone; in many theologies also, unveiling gestures are to be discovered behind the interpreting ones.

We find this replacement of I-Thou by an I-It in manifold forms in that new philosophy of religion which seeks to "save" religion. In it, the "I" of this relation steps ever more into the foreground as "subject" of "religious feeling," as profiter from a pragmatist decision to believe, and the like.

Much more important than all this, however, is an event penetrating to the innermost depth of the religious life, an event which may be described as the subjectivizing of the act of faith itself. Its essence can be grasped most clearly through the example of prayer.

We call prayer in the pregnant sense of the term that speech of man to God which, whatever else is asked, ultimately asks for the manifestation of the divine Presence, for this Presence becoming dialogically perceivable. The single presupposition of a genuine state of prayer is thus the readiness of the whole man for this Presence, simple-turned-towardness, unreserved spontaneity. This spontaneity, ascending from the roots, succeeds time and again in overcoming all that disturbs and diverts. But in this our stage of subjectivized reflection not only the concentration of the one who prays, but also his spontaneity, is assailed. The assailant is consciousness, the overconsciousness of this man here that he is praying, that he is *praying*, that *he* is praying. And the assailant appears to be invincible. The subjective knowledge of the one turning-toward about his turning-toward, this holding back of an I which does not enter into the action with the rest of the person, an I to which the action is an object—all this de-possesses the moment, takes away its spontaneity. The specifically modern man who has not yet let go of God knows what that means: he who is not present perceives no Presence.

One must understand this correctly: this is not a question of a special case of the known sickness of modern man, who must attend his own actions as spectator. It is the confession of the Absolute into which he brings his unfaithfulness to the Absolute, and it is the relation between the Absolute and him upon which this unfaithfulness works, in the midst of the statement of trust. And now he too who is seemingly holding fast to God becomes aware of the eclipsed Transcendence.

What is it that we mean when we speak of an eclipse of God which is even now taking place? Through this metaphor we make the tremendous assumption that we can glance up to God with our "mind's eye," or rather being's eye, as with our bodily eye to the sun, and that something can step between our existence and his as between the earth and the sun. That this glance of the being exists, wholly unillusory, yielding no images yet first making possible all images, no other court in the world attests than that of faith. It is not to be proved; it is only to be experienced; man has experienced it. And that other, that which steps in between, one also experiences, today. I have spoken of it since I have recognized it, and as exactly as my perception has allowed me.

The double nature of man, as the being that is both brought forth from "below" and sent from "above," results in the duality of his basic characteristics. These cannot be understood through the categories of the individual man existing-for-himself, but only through the categories of his existing as man-with-man. As a being who is sent, man exists over against the existing being before which he is placed. As a being who is brought forth, he finds himself beside all existing beings in the world, beside which he is set. The first of these categories has its living reality in the relation I-Thou, the second has its reality in the relation I-It. The second always brings us only to the aspects of an existing being, not to that being itself. Even the most intimate contact with another remains covered over by an aspect if the other has not become Thou for me. Only the first relation, that which establishes essential immediacy between me and an existing being, brings me precisely thereby not to an aspect of it, but to that being itself. To be sure, it brings me only to the existential meeting with it; it does not somehow put me in a position to view it objectively in its being. As soon as an objective viewing is established, we are given only an aspect and ever again only an aspect. But it is also only the relation I-Thou in which we can meet God at all, because of him, in absolute contrast to all other existing beings, no objective aspect can be attained. Even a vision yields no objective viewing, and he who strains to hold fast an afterimage after the cessation of the full I-Thou relation has already lost the vision.

It is not the case, however, that the I in both relations, I-Thou and I-It, is the same. Rather where and when the beings around one are seen and treated as objects of observation, reflection, use, perhaps also of solicitude or help, there and then another I is spoken, another I manifested, another I exists than where and when one stands with the whole of one's being over against another being and steps into an essential relation with him. Everyone who knows both in himself—and that is the life of man, that one comes to know both in himself and ever again both—knows whereof I speak. Both together build up human existence; it is only a question of which of the two is at any particular time the architect and which is his assistant. Rather, it is a question of whether the I-Thou relation remains the architect, for it is self-evident that it cannot be employed as assistant. If it does not command, then it is already disappearing.

In our age, the I-It relation, gigantically swollen, has usurped, practically uncontested, the mastery and the rule. The I of this relation, an I that possesses all, makes all, succeeds with all, this I that is unable to say Thou, unable to meet a being essentially, is the lord of the hour. This selfhood that has become omnipotent, with all the It around it, can naturally acknowledge neither God nor any genuine absolute which manifests itself to men as of non-human origin. It steps in between and shuts off from us the light of heaven.

Such is the nature of this hour. But what of the next? It is a modern super-stition that the character of an age acts as fate for the next. One lets it pre-scribe what is possible to do and hence what is permitted. One surely cannot swim against the stream, one says. But perhaps one can swim with a new stream whose source is still hidden? In another image, the I-Thou relation has gone into the catacombs—who can say with how much greater power it will step forth! Who can say when the I-It relation will be directed anew to its assisting place and activity!

The most important events in the history of that embodied possibility called man are the occasionally occurring beginnings of new epochs, determined by forces previously invisible or unregarded. Each age is, of course, a con-tinuation of the preceding one, but a continuation can be confirmation and it can be refutation.

Something is taking place in the depths that as yet needs no name. To-morrow even it may happen that it will be beckoned to from the heights, across the heads of the earthly archons. The eclipse of the light of God is no extinction; even tomorrow that which has stepped in between may give way.

JACQUES MARITAIN

Confession of Faith[1]

As a child I was brought up in "Liberal Protestantism." Later on I became acquainted with the different phases of secularistic thought. The scientist and phenomenist philosophy of my teachers at the Sorbonne at last made me de-spair of reason. At one time I thought I might be able to find complete certi-tude in the sciences, and Felix Le Dantec thought that my fiancée and I would become followers of his biological materialism. The best thing I owe to my studies at that time is that they let me meet, in the School of Sciences, the woman who since then has always, happily for me, been at my side in a perfect and blessed communion. Bergson was the first to answer our deep desire for metaphysical truth—he liberated in us the sense of the absolute.

Before being captured by St. Thomas Aquinas, I underwent some great in-fluences, those of Charles Péguy, Bergson, and Leon Bloy. A year after we met Bloy, my wife and I were baptized Catholics, and we chose him as our godfather.

It was after my conversion to Catholicism that I came to know St. Thomas. I had voyaged passionately among all the doctrines of modern philosophers and

1 From *The Social and Political Philosophy of Jacques Maritain*, edited by Joseph W. Evans and Leo R. Ward, copyright 1955 by Charles Scribner's Sons and re-printed with their permission.

had found in them nothing but deception and grandiose uncertainty. What I now experienced was like an illumination of reason. My vocation as philosopher became perfectly clear to me. *Woe to me if I do not thomisticize,* I wrote in one of my first books. And through thirty years of work and battles I have kept to this same path, with the feeling of sympathizing all the more profoundly with the researches, the discoveries and the agonies of modern thought, the more I tried to penetrate them with the light which comes to us from a wisdom worked out through the centuries, a wisdom resistant to the fluctuations of time.

In order to advance in this path we are obliged constantly to bring together singularly distant extremes, for no solution of our problems is found ready-made in the heritage of the ancients. We are also obliged to make a difficult sifting of the pure substance of truths which many a modern rejects in his loathing of the trashy opinions of the past, from all the dross, the prejudices, the out-of-date images and arbitrary constructions which many a traditionalist confuses with what is really worthy of being venerated by intelligence.

I have spoken of the different experiences through which I passed, because they gave me the occasion to try personally the state of mind of the idealist freethinker, of the inexperienced convert, and of the Christian who becomes aware, in proportion as his faith takes root, of the purifications to which that faith must be subjected. I was also able to obtain some experimental idea of what the anti-religious camp and the straddlers' camp are worth. Neither of them is worth very much. And the worst disgrace of the second camp is that it runs the risk of compromising along with itself the innocent and persecuted Church, the Mystical Body of Christ, whose essential life, *sine macula sine ruga,* is in the Truth and in the saints, and which travels towards its fullness through the weaknesses of its own and the ferocity of the world. In my view, God educates us through our deceptions and mistakes, in order to make us understand at last that we ought to believe only in Him and not in men—which readily brings one to marvel at all the good which is in men despite everything and at all the good they do in spite of themselves.

I have decidedly come to the conclusion that in practice there are only two ways to know the depths of things, or, if one wishes, two "wisdoms," each of them a kind of folly, though in opposite manners. One is the way of sinners, who in order to drain things to the dregs embrace the nothingness of which all things are made and thereby have a full experience of this world, in the evil of the world more than in its good. The other way is the way of the saints, who adhere to subsisting Goodness, maker of all things, and receive in love a full experience of God and of creation, and who stand surety for all the world by their suffering and compassion. Well, it is normal to hope that the disciples of vain wisdom, if they are not hardened by pride and if they are loyal to their own experience, will finally be saved "through fire" by the lovers of true wisdom. And if they should live to be converted, they will perhaps be harsher than others in censuring any of their brothers still in darkness, so that, after having long tasted the delights of the world, they will taste for a moment the delights of their virtues and will continue vain till the last day, till they enter eternity.

This is not the place to give an exposition of theses in speculative philosophy. I will only say that I consider Thomistic philosophy to be a living and present philosophy, with all the greater power to make conquests in new fields of discovery just because its principles are so firm and so organically bound together. Confronted with the succession of scientific hypotheses, some minds are surprised that anyone could find inspiration today in metaphysical principles acknowledged by Aristotle and Thomas Aquinas and rooted in the oldest intellectual heritage of the race. My reply is that the telephone and the radio do not prevent man from still having two arms, two legs and two lungs, or from falling in love and seeking happiness as did his faraway ancestors. Besides, truth recognizes no chronological criteria, and the art of the philosopher is not to be confused with the art of the great dressmakers.

On a deeper level, we must explain that progress in the sciences of phenomena, where the "problem" aspect is so characteristic, takes place chiefly by *substitution* of one theory for another which saved less well the known facts and phenomena; but in metaphysics and philosophy, where the "mystery" aspect is predominant, progress takes place chiefly by *deeper penetration*. Besides, the different philosophical systems, however ill founded they may be, constitute in some way, in their totality, a virtual and fluent philosophy, overlapping contrary formulations and unfriendly doctrines and carried along by the elements of truth they all contain. If, therefore, there exists among men a doctrinal organism entirely supported by true principles, it will incorporate—more or less tardily, due to the laziness of its defenders—it will progressively realize within itself this virtual philosophy, and this will thereby, and in a proportionate degree, take on form and organic arrangement. Such is my idea of progress in philosophy.

If I say next that the metaphysics which I hold to be founded on truth may be described as a critical realism and as a philosophy of intelligence and of being, or still more precisely as a philosophy of the *act of existing* regarded as the act and perfection of all perfections, these formulas, of course, will be of interest only to specialists. A brief reflection on the historical significance of modern philosophy will no doubt be more appropriate.

In the Middle Ages, philosophy was in fact ordinarily treated as an instrument in the service of theology. Culturally, it was not in the state required by its nature. The coming of a philosophical or lay wisdom which had completed its own formation for itself and according to its own finalities was therefore a response to an historical necessity. But unfortunately this work was brought about under the aegis of division and of a sectarian rationalism; Descartes *separated* philosophy from any higher wisdom, from anything in man which comes from above man. I am convinced that what the world and civilization have lacked in the intellectual order for three centuries has been a philosophy which would develop its autonomous exigencies in a Christian climate, a wisdom of reason not closed but open to the wisdom of grace. Today reason must battle an irrational deification of elemental and instinctive forces that threatens to ruin all civilization. In this struggle, reason's task is one of integration; understanding that intelligence is not the enemy of mystery, but lives on it, reason must come to terms with the irrational world of affectivity and instinct, as well as with the world of the will, of freedom and of love, and the suprarational world of grace and of divine life.

The dynamic harmony of the degrees of knowledge will at the same time become manifest. From this point of view, the problem proper to the age we are entering will be, it seems, to reconcile *science* and *wisdom*. The sciences themselves seem to invite intelligence to this work. We see them stripping themselves of the remains of materialistic and mechanistic metaphysics which for a time hid their true features. They call for a philosophy of nature, and the wonderful progress in contemporary physics restores to the scientist the sense of the mystery stammered by the atom and by the universe. A critique of knowledge formed in a genuinely realist and metaphysical spirit has a chance henceforth to be heard when it affirms the existence of structures of knowledge specifically and hierarchically distinct—distinct, but not separated—and shows that they correspond to original types of explanation which cannot be substituted one for another.

The Greeks recognized the great truth that contemplation is in itself superior to action. But they at once transformed this truth into a great error: they believed that the human race exists for a few intellectuals. As they saw it, there was a category of specialists, the philosophers, who lived a superhuman life, and the properly human life, namely, civil or political life, existed to serve them. To serve civil or political life, in turn, there was the subhuman life of labor, which in final analysis was the life of the slave. The lofty truth of the superiority of the contemplative life was thus bound to a contempt for labor and to the evil of slavery.

Christianity transfigured all this. It taught men that love is of more value than intelligence. It transformed the notion of contemplation, which henceforth does not stop in the intellect, but only in the love of God, the contemplated object. It restored to action its human significance as a service to our neighbor, and rehabilitated work by disclosing in it a value of natural redemption, as it were, and even a natural prefiguration of the communications of charity. It called to the contemplation of the saints and to perfection, not a few specialists or privileged persons, but all men, who are all bound proportionately by the law of work. Man is at once "homo faber" and "homo sapiens," and he is "homo faber" before truly and actually being "homo sapiens" and in order to become the latter. In this way Christianity saved, but by transforming and delivering from the error which tainted it, the Greek idea of the superiority of the contemplative life.

The saints' contemplation completes and consummates a natural aspiration to contemplation consubstantial to man, of which the sages of India and Greece especially give testimony. It is through love that the knowledge of divine things becomes experimental and fruitful. And precisely because this knowledge is the work of love in act, it also passes into action by virtue of the very generosity and abundance of love, which is gift of self. Then action proceeds from the superabundance of contemplation, and that is why, far from suppressing action or being opposed to it, contemplation vivifies it. It is in this sense, which relates to the essential generosity of the contemplation of love, that we must recognize with Bergson, in the superabundance and excess of the giving of self shown by the Christian mystics, the sign of their success in reaching the heroic summit of human life.

The pursuit of the highest contemplation and the pursuit of the highest freedom are two aspects of the same pursuit. In the order of spiritual life, man aspires to a perfect and absolute freedom, and therefore to a superhuman condition; sages of all times give evidence of this. The function of law is a function of protection and education of freedom, the function of a pedagogue. At the conclusion of this tutelage the perfect spiritual man is freed from every servitude, even, St. Paul says, from the servitude of the law, because he does spontaneously what is of the law and is simply one spirit and one love with the Creator.

To my way of thinking, the pursuit of freedom is also at the base of the social and political problem. But in the order of temporal life, it is not a divine freedom which is the object of our desires, but rather a freedom proportionate to the human condition and to the natural possibilities of our earthly existence. It is important not to deceive ourselves on the nature of the good thus pursued. It is not simply the preservation of each one's *freedom of choice*, nor the social community's *freedom of power*. The good in question is the *freedom of expansion* of human persons making up a people and participating in its good. Political society has as an end to develop conditions of life in common which, while assuring first of all the good and peace of the whole, will positively aid each person in the progressive conquest of this freedom of expansion, a freedom which consists above all in the flowering of moral and rational life.

Thus justice and friendship are the very foundations of society's life; and it is to truly human goods that society ought to subordinate all material goods, technical progress and the implements of power which also make up part of society's common good.

I believe that historical conditions and the yet backward state of human development make it difficult for social life fully to reach its end, and that in regard to the possibilities and demands which the Gospel brings to us in the socio-temporal order, we are still in a prehistoric age. As we see today in the psychoses of the masses which adore Stalin or Hitler, or dream of exterminating certain groups that they judge to be diabolical, in particular the Jews, doubtless because they are the people of God, human collectivities bear such a burden of willingly diseased animality that it will still require many centuries for the life of personality to be able truly to take on among the masses the fullness to which it aspires. But it still remains that the end towards which social life of itself tends is to procure the common good of the multitude in such a way that the concrete person, not merely in a privileged class but in the entire mass, may truly reach that measure of independence which belongs to civilized life and which is assured alike by the economic guarantees of work and property, by political rights, civic virtues and the cultivation of the mind.

These ideas are tied up with wider views which seem to me most properly designated by the expression *integral humanism*, and which involve a whole philosophy of modern history. Such a humanism, considering man in the integral wholeness of his natural and supernatural being and setting no a priori limits to the descent of the divine into man, may also be called a humanism of the Incarnation.

In the socio-temporal order it does not ask men to sacrifice themselves to the imperialism of race, of class or of nation. It asks them to sacrifice themselves to a better life for their brothers and to the concrete good of the community of human persons. That is why it cannot be less than an heroic humanism.

It has often been remarked that "bourgeois" liberalism, which tries to base everything on the individual taken as a little god and on his good pleasure, on an absolute freedom of ownership, of business and the pleasures of life, ends up fatally in statism. The rule of numbers produces the omnipotence of the State, of a ruminant or plutocratic State. Communism may be regarded as a reaction against this individualism. It claims to be orientated towards the absolute emancipation of man, who would thus become the god of history, but in reality this emancipation, supposing it were accomplished, would then be that of collective man, not that of the human person. Society as economic community would enslave the whole life of the person, because the essential work of civil society would be made to consist in economic functions, instead of subordinating this work to the freedom of expansion of persons: what the Communists propose as the emancipation of collective man would be the enslavement of human persons.

What of the anti-communist and anti-individualistic reactions of a totalitarian or dictatorial type? It is not in the name of the social community and the freedom of collective man, it is in the name of the sovereign dignity of the State, a state of the carnivorous type, or in the name of the spirit of a people, in the name of race or of blood, that they would annex man in his entirety to a social whole where the person of the ruler is the only one, properly speaking, to enjoy the privileges of personality. This is why totalitarian states, needing for themselves the total devotion of the person and having no sense of or respect for the person, inevitably seek a principle of human exaltation in myths of external grandeur and in the never-ending struggle for power and prestige. By its nature this tends to war and the self-destruction of the civilized community. If there are people in the Church—and they are fewer and fewer—who count on dictatorships of this kind to promote the religion of Christ and Christian civilization, they forget that the totalitarian phenomenon is an aberrant religious phenomenon in which an earthly mysticism devours every other mysticism whatever it may be, and will tolerate none besides itself.

Confronted with "bourgeois" liberalism, communism and totalitarian statism, what we need, I do not cease to say, is a new solution, one that is at the same time personalist and communal, one that sees human society as an organization of freedoms. We are thus brought to a conception of democracy, the community of free men, very different from that of Jean-Jacques Rousseau. We may call it *pluralist*, because it requires that the body politic guarantee the organic freedoms of the different spiritual families and different social bodies assembled within it, beginning with the basic natural community, the society of the family. The drama of modern democracies is that, under the appearance of an error—the deification of a fictitious individual entirely closed up in himself—they have without knowing it pursued a good thing: the expansion of the real person open to higher realities and to the common service of justice and friendship.

Personalist democracy holds that each is called, by virtue of the common dignity of human nature, to participate actively in political life, and that those who hold authority—which is a vital function in society and a real right to direct people—should be freely designated by the people. This is why personalist democracy sees in universal suffrage the first practical token by which a democratic society becomes aware of itself and which it may not in any case renounce. It has no better or more meaningful motto than the republican motto, understood as indicating, not an established condition in which man has only to be installed, but an end to be reached, a difficult and lofty goal to which man must tend by force of courage, justice and virtue. For freedom must be conquered, by the progressive elimination of the several forms of servitude, and it is not enough to proclaim equality of the fundamental rights of human persons, whatever one's race, one's religion, one's condition. This equality ought to pass in a real way into custom and into social structures and ought to yield fruit in a larger and larger participation by all in the common good of civilization. Finally, fraternity in the body politic requires that the loftiest and most generous of virtues, the love to which the Gospel has called our ungrateful species, pass into the very order of political life. A personalist democracy is not really conceivable without the super-elevations which nature and temporal civilizations receive, each in its own order, from the energies of the Christian leaven.

I am convinced that the coming of such a democracy, which presupposes that class antagonism has been overcome, demands that, by a genuine renewal of life and of justice, we truly go beyond "capitalism" and beyond socialism, each of which is vitiated by a materialistic conception of life. Nothing is more opposed to personalist democracy than fascist totalitarianism—whether social-nationalist or national-socialist; for it goes beyond "capitalism" only through the paroxysm of the evils it begets.

Let me remark that Christians are confronted today, in the socio-temporal order, with problems quite similar to those their sixteenth- and seventeenth-century ancestors encountered in the area of the philosophy of nature. At that time modern physics and astronomy, then in their beginnings, were simply one with philosophies set against tradition. The defenders of tradition did not know how to make the necessary distinctions. They took sides against what was to become modern science, at the same time that they took sides against the philosophical errors which at the start were parasitic on science. It took three centuries to get rid of this misunderstanding, if indeed the world is yet rid of it. It would be a sad story if we should be guilty today, in the field of practical and social philosophy, of like errors.

In the words of Pope Pius XI, the great scandal of the nineteenth century was the divorce of the working classes from the Church of Christ. In the temporal order, the moral secession of the working masses from the political community was a comparable tragedy. The awakening in the working masses of what the socialist vocabulary calls "class consciousness" appears to us as a great gain, so far as we see in it man's becoming aware of an offended and humiliated human dignity and of a vocation. But it has been chained to an historic calamity, because this awakening has been spoiled by the gospel of despair and of social warfare which is at the bottom of the Marxist idea of class struggle and the dictatorship of the proletariat. And it was precisely into this *secessionist* conception, whose protagonist was Marx and whose demand is that proletarians of all countries should recognize no other common good than that of their class, that the blindness of the possessing classes in the nineteenth century precipitated the working masses.

Whoever has pondered on these fundamental facts and on the history of the labor movement understands that the central problem of our times is the temporal and spiritual problem of the *reintegration of the masses*. In my view, it is only an artificial and illusory solution of this problem when the attempt is made, as in the case of German National Socialism, to manufacture happy slaves through violence linked with material ameliorations good in themselves but achieved in a spirit of domination, and with a psychotechnic solicitude vowed to satisfy and to benumb appetites. The fact is that one manufactures only unhappy slaves, robots of non-being.

However difficult, slow and painful it may be, the reintegration of the proletariat within the national community, not to exercise a class dictatorship in it, but to collaborate body and soul in the work of the community, will take place really, which means humanly, only by a recasting of social structures worked out in the spirit of justice. I am not naïve enough to believe that this reintegration can be accomplished without knocks and sacrifices, on the one hand as regards the well-being of the privileged sons of fortune and on the other as regards the theories and the destructive instincts of fanatical revolutionaries. But I am persuaded that it requires above all else the free cooperation of the workers' leaders (elites) and of the masses who follow them, and this cooperation must go along with a better general understanding of historical realities and with an awareness, not wiped out but heightened, of the human being's dignity as worker and citizen. In like manner the return of the masses to Christianity will be brought about only through love, I mean love stronger than death, the fire of the Gospel.

We shall never give up hope of a new Christendom, a new temporal order of Christian inspiration. Now the means should correspond to the end, and already are the end itself as in the state of movement and preparation. If this is so, it is clear that in order to prepare a Christian social order we must use Christian means, that is to say true means, just means, and these are means animated, even when they are of necessity harsh, by a genuine spirit of love. In two books published in 1930 and 1933 [2] I have insisted at length on these axiomatic truths. Nothing is more serious or scandalous than to see, as we have for some years seen in certain countries, iniquitous and barbarous means used by men in the name of Christian order and Christian civilization. It is a truth embedded in the very nature of things that Christendom will be renewed through Christian means or it will be completely eclipsed.

The present state of nations obliges us to declare that never has the spirit been so profoundly humiliated in the world. And yet pessimism in the end always dupes itself. It disregards the great law which may be called the law of the double movement involving the energy of history. While the wear and tear of time naturally dissipates and degrades the things of this world and the "energy of history," and this means the mass of human activity on which the movement of history depends, the creative forces which are characteristic of spirit and freedom and are a witness to them, forces which ordinarily find their point of application in the effort of the few—who are thereby bound to sacrifice—improve more and more the quality of this energy. This is exactly the work of the sons of God in history, it is the work of Christians if they do not belie their name.

People do not understand this work at all if they imagine that it aims at installing the world in a state from which all evil and all injustice would have disappeared. If this were the aim, it would be quite easy, considering the results, stupidly to condemn the Christian as utopian. The work the Christian has to do is to keep up and to increase in the world the internal tension and movement of slow and painful deliverance, a tension and movement due to the

[2] *Religion et culture; Du regime temporel et de la liberté.* (*Religion and Culture; Freedom in the Modern World.*)

invisible powers of truth and justice, of goodness and love, acting on the mass which is opposed to them. This work cannot be in vain, it assuredly bears its fruit.

Woe to the world should Christians turn their back on it, should they fail to do their work, which is to heighten here on earth the charge and tension of the spiritual; should they listen to blind leaders of the blind who seek the means to order and to good in things which of themselves lead to dissolution and death. We have no illusions about the misery of human nature and the malice of this world. But neither have we any illusions about the blindness and malfeasance of pseudo-realists who cultivate and exalt evil in order to fight evil, and who take the Gospel as a decorative myth which cannot be regarded seriously without wrecking the machinery of the world. They themselves, meantime, take it upon themselves to ruin, to distract, and to torment this unhappy world.

The ferment of the pharisees, against which Christ put us on our guard, is a permanent temptation for the religious conscience. Undoubtedly, this ferment will not be altogether driven out of the world till the end of history. Meantime, in the social as well as in the spiritual order, we must never let up the fight against it. However great may be the mass of evil which a mass of pharisaism means to oppose, the latter is always as great an evil, because the good it sets against that evil is a good which does not give life but kills, as does the letter without the spirit: it is a good which leaves God without resources in man.

One of the gravest lessons afforded us by the experience of life is that, in fact, in the practical conduct of most people, all those things which in themselves are good and very good—science, technical progress, culture, etc., and even the knowledge of moral laws, and religious faith itself, faith in the living God (which of itself demands the love of charity)—all these things, *without love and good will*, serve to make men all the more evil and the more unhappy. So far as religious faith is concerned, this was demonstrated in the Spanish civil war by the inhuman feelings that surged up in the "crusaders" as well as in the "reds," but were confirmed in the former in the sanctuary of the soul. What happens is that, without love and charity, man turns the best in him into an evil that is yet greater.

When one has understood this, he no longer puts his hope on earth in anything less than that good will of which the Gospel speaks—it speaks of good will, not of good velleity; he puts his hope in these obscure energies of a little real goodness which persists in making life germinate and regerminate in the secret depths of things. There is nothing more destitute, nothing more hidden, nothing nearer to the weakness of the infant. And there is no wisdom more fundamental or more effective than that simple and tenacious confidence, not in the means of violence, deceit and malice, which certainly are capable of crushing men and of triumphing, but which a grain of sand is nevertheless enough to cause to be smashed one against the other—but simple and tenacious confidence in the resources of personal courage to give oneself, and of good will set to do as one ought the tasks of every day. Through this disinterested spirit flows the power of nature and the Author of nature.

GEORGE HEDLEY

Frontiers of Religion[1]

Religion is probably the hardest subject in the world to approach objectively. By its very nature it appeals to and seizes upon the emotions of men and women—either positively or negatively. And not only its emotional content hampers exact learning. Since religion concerns itself with the invisible values of life, it depends especially on symbols for its expression—symbols as words themselves, or as other less explicit sights and sounds. That precise verbal statement of meaning which scholars yearn for is unattainable.

Nevertheless in recent years the scholarly study of religion as one of the fundamental ways of human acting, thinking, and feeling—and as our most rewarding way of reaching out beyond ourselves—has developed with a speed and a scope unparalleled in the past.

The literature, history, and psychology of religion have become separate disciplines. The search for meaning has led to a new and intense interest in the philosophy of religion, and in the exploration of symbolic means of religious expression—in liturgies, in the arts, and above all in theology. Even the emotional and symbolic limitations to what we call the "scientific method" of scholarship are leading to new understanding when studied in themselves.

Because scientific inquiry has been most highly developed in the West, it is within the Hebrew-Christian tradition that we look first for new knowledge about both the symbols and the substance of religion.

The documents come first in the story. It is true that some of the Hebrew prophets violently repudiated parts of the Hebrew Law, and that the early Christian Fathers held conflicting views, and conducted completely free debates, about the authorship of many of the books of the New Testament. As time passed, however, the Bible came to be regarded as monolithic, infallible, and sacrosanct. In effect, the medieval Church left it in the background of a scene whose fore-stage was occupied by a mixture (scarcely a combination) of official dogmas and unofficial legends. Protestant rejection of the Church as final authority led to a new emphasis upon the Scriptures, but only very slowly to new techniques in studying them.

The major leaders of Protestantism engaged in no slavish devotion to the

[1] From *Harper's Magazine*, CCXIII (November, 1956), 40-45. Copyright by *Harper's Magazine*. 1956. Reprinted by permission of the author.

letter of the Scriptures. Martin Luther to all intents and purposes dropped the books of St. James, Esther, and the Revelation from his canon. John Calvin admitted no relationship between the Jewish Sabbath and the Christian Sunday. John Wesley excised the imprecatory Psalms from his Psalter. Alexander Campbell, of the Bible-centered Disciples of Christ, in 1826 declared the King James translation to be "in many instances incorrect." It was easier, however, for the mass of Christians (including the majority of clerics) to rest upon a single authority than to investigate a plurality of problems. Thus for some three hundred years Protestantism in general assumed the Scriptures to be not only the Word of God, but also his words; and another century-plus has not disabused either the typical believer or the typical unbeliever of the misconception that this is the standard Christian position.

Rebuilding the Bible

Fortunately, most official schools of theology of the Protestant denominations have not remained captives of this type of anti-intellectualism. (The Roman Catholic path, for many years parallel and often pioneering, diverged sharply after 1907, when Pope Pius X condemned "modernism" in his encyclical *Pascendi*.) From the early nineteenth century onward inquiring minds had seized upon the Biblical writings and grappled with the problems of their actual authorships, dates, and purposes. By a generation ago a number of findings of Biblical scholarship had moved from the realm of opinion into that of settled conclusion.

The "five books of Moses," plus many of the other narrative materials in the Old Testament, came to be seen as a weaving together of four major strands dating variously from 850 to perhaps 350 B.C., and representing not one but many different views both of the purposes of God and of the history of man. The book of Isaiah was seen to consist of an eighth-century work of demolition and a sixth-century one of reconstruction, and interpolations and additions were recognized in almost all of the books of the prophets. In the New Testament the letters of St. Paul were rearranged into chronological sequence, with only nine of the traditional fourteen now regarded as authentic writings of the apostle himself. The Gospel of St. Mark was recognized as a basic literary source for those of Sts. Matthew and Luke, while the Fourth Gospel was identified as being probably a Greek restatement of an originally Jewish faith.

One Old Testament example will show the kind of clarifying that ensued. As the record stands ostensibly, Abraham decides to offer his son Isaac as a sacrifice, but at the last minute learns better. Long afterward (five hundred years?) Moses forbids human sacrifice as the worst of Canaanite abominations. Yet two hundred years later still, the judge Jephthah sacrifices his own daughter in fulfillment of a hasty vow and is applauded for his fidelity if not for his good judgment. How sorely the sequence has confused and embarrassed many a sincere but uninformed Sunday School teacher!

Critical dating of the documents immediately makes sense out of this chaos. The Jephthah episode (Judges 11:29-40), latest in reputed occurrence, turns out to be the earliest in its recording: about the middle of the ninth century B.C. A century later a sensitive pioneer in morality mildly suggests, in his tale of Abraham (Genesis 22:1-19), that human sacrifice scarcely is essential to please the God of the Hebrew family. Finally, after another two hundred years, the time is ripe for the jurists of the "second law" (Deuteronomy 12:31) to issue the flat prohibition which to their mind should have come from Moses. Criticism thus at once relieves the tender modern conscience, and straightens out the order in which conscience grew in the ancient past.

Less easy for modern minds to digest, but not less important for religio-historical understanding, have been such contributions as the first notable one made by the many-sided Albert Schweitzer. Ostensibly a study of existing "lives of Christ," Schweitzer's *Quest of the Historical Jesus* (German 1906, English 1910) turned out to be the statement of a new and revolutionary thesis about the framework of Jesus' thinking. Schweitzer saw the whole gospel record in the light of Judeo-Christian pessimism about the existing world order, and the correlative expectation of its immediate and cataclysmic ending. Jesus, contended the *enfant terrible* who has become the white-haired saint of Lambarene, took this popular Jewish position for granted and taught with it as his basic assumption.

This was fearfully upsetting to many scholars trained in the "liberal" Biblical tradition. They had made up their minds, long ago, that they were under no compulsion to agree with every view stated in the Bible. Many of them, however, had fallen into the habit of expecting that at least the important sections and persons of the Bible would agree with them. There are few today who would follow Schweitzer in making Jesus' belief in the imminent end of the world the touchstone for all his mission, but there are fewer who would deny that this element was present and important. The total effect, and a happy one for accurate evaluation and for religious insight as well, has been greatly to reduce the tendency to make of the man of Galilee a modern liberal Christian, and therefore to identify him the more clearly as a real citizen of Palestine in the first century.

The Dead Sea Scrolls

The first period of modern religious scholarship, within Protestantism, was heavily Bible-centered. The very study of the Bible, however, demonstrated that the Bible was at least as much a product as it was a producer. Attention then had to be turned to extra-Biblical factors.

In its application to religion, archaeology has clarified history and has amplified understanding. Numerous Canaanite artifacts have been found at what are considered "Israelite" levels in the Palestinian city-mounds, indicating that the Israelite conquest was one largely of interpenetration rather than of total genocide. Particularly common are terra-cotta figurines of the goddess Astarte, with sexual characteristics greatly exaggerated. One realizes, looking at these, that the Israelite and Jewish prophets had reason for their passionate protest against the survival of Canaanite fertility rites.

At several Palestinian sites small and identical weights labeled *pim* have been discovered. These have served to translate a previously obscure line in I Samuel 13:21, "and it was a *pim* for (sharpening) the mattocks," and have confirmed the judgment that Philistia was in the iron age before Israel had attained to it. In general archaeological evidence has made the Philistines come alive as a powerful and able people, long the victims of enemy propaganda (Israelite, Egyptian, and Assyrian) and of their own literary silence.

Another effect of Biblical archaeology, parallel to that in the classical field, has been to affirm a good deal of tradition which in early "critical" times had been regarded as completely unhistorical. The second excavation at Jericho, after World War I, revealed an almost total destruction of the city about the middle of the fifteenth century B.C. Fitted together with Canaanite complaints of marauding tribes referred to as "Habiri," this at once helped to support the Biblical account of the Israelite invasion of Palestine and to fix its date during the XVIIIth rather than the XIXth dynasty of Egypt, some two hundred years earlier than the previously accepted dating. In numerous cases the evidence of building, destruction, and rebuilding during the period of the Israelite and Jewish kingdoms substantiates and clarifies the narratives found in the books of the Kings.

Excavation in the Egyptian oases has revealed, through a mass of non-literary papyri, that the Greek of the New Testament was precisely the colloquial speech of the Levant in the Hellenistic age. This not only has served to establish the character of early Christianity as a religion appealing consciously and unpretentiously to the common man, but also has provided new and vivid renderings for many New Testament words and phrases. Jesus crucified is, in the letter to the Galatians, no longer merely "openly set forth" but publicly "placarded"; the Law as "schoolmaster" is a tutor-slave; St. Paul does not "buffet" his body but "punishes" it as in a prize ring; and "Be not anxious" turns into "Don't skin yourself."

The most sensational find of recent years, and quite possibly the most important, has been that of the so-called "Dead Sea Scrolls." It will be a long time before the full content of these materials can be known. It will take many times as long till the inevitable battles about their significance will have been fought out. Two points, however, now are reasonably clear.

One is that at least we have actual manuscripts of some of the Hebrew scriptures, dating from almost a thousand years before those of the traditional ("Masoretic") Hebrew text, so that we are much nearer to the original readings, whether of disputed passages or of those that up to now have been taken for granted. The other is that the first century accounts of a monastic community known as the "Essenes," found in the works of Philo and Josephus, are so closely paralleled in the new discoveries as to give enhanced authority and additional meaning to those ancient writings. The implication that Jesus was directly influenced by the Essenes, or that he may indeed have been a member of the sect, will require further and very careful examination. The general effect to date is to reinforce the judgment which scholars long have held, to the effect that the recorded teachings of Jesus were unique in selection and implementation rather than in invention.

Light from the Dark Ages

Another expansion of interest beyond the Bible has been that into the history of the Christian Church in its first fifteen centuries. To most of the early Protestants this had seemed a period of decline and apostasy, well to be forgotten. The reaction of the Counter Reformation long tended to make historical studies on the Roman Catholic side polemical rather than exploratory. Both antagonists now are doing better: the Protestants trying to identify the real nature of historic Catholic Christianity, the Romans applying the canons of literary and historical criticism to their own tradition. Partisan interests are feebler far than they were a half-century ago.

Christian scholars thus are newly aware, even if the Protestant laity isn't, that Christianity has not only a long history before Jesus, but also a long and critically important history after him. The teaching of the Church is rooted indeed in the New Testament, but its flowering and its fruits are not all to be found there. Many of them came long after, and new and sometimes surprising growth continues even yet to appear.

Taking its theology largely from the historian Gibbon and the novelist Merezhkovsky, recent liberalism had considered the theological disputing of the fourth century to be a senseless quarreling about trivia. Patient and inquiring reading of the Fathers of the Church, and of the memoranda and decrees of the ecumenical councils, has shown that there were not only individual jealousies, and local quarrels, and cultural clashes between regions, and not only honest differences of opinion among churchmen. There were also basic and important differences in estimates of value. The notable case is that of the Trinitarian controversy: what was the mutual relationship of the Father, the Son, and the Holy Ghost? Here the resolution of the dispute in favor of a single God, manifested in three kinds of appearance to humanity, gave to the Christian fellowship an organic unity which it scarcely could have achieved and maintained if the opposing view, declaring the separation of the divine "persons" and the subordination of the second and third of them, had secured the majority vote.

The Byzantine tradition, long ignored by both Roman Catholics and Protestants as a fatty degeneration of the Christian heart and mind, turns out on re-examination to be rich not only in art works but also in important types of religious experience and expression. The folk faith of the Ethiopians, issuing in the elaboration of the cult of the Virgin; the liturgical riches of Constanti-

nople and Alexandria and Malabar; the quiet quest of the Holy Ghost in the
monasteries of Mount Athos; the development of the great Russian churches
from a blending of Mediterranean domes and snow-covered gables: all these
have captured the interest of scholarship, and all have much yet to yield in
data and in comprehension.

To us the story of Western Christendom is more familiar, if not yet
familiar enough. Others than G. K. Chesterton and Hilaire Belloc are realizing
that the "Middle Ages" were not a void between classical antiquity and
modern times, but vital creators of the world we live in. The medieval
scholastics and mystics and heretics are being restudied and ever and again
re-interpreted. The "reformers before the Reformation," and the founders
of Protestant movements large and small, are better known than they were,
and will be known better still. The broad churchmen of England, the Socialists of America, the sects of the underprivileged on both sides of the Atlantic,
the modern monks of Einsiedeln and Solesme, the theologians of Halle and
Copenhagen and Göttingen and New York, are integral to the patterns of
religion in the West. None may be omitted if our knowledge and our understanding are to be at all complete.

Approach to the Heathen

Nor is the Judeo-Christian tradition by any means all. "Comparative Religion," which began in medieval polemics against Islam, no longer is a tendentious comparison of the Christian ideal with the non-Christian actual, to the
necessary advantage of Christianity. Intelligence and conscience here again
have combined to require a fairer and a more accurate approach. The nineteenth century saw a vast amount of first translating of Indian, Persian, Chinese, and Arabic religious writings, and the twentieth is digging deeper into
their meanings.

Embarrassing to those who had thought of Christianity as a strictly unique
revelation, but greatly illumining to those who inquire to learn, is the discovery of many and great resemblances between the Christian and the "heathen" scriptures. Not only did ancient Babylonia have a flood myth comparable to the Israelite one of Noah, but the arid plateau of Persia turned out
to have its own parallel in the "seven fatal winters." Nationalism and uni-
versalism appeared in the Hindu Vedas much as they did in the Jewish
Psalms, and monotheism was declared with the same rigor by Mohammed as
it had been by the second Isaiah.

Something like the "Golden Rule" turned out to be pretty nearly universal.
Religious loyalty, at whatever cost to the individual, was as ringingly urged
(if to our minds as puzzlingly expressed) in the *Bhagavad-Gita* as in the
Revelation of St. John. Confucius evidently would have been quite at home
sitting among the wise men who compiled the book of Proverbs, and Laotse
would have said, of the *Logos* of the Fourth Gospel, "This 'Word' is just

what I mean by the *Tao.*" Some deprecated these similarities as mere matters of chance. To others they were new and encouraging evidence that God has not left himself without a witness among any people, that human values and aspirations are essentially alike wherever men think intently and live seriously.

Identity is not all, and comparison with Christianity is not the only, nor the necessary, technique in the approach to the religions of the Orient. Not a few Occidentals, including a striking number of psychiatrists, have found Buddhism, in one or another of its myriad types of expression, to be the religious answer they personally want. Whether or not there is such conversion, there needs to be quite as much scholarly work done on the proliferation of Buddhist movements as there has been on the multiple forms of Christianity; and the complexities of Hinduism and Islam turn out to be scarcely fewer or less intricate.

A notable example of the study of an Oriental system in its own right is the work of Dr. D. T. Suzuki, of the Otani Buddhist College in Tokyo, on that immediate-apprehension form of Buddhism which is known as *Zen*. The late Dr. J. B. Pratt of Williams College remarked that "there are two kinds of cultured people; those who have read Professor Suzuki's works on Zen-Buddhism, and those who have not."

Unfortunately it is true that as yet there are relatively few adherents of the Eastern religions who have the thoroughgoing scholarship of a Suzuki, and who are willing to apply the canons of criticism sharply to their own traditions. The revised chronology of the sections to the Koran, established by Western scholars, is largely ignored by Moslems. The pluralism of Hindu religious origins is blanketed by most Hindu teachers in a clinging fog of philosophical monism. The Chinese in the past were prepared by the realism of their primary hero to be realistic about him, but there seems to be little objectivity toward the conservative Confucius today in the People's Republic. For the time being it appears that the West will have to continue its leadership in the scholarly study of the religions of the East.

What Makes a Mystic?

The implications of historical analysis—as applied to the Bible, to Church history, and to the story of religion in general—naturally present themselves also in the realm of personal religious faith and attitude. Perhaps the greatest single force in the recent development of humanistic studies has been the new science of psychology. Inevitably psychology has concerned itself with the phenomena of religion. The study of the psychology of religion has followed, as one would expect, the waves and currents of general psychological fashion. William James saw *The Varieties of Religious Experience* against the backdrop of his own somewhat romantic empiricism. The heyday of Watsonite behaviorism coincided with that of liberal modernism, whose mood combined a pedestrian factualism with a comfortable religious and ethical relativity. Freud changed all that; but then came Jung, and Künkel, and a host of others, to challenge the religious findings of Freud.

The psychologists of religion began to examine now not the works of official theologians, but those of the generally unofficial persons called "mystics." The psychological processes at work in these were visible enough, and could be readily described in the jargon of Vienna and Zurich. They could be described, but it turned out that they were not thereby explained. How these men and women had searched for God was evident, and not only in Europe but also in India and Japan. What they had found nevertheless refused to melt away. The psychology of religion had helped to interpret some aspects of religion, but it had no more disposed of religion than the psychology of art has abolished aesthetic experience. Scientific honesty and humility then compelled the judgment that the indemonstrable was not necessarily the nonexistent.

What seemed now to offer itself as an academic explanation, but what may be a cognate religious phenomenon, was that rigorous form of Protestant theological doctrine which bears the name of Karl Barth. The essence of Barthianism, described as "crisis theology" and more loosely as "neo-orthodoxy," is the proposition that man's encounter with the divine is at once absolute and indefinable: that there is no escaping it, but that there is no explaining it either. God is declared to be the "Wholly Other," by no means to be captured within the formulas of men, yet always confronting man with the ultimate in moral obligation. Soon it was recognized that this was just what John Calvin had insisted upon three hundred years before, in his doctrine of predestination and in his demand for total submission to the divine law; and so neo-orthodoxy appears today as an authentic neo-Calvinism.

Because the mystic usually has seemed so assured of his direct contact with infinite reality, and so little dependent upon the authoritative guidance of either Church or Scripture, most of the followers of Barth have refused to admit the validity of the mystic way. It is possible, however, to suppose the kinship which they have thought to deny. Confident as are the mystics of their experience, they are emphatic that it cannot be verbalized with any degree of precision. Both for them and for the Barthians, God is at once totally real and almost totally indescribable. For both, the conviction of divine reality rests not upon scientific demonstration but on immediate inner contact. For both, then, the objective judgment about the subjective is that what is called the subjective is real, whatever scientific objectivity may have to say about it.

These, then, are the inevitable polarities of religion: deity and humanity, intuition and research, spirit and body. Can there be a genuine nexus within each of the pairs? Or are we trapped forever in the abysses that lie between? The basic problem of religious scholarship seems to be the very problem of religion itself. Questing for answer, St. Anselm of Canterbury asked the question, *"Cur deus homo?"*—"Why a God-man?" The seeker of today continues to inquire, "How does God come to man?"

Anselm's reply from the late eleventh century, which is one directed to both forms of the question, seems curiously to lead toward our most advanced twentieth-century thinking; but we shall have to trace it by a somewhat circuitous route. The way is that of symbolism. We do not know God, says Anselm, as we know physical objects, nor even as we know many of our abstract ideas. When we try to think of God, therefore, we have to think in terms of what we do know: of ideas and objects that are in the range of our comprehension and description.

Symbol and Substance

This is the function of symbolism. It may be as crass as the clay Astarte, as clumsy as the Aztec goddess of the corn; or it may be as subtle and articulate as the finest-spun passages in St. Thomas' *Summa Theologica*. It is symbolism in either case, the use of something else in the effort to reflect and represent something, of the object to carry a value.

The danger of symbolism is obvious. It is idolatry. "These be thy gods, O Israel!" has been applicable not only to the golden calves of Aaron, but also to statues of St. Mary the Virgin, to the creeds of the Church, to days of fasting and festival, to the absolutist formulas of Midwestern fundamentalism. It always is idolatry to confuse the symbol with the reality.

The early Protestants saw this with reference to the images of the saints, though not all of them as to the phrasing of the Bible. The liberal modernists, more inclusively, tried to sweep away all symbols because in themselves they were not finally real. But thereby the Protestants exiled from their ken not only the churchly statues but also the noble army of martyrs whom they represented, and the modernists soon found themselves left with no reality that mattered. A childish use of symbolism had assumed a one-for-one correlation between the immediate and the ultimate. Surely it was a kind of adolescence that reduced the correlation to zero. At last a renewed adulthood has begun to supervene.

One effect of the realization that man does not get along without symbols, and cannot get along without them, has been a revival of interest in religious achitecture and in the procedures of public worship. The fields of liturgics, of Christian iconography and music, of hymnology, have been cultivated with an increasing discernment and a heightened enthusiasm. In one way these inquiries are factual and historical. In another they are psychological too, and ultimately philosophical in the fullest sense.

Even more importantly, the necessarily symbolic nature of every kind of religious utterance has become apparent. The historic creeds have come to mean not less, but more, as attention has turned from their apparent narration of events to their central assertion of meanings. "Modernist" embarrassment with evident crudities in the Biblical texts is yielding to a fresh appreciation of essential Biblical intentions. From the innocence of its childhood the Christian mind thus has moved, through the literalism of its schooldays, toward the sympathetic sophistication of the mentally and morally grown up.

This is where St. Anselm comes in. Why a God-man? The answer is myth, if we will; but it is the kind of myth that alone will lead us nearer to ultimate truth. The myth of the incarnation, "that God became man by necessity," is the nearest that man yet has come to bridging the gap between himself and the creative and sustaining force which undergirds all being. "The *Logos* became flesh, and dwelt among us." This is a considered philosophy. It is vaulting imagination. It is the core of the Christian faith.

Those of us who count ourselves Christian do not pretend that this central myth of ours includes all that is in the outer reality. The very limits of our knowledge, as marked out by scientific inquiry, prohibit any such claim; and religious intuition readily concurs. We nevertheless are persuaded that the actualities of human experience, and the symbolic nature of human thought, unite to drive us to this symbol of the God-man beyond all others, because it does more than any other to bring together the polarities of immediate and ultimate.

Historical, documentary, and psychological inquiry will go on to reap new harvests of learning, and philosophy and theology will continue to build new structures to contain them. None of these will avoid symbolism, both because they cannot and because our time is willing to rejoice in symbols once more. Nor within their inescapable symbolisms will they capture everything of the truth. What their history to date does argue is that the symbol of the eternal Christ revealed in the historic man Jesus is the one best designed to reflect the confrontation of finite man by the infinite God.

The Nature of Reality

❖◈

PLATO

The Allegory of the Cave[1]

Next, said I, here is a parable to illustrate the degrees in which our nature may be enlightened or unenlightened. Imagine the condition of men living in a sort of cavernous chamber underground, with an entrance open to the light

[1] From *The Republic*, translated by Francis MacDonald Cornford (Oxford: The Clarendon Press, 1941), pp. 227-231. Reprinted by permission of The Clarendon Press.

and a long passage all down the cave.[2] Here they have been from childhood, chained by the leg and also by the neck, so that they cannot move and can see only what is in front of them, because the chains will not let them turn their heads. At some distance higher up is the light of a fire burning behind them; and between the prisoners and the fire is a track[3] with a parapet built along it, like the screen at a puppet-show, which hides the performers while they show their puppets over the top.

I see, said he.

Now behind this parapet imagine persons carrying along various artificial objects, including figures of men and animals in wood or stone or other materials, which project above the parapet. Naturally, some of these persons will be talking, others silent.[4]

It is a strange picture, he said, and a strange sort of prisoners.

Like ourselves, I replied; for in the first place prisoners so confined would have seen nothing of themselves or of one another, except the shadows thrown by the fire-light on the wall of the Cave facing them, would they?

Not if all their lives they had been prevented from moving their heads.

And they would have seen as little of the objects carried past.

Of course.

Now, if they could talk to one another, would they not suppose that their words referred only to those passing shadows which they saw?[5]

Necessarily.

And suppose their prison had an echo from the wall facing them? When one of the people crossing behind them spoke, they could only suppose that the sound came from the shadow passing before their eyes.

No doubt.

In every way, then, such prisoners would recognize as reality nothing but the shadows of those artificial objects.[6]

---

[2] The *length* of the "way in" (*eisodos*) to the chamber where the prisoners sit is an essential feature, explaining why no daylight reaches them.

[3] The track crosses the passage into the cave at right angles, and is *above* the parapet built along it.

[4] A modern Plato would compare his Cave to an underground cinema, where the audience watch the play of shadows thrown by the film passing before a light at their backs. The film itself is only an image of "real" things and events in the world outside the cinema. For the film Plato has to substitute the clumsier apparatus of a procession of artificial objects carried on their heads by persons who are merely part of the machinery, providing for the movement of the objects and the sounds whose echo the prisoners hear. The parapet prevents these persons' shadows from being cast on the wall of the Cave.

[5] Adam's text and interpretation. The prisoners, having seen nothing but shadows, cannot think their words refer to the objects carried past behind their backs. For them shadows (images) are the only realities.

[6] The state of mind called *eikasia* in the previous chapter.

Inevitably.

Now consider what would happen if their release from the chains and the healing of their unwisdom should come about in this way. Suppose one of them set free and forced suddenly to stand up, turn his head, and walk with eyes lifted to the light; all these movements would be painful, and he would be too dazzled to make out the objects whose shadows he had been used to see. What do you think he would say, if someone told him that what he had formerly seen was meaningless illusion, but now, being somewhat nearer to reality and turned towards more real objects, he was getting a truer view? Suppose further that he were shown the various objects being carried by and were made to say, in reply to questions, what each of them was. Would he not be perplexed and believe the objects now shown him to be not so real as what he formerly saw?

Yes, not nearly so real.

And if he were forced to look at the fire-light itself, would not his eyes ache, so that he would try to escape and turn back to the things which he could see distinctly, convinced that they really were clearer than these other objects now being shown to him?

Yes.

And suppose someone were to drag him away forcibly up the steep and rugged ascent and not let him go until he had hauled him out into the sunlight, would he not suffer pain and vexation at such treatment, and, when he had come out into the light, find his eyes so full of its radiance that he could not see a single one of the things that he was now told were real?

Certainly he would not see them all at once.

He would need, then, to grow accustomed before he could see things in that upper world. At first it would be easiest to make out shadows, and then the images of men and things reflected in water, and later on the things themselves. After that, it would be easier to watch the heavenly bodies and the sky itself by night, looking at the light of the moon and stars rather than the Sun and the Sun's light in the day-time.

Yes, surely.

Last of all, he would be able to look at the Sun and contemplate its nature, not as it appears when reflected in water or any alien medium, but as it is in itself in its own domain.

No doubt.

And now he would begin to draw the conclusion that it is the Sun that produces the seasons and the course of the year and controls everything in the visible world, and moreover is in a way the cause of all that he and his companions used to see.

Clearly he would come at last to that conclusion.

Then if he called to mind his fellow prisoners and what passed for wisdom in his former dwelling-place, he would surely think himself happy in the change and be sorry for them. They may have had a practice of honouring and commending one another, with prizes for the man who had the keenest eye for the passing shadows and the best memory for the order in which they followed or accompanied one another, so that he could make a good guess as to which was going to come next.[7] Would our released prisoner be likely to covet those prizes or to envy the men exalted to honour and power in the Cave? Would he not feel like Homer's Achilles, that he would far sooner "be on earth as a hired servant in the house of a landless man" [8] or endure anything rather than go back to his old beliefs and live in the old way?

Yes, he would prefer any fate to such a life.

Now imagine what would happen if he went down again to take his former seat in the Cave. Coming suddenly out of the sunlight, his eyes would be filled with darkness. He might be required once more to deliver his opinion on those shadows, in competition with the prisoners who had never been released, while his eyesight was still dim and unsteady; and it might take some time to become used to the darkness. They would laugh at him and say that he had gone up only to come back with his sight ruined; it was worth no one's while even to attempt the ascent. If they could lay hands on the man who was trying to set them free and lead them up, they would kill him.[9]

Yes, they would.

Every feature in this parable, my dear Glaucon, is meant to fit our earlier analysis. The prison dwelling corresponds to the region revealed to us through the sense of sight, and the fire-light within it to the power of the Sun. The ascent to see the things in the upper world you may take as standing for the upward journey of the soul into the region of the intelligible; then you will be in possession of what I surmise, since that is what you wish to be told. Heaven knows whether it is true; but this, at any rate, is how it appears to me. In the world of knowledge, the last thing to be perceived and only with great difficulty is the essential Form of Goodness. Once it is perceived, the conclusion must follow that, for all things, this is the cause of whatever is right and good; in the visible world it gives birth to light and to the lord of light, while it is itself sovereign in the intelligible world and the parent of intelligence and truth. Without having had a vision of this Form no one can act with wisdom, either in his own life or in matters of state.

[7] The empirical politician, with no philosophic insight, but only a "knack of remembering what usually happens" (*Gorg.* 501 A). He has *eikasia* = conjecture as to what is likely (*eikos*).

[8] This verse, being spoken by the ghost of Achilles, suggests that the Cave is comparable with Hades.

[9] An allusion to the fate of Socrates.

RENÉ DESCARTES

A Discourse on Method[1]

I was then in Germany, attracted thither by the wars in that country, which have not yet been brought to a termination; and as I was returning to the army from the coronation of the emperor, the setting in of winter arrested me in a locality where, as I found no society to interest me, and was besides fortunately undisturbed by any cares or passions, I remained the whole day in seclusion, with full opportunity to occupy my attention with my own thoughts. Of these one of the very first that occurred to me was, that there is seldom so much perfection in works composed of many separate parts, upon which different hands had been employed, as in those completed by a single master. Thus it is observable that the buildings which a single archtect has planned and executed, are generally more elegant and commodious than those which several have attempted to improve, by making old walls serve for purposes for which they were not originally built. Thus also, those ancient cities which, from being at first only villages, have become, in course of time, large towns, are usually but ill laid out compared with the regularly constructed towns which a professional architect has freely planned on an open plain; so that although the several buildings of the former may often equal or surpass in beauty those of the latter, yet when one observes their indiscriminate juxtaposition, there a large one and here a small, and the consequent crookedness and irregularity of the streets, one is disposed to allege that chance rather than any human will guided by reason must have led to such an arrangement. And if we consider that nevertheless there have been at all times certain officers whose duty it was to see that private buildings contributed to public ornament, the difficulty of reaching high perfection with but the materials of others to operate on, will be readily acknowledged. In the same way I fancied that those nations which, starting from a semibarbarous state and advancing to civilization by slow degrees, have had their laws successively determined, and, as it were, forced upon them simply by experience of the hurtfulness of particular crimes and disputes, would by this process come to be possessed of less perfect institutions than those which, from the commencement of their association as communities, have followed the appointment of some wise legislator. It is thus quite certain that the constitution of the true religion, the ordinances of which are derived from God, must be incomparably superior to that of every other. And, to speak of human affairs, I believe that the past pre-eminence of Sparta was due not to the goodness of each of its laws in

[1] From A Discourse on Method (1637), by René Descartes, in The Method, Meditations, and Philosophy of Descartes, translated by John Veitch (New York: Tudor Publishing Co., n.d.), pp. 155-172, omitting Ch. 2.

particular, for many of these were very strange, and even opposed to good morals, but to the circumstance that, originated by a single individual, they all tended to a single end. In the same way I thought that the sciences contained in books (such of them at least as are made up of probable reasonings, without demonstrations), composed as they are of the opinions of many different individuals massed together, are farther removed from truth than the simple inferences which a man of good sense using his natural and unprejudiced judgment draws respecting the matters of his experience. And because we have all to pass through a state of infancy to manhood, and have been of necessity, for a length of time, governed by our desires and preceptors (whose dictates were frequently conflicting, while neither perhaps always counselled us for the best), I farther concluded that it is almost impossible that our judgments can be so correct or solid as they would have been, had our reason been mature from the moment of our birth, and had we always been guided by it alone.

It is true, however, that it is not customary to pull down all the houses of a town with the single design of rebuilding them differently, and thereby rendering the streets more handsome; but it often happens that a private individual takes down his own with the view of erecting it anew, and that people are even sometimes constrained to this when their houses are in danger of falling from age, or when the foundations are insecure. With this before me by way of example, I was persuaded that it would indeed be preposterous for a private individual to think of reforming a state by fundamentally changing it throughout, and overturning it in order to set it up amended; and the same I thought was true of any similar project for reforming the body of the sciences, or the order of teaching them established in the schools: but as for the opinions which up to that time I had embraced, I thought that I could not do better than resolve at once to sweep them wholly away, that I might afterwards be in a position to admit either others more correct, or even perhaps the same when they had undergone the scrutiny of reason. I firmly believed that in this way I should much better succeed in the conduct of my life, than if I built only upon old foundations, and leaned upon principles which, in my youth, I had taken upon trust. For although I recognized various difficulties in this undertaking, these were not, however, without remedy, nor once to be compared with such as attend the slightest reformation in public affairs. Large bodies, if once overthrown, are with great difficulty set up again, or even kept erect when once seriously shaken, and the fall of such is always disastrous. Then if there are any imperfections in the constitutions of states (and that many such exist the diversity of constitutions is alone sufficient to assure us), custom has without doubt materially smoothed their inconveniences, and has even managed to steer altogether clear of, or insensibly corrected a number which sagacity could not have provided against with equal effect; and, in fine, the defects are almost more tolerable than the change necessary for their removal; in the same manner that highways which wind among mountains, by being much frequented, become gradually so smooth and commodious, that it is much better to follow them than to seek a straighter path by climbing over the tops of rocks and descending to the bottoms of precipices.

Hence it is that I cannot in any degree approve of those restless and busy meddlers who, called neither by birth no fortune to take part in the management of public affairs, are yet always projecting reforms; and if I thought that this tract contained aught which might justify the suspicion that I was a victim of such folly, I would by no means permit its publication. I have never contemplated anything higher than the reformation of my own opinions, and basing them on a foundation wholly my own. And although my own satisfaction with my work has led me to present here a draft of it, I do not by any means therefore recommend to everyone else to make a similar attempt. Those whom God has endowed with a larger measure of genius will entertain, perhaps, designs still more exalted; but for the many I am much afraid lest even the present undertaking be more than they can safely venture to imitate. The single design to strip one's self of all past beliefs is one that ought not to be taken by every one. The majority of men is composed of two classes, for neither of which would this be at all a befitting resolution: in the first place, of those who with more than a due confidence in their own powers, are precipitate in their judgments and want the patience requisite for orderly and circumspect thinking; whence it happens, that if men of this class once take the liberty to doubt of their accustomed opinions, and quit the beaten highway, they will never be able to thread the byway that would lead them by a shorter course, and will lose themselves and continue to wander for life; in the second place, of those who, possessed of sufficient sense or modesty to determine that there are others who excel them in the power of discriminating between truth and error, and by whom they may be instructed, ought rather to content themselves with the opinions of such than trust for more correct to their own reason.

For my own part, I should doubtless have belonged to the latter class, had I received instruction from but one master, or had I never known the diversities of opinion that from time immemorial have prevailed among men of the greatest learning. But I had become aware, even so early as during my college life, that no opinion, however absurd and incredible, can be imagined, which has not been maintained by some one of the philosophers; and afterwards in the course of my travels I remarked that all those whose opinions are decidedly repugnant to ours are not on that account barbarians and savages, but on the contrary that many of these nations make an equally good, if not a better, use of their reason than we do. I took into account also the very different character which a person brought up from infancy in France or Germany exhibits, from that which, with the same mind originally, this individual would have possessed had he lived always among the Chinese or with savages, and the circumstance that in dress itself the fashion which pleased us ten years ago, and which may again, perhaps, be received into favour before ten years have gone, appears to us at this moment extravagant and ridiculous. I was thus led to infer that the ground of our opinions is far more custom and example than any certain knowledge. And, finally, although such be the ground of our opinions, I remarked that a plurality of suffrages is no guarantee of truth where it is at all of difficult discovery, as in such cases it is much more likely that it will be found by one than by many. I could, however, select from the crowd no one whose opinions seemed worthy of preference, and thus I found myself constrained, as it were, to use my own reason in the conduct of my life.

But like one walking alone and in the dark, I resolved to proceed so slowly and with such circumspection, that if I did not advance far, I would at least guard against falling. I did not even choose to dismiss summarily any of the opinions that had crept in my belief without having been introduced by reason, but first of all took sufficient time carefully to satisfy myself of the general nature of the task I was setting myself, and ascertain the true method by which to arrive at the knowledge of whatever lay within the compass of my powers.

Among the branches of philosophy, I had, at an earlier period, given some attention to logic, and among those of the mathematics to geometrical analysis and algebra—three arts or sciences which ought, as I conceived, to contribute something to my design. But, on examination, I found that, as for logic, its syllogisms and the majority of its other precepts are of avail rather in the communication of what we already know, or even as the art of Tully, in speaking without judgment of things of which we are ignorant, than in the investigation of the unknown; and although this science contains indeed a number of correct and very excellent precepts, there are, nevertheless, so many others, and these either injurious or superfluous, mingled with the former, that it is almost quite as difficult to effect a severance of the true from the false as it is to extract a Diana or a Minerva from a rough block of marble. Then as to the analysis of the ancients and the algebra of the moderns, besides that they embrace only matters highly abstract, and, to appearance, of no use, the former is so exclusively restricted to the consideration of figures, that it can exercise the understanding only on condition of greatly fatiguing the imagination; and, in the latter, there is so complete a subjection to certain rules and formulas, that there results an art full of confusion and obscurity calculated to embarrass, instead of a science fitted to cultivate the mind. By these considerations I was induced to seek some other method which would comprise the advantages of the three and be exempt from their defects. And as a multitude of laws often only hampers justice, so that a state is best governed when, with few laws, these are rigidly administered; in like manner, instead of the great number of precepts of which logic is composed, I believed that the four following would prove perfectly sufficient for me, provided I took the firm and unwavering resolution never in a single instance to fail to observe them.

The first was never to accept anything for true which I did not clearly know to be such; that is to say, carefully to avoid precipitancy and prejudice, and to comprise nothing more in my judgment than was presented to my mind so clearly and distinctly as to exclude all ground of doubt.

The second, to divide each of the difficulties under examination into as many parts as possible, and as might be necessary for its adequate solution.

The third, to conduct my thoughts in such order that, by commencing with objects the simplest and easiest to know, I might ascend by little and little, and, as it were, step by step, to the knowledge of the more complex; assigning in thought a certain order even to those objects which in their own nature do not stand in a relation of antecedence and sequence.

And the last, in every case to make enumerations so complete, and reviews so general, that I might be assured that nothing was omitted.

The long chains of simple and easy reasonings by means of which geometers are accustomed to reach the conclusions of their most difficult demonstrations, had led me to imagine that all things, to the knowledge of which man is competent, are mutually connected in the same way, and that there is nothing so far removed from us as to be beyond our reach, or so hidden that we cannot discover it, provided only we abstain from accepting the false for the true, and always preserve in our thoughts the order necessary for the deduction of one truth from another. And I had little difficulty in determining the objects with which it was necessary to commence, for I was already persuaded that it must be with the simplest and easiest to know, and, considering that of all those who have hitherto sought truth in the sciences, the mathematicians alone have been able to find any demonstrations, that is, any certain and evident reasons, I did not doubt but that such must have been the rule of their investigations. I resolved to commence, therefore, with the examination of the simplest objects, not anticipating, however, from this any other advantage than that to be found in accustoming my mind to the love and nourishment of truth, and to a distaste for all such reasonings as were unsound. But I had no intention on that account of attempting to master all the particular sciences commonly denominated mathematics: but observing that, however different their objects, they all agree in considering only the various relations or proportions subsisting among those objects, I thought it best for my purpose to consider these proportions in the most general form possible, without referring them to any objects in particular, except such as would most facilitate the knowledge of them, and without by any means restricting them to these, that afterwards I might thus be the better able to apply them to every other class of objects to which they are legitimately applicable. Perceiving further, that in order to understand these relations I should sometimes have to consider them one by one, and sometimes only to bear them in mind, or embrace them in the aggregate, I thought that, in order the better to consider them individually, I should view them as subsisting between straight lines, than which I could find no objects more simple, or capable of being more distinctly represented to my imagination and senses; and on the other hand, that in order to retain them in the memory, or embrace an aggregate of many,

I should express them by certain characters the briefest possible. In this way I believed that I could borrow all that was best both in geometrical analysis and in algebra, and correct all the defects of the one by help of the other.

And in point of fact, the accurate observance of these few precepts gave me, I take the liberty of saying, such ease in unravelling all the questions embraced in these two sciences, that in the two or three months I devoted to their examination, not only did I reach solutions of questions I had formerly deemed exceedingly difficult, but even as regards questions of the solution of which I continued ignorant, I was enabled, as it appeared to me, to determine the means whereby, and the extent to which, a solution was possible; results attributable to the circumstance that I commenced with the simplest and most general truths, and that thus each truth discovered was a rule available in the discovery of subsequent ones. Nor in this perhaps shall I appear too vain, if it be considered that, as the truth on any particular points is one, whoever apprehends the truth, knows all that on that point can be known. The child, for example, who has been instructed in the elements of arithmetic, and has made a particular addition, according to rule, may be assured that he has found, with respect to the sum of the numbers before him, all that in this instance is within the reach of human genius. Now, in conclusion, the method which teaches adherence to the true order, and an exact enumeration of all the conditions of the thing sought includes all that gives certitude to the rules of arithmetic.

But the chief ground of my satisfaction with this method, was the assurance I had of thereby exercising my reason in all matters, if not with absolute perfection, at least with the greatest attainable by me: besides, I was conscious that by its use my mind was becoming gradually habituated to clearer and more distinct conceptions of its objects; and I hoped also, from not having restricted this method to any particular matter, to apply it to the difficulties of the other sciences, with not less success than to those of algebra. I should not, however, on this account have ventured at once on the examination of all the difficulties of the sciences which presented themselves to me, for this would have been contrary to the order prescribed in the method, but observing that the knowledge of such is dependent on principles borrowed from philosophy, in which I found nothing certain, I thought it necessary first of all to endeavour to establish its principles. And because I observed, besides, that an inquiry of this kind was of all others of the greatest moment, and one in which precipitancy and anticipation in judgment were most to be dreaded, I thought that I ought not to approach it till I had reached a more mature age (being at that time but twenty-three), and had first of all employed much of my time in preparation for the work, as well by eradicating from my mind all the erroneous opinions I had up to that moment accepted, as by amassing variety of experience to afford materials for my reasonings, and by continually exercising myself in my chosen method with a view to increased skill in its application. . . .

I am in doubt as to the propriety of making my first meditations, in the place above mentioned, matter of discourse; for these are so metaphysical, and so uncommon, as not, perhaps, to be acceptable to every one. And yet, that it may be determined whether the foundations that I have laid are sufficiently secure, I find myself in a measure constrained to advert to them. I had long before remarked that, in relation to practice, it is sometimes necessary to adopt, as if above doubt, opinions which we discern to be highly uncertain, as has been already said; but as I then desired to give my attention solely to the search after truth, I thought that a procedure exactly the opposite was called for, and that I ought to reject as absolutely false all opinions in regard to which I could suppose the least ground for doubt, in order to ascertain whether after that there remained aught in my belief that was wholly indubitable. Accordingly, seeing that our senses sometimes deceived us, I was willing to suppose that there existed nothing really such as they presented to us; and because some men err in reasoning, and fall into paralogisms, even on the simplest matters of geometry, I, convinced that I was as open to error as any other, rejected as false all the reasonings I had hitherto taken for demonstrations; and finally, when I considered that the very same thoughts (presentations) which we experience when awake may also be experienced when we are asleep, while there is at that time not one of them true, I supposed that all the objects (presentations) that had ever entered into my mind when awake, had in them no more truth than the illusions of my dreams. But immediately upon this I observed that, whilst I thus wished to think that all was false, it was absolutely necessary that I, who thus thought, should be somewhat; and as I observed that this truth, I THINK, HENCE I AM, was so certain and of such evidence, that no ground of doubt, however extravagant, could be alleged by the sceptics capable of shaking it, I concluded that I might, without scruple, accept it as the first principle of the philosophy of which I was in search.

In the next place, I attentively examined what I was, and as I observed that I could suppose that I had no body, and that there was no world nor any place in which I might be; but that I could not therefore suppose that I was not; and that, on the contrary, from the very circumstance that I thought to doubt of the truth of other things, it most clearly and certainly followed that I was; while, on the other hand, if I had only ceased to think, although all the other objects which I had ever imagined had been in reality existent, I would have had no reason to believe that I existed; I thence concluded that I was a substance whose whole essence or nature consists only in thinking, and which, that it may exist, has need of no place, nor is dependent on any material thing; so that "I," that is to say, the mind by which I am what I am, is wholly distinct from the body, and is even more easily known than the latter, and is such, that although the latter were not, it would still continue to be all that it is.

After this I inquired in general into what is essential to the truth and certainty of a proposition; for since I had discovered one which I knew to be true, I thought that I must likewise be able to discover the ground of this certitude. And as I observed that in the words *I think, hence I am*, there is nothing at all which gives me assurance of their truth beyond this, that I see very clearly that in order to think it is necessary to exist, I concluded that I might take, as a general rule, the principle, that all the things which we very clearly and distinctly conceive are true, only observing, however, that there is some difficulty in rightly determining the objects which we distinctly conceive.

JOHN LOCKE

An Essay Concerning Human Understanding[1]

1. Every man being conscious to himself that he thinks; and that which his mind is applied about whilst thinking being the *ideas* that are there, it is past doubt that men have in their minds several ideas—such as are those expressed by the words *whiteness, hardness, sweetness, thinking, motion, man, elephant, army, drunkenness*, and others: it is in the first place then to be inquired, *How he comes by them?*

I know it is a received doctrine, that men have native ideas, and original characters, stamped upon their minds in their very first being. This opinion I have at large examined already; and, I suppose what I have said in the foregoing Book will be much more easily admitted, when I had shown whence the understanding may get all the ideas it has; and by what ways and degrees they may come into the mind;—for which I shall appeal to every one's own observation and experience.

2. Let us then suppose the mind to be, as we say, white paper, void of all characters, without any ideas:—How comes it to be furnished? Whence comes it by that vast store which the busy and boundless fancy of man has painted on it with an almost endless variety? Whence has it all the *materials* of reason and knowledge? To this I answer, in one word, from EXPERIENCE. In that all our knowledge is founded; and from that it ultimately derives itself. Our observation employed either about external sensible objects, or about the internal operations of our minds perceived and reflected on by ourselves, is that which supplies our understandings with all the *materials* of thinking. These two are the fountains of knowledge, from whence all the ideas we have, or can naturally have, do spring.

3. First, our Senses, conversant about particular sensible objects, do convey into the mind several distinct perceptions of things, according to those vari-

[1] *An Essay Concerning Human Understanding* (1690), ed., Alexander Campbell Fraser (Oxford: The Clarendon Press, 1894), Book II, Chap. I.

ous ways wherein those objects do affect them. And thus we come by those ideas we have of *yellow, white, heat, cold, soft, hard, bitter, sweet,* and all those which we call sensible qualities; which when I say the senses convey into the mind, I mean, they from external objects convey into the mind what produces there those perceptions. This great source of most of the ideas we have, depending wholly upon our senses, and derived by them to the understanding, I call SENSATION.

4. Secondly, the other fountain from which experience furnisheth the understanding with ideas is—the perception of the operations of our own mind within us, as it is employed about the ideas it has got;—which operations, when the soul comes to reflect on and consider, do furnish the understanding with another set of ideas, which could not be had from things without. And such are *perception, thinking, doubting, believing, reasoning, knowing, willing,* and all the different actings of our own minds;—which we being conscious of, and observing in ourselves, do from these receive into our understandings as distinct ideas as we do from bodies affecting our senses. This source of ideas every man has wholly in himself; and though it be not sense, as having nothing to do with external objects, yet it is very like it, and might properly enough be called *internal sense.* But as I call the other Sensation, so I call this REFLECTION, the ideas it affords being such only as the mind gets by reflecting on its own operations within itself. By reflection then, in the following part of this discourse, I would be understood to mean, that notice which the mind takes of its own operations, and the manner of them, by reason whereof there come to be ideas of these operations in the understanding. These two, I say, viz. external material things, as the objects of SENSATION, and the operations of our own minds within, as the objects of REFLECTION, are to me the only originals from whence all our ideas take their beginnings. The term *operations* here I use in a large sense, as comprehending not barely the actions of the mind about its ideas, but some sort of passions arising sometimes from them, such as is the satisfaction or uneasiness arising from any thought.

5. The understanding seems to me not to have the least glimmering of any ideas which it doth not receive from one of these two. *External objects* furnish the mind with the ideas of sensible qualities, which are all those different perceptions they produce in us; and *the mind* furnishes the understanding with ideas of its own operations.

These, when we have taken a full survey of them, and their several modes, [combinations, and relations,] we shall find to contain all our whole stock of ideas; and that we have nothing in our minds which did not come in one of these two ways. Let any one examine his own thoughts, and thoroughly search into his understanding; and then let him tell me, whether all the original ideas he has there, are any other than of the objects of his senses, or of the operations of his mind, considered as objects of his reflection. And how great a mass of knowledge soever he imagines to be lodged there, he will, upon taking a strict view, see that he has not any idea in his mind but what one of these two have imprinted;—though perhaps, with infinite variety compounded and enlarged by the understanding, as we shall see hereafter.

6. He that attentively considers the state of a child, at his first coming into the world, will have little reason to think him stored with plenty of ideas, that are to be the matter of his future knowledge. It is *by degrees* he comes to be furnished with them. And though the ideas of obvious and familiar qualities imprint themselves before the memory begins to keep a register of time and order, yet it is often so late before some unusual qualities come in the way, that there are few men that cannot recollect the beginning of their acquaintance with them. And if it were worth while, no doubt a child might be so ordered as to have but a very few, even of the ordinary ideas, till he were grown up to a man. But all that are born into the world, being surrounded with bodies that perpetually and diversely affect them, variety of ideas, whether care be taken of it or not, are imprinted on the minds of children. Light and colours are busy at hand everywhere, when the eye is but open; sounds and some tangible qualities fail not to solicit their proper senses, and force an entrance to the mind;—but yet, I think, it will be granted easily, that if a child were kept in a place where he never saw any other but black and white till he were a man, he would have no more ideas of scarlet or green, than he that from his childhood never tasted an oyster, or a pineapple, has of those particular relishes.

7. Men then come to be furnished with fewer or more simple ideas from without, according as the objects they converse with afford greater or less variety; and from the operations of their minds within, according as they more or less reflect on them. For, though he that contemplates the operations of his mind, cannot but have plain and clear ideas of them; yet, unless he turn his thoughts that way, and considers them *attentively*, he will no more have clear and distinct ideas of all the operations of his mind, and all that may be observed therein, than he will have all the particular ideas of any landscape, or of the parts and motions of a clock, who will not turn his eyes to it, and with attention heed all the parts of it. The picture, or clock may be so placed, that they may come in his way every day; but yet he will have but a confused idea of all the parts they are made up of, till he applies himself with attention, to consider them each in particular.

8. And hence we see the reason why it is pretty late before most children get ideas of the operations of their own minds; and some have not any very clear or perfect ideas of the greatest part of them all their lives. Because, though they pass there continually, yet, like floating visions, they make not deep impressions enough to leave in their mind clear, distinct, lasting ideas, till the understanding turns inward upon itself, reflects on its own operations, and makes them the objects of its own contemplation. Children, when they come first into it, are surrounded with a world of new things, which, by a constant solicitation of their senses, draw the mind constantly to them; forward to take notice of new, and apt to be delighted with the variety of

changing objects. Thus the first years are usually employed and diverted in looking abroad. Men's business in them is to acquaint themselves with what is to be found without; and so growing up in a constant attention to outward sensations, seldom make any considerable reflection on what passes within them, till they come to be of riper years; and some scarce ever at all.

WILLIAM JAMES

What Pragmatism Is[1]

Some years ago, being with a camping party in the mountains, I returned from a solitary ramble to find every one engaged in a ferocious metaphysical dispute. The *corpus* of the dispute was a squirrel—a live squirrel supposed to be clinging to one side of a tree-trunk; while over against the tree's opposite side a human being was imagined to stand. This human witness tries to get sight of the squirrel by moving rapidly round the tree, but no matter how fast he goes, the squirrel moves as fast in the opposite direction, and always keeps the tree between himself and the man, so that never a glimpse of him is caught. The resultant metaphysical problem now is this: *Does the man go round the squirrel or not?* He goes round the tree, sure enough, and the squirrel is on the tree; but does he go round the squirrel? In the unlimited leisure of the wilderness, discussion had been worn threadbare. Every one had taken sides and was obstinate; and the numbers on both sides were even. Each side, when I appeared, therefore appealed to me to make it a majority. Mindful of the scholastic adage that whenever you meet a contradiction you must make a distinction, I immediately sought and found one, as follows: "Which party is right," I said, "depends on what you *practically mean* by 'going round' the squirrel. If you mean passing from the north of him to the east, then to the south, then to the west, and then to the north of him again, obviously the man does go round him, for he occupies these successive positions. But if on the contrary you mean being first in front of him, then on the right of him, then behind him, then on his left, and finally in front again, it is quite obvious that the man fails to go round him, for by compensating movements the squirrel makes, he keeps his belly turned towards the man all the time, and his back turned away. Make the distinction, and there is no occasion for any further dispute. You are both right and both wrong, according as you conceive the verb 'to go round' in one practical fashion or the other."

    Although one or two of the hotter disputants called my speech a shuffling

1 From William James, *Pragmatism* (New York: Longmans, Green & Company, Inc., 1907, 1928), pp. 43-55. Reprinted by permission of Paul R. Reynolds & Son, 599 Fifth Avenue, New York 17, N.Y.

evasion, saying they wanted no quibbling or scholastic hair-splitting, but meant just plain honest English "round," the majority seemed to think that the distinction had assuaged the dispute.

I tell this trivial anecdote because it is a peculiarly simple example of what I wish now to speak of as *the pragmatic method*. The pragmatic method is primarily a method of settling metaphysical disputes that otherwise might be interminable. Is the world one or many?—fated or free?—material or spiritual?—here are notions either of which may or may not hold good of the world; and disputes over such notions are unending. The pragmatic method in such cases is to try to interpret each notion by tracing its respective practical consequences. What difference would it practically make to any one if this notion rather than that notion were true? If no practical difference whatever can be traced, then the alternatives mean practically the same thing, and all dispute is idle. Whenever a dispute is serious, we ought to be able to show some practical difference that must follow from one side or the other's being right.

A glance at the history of the idea will show you still better what pragmatism means. The term is derived from the same Greek word πραγμά, meaning action, from which our words "practice" and "practical" come. It was first introduced into philosophy by Mr. Charles Peirce in 1878. In an article entitled "How to Make Our Ideas Clear," in the *Popular Science Monthly* for January of that year, Mr. Peirce, after pointing out that our beliefs are really rules for action, said that, to develop a thought's meaning, we need only determine what conduct it is fitted to produce: that conduct is for us its sole significance. And the tangible fact at the root of all our thought-distinctions, however subtle, is that there is no one of them so fine as to consist in anything but a possible difference of practice. To attain perfect clearness in our thoughts of an object, then, we need only consider what conceivable effects of a practical kind the object may involve—what sensations we are to expect from it, and what reactions we must prepare. Our conception of these effects whether immediate or remote, is then for us the whole of our conception of the object, so far as that conception has positive significance at all.

This is the principle of Peirce, the principle of pragmatism. It lay entirely unnoticed by any one for twenty years, until I, in an address before Professor Howison's philosophical union at the University of California, brought it forward again and made a special application of it to religion. By that date (1898) the times seemed ripe for its reception. The word "pragmatism" spread, and at present it fairly spots the pages of the philosophic journals. On all hands we find the "pragmatic movement" spoken of, sometimes with respect, sometimes with contumely, seldom with clear understanding. It is evident that the term applies itself conveniently to a number of tendencies that hitherto have lacked a collective name, and that it has "come to stay."

To take in the importance of Peirce's principle, one must get accustomed to applying it to concrete cases. I found a few years ago that Ostwald, the illustrious Leipzig chemist, had been making perfectly distinct use of the principle of pragmatism in his lectures on the philosophy of science, though he had not called it by that name.

"All realities influence our practice," he wrote me, "and that influence is their meaning for us. I am accustomed to put questions to my classes in this way: In what respects would the world be different if this alternative or that were true? If I can find nothing that would become different, then the alternative has no sense."

That is, the rival views mean practically the same thing, and meaning, other than practical, there is for us none. Ostwald in a published lecture gives this example of what he means. Chemists have long wrangled over the inner constitution of certain bodies called "tautomerous." Their properties seemed equally consistent with the notion that an instable hydrogen atom oscillates inside of them, or that they are instable mixtures of two bodies. Controversy raged, but never was decided. "It would never have begun," says Ostwald, "if the combatants had asked themselves what particular experimental fact could have been made different by one or the other view being correct. For it would then have appeared that no difference of fact could possibly ensue; and the quarrel was as unreal as if, theorising in primitive times about the raising of dough by yeast, one party should have invoked a 'brownie,' while another insisted on an 'elf' as the true cause of the phenomenon."

It is astonishing to see how many philosophical disputes collapse into insignificance the moment you subject them to this simple test of tracing a concrete consequence. There can *be* no difference anywhere that doesn't *make* a difference elsewhere—no difference in abstract truth that doesn't express itself in a difference in concrete fact and in conduct consequent upon that fact, imposed on somebody, somehow, somewhere, and somewhen. The whole function of philosophy ought to be to find out what definite difference it will make to you and me, at definite instants of our life, if this world-formula or that world-formula be the true one.

There is absolutely nothing new in the pragmatic method. Socrates was an adept at it. Aristotle used it methodically. Locke, Berkeley, and Hume made momentous contributions to truth by its means. Shadworth Hodgson keeps insisting that realities are only what they are "known as." But these forerunners of pragmatism used it in fragments: they were a prelude only. Not until in our time has it generalized itself, become conscious of a universal mission, pretended to a conquering destiny. I believe in that destiny, and I hope I may end by inspiring you with my belief.

Pragmatism represents a perfectly familiar attitude in philosophy, the empiricist attitude, but it represents it, as it seems to me, both in a more radical and in a less objectionable form than it has ever yet assumed. A pragmatist turns his back resolutely and once for all upon a lot of inveterate habits dear to professional philosophers. He turns away from abstraction and insufficiency, from verbal solutions, from bad *a priori* reasons, from fixed principles, closed systems, and pretended absolutes and origins. He turns towards concreteness and adequacy, towards facts, towards action and towards power. That means the empiricist temper regnant and the rationalist temper sincerely given up. It means the open air and possibilities of nature, as against dogma, artificiality, and the pretence of finality in truth.

At the same time it does not stand for any special results. It is a method only. But the general triumph of that method would mean an enormous change in what I called in my last lecture the "temperament" of philosophy. Teachers of the ultra-rationalistic type would be frozen out, much as the courtier type is frozen out in republics, as the ultra-montane type of priest is frozen out in protestant lands. Science and metaphysics would come much nearer together, would in fact work absolutely hand in hand.

Metaphysics has usually followed a very primitive kind of quest. You know how men have always hankered after unlawful magic, and you know what a great part in magic *words* have always played. If you have his name, or the formula of incantation that binds him, you can control the spirit, genie, afrite, or whatever the power may be. Solomon knew the names of all the spirits, and having their names, he held them subject to his will. So the universe has always appeared to the natural mind as a kind of enigma, of which the key must be sought in the shape of some illuminating or power-bringing word or name. That word names the universe's *principle*, and to possess it is after a fashion to possess the universe itself. "God," "Matter," "Reason," "the Absolute," "Energy," are so many solving names. You can rest when you have them. You are at the end of your metaphysical quest.

But if you follow the pragmatic method you cannot look on any such word as closing your quest. You must bring out of each word its practical cash-value, set it at work within the stream of your experience. It appears less as a solution, then, than as a programme for more work, and more particularly as an indication of the ways in which existing realities may be *changed*.

Theories thus become instruments, not answers to enigmas, in which we can rest. We don't lie back upon them, we move forward, and, on occasion, make nature over again by their aid. Pragmatism unstiffens all our theories, limbers them up and sets each one at work. Being nothing essentially new, it harmonizes with many ancient philosophic tendencies. It agrees with nominalism, for instance, in always appealing to particulars; with utilitarianism in emphasizing practical aspects; with positivism in its disdain for verbal solutions, useless questions, and metaphysical abstractions.

All these, you see, are *anti-intellectualist* tendencies. Against rationalism as a pretension and a method pragmatism is fully armed and militant. But, at the outset, at least, it stands for no particular results. It has no dogmas, and no doctrines save its method. As the young Italian pragmatist Papini has well said, it lies in the midst of our theories like a corridor in a hotel. Innumerable chambers open out of it. In one you may find a man writing an atheistic volume; in the next some one on his knees praying for faith and strength; in a third a chemist investigating a body's properties; in a fourth a system of idealistic metaphysics is being excogitated; in a fifth the impossibility of metaphysics is being shown. But they all own the corridor, and all must pass through it if they want a practicable way of getting into or out of their respective rooms.

No particular results then, so far, but only an attitude of orientation, is what the pragmatic method means. *The attitude of looking away from first things, principles, "categories," supposed necessities; and of looking towards last things, fruits, consequences, facts.*

So much for the pragmatic method! You may say that I have been praising it rather than explaining it to you, but I shall presently explain it abundantly enough by showing how it works on some familiar problems. Meanwhile the word pragmatism has come to be used in a still wider sense, as meaning also a certain *theory of truth.* I mean to give a whole lecture to the statement of that theory, after first paving the way, so I can be very brief now. But brevity is hard to follow, so I ask for your redoubled attention for a quarter of an hour. If much remains obscure, I hope to make it clearer in the later lectures.

One of the most successfully cultivated branches of philosophy in our time is what is called inductive logic, the study of the conditions under which our sciences have evolved. Writers on this subject have begun to show a singular unanimity as to what the laws of nature and elements of fact mean when formulated by mathematicians, physicists, and chemists. When the first mathematical, logical, and natural uniformities, the first *laws,* were discovered, men were so carried away by the clearness, beauty, and simplification that resulted that they believed themselves to have deciphered authentically the eternal thoughts of the Almighty. His mind also thundered and reverberated in syllogisms. He also thought in conic sections, squares, and roots and ratios, and geometrized like Euclid. He made Kepler's laws for the planets to follow; he made velocity increase proportionally to the time in falling bodies; he made the law of the sines for light to obey when refracted; he established the classes, orders, families, and genera of plants and animals, and fixed the distances between them. He thought the archetypes of all things, and devised their variations; and when we rediscover any one of these his wondrous institutions, we seize his mind in its very literal intention.

But as the sciences have developed farther, the notion has gained ground that most, perhaps all, of our laws are only approximations. The laws themselves, moreover, have grown so numerous that there is no counting them; and so many rival formulations are proposed in all the branches of science that investigators have become accustomed to the notion that no theory is absolutely a transcript of reality, but that any one of them may from some point of view be useful. Their great use is to summarize old facts and to lead to new ones. They are only a man-made language, a conceptual shorthand, as some one calls them, in which we write our reports of nature; and languages, as is well known, tolerate much choice of expression and many dialects.

Thus human arbitrariness has driven divine necessity from scientific logic. If I mention the names of Sigwart, Mach, Ostwald, Pearson, Milhaud, Poincaré, Duhem, Heymans, those of you who are students will easily identify the tendency I speak of, and will think of additional names.

Riding now on the front of this wave of scientific logic, Messrs. Schiller and Dewey appear with their pragmatistic account of what truth everywhere signifies. Everywhere, these teachers say, "truth" in our ideas and beliefs means the same thing that it means in science. It means, they say, nothing but this, *that ideas (which themselves are but parts of our experience) become true just in so far as they help us to get into satisfactory relation with other parts of our experience*, to summarize them and get about among them by conceptual shortcuts instead of following the interminable succession of particular phenomena. Any idea upon which we can ride, so to speak; any idea that will carry us prosperously from any one part of our experience to any other part, linking things satisfactorily, working securely, simplifying, saving labour—is true for just so much, true in so far forth, true *instrumentally*. This is the "instrumental" view of truth taught so successfully at Chicago, the view that truth in our ideas means their power to "work," promulgated so brilliantly at Oxford.

Messrs. Dewey, Schiller, and their allies, in reaching this general conception of all truth, have only followed the example of geologists, biologists, and philologists. In the establishment of these other sciences, the successful stroke was always to take some simple process actually observable in operation—as denudation by weather, say, or variation from parental type, or change of dialect by incorporation of new words and pronunciations—and then to generalize it, making it apply to all times, and produce great results by summating its effects through the ages.

The observable process which Schiller and Dewey particularly singled out for generalization is the familiar one by which any individual settles into *new opinions*. The process here is always the same. The individual has a stock of old opinions already, but he meets a new experience that puts them to a strain. Somebody contradicts them; or in a reflective moment he discovers that they contradict each other; or he hears of facts with which they are incompatible; or desires arise in him which they cease to satisfy. The result is an inward trouble to which his mind till then had been a stranger, and from which he seeks to escape by modifying his previous mass of opinions. He saves as much of it as he can, for in this matter of belief we are all extreme conservatives. So he tries to change first this opinion, and then that (for they resist change very variously), until at last some new idea comes up which he can graft upon the ancient stock with a minimum of disturbance of the latter, some idea that mediates between the stock and the new experience and runs them into one another most felicitously and expediently.

This new idea is then adopted as the true one. It preserved the older stock of truths with a minimum of modification, stretching them just enough to make them admit the novelty, but conceiving that in ways as familiar as the case leaves possible. An *outrée* explanation, violating all our preconceptions, would never pass for a true account of a novelty. We should scratch round industriously till we found something less eccentric. The most violent revolutions in an individual's beliefs leave most of his old order standing. Time and space, cause and effect, nature and history, and one's own biography remain untouched. New truth is always a go-between, a smoother-over of transitions. It marries old opinion to new fact so as ever to show a minimum of jolt, a maximum of continuity. We hold a theory true just in proportion to its success in solving this "problem of maxima and minima." But success in solving this problem is eminently a matter of approximation. We say this theory solves it on the whole more satisfactorily than that theory; but that means more satisfactorily to ourselves, and individuals will emphasize their points of satisfaction differently. To a certain degree, therefore, everything here is plastic.

WILLIAM BARRETT

Existentialism as a
Symptom of Man's Contemporary Crisis[1]

Nowadays we speak quite easily and naturally of the crisis through which our civilization is passing. Without questioning the assumption that we are in the midst of a crisis, I should like to ask whether this feeling of crisis is not something inseparable from human life in any historical period. The more closely we examine the past, the more we find that it, too, is uneasy with its own sense of historical crisis and urgency. Sometimes, in retrospect, these crises look illusory, for mankind has survived some of its worst apprehensions; and then we have to remind ourselves that these men and women of the past felt that bygone crisis in their bones, with the same intimate uneasiness with which we feel ours. We begin to suspect that to live itself is to exist in crisis (more or less actual at any moment), and that only in periods of real historic somnolence and lethargy—real decadence, in short—has mankind been without a sense of crisis. No doubt, there are important differences of degree, and one age may be more plainly a period of breakdown than another; it would be folly to neglect such differences of degree, but the thought that crisis, or the

[1] From *Spiritual Problems in Contemporary Literature*, edited by Stanley R. Hopper (New York: Harper & Brothers, 1957), pp. 139-152. Reprinted by permission of Harper & Brothers.

sense of it is a permanent part of human life, does fortify us to see our own contemporary crisis in a much broader light—as a total human condition.

This thought will explain why I prefer to discuss existential philosophy as a symptom, rather than a solution, of our present crisis. For to the degree that we see our crisis as a total and concrete condition, to that degree we shall doubt that any philosophy, no matter how ambitious, can propose itself as the unique path of salvation. Anyone who has had any personal experience of a spiritual crisis will know that recovery does not come through the acquisition of any new abstract ideas. The progress from health to sickness is a change of being, rather than a change in thought. So, if we agree that our civilization is spiritually sick, we should also expect that the recovery will not come through any single set of ideas, or philosophy, but only through a transformation of our whole existence—thus requiring social, economic, and religious change. A new philosophy would be only a necessary *part* of this total change.

Moreover, it is the very characteristic of Existentialism as a philosophy that it must look with irony upon any system of thought that proposes itself as *the* solution for all of life's crises. Let us remember that Kierkegaard, the founder of Existentialism, began to philosophize with the purpose of discovering difficulties, rather than offering easy and readymade solutions. Existentialism as a philosophy attempts to make man aware of certain basic realities of his life. In this sense it seeks to increase, rather than minimize, our human difficulties. The business of finding solutions must come only after a man is aware of the whole depth, import, and, therefore, difficulty, of his human life.

I

This preliminary definition of existential philosophy will be understood better, if we contrast it with the usual kinds of philosophy now taught in our academies. The various schools of philosophy are distinguished from each other by different beliefs. Thus it comes about that a philosophy is understood as a set of beliefs, or propositions, to which a man gives intellectual assent. A man is said to have a philosophy, then, if he has a system of propositions which he holds to be true on purely intellectual or rational grounds. This is the understanding of philosophy that has prevailed particularly in our period of the departmentalization of all human knowledge. But Existentialism seeks to restore a much more primitive sense of the word, "philosophy," than this: namely, the ancient sense of philosophy as a concrete way of life, rather than an abstract set of propositions. Nietzsche, also an Existentialist, pointed out that for ancient man, and even the modern Oriental, the business of achieving a philosophy is one that engaged the whole man, his total being, and was not pursued simply as one specialized department of knowledge among others. Kierkegaard attacked the Hegelian professors of his time as being philosophers without any real philosophic existence: they had a system of propositions to teach, but the system itself was a means of forgetting the concrete realities of human life. For us in America today the philosopher is merely a "professional" savant among many others.

Existentialism, on the contrary, understands philosophy as a thing that is to be lived, and not merely a body of knowledge to be taught to pupils. I have said that Existentialism attempts to bring to human consciousness the basic, even banal, realities of human life: realities such as death, anxiety, choice, love, freedom, guilt, conscience, the willing acceptance of anxiety, etc., etc. In American academic philosophy today these are not the prevailing concepts: philosophers discuss concepts relating to science, knowledge, logic. Existential concepts are thought to belong to literature, perhaps to poetry. This rejection is an evidence of how far one particular tradition among the intellectual elite of our society has tended to set knowledge above life. If the philosopher exists professionally as a member of a department in a university, and if he accepts his role as one that deals with one special department of knowledge among others, then he is inevitably drawn to devote himself to those very special and technical problems that seem to be the peculiar province of the "expert." Our technological civilization has tended more and more to worship the expert, and the philosopher, assimilated to his civilization, strives more and more to justify his own professional existence by a high technical competence in the special problems of logic and philosophical analysis. The result is that a great deal of modern philosophy has tended to become divorced from life. Hence it is only natural that Existentialism, which struggles against this tendency, is looked on somewhat askance by a great many American philosophers.

All this has been by way of explaining why it seemed preferable to discuss Existentialism as a symptom, rather than a solution, of our contemporary crisis. But there has also been in the background of my remarks another, and much more drastic point, which will be substantiated by my further discussion, but can be announced now: the point, quite simply, that there is never a solution to any of life's crises. This is one of the cardinal points in existential philosophy itself. The word, "solution," belongs to the vocabulary of science and engineering, suggesting some kind of blueprint that would immediately deliver us from the pain and muddle of suffering, when, in fact, we know that our really deep crises in life are precisely those that we have to live through. Our deepest personal problems do not in the least resemble any problem of engineering, and it is the same, we suggest, with the sickness of civilization, even though the "cure" of a sick civilization might require vast exploits of engineering.

II

That movement in thought should be a symptom of its time, is not in the least a condemnation of this movement as a wild or trivial aberration. I am using the word, "symptom," in its simple and unprejudiced sense of a sign—

something that instructs us about the state of the organism from which it arises. Thus Existentialism has a great deal to teach us—which we might otherwise not know—about the condition of the Western civilization that has brought it to birth.

Most Americans connect Existentialism with the current French movement, and particularly with the name of its most brilliant publicist, Jean Paul Sartre. Sartre's is an agile and energetic mind, but his doctrine represents, I believe, a dilution of existential philosophy, and in any case does not take us back to its original sources. These lie in the nineteenth century, and the great innovators are Kierkegaard and Nietzsche—though the latter, unlike Kierkegaard, is not fully aware of his existential point of departure. Existential themes are treated in the fiction of Tolstoi and Dostoievski. In this century the two most important existential philosophers have been the German professors, Martin Heidegger and Karl Jaspers. To these names we might add the considerable figure of the Spanish philosopher, José Ortega y Gasset, who has described his philosophy as one of "vital reason," though it is fundamentally existential in its directions. These names should indicate that Existentialism is not a momentary intellectual fad, derived from the French, but a much wider and deeper movement in Western thought, having roots indeed in the profound upheavals of this civilization during the past two centuries. To see what these roots are, we may find it more convenient to turn, not to an abstruse text in philosophy, but to a work of literature that takes a simpler and more direct grasp of the issues involved: Tolstoi's great story, "The Death of Ivan Ilyich," which by this time has become something of a basic scripture for existential thought.

The plot of Tolstoi's story is slight and almost negligible. Ivan Ilyich is an amiable and undistinguished bourgeois, who has spent his whole life trying to be like everyone else in his social class: a successful and happy man, where happiness means only the absence of suffering. But one day Ivan Ilyich feels a pain in his side, which resists all treatment by doctors, and as his illness progresses, he suddenly realizes that he is going to die. For the first time in his life death becomes a reality for him. In the face of this awful presence, all his disguises fall away: confronting death for the first time in his life, he is also confronting himself for the first time. Hitherto in his life he had hid from himself amid the routine mechanisms of all his social, official, and familial functions. Now, as he is about to die, he asks himself the questions: Who am I? What has been the meaning of my life? In the end Ivan Ilyich dies content, because he has reached the point of knowing that the life he lived was empty, futile, and meaningless.

What Tolstoi is saying here, to put it now as a general thesis, is that modern life has alienated the individual from himself. The materialistic and rationalistic nineteenth century, with its emphasis upon all the bourgeois routines of life, has so externalized the individual that he has lost the feeling and the passion for his own personal existence. Modern man, Tolstoi is saying, has lost the meaning of life, and, as with Ivan Ilyich, it will take nothing less than the presence of death to restore this sense of life.

The sense of decadence haunts the nineteenth century, even at the moments of its most splendid optimism. There is a widespread uneasiness that life has lost its passion, intensity, and meaning; that there has been some secret decline in human vitality. Kierkegaard puts it as eloquently and compactly as one could wish:

> Let others complain that times are bad; I complain that they are petty because they lack passion. Men's thoughts are as flimsy as thin ice and men themselves as insignificant as the thin snow that covers it. Their thoughts are too petty to be sinful. A worm might consider such thoughts to be sinful, but not a man created in the image of God. Their pleasures are circumspect and boring; their passions, sleep; these materialistic souls fulfill their duties, but they collect their usury for it; they believe that although our Lord keeps His accounts in good order, they can hand Him counterfeit. Out with them! This is why my soul always hearkens back to Shakespeare and the Old Testament. There one feels that those who speak are men; there they hate; there they love; there they kill the enemy, curse their descendants for generations to come, there they sin.

This passage might almost have been written by Nietzsche, who launches his plea from the diametrically opposite anti-Christian pole. Modern man, says Nietzsche, lacks a goal, and his existence is, therefore, purposeless and nihilistic. Similar themes appear also in such diverse writers as Stendhal and Burckhardt.

The twentieth century has no reason to forget these fears. Our technological civilization has become even more involved with elaborate apparatus to catch and smother the individual. We have gone beyond the nineteenth century in the development of a fantastic mass culture—in radio, movies, and television —that stamps out all individual differences. Modern society has become more and more a mass society. Cities grow larger, crowds become more and more potent factors, and the individual threatened more than ever by anonymity in the mass. The image of modern man lies in T. S. Eliot's line: "Men and bits of paper, whirled by the cold wind." [2] These fears of the nineteenth century turn out to be prophetic for us: amid this general purposelessness of life, this mass drifting, we set ourselves the task of recapturing the sense and the meaning of life.

III

When Tolstoi speaks of a loss of the meaning of life, he is not referring to a loss of some rational explanation. Nor is the meaning that is to be restored

[2] T. S. Eliot, "Burnt Norton," *Collected Poems of T. S. Eliot, 1909-1935* (New York: Harcourt, Brace & World, Inc., 1936), p. 217.

an intellectual one, some new fact or discovery of the mind. On the contrary, the disorder in modern man that Tolstoi's story speaks of is a disorder in the more primitive and irrational, or non-rational, parts of man's being. Existentialism as a philosophy seeks to deal with these irrational parts of our existence in a way that philosophy has never done before, and by so doing gives reason itself a new place in the human hierarchy.

This is why existential philosophy has been frequently—and, I think, unjustly—criticized as anti-rational. One is not against reason, if one insists that the irrational is an inseparable part of life, and that it is precisely with the irrational parts of our being that modern civilization fails to deal adequately. This so-called "anti-rational" tendency in modern philosophy has now had a long history, from Rousseau to Bergson, Whitehead, and Heidegger in our century, and it embraces too many great names to be dismissed out of hand. Any future rationalism worth its salt will have to assimilate a great deal from these thinkers, and we ourselves would be less than rational, if we did not make an earnest effort to understand in detail how the irrational enters human life.

We gain some idea of the irrational character of life, if we turn back again to Tolstoi's "Ivan Ilyich." As death appears to Ivan Ilyich, it presents itself as something altogether unreasonable and incomprehensible. Immersed in the comfortable structure of his life, he sees this strange and dark intruder creep in to destroy everything. Yes, death is a banal fact, and we know that all men have to die; Ivan Ilyich knows all this with his head, but his heart cannot grasp the incomprehensible fact that he, Ivan Ilyich, should have to die. This bewilderment may strike us as childish, but it is Tolstoi's means of showing us how the irrational, like death, may fall upon us in the most incalculable and unpredictable way, upsetting all our plans for life.

Kierkegaard has expounded the presence of the irrational in another area of human life—in the act of choice or decision. We do not doubt that some decisions are more rational than others, and we may even speak of a decision as being the only rational choice under the circumstances. But is a rational choice one from which the irrational is ever completely excluded? Is any choice, however rational it be, free from the uncertain contingencies of risk and adventure? Of course, there are certain trivial choices that we make every day, and that we may reverse the next day, if we are proved wrong. But these are choices that do not commit us deeply, that leave us relatively disengaged from the consequences. As soon, however, as a choice cuts deeply; as soon as it commits our whole life in a certain direction; so soon, then, do the immense difficulties appear, the balance of probabilities becomes harder, and each alternative appears, however we may canvass its possibilities, as a leap into the unknown.

The choice that personally involved Kierkegaard happened to be the question whether or not to marry. Engaged to a young woman in Copenhagen, he desired marriage intensely, but he felt in himself also a certain religious mission that would prevent him from giving himself completely in marriage. The particular psychological facts involved here are important for an understanding of Kierkegaard's biography, but the peculiarly personal difficulties should not obscure for us the fact that the pathos of choice Kierkegaard faced is universal. There are, in short, choices in life that are irreversible. Kierkegaard could not have made an *experimental* choice of marriage, in the expectation that if it "did not work out"—to use the expression that has become common among us these days—he could return to his religious vocation and its tasks, for the vocation might have been lost through his marriage. On the other hand, if he renounced marriage experimentally, he could not hope to return to the young lady, should the other alternative not work out. She might not be there (as in fact she was not) when he returned. Love has to be seized at the moment it is offered; our indecision pollutes and destroys it.

All of this points to the fact that the situation of human choice is not at all a situation of scientific experiment. A situation is experimental in science when certain scientific controls have been established, so that through these controls we can repeat the experiment at any time and place we choose, and indeed repeat it indefinitely. The more precisely scientific the experiment becomes, the more its features of accidental particularity become refined away, and the easier it becomes to repeat it in all its detail. But our fundamental choices in life do not permit us this degree of control, because they do not permit us this degree of detachment. We have to choose here and now, and for the rest of our life, and the alternative we renounce is lost forever. We could be completely experimental about our own lives only if we were immortal, and so could repeat any situation or choice indefinitely.

But as death is real and our lives finite, every choice is also a renunciation, and this is why Kierkegaard speaks of the *pathos* of human choice. It was this sacrificial and pathetic aspect of choice that led Kierkegaard to his great polemic against the excessively rational philosophy of Hegel. The old adage puts the matter quite simply and adequately, "You cannot eat your cake and have it, too"; but Hegel devised a sophisticated dialectic by which it was possible to bring together two conflicting alternatives, thesis and antithesis, into a higher synthesis, so that the speculative philosopher, triumphing over life, could both have his cake and eat it, too. Such a reconciling of opposites is indeed possible in knowledge, where a more inclusive theory may embrace two conflicting alternatives; but it is not possible in life, where the suffering of renunciation cannot be altogether eliminated by reason. This opposition between knowledge and life has been one of the chief themes of Existentialism, as well as of a great deal of modern philosophy and literature.

IV

These two brief illustrations of the irrational—death and human choice—which cannot be altogether expunged from our existence, also illustrate that science, and scientific experiment, cannot take over the whole of life. The fear that science might devour the whole of human life has been a very powerful current of thought in the West, from William Blake onward. Indeed, from the Enlightenment in the eighteenth century to the present day, two deeply opposed attitudes toward science have dominated Western thinking: along with the great hope in science and its possibilities of human liberation, there has developed a great fear that science would somehow mechanize and impoverish human life. This fear of science cannot be dismissed simply as a crude popular superstition, for it embraces too many great names of our culture: Blake, Wordsworth, Kierkegaard, Nietzsche, Dostoievski, Tolstoi, Bergson. Our task, rather, should be to disengage the philosophical traits that characterize this fear of science at its deepest level.

One of the best expressions of the fear of science is found in the first part of Dostoievski's great novel, *Notes from Underground*. The hero is afraid of the scientific society of the future, in which human life can be rationally controlled and ordered, down to the very last detail. When human life is so scientifically precise and predictable, nobody would want to live it. Dostoievski's hero would prefer to smash this machine that would seek to contain him—out of sheer spite, as he puts it—to show that his human will in its liberty transcends the mathematically predictable, even if he has to show this in a destructive way. We come back thus to our principal point: what Dostoievski is saying, through his tormented and oppressed little hero, is that human life must be more than pure reason, and to attempt to reduce it to the latter is to destroy it, even if we make that reduction in the name of universal enlightenment.

It would be a mistake to consider the Underground Man as merely a sick and neurotic individual produced by the stresses of modern society. He is that, of course, but he is also a universal human character. We are all the Underground Man, to some degree or other. He is that dark side of our being, with which we must try to live in peace, and if we take lightly his fulminations against a human regime completely controlled by science and reason, we do so at our own risk.

As he is thus universal, the Underground Man reappears, and perhaps I may drive home my point by turning to the rather extraordinary position advanced in the nineteen hundred and twenties by I. A. Richards, the British critic and psychologist—a position that seems to me to express the extreme of hope that science will master life. (In justice to Richards, however, we must point out that at the time he was much more enamored of the possibilities of psychology than he is today.) Richards contended nothing less than this: that we can anticipate the time when psychological science will have advanced to the point where we can have, if we choose, whatever minds we desire. In the perfectly scientific utopia, in short, you could order your personality at a psychological laboratory the way you might order a prescription at a druggist's. Select your label, follow the prescription carefully, and you will have the personality, or the mind, that you want. Science which has performed so many miracles in the transformation of matter, and has found synthetic substitutes for almost everything, would here have found at last a substitute for life itself. In this psychological utopia it would be possible for a man to have a certain character without living through the risks, anxieties, and uncertain struggles that make it. We need not live to become a certain kind of being; science would provide it readymade.

We notice that this possibility that once inspired Richards with such hopes, is precisely the possibility against which Dostoievski's Underground Man rebels. Sick and resentful though he may be, the Underground Man at least insists upon having his own human life, rather than some mechanized substitute for it. The science of psychology has gone on developing since Richards's remark, but it is now further from maintaining any such utopian claims as once enchanted him. Among some circles in America, psychoanalysis may be regarded as a kind of magic, but not by the analysts themselves. Some people tend to think of psychoanalysis as a process in which the analyst, somewhat like a mechanic, overhauls the patient and gives him a new engine or set of works. But the serious analyst, while hoping to transform the neurotic patient's fundamental orientations toward life, insists that the patient can solve his problems only in actual life and not in the psychoanalytic session. Life has to be lived, there is no substitute for living—not even psychoanalysis.

Existential philosophy, in its insistence that the categories of life cannot be reduced to science, carries this point further. It may seem a rather trivial platitude to say that there can be no substitute for living, but the saying may not strike us as so platitudinous when we reflect upon the vast mechanized passivity that our civilization imposes upon so many of its members. In such circumstances the living rediscovery of certain banalities may represent an immense task and an immense triumph. Some of the greatest chapters in the history of philosophy are its discoveries of what lay obvious, but unnoticed, before every man's eyes. We may recall the great saying of Heraclitus, at the very dawn of philosophy in the sixth century B.C.: "Man is estranged from that with which he is most familiar, and he must continuously seek to rediscover it." This saying might serve as a very good motto for Existentialism. Among other things, it may make clear why the modern Existentialist, Heidegger, finds these early pre-Socratic Greeks his real forebears in the effort to confront human life and the whole life of nature with a primitive directness. The ancestry of existential philosophy thus turns out to be very ancient. I come back thus to a point made at the beginning, which should now be considerably clearer in its import: Existentialism, a modern movement in philosophy, is, in fact, an effort to recapture an old and very primitive sense of philosophy. Philosophy, here, is not the mere putting together of certain abstract propositions into a system; it is rather the concrete effort of the living individual to relate himself to his own life and the life of others around him. Quite literally, philosophy is a task that each individual has to perform for himself.

V

In this search for the primitive, Existentialism is in line with the most considerable movements in art and literature in this century. The word, "primitive," here is bound to arouse misunderstandings, if it is associated with the life of savages, barbarians, or big game hunters. Primitivism suggests to some the beat of tom-toms, Tahiti, maidens in sarongs, Gauguin; in short, an escape from modern civilization into the illusory simplicities of some South Sea island. These forms of primitivism have abounded, but they have always ended in a blind alley, because the desire for escape is itself a very nonprimitive state of being. I am using the word, "primitive," in a much more basic—I almost wrote primitive—sense: the primitive is the primary; and the valid search for the primitive is a search for the sources of our being which a too routinized civilization tends to obscure. In this sense, nearly all the art and literature that matter in the past half century have been primitive.

Modern painting and sculpture, for example, have really succeeded in creating a new kind of vision. In these works we stand in a new and more direct relation to colors, shapes, and forms. It is a vision of things at once simpler and more complex than the Western art of the past. In its distorting simplifications, bold arbitrary forms, it often resembles primitive art, from which indeed it has consciously drawn inspiration in certain cases, though it could not exist without the whole tradition of Western art. Moreover, the artist himself seems to stand in a new and direct relation to the very materials of his art: he seeks naïvely to assert the presence of his paint, stone, or metal, and his art is no longer a device to conceal or transcend this presence.

In literature, in writers such as D. H. Lawrence, James Joyce, and Thomas Mann, we find similar and diverging efforts to deal with the primitive. In his Joseph stories, Mann seeks to restore the primitive mythic consciousness to literature. James Joyce, in his last work, uses the most sophisticated literary technique, drawing upon the whole past of Western literature for its resources, in order to render the most unconscious, inarticulate, and primitive parts of human experience. Of these writers perhaps Lawrence is the most explicitly programmatic in his search for the primitive simplicities that he believes modern life to have lost. The organic unity of being that Lawrence seeks through sexual experience, is something that existential philosophers have sought in other directions. As T. S. Eliot reminds us, Lawrence was a man with an intense spiritual vocation, and his interest in sex was not at all a message of sex-for-sex's sake. Nevertheless, his proposed solution to the sickness of modern civilization seems to us today to be rather onesided. His perception of the sickness was real enough, but his prescription for cure represents a kind of impatient rush toward a solution. We are reminded, again, that when a sickness is total, the recovery can come only through development along many avenues of being at once.

This list could be swelled indefinitely to show that this struggle for rebirth is one of the great themes of modern culture. I have appended these brief indications to my main discussion only to point to the total historical context in which we must try to see the development of modern existential philosophy; and to suggest that this philosophy is not an eccentric movement, but lies in the main stream of modern culture. Existentialism makes clearer the human tasks that our epoch confronts. Unless we realize what the tasks are, we can hardly work significantly toward any solution at all.

Can Philosophy Save Civilization?

ÉTIENNE GILSON

The Breakdown of Modern Philosophy[1]

When Oswald Spengler first published *The Decline of the West*, many readers of his now famous book felt at variance with more than one of its conclusions; yet few among them would have thought of questioning the fact that the West was actually declining. Most of them had already known it for a long time. Not in the least because of the World War; on the contrary, the war had been a time of enthusiasm and complete self-dedication to a sacred cause, when old fears and solicitous misgivings as to the future of Western culture had been forgotten. I know that it is now fashionable to laugh at that sacred cause; yet there are still a few people who remember how they were then trying to redeem war by giving it a meaning and who remember what that meaning was. A certain idea of man and a corresponding ideal of social life were not to be allowed to perish. Yet it now seems clear that even at that time Western culture was steadily following its process of dissolution, and we know it from within, by a sort of immediate and personal experience. For we are the bearers of that culture; it cannot be dying, and dying in us, without our being aware of it.

In its broadest sense, what we call Western culture is essentially the culture of Greece, inherited from the Greeks by the Romans, transfused by the fathers of the church with the religious teachings of Christianity, and progressively enlarged by countless numbers of artists, writers, scientists, and philosophers from the beginning of the Middle Ages up to the first third of the

[1] From *The Unity of Philosophical Experience* by Étienne Gilson, copyright 1937 by Charles Scribner's Sons, and reprinted with their permission.

nineteenth century. It would be a waste of time to look for a turning point in its history—in the continuous stream of historical events every point is a turning point—but it can safely be assumed that the French Revolution marks the time when the more clear-sighted among the representatives of Western culture began to feel that there was something wrong with it. They offered various diagnoses, and they began to suggest remedies. For the reasons we have noted, Comte failed to provide Europe with a living dogma; his new scientific religion was stillborn, and he died, a self-appointed pope, with a very small number of disciples. On the whole, his Reformation was a failure, but Comte had at least seen clearly that the European crisis was essentially a crisis of Western culture: Can a social order, begotten by a common faith in the value of certain principles, keep on living when all faith in these principles is lost?

The meaning of that question will be illustrated best by a summary description of what may be called, for brevity's sake, the Western creed. Its most fundamental feature is a firm belief in the eminent dignity of man. The Greeks of classical times never wavered in their conviction that of all the things that can be found in nature, man is by far the highest, and that of all the things important for man to know, by far the most important is man. When Socrates, after unsuccessful attempts to deal with physical problems, made up his mind to dedicate himself to the exclusive study of man, he was making a momentous decision. "Know thyself" is not only the key to Greek culture but to the classical culture of the Western world as well. What the Greeks left to their successors was a vast body of knowledge, mainly related to man's nature and his various needs: logic, which is the science of how to think; several different philosophies, all of them culminating in ethics and politics, which are the sciences of how to live; remarkable specimens of history and political eloquence, related to the life of the city. As to what we today call positive science, the greatest achievements of the Greek genius were along the lines of mathematics, a knowledge which man draws from his own mind without submitting to the degrading tyranny of material facts, and medicine, whose proper object is to insure the well-being of the human body. And they stopped there, checked by an obscure feeling that the rest was not worth having, at least not at the price which the human mind would have to pay for it; its freedom from matter, its internal liberty.

Of the heirs to Greek culture it can truly be said that while they enlarged and deepened their heritage, they always respected its nature and never thought of displacing its center of gravity. When the Romans added the lofty structure of Roman law to it, man and the betterment of human life still remained their essential interest. As to Christianity, though it be true that God was its ultimate goal and its center of reference, the fact remains that it conceived man, created by God in His own image and likeness, as the most perfect of all earthly beings, with no higher duty than to achieve his own salvation. And why is man an image of God? Because, says St. Augustine, he has a mind. All the Greek philosophers would have gladly subscribed to that statement.

Hence the second fundamental feature of Western culture, which is a definite conviction that reason is the specific difference of man. Man is best described as a rational animal; deprive man of reason, and what is left is not man, but animal. This looks like a very commonplace statement; yet Western culture is dying wherever it has been forgotten, for the rational nature of man is the only conceivable foundation for a rational system of ethics. Morality is essentially normality; for a rational being to act and to behave either without reason or contrary to its dictates is to act and behave, not exactly as a beast, but as a beastly man, which is worse. For it is proper that a beast should act as a beast—that is, according to its own nature—but it is totally unfitting for a man to act as a beast, because that means the complete oblivion of his own nature, and hence his final destruction.

It is hardly possible to realize the continuity that prevails throughout the whole history of Western culture unless one keeps in mind the important part played by the church in the work of its transmission. The Greek and the Latin fathers of the church had so carefully preserved the classical notion of man that when St. Thomas Aquinas, in the thirteenth century, undertook to build up a complete exposition of the Christian truth, he did not scruple to borrow for his technical equipment from the pagan Aristotle, whose logic, physics, biology, ethics, and metaphysics were then transformed by his mediaeval disciple into as many elements of a Christian synthesis.

The Reformation of the sixteenth century was to wreck that stately edifice, whose two component elements then fell apart, Christianity on the one side, and Greek culture on the other. Yet not only Catholic humanists such as Erasmus but even Protestants such as Melanchthon immediately set about rebuilding it. Luther himself, despite his fierce attacks upon pagan culture, was fond of Ovid, and he always remained partial to Cicero. The humanists who, more or less consciously, swerved from Christianity to paganism were either going back to what seemed to them the pure doctrine of Aristotle or testing the truth value of the doctrines left by the Stoics and Epicureans. Throughout the Renaissance and until the middle of the nineteenth century, the classical tradition remained the common ground on which both pagans and Christians could still meet and carry on fruitful intellectual intercourse. Even the most brilliant scientific discoveries were made by men who, like Descartes, Pascal, Fermat, Leibnitz, and Newton, had learned little more at school than classical Latin, a philosophy which more or less resembled that of St. Thomas or Aristotle, and the elements of mathematics. So long as, and in so far as, science itself kept faith with its own nature, it remained the healthy exercise of reason, reason seeking to know, because knowing is its natural function. Even the most stupendous progress made by the physical and biological sciences entailed no disruption in the continuity of Western culture. While man remained in control of nature, culture could still survive. It was lost from the very moment nature began to control man.

Such a development was by no means inevitable, but the progressive growth of natural science had made it more and more probable. The growing interest taken by men in the practical results of science was in itself both natural and legitimate, but it helped them to forget that science is knowledge, and practical results but its by-products. Moreover, the constant accumulation of hitherto unknown facts and of their recently formulated laws was destroying the old balance between the human and the physical sciences, to the advantage of the latter. This, however, was not the main point. It lay rather in the fact that before their unexpected success in finding conclusive explanations of the material world, men had begun either to despise all disciplines in which such demonstrations could not be found or to rebuild those disciplines after the pattern of the physical sciences. As a consequence, metaphysics and ethics had to be ignored or, at least, replaced by new positive sciences; in either case, they would be eliminated.

A very dangerous move indeed, which accounts for the perilous position in which Western culture has now found itself. The European burned his old ships before making sure that the new ones would float. Moreover, the first article of the scientific creed is the acceptance of nature such as it is. Far from making up for the loss of philosophy, the discovery of the scientific substitutes for it leaves man alone with nature such as it is and obliges him to surrender to natural necessity. Philosophy is the only rational knowledge by which both science and nature can be judged. By reducing philosophy to pure science, man has not only abdicated his right to judge nature and to rule it, but he has also turned himself into a particular aspect of nature, subjected, like all the rest, to the necessary law which regulates its development. A world where accomplished facts are unto themselves their own justification is ripe for the most reckless social adventures. Its dictators can wantonly play havoc with human institutions and human lives, for dictatorships are facts, and they also are unto themselves their own justification.

ERICH FROMM

The Present Human Condition[1]

At the close of the middle ages, Western man seemed to be headed for the final fulfillment of his keenest dreams and visions. He freed himself from the authority of a totalitarian church, the weight of traditional thought, the geographical limitations of our but half-discovered globe. He built a new sci-

[1] From *The American Scholar*, XXV (Winter, 1955-56), 29-35. Copyright 1956 by Erich Fromm and reprinted with his permission.

ence which eventually has led to the release of hitherto unheard-of productive powers, and to the complete transformation of the material world. He created political systems which seem to guarantee the free and productive development of the individual; he reduced the time of work to such a level that man was free to enjoy hours of leisure to an extent his forefathers had hardly dreamed of.

Yet Where Are We Today?

The danger of an all-destructive war hangs over the head of humanity, a danger which is by no means overcome by the spirit of Geneva prevalent at the time of this writing. But even if man's political representatives have enough sanity left to avoid a war, man's condition is far from the fulfillment of the hopes of the sixteenth, seventeenth and eighteenth centuries.

Man's character has been molded by the demands of the world he has built with his own hands. In the eighteenth and nineteenth centuries, man's character orientation was essentially exploitative and hoarding. His course through life was determined by the desire to exploit others and to save his earnings to make further profit from them. In the twentieth century, man's character orientation is essentially a receptive and a marketing one. He is receptive in most of his leisure time. He is the eternal consumer; he "takes in" drink, food, cigarettes, lectures, sights, books, movies—all are consumed, swallowed. The world is one great object for his appetite, a big bottle, a big apple, a big breast. Man has become the suckler, the eternally expectant—and the eternally disappointed one.

If "privately," individually, modern man is a consumer, he is "publicly," in his active participation in his society, a trader. Our economic system is centered around the function of the market as determining the value of all commodities, and as the regulator of each one's share in the social product. Neither force nor tradition, as in previous periods of history, nor fraud or trickery govern man's economic activities. He is free to produce and to sell; market day is judgment day for the success of his efforts. Not only are commodities offered and sold on the market; labor itself has become a commodity, sold on the labor market under the same conditions of fair competition. But the market system has reached out farther than the economic sphere of commodities and labor. Man has transformed *himself* into a commodity, experiences his life as capital to be invested profitably; if he succeeds in this, he is "successful," and his life has meaning; if not, "he is a failure." His "value" lies in his salability, not in his human qualities of love and reason or in his artistic capacities. Hence his sense of his own value depends on extraneous factors, his success, the judgment of others. Hence he is dependent on these others, and his security lies in conformity, in never being more than two feet away from the herd.

However, it is not only the market which determines modern man's "public" character. Another factor, though one closely related to the market function, is the mode of industrial production. Enterprises become bigger and bigger; the number of people employed by these enterprises as workers or clerks grows incessantly; ownership is separated from management, and the industrial giants are governed by a professional bureaucracy which is mainly interested in the smooth functioning and in the expansion of their enterprise, rather than in profit per se.

What kind of man, then, does our society need in order to function smoothly? It needs men who co-operate smoothly in large groups; who want to consume more and more, and whose tastes are standardized and can be easily influenced and anticipated. It needs men who feel free and independent, who do not feel subject to any authority or principle or conscience, yet are willing to be commanded, to do what is expected, to fit unto the social machine without friction—men who can be guided without force, led without leaders, be prompted without any aim except the one to be on the move, to function, to go ahead. Modern capitalism has succeeded in producing this kind of man; he is the automaton, the alienated man. He is alienated in the sense that his acts and forces have become estranged from him; they stand above and against him, and rule him rather than being ruled by him. His life forces have flowed into things and institutions, and these things, having become idols, are not experienced as the result of his own efforts, but as something apart from him which he worships and to which he submits. Alienated man bows down before the works of his own hands. His idols represent his own life forces in an alienated form. Man does not experience himself as the active bearer of his own forces and riches, but as an impoverished "thing," dependent on other things—things outside himself, into which he has projected his living substance.

Man's social feelings are projected into the state. Just because he has made the state the embodiment of his own social feelings, he worships it and its symbols. He projects his sense of power, wisdom and courage into his leaders, and he worships them as his idols. As a worker, clerk or manager, modern man is alienated from his work. The worker has become an economic atom that dances to the tune of automatized management. He has no part in planning the work process, in its outcome; he is hardly ever in touch with the whole product. The manager, on the other hand, is in touch with the whole product, but he is alienated from it as something concrete and useful. His aim is to employ profitably the capital invested by others; the commodity is the abstractified embodiment of capital, not something which, as a concrete entity, matters to him. The manager has become a bureaucrat who handles things, figures and human beings as mere objects of his activity. Their manipulation is considered to be a concern with human relations, when actually one deals with the most inhuman relations—those between abstractified automatons.

Our consumption is equally alienated. It is determined by the advertising slogans, rather than by our palates, eyes or ears.

As a citizen, then, modern man is willing even to give his life for his fellow men; as a private individual, he is filled with an egotistical concern for himself. The meaninglessness and alienation of work result in a longing for complete laziness. Man hates his working life because it makes him feel a prisoner and a fraud. His ideal becomes absolute laziness, in which he will not have to make a move, where everything goes according to the Kodak slogan: "You press the button; we do the rest." This tendency is reinforced by the type of consumption necessary for the expansion of the inner market, leading to a principle which Huxley has very succinctly expressed in his *Brave New World*. One might epitomize the way many of us today have been conditioned from childhood with: "Never put off till tomorrow the fun you can have today." If I do not postpone the satisfaction of my wish (and I am conditioned only to wish for what I can get), I have no conflicts, no doubts; no decision has to be made; I am never alone with myself because I am always busy—either working or having fun. I have no need to be aware of myself as myself because I am constantly absorbed with consuming. I am a system of desires and satisfactions; I have to work in order to fulfill my desires, and these very desires are constantly stimulated and directed by the economic machine.

We claim that we pursue the aims of the Judaeo-Christian tradition, the love of God and of our neighbor. We are even told that we are going through a period of a promising religious renaissance. Nothing could be further from the truth. We use symbols belonging to a genuinely religious tradition, and transform them into formulas serving the purposes of alienated man. Religion becomes a self-help device for increasing one's own powers for success. God becomes a partner in business. The "Power of Positive Thinking" is the successor of "How to Make Friends and Influence People."

Love of man is a rare phenomenon too. Automatons do not love; alienated men do not care. What is praised by love experts and marriage counselors is a team relationship between two people who manipulate each other with the right techniques, and whose love is essentially a haven from an otherwise unbearable aloneness, an egotism à deux.

What, then, can be expected from the future? If one ignores those thoughts produced by our wishes, one has to admit, I am afraid, that the most likely possibility is still that the discrepancy between technical intelligence and reason will lead the world into an atomic war. The most likely outcome of such a war is the destruction of industrial civilization and the regression of the world to a primitive agrarian level. Or, if the destruction should not prove to be as thorough as many specialists in the field believe, the result will be the necessity for the victor to organize and dominate the whole world. This could be realized only by a centralized state based on force, and it would make little difference whether Moscow or Washington would be the seat of government.

But, unfortunately, even the avoidance of war does not in itself promise a bright future. In the development of both capitalism and communism as we

can visualize them in the next fifty or a hundred years, the process of autom-
atization and alienation will proceed. Both these systems are developing
managerial societies in which inhabitants are well fed and well clad, having
their wishes satisfied, and not having wishes that cannot be satisfied; automatons, who follow without force, who are guided without leaders, who make
machines that act like men and produce men who act like machines; men
whose reason deteriorates while their intelligence rises, thus creating the
dangerous situation of equipping man with the greatest material power without the wisdom to use it.

In spite of increasing production and comfort, man loses more and more the
sense of self, feels that his life is meaningless, even though such feeling is
largely unconscious. In the nineteenth century the problem was that *God is
dead*; in the twentieth century the problem is that *man is dead*. In the nineteenth century inhumanity meant cruelty; in the twentieth century it means
schizoid self-alienation. The danger of the past was that men became slaves.
The danger of the future is that men may become robots. True enough,
robots do not rebel. But given man's nature, robots cannot live and remain
sane. They become "golems"; they will destroy their world and themselves
because they cannot stand any longer the boredom of a meaningless life.

What is the alternative to war and robotism? Most fundamentally, perhaps,
the answer could be given by reversing Emerson's phrase: "Things are in the
saddle and ride mankind," and saying: "Put mankind in the saddle so that it
rides things." This is another way of saying that man must overcome the alienation which makes him an impotent and irrational worshiper of idols. This
means, if we remain in the psychological sphere, that he must overcome the
marketing and receptive orientation which dominates him now, and emerge
into the mature, productive orientation. He must acquire again a sense of self,
he must be capable of loving, and of making his work a meaningful and concrete activity. He must emerge from a materialistic orientation and arrive at a
level where spiritual values, love, truth and justice truly become of ultimate
concern to him. But any attempt to change only one section of life, the human
or spiritual one, is doomed to failure. In fact, any progress which occurs only
in one sphere is destructive of progress in all spheres. The gospel concerned
only with spiritual salvation led to the establishment of the Roman Catholic
Church; the French Revolution, with its exclusive concern with political reform, led to Robespierre and Napoleon; socialism, insofar as it was only concerned with economic change, led to Stalinism.

Applying this principle of simultaneous change to all spheres of life, we
must think of those economic and political changes which are necessary in order to overcome the psychological fact of alienation. We must retain the industrial method. But we must decentralize work and the state so as to give
them *human* proportions, and permit centralization only to an optimal point
which is necessary because of the requirements of industry. In the economic
sphere we need co-management of all who work in an enterprise to permit

their active and responsible participation. The new forms for such participation can be found. In the political sphere, we must return to the town meeting by creating thousands of small face-to-face groups which are well informed, which discuss, and whose decisions are integrated in a new "lower house." A cultural renaissance must combine work education for the young, adult education, and a new system of popular art and secular ritual throughout the whole nation.

Just as primitive man was helpless before the natural forces, modern man is helpless before the social and economic forces created by himself. He worships the works of his own hands, bowing to the new idols, yet swearing by the name of the God who commanded him to destroy all idols. Man can protect himself from the consequences of his own madness only by creating a sane society which conforms with the needs of man, needs which are rooted in the very conditions of his existence: a society in which man relates to man lovingly, in which he is rooted in bonds of brotherliness and solidarity, rather than in the ties of blood and soil; a society which gives him the possibility of transcending nature by creating rather than by destroying; one in which everyone gains a sense of self by experiencing himself as the subject of his powers rather than by conformity; one in which a system of orientation and devotion exists without man's needing to distort reality and to worship idols.

Building such a society means taking the next step; it means the end of "humanoid" history, the phase in which man has not become fully human. It does not mean the "end of days," the "completion," the state of perfect harmony in which no conflicts or problems confront man. On the contrary, it is man's fate that his existence is beset by contradictions which he is impelled to solve without ever solving them. When he has overcome the primitive state of human sacrifice, be it in the ritualistic form of the Aztecs or in the secular form of war; when he has been able to regulate his relationship with nature reasonably instead of blindly; when things have truly become his servants rather than his idols—he will be confronted with the truly human conflicts and problems. He will have to be adventuresome, courageous, imaginative, capable of suffering and of joy, but his powers will be in the service of life, and not in the service of death. The new phase of human history, if it comes to pass, will be a beginning, not an end.

Biographical Notes

ARISTOTLE (384–322 B.C.), versatile Greek philosopher, was a student of Plato. He was appointed by Philip of Macedon to tutor his son, Alexander the Great. Later he returned to Athens where he lectured to many disciples and wrote his numerous works on poetry, logic, natural science, politics, rhetoric, philosophy, and metaphysics. His influence, particularly great during the Middle Ages, continues to this day.

MATTHEW ARNOLD (1822–1888), critic of the strains in contemporary culture, in his poems voiced the doubts of an age "wandering between two worlds, one dead, the other powerless to be born"—the world of religious faith and the world of doubt engendered by science.

FRANCIS BACON (1561–1626), scientist, philosopher, and man of letters, became Lord Chancellor of England. His works, which have influenced the development of human thought and progress, include *The Advancement of Learning* (1605), *Instauratio Magna*, and *Novum Organum* (1627).

WILLIAM BARRETT (1913–), formerly editor of *Partisan Review*, is a member of the Department of Philosophy at New York University. He has also taught at the University of Illinois and at Brown University. Besides contributing to the periodicals, he has written *What is Existentialism?* (1947).

JACQUES BARZUN (1907–) was born in Paris and received his early education at a Paris lycée. Now a United States citizen, he has taught history at Columbia since 1937, from which he received his Ph.D. in 1932. Among his many books are *Teacher in America* (1945), *Berlioz and the Romantic Century* (1950), *God's Country and Mine* (1954), and *The House of Intellect* (1959).

CLAUDE BERNARD (1813–1878), French physiologist and opponent of "vitalism," carried out experimental investigation on nerves and chemical research. He discovered the function of the vasomotor nerves. His theory of the "interior environment" has been of major importance. Two of his books are *An Introduction to Experimental Medicine* (1865) and *General Physiology* (1872).

CARL BINGER (1889–), psychiatrist, graduated from Harvard College and took his M.D. at Harvard Medical School. He is consulting psychiatrist to the Harvard University Health Service and to the Medical Department of Radcliffe College. Among his books are *Personality in Arterial Hypertension* (1945), *More About Psychiatry* (1949) and *Emotional Problems of the Student* (1961).

MORRIS GILBERT BISHOP (1893–), scholar and teacher of Romance Languages at Cornell University, is also known as a satirist and humorist. He has published biographical and critical works on Cabeza de Vaca, Pascal, and Ronsard, and a number of volumes of humorous poems and sketches.

MORTON W. BLOOMFIELD (1913–), a graduate of McGill and Wisconsin, taught English at Ohio State University (1941–1961) and is now professor of English at Harvard. He is the author of *The Seven Deadly Sins* (1952).

DAVID BOROFF (1917–), who has studied at Brooklyn, Yale, and Columbia, is assistant professor of English at Washington Square College of New York University and a free-lance writer. He is the author of *Campus U.S.A.*

ROLLO WALTER BROWN (1880–), author and teacher, was born in Ohio. He has taught English at Carleton College and Harvard, lectured, contributed to magazines, and written a number of books, among which are *Next Door to a Poet*, *The Writer's Art*, and *Harvard Yard in the Golden Age*.

MARTIN BUBER (1878–), Jewish theologian and philosopher, is a native of Vienna. He has done much to interpret Judaism to contemporary America. The present selection is substantially a lecture which he delivered in 1951 at a number of American universities. Among his books are *I and Thou* (1923), *Israel and the World* (1948), *Good and Evil* (1952), *Pointing the Way* (1957), *I And Thou* (1958), and *Hasidism and Modern Man* (1958).

INGRAM BYWATER (1841–1914) was an English Hellenist and translator of Aristotle.

JAMES BRYANT CONANT (1893–), American scientist and educator, was formerly president of Harvard and Ambassador to the Republic of West Germany. In recent years Conant has devoted most of his time to a study of secondary education in America. He is the author of *The Chemistry of Organic Compounds* (1933), *Education and Liberty* (1953), *The Revolutionary Transformation of the American High School* (1959), and *Science and Common Sense* (1961).

AARON COPLAND (1900–) has composed numerous symphonies, sonatas, concertos, film scores, and opera. Among his more recent works are *Tender Land* (opera, 1954) and *Piano Fantasy* (1957).

ROBERT GORHAM DAVIS (1908–), a graduate of Harvard, is professor of English at Columbia University. The author of many critical essays and reviews, he has also published short stories.

RENÉ DESCARTES (1596–1650) was the French philosopher whose system did much to sweep aside the subtleties of medieval thinkers and thus to influence greatly the formation of the modern mind. A mathematician as well as a philosopher, Descartes aimed at the ideal of mathematical certitude in metaphysical problems. His principal works are *Discours de la Methode, Meditationes de Prima Philosophia*, and *Principia Philosophiae*.

JOHN DONNE (1573–1631), the famous Dean of St. Paul's and metaphysical poet, was born a Roman Catholic. After his conversion to the Anglican Church he took holy orders at the suggestion of King James I, who was pleased to grant him several preferments in the Church, culminating in the Deanship of St. Paul's. Though Donne in early youth was worldly, and wrote some of the most passionate love poetry in English literature, he became fervent in spirit and zealous for the Lord. His sermons, many of them preached before Charles I, are among the most eloquent in all English pulpit oratory. His *Devotions*, occasioned by a grave illness, were written in 1623. Donne is considered one of the greatest of English prose writers by many critics.

SIR ARTHUR STANLEY EDDINGTON (1882–1944), English physicist and astronomer, made distinguished contributions to astrophysics and the theory of relativity with such books as *Space, Time and Gravitation* (1920), *The Internal Constitution of the Stars* (1926), and *The Expanding Universe* (1933).

IRWIN EDMAN (1896–1954) received both his B.A. and Ph.D. at Columbia and taught there in the Department of Philosophy. A posthumous collection of his essays is entitled *The Uses of Philosophy* (1955).

T. S. ELIOT (1888–), born in St. Louis and a graduate of Harvard, became a British citizen in 1927. In addition to his poems, he has written criticism (much of it available in *Selected Essays*, 1950) and plays, of which *The Cocktail Party* (1950) is best known.

JEROME ELLISON (1907–), a graduate of Michigan, is a teacher of journalism at Indiana University. A founder of *Best Articles & Stories Magazine*, he has also been an editor of *Reader's Digest*.

WILLIAM FAULKNER (1897–), one of the foremost living American novelists, has published some twenty books of fiction, notably *The Sound and the Fury* (1931), *Light in August* (1932), and *The Town* (1957). In 1950 he was awarded the Nobel Prize for literature.

LESLIE A. FIEDLER (1917–), a graduate of The Universities of New York and Wisconsin, teaches English at Montana State University. He has written *An End of Innocence* (1955) and *Love and Death in the American Novel* (1960).

ABRAHAM FLEXNER (1866–1959), American educator and physician, was director of the Institute for Advanced Studies at Princeton from 1930 to 1939, and afterwards was its director emeritus. Associated with the General Education Board, he wrote many books on medical education and on higher education in the United States and Europe.

E. M. FORSTER (1879–), British novelist, is author of the celebrated *A Passage to India* (1924). He was educated at Cambridge, where he is now an Honorary Fellow of King's College. He is also author of *A Room with a View* (1908) and *Howard's End* (1910), as well as two books of short stories, *The Eternal Moment* (1928), and *The Celestial Omnibus* (1911).

MORRIS FREEDMAN (1920–), a graduate of the City College of New York (A.B.) and Columbia University (M.A., Ph.D.), has taught English at the University of New Mexico since 1955. A former editor of *Commentary*, he has written articles on contemporary American life and essays on Milton and Dryden.

SIGMUND FREUD (1856–1939), Viennese neurologist and psychologist and the founder of psychoanalysis, has exerted a profound influence upon modern art, literature, and philosophy as well as on psychology and medicine. He is best known for such writings as *The Interpretation of Dreams* (1913) and *A General Introduction to Psychoanalysis* (1920).

ERICH FROMM (1900–) was born in Frankfurt, Germany. Trained in psychoanalysis in Munich and at the Psychoanalytic Institute in Berlin, he has devoted his time since 1925 to work as a consultant psychologist and partly to theoretical work especially in the field of the application of psychoanalytic theory to problems of culture and society. A naturalized American citizen, he now teaches at the National University of Mexico. Among his books are *Escape from Freedom* (1941), *Man for Himself* (1947), *The Forgotten Language* (1951), and *The Sane Society* (1955).

JOHN KENNETH GALBRAITH (1908–), graduate of the Universities of Toronto and California, has served in many government posts and was appointed Ambassador to India in 1961. Two of his best known books are *The Affluent Society* (1958) and *The Liberal Hour* (1960).

ÉTIENNE GILSON (1884–), French philosopher and historian, was educated at the Sorbonne, where he has been professor of medieval philosophy. Since 1929 he has been director of the Institute of Medieval Studies at Toronto. A popular lecturer in English as well as French, he has frequently lectured in England and at universities in the United States. He is considered one of the most distinguished medievalists in the world. A devout Roman Catholic in religion, in philosophy he is a follower of St. Thomas Aquinas. Some of his books are *The Philosophy of St. Thomas Aquinas, The Unity of Philosophical Experience,* and *Christianity and Philosophy*.

CLEMENT GREENBERG (1909–), art critic and consultant, has written books on Joan Miro, Henri Matisse, and Jackson Pollock. *Art and Culture* (1961) is a collection of critical essays by him.

LEARNED HAND (1872–1961) was born at Albany and educated at Harvard and the Harvard Law School. He was Judge of the United States Circuit Court,

Second Circuit, from 1924 to 1951. The probity and wisdom of his decisions made other lawyers, as well as the public, revere him as the dean of the American bar.

WILLIAM HARVEY (1578–1657), English physiologist and physician to Charles I, was educated at Cambridge and Padua. A series of experiments, now regarded as classic, led to his discovery and description of the circulation of the blood. *On the Motion of the Heart and Blood in Animals* was published under a Latin title in 1628.

GEORGE P. HEDLEY (1899–), chaplain and professor of religion at Mills College, was born in China. Educated at the University of Southern California and at the Pacific School of Religion, Dr. Hedley is author of *Reconsiderations* (1942) and *The Christian Heritage in America* (1946).

GEOFFREY T. HELLMAN (1907–), a graduate of Yale, has been associated with *The New Yorker* since 1929, except for brief intervals with *Fortune* and *Life* and for governmental and military service during World War II.

GILBERT HIGHET (1906–), born in Scotland and a graduate of Glasgow and Oxford, came to the United States in 1937. A professor of Latin at Columbia, he is widely known for his radio and television talks. Among his books are *The Classical Tradition* (1949), *Poets in a Landscape* (1957), and *The Powers of Poetry* (1960).

ARCHIBALD A. HILL (1915–), a graduate of Pomona, Stanford, and Yale, has taught philology and linguistics at the University of Texas since 1955. His *Introduction to Linguistic Structures* appeared in 1958.

ALFRED EDWARD HOUSMAN (1859–1936), distinguished English poet and classical scholar, was educated at Oxford, where he failed to receive honors and took a pass degree. In 1892 he became professor of Latin at University College, London, and in 1911, professor of Latin at Cambridge. His "Introductory Lecture" was delivered upon the occasion of his becoming professor of Latin at University College. He edited Manilius, Juvenal, and Lucan. He ranks among the greatest classical scholars England has produced. But he is more highly esteemed by most readers for his three slender volumes of poems: *A Shropshire Lad* (1896), *Last Poems* (1922), and *More Poems* (1936).

ROBERT MAYNARD HUTCHINS (1899–), formerly president of the University of Chicago and now president of the Fund for the Republic, was educated at Oberlin and Yale. A controversial figure in American education, he has published many articles and books.

WILLIAM JAMES (1842–1910), educated in Europe and at the Harvard Medical School, became an internationally famous psychologist and philosopher. He founded at Harvard the first American psychology laboratory. He was the author of *Principles of Psychology*, *Pragmatism*, and *The Meaning of Truth*. With Charles S. Peirce, he founded the pragmatic school of philosophy.

THOMAS JEFFERSON (1743–1826) composed his own epitaph: "Here was buried Thomas Jefferson, Author of the Declaration of Independence, of the Statute of Virginia for Religious Freedom, and Father of the University of Virginia."

E. J. KAHN, JR. (1916–) graduated from Harvard in 1937, and in the same year began his career of writer and reporter in New York City. He served with the U.S. Army from 1941 to 1945. Among his books are *The Army Life* (1942), *Who, Me?* (1949), and *The Merry Partners* (1956).

CLYDE KLUCKHOHN (1905–1960), member of the Department of Anthropology at Harvard 1935–1960, first became interested in anthropology when he began to study the Navajos and other peoples of the Southwest. He traveled and studied in Europe, was chief of the Policy Division in the Far East of the O. W. I. Among his books were *To the Foot of the Rainbow* (1927), *Personality in Nature, Society and Culture* (1948), and *How the Soviet System Works* (1955).

ARTHUR KOESTLER (1905–), born in Hungary, has been a correspondent and a soldier in the French and British armies. Two of his books are the novel *Darkness at Noon* (1941) and *The Lotos and the Robot* (1960), essays on Yoga and Zen.

SUSANNE LANGER (1895–), a graduate of Radcliffe (A.B., A.M., Ph.D.), is professor of philosophy at Connecticut College. Her best known works are *Philosophy in a New Key* (1942) and its sequel *Feeling and Form* (1953). Recently she has written *Problems of Art* (1957).

JOHN LOCKE (1632–1704) was an English philosopher whose writings turned from the subtleties of Aristotle and the Schoolmen and helped point the modern world toward experimental science. Locke has been called the father of English empiricism, and his influence on the development of psychology, philosophy, education, and political science has been tremendous. His principal philosophical work is *An Essay Concerning Human Understanding*. His two *Treatises of Government* denied the divine right of kings and justified the Revolution of 1688, thus indirectly providing justification for the American Revolution. He was probably the most influential English thinker of the seventeenth century, and his influence is still felt in Western democracies.

F. L. LUCAS (1894–), fellow and lecturer of King's College, Cambridge, is the author of poems, criticism, fiction, and plays. Two of his books are *The Decline and Fall of the Romantic Ideal* (1936) and *The Art of Living: Four Eighteenth-Century Minds* (1959).

DWIGHT MACDONALD (1906–), a graduate of Yale, has been an editor of *The Partisan Review* and is a staff writer for *The New Yorker*. Two recent books are *Ford Foundation: The Men and the Millions* (1956) and *Parodies: An Anthology* (1960).

MARCUS AURELIUS ANTONINUS (121–180), Roman emperor and philosopher, was one of the greatest Stoics. His *Meditations*, written in Greek, consist of twelve books of sage advice on conduct and living. Learned and gentle, he nevertheless opposed Christianity, even to the extent of persecuting Christians.

JACQUES MARITAIN (1882–), Catholic philosopher, was born in Paris and educated at the University of Paris and at Rome. In 1906, he was converted to Roman Catholicism, and since then he has been widely regarded as one of the most influential Catholic spokesmen in the world. For many years he has specialized in the scholastic philosophy of St. Thomas Aquinas, upon which he has lectured at many of the great universities of the world. From 1948–1953 he was professor of philosophy at Princeton, and since 1953 he has been professor emeritus. Some of the most important of his many books are *The Person and the Common Good* (1947), *Existence and the Existent* (1948), *Man and the State* (1950), *The Range of Reason* (1952), *Creative Intuition in Art and Poetry* (1953), and *Approaches to God* (1954).

FRANK JEWETT MATHER, JR. (1868–1953) was a professor of art and archaeology at Princeton University. His specialty was Italian painting.

H. L. MENCKEN (1880–1956), critic, editor, and philologist, edited *The American Mercury* from 1924 until 1933, and long was associated with the *Baltimore Evening Sun*. His six series of *Prejudices* (1919–1927) exemplify his work as a critic, and *The American Language* (1918, with later revisions) is his philological masterpiece.

ARTHUR MILLER (1915–) graduated from Michigan in 1938. Most famous of his plays is *Death of a Salesman* (1949); others are *All My Sons* (1947), *The Crucible* (1953), and *View from the Bridge* (1955).

GEOFFREY MOORE (1920–), a graduate of Cambridge, has taught at six colleges and universities in the United States. Long active in BBC radio and television, he was appointed lecturer in American literature at the University of Manchester in 1955. He has written *Poetry Today* (1958).

MICHEL EYQUEM DE MONTAIGNE (1533–1592) was a French courtier and essayist. His *Essais*, important both for their matter and for their style, have exercised a considerable influence on the development of the essay in English literature.

THEODORE MORRISON (1901–), for many years director of English A at Harvard and now lecturer in English, is the author of several volumes of poetry and frequent critical papers. His books include *The Portable Chaucer* and a novel *To Make a World* (1957).

LEWIS MUMFORD (1895–) has written a number of books on American civilization. Though his most distinguished work has concerned architecture (as in *Sticks and Stones*, 1924, and *The City in History*, 1961), he has also made notable contributions in literary and cultural history (as in *The Golden Day*, 1926, and *The Brown Decades*, 1931) and in philosophical analysis (as in *Values for Survival*, 1946, *The Conduct of Life*, 1951, *The Human Prospect*, 1955, and *Transformations of Man*, 1956).

OGDEN NASH (1902–) has established himself as a leading humorous poet since *Hard Lines* appeared in 1931. Other titles are *The Face Is Familiar* (1940) and *The Christmas That Almost Wasn't* (1957). A recent collection is *Verses from 1929 On* (1959).

REINHOLD NIEBUHR (1892–), influential American theologian, studied at Elmhurst College (Illinois) and the Yale Divinity School. After graduation, he was ordained to the ministry of the Evangelical Synod of North America in 1915. Since 1930 he has taught theology at Union Theological Seminary in New York. His most important works are *Moral Man and Immoral Society* (1932), *Beyond Tragedy* (1937), *The Nature and Destiny of Man* (1941–43), *Discerning the Signs of the Times* (1946), and *Faith and History* (1949). He is one of contemporary Protestantism's most profound spokesmen.

GEORGE ORWELL is the pseudonym of Eric Blair (1904–1950), British essayist and novelist. Among his best known books are *Animal Farm* (1945) and *1984* (1949).

THOMAS PAINE (1737–1809), American political philosopher, encouraged the American Revolution by publishing *Common Sense*, which called for an immediate declaration of independence (January 10, 1776), and *The Crisis*, twelve issues of which appeared during the course of the war. He is also the author of *The Rights of Man* and *The Age of Reason*.

C. NORTHCOTE PARKINSON (1909–), educated at Cambridge, was Raffles Professor of History at the University of Malaya from 1950 to 1958. Among his books are *Parkinson's Law* (1957) and *Law and the Profits* (1960).

JOHN DOS PASSOS (1896–), novelist and essayist, first became known for his novel *Three Soldiers* in 1921. Many other novels have appeared, among them *The Big Money* (1936), *The Grand Design* (1949), and *Prospect of a Golden Age* (1959).

DONALD CULROSS PEATTIE (1898–) worked in the Department of Agriculture from 1922 to 1925. Since then, writing in the tradition of Agassiz and Thoreau, he has published many books on the natural scene in America, including *Audubon's America* (1940), *Lives of Destiny* (1954), and *Parade with Banners* (1957).

PLATO (428–347 B.C.), the Greek philosopher, was a pupil and admirer of Socrates. Most of his adult life was spent in teaching at Athens, his native city, and in the composition of his *Dialogues*, all of which are extant. The *Dialogues* are based on the teachings of Socrates, who figures largely in them as the conductor of the discussions.

DAVID M. POTTER (1910–), Coe Professor of American History at Yale University, has written many historical studies, the latest of which is *People of Plenty* (1954).

DAVID M. RIESMAN (1909–), Henry Ford Professor of Social Science at Harvard, was educated at Harvard College and Harvard Law School. After legal practice, he became a professor of the social science department at the University of Chicago in 1946. His most influential book is *The Lonely Crowd* (1950). Author of many articles, he has also written *Individualism Reconsidered and Other Essays* (1954) and *Constraint and Variety in American Education* (1956).

JAMES HARVEY ROBINSON (1863–1936), a native of Illinois, held degrees from Harvard and the University of Freiburg. For many years he was professor of history at Columbia, but resigned in 1917 as a protest against what he considered a suppression of academic freedom in the university. As a historian, his work has done much to change the emphasis of historical writing from wars, territorial changes, and treaties to the development of ideas and beliefs. He is the author of *The Mind in the Making, Introduction to the History of Western Europe*, and many other books.

LEONARD Q. ROSS is the pseudonym of Leo Calvin Rosten (1908–), who, after beginning an academic career as English teacher and student in the social sciences, has been largely associated with motion-picture projects (since 1937). From this latter part of his career has come *Hollywood: the Movie Colony—the Movie Makers* (1941). More recently he has edited *The Religions of America* (1955), and has written *The Return of H*y*m*a*n K*a*p*l*a*n* (1959).

CLINTON ROSSITER (1917–) was educated at Cornell and Princeton, where he took his Ph.D. in 1942. He has taught government at Cornell since 1946, and is currently chairman of the Department of Government there. He is author of *Constitutional Dictatorship* (1948), *Seedtime of the Republic* (1953), *Conservatism in America* (1955), *The First American Revolution* (1956), and *The American Presidency* (1956).

BERTRAND RUSSELL (1872–), philosopher and mathematician, was educated at Cambridge. He has taught mathematics and philosophy at Cambridge, Harvard, the University of Chicago, and the University of California at Los Angeles. He is co-author with Alfred North Whitehead of *Principia Mathematica* (1910–1913). Among his other books are *Introduction to Mathematical Philosophy* (1919), *The Analysis of Matter, Philosophical Essays, Marriage and*

Morals, Education and the Social Order. He has recently published *Night-mares of Eminent Persons* (1954), *Human Society in Ethics and Politics* (1955), and *The Wisdom of the West* (1959). His views on marriage and pacificism have at times involved him in controversies. Though he is an English nobleman, he refuses to use his title.

NATHANIEL SOUTHGATE SHALER (1841–1906), a Kentuckian by birth, was a distinguished American geologist. During most of his life he was identified with Harvard, and it was there that he studied with the great Louis Agassiz. He was graduated from Lawrence School of Science, Harvard, in 1862. After serving two years as an artillery officer in the Union Army, he taught at Harvard successively zoology, geology, and paleontology, becoming professor of geology in 1888, a position he held until his death. He was director of the Kentucky Geologic Survey. He wrote *A First Book in Geology, Aspects of the Earth, The Interpretation of Nature,* and *Man and Death.*

HARLOW SHAPLEY (1885–), distinguished American scientist, is Paine Professor of Astronomy emeritus at Harvard. He was educated at the University of Missouri and at Princeton, where he took his Ph.D. in 1913. Professor Shapley was director of the Harvard Observatory from 1921 to 1952. He is past president of the American Association for the Advancement of Science. Among his books are *Of Stars and Men* (1958).

GEORGE BERNARD SHAW (1856–1950), born in Dublin, joined the Fabian Society in London and wrote music, drama, and art criticism before turning to the stage. He was a socialist, satirist, and meliorist. His wit and stagecraft and his belief in a "Life Force" are evident in such different plays as *Candida* (1898), *Androcles and the Lion* (1912), and *St. Joan* (1924).

ALAN SIMPSON (1912–), a graduate of Oxford, is Dean of the College of the University of Chicago and Thomas E. Donnelly Professor of History. He has written *Puritanism in Old and New England* (1955).

CHARLES PERCY SNOW (1905–), British novelist and scientist, took his Ph.D. in physics at Cambridge and became a fellow of Corpus Christi College. During World War II, he was chief of scientific personnel for the Ministry of Labour. Among his novels are: *Time of Hope* (1950), *The Light and the Dark* (1948), *The Masters* (1951), and *The New Men* (1954). His recent non-fiction books are *The Two Cultures and the Scientific Revolution* (1960) and *Science and Government* (1961).

RANDALL STEWART (1896–) is professor of English and chairman of the department at Vanderbilt. Two of his books are *Nathaniel Hawthorne: A Biography* (1948) and *American Literature and Christian Doctrine* (1958).

FRANK SULLIVAN (1892–), a graduate of Cornell, is the author of humorous sketches collected under such titles as *A Pearl in Every Oyster* (1938), *A Rock in Every Snowball* (1946), *The Night the Old Nostalgia Burned Down* (1953), and *A Moose in the House* (1959).

JONATHAN SWIFT (1667–1745), greatest English prose satirist, was born in Dublin and educated at Trinity College. In addition to his masterpiece, *Travels into Several Remote Nations of the World*, commonly known as *Gulliver's Travels*, he is also the author of *A Tale of a Tub*, a brilliant satire on the divisions of the Christian Church, *The Battle of the Books*, *A Modest Proposal*, a masterpiece of irony, and *The Journal to Stella*, as well as a number of poems, most of which are humorous.

HAROLD TAYLOR (1914–), a graduate of the Universities of Toronto and London, served as president of Sarah Lawrence College from 1945 to 1959. Two of his books are *On Education and Freedom* (1954) and *Art and the Intellect* (1960).

HENRY DAVID THOREAU (1817–1862) called himself "a mystic, a transcendental philosopher, and a natural philosopher to boot." His dominant individualism is evident in his most famous book, *Walden* (1854). It also appears, but tempered by a belief in acting collectively "according to the spirit of our institutions," in the three John Brown speeches (1859–1860) and *Life Without Principle* (1863) as well as in the essay printed here.

THUCYDIDES (c. 471–c. 400 B.C.), greatest of the ancient historians, wrote *The History of the Peloponnesian War*. He served his native Athens as a commander in the Peloponnesian War.

JAMES THURBER (1894–1961), one of the best contemporary humorists and cartoonists, was educated at Ohio State University. After working on several newspapers, he joined the staff of *The New Yorker*, where he was for a time managing editor. Later he wrote the "Talk of the Town" for the same magazine. Until his death he was a frequent contributor to *The New Yorker*. He wrote *My Life and Hard Times* (1933), *Let Your Mind Alone* (1937), *The Male Animal* (1940), *Fables for Our Times* (1941), *My World—and Welcome to It!* (1944), and others.

ARNOLD TOYNBEE (1889–), influential British historian, has covered much of the history of East and West in a series of studies, and in 1954 completed his monumental ten-volume *A Study of History*. Director of Studies in the Royal Institute of International Affairs, he has lectured at universities on several continents. Some of his other books are *Civilization on Trial* (1948), *An Historian's Approach to Religion* (1956), *The World and the West* (1953), *East to West: A Journey Around the World* (1958), and *Hellenism* (1959).

LIONEL TRILLING (1905–) is the author of a novel, *The Middle of the Journey* (1947), and of short stories that have frequently been anthologized. Critical volumes by him include *E. M. Forster* (1943), *The Liberal Imagination*

(1950), and A *Gathering of Fugitives* (1956). He has been a professor of English at Columbia University since 1948.

FREDERICK JACKSON TURNER (1861–1932) taught history at the University of Wisconsin and at Harvard University. His carefully documented account of the frontiers of the discoverer and explorer, the missionary, soldier, trapper, and farmer constituted a new synthesis and a new point of view in American history.

BARRY ULANOV (1918–), a graduate of Columbia, teaches English at Barnard and contributes a column to *Down Beat*. In addition to biographies of Duke Ellington and Bing Crosby, some of his books are A *Handbook of Jazz* (1957) and *Death: A Book of Preparation and Consolation* (1959).

THORSTEIN VEBLEN (1857–1929), American teacher and economist, became a leading figure in the "institutional school" of economic theory and was in part responsible for the trend toward social control in the decade 1930–1940. *The Instinct of Workmanship* (1914) and *The Engineers and the Price System* (1921) are important books by him.

ROBERT PENN WARREN (1905–), a graduate of Vanderbilt and California and a Rhodes Scholar at Oxford, is a poet, critic, and novelist. Among his works are *Brother to Dragons* (1953), *Segregation: The Inner Conflict of the South* (1956), and *The Cave* (1959).

PHILIP WHEELWRIGHT (1901–), a graduate of Princeton (A.B., Ph.D.), has been professor of philosophy at the University of California at Riverside since 1954. Besides *The Burning Fountain*, he has written A *Critical Introduction to Ethics* (revised edition, 1949), *The Way of Philosophy* (1954), and *Heraclitus* (1959).

E. B. WHITE (1899–), essayist, lives at North Brooklyn, Maine. Born at Mt. Vernon, New York, he was educated at Cornell. He began his career as a reporter. Formerly a contributor to *Harper's*, he has been for a number of years a contributing editor of *The New Yorker*. In addition to his frequent contributions to magazines, he has written many books: *Is Sex Necessary?* (in collaboration with James Thurber), *One Man's Meat* (1944), *Stuart Little* (1945), *Charlotte's Web* (1952), and *The Second Tree from the Corner* (1953). In 1941 he edited A *Subtreasury of American Humor*.

ALFRED NORTH WHITEHEAD (1861–1947) was an English philosopher and mathematician. One of the most influential thinkers of the twentieth century, Whitehead taught at Trinity College, Cambridge, the University of London, and at Harvard. Among his books are *Principia Mathematica*, which he wrote with Bertrand Russell in 1910, *The Principles of Natural Knowledge* (1919), *Science and the Modern World* (1925), *Adventures of Ideas* (1933), and *Nature and Life* (1934).

JOHN WOOLMAN (1720–1772), Quaker preacher and author, was born in New Jersey, where he was apprenticed to a tailor. He traveled widely throughout the Colonies, visiting meetings of the Friends and denouncing slavery. His most famous work is his *Journal*, which gives an account of these activities. It has been frequently reprinted and is much praised for its style. Charles Lamb once suggested that aspiring writers "get Woolman's writings by heart."

FRANK LLOYD WRIGHT (1869–1959) began his illustrious career in 1893 at Chicago. *An Autobiography—Frank Lloyd Wright* (1932, rev. 1943) tells the long story of his struggle in establishing modern architecture.

PHILIP WYLIE (1902–), editor, columnist, and author of the popular "Crunch and Des" fishing stories, is also a satirist and moralist. His virulent criticisms of many aspects of American civilization appear in *Generation of Vipers* (1942), *Night unto Night* (1944), *An Essay on Morals* (1947), and *Tomorrow!* (1954).

Index

Introduction to Literature

❀◈◇

But Achilles raised him aloft. He crouched on the wonderful shield, on heroes and burning cities, on vineyards graven in gold, on every dear passion, every joy, on the entire image of the Mountain that he had discovered, encircled, like it, with an everlasting stream.

E. M. FORSTER, *The Celestial Omnibus*

Contents

I. Poems

Contents

II. Short Stories

III. Plays

I
Poems

❖◇❖

CATULLUS

Poem V

Vivamus, mea Lesbia, atque amemus,
rumoresque senum severiorum
omnes unius aestimemus assis.
soles occidere et redire possunt:
nobis cum semel occidit brevis lux,
nox est perpetua una dormienda.
da mi basia mille, deinde centum,
dein mille altera, dein secunda centum,
deinde usque altera mille, deinde centum
dein, cum milia multa fecerimus,
conturbabimus illa, ne sciamus,
aut nequis malus invidere possit,
cum tantum sciat esse basiorum.

To Celia

A Translation by Ben Jonson

Come, my Celia, let us prove,
While we can, the sports of love.
Time will not be ours for ever;
He, at length, our good will sever.
Spend not then his gifts in vain:
Suns that set may rise again
But if once we lose this light,
'Tis with us perpetual night.
Why should we defer our joys?
Fame and rumour are but toys.
Cannot we delude the eyes

Of a few poor household spies?
Or his easier eares beguile,
Thus removed by our wile?
'Tis no sin love's fruits to steal,
But the sweet thefts to reveal;
To be taken, to be seen,
These have crimes accounted been.

My Sweetest Lesbia

A Translation by Thomas Campion

My sweetest Lesbia, let us live and love;
And though the sager sort our deeds reprove,
Let us not weigh them. Heaven's great lamps do dive
Into their west, and straight again revive;
But, soon as once is set our little light,
Then must we sleep one ever-during night.

If all would lead their lives in love like me,
Then bloody swords and armour should not be;
No drum nor trumpet peaceful sleeps should move,
Unless alarm came from the camp of Love.
But fools do live and waste their little light,
And seek with pain their ever-during night.

When timely death my life and fortunes ends,
Let not my hearse be vext with mourning friends;
But let all lovers rich in triumph come,
And with sweet pastime grace my happy tomb.
And, Lesbia, close up thou my little light,
And crown with love my ever-during night.

HUGH KENNER

On Catullus's "Poem V" [1]

The point of the last three lines ["Let us confuse them thoroughly, so we won't
know, / Or so no ill-wisher can cast an evil eye on us, / Knowing that we ex-
changed so many kisses."] depends on the ancient superstition about exact

[1] From *The Art of Poetry* (New York, 1959), pp. 237-238. Copyright (1959) by
Hugh Kenner. Reprinted by permission of Holt, Rinehart and Winston, Inc.

numbers; if you reckon your blessings exactly, you invite disaster; and the power of the evil eye is fortified by a knowledge of exact figures. That this point is lost in an English poem is perhaps one reason why neither Campion nor Jonson tackles the second half of Catullus's lyric. Their object in any case is not to provide a substitute for the Latin; they can assume that their audience knows Catullus, and use him as a theme for variations.

Compare Campion's lines 1-6 with Jonson's lines 1-8. Which can you more easily imagine being spoken? Consider the habit of mind represented by phrases like "the sager sort" (line 2) and "heaven's great lamps" (line 3). Can one imagine anyone using such words? Do the images implied by "dive" and "revive" sharpen what Campion is saying, or are they merely rhymes? How vividly is Campion imagining the speaker and his emotions?

Jonson stays within Catullus's first six lines; Campion attempts to hitch them to a larger theme. By stanza 2 he is writing decorous lines on a theme; he has abandoned any dramatic pretense of speaking to the lady.

Why is death "timely" (line 13)? Because a word is needed to fill out the line? Is it a blank word? Does the facility with which it drops into place suggest that Campion's interests weren't particularly engaged with the emotions of lines 5-6? What does line 17 mean? Shut my eyes? Does the last line mean anything in particular?

How many words in the first stanza contribute nothing to the presentation of the matter? How many are positive drags upon it?

Campion's poem is a literary exercise; Jonson's none the less real for being in part a translation. The distinction between poets who draw on books and poets who draw on "life" is less simple than is sometimes assumed. There are many ways of using books. What does Jonson's debt to Catullus consist of?

Jonson has 109 words, Catullus but 66, and Jonson used only the first six lines of Catullus. Partly this reflects the fact that English won't compress like Latin, which can juxtapose "omnes" and "unius," "lux" and "nox," and convey complex meanings in single words like "dormienda" and "conturbabimus." Partly it reflects Jonson's intention of conferring on Catullus's hardness an ease that has its own pathos. If you try to stick close to Catullus's words and effects you get the kind of inflation represented by Campion's first stanza. Why?

Poem LI

> Ille mi par esse deo videtur,
> ille, si fas est, superare divos,
> qui sedens adversus identidem te
>   spectat et audit
> dulce ridentem, misero quod omnis
> eripit sensus mihi; nam simul te,
> Lesbia, aspexi, nihil est super mi
>   [vocis in ore]

lingua sed torpet, tenuis sub artus
flamma demanat, sonitu suopte
tintinant aures, gemina teguntur
    lumina nocte.

otium, Catulle, tibi molestum est:
✦ otio exsultas nimiumque gestis.
otium et reges prius et beatas
    perdidit urbes.

To Lesbia[1]

A Translation by Horace Gregory

He is changed to a god he who looks on her,
godlike he shines when he's seated beside her,
immortal joy to gaze and hear the fall of
    her sweet laughter.

All of my senses are lost and confounded;
Lesbia rises before me and trembling
I sink into earth and swift dissolution
    seizes my body.

Limbs are pierced with fire and the heavy tongue fails,
ears resound with noise of distant storms shaking
this earth, eyes gaze on stars that fall forever
    into deep midnight.

This languid madness destroys you Catullus,
long day and night shall be desolate, broken,
as long ago ancient kings and rich cities
    fell into ruin.

HORACE

Ode, I, xi

Tu ne quaesieris—scire nefas—quem mihi, quem tibi
finem di dederint, Leuconoë, nec Babylonios
temptaris numeros. ut melius, quicquid erit, pati!

[1] From *The Poems of Catullus* (New York: Grove Press, 1956). Copyright 1956
by Horace Gregory.

seu plures hiemes, seu tribuit Iuppiter ultimam,
quae nunc oppositis debilitat pumicibus mare
Tyrrhenum. sapias, vina liques, et spatio brevi
spem longam reseces. dum loquimur, fugerit invida
aetas: carpe diem, quam minimum credula postero.

Horace to Leuconoë

A Translation by E. A. Robinson[1]

I pray you not, Leuconoë, to pore
With unpermitted eyes on what may be
Appointed by the gods for you and me,
Nor on Chaldaean figures any more.
'T were infinitely better to implore
The present only:—whether Jove decree
More winters yet to come, or whether he
Make even this, whose hard, wave-eaten shore
Shatters the Tuscan seas to-day, the last—
Be wise withal, and rack your wine, nor fill
Your bosom with large hopes; for while I sing,
The envious close of time is narrowing;—
So seize the day, or ever it be past,
And let the morrow come for what it will.

Ode, II, x

Rectius vives, Licini, neque altum
semper urgendo neque, dum procellas
cautus horrescis, nimium premendo
   litus iniquum.
auream quisquis mediocritatem
deligit, tutus caret obsoleti
sordibus tecti, caret invidenda
   sobrius aula.
saepius ventis agitatur ingens
pinus et celsae graviore casu
decidunt turres feriuntque summos
   fulgura montis.
sperat infestis, metuit secundis
alteram sortem bene praeparatum
pectus. informes hiemes reductit
   Iuppiter; idem

[1] From *Children of the Night* (1897).

summovet. non, si male nunc, et olim
sic erit: quondam cithara tacentem
suscitat Musam neque semper arcum
    tendit Apollo.
rebus angustis animosus atque
fortis appare: sapienter idem
contrahes vento nimium secundo
    turgida vela.

The Golden Mean

A Translation by Sir Philip Sidney

You better sure shall live, not evermore
    Trying high seas; nor, while sea's rage you flee,
Pressing too much upon ill-harboured shore.

The golden mean who loves, lives safely free
From filth of foreworn house, and quiet lives,
    Releas'd from court, where envy needs must be.

The wind most oft the hugest pine tree grieves:
    The stately towers come down with greater fall:
The highest hills the bolt of thunder cleaves.

Evil haps do fill with hope, good haps appal
With fear of change, the courage well prepar'd:
    Foul winters, as they come, away they shall.

Though present times, and past with evils be snar'd,
    They shall not last: with cithern silent muse
Apollo wakes, and bow hath sometime spar'd.

In hard estate, with stout shows, valour use,
The same man still, in whom wisdom prevails;
In too full wind draw in thy swelling sails.

ANONYMOUS

Sir Patrick Spens

The king sits in Dumferling toune,
  Drinking the blude-reid wine:
"O whar will I get a guid sailor,
  To sail this schip of mine?"

Up and spak an eldern knicht,
  Sat at the kings richt kne:
"Sir Patrick Spens is the best sailor
  That sails upon the se."

The king has written a braid letter,
  And signd it wi his hand,
And sent it to Sir Patrick Spens,
  Was walking on the sand.   10

The first line that Sir Patrick red,
  A loud lauch lauched he;
The next line that Sir Patrick red,
  The teir blinded his ee.

"O wha is this has don this deid,
  This ill deid don to me,
To send me out this time o' the yeir,
  To sail upon the se!   20

"Mak hast, mak haste, my mirry men all,
  Our guid schip sails the morne."
"Oh say na sae, my master deir,
  For I feir a deadlie storme.

"Late late yestreen I saw the new moone,
  Wi the auld moone in hir arme,
And I feir, I feir, my deir master,
  That we will cum to harme."

O our Scots nobles wer richt laith
  To weet their cork-heild schoone,   30

Bot lang owre a' the play wer playd,
    Thair hats they swam aboone.

O lang, lang may their ladies sit,
    Wi thair fans into their hand,
Or eir they se Sir Patrick Spens
    Cum sailing to the land.

O lang, lang may the ladies stand,
    Wi thair gold kems in their hair,
Waiting for thair ain deir lords,
    For they'll se thame na mair.   40

Haf owre, half owre to Aberdour,
    It's fiftie fadom deip,
And thair lies guid Sir Patrick Spens,
    Wi the Scots lords at his feit.

MARK VAN DOREN

On *Sir Patrick Spens*[1]

Some versions of this old Scottish ballad are longer than we have it here, and many of them differ in other respects. A popular ballad has no author as we know the term; it may have had one once, but time and repetition have obscured his identity and altered his text—altered it in most cases by shortening it until it contains only the essentials of the tale it originally told. It was a song to be sung, and singers have an immemorial tendency to forget, to improvise, and to improve. The great virtue of any ballad is brevity—assuming, of course, a subject with enough drama in it to invite intensification by abridgement and omission.

The history of the present ballad is not our business here, though it is well to remember that longer versions of it speak of a voyage to Norway to bring back the king's daughter; of Sir Patrick's safe arrival there; of a quarrel between his nobles and the nobles of Norway, who accuse the Scots of staying too long and wasting their host's food and drink; of Sir Patrick's resolution to sail for Scotland even though he is advised that the sea is unsafe; of his sailing nevertheless; and of the wreck with which every version ends. The shipwreck was the

[1] From *Introduction to Poetry* (New York, 1951), pp. 127-129. With the permission of Holt, Rinehart and Winston, Inc. Copyright, 1951, by Holt, Rinehart and Winston, Inc.

heart of the ballad, as calamity is likely to be the stuff of any popular narrative.

The present version is the classic one, and serves best to show how a ballad should be constructed, and why it is so difficult for a single author in sophisticated times to capture the secret of the art. Line 41 is the only residue of the return voyage; otherwise we should suppose that the ship was wrecked soon after it first set sail, and indeed most readers do naturally suppose this. We shall suppose it too, and forget everything except the lines before us. They constitute a masterpiece of the ballad art, which is both a lyric and a narrative art since its aim is to sing—briefly, without taking breath—a human action, and to make it as moving as the sweetest song can be.

This song of Sir Patrick Spens is a series of lyric scenes with every transitional or explanatory passage left out. All we are told is that the king asks for a sailor; that an elder knight recommends Sir Patrick; that the king sends him an order and he receives it; that he laughs at first, then weeps at the thought of certain death, and wonders who has brought it on him; that nevertheless he rouses his crew, saying they will sail tomorrow; that one of them protests, foreseeing a storm; that they sail as scheduled; that the ship sinks, leaving only their hats on top of the water; and that their ladies will wait a long time for their return, seeing that they lie fifty fathoms deep, half way between somewhere and Aberdour. We are told, certainly, a great deal in eleven ballad stanzas; but that is the point. There could have been many more stanzas, and much more detail. As it is there seems to be nothing that we could do without; and everything we are given is musical and moving. Not merely is no mention made of the king's starting to talk as he drinks his blood-red wine, or of his decision to write a letter, or of Sir Patrick's resolution to overlook the danger he faces, or of who it is that has seen the old moon in the new moon's arms, or of the storm itself and the sinking of the ship. A hundred other items are equally ignored—everything, indeed, except that essence which cannot be ignored if the poem is to exist at all.

The genius responsible for our song wastes no time on things we cannot instantly and deeply feel. It is not the facts that matter, or the reasons for the facts; it is the feeling—the pity of it, seeing how well these men were aware that they would die. Twice only does the ballad develop anything at length, and both times it is something to that point: first, the premonition of the men, and last the sorrow of their wives. Out of the forty-four lines as many as sixteen (15-30) are devoted to the one and as many as twelve (33-44) to the other. More than half of the poem, that is to say, concentrates upon the tragedy; less than half provides us with its framework. We have the minimum of deed and the maximum of desolation.

The poet is thus left free to do with his words what words in narrative song can best do—namely, enchant us. The bluff king, the quiet and perhaps cunning old knight, and the courageous crew whose members speak their minds so clearly, create a heroic setting which magnifies the disaster, but it is

the disaster that moves us as only things both terrible and beautiful are able
to move men. All is beautiful here, but we may not be sure of this until the
last three stanzas, whose rhythmical, sweet movement, suggestive of a gentle
sea that will bring the king's ship smoothly in, helps also to create the ladies
with their fans and their gold combs who wait prettily for what the fair wind
and the bright waves have in store. We know, of course, that they will wait
forever; and so they seem to be doing as the poem closes. The repetitions in
lines 33, 37, and 41 have done their work; they have raised the music of this
narrative poem to the lyric level where all poetry, as poetry, is felt. The
narrative was necessary, and indeed if it had not been perfect we should not
be feeling what we feel in "fiftie fadom deip."

The art of poetry is the art of narrative too; no great lyric but tells its
story, regardless of how much action was left out; no poem studied in these
pages but somewhere—often in a middle stanza—reveals its concern with
humanity in motion. But the final success, as even Homer knew, is when
the story sings. That of Sir Patrick Spens sings in the memory of every
person who knows it, and sings in the words of the poem itself. This is why
there is no greater ballad, and possibly—for its length—no greater poem.

The Three Ravens

1. There were three ravens sat on a tree,
   Downe a downe, hay downe, hay downe
   There were three ravens sat on a tree,
   With a downe
   There were three ravens sat on a tree,
   They were as blacke as they might be.
   With a downe derrie, derrie, derrie, downe, downe.

2. The one of them said to his mate,
   "Where shall we our breakfast take?"

3. "Downe in yonder greene field,
   There lies a knight slain under his shield.

4. "His hounds they lie downe at his feete,
   So well they can their master keepe.

5. "His haukes they flie so eagerly,
   There's no fowle dare him come nie."

6. Downe there comes a fallow doe,
   As great with yong as she might goe.

7. She lift up his bloudy hed,
   And kist his wounds that were so red.

8. She got him up upon her backe,
   And carried him to earthen lake.

9. She buried him before the prime,
   She was dead herselfe ere even-song time.

10. God send every gentleman,
    Such haukes, such hounds, and such a leman.

The Twa Corbies

As I was walking all alane,
I herd twa corbies making a mane;
The tane unto the t' other say,
"Where sall we gang and dine to-day?"

"In behint yon auld fail dyke,
I wot there lies a new slain knight;
And naebody kens that he lies there,
But his hawk, his hound, and lady fair.

"His hound is to the hunting gane,
His hawk to fetch the wild-fowl hame,
His lady's ta'en another mate,
So we may mak our dinner sweet.

"Ye'll sit on his white hause-bane,
And I'll pike out his bonny blue een;
Wi ae lock o his gowden hair
We'll theek our nest when it grows bare.

"Mony a one for him makes mane,
But nane sall ken where he is gane;
Oer his white banes when they are bare,
The wind sall blaw for evermair."

The Wife of Usher's Well

There lived a wife at Usher's Well,
   And a wealthy wife was she;
She had three stout and stalwart sons,
   And sent them oer the sea.

They hadna been a week from her,
    A week but barely ane,
Whan word came to the carlin wife
    That her three sons were gane.

They hadna been a week from her,
    A week but barely three,   10
Whan word came to the carlin wife
    That her sons she'd never see.

"I wish the wind may never cease,
    Nor fashes in the flood,
Till my three sons come hame to me,
    In earthly flesh and blood."

It fell about the Martinmass,
    When nights are lang and mirk,
The carlin wife's three sons came hame,
    And their hats were o the birk.   20

It neither grew in syke nor ditch,
    Nor yet in ony sheugh;
But at the gates o Paradise,
    That birk grew fair eneugh.

"Blow up the fire, my maidens,
    Bring water from the well;
For a' my house shall feast this night,
    Since my three sons are well."

And she has made to them a bed,
    She's made it large and wide,   30
And she's taen her mantle her about,
    Sat down at the bed-side.

Up then crew the red, red cock,
    And up and crew the gray,
The eldest to the youngest said,
    " 'Tis time we were away."

The cock he hadna crawd but once,
    And clappd his wings at a',
When the youngest to the eldest said,
    "Brother, we must awa.   40

"The cock doth craw, the day doth daw,
    The channerin worm doth chide;
Gin we be mist out o our place,
    A sair pain we maun bide.

"Fare ye weel, my mother dear!
    Fareweel to barn and byre!
And fare ye weel, the bonny lass
    That kindles my mother's fire!"

Lord Randal

"O where hae ye been, Lord Randal, my son?
O where hae ye been, my handsome young man?"
"I hae been to the wild wood; mother, make my bed soon,
For I'm weary wi' hunting, and fain wald lie down."

"Where gat ye your dinner, Lord Randal, my son?
Where gat ye your dinner, my handsome young man?"
"I dined wi' my true-love; mother, make my bed soon,
For I'm weary wi' hunting, and fain wald lie down."

"What gat ye to your dinner, Lord Randal, my son?
What gat ye to your dinner, my handsome young man?"
"I gat eels boiled in broo; mother, make my bed soon,
For I'm weary wi' hunting, and fain wald lie down."

"What became of your bloodhounds, Lord Randal, my son?
What became of your bloodhounds, my handsome young man?"
"O they swelld and they died; mother, make my bed soon,
For I'm weary wi' hunting, and fain wald lie down."

"O I fear ye are poisoned, Lord Randal, my son!
O I fear ye are poisoned, my handsome young man!"
"O yes! I am poisoned; mother, make my bed soon,
For I'm sick at the heart, and I fain wald lie down."

Bonny Barbara Allan

It was in and about the Martinmas time,
    When the green leaves were a falling,
That Sir John Graeme, in the West Country,
    Fell in love with Barbara Allan.

He sent his man down through the town,
   To the place where she was dwelling:
"O haste and come to my master dear,
   Gin ye be Barbara Allan."

O hooly, hooly rose she up,
   To the place where he was lying,   10
And when she drew the curtain by,
   "Young man, I think you're dying."

"O it's I'm sick, and very, very sick,
   And 'tis a' for Barbara Allan;"
"O the better for me ye's never be,
   Tho your heart's blood were a spilling.

"O dinna ye mind, young man," said she,
   "When ye was in the tavern a drinking,
That ye made the healths gae round and round,
   And slighted Barbara Allan?"   20

He turnd his face unto the wall,
   And death was with him dealing:
"Adieu, adieu, my dear friends all,
   And be kind to Barbara Allan."

And slowly, slowly raise she up,
   And slowly, slowly left him,
And sighing said, she could not stay,
   Since death of life had reft him.

She had not gane a mile but twa,
   When she heard the dead-bell ringing,   30
And every jow that the dead-bell geid,
   It cry'd "Woe to Barbara Allan!"

"O mother, mother, make my bed!
   O make it soft and narrow!
My love has died for me today,
   I'll die for him tomorrow."

FRANÇOIS VILLON

Ballade des Dames du Temps Jadis

Dictes moy où, n'en quel pays,
Est Flora, la belle Rommaine;
Archipiades, ne Thaïs,
Qui fut sa cousine germaine;
Echo, parlant quant bruyt on maine
Dessus riviere ou sus estan,
Qui beauté ot trop plus qu'humaine.
Mais où sont les neiges d'antan!

Où est la tres sage Helloïs,
Pour qui fut chastré et puis moyne   10
Pierre Esbaillart à Saint-Denis?
Pour son amour ot cest essoyne.
Semblablement où est la royne
Qui commanda que Buridan
Fust geté en ung sac en Saine?
Mais où sont les neiges d'antan!

La royne Blanche comme lis,
Qui chantoit à voix de seraine;
Berte au grant pié, Biertris, Allis;
Haremburgis qui tint le Maine,   20
Et Jehanne, la bonne Lorraine,
Qu'Englois brulerent à Rouan;
Où sont elles, Vierge souvraine? . . .
Mais où sont les neiges d'antan!

ENVOI

Prince, n'enquerez de sepmaine
Où elles sont, ne de cest an,
Que se reffrain ne vous remaine.
Mais où sont les neiges d'antan!

The Ballad of Dead Ladies

A Translation by Dante Gabriel Rossetti

Tell me now in what hidden way is
　　Lady Flora the lovely Roman?
Where's Hipparchia, and where is Thaïs,
　　Neither of them the fairer woman?
　　Where is Echo, beheld of no man,
Only heard on river and mere—
　　She whose beauty was more than human? . . .
But where are the snows of yester-year?

Where's Héloïse, the learned nun,
　　For whose sake Abeillard, I ween,   10
Lost manhood and put priesthood on?
　　(From Love he won such dule and teen!)
　　And where, I pray you, is the Queen
Who willed that Buridan should steer
　　Sewed in a sack's mouth down the Seine? . . .
But where are the snows of yester-year?

White Queen Blanche, like a queen of lilies,
　　With a voice like any mermaiden—
Bertha Broadfoot, Beatrice, Alice,
　　And Ermengarde the lady of Maine—   20
　　And that good Joan whom Englishmen
At Rouen doomed and burned her there—
　　Mother of God, where are they then? . . .
But where are the snows of yester-year?

Nay, never ask this week, fair lord,
　　Where they are gone, nor yet this year,
Except with this for an overword—
　　But where are the snows of yester-year?

SIR THOMAS WYATT

The Lover Compareth His State to a Ship in Perilous Storm Tossed on the Sea

My galley charged with forgetfulness
Thorough sharp seas, in winter nights doth pass,
'Tween rock and rock; and eke my foe, alas,
That is my lord, steereth with cruelness,
And every hour, a thought in readiness,
As though that death were light in such a case.
An endless wind doth tear the sail apace
Of forced sighs, and trusty fearfulness.
A rain of tears, a cloud of dark disdain
Hath done the wearied cords great hinderance,
Wreathed with error, and with ignorance.
The stars be hid that led me to this pain;
  Drowned is reason that should be my comfort,
  And I remain, despairing of the port.

The Lover Showeth How He Is Forsaken of Such as He Sometime Enjoyed

They flee from me, that sometime did me seek,
With naked foot stalking within my chamber.
Once have I seen them gentle, tame, and meek,
That now are wild, and do not once remember
That sometime they have put themselves in danger
To take bread at my hand; and now they range,
Busily seeking in continual change.
  Thanked be fortune it hath been otherwise,
Twenty times better; but once especial,
In thin array, after a pleasant guise,
When her loose gown did from her shoulders fall,
And she me caught in her arms long and small,
And therewithal so sweetly did me kiss
And softly said, Dear heart, how like you this?
  It was no dream, for I lay broad awaking.

10

But all is turned now, through my gentleness,
Into a bitter fashion of forsaking;
And I have leave to go, of her goodness,
And she also to use newfangleness.
But since that I unkindly so am served,   20
How like you this? what hath she now deserved?

CHRISTOPHER MARLOWE

The Passionate Shepherd to His Love

Come live with me, and be my love;
And we will all the pleasures prove
That hills and valleys, dales and fields,
Woods, or steepy mountain yields.

And we will sit upon the rocks,
Seeing the shepherds feed their flocks
By shallow rivers, to whose falls
Melodious birds sing madrigals.

And I will make thee beds of roses,
And a thousand fragrant posies;   10
A cap of flowers, and a kirtle
Embroidered all with leaves of myrtle;

A gown made of the finest wool
Which from our pretty lambs we pull;
Fair-lined slippers for the cold,
With buckles of the purest gold;

A belt of straw and ivy-buds,
With coral clasps and amber studs;
And if these pleasures may thee move,
Come live with me, and be my love.   20

The shepherd-swains shall dance and sing
For thy delight each May morning;
If these delights thy mind may move,
Then live with me, and be my love.

SIR WALTER RALEGH

The Nymph's Reply

If all the world and love were young,
And truth in every shepherd's tongue,
These pretty pleasures might me move
To live with thee and be thy love.

Time drives the flocks from field to fold
When rivers rage and rocks grow cold,
And Philomel becometh dumb;
The rest complains of cares to come.

The flowers do fade, and wanton fields
To wayward winter reckoning yields;   10
A honey tongue, a heart of gall,
Is fancy's spring, but sorrow's fall.

Thy gowns, thy shoes, thy beds of roses,
Thy cap, thy kirtle, and thy posies
Soon break, soon wither, soon forgotten,—
In folly ripe, in reason rotten.

Thy belt of straw and ivy buds,
Thy coral clasps and amber studs,
All these in me no means can move
To come to thee and be thy love.   20

But could youth last and love still breed,
Had joys no date nor age no need,
Then these delights my mind might move
To live with thee and be thy love.

EDMUND SPENSER

Amoretti, XXXIV

Lyke as a ship, that through the Ocean wyde,
by conduct of some star doth make her way;
whenas a storme hath dimd her trusty guyde,

out of her course doth wander far astray!
So I, whose star, that wont with her bright ray
   me to direct, with cloudes is over cast,
   doe wander now, in darknesse and dismay,
   through hidden perils round about me plast.
Yet hope I well that, when this storme is past,
   my Helice, the lodestar of my lyfe,
   will shine again, and looke on me at last,
   with lovely light to cleare my cloudy grief.
Till then I wander carefull, comfortlesse,
   in secret sorrow, and sad pensivenesse.

Amoretti, LXX

Fresh spring the herald of loves mighty king,
   in whose cote-armour richly are displayd
   all sorts of flowers the which on earth do spring
   in goodly colours gloriously arrayd.
Goe to my love, where she is carelesse layd,
   yet in her winters bowre not well awake:
   tell her the joyous time wil not be staid
   unlesse she doe him by the forelock take.
Bid her therefore her selfe soone ready make,
   to wayt on love amongst his lovely crew:
   where every one that misseth then her make,
   shall be by him amearst with penance dew.
Make hast therefore sweet love, whilest it is prime,
   for none can call againe the passed time.

Amoretti, LXXV

One day I wrote her name upon the strand,
   but came the waves and washed it away:
   agayne I wrote it with a second hand,
   but came the tyde, and made my paynes his pray.
Vayne man, sayd she, that doest in vaine assay,
   a mortall thing so to immortalize,
   for I my selve shall lyke to this decay,
   and eek my name bee wyped out lykewize.
Not so, (quod I) let baser things devize
   to dy in dust, but you shall live by fame:
   my verse your vertues rare shall eternize,

and in the hevens wryte your glorious name.
Where whenas death shall all the world subdew,
our love shall live, and later life renew.

SIR PHILIP SIDNEY

Astrophel and Stella, I

Loving in truth, and fain in verse my love to show,
That she, dear she, might take some pleasure of my pain,
Pleasure might cause her read, reading might make her know,
Knowledge might pity win, and pity grace obtain,
I sought fit words to paint the blackest face of woe;
Studying inventions fine, her wits to entertain,
Oft turning others' leaves, to see if thence would flow
Some fresh and fruitful showers upon my sunburned brain.
But words came halting forth, wanting Invention's stay;
Invention, Nature's child, fled step-dame Study's blows;
And others' feet still seemed but strangers in my way.
Thus, great with child to speak, and helpless in my throes,
Biting my truant pen, beating myself for spite,
Fool, said my Muse to me, look in thy heart, and write.

Astrophel and Stella, XXXIX

Come, Sleep! O Sleep, the certain knot of peace,
The baiting-place of wit, the balm of woe,
The poor man's wealth, the prisoner's release,
Th' indifferent judge between the high and low;
With shield of proof shield me from out the prease
Of those fierce darts despair at me doth throw;
O make in me those civil wars to cease;
I will good tribute pay, if thou do so.
Take thou of me smooth pillows, sweetest bed,
A chamber deaf to noise and blind to light,
A rosy garland and a weary head;
And if these things, as being thine in right,
Move not thy heavy grace, thou shalt in me,
Livelier than elsewhere, Stella's image see.

Astrophel and Stella, CX

Leave me, O love which reachest but to dust;
And thou, my mind, aspire to higher things;
Grow rich in that which never taketh rust,
Whatever fades but fading pleasure brings.
Draw in thy beams, and humble all thy might
To that sweet yoke where lasting freedoms be;
Which breaks the clouds and opens forth the light,
That doth both shine and give us sight to see.
O take fast hold; let that light be thy guide
In this small course which birth draws out to death,
And think how evil becometh him to slide,
Who seeketh heav'n, and comes of heav'nly breath.
Then farewell, world; thy uttermost I see;
Eternal Love, maintain thy life in me.

WILLIAM SHAKESPEARE

Sonnet XXIX

When, in disgrace with fortune and men's eyes,
I all alone beweep my outcast state,
And trouble deaf heaven with my bootless cries
And look upon myself and curse my fate,
Wishing me like to one more rich in hope,
Featured like him, like him with friends possess'd,
Desiring this man's art and that man's scope,
With what I most enjoy contented least;
Yet in these thoughts myself almost despising,
Haply I think on thee,—and then my state,
Like to the lark at break of day arising
From sullen earth, sings hymns at heaven's gate;
  For thy sweet love remembered such wealth brings
  That then I scorn to change my state with kings.

Sonnet LX

Like as the waves make towards the pebbled shore,
So do our minutes hasten to their end;
Each changing place with that which goes before,

In sequent toil all forwards do contend.
Nativity, once in the main of light,
Crawls to maturity, wherewith being crowned,
Crooked eclipses 'gainst his glory fight,
And Time that gave doth now his gift confound.
Time doth transfix the flourish set on youth
And delves the parallels in beauty's brow,
Feeds on the rarities of nature's truth,
And nothing stands but for his scythe to mow:
  And yet to times in hope my verse shall stand,
  Praising thy worth, despite his cruel hand.

Sonnet LXXIII

That time of year thou mayst in me behold
When yellow leaves, or none, or few, do hang
Upon those boughs which shake against the cold,
Bare ruin'd choirs, where late the sweet birds sang.
In me thou see'st the twilight of such day
As after sunset fadeth in the west,
Which by and by black night doth take away,
Death's second self, that seals up all in rest.
In me thou see'st the glowing of such fire
That on the ashes of his youth doth lie,
As the death-bed whereon it must expire
Consum'd with that which it was nourish'd by.
  This thou perceivest, which makes thy love more strong,
  To love that well which thou must leave ere long.

Sonnet CXXIX

Th' expense of spirit in a waste of shame
Is lust in action; and till action, lust
Is perjur'd, murd'rous, bloody, full of blame,
Savage, extreme, rude, cruel, not to trust;
Enjoy'd no sooner but despised straight;
Past reason hunted, and no sooner had,
Past reason hated, as a swallowed bait
On purpose laid to make the taker mad;
Mad in pursuit, and in possession so;
Had, having, and in quest to have, extreme;
A bliss in proof—and prov'd, a very woe;
Before, a joy propos'd; behind, a dream.

All this the world well knows; yet none knows well
To shun the heaven that leads men to this hell.

Sonnet CXLVI

Poor soul, the center of my sinful earth,
Thrall to these rebel powers that thee array,
Why dost thou pine within and suffer dearth,
Painting thy outward walls so costly gay?
Why so large cost, having so short a lease,
Dost thou upon thy fading mansion spend?
Shall worms, inheritors of this excess,
Eat up thy charge? Is this thy body's end?
Then, soul, live thou upon thy servant's loss,
And let that pine to aggravate thy store;
Buy terms divine in selling hours of dross;
Within be fed, without be rich no more:
    So shalt thou feed on Death, that feeds on men,
    And Death once dead, there's no more dying then.

O Mistress Mine

O mistress mine, where are you roaming?
O, stay and hear, your true love's coming,
    That can sing both high and low:
Trip no further, pretty sweeting,
Journeys end in lovers meeting,
    Every wise man's son doth know.

What is love? 'Tis not hereafter;
Present mirth hath present laughter;
    What's to come is still unsure:
In delay there lies no plenty;
Then come kiss me, sweet and twenty,
    Youth's a stuff will not endure.

Fear No More

Fear no more the heat o' th' sun,
    Nor the furious winter's rages;
Thou thy worldly task hast done,

Home art gone, and ta'en thy wages:
Golden lads and girls all must,
As chimney-sweepers, come to dust.

Fear no more the frown o' th' great;
  Thou art past the tyrant's stroke;
Care no more to clothe and eat;
  To thee the reed is as the oak: 10
The sceptre, learning, physic, must
All follow this, and come to dust.

Fear no more the lightning-flash,
  Nor th' all-dreaded thunder-stone,
Fear not slander, censure rash;
  Thou hast finished joy and moan:
All lovers young, all lovers must
Consign to thee, and come to dust.

No exorciser harm thee!
  Nor no witchcraft charm thee!   20
Ghost unlaid forbear thee!
  Nothing ill come near thee!
Quiet consummation have;
And renowned be thy grave!

JOHN DONNE

Song

Go and catch a falling star,
  Get with child a mandrake root,
Tell me where all past years are,
  Or who cleft the devil's foot,
Teach me to hear mermaids singing,
Or to keep off envy's stinging,
    And find
    What wind
Serves to advance an honest mind.

If thou be'st born to strange sights,   10
  Things invisible to see,

Ride ten thousand days and nights
   Till age snow white hairs on thee,
Thou, when thou return'st, wilt tell me
All strange wonders that befell thee,
     And swear
     No where
Lives a woman true and fair.

If thou find'st one, let me know;
   Such a pilgrimage were sweet.   20
Yet do not; I would not go,
   Though at next door we might meet.
Though she were true when you met her,
And last till you write your letter,
     Yet she
     Will be
False, ere I come, to two or three.

The Good-Morrow

I wonder, by my troth, what thou and I
Did till we loved? were we not weaned till then?
But sucked on country pleasures, childishly?
Or snorted we in the seven sleepers' den?
'Twas so; but this, all pleasures fancies be.
If ever any beauty I did see,
Which I desired, and got, 'twas but a dream of thee.

And now good-morrow to our waking souls,
Which watch not one another out of fear;
For love all love of other sights controls,   10
And makes one little room an everywhere.
Let sea-discoverers to new worlds have gone;
Let maps to other, worlds on worlds have shown;
Let us possess one world; each hath one, and is one.

My face in thine eye, thine in mine appears,
And true plain hearts do in the faces rest;
Where can we find two better hemispheres
Without sharp north, without declining west?
Whatever dies, was not mixed equally;
If our two loves be one, or thou and I   20
Love so alike that none do slacken, none can die.

Holy Sonnet VII

At the round earth's imagined corners, blow
Your trumpets, angels, and arise, arise
From death, you numberless infinities
Of souls, and to your scattered bodies go;
All whom the flood did, and fire shall o'erthrow;
All whom war, dearth, age, agues, tyrannies,
Despair, law, chance, hath slain, and you whose eyes
Shall behold God, and never taste death's woe.
But let them sleep, Lord, and me mourn a space,
For, if above all these, my sins abound,
'Tis late to ask abundance of Thy grace,
When we are there; here on this lowly ground,
Teach me how to repent; for that's as good
As if Thou hadst sealed my pardon, with Thy blood.

REUBEN A. BROWER

On Donne's *Holy Sonnet VII*[1]

As I have hinted more than once, analysis of sound must always be kept in its place. Clearly, talk of sound in itself has little importance or meaning; and though tone in itself and metaphor in itself are abstractions of equally limited value, most readers will nevertheless regard a complete analysis of sound in a poem as a more violent distortion of their experience than a complete analysis of tone or metaphor. By choosing a well-known poem and by making a fairly complete interpretation of it, I hope to keep analysis of sound in its place and to balance the evils of overemphasis on any one design.

Donne's poem is conceived in two sharply contrasted situations and tones: the imagined judgment day in which the poet all but assumes the voice of God, and the meditation in which he speaks to his Lord in humble intimacy. The two dramatic lines and all they imply are brought to sharp focus in two words, "there" and "here." "There" is before God, at the Judgment, and recapitulates the vision of that tremendous day which Donne has so terribly

[1] From *The Fields of Light: An Experiment in Critical Reading.* Copyright 1951 by Oxford University Press, Inc. Used by permission.

pictured. The controlling metaphor, the key to Donne's attitude in the first eight lines of the sonnet, lies in his insistence on the numberless dead:

> I had not thought death had undone so many.

Characteristically, Donne goes over and over this impression: "numberlesse infinities . . . all . . . all these." The Lucretian clash of images in the opening lines, "at the round earths imagin'd corners," sets a vast geographic stage for the enumeration. The angels must blow, and the poet must call twice on the souls to "arise." To the vastness of space and the vastness of numbers is added the horrible inclusiveness of kinds:

> All whom the flood did, and fire shall o'erthrow,
> All whom warre, dearth, age, agues, tyrannies,
> Despaire, law, chance, hath slaine . . .

The gentleness of "let them sleep" marks the shift in tone and feeling to Donne's sense of his own sinfulness, which he measures in immediate relation to his vision:

> But let them sleepe, Lord, and mee mourne a space,
> For, if above all these, my sinnes abound,
> 'Tis late to aske abundance of thy grace,
> When wee are there . . .

The terrible recollection of "there" moves him to learn repentance "here." In the promise of atonement to those who repent he finds some assurance, and he speaks to his Lord (now Christ) in a tone that is everyday and even a little offhand, touched by the irreverence that is the sign of assured faith.

The continuity between the two dramatic situations and the contrasting attitudes lies mainly in our remembered sense of the grand and awful scene of the opening lines. But this continuity is in part rhythmic, for the bigness of movement which marks the octet is not wholly lost in the sestet. Both are single long sentences. In each there is a good deal of rather elaborate balancing of phrases and clauses, and in each the balancings are broken in ways that are perfectly harmonious with the dominant tone and feeling. In the octet, as the sense of all-inclusiveness increases, the balance is broken, the meter distintegrates in a series of continuous stresses and sharp pauses:

> All whom warre, dearth, age, agues, tyrannies,
> Despaire, law, chance, hath slaine, and you whose eyes . . .

The assonance and vowel alliteration in the first of these lines help us to keep a measured swing in reading, while the tumbling sounds, the confusion of meter to the ear fit exactly the helter-skelter gathering which Donne is describing. It is all mere accumulation. The sestet has breaks of another sort, the freely distributed pauses of reflective conversation, a movement thoroughly appropriate to the intimacy of Donne's prayer.

Nearly everywhere we can point out wonderfully nice adjustment of particular sound patterns to meaning. As the first of a number of instances of different
types, note "blow" at the end of line one,

> At the round earths imagin'd corners, blow . . .

The break, the rhyme and metrical stress, and the run-over of line and sense
have curious effects on our reading. We must stress rather loudly for accent
and rhyme and pause slightly for the break and for the coming rhyme. Yet
because of the continuing sense, because the command is incomplete, we
must extend the sound by keeping the voice steady and up. And the long "o"
gives a fine chance for "trumpeting." All of these "soundings" which the
word arrangement demands or allows are what we want for this

> Tuba mirum spargens sonum
> Per sepulchra regionum . . .[2]

This memorable sound serves as one of the links through which we feel the
immediacy of the opening scene in the second half of the poem.

The key to Donne's attitude, as we have seen, is first clearly revealed in
"all," a word which the reader comes down on with full force:

>   arise
> From death, you numberless infinities
> Of soules, and to your scattered bodies goe,
> All whom the flood did, and . . .

We must of course emphasize the word for sense, but a shift in meter forces
us to give an even greater stress and to mark a change in rhythm at the
moment of a change in intensity of feeling. Up until this point Donne has
begun each line in conventional iambic fashion, the ⏑ ⏑ ´ of the first line
being an accepted variation. The reversal of meter in "all" occurs at the first
critical moment in the poem's progress, just as the meaning of "numberlesse
infinities" begins to unfold. We have already noticed the irruption of stresses
in the lines that follow; we should observe also the increase in number to
seven in each. The resultant increase in time as we make each stress and
pause gives a spaciousness of measure to the ear just as the enumeration reaches
its climax in immensity.

Perhaps the most wonderful variation of all comes at the point where the
main dramatic lines and the main attitudes of the poem are most sharply
opposed:

> When wee are there; here on this lowly ground . . .

The reversal of accent increases the stress and makes us put in a pause for
the unaccented syllable we have lost; while "here" gets a further stress due

---

[2] "Trumpet scattering its wondrous sound among the tombs of the world." From
the thirteenth-century hymn "Dies Irae"; cf. I Corinthians, xv, 52.

to the chiasmus and the lack of a connective corresponding to "when." The extraordinary stress, the two blows of sound with a sharp break, is the sound equivalent for this crucial contrast in tone and feeling.

As we return to the lower key of the conclusion Donne gives us one of his pieces of coalescing sound,

> for that's as good
> As if thou'hadst seal'd my pardon, with thy blood.

He contracts, he elides, he brings consonants together of very similar sound, and accordingly we must telescope sounds in reading. The devices force and encourage us to relax our utterance as we do in casual speech. This is what we want to do, in order to move into the new tone and the new mood of assurance which we have at long length reached. The movement of drama in Donne's sonnet, from cosmic vision to private confession, is accompanied throughout by a movement of sound that is exquisitely adjusted to the moments of most significant change.

Holy Sonnet X

Death, be not proud, though some have called thee
Mighty and dreadful, for thou art not so;
For those whom thou think'st thou dost overthrow
Die not, poor Death; nor yet canst thou kill me.
From Rest and Sleep, which but thy pictures be,
Much pleasure, then from thee much more must flow;
And soonest our best men with thee do go,
Rest of their bones and souls' delivery!
Thou art slave to fate, chance, kings, and desperate men,
And dost with poison, war, and sickness dwell;
And poppy or charms can make us sleep as well
And better than thy stroke. Why swell'st thou then?
One short sleep past, we wake eternally,
And Death shall be no more: Death, thou shalt die!

The Anniversary

All kings and all their favorites,
All glory of honors, beauties, wits,
The sun itself, which makes times as they pass,
Is elder by a year now than it was
When thou and I first one another saw;
All other things to their destruction draw;

Only our love hath no decay;
This no to-morrow hath, nor yesterday;
Running, it never runs from us away,
But truly keeps his first, last, everlasting day.   10

Two graves must hide thine and my corse;
If one might, death were no divorce.
Alas, as well as other princes, we,
Who prince enough in one another be,
Must leave at last in death these eyes and ears,
Oft fed with true oaths, and with sweet salt tears;
But souls where nothing dwells but love,
All other thoughts being inmates, then shall prove
This, or a love increased there above,
When bodies to their graves, souls from their graves, remove.   20

And then we shall be thoroughly blest,
But we no more than all the rest;
Here upon earth we are kings, and none but we
Can be such kings, nor of such subjects be.
Who is so safe as we, where none can do
Treason to us, except one of us two?
True and false fears let us refrain;
Let us love nobly, and live, and add again
Years and years unto years, till we attain
To write threescore; this is the second of our reign.   30

The Bait

Come live with me and be my love,
And we will some new pleasures prove
Of golden sands and crystal brooks,
With silken lines and silver hooks.

There will the river whispering run,
Warm'd by thine eyes more than the sun,
And there th' enamor'd fish will stay,
Begging themselves they may betray.

When thou wilt swim in that live bath,
Each fish which every channel hath   10
Will amorously to thee swim,
Gladder to catch thee than thou him.

If thou to be so seen be'st loath,
By sun or moon, thou dark'nest both,
And if myself have leave to see,
I need not their light, having thee.

Let others freeze with angling reeds,
And cut their legs with shells and weeds,
Or treacherously poor fish beset
With strangling snare or windowy net;   20

Let coarse bold hands from slimy nest
The bedded fish in banks outwrest,
Or curious traitors, sleave-silk flies,
Bewitch poor fishes' wand'ring eyes.

For thee, thou need'st no such deceit
For thou thyself art thine own bait;
That fish that is not catch'd thereby,
Alas, is wiser far than I.

Hymn to God, My God, in My Sickness

Since I am coming to that holy room
    Where with thy choir of saints for evermore
I shall be made thy music, as I come
    I tune the instrument here at the door,
    And what I must do then, think here before.

Whilst my physicians by their love are grown
    Cosmographers, and I their map, who lie
Flat on this bed, that by them may be shown
    That this is my Southwest discovery
    Per fretum febris, by these straits to die,   10

I joy that in these straits I see my West.
    For though their currents yield return to none,
What shall my West hurt me? As West and East
    In all flat maps (and I am one) are one,
    So death doth touch the resurrection.

Is the Pacific Sea my home? Or are
    The Eastern riches? Is Jerusalem?
Anian and Magellan and Gibraltar,

All straits, and none but straits, are ways to them,
Whether where Japhet dwelt, or Cham or Shem.   20

We think that Paradise and Calvary,
Christ's Cross and Adam's tree, stood in one place.
Look, Lord, and find both Adams met in me;
As the first Adam's sweat surrounds my face,
May the last Adam's blood my soul embrace.

So in his purple wrapp'd, receive me, Lord,
By these his thorns give me his other crown;
And as to others' souls I preach'd thy word,
Be this my text, my sermon to mine own:
Therefore that he may raise, the Lord throws down.   30

BEN JONSON

Simplex Munditiis[1]

Still to be neat, still to be drest,
As you were going to a feast;
Still to be powdered, still perfumed:
Lady, it is to be presumed,
Though art's hid causes are not found,
All is not sweet, all is not sound.
Give me a look, give me a face
That makes simplicity a grace;
Robes loosely flowing, hair as free:
Such sweet neglect more taketh me
Than all th' adulteries of art;
They strike mine eyes, but not my heart.

Slow, Slow, Fresh Fount

Slow, slow, fresh fount, keep time with my salt tears;
Yet slower yet, oh faintly, gentle springs;
List to the heavy part the music bears,
Woe weeps out her division when she sings.

[1] The title, from Horace, Book I, Ode 5, means "in simple elegance."

Droop herbs and flowers,
Fall grief in showers;
Our beauties are not ours;
   Oh, I could still,
Like melting snow upon some craggy hill,
   Drop, drop, drop, drop,
Since nature's pride is now a withered daffodil.

The Triumph of Charis

See the chariot at hand here of Love,
   Wherein my Lady rideth!
Each that draws is a swan or a dove,
   And well the car Love guideth.
As she goes, all hearts do duty
      Unto her beauty;
And enamored, do wish, so they might
      But enjoy such a sight,
That they still were to run by her side,
Through swords, through seas, whither she would ride.   10

Do but look on her eyes, they do light
   All that Love's world compriseth!
Do but look on her hair, it is bright
   As Love's star when it riseth!
Do but mark, her forehead's smoother
      Than words that soothe her;
And from her arched brows, such a grace
      Sheds itself through the face
As alone there triumphs to the life
All the gain, all the good, of the elements' strife.   20

Have you seen but a bright lily grow
   Before rude hands have touched it?
Have you marked but the fall of the snow
   Before the soil hath smutched it?
Have you felt the wool of the beaver?
      Or swan's down ever?
Or have smelt o' the bud of the briar?
      Or the nard in the fire?
Or have tasted the bag of the bee?
Oh so white! Oh so soft! Oh so sweet is she!   30

ROBERT HERRICK

Delight in Disorder

A sweet disorder in the dress
Kindles in clothes a wantonness;
A lawn about the shoulders thrown
Into a fine distraction,
An erring lace, which here and there
Enthralls the crimson stomacher,
A cuff neglectful, and thereby
Ribands to flow confusedly,
A winning wave, deserving note,
In the tempestuous petticoat,
A careless shoe-string, in whose tie
I see a wild civility,
Do more bewitch me than when art
Is too precise in every part.

F. W. BATESON

On Herrick's "Delight in Disorder" [1]

The impression of a surprising richness, and almost grandeur (as of a painting by Titian), with a certain tantalizing quality, that Herrick's poem leaves, is primarily due to the skill with which he has exploited the ambiguous associations of the epithets. On the surface his subject is the "Delight in Disorder" of the title—a disorder, that is, of costume. But a second subject is hinted at, though not protruded: a delight in disorder, not of costume but of manners and morals. It is not only the clothes but the wearers too whom he would have *sweet, wanton, distracted, erring, neglectful, winning, tempestuous, wild,* and *bewitching* rather than *precise.* The poem, in fact, instead of being the mere *jeu d'esprit* that it would seem to be, is essentially a plea for paganism. There are three themes: (1) untidiness is becoming; (2) the clothes are the woman; (3) anti-Puritanism. But the success of the poem depends upon the fact that the themes are not isolated and contrasted but grow out of and into each other.

[1] From *English Poetry and English Language* (Oxford: The Clarendon Press, 1934), pp. 42-43. Reprinted by permission of Oxford University Press.

The suspension between the various meanings produces a range of reference that none of them would have alone.

Upon Julia's Clothes

Whenas in silks my Julia goes,
Then, then (methinks) how sweetly flows
The liquefaction of her clothes.
Next, when I cast mine eyes and see
That brave vibration each way free,
O how that glittering taketh me!

To the Virgins, to Make Much of Time

Gather ye rose-buds while ye may,
Old Time is still a-flying:
And this same flower that smiles today,
Tomorrow will be dying.

The glorious lamp of heaven, the Sun,
The higher he's a-getting
The sooner will his race be run,
And nearer he's to setting.

That age is best which is the first,
When youth and blood are warmer;
But being spent, the worse, and worst
Times still succeed the former.

Then be not coy, but use your time,
And while ye may, go marry;
For having lost but once your prime,
You may for ever tarry.

The Coming of Good Luck

So Good Luck came, and on my roof did light,
Like noiseless snow, or as the dew of night:
Not all at once, but gently, as the trees
Are, by the sun beams, tickled by degrees.

GEORGE HERBERT

The Pulley

When God at first made man,
Having a glass of blessings standing by,
Let us, said he, pour on him all we can.
Let the world's riches, which dispersèd lie,
    Contract into a span.

So strength first made a way,
Then beauty flowed, then wisdom, honor, pleasure.
When almost all was out, God made a stay,
Perceiving that alone of all his treasure
    Rest in the bottom lay.   10

For if I should, said he,
Bestow this jewel also on my creature,
He would adore my gifts instead of me,
And rest in nature, not the God of nature;
    So both should losers be.

Yet let him keep the rest,
But keep them with repining restlessness.
Let him be rich and weary, that at least,
If goodness lead him not, yet weariness
    May toss him to my breast.   20

The Collar

I struck the board, and cried, "No more; I will abroad!
What! shall I ever sigh and pine?
My lines and life are free; free as the road,
    Loose as the wind, as large as store.
      Shall I be still in suit?
Have I no harvest but a thorn
    To let me blood, and not restore
What I have lost with cordial fruit?
      Sure there was wine
Before my sighs did dry it; there was corn   10

Before my tears did drown it.
    Is the year only lost to me?
    Have I no bays to crown it,
No flowers, no garlands gay? all blasted,
       All wasted?
Not so, my heart, but there is fruit,
    And thou hast hands.
    Recover all thy sigh-blown age
On double pleasures; leave thy cold dispute
Of what is fit and not; forsake thy cage,   20
       Thy rope of sands,
Which petty thoughts have made; and made to thee
    Good cable, to enforce and draw,
       And be thy law,
While thou didst wink and wouldst not see.
       Away! take heed!
       I will abroad.
Call in thy death's-head there, tie up thy fears.
       He that forbears
       To suit and serve his need   30
       Deserves his load."
But as I raved, and grew more fierce and wild
       At every word,
Methought I heard one calling, "Child";
    And I replied, "My Lord."

Prayer

Prayer, the church's banquet, angels' age,
    God's breath in man returning to his birth,
    The soul in paraphrase, heart in pilgrimage,
The Christian plummet sounding heaven and earth;
Engine against the Almighty, sinner's tower,
    Reversèd thunder, Christ-side-piercing spear,
    The six days' world-transposing in an hour,
A kind of tune, which all things hear and fear;
Softness, and peace, and joy, and love, and bliss,
    Exalted manna, gladness of the best,
    Heaven in ordinary, man well dressed,
The Milky Way, the bird of Paradise,
    Church bells beyond the stars heard, the soul's blood,
    The land of spices, something understood.

JOHN MILTON

Lycidas

In This Monody the Author Bewails a Learned Friend, Unfortunately Drowned in His Passage from Chester on the Irish Seas, 1637; and, by Occasion, Foretells the Ruin of Our Corrupted Clergy, Then in Their Height.

Yet once more, O ye laurels, and once more,
Ye myrtles brown, with ivy never sere,
I come to pluck your berries harsh and crude,
And with forced fingers rude
Shatter your leaves before the mellowing year.
Bitter constraint, and sad occasion dear
Compels me to disturb your season due;
For Lycidas is dead, dead ere his prime,
Young Lycidas, and hath not left his peer.
Who would not sing for Lycidas? he knew   10
Himself to sing, and build the lofty rhyme.
He must not float upon his watery bier
Unwept, and welter to the parching wind,
Without the meed of some melodious tear.
    Begin, then, Sisters of the sacred well
That from beneath the seat of Jove doth spring;
Begin, and somewhat loudly sweep the string.
Hence with denial vain and coy excuse:
So may some gentle Muse
With lucky words favour my destined urn,   20
And as he passes turn,
And bid fair peace be to my sable shroud!
For we were nursed upon the self-same hill,
Fed the same flock, by fountain, shade, and rill.
    Together both, ere the high lawns appeared
Under the opening eyelids of the Morn,
We drove a-field, and both together heard
What time the gray-fly winds her sultry horn,
Battening our flocks with the fresh dews of night,
Oft till the star that rose, at evening, bright   30
Toward heaven's descent had sloped his westering wheel.
Meanwhile the rural ditties were not mute;

Tempered to the oaten flute,
Rough Satyrs danced, and Fauns with cloven heel
From the glad sound would not be absent long;
And old Damoetas loved to hear our song.

But, oh! the heavy change, now thou art gone,
Now thou art gone and never must return!
Thee, Shepherd, thee the woods and desert caves,
With wild thyme and the gadding vine o'ergrown,   40
And all their echoes, mourn.
The willows, and the hazel copses green,
Shall now no more be seen
Fanning their joyous leaves to thy soft lays.
As killing as the canker to the rose,
Or taint-worm to the weanling herds that graze,
Or frost to flowers, that their gay wardrobe wear,
When first the white-thorn blows;
Such, Lycidas, thy loss to shepherd's ear.

Where were ye, Nymphs, when the remorseless deep   50
Closed o'er the head of your loved Lycidas?
For neither were ye playing on the steep
Where your old bards, the famous Druids, lie,
Nor on the shaggy top of Mona high,
Nor yet where Deva spreads her wizard stream.
Ay me! I fondly dream
"Had ye been there"—for what could that have done?
What could the Muse herself that Orpheus bore,
The Muse herself, for her enchanting son,
Whom universal nature did lament,   60
When, by the rout that made the hideous roar,
His gory visage down the stream was sent,
Down the swift Hebrus to the Lesbian shore?

Alas! what boots it with uncessant care
To tend the homely, slighted, shepherd's trade,
And strictly meditate the thankless Muse?
Were it not better done, as others use,
To sport with Amaryllis in the shade,
Or with the tangles of Neaera's hair?
Fame is the spur that the clear spirit doth raise   70
(That last infirmity of noble mind)
To scorn delights, and live laborious days;
But the fair guerdon when we hope to find,
And think to burst out into sudden blaze,
Comes the blind Fury with the abhorrèd shears,
And slits the thin-spun life. "But not the praise,"

Phoebus replied, and touched my trembling ears:
"Fame is no plant that grows on mortal soil,
Nor in the glistering foil
Set off to the world, nor in broad rumour lies,   80
But lives and spreads aloft by those pure eyes,
And perfect witness of all-judging Jove;
As he pronounces lastly on each deed,
Of so much fame in heaven expect thy meed."
   O fountain Arethuse, and thou honoured flood,
Smooth-sliding Mincius, crowned with vocal reeds,
That strain I heard was of a higher mood.
But now my oat proceeds,
And listens to the Herald of the Sea
That came in Neptune's plea.   90
He asked the waves, and asked the felon winds,
What hard mishap hath doomed this gentle swain?
And questioned every gust of rugged wings
That blows from off each beakèd promontory.
They knew not of his story;
And sage Hippotades their answer brings;
That not a blast was from his dungeon strayed,
The air was calm, and on the level brine
Sleep Panope with all her sisters played.
It was that fatal and perfidious bark,   100
Built in the eclipse, and rigged with curses dark,
That sunk so low that sacred head of thine.
   Next, Camus, reverend sire, went footing slow,
His mantle hairy, and his bonnet sedge,
Inwrought with figures dim, and on the edge
Like to that sanguine flower inscribed with woe.
"Ah! who hath reft," quoth he, "my dearest pledge?"
Last came, and last did go,
The Pilot of the Galilean Lake;
Two massy keys he bore of metals twain   110
(The golden opes, the iron shuts amain).
He shook his mitred locks, and stern bespake:—
"How well could I have spared for thee, young swain,
Enow of such as, for their bellies' sake,
Creep, and intrude, and climb into the fold!
Of other care they little reckoning make
Than how to scramble at the shearers' feast,
And shove away the worthy bidden guest.
Blind mouths! that scarce themselves know how to hold
A sheep-hook, or have learnt aught else the least   120

That to the faithful herdman's art belongs!
What recks it them? What need they? They are sped;
And, when they list, their lean and flashy songs
Grate on their scrannel pipes of wretched straw;
The hungry sheep look up, and are not fed,
But, swoln with wind and the rank mist they draw,
Rot inwardly, and foul contagion spread;
Besides what the grim wolf with privy paw
Daily devours apace, and nothing said.
But that two-handed engine at the door   130
Stands ready to smite once, and smite no more."
    Return, Alpheus; the dread voice is past
That shrunk thy streams; return, Sicilian Muse,
And call the vales, and bid them hither cast
Their bells and flowerets of a thousand hues.
Ye valleys low, where the mild whispers use
Of shades, and wanton winds, and gushing brooks,
On whose fresh lap the swart star sparely looks,
Throw hither all your quaint enamelled eyes,
That on the green turf suck the honeyed showers,   140
And purple all the ground with vernal flowers.
Bring the rathe primrose that forsaken dies,
The tufted crow-toe, and pale jessamine,
The white pink, and the pansy freaked with jet,
The glowing violet,
The musk rose, and the well-attired woodbine,
With cowslips wan that hang the pensive head,
And every flower that sad embroidery wears;
Bid amaranthus all his beauty shed,
And daffadillies fill their cups with tears,   150
To strew the laureate hearse where Lycid lies.
For so, to interpose a little ease,
Let our frail thoughts dally with false surmise.
Ay me! whilst thee the shores and sounding seas
Wash far away, where'er thy bones are hurled;
Whether beyond the stormy Hebrides,
Where thou perhaps under the whelming tide
Visit'st the bottom of the monstrous world;
Or whether thou, to our moist vows denied,
Sleep'st by the fable of Bellerus old,   160
Where the great Vision of the guarded mount
Looks toward Namancos and Bayona's hold.
Look homeward, Angel, now, and melt with ruth:
And, O ye dolphins, waft the hapless youth.

Weep no more, woeful shepherds, weep no more,
For Lycidas, your sorrow, is not dead,
Sunk though he be beneath the watery floor.
So sinks the day-star in the ocean bed,
And yet anon repairs his drooping head,
And tricks his beams, and with new-spangled ore   170
Flames in the forehead of the morning sky:
So Lycidas sunk low, but mounted high,
Through the dear might of Him that walked the waves,
Where, other groves and other streams along,
With nectar pure his oozy locks he laves,
And hears the unexpressive nuptial song,
In the blest kingdoms meek of joy and love.
There entertain him all the Saints above,
In solemn troops, and sweet societies,
That sing, and singing in their glory move,   180
And wipe the tears for ever from his eyes.
Now, Lycidas, the shepherds weep no more;
Henceforth thou art the Genius of the shore,
In thy large recompense, and shalt be good
To all that wander in that perilous flood.
    Thus sang the uncouth swain to the oaks and rills,
While the still morn went out with sandals grey:
He touched the tender stops of various quills,
With eager thought warbling his Doric lay:
And now the sun had stretched out all the hills,   190
And now was dropt into the western bay;
At last he rose, and twitched his mantle blue:
To-morrow to fresh woods, and pastures new.

On His Being Arrived to the Age of Twenty-Three

How soon hath time, the subtle thief of youth,
    Stolen on his wing my three and twentieth year!
    My hasting days fly on with full career,
    But my late spring no bud or blossom shew'th.
Perhaps my semblance might deceive the truth,
    That I to manhood am arrived so near,
    And inward ripeness doth much less appear,
    That some more timely-happy spirits endu'th.
Yet be it less or more, or soon or slow,
    It shall be still in strictest measure even
    To that same lot, however mean or high,

Toward which Time leads me, and the will of Heaven.
    All is, if I have grace to use it so,
    As ever in my great Task-master's eye.

On His Blindness

When I consider how my light is spent
    Ere half my days in this dark world and wide,
    And that one talent which is death to hide
    Lodged with me useless, though my soul more bent
To serve therewith my Maker, and present
    My true account, lest He returning chide,
    "Doth God exact day-labor, light denied?"
    I fondly ask. But Patience, to prevent
That murmur, soon replies, "God doth not need
    Either man's work or his own gifts. Who best
    Bear his mild yoke, they serve him best. His state
Is kingly: thousands at his bidding speed,
    And post o'er land and ocean without rest;
    They also serve who only stand and wait."

SIR JOHN SUCKLING

Why So Pale and Wan?

Why so pale and wan, fond lover?
    Prithee, why so pale?
Will, when looking well can't move her,
    Looking ill prevail?
    Prithee, why so pale?

Why so dull and mute, young sinner?
    Prithee, why so mute?
Will, when speaking well can't win her,
    Saying nothing do't?
    Prithee, why so mute?

Quit, quit for shame! This will not move,
    This cannot take her.
If of herself she will not love,

Nothing can make her:
The devil take her!

The Constant Lover

Out upon it, I have loved
   Three whole days together!
And am like to love three more,
   If it prove fair weather.

Time shall moult away his wings,
   Ere he shall discover
In the whole wide world again
   Such a constant lover.

But the spite on't is, no praise
   Is due at all to me:
Love with me had made no stays,
   Had it any been but she.

Had it any been but she,
   And that very face,
There had been at least ere this
   A dozen dozen in her place.

ANDREW MARVELL

To His Coy Mistress

Had we but world enough, and time,
This coyness, Lady, were no crime.
We would sit down and think which way
To walk and pass our long love's day.
Thou by the Indian Ganges' side
Shouldst rubies find; I by the tide
Of Humber would complain. I would
Love you ten years before the Flood,
And you should, if you please, refuse
Till the conversion of the Jews.
My vegetable love should grow

10

Vaster than empires, and more slow;
An hundred years should go to praise
Thine eyes and on thy forehead gaze;
Two hundred to adore each breast,
But thirty thousand to the rest;
An age at least to every part,
And the last age should show your heart.
For, Lady, you deserve this state,
Nor would I love at lower rate.   20
    But at my back I always hear
Time's winged chariot hurrying near;
And yonder all before us lie
Deserts of vast eternity.
Thy beauty shall no more be found,
Nor, in thy marble vault, shall sound
My echoing song; then worms shall try
That long preserved virginity,
And your quaint honor turn to dust,
And into ashes all my lust: 30
The grave's a fine and private place,
But none, I think, do there embrace.
    Now therefore, while the youthful hue
Sits on thy skin like morning dew,
And while thy willing soul transpires
At every pore with instant fires,
Now let us sport us while we may,
And now, like amorous birds of prey,
Rather at once our time devour
Than languish in his slow-chapped power.   40
Let us roll all our strength and all
Our sweetness up into one ball,
And tear our pleasures with rough strife
Thorough the iron gates of life:
Thus, though we cannot make our sun
Stand still, yet we will make him run.

A Dialogue Between the Soul and Body

SOUL

Oh, who shall from this dungeon raise
A soul enslaved so many ways?
With bolts of bones; that fettered stands
In feet, and manacled in hands;

Here blinded with an eye, and there
Deaf with the drumming of an ear;
A soul hung up, as 'twere, in chains
Of nerves and arteries and veins;
Tortured, besides each other part,
In a vain head and double heart.   10

BODY

Oh, who shall me deliver whole
From bonds of this tyrannic soul?
Which, stretched upright, impales me so
That mine own precipice I go;
And warms and moves this needless frame,
A fever could but do the same.
And, wanting where its spite to try,
Has made me live to let me die.
A body that could never rest,
Since this ill spirit it possessed.   20

SOUL

What magic could me thus confine
Within another's grief to pine?
Where whatsoever it complain,
I feel, that cannot feel, the pain.
And all my care itself employs,
That to preserve which me destroys.
Constrained not only to endure
Diseases, but, what's worse, the cure;
And ready oft the port to gain,
Am shipwrecked into health again.   30

BODY

But physic yet could never reach
The maladies thou me dost teach:
Whom first the cramp of hope does tear,
And then the palsy shakes of fear;
The pestilence of love does heat,
Or hatred's hidden ulcer eat.
Joy's cheerful madness does perplex,
Or sorrow's other madness vex;
Which knowledge forces me to know,
And memory will not forgo.   40
What but a soul could have the wit
To build me up for sin so fit?

So architects do square and hew
Green trees that in the forest grew.

JOHN DRYDEN

Can Life Be a Blessing?

I

Can life be a blessing,
   Or worth the possessing,
Can life be a blessing if love were away?
   Ah no! though our love all night keep us waking,
And though he torment us with cares all the day,
   Yet he sweetens, he sweetens our pains in the taking,
There's an hour at the last, there's an hour to repay.

II

In ev'ry possessing,
   The ravishing blessing,
In ev'ry possessing the fruit of our pain,
   Poor lovers forget long ages of anguish,
What e'er they have suffer'd and done to obtain;
   'Tis a pleasure, a pleasure to sigh and to languish,
When we hope, when we hope to be happy again.

A Song for St. Cecilia's Day

1687

From harmony, from heav'nly harmony,
   This universal frame began;
   When Nature underneath a heap
      Of jarring atoms lay,
   And could not heave her head,
The tuneful voice was heard from high:
   "Arise, ye more than dead."
Then cold and hot and moist and dry
In order to their stations leap,
      And Music's pow'r obey.   10
From harmony, from heav'nly harmony,

This universal frame began:
From harmony to harmony
Through all the compass of the notes it ran,
The diapason closing full in man.

What passion cannot Music raise and quell!
    When Jubal struck the corded shell,
    His listening brethren stood around,
    And, wond'ring, on their faces fell
    To worship that celestial sound.
Less than a god they thought there could not dwell   20
    Within the hollow of that shell
    That spoke so sweetly and so well.
What passion cannot Music raise and quell!

    The trumpet's loud clangor
        Excites us to arms
    With shrill notes of anger
        And mortal alarms.
    The double, double, double beat
        Of the thundering drum   30
        Cries: "Hark! the foes come;
Charge, charge, 'tis too late to retreat!"

    The soft complaining flute
        In dying notes discovers
        The woes of hopeless lovers,
Whose dirge is whispered by the warbling lute.

    Sharp violins proclaim
Their jealous pangs and desperation,
Fury, frantic indignation,
Depth of pains, and height of passion,
    For the fair, disdainful dame.   40

But oh! what art can teach,
What human voice can reach
    The sacred organ's praise?
    Notes inspiring holy love,
Notes that wing their heavenly ways
    To mend the choirs above.

Orpheus could lead the savage race;
And trees unrooted left their place,

Sequacious of the lyre;
But bright Cecilia raised the wonder higher:
When to her organ vocal breath was given,
An angel heard, and straight appeared,
    Mistaking earth for heaven.

GRAND CHORUS

As from the power of sacred lays
    The spheres began to move,
And sung the great Creator's praise
    To all the blessed above;
So when the last and dreadful hour
This crumbling pageant shall devour,
The trumpet shall be heard on high,
The dead shall live, the living die,
And Music shall untune the sky.

60

SIR CHARLES SEDLEY

Song

Phillis is my only Joy,
    Faithless as the Winds or Seas;
Sometimes coming, sometimes coy,
    Yet she never fails to please;
        If with a Frown
        I am cast down,
        Phillis smiling,
        And beguiling,
Makes me happier than before.

Tho', alas, too late I find,
    Nothing can her Fancy fix;
Yet the Moment she is kind,
    I forgive her all her Tricks;
        Which, tho' I see,
        I can't get free;
        She deceiving,
        I believing;
What need Lovers wish for more?

JOHN WILMOT, EARL OF ROCHESTER

Upon His Leaving His Mistress

I

'Tis not that I am weary grown
Of being yours, and yours alone:
But with what Face can I incline,
To damn you to be only mine?
You, who some kinder Pow'r did fashion,
By Merit, and by Inclination,
The Joy at least of a whole Nation.

II

Let meaner Spirits of your Sex,
With humble Aims their Thoughts perplex:
And boast, if, by their Arts they can   10
Contrive to make *one* happy Man.
While, mov'd by an impartial Sense,
Favours, like Nature, you dispence,
With universal Influence.

III

See the kind Seed-receiving Earth,
To every Grain affords a Birth:
On her no Show'rs unwelcome fall,
Her willing Womb retains 'em all.
And shall my *Caelia* be confin'd?
No, live up to thy mighty Mind;   20
And be the Mistress of Mankind.

Love and Life, A Song

All my past life is mine no more;
    The flying hours are gone,
Like transitory dreams given o'er,
Whose images are kept in store
    By memory alone.

The time that is to come is not;
    How can it then be mine?

The present moment's all my lot;
And that, as fast as it is got,
   Phillis, is only thine.

Then talk not of inconstancy,
   False hearts, and broken vows;
If I by miracle can be
This live-long minute true to thee,
   'Tis all that heaven allows.

MATTHEW PRIOR

An Epitaph (1718)

Stet quicunque volet potens
Aulae culmine lubrico, &c.[1]

Interr'd beneath this Marble Stone,
Lie Saunt'ring Jack, and Idle Joan.
While rolling Threescore Years and One
Did round this Globe their Courses run;
If Human Things went Ill or Well;
If changing Empires rose or fell;
The Morning past, the Evening came,
And found this Couple still the same.
They Walk'd and Eat, good Folks: What then?
Why then They Walk'd and Eat again;   10
They soundly slept the Night away:
They did just Nothing all the Day:
And having bury'd Children Four,
Wou'd not take Pains to try for more.
Nor Sister either had, nor Brother:
They seem'd just Tally'd for each other.

   Their Moral and Oeconomy
Most perfectly They made agree:
Each Virtue kept it's proper Bound,
Nor Trespass'd on the other's Ground.   20

[1] Let him stand who will, in pride of power, on empire's slippery height; [let me be filled with sweet repose. . . .] —Seneca, *Thyestes* (as translated by Maynard Mack).

Nor Fame, nor Censure They regarded:
They neither Punish'd, nor Rewarded.
He car'd not what the Footmen did:
Her Maids She neither prais'd, nor chid:
So ev'ry Servant took his Course;
And bad at First, They all grew worse.
Slothful Disorder fill'd His Stable;
And sluttish Plenty deck'd Her Table.
Their Beer was strong; Their Wine was *Port*;
Their Meal was large; Their Grace was short.   30
They gave the Poor the Remnant-meat,
Just when it grew not fit to eat.

    They paid the Church and Parish-Rate;
And took, but read not the Receit:
For which They claim'd their *Sunday's* Due,
Of slumb'ring in an upper Pew.

    No Man's Defects sought They to know;
So never made Themselves a Foe.
No Man's good Deeds did They commend;
So never rais'd Themselves a Friend.   40
Nor cherish'd They Relations poor:
That might decrease Their present Store:
Nor Barn nor House did they repair:
That might oblige Their future Heir.

    They neither Added, nor Confounded:
They neither Wanted, nor Abounded.
Each *Christmas* They Accompts did clear;
And wound their Bottom round the Year.
Nor Tear, nor Smile did They imploy
At News of Public Grief, or Joy.   50
When Bells were Rung, and Bonfires made;
If ask'd, They ne'er deny'd their Aid:
Their Jugg was to the Ringers carry'd;
Who ever either Dy'd, or Marry'd.
Their Billet at the Fire was found;
Who ever was Depos'd, or Crown'd.

    Nor Good, Nor Bad, nor Fools, nor Wise;
They wou'd not learn, nor cou'd advise:
Without Love, Hatred, Joy, or Fear,
They led—a kind of—as it were: 60

Nor Wish'd, nor Car'd, nor Laugh'd, nor Cry'd:
And so They liv'd; and so They dy'd.

JONATHAN SWIFT

A Description of a City Shower

Careful Observers may fortel the Hour
(By sure Prognosticks) when to dread a Show'r:
While Rain depends, the pensive Cat gives o'er
Her Frolicks, and pursues her Tail no more.
Returning Home at Night, you'll find the Sink
Strike your offended Sense with double Stink.
If you be wise, then go not far to Dine,
You'll spend in Coach-hire more than save in Wine.
A Coming Show'r your shooting Corns presage,
Old Arches throb, your hollow Tooth will rage.   10
Sauntring in Coffee-house is *Dulman* seen;
He damns the Climate, and complains of Spleen.
     Mean while the South rising with dabbled Wings,
A Sable Cloud a-thwart the Welkin flings,
That swill'd more Liquor than it could contain,
And like a Drunkard gives it up again.
Brisk *Susan* whips her Linen from the Rope,
While the first drizzling Show'r is born aslope,
Such is that Sprinkling which some careless Quean
Flirts on you from her Mop, but not so clean.   20
You fly, invoke the Gods; then turning, stop
To rail; she singing, still whirls on her Mop.
Not yet, the Dust had shun'd th' unequal Strife,
But aided by the Wind, fought still for Life;
And wafted with its Foe by violent Gust,
'Twas doubtful which was Rain, and which was Dust.
Ah! where must needy Poet seek for Aid,
When Dust and Rain at once his Coat invade;
His only Coat, where Dust confus'd with Rain,
Roughen the Nap, and leave a mingled Stain.   30
     Now in contiguous Drops the Flood comes down,
Threat'ning with Deluge this *Devoted* Town.
To Shops in Crouds the dagged Females fly,
Pretend to cheapen Goods, but nothing buy.

The Templer spruce, while ev'ry Spout's a-broach,
Stays till 'tis fair, yet seems to call a Coach.
The tuck'up Sempstress walks with hasty Strides,
While Streams run down her oil'd Umbrella's Sides.
Here various Kinds by various Fortunes led,
Commence Acquaintance underneath a Shed.
Triumphant Tories, and desponding Whigs,   40
Forget their Fewds, and join to save their Wigs.
Box'd in a Chair the Beau impatient sits,
While Spouts run clatt'ring o'er the Roof by Fits;
And ever and anon with frightful Din
The Leather sounds, he trembles from within.
So when *Troy* Chair-men bore the Wooden Steed,
Pregnant with *Greeks*, impatient to be freed,
(Those Bully *Greeks*, who, as the Moderns do,
Instead of paying Chair-men, run them thro'.)
Laoco'n struck the Outside with his Spear,   50
And each imprison'd Hero quak'd for Fear.
  Now from all Parts the swelling Kennels flow,
And bear their Trophies with them as they go:
Filth of all Hues and Odours seem to tell
What Street they sail'd from, by their Sight and Smell.
They, as each Torrent drives, with rapid Force
From *Smithfield*, or St. *Pulchre*'s shape their Course,
And in huge Confluent join at *Snow-Hill* Ridge,
Fall from the *Conduit* prone to *Holborn-Bridge*.   60
Sweepings from Butchers Stalls, Dung, Guts, and Blood,
Drown'd Puppies, stinking Sprats, all drench'd in Mud,
Dead Cats and Turnip-Tops come tumbling down the Flood.

ALEXANDER POPE

To a Young Lady: On Her Leaving the Town After the Coronation

As some fond Virgin, whom her mother's care
Drags from the Town to wholesome Country air,
Just when she learns to roll a melting eye,
And hear a spark, yet think no danger nigh;
From the dear man unwilling she must sever,

Yet takes one kiss before she parts forever:
Thus from the world fair Zephalinda flew,
Saw others happy, and with sighs withdrew;
Not that their pleasures caus'd her discontent,
She sigh'd not that they stay'd, but that she went.   10
  She went, to plain-work and to purling brooks,
Old-fashioned halls, dull Aunts, and croaking rooks:
She went from op'ra, park, assembly, play,
To morning walks, and pray'rs three hours a day;
To part her time 'twixt reading and bohea,
To muse, and spill her solitary tea,
Or o'er cold coffee trifle with the spoon,
Count the slow clock, and dine exact at noon;
Divert her eyes with pictures in the fire,
Hum half a tune, tell stories to the squire;   20
Up to her godly garret after sev'n,
There starve and pray, for that's the way to heav'n.
  Some Squire, perhaps, you take delight to rack;
Whose game is Whisk, whose treat a toast in sack;
Who visits with a gun, presents you birds,
Then gives a smacking buss, and cries,—No words!
Or with his hound comes hollowing from the stable,
Makes love with nods, and knees beneath a table;
Whose laughs are hearty, tho' his jests are coarse,
And loves you best of all things—but his horse.   30
  In some fair ev'ning, on your elbow laid,
You dream of Triumphs in the rural shade;
In pensive thought recall the fancy'd scene,
See Coronations rise on ev'ry green;
Before you pass th' imaginary sights
Of Lords, and Earls, and Dukes, and garter'd Knights,
While the spread fan o'ershades your closing eyes;
Then give one flirt, and all the vision flies.
Thus vanish sceptres, coronets, and balls,
And leave you in lone woods, or empty walls.   40
  So when your Slave, at some dear idle time,
(Not plagu'd with head-aches, or the want of rhyme)
And while he seems to study, thinks of you;
Just when his fancy points your sprightly eyes,
Or sees the blush of Parthenissa rise,
Gay pats my shoulder, and you vanish quite,
Streets, Chairs, and Coxcombs rush upon my sight;
Vex'd to be still in town, I knit my brow,
Look sour, and hum a song—as you may now.

Moral Essay, II

TO A LADY, OF THE CHARACTERS OF WOMEN

Nothing so true as what you once let fall,
"Most Women have no Characters at all."
Matter too soft a lasting mark to bear,
And best distinguished by black, brown, or fair.

    How many pictures of one Nymph we view,
All how unlike each other, all how true!
Arcadia's Countess, here, in ermined pride,
Is, there, Pastora by a fountain side.
Here Fannia, leering on her own good man,
And there, a naked Leda with a Swan.   10
Let then the Fair one beautifully cry,
In Magdalen's loose hair, and lifted eye,
Or drest in smiles of sweet Cecilia shine,
With simp'ring Angels, Palms, and Harps divine;
Whether the Charmer sinner it, or saint it,
If Folly grow romantic, I must paint it.

    Come then, the colours and the ground prepare!
Dip in the Rainbow, trick her off in Air;
Choose a firm Cloud, before it fall, and in it
Catch, ere she change, the Cynthia of this minute.   20

    Rufa, whose eye quick-glancing o'er the Park,
Attracts each light gay meteor of a Spark,
Agrees as ill with Rufa studying Locke,
As Sappho's diamonds with her dirty smock;
Or Sappho at her toilet's greasy task,
With Sappho fragrant at an evening Masque:
So morning Insects that in muck begun,
Shine, buzz, and fly-blow in the setting-sun.

    How soft is Silia! fearful to offend;
The Frail one's advocate, the Weak one's friend: 30
To her, Calista proved her conduct nice;
And good Simplicius asks of her advice.
Sudden, she storms! she raves! You tip the wink,
But spare your censure; Silia does not drink.
All eyes may see from what the change arose,
All eyes may see—a Pimple on her nose.

    Papillia, wedded to her am'rous spark,
Sighs for the shades—"How charming is a Park!"
A Park is purchased, but the Fair he sees

All bathed in tears—"Oh, odious, odious Trees!"   40
    Ladies, like variegated Tulips, show;
'Tis to their Changes half their charms we owe;
Fine by defect, and delicately weak,
Their happy Spots the nice admirer take,
'Twas thus Calypso once each heart alarmed,
Awed without Virtue, without Beauty charmed;
Her tongue bewitched as oddly as her Eyes,
Less Wit than Mimic, more a Wit than wise;
Strange graces still, and stranger flights she had,
Was just not ugly, and was just not mad;   50
Yet ne'er so sure our passion to create,
As when she touched the brink of all we hate.
    Narcissa's nature, tolerably mild,
To make a wash, would hardly stew a child;
Has even been proved to grant a Lover's prayer,
And paid a Tradesman once to make him stare;
Gave alms at Easter, in a Christian trim,
And made a Widow happy, for a whim.
Why then declare Good-nature is her scorn,
When 'tis by that alone she can be borne?   60
Why pique all mortals, yet affect a name?
A fool to Pleasure, yet a slave to Fame:
Now deep in Taylor and the Book of Martyrs,
Now drinking citron with his Grace and Chartres:
Now Conscience chills her, and now Passion burns;
And Atheism and Religion take their turns;
A very Heathen in the carnal part,
Yet still a sad, good Christian at her heart.
    See Sin in State, majestically drunk;
Proud as a Peeress, prouder as a Punk;   70
Chaste to her Husband, frank to all beside,
A teeming Mistress, but a barren Bride.
What then? let Blood and Body bear the fault,
Her Head's untouched, that noble Seat of Thought:
Such this day's doctrine—in another fit
She sins with Poets through pure Love of Wit.
What has not fired her bosom or her brain?
Cæsar and Tall-boy, Charles and Charlemagne.
As Helluo, late Dictator of the Feast,
The Nose of Hautgout, and the Tip of Taste,   80
Critiqued your wine, and analysed your meat,
Yet on plain Pudding deigned at home to eat;
So Philomedé, lect'ring all mankind

On the soft Passion, and the Taste refined,
Th' Address, the Delicacy—stoops at once,
And makes her hearty meal upon a Dunce.
      Flavia's a Wit, has too much sense to Pray;
To Toast our wants and wishes, is her way;
Nor asks of God, but of her Stars, to give
The mighty blessing, "While we live, to live."   90
Then all for Death, that Opiate of the soul!
Lucretia's dagger, Rosamonda's bowl.
Say, what can cause such impotence of mind?
A spark too fickle, or a Spouse too kind.
Wise Wretch! with Pleasures too refined to please;
With too much Spirit to be e'er at ease;
With too much Quickness ever to be taught;
With too much Thinking to have common Thought:
You purchase Pain with all that Joy can give,
And die of nothing but a Rage to live.   100
      Turn then from Wits; and look on Simo's Mate,
No Ass so meek, no Ass so obstinate.
Or her, that owns her Faults, but never mends,
Because she's honest, and the best of Friends.
Or her, whose life the Church and Scandal share,
For ever in a Passion, or a Prayer.
Or her, who laughs at Hell, but (like her Grace)
Cries, "Ah! how charming, if there's no such place!"
Or who in sweet vicissitude appears
Or Mirth and Opium, Ratafie and Tears,   110
The daily Anodyne, and nightly Draught,
To kill those foes to Fair ones, Time and Thought.
Woman and Fool are two hard things to hit;
For true No-meaning puzzles more than Wit.
      But what are these to great Atossa's mind?
Scarce once herself, by turns all Womankind!
Who, with herself, or others, from her birth
Finds all her life one warfare upon earth:
Shines in exposing Knaves, and painting Fools,
Yet is, whate'er she hates and ridicules.   120
No Thought advances, but her Eddy Brain
Whisks it about, and down it goes again.
Full sixty years the World has been her Trade,
The wisest Fool much Time has ever made.
From loveless youth to unrespected age,
No passion gratified except her Rage.
So much the Fury still out-ran the Wit,

The Pleasure missed her, and the Scandal hit.
Who breaks with her, provokes Revenge from Hell,
But he's a bolder man who dares be well.   130
Her every turn with Violence pursued,
Nor more a storm her Hate than Gratitude:
To that each Passion turns, or soon or late;
Love, if it makes her yield, must make her hate:
Superiors? death! and Equals? what a curse!
But an Inferior not dependant? worse.
Offend her, and she knows not to forgive;
Oblige her, and she'll hate you while you live:
But die, and she'll adore you—Then the Bust
And Temple rise—then fall again to dust.   140
Last night, her Lord was all that's good and great;
A Knave this morning, and his Will a Cheat.
Strange! by the Means defeated of the Ends,
By Spirit robbed of Power, by Warmth of Friends,
By Wealth of Followers! without one distress
Sick of herself through very selfishness!
Atossa, cursed with every granted prayer,
Childless with all her Children, wants an Heir.
To Heirs unknown descends th' unguarded store,
Or wanders, Heaven-directed, to the Poor.   150
   Pictures like these, dear Madam, to design,
Asks no firm hand, and no unerring line;
Some wand'ring touches, some reflected light,
Some flying stroke alone can hit 'em right:
For how should equal Colours do the knack?
Chameleons who can paint in white and black?
   "Yet Chloe sure was formed without a spot"—
Nature in her then erred not, but forgot.
"With every pleasing, every prudent part,
Say, what can Chloe want?"—She wants a Heart.   160
She speaks, behaves, and acts just as she ought;
But never, never, reached one gen'rous Thought.
Virtue she finds too painful an endeavour,
Content to dwell in Decencies for ever.
So very reasonable, so unmoved,
As never yet to love, or to be loved.
She, while her Lover pants upon her breast,
Can mark the figures on an Indian chest;
And when she sees her Friend in deep despair,
Observes how much a Chintz exceeds Mohair.   170
Forbid it Heaven, a Favour or a Debt
She e'er should cancel—but she may forget.

Safe is your Secret still in Chloe's ear;
But none of Chloe's shall you ever hear.
Of all her Dears she never slandered one,
But cares not if a thousand are undone.
Would Chloe know if you're alive or dead?
She bids her Footman put it in her head.
Chloe is prudent—Would you too be wise?
Then never break your heart when Chloe dies.

One certain Portrait may (I grant) be seen,   180
Which Heaven has varnished out, and made a *Queen*:
THE SAME FOR EVER! and described by all
With Truth and Goodness, as with Crown and Ball.
Poets heap Virtues, Painters Gems at will,
And shew their zeal, and hide their want of skill.
'Tis well—but, Artists! who can paint or write,
To draw the Naked is your true delight.
That robe of Quality so struts and swells,
None see what Parts of Nature it conceals:
Th' exactest traits of Body or of Mind,   190
We owe to models of an humble kind.
If QUEENSBURY to strip there's no compelling,
'Tis from a Handmaid we must take a Helen,
From Peer or Bishop 'tis no easy thing
To draw the man who loves his God, or King:
Alas! I copy (or my draught would fail)
From honest Mah'met, or plain Parson Hale.

But grant, in Public Men sometimes are shown,
A Woman's seen in Private life alone:
Our bolder Talents in full light displayed;   200
Your virtues open fairest in the shade.
Bred to disguise, in Public 'tis you hide;
There, none distinguish 'twixt your Shame or Pride,
Weakness or Delicacy; all so nice,
That each may seem a Virtue, or a Vice.

In Men, we various Ruling Passions find;
In Women, two almost divide the kind;
Those, only fixed, they first or last obey,
The Love of Pleasure, and the Love of Sway.

That, Nature gives; and where the lesson taught   210
Is but to please, can Pleasure seem a fault?
Experience, this; by Man's oppression curst,
They seek the second not to lose the first.

Men, some to Business, some to Pleasure take;
But every Woman is at heart a Rake:
Men, some to Quiet, some to public Strife;

But every Lady would be Queen for life.
   Yet mark the fate of a whole Sex of Queens!
Power all their end, but Beauty all the means: 220
In Youth they conquer, with so wild a rage,
As leaves them scarce a subject in their Age:
For foreign glory, foreign joy, they roam;
No thought of peace or happiness at home.
But Wisdom's triumph is well-timed Retreat,
As hard a science to the Fair as Great!
Beauties, like Tyrants, old and friendless grown,
Yet hate repose, and dread to be alone,
Worn out in public, weary every eye,
Nor leave one sigh behind them when they die.   230
   Pleasures the sex, as children Birds, pursue,
Still out of reach, yet never out of view;
Sure, if they catch, to spoil the Toy at most,
To covet flying, and regret when lost:
At last, to follies Youth could scarce defend,
It grows their Age's prudence to pretend;
Ashamed to own they gave delight before,
Reduced to feign it, when they give no more:
As Hags hold Sabbaths, less for joy than spite,
So these their merry, miserable Night;   240
Still round and round the Ghosts of Beauty glide,
And haunt the places where their Honour died.
   See how the World its Veterans rewards!
A Youth of Frolics, an old Age of Cards;
Fair to no purpose, artful to no end,
Young without Lovers, old without a Friend;
A Fop their Passion, but their Prize a Sot;
Alive, ridiculous, and dead, forgot!
   Ah! Friend! to dazzle let the Vain design;
To raise the Thought, and touch the Heart be thine!   250
That Charm shall grow, while what fatigues the Ring,
Flaunts and goes down, an unregarded thing:
So when the Sun's broad beam has tired the sight,
All mild ascends the Moon's more sober light,
Serene in Virgin Modesty she shines,
And unobserved the glaring Orb declines.
   Oh! blest with Temper, whose unclouded ray
Can make to-morrow cheerful as to-day;
She, who can love a Sister's charms, or hear
Sighs for a daughter with unwounded ear;   260
She, who ne'er answers till a Husband cools,
Or, if she rules him, never shews she rules;

Charms by accepting, by submitting sways,
Yet has her humour most, when she obeys;
Let Fops or Fortune fly which way they will;
Disdains all loss of Tickets, or Codille:
Spleen, Vapours, or Small-pox, above them all,
And Mistress of herself, though China fall.
    And yet, believe me, good as well as ill,
Woman's at best a Contradiction still. 270
Heaven, when it strives to polish all it can
Its last best work, but forms a softer Man;
Picks from each sex, to make the Fav'rite blest,
Your love of Pleasure, or desire of Rest:
Blends, in exception to all general rules,
Your Taste of Follies, with our Scorn of Fools:
Reserve with Frankness, Art with Truth allied,
Courage with Softness, Modesty with Pride;
Fixed Principles, with Fancy ever new;
Shakes all together, and produces—You. 280
    Be this a Woman's Fame: with this unblest,
Toasts live a scorn, and Queens may die a jest.
This Phœbus promised (I forget the year)
When those blue eyes first opened on the sphere;
Ascendant Phœbus watched that hour with care,
Averted half your Parents' simple Prayer;
And gave you Beauty, but denied the Pelf
That buys your sex a Tyrant o'er itself.
The gen'rous God, who Wit and Gold refines,
And ripens Spirits as he ripens Mines,
Kept Dross for Duchesses, the world shall know it, 290
To you gave Sense, Good-humour, and a Poet.

HALLETT D. SMITH

On Pope's "Moral Essay, II"[1]

The subtitle "Of the Characters of Women" describes generally Pope's poem, but the first five-sixths of the epistle is a satirical portrait gallery in verse, and the last part is an enthusiastic favorable portrait—a compliment to the Lady of the title, Martha Blount. Pope contrasts her character, manner,

[1] From *The Critical Reader*, edited by Wallace Douglas, Roy Lamson, and Hallett Smith (New York, 1949), pp. 25-31. By permission of W. W. Norton & Company, Inc. Copyright, 1949, by W. W. Norton & Company, Inc.

and disposition to an array of eighteenth-century court women. No one in the group is named except the Duchess of Queensbury (line 193), but they are given distinguishing classical names, some of which suggest particular features or qualities.

The poem develops as a series of illustrations of the truth of Martha Blount's remark, "Most women have no characters at all." What this means is that women, unlike men, are not controlled by a ruling passion or principle; they are changeable, self-contradictory, inconsistent. Any definite description you apply to a woman is immediately contradicted by something else in her behavior or temperament. This complaint, by no means original with Pope or Martha Blount, of course, is made fresh and vivid by the metaphor of painting portraits. Most society ladies, says Pope, have to be portrayed in a series of roles—as a countess in court costume and as a shepherdess; as a good and loving wife and as the naked pagan Leda with her swan-lover; as the immoral Magdalen and the pure St. Cecilia. How then is the poet to capture them in a single verse portrait apiece? This is the all but impossible task Pope sets himself, and the answer he gives to the question of how to do it develops the painting metaphor and incidentally characterizes his own style and manner:

> Come then, the colours and the ground prepare!
> Dip in the rainbow, trick her off in air;
> Choose a firm cloud, before it fall, and in it
> Catch, ere she change, the Cynthia of this minute. (17-20)

The idea that the material itself is evanescent is of course a phrasing of the main theme, but the suggestion that the treatment is to be all delicate and airy is in part a deliberate deception of the reader: he is all the more shocked when he finds that very frequently the ladies are sketched not with cloud-stuff and rainbow tints, but with acid, sharply and firmly etched. But Pope's model in this poem and others like it is Horace, and the epistles of Horace are satires which are never heavy-footed and violent, but witty, urbane, and smooth. The conventional "epistle" or letter gives an air of informality, and the poet is not setting himself up as the formal indignant castigator of the vices and follies of mankind. The instrument of this kind of satirist is the rapier and not the whip.

But neither "rapier" nor "paintbrush" adequately conveys an idea of Pope's technique. It is first of all a kind of thinking, and the intellectual power of the poem should not be underestimated. Take Calypso, for example, she who

> once each heart alarm'd,
> Awed without virtue, without beauty charm'd; (45-46)

what is the mysterious source of her attractiveness? If she is neither good nor beautiful, what is it that she has? Pope pretends that it is a mystery, but he shows by his manner of describing it that he knows that we are sometimes drawn or attracted by those things that are just this side of the repulsive:

> Strange graces still, and stranger flights she had,
> Was just not ugly, and was just not mad;
> Yet ne'er so sure our passion to create,
> As when she touch'd the brink of all we hate. (49-52)

For all the emphasis on female vanity, on social foibles, on fashionable affectations, this epistle is fundamentally a Moral Essay; it probes deeply into the relationship between motives and deeds. Narcissa is not a "bad" woman; she wouldn't stew a child, in the fashion of witches making their broth, just to prepare a cosmetic "wash" for her face; she is even generous, if you recite some of her deeds—but what about the motives? She

> Has ev'n been prov'd to grant a lover's pray'r,
> And paid a tradesman once to make him stare;
> Gave alms at Easter, in a Christian trim,
> And made a widow happy, for a whim. (55-58)

As a matter of fact, she is another example of that combination of irreconcilable opposites which constitutes the female character:

> Now conscience chills her, and now passion burns;
> And atheism and religion take their turns;
> A very heathen in the carnal part,
> Yet still a sad, good Christian at her heart. (65-68)

Pope's moral insight is exhibited even more impressively in the rhetoric and logical syntax of passages which appear on the surface to be mere wit:

> See Sin in state, majestically drunk;
> Proud as a peeress, prouder as a punk; (69-70)

Here the paradox in the phrase "majestically drunk" not only expresses contempt for the degradation of majestic qualities in drunkenness; it also prepares the reader's mind for some such phrase as "drunk as a lord." And the phrase follows, satisfyingly: "Proud as a peeress," but by a verbal trick Pope converts what seems like a superlative into a mere positive, and the comparative "prouder as a punk" explodes in a marvelous anticlimax. The rhetorical progression in the description of Flavia, the epicurean, reveals the same degree of profundity:

> Wise wretch! with pleasures too refin'd to please;
> With too much spirit to be e'er at ease;
> With too much quickness ever to be taught;
> With too much thinking to have common thought;
> You purchase pain with all that joy can give,
> And die of nothing but a rage to live. (95-100)

The thrice-repeated "with too much . . ." and the metaphor of purchasing develop a sense of opulence and wealth to give a terrible significance to the word "nothing" in the last line.

To temper this moral seriousness and to keep the poem on the level of the

well-bred, cultivated letter from one friend to another, to suggest a tone of
gallant frankness rather than zealous misogyny, Pope returns, after one hundred and fifty lines, to a comment on his technique:

> Pictures like these, dear Madam, to design,
> Asks no firm hand, and no unerring line;
> Some wand'ring touches, some reflected light,
> Some flying stroke alone can hit 'em right: (151-154)

Any analysis of Pope's style might take this passage as its point of departure. Is
there really no firm hand or unerring line in these portraits? Are they really
just flying strokes?

The versification of this poem is of course connected with its wit. But the
iambic pentameter couplet which Pope so polished and developed, which he
made so capable of variety and so fluent in a poem of almost three hundred
lines, is not to be considered the source of the wit. It is the sharpening of something which already cuts. So many illustrations offer themselves to show Pope's
skill in the technique of versification that it is hard to make a choice. Is he most
remarkable for his variation of the normal iambic movement to make a sudden
special effect, as in the second line of

> A very heathen in the carnal part,
> Yet still a sad, good Christian at her heart. (67-68)

or is he to be praised for the compactness of his summarizing couplets, when he
conveys the matter of an epic in an epigram?

> From loveless youth to unrespected age,
> No passion gratified except her rage. (125-126)

One might point out the extraordinary precision in the choice of the specific
detail to contrast with a general emotion:

> She, while her lover pants upon her breast,
> Can mark the figures on an Indian chest;
> And when she sees her friend in deep despair,
> Observes how much a chintz exceeds mohair. (167-170)

This is in reality a perfect realization of balance, intellectually and imaginatively, and the same poise is evident in Pope's prosody. The quotability of his
general statements is often due to this balance:

> In men, we various ruling passions find;
> In women, two almost divide the kind;
> Those, only fix'd, they first or last obey,
> The love of pleasure, and the love of sway. (207-210)

Here the unbalance of the third line, in the placing of caesuras, prepares the
ear for the satisfaction of the perfect balance of the fourth, and even the paral-

lel structure of the first and second lines, with the early caesura, has its effect on the last line.

The end of the poem, progressing from the character of "Queensbury" through some general reflections on the female sex, leads up to the good advice and gallant compliment paid to Martha Blount. Yet in paying this compliment Pope does not retract his general contention about the contradictions in feminine character; he only makes it clear that one combination of disparate traits, the best from each sex, has resulted in the creation of an ideal woman and friend. As the poet makes his exit, he separates Martha Blount from the women of the world he has been describing. She has beauty but not wealth; hence she is unspoiled. And in the final lines, as he shows the compensations for lack of wealth, he produces the same retarding effect in the last line that we are accustomed to at the end of a piece of music:

> The gen'rous god, who wit and gold refines,
> And ripens spirits as he ripens mines,
> Kept dross for duchesses, the world shall know it,
> To you gave sense, good-humour, and a poet. (289-292)

Anyone who walks through an art gallery and looks at the portraits of eighteenth-century ladies by Lely, Kneller and Reynolds is not quite satisfied until he goes up to the pictures of the ladies, in their roles as the goddess Diana, the Tragic Muse, or St. Cecilia, to read on the little brass plates the names of the actual subjects of the pictures. So, in Pope's poem, it may be of some interest to know that Philomede is supposed to represent Henrietta, Duchess of Marlborough, in succession to her father, the first Duke; Atossa is traditionally supposed to be Sarah, Duchess of Marlborough, widow of the first Duke; Chloe is thought to be the Countess of Suffolk (Mrs. Howard), a neighbor of Pope's at Twickenham and formerly mistress to King George II. There is some point to "dross for *duchesses*" in the next-to-last line.

THOMAS GRAY

Elegy Written in a Country Churchyard

> The curfew tolls the knell of parting day,
>   The lowing herd wind slowly o'er the lea,
> The ploughman homeward plods his weary way,
>   And leaves the world to darkness and to me.
>
> Now fades the glimmering landscape on the sight,
>   And all the air a solemn stillness holds,

Save where the beetle wheels his droning flight,
  And drowsy tinklings lull the distant folds;

Save that from yonder ivy-mantled tower
  The moping owl does to the moon complain   10
Of such, as wandering near her secret bower,
  Molest her ancient solitary reign.

Beneath those rugged elms, that yew-tree's shade,
  Where heaves the turf in many a moldering heap,
Each in his narrow cell forever laid,
  The rude forefathers of the hamlet sleep.

The breezy call of incense-breathing morn,
  The swallow twittering from the straw-built shed,
The cock's shrill clarion, or the echoing horn,
  No more shall rouse them from their lowly bed.   20

For them no more the blazing hearth shall burn,
  Or busy housewife ply her evening care;
No children run to lisp their sire's return,
  Or climb his knees the envied kiss to share.

Oft did the harvest to their sickle yield;
  Their furrow oft the stubborn glebe has broke;
How jocund did they drive their team afield!
  How bowed the woods beneath their sturdy stroke!

Let not Ambition mock their useful toil,
  Their homely joys, and destiny obscure;   30
Nor Grandeur hear with a disdainful smile
  The short and simple annals of the poor.

The boast of heraldry, the pomp of power,
  And all that beauty, all that wealth e'er gave,
Awaits alike th' inevitable hour:
  The paths of glory lead but to the grave.

Nor you, ye proud, impute to these the fault,
  If Memory o'er their tomb no trophies raise,
Where through the long-drawn aisle and fretted vault
  The pealing anthem swells the note of praise.   40

Can storied urn or animated bust
  Back to its mansion call the fleeting breath?

Can Honor's voice provoke the silent dust,
    Or Flattery soothe the dull cold ear of Death?

Perhaps in this neglected spot is laid
    Some heart once pregnant with celestial fire;
Hands that the rod of empire might have swayed,
    Or waked to ecstasy the living lyre.

But Knowledge to their eyes her ample page,
    Rich with the spoils of time, did ne'er unroll;   50
Chill Penury repressed their noble rage,
    And froze the genial current of the soul.

Full many a gem of purest ray serene,
    The dark unfathomed caves of ocean bear;
Full many a flower is born to blush unseen,
    And waste its sweetness on the desert air.

Some village Hampden, that with dauntless breast
    The little tyrant of his fields withstood;
Some mute inglorious Milton here may rest,
    Some Cromwell, guiltless of his country's blood.   60

Th' applause of listening senates to command,
    The threats of pain and ruin to despise,
To scatter plenty o'er a smiling land,
    And read their history in a nation's eyes,

Their lot forbade; nor circumscribed alone
    Their growing virtues, but their crimes confined.
Forbade to wade through slaughter to a throne,
    And shut the gates of mercy on mankind;

The struggling pangs of conscious truth to hide,
    To quench the blushes of ingenuous shame,   70
Or heap the shrine of Luxury and Pride
    With incense kindled at the Muse's flame.

Far from the madding crowd's ignoble strife,
    Their sober wishes never learned to stray;
Along the cool sequestered vale of life
    They kept the noiseless tenor of their way.

Yet ev'n these bones from insult to protect,
    Some frail memorial still erected nigh,

With uncouth rhymes and shapeless sculpture decked,
   Implores the passing tribute of a sigh.   80

Their name, their years, spelt by th' unlettered Muse,
   The place of fame and elegy supply;
And many a holy text around she strews,
   That teach the rustic moralist to die.

For who, to dumb forgetfulness a prey,
   This pleasing anxious being e'er resigned,
Left the warm precincts of the cheerful day,
   Nor cast one longing lingering look behind?

On some fond breast the parting soul relies,
   Some pious drops the closing eye requires;   90
Ev'n from the tomb the voice of Nature cries,
   Ev'n in our ashes live their wonted fires.

For thee, who mindful of th' unhonored dead
   Dost in these lines their artless tale relate;
If chance, by lonely contemplation led,
   Some kindred spirit shall inquire thy fate,

Haply some hoary-headed swain may say,
   "Oft have we seen him at the peep of dawn
Brushing with hasty steps the dews away
   To meet the sun upon the upland lawn.   100

"There at the foot of yonder nodding beech
   That wreathes its old fantastic roots so high,
His listless length at noontide would he stretch,
   And pore upon the brook that babbles by.

"Hard by yon wood, now smiling as in scorn,
   Muttering his wayward fancies he would rove;
Now drooping, woeful-wan, like one forlorn,
   Or crazed with care, or crossed in hopeless love.

"One morn I missed him on the customed hill,
   Along the heath, and near his favorite tree;   110
Another came; nor yet beside the rill,
   Nor up the lawn, nor at the wood was he;

"The next, with dirges due, in sad array,
   Slow through the church-way path we saw him borne.

Approach and read (for thou canst read) the lay,
  Graved on the stone beneath yon agèd thorn."

THE EPITAPH

Here rests his head upon the lap of earth,
  A youth to Fortune and to Fame unknown;
Fair Science frowned not on his humble birth,
  And Melancholy marked him for her own.   120

Large was his bounty, and his soul sincere;
  Heaven did a recompense as largely send:
He gave to Misery all he had, a tear;
  He gained from Heaven ('twas all he wished) a friend.

No farther seek his merits to disclose,
  Or draw his frailties from their dread abode,
(There they alike in trembling hope repose)
  The bosom of his Father and his God.

WILLIAM BLAKE

The Lamb

Little Lamb, who made thee?
  Dost thou know who made thee?
Gave thee life, and bid thee feed,
By the stream and o'er the mead;
Gave thee clothing of delight,
Softest clothing, woolly, bright;
Gave thee such a tender voice,
Making all the vales rejoice?
  Little Lamb, who made thee?
  Dost thou know who made thee?

  Little Lamb, I'll tell thee,
  Little Lamb, I'll tell thee:
He is callèd by thy name,
For He calls Himself a Lamb,
He is meek, and He is mild;
He became a little child.
I a child, and thou a lamb,

We are callèd by His name.
Little Lamb, God bless thee!
Little Lamb, God bless thee!

The Tiger

Tiger! Tiger! burning bright
In the forests of the night,
What immortal hand or eye
Could frame thy fearful symmetry?

In what distant deeps or skies
Burnt the fire of thine eyes?
On what wings dare he aspire?
What the hand dare seize the fire?

And what shoulder, and what art,
Could twist the sinews of thy heart?   10
And when thy heart began to beat,
What dread hand? and what dread feet?

What the hammer? what the chain?
In what furnace was thy brain?
What the anvil? what dread grasp
Dare its deadly terrors clasp?

When the stars threw down their spears
And watered heaven with their tears,
Did he smile his work to see?
Did he who made the Lamb make thee?   20

Tiger! Tiger! burning bright
In the forests of the night,
What immortal hand or eye
Dare frame thy fearful symmetry?

London

I wander through each chartered street,
Near where the chartered Thames does flow,
And mark in every face I meet
Marks of weakness, marks of woe.

In every cry of every man,
In every infant's cry of fear,
In every voice, in every ban,
The mind-forged manacles I hear:

How the chimney-sweeper's cry
Every blackening church appalls,
And the hapless soldier's sigh
Runs in blood down palace walls.

But most, through midnight streets I hear
How the youthful harlot's curse
Blasts the new-born infant's tear,
And blights with plagues the marriage hearse.

M. L. ROSENTHAL AND A. J. M. SMITH

On Blake's "London" [1]

"London," at first, seems an expression of outright rejection. Blake sees not merely unrealized potentialities but deathly pain—"weakness" and "woe"—everywhere. Each face, each voice, reminds him of the frustrations, lies, and cruelty of the city's life in the early years of the Industrial Revolution. The pathetic little chimney-sweeps make religion and morality seem arrant hypocrisy; the suffering of soldiers belies the benevolence of governments and rulers; the cursing street-harlots force him to think of the perversion of marital happiness which their existence means. (The final lines compress references to illegitimate birth, syphilis, and the ugliness which seems to the speaker to have blighted love in all its aspects; the compression is achieved by a series of related outbursts of sound and image, culminating in the paradoxical "Marriage hearse" which brings the poem to its tragic close.)

Yet to feel so strongly on the subject of the "chartering"—the parceling out for hire and profit—of the city while the potentialities for joy and love are thwarted is to have a humane vision of the right relations between man and man, man and woman, and man and God. The corruption of society, the failure of Church and State, the perversion of love can arouse savage condemnation only in someone with a blazing concern for those right relations. Thus, "London," in the very vehemence of its description and its rejection of all that has blighted human life and affection, gives us a pure affirmation of their intrinsic

[1] From *Exploring Poetry* (New York: The Macmillan Company, 1955), pp. 694-695. Copyright, 1955, The Macmillan Company. Reprinted by permission.

beauty. Blake views evil and suffering in the light of his concept of *love* as the great creative force. His "London" exemplifies the way in which many poems of stature imply critical and affirmative attitudes at one and the same time. The importance of such "opposite implication" must be recognized if we are to understand the real functions of much of the paradoxical, ironic, ambiguous, and mystical language of poetry. Blake's method here is to give us images that paint the harsh truth as tragically and nakedly as possible, and yet are also unmistakable emblems of what is valued most (freedom, health, joy, enlightenment, the happiness of children, peace, and innocent sexual love).

To the Accuser Who Is the God of This World

Truly, My Satan, thou art but a Dunce,
And dost not know the Garment from the Man.
Every Harlot was a Virgin once,
Nor can'st thou ever change Kate into Nan.

Tho' thou art Worship'd by the Names Divine
Of Jesus & Jehovah, thou art still
The Son of Morn in weary Night's decline,
The lost Traveller's Dream under the Hill.

Stanzas from Milton

And did those feet in ancient time
Walk upon England's mountain green?
And was the holy Lamb of God
On England's pleasant pastures seen?

And did the Countenance Divine
Shine forth upon our clouded hills?
And was Jerusalem builded here
Among these dark Satanic mills?

Bring me my bow of burning gold!
Bring me my arrows of desire!
Bring me my spear! O clouds, unfold!
Bring me my chariot of fire!

I will not cease from mental fight,
Nor shall my sword sleep in my hand,
Till we have built Jerusalem
In England's green and pleasant land.

ROBERT BURNS

Ye Flowery Banks

Ye flowery banks o' bonie Doon,
     How can ye blume sae fair?
How can ye chant, ye little birds,
     And I sae fu' o' care?

Thou'll break my heart, thou bonie bird,
     That sings upon the bough;
Thou minds me o' the happy days
     When my fause luve was true!

Thou'll break my heart, thou bonie bird,
     That sings beside thy mate;
For sae I sat, and sae I sang,   10
     And wist na o' my fate!

Aft hae I roved by bonie Doon
     To see the woodbine twine,
And ilka bird sang o' its luve,
     And sae did I o' mine.

Wi' lightsome heart I pu'd a rose
     Frae aff its thorny tree;
And my fause luver staw my rose,
     But left the thorn wi' me.   20

Mary Morison

I

O Mary, at thy window be!
     It is the wished, the trysted hour.
Those smiles and glances let me see,
     That make the miser's treasure poor.
     How blythely wad I bide the stoure,
A weary slave frae sun to sun,
     Could I the rich reward secure—
The lovely Mary Morison!

II

Yestreen, when to the trembling string
   The dance gaed thro' the lighted ha',   10
To thee my fancy took its wing,
   I sat, but neither heard or saw:
   Tho' this was fair, and that was braw,
And yon the toast of a' the town,
   I sighed and said amang them a':—
"Ye are na Mary Morison!"

III

O Mary, canst thou wreck his peace
   Wha for thy sake wad gladly die?
Or canst thou break that heart of his
   Whase only faut is loving thee?   20
   If love for love thou wilt na gie,
At least be pity to me shown:
   A thought ungentle canna be
The thought o' Mary Morison.

WILLIAM WORDSWORTH

The Solitary Reaper

Behold her, single in the field,
Yon solitary Highland lass!
Reaping and singing by herself;
Stop here, or gently pass!
Alone she cuts and binds the grain,
And sings a melancholy strain;
O listen! for the vale profound
Is overflowing with the sound.

No nightingale did ever chaunt
More welcome notes to weary bands   10
Of travelers in some shady haunt,
Among Arabian sands:
A voice so thrilling ne'er was heard
In springtime from the cuckoo-bird,
Breaking the silence of the seas
Among the farthest Hebrides.

Will no one tell me what she sings?—
Perhaps the plaintive numbers flow
For old, unhappy, far-off things,
And battles long ago: 20
Or is it some more humble lay,
Familiar matter of today?
Some natural sorrow, loss, or pain,
That has been, and may be again?

Whate'er the theme, the maiden sang
As if her song could have no ending;
I saw her singing at her work,
And o'er the sickle bending;—
I listened, motionless and still;
And, as I mounted up the hill,   30
The music in my heart I bore,
Long after it was heard no more.

W. K. WIMSATT, JR.

On Wordsworth's "The Solitary Reaper" [1]

Character is one type of concrete universal; there are other types, as many perhaps as the central terms of criticism; but most can be learned I believe by examination of metaphor—the structure most characteristic of concentrated poetry. The language of poets, said Shelley, "is vitally metaphorical: that is, it marks the before unapprehended relations of things and perpetuates their apprehension." Wordsworth spoke of the abstracting and modifying powers of the imagination. Aristotle said that the greatest thing was the use of metaphor, because it meant an eye for resemblances. Even the simplest form of metaphor or simile ("My love is like a red, red rose") presents us with a special and creative, in fact a concrete, kind of abstraction different from that of science. For behind a metaphor lies a resemblance between two classes, and hence a more general third class. This class is unnamed and most likely remains unnamed and is apprehended only through the metaphor. It is a new conception for which there is no other expression. Keats discovering Homer is like a traveler in the realms of gold, like an astronomer who discovers a planet, like Cortez gazing at the Pacific. The title of the sonnet, "On First Looking into Chapman's Homer," seems to furnish not so much the subject of the poem as a fourth member of

[1] From *The Verbal Icon* (Lexington: The University of Kentucky Press, 1954). Reprinted by permission.

a central metaphor, the real subject of the poem being an abstraction, a certain kind of thrill in discovering, for which there is no name and no other description, only the four members of the metaphor pointing, as to the center of their pattern. The point of the poem seems to lie somewhere outside both vehicle and tenor.

To take a more complicated instance, Wordsworth's "Solitary Reaper" has the same basic metaphorical structure, the girl alone reaping and singing, and the two bird images, the nightingale in Arabian sands and the cuckoo among the Hebrides, the three figures serving the parallel or metaphorical function of bringing out the abstraction of loneliness, remoteness, mysterious charm in the singing. But there is also a kind of third-dimensional significance, in the fact that one bird is far out in the northern sea, the other far off in southern sands, a fact which is not part of the comparison between the birds and the girl. By an implication cutting across the plane of logic of the metaphor, the girl and the two birds suggest extension in space, universality and world communion— an effect supported by other details of the poem such as the overflowing of the vale profound, the mystery of the Erse song, the bearing of the song away in the witness' heart, the past and future themes which the girl may be singing. Thus a central abstraction is created, of communion, telepathy in solitude, the prophetic soul of the wide world dreaming on things to come—an abstraction which is the effect not wholly of the metaphor elaborated logically (in a metaphysical way) but of a working on two axes, by association rather than by logic, by a three-dimensional complexity of structure.

I Wandered Lonely as a Cloud

    I wandered lonely as a cloud
    That floats on high o'er vales and hills,
    When all at once I saw a crowd,
    A host, of golden daffodils;
    Beside the lake, beneath the trees,
    Fluttering and dancing in the breeze.

    Continuous as the stars that shine
    And twinkle on the milky way,
    They stretched in never-ending line
    Along the margin of a bay: 10
    Ten thousand saw I at a glance,
    Tossing their heads in sprightly dance.

    The waves beside them danced; but they
    Out-did the sparkling waves in glee:
    A poet could not but be gay

In such a jocund company:
I gazed—and gazed—but little thought
What wealth the show to me had brought:

For oft, when on my couch I lie
In vacant or in pensive mood,   20
They flash upon that inward eye
Which is the bliss of solitude;
And then my heart with pleasure fills,
And dances with the daffodils.

FREDERICK A. POTTLE

On Wordsworth's "I Wandered Lonely as a Cloud" [1]

What are we to make of Wordsworth's boast that he endeavored at all times
to look steadily at his subject? I shall try to answer the question by tracing the
steps he followed in writing one of his most famous poems, "I Wandered
Lonely as a Cloud," commonly (though with no authority from Wordsworth)
called "Daffodils." The starting point is the entry in Dorothy's journal for April
15, 1802. That entry is fairly long, but it is all good reading; and I have my
reasons for not eliminating any of it.

"It was a threatening, misty morning, but mild. We set off after dinner
from Eusemere. Mrs. Clarkson went a short way with us, but turned back. The
wind was furious, and we thought we must have returned. We first rested in
the large boat-house, then under a furze bush opposite Mr. Clarkson's. Saw the
plough going in the field. The wind seized our breath. The Lake was rough.
There was a boat by itself floating in the middle of the bay below Water
Millock. We rested again in the Water Millock Lane. The hawthorns are black
and green, the birches here and there greenish, but there is yet more of purple
to be seen on the twigs. We got over into a field to avoid some cows—people
working. A few primroses by the roadside—woodsorrel flower, the anemone,
scentless violets, strawberries, and that starry, yellow flower which Mrs. C. calls
pile wort. When we were in the woods beyond Gowbarrow Park we saw a few
daffodils close to the water-side. We fancied that the lake had floated the seeds
ashore, and that the little colony had so sprung up. But as we went along there
were more and yet more; and at last, under the boughs of the trees, we saw
that there was a long belt of them along the shore, about the breadth of a

[1] From *The Yale Review*, XL (Autumn, 1950), 29-35. Copyright, 1950, Yale
University Press. Reprinted by permission of the author and the Yale University
Press.

country turnpike road. I never saw daffodils so beautiful. They grew among the mossy stones about and about them; some rested their heads upon these stones as on a pillow for weariness; and the rest tossed and reeled and danced, and seemed as if they verily laughed with the wind, that blew upon them over the lake; they looked so gay, ever glancing, ever changing. This wind blew directly over the lake to them. There was here and there a little knot, and a few stragglers a few yards higher up; but they were so few as not to disturb the simplicity, unity, and life of that one busy highway. We rested again and again. The bays were stormy, and we heard the waves at different distances, and in the middle of the water, like the sea. Rain came on—we were wet when we reached Luff's, but we called in. Luckily all was cheerless and gloomy, so we faced the storm—we *must* have been wet if we had waited—put on dry clothes at Dobson's. I was very kindly treated by a young woman, the landlady looked sour, but it is her way. She gave us a goodish supper, excellent ham and potatoes. We paid 7/– when we came away. William was sitting by a bright fire when I came downstairs. He soon made his way to the library, piled up in a corner of the window. He brought out a volume of Enfield's *Speaker,* another miscellany, and an odd volume of Congreve's plays. We had a glass of warm rum and water. We enjoyed ourselves, and wished for Mary. It rained and blew, when we went to bed. N.B. Deer in Gowbarrow Park like skeletons."

I said this was the starting point, for it is as near the raw matter of the poem as we can get. The true raw matter was certain perceptions—visual, auditory, tactile—which Wordsworth and his sister had on that windy April morning; and those we have no way of recovering. In Dorothy's entry this raw matter has already been grasped and shaped by a powerful imagination, and it has been verbalized. The entry is not a poem, because it contains a good deal of true but inconsequential statement (the rum and water, the volume of Congreve), but much of it is prefabricated material for a poem. And the fact is (though this is doctrine little heard of among men) that Wordsworth made grateful use of prefabricated material whenever he could get it of the right sort. As Professor Lane Cooper showed us long ago, he went regularly to books of travel for material of the right sort, but his best source was his sister's journal.

The function of the Imagination, as Wordsworth and Coleridge insisted, is, at the first level, to make sense out of the undifferentiated manifold of sensation by organizing it into individual objects or things; at the second, and specifically poetic, level, to reshape this world of common perception in the direction of a unity that shall be even more satisfactory and meaningful. Dorothy has made extensive use of the secondary or poetic imagination. Notice the devices by which she has unified and made sense of the experience of the daffodils. First, and most important, she has endowed them with human qualities. They are a social group engaged in busy concerted activity. The notion of the social group, the crowd (she does not actually use the word) is reinforced by her further figure of stragglers. Secondly, besides being active, the crowd of daffodils is happy: they look gay, they toss and reel and dance (their very activity is sport) and seem verily to laugh. And thirdly, some of the crowd have danced so hard that they are tired: they rest their heads upon the stones as on pillows.

Wordsworth recollected the scene in tranquillity and wrote his poem a full two years afterwards. He fixes on Dorothy's fine central perception of "the simplicity, unity, and life of that one busy highway," and condenses it into the one word "crowd." He takes over, too, her impression that the daffodils were "dancing," that they were "gay," that they were even "laughing." Ever since 1807, when Wordsworth published this poem, daffodils have danced and laughed, but there is nothing inevitable about it. The Greek myth of Narcissus is not exactly hilarious; and even Herrick, when he looked at a daffodil, saw something far from jocund:

> When a daffodill I see
> Hanging down his head t'wards me,
> Guesse I may, what I must be:
> First, I shall decline my head;
> Secondly, I shall be dead;
> Lastly, safely buryed.

The literal, positivistic, "scientific" fact was that Wordsworth and his sister saw a large bed of wild daffodils beside a lake, agitated by a strong, cold spring wind. The rest is all the work of the imagination.

The mark of the poetic imagination is to simplify: to make the manifold of sensation more meaningful by reducing it to a number of objects which can actually be contemplated. Wordsworth continues Dorothy's process of simplification: he eliminates the bitterness of the wind, which is so prominent in her account; reduces the wind, in fact, to a breeze. It may appear here that he has simplified more than was necessary or wise. Shakespeare, in the most famous lines ever written about daffodils, kept the wind:

> Daffodils
> That come before the swallow dares, and take
> The winds of March with beauty.

Admittedly, it is a higher mode. Wordsworth, on some occasions, would have kept the wind, too; but to have kept it here would have made a more complex —if you will, a more tragic—poem than he felt like writing. He felt this poem as something very simple and very pure; when he came to publish it, he put it in a group called "Moods of My Own Mind." But he is impartial; as he throws out matter on the one hand because it is too serious, so he eliminates matter on the other because it is too playful. The prettiest thing in Dorothy's realization—her image of the daffodils pillowing their heads on the stones—drops out. He dispenses too with Dorothy's stragglers. He fastens on her central image of the dancing, laughing crowd, and lets everything else go.

But now the idea of the crowd calls for a modification, and a modification of a fundamental sort. The social glee of the crowd can be made more significant if it is set over against solitary joy; and so in the poem he makes himself solitary, which in literal fact he was not. He now has what for him is a promising situation. The solitariness of the poet and the sociability of the daffodils are set up as poles between which the poem discharges itself. I have said that the situation is for him a promising one. Everyone knows of Wordsworth's love of solitude, his conviction that the highest experiences came to him when he was alone. What we need constantly to remind ourselves of is that his theory assigned an only slightly lower value to the love of men in societies. (The subtitle of Book VIII of "The Prelude" is "Love of Nature Leading to Love of Mankind.") The trouble was that, though he had the best of intentions, he could never handle close-packed, present, human crowds in the mode of Imagination. If he were to grasp the life of a great city imaginatively, it had to be at night or early in the morning, while the streets were deserted; or at least in bad weather, when few people were abroad.

But in the figure of a bed of daffodils endowed with human characteristics, he can handle with feelings of approval and exhilaration the concept of a crowd, of ten thousand individuals packed close together. He begins and ends solitary: at the beginning, we may assume, filled with joy, but a joy somewhat solemn, somewhat cold and remote, as the symbol of the cloud indicates. He is surprised by the sensation of mere unmixed human gaiety and light-heartedness, yields to it, and finds it good; so good that ever after he can derive refreshment from the memory of the experience.

The progress towards explicit identification of the symbol is gradual. In the first stanza the flowers are "fluttering" (literal: the flowers are moved by the breeze); then "dancing" (the flowers are self-moved). By the end of the second stanza they are "tossing their heads in sprightly dance." (The flowers are self-moved and are having a wonderful time. "Dance" is the key-word: it occurs in either the last or the first line of each stanza.) Finally, but not till the third stanza is reached, we get the quite explicit series "glee," "gay," "jocund," "pleasure." Wordsworth is always (or almost always) explicit in this fashion: he tells you just how you are expected to take his figures. Of course it is the figures that do the work. No one can make us joyful by merely using the word "joy" or any of its synonyms. But there is impressive agreement among readers of all periods that by giving us a simple figure, reinforcing it by certain devices of varied iteration, and explicitly interpreting it, Wordsworth does evoke the emotion of joy.

We can now see what Wordsworth meant by looking steadily at his subject. So far as his subject is expressed in imagery drawn from nature (and that means in all his best poetry), there is implied a lifelong habit of close, detailed, and accurate observation of the objects composing the external universe. By "accurate" I mean something the same thing as "naturalistic," but not entirely so. Wordsworth scorned the merely analytic vision of the naturalist ("One that would peep and botanize Upon his mother's grave"), because in his opinion that kind of apprehension empties the object of life and meaning by detaching it from its ground. "His theme is nature *in solido*," as Whitehead pointed out, "that is to say, he dwells on that mysterious presence of surrounding things, which imposes itself on any separate element that we set up as an individual for its own sake. He always grasps the whole of nature as involved in the tonality of the particular instance." But, except for those portions of the scientist's vision which require (let us say) dissection and magnification, there is little in the scientist's vision that Wordsworth misses. A *merely* matter-of-fact, an *exclusively* positivistic view of nature fills him with anger, but his own apprehension includes the matter-of-fact view without denying any of it. Dr. Leavis has perhaps put this more intelligibly when he remarks, as the chief virtue of Wordsworth's poetry, a "firm hold upon the world of common perception," though I myself should like to modify it, "in the mode of perception which has been common in Western civilization since some time in the late eighteenth century." In a literal, physiological sense, Wordsworth did look steadily at the natural objects that appear in his poetry.

Ode on Intimations of Immortality from Recollections of Early Childhood

The Child is father of the man;
And I could wish my days to be
Bound each to each by natural piety.

1

There was a time when meadow, grove, and stream,
        The earth, and every common sight,
            To me did seem
            Appareled in celestial light,
The glory and the freshness of a dream.
It is not now as it hath been of yore;—
            Turn wheresoe'er I may,
                By night or day,
The things which I have seen I now can see no more.

2

            The Rainbow comes and goes,
            And lovely is the Rose;
            The Moon doth with delight
    Look round her when the heavens are bare;
            Waters on a starry night

10

Are beautiful and fair;
    The sunshine is a glorious birth;
    But yet I know, where'er I go,
That there hath passed away a glory from the earth.

3

Now, while the birds thus sing a joyous song,
    And while the young lambs bound   20
      As to the tabor's sound,
To me alone there came a thought of grief:
A timely utterance gave that thought relief,
    And I again am strong:
The cataracts blow their trumpets from the steep;
No more shall grief of mine the season wrong;
I hear the Echoes through the mountains throng,
The Winds come to me from the fields of sleep,
    And all the earth is gay;
      Land and sea   30
  Give themselves up to jollity,
    And with the heart of May
  Doth every Beast keep holiday;—
      Thou Child of Joy,
Shout round me, let me hear thy shouts, thou happy Shepherd-boy!

4

Ye blessèd Creatures, I have heard the call
    Ye to each other make; I see
The heavens laugh with you in your jubilee;
    My heart is at your festival,
    My head hath its coronal,   40
The fulness of your bliss, I feel—I feel it all.
    Oh, evil day! if I were sullen
    While Earth herself is adorning,
      This sweet May-morning,
    And the Children are culling
      On every side,
In a thousand valleys far and wide,
Fresh flowers; while the sun shines warm,
And the Babe leaps up on his Mother's arm—
    I hear, I hear, with joy I hear!   50
    —But there's a Tree, of many, one,
A single Field which I have looked upon,
Both of them speak of something that is gone:
    The Pansy at my feet

Doth the same tale repeat:
Whither is fled the visionary gleam?
Where is it now, the glory and the dream?

5

Our birth is but a sleep and a forgetting:
The Soul that rises with us, our life's Star,
  Hath had elsewhere its setting,
   And cometh from afar: 60
  Not in entire forgetfulness,
  And not in utter nakedness,
But trailing clouds of glory do we come
  From God, who is our home:
Heaven lies about us in our infancy!
Shades of the prison-house begin to close
  Upon the growing Boy,
But he beholds the light, and whence it flows
  He sees it in his joy;
The Youth, who daily farther from the east   70
  Must travel, still is Nature's priest,
  And by the vision splendid
  Is on his way attended;
At length the Man perceives it die away,
And fade into the light of common day.

6

Earth fills her lap with pleasures of her own;
Yearnings she hath in her own natural kind,
And even with something of a Mother's mind,
  And no unworthy aim,
  The homely Nurse doth all she can   80
To make her Foster-child, her Inmate Man,
  Forget the glories he hath known,
And that imperial palace whence he came.

7

Behold the Child among his new-born blisses,
A six years' Darling of a pigmy size!
See, where 'mid work of his own hand he lies,
Fretted by sallies of his mother's kisses,
With light upon him from his father's eyes!
See, at his feet, some little plan or chart,
Some fragment from his dream of human life,   90
Shaped by himself with newly-learnèd art;

A wedding or a festival,
A mourning or a funeral,
  And this hath now his heart,
And unto this he frames his song:
  Then will he fit his tongue
To dialogues of business, love, or strife;
  But it will not be long
  Ere this be thrown aside,
  And with new joy and pride   100
The little Actor cons another part;
Filling from time to time his "humorous stage"
With all the Persons, down to palsied Age,
That Life brings with her in her equipage;
  As if his whole vocation
  Were endless imitation.

8

Thou, whose exterior semblance doth belie
  Thy Soul's immensity;
Thou best Philosopher, who yet dost keep   110
Thy heritage, thou Eye among the blind,
That, deaf and silent, read'st the eternal deep,
Haunted forever by the eternal mind—
  Mighty Prophet! Seer blest!
  On whom those truths do rest,
Which we are toiling all our lives to find,
In darkness lost, the darkness of the grave;
Thou, over whom thy Immortality
Broods like the Day, a Master o'er a Slave,
A Presence which is not to be put by;   120
Thou little Child, yet glorious in the might
Of heaven-born freedom on thy being's height,
Why with such earnest pains dost thou provoke
The years to bring the inevitable yoke,
Thus blindly with thy blessedness at strife?
Full soon thy Soul shall have her earthly freight,
And custom lie upon thee with a weight,
Heavy as frost, and deep almost as life!

9

O joy! that in our embers
Is something that doth live,   130
That Nature yet remembers
What was so fugitive!

The thought of our past years in me doth breed
Perpetual benediction: not indeed
For that which is most worthy to be blest,
Delight and liberty, the simple creed
Of Childhood, whether busy or at rest,
With new-fledged hope still fluttering in his breast:—
    —Not for these I raise
      The song of thanks and praise;   140
   But for those obstinate questionings
    Of sense and outward things,
    Fallings from us, vanishings;
    Blank misgivings of a creature
Moving about in worlds not realized,
High instincts, before which our mortal nature
Did tremble like a guilty thing surprised:
    But for those first affections,
    Those shadowy recollections,
      Which, be they what they may,   150
Are yet the fountain-light of all our day,
Are yet a master-light of all our seeing;
   Uphold us, cherish, and have power to make
Our noisy years seem moments in the being
Of the eternal Silence: truths that wake,
      To perish never;
Which neither listlessness, nor mad endeavor,
      Nor man nor boy,
Nor all that is at enmity with joy,
Can utterly abolish or destroy!   160
   Hence, in a season of calm weather
     Though inland far we be,
Our souls have sight of that immortal sea
    Which brought us hither;
   Can in a moment travel thither—
And see the children sport upon the shore,
And hear the mighty waters rolling evermore.

       10

Then, sing ye birds, sing, sing a joyous song!
    And let the young lambs bound
    As to the tabor's sound!
  We, in thought, will join your throng,   170
    Ye that pipe and ye that play,
    Ye that through your hearts to-day
    Feel the gladness of the May!

What though the radiance which was once so bright
Be now for ever taken from my sight,
  Though nothing can bring back the hour
Of splendor in the grass, of glory in the flower;
   We will grieve not, rather find
   Strength in what remains behind;   180
   In the primal sympathy
   Which having been must ever be;
   In the soothing thoughts that spring
   Out of human suffering;
   In the faith that looks through death,
In years that bring the philosophic mind.

11

And O, ye Fountains, Meadows, Hills, and Groves,
Forbode not any severing of our loves!
Yet in my heart of hearts I feel your might;
I only have relinquished one delight   190
To live beneath your more habitual sway:
I love the brooks which down their channels fret
Even more than when I tripped lightly as they;
The innocent brightness of a new-born day
   Is lovely yet;

The clouds that gather round the setting sun
Do take a sober coloring from an eye
That hath kept watch o'er man's mortality;
Another race hath been, and other palms are won.
Thanks to the human heart by which we live, 200
Thanks to its tenderness, its joys, and fears,
To me the meanest flower that blows can give
Thoughts that do often lie too deep for tears.

The World Is Too Much with Us

The world is too much with us: late and soon,
Getting and spending, we lay waste our powers:
Little we see in Nature that is ours;
We have given our hearts away, a sordid boon!
This Sea that bares her bosom to the moon;
The winds that will be howling at all hours,
And are up-gathered now like sleeping flowers;
For this, for everything, we are out of tune;
It moves us not.—Great God! I'd rather be

A pagan suckled in a creed outworn;
So might I, standing on this pleasant lea,
Have glimpses that would make me less forlorn;
Have sight of Proteus rising from the sea;
Or hear old Triton blow his wreathèd horn.

SAMUEL T. COLERIDGE

Kubla Khan; or, A Vision in a Dream

A FRAGMENT

In Xanadu did Kubla Khan
A stately pleasure-dome decree:
Where Alph, the sacred river, ran
    Through caverns measureless to man
        Down to a sunless sea.
So twice five miles of fertile ground
With walls and towers were girdled round:
And here were gardens bright with sinuous rills,
Where blossomed many an incense-bearing tree;
And here were forests ancient as the hills,   10
Enfolding sunny spots of greenery.

But oh! that deep romantic chasm which slanted
Down the green hill athwart a cedarn cover!
A savage place! as holy and enchanted
As e'er beneath a waning moon was haunted
By woman wailing for her demon-lover!
And from this chasm, with ceaseless turmoil seething,
As if this earth in fast thick pants were breathing,
A mighty fountain momently was forced:
Amid whose swift half-intermitted burst   20
Huge fragments vaulted like rebounding hail,
Or chaffy grain beneath the thresher's flail:
And 'mid these dancing rocks at once and ever
It flung up momently the sacred river.
Five miles meandering with a mazy motion
Through wood and dale the sacred river ran,
Then reached the caverns measureless to man,
And sank in tumult to a lifeless ocean:
And 'mid this tumult Kubla heard from far
Ancestral voices prophesying war!   30

The shadow of the dome of pleasure
Floated midway on the waves;
Where was heard the mingled measure
From the fountain and the caves.
It was a miracle of rare device,
A sunny pleasure-dome with caves of ice!

A damsel with a dulcimer
In a vision once I saw:
It was an Abyssinian maid,
And on her dulcimer she played,   40
Singing of Mount Abora.
Could I revive within me,
Her symphony and song,
To such a deep delight 'twould win me,
That with music loud and long,
I would build that dome in air,
That sunny dome! those caves of ice!
And all who heard should see them there,
And all should cry, Beware! Beware!
His flashing eyes, his floating hair!   50
Weave a circle round him thrice,
And close your eyes with holy dread,
For he on honey-dew hath fed,
And drunk the milk of Paradise.

GEORGE GORDON, LORD BYRON

The Destruction of Sennacherib

The Assyrian came down like the wolf on the fold,
And his cohorts were gleaming in purple and gold;
And the sheen of their spears was like stars on the sea,
When the blue wave rolls nightly on deep Galilee.

Like the leaves of the forest when Summer is green,
That host with their banners at sunset were seen:
Like the leaves of the forest when Autumn hath blown,
That host on the morrow lay withered and strown.

For the Angel of Death spread his wings on the blast,
And breathed in the face of the foe as he passed;   10

And the eyes of the sleepers waxed deadly and chill,
And their hearts but once heaved, and for ever grew still!

And there lay the steed with his nostril all wide,
But through it there rolled not the breath of his pride;
And the foam of his gasping lay white on the turf,
And cold as the spray of the rock-beating surf.

And there lay the rider distorted and pale,
With the dew on his brow, and the rust on his mail:
And the tents were all silent, the banners alone,
The lances unlifted, the trumpet unblown.   20

And the widows of Ashur are loud in their wail,
And the idols are broke in the temple of Baal;
And the might of the Gentile, unsmote by the sword,
Hath melted like snow in the glance of the Lord!

Don Juan

CANTO THE SECOND

1

Oh ye! who teach the ingenuous youth of nations,
　　Holland, France, England, Germany, or Spain,
I pray ye flog them upon all occasions,
　　It mends their morals, never mind the pain:
The best of mothers and of educations
　　In Juan's case were but employ'd in vain,
Since, in a way that's rather of the oddest, he
Became divested of his native modesty.

2

Had he but been placed at a public school,
　　In the third form, or even in the fourth,
His daily task had kept his fancy cool,   10
　　At least, had he been nurtured in the north;
Spain may prove an exception to the rule,
　　But then exceptions always prove its worth—
A lad of sixteen causing a divorce
Puzzled his tutors very much, of course.

3

I can't say that it puzzles me at all,
    If all things be consider'd; first, there was
His lady-mother, mathematical,
    A——never mind;—his tutor, an old ass;   20
A pretty woman—(that's quite natural,
    Or else the thing had hardly come to pass)
A husband rather old, not much in unity
With his young wife—a time, and opportunity.

4

Well—well; the world must turn upon its axis,
    And all mankind turn with it, heads or tails,
And live and die, make love and pay our taxes,
    And as the veering wind shifts, shift our sails;
The king commands us, and the doctor quacks us,
    The priest instructs, and so our life exhales,   30
A little breath, love, wine, ambition, fame,
Fighting, devotion, dust,—perhaps a name.

5

I said, that Juan had been sent to Cadiz—
    A pretty town, I recollect it well—
'Tis there the mart of the colonial trade is,
    (Or was, before Peru learn'd to rebel,)
And such sweet girls—I mean, such graceful ladies,
    Their very walk would make your bosom swell;
I can't describe it, though so much it strike,
Nor liken it—I never saw the like: 40

6

An Arab horse, a stately stag, a barb
    New-broke, a cameleopard, a gazelle,
No—none of these will do—and then their garb,
    Their veil and petticoat—Alas! to dwell
Upon such things would very near absorb
    A canto—then their feet and ankles,—well,
Thank Heaven I've got no metaphor quite ready,
(And so, my sober Muse—come, let's be steady—

7

Chaste Muse!—well, if you must, you must)—the veil
    Thrown back a moment with the glancing hand,   50
While the o'erpowering eye, that turns you pale,

Flashes into the heart:—All sunny land
Of love! when I forget you, may I fail
   To——say my prayers—but never was there plann'd
A dress through which the eyes give such a volley,
Excepting the Venetian Fazzioli.

8

But to our tale: the Donna Inez sent
   Her son to Cadiz only to embark;
To stay there had not answer'd her intent,
   But why?—we leave the reader in the dark—   60
'Twas for a voyage the young man was meant,
   As if a Spanish ship were Noah's ark,
To wean him from the wickedness of earth,
And send him like a dove of promise forth.

9

Don Juan bade his valet pack his things
   According to direction, then received
A lecture and some money: for four springs
   He was to travel; and though Inez grieved
(As every kind of parting has its stings),
   She hoped he would improve—perhaps believed: 70
A letter, too, she gave (he never read it)
Of good advice—and two or three of credit.

10

In the mean time, to pass her hours away,
   Brave Inez now set up a Sunday school
For naughty children, who would rather play
   (Like truant rogues) the devil, or the fool;
Infants of three years old were taught that day,
   Dunces were whipt, or set upon a stool:
The great success of Juan's education
Spurr'd her to teach another generation.   80

11

Juan embark'd—the ship got under way,
   The wind was fair, the water passing rough;
A devil of a sea rolls in that bay,
   As I, who've cross'd it oft, know well enough;
And, standing upon deck, the dashing spray
   Flies in one's face, and makes it weather-tough:
And there he stood to take, and take again,
His first—perhaps his last—farewell of Spain.

12

I can't but say it is an awkward sight
    To see one's native land receding through   90
The growing waters; it unmans one quite,
    Especially when life is rather new:
I recollect Great Britain's coast looks white,
    But almost every other country's blue,
When gazing on them, mystified by distance,
We enter on our nautical existence.

13

So Juan stood, bewilder'd on the deck:
    The wind sung, cordage strain'd, and sailors swore,
And the ship creak'd, the town became a speck,
    From which away so fair and fast they bore.   100
The best of remedies is a beef-steak
    Against sea-sickness; try it, sir, before
You sneer, and I assure you this is true,
For I have found it answer—so may you.

14

Don Juan stood, and, gazing from the stern,
    Beheld his native Spain receding far:
First partings form a lesson hard to learn,
    Even nations feel this when they go to war;
There is a sort of unexprest concern,
    A kind of shock that sets one's heart ajar: 110
At leaving even the most unpleasant people
And places, one keeps looking at the steeple.

15

But Juan had got many things to leave,
    His mother, and a mistress, and no wife,
So that he had much better cause to grieve
    Than many persons more advanced in life;
And if we now and then a sigh must heave
    At quitting even those we quit in strife,
No doubt we weep for those the heart endears—
That is, till deeper griefs congeal our tears.   120

16

So Juan wept, as wept the captive Jews
    By Babel's waters, still remembering Sion:

I'd weep,—but mine is not a weeping Muse,
  And such light griefs are not a thing to die on;
Young men should travel, if but to amuse
  Themselves; and the next time their servants tie on
Behind their carriages their new portmanteau,
Perhaps it may be lined with this my canto.

17

And Juan wept, and much he sigh'd and thought,
  While his salt tears dropp'd into the salt sea,   130
"Sweets to the sweet"; (I like so much to quote;
  You must excuse this extract,—'t is where she,
The Queen of Denmark, for Ophelia brought
  Flowers to the grave;) and, sobbing often, he
Reflected on his present situation,
And seriously resolved on reformation.

18

"Farewell, my Spain! a long farewell!" he cried,
  "Perhaps I may revisit thee no more,
But die, as many an exiled heart hath died,
  Of its own thirst to see again thy shore: 140
Farewell, where Guadalquivir's waters glide!
  Farewell, my mother! and, since all is o'er,
Farewell, too, dearest Julia!—(here he drew
Her letter out again, and read it through.)

19

"And oh! if e'er I should forget, I swear—
  But that's impossible, and cannot be—
Sooner shall this blue ocean melt to air,
  Sooner shall earth resolve itself to sea,
Than I resign thine image, oh, my fair!
  Or think of anything, excepting thee;   150
A mind diseased no remedy can physic—
(Here the ship gave a lurch, and he grew sea-sick.)

20

"Sooner shall heaven kiss earth—(here he fell sicker)
  Oh, Julia! what is every other woe?—
(For God's sake let me have a glass of liquor;
  Pedro, Battista, help me down below.)
Julia, my love—(you rascal, Pedro, quicker)—
  Oh, Julia!—(this curst vessel pitches so)—

Beloved Julia, hear me still beseeching!"
(Here he grew inarticulate with retching.)   160

21

He felt that chilling heaviness of heart,
    Or rather stomach, which, alas! attends,
Beyond the best apothecary's art,
    The loss of love, the treachery of friends,
Or death of those we dote on, when a part
    Of us dies with them as each fond hope ends:
No doubt he would have been much more pathetic,
But the sea acted as a strong emetic.

22

Love's a capricious power: I've known it hold
    Out through a fever caused by its own heat,   170
But be much puzzled by a cough and cold,
    And find a quinsy very hard to treat;
Against all noble maladies he's bold,
    But vulgar illnesses don't like to meet,
Nor that a sneeze should interrupt his sigh,
Nor inflammations redden his blind eye.

23

But worst of all is nausea, or a pain
    About the lower region of the bowels;
Love, who heroically breathes a vein,
    Shrinks from the application of hot towels,   180
And purgatives are dangerous to his reign,
    Sea-sickness death: his love was perfect, how else
Could Juan's passion, while the billows roar,
Resist his stomach, ne'er at sea before?

PERCY BYSSHE SHELLEY

Ozymandias

I met a traveller from an antique land
Who said: "Two vast and trunkless legs of stone
Stand in the desert. Near them, on the sand,
Half sunk, a shattered visage lies, whose frown,
And wrinkled lip, and sneer of cold command,

Tell that its sculptor well those passions read
Which yet survive, stamped on these lifeless things,
The hand that mocked them, and the heart that fed:
And on the pedestal these words appear:
'My name is Ozymandias, king of kings:
Look on my works, ye Mighty, and despair!'
Nothing beside remains. Round the decay
Of that colossal wreck, boundless and bare
The lone and level sands stretch far away."

Ode to the West Wind

1

O wild West Wind, thou breath of Autumn's being,
Thou, from whose unseen presence the leaves dead
Are driven, like ghosts from an enchanter fleeing,

Yellow, and black, and pale, and hectic red,
Pestilence-stricken multitudes: O thou,
Who chariotest to their dark wintry bed

The wingèd seeds, where they lie cold and low,
Each like a corpse within its grave, until
Thine azure sister of the spring shall blow

Her clarion o'er the dreaming earth, and fill   10
(Driving sweet buds like flocks to feed in air)
With living hues and odors plain and hill:

Wild Spirit, which art moving everywhere;
Destroyer and preserver; hear, oh hear!

2

Thou on whose stream, 'mid the steep sky's commotion,
Loose clouds like earth's decaying leaves are shed,
Shook from the tangled boughs of Heaven and Ocean,

Angels of rain and lightning: there are spread
On the blue surface of thine airy surge,
Like the bright hair uplifted from the head   20

Of some fierce Maenad, even from the dim verge
Of the horizon to the zenith's height
The locks of the approaching storm. Thou dirge

Of the dying year, to which this closing night
Will be the dome of a vast sepulchre,
Vaulted with all thy congregated might

Of vapours, from whose solid atmosphere
Black rain, and fire, and hail will burst: O, hear!

3

Thou who didst waken from his summer dreams
The blue Mediterranean, where he lay,   30
Lulled by the coil of his crystalline streams,

Beside a pumice isle in Baiæ's bay,
And saw in sleep old palaces and towers
Quivering within the wave's intenser day,

All overgrown with azure moss and flowers
So sweet, the sense faints picturing them! Thou
For whose path the Atlantic's level powers

Cleave themselves into chasms, while far below
The sea-blooms and the oozy woods which wear
The sapless foliage of the ocean, know   40

Thy voice, and suddenly grow gray with fear,
And tremble and despoil themselves: O hear!

4

If I were a dead leaf thou mightest bear;
If I were a swift cloud to fly with thee;
A wave to pant beneath thy power, and share

The impulse of thy strength, only less free
Than thou, O, uncontrollable! If even
I were as in my boyhood, and could be

The comrade of thy wanderings over heaven,
As then, when to outstrip thy skiey speed   50
Scarce seemed a vision; I would ne'er have striven

As thus with thee in prayer in my sore need,
Oh! lift me as a wave, a leaf, a cloud!
I fall upon the thorns of life! I bleed!

A heavy weight of hours has chained and bowed
One too like thee: tameless, and swift, and proud.

5

Make me thy lyre, even as the forest is:
What if my leaves are falling like its own!
The tumult of thy mighty harmonies

Will take from both a deep, autumnal tone,   60
Sweet though in sadness. Be thou, Spirit fierce,
My spirit! Be thou me, impetuous one!

Drive my dead thoughts over the universe
Like withered leaves to quicken a new birth!
And, by the incantation of this verse,

Scatter, as from an unextinguished hearth
Ashes and sparks, my words among mankind!
Be through my lips to unawakened earth

The trumpet of a prophecy! O, Wind,
If Winter comes, can Spring be far behind?   70

To a Skylark

Hail to thee, blithe spirit!
    Bird thou never wert,
That from heaven, or near it,
    Pourest thy full heart
In profuse strains of unpremeditated art.

Higher still and higher
    From the earth thou springest
Like a cloud of fire;
    The blue deep thou wingest,
And singing still dost soar, and soaring ever singest.   10

In the golden lightning
    Of the sunken sun,
O'er which clouds are bright'ning,
    Thou does float and run;
Like an unbodied joy whose race is just begun.

The pale purple even
  Melts around thy flight;
Like a star of heaven
  In the broad daylight
Thou art unseen, but yet I hear thy shrill delight,   20

Keen as are the arrows
  Of that silver sphere,
Whose intense lamp narrows
  In the white dawn clear,
Until we hardly see, we feel that it is there.

All the earth and air
  With thy voice is loud,
As, when night is bare,
  From one lonely cloud
The moon rains out her beams, and heaven is overflowed.   30

What thou art we know not;
  What is most like thee?
From rainbow clouds there flow not
  Drops so bright to see
As from thy presence showers a rain of melody.

Like a poet hidden
  In the light of thought,
Singing hymns unbidden,
  Till the world is wrought
To sympathy with hopes and fears it heeded not: 40

Like a highborn maiden
  In a palace tower,
Soothing her love-laden
  Soul in secret hour
With music sweet as love, which overflows her bower:

Like a glowworm golden
  In a dell of dew,
Scattering unbeholden
  Its aërial hue
Among the flowers and grass which screen it from the view: 50

Like a rose embowered
  In its own green leaves,

By warm winds deflowered,
  Till the scent it gives
Makes faint with too much sweet these heavy-wingèd thieves.

  Sound of vernal showers
    On the twinkling grass,
  Rain-awakened flowers,
    All that ever was
Joyous and clear and fresh, thy music doth surpass.   60

  Teach us, sprite or bird,
    What sweet thoughts are thine;
  I have never heard
    Praise of love or wine
That panted forth a flood of rapture so divine.

  Chorus Hymeneal,
    Or triumphal chaunt,
  Matched with thine would be all
    But an empty vaunt,
A thing wherein we feel there is some hidden want.   70

  What objects are the fountains
    Of thy happy strain?
  What fields, or waves, or mountains?
    What shapes of sky or plain?
What love of thine own kind? what ignorance of pain?

  With thy clear keen joyance
    Languor cannot be:
  Shadow of annoyance
    Never came near thee:
Thou lovest, but ne'er knew love's sad satiety.   80

  Waking or asleep,
    Thou of death must deem
  Things more true and deep
    Than we mortals dream,
Or how could thy notes flow in such a crystal stream?

  We look before and after,
    And pine for what is not:
  Our sincerest laughter

With some pain is fraught;
Our sweetest songs are those that tell of saddest thought.   90

    Yet if we could scorn
      Hate and pride and fear;
    If we were things born
      Not to shed a tear,
I know not how thy joy we ever should come near.

    Better than all measures
      Of delightful sound,
    Better than all treasures
      That in books are found,
Thy skill to poet were, thou scorner of the ground!   100

    Teach me half the gladness
      That thy brain must know,
    Such harmonious madness
      From my lips would flow,
The world should listen then, as I am listening now.

JOHN KEATS

On First Looking into Chapman's Homer

Much have I travelled in the realms of gold,
    And many goodly states and kingdoms seen;
    Round many western islands have I been
Which bards in fealty to Apollo hold.
Oft of one wide expanse had I been told,
    That deep-browed Homer ruled as his demesne:
    Yet did I never breathe its pure serene
Till I heard Chapman speak out loud and bold:
Then felt I like some watcher of the skies
    When a new planet swims into his ken;
Or like stout Cortez when with eagle eyes
    He stared at the Pacific—and all his men
Looked at each other with a wild surmise—
    Silent, upon a peak in Darien.

Bright Star, Would I Were Stedfast as Thou Art

Bright star, would I were stedfast as thou art—
Not in lone splendor hung aloft the night,
And watching, with eternal lids apart,
Like nature's patient sleepless Eremite,
The moving waters at their priest-like task
Of pure ablution round earth's human shores,
Or gazing on the new soft fallen mask
Of snow upon the mountains and the moors:
No—yet still stedfast, still unchangeable,
Pillowed upon my fair love's ripening breast
To feel for ever its soft fall and swell,
Awake for ever in a sweet unrest;
Still, still to hear her tender-taken breath,
And so live ever—or else swoon to death.

La Belle Dame sans Merci

Oh, what can ail thee, knight-at-arms,
    Alone and palely loitering?
The sedge has withered from the lake,
    And no birds sing.

Oh, what can ail thee, knight-at-arms,
    So haggard and so woe-begone?
The squirrel's granary is full,
    And the harvest's done.

I see a lily on thy brow,
    With anguish moist and fever dew;
And on thy cheeks a fading rose
    Fast withereth too.

"I met a lady in the meads,
    Full beautiful—a faery's child;
Her hair was long, her foot was light,
    And her eyes were wild.

"I made a garland for her head,
    And bracelets too, and fragrant zone;

10

She looked at me as she did love,
    And made sweet moan.   20

"I set her on my pacing steed,
    And nothing else saw all day long;
For sideways would she lean, and sing
    A faery's song.

"She found me roots of relish sweet,
    And honey wild, and manna-dew,
And sure in language strange she said,
    'I love thee true.'

"She took me to her elfin grot,
    And there she wept, and sighed full sore,   30
And there I shut her wild, wild eyes,
    With kisses four.

"And there she lullèd me asleep,
    And there I dreamed—ah! woe betide!—
The latest dream I ever dreamed
    On the cold hill side.

"I saw pale kings and princes too,
    Pale warriors, death-pale were they all,
They cried—'La Belle Dame sans Merci
    Hath thee in thrall!'   40

"I saw their starved lips in the gloam,
    With horrid warning gapèd wide;
And I awoke, and found me here
    On the cold hill's side.

"And this is why I sojourn here
    Alone and palely loitering,
Though the sedge is withered from the lake,
    And no birds sing."

Ode to a Nightingale

My heart aches, and a drowsy numbness pains
    My sense, as though of hemlock I had drunk,
Or emptied some dull opiate to the drains
    One minute past, and Lethe-wards had sunk:

'Tis not through envy of thy happy lot,
But being too happy in thine happiness—
That thou, light-wingèd Dryad of the trees,
In some melodious plot
Of beechen green, and shadows numberless,
Singest of summer in full-throated ease.   10

O, for a draught of vintage! that hath been
Cooled a long age in the deep-delvèd earth,
Tasting of Flora and the country green,
Dance, and Provençal song, and sunburnt mirth!
O for a beaker full of the warm South,
Full of the true, the blushful Hippocrene,
With beaded bubbles winking at the brim,
And purple-stainèd mouth;
That I might drink, and leave the world unseen,
And with thee fade away into the forest dim: 20

Fade far away, dissolve, and quite forget
What thou among the leaves hast never known,
The weariness, the fever, and the fret
Here, where men sit and hear each other groan;
Where palsy shakes a few, sad, last gray hairs,
Where youth grows pale, and specter-thin, and dies;
Where but to think is to be full of sorrow
And leaden-eyed despairs,
Where Beauty cannot keep her lustrous eyes,
Or new Love pine at them beyond tomorrow.   30

Away! away! for I will fly to thee,
Not charioted by Bacchus and his pards,
But on the viewless wings of Poesy,
Though the dull brain perplexes and retards:
Already with thee! tender is the night,
And haply the Queen-Moon is on her throne,
Clustered around by all her starry Fays;
But here there is no light,
Save what from heaven is with the breezes blown
Through verdurous glooms and winding mossy ways.   40

I cannot see what flowers are at my feet,
Nor what soft incense hangs upon the boughs,
But, in embalmèd darkness, guess each sweet
Wherewith the seasonable month endows
The grass, the thicket, and the fruit-tree wild;

White hawthorn, and the pastoral eglantine;
  Fast fading violets covered up in leaves;
      And mid-May's eldest child.
The coming musk-rose, full of dewy wine,
  The murmurous haunt of flies on summer eves.   50

Darkling I listen; and, for many a time,
  I have been half in love with easeful Death,
Called him soft names in many a musèd rime,
  To take into the air my quiet breath;
Now more than ever seems it rich to die,
  To cease upon the midnight with no pain,
    While thou art pouring forth thy soul abroad
      In such an ecstasy!
Still wouldst thou sing, and I have ears in vain—
  To thy high requiem become a sod.   60

Thou wast not born for death, immortal Bird!
  No hungry generations tread thee down;
The voice I hear this passing night was heard
  In ancient days by emperor and clown:
Perhaps the self-same song that found a path
  Through the sad heart of Ruth, when, sick for home,
    She stood in tears amid the alien corn;
      The same that oft-times hath
Charmed magic casements, opening on the foam
  Of perilous seas, in faery lands forlorn.   70

Forlorn! the very word is like a bell
  To toll me back from thee to my sole self,
Adieu! the fancy cannot cheat so well
  As she is famed to do, deceiving elf.
Adieu! adieu! thy plaintive anthem fades
  Past the near meadows, over the still stream,
    Up the hillside; and now 'tis buried deep
      In the next valley glades:
Was it a vision, or a waking dream?
  Fled is that music—Do I wake or sleep?   80

Ode on a Grecian Urn

1

Thou still unravished bride of quietness,
  Thou foster-child of silence and slow time,

Sylvan historian, who canst thus express
　A flowery tale more sweetly than our rhyme:
What leaf-fringed legend haunts about thy shape
　Of deities or mortals, or of both,
　　In Tempe or the dales of Arcady?
What men or gods are these? What maidens loth?
　What mad pursuit? What struggle to escape?
　　What pipes and timbrels? What wild ecstasy?   10

2

Heard melodies are sweet, but those unheard
　Are sweeter; therefore, ye soft pipes, play on;
Not to the sensual ear, but, more endeared,
　Pipe to the spirit ditties of no tone:
Fair youth, beneath the trees, thou canst not leave
　Thy song, nor ever can those trees be bare;
　　Bold Lover, never, never canst thou kiss,
Though winning near the goal—yet, do not grieve;
　She cannot fade, though thou hast not thy bliss,
　　Forever wilt thou love, and she be fair!   20

3

Ah, happy, happy boughs! that cannot shed
　Your leaves, nor ever bid the Spring adieu;
And, happy melodist, unwearied,
　Forever piping songs forever new;
More happy love! more happy, happy love!
　Forever warm and still to be enjoyed,
　　Forever panting, and forever young;
All breathing human passion far above,
　That leaves a heart high-sorrowful and cloyed,
　　A burning forehead, and a parching tongue.   30

4

Who are these coming to the sacrifice?
　To what green altar, O mysterious priest,
Lead'st thou that heifer lowing at the skies,
　And all her silken flanks with garlands dressed?
What little town by river or sea shore,
　Or mountain-built with peaceful citadel,
　　Is emptied of this folk, this pious morn?
And, little town, thy streets for ever more
　Will silent be; and not a soul to tell
　　Why thou are desolate, can e'er return.   40

5

O Attic shape! Fair attitude! with brede
    Of marble men and maidens overwrought,
With forest branches and the trodden weed;
    Thou, silent form, dost tease us out of thought
As doth eternity: Cold Pastoral!
    When old age shall this generation waste,
        Thou shalt remain, in midst of other woe
Than ours, a friend to man, to whom thou say'st,
    "Beauty is truth, truth beauty,"—that is all
        Ye know on earth, and all ye need to know.   50

To Autumn

Season of mists and mellow fruitfulness,
    Close bosom-friend of the maturing sun;
Conspiring with him how to load and bless
    With fruit the vines that round the thatch-eaves run;
To bend with apples the mossed cottage-trees,
    And fill all fruit with ripeness to the core;
        To swell the gourd, and plump the hazel shells
    With a sweet kernel; to set budding more,
And still more, later flowers for the bees,
Until they think warm days will never cease,   10
        For Summer has o'er-brimmed their clammy cells.

Who hath not seen thee oft amid thy store?
    Sometimes whoever seeks abroad may find
Thee sitting careless on a granary floor,
    Thy hair soft-lifted by the winnowing wind;
Or on a half-reaped furrow sound asleep,
    Drowsed with the fume of poppies, while thy hook
        Spares the next swath and all its twinèd flowers:
And sometimes like a gleaner thou dost keep
    Steady thy laden head across a brook;   20
    Or by a cider-press, with patient look,
        Thou watchest the last oozings hours by hours.

Where are the songs of Spring? Ay, where are they?
    Think not of them, thou hast thy music too,—
While barrèd clouds bloom the soft-dying day,
    And touch the stubble-plains with rosy hue;

> Then in a wailful choir the small gnats mourn
> Among the river sallows, borne aloft
> Or sinking as the light wind lives or dies;
> And full-grown lambs loud bleat from hilly bourn;   30
> Hedge-crickets sing; and now with treble soft
> The red-breast whistles from a garden-croft;
> And gathering swallows twitter in the skies.

LEONARD UNGER AND

WILLIAM VAN O'CONNOR

On Keats' "To Autumn" [1]

The poem opens with an apostrophe to the season and with a description of natural objects at their richest and ripest stage. The details about the fruit, the flowers, and the bees constitute a lush and colorful picture of autumn and the effects of the "maturing sun." In the final lines of the first stanza, however, slight implications about the passage of time begin to operate. The flowers are called "later," the bees are assumed to think that "warm days will never cease," and there is a reference to the summer which has already passed.

In the second stanza an imaginative element enters the description, and we get a personification of the season in several appropriate postures and settings. As this stanza proceeds, the implications of the descriptive details become increasingly strong. For example, autumn is now seen, not as setting the flowers to budding, but as already bringing some of them to an end, although it "spares the next swath." Autumn has become a "gleaner." The whole stanza presents the paradoxical qualities of autumn, its aspects both of lingering and passing. This is especially true of the final image of the stanza. Autumn is the season of dying as well as of fulfilling. Hence it is with *"patient* look" that she (or he?) watches "the last oozings hours by hours." Oozing, or a steady dripping, is, of course, not unfamiliar as a symbol of the passage of time.

It is in the last stanza that the theme emerges most conspicuously. The opening question implies that the season of youth and rebirth, with its beauties of sight and sound, has passed, and that the season of autumn is passing. But autumn, too, *while* it lasts—"While barred clouds bloom the soft-dying day"—has its beauties, its music, as Keats's poem demonstrates. The imagery of the last stanza contrasts significantly with that of the first, and the final development of the poem adds meaning to its earlier portions. The slight implications are confirmed. We may recall that *maturing* means aging and end-

[1] From *Poems for Study* (New York, 1953), pp. 455-456. Copyright 1953 by Leonard Unger and William Van O'Connor. Reprinted by permission of Holt, Rinehart and Winston, Inc.

ing as well as ripening. The earlier imagery is, of course, that of ripeness. But the final imagery is more truly autumnal. The first words used to describe the music of autumn are "wailful" and "mourn." The opening stanza suggests the height of day, when the sun is strong and the bees are gathering honey from the open flowers. But in the last stanza, after the passing of "hours and hours," we have "the soft-dying day," the imagery of sunset and deepening twilight, when the clouds impart their glow to the day and the plains. The transitive, somewhat rare use of the verb "bloom," with its springlike associations, is perhaps surprising, and certainly appropriate and effective in suggesting the tensions of the theme, in picturing a beauty that is lingering, but *only* lingering. The conjunction of "rosy hue" and "stubble-plains" has the same significant incongruity, although the image is wholly convincing and actual in its reference. While the poem is more descriptive and suggestive than dramatic, its latent theme of transitoriness and mortality is symbolically dramatized by the passing course of the day. All these characteristics of the poem are to be found in its final image: "And gathering swallows twitter in the skies." Here we have the music of autumn. And our attention is directed toward the darkening skies. Birds habitually gather in flocks toward nightfall, particularly when they are preparing to fly south at the approach of winter. But they are still gathering. The day, the season, are "soft-dying" and are both the reality and the symbol of life as most intensely and poignantly beautiful when viewed from this melancholy perspective.

The poem has an obvious structure insofar as it is a coherent description. Its structure, however, is not simple in the sense of being merely continuous. For example, the course of the day parallels the development of the poem. And an awareness of the theme gives even greater significance to the structure, for the theme emerges with increasing clarity and fullness throughout the poem until the very last line. Because the theme is always in the process of emerging without ever shaking off the medium in which it is developed, the several parts of the poem have a relationship to each other beyond their progression in a single direction. The gathering swallows return some borrowed meaning to the soft-dying day with substantial interest, and the whole last stanza negotiates with the first in a similar relationship.

HEINRICH HEINE

Du schönes Fischermädchen

Du schönes Fischermädchen,
Treibe den Kahn ans Land;
Komm zu mir und setze dich nieder,
Wir kosen Hand in Hand.

Leg an mein Herz dein Köpfchen,
Und fürchte dich nicht zu sehr,
Vertraust du dich doch sorglos
Täglich dem wilden Meer.

Mein Herz gleicht ganz dem Meere,
Hat Sturm und Ebb und Flut,
Und manche schöne Perle
In seiner Tiefe ruht.

Oh Lovely Fishermaiden[1]

A Translation by Louis Untermeyer

Oh lovely fishermaiden,
   Come, bring your boat to land;
And we will sit together
   And whisper, hand in hand.

O rest upon my bosom,
   And fear no harm from me.
You give your body daily,
   Unfearing to the sea.

My heart is like the ocean
   With storm and ebb and flow—
And many a pearly treasure
   Burns in the depths below.

Zu fragmentarisch ist Welt und Leben

Zu fragmentarisch ist Welt und Leben!
Ich will mich zum deutschen Professor begeben.
Der weiss das Leben zusammenzusetzen,
Und er macht ein verständlich System daraus;
Mit seinen Nachtmützen und Schlafrockfetzen
Stopft er die Lücken des Weltenbaus.

The World and This Life Are So Scattered [1]

A Translation by Charles G. Leland

> This world and this life are so scattered, they try me,
>   And so to a German professor I'll hie me.
> He can well put all the fragments together
>   Into a system convenient and terse;
> While with his night-cap and dressing-robe tatters
>   He'll stop up the chink of the wide Universe.

RALPH WALDO EMERSON

Days

> Daughters of Time, the hypocritic Days,
> Muffled and dumb like barefoot dervishes,
> And marching single in an endless file,
> Bring diadems and fagots in their hands.
> To each they offer gifts after his will,
> Bread, kingdoms, stars, and sky that holds them all.
> I, in my pleachèd garden, watched the pomp,
> Forgot my morning wishes, hastily
> Took a few herbs and apples, and the Day
> Turned and departed silent. I, too late,
> Under her solemn fillet saw the scorn.

Hamatreya

> Bulkeley, Hunt, Willard, Hosmer, Meriam, Flint
> Possessed the land which rendered to their toil
> Hay, corn, roots, hemp, flax, apples, wool and wood.
> Each of these landlords walked amidst his farm,
> Saying, " 'Tis mine, my children's and my name's.
> How sweet the west wind sounds in my own trees!
> How graceful climb those shadows on my hill!
> I fancy these pure waters and the flags

[1] In the original version of this translation Leland retained the German title.

Know me, as does my dog: we sympathize;
And, I affirm, my actions smack of the soil."   10

Where are these men? Asleep beneath their grounds:
And strangers, fond as they, their furrows plough.
Earth laughs in flowers, to see her boastful boys
Earth-proud, proud of the earth which is not theirs;
Who steer the plough, but cannot steer their feet
Clear of the grave.
They added ridge to valley, brook to pond,
And sighed for all that bounded their domain;
"This suits me for a pasture; that's my park;
We must have clay, lime, gravel, granite-ledge,   20
And misty lowland, where to go for peat.
The land is well,—lies fairly to the south.
'Tis good, when you have crossed the sea and back,
To find the sitfast acres where you left them."
Ah! the hot owner sees not Death, who adds
Him to his land, a lump of mould the more.
Hear what the Earth says:—

EARTH-SONG

"Mine and yours;
Mine, not yours.
Earth endures;
Stars abide—   30
Shine down in the old sea;
Old are the shores;
But where are old men?
I who have seen much,
Such have I never seen.

"The lawyer's deed
Ran sure,
In tail,
To them, and to their heirs
Who shall succeed,   40
Without fail,
Forevermore.

"Here is the land,
Shaggy with wood.
With its old valley,
Mound and flood.

But the heritors?—
Fled like the flood's foam.
The lawyer, and the laws,
And the kingdom,
Clean swept herefrom.

"They called me theirs,
Who so controlled me;
Yet every one
Wished to stay, and is gone,
How am I theirs,
If they cannot hold me,
But I hold them?"

When I heard the Earth-song
I was no longer brave,
My avarice cooled
Like lust in the chill of the grave.

Brahma

If the red slayer thinks he slays,
    Or if the slain think he is slain,
They know not well the subtle ways
    I keep, and pass, and turn again.

Far or forgot to me is near;
    Shadow and sunlight are the same;
The vanished gods to me appear;
    And one to me are shame and fame.

They reckon ill who leave me out;
    When me they fly, I am the wings;
I am the doubter and the doubt,
    And I the hymn the Brahmin sings.

The strong gods pine for my abode,
    And pine in vain the sacred Seven;
But thou, meek lover of the good!
    Find me, and turn thy back on heaven.

ELIZABETH BARRETT BROWNING

Sonnet from the Portuguese, XLIII

How do I love thee? Let me count the ways.
I love thee to the depth and breadth and height
My soul can reach, when feeling out of sight
For the ends of Being and ideal Grace.
I love thee to the level of every day's
Most quiet need, by sun and candlelight.
I love thee freely, as men strive for Right;
I love thee purely, as they turn from Praise.
I love thee with the passion put to use
In my old griefs, and with my childhood's faith.
I love thee with a love I seemed to lose
With my lost saints,—I love thee with the breath,
Smiles, tears, of all my life!—and, if God choose,
I shall but love thee better after death.

ROBERT B. HEILMAN

On E. B. Browning's
"Sonnet from the Portuguese, XLIII" [1]

"How do I love thee?" is a theme on which both Elizabeth Barrett Browning and Goneril, daughter of Lear, expressed themselves in pentameters—with certain recognizable similarities. Goneril says (*King Lear*, I, i, 56-62):

Dearer than eye-sight, space, and liberty;
Beyond what can be valued, rich or rare;
No less than life, with grace, health, beauty, honour . . . .

E.B.B. says (*Sonnets from the Portuguese*, XLIII):

I love thee to the depth and breadth and height
My soul can reach, when feeling out of sight
For the ends of Being and ideal Grace . . . .
I love thee freely, as men strive for Right;
I love thee purely, as they turn from Praise.

[1] From *The Explicator*, IV (October, 1945), 3. Reprinted by permission of the author and of the Editors of *The Explicator*.

There is a notable insistence on spaciousness in each protestation; Goneril disdains even the rich and rare, and E.B.B. conspicuously selects intangibles to express degree; both find a measure in Grace; and presumably striving for Right and turning from Praise are the equivalent of honor. Health and beauty are perhaps a bit more pretentious than "the level of every day's/Most quiet need." But Goneril loves "As much as child e'er loved," and E.B.B., "with my childhood's faith." Goneril's love "makes breath poor and speech unable"; E.B.B. loves "with the breath,/Smiles, tears of all my life!" and anticipates loving "better after death." Goneril likewise hyperbolizes; she loves "more than words can wield the matter" and "beyond all matter of so much. . . ."

Goneril wished to give the unperceptive Lear an impression of sincerity; E.B.B., no doubt, looked in her heart and wrote. Yet, except for a detail or two added by E.B.B., both said much the same thing. What comes out of this is a lesson in verse-technique: the piling up of abstractions and generalizations not only does not carry conviction but gives a positive effect of insincerity. E.B.B.'s sonnet is as embarrassing as all platform rhetoric; she can find no images to realize, to prove, her experience. Ironically, she relies upon personal sincerity to give body to her words, whereas Goneril relies upon comparable words to suggest a body of sincerity. Shakespeare succeeded in his intention, for Goneril took in only Lear; in days of sharp awareness of poetic techniques, E.B.B. should not be taking in anybody. Shakespeare's method in Goneril's speech underlines a basic tenet of modern poetic criticism.

With the gusty protestations quoted above, compare Cordelia's single image and understatement (with the real emphasis ironically concealed in *bond*—a word which Lear fails entirely to understand):

> I cannot heave
> My heart into my mouth: I love your majesty
> According to my bond . . . .

Shakespeare knew precisely what kind of language to use for each sister. E.B.B. could have learned from him.

HENRY   WADSWORTH   LONGFELLOW

Snow-Flakes

> Out of the bosom of the Air,
>   Out of the cloud-folds of her garments shaken,
> Over the woodlands brown and bare,
>   Over the harvest-fields forsaken,
>   Silent, and soft, and slow
>   Descends the snow.

Even as our cloudy fancies take
   Suddenly shape in some divine expression,
Even as the troubled heart doth make
   In the white countenance confession,
     The troubled sky reveals
     The grief it feels.

This is the poem of the air,
   Slowly in silent syllables recorded;
This is the secret of despair,
   Long in its cloudy bosom hoarded,
     Now whispered and revealed
     To wood and field.

The Tide Rises, the Tide Falls

The tide rises, the tide falls,
The twilight darkens, the curlew calls;
Along the sea-sands damp and brown
The traveller hastens toward the town,
   And the tide rises, the tide falls.

Darkness settles on roofs and walls,
But the sea, the sea in the darkness calls;
The little waves, with their soft, white hands,
Efface the footprints in the sands,
   And the tide rises, the tide falls.

The morning breaks; the steeds in their stalls
Stamp and neigh, as the hostler calls;
The day returns, but nevermore
Returns the traveller to the shore,
   And the tide rises, the tide falls.

EDGAR ALLAN POE

The City in the Sea

Lo! Death has reared himself a throne
In a strange city lying alone
Far down within the dim West,

Where the good and the bad and the worst and the best
Have gone to their eternal rest.
There shrines and palaces and towers
(Time-eaten towers that tremble not!)
Resemble nothing that is ours.
Around, by lifting winds forgot,
Resignedly beneath the sky   10
The melancholy waters lie.

No rays from the holy heaven come down
On the long night-time of that town;
But light from out the lurid sea
Streams up the turrets silently—
Gleams up the pinnacles far and free—
Up domes—up spires—up kingly halls—
Up fanes—up Babylon-like walls—
Up shadowy long-forgotten bowers
Of sculptured ivy and stone flowers—   20
Up many and many a marvelous shrine
Whose wreathèd friezes intertwine
The viol, the violet, and the vine.

Resignedly beneath the sky
The melancholy waters lie.
So blend the turrets and shadows there
That all seem pendulous in air,
While from a proud tower in the town
Death looks gigantically down.
There open fanes and gaping graves   30
Yawn level with the luminous waves;
But not the riches there that lie
In each idol's diamond eye—
Not the gaily-jeweled dead
Tempt the waters from their bed;
For no ripples curl, alas!
Along that wilderness of glass—
No swellings tell that winds may be
Upon some far-off happier sea—
No heavings hint that winds have been   40
On seas less hideously serene.

But lo, a stir is in the air!
The wave—there is a movement there!
As if the towers had thrust aside,
    In slightly sinking, the dull tide—

As if their tops had feebly given
A void within the filmy Heaven.
The waves have now a redder glow—
The hours are breathing faint and low—
And when, amid no earthly moans,   50
Down, down that town shall settle hence,
Hell, rising from a thousand thrones,
Shall do it reverence.

To Helen

Helen, thy beauty is to me
  Like those Nicèan barks of yore,
That gently, o'er a perfumed sea,
  The weary, way-worn wanderer bore
  To his own native shore.

On desperate seas long wont to roam,
  Thy hyacinth hair, thy classic face,
Thy Naiad airs have brought me home
  To the glory that was Greece
And the grandeur that was Rome.

Lo! in yon brilliant window-niche
  How statue-like I see thee stand,
  The agate lamp within thy hand!
Ah, Psyche, from the regions which
  Are Holy Land!

The Valley of Unrest

Once it smiled a silent dell
Where the people did not dwell;
They had gone unto the wars,
Trusting to the mild-eyed stars,
Nightly, from their azure towers,
To keep watch above the flowers,
In the midst of which all day
The red sun-light lazily lay.
Now each visitor shall confess
The sad valley's restlessness.   10
Nothing there is motionless—
Nothing save the airs that brood

Over the magic solitude.
Ah, by no wind are stirred those trees
That palpitate like the chill seas
Around the misty Hebrides!
Ah, by no wind those clouds are driven
That rustle through the unquiet Heaven
Uneasily, from morn till even,
Over the violets there that lie   20
In myriad types of the human eye—
Over the lilies there that wave
And weep above a nameless grave!
They wave:—from out their fragment tops
Eternal dews come down in drops.
They weep:—from off their delicate stems
Perennial tears descend in gems.

ROY P. BASLER

On Poe's "The Valley of Unrest"[1]

The imagery and music of the poem, as well as the definitive significance of the
word "unrest" in the title, suggest symbolism of a psychic state or condition.
The general emotional import of the poem has been recognized even by orthodox commentators who tend to identify the valley in supernatural terms as
the "place of departed spirits" (Campbell). Although the symbolism is not
as explicitly allegorical as in "The Haunted Palace," instructive comparison
may be made of the contrasting psychic states symbolized in each: sanity and
insanity on the conscious level in "The Haunted Palace," expression and repression on the unconscious level in "The Valley of Unrest."

In the first part ("*Once*"), the silent peaceful valley where the people did
not dwell because they had gone into the outer world to war against their
enemies, we have a symbol of the psychic state in which emotion, finding an
objective, conscious activity under the approval of the superego, is *expressed*.
The silent dell is the psyche's secret retreat, safe because unknown to the
"enemy" in the outer world, but open to discovery by an "enemy" who defeats
hate by turning it to love.

In the second part ("*Now*"), the troubled and restless valley, haunted by
revenants of its former inhabitants (*i.e.*, dream images), symbolized appro-

[1] From *The Explicator*, V (December, 1946), 25. Reprinted by permission of the
author and of the Editors of *The Explicator*. The above article also appears in
the author's book *Sex, Symbolism, and Psychology in Literature*, published by
Rutgers University Press, 1948.

priately as motion without apparent cause, we have a symbol of the unconscious when emotion, denied objective play by the disapproval of the superego, is *repressed*. In the symbol of fear (eternal watchfulness) resented in "the violets there that lie/ In myriad types of the human eye," and the symbol of sorrow in "the lilies there that wave/ And weep above a nameless grave," we have the dual reaction of the psyche to repression—eternal sorrow for the dead (repressed) emotion whose betrayal of the secret valley made a martyrdom necessary, and eternal fear that the valley may be discovered again. The grave is nameless, because as key symbol of the act of repression (to repress is simply to will the censored feeling out of existence so far as consciousness is concerned) it is not consciously recognized for what it is. Poe presents the mysterious valley and grave as seen by "each visitor" (*i.e.*, perceptions on the part of the conscious ego, which occasionally under emotional stress penetrate the realm of the id; note that in the 1831 version "each visitor" is merely "the unhappy," and that in "Ulalume" and other poems of the unconscious Poe presents similar transient, halfway glimpses of the meaning of dreamland under emotional stress). The valley is perceived, but not understood, by the stranger to the realm.

The final version of the poem has an almost purely psychological symbolism where the earlier versions convey a suggestion of traditional moralistic myth. The introductory lines of the 1831 version, which Poe abandoned, link the story of the valley to a hypothetical Syriac myth with suggestions of "Satan's dart" and a "broken heart" as more or less specific hints of guilt related not to a "nameless grave," but merely to "a grave" in the 1831 version, and to "the old forgotten grave" in the *Southern Literary Messenger* version. In the final version the sense of guilt underlying the symbolism is left entirely to the reader's inference, and the imagery conveys primarily the sense of repression and psychic unrest. This shift parallels in interesting fashion Poe's changes of "The Doomed City" to "The City of Sin" to "The City in the Sea," and I believe indicates a growing awareness on Poe's part of the primarily psychological import of his symbols.

The nameless grave contains buried love, and the haunting awareness of this truth, vaguely apprehended by almost any reader, is grounded in universal human experience that repression creates in the unconscious a psychic "place of departed spirits" troubled by an intolerably real though undefined unrest.

ALFRED LORD TENNYSON

Ulysses

> It little profits that an idle king,
> By this still hearth, among these barren crags,
> Matched with an agèd wife, I mete and dole

Unequal laws unto a savage race
That hoard and sleep and feed, and know not me.
I cannot rest from travel; I will drink
Life to the lees. All times I have enjoyed
Greatly, have suffered greatly, both with those
That loved me, and alone; on shore, and when
Thro' scudding drifts the rainy Hyades   10
Vext the dim sea. I am become a name;
For always roaming with a hungry heart
Much have I seen and known—cities of men
And manners, climates, councils, governments,
Myself not least, but honored of them all—
And drunk delight of battle with my peers,
Far on the ringing plains of windy Troy.
I am a part of all that I have met;
Yet all experience is an arch wherethro'
Gleams that untravelled world, whose margin fades   20
For ever and for ever when I move.
How dull it is to pause, to make an end,
To rust unburnished, not to shine in use!
As though to breathe were life! Life piled on life
Were all too little, and of one to me
Little remains; but every hour is saved
From that eternal silence, something more,
A bringer of new things; and vile it were
For some three suns to store and hoard myself,
And this grey spirit yearning in desire   30
To follow knowledge like a sinking star,
Beyond the utmost bound of human thought.
    This is my son, mine own Telemachus,
To whom I leave the sceptre and the isle—
Well-loved of me, discerning to fulfil
This labor, by slow prudence to make mild
A rugged people, and through soft degrees
Subdue them to the useful and the good.
Most blameless is he, centered in the sphere
Of common duties, decent not to fail   40
In offices of tenderness, and pay
Meet adoration to my household gods,
When I am gone. He works his work, I mine.
    There lies the port; the vessel puffs her sail;
There gloom the dark, broad seas. My mariners,
Souls that have toiled, and wrought, and thought with me—
That ever with a frolic welcome took

The thunder and the sunshine, and opposed
Free hearts, free foreheads—you and I are old;
Old age has yet his honor and his toil.
Death closes all; but something ere the end,   50
Some work of noble note, may yet be done,
Not unbecoming men that strove with gods.
The lights begin to twinkle from the rocks;
The long day wanes; the slow moon climbs; the deep
Moans round with many voices. Come, my friends,
'Tis not too late to seek a newer world.
Push off, and sitting well in order smite
The sounding furrows; for my purpose holds
To sail beyond the sunset, and the baths   60
Of all the western stars, until I die.
It may be that the gulfs will wash us down;
It may be we shall touch the Happy Isles,
And see the great Achilles, whom we knew.
Though much is taken, much abides; and though
We are not now that strength which in old days
Moved earth and heaven; that which we are, we are—
One equal temper of heroic hearts,
Made weak by time and fate, but strong in will
To strive, to seek, to find, and not to yield.   70

Tears, Idle Tears

Tears, idle tears, I know not what they mean,
Tears from the depth of some divine despair
Rise in the heart, and gather to the eyes,
In looking on the happy Autumn-fields,
And thinking of the days that are no more.

Fresh as the first beam glittering on a sail,
That brings our friends up from the underworld,
Sad as the last which reddens over one
That sinks with all we love below the verge;
So sad, so fresh, the days that are no more.   10

Ah, sad and strange as in dark summer dawns
The earliest pipe of half-awaken'd birds
To dying ears, when unto dying eyes
The casement slowly grows a glimmering square;
So sad, so strange, the days that are no more.

Dear as remember'd kisses after death,
And sweet as those by hopeless fancy feign'd
On lips that are for others; deep as love,
Deep as first love, and wild with all regret;
O Death in Life, the days that are no more!   20

CLEANTH BROOKS

On Tennyson's "Tears, Idle Tears" [1]

Any account of the poem may very well begin with a consideration of the nature of the tears. Are they *idle* tears? Or are they not rather the most meaningful of tears? Does not the very fact that they are "idle" (that is, tears occasioned by no immediate grief) become in itself a guarantee of the fact that they spring from a deeper, more universal cause?

It would seem so, and that the poet is thus beginning his poem with a paradox. For the third line of the poem indicates that there is no doubt in the speaker's mind about the origin of the tears in some divine despair. They "rise in the heart"—for all that they have been first announced as "idle."

But the question of whether Tennyson is guilty of (or to be complimented upon) a use of paradox may well wait upon further discussion. At this point in our commentary, it is enough to observe that Tennyson has chosen to open his poem with some dramatic boldness—if not with the bold step of equating "idle" with "from the depth of some divine despair," then at least with a bold and violent reversal of the speaker's first characterization of his tears.

The tears "rise in the heart" as the speaker looks upon a scene of beauty and tranquillity. Does looking on the "happy Autumn-fields" bring to mind the days that are no more? The poet does not say so. The tears rise to the eyes in looking on the happy "Autumn-fields" *and* thinking on the days that are no more. The poet himself does not stand responsible for any closer linkage between these actions, though, as a matter of fact, most of us will want to make a closer linkage here. For, if we change "happy Autumn-fields," say, to "happy April-fields," the two terms tend to draw apart. The fact that the fields are autumn-fields which, though happy, point back to something which is over—which is finished —*does* connect them with the past and therefore properly suggests to the observer thoughts about that past.

To sum up: the first stanza has a unity, but it is not a unity which finds its sanctions in the ordinary logic of language. Its sanctions are to be found in the dramatic context, and, to my mind, there alone. Indeed, the stanza suggests the play of the speaker's mind as the tears unexpectedly start, tears for which there

[1] From *The Well Wrought Urn*. Copyright, 1947, by Cleanth Brooks. Reprinted by permission of Harcourt, Brace and Company, Inc.

is no apparent occasion, and as he searches for an explanation of them. He calls them "idle," but, even as he says "I know not what they mean," he realizes that they must spring from the depths of his being—is willing, with his very next words, to associate them with "some divine despair." Moreover, the real occasion of the tears, though the speaker himself comes to realize it only as he approaches the end of the stanza, is the thought about the past. It is psychologically and dramatically right, therefore, that the real occasion should be stated explicitly only with the last line of the stanza.

This first stanza, then, recapitulates the surprise and bewilderment in the speaker's own mind, and sets the problem which the succeeding stanzas are to analyze. The dramatic effect may be described as follows: the stanza seems, not a meditated observation, but a speech begun impulsively—a statement which the speaker has begun before he knows how he will end it.

In the second stanza we are not surprised to have the poet characterize the days that are no more as "sad," but there is some shock in hearing him apply to them the adjective "fresh." Again, the speaker does not pause to explain: the word "fresh" actually begins the stanza. Yet the adjective justifies itself.

The past is fresh as with a dawn freshness—as fresh as the first beam glittering on the sail of an incoming ship. The ship is evidently expected; it brings friends, friends "up from the underworld." On the surface, the comparison is innocent: the "underworld" is merely the antipodes, the world which lies below the horizon—an underworld in the sense displayed in old-fashioned geographies with their sketches illustrating the effects of the curvature of the earth. The sails, which catch the light and glitter, will necessarily be the part first seen of any ship which is coming "up" over the curve of the earth.

But the word "underworld" will necessarily suggest the underworld of Greek mythology, the realm of the shades, the abode of the dead. The attempt to characterize the freshness of the days that are no more has, thus, developed, almost imperceptibly, into a further characterization of the days themselves as belonging, not to our daylight world, but to an "underworld." This suggestion is, of course, strengthened in the lines that follow in which the ship metaphor is reversed so as to give us a picture of sadness: evening, the last glint of sunset light on the sail of a ship.

> That sinks with all we love below the verge.

The conjunction of the qualities of sadness and freshness is reinforced by the fact that the same basic symbol—the light on the sails of a ship hull down— has been employed to suggest both qualities. With the third stanza, the process is carried one stage further: the two qualities (with the variant of "strange" for "fresh") are explicitly linked together:

> Ah, sad and strange as in dark summer dawns. . . .

And here the poet is not content to suggest the qualities of sadness and strangeness by means of two different, even if closely related, figures. In this third stanza the special kind of sadness and strangeness is suggested by one and the same figure.

It is a figure developed in some detail. It, too, involves a dawn scene, though ironically so, for the beginning of the new day is to be the beginning of the long night for the dying man. The dying eyes, the poem suggests, have been for some time awake—long enough to have had time to watch the

> . . . casement slowly [grow] a glimmering square. . . .

The dying man, soon to sleep the lasting sleep, is more fully awake than the "half-awaken'd birds" whose earliest pipings come to his dying ears. We know why these pipings are sad; but why are they *strange*? Because to the person hearing a bird's song for the last time, it will seem that he has never before really heard one. The familiar sound will take on a quality of unreality—of strangeness.

If this poem were merely a gently melancholy reverie on the sweet sadness of the past, Stanzas II and III would have no place in the poem. But the poem is no such reverie: the images from the past rise up with a strange clarity and sharpness that shock the speaker. Their sharpness and freshness account for the sudden tears and for the psychological problem with which the speaker wrestles in the poem. If the past would only remain melancholy but dimmed, sad but worn and familiar, we should have no problem and no poem. At least, we should not have *this* poem; we should certainly not have the intensity of the last stanza.

That intensity, if justified, must grow out of a sense of the apparent nearness and intimate presence of what is irrevocably beyond reach: the days that are no more must be more than the conventional "dear, dead days beyond recall." They must be beyond recall, yet alive—tantalizingly vivid and near. It is only thus that we can feel the speaker justified in calling them

> Dear as remember'd kisses after death,
> And sweet as those by hopeless fancy feign'd
> On lips that are for others. . . .

It is only thus that we can accept the culminating paradox of

> O Death in Life, the days that are no more.

We have already observed, in the third stanza, how the speaker compares the strangeness and sadness of the past to the sadness of the birds' piping as it sounds to dying ears. There is a rather brilliant ironic contrast involved in the comparison. The speaker, a living man, in attempting to indicate how sad and strange to him are the days of the past, says that they are as sad and strange as is the natural activity of the awakening world to the man who is dying: the dead past seems to the living man as unfamiliar and fresh in its sadness as the living present seems to the dying man. There is more here, however, than a mere, ironic reversal of roles; in each case there is the sense of being irrevocably barred out from the known world.

This ironic contrast, too, accounts for the sense of desperation which runs through the concluding lines of the poem. The kisses feigned by "hopeless fancy" are made the more precious because of the very hopelessness; but memory takes on the quality of fancy. It is equally hopeless—the kisses can as little be renewed as those "feign'd/ On lips that are for others" can be obtained. The realized past has become as fabulous as the unrealizable future. The days that are no more are as dear as the one, as sweet as the other, the speaker says; and it does not matter whether we compare them to the one or to the other or to both: it comes to the same thing.

But the days that are no more are not merely "dear" and "sweet"; they are "deep" and "wild." Something has happened to the grammar here. How can the days be "deep as love" or "wild with all regret"? And what is the status of the exclamation "O Death in Life"? Is it merely a tortured cry like "O God! the days that are no more"? Or is it a loose appositive: "the days that are no more are a kind of death in life?"

The questions are not asked in a censorious spirit, as if there were no justification for Tennyson's license here. But it is important to see how much license the poem requires, and the terms on which the reader decides to accord it justification. What one finds on closer examination is not muddlement but richness. But it is a richness achieved through principles of organization which many an admirer of the poet has difficulty in allowing to the "obscure" modern poet.

For example, how can the days of the past be *deep*? Here, of course, the problem is not very difficult. The past is buried within one: the days that are no more constitute the deepest level of one's being, and the tears that arise from thinking on them may be said to come from the "depth of some divine despair." But how can the days be "wild with all regret"? The extension demanded here is more ambitious. In matter of fact, it is the speaker, the man, who is made wild with regret by thinking on the days.

One can, of course, justify the adjective as a transferred epithet on the model of Vergil's *maestum timorem*; and perhaps this was Tennyson's own conscious justification (if, indeed, the need to justify it ever occurred to him). But one can make a better case than a mere appeal to the authority of an established literary convention. There is a sense in which the man and the remembered days are one and the same. A man is the sum of his memories. The adjective which applies to the man made wild with regret can apply to those memories which make him wild with regret. For, does the man charge the memories with his own passion, or is it the memories that give the emotion to him? If we pursue the matter far enough, we come to a point where the distinction lapses. Perhaps I should say, more accurately, adopting the metaphor of the poem itself, we *descend* to a depth where the distinction lapses. The days that are no more are *deep* and *wild*, buried but not dead—below the surface and unthought of, yet at the deepest core of being, secretly alive.

The past *should* be tame, fettered, brought to heel; it is not. It is capable of breaking forth and coming to the surface. The word "wild" is bold, therefore, but justified. It reasserts the line of development which has been maintained throughout the earlier stanzas: "fresh," "strange," and now "wild"—all adjectives which suggest passionate, irrational life. The word "wild," thus, not only pulls into focus the earlier paradoxes, but is the final stage in the preparation for the culminating paradox, "O Death in Life."

The last stanza evokes an intense emotional response from the reader. The claim could hardly be made good by the stanza taken in isolation. The stanza leans heavily upon the foregoing stanzas, and the final paradox draws heavily upon the great metaphors in stanzas II and III. This is as it should be. The justification for emphasizing the fact here is this: the poem, for all its illusion of impassioned speech—with the looseness and *apparent* confusion of unpremeditated speech—is very tightly organized. It represents an organic structure; and the intensity of the total effect is a reflection of the total structure.

The reader, I take it, will hardly be disposed to quarrel with the general statement of the theme of the poem as it is given in the foregoing account; and he will probably find himself in accord with this general estimate of the poem's value. But the reader may well find that the amount of attention given to the structure of the poem is irrelevant, if not positively bad. In particular, he may find the emphasis on paradox, ambiguity, and ironic contrast displeasing. He has not been taught to expect these in Tennyson, and he has had the general impression that the presence of these qualities represents the intrusion of alien, "unpoetic" matter.

I have no wish to intellectualize the poem—to make conscious and artful what was actually spontaneous and simple. Nevertheless, the qualities of ironic contrast and paradox *do* exist in the poem; and they *do* have a relation to the poem's dramatic power.

ROBERT BROWNING

My Last Duchess

FERRARA

That's my last Duchess painted on the wall,
Looking as if she were alive. I call
That piece a wonder, now: Frà Pandolf's hands
Worked busily a day, and there she stands.
Will't please you sit and look at her? I said
"Frà Pandolf" by design, for never read
Strangers like you that pictured countenance,
The depth and passion of its earnest glance
But to myself they turned (since none puts by
The curtain I have drawn for you, but I)   10
And seemed as they would ask me, if they durst,

How such a glance came there; so, not the first
Are you to turn and ask thus. Sir, 'twas not
Her husband's presence only, called that spot
Of joy into the Duchess' cheek: perhaps
Frà Pandolf chanced to say, "Her mantle laps
Over my lady's wrist too much," or "Paint
Must never hope to reproduce the faint
Half-flush that dies along her throat": such stuff
Was courtesy, she thought, and cause enough   20
For calling up that spot of joy. She had
A heart—how shall I say?—too soon made glad,
Too easily impressed: she liked whate'er
She looked on, and her looks went everywhere.
Sir, 'twas all one! My favor at her breast,
The dropping of the daylight in the West,
The bough of cherries some officious fool
Broke in the orchard for her, the white mule
She rode with round the terrace—all and each
Would draw from her alike the approving speech,   30
Or blush, at least. She thanked men,—good! but thanked
Somehow—I know not how—as if she ranked
My gift of a nine-hundred-years-old name
With anybody's gift. Who'd stoop to blame
This sort of trifling? Even had you skill
In speech—(which I have not)—to make your will
Quite clear to such an one, and say, "Just this
Or that in you disgusts me; here you miss,
Or there exceed the mark"—and if she let
Herself be lessoned so, nor plainly set   40
Her wits to yours, forsooth, and made excuse,
—E'en then would be some stooping; and I choose
Never to stoop. Oh sir, she smiled, no doubt,
Whene'er I passed her; but who passed without
Much the same smile? This grew; I gave commands;
Then all smiles stopped together. There she stands
As if alive. Will't please you rise? We'll meet
The company below, then. I repeat,
The Count your master's known munificence
Is ample warrant that no just pretence   50
Of mine for dowry will be disallowed;
Though his fair daughter's self, as I avowed
At starting, is my object. Nay, we'll go
Together down, sir. Notice Neptune, though,
Taming a sea-horse, thought a rarity,
Which Claus of Innsbruck cast in bronze for me!

Home-Thoughts, from the Sea

Noby, nobly Cape Saint Vincent to the northwest died away;
Sunset ran, one glorious blood-red, reeking into Cadiz Bay;
Bluish 'mid the burning water, full in face Trafalgar lay;
In the dimmest northeast distance dawned Gibraltar grand and gray;
"Here and here did England help me; how can I help England?"—say,
Whoso turns as I, this evening, turn to God to praise and pray,
While Jove's planet rises yonder, silent over Africa.

FREDERICK L. GWYNN

On Browning's "Home-Thoughts, from the Sea" [1]

The poem stems from Browning's admiration for Lord Nelson, whom he also honors in the 1845 companion poem, "Here's to Nelson's Memory." Cape Saint Vincent, Cadiz Bay, and Trafalgar are all sites of Nelsonian naval activity, although it was Nelson's superior, Sir John Jervis, who was made Earl Saint Vincent for defeating 27 Spanish ships off the Portuguese cape, and it was Sir Francis Drake who "singed the King of Spain's beard" more memorably in Cadiz Bay in 1587. The British took Gibraltar in 1704 and kept it against many Spanish attacks, especially the Great Siege of 1779-1783. Browning, proceeding along the coast of Spain in 1844, indeed looked back on colorful occasions when England could be said to have helped him.

These rich allusions are important to the poem; but even for non-British readers who may be ignorant of or indifferent to such richness, the piece succeeds by dint of its unique structure. The application of the rollicking trochees of "Locksley Hall" to a brief lyric, the restriction to a single rhyme for the seven end-stopped lines, the stress on the last syllable of the poem as an expected yet unexpected long *a*, the piling up of alliteration in every line except the last, the consonantal or assonantal linking of almost every word in the poem—these are bold devices that come off here without inviting parody. But there is more to it. It is possibly a coincidence that the first four lines contain ten words each, but not a coincidence that they are all descriptive, that each presents a separate geographical item, and that each ends with a semicolon to stress the parallelism. Lines 5-6 contain thirteen words each; both lines are personal, and comprise a continuous rather than a parallel line of thought. And the final line stands further by itself in having only eight words.

What is most substantial and subtle about the poem is the poet's uncharac-

[1] From The Explicator, XII (November, 1953), 12. Reprinted by permission of the author and of the Editors of The Explicator.

teristic use of sensuous metaphor and of unobtrusive but ranging symbol. The *blood-red* sun is *reeking* (*NED*, v^1 2c) into the peaceful scene; the water is *burning*; and in the midst of sunset, Gibraltar has *dawned*. The contrasting aspect of these few metaphors is carried out in much of the imagery and diction, with occasional irony. The *Northwest* is opposed to the *Northeast* and to the Southeast (*Africa*), and this compass contrast is underlined by the fact that where Cape Saint Vincent *died* and the sun *set* and *ran* down *into*, Gibraltar *dawned* and Jupiter *rises* . . . *over Africa*. (On the cosmic level, the sun went down but the planet comes up.) Where the Christian Saint Vincent (in the form of his geographical cape) *Nobly, nobly* . . . *died* with the martyr's éclat, the pagan Jove *rises* . . . *silent*. The sun's light is liquid *blood* in the liquid *Bay*, and it sets the *water* on fire (*burning*). Cape Trafalgar is *Bluish 'mid the burning* (blue and red), as well as being *full in* [the speaker's] *face*, whereas Gibraltar is *gray* and *In the dimmest* . . . *distance*. Gibraltar's *distance* is opposed to *here*. The country *England* is explicitly contrasted to the person *me* and implicitly contrasted to the continent *Africa*. The speaker is turning to God for opposing reasons—to *praise* and to *pray*. *Say* opposes *silent*.

Submerged in this imagery are the three most important contrasts of the poem, all symbolic. The first depends on seeing the two capes, the bay, the *grand* rock, the *glorious* sun, and the continent as large and abiding objects in nature. The second depends on associating the first three geographical names with the greatest of naval heroes, Lord Nelson. (Although Nelson was also "the hero of the Nile," I cannot believe that *Africa* should call up this fact.) The speaker feels small and impotent in comparison to nature, Nelson, and the scenes of victory, and this leads him to ask the central question of the poem, which is unanswered. (*Say* is not a request for an answer, but an exhortation to others to ask the same question.) Ordinary individual mortals have little power —as opposed to heroes like Nelson and enduring immensities like sea-coasts and England and God. The last line, which provides the third major contrast, rounds off the poem with an elevated image of superhuman immensity: *Jove* connotes ancient divinity; his *planet*, the cosmos; the fact that it is *silent*, the inscrutability of the cosmos; all these oppose *Africa*, which symbolizes this dark world.

With such a magnificent poem, Browning's only lapse was to tack on the sentimental title and pair it with the jejune "Home-Thoughts, from Abroad." For the theme of the sea poem is not nostalgia, but the awareness of magnitude.

The Bishop Orders His Tomb at St. Praxed's Church

ROME, 15—

Vanity, saith the preacher, vanity!
Draw round my bed: is Anselm keeping back?
Nephews—sons mine . . . ah God, I know not! Well—
She, men would have to be your mother once,

Old Gandolf envied me, so fair she was!
What's done is done, and she is dead beside,
Dead long ago, and I am Bishop since,
And as she died so must we die ourselves,
And thence ye may perceive the world's a dream.
Life, how and what is it? As here I lie   10
In this state-chamber, dying by degrees,
Hours and long hours in the dead night, I ask,
"Do I live, am I dead?" Peace, peace seems all.
Saint Praxed's ever was the church for peace;
And so, about this tomb of mine. I fought
With tooth and nail to save my niche, ye know:
—Old Gandolf cozened me, despite my care;
Shrewd was that snatch from out the corner South
He graced his carrion with, God curse the same!
Yet still my niche is not so cramped but thence   20
One sees the pulpit o' the epistle-side,
And somewhat of the choir, those silent seats,
And up into the aery dome where live
The angels, and a sunbeam's sure to lurk:
And I shall fill my slab of basalt there,
And 'neath my tabernacle take my rest,
With those nine columns round me, two and two,
The odd one at my feet where Anselm stands:
Peach-blossom marble all, the rare, the ripe
As fresh-poured red wine of a mighty pulse.   30
—Old Gandolf with his paltry onion-stone,
Put me where I may look at him! True peach,
Rosy and flawless: how I earned the prize!
Draw close: that conflagration of my church
—What then? So much was saved if aught were missed!
My sons, ye would not be my death? Go dig
The white-grape vineyard where the oil-press stood,
Drop water gently till the surface sink,
And if ye find . . . Ah God, I know not, I! . . .
Bedded in store of rotten fig-leaves soft,   40
And corded up in a tight olive-frail,
Some lump, ah God, of *lapis lazuli*,
Big as a Jew's head cut off at the nape,
Blue as a vein o'er the Madonna's breast . . .
Sons, all have I bequeathed you, villas, all,
That brave Frascati villa with its bath,
So, let the blue lump poise between my knees,
Like God the Father's globe on both his hands
Ye worship in the Jesu Church so gay,

For Gandolf shall not choose but see and burst! 50
Swift as a weaver's shuttle fleet our years:
Man goeth to the grave, and where is he?
Did I say basalt for my slab, sons? Black—
'Twas ever antique-black I meant! How else
Shall ye contrast my frieze to come beneath?
The bas-relief in bronze ye promised me,
Those Pans and Nymphs ye wot of, and perchance
Some tripod, thyrsus, with a vase or so,
The Saviour at his sermon on the mount,
Saint Praxed in a glory, and one Pan 60
Ready to twitch the Nymph's last garment off,
And Moses with the tables . . . but I know
Ye mark me not! What do they whisper thee,
Child of my bowels, Anselm? Ah, ye hope
To revel down my villas while I gasp
Bricked o'er with beggar's mouldy travertine
Which Gandolf from his tomb-top chuckles at!
Nay, boys, ye love me—all of jasper, then!
'Tis jasper ye stand pledged to, lest I grieve.
My bath must needs be left behind, alas! 70
One block, pure green as a pistachio-nut,
There's plenty jasper somewhere in the world—
And have I not Saint Praxed's ear to pray
Horses for ye, and brown Greek manuscripts,
And mistresses with great smooth marbly limbs?
—That's if ye carve my epitaph aright,
Choice Latin, picked phrase, Tully's every word,
No gaudy ware like Gandolf's second line—
Tully, my masters? Ulpian serves his need!
And then how I shall lie through centuries, 80
And hear the blessed mutter of the mass,
And see God made and eaten all day long,
And feel the steady candle-flame, and taste
Good strong thick stupefying incense-smoke!
For as I lie here, hours of the dead night,
Dying in state and by such slow degrees,
I fold my arms as if they clasped a crook,
And stretch my feet forth straight as stone can point,
And let the bedclothes, for a mort-cloth, drop
Into great laps and folds of sculptor's-work: 90
And as yon tapers dwindle, and strange thoughts
Grow, with a certain humming in my ears,
About the life before I lived this life,
And this life too, popes, cardinals and priests.

Saint Praxed at his sermon on the mount,
Your tall pale mother with her talking eyes,
And new-found agate urns as fresh as day,
And marble's language, Latin pure, discreet,
—Aha, ELUCESCEBAT quoth our friend?
No Tully, said I, Ulpian at the best!   100
Evil and brief hath been my pilgrimage.
All *lapis*, all sons! Else I give the Pope
My villas! Will ye ever eat my heart?
Ever your eyes were as a lizard's quick,
They glitter like your mother's for my soul,
Or ye would heighten my impoverished frieze,
Piece out its starved design, and fill my vase
With grapes, and add a visor and a Term,
And to the tripod ye would tie a lynx
That in his struggle throws the thyrsus down,   110
To comfort me on my entablature
Whereon I am to lie till I must ask
"Do I live, am I dead?" There, leave me, there!
For ye have stabbed me with ingratitude
To death—ye wish it—God, ye wish it! Stone—
Gritstone, a-crumble! Clammy squares which sweat
As if the corpse they keep were oozing through—
And no more *lapis* to delight the world!
Well, go! I bless ye. Fewer tapers there,
But in a row: and, going, turn your backs   120
—Ay, like departing altar-ministrants,
And leave me in my church, the church for peace,
That I may watch at leisure if he leers—
Old Gandolf—at me, from his onion-stone,
As still he envied me, so fair she was!

WALT WHITMAN[1]

One's-Self I Sing

One's-self I sing, a simple separate person,
Yet utter the word Democratic, the word En-Masse.
Of physiology from top to toe I sing,

[1] Reprinted from *Walt Whitman: Leaves of Grass and Selected Prose*, edited by Sculley Bradley, "Rinehart Editions" (New York: Holt, Rinehart and Winston, Inc., 1949).

Not physiognomy alone nor brain alone is worthy for the Muse,
    I say the Form complete is worthier far,
The Female equally with the Male I sing.

Of Life immense in passion, pulse, and power,
Cheerful, for freest action form'd under the laws divine,
The Modern Man I sing.

When Lilacs Last in the Dooryard Bloom'd

1

When lilacs last in the dooryard bloom'd,
And the great star early droop'd in the western sky in the night,
I mourn'd, and yet shall mourn with ever-returning spring.

Ever-returning spring, trinity sure to me you bring,
Lilac blooming perennial and drooping star in the west,
And thought of him I love.

2

O powerful western fallen star!
O shades of night—O moody, tearful night!
O great star disappear'd—O the black murk that hides the star!
O cruel hands that hold me powerless—O helpless soul of me!   10
O harsh surrounding cloud that will not free my soul.

3

In the dooryard fronting an old farm-house near the white-wash'd palings,
Stands the lilac-bush tall-growing with heart-shaped leaves of rich green,
With many a pointed blossom rising delicate, with the perfume strong I love,
With every leaf a miracle—and from this bush in the dooryard,
With delicate-color'd blossoms and heart-shaped leaves of rich green,
A sprig with its flower I break.

4

In the swamp in secluded recesses,
A shy and hidden bird is warbling a song.

Solitary the thrush,   20
The hermit withdrawn to himself, avoiding the settlements,
Sings by himself a song.
Song of the bleeding throat,
Death's outlet song of life, (for well dear brother I know,
If thou wast not granted to sing thou would'st surely die.)

5

Over the breast of the spring, the land, amid cities,
Amid lanes and through old woods, where lately the violets peep'd from the
    ground spotting the gray debris,
Amid the grass in the fields each side of the lanes, passing the endless grass,
Passing the yellow-spear'd wheat, every grain from its shroud in the dark-
    brown fields uprisen,
Passing the apple-tree blows of white and pink in the orchards,   30
Carrying a corpse to where it shall rest in the grave,
Night and day journeys a coffin.

6

Coffin that passes through lanes and streets,
Through day and night with the great cloud darkening the land,
With the pomp of the inloop'd flags with the cities draped in black,
With the show of the States themselves as of crape-veil'd women standing,
With processions long and winding and the flambeaus of the night,
With the countless torches lit, with the silent sea of faces and the unbared
    heads,
With the waiting depot, the arriving coffin, and the sombre faces,
With dirges through the night, with the thousand voices rising strong and
    solemn,   40
With all the mournful voices of the dirges pour'd around the coffin,
The dim-lit churches and the shuddering organs—where amid these you
    journey,
With the tolling, tolling bells' perpetual clang,
Here, coffin that slowly passes,
I give you my sprig of lilac.

7

(Nor for you, for one alone,
Blossoms and branches green to coffins all I bring,
For fresh as the morning, thus would I chant a song for you, O sane and
    sacred death.

All over bouquets of roses,
O death, I cover you over with roses and early lilies,   50
But mostly and now the lilac that blooms the first,
Copious I break, I break the sprigs from the bushes,
With loaded arms I come, pouring for you,
For you and the coffins all of you, O death.)

8

O western orb sailing the heaven,
Now I know what you must have meant as a month since I walk'd,
As I walk'd in silence the transparent shadowy night,
As I saw you had something to tell as you bent to me night after night,
As you droop'd from the sky low down as if to my side, (while the other stars
    all look'd on,)
As we wander'd together the solemn night, (for something I know not what
    kept me from sleep,)
As the night advanced, and I saw on the rim of the west how full you were of
    woe,
As I stood on the rising ground in the breeze in the cool transparent night,
As I watch'd where you pass'd and was lost in the netherward black of the
    night,
As my soul in its trouble dissatisfied sank, as where yon sad orb,
Concluded, dropt in the night, and was gone.

9

Sing on there in the swamp,
O singer bashful and tender, I hear your notes, I hear your call,
I hear, I come presently, I understand you,
But a moment I linger, for the lustrous star has detain'd me,
The star my departing comrade holds and detains me.

10

O how shall I warble myself for the dead one there I loved?
And how shall I deck my song for the large sweet soul that has gone?
And what shall my perfume be for the grave of him I love?
Sea-winds blown from east and west,
Blown from the Eastern sea and blown from the Western sea, till there on
    the prairies meeting,
These and with these and the breath of my chant,
I'll perfume the grave of him I love.

11

O what shall I hang on the chamber walls?
And what shall the pictures be that I hang on the walls,
To adorn the burial-house of him I love?

Pictures of growing spring and farms and homes,
With the Fourth-month eve at sundown, and the gray smoke lucid and bright,
With floods of the yellow gold of the gorgeous, indolent, sinking sun,
    burning, expanding the air,

With the fresh sweet herbage under foot, and the pale green leaves of the
  trees prolific,
In the distance the flowing glaze, the breast of the river, with a wind-dapple
  here and there,
With ranging hills on the banks, with many a line against the sky, and
  shadows,
And the city at hand with dwellings so dense, and stacks of chimneys,
And all the scenes of life and the workshops, and the workmen homeward
  returning.

12

Lo, body and soul—this land,
My own Manhattan with spires, and the sparkling and hurrying tides, and
  the ships,   90
The varied and ample land, the South and the North in the light, Ohio's
  shores and flashing Missouri,
And ever the far-spreading prairies cover'd with grass and corn.

Lo, the most excellent sun so calm and haughty,
The violet and purple morn with just-felt breezes,
The gentle soft-born measureless light,
The miracle spreading bathing all, the fulfill'd noon,
The coming eve delicious, the welcome night and the stars,
Over my cities shining all, enveloping man and land.

13

Sing on, sing on you gray-brown bird,
Sing from the swamps, the recesses, pour your chant from the bushes,   100
Limitless out of the dusk, out of the cedars and pines.

Sing on dearest brother, warble your reedy song,
Loud human song, with voice of uttermost woe.

O liquid and free and tender!
O wild and loose to my soul—O wondrous singer!
You only I hear—yet the star holds me, (but will soon depart,)
Yet the lilac with mastering odor holds me.

14

Now while I sat in the day and look'd forth,
In the close of the day with its light and the fields of spring, and the farmers
  preparing their crops,
In the large unconscious scenery of my land with its lakes and forests,   110
In the heavenly aerial beauty (after the perturb'd winds and the storms,)

Under the arching heavens of the afternoon swift passing, and the voices of
    children and women,
The many-moving sea-tides, and I saw the ships how they sail'd,
And the summer approaching with richness, and the fields all busy with
    labor,
And the infinite separate houses, how they all went on, each with its meals
    and minutia of daily usages,
And the streets how their throbbings throbb'd, and the cities pent—lo, then
    and there,
Falling upon them all and among them all, enveloping me with the rest,
Appear'd the cloud, appear'd the long black trail,
And I knew death, its thought, and the sacred knowledge of death.

Then with the knowledge of death as walking one side of me,   120
And the thought of death close-walking the other side of me,
And I in the middle as with companions, and as holding the hands of
    companions,
I fled forth to the hiding receiving night that talks not,
Down to the shores of the water, the path by the swamp in the dimness,
To the solemn shadowy cedars and ghostly pines so still.

And the singer so shy to the rest receiv'd me,
The gray-brown bird I know receiv'd us comrades three,
And he sang the carol of death, and a verse for him I love.

From deep secluded recesses,
From the fragrant cedars and the ghostly pines so still   130
Came the carol of the bird.

And the charm of the carol rapt me,
As I held as if by their hands my comrades in the night,
And the voice of my spirit tallied the song of the bird.

Come lovely and soothing death,
Undulate round the world, serenely arriving, arriving,
In the day, in the night, to all, to each,
Sooner or later delicate death.

Prais'd be the fathomless universe,
For life and joy, and for objects and knowledge curious,   140
And for love, sweet love—but praise! praise! praise!
For the sure-enwinding arms of cool-enfolding death.

Dark mother always gliding near with soft feet,
Have none chanted for thee a chant of fullest welcome?

Then I chant it for thee, I glorify thee above all,
I bring thee a song that when thou must indeed come, come unfalteringly.

Approach, strong deliveress,
When it is so, when thou hast taken them I joyously sing the dead,
Lost in the loving floating ocean of thee,
Laved in the flood of thy bliss O death.   150

From me to thee glad serenades,
Dances for thee I propose saluting thee, adornments and feastings for thee,
And the sights of the open landscape and the high-spread sky are fitting,
And life and the fields, and the huge and thoughtful night.

The night in silence under many a star,
The ocean shore and the husky whispering wave whose voice I know,
And the soul turning to thee O vast and well-veil'd death,
And the body gratefully nestling close to thee.

Over the tree-tops I float thee a song,
Over the rising and sinking waves, over the myriad fields and the prairies
*   wide,*   160
Over the dense-pack'd cities all and the teeming wharves and ways,
I float this carol with joy, with joy to thee O death.

15

To the tally of my soul,
Loud and strong kept up the gray-brown bird,
With pure deliberate notes spreading filling the night.

Loud in the pines and cedars dim,
Clear in the freshness moist and the swamp-perfume,
And I with my comrades there in the night.

While my sight that was bound in my eyes unclosed,
As to long panoramas of visions.   170

And I saw askant the armies,
I saw as in noiseless dreams hundreds of battle-flags,
Borne through the smoke of the battles and pierc'd with missiles I saw them,
And carried hither and yon through the smoke, and torn and bloody,
And at last but a few shreds left on the staffs, (and all in silence,)
And the staffs all splinter'd and broken.

I saw battle-corpses, myriads of them,
And the white skeletons of young men, I saw them,

I saw the debris and debris of all the slain soldiers of the war,
But I saw they were not as was thought,   180
They themselves were fully at rest, they suffer'd not,
The living remain'd and suffer'd, the mother suffer'd,
And the wife and the child and the musing comrade suffer'd,
And the armies that remain'd suffer'd.

16

Passing the visions, passing the night,
Passing, unloosing the hold of my comrades' hands,
Passing the song of the hermit bird and the tallying song of my soul,
Victorious song, death's outlet song, yet varying ever-altering song,
As low and wailing, yet clear the notes, rising and falling, flooding the night,
Sadly sinking and fainting, as warning and warning, and yet again bursting
    with joy,
Covering the earth and filling the spread of the heaven,   190
As that powerful psalm in the night I heard from recesses,
Passing, I leave thee lilac with heart-shaped leaves,
I leave thee there in the door-yard, blooming, returning with spring.

I cease from my song for thee,
From my gaze on thee in the west, fronting the west, communing with thee,
O comrade lustrous with silver face in the night.

Yet each to keep and all, retrievements out of the night,
The song, the wondrous chant of the gray-brown bird,
And the tallying chant, the echo arous'd in my soul,   200
With the lustrous and drooping star with the countenance full of woe,
With the holders holding my hand nearing the call of the bird,
Comrades mine and I in the midst, and their memory ever to keep, for the
    dead I loved so well,
For the sweetest, wisest soul of all my days and lands—and this for his dear
    sake,
Lilac and star and bird twined with the chant of my soul,
There in the fragrant pines and the cedars dusk and dim.

To a Locomotive in Winter

Thee for my recitative,
Thee in the driving storm even as now, the snow, the winter-day declining,
Thee in thy panoply, thy measur'd dual throbbing and thy beat convulsive,
Thy black cylindric body, golden brass and silvery steel,

Thy ponderous side-bars, parallel and connecting rods, gyrating, shuttling at
    thy sides,
Thy metrical, now swelling pant and roar, now tapering in the distance,
Thy great protruding head-light fix'd in front,
Thy long, pale, floating vapor-pennants, tinged with delicate purple,
The dense and murky clouds out-belching from thy smoke-stack,
Thy knitted frame, thy springs and valves, the tremulous twinkle of thy
    wheels,   10
Thy train of cars behind, obedient, merrily following,
Through gale or calm, now swift, now slack, yet steadily careering;
Type of the modern—emblem of motion and power—pulse of the continent,
For once come serve the Muse and merge in verse, even as here I see thee,
With storm and buffeting gusts of wind and falling snow,
By day thy warning ringing bell to sound its notes,
By night thy silent signal lamps to swing.

Fierce-throated beauty!
Roll through my chant with all thy lawless music, thy swinging lamps at
    night,
Thy madly-whistled laughter, echoing, rumbling like an earthquake, rousing
    all,   20
Law of thyself complete, thine own track firmly holding,
(No sweetness debonair of tearful harp or glib piano thine,)
Thy trills of shrieks by rocks and hills return'd,
Launch'd o'er the prairies wide, across the lakes,
To the free skies unpent and glad and strong.

Spirit That Form'd This Scene

Written in Platte Cañon, Colorado

Spirit that form'd this scene,
These tumbled rock-piles grim and red,
These reckless heaven-ambitious peaks,
These gorges, turbulent-clear streams, this naked freshness,
These formless wild arrays, for reasons of their own,
I know thee, savage spirit—we have communed together,
Mine too such wild arrays, for reasons of their own;
Was't charged against my chants they had forgotten art?
To fuse within themselves its rules precise and delicatesse?
The lyrist's measur'd beat, the wrought-out temple's grace—column and
    polish'd arch forgot?

But thou that revelest here—spirit that form'd this scene,
They have remember'd thee.

CHARLES BAUDELAIRE

Au Lecteur

La sottise, l'erreur, le péché, la lésine,
Occupent nos esprits et travaillent nos corps,
Et nous alimentons nos aimables remords,
Comme les mendiants nourrissent leur vermine.

Nos péchés sont têtus, nos repentirs sont lâches;
Nous nous faisons payer grassement nos aveux,
Et nous rentrons gaiement dans le chemin bourbeux,
Croyant par de vils pleurs laver toutes nos taches.

Sur l'oreiller du mal c'est Satan Trismégiste
Qui berce longuement notre esprit enchanté,   10
Et le riche métal de notre volonté
Est tout vaporisé par ce savant chimiste.

C'est le Diable qui tient les fils qui nous remuent!
Aux objets répugnants nous trouvons des appas;
Chaque jour vers l'Enfer nous descendons d'un pas,
Sans horreur, à travers des ténèbres qui puent.

Ainsi qu'un débauché pauvre qui baise et mange
Le sein martyrisé d'une antique catin,
Nous volons au passage un plaisir clandestin
Que nous pressons bien fort comme une vieille orange.   20

Serré, fourmillant, comme un million d'helminthes,
Dans nos cerveaux ribote un peuple de Démons,
Et, quand nous respirons, la Mort dans nos poumons
Descend, fleuve invisible, avec de sourdes plaintes.

Si le viol, le poison, le poignard, l'incendie,
N'ont pas encor brodé de leurs plaisants dessins
Le canevas banal de nos piteux destins,
C'est que notre âme, hélas! n'est pas assez hardie.

Mais parmi les chacals, les panthères, les lices,
Les singes, les scorpions, les vautours, les serpents,   30
Les monstres glapissants, hurlants, grognants, rampants,
Dans la ménagerie infâme de nos vices,

Il en est un plus laid, plus méchant, plus immonde!
Quoiqu'il ne pousse ni grands gestes ni grands cris,
Il ferait volontiers de la terre un débris
Et dans un bâillement avalerait le monde;

C'est l'Ennui!—l'oeil chargé d'un pleur involontaire,
Il rêve d'échafauds en fumant son houka.
Tu le connais, lecteur, ce monstre délicat,
—Hypocrite lecteur,—mon semblable,—mon frère!   40

To the Reader[1]

A Translation by C. F. MacIntyre

By folly, error, stinginess, and vice
our flesh is worked, our souls inhabited,
and all our dear remorses are well fed,
as beggars nourish their own fleas and lice.

Our sins are stubborn, our repentance mean;
pretending to pay fatly what we vowed,
we run back gaily to the muddy road,
thinking with cheap tears to wash off the stain.

On the pillow of evil, Satan Trismegist
a long time cradles our enchanted souls,   10
and the all-precious metal of our will
is turned to fumes by this wise alchemist.

We find allurement in repugnant things;
unawed, each day another step we sink
toward Hell, across tenebrous depths that stink.
It is the Devil pulls the leading-strings!

Like a mean lecher kissing and sucking thin
the martyred breast of some poor ancient tart,

[1] *One Hundred Poems from Les Fleurs du Mal* (Berkeley: University of California Press, 1947). In his original translation, MacIntyre retained the French title.

we steal in passing any furtive sport
and squeeze it, like an orange, to the skin.

20

Swarming and crowding, like a million worms,
the Demons in our brain are on a spree,
and when we breathe, in our lungs quietly
Death's unseen river flows and dully mourns.

If poison, dagger, arson, and the rough
assault of rape have not with droll designs
adorned the vulgar canvas doom assigns,
it is because our soul's not bold enough.

But among jackals, panthers, and hound-bitches,
monkeys and vultures, scorpions and serpents,
the yelping, roaring, growling monsters, rampant
in the infamous menagerie of our vices,

30

is one more vicious, ugly, and perverse!
Though he makes no great gesture, no loud cry,
he would glady turn our earth into debris
and in a yawn engulf the universe;

Ennui!—his unwilling tears brim over
as, pulling at his hookah, he dreams of scaffolds.
You know him, reader, this fastidious scoundrel,
—hypocritical reader, my fellow, my brother!

40

Le Balcon

Mère des souvenirs, maîtresse des maîtresses,
O toi, tous mes plaisirs! ô toi, tous mes devoirs!
Tu te rappelleras la beauté des caresses,
La douceur du foyer et le charme des soirs,
Mère des souvenirs, maîtresse des maîtresses!

Les soirs illuminés par l'ardeur du charbon,
Et les soirs au balcon, voilés de vapeurs roses.
Que ton sein m'était doux! que ton cœur m'était bon!
Nous avons dit souvent d'impérissables choses
Les soirs illuminés par l'ardeur du charbon.

10

Que les soleils sont beaux dans les chaudes soirées!
Que l'espace est profond! que le cœur est puissant!

En me penchant vers toi, reine des adorées,
Je croyais respirer le parfum de ton sang.
Que les soleils sont beaux dans les chaudes soirées!

La nuit s'épaississait ainsi qu'une cloison,
Et mes yeux dans le noir devinaient tes prunelles,
Et je buvais ton souffle, ô douceur, ô poison!
Et tes pieds s'endormaient dans mes mains fraternelles.
La nuit s'épaississait ainsi qu'une cloison.   20

Je sais l'art d'évoquer les minutes heureuses,
Et revis mon passé blotti dans tes genoux.
Car à quoi bon chercher tes beautés langoureuses
Ailleurs qu'en ton cher corps et qu'en ton cœur si doux?
Je sais l'art d'évoquer les minutes heureuses!

Ces serments, ces parfums, ces baisers infinis,
Renaîtront-ils d'un gouffre interdit à nos sondes,
Comme montent au ciel les soleils rajeunis
Après s'être lavés au fond des mers profondes?
—O serments! ô parfums! ô baisers infinis!   30

The Balcony[1]

A Translation by C. F. MacIntyre

Mother of memories, mistress of mistresses,
O you, all my devoirs, all my delights!
you will recall the joy of our caresses,
the pleasant fireside and the charm of night,
mother of memories, mistress of mistresses!

the evenings lighted by the glowing embers,
or on the balcony, by rose-mists obscured.
How sweet your breast was, and your heart was tender!
We often said imperishable words
on evenings lighted by the glowing embers.   10

What splendid sunsets on those summer evenings!
So powerful is the heart, how vast space looms!
Queen of the adored, toward you leaning,

[1] *One Hundred Poems from Les Fleurs du Mal* (Berkeley: University of California Press, 1947). In his original translation, MacIntyre retained the French title.

I thought I breathed your very blood's perfume.
What splendid sunsets on those summer evenings!

Then the night closed round like a bulwark,
I drank your soft breath, poisonous and sweet,
my eyes divined your sloe-eyes in the dark,
and in my brother-hands I held your feet.
Then the night closed round like a bulwark.   20

I know the art to evoke such happy hours,
and live again my past, head on your knees.
What good to seek your beauty's languorous flowers
save in your heart and body's mysteries?
I know the art to evoke such happy hours!

All those perfumes, those vows, those infinite kisses,
will they be reborn from a depth we cannot sound,
as the renewed sun climbs from night's abysses
after being bathed in oceans most profound?
—O vows and perfumes! Oh, those infinite kisses!   30

MATTHEW ARNOLD

The Scholar-Gypsy

Go, for they call you, shepherd, from the hill;
  Go, shepherd, and untie the wattled cotes!
    No longer leave thy wistful flock unfed,
    Nor let thy bawling fellows rack their throats,
    Nor the cropped herbage shoot another head.
      But when the fields are still,
  And the tired men and dogs all gone to rest,
    And only the white sheep are sometimes seen
    Cross and recross the strips of moon-blanched green,
  Come, shepherd, and again begin the quest!   10

Here, where the reaper was at work of late—
  In this high field's dark corner, where he leaves
    His coat, his basket, and his earthen cruse,
  And in the sun all morning binds the sheaves,
    Then here, at noon, comes back his stores to use—
      Here will I sit and wait,

While to my ear from uplands far away
    The bleating of the folded flocks is borne,
        With distant cries of reapers in the corn—
    All the live murmur of a summer's day.   20

Screened is this nook o'er the high, half-reaped field,
    And here till sun-down, shepherd! will I be.
        Through the thick corn the scarlet poppies peep,
        And round green roots and yellowing stalks I see
            Pale pink convolvulus in tendrils creep;
                And air-swept lindens yield
    Their scent, and rustle down their perfumed showers
        Of bloom on the bent grass where I am laid,
        And bower me from the August sun with shade;
    And the eye travels down to Oxford's towers.   30

And near me on the grass lies Glanvil's book—
    Come, let me read the oft-read tale again!
        The story of the Oxford scholar poor,
        Of pregnant parts and quick inventive brain,
            Who, tired of knocking at preferment's door,
                One summer-morn forsook
    His friends, and went to learn the gypsy-lore,
        And roamed the world with that wild brotherhood,
        And came, as most men deemed, to little good,
    But came to Oxford and his friends no more.   40

But once, years after, in the country-lanes,
    Two scholars, whom at college erst he knew,
        Met him, and of his way of life inquired;
        Whereat he answered that the gypsy-crew,
            His mates, had arts to rule as they desired
                The workings of men's brains,
    And they can bind them to what thoughts they will.
        "And I," he said, "the secret of their art,
        When fully learned, will to the world impart;
    But it needs heaven-sent moments for this skill."   50

This said, he left them, and returned no more.—
    But rumors hung about the country-side,
        That the lost scholar long was seen to stray,
        Seen by rare glimpses, pensive and tongue-tied,
            In hat of antique shape, and cloak of gray,
                The same the gypsies wore.
    Shepherds had met him on the Hurst in spring;

At some lone alehouse in the Berkshire moors,
  On the warm ingle-bench, the smock-frocked boors
Had found him seated at their entering.   60

But, 'mid their drink and clatter, he would fly.
And I myself seem half to know thy looks,
  And put the shepherds, wanderer! on thy trace;
And boys who in lone wheatfields scare the rooks
  I ask if thou hast passed their quiet place;
    Or in my boat I lie
Moored to the cool bank in the summer-heats,
  'Mid wide grass meadows which the sunshine fills,
  And watch the warm, green-muffled Cumner hills,
And wonder if thou haunt'st their shy retreats.   70

For most, I know, thou lov'st retired ground!
  Thee at the ferry Oxford riders blithe,
    Returning home on summer-nights, have met
Crossing the stripling Thames at Bab-lock-hithe,
    Trailing in the cool stream thy fingers wet,
      As the punt's rope chops round;
And leaning backward in a pensive dream,
    And fostering in thy lap a heap of flowers
    Plucked in shy fields and distant Wychwood bowers,
And thine eyes resting on the moonlit stream.   80

And then they land, and thou art seen no more!—
  Maidens, who from the distant hamlets come
    To dance around the Fyfield elm in May,
Oft through the darkening fields have seen thee roam,
    Or cross a stile into the public way.
      Oft thou hast given them store
Of flowers—the frail-leafed, white anemone,
    Dark bluebells drenched with dews of summer eves.
    And purple orchises with spotted leaves—
But none hath words she can report of thee.   90

And, above Godstow Bridge, when hay-time's here
  In June, and many a scythe in sunshine flames,
    Men who through those wide fields of breezy grass
Where black-winged swallows haunt the glittering Thames,
    To bathe in the abandoned lasher pass,
      Have often passed thee near
Sitting upon the river bank o'ergrown;
    Marked thine outlandish garb, thy figure spare,

Thy dark vague eyes, and soft abstracted air—
But, when they came from bathing, thou wast gone!   100

At some lone homestead in the Cumner hills,
   Where at her open door the housewife darns,
     Thou hast been seen, or hanging on a gate
To watch the threshers in the mossy barns.
     Children, who early range these slopes and late
       For cresses from the rills,
   Have known thee eying, all an April-day,
     The springing pastures and the feeding kine;
     And marked thee, when the stars come out and shine,
Through the long dewy grass move slow away.   110

In autumn, on the skirts of Bagley Wood—
   Where most the gypsies by the turf-edged way
     Pitch their smoked tents, and every bush you see
With scarlet patches tagged and shreds of gray,
     Above the forest-ground called Thessaly—
       The blackbird, picking food,
   Sees thee, nor stops his meal, nor fears at all;
     So often has he known thee past him stray,
     Rapt, twirling in thy hand a withered spray,
And waiting for the spark from heaven to fall.   120

And once, in winter, on the causeway chill
   Where home through flooded fields foot-travelers go,
     Have I not passed thee on the wooden bridge,
Wrapped in thy cloak and battling with the snow,
     Thy face tow'rd Hinksey and its wintry ridge?
       And thou hast climbed the hill,
   And gained the white brow of the Cumner range;
     Turned once to watch, while thick the snowflakes fall,
     The line of festal light in Christ-Church hall—
Then sought thy straw in some sequestered grange.   130

But what—I dream! Two hundred years are flown
   Since first thy story ran through Oxford halls,
     And the grave Glanvil did the tale inscribe
That thou wert wandered from the studious walls
     To learn strange arts, and join a gypsy tribe;
       And thou from earth art gone
   Long since, and in some quiet churchyard laid—
     Some country-nook, where o'er thy unknown grave
     Tall grasses and white flowering nettles wave,
Under a dark, red-fruited yew-tree's shade.   140

For what wears out the life of mortal men?
—No, no, thou hast not felt the lapse of hours!
'Tis that from change to change their being rolls;
'Tis that repeated shocks, again, again,
  Exhaust the energy of strongest souls
    And numb the elastic powers,
Till having used our nerves with bliss and teen,
  And tired upon a thousand schemes our wit,
  To the just-pausing Genius we remit
Our worn-out life, and are—what we have been.   150

Thou hast not lived, why should'st thou perish, so?
  Thou hadst *one* aim, *one* business, *one* desire;
    Else wert thou long since numbered with the dead!
  Else hadst thou spent, like other men, thy fire!
    The generations of thy peers are fled,
      And we ourselves shall go;
  But thou possessest an immortal lot,
    And we imagine thee exempt from age
    And living as thou liv'st on Glanvil's page,
  Because thou hadst—what we, alas! have not.   160

For early didst thou leave the world, with powers
  Fresh, undiverted to the world without,
    Firm to their mark, not spent on other things;
  Free from the sick fatigue, the languid doubt,
    Which much to have tried, in much been baffled, brings.
      O life unlike to ours!
  Who fluctuate idly without term or scope,
    Of whom each strives, nor knows for what he strives,
    And each half lives a hundred different lives;
  Who wait like thee, but not, like thee, in hope.   170

Thou waitest for the spark from heaven! and we,
  Light half-believers of our casual creeds,
    Who never deeply felt, nor clearly willed,
  Whose insight never has borne fruit in deeds,
    Whose vague resolves never have been fulfilled;
      For whom each year we see
  Breeds new beginnings, disappointments new;
    Who hesitate and falter life away,
    And lose tomorrow the ground won today—
  Ah! do not we, wanderer! await it too?   180

Yes, we await it!—but it still delays,
  And then we suffer! and amongst us one,

Who most hast suffered, takes dejectedly
His seat upon the intellectual throne;
  And all his store of sad experience he
    Lays bare of wretched days;
Tells us his misery's birth and growth and signs,
  And how the dying spark of hope was fed,
  And how the breast was soothed, and how the head,
And all his hourly varied anodynes.   190

This for our wisest! and we others pine,
  And wish the long unhappy dream would end,
    And waive all claim to bliss, and try to bear;
  With close-lipped patience for our only friend,
    Sad patience, too near neighbor to despair—
      But none has hope like thine!
Thou through the fields and through the woods dost stray,
  Roaming the country-side, a truant boy,
  Nursing thy project in unclouded joy,
And every doubt long blown by time away.   200

O born in days when wits were fresh and clear,
  And life ran gayly as the sparkling Thames;
    Before this strange disease of modern life,
  With its sick hurry, its divided aims,
    Its head o'ertaxed, its palsied hearts, was rife—
      Fly hence, our contact fear!
Still fly, plunge deeper in the bowering wood!
  Averse, as Dido did with gesture stern
  From her false friend's approach in Hades turn,
Wave us away, and keep thy solitude!   210

Still nursing the unconquerable hope,
  Still clutching the inviolable shade,
    With a free, onward impulse brushing through,
  By night, the silvered branches of the glade—
    Far on the forest-skirts, where none pursue,
      On some mild pastoral slope
Emerge, and resting on the moonlit pales
  Freshen thy flowers as in former years
  With dew, or listen with enchanted ears,
From the dark dingles, to the nightingales!   220

But fly our paths, our feverish contact fly!
  For strong the infection of our mental strife,
    Which, though it gives no bliss, yet spoils for rest;

And we should win thee from thy own fair life,
  Like us distracted, and like us unblest.
    Soon, soon thy cheer would die,
Thy hopes grow timorous, and unfixed thy powers,
  And thy clear aims be cross and shifting made;
  And then thy glad perennial youth would fade,
Fade, and grow old at last, and die like ours. 230

Then fly our greetings, fly our speech and smiles!
  —As some grave Tyrian trader, from the sea,
    Descried at sunrise an emerging prow
Lifting the cool-haired creepers stealthily,
    The fringes of a southward-facing brow
      Among the Ægæan isles;
And saw the merry Grecian coaster come,
  Freighted with amber grapes, and Chian wine,
  Green, bursting figs, and tunnies steeped in brine—
And knew the intruders on his ancient home. 240

The young light-hearted masters of the waves—
  And snatched his rudder, and shook out more sail;
    And day and night held on indignantly
O'er the blue Midland waters with the gale,
    Betwixt the Syrtes and soft Sicily,
      To where the Atlantic raves
Outside the western straits; and unbent sails
  There, where down cloudy cliffs, through sheets of foam,
  Shy traffickers, the dark Iberians come;
And on the beach undid his corded bales. 250

EMILY DICKINSON

I Felt a Funeral in My Brain[1]

I felt a funeral in my brain,
And mourners, to and fro,
Kept treading, treading, till it seemed
That sense was breaking through.

[1] The text is that of *The Poems of Emily Dickinson*, edited by Thomas H. John-son, but the punctuation is derived from earlier editions. Reprinted by permission of the publishers from *The Poems of Emily Dickinson*, edited by Thomas H. John-son (Cambridge, Mass.: The Belknap Press of Harvard University Press). Copy-right 1951, 1955, by the President and Fellows of Harvard College.

And when they all were seated,
A service like a drum
Kept beating, beating, till I thought
My mind was going numb.

And then I heard them lift a box,
And creak across my soul   10
With those same boots of lead, again.
Then space began to toll

As all the heavens were a bell,
And Being but an ear,
And I and silence some strange race,
Wrecked, solitary, here.

And then a plank in reason broke,
And I dropped down and down
And hit a world at every plunge
And finished knowing, then.   20

Reverse Cannot Befall [1]

Reverse cannot befall
That fine Prosperity
Whose Sources are interior.
As soon, Adversity

A Diamond overtake
In far Bolivian Ground.
Misfortune hath no implement
Could mar it, if it found.

CHARLES R. ANDERSON

On Dickinson's "Reverse Cannot Befall" [2]

The temptation to find parallels between Emily Dickinson and Emerson are
particularly strong in the matter of self-reliance, but it can lead to serious misunderstanding of her meanings. Though she was deeply concerned with the

[1] From *The Complete Poems of Emily Dickinson*. Copyright 1914, 1942 by
Martha Dickinson Bianchi, by permission of Little, Brown and Company, and
the President and Fellows of Harvard College.
[2] From *The Explicator*, XVIII (May, 1960), 46. Reprinted by permission of the
author and of the Editors of *The Explicator*.

problem, she never tried to make it into a philosophical doctrine. Instead, she made a fine poem out of the idea. The paired abstractions, "Prosperity" and "Adversity," are made concrete in the diamond mines of Bolivia and the chances of their being overtaken by reverses. For a contemporary reader these words would have set up ironic references to the financial panic of 1857 from which the country had not yet recovered at the time this poem was written, a few years later. But the prosperity she is advocating is clearly spiritual, for its "Sources are interior."

This is a far cry from the self-reliance of the Transcendentalists, however, which was based on the doctrine of indwelling spirit that enables man to rely on his own divinity. It is when Emerson dropped the terminology of mysticism for the sharper language of the stoic—as in the essay on "Self-Reliance" (Trust thyself: every heart vibrates to that iron string)—that he seems nearest to Dickinson. She recognized this particular kinship when presenting a friend with a volume of his prose, saying: "I am bringing a little Granite Book you can lean upon." She uses the same New England referent for self-reliance, "That Granitic Base," in a poem beginning "On a Columnar Self—/How ample to rely." But she explicitly discriminates it from reliance on any god within:

> Suffice Us—for a Crowd—
> Ourself—and Rectitude—
> And that Assembly—not far off
> From furthest Spirit—God—

The self is its own Rock of Ages. God is not immanent spirit but an "Assembly," or, as a variant line reads, "That Companion—not far off." How far off? and how helpful a companion? She does not say, for this is hardly an orthodox concept of deity either. She was no more Calvinist than she was Transcendentalist in her belief about the relation between man and God.

In the principal poem under consideration the very hardness of her image, "A Diamond," suggests a discipline of mind and will rather than any vague reliance on the infallibility of the intuition for finding the god within. "Diamond" is also a brilliant image for the soul, crystal pure, of dazzling white light, and small enough in this context for the invisible; for if the body is to the soul as a Bolivian mountain to a diamond, then the soul approaches the vanishing point. (Her slip of "Bolivian" for "Brazilian," probably caused by her fascination with the spectacular silver mines of Potosi, is irrelevant.) But this is a very secular image for the soul, and there is no oversoul for it to gain strength from. This is a single gem that stands alone, gaining its compactness and indestructibility from resistance to the vast pressures of the earth. It is her metaphor for the integrated self that, hidden deep within, will endure; even if found out by misfortune, no instrument of this world's pain and suffering can "mar" it. Such is a man's interior jewel, and "Reverse cannot befall" him who possesses it.

'Twas Like a Maelstrom[1]

'Twas like a maelstrom, with a notch,
That nearer every day
Kept narrowing its boiling wheel
Until the agony

Toyed coolly with the final inch
Of your delirious hem,
And you dropped, lost, when something broke
And let you from a dream;

As if a goblin with a gauge
Kept measuring the hours,   10
Until you felt your second
Weigh helpless in his paws,

And not a sinew, stirred, could help,
And sense was getting numb,
When God remembered, and the fiend
Let go then, overcome;

As if your sentence stood pronounced,
And you were frozen led
From dungeon's luxury of doubt
To gibbets and the dead;   20

And when the film had stitched your eyes,
A creature gasped "Reprieve!"
Which anguish was the utterest then,
To perish, or to live?

A Solemn Thing Within the Soul

A solemn thing within the soul
To feel itself get ripe
And golden hang, while farther up

The Maker's ladders stop,
And in the orchard far below
You hear a being drop;

A wonderful, to feel the sun
Still toiling at the cheek
You thought was finished;
Cool of eye, and critical of work,
He shifts the stem a little
To give your core a look;

But solemnest to know
Your chance in harvest moves
A little nearer; every sun
The single, to some lives.

Because I Could Not Stop for Death

Because I could not stop for Death,
He kindly stopped for me;
The carriage held but just ourselves
And Immortality.

We slowly drove, he knew no haste,
And I had put away
My labor and my leisure too,
For his civility.

We passed the school where children strove
At recess in a ring;
We passed the fields of gazing grain,
We passed the setting sun—

10

Or rather he passed us;
The dews drew quivering and chill,
For only gossamer my gown,
My tippet only tulle.

We paused before a house that seemed
A swelling of the ground;
The roof was scarcely visible,
The cornice in the ground.

20

Since then, 'tis centuries; and yet
Feels shorter than the day
I first surmised the horses' heads
Were toward eternity.

THOMAS HARDY

The Darkling Thrush[1]

I leant upon a coppice gate
    When Frost was specter-gray,
And Winter's dregs made desolate
    The weakening eye of day.
The tangled bine-stems scored the sky
    Like strings of broken lyres,
And all mankind that haunted nigh
    Had sought their household fires.

The land's sharp features seemed to be
    The Century's corpse outleant,   10
His crypt the cloudy canopy,
    The wind his death-lament.
The ancient pulse of germ and birth
    Was shrunken hard and dry,
And every spirit upon earth
    Seemed fervorless as I.

At once a voice arose among
    The bleak twigs overhead
In a full-hearted evensong
    Of joy illimited;   20
An aged thrush, frail, gaunt, and small,
    In blast-beruffled plume,
Had chosen thus to fling his soul
    Upon the growing gloom.

So little cause for carolings
    Of such ecstatic sound
Was written on terrestrial things

Afar or nigh around,
That I could think there trembled through
His happy good-night air
Some blessed Hope, whereof he knew
And I was unaware.

Drummer Hodge[1]

They throw in Drummer Hodge to rest
Uncoffined—just as found:
His landmark is a kopje-crest
That breaks the veldt around;
And foreign constellations west
Each night above his mound.

Young Hodge the Drummer never knew—
Fresh from his Wessex home—
The meaning of the broad Karoo,
The Bush, the dusty loam,
And why uprose to nightly view
Strange stars amid the gloam.

Yet portion of that unknown plain
Will Hodge forever be;
His homely Northern breast and brain
Grow to some Southern tree,
And strange-eyed constellations reign
His stars eternally.

The Convergence of the Twain[2]

Lines on the Loss of the "Titanic"

I

In a solitude of the sea
Deep from human vanity,
And the Pride of Life that planned her, stilly couches she.

[1] From *Collected Poems by Thomas Hardy*. Copyright 1925 by The Macmillan Company and used with their permission.
[2] From *The Collected Poems of Thomas Hardy*. Copyright, 1925, The Macmillan Company. Reprinted by permission of The Macmillan Company; the trustees of the Hardy estate; Macmillan & Co., Ltd., London; and The Macmillan Company of Canada, Limited.

II

Steel chambers, late the pyres
Of her salamandrine fires,
Cold currents thrid, and turn to rhythmic tidal lyres.

III

Over the mirrors meant
To glass the opulent
The sea-worm crawls—grotesque, slimed, dumb, indifferent.

IV

Jewels in joy designed
To ravish the sensuous mind
Lie lightless, all their sparkles bleared and black and blind.

V

Dim moon-eyed fishes near
Gaze at the gilded gear
And query: "What does this vaingloriousness down here?"

VI

Well: while was fashioning
This creature of cleaving wing,
The Immanent Will that stirs and urges everything

VII

Prepared a sinister mate
For her—so gaily great
A Shape of Ice, for the time far and dissociate.

VIII

And as the smart ship grew
In stature, grace, and hue,
In shadowy silent distance grew the Iceberg too.

IX

Alien they seemed to be;
No mortal eye could see
The intimate welding of their later history,

X

Or sign that they were bent
By paths coincident
On being anon twin halves of one august event,

XI

Till the Spinner of the Years
  Said "Now!" And each one hears,
And consummation comes, and jars two hemispheres.

GERARD MANLEY HOPKINS[1]

God's Grandeur

The world is charged with the grandeur of God.
  It will flame out, like shining from shook foil;
  It gathers to a greatness, like the ooze of oil
Crushed. Why do men then now not reck his rod?

Generations have trod, have trod, have trod;
  And all is seared with trade; bleared, smeared with toil;
  And wears man's smudge and shares man's smell: the soil
Is bare now, nor can foot feel, being shod.

And for all this, nature is never spent;
  There lives the dearest freshness deep down things;
And though the last lights off the black West went
  Oh, morning, at the brown brink eastward, springs—
Because the Holy Ghost over the bent
  World broods with warm breast and with ah! bright wings.

The Windhover

TO CHRIST OUR LORD

  I caught this morning morning's minion, king-
    dom of daylight's dauphin, dapple-dawn-drawn Falcon, in his riding
  Of the rolling level underneath him steady air, and striding
High there, how he rung upon the rein of a wimpling wing
In his ecstasy! then off, off forth on swing,
  As a skate's heel sweeps smooth on a bow-bend: the hurl and gliding
  Rebuffed the big wind. My heart in hiding
Stirred for a bird,—the achieve of, the mastery of the thing!

1 From *Poems of Gerard Manley Hopkins*. By permission of the Oxford University Press, London, publishers.

Brute beauty and valor and act, oh, air, pride, plume, here
    Buckle! AND the fire that breaks from thee then, a billion
Times told lovelier, more dangerous, O my chevalier!

    No wonder of it: shéer plód makes plow down sillion
Shine, and blue-bleak embers, ah my dear,
    Fall, gall themselves, and gash gold-vermilion.

ELISABETH SCHNEIDER

On Hopkins' "The Windhover" [1]

On "The Windhover" I am disposed to be dogmatic. The poem conveys one
direct meaning, and only one in which all the parts of the poem and all the
images find a place. Belt buckles and buckles in armor are not part of it; they
belong to some other poem, "in another country." Hopkins willingly employed
puns when double meaning might be "to one thing wrought" but not when two
meanings fractured a poem. The instinct of critics to hover around the word
buckle is nevertheless sound, for that word is the structural center, the pivot on
which the sonnet turns.

Something buckles and something breaks through. Readers who buckle belts
neglect the second half of this statement, though Hopkins capitalized the AND
between the parts. It will not do to take *buckle* as an imperative either, as many
writers do, for that leaves AND hanging loose and destroys the sentence. It is
neither armor nor belt, nor Mr. Empson's bicycle wheel, that buckles or breaks;
the pivotal image is of a higher order of magnitude. Deck or bulkheads of a
ship buckle before fire breaks through; walls of a building buckle before they
crash or burn. In "The Windhover" the whole material world buckles, "AND
the fire" of the spiritual world—or Christ—"breaks" through. *Buckle* and
break control the sestet as it subsides from the climax of spiritual illumination
to the everyday imagery of the conclusion.

"The Windhover" is one of several variations on a theme that occupied
Hopkins in 1877. Other sonnets, particularly "The Starlight Night" and
"Spring," display the same pattern of thought: a progression from the concrete beauty of nature described in the octave, to its spiritual meaning or
analogue in the sestet. As is so often true in Hopkins, the plan is simple and
straightforward; only the execution is complex.

"The Windhover" is addressed "To Christ Our Lord," and though Christ
is not mentioned till the tenth line, He is prepared for in the first by epithets
given to the falcon—morning's favorite (minion), "kingdom of daylight's"

[1] From *The Explicator*, XVIII (January, 1960), 22. Reprinted by permission of
the author and of the Editors of *The Explicator*.

crown prince—the Son, not the King or Father. *Dauphin* is more than an automatic bit of alliteration; it counts for the meaning and for unity. The falcon
is an analogue, however, not a symbol of Christ. Though the power and beauty
of its flight make it prince of the morning scene, it is not more than a bird,
and it is described throughout the octave in the language of the material world.
But the sight of it awakens the poet: "My heart [which had been] in hiding
stirred." Beneath the word *hiding* I hear *hibernating*, but that may be an accidental personal association; at any rate, the poet's heart had been stagnant and
perhaps reluctant to be moved (cf. *Letters* I, 66). Its awakening preludes the
turn of the sonnet.

In the ninth line, the particularities of bird and morning are drained away,
leaving abstractions and universals to represent the power and beauty in nature.
This material world, so abstracted—"brute beauty and valour and act, oh, air,
pride, plume"—"here [at this point, now] buckle[s]," and as it collapses before
the poet's vision, the fire of Christ "breaks" through, "a billion times" more
lovely and more dangerous. Only now does the poet address Christ directly:
"the fire that breaks from thee then . . . O my chevalier." The image in
Hopkins' mind probably derives from the crackling of timbers or plates in a
fire at sea, a kind of disaster with which his father was professionally concerned
and which from time to time furnished Hopkins himself, landsman though
he was, with a surprising quantity of imagery. Such an image gives double
significance to the epithet *dangerous*, applied immediately afterwards to Christ.
From this point on, tension relaxes and the pitch drops to a quiet conclusion
with the imagery remaining under the shadow of *buckle* and *break*. "No wonder" this transformation occurs, Hopkins says, when the *breaking open* of the
most drab things in life may reveal brightness within. Mere labor of plowing
breaks open the earth and transforms dull clod into shining furrow ("the near
hill glistening with very bright newly turned sods," he noted in his journal);
and "blue-bleak" coals of an apparently dead fire fall and break apart to show
bright living fire within.

In the outline of its thought, then, "The Windhover" is simple and strict.
Its complexities lie, on the one hand, in the elaboration of the visual imagery
interwoven with elaborately echoing patterns of sound, and, on the other, in
the play between two counterpointed sets of opposites. The first is the opposition of the material and the spiritual which mark the two parts of the sonnet
and are expressly brought together by the dauphin-Son parallel and more essentially by the primary theme of the poet's being stirred by one into more intense
awareness of the other. The second pair of opposites appear in more shadowy
form. The opposition of beauty and terror (or pain), present in so much of
Hopkins' writing, runs through the poem without any reconciling of the two,
though they are brought together in an uneasy harmony through the idea of
power in the "mastery" of the bird and the "lovelier, more dangerous" fire of
Christ. These opposites, however, are not evenly balanced in the poem: the
terror or pain is no more than an undertone, reflected in one epithet of Christ,
in the "gall" and "gash" of the close, possibly in the predatory character as well

as the daring of the hawk and in the poet's "hiding" heart. The unresolved suggestions of terror and pain give an edge to the overriding spirit of breathless admiration.

These complexities are enough. Richness of symbolic meaning cannot be had merely by reading into the poem a mechanical, dictionary-flavored ambiguity in *buckle*. For the interpretation of "The Windhover" at least, an inveterate commitment to irony and paradox is apt to defeat itself by producing only disjointed structure and discordant associations that destroy, by neutralizing, the resonance of the poem. Quite a good deal of the resonance of "The Windhover" comes from simplicity of theme, clarity of structure, and directness of movement. This is true even though the final effect is of an extremely complex poem.

Pied Beauty

Glory be to God for dappled things—
    For skies of couple-color as a brinded cow;
      For rose-moles all in stipple upon trout that swim;
Fresh-firecoal chestnut-falls; finches' wings;
    Landscape plotted and pieced—fold, fallow, and plow;
      And áll trádes, their gear and tackle and trim.

All things counter, original, spare, strange;
    Whatever is fickle, freckled (who knows how?)
      With swift, slow; sweet, sour; adazzle, dim;
He fathers-forth whose beauty is past change:
      Praise him.

I Wake and Feel the Fell of Dark

I wake and feel the fell of dark, not day.
What hours, O what black hoùrs we have spent
This night! what sights you, heart, saw; ways you went!
And more must, in yet longer light's delay.
    With witness I speak this. But where I say
Hours I mean years, mean life. And my lament
Is cries countless, cries like dead letters sent
To dearest him that lives alas! away.

    I am gall, I am heartburn. God's most deep decree
Bitter would have me taste: my taste was me;
Bones built in me, flesh filled, blood brimmed the curse.
Selfyeast of spirit a dull dough sours. I see

The lost are like this, and their scourge to be
As I am mine, their sweating selves; but worse.

A. E. HOUSMAN

Be Still, My Soul, Be Still [1]

Be still, my soul, be still; the arms you bear are brittle,
  Earth and high heaven are fixt of old and founded strong.
Think rather,—call to thought, if now you grieve a little,
  The days when we had rest, O soul, for they were long.

Men loved unkindness then, but lightless in the quarry
  I slept and saw not; tears fell down, I did not mourn;
Sweat ran and blood sprang out and I was never sorry:
  Then it was well with me, in days ere I was born.

Now, and I muse for why and never find the reason,
  I pace the earth, and drink the air, and feel the sun.
Be still, be still, my soul; it is but for a season:
  Let us endure an hour and see injustice done.

Ay, look: high heaven and earth ail from the prime foundation;
  All thoughts to rive the heart are here, and all are vain:
Horror and scorn and hate and fear and indignation—
  Oh why did I awake? when shall I sleep again?

Loveliest of Trees [1]

Loveliest of trees, the cherry now
Is hung with bloom along the bough,
And stands about the woodland ride
Wearing white for Eastertide.

Now, of my threescore years and ten,
Twenty will not come again,

And take from seventy springs a score,
It only leaves me fifty more.

And since to look at things in bloom
Fifty springs are little room,
About the woodlands I will go
To see the cherry hung with snow.

On Wenlock Edge[1]

On Wenlock Edge the wood's in trouble;
His forest fleece the Wrekin heaves;
The gale, it plies the saplings double,
And thick on Severn snow the leaves.

'Twould blow like this through holt and hanger
When Uricon the city stood:
'Tis the old wind in the old anger,
But then it threshed another wood.

Then, 'twas before my time, the Roman
At yonder heaving hill would stare: 10
The blood that warms an English yeoman,
The thoughts that hurt him, they were there.

There, like the wind through woods in riot,
Through him the gale of life blew high;
The tree of man was never quiet:
Then 'twas the Roman, now 'tis I.

The gale, it plies the saplings double,
It blows so hard, 'twill soon be gone:
To-day the Roman and his trouble
Are ashes under Uricon.   20

Terence, This Is Stupid Stuff[1]

"Terence, this is stupid stuff:
You eat your victuals fast enough;
There can't be much amiss, 'tis clear,

[1] From *The Collected Poems of A. E. Housman.* Copyright, 1940, by Holt, Rinehart and Winston, Inc. By permission of the publishers.

To see the rate you drink your beer.
But oh, good Lord, the verse you make,
It gives a chap the belly-ache.
The cow, the old cow, she is dead;
It sleeps well, the hornèd head:
We poor lads, 'tis our turn now
To hear such tunes as killed the cow.   10
Pretty friendship 'tis to rhyme
Your friends to death before their time
Moping melancholy mad:
Come, pipe a tune to dance to, lad."

  Why, if 'tis dancing you would be,
There's brisker pipes than poetry.
Say, for what were hop-yards meant,
Or why was Burton built on Trent?
Oh, many a peer of England brews
Livelier liquor than the Muse,   20
And malt does more than Milton can
To justify God's ways to man.
Ale, man, ale's the stuff to drink
For fellows whom it hurts to think:
Look into the pewter pot
To see the world as the world's not.
And faith, 'tis pleasant till 'tis past:
The mischief is that 'twill not last.
Oh, I have been to Ludlow fair
And left my necktie God knows where,   30
And carried half-way home, or near,
Pints and quarts of Ludlow beer:
Then the world seemed none so bad,
And I myself a sterling lad;
And down in lovely muck I've lain,
Happy till I woke again.
Then I saw the morning sky:
Heigho, the tale was all a lie;
The world, it was the old world yet,
I was I, my things were wet,   40
And nothing now remained to do
But begin the game anew.

  Therefore, since the world has still
Much good, but much less good than ill,
And while the sun and moon endure
Luck's a chance, but trouble's sure,

I'd face it as a wise man would,
And train for ill and not for good.
'Tis true, the stuff I bring for sale
Is not so brisk a brew as ale: 50
Out of a stem that scored the hand
I wrung it in a weary land.
But take it: if the smack is sour,
The better for the embittered hour;
It should do good to heart and head
When your soul is in my soul's stead;
And I will friend you, if I may,
In the dark and cloudy day.

There was a king reigned in the East:
There, when kings will sit to feast,   60
They get their fill before they think
With poisoned meat and poisoned drink.
He gathered all that springs to birth
From the many-venomed earth;
First a little, thence to more,
He sampled all her killing store;
And easy, smiling, seasoned sound,
Sate the king when healths went round.
They put arsenic in his meat
And stared aghast to watch him eat;   70
They poured strychnine in his cup
And shook to see him drink it up:
They shook, they stared as white's their shirt:
Them it was their poison hurt.
—I tell the tale that I heard told.
Mithridates, he died old.

WILLIAM BUTLER YEATS

A Prayer for My Daughter[1]

Once more the storm is howling, and half hid
Under this cradle-hood and coverlid
My child sleeps on. There is no obstacle

[1] From *The Collected Poems of W. B. Yeats.* Copyright, 1933. By permission of
The Macmillan Company, publishers.

But Gregory's wood and one bare hill
Whereby the haystack- and roof-levelling wind,
Bred on the Atlantic, can be stayed;
And for an hour I have walked and prayed
Because of the great gloom that is in my mind.

I have walked and prayed for this young child an hour
And heard the sea-wind scream upon the tower,   10
And under the arches of the bridge, and scream
In the elms above the flooded stream;
Imagining in excited reverie
That the future years had come,
Dancing to a frenzied drum,
Out of the murderous innocence of the sea.

May she be granted beauty and yet not
Beauty to make a stranger's eye distraught,
Or hers before a looking-glass for such,
Being made beautiful overmuch,   20
Consider beauty a sufficient end,
Lose natural kindness and maybe
The heart-revealing intimacy
That chooses right, and never find a friend.

Helen being chosen found life flat and dull
And later had much trouble from a fool,
While that great Queen, that rose out of the spray,
Being fatherless could have her way
Yet chose a bandy-leggèd smith for man.
It's certain that fine women eat   30
A crazy salad with their meat
Whereby the Horn of Plenty is undone.

In courtesy I'd have her chiefly learned;
Hearts are not had as a gift but hearts are earned
By those that are not entirely beautiful;
Yet many, that have played the fool
For beauty's very self, has charm made wise,
And many a poor man that has roved,
Loved and thought himself beloved,
From a glad kindness cannot take his eyes.   40

May she become a flourishing hidden tree
That all her thoughts may like the linnet be,

And have no business but dispensing round
Their magnanimities of sound.
Nor but in merriment begin a chase,
Nor but in merriment a quarrel.
O may she live like some green laurel
Rooted in one dear perpetual place.

My mind, because the minds that I have loved,
The sort of beauty that I have approved,   50
Prosper but little, has dried up of late,
Yet knows that to be choked with hate
May well be of all evil chances chief.
If there's no hatred in a mind
Assault and battery of the wind
Can never tear the linnet from the leaf.

An intellectual hatred is the worst,
So let her think opinions are accursed.
Have I not seen the loveliest woman born
Out of the mouth of Plenty's horn,   60
Because of her opinionated mind
Barter that horn and every good
By quiet natures understood
For an old bellows full of angry wind?

Considering that, all hatred driven hence,
The soul recovers radical innocence
And learns at last that it is self-delighting,
Self-appeasing, self-affrighting,
And that its own sweet will is Heaven's will;
She can, though every face should scowl   70
And every windy quarter howl
Of every bellows burst, be happy still.

And may her bridegroom bring her to a house
Where all's accustomed, ceremonious;
For arrogance and hatred are the wares
Peddled in the thoroughfares.
How but in custom and in ceremony
Are innocence and beauty born?
Ceremony's name for the rich horn,
And custom for the spreading laurel tree.   80

Sailing to Byzantium[1]

That is no country for old men. The young
In one another's arms, birds in the trees,
—Those dying generations—at their song,
The salmon-falls, the mackerel-crowded seas,
Fish, flesh, or fowl, commend all summer long
Whatever is begotten, born, and dies.
Caught in that sensual music all neglect
Monuments of unaging intellect.

An aged man is but a paltry thing,
A tattered coat upon a stick, unless   10
Soul clap its hands and sing, and louder sing
For every tatter in its mortal dress,
Nor is there singing school but studying
Monuments of its own magnificence;
And therefore I have sailed the seas and come
To the holy city of Byzantium.

O sages standing in God's holy fire
As in the gold mosaic of a wall,
Come from the holy fire, perne in a gyre,
And be the singing-masters of my soul.   20
Consume my heart away, sick with desire
And fastened to a dying animal
It knows not what it is; and gather me
Into the artifice of eternity.

Once out of nature I shall never take
My bodily form from any natural thing.
But such a form as Grecian goldsmiths make
Of hammered gold and gold enamelling
To keep a drowsy Emperor awake;
Or set upon a golden bough to sing   30
To lords and ladies of Byzantium
Of what is past, or passing, or to come.

[1] From *The Collected Poems of W. B. Yeats*. Copyright, 1933. By permission of
The Macmillan Company, publishers.

Byzantium[1]

The unpurged images of day recede;
The Emperor's drunken soldiery are abed;
Night resonance recedes, night-walkers' song
After great cathedral gong;
A starlit or a moonlit dome disdains
All that man is,
All mere complexities,
The fury and the mire of human veins.

Before me floats an image, man or shade,
Shade more than man, more image than a shade;   10
For Hades' bobbin bound in mummy-cloth
May unwind the winding path;
A mouth that has no moisture and no breath
Breathless mouths may summon;
I hail the superhuman;
I call it death-in-life and life-in-death.

Miracle, bird or golden handiwork,
More miracle than bird or handiwork,
Planted on the star-lit golden bough,
Can like the cocks of Hades crow,   20
Or, by the moon embittered, scorn aloud
In glory of changeless metal
Common bird or petal
And all complexities of mire or blood.

At midnight on the Emperor's pavement flit
Flames that no faggot feeds, nor steel has lit,
Nor storm disturbs, flames begotten of flame,
Where blood-begotten spirits come
And all complexities of fury leave,
Dying into a dance,   30
An agony of trance,
An agony of flame that cannot singe a sleeve.

Astraddle on the dolphin's mire and blood,
Spirit after spirit! The smithies break the flood,

1 From *The Collected Poems of W. B. Yeats.* Reprinted by permission of Mrs.
Yeats, The Macmillan Company, The Macmillan Company of Canada, Ltd., and
A. P. Watt & Son

> The golden smithies of the Emperor!
> Marbles of the dancing floor
> Break bitter furies of complexity,
> Those images that yet
> Fresh images beget,
> That dolphin-torn, that gong-tormented sea.   40

RICHARD ELLMANN

On Yeats's "Byzantium" [1]

"Byzantium" is a dramatic example of Yeats's handling of the image, and a difficult one. At first the poet appears to distinguish between two meanings of the word. In the beginning stanza, "The unpurged images of day recede." These day-time images, which the poet so immediately dismisses, are apparently the ordinary objects of experience which make up the external world. Only at the end of the poem do we learn that they are made of the same stuff as the night-time images, one of which he now proceeds to invoke:

> Before me floats an image, man or shade,
> Shade more than man, more image than a shade.

Such images seem at first to be far removed from life, since they are identifiable neither with the living man nor his ghostly substitute.

How may the poet grasp these images, as he must do if his poetry is to go below the superficies of day? Yeats answers with two powerful affirmations:

> For Hades' bobbin bound in mummy-cloth
> May unwind the winding path;
> A mouth that has no moisture and no breath
> Breathless mouths may summon. . . .

Hades' bobbin is the soul, which comes from the underworld and eventually returns there until its rebirth. In life it winds up the mummy-cloth of experience, a funereal term used because in the poem life is paradoxically regarded as a surrender of the soul's freedom and therefore as a kind of imprisonment or death. On returning to Hades the soul unwinds the cloth—"the winding path" of nature—like a bobbin unwinding thread. But, says the poet, even during life, at moments of "breathless" inspiration, we escape from ourselves and our past and summon the deathless, lifeless image which "has no moisture and no breath."

[1] From *The Identity of Yeats* (New York: Oxford University Press, 1954), pp. 219-222. Used by permission of Oxford University Press, Inc.

> I hail the superhuman;
> I call it death-in-life and life-in-death.

From the point of view of this life, such images are dead; but from a more detached vantage-point, it is they that are immortal, and the living who have no genuine life.

In the next stanza the poet's eye fastens on another super-human image; by apostrophizing it as "miracle, bird, or golden handiwork," he locates it more precisely in the world of art. He thinks of it as having a bird's shape, and as either crowing like cocks of Hades or scorning other birds and life. Yeats had learned from Eugénie Strong's *Apotheosis and After Life* that the cock, as herald of the sun, became "by an easy transition the herald of rebirth" on Roman tombstones. Since in this poem he accepts reincarnation, he is distinguishing here between the birds that sing the common strain of the continuing cycle of human lives and those that scorn the cycle and sing only of escape from it; here were the two directions of his own art.

There follows a sudden revelation of the process by which such images are hammered out, by the Byzantine smithies of the imagination, into their purest form:

> At midnight on the Emperor's pavement flit
> Flames that no faggot feeds, nor steel has lit,
> Nor storm disturbs, flames begotten of flame,
> Where blood-begotten spirits come
> And all complexities of fury leave,
> Dying into a dance,
> An agony of trance,
> An agony of flame that cannot singe a sleeve.

Begotten by the living, they have to be immortalized by fire. Some aspects of their perfected state are clarified in notes which Yeats made for *A Vision* two years before writing "Byzantium":

> At first we are subject to Destiny . . . but the point in the Zodiac where the whirl becomes a sphere once reached, we may escape from the constraint of our nature and from that of external things, entering upon a state where all fuel has become flame, where there is nothing but the state itself, nothing to constrain it or end it. We attain it always in the creation or enjoyment of a work of art, but that moment though eternal in the Daimon passes from us because it is not an attainment of our whole being. Philosophy has always explained its moment of moments in much the same way; nothing can be added to it, nothing taken away; that all progressions are full of illusion, that everything is born there like a ship in full sail.

By equating the perfection of the afterlife with every metaphysical perfection the philosophers have conceived and with the perfection of art wrought "in nature's spite," Yeats avoids mere estheticism and justifies the description in "Byzantium" which treats the passage of the spirits of the dead to the other world and their purification there as synonymous with the purgative process which a work of art undergoes. These processes are among those which Yeats makes equivalent and symbolical of one another.

But the fires of the imaginations have a characteristic which distinguishes them from the fires of this world: they burn and do not burn. They are all-powerful to purge images of any experiential dross, but impotent to singe a sleeve. In a position of prominence in the poem, the last line of the above stanza, Yeats casts one of the many backward glances in his poetry, directing it here towards the life of action that the spirit or image is transcending. At the very moment that he heralds the purgative process, he reminds us that the purgation can occur only outside action, for there it has no power. The same reflection causes him, at the end of the poem, to express not his admiration for the completed work, as might be expected, but his wonder at the spawning images, covered with the mire of experience, in which the work began:

> Marbles of the dancing-floor
> Break bitter furies of complexity,
> These images that yet
> Fresh images beget,
> That dolphin-torn, that gong-tormented sea

Ecstatic before the perfection of the creative process, the poet still yields a little to the fascination for the imperfect and unpurged images not yet arrived at Byzantium.

Crazy Jane Talks with the Bishop[1]

> I met the Bishop on the road
> And much said he and I.
> 'Those breasts are flat and fallen now,
> Those veins must soon be dry;
> Live in a heavenly mansion,
> Not in some foul sty.'
>
> 'Fair and foul are near of kin,
> And fair needs foul,' I cried.
> 'My friends are gone, but that's a truth
> Nor grave nor bed denied,
> Learned in bodily lowliness
> And in the heart's pride.

[1] From *The Collected Poems of W. B. Yeats.* Copyright 1933 by The Macmillan Company and used with their permission.

'A woman can be proud and stiff
When on love intent;
But Love has pitched his mansion in
The place of excrement;
For nothing can be sole or whole
That has not been rent.'

E. A. ROBINSON

How Annandale Went Out[1]

"They called it Annandale—and I was there
To flourish, to find words, and to attend:
Liar, physician, hypocrite, and friend,
I watched him; and the sight was not so fair
As one or two that I have seen elsewhere:
An apparatus not for me to mend—
A wreck, with hell between him and the end,
Remained of Annandale; and I was there.

"I knew the ruin as I knew the man;
So put the two together, if you can,
Remembering the worst you know of me.
Now view yourself as I was, on the spot—
With a slight kind of engine. Do you see?
Like this . . . You wouldn't hang me? I thought not."

Mr. Flood's Party[2]

Old Eben Flood, climbing alone one night
Over the hill between the town below
And the forsaken upland hermitage
That held as much as he should ever know
On earth again of home, paused warily.
The road was his with not a native near;
And Eben, having leisure, said aloud,
For no man else in Tilbury Town to hear:

[1] Reprinted from *The Town Down the River*. Copyright, 1910, by Charles
Scribner's Sons and reprinted with their permission.
[2] From *Avon's Harvest*. Copyright, 1921, by The Macmillan Company. By permission of The Macmillan Company, publishers.

"Well, Mr. Flood, we have the harvest moon
Again, and we may not have many more;
The bird is on the wing, the poet says,
And you and I have said it here before.
Drink to the bird." He raised up to the light
The jug that he had gone so far to fill,
And answered huskily: "Well, Mr. Flood,
Since you propose it, I believe I will."

Alone, as if enduring to the end
A valiant armor of scarred hopes outworn,
He stood there in the middle of the road
Like Roland's ghost winding a silent horn.
Below him, in the town among the trees,
Where friends of other days had honored him,
A phantom salutation of the dead
Rang thinly till old Eben's eyes were dim.

Then, as a mother lays her sleeping child
Down tenderly, fearing it may awake,
He set the jug down slowly at his feet
With trembling care, knowing that most things break,
And only when assured that on firm earth
It stood, as the uncertain lives of men
Assuredly did not, he paced away,
And with his hand extended paused again:

"Well, Mr. Flood, we have not met like this
In a long time; and many a change has come
To both of us, I fear, since last it was
We had a drop together. Welcome home!"
Convivially returning with himself,
Again he raised the jug up to the light;
And with an acquiescent quaver said:
"Well, Mr. Flood, if you insist, I might.

"Only a very little, Mr. Flood—
For auld lang syne. No more, sir; that will do."
So, for the time, apparently it did,
And Eben evidently thought so too;
For soon amid the silver loneliness
Of night he lifted up his voice and sang,
Secure, with only two moons listening,
Until the whole harmonious landscape rang—

"For auld lang syne." The weary throat gave out,
The last word wavered; and the song being done,   50
He raised again the jug regretfully
And shook his head, and was again alone.
There was not much that was ahead of him,
And there was nothing in the town below—
Where strangers would have shut the many doors
That many friends had opened long ago.

STEPHEN CRANE[1]

War Is Kind

Do not weep, maiden, for war is kind.
Because your lover threw wild hands toward the sky
And the affrighted steed ran on alone,
Do not weep.
War is kind.

Hoarse, booming drums of the regiment,
Little souls who thirst for fight,
These men were born to drill and die.
The unexplained glory flies above them,
Great is the battle-god, great, and his kingdom—   10
A field where a thousand corpses lie.

Do not weep, babe, for war is kind.
Because your father tumbled in the yellow trenches,
Raged at his breast, gulped and died,
Do not weep.
War is kind.

Swift blazing flag of the regiment,
Eagle with crest of red and gold,
These men were born to drill and die.
Point for them the virtue of slaughter,   20
Make plain to them the excellence of killing
And a field where a thousand corpses lie.

Mother whose heart hung humble as a button
On the bright splendid shroud of your son,

1 Reprinted from *Stephen Crane: The Red Badge of Courage and Selected Prose and Poetry*, edited by William M. Gibson, "Rinehart Editions" (New York: Holt, Rinehart and Winston, Inc., 1956).

Do not weep.
War is kind.

Should the Wide World Roll Away

Should the wide world roll away,
Leaving black terror,
Limitless night,
Nor God, nor man, nor place to stand
Would be to me essential
If thou and thy white arms were there,
And the fall to doom a long way.

Well, Then, I Hate Thee

*"And the sins of the fathers shall be visited upon
the heads of the children, even unto the third
and fourth generation of them that hate me."*

Well, then, I hate Thee, unrighteous picture;
Wicked image, I hate Thee;
So, strike with Thy vengeance
The heads of those little men
Who come blindly.
It will be a brave thing.

ROBERT FROST

Reluctance[1]

Out through the fields and the woods
    And over the walls I have wended;
I have climbed the hills of view
    And looked at the world, and descended,
I have come by the highway home,
    And lo, it is ended.

The leaves are all dead on the ground,
　　Save those that the oak is keeping
To ravel them one by one
　　And let them go scraping and creeping　　　　　　10
Out over the crusted snow,
　　When others are sleeping.

And the dead leaves lie huddled and still,
　　No longer blown hither and thither;
The last lone aster is gone;
　　The flowers of the witch-hazel wither;
The heart is still aching to seek,
　　But the feet question "Whither?"

Ah, when to the heart of man
　　Was it ever less than a treason　　　　　　　　20
To go with the drift of things,
　　To yield with a grace to reason,
And bow and accept the end
　　Of a love or a season?

The Road Not Taken[1]

Two roads diverged in a yellow wood,
And sorry I could not travel both
And be one traveler, long I stood
And looked down one as far as I could
To where it bent in the undergrowth;

Then took the other, as just as fair,
And having perhaps the better claim,
Because it was grassy and wanted wear;
Though as for that the passing there
Had worn them really about the same,　　　　　　　10

And both that morning equally lay
In leaves no step had trodden black.
Oh, I kept the first for another day!
Yet knowing how way leads on to way,
I doubted if I should ever come back.

I shall be telling this with a sigh
Somewhere ages and ages hence:
Two roads diverged in a wood, and I—
I took the one less traveled by,
And that has made all the difference.   20

Fire and Ice[1]

Some say the world will end in fire;
Some say in ice.
From what I've tasted of desire
I hold with those who favor fire.
But if it had to perish twice,
I think I know enough of hate
To know that for destruction ice
Is also great
And would suffice.

Stopping by Woods on a Snowy Evening[1]

Whose woods these are I think I know.
His house is in the village though;
He will not see me stopping here
To watch his woods fill up with snow.

My little horse must think it queer
To stop without a farmhouse near
Between the woods and frozen lake
The darkest evening of the year.

He gives his harness bells a shake
To ask if there is some mistake.
The only other sound's the sweep
Of easy wind and downy flake.

The woods are lovely, dark and deep.
But I have promises to keep,

And miles to go before I sleep,
And miles to go before I sleep.

JOHN HOLMES

On Frost's "Stopping by Woods on a Snowy Evening"[1]

1 From *Preface to Poetry* by Charles W. Cooper and John Holmes. Copyright, 1946, by Harcourt, Brace & World, Inc.
Facsimile of the last three stanzas of "Stopping by Woods on a Snowy Evening" by Robert Frost. By permission of Holt, Rinehart and Winston, Inc.

This facsimile is a reproduction of the last three stanzas of "Stopping by Woods on a Snowy Evening" as Robert Frost worked it out. We know from the poet that he had just written the long poem, "New Hampshire," in one all-night unbroken stretch of composition, and that he then turned a page of his workbook and wrote this short poem without stopping. This fact has interesting implications. "New Hampshire" is a discourse in the idiomatic blank verse that is so peculiarly Frost's own style—the rhythms of natural speech matched to the strict but inconspicuous iambic pentameter, the beat always discernible but never formal. It is reasonable to suppose that after the hours spent in writing the long poem, in its loosened but never loose manner, he was ready, unconsciously, for a poem in strict pattern. He had also obviously had in his head for some time the incident on which the short poem was to be based, as well as the use he wished to make of it. He committed himself, as he has said, to the four-stress iambic line and to the *aaba* rime-scheme, in the first stanza, which he wrote rapidly and did not revise. He knew what he had seen, and he knew how he wanted to write it.

> Whose woods these are I think I know.
> His house is in the village though;
> He will not see me stopping here
> To watch his woods fill up with snow.

"That went off so easily I was tempted into the added difficulty of picking up my 3 for my 1-2-4 to go on with in the second stanza. I was amused and scared at what that got me into," Frost says. The facsimile shows what it got him into, how he got out of it, and how he achieved the poem as it meant itself to be written.

It began with what was the actual experience of stopping at night by some dark woods in winter, and the fact that there were two horses. He remembered what he saw then. "The steaming horses think it queer." But the poem needs truth more than fact, and he cancels the line, and begins again, "The horse begins to think it queer," but doesn't like the word "begins," needing in the allowed space a word that will particularize the horse, so writes "The little horse must think it queer." Now he runs into a grammatical difficulty, which must somehow be solved before he gets on into the poem he already feels sure of. "I launched into the construction 'My little horse must think it queer that we should stop.' I didn't like omitting the 'that' and I had no room for 'should.' I had the luck to get out of it with the infinitive." This groping and warming-up has a kind of impatience, an urgency to get on with the poem, but not until all the parts are right. At this point the poet knew and did not know how the poem would end. He knew the feel, and the sense, and almost everything about the form—certainly enough to know when he got off the track.

Whether he revised the third line here or later we cannot know. But we can see in several places in this poem his changes toward particularization. The line "Between a forest and a lake" is a notation, and "Between the woods and frozen lake" is a finished line of poetry. "A forest" is too big, too vague, but "the woods" is definite, and bounded; you get lost in a forest, but you can walk through and out of the woods, and probably you know who owns it —Vermonters do, as he has said in the first stanza. "A lake" has not the specific condition or picture of "frozen lake." This sort of revision, or what Frost calls, "touching up," is what makes a poem—this, plus the first inspiration. Either one, without the other, is unlikely to make a good poem.

The next stanza comes easier, because the rime-scheme has been determined, and one unexpected obstacle has been overcome. But once more there is a delay, as the poet makes a decision as to the "he" or "she"—and the more important and more interesting about the falling snow. In writing "downy flake" for "fall of flake" the gain is great not only for accuracy of feeling and fact, but also for the music of the lines. The simple alliteration in "fall of flake" is canceled in favor of the word, one word, "downy," which blends with the vowel-chords a poet half-consciously makes and modulates as he goes. In this instance, it half-chimes with "sounds" and adds a rounder, fuller, and yet quieter tone.

Now the carry-over rime is "sweep," a fortunate one, really, and important to the final solution of the rime-scheme. It is not too much to assume, knowing all we know about the circumstances of the writing of this poem—the all-night composition of "New Hampshire," and the sudden urge to catch and shape still another saved idea—that the darker, more confident, more rapid strokes of the pen show the poet's growing excitement. The end is in sight. The thing he believed could happen will happen, surely now, and he must hurry to get it onto the page. This is the real moment of power, and any poet's greatest satisfaction.

"The woods are lovely dark and deep/But I have promises to keep." The first two lines of the last stanza come fast, and flow beautifully, the crest of the poem's emotion and its music. We cannot know whether he had held them in his head, or had swept up to and into them as he felt the destined pattern fulfilling itself.

Then, with success in sight, there comes an awkward and unexpected stumble. He writes, "That bid me give the reins a shake," which may have been the fact and the action. But the rime is wrong. Not only has the rime been used in the previous stanza, but so has the image of the horse shaking his head and reins. Things are moving fast now, no doubt impatiently, but certainly with determination, shown in the heavy black lines of abrupt cancellation. He strikes out "me give the reins a shake," and writes above it, so the line will read, "That bid me on, and there are miles," and then the whole thing comes through! Of course! "Miles to go . . . ?"

That's what it was supposed to be—the feeling of silence and dark, almost overpowering the man, but the necessity of going on. "And miles to go before I sleep." Then the triumph in the whole thing, the only right and perfect last line, solving the problem of the carried-over rime, keeping the half-tranced state, and the dark, and the solitude, and man's great effort to be responsible man . . . the repetition of that line.

"Stopping by Woods on a Snowy Evening," can be studied as perfected structure, with the photostat manuscript to show that art is not, though it must always appear to be, effortless. It can be thought of as a picture: the whites, grays, and blacks of the masses and areas of lake, field, and woods, with the tiny figure of the man in the sleigh, and the horse. And it can be thought of as a statement of man's everlasting responsibility to man; though the dark and nothingness tempt him to surrender, he will not give in. It is interesting to compare this poem with two later pieces of Frost's, in which he uses the same image, "Desert Places," and "Come In," none alike, all on the first level of his poetry, and all three built on the image of the pull of wildness and lawlessness against man's conscious will and the promises he has made to be kept.

After Apple-Picking

My long two-pointed ladder's sticking through a tree
Toward heaven still,
And there's a barrel that I didn't fill
Beside it, and there may be two or three
Apples I didn't pick upon some bough.
But I am done with apple-picking now.
Essence of winter sleep is on the night,
The scent of apples: I am drowsing off.
I cannot rub the strangeness from my sight
I got from looking through a pane of glass   10
I skimmed this morning from the drinking trough
And held against the world of hoary grass.
It melted, and I let it fall and break.
But I was well
Upon my way to sleep before it fell,
And I could tell
What form my dreaming was about to take.
Magnified apples appear and disappear,
Stem-end and blossom-end,
And every fleck of russet showing clear.   20
My instep arch not only keeps the ache,
It keeps the pressure of a ladder-round.
I feel the ladder sway as the boughs bend.
And I keep hearing from the cellar bin

The rumbling sound
Of load on load of apples coming in.
For I have had too much
Of apple-picking: I am overtired
Of the great harvest I myself desired.
There were ten thousand fruit to touch,   30
Cherish in hand, lift down, and not let fall.
For all
That struck the earth,
No matter if not bruised or spiked with stubble,
Went surely to the cider-apple heap
As of no worth.
One can see what will trouble
This sleep of mine, whatever sleep it is.
Were he not gone,
The woodchuck could say whether it's like his   40
Long sleep, as I describe its coming on,
Or just some human sleep.

RAINER MARIA RILKE

Der Panther[1]

Sein Blick ist vom Vorübergehn der Stäbe
so müd geworden, dass er nichts mehr hält.
Ihm ist, als ob es tausend Stäbe gäbe
und hinter tausend Stäben keine Welt.

Der weiche Gang geschmeidig starker Schritte,
der sich im allerkleinsten Kreise dreht,
ist wie ein Tanz von Kraft um eine Mitte,
in der betäubt ein grosser Wille steht.

Nur manchmal schiebt der Vorhang der Pupille
sich lautlos auf—. Dann geht ein Bild hinein,
geht durch der Glieder angespannte Stille—
und hört im Herzen auf zu sein.

[1] From *Neue Gedichte* (Zweigstelle Wiesbaden: Insel-Verlag Anton Kippenberg, n.d.). Reprinted by permission of the publishers.

The Panther[1]

A Translation by Jessie Lemont

His weary glance, from passing by the bars,
Has grown into a dazed and vacant stare;
It seems to him there are a thousand bars
And out beyond those bars the empty air.

The pad of his strong feet, that ceaseless sound
Of supple tread behind the iron bands,
Is like a dance of strength circling around,
While in the circle, stunned, a great will stands.

But there are times the pupils of his eyes
Dilate, the strong limbs stand alert, apart,
Tense with the flood of visions that arise
Only to sink and die within his heart.

Letzter Abend [2]

Und Nacht und fernes Fahren; denn der Train
des ganzen Heeres zog am Park vorüber.
Er aber hob den Blick vom Clavecin
und spielte noch und sah zu ihr hinüber

beinah, wie man in einen Spiegel schaut:
so sehr erfüllt von seinen jungen Zügen
und wissend, wie sie seine Trauer trügen,
schön und verführender bei jedem Laut.

Doch plötzlich war's, als ob sich das verwische:
sie stand wie mühsam in der Fensternische
und hielt des Herzens drängendes Geklopf.

Sein Spiel gab nach. Von draussen wehte Frische.
Und seltsam fremd stand auf dem Spiegeltische
der schwarze Tschako mit dem Totenkopf.

[1] From *Poems of Rainer Maria Rilke* (New York, 1943). Copyright 1943,
Columbia University Press.
[2] From *Neue Gedichte*.

Last Evening[1]

A Translation by Jessie Lemont

Night and the distant rumbling; for the train
Of the whole army passed by the park.
But he raised his eyes from the clavichord again,
And gazed at her, and played on in the dark,

Almost like a man who looks once more
Into a mirror filled with his young face,
Knowing the sorrow that his features bore
Made beautifully seductive with the grace

Of music. Then suddenly the scene was gone:
And sadly at the window, in her grief
She held the beating of her heart instead.

He played no more. The dawn wind blew each leaf.
And on the mirror table—strange—alone—
Stood the black shako with the white death's-head.

ANTONIO MACHADO

Del Camino, IX[2]

Crear fiestas de amores
en nuestro amor pensamos,
quemar nuevos aromas
en montes no pisados,

y guardar el secreto
de nuestros rostros pálidos,
porque en las bacanales de la vida
vacías nuestras copas conservamos,

1 From *Poems of Rainer Maria Rilke.*
2 From *Obras Completas de Manuel y Antonio Machado* (Madrid: n.d.). Copyright by the heirs of Manuel y Antonio Machado.

mientras con eco de cristal y espuma
ríen los zumos de la vid dorados.

Un pájaro escondido entre las ramas
del parque solitario,
silba burlón . . . .
                        Nosotros exprimimos
la penumbra de un sueño en nuestro vaso . . . .
Y algo, que es tierra en nuestra carne, siente
la humedad del jardín como un halago.

Of the Road [1]

A Translation by John Dos Passos

We think to create festivals
of love out of our love,
to burn new incense
on untrodden mountains;
and to keep the secret
of our pale faces,
and why in the bacchanals of life
we carry empty glasses,
while with tinkling echoes and laughing
foams the gold must of the grape. . . .
A hidden bird among the branches
of the solitary park
whistles mockery. . . . We feel
the shadow of a dream in our wine-glass,
and something that is earth in our flesh
feels the dampness of the garden like a caress.

Campos de Soria, IV [2]

¡Las figuras del campo sobre el cielo!
Dos lentos bueyes aran
en un alcor, cuando el otoño empieza,
y entre las negras testas doblegadas

---

[1] From *Rosinante to the Road* by John Dos Passos. Copyright, 1923. In the original version of this translation, the poem is untitled.
[2] From *Obras Completas de Manuel y Antonio Machado*.

bajo el pesado yugo,
pende un cesto de juncos y retama,
que es la cuna de un niño;
y tras la yunta marcha
un hombre que se inclina hacia la tierra,
y una mujer que en las abiertas zanjas
arroja la semilla.
Bajo una nube de carmín y llama,
en el oro flúido y verdinoso
del Poniente, las sombras se agigantan.

Fields of Soria[1]

A Translation by John Dos Passos

Figures in the fields against the sky!
Two slow oxen plow
on a hillside early in autumn,
and between the black heads bent down
under the weight of the yoke,
hangs and sways a basket of reeds,
a child's cradle;
And behind the yoke stride
a man who leans towards the earth
and a woman who, into the open furrows,
throws the seed.
Under a cloud of carmine and flame,
in the liquid green gold of the setting,
their shadows grow monstrous.

WALLACE STEVENS[2]

Sunday Morning

Complacencies of the peignoir, and late
Coffee and oranges in a sunny chair,
And the green freedom of a cockatoo

Upon a rug mingle to dissipate
The holy hush of ancient sacrifice.
She dreams a little, and she feels the dark
Encroachment of that old catastrophe,
As a calm darkens among water-lights.
The pungent oranges and bright, green wings
Seem things in some procession of the dead,   10
Winding across wide water, without sound.
The day is like wide water, without sound,
Stilled for the passing of her dreaming feet
Over the seas, to silent Palestine,
Dominion of the blood and sepulchre.

2

Why should she give her bounty to the dead?
What is divinity if it can come
Only in silent shadows and in dreams?
Shall she not find in comforts of the sun,
In pungent fruit and bright, green wings, or else   20
In any balm or beauty of the earth,
Things to be cherished like the thought of heaven?
Divinity must live within herself:
Passions of rain, or moods in falling snow;
Grieving in loneliness, or unsubdued
Elations when the forest blooms; gusty
Emotions on wet roads on autumn nights;
All pleasures and all pains, remembering
The bough of summer and the winter branch.
These are the measures destined for her soul.   30

3

Jove in the clouds had his inhuman birth.
No mother suckled him, no sweet land gave
Large-mannered motions to his mythy mind.
He moved among us, as a muttering king,
Magnificent, would move among his hinds,
Until our blood, commingling, virginal,
With heaven, brought such requital to desire
The very hinds discerned it, in a star.
Shall our blood fail? Or shall it come to be
The blood of paradise? And shall the earth   40
Seem all of paradise that we shall know?
The sky will be much friendlier then than now,
A part of labor and a part of pain,

And next in glory to enduring love,
Not this dividing and indifferent blue.

4

She says, "I am content when wakened birds,
Before they fly, test the reality
Of misty fields, by their sweet questionings;
But when the birds are gone, and their warm fields
Return no more, where, then, is paradise?"   50
There is not any haunt of prophecy,
Nor any old chimera of the grave,
Neither the golden underground, nor isle
Melodious, where spirits gat them home,
Nor visionary south, nor cloudy palm
Remote on heaven's hill, that has endured
As April's green endures; or will endure
Like her remembrance of awakened birds,
Or her desire for June and evening, tipped
By the consummation of the swallow's wings.   60

5

She says, "But in contentment I still feel
The need of some imperishable bliss."
Death is the mother of beauty; hence from her,
Alone, shall come fulfilment to our dreams
And our desires. Although she strews the leaves
Of sure obliteration on our paths,
The path sick sorrow took, the many paths
Where triumph rang its brassy phrase, or love
Whispered a little out of tenderness,
She makes the willow shiver in the sun   70
For maidens who were wont to sit and gaze
Upon the grass, relinquished to their feet.
She causes boys to pile new plums and pears
On disregarded plate. The maidens taste
And stray impassioned in the littering leaves.

6

Is there no change of death in paradise?
Does ripe fruit never fall? Or do the boughs
Hang always heavy in that perfect sky,
Unchanging, yet so like our perishing earth,
With rivers like our own that seek for seas   80

They never find, the same receding shores
That never touch with inarticulate pang?
Why set the pear upon those river-banks
Or spice the shores with odors of the plum?
Alas, that they should wear our colors there,
The silken weavings of our afternoons,
And pick the strings of our insipid lutes!
Death is the mother of beauty, mystical,
Within whose burning bosom we devise
Our earthly mothers waiting, sleeplessly.   90

7

Supple and turbulent, a ring of men
Shall chant in orgy on a summer morn
Their boisterous devotion to the sun,
Not as a god, but as a god might be,
Naked among them, like a savage source.
Their chant shall be a chant of paradise,
Out of their blood, returning to the sky;
And in their chant shall enter, voice by voice,
The windy lake wherein their lord delights,
The trees, like serafin, and echoing hills,   100
That choir among themselves long afterward.
They shall know well the heavenly fellowship
Of men that perish and of summer morn.
And whence they came and whither they shall go
The dew upon their feet shall manifest.

8

She hears, upon that water without sound,
A voice that cries, "The tomb in Palestine
Is not the porch of spirits lingering.
It is the grave of Jesus, where he lay."
We live in an old chaos of the sun,   110
Or old dependency of day and night,
Or island solitude, unsponsored, free,
Of that wide water, inescapable.
Deer walk upon our mountains, and the quail
Whistle about us their spontaneous cries;
Sweet berries ripen in the wilderness;
And, in the isolation of the sky,
At evening, casual flocks of pigeons make
Ambiguous undulations as they sink,
Downward to darkness, on extended wings.   120

YVOR WINTERS

On Stevens' "Sunday Morning" [1]

His fundamental ideas are stated in "Sunday Morning," an early poem, and in some ways his greatest. The poem consists of eight stanzas in blank verse, each containing fifteen lines, and it presents a clear and fairly coherent argument.

The first stanza sets the stage and identifies the protagonist. We are given a woman, at home on a Sunday morning, meditating on the meaning of death. The second stanza asks the question which provides the subject of the poem; it asks what divinity this woman may be thought to possess as a recompense for her ultimate surrender to death; and having asked the question, it replies that her divinity, which must live within herself, consists wholly in her emotions—not in her understanding of the emotions, but in the emotions as a good in themselves. This answer is not quite the orthodox romantic answer, which would offer us in the emotions either a true guide to virtue or a more or less mystical experience leading to some kind of union with some kind of deity. Any philosophy which offers the cultivation of the emotions as an end in itself, I suppose, is a kind of hedonism. In any event, that is the kind of philosophy which we find here.

The third stanza, by means of the allegory of Jove and his human loves, through his union with whom he crossed the heavenly strain upon the human, implies that man has a capacity which may at least figuratively be termed divine; the stanza is a subordinate commentary on the one preceding; and does not really advance the argument.

In the fourth stanza, however, the argument moves forward. The protagonist objects to the concept which has been offered her; she states that the beauties of this life are transient and that she longs to believe in a Paradise beyond them. The remainder of the stanza, and the greater part of it, is the poet's reply: in a passage of great rhetorical power, he denies the possibility of Paradise, at the same time that he communicates through the feeling of his language a deep nostalgic longing to accept the ideas which he is rejecting. In the first two lines of the fifth stanza, the woman repeats her objection, and the poet then replies with an explanation of the function of death: it is our awareness of the imminence of death which heightens our emotions and sharpens our perceptions; our knowledge of life's transience stimulates our perception of life's beauty.

In the sixth stanza the poet considers an hypothetical paradise, and, since he can imagine it only in terms of a projection of the good life as the hedonist understands the good life, he deduces that paradise would become tedious and insipid: we have in this stanza the first sharp vision of the ennui which is to

[1] From *The Anatomy of Nonsense*. Copyright, 1948, by New Directions.

obsess the later work of the poet and which is ultimately to wreck his talent, an ennui arising from the fact that emotion is not a good in itself, but that if cultivated for itself alone is merely a pleasant diversion so long as the novelty of a given experience endures, at most as long as new experiences can give us the illusion of novel excitement, and then becomes a disease of the spirit, a state of indifferency in which there is neither novelty nor significance.

The seventh stanza presents a vision of a future race of men engaged in a religous ritual, the generating principle of which is their joy in the world as it is given them and their sense of brotherhood as "men that perish." The stanza contains suggestions of a pantheism which goes beyond the bounds of a strict hedonism, but they are merely suggestions and they appear nowhere else. The eighth and last stanza begins by denying the immortality of Jesus, and by implication, of man; and it places the protagonist finally and irretrievably on a small but beautiful planet, floating like a tropical island in boundless space, "in an old chaos of the sun."

This summary, even as summaries go, is extremely skeletalized. It has been my intention, here, merely to isolate the hedonistic theme for future consideration; the theme is not thus isolated in the poem, but is complicated by its interconnections with other human problems from which not even a hedonist can escape. Whatever the defects of the hedonistic theme, and with the possible but by no means certain exception of a few short poems by Stevens and of two or three poems by E. A. Robinson, "Sunday Morning" is probably the greatest American poem of the twentieth century and is certainly one of the greatest contemplative poems in English: in a blank verse which differs, in its firmness of structure and incalculable sensitivity of detail, from all other blank verse of our time save that of a few poems by Hart Crane which were in some measure modeled upon it, it renders the acute uncertainty of what we are inclined to consider the modern mind, but it does so with no uncertainty of method or of statement; it renders an acute consciousness of the imminence of death, of the sensory and emotional richness of life on this bewildering planet, and of the heroic magnificence of the religious myths which are lost to the poet and to many of the rest of us, except as memories of things long past. If Stevens' career had stopped with this poem, or a few years thereafter, it might seem an unnecessary unkindness to insist upon the limitations of understanding which the poem discloses; but those limitations appear very obviously in a few later poems, and they seem to me to be very clearly related to the rapid and tragic decay of the poet's style. As a poet in early maturity, Stevens brought to this subject a style which was the result of a fine native gift enriched by the study of English blank verse; the subject, once formulated, and accepted as a guide to life and to expression, destroyed the style in less than two decades. In "Sunday Morning" itself, we detect the limitations of the subject only by rational analysis; in the later work we see the effect of those limitations. . . .

Some of the virtues of "Sunday Morning" I have indicated in very general terms, but one cannot turn from the poem that may be the greatest American work of our century without considering briefly some of its more haunting beauties, if it be only as an act of piety.

I have already quoted the final stanza of the poem, and its beauty should be obvious; yet as removed from its context, the stanza loses much of its complexity. The "water without sound," and "wide water inescapable," is not only an image representing infinite space; it is an image, established in the first stanza, representing a state of mind, a kind of bright and empty beatitude, over which the thought of death may darken suddenly and without warning:

> She dreams a little, and she feels the dark
> Encroachment of that old catastrophe,
> As a calm darkens among water-lights.

The language has the greatest possible dignity and subtlety, combined with perfect precision. The imminence of absolute tragedy is felt and recorded, but the integrity of the feeling mind is maintained. The mind perceives, as by a kind of metaphysical sense, the approach of invading impersonality, yet knowing the invasion to be inevitable and its own identity, while that identity lasts, the only source of any good whatever, maintains that identity in its full calm and clarity, that nothing may be sacrificed without need. This combination of calm and terror, in dealing with this particular theme, will be found in only one other poet in English, in Shakespeare as one finds him in a few of the more metaphysical sonnets. The calm clarity of tone enables the poet to deal with a variety of kinds of feeling which would be impossible were the terror emphasized for a moment at any point, were the complete and controlled unity of the experiencing mind for a moment disordered by its own perceptions. The same poem, for example, is able to contain the following lines, of a sweetness and of an illusory simplicity which again are scarcely less than Shakespearean:

> She says, "I am content when wakened birds,
> Before they fly, test the reality
> Of misty fields, by their sweet questionings;
> But when the birds are gone, and their warm fields
> Return no more, where, then, is paradise?"

And out of this passage proceeds the great lament for the lost myths, which I have already mentioned. This passage and others similar, though beautiful in themselves, are a preparation for the descriptive lines in the last stanza, and when we finally come to those lines, they are weighted with meaning and feeling accumulated from all that has gone before. It is difficult for this reason to quote from the poem for the purpose of illustrating its beauty.

One aspect of the poem may perhaps be mentioned, however, with some small profit, and it may best be indicated, I believe, through a brief comparison with Bryant's "Thanatopsis." Bryant's poem is a great poem and is worthy of the comparison, and its resemblance to Stevens' poem in certain ways is both surprising and illuminating. Both poems are semididactic meditations on death, written in a firm but simplified Miltonic blank verse, the verse of Stevens, possibly, being somewhat smoothed and softened by the intervention of Tennyson. Both poems are pagan in their view: but that of Bryant, the New Englander of the early 19th century, is essentially stoical, whereas that of Stevens, the Pennsylvanian of the 20th century, is Epicurean. Both poems find man, a spiritual being, isolated in a physical universe: but for Bryant that universe is the Earth, hairy, vast, and almost against the eye; for Stevens it is the tropical Pacific of infinity, in which the earth appears as an infinitesimal floating island.

Sea Surface Full of Clouds

I

In that November off Tehuantepec,
The slopping of the sea grew still one night
And in the morning summer hued the deck

And made one think of rosy chocolate
And gilt umbrellas. Paradisal green
Gave suavity to the perplexed machine

Of ocean, which like limpid water lay.
Who, then, in that ambrosial latitude
Out of the light evolved the moving blooms,

Who, then, evolved the sea-blooms from the clouds   10
Diffusing balm in that Pacific calm?
C'était mon enfant, mon bijou, mon âme.

The sea-clouds, whitened far below the calm
And moved, as blooms move, in the swimming green
And in its watery radiance, while the hue

Of heaven in an antique reflection rolled
Round those flotillas. And sometimes the sea
Poured brilliant iris on the glistening blue.

II

In that November off Tehuantepec
The slopping of the sea grew still one night.   20
At breakfast jelly yellow streaked the deck

And made one think of chop-house chocolate
And sham umbrellas. And a sham-like green
Capped summer-seeming on the tense machine

Of ocean, which in sinister flatness lay.
Who, then, beheld the rising of the clouds
That strode submerged in that malevolent sheen,

Who saw the mortal massives of the blooms
Of water moving on the water-floor?
C'était mon frère du ciel, ma vie, mon or.   30

The gongs rang loudly as the windy blooms
Hoo-hooed it in the darkened ocean-blooms.
The gongs grew still. And then blue heaven spread

Its crystalline pendentives on the sea
And the macabre of the water-glooms,
In an enormous undulation fled.

III

In that November off Téhuantepec,
The slopping of the sea grew still one night,
And a pale silver patterned on the deck

Made one think of porcelain chocolate   40
And pied umbrellas. An uncertain green,
Piano-polished, held the tranced machine

Of ocean, as a prelude holds and holds.
Who, seeing silver petals of white blooms
Unfolding in the water, feeling sure

Of the milk within the saltiest spurge, heard, then,
The sea unfolding in the sunken clouds?
Oh! C'était mon extase et mon amour.

So deeply sunken were they that the shrouds,
The shrouding shadows, made the petals black   50
Until the rolling heaven made them blue,

A blue beyond the rainy hyacinth,
And smiting the crevasses of the leaves
Deluged the ocean with a sapphire hue.

IV

In that November off Tehuantepec
The night-long slopping of the sea grew still.
A mallow morning dozed upon the deck

And made one think of musky chocolate
And frail umbrellas. A too-fluent green
Suggested malice in the dry machine   60

Of ocean, pondering dank stratagem.
Who then beheld the figures of the clouds,
Like blooms secluded in the thick marine?

Like blooms? Like damasks that were shaken off
From the loosed girdles in the spangling must.
C'était ma foi, la nonchalance divine.

The nakedness would rise and suddenly turn
Salt masks of beard and mouths of bellowing,
Would— But more suddenly the heaven rolled

Its bluest sea-clouds in the thinking green   70
And the nakedness became the broadest blooms,
Mile-mallows that a mallow sun cajoled.

V

In that November off Tehuantepec
Night stilled the slopping of the sea. The day
Came, bowing and voluble, upon the deck,

Good clown. . . . One thought of Chinese chocolate
And large umbrellas. And a motley green
Followed the drift of the obese machine

Of ocean, perfected in indolence.
What pistache one, ingenious and droll,   80
Beheld the sovereign clouds as jugglery

And the sea as turquoise-turbaned Sambo, neat
At tossing saucers—cloudy-conjuring sea?
C'était mon esprit bâtard, l'ignominie.

The sovereign clouds came clustering. The conch
Of loyal conjuration trumped. The wind
Of green blooms turning crisped the motley hue

To clearing opalescence. Then the sea
And heaven rolled as one and from the two
Came fresh transfigurings of freshest blue.   90

The Emperor of Ice-Cream

Call the roller of big cigars,
The muscular one, and bid him whip
In kitchen cups concupiscent curds.
Let the wenches dawdle in such dress
As they are used to wear, and let the boys
Bring flowers in last month's newspapers.
Let be be finale of seem.
The only emperor is the emperor of ice-cream.

Take from the dresser of deal,
Lacking the three glass knobs, that sheet
On which she embroidered fantails once
And spread it so as to cover her face.
If her horny feet protrude, they come
To show how cold she is, and dumb.
Let the lamp affix its beam.
The only emperor is the emperor of ice-cream.

Of Hartford in a Purple Light

A long time you have been making the trip
From Havre to Hartford, Master Soleil,
Bringing the lights of Norway and all that.

A long time the ocean has come with you,
Shaking the water off, like a poodle,
That splatters incessant thousands of drops,

Each drop a petty tricolor. For this,
The aunts in Pasadena, remembering,
Abhor the plaster of the western horses,

Souvenirs of museums. But, Master, there are   10
Lights masculine and lights feminine.
What is this purple, this parasol,

This stage-light of the Opera?
It is like a region full of intonings.
It is Hartford seen in a purple light.

A moment ago, light masculine,
Working, with big hands, on the town,
Arranged its heroic attitudes.

But now as in an amour of women
Purple sets purple round. Look, Master,   20
See the river, the railroad, the cathedral . . .

When male light fell on the naked back
Of the town, the river, the railroad *were* clear.
Now, every muscle slops away.

Hi! Whisk it, poodle, flick the spray
Of the ocean, ever-freshening,
On the irised hunks, the stone bouquet.

WILLIAM CARLOS WILLIAMS[1]

Poem

By the road to the contagious hospital,
under the surge of the blue
mottled clouds driven from the
northeast—cold wind. Beyond, the
waste of broad, muddy fields,
brown with dried weeds, standing and fallen,

patches of standing water,
the scattering of tall trees.

All along the road the reddish,
purplish, forked, upstanding, twiggy   10
stuff of brushes and small trees
with dead, brown leaves under them
leafless vines—

Lifeless in appearance, sluggish,
dazed spring approaches—

1 From *The Collected Poems of William Carlos Williams*. Copyright 1938 by William Carlos Williams, published by New Directions.

They enter the new world naked,
cold, uncertain of all
save that they enter. All about them
the cold, familiar wind—

Now the grass, tomorrow   20
the stiff curl of wild-carrot leaf.

One by one objects are defined—
It quickens: clarity, outline of leaf,

But now the stark dignity of
entrance— Still, the profound change
has come upon them; rooted, they
grip down and begin to awaken.

The Yachts

contend in a sea which the land partly encloses
shielding them from the too heavy blows
of an ungoverned ocean which when it chooses

tortures the biggest hulls, the best man knows
to pit against its beating, and sinks them pitilessly.
Mothlike in mists, scintillant in the minute

brilliance of cloudless days, with broad bellying sails
they glide to the wind tossing green water
from their sharp prows while over them the crew crawls

ant-like, solicitously grooming them, releasing,   10
making fast as they turn, lean far over and having
caught the wind again, side by side, head for the mark.

In a well guarded arena of open water surrounded by
lesser and greater craft which, sycophant, lumbering
and flittering follow them, they appear youthful, rare

as the light of a happy eye, live with the grace
of all that in the mind is feckless, free and
naturally to be desired. Now the sea which holds them

is moody, lapping their glossy sides, as if feeling
for some slightest flaw but fails completely.   20
Today no race. Then the wind comes again. The yachts

move, jockeying for a start, the signal is set and they
are off. Now the waves strike at them but they are too
well made, they slip through, they take in canvas.

Arms with hands grasping seek to clutch at the prows.
Bodies thrown recklessly in the way are cut aside.
It is a sea of faces about them in agony, in despair

until the horror of the race dawns staggering the mind,
the whole sea become an entanglement of watery bodies
lost to the world bearing what they cannot hold. Broken,   30

beaten, desolate, reaching from the dead to be taken up
they cry out, failing, failing! their cries rising
in waves still as the skillful yachts pass over.

MARIANNE MOORE

See in the Midst of Fair Leaves[1]

and much fruit, the swan—
one line of the mathematician's
sign greater-than drawn
to an apex where the lake is
met by the weight on it; or an angel
standing in the sun; how well
armed, how manly;

and promenading
in sloughs of despond, a monster,
man when human nothing
more, grown to immaturity,
punishing debtors, seeking his due as
an arrow turned inward has
no chance of peace.

[1] From *What Are Years?* Reprinted by permission of The Macmillan Company,
copyright, 1941.

DANIEL G. HOFFMAN

On Moore's "See in the Midst of Fair Leaves" [1]

In her notes to *What Are Years* Miss Marianne Moore refers to *Daniel* IV, 12 as the source of her phrase, "See in the Midst of Fair Leaves and much fruit." In verses 20-22, Daniel explains to Nebuchadnezzar the meaning of the latter's dream:

> The tree that thou sawest, which grew, and was strong, whose height reached unto heaven, and the sight thereof to all the earth; whose leaves were fair, and the fruit thereof much, and in it was meat for all; under which the beasts of the field dwelt, and upon whose branches the fowls of heaven had their habitation; it is thou, O king, that art grown and become strong: for thy greatness is grown, and reacheth unto heaven, and thy dominion to the ends of the earth.

In her poem the tree is paradigm both of the abundance of the world, and of the growth of man's power till he challenges or ignores the power of God. The swan is seen in the midst of the tree's abundance.

Afloat on the lake which is overhung by the tree, this swan is seen as the upper half of the mathematical symbol, "greater-than"; the lower half, of course, is formed by the reflection of the swan's long slanting neck "where the lake is met by the weight on it." The second half, without which the swan is nothing, is formed by his interaction with Nature. This mathematical sign is an abstraction representing abundance, just as the King's dream-tree flowers into the particulars of abundance: fruit, shade, shelter.

"An angel standing in the sun"; the swan now stands in shallow water and spreads its majestic wings: "how well armed, how manly." The bird partakes of all three orders of creation: bestial, human, and angelic, like the butterfly in "HALF DEITY half worm."

In lines 8-9 the angelic, manly swan suddenly becomes "a monster." Miss Moore is always just to nature, and here she records the disenchantment of her observer who watches the swan in its imperious gesture, wings spread to the sun, suddenly transformed into an ungainly loutish bird that walks about in mud. ". . . promenading in sloughs of despond" expresses the tension between the well-armed angel and the monster. The bird still retains a vestige of its lost dignity; and swans actually do walk with incongruous ceremoniousness. The monstrous swan now represents Nebuchadnezzar himself, who also had stood well-armed and manly in the sun, only to root in the muddy grass among the oxen, a monster.

[1] From *The Explicator*, X (March, 1952), 34. By permission of the author and of the Editors of *The Explicator*.

The remainder of the poem attributes the fall of man to selfhood. Man, "grown to immaturity," wastes his life-force in "punishing debtors, seeking his due"—asserting the power of the self alone. Like the arrow turned upon itself, he has "no chance of peace." What would bring him peace is, I believe, omitted from the poem in the same way that it was omitted from Nebuchadnezzar's dream: realization of his dependence upon God. If this surmise is so, then Miss Moore has left out God because to have included Him would have given man the peace he lacks. It is interesting to note that the entire poem is all one sentence—a rhetorical device which Miss Moore may have adopted to reflect the indivisibility of angel, man, and monster in the restless human spirit.

What Are Years? [1]

What is our innocence,
what is our guilt? All are
     naked, none is safe. And whence
is courage: the unanswered question,
the resolute doubt,—
dumbly calling, deafly listening—that
in misfortune, even death,
     encourages others
     and in its defeat, stirs

     the soul to be strong? He   10
sees deep and is glad, who
     accedes to mortality
and in his imprisonment, rises
upon himself as
the sea in a chasm, struggling to be
free and unable to be,
     in its surrendering
     finds its continuing.

     So he who strongly feels,
behaves. The very bird,   20
     grown taller as he sings, steels
his form straight up. Though he is captive,
his mighty singing
says, satisfaction is a lowly
thing, how pure a thing is joy.
     This is mortality,
     this is eternity.

[1] From *What Are Years?* Copyright, 1941, The Macmillan Company. Reprinted by permission.

The Wood-Weasel [1]

> emerges daintily, the skunk—
> don't laugh—in sylvan black and white chipmunk
> regalia. The inky thing
> adaptively whited with glistening
> goat-fur, is wood-warden. In his
> ermined well-cuttlefished-inked wool, he is
> determination's totem. Out-
> lawed? His sweet face and powerful feet go about
> in chieftain's coat of Chilcat cloth.
> He is his own protection from the moth,
>
> noble little warrior. That
> otter-skin on it, the living pole-cat,
> smothers anything that stings. Well,—
> this same weasel's playful and his weasel
> associates are too. Only
> WOOD-weasels shall associate with me.

T. S. ELIOT

The Love Song of J. Alfred Prufrock [2]

> *S'io credesse che mia risposta fosse*
> *A persona che mai tornasse al mondo,*
> *Questa fiamma staria senza piu scosse.*
> *Ma percioccbe giammai di questo fondo*
> *Non torno vivo alcun, s'i' odo il vero,*
> *Senza tema d'infamia ti rispondo.* [3]

[1] From *Collected Poems.* Copyright 1944 by Marianne Moore. Used by permission of The Macmillan Company.
[2] From *Collected Poems 1909-1935* by T. S. Eliot, copyright 1936, by Harcourt, Brace & World, Inc.
[3] "If I thought my answer were to one who ever could return to the world, this flame should shake no more; but since none ever did return alive from this depth, if what I hear be true, without fear of infamy I answer thee."—*Inferno,* XXVII, 61-66.

Let us go then, you and I,
When the evening is spread out against the sky
Like a patient etherized upon a table;
Let us go, through certain half-deserted streets,
The muttering retreats
Of restless nights in one-night cheap hotels
And sawdust restaurants with oyster-shells:
Streets that follow like a tedious argument
Of insidious intent
To lead you to an overwhelming question. . . .   10
Oh, do not ask, "What is it?"
Let us go and make our visit.

In the room the women come and go
Talking of Michelangelo.

The yellow fog that rubs its back upon the window-panes,
The yellow smoke that rubs its muzzle on the window-panes
Licked its tongue into the corners of the evening,
Lingered upon the pools that stand in drains,
Let fall upon its back the soot that falls from chimneys,
Slipped by the terrace, made a sudden leap,   20
And seeing that it was a soft October night,
Curled once about the house, and fell asleep.
And indeed there will be time
For the yellow smoke that slides along the street
Rubbing its back upon the window-panes;
There will be time, there will be time
To prepare a face to meet the faces that you meet;
There will be time to murder and create,
And time for all the works and days of hands
That lift and drop a question on your plate;
Time for you and time for me,   30
And time yet for a hundred indecisions,
And for a hundred visions and revisions,
Before the taking of a toast and tea.

In the room the women come and go
Talking of Michelangelo.

And indeed there will be time
To wonder, "Do I dare?" and, "Do I dare?"
Time to turn back and descend the stair,
With a bald spot in the middle of my hair—   40

(They will say: "How his hair is growing thin!")
My morning coat, my collar mounting firmly to the chin,
My necktie rich and modest, but asserted by a simple pin—
(They will say: "But how his arms and legs are thin!")
Do I dare
Disturb the universe?
In a minute there is time
For decisions and revisions which a minute will reverse.

For I have known them all already, known them all:
Have known the evenings, mornings, afternoons,   50
I have measured out my life with coffee spoons;
I know the voices dying with a dying fall
Beneath the music from a farther room.
        So how should I presume?
And I have known the eyes already, known them all—
The eyes that fix you in a formulated phrase,
And when I am formulated, sprawling on a pin,
When I am pinned and wriggling on the wall,
Then how should I begin
To spit out all the butt-ends of my days and ways?   60
    And how should I presume?

And I have known the arms already, known them all—
Arms that are braceleted and white and bare
(But in the lamplight, downed with light brown hair!)
Is it perfume from a dress
That makes me so digress?
Arms that lie along a table, or wrap about a shawl.
        And should I then presume?
        And how should I begin?

Shall I say, I have gone at dusk through narrow streets   70
And watched the smoke that rises from the pipes
Of lonely men in shirt-sleeves, leaning out of windows? . . . .

I should have been a pair of ragged claws
Scuttling across the floors of silent seas.

And the afternoon, the evening, sleeps so peacefully!
Smoothed by long fingers,
Asleep . . . tired . . . or it malingers,

Stretched on the floor, here beside you and me.
Should I, after tea and cakes and ices,
Have the strength to force the moment to its crisis?   80
But though I have wept and fasted, wept and prayed,
Though I have seen my head (grown slightly bald) brought in upon a
    platter,
I am no prophet—and here's no great matter;
I have seen the moment of my greatness flicker,
And I have seen the eternal Footman hold my coat, and snicker,
And in short, I was afraid.

And would it have been worth it, after all,
After the cups, the marmalade, the tea,
Among the porcelain, among some talk of you and me,
Would it have been worth while,   90
To have bitten off the matter with a smile,
To have squeezed the universe into a ball
To roll it toward some overwhelming question,
To say: "I am Lazarus, come from the dead,
Come back to tell you all, I shall tell you all"—
If one, settling a pillow by her head,
    Should say: "That is not what I meant at all;
    That is not it, at all."

And would it have been worth it, after all,
Would it have been worth while,   100
After the sunsets and the dooryards and the sprinkled streets,
After the novels, after the teacups, after the skirts that trail along the
    floor—
And this, and so much more?—
It is impossible to say just what I mean!
But as if a magic lantern threw the nerves in patterns on a screen:
Would it have been worth while
If one, settling a pillow or throwing off a shawl,
And turning toward the window, should say:
    "That is not it at all,
    That is not what I meant, at all."   110

No! I am not Prince Hamlet, nor was meant to be;
Am an attendant lord, one that will do
To swell a progress, start a scene or two,
Advise the prince; no doubt, an easy tool,

Deferential, glad to be of use,
Politic, cautious, and meticulous;
Full of high sentence, but a bit obtuse;
At times, indeed, almost ridiculous—
Almost, at times, the Fool.

I grow old. . . . I grow old. . . .   120
I shall wear the bottoms of my trousers rolled.

Shall I part my hair behind? Do I dare to eat a peach?
I shall wear white flannel trousers, and walk upon the beach.
I have heard the mermaids singing, each to each.

I do not think that they will sing to me.

I have seen them riding seaward on the waves
Combing the white hair of the waves blown back
When the wind blows the water white and black.

We have lingered in the chambers of the sea
By sea-girls wreathed with seaweed red and brown   130
Till human voices wake us, and we drown.

Cousin Nancy[1]

Miss Nancy Ellicott
Strode across the hills and broke them,
Rode across the hills and broke them—
The barren New England hills—
Riding to hounds
Over the cow-pasture.

Miss Nancy Ellicott smoked
And danced all the modern dances;
And her aunts were not quite sure how they felt about it,
But they knew that it was modern.

Upon the glazen shelves kept watch
Matthew and Waldo, guardians of the faith,
The army of unalterable law.

1 From *Collected Poems* 1909-1935 by T. S. Eliot, copyright 1936, by Harcourt,
Brace and World, Inc.

Sweeney among the Nightingales[1]

ὤμοι, πέπληγμαι καιρίαν πληγὴν ἔσω.[2]

Apeneck Sweeney spreads his knees
Letting his arms hang down to laugh,
The zebra stripes along his jaw
Swelling to maculate giraffe.

The circles of the stormy moon
Slide westward toward the River Plate,
Death and the Raven drift above
And Sweeney guards the hornèd gate.

Gloomy Orion and the Dog
Are veiled; and hushed the shrunken seas;   10
The person in the Spanish cape
Tries to sit on Sweeney's knees

Slips and pulls the table cloth
Overturns a coffee-cup,
Reorganised upon the floor
She yawns and draws a stocking up;

The silent man in mocha brown
Sprawls at the window-sill and gapes;
The waiter brings in oranges
Bananas figs and hothouse grapes.   20

The silent vertebrate in brown
Contracts and concentrates, withdraws;
Rachel née Rabinovitch
Tears at the grapes with murderous paws;

She and the lady in the cape
Are suspect, thought to be in league;
Therefore the man with heavy eyes
Declines the gambit, shows fatigue,

[1] From *Collected Poems* 1909-1935 by T. S. Eliot, copyright 1936, by Harcourt,
Brace and World, Inc.
[2] "Woe's me, I'm stricken a mortal blow within."—*Agamemnon*, line 1341.

Leaves the room and reappears
Outside the window, leaning in,   30
Branches of wisteria
Circumscribe a golden grin;

The host with someone indistinct
Converses at the door apart,
The nightingales are singing near
The Convent of the Sacred Heart,

And sang within the bloody wood
When Agamemnon cried aloud,
And let their liquid siftings fall
To stain the stiff dishonoured shroud.   40

Macavity: The Mystery Cat[1]

Macavity's a Mystery Cat: he's called the Hidden Paw—
For he's the master criminal who can defy the Law.
He's the bafflement of Scotland Yard, the Flying Squad's despair:
For when they reach the scene of crime—*Macavity's not there!*

Macavity, Macavity, there's no-one like Macavity,
He's broken every human law, he breaks the law of gravity.
His powers of levitation would make a fakir stare,
And when you reach the scene of crime—*Macavity's not there!*
You may seek him in the basement, you may look up in the air—
But I tell you once and once again, *Macavity's not there!*   10

Macavity's a ginger cat, he's very tall and thin;
You would know him if you saw him, for his eyes are sunken in.
His brow is deeply lined with thought, his head is highly domed;
His coat is dusty from neglect, his whiskers are uncombed.
He sways his head from side to side, with movements like a snake;
And when you think he's half asleep, he's always wide awake.

Macavity, Macavity, there's no-one like Macavity,
For he's a fiend in feline shape, a monster of depravity.
You may meet him in a by-street, you may see him in the square—
But when a crime's discovered, then *Macavity's not there!*   20

[1] From *Old Possum's Book of Practical Cats*, copyright, 1939, by T. S. Eliot.
Reprinted by permission of Harcourt, Brace & World, Inc.

He's outwardly respectable. (They say he cheats at cards.)
And his footprints are not found in any file of Scotland Yard's.
And when the larder's looted, or the jewel-case is rifled,
Or when the milk is missing, or another Peke's been stifled,
Or the greenhouse glass is broken, and the trellis past repair—
Ay, there's the wonder of the thing! *Macavity's not there!*

And when the Foreign Office finds a Treaty's gone astray,
Or the Admiralty lose some plans and drawings by the way,
There may be a scrap of paper in the hall or on the stair—
But it's useless to investigate—*Macavity's not there!*   30
And when the loss has been disclosed, the Secret Service say:
'It *must* have been Macavity!'—but he's a mile away.
You'll be sure to find him resting, or a-licking of his thumbs,
Or engaged in doing complicated long division sums.

Macavity, Macavity, there's no-one like Macavity,
There never was a Cat of such deceitfulness and suavity.
He always has an alibi, and one or two to spare:
At whatever time the deed took place—MACAVITY WASN'T THERE!
And they say that all the Cats whose wicked deeds are widely known
(I might mention Mungojerrie, I might mention Griddlebone)   40
Are nothing more than agents for the Cat who all the time
Just controls their operations: the Napoleon of Crime!

Burnt Norton[1]

I

Time present and time past
Are both perhaps present in time future,
And time future contained in time past.
If all time is eternally present
All time is unredeemable.
What might have been is an abstraction
Remaining a perpetual possibility
Only in a world of speculation.
What might have been and what has been
Point to one end, which is always present.   10
Footfalls echo in the memory
Down the passage which we did not take
Towards the door we never opened

Into the rose-garden. My words echo
Thus, in your mind.
                          But to what purpose
Disturbing the dust on a bowl of rose-leaves
I do not know.
                    Other echoes
Inhabit the garden. Shall we follow?   20
Quick, said the bird, find them, find them,
Round the corner. Through the first gate,
Into our first world, shall we follow
The deception of the thrush? Into our first world.
There they were, dignified, invisible,
Moving without pressure, over the dead leaves,
In the autumn heat, through the vibrant air,
And the bird called, in response to
The unheard music hidden in the shrubbery,
And the unseen eyebeam crossed, for the roses   30
Had the look of flowers that are looked at.
There they were as our guests, accepted and accepting.
So we moved, and they, in a formal pattern,
Along the empty alley, into the box circle,
To look down into the drained pool.
Dry the pool, dry concrete, brown-edged,
And the pool was filled with water out of sunlight,
And the lotus rose, quietly, quietly,
The surface glittered out of heart of light,
And they were behind us, reflected in the pool,   40
Then a cloud passed, and the pool was empty.
Go, said the bird, for the leaves were full of children,
Hidden, excitedly, containing laughter.
Go, go, go, said the bird: human kind
Cannot bear very much reality.
Time past and time future
What might have been and what has been
Point to one end, which is always present.

                              II

Garlic and sapphires in the mud
Clot the bedded axle-tree.   50
The trilling wire in the blood
Sings below inveterate scars
And reconciles forgotten wars.
The dance along the artery
The circulation of the lymph

Are figured in the drift of stars
Ascend to summer in the tree
We move above the moving tree
In light upon the figured leaf
And hear upon the sodden floor   60
Below, the boarhound and the boar
Pursue their pattern as before
But reconciled among the stars.

At the still point of the turning world. Neither flesh nor fleshless;
Neither from nor towards; at the still point, there the dance is,
But neither arrest nor movement. And do not call it fixity,
Where past and future are gathered. Neither movement from nor towards,
Neither ascent nor decline. Except for the point, the still point,
There would be no dance, and there is only the dance.
I can only say, *there* we have been: but I cannot say where.   70
And I cannot say, how long, for that is to place it in time.

The inner freedom from the practical desire,
The release from action and suffering, release from the inner
And the outer compulsion, yet surrounded
By a grace of sense, a white light still and moving,
Erhebung without motion, concentration
Without elimination, both a new world
And the old made explicit, understood
In the completion of its partial ecstasy,
The resolution of its partial horror.   80
Yet the enchainment of past and future
Woven in the weakness of the changing body,
Protects mankind from heaven and damnation
Which flesh cannot endure.
                              Time past and time future
Allow but a little consciousness.
To be conscious is not to be in time
But only in time can the moment in the rose-garden,
The moment in the arbour where the rain beat,
The moment in the draughty church at smokefall   90
Be remembered; involved with past and future.
Only through time time is conquered.

                              III

Here is a place of disaffection
Time before and time after
In a dim light: neither daylight

Investing form with lucid stillness
Turning shadow into transient beauty
With slow rotation suggesting permanence
Nor darkness to purify the soul
Emptying the sensual with deprivation   100
Cleansing affection from the temporal.
Neither plenitude nor vacancy. Only a flicker
Over the strained time-ridden faces
Distracted from distraction by distraction
Filled with fancies and empty of meaning
Tumid apathy with no concentration
Men and bits of paper, whirled by the cold wind
That blows before and after time,
Wind in and out of unwholesome lungs
Time before and time after.   110
Eructation of unhealthy souls
Into the faded air, the torpid
Driven on the wind that sweeps the gloomy hills of London,
Hampstead and Clerkenwell, Campden and Putney,
Highgate, Primrose and Ludgate. Not here
Not here the darkness, in this twittering world.

Descend lower, descend only
Into the world of perpetual solitude,
World not world, but that which is not world,
Internal darkness, deprivation   120
And destitution of all property,
Desiccation of the world of sense,
Evacuation of the world of fancy,
Inoperancy of the world of spirit;
This is the one way, and the other
Is the same, not in movement
But abstention from movement; while the world **moves**
In appetency, on its metalled ways
Of time past and time future.

IV

Time and the bell have buried the day,   130
The black cloud carries the sun away.
Will the sunflower turn to us, will the clematis
Stray down, bend to us; tendril and spray
Clutch and cling?
Chill
Fingers of yew be curled

Down on us? After the kingfisher's wing
Has answered light to light, and is silent, the light is still
At the still point of the turning world.

V

Words move, music moves
Only in time; but that which is only living   140
Can only die. Words, after speech, reach
Into the silence. Only by the form, the pattern,
Can words or music reach
The stillness, as a Chinese jar still
Moves perpetually in its stillness.
Not the stillness of the violin, while the note lasts,
Not that only, but the co-existence,
Or say that the end precedes the beginning,
And the end and the beginning were always there   150
Before the beginning and after the end.
And all is always now. Words strain,
Crack and sometimes break, under the burden,
Under the tension, slip, slide, perish,
Decay with imprecision, will not stay in place,
Will not stay still. Shrieking voices
Scolding, mocking, or merely chattering,
Always assail them. The Word in the desert
Is most attacked by voices of temptation,
The crying shadow in the funeral dance,   160
The loud lament of the disconsolate chimera.

The detail of the pattern is movement,
As in the figure of the ten stairs.
Desire itself is movement
Not in itself desirable;
Love is itself unmoving,
Only the cause and end of movement,
Timeless, and undesiring
Except in the aspect of time
Caught in the form of limitation
Between un-being and being.   170
Sudden in a shaft of sunlight
Even while the dust moves
There rises the hidden laughter
Of children in the foliage
Quick now, here, now, always—

> Ridiculous the waste sad time
> Stretching before and after.

ELIZABETH DREW

On Eliot's "Burnt Norton" [1]

The poem opens with a passage of musing commentary on the nature of experience in time, with three self-contained propositions, and then a statement of what is really the substance and conclusion of all four poems [the *Four Quartets*]. First there is the usual concept of time as progression, and events as a sequence of cause and effect:

> Time present and time past
> Are both perhaps present in time future,
> And time future contained in time past.

Then there is the concept of time as "eternally present," with the comment that if that is so, it makes time "unredeemable"; nothing can be altered, we can't bring back the past. This statement is left as it is for the moment: it is developed in the later poems and shown to be a half truth only. Finally there is a third category of experience "what might have been"—the potential. This is "perpetual," but exists only "in a world of speculation." The three aspects of time are then reduced to the central truth:

> What might have been and what has been
> Point to one end, which is always present.

This is the first entrance of subtle ambiguity in the language, with its two-faced meanings of *point, end* and *present*. As a summing up of time as progression, it says that what has been (the past) and what might have been (the potentialities of the past) point to the present as their conclusion: that is what they have produced. As a summing up of the second idea of the eternal present as a "point," it says that what that points to is both that the present moment is the only actuality, and that what to do in the present is an *aim* or purpose which is always present with us.

Then the pure abstraction modulates into a transition passage. "What might have been" is translated into the sensuous embodiment of the echoing footfalls down the imaginary passage to the closed door into the rose-garden. "My words echo / Thus your mind," says the poet. He may be addressing the reader and

[1] "Burnt Norton" is reprinted with the permission of Charles Scribner's Sons from *T. S. Eliot: The Design of His Poetry*, pp. 151–162, by Elizabeth Drew.

suggesting that such experiences are common to all; or the echoes may be in the mind of the woman in the imaginary scene. Then he returns to the symbolic presentation of the past as "dust on a bowl of rose-leaves." What *purpose* can such disturbing memories have, since the past is unredeemable, its pattern unalterable?

The rhythm quickens to a sense of breathless expectancy and creates the sense of the mind darting about, confusing the logic of temporal and spatial happenings in its own spontaneous flight into "the garden." The interpretation of the lovely scene in the rose-garden itself must depend on personal readings. Many people seem to feel it as a memory of childhood, taking "our first world" to mean that. I interpret the whole passage in the light of the line between the conclusion of the development of all the themes and the final recapitulation at the end of *Little Gidding*: "With the drawing of this Love and the voice of this Calling." That transfigures the bird and the roses of *Burnt Norton* into the dove of *Little Gidding* and the rose of fire and light at the end of that poem: that is, nature becomes a symbol of a spiritual truth which transcends it. By the end of the poems "our first world" and the children in the leaves hold a suggestion of the age of innocence in the Garden of Eden, before the pattern of perfect relationship between God, man and nature was clouded and darkened. Here, in *Burnt Norton*, a transcendence of nature is brought about by the experience being "an airy nothing" given "a local habitation," and by its fusion of nature and man into perfect inter-relationship. But the experience itself—that of *this* love and *this* calling—seems to me to be that of love as a part of the natural world, the "first world" of our development as human beings, the first "gate" on the way. The voice of the thrush is "deception," partly because the whole thing is unseen and unheard by the outward senses, and partly because the experience, though it is one of the moments of "reality," contains only a partial revelation of it, since its centre is in the sense world.

The vision is created in flowing, free and melodious rhythms, its invisible and inaudible quality mysteriously carried by the clearest pictures and verse music. The actual setting in place and time is an autumn scene, but the echoing footfalls of memory and might-have-been enter the deserted rose-garden and people it with life from an inner world. The voice of the bird calls in response to "unheard music" in the shrubbery; the unseen figures *must* be there "for the roses had the look of flowers that are looked at." The roses (the emblems of earthly love) and the dream figures from the past are blended into an inseparable union of giving and receiving, "accepted and accepting." With that the scene groups itself round a symbolic centre "in a formal pattern." The roses and the figures move, concentrating the "point" of vision from the garden to the evergreen "box circle" and thence to the pool and the lotos. The actual deserted drained pool, and its emotional counterpart in the hardness and dryness and neutral shades of the actuality of life, are suddenly transformed into the exquisite moment:

And the pool was filled with water out of sunlight,
And the lotos rose, quietly, quietly,
The surface glittered out of heart of light,
And they were behind us, reflected in the pool.

Here in natural terms, in the autumn "vibrant air" is the parallel with what in *Little Gidding* is the "mid-winter spring" of the pentecostal fire, which is "not in the scheme of generation." Here, nature and man seem part of an indestructible unity and harmony which *is* within the scheme of generation; the golden cup of the lotos and the surface of the pool receiving their glittering light from the physical sun; the human figures and the roses reflected in the water; the fading leaves full of children "hidden excitedly, containing laughter." The vision is that of an ecstasy of fulfillment at the human and natural level, which is a beautiful "reality," though not the ultimate one. It is blotted out by the cloud, the bird says "Go, go, go"—leave *that* garden—and we are brought back from the vision to the grave statement of the opening, that all things "point to one end, which is always present."

The lovely dancing lyric at the opening of the second movement is obviously based on the Heraclitean idea of the perpetual strife which resolves itself into beautiful harmony. The apparently conflicting and the apparently static are all part of an eternal moving pattern, existing simultaneously in all the elements in nature and linking them in a dynamic whole. The only inanimate thing is "the bedded axle-tree," maybe a relic of some chariot or gun-carriage in a "forgotten war," but reminding us of the symbol of the wheel. From the bright stones under it and the bright flowers around it, from under the "sodden floor" up to the stars, there streams up and down this uninterrupted energy of strife, forming itself into harmonious living patterns; singing, dancing, circulating, and having their final meaning in "the stars," the reflection of the Heraclitean "fire." Even the rather horrible strife of pursuer and pursued, the boarhound and the boar, is constellated (like the warring of the Olympian gods?) into an eternally subsisting order.

But then there is a complete change of rhythm. Heraclitus' system had no still point, which makes his dance very different. His concept of reconciliation is that of perpetual sustaining tension between opposites and not of a centre of resolution. How then define this centre dispassionately, rationally? In place of the crowding, swift images creating the ever-changing configurations of natural forces, the rhythm becomes slow, the vocabulary abstract, the method analytical. But the poet finds the language of logic inadequate here. The still point can be approached only through paradox and negation. It is nothing that can be measured in terms of time, or of movement and fixity, of body or spirit, of ascent and descent. And yet it cannot be detached from these things, because though it is the point where there is no movement, it controls all the movement, and it is only through the measured movements that its presence can be known. It exists, but cannot be captured in a *where* or *when*.

Breaking off the effort at definition by negation and exclusion, the next sequence, continuing the analytical approach, describes in positive terms the *quality* of the experience, which has been given direct sensuous revelation in the vision in the rose-garden. It is a feeling of detachment from the ego and its conflicts, with a sense of grace and illumination and combined stillness and movement; a keeping of personal identity, and of the world of human experience, and yet an expansion beyond it and an elevation above it. Above all a sense of *wholeness*, in which the fragmentary nature of human experience, its partial ecstasy, and its partial horror, are completed and resolved and given *meaning*. Yet man, because he is human, cannot live at the level of the apprehension of wholeness. "Woven in the weakness of the changing body" are the inextricable strands which chain him to time and change. But the chains protect him too. They protect him from more than glimpses of absolute good or evil, ecstasy or agony, "which flesh cannot endure"—whose *duration* would cost man his humanity, since time and change are the laws of his being. He has these moments of ecstasy when he seems to transcend time and conquer it, but it is only within the pattern of time that they can be seen to be a part of a timeless pattern.

The third movement introduces the theme which is in absolute contrast to that of life as part of an ordered natural process, and of life as a pattern of inner relationships centred in the still point, and pointed towards it. It is that of life with no centre, no ordered direction, no organic relationships. Eliot creates these antitheses into a passage where images of them and the language in which they are described produce the most immediate and concrete sensations. On the one hand we feel the true emotional oppositions, by any of which the still point may be reached and which are as patterned as the natural images which symbolize them; on the other all the confusion and fragmentariness and negative neutrality of the dim "place of disaffection." That word itself at once condenses a complex of ideas of the cause and effect of the condition. It carries connotations of discontent; of the diminution and alienation of affection; and of disorder. The next lines contrast the oppositions which are rendered *lucid* by the sense of pattern, with the disaffection and dimness, which are

> neither daylight
> Investing form with lucid stillness
> Turning shadow into transient beauty
> With slow rotation suggesting permanence
> Nor darkness to purify the soul
> Emptying the sensual with deprivation
> Cleansing affection from the temporal.
> Neither plenitude nor vacancy.

The London scene which follows continues the parallels. Instead of creative tension there is *strain* on the "time-ridden faces / Distracted from distraction by distraction." Instead of light or dark, a *flicker* and *faded air* and *gloomy hills*; instead of plenitude or vacancy, the faces "filled with fancies and empty of meaning"; instead of wholeness, *unwholesome* lungs, *unhealthy* souls; instead of permanence and lucid stillness, the *tumid apathy* of the *torpid*; instead of measured movement the "men and bits of paper, whirled by the cold wind."

From all "this twittering world" of dim light and dim humanity, the poet turns to the creative "way down" into the inner darkness and isolation and silence, to the vacancy which is not "empty of meaning," but empty of self. It is "deprivation / And destitution of all property," the active forsaking of the ego, the way of withdrawal from the worlds of both sense and spirit, the disciplined "abstention from movement";

> while the world moves
> In appetency, on its metalled ways
> Of time past and time future.

Here again in *appetency* there is a great concentration of meaning. Not only the sense of conscious and unconscious compulsive drives, but the reminder of the Lamarckian doctrine that changes in the desires and needs of an organism result in adaptive modifications of its structure. So that the "metalled ways" on which the urban world now moves, suggest not only a picture of it as a vast network of roads and railways leading nowhere, but the whole quality of the mechanistic culture of today and its possible consequences for the future of the race.

After the formal declaration and loaded latinized language of the third movement, the short lyric of the fourth takes us back to the memory of the vision in the garden, but in a very different mood. There, there was the ecstatic assurance of lucid pattern uniting nature and man. This was reinforced by the lyric emphasizing the dynamic order of the natural world and the passages of analysis describing the order of the world of spirit. Against this was the disorder of the modern city. From this the poet turned to a discipline of spiritual negation and a conquest of sense. But that is a voluntary darkness and emptiness; there is a return from it to the world which had been renounced. What of the involuntary defeat of the darkness and silence of death, which is the inevitable end of "the changing body"? With mingled horror and hope the poet questions its meaning.

> Time and the bell have buried the day,
> The black cloud carries the sun away.

The day and all that daylight brought, "investing form with lucid stillness" and the sense of permanent moving pattern, is "buried"; its lucid stillness destroyed by the black cloud and the death knell. The only sense of movement is the carrying away of the sun by the cloud, not only obscuring but *removing* the unmoving centre of the universe as we know it. This fact brings at one level sensations of pure terror. The words *bury, cloud, clutch, cling, curled fingers*, and the isolation of *chill* as a line in itself, suggest obliteration, dark cold extinction, strangulation by forces against which man is helpless. Will the only centre of life then be the nourishment our rotting bodies supply to the loveliness of flowers and trees? But there is another tone of gentler questioning. To pass into the pattern of nature expressed in the turning of the sunflower; in the tendrils and sprays of the clematis straying down, bending, clutching and clinging; in the curled fingers of the yew, has its own beauty. But will it be all? The tones of both horror and tender regret in the question are answered by the flashing image of the kingfisher in relation to the source of natural light, and its parallel in terms of the spirit.

> After the kingfisher's wing
> Has answered light to light, and is silent, the light is still
> At the still point of the turning world.

The opposition of the movement of the kingfisher's wing and silence, in the last image, leads on to the next subject, the union of movement and stillness in a work of art and its parallel with the worlds of time and the still point. The poet shifts again to analytical discourse, this time in flowing speech rhythms. Again we have the two worlds of the temporal and the unchanging contrasted. The actuality of poetry and music to eye and ear is a series of progressions in a temporal sequence. But if they existed only in that dimension they would die like the flower and the kingfisher. Their "reality" is a matter of dynamic relationships, a structure where every part is involved with every other part to form an indivisible whole. The temporal sequence is co-existent with the unchanging pattern, all held together in a vital tension of sound and meaning. Carrying on the image of the whole as a system of tensions, he says:

> Words strain,
> Crack and sometimes break, under the burden,
> Under the tension, slip, slide, perish,
> Decay with imprecision, will not stay in place,
> Will not stay still. Shrieking voices
> Scolding, mocking, or merely chattering,
> Always assail them.

We shift almost imperceptibly from the abstract discussion of an intellectual aesthetic to the immediate reminder that this is by way of illustration of something else. The theme is not primarily a matter of aesthetics or physics. The burden is not only the weight on a word. The *imprecision* is linked with the concrete *decay*, the loss of tension with the concrete *slip, slide, perish*. The abstract stillness and movement of poetic "form" is invaded by the discordant, irrelevant "voices." In the last image the sense of *disorder* is suddenly intensified and its menace as the enemy of pattern and permanence is created in the word *assail*. Then "words" become the Word and we are translated from art to life.

> The Word in the desert
> Is most attacked by voices of temptation,
> The crying shadow in the funeral dance,
> The loud lament of the disconsolate chimera.

The temptation, the *attack* on creative order, becomes the wonderful complex imagery of the last two lines, where the harmonious dance is disturbed by "the funeral dance," and where noise, darkness, self-pity and self-deception invade the stillness. "The disconsolate chimera" is another of those strokes of genius where the words absorb and radiate implications. *Disconsolate*, recalling the earlier *disaffection*, carries the meaning of comfortless and melancholy, while *chimera* is both an empty, meaningless fancy and the incongruously composed monster slain by Bellerophon. Every aspect of the meanings fuse, and the *loud lament* and the *crying shadow* again enforce the sense of discord, pain and confused darkness of the temptation.

The recapitulation of the whole poem moves in a measure of short fluent lines, which is used again at the conclusion of *The Dry Salvages* and *Little Gidding*. The pattern of dynamic tensions sustaining life, which in the natural world was "figured in the drift of stars" and down to the garlic and the mud, is, in the world of spirit "the figure of the ten stairs." This is a reference to St. John of the Cross, who pictured the discipline of contemplation as a ladder of ten steps "which the soul is ascending and descending continually in ecstasy and humiliation until it has acquired perfect habits." The summit of the ladder and what it rests upon is God as Love, and for a moment we are taken outside of both the turning world and the pattern whose centre is the still point, to the unmoved mover who exists untouched by the temporal, by the "form of limitation" decreed by life. Love in its human aspect cannot rid itself entirely of the element of desire. It can reach only to the moment of "reality" in the rose-garden, when, for a brief instant, nature and spirit glittered together "out of heart of light." Swiftly we are transported back to that ecstasy—

> Sudden in a shaft of sunlight
> Even while the dust moves
> There rises the hidden laughter
> Of children in the foliage
> Quick now, here, now, always—

The "purpose" of the disturbance of the dust on the bowl of rose-leaves is now clear. It is a reminder that every moment of time can be transfigured by the apprehension of the timeless pattern and the sharing of its vitality. The release, the "grace of sense," the spontaneous, joyous illumination, comes like the "dancing arrow" of bird flight, flashes in the here and now—and is gone— leaving the sense of the combined unimportance and unworthiness and mockery of "the aspect of time."

Ridiculous the waste sad time
Stretching before and after.

JOHN CROWE RANSOM

Blue Girls[1]

Twirling your blue skirts, traveling the sward
Under the towers of your seminary,
Go listen to your teachers old and contrary
Without believing a word.

Tie the white fillets then about your lustrous hair
And think no more of what will come to pass
Than bluebirds that go walking on the grass
And chattering on the air.

Practice your beauty, blue girls, before it fail;
And I will cry with my loud lips and publish
Beauty which all our power shall never establish,
It is so frail.

For I could tell you a story which is true:
I know a lady with a terrible tongue,
Blear eyes fallen from blue,
All her perfections tarnished—and yet it is not long
Since she was lovelier than any of you.

ARCHIBALD MACLEISH[2]

The End of the World

Quite unexpectedly as Vasserot
The armless ambidextrian was lighting
A match between his great and second toe

And Ralph the lion was engaged in biting
The neck of Madame Sossman while the drum
Pointed, and Teeny was about to cough
In waltz-time swinging Jocko by the thumb—
Quite unexpectedly the top blew off:

And there, there overhead, there, there, hung over
Those thousands of white faces, those dazed eyes,
There in the starless dark, the poise, the hover,
There with vast wings across the canceled skies,
There in the sudden blackness, the black pall
Of nothing, nothing, nothing—nothing at all.

You, Andrew Marvell

And here face down beneath the sun
And here upon earth's noonward height
To feel the always coming on
The always rising of the night

To feel creep up the curving east
The earthly chill of dusk and slow
Upon those under lands the vast
And ever climbing shadow grow

And strange at Ecbatan the trees
Take leaf by leaf the evening strange   10
The flooding dark about their knees
The mountains over Persia change

And now at Kermanshah the gate
Dark empty and the withered grass
And through the twilight now the late
Few travelers in the westward pass

And Baghdad darken and the bridge
Across the silent river gone
And through Arabia the edge
Of evening widen and steal on   20

And deepen on Palmyra's street
The wheel rut in the ruined stone
And Lebanon fade out and Crete
High through the clouds and overblown

And over Sicily the air
Still flashing with the landward gulls
And loom and slowly disappear
The sails above the shadowy hulls

And Spain go under and the shore
Of Africa the gilded sand
And evening vanish and no more
The low pale light across that land

Nor now the long light on the sea
And here face downward in the sun
To feel how swift how secretly
The shadow of the night comes on . . .

30

E. E. CUMMINGS

I [1]

     in Just-
     spring   when the world is mud-
     luscious the little
     lame baloonman

     whistles   far   and wee

     and eddieandbill come
     running from marbles and
     piracies and it's
     spring

     when the world is puddle-wonderful

10

     the queer
     old baloonman whistles
     far   and   wee
     and bettyandisbel come dancing

     from hop-scotch and jump-rope and

it's
spring
and
   the

        goat-footed

baloonMan   whistles
far
and
wee

II [1]

Space being(don't forget to remember)Curved
(and that reminds me who said o yes Frost
Something there is which isn't fond of walls)

an electromagnetic(now I've lost
the)Einstein expanded Newton's law preserved
conTinuum(but we read that beFore)

of Course life being just a Reflex you
know since Everything is Relative or

to sum it All Up god being Dead(not to

mention inTerred)
             LONG LIVE that Upwardlooking
Serene Illustrious and Beatific
Lord of Creation,MAN:
                at a least crooking
of Whose compassionate digit,earth's most terrific

quadruped swoons into billiardBalls!

III [1]

mr u will not be missed
who as an anthologist

20

sold the many on the few
not excluding mr u

IV [1]

if everything happens that can't be done
(and anything's righter
than books
could plan)
the stupidest teacher will almost guess
(with a run
skip
around we go yes)
there's nothing as something as one

one hasn't a why or because or although   10
(and buds know better
than books
don't grow)
one's anything old being everything new
(with a what
which
around we come who)
one's everyanything so

so world is a leaf so tree is a bough
(and birds sing sweeter   20
than books
tell how)
so here is away and so your is a my
(with a down
up
around again fly)
forever was never till now

now i love you and you love me
(and books are shuter
than books   30
can be)
and deep in the high that does nothing but fall
(with a shout

each
around we go all)
there's somebody calling who's we

we're anything brighter than even the sun
(we're everything greater
than books
might mean)   40
we're everyanything more than believe
(with a spin
leap
alive we're alive)
we're wonderful one times one

HART CRANE[1]

At Melville's Tomb

Often beneath the wave, wide from this ledge
The dice of drowned men's bones he saw bequeath
An embassy. Their numbers as he watched,
Beat on the dusty shore and were obscured.

And wrecks passed without sound of bells,
The calyx of death's bounty giving back
A scattered chapter, livid hieroglyph,
The portent wound in corridors of shells.

Then in the circuit calm of one vast coil,
Its lashings charmed and malice reconciled,
Frosted eyes there were that lifted altars;
And silent answers crept across the stars.

Compass, quadrant and sextant contrive
No farther tides . . . High in the azure steeps
Monody shall not wake the mariner.
This fabulous shadow only the sea keeps.

HART CRANE AND HARRIET MONROE

On Crane's "At Melville's Tomb" [1]

Apropos of the poem "At Melville's Tomb," printed in the verse section of this number, the following correspondence between its author and the editor, printed with the consent of both, may be of interest to our readers.

From the editor to Mr. Crane:

Take me for a hard-boiled unimaginative unpoetic reader, and tell me how *dice* can *bequeath an embassy* (or anything else); and how a *calyx* (*of death's bounty* or anything else) can give back a *scattered chapter, livid hieroglyph*; and how, if it does, such a *portent* can be *wound in corridors* (of shells or anything else).

And so on. I find your image of *frosted eyes lifting altars* difficult to visualize. Nor do compass, quadrant and sextant *contrive* tides, they merely record them, I believe.

All this may seem impertinent, but is not so intended. Your ideas and rhythms interest me, and I am wondering by what process of reasoning you would justify this poem's succession of champion mixed metaphors, of which you must be conscious. The packed line should pack its phrases in orderly relation, it seems to me, in a manner tending to clear confusion instead of making it worse confounded.

But pardon me—you didn't ask for criticism. Of course, I should not venture upon these remarks if I were not much interested.

From Mr. Crane to the editor:

Your good nature and manifest interest in writing me about the obscurities apparent in my Melville poem certainly prompt a wish to clarify my intentions in that poem as much as possible. But I realize that my explanations will not be very convincing. For a paraphrase is generally a poor substitute for any organized conception that one has fancied he has put into the more essentialized form of the poem itself.

At any rate, and though I imagine us to have considerable differences of opinion regarding the relationship of poetic metaphor to ordinary logic (I judge this from the angle of approach you use toward portions of the poem), I hope my answers will not be taken as a defense of merely certain faulty lines. I am really much more interested in certain theories of metaphor and technique

[1] From *Poetry: A Magazine of Verse*, XXIX (October, 1926), 34-41. Whole article, "A Discussion with Hart Crane." Reprinted by permission of the authors and the publisher.

involved generally in poetics, than I am concerned in vindicating any particular perpetrations of my own.

My poem may well be elliptical and actually obscure in the ordering of its content, but in your criticism of this very possible deficiency you have stated your objections in terms that allow me, at least for the moment, the privilege of claiming your ideas and ideals as theoretically, at least, quite outside the issues of my own aspirations. To put it more plainly, as a poet I may very possibly be more interested in the so-called illogical impingements of the connotations of words on the consciousness (and their combinations and interplay in metaphor on this basis) than I am interested in the preservation of their logically rigid significations at the cost of limiting my subject matter and perceptions involved in the poem.

This may sound as though I merely fancied juggling words and images until I found something novel, or esoteric; but the process is much more predetermined and objectified than that. The nuances of feeling and observation in a poem may well call for certain liberties which you claim the poet has no right to take. I am simply making the claim that the poet does have that authority, and that to deny it is to limit the scope of the medium so considerably as to outlaw some of the richest genius of the past.

This argument over the dynamics of metaphor promises as active a future as has been evinced in the past. Partaking so extensively as it does of the issues involved in the propriety or non-propriety of certain attitudes toward subject matter, etc., it enters the critical distinctions usually made between "romantic," "classic" as an organic factor. It is a problem that would require many pages to state adequately—merely from my own limited standpoint on the issues. Even this limited statement may prove onerous reading, and I hope you will pardon me if my own interest in the matter carries me to the point of presumption.

Its paradox, of course, is that its apparent illogic operates so logically in conjunction with its context in the poem as to establish its claim to another logic, quite independent of the original definition of the word or phrase or image thus employed. It implies (this *inflection* of language) a previous or prepared receptivity to its stimulus on the part of the reader. The reader's sensibility simply responds by identifying this inflection of experience with some event in his own history or perceptions—or rejects it altogether. The logic of metaphor is so organically entrenched in pure sensibility that it can't be thoroughly traced or explained outside of historical sciences, like philology and anthropology. This "pseudo-statement," as I. A. Richards calls it in an admirable essay touching our contentions in last July's *Criterion*, demands completely other faculties of recognition than the pure rationalistic associations permit. Much fine poetry may be completely rationalistic in its use of symbols, but there is much great poetry of another order which will yield the reader very little when inspected under the limitation of such arbitrary concerns as are manifested in your judgment of the Melville poem, especially when you constitute such requirements of ordinary logical relationship between word and word as irreducible.

I don't wish to enter here defense of the particular symbols employed in my own poem, because, as I said, I may well have failed to supply the necessary emotional connectives to the content featured. But I would like to counter a question or so of yours with a similar question. Here the poem is less dubious in quality than my own, and as far as the abstract pertinacity of question and its immediate consequences are concerned the point I'm arguing about can be better demonstrated. Both quotations are familiar to you, I'm sure.

You ask me how a *portent* can possibly be wound in a *shell*. Without attempting to answer this for the moment, I ask you how Blake could possibly say that "a *sigh* is a *sword* of an Angel King." You ask me how *compass, quadrant and sextant* "contrive" tides. I ask you how Eliot can possibly believe that "Every street *lamp* that I pass *beats* like a fatalistic *drum!*" Both of my metaphors may fall down completely. I'm not defending their actual value in themselves; but your criticism of them in each case was leveled at an illogicality of relationship between symbols, which similar fault you must have either overlooked in case you have ever admired the Blake and Eliot lines, or have there condoned them on account of some more ultimate convictions pressed on you by the impact of the poems in their entirety.

It all comes to the recognition that emotional dynamics are not to be confused with any absolute order of rationalized definitions; ergo, in poetry the *rationale* of metaphor belongs to another order of experience than science, and is not to be limited by a scientific and arbitrary code of relationships either in verbal inflections or concepts.

There are plenty of people who have never accumulated a sufficient series of reflections (and these of a rather special nature) to perceive the relation between a *drum* and a *street lamp—via* the *unmentioned* throbbing of the heart and nerves in a distraught man which *tacitly* creates the reason and "logic" of the Eliot metaphor. They will always have a perfect justification for ignoring those lines and to claim them obscure, excessive, etc., until by some experience of their own the words accumulate the necessary connotations to complete their connection. It is the same with the "patient etherized upon a table," isn't it? Surely that line must lack all eloquence to many people who, for instance, would delight in agreeing that the sky was like a dome of many-colored glass.

If one can't count on some such bases in the reader now and then, I don't see how the poet has any chance to ever get beyond the simplest conceptions of emotion and thought, of sensation and lyrical sequence. If the poet is to be held completely to the already evolved and exploited sequences of imagery and logic —what field of added consciousness and increased perceptions (the actual province of poetry, if not lullabies) can be expected when one has to relatively return to the alphabet every breath or so? In the minds of people who have sensitively read, seen and experienced a great deal, isn't there a terminology something like short-hand as compared to usual description and dialectics, which the artist ought to be right in trusting as a reasonable connective agent toward fresh concepts, more inclusive evaluations? The question is more important to me than it perhaps ought to be; but as long as poetry is written, an audience, however small, is implied, and there remains the question of an active or an inactive imagination as its characteristic.

It is of course understood that a street-lamp simply can't beat with a sound like a drum; but it often happens that images, themselves totally dissociated, when joined in the circuit of a particular emotion located with specific relation to both of them, conduce to great vividness and accuracy of statement in defining that emotion.

Not to rant on forever, I'll beg your indulgence and come at once to the explanations you requested on the Melville poem:

> The dice of drowned men's bones he saw bequeath
> An embassy.

Dice bequeath an embassy, in the first place, by being ground (in this connection only, of course) in little cubes from the bones of drowned men by the action of the sea, and are finally thrown up on the sand, having "numbers" but no identification. These being the bones of dead men who never completed their voyage, it seems legitimate to refer to them as the only surviving evidence of certain messages undelivered, mute evidence of certain things, experiences that the dead mariners might have had to deliver. Dice as a symbol of chance and circumstance is also implied.

> The calyx of death's bounty giving back, etc.

This calyx refers in a double ironic sense both to a cornucopia and the vortex made by a sinking vessel. As soon as the water has closed over a ship this whirlpool sends up broken spars, wreckage, etc., which can be alluded to as *livid hieroglyphs*, making a *scattered chapter* so far as any complete record of the recent ship and her crew is concerned. In fact, about as much definite knowledge might come from all this as anyone might gain from the roar of his own veins, which is easily heard (haven't you ever done it?) by holding a shell close to one's ear.

> Frosted eyes lift altars.

Refers simply to a conviction that a man, not knowing perhaps a definite god yet being endowed with a reverence for deity—such a man naturally postulates a deity somehow, and the altar of that deity by the very *action* of the eyes *lifted* in searching.

> Compass, quadrant and sextant contrive no farther tides.

Hasn't it often occurred that instruments originally invented for record and computation have inadvertently so extended the concepts of the entity they were invented to measure (concepts of space, etc.) in the mind and imagination that employed them, that they may metaphorically be said to have extended the original boundaries of the entity measured? This little bit of "relativity" ought not to be discredited in poetry now that scientists are proceeding to measure the universe on principles of pure *ratio*, quite as metaphorical, so far as previous standards of scientific methods extended, as some of the axioms in *Job*.

I may have completely failed to provide any clear interpretation of these symbols in their context. And you will no doubt feel that I have rather heatedly explained them for anyone who professes no claims for their particular value. I hope, at any rate, that I have clarified them enough to suppress any suspicion that their obscurity derives from a lack of definite intentions in the subject-matter of the poem. The execution is another matter, and you must be accorded a superior judgment to mine in that regard.

From the editor to Mr. Crane:

No doubt our theories and ideals in the art differ more or less fundamentally, yet I would not deny to the poet the right to take certain of the liberties you claim. I think he can take as many as he succeeds with without mystifying his particular audience; for mystery is good, but not mystification.

I think that in your poem certain phrases carry to an excessive degree the "dynamics of metaphor"—they telescope three or four images together by mental leaps (I fear my own metaphors are getting mixed!) which the poet, knowing his ground, can take safely, but which the most sympathetic reader cannot take unless the poet leads him by the hand with some such explanation as I find in your letter. I refer to such phrases as my letter quoted, except that I think I was over-exacting in criticizing the "quadrant and sextant" line. Accepting as I do much of what you say about "the illogical impingements of the connotations of words on the consciousness, and their combinations and interplay in metaphor," I must admit that these phrases in your poem are for me too elliptical to produce any effect but mystification (this until you explained them).

I don't get this effect from Blake or Eliot in the lines you quote or others that I have read. I am not familiar with Blake's symbolic poems but now, opening Prof. Pierce's volume of selections from them, I find in their use of metaphor a singular simplicity and clarity. He deals with magnificent mysteries, but presents them in flaming images like

> what time I bound my sandals
> On to walk forward through eternity.

I find here no crowded and tortured lines.

My argument comes down, I suppose, rather to your practice than your theory. Or, more specifically, your practice strains your theory by carrying it, with relentless logic, to a remote and exaggerated extreme. You find me testing metaphors, and poetic concept in general, too much by logic, whereas I find you pushing logic to the limit in a painfully intellectual search for emotion, for poetic motive. Your poem reeks with brains—it is thought out, worked out, sweated out. And the beauty which it seems entitled to is tortured and lost.

In all this I may be entirely wrong, and I am aware that a number of poets and critics would think so. Yvor Winters, for example, in a recent letter, speaks of your *Marriage of Faustus and Helen* in *Secession* 7 as "one of the great poems

of our time, as great as the best of Stevens or Pound or Eliot." Well, I cannot
grant it such a rank.

The editor would rather not have the last word, but as Mr. Crane contributes
no further to the discussion, we must pass it on to our readers.

Voyages: II

—And yet this great wink of eternity,
Of rimless floods, unfettered leewardings,
Samite sheeted and processioned where
Her undinal vast belly moonward bends,
Laughing the wrapt inflections of our love;

Take this Sea, whose diapason knells
On scrolls of silver snowy sentences,
The sceptered terror of whose sessions rends
As her demeanors motion well or ill,
All but the pieties of lovers' hands.   10

And onward, as bells off San Salvador
Salute the crocus lusters of the stars,
In these poinsettia meadows of her tides,—
Adagios of islands, O my Prodigal,
Complete the dark confessions her veins spell.

Mark how her turning shoulders wind the hours,
And hasten while her penniless rich palms
Pass superscription of bent foam and wave,—
Hasten, while they are true,—sleep, death, desire,
Close round one instant in one floating flower.   20

Bind us in time, O seasons clear, and awe.
O minstrel galleons of Carib fire,
Bequeath us to no earthly shore until
Is answered in the vortex of our grave
The seal's wide spindrift gaze toward paradise.

The Air Plant

GRAND CAYMAN, W. I.

This tuft that thrives on saline nothingness,
Inverted octopus with heavenward arms

Thrust parching from a palm-bole hard by the cove—
A bird almost—of almost bird alarms,

Is pulmonary to the wind that jars
Its tentacles, horrific in the lurch.
The lizard's throat, held bloated for a fly,
Balloons but warily from this throbbing perch.

The needles and hacksaws of cactus bleed
A milk of earth when stricken off the stalk;
But this—defenseless, thornless, sheds no blood,
Scarce shadow even—but the air's thin talk.

Angelic Dynamo! Ventriloquist of the Blue!
While beachward creeps the shark-swept Spanish Main.
By what conjunctions do the winds appoint
Its apotheosis, at last—the hurricane!

OGDEN NASH

Very Like a Whale[1]

One thing that literature would be greatly the better for
Would be a more restricted employment by authors of simile and metaphor.
Authors of all races, be they Greeks, Romans, Teutons or Celts,
Can't seem just to say that anything is the thing it is but have to go out of
    their way to say that it is like something else.
What does it mean when we are told
That the Assyrian came down like a wolf on the fold?
In the first place, George Gordon Byron had had enough experience
To know that it probably wasn't just one Assyrian, it was a lot of Assyrians.
However, as too many arguments are apt to induce apoplexy and thus hinder
    longevity,
We'll let it pass as one Assyrian for the sake of brevity.   10
Now then, this particular Assyrian, the one whose cohorts were gleaming in
    purple and gold,
Just what does the poet mean when he says he came down like a wolf on the
    fold?

[1] From *Many Long Years Ago.* By permission of Little, Brown and Company.
Copyright, 1935, by Ogden Nash.

In heaven and earth more than is dreamed of in our philosophy there are a
    great many things,
But I don't imagine that among them there is a wolf with purple and gold
    cohorts or purple and gold anythings.
No, no, Lord Byron, before I'll believe that this Assyrian was actually like a
    wolf I must have some kind of proof;
Did he run on all fours and did he have a hairy tail and a big red mouth and
    big white teeth and did he say Woof woof woof?
Frankly I think it very unlikely, and all you were entitled to say, at the very
    most,
Was that the Assyrian cohorts came down like a lot of Assyrian cohorts about
    to destroy the Hebrew host.
But that wasn't fancy enough for Lord Byron, oh dear me no, he had to invent
    a lot of figures of speech and then interpolate them.
With the result that whenever you mention Old Testament soldiers to people
    they say Oh yes, they're the ones that a lot of wolves dressed up in gold
    and purple ate them.   20
That's the kind of thing that's being done all the time by poets, from Homer
    to Tennyson;
They're always comparing ladies to lilies and veal to venison,
And they always say things like that the snow is a white blanket after a winter
    storm.
Oh it is, is it, all right then, you sleep under a six-inch blanket of snow and
    I'll sleep under a half-inch blanket of unpoetical blanket material and
    we'll see which one keeps warm,
And after that maybe you'll begin to comprehend dimly
What I mean by too much metaphor and simile.

The Purist[1]

    I give you now Professor Twist,
    A conscientious scientist.
    Trustees exclaimed, "He never bungles!"
    And sent him off to distant jungles.
    Camped on a tropic riverside,
    One day he missed his loving bride.
    She had, the guide informed him later,
    Been eaten by an alligator.
    Professor Twist could not but smile.
    "You mean," he said, "a crocodile."

W. H. AUDEN

Musée des Beaux Arts[1]

About suffering they were never wrong,
The Old Masters: how well they understood
Its human position; how it takes place
While someone else is eating or opening a window or just walking dully along;
How, when the aged are reverently, passionately waiting
For the miraculous birth, there always must be
Children who did not specially want it to happen, skating
On a pond at the edge of the wood:
They never forgot
That even the dreadful martyrdom must run its course   10
Anyhow in a corner, some untidy spot
Where the dogs go on with their doggy life and the torturer's horse
Scratches its innocent behind on a tree.

In Brueghel's *Icarus*, for instance: how everything turns away
Quite leisurely from the disaster; the ploughman may
Have heard the splash, the forsaken cry,
But for him it was not an important failure; the sun shone
As it had to on the white legs disappearing into the green
Water; and the expensive delicate ship that must have seen
Something amazing, a boy falling out of the sky,   20
Had somewhere to get to and sailed calmly on.

Petition[2]

Sir, no man's enemy, forgiving all
But will his negative inversion, be prodigal:
Send to us power and light, a sovereign touch
Curing the intolerable neural itch,
The exhaustion of weaning, the liar's quinsy,
And the distortions of ingrown virginity.
Prohibit sharply the rehearsed response
And gradually correct the coward's stance;

Cover in time with beams those in retreat
That, spotted, they turn though the reverse were great;
Publish each healer that in city lives
Or country houses at the end of drives;
Harrow the house of the dead; look shining at
New styles of architecture, a change of heart.

In Memory of W. B. Yeats[1]

d. Jan. 1939

I

He disappeared in the dead of winter:
The brooks were frozen, the air-ports almost deserted,
And snow disfigured the public statues;
The mercury sank in the mouth of the dying day.
O all the instruments agree
The day of his death was a dark cold day.

Far from his illness
The wolves ran on through the evergreen forests,
The peasant river was untempted by the fashionable quays;
By mourning tongues   10
The death of the poet was kept from his poems.

But for him it was his last afternoon as himself,
An afternoon of nurses and rumours;
The provinces of his body revolted,
The squares of his mind were empty,
Silence invaded the suburbs,
The current of his feeling failed: he became his admirers.

Now he is scattered among a hundred cities
And wholly given over to unfamiliar affections;
To find his happiness in another kind of wood   20
And he punished under a foreign code of conscience.
The words of a dead man
Are modified in the guts of the living.

But in the importance and noise of to-morrow
When the brokers are roaring like beasts on the floor of the Bourse,
And the poor have the sufferings to which they are fairly accustomed,
And each in the cell of himself is almost convinced of his freedom;
A few thousand will think of this day
As one thinks of a day when one did something slightly unusual.

O all the instruments agree   30
The day of his death was a dark cold day.

II

You were silly like us: your gift survived it all;
The parish of rich women, physical decay,
Yourself; mad Ireland hurt you into poetry.
Now Ireland has her madness and her weather still,
For poetry makes nothing happen: it survives
In the valley of its saying where executives
Would never want to tamper; it flows south
From ranches of isolation and the busy griefs,
Raw towns that we believe and die in; it survives,   40
A way of happening, a mouth.

III

Earth, receive an honoured guest;
William Yeats is laid to rest:
Let the Irish vessel lie
Emptied of its poetry.

Time that is intolerant
Of the brave and innocent,
And indifferent in a week
To a beautiful physique,

Worships language and forgives   50
Everyone by whom it lives;
Pardons cowardice, conceit,
Lays its honours at their feet.

Time that with this strange excuse
Pardoned Kipling and his views,
And will pardon Paul Claudel,
Pardons him for writing well.

In the nightmare of the dark
All the dogs of Europe bark,

And the living nations wait,   60
Each sequestered in its hate;

Intellectual disgrace
Stares from every human face,
And the seas of pity lie
Locked and frozen in each eye.

Follow, poet, follow right
To the bottom of the night,
With your unconstraining voice
Still persuade us to rejoice;

With the farming of a verse   70
Make a vineyard of the curse,
Sing of human unsuccess
In a rapture of distress;

In the deserts of the heart
Let the healing fountain start,
In the prison of his days
Teach the free man how to praise.

Under Which Lyre[1]

A Reactionary Tract for the Times
Phi Beta Kappa Poem. Harvard. 1946

Ares at last has quit the field,
The bloodstains on the bushes yield
    To seeping showers,
And in their convalescent state
The fractured towns associate
    With summer flowers.

Encamped upon the college plain
Raw veterans already train
    As freshman forces;
Instructors with sarcastic tongue   10
Shepherd the battle-weary young
    Through basic courses.

Among bewildering appliances
For mastering the arts and sciences
    They stroll or run,
And nerves that never flinched at slaughter
Are shot to pieces by the shorter
    Poems of Donne.

Professors back from secret missions
Resume their proper eruditions,   20
    Though some regret it;
They like their dictaphones a lot,
They met some big wheels, and do not
    Let you forget it.

But Zeus' inscrutable decree
Permits the will-to-disagree
    To be pandemic,
Ordains that vaudeville shall preach
And every commencement speech
    Be a polemic.   30

Let Ares doze, that other war
Is instantly declared once more
    'Twixt those who follow
Precocious Hermes all the way
And those who without qualms obey
    Pompous Apollo.

Brutal like all Olympic games,
Though fought with smiles and Christian names
    And less dramatic,
This dialectic strife between   40
The civil gods is just as mean,
    And more fanatic.

What high immortals do in mirth
Is life and death on Middle Earth;
    Their a-historic
Antipathy forever gripes
All ages and somatic types,
    The sophomoric

Who face the future's darkest hints
With giggles or with prairie squints   50
    As stout as Cortez,

And those who like myself turn pale
As we approach with ragged sail
     The fattening forties.

The sons of Hermes love to play,
And only do their best when they
     Are told they oughtn't;
Apollo's children never shrink
From boring jobs but have to think
     Their work important.   60

Related by antithesis,
A compromise between us is
     Impossible:
Respect perhaps but friendship never:
Falstaff the fool confronts forever
     The prig Prince Hal.

If he would leave the self alone,
Apollo's welcome to the throne,
     Fasces and falcons;
He loves to rule, has always done it;   70
The earth would soon, did Hermes run it,
     Be like the Balkans.

But jealous of our god of dreams,
His common-sense in secret schemes
     To rule the heart;
Unable to invent the lyre,
Creates with simulated fire
     Official art.

And when he occupies a college,
Truth is replaced by Useful Knowledge;   80
     He pays particular
Attention to Commercial Thought,
Public Relations, Hygiene, Sport,
     In his curricula.

Athletic, extrovert and crude,
For him, to work in solitude
     Is the offence,
The goal a populous Nirvana:
His shield bears this device: *Mens sana*
     Qui mal y pense.   90

Today his arms, we must confess,
From Right to Left have met success,
 His banners wave
From Yale to Princeton, and the news
From Broadway to the Book Reviews
 Is very grave.

His radio Homers all day long
In over-Whitmanated song
 That does not scan,
With adjectives laid end to end,
Extol the doughnut and commend
 The Common Man.

His, too, each homely lyric thing
On sport or spousal love or spring
 Or dogs or dusters,
Invented by some court-house bard
For recitation by the yard
 In filibusters.

To him ascend the prize orations
And sets of fugal variations
 On some folk-ballad,
While dietitians sacrifice
A glass of prune-juice or a nice
 Marsh-mallow salad.

Charged with his compound of sensational
Sex plus some undenominational
 Religious matter,
Enormous novels by co-eds
Rain down on our defenceless heads
 Till our teeth chatter.

In fake Hermetic uniforms
Behind our battle-line, in swarms
 That keep alighting,
His existentialists declare
That they are in complete despair,
 Yet go on writing.

No matter; He shall be defied;
White Aphrodite is on our side:
 What though his threat

100

110

120

To organize us grow more critical?   130
Zeus willing, we, the unpolitical,
      Shall beat him yet.

Lone scholars, sniping from the walls
Of learned periodicals,
      Our facts defend,
Our intellectual marines,
Landing in little magazines
      Capture a trend.

By night our student Underground
At cocktail parties whisper round   140
      From ear to ear;
Fat figures in the public eye
Collapse next morning, ambushed by
      Some witty sneer.

In our morale must lie our strength:
So, that we may behold at length
      Routed Apollo's
Battalions melt away like fog,
Keep well the Hermetic Decalogue,
      Which runs as follows:—   150

Thou shalt not do as the dean pleases,
Thou shalt not write thy doctor's thesis
      On education,
Thou shalt not worship projects nor
Shalt thou or thine bow down before
      Administration.

Thou shalt not answer questionnaires
Or quizzes upon World-Affairs,
      Nor with compliance
Take any test. Thou shalt not sit   160
With statisticians nor commit
      A social science.

Thou shalt not be on friendly terms
With guys in advertising firms,
      Nor speak with such
As read the Bible for its prose,
Nor, above all, make love to those
      Who wash too much.

Thou shalt not live within thy means
Nor on plain water and raw greens.
    If thou must choose
Between the chances, choose the odd;
Read *The New Yorker*, trust in God;
    And take short views.

170

STEPHEN SPENDER

The Express[1]

After the first powerful plain manifesto
The black statement of pistons, without more fuss
But gliding like a queen, she leaves the station.
Without bowing and with restrained unconcern
She passes the houses which humbly crowd outside,
The gasworks and at last the heavy page
Of death, printed by gravestones in the cemetery.
Beyond the town there lies the open country
Where, gathering speed, she acquires mystery,
The luminous self-possession of ships on ocean.
It is now she begins to sing—at first quite low
Then loud, and at last with a jazzy madness—
The song of her whistle screaming at curves,
Of deafening tunnels, brakes, innumerable bolts.
And always light, aerial, underneath
Goes the elate metre of her wheels.
Streaming through metal landscape on her lines
She plunges new eras of wild happiness
Where speed throws up strange shapes, broad curves
And parallels clean like the steel of guns.
At last, further than Edinburgh or Rome,
Beyond the crest of the world, she reaches night
Where only a low streamline brightness
Of phosphorus on the tossing hills is white.
Ah, like a comet through flame she moves entranced
Wrapt in her music no bird song, no, nor bough
Breaking with honey buds, shall ever equal.

10

20

The Landscape near an Aerodrome[1]

More beautiful and soft than any moth
With burring furred antennae feeling its huge path
Through dusk, the air-liner with shut-off engines
Glides over suburbs and the sleeves set trailing tall
To point the wind. Gently, broadly, she falls,
Scarcely disturbing charted currents of air.

Lulled by descent, the travelers across sea
And across feminine land indulging its easy limbs
In miles of softness, now let their eyes trained by watching
Penetrate through dusk the outskirts of this town   10
Here where industry shows a fraying edge.
Here they may see what is being done.

Beyond the winking masthead light
And the landing-ground, they observe the outposts
Of work: chimneys like lank black fingers
Or figures frightening and mad: and squat buildings
With their strange air behind trees, like women's faces
Shattered by grief. Here where few houses
Moan with faint light behind their blinds
They remark the unhomely sense of complaint, like a dog   20
Shut out and shivering at the foreign moon.

In the last sweep of love, they pass over fields
Behind the aerodrome, where boys play all day
Hacking dead grass: whose cries, like wild birds,
Settle upon the nearest roofs
But soon are hid under the loud city.

Then, as they land, they hear the tolling bell
Reaching across the landscape of hysteria
To where, larger than all the charcoaled batteries
And imaged towers against the dying sky,   30
Religion stands, the church blocking the sun.

KARL SHAPIRO

University[1]

To hurt the Negro and avoid the Jew
Is the curriculum. In mid-September
The entering boys, identified by hats,
Wander in a maze of mannered brick
   Where boxwood and magnolia brood
   And columns with imperious stance
   Like rows of ante-bellum girls
      Eye them, outlanders.

In whited cells, on lawns equipped for peace,
Under the arch, and lofty banister,   10
Equals shake hands, unequals blankly pass;
The exemplary weather whispers, "Quiet, quiet!"
   And visitors on tiptoe leave
   For the raw North, the unfinished West
   As the young, detecting an advantage,
      Practice a face.

Where, on their separate hill, the colleges,
Like manor houses of an older law,
Gaze down embankments on a land in fee,
The Deans, dry spinsters over family plate,   20
   Ring out the English name like coin,
   Humor the snob and lure the lout.
   Within the precincts of this world
      Poise is a club.

But on the neighboring range, misty and high,
The past is absolute; some luckless race
Dull with inbreeding and conformity
Wears out its heart, and comes barefoot and bad
   For charity or jail. The scholar
   Sanctions their obsolete disease;   30
   The gentleman revolts with shame
      At his ancestor.

[1] From *Poems 1940-1953*. Copyright 1942 by Karl Shapiro. Reprinted by permission of Random House, Inc.

And the true nobleman, once a democrat,
Sleeps on his private mountain. He was one
Whose thought was shapely and whose dream was broad;
This school he held his art and epitaph.
    But now it takes from him his name,
    Falls open like a dishonest look,
    And shows us, rotted and endowed,
      Its senile pleasure.   40

Auto Wreck[1]

Its quick soft silver bell beating, beating,
And down the dark one ruby flare
Pulsing out red light like an artery,
The ambulance at top speed floating down
Past beacons and illuminated clocks
Wings in a heavy curve, dips down,
And brakes speed, entering the crowd.
The doors leap open, emptying light;
Stretchers are laid out, the mangled lifted
And stowed into the little hospital.   10
Then the bell, breaking the hush, tolls once,
And the ambulance with its terrible cargo
Rocking, slightly rocking, moves away,
As the doors, an afterthought, are closed.

We are deranged, walking among the cops
Who sweep glass and are large and composed.
One is still making notes under the light.
One with a bucket douches ponds of blood
Into the street and gutter.
One hangs lanterns on the wrecks that cling,   20
Empty husks of locusts, to iron poles.

Our throats were tight as tourniquets,
Our feet were bound with splints, but now
Like convalescents intimate and gauche,
We speak through sickly smiles and warn
With the stubborn saw of common sense,
The grim joke and the banal resolution.
The traffic moves around with care,

1 From *Poems 1940-1953*. Copyright 1942 by Karl Shapiro. Reprinted by permission of Random House, Inc.

But we remain, touching a wound
That opens to our richest horror.　　　　　　　　30

Already old, the question Who shall die?
Becomes unspoken Who is innocent?
For death in war is done by hands;
Suicide has cause and still birth, logic.
But this invites the occult mind,
Cancels our physics with a sneer,
And spatters all we knew of dénouement
Across the expedient and wicked stones.

Recapitulation, XIV [1]

"Doctor, doctor, a little of your love
　　And a little of your skill,
I can no longer sight my gun,
　　No longer can I kill."

"Soldier, soldier, I cannot find the cause
　　And I will not set you free,
But take this pill and go your way
　　To your own company."

"Chaplain, chaplain, a little of your love
　　And a little of your grace,
I can no longer think my thoughts　　　　　　10
　　Nor bear the demon's face."

"My son, my son, I cannot find the cause
　　And I will not set you free,
But take this book and go your way
　　To your own company."

"Captain, captain, a little of your love
　　And likewise of your loyalty,
I can no longer land at dawn
　　Nor ride the troopship sea."　　　　　　　20

"Soldier, soldier, I cannot find the cause
　　And I will not set you free

But take this leave and go your way
    To your own company."

With doctor's pill and chaplain's book
    And captain's furlough free,
The soldier went and hanged himself
    On a Signal Corps cross-tree.

O soldier, soldier, where now are your eyes
    That once so much did see?   30
The vultures have plucked them from his face
    Just over our company.

DYLAN THOMAS

The Force That Through the Green Fuse
Drives the Flower[1]

The force that through the green fuse drives the flower
Drives my green age; that blasts the roots of trees
Is my destroyer.
And I am dumb to tell the crooked rose
My youth is bent by the same wintry fever.

The force that drives the water through the rocks
Drives my red blood; that dries the mouthing streams
Turns mine to wax.
And I am dumb to mouth unto my veins
How at the mountain spring that same mouth sucks.   10

The hand that whirls the water in the pool
Stirs the quicksand; that ropes the blowing wind
Hauls my shroud sail.
And I am dumb to tell the hanging man
How of my clay is made the hangman's lime.

The lips of time leech to the fountain head;
Love drips and gathers, but the fallen blood
Shall calm her sores.

[1] From *Selected Writings*. Copyright, 1939, 1946, by New Directions.

> And I am dumb to tell a weather's wind
> How time has ticked a heaven round the stars.   20
> And I am dumb to tell the lover's tomb
> How at my sheet goes the same crooked worm.

G. GIOVANNINI

On Thomas' "The Force That Through the Green Fuse Drives the Flower" [1]

Thomas' poem has a highly wrought and closely knit metaphorical surface carefully disguising meaning, and in such poetry what is extracted as basic meaning may be only another surface disguising a meaning felt rather than understood conceptually. The explication which follows attempts to uncover the meaning next to the metaphorical surface of Thomas' poem, and it leaves to one side the felt implications, largely Freudian, which commentators have found in his early verse.

The character speaking in the poem is a youth ("my green age") who discovers that life predicates death, and stands bewildered and inarticulate ("I am dumb") before man and nature informed by a paradoxical principle. The meaning is a variation on an old theme: life (and love) cankered by death (cf. Blake's "The Sick Rose"). The variation consists of the predication that life and death issue from the same cause—"The force" in the poem, a force in an obscure way associated with God; for in the first line of stanza 2 there is an oblique allusion to *Exodus*, xvii, 6, where God draws water out of a rock, and in the first line of stanza 3 an allusion to *John*, v, 4, where the angel of God stirs the water in the pool of Bethesda. The theme may be seen developed in the first three lines of each of the first three stanzas in a powerful manner by a statement immediately followed, after the semicolon, by a counterstatement. The life-giving force driving through the stem ("green fuse") of the flower and the youth's body also "blasts" the tree (the verb echoes "fuse" now understood in its literal sense) and kills the man. The syntactic pattern of the first three lines carries the paradoxical meaning; for the counterstatement (death) is grammatically a coordinate and integral part of the statement (life), a conjunction of a meaningful kind seen in small in the phrases (e.g., the oxymoron "wintry fever"). This same pattern and meaning are repeated exactly in the next two stanzas. The force driving the water, traditionally a symbol of life, and the blood also dries the streams at their source ("mouthing") and congeals in

[1] From *The Explicator*, VIII (June, 1950), 59-60. By permission of the authors and of the Editors of *The Explicator*.

death the speaker's life-streams ("turns mine to wax"). In the third stanza the dynamism of the force, now "The hand," is in terms of rapid movement (whirlpool), and of swift time; for "The hand that whirls" seems to suggest a clock, and "quicksand" the swift passage of time as in an hour glass. But the same force checks ("ropes") the movement of the wind and kills ("Hauls my shroud sail"). In the fourth stanza the syntactic pattern is varied a little, and so is the meaning, the paradox of life-death being here translated as love-death. The theme is developed in its cosmic aspects: creation ("The lips of time") passionately sucks ("leech") its being from a source, and love "gathers," possibly in the sense in which Hopkins uses the verb in "God's Grandeur": "The world is charged with the grandeur of God . . . It gathers to a greatness." But with reference to the counterstatement, where death ("fallen blood") again appears, "gathers" has an appropriate medical sense: love is imaged as a swollen suppurating wound, from which the issue of blood signifies the stillness of death ("Shall calm her sores").

The refrain, "And I am dumb," functions as illustration everywhere except in the fourth stanza: the speaker carries death within him; for though he is young and avidly experiences life ("at the mountain spring the same mouth sucks"), his body bends toward death, it is attacked by the "crooked worm" and is the making of the quicklime of the grave ("hangman's lime"). The refrain in the fourth stanza refers not to death, but to the ecstasy of love ticking "a heaven round the stars"; but the meaning here is countered by death in the final refrain which immediately follows, and the poem ends effectively with the two sides of the thematic paradox formally and precisely juxtaposed. All the refrains have in common the sense of the speaker's isolation, of his inability to communicate and establish a sympathetic contact with an inexplicable universe. The isolation is intense; for in the second refrain the young man is unable to communicate even with himself ("dumb to mouth unto my veins"). The theme of this poem is more succinctly and abstractly stated in a passage from Thomas' "A Process in the Weather": "the womb Drives in a death as life leaks out"—a theme which can be glossed by Donne's sermon *Death's Duell* (cf. J. L. Sweeney, Intro., Thomas' *Selected Writings*): "wee celebrate our own funeralls with cries, even at our birth."

S. F. JOHNSON

Thomas' "force" is a generalized *élan vital,* the natural vitality that both creates and destroys us. Human change is but a small part of the great cycle of natural change and is effected by the same simple cause. The opening lines of each stanza present four variations on this implied theme; the two-line refrains stress the limits of human communication by detailing the senses in which even a poet is "dumb."

I. The force is an explosive. Stalks of plants are fuses through which the explosive power is driven; flowers and foliage are products of an explosion which creates on condition of mortality. The poet is "green" (young) and, unlike non-human organisms, is aware that birth is the beginning of death. The refrain emphasizes his humanity, his ability to communicate complex meanings only to other humans. Here the explosive image is translated into human terms (fever). Fever is wintry since it hastens human age and death just as the first frost hastens vegetative age and death.

II. The vitality of growing things is extended to inanimate nature, where again the same force drives and dries (the omission of a phoneme is the difference between life and death). The poet's streams are blood-streams; the pliability and stickiness of wax applies equally to the coagulation of the blood at death and to the drying-up of mud in a stream-bed. Refrain: the force is personified as a mouth (connecting with "leech" in stanza 4). "Mouth" is used in three ways here ("tell" is altered in this refrain alone in order to give scope to the play on words): streams "mouth" into larger streams, into the sea; the poet "mouths" (declaims) to those who can (will) hear him; the "mouth," adapted to giving out and taking in, symbolizes the elemental force that creates and destroys.

III. The force, here as the hand of God, keeps the elements in motion: water, earth, and air, connecting with fire in stanza 1. Of course it controls the poet, now a ship, consistent with the sea imagery of the stanza; the sail, the activated part, is the libido. Refrain: the poet can communicate only with the living, part of whose clay, in various excremental forms, has long since re-entered the natural cycle and helped compose its products.

IV. The force is time itself. The mouth symbol is developed in the verb "leech." The reduction of the life-force from anthropomorphic God to a voracious, blind mouth emphasizes the naturalistic attitude in the poem. Time's leeching lips are juxtaposed with love, the only emotion named in the poem. Love acts in such a way as to place it, with the life-force, at the very pulse of life; it drips and gathers, like blood at a leech wound, subject to the involuntary pulsation of all nature. The supposedly beneficial effects of blood-letting are paralleled with the calming effect of the sexual manifestation of love. The refrain contrasts chillingly with the warmth of love and emphasizes man's small place in the well-integrated, clockwork universe.

Refrain: The facts of death support the poet's consistent view of man's place in nature. The refrain tightens the poem by drawing on the power of earlier elements (lover's tomb and hanging man, crooked worm and crooked rose, worm and leech, sheet and shroud sail) and by reiterating the central notion that everything is subject to decay.

The poem is saved from sentimentality, a risk it runs, by its tightly consistent attitude, which unifies images drawn from widely disparate spheres. The vocabulary, as in most of Thomas' poems, is largely restricted to common Anglo-Saxon words, predominantly monosyllabic, arranged in a pattern so slowly paced that the reader is forced to explore the range of meanings of these words, revitalized by their unusual contexts. The poet is not dumb to tell his readers what he is about: "from the first declension of the flesh I learnt man's tongue . . . To shade and knit anew the patch of words Left by the dead who . . . Need no word's warmth" (from "Love's First Fever"); "I write . . . Not for the towering dead . . . But for the lovers . . . Who pay no praise or wages Nor heed my craft or art" ("In My Craft").

Fern Hill [1]

Now as I was young and easy under the apple boughs
About the lilting house and happy as the grass was green.
   The night above the dingle starry,
     Time let me hail and climb
    Golden in the heydays of his eyes.
And honoured among wagons I was prince of the apple towns
And once below a time I lordly had the trees and leaves
     Trail with daisies and barley
    Down the rivers of the windfall light.

And as I was green and carefree, famous among barns   10
About the happy yard and singing as the farm was home,
   In the sun that is young once only,
     Time let me play and be
    Golden in the mercy of his means,
And green and golden I was huntsman and herdsman, the calves
Sang to my horn, the foxes on the hills barked clear and cold,
     And the sabbath rang slowly
    In the pebbles of the holy streams.

All the sun long it was running, it was lovely, the hay—
Fields high as the house, the tunes from the chimneys, it was air   20
     And playing, lovely and watery
      And fire green as grass.
   And nightly under the simple stars
As I rode to sleep the owls were bearing the farm away,
All the moon long I heard, blessed among stables, the nightjars
     Flying with the ricks and the horses
      Flashing into the dark.

And then to awake, and the farm, like a wanderer white
  With the dew, come back, the cock on his shoulder: it was all

Shining, it was Adam and maiden,
  The sky gathered again
And the sun grew round that very day.
So it must have been after the birth of the simple light
In the first, spinning place, the spellbound horses walking warm
  Out of the whinnying green stable
    On to the fields of praise.

And honoured among foxes and pheasants by the gay house
Under the new made clouds and happy as the heart was long,
  In the sun born over and over,
    I ran my heedless ways,
  My wishes raced through the house-high hay
And nothing I cared at my sky blue trades, that time allows
In all his tuneful turning so few and such morning songs
  Before the children green and golden
    Follow him out of grace.

Nothing I cared, in the lamb white days, that time would take me
Up to the swallow thronged loft by the shadow of my hand,
  In the moon that is always rising,
    Nor that riding to sleep
  I should hear him fly with the high fields
And wake to the farm forever fled from the childless land.
O as I was young and easy in the mercy of his means,
  Time held me green and dying
  Though I sang in my chains like the sea.

A Refusal to Mourn the Death, by Fire,
of a Child in London[1]

Never until the mankind making
Bird beast and flower
Fathering and all humbling darkness
Tells with silence the last light breaking
And the still hour
Is come of the sea tumbling in harness

And I must enter again the round
Zion of the water bead

And the synagogue of the ear of corn
Shall I let pray the shadow of a sound   10
Or sow my salt seed
In the least valley of sackcloth to mourn

The majesty and burning of the child's death.
I shall not murder
The mankind of her going with a grave truth
Nor blaspheme down the stations of the breath
With any further
Elegy of innocence and youth.

Deep with the first dead lies London's daughter,
Robed in the long friends,   20
The grains beyond age, the dark veins of her mother,
Secret by the unmourning water
Of the riding Thames.
After the first death, there is no other.

RANDALL JARRELL

The Death of the Ball Turret Gunner[1]

From my mother's sleep I fell into the State,
And I hunched in its belly till my wet fur froze.
Six miles from earth, loosed from its dream of life,
I woke to black flak and the nightmare fighters.
When I died they washed me out of the turret with a hose.

ROBERT LOWELL

Where the Rainbow Ends[2]

I saw the sky descending, black and white,
Not blue, on Boston where the winters wore
The skulls to jack-o'-lanterns on the slates,

[1] From *Selected Poems of Randall Jarrell* (1955). First published in *Little Friend,
Little Friend.* Copyright 1945, 1951 by Randall Jarrell. Reprinted by permission
of Alfred A. Knopf, Inc.
[2] From *Lord Weary's Castle,* copyright, 1944, 1946, by Robert Lowell. Reprinted
by permission of Harcourt, Brace & World, Inc.

And Hunger's skin-and-bone retrievers tore
The chickadee and shrike. The thorn tree waits
Its victim and tonight
The worms will eat the deadwood to the foot
Of Ararat: the scythers, Time and Death,
Helmed locusts, move upon the tree of breath;
The wild ingrafted olive and the root   10

Are withered, and a winter drifts to where
The Pepperpot, ironic rainbow, spans
Charles River and its scales of scorched-earth miles
I saw my city in the Scales, the pans
Of judgment rising and descending. Piles
Of dead leaves char the air—
And I am a red arrow on this graph
Of Revelations. Every dove is sold.
The Chapel's sharp-shinned eagle shifts its hold
On serpent-Time, the rainbow's epitaph.   20

In Boston serpents whistle at the cold.
The victim climbs the altar steps and sings:
"Hosannah to the lion, lamb, and beast
Who fans the furnace-face of IS with wings:
I breathe the ether of my marriage feast."
At the high altar, gold
And a fair cloth. I kneel and the wings beat
My cheek. What can the dove of Jesus give
You now but wisdom, exile? Stand and live,
The dove has brought an olive branch to eat.   30

Mr. Edwards and the Spider[1]

I saw the spiders marching through the air,
Swimming from tree to tree that mildewed day
In latter August when the hay
Came creaking to the barn. But where
The wind is westerly,
Where gnarled November makes the spiders fly
Into the apparitions of the sky,

They purpose nothing but their ease and die
Urgently beating east to sunrise and the sea;

What are we in the hands of the great God?   10
It was in vain you set up thorn and briar
    In battle array against the fire
    And treason crackling in your blood;
        For the wild thorns grow tame
And will do nothing to oppose the flame;
Your lacerations tell the losing game,
You play against a sickness past your cure.
How will the hands be strong? How will the heart endure?

A very little thing, a little worm,
Or hourglass-blazoned spider, it is said,   20
    Can kill a tiger. Will the dead
    Hold up his mirror and affirm
        To the four winds the smell
And flash of his authority? It's well
If God who holds you to the pit of hell,
Much as one holds a spider, will destroy,
Baffle and dissipate your soul. As a small boy

On Windsor Marsh, I saw the spider die
When thrown into the bowels of fierce fire:
    There's no long struggle, no desire   30
    To get up on its feet and fly—
        It stretches out its feet
And dies. This is the sinner's last retreat;
Yes, and no strength exerted on the heat
Then sinews the abolished will, when sick
And full of burning, it will whistle on a brick.

But who can plumb the sinking of that soul?
Josiah Hawley, picture yourself cast
    Into a brick-kiln where the blast
    Fans your quick vitals to a coal—   40
        If measured by a glass,
How long would it seem burning! Let there pass
A minute, ten, ten trillion; but the blaze
Is infinite, eternal: this is death,
To die and know it. This is the Black Widow, death.

WALKER GIBSON[1]

Billiards

Late of the jungle, wild and dim,
Sliced from the elephant's ivory limb,
Painted, polished, here these spheres
Rehearse their civilized careers—
Trapped in a geometric toil,
Exhibit impact and recoil
Politely, in a farce of force.
And let's have no absurd remorse,
But praise the complicated plan
That organizes beast and man
In patterns so superbly styled,
Late of the jungle, dim and wild.

The Killer Too

Kill or be killed, the sergeant cried,
Discriminating Die from Live,
And spoke the truth. And also lied,
Positing false alternative

And false distinction: you or you.
For both the quick and quiet of breath
Participate. The killer too
Incurs a penalty of death,

And even as the bombardier
In his glass house saw ack-ack bloom
Like flowers of evil on his bier,
His own bombs burst on his own tomb.

[1] From *The Reckless Spenders* (Bloomington: Indiana University Press, 1954).
Copyright, 1954, Walker Gibson.

HOWARD NEMEROV

The Salt Garden[1]

for S.M.S.

A good house, and ground whereon
With an amateur's toil
Both lawn and garden have been won
From a difficult, shallow soil
That, now inland, was once the shore
And once, maybe, the ocean floor.
Much patience, and some sweat,
Have made the garden green,
An even green the lawn.
Turnip and bean and violet   10
In a decent order set,
Grow, flourish and are gone;
Even the ruins of stalk and shell,
The vine when it goes brown,
Look civil and die well.
Sometimes in the late afternoon
I sit out with my wife,
Watching the work that we have done
Bend in the salt wind,
And think that here our life   20
Might be a long and happy one;
Though restless over the sand
The ocean's wrinkled green
Maneuvers in its sleep,
And I despise what I had planned,
Every work of the hand,
For what can man keep?

II

Restless, rising at dawn,
I saw the great gull come from the mist
To stand upon the lawn.   30
And there he shook his savage wing
To quiet, and stood like a high priest

[1] From *The Salt Garden* (Boston: Little, Brown and Company, 1955). Reprinted by permission of Howard Nemerov.

Bird-masked, mantled in grey.
Before his fierce austerity
My thought bowed down, imagining
The wild sea lanes he wandered by
And the wild waters where he slept
Still as a candle in the crypt.
Noble, and not courteous,
He stared upon my green concerns,   40
Then, like a merchant prince
Come to some poor province,
Who, looking all about, discerns
No spice, no treasure house,
Nothing that can be made
Delightful to his haughty trade,
And so spreads out his sail,
Leaving to savage men
Their miserable regimen;
So did he rise, making a gale   50
About him by his wings,
And fought his huge freight into air
And vanished seaward with a cry—
A strange tongue but the tone clear.
He faded from my troubled eye
There where the ghostly sun
Came from the mist.
               When he was gone
I turned back to the house
And thought of wife, of child,
And of my garden and my lawn   60
Serene in the wet dawn;
And thought that image of the wild
Wave where it beats the air
Had come, brutal, mysterious,
To teach the tenant gardener,
Green fellow of this paradise,
Where his salt dream lies.

The Sanctuary[1]

Over a ground of slate and light gravel,
Clear water, so shallow that one can see
The numerous springs moving their mouths of sand;

[1] From *The Salt Garden* (Boston: Little, Brown and Company, 1955). Reprinted by permission of Howard Nemerov.

And the dark trout are clearly to be seen,
Swimming this water which is color of air
So that the fish appear suspended nowhere and
In nothing. With a delicate bend and reflex
Of their tails the trout slowly glide
From the shadowy side into the light, so clear,
And back again into the shadows; slow   10
And so definite, like thoughts emerging
Into a clear place in the mind, then going back,
Exchanging shape for shade. Now and again
One fish slides into the center of the pool
And hangs between the surface and the slate
For several minutes without moving, like
A silence in a dream; and when I stand
At such a time, observing this, my life
Seems to have been suddenly moved a great
Distance away on every side, as though   20
The quietest thought of all stood in the pale
Watery light alone, and was no more
My own than the speckled trout I stare upon
All but unseeing. Even at such times
The mind goes on transposing and revising
The elements of its long allegory
In which the anagoge is always death;
And while this vision blurs with empty tears,
I visit, in the cold pool of the skull,
A sanctuary where the slender trout   30
Feed on my drowned eyes. . . . Until this trout
Pokes through the fabric of the surface to
Snap up a fly. As if a man's own eyes
Raised welts upon the mirror whence they stared,
I find this world again in focus, and
This fish, a shadow dammed in artifice,
Swims to the furthest shadows out of sight
Though not, in time's ruining stream, out of mind.

Life Cycle of Common Man[1]

Roughly figured, this man of moderate habits,
This average consumer of the middle class,
Consumed in the course of his average life span

[1] From *New & Selected Poems* (Chicago: The University of Chicago Press, 1960). Reprinted by permission of Howard Nemerov.

Just under half a million cigarettes,
Four thousand fifths of gin and about
A quarter as much vermouth; he drank
Maybe a hundred thousand cups of coffee,
And counting his parents' share it cost
Something like half a million dollars
To put him through life. How many beasts						10
Died to provide him with meat, belts and shoes
Cannot be certainly said.
                        But anyhow,
It is in this way that a man travels through time,
Leaving behind him a lengthening trail
Of empty bottles and bones, of broken shoes,
Frayed collars and worn out or outgrown
Diapers and dinnerjackets, silk ties and slickers.

Given the energy and security thus achieved,
He did . . . ? What? The usual things, of course,
The eating, dreaming, drinking, and begetting,						20
And he worked for the money which was to pay
For the eating, et cetera, which were necessary
If he were to go on working for the money, et cetera,
But chiefly he talked. As the bottles and bones
Accumulated behind him, the words proceeded
Steadily from the front of his face as he
Advanced into silence and made it verbal.
Who can tally the tale of his words? A lifetime
Would barely suffice for their repetition;
If you merely printed all his commas the result						30
Would be a very large volume, and the number of times
He said "thank you" or "very little sugar, please,"
Would stagger the imagination. There were also
Witticisms, platitudes, and statements beginning
"It seems to me" or "As I always say."

Consider the courage in all that, and behold the man
Walking into deep silence, with the ectoplastic
Cartoon's balloon of speech proceeding
Steadily out of the front of his face, the words
Borne along on the breath which is his spirit						40
Telling the numberless tale of his untold Word
Which makes the world his apple, and forces him to eat.

The Fall Again[1]

It is the Old Man through the sleeping town
Comes oil dark to a certain lip, and breaks
By the white rain's beard the word he speaks,
A drunken Babel that stuns on a stone
And leaps in shatterings of light against
Its pouring fall, and falls again to spill
Asleep its darkening strength along the kill
On those great sinews' curves twisted and tensed.

Between the vineyard and the drunken dark,
O sorrow, there the rainbow shines no more,
There promises are broken in the roar
Of that Old Man, the staggered Patriarch
And whitebeard falling naked to the floor
Ashamed, who was himself both Flood and Ark.

RICHARD WILBUR

Still, Citizen Sparrow[2]

Still, citizen sparrow, this vulture which you call
Unnatural, let him but lumber again to air
Over the rotten office, let him bear
The carrion ballast up, and at the tall

Tip of the sky lie cruising. Then you'll see
That no more beautiful bird is in heaven's height,
No wider more placid wings, no watchfuller flight;
He shoulders nature there, the frightfully free,

The naked-headed one. Pardon him, you
Who dart in the orchard aisles, for it is he   10
Devours death, mocks mutability,
Has heart to make an end, keeps nature new.

1 From *Northwestern Tri-Quarterly*, Fall, 1960. Reprinted by permission of How-ard Nemerov.
2 From *Ceremony, and Other Poems*. Copyright, 1950, by Richard Wilbur. Re-printed by permission of Harcourt, Brace & World, Inc.

Thinking of Noah, childheart, try to forget
How for so many bedlam hours his saw
Soured the song of birds with its wheezy gnaw,
And the slam of his hammer all the day beset

The people's ears. Forget that he could bear
To see the towns like coral under the keel,
And the fields so dismal deep. Try rather to feel
How high and weary it was, on the waters where   20

He rocked his only world, and everyone's.
Forgive the hero, you who would have died
Gladly with all you knew; he rode that tide
To Ararat; all men are Noah's sons.

A Simile for Her Smile[1]

Your smiling, or the hope, the thought of it,
Makes in my mind such pause and abrupt ease
As when the highway bridgegates fall,
Balking the hasty traffic, which must sit
On each side massed and staring, while
Deliberately the drawbridge starts to rise:

Then horns are hushed, the oilsmoke rarefies,
Above the idling motors one can tell
The packet's smooth approach, the slip,
Slip of the silken river past the sides,
The ringing of clear bells, the dip
And slow cascading of the paddle wheel.

Parable[1]

I read how Quixote in his random ride
Came to a crossing once, and lest he lose
The purity of chance, would not decide

Whither to fare, but wished his horse to choose.
For glory lay wherever he might turn.
His head was light with pride, his horse's shoes

Were heavy, and he headed for the barn.

Mind [1]

Mind in the purest play is like some bat
That beats about in caverns all alone,
Contriving by a kind of senseless wit
Not to conclude against a wall of stone.

It has no need to falter or explore;
Darkly it knows what obstacles are there,
And so may weave and flitter, dip and soar
In perfect courses through the blackest air.

And has this simile a like perfection?
The mind is like a bat. Precisely. Save
That in the very happiest intellection
A graceful error may correct the cave.

Short Stories

✦◈✦

NATHANIEL HAWTHORNE

Young Goodman Brown[1]

Young Goodman Brown came forth at sunset into the street at Salem village; but put his head back, after crossing the threshold, to exchange a parting kiss with his young wife. And Faith, as the wife was aptly named, thrust her own pretty head into the street, letting the wind play with the pink ribbons of her cap while she called to Goodman Brown.

"Dearest heart," whispered she, softly and rather sadly, when her lips were close to his ear, "prithee put off your journey until sunrise and sleep in your own bed to-night. A lone woman is troubled with such dreams and such thoughts that she's afeared of herself sometimes. Pray tarry with me this night, dear husband, of all nights in the year."

"My love and my Faith," replied young Goodman Brown, "of all nights in the year, this one night must I tarry away from thee. My journey, as thou callest it, forth and back again, must needs be done 'twixt now and sunrise. What, my sweet, pretty wife, dost thou doubt me already, and we but three months married?"

"Then God bless you!" said Faith, with the pink ribbons; "and may you find all well when you come back."

"Amen!" cried Goodman Brown. "Say thy prayers, dear Faith, and go to bed at dusk, and no harm will come to thee."

So they parted; and the young man pursued his way until, being about to turn the corner by the meeting-house, he looked back and saw the head of Faith still peeping after him with a melancholy air, in spite of her pink ribbons.

"Poor little Faith!" thought he, for his heart smote him. "What a wretch am I to leave her on such an errand! She talks of dreams, too. Methought as she spoke there was trouble in her face, as if a dream had warned her what work is

[1] First printed in the New-England Magazine, 1835.

269

to be done to-night. But no, no; 'twould kill her to think it. Well, she's a blessed angel on earth; and after this one night I'll cling to her skirts and follow her to heaven."

With this excellent resolve for the future, Goodman Brown felt himself justified in making more haste on his present evil purpose. He had taken a dreary road, darkened by all the gloomiest trees of the forest, which barely stood aside to let the narrow path creep through, and closed immediately behind. It was all as lonely as could be; and there is this peculiarity in such a solitude, that the traveller knows not who may be concealed by the innumerable trunks and the thick boughs overhead; so that with lonely footsteps he may yet be passing through an unseen multitude.

"There may be a devilish Indian behind every tree," said Goodman Brown to himself; and he glanced fearfully behind him as he added, "What if the devil himself should be at my very elbow!"

His head being turned back, he passed a crook of the road, and, looking forward again, beheld the figure of a man, in grave and decent attire, seated at the foot of an old tree. He arose at Goodman Brown's approach and walked onward side by side with him.

"You are late, Goodman Brown," said he. "The clock of the Old South was striking as I came through Boston, and that is full fifteen minutes agone."

"Faith kept me back a while," replied the young man, with a tremor in his voice, caused by the sudden appearance of his companion, though not wholly unexpected.

It was now deep dusk in the forest, and deepest in that part of it where these two were journeying. As nearly as could be discerned, the second traveller was about fifty years old, apparently in the same rank of life as Goodman Brown, and bearing a considerable resemblance to him, though perhaps more in expression than features. Still they might have been taken for father and son. And yet, though the elder person was as simply clad as the younger, and as simple in manner too, he had an indescribable air of one who knew the world, and who would not have felt abashed at the governor's dinner table or in King William's court, were it possible that his affairs should call him thither. But the only thing about him that could be fixed upon as remarkable was his staff, which bore the likeness of a great black snake, so curiously wrought that it might almost be seen to twist and wriggle itself like a living serpent. This, of course, must have been an ocular deception, assisted by the uncertain light.

"Come, Goodman Brown," cried his fellow-traveller, "this is a dull pace for the beginning of a journey. Take my staff, if you are so soon weary."

"Friend," said the other, exchanging his slow pace for a full stop, "having kept covenant by meeting thee here, it is my purpose now to return whence I came. I have scruples touching the matter thou wot'st of."

"Sayest thou so?" replied he of the serpent, smiling apart. "Let us walk on, nevertheless, reasoning as we go; and if I convince thee not thou shalt turn back. We are but a little way in the forest yet."

"Too far! too far!" exclaimed the goodman, unconsciously resuming his walk. "My father never went into the woods on such an errand, nor his father before him. We have been a race of honest men and good Christians since the days of the martyrs; and shall I be the first of the name of Brown that ever took this path and kept——"

"Such company, thou wouldst say," observed the elder person, interpreting his pause. "Well said, Goodman Brown! I have been as well acquainted with your family as with ever a one among the Puritans; and that's no trifle to say. I helped your grandfather, the constable, when he lashed the Quaker woman so smartly through the streets of Salem; and it was I that brought your father a pitch-pine knot, kindled at my own hearth, to set fire to an Indian village, in King Philip's war. They were my good friends, both; and many a pleasant walk have we had along this path, and returned merrily after midnight. I would fain be friends with you for their sake."

"If it be as thou sayest," replied Goodman Brown, "I marvel they never spoke of these matters; or, verily, I marvel not, seeing that the least rumor of the sort would have driven them from New England. We are a people of prayer, and good works to boot, and abide no such wickedness."

"Wickedness or not," said the traveller with the twisted staff, "I have a very general acquaintance here in New England. The deacons of many a church have drunk the communion wine with me; the selectmen of divers towns make me their chairman; and a majority of the Great and General Court are firm supporters of my interest. The governor and I, too——But these are state secrets."

"Can this be so?" cried Goodman Brown, with a stare of amazement at his undisturbed companion. "Howbeit, I have nothing to do with the governor and council; they have their own ways, and are no rule for a simple husbandman like me. But, were I to go on with thee, how should I meet the eye of that good old man, our minister, at Salem village? Oh, his voice would make me tremble both Sabbath day and lecture day."

Thus far the elder traveller had listened with due gravity; but now burst into a fit of irrepressible mirth, shaking himself so violently that his snake-like staff actually seemed to wriggle in sympathy.

"Ha! ha! ha!" shouted he again and again; then composing himself, "Well, go on, Goodman Brown, go on; but, prithee, don't kill me with laughing."

"Well, then, to end the matter at once," said Goodman Brown, considerably nettled, "there is my wife, Faith. It would break her dear little heart; and I'd rather break my own."

"Nay, if that be the case," answered the other, "e'en go thy ways, Goodman Brown. I would not for twenty old women like the one hobbling before us that Faith should come to any harm."

As he spoke he pointed his staff at a female figure on the path, in whom Goodman Brown recognized a very pious and exemplary dame, who had taught him his catechism in youth, and was still his moral and spiritual adviser, jointly with the minister and Deacon Gookin.

"A marvel, truly, that Goody Cloyse should be so far in the wilderness at nightfall," said he. "But with your leave, friend, I shall take a cut through the woods until we have left this Christian woman behind. Being a stranger to you, she might ask whom I was consorting with and whither I was going."

"Be it so," said his fellow-traveller. "Betake you to the woods, and let me keep the path."

Accordingly the young man turned aside, but took care to watch his companion, who advanced softly along the road until he had come within a staff's length of the old dame. She, meanwhile, was making the best of her way, with singular speed for so aged a woman, and mumbling some indistinct words—a prayer, doubtless—as she went. The traveller put forth his staff and touched her withered neck with what seemed the serpent's tail.

"The devil!" screamed the pious old lady.

"Then Goody Cloyse knows her old friend?" observed the traveller, confronting her and leaning on his writhing stick.

"Ah, forsooth, and is it your worship indeed?" cried the good dame. "Yea, truly it is, and in the very image of my old gossip, Goodman Brown, the grandfather of the silly fellow that now is. But—would your worship believe it?—my broomstick hath strangely disappeared, stolen, as I suspect, by that unhanged witch, Goody Cory, and that, too, when I was all anointed with the juice of smallage, and cinquefoil, and wolf's bane—"

"Mingled with fine wheat and the fat of a new-born babe," said the shape of old Goodman Brown.

"Ah, your worship knows the recipe," cried the old lady, cackling aloud. "So, as I was saying, being all ready for the meeting, and no horse to ride on, I made up my mind to foot it; for they tell me there is a nice young man to be taken into communion to-night. But now your good worship will lend me your arm, and we shall be there in a twinkling."

"That can hardly be," answered her friend. "I may not spare you my arm, Goody Cloyse; but here is my staff, if you will."

So saying, he threw it down at her feet, where, perhaps, it assumed life, being one of the rods which its owner had formerly lent to the Egyptian magi. Of this fact, however, Goodman Brown could not take cognizance. He had cast up his eyes in astonishment, and, looking down again, beheld neither Goody Cloyse nor the serpentine staff, but his fellow-traveller alone, who waited for him as calmly as if nothing had happened.

"That old woman taught me my catechism," said the young man; and there was a world of meaning in this simple comment.

They continued to walk onward, while the elder traveller exhorted his companion to make good speed and persevere in the path, discoursing so aptly that his arguments seemed rather to spring up in the bosom of his auditor than to be suggested by himself. As they went, he plucked a branch of maple to serve for a walking stick, and began to strip it of the twigs and little boughs, which were wet with evening dew. The moment his fingers touched them they became strangely withered and dried up as with a week's sunshine. Thus the pair proceeded, at a good free pace, until suddenly, in a gloomy hollow of the road, Goodman Brown sat himself down on the stump of a tree and refused to go any farther.

"Friend," said he, stubbornly, "my mind is made up. Not another step will I budge on this errand. What if a wretched old woman do choose to go to the devil when I thought she was going to heaven: is that any reason why I should quit my dear Faith and go after her?"

"You will think better of this by and by," said his acquaintance, composedly. "Sit here and rest yourself a while; and when you feel like moving again, there is my staff to help you along."

Without more words, he threw his companion the maple stick, and was as speedily out of sight as if he had vanished into the deepening gloom. The young man sat a few moments by the roadside, applauding himself greatly, and thinking with how clear a conscience he should meet the minister in his morning walk, nor shrink from the eye of good old Deacon Gookin. And what calm sleep would be his that very night, which was to have been spent so wickedly, but so purely and sweetly now, in the arms of Faith! Amidst these pleasant and praiseworthy meditations, Goodman Brown heard the tramp of horses along the road, and deemed it advisable to conceal himself within the verge of the forest, conscious of the guilty purpose that had brought him thither, though now so happily turned from it.

On came the hoof tramps and the voices of the riders, two grave old voices, conversing soberly as they drew near. These mingled sounds appeared to pass along the road, within a few yards of the young man's hiding-place; but, owing doubtless to the depth of the gloom at that particular spot, neither the travellers nor their steeds were visible. Though their figures brushed the small boughs by the wayside, it could not be seen that they intercepted, even for a moment, the faint gleam from the strip of bright sky athwart which they must have passed. Goodman Brown alternately crouched and stood on tiptoe, pulling aside the branches and thrusting forth his head as far as he durst without discerning so much as a shadow. It vexed him the more, because he could have sworn, were such a thing possible, that he recognized the voices of the minister and Deacon Gookin, jogging along quietly, as they were wont to do, when bound to some ordination or ecclesiastical council. While yet within hearing, one of the riders stopped to pluck a switch.

"Of the two, reverend sir," said the voice like the deacon's, "I had rather miss an ordination dinner than to-night's meeting. They tell me that some of our community are to be here from Falmouth and beyond, and others from Connecticut and Rhode Island, besides several of the Indian powwows, who, after their fashion, know almost as much deviltry as the best of us. Moreover, there is a goodly young woman to be taken into communion."

"Mighty well, Deacon Gookin!" replied the solemn old tones of the minister. "Spur up, or we shall be late. Nothing can be done, you know, until I get on the ground."

The hoofs clattered again; and the voices, talking so strangely in the empty air, passed on through the forest, where no church had ever been gathered or solitary Christian prayed. Whither, then, could these holy men be journeying so deep into the heathen wilderness? Young Goodman Brown caught hold of a tree for support, being ready to sink down on the ground, faint and overburdened with the heavy sickness of his heart. He looked up to the sky, doubting whether there really was a heaven above him. Yet there was the blue arch, and the stars brightening in it.

"With heaven above and Faith below, I will yet stand firm against the devil!" cried Goodman Brown.

While he still gazed upward into the deep arch of the firmament and had lifted his hands to pray, a cloud, though no wind was stirring, hurried across the zenith and hid the brightening stars. The blue sky was still visible, except directly overhead, where this black mass of cloud was sweeping swiftly northward. Aloft in the air, as if from the depths of the cloud, came a confused and doubtful sound of voices. Once the listener fancied that he could distinguish the accents of townspeople of his own, men and women, both pious and ungodly, many of whom he had met at the communion table, and had seen others rioting at the tavern. The next moment, so indistinct were the sounds, he doubted whether he had heard aught but the murmur of the old forest, whispering without a wind. Then came a stronger swell of those familiar tones, heard daily in the sunshine at Salem village, but never until now from a cloud of night. There was one voice, of a young woman, uttering lamentations, yet with an uncertain sorrow, and entreating for some favor, which, perhaps, it would grieve her to obtain; and all the unseen multitude, both saints and sinners, seemed to encourage her onward.

"Faith!" shouted Goodman Brown, in a voice of agony and desperation; and the echoes of the forest mocked him, crying, "Faith! Faith!" as if bewildered wretches were seeking her all through the wilderness.

The cry of grief, rage, and terror was yet piercing the night, when the unhappy husband held his breath for a response. There was a scream, drowned immediately in a louder murmur of voices, fading into far-off laughter, as the dark cloud swept away, leaving the clear and silent sky above Goodman Brown. But something fluttered lightly down through the air and caught on the branch of a tree. The young man seized it, and beheld a pink ribbon.

"My Faith is gone!" cried he, after one stupefied moment. "There is no good on earth; and sin is but a name. Come, devil; for to thee is this world given."

And, maddened with despair, so that he laughed loud and long, did Goodman Brown grasp his staff and set forth again, at such a rate that he seemed to fly along the forest path rather than to walk or run. The road grew wilder and drearier and more faintly traced, and vanished at length, leaving him in the heart of the dark wilderness, still rushing onward with the instinct that guides mortal man to evil. The whole forest was peopled with frightful sounds—the creaking of the trees, the howling of wild beasts, and the yell of Indians; while sometimes the wind tolled like a distant church bell, and sometimes gave a broad roar around the traveller, as if all Nature were laughing him to scorn. But he was himself the chief horror of the scene, and shrank not from its other horrors.

"Ha! ha! ha!" roared Goodman Brown when the wind laughed at him. "Let us hear which will laugh loudest. Think not to frighten me with your deviltry. Come witch, come wizard, come Indian powwow, come devil himself, and here comes Goodman Brown. You may as well fear him as he fear you."

In truth, all through the haunted forest there could be nothing more frightful than the figure of Goodman Brown. On he flew among the black pines, brandishing his staff with frenzied gestures, now giving vent to an inspiration of horrid blasphemy, and now shouting forth such laughter as set all the echoes of the forest laughing like demons around him. The fiend in his own shape is less hideous than when he rages in the breast of man. Thus sped the demoniac on his course, until, quivering among the trees, he saw a red light before him, as when the felled trunks and branches of a clearing have been set on fire, and throw up their lurid blaze against the sky, at the hour of midnight. He paused, in a lull of the tempest that had driven him onward, and heard the swell of what seemed a hymn, rolling solemnly from a distance with the weight of many voices. He knew the tune; it was a familiar one in the choir of the village meeting-house. The verse died heavily away, and was lengthened by a chorus, not of human voices, but of all the sounds of the benighted wilderness pealing in awful harmony together. Goodman Brown cried out, and his cry was lost to his own ear by its unison with the cry of the desert.

In the interval of silence he stole forward until the light glared full upon his eyes. At one extremity of an open space, hemmed in by the dark wall of the forest, arose a rock, bearing some rude, natural resemblance either to an altar or a pulpit, and surrounded by four blazing pines, their tops aflame, their stems untouched, like candles at an evening meeting. The mass of foliage that had overgrown the summit of the rock was all on fire, blazing high into the night and fitfully illuminating the whole field. Each pendent twig and leafy festoon was in a blaze. As the red light arose and fell, a numerous congregation alternately shone forth, then disappeared in shadow, and again grew, as it were, out of the darkness, peopling the heart of the solitary woods at once.

"A grave and dark-clad company," quoth Goodman Brown.

In truth they were such. Among them, quivering to and fro between gloom and splendor, appeared faces that would be seen next day at the council board of the province, and others which, Sabbath after Sabbath, looked devoutly heavenward, and benignantly over the crowded pews, from the holiest pulpits in the land. Some affirm that the lady of the governor was there. At least there were high dames well known to her, and wives of honored husbands, and widows, a great multitude, and ancient maidens, all of excellent repute, and fair young girls, who trembled lest their mothers should espy them. Either the sudden gleams of light flashing over the obscure field bedazzled Goodman Brown, or he recognized a score of the church members of Salem village famous for their especial sanctity. Good old Deacon Gookin had arrived, and waited at the skirts of that venerable saint, his revered pastor. But, irreverently consorting with these grave, reputable, and pious people, these elders of the church, these chaste dames and dewy virgins, there were men of dissolute lives and women of spotted fame, wretches given over to all mean and filthy vice, and suspected even of horrid crimes. It was strange to see that the good shrank not from the wicked, nor were the sinners abashed by the saints. Scattered also among their pale-faced enemies were the Indian priests, or powwows, who had often scared their native forest with more hideous incantations than any known to English witchcraft.

"But where is Faith?" thought Goodman Brown; and, as hope came into his heart, he trembled.

Another verse of the hymn arose, a slow and mournful strain, such as the pious love, but joined to the words which expressed all that our nature can conceive of sin, and darkly hinted at far more. Unfathomable to mere mortals is the lore of fiends. Verse after verse was sung; and still the chorus of the desert swelled between like the deepest tone of a mighty organ; and with the final peal of that dreadful anthem there came a sound, as if the roaring wind, the rushing streams, the howling beasts, and every other voice of the unconcerted wilderness were mingling and according with the voice of guilty man in homage to the prince of all. The four blazing pines threw up a loftier flame, and obscurely discovered shapes and visages of horror on the smoke wreaths above the impious assembly. At the same moment the fire on the rock shot redly forth and formed a glowing arch above its base, where now appeared a figure. With reverence be it spoken, the figure bore no slight similitude, both in garb and manner, to some grave divine of the New England churches.

"Bring forth the converts!" cried a voice that echoed through the field and rolled into the forest.

At the word, Goodman Brown stepped forth from the shadow of the trees and approached the congregation, with whom he felt a loathful brotherhood by the sympathy of all that was wicked in his heart. He could have well-nigh sworn that the shape of his own dead father beckoned him to advance, looking downward from a smoke wreath, while a woman, with dim features of despair, threw out her hand to warn him back. Was it his mother? But he had no power to retreat one step, nor to resist, even in thought, when the minister and good old Deacon Gookin seized his arms and led him to the blazing rock. Thither came also the slender form of a veiled female, led between Goody Cloyse, that pious teacher of the catechism, and Martha Carrier, who had received the devil's promise to be queen of hell. A rampant hag was she. And there stood the proselytes beneath the canopy of fire.

"Welcome, my children," said the dark figure, "to the communion of your race. Ye have found thus young your nature and your destiny. My children, look behind you!"

They turned; and flashing forth, as it were, in a sheet of flame, the fiend worshippers were seen; the smile of welcome gleamed darkly on every visage.

"There," resumed the sable form, "are all whom ye have reverenced from youth. Ye deemed them holier than yourselves, and shrank from your own sin, contrasting it with their lives of righteousness and prayerful aspirations heavenward. Yet here are they all in my worshipping assembly. This night it shall be granted you to know their secret deeds: how hoary-bearded elders of the church have whispered wanton words to the young maids of their households; how many a woman, eager for widows' weeds, has given her husband a drink at bedtime and let him sleep his last sleep in her bosom; how beardless youths have made haste to inherit their fathers' wealth; and how fair damsels—blush not, sweet ones—have dug little graves in the garden, and bidden me, the sole guest, to an infant's funeral. By the sympathy of your human hearts for sin ye shall scent out all the places—whether in church, bedchamber, street, field, or forest where crime has been committed, and shall exult to behold the whole earth one stain of guilt, one mighty blood spot. Far more than this. It shall be yours to penetrate, in every bosom, the deep mystery of sin, the fountain of all wicked arts, and which inexhaustibly supplies more evil impulses than human power—than my power at its utmost—can make manifest in deeds. And now, my children, look upon each other."

They did so; and, by the blaze of the hell-kindled torches, the wretched man beheld his Faith, and the wife her husband, trembling before that unhallowed altar.

"Lo, there ye stand, my children," said the figure, in a deep and solemn tone, almost sad with its despairing awfulness, as if his once angelic nature could yet mourn for our miserable race. "Depending upon one another's hearts, ye had still hoped that virtue were not all a dream. Now are ye undeceived. Evil is the nature of mankind. Evil must be your only happiness. Welcome again, my children, to the communion of your race."

"Welcome," repeated the fiend worshippers, in one cry of despair and triumph.

And there they stood, the only pair, as it seemed, who were yet hesitating on the verge of wickedness in this dark world. A basin was hollowed, naturally, in the rock. Did it contain water, reddened by the lurid light? or was it blood? or, perchance, a liquid flame? Herein did the shape of evil dip his hand and prepare to lay the mark of baptism upon their foreheads, that they might be partakers of the mystery of sin, more conscious of the secret guilt of others, both in deed and thought, than they could now be of their own. The husband cast one look at his pale wife, and Faith at him. What polluted wretches would the next glance show them to each other, shuddering alike at what they disclosed and what they saw!

"Faith! Faith!" cried the husband, "look up to heaven, and resist the wicked one."

Whether Faith obeyed he knew not. Hardly had he spoken when he found himself amid calm night and solitude, listening to a roar of the wind which died heavily away through the forest. He staggered against the rock, and felt it chill and damp; while a hanging twig, that had been all on fire, besprinkled his cheek with the coldest dew.

The next morning young Goodman Brown came slowly into the street of Salem village, staring around him like a bewildered man. The good old minister was taking a walk along the graveyard to get an appetite for breakfast and meditate his sermon, and bestowed a blessing, as he passed, on Goodman Brown. He shrank from the venerable saint as if to avoid an anathema. Old Deacon Gookin was at domestic worship, and the holy words of his prayer were heard through the open window. "What God doth the wizard pray to?" quoth Goodman Brown. Goody Cloyse, that excellent old Christian, stood in the early sunshine at her own lattice, catechizing a little girl who had brought her a pint of morning's milk. Goodman Brown snatched away the child as from the grasp of the fiend himself. Turning the corner by the meeting-house, he spied the head of Faith, with the pink ribbons, gazing anxiously forth, and bursting into such joy at sight of him that she skipped along the street and almost kissed her husband before the whole village. But Goodman Brown looked sternly and sadly into her face, and passed on without a greeting.

Had Goodman Brown fallen asleep in the forest and only dreamed a wild dream of a witch-meeting?

Be it so if you will; but, alas! it was a dream of evil omen for young Goodman Brown. A stern, a sad, a darkly meditative, a distrustful, if not a desperate man did he become from the night of that fearful dream. On the Sabbath day, when the congregation were singing a holy psalm, he could not listen because an anthem of sin rushed loudly upon his ear and drowned all the blessed strain. When the minister spoke from the pulpit with power and fervid eloquence, and, with his hand on the open Bible, of the sacred truths of our religion, and of saint-like lives and triumphant deaths, and of future bliss or misery unutterable, then did Goodman Brown turn pale, dreading lest the roof should thunder down upon the gray blasphemer and his hearers. Often, awaking suddenly at midnight, he shrank from the bosom of Faith; and at morning or eventide, when the family knelt down at prayer, he scowled and muttered to himself, and gazed sternly at his wife, and turned away. And when he had lived long, and was borne to his grave a hoary corpse, followed by Faith, an aged woman, and children and grandchildren, a goodly procession, besides neighbors not a few, they carved no hopeful verse upon his tombstone, for his dying hour was gloom.

RICHARD HARTER FOGLE

On Hawthorne's "Young Goodman Brown" [1]

"Young Goodman Brown" is generally felt to be one of Hawthorne's more difficult tales, from the ambiguity of the conclusions which may be drawn from it. Its hero, a naïve young man who accepts both society in general and his fellow men as individuals at their own valuation, is in one terrible night confronted with the vision of human evil, and is ever afterwards "a stern, a sad, a darkly meditative, a distrustful, if not a desperate man . . .", whose "dying hour was gloom." So far we are clear enough, but there are confusing factors. In the first place, are the events of the night merely subjective, a dream, or do they actually occur? Again, at the crucial point in his ordeal Goodman Brown summons the strength to cry to his wife Faith, "look up to heaven, and resist the evil one." It would appear from this that he had successfully resisted the supreme temptation—but evidently he is not therefore saved. Henceforth, "on the Sabbath day, when the congregation were singing a holy psalm, he could not listen because an anthem of sin rushed loudly upon his ear and drowned all the blessed strain." On the other hand he is not wholly lost, for he is only at intervals estranged from "the bosom of Faith." Has Hawthorne failed to control the implications of his allegory?

I should say rather that these ambiguities of meaning are intentional, an integral part of his purpose. He does not wish to propose flatly that man is primarily evil; rather he has a gnawing fear that this might indeed be true. "Come, devil; for to thee is this world given," exclaims Goodman Brown at the height of his agony. But he finds strength to resist the devil, and in the ambiguous conclusion he does not entirely reject his former faith. His trial, then, comes not from the certainty but from the dread of Evil. Hawthorne poses the dangerous question of the relations of Good and Evil in man but withholds his answer. Nor does he permit himself to determine whether the events of the night of trial are real or the mere figment of a dream.

These ambiguities he conveys and fortifies by what Yvor Winters has called "the formula of alternative possibilities," and F. O. Matthiessen "the device of multiple choice," in which are suggested two or more interpretations

[1] From *Hawthorne's Fiction: The Light and the Dark* (Norman: University of Oklahoma Press, 1952), pp. 15-32. Copyright, 1952, by University of Oklahoma Press. Used by permission.

of a single action or event. Perhaps the most striking instance of the use of this device in "Young Goodman Brown" is the final word on the reality of the hero's night experience:

> Had Goodman Brown fallen asleep in the forest and only dreamed a wild dream of a witch-meeting?
>
> *Be it so if you will;*[2] but alas! it was a dream of evil omen for young Goodman Brown.

This device of multiple choice, or ambiguity, is the very essence of Hawthorne's tale. Nowhere does he permit us a simple meaning, a merely single interpretation. At the outset young Goodman Brown leaves the arms of his wife Faith and the safe limits of Salem to keep a mysterious appointment in the forest. Soon he encounters his guide, a man "in grave and decent attire," commonplace enough save for an indefinable air of acquaintanceship with the great world. ". . . the only thing about him that could be fixed upon as re-markable was his staff, which bore the likeness of a great black snake, so curiously wrought that it might almost be seen to twist and wriggle itself like a living serpent. *This, of course, must have been an ocular deception, assisted by the uncertain light.*"

This man is, of course, the Devil, who seeks to lure the still-reluctant good-man to a witch-meeting. In the process he progressively undermines the young man's faith in the institutions and the men whom he has heretofore revered. First Goody Cloyse, "a very pious and exemplary dame, who had taught him his catechism in youth, and was still his moral and spiritual adviser," is shown to have more than casual acquaintance with the Devil—to be, in fact, a witch. Goodman Brown is shaken, but still minded to turn back and save himself. He is then faced with a still harder test. Just as he is about to return home, filled with self-applause, he hears the tramp of horses along the road:

> On came the hoof tramps and the voices of the riders, two grave old voices, conversing soberly as they drew near. These mingled sounds appeared to pass along the road, within a few yards of the young man's hiding-place; *but, owing doubtless to the depth of the gloom at that particular spot, neither the travellers nor their steeds were visible. Though their figures brushed the small boughs by the wayside, it could not be seen that they intercepted, even for a moment, the faint gleam from the strip of bright sky athwart which they must have passed.* It vexed him the more, because he could have sworn, *were such a thing possible,* that he recognized the voices of the minister and Dea-con Gookin, jogging along quietly, as they were wont to do, when bound to some ordination or ecclesiastical council.

The conversation of the minister and the deacon makes it only too clear that they also are in league with the Devil. Yet Goodman Brown, although now

---

2 This and all subsequent italics are mine. [Richard Harter Fogle]

even more deeply dismayed, still resolves to stand firm, heartened by the blue arch of the sky and the stars brightening in it. At that moment a cloud, "though no wind was stirring," hides the stars, and he hears a confused babble of voices. "*Once the listener fancied that he could distinguish* the accents of townspeople of his own. . . . The next moment, so indistinct were the sounds, *he doubted whether he had heard aught* but the murmur of the old forest, whispering without a wind." But to his horror he believes that he hears the voice of his wife Faith, uttering only weak and insincere objections as she is borne through the air to the witch-meeting.

Now comes an event which at first would appear to break the chain of ambiguities, for Goodman Brown's suspicions seem concretely verified. A pink ribbon, which he remembers having seen in his wife's hair, comes fluttering down into his grasp. This ribbon, apparently a solid object like the fatal handkerchief in *Othello*, seems out of keeping with the atmosphere of doubt which has enveloped the preceding incidents. Two considerations, however, make it possible to account for its appearance. One is that if Goodman Brown is dreaming the ribbon may be taken as part and parcel of his dream. It is to be noted that this pink ribbon appears in his wife's hair once more as she meets him on his return to Salem the next morning. The other is that for the moment the ribbon vanishes from the story, melting into its shadowy background. Its impact is merely temporary.

Be it as you will, as Hawthorne would say. At any rate, the effect on Goodman Brown is instantaneous and devastating. Casting aside all further scruples, he rages through the wild forest to the meeting of witches, for the time at least fully accepting the domination of Evil. He soon comes upon a large gathering, alternately shadowy and clear in the flickering red light of four blazing pines above a central rock.

> Among them, *quivering to and fro between gloom and splendor*, appeared faces that would be seen next day at the council board of the province, and others which, Sabbath after Sabbath, looked devoutly heavenward, and benignantly over the crowded pews, from the holiest pulpits in the land. *Some affirm that* the lady of the governor was there. . . . *Either the sudden gleams of light flashing over the obscure field bedazzled Goodman Brown, or he recognized* a score of the church members of Salem village famous for their especial sanctity.

Before this company steps out a presiding figure who bears "with reverence be it spoken . . . *no slight similitude*, both in garb and manner, to some grave divine of the New England churches," and calls forth the "converts." At the word young Goodman Brown comes forward. "*He could have well-nigh sworn that* the shape of his own dead father beckoned him to advance, looking downward from a smoke wreath, while a woman, with dim features of despair, threw out her hand to warn him back. *Was it his mother?*" But he is quickly seized and led to the rock, along with a veiled woman whom he dimly discerns to be his wife Faith. The two are welcomed by the dark and ambiguous leader into the fraternity of Evil, and the final, irretrievable step is prepared.

A basin was hollowed, naturally, in the rock. *Did it contain water, reddened by the lurid light? or was it blood? or perchance, a liquid flame?* Herein did the shape of evil dip his hand and prepare to lay the mark of baptism upon their foreheads, that they might be partakers of the mystery of sin, more conscious of the secret guilt of others, both in deed and thought, than they could now be of their own. The husband cast one look at his pale wife, and Faith at him. What polluted wretches would the next glance show them to each other, shuddering alike at what they disclosed and what they saw!

"Faith! Faith!" cried the husband, "look up to heaven, and resist the wicked one."

Whether Faith obeyed he knew not.

Hawthorne then concludes with the central ambiguity, which we have already noticed, whether the events of the night were actual or a dream. The uses of this device, if so it may be called, are multiple in consonance with its nature. Primarily it offers opportunity for freedom and richness of suggestion. By it Hawthorne is able to suggest something of the density and incalculability of life, the difficulties which clog the interpretation of even the simplest incidents, the impossibility of achieving a single and certain insight into the actions and motives of others. This ambiguity adds depth and tone to Hawthorne's thin and delicate fabric. It covers the bareness of allegory, imparting to its one-to-one equivalence of object and idea a wider range of allusiveness, a hint of rich meaning still untapped. By means of it the thesis of "Young Goodman Brown" is made to inhere firmly in the situation, and the reader himself must extract it to interpret. Hawthorne refuses to limit himself to a single and doctrinaire conclusion, proceeding instead by indirection. Further, this ambiguity permits the author to make free of the two opposed worlds of actuality and imagination without incongruity or the need to commit himself entirely to either. While avoiding a frontal attack upon the reader's feeling for everyday verisimilitude, it affords the author license of fancy. It allows him to draw upon sources of legend and superstition which still strike a responsive chord in us and possess something of the validity of universal symbols. Hawthorne's own definition of romance may very aptly be applied to his use of ambiguity: it gives him scope "so [to] manage his atmospherical medium as to bring out or mellow the lights and deepen and enrich the shadows of the picture."

Above all, the separate instances of the "multiple choice device" organically unite to reproduce in the reader's mind the feel of the central ambiguity of theme—the horror of the hero's doubt. Goodman Brown, a simple and pious nature, is wrecked as a result of the disappearance of the fixed poles of his belief. His orderly cosmos dissolves into chaos as church and state, the twin pillars of his society, are hinted to be rotten, with their foundations undermined. The yearning for certainty is basic to his spirit—and he is left without even the comfort of a firm reliance in the Devil. His better qualities avail him in his desperation little more than the inner evil which prompted him to court temptation, for they prevent him from seeking the only remaining refuge—the confraternity of Sin. Henceforth he is fated to battle with shadows, to struggle with limed feet toward a redemption which must forever elude him, since he has lost the vision of Good while rejecting the opportunity to embrace Evil fully. Individual instances of ambiguity, then, merge and coalesce in the theme itself to produce an all-pervading atmosphere of uneasiness and anguished doubt.

Ambiguity alone, however, is not a satisfactory aesthetic principle. Flexibility, suggestiveness, allusiveness, variety—all these are without meaning if there is no pattern from which to vary, no center from which to radiate. And, indeed, ambiguity of itself will not adequately account for the individual phenomenon of "Young Goodman Brown." The deliberate haziness and multiple implications of its meaning are counter-balanced by the firm clarity of its technique, in structure and in style.

This clarity is embodied in the lucid simplicity of the basic action; in the skillful foreshadowing by which the plot is bound together; in the balance of episode and scene; in the continuous use of contrast; in the firmness and selectivity of Hawthorne's pictorial composition; in the carefully arranged climactic order of incident and tone; in the detachment and irony of Hawthorne's attitude; and finally in the purity, the grave formality, and the rhetorical balance of the style. His amalgamation of these elements reveals consummate artistic economy in fitting the means to the attempted ends.

The general framework of the story has a large simplicity. At sunset Goodman Brown leaves his wife Faith and the safe confines of Salem, spends the night in the forest, and at dawn returns a changed man. Within this simple pattern, plot and allegory unfold symmetrically and simultaneously. The movement of "Young Goodman Brown" is the single revolution of a wheel, which turns full circle upon itself. Apart from this basic structure, the action is also given form by the device of foreshadowing, through which the entire development of the plot is made implicit in the opening paragraph. Faith is troubled by her husband's expedition and begs him to put it off till sunrise. " 'My love and my Faith,' replied young Goodman Brown, 'of all nights in the year, this one night must I tarry away from thee. My journey . . . forth and back again, must needs be done 'twixt now and sunrise.' " They part, but looking back Brown sees "the head of Faith still peeping after him with a melancholy air, in spite of her pink ribbons."

"Poor little Faith!" thought he, for his heart smote him. "What a wretch am I to leave her on such an errand! She talks of dreams, too. Methought as she spoke there was trouble in her face, as if a dream had warned her what work is to be done to-night. But no, no; 'twould kill her to think of it. Well, she's a blessed angel on earth; and after this one night I'll cling to her skirts and follow her to heaven."

This speech is in several respects clumsy, obvious, and melodramatic; but beneath the surface is a deeper layer. The persuasive ambiguity of the story is foreshadowed in the subtle emphasizing of the dream motif, which paves the way for the ultimate uncertainty whether the incidents of the night are dream or reality; and in his simple-minded aspirations to " 'cling to her skirts and follow her to heaven' " Goodman Brown is laying an ironic foundation for his later horror of doubt. A broader irony is apparent, in the light of later events, in the general emphasis upon Faith's angelic goodness.

Hawthorne's seemingly casual references to Faith's pink ribbons, which are mentioned three times in the opening paragraphs, are likewise far from artless. These ribbons, as we have seen, are an important factor in the plot, and as an emblem of heavenly faith their color gradually deepens into the liquid flame or blood of the baptism into sin.

Another instance of Hawthorne's careful workmanship is his architectural balance of episodes or scenes. The encounter with Goody Cloyse, the female hypocrite and sinner, is set off against the conversation of the minister and Deacon Gookin immediately afterward. The exact correspondence of the two episodes is brought into high relief by two balancing speeches. Goody Cloyse has lost her broomstick, and must perforce walk to the witch-meeting—a sacrifice she is willing to make since " 'they tell me there is a nice young man to be taken into communion to-night.' " A few minutes later Deacon Gookin remarks that " 'there is a goodly young woman to be taken into communion.' " A still more significant example of this balance is contained in the full swing of the wheel—in the departure at sunset and the return at sunrise. At the beginning of the story Brown takes leave of "Faith with the pink ribbons," turns the corner by the meetinghouse, and leaves the town; in the conclusion

. . . Young Goodman Brown came slowly into the street of Salem village, staring around him like a bewildered man. The good old minister was taking a walk along the graveyard to get an appetite for breakfast and meditate his sermon, and bestowed a blessing, as he passed, on Goodman Brown. He shrank from the venerable saint as if to avoid an anathema. Old Deacon Gookin was at domestic worship, and the holy words of his prayer were heard through the open window. "What God doth the wizard pray to?" quoth Goodman Brown. Goody Cloyse, that excellent old Christian, stood in the early sunshine at her own lattice, catechizing a little girl who had brought her a pint of morning's milk. Goodman Brown snatched the child away as from the grasp of the fiend himself. Turning the corner by the meeting-house, he spied the head of Faith, with the pink ribbons, gazing anxiously forth, and bursting into such joy at the sight of him that she skipped along the street and almost kissed her husband before the whole village. But Goodman Brown looked sternly and sadly into her face, and passed on without a greeting.

The exact parallel between the earlier and the later situations serves to dramatize intensely the change which the real or fancied happenings of the night brought about in Goodman Brown.

Contrast, a form of balance, is still more prominent in "Young Goodman Brown" than the analogy of scene and episode which I have mentioned. The broad antitheses of day and night, town and forest, both of which signify in general a sharp dualism of Good and Evil, are supplemented by a color contrast of red and black at the witch meeting, by the swift transition of the forest scene from leaping flame to damp and chill, and by the consistent cleavage between outward decorum and inner corruption in the characters.

The symbols of Day and Night, of Town and Forest, are almost indistinguishable in meaning. Goodman Brown leaves the limits of Salem at dusk and reenters them at sunrise; he spends the intervening night in the forest. Day and the Town are clearly emblematic of Good, of the seemly outward appearance of human convention and society. They stand for the safety of an unquestioning and unspeculative faith. Oddly enough, in the daylight of the Salem streets Goodman Brown is too simple and straightforward to be interesting and is somewhat distasteful in his boundless reverence for such unspectacular worthies as the minister, the deacon, and Goody Cloyse. Night and the Forest, symbols of doubt and wandering, are the domains of the Evil One, where the dark subterranean forces of the human spirit riot unchecked. By the dramatic necessities of the plot Brown is a larger figure in the Forest of Evil and at the witch-meeting than he is within the safe bounds of the town.

The contrast of the red of fire and blood and the black of night and forest at the witch-meeting has a different import. As the flames rise and fall, the faces of the worshipers of Evil are alternately seen in clear outline and in deep shadow, and all the details of the scene are at one moment revealed, the next obscured. It seems, then, that red represents Sin or Evil, plain and unequivocal; black represents that doubt of the reality of either Evil or Good which tortures Goodman Brown. A further contrast follows in the swift transformation of scene, when young Goodman Brown finds himself "amid calm night and solitude. . . . He staggered against the rock, and felt it chill and damp; while a hanging twig, that had been all on fire, besprinkled his cheek with the coldest dew."

Most pervasive of the contrasts in "Young Goodman Brown" is the consistent discrepancy between appearance and reality, which helps to produce the heavy atmosphere of doubt and shadow. The church is represented by the highly respectable figures of Goody Cloyse, the minister, and Deacon Gookin, who in the forest are witch and wizards. The devil appears in the guise of Brown's grandfather. As the good man approaches the meeting, his ears are greeted by "the swell of what seemed a hymn, rolling solemnly from a distance with the weight of many voices. He knew the tune; it was a familiar one in the choir of the village meeting-house." The Communion of Sin is, in fact, the faithful counterpart of a grave and pious ceremony at a Puritan meetinghouse. "At one extremity of an open space, hemmed in by the dark wall of the forest, arose a rock, bearing some rude, natural resemblance either to an altar or a pulpit, and surrounded by four blazing pines, their tops aflame, their stems untouched, like candles at an evening meeting." The worshipers are "a numerous congregation," Satan resembles some grave divine, and the initiation into sin takes the form of a baptism.

Along with this steady use of contrast in the Sabbath scene should be noticed the firmly composed pictorial quality. The rock, the center of the picture, is lighted by blazing pines. The chief actors are, as it were, spotlighted in turn as they advance to the rock, while the congregation is generalized in the dimmer light at the outer edges. The whole composition is simple and definite, in contrast to the ambiguity occasioned by the rise and fall of the flame, in which the mass of the worshipers alternately shines forth and disappears in shadow.

The clarity and simple structural solidity of "Young Goodman Brown" evinces itself in its tight dramatic framework. Within the basic form of the turning wheel the story further divides into four separate scenes, the first and last of which, are, of course, the balancing departure from and return to Salem. The night in the forest falls naturally into two parts: the temptation by the Devil and the witch-meeting. These two scenes, particularly the first, make full and careful use of the dramatic devices of suspense and climactic arrangement, and Hawthorne manipulates his materials to divide them as sharply as by a dropped curtain.

The temptation at first has the stylized and abstract delicacy of Restoration comedy or of the formalized seductions of Molière's *Don Juan*. The simple goodman, half-eager and half-reluctant, is wholly at the mercy of Satan, who leads him step by step to the inevitable end. The lightly ironic tone of the earlier part of this scene is reinforced by the inherent irony of the situation, which elicits a double meaning at every turn.

"Come, Goodman Brown," cried his fellow-traveller, "this is a dull pace for the beginning of a journey. Take my staff, if you are so soon weary."

"Friend," said the other, exchanging his slow pace for a full stop, "having kept covenant by meeting thee here, it is my purpose now to return whence I came. I have scruples touching the matter thou wot'st of."

"Sayest thou so?" replied he of the serpent, smiling apart. "Let us walk on, nevertheless, reasoning as we go; and if I convince thee not thou shalt turn back. We are but a little way in the forest yet."

Then commences a skillful and relentless attack on all the values which Goodman Brown has lived by. His reverence for his Puritan ancestors, "a people of prayer, and good works to boot," is speedily turned against him as the Devil claims them for tried and dear companions. Next comes the encounter with Goody Cloyse, who taught the young man his catechism. Brown is sorely cast down, but at length sturdily concludes, "What if a wretched old woman do choose to go to the devil when I thought she was going to heaven:

is that any reason why I should quit my dear Faith and go after her?" But no sooner has he rallied from this blow than he is hit by another, still more shrewdly placed: he hears the voices of the minister and Deacon Gookin, and from their conversation gathers that they are bound for the meeting and are eagerly anticipating it. This is almost the final thrust, but still Brown holds out. " 'With heaven above, and Faith below, I will yet stand firm against the devil!' " he cries, only to be utterly overthrown by the sound of his wife's voice and the crushing evidence of the pink ribbon.

The style has gradually deepened and intensified with the carefully graduated intensity of the action, and now Hawthorne lets it out full. Nature is made at once to sympathize with and to mock the anguished chaos in Goodman Brown; in his rage the hero is both united with and opposed to the forest and the wind. The symphony of sound, which began with the confused babble of voices in the sky as Faith and her witch-attendants swept overhead, rises to a wild crescendo.

> And, maddened with despair, so that he laughed loud and long, did Goodman Brown grasp his staff and set forth again, at such a rate that he seemed to fly along the forest path rather than to walk or run. The road grew wilder and drearier and more faintly traced, and vanished at length, leaving him in the heart of the dark wilderness, still rushing onward with the instinct that guides mortal man to evil. The whole forest was peopled with frightful sounds—the creaking of the trees, the howling of wild beasts, and the yell of Indians; while sometimes the wind tolled like a distant church bell, and sometimes gave a broad roar around the traveller, as if all Nature were laughing him to scorn. But he was himself the chief horror of the scene, and shrank not from its other horrors.

After ascending to this climax Hawthorne disengages himself and separates his scenes by the simple expedient of shifting his view from the hero to the hero's surroundings. Goodman Brown is a mere onlooker at the witch-meeting until the moment comes for him to step forward for his baptism into sin. Up to that point Satan usurps the stage. The eye is first directed to the central rock-altar, then to the four blazing pines which light it. Next there is the impression of a large assembly, vaguely seen in the fitful firelight. Finally the figure of Satan appears at the base of the rock, framed in an arch of flame. Only when he is summoned are we once more fully aware of Goodman Brown, as he stands at the altar by his wife. A moment later comes the second climax, when Brown calls upon his wife to " 'look up to heaven, and resist the wicked one' " —cut off abruptly by anticlimax as the meeting vanishes in a roaring wind, and Brown leaning against the rock finds it chill and damp to his touch.

The satisfaction one feels in the clean line of the story's structure is enhanced by Hawthorne's steady detachment from his materials, an attitude which deepens the impression of classic balance, which in turn stands against the painful ambiguity of the theme. Even the full tone of the most intense scenes, as the one in which Goodman Brown rushes through the forest, is tempered by restraint. The participant is overweighted by the calm, impartial (though not unfeeling) spectator; Hawthorne does not permit himself to become identified with his hero. He displays young Goodman Brown not in and for the hero himself, but always in relation to the whole situation and set of circumstances. This detachment of attitude is plainest in the almost continuous irony, unemphatic but nonetheless relentless: an irony organically related to the ever-present ambiguities of the situation, but most evident in sustained tone. Thus, after recording Goodman Brown's aspiration to " 'cling to Faith's skirts and follow her to heaven,' " the author adds with deadly calm, "With this excellent resolve for the future, Goodman Brown felt himself justified in making more haste on his present evil purpose."

This detachment is implicit in the quiet, the abstractness, and the gravity of Hawthorne's style, which is everywhere formal and exactly, though subtly, cadenced. It throws a light and idealizing veil over the action and maintains an aesthetic distance, while hinting at the ugliness it covers. The difference between the saying and the thing said provides dramatic tension. Note, for example, the grave decorum, the eighteenth-century stateliness, and the perverted courtliness of Satan's welcome to young Brown and Faith:

> This night it shall be granted you to know their secret deeds: how hoary-
> bearded elders of the church have whispered wanton words to the young
> maids of their households; how many a woman, eager for widows' weeds, has
> given her husband a drink at bedtime and let him sleep his last sleep in her
> bosom; how beardless youths have made haste to inherit their fathers' wealth;
> and how fair damsels—blush not, sweet ones—have dug little graves in the
> garden, and bidden me, the sole guest, to an infant's funeral.

The steady procession of measured, ceremonious generalizations—"hoary-bearded elders," "wanton words," "beardless youths," "fair damsels," and so on—is in radical contrast to the implication of the meaning; and the grisly archness of "blush not, sweet ones" is suggestive in its incongruity.

In "Young Goodman Brown," then, Hawthorne has achieved that reconciliation of opposites which Coleridge considered the highest art. The combination of clarity of technique—embodied in simplicity and balance of structure, in firm pictorial composition, in contrast and climatic arrangement, in irony and detachment—with ambiguity of meaning, as signalized by the "device of multiple choice," in its interrelationships produces the story's characteristic effect. By means of these two elements Hawthorne reconciles oneness of action with multiplicity of suggestion and enriches the bareness of systematic allegory. Contrarily, by them he avoids lapsing into mere speculation without substance or form. The phantasmagoric light and shadow of the rising and falling fire, which obscures and softens the clear, hard outline of the witch-meeting, is an image which will stand for the essential effect of the story itself, an effect compacted of ambiguity and clarity harmoniously interfused.

EDGAR ALLAN POE

The Masque of the Red Death[1]

The "Red Death" had long devastated the country. No pestilence had ever been so fatal, or so hideous, blood was its avatar and its seal—the redness and the horror of blood. There were sharp pains, and sudden dizziness, and then profuse bleeding at the pores, with dissolution. The scarlet stains upon the body, and especially upon the face, of the victim were the pest ban which shut him out from the aid and from the sympathy of his fellow-men. And the whole seizure, progress, and termination of the disease were the incidents of half an hour.

But the Prince Prospero was happy and dauntless and sagacious. When his dominions were half depopulated, he summoned to his presence a thousand hale and lighthearted friends from among the knights and dames of his court, and with these retired to the deep seclusion of one of his castellated abbeys. This was an extensive and magnificent structure, the creation of the Prince's own eccentric yet august taste. A strong and lofty wall girdled it in. This wall had gates of iron. The courtiers, having entered, brought furnaces and massy hammers, and welded the bolts. They resolved to leave means neither of ingress or egress to the sudden impulses of despair or of frenzy from within. The abbey was amply provisioned. With such precautions the courtiers might bid defiance to contagion. The external world could take care of itself. In the meantime it was folly to grieve, or to think. The Prince had provided all the appliances of pleasure. There were buffoons, there were improvisatori, there were ballet dancers, there were musicians, there was Beauty, there was wine. All these and security were within. Without was the "Red Death."

It was toward the close of the fifth or sixth month of his seclusion, and while the pestilence raged most furiously abroad, that the Prince Prospero entertained his thousand friends at a masked ball of the most unusual magnificence.

It was a voluptuous scene, that masquerade. But first let me tell of the rooms in which it was held. There were seven—an imperial suite. In many palaces, however, such suites form a long and straight vista, while the folding-doors slide back nearly to the walls on either hand, so that the view of the whole extent is scarcely impeded. Here the case was very different, as might have been expected from the Prince's love of the bizarre. The apartments were so irregularly disposed that the vision embraced but little more than one at a time. There was a sharp turn at every twenty or thirty yards, and at each turn a novel effect. To the right and left, in the middle of each wall, a tall and

[1] First printed in Graham's Magazine, in 1842.

narrow Gothic window looked out upon a closed corridor which pursued the windings of the suite. These windows were of stained glass, whose color varied in accordance with the prevailing hue of the decorations of the chamber into which it opened. That at the eastern extremity was hung, for example, in blue—and vividly blue were its windows. The second chamber was purple in its ornaments and tapestries, and here the panes were purple. The third was green throughout, and so were the casements. The fourth was furnished and lighted with orange, the fifth with white, the sixth with violet. The seventh apartment was closely shrouded in black velvet tapestries that hung all over the ceiling and down the walls, falling in heavy folds upon a carpet of the same material and hue. But, in this chamber only, the color of the windows failed to correspond with the decorations. The panes here were scarlet—a deep blood-color. Now in no one of the seven apartments was there any lamp or candelabrum, amid the profusion of golden ornaments that lay scattered to and fro or depended from the roof. There was no light of any kind emanating from lamp or candle within the suite of chambers. But in the corridors that followed the suite there stood, opposite to each window, a heavy tripod, bearing a brazier of fire, that projected its rays through the tinted glass and so glaringly illumined the room. And thus were produced a multitude of gaudy and fantastic appearances. But in the western or black chamber the effect of the firelight that streamed upon the dark hangings through the blood-tinted panes was ghastly in the extreme, and produced so wild a look upon the countenances of those who entered that there were few of the company bold enough to set foot within its precincts at all.

It was in this apartment, also, that there stood against the western wall a gigantic clock of ebony. Its pendulum swung to and fro with a dull, heavy, monotonous clang; and when the minute hand made the circuit of the face, and the hour was to be stricken, there came from the brazen lungs of the clock a sound which was clear and loud and deep and exceedingly musical, but of so peculiar a note and emphasis that, at each lapse of an hour, the musicians of the orchestra were contrained to pause, momentarily, in their performance to hearken to the sound; and thus the waltzers perforce ceased their evolutions; and there was a brief disconcert of the whole gay company; and, while the chimes of the clock yet rang, it was observed that the giddiest grew pale, and the more aged and sedate passed their hands over their brows as if in confused revery or meditation. But when the echoes had fully ceased, a light laughter at once pervaded the assembly; the musicians looked at each other and smiled as if at their own nervousness and folly, and made whispering vows, each to the other, that the next chiming of the clock should produce in them no similar emotion and then, after the lapse of sixty minutes (which embrace three thousand and six hundred seconds of the Time that flies) there came yet another chiming of the clock, and then were the same disconcert and tremulousness and meditation as before.

But, in spite of these things, it was a gay and magnificent revel. The tastes of the Prince were peculiar. He had a fine eye for colors and effects. He disregarded the *decora* of mere fashion. His plans were bold and fiery, and his conceptions glowed with barbaric luster. There are some who would have thought him mad. His followers felt that he was not. It was necessary to hear and see and touch him to be *sure* that he was not.

He had directed, in great part, the movable embellishments of the seven chambers, upon occasion of this great *fête*; and it was his own guiding taste which had given character to the masqueraders. Be sure they were grotesque. There were much glare and glitter and piquancy and phantasm—much of what has been since seen in *Hernani*. There were arabesque figures with unsuited limbs and appointments. There were delirious fancies such as the madman fashions. There was much of the beautiful, much of the wanton, much of the bizarre, something of the terrible, and not a little of that which might have excited disgust. To and fro in the seven chambers there stalked, in fact, a multitude of dreams. And these—the dreams—writhed in and about, taking hue from the rooms, and causing the wild music of the orchestra to seem as the echo of their steps. And, anon, there strikes the ebony clock which stands in the hall of the velvet. And then, for a moment, all is still, and all is silent save the voice of the clock. The dreams are stiff-frozen as they stand. But the echoes of the chime die away—they have endured but an instant—and a light, half-subdued laughter floats after them as they depart. And now again the music swells, and the dreams live, and writhe to and fro more merrily than ever, taking hue from the many tinted windows through which stream the rays from the tripods. But to the chamber which lies most westwardly of the seven, there are now none of the maskers who venture; for the night is waning away, and there flows a ruddier light through the blood-colored panes; and the blackness of the sable drapery appalls; and to him whose foot falls upon the sable carpet, there comes from the near clock of ebony a muffled peal more solemnly emphatic than any which reaches *their* ears who indulge in the more remote gayeties of the other apartments.

But these other apartments were densely crowded, and in them beat feverishly the heart of life. And the revel went whirlingly on, until at length there commenced the sounding of midnight upon the clock. And then the music ceased, as I have told; and the evolutions of the waltzers were quieted; and there was an uneasy cessation of all things as before. But now there were twelve strokes to be sounded by the bell of the clock; and thus it happened, perhaps, that more of thought crept, with more of time, into the meditations of the thoughtful among those who reveled. And thus, too, it happened, perhaps, that before the last echoes of the last chime had utterly sunk into silence, there were many individuals in the crowd who had found leisure to become aware of the presence of a masked figure which had arrested the attention of no single individual before. And the rumor of this new presence having spread itself whisperingly around, there arose at length from the whole company a buzz, or murmur, expressive of disapprobation and surprise—then, finally, of terror, of horror, and of disgust.

In an assembly of phantasms such as I have painted, it may well be supposed that no ordinary appearance could have excited such sensation. In truth the masquerade license of the night was nearly unlimited; but the figure in question had out-Heroded Herod, and gone beyond the bounds of even the Prince's indefinite decorum. There are chords in the hearts of the most reckless which cannot be touched without emotion. Even with the utterly lost, of whom life and death are equally jests, there are matters of which no jest can be made. The whole company, indeed, seemed now deeply to feel that in the costume and bearing of the stranger neither wit nor propriety existed. The figure was tall and gaunt, and shrouded from head to foot in the habiliments of the grave. The mask which concealed the visage was made so nearly to resemble the countenance of a stiffened corpse that the closest scrutiny must have had difficulty in detecting the cheat. And yet all this might have been endured, if not approved, by the mad revelers around. But the mummer had gone so far as to assume the type of the Red Death. His vesture was dabbed in *blood*—and his broad brow, with all the features of the face, was besprinkled with the scarlet horror.

When the eyes of Prince Prospero fell upon this spectral image (which with a slow and solemn movement, as if more fully to sustain its *rôle*, stalked to and fro among the waltzers) he was seen to be convulsed, in the first moment, with a strong shudder either of terror or distaste; but, in the next, his brow reddened with rage.

"Who dares?" he demanded hoarsely of the courtiers who stood near him— "who dares insult us with this blasphemous mockery? Seize him and unmask him—that we may know whom we have to hang at sunrise, from the battlements."

It was in the eastern or blue chamber in which stood the Prince Prospero as he uttered these words. They rang throughout the seven rooms loudly and clearly—for the Prince was a bold and robust man, and the music had become hushed at the waving of his hand.

It was in the blue room where stood the Prince, with a group of pale courtiers by his side. At first, as he spoke, there was a slight rushing movement of this group in the direction of the intruder, who at the moment was also near at hand, and now, with deliberate and stately step, made closer approach to the speaker. But from a certain nameless awe with which the mad assumptions of the mummer had inspired the whole party, there were found none who put forth hand to seize him; so that, unimpeded, he passed within a yard of the Prince's person; and while the vast assembly, as if with one impulse, shrank from the centers of the rooms to the walls, he made his way uninterruptedly, but with the same solemn and measured step which had distinguished him from the first, through the blue chamber to the purple— through the purple to the green—through the green to the orange— through this again to the white and even thence to the violet, ere a decided movement had been made to arrest him. It was then, however, that the Prince Prospero, maddening with rage and the shame of his own momentary cowardice, rushed hurriedly through the six chambers, while none followed him, on account of a deadly terror that had seized upon all. He bore aloft a drawn dagger, and had approached, in rapid impetuosity, to within three or four feet of the retreating figure, when the latter, having attained the extremity of the velvet apartment, turned suddenly and confronted his pursuer. There was a sharp cry—and the dagger dropped gleaming upon the sable carpet, upon which, instantly afterwards, fell prostrate in death the Prince Prospero. Then, summoning the wild courage of despair, a throng of the revelers at once threw themselves into the black apartment, and, seizing the mummer, whose tall figure stood erect and motionless within the shadow of the ebony clock, gasped in unutterable horror at finding the grave cerements and corpse-like mask, which they handled with so violent a rudeness, untenanted by any tangible form.

And now was acknowledged the presence of the Red Death. He had come like a thief in the night. And one by one dropped the revelers in the blood-bedewed halls of their revel, and died each in the despairing posture of his fall. And the life of the ebony clock went out with that of the last of the gay. And the flames of the tripods expired. And Darkness and Decay and the Red Death held illimitable dominion over all.

WALTER BLAIR

On Poe's "The Masque of the Red Death" [1]

Poe's theories about incident and tone in the tale suggest a way of considering how, in his own stories, he achieved the kind of reconciliation he believed inevitable between theory and practice. Let us consider, for instance, in the light of these theories, one of his most famous tales, "The Masque of the Red Death."

A change of the sort typical of Poe—one in the feelings of the characters —occurs in this story. At the beginning the courtiers are "hale and light hearted," but they shortly manifest uneasiness by retiring to the secluded abbey and barring the door to "the sudden impulses of despair or of frenzy." In the final pages they are inspired by "nameless awe," and their only act is prompted by "the wild courage of despair." The prince is so characterized that his growing fright contributes to the graduation of this climactic development: he is "happy and dauntless," "bold and robust," capable of making

[1] From "Poe's Conception of Incident and Tone in the Tale," *Modern Philology*, XLI (May, 1944), 236-240. Reprinted by permission of The University of Chicago Press. The essay is a conscious attempt to criticize Poe's story in the light of his theory of fiction.

"bold and fiery plans." Yet, near the end, even this courageous man suffers "momentary cowardice"; and, when he is overcome by the terrible Red Death, the courtiers are "grasped in unutterable horror."

Paralleling this development, characteristically enough, are a series of backgrounds and happenings so selected and arranged as to account for these mounting fears. The raging plague, though it is apparently shut out when the prince and his friends bar the doors of the abbey, nevertheless contributes its element of menace from the start. But the chief scene (in the theatrical sense of the word), beginning in the third paragraph, is the masque during which, by degrees, feverish gaiety gives way to abject terror. This part of the narrative falls into three divisions, in which are inspired, respectively, physical disquiet, fear of the aberrations of the mind, and, finally, horror aroused by the supernatural.

Poe tells first of the decorative scheme—the seven rooms, so arranged as to play upon any claustrophobia the reader may feel as he identifies himself with characters whose vision is limited by walls of single rooms which themselves are in an abbey shut off from the world by welded iron doors. Light and color in each of these rooms are abnormal and disquieting, and into the seventh room—most disquieting of all—"few of the company are bold enough to set foot." Hearing as well as sight is disturbed: the sound which issues from the ebony clock as its pendulum swings is a "dull, heavy, monotonous clang"; and, when the hour strikes, the "peculiar note and emphasis" of the chime stops the music and makes even the giddiest courtiers momentarily turn pale.

From such purely physical details, the account moves to the rumored madness of the prince by a neat transition: "It was necessary to hear and see and touch him to be *sure* that he was not mad." Mad or not, when Prospero makes plans for the ball, mental as well as physical distortion is suggested. "Grotesque," "phantasm," "arabesque," "delirious fancies such as the madman fashions," "much of the *bizarre*, something of the terrible, and not a little of that which might have excited disgust"—such words as these tell of the dreamlike figures moving through the rooms. And, now, "there are none of the masquers who venture" into the seventh room.

For in this room, says the author, introducing the supernatural note to prevail until the end, "the night is waning. . . . and there flows a ruddier light through the blood-colored panes. . . . and to him whose foot falls upon the sable carpet, there comes from the near clock a muffled peal more solemnly emphatic than any which reaches *their* ears who indulge in the more remote gayeties of the other apartments." The ruddier light can have only a supernatural explanation, since the time is not yet midnight; and there is no natural reason for the change in the sound of the clock. Now the clock strikes twelve, and, during the time it strikes, many first see the strange figure who causes the company to feel and voice "disapprobation and surprise," then "terror. . . . horror. . . . disgust." Seeing this figure habited as the Red Death, the pale courtiers shrink back, and even the brave prince is paralyzed by momentary cowardice. Prospero in time, though, finds courage enough to follow the figure to the seventh room; and there he dies. "Summoning the wild courage of despair," the courtiers follow and seize the figure. Finding "the grave-cerements and corpse-like masks . . . untenanted by any tangible form," they "gasp in unutterable horror." But even this high mark in the depiction of the supernatural is surpassed by the final paragraph as it tells of the death not only of animate beings but of inanimate objects as well: "And the life of the ebony clock went out with that of the last of the gay. And the flames of the tripods expired. And Darkness and Decay and the Red Death held illimitable dominion over all."

Since this is a tale of mounting terror, it is so wrought, Poe probably would say, as to excite the heart. The selection and arrangement of incidents, as has been shown, is such as to achieve this effect. Variety in the tone helps make the concluding terror impressive. As in "The Raven," the author avails himself of the force of contrast: he does this by portraying the figures at the masque in terms of the grotesque, thus heightening the effect of the more serious tone at the conclusion. The tone, too, in portions of the story, is such as to present many details with appropriate "homeliness." Consider the particularized description of the mysterious figure:

. . . . tall and gaunt and shrouded from head to foot in the habiliments of the grave. The mask. . . . was made so nearly to resemble the countenance of a stiffened corpse that the closest scrutiny must have had difficulty detecting the cheat. . . . His vesture was dabbed in *blood*—and his broad brow, with all the features of the face, was besprinkled with the scarlet horror.

Such vivid details, reminiscent in their particularity of lines in "The Wreck of the Hesperus," bring, to use Poe's words in his criticism of Longfellow, "If not positive disgust," "thrilling horror."

But elsewhere in most of the tale there is that indefiniteness, that suggestiveness—of image, of sensation, and of meaning—calculated to elevate the soul. The use in the tale, after the business-like diction of the opening paragraphs, of "the quaint in phraseology"—may be expected to have an effect similar to that of the archaic diction of the old English poets, which creates in admirers of such poets "a sense of dreamy, wild, indefinite, and . . . indefinable delight." And when the rooms in which the revel is held are described only in terms of color and light, their only mentioned furnishing being the ebony clock, the omission of so many details "stirs the spirit more pleasantly than the most elaborate picture." And often the author, like Margaret Fuller, describes rather by showing effect than by depicting directly, as in the portrayal of the bizarre figures as "delirious fancies" and "a multitude of dreams," or in calling blood "the scarlet horror."

Such phrases serve also, of course, to portray sensations suggestively, since they are attached not to the courtiers but to what they see. Other devices are helpful to the achievement of the same end. The fear stirred by the clock is

hinted in words which link human qualities with this inanimate thing: when
it chimes, the hour is "stricken," and the "voice of the clock" comes from its
"brazen lungs" in a "solemnly emphatic" fashion. Actions suggest emotions
indirectly, as when the courtiers weld shut the iron door; when few, then none,
of the masquers venture into the seventh chamber; when, after "a slight rushing movement" toward the intruder, none of the courtiers puts forth a hand to
seize him. The resemblance of the seventh room to a coffin is simply hinted at
in the first description and in subsequent references to the "most westerly"
chamber, "the hall of velvet," "the velvet apartment," and "the black apartment." And, at the very end of the story, emotions are vaguely denoted—"a
certain nameless awe" and "unutterable horror."

The soul will also be stirred, presumably, by the undercurrent of meaning
which runs half-hidden through "The Masque of the Red Death." An allegorical signification, suggested by the tone, may be articulated. In such a
signification the seven chambers progressing from east to west—from blue to
black—connote the seven ages of man from the blue of the dawn of life to the
black of its night. The prince and the courtiers stand for the living, who
vainly seek to bar out and forget death by being gay and carefree, imagining
"it is folly to grieve or to think." But death walks the earth like a plague, certain, in the end, to conquer all, and the courtiers are deceived when they believe that "with such precautions they may bid defiance to contagion." Like
all men, they cannot repeat the opening words of the old saw, "Eat, drink
and be merry," without adding the conclusion.

The tone, then, implies analogies which are suggestive of hidden meanings.
But to say, as one very discerning critic of Poe does, that the tale "reproduces
in a synthetic vision the inevitable victory of Death over Humanity," is to
formulate a meaning more definitely than Poe would consider proper in the
tale itself. In accordance with Poe's demand for ambiguity, he allows such a
"moral" to be nothing more than a generally hidden undercurrent, and the
last paragraph ends on a note inconsistent with such a meaning—a note which
Poe doubtless would hold is suggestive of implications which cannot be made
explicit this side of eternity.

However, it is improper, in an important sense, thus to consider separately
incident and tone, since in Poe's opinion, if a tale is well constructed, they
will be so integrated as to co-operate from the beginning to carry the tale
inevitably to its denouement. It should be noticed, therefore, that the opening
paragraphs not only introduce the incidents by setting forth the initial situation: they also introduce the word-symbols which are to have cumulative
analogical significance—death and inexorable time, on the one hand, and life
and the gaiety which seeks to kill time by forgetting it, on the other. The
whole story which follows shows these two forces at grips and more and more
definitely points forward to the inevitable and meaningful triumph of one of
the forces.

The second paragraph shows Prospero and his party apparently successful in their escape from the plague: "buffoons, ... improvisatori, ... ballet-dancers, ... musicians, ... Beauty, ... wine. All these and security were within." But the last short sentence of the long paragraph again mentions the lurking enemy: "Without was the 'Red Death.' " Then, as the scene of the ball is described, the vague hint emerges that the escape is a wish rather than an actuality. The black velvet curtains, the blood-red light, and the clock which ticks the time in the seventh room, and the fear engendered in the hearts of the courtiers by the room, initiate the connotation by that room of the inescapable Red Death.

With such analogies ambiguously suggested, the incidents and tone operate simultaneously in a fashion comparable to that of a ballet. There are moments of gaiety, and then the clock strikes in the seventh room, and, inevitably, the courtiers are constrained to remember Death and Time, which are more and more definitely identified with that room:

> The musicians . . . . were constrained to pause, momentarily, in their performance, to hearken to the sound; and thus the waltzers perforce ceased their evolutions; and there was a brief disconcert of the whole gay company, and, while the chimes of the clock yet rang . . . . the giddiest grew pale, and the more aged and sedate passed their hands over their brows as if in confused reverie and meditation.

When the chimes cease, the musicians vow that they will not allow the clock again to disturb them. However, "after the lapse of sixty minutes (which embrace three thousand and six hundred seconds of the Time that flies)," there comes another chiming of the clock, and "the same disconcert and tremulousness and meditation as before." The parenthetical expression suggests more clearly than before an analogical significance for the clock, and the action and inaction of the dancers acquire accordant significance. The dance resumes, this time with the bizarre figures conjured up by Prospero moving through the rooms. But, when the clock chimes, even these do not bring forgetfulness. And the pause which now follows is, more clearly than in previous pauses, like an instant of death: "for a moment, all is still, and all is silent save the voice of the clock. The dreams are stiff-frozen as they stand." "And now again," continues the story, "the music swells, and the dreams live, and writhe to and fro more merrily than ever. . . . But. . . ." and again the story turns to the room of the clock. The coming of midnight, the hour associated with death and with the walking of the earth by uneasy spirits, is made to coincide with the discovery of the shrouded figure:

> The music ceased . . . . ; and the evolutions of the waltzers were quieted and there was an uneasy cessation of all things. . . . . But now there were twelve strokes . . . . ; and thus . . . . more of thought crept, with more of time, into the meditations of the thoughtful among those who revelled. And thus, too, it happened, perhaps, that before the last echoes . . . . had ut-

terly sunk into silence, ... many . . . . had found leisure to become aware of the presence of a masked figure who had arrested the attention of no single individual before.

The figure, thus appearing during a pause in music and motion and unwillingly acknowledged as a presence by the courtiers, is the Red Death. He is first viewed in the room most remote from the velvet chamber—the blue room. At first the revelers who have sought to forget and avoid death, as well as the brave prince, shrink from this explicitly symbolical masked figure. Then, when he moves with "solemn and measured step" more appropriate for a funeral than for a dance—when he moves through the seven chambers, the prince and courtiers, as if drawn by fate, follow him to "the black apartment." They see the prince die "within the shadow of the ebony clock," and now is "acknowledged the presence of the Red Death." And "the life of the ebony clock goes out with that of the last of the gay." Thus incident and tone work together from the start of the tale to its inevitable conclusion to achieve a unified effect.

LEO TOLSTOY

How Much Land Does a Man Need? [1]

An elder sister came to visit her younger sister in the country. The elder was married to a shopkeeper in town, the younger to a peasant in the village. As the sisters sat over their tea talking, the elder began to boast of the advantages of town life, saying how comfortably they lived there, how well they dressed, what fine clothes her children wore, what good things they ate and drank, and how she went to the theater, promenades, and entertainments.

The younger sister was piqued, and in turn disparaged the life of a shopkeeper, and stood up for that of a peasant.

"I wouldn't change my way of life for yours," said she. "We may live roughly, but at least we're free from worry. You live in better style than we do, but though you often earn more than you need, you're very likely to lose all you have. You know the proverb, 'Loss and gain are brothers twain.' It often happens that people who're wealthy one day are begging their bread the next. Our way is safer. Though a peasant's life is not a rich one, it's long. We'll never grow rich, but we'll always have enough to eat."

The elder sister said sneeringly:

"Enough? Yes, if you like to share with the pigs and the calves! What do you

[1] From *Twenty-Three Tales* by Leo Tolstoy, translated by Louise and Aylmer Maude. Reprinted by permission of Oxford University Press, London.

know of elegance or manners! However much your good man may slave, you'll die as you live—in a dung heap—and your children the same."

"Well, what of that?" replied the younger sister. "Of course our work is rough and hard. But on the other hand, it's sure, and we need not bow to anyone. But you, in your towns, are surrounded by temptations; today all may be right, but tomorrow the Evil One may tempt your husband with cards, wine, or women, and all will go to ruin. Don't such things happen often enough?"

Pahom, the master of the house, was lying on the top of the stove and he listened to the women's chatter.

"It is perfectly true," thought he. "Busy as we are from childhood tilling mother earth, we peasants have no time to let any nonsense settle in our heads. Our only trouble is that we haven't land enough. If I had plenty of land, I shouldn't fear the Devil himself!"

The women finished their tea, chatted a while about dress, and then cleared away the tea things and lay down to sleep.

But the Devil had been sitting behind the stove, and had heard all that had been said. He was pleased that the peasant's wife had led her husband into boasting, and that he had said that if he had plenty of land he would not fear the Devil himself.

"All right," thought the Devil. "We'll have a tussle. I'll give you land enough; and by means of that land I'll get you into my power."

II

Close to the village there lived a lady, a small landowner who had an estate of about three hundred acres. She had always lived on good terms with the peasants until she engaged as her manager an old soldier, who took to burdening the people with fines. However careful Pahom tried to be, it happened again and again that now a horse of his got among the lady's oats, now a cow strayed into her garden, now his calves found their way into her meadows —and he always had to pay a fine.

Pahom paid up, but grumbled, and, going home in a temper, was rough with his family. All through that summer Pahom had much trouble because of this manager, and he was actually glad when winter came and the cattle had to be stabled. Though he grudged the fodder when they could no longer graze on the pasture land, at least he was free from anxiety about them.

In the winter the news got about that the lady was going to sell her land and that the keeper of the inn on the high road was bargaining for it. When the peasants heard this they were very much alarmed.

"Well," thought they, "if the innkeeper gets the land, he'll worry us with fines worse than the lady's manager. We all depend on that estate."

So the peasants went on behalf of their village Council and asked the lady not to sell the land to the innkeeper, offering her a better price for it themselves. The lady agreed to let them have it. Then the peasants tried to arrange for the village Council to buy the whole estate, so that it might be held by them all in common. They met twice to discuss it, but could not settle the matter; the Evil One sowed discord among them and they could not agree. So they decided to buy the land individually, each according to his means; and the lady agreed to this plan as she had to the other.

Presently Pahom heard that a neighbor of his was buying fifty acres, and that the lady had consented to accept one half in cash and to wait a year for the other half. Pahom felt envious.

"Look at that," thought he, "the land is all being sold, and I'll get none of it." So he spoke to his wife.

"Other people are buying," said he, "and we must also buy twenty acres or so. Life is becoming impossible. That manager is simply crushing us with his fines."

So they put their heads together and considered how they could manage to buy it. They had one hundred rubles laid by. They sold a colt and one half of their bees, hired out one of their sons as a farm hand, and took his wages in advance; borrowed the rest from a brother-in-law, and so scraped together half the purchase money.

Having done this, Pahom chose a farm of forty acres, some of it wooded, and went to the lady to bargain for it. They came to an agreement, and he shook hands with her upon it and paid her a deposit in advance. Then they went to town and signed the deeds, he paying half the price down, and undertaking to pay the remainder within two years.

So now Pahom had land of his own. He borrowed seed, and sowed it on the land he had bought. The harvest was a good one, and within a year he had managed to pay off his debts both to the lady and to his brother-in-law. So he became a landowner, plowing and sowing his own land, making hay on his own land, cutting his own trees, and feeding his cattle on his own pasture. When he went out to plow his fields, or to look at his growing corn, or at his grass meadows, his heart would fill with joy. The grass that grew and the flowers that bloomed there seemed to him unlike any that grew elsewhere. Formerly, when he had passed by that land, it had appeared the same as any other land, but now it seemed quite different.

III

So Pahom was well contented, and everything would have been right if the neighboring peasants would only not have trespassed on his wheatfields and meadows. He appealed to them most civilly, but they still went on: now the herdsmen would let the village cows stray into his meadows, then horses from the night pasture would get among his corn. Pahom turned them out again and again, and forgave their owners, and for a long time he forbore to prosecute anyone. But at last he lost patience and complained to the District Court. He knew it was the peasants' want of land, and no evil intent on their part, that caused the trouble, but he thought:

"I can't go on overlooking it, or they'll destroy all I have. They must be taught a lesson."

So he had them up, gave them one lesson, and then another, and two or three of the peasants were fined. After a time Pahom's neighbors began to bear him a grudge for this, and would now and then let their cattle on to his land on purpose. One peasant even got into Pahom's wood at night and cut down five young lime trees for their bark. Pahom, passing through the wood one day, noticed something white. He came nearer and saw the stripped trunks lying on the ground, and close by stood the stumps where the trees had been. Pahom was furious.

"If he'd only cut one here and there it would have been bad enough," thought Pahom, "but the rascal has actually cut down a whole clump. If I could only find out who did this, I'd get even with him."

He racked his brains as to who it could be. Finally he decided: "It must be Simon—no one else could have done it." So he went to Simon's homestead to have a look around, but he found nothing, and only had an angry scene. However, he now felt more certain than ever that Simon had done it, and he lodged a complaint. Simon was summoned. The case was tried, and retried, and at the end of it all Simon was acquitted, there being no evidence against him. Pahom felt still more aggrieved, and let his anger loose upon the Elder and the Judges.

"You let thieves grease your palms," said he. "If you were honest folk yourselves you wouldn't let a thief go free."

So Pahom quarreled with the judges and with his neighbors. Threats to burn his hut began to be uttered. So though Pahom had more land, his place in the community was much worse than before.

About this time a rumor got about that many people were moving to new parts.

"There's no need for me to leave my land," thought Pahom. "But some of the others may leave our village and then there'd be more room for us. I'd take over their land myself and make my estates somewhat bigger. I could then live more at ease. As it is, I'm still too cramped to be comfortable."

One day Pahom was sitting at home, when a peasant, passing through the village, happened to drop in. He was allowed to stay the night, and supper was given him. Pahom had a talk with this peasant and asked him where he came from. The stranger answered that he came from beyond the Volga, where he had been working. One word led to another, and the man went on to say that many people were settling in those parts. He told how some people from his village had settled there. They had joined the community there and had had twenty-five acres per man granted them. The land was so good, he said, that the rye sown on it grew as high as a horse, and so thick that five cuts of a sickle made a sheaf. One peasant, he said, had brought nothing with him but his bare hands, and now he had six horses and two cows of his own.

Pahom's heart kindled with desire.

"Why should I suffer in this narrow hole, if one can live so well elsewhere?" he thought. "I'll sell my land and my homestead here, and with the money I'll start afresh over there and get everything new. In this crowded place one is always having trouble. But I must first go and find out all about it myself."

Toward summer he got ready and started out. He went down the Volga on a steamer to Samara, then walked another three hundred miles on foot, and at last reached the place. It was just as the stranger had said. The peasants had plenty of land: every man had twenty-five acres of communal land given him for his use, and anyone who had money could buy, besides, at a ruble-and-a-half an acre, as much good freehold land as he wanted.

Having found out all he wished to know, Pahom returned home as autumn came on, and began selling off his belongings. He sold his land at a profit, sold his homestead and all his cattle, and withdrew from membership in the village. He only waited till the spring, and then started with his family for the new settlement.

IV

As soon as Pahom and his family reached their new abode, he applied for admission into the Council of a large village. He stood treat to the Elders and obtained the necessary documents. Five shares of communal land were given him for his own and his sons' use: that is to say—125 acres (not all together, but in different fields) besides the use of the communal pasture. Pahom put up the buildings he needed and bought cattle. Of the communal land alone he had three times as much as at his former home, and the land was good wheat-land. He was ten times better off than he had been. He had plenty of arable land and pasturage, and could keep as many head of cattle as he liked.

At first, in the bustle of building and settling down, Pahom was pleased with it all, but when he got used to it he began to think that even here he hadn't enough land. The first year he sowed wheat on his share of the communal land and had a good crop. He wanted to go on sowing wheat, but had not enough communal land for the purpose, and what he had already used was not available, for in those parts wheat is sown only on virgin soil or on fallow land. It is sown for one or two years, and then the land lies fallow till it is again overgrown with steppe grass. There were many who wanted such land, and there was not enough for all, so that people quarreled about it. Those who were better off wanted it for growing wheat, and those who were poor wanted it to let to dealers, so that they might raise money to pay their taxes. Pahom wanted to sow more wheat, so he rented land from a dealer for a year. He sowed much wheat and had a fine crop, but the land was too far from the village—the wheat had to be carted more than ten miles. After a time Pahom noticed that some peasant-dealers were living on separate farms and were growing wealthy, and he thought:

"If I were to buy some freehold land and have a homestead on it, it would be a different thing altogether. Then it would all be fine and close together."

The question of buying freehold land recurred to him again and again.

He went on in the same way for three years, renting land and sowing wheat.

The seasons turned out well and the crops were good, so that he began to lay by money. He might have gone on living contentedly, but he grew tired of having to rent other people's land every year, and having to scramble for it. Wherever there was good land to be had, the peasants would rush for it and it was taken up at once, so that unless you were sharp about it you got none. It happened in the third year that he and a dealer together rented a piece of pasture land from some peasants, and they had already plowed it up, when there was some dispute and the peasants went to law about it, and things fell out so that the labor was all lost.

"If it were my own land," thought Pahom, "I should be independent, and there wouldn't be all this unpleasantness."

So Pahom began looking out for land which he could buy, and he came across a peasant who had bought thirteen hundred acres, but having got into difficulties was willing to sell again cheap. Pahom bargained and haggled with him, and at last they settled the price at fifteen hundred rubles, part in cash and part to be paid later. They had all but clinched the matter when a passing dealer happened to stop at Pahom's one day to get feed for his horses. He drank tea with Pahom, and they had a talk. The dealer said that he was just returning from the land of the Bashkirs, far away, where he had bought thirteen thousand acres of land, all for a thousand rubles. Pahom questioned him further, and the dealer said:

"All one has to do is to make friends with the chiefs. I gave away about one hundred rubles' worth of silk robes and carpets, besides a case of tea, and I gave wine to those who would drink it; and I got the land for less than three kopecks an acre." And he showed Pahom the title deed, saying:

"The land lies near a river, and the whole steppe is virgin soil."

Pahom plied him with questions, and the dealer said:

"There's more land there than you could cover if you walked a year, and it all belongs to the Bashkirs. They're as simple as sheep, and land can be got almost for nothing."

"There, now," thought Pahom, "with my one thousand rubles, why should I get only thirteen hundred acres, and saddle myself with a debt besides? If I take it out there, I can get more than ten times as much for my money."

V

Pahom inquired how to get to the place, and as soon as the grain dealer had left him, he prepared to go there himself. He left his wife to look after the homestead, and started on his journey, taking his hired man with him. They stopped at a town on their way and bought a case of tea, some wine, and other presents, as the grain dealer had advised.

On and on they went until they had gone more than three hundred miles, and on the seventh day they came to a place where the Bashkirs had pitched their round tents. It was all just as the dealer had said. The people lived on the steppe, by a river, in felt-covered tents. They neither tilled the ground nor ate bread. Their cattle and horses grazed in herds on the steppe. The colts were tethered behind the tents, and the mares were driven to them twice a day. The mares were milked, and from the milk kumiss was made. It was the women who prepared the kumiss, and they also made cheese. As far as the men were concerned, drinking kumiss and tea, eating mutton, and playing on their pipes was all they cared about. They were all stout and merry, and all the summer long they never thought of doing any work. They were quite ignorant, and knew no Russian, but were good-natured enough.

As soon as they saw Pahom, they came out of their tents and gathered around the visitor. An interpreter was found, and Pahom told them he had come about some land. The Bashkirs seemed very glad; they took Pahom and led him into one of the best tents, where they made him sit on some down cushions placed on a carpet, while they sat around him. They gave him some tea and kumiss, and had a sheep killed, and gave him mutton to eat. Pahom took presents out of his cart and distributed them among the Bashkirs, and divided the tea amongst them. The Bashkirs were delighted. They talked a great deal among themselves, and then told the interpreter what to say.

"They wish to tell you," said the interpreter, "that they like you, and that it's our custom to do all we can to please a guest and to repay him for his gifts. You have given us presents, now tell us which of the things we possess please you best, that we may present them to you."

"What pleases me best here," answered Pahom, "is your land. Our land is crowded and the soil is worn out, but you have plenty of land, and it is good land. I never saw the likes of it."

The interpreter told the Bashkirs what Pahom had said. They talked among themselves for a while. Pahom could not understand what they were saying, but saw that they were much amused and heard them shout and laugh. Then they were silent and looked at Pahom while the interpreter said:

"They wish me to tell you that in return for your presents they will gladly give you as much land as you want. You have only to point it out with your hand and it is yours."

The Bashkirs talked again for a while and began to dispute. Pahom asked what they were disputing about, and the interpreter told him that some of them thought they ought to ask their Chief about the land and not act in his absence, while others thought there was no need to wait for his return.

V I

While the Bashkirs were disputing, a man in a large fox-fur cap appeared on the scene. They all became silent and rose to their feet. The interpreter said: "This is our Chief himself."

Pahom immediately fetched the best dressing gown and five pounds of tea, and offered these to the Chief. The Chief accepted them, and seated himself in the place of honor. The Bashkirs at once began telling him something. The Chief listened for a while, then made a sign with his head for them to be silent, and addressing himself to Pahom, said in Russian:

"Well, so be it. Choose whatever piece of land you like; we have plenty of it."

"How can I take as much as I like?" thought Pahom. "I must get a deed to make it secure, or else they may say: 'It is yours,' and afterward may take it away again."

"Thank you for your kind words," he said aloud. "You have much land, and I only want a little. But I should like to be sure which portion is mine. Could it not be measured and made over to me? Life and death are in God's hands. You good people give it to me, but your children might wish to take it back again."

"You are quite right," said the Chief. "We will make it over to you."

"I heard that a dealer had been here," continued Pahom, "and that you gave him a little land, too, and signed title deeds to that effect. I should like to have it done in the same way."

The Chief understood.

"Yes," replied he, "that can be done quite easily. We have a scribe, and we will go to town with you and have the deed properly sealed."

"And what will be the price?" asked Pahom.

"Our price is always the same: one thousand rubles a day."

Pahom did not understand.

"A day? What measure is that? How many acres would that be?"

"We do not know how to reckon it out," said the Chief. "We sell it by the day. As much as you can go around on your feet in a day is yours, and the price is one thousand rubles a day."

Pahom was surprised.

"But in a day you can get around a large tract of land," he said.

The Chief laughed.

"It will all be yours!" said he. "But there is one condition: If you don't return on the same day to the spot whence you started, your money is lost."

"But how am I to mark the way that I have gone?"

"Why, we shall go to any spot you like, and stay there. You must start from that spot and make your round, taking a spade with you. Wherever you think necessary, make a mark. At every turning, dig a hole and pile up the turf; then afterward we will go around with a plow from hole to hole. You may make as large a circuit as you please, but before the sun sets you must return to the place you started from. All the land you cover will be yours."

Pahom was delighted. It was decided to start early next morning. They talked a while, and after drinking some more kumiss and eating some more mutton, they had tea again, and then the night came on. They gave Pahom a feather bed to sleep on, and the Bashkirs dispersed for the night, promising to assemble the next morning at daybreak and ride out before sunrise to the appointed spot.

VII

Pahom lay on the feather bed, but could not sleep. He kept thinking about the land.

"What a large tract I'll mark off!" thought he, "I can easily do thirty-five miles in a day. The days are long now, and within a circuit of thirty-five miles what a lot of land there will be! I'll sell the poorer land, or let it to peasants, but I'll pick out the best and farm it myself. I'll buy two ox teams and hire two more laborers. About a hundred and fifty acres shall be plow-land, and I'll pasture cattle on the rest."

Pahom lay awake all night, and dozed off only just before dawn. Hardly were his eyes closed when he had a dream. He thought he was lying in that same tent and heard somebody chuckling outside. He wondered who it could be, and rose and went out, and he saw the Bashkir Chief sitting in front of the tent holding his sides and rolling about with laughter. Going nearer to the Chief, Pahom asked: "What are you laughing at?" But he saw that it was no longer the Chief but the grain dealer who had recently stopped at his house and had told him about the land. Just as Pahom was going to ask: "Have you been here long?" he saw that it was not the dealer, but the peasant who had come up from the Volga long ago, to Pahom's old home. Then he saw that it was not the peasant either, but the Devil himself with hoofs and horns, sitting there and chuckling, and before him lay a man, prostrate on the ground, barefooted, with only trousers and a shirt on. And Pahom dreamed that he looked more attentively to see what sort of man it was lying there, and he saw that the man was dead, and that it was himself. Horror-struck, he awoke.

"What things one dreams about!" thought he.

Looking around he saw through the open door that the dawn was breaking.

"It's time to wake them up," thought he. "We ought to be starting."

He got up, roused his man (who was sleeping in his cart), bade him harness, and went to call the Bashkirs.

"It's time to go to the steppe to measure the land," he said.

The Bashkirs rose and assembled, and the Chief came, too. Then they began drinking kumiss again, and offered Pahom some tea, but he would not wait.

"If we are to go, let's go. It's high time," said he.

VIII

The Bashkirs got ready and they all started: some mounted on horses and some in carts. Pahom drove in his own small cart with his servant and took a

spade with him. When they reached the steppe, the red dawn was beginning to kindle. They ascended a hillock (called by the Bashkirs a *shikhan*)
and, dismounting from their carts and their horses, gathered in one spot. The
Chief came up to Pahom and, stretching out his arm toward the plain:

"See," said he, "all this, as far as your eye can reach, is ours. You may
have any part of it you like."

Pahom's eyes glistened: it was all virgin soil, as flat as the palm of your
hand, as black as the seed of a poppy, and in the hollows different kinds of
grasses grew breast-high.

The Chief took off his fox-fur cap, placed it on the ground, and said:

"This will be the mark. Start from here, and return here again. All the
land you go around shall be yours."

Pahom took out his money and put it on the cap. Then he took off his
outer coat, remaining in his sleeveless undercoat. He unfastened his girdle
and tied it tight below his stomach, put a little bag of bread into the breast
of his coat, and, tying a flask of water to his girdle, he drew up the tops of
his boots, took the spade from his man, and stood ready to start. He considered for some moments which way he had better go—it was tempting
everywhere.

"No matter," he concluded, "I'll go toward the rising sun."

He turned his face to the east, stretched himself, and waited for the sun
to appear above the rim.

"I must lose no time," he thought, "and it's easier walking while it's still
cool."

The sun's rays had hardly flashed above the horizon when Pahom, carrying
the spade over his shoulder, went down into the steppe.

Pahom started walking neither slowly nor quickly. After having gone a
thousand yards he stopped, dug a hole, and placed pieces of turf one on
another to make it more visible. Then he went on; and now that he had
walked off his stiffness he quickened his pace. After a while he dug another
hole.

Pahom looked back. The hillock could be distinctly seen in the sunlight,
with the people on it, and the glittering iron rims of the cartwheels. At a
rough guess Pahom concluded that he had walked three miles. It was growing warmer; he took off his undercoat, slung it across his shoulder, and went
on again. It had grown quite warm now; he looked at the sun—it was time
to think of breakfast.

"The first shift is done, but there are four in a day, and it's too soon yet to
turn. But I'll just take off my boots," said he to himself.

He sat down, took off his boots, stuck them into his girdle, and went on.
It was easy walking now.

"I'll go on for another three miles," thought he, "and then turn to the left.
This spot is so fine that it would be a pity to lose it. The further one goes,
the better the land seems."

He went straight on for a while, and when he looked around, the hillock was scarcely visible and the people on it looked like black ants, and he could just see something glistening there in the sun.

"Ah," thought Pahom, "I have gone far enough in this direction; it's time to turn. Besides, I'm in a regular sweat, and very thirsty."

He stopped, dug a large hole, and heaped up pieces of turf. Next he untied his flask, had a drink, and then turned sharply to the left. He went on and on; the grass was high, and it was very hot.

Pahom began to grow tired: he looked at the sun and saw that it was noon.

"Well," he thought, "I must have a rest."

He sat down, and ate some bread and drank some water; but he did not lie down, thinking that if he did he might fall asleep. After sitting a little while, he went on again. At first he walked easily; the food had strengthened him; but it had become terribly hot and he felt sleepy. Still he went on, thinking: "An hour to suffer, a lifetime to live."

He went a long way in this direction also, and was about to turn to the left again, when he perceived a damp hollow: "It would be a pity to leave that out," he thought. "Flax would do well there." So he went on past the hollow and dug a hole on the other side of it before he made a sharp turn. Pahom looked toward the hillock. The heat made the air hazy: it seemed to be quivering, and through the haze the people on the hillock could scarcely be seen.

"Ah," thought Pahom, "I have made the sides too long; I must make this one shorter." And he went along the third side, stepping faster. He looked at the sun: it was nearly halfway to the horizon, and he had not yet done two miles of the third side of the square. He was still ten miles from the goal.

"No," he thought, "though it will make my land lopsided, I must hurry back in a straight line now. I might go too far, and as it is I have a great deal of land."

So Pahom hurriedly dug a hole and turned straight toward the hillock.

IX

Pahom went straight toward the hillock, but he now walked with difficulty. He was exhausted from the heat, his bare feet were cut and bruised, and his legs began to fail. He longed to rest, but it was impossible if he meant to get back before sunset. The sun waits for no man, and it was sinking lower and lower.

"Oh, Lord," he thought, "if only I have not blundered trying for too much! What if I am too late?"

He looked toward the hillock and at the sun. He was still far from his goal, and the sun was already near the rim of the sky.

Pahom walked on and on; it was very hard walking, but he went quicker and quicker. He pressed on, but was still far from the place. He began running, threw away his coat, his boots, his flask, and his cap, and kept only the spade which he used as a support.

"What am I to do?" he thought again. "I've grasped too much and ruined the whole affair. I can't get there before the sun sets."

And this fear made him still more breathless. Pahom kept on running; his soaking shirt and trousers stuck to him, and his mouth was parched. His breast was working like a blacksmith's bellows, his heart was beating like a hammer, and his legs were giving way as if they did not belong to him. Pahom was seized with terror lest he should die of the strain.

Though afraid of death, he could not stop.

"After having run all that way they will call me a fool if I stop now," thought he.

And he ran on and on, and drew near and heard the Bashkirs yelling and shouting to him, and their cries inflamed his heart still more. He gathered his last strength and ran on.

The sun was close to the rim of the sky and, cloaked in mist, looked large, and red as blood. Now, yes, now, it was about to set! The sun was quite low, but he was also quite near his goal. Pahom could already see the people on the hillock waving their arms to make him hurry. He could see the fox-fur cap on the ground and the money in it, and the Chief sitting on the ground holding his sides. And Pahom remembered his dream.

"There's plenty of land," thought he, "but will God let me live on it? I have lost my life, I have lost my life! Never will I reach that spot!"

Pahom looked at the sun, which had reached the earth: one side of it had already disappeared. With all his remaining strength he rushed on, bending his body forward so that his legs could hardly follow fast enough to keep him from falling. Just as he reached the hillock it suddenly grew dark. He looked up—the sun had already set!

He gave a cry: "All my labor has been in vain," thought he, and was about to stop, but he heard the Bashkirs still shouting, and remembered that though to him, from below, the sun seemed to have set, they on the hillock could still see it. He took a long breath and ran up the hillock. It was still light there. He reached the top and saw the cap. Before it sat the Chief, laughing and holding his sides. Again Pahom remembered his dream, and he uttered a cry: his legs gave way beneath him, he fell forward and reached the cap with his hands.

"Ah, that's a fine fellow!" exclaimed the Chief. "He has gained much land!"

Pahom's servant came running up and tried to raise him, but he saw that blood was flowing from his mouth. Pahom was dead.

The Bashkirs clicked their tongues to show their pity.

His servant picked up the spade and dug a grave long enough for Pahom to lie in, and buried him in it.

Six feet from his head to his heels was all he needed.

HENRY JAMES

The Great Good Place[1]

I

George Dane had opened his eyes to a bright new day, the face of nature well washed by last night's downpour and shining as with high spirits, good resolutions, lively intentions—the great glare of recommencement in short fixed in his patch of sky. He had sat up late to finish work—arrears over-whelming, then at last had gone to bed with the pile but little reduced. He was now to return to it after the pause of the night; but he could only look at it, for the time, over the bristling hedge of letters planted by the early postman an hour before and already, on the customary table by the chimney-piece, formally rounded and squared by his systematic servant. It was some-thing too merciless, the domestic perfection of Brown. There were news-papers on another table, ranged with the same rigour of custom, newspapers too many—what could any creature want of so much news?—and each with its hand on the neck of the other, so that the row of their bodiless heads was like a series of decapitations. Other journals, other periodicals of every sort, folded and in wrappers, made a huddled mound that had been growing for several days and of which he had been wearily, helplessly aware. There were new books, also in wrappers as well as disenveloped and dropped again —books from publishers, books from authors, books from friends, books from enemies, books from his own bookseller, who took, it sometimes struck him, inconceivable things for granted. He touched nothing, approached nothing, only turned a heavy eye over the work, as it were, of the night—the fact, in his high wide-windowed room, where duty shed its hard light into every corner, of the still unashamed admonitions. It was the old rising tide, and it rose and rose even under a minute's watching. It had been up to his shoulders last night—it was up to his chin now.

Nothing had *gone*, had passed on while he slept—everything had stayed; nothing, that he could yet feel, had died—so naturally, one would have thought; many things on the contrary had been born. To let them alone, these things, the new things, let them utterly alone and see if that, by chance, wouldn't somehow prove the best way to deal with them: this fancy brushed his face for a moment as a possible solution, just giving it, as so often before, a cool wave of air. Then he knew again as well as ever that leaving was difficult, leaving impossible—that the only remedy, the true soft effacing sponge, would be to *be* left, to be forgotten. There was no footing on which a man who had ever liked life—liked it at any rate as *he* had—could now

[1] From *The Soft Side* (New York: The Macmillan Company, 1900). Reprinted by permission of Paul R. Reynolds & Son.

escape it. He must reap as he had sown. It was a thing of meshes; he had simply gone to sleep under the net and had simply waked up there. The net was too fine; the cords crossed each other at spots too near together, making at each a little tight hard knot that tired fingers were this morning too limp and too tender to touch. Our poor friend's touched nothing—only stole significantly into his pockets as he wandered over to the window and faintly gasped at the energy of nature. What was most overwhelming was that she herself was so ready. She had soothed him rather, the night before, in the small hours by the lamp. From behind the drawn curtain of his study the rain had been audible and in a manner merciful; washing the window in a steady flood, it had seemed the right thing, the retarding interrupting thing, the thing that, if it would only last, might clear the ground by floating out to a boundless sea the innumerable objects among which his feet stumbled and strayed. He had positively laid down his pen as on a sense of friendly pressure from it. The kind full swish had been on the glass when he turned out his lamp; he had left his phrase unfinished and his papers lying quite as for the flood to bear them away in its rush. But there still on the table were the bare bones of the sentence—and not all of those; the single thing borne away and that he could never recover was the missing half that might have paired with it and begotten a figure.

Yet he could at last only turn back from the window; the world was everywhere, without and within, and the great staring egotism of its health and strength wasn't to be trusted for tact or delicacy. He faced about precisely to meet his servant and the absurd solemnity of two telegrams on a tray. Brown ought to have kicked them into the room—then he himself might have kicked them out.

"And you told me to remind you, sir—"

George Dane was at last angry. "Remind me of nothing!"

"But you insisted, sir, that I was to insist!"

He turned away in despair, using a pathetic quaver at absurd variance with his words: "If you insist, Brown, I'll kill you!" He found himself anew at the window, whence, looking down from his fourth floor, he could see the vast neighbourhood, under the trumpet-blare of the sky, beginning to rush about. There was a silence, but he knew Brown hadn't left him—knew exactly how straight and serious and stupid and faithful he stood there. After a minute he heard him again.

"It's only because, sir, you know, sir, you can't remember—"

At this Dane did flash round; it was more than at such a moment he could bear. "Can't remember, Brown? I can't forget. That's what's the matter with me."

Brown looked at him with the advantage of eighteen years of consistency. "I'm afraid you're not well, sir."

Brown's master thought. "It's a shocking thing to say, but I wish to heaven I weren't! It would be perhaps an excuse."

Brown's blankness spread like the desert. "To put them off?"

"Ah!". The sound was a groan; the plural pronoun, *any* pronoun, so mis-
timed. "Who is it?"

"Those ladies you spoke of—to luncheon."

"Oh!" The poor man dropped into the nearest chair and stared a while at
the carpet. It was very complicated.

"How many will there be, sir?" Brown asked.

"Fifty!"

"Fifty, sir?"

Our friend, from his chair, looked vaguely about; under his hand were the
telegrams, still unopened, one of which he now tore asunder. " 'Do hope you
sweetly won't mind, today, 1.30, my bringing poor dear Lady Mullet, who's
so awfully bent,' " he read to his companion.

His companion weighed it. "How many does *she* make, sir?"

"Poor dear Lady Mullet? I haven't the least idea."

"Is she—a—deformed, sir?" Brown enquired, as if in this case she might
make more.

His master wondered, then saw he figured some personal curvature. "No:
she's only bent on coming!" Dane opened the other telegram and again read
out: " 'So sorry it's at eleventh hour impossible, and count on you here, as
very greatest favour, at two sharp instead.' "

"How many does *that* make?" Brown imperturbably continued.

Dane crumpled up the two missives and walked with them to the waste-
paper basket, into which he thoughtfully dropped them. "I can't say. You
must do it all yourself. I shan't be there."

It was only on this that Brown showed an expression. "You'll go instead—"

"I'll go instead!" Dane raved.

Brown, however, had had occasion to show before that *he* would never
desert their post. "Isn't that rather sacrificing the three?" Between respect
and reproach he paused.

"*Are* there three?"

"I lay for four in all."

His master had at any rate caught his thought. "Sacrificing the three to the
one, you mean? Oh I'm not going to *her!*"

Brown's famous "thoroughness"—his great virtue—had never been so
dreadful. "Then where *are* you going?"

Dane sat down to his table and stared at his ragged phrase. " '*There* is a
happy land—far far away!' " He chanted it like a sick child and knew that
for a minute Brown never moved. During this minute he felt between his
shoulders the gimlet of criticism.

"Are you quite sure you're all right?"

"It's my certainty that overwhelms me, Brown. Look about you and judge.
Could anything be more 'right,' in the view of the envious world, than everything that surrounds us here: that immense array of letters, notes, circulars:

that pile of printers' proofs, magazines and books; these perpetual telegrams, these impending guests, this retarded, unfinished and interminable work? What could a man want more?"

"Do you mean there's too much, sir?"—Brown had sometimes these flashes.

"There's too much. There's too much. But *you* can't help it, Brown."

"No, sir," Brown assented. "Can't *you?*"

"I'm thinking—I must see. There are hours—!" Yes, there were hours, and this was one of them: he jerked himself up for another turn in his labyrinth, but still not touching, not even again meeting, his admonisher's eye. If he was a genius for any one he was a genius for Brown; but it was terrible what that meant, being a genius for Brown. There had been times when he had done full justice to the way it kept him up; now, however, it was almost the worst of the avalanche. "Don't trouble about me," he went on insincerely and looking askance through his window again at the bright and beautiful world. "Perhaps it will rain—that *may* not be over. I do love the rain," he weakly pursued. "Perhaps, better still, it will snow."

Brown now had indeed a perceptible expression, and the expression was of fear. "Snow, sir—the end of May?" Without pressing this point he looked at his watch. "You'll feel better when you've had breakfast."

"I dare say," said Dane, whom breakfast struck in fact as a pleasant alternative to opening letters. "I'll come in immediately."

"But without waiting—?"

"Waiting for what?"

Brown at last, under his apprehension, had his first lapse from logic, which he betrayed by hesitating in the evident hope his companion might by a flash of remembrance relieve him of an invidious duty. But the only flashes now were the good man's own. "You say you can't forget, sir; but you do forget—"

"Is it anything very horrible?" Dane broke in.

Brown hung fire. "Only the gentleman you told me you had asked—"

Dane again took him up; horrible or not it came back—indeed its mere coming back classed it. "To breakfast today? It *was* today; I see." It came back, yes, came back; the appointment with the young man—he supposed him young—whose letter, the letter about—what was it?—had struck him. "Yes, yes; wait, wait."

"Perhaps he'll do you good, sir," Brown suggested.

"Sure to—sure to. All right!" Whatever he might do he would at least prevent some other doing: that was present to our friend as, on the vibration of the electric bell at the door of the flat, Brown moved away. Two things in the short interval that followed were present to Dane: his having utterly forgotten the connexion, the whence, whither and why of his guest; and his continued disposition not to touch—no, not with the finger. Ah if he might *never* again touch! All the unbroken seals and neglected appeals lay there while, for a pause he couldn't measure, he stood before the chimney-piece with his hands still in his pockets. He heard a brief exchange of words in the hall, but never afterwards recovered the time taken by Brown to reappear, to precede and announce another person—a person whose name somehow failed to reach Dane's ear. Brown went off again to serve breakfast, leaving host and guest confronted. The duration of this first stage also, later on, defied measurement; but that little mattered, for in the train of what happened came promptly the second, the third, the fourth, the rich succession of the others. Yet what happened was but that Dane took his hand from his pocket, held it straight out and felt it taken. Thus indeed, if he had wanted never again to touch, it was already done.

II

He might have been a week in the place—the scene of his new consciousness—before he spoke at all. The occasion of it then was that one of the quiet figures he had been idly watching drew at last nearer and showed him a face that was the highest expression—to his pleased but as yet slightly confused perception—of the general charm. What *was* the general charm? He couldn't, for that matter, easily have phrased it; it was such an abyss of negatives, such an absence of positives and of everything. The oddity was that after a minute he was struck as by the reflexion of his own very image in this first converser seated with him, on the easy bench, under the high clear portico and above the wide far-reaching garden, where the things that most showed in the greenness were the surface of still water and the white note of old statues. The absence of everything was, in the aspect of the Brother who had thus informally joined him—a man of his own age, tired distinguished modest kind—really, as he could soon see, but the absence of what he didn't want. He didn't want, for the time, anything but just to *be* there, to steep in the bath. He was in the bath yet, the broad deep bath of stillness. They sat in it together now with the water up to their chins. He hadn't had to talk, he hadn't had to think, he had scarce even had to feel. He had been sunk that way before, sunk—when and where?—in another flood; only a flood of rushing waters in which bumping and gasping were all. *This* was a current so slow and so tepid that one floated practically without motion and without chill. The break of silence was not immediate, though Dane seemed indeed to feel it begin before a sound passed. It could pass quite sufficiently without words that he and his mate were Brothers, and what that meant.

He wondered, but with no want of ease—for want of ease was impossible —if his friend found in *him* the same likeness, the proof of peace, the gage of what the place could do. The long afternoon crept to its end; the shadows fell further and the sky glowed deeper; but nothing changed—nothing *could* change—in the element itself. It was a conscious security. It was wonderful! Dane had lived into it, but he was still immensely aware. He would have been sorry to lose that, for just this fact as yet, the blest fact of consciousness, seemed the greatest thing of all. Its only fault was that, being in itself such an occupation, so fine an unrest in the heart of gratitude, the life of the day all went to it. But what even then was the harm? He had come only to come, to take what he found. This was the part where the great cloister, enclosed externally on three sides and probably the largest lightest fairest effect, to his charmed sense, that human hands could ever have expressed in dimensions of length and breadth, opened to the south its splendid fourth quarter, turned to the great view an outer gallery that combined with the rest of the portico to form a high dry loggia, such as he a little pretended to himself he had, in the Italy of old days, seen in old cities, old convents, old villas. This recalled disposition of some great abode of an Order, some mild Monte Cassino, some Grande Chartreuse more accessible, was his main term of comparison; but he knew he had really never anywhere beheld anything at once so calculated and so generous.

Three impressions in particular had been with him all the week, and he could but recognise in silence their happy effect on his nerves. How it was all managed he couldn't have told—he had been content moreover till now with his ignorance of cause and pretext; but whenever he chose to listen with a certain intentness he made out as from a distance the sound of slow sweet bells. How could they be so far and yet so audible? How could they be so near and yet so faint? How above all could they be, in such an arrest of life, be, to *time* things, so frequent? The very essence of the bliss of Dane's whole change had been precisely that there was nothing now to time. It was the same with the slow footsteps that, always within earshot to the vague attention, marked the space and the leisure, seemed, in long cool arcades, lightly to fall and perpetually to recede. This was the second impression, and it melted into the third, as, for that matter, every form of softness, in the great good place, was but a further turn, without jerk or gap, of the endless roll of serenity. The quiet footsteps were quiet figures; the quiet figures that, to the eye, kept the picture human and brought its perfection within reach. This perfection, he felt on the bench by his friend, was now more within reach than ever. His friend at last turned to him a look different from the looks of friends in London clubs.

"The thing was to find it out!"

It was extraordinary how this remark fitted into his thought. "Ah wasn't it? And when I think," said Dane, "of all the people who haven't and who never will!" He sighed over these unfortunates with a tenderness that, in its degree, was practically new to him, feeling too how well his companion would know the people he meant. He only meant some, but they were all who'd want it; though of these, no doubt—well, for reasons, for things that, in the world, he had observed—there would never be too many. Not all perhaps who wanted would really find; but none at least would find who didn't really want. And then what the need would have to have been first! What it at first had had to be for himself! He felt afresh, in the light of his companion's face, what it might still be even when deeply satisfied, as well as what communication was established by the mere common knowledge of it.

"Every man must arrive by himself and on his own feet—isn't that so? We're Brothers here for the time, as in a great monastery, and we immediately think of each other and recognise each other as such; but we must have first got here as we can, and we meet after long journeys by complicated ways. Moreover we meet—don't we?—with closed eyes."

"Ah don't speak as if we were dead!" Dane laughed.

"I shan't mind death if it's like this," his friend replied.

It was too obvious, as Dane gazed before him, that one wouldn't; but after a moment he asked with the first articulation as yet of his most elementary wonder: "Where is it?"

"I shouldn't be surprised if it were much nearer than one ever suspected."

"Nearer 'town,' do you mean?"

"Nearer everything—nearer every one."

George Dane thought. "Would it be somewhere for instance down in Surrey?"

His Brother met him on this with a shade of reluctance. "Why should we call it names? It must have a climate, you see."

"Yes," Dane happily mused; "without that—!" All it so securely did have overwhelmed him again, and he couldn't help breaking out: "What is it?"

"Oh it's positively a part of our ease and our rest and our change, I think, that we don't at all know and that we may really call it, for that matter, anything in the world we like—the thing for instance we love it most for being."

"I know what I call it," said Dane after a moment. Then as his friend listened with interest: "Just simply 'The Great Good Place.' "

"I see—what can you say more? I've put it to myself perhaps a little differently." They sat there as innocently as small boys confiding to each other the names of toy animals. " 'The Great Want Met.' "

"Ah yes—that's it!"

"Isn't it enough for us that it's a place carried on for our benefit so admirably that we strain our ears in vain for a creak of the machinery? Isn't it enough for us that it's simply a thorough hit?"

"Ah a hit!" Dane benignantly murmured.

"It does for us what it pretends to do," his companion went on; "the mystery isn't deeper than that. The thing's probably simple enough in fact, and on a thoroughly practical basis; only it has had its origin in a splendid thought, in a real stroke of genius."

"Yes," Dane returned, "in a sense—on somebody or other's part—so exquisitely personal!"

"Precisely—it rests, like all good things, on experience. The 'great want' comes home—that's the great thing it does! On the day it came home to the right mind this dear place was constituted. It always moreover in the long run *has* been met—it always must be. How can it not require to be, more and more, as pressure of every sort grows?"

Dane, with his hands folded in his lap, took in these words of wisdom. "Pressure of every sort *is* growing!" he placidly observed.

"I see well enough what that fact has done to *you*," his Brother declared.

Dane smiled. "I couldn't have borne it longer. I don't know what would have become of me."

"I know what would have become of *me*."

"Well, it's the same thing."

"Yes," said Dane's companion, "it's doubtless the same thing." On which they sat in silence a little, seeming pleasantly to follow, in the view of the green garden, the vague movements of the monster—madness, surrender, collapse—they had escaped. Their bench was like a box at the opera. "And I may perfectly, you know," the Brother pursued, "have seen you before. I may even have known you well. We don't know."

They looked at each other again serenely enough, and at last Dane said: "No, we don't know."

"That's what I meant by our coming with our eyes closed. Yes—there's something out. There's a gap, a link missing, the great hiatus!" the Brother laughed. "It's as simple a story as the old, old rupture—the break that lucky Catholics have always been able to make, that they're still, with their innumerable religious houses, able to make, by going into 'retreat.' I don't speak of the pious exercises—I speak only of the material simplification. I don't speak of the putting off of one's self; I speak only—if one has a self worth sixpence—of the getting it back. The place, the time, the way were, for those of the old persuasion, always there—are indeed practically there for them as much as ever. They can always get off—the blessed houses receive. So it was high time that we—we of the great Protestant peoples, still more, if possible, in the sensitive individual case, overscored and overwhelmed, still more congested with mere quantity and prostituted, through our 'enterprise,' to mere profanity—should learn how to get off, should find somewhere *our* retreat and remedy. There was such a huge chance for it!"

Dane laid his hand on his companion's arm. "It's charming how when we speak for ourselves we speak for each other. That was exactly what I said!" He had fallen to recalling from over the gulf the last occasion.

The Brother, as if it would do them both good, only desired to draw him out. "What you 'said'—?"

"To *him*—that morning." Dane caught a far bell again and heard a slow footstep. A quiet presence passed somewhere—neither of them turned to look. What was little by little more present to him was the perfect taste. It was supreme—it was everywhere. "I just dropped my burden—and he received it."

"And was it very great?"

"Oh such a load!" Dane said with gaiety.

"Trouble, sorrow, doubt?"

"Oh no—worse than that!"

"Worse?"

" 'Success'—the vulgarest kind!" He mentioned it now as with amusement.

"Ah I know that too! No one in future, as things are going, will be able to face success."

"Without something of this sort—never. The better it is the worse—the greater the deadlier. But my one pain here," Dane continued, "is in thinking of my poor friend."

"The person to whom you've already alluded?"

He tenderly assented. "My substitute in the world. Such an unutterable benefactor. He turned up that morning when everything had somehow got on my nerves, when the whole great globe indeed, nerves or no nerves, seemed to have appallingly squeezed itself into my study and to be bent on simply swelling there. It wasn't a question of nerves, it was a mere question of the dislodgement and derangement of everything—of a general submersion by our eternal too much. I didn't know *où donner de la tête*—I couldn't have gone a step further."

The intelligence with which the Brother listened kept them as children feeding from the same bowl. "And then you got the tip?"

"I got the tip!" Dane happily sighed.

"Well, we all get it. But I dare say differently."

"Then how did *you*—?"

The Brother hesitated, smiling. "You tell me first."

III

"Well," said George Dane, "it was a young man I had never seen—a man at any rate much younger than myself—who had written to me and sent me some article, some book. I read the stuff, was much struck with it, told him so and thanked him—on which of course I heard from him again. Ah *that*—!" Dane comically sighed. "He asked me things—his questions were interesting; but to save time and writing I said to him: 'Come to see me—we can talk a little; but all I can give you is half an hour at breakfast.' He arrived to the minute on a day when more than ever in my life before I seemed, as it happened, in the endless press and stress, to have lost possession of my soul and to be surrounded only with the affairs of other people, smothered in mere irrelevant importunity. It made me literally ill—made me feel as I had never felt that should I once really for an hour lose hold of the thing itself, the thing that did matter and that I was trying for, I should never recover it again. The wild waters would close over me and I should drop straight to the dark depths where the vanquished dead lie."

"I follow you every step of your way," said the friendly Brother. "The wild waters, you mean, of our horrible time."

"Of our horrible time precisely. Not of course—as we sometimes dream —of any other."

"Yes, any other's only a dream. We really know none but our own."

"No, thank God—that's enough," Dane contentedly smiled. "Well, my young man turned up, and I hadn't been a minute in his presence before making out that practically it would be in him somehow or other to help me. He came to me with envy, envy extravagant—really passionate. I was, heaven save us, the great 'success' for him; he himself was starved and broken and beaten. How can I say what passed between us?—it was so strange, so swift, so much a matter, from one to the other, of instant perception and agreement. He was so clever and haggard and hungry!"

"Hungry?" the Brother asked.

"I don't mean for bread, though he had none too much, I think, even of that. I mean for—well, what I had and what I was a monument of to him as I stood there up to my neck in preposterous evidence. He, poor chap, had been for ten years serenading closed windows and had never yet caused a shutter to show that it stirred. My dim blind was the first raised to him an inch; my reading of his book, my impression of it, my note and my invitation, formed literally the only response ever dropped into his dark alley. He saw in my littered room, my shattered day, my bored face and spoiled temper —it's embarrassing, but I must tell you—the very proof of my pudding, the very blaze of my glory. And he saw in my repletion and my 'renown'—deluded innocent!—what he had yearned for in vain."

"What he had yearned for was to be you," said the Brother. Then he added: "I see where you're coming out."

"At my saying to him by the end of five minutes: 'My dear fellow, I wish you'd just try it—wish you'd for a while just be me!' You go straight to the mark, good Brother, and that was exactly what occurred—extraordinary though it was that we should both have understood. I saw what he could give, and he did too. He saw moreover what I could take; in fact what he saw was wonderful."

"He must be very remarkable!" Dane's converser laughed.

"There's no doubt of it whatever—far more remarkable than I. That's just the reason why what I put to him in joke—with a fantastic desperate irony —became, in his hands, with his vision of his chance, the blessed means and measure of my sitting on this spot in your company. 'Oh if I could just shift it all—make it straight over for an hour to other shoulders! If there only were a pair!'—that's the way I put it to him. And then at something in his face, 'Would you, by a miracle, undertake it?' I asked. I let him know all it meant—how it meant that he should at that very moment step in. It meant that he should finish my work and open my letters and keep my engagements and be subject, for better or worse, to my contacts and complications. It meant that he should live with my life and think with my brain and write with my hand and speak with my voice. It meant above all that I should get off. He accepted with greatness—rose to it like a hero. Only he said: 'What will become of *you?*' "

"There was the rub!" the Brother admitted.

"Ah but only for a minute. He came to my help again," Dane pursued, "when he saw I couldn't quite meet that, could at least only say that I wanted to think, wanted to cease, wanted to do the thing itself—the thing that mattered and that I was trying for, miserable me, and that thing only —and therefore wanted first of all really to *see* it again, planted out, crowded out, frozen out as it now so long had been. 'I know what you want,' he after a moment quietly remarked to me. 'Ah what I want doesn't exist!' 'I know what you want,' he repeated. At that I began to believe him."

"Had you any idea yourself?" the Brother's attention breathed.

"Oh yes," said Dane, "and it was just my idea that made me despair. There it was as sharp as possible in my imagination and my longing—there it was so utterly *not* in the fact. We were sitting together on my sofa as we waited for breakfast. He presently laid his hand on my knee—showed me a face that the sudden great light in it had made, for me, indescribably beautiful. 'It exists—it exists,' he at last said. And so I remember we sat a while and looked at each other, with the final effect of my finding that I absolutely believed him. I remember we weren't at all solemn—we smiled with the joy of discoveries. He was as glad as I—he was tremendously glad. That came out in the whole manner of his reply to the appeal that broke from me: 'Where is it then in God's name? Tell me without delay where it is!' "

The Brother had bent such a sympathy! "He gave you the address?"

"He was thinking it out—feeling for it, catching it. He has a wonderful head of his own and must be making of the whole thing, while we sit here patching and gossiping, something much better than ever I did. The mere sight of his face, the sense of his hand on my knee, made me, after a little, feel that he not only knew what I wanted but was getting nearer to it than I could have got in ten years. He suddenly sprang up and went over to my study-table—sat straight down there as if to write me my prescription or my passport. Then it was—at the mere sight of his back, which was turned to me—that I felt the spell work. I simply sat and watched him with the queerest deepest sweetest sense in the world—the sense of an ache that had stopped. All life was lifted; I myself at least was somehow off the ground. He was already where I had been."

"And where were you?" the Brother amusedly asked.

"Just on the sofa always, leaning back on the cushion and feeling a delicious ease. He was already me."

"And who were *you?*" the Brother continued.

"Nobody. That was the fun."

"That *is* the fun," said the Brother with a sigh like soft music.

Dane echoed the sigh, and, as nobody talking with nobody, they sat there together still and watched the sweet wide picture darken into tepid night.

I V

At the end of three weeks—so far as time was distinct—Dane began to feel there was something he had recovered. It was the thing they never named—partly for want of the need and partly for lack of the word; for what indeed was the description that would cover it all? The only real need was to know it, to see it in silence. Dane had a private practical sign for it, which, however, he had appropriated by theft—"the vision and the faculty divine." That doubtless was a flattering phrase for his idea of his genius; the genius was at all events what he had been in danger of losing and had at last held by a thread that might at any moment have broken. The change was that little by little his hold had grown firmer, so that he drew in the line—more and more each day—with a pull he was delighted to find it would bear. The mere dream-sweetness of the place was superseded; it was more and more a world of reason and order, of sensible visible arrangement. It ceased to be strange—it was high triumphant clearness. He cultivated, however, but vaguely the question of where he was, finding it near enough the mark to be almost sure that if he wasn't in Kent he was then probably in Hampshire. He paid for everything but that—that wasn't one of the items. Payment, he had soon learned, was definite; it consisted of sovereigns and shillings—just like those of the world he had left, only parted with more ecstatically—that he committed, in his room, to a fixed receptacle and that were removed in his absence by one of the unobtrusive effaced agents (shadows projected on the hours like the noiseless march of the sundial) that were always at work. The scene had whole sides that reminded and resembled, and a pleased resigned perception of these things was at once the effect and the cause of its grace.

Dane picked out of his dim past a dozen halting similes. The sacred silent convent was one; another was the bright country-house. He did the place no outrage to liken it to an hotel; he permitted himself on occasion to feel it suggest a club. Such images, however, but flickered and went out—they lasted only long enough to light up the difference. An hotel without noise, a club without newspapers—when he turned his face to what it was "without" the view opened wide. The only approach to a real analogy was in himself and his companions. They were brothers, guests, members; they were even, if one liked—and they didn't in the least mind what they were called—"regular boarders." It wasn't they who made the conditions, it was the conditions that made them. These conditions found themselves accepted, clearly, with an appreciation, with a rapture, it was rather to be called, that proceeded, as the very air that pervaded them and the force that sustained, from their quiet and noble assurance. They combined to form the large simple idea of a general refuge—an image of embracing arms, of liberal accommodation. What was the effect really but the poetisation by perfect taste of a type common enough? There was no daily miracle; the perfect taste, with the aid of space, did the trick. What underlay and overhung it all, better yet, Dane mused, was some original inspiration, but confirmed, unquenched, some happy thought of an individual breast. It had been born somehow and somewhere —it had had to insist on being—the blest conception. The author might remain in the obscure for that was part of the perfection: personal service so hushed and regulated that you scarce caught it in the act and only knew it by its results. Yet the wise mind was everywhere—the whole thing infallibly centred at the core in a consciousness. And what a consciousness it had been, Dane thought, a consciousness how like his own! The wise mind had felt, the wise mind had suffered; then, for all the worried company of minds, the wise mind had seen a chance. Of the creation thus arrived at you could none the less never have said if it were the last echo of the old or the sharpest note of the modern.

Dane again and again, among the far bells and the soft footfalls, in cool cloister and warm garden, found himself wanting not to know more and yet liking not to know less. It was part of the high style and the grand manner that there was no personal publicity, much less any personal reference. Those things were in the world—in what he had left; there was no vulgarity here of credit or claim or fame. The real exquisite was to be without the complication of an identity, and the greatest boon of all, doubtless, the solid security, the clear confidence one could feel in the keeping of the contract. That was what had been most in the wise mind—the importance of the absolute sense, on the part of its beneficiaries, that what was offered was guaranteed. They had no concern but to pay—the wise mind knew what they paid for. It was present to Dane each hour that he could never be overcharged. Oh the deep deep bath, the soft cool plash in the stillness!—this, time after time, as if under regular treatment, a sublimated German "cure," was the vivid name for his luxury. The inner life woke up again, and it was the inner life, for people of his generation, victims of the modern madness, mere maniacal extension and motion, that was returning health. He had talked of independence and written of it, but what a cold flat word it had been! This was the wordless fact itself—the uncontested possession of the long sweet stupid day. The fragrance of flowers just wandered through the void, and the quiet recurrence of delicate plain fare in a high, clean refectory where the soundless simple service was a triumph of art. That, as he analysed, remained the constant explanation: all the sweetness and serenity were created calculated things. He analysed, however, but in a desultory way and with a positive delight in the residuum of mystery that made for the great agent in the background the innermost shrine of the idol of a temple; there were odd moments for it, mild meditations when, in the broad cloister of peace or some garden-nook where the air was light, a special glimpse of beauty or reminder of felicity seemed, in passing, to hover and linger. In the mere ecstasy of change that had at first possessed him he hadn't discriminated— had only let himself sink, as I have mentioned, down to hushed depths. Then had come the slow soft stages of intelligence and notation, more marked and more fruitful perhaps after that long talk with his mild mate in the twilight, and seeming to wind up the process by putting the key into his hand. This key, pure gold, was simply the cancelled list. Slowly and blissfully he read into the general wealth of his comfort all the particular absences of which it was composed. One by one he touched, as it were, all the things it was such rapture to be without.

It was the paradise of his own room that was most indebted to them—a great square fair chamber, all beautified with omissions, from which, high up, he looked over a long valley to a far horizon, and in which he was vaguely and pleasantly reminded of some old Italian picture, some Carpaccio or some early Tuscan, the representation of a world without newspapers and letters, without telegrams and photographs, without the dreadful fatal too much. There, for a blessing, he *could* read and write; there above all he could do nothing—he could live. And there were all sorts of freedoms—always, for the occasion, the particular right one. He could bring a book from the library—he could bring two, he could bring three. An effect produced by the charming place was that for some reason he never wanted to bring more. The library was a benediction—high and clear and plain like everything else, but with something, in all its arched amplitude, unconfused and brave and gay. He should never forget, he knew, the throb of immediate perception with which he first stood there, a single glance round sufficing so to show him that it would give him what for years he had desired. He had not had detachment, but there was detachment here—the sense of a great silver bowl from which he could ladle up the melted hours. He strolled about from wall to wall, too pleasantly in tune on that occasion to sit down punctually or to choose; only recognising from shelf to shelf every dear old book that he had had to put off or never returned to; every deep distinct voice of another time that in the hubbub of the world, he had had to take for lost and unheard. He came back of course soon, came back every day; enjoyed there, of all the rare strange moments, those that were at once most quickened and most caught—moments in which every apprehension counted double and every act of the mind was a lover's embrace. It was the quarter he perhaps, as the days went on, liked best; though indeed it only shared with the rest of the place, with every aspect to which his face happened to be turned, the power to remind him of the masterly general care.

There were times when he looked up from his book to lose himself in the mere tone of the picture that never failed at any moment or at any angle. The picture was always there, yet was made up of things common enough. It was in the way an open window in a broad recess let in the pleasant morning; in the way the dry air pricked into faint freshness the gilt of old bindings; in the way an empty chair beside a table unlittered showed a volume just laid down; in the way a happy Brother—as detached as one's self and with his innocent back presented—lingered before a shelf with the slow sound of turned pages. It was a part of the whole impression that, by some extraordinary law, one's vision seemed less from the facts than the facts from one's vision; that the elements were determined at the moment by the

moment's need or the moment's sympathy. What most prompted this reflexion was the degree in which Dane had after a while a consciousness of
company. After that talk with the good Brother on the bench there were
other good Brothers in other places—always in cloister or garden some figure
that stopped if he himself stopped and with which a greeting became, in the
easiest way in the world, a sign of the diffused amenity and the consecrating
ignorance. For always, always, in all contacts, was the balm of a happy blank.
What he had felt the first time recurred: the friend was always new and yet
at the same time—it was amusing, not disturbing—suggested the possibility
that he might be but an old one altered. That was only delightful—as positively delightful in the particular, the actual conditions as it might have
been the reverse in the conditions abolished. These others, the abolished,
came back to Dane at last so easily that he could exactly measure each
difference, but with what he had finally been hustled on to hate in them
robbed of its terror in consequence of something that had happened. What
had happened was that in tranquil walks and talks the deep spell had worked
and he had got his soul again. He had drawn in by this time, with his
lightened hand, the whole of the long line, and that fact just dangled at the
end. He could put his other hand on it, he could unhook it, he was once more
in possession. This, as it befell, was exactly what he supposed he must have
said to a comrade beside whom, one afternoon in the cloister, he found himself measuring steps.

"Oh it comes—comes of itself, doesn't it, thank goodness?—just by the
simple fact of finding room and time!"

The comrade was possibly a novice or in a different stage from his own;
there was at any rate a vague envy in the recognition that shone out of the
fatigued yet freshened face. "It has come to *you* then?—you've got what you
wanted?" That was the gossip and interchange that could pass to and fro.
Dane, years before, had gone in for three months of hydropathy, and there
was a droll echo, in this scene, of the old questions of the water-cure, the
questions asked in the periodical pursuit of the "reaction"—the ailment, the
progress of each, the action of the skin and the state of the appetite. Such
memories worked in now—all familiar reference, all easy play of mind; and
among them our friends, round and round, fraternised ever so softly till, suddenly stopping short, Dane, with a hand on his companion's arm, broke into
the happiest laugh he had yet sounded.

v

"Why it's raining!" And he stood and looked at the splash of the shower
and the shine of the wet leaves. It was one of the summer sprinkles that
bring out sweet smells.

"Yes—but why not?" his mate demanded.

"Well—because it's so charming. It's so exactly right."

"But everything *is*. Isn't that just why we're here?"

"Just exactly," Dane said; "only I've been living in the beguiled supposition that we've somehow or other a climate."

"So have I, so I dare say has every one. Isn't that the blest moral?—that we live in beguiled suppositions. They come so easily here, where nothing contradicts them." The good Brother looked placidly forth—Dane could identify his phase. "A climate doesn't consist in its never raining, does it?"

"No, I dare say not. But somehow the good I've got has been half the great easy absence of all that friction of which the question of weather mostly forms a part—has been indeed largely the great easy perpetual air-bath."

"Ah yes—that's not a delusion; but perhaps the sense comes a little from our breathing an emptier medium. There are fewer things *in* it! Leave people alone, at all events, and the air's what they take to. Into the closed and the stuffy they have to be driven. I've had too—I think we must all have—a fond sense of the south."

"But imagine it," said Dane, laughing, "in the beloved British islands and so near as we are to Bradford!"

His friend was ready enough to imagine. "To Bradford?" he asked, quite unperturbed. "How near?"

Dane's gaiety grew. "Oh it doesn't matter!"

His friend, quite unmystified, accepted it. "There are things to puzzle out —otherwise it would be dull. It seems to me one can puzzle them."

"It's because we're so well disposed," Dane said.

"Precisely—we find good in everything."

"In everything," Dane went on. "The conditions settle that—they determine us."

They resumed their stroll, which evidently represented on the good Brother's part infinite agreement. "Aren't they probably in fact very simple?" he presently enquired. "Isn't simplification the secret?"

"Yes, but applied with a tact!"

"There it is. The thing's so perfect that it's open to as many interpretations as any other great work—a poem of Goethe, a dialogue of Plato, a symphony of Beethoven."

"It simply stands quiet, you mean," said Dane, "and lets us call it names?"

"Yes, but all such loving ones. We're 'staying' with some one—some delicious host or hostess who never shows."

"It's liberty-hall—absolutely," Dane assented.

"Yes—or a convalescent home."

To this, however, Dane demurred. "Ah that, it seems to me, scarcely puts it. You weren't *ill*—were you? I'm very sure I really wasn't. I was only, as the world goes, too 'beastly well'!"

The good Brother wondered. "But if we couldn't keep it up—?"

"We couldn't keep it *down*—that was all the matter!"

"I see—I see." The good Brother sighed contentedly; after which he brought out again with kindly humour: "It's a sort of kindergarten!"

"The next thing you'll be saying that we're babes at the breast!"

"Of some great mild invisible mother who stretches away into space and whose lap's the whole valley—?"

"And her bosom"—Dane completed the figure—"the noble eminence of our hill? That will do; anything will do that covers the essential fact."

"And what do you call the essential fact?"

"Why that—as in old days on Swiss lakesides—we're *en pension*."

The good Brother took this gently up. "I remember—I remember: seven francs a day without wine! But alas it's more than seven francs here."

"Yes, it's considerably more," Dane had to confess. "Perhaps it isn't particularly cheap."

"Yet should you call it particularly dear?" his friend after a moment enquired.

George Dane had to think. "How do I know, after all? What practice has one ever had in estimating the inestimable? Particular cheapness certainly isn't the note we feel struck all round; but don't we fall naturally into the view that there *must* be a price to anything so awfully sane?"

The good Brother in his turn reflected. "We fall into the view that it must pay—that it does pay."

"Oh yes; it does pay!" Dane eagerly echoed. "If it didn't it wouldn't last. It has *got* to last of course!" he declared.

"So that we can come back?"

"Yes—think of knowing that we shall be able to!"

They pulled up again at this and, facing each other, thought of it, or at any rate pretended to; for what was really in their eyes was the dread of a loss of the clue. "Oh when we want it again we shall find it," said the good Brother. "If the place really pays it will keep on."

"Yes, that's the beauty; that it isn't, thank goodness, carried on only for love."

"No doubt, no doubt; and yet, thank goodness, there's love in it too." They had lingered as if, in the mild moist air, they were charmed with the patter of the rain and the way the garden drank it. After a little, however, it did look rather as if they were trying to talk each other out of a faint small fear. They saw the increasing rage of life and the recurrent need, and they wondered proportionately whether to return to the front when their hour should sharply strike would be the end of the dream. Was this a threshold perhaps, after all, that could only be crossed one way? They must return to the front sooner or later—that was certain: for each his hour would strike. The flower would have been gathered and the trick played—the sands would in short have run.

There, in its place, *was* life—with all its rage; the vague unrest of the need for action knew it again, the stir of the faculty that had been refreshed and reconsecrated. They seemed each, thus confronted, to close their eyes a moment for dizziness; then they were again at peace and the Brother's confidence rang out. "Oh we shall meet!"

"Here, do you mean?"

"Yes—and I dare say in the world too."

"But we shan't recognise or know," said Dane.

"In the world, do you mean?"

"Neither in the world nor here."

"Not a bit—not the least little bit, you think?"

Dane turned it over. "Well, so is it that it seems to me all best to hang together. But we shall see."

His friend happily concurred. "We shall see." And at this, for farewell, the Brother held out his hand.

"You're going?" Dane asked.

"No, but I thought you were."

It was odd, but at this Dane's hour seemed to strike—his consciousness to crystallise. "Well, I am. I've got it. You stay?" he went on.

"A little longer."

Dane hesitated. "You haven't yet got it?"

"Not altogether—but I think it's coming."

"Good!" Dane kept his hand, giving it a final shake, and at that moment the sun glimmered again through the shower, but with the rain still falling on the hither side of it and seeming to patter even more in the brightness. "Hallo—how charming!"

The Brother looked a moment from under the high arch—then again turned his face to our friend. He gave this time his longest happiest sigh. "Oh it's all right!"

But why was it, Dane after a moment found himself wondering, that in the act of separation his own hand was so long retained? Why but through a queer phenomenon of change, on the spot, in his companion's face—change that gave it another, but an increasing and above all a much more familiar identity, an identity not beautiful, but more and more distinct, an identity with that of his servant, with the most conspicuous, the physiognomic seat of the public propriety of Brown? To this anomaly his eyes slowly opened; it was not his good Brother, it was verily Brown who possessed his hand. If his eyes had to open it was because they had been closed and because Brown appeared to think he had better wake up. So much as this Dane took in, but the effect of his taking it was a relapse into darkness, a recontraction of the lids just prolonged enough to give Brown time, on a second thought, to withdraw his touch and move softly away. Dane's next consciousness was that of the desire to make sure he was away, and this desire had somehow the result of dissipating the obscurity. The obscurity was completely gone by the time he had made out that the back of a person writing at his study-table was presented to him. He recognised a portion of a figure that he had somewhere described to somebody—the intent shoulders of the unsuccessful young man who had come that bad morning to breakfast. It was strange, he at last mused, but the young man was still there. How long had he stayed—days, weeks, months? He was exactly in the position in which Dane had last seen him. Everything—stranger still—was exactly in that position; everything at

least but the light of the window, which came in from another quarter and
showed a different hour. It wasn't after breakfast now; it was after—well,
what? He suppressed a gasp—it was after everything. And yet—quite literally
—there were but two other differences. One of these was that if he was still
on the sofa he was now lying down; the other was the patter on the glass that
showed him how the rain—the great rain of the night—had come back. It
was the rain of the night, yet when had he last heard it? But two minutes
before? Then how many were there before the young man at the table, who
seemed intensely occupied, found a moment to look round at him and, on
meeting his open eyes, get up and draw near?

"You've slept all day," said the young man.

"All day?"

The young man looked at his watch. "From ten to six. You were extraordinarily tired. I just after a bit let you alone, and you were soon off." Yes, that
was it; he had been "off"—off, off, off. He began to fit it together: while he
had been off the young man had been on. But there were still some few
confusions; Dane lay looking up. "Everything's done," the young man continued.

"Everything?"

"Everything."

Dane tried to take it all in, but was embarrassed and could only say weakly
and quite apart from the matter: "I've been so happy!"

"So have I," said the young man. He positively looked so; seeing which
George Dane wondered afresh, and then in his wonder read it indeed quite
as another face, quite, in a puzzling way, as another person's. Every one was a
little some one else. While he asked himself who else then the young man was,
this benefactor, struck by his appealing stare, broke again into perfect cheer.
"It's all right!" that answered Dane's question; the face was the face turned
to him by the good Brother there in the portico while they listened together
to the rustle of the shower. It was all queer, but all pleasant and all distinct,
so distinct that the last words in his ear—the same from both quarters—appeared the effect of a single voice. Dane rose and looked about his room,
which seemed disencumbered, different, twice as large. It *was* all right.

CLIFTON FADIMAN

On James's "The Great Good Place" [1]

James's remarks on this beautiful story should, I presume, preclude my own.
To its spirit, he thought, "any gloss or comment would be a tactless challenge.
It embodies a calculated effect, and to plunge into it, I find, even for a be-
guiled glance—a course I indeed recommend—is to have left all else out-

[1] Copyright 1945 by Random House, Inc. Reprinted from *The Short Stories of
Henry James*, edited by Clifton Fadiman, by permission.

side." This is true enough but it is almost equally true of *any* James story that "embodies a calculated effect." In extenuation of these "tactless challenges," I fear I can plead only that there is no obligation to read them, and that, if read, they will prove harmless.

Like *The Pilgrim's Progress* or *The Divine Comedy* "The Great Good Place" is a criticism of a whole culture, though developed on a miniature scale. Like them, too, it forsakes completely the methods of realism; like them, it invents a world. In this tiny bit of ordered dreamwork James points, however obliquely, to the essential vacuity of modern living. Only those infatuated with the twentieth century, only the gadget-men, the accumulators, will fail to make some response, however feeble, to "The Great Good Place." But it will haunt the others like a dream which, despite its oddity, seems to offer the serene answer to our deepest and most desperate prayer.

One good way to feel this story is to read it, as I chance just to have done, after listening to Mozart. The Mozartian note—perfection achieved with essentials—is precisely *not* the note of our time. We are anti-Mozartian in many ways but primarily in our passion for organizing non-essentials, both material and mental. Dimly conscious that we have lost a few simple things, we cover over our sense of loss by distributing as widely and as ingeniously as possible a million complicated things. Unable to derive satisfaction from stillness we develop speeds of almost cometary order. No longer certain what it is that makes one man better than another, we solve the problem by grading people according to the number and variety of their possessions.

The consequence of what James in this story calls "the modern madness, mere maniacal extension and motion" is a special form of lunacy known as being "under pressure." The sense of pressure has little to do with overwork or specific worries. Rather is it identical with the whole pattern of our lives, based on "getting somewhere" or "getting something." It comes about because we are engaged in doing something unnatural. We are neglecting, we are denying man's rational mind.

"The Great Good Place" is James's try—and a successful one—at putting all these truisms in the form of a fairy tale. His novelist has done what we all do: he has permitted himself to get so "involved" that he no longer knows who or what he is. He has too much of everything—success, friends, guests, work, appointments. His life is "full" or rather crowded. That is to say, it is devoid of any principle of clarity. There is no Mozart in it.

The Great Good Place is the world of Mozart's music, "all beautiful with omissions." It is not—this is the whole point—a mere refuge, an escape-hole. On the contrary it is "real life"—the life of achievement, success, accumulation and motion that is the escape. It is the escape from the mind, the escape from reflection, the escape from a recognition of one's own personality. The Great Good Place is simply ordered reality, stripped truth. Wherever the mind comes into its own, that is the Great Good Place. As the Brother says, "I don't speak of the putting off of one's self; I speak only—if one has a self worth sixpence—of the getting it back."

Note that the Place is no ethereal heaven—James is almost devoid of any religious sense—but a theoretically achievable Utopia. It is "an hotel without noise, a club without newspapers." You even have to pay for service. The Place is what our civilization could be if we did not persist in taking wrong turnings, if we divested ourselves of things, if our conception of time were not based on the date-pad and the appointment-book, if we had not forgotten the know-thyself of the Greeks, if we could rediscover the private life.

To my mind "The Great Good Place" is, of the seventeen stories in this collection [of *The Short Stories of Henry James*], the one most densely charged with contemporary application.

GUY DE MAUPASSANT

The Jewels[1]

M. Lantin met the girl at a party given by the assistant to the head of his office and fell in love with her.

She was the daughter of a provincial tax-collector who had died several years previously. After his death she had come to Paris with her mother, who often visited in several bourgeois families in her quarter in the hope of getting her daughter married off. They were poor and honorable, quiet and gentle. The girl seemed to be the perfect type of respectable young woman to whom every wise young man dreams of entrusting his future. Her unassuming beauty had a charm of angelic modesty, and the imperceptible smile which never left her lips seemed to be a reflection of the purity of her heart.

Everyone sang her praises: all of those who knew her kept repeating: "Happy will be the man who wins her. He could never find a better wife."

M. Lantin, at that time, was chief clerk in the Ministry of the Interior, with an annual salary of three thousand five hundred francs. He asked for her hand and married her.

He was unbelievably happy with her. She managed his household with such clever economy that they seemed to live in luxury. There were no attentions, no blandishments, no caresses which she did not lavish on her husband; and the attraction of her person was so great that, even six years after their first meeting, he loved her still more than he did in the first days.

He found only two faults with her: her love for the theatre and her great fondness for imitation jewelry.

Her friends (she was acquainted with the wives of several petty functionaries) always procured for her loges for the fashionable plays and sometimes even for the premières; and she dragged along her husband to these amusements whether he wanted to go or not. They tired him frightfully after his

[1] Translated by Marion E. Porter and Louis G. Locke.

day of work at the office. Then he began to beg her to go to the theatre with some lady of her acquaintance who might be willing to accompany her home afterwards. It took a long time for her to give in, since she did not think that was the proper thing to do. Finally, to please her husband, she gave in, and he was infinitely grateful.

Now, her love for the theatre soon made her feel the need of adorning herself. Her gowns remained quite simple, it is true, and, though unpretentious, in good taste; and her gentle, irresistible grace, humble and smiling, seemed to be enhanced by the simplicity of these dresses. She, however, acquired the habit of wearing two large rhinestone earrings which simulated diamonds, and she wore necklaces of false pearls, bracelets of imitation gold, and combs set with various cut glasses designed to play the rôle of precious stones.

Her husband, who was somewhat shocked by this love for costume jewelry, often said: "My dear, when one does not have the means of paying for real jewels, one does not go in public ornamented with anything except one's own beauty and grace. Those are the rarest jewels."

But she smiled gently and said: "What does it matter? I like them. They are my vice. Of course, you are right; but one cannot remake oneself. I would have adored jewels!"

And she rolled over her fingers the pearl necklaces, flashed the facets of cut crystals in the light, repeating: "Just look how well made this is. You might swear that it is the real thing."

He smiled as he said: "You have Bohemian tastes."

Sometimes, in the evening when they were alone before the fire, she would bring to the table where they were having tea, the leather box in which she kept her "baubles," as M. Lantin called them; and she would examine the imitation jewelry with passionate attention as if she were tasting some secret and profound joy; and she would insist on putting a necklace around her husband's neck, after which she would laugh heartily and cry: "How funny you are!" Then she would throw herself into his arms and kiss him recklessly.

After going to the Opera one winter night, she returned home shivering with cold. The next morning she was coughing. A week later she died of pneumonia.

Lantin almost followed her into the tomb. His despair was so terrible that his hair turned white within a month. He wept from morning to evening, his soul rent by an intolerable suffering, haunted by the memory, by the smile, the voice, the charm of the dead woman.

Time did not soften his grief. Often during the hours at his office, when his colleagues came to chat about the affairs of the day, one might see his cheeks suddenly swell, his nose wrinkle up, and his eyes fill with tears; he would make a frightful face and begin to sob.

He had kept his wife's room intact and every day he would shut himself up in it to think about her; all the furniture, even her clothes, remained in their places as they had been on her last day.

But life was becoming hard for him. His pay, which, when managed by his wife, had been adequate for all the needs of his household, was now becoming insufficient for him alone. And he wondered with helpless amazement how she had always managed to provide him with excellent wines and delicate foods which he could no longer obtain with his modest resources.

He made a few debts and chased money in the manner of people who are reduced to living by their wits. Finding himself without a sou one morning an entire week before the end of the month, he thought of selling something; and all at once the thought came to him that he might dispose of his wife's "baubles," for he had kept in the bottom of his heart a kind of grudge against these "eye-deceivers" which used to irritate him so much. The very sight of them each day somewhat spoiled his memory of his beloved.

He sought a long time in the pile of tawdry jewelry which she had left behind, for she had obstinately kept on buying these things up to the last days of her life, bringing home some new piece almost every evening. Finally he decided on the great necklace which she seemed to prefer and which he thought might be worth, at least six or eight francs, for it was really very carefully made for artificial jewelry.

He put it in his pocket and left for the office, following the boulevards on which he hoped to find a jeweler's shop which he might feel confident enough to enter.

He finally saw one and went in, a bit ashamed at displaying his poverty by trying to sell a thing of so little value.

"Sir," he said to the merchant, "I would like to know at what you value this piece."

The man took the object, examined it, turned it over, tried its weight, looked at it through his glass, called his clerk, said something to him in a low voice, placed the necklace back on the counter and looked at it from a distance in order to judge its effect better.

M. Lantin, disturbed by all this ceremony, was about to open his mouth to declare: "Oh! I know it is of no value," when the jeweler delivered his pronouncement:

"Sir, that is worth between twelve and fifteen thousand francs; but I could buy it only upon the condition that you inform me as to exactly where it comes from."

The widower opened his eyes wide in amazement and gaped in astonishment, not understanding. He finally stammered: "You say . . . ? You are sure?" The other failed to understand the cause of his astonishment, and said drily: "You can try elsewhere to see if anyone will give you more. As far as I am concerned, that is worth fifteen thousand, at the most. You can come back to see me if you can not find anything better."

M. Lantin, completely stupefied, took up his necklace and left, obeying a confused need to be alone and to think.

But as soon as he was in the street, he was seized by a need to laugh, and he thought: "That fool! Oh, the fool! What if I had taken him at his word? There's a jeweler who can't distinguish between the false and the real."

And he went to another merchant at the entrance of the rue de la Paix. As soon as he saw the jewel, the goldsmith cried:

"Ah! indeed; I am well acquainted with that necklace; it comes from my shop."

Lantin, very disturbed, asked:

"How much is it worth?"

"Sir, I sold it for twenty-five thousand. I am ready to buy it back for eighteen thousand as soon as you have indicated to me just how it happens to be in your possession. I need that information in order to obey the law."

This time M. Lantin sat down paralyzed with amazement. He answered: "Why . . . why, examine it carefully, sir. I had thought until now that it was . . . artificial."

The jeweler replied: "Will you tell me your name, sir?"

"Certainly. My name is Lantin, I am an employee at the Ministry of the Interior, and I live at 16, rue des Martyrs."

The merchant opened his registers, looked in them, and said: "This necklace was in fact sent to the address of Mme. Lantin at 16, rue des Martyrs, on the 20th of July, 1876."

And the two men looked into each other's eyes, the government employee dumb with amazement and the jeweler sensing a thief.

The latter replied, "Will you leave this piece with me for just twenty-four hours? I will give you a receipt for it."

Lantin stammered: "Why yes, certainly." And he departed, folding the receipt which he placed in his pocket.

Then he crossed the street, went up it, saw that he had gone the wrong way, went back down to the Tuileries, crossed the Seine, recognized that he had made another error, returned to the Champs Élysées. His head was completely void of clear ideas. He tried to reason, to understand. His wife had not been able to buy an object of such value. No, certainly not. Why then it was a gift! A gift! A gift from whom? Why?

He had stopped in the middle of the avenue and stood there. A horrible doubt came over him. She? Why then all the other jewels were also gifts! It seemed to him that the earth was shaking; that a tree in front of him was falling; he stretched out his arms and collapsed, unconscious.

He regained consciousness in a pharmacist's shop where some passers-by had carried him. He got somebody to take him home and he shut himself up.

He wept desperately until night, biting a handkerchief to keep from crying out. Then he went to bed overwhelmed with fatigue and sorrow, and he slept soundly and dreamlessly.

A ray of sunlight awakened him and he got up slowly to go to the office. It was hard to work after such shattering experiences. He thought then that he might apologize to his chief; and he wrote to him. Then he thought that he must return to the jeweler's; and shame made him blush. He thought it over for a long time. He could not leave the necklace at that man's shop; he dressed and went out.

It was a beautiful day, the blue sky covering the city seemed to smile. Idlers were strolling about with their hands in their pockets.

Lantin said to himself as he watched them pass: "How happy a person must be who has money. With money one can even shake off grief; one can go where one wants; one can travel, have a good time. Oh! if I were only rich!"

He realized that he was hungry since he had not eaten for forty-eight hours. But his pockets were empty. "Eighteen thousand francs! *That* was a sum!"

He reached the rue de la Paix and began to pace back and forth on the sidewalk across from the shop. Eighteen thousand francs! Twenty times he tried to enter, but shame stopped him.

He was hungry, however, very hungry and did not have a *sou*. All of a sudden he made up his mind, crossed the street at a run, so as not to give himself time to think, and dashed into the jeweler's shop.

As soon as the merchant saw him he rushed forward, offered him a chair with a kind of smiling politeness. The clerks came forward, giving Lantin sidewise glances, with gaiety in their eyes and on their lips.

The jeweler declared: "I have made the necessary inquiries, sir, and if you are still willing, I am prepared to pay you the sum which I proposed to you."

The government employee stammered: "Why certainly."

The jeweler took eighteen large banknotes from a drawer, counted them, handed them to Lantin who signed a receipt and tremblingly placed the money in his pocket.

Then, as he was about to leave, he turned toward the merchant, who was still smiling and, lowering his eyes, said: "I . . . I have other jewels . . . which came to me . . . from the same source. Would you care to buy them also?"

The merchant bowed: "Why certainly, sir."

One of the clerks left the room in order to laugh more freely; another blew his nose loudly.

Lantin, impassive, blushing and serious, said: "I shall bring them to you."

And he took a cab in order to go and get the jewels.

When he came back to the merchant's an hour later, he had not yet had lunch. They began to examine the jewelry piece by piece, evaluating each one. Almost all of them came from that shop.

Lantin was now disposed to argue about the evaluation, he would become angry, he demanded that he be shown the ledgers, and spoke louder as the sum increased.

The large diamond earrings were worth twenty thousand francs, the bracelets thirty-five thousand, the brooches, rings and lockets sixteen thousand, an emerald and sapphire necklace fourteen thousand; a diamond solitaire on a gold chain forty thousand—the lot reached the figure of a hundred and ninety-six thousand francs.

The jeweler declared with bantering good humor: "All that comes from a person whose savings were put in jewels."

Lantin said seriously: "That is as good a way as any of investing money." And he left after deciding with the purchaser that another evaluation would be made the next day.

When he was in the street, he looked at the Colonne Vendôme with the desire to climb it in high good spirits. He felt that he was light enough to play leap frog with the statue of Napoleon which is on top of it.

He went to Voisin's for lunch and drank wine which cost twenty francs per bottle.

Then he took a cab and had a ride through the Bois de Boulogne. He looked at the other carriages somewhat scornfully, assailed with the desire to cry out to all whom he passed: "I, too, am rich. I have two hundred thousand francs!"

He remembered the office. He had the driver take him there, entered his chief's office deliberately, and announced:

"I come, sir, to hand you my resignation. I have inherited three hundred thousand francs." He shook hands with his former colleagues and told them confidentially of his plans for his new life; then he dined at the café Anglais.

Finding himself beside a gentleman who seemed distinguished, he could not resist the desire to confide in him, with a certain coquettishness, that he had just inherited four hundred thousand francs.

For the first time in his life he was not bored at the theatre and he spent the night with some girls.

Six months later he remarried. His second wife was very respectable, but of a difficult disposition. She made him suffer a lot.

ANTON CHEKHOV

Gooseberries[1]

The sky had been overcast since early morning; it was a still day, not hot, but tedious, as it usually is when the weather is gray and dull, when clouds have been hanging over the fields for a long time, and you wait for the rain that does not come. Ivan Ivanych, a veterinary, and Burkin, a high school teacher, were already tired with walking, and the plain seemed endless to them. Far ahead

[1] From *The Portable Chekhov*, translated by Avrahm Yarmolinsky. Copyright 1947 by The Viking Press, Inc. and reprinted by their permission.

were the scarcely visible windmills of the village of Mironositzkoe; to the right lay a range of hills that disappeared in the distance beyond the village, and both of them knew that over there were the river, and fields, green willows, homesteads, and if you stood on one of the hills, you could see from there another vast plain, telegraph poles, and a train that from afar looked like a caterpillar crawling, and in clear weather you could even see the town. Now, when it was still and when nature seemed mild and pensive, Ivan Ivanych and Burkin were filled with love for this plain, and both of them thought what a beautiful land it was.

"Last time when we were in Elder Prokofy's barn," said Burkin, "you were going to tell me a story."

"Yes; I wanted to tell you about my brother."

Ivan Ivanych heaved a slow sigh and lit his pipe before beginning his story, but just then it began to rain. And five minutes later there was a downpour, and it was hard to tell when it would be over. The two men halted, at a loss; the dogs, already wet, stood with their tails between their legs and looked at them feelingly.

"We must find shelter somewhere," said Burkin. "Let's go to Alyohin's; it's quite near."

"Let's."

They turned aside and walked across a mown meadow, now going straight ahead, now bearing to the right, until they reached the road. Soon poplars came into view, a garden, then the red roofs of barns; the river gleamed, and the view opened on a broad expanse of water with a mill and a white bathing-cabin. That was Sofyino, Alyohin's place.

The mill was going, drowning out the sound of the rain; the dam was shaking. Wet horses stood near the carts, their heads drooping, and men were walking about, their heads covered with sacks. It was damp, muddy, dreary; and the water looked cold and unkind. Ivan Ivanych and Burkin felt cold and messy and uncomfortable through and through; their feet were heavy with mud and when, having crossed the dam, they climbed up to the barns, they were silent as though they were cross with each other.

The noise of a winnowing-machine came from one of the barns, the door was open, and clouds of dust were pouring from within. On the threshold stood Alyohin himself, a man of forty, tall and rotund, with long hair, looking more like a professor or an artist than a gentleman farmer. He was wearing a white blouse, badly in need of washing, that was belted with a rope, and drawers, and his high boots were plastered with mud and straw. His eyes and nose were black with dust. He recognized Ivan Ivanych and Burkin and was apparently very glad to see them.

"Please go up to the house, gentlemen," he said, smiling; "I'll be there directly, in a moment."

It was a large structure of two stories. Alyohin lived downstairs in what was formerly the stewards' quarters: two rooms that had arched ceilings and small windows; the furniture was plain, and the place smelled of rye bread, cheap vodka, and harness. He went into the showy rooms upstairs only rarely, when he had guests. Once in the house, the two visitors were met by a chambermaid, a young woman so beautiful that both of them stood still at the same moment and glanced at each other.

"You can't imagine how glad I am to see you, gentlemen," said Alyohin, joining them in the hall. "What a surprise! Pelageya," he said, turning to the chambermaid, "give the guests a change of clothes. And, come to think of it, I will change, too. But I must go and bathe first, I don't think I've had a wash since spring. Don't you want to go into the bathing-cabin? In the meanwhile things will be got ready here."

The beautiful Pelageya, with her soft, delicate air, brought them bath towels and soap, and Alyohin went to the bathing-cabin with his guests.

"Yes, it's a long time since I've bathed," he said, as he undressed. "I've an excellent bathing-cabin, as you see—it was put up by my father—but somehow I never find time to use it." He sat down on the steps and lathered his long hair and neck, and the water around him turned brown.

"I say—" observed Ivan Ivanych significantly, looking at his head.

"I haven't had a good wash for a long time," repeated Alyohin, embarrassed, and soaped himself once more; the water about him turned dark-blue, the color of ink.

Ivan Ivanych came out of the cabin, plunged into the water with a splash and swam in the rain, thrusting his arms out wide; he raised waves on which white lilies swayed. He swam out to the middle of the river and dived and a minute later came up in another spot and swam on and kept diving, trying to touch bottom. "By God!" he kept repeating delightedly, "by God!" He swam to the mill, spoke to the peasants there, and turned back and in the middle of the river lay floating, exposing his face to the rain. Burkin and Alyohin were already dressed and ready to leave, but he kept on swimming and diving. "By God!" he kept exclaiming. "Lord, have mercy on me."

"You've had enough!" Burkin shouted to him.

They returned to the house. And only when the lamp was lit in the big drawing room upstairs, and the two guests, in silk dressing-gowns and warm slippers, were lounging in armchairs, and Alyohin himself, washed and combed, wearing a new jacket, was walking about the room, evidently savoring the warmth, the cleanliness, the dry clothes and light footwear, and when pretty Pelageya, stepping noiselessly across the carpet and smiling softly, brought in a tray with tea and jam, only then did Ivan Ivanych begin his story, and it was as though not only Burkin and Alyohin were listening, but also the ladies, old and young, and the military men who looked down upon them, calmly and severely, from their gold frames.

"We are two brothers," he began, "I, Ivan Ivanych, and my brother, Nikolay Ivanych, who is two years my junior. I went in for a learned profession and became a veterinary; Nikolay at nineteen began to clerk in a provincial branch of the Treasury. Our father was a *kantonist*,[2] but he rose to be an officer and so a nobleman, a rank that he bequeathed to us together with a small estate. After his death there was a lawsuit and we lost the estate to creditors, but be that as it may, we spent our childhood in the country. Just like peasant children we passed days and nights in the fields and the woods, herded horses, stripped bast from the trees, fished, and so on. And, you know, whoever even once in his life has caught a perch or seen thrushes migrate in the autumn, when on clear, cool days they sweep in flocks over the village, will never really be a townsman and to the day of his death will have a longing for the open. My brother was unhappy in the government office. Years passed, but he went on warming the same seat, scratching away at the same papers, and thinking of one and the same thing: how to get away to the country. And little by little this vague longing turned into a definite desire, into a dream of buying a little property somewhere on the banks of a river or a lake.

"He was a kind and gentle soul and I loved him, but I never sympathized with his desire to shut himself up for the rest of his life on a little property of his own. It is a common saying that a man needs only six feet of earth. But six feet is what a corpse needs, not a man. It is also asserted that if our educated class is drawn to the land and seeks to settle on farms, that's a good thing. But these farms amount to the same six feet of earth. To retire from the city, from the struggle, from the hubbub, to go off and hide on one's own farm—that's not life, it is selfishness, sloth, it is a kind of monasticism, but monasticism without works. Man needs not six feet of earth, not a farm, but the whole globe, all of Nature, where unhindered he can display all the capacities and peculiarities of his free spirit.

"My brother Nikolay, sitting in his office, dreamed of eating his own *shchi*, which would fill the whole farmyard with a delicious aroma, of picnicking on the green grass, of sleeping in the sun, of sitting for hours on the seat by the gate gazing at field and forest. Books on agriculture and the farming items in almanacs were his joy, the delight of his soul. He liked newspapers too, but the only things he read in them were advertisements of land for sale, so many acres of tillable land and pasture, with house, garden, river, mill, and millpond. And he pictured to himself garden paths, flowers, fruit, bird-houses with starlings in them, crucians in the pond, and all that sort of thing, you know. These imaginary pictures varied with the advertisements he came upon, but somehow gooseberry bushes figured in every one of them. He could not picture to himself a single country-house, a single rustic nook, without gooseberries.

"'Country life has its advantages,' he used to say. 'You sit on the veranda having tea, and your ducks swim in the pond, and everything smells delicious and—the gooseberries are ripening.'

"He would draw a plan of his estate and invariably it would contain the

[2] The son of a private, registered at birth in the army and trained in a military school.

following features: a) the master's house; b) servants' quarters; c) kitchen-garden; d) a gooseberry patch. He lived meagerly: he deprived himself of food and drink; he dressed God knows how, like a beggar, but he kept on saving and salting money away in the bank. He was terribly stingy. It was painful for me to see it, and I used to give him small sums and send him something on holidays, but he would put that away too. Once a man is possessed by an idea, there is no doing anything with him.

"Years passed. He was transferred to another province, he was already past forty, yet he was still reading newspaper advertisements and saving up money. Then I heard that he was married. Still for the sake of buying a property with a gooseberry patch he married an elderly, homely widow, without trace of affection for her, but simply because she had money. After marrying her, he went on living parsimoniously, keeping her half-starved, and he put her money in the bank in his own name. She had previously been the wife of a postmaster, who had got her used to pies and cordials. This second husband did not even give her enough black bread. She began to sicken, and some three years later gave up the ghost. And, of course, it never for a moment occurred to my brother that he was to blame for her death. Money, like vodka, can do queer things to a man. Once in our town a merchant lay on his deathbed; before he died, he ordered a plateful of honey and he ate up all his money and lottery tickets with the honey, so that no one should get it. One day when I was inspecting a drove of cattle at a railway station, a cattle dealer fell under a locomotive and it sliced off his leg. We carried him in to the infirmary, the blood was gushing from the wound—a terrible business, but he kept begging us to find his leg and was very anxious about it: he had twenty rubles in the boot that was on that leg, and he was afraid they would be lost."

"That's a tune from another opera," said Burkin.

Ivan Ivanych paused a moment and then continued:

"After his wife's death, my brother began to look around for a property. Of course, you may scout about for five years and in the end make a mistake, and buy something quite different from what you have been dreaming of. Through an agent my brother bought a mortgaged estate of three hundred acres with a house, servants' quarters, a park, but with no orchard, no gooseberry patch, no duck-pond. There was a stream, but the water in it was the color of coffee, for on one of its banks there was a brickyard and on the other a glue factory. But my brother was not at all disconcerted: he ordered a score of gooseberry bushes, planted them, and settled down to the life of a country gentleman.

"Last year I paid him a visit. I thought I would go and see how things were with him. In his letter to me my brother called his estate 'Chumbaroklov Waste, or Himalaiskoe' (our surname was Chimsha-Himalaisky). I reached the place in the afternoon. It was hot. Everywhere there were ditches, fences, hedges, rows of fir trees, and I was at a loss as to how to get to the yard and where to leave my horse. I made my way to the house and was met by a fat dog with reddish hair that looked like a pig. It wanted to bark, but was too lazy. The cook, a fat, bare-legged woman, who also looked like a pig, came out of the kitchen and said that the master was resting after dinner. I went in to see my brother, and found him sitting up in bed, with a quilt over his knees. He had grown older, stouter, flabby; his cheeks, his nose, his lips jutted out: it looked as though he might grunt into the quilt at any moment.

"We embraced and dropped tears of joy and also of sadness at the thought that the two of us had once been young, but were now gray and nearing death. He got dressed and took me out to show me his estate.

"'Well, how are you getting on here?' I asked.

"'Oh, all right, thank God. I am doing very well.'

"He was no longer the poor, timid clerk he used to be but a real landowner, a gentleman. He had already grown used to his new manner of living and developed a taste for it. He ate a great deal, steamed himself in the bath-house, was growing stout, was already having a lawsuit with the village commune and the two factories and was very much offended when the peasants failed to address him as 'Your Honor.' And he concerned himself with his soul's welfare too in a substantial, upper-class manner, and performed good deeds not simply, but pompously. And what good works! He dosed the peasants with bicarbonate and castor oil for all their ailments and on his name day he had a thanksgiving service celebrated in the center of the village, and then treated the villagers to a gallon of vodka, which he thought was the thing to do. Oh, those horrible gallons of vodka! One day a fat landowner hauls the peasants up before the rural police officer for trespassing, and the next, to mark a feast day, treats them to a gallon of vodka, and they drink and shout 'Hurrah' and when they are drunk bow down at his feet. A higher standard of living, over-eating and idleness develop the most insolent self-conceit in a Russian. Niko-lay Ivanych, who when he was a petty official was afraid to have opinions of his own even if he kept them to himself, now uttered nothing but incon-trovertible truths and did so in the tone of a minister of state: 'Education is necessary, but the masses are not ready for it; corporal punishment is gen-erally harmful, but in some cases it is useful and nothing else will serve.'

"'I know the common people, and I know how to deal with them,' he would say. 'They love me. I only have to raise my little finger, and they will do anything I want.'

"And all this, mark you, would be said with a smile that bespoke kindness and intelligence. Twenty times over he repeated: 'We, of the gentry,' 'I, as a member of the gentry.' Apparently he no longer remembered that our grandfather had been a peasant and our father just a private. Even our sur-name, 'Chimsha-Himalaisky,' which in reality is grotesque, seemed to him sonorous, distinguished, and delightful.

"But I am concerned now not with him, but with me. I want to tell you about the change that took place in me during the few hours that I spent on his estate. In the evening when we were having tea, the cook served a plateful of gooseberries. They were not bought, they were his own gooseberries, the first ones picked since the bushes were planted. My brother gave a laugh and for a minute looked at the gooseberries in silence, with tears in his eyes—he could not speak for excitement. Then he put the one berry in his mouth, glanced at me with the triumph of a child who has at last been given a toy he was longing for and said: 'How tasty!' And he ate the gooseberries greedily, and kept repeating: 'Ah, how delicious! Do taste them!'

"They were hard and sour, but as Pushkin has it,

> The falsehood that exalts we cherish more
> Than meaner truths that are a thousand strong.

I saw a happy man, one whose cherished dream had so obviously come true, who had attained his goal in life, who had got what he wanted, who was satisfied with his lot and with himself. For some reason an element of sadness had always mingled with my thoughts of human happiness, and now at the sight of a happy man I was assailed by an oppressive feeling bordering on despair. It weighed on me particularly at night. A bed was made up for me in a room next to my brother's bedroom, and I could hear that he was wakeful, and that he would get up again and again, go to the plate of gooseberries and eat one after another. I said to myself: how many contented, happy people there really are! What an overwhelming force they are! Look at life: the insolence and idlensss of the strong, the ignorance and brutishness of the weak, horrible poverty everywhere, overcrowding, degeneration, drunkenness, hypocrisy, lying— Yet in all the houses and on all the streets there is peace and quiet; of the fifty thousand people who live in our town there is not one who would cry out, who would vent his indignation aloud. We see the people who go to market, eat by day, sleep by night, who babble nonsense, marry, grow old, good-naturedly drag their dead to the cemetery, but we do not see or hear those who suffer, and what is terrible in life goes on somewhere behind the scenes. Everything is peaceful and quiet and only mute statistics protest: so many people gone out of their minds, so many gallons of vodka drunk, so many children dead from malnutrition— And such a state of things is evidently necessary; obviously the happy man is at ease only because the unhappy ones bear their burdens in silence, and if there were not this silence, happiness would be impossible. It is a general hypnosis. Behind the door of every contented, happy man there ought to be someone standing with a little hammer and continually reminding him with a knock that there are unhappy people, that however happy he may be, life will sooner or later show him its claws, and trouble will come to him—illness, poverty, losses, and then no one will see or hear him, just as now he neither sees nor hears others. But there is no man with a hammer. The happy man lives at his ease, faintly fluttered by small daily cares, like an aspen in the wind—and all is well.

"That night I came to understand that I too had been contented and happy," Ivan Ivanych continued, getting up. "I too over the dinner table or

out hunting would hold forth on how to live, what to believe, the right way
to govern the people. I too would say that learning was the enemy of darkness,
that education was necessary but that for the common people the three R's
were sufficient for the time being. Freedom is a boon, I used to say, it is as
essential as air, but we must wait awhile. Yes, that's what I used to say, and now
I ask: Why must we wait?" said Ivan Ivanych, looking wrathfully at Burkin.
"Why must we wait, I ask you? For what reason? I am told that nothing can be
done all at once, that every idea is realized gradually, in its own time. But
who is it that says so? Where is the proof that it is just? You cite the natural
order of things, the law governing all phenomena, but is there law, is there
order in the fact that I, a living, thinking man, stand beside a ditch and
wait for it to close up of itself or fill up with silt, when I could jump over it or
throw a bridge across it? And again, why must we wait? Wait, until we have
no strength to live, and yet we have to live and are eager to live!

"I left my brother's place early in the morning, and ever since then it has become intolerable for me to stay in town. I am oppressed by the peace and the
quiet, I am afraid to look at the windows, for there is nothing that pains me
more than the spectacle of a happy family sitting at table having tea. I am an
old man now and unfit for combat, I am not even capable of hating. I can only
grieve inwardly, get irritated, worked up, and at night my head is ablaze with
the rush of ideas and I cannot sleep. Oh, if I were young!"

Ivan Ivanych paced up and down the room excitedly and repeated, "If I were
young!"

He suddenly walked up to Alyohin and began to press now one of his hands,
now the other.

"Pavel Konstantinych," he said imploringly, "don't quiet down, don't
let yourself be lulled to sleep! as long as you are young, strong, alert, do not
cease to do good! There is no happiness and there should be none, and if life
has a meaning and a purpose, that meaning and purpose is not our happiness
but something greater and more rational. Do good!"

All this Ivan Ivanych said with a pitiful, imploring smile, as though he
were asking a personal favor.

Afterwards all three of them sat in armchairs in different corners of the
drawing room and were silent. Ivan Ivanych's story satisfied neither Burkin nor
Alyohin. With the ladies and generals looking down from the golden frames,
seeming alive in the dim light, it was tedious to listen to the story of the
poor devil of a clerk who ate gooseberries. One felt like talking about elegant
people, about women. And the fact that they were sitting in a drawing room
where everything—the chandelier under its cover, the armchairs, the carpets
underfoot—testified that the very people who were now looking down from
the frames had once moved about here, sat and had tea, and the fact that
lovely Pelageya was noiselessly moving about—that was better than any story.

Alyohin was very sleepy; he had gotten up early, before three o'clock in the
morning, to get some work done, and now he could hardly keep his eyes

open, but he was afraid his visitors might tell an interesting story in his absence, and he would not leave. He did not trouble to ask himself if what Ivan Ivanych had just said was intelligent or right. The guests were not talking about groats, or hay, or tar, but about something that had no direct bearing on his life, and he was glad of it and wanted them to go on.

"However, it's bedtime," said Burkin, rising. "Allow me to wish you good night."

Alyohin took leave of his guests and went downstairs to his own quarters, while they remained upstairs. They were installed for the night in a big room in which stood two old wooden beds decorated with carvings and in the corner was an ivory crucifix. The wide cool beds which had been made by the lovely Pelageya gave off a pleasant smell of clean linen.

Ivan Ivanych undressed silently and got into bed.

"Lord forgive us sinners!" he murmured, and drew the bedclothes over his head.

His pipe, which lay on the table, smelled strongly of burnt tobacco, and Burkin, who could not sleep for a long time, kept wondering where the unpleasant odor came from.

The rain beat against the window panes all night.

MARK SCHORER

On Chekhov's "Gooseberries" [1]

In Chekhov's "Gooseberries," we begin once more with the direct, anecdotal convention: " '. . . you were going to tell me a story' ". . . ". . . only then did Ivan Ivanych begin his story . . . 'We are two brothers,' he began." But how remarkably everything here has opened up to give us a wide and richly detailed view of human life and then gently closed down and framed that view for us! And when we finish the story (perhaps not after the first reading, but after the third or fourth) we are left not with a sharp jab at our nervous system but with vastly more. How does Chekhov accomplish that more? How does he get from a sketch to a short story, from the convention of the anecdote to the full, evocative beauty of form?

His anecdote is itself "framed." The anecdote is placed within a surrounding action and a surrounding atmosphere, and the first observation to be made is the interplay between the framing action and the framed anecdote, the way that each illuminates the other, gives the other its significance. It is a story that moves by counterpoint, and its formal and therefore its thematic

[1] Mark Schorer, ed., *The Story: A Critical Anthology.* © 1950. Prentice-Hall, Inc., Englewood Cliffs, N. J. Reprinted by permission.

beauty exists in the interwoven harmonies, the two strains of present events (the action) and remembered events (the anecdote).

Two men are walking in the country, we are told, and the essential contrast of the story is announced at once, there, in the opening paragraph. First we are presented with a landscape that is tedious, gray, and dull, and with two men who are weary, and weary of it; then, at the end of the paragraph, by some magical elision, the same landscape has become attractive, "mild and pensive," and the men are aware of their deep affection for it. The contradiction is not in the landscape, for that has not changed (the rain has not even begun), but in the varieties and waverings of human response to facts, which emotions apparently create.

The men seek shelter from the rain at the farm of a friend, and the farm is like most farms—dirty. The mill is working, the horses are wet, the hired hands are drenched, their heads in sacks, everything is "damp, muddy, dreary." The owner is a model of filth and the rooms he lives in are sordid. The visitors are miserably uncomfortable. Then comes that remarkable scene of the bath. Alyohin begins to wash off his several seasons of dirt, and suddenly the chief character, Ivan, leaps into that river whose waters only a few moments before had "looked cold and unkind," and, with the most marvelous emotional release and physical pleasure, swims and shouts in the rain. Then, when the three of them are clean, dry, and comfortable, they go into the house and to the drawing room upstairs. Upstairs is different from downstairs, as pleasure is different from pain, or dreams different from reality, or emotions different from the facts to which they are responses. Still, upstairs and downstairs are parts of the same house. Upstairs, the anecdote at last begins.

The anecdote has to do with another farmer, Ivan's brother, a drudging clerk who all his life aspired to be a landed gentleman and ended as a perfectly happy, perfect parody of a landed gentleman, ecstatic in his failure. To an outside eye, Ivan's, for example, there is no relation whatever between the drab actuality of Nikolay's farm and Nikolay's dream of it, but to that dream, meanwhile, Nikolay has sacrificed years of effort, all comfort, a moral sense, and a woman's life. That is the first large irony of the anecdote: that all these human actualities should have been thrown so willingly into the trough of this dream. The second is that this dream, in which Nikolay is so happy, is a miserable actuality, in which even the gooseberries are inedible, except, of course, to Nikolay. But there are intermediate ironies—the two boys had been raised as peasant children, and therefore, we are told, they love the country, a large unlikelihood; Ivan does not believe that one can "retire" from the world, for man, a free being, needs the challenge of the world to prove his freedom, yet there are the examples of Nikolay, supremely happy out of it, and Ivan himself, in it, and hardly so. There are other such ironies, but the great one is of course in the fact that the reality of Alyohin's farm, apart from that upstairs room where Ivan is talking, is much like that of Nikolay's, and the two descriptions, of Alyohin's first appearance on his farm in the frame story, and of Nikolay's in the anecdote, should be observed for their similarity. This similarity Ivan does not see, as he spins out his tale in the upstairs drawing room, as he announces the contrast he felt (and told his brother of) between youth, with its potentialities of fulfillment, and death, with its frustrating finality. So he concludes with the observation that happiness is a form of blindness, of illusion, a perception that came to him on his brother's farm and that changed him ("I want to tell you about the change that took place in me"), and then, after adjuring his host to make something noble of his life, to do good, so that he will not have to live in the regret of lost dreams, Ivan himself reverses his position (as he did at the river) and tells us how now he must always wish to live in the country—that is, in an illusion of the country.

Then the anecdote lapses back into its frame, the actuality. Who has cared so far? Not Alyohin, not Burkin, they have been disappointed in the tale. But the pictures seem to have been listening, the ghosts, the noble shades, the unrealities. For Alyohin, the tale has been a fantasy, it has "had no direct bearing on his life, and he was glad of it"; it has been a "story." Burkin suggests bed, and Alyohin goes back downstairs to the sordid actuality. Ivan falls asleep, but Burkin is disturbed for a long time by the smell of Ivan's pipe, which he cannot identify. It is the smell of some lingering falsehood, of Ivan's story, in fact, which tried at once to prove and disprove its point. The frame of the story—the landscape, the arrival, the farm, the bath and the swim, the downstairs and the upstairs rooms, the sleep at last—all these have proved the proving-disproving attempt. The frame has judged the anecdote; its actuality reveals the confusion of fact and dream in the anecdote it contains. The story is like Ivan's wished-for hammer: it knocks at the door of our consciousness, telling us of the lovely vanity of human wishes, or of the way that wishes transform the world into vain loveliness.

Why, at the end of the story, is it still raining?

STEPHEN CRANE

The Bride Comes to Yellow Sky[1]

I

The great Pullman was whirling onward with such dignity of motion that a glance from the window seemed simply to prove that the palms of Texas were pouring eastward. Vast flats of green grass, dull-hued spaces of mesquite and

[1] From *Stephen Crane: The Red Badge of Courage and Selected Prose and Poetry*, edited by William M. Gibson, "Rinehart Editions" (New York: Holt, Rinehart and Winston, Inc., 1956), pp. 109-121.

cactus, little groups of frame houses, woods of light and tender trees, all were sweeping into the east, sweeping over the horizon, a precipice.

A newly married pair had boarded this coach at San Antonio. The man's face was reddened from many days in the wind and sun, and a direct result of his new black clothes was that his brick-colored hands were constantly performing in a most conscious fashion. From time to time he looked down respectfully at his attire. He sat with a hand on each knee, like a man waiting in a barber's shop. The glances he devoted to other passengers were furtive and shy.

The bride was not pretty, nor was she very young. She wore a dress of blue cashmere, with small reservations of velvet here and there, and with steel buttons abounding. She continually twisted her head to regard her puff sleeves, very stiff, straight, and high. They embarrassed her. It was quite apparent that she had cooked, and that she expected to cook, dutifully. The blushes caused by the careless scrutiny of some passengers as she had entered the car were strange to see upon this plain, under-class countenance, which was drawn in placid, almost emotionless lines.

They were evidently very happy. "Ever been in a parlor-car before?" he asked, smiling with delight.

"No," she answered; "I never was. It's fine, ain't it?"

"Great! And then after a while we'll go forward to the diner, and get a big lay-out. Finest meal in the world. Charge a dollar."

"Oh, do they?" cried the bride. "Charge a dollar? Why, that's too much— for us—ain't it, Jack?"

"Not this trip, anyhow," he answered bravely. "We're going to go the whole thing."

Later he explained to her about the trains. "You see, it's a thousand miles from one end of Texas to the other; and this train runs right across it, and never stops but four times." He had the pride of an owner. He pointed out to her the dazzling fittings of the coach; and in truth her eyes opened wider as she contemplated the sea-green figured velvet, the shining brass, silver, and glass, the wood that gleamed as darkly brilliant as the surface of a pool of oil. At one end a bronze figure sturdily held a support for a separated chamber, and at convenient places on the ceiling were frescos in olive and silver.

To the minds of the pair, their surroundings reflected the glory of their marriage that morning in San Antonio; this was the environment of their new estate; and the man's face in particular beamed with an elation that made him appear ridiculous to the negro porter. This individual at times surveyed them from afar with an amused and superior grin. On other occasions he bullied them with skill in ways that did not make it exactly plain to them that they were being bullied. He subtly used all the manners of the most unconquerable kind of snobbery. He oppressed them; but of this oppression they had small knowledge, and they speedily forgot that infrequently a number of travellers covered them with stares of derisive enjoyment. Historically there was supposed to be something infinitely humorous in their situation.

"We are due in Yellow Sky at 3:42," he said, looking tenderly into her eyes.

"Oh, are we?" she said, as if she had not been aware of it. To evince surprise at her husband's statement was part of her wifely amiability. She took from a pocket a little silver watch; and as she held it before her, and stared at it with a frown of attention, the new husband's face shone.

"I bought it in San Anton' from a friend of mine," he told her gleefully.

"It's seventeen minutes past twelve," she said, looking up at him with a kind of shy and clumsy coquetry. A passenger, noting this play, grew excessively sardonic, and winked at himself in one of the numerous mirrors.

At last they went to the dining-car. Two rows of negro waiters, in glowing white suits, surveyed their entrance with the interest, and also the equanimity, of men who had been forewarned. The pair fell to the lot of a waiter who happened to feel pleasure in steering them through their meal. He viewed them with the manner of a fatherly pilot, his countenance radiant with benevolence. The patronage, entwined with the ordinary deference, was not plain to them. And yet, as they returned to their coach, they showed in their faces a sense of escape.

To the left, miles down a long purple slope, was a little ribbon of mist where moved the keening Rio Grande. The train was approaching it at an angle, and the apex was Yellow Sky. Presently it was apparent that, as the distance from Yellow Sky grew shorter, the husband became commensurately restless. His brick-red hands were most insistent in their prominence. Occasionally he was even rather absent-minded and far-away when the bride leaned forward and addressed him.

As a matter of truth, Jack Potter was beginning to find the shadow of a deed weigh upon him like a leaden slab. He, the town marshal of Yellow Sky, a man known, liked, and feared in his corner, a prominent person, had gone to San Antonio to meet a girl he believed he loved, and there, after the usual prayers, had actually induced her to marry him, without consulting Yellow Sky for any part of the transaction. He was now bringing his bride before an innocent and unsuspecting community.

Of course people in Yellow Sky married as it pleased them, in accordance with a general custom; but such was Potter's thought of his duty to his friends, or of their idea of his duty, or of an unspoken form which does not control men in these matters, that he felt he was heinous. He had committed an extraordinary crime. Face to face with this girl in San Antonio, and spurred by his sharp impulse, he had gone headlong over all the social hedges. At San Antonio he was like a man hidden in the dark. A knife to sever any friendly duty, any form, was easy to his hand in that remote city. But the hour of Yellow Sky—the hour of daylight—was approaching.

He knew full well that his marriage was an important thing to his town. It could only be exceeded by the burning of the new hotel. His friends could not forgive him. Frequently he had reflected on the advisability of telling them by telegraph, but a new cowardice had been upon him. He feared to do it. And now the train was hurrying him toward a scene of amazement, glee, and reproach. He glanced out of the window at the line of haze swinging slowly in toward the train.

Yellow Sky had a kind of brass band, which played painfully, to the delight of the populace. He laughed without heart as he thought of it. If the citizens could dream of his prospective arrival with his bride, they would parade the band at the station and escort them, amid cheers and laughing congratulations, to his adobe home.

He resolved that he would use all the devices of speed and plains-craft in making the journey from the station to his house. Once within that safe citadel, he could issue some sort of vocal bulletin, and then not go among the citizens until they had time to wear off a little of their enthusiasm.

The bride looked anxiously at him. "What's worrying you, Jack?"

He laughed again. "I'm not worrying, girl; I'm only thinking of Yellow Sky."

She flushed in comprehension.

A sense of mutual guilt invaded their minds and developed a finer tenderness. They looked at each other with eyes softly aglow. But Potter often laughed the same nervous laugh; the flush upon the bride's face seemed quite permanent.

The traitor to the feelings of Yellow Sky narrowly watched the speeding landscape. "We're nearly there," he said.

Presently the porter came and announced the proximity of Potter's home. He held a brush in his hand, and, with all his airy superiority gone, he brushed Potter's new clothes as the latter slowly turned this way and that way. Potter fumbled out a coin and gave it to the porter, as he had seen others do. It was a heavy and muscle-bound business, as that of a man shoeing his first horse.

The porter took their bag, and as the train began to slow they moved forward to the hooded platform of the car. Presently the two engines and their long string of coaches rushed into the station of Yellow Sky.

"They have to take water here," said Potter, from a constricted throat and in mournful cadence, as one announcing death. Before the train stopped his eye had swept the length of the platform, and he was glad and astonished to see there was none upon it but the station-agent, who, with a slightly hurried and anxious air, was walking toward the water-tanks. When the train had halted, the porter alighted first, and placed in position a little temporary step.

"Come on, girl," said Potter, hoarsely. As he helped her down they each laughed on a false note. He took the bag from the Negro, and bade his wife cling to his arm. As they slunk rapidly away, his hang-dog glance perceived that they were unloading the two trunks, and also that the station-agent, far ahead near the baggage-car, had turned and was running toward him, making gestures. He laughed, and groaned as he laughed, when he noted the first effect of his marital bliss upon Yellow Sky. He gripped his wife's arm firmly to his side, and they fled. Behind them the porter stood, chuckling fatuously.

II

The California express on the Southern Railway was due at Yellow Sky in twenty-one minutes. There were six men at the bar of the Weary Gentleman saloon. One was a drummer who talked a great deal and rapidly; three were Texans who did not care to talk at that time; and two were Mexican sheepherders, who did not talk as a general practice in the Weary Gentleman saloon. The barkeeper's dog lay on the board walk that crossed in front of the door. His head was on his paws, and he glanced drowsily here and there with the constant vigilance of a dog that is kicked on occasion. Across the sandy street were some vivid green grass-plots, so wonderful in appearance, amid the sands that burned near them in a blazing sun, that they caused a doubt in the mind. They exactly resembled the grass mats used to represent lawns on the stage. At the cooler end of the railway station, a man without a coat sat in a tilted chair and smoked his pipe. The fresh-cut bank of the Rio Grande circled near the town, and there could be seen beyond it a great plum-colored plain of mesquite.

Save for the busy drummer and his companions in the saloon, Yellow Sky was dozing. The new-comer leaned gracefully upon the bar, and recited many tales with the confidence of a bard who has come upon a new field.

"—and at the moment that the old man fell downstairs with the bureau in his arms, the old woman was coming up with two scuttles of coal, and of course—"

The drummer's tale was interrupted by a young man who suddenly appeared in the open door. He cried: "Scratchy Wilson's drunk, and has turned loose with both hands." The two Mexicans at once set down their glasses and faded out of the rear entrance of the saloon.

The drummer, innocent and jocular, answered: "All right, old man. S'pose he has? Come in and have a drink, anyhow."

But the information had made such an obvious cleft in every skull in the room that the drummer was obliged to see its importance. All had become instantly solemn. "Say," said he, mystified, "what is this?" His three companions made the introductory gesture of eloquent speech; but the young man at the door forestalled them.

"It means, my friend," he answered, as he came into the saloon, "that for the next two hours this town won't be a health resort."

The barkeeper went to the door, and locked and barred it; reaching out of the window, he pulled in heavy wooden shutters, and barred them. Immediately a solemn, chapel-like gloom was upon the place. The drummer was looking from one to another.

"But say," he cried, "what is this, anyhow? You don't mean there is going to be a gun-fight?"

"Don't know whether there'll be a fight or not," answered one man, grimly; "but there'll be some shootin'—some good shootin'."

The young man who had warned them waved his hand. "Oh, there'll be a fight fast enough, if any one wants it. Anybody can get a fight out there in the street. There's a fight just waiting."

The drummer seemed to be swayed between the interest of a foreigner and a perception of personal danger.

"What did you say his name was?" he asked.

"Scratchy Wilson," they answered in chorus.

"And will he kill anybody? What are you going to do? Does this happen often? Does he rampage around like this once a week or so? Can he break in that door?"

"No; he can't break down that door," replied the barkeeper. "He's tried it three times. But when he comes you'd better lay down on the floor, stranger. He's dead sure to shoot at it, and a bullet may come through."

Thereafter the drummer kept a strict eye upon the door. The time had not yet been called for him to hug the floor, but, as a minor precaution, he sidled near to the wall. "Will he kill anybody?" he said again.

The men laughed low and scornfully at the question.

"He's out to shoot, and he's out for trouble. Don't see any good in experimentin' with him."

"But what do you do in a case like this? What do you do?"

A man responded: "Why, he and Jack Potter——"

"But," in chorus the other men interrupted, "Jack Potter's in San Anton'."

"Well, who is he? What's he got to do with it?"

"Oh, he's the town marshal. He goes out and fights Scratchy when he gets on one of these tears."

"Wow!" said the drummer, mopping his brow. "Nice job he's got."

The voices had toned away to mere whisperings. The drummer wished to ask further questions, which were born of an increasing anxiety and bewilderment; but when he attempted them, the men merely looked at him in irritation and motioned him to remain silent. A tense waiting hush was upon them. In the deep shadows of the room their eyes shone as they listened for sounds from the street. One man made three gestures at the barkeeper; and the latter, moving like a ghost, handed him a glass and a bottle. The man poured a full glass of whisky, and set down the bottle noiselessly. He gulped the whisky in a swallow, and turned again toward the door in immovable silence. The drummer saw that the barkeeper, without a sound, had taken a Winchester from beneath the bar. Later he saw this individual beckoning to him, so he tiptoed across the room.

"You better come with me back of the bar."

"No, thanks," said the drummer, perspiring; "I'd rather be where I can make a break for the back door."

Whereupon the man of bottles made a kindly but peremptory gesture. The drummer obeyed it, and, finding himself seated on a box with his head below the level of the bar, balm was laid upon his soul at sight of various zinc and copper fittings that bore a resemblance to armor-plate. The barkeeper took a seat comfortably upon an adjacent box.

"You see," he whispered, "this here Scratchy Wilson is a wonder with a gun—a perfect wonder; and when he goes on the wartrail, we hunt our holes—naturally. He's about the last one of the old gang that used to hang out along the river here. He's a terror when he's drunk. When he's sober he's all right—kind of simple—wouldn't hurt a fly—nicest fellow in town. But when he's drunk—whoo!"

There were periods of stillness. "I wish Jack Potter was back from San Anton'," said the barkeeper. "He shot Wilson up once—in the leg—and he would sail in and pull out the kinks in this thing."

Presently they heard from a distance the sound of a shot, followed by three wild yowls. It instantly removed a bond from the men in the darkened saloon. There was a shuffling of feet. They looked at each other. "Here he comes," they said.

III

A man in a maroon-colored flannel shirt, which had been purchased for purposes of decoration, and made principally by some Jewish women on the East Side of New York, rounded a corner and walked into the middle of the main street of Yellow Sky. In either hand the man held a long, heavy, blue-black revolver. Often he yelled, and these cries rang through a semblance of a deserted village, shrilly flying over the roofs in a volume that seemed to have no relation to the ordinary vocal strength of a man. It was as if the surrounding stillness formed the arch of a tomb over him. These cries of ferocious challenge rang against walls of silence. And his boots had red tops with gilded imprints, of the kind beloved in winter by little sledding boys on the hillsides of New England.

The man's face flamed in a rage begot of whiskey. His eyes, rolling, and yet keen for ambush, hunted the still doorways and windows. He walked with the creeping movement of the midnight cat. As it occurred to him, he roared menacing information. The long revolvers in his hands were as easy as straws; they were moved with an electric swiftness. The little fingers of each hand played sometimes in a musician's way. Plain from the low collar of the shirt, the cords of his neck straightened and sank, straightened and sank, as passion moved him. The only sounds were his terrible invitations. The calm adobes preserved their demeanor at the passing of this small thing in the middle of the street.

There was no offer of fight—no offer of fight. The man called to the sky. There were no attractions. He bellowed and fumed and swayed his revolvers here and everywhere.

The dog of the barkeeper of the Weary Gentleman saloon had not appreciated the advance of events. He yet lay dozing in front of his master's door. At sight of the dog, the man paused and raised his revolver humorously. At sight of the man, the dog sprang up and walked diagonally away, with a sullen head, and growling. The man yelled, and the dog broke into a gallop. As it was about to enter an alley, there was a loud noise, a whistling, and something spat the ground directly before it. The dog screamed, and, wheeling in terror, galloped headlong in a new direction. Again there was a noise, a whistling, and sand was kicked viciously before it. Fear-stricken, the dog turned and flurried like an animal in a pen. The man stood laughing, his weapons at his hips.

Ultimately the man was attracted by the closed door of the Weary Gentleman saloon. He went to it and, hammering with a revolver, demanded drink.

The door remaining imperturbable, he picked a bit of paper from the walk, and nailed it to the framework with a knife. He then turned his back contemptuously upon this popular resort and, walking to the opposite side of the street and spinning there on his heel quickly and lithely, fired at the bit of paper. He missed it by a half-inch. He swore at himself, and went away. Later he comfortably fusilladed the windows of his most intimate friend. The man was playing with this town; it was a toy for him.

But still there was no offer of fight. The name of Jack Potter, his ancient antagonist, entered his mind, and he concluded that it would be a glad thing if he should go to Potter's house, and by bombardment induce him to come out and fight. He moved in the direction of his desire, chanting Apache scalp-music.

When he arrived at it, Potter's house presented the same still front as had the other adobes. Taking up a strategic position, the man howled a challenge. But this house regarded him as might a great stone god. It gave no sign. After a decent wait, the man howled further challenges, mingling with them wonderful epithets.

Presently there came the spectacle of a man churning himself into deepest rage over the immobility of a house. He fumed at it as the winter wind attacks a prairie cabin in the North. To the distance there should have gone the sound of a tumult like the fighting of two hundred Mexicans. As necessity bade him, he paused for breath or to reload his revolvers.

IV

Potter and his bride walked sheepishly and with speed. Sometimes they laughed together shamefacedly and low.

"Next corner, dear," he said finally.

They put forth the efforts of a pair walking bowed against a strong wind. Potter was about to raise a finger to point the first appearance of the new home when, as they circled the corner, they came face to face with a man in a maroon-colored shirt, who was feverishly pushing cartridges into a large revolver. Upon the instant the man dropped his revolver to the ground and, like lightning, whipped another from its holster. The second weapon was aimed at the bridegroom's chest.

There was a silence. Potter's mouth seemed to be merely a grave for his tongue. He exhibited an instinct to at once loosen his arm from the woman's grip, and he dropped the bag to the sand. As for the bride, her face had gone as yellow as old cloth. She was a slave to hideous rites, gazing at the apparitional snake.

The two men faced each other at a distance of three paces. He of the revolver smiled with a new and quiet ferocity.

"Tried to sneak up on me," he said. "Tried to sneak up on me!" His eyes grew more baleful. As Potter made a slight movement, the man thrust his revolver venomously forward. "No; don't you do it, Jack Potter. Don't you move a finger toward a gun just yet. Don't you move an eyelash. The time has come for me to settle with you, and I'm goin' to do it my own way, and loaf along with no interferin'. So if you don't want a gun bent on you, just mind what I tell you."

Potter looked at his enemy. "I ain't got a gun on me, Scratchy," he said. "Honest, I ain't." He was stiffening and steadying, but yet somewhere at the back of his mind a vision of the Pullman floated: the sea-green figured velvet, the shining brass, silver, and glass, the wood that gleamed as darkly brilliant as the surface of a pool of oil—all the glory of the marriage, the environment of the new estate. "You know I fight when it comes to fighting, Scratchy Wilson; but I ain't got a gun on me. You'll have to do all the shootin' yourself."

His enemy's face went livid. He stepped forward, and lashed his weapon to and fro before Potter's chest. "Don't you tell me you ain't got no gun on you, you whelp. Don't tell me no lie like that. There ain't a man in Texas ever seen you without no gun. Don't take me for no kid." His eyes blazed with light, and his throat worked like a pump.

"I ain't takin' you for no kid," answered Potter. His heels had not moved an inch backward. "I'm takin' you for a damn fool. I tell you I ain't got a gun, and I ain't. If you're goin' to shoot me up, you better begin now; you'll never get a chance like this again."

So much enforced reasoning had told on Wilson's rage; he was calmer. "If you ain't got a gun, why ain't you got a gun?" he sneered. "Been to Sunday-school?"

"I ain't got a gun because I've just come from San Anton' with my wife. I'm married," said Potter. "And if I'd thought there was going to be any galoots like you prowling around when I brought my wife home, I'd had a gun, and don't you forget it."

"Married!" said Scratchy, not at all comprehending.

"Yes, married. I'm married," said Potter, distinctly.

"Married?" said Scratchy. Seemingly for the first time, he saw the drooping, drowning woman at the other man's side. "No!" he said. He was like a creature allowed a glimpse of another world. He moved a pace backward, and his arm, with the revolver, dropped to his side. "Is this the lady?" he asked.

"Yes; this is the lady," answered Potter.

There was another period of silence.

"Well," said Wilson at last, slowly, "I s'pose it's all off now."

"It's all off if you say so, Scratchy. You know I didn't make the trouble."
Potter lifted his valise.

"Well, I 'low it's off, Jack," said Wilson. He was looking at the ground.
"Married!" He was not a student of chivalry; it was merely that in the
presence of this foreign condition he was a simple child of the earlier plains.
He picked up his starboard revolver, and, placing both weapons in their hol-
sters, he went away. His feet made funnel-shaped tracks in the heavy sand.

THOMAS MANN

Gladius Dei[1]

Munich was radiant. Above the gay squares and white columned temples,
the classicistic monuments and the baroque churches, the leaping fountains, the palaces and parks of the Residence there stretched a sky of luminous blue silk. Well-arranged leafy vistas laced with sun and shade lay
basking in the sunshine of a beautiful day in early June.

There was a twittering of birds and a blithe holiday spirit in all the little
streets. And in the squares and past the rows of villas there swelled, rolled,
and hummed the leisurely, entertaining traffic of that easy-going, charming
town. Travellers of all nationalities drove about in the slow little droshkies,
looking right and left in aimless curiosity at the house-fronts; they mounted
and descended museum stairs. Many windows stood open and music was
heard from within: practising on piano, cello, or violin—earnest and well-
meant amateur efforts; while from the Odeon came the sound of serious work
on several grand pianos.

Young people, the kind that can whistle the Nothung motif, who fill the pit
of the Schauspielhaus every evening, wandered in and out of the University
and Library with literary magazines in their coat pockets. A court carriage
stood before the Academy, the home of the plastic arts, which spreads its
white wings between the Türkenstrasse and the Siegestor. And colourful
groups of models, picturesque old men, women and children in Albanian
costume, stood or lounged at the top of the balustrade.

Indolent, unhurried sauntering was the mode in all the long streets of the
northern quarter. There life is lived for pleasanter ends than the driving greed
of gain. Young artists with little round hats on the backs of their heads, flowing cravats and no canes—carefree bachelors who paid for their lodgings with
colour-sketches—were strolling up and down to let the clear blue morning play

[1] From *Stories of Three Decades*, translated from the German by H. T. Lowe-
Porter. By permission of Alfred A. Knopf, Inc. Copyright 1936 by Alfred A.
Knopf, Inc.

upon their mood, also to look at the little girls, the pretty, rather plump type, with the brunette bandeaux, the too large feet, and the unobjectionable morals. Every fifth house had studio windows blinking in the sun. Sometimes a fine piece of architecture stood out from a middle-class row, the work of some imaginative young architect; a wide front with shallow bays and decorations in a bizarre style very expressive and full of invention. Or the door to some monotonous façade would be framed in a bold improvisation of flowing lines and sunny colours, with bacchantes, naiads, and rosy-skinned nudes.

It was always a joy to linger before the windows of the cabinetmakers and the shops for modern articles *de luxe*. What a sense for luxurious nothings and amusing, significant line was displayed in the shape of everything! Little shops that sold picture-frames, sculptures, and antiques there were in endless number; in their windows you might see those busts of Florentine women of the Renaissance, so full of noble poise and poignant charm. And the owners of the smallest and meanest of these shops spoke of Mino da Fiesole and Donatello as though he had received the rights of reproduction from them personally.

But on the Odeonsplatz, in view of the mighty loggia with the spacious mosaic pavement before it, diagonally opposite to the Regent's palace, people were crowding round the large windows and glass show-cases of the big art-shop owned by M. Blüthenzweig. What a glorious display! There were reproductions of the masterpieces of all the galleries in the world, in costly decorated and tinted frames, the good taste of which was precious in its very simplicity. There were copies of modern paintings, works of a joyously sensuous fantasy, in which the antiques seemed born again in humorous and realistic guise; bronze nudes and fragile ornamental glassware; tall, thin earthenware vases with an iridescent glaze produced by a bath in metal steam: *éditions de luxe* which were triumphs of modern binding and presswork, containing the works of the most modish poets, set out with every possible advantage of sumptuous elegance. Cheek by jowl with these, the portraits of artists, musicians, philosophers, actors, writers, displayed to gratify the public taste for personalities.—In the first window, next the book-shop, a large picture stood on an easel, with a crowd of people in front of it, a fine sepia photograph in a wide old-gold frame, a very striking reproduction of the sensation at this year's great international exhibition, to which public attention is always invited by means of effective and artistic posters stuck up everywhere on hoardings among concert programmes and clever advertisements of toilet preparations.

If you looked into the windows of the book-shop, your eye met such titles as *Interior Decoration Since the Renaissance*, *The Renaissance in Modern Decorative Art*, *The Book as Work of Art*, *The Decorative Arts*, *Hunger for Art*, and many more. And you would remember that these thought-provoking pamphlets were sold and read by the thousand and that discussions on these subjects were the preoccupation of all the salons.

You might be lucky enough to meet in person one of the famous fair ones whom less fortunate folk know only through the medium of art; one of those rich and beautiful women whose Titian-blond colouring Nature's most sweet and cunning hand did *not* lay on, but whose diamond parures and beguiling charms had received immortality from the hand of some portrait-painter of genius and whose love-affairs were the talk of the town. These were the queens of the artist balls at carnival-time. They were a little painted, a little made up, full of haughty caprices, worthy of adoration, avid of praise. You might see a carriage rolling up the Ludwigstrasse, with such a great painter and his mistress inside. People would be pointing out the sight, standing still to gaze after the pair. Some of them would curtsy. A little more and the very policemen would stand attention.

Art flourished, art swayed the destinies of the town, art stretched above it her rose-bound sceptre and smiled. On every hand obsequious interest was displayed in her prosperity, on every hand she was served with industry and devotion. There was a downright cult of line, decoration, form, significance, beauty. Munich was radiant.

A youth was coming down the Schellingstrasse. With the bells of cyclists ringing about him he strode across the wooden pavement towards the broad façade of Ludwigskirche. Looking at him it was as though a shadow passed across the sky, or cast over the spirit some memory of melancholy hours. Did he not love the sun which bathed the lovely city in its festal light? Why did he walk wrapped in his own thoughts, his eyes directed on the ground?

No one in that tolerant and variety-loving town would have taken offence at his wearing no hat; but why need the hood of his ample black cloak have been drawn over his head, shadowing his low, prominent, and peaked forehead, covering his ears and framing his haggard cheeks? What pangs of conscience, what scruples and self-tortures had so availed to hollow out these cheeks? It is frightful, on such a sunny day, to see care sitting in the hollows of the human face. His dark brows thickened at the narrow base of his hooked and prominent nose. His lips were unpleasantly full, his eyes brown and close-lying. When he lifted them, diagonal folds appeared on the peaked brow. His gaze expressed knowledge, limitation, and suffering. Seen in profile his face was strikingly like an old painting preserved at Florence in a narrow cloister cell whence once a frightful and shattering protest issued against life and her triumphs.

Hieronymus walked along the Schellingstrasse with a slow, firm stride, holding his wide cloak together with both hands from inside. Two little girls, two of those pretty, plump little creatures with the bandeaux, the big feet, and the unobjectionable morals, strolled towards him arm in arm, on pleasure bent. They poked each other and laughed, they bent double with laughter, they even broke into a run and ran away still laughing, at his hood and his face. But he paid them no heed. With bent head, looking neither to the right nor to the left, he crossed the Ludwigstrasse and mounted the church steps.

The great wings of the middle portal stood wide open. From somewhere within the consecrated twilight, cool, dank, incense-laden, there came a pale red glow. An old woman with inflamed eyes rose from a prayer-stool and slipped on crutches through the columns. Otherwise the church was empty.

Hieronymus sprinkled brow and breast at the stoup, bent the knee before the high altar, and then paused in the centre nave. Here in the church his stature seemed to have grown. He stood upright and immovable; his head was flung up and his great hooked nose jutted domineeringly above the thick lips. His eyes no longer sought the ground, but looked straight and boldly into the distance, at the crucifix on the high altar. Thus he stood awhile, then retreating he bent the knee again and left the church.

He strode up the Ludwigstrasse, slowly, firmly, with bent head, in the centre of the wide unpaved road, towards the mighty loggia with its statues. But arrived at the Odeonsplatz, he looked up, so that the folds came out on his peaked forehead, and checked his step, his attention being called to the crowd at the windows of the big art-shop of M. Blüthenzweig.

People moved from window to window, pointed out to each other the treasures displayed and exchanging views as they looked over one another's shoulders. Hieronymus mingled among them and did as they did, taking in all these things with his eyes, one by one.

He saw the reproductions of masterpieces from all the galleries in the world, the priceless frames so precious in their simplicity, the Renaissance sculpture, the bronze nudes, the exquisitely bound volumes, the iridescent vases, the portraits of artists, musicians, philosophers, actors, writers; he looked at everything and turned a moment of his scrutiny upon each object. Holding his mantle closely together with both hands from inside, he moved his hood-covered head in short turns from one thing to the next, gazing at each awhile with a dull, inimical, and remotely surprised air, lifting the dark brows which grew so thick at the base of the nose. At length he stood in front of the last window, which contained the startling picture. For a while he looked over the shoulders of people before him and then in his turn reached a position directly in front of the window.

The large red-brown photograph in the choice old-gold frame stood on an easel in the centre. It was a Madonna, but an utterly unconventional one, a work of entirely modern feeling. The figure of the Holy Mother was revealed as enchantingly feminine and beautiful. Her great smouldering eyes were rimmed with darkness; and her delicate and strangely smiling lips were half-parted. Her slender fingers held in a somewhat nervous grasp the hips of the Child, a nude boy of pronounced, almost primitive leanness. He was playing with her breast and glancing aside at the beholder with a wise look in his eyes.

Two other youths stood near Hieronymus, talking about the picture. They were two young men with books under their arms, which they had fetched from the Library, or were taking thither. Humanistically educated people, that is, equipped with science and with art.

"The little chap is in luck, devil take me!" said one.

"He seems to be trying to make one envious," replied the other. "A bewildering female!"

"A female to drive a man crazy! Gives you funny ideas about the Immaculate Conception."

"No, she doesn't look exactly immaculate. Have you seen the original?"

"Of course; I was quite bowled over. She makes an even more aphrodisiac impression in colour. Especially the eyes."

"The likeness is pretty plain."

"How so?"

"Don't you know the model? Of course he used his little dressmaker. It is almost a portrait, only with a lot more emphasis on the corruptible. The girl is more innocent."

"I hope so. Life would be altogether too much of a strain if there were many like this *mater amata*."

"The Pinakothek has bought it."

"Really? Well, well! They knew what they were about, anyhow. The treatment of the flesh and the flow of the linen garment are really first-class."

"Yes, an incredibly gifted chap."

"Do you know him?"

"A little. He will have a career, that is certain. He has been invited twice by the Prince Regent."

This last was said as they were taking leave of each other.

"Shall I see you this evening at the theatre?" asked the first. "The Dramatic Club is giving Machiavelli's *Mandragola*."

"Oh, bravo! That will be great, of course. I had meant to go to the Variété, but I shall probably choose our stout Niccolò after all. Good-bye."

They parted, going off to right and left. New people took their places and looked at the famous picture. But Hieronymus stood where he was, motionless, with his head thrust out; his hands clutched convulsively at the mantle as they held it together from inside. His brows were no longer lifted with that cool and unpleasantly surprised expression; they were drawn and darkened; his cheeks, half-shrouded in the black hood, seemed more sunken than ever and his thick lips had gone pale. Slowly his head dropped lower and lower, so that finally his eyes stared upwards at the work of art, while the nostrils of his great nose dilated.

Thus he remained for perhaps a quarter of an hour. The crowd about him melted away, but he did not stir from the spot. At last he turned slowly on the balls of his feet and went hence.

But the picture of the Madonna went with him. Always and ever, whether in his hard and narrow little room or kneeling in the cool church, it stood before his outraged soul, with its smouldering, dark-rimmed eyes, its riddling smiling lips—stark and beautiful. And no prayer availed to exorcise it.

But the third night it happened that a command and summons from on high came to Hieronymus, to intercede and lift his voice against the frivolity, blasphemy, and arrogance of beauty. In vain like Moses he protested that he had not the gift of tongues. God's will remained unshaken; in a loud voice He demanded that the faint-hearted Hieronymus go forth to sacrifice amid the jeers of the foe.

And since God would have it so, he set forth one morning and wended his way to the great art-shop of M. Blüthenzweig. He wore his hood over his head and held his mantle together in front from inside with both hands as he went.

The air had grown heavy, the sky was livid and thunder threatened. Once more crowds were besieging the show-cases at the art-shop and especially the window where the photograph of the Madonna stood. Hieronymus cast one brief glance thither; then he pushed up the latch of the glass door hung with placards and art magazines. "As God wills," said he, and entered the shop.

A young girl was somewhere at the desk writing in a big book. She was a pretty brunette thing with bandeaux of hair and big feet. She came up to him and asked pleasantly what he would like.

"Thank you," said Hieronymus in a low voice and looked her earnestly in the face, with diagonal wrinkles in his peaked brow. "I would speak not to you but to the owner of this shop, Herr Blüthenzweig."

She hesitated a little, turned away, and took up her work once more. He stood there in the middle of the shop.

Instead of the single specimens in the show-windows there was here a riot and a heaping-up of luxury, a fullness of colour, line, form, style, invention, good taste, and beauty. Hieronymus looked slowly round him, drawing his mantle close with both hands.

There were several people in the shop besides him. At one of the broad tables running across the room sat a man in a yellow suit, with a black goat's beard, looking at a portfolio of French drawings, over which he now and then emitted a bleating laugh. He was being waited on by an undernourished and vegetarian young man, who kept on dragging up fresh portfolios. Diagonally opposite the bleating man sat an elegant old dame, examining art embroideries with a pattern of fabulous flowers in pale tones standing together on tall perpendicular stalks. An attendant hovered about her too. A leisurely Englishman in a travelling-cap, with his pipe in his mouth, sat at another table. Cold and smooth-shaven, of indefinite age, in his good English clothes, he sat examining bronzes brought to him by M. Blüthenzweig in person. He was holding up by the head the dainty figure of a nude young girl, immature and delicately articulated, her hands crossed in coquettish innocence upon her breast. He studied her thoroughly, turning her slowly about. M. Blüthenzweig, a man with a short, heavy brown beard and bright brown eyes of exactly the same colour, moved in a semicircle round him, rubbing his hands, praising the statuette with all the terms his vocabulary possessed.

"A hundred and fifty marks, sir," he said in English. "Munich art—very charming, in fact. Simply full of charm, you know. Grace itself. Really extremely pretty, good, admirable, in fact." Then he thought of some more and went on: "Highly attractive, fascinating." Then he began again from the beginning.

His nose lay a little flat on his upper lip, so that he breathed constantly with a slight sniff into his moustache. Sometimes he did this as he approached a customer, stooping over as though he were smelling at him. When Hieronymus entered, M. Blüthenzweig had examined him cursorily in this way, then devoted himself again to his Englishman.

The elegant old dame made her selection and left the shop. A man entered. M. Blüthenzweig sniffed briefly at him as though to scent out his capacity to buy and left him to the young bookkeeper. The man purchased a faïence bust of young Piero de' Medici, son of Lorenzo, and went out again. The Englishman began to depart. He had acquired the statuette of the young girl and left amid bowings from M. Blüthenzweig. Then the art-dealer turned to Hieronymus and came forward.

"You wanted something?" he said, without any particular courtesy.

Hieronymus held his cloak together with both hands and looked the other in the face almost without winking an eyelash. He parted his big lips slowly and said:

"I have come to you on account of the picture in the window there, the big photograph, the Madonna." His voice was thick and without modulation.

"Yes, quite right," said M. Blüthenzweig briskly and began rubbing his hands. "Seventy marks in the frame. It is unfadable—a first-class reproduction. Highly attractive and full of charm."

Hieronymus was silent. He nodded his head in the hood and shrank a little into himself as the dealer spoke. Then he drew himself up again and said:

"I would remark to you first of all that I am not in the position to purchase anything, nor have I the desire. I am sorry to have to disappoint your expectations. I regret if it upsets you. But in the first place I am poor and in the second I do not love the things you sell. No, I cannot buy anything."

"No? Well, then?" asked M. Blüthenzweig, sniffing a good deal. "Then may I ask—"

"I suppose," Hieronymus went on, "that being what you are you look down on me because I am not in a position to buy."

"Oh—er—not at all," said M. Blüthenzweig. "Not at all. Only—"

"And yet I beg you to hear me and give some consideration to my words."

"Consideration to your words. H'm—may I ask—"

"You may ask," said Hieronymus, "and I will answer you. I have come to beg you to remove that picture, the big photograph, the Madonna, out of your window and never display it again."

M. Blüthenzweig looked awhile dumbly into Hieronymus's face—as though he expected him to be abashed at the words he had just uttered. But as this did not happen he gave a violent sniff and spoke himself:

"Will you be so good as to tell me whether you are here in any official capacity which authorizes you to dictate to me, or what does bring you here?"

"Oh, no," replied Hieronymus, "I have neither office nor dignity from the state. I have no power on my side, sir. What brings me hither is my conscience alone."

M. Blüthenzweig, searching for words, snorted violently into his moustache. At length he said:

"Your conscience . . . well, you will kindly understand that I take not the faintest interest in your conscience." With which he turned round and moved quickly to his desk at the back of the shop, where he began to write. Both attendants laughed heartily. The pretty Fräulein giggled over her account-book. As for the yellow gentleman with the goat's beard, he was evidently a foreigner, for he gave no sign of comprehension but went on studying the French drawings and emitting from time to time his bleating laugh.

"Just get rid of the man for me," said M. Blüthenzweig shortly over his shoulder to his assistant. He went on writing. The poorly paid young vegetarian approached Hieronymus, smothering his laughter, and the other salesman came up too.

"May we be of service to you in any other way?" the first asked mildly. Hieronymus fixed him with his glazed and suffering eyes.

"No," he said, "you cannot. I beg you to take the Madonna picture out of the window, at once and forever."

"But—why?"

"It is the Holy Mother of God," said Hieronymus in a subdued voice.

"Quite. But you have heard that Herr Blüthenzweig is not inclined to accede to your request."

"We must bear in mind that it is the Holy Mother of God," said Hieronymus again and his head trembled on his neck.

"So we must. But should we not be allowed to exhibit any Madonnas—or paint any?"

"It is not that," said Hieronymus, almost whispering. He drew himself up and shook his head energetically several times. His peaked brow under the hood was entirely furrowed with long, deep cross-folds. "You know very well that it is vice itself that is painted there—naked sensuality. I was standing near two simple young people and overheard with my own ears that it led them astray upon the doctrine of the Immaculate Conception."

"Oh, permit me—that is not the point," said the young salesman, smiling. In his leisure hours he was writing a brochure on the modern movement in

art and was well qualified to conduct a cultured conversation. "The picture
is a work of art," he went on, "and one must measure it by the appropriate
standards as such. It has been very highly praised on all hands. The state has
purchased it."

"I know that the state has purchased it," said Hieronymus. "I also know
that the artist has twice dined with the Prince Regent. It is common talk—
and God knows how people interpret the fact that a man can become famous
by such work as this. What does such a fact bear witness to? To the blindness
of the world, a blindness inconceivable, if not indeed shamelessly hypocritical.
This picture has its origin in sensual lust and is enjoyed in the same—is that
true or not? Answer me! And you too answer me, Herr Blüthenzweig!"

A pause ensued. Hieronymus seemed in all seriousness to demand an answer to his question, looking by turns at the staring attendants and the round
back M. Blüthenzweig turned upon him, with his own piercing and anguish-
ing brown eyes. Silence reigned. Only the yellow man with the goat's beard,
bending over the French drawings, broke it with his bleating laugh.

"It is true," Hieronymus went on in a hoarse voice that shook with his profound indignation. "You do not dare deny it. How then can honour be done
to its creator, as though he had endowed mankind with a new ideal possession?
How can one stand before it and surrender unthinkingly to the base enjoyment which it purveys, persuading oneself in all seriousness that one is yielding to a noble and elevated sentiment, highly creditable to the human race?
Is this reckless ignorance or abandoned hypocrisy? My understanding falters,
it is completely at a loss when confronted by the absurd fact that a man can
achieve renown on this earth by the stupid and shameless exploitation of the
animal instincts. Beauty? What is beauty? What forces are they which use
beauty as their tool today—and upon what does it work? No one can fail to
know this, Herr Blüthenzweig. But who, understanding it clearly, can fail to
feel disgust and pain? It is criminal to play upon the ignorance of the immature, the lewd, the brazen, and the unscrupulous by elevating beauty into
an idol to be worshipped, to give it even more power over those who know
not affliction and have no knowledge of redemption. You are unknown to me,
and you look at me with black looks—yet answer me! Knowledge, I tell you, is
the profoundest torture in the world; but it is the purgatory without whose
purifying pangs no soul can reach salvation. It is not infantile, blasphemous
shallowness that can save us, Herr Blüthenzweig; only knowledge can avail,
knowledge in which the passions of our loathsome flesh die away and are
quenched."

Silence.—The yellow man with the goat's beard gave a sudden little bleat.

"I think you really must go now," said the underpaid assistant mildly.

But Hieronymus made no move to do so. Drawn up in his hooded cape, he
stood with blazing eyes in the center of the shop and his thick lips poured out
condemnation in a voice that was harsh and rusty and clanking.

"Art, you cry; enjoyment, beauty! Enfold the world in beauty and endow all things with the noble grace of style!—Profligate, away! Do you think to wash over with lurid colours the misery of the world? Do you think with the sounds of feasting and music to drown out the voice of the tortured earth? Shameless one, you err! God lets not Himself be mocked, and your impudent deification of the glistering surface of things is an abomination in His eyes. You tell me that I blaspheme art. I say to you that you lie. I do not blaspheme art. Art is no conscienceless delusion, lending itself to reinforce the allurements of the fleshly. Art is the holy torch which turns its light upon all the frightful depths, all the shameful and woeful abysses of life; art is the godly fire laid to the world that, being redeemed by pity, it may flame up and dissolve altogether with its shames and torments.—Take it out, Herr Blüthenzweig, take away the work of that famous painter out of your window —you would do well to burn it with a hot fire and strew its ashes to the four winds—yes, to all the four winds—"

His harsh voice broke off. He had taken a violent backwards step, snatched one arm from his black wrappings, and stretched it passionately forth, gesturing towards the window with a hand that shook as though palsied. And in this commanding attitude he paused. His great hooked nose seemed to jut more than ever, his dark brows were gathered so thick and high that folds crowded upon the peaked forehead shaded by the hood; a hectic flush mantled his hollow cheeks.

But at this point M. Blüthenzweig turned round. Perhaps he was outraged by the idea of burning his seventy-mark reproduction; perhaps Hieronymus's speech had completely exhausted his patience. In any case he was a picture of stern and righteous anger. He pointed with his pen to the door of the shop, gave several short, excited snorts into his moustache, struggled for words, and uttered with the maximum of energy those which he found:

"My fine fellow, if you don't get out at once I will have my packer help you —do you understand?"

"Oh, you cannot intimidate me, you cannot drive me away, you cannot silence my voice!" cried Hieronymus as he clutched his cloak over his chest with his fists and shook his head doughtily. "I know that I am single-handed and powerless, but yet I will not cease until you hear me, Herr Blüthenzweig! Take the picture out of your window and burn it even today! Ah, burn not it alone! Burn all these statues and busts, the sight of which plunges the beholder into sin! Burn these vases and ornaments, these shameless revivals of paganism, these elegantly bound volumes of erotic verse! Burn everything in your shop, Herr Blüthenzweig, for it is a filthiness in God's sight. Burn it, burn it!" he shrieked, beside himself, describing a wild, all-embracing circle with his arm. "The harvest is ripe for the reaper, the measure of the age's shamelessness is full—but I say unto you—"

"Krauthuber!" Herr Blüthenzweig raised his voice and shouted towards a door at the back of the shop. "Come in here at once!"

And in answer to the summons there appeared upon the scene a massive overpowering presence, a vast and awe-inspiring, swollen human bulk, whose limbs merged into each other like links of sausage—a gigantic son of the people, malt-nourished and immoderate, who weighed in, with puffings, bursting with energy, from the packing-room. His appearance in the upper reaches of his form was notable for a fringe of walrus beard; a hide apron fouled with paste covered his body from the waist down, and his yellow shirt-sleeves were rolled back from his heroic arms.

"Will you open the door for this gentleman, Krauthuber?" said M. Blüthenzweig; "and if he should not find the way to it, just help him into the street."

"Huh," said the man, looking from his enraged employer to Hieronymus and back with his little elephant eyes. It was a heavy monosyllable, suggesting reserve force restrained with difficulty. The floor shook with his tread as he went to the door and opened it.

Hieronymus had grown very pale. "Burn—" he shouted once more. He was about to go on when he felt himself turned round by an irresistible power, by a physical preponderance to which no resistance was even thinkable. Slowly and inexorably he was propelled towards the door.

"I am weak," he managed to ejaculate. "My flesh cannot bear the force . . . it cannot hold its ground, no . . . but what does that prove? Burn—"

He stopped. He found himself outside the art-shop. M. Blüthenzweig's giant packer had let him go with one final shove, which set him down on the stone threshold of the shop, supporting himself with one hand. Behind him the door closed with a rattle of glass.

He picked himself up. He stood erect, breathing heavily, and pulled his cloak together with one fist over his breast, letting the other hand down inside. His hollow cheeks had a grey pallor; the nostrils of his great hooked nose opened and closed; his ugly lips were writhen in an expression of hatred and despair and his red-rimmed eyes wandered over the beautiful square like those of a man in a frenzy.

He did not see that people were looking at him with amusement and curiosity. For what he beheld upon the mosaic pavement before the great loggia were all the vanities of this world: the masked costumes of the artist balls, the decorations, vases and art objects, the nude statues, the female busts, the picturesque rebirths of the pagan age, the portraits of famous beauties by the hands of masters, the elegantly bound erotic verse, the art brochures—all these he saw heaped in a pyramid and going up in crackling flames amid loud exultations from the people enthralled by his own frightful words. A yellow background of cloud had drawn up over the Theatinerstrasse, and from it issued wild rumblings; but what he saw was a burning fiery sword, towering in sulphurous light above the joyous city.

"*Gladius Dei super terram* . . ." his thick lips whispered; and drawing himself still higher in his hooded cloak while the hand hanging down inside it twitched convulsively, he murmured, quaking: "*cito et velociter!*" [1]

[1] "O Sword of the Lord, [smite] the earth . . . swiftly and sharply!"

E. M. FORSTER

The Celestial Omnibus[1]

The boy who resided at Agathox Lodge, 28 Buckingham Park Road, Surbiton, had often been puzzled by the old sign-post that stood almost opposite. He asked his mother about it, and she replied that it was a joke, and not a very nice one, which had been made many years back by some naughty young men, and that the police ought to remove it. For there were two strange things about this sign-post; firstly, it pointed up a blank alley, and, secondly, it had painted on it, in faded characters, the words, "To Heaven."

"What kind of young men were they?" he asked.

"I think your father told me that one of them wrote verses, and was expelled from the University and came to grief in other ways. Still, it was a long time ago. You must ask your father about it. He will say the same as I do, that it was put up as a joke."

"So it doesn't mean anything at all?"

She sent him upstairs to put on his best things, for the Bonses were coming to tea, and he was to hand the cakestand.

It struck him, as he wrenched on his tightening trousers, that he might do worse than ask Mr. Bons about the sign-post. His father, though very kind, always laughed at him—shrieked with laughter whenever he or any other child asked a question or spoke. But Mr. Bons was serious as well as kind. He had a beautiful house and lent one books, he was a churchwarden, and a candidate for the County Council; he had donated to the Free Library enormously, he presided over the Literary Society, and had Members of Parliament to stop with him—in short, he was probably the wisest person alive.

Yet even Mr. Bons could only say that the sign-post was a joke—the joke of a person named Shelley.

"Of course!" cried the mother; "I told you so, dear. That was the name."

"Had you ever heard of Shelley?" asked Mr. Bons.

"No," said the boy, and hung his head.

"But is there no Shelley in the house?"

"Why, yes!" exclaimed the lady, in much agitation. "Dear Mr. Bons, we aren't such Philistines as that. Two at the least. One a wedding present, and the other, smaller print, in one of the spare rooms."

"I believe we have seven Shelleys," said Mr. Bons, with a slow smile. Then he brushed the cake crumbs off his stomach, and, together with his daughter. rose to go.

The boy, obeying a wink from his mother, saw them all the way to the

[1] From *The Celestial Omnibus*. By permission of Alfred A. Knopf, Inc., and Sedgwick & Jackson Ltd., of London, England. Copyright 1947 by Alfred A. Knopf, Inc.

garden gate, and when they had gone, he did not at once return to the house, but gazed for a little up and down Buckingham Park Road.

His parents lived at the right end of it. After No. 39 the quality of the houses dropped very suddenly, and 64 had not even a separate servants' entrance. But at the present moment the whole road looked rather pretty, for the sun had just set in splendour, and the inequalities of rent were drowned in a saffron afterglow. Small birds twittered, and the breadwinners' train shrieked musically down through the cutting—that wonderful cutting which has drawn to itself the whole beauty out of Surbiton, and clad itself, like any Alpine valley, with the glory of the fir and the silver birch and the primrose. It was this cutting that had first stirred desires within the boy— desires for something just a little different, he knew not what, desires that would return whenever things were sunlit, as they were this evening, running up and down inside him, up and down, up and down, till he would feel quite unusual all over, and as likely as not would want to cry. This evening he was even sillier, for he slipped across the road towards the sign-post and began to run up the blank alley.

The alley runs between high walls—the walls of the gardens of "Ivanhoe" and "Bella Vista," respectively. It smells a little all the way, and is scarcely twenty yards long, including the turn at the end. So not unnaturally the boy soon came to a standstill. "I'd like to kick that Shelley," he exclaimed, and glanced idly at a piece of paper which was pasted on the wall. Rather an odd piece of paper, and he read it carefully before he turned back. This is what he read:

S. AND C.R.C.C.
ALTERATION IN SERVICE
Owing to lack of patronage the Company are regretfully compelled to suspend the hourly service, and to retain only the
Sunrise and Sunset Omnibuses,
which will run as usual. It is to be hoped that the public will patronize an arrangement which is intended for their convenience. As an extra inducement, the Company will, for the first time, now issue
Return Tickets!
(available one day only), which may be obtained of the driver. Passengers are again reminded that *no tickets are issued at the other end*, and that no complaints in this connection will receive consideration from the Company. Nor will the Company be responsible for any negligence or stupidity on the part of Passengers, nor for Hailstorms, Lightning, Loss of Tickets, nor any Act of God.

For the Direction.

Now he had never seen this notice before, nor could he imagine where the omnibus went to. S. of course was for Surbiton, and R.C.C. meant Road Car Company. But what was the meaning of the other C.? Coombe and

Malden, perhaps, or possibly "City." Yet it could not hope to compete with the South-Western. The whole thing, the boy reflected, was run on hopelessly unbusinesslike lines. Why no tickets from the other end? And what an hour to start! Then he realized that unless the notice was a hoax, an omnibus must have been starting just as he was wishing the Bonses goodbye. He peered at the ground through the gathering dusk, and there he saw what might or might not be the marks of wheels. Yet nothing had come out of the alley. And he had never seen an omnibus at any time in the Buckingham Park Road. No: it must be a hoax, like the sign-post, like the fairy tales, like the dreams upon which he would wake suddenly in the night. And with a sigh he stepped from the alley—right into the arms of his father.

Oh, how his father laughed! "Poor, poor Popsey!" he cried. "Diddums! Diddums! Diddums think he'd walky-palky up to Evink!" And his mother, also convulsed with laughter, appeared on the steps of Agathox Lodge.

"Don't Bob!" she gasped. "Don't be so naughty! Oh, you'll kill me! Oh, leave the boy alone!"

But all that evening the joke was kept up. The father implored to be taken too. Was it a very tiring walk? Need one wipe one's shoes on the door-mat? And the boy went to bed feeling faint and sore, and thankful for only one thing—that he had not said a word about the omnibus. It was a hoax, yet through his dreams it grew more and more real, and the streets of Surbiton, through which he saw it driving, seemed instead to become hoaxes and shadows. And very early in the morning he woke with a cry, for he had had a glimpse of its destination.

He struck a match, and its light fell not only on his watch but also on his calendar, so that he knew it to be half-an-hour to sunrise. It was pitch dark, for the fog had come down from London in the night, and all Surbiton was wrapped in its embraces. Yet he sprang out and dressed himself, for he was determined to settle once for all which was real: the omnibus or the streets. "I shall be a fool one way or the other," he thought, "until I know." Soon he was shivering in the road under the gas lamp that guarded the entrance to the alley.

To enter the alley itself required some courage. Not only was it horribly dark, but he now realized that it was an impossible terminus for an omnibus. If it had not been for a policeman, whom he heard approaching through the fog, he would never have made the attempt. The next moment he had made the attempt and failed. Nothing. Nothing but a blank alley and a very silly boy gaping at its dirty floor. It *was* a hoax. "I'll tell papa and mamma," he decided. "I deserve it. I deserve that they should know. I am too silly to be alive." And he went back to the gate of Agathox Lodge.

There he remembered that his watch was fast. The sun was not risen; it would not rise for two minutes. "Give the bus every chance," he thought cynically, and returned into the alley.

But the omnibus was there.

II

It had two horses, whose sides were still smoking from their journey, and its two great lamps shone through the fog against the alley's walls, changing their cobwebs and moss into tissues of fairyland. The driver was huddled up in a cape. He faced the blank wall, and how he had managed to drive in so neatly and so silently was one of the many things that the boy never discovered. Nor could he imagine how ever he would drive out.

"Please," his voice quavered through the foul brown air, "please, is that an omnibus?"

"Omnibus est," said the driver, without turning round. There was a moment's silence. The policeman passed, coughing, by the entrance of the alley. The boy crouched in the shadow, for he did not want to be found out. He was pretty sure, too, that it was a Pirate; nothing else, he reasoned, would go from such odd places and at such odd hours.

"About when do you start?" He tried to sound nonchalant.

"At sunrise."

"How far do you go?"

"The whole way."

"And can I have a return ticket which will bring me all the way back?"

"You can."

"Do you know, I half think I'll come." The driver made no answer. The sun must have risen, for he unhitched the brake. And scarcely had the boy jumped in before the omnibus was off.

How? Did it turn? There was no room. Did it go forward? There was a blank wall. Yet it was moving—moving at a stately pace through the fog, which had turned from brown to yellow. The thought of warm bed and warmer breakfast made the boy feel faint. He wished he had not come. His parents would not have approved. He would have gone back to them if the weather had not made it impossible. The solitude was terrible; he was the only passenger. And the omnibus, though well-built, was cold and somewhat musty. He drew his coat round him, and in so doing chanced to feel his pocket. It was empty. He had forgotten his purse.

"Stop!" he shouted. "Stop!" And then, being of a polite disposition, he glanced up at the painted notice-board so that he might call the driver by name. "Mr. Browne! stop; oh, do please stop!"

Mr. Browne did not stop, but he opened a little window and looked in at the boy. His face was a surprise, so kind it was and modest.

"Mr. Browne, I've left my purse behind. I've not got a penny. I can't pay for the ticket. Will you take my watch, please? I am in the most awful hole."

"Tickets on this line," said the driver, "whether single or return, can be purchased by coinage from no terrene mint. And a chronometer, though it had solaced the vigils of Charlemagne, or measured the slumbers of Laura, can acquire by no mutation the double-cake that charms the fangless Cerberus of Heaven!" So saying, he handed in the necessary ticket, and, while the boy said "Thank you," continued, "Titular pretensions, I know it well, are vanity. Yet they merit no censure when uttered on a laughing lip, and in an homonymous world are in some sort useful, since they do serve to distinguish one Jack from his fellow. Remember me, therefore, as Sir Thomas Browne."

"Are you a Sir? Oh, sorry!" He had heard of these gentlemen drivers. "It *is* good of you about the ticket. But if you go on at this rate, however does your bus pay?"

"It does not pay. It was not intended to pay. Many are the faults of my equipage; it is compounded too curiously of foreign woods; its cushions tickle erudition rather than promote repose; and my horses are nourished not on the evergreen pastures of the moment, but on the dried bents and clovers of Latinity. But that it pays!—that error at all events was never intended and never attained."

"Sorry again," said the boy rather hopelessly. Sir Thomas looked sad, fearing that, even for a moment, he had been the cause of sadness. He invited the boy to come up and sit beside him on the box, and together they journeyed on through the fog, which was now changing from yellow to white. There were no houses by the road; so it must be either Putney Heath or Wimbledon Common.

"Have you been a driver always?"

"I was a physician once."

"But why did you stop? Weren't you good?"

"As a healer of bodies I had scant success, and several score of my patients preceded me. But as the healer of the spirit I have succeeded beyond my hopes and my deserts. For though my draughts were not better nor subtler than those of other men, yet, by reason of the cunning goblets wherein I offered them, the queasy soul was ofttimes tempted to sip and be refreshed."

"The queasy soul," the boy murmured; "if the sun sets with trees in front of it, and you suddenly come strange all over, is that a queasy soul?"

"Have you felt that?"

"Why, yes."

After a pause he told the boy a little, a very little, about the journey's end. But they did not chatter much, for the boy, when he liked a person, would as soon sit silent in his company as speak, and this, he discovered, was also the mind of Sir Thomas Browne and of many others with whom he was to be acquainted. He heard, however, about the young man Shelley, who was now quite a famous person, with a carriage of his own, and about some of the other drivers who are in the service of the Company. Meanwhile the light grew stronger, though the fog did not disperse. It was now more like mist than fog, and at times would travel quickly across them, as if it was part of a cloud. They had been ascending, too, in a most puzzling way; for over two hours the horses had been pulling against the collar, and even if it were Richmond Hill they ought to have been at the top long ago. Perhaps it was Epsom, or even the North Downs; yet the air seemed keener than that which blows on either. And as to the name of their destination, Sir Thomas **Browne** was silent.

Crash!

"Thunder, by Jove!" said the boy, "and not so far off either. Listen to the echoes! It's more like mountains."

He thought, not very vividly, of his father and mother. He saw them sitting down to sausages and listening to the storm. He saw his own empty place. Then there would be questions, alarms, theories, jokes, consolations. They would expect him back at lunch. To lunch he would not come, nor to tea, but he would be in for dinner, and so his day's truancy would be over. If he had had his purse he would have bought them presents—not that he should have known what to get them.

Crash!

The peal and the lightning came together. The cloud quivered as if it were alive, and torn streamers of mist rushed past. "Are you afraid?" asked Sir Thomas Browne.

"What is there to be afraid of? Is it much farther?"

The horses of the omnibus stopped just as a ball of fire burst up and exploded with a ringing noise that was deafening but clear, like the noise of a blacksmith's forge. All the cloud was shattered.

"Oh, listen, Sir Thomas Browne! No, I mean look; we shall get a view at last. No, I mean listen; that sounds like a rainbow!"

The noise had died into the faintest murmur, beneath which another murmur grew, spreading stealthily, steadily, in a curve that widened but did not vary. And in widening curves a rainbow was spreading from the horses' feet into the dissolving mists.

"But how beautiful! What colours! Where will it stop? It is more like the rainbows you can tread on. More like dreams."

The colour and the sound grew together. The rainbow spanned an enormous gulf. Clouds rushed under it and were pierced by it, and still it grew, reaching forward, conquering the darkness, until it touched something that seemed more solid than a cloud.

The boy stood up. "What is that out there?" he called. "What does it rest on, out at that other end?"

In the morning sunshine a precipice shone forth beyond the gulf. A precipice—or was it a castle? The horses moved. They set their feet upon the rainbow.

"Oh, look!" the boy shouted. "Oh, listen! Those caves—or are they gateways? Oh, look between those cliffs at those ledges. I see people! I see trees!"

"Look also below," whispered Sir Thomas. "Neglect not the diviner Acheron."

The boy looked below, past the flames of the rainbow that licked against their wheels. The gulf also had cleared, and in its depths there flowed an everlasting river. One sunbeam entered and struck a green pool, and as they passed over he saw three maidens rise to the surface of the pool, singing, and playing with something that glistened like a ring.

"You down in the water—" he called.

They answered, "You up on the bridge—" There was a burst of music. "You up on the bridge, good luck to you. Truth in the depth, truth on the height."

"You down in the water, what are you doing?"

Sir Thomas Browne replied: "They sport in the mancipiary possession of their gold"; and the omnibus arrived.

III

The boy was in disgrace. He sat locked up in the nursery of Agathox Lodge, learning poetry for a punishment. His father had said, "My boy! I can pardon anything but untruthfulness," and had caned him, saying at each stroke, "There is *no* omnibus, *no* driver, *no* bridge, *no* mountain; you are a *truant*, a *gutter snipe*, a *liar*." His father could be very stern at times. His mother had begged him to say he was sorry. But he could not say that. It was the greatest day of his life, in spite of the caning and the poetry at the end of it.

He had returned punctually at sunset—driven not by Sir Thomas Browne, but by a maiden lady who was full of quiet fun. They had talked of omnibuses and also of barouche landaus. How far away her gentle voice seemed now! Yet it was scarcely three hours since he had left her up the alley.

His mother called through the door. "Dear, you are to come down and to bring your poetry with you."

He came down, and found that Mr. Bons was in the smoking-room with his father. It had been a dinner party.

"Here is the great traveller!" said his father grimly. "Here is the young gentleman who drives in an omnibus over rainbows, while young ladies sing to him." Pleased with his wit, he laughed.

"After all," said Mr. Bons, smiling, "there is something a little like it in Wagner. It is odd how, in quite illiterate minds, you will find glimmers of Artistic Truth. The case interests me. Let me plead for the culprit. We have all romanced in our time, haven't we?"

"Hear how kind Mr. Bons is," said his mother, while his father said, "Very well. Let him say his Poem, and that will do. He is going away to my sister on Tuesday, and *she* will cure him of this alley-slopering." (Laughter.) "Say your Poem."

The boy began. " 'Standing aloof in giant ignorance.' "

His father laughed again—roared. "One for you, my son! 'Standing aloof in giant ignorance!' I never knew these poets talked sense. Just describes you. Here, Bons, you go in for poetry. Put him through it, will you, while I fetch up the whisky?"

"Yes, give me the Keats," said Mr. Bons. "Let him say his Keats to me."

So for a few moments the wise man and the ignorant boy were left alone in the smoking-room.

" 'Standing aloof in giant ignorance, of thee I dream and of the Cyclades, as one who sits ashore and longs perchance to visit—'."

"Quite right. To visit what?"

" 'To visit dolphin coral in deep seas,' " said the boy, and burst into tears.

"Come, come! why do you cry?"

"Because—because all these words that only rhymed before, now that I've come back they're me."

Mr. Bons laid the Keats down. The case was more interesting than he had expected. "*You?*" he exclaimed. "This sonnet, *you?*"

"Yes—and look further on: 'Aye, on the shores of darkness there is light, and precipices show untrodden green.' It *is* so, sir. All these things are true."

"I never doubted it," said Mr. Bons, with closed eyes.

"You—then you believe me? You believe in the omnibus and the driver and the storm and that return ticket I got for nothing and—"

"Tut, tut! No more of your yarns, my boy. I meant that I never doubted the essential truth of Poetry. Some day, when you have read more, you will understand what I mean."

"But, Mr. Bons, it *is* so. There *is* light upon the shores of darkness. I have seen it coming. Light and a wind."

"Nonsense," said Mr. Bons.

"If I had stopped! They tempted me. They told me to give up my ticket—for you cannot come back if you lose your ticket. They called from the river for it, and indeed I was tempted, for I have never been so happy as among those precipices. But I thought of my mother and father, and that I must fetch them. Yet they will not come, though the road starts opposite our house. It has all happened as the people up there warned me, and Mr. Bons has disbelieved me like everyone else. I have been caned. I shall never see that mountain again."

"What's that about me?" said Mr. Bons, sitting up in his chair very suddenly.

"I told them about you, and how clever you were, and how many books you had and they said 'Mr. Bons will certainly disbelieve you.' "

"Stuff and nonsense, my young friend. You grow impertinent. I—well—I will settle the matter. Not a word to your father. I will cure you. Tomorrow evening I will myself call here to take you for a walk, and at sunset we will go up this alley opposite and hunt for your omnibus, you silly little boy."

His face grew serious, for the boy was not disconcerted, but leapt about the room singing, "Joy! joy! I told them you would believe me. We will drive together over the rainbow. I told them that you would come." After all, could there be anything in the story? Wagner? Keats? Shelley? Sir Thomas Browne? Certainly the case was interesting.

And on the morrow evening, though it was pouring with rain, Mr. Bons did not omit to call at Agathox Lodge.

The boy was ready, bubbling with excitement, and skipping about in a way that rather vexed the President of the Literary Society. They took a turn down Buckingham Park Road, and then—having seen that no one was watching them—slipped up the alley. Naturally enough (for the sun was setting) they ran straight against the omnibus.

"Good heavens!" exclaimed Mr. Bons. "Good gracious heavens!"

It was not the omnibus in which the boy had driven first, nor yet that in which he had returned. There were three horses—black, gray, and white, the gray being the finest. The driver, who turned round at the mention of goodness and of heaven, was a sallow man with terrifying jaws and sunken eyes. Mr. Bons, on seeing him, gave a cry as if of recognition, and began to tremble violently.

The boy jumped in.

"Is it possible?" cried Mr. Bons. "Is the impossible possible?"

"Sir; come in, sir. It is such a fine omnibus. Oh, here is his name—Dan someone."

Mr. Bons sprang in too. A blast of wind immediately slammed the omnibus door, and the shock jerked down all the omnibus blinds, which were very weak on their springs.

"Dan . . . Show me. Good gracious heavens! We're moving."

"Hooray!" said the boy.

Mr. Bons became flustered. He had not intended to be kidnapped. He could not find the door-handle nor push up the blinds. The omnibus was quite dark, and by the time he had struck a match, night had come on outside also. They were moving rapidly.

"A strange, a memorable adventure," he said, surveying the interior of the omnibus, which was large, roomy, and constructed with extreme regularity, every part exactly answering to every other part. Over the door (the handle of which was outside) was written "Lasciate ogni baldanza voi che entrate" —at least, that was what was written, but Mr. Bons said that it was Lashy arty something, and that baldanza was a mistake for speranza. His voice sounded as if he was in church. Meanwhile, the boy called to the cadaverous driver for two return tickets. They were handed in without a word. Mr. Bons covered his face with his hand and again trembled. "Do you know who that is!" he whispered, when the little window had shut upon them. "It is the impossible."

"Well, I don't like him as much as Sir Thomas Browne, though I shouldn't be surprised if he had even more in him."

"More in him?" He stamped irritably. "By accident you have made the greatest discovery of the century, and all you can say is that there is more in this man. Do you remember those vellum books in my library, stamped with red lilies? This—sit still, I bring you stupendous news!—*this is the man who wrote them.*"

The boy sat quite still. "I wonder if we shall see Mrs. Gamp?" he asked, after a civil pause.

"Mrs.—?"

"Mrs. Gamp and Mrs. Harris. I like Mrs. Harris. I came upon them quite suddenly. Mrs. Gamp's handboxes have moved over the rainbow so badly. All the bottoms have fallen out, and two of the pippins off her bedspread tumbled into the stream."

"Out there sits the man who wrote my vellum books!" thundered Mr. Bons, "and you talk to me of Dickens and of Mrs. Gamp?"

"I know Mrs. Gamp so well," he apologized. "I could not help being glad to see her. I recognized her voice. She was telling Mrs. Harris about Mrs. Prig."

"Did you spend the whole day in her elevating company?"

"Oh, no. I raced. I met a man who took me out beyond to a race-course. You run, and there are dolphins out at sea."

"Indeed. Do you remember the man's name?"

"Achilles. No; he was later. Tom Jones."

Mr. Bons sighed heavily. "Well, my lad, you have made a miserable mess of it. Think of a cultured person with your opportunities! A cultured person would have known all these characters and known what to have said to each. He would not have wasted his time with a Mrs. Gamp or a Tom Jones. The creations of Homer, of Shakespeare, and of Him who drives us now, would alone have contented him. He would not have raced. He would have asked intelligent questions."

"But, Mr. Bons," said the boy humbly, "you will be a cultured person. I told them so."

"True, true, and I beg you not to disgrace me when we arrive. No gossiping. No running. Keep close to my side, and never speak to these Immortals unless they speak to you. Yes, and give me the return tickets. You will be losing them."

The boy surrendered the tickets, but felt a little sore. After all, he had found the way to this place. It was hard first to be disbelieved and then to be lectured. Meanwhile, the rain had stopped, and moonlight crept into the omnibus through the cracks in the blinds.

"But how is there to be a rainbow?" cried the boy.

"You distract me," snapped Mr. Bons. "I wish to meditate on beauty. I wish to goodness I was with a reverent and sympathetic person."

The lad bit his lip. He made good resolutions. He would imitate Mr. Bons all the visit. He would not laugh, or run, or sing, or do any of the vulgar things that must have disgusted his new friends last time. He would be very careful to pronounce their names properly, and to remember who knew whom. Achilles did not know Tom Jones—at least, so Mr. Bons said. The Duchess of Malfi was older than Mrs. Gamp—at least, so Mr. Bons said. He would be self-conscious, reticent, and prim. He would never say he liked anyone. Yet, when the blind flew up at a chance touch of his head, all these good resolutions went to the winds, for the omnibus had reached the summit of a moonlit hill, and there was the chasm, and there, across it, stood the old precipices, dreaming, with their feet in the everlasting river. He exclaimed, "The mountain! Listen to the new tune in the water! Look at the camp fires in the ravines," and Mr. Bons, after a hasty glance, retorted, "Water? Camp fires? Ridiculous rubbish. Hold your tongue. There is nothing at all."

Yet, under his eyes, a rainbow formed, compounded not of sunlight and storm, but of moonlight and the spray of the river. The three horses put their feet upon it. He thought it the finest rainbow he had seen, but did not dare to say so, since Mr. Bons said that nothing was there. He leant out—the window had opened—and sang the tune that rose from the sleeping waters.

"The prelude of Rhinegold?" said Mr. Bons suddenly. "Who taught you these *leit motifs*?" He, too, looked out of the window. Then he behaved very oddly. He gave a choking cry and fell back onto the omnibus floor. He writhed and kicked. His face was green.

"Does the bridge make you dizzy?" the boy asked.

"Dizzy!" gasped Mr. Bons. "I want to go back. Tell the driver."

But the driver shook his head.

"We are nearly there," said the boy. "They are asleep. Shall I call? They will be so pleased to see you, for I have prepared them."

Mr. Bons moaned. They moved over the lunar rainbow, which ever and ever broke away behind their wheels. How still the night was! Who would be sentry at the Gate?

"I am coming," he shouted, again forgetting the hundred resolutions. "I am returning—I, the boy."

"The boy is returning," cried a voice to other voices, who repeated, "The boy is returning."

"I am bringing Mr. Bons with me."

Silence.

"I should have said Mr. Bons is bringing me with him."

Profound silence.

"Who stands sentry?"

"Achilles."

And on the rocky causeway, close to the springing of the rainbow bridge, he saw a young man who carried a wonderful shield.

"Mr. Bons, it is Achilles, armed."

"I want to go back," said Mr. Bons.

The last fragment of the rainbow melted, the wheels sang upon the living rock, the door of the omnibus burst open. Out leapt the boy—he could not resist—and sprang to meet the warrior, who, stooping suddenly, caught him on his shield.

"Achilles!" he cried, "let me get down, for I am ignorant and vulgar, and I must wait for that Mr. Bons of whom I told you yesterday."

But Achilles raised him aloft. He crouched on the wonderful shield, on heroes and burning cities, on vineyards graven in gold, on every dear passion, every joy, on the entire image of the Mountain that he had discovered, encircled, like it, with an everlasting stream. "No, no," he protested, "I am not worthy. It is Mr. Bons who must be up here."

But Mr. Bons was whimpering, and Achilles trumpeted and cried, "Stand upright upon my shield!"

"Sir, I did not mean to stand! something made me stand. Sir, why do you delay? Here is only the great Achilles, whom you knew."

Mr. Bons screamed, "I see no one. I see nothing. I want to go back." Then he cried to the driver, "Save me! Let me stop in your chariot. I have honoured you. I have quoted you. I have bound you in vellum. Take me back to my world."

The driver replied, "I am the means and not the end. I am the food and not the life. Stand by yourself, as that boy has stood. I cannot save you. For poetry is a spirit; and they that would worship it must worship in spirit and in truth."

Mr. Bons—he could not resist—crawled out of the beautiful omnibus. His face appeared, gaping horribly. His hands followed, one gripping the step, the other beating the air. Now his shoulders emerged, his chest, his stomach. With a shriek of "I see London," he fell—fell against the hard, moonlit rock, fell into it as if it were water, fell through it, vanished, and was seen by the boy no more.

"Where have you fallen to, Mr. Bons? Here is a procession arriving to honour you with music and torches. Here come the men and women whose names you know. The mountain is awake, the river is awake, over the race course the sea is awaking those dolphins, and it is all for you. They want you—"

There was the touch of fresh leaves on his forehead. Someone had crowned him.

ΤΕΛΟΣ [2]

✠

From the *Kingston Gazette, Surbiton Times,* and *Raynes Park Observer.* The body of Mr. Septimus Bons has been found in a shockingly mutilated condition in the vicinity of the Bermondsey gas-works. The deceased's pockets contained a sovereign-purse, a silver cigar-case, a bijou pronouncing dic-

[2] End.

tionary, and a couple of omnibus tickets. The unfortunate gentleman had apparently been hurled from a considerable height. Foul play is suspected, and a thorough investigation is pending by the authorities.

JAMES JOYCE

A Little Cloud [1]

Eight years before he had seen his friend off at the North Wall and wished him godspeed. Gallaher had got on. You could tell that at once by his travelled air, his well-cut tweed suit, and fearless accent. Few fellows had talents like his and fewer still could remain unspoiled by such success. Gallaher's heart was in the right place and he had deserved to win. It was something to have a friend like that.

Little Chandler's thoughts ever since lunchtime had been of his meeting with Gallaher, of Gallaher's invitation and of the great city London where Gallaher lived. He was called Little Chandler because, though he was but slightly under the average stature, he gave one the idea of being a little man. His hands were white and small, his frame was fragile, his voice was quiet and his manners were refined. He took the greatest care of his fair silken hair and moustache and used perfume discreetly on his handkerchief. The halfmoons of his nails were perfect and when he smiled you caught a glimpse of a row of childish white teeth.

As he sat at his desk in the King's Inns he thought what changes those eight years had brought. The friend whom he had known under a shabby and necessitous guise had become a brilliant figure on the London Press. He turned often from his tiresome writing to gaze out of the office window. The glow of a late autumn sunset covered the grass plots and walks. It cast a shower of kindly golden dust on the untidy nurses and decrepit old men who drowsed on the benches; it flickered upon all the moving figures—on the children who ran screaming along the gravel paths and on everyone who passed through the gardens. He watched the scene and thought of life; and (as always happened when he thought of life) he became sad. A gentle melancholy took possession of him. He felt how useless it was to struggle against fortune, this being the burden of wisdom which the ages had bequeathed to him.

He remembered the books of poetry upon his shelves at home. He had bought them in his bachelor days and many an evening, as he sat in the little room off the hall, he had been tempted to take one down from the bookshelf and read out something to his wife. But shyness had always held him back; and so the books had remained on their shelves. At times he repeated lines to himself and this consoled him.

When his hour had struck he stood up and took leave of his desk and of his fellow-clerks punctiliously. He emerged from under the feudal arch of the King's Inns, a neat modest figure, and walked swiftly down Henrietta Street. The golden sunset was waning and the air had grown sharp. A horde of grimy children populated the street. They stood or ran in the roadway or crawled up the steps before the gaping doors or squatted like mice upon the thresholds. Little Chandler gave them no thought. He picked his way deftly through all that minute vermin-like life and under the shadow of the gaunt spectral mansions in which the old nobility of Dublin had roystered. No memory of the past touched him, for his mind was full of a present joy.

He had never been in Corless's but he knew the value of the name. He knew that people went there after the theatre to eat oysters and drink liqueurs; and he had heard that the waiters there spoke French and German. Walking swiftly by at night he had seen cabs drawn up before the door and richly dressed ladies, escorted by cavaliers, alight and enter quickly. They wore noisy dresses and many wraps. Their faces were powdered and they caught up their dresses, when they touched earth, like alarmed Atalantas. He had always passed without turning his head to look. It was his habit to walk swiftly in the street even by day and whenever he found himself in the city late at night he hurried on his way apprehensively and excitedly. Sometimes, however, he courted the causes of his fear. He chose the darkest and narrowest streets and, as he walked boldly forward, the silence that was spread about his footsteps troubled him, the wandering, silent figures troubled him; and at times a sound of low fugitive laughter made him tremble like a leaf.

He turned to the right towards Capel Street. Ignatius Gallaher on the London Press! Who would have thought it possible eight years before? Still, now that he reviewed the past, Little Chandler could remember many signs of future greatness in his friend. People used to say that Ignatius Gallaher was wild. Of course, he did mix with a rakish set of fellows at that time, drank freely and borrowed money on all sides. In the end he had got mixed up in some shady affair, some money transaction: at least, that was one version of his flight. But nobody denied him talent. There was always a certain . . . something in Ignatius Gallaher that impressed you in spite of yourself. Even when he was out at elbows and at his wits' end for money he kept up a bold face. Little Chandler remembered (and the remembrance brought a slight flush of pride to his cheek) one of Ignatius Gallaher's sayings when he was in a tight corner:

"Half time now, boys," he used to say lightheartedly. "Where's my considering cap?"

That was Ignatius Gallaher all out; and, damn it, you couldn't but admire him for it.

Little Chandler quickened his pace. For the first time in his life he felt himself superior to the people he passed. For the first time his soul revolted against the dull inelegance of Capel Street. There was no doubt about it: if you wanted to succeed you had to go away. You could do nothing in Dublin. As he crossed Grattan Bridge he looked down the river towards the lower quays and pitied the poor stunted houses. They seemed to him a band of tramps, huddled together along the river-banks, their old coats covered with dust and soot, stupefied by the panorama of sunset and waiting for the first chill of night to bid them arise, shake themselves and be gone. He wondered whether he could write a poem to express his idea. Perhaps Gallaher might be able to get it into some London paper for him. Could he write something original? He was not sure what idea he wished to express but the thought that a poetic moment had touched him took life within him like an infant hope. He stepped onward bravely.

Every step brought him nearer to London, farther from his own sober inartistic life. A light began to tremble on the horizon of his mind. He was not so old—thirty-two. His temperament might be said to be just at the point of maturity. There were so many different moods and impressions that he wished to express in verse. He felt them within him. He tried to weigh his soul to see if it was a poet's soul. Melancholy was the dominant note of his temperament, he thought, but it was a melancholy tempered by recurrences of faith and resignation and simple joy. If he could give expression to it in a book of poems perhaps men would listen. He would never be popular: he saw that. He could not sway the crowd but he might appeal to a little circle of kindred minds. The English critics, perhaps, would recognise him as one of the Celtic school by reason of the melancholy tone of his poems; besides that, he would put in allusions. He began to invent sentences and phrases from the notice which his book would get. "Mr. Chandler has the gift of *easy and graceful verse.*" . . . "A *wistful sadness pervades these poems.*" . . . "*The Celtic note.*" It was a pity his name was not more Irish-looking. Perhaps it would be better to insert his mother's name before the surname: Thomas Malone Chandler, or better still: T. Malone Chandler. He would speak to Gallaher about it.

He pursued his revery so ardently that he passed his street and had to turn back. As he came near Corless's his former agitation began to overmaster him and he halted before the door in indecision. Finally he opened the door and entered.

The light and noise of the bar held him at the doorway for a few moments. He looked about him, but his sight was confused by the shining of many red and green wine-glasses. The bar seemed to him to be full of people and he felt that the people were observing him curiously. He glanced quickly to right and left (frowning slightly to make his errand appear serious), but when his sight cleared a little he saw that nobody had turned to look at him: and there, sure enough, was Ignatius Gallaher leaning with his back against the counter and his feet planted far apart.

"Hallo, Tommy, old hero, here you are! What is it to be? What will you have? I'm taking whisky: better stuff than we get across the water. Soda? Lithia? No mineral? I'm the same. Spoils the flavour. . . . Here, *garçon*, bring us two halves of malt whisky, like a good fellow. . . . Well, and how have you been pulling along since I saw you last? Dear God, how old we're getting! Do you see any signs of aging in me—eh, what? A little grey and thin on the top—what?"

Ignatius Gallaher took off his hat and displayed a large closely cropped head. His face was heavy, pale and clean-shaven. His eyes, which were of bluish slate-colour, relieved his unhealthy pallor and shone out plainly above the vivid orange tie he wore. Between these rival features the lips appeared very long and shapeless and colourless. He bent his head and felt with two sympathetic fingers the thin hair at the crown. Little Chandler shook his head as a denial. Ignatius Gallaher put on his hat again.

"It pulls you down," he said, "press life. Always hurry and scurry, looking for copy and sometimes not finding it: and then, always to have something new in your stuff. Damn proofs and printers, I say, for a few days. I'm deuced glad, I can tell you, to get back to the old country. Does a fellow good, a bit of a holiday. I feel a ton better since I landed again in dear dirty Dublin. . . . Here you are, Tommy. Water? Say when."

Little Chandler allowed his whisky to be very much diluted.

"You don't know what's good for you, my boy," said Ignatius Gallaher. "I drink mine neat."

"I drink very little as a rule," said Little Chandler modestly. "An odd half-one or so when I meet any of the old crowd: that's all."

"Ah, well," said Ignatius Gallaher, cheerfully, "here's to us and to old times and old acquaintance."

They clinked glasses and drank the toast.

"I met some of the old gang today," said Ignatius Gallaher. "O'Hara seems to be in a bad way. What's he doing?"

"Nothing," said Little Chandler. "He's gone to the dogs."

"But Hogan has a good sit, hasn't he?"

"Yes; he's in the Land Commission."

"I met him one night in London and he seemed to be very flush. . . . Poor O'Hara! Boose, I suppose?"

"Other things, too," said Little Chandler shortly.

Ignatius Gallaher laughed.

"Tommy," he said, "I see you haven't changed an atom. You're the very same serious person that used to lecture me on Sunday mornings when I had a sore head and a fur on my tongue. You'd want to knock about a bit in the world. Have you never been anywhere even for a trip?"

"I've been to the Isle of Man," said Little Chandler.

Ignatius Gallaher laughed.

"The Isle of Man!" he said. "Go to London or Paris: Paris, for choice. That'd do you good."

"Have you seen Paris?"

"I should think I have! I've knocked about there a little."

"And is it really so beautiful as they say?" asked Little Chandler.

He sipped a little of his drink while Ignatius Gallaher finished his boldly.

"Beautiful?" said Ignatius Gallaher, pausing on the word and on the flavour of his drink. "It's not so beautiful, you know. Of course, it is beautiful. . . . But it's the life of Paris; that's the thing. Ah, there's no city like Paris for gaiety, movement, excitement. . . ."

Little Chandler finished his whisky and, after some trouble, succeeded in catching the barman's eye. He ordered the same again.

"I've been to the Moulin Rouge," Ignatius Gallaher continued when the barman had removed their glasses, "and I've been to all the Bohemian cafés. Hot stuff! Not for a pious chap like you, Tommy."

Little Chandler said nothing until the barman returned with two glasses: then he touched his friend's glass lightly and reciprocated the former toast. He was beginning to feel somewhat disillusioned. Gallaher's accent and way of expressing himself did not please him. There was something vulgar in his friend which he had not observed before. But perhaps it was only the result of living in London amid the bustle and competition of the Press. The old personal charm was still there under this new gaudy manner. And, after all, Gallaher had lived, he had seen the world. Little Chandler looked at his friend enviously.

"Everything in Paris is gay," said Ignatius Gallaher. "They believe in enjoying life—and don't you think they're right? If you want to enjoy yourself properly you must go to Paris. And, mind you, they've a great feeling for the Irish there. When they heard I was from Ireland they were ready to eat me, man."

Little Chandler took four or five sips from his glass.

"Tell me," he said, "is it true that Paris is so . . . immoral as they say?"

Ignatius Gallaher made a catholic gesture with his right arm.

"Every place is immoral," he said. "Of course you do find spicy bits in Paris. Go to one of the students' balls, for instance. That's lively, if you like, when the *cocottes* begin to let themselves loose. You know what they are, I suppose?"

"I've heard of them," said Little Chandler.

Ignatius Gallaher drank off his whisky and shook his head.

"Ah," he said, "you may say what you like. There's no woman like the Parisienne—for style, for go."

"Then it is an immoral city," said Little Chandler, with timid insistence —"I mean, compared with London or Dublin?"

"London!" said Ignatius Gallaher. "It's six of one and half-a-dozen of the other. You ask Hogan, my boy. I showed him a bit about London when he was over there. He'd open your eye. . . . I say, Tommy, don't make punch of that whisky: liquor up."

"No, really. . . ."

"O, come on, another one won't do you any harm. What is it? The same again, I suppose?"

"Well . . . all right."

"*François*, the same again. . . . Will you smoke, Tommy?"

Ignatius Gallaher produced his cigar-case. The two friends lit their cigars and puffed at them in silence until their drinks were served.

"I'll tell you my opinion," said Ignatius Gallaher, emerging after some time from the clouds of smoke in which he had taken refuge, "it's a rum world. Talk of immorality! I've heard of cases—what am I saying?—I've known them: cases of . . . immorality. . . ."

Ignatius Gallaher puffed thoughtfully at his cigar and then, in a calm historian's tone, he proceeded to sketch for his friend some pictures of the corruption which was rife abroad. He summarised the vices of many capitals and seemed inclined to award the palm to Berlin. Some things he could not vouch for (his friends had told him), but of others he had had personal experience. He spared neither rank nor caste. He revealed many of the secrets of religious houses on the Continent and described some of the practices which were fashionable in high society and ended by telling, with details, a story about an English duchess—a story which he knew to be true. Little Chandler was astonished.

"Ah, well," said Ignatius Gallaher, "here we are in old jog-along Dublin where nothing is known of such things."

"How dull you must find it," said Little Chandler, "after all the other places you've seen!"

"Well," said Ignatius Gallaher, "it's a relaxation to come over here, you know. And, after all, it's the old country, as they say, isn't it? You can't help having a certain feeling for it. That's human nature. . . . But tell me something about yourself. Hogan told me you had . . . tasted the joys of connubial bliss. Two years ago, wasn't it?"

Little Chandler blushed and smiled.

"Yes," he said. "I was married last May twelve months."

"I hope it's not too late in the day to offer my best wishes," said Ignatius Gallaher. "I didn't know your address or I'd have done so at the time."

He extended his hand, which Little Chandler took.

"Well, Tommy," he said, "I wish you and yours every joy in life, old chap, and tons of money, and may you never die till I shoot you. And that's the wish of a sincere friend, an old friend. You know that?"

"I know that," said Little Chandler.

"Any youngsters?" said Ignatius Gallaher.

Little Chandler blushed again.

"We have one child," he said.

"Son or daughter?"

"A little boy."

Ignatius Gallaher slapped his friend sonorously on the back.

"Bravo," he said, "I wouldn't doubt you, Tommy."

Little Chandler smiled, looked confusedly at his glass and bit his lower lip with three childishly white front teeth.

"I hope you'll spend an evening with us," he said, "before you go back. My wife will be delighted to meet you. We can have a little music and—"

"Thanks awfully, old chap," said Ignatius Gallaher, "I'm sorry we didn't meet earlier. But I must leave tomorrow night."

"Tonight, perhaps . . . ?"

"I'm awfully sorry, old man. You see I'm over here with another fellow, clever young chap he is too, and we arranged to go to a little card-party. Only for that. . . ."

"O, in that case. . . ."

"But who knows?" said Ignatius Gallaher considerately. "Next year I may take a little skip over here now that I've broken the ice. It's only a pleasure deferred."

"Very well," said Little Chandler, "the next time you come we must have an evening together. That's agreed now, isn't it?"

"Yes, that's agreed," said Ignatius Gallaher. "Next year if I come, parole d'honneur."

"And to clinch the bargain," said Little Chandler, "we'll just have one more now."

Ignatius Gallaher took out a large gold watch and looked at it.

"Is it to be the last?" he said. "Because you know, I have an a.p."

"O, yes, positively," said Little Chandler.

"Very well, then," said Ignatius Gallaher, "let us have another one as a deoc an doruis—that's good vernacular for a small whisky, I believe."

Little Chandler ordered the drinks. The blush which had risen to his face a few moments before was establishing itself. A trifle made him blush at any time: and now he felt warm and excited. Three small whiskies had gone to his head and Gallaher's strong cigar had confused his mind, for he was a delicate and abstinent person. The adventure of meeting Gallaher after eight years, of finding himself with Gallaher in Corless's surrounded by lights and noise, of listening to Gallaher's stories and of sharing for a brief space Gallaher's vagrant and triumphant life, upset the equipoise of his sensitive nature. He felt acutely the contrast between his own life and his friend's, and it seemed to him unjust. Gallaher was his inferior in birth and education. He was sure that he could do something better than his friend had ever done, or could ever do, something higher than mere tawdry journalism if he only got the chance. What was it that stood in his way? His unfortunate timidity! He wished to vindicate himself in some way, to assert his manhood. He saw behind Gallaher's refusal of his invitation. Gallaher was only patronising him by his friendliness just as he was patronising Ireland by his visit.

The barman brought their drinks. Little Chandler pushed one glass towards his friend and took up the other boldly.

"Who knows?" he said, as they lifted their glasses. "When you come next year I may have the pleasure of wishing long life and happiness to Mr. and Mrs. Ignatius Gallaher."

Ignatius Gallaher in the act of drinking closed one eye expressively over the rim of his glass. When he had drunk he smacked his lips decisively, set down his glass and said:

"No blooming fear of that, my boy. I'm going to have my fling first and see a bit of life and the world before I put my head in the sack—if I ever do."

"Some day you will," said Little Chandler calmly.

Ignatius Gallaher turned his orange tie and slate-blue eyes full upon his friend.

"You think so?" he said.

"You'll put your head in the sack," repeated Little Chandler stoutly, "like everyone else if you can find the girl."

He had slightly emphasised his tone and he was aware that he had betrayed himself; but, though the colour had heightened in his cheek, he did not flinch from his friend's gaze. Ignatius Gallaher watched him for a few moments and then said:

"If ever it occurs, you may bet your bottom dollar there'll be no mooning and spooning about it. I mean to marry money. She'll have a good fat account at the bank or she won't do for me."

Little Chandler shook his head.

"Why, man alive," said Ignatius Gallaher, vehemently, "do you know what it is? I've only to say the word and tomorrow I can have the woman and the cash. You don't believe it? Well, I know it. There are hundreds—what am I saying?—thousands of rich Germans and Jews, rotten with money, that'd only be too glad. . . . You wait a while, my boy. See if I don't play my cards properly. When I go about a thing I mean business, I tell you. You just wait."

He tossed his glass to his mouth, finished his drink and laughed loudly. Then he looked thoughtfully before him and said in a calmer tone:

"But I'm in no hurry. They can wait. I don't fancy tying myself up to one woman, you know."

He imitated with his mouth the act of tasting and made a wry face.

"Must get a bit stale, I should think," he said.

Little Chandler sat in the room off the hall, holding a child in his arms. To save money they kept no servant but Annie's young sister Monica came for an hour or so in the morning and an hour or so in the evening to help. But Monica had gone home long ago. It was a quarter to nine. Little Chandler had come home late for tea and, moreover, he had forgotten to bring Annie home the parcel of coffee from Bewley's. Of course she was in a bad humour and gave him short answers. She said she would do without any tea but when it came near the time at which the shop at the corner closed she decided to go out herself for a quarter of a pound of tea and two pounds of sugar. She put the sleeping child deftly in his arms and said:

"Here. Don't waken him."

A little lamp with a white china shade stood upon the table and its light fell over a photograph which was enclosed in a frame of crumpled horn. It was Annie's photograph. Little Chandler looked at it, pausing at the thin tight lips. She wore the pale blue summer blouse which he had brought her home as a present one Saturday. It had cost him ten and elevenpence; but what an agony of nervousness it had cost him! How he had suffered that day, waiting at the shop door until the shop was empty, standing at the counter and trying to appear at his ease while the girl piled ladies' blouses before him, paying at the desk and forgetting to take up the odd penny of his change, being called back by the cashier, and finally, striving to hide his blushes as he left the shop by examining the parcel to see if it were securely tied. When he brought the blouse home Annie kissed him and said it was very pretty and stylish; but when she heard the price she threw the blouse on the table and said it was a regular swindle to charge ten and elevenpence for it. At first she wanted to take it back but when she tried it on she was delighted with it, especially with the make of the sleeves, and kissed him and said he was very good to think of her.

Hm! . . .

He looked coldly into the eyes of the photograph and they answered coldly. Certainly they were pretty and the face itself was pretty. But he found something mean in it. Why was it so unconscious and ladylike? The composure of the eyes irritated him. They repelled him and defied him: there was no passion in them, no rapture. He thought of what Gallaher had said about rich Jewesses. Those dark Oriental eyes, he thought, how full they are of passion, of voluptuous longing! . . . Why had he married the eyes in the photograph?

He caught himself up at the question and glanced nervously round the room. He found something mean in the pretty furniture which he had bought for his house on the hire system. Annie had chosen it herself and it reminded him of her. It too was prim and pretty. A dull resentment against his life awoke within him. Could he not escape from his little house? Was it too late for him to try to live bravely like Gallaher? Could he go to London? There was the furniture still to be paid for. If he could only write a book and get it published, that might open the way for him.

A volume of Byron's poems lay before him on the table. He opened it cautiously with his left hand lest he should waken the child and began to read the first poem in the book:

> "Hushed are the winds and still the evening gloom,
> Not e'en a Zephyr wanders through the grove,
> Whilst I return to view my Margaret's tomb
> And scatter flowers on the dust I love."

He paused. He felt the rhythm of the verse about him in the room. How melancholy it was! Could he, too, write like that, express the melancholy of his soul in verse? There were so many things he wanted to describe: his sensation of a few hours before on Grattan Bridge, for example. If he could get back again into that mood. . . .

The child awoke and began to cry. He turned from the page and tried to hush it: but it would not be hushed. He began to rock it to and fro in his arms but its wailing cry grew keener. He rocked it faster while his eyes began to read the second stanza:

> "Within this narrow cell reclines her clay,
> That clay where once . . ."

It was useless. He couldn't read. He couldn't do anything. The wailing of the child pierced the drum of his ear. It was useless, useless! He was a prisoner for life. His arms trembled with anger and suddenly bending to the child's face he shouted:

"Stop!"

The child stopped for an instant, had a spasm of fright and began to scream. He jumped up from his chair and walked hastily up and down the room with the child in his arms. It began to sob piteously, losing its breath for four or five seconds, and then bursting out anew. The thin walls of the room echoed the sound. He tried to soothe it but it sobbed more convulsively. He looked at the contracted and quivering face of the child and began to be alarmed. He counted seven sobs without a break between them and caught the child to his breast in fright. If it died! . . .

The door was burst open and a young woman ran in, panting.

"What is it? What is it?" she cried.

The child, hearing its mother's voice, broke out into a paroxysm of sobbing.

"It's nothing, Annie . . . it's nothing. . . . He began to cry . . ."

She flung her parcels on the floor and snatched the child from him.

"What have you done to him?" she cried, glaring into his face.

Little Chandler sustained for one moment the gaze of her eyes and his heart closed together as he met the hatred in them. He began to stammer:

"It's nothing. . . . He . . . he began to cry. . . . I couldn't . . . I didn't do anything. . . . What?"

Giving no heed to him she began to walk up and down the room, clasping the child tightly in her arms and murmuring:

"My little man! My little mannie! Was 'ou frightened, love? . . . There now, love. There now! . . . Lambabaun! Mamma's little lamb of the world! . . . There now!"

Little Chandler felt his cheeks suffused with shame and he stood back out of the lamplight. He listened while the paroxysm of the child's sobbing grew less and less; and tears of remorse started to his eyes.

FRANZ KAFKA

A Country Doctor[1]

I was in great perplexity; I had to start on an urgent journey; a seriously ill patient was waiting for me in a village ten miles off; a thick blizzard of snow filled all the wide spaces between him and me; I had a gig, a light gig with big wheels, exactly right for our country roads; muffed in furs, my bag of instruments in my hand, I was in the courtyard all ready for the journey; but there was no horse to be had, no horse. My own horse had died in the night, worn out by the fatigues of this icy winter; my servant girl was now running round the village trying to borrow a horse; but it was hopeless, I knew it, and I stood there forlornly, with the snow gathering more and more thickly upon me, more and more unable to move. In the gateway the girl appeared, alone, and waved the lantern; of course, who would lend a horse at this time for such a journey? I strode through the courtway once more; I could see no way out; in my confused distress I kicked at the dilapidated door of the year-long uninhabited pigsty. It flew open and flapped to and fro on its hinges. A steam and smell as of horses came out of it. A dim stable lantern was swinging inside from a rope. A man, crouching on his hams in that low space, showed an open blue-eyed face. "Shall I yoke up?" he asked, crawling out on all fours. I did not know what to say and merely stooped down to see what else was in the sty. The servant girl standing beside me. "You never know what you're going to find in your own house," she said, and we both laughed. "Hey there, Brother, hey there, Sister!" called the groom, and two horses, enormous creatures with powerful flanks, one after the other, their legs tucked close to their bodies, each well-shaped head lowered like a camel's, by sheer strength of buttocking squeezed out through the door hole which they filled entirely. But at once they were standing up, with their long legs and their bodies steaming thickly. "Give him a hand," I said, and the

[1] From *The Penal Colony*, translated by Willa and Edwin Muir. By permission of Schocken Books, New York. Copyright by Schocken Books, New York.

willing girl hurried to help the groom with the harnessing. Yet hardly was she beside him when the groom clipped hold of her and pushed his face against hers. She screamed and fled back to me; on her cheek stood out in red the marks of two rows of teeth. "You brute," I yelled in fury, "do you want a whipping?" but in the same moment reflected that the man was a stranger; that I did not know where he came from, and that of his own free will he was helping me out when everyone else had failed me. As if he knew my thoughts he took no offense at my threat but, still busied with the horses, only turned round once towards me. "Get in," he said then, and indeed: everything was ready. A magnificent pair of horses, I observed, such as I had never sat behind, and I climbed in happily. "But I'll drive, you don't know the way," I said. "Of course," said he, "I'm not coming with you anyway, I'm staying with Rose." "No," shrieked Rose, fleeing into the house with a justified presentiment that her fate was inescapable; I heard the door chain rattle as she put it up; I heard the key turn in the lock; I could see, moreover, how she put out the lights in the entrance hall and in further flight all through the rooms to keep herself from being discovered. "You're coming with me," I said to the groom, "or I won't go, urgent as my journey is. I'm not thinking of paying for it by handing the girl over to you." "Gee up!" he said; clapped his hands; the gig whirled off like a log in a freshet; I could just hear the door of my house splitting and bursting as the groom charged at it and then I was deafened and blinded by a storming rush that steadily buffeted all my senses. But this only for a moment, since, as if my patient's farmyard had opened out just before my courtyard gate, I was already there; the horses had come quietly to a standstill; the blizzard had stopped; the moonlight all around; my patient's parents hurried out of the house, his sister behind them; I was almost lifted out of the gig; from their confused ejaculations I gathered not a word; in the sick room the air was almost unbreathable; the neglected stove was smoking; I wanted to push open a window; but first I had to look at my patient. Gaunt, without any fever, not cold, not warm, with vacant eyes, without a shirt, the youngster heaved himself up from under the feather bedding, threw his arms around my neck, and whispered in my ear: "Doctor, let me die." I glanced round the room; no one had heard it; the parents were leaning forward in silence waiting for my verdict; the sister had set a chair for my handbag; I opened the bag and hunted among my instruments; the boy kept clutching at me from his bed to remind me of his entreaty; I picked up a pair of tweezers, examined them in the candlelight and laid them down again. "Yes," I thought blasphemously, "in cases like this the gods are helpful, send the missing horse, add to it a second because of the urgency, and to crown everything bestow even a groom—" And only now did I remember Rose again; what was I to do, how could I rescue her, how could I pull her away from under that groom at ten miles' distance, with a team of horses I couldn't control. These horses, now, they had somehow slipped the reins loose, pushed the window open from the outside, I did not know how; each of them had stuck a head in at a window and, quite unmoved by the startled cries of the family, stood eyeing the patient. "Better go back at once," I thought, as if the horses were summoning me to the return journey, yet I permitted the patient's sister, who fancied that I was dazed by the heat, to take my fur coat from me. A glass of rum was poured out for me, the old man clapped me on the shoulder, a familiarity justified by this offer of his treasure. I shook my head; in the narrow confines of the old man's thoughts I felt ill; that was my only reason for refusing the drink. The mother stood by the bedside and cajoled me towards it. I yielded, and, while one of the horses whinnied loudly to the ceiling, laid my head to the boy's breast, which shivered under my wet beard. I confirmed what I already knew; the boy was quite sound, something a little wrong with his circulation, saturated with coffee by his solicitous mother, but sound and best turned out of bed with one shove. I am no world reformer and so I let him lie. I was the district doctor and I did my duty to the uttermost, to the point where it became almost too much. I was badly paid and yet generous and helpful to the poor. I had still to see that Rose was all right, and then the boy might have his way and I wanted to die too. What was I doing there in that endless winter! My horse was dead, and not a single person in the village would lend me another. I had to get my team out of the pigsty; if they hadn't chanced to be horses I should have had to travel with swine. That was how it was. And I nodded to the family. They knew nothing about it, and, had they known, would not have believed it. To write prescriptions is easy, but to come to an understanding with people is hard. Well, this should be the end of my visit, I had once more been called out needlessly, I was used to that, the whole district made my life a torment with my night bell, but that I should have to sacrifice Rose this time as well, the pretty girl who had lived in my house for years almost without my noticing her—that sacrifice was too much to ask, and I had somehow to get it reasoned out in my head with the help of what craft I could muster, in order not to let fly at this family, which with the best will in the world could not restore Rose to me. But as I shut my bag and put an arm out for my fur coat, the family meanwhile standing together, the father sniffing at the glass of rum in his hand, the mother, apparently disappointed in me—why, what do people expect?—biting her lips with tears in her eyes, the sister fluttering a blood-soaked towel, I was somehow ready to admit conditionally that the boy might be ill after all. I went towards him, he welcomed me smiling as if I were bringing him the most nourishing invalid broth—ah, now both horses were whinnying together; the noise, I suppose, was ordained by heaven to assist my examination of the patient—and this time I discovered that the boy was indeed ill. In his right side, near the hip, was an open wound as big as the palm of my hand. Rose-red, in many variations of shade, dark in the hollows, lighter at the edges, softly granulated, with irregular clots of blood, open as a surface mine to the daylight. That was how it looked from a distance. But on a closer inspection there was another complication. I could not help a low whistle of surprise. Worms, as thick and as long as my little finger, themselves rose-red and blood-spotted as well, were wriggling from their fastness in the interior of the wound towards the light, with small white heads and many little legs. Poor boy, you were past helping. I had discovered your great wound; this blossom in your side was destroying you. The family was pleased; they saw me busying myself; the sister told the mother, the mother the father, the father told several guests who were coming in, through the moonlight at the open door, walking on tiptoe, keeping their balance with outstretched arms. "Will you save me?" whispered the boy with a sob, quite blinded by the life within his wound. That is what people are like in my district. Always expecting the impossible from the doctor. They have lost their ancient beliefs; the parson sits at home and unravels his vestments, one after another; but the doctor is supposed to be omnipotent with his merciful surgeon's hand. Well, as it pleases them; I have not thrust my services on them; if they misuse me for sacred ends, I let that happen to me too; what better do I want, old country doctor that I am, bereft of my servant girl! And so they came, the family and the village elders, and stripped my clothes off me; a school choir with the teacher at the head of it stood before the house and sang these words to an utterly simple tune:

> Strip his clothes off, then he'll heal us,
> If he doesn't, kill him dead!
> Only a doctor, only a doctor.

Then my clothes were off and I looked at the people quietly, my fingers in my beard and my head cocked to one side. I was altogether composed and equal to the situation and remained so, although it was no help to me, since they now took me by the head and feet and carried me to the bed. They laid me down in it next to the wall, on the side of the wound. Then they all left the room; the door was shut; the singing stopped; clouds covered the moon; the bedding was warm around me; the horses' heads in the opened windows wavered like shadows. "Do you know," said a voice in my ear, "I have very little confidence in you. Why, you were only blown in here, you didn't come on your own feet. Instead of helping me, you're cramping me on my death bed. What I'd like best is to scratch your eyes out." "Right," I said, "it's a shame. And yet I am a doctor. What am I to do? Believe me, it is not too easy for me either." "Am I supposed to be content with this apology? Oh, I must be, I can't help it. I always have to put up with things. A fine wound is all I brought into the world; that was my sole endowment." "My young friend," said I, "your mistake is: you have not a wide enough view. I have been in all the sickrooms, far and wide, and I tell you: your wound is not so bad. Done in a tight corner with two strokes of the ax. Many a one proffers his side and can hardly hear the ax in the forest, far less that it is coming nearer to him." "Is that really so, or are you deluding me in my fever?" "It is really so, take the word of honor of an official doctor." And he took it and lay still. But now it was time for me to think of escaping. The horses were still standing faithfully in their places. My clothes, my fur coat, my bag were quickly collected; I didn't want to waste time dressing; if the horses raced home as they had come, I should only be springing, as it were, out of this bed into my own. Obediently a horse backed away from the window; I threw my bundle into the gig; the fur coat missed its mark and was caught on a hook only by the sleeve. Good enough. I swung myself on to the horse. With the reins loosely trailing, one horse barely fastened to the other, the gig swaying behind, my fur coat last of all in the snow. "Geeup!" I said, but there was no galloping; slowly, like old men, we crawled through the snowy wastes; a long time echoed behind us the new but faulty song of the children:

> O be joyful, all you patients,
> The doctor's laid in bed beside you!

Never shall I reach home at this rate; my flourishing practice is done for; my successor is robbing me, but in vain, for he cannot take my place; in my house the disgusting groom is raging; Rose is the victim; I do not want to think about it any more. Naked, exposed to the frost of this most unhappy of ages, with an earthly vehicle, unearthly horses, old man that I am, I wander astray. My fur coat is hanging from the back of the gig, but I cannot reach it, and none of my limber pack of patients lifts a finger. Betrayed! Betrayed! A false alarm on the night bell once answered—it cannot be made good, not ever.

MARGARET CHURCH

On Kafka's "A Country Doctor" [1]

"A Country Doctor," like *The Trial* and *The Castle*, is a quest. It centers around the theme of the alienation and frustrations of man in seeking a goal, in this story of those isolated (country) few who seek to help others. Also implied is the false pride of these self-appointed helpers. The doctor's horse is dead; a blizzard rages. The only person who stands by him is his servant girl Rose. Fate conjures up in answer to the doctor's need a demonic pair of horses and a demonic groom. He must sacrifice Rose to the groom if he is to reach his patient. Those who would do good must often, ironically enough, utilize evil in order to accomplish their ends.

He arrives at the patient's house. Further frustration comes, however, when the boy begs that he may be left to die. Those whom we want to help do not even wish it. The heads of the demonic horses thrust into the room constantly remind the doctor (symbolically as well as actually) of his sacrifice of Rose, and he is tempted to leave his quest in order to save her. He is about to depart,

[1] From *The Explicator*, XVI (May, 1958), 45. By permission of the author and of the Editors of *The Explicator*.

thinking "he has been called out needlessly," when he discovers on second examination a large wound in the boy's side, and he knows that he is past helping. Now that he knows he cannot save the boy, the boy, of course, begs to be saved.

The wound is the wound of evil in the side of innocence, for instance, the wound (Rose-red) which the groom makes when he bites the servant girl. The wound is also paradoxically "the Rose"—beauty and goodness which "inflict themselves" on sinful man. Thus the boy exclaims that his wound is all he has to contribute, for he selfishly cherishes the sacrificial nature of his role and the beauty of the roselike wound which stems from his sacrifice.

At the doctor's realization of his inability to cure the boy, the villagers (society or our censors) punish him by stripping him of his clothes, his dignity, and laying him beside the boy, on the same level as the one he would help. Only now is he able to offer the succor he could not give when he had placed himself in a superior position. He tells the boy that one's wounds, the inroads of evil and guilt, are only a matter of perspective: "your mistake is: you have not a wide enough view."

He returns home on the now slowly moving horses (time is an inner affair) bereft of his clothes, his coat, naked, exposed. Still not cured of his pride, he feels betrayed, that the call has been a false alarm. As in Kafka's *The Trial* and *The Castle*, the efforts of the hero avail nothing, for fate (the officials of the novels) is indifferent.

Any interpretation of Kafka requires a point of view toward his works. It is not possible, in this author's opinion, to interpret him in a narrowly religious sense, for instance. On one level, the wound is, perhaps, the wound in the side of Christ. But Kafka's preoccupation with sin and guilt is more general. Likewise the symbolism should not be interpreted in too narrow a Freudian sense. The heads of the horses thrust through the window or the worms in the wound may be phallic in significance, but the action of Kafka's work takes place in a more general area. He writes, in fact, of all human experience and thought, leaving the reader with a wide range of interpretation.

WILLIAM CARLOS WILLIAMS

Jean Beicke[1]

During a time like this, they kid a lot among the doctors and nurses on the obstetrical floor because of the rushing business in new babies that's pretty nearly always going on up there. It's the Depression, they say, nobody has

[1] From *Make Light of It*. Reprinted by permission of Random House, Inc. Copyright, 1933, by William Carlos Williams.

any money so they stay home nights. But one bad result of this is that in the children's ward, another floor up, you see a lot of unwanted children.

The parents get them into the place under all sort of pretexts. For instance, we have two premature brats, Navarro and Cryschka, one a boy and one a girl; the mother died when Cryschka was born, I think. We got them within a few days of each other, one weighing four pounds and one a few ounces more. They dropped down below four pounds before we got them going but there they are; we had a lot of fun betting on their daily gains in weight but we still have them. They're in pretty good shape though now. Most of the kids that are left that way get along swell. The nurses grow attached to them and get a real thrill when they begin to pick up. It's great to see. And the parents sometimes don't even come to visit them, afraid we'll grab them and make them take the kids out, I suppose.

A funny one is a little Hungarian Gypsy girl that's been up there for the past month. She was about eight weeks old maybe when they brought her in with something on her lower lip that looked like a chancre. Everyone was interested but the Wassermann was negative. It turned out finally to be nothing but a peculiarly situated birthmark. But that kid is still there too. Nobody can find the parents. Maybe they'll turn up some day.

Even when we do get rid of them, they often come back in a week or so—sometimes in terrible condition, full of impetigo, down in weight—everything we'd done for them to do over again. I think it's deliberate neglect in most cases. That's what happened to this little Gypsy. The nurse was funny after the mother had left the second time. I couldn't speak to her, she said. I just couldn't say a word I was so mad. I wanted to slap her.

We had a couple of Irish girls a while back named Cowley. One was a red head with beautiful wavy hair and the other a straight haired blonde. They really were good looking and not infants at all. I should say they must have been two and three years old approximately. I can't imagine how the parents could have abandoned them. But they did. I think they were habitual drunkards and may have had to beat it besides on short notice. No fault of theirs maybe.

But all these are, after all, not the kind of kids I have in mind. The ones I mean are those they bring in stinking dirty, and I mean stinking. The poor brats are almost dead sometimes, just living skeletons, almost, wrapped in rags, their heads caked with dirt, their eyes stuck together with pus and their legs all excoriated from the dirty diapers no one has had the interest to take off them regularly. One poor little tot we have now with a thin purplish skin and big veins standing out all over its head had a big sore place in the fold of its neck under the chin. The nurse told me that when she started to undress it it had on a shirt with a neckband that rubbed right into that place. Just dirt. The mother gave a story of having had it in some sort of home in Paterson. We couldn't get it straight. We never try. What the hell? We take 'em and try to make something out of them.

Sometimes, you'd be surprised, some doctor has given the parents a ride before they bring the child to the clinic. You wouldn't believe it. They clean 'em out, maybe for twenty-five dollars—they maybe had to borrow—and then tell 'em to move on. It happens. Men we all know too. Pretty bad. But what can you do?

And sometimes the kids are not only dirty and neglected but sick, ready to die. You ought to see those nurses work. You'd think it was the brat of their best friend. They handle those kids as if they were worth a million dollars. Not that some nurses aren't better than others but in general they break their hearts over those kids, many times, when I, for one, wish they'd never get well.

I often kid the girls. Why not? I look at some miserable specimens they've dolled up for me when I make the rounds in the morning and I tell them: Give it an enema, maybe it will get well and grow up into a cheap prostitute or something. The country needs you, brat. I once proposed that we have a mock wedding between a born garbage hustler we'd saved and a little female with a fresh mug on her that would make anybody smile.

Poor kids! You really wonder sometimes if medicine isn't all wrong to try to do anything for them at all. You actually want to see them pass out, especially when they're deformed or—they're awful sometimes. Every one has rickets in an advanced form, scurvy too, flat chests, spindly arms and legs. They come in with pneumonia, a temperature of a hundred and six, maybe, and before you can do a thing, they're dead.

This little Jean Beicke was like that. She was about the worst you'd expect to find anywhere. Eleven months old. Lying on the examining table with a blanket half way up her body, stripped, lying there, you'd think it a five months baby, just about that long. But when the nurse took the blanket away, her legs kept on going for a good eight inches longer. I couldn't get used to it. I covered her up and asked two of the men to guess how long she was. Both guessed at least half a foot too short. One thing that helped the illusion besides her small face was her arms. They came about to her hips. I don't know what made that. They should come down to her thighs, you know.

She was just skin and bones but her eyes were good and she looked straight at you. Only if you touched her anywhere, she started to whine and then cry with a shrieking, distressing sort of cry that no one wanted to hear. We handled her as gently as we knew how but she had to cry just the same.

She was one of the damnedest looking kids I've ever seen. Her head was all up in front and flat behind, I suppose from lying on the back of her head so long the weight of it and the softness of the bones from the rickets had just flattened it out and pushed it up forward. And her legs and arms seemed loose on her like the arms and legs of some cheap dolls. You could bend her feet up on her shins absolutely flat—but there was no real deformity, just all loosened up. Nobody was with her when I saw her though her mother had brought her in.

It was about ten in the evening, the interne had asked me to see her because she had a stiff neck, and how! and there was some thought of meningitis—perhaps infantile paralysis. Anyhow, they didn't want her to go through the night without at least a lumbar puncture if she needed it. She had a fierce cough and a fairly high fever. I made it out to be a case of broncho-pneumonia with meningismus but no true involvement of the central nervous system. Besides she had inflamed ear drums.

I wanted to incise the drums, especially the left, and would have done it only the night superintendent came along just then and made me call the ear man on service. You know. She also looked to see if we had an operative release from the parents. There was. So I went home, the ear man came in a while later and opened the ears—a little bloody serum from both sides and that was that.

Next day we did a lumbar puncture, tapped the spine that is, and found clear fluid with a few lymphocytes in it, nothing diagnostic. The X-ray of the chest clinched the diagnosis of broncho-pneumonia, there was an extensive involvement. She was pretty sick. We all expected her to die from exhaustion before she'd gone very far.

I had to laugh every time I looked at the brat after that, she was such a funny looking one but one thing that kept her from being a total loss was that she did eat. Boy! how that kid could eat! As sick as she was she took her grub right on time every three hours, a big eight ounce bottle of whole milk and digested it perfectly. In this depression you got to be such a hungry baby, I heard the nurse say to her once. It's a sign of intelligence, I told her. But anyway, we all got to be crazy about Jean. She'd just lie there and eat and sleep. Or she'd lie and look straight in front of her by the hour. Her eyes were blue, a pale sort of blue. But if you went to touch her, she'd begin to scream. We just didn't, that's all, unless we absolutely had to. And she began to gain in weight. Can you imagine that? I suppose she had been so terribly run down that food, real food, was an entirely new experience to her. Anyway she took her food and gained on it though her temperature continued to run steadily around between a hundred and three and a hundred and four for the first eight or ten days. We were surprised.

When we were expecting her to begin to show improvement, however, she didn't. We did another lumbar puncture and found fewer cells. That was fine and the second X-ray of the chest showed it somewhat improved also. That wasn't so good though, because the temperature still kept up and we had no way to account for it. I looked at the ears again and thought they ought to be opened once more. The ear man disagreed but I kept after him and next day he did it to please me. He didn't get anything but a drop of serum on either side.

Well, Jean didn't get well. We did everything we knew how to do except the right thing. She carried on for another two—no I think it was three—weeks longer. A couple of times her temperature shot up to a hundred and eight. Of course we knew then it was the end. We went over her six or eight times, three or four of us, one after the other, and nobody thought to take an X-ray of the mastoid regions. It was dumb, if you want to say it, but there wasn't a sign of anything but the history of the case to point to it. The ears had been opened early, they had been watched carefully, there was no discharge to speak of at any time and from the external examination, the mastoid processes showed no change from the normal. But that's what she died of, acute purulent mastoiditis of the left side, going on to involvement of the left lateral sinus and finally the meninges. We might, however, have taken a culture of the pus when the ear was first opened and I shall always, after this, in suspicious cases. I have been told since that if you get a virulent bug like the streptococcus mucosus capsulatus it's wise at least to go in behind the ear for drainage if the temperature keeps up. Anyhow she died.

I went in when she was just lying there gasping. Somehow or other, I hated to see that kid go. Everybody felt rotten. She was such a scrawny, misshapen, worthless piece of humanity that I had said many times that somebody ought to chuck her in the garbage chute—but after a month watching her suck up her milk and thrive on it—and to see those alert blue eyes in that face—well, it wasn't pleasant. Her mother was sitting by the bed crying quietly when I came in, the morning of the last day. She was a young woman, didn't look more than a girl, she just sat there looking at the child and crying without a sound.

I expected her to begin to ask me questions with that look on her face all doctors hate—but she didn't. I put my hand on her shoulder and told her we had done everything we knew how to do for Jean but that we really didn't know what, finally, was killing her. The woman didn't make any sign of hearing me. Just sat there looking in between the bars of the crib. So after a moment watching the poor kid beside her, I turned to the infant in the next crib to go on with my rounds. There was an older woman there looking in at that baby also—no better off than Jean, surely. I spoke to her, thinking she was the mother of this one, but she wasn't.

Before I could say anything, she told me she was the older sister of Jean's mother and that she knew that Jean was dying and that it was a good thing. That gave me an idea—I hated to talk to Jean's mother herself—so I beckoned the woman to come out into the hall with me.

I'm glad she's going to die, she said. She's got two others home, older, and her husband has run off with another woman. It's better off dead—never was any good anyway. You know her husband came down from Canada about a year and a half ago. She seen him and asked him to come back and live with her and the children. He come back just long enough to get her pregnant with this one then he left her again and went back to the other woman. And I suppose knowing she was pregnant, and suffering, and having no money and nowhere to get it, she was worrying and this one never was formed right. I seen it as soon as it was born. I guess the condition she was in was the cause. She's got enough to worry about now without this one. The husband's gone to Canada again and we can't get a thing out of him. I been keeping them, but we can't do much more. She'd work if she could find anything but what can you do with three kids in times like this? She's got a boy nine years old but her mother-in-law sneaked it away from her and now he's with his father in Canada. She worries about him too, but that don't do no good.

Listen, I said, I want to ask you something. Do you think she'd let us do an autopsy on Jean if she dies? I hate to speak to her of such a thing now but to tell the truth, we've worked hard on that poor child and we don't exactly know what is the trouble. We know that she's had pneumonia but that's been getting well. Would you take it up with her for me, if—of course—she dies.

Oh, she's gonna die all right, said the woman. Sure, I will. If you can learn anything, it's only right. I'll see that you get the chance. She won't make any kick, I'll tell her.

Thanks, I said.

The infant died about five in the afternoon. The pathologist was dog-tired from a lot of extra work he'd had to do due to the absence of his assistant on her vacation so he put off the autopsy till next morning. They packed the body in ice in one of the service hoppers. It worked perfectly.

Next morning they did the postmortem. I couldn't get the nurse to go down to it. I may be a sap, she said, but I can't do it, that's all. I can't. Not when I've taken care of them. I feel as if they're my own.

I was amazed to see how completely the lungs had cleared up. They were almost normal except for a very small patch of residual pneumonia here and there which really amounted to nothing. Chest and abdomen were in excellent shape, otherwise, throughout—not a thing aside from the negligible pneumonia. Then he opened the head.

It seemed to me the poor kid's convolutions were unusually well developed. I kept thinking it's incredible that that complicated mechanism of the brain has come into being just for this. I never can quite get used to an autopsy.

The first evidence of the real trouble—for there had been no gross evidence of meningitis—was when the pathologist took the brain in his hand and made the long steady cut which opened up the left lateral ventricle. There was just a faint color of pus on the bulb of the choroid plexus there. Then the diagnosis all cleared up quickly. The left lateral sinus was completely thrombosed and on going into the left temporal bone from the inside the mastoid process was all broken down.

I called up the ear man and he came down at once. A clear miss, he said. I think if we'd gone in there earlier, we'd have saved her.

For what? said I. Vote the straight Communist ticket.

Would it make us any dumber? said the ear man.

D. H. LAWRENCE

Tickets, Please[1]

There is in the Midlands a single-line tramway system which boldly leaves
the county town and plunges off into the black, industrial countryside, up hill
and down dale, through the long, ugly villages of workmen's houses, over
canals and railways, past churches perched high and nobly over the smoke
and shadows through stark, grimy, cold little market-places, tilting away in a
rush past cinemas and shops down to the hollow where the collieries are, then
up again, past a little rural church, under the ash trees, on in a rush to the
terminus, the last little ugly place of industry, the cold little town that
shivers on the edge of the wild, gloomy country beyond. There the green and
creamy coloured tram-car seems to pause and purr with curious satisfaction.
But in a few minutes—the clock on the turret of the Co-operative Wholesale
Society's Shops gives the time—away it starts once more on the adventure.
Again there are the reckless swoops downhill, bouncing the loops: again the
chilly wait in the hill-top market-place: again the breathless slithering round
the precipitous drop under the church: again the patient halts at the loops,
waiting for the outcoming car: so on and on, for two long hours, till at last the
city looms beyond the fat gas-works, the narrow factories draw near, we are
in the sordid streets of the great town, once more we sidle to a standstill at
our terminus, abashed by the great crimson and cream-coloured city cars, but
still perky, jaunty, somewhat dare-devil, green as a jaunty sprig of parsley out
of a black colliery garden.

To ride on these cars is always an adventure. Since we are in war-time, the
drivers are men unfit for active service: cripples and hunchbacks. So they
have the spirit of the devil in them. The ride becomes a steeple-chase. Hur-
ray! we have leapt in a clear jump over the canal bridges—now for the four-
lane corner. With a shriek and a trail of sparks we are clear again. To be sure,
a tram often leaps the rails—but what matter! It sits in a ditch till other
trams come to haul it out. It is quite common for a car, packed with one solid
mass of living people, to come to a dead halt in the midst of unbroken
blackness, the heart of nowhere on a dark night, and for the driver and the
girl conductor to call, "All get off—car's on fire!" Instead, however, of rushing out in a panic, the passengers stolidly reply: "Get on—get on! We're not
coming out. We're stopping where we are. Push on, George." So till flames
actually appear.

[1] From *The Portable D. H. Lawrence* edited by Diana Trilling. Copyright 1922
by Thomas Seltzer, Inc., 1950 by Frieda Lawrence. Reprinted by permission of
The Viking Press, Inc.

The reason for this reluctance to dismount is that the nights are howlingly cold, black, and windswept, and a car is a haven of refuge. From village to village the miners travel, for a change of cinema, of girl, of pub. The trams are desperately packed. Who is going to risk himself in the black gulf outside, to wait perhaps an hour for another tram, then to see the forlorn notice "Depot Only," because there is something wrong! or to greet a unit of three bright cars all so tight with people that they sail past with a howl of derision. Trams that pass in the night.

This, the most dangerous tram-service in England, as the authorities themselves declare, with pride, is entirely conducted by girls, and driven by rash young men, a little crippled, or by delicate young men, who creep forward in terror. The girls are fearless young hussies. In their ugly blue uniform, skirts up to their knees, shapeless old peaked caps on their heads, they have all the sang-froid of an old non-commissioned officer. With a tram packed with howling colliers, roaring hymns downstairs and a sort of antiphony of obscenities upstairs, the lasses are perfectly at their ease. They pounce on the youths who try to evade their ticket-machine. They push off the men at the end of their distance. They are not going to be done in the eye—not they. They fear nobody—and everybody fears them.

"Hello, Annie!"

"Hello, Ted!"

"Oh, mind my corn, Miss Stone. It's my belief you've got a heart of stone, for you've trod on it again."

"You should keep it in your pocket," replies Miss Stone, and she goes sturdily upstairs in her high boots.

"Tickets, please."

She is peremptory, suspicious, and ready to hit first. She can hold her own against ten thousand. The step of that tram-car is her Thermopylæ.

Therefore, there is a certain wild romance aboard these cars—and in the sturdy bosom of Annie herself. The time for soft romance is in the morning, between ten o'clock and one, when things are rather slack: that is, except market-day and Saturday. Thus Annie has time to look about her. Then she often hops off her car and into a shop where she has spied something, while the driver chats in the main road. There is very good feeling between the girls and the drivers. Are they not companions in peril, shipments aboard this careering vessel of a tram-car, for ever rocking on the waves of a stormy land.

Then, also, during the easy hours, the inspectors are most in evidence. For some reason, everybody employed in this tram-service is young: there are no grey heads. It would not do. Therefore the inspectors are of the right age, and one, the chief, is also good-looking. See him stand on a wet, gloomy morning, in his long oilskin, his peaked cap well down over his eyes, waiting to board a car. His face is ruddy, his small brown moustache is weathered, he has a faint impudent smile. Fairly tall and agile, even in his waterproof, he springs aboard a car and greets Annie.

"Hello, Annie! Keeping the wet out?"

"Trying to."

There are only two people in the car. Inspecting is soon over. Then for a long and impudent chat on the footboard, a good, easy, twelve-mile chat.

The inspector's name is John Thomas Raynor—always called John Thomas, except sometimes, in malice, Coddy. His face sets in fury when he is addressed, from a distance, with this abbreviation. There is considerable scandal about John Thomas in half a dozen villages. He flirts with the girl conductors in the morning and walks out with them in the dark night, when they leave their tram-car at the depot. Of course, the girls quit the service frequently. Then he flirts and walks out with the newcomer: always providing she is sufficiently attractive, and that she will consent to walk. It is remarkable, however, that most of the girls are quite comely, they are all young, and this roving life aboard the car gives them a sailor's dash and recklessness. What matter how they behave when the ship is in port. Tomorrow they will be aboard again.

Annie, however, was something of a Tartar, and her sharp tongue had kept John Thomas at arm's length for many months. Perhaps, therefore, she liked him all the more: for he always came up smiling, with impudence. She watched him vanquish one girl, then another. She could tell by the movement of his mouth and eyes, when he flirted with her in the morning, that he had been walking out with this lass, or the other, the night before. A fine cock-of-the-walk he was. She could sum him up pretty well.

In this subtle antagonism they knew each other like old friends, they were as shrewd with one another almost as man and wife. But Annie had always kept him sufficiently at arm's length. Besides, she had a boy of her own.

The Statutes fair, however, came in November, at Bestwood. It happened that Annie had the Monday night off. It was a drizzling ugly night, yet she dressed herself up and went to the fair ground. She was alone, but she expected soon to find a pal of some sort.

The roundabouts were veering round and grinding out their music, the side shows were making as much commotion as possible. In the cocoanut shies there were no cocoanuts, but artificial war-time substitutes, which the lads declared were fastened into the irons. There was a sad decline in brilliance and luxury. None the less, the ground was muddy as ever, there was the same crush, the press of faces lighted up by the flares and the electric lights, the same smell of naphtha and a few fried potatoes, and of electricity.

Who should be the first to greet Miss Annie, on the show ground, but John Thomas. He had a black overcoat buttoned up to his chin, and a tweed cap pulled down over his brows, his face between was ruddy and smiling and handy as ever. She knew so well the way his mouth moved.

She was very glad to have a "boy." To be at the Statutes without a fellow was no fun. Instantly, like the gallant he was, he took her on the Dragons, grim-toothed, roundabout switchbacks. It was not nearly so exciting as a tram-car actually. But, then, to be seated in a shaking green dragon, uplifted above the sea of bubble faces, careering in a rickety fashion in the lower heavens, whilst John Thomas leaned over her, his cigarette in his mouth, was after all the right style. She was a plump, quick, alive little creature. So she was quite excited and happy.

John Thomas made her stay on for the next round. And therefore she could hardly for shame repulse him when he put his arm round her and drew her a little nearer to him, in a very warm and cuddly manner. Besides, he was fairly discreet, he kept his movement as hidden as possible. She looked down and saw that his red, clean hand was out of sight of the crowd. And they knew each other so well. So they warmed up to the fair.

After the dragons they went on the horses. John Thomas paid each time, so she could but be complaisant. He, of course, sat astride on the outer horse—named "Black Bess"—and she sat sideways, towards him, on the inner horse—named "Wildfire." But of course John Thomas was not going to sit discreetly on "Black Bess," holding the brass bar. Round they spun and heaved, in the light. And round he swung on his wooden steed, flinging one leg across her mount, and perilously tipping up and down, across the space, half lying back, laughing at her. He was perfectly happy; she was afraid her hat was on one side, but she was excited.

He threw quoits on a table and won for her two large, pale-blue hat-pins. And then, hearing the noise of the cinemas, announcing another performance, they climbed the boards and went in.

Of course, during these performances pitch darkness falls from time to time, when the machine goes wrong. Then there is a wild whooping, and a loud smacking of simulated kisses. In these moments John Thomas drew Annie towards him. After all, he had a wonderfully warm, cosy way of holding a girl with his arm, he seemed to make such a nice fit. And after all, it was pleasant to be so held: so very comforting and cosy and nice. He leaned over her and she felt his breath on her hair; she knew he wanted to kiss her on the lips. And after all, he was so warm and she fitted in to him so softly. After all, she wanted him to touch her lips.

But the light sprang up; she also started electrically, and put her hat straight. He left his arm lying nonchalantly behind her. Well, it was fun, it was exciting to be at the Statutes with John Thomas.

When the cinema was over they went for a walk across the dark, damp fields. He had all the arts of love-making. He was especially good at holding a girl, when he sat with her on a stile in the black, drizzling darkness. He seemed to be holding her in space, against his own warmth and gratification. And his kisses were soft and slow and searching.

So Annie walked out with John Thomas, though she kept her own boy dangling in the distance. Some of the tram-girls chose to be huffy. But there, you must take things as you find them, in this life.

There was no mistake about it, Annie liked John Thomas a good deal. She felt so rich and warm in herself whenever he was near. And John Thomas really liked Annie more than usual. The soft, melting way in which she could flow into a fellow, as if she melted into his very bones, was something rare and good. He fully appreciated this.

But with a developing acquaintance there began a developing intimacy. Annie wanted to consider him a person, a man; she wanted to take an intelligent interest in him, and to have an intelligent response. She did not want a mere nocturnal presence, which was what he was so far. And she prided herself that he could not leave her.

Here she made a mistake. John Thomas intended to remain a nocturnal presence; he had no idea of becoming an all-round individual to her. When she started to take an intelligent interest in him and his life and his character, he sheered off. He hated intelligent interest. And he knew that the only way to stop it was to avoid it. The possessive female was aroused in Annie. So he left her.

It is no use saying she was not surprised. She was at first startled, thrown out of her count. For she had been so *very* sure of holding him. For a while she was staggered, and everything became uncertain to her. Then she wept with fury, indignation, desolation, and misery. Then she had a spasm of despair. And then, when he came, still impudently, on to her car, still familiar, but letting her see by the movement of his head that he had gone away to somebody else for the time being and was enjoying pastures new, then she determined to have her own back.

She had a very shrewd idea what girls John Thomas had taken out. She went to Nora Purdy. Nora was a tall, rather pale, but well-built girl, with beautiful yellow hair. She was rather secretive.

"Hey!" said Annie, accosting her; then softly, "Who's John Thomas on with now?"

"I don't know," said Nora.

"Why tha does," said Annie, ironically lapsing into dialect. "Tha knows as well as I do."

"Well, I do, then," said Nora. "It isn't me, so don't bother."

"It's Cissy Meakin, isn't it?"

"It is, for all I know."

"Hasn't he got a face on him!" said Annie. "I don't half like his cheek. I could knock him off the footboard when he comes round at me."

"He'll get dropped-on one of these days," said Nora.

"Ay, he will when somebody makes up their mind to drop it on him. I should like to see him taken down a peg or two, shouldn't you?"

"I shouldn't mind," said Nora.

"You've got quite as much cause to as I have," said Annie. "But we'll drop on him one of these days, my girl. What? Don't you want to?"

"I don't mind," said Nora.

But as a matter of fact, Nora was much more vindictive than Annie.

One by one Annie went the round of the old flames. It so happened that Cissy Meakin left the tramway service in quite a short time. Her mother made her leave. Then John Thomas was on the qui-vive. He cast his eyes over his old flock. And his eyes lighted on Annie. He thought she would be safe now. Besides, he liked her.

She arranged to walk home with him on Sunday night. It so happened that her car would be in the depot at half-past nine: the last car would come in at ten-fifteen. So John Thomas was to wait for her there.

At the depot the girls had a little waiting-room of their own. It was quite rough, but cosy, with a fire and an oven and a mirror, and table and wooden chairs. The half dozen girls who knew John Thomas only too well had arranged to take service this Sunday afternoon. So, as the cars began to come in, early, the girls dropped into the waiting-room. And instead of hurrying off home, they sat around the fire and had a cup of tea. Outside was the darkness and lawlessness of war-time.

John Thomas came on the car after Annie, at about a quarter to ten. He poked his head easily into the girls' waiting-room.

"Prayer-meeting?" he asked.

"Ay," said Laura Sharp. "Ladies only."

"That's me!" said John Thomas. It was one of his favourite exclamations.

"Shut the door, boy," said Muriel Baggaley.

"On which side of me?" said John Thomas.

"Which tha likes," said Polly Birkin.

He had come in and closed the door behind him. The girls moved in their circle, to make a place for him near the fire. He took off his great-coat and pushed back his hat.

"Who handles the teapot?" he said.

Nora Purdy silently poured him out a cup of tea.

"Want a bit o' my bread and drippin'?" said Muriel Baggaley to him.

"Ay, give us a bit."

And he began to eat his piece of bread.

"There's no place like home, girls," he said.

They all looked at him as he uttered this piece of impudence. He seemed to be sunning himself in the presence of so many damsels.

"Especially if you're not afraid to go home in the dark," said Laura Sharp.

"Me! By myself I am."

They sat till they heard the last tram come in. In a few minutes Emma Houselay entered.

"Come on, my old duck!" cried Polly Birkin.

"It *is* perishing," said Emma, holding her fingers to the fire.

"But—I'm afraid to, go home in, the dark," sang Laura Sharp, the tune having got into her mind.

"Who're you going with tonight, John Thomas?" asked Muriel Baggaley, coolly.

"Tonight?" said John Thomas. "Oh, I'm going home by myself tonight—all on my lonely-O."

"That's me!" said Nora Purdy, using his own ejaculation.

The girls laughed shrilly.

"Me as well, Nora," said John Thomas.

"Don't know what you mean," said Laura.

"Yes, I'm toddling," said he, rising and reaching for his overcoat.

"Nay," said Polly. "We're all here waiting for you."

"We've got to be up in good time in the morning," he said in the benevolent official manner.

They all laughed.

"Nay," said Muriel. "Don't leave us all lonely, John Thomas. Take one!"

"I'll take the lot, if you like," he responded gallantly.

"That you won't, either," said Muriel. "Two's company; seven's too much of a good thing."

"Nay—take one," said Laura. "Fair and square, all above board, and say which."

"Ay," cried Annie, speaking for the first time. "Pick, John Thomas; let's hear thee."

"Nay," he said. "I'm going home quiet tonight. Feeling good, for once."

"Whereabouts?" said Annie. "Take a good un, then. But tha's got to take one of us!"

"Nay, how can I take one," he said, laughing uneasily. "I don't want to make enemies."

"You'd only make one," said Annie.

"The chosen one," added Laura.

"Oh, my! Who said girls!" exclaimed John Thomas, again turning, as if to escape. "Well—good-night."

"Nay, you've got to make your pick," said Muriel. "Turn your face to the wall and say which one touches you. Go on—we shall only just touch your back—one of us. Go on—turn your face to the wall, and don't look, and say which one touches you."

He was uneasy, mistrusting them. Yet he had not the courage to break away. They pushed him to a wall and stood him there with his face to it. Behind his back they all grimaced, tittering. He looked so comical. He looked around uneasily.

"Go on!" he cried.

"You're looking—you're looking!" they shouted.

He turned his head away. And suddenly, with a movement like a swift cat, Annie went forward and fetched him a box on the side of the head that set his cap flying, and himself staggering. He started round.

But at Annie's signal they all flew at him, slapping him, pinching him, pulling his hair, though more in fun than in spite or anger. He, however, saw red. His blue eyes flamed with strange fear as well as fury, and he butted through the girls to the door. It was locked. He wrenched at it. Roused, alert, the girls stood round and looked at him. He faced them, at bay. At that moment they were rather horrifying to him, as they stood in their short uniforms. He was distinctly afraid.

"Come on, John Thomas! Come on! Choose!" said Annie.

"What are you after? Open the door," he said.

"We sha'n't—not till you've chosen!" said Muriel.

"Chosen what?" he said.

"Chosen the one you're going to marry," she replied.

He hesitated a moment.

"Open the blasted door," he said, "and get back to your senses." He spoke with official authority.

"You've got to choose!" cried the girls.

"Come on!" cried Annie, looking him in the eye. "Come on! Come on!"

He went forward, rather vaguely. She had taken off her belt, and swinging it, she fetched him a sharp blow over the head with the buckle end. He sprang and seized her. But immediately the other girls rushed upon him, pulling and tearing and beating him. Their blood was now thoroughly up. He was their sport now. They were going to have their own back, out of him. Strange, wild creatures, they hung on him and rushed at him to bear him down. His tunic was torn right up the back, Nora had hold at the back of his collar, and was actually strangling him. Luckily the button burst. He struggled in a wild frenzy of fury and terror, almost mad terror. His tunic was simply torn off his back, his shirt-sleeves were torn away, his arms were naked. The girls rushed at him, clenched their hands on him and pulled at him: or they rushed at him and pushed him, butted him with all their might: or they struck him wild blows. He ducked and cringed and struck sideways. They became more intense.

At last he was down. They rushed on him, kneeling on him. He had neither breath nor strength to move. His face was bleeding with a long scratch, his brow was bruised.

Annie knelt on him, the other girls knelt and hung on to him. Their faces were flushed, their hair wild, their eyes were all glittering strangely. He lay at last quite still, with face averted, as an animal lies when it is defeated and at the mercy of the captor. Sometimes his eye glanced back at the wild faces of the girls. His breast rose heavily, his wrists were torn.

"Now, then, my fellow!" gasped Annie at length. "Now then—now——"

At the sound of her terrifying, cold triumph, he suddenly started to struggle as an animal might, but the girls threw themselves upon him with unnatural strength and power, forcing him down.

"Yes—now, then!" gasped Annie at length.

And there was a dead silence, in which the thud of heart-beating was to be heard. It was a suspense of pure silence in every soul.

"Now you know where you are," said Annie.

The sight of his white, bare arm maddened the girls. He lay in a kind of trance of fear and antagonism. They felt themselves filled with supernatural strength.

Suddenly Polly started to laugh—to giggle wildly—helplessly—and Emma and Muriel joined in. But Annie and Nora and Laura remained the same, tense, watchful, with gleaming eyes. He winced away from these eyes.

"Yes," said Annie, in a curious low tone, secret and deadly. "Yes! You've got it now! You know what you've done, don't you? You know what you've done."

He made no sound nor sign, but lay with bright, averted eyes, and averted, bleeding face.

"You ought to be *killed*, that's what you ought," said Annie tensely. "You ought to be *killed*." And there was a terrifying lust in her voice.

Polly was ceasing to laugh, and giving long-drawn oh-h-hs and sighs as she came to herself.

"He's got to choose," she said vaguely.

"Oh, yes, he has," said Laura, with vindictive decision.

"Do you hear—do you hear?" said Annie. And with a sharp movement that made him wince, she turned his face to her.

"Do you hear?" she repeated, shaking him.

But he was quite dumb. She fetched him a sharp slap on the face. He started, and his eyes widened. Then his face darkened with defiance, after all.

"Do you hear?" she repeated.

He only looked at her with hostile eyes.

"Speak!" she said, putting her face devilishly near his.

"What?" he said, almost overcome.

"You've got to *choose*!" she cried, as if it were some terrible menace, and as if it hurt her that she could not exact more.

"What?" he said in fear.

"Choose your girl, Coddy. You've got to choose her now. And you'll get your neck broken if you play any more of your tricks, my boy. You're settled now."

There was a pause. Again he averted his face. He was cunning in his overthrow. He did not give in to them really—no, not if they tore him to bits.

"All right, then," he said, "I choose Annie." His voice was strange and full of malice. Annie let go of him as if he had been a hot coal.

"He's chosen Annie!" said the girls in chorus.

"Me!" cried Annie. She was still kneeling, but away from him. He was still lying prostrate, with averted face. The girls grouped uneasily around.

"Me!" repeated Annie, with a terrible bitter accent.

Then she got up, drawing away from him with strange disgust and bitterness.

"I wouldn't touch him," she said.

But her face quivered with a kind of agony, she seemed as if she would fall. The other girls turned aside. He remained lying on the floor, with his torn clothes and bleeding, averted face.

"Oh, if he's chosen——" said Polly.

"I don't want him—he can choose again," said Annie, with the same rather bitter hopelessness.

"Get up," said Polly, lifting his shoulder. "Get up."

He rose slowly, a strange, ragged, dazed creature. The girls eyed him from a distance, curiously, furtively, dangerously.

"Who wants him?" cried Laura roughly.

"Nobody," they answered with contempt. Yet each one of them waited for him to look at her, hoped he would look at her. All except Annie, and something was broken in her.

He, however, kept his face closed and averted from them all. There was a silence of the end. He picked up the torn pieces of his tunic, without knowing what to do with them. The girls stood about uneasily, flushed, panting, tidying their hair and their dress unconsciously, and watching him. He looked at none of them. He espied his cap in a corner and went and picked it up. He put it on his head, and one of the girls burst into a shrill, hysteric laugh at the sight he presented. He, however, took no heed but went straight to where his overcoat hung on a peg. The girls moved away from contact with him as if he had been an electric wire. He put on his coat and buttoned it down. Then he rolled his tunic-rags into a bundle, and stood before the locked door, dumbly.

"Open the door, somebody," said Laura.

"Annie's got the key," said one.

Annie silently offered the key to the girls. Nora unlocked the door.

"Tit for tat, old man," she said. "Show yourself a man, and don't bear a grudge."

But without a word or sign he had opened the door and gone, his face closed, his head dropped.

"That'll learn him," said Laura.

"Coddy!" said Nora.

"Shut up, for God's sake!" cried Annie fiercely, as if in torture.

"Well, I'm about ready to go, Polly. Look sharp!" said Muriel.

The girls were all anxious to be off. They were tidying themselves hurriedly, with mute, stupefied faces.

KATHERINE ANNE PORTER

That Tree[1]

He had really wanted to be a cheerful bum lying under a tree in a good climate, writing poetry. He wrote bushel basketsful of poetry and it was all no good and he knew it, even while he was writing it. Knowing his poetry was no good did not take away much from his pleasure in it. He would have enjoyed just that kind of life: no respectability, no responsibility, no money to speak of, wearing worn-out sandals and a becoming, if probably ragged, blue shirt, lying under a tree writing poetry. That was why he had come to Mexico in the first place. He had felt in his bones that it was the country for him. Long after he had become quite an important journalist, an authority on Latin-American revolutions and a best seller, he confessed to any friends and acquaintances who would listen to him—he enjoyed this confession, it gave him a chance to talk about the thing he believed he loved best, the idle free romantic life of a poet—that the day Miriam kicked him out was the luckiest day of his life. She had left him, really, packing up suddenly in a cold quiet fury, stabbing him with her elbows when he tried to get his arms around her, now and again cutting him to the bone with a short sentence expelled through her clenched teeth; but he felt that he had been, as he always explained, kicked out. She had kicked him out and it had served him right.

The shock had brought him to himself as if he had been surprised out of a long sleep. He had sat quite benumbed in the bare clean room, among the straw mats and the painted Indian chairs Miriam hated, in the sudden cold silence, his head in his hands, nearly all night. It hadn't even occurred to him to lie down. It must have been almost daylight when he got up stiff in every joint from sitting still so long, and though he could not say he had been thinking yet he had formed a new resolution. He had started out, you might almost say that very day, to make a career for himself in journalism. He couldn't say why he had hit on that, except that the word would impress his wife, the work was just intellectual enough to save his self-respect, such as it was, and even to him it seemed a suitable occupation for a man such as he had suddenly become, bent on getting on in the world of affairs. Nothing ever happens suddenly to anyone, he observed, as if the thought had just occurred to him; it had been coming on probably for a long time, sneaking up on him when he wasn't looking. His wife had called him "Parasite!" She had said "Ne'er-do-well!" and as she repeated these things for what proved to be the last time, it struck him she had said them often before, when he had not listened to her

[1] From *Flowering Judas and Other Stories* by Katherine Anne Porter, copyright, 1930, 1935, by Katherine Anne Porter. Reprinted by permission of Harcourt, Brace & World, Inc.

with the ear of his mind. He translated these relatively harmless epithets instantly into their proper synonyms of Loafer! and Bum! Miriam had been a schoolteacher, and no matter what her disappointments and provocations may have been, you could not expect her easily to forget such discipline. She had got into a professional habit of primness; besides, she was a properly brought-up girl, not a prissy bore, not at all, but a—well, there you are, a nicely brought-up Middle-Western girl, who took life seriously. And what can you do about that? She was sweet and gay and full of little crazy notions, but she never gave way to them honestly, or at least never at the moment when they might have meant something. She was never able to see the amusing side of a threatening situation which, taken solemnly, would ruin everything. No, her sense of humor never worked for salvation. It was just an extra frill on what would have been a good time anyhow.

He wondered if anybody had ever thought—oh, well, of course everybody else had, he was always making marvelous discoveries that other people had known all along—how impossible it is to explain or to make other eyes see the special qualities in the person you love. There was such a special kind of beauty in Miriam. In certain lights and moods he simply got a clutch in the pit of his stomach when he looked at her. It was something that could happen at any hour of the day, in the midst of the most ordinary occupations. He thought there was something to be said for living with one person day and night the year round. It brings out the worst, but it brings out the best, too, and Miriam's best was pretty damn swell. He couldn't describe it. It was easy to talk about her faults. He remembered all of them, he could add them up against her like rows of figures in a vast unpaid debt. He had lived with her for four years, and even now sometimes he woke out of a sound sleep in a sweating rage with himself, asking himself again why he had ever wasted a minute on her. She wasn't beautiful in his style. He confessed to a weakness for the kind that knocks your eye out. Her notion of daytime dress was a tailored suit with a round-collared blouse and a little felt hat like a bent shovel pulled down over her eyes. In the evening she put on a black dinner dress, positively disappeared into it. But she did her hair well and had the most becoming nightgowns he ever saw. You could have put her mind in a peanut shell. She hadn't temperament of the kind he had got used to in the Mexican girls. She did not approve of his use of the word temperament, either. She thought it was a kind of occupational disease among artists, or a trick they practiced to make themselves interesting. In any case, she distrusted artists and she distrusted temperament. But there was something about her. In cold blood he could size her up to himself, but it made him furious if anyone even hinted a criticism against her. His second wife had made a point of being catty about Miriam. In the end he could almost be willing to say this had led to his second divorce. He could not bear hearing Miriam called a mousy little nitwit—at least not by *that* woman. . . .

They both jumped nervously at an explosion in the street, the backfire of an automobile.

"Another revolution," said the fat scarlet young man in the tight purplish suit, at the next table. He looked like a parboiled sausage ready to burst from its skin. It was the oldest joke since the Mexican Independence, but he was trying to look as if he had invented it. The journalist glanced back at him over a sloping shoulder. "Another of those smart-cracking newspaper guys," he said in a tough voice, too loudly on purpose, "sitting around the Hotel Regis lobby wearing out the spittoons."

The smart-cracker swelled visibly and turned a darker red. "Who do you think you're talking about, you banjo-eyed chinless wonder, you?" he asked explicitly, spreading his chest across the table.

"Somebody way up, no doubt," said the journalist, in his natural voice, "somebody in with the government, I'll bet."

"Dyuhwana fight?" asked the newspaperman, trying to unwedge himself from between the table and his chair, which sat against the wall.

"Oh, I don't mind," said the journalist, "if you don't."

The newspaper man's friends laid soothing paws all over him and held him down. "Don't start anything with that shrimp," said one of them, his wet pink eyes trying to look sober and responsible. "For crisesake, Joe, can't you see he's about half your size and a feeb to boot? You wouldn't hit a feeb, now, Joe, would you?"

"I'll feeb him," said the newspaper man, wiggling faintly under restraint.

"Señores'n, señores'n," urged the little Mexican waiter, "there are respectable ladies and gentlemen present. Please, a little silence and correct behavior, please."

"Who the hell are you, anyhow?" the newspaper man asked the journalist, from under his shelter of hands, around the thin form of the waiter.

"Nobody you'd wanta know, Joe," said another of his pawing friends. "Pipe down now before these greasers turn in a general alarm. You know how liable they are to go off when you least expect it. Pipe down, now, Joe, now you just remember what happened the last time, Joe. Whaddayah care, anyhow?"

"Señores'n," said the little waiter, working his thin outspread mahogany colored hands up and down alternately as if they were on sticks, "it is necessary it must cease or the señores'n must remove themselves."

It did cease. It seemed to evaporate. The four newspaper men at the next table subsided, cluttered in a circle with their heads together, muttering into their highballs. The journalist turned back, ordered another round of drinks, and went on talking, in a low voice.

He had never liked this café, never had any luck in it. Something always happened here to spoil his evening. If there was one brand of bum on earth he despised, it was a newspaper bum. Or anyhow the drunken illiterates the United Press and Associated Press seemed to think were good enough for Mexico and South America. They were always getting mixed up in affairs that were none of their business, and they spent their time trying to work up trouble somewhere so they could get a story out of it. They were always having to be thrown out on their ears by the government. He just happened to know that the bum at the next table was about due to be deported. It had been pretty safe to make that crack about how he was no doubt way up in Mexican official esteem. . . . He thought that would remind him of something, all right.

One evening he had come here with Miriam for dinner and dancing, and at the very next table sat four fat generals from the North, with oxhorn mustaches and big bellies and big belts full of cartridges and pistols. It was in the old days just after Obregón had taken the city, and the town was crawling with generals. They infested the steam baths, where they took off their soiled campaign harness and sweated away the fumes of tequila and fornication, and they infested the cafés to get drunk again on champagne, and pick up the French whores who had been imported for the festivities of the presidential inauguration. These four were having an argument very quietly, their mean little eyes boring into each other's faces. He and his wife were dancing within arm's length of the table when one of the generals got up suddenly, tugging at his pistol, which stuck, and the other three jumped and grabbed him, all without a word; everybody in the place saw it at once. So far there was nothing unusual. The point was, every right-minded Mexican girl just seized her man firmly by the waist and spun him around until his back was to the generals, holding him before her like a shield, and there the whole roomful had stood frozen for a second, the music dead. His wife Miriam had broken from him and hidden under a table. He had to drag her out by the arm before everybody. "Let's have another drink," he said, and paused, looking around him as if he saw again the place as it had been on that night nearly ten years before. He blinked, and went on. It had been the most utterly humiliating moment of his whole blighted life. He had thought he couldn't survive to pick up their things and get her out of there. The generals had all sat down again and everybody went on dancing as though nothing had happened. . . . Indeed, nothing had happened to anyone except himself.

He tried, for hours that night and on and on for nearly a year, to explain to her how he felt about it. She could not understand at all. Sometimes she said it was all perfect nonsense. Or she remarked complacently that it had never occurred to her to save her life at his expense. She thought such tricks were all very well for the Mexican girls who had only one idea in their heads, and any excuse would do to hold a man closer than they should, but she could not, could *not*, see why he should expect her to imitate them. Besides, she had felt safer under the table. It was her first and only thought. He told her a bullet might very well have gone through the wood; a plank was no protection at all, a human torso was as good as a feather pillow to stop a bullet. She kept saying it simply had not occurred to her to do anything else, and that it really had nothing at all to do with him. He could never make her see his point of view for one moment. It should have had something to do with him. All those Mexican girls were born knowing what they should do and they did it instantly, and Miriam had merely proved once for all that her instincts were out of tune. When she tightened her mouth to bite her lip and say "Instincts!" she could make it sound like the most obscene word in any language. It was a shocking word. And she did not stop there. At last she said, she hadn't the faintest interest in what Mexican girls were born for, but she had no intention of wasting her life flattering male vanity. "Why should I trust you in anything?" she asked. "What reason have you given me to trust you?"

He was surprised at the change in her since he had first met her in Minneapolis. He chose to believe this change had been caused by her teaching school. He told her he thought it the most deadly occupation there was and a law should be passed prohibiting pretty women under thirty-five years of age from taking it up. She reminded him they were living on the money she had earned at it. They had been engaged for three years, a chaste long-distance engagement which he considered morbid and unnatural. Of course he had to do something to wear away the time, so while she was in Minneapolis saving her money and filling a huge trunk with household linen, he had been living in Mexico City with an Indian girl who posed for a set of painters he knew. He had a job teaching English in one of the technical schools—damned odd, he had been a schoolteacher too, but he never thought of it just that way until this minute—and he lived very comfortably with the Indian girl on his wages, for naturally the painters did not pay her for posing. The Indian girl divided her time cheerfully between the painters, the cooking pot, and his bed, and she managed to have a baby without interrupting any of these occupations for more than a few days. Later on she was taken up by one of the more famous and successful painters, and grew very sophisticated and a "character," but at that time she was still simple and nice. She took, later on, to wearing native art-jewelry and doing native dances in costume, and learned to paint almost as well as a seven-year-old child; "you know," he said, "the primitive style." Well, by that time, he was having troubles of his own. When the time came for Miriam to come out and marry him—the whole delay, he realized afterward, was caused by Miriam's expansive notions of what a bride's outfit should be—the Indian girl had gone away very cheerfully, too cheerfully, in fact, with a new man. She had come back in three days to say she was at last going to get married honestly, and she felt he should give her the furniture for a dowry. He had helped her pile the stuff on the backs of two Indian carriers, and the girl had walked away with the baby's head dangling out of her shawl. For just a moment when he saw the baby's face, he had an odd feeling. "That's mine," he said to himself, and added at once, "perhaps." There was no way of knowing, and it certainly looked like any other little shock-haired Indian baby. Of course the girl had not got married; she had never even thought of it.

When Miriam arrived, the place was almost empty, because he had not been able to save a peso. He had a bed and a stove, and the walls were decorated with drawings and paintings by his Mexican friends, and there was a litter of painted gourds and carved wood and pottery in beautiful colors. It didn't seem so bad to him, but Miriam's face, when she stepped into the first room, was, he had to admit, pretty much of a study. She said very little, but she began to be unhappy about a number of things. She cried intermittently for the first few weeks, for the most mysterious and far-fetched causes. He would wake in the night and find her crying hopelessly. When she sat down to coffee in the morning she would lean her head on her hands and cry. "It's nothing, nothing really," she would tell him. "I don't know what is the matter. I just want to cry." He knew now what was the matter. She had come all that way to marry after three years' planning, and she couldn't see herself going back and facing the music at home. This mood had not lasted, but it made a fairly dreary failure of their honeymoon. She knew nothing about the Indian girl, and believed, or professed to believe, that he was virgin as she was at their marriage. She hadn't much curiosity and her moral standards were severe, so it was impossible for him ever to take her into his confidence about his past. She simply took it for granted in the most irritating way that he hadn't any past worth mentioning except the three years they were engaged, and that, of course, they shared already. He had believed that all virgins, however austere their behavior, were palpitating to learn about life, were you might say hanging on an eyelash until they arrived safely at initiation within the secure yet libertine advantages of marriage. Miriam upset this theory as in time she upset most of his theories. His intention to play the rôle of a man of the world educating an innocent but interestingly teachable bride was nipped in the bud. She was not at all teachable and she took no trouble to make herself interesting. In their most intimate hours her mind seemed elsewhere, gone into some darkness of its own, as if a prior and greater shock of knowledge had forestalled her attention. She was not to be won, for reasons of her own which she would not or could not give. He could not even play the rôle of a poet. She was not interested in his poetry. She preferred Milton, and she let him know it. She let him know also that she believed their mutual sacrifice of virginity was the most important act of their marriage, and this sacred rite once achieved, the whole affair had descended to a pretty low plane. She had a terrible phrase about "walking the chalk line" which she applied to all sorts of situations. One walked, as never before, the chalk line in marriage; there seemed to be a chalk line drawn between them as they lay together.

The thing that finally got him down was Miriam's devilish inconsistency. She spent three mortal years writing him how dull and dreadful and commonplace her life was, how sick and tired she was of petty little conventions and amusements, how narrow-minded everybody around her was, how she longed to live in a beautiful dangerous place among interesting people who painted and wrote poetry, and how his letters came into her stuffy little world like a breath of free mountain air, and all that. "For God's sake," he said to his guest, "let's have another drink." Well, he had something of a notion he was freeing a sweet bird from a cage. Once freed, she would perch gratefully on his hand. He wrote a poem about a caged bird set free, dedicated it to her and sent her a copy. She forgot to mention it in her next letter. Then she came out with a two-hundred-pound trunk of linen and enough silk underwear to last her a lifetime, you might have supposed, expecting to settle down in a modern steam-heated flat and have nice artistic young couples from the American colony in for dinner Wednesday evenings. No wonder her face had changed at the first glimpse of her new home. His Mexican friends had scattered flowers all over the place, tied bunches of carnations on the door knobs, almost carpeted the floor with red roses, pinned posies of small bright blooms on the sagging cotton curtains, spread a coverlet of gardenias on the lumpy bed, and had disappeared discreetly, leaving gay reassuring messages scribbled here and there, even on the white plastered walls. . . . She had walked through with a vague look of terror in her eyes, pushing back the wilting flowers with her advancing feet. She swept the gardenias aside to sit on the edge of the bed, and she had said not a word. Hail, Hymen! What next?

He had lost his teaching job almost immediately. The Minister of Education, who was a patron of the school superintendent, was put out of office suddenly, and naturally, every soul in his party down to the school janitors went out with him, and there you were. After a while you learn to take such things calmly. You wait until your man gets back in the saddle or you work up an alliance with the new one. . . . Whichever. . . . Meanwhile the change and movement made such a good show you almost forgot the effect it had on your food supply. Miriam was not interested in politics or the movements of local history. She could see nothing but that he had lost his job. They lived on Miriam's savings eked out with birthday checks and Christmas checks from her father, who threatened constantly to come for a visit, in spite of Miriam's desperate letters warning him that the country was appalling, and the climate would most certainly ruin his health. Miriam went on holding her nose when she went to the markets, trying to cook wholesome civilized American food over a charcoal brasier, and doing the washing in the patio over a stone tub with a cold water tap; and everything that had seemed so jolly and natural and inexpensive with the Indian girl was too damnifying and costly for words with Miriam. Her money melted away and they got nothing for it.

She would not have an Indian servant near her; they were dirty and besides how could she afford it? He could not see why she despised and resented housework so, especially since he offered to help. He had thought it rather a picnic to wash a lot of gayly colored Indian crockery outdoors in the sunshine, with the bougainvillea climbing up the wall and the heaven tree in full bloom. Not Miriam. She despised him for thinking it a picnic. He remembered for the first time his mother doing the housework when he was a child. There were half a dozen assorted children, her work was hard and endless, but she went about it with a quiet certainty, a happy absorbed look on her face, as if her hands were working automatically while her imagination was away playing somewhere. "Ah, your mother," said his wife, without any particular emphasis. He felt horribly injured, as if she was insulting his mother and calling down a curse on her head for bringing such a son into the world. No doubt about it, Miriam had force. She could make her personality, which no one need really respect, felt in a bitter, sinister way. She had a background, and solid earth under her feet, and a point of view and a strong spine: even when she danced with him he could feel her tense controlled hips and her locked knees, which gave her dancing a most attractive strength and lightness without any yielding at all. She had her points, all right, like a good horse, but she had missed being beautiful. It wasn't in her. He began to cringe when she reminded him that if he were an invalid she would cheerfully work for him and take care of him, but he appeared to be in the best of health, he was not even looking for a job, and he was still writing that poetry, which was the last straw. She called him a failure. She called him worthless and shiftless and trifling and faithless. She showed him her ruined hands and asked him what she had to look forward to, and told him again, and again, that she was not used to associating with the simply indescribably savage and awful persons who kept streaming through the place. Moreover, she had no intention of getting used to it. He tried to tell her that these persons were the best painters and poets and what-alls in Mexico, that she should try to appreciate them; these were the artists he had told her about in his letters. She wanted to know why Carlos never changed his shirt. "I told her," said the journalist, "it was because probably he hadn't got any other shirt." And why was Jaime such a glutton, leaning over his plate and wolfing his food? Because he was famished, no doubt. It was precisely that she could not understand. Why didn't they go to work and make a living? It was no good trying to explain to her his Franciscan notions of holy Poverty as being the natural companion for the artist. She said, "So you think they're being poor on purpose? Nobody but you would be such a fool." Really, the things that girl said. And his general impression of her was that she was silent as a cat. He went on in his pawky way trying to make clear to her his mystical faith in these men who went ragged and hungry because they had chosen once for all between what he called in all seriousness their souls, and this world. Miriam knew better. She knew they were looking for the main chance. "She was abominably, obscenely right. How I hate that woman, I hate her as I hate no one else. She assured me they were not so stupid as I thought; and I lived to see Jaime take up with a rich old woman, and Ricardo decide to turn film actor, and Carlos sitting easy with a government job, painting revolutionary frescoes to order, and I asked myself, Why shouldn't a man survive in any way he can?" But some fixed point of feeling in him refused to be convinced, he had a sackful of romantic notions about artists and their destiny and he was left holding it. Miriam had seen through them with half an eye, and how he

wished he might have thought of a trick to play on her that would have finished her for life. But he had not. They all in turn ran out on him and in the
end he had run out too. "So you see, I don't feel any better about doing what I
did finally do, but I can say I am not unusual. That I can say. The trouble was
that Miriam was right, damn her. I am not a poet, my poetry is filthy, and I had
notions about artists that I must have got out of books. . . . You know, a
race apart, dedicated men much superior to common human needs and
ambitions. . . . I mean I thought art was a religion. . . . I mean that when
Miriam kept saying . . ."

What he meant was that all this conflict began to damage him seriously.
Miriam had become an avenging fury, yet he could not condemn her. Hate
her, yes, that was almost too simple. His old-fashioned respectable middle-
class hard-working American ancestry and training rose up in him and fought
on Miriam's side. He felt he had broken about every bone in him to get away
from them and live them down, and here he had been overtaken at last and
beaten into resignation that had nothing to do with his mind or heart. It
was as if his blood stream had betrayed him. The prospect of taking a job and
being a decent little clerk with shiny pants and elbows—for he couldn't think
of a job in any other terms—seemed like a kind of premature death which
would not even compensate him with loss of memory. He didn't do anything
about it at all. He did odd jobs and picked up a little money, but never
enough. He could see her side of it, at least he tried hard to see it. When it came
to a showdown, he hadn't a single argument in favor of his way of life that
would hold water. He had been trying to live and think in a way that he
hoped would end by making a poet of him, but it hadn't worked. That was the
long and short of it. So he might have just gone on to some unimaginably
sordid end if Miriam, after four years: four years? yes, good God, four years
and one month and eleven days, had not written home for money, packed up
what was left of her belongings, called him a few farewell names, and left.
She had been shabby and thin and wild-looking for so long he could not remember ever having seen her any other way, yet all at once her profile in the
doorway was unrecognizable to him.

So she went, and she did him a great favor without knowing it. He had
fallen into the cowardly habit of thinking their marriage was permanent, no
matter how evil it might be, that they loved each other, and so it did not
matter what cruelties they committed against each other, and he had developed
a real deafness to her words. He was unable, towards the end, either to see her
or hear her. He realized this afterward, when remembered phrases and expressions of her eyes and mouth began to eat into his marrow. He was grateful
to her. If she had not gone, he might have loitered on, wasting his time trying
to write poetry, hanging around dirty picturesque little cafés with a fresh set
of clever talkative poverty-stricken young Mexicans who were painting or
writing or talking about getting ready to paint or write. His faith had renewed itself; these fellows were pure artists—they would never sell out.

They were not bums, either. They worked all the time at something to do with Art. "Sacred Art," he said, "our glasses are empty again."

But try telling anything of the kind to Miriam. Somehow he had never got to that tree he meant to lie down under. If he had, somebody would certainly have come around and collected rent for it, anyhow. He had spent a good deal of time lying under tables at Dinty Moore's or the Black Cat with a gang of Americans like himself who were living a free life and studying the native customs. He was rehearsing, he explained to Miriam, hoping for once she would take a joke, for lying under a tree later on. It didn't go over. She would have died with her boots on before she would have cracked a smile at that. So then. . . . He had gone in for a career in the hugest sort of way. It had been easy. He hardly could say now just what his first steps were, but it had been easy. Except for Miriam, he would have been a lousy failure, like those bums at Dinty Moore's, still rolling under the tables, studying the native customs. He had gone in for a career in journalism and he had made a good thing of it. He was a recognized authority on revolutions in twenty-odd Latin-American countries, and his sympathies happened to fall in exactly right with the high-priced magazines of a liberal humanitarian slant which paid him well for telling the world about the oppressed peoples. He could really write, too; if he did say so, he had a prose style of his own. He had made the kind of success you can clip out of newspapers and paste in a book, you can count it and put it in the bank, you can eat and drink and wear it, and you can see it in other people's eyes at tea and dinner parties. Fine, and now what? On the strength of all this he had got married again. Twice, in fact, and divorced twice. That made three times, didn't it? That was plenty. He had spent a good deal of time and energy doing all sorts of things he didn't care for in the least to prove to his first wife, who had been a twenty-three-year-old schoolteacher in Minneapolis, Minnesota, that he was not just merely a bum, fit for nothing but lying under a tree—if he had ever been able to locate that ideal tree he had in his mind's eye—writing poetry and enjoying his life.

Now he had done it. He smoothed out the letter he had been turning in his hands and stroked it as if it were a cat. He said, "I've been working up to the climax all this time. You know, good old surprise technique. Now then, get ready."

Miriam had written to him, after these five years, asking him to take her back. And would you believe it, he was going to break down and do that very thing. Her father was dead, she was terribly lonely, she had had time to think everything over, she believed herself to blame for a great many things, she loved him truly and she always had, truly; she regretted, oh, everything, and hoped it was not too late for them to make a happy life together once more. . . . She had read everything she could find of his in print, and she loved all of it. He had that very morning sent by cable the money for her to travel on, and he was going to take her back. She was going to live again in a Mexican house without any conveniences and she was not going to have a modern flat

She was going to take whatever he chose to hand her, and like it. And he wasn't going to marry her again, either. Not he. If she wanted to live with him on these terms, well and good. If not, she could just go back once more to that school of hers in Minneapolis. If she stayed, she would walk a chalk line, all right, one she hadn't drawn for herself. He picked up a cheese knife and drew a long sharp line in the checkered tablecloth. She would, believe him, walk *that*.

The hands of the clock pointed half past two. The journalist swallowed the last of his drink and went on drawing more cross-patches on the table-cloth with a relaxed hand. His guest wished to say, "Don't forget to invite me to your wedding," but thought better of it. The journalist raised his twitching lids and swung his half-focused eyes upon the shadow opposite and said, "I suppose you think I don't know——"

His guest moved to the chair edge and watched the orchestra folding up for the night. The café was almost empty. The journalist paused, not for an answer, but to give weight to the important statement he was about to make.

"I don't know what's happening, this time," he said, "don't deceive yourself. This time, I know." He seemed to be admonishing himself before a mirror.

JAMES THURBER

The Secret Life of Walter Mitty[1]

"We're going through!" The Commander's voice was like thin ice breaking. He wore his full-dress uniform, with the heavily braided white cap pulled down rakishly over one cold gray eye. "We can't make it, sir. It's spoiling for a hurricane, if you ask me." "I'm not asking you, Lieutenant Berg," said the Commander. "Throw on the power lights! Rev her up to 8,500! We're going through!" The pounding of the cylinders increased; ta-pocketa-pocketa-pocketa-*pocketa-pocketa*. The Commander stared at the ice forming on the pilot window. He walked over and twisted a row of complicated dials. "Switch on No. 8 auxiliary!" he shouted. "Switch on No. 8 auxiliary!" repeated Lieutenant Berg. "Full strength in No. 3 turret!" shouted the Commander. "Full strength in No. 3 turret!" The crew, bending to their various tasks in the huge, hurtling eight-engined Navy hydroplane, looked at each other and grinned. "The Old Man'll get us through," they said to one another. "The Old Man ain't afraid of Hell!" . . .

"Not so fast! You're driving too fast!" said Mrs. Mitty. "What are you driving so fast for?"

"Hmm?" said Walter Mitty. He looked at his wife, in the seat beside him,

[1] Reprinted by permission of the author. Copyright, 1939, by James Thurber. Originally published in The New Yorker.

with shocked astonishment. She seemed grossly unfamiliar, like a strange woman who had yelled at him in a crowd. "You were up to fifty-five," she said. "You know I don't like to go more than forty. You were up to fifty-five." Walter Mitty drove on toward Waterbury in silence, the roaring of the SN-202 through the worst storm in twenty years of Navy flying fading in the remote, intimate airways of his mind. "You're tensed up again," said Mrs. Mitty. "It's one of your days. I wish you'd let Dr. Renshaw look you over."

Walter Mitty stopped the car in front of the building where his wife went to have her hair done. "Remember to get those overshoes while I'm having my hair done," she said. "I don't need overshoes," said Mitty. She put her mirror back into her bag. "We've been all through that," she said, getting out of the car. "You're not a young man any longer." He raced the engine a little. "Why don't you wear your gloves? Have you lost your gloves?" Walter Mitty reached in a pocket and brought out the gloves. He put them on, but after she had turned and gone into the building and he had driven on to a red light, he took them off again. "Pick it up, brother!" snapped a cop as the light changed, and Mitty hastily pulled on his gloves and lurched ahead. He drove around the streets aimlessly for a time, and then he drove past the hospital on his way to the parking lot.

. . . . "It's the millionaire banker, Wellington McMillan," said the pretty nurse. "Yes?" said Walter Mitty, removing his gloves slowly. "Who has the case?" "Dr. Renshaw and Dr. Benbow, but there are two specialists here, Dr. Remington from New York and Dr. Pritchard-Mitford from London. He flew over." A door opened down a long, cool corridor and Dr. Renshaw came out. He looked distraught and haggard. "Hello, Mitty," he said. "We're having the devil's own time with McMillan, the millionaire banker and close personal friend of Roosevelt. Obstreosis of the ductal tract. Tertiary. Wish you'd take a look at him." "Glad to," said Mitty.

In the operating room there were whispered introductions: "Dr. Remington, Dr. Mitty. Dr. Pritchard-Mitford, Dr. Mitty." "I've read your book on strepto-thricosis," said Pritchard-Mitford, shaking hands. "A brilliant performance, sir." "Thank you," said Walter Mitty. "Didn't know you were in the States, Mitty," grumbled Remington. "Coals to Newcastle, bringing Mitford and me up here for a tertiary." "You are very kind," said Mitty. A huge, complicated machine, connected to the operating table, with many tubes and wires, began at this moment to go pocketa-pocketa-pocketa. "The new anaesthetizer is giving away!" shouted an interne. "There is no one in the East who knows how to fix it!" "Quiet, man!" said Mitty, in a low, cool voice. He sprang to the machine, which was now going pocketa-pocketa-queep-pocketa-queep. He began fingering delicately a row of glistening dials. "Give me a fountain pen!" he snapped. Someone handed him a fountain pen. He pulled a faulty piston out of the machine and inserted the pen in its place. "That will hold for ten minutes," he said. "Get on with the operation." A nurse hurried over and whispered to Renshaw, and Mitty saw the man turn pale. "Coreopsis has set in," said Renshaw nervously. "If you would take over, Mitty?" Mitty looked at him and at the craven figure of Benbow, who drank, and at the grave, uncertain faces of the two great specialists. "If you wish," he said. They slipped a white gown on him; he adjusted a mask and drew on thin gloves; nurses handed him shining . . . .

"Back it up, Mac! Look out for that Buick!" Walter Mitty jammed on the brakes. "Wrong lane, Mac," said the parking-lot attendant, looking at Mitty closely. "Gee. Yeh," muttered Mitty. He began cautiously to back out of the lane marked "Exit Only." "Leave her sit there," said the attendant. "I'll put her away." Mitty got out of the car. "Hey, better leave the key." "Oh," said Mitty, handing the man the ignition key. The attendant vaulted into the car, backed it up with insolent skill, and put it where it belonged.

They're so damn cocky, thought Walter Mitty, walking along Main Street; they think they know everything. Once he had tried to take his chains off, outside New Milford, and he had got them wound around the axles. A man had had to come out in a wrecking car and unwind them, a young, grinning garageman. Since then Mrs. Mitty always made him drive to a garage to have the chains taken off. The next time, he thought, I'll wear my right arm in a sling; they won't grin at me then. I'll have my right arm in a sling and they'll see I couldn't possibly take the chains off myself. He kicked at the slush on the sidewalk. "Overshoes," he said to himself, and he began looking for a shoe store.

When he came out into the street again, with the overshoes in a box under his arm, Walter Mitty began to wonder what the other thing was his wife had told him to get. She had told him twice before they set out from their house for Waterbury. In a way he hated these weekly trips to town—he was always getting something wrong. Kleenex, he thought, Squibb's, razor blades? No. Toothpaste, toothbrush, bicarbonate, carborundum, initiative and referendum? He gave up. But she would remember it. "Where's that what's-its-name?" she would ask. "Don't tell me you forgot the what's-its-name." A newsboy went by shouting something about the Waterbury trial.

. . . "Perhaps this will refresh your memory." The District Attorney suddenly thrust a heavy automatic at the quiet figure on the witness stand. "Have you ever seen this before?" Walter Mitty took the gun and examined it expertly. "This is my Webley-Vickers 50.80," he said calmly. An excited buzz ran around the courtroom. The Judge rapped for order. "You are a crack shot with any sort of firearms, I believe?" said the District Attorney, insinuatingly. "Objection!" shouted Mitty's attorney. "We have shown that the defendant could not have fired the shot. We have shown that he wore his right arm in a sling on the night of the fourteenth of July." Walter Mitty raised his hand briefly and the bickering attorneys were stilled. "With any known make of gun," he said evenly, "I could have killed Gregory Fitzhurst at three hundred feet *with my left hand*." Pandemonium broke loose in the courtroom. A woman's scream rose above the bedlam and suddenly a lovely, dark-haired girl was in Walter Mitty's arms. The District Attorney struck at her savagely. Without rising from his chair, Mitty let the man have it on the point of the chin. "You miserable cur!"

"Puppy biscuit," said Walter Mitty. He stopped walking and the buildings of Waterbury rose up out of the misty courtroom and surrounded him again. A woman who was passing laughed. "He said 'Puppy biscuit,'" she said to her companion. "That man said 'Puppy biscuit' to himself." Walter Mitty hurried on. He went into an A. & P., not the first one he came to but a smaller one farther up the street. "I want some biscuit for small, young dogs," he said to the clerk. "Any special brand, sir?" The greatest pistol shot in the world thought a moment. "It says 'Puppies Bark for It' on the box," said Walter Mitty.

His wife would be through at the hairdresser's in fifteen minutes, Mitty saw in looking at his watch, unless they had trouble drying it; sometimes they had trouble drying it. She didn't like to get to the hotel first; she would want him to be there waiting for her as usual. He found a big leather chair in the lobby, facing a window, and he put the overshoes and the puppy biscuit on the floor beside it. He picked up an old copy of *Liberty* and sank down into the chair. "Can Germany Conquer the World Through the Air?" Walter Mitty looked at the pictures of bombing planes and of ruined streets.

. . . "The cannonading has got the wind up in young Raleigh, sir," said the sergeant. Captain Mitty looked up at him through tousled hair. "Get him to bed," he said wearily, "with the others. I'll fly alone." "But you can't, sir," said the sergeant anxiously. "It takes two men to handle that bomber and the Archies are pounding hell out of the air. Von Richtman's circus is between here and Saulier." "Somebody's got to get the ammunition dump," said Mitty. "I'm going over. Spot of brandy?" He poured a drink for the sergeant and one for himself. War thundered and whined around the dugout and battered at the door. There was a rending of wood, and splinters flew through the room. "A bit of a near thing," said Captain Mitty carelessly. "The box barrage is closing in," said the sergeant. "We only live once, Sergeant," said Mitty, with his faint, fleeting smile. "Or do we?" He poured another brandy and tossed it off. "I never see a man could hold his brandy like you, sir," said the sergeant. "Begging your pardon, sir." Captain Mitty stood up and strapped on his huge Webley-Vickers automatic. "It's forty kilometers through hell, sir," said the sergeant. Mitty finished one last brandy. "After all," he said softly, "what isn't?" The pounding of the cannon increased; there was the rat-tat-tatting of machine guns, and from somewhere came the menacing pocketa-pocketa-pocketa of the new flame-throwers. Walter Mitty walked to the door of the dugout humming, "Auprès de Ma Blonde." He turned and waved to the sergeant. "Cheerio!" he said. . . . .

Something struck his shoulder. "I've been looking all over this hotel for you," said Mrs. Mitty. "Why do you have to hide in this old chair? How did you expect me to find you?" "Things close in," said Walter Mitty vaguely. "What?" Mrs. Mitty said. "Did you get the what's-its-name? The puppy biscuit? What's in that box?" "Overshoes," said Mitty. "Couldn't you have put them on in the store?" "I was thinking," said Walter Mitty. "Does it ever occur to you that I am sometimes thinking?" She looked at him. "I'm going to take your temperature when I get you home," she said.

They went out through the revolving doors that made a faintly derisive whistling sound when you pushed them. It was two blocks to the parking lot. At the drugstore on the corner she said, "Wait here for me. I forgot something. I won't be a minute." She was more than a minute. Walter Mitty lighted a cigarette. It began to rain, rain with sleet in it. He stood up against the wall of the drugstore, smoking. . . . He put his shoulders back and his heels together. "To hell with the handkerchief," said Walter Mitty scornfully. He took one last drag on his cigarette and snapped it away. Then, with that faint, fleeting smile playing about his lips, he faced the firing squad; erect and motionless, proud and disdainful. Walter Mitty the Undefeated, inscrutable to the last.

F. SCOTT FITZGERALD

Babylon Revisited [1]

I

"And where's Mr. Campbell?" Charlie asked.

"Gone to Switzerland. Mr. Campbell's a pretty sick man, Mr. Wales."

"I'm sorry to hear that. And George Hardt?" Charlie inquired.

"Back in America, gone to work."

"And where is the Snow Bird?"

"He was in here last week. Anyway, his friend, Mr. Schaeffer, is in Paris."

Two familiar names from the long list of a year and a half ago. Charlie scribbled an address in his note book and tore out the page.

"If you see Mr. Schaeffer, give him this," he said. "It's my brother-in-law's address. I haven't settled on a hotel yet."

He was not really disappointed to find Paris was so empty. But the stillness in the Ritz bar was strange and portentous. It was not an American bar any more—he felt polite in it, and not as if he owned it. It had gone back into France. He felt the stillness from the moment he got out of the taxi and saw the doorman, usually in a frenzy of activity at this hour, gossiping with a *chasseur* by the servants' entrance.

Passing through the corridor, he heard only a single, bored voice in the once-

[1] "Babylon Revisited" (Copyright 1931 The Curtis Publishing Company; renewal copyright © 1959 Frances Scott Fitzgerald Lanahan) is reprinted with the permission of Charles Scribner's Sons from *Taps at Reveille* by F. Scott Fitzgerald.

clamorous women's room. When he turned into the bar he travelled the twenty feet of green carpet with his eyes fixed straight ahead by old habit; and then, with his foot firmly on the rail, he turned and surveyed the room, encountering only a single pair of eyes that fluttered up from a newspaper in the corner. Charlie asked for the head barman, Paul, who in the latter days of the bull market had come to work in his own custom-built car—disembarking, however, with due nicety at the nearest corner. But Paul was at his country house today and Alix giving him information.

"No, no more," Charlie said, "I'm going slow these days."

Alix congratulated him: "You were going pretty strong a couple of years ago."

"I'll stick to it all right," Charlie assured him. "I've stuck to it for over a year and a half now."

"How do you find conditions in America?"

"I haven't been to America for months. I'm in business in Prague, representing a couple of concerns there. They don't know about me down there."

Alix smiled.

"Remember the night of George Hardt's bachelor dinner here?" said Charlie. "By the way, what's become of Claude Fessenden?"

Alix lowered his voice confidentially: "He's in Paris, but he doesn't come here any more. Paul doesn't allow it. He ran up a bill of thirty thousand francs, charging all his drinks and his lunches, and usually his dinner, for more than a year. And when Paul finally told him he had to pay, he gave him a bad check."

Alix shook his head sadly.

"I don't understand it, such a dandy fellow. Now he's all bloated up—" He made a plump apple of his hands.

Charlie watched a group of strident queens installing themselves in a corner.

"Nothing affects them," he thought. "Stocks rise and fall, people loaf or work, but they go on forever." The place oppressed him. He called for the dice and shook with Alix for the drink.

"Here for long, Mr. Wales?"

"I'm here for four or five days to see my little girl."

"Oh-h! You have a little girl?"

Outside, the fire-red, gas-blue, ghost-green signs shone smokily through the tranquil rain. It was late afternoon and the streets were in movement; the *bistros* gleamed. At the corner of the Boulevard des Capucines he took a taxi. The Place de la Concorde moved by in pink majesty; they crossed the logical Seine, and Charlie felt the sudden provincial quality of the Left Bank.

Charlie directed his taxi to the Avenue de l'Opera, which was out of his way. But he wanted to see the blue hour spread over the magnificent façade, and imagine that the cab horns, playing endlessly the first few bars of *Le Plus que Lent*, were the trumpets of the Second Empire. They were closing the iron grill in front of Brentano's Book-store, and people were already at dinner behind the trim little bourgeois hedge of Duval's. He had never eaten at a really cheap restaurant in Paris. Five-course dinner, four francs fifty, eighteen cents, wine included. For some odd reason he wished that he had.

As they rolled on to the Left Bank and he felt its sudden provincialism, he thought, "I spoiled this city for myself. I didn't realize it, but the days came along one after another, and then two years were gone, and everything was gone, and I was gone."

He was thirty-five, and good to look at. The Irish mobility of his face was sobered by a deep wrinkle between his eyes. As he rang his brother-in-law's bell in the Rue Palatine, the wrinkle deepened till it pulled down his brows; he felt a cramping sensation in his belly. From behind the maid who opened the door darted a lovely little girl of nine who shrieked "Daddy!" and flew up, struggling like a fish, into his arms. She pulled his head around by one ear and set her cheek against his.

"My old pie," he said.

"Oh, daddy, daddy, daddy, daddy, dads, dads, dads!"

She drew him into the salon, where the family waited, a boy and girl his daughter's age, his sister-in-law and her husband. He greeted Marion with his voice pitched carefully to avoid either feigned enthusiasm or dislike, but her response was more frankly tepid, though she minimized her expression of unalterable distrust by directing her regard toward his child. The two men clasped hands in a friendly way and Lincoln Peters rested his for a moment on Charlie's shoulder.

The room was warm and comfortably American. The three children moved intimately about, playing through the yellow oblongs that led to other rooms; the cheer of six o'clock spoke in the eager smacks of the fire and the sounds of French activity in the kitchen. But Charlie did not relax; his heart sat up rigidly in his body and he drew confidence from his daughter, who from time to time came close to him, holding in her arms the doll he had brought.

"Really extremely well," he declared in answer to Lincoln's question. "There's a lot of business there that isn't moving at all, but we're doing even better than ever. In fact, damn well. I'm bringing my sister over from America next month to keep house for me. My income last year was bigger than it was when I had money. You see, the Czechs——"

His boasting was for a specific purpose; but after a moment, seeing a faint restiveness in Lincoln's eye, he changed the subject:

"Those are fine children of yours, well brought up, good manners."

"We think Honoria's a great little girl too."

Marion Peters came back from the kitchen. She was a tall woman with worried eyes, who had once possessed a fresh American loveliness. Charlie had never been sensitive to it and was always surprised when people spoke of how pretty she had been. From the first there had been an instinctive antipathy between them.

"Well, how do you find Honoria?" she asked.

"Wonderful. I was astonished how much she's grown in ten months. All the children are looking well."

"We haven't had a doctor for a year. How do you like being back in Paris?"

"It seems very funny to see so few Americans around."

"I'm delighted," Marion said vehemently. "Now at least you can go into a store without their assuming you're a millionaire. We've suffered like everybody, but on the whole it's a good deal pleasanter."

"But it was nice while it lasted," Charlie said. "We were a sort of royalty, almost infallible, with a sort of magic around us. In the bar this afternoon"—he stumbled, seeing his mistake—"there wasn't a man I knew."

She looked at him keenly. "I should think you'd have had enough of bars."

"I only stayed a minute. I take one drink every afternoon, and no more."

"Don't you want a cocktail before dinner?" Lincoln asked.

"I take only one drink every afternoon, and I've had that."

"I hope you keep to it," said Marion.

Her dislike was evident in the coldness with which she spoke, but Charlie only smiled; he had larger plans. Her very aggressiveness gave him an advantage, and he knew enough to wait. He wanted them to initiate the discussion of what they knew had brought him to Paris.

At dinner he couldn't decide whether Honoria was most like him or her mother. Fortunate if she didn't combine the traits of both that had brought them to disaster. A great wave of protectiveness went over him. He thought he knew what to do for her. He believed in character; he wanted to jump back a whole generation and trust in character again as the eternally valuable element. Everything wore out.

He left soon after dinner, but not to go home. He was curious to see Paris by night with clearer and more judicious eyes than those of other days. He bought a *strapontin* for the Casino and watched Josephine Baker go through her chocolate arabesques.

After an hour he left and strolled toward Montmartre, up the Rue Pigalle into the Place Blanche. The rain had stopped and there were a few people in evening clothes disembarking from taxis in front of cabarets, and *cocottes* prowling singly or in pairs, and many Negroes. He passed a lighted door from which issued music, and stopped with the sense of familiarity; it was Bricktop's, where he had parted with so many hours and so much money. A few doors farther on he found another ancient rendezvous and incautiously put his head inside. Immediately an eager orchestra burst into sound, a pair of professional dancers leaped to their feet and a maître d'hôtel swooped toward him, crying, "Crowd just arriving, sir!" But he withdrew quickly.

"You have to be damn drunk," he thought.

Zelli's was closed, the bleak and sinister cheap hotels surrounding it were dark; up in the Rue Blanche there was more light and a local, colloquial French crowd. The Poet's Cave had disappeared, but the two great mouths of the Café of Heaven and the Café of Hell still yawned—even devoured, as he watched, the meagre contents of a tourist bus—a German, a Japanese, and an American couple who glanced at him with frightened eyes.

So much for the effort and ingenuity of Montmartre. All the catering to vice and waste was on an utterly childish scale, and he suddenly realized the meaning of the word "dissipate"—to dissipate into thin air; to make nothing out of something. In the little hours of the night every move from place to place was an enormous human jump, an increase of paying for the privilege of slower and slower motion.

He remembered thousand-franc notes given to an orchestra for playing a single number, hundred-franc notes tossed to a doorman for calling a cab.

But it hadn't been given for nothing.

It had been given, even the most wildly squandered sum, as an offering to destiny that he might not remember the things most worth remembering, the things that now he would always remember—his child taken from his control, his wife escaped to a grave in Vermont.

In the glare of a *brasserie* a woman spoke to him. He bought her some eggs and coffee, and then, eluding her encouraging stare, gave her a twenty-franc note and took a taxi to his hotel.

II

He woke upon a fine fall day—football weather. The depression of yesterday was gone and he liked the people on the streets. At noon he sat opposite Honoria at Le Grand Vatel, the only restaurant he could think of not reminiscent of champagne dinners and long luncheons that began at two and ended in a blurred and vague twilight.

"Now, how about vegetables? Oughtn't you to have some vegetables?"

"Well, yes."

"Here's *épinards* and *chou-fleur* and carrots and *haricots*."

"I'd like *chou-fleur*."

"Wouldn't you like to have two vegetables?"

"I usually only have one at lunch."

The waiter was pretending to be inordinately fond of children. *"Qu'elle est mignonne la petite? Elle parle exactement comme une française."*

"How about dessert? Shall we wait and see?"

The waiter disappeared. Honoria looked at her father expectantly.

"What are we going to do?"

"First, we're going to that toy store in the Rue Saint-Honoré and buy you anything you like. And then we're going to the vaudeville at the Empire."

She hesitated. "I like it about the vaudeville, but not the toy store."

"Why not?"

"Well, you brought me this doll." She had it with her. "And I've got lots of things. And we're not rich any more, are we?"

"We never were. But today you are to have anything you want."

"All right," she agreed resignedly.

When there had been her mother and a French nurse he had been inclined to be strict; now he extended himself, reached out for a new tolerance; he must be both parents to her and not shut any of her out of communication.

"I want to get to know you," he said gravely. "First let me introduce myself. My name is Charles J. Wales, of Prague."

"Oh, daddy!" her voice cracked with laughter.

"And who are you, please?" he persisted, and she accepted a rôle immediately: "Honoria Wales, Rue Palatine, Paris."

"Married or single?"

"No, not married. Single."

He indicated the doll. "But I see you have a child, madame."

Unwilling to disinherit it, she took it to her heart and thought quickly: "Yes, I've been married, but I'm not married now. My husband is dead."

He went on quickly, "And the child's name?"

"Simone. That's after my best friend at school."

"I'm very pleased that you're doing so well at school."

"I'm third this month," she boasted. "Elsie"—that was her cousin—"is only about eighteenth, and Richard is about at the bottom."

"You like Richard and Elsie, don't you?"

"Oh, yes. I like Richard quite well and I like her all right."

Cautiously and casually he asked: "And Aunt Marion and Uncle Lincoln—which do you like best?"

"Oh, Uncle Lincoln, I guess."

He was increasingly aware of her presence. As they came in, a murmur of ". . . adorable" followed them, and now the people at the next table bent all their silences upon her, staring as if she were something no more conscious than a flower.

"Why don't I live with you?" she asked suddenly. "Because mamma's dead?"

"You must stay here and learn more French. It would have been hard for daddy to take care of you so well."

"I don't really need much taking care of any more. I do everything for myself."

Going out of the restaurant, a man and a woman unexpectedly hailed him.

"Well, the old Wales!"

"Hello there, Lorraine. . . . Dunc."

Sudden ghosts out of the past: Duncan Schaeffer, a friend from college. Lorraine Quarrles, a lovely, pale blonde of thirty; one of a crowd who had helped them make months into days in the lavish times of three years ago.

"My husband couldn't come this year," she said, in answer to his question. "We're poor as hell. So he gave me two hundred a month and told me I could do my worst on that. . . . This your little girl?"

"What about coming back and sitting down?" Duncan asked.

"Can't do it." He was glad for an excuse. As always, he felt Lorraine's passionate, provocative attraction, but his own rhythm was different now.

"Well, how about dinner?" she asked.

"I'm not free. Give me your address and let me call you."

"Charlie, I believe you're sober," she said judicially. "I honestly believe he's sober, Dunc. Pinch him and see if he's sober."

Charlie indicated Honoria with his head. They both laughed.

"What's your address?" said Duncan sceptically.

He hesitated, unwilling to give the name of his hotel.

"I'm not settled yet. I'd better call you. We're going to see the vaudeville at the Empire."

"There! That's what I want to do," Lorraine said. "I want to see some clowns and acrobats and jugglers. That's just what we'll do, Dunc."

"We've got to do an errand first," said Charlie. "Perhaps we'll see you there."

"All right, you snob. . . . Good-by, beautiful little girl."

"Good-by."

Honoria bobbed politely.

Somehow, an unwelcome encounter. They liked him because he was functioning, because he was serious; they wanted to see him, because he was stronger than they were now, because they wanted to draw a certain sustenance from his strength.

At the Empire, Honoria proudly refused to sit upon her father's folded coat. She was already an individual with a code of her own, and Charlie was more and more absorbed by the desire of putting a little of himself into her before she crystallized utterly. It was hopeless to try to know her in so short a time.

Between the acts they came upon Duncan and Lorraine in the lobby where the band was playing.

"Have a drink?"

"All right, but not up at the bar. We'll take a table."

"The perfect father."

Listening abstractedly to Lorraine, Charlie watched Honoria's eyes leave their table, and he followed them wistfully about the room, wondering what they saw. He met her glance and she smiled.

"I liked that lemonade," she said.

What had she said? What had he expected? Going home in a taxi afterward, he pulled her over until her head rested against his chest.

"Darling, do you ever think about your mother?"

"Yes, sometimes," she answered vaguely.

"I don't want you to forget her. Have you got picture of her?"

"Yes, I think so. Anyhow, Aunt Marion has. Why don't you want me to forget her?"

"She loved you very much."

"I loved her too."

They were silent for a moment.

"Daddy, I want to come and live with you," she said suddenly. His heart leaped; he had wanted it to come like this.

"Aren't you perfectly happy?"

"Yes, but I love you better than anybody. And you love me better than anybody, don't you, now that mummy's dead?"

"Of course I do. But you won't always like me best, honey. You'll grow up and meet somebody your own age and go marry him and forget you ever had a daddy."

"Yes, that's true," she agreed tranquilly.

He didn't go in. He was coming back at nine o'clock and he wanted to keep himself fresh and new for the thing he must say then.

"When you're safe inside, just show yourself in that window."

"All right. Good-bye, dads, dads, dads, dads."

He waited in the dark street until she appeared, all warm and glowing, in the window above and kissed her fingers out into the night.

III

They were waiting. Marion sat behind the coffee service in a dignified black dinner dress that just faintly suggested mourning. Lincoln was walking up and down with the animation of one who had already been talking. They were as anxious as he was to get into the question. He opened it almost immediately:

"I suppose you know what I want to see you about—why I really came to Paris."

Marion played with the black stars on her necklace and frowned.

"I'm awfully anxious to have a home," he continued. "And I'm awfully anxious to have Honoria in it. I appreciate your taking in Honoria for her mother's sake, but things have changed now"—he hesitated and then continued more forcibly—"changed radically with me, and I want to ask you to reconsider the matter. It would be silly for me to deny that about three years ago I was acting badly——"

Marion looked up at him with hard eyes.

"—but all that's over. As I told you, I haven't had more than a drink a day for over a year, and I take that drink deliberately, so that the idea of alcohol won't get too big in my imagination. You see the idea?"

"No," said Marion succinctly.

"It's a sort of stunt I set myself. It keeps the matter in proportion."

"I get you," said Lincoln. "You don't want to admit it's got any attraction for you."

"Something like that. Sometimes I forget and don't take it. But I try to take it. Anyhow, I couldn't afford to drink in my position. The people I represent are more than satisfied with what I've done, and I'm bringing my sister over from Burlington to keep house for me, and I want awfully to have Honoria too. You know that even when her mother and I weren't getting along well we never let anything that happened touch Honoria. I know she's fond of me and I know I'm able to take care of her and—well, there you are. How do you feel about it?"

He knew that now he would have to take a beating. It would last an hour or two hours, and it would be difficult, but if he modulated his inevitable resentment to the chastened attitude of the reformed sinner, he might win his point in the end.

Keep your temper, he told himself. You don't want to be justified. You want Honoria.

Lincoln spoke first: "We've been talking it over ever since we got your letter last month. We're happy to have Honoria here. She's a dear little thing, and we're glad to be able to help her, but of course that isn't the question——"

Marion interrupted suddenly. "How long are you going to stay sober, Charlie?" she asked.

"Permanently, I hope."

"How can anybody count on that?"

"You know I never did drink heavily until I gave up business and came over here with nothing to do. Then Helen and I began to run around with——"

"Please leave Helen out of it. I can't bear to hear you talk about her like that."

He stared at her grimly; he had never been certain how fond of each other the sisters were in life.

"My drinking only lasted about a year and a half—from the time we came over until I—collapsed."

"It was time enough."

"It was time enough," he agreed.

"My duty is entirely to Helen," she said. "I try to think what she would have wanted me to do. Frankly, from the night you did that terrible thing you haven't really existed for me. I can't help that. She was my sister."

"Yes."

"When she was dying, she asked me to look out for Honoria. If you hadn't been in a sanitarium then, it might have helped matters."

He had no answer.

"I'll never in my life be able to forget the morning when Helen knocked at my door, soaked to the skin and shivering, and said you'd locked her out."

Charlie gripped the sides of the chair. This was more difficult than he expected; he wanted to launch out into a long expostulation and explanation, but he only said: "The night I locked her out——" and she interrupted, "I don't feel up to going over that again."

After a moment's silence Lincoln said: "We're getting off the subject. You want Marion to set aside her legal guardianship and give you Honoria. I think the main point for her is whether she has confidence in you or not."

"I don't blame Marion," Charlie said slowly, "but I think she can have entire confidence in me. I had a good record up to three years ago. Of course, it's
within human possibilities I might go wrong any time. But if we wait much
longer I'll lose Honoria's childhood and my chance for a home." He shook
his head, "I'll simply lose her, don't you see?"

"Yes, I see," said Lincoln.

"Why didn't you think of all this before?" Marion asked.

"I suppose I did, from time to time, but Helen and I were getting along
badly. When I consented to the guardianship, I was flat on my back in a sanitarium and the market had cleaned me out. I knew I'd acted badly, and I
thought if it would bring any peace to Helen, I'd agree to anything. But now
it's different. I'm functioning, I'm behaving damn well, so far as——"

"Please don't swear at me," Marion said.

He looked at her, startled. With each remark the force of her dislike became more and more apparent. She had built up all her fear of life into one
wall and faced it toward him. This trivial reproof was possibly the result of
some trouble with the cook several hours before. Charlie became increasingly
alarmed at leaving Honoria in this atmosphere of hostility against himself;
sooner or later it would come out, in a word here, a shake of the head there,
and some of that distrust would be irrevocably implanted in Honoria. But he
pulled his temper down out of his face and shut it up inside him; he had a
point, for Lincoln realized the absurdity of Marion's remark and asked her
lightly since when she had objected to the word "damn."

"Another thing," Charlie said: "I'm able to give her certain advantages now.
I'm going to take a French governess to Prague with me. I've got a lease on a
new apartment——"

He stopped, realizing that he was blundering. They couldn't be expected to
accept with equanimity the fact that his income was again twice as large as
their own.

"I suppose you can give her more luxuries than we can," said Marion.
"When you were throwing away money we were living along watching every
ten francs. . . . I suppose you'll start doing it again."

"Oh, no," he said. "I've learned. I worked hard for ten years, you know—
until I got lucky in the market, like so many people. Terribly lucky. It didn't
seem any use working any more, so I quit. It won't happen again."

There was a long silence. All of them felt their nerves straining, and for the
first time in a year Charlie wanted a drink. He was sure now that Lincoln
Peters wanted him to have his child.

Marion shuddered suddenly; part of her saw that Charlie's feet were planted
on the earth now, and her own maternal feeling recognized the naturalness of
his desire; but she had lived for a long time with a prejudice—a prejudice
founded on a curious disbelief in her sister's happiness, and which, in the
shock of one terrible night, had turned to hatred for him. It had all happened
at a point in her life where the discouragement of ill health and adverse cir-

cumstances made it necessary for her to believe in tangible villainy and a tangible villain.

"I can't help what I think!" she cried out suddenly. "How much you were responsible for Helen's death, I don't know. It's something you'll have to square with your own conscience."

An electric current of agony surged through him; for a moment he was almost on his feet, an unuttered sound echoing in his throat. He hung on to himself for a moment, another moment.

"Hold on there," said Lincoln uncomfortably. "I never thought you were responsible for that."

"Helen died of heart trouble," Charlie said dully.

"Yes, heart trouble." Marion spoke as if the phrase had another meaning for her.

Then, in the flatness that followed her outburst, she saw him plainly and she knew he had somehow arrived at control over the situation. Glancing at her husband, she found no help from him, and as abruptly as if it were a matter of no importance, she threw up the sponge.

"Do what you like!" she cried, springing up from her chair. "She's your child. I'm not the person to stand in your way. I think if it were my child I'd rather see her—" She managed to check herself. "You two decide it. I can't stand this. I'm sick. I'm going to bed."

She hurried from the room; after a moment Lincoln said:

"This has been a hard day for her. You know how strongly she feels—" His voice was almost apologetic: "When a woman gets an idea in her head."

"Of course."

"It's going to be all right. I think she sees now that you—can provide for the child, and so we can't very well stand in your way or Honoria's way."

"Thank you, Lincoln."

"I'd better go along and see how she is."

"I'm going."

He was still trembling when he reached the street, but a walk down the Rue Bonaparte to the *quais* set him up, and as he crossed the Seine, fresh and new by the *quai* lamps, he felt exultant. But back in his room he couldn't sleep. The image of Helen haunted him. Helen whom he had loved so until they had senselessly begun to abuse each other's love, tear it into shreds. On that terrible February night that Marion remembered so vividly, a slow quarrel had gone on for hours. There was a scene at the Florida, and then he attempted to take her home, and then she kissed young Webb at a table; after that there was what she had hysterically said. When he arrived home alone he turned the key in the lock in wild anger. How could he know she would arrive an hour later alone, that there would be a snowstorm in which she wandered about in slippers, too confused to find a taxi? Then the aftermath, her escaping pneumonia by a miracle, and all the attendant horror. They were "reconciled," but that was the beginning of the end, and Marion, who had seen with her own eyes and who imagined it to be one of many scenes from her sister's martyrdom, never forgot.

Going over it again brought Helen nearer, and in the white, soft light that steals upon half sleep near morning he found himself talking to her again. She said that he was perfectly right about Honoria and that she wanted Honoria to be with him. She said she was glad he was being good and doing better. She said a lot of other things—very friendly things—but she was in a swing in a white dress, and swinging faster and faster all the time, so that at the end he could not hear clearly all that she said.

IV

He woke up feeling happy. The door of the world was open again. He made plans, vistas, futures for Honoria and himself, but suddenly he grew sad, remembering all the plans he and Helen had made. She had not planned to die. The present was the thing—work to do and someone to love. But not to love too much, for he knew the injury that a father can do to a daughter or a mother to a son by attaching them too closely: afterward, out in the world, the child would seek in the marriage partner the same blind tenderness and, failing probably to find it, turn against love and life.

It was another bright, crisp day. He called Lincoln Peters at the bank where he worked and asked if he could count on taking Honoria when he left for Prague. Lincoln agreed that there was no reason for delay. One thing—the legal guardianship. Marion wanted to retain that a while longer. She was upset by the whole matter, and it would oil things if she felt that the situation was still in her control for another year. Charlie agreed, wanting only the tangible, visible child.

Then the question of a governess. Charlie sat in a gloomy agency and talked to a cross Bernaise and to a buxom Breton peasant, neither of whom he could have endured. There were others whom he would see tomorrow.

He lunched with Lincoln Peters at Griffons, trying to keep down his exultation.

"There's nothing quite like your own child," Lincoln said. "But you understand how Marion feels too."

"She's forgotten how hard I worked for seven years there," Charlie said. "She just remembers one night."

"There's another thing," Lincoln hesitated. "While you and Helen were tearing around Europe throwing money away, we were just getting along. I didn't touch any of the prosperity because I never got ahead enough to carry anything but my insurance. I think Marion felt there was some kind of injustice in it—you not even working toward the end, and getting richer and richer."

"It went just as quick as it came," said Charlie.

"Yes, a lot of it stayed in the hands of *chasseurs* and saxophone players and maîtres d'hôtel—well, the big party's over now. I just said that to explain

Marion's feeling about those crazy years. If you drop in about six o'clock to-night before Marion's too tired, we'll settle the details on the spot."

Back at his hotel, Charlie found a *pneumatique* that had been redirected from the Ritz bar where Charlie had left his address for the purpose of find-ing a certain man.

DEAR CHARLIE: You were so strange when we saw you the other day that I wondered if I did something to offend you. If so, I'm not conscious of it. In fact, I have thought about you too much for the last year, and it's always been in the back of my mind that I might see you if I came over here. We *did* have such good times that crazy spring, like the night you and I stole the butcher's tricycle, and the time we tried to call on the president and you had the old derby rim and the wire cane. Everybody seems so old lately, but I don't feel old a bit. Couldn't we get together some time today for old time's sake? I've got a vile hang-over for the moment, but will be feeling better this afternoon and will look for you about five in the sweat-shop at the Ritz.

Always devotedly,
LORRAINE.

His first feeling was one of awe that he had actually, in his mature years, stolen a tricycle and pedalled Lorraine all over the Étoile between the small hours and dawn. In retrospect it was a nightmare. Locking out Helen didn't fit in with any other act of his life, but the tricycle incident did—it was one of many. How many weeks or months of dissipation to arrive at that condition of utter irresponsibility?

He tried to picture how Lorraine had appeared to him then—very attrac-tive; Helen was unhappy about it, though she said nothing. Yesterday, in the restaurant, Lorraine had seemed trite, blurred, worn away. He emphatically did not want to see her, and he was glad Alix had not given away his hotel ad-dress. It was a relief to think, instead, of Honoria, to think of Sundays spent with her and of saying good morning to her and of knowing she was there in his house at night, drawing her breath in the darkness.

At five he took a taxi and bought presents for all the Peters—a piquant cloth doll, a box of Roman soldiers, flowers for Marion, big linen handker-chiefs for Lincoln.

He saw, when he arrived in the apartment, that Marion had accepted the inevitable. She greeted him now as though he were a recalcitrant member of the family rather than a menacing outsider. Honoria had been told she was going; Charlie was glad to see that her tact made her conceal her excessive happiness. Only on his lap did she whisper her delight and the question "When?" before she slipped away with the other children.

He and Marion were alone for a minute in the room, and on an impulse he spoke out boldly:

"Family quarrels are bitter things. They don't go according to any rules. They're not like aches or wounds; they're more like splits in the skin that won't heal because there's not enough material. I wish you and I could be on better terms."

"Some things are hard to forget," she answered. "It's a question of confidence." There was no answer to this and presently she asked, "When do you propose to take her?"

"As soon as I can get a governess. I hoped the day after tomorrow."

"That's impossible. I've got to get her things in shape. Not before Saturday."

He yielded. Coming back into the room, Lincoln offered him a drink.

"I'll take my daily whisky," he said.

It was warm here, it was a home, people together by a fire. The children felt very safe and important; the mother and father were serious, watchful. They had things to do for the children more important than his visit here. A spoonful of medicine was, after all, more important than the strained relations between Marion and himself. They were not dull people, but they were very much in the grip of life and circumstances. He wondered if he couldn't do something to get Lincoln out of his rut at the bank.

A long peal at the door-bell; the *bonne de toute faire* passed through and went down the corridor. The door opened upon another long ring, and then voices, and the three in the salon looked up expectantly; Richard moved to bring the corridor within his range of vision, and Marion rose. Then the maid came back along the corridor, closely followed by the voices, which developed under the light into Duncan Schaeffer and Lorraine Quarrles.

They were gay, they were hilarious, they were roaring with laughter. For a moment Charlie was astounded; unable to understand how they ferreted out the Peters' address.

"Ah-h-h!" Duncan wagged his finger roguishly at Charlie. "Ah-h-h!"

They both slid down another cascade of laughter. Anxious and at a loss, Charlie shook hands with them quickly and presented them to Lincoln and Marion. Marion nodded, scarcely speaking. She had drawn back a step toward the fire; her little girl stood beside her, and Marion put an arm about her shoulder.

With growing annoyance at the intrusion, Charlie waited for them to explain themselves. After some concentration Duncan said:

"We came to invite you out to dinner. Lorraine and I insist that all this shishi, cagy business 'bout your address got to stop."

Charlie came closer to them, as if to force them backward down the corridor.

"Sorry, but I can't. Tell me where you'll be and I'll phone you in half an hour."

This made no impression. Lorraine sat down suddenly on the side of a chair, and focusing her eyes on Richard, cried, "Oh, what a nice little boy! Come here, little boy." Richard glanced at his mother, but did not move. With a perceptible shrug of her shoulders, Lorraine turned back to Charlie:

"Come and dine. Sure your cousins won' mine. See you so sel'om. Or solemn."

"I can't," said Charlie sharply. "You two have dinner and I'll phone you."

Her voice became suddenly unpleasant. "All right, we'll go. But I remember once when you hammered on my door at four A.M. I was enough of a good sport to give you a drink. Come on, Dunc."

Still in slow motion, with blurred, angry faces, with uncertain feet, they retired along the corridor.

"Good night," Charlie said.

"Good night!" responded Lorraine emphatically.

When he went back into the salon Marion had not moved, only now her son was standing in the circle of her other arm. Lincoln was still swinging Honoria back and forth like a pendulum from side to side.

"What an outrage!" Charlie broke out. "What an absolute outrage!"

Neither of them answered. Charlie dropped into an arm chair, picked up his drink, set it down again and said:

"People I haven't seen for two years having the colossal nerve——"

He broke off. Marion had made the sound "Oh!" in one swift, furious breath, turned her body from him with a jerk and left the room.

Lincoln set down Honoria carefully.

"You children go in and start your soup," he said, and when they obeyed, he said to Charlie:

"Marion's not well and she can't stand shocks. That kind of people make her really physically sick."

"I didn't tell them to come here. They wormed your name out of somebody. They deliberately——"

"Well, it's too bad. It doesn't help matters. Excuse me a minute."

Left alone, Charlie sat tense in his chair. In the next room he could hear the children eating, talking in monosyllables, already oblivious to the scene between their elders. He heard a murmur of conversation from a farther room and then the ticking bell of a telephone receiver picked up, and in a panic he moved to the other side of the room and out of earshot.

In a minute Lincoln came back. "Look here, Charlie. I think we'd better call off dinner for tonight. Marion's in bad shape."

"Is she angry with me?"

"Sort of," he said, almost roughly. "She's not strong and——"

"You mean she's changed her mind about Honoria?"

"She's pretty bitter right now. I don't know. You phone me at the bank tomorrow."

"I wish you'd explain to her I never dreamed these people would come here. I'm just as sore as you are."

"I couldn't explain anything to her now."

Charlie got up. He took his coat and hat and started down the corridor.

Then he opened the door of the dining room and said in a strange voice, "Good night, children."

Honoria rose and ran around the table to hug him.

"Good night, sweetheart," he said vaguely, and then trying to make his voice more tender, trying to conciliate something, "Good night, dear children."

V

Charlie went directly to the Ritz bar with the furious idea of finding Lorraine and Duncan, but they were not there, and he realized that in any case there was nothing he could do. He had not touched his drink at the Peters', and now he ordered a whisky-and-soda. Paul came over to say hello.

"It's a great change," he said sadly. "We do about half the business we did. So many fellows I hear about back in the States lost everything, maybe not in the first crash, but then in the second. Your friend George Hardt lost every cent, I hear. Are you back in the States?"

"No, I'm in business in Prague."

"I heard that you lost a lot in the crash."

"I did," and he added grimly, "but I lost everything I wanted in the boom."

"Selling short."

"Something like that."

Again the memory of those days swept over him like a nightmare—the people they had met travelling; then people who couldn't add a row of figures or speak a coherent sentence. The little man Helen had consented to dance with at the ship's party, who had insulted her ten feet from the table; the women and girls carried screaming with drink or drugs out of public places——

—The men who locked their wives out in the snow, because the snow of twenty-nine wasn't real snow. If you didn't want it to be snow, you just paid some money.

He went to the phone and called the Peters' apartment; Lincoln answered.

"I called up because this thing is on my mind. Has Marion said anything definite?"

"Marion's sick," Lincoln answered shortly. "I know this thing isn't altogether your fault, but I can't have her go to pieces about it. I'm afraid we'll have to let it slide for six months; I can't take the chance of working her up to this state again."

"I see."

"I'm sorry, Charlie."

He went back to his table. His whisky glass was empty, but he shook his head when Alix looked at it questioningly. There wasn't much he could do now except send Honoria some things; he would send her a lot of things tomorrow. He thought rather angrily that this was just money—he had given so many people money. . . .

"No, no more," he said to another waiter. "What do I owe you?"

He would come back some day; they couldn't make him pay forever. But he wanted his child, and nothing was much good now, beside that fact. He wasn't young any more, with a lot of nice thoughts and dreams to have by himself. He was absolutely sure Helen wouldn't have wanted him to be so alone.

WILLIAM FAULKNER

Barn Burning[1]

The store in which the Justice of the Peace's court was sitting smelled of cheese. The boy, crouched on his nail keg at the back of the crowded room, knew he smelled cheese, and more: from where he sat he could see the ranked shelves close-packed with the solid, squat, dynamic shapes of tin cans whose labels his stomach read, not from the lettering which meant nothing to his mind but from the scarlet devils and the silver curve of fish—this, the cheese which he knew he smelled and the hermetic meat which his intestines believed he smelled coming in intermittent gusts momentary and brief between the other constant one, the smell and sense just a little of fear because mostly of despair and grief, the old fierce pull of blood. He could not see the table where the Justice sat and before which his father and his father's enemy (*our enemy* he thought in that despair; *ourn! mine and hisn both! He's my father!*) stood, but he could hear them, the two of them that is, because his father had said no word yet:

"But what proof have you, Mr. Harris?"

"I told you. The hog got into my corn. I caught it up and sent it back to him. He had no fence that would hold it. I told him so, warned him. The next time I put the hog in my pen. When he came to get it I gave him enough wire to patch up his pen. The next time I put the hog up and kept it. I rode down to his house and saw the wire I gave him still rolled on to the spool in his yard. I told him he could have the hog when he paid me a dollar pound fee. That evening a nigger came with the dollar and got the hog. He was a strange nigger. He said, 'He say to tell you wood and hay kin burn.' I said, 'What?' 'That whut he say to tell you,' the nigger said. 'Wood and hay kin burn.' That night my barn burned. I got the stock out but I lost the barn."

"Where is the nigger? Have you got him?"

"He was a strange nigger, I tell you. I don't know what became of him."

"But that's not proof. Don't you see that's not proof?"

"Get that boy up here. He knows." For a moment the boy thought too

[1] Copyright 1939 by William Faulkner. Reprinted from *Collected Stories of William Faulkner* by permission of Random House, Inc.

that the man meant his older brother until Harris said, "Not him. The little one. The boy," and, crouching, small for his age, small and wiry like his father, in patched and faded jeans even too small for him, with straight, un-combed, brown hair and eyes gray and wild as storm scud, he saw the men between himself and the table part and become a lane of grim faces, at the end of which he saw the Justice, a shabby, collarless, graying man in specta-cles, beckoning him. He felt no floor under his bare feet; he seemed to walk beneath the palpable weight of the grim turning faces. His father, stiff in his black Sunday coat donned not for the trial but for the moving, did not even look at him. *He aims for me to lie,* he thought, again with that frantic grief and despair. *And I will have to do hit.*

"What's your name, boy?" the Justice said.

"Colonel Sartoris Snopes," the boy whispered.

"Hey?" the Justice said. "Talk louder. Colonel Sartoris? I reckon anybody named for Colonel Sartoris in this country can't help but tell the truth, can they?" The boy said nothing. *Enemy! Enemy!* he thought; for a moment he could not even see, could not see that the Justice's face was kindly nor dis-cern that his voice was troubled when he spoke to the man named Harris: "Do you want me to question this boy?" But he could hear, and during those subsequent long seconds while there was absolutely no sound in the crowded little room save that of quiet and intent breathing it was as if he had swung outward at the end of a grape vine, over a ravine, and at the top of the swing had been caught in a prolonged instant of mesmerized gravity, weightless in time.

"No!" Harris said violently, explosively. "Damnation! Send him out of here!" Now time, the fluid world, rushed beneath him again, the voices com-ing to him again through the smell of cheese and sealed meat, the fear and despair and the old grief of blood:

"This case is closed. I can't find against you, Snopes, but I can give you advice. Leave this country and don't come back to it."

His father spoke for the first time, his voice cold and harsh, level, without emphasis: "I aim to. I don't figure to stay in a country among people who . . ." he said something unprintable and vile, addressed to no one.

"That'll do," the Justice said. "Take your wagon and get out of this coun-try before dark. Case dismissed."

His father turned, and he followed the stiff black coat, the wiry figure walking a little stiffly from where a Confederate provost's man's musket ball had taken him in the heel on a stolen horse thirty years ago, followed the two backs now, since his older brother had appeared from somewhere in the crowd, no taller than the father but thicker, chewing tobacco steadily, be-tween the two lines of grim-faced men and out of the store and across the worn gallery and down the sagging steps and among the dogs and half-grown boys in the mild May dust, where as he passed a voice hissed:

"Barn burner!"

Again he could not see, whirling; there was a face in a red haze, moon-like, bigger than the full moon, the owner of it half again his size, he leaping in the red haze toward the face, feeling no blow, feeling no shock when his head struck the earth, scrabbling up and leaping again, feeling no blow this time either and tasting no blood, scrabbling up to see the other boy in full flight and himself already leaping into pursuit as his father's hand jerked him back, the harsh, cold voice speaking above him: "Go get in the wagon."

It stood in a grove of locusts and mulberries across the road. His two hulking sisters in their Sunday dresses and his mother and her sister in calico and sunbonnets were already in it, sitting on and among the sorry residue of the dozen and more movings which even the boy could remember—the battered stove, the broken beds and chairs, the clock inlaid with mother-of-pearl, which would not run, stopped at some fourteen minutes past two o'clock of a dead and forgotten day and time, which had been his mother's dowry. She was crying, though when she saw him she drew her sleeve across her face and began to descend from the wagon. "Get back," the father said.

"He's hurt. I got to get some water and wash his . . ."

"Get back in the wagon," his father said. He got in too, over the tail-gate. His father mounted to the seat where the older brother already sat and struck the gaunt mules two savage blows with the peeled willow, but without heat. It was not even sadistic; it was exactly that same quality which in later years would cause his descendants to over-run the engine before putting a motor car into motion, striking and reining back in the same movement. The wagon went on, the store with its quiet crowd of grimly watching men dropped behind; a curve in the road hid it. *Forever* he thought. *Maybe he's done satisfied now, now that he has* . . . stopping himself, not to say it aloud even to himself. His mother's hand touched his shoulder.

"Does hit hurt?" she said.

"Naw," he said. "Hit don't hurt. Lemme be."

"Can't you wipe some of the blood off before hit dries?"

"I'll wash to-night," he said. "Lemme be, I tell you."

The wagon went on. He did not know where they were going. None of them ever did or ever asked, because it was always somewhere, always a house of sorts waiting for them a day or two days or even three days away. Likely his father had already arranged to make a crop on another farm before he . . . Again he had to stop himself. He (the father) always did. There was something about his wolflike independence and even courage when the advantage was at least neutral which impressed strangers, as if they got from his latent ravening ferocity not so much a sense of dependability as a feeling that his ferocious conviction in the rightness of his own actions would be of advantage to all whose interest lay with his.

That night they camped, in a grove of oaks and beeches where a spring ran. The nights were still cool and they had a fire against it, of a rail lifted from a nearby fence and cut into lengths—a small fire, neat, niggard almost, a shrewd fire; such fires were his father's habit and custom always, even in freezing weather. Older, the boy might have remarked this and wondered why not a big one; why should not a man who had not only seen the waste and extravagance of war, but who had in his blood an inherent voracious prodigality with material not his own, have burned everything in sight? Then he might have gone a step farther and thought that that was the reason: that niggard blaze was the living fruit of nights passed during those four years in the woods hiding from all men, blue or gray, with his strings of horses (captured horses, he called them). And older still, he might have divined the true reason: that the element of fire spoke to some deep mainspring of his father's being, as the element of steel or of power spoke to other men, as the one weapon for the preservation of integrity, else breath were not worth the breathing, and hence to be regarded with respect and used with discretion.

But he did not think this now and he had seen those same niggard blazes all his life. He merely ate his supper beside it and was already half asleep over his iron plate when his father called him, and once more he followed the stiff back, the stiff and ruthless limp, up the slope and on to the starlit road where, turning, he could see his father against the stars but without face or depth—a shape black, flat, and bloodless as though cut from tin in the iron folds of the frockcoat which had not been made for him, the voice harsh like tin and without heat like tin:

"You were fixing to tell them. You would have told him." He didn't answer. His father struck him with the flat of his hand on the side of the head, hard but without heat, exactly as he had struck the two mules at the store, exactly as he would strike either of them with any stick in order to kill a horse fly, his voice still without heat or anger: "You're getting to be a man. You got to learn. You got to learn to stick to your own blood or you ain't going to have any blood to stick to you. Do you think either of them, any man there this morning, would? Don't you know all they wanted was a chance to get at me because they knew I had them beat? Eh?" Later, twenty years later, he was to tell himself, "If I had said they wanted only truth, justice, he would have hit me again." But now he said nothing. He was not crying. He just stood there. "Answer me," his father said.

"Yes," he whispered. His father turned.

"Get on to bed. We'll be there tomorrow."

To-morrow they were there. In the early afternoon the wagon stopped before a paintless two-room house identical almost with the dozen others it had stopped before even in the boy's ten years, and again, as on the other dozen occasions, his mother and aunt got down and began to unload the wagon, although his two sisters and his father and brother had not moved.

"Likely hit ain't fitten for hawgs," one of the sisters said.

"Nevertheless, fit it will and you'll hog it and like it," his father said. "Get out of them chairs and help your Ma unload."

The two sisters got down, big, bovine, in a flutter of cheap ribbons; one of them drew from the jumbled wagon bed a battered lantern, the other a worn broom. His father handed the reins to the older son and began to climb stiffly over the wheel. "When they get unloaded, take the team to the barn and feed them." Then he said, and at first the boy thought he was still speaking to his brother: "Come with me."

"Me?" he said.

"Yes," his father said. "You."

"Abner," his mother said. His father paused and looked back—the harsh level stare beneath the shaggy, graying, irascible brows.

"I reckon I'll have a word with the man that aims to begin to-morrow owning me body and soul for the next eight months."

They went back up the road. A week ago—or before last night, that is—he would have asked where they were going, but not now. His father had struck him before last night but never before had he paused afterward to explain why; it was as if the blow and the following calm, outrageous voice still rang, repercussed, divulging nothing to him save the terrible handicap of being young, the light weight of his few years, just heavy enough to prevent his soaring free of the world as it seemed to be ordered but not heavy enough to keep him footed solid in it, to resist it and try to change the course of its events.

Presently he could see the grove of oaks and cedars and the other flowering trees and shrubs where the house would be, though not the house yet. They walked beside a fence massed with honeysuckle and Cherokee roses and came to a gate swinging open between two brick pillars, and now, beyond a sweep of drive, he saw the house for the first time and at that instant he forgot his father and the terror and despair both, and even when he remembered his father again (who had not stopped) the terror and despair did not return. Because, for all the twelve movings, they had sojourned until now in a poor country, a land of small farms and fields and houses, and he had never seen a house like this before. *Hit's big as a courthouse* he thought quietly, with a surge of peace and joy whose reason he could not have thought into words, being too young for that: *They are safe from him. People whose lives are a part of this peace and dignity are beyond his touch, he no more to them than a buzzing wasp: capable of stinging for a little moment but that's all; the spell of this peace and dignity rendering even the barns and stable and cribs which belong to it impervious to the puny flames he might contrive . . .* this, the peace and joy, ebbing for an instant as he looked again at the stiff black back, the stiff and implacable limp of the figure which was not dwarfed by the house, for the reason that it had never looked big anywhere and which now, against the serene columned backdrop, had more than ever that impervious quality of something cut ruthlessly from tin, depthless, as though, sidewise to the sun, it would cast no shadow. Watching him, the boy remarked the absolutely undeviating course which his father held and saw the stiff foot come squarely down in a pile of fresh droppings where a horse had stood in the drive and which his father could have avoided by a simple change of stride. But it ebbed only for a moment, though he could not have thought this into words either, walking on in the spell of the house, which he could even want but without envy, without sorrow, certainly never with that ravening and jealous rage which unknown to him walked in the ironlike black coat before him: *Maybe he will feel it too. Maybe it will even change him now from what maybe he couldn't help but be.*

They crossed the portico. Now he could hear his father's stiff foot as it came down on the boards with clocklike finality, a sound out of all proportion to the displacement of the body it bore and which was not dwarfed either by the white door before it, as though it had attained to a sort of vicious and ravening minimum not to be dwarfed by anything—the flat, wide, black hat, the formal coat of broadcloth which had once been black but which had now that friction-glazed greenish cast of the bodies of old house flies, the lifted sleeve which was too large, the lifted hand like a curled claw. The door opened so promptly that the boy knew the Negro must have been watching them all the time, an old man with neat grizzled hair, in a linen jacket, who stood barring the door with his body, saying, "Wipe yo foots, white man, fo you come in here. Major ain't home nohow."

"Get out of my way, nigger," his father said, without heat too, flinging the door back and the Negro also and entering, his hat still on his head. And now the boy saw the prints of the stiff foot on the doorjamb and saw them appear on the pale rug behind the machinelike deliberation of the foot which seemed to bear (or transmit) twice the weight which the body compassed. The Negro was shouting "Miss Lula! Miss Lula!" somewhere behind them, then the boy, deluged as though by a warm wave by a suave turn of carpeted stair and a pendant glitter of chandeliers and a mute gleam of gold frames, heard the swift feet and saw her too, a lady—perhaps he had never seen her like before either—in a gray, smooth gown with lace at the throat and an apron tied at the waist and the sleeves turned back, wiping cake or biscuit dough from her hands with a towel as she came up the hall, looking not at his father at all but at the tracks on the blond rug with an expression of incredulous amazement.

"I tried," the Negro cried. "I tole him to . . . ."

"Will you please go away?" she said in a shaking voice. "Major de Spain is not at home. Will you please go away?"

His father had not spoken again. He did not speak again. He did not even look at her. He just stood stiff in the center of the rug, in his hat, the shaggy iron-gray brows twitching slightly above the pebble-colored eyes as he appeared to examine the house with brief deliberation. Then with the same deliberation he turned; the boy watched him pivot on the good leg and saw the stiff foot drag round the arc of the turning, leaving a final long and fading smear. His father never looked at it, he never once looked down at the rug. The Negro held the door. It closed behind them, upon the hysteric and indistinguishable woman-wail. His father stopped at the top of the steps and scraped his boot clean on the edge of it. At the gate he stopped again. He stood for a moment, planted stiffly on the stiff foot, looking back at the house. "Pretty and white, ain't it?" he said. "That's sweat. Nigger sweat. Maybe it ain't white enough yet to suit him. Maybe he wants to mix some white sweat with it."

Two hours later the boy was chopping wood behind the house within which his mother and aunt and the two sisters (the mother and aunt, not the two girls, he knew that; even at this distance and muffled by walls the flat loud voices of the two girls emanated an incorrigible idle inertia) were setting up the stove to prepare a meal, when he heard the hooves and saw the linen-clad man on a fine sorrel mare, whom he recognized even before he saw the rolled rug in front of the Negro youth following on a fat bay carriage horse—a suffused, angry face vanishing, still at full gallop, beyond the corner of the house where his father and brother were sitting in the two tilted chairs; and a moment later, almost before he could have put the axe down, he heard the hooves again and watched the sorrel mare go back out of the yard, already galloping again. Then his father began to shout one of the sisters' names, who presently emerged backward from the kitchen door dragging the rolled rug along the ground by one end while the other sister walked behind it.

"If you ain't going to tote, go on and set up the wash pot," the first said.

"You, Sarty!" the second shouted. "Set up the wash pot!" His father appeared at the door, framed against that shabbiness, as he had been against that other bland perfection, impervious to either, the mother's anxious face at his shoulder.

"Go on," the father said. "Pick it up." The two sisters stooped, broad, lethargic; stooping, they presented an incredible expanse of pale cloth and a flutter of tawdry ribbons.

"If I thought enough of a rug to have to git hit all the way from France I wouldn't keep hit where folks coming in would have to tromp on hit," the first said. They raised the rug.

"Abner," the mother said. "Let me do it."

"You go back and git dinner," his father said. "I'll tend to this."

From the woodpile through the rest of the afternoon the boy watched them, the rug spread flat in the dust beside the bubbling wash-pot, the two sisters stooping over it with that profound and lethargic reluctance, while the father stood over them in turn, implacable and grim, driving them though never raising his voice again. He could smell the harsh homemade lye they were using; he saw his mother come to the door once and look toward them with an expression not anxious now but very like despair; he saw his father turn, and he fell to with the axe and saw from the corner of his eye his father raise from the ground a flattish fragment of field stone and examine it and return to the pot, and this time his mother actually spoke: "Abner. Abner. Please don't. Please, Abner."

Then he was done too. It was dusk; the whippoorwills had already begun. He could smell coffee from the room where they would presently eat the cold food remaining from the mid-afternoon meal, though when he entered the house he realized they were having coffee again probably because there was a fire on the hearth, before which the rug now lay spread over the backs of the two chairs. The tracks of his father's foot were gone. Where they had been were now long, water-cloudy scoriations resembling the sporadic course of a lilliputian mowing machine.

It still hung there while they ate the cold food and then went to bed, scattered without order or claim up and down the two rooms, his mother in one bed, where his father would later lie, the older brother in the other, himself, the aunt, and the two sisters on pallets on the floor. But his father was not in bed yet. The last thing the boy remembered was the depthless, harsh silhouette of the hat and coat bending over the rug and it seemed to him that he had not even closed his eyes when the silhouette was standing over him, the fire almost dead behind it, the stiff foot prodding him awake. "Catch up the mule," his father said.

When he returned with the mule his father was standing in the black door, the rolled rug over his shoulder. "Ain't you going to ride?" he said.

"No. Give me your foot."

He bent his knee into his father's hand, the wiry, surprising power flowed smoothly, rising, he rising with it, on to the mule's bare back (they had owned a saddle once; the boy could remember it though not when or where) and with the same effortlessness his father swung the rug up in front of him. Now in the starlight they retraced the afternoon's path, up the dusty road rife with honeysuckle, through the gate and up the black tunnel of the drive to the lightless house, where he sat on the mule and felt the rough warp of the rug drag across his thighs and vanish.

"Don't you want me to help?" he whispered. His father did not answer and now he heard again that stiff foot striking the hollow portico with that wooden and clocklike deliberation, that outrageous overstatement of the weight it carried. The rug, hunched, not flung (the boy could tell that even in the darkness) from his father's shoulder struck the angle of wall and floor with a sound unbelievably loud, thunderous, then the foot again, unhurried and enormous; a light came on in the house and the boy sat, tense, breathing steadily and quietly and just a little fast, though the foot itself did not increase its beat at all, descending the steps now; now the boy could see him.

"Don't you want to ride now?" he whispered. "We kin both ride now," the light within the house altering now, flaring up and sinking. *He's coming down the stairs now*, he thought. He had already ridden the mule up beside the horse block; presently his father was up behind him and he doubled the reins over and slashed the mule across the neck, but before the animal could begin to trot the hard, thin arm came round him, the hard, knotted hand jerking the mule back to a walk.

In the first red rays of the sun they were in the lot, putting plow gear on the mules. This time the sorrel mare was in the lot before he heard it at all, the rider collarless and even bareheaded, trembling, speaking in a shaking voice as the woman in the house had done, his father merely looking up once before stooping again to the hame he was buckling, so that the man on the mare spoke to his stooping back:

"You must realize you have ruined that rug. Wasn't there anybody here, any of your women . . ." he ceased, shaking, the boy watching him, the older brother leaning now in the stable door, chewing, blinking slowly and steadily at nothing apparently. "It cost a hundred dollars. But you never had a hundred dollars. You never will. So I'm going to charge you twenty bushels of corn against your crop. I'll add it in your contract and when you come to the commissary you can sign it. That won't keep Mrs. de Spain quiet but maybe it will teach you to wipe your feet off before you enter her house again."

Then he was gone. The boy looked at his father, who still had not spoken or even looked up again, who was now adjusting the logger-head in the hame.

"Pap," he said. His father looked at him—the inscrutable face, the shaggy brows beneath which the gray eyes glinted coldly. Suddenly the boy went toward him, fast, stopping as suddenly. "You done the best you could!" he cried. "If he wanted hit done different why didn't he wait and tell you how? He won't git no twenty bushels! He won't git none! We'll gether hit and hide hit! I kin watch . . ."

"Did you put the cutter back in that straight stock like I told you?"

"No, sir," he said.

"Then go do it."

That was Wednesday. During the rest of that week he worked steadily, at what was within his scope and some which was beyond it, with an industry that did not need to be driven nor even commanded twice; he had this from his mother, with the difference that some at least of what he did he liked to do, such as splitting wood with the half-size axe which his mother and aunt had earned, or saved money somehow, to present him with at Christmas. In company with the two older women (and on one afternoon, even one of the sisters), he built pens for the shoat and the cow which were a part of his father's contrast with the landlord, and one afternoon, his father being absent, gone somewhere on one of the mules, he went to the field.

They were running a middle buster now, his brother holding the plow straight while he handled the reins, and walking beside the straining mule, the rich black soil shearing cool and damp against his bare ankles, he thought *Maybe this is the end of it. Maybe even that twenty bushels that seems hard to have to pay for just a rug will be a cheap price for him to stop forever and always from being what he used to be*; thinking, dreaming now, so that his brother had to speak sharply to him to mind the mule: *Maybe he even won't collect the twenty bushels. Maybe it will all add up and balance and vanish—corn, rug, fire; the terror and grief, the being pulled two ways like between two teams of horses—gone, done with for ever and ever.*

Then it was Saturday; he looked up from beneath the mule he was harnessing and saw his father in the black coat and hat. "Not that," his father said. "The wagon gear." And then, two hours later, sitting in the wagon bed behind his father and brother on the seat, the wagon accomplished a final curve, and he saw the weathered paintless store with its tattered tobacco- and patent-medicine posters and the tethered wagons and saddle animals below the gallery. He mounted the gnawed steps behind his father and brother, and there again was the lane of quiet, watching faces for the three of them to walk through. He saw the man in spectacles sitting at the plank table and he did not need to be told this was a Justice of the Peace; he sent one glare of fierce, exultant, partisan defiance at the man in collar and cravat now, whom he had seen but twice before in his life, and that on a galloping horse, who now wore on his face an expression not of rage but of amazed unbelief which the boy could not have known was at the incredible circumstance of being sued by one of his own tenants, and came and stood against his father and cried at the Justice: "He ain't done it! He ain't burnt . . ."

"Go back to the wagon," his father said.

"Burnt?" the Justice said. "Do I understand this rug was burned too?"

"Does anybody here claim it was?" his father said. "Go back to the wagon." But he did not, he merely retreated to the rear of the room, crowded as that other had been, but not to sit down this time, instead, to stand pressing among the motionless bodies, listening to the voices:

"And you claim twenty bushels of corn is too high for the damage you did to the rug?"

"He brought the rug to me and said he wanted the tracks washed out of it. I washed the tracks out and took the rug back to him."

"But you didn't carry the rug back to him in the same condition it was in before you made the tracks on it."

His father did not answer, and now for perhaps half a minute there was no sound at all save that of breathing, the faint, steady suspiration of complete and intent listening.

"You decline to answer that, Mr. Snopes?" Again his father did not answer. "I'm going to find against you, Mr. Snopes. I'm going to find that you were responsible for the injury to Major de Spain's rug and hold you liable for it. But twenty bushels of corn seems a little high for a man in your circumstances to have to pay. Major de Spain claims it cost a hundred dollars. October corn will be worth about fifty cents. I figure that if Major de Spain can stand a ninety-five dollar loss on something he paid cash for, you can stand a five-dollar loss you haven't earned yet. I hold you in damages to Ma-

jor de Spain to the amount of ten bushels of corn over and above your contract with him, to be paid to him out of your crop at gathering time. Court
adjourned."

It had taken no time hardly, the morning was but half begun. He thought
they would return home and perhaps back to the field, since they were late,
far behind all other farmers. But instead his father passed on behind the
wagon, merely indicating with his hand for the older brother to follow with
it, and crossed the road toward the blacksmith shop opposite, pressing on
after his father, overtaking him, speaking, whispering up at the harsh, calm
face beneath the weathered hat: "He won't git no ten bushels neither. He
won't git one. We'll . . ." until his father glanced for an instant down at
him, the face absolutely calm, the grizzled eyebrows tangled above the cold
eyes, the voice almost pleasant, almost gentle:

"You think so? Well, we'll wait till October anyway."

The matter of the wagon—the setting of a spoke or two and the tightening
of the tires—did not take long either, the business of the tires accomplished
by driving the wagon into the spring branch behind the shop and letting it
stand there, the mules nuzzling into the water from time to time, and the
boy on the seat with the idle reins, looking up the slope and through the
sooty tunnel of the shed where the slow hammer rang and where his father
sat on an upended cypress bolt, easily, either talking or listening, still sitting
there when the boy brought the dripping wagon up out of the branch and
halted it before the door.

"Take them on to the shade and hitch," his father said. He did so and returned. His father and the smith and a third man squatting on his heels inside the door were talking, about crops and animals; the boy, squatting too
in the ammoniac dust and hoof-parings and scales of rust, heard his father
tell a long and unhurried story out of the time before the birth of the older
brother even when he had been a professional horsetrader. And then his father
came up beside him where he stood before a tattered last year's circus poster
on the other side of the store, gazing rapt and quiet at the scarlet horses, the incredible poisings and convolutions of tulle and tights and the painted leers of
comedians, and said, "It's time to eat."

But not at home. Squatting beside his brother against the front wall, he
watched his father emerge from the store and produce from a paper sack a
segment of cheese and divide it carefully and deliberately into three with
his pocket knife and produce crackers from the same sack. They all three
squatted on the gallery and ate, slowly, without talking; then in the store
again, they drank from a tin dipper tepid water smelling of the cedar bucket
and of living beech trees. And still they did not go home. It was a horse lot
this time, a tall rail fence upon and along which men stood and sat and out
of which one by one horses were led, to be walked and trotted and then
cantered back and forth along the road while the slow swapping and buying
went on and the sun began to slant westward, they—the three of them—

watching and listening, the older brother with his muddy eyes and his steady, inevitable tobacco, the father commenting now and then on certain of the animals, to no one in particular.

It was after sundown when they reached home. They ate supper by lamplight, then, sitting on the doorstep, the boy watched the night fully accomplish, listening to the whippoorwills and the frogs, when he heard his mother's voice: "Abner! No! No! Oh, God. Oh, God. Abner!" and he rose, whirled, and saw the altered light through the door where a candle stub now burned in a bottle neck on the table and his father, still in the hat and coat, at once formal and burlesque as though dressed carefully for some shabby and ceremonial violence, emptying the reservoir of the lamp back into the five-gallon kerosene can from which it had been filled, while the mother tugged at his arm until he shifted the lamp to the other hand and flung her back, not savagely or viciously, just hard, into the wall, her hands flung out against the wall for balance, her mouth open and in her face the same quality of hopeless despair as had been in her voice. Then his father saw him standing in the door.

"Go to the barn and get that can of oil we were oiling the wagon with," he said. The boy did not move. Then he could speak.

"What . . ." he cried. "What are you . . ?"

"Go get that oil," his father said. "Go."

Then he was moving, running, outside the house, toward the stable: this the old habit, the old blood which he had not been permitted to choose for himself, which had been bequeathed him willy nilly and which had run for so long (and who knew where, battening on what of outrage and savagery and lust) before it came to him. *I could keep on*, he thought. *I could run on and on and never look back, never need to see his face again. Only I can't. I can't*, the rusted can in his hand now, the liquid sploshing in it as he ran back to the house and into it, into the sound of his mother's weeping in the next room, and handed the can to his father.

"Ain't you going to even send a nigger?" he cried. "At least you sent a nigger before!"

This time his father didn't strike him. The hand came even faster than the blow had, the same hand which had set the can on the table with almost excruciating care flashing from the can toward him too quick for him to follow it, gripping him by the back of his shirt and on to tiptoe before he had seen it quit the can, the face stooping at him in breathless and frozen ferocity, the cold, dead voice speaking over him to the older brother who leaned against the table, chewing with that steady, curious, sidewise motion of cows:

"Empty the can into the big one and go on. I'll catch up with you."

"Better tie him up to the bedpost," the brother said.

"Do like I told you," the father said. Then the boy was moving, his bunched shirt and the hard, bony hand between his shoulder-blades, his toes just touching the floor, across the room and into the other one, past the sisters sitting with spread heavy thighs in the two chairs over the cold hearth, and to where his mother and aunt sat side by side on the bed, the aunt's arms about his mother's shoulders.

"Hold him," the father said. The aunt made a startled movement. "Not you," the father said. "Lennie. Take hold of him. I want to see you do it." His mother took him by the wrist. "You'll hold him better than that. If he gets loose don't you know what he is going to do? He will go up yonder." He jerked his head toward the road. "Maybe I'd better tie him."

"I'll hold him," his mother whispered.

"See you do then." Then his father was gone, the stiff foot heavy and measured upon the boards, ceasing at last.

Then he began to struggle. His mother caught him in both arms, he jerking and wrenching at them. He would be stronger in the end, he knew that. But he had no time to wait for it. "Lemme go!" he cried. "I don't want to have to hit you!"

"Let him go!" the aunt said. "If he don't go, before God, I am going up there myself!"

"Don't you see I can't?" his mother cried. "Sarty! Sarty! No! No! Help me, Lizzie!"

Then he was free. His aunt grasped at him but it was too late. He whirled, running, his mother stumbled forward on to her knees behind him, crying to the nearer sister: "Catch him, Net! Catch him!" But that was too late too, the sister (the sisters were twins, born at the same time, yet either of them now gave the impression of being, encompassing as much living meat and volume and weight as any other two of the family) not yet having begun to rise from the chair, her head, face, alone merely turned, presenting to him in the flying instant an astonishing expanse of young female features untroubled by any surprise even, wearing only an expression of bovine interest. Then he was out of the room, out of the house, in the mild dust of the starlit road and the heavy rifeness of honeysuckle, the pale ribbon unspooling with terrific slowness under his running feet, reaching the gate at last and turning in, running, his heart and lungs drumming, on up the drive toward the lighted house, the lighted door. He did not knock, he burst in, sobbing for breath, incapable for the moment of speech; he saw the astonished face of the Negro in the linen jacket without knowing when the Negro had appeared.

"De Spain!" he cried, panted. "Where's . . ." then he saw the white man too emerging from a white door down the hall. "Barn!" he cried. "Barn!"

"What?" the white man said. "Barn?"

"Yes!" the boy cried. "Barn!"

"Catch him!" the white man shouted.

But it was too late this time too. The Negro grasped his shirt, but the entire sleeve, rotten with washing, carried away, and he was out that door too and in the drive again, and had actually never ceased to run even while he was screaming into the white man's face.

Behind him the white man was shouting, "My horse! Fetch my horse!" and he thought for an instant of cutting across the park and climbing the fence into the road, but he did not know the park nor how high the vine-massed fence might be and he dared not risk it. So he ran on down the drive, blood and breath roaring; presently he was in the road again though he could not see it. He could not hear either: the galloping mare was almost upon him before he heard her, and even then he held his course, as if the very urgency of his wild grief and need must in a moment more find him wings, waiting until the ultimate instant to hurl himself aside and into the weed-choked roadside ditch as the horse thundered past and on, for an instant in furious silhouette against the stars, the tranquil early summer night sky which, even before the shape of the horse and rider vanished, stained abruptly and violently upward: a long, swirling roar incredible and soundless, blotting the stars, and he springing up and into the road again, running again, knowing it was too late yet still running even after he heard the shot and an instant later, two shots, pausing now without knowing he had ceased to run, crying "Pap! Pap!", running again before he knew he had begun to run, stumbling, tripping over something and scrabbling up again without ceasing to run, looking backward over his shoulder at the glare as he got up, running on among the invisible trees, panting, sobbing, "Father! Father!"

At midnight he was sitting on the crest of a hill. He did not know it was midnight and he did not know how far he had come. But there was no glare behind him now and he sat now, his back toward what he had called home for four days anyhow, his face toward the dark woods which he would enter when breath was strong again, small, shaking steadily in the chill darkness, hugging himself into the remainder of his thin, rotten shirt, the grief and despair now no longer terror and fear but just grief and despair. *Father. My father*, he thought. "He was brave!" he cried suddenly, aloud but not loud, no more than a whisper: "He was! He was in the war! He was in Colonel Sartoris' cav'ry!" not knowing that his father had gone to that war a private in the fine old European sense, wearing no uniform, admitting the authority of and giving fidelity to no man or army or flag, going to war as Malbrouck himself did: for booty—it meant nothing and less than nothing to him if it were enemy booty or his own.

The slow constellations wheeled on. It would be dawn and then sun-up after a while and he would be hungry. But that would be to-morrow and now he was only cold, and walking would cure that. His breathing was easier now and he decided to get up and go on, and then he found that he had been asleep because he knew it was almost dawn, the night almost over. He could tell that from the whippoorwills. They were everywhere now among the dark trees below him, constant and inflectioned and ceaseless, so that, as the instant for giving over to the day birds drew nearer and nearer, there was no interval at all between them. He got up. He was a little stiff, but walking would cure that too as it would the cold, and soon there would be the sun.

He went on down the hill, toward the dark woods within which the liquid silver voices of the birds called unceasing—the rapid and urgent beating of the urgent and quiring heart of the late spring night. He did not look back.

ERNEST HEMINGWAY

The Short Happy Life of Francis Macomber[1]

It was now lunch time and they were all sitting under the double green fly of the dining tent pretending that nothing had happened.

"Will you have lime juice or lemon squash?" Macomber asked.

"I'll have a gimlet," Robert Wilson told him.

"I'll have a gimlet too. I need something," Macomber's wife said.

"I suppose it's the thing to do," Macomber agreed. "Tell him to make three gimlets."

The mess boy had started them already, lifting the bottles out of the canvas cooling bags that sweated wet in the wind that blew through the trees that shaded the tents.

"What had I ought to give them?" Macomber asked.

"A quid would be plenty," Wilson told him. "You don't want to spoil them."

"Will the headman distribute it?"

"Absolutely."

Francis Macomber had, half an hour before, been carried to his tent from the edge of the camp in triumph on the arms and shoulders of the cook, the personal boys, the skinner and the porters. The gun-bearers had taken no part in the demonstration. When the native boys put him down at the door of his tent, he had shaken all their hands, received their congratulations, and then gone into the tent and sat on the bed until his wife came in. She did not speak to him when she came in and he left the tent at once to wash his face and hands in the portable wash basin outside and go over to the dining tent to sit in a comfortable canvas chair in the breeze and the shade.

"You've got your lion," Robert Wilson said to him, "and a damned fine one too."

Mrs. Macomber looked at Wilson quickly. She was an extremely handsome and well-kept woman of the beauty and social position which had, five years before, commanded five thousand dollars as the price of endorsing, with

[1] "The Short Happy Life of Francis Macomber" (Copyright 1936 Ernest Hemingway) is reprinted with the permission of Charles Scribner's Sons from *The Fifth Column and the First Forty-Nine Stories* by Ernest Hemingway.

photographs, a beauty product which she had never used. She had been married to Francis Macomber for eleven years.

"He is a good lion, isn't he?" Macomber said. His wife looked at him now. She looked at both these men as though she had never seen them before.

One, Wilson, the white hunter, she knew she had never truly seen before. He was about middle height with sandy hair, a stubby mustache, a very red face and extremely cold blue eyes with faint white wrinkles at the corners that grooved merrily when he smiled. He smiled at her now and she looked away from his face at the way his shoulders sloped in the loose tunic he wore with the four big cartridges held in loops where the left breast pocket should have been, at his big brown hands, his old slacks, his very dirty boots and back to his red face again. She noticed where the baked red of his face stopped in a white line that marked the circle left by his Stetson hat that hung now from one of the pegs of the tent pole.

"Well, here's to the lion," Robert Wilson said. He smiled at her again and, not smiling, she looked curiously at her husband.

Francis Macomber was very tall, very well built if you did not mind that length of bone, dark, his hair cropped like an oarsman, rather thin-lipped, and was considered handsome. He was dressed in the same sort of safari clothes that Wilson wore except that his were new, he was thirty-five years old, kept himself very fit, was good at court games, had a number of big-game fishing records, and had just shown himself, very publicly, to be a coward.

"Here's to the lion," he said. "I can't ever thank you for what you did."

Margaret, his wife, looked away from him and back to Wilson.

"Let's not talk about the lion," she said.

Wilson looked over at her without smiling and now she smiled at him.

"It's been a very strange day," she said. "Hadn't you ought to put your hat on even under the canvas at noon? You told me that, you know."

"Might put it on," said Wilson.

"You know you have a very red face, Mr. Wilson," she told him and smiled again.

"Drink," said Wilson.

"I don't think so," she said. "Francis drinks a great deal, but his face is never red."

"It's red today," Macomber tried a joke.

"No," said Margaret. "It's mine that's red today. But Mr. Wilson's is always red."

"Must be racial," said Wilson. "I say, you wouldn't like to drop my beauty as a topic, would you?"

"I've just started on it."

"Let's chuck it," said Wilson.

"Conversation is going to be so difficult," Margaret said.

"Don't be silly, Margot," her husband said.

"No difficulty," Wilson said. "Got a damn fine lion."

Margot looked at them both and they both saw that she was going to cry. Wilson had seen it coming for a long time and he dreaded it. Macomber was past dreading it.

"I wish it hadn't happened. Oh, I wish it hadn't happened," she said and started for her tent. She made no noise of crying but they could see that her shoulders were shaking under the rose-colored, sun-proofed shirt she wore.

"Women upset," said Wilson to the tall man. "Amounts to nothing. Strain on the nerves and one thing'n another."

"No," said Macomber. "I suppose that I rate that for the rest of my life now."

"Nonsense. Let's have a spot of giant killer," said Wilson. "Forget the whole thing. Nothing to it anyway."

"We might try," said Macomber. "I won't forget what you did for me though."

"Nothing," said Wilson. "All nonsense."

So they sat there in the shade where the camp was pitched under some wide-topped acacia trees with a boulder-strewn cliff behind them, and a stretch of grass that ran to the bank of a boulder-filled stream in front with forest beyond it, and drank their just-cool lime drinks and avoided one another's eyes while the boys set the table for lunch. Wilson could tell that the boys all knew about it now and when he saw Macomber's personal boy looking curiously at his master while he was putting dishes on the table he snapped at him in Swahili. The boy turned away with his face blank.

"What were you telling him?" Macomber asked.

"Nothing. Told him to look alive or I'd see he got about fifteen of the best."

"What's that? Lashes?"

"It's quite illegal," Wilson said. "You're supposed to fine them."

"Do you still have them whipped?"

"Oh, yes. They could raise a row if they chose to complain. But they don't. They prefer it to the fines."

"How strange!" said Macomber.

"Not strange, really," Wilson said. "Which would you rather do? Take a good birching or lose your pay?"

Then he felt embarrassed at asking it and before Macomber could answer he went on, "We all take a beating every day, you know, one way or another."

This was no better. "Good God," he thought. "I am a diplomat, aren't I?"

"Yes, we take a beating," said Macomber, still not looking at him. "I'm awfully sorry about that lion business. It doesn't have to go any further, does it? I mean no one will hear about it, will they?"

"You mean will I tell it at the Mathaiga Club?" Wilson looked at him now coldly. He had not expected this. So he's a bloody four-letter man as well as a bloody coward, he thought. I rather liked him too until today. But how is one to know about an American?

"No," said Wilson. "I'm a professional hunter. We never talk about our clients. You can be quite easy on that. It's supposed to be bad form to ask us not to talk though."

He had decided now that to break would be much easier. He would eat, then, by himself and could read a book with his meals. They would eat by themselves. He would see them through the safari on a very formal basis— what was it the French called it? Distinguished consideration—and it would be a damn sight easier than having to go through this emotional trash. He'd insult him and make a good clean break. Then he could read a book with his meals and he'd still be drinking their whisky. That was the phrase for it when a safari went bad. You ran into another white hunter and you asked, "How is everything going?" and he answered, "Oh, I'm still drinking their whisky," and you knew everything had gone to pot.

"I'm sorry," Macomber said and looked at him with his American face that would stay adolescent until it became middle-aged, and Wilson noted his crew-cropped hair, fine eyes only faintly shifty, good nose, thin lips and handsome jaw. "I'm sorry I didn't realize that. There are lots of things I don't know."

So what could he do, Wilson thought. He was all ready to break it off quickly and neatly and here the beggar was apologizing after he had just insulted him. He made one more attempt. "Don't worry about me talking," he said. "I have a living to make. You know in Africa no woman ever misses her lion and no white man ever bolts."

"I bolted like a rabbit," Macomber said.

Now what in hell were you going to do about a man who talked like that, Wilson wondered.

Wilson looked at Macomber with his flat, blue, machine-gunner's eyes and the other smiled back at him. He had a pleasant smile if you did not notice how his eyes showed when he was hurt.

"Maybe I can fix it up on Buffalo," he said. "We're after them next, aren't we?"

"In the morning if you like," Wilson told him. Perhaps he had been wrong. This was certainly the way to take it. You most certainly could not tell a damned thing about an American. He was all for Macomber again. If you could forget the morning. But, of course, you couldn't. The morning had been about as bad as they come.

"Here comes the Memsahib," he said. She was walking over from her tent looking refreshed and cheerful and quite lovely. She had a very perfect oval face, so perfect that you expected her to be stupid. But she wasn't stupid, Wilson thought, no, not stupid.

"How is the beautiful red-faced Mr. Wilson? Are you feeling better, Francis, my pearl?"

"Oh, much," said Macomber.

"I've dropped the whole thing," she said, sitting down at the table. "What importance is there to whether Francis is any good at killing lions? That's not his trade. That's Mr. Wilson's trade. Mr. Wilson is really very impressive killing anything. You do kill anything, don't you?"

"Oh, anything," said Wilson. "Simply anything." They are, he thought, the hardest in the world; the hardest, the cruelest, the most predatory and the most attractive and their men have softened or gone to pieces nervously as they have hardened. Or is it that they pick men they can handle? They can't know that much at the age they marry, he thought. He was grateful that he had gone through his education on American women before now because this was a very attractive one.

"We're going after buff in the morning," he told her.

"I'm coming," she said.

"No, you're not."

"Oh, yes, I am. Mayn't I, Francis?"

"Why not stay in camp?"

"Not for anything," she said. "I wouldn't miss something like today for anything."

When she left, Wilson was thinking, when she went off to cry, she seemed a hell of a fine woman. She seemed to understand, to realize, to be hurt for him and for herself and to know how things really stood. She is away for twenty minutes and now she is back, simply enamelled in that American female cruelty. They are the damnedest women. Really the damnedest.

"We'll put on another show for you tomorrow," Francis Macomber said.

"You're not coming," Wilson said.

"You're very mistaken," she told him. "And I want so to see you perform again. You were lovely this morning. That is if blowing things' heads off is lovely."

"Here's the lunch," said Wilson. "You're very merry, aren't you?"

"Why not? I didn't come out here to be dull."

"Well, it hasn't been dull," Wilson said. He could see the boulders in the river and the high bank beyond with the trees and he remembered the morning.

"Oh, no," she said. "It's been charming. And tomorrow. You don't know how I look forward to tomorrow."

"That's eland he's offering you," Wilson said.

"They're the big cowy things that jump like hares, aren't they?"

"I suppose that describes them," Wilson said.

"It's very good meat," Macomber said.

"Did you shoot it, Francis?" she asked.

"Yes."

"They're not dangerous, are they?"

"Only if they fall on you," Wilson told her.

"I'm so glad."

"Why not let up on the bitchery just a little, Margot," Macomber said, cutting the eland steak and putting some mashed potato, gravy and carrot on the down-turned fork that tined through the piece of meat.

"I suppose I could," she said, "since you put it so prettily."

"Tonight we'll have champagne for the lion," Wilson said. "It's a bit too hot at noon."

"Oh, the lion," Margot said. "I'd forgotten the lion!"

So, Robert Wilson thought to himself, she *is* giving him a ride, isn't she? Or do you suppose that's her idea of putting up a good show? How should a woman act when she discovers her husband is a bloody coward? She's damn cruel but they're all cruel. They govern, of course, and to govern one has to be cruel sometimes. Still, I've seen enough of their damn terrorism.

"Have some more eland," he said to her politely.

That afternoon, late, Wilson and Macomber went out in the motor car with the native driver and the two gun-bearers. Mrs. Macomber stayed in the camp. It was too hot to go out, she said, and she was going with them in the early morning. As they drove off Wilson saw her standing under the big tree, looking pretty rather than beautiful in her faintly rosy khaki, her dark hair drawn back off her forehead and gathered in a knot low on her neck, her face as fresh, he thought, as though she were in England. She waved to them as the car went off through the swale of high grass and curved around through the trees into the small hills of orchard bush.

In the orchard bush they found a herd of impala, and leaving the car they stalked one old ram with long, wide-spread horns and Macomber killed it with a very creditable shot that knocked the buck down at a good two hundred yards and sent the herd off bounding wildly and leaping over one another's backs in long, leg-drawn-up leaps as unbelievable and as floating as those one makes sometimes in dreams.

"That was a good shot," Wilson said. "They're a small target."

"Is it a worth-while head?" Macomber asked.

"It's excellent," Wilson told him. "You shoot like that and you'll have no trouble."

"Do you think we'll find buffalo tomorrow?"

"There's a good chance of it. They feed out early in the morning and with luck we may catch them in the open."

"I'd like to clear away that lion business," Macomber said. "It's not very pleasant to have your wife see you do something like that."

I should think it would be even more unpleasant to do it, Wilson thought, wife or no wife, or to talk about it having done it. But he said, "I wouldn't think about that any more. Any one could be upset by his first lion. That's all over."

But that night after dinner and a whisky and soda by the fire before going to bed, as Francis Macomber lay on his cot with the mosquito bar over him and listened to the night noises it was not all over. It was neither all over nor was it beginning. It was there exactly as it happened with some parts of it indelibly emphasized and he was miserably ashamed at it. But more than shame he felt cold, hollow fear in him. The fear was still there like a cold slimy hollow in all the emptiness where once his confidence had been and it made him feel sick. It was still there with him now.

It had started the night before when he had wakened and heard the lion roaring somewhere up along the river. It was a deep sound and at the end there were sort of coughing grunts that made him seem just outside the tent, and when Francis Macomber woke in the night to hear it he was afraid. He could hear his wife breathing quietly, asleep. There was no one to tell he was afraid, nor to be afraid with him, and, lying alone, he did not know the Somali proverb that says a brave man is always frightened three times by a lion; when he first sees his track, when he first hears him roar and when he first confronts him. Then while they were eating breakfast by lantern light out in the dining tent, before the sun was up, the lion roared again and Francis thought he was just at the edge of camp.

"Sounds like an old-timer," Robert Wilson said, looking up from his kippers and coffee. "Listen to him cough."

"Is he very close?"

"A mile or so up the stream."

"Will we see him?"

"We'll have a look."

"Does his roaring carry that far? It sounds as though he were right in camp."

"Carries a hell of a long way," said Robert Wilson. "It's strange the way it carries. Hope he's a shootable cat. The boys said there was a very big one about here."

"If I get a shot, where should I hit him," Macomber asked, "to stop him?"

"In the shoulders," Wilson said. "In the neck if you can make it. Shoot for bone. Break him down."

"I hope I can place it properly," Macomber said.

"You shoot very well," Wilson told him. "Take your time. Make sure of him. The first one in is the one that counts."

"What range will it be?"

"Can't tell. Lion has something to say about that. Don't shoot unless it's close enough so you can make sure."

"At under a hundred yards?" Macomber asked.

Wilson looked at him quickly.

"Hundred's about right. Might have to take him a bit under. Shouldn't chance a shot at much over that. A hundred's a decent range. You can hit him wherever you want at that. Here comes the Memsahib."

"Good morning," she said. "Are we going after that lion?"

"As soon as you deal with your breakfast," Wilson said. "How are you feeling?"

"Marvellous," she said. "I'm very excited."

"I'll just go and see that everything is ready," Wilson went off. As he left the lion roared again.

"Noisy beggar," Wilson said. "We'll put a stop to that."

"What's the matter, Francis?" his wife asked him.

"Nothing," Macomber said.

"Yes, there is," she said. "What are you upset about?"

"Nothing," he said.

"Tell me," she looked at him. "Don't you feel well?"

"It's that damned roaring," he said. "It's been going on all night, you know."

"Why didn't you wake me," she said. "I'd love to have heard it."

"I've got to kill the damned thing," Macomber said, miserably.

"Well, that's what you're out here for, isn't it?"

"Yes. But I'm nervous. Hearing the thing roar gets on my nerves."

"Well then, as Wilson said, kill him and stop his roaring."

"Yes, darling," said Francis Macomber. "It sounds easy, doesn't it?"

"You're not afraid, are you?"

"Of course not. But I'm nervous from hearing him roar all night."

"You'll kill him marvellously," she said. "I know you will. I'm awfully anxious to see it."

"Finish your breakfast and we'll be starting."

"It's not light yet," she said. "This is a ridiculous hour."

Just then the lion roared in a deep-chested moaning, suddenly guttural, ascending vibration that seemed to shake the air and ended in a sigh and a heavy, deep-chested grunt.

"He sounds almost here," Macomber's wife said.

"My God," said Macomber. "I hate that damned noise."

"It's very impressive."

"Impressive. It's frightful."

Robert Wilson came up then carrying his short, ugly, shockingly big-bored .505 Gibbs and grinning.

"Come on," he said. "Your gun-bearer has your Springfield and the big gun. Everything's in the car. Have you solids?"

"Yes."

"I'm ready," Mrs. Macomber said.

"Must make him stop that racket," Wilson said. "You get in front. The Memsahib can sit back here with me."

They climbed into the motor car and, in the gray first daylight, moved off up the river through the trees. Macomber opened the breech of his rifle and saw he had metal-cased bullets, shut the bolt and put the rifle on safety. He saw his hand was trembling. He felt in his pocket for more cartridges and moved his fingers over the cartridges in the loops of his tunic front. He turned back to where Wilson sat in the rear seat of the doorless, box-bodied motor car beside his wife, them both grinning with excitement, and Wilson leaned forward and whispered.

"See the birds dropping. Means the old boy has left his kill."

On the far bank of the stream Macomber could see, above the trees, vultures circling and plummeting down.

"Chances are he'll come to drink along here," Wilson whispered. "Before he goes to lay up. Keep an eye out."

They were driving slowly along the high bank of the stream which here cut deeply to its boulder-filled bed, and they wound in and out through big trees as they drove. Macomber was watching the opposite bank when he felt Wilson take hold of his arm. The car stopped.

"There he is," he heard the whisper. "Ahead and to the right. Get out and take him. He's a marvellous lion."

Macomber saw the lion now. He was standing alone almost broadside, his great head up and turned toward them. The early morning breeze that blew toward them was just stirring his dark mane, and the lion looked huge, silhouetted on the rise of bank in the gray morning light, his shoulders heavy, his barrel of a body bulking smoothly.

"How far is he?" asked Macomber, raising his rifle.

"About seventy-five. Get out and take him."

"Why not shoot from where I am?"

"You don't shoot them from cars," he heard Wilson saying in his ear. "Get out. He's not going to stay there all day."

Macomber stepped out of the curved opening at the side of the front seat, onto the step and down onto the ground. The lion still stood looking majestically and coolly toward this object that his eyes showed only in silhouette, bulking like some super-rhino. There was no man smell carried toward him and he watched the object, moving his great head a little from side to side. Then watching the object, not afraid, but hesitating before going down the bank to drink with such a thing opposite him, he saw a man figure detach itself from it and he turned his heavy head and swung away toward the cover of the trees as he heard a cracking crash and felt the slam of a .30-06 220-grain solid bullet that bit his flank and ripped in sudden hot scalding nausea through his stomach. He trotted, heavy, big-footed, swinging wounded fullbellied, through the trees toward the tall grass and cover, and the crash came again to go past him ripping the air apart. Then it crashed again and he felt the blow as it hit his lower ribs and ripped on through, blood sudden hot and frothy in his mouth, and he galloped toward the high grass where he could crouch and not be seen and make them bring the crashing thing close enough so he could make a rush and get the man that held it.

Macomber had not thought how the lion felt as he got out of the car. He only knew his hands were shaking and as he walked away from the car it was almost impossible for him to make his legs move. They were stiff in the thighs, but he could feel the muscles fluttering. He raised the rifle, sighted on the junction of the lion's head and shoulders and pulled the trigger. Nothing happened though he pulled until he thought his finger would break. Then he knew he had the safety on and as he lowered the rifle to move the safety over he moved another frozen pace forward, and the lion seeing his silhouette now clear of the silhouette of the car, turned and started off at a trot, and, as Macomber fired, he heard a whunk that meant that the bullet was home; but the lion kept on going. Macomber shot again and every one saw the bullet throw a spout of dirt beyond the trotting lion. He shot again, remembering to lower his aim, and they all heard the bullet hit, and the lion went into a gallop and was in the tall grass before he had the bolt pushed forward.

Macomber stood there feeling sick at his stomach, his hands that held the Springfield still cocked, shaking, and his wife and Robert Wilson were standing by him. Beside him too were the two gun-bearers chattering in Wakamba.

"I hit him," Macomber said. "I hit him twice."

"You gut-shot him and you hit him somewhere forward," Wilson said without enthusiasm. The gun-bearers looked very grave. They were silent now.

"You may have killed him," Wilson went on. "We'll have to wait a while before we go in to find out."

"What do you mean?"

"Let him get sick before we follow him up."

"Oh," said Macomber.

"He's a hell of a fine lion," Wilson said cheerfully. "He's gotten into a bad place though."

"Why is it bad?"

"Can't see him until you're on him."

"Oh," said Macomber.

"Come on," said Wilson. "The Memsahib can stay here in the car. We'll go to have a look at the blood spoor."

"Stay here, Margot," Macomber said to his wife. His mouth was very dry and it was hard for him to talk.

"Why?" she asked.

"Wilson says so."

"We're going to have a look," Wilson said. "You stay here. You can see even better from here."

"All right."

Wilson spoke in Swahili to the driver. He nodded and said, "Yes, Bwana."

Then they went down the steep bank and across the stream, climbing over and around the boulders and up the other bank, pulling up by some projecting roots, and along it until they found where the lion had been trotting when

Macomber first shot. There was dark blood on the short grass that the gun-bearers pointed out with grass stems, and that ran away behind the river bank trees.

"What do we do?" asked Macomber.

"Not much choice," said Wilson. "We can't bring the car over. Bank's too steep. We'll let him stiffen up a bit and then you and I'll go in and have a look for him."

"Can't we set the grass on fire?" Macomber asked.

"Too green."

"Can't we send beaters?"

Wilson looked at him appraisingly. "Of course we can," he said. "But it's just a touch murderous. You see we know the lion's wounded. You can drive an unwounded lion—he'll move on ahead of a noise—but a wounded lion's going to charge. You can't see him until you're right on him. He'll make himself perfectly flat in cover you wouldn't think would hide a hare. You can't very well send boys in there to that sort of a show. Somebody bound to get mauled."

"What about the gun-bearers?"

"Oh, they'll go with us. It's their *shauri*. You see, they signed on for it. They don't look too happy though, do they?"

"I don't want to go in there," said Macomber. It was out before he knew he'd said it.

"Neither do I," said Wilson very cheerily. "Really no choice though." Then, as an afterthought, he glanced at Macomber and saw suddenly how he was trembling and the pitiful look on his face.

"You don't have to go in, of course," he said. "That's what I'm hired for, you know. That's why I'm so expensive."

"You mean, you'd go in by yourself? Why not leave him there?"

Robert Wilson, whose entire occupation had been with the lion and the problem he presented, and who had not been thinking about Macomber except to note that he was rather windy, suddenly felt as though he had opened the wrong door in a hotel and seen something shameful.

"What do you mean?"

"Why not just leave him?"

"You mean pretend to ourselves he hasn't been hit?"

"No. Just drop it."

"It isn't done."

"Why not?"

"For one thing, he's certain to be suffering. For another, some one else might run onto him."

"I see."

"But you don't have to have anything to do with it."

"I'd like to," Macomber said. "I'm just scared, you know."

"I'll go ahead when we go in," Wilson said, "with Kongoni tracking. You keep behind me and a little to one side. Chances are we'll hear him growl. If we see him we'll both shoot. Don't worry about anything. I'll keep you backed up. As a matter of fact, you know, perhaps you'd better not go. It might be much better. Why don't you go over and join the Memsahib while I just get it over with?"

"No, I want to go."

"All right," said Wilson. "But don't go in if you don't want to. This is my *shauri* now, you know."

"I want to go," said Macomber.

They sat under a tree and smoked.

"Want to go back and speak to the Memsahib while we're waiting?" Wilson asked.

"No."

"I'll just step back and tell her to be patient."

"Good," said Macomber. He sat there, sweating under his arms, his mouth dry, his stomach hollow feeling, wanting to find courage to tell Wilson to go on and finish off the lion without him. He could not know that Wilson was furious because he had not noticed the state he was in earlier and sent him back to his wife. While he sat there Wilson came up. "I have your big gun," he said. "Take it. We've given him time, I think. Come on."

Macomber took the big gun and Wilson said:

"Keep behind me and about five yards to the right and do exactly as I tell you." Then he spoke in Swahili to the two gun-bearers who looked the picture of gloom.

"Let's go," he said.

"Could I have a drink of water?" Macomber asked. Wilson spoke to the older gun-bearer, who wore a canteen on his belt, and the man unbuckled it, unscrewed the top and handed it to Macomber, who took it noticing how heavy it seemed and how hairy and shoddy the felt covering was in his hand. He raised it to drink and looked ahead at the high grass with the flat-topped trees behind it. A breeze was blowing toward them and the grass rippled gently in the wind. He looked at the gun-bearer and he could see the gun-bearer was suffering too with fear.

Thirty-five yards into the grass the big lion lay flattened out along the ground. His ears were back and his only movement was a slight twitching up and down of his long, black-tufted tail. He had turned at bay as soon as he had reached this cover and he was sick with the wound through his full belly, and weakening with the wound through his lungs that brought a thin foamy red to his mouth each time he breathed. His flanks were wet and hot and flies were on the little openings the solid bullets had made in his tawny hide, and his big yellow eyes, narrowed with hate, looked straight ahead, only blinking when the pain came as he breathed, and his claws dug in the soft baked earth. All of him, pain, sickness, hatred and all of his remaining strength, was tightening into an absolute concentration for a rush. He could hear the men talking and he waited, gathering all of himself into this preparation for a charge as soon as the men would come into the grass. As he heard their voices his tail stiffened to twitch up and down, and, as they came into the edge of the grass, he made a coughing grunt and charged.

Kongoni, the old gun-bearer, in the lead watching the blood spoor, Wilson watching the grass for any movement, his big gun ready, the second gun-bearer looking ahead and listening, Macomber close to Wilson, his rifle cocked, they had just moved into the grass when Macomber heard the blood-choked coughing grunt, and saw the swishing rush in the grass. The next thing he knew he was running; running wildly, in panic in the open, running toward the stream.

He heard the *ca-ra-wong!* of Wilson's rifle, and again in a second crashing *carawong!* and turning saw the lion, horrible-looking now, with half his head seeming to be gone, crawling toward Wilson in the edge of the tall grass while the red-faced man worked the bolt on the short ugly rifle and aimed carefully as another blasting *carawong!* came from the muzzle, and the crawling, heavy, yellow bulk of the lion stiffened and the huge, mutilated head slid forward and Macomber, standing by himself in the clearing where he had run, holding a loaded rifle, while two black men and a white man looked back at him in contempt, knew the lion was dead. He came toward Wilson, his tallness all seeming a naked reproach, and Wilson looked at him and said:

"Want to take pictures?"

"No," he said.

That was all any one had said until they reached the motor car. Then Wilson had said:

"Hell of a fine lion. Boys will skin him out. We might as well stay here in the shade."

Macomber's wife had not looked at him nor he at her and he had sat by her in the back seat with Wilson sitting in the front seat. Once he had reached over and taken his wife's hand without looking at her and she had removed her hand from his. Looking across the stream to where the gun-bearers were skinning out the lion he could see that she had been able to see the whole thing. While they sat there his wife had reached forward and put her hand on Wilson's shoulder. He turned and she had leaned forward over the low seat and kissed him on the mouth.

"Oh, I say," said Wilson, going redder than his natural baked color.

"Mr. Robert Wilson," she said. "The beautiful red-faced Mr. Robert Wilson."

Then she sat down beside Macomber again, and looked away across the stream to where the lion lay, with uplifted, white-muscled, tendon-marked naked forearms, and white bloating belly, as the black men fleshed away the skin. Finally the gun-bearers brought the skin over, wet and heavy, and climbed in behind with it, rolling it up before they got in, and the motor car started. No one had said anything more until they were back in camp.

That was the story of the lion. Macomber did not know how the lion had felt before he started his rush, nor during it when the unbelievable smash of the .505 with a muzzle velocity of two tons had hit him in the mouth, nor what kept him coming after that, when the second dripping crash had smashed his hind quarters and he had come crawling on toward the crashing, blasting thing that had destroyed him. Wilson knew something about it and only expressed it by saying, "Damned fine lion," but Macomber did not know how Wilson felt about things either. He did not know how his wife felt except that she was through with him.

His wife had been through with him before but it never lasted. He was very wealthy, and would be much wealthier, and he knew she would not leave him ever now. That was one of the few things that he really knew. He knew about that, about motorcycles—that was earliest—about motor cars, about duck-shooting, about fishing, trout, salmon and big-sea, about sex in books, many books, too many books, about all court games, about dogs, not much about horses, about hanging on to his money, about most of the other things his world dealt in, and about his wife not leaving him. His wife had been a great beauty and she was still a great beauty in Africa, but she was not a great enough beauty any more at home to be able to leave him and better herself and she knew it and he knew it. She had missed the chance to leave him and he knew it. If he had been better with women she would probably have started to worry about him getting another new, beautiful wife; but she knew too much about him to worry about him either. Also, he had always had a great tolerance which seemed the nicest thing about him if it were not the most sinister.

All in all they were known as a comparatively happily married couple, one of those whose disruption is often rumored but never occurs, and as the society columnist put it, they were adding more than a spice of *adventure* to their much envied and ever-enduring *Romance* by a *Safari* in what was known as *Darkest Africa* until the Martin Johnsons lighted it on so many silver screens where they were pursuing *Old Simba* the lion, the buffalo, *Tembo* the elephant and as well collecting specimens for the Museum of Natural History. This same columnist had reported them *on the verge* at least three times in the past and they had been. But they always made it up. They had a sound basis of union. Margot was too beautiful for Macomber to divorce her and Macomber had too much money for Margot ever to leave him.

It was now about three o'clock in the morning and Francis Macomber, who had been asleep a little while after he had stopped thinking about the lion, wakened and then slept again, woke suddenly, frightened in a dream of the bloody-headed lion standing over him, and listening while his heart pounded, he realized that his wife was not in the other cot in the tent. He lay awake with that knowledge for two hours.

At the end of that time his wife came into the tent, lifted her mosquito bar and crawled cozily into bed.

"Where have you been?" Macomber asked in the darkness.

"Hello," she said. "Are you awake?"

"Where have you been?"

"I just went out to get a breath of air."

"You did, like hell."

"What do you want me to say, darling?"

"Where have you been?"

"Out to get a breath of air."

"That's a new name for it. You *are* a bitch."

"Well, you're a coward."

"All right," he said. "What of it?"

"Nothing as far as I'm concerned. But please let's not talk, darling, because I'm very sleepy."

"You think that I'll take anything."

"I know you will, sweet."

"Well, I won't."

"Please, darling, let's not talk. I'm so very sleepy."

"There wasn't going to be any of that. You promised there wouldn't be."

"Well, there is now," she said sweetly.

"You said if we made this trip that there would be none of that. You promised."

"Yes, darling. That's the way I meant it to be. But the trip was spoiled yesterday. We don't have to talk about it, do we?"

"You don't wait long when you have an advantage, do you?"

"Please let's not talk. I'm so sleepy, darling."

"I'm going to talk."

"Don't mind me then, because I'm going to sleep." And she did.

At breakfast they were all three at the table before daylight and Francis Macomber found that, of all the men that he had hated, he hated Robert Wilson the most.

"Sleep well?" Wilson asked in his throaty voice, filling a pipe.

"Did you?"

"Topping," the white hunter told him.

You bastard, thought Macomber, you insolent bastard.

So she woke him when she came in, Wilson thought, looking at them both with his flat, cold eyes. Well, why doesn't he keep his wife where she belongs? What does he think I am, a bloody plaster saint? Let him keep her where she belongs. It's his own fault.

"Do you think we'll find buffalo?" Margot asked, pushing away a dish of apricots.

"Chance of it," Wilson said and smiled at her. "Why don't you stay in camp?"

"Not for anything," she told him.

"Why not order her to stay in camp?" Wilson said to Macomber.

"You order her," said Macomber coldly.

"Let's not have any ordering, nor," turning to Macomber, "any silliness, Francis," Margot said quite pleasantly.

"Are you ready to start?" Macomber asked.

"Any time," Wilson told him. "Do you want the Memsahib to go?"

"Does it make any difference whether I do or not?"

The hell with it, thought Robert Wilson. The utter complete hell with it. So this is what it's going to be like. Well, this is what it's going to be like, then.

"Makes no difference," he said.

"You're sure you wouldn't like to stay in camp with her yourself and let me go out and hunt the buffalo?" Macomber asked.

"Can't do that," said Wilson. "Wouldn't talk rot if I were you."

"I'm not talking rot. I'm disgusted."

"Bad word, disgusted."

"Francis, will you please try to speak sensibly?" his wife asked.

"I speak too damned sensibly," Macomber said. "Did you ever eat such filthy food?"

"Something wrong with the food?" asked Wilson quietly.

"No more than with everything else."

"I'd pull yourself together, laddybuck," Wilson said very quietly. "There's a boy waits at table that understands a little English."

"The hell with him."

Wilson stood up and puffing on his pipe strolled away, speaking a few words in Swahili to one of the gun-bearers who was standing waiting for him. Macomber and his wife sat on at the table. He was staring at his coffee cup.

"If you make a scene I'll leave you, darling," Margot said quietly.

"No, you won't."

"You can try it and see."

"You won't leave me."

"No," she said. "I won't leave you and you'll behave yourself."

"Behave myself? That's a way to talk. Behave myself."

"Yes. Behave yourself."

"Why don't *you* try behaving?"

"I've tried it so long. So very long."

"I hate that red-faced swine," Macomber said. "I loathe the sight of him."

"He's really *very* nice."

"Oh, *shut up*," Macomber almost shouted. Just then the car came up and stopped in front of the dining tent and the driver and the two gun-bearers got out. Wilson walked over and looked at the husband and wife sitting there at the table.

"Going shooting?" he asked.

"Yes," said Macomber, standing up. "Yes."

"Better bring a woolly. It will be cool in the car," Wilson said.

"I'll get my leather jacket," Margot said.

"The boy has it," Wilson told her. He climbed into the front with the driver and Francis Macomber and his wife sat, not speaking, in the back seat.

Hope the silly beggar doesn't take a notion to blow the back of my head off, Wilson thought to himself. Women *are* a nuisance on safari.

The car was grinding down to cross the river at a pebbly ford in the gray daylight and then climbed, angling up the steep bank, where Wilson had ordered a way shovelled out the day before so they could reach the parklike wooded rolling country on the far side.

It was a good morning, Wilson thought. There was a heavy dew and as the wheels went through the grass and low bushes he could smell the odor of the crushed fronds. It was an odor like verbena and he liked this early morning smell of the dew, the crushed bracken and the look of the tree trunks showing black through the early morning mist, as the car made its way through the untracked, parklike country. He had put the two in the back seat out of his mind now and was thinking about buffalo. The buffalo that he was after stayed in the daytime in a thick swamp where it was impossible to get a shot, but in the night they fed out into an open stretch of country and if he could come between them and their swamp with the car, Macomber would have a good chance at them in the open. He did not want to hunt buff with Macomber in thick cover. He did not want to hunt buff or anything else with Macomber at all, but he was a professional hunter and he had hunted with some rare ones in his time. If they got buff today there would only be rhino to come and the poor man would have gone through his dangerous game and things might pick up. He'd have nothing more to do with the woman and Macomber would get over that too. He must have gone through plenty of that before by the look of things. Poor beggar. He must have a way of getting over it. Well, it was the poor sod's own bloody fault.

He, Robert Wilson, carried a double size cot on safari to accommodate any windfalls he might receive. He had hunted for a certain clientele, the international, fast, sporting set, where the women did not feel they were getting their money's worth unless they had shared that cot with the white hunter. He despised them when he was away from them although he liked some of them well enough at the time, but he made his living by them; and their standards were his standards as long as they were hiring him.

They were his standards in all except the shooting. He had his own standards about the killing and they could live up to them or get some one else to hunt them. He knew, too, that they all respected him for this. This Macomber was an odd one though. Damned if he wasn't. Now the wife. Well, the wife. Yes, the wife. Hm, the wife. Well he'd dropped all that. He looked around at them. Macomber sat grim and furious. Margot smiled at him. She looked younger today, more innocent and fresher and not so professionally beautiful. What's in her heart God knows, Wilson thought. She hadn't talked much last night. At that it was a pleasure to see her

The motor car climbed up a slight rise and went on through the trees and then out into a grassy prairie-like opening and kept in the shelter of the trees along the edge, the driver going slowly and Wilson looking carefully out across the prairie and all along its far side. He stopped the car and studied the opening with his field glasses. Then he motioned to the driver to go on and the car moved slowly along, the driver avoiding wart-hog holes and driving around the mud castles ants had built. Then, looking across the opening, Wilson suddenly turned and said,

"By God, there they are!"

And looking where he pointed, while the car jumped forward and Wilson spoke in rapid Swahili to the driver, Macomber saw three huge, black animals looking almost cylindrical in their long heaviness, like big black tank cars, moving at a gallop across the far edge of the open prairie. They moved at a stiff-necked, stiff bodied gallop and he could see the upswept wide black horns on their heads as they galloped heads out; the heads not moving.

"They're three old bulls," Wilson said. "We'll cut them off before they get to the swamp."

The car was going a wild forty-five miles an hour across the open and as Macomber watched, the buffalo got bigger and bigger until he could see the gray, hairless, scabby look of one huge bull and how his neck was a part of his shoulders and the shiny black of his horns as he galloped a little behind the others that were strung out in that steady plunging gait; and then, the car swaying as though it had just jumped a road, they drew up close and he could see the plunging hugeness of the bull, and the dust in his sparsely haired hide, the wide boss of horn and his outstretched, wide-nostrilled muzzle, and he was raising his rifle when Wilson shouted, "Not from the car, you fool!" and he had no fear, only hatred, of Wilson, while the brakes clamped on and the car skidded, plowing sideways to an almost stop and Wilson was out on one side and he on the other, stumbling as his feet hit the still speeding-by of the earth, and then he was shooting at the bull as he moved away, hearing the bullets whunk into him, emptying his rifle at him as he moved steadily away, finally remembering to get his shots forward into the shoulder, and as he fumbled to re-load, he saw the bull was down. Down on his knees, his big head tossing, and seeing the other two still galloping he shot at the leader and hit him. He shot again and missed and he heard the *carawonging* roar as Wilson shot and saw the leading bull slide forward onto his nose.

"Get that other," Wilson said. "Now you're shooting!"

But the other bull was moving steadily at the same gallop and he missed, throwing a spout of dirt, and Wilson missed and the dust rose in a cloud and Wilson shouted, "Come on. He's too far!" and grabbed his arm and they were in the car again, Macomber and Wilson hanging on the sides and rocketing swayingly over the uneven ground, drawing up on the steady, plunging, heavy-necked, straight-moving gallop of the bull.

They were behind him and Macomber was filling his rifle, dropping shells onto the ground, jamming it, clearing the jam, then they were almost up with the bull when Wilson yelled "Stop," and the car skidded so that it almost swung over and Macomber fell forward onto his feet, slammed his bolt forward and fired as far forward as he could aim into the galloping, rounded black back, aimed and shot again, then again, then again and the bullets, all of them hitting, had no effect on the buffalo that he could see. Then Wilson shot, the roar deafening him, and he could see the bull stagger. Macomber shot again, aiming carefully, and down he came, onto his knees.

"All right," Wilson said. "Nice work. That's the three."

Macomber felt a drunken elation.

"How many times did you shoot?" he asked.

"Just three," Wilson said. "You killed the first bull. The biggest one. I helped you finish the other two. Afraid they might have got into cover. You had them killed. I was just mopping up a little. You shot damn well."

"Let's go to the car," said Macomber. "I want a drink."

"Got to finish off that buff first," Wilson told him. The buffalo was on his knees and he jerked his head furiously and bellowed in pig-eyed, roaring rage as they came toward him.

"Watch he doesn't get up," Wilson said. Then, "Get a little broadside and take him in the neck just behind the ear."

Macomber aimed carefully at the center of the huge, jerking, rage-driven neck and shot. At the shot the head dropped forward.

"That does it," said Wilson. "Got the spine. They're a hell of a looking thing, aren't they?"

"Let's get the drink," said Macomber. In his life he had never felt so good.

In the car Macomber's wife sat very white faced. "You were marvellous, darling," she said to Macomber. "What a ride."

"Was it rough?" Wilson asked.

"It was frightful. I've never been more frightened in my life."

"Let's all have a drink," Macomber said.

"By all means," said Wilson. "Give it to the Memsahib." She drank the neat whisky from the flask and shuddered a little when she swallowed. She handed the flask to Macomber who handed it to Wilson.

"It was frightfully exciting," she said. "It's given me a dreadful headache. I didn't know you were allowed to shoot them from cars though."

"No one shot from cars," said Wilson coldly.

"I mean chase them."

"Wouldn't ordinarily," Wilson said. "Seemed sporting enough to me while we were doing it. Taking more chance driving that way across the plain full of holes and one thing and another than hunting on foot. Buffalo could have charged us each time we shot if he liked. Gave him every chance. Wouldn't mention it to any one though. It's illegal if that's what you mean."

"It seemed very unfair to me," Margot said, "chasing those big helpless things in a motor car."

"Did it?" said Wilson.

"What would happen if they heard about it in Nairobi?"

"I'd lose my license for one thing. Other unpleasantnesses," Wilson said, taking a drink from the flask. "I'd be out of business."

"Really?"

"Yes, really."

"Well," said Macomber, and he smiled for the first time all day. "Now she has something on you."

"You have such a pretty way of putting things, Francis," Margot Macomber said. Wilson looked at them both. If a four-letter man marries a five-letter woman, he was thinking, what number of letters would their children be? What he said was, "We lost a gun-bearer. Did you notice it?"

"My God, no," Macomber said.

"Here he comes," Wilson said. "He's all right. He must have fallen off when we left the first bull."

Approaching them was the middle-aged gun-bearer, limping along in his knitted cap, khaki tunic, shorts and rubber sandals, gloomy-faced and disgusted looking. As he came up he called out to Wilson in Swahili and they all saw the change in the white hunter's face.

"What does he say?" asked Margot.

"He says the first bull got up and went into the bush," Wilson said with no expression in his voice.

"Oh," said Macomber blankly.

"Then it's going to be just like the lion," said Margot, full of anticipation.

"It's not going to be a damned bit like the lion," Wilson told her. "Did you want another drink, Macomber?"

"Thanks, yes," Macomber said. He expected the feeling he had had about the lion to come back but it did not. For the first time in his life he really felt wholly without fear. Instead of fear he had a feeling of definite elation.

"We'll go and have a look at the second bull," Wilson said. "I'll tell the driver to put the car in the shade."

"What are you going to do?" asked Margot Macomber.

"Take a look at the buff," Wilson said.

"I'll come."

"Come along."

The three of them walked over to where the second buffalo bulked blackly in the open, head forward on the grass, the massive horns swung wide.

"He's a very good head," Wilson said. "That's close to a fifty-inch spread."

Macomber was looking at him with delight.

"He's hateful looking," said Margot. "Can't we go into the shade?"

"Of course," Wilson said. "Look," he said to Macomber, and pointed. "See that patch of bush?"

"Yes."

"That's where the first bull went in. The gun-bearer said when he fell off the bull was down. He was watching us helling along and the other two buff galloping. When he looked up there was the bull up and looking at him. Gunbearer ran like hell and the bull went off slowly into that bush."

"Can we go in after him now?" asked Macomber eagerly.

Wilson looked at him appraisingly. Damned if this isn't a strange one, he thought. Yesterday he's scared sick and today he's a ruddy fire-eater.

"No, we'll give him a while."

"Let's please go into the shade," Margot said. Her face was white, and she looked ill.

They made their way to the car where it stood under a single, wide-spreading tree and all climbed in.

"Chances are he's dead in there," Wilson remarked. "After a little we'll have a look."

Macomber felt a wild unreasonable happiness that he had never known before.

"By God, that was a chase," he said. "I've never felt any such feeling. Wasn't it marvellous, Margot?"

"I hated it."

"Why?"

"I hated it," she said bitterly. "I loathed it."

"You know I don't think I'd ever be afraid of anything again," Macomber said to Wilson. "Something happened in me after we first saw the buff and started after him. Like a dam bursting. It was pure excitement."

"Cleans out your liver," said Wilson. "Damn funny things happen to people."

Macomber's face was shining. "You know something did happen to me," he said. "I feel absolutely different."

His wife said nothing and eyed him strangely. She was sitting far back in the seat and Macomber was sitting forward talking to Wilson who turned sideways talking over the back of the front seat.

"You know, I'd like to try another lion," Macomber said. "I'm really not afraid of them now. After all, what can they do to you?"

"That's it," said Wilson. "Worst one can do is kill you. How does it go? Shakespeare. Damned good. See if I can remember. Oh, damned good. Used to quote it to myself at one time. Let's see. 'By my troth, I care not; a man can die but once; we owe God a death and let it go which way it will he that dies this year is quit for the next.' Damned fine, eh?"

He was very embarrassed, having brought out this thing he had lived by, but he had seen men come of age before and it always moved him. It was not a matter of their twenty-first birthday.

It had taken a strange chance of hunting, a sudden precipitation into action without opportunity for worrying beforehand, to bring this about with Macomber, but regardless of how it had happened it had most certainly happened. Look at the beggar now, Wilson thought. It's that some of them stay little boys so long, Wilson thought. Sometimes all their lives. Their figures stay boyish when they're fifty. The great American boy-men. Damned strange people. But he liked this Macomber now. Damned strange fellow. Probably meant the end of cuckoldry too. Well, that would be a damned good thing. Damned good thing. Beggar had probably been afraid all his life. Don't know what started it. But over now. Hadn't had time to be afraid with the buff. That and being angry too. Motor car too. Motor cars made it familiar. Be a damn fire eater now. He'd seen it in the war work the same way. More of a change than any loss of virginity. Fear gone like an operation. Something else grew in its place. Main thing a man had. Made him into a man. Women knew it too. No bloody fear.

From the far corner of the seat Margot Macomber looked at the two of them. There was no change in Wilson. She saw Wilson as she had seen him the day before when she had first realized what his great talent was. But she saw the change in Francis Macomber now.

"Do you have that feeling of happiness about what's going to happen?" Macomber asked, still exploring his new wealth.

"You're not supposed to mention it," Wilson said, looking in the other's face. "Much more fashionable to say you're scared. Mind you, you'll be scared too, plenty of times."

"But you *have* a feeling of happiness about action to come?"

"Yes," said Wilson. "There's that. Doesn't do to talk too much about all this. Talk the whole thing away. No pleasure in anything if you mouth it up too much."

"You're both talking rot," said Margot. "Just because you've chased some helpless animals in a motor car you talk like heroes."

"Sorry," said Wilson. "I have been gassing too much." She's worried about it already, he thought.

"If you don't know what we're talking about why not keep out of it?" Macomber asked his wife.

"You've gotten awfully brave, awfully suddenly," his wife said contemptuously, but her contempt was not secure. She was very afraid of something.

Macomber laughed, a very natural hearty laugh. "You know I *have*," he said. "I really have."

"Isn't it sort of late?" Margot said bitterly. Because she had done the best she could for many years back and the way they were together now was no one person's fault.

"Not for me," said Macomber.

Margot said nothing but sat back in the corner of the seat.

"Do you think we've given him time enough?" Macomber asked Wilson cheerfully.

"We might have a look," Wilson said. "Have you any solids left?"

"The gun-bearer has some."

Wilson called in Swahili and the older gun-bearer, who was skinning out one of the heads, straightened up, pulled a box of solids out of his pocket and brought them over to Macomber, who filled his magazine and put the remaining shells in his pocket.

"You might as well shoot the Springfield," Wilson said. "You're used to it. We'll leave the Mannlicher in the car with the Memsahib. Your gun-bearer can carry your heavy gun. I've this damned cannon. Now let me tell you about them." He had saved this until the last because he did not want to worry Macomber. "When a buff comes he comes with his head high and thrust straight out. The boss of the horns covers any sort of a brain shot. The only shot is straight into the nose. The only other shot is into his chest or, if you're to one side, into the neck or the shoulders. After they've been hit once they take a hell of a lot of killing. Don't try anything fancy. Take the easiest shot there is. They've finished skinning out that head now. Should we get started?"

He called to the gun-bearers, who came up wiping their hands, and the older one got into the back.

"I'll only take Kongoni," Wilson said. "The other can watch to keep the birds away."

As the car moved slowly across the open space toward the island of brushy trees that ran in a tongue of foliage along a dry water course that cut the open swale, Macomber felt his heart pounding and his mouth was dry again, but it was excitement, not fear.

"Here's where he went in," Wilson said. Then to the gun-bearer in Swahili, "Take the blood spoor."

The car was parallel to the patch of bush. Macomber, Wilson and the gun-bearer got down. Macomber, looking back, saw his wife, with the rifle by her side, looking at him. He waved to her and she did not wave back.

The brush was very thick ahead and the ground was dry. The middle-aged gun-bearer was sweating heavily and Wilson had his hat down over his eyes and his red neck showed just ahead of Macomber. Suddenly the gun-bearer said something in Swahili to Wilson and ran forward.

"He's dead in there," Wilson said. "Good work," and he turned to grip Macomber's hand and as they shook hands, grinning at each other, the gun-bearer shouted wildly and they saw him coming out of the bush sideways, fast as a crab, and the bull coming, nose out, mouth tight closed, blood dripping, massive head straight out, coming in a charge, his little pig eyes bloodshot as he looked at them. Wilson, who was ahead, was kneeling shooting, and Macomber, as he fired, unhearing his shot in the roaring of Wilson's gun, saw fragments like slate burst from the huge boss of the horns, and the head jerked, he shot again at the wide nostrils and saw the horn jolt again and fragments fly, and he did not see Wilson now and, aiming carefully, shot again with the buffalo's huge bulk almost on him and his rifle almost level with the on-coming head, nose out, and he could see the little wicked eyes and the head started to lower and he felt a sudden white-hot, blinding flash explode inside his head and that was all he ever felt.

Wilson had ducked to one side to get in a shoulder shot. Macomber had stood solid and shot for the nose, shooting a touch high each time and hitting the heavy horns, splintering and chipping them like hitting a slate roof, and Mrs. Macomber, in the car, had shot at the buffalo with the 6.5 Mannlicher as it seemed about to gore Macomber and had hit her husband about two inches up and a little to one side of the base of his skull.

Francis Macomber lay now, face down, not two yards from where the buffalo lay on his side and his wife knelt over him with Wilson beside her.

"I wouldn't turn him over," Wilson said.

The woman was crying hysterically.

"I'd get back in the car," Wilson said. "Where's the rifle?"

She shook her head, her face contorted. The gun-bearer picked up the rifle.

"Leave it as it is," said Wilson. Then, "Go get Abdulla so that he may witness the manner of the accident."

He knelt down, took a handkerchief from his pocket, and spread it over Francis Macomber's crew-cropped head where it lay. The blood sank into the dry, loose earth.

Wilson stood up and saw the buffalo on his side, his legs out, his thinly-haired belly crawling with ticks. "Hell of a good bull," his brain registered automatically. "A good fifty inches, or better. Better." He called to the driver and told him to spread a blanket over the body and stay by it. Then he walked over to the motor car where the woman sat crying in the corner.

"That was a pretty thing to do," he said in a toneless voice. "He *would* have left you too."

"Stop it," she said.

"Of course it's an accident," he said. "I know that."

"Stop it," she said.

"Don't worry," he said. "There will be a certain amount of unpleasantness but I will have some photographs taken that will be very useful at the inquest. There's the testimony of the gun-bearers and the driver too. You're perfectly all right."

"Stop it," she said.

"There's a hell of a lot to be done," he said. "And I'll have to send a truck off to the lake to wireless for a plane to take the three of us into Nairobi. Why didn't you poison him? That's what they do in England."

"Stop it. Stop it. Stop it," the woman cried.

Wilson looked at her with his flat blue eyes.

"I'm through now," he said. "I was a little angry. I'd begun to like your husband."

"Oh, please stop it," she said. "Please, please stop it."

"That's better," Wilson said. "Please is much better. Now I'll stop."

RONALD S. CRANE

Observations on a Story by Hemingway[1]

My dear M——:

I am very grateful to you for sending me the three papers on "The Short Happy Life of Francis Macomber." I have read them with much interest, and with only two major reservations.

One of these has to do with your attempt to interpret Macomber as an "Aristotelian" tragic hero. This came as somewhat of a surprise to me after your earlier statements about the plot. With these I would largely agree. Like you I think that the action begins with Macomber "in his lowest condition" and proceeds to his achievement, for a brief moment before his death, of a "happiness" greater than he had ever known before; as you put it, he is transformed from an *object* into a *man*. The essential change is thus not one of fortune but of moral character, the word "happy" in the title having the ethical connotation given it in Aristotle's definition of "happiness" as activity in accordance with virtue. For such a change the appropriate response of the reader is obviously a pleasurable rather than a painful one, i.e., some degree of rejoicing dependent on the depth of "unhappiness" from which the man has risen, and on the suddenness of the change. That something like this is what we are intended to feel for Macomber is suggested by the reactions of Wilson in the paragraph beginning, "He was very embarrassed" and in his remark at the end to Margot, "I'd begun to like your husband."

All this you say or imply in the concluding paragraphs of your first section, and here at least you don't treat Macomber's death as a tragic catastrophe, though I think you fail to make sufficiently clear what its relation is to the "emotional satisfaction" of which you correctly say that the "change in Macomber's life is . . . a principal cause." Plainly the answer turns in part on how we construe the act of Margot which brings her husband's "short happy life" to a sudden end; and I am puzzled by W——'s contentions, with which you appear to agree, that Hemingway meant to leave us in doubt whether the killing was accident or murder and that this very uncertainty constitutes "the finest artistic touch in the story." I should say, on the contrary, that if "suspension of judgment" about the cause of Macomber's death is the in-

---

[1] This letter was written in 1949 to a former student who had sent me copies of the *English* "A" *Analyst* (a private publication of the English staff of Northwestern University, Evanston, Illinois) containing essays by himself and two of his colleagues on Ernest Hemingway's "The Short Happy Life of Francis Macomber." The letter was subsequently published in No. 16 of the *Analyst*, from which it is here reprinted with some changes and the substitution of initials for names, by the kind permission of the editors.

tended final state of mind of the reader, then Hemingway has bungled his job. For the climactic emotion in that case becomes a species of wonder, much as in trick stories like "The Lady and the Tiger"; our attention, moreover, is shifted away from Macomber, who up to this point has been the major object of our feelings, and concentrated on Margot, who is suddenly turned into a lady of mystery, with the result that all the reiterated signs of her emotions and intentions during the buffalo hunt become retrospectively ambiguous; and, finally, the doubt about Margot is extended to Wilson, who certainly gives every appearance of being certain about the facts—and what then becomes of our confidence in him as a trustworthy chorus which has been built up through the story? Can we suppose that now, and for the first time, he is wrong in his judgment of Margot? But the whole idea is untenable except on the supposition that Hemingway was no artist or a deliberately irresponsible one.

In spite of the narrator's statement that "Mrs. Macomber . . . had shot at the buffalo," etc., I think we can no less easily rule out the possibility of accident. For, to begin with, the theory of accident implies an intention on Margot's part to save Macomber's life, and such an intention doesn't accord either with what we have been led to believe about her character from the beginning or with the clear indications of her growing hatred for her husband in the immediately preceding scene; and, for another thing, it implies that the outcome of her act was determined merely by chance, and there are no previous instances of this sort of probability in the story. (This last objection can also be brought against E——'s suggestion of "unconscious motivation"; where in the narrative up to this point are the motives of the agents ever presented except as conscious ones deriving from relatively simple states of passion?) But there is also a further and more important objection, which will appear when you ask how our feelings would be affected if we really thought that the killing of Macomber was accidental. Wouldn't the inevitable effect be to arouse some degree of pity for Margot at least at the moment when we see her "crying hysterically" over her husband's body, and hence to make us resent the rough handling of her by Wilson? But I can't think that any reader ever reacted in this way; and we don't so react because we never seriously entertain, as we are reading the story, the notion of accident.

We must suppose, then, either that Hemingway didn't know his business or that Macomber was murdered by his wife. But if he was murdered, why do we continue to feel toward him at the end of the story the "emotional satisfaction" which I agree with you is the effect on us of his final achievement of courage? Or why is it that, although we experience a painful shock when we come abruptly, at the end of the sentence telling us of his victorious stand against the buffalo, to the clause "and he felt . . . ," the shock we then feel is momentary only and the pain never becomes the pity which we normally feel for victims of murder when they are good men whom we know vividly?

I think the reason is partly to be found in certain tricks of technique by which, in the first place, our attention is centered so wholly on Macomber and the buffalo during the last stages of the hunt that we don't think of danger from any other source, and by which, in the second place, as soon as Macomber has fallen, our thoughts are turned away from him to Wilson and Margot. But the causes lie also in the plot itself. We tend to feel pity at the murder of anyone whose destruction seems to involve waste or who appears to have un- exhausted possibilities of "happiness" or possibilities of greater "happiness" in the future. But Macomber is clearly not so conceived. Within the story he is only (a) the ineffective husband of a "predatory" wife and (b) such a man engaged in an African *safari*—in short, one who satisfies completely all our expectations and hopes when he finally dominates Margot and acts without fear as a hunter. Once this climax is reached he has done the best that is in him, and we have no active desire that he should live on; or rather, as you shrewdly suggest, we take his death as in some sense necessary to our full appreciation of his victory over himself—he is so ordinary a creature that had he survived, the perfection of the moment might well have been spoiled. Again, no matter how nobly a man acts on the eve of his death, we still pity him as long as we think of his courageous act as something done in spite of a natural human aversion to dying. But this is ruled out for Macomber by the very nature of his victory over his previous fear, and here once more, as you point out, Wilson serves as chorus (cf. his words in the passage beginning " 'You know, I'd like to try another lion,' Macomber said"). Finally, not only is Macomber's death part of his moral triumph, it marks also the complete and deserved defeat of his wife; she has got rid of her husband only to fall under the power of Wilson; and our satisfaction at this, aroused in the con- cluding dialogue, effectively counteracts our momentary shock at the murder.

But if all this is true, isn't it quite misleading to analogize Macomber to the "Aristotelian" tragic hero? I should have thought that you would have been more struck by the essential differences between the two than by their super- ficial likenesses as protagonists who suffer death in serious actions. "Tragedy," as Aristotle defines it in *Poetics* 13 and 14, is a very special plot-form, which has been fully achieved, I think, only by a few of the Greeks and by Shakes- peare in some of his major works, notably *Hamlet, King Lear*, and *Othello*. Its distinguishing pleasure is a catharsis of fear and pity, the peculiar "tragic" quality of which is determined by the other causes which Aristotle specifies in these two chapters. The formal cause is a change of fortune rather than of character (though this may also be involved) from good to bad, resulting from an unjust deed, productive of great pain and suffering, committed by the protagonist on a friend or friends, as a consequence of which the protagonist himself is ruined; the material cause is a hero of the intermediate type, not bad but not "preeminently virtuous and just," though within these limits better rather than worse, and also preferably (for then the change will seem all the more impressive) one who enjoys at the beginning great "reputation and prosperity"; and the efficient cause, located in the moral choices of the protagonist, is a course of action motivated not by evil intent but by *hamartia*, i.e., a fundamental error with respect to the circumstances of the situation which is yet compatible with goodness of character, so that though the hero acts voluntarily, the evil results of his acts are non-voluntary and he himself suffers more deeply than any of his victims. When all these conditions are fulfilled in the construction of a plot, the effect for the normally sensitive spectator is tragic fear and pity; and this effect will be enhanced if the change of fortune comes about suddenly and unexpectedly (peripety) and is accompanied or followed by a change from ignorance to knowledge that reverses the attitudes of the major characters to one another and also, in the best tragedies, to themselves (discovery).

But how completely different from this is the plot-form of "The Short Happy Life"! The change upon which the effect depends is, as I have said, not a change of fortune from good to bad but of character from bad to good. It comes about as a result of action by the hero (in the buffalo hunt) which involves no injustice, has no destructive effects on any one who is dear to him, and proceeds not from error concerning the circumstances but from a wholly praiseworthy cause, his conquest of fear. The decision to go on the hunting trip may have been, as you suggest, a mistake; but it is merely one of the given conditions of the plot, not a primary factor in its development or in the determination of our emotions before and at the climax, as is always the case with tragic *hamartia*. Macomber's suffering before the buffalo hunt, moreover, has its source not in any sense of erroneous or misdirected action (as in Oedipus or Hamlet) but in shame at his own bad conduct in the face of the lion. The only mistake that functions in the plot is that of Margot, for which she pays in the end; but this is not "tragic" either in its motivation or in its results for Macomber; and Margot, in any case, is not the protagonist. (If she had been, a very different plot-form would have resulted, but it would not have been "tragic" either.) The only thing, in short, that Hemingway's tale has in common with tragedy, in Aristotle's sense, is that issues of life and death are involved in the change it depicts. But they are involved in such a way that we do not experience fear for Macomber as he proceeds to assert his newfound courage or pity for him when he falls.

Parenthetically, I think that the antecedents and circumstances of the lion hunt are also "conditions"; the action proper begins with the immediate consequences of the incident in Margot's act of kissing Wilson and in Macomber's shame. There is therefore, it seems to me, only one formal peripety—Macomber's unexpected coming of age; the murder is a peripety only in a material sense, its formal significance, as I said before, being inseparable from that of Macomber's final act. Because of the nature of the action the only possible kind of discovery is self-discovery, and this occurs when Macomber recognizes that he no longer fears death. There are plenty of "discoveries" to the reader besides the one you mention, but these are not discoveries in a poetic sense, since they proceed not from the events of the plot but from Hemingway's decisions as to what he must disclose to the reader and when.

My second chief reservation about the essays concerns the adequacy of the analytical apparatus employed in them. A critic, I should think, ought to be able, among other things, to say how successful artistically—i.e., as a constructed whole—"The Short Happy Life" really is and to give relevant reasons for his judgment; and this necessitates his finding answers to three main questions: how good is Hemingway's plot relatively to the kind of pleasure intended? how effectively is it brought before the reader in the words of the story? and how well adjusted to the specific requirements of the plot are the subordinate parts of characterization, thought, and language.

Of these three questions only the first is touched upon in the essays, and it is dealt with for the most part in a fashion that doesn't permit of a critical appraisal of the story. Except for one place in your paper, the three of you are more concerned with the underlying matter of Hemingway's plot than with the plot itself considered as an artistic construction. It is true that you all look for the form of this matter, i.e., what holds its successive parts together; but the direction in which you look for it takes you away from the story itself viewed as a sequential whole with a particularized system of suspense and surprise, and leads to the discovery not of a plot, in the strict sense of the principle that organizes the action and gives to it its peculiar emotional quality, but of some general "pattern" of human conduct in terms of which the things done and thought by Hemingway's characters can be made abstractly intelligible. For E—— the pattern is given by his conception of Macomber as a neurotic egoist who finally frees himself "from the incubus of his heroic self-portrait"; and he has some difficulty in adjusting to this what he calls "the most complicated dilemma of the story," the question whether the Macomber marriage is or is not "spiritually dead." For W—— the story is essentially an instance of the behavior of "predatory" creatures seeking "advantages" over one another in a "predatory" world. For you the dominant pattern is one which you take to be central in many or most of Hemingway's writings: the problem of how different kinds of men face death. The three of you come out, in other words, in spite of your protests of mutual agreement, with three perceptibly different "plots"! I don't doubt that the story rests on a material substrate of ideas and unconscious associations that can be interpreted, without doing complete violence to the text, in some or perhaps all of these ways. A plot, however, is more than its substrate of ideas or beliefs; it is the form that actually synthesizes the materials and successive incidents of an individual story and hence, as we infer it progressively from the writer's words, determines the sequence of our emotions with respect to the characters and the changes they undergo.

The difficulty, I think, is that the essays tend to approach the story in terms of preestablished formulae applicable to many stories rather than by way of close attention to the successive effects which Hemingway, in this story, is engaged in producing. You are something of an exception, as I have said, and as a result you come nearer to seeing what the form of the story is (in the sense of the working on us of its particularized action) than do your colleagues, who seem to me to be talking about the plot in more or less complete separation from the special sequence of emotions which is at once its artistic end and the principal source of the criteria whereby, at least as a constructed whole, it ought to be judged. I wish, however, that you had elaborated your insight in relation to the peculiar correlation of character and event that produces the effect you recognize and had then gone on to say something about how successful, in the light of its form, you think Hemingway's construction is.

On the first point something might be made of an aspect of the story that struck me when I reread it the other day. Part of the effect depends, I think, on the fact that there had been a long literary tradition of characters like Macomber, i.e., cuckolds in subjection to their wives who are also, in moments of physical danger, cowards. For the most part, until the middle of the nineteenth century, such characters had been comic butts. Then, in various novels and plays, their traits and actions were employed to produce "naturalistic" effects of sordidness or the like. In the twentieth century they (and other similar characters, like alcoholics and ineffectives generally) have often been given the status of protagonists in serious plots, in which a certain impression of nobility is achieved by making them unexpectedly act or speak like heroes. I think this is Hemingway's central idea in "The Short Happy Life," as something not greatly different is Eliot's idea in "Prufrock" and Graham Greene's in *The Confidential Agent*. On this view of the story, the function of Wilson in the plot, as distinguished from his technical function as chorus, becomes evident: part of Macomber's triumph is the admiration his action elicits from his latest cuckolder! And so too with Margot. The state of her marriage is not a problem in the sense of being material to the unifying suspense—it is merely one of the prior conditions of the action; and Margot's role in the plot is threefold: she is a sign of her husband's initial degradation, the immediate occasion of the hate which frees him from fear, and finally the instrument that makes his heroism complete.

As for the virtues and weaknesses of the plot, I should like to have had your opinion on two points. One is the manner in which Margot's shooting of her husband is related to the previous events. The moral probability is strong enough, but what about the probability that she will have the gun? Is it good enough to support the intended seriousness of the final effect? The other point is more important. I have often thought that the power of the story is considerably attenuated by the fact that the change in Macomber, which ought to have something of the quality of a miracle (it surprises and embarrasses Wilson), is rather too easily foreseeable from the beginning. Macomber has begun as an abject coward and a slave to Margot: what else can he now do except what he does—namely, get over his fear and in so doing emancipate himself from his wife? I grant that there is plenty of suspense during the buffalo hunt, but it turns only on the physical danger, not at all on the complexity of the central action. The plots of the best short stories are not as obvious as this. And there is finally the question of how seriously, in the moral sense, we can take the action as a whole in spite of its fatal ending. Macomber himself, I can't help thinking, is too commonplace a creature to excite in us any strong wishes, on his own account as an individual, that he should rise from the low state in which we first see him. I agree with you that we feel a certain "emotional satisfaction" when he does, but I wonder if this is not to be accounted for by a combination of two things that have little to do with the particularity of his character: our general disposition to take pleasure in any sudden access of virtue in human beings even when, as persons, they are indifferent to us; and our detestation of Margot and consequent desire that that should happen in the story which would most frustrate and displease her. The effect produced by the change in Macomber is thus of the relatively inferior order which we properly call "sentimental"; it is certainly, for me at least, less "serious" than is (say) the generically similar effect aroused by the emergence of good sense in Jane Austen's Emma!

For an adequate judgment of Hemingway's success, however, it is necessary to go beyond the plot and, holding this constant, to ask about how the story is told. This, you will see, is our old problem of representation as distinct from what is represented. It concerns all the devices a writer employs, vis-à-vis his audience, for the sake of inducing a proper judgment of the emotional quality, the probability, or the importance of the things going on in his plot when this would not be evident from a simple and direct presentation of them. The sources from which the devices derive are common to rhetoric and poetics, but since the final end to be served is a certain poetic pleasure determined primarily by the construction of the plot, the criteria for judging the success of any representational device must be drawn from a prior consideration of what the plot and its peculiar "power" are intended to be. You were right therefore to center your first discussion of Hemingway's tale on its action; what I regret is that you did not then proceed to the further question of how well the plot-form, as you conceive it, is clarified and sustained by the narrative.

Looked at from this point of view, "The Short Happy Life" is not, it seems to me, one of Hemingway's most expert jobs. Consider the manner in which Macomber's behavior during the lion hunt is made clear to us. We see it first in terms of the effects of his cowardice on himself, his wife, and Wilson (to say nothing of the servants), and then, in a "flashback" that takes off from Macomber's thoughts that night, we are given the incident itself in full and vivid detail. As an expedient for forcing us to attend closely to what has happened before the story proper begins, this inverted order of narration is effective enough, though a bit shopworn. But think of what the result is for our opinion of the hero. If the story is indeed one in which Macomber passes suddenly (in your phrase) "from *object* to *man*" and if the function of Wilson, in connection with this, is to provide the "norm" by which we are intended to evaluate the change, then clearly nothing should be done in the narrative that will obscure this view of the case. Now I think we do become more or less convinced during the opening scene that Macomber is "less of a man and more of an object than ever before" and that Wilson, if not Margot, is probably right in judging him as severely as he does. But then we learn for ourselves what has actually happened earlier in the day, and I think he would be a rather exceptional reader who could feel quite sure that, if he were put into the same fearsome circumstances as Macomber, and with no more previous experience with African lions, he would not, like Macomber, suddenly find himself "running wildly, in panic in the open, running toward the stream." It may be, as you suggest, that Hemingway wishes us to think of Macomber, in this situation, as "less . . . even as an *object*, than the lion itself"; and this may be the reason for the otherwise somewhat arbitrary glimpses he gives us into the lion's thoughts. But if so, the device surely misses the mark, with the result that so far from thinking that Wilson's previously indicated contempt has been warranted by the facts, we now tend to feel that he and his professional code are below humanity in a sense in which Macomber's regrettable but wholly natural "cowardice" is not. I repeat that I don't think this is a part of the plot as Hemingway conceived it; about that you seem to me to be right. But certainly to the extent that you are right, Hemingway is wrong! Either he should not have told the story of the lion hunt at all or he should have told it in such a way as to confirm rather than contradict the impression of Macomber's initial moral state which he had been careful to fix in our minds at the start.

It seems to me also that in several portions of his narrative Hemingway has resorted too much to inferior and makeshift devices for keeping the reader aware of what is going on. What we are led to expect from the opening pages is an objective and dramatic rendering of events in the manner, for instance, of "The Killers," and I can see no reason why the whole story could not have been told in this way. The device is modified, however, in the course of the first scene, by the singling out of Wilson as a kind of observer-chorus whose inferences and judgments about Macomber and Margot are given to us in brief asides. This has some obvious advantages, and entails no great sacrifice of that economy of representation on which Hemingway has always prided himself; and if he had been content to do the later scenes in a technique consistent with this beginning, there would be nothing more to say. But then comes the scene of the lion hunt as recollected by Macomber lying in his cot, and here the crudities begin. Observe the flat narrative statements about how Macomber felt as he listened to the night noises; the shift to the lion's perceptions when the motor car reached the place and the later return to these as the beast is about to spring; the amateurish "He could not know that Wilson was furious because he had not noticed . . ."; and lastly the two paragraphs on the marriage, in which Macomber's reflections are allowed to merge, not imperceptibly, into mere historical report.

And what is done in the final scene of the buffalo hunt is even worse, except that we are spared a look into the buffalo's mind. The scene starts in the manner of the first, with Wilson as chorus in an otherwise dramatic rendering.

But this method presently breaks down, and we get many direct statements of thought and feeling not only for Macomber but, in one or two places toward the end, even for Margot, who has hitherto been merely heard and seen (cf. "but her contempt was not secure. She was very afraid of something" and "Because she had done the best she could for many years back and the way they were together was no one person's fault"). Most of these statements seem to me superfluous in view of what is obviously going on, or, when they serve a purpose, to be clumsy explicit notations of things that could be better shown dramatically. The worst are the reiterated assertions, in the narrator's flat prose, of Macomber's "happiness": "he had no fear, only hatred of Wilson"; "Macomber felt a drunken elation"; "In his life he had never felt so good"; "For the first time in his life he really felt wholly without fear. Instead of fear he had a feeling of definite elation"; etc. Hemingway at his best would have left all this to the reader's inference, as he does similar things in "The Killers," and he would never have printed a passage like the following:

> Macomber felt a wild unreasonable happiness that he had never known before.
> "By God, that was a chase," he said. "I've never felt any such feeling. Wasn't it marvellous, Margot?"

There is in all this little of the concision we appreciate in Hemingway's better work, and the result is a watering down of the effect proper to this crucial part of the story; there is a certain jarring incongruity, too, between the commonplace flavor of Macomber's thoughts as the narrator states them and the relatively heroic quality of his actions. I can explain these lapses only by supposing that, having begun to write like himself in the opening section, Hemingway then suddenly became conscious of the limited intelligence, in matters of art, of his prospective readers in the *Cosmopolitan* magazine!

I had intended to say something finally about the last of my three critical topics—the handling of the parts other than plot. But to do so I should have to read the story again, and I am somewhat tired of it, and it is hot, and I have already written more than a single letter ought to contain.

FRANK O'CONNOR

Legal Aid [1]

Delia Carty came of a very respectable family. It was going as maid to the O'Gradys of Pouladuff that ruined her. That whole family was slightly touched. The old man, a national teacher, was hardly ever at home, and the

[1] From *The Stories of Frank O'Connor* (New York: Alfred A. Knopf, Inc., 1951). Copyright, 1951, 1952, by Frank O'Connor. Reprinted by permission.

daughters weren't much better. When they weren't away visiting, they had people visiting them, and it was nothing to Delia to come in late at night and find one of them plastered round some young fellow on the sofa.

That sort of thing isn't good for any young girl. Like mistress like maid; inside six months she was smoking, and within a year she was carrying on with one Tom Flynn, a farmer's son. Her father, a respectable, hardworking man, knew nothing about it, for he would have realized that she was no match for one of the Flynns, and even if Tom's father, Ned, had known, he would never have thought it possible that any labourer's daughter could imagine herself a match for Tom.

Not, God knows, that Tom was any great catch. He was a big uncouth galoot who was certain that love-making, like drink, was one of the simple pleasures his father tried to deprive him of, out of spite. He used to call at the house while the O'Gradys were away, and there would be Delia in one of Eileen O'Grady's frocks and with Eileen O'Grady's lipstick and powder on, doing the lady over the tea things in the parlour. Throwing a glance over his shoulder in case anyone might spot him, Tom would heave himself onto the sofa with his boots over the end.

"Begod, I love sofas," he would say with simple pleasure.

"Put a cushion behind you," Delia would say.

"Oh, begod," Tom would say, making himself comfortable, "if ever I have a house of my own 'tis unknown what sofas and cushions I'll have. Them teachers must get great money. What the hell do they go away at all for?"

Delia loved making the tea and handing it out like a real lady, but you couldn't catch Tom out like that.

"Ah, what do I want tay for?" he would say with a doubtful glance at the cup. "Haven't you any whisky? Ould O'Grady must have gallons of it. . . . Leave it there on the table. Why the hell don't they have proper mugs with handles a man could get a grip on? Is that taypot silver? Pity I'm not a teacher!"

It was only natural for Delia to show him the bedrooms and the dressing-tables with the three mirrors, the way you could see yourself from all sides, but Tom, his hands under his head, threw himself with incredulous delight on the low double bed and cried: "Springs! Begod, 'tis like a car!"

What the springs gave rise to was entirely the O'Gradys' fault since no one but themselves would have left a house in a lonesome part to a girl of nineteen to mind. The only surprising thing was that it lasted two years without Delia showing any signs of it. It probably took Tom that time to find the right way.

But when he did he got into a terrible state. It was hardly in him to believe that a harmless poor devil like himself whom no one ever bothered his head about could achieve such unprecedented results on one girl, but when he understood it he knew only too well what the result of it would be. His father would first beat hell out of him and then throw him out and leave the farm to his nephews. There being no hope of conciliating his father, Tom turned his attention to God, who, though supposed to share Ned Flynn's views about fellows and girls, had some nature in Him. Tom stopped seeing Delia, to persuade God that he was reforming and to show that anyway it wasn't his fault. Left alone he could be a decent, good-living young fellow, but the Carty girl was a forward, deceitful hussy who had led him on instead of putting him off the way any well-bred girl would do. Between lipsticks, sofas, and tay in the parlour, Tom put it up to God that it was a great wonder she hadn't got him into worse trouble.

Delia had to tell her mother, and Mrs. Carty went to Father Corcoran to see could he induce Tom to marry her. Father Corcoran was a tall, testy old man who, even at the age of sixty-five, couldn't make out for the life of him what young fellows saw in girls, but if he didn't know much about lovers he knew a lot about farmers.

"Wisha, Mrs. Carty," he said crankily, "how could I get him to marry her? Wouldn't you have a bit of sense? Some little financial arrangement, maybe, so that she could leave the parish and not be a cause of scandal—I might be able to do that."

He interviewed Ned Flynn, who by this time had got Tom's version of the story and knew financial arrangements were going to be the order of the day unless he could put a stop to them. Ned was a man of over six foot with a bald brow and a smooth unlined face as though he never had a care except his general concern for the welfare of humanity which made him look so abnormally thoughtful. Even Tom's conduct hadn't brought a wrinkle to his brow.

"I don't know, father," he said, stroking his bald brow with a dieaway air, "I don't know what you could do at all."

"Wisha, Mr. Flynn," said the priest who, when it came to the pinch, had more nature than twenty Flynns, "wouldn't you do the handsome thing and let him marry her before it goes any farther?"

"I don't see how much farther it could go, father," said Ned.

"It could become a scandal."

"I'm afraid 'tis that already, father."

"And after all," said Father Corcoran, forcing himself to put in a good word for one of the unfortunate sex whose very existence was a mystery to him, "is she any worse than the rest of the girls that are going? Bad is the best of them, from what I see, and Delia is a great deal better than most."

"That's not my information at all, father," said Ned, looking like "The Heart Bowed Down."

"That's a very serious statement, Mr. Flynn," said Father Corcoran, giving him a challenging look.

"It can be proved, father," said Ned gloomily. "Of course I'm not denying the boy was foolish, but the cleverest can be caught."

"You astonish me, Mr. Flynn," said Father Corcoran who was beginning to realize that he wasn't even going to get a subscription. "Of course I can't contradict you, but 'twill cause a terrible scandal."

"I'm as sorry for that as you are, father," said Ned, "but I have my son's future to think of."

Then, of course, the fun began. Foolish to the last, the O'Gradys wanted to keep Delia on till it was pointed out to them that Mr. O'Grady would be bound to get the blame. After this, her father had to be told. Dick Carty knew exactly what became a devoted father, and he beat Delia till he had to be hauled off her by the neighbours. He was a man who loved to sit in his garden reading his paper; now he felt he owed it to himself not to be seen enjoying himself, so instead he sat over the fire and brooded. The more he brooded the angrier he became. But seeing that, with the best will in the world, he could not beat Delia every time he got angry, he turned his attention to the Flynns. Ned Flynn, that contemptible bosthoon, had slighted one of the Cartys in a parish where they had lived for hundreds of years with unblemished reputations; the Flynns, as everyone knew, being mere upstarts and outsiders without a date on their gravestones before 1850—nobodies!

He brought Delia to see Jackie Canty, the solicitor in town. Jackie was a little jenny-ass of a man with thin lips, a pointed nose, and a pince-nez that wouldn't stop in place, and he listened with grave enjoyment to the story of Delia's misconduct. "And what happened then, please?" he asked in his shrill singsong, looking at the floor and trying hard not to burst out into a giggle of delight. "The devils!" he thought. "The devils!" It was as close as Jackie was ever likely to get to the facts of life, an opportunity not to be missed.

"Anything in writing?" he sang, looking at her over the pince-nez. "Any letters? Any documents?"

"Only a couple of notes I burned," said Delia, who thought him a very queer man, and no wonder.

"Pity!" Jackie said with an admiring smile. "A smart man! Oh, a very smart man!"

"Ah, 'tisn't that at all," said Delia uncomfortably, "only he had no occasion for writing."

"Ah, Miss Carty," cried Jackie in great indignation, looking at her challengingly through the specs while his voice took on a steely ring, "a gentleman in love always finds plenty of occasion for writing. He's a smart man; your father might succeed in an action for seduction, but if 'tis defended 'twill be a dirty case."

"Mr. Canty," said her father solemnly, "I don't mind how dirty it is so long as I get justice." He stood up, a powerful man of six feet, and held up his clenched fist. "Justice is what I want," he said dramatically. "That's the sort I am. I keep myself to myself and mind my own business, but give me a cut, and I'll fight in a bag, tied up."

"Don't forget that Ned Flynn has the money, Dick," wailed Jackie.

"Mr. Canty," said Dick with a dignity verging on pathos, "you know me?"

"I do, Dick, I do."

"I'm living in this neighbourhood, man and boy, fifty years, and I owe nobody a ha-penny. If it took me ten years, breaking stones by the road, I'd pay it back, every penny."

"I know, Dick, I know," moaned Jackie. "But there's other things as well. There's your daughter's reputation. Do you know what they'll do? They'll go into court and swear someone else was the father."

"Tom could never say that," Delia cried despairingly. "The tongue would rot in his mouth."

Jackie had no patience at all with this chit of a girl, telling him his business. He sat back with a weary air, his arm over the back of his chair.

"That statement has no foundation," he said icily. "There is no record of any such thing happening a witness. If there was, the inhabitants of Ireland would have considerably less to say for themselves. You would be surprised the things respectable people will say in the witness box. Rot in their mouths indeed! Ah, dear me, no. With documents, of course, it would be different, but it is only our word against theirs. Can it be proved that you weren't knocking round with any other man at this time, Miss Carty?"

"Indeed, I was doing nothing of the sort," Delia said indignantly. "I swear to God I wasn't, Mr. Canty. I hardly spoke to a fellow the whole time, only when Tom and myself might have a row and I'd go out with Timmy Martin."

"Timmy Martin!" Canty cried dramatically, pointing an accusing finger at her. "There is their man!"

"But Tom did the same with Betty Daly," cried Delia on the point of tears, "and he only did it to spite me. I swear there was nothing else in it, Mr. Canty, nor he never accused me of it."

"Mark my words," chanted Jackie with a mournful smile, "he'll make up for lost time now."

In this he showed considerably more foresight than Delia gave him credit for. After the baby was born and the action begun, Tom and his father went to town to see their solicitor, Peter Humphreys. Peter, who knew all he wanted to know about the facts of life, liked the case much less than Jackie. A cross-eyed, full-blooded man who had made his money when law was about land, not love, he thought it a terrible comedown. Besides, he didn't think it nice to be listening to such things.

"And so, according to you, Timmy Martin is the father?" he asked Tom.

"Oh, I'm not swearing he is," said Tom earnestly, giving himself a heave in his chair and crossing his legs. "How the hell could I? All I am saying is that I wasn't the only one, and what's more she boasted about it. Boasted about it, begod!" he added with a look of astonishment at such female depravity.

"Before witnesses?" asked Peter, his eyes doing a double cross with hopelessness.

"As to that," replied Tom with great solemnity, looking over his shoulder for an open window he could spit through, "I couldn't swear."

"But you understood her to mean Timmy Martin?"

"I'm not accusing Timmy Martin at all," said Tom in great alarm, seeing how the processes of law were tending to involve him in a row with the Martins, who were a turbulent family with ways of getting their own back unknown to any law. "Timmy Martin is one man she used to be round with. It might be Timmy Martin or it might be someone else, or what's more," he added with the look of a man who has had a sudden revelation, "it might be more than one." He looked from Peter to his father and back again to see what effect the revelation was having, but like other revelations it didn't seem to be going down too well. "Begod," he said, giving himself another heave, "it might be any God's number. . . . But, as to that," he added cautiously, "I wouldn't like to swear."

"Nor indeed, Tom," said his solicitor with a great effort at politeness, "no one would advise you. You'll want a good counsel."

"Begod, I suppose I will," said Tom with astonished resignation before the idea that there might be people in the world bad enough to doubt his word.

There was great excitement in the village when it became known that the Flynns were having the Roarer Cooper as counsel. Even as a first-class variety turn Cooper could always command attention, and everyone knew that the rights and wrongs of the case would be relegated to their proper position while the little matter of Eileen O'Grady's best frock received the attention it deserved.

On the day of the hearing the court was crowded. Tom and his father were sitting at the back with Peter Humphreys, waiting for Cooper, while Delia and her father were talking to Jackie Canty and their own counsel, Ivers. He was a well-built young man with a high brow, black hair, and half-closed, red-tinged sleepy eyes. He talked in a bland drawl.

"You're not worrying, are you?" he asked Delia kindly. "Don't be a bit afraid. . . . I suppose there's no chance of them settling, Jackie?"

"Musha, what chance would there be?" Canty asked scoldingly. "Don't you know yourself what sort they are?"

"I'll have a word with Cooper myself," said Ivers. "Dan isn't as bad as he looks." He went to talk to a coarse-looking man in wig and gown who had just come in. To say he wasn't as bad as he looked was no great compliment. He had a face that was almost a square, with a big jaw and blue eyes in wicked little slits that made deep dents across his cheekbones.

"What about settling this case of ours, Dan?" Ivers asked gently.

Cooper didn't even return his look; apparently he was not responsive to charm.

"Did you ever know me to settle when I could fight?" he growled.

"Not when you could fight your match," Ivers said, without taking offence. "You don't consider that poor girl your match?"

"We'll soon see what sort of girl she is," replied Cooper complacently as his eyes fell on the Flynns. "Tell me," he whispered, "what did she see in my client?"

"What you saw yourself when you were her age, I suppose," said Ivers. "You don't mean there wasn't a girl in a tobacconist's shop that you thought came down from heaven with the purpose of consoling you?"

"She had nothing in writing," Cooper replied gravely. "And, unlike your client, I never saw double."

"You don't believe that yarn, do you?"

"That's one of the things I'm going to inquire into."

"I can save you the trouble. She was too fond of him."

"Hah!" snorted Cooper as though this were a good joke. "And I suppose that's why she wants the cash."

"The girl doesn't care if she never got a penny. Don't you know yourself what's behind it? A respectable father. Two respectable fathers! The trouble about marriage in this country, Dan Cooper, is that the fathers always insist on doing the coorting."

"Hah!" grunted Cooper, rather more uncertain of himself. "Show me this paragon of the female sex, Ivers."

"There in the brown hat beside Canty," said Ivers without looking round. "Come on, you old devil, and stop trying to pretend you're Buffalo Bill. It's enough going through what she had to go through. I don't want her to go through any more."

"And why in God's name do you come to me?" Cooper asked in sudden indignation. "What the hell do you take me for? A Society for Protecting Fallen Women? Why didn't the priest make him marry her?"

"When the Catholic Church can make a farmer marry a labourer's daughter the kingdom of God will be at hand," said Ivers. "I'm surprised at you, Dan Cooper, not knowing better at your age."

"And what are the neighbours doing here if she has nothing to hide?"

"Who said she had nothing to hide?" Ivers asked lightly, throwing in his hand. "Haven't you daughters of your own? You know she played the fine lady in the O'Gradys' frocks. If 'tis any information to you she wore their jewellery as well."

"Ivers, you're a young man of great plausibility," said Cooper, "but you can spare your charm on me. I have my client's interests to consider. Did she sleep with the other fellow?"

"She did not."

"Do you believe that?"

"As I believe in my own mother."

"The faith that moves mountains," Cooper said despondently. "How much are ye asking?"

"Two hundred and fifty," replied Ivers, shaky for the first time.

"Merciful God Almighty!" moaned Cooper, turning his eyes to the ceiling.

"As if any responsible Irish court would put that price on a girl's virtue. Still, it might be as well. I'll see what I can do."

He moved ponderously across the court and with two big arms outstretched like wings shepherded out the Flynns.

"Two hundred and fifty pounds?" gasped Ned, going white. "Where in God's name would I get that money?"

"My dear Mr. Flynn," Cooper said with coarse amiability, "that's only half the yearly allowance his Lordship makes the young lady that obliges him, and she's not a patch on that girl in court. After a lifetime of experience I can assure you that for two years' fornication with a fine girl like that you won't pay a penny less than five hundred."

Peter Humphreys's eyes almost grew straight with the shock of such reckless slander on a blameless judge. He didn't know what had come over the Roarer. But that wasn't the worst. When the settlement was announced and the Flynns were leaving he went up to them again.

"You can believe me when I say you did the right thing, Mr. Flynn," he said. "I never like cases involving good-looking girls. Gentlemen of his Lordship's age are terribly susceptible. But tell me, why wouldn't your son marry her now as he's about it?"

"Marry her?" echoed Ned, who hadn't yet got over the shock of having to pay two hundred and fifty pounds and costs for a little matter he could have compounded for with Father Corcoran for fifty. "A thing like that!"

"With two hundred and fifty pounds, man?" snarled Cooper. "'Tisn't every day you'll pick up a daughter-in-law with that. . . . What do you say to the girl yourself?" he asked Tom.

"Oh, begod, the girl is all right," said Tom.

Tom looked different. It was partly relief that he wouldn't have to perjure himself, partly astonishment at seeing his father so swiftly overthrown. His face said: "The world is wide."

"Ah, Mr. Flynn, Mr. Flynn," whispered Cooper scornfully, "sure you're not such a fool as to let all that good money out of the family?"

Leaving Ned gasping, he went on to where Dick Carty, aglow with pride and malice, was receiving congratulations. There were no congratulations for Delia who was standing near him. She felt a big paw on her arm and looked up to see the Roarer.

"Are you still fond of that boy?" he whispered.

"I have reason to be, haven't I?" she retorted bitterly.

"You have," he replied with no great sympathy. "The best. I got you that money so that you could marry him if you wanted to. Do you want to?"

Her eyes filled with tears as she thought of the poor broken china of an idol that was being offered her now.

"Once a fool, always a fool," she said sullenly.

"You're no fool at all, girl," he said, giving her arm an encouraging squeeze.

"You might make a man of him yet. I don't know what the law in this country is coming to. Get him away to hell out of this till I find Michael Ivers and get him to talk to your father."

The two lawyers made the match themselves at Johnny Desmond's pub, and Johnny said it was like nothing in the world so much as a mission, with the Roarer roaring and threatening hellfire on all concerned, and Michael Ivers piping away about the joys of heaven. Johnny said it was the most instructive evening he ever had. Ivers was always recognized as a weak man so the marriage did him no great harm, but of course it was a terrible comedown for a true Roarer, and Cooper's reputation has never been the same since then.

EUDORA WELTY

Why I Live at the P.O.[1]

I was getting along fine with Mama, Papa-Daddy and Uncle Rondo until my sister Stella-Rondo just separated from her husband and came back home again. Mr. Whitaker! Of course I went with Mr. Whitaker first, when he first appeared here in China Grove, taking "Pose Yourself" photos, and Stella-Rondo broke us up. Told him I was one-sided. Bigger on one side than the other, which is a deliberate, calculated falsehood: I'm the same. Stella-Rondo is exactly twelve months to the day younger than I am and for that reason she's spoiled.

She's always had anything in the world she wanted and then she'd throw it away. Papa-Daddy gave her this gorgeous Add-a-Pearl necklace when she was eight years old and she threw it away playing baseball when she was nine, with only two pearls.

So as soon as she got married and moved away from home the first thing she did was separate! From Mr. Whitaker! This photographer with the popeyes she said she trusted. Came home from one of those towns up in Illinois and to our complete surprise brought this child of two.

Mama said she like to made her drop dead for a second. "Here you had this marvelous blonde child and never so much as wrote your mother a word about it," says Mama. "I'm thoroughly ashamed of you." But of course she wasn't.

Stella-Rondo just calmly takes off this *hat*, I wish you could see it. She says, "Why, Mama, Shirley-T.'s adopted, I can prove it."

"How?" says Mama, but all I says was, "H'm!" There I was over the hot stove, trying to stretch two chickens over five people and a completely unexpected child into the bargain, without one moment's notice.

"What do you mean—'H'm!'?" says Stella-Rondo, and Mama says, "I heard that, Sister."

I said that oh, I didn't mean a thing, only that whoever Shirley-T. was, she was the spit-image of Papa-Daddy if he'd cut off his beard, which of course he'd never do in the world. Papa-Daddy's Mama's papa and sulks.

Stella-Rondo got furious! She said, "Sister, I don't need to tell you you got a lot of nerve and always did have and I'll thank you to make no future reference to my adopted child whatsoever."

"Very well," I said. "Very well, very well. Of course I noticed at once she looks like Mr. Whitaker's side too. That frown. She looks like a cross between Mr. Whitaker and Papa-Daddy."

"Well, all I can say is she isn't."

"She looks exactly like Shirley Temple to me," says Mama, but Shirley-T. just ran away from her.

So the first thing Stella-Rondo did at the table was turn Papa-Daddy against me.

"Papa-Daddy," she says. He was trying to cut up his meat. "Papa-Daddy!" I was taken completely by surprise. Papa-Daddy is about a million years old and's got this long-long beard. "Papa-Daddy, Sister says she fails to understand why you don't cut off your beard."

So Papa-Daddy l-a-y-s down his knife and fork! He's real rich. Mama says he is, he says he isn't. So he says, "Have I heard correctly? You don't understand why I don't cut off my beard?"

"Why," I says, "Papa-Daddy, of course I understand; I did not say any such of a thing, the idea!"

He says, "Hussy!"

I says, "Papa-Daddy, you know I wouldn't any more want you to cut off your beard than the man in the moon. It was the farthest thing from my mind! Stella-Rondo sat there and made that up while she was eating breast of chicken."

But he says, "So the postmistress fails to understand why I don't cut off my beard. Which job I got you through my influence with the government. 'Bird's nest'—is that what you call it?"

Not that it isn't the next to smallest P.O. in the entire state of Mississippi.

I says, "Oh, Papa-Daddy," I says, "I didn't say any such of a thing, I never dreamed it was a bird's nest, I have always been grateful though this is the next to smallest P.O. in the state of Mississippi, and I do not enjoy being referred to as a hussy by my own grandfather."

But Stella-Rondo says, "Yes, you did say it too. Anybody in the world could of heard you, that had ears."

"Stop right there," says Mama, looking at *me*.

So I pulled my napkin straight back through the napkin ring and left the table.

As soon as I was out of the room Mama says, "Call her back, or she'll starve to death," but Papa-Daddy says, "This is the beard I started growing on the coast when I was fifteen years old." He would of gone on till nightfall if Shirley-T. hadn't lost the Milky Way she ate in Cairo.

So Papa-Daddy says, "I am going out and lie in the hammock, and you can all sit here and remember my words: I'll never cut off my beard as long as I live, even one inch, and I don't appreciate it in you at all." Passed right by me in the hall and went straight out and got in the hammock.

It would be a holiday. It wasn't five minutes before Uncle Rondo suddenly appeared in the hall in one of Stella-Rondo's flesh-colored kimonos, all cut on the bias, like something Mr. Whitaker probably thought was gorgeous.

"Uncle Rondo!" I says. "I didn't know who that was! Where are you going?"

"Sister," he says, "get out of my way, I'm poisoned."

"If you're poisoned stay away from Papa-Daddy," I says. "Keep out of the hammock. Papa-Daddy will certainly beat you on the head if you come within forty miles of him. He thinks I deliberately said he ought to cut off his beard after he got me the P.O., and I've told him and told him and told him, and he acts like he just don't hear me. Papa-Daddy must of gone stone deaf."

"He picked a fine day to do it then," says Uncle Rondo, and before you could say "Jack Robinson" flew out in the yard.

What he'd really done, he'd drunk another bottle of that prescription. He does it every single Fourth of July as sure as shooting, and it's horribly expensive. Then he falls over in the hammock and snores. So he insisted on zigzagging right on out to the hammock, looking like a half-wit.

Papa-Daddy woke up with this horrible yell and right there without moving an inch he tried to turn Uncle Rondo against me. I heard every word he said. Oh, he told Uncle Rondo I didn't learn to read till I was eight years old and he didn't see how in the world I ever got the mail put up at the P.O., much less read it all, and he said if Uncle Rondo could only fathom the lengths he had gone to get me that job! And he said on the other hand he thought Stella-Rondo had a brilliant mind and deserved credit for getting out of town. All the time he was just lying there swinging as pretty as you please and looping out his beard, and poor Uncle Rondo was *pleading* with him to slow down the hammock, it was making him as dizzy as a witch to watch it. But that's what Papa-Daddy likes about a hammock. So Uncle Rondo was too dizzy to get turned against me for the time being. He's Mama's only brother and is a good case of a one-track mind. Ask anybody. A certified pharmacist.

Just then I heard Stella-Rondo raising the upstairs window. While she was married she got this peculiar idea that it's cooler with the windows shut and locked. So she has to raise the window before she can make a soul hear her outdoors.

So she raises the window and says, "*Oh!*" You would have thought she was mortally wounded.

Uncle Rondo and Papa-Daddy didn't even look up, but kept right on with what they were doing. I had to laugh.

I flew up the stairs and threw the door open! I says, "What in the wide world's the matter, Stella-Rondo? You mortally wounded?"

"No," she says, "I am not mortally wounded but I wish you would do me the favor of looking out that window there and telling me what you see."

So I shade my eyes and look out the window.

"I see the front yard," I says.

"Don't you see any human beings?" she says.

"I see Uncle Rondo trying to run Papa-Daddy out of the hammock," I says. "Nothing more. Naturally, it's so suffocating-hot in the house, with all the windows shut and locked, everybody who cares to stay in their right mind will have to go out and get in the hammock before the Fourth of July is over."

"Don't you notice anything different about Uncle Rondo?" asks Stella-Rondo.

"Why, no, except he's got on some terrible-looking flesh-colored contraption I wouldn't be found dead in, is all I can see," I says.

"Never mind, you won't be found dead in it, because it happens to be part of my trousseau, and Mr. Whitaker took several dozen photographs of me in it," says Stella-Rondo. "What on earth could Uncle Rondo *mean* by wearing part of my trousseau out in the broad open daylight without saying so much as 'Kiss my foot,' *knowing* I only got home this morning after my separation and hung my negligee up on the bathroom door, just as nervous as I could be?"

"I'm sure I don't know, and what do you expect me to do about it?" I says. "Jump out the window?"

"No, I expect nothing of the kind. I simply declare that Uncle Rondo looks like a fool in it, that's all," she says. "It makes me sick to my stomach."

"Well, he looks as good as he can," I says. "As good as anybody in reason could." I stood up for Uncle Rondo, please remember. And I said to Stella-Rondo, "I think I would do well not to criticize so freely if I were you and came home with a two-year-old child I had never said a word about, and no explanation whatever about my separation."

"I asked you the instant I entered this house not to refer one more time to my adopted child, and you gave me your word of honor you would not," was all Stella-Rondo would say, and started pulling out every one of her eyebrows with some cheap Kress tweezers.

So I merely slammed the door behind me and went down and made some green-tomato pickle. Somebody had to do it. Of course Mama had turned both the niggers loose; she always said no earthly power could hold one anyway on the Fourth of July, so she wouldn't even try. It turned out that Jaypan fell in the lake and came within a very narrow limit of drowning.

So Mama trots in. Lifts up the lid and says, "H'm! Not very good for your Uncle Rondo in his precarious condition, I must say. Or poor little adopted Shirley-T. Shame on you!"

That made me tired. I says, "Well, Stella-Rondo had better thank her lucky stars it was her instead of me came trotting in with that very peculiar-looking child. Now if it had been me that trotted in from Illinois and brought a peculiar-looking child of two, I shudder to think of the reception I'd of got, much less controlled the diet of an entire family."

"But you must remember, Sister, that you were never married to Mr. Whitaker in the first place and didn't go up to Illinois to live," says Mama, shaking a spoon in my face. "If you had I would of been just as overjoyed to see you and your little adopted girl as I was to see Stella-Rondo, when you wound up with your separation and came on back home."

"You would not," I says.

"Don't contradict me, I would," says Mama.

But I said she couldn't convince me though she talked till she was blue in the face. Then I said, "Besides, you know as well as I do that that child is not adopted."

"She most certainly is adopted," says Mama, stiff as a poker.

I says, "Why, Mama, Stella-Rondo had her just as sure as anything in this world, and just too stuck up to admit it."

"Why, Sister," said Mama. "Here I thought we were going to have a pleasant Fourth of July, and you start right out not believing a word your own baby sister tells you!"

"Just like Cousin Annie Flo. Went to her grave denying the facts of life," I reminded Mama.

"I told you if you ever mentioned Annie Flo's name I'd slap your face," says Mama, and slaps my face.

"All right, you wait and see," I says.

"I," says Mama, "I prefer to take my children's word for anything when it's humanly possible." You ought to see Mama, she weighs two hundred pounds and has real tiny feet.

Just then something perfectly horrible occurred to me.

"Mama," I says, "can that child talk?" I simply had to whisper! "Mama, I wonder if that child can be—you know—in any way? Do you realize," I says, "that she hasn't spoken one single, solitary word to a human being up to the minute? This is the way she looks," I says, and I looked like this.

Well, Mama and I just stood there and stared at each other. It was horrible!

"I remember well that Joe Whitaker frequently drank like a fish," says Mama. "I believed to my soul he drank chemicals." And without another word she marches to the foot of the stairs and calls Stella-Rondo.

"Stella-Rondo? O-o-o-o-o! Stella-Rondo!"

"What?" says Stella-Rondo from upstairs. Not even the grace to get up off the bed.

"Can that child of yours talk?" asks Mama.

Stella-Rondo says, "Can she what?"

"Talk! Talk!" says Mama. "Burdyburdyburdyburdy!"

So Stella-Rondo yells back, "Who says she can't talk?"

"Sister says so," says Mama.

"You didn't have to tell me, I know whose word of honor don't mean a thing in this house," says Stella-Rondo.

And in a minute the loudest Yankee voice I ever heard in my life yells out, "OE'm Pop-OE the Sailor-r-r-r Ma-a-an!" and then somebody jumps up and down in the upstairs hall. In another second the house would of fallen down.

"Not only talks, she can tap-dance!" calls Stella-Rondo. "Which is more than some people I won't name can do."

"Why, the little precious darling thing!" Mama says, so surprised. "Just as smart as she can be!" Starts talking baby talk right there. Then she turns on me. "Sister, you ought to be thoroughly ashamed! Run upstairs this instant and apologize to Stella-Rondo and Shirley-T."

"Apologize for what?" I says. "I merely wondered if the child was normal, that's all. Now that she's proved she is, why, I have nothing further to say."

But Mama just turned on her heel and flew out, furious. She ran right upstairs and hugged the baby. She believed it was adopted. Stella-Rondo hadn't done a thing but turn her against me from upstairs while I stood there helpless over the hot stove. So that made Mama, Papa-Daddy and the baby all on Stella-Rondo's side.

Next, Uncle Rondo.

I must say that Uncle Rondo has been marvelous to me at various times in the past and I was completely unprepared to be made to jump out of my skin, the way it turned out. Once Stella-Rondo did something perfectly horrible to him—broke a chain letter from Flanders Field—and he took the radio back he had given her and gave it to me. Stella-Rondo was furious! For six months we all had to call her Stella instead of Stella-Rondo, or she wouldn't answer. I always thought Uncle Rondo had all the brains of the entire family. Another time he sent me to Mammoth Cave, with all expenses paid.

But this would be the day he was drinking that prescription, the Fourth of July.

So at supper Stella-Rondo speaks up and says she thinks Uncle Rondo ought to try to eat a little something. So finally Uncle Rondo said he would try a little cold biscuits and ketchup, but that was all. So *she* brought it to him.

"Do you think it wise to disport with ketchup in Stella-Rondo's flesh-colored kimono?" I says. Trying to be considerate! If Stella-Rondo couldn't watch out for her trousseau, somebody had to.

"Any objections?" asks Uncle Rondo, just about to pour out all the ketchup.

"Don't mind what she says, Uncle Rondo," says Stella-Rondo. "Sister has been devoting this solid afternoon to sneering out my bedroom window at the way you look."

"What's that?" says Uncle Rondo. Uncle Rondo has got the most terrible temper in the world. Anything is liable to make him tear the house down if it comes at the wrong time.

So Stella-Rondo says, "Sister says, 'Uncle Rondo certainly does look like a fool in that pink kimono!'"

Do you remember who it was really said that?

Uncle Rondo spills out all the ketchup and jumps out of his chair and tears off the kimono and throws it down on the dirty floor and puts his foot on it. It had to be sent all the way to Jackson to the cleaners and re-pleated.

"So that's your opinion of your Uncle Rondo, is it?" he says. "I look like a fool, do I? Well, that's the last straw. A whole day in this house with nothing to do, and then to hear you come out with a remark like that behind my back!"

"I didn't say any such of a thing, Uncle Rondo," I says, "and I'm not saying who did, either. Why, I think you look all right. Just try to take care of yourself and not talk and eat at the same time," I says. "I think you better go lie down."

"Lie down my foot," says Uncle Rondo. I ought to of known by that he was fixing to do something perfectly horrible.

So he didn't do anything that night in the precarious state he was in—just played Casino with Mama and Stella-Rondo and Shirley-T. and gave Shirley-T. a nickel with a head on both sides. It tickled her nearly to death, and she called him "Papa." But at 6:30 A.M. the next morning, he threw a whole five-cent package of some unsold one-inch firecrackers from the store as hard as he could into my bedroom and they every one went off. Not one bad one in the string. Anybody else, there'd be one that wouldn't go off.

Well, I'm just terribly susceptible to noise of any kind, the doctor has always told me I was the most sensitive person he had ever seen in his whole life, and I was simply prostrated. I couldn't eat! People tell me they heard it as far as the cemetery, and old Aunt Jep Patterson, that had been holding her own so good, thought it was Judgment Day and she was going to meet her whole family. It's usually so quiet here.

And I'll tell you it didn't take me any longer than a minute to make up my mind what to do. There I was with the whole entire house on Stella-Rondo's side and turned against me. If I have anything at all I have pride.

So I just decided I'd go straight down to the P.O. There's plenty of room there in the back, I says to myself.

Well! I made no bones about letting the family catch on to what I was up to. I didn't try to conceal it.

The first thing they knew, I marched in where they were all playing Old

Maid and pulled the electric oscillating fan out by the plug, and everything got real hot. Next I snatched the pillow I'd done the needlepoint on right off the davenport from behind Papa-Daddy. He went "Ugh!" I beat Stella-Rondo up the stairs and finally found my charm bracelet in her bureau drawer under a picture of Nelson Eddy.

"So that's the way the land lies," says Uncle Rondo. There he was, piecing on the ham. "Well, Sister, I'll be glad to donate my army cot if you got any place to set it up, providing you'll leave right this minute and let me get some peace." Uncle Rondo was in France.

"Thank you kindly for the cot and 'peace' is hardly the word I would select if I had to resort to firecrackers at 6:30 A.M. in a young girl's bedroom," I says back to him. "And as to where I intend to go, you seem to forget my position as postmistress of China Grove, Mississippi," I says. "I've always got the P.O."

Well, that made them all sit up and take notice.

I went out front and started digging up some four-o'clocks to plant around the P.O.

"Ah-ah-ah!" says Mama, raising the window. "Those happen to be my four-o'clocks. Everything planted in that star is mine. I've never known you to make anything grow in your life."

"Very well," I says. "But I take the fern. Even you, Mama, can't stand there and deny that I'm the one watered that fern. And I happen to know where I can send in a box top and get a packet of one thousand mixed seeds, no two the same kind, free."

"Oh, where?" Mama wants to know.

But I says, "Too late. You 'tend to your house, and I'll 'tend to mine. You hear things like that all the time if you know how to listen to the radio. Perfectly marvelous offers. Get anything you want free."

So I hope to tell you I marched in and got that radio, and they could of all bit a nail in two, especially Stella-Rondo, that it used to belong to, and she well knew she couldn't get it back, I'd sue for it like a shot. And I very politely took the sewing-machine motor I helped pay the most on to give Mama for Christmas back in 1929, and a good big calendar, with the first-aid remedies on it. The thermometer and the Hawaiian ukulele certainly were rightfully mine, and I stood on the step-ladder and got all my watermelon-rind preserves and every fruit and vegetable I'd put up, every jar. Then I began to pull the tacks out of the bluebird wall vases on the archway to the dining room.

"Who told you you could have those, Miss Priss?" says Mama, fanning as hard as she could.

"I bought 'em and I'll keep track of 'em," I says. "I'll tack 'em up one on each side the post-office window, and you can see 'em when you come to ask me for your mail, if you're so dead to see 'em."

"Not I! I'll never darken the door to that post office again if I live to be a hundred," Mama says. "Ungrateful child! After all the money we spent on you at the Normal."

"Me either," says Stella-Rondo. "You can just let my mail lie there and *rot*, for all I care. I'll never come and relieve you of a single, solitary piece."

"I should worry," I says. "And who you think's going to sit down and write you all those big fat letters and postcards, by the way? Mr. Whitaker? Just because he was the only man ever dropped down in China Grove and you got him—unfairly—is he going to sit down and write you a lengthy correspondence after you come home giving no rhyme nor reason whatsoever for your separation and no explanation for the presence of that child? I may not have your brilliant mind, but I fail to see it."

So Mama says, "Sister, I've told you a thousand times that Stella-Rondo simply got homesick, and this child is far too big to be hers," and she says, "Now, why don't you all just sit down and play Casino?"

Then Shirley-T. sticks out her tongue at me in this perfectly horrible way. She has no more manners than the man in the moon. I told her she was going to cross her eyes like that some day and they'd stick.

"It's too late to stop me now," I says. "You should have tried that yesterday. I'm going to the P.O. and the only way you can possibly see me is to visit me there."

So Papa-Daddy says, "You'll never catch me setting foot in that post office, even if I should take a notion into my head to write a letter some place." He says, "I won't have you reachin' out of that little old window with a pair of shears and cuttin' off any beard of mine. I'm too smart for you!"

"We all are," says Stella-Rondo.

But I said, "If you're so smart, where's Mr. Whitaker?"

So then Uncle Rondo says, "I'll thank you from now on to stop reading all the orders I get on postcards and telling everybody in China Grove what you think is the matter with them," but I says, "I draw my own conclusions and will continue in the future to draw them." I says, "If people want to write their inmost secrets on penny postcards, there's nothing in the wide world you can do about it, Uncle Rondo."

"And if you think we'll ever *write* another postcard you're sadly mistaken," says Mama.

"Cutting off your nose to spite your face then," I says. "But if you're all determined to have no more to do with the U.S. mail, think of this: What will Stella-Rondo do now, if she wants to tell Mr. Whitaker to come after her?"

"Wah!" says Stella-Rondo. I knew she'd cry. She had a conniption fit right there in the kitchen.

"It will be interesting to see how long she holds out," I says. "And now—I am leaving."

"Good-bye," says Uncle Rondo.

"Oh, I declare," says Mama, "to think that a family of mine should quarrel on the Fourth of July, or the day after, over Stella-Rondo leaving old Mr. Whitaker and having the sweetest little adopted child! It looks like we'd all be glad!"

"Wah!" says Stella-Rondo, and has a fresh conniption fit.

"*He* left *her*—you mark my words," I says. "That's Mr. Whitaker. I know Mr. Whitaker. After all, I knew him first. I said from the beginning he'd up and leave her. I foretold every single thing that's happened."

"Where did he go?" asks Mama.

"Probably to the North Pole, if he knows what's good for him," I says.

But Stella-Rondo just bawled and wouldn't say another word. She flew to her room and slammed the door.

"Now look what you've gone and done, Sister," says Mama. "You go apologize."

"I haven't got time, I'm leaving," I says.

"Well, what are you waiting around for?" asks Uncle Rondo.

So I just picked up the kitchen clock and marched off, without saying "Kiss my foot" or anything, and never did tell Stella-Rondo good-bye.

There was a nigger girl going along on a little wagon right in front.

"Nigger girl," I says, "come help me haul these things down the hill, I'm going to live in the post office."

Took her nine trips in her express wagon. Uncle Rondo came out on the porch and threw her a nickel.

And that's the last I've laid eyes on any of my family or my family laid eyes on me for five solid days and nights. Stella-Rondo may be telling the most horrible tales in the world about Mr. Whitaker, but I haven't heard them. As I tell everybody, I draw my own conclusions.

But oh, I like it here. It's ideal, as I've been saying. You see, I've got everything cater-cornered, the way I like it. Hear the radio? All the war news. Radio, sewing machine, book ends, ironing board and that great big piano lamp—peace, that's what I like. Butter-bean vines planted all along the front where the strings are.

Of course, there's not much mail. My family are naturally the main people in China Grove, and if they prefer to vanish from the face of the earth, for all the mail they get or the mail they write, why I'm not going to open my mouth. Some of the folks here in town are taking up for me and some turned against me. I know which is which. There are always people who will quit buying stamps just to get on the right side of Papa-Daddy.

But here I am, and here I'll stay. I want the world to know I'm happy.

And if Stella-Rondo should come to me this minute, on bended knees, and *attempt* to explain the incidents of her life with Mr. Whitaker, I'd simply put my fingers in both my ears and refuse to listen.

BERNARD MALAMUD

A Summer's Reading[1]

George Stoyonovich was a neighborhood boy who had quit high school on an impulse when he was sixteen, run out of patience, and though he was ashamed everytime he went looking for a job, when people asked him if he had finished and he had to say no, he never went back to school. This summer was a hard time for jobs and he had none. Having so much time on his hands, George thought of going to summer school, but the kids in his classes would be too young. He also considered registering in a night high school, only he didn't like the idea of the teachers always telling him what to do. He felt they had not respected him. The result was he stayed off the streets and in his room most of the day. He was close to twenty and had needs with the neighborhood girls, but no money to spend, and he couldn't get more than an occasional few cents because his father was poor, and his sister Sophie, who resembled George, a tall bony girl of twenty-three, earned very little and what she had she kept for herself. Their mother was dead, and Sophie had to take care of the house.

Very early in the morning George's father got up to go to work in a fish market. Sophie left at about eight for her long ride in the subway to a cafeteria in the Bronx. George had his coffee by himself, then hung around in the house. When the house, a five-room railroad flat above a butcher store, got on his nerves he cleaned it up—mopped the floors with a wet mop and put things away. But most of the time he sat in his room. In the afternoons he listened to the ball game. Otherwise he had a couple of old copies of the *World Almanac* he had bought long ago, and he liked to read in them and also the magazines and newspapers that Sophie brought home, that had been left on the tables in the cafeteria. They were mostly picture magazines about movie stars and sports figures, also usually the *News* and *Mirror*. Sophie herself read whatever fell into her hands, although she sometimes read good books.

She once asked George what he did in his room all day and he said he read a lot too.

"Of what besides what I bring home? Do you ever read any worthwhile books?"

"Some," George answered, although he really didn't. He had tried to read a book or two that Sophie had in the house but found he was in no mood for them. Lately he couldn't stand made-up stories, they got on his nerves. He

1 From *The Magic Barrel*. Copyright 1956, 1958 by Bernard Malamud. Used by permission of the publishers, Farrar, Straus and Cudahy, Inc. The story originally appeared in *The New Yorker*.

wished he had some hobby to work at—as a kid he was good in carpentry, but where could he work at it? Sometimes during the day he went for walks, but mostly he did his walking after the hot sun had gone down and it was cooler in the streets.

In the evening after supper George left the house and wandered in the neighborhood. During the sultry days some of the storekeepers and their wives sat in chairs on the thick, broken sidewalks in front of their shops, fanning themselves, and George walked past them and the guys hanging out on the candy store corner. A couple of them he had known his whole life, but nobody recognized each other. He had no place special to go, but generally, saving it till the last, he left the neighborhood and walked for blocks till he came to a darkly lit little park with benches and trees and an iron railing, giving it a feeling of privacy. He sat on a bench here, watching the leafy trees and the flowers blooming on the inside of the railing, thinking of a better life for himself. He thought of the jobs he had had since he had quit school—delivery boy, stock clerk, runner, lately working in a factory—and he was dissatisfied with all of them. He felt he would someday like to have a good job and live in a private house with a porch, on a street with trees. He wanted to have some dough in his pocket to buy things with, and a girl to go with, so as not to be so lonely, especially on Saturday nights. He wanted people to like and respect him. He thought about these things often but mostly when he was alone at night. Around midnight he got up and drifted back to his hot and stony neighborhood.

One time while on his walk George met Mr. Cattanzara coming home very late from work. He wondered if he was drunk but then could tell he wasn't. Mr. Cattanzara, a stocky, bald-headed man who worked in a change booth on an IRT station, lived on the next block after George's, above a shoe repair store. Nights, during the hot weather, he sat on his stoop in an undershirt, reading the New York Times in the light of the shoemaker's window. He read it from the first page to the last, then went up to sleep. And all the time he was reading the paper, his wife, a fat woman with a white face, leaned out of the window, gazing into the street, her thick white arms folded under her loose breast, on the window ledge.

Once in a while Mr. Cattanzara came home drunk, but it was a quiet drunk. He never made any trouble, only walked stiffly up the street and slowly climbed the stairs into the hall. Though drunk, he looked the same as always, except for his tight walk, the quietness, and that his eyes were wet. George liked Mr. Cattanzara because he remembered him giving him nickels to buy lemon ice with when he was a squirt. Mr. Cattanzara was a different type than those in the neighborhood. He asked different questions than the others when he met you, and he seemed to know what went on in all the newspapers. He read them, as his fat sick wife watched from the window.

"What are you doing with yourself this summer, George?" Mr. Cattanzara asked. "I see you walkin' around at nights."

George felt embarrassed. "I like to walk."

"What are you doin' in the day now?"

"Nothing much just right now. I'm waiting for a job." Since it shamed him to admit he wasn't working, George said, "I'm staying home—but I'm reading a lot to pick up my education."

Mr. Cattanzara looked interested. He mopped his hot face with a red handkerchief.

"What are you readin'?"

George hesitated, then said, "I got a list of books in the library once, and now I'm gonna read them this summer." He felt strange and a little unhappy saying this, but he wanted Mr. Cattanzara to respect him.

"How many books are there on it?"

"I never counted them. Maybe around a hundred."

Mr. Cattanzara whistled through his teeth.

"I figure if I did that," George went on earnestly, "it would help me in my education. I don't mean the kind they give you in high school. I want to know different things than they learn there, if you know what I mean."

The change maker nodded. "Still and all, one hundred books is a pretty big load for one summer."

"It might take longer."

"After you're finished with some, maybe you and I can shoot the breeze about them?" said Mr. Cattanzara.

"When I'm finished," George answered.

Mr. Cattanzara went home and George continued on his walk. After that, though he had the urge to, George did nothing different from usual. He still took his walks at night, ending up in the little park. But one evening the shoemaker on the next block stopped George to say he was a good boy, and George figured that Mr. Cattanzara had told him all about the books he was reading. From the shoemaker it must have gone down the street, because George saw a couple of people smiling kindly at him, though nobody spoke to him personally. He felt a little better around the neighborhood and liked it more, though not so much he would want to live in it forever. He had never exactly disliked the people in it, yet he had never liked them very much either. It was the fault of the neighborhood. To his surprise, George found out that his father and Sophie knew about his reading too. His father was too shy to say anything about it—he was never much of a talker in his whole life —but Sophie was softer to George, and she showed him in other ways she was proud of him.

As the summer went on George felt in a good mood about things. He cleaned the house every day, as a favor to Sophie, and he enjoyed the ball games more. Sophie gave him a buck a week allowance, and though it still wasn't enough and he had to use it carefully, it was a helluva lot better than just having two bits now and then. What he bought with the money —cigarettes mostly, an occasional beer or movie ticket—he got a big kick out of. Life wasn't so bad if you knew how to appreciate it. Occasionally he bought a paperback book from the newsstand, but he never got around to reading it, though he was glad to have a couple of books in his room. But he read thoroughly Sophie's magazines and newspapers. And at night was the most enjoyable time, because when he passed the storekeepers sitting outside their stores, he could tell they regarded him highly. He walked erect, and though he did not say much to them, or they to him, he could feel approval on all sides. A couple of nights he felt so good that he skipped the park at the end of the evening. He just wandered in the neighborhood, where people had known him from the time he was a kid playing punchball whenever there was a game of it going; he wandered there, then came home and got undressed for bed, feeling fine.

For a few weeks he had talked only once with Mr. Cattanzara, and though the change maker had said nothing more about the books, asked no questions, his silence made George a little uneasy. For a while George didn't pass in front of Mr. Cattanzara's house anymore, until one night, forgetting himself, he approached it from a different direction than he usually did when he did. It was already past midnight. The street, except for one or two people, was deserted, and George was surprised when he saw Mr. Cattanzara still reading his newspaper by the light of the street lamp overhead. His impulse was to stop at the stoop and talk to him. He wasn't sure what he wanted to say, though he felt the words would come when he began to talk; but the more he thought about it, the more the idea scared him, and he decided he'd better not. He even considered beating it home by another street, but he was too near Mr. Cattanzara, and the change maker might see him as he ran, and get annoyed. So George unobtrusively crossed the street, trying to make it seem as if he had to look in a store window on the other side, which he did, and then went on, uncomfortable at what he was doing. He feared Mr. Cattanzara would glance up from his paper and call him a dirty rat for walking on the other side of the street, but all he did was sit there, sweating through his undershirt, his bald head shining in the dim light as he read his *Times*, and upstairs his fat wife leaned out of the window, seeming to read the paper along with him. George thought she would spy him and yell out to Mr. Cattanzara, but she never moved her eyes off her husband.

George made up his mind to stay away from the change maker until he had got some of his softback books read, but when he started them and saw they were mostly story books, he lost his interest and didn't bother to finish them. He lost his interest in reading other things too. Sophie's magazines and newspapers went unread. She saw them piling up on a chair in his room and asked why he was no longer looking at them, and George told her it was because of all the other reading he had to do. Sophie said she had guessed that was it. So for most of the day, George had the radio on, turning to music when he was sick of the human voice. He kept the house fairly neat, and Sophie said nothing on the days when he neglected it. She was still kind and gave him his extra buck, though things weren't so good for him as they had been before.

But they were good enough, considering. Also his night walks invariably picked him up, no matter how bad the day was. Then one night George saw Mr. Cattanzara coming down the street toward him. George was about to turn and run but he recognized from Mr. Cattanzara's walk that he was drunk, and if so, probably he would not even bother to notice him. So George kept on walking straight ahead until he came abreast of Mr. Cattanzara and though he felt wound up enough to pop into the sky, he was not surprised when Mr. Cattanzara passed him without a word, walking slowly, his face and body stiff. George drew a breath in relief at his narrow escape, when he heard his name called, and there stood Mr. Cattanzara at his elbow, smelling like the inside of a beer barrel. His eyes were sad as he gazed at George, and George felt so intensely uncomfortable he was tempted to shove the drunk aside and continue on his walk.

But he couldn't act that way to him, and, besides, Mr. Cattanzara took a nickel out of his pants pocket and handed it to him.

"Go buy yourself a lemon ice, Georgie."

"It's not that time anymore, Mr. Cattanzara," George said, "I am a big guy now."

"No, you ain't," said Mr. Cattanzara, to which George made no reply he could think of.

"How are all your books comin' along now?" Mr. Cattanzara asked. Though he tried to stand steady, he swayed a little.

"Fine, I guess," said George, feeling the red crawling up his face.

"You ain't sure?" The change maker smiled slyly, a way George had never seen him smile.

"Sure, I'm sure. They're fine."

Though his head swayed in little arcs, Mr. Cattanzara's eyes were steady. He had small blue eyes which could hurt if you looked at them too long.

"George," he said, "name me one book on that list that you read this summer, and I will drink to your health."

"I don't want anybody drinking to me."

"Name me one so I can ask you a question on it. Who can tell, if it's a good book maybe I might wanna read it myself."

George knew he looked passable on the outside, but inside he was crumbling apart.

Unable to reply, he shut his eyes, but when—years later—he opened them, he saw that Mr. Cattanzara had, out of pity, gone away, but in his ears he still heard the words he had said when he left: "George, don't do what I did."

The next night he was afraid to leave his room, and though Sophie argued with him he wouldn't open the door.

"What are you doing in there?" she asked.

"Nothing."

"Aren't you reading?"

"No."

She was silent a minute, then asked, "Where do you keep the books you read? I never see any in your room outside of a few cheap trashy ones."

He wouldn't tell her.

"In that case you're not worth a buck of my hard-earned money. Why should I break my back for you? Go on out, you bum, and get a job."

He stayed in his room for almost a week, except to sneak into the kitchen when nobody was home. Sophie railed at him, then begged him to come out, and his old father wept, but George wouldn't budge, though the weather was terrible and his small room stifling. He found it very hard to breathe, each breath was like drawing a flame into his lungs.

One night, unable to stand the heat anymore, he burst into the street at one A.M., a shadow of himself. He hoped to sneak to the park without being seen, but there were people all over the block, wilted and listless, waiting for a breeze. George lowered his eyes and walked, in disgrace, away from them, but before long he discovered they were still friendly to him. He figured Mr. Cattanzara hadn't told on him. Maybe when he woke up out of his drunk the next morning, he had forgotten all about meeting George. George felt his confidence slowly come back to him.

That same night a man on a street corner asked him if it was true that he had finished reading so many books, and George admitted he had. The man said it was a wonderful thing for a boy his age to read so much.

"Yeah," George said, but he felt relieved. He hoped nobody would mention the books anymore, and when, after a couple of days, he accidentally met Mr. Cattanzara again, he didn't, though George had the idea he was the one who had started the rumor that he had finished all the books.

One evening in the fall, George ran out of his house to the library, where he hadn't been in years. There were books all over the place, wherever he looked, and though he was struggling to control an inward trembling, he easily counted off a hundred, then sat down at a table to read.

III

Plays

✿◇

SOPHOCLES

Oedipus the King

A Translation by David Grene[1]

CHARACTERS

OEDIPUS, *King of Thebes*
JOCASTA, *Queen of Thebes; wife of*
  Oedipus; widow of Laius,
  the late King
PRIEST OF ZEUS
CREON, *brother of Jocasta*
TEIRESIAS, *a blind prophet*

A MESSENGER, *from Corinth*
A HERDSMAN, *formerly in the*
  service of Laius
SECOND MESSENGER
CHORUS *of Theban elders*
A CROWD *of suppliants, men,*
  women, and children

SCENE: *In front of the palace of* OEDIPUS *at Thebes. To the right of the stage near the altar stands the* PRIEST *with a crowd of suppliants of all ages.* OEDIPUS *emerges from the central door.*

OEDIPUS. Children, young sons and daughters of old Cadmus,
why do you sit here with your suppliant crowns?
The town is heavy with a mingled burden
of sounds and smells, of groans and hymns and incense;
I did not think it fit that I should hear
of this from messengers but came myself,—
I Oedipus whom all men call the Great.

[*He turns to the* PRIEST.]

You're old and they are young; come, speak for them.
What do you fear or want, that you sit here
suppliant? Indeed I'm willing to give all

[1] David Grene, *Three Greek Tragedies.* Copyright, 1942, by The University of Chicago Press. Used by permission.

Courtesy of A. Rogers, Central Photography, Toronto.

(*Top*) *Oedipus the King* from the filming of the Stratford production directed by Tyrone Guthrie and produced by Leonard Kipnis; (*center*) *Blood Wedding*, from a New Stages production, Bleecker Street Playhouse, February 6, 1949; (*bottom*) *The Infernal Machine*, from the 1958 Phoenix Theatre production.

Courtesy of the Phoenix Theatre.

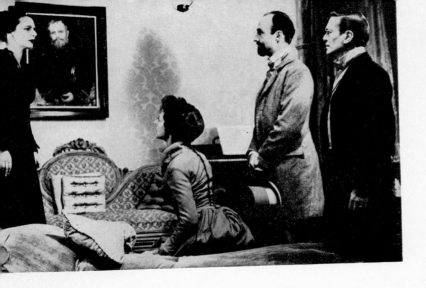

(Top) Hedda Gabler, from the David Ross production staged at the Fourth Street Theatre, September, 1960; (center) Candida, from the 1942 benefit production for the Army Emergency Fund and the Navy Relief Society; (bottom) The Long Voyage Home, from the Argosy production directed by John Ford and filmed at the Walter Wanger Studios.

that you may need; I would be very hard
should I not pity suppliants like these.

    PRIEST.   O ruler of my country, Oedipus,
you see our company around the altar;
you see our ages; some of us, like these,
who cannot yet fly far, and some of us
heavy with age; these children are the chosen
among the young, and I the priest of Zeus.
Within the market place sit others crowned
with suppliant garlands, at the double shrine
of Pallus and the temple where Ismenus
gives oracles by fire. King, you yourself
have seen our city reeling like a wreck
already; it can scarcely lift its prow
out of the depths, out of the bloody surf.
A blight is on the fruitful plants of the earth,
a blight is on the cattle in the fields,
a blight is on our women that no children
are born to them; a God that carries fire,
a deadly pestilence, is in our town,
strikes us and spares not, and the house of Cadmus
is emptied of its people while black Death
grows rich in groaning and in lamentation.
We have not come as suppliants to this altar
because we thought of you as of a God,
but rather judging you the first of men
in all the chances of this life and when
we mortals have to do with more than man.
You came and by your coming saved our city,
freed us from tribute which we paid of old
to the Sphinx, cruel singer. This you did
in virtue of no knowledge we could give you,
in virtue of no teaching; it was God
that aided you, men say, and you are held
with God's assistance to have saved our lives.
Now Oedipus, whom all men call the Greatest,
here falling at your feet we all entreat you,
find us some strength for rescue.
Perhaps you'll hear a wise word from some God,
perhaps you will learn something from a man
(for I have seen that for the skilled of practice
the outcome of their counsels live the most).
Noblest of men, go, and raise up our city,
go,—and give heed. For now this land of ours

calls you its savior since you saved it once.
So, let us never speak about your reign
as of a time when first our feet were set
secure on high, but later fell to ruin.
Raise up our city, save it and raise it up.
Once you have brought us luck with happy omen;
be no less now in fortune.
If you will rule this land, as now you rule it,
better to rule it full of men than empty.
For neither town nor ship is anything
when empty, and none live in it together.

    OEDIPUS.   Poor children! You have come to me entreating,
but I have known the story before you told it
only too well. I know you are all sick,
yet there is not one of you, sick though you are,
that is as sick as I myself.
Your several sorrows each have single scope
and touch but one of you. My spirit groans
for city and myself and you at once.
You have not roused me like a man from sleep;
know that I have given many tears to this,
gone many ways wandering in thought,
but as I thought I found only one remedy
and that I took. I sent Menoeceus' son
Creon, Jocasta's brother, to Apollo,
to his Pythian temple,
that he might learn there by what act or word
I could save this city. As I count the days,
it vexes me what ails him; he is gone
far longer than he needed for the journey.
But when he comes, then, may I prove a villain,
if I shall not do all the God commands.

    PRIEST.   Thanks for your gracious words. Your servants here
signal that Creon is this moment coming.

    OEDIPUS.   His face is bright. O holy Lord Apollo,
grant that his news too may be bright for us
and bring us safety.

    PRIEST.   It is happy news,
I think, for else his head would not be crowned
with sprigs of fruitful laurel.

    OEDIPUS.   We will know soon,
he's within hail. Lord Creon, my good brother,
what is the word you bring us from the God?

[CREON *enters.*]

CREON.   A good word,— for things hard to bear themselves
if in the final issue all is well
I count complete good fortune.

OEDIPUS.   What do you mean?
What you have said so far
leaves me uncertain whether to trust or fear.

CREON.   If you will hear my news before these others
I am ready to speak, or else to go within.

OEDIPUS.   Speak it to all;
the grief I bear, I bear it more for these
than for my own heart.

CREON.   I will tell you, then,
what I heard from the God.
King Phoebus in plain words commanded us
to drive out a pollution from our land,
pollution grown ingrained within the land;
drive it out, said the God, not cherish it,
till it's past cure.

OEDIPUS.   What is the rite
of purification? How shall it be done?

CREON.   By banishing a man, or expiation
of blood by blood, since it is murder guilt
which holds our city in this storm of death.

OEDIPUS.   Who is this man whose fate the God pronounces?

CREON.   My Lord, before you piloted the state
we had a king called Laius.

OEDIPUS.   I know of him by hearsay. I have not seen him.

CREON.   The God commanded clearly: let some one
punish with force this dead man's murderers.

OEDIPUS.   Where are they in the world? Where would a trace
of this old crime be found? It would be hard
to guess where.

CREON.   The clue is in this land;
that which is sought is found;
the unheeded thing escapes:
so said the God.

OEDIPUS.   Was it at home,
or in the country that death came upon him,
or in another country travelling?

CREON.   He went, he said himself, upon an embassy,
but never returned when he set out from home.

OEDIPUS.   Was there no messenger, no fellow traveller

who knew what happened? Such a one might tell
something of use.

    CREON.   They were all killed save one. He fled in terror
and he could tell us nothing in clear terms
of what he knew, nothing, but one thing only.

    OEDIPUS.   What was it?
If we could even find a slim beginning
in which to hope, we might discover much.

    CREON.   This man said that the robbers they encountered
were many and the hands that did the murder
were many; it was no man's single power.

    OEDIPUS.   How could a robber dare a deed like this
were he not helped with money from the city,
money and treachery?

    CREON.   That indeed was thought.
But Laius was dead and in our trouble
there was none to help.

    OEDIPUS.   What trouble was so great to hinder you
inquiring out the murder of your king?

    CREON.   The riddling Sphinx induced us to neglect
mysterious crimes and rather seek solution
of troubles at our feet.

    OEDIPUS.   I will bring this to light again. King Phoebus
fittingly took this care about the dead,
and you too fittingly.
And justly you will see in me an ally,
a champion of my country and the God.
For when I drive pollution from the land
I will not serve a distant friend's advantage,
but act in my own interest. Whoever
he was that killed the king may readily
wish to dispatch me with his murderous hand;
so helping the dead king I help myself.
Come children, take your suppliant boughs and go;
up from the altars now. Call the assembly
and let it meet upon the understanding
that I'll do everything. God will decide
whether we prosper or remain in sorrow.

    PRIEST.   Rise, children—it was this we came to seek,
which of himself the king now offers us.
May Phoebus who gave us the oracle
come to our rescue and stay the plague.

    [*Exeunt. Enter* CHORUS OF THEBAN ELDERS.]

Strophe 1

CHORUS.   What is the sweet spoken word of God from the shrine of Pytho
rich in gold
that has come to glorious Thebes?
I am stretched on the rack of doubt, and terror and trembling hold
my heart, O Delian Healer, and I worship full of fears
for what doom you will bring to pass, new or renewed in the revolving years.
Speak to me, immortal voice,
child of golden Hope.

Antistrophe 1

First I call on you, Athene, deathless daughter of Zeus,
and Artemis, Earth Upholder,
who sits in the midst of the market place in the throne which men call Fame,
and Phoebus, the Far Shooter, three averters of Fate,
come to us now, if ever before, when ruin rushed upon the state,
you drove destruction's flame away
out of our land.

Strophe 2

Our sorrows defy number;
all the ship's timbers are rotten;
taking of thought is no spear for the driving away of the plague.
There are no growing children in this famous land;
there are no women staunchly bearing the pangs of childbirth.
You may see them one with another, like birds swift on the wing,
quicker than fire unmastered,
speeding away to the coast of the Western God.

Antistrophe 2

In the unnumbered deaths
of its people the city dies;
those children that are born lie dead on the naked earth
unpitied, spreading contagion of death; and grey haired mothers and wives
everywhere stand at the altar's edge, suppliant, moaning;
the hymn to the healing God rings out but with it the wailing voices are
   blended.
From these our sufferings grant us, O golden Daughter of Zeus,
glad-faced deliverance.

Strophe 3

There is no clash of brazen shields but our fight is with the War God,
a War God ringed with the cries of men, a savage God who burns us;

grant that he turn in racing course backwards out of our country's bounds
to the great palace of Amphitrite or where the waves of the Thracian sea
deny the stranger safe anchorage.
Whatsoever escapes the night
at last the light of day revisits;
so smite the War God, Father Zeus,
beneath your thunderbolt,
for you are the Lord of the lightning, the lightning that
carries fire.

Antistrophe 3

And your unconquered arrow shafts, winged by the golden corded bow,
Lycean king, I beg to be at our side for help;
and the gleaming torches of Artemis with which she scours the Lycean hills,
and I call on the God with the turban of gold, who gave his name to this
    country of ours,
the Bacchic God with the wine flushed face,
Evian One, who travel
with the Maenad company,
combat the God that burns us
with your torch of pine;
for the God that is our enemy is a God unhonoured among the Gods.

[OEDIPUS *returns*.]

OEDIPUS.   For what you ask me—if you will hear my words,
and hearing welcome them and fight the plague,
you will find strength and lightening of your load.

Hark to me; what I say to you, I say
as one that is a stranger to the story
as stranger to the deed. For I would not
be far upon the track if I alone
were tracing it without a clue. But now,
since after all was finished, I became
a citizen among you, citizens—
now I proclaim to all the men of Thebes:
whoso among you knows the murderer
by whose hand Laius, son of Labdacus,
died—I command him to tell everything
to me,—yes, though he fears himself to take the blame
on his own head; for bitter punishment
he shall have none, but leave this land unharmed.
Or if he knows the murderer, another,
a foreigner, still let him speak the truth.

For I will pay him and be grateful, too.
But if you shall keep silence, if perhaps
some one of you, to shield a guilty friend,
or for his own sake shall reject my words—
hear what I shall do then:
I forbid that man, whoever he be, my land,
my land where I hold sovereignty and throne;
and I forbid any to welcome him
or cry him greeting or make him a sharer
in sacrifice or offering to the Gods,
or give him water for his hands to wash.
I command all to drive him from their homes,
since he is our pollution, as the oracle
of Pytho's God proclaimed him now to me.
So I stand forth a champion of the God
and of the man who died.
Upon the murderer I invoke this curse—
whether he is one man and all unknown,
or one of many—may he wear out his life
in misery to miserable doom!
If with my knowledge he lives at my hearth
I pray that I myself may feel my curse.

Even were this no matter of God's ordinance
it would not fit you so to leave it lie,
unpurified, since a good man is dead
and one that was a king. Search it out.
Since I am now the holder of his office,
and have his bed and wife that once was his,
and had his line not been unfortunate
we would have common children—(fortune leaped
upon his head)—because of all these things,
I fight in his defence as for my father,
and I shall try all means to take the murderer
of Laius the son of Labdacus
the son of Polydorus and before him
of Cadmus and before him of Agenor.
Those who do not obey me, may the Gods
grant no crops springing from the ground they plough
nor children to their women! May a fate
like this, or one still worse than this consume them!
For you whom these words please, the other Thebans,
may Justice as your ally and all the Gods
live with you, blessing you now and for ever!

CHORUS.   As you have held me to my oath, I speak:
I neither killed the king nor can declare
the killer; but since Phoebus set the quest
it is his part to tell who the man is.

OEDIPUS.   Right; but to put compulsion on the Gods
against their will—no man has strength for that.

CHORUS.   May I then say what I think second best?

OEDIPUS.   If there's a third best, too, spare not to tell it.

CHORUS.   I know that what the Lord Teiresias
sees, is most often what the Lord Apollo
sees. If you should inquire of this from him
you might find out most clearly.

OEDIPUS.   Even in this my actions have not been sluggard.
On Creon's word I have sent two messengers
and why the prophet is not here already
I have been wondering.

CHORUS.   His skill apart
there is besides only an old faint story.

OEDIPUS.   What is it?
I seize on every story.

CHORUS.   It was said
that he was killed by certain wayfarers.

OEDIPUS.   I heard that, too, but no one saw the killer.

CHORUS.   Yet if he has a share of fear at all,
his courage will not stand firm, hearing your curse.

OEDIPUS.   The man who in the doing did not shrink
will fear no word.

CHORUS.   Here comes his prosecutor:
led by your men the godly prophet comes
in whom alone of mankind truth is native.

[*Enter* TEIRESIAS, *led by a little boy.*]

OEDIPUS.   Teiresias, you are versed in everything,
things teachable and things not to be spoken,
things of the heaven and earth-creeping things.
You have no eyes but in your mind you know
with what a plague our city is afflicted.
My lord, in you alone we find a champion,
in you alone one that can rescue us.
Perhaps you have not heard the messengers,
but Phoebus sent in answer to our sending
an oracle declaring that our freedom
from this disease would only come when we
should learn the names of those who killed King Laius,

and kill them or expel from our country.
Do not begrudge us oracles from birds,
or any other way of prophecy
within your skill; save yourself and the city,
save me; redeem the debt of our pollution
that lies on us because of this dead man.
We are in your hands; it is the finest task
to help another when you have means and power.

TEIRESIAS.   Alas, how terrible is wisdom when
it brings no profit to the man that's wise!
This I knew well, but had forgotten it,
else I would not have come here.

OEDIPUS.   What is this?
How sad you are now you have come!

TEIRESIAS.   Let me
go home. It will be easiest for us both
to bear our several destinies to the end
if you will follow my advice.

OEDIPUS.   You'd rob us
of this your gift of prophecy? You talk
as one who had no care for law nor love
for Thebes who reared you.

TEIRESIAS.   Yes, but I see that even your own words
miss the mark; therefore I must fear for mine.

OEDIPUS.   For God's sake if you know of anything,
do not turn from us; all of us kneel to you,
all of us here, your suppliants.

TEIRESIAS.   All of you here know nothing. I will not
bring to the light of day my troubles, mine—
rather than call them yours.

OEDIPUS.   What do you mean?
You know of some thing but refuse to speak.
Would you betray us and destroy the city?

TEIRESIAS.   I will not bring this pain upon us both,
neither on you nor on myself. Why is it
you question me and waste your labour? I
will tell you nothing.

OEDIPUS.   You would provoke a stone? Tell us, you villain,
tell us, and do not stand there quietly
unmoved and balking at the final issue.

TEIRESIAS.   You blame my temper but you do not see
your own that lives within you; it is me
you chide.

OEDIPUS.   Who would not feel his temper rise

at words like these with which you shame our city?

TEIRESIAS. Of themselves things will come, although I hide them and breathe no word of them.

OEDIPUS. Since they will come tell them to me.

TEIRESIAS. I will say nothing further. Against this answer let your temper rage as wildly as you will.

OEDIPUS. Indeed I am so angry I shall not hold back a jot of what I think. For I would have you know I think you were complotter of the deed and doer of the deed save in so far as for the actual killing. Had you had eyes I would have said alone you murdered him.

TEIRESIAS. Yes? Then I warn you faithfully to keep the letter of your proclamation and from this day forth to speak no word of greeting to these nor me; you are the land's pollution.

OEDIPUS. How shamelessly you started up this taunt! How do you think you will escape?

TEIRESIAS. I have. I have escaped; the truth is what I cherish and that's my strength.

OEDIPUS. And who has taught you truth? Not your profession surely!

TEIRESIAS. You have taught me, for you have made me speak against my will.

OEDIPUS. Speak what? Tell me again that I may learn it better.

TEIRESIAS. Did you not understand before or would you provoke me into speaking?

OEDIPUS. I did not grasp it, not so to call it known. Say it again.

TEIRESIAS. I say you are the murderer of the king whose murderer you seek.

OEDIPUS. Not twice you shall not say calumnies like this and stay unpunished.

TEIRESIAS. Shall I say more to tempt your anger more?

OEDIPUS. As much as you desire; it will be said in vain.

TEIRESIAS. I say that with those you love best you live in foulest shame unconsciously and do not see where you are in calamity.

OEDIPUS. Do you imagine you can always talk

like this, and live to laugh at it hereafter?

TEIRESIAS.   Yes, if the truth has anything of strength.

OEDIPUS.   It has, but not for you; it has no strength
for you because you are blind in mind and ears
as well as in your eyes.

TEIRESIAS.   You are a poor wretch
to taunt me with the very insults which
everyone soon will heap upon yourself.

OEDIPUS.   Your life is one long night so that you cannot
hurt me or any other who sees the light.

TEIRESIAS.   It is not fate that I should be your ruin,
Apollo is enough; it is his care
to work this out.

OEDIPUS.   Was this your own design
or Creon's?

TEIRESIAS.   Creon is no hurt to you,
but you are to yourself.

OEDIPUS.   Wealth, sovereignty and skill outmatching skill
for the contrivance of an envied life,
great store of jealousy fill your treasury chests,
if my friend Creon, friend from the first and loyal,
thus secretly attacks me, secretly
desires to drive me out and secretly
suborns this juggling, trick devising quack,
this wily beggar who has only eyes
for his own gains, but blindness in his skill.
For, tell me, where have you seen clear, Teiresias,
with your prophetic eyes? When the dark singer,
the Sphinx, was in your country, did you speak
word of deliverance to its citizens?
And yet the riddle's answer was not the province
of a chance comer. It was a prophet's task
and plainly you had no such gift of prophecy
from birds nor otherwise from any God
to glean a word of knowledge. But I came,
Oedipus, who knew nothing, and I stopped her.
I solved the riddle by my wit alone.
Mine was no knowledge got from birds. And now
you would expel me,
because you think that you will find a place
by Creon's throne. I think you will be sorry,
both you and your accomplice, for your plot
to drive me out. And did I not regard you
as an old man, some suffering would have taught you

that **what** was in your heart was treason.

CHORUS.   We look at this man's words and yours, my king,
and we find both have spoken them in anger.
We need no angry words but only thought
how we may best hit the God's meaning for us.

TEIRESIAS.   If you are king, at least I have the right
no less to speak in my defence against you.
Of that much I am master. I am no slave
of yours, but Loxias', and so I shall not
enroll myself with Creon for my patron.
Since you have taunted me with being blind,
here is my word for you.
You have your eyes but see not where you are
in sin, nor where you live, nor whom you live with.
Do you know who your parents are? Unknowing
you are an enemy to kith and kin
in death, beneath the earth, and in this life.
A deadly-footed, double-striking curse,
from father and mother both, shall drive you forth
out of this land, with darkness on your eyes,
that now have such straight vision. Shall there be
a place will not be harbour to your cries,
a corner of Cithaeron will not ring
in echo to your cries, soon, soon,—
when you shall learn the secret of your marriage,
which steered you to a haven in this house,—
haven no haven, after lucky voyage?
And of the multitude of other evils
establishing a grim equality
between you and your children, you know nothing.
So, muddy with contempt my words and Creon's!
there is no man shall perish as you shall.

OEDIPUS.   Is it endurable that I should hear
such words from him? Go and a curse go with you!
Quick, home with you! Out of my house at once!

TEIRESIAS.   I would not have come either had you not called me.

OEDIPUS.   I did not know then you would talk like a fool—
or it would have been long before I called you.

TEIRESIAS.   I am a fool then, as it seems to you—
but to the parents who have bred you, wise.

OEDIPUS.   What parents? Stop! Who are they of all the world?

TEIRESIAS.   This day will show your birth and bring your ruin.

OEDIPUS.   How needlessly your riddles darken everything.

TEIRESIAS.   But it's in riddle-answering you are strongest.

OEDIPUS.   Yes. Taunt me where you will find me great.
TEIRESIAS.   It is this very luck that has destroyed you.
OEDIPUS.   I do not care, if it has served this city.
TEIRESIAS.   Well, I will go. Come, boy, lead me away.
OEDIPUS.   Yes, lead him off. So long as you are here,
you'll be a stumbling block and a vexation;
once gone, you will not trouble me again.

TEIRESIAS.   I have said
what I came here to say not fearing your
countenance: there is no way you can hurt me.
I tell you, king, this man, this murderer
(whom you have long declared you are in search of,
indicting him in threatening proclamation
as murderer of Laius)—he is here.
In name he is a stranger among citizens
but soon he will be shown to be a citizen
true native Theban, and he'll have no joy
of the discovery: blindness for sight
and beggary for riches his exchange,
he shall go journeying to a foreign country
tapping his way before him with a stick.
He shall be proved father and brother both
to his own children in his house; to her
that gave him birth, a son and husband both;
a fellow sower in his father's bed
with that same father that he murdered.
Go within, reckon that out, and if you find me
mistaken, say I have no skill in prophecy.

[*Exeunt separately* TEIRESIAS *and* OEDIPUS.]

Strophe 1

CHORUS.   Who is the man proclaimed
by Delphi's prophetic rock
as the bloody-handed murderer,
the doer of deeds that none dares name?
Now is the time for him to run
with a stronger foot
than Pegasus
for the child of Zeus leaps in arms upon him
with fire and the lightning bolt,
and terribly close on his heels
are the Fates that never miss.

Antistrophe 1

Lately from snowy Parnassus
clearly the voice flashed forth,
bidding each Theban track him down,
the unknown murderer.
In the savage forests he lurks and in
the caverns like
the mountain bull.
He is sad and lonely, and lonely his feet
that carry him far from the navel of earth;
but its prophecies, ever living,
flutter around his head.

Strophe 2

The augur has spread confusion
terrible confusion;
I do not approve what was said
nor can I deny it.
I do not know what to say;
I am in a flutter of foreboding;
I never heard in the present
nor past of a quarrel between
the sons of Labdacus and Polybus,
that I might bring as proof
in attacking the popular fame
of Oedipus, seeking
to take vengeance for undiscovered
death in the line of Labdacus.

Antistrophe 2

Truly Zeus and Apollo are wise
and in human things all-knowing;
but amongst men there is no
distinct judgment, between the prophet
and me—which of us is right.
One man may pass another in wisdom
but I would never agree
with those that find fault with the king
till I should see the word
proved right beyond doubt. For once
in visible form the Sphinx
came on him and all of us

saw his wisdom and in that test
he saved the city. So he will not be condemned by my mind.

[*Enter* CREON.]

CREON.   Citizens, I have come because I heard
deadly words spread about me, that the king
accuses me. I cannot take that from him.
If he believes that in these present troubles
he has been wronged by me in word or deed
I do not want to live on with the burden
of such a scandal on me. The report
injures me doubly and most vitally—
for I'll be called a traitor to my city
and traitor also to my friends and you.

CHORUS.   Perhaps it was a sudden gust of anger
that forced that insult from him, and no judgment.

CREON.   But did he say that it was in compliance
with schemes of mine that the seer told him lies?

CHORUS.   Yes, he said that, but why, I do not know.

CREON.   Were his eyes straight in his head? Was his mind right
when he accused me in this fashion?

CHORUS.   I do not know; I have no eyes to see
what princes do. Here comes the king himself.

[*Enter* OEDIPUS.]

OEDIPUS.   You, sir, how is it you come here? Have you so much
brazen-faced daring that you venture in
my house although you are proved manifestly
the murderer of that man, and though you tried,
openly, highway robbery of my crown?
For God's sake, tell me what you saw in me,
what cowardice or what stupidity,
that made you lay a plot like this against me?
Did you imagine I should not observe
the crafty scheme that stole upon me or
seeing it, take no means to counter it?
Was it not stupid of you to make the attempt,
to try to hunt down royal power without
the people at your back or friends? For only
with the people at your back or money can
the hunt end in the capture of a crown.

CREON.   Do you know what you're doing? Will you listen
to words to answer yours, and then pass judgment?

OEDIPUS.   You're quick to speak, but I am slow to grasp you,
for I have found you dangerous,—and my foe.

CREON.   First of all hear what I shall say to that.

OEDIPUS.   At least don't tell me that you are not guilty.

CREON.   If you believe you cherish something fine
in obstinacy without brains, you're wrong.

OEDIPUS.   And you are wrong if you believe that one,
a criminal, will not be punished only
because he is my kinsman.

CREON.   This is but just—
but tell me, then, of what offense I'm guilty?

OEDIPUS.   Did you or did you not urge me to send
to this prophetic mumbler?

CREON.   I did indeed,
and I shall stand by what I told you.

OEDIPUS.   How long ago is it since Laius. . . .

CREON.   What about Laius? I don't understand.

OEDIPUS.   Vanished—died—was murdered?

CREON.   It is long,
a long, long time to reckon.

OEDIPUS.   Was this prophet
in the profession then?

CREON.   He was, and honoured
as highly as he is today.

OEDIPUS.   At that time did he say a word about me?

CREON.   Never, at least when I was near him.

OEDIPUS.   You never made a search for the dead man?

CREON.   We searched, indeed, but never learned of anything.

OEDIPUS.   Why did our wise old friend not say this then?

CREON.   I don't know; and when I know nothing, I
usually hold my tongue.

OEDIPUS.   You know this much,
and can declare this much if you are loyal.

CREON.   What is it? If I know I'll not deny it.

OEDIPUS.   That he would not have said that I killed Laius
had he not met you first.

CREON.   You know yourself
whether he said this, but I demand that I
should hear as much from you as you from me.

OEDIPUS.   Then hear,—I'll not be proved a murderer.

CREON.   Well, then. You're married to my sister.

OEDIPUS.   Yes,
that I am not disposed to deny.

CREON.   You rule

this country giving her an equal share
in the government?

OEDIPUS.　　　　　Yes, everything she wants
she has from me.

CREON.　　　And I, as thirdsman to you,
am rated as the equal of you two?

OEDIPUS.　Yes, and it's there you've proved yourself false friend.

CREON.　Not if you will reflect on it as I do.
Consider, first, if you think anyone
would choose to rule and fear rather than rule
and sleep untroubled by a fear if power
were equal in both cases. I, at least,
I was not born with such a frantic yearning
to be a king—but to do what kings do.
And so it is with every one who has learned
wisdom and self-control. As it stands now,
the prizes are all mine—and without fear.
But if I were the king myself, I must
do much that went against the grain.
How should despotic rule seem sweeter to me
than painless power and an assured authority?
I am not so besotted yet that I
want other honours than those that come with profit.
Now every man's my pleasure; every man greets me;
now those who are your suitors fawn on me,—
success for them depends upon my favour.
Why should I let all this go to win that?
My mind would not be traitor if it's wise;
I am no treason-lover, of my nature,
nor would I ever dare to join a plot.
Prove what I say. Go to the oracle
at Pytho and inquire about the answers,
if they are as I told you. For the rest,
if you discover I laid any plot
together with the seer, kill me, I say,
not only by your vote but by my own.
But do not charge me on obscure opinion
without some proof to back it. It's not just
lightly to count your knaves as honest men,
nor honest men as knaves. To throw away
an honest friend is, as it were, to throw
your life away, which a man loves the best.
In time you will know all with certainty;
time is the only test of honest men,

one day is space enough to know a rogue.

CHORUS.   His words are wise, king, if one fears to fall.
Those who are quick of temper are not safe.

OEDIPUS.   When he that plots against me secretly
moves quickly, I must quickly counterplot.
If I wait taking no decisive measure
his business will be done, and mine be spoiled.

CREON.   What do you want to do then? Banish me?

OEDIPUS.   No, certainly; kill you, not banish you.

CREON.   I do not think that you've your wits about you.

OEDIPUS.   For my own interests, yes.

CREON.   But for mine, too,
you should think equally.

OEDIPUS.   You are a rogue.

CREON.   Suppose you do not understand?

OEDIPUS.   But yet
I must be ruler.

CREON.   Not if you rule badly.

OEDIPUS.   O, city, city!

CREON.   I too have some share
in the city; it is not yours alone.

CHORUS.   Stop, my lords! Here—and in the nick of time
I see Jocasta coming from the house;
with her help lay the quarrel that now stirs you.

[*Enter* JOCASTA.]

JOCASTA.   For shame! Why have you raised this foolish squabbling
brawl? Are you not ashamed to air your private
griefs when the country's sick? Go in, you, Oedipus,
and you, too, Creon, into the house. Don't magnify
your nothing troubles.

CREON.   Sister, Oedipus,
your husband, thinks he has the right to do
terrible wrongs—he has but to choose between
two terrors: banishing or killing me.

OEDIPUS.   He's right, Jocasta; for I find him plotting
with knavish tricks against my person.

CREON.   That God may never bless me! May I die
accursed, if I have been guilty of
one tittle of the charge you bring against me!

JOCASTA.   I beg you, Oedipus, trust him in this,
spare him for the sake of this his oath to God,
for my sake, and the sake of those who stand here.

CHORUS.   Be gracious, be merciful,

we beg of you.

OEDIPUS. In what would you have me yield?

CHORUS. He has been no silly child in the past.
He is strong in his oath now.
Spare him.

OEDIPUS. Do you know what you ask?

CHORUS. Yes.

OEDIPUS. Tell me then.

CHORUS. He has been your friend before all men's eyes; do not cast
him away dishonoured on an obscure conjecture.

OEDIPUS. I would have you know that this request of yours
really requests my death or banishment.

CHORUS. May the Sun God, king of Gods, forbid! May I die without
God's blessing, without friends' help, if I had any such
thought. But my spirit is broken by my unhappiness for my
wasting country; and this would but add troubles amongst
ourselves to the other troubles.

OEDIPUS. Well, let him go then—if I must die ten times for it,
or be sent out dishonoured into exile.
It is your lips that prayed for him I pitied,
not his; wherever he is, I shall hate him.

CREON. I see you sulk in yielding and you're dangerous
when you are out of temper; natures like yours
are justly heaviest for themselves to bear.

OEDIPUS. Leave me alone! Take yourself off, I tell you.

CREON. I'll go, you have not known me, but they have,
and they have known my innocence.

[*Exit.*]

CHORUS. Won't you take him inside, lady?

JOCASTA. Yes, when I've found out what was the matter.

CHORUS. There was some misconceived suspicion of a story, and on
the other side the sting of injustice.

JOCASTA. So, on both sides?

CHORUS. Yes.

JOCASTA. What was the story?

CHORUS. I think it best, in the interests of the country, to leave it
where it ended.

OEDIPUS. You see where you have ended, straight of judgment
although you are, by softening my anger.

CHORUS. Sir, I have said before and I say again—be sure that I would
have been proved a madman, bankrupt in sane council, if I
should put you away, you who steered the country I love
safely when she was crazed with troubles. God grant that

now, too, you may prove a fortunate guide for us.

JOCASTA.   Tell me, my lord, I beg of you, what was it
that roused your anger so?

OEDIPUS.   Yes, I will tell you.
I honour you more than I honour them.
It was Creon and the plots he laid against me.

JOCASTA.   Tell me—if you can clearly tell the quarrel—

OEDIPUS.   Creon says
that I'm the murderer of Laius.

JOCASTA.   Of his own knowledge or on information?

OEDIPUS.   He sent this rascal prophet to me, since
he keeps his own mouth clean of any guilt.

JOCASTA.   Do not concern yourself about this matter;
listen to me and learn that human beings
have no part in the craft of prophecy.
Of that I'll show you a short proof.
There was an oracle once that came to Laius,—
I will not say that it was Phoebus' own,
but it was from his servants—and it told him
that it was fate that he should die a victim
at the hands of his own son, a son to be born
of Laius and me. But, see now, he,
the king, was killed by foreign highway robbers
at a place where three roads meet—so goes the story;
and for the son—before three days were out
after his birth King Laius pierced his ankles
and by the hands of others cast him forth
upon a pathless hillside. So Apollo
failed to fulfill his oracle to the son,
that he should kill his father, and to Laius
also proved false in that thing he feared,
death at his son's hands, never came to pass.
So clear in this case were the oracles,
so clear and false. Give them no heed, I say:
what God discovers need of, easily
he shows to us himself.

OEDIPUS.   O dear Jocasta,
as I hear this from you, there comes upon me
a wandering of the soul—I could run mad.

JOCASTA.   What trouble is it, that you turn again
and speak like this?

OEDIPUS.   I thought I heard you say
that Laius was killed at a crossroads.

JOCASTA.   Yes, that was how the story went and still

that word goes round.

OEDIPUS.   Where is this place, Jocasta,
where he was murdered?

JOCASTA.   Phocis is the country
and the road splits there, one of two roads from Delphi,
another comes from Daulia.

OEDIPUS.   How long ago is this?

JOCASTA.   The news came to the city just before
you became king and all men's eyes looked to you.
What is it, Oedipus, that's in your mind?

OEDIPUS.   Don't ask me yet—tell me of Laius—
how did he look? How old or young was he?

JOCASTA.   He was a tall man and his hair was grizzled
already—nearly white—and in his form
not unlike you.

OEDIPUS.   O God, I think I have
called curses on myself in ignorance.

JOCASTA.   What do you mean? I am terrified
when I look at you.

OEDIPUS.   I have a deadly fear
that the old seer had eyes. You'll show me more
if you can tell me one more thing.

JOCASTA.   I will.
I'm frightened,—but if I can understand,
I'll tell you all you ask.

OEDIPUS.   How was his company?
Had he few with him when he went this journey,
or many servants, as would suit a prince?

JOCASTA.   In all there were but five, and among them
a herald; and one carriage for the king.

OEDIPUS.   It's plain—it's plain—who was it told you this?

JOCASTA.   The only servant that escaped safe home.

OEDIPUS.   Is he at home now?

JOCASTA.   No, when he came home again
and saw you king and Laius was dead,
he came to me and touched my hand and begged
that I should send him to the fields to be
my shepherd and so he might see the city
as far off as he might. So I
sent him away. He was an honest man,
as slaves go, and was worthy of far more
than what he asked of me.

OEDIPUS.   O, how I wish that he could come back quickly!

JOCASTA.   He can. Why is your heart so set on this?

OEDIPUS.   O dear Jocasta, I am full of fears
that I have spoken far too much; and therefore
I wish to see this shepherd.

JOCASTA.   He will come;
but, Oedipus, I think I'm worthy too
to know what is it that disquiets you.

OEDIPUS.   It shall not be kept from you, since my mind
has gone so far with its forebodings. Whom
should I confide in rather than you, who is there
of more importance to me who have passed
through such a fortune?
Polybus was my father, king of Corinth,
and Merope, the Dorain, my mother.
I was held greatest of the citizens
in Corinth till a curious chance befell me
as I shall tell you—curious, indeed,
but hardly worth the store I set upon it.
There was a dinner and at it a man,
a drunken man, accused me in his drink
of being bastard. I was furious
but held my temper under for that day.
Next day I went and taxed my parents with it;
they took the insult very ill from him,
the drunken fellow who had uttered it.
So I was comforted for their part, but
still this thing rankled always, for the story
crept about widely. And I went at last
to Pytho, though my parents did not know.
But Phoebus sent me home again unhonoured
in what I came to learn, but he foretold
other and desperate horrors to befall me,
that I was fated to lie with my mother,
and show to daylight an accursed breed
which men would not endure, and I was doomed
to be murderer of the father that begot me.
When I heard this I fled, and in the days
that followed I would measure from the stars
the whereabouts of Corinth—yes, I fled
to somewhere where I should not see fulfilled
the infamies told in that dreadful oracle.
And as I journeyed I came to the place
where, as you say, this king met with his death.
Jocasta, I will tell you the whole truth.
When I was near the branching of the crossroads,

going on foot, I was encountered by
a herald and a carriage with a man in it,
just as you tell me. He that led the way
and the old man himself wanted to thrust me
out of the road by force. I became angry
and struck the coachman who was pushing me.
When the old man saw this he watched his moment,
and as I passed he struck me from his carriage,
full on the head with his two pointed goad.
But he was paid in full and presently
my stick had struck him backwards from the car
and he rolled out of it. And then I killed them
all. If it happened there was any tie
of kinship twixt this man and Laius,
who is then now more miserable than I,
what man on earth so hated by the Gods,
since neither citizen nor foreigner
may welcome me at home or even greet me,
but drive me out of doors? And it is I,
I and no other have so cursed myself.
And I pollute the bed of him I killed
by the hands that killed him. Was I not born evil?
Am I not utterly unclean? I had to fly
and in my banishment not even see
my kindred nor set foot in my own country,
or otherwise my fate was to be yoked
in marriage with my mother and kill my father,
Polybus who begot me and had reared me.
Would not one rightly judge and say that on me
these things were sent by some malignant God?
O no, no, no—O holy majesty
of God on high, may I not see that day!
May I be gone out of men's sight before
I see the deadly taint of this disaster
come upon me.

CHORUS.   Sir, we too fear these things. But until you see this man face to face and hear his story, hope.

OEDIPUS.   Yes, I have just this much of hope—to wait until the herdsman comes.

JOCASTA.   And when he comes, what do you want with him?

OEDIPUS.   I'll tell you; if I find that his story is the same as yours, I at least will be clear of this guilt.

JOCASTA.   Why what so particularly did you learn from my story?

OEDIPUS.   You said that he spoke of highway *robbers* who killed Laius. Now

if he uses the same number, it was not I who killed him. One man cannot be
the same as many. But if he speaks of a man travelling alone, then clearly the
burden of the guilt inclines towards me.

JOCASTA.   Be sure, at least, that this was how he told the story. He cannot
unsay it now, for every one in the city heard it—not I alone. But, Oedipus, even
if he diverges from what he said then, he shall never prove that the murder of
Laius squares rightly with the prophecy—for Loxias declared that the king
should be killed by his own son. And that poor creature did not kill him surely,
—for he died himself first. So as far as prophecy goes, henceforward I shall not
look to the right hand or the left.

OEDIPUS.   Right. But yet, send some one for the peasant to bring him here;
do not neglect it.

JOCASTA.   I will send quickly. Now let me go indoors. I will do nothing
except what pleases you.

[*Exeunt.*]

Strophe 1

CHORUS.   May destiny ever find me
pious in word and deed
prescribed by the laws that live on high:
laws begotten in the clear air of heaven,
whose only father is Olympus;
no mortal nature brought them to birth,
no forgetfulness shall lull them to sleep;
for God is great in them and grows not old.

Antistrophe 1

Insolence breeds the tyrant, insolence
if it is glutted with a surfeit, unseasonable, unprofitable,
climbs to the roof-top and plunges
sheer down to the ruin that must be,
and there its feet are no service.
But I pray that the God may never
abolish the eager ambition that profits the state.
For I shall never cease to hold the God as our protector.

Strophe 2

If a man walks with haughtiness
of hand or word and gives no heed
to Justice and the shrines of Gods
despises—may an evil doom
smite him for his ill-starred pride of heart!—
if he reaps gains without justice

and will not hold from impiety
and his fingers itch for untouchable things.
When such things are done, what man shall contrive
to shield his soul from the shafts of the God?
When such deeds are held in honour,
why should I honour the Gods in the dance?

Antistrophe 2

No longer to the holy place,
to the navel of earth I'll go
to worship, nor to Abae
nor to Olympia,
unless the oracles are proved to fit,
for all men's hands to point at.
O Zeus, if you are rightly called
the sovereign lord, all-mastering,
let this not escape you nor your ever-living power!
The oracles concerning Laius
are old and dim and men regard them not.
Apollo is nowhere clear in honour; God's service perishes.

[*Enter* JOCASTA, *carrying garlands.*]

JOCASTA.   Princes of the land, I have had the thought to go
to the Gods' temples, bringing in my hand
garlands and gifts of incense, as you see.
For Oedipus excites himself too much
at every sort of trouble, not conjecturing,
like a man of sense, what will be from what was,
but he is always at the speaker's mercy,
when he speaks terrors. I can do no good
by my advice, and so I came as suppliant
to you, Lycaean Apollo, who are nearest.
These are the symbols of my prayer and this
my prayer: grant us escape free of the curse.
Now when we look to him we are all afraid;
he's pilot of our ship and he is frightened.

[*Enter a* MESSENGER.]

MESSENGER.   Might I learn from you, sirs, where is the house of Oedipus?
Or best of all, if you know, where is the king himself?

CHORUS.   This is his house and he is within doors. This lady is his wife and
mother of his children.

MESSENGER.   God bless you, lady, and God bless your household! God bless
Oedipus' noble wife!

JOCASTA.   God bless you, sir, for your kind greeting! What do you want of us that you have come here? What have you to tell us?

MESSENGER.   Good news, lady. Good for your house and for your husband.

JOCASTA.   What is your news? Who sent you to us?

MESSENGER.   I come from Corinth and the news I bring will give you pleasure. Perhaps a little pain too.

JOCASTA.   What is this news of double meaning?

MESSENGER.   The people of the Isthmus will choose Oedipus to be their king. That is the rumour there.

JOCASTA.   But isn't their king still old Polybus?

MESSENGER.   No. He is in his grave. Death has got him.

JOCASTA.   Is that the truth? Is Oedipus' father dead?

MESSENGER.   May I die myself if it be otherwise!

JOCASTA. [*To a servant.*]   Be quick and run to the King with the news! O oracles of the Gods, where are you now? It was from this man Oedipus fled, lest he should be his murderer! And now he is dead, in the course of nature, and not killed by Oedipus.

[*Enter* OEDIPUS.]

OEDIPUS.   Dearest Jocasta, why have you sent for me?

JOCASTA.   Listen to this man and when you hear reflect what is the outcome of the holy oracles of the Gods.

OEDIPUS.   Who is he? What is his message for me?

JOCASTA.   He is from Corinth and he tells us that your father Polybus is dead and gone.

OEDIPUS.   What's this you say, sir? Tell me yourself.

MESSENGER.   Since this is the first matter you want clearly told: Polybus has gone down to death. You may be sure of it.

OEDIPUS.   By treachery or sickness?

MESSENGER.   A small thing will put old bodies asleep.

OEDIPUS.   So he died of sickness, it seems,—poor old man!

MESSENGER.   Yes, and of age—the long years he had measured.

OEDIPUS.   Ha! Ha! O dear Jocasta, why should one
look to the Pythian hearth? Why should one look
to the birds screaming overhead? They prophesied
that I should kill my father! But he's dead,
and hidden deep in earth, and I stand here
who never laid a hand on spear against him,—
unless perhaps he died of longing for me,
and thus I am his murderer. But they,
the oracles, as they stand—he's taken them
away with him, they're dead as he himself is,
and worthless.

JOCASTA.   That I told you before now.

OEDIPUS.   You did, but I was misled by my fear.

JOCASTA.   Then lay no more of them to heart, not one.

OEDIPUS.   But surely I must fear my mother's bed?

JOCASTA.   Why should man fear since chance is all in all
for him, and he can clearly foreknow nothing?
Best to live lightly, as one can, unthinkingly.
As to your mother's marriage bed,—don't fear it.
Before this, in dreams too, as well as oracles,
many a man has lain with his own mother.
But he to whom such things are nothing bears
his life most easily.

OEDIPUS.   All that you say would be said perfectly
if she were dead; but since she lives I must
still fear, although you talk so well, Jocasta.

JOCASTA.   Still in your father's death there's light of comfort?

OEDIPUS.   Great light of comfort; but I fear the living.

MESSENGER.   Who is the woman that makes you afraid?

OEDIPUS.   Merope, old man, Polybus' wife.

MESSENGER.   What about her frightens the queen and you?

OEDIPUS.   A terrible oracle, stranger, from the Gods.

MESSENGER.   Can it be told? Or does the sacred law
forbid another to have knowledge of it?

OEDIPUS.   O no! Once on a time Loxias said
that I should lie with my own mother and
take on my hands the blood of my own father.
And so for these long years I've lived away
from Corinth; it has been to my great happiness;
but yet it's sweet to see the face of parents.

MESSENGER.   This was the fear which drove you out of Corinth?

OEDIPUS.   Old man, I did not wish to kill my father.

MESSENGER.   Why should I not free you from this fear, sir,
since I have come to you in all goodwill?

OEDIPUS.   You would not find me thankless if you did.

MESSENGER.   Why, it was just for this I brought the news,—
to earn your thanks when you had come safe home.

OEDIPUS.   No, I will never come near my parents.

MESSENGER.   Son,
it's very plain you don't know what you're doing.

OEDIPUS.   What do you mean, old man? For God's sake, tell me.

MESSENGER.   If your homecoming is checked by fears like these.

OEDIPUS.   Yes, I'm afraid that Phoebus may prove right.

MESSENGER.   The murder and the incest?

OEDIPUS.   Yes, old man,
that is my constant terror.

MESSENGER.   Do you know
that all your fears are empty?

OEDIPUS.   How is that,
if they are father and mother and I their son?

MESSENGER.   Because Polybus was no kin to you in blood.

OEDIPUS.   What, was not Polybus my father?

MESSENGER.   No more than I but just so much.

OEDIPUS.   How can
my father be my father as much as one
that's nothing to me?

MESSENGER.   Neither he nor I
begat you.

OEDIPUS.   Why then did he call me son?

MESSENGER.   A gift he took you from these hands of mine.

OEDIPUS.   Did he love so much what he took from another's hand?

MESSENGER.   His childlessness before persuaded him.

OEDIPUS.   Was I a child you bought or found when I
was given to him?

MESSENGER.   On Cithaeron's slopes
in the twisting thickets you were found.

OEDIPUS.   And why
were you a traveller in those parts?

MESSENGER.   I was
in charge of mountain flocks.

OEDIPUS.   You were a shepherd?
A hireling vagrant?

MESSENGER.   Yes, but at least at that time
the man that saved your life, son.

OEDIPUS.   What ailed me when you took me in your arms?

MESSENGER.   In that your ankles should be witnesses.

OEDIPUS.   Why do you speak of that old pain?

MESSENGER.   I loosed you;
the tendons of your feet were pierced and fettered,—

OEDIPUS.   My swaddling clothes brought me a rare disgrace.

MESSENGER.   So that from this you're called your present name.

OEDIPUS.   Was this my father's doing or my mother's?
For God's sake, tell me.

MESSENGER.   I don't know, but he
who gave you to me has more knowledge than I.

OEDIPUS.   You yourself did not find me then? You took me
from someone else?

MESSENGER.   Yes, from another shepherd.

OEDIPUS.   Who was he? Do you know him well enough
to tell?

MESSENGER.   He was called Laius' man.

OEDIPUS.   You mean the king who reigned here in the old days?

MESSENGER.   Yes, he was that man's shepherd.

OEDIPUS.   Is he alive still, so that I could see him?

MESSENGER.   You who live here would know that best.

OEDIPUS.   Do any of you here know of this shepherd whom he speaks about in town or in the fields? Tell me. It's time that this was found out once for all.

CHORUS.   I think he is none other than the peasant whom you have sought to see already; but Jocasta here can tell us best of that.

OEDIPUS.   Jocasta, do you know about this man whom we have sent for? Is he the man he mentions?

JOCASTA.   Why ask of whom he spoke? Don't give it heed; nor try to keep in mind what has been said. It will be wasted labour.

OEDIPUS.   With such clues I could not fail to bring my birth to light.

JOCASTA.   I beg you—do not hunt this out—I beg you, if you have any care for your own life. What I am suffering is enough.

OEDIPUS.   Keep up your heart, Jocasta. Though I'm proved a slave, thrice slave, and though my mother is thrice slave, you'll not be shown to be of lowly lineage.

JOCASTA.   O be persuaded by me, I entreat you; do not do this.

OEDIPUS.   I will not be persuaded to let be the chance of finding out the whole thing clearly.

JOCASTA.   It is because I wish you well that I give you this counsel—and it's the best counsel.

OEDIPUS.   Then the best counsel vexes me, and has for some while since.

JOCASTA.   O Oedipus, God help you! God keep you from the knowledge of who you are!

OEDIPUS.   Here, some one, go and fetch the shepherd for me; and let her find her joy in her rich family!

JOCASTA.   O Oedipus, unhappy Oedipus! that is all I can call you, and the last thing that I shall ever call you.

[*Exit.*]

CHORUS.   Why has the queen gone, Oedipus, in wild
grief rushing from us? I am afraid that trouble
will break out of this silence.

OEDIPUS.   Break out what will! I at least shall be
willing to see my ancestry, though humble.
Perhaps she is ashamed of my low birth,
for she has all a woman's high-flown pride.
But I account myself a child of Fortune,
beneficent Fortune, and I shall not be
dishonoured. She's the mother from whom I spring;
the months, my brothers, marked me, now as small,
and now again as mighty. Such is my breeding,
and I shall never prove so false to it,
as not to find the secret of my birth.

Strophe

CHORUS.   If I am a prophet and wise of heart
you shall not fail, Cithaeron,
by the limitless sky, you shall not!—
to know at tomorrow's full moon that Oedipus honours you as native to him
    and mother and nurse at once;
and that you are honoured in dancing by us, as finding favour in sight of our
    king.
Apollo, to whom we cry, find these things pleasing!

Antistrophe

Who was it bore you, child? One of
the long-lived nymphs who lay with Pan—
the father who treads the hills?
Or was she a bride of Loxias, your mother? The grassy slopes
are all of them dear to him. Or perhaps Cyllene's king
or the Bacchants' God that lives on the tops
of the hills received you a gift from some
one of the Helicon Nymphs, with whom he mostly plays?

[*Enter an old man, led by* OEDIPUS' *servants.*]

OEDIPUS.   If some one like myself who never met him
may make a guess,—I think this is the herdsman,
whom we were seeking. His old age is consonant
with the other. And besides, the men who bring him
I recognize as my own servants. You
perhaps may better me in knowledge since

Sophocles					539

you've seen the man before.

CHORUS.					You can be sure
I recognize him. For if Laius
had ever an honest shepherd, this was he.

OEDIPUS.   You, sir, from Corinth, I must ask you first,
is this the man you spoke of?

MESSENGER.				This is he
before your eyes.

OEDIPUS.   Old man, look here at me
and tell me what I ask you. Were you ever
a servant of King Laius?

HERDSMAN.			I was,—
no slave he bought but reared in his own house.

OEDIPUS.   What did you do as work? How did you live?

HERDSMAN.   Most of my life was spent among the flocks.

OEDIPUS.   In what part of the country did you live?

HERDSMAN.   Cithaeron and the places near to it.

OEDIPUS.   And somewhere there perhaps you knew this man?

HERDSMAN.   What was his occupation? Who?

OEDIPUS.				This man here,
have you had any dealings with him?

HERDSMAN.				No—
not such that I can quickly call to mind.

MESSENGER.   That is no wonder, master. But I'll make him remember that
he does not know. For I know, that he well knows the country of Cithaeron,
how he with two flocks, I with one kept company for three years—each year
half a year—from spring till autumn time and then when winter came I drove
my flocks to our fold home again and he to Laius' steadings. Well—am I right
or not in what I said we did?

HERDSMAN.   You're right—although it's a long time ago.

MESSENGER.   Do you remember giving me a child
to bring up as my foster child?

HERDSMAN.		What's this?
Why do you ask this question?

MESSENGER.			Look, old man,
here he is—here's the man who was that child!

HERDSMAN.   Death take you! Won't you hold your tongue?

OEDIPUS.					No, no,
do not find fault with him, old man. Your words
are more at fault than his.

HERDSMAN.			O best of masters,
how do I give offense?

OEDIPUS.		When you refuse
to speak about the child of whom he asks you.

HERDSMAN.   He speaks out of his ignorance, without meaning.

OEDIPUS.   If you'll not talk to gratify me, you
will talk with pain to urge you.

HERDSMAN.   O please, sir,
don't hurt an old man, sir.

OEDIPUS. [*To the servants.*]   Here, one of you,
twist his hands behind him.

HERDSMAN.   Why, God help me, why?
What do you want to know?

OEDIPUS.   You gave a child
to him,—the child he asked you of?

HERDSMAN.   I did.
I wish I'd died the day I did.

OEDIPUS.   You will
unless you tell me truly.

HERDSMAN.   And I'll die
far worse if I should tell you.

OEDIPUS.   This fellow
is bent on more delays, as it would seem.

HERDSMAN.   O no, no! I have told you that I gave it.

OEDIPUS.   Where did you get this child from? Was it your own
or did you get it from another?

HERDSMAN.   Not
my own at all; I had it from some one.

OEDIPUS.   One of these citizens? or from what house?

HERDSMAN.   O master, please—I beg you, master, please
don't ask me more.

OEDIPUS.   You're a dead man if I
ask you again.

HERDSMAN.   It was one of the children
of Laius.

OEDIPUS.   A slave? Or born in wedlock?

HERDSMAN.   O God, I am on the brink of frightful speech.

OEDIPUS.   And I of frightful hearing. But I must hear.

HERDSMAN.   The child was called his child; but she within,
your wife would tell you best how all this was.

OEDIPUS.   *She* gave it to you?

HERDSMAN.   Yes, she did, my lord.

OEDIPUS.   To do what with it?

HERDSMAN.   Make away with it.

OEDIPUS.   She was so hard—its mother?

HERDSMAN.   Aye, through fear
of evil oracles.

OEDIPUS.   Which?

HERDSMAN.   They said that he
should kill his parents.

OEDIPUS.   How was it that you
gave it away to this old man?

HERDSMAN.   O master,
I pitied it, and thought that I could send it
off to another country and this man
was from another country. But he saved it
for the most terrible troubles. If you are
the man he says you are, you're bred to misery.

OEDIPUS.   O, O, O, they will all come,
all come out clearly! Light of the sun, let me
look upon you no more after today!
I who first saw the light bred of a match
accursed, and accursed in my living
with them I lived with, cursed in my killing.

[Exeunt all but the CHORUS.]

Strophe 1

CHORUS.   O generations of men, how I
count you as equal with those who live
not at all!
what man, what man on earth wins more
of happiness than a seeming
and after that turning away?
Oedipus, you are my pattern of this,
Oedipus, you and your fate!
Luckless Oedipus, whom of all men
I envy not at all.

Antistrophe 1

Inasmuch as he shot his bolt
beyond the others and won the prize
of happiness complete—
O Zeus—and killed and reduced to nought
the hooked taloned maid of the riddling speech,
standing a tower against death for my land:
hence he was called my king and hence
was honoured the highest of all
honours; and hence he ruled
in the great city of Thebes.

Strophe 2

But now whose tale is more miserable?
Who is there lives with a savager fate?
Whose troubles so reverse his life as his?
O Oedipus, the famous prince
for whom a great haven
the same both as father and son
sufficed for generation,
how, O how, have the furrows ploughed
by your father endured to bear you, poor wretch,
and hold their peace so long?

Antistrophe 2

Time who sees all has found you out
against your will; judges your marriage accursed,
begetter and begot at one in it.

O child of Laius,
would I had never seen you,
I weep for you and cry
a dirge of lamentation.
To speak directly, I drew my breath
from you at the first and so now I lull
my mouth to sleep with your name.

[*Enter a* SECOND MESSENGER.]

SECOND MESSENGER.   O Princes always honoured by our country,
what deeds you'll hear of and what horrors see
what grief you'll feel, if you as true born Thebans
care for the house of Labdacus's sons.
Phasis nor Ister cannot purge this house,
I think, with all their streams, such things
it hides, such evils shortly will bring forth
into the light, whether they will or not;
and troubles hurt the most
when they prove self-inflicted.
    CHORUS.   What we had known before did not fall short
of bitter groaning's worth; what's more to tell?
    SECOND MESSENGER.   Shortest to hear and tell—our glorious queen
Jocasta's dead.
    CHORUS.   Unhappy woman! How?
    SECOND MESSENGER.   By her own hand. The worst of what was done

you cannot know. You did not see the sight.
Yet in so far as I remember it
you'll hear the end of our unlucky queen.
When she came raging into the house she went
straight to her marriage bed, tearing her hair
with both her hands, and crying upon Laius
long dead—Do you remember, Laius,
that night long past which bred a child for us
to send you to your death and leave
a mother making children with her son?
And then she groaned and cursed the bed in which
she brought forth husband by her husband, children
by her own child, an infamous double bond.
How after that she died I do not know,—
for Oedipus distracted us from seeing.
He burst upon us shouting and we looked
to him as he paced frantically around,
begging us always: Give me a sword, I say,
to find this wife no wife, this mother's womb,
this field of double sowing whence I sprang
and where I sowed my children! As he raved
some god showed him the way—none of us there.
Bellowing terribly and led by some
invisible guide he rushed on the two doors,—
wrenching the hollow bolts out of their sockets,
he charged inside. There, there, we saw his wife
hanging, the twisted rope around her neck.
When he saw her, he cried out fearfully
and cut the dangling noose. Then, as she lay,
poor woman, on the ground, what happened after,
was terrible to see. He tore the brooches—
the gold chased brooches fastening her robe—
away from her and lifting them up high
dashed them on his own eyeballs, shrieking out
such things as: they will never see the crime
I have committed or had done upon me!
Dark eyes, now in the days to come look on
forbidden faces, do not recognize
those whom you long for—with such imprecations
he struck his eyes again and yet again
with the brooches. And the bleeding eyeballs gushed
and stained his beard—no sluggish oozing drops
but a black rain and bloody hail poured down.

So it has broken—and not on one head
but troubles mixed for husband and for wife.
The fortune of the days gone by was true
good fortune—but today groans and destruction
and death and shame—of all ills can be named
not one is missing.

    CHORUS.   Is he now in any ease from pain?

    SECOND MESSENGER.   **He shouts**
for some one to unbar the doors and show him
to all the men of Thebes, his father's killer,
his mother's—no I cannot say the word,
it is unholy—for he'll cast himself,
out of the land, he says, and not remain
to bring a curse upon his house, the curse
he called upon it in his proclamation. But
he wants for strength, aye, and some one to guide him;
his sickness is too great to bear. You, too,
will be shown that. The bolts are opening.
Soon you will see a sight to waken pity
even in the horror of it.

    [*Enter the blinded* OEDIPUS.]

    CHORUS.   This is a terrible sight for men to see!
I never found a worse!
Poor wretch, what madness came upon you!
What evil spirit leaped upon your life
to your ill-luck—a leap beyond man's strength!
Indeed I pity you, but I cannot
look at you, though there's much I want to ask
and much to learn and much to see.
I shudder at the sight of you.

    OEDIPUS.   O, O,
where am I going? Where is my voice
borne on the wind to and fro?
Spirit, how far have you sprung?

    CHORUS.   To a terrible place whereof men's ears
may not hear, nor their eyes behold it.

    OEDIPUS.   Darkness!
Horror of darkness enfolding, resistless, unspeakable visitant sped by an ill
    wind in haste!
madness and stabbing pain and memory
of evil deeds I have done!

    CHORUS.   In such misfortunes it's no wonder
if double weighs the burden of your grief.

OEDIPUS.   My friend,
you are the only one steadfast, the only one that attends on me;
you still stay nursing the blind man.
Your care is not unnoticed. I can know
your voice, although this darkness is my world.

CHORUS.   Doer of dreadful deeds, how did you dare
so far to do despite to your own eyes?
what spirit urged you to it?

OEDIPUS.   It was Apollo, friends, Apollo,
that brought this bitter bitterness, my sorrows to completion.
But the hand that struck me
was none but my own.
Why should I see
whose vision showed me nothing sweet to see?

CHORUS.   These things are as you say.

OEDIPUS.   What can I see to love?
What greeting can touch my ears with joy?
Take me away, and haste—to a place out of the way!
Take me away, my friends, the greatly miserable,
the most accursed, whom God too hates
above all men on earth!

CHORUS.   Unhappy in your mind and your misfortune,
would I had never known you!

OEDIPUS.   Curse on the man who took
the cruel bonds from off my legs, as I lay in the field.
He stole me from death and saved me,
no kindly service.
Had I died then
I would not be so burdensome to friends.

CHORUS.   I, too, could have wished it had been so.

OEDIPUS.   Then I would not have come
to kill my father and marry my mother infamously.
Now I am godless and child of impurity,
begetter in the same seed that created my wretched self.
If there is any ill worse than ill,
that is the lot of Oedipus.

CHORUS.   I cannot say your remedy was good;
you would be better dead than blind and living.

OEDIPUS.   What I have done here was best done—don't tell me
otherwise, do not give me further counsel.
I do not know with what eyes I could look
upon my father when I die and go
under the earth, nor yet my wretched mother—
those two to whom I have done things deserving

worse punishment than hanging. Would the sight
of children, bred as mine are, gladden me?
No, not these eyes, never. And my city,
its towers and sacred places of the Gods,
of these I robbed my miserable self
when I commanded all to drive *him* out,
the criminal since proved by God impure
and of the race of Laius.
To this guilt I bore witness against myself—
with what eyes shall I look upon my people?
No. If there were a means to choke the fountain
of hearing I would not have stayed my hand
from locking up my miserable carcase,
seeing and hearing nothing; it is sweet
to keep our thoughts out of the range of hurt.

Cithaeron, why did you receive me? why
having received me did you not kill me straight?
And so I had not shown to men my birth.

O Polybus and Corinth and the house,
the old house that I used to call my father's—
what fairness you were nurse to, and what foulness
festered beneath! Now I am found to be
a sinner and a son of sinners. Crossroads,
and hidden glade, oak and the narrow way
at the crossroads, that drank my father's blood
offered you by my hands, do you remember
still what I did as you looked on, and what
I did when I came here? O marriage, marriage!
you bred me and again when you had bred
bred children of your child and showed to men
brides, wives and mothers and the foulest deeds
that can be in this world of ours.

Come—it's unfit to say what is unfit
to do.—I beg of you in God's name hide me
somewhere outside your country, yes, or kill me,
or throw me into the sea, to be forever
out of your sight. Approach and deign to touch me
for all my wretchedness, and do not fear.
No man but I can bear my evil doom.

   CHORUS.   Here Creon comes in fit time to perform
or give advice in what you ask of us.

Creon is left sole ruler in your stead.

OEDIPUS.   Creon! Creon! What shall I say to him?
How can I justly hope that he will trust me?
In what is past I have been proved towards him
an utter liar.

[*Enter* CREON.]

CREON.   Oedipus, I've come
not so that I might laugh at you nor taunt you
with evil of the past. But if you still
are without shame before the face of men
reverence at least the flame that gives all life,
our Lord the Sun, and do not show unveiled
to him pollution such that neither land
nor holy rain nor light of day can welcome.

[*To a servant.*]

Be quick and take him in. It is most decent
that only kin should see and hear the troubles
of kin.

OEDIPUS.   I beg you, since you've torn me from
my dreadful expectations and have come
in a most noble spirit to a man
that has used you vilely—do a thing for me.
I shall speak for your own good, not for my own.

CREON.   What do you need that you would ask of me?

OEDIPUS.   Drive me from here with all the speed you can to where I may
not hear a human voice.

CREON.   Be sure, I would have done this had not I
wished first of all to learn from the God the course
of action I should follow.

OEDIPUS.   But his word
has been quite clear to let the parricide,
the sinner, die.

CREON.   Yes, that indeed was said.
But in the present need we had best discover
what we should do.

OEDIPUS.   And will you ask about
a man so wretched?

CREON.   Now even you will trust
the god.

OEDIPUS.   So. I command you—and will beseech you—
to her that lies inside that house give burial
as you would have it; she is yours and rightly

you will perform the rites for her. For me—
never let this my father's city have me
living a dweller in it. Leave me live
in the mountains where Cithaeron is, that's called
my mountain, which my mother and my father
while they were living would have made my tomb.
So I may die by their decree who sought
indeed to kill me. Yet I know this much:
no sickness and no other thing will kill me.
I would not have been saved from death if not
for some strange evil fate. Well, let my fate
go where it will.
　　　　　Creon, you need not care
about my sons; they're men and so wherever
they are, they will not lack a livelihood.
But my two girls—so sad and pitiful—
whose table never stood apart from mine,
and everything I touched they always shared—
O Creon, have a thought for them! And most
I wish that you might suffer me to touch them
and sorrow with them.

　　　[*Enter* ANTIGONE *and* ISMENE, OEDIPUS' *two daughters.*]

O my lord! O true noble Creon! Can I
really be touching them, as when I saw?
What shall I say?
Yes, I can hear them sobbing—my two darlings!
and Creon has had pity and has sent me
what I loved most?
Am I right?
　　　CREON.　You're right: it was I gave you this
because I knew from old days how you loved them
as I see now.
　　　OEDIPUS.　God bless you for it, Creon,
and may God guard you better on your road
than he did me!
　　　　　　O children,
where are you? Come here, come to my hands,
a brother's hands which turned your father's eyes,
those bright eyes you knew once, to what you see,
a father seeing nothing, knowing nothing,
begetting you from his own source of life.
I weep for you—I cannot see your faces—
I weep when I think of the bitterness

there will be in your lives, how you must live
before the world. At what assemblages
of citizens will you make one? to what
gay company will you go and not come home
in tears instead of sharing in the holiday?
And when you're ripe for marriage, who will he be,
the man who'll risk to take such infamy
as shall cling to my children, to bring hurt
on them and those that marry with them? What
curse is not there? "Your father killed his father
and sowed the seed where he had sprung himself
and begot you out of the womb that held him."
These insults you will hear. Then who will marry you?
No one, my children; clearly you are doomed
to waste away in barrenness unmarried.
Son of Menoeceus, since you are all the father
left these two girls, and we, their parents, both
are dead to them—do not allow them wander
like beggars, poor and husbandless.
They are of your own blood.
And do not make them equal with myself
in wretchedness; for you can see them now
so young, so utterly alone, save for you only.
Touch my hand, noble Creon, and say yes.
If you were older, children, and were wiser,
there's much advice I'd give you. But as it is,
let this be what you pray: give me a life
wherever there is opportunity
to live, and better life than was my father's.

CREON. Your tears have had enough of scope; now go within the house.

OEDIPUS. I must obey, though bitter of heart.

CREON.   In season, all is good.

OEDIPUS. Do you know on what conditions I obey?

CREON.   You tell me them,
and I shall know them when I hear.

OEDIPUS.   That you shall send me out
to live away from Thebes.

CREON.   That gift you must ask of the God.

OEDIPUS. But I'm now hated by the Gods.

CREON.   So quickly you'll obtain your prayer.

OEDIPUS. You consent then?

CREON.   What I do not mean, I do not use to say.

OEDIPUS. Now lead me away from here.

CREON. Let go the children, then, and come.

OEDIPUS.   Do not take them from me.

CREON.   Do not seek to be master in everything,
for the things you mastered did not follow you throughout your life.

[As CREON and OEDIPUS go out.]

CHORUS.   You that live in my ancestral Thebes, behold this Oedipus,—
him who knew the famous riddles and was a man most masterful;
not a citizen who did not look with envy on his lot—
See him now and see the breakers of misfortune swallow him!
Look upon that last day always. Count no mortal happy till
he has passed the final limit of his life secure from pain.

HENRIK IBSEN

Hedda Gabler[1]

A Translation by Eva Le Gallienne

CHARACTERS

GEORGE TESMAN

HEDDA TESMAN, *his wife*

MISS JULIA TESMAN, *his aunt*

EILERT LØVBORG

MRS. THEA ELVSTED

JUDGE BRACK

BERTA, *servant at the Tesmans'*

ACT ONE

SCENE: *A large handsomely-furnished drawing-room, decorated in dark colours. In the back wall a wide opening with portières that are drawn back. This opening leads to a smaller room decorated in the same style as the drawing-room. In the right-hand wall of the front room is a folding-door leading to the hall. In the wall opposite, on the left, a glass door, its hangings also drawn back. Through the panes can be seen part of a veranda and trees covered in autumn foliage. Standing well forward is an oval table, with a cover on it and surrounded by chairs. By the wall on the right stands a wide stove of dark porcelain, a high-backed armchair, an upholstered footstool and two tabourets. A small sofa fits into the right-hand corner with a small round table in front of it. Down left, standing slightly away from the wall, another sofa. Above the glass door, a piano. On either side of the opening in the back wall two étagères with terra-cotta and majolica ornaments. Against the back wall of the inner room a sofa, a table, and a couple of chairs. Above the sofa hangs the portrait of a handsome elderly man in the uniform of a general. Over the table a hanging-lamp with an opalescent glass shade. A number of bouquets of flowers are arranged about the drawing-room in vases and glasses. Others lie on the various tables. The floors in both rooms are covered with thick carpets. It is morning. The sun shines through the glass door.*

MISS JULIA TESMAN, wearing a hat and carrying a parasol, enters from the hall followed by BERTA, who carries a bouquet wrapped in paper. MISS TESMAN is a good and pleasant-looking lady of about 65. Simply but nicely dressed in a grey tailor-made. BERTA is a maid getting on in years, plain and rather countrified in appearance.

---

[1] *Hedda Gabler* by Henrik Ibsen in an English translation by Eva Le Gallienne, copyright 1953 by Eva Le Gallienne. Reprinted by permission of Random House, Inc.

MISS TESMAN. [*Stops just inside the door, listens, and says softly.*]   Good gracious! They're not even up—I do believe!

BERTA. [*Also speaks softly.*]   That's what I told you, Miss Julia. The steamer got in so late last night; and the young mistress had such a lot of unpacking to do before she could get to bed.

MISS TESMAN.   Well—let them sleep as long as they like. But when they do get up, they'll certainly need a breath of fresh air. [*She goes to the glass door and opens it wide.*]

BERTA. [*At the table uncertain what to do with the bouquet in her hand.*] There's not a bit of room left anywhere. I'll just put them down here, Miss Julia. [*Puts the bouquet down on the piano.*]

MISS TESMAN.   So now you have a new mistress, Berta. Heaven knows it was hard enough for me to part with you.

BERTA. [*On the verge of tears.*]   Don't think it wasn't hard for me too, Miss Julia; after all those happy years I spent with you and Miss Rina.

MISS TESMAN.   We'll just have to make the best of it, Berta. Master George needs you—he really does. You've looked after him ever since he was a little boy.

BERTA.   That's true, Miss Julia; but I can't help worrying about Miss Rina lying there helpless, poor thing; how *will* she manage? That new maid will never learn to take proper care of an invalid!

MISS TESMAN.   I'll soon be able to train her; and until then, I'll do most of the work myself—so don't you worry about my poor sister, Berta.

BERTA.   But, there's something else, Miss Julia—you see, I'm so afraid I won't be able to please the young mistress.

MISS TESMAN.   Well—there may be one or two things, just at first——

BERTA.   She'll be very particular, I expect——

MISS TESMAN.   That's only natural—after all, she's General Gabler's daughter. She was used to being spoiled when her father was alive. Do you remember how we used to see her galloping by? How smart she looked in her riding clothes!

BERTA.   Indeed I do remember, Miss Julia! Who would ever have thought that she and Master George would make a match of it!

MISS TESMAN.   God moves in mysterious ways——! But, by the way, Berta— before I forget—you mustn't say Master George any more—it's Doctor Tesman!

BERTA.   I know, Miss Julia. That was one of the very first things the young mistress told me last night. So it's really true, Miss Julia?

MISS TESMAN.   Yes, it is indeed! He was made a doctor by one of the foreign universities while he was abroad. It was a great surprise to me; I knew nothing about it until he told me last night on the pier.

BERTA.   Well—he's clever enough for anything, he is! But I never thought he'd go in for doctoring people!

MISS TESMAN.   It's not *that* kind of a doctor, Berta! [*Nods significantly.*] But later on, you may have to call him something even grander!

BERTA.   Really, Miss Julia? Now what could that be?

MISS TESMAN. [*Smiles.*] Wouldn't you like to know! [*Moved.*] I wonder what my poor brother would say if he could see what a great man his little boy has become. [*Looking around.*] But, what's this, Berta? Why have you taken all the covers off the furniture?

BERTA. The young mistress told me to. She said she couldn't bear them.

MISS TESMAN. Perhaps she intends to use this as the living-room?

BERTA. I think maybe she does, Miss Julia; though Master George—I mean the Doctor—said nothing about it.

[GEORGE TESMAN *enters the inner room from right, singing gaily. He carries an unstrapped empty suitcase. He is a young-looking man of 33, medium height. Rather plump, a pleasant, round, open face. Blond hair and beard, wears spectacles. Rather carelessly dressed in comfortable lounging clothes.*]

MISS TESMAN. Good morning—good morning, my dear George!

TESMAN. [*At the opening between the rooms.*] Aunt Julia! Dear Aunt Julia! [*Goes to her and shakes her warmly by the hand.*] Way out here—so early in the morning—eh?

MISS TESMAN. I had to come and see how you were getting on.

TESMAN. In spite of going to bed so late?

MISS TESMAN. My dear boy—as if that mattered to me!

TESMAN. You got home all right from the pier—eh?

MISS TESMAN. Quite all right, dear, thank you. Judge Brack was kind enough to see me safely to my door.

TESMAN. We were so sorry we couldn't give you a lift—but Hedda had such a fearful lot of luggage——

MISS TESMAN. Yes—she did seem to have quite a bit!

BERTA. [*To* TESMAN.] Should I ask the Mistress if there's anything I can do for her, sir?

TESMAN. No thank you, Berta—there's no need. She said she'd ring if she wanted anything.

BERTA. [*Starting right.*] Very good, sir.

TESMAN. [*Indicates suitcase.*] You might just take that suitcase with you.

BERTA. [*Taking it.*] Yes, sir. I'll put it in the attic. [*She goes out by the hall door.*]

TESMAN. Do you know, Aunt Julia—I had that whole suitcase full of notes? It's unbelievable how much I found in all the archives I examined; curious old details no one had any idea existed.

MISS TESMAN. You don't seem to have wasted your time on your wedding-trip!

TESMAN. Indeed I haven't!—But do take off your hat, Aunt Julia—let me help you—eh?

MISS TESMAN. [*While he does so.*] How sweet of you! This is just like the old days when you were still with us!

TESMAN. [*He turns the hat round in his hands looking at it admiringly from all sides.*] That's a very elegant hat you've treated yourself to.

MISS TESMAN. I bought that on Hedda's account.

TESMAN. On Hedda's account—eh?

MISS TESMAN. Yes—I didn't want her to feel ashamed of her old aunt—in case we should happen to go out together.

TESMAN. [*Patting her cheek.*] What a dear you are, Aunt Julia—always thinking of everything! [*Puts the hat down on a chair near the table.*] And now let's sit down here on the sofa and have a cosy little chat till Hedda comes.

[*They sit down. She leans her parasol in the corner of the sofa.*]

MISS TESMAN. [*Takes both his hands and gazes at him.*] I can't tell you what a joy it is to have you home again, George.

TESMAN. And it's a joy for me to see you again, dear Aunt Julia. You've been as good as a father and mother to me—I can never forget that!

MISS TESMAN. I know dear—you'll always have a place in your heart for your poor old aunts.

TESMAN. How *is* Aunt Rina—eh? Isn't she feeling a little better?

MISS TESMAN. No dear. I'm afraid she'll never be any better, poor thing! But I pray God I may keep her with me a little longer—for now that I haven't you to look after any more, I don't know what will become of me when she goes.

TESMAN. [*Pats her on the back.*] There, there, there!

MISS TESMAN. [*With a sudden change of tone.*] You know, I can't get used to thinking of you as a married man, George. And to think that you should have been the one to carry off Hedda Gabler—the fascinating Hedda Gabler—who was always surrounded by so many admirers!

TESMAN. [*Hums a little and smiles complacently.*] Yes—I wouldn't be surprised if some of my friends were a bit jealous of me—eh?

MISS TESMAN. And then this wonderful wedding-trip! Five—nearly six months!

TESMAN. Of course, you must remember, the trip was also of great value to me in my research work. I can't begin to tell you all the archives I've been through—and the many books I've read!

MISS TESMAN. I can well believe it! [*More confidently, lowering her voice.*] But George, dear, are you sure you've nothing—well—nothing *special* to tell me?

TESMAN. About our trip?

MISS TESMAN. Yes.

TESMAN. I can't think of anything I didn't write you about. I had a Doctor's degree conferred on me—but I told you that last night.

MISS TESMAN. Yes, yes—you told me about that. But what I mean is—haven't you any—well—any expectations?

TESMAN. Expectations?

MISS TESMAN. Yes, George. Surely you can talk frankly to your old aunt?

TESMAN. Well, of course I have expectations!

MISS TESMAN. Well?

TESMAN. I have every expectation of becoming a professor one of these days!

MISS TESMAN.   A professor—yes, yes, I know dear—but——

TESMAN.   In fact I'm certain of it. But you know that just as well as I do, Aunt Julia.

MISS TESMAN. [*Chuckling.*]   Of course I do, dear—you're quite right. [*Changing the subject.*] But we were talking about your journey—it must have cost a great deal of money, George!

TESMAN.   Well, you see, the scholarship I had was pretty ample—that went a good way.

MISS TESMAN.   Still—I don't see how it could have been ample enough for two—especially travelling with a lady—they say that makes it ever so much more expensive.

TESMAN.   It does make it a bit more expensive—but Hedda simply had to have this trip—she really had to—it was the fashionable thing to do.

MISS TESMAN.   I know—nowadays it seems a wedding has to be followed by a wedding-trip. But tell me George—have you been over the house yet?

TESMAN.   I have indeed! I've been up since day-break!

MISS TESMAN.   What do you think of it?

TESMAN.   It's splendid—simply splendid! But it seems awfully big—what on earth shall we do with all those empty rooms?

MISS TESMAN. [*Laughingly.*]   Oh, my dear George—I expect you'll find plenty of use for them—a little later on.

TESMAN.   Yes, you're right, Aunt Julia—as I get more and more books—eh?

MISS TESMAN.   Of course, my dear boy—it was your books I was thinking of!

TESMAN.   I'm especially pleased for Hedda's sake. She had her heart set on this house—it belonged to Secretary Falk you know—even before we were engaged, she used to say it was the one place she'd really like to live in.

MISS TESMAN.   But I'm afraid you'll find all this very expensive, my dear George—very expensive!

TESMAN. [*Looks at her a little despondently.*]   Yes, I suppose so. How much do you really think it will cost? I mean approximately—eh?

MISS TESMAN.   That's impossible to say until we've seen all the bills.

TESMAN.   Judge Brack wrote Hedda that he'd been able to secure very favourable terms for me.

MISS TESMAN.   But you mustn't worry about it, my dear boy—for one thing, I've given security for all the furniture and the carpets.

TESMAN.   Security? You, dear Aunt Julia? What sort of security?

MISS TESMAN.   A mortgage on our annuity.

TESMAN. [*Jumps up.*]   What!

MISS TESMAN.   I didn't know what else to do.

TESMAN. [*Standing before her.*]   You must be mad, Aunt Julia—quite mad! That annuity is all that you and Aunt Rina have to live on!

MISS TESMAN.   Don't get so excited about it! It's only a matter of form, Judge Brack says. He was kind enough to arrange the whole matter for me.

TESMAN.   That's all very well—but still——!

MISS TESMAN.   And from now on you'll have your own salary to depend on—and even if we should have to help out a little, just at first—it would only be the greatest pleasure to us!

TESMAN.   Isn't that just like you, Aunt Julia! Always making sacrifices for me.

MISS TESMAN. [*Rises and places her hands on his shoulders.*]   The only happiness I have in the world is making things easier for you, my dear boy. We've been through some bad times, I admit—but now we've reached the goal and we've nothing to fear.

TESMAN. [*Sits down beside her again.*]   Yes—it's amazing how everything's turned out for the best!

MISS TESMAN.   Now there's no one to stand in your way—even your most dangerous rival has fallen. Well, he made his bed—let him lie on it, poor misguided creature.

TESMAN.   Has there been any news of Eilert—since I went away, I mean?

MISS TESMAN.   They say he's supposed to have published a new book.

TESMAN.   Eilert Løvborg! A new book? Recently—eh?

MISS TESMAN.   That's what they say—but I shouldn't think any book of his would be worth much. It'll be a very different story when *your* new book appears. What's it to be about, George?

TESMAN.   It will deal with the Domestic Industries of Brabant during the Middle Ages.

MISS TESMAN.   Fancy being able to write about such things!

TESMAN.   Of course it'll be some time before the book is ready—I still have to arrange and classify all my notes, you see.

MISS TESMAN.   Yes—collecting and arranging—no one can compete with you in that! You're not your father's son for nothing!

TESMAN.   I can't wait to begin! Especially now that I have my own comfortable home to work in.

MISS TESMAN.   And best of all—you have your wife! The wife you longed for!

TESMAN. [*Embracing her.*]   Yes, you're right, Aunt Julia—Hedda! She's the most wonderful part of it all! [*Looks towards opening between the rooms.*] But here she comes—eh?

[HEDDA *enters from the left through the inner room. She is a woman of 29. Her face and figure show breeding and distinction. Her complexion is pale and opaque. Her eyes are steel-grey and express a cold, unruffled repose. Her hair is an agreeable medium-brown, but not especially abundant. She wears a tasteful, somewhat loose-fitting négligée.*]

MISS TESMAN. [*Goes to meet* HEDDA.]   Good morning, Hedda dear—and welcome home!

HEDDA. [*Gives her her hand.*]   Good morning, my dear Miss Tesman. What an early visitor you are—how kind of you!

MISS TESMAN. [*Seems slightly embarrassed.*]   Not at all. And did the bride sleep well in her new home?

HEDDA. Thank you—fairly well.

TESMAN. [*Laughing.*] Fairly well! I like that, Hedda! You were sleeping like a log when I got up!

HEDDA. Yes—fortunately. You know, Miss Tesman, one has to adapt oneself gradually to new surroundings. [*Glancing towards the left.*] Good heavens—what a nuisance! That maid's opened the window and let in a whole flood of sunshine!

MISS TESMAN. [*Starts towards door.*] Well—we'll just close it then!

HEDDA. No, no—don't do that! George, dear, just draw the curtains, will you? It'll give a softer light.

TESMAN. [*At the door.*] There, Hedda! Now you have both shade and fresh air!

HEDDA. Heaven knows we need some fresh air, with all these stacks of flowers! But do sit down, my dear Miss Tesman.

MISS TESMAN. No—many thanks! Now that I know everything's all right here, I must be getting home to my poor sister.

TESMAN. Do give her my best love, Aunt Julia—and tell her I'll drop in and see her later in the day.

MISS TESMAN. Yes, dear, I'll do that. . . . Oh! I'd almost forgotten [*Feeling in the pocket of her dress.*] I've brought something for you!

TESMAN. What can that be, Aunt Julia—eh?

MISS TESMAN. [*Produces a flat parcel wrapped in newspaper and presents him with it.*] Look, dear!

TESMAN. [*Opens the parcel.*] Oh, Aunt Julia! You really kept them for me! Isn't that touching, Hedda—eh?

HEDDA. [*By the étagère on the right.*] Well, what is it, dear?

TESMAN. My slippers, Hedda! My old bedroom slippers!

HEDDA. Oh yes—I remember. You often spoke of them on our journey.

TESMAN. I can't tell you how I've missed them! [*Goes up to her.*] Do have a look at them, Hedda——

HEDDA. [*Going towards stove.*] I'm really not very interested, George——

TESMAN. [*Following her.*] Dear Aunt Rina embroidered them for me during her illness. They have so many memories for me——

HEDDA. [*At the table.*] Scarcely for me, George.

MISS TESMAN. Of course not, George! They mean nothing to Hedda.

TESMAN. I only thought, now that she's one of the family——

HEDDA. [*Interrupting.*] We shall never get on with this servant, George!

MISS TESMAN. Not get on with Berta?

TESMAN. Hedda dear, what do you mean?

HEDDA. [*Pointing.*] Look! She's left her old hat lying about on the table.

TESMAN. [*Flustered—dropping the slippers on the floor.*] Why—Hedda——!

HEDDA. Just imagine if someone were to come in and see it!

TESMAN. But, Hedda! That's Aunt Julia's hat!

HEDDA. Oh! Is it?

MISS TESMAN. [*Picks up the hat.*]   Yes, indeed it is! And what's more it's not old—little Mrs. Tesman!

HEDDA.   I really didn't look at it very closely, Miss Tesman.

MISS TESMAN. [*Puts on the hat.*]   This is the very first time I've worn it!

TESMAN.   And it's a lovely hat, too—quite a beauty!

MISS TESMAN.   Oh, it isn't as beautiful as all that. [*Looking round.*] Where's my parasol? [*Takes it.*] Ah—here it is! [*Mutters.*] For this is mine too—not Berta's.

TESMAN.   A new hat and a new parasol—just think, Hedda!

HEDDA.   Most handsome and lovely, I'm sure!

TESMAN.   Yes—isn't it, eh? But do take a good look at Hedda—see how lovely *she* is!

MISS TESMAN.   Hedda was always lovely, my dear boy—that's nothing new. [*She nods and goes towards the right.*]

TESMAN. [*Following her.*]   But don't you think she's looking especially well? I think she's filled out a bit while we've been away.

HEDDA. [*Crossing the room.*]   Oh, do be quiet! . . .

MISS TESMAN. [*Who has stopped and turned towards them.*]   Filled out?

TESMAN.   Of course, you can't notice it so much in that loose dress—but I have certain opportunities——

HEDDA. [*Stands at the glass door—impatiently.*]   You have no opportunities at all, George——

TESMAN.   I think it must have been the mountain air in the Tyrol——

HEDDA. [*Curtly interrupting.*]   I'm exactly as I was when we left!

TESMAN.   That's what you say—but I don't agree with you! What do you think, Aunt Julia?

MISS TESMAN. [*Gazing at her with folded hands.*]   Hedda is lovely—lovely! [*Goes to her, takes her face in her hands and gently kisses the top of her head.*] God bless and keep you, Hedda Tesman, for George's sake!

HEDDA. [*Quietly freeing herself.*]   Please! Oh, please let me go!

MISS TESMAN. [*With quiet emotion.*]   I shan't let a day pass without coming to see you!

TESMAN.   That's right, Aunt Julia!

MISS TESMAN.   Good-bye, dearest Hedda—good-bye!

[*She goes out by the hall door.* TESMAN *sees her out. The door remains half-open.* TESMAN *can be heard repeating his greetings to* AUNT RINA *and his thanks for the bedroom slippers. Meanwhile,* HEDDA *paces about the room, raises her arms and clenches her hands as though in desperation. She flings back the curtains of the glass-door and stands gazing out. In a moment* TESMAN *returns and closes the door behind him.*]

TESMAN. [*Picking up the slippers from the floor.*]   What are you looking at, Hedda?

HEDDA. [*Once more calm and controlled.*]   I'm just looking at the leaves—they're so yellow—so withered.

TESMAN. [*Wraps up the slippers and puts them on the table.*] Well, we're well into September now.

HEDDA. [*Again restless.*] God, yes! September—September already!

TESMAN. Didn't you think Aunt Julia was a little strange? Almost solemn, I thought. What do you suppose was the matter with her—eh?

HEDDA. Well, you see, I scarcely know her. Isn't she always like that?

TESMAN. No, not as she was today.

HEDDA. [*Leaving the glass door.*] Perhaps she was annoyed about the hat.

TESMAN. Oh, not specially—perhaps just for a moment——

HEDDA. [*Crosses over towards the fireplace.*] Such a peculiar way to behave —flinging one's hat about in the drawing-room—one doesn't do that sort of thing.

TESMAN. I'm sure Aunt Julia won't do it again.

HEDDA. I shall manage to make my peace with her. When you see her this afternoon, George, you might ask her to come and spend the evening here.

TESMAN. Yes, I will, Hedda. And there's another thing you could do that would give her so much pleasure.

HEDDA. Well—what's that?

TESMAN. If you could only be a little more affectionate with her—just for my sake—eh?

HEDDA. I shall try to call her Aunt—but that's really all I can do.

TESMAN. Very well. I just thought, now that you belong to the family——

HEDDA. I really don't see why, George—— [*She goes up towards the centre opening.*]

TESMAN. [*After a short pause.*] Is there anything the matter with you, Hedda, eh?

HEDDA. No, nothing. I'm just looking at my old piano. It doesn't seem to fit in with the rest of the furniture.

TESMAN. The first time I draw my salary, we'll see about exchanging it.

HEDDA. Exchange it! Why exchange it? I don't want to part with it. Why couldn't we put it in the inner room and get a new one for here? That is, of course, when we can afford it.

TESMAN. [*Slightly taken aback.*] Yes, I suppose we could do that.

HEDDA. [*Takes up the bouquet from the piano.*] These flowers weren't here last night when we arrived.

TESMAN. I expect Aunt Julia brought them for you.

HEDDA. [*Examines the bouquet.*] Here's a card. [*Takes out a card and reads it.*] 'Shall return later in the day.' Can you guess who it's from?

TESMAN. No. Tell me.

HEDDA. From Mrs. Elvsted.

TESMAN. Really! Sheriff Elvsted's wife. The former Miss Rysing.

HEDDA. Exactly. The girl with that irritating mass of hair—she was always showing off. I've heard she was an old flame of yours, George?

TESMAN. [*Laughs.*] Oh, that didn't last long, and it was before I met you, Hedda. Fancy her being in town.

HEDDA. Funny that she should call on us. I haven't seen her for years. Not since we were at school together.

TESMAN. I haven't seen her, either, for ever so long. I wonder how she can stand living in that remote, dreary place.

HEDDA. I wonder! [*After a moment's thought, says suddenly.*] Tell me, George, doesn't Eilert Løvborg live somewhere near there?

TESMAN. Yes, I believe he does. Somewhere in that neighborhood.

BERTA. [*Enters by the hall-door.*] That lady, ma'am, who left some flowers a little while ago is back again. [*Pointing.*] The flowers you have in your hand, ma'am.

HEDDA. Oh, is she? Very well, ask her to come in.

[BERTA *opens the door for* MRS. ELVSTED *and exits.* MRS. ELVSTED *is a fragile woman with soft pretty features. Her large, round, light-blue eyes are slightly prominent and have a timid, questioning look. Her hair is unusually fair, almost white-gold and extremely thick and wavy. She is a couple of years younger than* HEDDA. *She wears a dark visiting-dress, in good taste but not in the latest fashion.*]

HEDDA. [*Graciously goes to meet her.*] How do you do, my dear Mrs. Elvsted? How delightful to see you again after all these years.

THEA. [*Nervously, trying to control herself.*] Yes, it's a very long time since we met.

TESMAN. [*Gives her his hand.*] And we haven't met for a long time, either, eh?

HEDDA. Thank you for your lovely flowers.

THEA. Oh, don't mention it. I would have come to see you yesterday, but I heard you were away.

TESMAN. Have you just arrived in town, eh?

THEA. Yes, I got here yesterday morning. I was so upset not to find you at home.

HEDDA. Upset! But why, my dear Mrs. Elvsted?

TESMAN. But, my dear Mrs. Rysing—eh, Mrs. Elvsted, I mean——

HEDDA. I hope you're not in any trouble.

THEA. Well, yes, I am, and I know no one else in town that I could possibly turn to——

HEDDA. [*Puts the bouquet down on the table.*] Come, let's sit down here on the sofa——

THEA. I'm really too nervous to sit down.

HEDDA. Of course you're not. Come along now—— [*She draws* MRS. ELVSTED *down to the sofa and sits beside her.*]

TESMAN. Well, Mrs. Elvsted?

HEDDA. Has anything gone wrong at home?

THEA. Well, eh—yes, and no. I do hope you won't misunderstand me.

HEDDA. Perhaps you'd better tell us all about it, Mrs. Elvsted.

TESMAN. I suppose that's what you've come for, eh?

THEA. Yes, of course. Well, first of all—— But perhaps you've already heard—Eilert Løvborg is in town, too.

HEDDA. Løvborg!

TESMAN. What! Eilert Løvborg has come back! Think of that, Hedda!

HEDDA. Good heavens, yes, I heard it!

THEA. He's been here for a week. A whole week. I'm so afraid he'll get into trouble——

HEDDA. But, my dear Mrs. Elvsted, why should you be so worried about him?

THEA. [Gives her a startled look and speaks hurriedly.] Well, you see—he's the children's tutor.

HEDDA. Your children's?

THEA. No. My husband's. I have none.

HEDDA. Oh, your stepchildren's then?

THEA. Yes.

TESMAN. [With some hesitation.] Was he—I don't quite know how to put it—was he dependable enough to fill such a position, eh?

THEA. For the last two years his conduct has been irreproachable.

TESMAN. Has it, really? Think of that, Hedda!

HEDDA. Yes, yes, yes! I heard it.

THEA. Irreproachable in every respect, I assure you, but still I know how dangerous it is for him to be here in town all alone, and he has quite a lot of money with him. I can't help being worried to death about him.

TESMAN. But why did he come here? Why didn't he stay where he was? With you and your husband, eh?

THEA. After his book was published he felt too restless to stay on with us.

TESMAN. Oh, yes, of course. Aunt Julia told me he had published a new book.

THEA. Yes, a wonderful book. A sort of outline of civilization. It came out a couple of weeks ago. It's sold marvellously. Made quite a sensation.

TESMAN. Has it really? Then I suppose it's something he wrote some time ago—during his better years.

THEA. No, no. He's written it all since he's been with us.

TESMAN. Well, isn't that splendid, Hedda? Think of that!

THEA. Yes, if only he'll keep it up.

HEDDA. Have you seen him here in town?

THEA. Not yet. I had great trouble finding out his address, but this morning I got it at last.

HEDDA. [Gives her a searching look.] But doesn't it seem rather odd of your husband to——

THEA. [*With a nervous start.*]   Of my husband—what?

HEDDA.   Well—to send you on such an errand. Why didn't he come himself to look after his friend?

THEA.   Oh, no. My husband is much too busy. And besides, I had some shopping to do.

HEDDA. [*With a slight smile.*]   Oh, I see!

THEA. [*Rising quickly and uneasily.*]   I implore you, Mr. Tesman, be good to Eilert Løvborg if he should come to see you. I'm sure he will. You were such great friends in the old days, and after all, you're both interested in the same studies. You specialize in the same subjects—as far as I can understand.

TESMAN.   Yes, we used to, at any rate.

THEA.   That's why I'd be grateful if you two would—well—keep an eye on him. You will do that, won't you, Mr. Tesman?

TESMAN.   I'd be delighted to, Mrs. Rysing.

HEDDA.   Elvsted!

TESMAN.   I'd be delighted to do anything in my power to help Eilert. You can rely on me.

THEA. [*Presses his hands.*]   Oh, how very kind of you! I can't thank you enough. . . . [*Frightened.*] You see, my husband is so very fond of him.

HEDDA. [*Rises.*]   Yes—I see. I think you should write to him, George. He may not care to come of his own accord.

TESMAN.   Perhaps that would be the right thing to do, Hedda, eh?

HEDDA.   Yes. The sooner the better. Why not at once?

THEA. [*Imploringly.*]   Oh, yes, please do!

TESMAN.   I'll write him this minute. Have you his address, Mrs. Ry—— Elvsted?

THEA. [*Takes a slip of paper from her pocket and gives it to him.*]   Here it is.

TESMAN.   Splendid. Then I'll go in. [*Looks around.*] Oh—I mustn't forget my slippers. Ah! Here they are. [*Takes the parcel and starts to go.*]

HEDDA.   Mind you write him a nice friendly letter, George, and a good long one, too.

TESMAN.   I most certainly will.

THEA.   But don't let him know that I suggested it!

TESMAN.   Of course not! That goes without saying, eh? [*He goes out right, through the inner room.*]

HEDDA. [*Smilingly goes to* MRS. ELVSTED *and says in a low voice.*]   There! Now we've killed two birds with one stone.

THEA.   What do you mean?

HEDDA.   Couldn't you see that I wanted to get rid of him?

THEA.   Yes, to write the letter.

HEDDA.   And so that I could talk to you alone.

THEA. [*Bewildered.*]   About the same thing?

HEDDA.   Precisely.

THEA. [*Apprehensively.*] But there's nothing else to tell, Mrs. Tesman. Absolutely nothing.

HEDDA. Of course there is. I can see that. There's a great *deal* more to tell. Come along. Sit down. We'll have a nice friendly talk.

[*She forces* MRS. ELVSTED *down into the armchair by the stove and seats herself on one of the tabourets.*]

THEA. [*Anxiously looking at her watch.*] But, really, Mrs. Tesman, I was just thinking of going——

HEDDA. Oh, you can't be in such a hurry. Come along, now——I want to know all about your life at home.

THEA. I prefer not to speak about that.

HEDDA. But to me, dear! After all, we went to school together.

THEA. Yes, but you were in a higher class, and I was always so dreadfully afraid of you then.

HEDDA. Afraid of me!

THEA. Yes, dreadfully. When we met on the stairs you always used to pull my hair.

HEDDA. Did I, really!

THEA. Yes. And once you said you were going to burn it all off.

HEDDA. I was just teasing you, of course!

THEA. I was so silly in those days, and afterwards we drifted so far apart. We lived in such different worlds. . . .

HEDDA. Well, then we must drift together again. At school we always called each other by our first names. Why shouldn't we now?

THEA. I think you're mistaken——

HEDDA. Of course not. I remember it distinctly. We were *great* friends! [*Draws her stool near to* MRS. ELVSTED *and kisses her on the cheek.*] So you must call me Hedda.

THEA. [*Pressing her hands and patting them.*] You're so kind and understanding. I'm not used to kindness.

HEDDA. And I shall call you my darling little Thora.

THEA. My name is Thea.

HEDDA. Yes, yes, of course, I meant Thea! [*Looking at her compassionately.*] So my darling little Thea——you mean they're not kind to you at home?

THEA. If only I had a home! But I haven't. I never had one.

HEDDA. [*Gives her a quick look.*] I suspected something of the sort.

THEA. [*Gazing helplessly before her.*] Ah!

HEDDA. Tell me, Thea——I'm a little vague about it. When you first went to the Elvsteds', you were engaged as housekeeper, weren't you?

THEA. I was supposed to go as governess, but Mrs. Elvsted——the first Mrs. Elvsted, that is——was an invalid, and rarely left her room, so I had to take charge of the house as well.

HEDDA. And, eventually, you became mistress of the house?

THEA. [*Sadly.*] Yes, I did.

HEDDA. How long ago was that?

THEA. That I married him?

HEDDA. Yes.

THEA. Five years ago.

HEDDA. Yes, that's right.

THEA. Oh, those five years, especially the last two or three of them—If only you knew, Mrs. Tesman!

HEDDA. [*Slaps her lightly on the hand.*] Mrs. Tesman! Thea!

THEA. I'll try—You have no idea, Hedda—

HEDDA. [*Casually.*] Eilert Løvborg's lived near you about three years, hasn't he?

THEA. [*Looks at her doubtfully.*] Eilert Løvborg? Why, yes, he has.

HEDDA. Had you met him before, here in town?

THEA. No, not really—I knew him by his name, of course.

HEDDA. But I suppose up there you saw a good deal of him.

THEA. Yes, he came to our house every day. He gave the children lessons, you see. I had so much to do; I couldn't manage that, as well.

HEDDA. No. Of course not. And I suppose your husband's away from home a good deal.

THEA. Yes. Being sheriff, he often has to travel about his district.

HEDDA. [*Leans against the arm of the chair.*] Now, my dear darling little Thea, I want you to tell me everything—exactly as it is.

THEA. Well, then you must question me.

HEDDA. Tell me—what sort of a man is your husband, Thea? To live with, I mean. Is he kind to you?

THEA. [*Evasively.*] He probably thinks he is.

HEDDA. But isn't he much too old for you, dear? There must be at least twenty years between you.

THEA. [*Irritably.*] Yes, that makes it all the harder. We haven't a thought in common. Nothing, in fact.

HEDDA. But, I suppose he's fond of you in his own way.

THEA. Oh, I don't know. I think he finds me useful. And then it doesn't cost much to keep me. I'm not expensive.

HEDDA. That's stupid of you.

THEA. [*Shakes her head.*] It couldn't be otherwise. Not with him. I don't believe he really cares about anyone but himself. And perhaps a little for the children.

HEDDA. And for Eilert Løvborg, Thea?

THEA. [*Looking at her.*] Eilert Løvborg? What makes you say that?

HEDDA. Well, it's obvious!—After all, he's sent you all this way into town, simply to look for him!—[*With the trace of a smile.*] Wasn't that what you told George?

THEA. [*With a nervous twitch.*] Yes, I suppose I did. [*Vehemently but in a low voice.*] Oh, I might as well tell you the truth. It's bound to come out sooner or later.

HEDDA. What——?

THEA. Well, then—my husband knew nothing about my coming here.

HEDDA. Your husband didn't know!

THEA. No, of course not. He was away himself at the time. I couldn't stand it any longer, Hedda. I simply couldn't. I felt so alone, so deserted——

HEDDA. Yes, yes—well?

THEA. So I packed a few of my things—just those I needed most—I didn't say a word to anyone. I simply left the house.

HEDDA. Just like that!

THEA. Yes, and took the next train to town.

HEDDA. But, Thea, my darling! How did you dare do such a thing?

THEA. [*Rises and walks about the room.*] What else could I possibly do?

HEDDA. But what will your husband say when you go home again?

THEA. [*At the table, looks at her.*] Back to him!

HEDDA. Well, of course.

THEA. I shall never go back to him again.

HEDDA. [*Rises and goes towards her.*] You mean you've actually left your home for good?

THEA. I saw nothing else to do.

HEDDA. But to leave like that, so openly——

THEA. You can't very well *hide* a thing like that!

HEDDA. But what will people say about you, Thea?

THEA. They can say whatever they like. [*Sits on the sofa wearily and sadly.*] I only did what I had to do.

HEDDA. [*After a short silence.*] What are your plans now?

THEA. I don't know yet. All I know is that I must live near Eilert Løvborg, if I'm to live at all.

HEDDA. [*Takes a chair from the table, sits down near* MRS. ELVSTED *and strokes her hands.*] Tell me, Thea—how did this friendship start between you and Eilert Løvborg?

THEA. It grew gradually. I began to have a sort of power over him.

HEDDA. Really?

THEA. Yes. After a while he gave up his old habits. Oh, not because I asked him to—I never would have dared do that. But I suppose he realized how unhappy they made me, and so he dropped them.

HEDDA. [*Concealing a scornful smile.*] So, my darling little Thea, you've actually reformed him!

THEA. Well, *he* says so, at any rate, and in return he's made a human being out of me. Taught me to think and understand so many things.

HEDDA. Did he give you lessons, too, then?

THEA. Not lessons, exactly, but he talked to me, explained so much to me —and the most wonderful thing of all was when he finally allowed me to share in his work. Allowed me to help him.

HEDDA. He did, did he?

THEA. Yes. He wanted me to be a part of everything he wrote.

HEDDA. Like two good comrades!

THEA. [*Brightly.*] Comrades! Why, Hedda, that's exactly what *he* says! I ought to be so happy, but somehow I'm not. I'm so afraid it may not last.

HEDDA. You're not very sure of him, then?

THEA. [*Gloomily.*] I sometimes feel a shadow between Løvborg and me—a woman's shadow.

HEDDA. [*Looks at her intently.*] Who could that be?

THEA. I don't know. Someone he knew long ago. Someone he's never been able to forget.

HEDDA. Has he told you anything about her?

THEA. He spoke of her once—quite vaguely.

HEDDA. What did he say?

THEA. He said that when they parted she threatened to shoot him.

HEDDA. [*With cold composure.*] What nonsense! No one does that sort of thing here!

THEA. I know. That's why I think it must have been that red-haired cabaret singer he was once——

HEDDA. Very likely.

THEA. They say she used to go about with loaded pistols.

HEDDA. Then of course it must have been she.

THEA. [*Wringing her hands.*] But, Hedda, they say she's here now—in town, again! I'm so worried I don't know what to do!

HEDDA. [*With a glance towards inner room.*] Sh! Here comes Tesman. Not a word to him. All this is between us.

THEA. [*Jumps up.*] Yes, yes, of course.

[GEORGE TESMAN, *a letter in his hand, enters from the right through the inner room.*]

TESMAN. Well, here is the letter signed and sealed!

HEDDA. Splendid! Mrs. Elvsted was just leaving, George. Wait a minute! I'll go with you as far as the garden gate.

TESMAN. Do you think Berta could post this for me, dear?

HEDDA. [*Takes the letter.*] I'll tell her to.

[BERTA *enters from the hall.*]

BERTA. Judge Brack wishes to know if you will see him, ma'am.

HEDDA. Yes. Show him in. And post this letter, will you?

BERTA. [*Taking the letter.*] Certainly, ma'am.

[*She opens the door for* JUDGE BRACK *and goes out. The* JUDGE *is a man of 45. Thick-set but well-built and supple in his movements. His face is rounded and his profile aristocratic. His short hair is still almost black and carefully*

*dressed. His eyes are bright and sparkling. His eye-brows thick. His mous-
tache also thick with short-cut ends. He wears a smart walking-suit, slightly
youthful for his age. He uses an eye-glass, which he lets drop from time
to time.*]

BRACK. [*Bowing, hat in hand.*] May one venture to call so early in the day?

HEDDA. Of course one may.

TESMAN. [*Shakes hands with him.*] You know you're always welcome. [*Introduces him.*] Judge Brack, Miss Rysing.

HEDDA. Ah!

BRACK. [*Bows.*] Delighted.

HEDDA. [*Looks at him and laughs.*] What fun to have a look at you by daylight, Judge.

BRACK. Do you find me—altered?

HEDDA. A little younger, I think.

BRACK. [*Laughs and goes down to fireplace.*] I thank you, most heartily.

TESMAN. But what do you say to Hedda, eh? Doesn't she look flourishing?
She's positively——

HEDDA. For heaven's sake, leave me out of it, George! You'd far better thank
Judge Brack for all the trouble he's taken.

BRACK. Oh, don't mention it. It was a pleasure, I assure you.

HEDDA. Yes, you're a loyal soul; but I mustn't keep Mrs. Elvsted waiting.
Excuse me, Judge. I'll be back directly.

[*Exchange of greetings.* MRS. ELVSTED *and* HEDDA *go out through the hall
door.*]

BRACK. Well, I hope your wife's pleased with everything.

TESMAN. We really can't thank you enough. Of course she wants to rearrange things a bit, and she talks of buying a few additional trifles.

BRACK. Is that so?

TESMAN. But you needn't bother about that. Hedda will see to that herself.
Why don't we sit down, eh?

BRACK. [*Sits at table.*] Thanks. Just for a moment—There's something I
must talk to you about, my dear Tesman.

TESMAN. Yes, the expenses, eh? [*Sits down.*] I suppose it's time we got
down to business.

BRACK. Oh, that's not so very pressing. Though perhaps it would have been
wiser to be a bit more economical.

TESMAN. But that would have been out of the question. You know Hedda,
Judge. After all, she's been used to a certain standard of living——

BRACK. Yes, that's just the trouble.

TESMAN. Fortunately, it won't be long before I receive my appointment.

BRACK. Well, you see—such things sometimes hang fire.

TESMAN. Have you heard anything further, eh?

BRACK. Nothing really definite. [*Interrupts himself.*] But, by the way, I
have one bit of news for you.

TESMAN. Well?

BRACK. Your old friend, Eilert Løvborg is back in town.

TESMAN. I've heard that already.

BRACK. Really? Who told you?

TESMAN. That lady who went out with Hedda.

BRACK. Oh yes, what was her name? I didn't quite catch it.

TESMAN. Mrs. Elvsted.

BRACK. Oh yes, the sheriff's wife. Of course. Løvborg's been living near them these past few years.

TESMAN. And, just think, I'm delighted to hear he's quite a reformed character.

BRACK. Yes, so they say.

TESMAN. And he's published a new book, eh?

BRACK. Indeed he has.

TESMAN. I hear it's made quite a sensation.

BRACK. A most unusual sensation.

TESMAN. Think of that. I'm delighted to hear it. A man of such extraordinary gifts. I felt so sorry to think he'd gone completely to rack and ruin!

BRACK. Well—everybody thought so.

TESMAN. I wonder what he'll do now—how on earth will he manage to make a living?

[During these last words HEDDA has re-entered by the hall door.]

HEDDA. [To BRACK with a scornful laugh.] Isn't that just like Tesman, Judge? Always worrying about how people are going to make their living.

TESMAN. We were just talking about Eilert Løvborg, dear.

HEDDA. [Giving him a quick glance. Seats herself in the armchair by the stove and asks casually.] What's the matter with him?

TESMAN. That money he inherited—he's undoubtedly squandered that long ago. And he can't very well write a new book every year, eh? So why shouldn't I wonder what's to become of him?

BRACK. Perhaps I can give you some information on the subject.

TESMAN. Indeed?

BRACK. You must remember that his relatives have a great deal of influence.

TESMAN. But they washed their hands of him long ago.

BRACK. At one time he was considered the hope of the family.

TESMAN. At one time, perhaps. But he soon put an end to that.

HEDDA. Who knows? [With a slight smile.] I hear they've quite reformed him up at the Elvsted's.

BRACK. And then there's his new book, of course.

TESMAN. Yes, that's true. Let's hope things will turn out well for him. I've just written him a note. I asked him to come and see me this evening, Hedda, dear.

BRACK. But you're coming to my stag-party this evening. You promised me last night on the pier.

HEDDA. Had you forgotten, Tesman!

TESMAN. Yes, I really had.

BRACK. In any case, I think you can be pretty sure he won't come.

TESMAN. Why shouldn't he?

BRACK. [*With a slight hesitation, rises and leans against the back of the chair.*] My dear Tesman, and you, too, Mrs. Tesman, I think it's only right that I should inform you of something that——

TESMAN. That concerns Eilert, eh?

BRACK. Yes, you as well as him.

TESMAN. [*Jumps up anxiously.*] But, my dear Judge, what is it?

BRACK. I think you should be prepared to find your appointment deferred —rather longer than you desired or expected.

TESMAN. Has anything happened to prevent it, eh?

BRACK. The nomination may depend on the result of a competition.

TESMAN. A competition! Think of that, Hedda. But who would my competitor be? Surely not——?

BRACK. Yes. Eilert Løvborg. Precisely.

[HEDDA *leans further back in the armchair with an ejaculation.*]

TESMAN. No, no! It's impossible! It's utterly inconceivable, eh?

BRACK. It may come to that, all the same.

TESMAN. But, Judge Brack, this would be incredibly unfair to me. [*Waving his arms.*] Just think, I'm a married man! We married on these prospects, Hedda and I. Think of the money we've spent, and we've borrowed from Aunt Julia, too! Why, they practically promised me the appointment, eh?

BRACK. Don't get so excited. You'll probably get the appointment all the same, only you'll have to compete for it.

HEDDA. [*Sits motionless in the armchair.*] Just think, George, it will have such a sporting interest.

TESMAN. Dearest Hedda, how can you be so indifferent about it?

HEDDA. [*As before.*] Indifferent! I'm not in the least indifferent. I can hardly wait to see which of you will win.

BRACK. In any case, I thought it better to warn you, Mrs. Tesman! Perhaps under the circumstances, you'd better go easy on those 'additional trifles' you're thinking of buying.

HEDDA. I don't see how this could possibly make any difference, my dear Judge.

BRACK. Really? Then I've no more to say. Good-bye. I'll call for you later on my way back from my afternoon walk.

TESMAN. Yes, yes—I'm so upset—my head's in a whirl!

HEDDA. [*Still reclining holds out her hand to him.*] I shall hope to see you later, Judge.

BRACK. Thank you, Mrs. Tesman. Good-bye.

TESMAN. [*Accompanies him to the door.*] Good-bye, my dear Judge. You really must excuse me——

[JUDGE *goes out by the hall door.*]

TESMAN. [*Pacing the room.*]   Oh, Hedda, Hedda, one should never rush into adventures, eh?

HEDDA. [*Looks at him and smiles.*]   Do you do that, George?

TESMAN.   What else can you call it? To get married and settle down on mere expectations, eh?

HEDDA.   You may be right.

TESMAN.   Well, at least we have our lovely home, Hedda, eh? The home we both dreamt of.

HEDDA. [*Rises slowly and wearily.*]   I'd counted on doing a lot of entertaining. That was part of the agreement, I thought. We were to keep open house.

TESMAN.   I'd been so looking forward to it, Hedda dear. To see you, a brilliant hostess, surrounded by distinguished guests—— Well, we'll just have to make the best of it for the time being, dear—— Be happy in one another— We can always invite Aunt Julia in now and then. But I wanted it to be so different for you, Hedda. So very different.

HEDDA.   I suppose this means I'll have to do without my butler.

TESMAN.   Yes, I'm afraid a butler is quite out of the question!

HEDDA.   You promised me a saddle-horse, remember? I suppose *that's* out of the question, too?

TESMAN.   I'm afraid so, Hedda.

HEDDA. [*Walks about the room.*]   Well, at least I have one thing to amuse myself with.

TESMAN. [*Beaming.*]   Thank heaven for that. What is it, Hedda, eh?

HEDDA. [*At centre opening—looks at him with suppressed scorn.*]   My pistols, George.

TESMAN.   Your pistols!

HEDDA. [*With cold eyes.*]   General Gabler's pistols. [*She goes out through the inner room to the left.*]

TESMAN. [*Rushes to the centre opening and calls after her.*]   Oh, Hedda, darling, please don't touch those dangerous things. For my sake, Hedda, eh?

End of Act One

Act Two

SCENE: *The room at the Tesmans' as in the first act. Only the piano has been removed and replaced by an elegant little writing-table with bookshelves. A smaller table has been placed by the sofa left. Most of the bouquets have been removed.* MRS. ELVSTED'S *bouquet stands on the large table downstage. It is afternoon.*

HEDDA, *dressed to receive callers, is alone in the room. She stands by the open glass-door loading a pistol. The matching pistol lies in an open pistol-case on the writing-table.*

HEDDA. [*Looks down into the garden and calls out.*] Welcome back, Judge!

BRACK. [*Is heard calling below at a distance.*] Thank you, Mrs. Tesman.

HEDDA. [*Raises the pistol and takes aim.*] Now, I'm going to shoot you, Judge!

BRACK. [*From below.*] No, no, don't aim at me like that!

HEDDA. That's what you get for sneaking in the back way. [*She fires.*]

BRACK. [*Nearer.*] Have you gone quite mad?

HEDDA. So sorry. Did I hit you by any chance?

BRACK. [*Still from outside.*] I wish you'd stop all this nonsense.

HEDDA. Come along, Judge, I'll let you pass.

[JUDGE BRACK, *dressed as for a men's party, comes in through the glass-door. Over his arm he carries a light overcoat.*]

BRACK. So you're still fooling with those pistols. What are you shooting at?

HEDDA. Just killing time. Shooting up into the blue.

BRACK. [*Gently takes the pistol out of her hand.*] Allow me. [*Examines it.*] Hm . . . I know this pistol . . . I've seen it before. [*Looks around.*] Where's the case for it? Ah, here! [*Places the pistol in its case and closes it.*] So that game is finished for today.

HEDDA. What in heaven's name am I to do with myself all day long!

BRACK. Haven't you had any visitors?

HEDDA. [*Closes the glass-door.*] Not one. I suppose all our friends are still out of town.

BRACK. Isn't Tesman home?

HEDDA. [*At the writing-table. Putting the pistol-case away in a drawer.*] No. He rushed off to his aunts' directly after lunch. He didn't expect you so early, Judge.

BRACK. Fancy my not thinking of that—That was stupid of me.

HEDDA. [*Turns her head and looks at him.*] Why stupid?

BRACK. Because I should have come even earlier.

HEDDA. [*Crossing the room.*] Then you'd have found no one to receive you, for I've been dressing ever since lunch.

BRACK. But isn't there a little crack in the door through which one might converse?

HEDDA. No. You forgot to provide one, Judge.

BRACK. Again stupid of me.

HEDDA. We must just sit here and wait until Tesman comes—He may not be back for some time.

BRACK. Never mind. I shan't be impatient.

[HEDDA *sits in the corner of the sofa.* BRACK *lays his overcoat over the back of the nearest chair and sits down, but keeps his hat in his hand. A short pause. They look at each other.*]

HEDDA. Well?

BRACK. [*In the same tone.*] Well?

HEDDA. I spoke first.

BRACK. [*Slightly bending forward.*] Let's have a really pleasant little talk, Mrs.—Hedda.

HEDDA. [*Leaning farther back on the sofa.*] It seems ages since our last one, doesn't it, Judge? Of course, I don't count the few words we had last night and this morning.

BRACK. I know—You mean a *real* talk. Just a 'twosome.'

HEDDA. Yes, that's it.

BRACK. Every single day I've wished you were home again.

HEDDA. I've wished that, too.

BRACK. You have? Really, Mrs. Hedda? And I thought you were having such a good time on your journey.

HEDDA. Ha!

BRACK. Tesman's letters led me to think so.

HEDDA. Oh, well, Tesman! You know Tesman, my dear Judge! His idea of bliss is grubbing about in a lot of dirty bookshops and making endless copies of antiquated manuscripts.

BRACK. [*With a touch of malice.*] Well, after all, that's his vocation in life, you know. Or a large part of it.

HEDDA. Yes, if it's one's vocation, I suppose that makes it different, but as for me! Oh, my dear Judge, I can't tell you how bored I've been!

BRACK. [*Sympathetically.*] Are you really serious?

HEDDA. Of course. Surely you can understand? How would *you* like to spend six whole months without meeting a soul you could really talk to?

BRACK. I shouldn't like it at all.

HEDDA. But the most unendurable thing of all was——

BRACK. What?

HEDDA. To be everlastingly with one and the same person.

BRACK. [*With a nod of agreement.*] Morning, noon, and night, at all possible times.

HEDDA. I said 'everlastingly.'

BRACK. But with our good Tesman, I should have thought one might——

HEDDA. Tesman is a specialist, my dear Judge.

BRACK. Undeniably.

HEDDA. And specialists are not amusing travelling companions—Not for long, at any rate.

BRACK. Not even the specialist you happen to love?

HEDDA. Ugh! Don't use that revolting word!

BRACK. [*Startled.*] What? What's that, Mrs. Hedda?

HEDDA. [*Half laughing, half in irritation.*] Just you try it! Nothing but the history of civilization morning, noon, and night.

BRACK. Everlastingly.

HEDDA. And then all this business about the domestic industries of Brabant during the Middle Ages. That's the most maddening part of it all.

BRACK. [*Looks at her searchingly.*] But, tell me, in that case, how did it happen that you——?

HEDDA. Married Tesman, you mean? Is there anything so very odd in that?

BRACK. Both yes and no, Mrs. Hedda.

HEDDA. I had danced myself tired, my dear Judge—and I wasn't getting any younger. [*With a slight shudder.*] But I won't talk about that. I won't even think about it.

BRACK. You certainly have no cause.

HEDDA. [*Watching him intently.*] And one must admit that George Tesman is a thoroughly worthy man.

BRACK. A worthy, dependable man. There can be no question of that.

HEDDA. And I don't see anything especially—*funny* about him, do you?

BRACK. Funny? No—o,—not really. No, I wouldn't say that.

HEDDA. After all, he's a distinguished scholar. Who knows? He may still go far.

BRACK. [*Looks at her uncertainly.*] I thought you believed like everyone else that some day he'd become a really famous man.

HEDDA. [*In a tired voice.*] Yes, so I did. And then since he was so absolutely bent on supporting me, I really didn't see why I shouldn't accept his offer.

BRACK. No, if you look at it from that point of view——

HEDDA. Well, that was more than some of my other admirers were prepared to do, my dear Judge.

BRACK. [*Laughs.*] I can't answer for the others, of course. You know, that generally speaking, I have a great respect for the state of matrimony, but I confess, that as an individual——

HEDDA. [*Jokingly.*] I never had any hopes as far as you were concerned.

BRACK. All I ask of life is to know a few people intimately. A few nice people whom I can help and advise, in whose houses I can come and go as a trusted friend.

HEDDA. Of the—master of the house, you mean?

BRACK. [*With a bow.*] Well, preferably, of the mistress. But of the master, too, of course! I find such a triangular friendship, if I may call it so, a great convenience to all concerned.

HEDDA. Yes, God knows, a third person would have been welcome on our journey. Oh, those infernal tête-à-têtes!

BRACK. Cheer up! Your wedding trip is over now.

HEDDA. [*Shaking her head.*] Not by a long shot. No, we've only stopped at a station on the line.

BRACK. Then the thing to do is to jump out and stretch oneself a bit, Mrs. Hedda.

HEDDA. I never jump out.

BRACK. Why not?

HEDDA. There's always someone there waiting to——

BRACK. [*Laughing.*] Stare at your legs, you mean?

HEDDA. Precisely.

BRACK. Well, good heavens——

HEDDA. [*With a gesture of distaste.*] I don't like that sort of thing. I'd rather keep my seat and continue the tête-à-tête.

BRACK. But if a third person were to jump in and join the couple?

HEDDA. Ah!—But *that's* quite a different thing!

BRACK. A trusted, understanding friend.

HEDDA. Gay and entertaining in a variety of ways?

BRACK. And not a bit of a specialist.

HEDDA. [*With an audible sigh.*] That would certainly be a great relief!

BRACK. [*Hears the front door open and glances in that direction.*] The triangle is completed.

HEDDA. [*In a half-tone.*] And on goes the train.

[GEORGE TESMAN *enters from the hall. He wears a grey walking-suit and a soft felt hat. He carries a great number of paper-bound books under his arm and in his pockets.*]

TESMAN. [*Goes up to the table beside the corner sofa.*] Pooh! It's a warm job to carry all these books, Hedda. [*Puts them down.*] I'm positively perspiring! [HEDDA *makes a scarcely audible ejaculation: 'How charming, George!'* TESMAN *puts some of the books down on the table.*] Oh, you're here already, Judge. Berta didn't tell me.

BRACK. [*Rising.*] I came in through the garden.

HEDDA. What are all those books, George?

TESMAN. [*Thumbing through the books.*] They're some new books on my special subject. I simply had to have them.

HEDDA. Your special subject, George?

BRACK. On his special subject, Mrs. Tesman.

[BRACK *and* HEDDA *exchange a confidential smile.*]

HEDDA. Do you need still more books on your special subject, George?

TESMAN. One can never have too many, Hedda. One *must* keep up with all the new publications.

HEDDA. Yes, I suppose one must.

TESMAN. [*Searching among the books.*] Look, I got Eilert Løvborg's new book, too. [*Offers it to her.*] Would you care to have a look at it, Hedda, eh?

HEDDA. No, thank you—well, perhaps a little later, George.

TESMAN. I glanced through it on my way home.

BRACK. What do you think of it? As a specialist, I mean.

TESMAN. He handles his subject with the greatest restraint. That is what struck me most—It's quite remarkable. He never wrote like that before. [*Gathers the books together.*] I'll just take these into my study. I'm longing to cut the leaves. And then I suppose I'd better change, though we needn't go just yet, eh?

BRACK. Oh, no. There's not the slightest hurry.

TESMAN. Then I'll take my time. [*Starts to go out with the books but stops and turns at centre opening.*] Oh, by the way, Hedda, Aunt Julia is afraid she can't come to see you this evening.

HEDDA.   Oh? Why not? Is she still annoyed about the hat?

TESMAN.   Of course not. That wouldn't be a bit like her! No, but you see, Aunt Rina's very ill.

HEDDA.   She always is.

TESMAN.   Yes, but today she's worse than ever, poor thing!

HEDDA.   Then she'll need her sister with her. That's only natural. I shall have to try and bear it.

TESMAN.   I can't tell you how delighted Aunt Julia was to see you looking so well, so positively flourishing.

HEDDA.   [In a half-tone, rising.]   Oh, those eternal aunts!

TESMAN.   What did you say, dear?

HEDDA.   [Going to the glass-door.]   Nothing—Nothing—Nothing!

TESMAN.   Very well, Hedda—eh? [He goes out right, through the inner room.]

BRACK.   What was that you said about a hat?

HEDDA.   Oh, it was just something that happened this morning. Miss Tesman had taken off her hat and put it down on the table. [Looks at him and smiles.] And I pretended to think it was the servant's.

BRACK. [Shakes his head.]   Why, my dear Mrs. Hedda. How could you do such a thing to that nice old lady?

HEDDA. [Walks nervously about the room.]   My dear Judge, I really don't know. I suddenly get impulses like that and I simply can't control them. [Flings herself down in the armchair by the stove.] I don't know how to explain it myself.

BRACK. [Behind the armchair.]   You're not really happy. I think that's the explanation.

HEDDA. [Gazing straight before her.]   I can't imagine why I should be— happy? Can you tell me?

BRACK.   Well, to begin with; here you are, in the very house you always longed to live in.

HEDDA. [Looks up at him and laughs.]   You really believe in that fairy-tale?

BRACK.   Wasn't it true, then?

HEDDA.   I'll tell you how it happened: last summer I made use of Tesman to see me home from parties.

BRACK.   Unfortunately, my way lay in a different direction.

HEDDA.   Yes, you were going in a different direction then, weren't you, Judge?

BRACK. [Laughs.]   Shame on you, Mrs. Hedda! And so you and Tesman——?

HEDDA.   Well, one evening we happened to pass by this house. Tesman, poor thing, was turning and twisting and couldn't think of anything to say.—I really felt sorry for the poor learned wretch.

BRACK. [Smiles sceptically.]   Sorry! You!

HEDDA.   Yes, I really did. I felt sorry for him. And so just to make conversation, to help him out a bit, I was foolish enough to say what a charming house this was, and how I should love to live in it.

BRACK. No more than that?

HEDDA. Not *that* evening.

BRACK. But afterwards?

HEDDA. Afterwards!—Afterwards my foolishness was not without consequences, my dear Judge.

BRACK. Yes—Unfortunately, that happens all too often.

HEDDA. Thanks! So, you see it was this fictitious enthusiasm for Secretary Falk's Villa that really brought Tesman and me together. It was the immediate cause of our engagement, our wedding, our wedding journey, and all the rest of it. Well, my dear Judge, they say as you make your bed, so you must lie.

BRACK. This is really priceless! So I suppose you didn't really care a rap about the house?

HEDDA. No, God knows, I didn't!

BRACK. Still, now that we've made it so attractive and comfortable for you——

HEDDA. To me it smells of lavender and dried rose leaves. What might be called the 'Aunt Julia atmosphere'.

BRACK. [*Laughs.*] No. That's probably a legacy from the late Mrs. Falk.

HEDDA. Yes! Yes, you're right! There is a touch of decay about it. [*She clasps her hands behind her head, leans back in the chair and looks at him.*] Oh, my dear Judge, my dear Judge! How incredibly I shall bore myself here!

BRACK. Why shouldn't you, too, find some sort of vocation in life, Mrs. Hedda?

HEDDA. A vocation—that would attract me?

BRACK. Preferably, yes.

HEDDA. God only knows what kind of a vocation that would be! I often wonder whether—— [*Breaks off.*] But that wouldn't be any good, either.

BRACK. What? Tell me.

HEDDA. I was wondering whether I could get George to go into politics.

BRACK. [*Laughs.*] Tesman? No, really! I'm afraid political life would be the last thing in the world for him.

HEDDA. I know you're probably right; but I could try and get him into it all the same.

BRACK. But what satisfaction would it be to you unless he were successful at it? Why should you want to drive him into it?

HEDDA. Because I'm *bored*, I tell you. [*After a pause.*] So you think it quite out of the question for George ever to become—let's say—Secretary of State?

BRACK. Ha, ha! Mrs. Hedda. You must remember, apart from anything else, to become anything of that sort he'd have to be a fairly rich man.

HEDDA. [*Rises impatiently.*] There you are. Money! Always money! [*Crosses the room.*] It's this genteel poverty that makes life so hideous, so utterly ludicrous.

BRACK. Now I should say the fault lies elsewhere.

HEDDA. Where then?

BRACK. I don't believe you've ever really been stirred by anything in life.

HEDDA. Anything serious, you mean?

BRACK. If you like. But I expect it will come.

HEDDA. [*Tossing her head.*] If you're thinking about that ridiculous professorship, that's George's own affair. I assure you I shan't give a thought to that!

BRACK. I dare say. But suppose you should suddenly find yourself faced with what's known in solemn language, as a grave responsibility—[*smiling*] a *new* responsibility, Mrs. Hedda.

HEDDA. [*Angrily.*] Be quiet! Nothing of that sort will ever happen to me.

BRACK. [*Cautiously.*] We'll talk of this again a year from now, at the very latest.

HEDDA. [*Curtly.*] That sort of thing doesn't appeal to me, Judge. I'm not fitted for it.—No responsibilities for me!

BRACK. What makes you think you're less fitted than the majority of women? Why should you deliberately turn away from duties——?

HEDDA. [*At the glass-door.*] Be quiet, I tell you! I sometimes think there's only one thing in this world I'm really fitted for.

BRACK. [*Nearer to her.*] What's that, if I may ask?

HEDDA. [*Looking out.*] Boring myself to death! Now you know it. [*Turns, looks towards the inner room, and laughs.*] Ah! I thought so—here comes the professor!

BRACK. [*Softly, warningly.*] Now, now! Mrs. Hedda!—

[GEORGE TESMAN, *dressed for the party, his gloves and hat in his hands, enters from the right through the inner room.*]

TESMAN. Oh, Hedda, has any message come from Eilert, eh?

HEDDA. No.

TESMAN. Then he'll be here presently, you'll see.

BRACK. You really think he'll come?

TESMAN. I'm almost sure of it. What you told us this morning was probably just a rumour.

BRACK. Do you think so?

TESMAN. At any rate, Aunt Julia didn't believe for a moment that he would ever stand in my way again. Think of that!

BRACK. Well, then, there's nothing to worry about.

TESMAN. [*Puts his hat and gloves down on a chair, right.*] I'd like to wait for him as long as possible, though.

BRACK. We've plenty of time. My guests won't arrive before seven or half-past.

TESMAN. Meanwhile, we can keep Hedda company and see what happens, eh?

HEDDA. [*Puts BRACK's overcoat and hat on the corner sofa.*] And if the worst comes to the worst, Mr. Løvborg can spend the evening with me.

BRACK. What do you mean by 'the worst'?

HEDDA.   I mean—if he refuses to go with you and Tesman.

TESMAN. [*Looks at her dubiously.*]   But, Hedda, dear, do you think it would
be quite the thing for him to stay here with you, eh? Remember, Aunt Julia
isn't coming.

HEDDA.   No, but Mrs. Elvsted is. We three can have a cup of tea together.

TESMAN.   Oh, well, then it would be *quite* all right.

BRACK. [*Smiling.*]   It might perhaps be the best thing for him, too.

HEDDA.   Why the 'best thing', Judge?

BRACK.   Well you know how rude you are about my stag-parties, Mrs. Tesman. You always say they're only safe for men of the strictest principles.

HEDDA.   I'm sure Mr. Løvborg's principles are strict enough now. A converted sinner——

[BERTA *appears at the hall door.*]

BERTA.   There's a gentleman asking to see you, ma'am.

HEDDA.   Oh, yes—show him in.

TESMAN. [*Softly.*]   It must be Eilert. Think of that! [EILERT LØVBORG *enters
from the hall. He is slim and lean. The same age as* TESMAN *he looks older, as
though worn out by life. Hair and beard dark brown; a long, pale face, but with
patches of colour on the cheekbones; he wears a well-cut black visiting suit, obviously new. He carries dark gloves and a silk hat. He stands near the door and
makes a rapid bow. He seems slightly embarrassed.*] [*Goes to him and shakes
him by the hand.*] Welcome, my dear Eilert. So at last we meet again!

LØVBORG. [*Speaks in a hushed voice.*]   Thanks for your letter, George. [*Approaches* HEDDA.] May I shake hands with you, too, Mrs. Tesman?

HEDDA. [*Takes his hand.*]   How do you do, Mr. Løvborg, I'm delighted to see
you. [*She motions with her hand.*] I don't know if you two gentlemen——

LØVBORG. [*With a slight bow.*]   Judge Brack, I believe.

BRACK. [*Bows likewise.*]   Yes, I've had the pleasure, some years ago.

TESMAN. [*To* LØVBORG *with his hands on his shoulders.*]   And now, Eilert,
you must make yourself at home, mustn't he, Hedda? I hear you're going to
settle in town again, eh?

LØVBORG.   Yes, I am.

TESMAN.   Well, that's splendid. I just got your new book, Eilert, but I
haven't had time to read it yet.

LØVBORG.   I wouldn't bother to, if I were you.

TESMAN.   Why, what do you mean?

LØVBORG.   It's pretty thin stuff.

TESMAN.   Just think! How can you say that?

BRACK.   It's been enormously praised, I hear.

LØVBORG.   That was exactly what I wanted, so I put nothing in it that anyone could take exception to.

BRACK.   Very wise of you.

TESMAN.   But my dear Eilert——

LØVBORG.   You see, I'm determined to make a fresh start; to win a real
position for myself.

TESMAN. [*Slightly embarrassed.*]   Oh, so that's what you plan to do, eh?

LØVBORG. [*Smiles, puts down his hat, and takes a parcel wrapped in paper from his coat pocket.*]   But when this one appears, George Tesman, you'll have to read it, for this is a real book. Every ounce of my true self is in this.

TESMAN.   Really! What's it about?

LØVBORG.   It's the sequel.

TESMAN.   Sequel? Sequel of what?

LØVBORG.   Of the other book.

TESMAN.   You mean, the new one?

LØVBORG.   Yes, of course.

TESMAN.   But, my dear Eilert, surely that comes right down to our time, doesn't it?

LØVBORG.   Yes, but this deals with the future.

TESMAN.   With the future. But good heavens, we know nothing about the future!

LØVBORG.   There's a thing or two to be said about it all the same. [*Opens the parcel.*] Look here——

TESMAN.   That's not your handwriting.

LØVBORG.   No, I dictated it. [*Thumbs through the pages.*] It falls into two sections. The first deals with the civilizing forces of the future and the second [*Turning to the pages towards the end*] forecasts the probable lines of development.

TESMAN.   How remarkable! I should have never thought of writing anything of that sort.

HEDDA. [*At the glass-door, drumming on the pane.*]   No, I daresay not.

LØVBORG. [*Puts the manuscript back in its wrapping and lays it on the table.*] I brought it with me; I thought I might read you a bit of it this evening.

TESMAN.   That was very kind of you, Eilert, but this evening—— [*Glancing at* BRACK.] I don't see how we can manage it——

LØVBORG.   Well, then some other time. There's no hurry.

BRACK.   The fact is, Mr. Løvborg, I'm giving a little party this evening to celebrate Tesman's return.

LØVBORG. [*Looking for his hat.*]   Oh, then I mustn't detain you.

BRACK.   No, but wait. I'd be delighted if you would give me the pleasure of your company.

LØVBORG. [*Curtly and decisively.*]   I'm sorry. I can't. Thank you very much.

BRACK.   Oh, nonsense! Do, come. We shall be quite a select little circle, and I can assure you, we shall have a 'jolly time' as Mrs. Hed—Mrs. Tesman puts it.

LØVBORG.   I don't doubt that, but nevertheless——

BRACK.   And you could bring your manuscript with you and read it to Tesman at my house. I could give you a room all to yourselves.

TESMAN.   Yes, think of that, Eilert. Why shouldn't you do that, eh?

HEDDA. [*Interposing.*]   But, George dear, if Mr. Løvborg says he doesn't want to go, I'm sure Mr. Løvborg would much prefer to stay here and have supper with me.

LØVBORG. [*Looking at her.*]   With you, Mrs. Tesman?

HEDDA.   Mrs. Elvsted will be here, too.

LØVBORG.   Oh—[*Casually.*] I saw her for a moment today.

HEDDA.   Oh, did you? Well, she's spending the evening here. So you see, you're almost obliged to stay, Mr. Løvborg. Otherwise, Mrs. Elvsted will have no one to see her home.

LØVBORG.   That's true. Many thanks. In that case, I will stay, Mrs. Tesman.

HEDDA.   Splendid! I'll just give one or two orders to the servant.

[*She goes to the hall door and rings.* BERTA *enters.* HEDDA *talks to her in a whisper and points to the inner room.* BERTA *nods and goes out.*]

TESMAN. [*During the above, to* EILERT LØVBORG.]   Tell me, Eilert, is it this new subject, the future, that you are going to lecture about?

LØVBORG.   Yes.

TESMAN.   They told me at the bookstore that you were planning a series of lectures.

LØVBORG.   Yes, I am. I hope you've no objection.

TESMAN.   No, of course not, but——

LØVBORG.   I can quite see that it might interfere with your plans.

TESMAN. [*Depressed.*]   I can't very well expect you, out of consideration for me, to——

LØVBORG.   But, of course, I'll wait until you receive your appointment.

TESMAN.   What! You'll wait! Then—then you're not going to compete with me, eh?

LØVBORG.   No. I only want people to realize that I *could* have—a sort of moral victory, if you like.

TESMAN.   Why, bless my soul, then Aunt Julia was right after all! I was sure of it. Hedda, just think, Eilert is not going to stand in our way!

HEDDA. [*Curtly.*]   Our way! Do please leave me out of it, George.

[*She goes up towards the inner room where* BERTA *is arranging a tray with decanters and glasses on the table.* HEDDA *nods approvingly and comes forward again.* BERTA *goes out.*]

TESMAN. [*During the above.*]   What do you say to this, Judge, eh?

BRACK.   Well, I say a moral victory may be all very fine but——

TESMAN.   Yes, certainly but all the same——

HEDDA. [*Looks at* TESMAN *with a cold smile.*]   You stand there looking absolutely thunderstruck, George.

TESMAN.   Well, you know, I almost believe I am.

HEDDA. [*Pointing to the inner room.*]   And now, gentlemen, won't you have a glass of cold punch before you go?

BRACK. [*Looks at his watch.*]   A sort of stirrup cup, you mean. Yes, that's not a bad idea.

TESMAN.   A capital idea, Hedda. Just the thing. Now that a heavy weight has been lifted off my mind——

HEDDA.   You'll join them, Mr. Løvborg?

LØVBORG. [*With a gesture of refusal.*]   No, thank you, nothing for me.

BRACK.   Why, surely, cold punch is not poison.

LØVBORG.   Perhaps not for everyone.

HEDDA.   Well, then, you two go in and I'll sit here and keep Mr. Løvborg company.

TESMAN.   Yes, do, Hedda, dear.

[*He and* BRACK *go into the inner room, sit down, drink punch, smoke ciga-rettes, and carry on an animated conversation during the following.* EILERT LØVBORG *remains standing by the stove.* HEDDA *goes to the writing-table.*]

HEDDA. [*In a raised voice.*]   Perhaps you'd like to look at some snapshots, Mr. Løvborg. You know, Tesman and I did some sightseeing in the Tyrol, on our way home. I'd so love to show you—— [*She brings over an album which she lays on the table by the sofa, in the further corner of which she seats herself.* EILERT LØVBORG *approaches, then stops and stands looking at her. He then takes a chair and sits on her left with his back to the inner room.*] [*She opens the album.*] Do you see this group of mountains, Mr. Løvborg? It's the Ortlar group—Oh, yes, Tesman has written the name underneath. 'The Ortlar group near Meran.'

LØVBORG. [*Who has never taken his eyes off her, says softly and slowly.*] Hedda Gabler——

HEDDA. [*Gives him a hasty look.*]   Sh!

LØVBORG. [*Repeats softly.*]   Hedda Gabler——

HEDDA. [*Looking at the album.*]   That was my name in the old days, when you and I knew each other.

LØVBORG.   Then I must learn never to say Hedda Gabler again? Never as long as I live?

HEDDA. [*Turning over the pages.*]   Yes, I'm afraid you must.

LØVBORG. [*In an indignant tone.*]   Hedda Gabler married! And married to George Tesman!

HEDDA.   Such is life!

LØVBORG.   Oh, Hedda, Hedda, how could you throw yourself away like that?

HEDDA. [*Looks at him sharply.*]   I won't have you say such things.

LØVBORG.   Why shouldn't I? [TESMAN *comes into the room and goes towards the sofa.*]

HEDDA. [*Hears him coming and says in a casual tone.*]   And this, Mr. Løv-borg, is a view from the Ampezzodalen. Just look at those peaks. [*Looks up at* TESMAN *affectionately.*] Oh, George, dear, what's the name of these curious peaks?

TESMAN.   Let me see—oh, those are the Dolomites.

HEDDA.   Oh, yes, those are the Dolomites, Mr. Løvborg.

TESMAN.   Hedda, dear, are you sure you wouldn't like me to bring some punch.—For yourself, at any rate, eh?

HEDDA.   Yes, I think I will have some, dear. And perhaps a few biscuits.

TESMAN.   A cigarette?

HEDDA.   No, I think not, dear.

TESMAN.   Very well. [*He goes into the inner room again and out to the right.* BRACK *sits in the inner room, occasionally keeping an eye on* HEDDA *and* LØV-BORG.]

LØVBORG. [*Softly as before.*]   Answer me, Hedda. How could you do it?

HEDDA. [*Apparently absorbed in the album.*]   If you go on calling me Hedda, I won't talk to you.

LØVBORG.   Can't I say Hedda even when we're alone?

HEDDA.   No. You may think it, but you mustn't say it.

LØVBORG.   I understand. It offends your love for George Tesman.

HEDDA. [*Glances at him and smiles.*]   Love? How funny you are!

LØVBORG.   It's not love, then?

HEDDA.   All the same, no unfaithfulness, remember.

LØVBORG.   Hedda, answer me just one thing.

HEDDA.   Sh! [TESMAN *comes from the inner room carrying a small tray.*]

TESMAN.   Here you are! Doesn't this look tempting? [*He puts the tray down on the table.*]

HEDDA.   Why do you bring it yourself, George?

TESMAN. [*Filling the glasses.*]   I think it's such fun to wait on you, Hedda.

HEDDA.   But you've poured out two glasses. Mr. Løvborg said he wouldn't have any.

TESMAN.   I know. But Mrs. Elvsted will be here soon, won't she?

HEDDA.   Oh, yes, of course, Mrs. Elvsted——

TESMAN.   Have you forgotten her, eh?

HEDDA.   Yes, you know we were so engrossed in these photographs. Oh, George, dear, do you remember this little village?

TESMAN.   Yes, of course I do. It's the one just below the Brenner Pass. Don't you remember? We spent the night there.

HEDDA.   Oh, yes. And met that gay party of tourists.

TESMAN.   Yes, that was the place. Just think, if only we could have had you with us, Eilert, eh?

[*He goes back to the inner room and sits down with* JUDGE BRACK.]

LØVBORG.   Answer me this one thing, Hedda.

HEDDA.   Well?

LØVBORG.   Was there no love in your feeling for *me*, either? Not the slightest touch of love?

HEDDA.   I wonder—To me it seems that we were just two good comrades, two thoroughly intimate friends. [*Smiles.*] You especially were exceedingly frank!

LØVBORG.   It was you who made me so.

HEDDA.   You know, as I look back on it all, I realize there was something very beautiful, something fascinating, something daring—yes, daring—in that secret intimacy, that comradeship no living soul suspected.

LØVBORG.   Yes, there was, wasn't there, Hedda? Do you remember when I used to come to your home in the afternoon and the General sat over at the window reading his paper, with his back towards us——

HEDDA.   We two sat on the corner sofa——

LØVBORG.   Always the same illustrated paper before us——

HEDDA.   For want of an album, yes!

LØVBORG.   Do you remember, Hedda, all those wild things I confessed to you? Things no one suspected at this time—my days and nights of passion and frenzy, of drinking and madness—— How did you make me talk like that, Hedda? By what power?

HEDDA.   Power?

LØVBORG.   Yes. How else can one explain it? And all those devious questions you used to ask——

HEDDA.   Questions you understood so perfectly——

LØVBORG.   How could you bring yourself to ask such questions? So candidly, so boldly?

HEDDA.   In a devious way, if you please.

LØVBORG.   Yes, but boldly, all the same.

HEDDA.   How could you bring yourself to answer them, Mr. Løvborg?

LØVBORG.   That's just what I can't understand. There must have been love at the bottom of it. Perhaps you felt that by making me confess like that you were somehow washing away my sins.

HEDDA.   No, not quite.

LØVBORG.   What was your motive, then?

HEDDA.   Isn't it quite easy to understand, that a young girl, especially if it can be done in secret——

LØVBORG.   Well?

HEDDA.   Should be tempted to investigate a forbidden world. A world she's supposed to know nothing about?

LØVBORG.   So that was it.

HEDDA.   That had a lot to do with it, I think.

LØVBORG.   I see; we were both greedy for life. That made us comrades. But why did it end?

HEDDA.   You were to blame for that!

LØVBORG.   You broke with me.

HEDDA.   I realized the danger; you wanted to spoil our intimacy—to drag it down to reality. You talk of my boldness, my candour—why did you try to abuse them?

LØVBORG.   [Clenching his hands.] Why didn't you do as you said? Why didn't you shoot me?

HEDDA.   Because . . . I have such a fear of scandal.

LØVBORG.   Yes, Hedda, you are a coward at heart.

HEDDA.   A terrible coward. [With a change of tone.] But after all, it was a lucky thing for you. You found ample consolation at the Elvsteds'.

LØVBORG.   I know Thea has confided in you.

HEDDA.   And I suppose you've confided in her—about us?

LØVBORG.   Not a word. She's too stupid to understand that.

HEDDA.   Stupid?

LØVBORG.   About that sort of thing—yes.

HEDDA.   And I am a coward. [*Leans towards him, without looking him in the eye, says softly.*] Now I'll confide something to you.

LØVBORG. [*Intensely.*]   Well?

HEDDA.   My not daring to shoot you——

LØVBORG.   Yes?

HEDDA.   That was not my greatest cowardice that evening.

LØVBORG. [*Looks at her a moment, understands, and whispers passionately.*] Oh, Hedda, Hedda Gabler! I begin to understand the real meaning of our comradeship. You and I!—— You see, it *was* your craving for life——

HEDDA. [*Softly, with a keen look.*]   Be careful! Believe nothing of the sort. [*It has begun to get dark. The hall door is opened by* BERTA.] [*Closes the album with a bang and calls out smilingly.*] At last! Thea darling!—[MRS. ELVSTED *enters from the hall. She is in evening dress. The door is closed behind her.* HEDDA, *still on the sofa, stretches out her arms towards her.*] Darling little Thea, I thought you were never coming!

[*In passing,* MRS. ELVSTED *lightly greets the gentlemen in the inner room, then goes to the table and gives* HEDDA *her hand.* EILERT LØVBORG *rises. He and* MRS. ELVSTED *greet each other with a silent nod.*]

THEA.   Shouldn't I go and say good evening to your husband?

HEDDA. [*Puts her arm round* THEA *and leads her towards sofa.*]   No, we needn't bother about them. I expect they'll soon be off.

THEA.   Are they going out?

HEDDA.   Yes. To a wild party!

THEA. [*Quickly. To* LØVBORG.]   You're not going, are you?

LØVBORG.   No.

HEDDA.   No. Mr. Løvborg is staying here with us.

[LØVBORG *sits down again on the sofa.*]

THEA. [*Takes a chair and starts to sit beside him.*]   Oh, how nice it is to be here!

HEDDA.   No, no, little Thea, not there! You be a good girl and sit here, next to me. I'll sit between you.

THEA.   Just as you like.

[*She goes round the table and sits on the sofa to* HEDDA's *right.* LØVBORG *sits down again.*]

LØVBORG. [*To* HEDDA, *after a short pause.*]   Isn't she lovely to look at?

HEDDA. [*Lightly stroking her hair.*]   Only to look at?

LØVBORG.   We're two real comrades, she and I. We have absolute faith in each other. We can talk with perfect frankness.

HEDDA.   Not in a devious way, Mr. Løvborg.

LØVBORG. Well——

THEA. [*Softly, clinging to* HEDDA.] Oh, I'm so happy, Hedda! You know—
he actually says I've inspired him in his work.

HEDDA. [*Looks at her and smiles.*]   Does he really, dear?

LØVBORG.   And then she has such courage, Mrs. Tesman.

THEA.   Good heavens, courage!

LØVBORG.   Tremendous courage where your comrade is concerned.

HEDDA.   God, yes, courage! If one only had that!

LØVBORG.   What then?

HEDDA.   Then life might perhaps be endurable, after all. . . . [*With a sudden change of tone.*] Now, my darling little Thea, you must have a nice glass
of cold punch.

THEA.   No, thank you. I never take anything like that.

HEDDA.   Then how about you, Mr. Løvborg?

LØVBORG.   I don't either, thank you.

THEA.   No, he doesn't either.

HEDDA. [*Looks at him intently.*]   But if I want you to.

LØVBORG.   It makes no difference.

HEDDA. [*Laughs.*]   Poor me! Have I no power over you at all, then?

LØVBORG.   Not in that respect.

HEDDA.   No, but seriously. I really think you ought to take it for your own
sake.

THEA.   Why, Hedda——

LØVBORG.   How do you mean?

HEDDA.   People might begin to suspect that you weren't quite sure, quite
confident of yourself.

THEA. [*Softly.*]   Don't, Hedda.

LØVBORG.   People may suspect whatever they like.

THEA. [*Happily.*]   Yes, let them.

HEDDA.   You should have seen Judge Brack's face a moment ago. . . .

LØVBORG.   Indeed?

HEDDA.   His contemptuous smile when you didn't dare join them in there.

LØVBORG.   Didn't dare! I simply preferred to stay here and talk to you.

THEA.   That's natural enough, Hedda.

HEDDA.   That's not what Judge Brack thought. You should have seen him
smile and look at Tesman when you didn't dare go to his ridiculous little party.

LØVBORG.   Didn't dare! You say I didn't dare!

HEDDA.   No, I don't say it—but that's how Judge Brack looks at it.

LØVBORG.   Well, let him.

HEDDA.   So you're not going with them?

LØVBORG.   No, I'm staying here with you and Thea.

THEA.   Yes, Hedda, of course, he is.

HEDDA. [*Smiles and nods approvingly to* LØVBORG.]   There, you see! Firm as a rock. Faithful to all good principles now and for ever. That's how a man should be. [*Turns to* MRS. ELVSTED *and says with a caress.*] What did I tell you this morning, Thea? Didn't I tell you not to be upset?

LØVBORG. [*Amazed.*]   Upset?

THEA. [*Terrified.*]   Hedda——! *Please*, Hedda!

HEDDA.   You see? Now are you convinced? You haven't the slightest reason to be so anxious and worried. . . . There! Now we can all three enjoy ourselves.

LØVBORG. [*With a start.*]   What does all this mean, Mrs. Tesman?

THEA.   Oh God! What are you doing, Hedda?

HEDDA.   Be careful! That horrid Judge is watching you.

LØVBORG.   So you were anxious and worried on my account?

THEA. [*Softly, miserably.*]   Oh, Hedda, you've ruined everything.

LØVBORG. [*Looks at her intently for a moment. His face is distorted.*]   Well, my comrade! So that's all your faith amounts to!

THEA. [*Imploringly.*]   You *must* listen to me, Eilert——

LØVBORG. [*Takes one of the glasses of punch, raises it, and says in a low, hoarse voice.*]   Your health, Thea! [*He empties the glass, puts it down, and takes the second one.*]

THEA. [*Softly.*]   Hedda, Hedda, how could you do this?

HEDDA.   I do it? Are you crazy?

LØVBORG.   And your health, too, Mrs. Tesman. Thanks for the truth. Long live the truth! [*He empties the glass and is about to fill it again.*]

HEDDA. [*Lays her hand on his arm.*]   There, there! No more for the present. You're going to the party, remember.

LØVBORG. [*Putting down the glass.*]   Now, Thea, be honest with me.

THEA.   Yes?

LØVBORG.   Did your husband know you came after me?

THEA. [*Wringing her hands.*]   Eilert! . . .

LØVBORG.   It was arranged between you, wasn't it, that you should come to town and keep an eye on me. I dare say the old man suggested it himself. No doubt he needed my help in the office. Or perhaps it was at the card table he missed me.

THEA. [*Softly, in great distress.*]   Eilert! Eilert!

LØVBORG. [*Seizes the glass and is about to fill it.*]   Let's drink to the old sheriff, too!

HEDDA. [*Preventing him.*]   No more now. Remember you're going to read your manuscript to George.

LØVBORG. [*Calmly, putting down the glass.*]   I'm behaving like a fool, Thea. Try and forgive me, my dear, dear comrade. You'll see—I'll prove to you—I'll prove to everyone, that I'm all right again. I'm back on my feet. Thanks to you, Thea.

THEA. [*Radiant.*]   Oh, thank God!

[*In the meantime* BRACK *has looked at his watch. He and* TESMAN *rise and come into the drawing-room.*]

BRACK. [*Takes up his hat and overcoat.*] Well, Mrs. Tesman, it's time to go.

HEDDA. I suppose it is, Judge.

LØVBORG. [*Rising.*] I've decided to join you, Judge.

THEA. [*Softly, imploringly.*] Oh, Løvborg, don't!

HEDDA. [*Pinching her arm.*] Sh! They'll hear you.

LØVBORG. [*To* BRACK.] Since you were kind enough to invite me.

BRACK. You've changed your mind?

LØVBORG. Yes, if you don't mind.

BRACK. I'm delighted.

LØVBORG. [*Putting the manuscript in his pocket, to* TESMAN.] I should like to show you one or two things before the manuscript goes to press.

TESMAN. Just think, how delightful! But, Hedda, dear, in that case, how is Mrs. Elvsted to get home?

HEDDA. Oh, we shall manage, somehow.

LØVBORG. [*Looking towards the ladies.*] Mrs. Elvsted? Of course, I'll come back and fetch her. [*Comes nearer.*] Around ten o'clock, Mrs. Tesman. Will that do?

HEDDA. That will be splendid, Mr. Løvborg.

TESMAN. Well, then that's settled. But you mustn't expect me so early, Hedda.

HEDDA. Oh, you can stay as long as you like, George.

THEA. [*With suppressed anxiety.*] Well, then, Mr. Løvborg, I'll wait here till you come.

LØVBORG. [*With his hat in his hand.*] That's understood, Mrs. Elvsted.

BRACK. Well, gentlemen, shall we start? I hope we're going to have a very jolly time, as a certain fair lady puts it.

HEDDA. If only the fair lady could be there, unseen, Judge.

BRACK. Why unseen?

HEDDA. So as to share a little in your unbridled fun.

BRACK. [*Laughs.*] I shouldn't advise the fair lady to try it.

TESMAN. [*Also laughing.*] Come. You're a nice one, Hedda. Think of that!

BRACK. Well, good-bye. Good-bye, ladies!

LØVBORG. [*Bowing.*] About ten o'clock then.

HEDDA. Yes, Mr. Løvborg!

[BRACK, LØVBORG, *and* TESMAN *go out by the hall door. Simultaneously,* BERTA *comes in from the inner room with a lighted lamp which she puts on the drawing-room table; she goes out again through the inner room.*]

THEA. [*Who has risen and paces restlessly about the room.*] Hedda, what will come of all this!

HEDDA. At ten o'clock he will be here, with vine leaves in his hair. Flushed and fearless.

THEA.   If I could only believe that——

HEDDA.   And then, you see, he will have regained confidence in himself. He'll be a free man for ever and ever.

THEA.   Pray God you may be right.

HEDDA.   I am right! It will be as I say. [*Rises and approaches her.*] Doubt him as much as you like. I believe in him. Now we shall see——

THEA.   You have some hidden reason for all this, Hedda.

HEDDA.   Yes, I have. For once in my life I want the power to shape a human destiny.

THEA.   But surely, you have that?

HEDDA.   I haven't. I never have had.

THEA.   But what about your husband?

HEDDA.   Do you think he's worth bothering about! If you could only understand how poor I am; and that you should be allowed to be so rich!—[*She flings her arms round her passionately.*] I think I shall have to burn your hair off, after all!

THEA.   Let me go! Let me go! I'm afraid of you, Hedda!

BERTA. [*At the centre opening.*]   Supper's ready, ma'am.

HEDDA.   Very well, we're coming.

THEA.   No, no! I'd rather go home alone. Now—at once!

HEDDA.   Nonsense! You'll do nothing of the sort, you silly little thing. You'll have some supper and a nice cup of tea and then at ten o'clock Eilert Løvborg will be here with vine leaves in his hair——

[*She almost drags* MRS. ELVSTED *towards the centre opening.*]

End of Act Two

Act Three

SCENE: *The room at the Tesmans'. The portières of the centre opening are closed as well as the curtains of the glass-door. The shaded lamp on the table is turned low. In the stove, of which the door stands open, there has been a fire which is now nearly burnt out.*

MRS. ELVSTED, *wrapped in a large shawl, reclines in the armchair close to the stove with her feet on a footstool.* HEDDA *lies asleep on the sofa, covered with a rug.*

THEA. [*After a pause, suddenly straightens up in her chair and listens eagerly. Then she sinks back wearily and says softly and plaintively.*]   Not yet—Oh God!—Oh God!—Not yet——

[BERTA *slips cautiously in by the hall door. She has a letter in her hand.*]

THEA. [*Turns and whispers eagerly.*]   Did someone come?

BERTA. [*Softly.*]   A girl just brought this letter, ma'am.

THEA. [*Quickly, stretching out her hand.*]   A letter! Give it to me!

BERTA.   It's for Dr. Tesman, ma'am.

THEA. Oh.

BERTA. Miss Tesman's maid brought it. I'll just put it on the table.

THEA. Yes, do.

BERTA. [*Puts down the letter.*] I think I'd better put out the lamp, ma'am.

THEA. You might as well—it must be nearly daylight.

BERTA. [*Puts out the lamp.*] It *is* daylight, ma'am.

THEA. So it is! Broad daylight—and no one's come home yet!

BERTA. Lord bless you, ma'am—I thought something like this would happen.

THEA. You did?

BERTA. Yes—when I saw them go off with a—certain gentleman, last night —we used to hear plenty about him in the old days.

THEA. Sh! Not so loud! You'll wake Mrs. Tesman——

BERTA. [*Looks towards the sofa and sighs.*] Yes, you're right—let her sleep, poor thing. Shall I make up the fire, ma'am?

THEA. Thank you—you needn't trouble——

BERTA. Very well, ma'am. [*She goes out softly by the hall door.*]

HEDDA. [*Wakes at the closing of the door and looks up.*] What—what was that?

THEA. It was just the maid——

HEDDA. [*Looks round her.*] What are we doing in here? Oh yes! Now I remember! [*She sits up on the sofa, stretches herself, and rubs her eyes.*] What's the time, Thea?

THEA. [*Looks at her watch.*] It's past seven.

HEDDA. When did George get home?

THEA. He hasn't come.

HEDDA. Not home yet?

THEA. [*Rising.*] No one has come.

HEDDA. And we were fools enough to sit up half the night—watching and waiting!

THEA. [*Wringing her hands.*] And waiting in such terrible anxiety!

HEDDA. [*Yawns, and says with her hand in front of her mouth.*] Well—we might have spared ourselves the trouble.

THEA. Did you manage to get a little sleep?

HEDDA. Yes, I believe I slept quite well—didn't you?

THEA. I couldn't, Hedda—I couldn't possibly!

HEDDA. [*Rises and goes towards her.*] There, there! There's nothing to worry about! It's easy to see what's happened.

THEA. What—tell me!

HEDDA. Brack's party probably dragged on for hours——

THEA. I expect that's true, but still——

HEDDA. —and probably Tesman didn't want to come home and wake me up in the middle of the night—perhaps he was in no condition to show himself, after the famous party.

THEA. But where could he have gone?

HEDDA. To his aunts', of course!——I expect he went there to sleep it off. They always keep his old room ready for him.

THEA. No, he can't be there. That letter just came for him, from Miss Tesman.

HEDDA. Letter? [*Looks at the address.*] Oh yes! It's from Aunt Julia. Well—then I suppose he stayed at Judge Brack's. As for Eilert Løvborg—he is sitting with vine leaves in his hair, reading his manuscript.

THEA. You're talking nonsense, Hedda! You know you don't believe a word of it——

HEDDA. What a little ninny you are, Thea!

THEA. Yes, I'm afraid I am——

HEDDA. And how dreadfully tired you look!

THEA. I am—dreadfully tired.

HEDDA. Now you do exactly as I tell you! You go into my room—lie down on the bed—and get a little rest.

THEA. No, no!—I'd never be able to sleep.

HEDDA. Of course you would.

THEA. Besides, your husband should be back soon; I must find out at once——

HEDDA. I'll tell you the moment he arrives——

THEA. You promise, Hedda?

HEDDA. Yes—you can count on me—Go on in now, and have a good sleep.

THEA. Thanks—I will try. [*She goes out through the inner room.*]

[HEDDA *goes to the glass-door and opens the curtains. Bright daylight streams into the room. She takes a small mirror from the writing-table, looks at herself in it, and tidies her hair. Then she goes to the hall door and rings the bell. A few moments later* BERTA *appears at the hall door.*]

BERTA. Did you ring, ma'am?

HEDDA. Yes—do something to the fire—I'm absolutely frozen.

BERTA. Certainly, ma'am—I'll make it up at once. [*She rakes the embers together and puts on a piece of wood. She stops and listens.*] That was the front door, ma'am.

HEDDA. See who it is—I'll look after the fire.

BERTA. It'll soon burn up, ma'am.

[*She goes out by the hall door.* HEDDA *kneels on the footstool and puts several pieces of wood in the stove. After a short pause* GEORGE TESMAN *comes in from the hall. He looks tired and rather serious. He tiptoes up towards the centre opening and is about to slip through the curtains.*]

HEDDA. [*At the stove, without looking up.*] Good morning, George!

TESMAN. [*Turns.*] Hedda! [*Approaches her.*] Good heavens—are you up so early, eh?

HEDDA. Yes, I'm up very early today, George.

TESMAN. And I was sure you'd still be sound asleep—think of that, Hedda!

HEDDA. Sh! Don't talk so loud. You'll wake Mrs. Elvsted.

TESMAN. Did Mrs. Elvsted stay here all night?

HEDDA. Naturally—since no one came to call for her.

TESMAN. No—I suppose not——

HEDDA. [Closes the stove door and rises.] Well—did you enjoy yourselves?

TESMAN. Were you worried about me, Hedda, eh?

HEDDA. That would never occur to me—I asked if you'd enjoyed yourselves?

TESMAN. Yes, we really did, Hedda. Especially at first—you see, Eilert read me part of his book. We got there quite early, think of that—and Brack had all sorts of arrangements to make, so Eilert read to me.

HEDDA. [Sits to the right of table.] Yes?—Well?

TESMAN. [Sits on a stool near the stove.] Hedda, you can't conceive what a book it will be! I believe it's one of the most remarkable things that has ever been written. Think of that!

HEDDA. I'm really not very interested, George.

TESMAN. I've something to confess, Hedda—after he'd finished reading, I had such a horrid feeling——

HEDDA. A horrid feeling, George?

TESMAN. Yes. I felt quite jealous of Eilert, because he'd been able to write such a book. Just think, Hedda.

HEDDA. Yes, yes! I am thinking!

TESMAN. It's really appalling, that he with all his great gifts, should be so utterly incorrigible!

HEDDA. Because he has more daring than any of the rest of you?

TESMAN. It's not that, Hedda—he's utterly incapable of moderation.

HEDDA. Well—tell me what happened.

TESMAN. There's only one word to describe it, Hedda—it was an orgy!

HEDDA. Did he have vine leaves in his hair?

TESMAN. Vine leaves? No, I didn't see any vine leaves—but he made a long incoherent speech in honour of the woman who had inspired him in his work —that was the phrase he used.

HEDDA. Did he mention her name?

TESMAN. No, he didn't. But I can't help thinking he meant Mrs. Elvsted— just you see!

HEDDA. Where did you part?

TESMAN. When the party finally broke up—there were only a few of us left—so we came away together. Brack came with us too—he wanted a breath of fresh air; and then we decided we had better take Eilert home—he was in pretty bad shape, you see.

HEDDA. Yes, I dare say.

TESMAN. And then, the strangest thing happened, Hedda—the most tragic thing! I'm really almost ashamed to tell you about it—for Eilert's sake——

HEDDA.   Oh, do go on, George!

TESMAN.   Well—as we were nearing town, you see—I happened to drop a little behind the others—only for a minute or two—think of that!

HEDDA.   Yes, yes!—Well?

TESMAN.   And then, as I hurried after them, what do you think I found on the sidewalk, eh?

HEDDA.   How should I know?

TESMAN.   You mustn't say a word about it to anyone, Hedda—do you hear? Promise me—for Eilert's sake.

HEDDA.   Yes, George!

TESMAN.   [*Takes a parcel wrapped in paper from his pocket.*] Just think, dear—I found this.

HEDDA.   Isn't that the parcel he had with him yesterday?

TESMAN.   Yes. It's his precious, irreplaceable manuscript. He had lost it, and hadn't even noticed it. Isn't it tragic, Hedda, that——

HEDDA.   Why didn't you give it back to him at once?

TESMAN.   I didn't dare trust him with it, in the condition he was in.

HEDDA.   Did you tell any of the others you'd found it?

TESMAN.   Certainly not! I didn't want them to know—for Eilert's sake, you see.

HEDDA.   Then no one knows that Eilert Løvborg's manuscript is in your possession?

TESMAN.   No—and no one must know it.

HEDDA.   What did you say to him afterwards?

TESMAN.   I didn't get a chance to talk to him again; he and two or three of the others gave us the slip and disappeared—think of that!

HEDDA.   I suppose they took him home then.

TESMAN.   Yes, I suppose they did—and Brack went home too.

HEDDA.   And where have you been gallivanting ever since?

TESMAN.   Someone suggested we should go back to his house and have an early breakfast there—or perhaps it should be called a late supper—eh? And now—as soon as I have had a little rest and poor Eilert has had a chance to recover himself a bit—I must take this back to him.

HEDDA.   [*Stretching out her hand for the parcel.*]   No, George—don't give it back to him—not right away, I mean. Let me read it first.

TESMAN.   No, dearest Hedda, I daren't do that. I really dare not.

HEDDA.   You dare not, George?

TESMAN.   Think of the state he'll be in when he wakes up and can't find his manuscript! There's no copy of it, Hedda—think of that! He told me so himself.

HEDDA.   [*Looks at him searchingly.*]   Tell me, George—would it be quite impossible to write such a thing over again?

TESMAN.   Oh, I should think so, Hedda. You see, it's the inspiration. . . .

HEDDA. Yes, of course—the inspiration. . . . I suppose it depends on that. [*Lightly.*] By the way, George, here's a letter for you.

TESMAN. Just think——

HEDDA. [*Hands it to him.*] It came just a little while ago.

TESMAN. It's from Aunt Julia, Hedda! What can it be? [*He puts the parcel down on the other stool, opens the letter, glances through it, and jumps up.*] Oh, Hedda—she says Aunt Rina is dying, poor thing.

HEDDA. Well—we were expecting that.

TESMAN. And that I must hurry, if I want to see her again—I'll just run over and see them at once.

HEDDA. [*Suppressing a smile.*] Will you run, George?

TESMAN. Oh, my dearest Hedda—if you could only bring yourself to come with me! Just think!

HEDDA. [*Rising. Rejects the idea wearily.*] No, no! Don't ask me to do that! I'll have nothing to do with sickness or death. I loathe anything ugly.

TESMAN. Well then, in that case—— [*Rushing about.*] My hat?—My over-coat?—Oh, in the hall. I do hope I won't be too late, Hedda—eh?

HEDDA. Well, after all—if you run, George——! [BERTA *enters by the hall door.*]

BERTA. Judge Brack is here, sir—and wishes to know if you'll see him?

TESMAN. At this hour? No, no! I can't possibly——

HEDDA. But I'll see him. [*To* BERTA.] Ask him to come in, Berta. [BERTA *goes.*] [*Rapidly, in a whisper.*] George!—the manuscript! [*She snatches it up from the stool.*]

TESMAN. Yes, give it to me!

HEDDA. No, no. I'll keep it here till you come back.

[*She goes over to the writing-table and puts it in the bookcase.* TESMAN *in a frenzy of haste can't get his gloves on.* BRACK *enters from the hall.*]

HEDDA. [*Nodding to him.*] You're certainly an early bird, Judge.

BRACK. I am, aren't I? [*To* TESMAN.] Where are you off to in such a hurry?

TESMAN. I must rush off to my aunts'. Just think, Aunt Rina is dying, poor thing.

BRACK. Dear me, is she? Then don't let me detain you; every moment may be precious.

TESMAN. Yes, I really must run—good-bye, good-bye, Hedda—— [*He rushes out by the hall door.*]

HEDDA. [*Approaching* BRACK.] I hear the party was more than usually jolly last night, Judge.

BRACK. Yes, I've been up all night—haven't even changed my clothes.

HEDDA. So I see——

BRACK. What has Tesman told you of last night's adventures?

HEDDA. Oh, nothing much; some dreary tale about going to someone's house and having breakfast.

BRACK. Yes, I've heard about that breakfast party—but Eilert Løvborg wasn't with them, was he?

HEDDA. No—he'd been escorted home.

BRACK. By Tesman, you mean?

HEDDA. No—by some of the others.

BRACK. [*Smiling.*] George Tesman is certainly a naïve creature, Mrs. Hedda.

HEDDA. Yes, God knows he is! But, you're very mysterious—what else happened last night?

BRACK. Oh, a number of things——

HEDDA. Do sit down, Judge, and tell me all about it! [*She sits to the left of the table.* BRACK *sits near her, at the long side of the table.*]—— Well?

BRACK. I had special reasons for keeping an eye on my guests—or rather some of my guests—last night.

HEDDA. One of them being Eilert Løvborg, I suppose.

BRACK. Frankly—yes.

HEDDA. This sounds quite thrilling, Judge!

BRACK. Do you know where he and some of the others spent the rest of the night?

HEDDA. No. Do tell me—if it's not quite unmentionable!

BRACK. No. It's by no means unmentionable. Well—they turned up at an extremely gay party.

HEDDA. A *very* jolly party, Judge?

BRACK. An excessively jolly one!

HEDDA. Do go on!

BRACK. Løvborg, as well as the others, had been invited some time ago. I knew all about it. But he had refused the invitation, for he had become a reformed character, as you know——

HEDDA. At the Elvsteds', yes. But he went all the same?

BRACK. Well, you see, Mrs. Hedda, he became somewhat inspired at my place last night——

HEDDA. Yes. I heard he was . . . inspired.

BRACK. Rather violently inspired, in fact—and so, he changed his mind. We men are not always as high-principled as perhaps we should be.

HEDDA. I'm sure you are an exception, Judge. But to get back to Eilert Løvborg——

BRACK. So—to make a long story short—he did finally turn up at Mlle. Diana's residence.

HEDDA. Mlle. Diana?

BRACK. Yes, it was she who was giving the party—to a very select circle of her friends and admirers.

HEDDA. Is she that red-haired woman?

BRACK. Precisely.

HEDDA. A sort of . . . singer?

BRACK. Yes—in her leisure moments. She is also a mighty huntress—of men. You must have heard of her, Mrs. Hedda. In the days of his glory Eilert Løvborg was one of her most enthusiastic protectors.

HEDDA. But how did all this end, Judge?

BRACK. In a none-too-friendly fashion, it seems. After greeting him most tenderly, Mlle. Diana finally proceeded to tear his hair out!

HEDDA. What?—Løvborg's?

BRACK. Yes. It seems he accused her, or her friends, of having robbed him. He kept insisting some valuable notebook had disappeared—as well as various other things. In short, he raised quite a terrific row.

HEDDA. What did all this lead to?

BRACK. It lead to a general free-for-all, in which the women as well as the men took part. Fortunately the police at last appeared on the scene.

HEDDA. The police?

BRACK. Yes. I'm afraid it may prove an expensive amusement for Eilert Løvborg—crazy lunatic that he is!

HEDDA. How?

BRACK. They say he made a violent resistance—half-killed one policeman, and tore another one's coat off his back. So they marched him off to the police station.

HEDDA. Where did you hear all this?

BRACK. From the police themselves.

HEDDA. [Gazing straight before her.] So that's what happened! Then, after all, he had no vine leaves in his hair!

BRACK. Vine leaves, Mrs. Hedda?

HEDDA. [With a change of tone.] Tell me, Judge—why should you be so interested in spying on Løvborg in this way?

BRACK. In the first place—I am not entirely indifferent to the fact that during the investigation it will be known that he came directly from my house.

HEDDA. You mean, the case will go to court?

BRACK. Naturally. However—be that as it may. But I felt it my duty, as a friend of the family, to give you and Tesman a full account of his nocturnal exploits.

HEDDA. For what reason, Judge?

BRACK. Because I have a shrewd suspicion that he means to use you as a sort of . . . screen.

HEDDA. Whatever makes you think that?

BRACK. After all—we're not completely blind, Mrs. Hedda. You watch! This Mrs. Elvsted—she'll be in no great hurry to leave town.

HEDDA. Well—supposing there were something between them—there must be plenty of other places where they could meet.

BRACK. Not a single home. From now on, every respectable house will be closed to Eilert Løvborg.

HEDDA. And mine ought to be too, you mean?

BRACK. Yes. I admit it would be more than painful to me if he should be welcome here. If this undesirable and superfluous person should be allowed to force his way into the——

HEDDA.   —the Triangle?

BRACK.   Precisely. It would simply mean that I should find myself homeless.

HEDDA.   [*Looks at him with a smile.*]   I see. So you want to be Cock-of-the-walk, Judge. That is your aim.

BRACK.   [*Nods slowly and speaks in a low voice.*]   Yes—that is my aim; and for that I will fight with every weapon I can command.

HEDDA.   [*Her smile vanishing.*]   I wonder, Judge, now one comes to think of it, if you're not rather a dangerous person.

BRACK.   Do you think so?

HEDDA.   I'm beginning to think so. And I'm exceedingly glad that you have no sort of hold over me.

BRACK.   [*Laughs ambiguously.*]   Well, well, Mrs. Hedda—perhaps you're right. If I had, who knows what I might be capable of.

HEDDA.   Come now! Come, Judge! That sounds almost like a threat.

BRACK.   [*Rising.*]   Not at all! For the Triangle, it seems to me, ought, if possible, to be based on mutual understanding.

HEDDA.   There I entirely agree with you.

BRACK.   Well—now I've said all I had to say—I'd better be off. Good-bye, Mrs. Hedda [*Crossing towards the glass-door.*]

HEDDA.   [*Rising.*]   Are you going through the garden, Judge?

BRACK.   Yes, it's a short cut for me.

HEDDA.   Yes—and then it's the back way, isn't it?

BRACK.   Very true; I've no objection to back ways. They are rather intriguing at times.

HEDDA.   When there's shooting going on, you mean?

BRACK.   [*At the glass-door, laughingly.*]   People don't shoot their tame poultry, I fancy.

HEDDA.   [*Also laughing.*]   And certainly not the Cock-of-the-walk, Judge! Good-bye!——

[*They exchange laughing nods of farewell. He goes. She closes the glass-door after him.* HEDDA, *now serious, stands looking out. She goes up and peeps through the portières into the inner room. Then goes to the writing-table, takes* LØVBORG's *parcel from the bookcase, and is about to examine it.* BERTA *is heard speaking loudly in the hall.* HEDDA *turns and listens. She hurriedly locks the parcel in the drawer and puts the key on the inkstand.* EILERT LØV-BORG, *wearing his overcoat and carrying his hat in his hand, tears open the hall door. He looks somewhat confused and excited.*]

LØVBORG.   [*Turns towards the hall.*]   I will go in, I tell you! [*He closes the door, turns, sees* HEDDA, *at once controls himself and bows.*]

HEDDA.   [*At the writing-table.*]   Well, Mr. Løvborg! Isn't it rather late to call for Thea?

LØVBORG.   And rather early to call on you—forgive me.

HEDDA.   How do you know Thea's still here?

LØVBORG.   They told me at her lodgings, she'd been out all night.

HEDDA. [*Goes to the table.*]   Did you notice anything odd in their manner when they told you that?

LØVBORG. [*Looks at her inquiringly.*]   Anything odd?

HEDDA.   Didn't they seem to think it—a little—queer?

LØVBORG. [*Suddenly understanding.*]   Oh, of course! I see what you mean. I suppose I'm dragging her down with me—— However, I didn't notice anything. I suppose Tesman isn't up yet?

HEDDA.   No—I don't think so——

LØVBORG.   When did he get home?

HEDDA.   Oh, very late.

LØVBORG.   Did he tell you anything?

HEDDA.   He just said it had all been very jolly at Judge Brack's.

LØVBORG.   Nothing else?

HEDDA.   No, I don't believe so. In any case, I was so dreadfully sleepy——

[MRS. ELVSTED *comes in through the portières from the inner room. She goes to him.*]

THEA.   Eilert! At last!

LØVBORG.   Yes—at last—and too late!

THEA. [*Looks at him anxiously.*]   What is too late?

LØVBORG.   Everything's too late now—it's all up with me.

THEA.   No, no! You mustn't say that!

LØVBORG.   You'll say the same when you hear——

THEA.   I don't want to hear anything!

HEDDA.   Perhaps you'd rather talk to her alone? I'll leave you.

LØVBORG.   No! Stay, please—I beg of you!

THEA.   But I don't want to hear anything, I tell you.

LØVBORG.   I don't intend to talk about last night, Thea——

THEA.   No?

LØVBORG.   No. I just want to tell you that now we must part.

THEA.   Part?

HEDDA. [*Involuntarily.*]   I knew it!

LØVBORG.   I no longer have any use for you, Thea.

THEA.   How can you say that! No more use for me? You'll let me go on helping you—we'll go on working together, Eilert?

LØVBORG.   I shall do no more work, from now on.

THEA. [*Despairingly.*]   Then, what shall I have to live for?

LØVBORG.   You must try and live as though you'd never known me.

THEA.   But you know I can't do that!

LØVBORG.   You must try, Thea. You must go home again.

THEA. [*Protesting vehemently.*]   Never! I won't leave you! I won't allow you to drive me away. We must be together when the book appears.

HEDDA. [*Whispers, in suspense.*]   Ah yes—the book!

LØVBORG. [*Looks at her.*]   My book and Thea's—for that's what it is.

THEA.   Yes—that's true; I feel that. That's why we must be together when it's published. I want to see you showered with praise and honours—and, the joy! I want to share that with you too!

LØVBORG.   Our book will not be published, Thea.

THEA.   Not published?

LØVBORG.   No. It never can be.

THEA.   [*Anxiously, with foreboding.*]   Løvborg—what have you done with the manuscript?

HEDDA.   [*Watches him intently.*]   Yes—the manuscript?

THEA.   Where is it?

LØVBORG.   Thea! Don't ask me about it!

THEA.   Yes—I must know—I have a right to know.

LØVBORG.   Very well, then!—I've torn it into a thousand pieces!

THEA.   [*Cries out.*]   No—no!

HEDDA.   [*Involuntarily.*]   But that's not——

LØVBORG.   [*Looks at her.*]   Not true, you think?

HEDDA.   [*Controlling herself.*]   Of course it must be—if you say so! But it sounds so utterly incredible!

LØVBORG.   It's true all the same.

THEA.   [*Wringing her hands.*]   Torn his own work to pieces!—Oh, God, Hedda.

LØVBORG.   I've torn my life to pieces—why shouldn't I tear up my work as well!

THEA.   And you did this last night?

LØVBORG.   Yes. I tore it into a thousand pieces. I scattered them far out on the fjord. I watch them drift on the cool sea-water—drift with the current and the wind. In a little while they'll sink, deeper and deeper—just as I shall, Thea.

THEA.   Løvborg—this thing you've done to the book—it's as though you'd killed a little child.

LØVBORG.   You're right—it was child-murder.

THEA.   Then—how could you?—it was my child too.

HEDDA.   [*Almost inaudibly.*]   The child——

THEA.   [*Breathes heavily.*]   It's all over then—I'll go now, Hedda.

HEDDA.   But you won't be leaving town?

THEA.   I don't know what I'll do—there's nothing but darkness before me. [*She goes out by the hall door.*]

HEDDA.   [*Stands waiting a moment.*]   Then—you're not going to see her home, Mr. Løvborg?

LØVBORG.   I?—— Do you want people to see her with *me*?

HEDDA.   Of course, I don't know what else may have happened last night— but is it so utterly irreparable?

LØVBORG.   It won't end with last night—I know that only too well; and the trouble is, that kind of life no longer appeals to me. I have no heart to start it again—she's somehow broken my courage—my defiant spirit!

HEDDA. [*Gazes before her.*] To think that that pretty little fool should have influenced a man's destiny! [*Looks at him.*] Still, I don't see how you could be so heartless.

LØVBORG. Don't say that!

HEDDA. What do you expect me to say! You've destroyed her whole purpose in life—isn't that being heartless?

LØVBORG. Hedda—to you I can tell the truth.

HEDDA. The truth?

LØVBORG. First, promise me—give me your word—that Thea will never know.

HEDDA. I give you my word.

LØVBORG. Good. There was no truth in what I said just now——

HEDDA. You mean—about the manuscript?

LØVBORG. Yes. I didn't tear it to pieces or scatter it on the fjord——

HEDDA. Where is it then?

LØVBORG. But I have destroyed it, Hedda—utterly destroyed it!

HEDDA. I don't understand.

LØVBORG. Just now, Thea said I had killed our child——

HEDDA. Yes—so she did——

LØVBORG. One can do worse things to a child than kill it—I wanted to spare Thea the truth——

HEDDA. What do you mean?

LØVBORG. I couldn't bring myself to tell her; I couldn't say to her: Thea, I spent last night in a frenzy of drinking—I took our child with me, dragged it round with me to all sorts of obscene and loathsome places—and I lost our child—lost it! God only knows what's become of it—or who's got hold of it!

HEDDA. But, when you come right down to it, this was only a book——

LØVBORG. Thea's pure soul was in that book.

HEDDA. Yes—so I understand.

LØVBORG. Then you must also understand why no future is possible for us.

HEDDA. What will you do now?

LØVBORG. Nothing. I want to make an end of it. The sooner the better.

HEDDA. [*Takes a step towards him.*] If you do make an end of it, Eilert Løvborg—let it be beautiful!

LØVBORG. [*Smiles.*] Beautiful! Shall I put vine leaves in my hair, as you wanted me to in the old days?

HEDDA. No—I don't believe in vine leaves any more. But—for once—let it be beautiful! Good-bye—you must go now—you mustn't come here any more.

LØVBORG. Good-bye, Mrs. Tesman. Remember me to George Tesman. [*He's on the point of going.*]

HEDDA. No, wait!—I want you to take something of mine with you—as a token——

[*She goes to the writing-table, opens the drawer, and the pistol-case. Goes back to* LØVBORG, *carrying one of the pistols.*]

LØVBORG. [*Looks at her.*]   This? Is this the token?

HEDDA. [*Nods slowly.*]   Do you remember it? It was aimed at you once.

LØVBORG.   You should have used it then.

HEDDA.   Take it—Use it now!

LØVBORG. [*Puts the pistol in his inner pocket.*]   Thanks.

HEDDA.   But let it be—beautiful, Eilert Løvborg! Promise me that!

LØVBORG.   Good-bye, Hedda Gabler.

[*He goes out by the hall door.* HEDDA *listens at the door a moment. Then she goes to the writing-table and takes out the parcel with the manuscript, peeps inside the cover, half takes out a few sheets of paper and looks at them. Then she takes the parcel over to the armchair by the stove and sits down. She has the parcel in her lap. In a moment she opens the stove door, then opens the parcel.*]

HEDDA. [*She throws part of the manuscript in the fire and whispers to herself.*] Your child, Thea—your child and Eilert Løvborg's. Darling little Thea, with the curly golden hair. [*Throws more of the manuscript into the stove.*] I'm burning your child, Thea. [*Throws in the rest of the manuscript.*] I'm burning it—burning it——

Curtain

Act Four

SCENE: *The same room at the* TESMAN'S. *It is evening. The drawing-room is dark. In the inner room the hanging lamp over the table is lighted. The curtains are drawn over the glass-doors.* HEDDA, *dressed in black, paces back and forth in the dark room. Then she goes up into the inner room and off left. A few chords are heard on the piano. She appears again and returns to the drawing-room.* BERTA *enters from the right, through the inner room, carrying a lighted lamp which she puts down on the table by the corner sofa in the drawing-room. Her eyes are red with weeping and she has black ribbons on her cap. She goes out right, quietly and circumspectly.* HEDDA *goes to the glass-door, pulls the curtains aside a little, and peers out into the darkness. After a moment* MISS TESMAN *comes in from the hall. She is in mourning and wears a hat and veil.* HEDDA *goes towards her and holds out her hand.*]

MISS TESMAN.   Well, Hedda, here I am, all dressed in black! My poor sister has found rest at last!

HEDDA.   As you see, I have heard already. Tesman sent me a note.

MISS TESMAN.   He promised he would. I wish Rina hadn't left us just now—this is not the time for Hedda's house to be a house of mourning.

HEDDA. [*Changing the subject.*]   It is good to know she died peacefully, Miss Tesman.

MISS TESMAN. Yes, her end was so calm, so beautiful. And thank heaven, she had the joy of seeing George once more—and bidding him good-bye.—He is not home yet?

HEDDA. No. He wrote me he might be detained. But do sit down, Miss Tesman.

MISS TESMAN. No, thank you, my dearest Hedda. I should like nothing better, but I have so much to do. I must prepare my darling sister for her burial. She must look her very sweetest when they carry her to her grave.

HEDDA. Can I do anything to help?

MISS TESMAN. Oh, no, you mustn't think of that! This is no time for Hedda Tesman to take part in such sad work. Nor let her thoughts dwell on it either——

HEDDA. H'm—one's thoughts——!

MISS TESMAN. [*Continuing the theme.*] How strange life is! At home we shall be sewing a shroud; and soon I expect there will be sewing here, too—but of a different kind, thank God!

[GEORGE TESMAN *enters by the hall door.*]

HEDDA. Well! Here you are at last!

TESMAN. You here, Aunt Julia? With Hedda? Think of that!

MISS TESMAN. I am just going, my dear boy. Did you get everything done?

TESMAN. I'm afraid I forgot half of it. I'll have to run over and see you in the morning. Today my brain's in a whirl! I can't keep my thoughts together.

MISS TESMAN. But, my dear George, you mustn't take it so much to heart.

TESMAN. How do you mean?

MISS TESMAN. We must be glad for her sake—glad that she has found rest at last.

TESMAN. Oh yes, of course—you are thinking of Aunt Rina.

HEDDA. I'm afraid it will be very lonely for you now, Miss Tesman.

MISS TESMAN. It will be at first—but I won't let poor Rina's room stay empty for long.

TESMAN. Really? Who will you put in it—eh?

MISS TESMAN. One can always find some poor invalid who needs to be taken care of.

HEDDA. Would you really take such a burden on yourself again?

MISS TESMAN. A burden? Heaven forgive you, child, it has been no burden to me.

HEDDA. But it's different with a stranger!

MISS TESMAN. I simply must have someone to live for—and one soon makes friends with sick folks; and perhaps some day there may be something in this house to keep an old aunt busy.

HEDDA. Oh, please don't trouble about us!

TESMAN. Just think! What a wonderful time we three might have together if——

HEDDA. If——?

TESMAN. [*Uneasy.*]   Nothing. Let's hope things will work out for the best—eh?

MISS TESMAN.   Well, well, I daresay you two want to have a little talk. [*Smiling.*] And perhaps Hedda may have something to tell you, George. Good-bye! I must go home to poor Rina. [*Turning at the door.*] How strange it is to think that now Rina is with my poor brother, as well as with me.

TESMAN.   Yes, think of that, Aunt Julia! Eh?

[MISS TESMAN *goes out by the hall door.*]

HEDDA. [HEDDA *gives* TESMAN *a cold, searching look.*]   Aunt Rina's death seems to affect you more than it does Aunt Julia.

TESMAN.   Oh, it's not that alone. It's Eilert I am so terribly upset about.

HEDDA. [*Quickly.*]   Have you heard anything new?

TESMAN.   I called on him this afternoon. I wanted to tell him the manuscript was safe.

HEDDA.   Did you see him?

TESMAN.   No, he wasn't home. But later, I met Mrs. Elvsted and she said he had been here, early this morning.

HEDDA.   Yes, directly after you had left.

TESMAN.   And he said that he had torn his manuscript to pieces, eh?

HEDDA.   That is what he said.

TESMAN.   Good heavens, he must have gone completely mad! I suppose in that case you didn't dare give it back to him, Hedda.

HEDDA.   No, he didn't get it.

TESMAN.   But of course you told him that we had it?

HEDDA.   No. Did you tell Mrs. Elvsted?

TESMAN.   No, I thought I had better not. But you ought to have told him. Just think—he might do himself some injury. Give me the manuscript. I'll run over with it at once. Where is it, Hedda? Eh?

HEDDA. [*Cold and motionless, leaning against the armchair.*]   I haven't got it any longer.

TESMAN.   Haven't got it? What in the world do you mean?

HEDDA.   I've burnt it—every word of it.

TESMAN. [*Starts up in terror.*]   Burnt! Burnt Eilert's manuscript!

HEDDA.   Don't shout so loud. The servant might hear you.

TESMAN.   Burnt! Why, good God——! No, no, no! It's utterly impossible!

HEDDA.   It's true, all the same.

TESMAN.   Do you realize what you have done, Hedda? It is unlawful appropriation of lost property. Think of that! Just ask Judge Brack, he will tell you what that means.

HEDDA.   It would be wiser not to speak of it—either to Judge Brack or to anyone else.

TESMAN.   But how could you do anything so unheard of? What put it into your head? What possessed you? Do answer me——

HEDDA. [*Suppressing a scarcely perceptible smile.*] I did it for your sake, George!

TESMAN. For my sake!

HEDDA. This morning when you told me that he had read it to you——

TESMAN. Yes, yes—what then?

HEDDA. You admitted that you were jealous of his work.

TESMAN. Of course, I didn't mean that literally.

HEDDA. All the same—I could not bear the thought of anyone putting you in the shade.

TESMAN. [*In an outburst of mingled doubt and joy.*] Hedda? Is this true? But—but—I have never known you to show your love like that before. Think of that!

HEDDA. Then—perhaps I'd better tell you that—just now—at this time—— [*Violently breaking off.*] No, no; ask Aunt Julia. She will tell you all about it.

TESMAN. Oh, I almost think I understand, Hedda. [*Clasping his hands together.*] Great heavens! Do you really mean it, eh?

HEDDA. Don't shout so loud. The servants will hear——

TESMAN. [*Laughing with irrepressible joy.*] The servants——? Why how absurd you are, Hedda! It is only my dear old Berta! Why, I'll run out and tell her myself!

HEDDA. [*Clenching her hands in despair.*] Oh God, I shall die—I shall die of all this——!

TESMAN. Of what, Hedda? What is it? Eh?

HEDDA. [*Coldly, controlling herself.*] It's all so ludicrous—George!

TESMAN. Ludicrous! That I should be overjoyed at the news? Still, after all, perhaps I had better not tell Berta.

HEDDA. Why not that—with all the rest?

TESMAN. No, no I won't tell her yet. But I must certainly tell Aunt Julia. Oh, she will be so happy—so happy!

HEDDA. When she hears that I've burnt Eilert Løvborg's manuscript—for your sake?

TESMAN. No, of course not—nobody must know about the manuscript. But I will certainly tell her how dearly you love me, Hedda. She must share that joy with me. I wonder, now, whether this sort of thing is usual in young wives? Eh?

HEDDA. Why not ask Aunt Julia that, too?

TESMAN. I will, indeed, some time or other. [*Again agitated and concerned.*] But the manuscript. Good God!—the manuscript! I can't bear to think what poor Eilert will do now!

[MRS. ELVSTED, *dressed as on her first visit, wearing a hat and coat, comes in from the hall door.*]

THEA. [*She greets them hurriedly, and says in evident agitation.*] Hedda, dear—please forgive my coming back so soon.

HEDDA. What is it, Thea? What has happened?

TESMAN.   Is it something to do with Eilert Løvborg, eh?

THEA.   Yes; I am terribly afraid he has met with some accident.

HEDDA. [*Seizes her arm.*]   Ah!—You think so?

TESMAN.   Why should you think that, Mrs. Elvsted?

THEA.   When I got back to my lodgings—I heard them talking about him. —There are all sorts of strange rumours——

TESMAN.   Yes, I've heard them too! And yet I can bear witness that he went straight home last night. Think of that!

HEDDA.   What sort of things did they say?

THEA.   Oh, I couldn't quite make it out. Either they knew nothing definite or—in any case, they stopped talking the moment I came in, and I didn't dare question them.

TESMAN. [*Moving about the room uneasily.*]   We must only hope you misunderstood them, Mrs. Elvsted.

THEA.   No, I am sure they were talking about him—they said something about a hospital or——

TESMAN.   Hospital?

HEDDA.   No, no! That's impossible!

THEA.   Oh, I am so terribly afraid for him. I finally went to his house to ask after him!

HEDDA.   You went there yourself, Thea?

THEA.   What else could I do? I couldn't bear the suspense any longer.

TESMAN.   But you didn't find him—eh?

THEA.   No. And the people there knew nothing about him. They said he hadn't been home since yesterday afternoon.

TESMAN.   Yesterday! just think—how could they say that?

THEA.   I am sure something terrible must have happened to him!

TESMAN.   Hedda, dear—supposing I run over and make some inquiries——?

HEDDA.   No, no! Please don't mix yourself up in this affair.

[JUDGE BRACK, *hat in hand, enters by the hall door which* BERTA *opens and closes behind him. He looks grave and bows silently.*]

TESMAN.   Oh, it's you, my dear Judge—eh?

BRACK.   Yes, it's imperative that I see you at once.

TESMAN.   I can see you have heard the news about Aunt Rina?

BRACK.   Yes, that among other things.

TESMAN.   Isn't it sad? Eh?

BRACK.   Well, my dear Tesman, that depends on how you look at it.

TESMAN. [*Looks at him doubtfully.*]   Has anything else happened?

BRACK.   Yes.

HEDDA. [*Intensely.*]   Anything sad, Judge?

BRACK.   That, too, depends on how you look at it, Mrs. Tesman.

THEA. [*In an involuntary outburst.*]   Oh! It's something about Eilert Løvborg!

BRACK. [*Glancing at her.*]   What makes you think that, Mrs. Elvsted? Perhaps you have already heard something——?

THEA. [*Confused.*]   No, no, nothing at all—but——

TESMAN.   Well, for heaven's sake, tell us. What is it?

BRACK. [*Shrugging his shoulders.*]   Well, I am sorry to say, Eilert Løvborg has been taken to the hospital—they say he is dying.

THEA. [*Cries out.*]   Oh God! God!

TESMAN.   To the hospital!! And dying——

HEDDA. [*Involuntarily.*]   So soon then——

THEA. [*Tearfully.*]   And we parted in anger, Hedda!

HEDDA. [*In a whisper.*]   Thea—Thea—be careful!

THEA. [*Not heeding her.*]   I must go to him! I must see him alive!

BRACK.   I'm afraid it is useless, Mrs. Elvsted. No one is allowed to see him.

THEA.   But at least tell me what happened to him? What is it?

TESMAN.   He didn't try to kill himself—eh?

HEDDA.   Yes—I am sure he did!

TESMAN.   Hedda, how can you——?

BRACK. [*Not taking his eyes off her.*]   Unfortunately, you have guessed quite correctly, Mrs. Tesman.

THEA.   Oh, how horrible!

TESMAN.   Killed himself!—Think of that!

HEDDA.   Shot himself!

BRACK.   You are right again, Mrs. Tesman.

THEA. [*Trying to control herself.*]   When did it happen, Judge Brack?

BRACK.   This afternoon—between three and four.

TESMAN.   But, where did it happen? Eh?

BRACK. [*With a slight hesitation.*]   Where? Well—I suppose at his lodgings.

THEA.   No, it couldn't have been there—for I was there myself between six and seven.

BRACK.   Well, then, somewhere else—I don't know exactly. I only know that he was found—he had shot himself . . . through the heart.

THEA.   How horrible! That he should die like that!

HEDDA. [*To* BRACK.]   Through the heart?

BRACK.   Yes—as I told you.

HEDDA.   Through the heart——

TESMAN.   It's absolutely fatal, you say?

BRACK.   Absolutely! Most likely it is already over.

THEA.   Over—all over—oh Hedda!

TESMAN.   You're quite positive of this? Who told you—eh?

BRACK. [*Curtly.*]   One of the police.

HEDDA. [*Loud.*]   At last, a deed worth doing!

TESMAN. [*Terrified.*]   Good heavens, what are you saying, Hedda?

HEDDA.   I say, there is beauty in this.

BRACK. H'm, Mrs. Tesman——

TESMAN. Beauty! Think of that!

THEA. Oh, Hedda, how can you talk of beauty in such a case?

HEDDA. Eilert Løvborg has made up his own account with life. He had the courage to do—the one right thing.

THEA. No; no! You mustn't believe that! He did it in delirium!

TESMAN. In despair.

HEDDA. No! No! He didn't—I'm sure of that!

THEA. I tell you he must have been delirious—as he was when he tore up our manuscript!

BRACK. [*With a start.*] The manuscript? He tore up the manuscript?

THEA. Yes. Last night.

TESMAN. [*In a low whisper.*] Oh, Hedda, we'll never get over this!

BRACK. H'm—how very extraordinary.

TESMAN. [*Pacing the room.*] To think of Eilert dead!—And his book destroyed too—his book that would have made him famous!

THEA. If only there were some way of saving it——

TESMAN. Yes, if only there were!—There's nothing I wouldn't give——

THEA. Perhaps there is a way, Mr. Tesman.

TESMAN. What do you mean?

THEA. [*Searches in the pocket of her dress.*] Look! I have kept all the notes he used to dictate from——

HEDDA. [*Takes a step towards her.*] Ah——!

TESMAN. You have, Mrs. Elvsted?—Eh?

THEA. Yes. I took them with me when I left home—they're here in my pocket——

TESMAN. Do let me see them!

THEA. [*Hands him a bundle of scraps of paper.*] I'm afraid they are dreadfully mixed up——

TESMAN. Perhaps, together, we might be able to sort them out—just think!

THEA. We could try at any rate——

TESMAN. We'll do it!—we *must* do it—I'll devote my life to it!

HEDDA. You, George? Your life?

TESMAN. Or at least, all the time I can spare. My own work will simply have to wait—I owe this to Eilert's memory . . . you understand, Hedda, eh?

HEDDA. You may be right.

TESMAN. Now, my dear Mrs. Elvsted, we must pull ourselves together—it is no good brooding over what has happened. Eh? We must try and control our grief as much as possible——

THEA. Yes, you're right, Mr. Tesman, I *will* try——

TESMAN. That's splendid! Now then, let's see—we must go through the notes at once—Where shall we sit? Here? No, no we'd better go in there—excuse me, Judge—Come along, Mrs. Elvsted!

THEA. Oh! If only it were possible——

[TESMAN *and* MRS. ELVSTED *go into the inner room. She takes off her hat and coat. They sit at the table under the hanging lamp and become absorbed in examining the papers.* HEDDA *goes towards the stove and sits down in the armchair. After a moment* BRACK *joins her.*]

HEDDA. [*In a low voice.*]   Oh, what a sense of freedom there is in this act of Eilert Løvborg's.

BRACK.   Freedom, Mrs. Hedda? Of course, it is freedom for him.

HEDDA.   I mean for me. It gives me a sense of freedom to know that an act of deliberate courage is still possible in this world—an act of spontaneous beauty.

BRACK. [*Smiles.*]   H'm—my dear Mrs. Hedda——

HEDDA.   Oh, I know what you are going to say. For you are a specialist, too, in a way—just like—well, you know.

BRACK. [*Looks at her intently.*]   Eilert Løvborg meant more to you than you are willing to admit—even to yourself. Or am I mistaken?

HEDDA.   I don't answer such questions. I know that Eilert Løvborg had the courage to live his life as he saw it—and to end it in beauty. He had the strength and the will to break with life—while still so young.

BRACK.   It pains me to do so, Mrs. Hedda—but I fear I must rob you of this beautiful illusion.

HEDDA.   Illusion?

BRACK.   It would soon be destroyed, in any case.

HEDDA.   What do you mean?

BRACK.   He did not shoot himself—of his own accord.

HEDDA.   Not of his own——?

BRACK.   No; the thing did not happen exactly as I told it.

HEDDA. [*In suspense.*]   You've concealed something? What is it?

BRACK.   For poor Mrs. Elvsted's sake, I slightly changed the facts.

HEDDA.   What are the facts, then?

BRACK.   First, that he is already dead.

HEDDA.   At the hospital.

BRACK.   Yes—without regaining consciousness.

HEDDA.   What else have you concealed?

BRACK.   That—the tragedy did not happen at his lodgings——

HEDDA.   That makes no difference——

BRACK.   Doesn't it? Not even if I tell you that Eilert Løvborg was found shot in—in Mademoiselle Diana's boudoir?

HEDDA. [*Attempts to jump up but sinks back again.*]   That is impossible, Judge. He couldn't have gone there again today.

BRACK.   He was there this afternoon. He went there to claim something he said they had taken from him—talked wildly about a lost child——

HEDDA.   Ah—that was why——

BRACK.   I thought he must have meant the manuscript. But now I hear he destroyed that himself. So I suppose it must have been his pocketbook.

HEDDA.   Yes—probably. So, he was found—there.

BRACK.   Yes. With a discharged pistol in his breast pocket. He had wounded himself mortally.

HEDDA.   Through the heart!—Yes!

BRACK.   No—in the bowels.

HEDDA.   [*Looks at him with an expression of loathing.*]   How horrible! Everything I touch becomes ludicrous and despicable!—It's like a curse!

BRACK.   There is something else, Mrs. Hedda—something rather ugly——

HEDDA.   What is that?

BRACK.   The pistol he carried——

HEDDA.   [*Breathless.*]   What of it?

BRACK.   He must have stolen it.

HEDDA.   [*Leaps up.*]   That is not true! He didn't steal it!

BRACK.   No other explanation is possible. He *must* have stolen it—hush!

[TESMAN *and* MRS. ELVSTED *have risen from the table in the inner room and come into the drawing-room.*]

TESMAN.   [*His hands full of papers.*]   Hedda, dear, it is almost impossible to see under that lamp. Just think!

HEDDA.   Yes, I am thinking.

TESMAN.   Do you think you'd let us use your desk, eh?

HEDDA.   Of course—no, wait! Just let me clear it first.

TESMAN.   Oh, you needn't trouble, Hedda. There's plenty of room.

HEDDA.   No, no! Let me do as I say. I will put all these things in on the piano.

[*She has taken something covered with sheet-music from under the bookcase, puts some added pieces of music on it, and carries the whole lot into the inner room and off left.* TESMAN *arranges the scraps of paper on the writing-table and moves the lamp from the corner table over to it. He and* MRS. ELVSTED *sit down and resume their work.* HEDDA *returns.*]

HEDDA.   [*Stands behind* MRS. ELVSTED's *chair, gently ruffling her hair.*]   Well, darling little Thea—how are you getting on with Eilert Løvborg's memorial?

THEA.   [*Looks up at her with a disheartened expression.*]   I'm afraid it's all very difficult——

TESMAN.   We *must* manage it. We've simply got to do it! And you know sorting out and arranging other people's papers—that's something I'm particularly good at——

[HEDDA *crosses to the stove and sits down on one of the stools.* BRACK *stands over her leaning on the armchair.*]

HEDDA.   [*In a whisper.*]   What was that you said about the pistol?

BRACK.   [*Softly.*]   That he must have stolen it.

HEDDA.   Why stolen?

BRACK.   Because any other explanation ought to be out of the question, Mrs. Hedda.

HEDDA. Indeed?

BRACK. [*Glancing at her*.]   Of course, Eilert Løvborg was here this morning. Wasn't he?

HEDDA. Yes.

BRACK. Were you alone with him?

HEDDA. Yes—for a little while.

BRACK. Did you leave the room while he was here?

HEDDA. No.

BRACK. Try to remember. Are you *sure* you didn't leave the room—even for a moment?

HEDDA. I might have gone into the hall—just for a moment——

BRACK. And where was your pistol-case?

HEDDA. It was put away in——

BRACK. Well, Mrs. Hedda?

HEDDA. It was over there on the desk.

BRACK. Have you looked since to see if both pistols are there?

HEDDA. No.

BRACK. Well, you needn't. I saw the pistol Løvborg had with him, and I recognized it at once as the one I had seen yesterday—and before that too.

HEDDA. Have you got it by any chance?

BRACK. No, the police have it.

HEDDA. What will the police do with it?

BRACK. Search until they find the owner.

HEDDA. Do you think they will succeed?

BRACK. [*Bends over her and whispers*.]   No, Hedda Gabler, not so long as I keep silent.

HEDDA. [*Gives him a frightened look*.]   And if you do *not* keep silent—what then?

BRACK. [*Shrugs his shoulders*.]   One could always declare that the pistol was stolen.

HEDDA. [*Firmly*.]   It would be better to die!

BRACK. [*Smiling*.]   One *says* such things—but one doesn't *do* them.

HEDDA. [*Without answering*.]   And if the pistol were not stolen and the police find the owner? What then?

BRACK. Well, Hedda—then—think of the scandal!

HEDDA. The scandal!

BRACK. The scandal, yes—of which you are so terrified. You'd naturally have to appear in court—both you and Mademoiselle Diana. She would have to explain how the thing happened—whether it was an accident or murder. Did he threaten to shoot her, and did the pistol go off then—or did she grab the pistol, shoot him, afterwards putting it back into his pocket. She might have done that, for she is a hefty woman, this—Mademoiselle Diana.

HEDDA. What have I to do with all this repulsive business?

BRACK. Nothing. But you will have to answer the question: Why did you give Eilert Løvborg the pistol? And what conclusion will people draw from the fact that you did give it to him?

HEDDA. [*Bowing her head.*] That is true. I didn't think of that.

BRACK. Well, fortunately, there is no danger as long as I keep silent.

HEDDA. [*Looks up at him.*] That means you have me in your power, Judge! You have me at your beck and call from now on.

BRACK. [*Whispers softly.*] Dearest Hedda—believe me—I shall not abuse my advantage.

HEDDA. I am in your power, all the same. Subject to your commands and wishes. No longer free—not free! . . . [*Rises impetuously.*] No, I won't endure that thought. Never!

BRACK. [*Looks at her half mockingly.*] People manage to get used to the inevitable.

HEDDA. [*Returns his look.*] Yes, perhaps. [*She crosses to the writing-table. Suppressing an involuntary smile and imitating* TESMAN's *intonations.*] Well? How's it going, George, eh?

TESMAN. Heaven knows, dear. In any case, it will take months to do.

HEDDA. [*As before.*] Think of that! [*She runs her fingers softly through* MRS. ELVSTED's *hair.*] Doesn't it seem strange to you, Thea? Here you are working with Tesman—as you used to work with Eilert Løvborg?

THEA. If I could only inspire your husband in the same way!

HEDDA. Oh, no doubt that will come—in time.

TESMAN. You know, Hedda—I'm really beginning to feel something of the sort! Why don't you go and talk to Judge Brack again?

HEDDA. Is there nothing at all—I can do to help?

TESMAN. No, thank you. Not a thing. [*Turning his head.*] You'll have to keep Hedda company from now on, my dear Judge.

BRACK. [*With a glance at Hedda.*] It will give me the greatest of pleasure!

HEDDA. Thanks. But this evening I feel a little tired. I will go and lie down on the sofa for a little while.

TESMAN. Yes, do that dear—eh?

[HEDDA *goes into the inner room and closes the portières after her. A short pause. Suddenly she is heard playing a wild dance-tune on the piano.*]

THEA. [*Starts up from her chair.*] Oh—what's that?

TESMAN. [*Runs to the centre opening.*] Dearest Hedda, don't play dance music tonight! Think of Aunt Rina! And of poor Eilert!

HEDDA. [*Sticks her head out between the curtains.*] And of Aunt Julia. And of all the rest of them—Never mind—From now on, I promise to be quiet. [*She closes the curtains again.*]

TESMAN. [*At the writing-table.*] I don't think it is good for her to see us at this distressing work; I have an idea, Mrs. Elvsted. You can move over to Aunt Julia's and then I'll come over in the evenings and we'll work there. Eh?

THEA. Perhaps that would be the best thing to do.

HEDDA. [*From the inner room.*]   I can hear what you are saying, Tesman. What am I to do with all those long evenings—here—by myself?

TESMAN. [*Turning over the papers.*]   Oh, I am sure Judge Brack will be kind enough to drop in and see you.

BRACK. [*In the armchair, calls out gaily.*]   Every single evening, with the very greatest of pleasure, Mrs. Tesman! I'm sure we'll have a very jolly time together, we two.

HEDDA. [*In a loud, clear voice.*]   Yes, that's what you hope, Judge, isn't it? —Now that you are cock-of-the-walk——

[*A shot is heard within.* TESMAN, MRS. ELVSTED, *and* BRACK *leap to their feet.*]

TESMAN.   Now she is playing with those pistols again.

[*He throws back the portières and runs in, followed by* MRS. ELVSTED. HEDDA *lies stretched out on the sofa, dead. Confusion and cries.* BERTA, *alarmed, comes in from the right.*]

TESMAN. [*Cries out, to* BRACK.]   Shot herself! Shot herself in the temple! Think of that!

BRACK. [*Sinks into the armchair, half-fainting.*]   Good God!—but—people don't *do* such things!

Curtain

BERNARD SHAW

Candida[1]

1895

CHARACTERS

THE REVEREND JAMES MAVOR MORELL   CANDIDA MORELL

MISS PROSERPINE GARNETT   MR BURGESS

THE REVEREND ALEXANDER MILL   EUGENE MARCHBANKS

ACT ONE

SCENE: *A fine morning in October 1894 in the north east quarter of London, a vast district miles away from the London of Mayfair and St. James's, and much less narrow, squalid, fetid and airless in its slums. It is strong in unfashionable middle class life: wide-streeted; myriad-populated; well served with ugly iron urinals, Radical clubs, and tram lines carrying a perpetual stream of yellow cars; enjoying in its main thoroughfares the luxury of grass-grown "front gardens" untrodden by the foot of man save as to the path from the gate to the hall door; blighted by a callously endured monotony of miles and miles of unlovely brick houses, black iron railings, stony pavements, slated roofs, and respectably ill dressed or disreputably worse dressed people, quite accustomed to the place, and mostly plodding uninterestedly about somebody else's work. The little energy and eagerness that crop up shew themselves in cockney cupidity and business "push." Even the policemen and the chapels are not infrequent enough to break the monotony. The sun is shining cheerfully: there is no fog; and though the smoke effectually prevents anything, whether faces and hands or bricks and mortar, from looking fresh and clean, it is not hanging heavily enough to trouble a Londoner.*

This desert of unattractiveness has its oasis. Near the outer end of the Hackney Road is a park of 217 acres, fenced in, not by railings, but by a wooden paling, and containing plenty of greensward, trees, a lake for bathers, flower beds which are triumphs of the admired cockney art of carpet gardening, and a sandpit, originally imported from the seaside for the delight of children, but speedily deserted on its becoming a natural vermin preserve for all the petty fauna of Kingsland, Hackney, and Hoxton. A bandstand, an unfurnished forum for religious, anti-religious, and political orators, cricket pitches, a gymnasium, and an old fashioned stone kiosk are among its attractions. Wherever the prospect is bounded by trees or rising green grounds, it is a pleasant place. Where the ground stretches flat to the grey palings, with

[1] Reprinted by arrangement with The Public Trustee and The Society of Authors.

bricks and mortar, sky signs, crowded chimneys and smoke beyond, the prospect makes it desolate and sordid.

The best view of Victoria Park is commanded by the front window of St. Dominic's Parsonage, from which not a brick is visible. The parsonage is semi-detached, with a front garden and a porch. Visitors go up the flight of steps to the porch: tradespeople and members of the family go down by a door under the steps to the basement, with a breakfast room, used for all meals, in front, and the kitchen at the back. Upstairs, on the level of the hall door, is the drawingroom, with its large plate glass window looking out on the park. In this, the only sitting room that can be spared from the children and the family meals, the parson, the REVEREND JAMES MAVOR MORELL, *does his work. He is sitting in a strong round backed revolving chair at the end of a long table, which stands across the window, so that he can cheer himself with a view of the park over his left shoulder. At the opposite end of the table, adjoining it, is a little table only half as wide as the other, with a typewriter on it. His typist is sitting at this machine, with her back to the window. The large table is littered with pamphlets, journals, letters, nests of drawers, an office diary, postage scales and the like. A spare chair for visitors having business with the parson is in the middle, turned to his end. Within reach of his hand is a stationery case, and a photograph in a frame. The wall behind him is fitted with bookshelves, on which an adept eye can measure the parson's casuistry and divinity by Maurice's Theological Essays and a complete set of Browning's poems, and the reformer's politics by a yellow backed Progress and Poverty, Fabian Essays, A Dream of John Ball, Marx's Capital, and half a dozen other literary landmarks in Socialism. Facing him on the other side of the room, near the typewriter, is the door. Further down opposite the fireplace, a bookcase stands on a cellaret, with a sofa near it. There is a generous fire burning; and the hearth, with a comfortable armchair and a black japanned flower-painted coal scuttle at one side, a miniature chair for children on the other, a varnished wooden mantelpiece, with neatly moulded shelves, tiny bits of mirror let into the panels, a traveling clock in a leather case (the inevitable wedding present), and on the wall above a large autotype of the chief figure in Titian's Assumption of the Virgin, is very inviting. Altogether the room is the room of a good housekeeper, vanquished, as far as the table is concerned, by an untidy man, but elsewhere mistress of the situation. The furniture, in its ornamental aspect, betrays the style of the advertised "drawingroom suite" of the pushing suburban furniture dealer; but there is nothing useless or pretentious in the room, money being too scarce in the house of an east end parson to be wasted on snobbish trimmings.*

The REVEREND JAMES MAVOR MORELL *is a Christian Socialist clergyman of the Church of England, and an active member of the Guild of St Matthew and the Christian Social Union. A vigorous, genial, popular man of forty, robust and good looking, full of energy, with pleasant, hearty, consid-*

erate manners, and a sound unaffected voice, which he uses with the clean athletic articulation of a practised orator, and with a wide range and perfect command of expression. He is a first-rate clergyman, able to say what he likes to whom he likes, to lecture people without setting himself up against them, to impose his authority on them without humiliating them, and, on occasion, to interfere in their business without impertinence. His well-spring of enthusiasm and sympathetic emotion has never run dry for a moment: he still eats and sleeps heartily enough to win the daily battle between exhaustion and recuperation triumphantly. Withal, a great baby, pardonably vain of his powers and unconsciously pleased with himself. He has a healthy complexion: good forehead, with the brows somewhat blunt, and the eyes bright and eager, mouth resolute but not particularly well cut, and a substantial nose, with the mobile spreading nostrils of the dramatic orator, void, like all his features, of subtlety.

The typist, MISS PROSERPINE GARNETT, *is a brisk little woman of about 30, of the lower middle class, neatly but cheaply dressed in a black merino skirt and a blouse, notably pert and quick of speech, and not very civil in her manner, but sensitive and affectionate. She is clattering away busily at her machine whilst* MORELL *opens the last of his morning's letters. He realizes its contents with a comic groan of despair.*

PROSERPINE.   Another lecture?

MORELL.   Yes. The Hoxton Freedom Group want me to address them on Sunday morning. [*He lays great emphasis on Sunday, this being the unreasonable part of the business.*] What are they?

PROSERPINE.   Communist Anarchists, I think.

MORELL.   Just like Anarchists not to know that they cant have a parson on Sunday! Tell them to come to church if they want to hear me: it will do them good. Say I can come on Mondays and Thursdays only. Have you the diary there?

PROSERPINE.   [*Taking up the diary.*]   Yes.

MORELL.   Have I any lecture on for next Monday?

PROSERPINE.   [*Referring to diary.*]   Tower Hamlets Radical Club.

MORELL.   Well, Thursday then?

PROSERPINE.   English Land Restoration League.

MORELL.   What next?

PROSERPINE.   Guild of St Matthew on Monday. Independent Labor Party, Greenwich Branch, on Thursday. Monday, Social-Democratic Federation, Mile End Branch. Thursday, first Confirmation class. [*Impatiently.*] Oh, I'd better tell them you cant come. Theyre only half a dozen ignorant and conceited costermongers without five shillings between them.

MORELL. [*Amused.*]   Ah; but you see theyre near relatives of mine.

PROSERPINE. [*Staring at him.*]   Relatives of y o u r s!

MORELL.   Yes: we have the same father—in Heaven.

PROSERPINE. [*Relieved.*]   Oh, is that all?

MORELL. [*With a sadness which is a luxury to a man whose voice expresses it so finely.*]   Ah, you dont believe it. Everybody says it: nobody believes it: nobody. [*Briskly, getting back to business.*] Well, well! Come, Miss Proserpine: cant you find a date for the costers? What about the 25th? That was vacant the day before yesterday.

PROSERPINE. [*Referring to diary.*]   Engaged. The Fabian Society.

MORELL.   Bother the Fabian Society! Is the 28th gone too?

PROSERPINE.   City dinner. Youre invited to dine with the Founders' Company.

MORELL.   Thatll do: I'll go to the Hoxton Group of Freedom instead. [*She enters the engagement in silence, with implacable disparagement of the Hoxton Anarchists in every line of her face.* MORELL *bursts open the cover of a copy of* The Church Reformer, *which has come by post, and glances through Mr Stewart Headlam's leader and the Guild of St Matthew news. These proceedings are presently enlivened by the appearance of* MORELL'S *curate, the* REVEREND ALEXANDER MILL, *a young gentleman gathered by* MORELL *from the nearest University settlement, whither he had come from Oxford to give the east end of London the benefit of his university training. He is a conceitedly well intentioned, enthusiastic, immature novice, with nothing positively unbearable about him except a habit of speaking with his lips carefully closed a full half inch from each corner for the sake of a finicking articulation and a set of university vowels, this being his chief means so far of bringing his Oxford refinement (as he calls his habits) to bear on Hackney vulgarity.* MORELL, *whom he has won over by a doglike devotion, looks up indulgently from* The Church Reformer, *and remarks.*] Well, Lexy? Late again, as usual!

LEXY.   I'm afraid so. I wish I could get up in the morning.

MORELL. [*Exulting in his own energy.*]   Ha! Ha! [*Whimsically.*] Watch and pray, Lexy: watch and pray.

LEXY.   I know. [*Rising wittily to the occasion.*] But how can I watch and pray when I am asleep? Isnt that so, Miss Prossy? [*He makes for the warmth of the fire.*]

PROSERPINE. [*Sharply.*]   Miss Garnett, if you please.

LEXY.   I beg your pardon. Miss Garnett.

PROSERPINE.   Youve got to do all the work today.

LEXY. [*On the hearth.*]   Why?

PROSERPINE.   Never mind why. It will do you good to earn your supper before you eat it, for once in a way, as I do. Come! dont dawdle. You should have been off on your rounds half an hour ago.

LEXY. [*Perplexed.*]   Is she in earnest, Morell?

MORELL. [*In the highest spirits: his eyes dancing.*]   Yes. I am going to dawdle today.

LEXY.   You! You dont know how.

MORELL. [*Rising.*]   Ha! ha! Dont I? I'm going to have this morning all to myself. My wife's coming back: she's due here at 11.45.

LEXY. [*Surprised.*]   Coming back already! with the children? I thought they were to stay to the end of the month.

MORELL.   So they are: she's only coming up for two days, to get some flannel things for Jimmy, and to see how we're getting on without her.

LEXY. [*Anxiously.*]   But, my dear Morell, if what Jimmy and Fluffy had was scarlatina, do you think it wise—

MORELL.   Scarlatina! Rubbish! it was German measles. I brought it into the house myself from the Pycroft Street school. A parson is like a doctor, my boy: he must face infection as a soldier must face bullets. [*He claps* LEXY *manfully on the shoulders.*] Catch the measles if you can, Lexy: she'll nurse you; and what a piece of luck that will be for you! Eh?

LEXY. [*Smiling uneasily.*]   It's so hard to understand you about Mrs Morell—

MORELL. [*Tenderly.*]   Ah, my boy, get married: get married to a good woman; and then youll understand. Thats a foretaste of what will be best in the Kingdom of Heaven we are trying to establish on earth. That will cure you of dawdling. An honest man feels that he must pay Heaven for every hour of happiness with a good spell of hard unselfish work to make others happy. We have no more right to consume happiness without producing it than to consume wealth without producing it. Get a wife like my Candida; and youll always be in arrear with your repayment. [*He pats* LEXY *affectionately and moves to leave the room.*]

LEXY.   Oh, wait a bit: I forgot. [MORELL *halts and turns with the door knob in his hand.*] Your father-in-law is coming round to see you.

[MORELL, *surprised and not pleased, shuts the door again, with a complete change of manner.*]

MORELL.   Mr Burgess?

LEXY.   Yes. I passed him in the park, arguing with somebody. He asked me to let you know that he was coming.

MORELL. [*Half incredulous.*]   But he hasnt called here for three years. Are you sure, Lexy? Youre not joking, are you?

LEXY. [*Earnestly.*]   No sir, really.

MORELL. [*Thoughtfully.*]   Hm! Time for him to take another look at Candida before she grows out of his knowledge. [*He resigns himself to the inevitable, and goes out.*]

[LEXY *looks after him with beaming worship.* MISS GARNETT, *not being able to shake* LEXY, *relieves her feelings by worrying the typewriter.*]

LEXY.   What a good man! What a thorough loving soul he is! [*He takes* MORELL's *place at the table, making himself very comfortable as he takes out a cigaret.*]

PROSERPINE. [*Impatiently, pulling the letter she has been working at off the typewriter and folding it.*]   Oh, a man ought to be able to be fond of his wife without making a fool of himself about her.

LEXY. [*Shocked.*]   Oh, Miss Prossy!

PROSERPINE. [*Snatching at the stationery case for an envelope, in which she encloses the letter as she speaks.*] Candida here, and Candida there, and Candida everywhere! [*She licks the envelope.*] It's enough to drive anyone out of their s e n s e s [*Thumping the envelope to make it stick*] to hear a woman raved about in that absurd manner merely because she's got good hair and a tolerable figure.

LEXY. [*With reproachful gravity.*] I think her extremely beautiful, Miss Garnett, [*He takes the photograph up; looks at it; and adds, with even greater impressiveness*] e x t r e m e l y beautiful. How fine her eyes are!

PROSERPINE. Her eyes are not a bit better than mine: now! [*He puts down the photograph and stares austerely at her.*] And you know very well you think me dowdy and second rate enough.

LEXY. [*Rising majestically.*] Heaven forbid that I should think of any of God's creatures in such a way! [*He moves stiffly away from her across the room to the neighborhood of the bookcase.*]

PROSERPINE. [*Sarcastically.*] Thank you. Thats very nice and comforting.

LEXY. [*Saddened by her depravity.*] I had no idea you had any feeling against Mrs Morell.

PROSERPINE. [*Indignantly.*] I have no feeling against her. She's very nice, very good-hearted: I'm very fond of her, and can appreciate her real qualities far better than any man can. [*He shakes his head sadly. She rises and comes at him with intense pepperiness.*] You dont believe me? You think I'm jealous? Oh, what a knowledge of the human heart you have, Mr Lexy Mill! How well you know the weaknesses of Woman, dont you? It must be so nice to be a man and have a fine penetrating intellect instead of mere emotions like us, and to know that the reason we dont share your amorous delusions is that we're all jealous of one another! [*She abandons him with a toss of her shoulders, and crosses to the fire to warm her hands.*]

LEXY. Ah, if you women only had the same clue to Man's strength that you have to his weakness, Miss Prossy, there would be no Woman Question.

PROSERPINE. [*Over her shoulder, as she stoops, holding her hands to the blaze.*] Where did you hear Morell say that? You didnt invent it yourself: youre not clever enough.

LEXY. Thats quite true. I am not ashamed of owing him that, as I owe him so many other spiritual truths. He said it at the annual conference of the Women's Liberal Federation. Allow me to add that though they didnt appreciate it, I, a mere man, did. [*He turns to the bookcase again, hoping that this may leave her crushed.*]

PROSERPINE. [*Putting her hair straight at a panel of mirror in the mantelpiece.*] Well, when you talk to me, give me your own ideas, such as they are, and not his. You never cut a poorer figure than when you are trying to imitate him.

LEXY. [*Stung.*] I try to follow his example, not to imitate him.

PROSERPINE. [*Coming at him again on her way back to her work.*] Yes, you do: you i m i t a t e him. Why do you tuck your umbrella under your left arm instead of carrying it in your hand like anyone else? Why do you walk with your chin stuck out before you, hurrying along with that eager look in your eyes? you! who never get up before half past nine in the morning. Why do you say "knoaledge" in church, though you always say "knolledge" in private conversation! Bah! do you think I dont know? [She goes back to the typewriter.] Here! come and set about your work: weve wasted enough time for one morning. Here's a copy of the diary for today. [She hands him a memorandum.]

LEXY. [Deeply offended.] Thank you. [He takes it and stands at the table with his back to her, reading it. She begins to transcribe her shorthand notes on the typewriter without troubling herself about his feelings.]

The door opens; and MR. BURGESS enters unannounced. He is a man of sixty, made coarse and sordid by the compulsory selfishness of petty commerce, and later on softened into sluggish bumptiousness by overfeeding and commercial success. A vulgar ignorant guzzling man, offensive and contemptuous to people whose labor is cheap, respectful to wealth and rank, and quite sincere and without rancor or envy in both attitudes. The world has offered him no decently paid work except that of a sweater; and he has become, in consequence, somewhat hoggish. But he has no suspicion of this himself, and honestly regards his commercial prosperity as the inevitable and socially wholesome triumph of the ability, industry, shrewdness, and experience in business of a man who in private is easygoing, affectionate, and humorously convivial to a fault. Corporeally he is podgy, with a snoutish nose in the centre of a flat square face, a dust colored beard with a patch of grey in the centre under his chin, and small watery blue eyes with a plaintively sentimental expression, which he transfers easily to his voice by his habit of pompously intoning his sentences.

BURGESS. [Stopping on the threshold, and looking round.] They told me Mr Morell was here.

PROSERPINE. [Rising.] I'll fetch him for you.

BURGESS. [Staring disappointedly at her.] Youre not the same young lady as hused to typewrite for him?

PROSERPINE. No.

BURGESS. [Grumbling on his way to the hearthrug.] No: she was young-er [MISS GARNETT stares at him; then goes out, slamming the door.] Startin on your rounds, Mr Mill?

LEXY. [Folding his memorandum and pocketing it.] Yes: I must be off presently.

BURGESS. [Momentously.] Dont let me detain you, Mr Mill. What I come about is p r i v a t e between me and Mr Morell.

LEXY. [Huffily.] I have no intention of intruding, I am sure, Mr. Burgess. G o o d morning.

BURGESS. [Patronizingly.] Oh, good morning to you.

[MORELL *returns as* LEXY *is making for the door.*]

MORELL. [*To* LEXY.]   Off to work?

LEXY.   Yes, sir.

MORELL.   Take my silk handkerchief and wrap your throat up. Theres a cold wind. Away with you.

[LEXY, *more than consoled for* BURGESS's *rudeness, brightens up and goes out.*]

BURGESS.   Spoilin your korates as usu'l, James. Good mornin. When a pay a man, an' 'is livin depens on me, I keep him in 'is place.

MORELL. [*Rather shortly.*]   I always keep my curates in their places as my helpers and comrades. If you get as much work out of your clerks and ware-housemen as I do out of my curates, you must be getting rich pretty fast. Will you take your old chair.

[*He points with curt authority to the armchair beside the fireplace; then takes the spare chair from the table and sits down at an unfamiliar distance from his visitor.*]

BURGESS. [*Without moving.*]   Just the same as hever, James!

MORELL.   When you last called—it was about three years ago, I think—you said the same thing a little more frankly. Your exact words then were "Just as big a fool as ever, James!"

BURGESS. [*Soothingly.*]   Well, praps I did; but [*With conciliatory cheerful-ness*] I meant no hoffence by it. A clorgyman is privileged to be a bit of a fool, you know: it's only becomin in 'is profession that he should. Anyhow, I come here, not to rake up hold differences, but to let bygones be bygones. [*Suddenly becoming very solemn, and approaching* MORELL.] James: three years ago, you done me a hil turn. You done me hout of a contrac; and when I gev you arsh words in my natral disappointment, you turned my daughrter again me. Well, Ive come to hact the part of a Kerischin. [*Offering his hand.*] I forgive you, James.

MORELL. [*Starting up.*]   Confound your impudence!

BURGESS. [*Retreating, with almost lachrymose deprecation of this treatment.*] Is that becomin language for a clorgyman, James? And you so particlar, too!

MORELL. [*Hotly.*]   No, sir: it is not becoming language for a clergyman. I used the wrong word. I should have said damn your impudence: thats what St Paul or any honest priest would have said to you. Do you think I have for-gotten that tender of yours for the contract to supply clothing to the workhouse?

BURGESS. [*In a paroxysm of public spirit.*]   I hacted in the hinterest of the ratepayers, James. It was the lowest tender: you carnt deny that.

MORELL.   Yes, the lowest, because you paid worse wages than any other employer—starvation wages—aye, worse than starvation wages—to the women who made the clothing. Your wages would have driven them to the streets to keep body and soul together. [*Getting angrier and angrier.*] Those women were my parishioners. I shamed the Guardians out of accepting your tender: I shamed the ratepayers out of letting them do it: I shamed everybody but you. [*Boiling over.*] How dare you, sir, come here and offer to forgive me, and talk about your daughter, and—

BURGESS.   Heasy, James! heasy! heasy! Dont git hinto a fluster about nothink. Ive howned I was wrong.

MORELL.   Have you? I didnt hear you.

BURGESS.   Of course I did. I hown it now. Come: I harsk your pardon for the letter I wrote you. Is that enough?

MORELL.   [*Snapping his fingers.*]   Thats nothing. Have you raised the wages?

BURGESS.   [*Triumphantly.*]   Yes.

MORELL.   What!

BURGESS.   [*Unctuously.*]   Ive turned a moddle hemployer. I dont hemploy no women now: theyre all sacked; and the work is done by machinery. Not a man 'as less than sixpence a *hour*; and the skilled ands gits the Trade Union rate. [*Proudly.*] What ave you say to me now?

MORELL.   [*Overwhelmed.*]   Is it possible! Well, theres more joy in heaven over one sinner that repenteth!—[*Going to Burgess with an explosion of apologetic cordiality.*] My dear Burgess: how splendid of you! I most heartily beg your pardon for my hard thoughts. [*Grasping his hand.*] And now, dont you feel the better for the change? Come! confess! youre happier. You look happier.

BURGESS.   [*Ruefully.*]   Well, praps I do. I spose I must, since you notice it. At all events, I git my contrax assepted by the County Council. [*Savagely.*] They dussent ave nothing to do with me unless I paid fair wages: curse em for a parcel o meddlin fools!

MORELL.   [*Dropping his hand, utterly discouraged.*]   So that was why you raised the wages! [*He sits down moodily.*]

BURGESS.   [*Severely, in spreading, mounting tones.*]   Woy helse should I do it? What does it lead to but drink and huppishness in workin men? [*He seats himself magisterially in the easy chair.*] It's hall very well for you, James: it gits you hinto the papers and makes a great man of you; but you never think of the arm you do, puttin money into the pockets of workin men that they dunno ow to spend, and takin it from people that might be makin a good huse on it.

MORELL.   [*With a heavy sigh, speaking with cold politeness.*]   What is your business with me this morning? I shall not pretend to believe that you are here merely out of family sentiment.

BURGESS.   [*Obstinately.*]   Yes I ham: just family sentiment and nothink helse.

MORELL.   [*With weary calm.*]   I dont believe you.

BURGESS.   [*Rising threateningly.*]   Dont say that to me again, James Mavor Morell.

MORELL.   [*Unmoved.*]   I'll say it just as often as may be necessary to convince you that it's true. I dont believe you.

BURGESS.   [*Collapsing into an abyss of wounded feeling.*]   Oh, well, if youre detormined to be hunfriendly, I spose I'd better go. [*He moves reluctantly to-wards the door.* MORELL *makes no sign. He lingers.*] I didnt hexpect to find a hunforgivin spirit in you, James. [MORELL *still not responding, he takes a few more reluctant steps doorwards. Then he comes back, whining.*] We huseter git on well enough, spite of our different hopinions. Woy are you so changed to me? I give you my word I come here in peeorr [pure] frenliness, not wishin to be hon bad terms with my hown daughrter's usban. Come, James: be a Keris-chin, and shake ands. [*He puts his hand sentimentally on* MORELL's *shoulder.*]

MORELL. [*Looking up at him thoughtfully.*]   Look here, Burgess. Do you want to be as welcome here as you were before you lost that contract?

BURGESS.   I do, James. I do—honest.

MORELL.   Then why dont you behave as you did then?

BURGESS. [*Cautiously removing his hand.*]   Ow d'y' mean?

MORELL.   I'll tell you. You thought me a young fool then.

BURGESS. [*Coaxingly.*]   No I didn't, James. I—

MORELL. [*Cutting him short.*]   Yes, you did. And I thought you an old scoundrel.

BURGESS. [*Most vehemently deprecating this gross self-accusation on* MORELL's *part.*]   No you didnt, James. Now you do yourself a hinjustice.

MORELL.   Yes I did. Well, that did not prevent our getting on very well together. God made you what I call a scoundrel as He made me what you call a fool. [*The effect of this observation on* BURGESS *is to remove the keystone of his moral arch. He becomes bodily weak, and, with his eyes fixed on* MORELL *in a helpless stare, puts out his hand apprehensively to balance himself, as if the floor had suddenly sloped under him.* MORELL *proceeds, in the same tone of quiet conviction.*] It was not for me to quarrel with His handiwork in the one case more than in the other. So long as you come here honestly as a self-respecting, thorough, convinced scoundrel, justifying your scoundrelism and proud of it, you are welcome. But [*And now* MORELL's *tone becomes formid-able; and he rises and strikes the back of the chair for greater emphasis*] I wont have you here snivelling about being a model employer and a converted man when youre only an apostate with your coat turned for the sake of a County Council contract. [*He nods at him to enforce the point; then goes to the hearth-rug, where he takes up a comfortably commanding position with his back to the fire, and continues.*] No: I like a man to be true to himself, even in wickedness. Come now: either take your hat and go; or else sit down and give me a good scoundrelly reason for wanting to be friends with me. [BURGESS, *whose emotions have subsided sufficiently to be expressed by a dazed grin, is relieved by this concrete proposition. He ponders it for a moment, and then, slowly and very modestly, sits down in the chair* MORELL *has just left.*] Thats right. Now out with it.

BURGESS. [*Chuckling in spite of himself.*]   Well, you orr a queer bird, James, and no mistake. But [*Almost enthusiastically*] one carnt elp likin you: besides, as I said afore, of course one dont take hall a clorgyman says seriously, or the world couldnt go on. Could it now? [*He composes himself for graver discourse, and, turning his eyes on* MORELL, *proceeds with dull seriousness.*] Well, I dont mind tellin you, since it's your wish we should be free with one another, that I did think you a bit of a fool once; but I'm beginnin to think that praps I was be'ind the times a bit.

MORELL. [*Exultant.*]   Aha! Youre finding that out at last, are you?

BURGESS. [*Portentously.*]   Yes: times 'es changed mor'n I could a believed. Five yorr [year] ago, no sensible man would a thought o takin hup with your hidears. I hused to wonder you was let preach at all. Why, I know a clorgyman what 'as bin kep hout of his job for yorrs by the Bishop o London, although the pore feller's not a bit more religious than you are. But today, if henyyone was to horffer to bet me a thousan poun that youll hend by bein a bishop yourself, I dussent take the bet. [*Very impressively.*] You and your crew are gittin hinfluential: I can see that. Theyll ave to give you somethink someday, if it's honly to stop your mouth. You ad the right instinc arter all, James: the line you took is the payin line in the long run for a man o your sort.

MORELL. [*Offering his hand with thorough decision.*]   Shake hands, Burgess. Now youre talking honestly. I dont think theyll make me a bishop; but if they do, I'll introduce you to the biggest jobbers I can get to come to my dinner parties.

BURGESS. [*Who has risen with a sheepish grin and accepted the hand of friendship.*]   You will ave your joke, James. Our quarrel's made up now, ain it?

A WOMAN'S VOICE.   Say yes, James.

Startled, they turn quickly and find that CANDIDA *has just come in, and is looking at them with an amused maternal indulgence which is her characteristic expression. She is a woman of 33, well built, well nourished, likely, one guesses, to become matronly later on, but now quite at her best, with the double charm of youth and motherhood. Her ways are those of a woman who has found that she can always manage people by engaging their affection, and who does so frankly and instinctively without the smallest scruple. So far, she is like any other pretty woman who is just clever enough to make the most of her sexual attractions for trivially selfish ends; but* CANDIDA'S *serene brow, courageous eyes, and well set mouth and chin signify largeness of mind and dignity of character to ennoble her cunning in the affections. A wise-hearted observer, looking at her, would at once guess that whoever had placed the Virgin of the Assumption over her hearth did so because he fancied some spiritual resemblance between them, and yet would not suspect either her husband or herself of any such idea, or indeed of any concern with the art of Titian. Just now she is in bonnet and mantle, carrying a strapped rug with her umbrella stuck through it, a handbag, and a supply of illustrated papers.*]

MORELL. [*Shocked at his remissness.*]   Candida! Why—[*He looks at his watch, and is horrified to find it so late.*] My darling! [*Hurrying to her and seizing the rug strap, pouring forth his remorseful regrets all the time.*] I intended to meet you at the train. I let the time slip. [*Flinging the rug on the sofa.*] I was so engrossed by— [*Returning to her*] —I forgot—oh! [*He embraces her with penitent emotion.*]

BURGESS. [*A little shamefaced and doubtful of his reception.*]   How orr you, Candy? [*She, still in* MORELL's *arms, offers him her cheek, which he kisses.*] James and me is come to a nunnerstannin. A honorable unnerstannin. Ain we, James?

MORELL. [*Impetuously.*]   Oh bother your understanding! youve kept me late for Candida. [*With compassionate fervor.*] My poor love: how did you manage about the luggage? How—

CANDIDA. [*Stopping him and disengaging herself.*]   There! there! there! I wasnt alone. Eugene has been down with us; and we travelled together.

MORELL. [*Pleased.*]   Eugene!

CANDIDA.   Yes: he's struggling with my luggage, poor boy. Go out, dear, at once; or he'll pay for the cab; and I dont want that. [MORELL *hurries out.* CANDIDA *puts down her handbag; then takes off her mantle and bonnet and puts them on the sofa with the rug, chatting meanwhile.*] Well, papa: how are you getting on at home?

BURGESS.   The ouse aint worth livin in since you left it, Candy. I wish youd come round and give the gurl a talkin to. Who's this Eugene thats come with you?

CANDIDA.   Oh, Eugene's one of James' discoveries. He found him sleeping on the Embankment last June. Havnt you noticed our new picture? [*Pointing to the Virgin.*] He gave us that.

BURGESS. [*Incredulously.*]   Garn! D'you mean to tell me—your hown father! —that cab touts or such like, orf the Embankment, buys pictures like that? [*Severely.*] Dont deceive me, Candy: it's a 'Igh Church picture; and James chose it hisself.

CANDIDA.   Guess again. Eugene isnt a cab tout.

BURGESS.   Then what is he? [*Sarcastically.*] A nobleman, I spose.

CANDIDA. [*Nodding delightedly.*]   Yes. His uncle's a peer! A real live earl.

BURGESS. [*Not daring to believe such good news.*]   No!

CANDIDA.   Yes. He had a seven day bill for £55 in his pocket when James found him on the Embankment. He thought he couldnt get any money for it until the seven days were up; and he was too shy to ask for credit. Oh, he's a dear boy! We are very fond of him.

BURGESS. [*Pretending to belittle the aristocracy, but with his eyes gleaming.*] Hm! I thort you wouldnt git a hearl's nevvy visitin in Victawriar Pawrk unless he were a bit of a flat. [*Looking again at the picture.*] Of course I dont old with that picture, Candy; but still it's a 'igh class fust rate work of ort: I can see that. Be sure you hintrodooce me to im, Candy. [*He looks at his watch anxiously.*] I can ony stay about two minutes.

MORELL *comes back with* EUGENE, *whom* BURGESS *contemplates moist-eyed with enthusiasm. He is a strange, shy youth of eighteen, slight, effeminate, with a delicate childish voice, and a hunted tormented expression and shrink-*

*ing manner that shew the painful sensitiveness of very swift and acute appre-
hensiveness in youth, before the character has grown to its full strength.
Miserably irresolute, he does not know where to stand or what to do. He is
afraid of* BURGESS, *and would run away into solitude if he dared; but the very
intensity with which he feels a perfectly commonplace position comes from
excessive nervous force; and his nostrils, mouth, and eyes betray a fiercely
petulant wilfulness, as to the bent of which his brow, already lined with pity,
is reassuring. He is so uncommon as to be almost unearthly; and to prosaic
people there is something noxious in this unearthliness, just as to poetic
people there is something angelic in it. His dress is anarchic. He wears an
old blue serge jacket, unbuttoned, over a woollen lawn tennis shirt, with a
silk handkerchief for a cravat, trousers matching the jacket, and brown canvas
shoes. In these garments he has apparently lain in the heather and waded
through the waters; and there is no evidence of his having ever brushed them.*

*As he catches sight of a stranger on entering, he stops, and edges along the
wall on the opposite side of the room.*

MORELL. [*As he enters.*]   Come along: you can spare us quarter of an hour
at all events. This is my father-in-law. Mr Burgess—Mr Marchbanks.

MARCHBANKS. [*Nervously backing against the bookcase.*]   Glad to meet you,
sir.

BURGESS. [*Crossing to him with great heartiness, whilst* MORELL *joins* CANDIDA
at the fire.]   Glad to meet y o u, I'm shore, Mr Morchbanks. [*Forcing him to
shake hands.*] Ow do you find yoreself this weather? Ope you aint lettin James
put no foolish ideas into your ed?

MARCHBANKS.   Foolish ideas? Oh, you mean Socialism? No.

BURGESS.   Thats right. [*Again looking at his watch.*] Well, I must go now:
theres no elp for it. Yore not comin my way, orr you, Mr Morchbanks?

MARCHBANKS.   Which way is that?

BURGESS.   Victawriar Pawrk Station. Theres a city train at 12.25.

MORELL.   Nonsense. Eugene will stay to lunch with us, I expect.

MARCHBANKS. [*Anxiously excusing himself.*]   No—I—I—

BURGESS.   Well, well, I shornt press you: I bet youd rather lunch with
Candy. Some night, I ope, youll come and dine with me at my club, the Freeman Founders in Nortn Folgit. Come: say you will!

MARCHBANKS.   Thank you, Mr Burgess. Where is Norton Folgate? Down in
Surrey, isnt it?

[BURGESS, *inexpressibly tickled, begins to splutter with laughter.*]

CANDIDA. [*Coming to the rescue.*]   Youll lose your train, papa, if you dont
go at once. Come back in the afternoon and tell Mr Marchbanks where to find
the club.

BURGESS. [*Roaring with glee.*]   Down in Surrey! Har, har! thats not a bad
one. Well, I never met a man as didnt know Nortn Folgit afore. [*Abashed at
his own noisiness.*] Goodbye, Mr Morchbanks: I know yore too ighbred to take
my pleasantry in bad part. [*He again offers his hand.*]

MARCHBANKS. [*Taking it with a nervous jerk.*]   Not at all.

BURGESS.   Bye, bye, Candy. I'll look in again later on. So long, James.

MORELL.   Must you go?

BURGESS.   Dont stir. [*He goes out with unabated heartiness.*]

MORELL.   Oh, I'll see you off. [*He follows him.*]

[EUGENE *stares after them apprehensively, holding his breath until* BURGESS *disappears.*]

CANDIDA. [*Laughing.*]   Well, Eugene? [*He turns with a start, and comes eagerly towards her, but stops irresolutely as he meets her amused look.*] What do you think of my father?

MARCHBANKS.   I—I hardly know him yet. He seems to be a very nice old gentleman.

CANDIDA. [*With gentle irony.*]   And youll go to the Freeman Founders to dine with him, wont you?

MARCHBANKS. [*Miserably, taking it quite seriously.*]   Yes, if it will please you.

CANDIDA. [*Touched.*]   Do you know, you are a very nice boy, Eugene, with all your queerness. If you had laughed at my father I shouldnt have minded; but I like you ever so much better for being nice to him.

MARCHBANKS.   Ought I to have laughed? I noticed that he said something funny; but I am so ill at ease with strangers; and I never can see a joke. I'm very sorry. [*He sits down on the sofa, his elbows on his knees and his temples between his fists, with an expression of hopeless suffering.*]

CANDIDA. [*Bustling him goodnaturedly.*]   Oh come! You great baby, you! You are worse than usual this morning. Why were you so melancholy as we came along in the cab?

MARCHBANKS.   Oh, that was nothing. I was wondering how much I ought to give the cabman. I know it's utterly silly; but you dont know how dreadful such things are to me—how I shrink from having to deal with strange people. [*Quickly and reassuringly.*] But it's all right. He beamed all over and touched his hat when Morell gave him two shillings. I was on the point of offering him ten.

[MORELL *comes back with a few letters and newspapers which have come by the midday post.*]

CANDIDA.   Oh, James dear, he was going to give the cabman ten shillings! ten shillings for a three minutes drive! Oh dear!

MORELL. [*At the table, glancing through the letters.*]   Never mind her, Marchbanks. The overpaying instinct is a generous one: better than the underpaying instinct, and not so common.

MARCHBANKS. [*Relapsing into dejection.*]   No: cowardice, incompetence. Mrs Morrell's quite right.

CANDIDA.   Of course she is. [*She takes up her hand-bag.*] And now I must leave you to James for the present. I suppose you are too much of a poet to know the state a woman finds her house in when she's been away for three weeks. Give me my rug. [EUGENE *takes the strapped rug from the couch, and gives it to her. She takes it in her left hand, having the bag in her right.*] Now hang my cloak across my arm. [*He obeys.*] Now my hat. [*He puts it into the hand which has the bag.*] Now open the door for me. [*He hurries before her and opens the door.*] Thanks. [*She goes out; and* MARCHBANKS *shuts the door.*]

MORELL. [*Still busy at the table.*] Youll stay to lunch, Marchbanks, of course.

MARCHBANKS. [*Scared.*] I mustnt. [*He glances quickly at* MORELL, *but at once avoids his frank look, and adds, with obvious disingenuousness.*] I mean I cant.

MORELL. You mean you wont.

MARCHBANKS. [*Earnestly.*] No: I should like to, indeed. Thank you very much. But—but—

MORELL. But—but—but—but—Bosh! If youd like to stay, stay. If youre shy, go and take a turn in the park and write poetry until half past one; and then come in and have a good feed.

MARCHBANKS. Thank you, I should like that very much. But I really mustnt. The truth is, Mrs Morell told me not to. She said she didnt think youd ask me to stay to lunch, but that I was to remember, if you did, that you didnt really want me to. [*Plaintively.*] She said I'd understand; but I dont. Please dont tell her I told you.

MORELL. [*Drolly.*] Oh, is that all? Wont my suggestion that you should take a turn in the park meet the difficulty?

MARCHBANKS. How?

MORELL. [*Exploding good-humoredly.*] Why, you duffer—[*But this boisterousness jars himself as well as* EUGENE. *He checks himself.*] No: I wont put it in that way. [*He comes to* EUGENE *with affectionate seriousness.*] My dear lad: in a happy marriage like ours, there is something very sacred in the return of the wife to her home. [MARCHBANKS *looks quickly at him, half anticipating his meaning.*] An old friend or a truly noble and sympathetic soul is not in the way on such occasions; but a chance visitor is. [*The hunted horror-stricken expression comes out with sudden vividness in* EUGENE'S *face as he understands.* MORELL, *occupied with his own thoughts, goes on without noticing this.*] Candida thought I would rather not have you here; but she was wrong. I'm very fond of you, my boy; and I should like you to see for yourself what a happy thing it is to be married as I am.

MARCHBANKS. Happy! Y o u r marriage! You think that! You believe that!

MORELL. [*Buoyantly.*] I know it, my lad. Larochefoucauld said that there are convenient marriages but no delightful ones. You dont know the comfort of seeing through and through a thundering liar and rotten cynic like that fellow. Ha! Ha! Now, off with you to the park, and write your poem. Half past one, sharp, mind: we never wait for anybody.

MARCHBANKS. [*Wildly.*] No: stop: you shant. I'll force it into the light.

MORELL. [*Puzzled.*] Eh? Force what?

MARCHBANKS. I must speak to you. There is something that must be settled between us.

MORELL. [*With a whimsical glance at his watch.*] Now?

MARCHBANKS. [*Passionately.*] Now. Before you leave this room. [*He retreats a few steps, and stands as if to bar* MORELL'S *way to the door.*]

MORELL. [*Without moving, and gravely, perceiving now that there is something serious the matter.*] I'm not going to leave it, my dear boy: I thought y o u were. [EUGENE, *baffled by his firm tone, turns his back on him, writhing with anger.* MORELL *goes to him and puts his hand on his shoulder strongly and kindly, disregarding his attempt to shake it off.*] Come: sit down quietly; and tell me what it is. And remember: we are friends, and need not fear that either of us will be anything but patient and kind to the other, whatever we may have to say.

MARCHBANKS. [*Twisting himself round on him.*] Oh, I am not forgetting myself: I am only [*Covering his face desperately with his hands*] full of horror. [*Then, dropping his hands, and thrusting his face forward fiercely at* MORELL, *he goes on threateningly.*] You shall see whether this is a time for patience and kindness. [MORELL, *firm as a rock, looks indulgently at him.*] Dont look at me in that self-complacent way. You think yourself stronger than I am; but I shall stagger you if you have a heart in your breast.

MORELL. [*Powerfully confident.*] Stagger me, my boy. Out with it.

MARCHBANKS. First—

MORELL. First?

MARCHBANKS. I love your wife.

[MORELL *recoils, and, after staring at him for a moment in utter amazement, bursts into uncontrollable laughter.* EUGENE *is taken aback, but not disconcerted; and he soon becomes indignant and contemptuous.*]

MORELL. [*Sitting down to have his laugh out.*] Why, my dear child, of course you do. Everybody loves her: they cant help it. I like it. But [*Looking up jocosely at him*] I say, Eugene: do you think yours is a case to be talked about? Youre under twenty: she's over thirty. Doesnt it look rather too like a case of calf love?

MARCHBANKS. [*Vehemently.*] You dare say that of her! You think that way of the love she inspires! It is an insult to her!

MORELL. [*Rising quickly, in an altered tone.*] To her! Eugene: take care. I have been patient. I hope to remain patient. But there are some things I wont allow. Dont force me to shew you the indulgence I should shew to a child. Be a man.

MARCHBANKS. [*With a gesture as if sweeping something behind him.*] Oh, let us put aside all that cant. It horrifies me when I think of the doses of it she has had to endure in all the weary years during which you have selfishly and blindly sacrificed her to minister to your self-sufficiency: y o u! [*Turning on him*] who have not one thought—one sense—in common with her.

MORELL. [*Philosophically.*]   She seems to bear it pretty well. [*Looking him straight in the face.*] Eugene, my boy: you are making a fool of yourself: a very great fool of yourself. Theres a piece of wholesome plain speaking for you. [*He knocks in the lesson with a nod in his old way, and posts himself on the hearth-rug, holding his hands behind him to warm them.*]

MARCHBANKS.   Oh, do you think I dont know all that? Do you think that the things people make fools of themselves about are any less real and true than the things they behave sensibly about? [MORELL's *gaze wavers for the first time. He forgets to warm his hands, and stands listening, startled and thoughtful.*] They are more true: they are the only things that are true. You are very calm and sensible and moderate with me because you can see that I am a fool about your wife; just as no doubt that old man who was here just now is very wise over your Socialism, because he sees that y o u are a fool about it. [MORELL's *perplexity deepens markedly. Eugene follows up his advantage, plying him fiercely with questions.*] Does that prove you wrong? Does your complacent superiority to me prove that *I* am wrong?

MORELL.   Marchbanks: some devil is putting these words into your mouth. It is easy—terribly easy—to shake a man's faith in himself. To take advantage of that to break a man's spirit is devil's work. Take care of what you are doing. Take care.

MARCHBANKS. [*Ruthlessly.*]   I know. I'm doing it on purpose. I told you I should stagger you.

[*They confront one another threateningly for a moment. Then* MORELL *recovers his dignity.*]

MORELL. [*With noble tenderness.*]   Eugene: listen to me. Some day, I hope and trust, you will be a happy man like me. [EUGENE *chafes intolerably, repudiating the worth of his happiness.* MORELL, *deeply insulted, controls himself with fine forbearance, and continues steadily, with great artistic beauty of delivery.*] You will be married; and you will be working with all your might and valor to make every spot on earth as happy as your own home. You will be one of the makers of the Kingdom of Heaven on earth; and—who knows?—you may be a master builder where I am only a humble journeyman; for dont think, my boy, that I cannot see in you, young as you are, promise of higher powers than I can ever pretend to. I well know that it is in the poet that the holy spirit of man—the god within him—is most godlike. It should make you tremble to think of that—to think that the heavy burthen and great gift of a poet may be laid upon you.

MARCHBANKS. [*Unimpressed and remorseless, his boyish crudity of assertion telling sharply against* MORELL's *oratory.*] It does not make me tremble. It is the want of it in others that makes me tremble.

MORELL. [*Redoubling his force of style under the stimulus of his genuine feeling and* EUGENE's *obduracy.*]   Then help to kindle it in them—in me—not to extinguish it. In the future, when you are as happy as I am, I will be your true brother in the faith. I will help you to believe that God has given us a world that nothing but our own folly keeps from being a paradise. I will help you to believe that every stroke of your work is sowing happiness for the great harvest that all—even the humblest—shall one day reap. And last, but trust me, not least, I will help you to believe that your wife loves you and is happy in her home. We need such help, Marchbanks: we need it greatly and always. There are so many things to make us doubt, if once we let our understanding be troubled. Even at home, we sit as if in camp, encompassed by a hostile army of doubts. Will you play the traitor and let them in on me?

MARCHBANKS. [Looking round wildly.] Is it like this for her here always? A woman, with a great soul, craving for reality, truth, freedom; and being fed on metaphors, sermons, stale perorations, mere rhetoric. Do you think a woman's soul can live on your talent for preaching?

MORELL. [Stung.] Marchbanks: you make it hard for me to control myself. My talent is like yours insofar as it has any real worth at all. It is the gift of finding words for divine truth.

MARCHBANKS. [Impetuously.] It's the gift of the gab, nothing more and nothing less. What has your knack of fine talking to do with the truth, any more than playing the organ has? Ive never been in your church; but Ive been to your political meetings; and Ive seen you do whats called rousing the meeting to enthusiasm: that is, you excited them until they behaved exactly as if they were drunk. And their wives looked on and saw what fools they were. Oh, it's an old story: youll find it in the Bible. I imagine King David, in his fits of enthusiasm, was very like you. [Stabbing him with the words.] "But his wife despised him in her heart."

MORELL. [Wrathfully.] Leave my house. Do you hear? [He advances on him threateningly.]

MARCHBANKS. [Shrinking back against the couch.] Let me alone. Dont touch me. [MORELL grasps him powerfully by the lapel of his coat: he cowers down on the sofa and screams passionately.] Stop, Morell: if you strike me, I'll kill myself: I wont bear it. [Almost in hysterics.] Let me go. Take your hand away.

MORELL. [With slow emphatic scorn.] You little snivelling cowardly whelp. [He releases him.] Go, before you frighten yourself into a fit.

MARCHBANKS. [On the sofa, gasping, but relieved by the withdrawal of MORELL's hand.] I'm not afraid of you: it's you who are afraid of me.

MORELL. [Quietly, as he stands over him.] It looks like it, doesn't it?

MARCHBANKS. [With petulant vehemence.] Yes, it does. [MORELL turns away contemptuously. EUGENE scrambles to his feet and follows him.] You think because I shrink from being brutally handled—because [With tears in his voice] I can do nothing but cry with rage when I am met with violence—because I cant lift a heavy trunk down from the top of a cab like you—because I cant fight you for your wife as a drunken navvy would: all that makes you think I'm afraid of you. But youre wrong. If I havent got what you call British pluck, I havent British cowardice either: I'm not afraid of a clergyman's ideas.

I'll fight your ideas. I'll rescue her from her slavery to them. I'll pit my own ideas against them. You are driving me out of the house because you darent let her choose between your ideas and mine. You are afraid to let me see her again. [MORELL, angered, turns suddenly on him. He flies to the door in involuntary dread.] Let me alone, I say. I'm going.

MORELL. [With cold scorn.] Wait a moment: I am not going to touch you: dont be afraid. When my wife comes back she will want to know why you have gone. And when she finds that you are never going to cross our threshold again, she will want to have that explained too. Now I dont wish to distress her by telling her that you have behaved like a blackguard.

MARCHBANKS. [Coming back with renewed vehemence.] You shall. You must. If you give any explanation but the true one, you are a liar and a coward. Tell her what I said; and how you were strong and manly, and shook me as a terrier shakes a rat; and how I shrank and was terrified; and how you called me a snivelling little whelp and put me out of the house. If you dont tell her, I will: I'll write it to her.

MORELL. [Puzzled.] Why do you want her to know this?

MARCHBANKS. [With lyric rapture.] Because she will understand me, and know that I understand her. If you keep back one word of it from her—if you are not ready to lay the truth at her feet as I am—then you will know to the end of your days that she really belongs to me and not to you. Goodbye. [Going.]

MORELL. [Terribly disquieted.] Stop: I will not tell her.

MARCHBANKS. [Turning near the door.] Either the truth or a lie you m u s t tell her, if I go.

MORELL. [Temporizing.] Marchbanks: it is sometimes justifiable—

MARCHBANKS. [Cutting him short.] I know: to lie. It will be useless. Goodbye, Mr Clergyman.

[As he turns finally to the door, it opens and CANDIDA enters in her housekeeping dress.]

CANDIDA. Are you going, Eugene? [Looking more observantly at him.] Well, dear me, just look at you, going out into the street in that state! You are a poet, certainly. Look at him, James! [She takes him by the coat, and brings him forward, shewing him to MORELL.] Look at his collar! look at his tie! look at his hair! One would think somebody had been throttling you. [EUGENE instinctively tries to look round at MORELL; but she pulls him back.] Here! Stand still. [She buttons his collar; ties his neckerchief in a bow; and arranges his hair.] There! Now you look so nice that I think youd better stay to lunch after all, though I told you you musnt. It will be ready in half an hour. [She puts a final touch to the bow. He kisses her hand.] Don't be silly.

MARCHBANKS. I want to stay, of course; unless the reverend gentleman your husband has anything to advance to the contrary.

CANDIDA. Shall he stay, James, if he promises to be a good boy and help me to lay the table?

MORELL. [Shortly.] Oh yes, certainly: he had better. [He goes to the table and pretends to busy himself with his papers there.]

MARCHBANKS. [Offering his arm to CANDIDA.] Come and lay the table. [She takes it. They go to the door together. As they pass out he adds.] I am the happiest of mortals.

MORELL. So was I—an hour ago.

ACT TWO

SCENE: The same day later in the afternoon. The same room. The chair for visitors has been replaced at the table. MARCHBANKS, alone and idle, is trying to find out how the typewriter works. Hearing someone at the door, he steals guiltily away to the window and pretends to be absorbed in the view. MISS GARNETT, carrying the notebook in which she takes down MORELL'S letters in shorthand from his dictation, sits down at the typewriter and sets to work transcribing them, much too busy to notice EUGENE. When she begins the second line she stops and stares at the machine. Something wrong evidently.

PROSERPINE. Bother! Youve been meddling with my typewriter, Mr Marchbanks; and theres not the least use in your trying to look as if you hadnt.

MARCHBANKS. [Timidly.] I'm very sorry, Miss Garnett. I only tried to make it write. [Plaintively.] But it wouldnt.

PROSERPINE. Well, youve altered the spacing

MARCHBANKS. [Earnestly.] I assure you I didnt. I didnt indeed. I only turned a little wheel. It gave a sort of click.

PROSERPINE. Oh, now I understand. [She restores the spacing, talking volubly all the time.] I suppose you thought it was a sort of barrel-organ. Nothing to do but turn the handle, and it would write a beautiful love letter for you straight off, eh?

MARCHBANKS. [Seriously.] I suppose a machine c o u l d be made to write love letters. Theyre all the same, arnt they?

PROSERPINE. [Somewhat indignantly: any such discussion, except by way of pleasantry, being outside her code of manners.] How do I know? Why do you ask m e?

MARCHBANKS. I beg your pardon. I thought clever people—people who can do business and write letters and that sort of thing—always had to have love affairs to keep them from going mad.

PROSERPINE. [Rising, outraged.] Mr Marchbanks! [She looks severely at him, and marches majestically to the bookcase.]

MARCHBANKS. [Approaching her humbly.] I hope I havnt offended you. Perhaps I shouldnt have alluded to your love affairs.

PROSERPINE. [Plucking a blue book from the shelf and turning sharply on *him.*] I havnt any love affairs. How dare you say such a thing? The idea! [*She tucks the book under her arm, and is flouncing back to her machine when he addresses her with awakened interest and sympathy.*]

MARCHBANKS.   Really! Oh, then you are shy, like me.

PROSERPINE.   Certainly I am not shy. What do you mean?

MARCHBANKS. [*Secretly.*]   You must be: that is the reason there are so few love affairs in the world. We all go about longing for love: it is the first need of our natures, the first prayer of our hearts; but we dare not utter our longing: we are too shy. [*Very earnestly.*] Oh, Miss Garnett, what would you not give to be without fear, without shame—

PROSERPINE. [*Scandalized.*]   Well, upon my word!

MARCHBANKS. [*With petulant impatience.*]   Ah, dont say those stupid things to me: they dont deceive me: what use are they? Why are you afraid to be your real self with me? I am just like you.

PROSERPINE.   Like m e! Pray are you flattering me or flattering yourself? I dont feel quite sure which. [*She again tries to get back to her work.*]

MARCHBANKS. [*Stopping her mysteriously.*]   Hush! I go about in search of love; and I find it in unmeasured stores in the bosoms of others. But when I try to ask for it, this horrible shyness strangles me; and I stand dumb, or worse than dumb, saying meaningless things: foolish lies. And I see the affection I am longing for given to dogs and cats and pet birds, because they come and ask for it. [*Almost whispering.*] It must be asked for: it is like a ghost: it cannot speak unless it is first spoken to. [*At his usual pitch, but with deep melancholy.*] All the love in the world is longing to speak; only it dare not, because it is shy! shy! shy! That is the world's tragedy. [*With a deep sigh he sits in the visitors' chair and buries his face in his hands.*]

PROSERPINE. [*Amazed, but keeping her wits about her: her point of honor in encounters with strange young men.*]   Wicked people get over that shyness occasionally, dont they?

MARCHBANKS. [*Scrambling up almost fiercely.*]   Wicked people means people who have no love: therefore they have no shame. They have the power to ask love because they dont need it: they have the power to offer it because they have none to give. [*He collapses into his seat, and adds, mournfully.*] But we, who h a v e love, and long to mingle it with the love of others: we cannot utter a word. [*Timidly.*] You find that, dont you?

PROSERPINE.   Look here: if you dont stop talking like this, I'll leave the room, Mr Marchbanks: I really will. It's not proper.

[*She resumes her seat at the typewriter, opening the blue book and preparing to copy a passage from it.*]

MARCHBANKS. [*Hopelessly.*]   Nothing thats worth saying is proper. [*He rises, and wanders about the room in his lost way.*] I cant understand you, Miss Garnett. What am I to talk about?

PROSERPINE. [*Snubbing him.*]   Talk about indifferent things. Talk about the weather.

MARCHBANKS. Would you talk about indifferent things if a child were by, crying bitterly with hunger?

PROSERPINE. I suppose not.

MARCHBANKS. Well: *I* cant talk about indifferent things with my heart crying bitterly in i t s hunger.

PROSERPINE. Then hold your tongue.

MARCHBANKS. Yes: that is what it always comes to. We hold our tongues. Does that stop the cry of your heart? for it does cry: doesnt it? It must, if you have a heart.

PROSERPINE. [*Suddenly rising with her hand pressed on her heart.*] Oh, it's no use trying to work while you talk like that. [*She leaves her little table and sits on the sofa. Her feelings are keenly stirred.*] It's no business of yours whether my heart cries or not; but I have a mind to tell you, for all that.

MARCHBANKS. You neednt. I know already that it must.

PROSERPINE. But mind! if you ever say I said so, I'll deny it.

MARCHBANKS. [*Compassionately.*] Yes, I know. And so you havnt the courage to tell him?

PROSERPINE. [*Bouncing up.*] H i m! Who?

MARCHBANKS. Whoever he is. The man you love. It might be anybody. The curate, Mr Mill, perhaps.

PROSERPINE. [*With disdain.*] Mr Mill!!! A fine man to break my heart about, indeed! I'd rather have y o u than Mr Mill.

MARCHBANKS. [*Recoiling.*] No, really: I'm very sorry; but you mustnt think of that. I—

PROSERPINE. [*Testily, going to the fire-place and standing at it with her back to him.*] Oh, dont be frightened: it's not you. It's not any one particular person.

MARCHBANKS. I know. You feel that you could love anybody that offered—

PROSERPINE. [*Turning, exasperated.*] Anybody that offered! No, I do not. What do you take me for?

MARCHBANKS. [*Discouraged.*] No use. You wont make me r e a l answers: only those things that everybody says. [*He strays to the sofa and sits down disconsolately*].

PROSERPINE. [*Nettled at what she takes to be a disparagement of her manners by an aristocrat.*] Oh well, if you want original conversation, youd better go and talk to yourself.

MARCHBANKS. That is what all the poets do: they talk to themselves out loud; and the world overhears them. But it's horribly lonely not to hear someone else talk sometimes.

PROSERPINE. Wait until Mr Morell comes. H e ' l l talk to you. [MARCHBANKS *shudders.*] Oh, you neednt make wry faces over him: he can talk better than you. [*With temper.*] He'd talk your little head off. [*She is going back angrily to her place, when he, suddenly enlightened, springs up and stops her.*]

MARCHBANKS. Ah! I understand now.

PROSERPINE. [*Reddening.*]   What do you understand?

MARCHBANKS.   Your secret. Tell me: is it really and truly possible for a woman to love him?

PROSERPINE. [*As if this were beyond all bounds.*]   Well!!

MARCHBANKS. [*Passionately.*]   No: answer me. I want to know: I m u s t know. *I* cant understand it. I can see nothing in him but words, pious resolutions, what people call goodness. You cant love that.

PROSERPINE. [*Attempting to snub him by an air of cool propriety.*]   I simply dont know what youre talking about. I dont understand you.

MARCHBANKS. [*Vehemently.*]   You do. You lie.

PROSERPINE.   Oh!

MARCHBANKS.   You d o understand; and you k n o w. [*Determined to have an answer.*] Is it possible for a woman to love him?

PROSERPINE. [*Looking him straight in the face.*]   Yes. [*He covers his face with his hands.*] Whatever is the matter with you! [*He takes down his hands. Frightened at the tragic mask presented to her, she hurries past him at the utmost possible distance, keeping her eyes on his face until he turns from her and goes to the child's chair beside the hearth, where he sits in the deepest dejection. As she approaches the door, it opens and* BURGESS *enters. Seeing him, she ejaculates* Praise heaven! here's somebody *and feels safe enough to resume her place at her table. She puts a fresh sheet of paper into the typewriter as* BURGESS *crosses to* EUGENE.]

BURGESS. [*Bent on taking care of the distinguished visitor.*]   Well: so this is the way they leave you to yoreself, Mr Morchbanks. Ive come to keep you company. [MARCHBANKS *looks up at him in consternation, which is quite lost on him.*] James is receivin a deppitation in the dinin room; and Candy is hupstairs heducating of a young stitcher gurl she's hinterested in. [*Condolingly.*] You must find it lonesome here with no one but the typist to talk to. [*He pulls round the easy chair, and sits down.*]

PROSERPINE. [*Highly incensed.*]   He'll be all right now that he has the advantage of y o u r polished conversation: thats one comfort, anyhow. [*She begins to typewrite with clattering asperity.*]

BURGESS. [*Amazed at her audacity.*]   Hi was not addressin myself to you, young woman, that I'm awerr of.

PROSERPINE.   Did you ever see worse manners, Mr Marchbanks?

BURGESS. [*With pompous severity.*]   Mr Morchbanks is a gentleman, and knows his place, which is more than some people do.

PROSERPINE. [*Fretfully.*]   It's well you and I are not ladies and gentlemen: I'd talk to you pretty straight if Mr Marchbanks wasnt here. [*She pulls the letter out of the machine so crossly that it tears.*] There! now I've spoiled this letter! have to be done all over again! Oh, I cant contain myself: silly old fathead!

BURGESS. [*Rising, breathless with indignation.*]   Ho! I'm a silly ole fat'ead, am I? Ho, indeed [*Gasping*]! Hall right, my gurl! Hall right. You just wait till I tell that to yore hemployer. Youll see. I'll teach you: see if I dont.

PROSERPINE. [*Conscious of having gone too far.*]   I—

BURGESS. [*Cutting her short.*]   No: youve done it now. No huse a-talkin to me. I'll let you know who I am. [PROSERPINE *shifts her paper carriage with a defiant bang, and disdainfully goes on with her work.*] Dont you take no notice of her, Mr Morchbanks. She's beneath it. [*He loftily sits down again.*]

MARCHBANKS. [*Miserably nervous and disconcerted.*]   Hadnt we better change the subject? I—I dont think Miss Garnett meant anything.

PROSERPINE. [*With intense conviction.*]   Oh, didnt I though, j u s t!

BURGESS.   I wouldnt demean myself to take notice on her.

[*An electric bell rings twice.*]

PROSERPINE. [*Gathering up her notebook and papers.*]   Thats for me. [*She hurries out.*]

BURGESS. [*Calling after her.*]   Oh, we can spare you. [*Somewhat relieved by the triumph of having the last word, and yet half inclined to try to improve on it, he looks after her for a moment; then subsides into his seat by* EUGENE, *and addresses him very confidentially.*]   Now we're alone, Mr Morchbanks, let me give you a friendly int that I wouldnt give to heverybody. Ow long ave you known my son-in-law James ere?

MARCHBANKS.   I dont know. I never can remember dates. A few months, perhaps.

BURGESS.   Ever notice hennythink queer about him?

MARCHBANKS.   I dont think so.

BURGESS. [*Impressively.*]   No more you wouldnt. Thats the danger on it. Well, he's mad.

MARCHBANKS.   Mad!

BURGESS.   Mad as a Morch 'are. You take notice on him and youll see.

MARCHBANKS. [*Uneasily.*]   But surely that is only because his opinions—

BURGESS. [*Touching him on the knee with his forefinger, and pressing it to hold his attention.*]   Thats the same what I hused to think, Mr Morchbanks. Hi thought long enough that it was ony his opinions; though, mind you, hopinions becomes vury serious things when people takes to hactin on em as e does. But thats not what I go on. [*He looks round to make sure that they are alone, and bends over to* EUGENE's *ear.*] What do you think he sez to me this mornin in this very room?

MARCHBANKS.   What?

BURGESS.   He sez to me—this is as sure as we're sitting here now—he sez "I'm a fool," he sez; "and yore a scounderl." Me a scounderl, mind you! And then shook ands with me on it, as if it was to my credit! Do you mean to tell me as that man's sane?

MORELL. [*Outside, calling to* PROSERPINE *as he opens the door.*]   Get all their names and addresses, Miss Garnett.

PROSERPINE. [*In the distance.*]   Yes, Mr Morell.

[MORELL *comes in, with the deputation's documents in his hands.*]

BURGESS. [*Aside to* MARCHBANKS.]   Yorr he is. Just you keep your heye on im and see. [*Rising momentously.*] I'm sorry, James, to ave to make a complaint to you. I dont want to do it; but I feel I oughter, as a matter o right and dooty.

MORELL.   Whats the matter?

BURGESS.   Mr Morchbanks will bear me hout: he was a witness. [*Very solemly.*] Yore young woman so far forgot herself as to call me a silly ole fat'ead.

MORELL.   [*With tremendous heartiness.*]   Oh, now, isnt that e x a c t l y like Prossy? She's so frank: she cant contain herself! Poor Prossy! Ha! ha!

BURGESS.   [*Trembling with rage.*]   And do you hexpec me to put up with it from the like of er?

MORELL.   Pooh, nonsense! you cant take any notice of it. Never mind. [*He goes to the cellaret and puts the papers into one of the drawers.*]

BURGESS.   Oh, Hi dont mind. Hi'm above it. But is it r i g h t? thats what I want to know. Is it right?

MORELL.   Thats a question for the Church, not for the laity. Has it done you any harm? thats the question for you, eh? Of course it hasnt. Think no more of it. [*He dismisses the subject by going to his place at the table and setting to work at his correspondence.*]

BURGESS. [*Aside to* MARCHBANKS.]   What did I tell you? Mad as a atter. [*He goes to the table and asks, with the sickly civility of a hungry man.*] When's dinner, James?

MORELL.   Not for a couple of hours yet.

BURGESS. [*With plaintive resignation.*]   Gimme a nice book to read over the fire, will you, James: thur's a good chap.

MORELL.   What sort of book? A good one?

BURGESS. [*With almost a yell of remonstrance.*]   Nah-oo! Summat pleasant, just to pass the time. [MORELL *takes an illustrated paper from the table and offers it. He accepts it humbly.*] Thank yer, James. [*He goes back to the big chair at the fire, and sits there at his ease, reading.*]

MORELL. [*As he writes.*]   Candida will come to entertain you presently. She has got rid of her pupil. She is filling the lamps.

MARCHBANKS. [*Starting up in the wildest consternation.*]   But that will soil her hands. I cant bear that, Morell: it's a shame. I'll go and fill them. [*He makes for the door.*]

MORELL.   Youd better not. [MARCHBANKS *stops irresolutely.*] She'd only set you to clean my boots, to save me the trouble of doing it myself in the morning.

BURGESS. [*With grave disapproval.*]   Dont you keep a servant now, James?

MORELL.   Yes; but she isnt a slave; and the house looks as if I kept three. That means that everyone has to lend a hand. It's not a bad plan: Prossy and I can talk business after breakfast while we're washing up. Washing up's no trouble when there are two people to do it.

MARCHBANKS.   [*Tormentedly.*]   Do you think every woman is as coarse-grained as Miss Garnett?

BURGESS. [*Emphatically.*]   Thats quite right, Mr Morchbanks: thats q u i t e right. She is corsegrained.

MORELL. [*Quietly and significantly.*]   Marchbanks!

MARCHBANKS.   Yes?

MORELL.   How many servants does your father keep?

MARCHBANKS. [*Pettishly.*]   Oh, I dont know. [*He moves to the sofa, as if to get as far as possible from* MORELL'S *questioning, and sits down in great agony of spirit, thinking of the paraffin.*]

MORELL. [*Very gravely.*]   So many that you dont know! [*More aggressively.*] When theres anything coarsegrained to be done, you just ring the bell and throw it on to somebody else, eh?

MARCHBANKS.   Oh, dont torture me. You dont even ring the bell. But your wife's beautiful fingers are dabbling in paraffin oil while you sit here comfortably preaching about it: everlasting preaching! preaching! words! words! words!

BURGESS. [*Intensely appreciating this retort.*]   Har, har! Devil a better! [*Radiantly.*] Ad you there, James, straight.

[CANDIDA *comes in, well aproned, with a reading lamp trimmed, filled, and ready for lighting. She places it on the table near* MORELL, *ready for use.*]

CANDIDA. [*Brushing her finger tips together with a slight twitch of her nose.*] If you stay with us, Eugene, I think I will hand over the lamps to you.

MARCHBANKS.   I will stay on condition that you hand over all the rough work to me.

CANDIDA.   Thats very gallant; but I think I should like to see how you do it first. [*Turning to* MORELL.] James: youve not been looking after the house properly.

MORELL.   What have I done—or not done—my love?

CANDIDA. [*With serious vexation.*]   My own particular pet scrubbing brush has been used for blackleading. [*A heartbreaking wail bursts from* MARCHBANKS. BURGESS *looks round, amazed.* CANDIDA *hurries to the sofa.*] Whats the matter? Are you ill, Eugene?

MARCHBANKS.   No: not ill. Only horror! horror! horror! [*He bows his head on his hands.*]

BURGESS. [*Shocked.*]   What! Got the orrors, Mr Morchbanks! Oh, thats bad, at your age. You must leave it off grajally.

CANDIDA. [*Reassured.*]   Nonsense, papa! It's only poetic horror, isnt it, Eugene? [*Petting him.*]

BURGESS. [*Abashed.*]   Oh, poetic orror, is it? I beg your pordon, I'm shore. [*He turns to the fire again, deprecating his hasty conclusion.*]

CANDIDA.   What is it, Eugene? the scrubbing brush? [*He shudders.*] Well, there! never mind. [*She sits down beside him.*] Wouldnt you like to present me with a nice new one, with an ivory back inlaid with mother-of-pearl?

MARCHBANKS. [*Softly and musically, but sadly and longingly.*]   No, not a scrubbing brush, but a boat: a tiny shallop to sail away in, far from the world, where the marble floors are washed by the rain and dried by the sun; where the south wind dusts the beautiful green and purple carpets. Or a chariot! to carry us up into the sky, where the lamps are stars, and dont need to be filled with paraffin oil every day.

MORELL. [*Harshly.*]   And where there is nothing to do but to be idle, selfish, and useless.

CANDIDA. [*Jarred.*]   Oh, James! how could you spoil it all?

MARCHBANKS. [*Firing up.*]   Yes, to be idle, selfish, and useless: that is, to be beautiful and free and happy: hasnt every man desired that with all his soul for the woman he loves? Thats my ideal: whats yours, and that of all the dreadful people who live in these hideous rows of houses? Sermons and scrubbing brushes! With you to preach the sermon and your wife to scrub.

CANDIDA. [*Quaintly.*]   He cleans the boots, Eugene. You will have to clean them to-morrow for saying that about him.

MARCHBANKS.   Oh, dont talk about boots! Your feet should be beautiful on the mountains.

CANDIDA.   My feet would not be beautiful on the Hackney Road without boots.

BURGESS. [*Scandalized.*]   Come, Candy! dont be vulgar. Mr Morchbanks aint accustomed to it. Youre givin him the orrors again. I mean the poetic ones.

[MORELL *is silent. Apparently he is busy with his letters: really he is puzzling with misgiving over his new and alarming experience that the surer he is of his moral thrusts, the more swiftly and effectively* EUGENE *parries them. To find himself beginning to fear a man whom he does not respect afflicts him bitterly.*]

[MISS GARNETT *comes in with a telegram.*]

PROSERPINE. [*Handing the telegram to* MORELL.]   Reply paid. The boy's waiting. [*To* CANDIDA, *coming back to her machine and sitting down.*] Maria is ready for you now in the kitchen, Mrs Morell. [CANDIDA *rises.*] The onions have come.

MARCHBANKS. [*Convulsively.*]   Onions!

CANDIDA.   Yes, onions. Not even Spanish ones: nasty little red onions. You shall help me to slice them. Come along.

[*She catches him by the wrist and runs out, pulling him after her.* BURGESS *rises in consternation, and stands aghast on the hearth-rug, staring after them.*]

BURGESS.   Candy didnt oughter andle a hearl's nevvy like that. It's goin too fur with it. Lookee ere, James: do e often git taken queer like that?

MORELL. [*Shortly, writing a telegram.*]   I dont know.

BURGESS. [*Sentimentally.*]   He talks very pretty. I awlus had a turn for a bit of poetry. Candy takes arter me that-a-way. Huseter make me tell er fairy stories when she was ony a little kiddy not that igh. [*Indicating a stature of two feet or thereabouts.*]

MORELL. [*Preoccupied.*]   Ah, indeed. [*He blots the telegram and goes out.*]

PROSERPINE. Used you to make the fairy stories up out of your own head?
[BURGESS, *not deigning to reply, strikes an attitude of the haughtiest disdain on the hearth-rug.*]

PROSERPINE. [*Calmly.*] I should never have supposed you had it in you. By the way, I'd better warn you, since youve taken such a fancy to Mr Marchbanks. He's mad.

BURGESS. Mad! What! Im too!!

PROSERPINE. Mad as a March hare. He did frighten me, I can tell you, just before you came in that time. Havnt you noticed the queer things he says?

BURGESS. So thats what the poetic orrors means. Blame me if it didnt come into my ed once or twyst that he was a bit horff 'is chump! [*He crosses the room to the door, lifting up his voice as he goes.*] Well, this is a pretty sort of asylum for a man to be in, with no one but you to take care of him!

PROSERPINE. [*As he passes her.*] Yes, what a dreadful thing it would be if anything happened to y o u!

BURGESS. [*Loftily.*] Dont you haddress no remarks to me. Tell your hemployer that Ive gone into the gorden for a smoke.

PROSERPINE. [*Mocking.*] Oh!
[*Before* BURGESS *can retort,* MORELL *comes back.*]

BURGESS. [*Sentimentally.*] Goin for a turn in the gording to smoke, James.

MORELL. [*Brusquely.*] Oh, all right, all right. [BURGESS *goes out pathetically in the character of a weary old man.* MORELL *stands at the table, turning over his papers, and adding, across to* PROSERPINE, *half humorously, half absently.*] Well, Miss Prossy, why have you been calling my father-in-law names?

PROSERPINE. [*Blushing fiery red, and looking quickly up at him, half scared, half reproachful.*] I—[*She bursts into tears.*]

MORELL. [*With tender gaiety, leaning across the table towards her, and consoling her.*] Oh, come! come! come! Never mind, Pross: he i s a silly old fathead, isnt he?

[*With an explosive sob, she makes a dash at the door, and vanishes, banging it.* MORELL, *shaking his head resignedly, sighs, and goes wearily to his chair, where he sits down and sets to work, looking old and careworn.*

CANDIDA *comes in. She has finished her household work and taken off the apron. She at once notices his dejected appearance, and posts herself quietly at the visitors' chair, looking down at him attentively. She says nothing.*]

MORELL. [*Looking up, but with his pen raised ready to resume his work.*] Well? Where is Eugene?

CANDIDA. Washing his hands in the scullery under the tap. He will make an excellent cook if he can only get over his dread of Maria.

MORELL. [*Shortly.*] Ha! No doubt. [*He begins writing again.*]

CANDIDA. [*Going nearer, and putting her hand down softly on his to stop him as she says.*] Come here, dear. Let me look at you. [*He drops his pen and yields himself to her disposal. She makes him rise, and brings him a little away from the table, looking at him critically all the time.*] Turn your face to the light.

[*She places him facing the window.*] My boy is not looking well. Has he been overworking?

MORELL.   Nothing more than usual.

CANDIDA.   He looks very pale, and grey, and wrinkled, and old. [*His melancholy deepens; and she attacks it with wilful gaiety.*] Here: [*Pulling him towards the easy chair*] youve done enough writing for to-day. Leave Prossy to finish it. Come and talk to me.

MORELL.   But—

CANDIDA. [*Insisting.*]   Yes, I m u s t be talked to. [*She makes him sit down, and seats herself on the carpet beside his knee.*] Now [*Patting his hand*] youre beginning to look better already. Why must you go out every night lecturing and talking? I hardly have one evening a week with you. Of course what you say is all very true; but it does no good: they dont mind what you say to them one little bit. They think they agree with you; but whats the use of their agreeing with you if they go and do just the opposite of what you tell them the moment your back is turned? Look at our congregation at St Dominic's! Why do they come to hear you talking about Christianity every Sunday? Why, just because theyve been so full of business and money-making for six days that they want to forget all about it and have a rest on the seventh; so that they can go back fresh and make money harder than ever! You positively help them at it instead of hindering them.

MORELL. [*With energetic seriousness.*]   You know very well, Candida, that I often blow them up soundly for that. And if there is nothing in their churchgoing but rest and diversion, why dont they try something more amusing? more self-indulgent? There must be some good in the fact that they prefer St Dominic's to worse places on Sundays.

CANDIDA.   Oh, the worse places arnt open; and even if they were, they darent be seen going to them. Besides, James dear, you preach so splendidly that it's as good as a play for them. Why do you think the women are so enthusiastic?

MORELL. [*Shocked.*]   Candida!

CANDIDA.   Oh, I know. You silly boy: you think it's your Socialism and your religion; but if it were that, theyd do what you tell them instead of only coming to look at you. They all have Prossy's complaint.

MORELL.   Prossy's complaint! What do you mean, Candida?

CANDIDA.   Yes, Prossy, and all the other secretaries you ever had. Why does Prossy condescend to wash up the things, and to peel potatoes and abase herself in all manner of ways for six shillings a week less than she used to get in a city office? She's in love with you, James: thats the reason. Theyre all in love with you. And you are in love with preaching because you do it so beautifully. And you think it's all enthusiasm for the kingdom of Heaven on earth; and so do they. You dear silly!

MORELL.   Candida: what dreadful! what soul-destroying cynicism! Are you jesting? Or—can it be?—are you jealous?

CANDIDA. [*With curious thoughtfulness.*]   Yes, I feel a little jealous sometimes.

MORELL. [*Incredulously.*]   Of Prossy?

CANDIDA. [*Laughing.*]   No, no, no, no. Not jealous o f anybody. Jealous f o r somebody else, who is not loved as he ought to be.

MORELL.   Me?

CANDIDA.   You! Why, youre spoiled with love and worship: you get far more than is good for you. No: I mean Eugene.

MORELL. [*Startled.*]   Eugene!

CANDIDA.   It seems unfair that all the love should go to you, and none to him; although he needs it so much more than you do. [*A convulsive movement shakes him in spite of himself.*] Whats the matter? Am I worrying you?

MORELL. [*Hastily.*]   Not at all. [*Looking at her with troubled intensity.*] You know that I have perfect confidence in you, Candida.

CANDIDA.   You vain thing! Are you so sure of your irresistible attractions?

MORELL.   Candida; you are shocking me. I never thought of my attractions. I thought of your goodness, of your purity. That is what I confide in.

CANDIDA.   What a nasty uncomfortable thing to say to me! Oh, you are a clergyman, James: a thorough clergyman!

MORELL. [*Turning away from her, heart-stricken.*]   So Eugene says.

CANDIDA. [*With lively interest, leaning over to him with her arms on his knee.*] Eugene's always right. He's a wonderful boy: I have grown fonder and fonder of him all the time I was away. Do you know, James, that though he has not the least suspicion of it himself, he is ready to fall madly in love with me?

MORELL. [*Grimly.*]   Oh, he has no suspicion of it himself, hasnt he?

CANDIDA.   Not a bit. [*She takes her arms from his knee, and turns thought-fully, sinking into a more restful attitude with her hands in her lap.*] Some day he will know: when he is grown up and experienced, like you. And he will know that I must have known. I wonder what he will think of me then.

MORELL.   No evil, Candida. I hope and trust, no evil.

CANDIDA. [*Dubiously.*]   That will depend.

MORELL. [*Bewildered.*]   Depend!

CANDIDA. [*Looking at him.*]   Yes: it will depend on what happens to him. [*He looks vacantly at her.*] Dont you see? It will depend on how he comes to learn what love really is. I mean on the sort of woman who will teach it to him.

MORELL. [*Quite at a loss.*]   Yes. No. I dont know what you mean.

CANDIDA. [*Explaining.*]   If he learns it from a good woman, then it will be all right: he will forgive me.

MORELL.   Forgive?

CANDIDA.   But supose he learns it from a bad woman, as so many men do, especially poetic men, who imagine all women are angels! Suppose he only discovers the value of love when he has thrown it away and degraded himself in his ignorance! Will he forgive me then, do you think?

MORELL.   Forgive you for what?

CANDIDA. [*Realizing how stupid he is, and a little disappointed, though quite tenderly so.*] Dont you understand? [*He shakes his head. She turns to him again, so as to explain with the fondest intimacy.*] I mean, will he forgive me for not teaching him myself? For abandoning him to the bad women for the sake of my goodness, of my purity, as you call it? Ah, James, how little you understand me, to talk of your confidence in my goodness and purity! I would give them both to poor Eugene as willingly as I would give my shawl to a beggar dying of cold, if there were nothing else to restrain me. Put your trust in my love for you, James; for if that went, I should care very little for your sermons: mere phrases that you cheat yourself and others with every day. [*She is about to rise.*]

MORELL.   H i s words!

CANDIDA. [*Checking herself quickly in the act of getting up.*] Whose words?

MORELL.   Eugene's.

CANDIDA. [*Delighted.*] He is always right. He understands you; he understands me; he understands Prossy; and you, darling, you understand nothing. [*She laughs, and kisses him to console him. He recoils as if stabbed, and springs up.*]

MORELL.   How can you bear to do that when—Oh, Candida [*With anguish in his voice*] I had rather you had plunged a grappling iron into my heart than given me that kiss.

CANDIDA. [*Amazed.*]   My dear: whats the matter?

MORELL. [*Frantically waving her off.*]   Dont touch me.

CANDIDA.   James!!!

[*They are interrupted by the entrance of* MARCHBANKS *with* BURGESS, *who stop near the door, staring.*]

MARCHBANKS.   Is anything the matter?

MORELL. [*Deadly white, putting an iron constraint on himself.*]   Nothing but this: that either you were right this morning, or Candida is mad.

BURGESS. [*In loudest protest.*]   What! Candy mad too! Oh, come! come! come! [*He crosses the room to the fireplace, protesting as he goes, and knocks the ashes out of his pipe on the bars.*]

[MORELL *sits down at his table desperately, leaning forward to hide his face, and interlacing his fingers rigidly to keep them steady.*]

CANDIDA. [*To* MORELL, *relieved and laughing.*]   Oh, youre only shocked! Is that all? How conventional all you unconventional people are! [*She sits gaily on the arm of the chair.*]

BURGESS.   Come: be'ave yourself, Candy. Whatll Mr Morchbanks think of you?

CANDIDA.   This comes of James teaching me to think for myself, and never to hold back out of fear of what other people may think of me. It works beautifully as long as I think the same things as he does. But now! because I have just thought something different! look at him! Just look! [*She points to* MORELL, *greatly amused.*]

[EUGENE *looks, and instantly presses his hand on his heart, as if some pain had shot through it. He sits down on the sofa like a man witnessing a tragedy.*]

BURGESS. [*On the hearthrug.*]   Well, James, you certnly haint as himpressive lookin as usu'l.

MORELL. [*With a laugh which is half a sob.*]   I suppose not. I beg all your pardons: I was not conscious of making a fuss. [*Pulling himself together.*] Well, well, well, well, well! [*He sets to work at his papers again with resolute cheerfulness.*]

CANDIDA. [*Going to the sofa and sitting beside* MARCHBANKS, *still in a bantering humor.*]   Well, Eugene: why are you so sad? Did the onions make you cry?

MARCHBANKS. [*Aside to her.*]   It is your cruelty. I hate cruelty. It is a horrible thing to see one person make another suffer.

CANDIDA. [*Petting him ironically.*]   Poor boy! have I been cruel? Did I make it slice nasty little red onions?

MARCHBANKS. [*Earnestly.*]   Oh, stop, stop: I dont mean myself. You have made him suffer frightfully. I feel his pain in my own heart. I know that it is not your fault: it is something that must happen; but dont make light of it. I shudder when you torture him and laugh.

CANDIDA. [*Incredulously.*]   I torture James! Nonsense, Eugene: how you exaggerate! Silly! [*She rises and goes to the table, a little troubled.*] Dont work any more, dear. Come and talk to us.

MORELL. [*Affectionately but bitterly.*]   Ah no: I cant talk. I can only preach.

CANDIDA. [*Caressing his hand.*]   Well, come and preach.

BURGESS. [*Strongly remonstrating.*]   Aw no, Candy. 'Ang it all! [LEXY MILL *comes in, anxious and important.*]

LEXY. [*Hastening to shake hands with* CANDIDA.]   How do you do, Mrs Morell? So glad to see you back again.

CANDIDA.   Thank you, Lexy. You know Eugene, dont you?

LEXY.   Oh yes. How do you do, Marchbanks?

MARCHBANKS.   Quite well, thanks.

LEXY. [*To* MORELL.]   Ive just come from the Guild of St Matthew. They are in the greatest consternation about your telegram.

CANDIDA.   What did you telegraph about, James?

LEXY. [*To* CANDIDA.]   He was to have spoken for them tonight. Theyve taken the large hall in Mare Street and spent a lot of money on posters. Morell's telegram was to say he couldnt come. It came on them like a thunderbolt.

CANDIDA. [*Surprised, and beginning to suspect something wrong.*]   Given up an engagement to speak!

BURGESS.   Fust time in his life, I'll bet. Ain it, Candy?

LEXY. [*To* MORELL.]   They decided to send an urgent telegram to you asking whether you could not change your mind. Have you received it?

MORELL. [*With restrained impatience.*] Yes, yes: I got it.

LEXY.   It was reply paid.

MORELL.   Yes, I know. I answered it. I cant go.

CANDIDA.   But why, James?

MORELL. [*Almost fiercely.*]   Because I dont choose. These people forget that I am a man: they think I am a talking machine to be turned on for their pleasure every evening of my life. May I not have o n e night at home, with my wife, and my friends?

[*They are all amazed at this outburst, except* EUGENE. *His expression remains unchanged.*]

CANDIDA.   Oh, James, you mustnt mind what I said about that. And if you dont go youll have an attack of bad conscience to-morrow.

LEXY. [*Intimidated, but urgent.*]   I know, of course, that they make the most unreasonable demands on you. But they have been telegraphing all over the place for another speaker; and they can get nobody but the President of the Agnostic League.

MORELL. [*Promptly.*]   Well, an excellent man. What better do they want?

LEXY.   But he always insists so powerfully on the divorce of Socialism from Christianity. He will undo all the good we have been doing. Of course you know best; but—[*He shrugs his shoulders and wanders to the hearth beside* BURGESS.]

CANDIDA. [*Coaxingly.*]   Oh, d o go, James. We'll all go.

BURGESS. [*Grumblingly.*]   Look 'ere, Candy! I say! Let's stay at home by the fire, comfortable. He wont need to be more'n a couple-o-hour away.

CANDIDA.   Youll be just as comfortable at the meeting. We'll all sit on the platform and be great people.

EUGENE. [*Terrified.*]   Oh please dont let us go on the platform. No: everyone will stare at us: I couldnt. I'll sit at the back of the room.

CANDIDA.   Dont be afraid. Theyll be too busy looking at James to notice you.

MORELL.   Prossy's complaint, Candida! Eh?

CANDIDA. [*Gaily.*]   Yes: Prossy's complaint.

BURGESS. [*Mystified.*]   Prossy's complaint! What are you talkin about, James?

MORELL. [*Not heeding him, rises; goes to the door; and holds it open, calling in a commanding tone.*]   Miss Garnett.

PROSERPINE. [*In the distance.*]   Yes, Mr Morell. Coming.

[*They all wait, except* BURGESS, *who turns stealthily to* LEXY.]

BURGESS.   Listen ere, Mr Mill. Whats Prossy's complaint? Whats wrong with er?

LEXY. [*Confidentially.*]   Well, I dont exactly know; but she spoke very strangely to me this morning. I'm afraid she's a little out of her mind sometimes.

BURGESS. [*Overwhelmed.*]   Why, it must be catchin! Four in the same ouse!

PROSERPINE. [*Appearing on the threshold.*]   What is it, Mr Morell?

MORELL.   Telegraph to the Guild of St Matthew that I am coming.

PROSERPINE. [*Surprised.*]   Dont they expect you?

MORELL. [*Peremptorily.*]   Do as I tell you.

[PROSERPINE, *frightened, sits down at her typewriter, and obeys.* MORELL, *now unaccountably resolute and forceful, goes across to* BURGESS. CANDIDA *watches his movements with growing wonder and misgiving.*]

MORELL.   Burgess: you dont want to come.

BURGESS.   Oh, dont put it like that, James. It's ony that it aint Sunday, you know.

MORELL.   I'm sorry. I thought you might like to be introduced to the chairman. He's on the Works Committee of the County Council, and has some influence in the matter of contracts. [BURGESS *wakes up at once.*]   Youll come?

BURGESS.   [*With enthusiasm.*]   Cawrse I'll come, James. Aint it awlus a pleasure to ear you!

MORELL.   [*Turning to* PROSSY.]   I shall want you to take some notes at the meeting, Miss Garnett, if you have no other engagement. [*She nods, afraid to speak.*] You are coming, Lexy, I suppose?

LEXY.   Certainly.

CANDIDA.   We're all coming, James.

MORELL.   No: you are not coming; and Eugene is not coming. You will stay here and entertain him—to celebrate your return home. [EUGENE *rises, breathless.*]

CANDIDA.   But, James—

MORELL.   [*Authoritatively.*]   I insist. You do not want to come; and he does not want to come. [CANDIDA *is about to protest.*] Oh, dont concern yourselves: I shall have plenty of people without you: your chairs will be wanted by unconverted people who have never heard me before.

CANDIDA.   [*Troubled.*]   Eugene: wouldnt you like to come?

MORELL.   I should be afraid to let myself go before Eugene: he is so critical of sermons. [*Looking at him.*] He knows I am afraid of him: he told me as much this morning. Well, I shall shew him how much afraid I am by leaving him here in your custody, Candida.

MARCHBANKS.   [*To himself, with vivid feeling.*]   Thats brave. Thats beautiful.

CANDIDA.   [*With anxious misgiving.*]   But—but— Is anything the matter, James? [*Greatly troubled.*] I cant understand—

MORELL.   [*Taking her tenderly in his arms and kissing her on the forehead.*] Ah, I thought it was *I* who couldnt understand, dear.

ACT THREE

SCENE: *Past ten in the evening. The curtains are drawn, and the lamps lighted. The typewriter is in its case: the large table has been cleared and tidied: everything indicates that the day's work is over.*

CANDIDA *and* MARCHBANKS *are sitting by the fire. The reading lamp is on the mantelshelf above* MARCHBANKS, *who is in the small chair, reading aloud. A little pile of manuscripts and a couple of volumes of poetry are on the carpet beside him.* CANDIDA *is in the easy chair. The poker, a light brass one, is upright in her hand. Leaning back and looking intently at the point of it, with her feet stretched towards the blaze, she is in a waking dream, miles away from her surroundings and completely oblivious of* EUGENE.

MARCHBANKS. [*Breaking off in his recitation.*]   Every poet that ever lived has put that thought into a sonnet. He must: he cant help it. [*He looks to her for assent, and notices her absorption in the poker.*]   Havnt you been listening? [*No response.*] Mrs Morell!

CANDIDA. [*Starting.*]   Eh?

MARCHBANKS.   Havnt you been listening?

CANDIDA. [*With a guilty excess of politeness.*]   Oh yes. It's very nice. Go on, Eugene. I'm longing to hear what happens to the angel.

MARCHBANKS. [*Letting the manuscript drop from his hand to the floor.*]   I beg your pardon for boring you.

CANDIDA.   But you are not boring me, I assure you. P l e a s e go on. Do, Eugene.

MARCHBANKS.   I finished the poem about the angel quarter of an hour ago. Ive read you several things since.

CANDIDA. [*Remorsefully.*]   I'm so sorry, Eugene. I think the poker must have hypnotized me. [*She puts it down.*]

MARCHBANKS.   It made me horribly uneasy.

CANDIDA.   Why didnt you tell me? I'd have put it down at once.

MARCHBANKS.   I was afraid of making you uneasy too. It looked as if it were a weapon. If I were a hero of old I should have laid my drawn sword between us. If Morell had come in he would have thought you had taken up the poker because there was no sword between us.

CANDIDA. [*Wondering.*]   What? [*With a puzzled glance at him.*]   I cant quite follow that. Those sonnets of yours have perfectly addled me. Why should there be a sword between us?

MARCHBANKS. [*Evasively.*]   Oh, never mind. [*He stoops to pick up the manuscript.*]

CANDIDA.   Put that down again, Eugene. There are limits to my appetite for poetry: even your poetry. Youve been reading to me for more than two hours, ever since James went out. I want to talk.

MARCHBANKS. [*Rising, scared.*]   No: I mustnt talk. [*He looks round him in his lost way, and adds, suddenly.*] I think I'll go out and take a walk in the park. [*He makes for the door.*]

CANDIDA.   Nonsense: it's closed long ago. Come and sit down on the hearth-rug, and talk moonshine as you usually do. I want to be amused. Dont you want to?

MARCHBANKS. [*Half in terror, half enraptured.*]   Yes.

CANDIDA. Then come along. [*She moves her chair back a little to make room.*]

[*He hesitates; then timidly stretches himself on the hearth-rug, face upwards, and throws back his head across her knees, looking up at her.*]

MARCHBANKS. Oh, Ive been so miserable all the evening, because I was doing right. Now I'm doing wrong; and I'm happy.

CANDIDA. [*Tenderly amused at him.*] Yes: I'm sure you feel a great grown-up wicked deceiver. Quite proud of yourself, arnt you?

MARCHBANKS. [*Raising his head quickly and turning a little to look round at her.*] Take care. I'm ever so much older than you, if you only knew. [*He turns quite over on his knees, with his hands clasped and his arms on her lap, and speaks with growing impulse, his blood beginning to stir.*] May I say some wicked things to you?

CANDIDA. [*Without the least fear or coldness, and with perfect respect for his passion, but with a touch of her wise-hearted maternal humor.*] No. But you may say anything you really and truly feel. Anything at all, no matter what it is. I am not afraid, so long as it is your real self that speaks, and not a mere attitude: a gallant attitude, or a wicked attitude, or even a poetic attitude. I put you on your honor and truth. Now say whatever you want to.

MARCHBANKS. [*The eager expression vanishing utterly from his lips and nostrils as his eyes light up with pathetic spirituality.*] Oh, now I cant say anything: all the words I know belong to some attitude or other—all except one.

CANDIDA. What one is that?

MARCHBANKS. [*Softly, losing himself in the music of the name.*] Candida, Candida, Candida, Candida, Candida. I must say that now, because you have put me on my honor and truth; and I never think or feel Mrs Morell: it is always Candida.

CANDIDA. Of course. And what have you to say to Candida?

MARCHBANKS. Nothing but to repeat your name a thousand times. Dont you feel that every time is a prayer to you?

CANDIDA. Does it make you happy to be able to pray?

MARCHBANKS. Yes, very happy.

CANDIDA. Well, that happiness is the answer to your prayer. Do you want anything more?

MARCHBANKS. No: I have come into heaven, where want is unknown.

[MORELL *comes in. He halts on the threshold, and takes in the scene at a glance.*]

MORELL. [*Grave and self-contained.*] I hope I dont disturb you.

[CANDIDA *starts up violently, but without the smallest embarrassment, laughing at herself.* EUGENE, *capsized by her sudden movement, recovers himself without rising, and sits on the rug hugging his ankles, also quite unembarrassed.*]

CANDIDA. Oh, James, how you startled me! I was so taken up with Eugene that I didnt hear your latchkey. How did the meeting go off? Did you speak well?

MORELL.   I have never spoken better in my life.

CANDIDA.   That was first rate! How much was the collection?

MORELL.   I forgot to ask.

CANDIDA.   [*To* EUGENE.] He must have spoken splendidly, or he would never have forgotten that. [*To* MORELL.] Where are all the others?

MORELL.   They left long before I could get away: I thought I should never escape. I believe they are having supper somewhere.

CANDIDA. [*In her domestic business tone.*]   Oh, in that case, Maria may go to bed. I'll tell her. [*She goes out to the kitchen.*]

MORELL. [*Looking sternly down at* MARCHBANKS.]   Well?

MARCHBANKS. [*Squatting grotesquely on the hearth-rug, and actually at ease with* MORELL: *even impishly humorous.*] Well?

MORELL.   Have you anything to tell me?

MARCHBANKS.   Only that I have been making a fool of myself here in private whilst you have been making a fool of yourself in public.

MORELL.   Hardly in the same way, I think.

MARCHBANKS. [*Eagerly, scrambling up.*]   The very, very v e r y same way. I have been playing the Good Man. Just like you. When you began your heroics about leaving me here with Candida—

MORELL. [*Involuntarily.*]   Candida!

MARCHBANKS.   Oh yes: Ive got that far. But dont be afraid. Heroics are infectious: I caught the disease from you. I swore not to say a word in your absence that I would not have said a month ago in your presence.

MORELL.   Did you keep your oath?

MARCHBANKS. [*Suddenly perching himself on the back of the easy chair.*]   It kept itself somehow until about ten minutes ago. Up to that moment I went on desperately reading to her—reading my own poems—anybody's poems—to stave off a conversation. I was standing outside the gate of Heaven, and refusing to go in. Oh, you cant think how heroic it was, and how uncomfortable! Then—

MORELL. [*Steadily controlling his suspense.*]   Then?

MARCHBANKS. [*Prosaically slipping down into a quite ordinary attitude on the seat of the chair.*]   Then she couldnt bear being read to any longer.

MORELL.   And you approached the gate of Heaven at last?

MARCHBANKS.   Yes.

MORELL.   Well? [*Fiercely.*] Speak, man: have you no feeling for me?

MARCHBANKS. [*Softly and musically.*]   Then she became an angel; and there was a flaming sword that turned every way, so that I couldnt go in; for I saw that that gate was really the gate of Hell.

MORELL. [*Triumphantly.*]   She repulsed you!

MARCHBANKS. [*Rising in wild scorn.*]   No, you fool: if she had done that I should never have seen that I was in Heaven already. Repulsed me! You think that would have saved us! virtuous indignation! Oh, you are not worthy to live in the same world with her. [*He turns away contemptuously to the other side of the room.*]

MORELL. [*Who has watched him quietly without changing his place.*] Do you think you make yourself more worthy by reviling me, Eugene?

MARCHBANKS.   Here endeth the thousand and first lesson. Morell: I dont think much of your preaching after all: I believe I could do it better myself. The man I want to meet is the man that Candida married.

MORELL.   The man that—? Do you mean me?

MARCHBANKS.   I dont mean the Reverend James Mavor Morell, moralist and windbag. I mean the real man that the Reverend James must have hidden somewhere inside his black coat: the man that Candida loved. You cant make a woman like Candida love you by merely buttoning your collar at the back instead of in front.

MORELL. [*Boldly and steadily.*]   When Candida promised to marry me, I was the same moralist and windbag you now see. I wore my black coat; and my collar was buttoned behind instead of in front. Do you think she would have loved me any the better for being insincere in my profession?

MARCHBANKS. [*On the sofa, hugging his ankles.*]   Oh, she forgave you, just as she forgives me for being a coward, and a weakling, and what you call a snivelling little whelp and all the rest of it. [*Dreamily.*] A woman like that has divine insight: she loves our souls, and not our follies and vanities and illusions, nor our collars and coats, nor any other of the rags and tatters we are rolled up in. [*He reflects on this for an instant; then turns intently to question* MORELL.] What I want to know is how you got past the flaming sword that stopped me.

MORELL.   Perhaps because I was not interrupted at the end of ten minutes.

MARCHBANKS. [*Taken aback.*]   What!

MORELL.   Man can climb to the highest summits; but he cannot dwell there long.

MARCHBANKS. [*Springing up.*]   It's false: there can he dwell for ever, and there only. It's in the other moments that he can find no rest, no sense of the silent glory of life. Where would you have me spend my moments, if not on the summits?

MORELL.   In the scullery, slicing onions and filling lamps.

MARCHBANKS.   Or in the pulpit, scrubbing cheap earthenware souls?

MORELL.   Yes, that too. It was there that I earned my golden moment, and the right, in that moment, to ask her to love me. I did not take the moment on credit; nor did I use it to steal another man's happiness.

MARCHBANKS. [*Rather disgustedly, trotting back towards the fireplace.*]   I have no doubt you conducted the transaction as honestly as if you were buying a pound of cheese. [*He stops on the brink of the hearth-rug, and adds, thoughtfully, to himself, with his back turned to* MORELL.] I could only go to her as a beggar.

MORELL. [*Starting.*]   A beggar dying of cold! asking for her shawl!

MARCHBANKS. [*Turning, surprised.*] Thank you for touching up my poetry. Yes, if you like: a beggar dying of cold, asking for her shawl.

MORELL. [*Excitedly.*] And she refused. Shall I tell you why she refused? I c a n tell you, on her own authority. It was because of—

MARCHBANKS. She didnt refuse.

MORELL. Not!

MARCHBANKS. She offered me all I chose to ask for: her shawl, her wings, the wreath of stars on her head, the lilies in her hand, the crescent moon beneath her feet—

MORELL. [*Seizing him.*] Out with the truth, man: my wife is my wife: I want no more of your poetic fripperies. I know well that if I have lost her love and you have gained it, no law will bind her.

MARCHBANKS. [*Quaintly, without fear or resistance.*] Catch me by the shirt collar, Morell: she will arrange it for me afterwards as she did this morning. [*With quiet rapture.*] I shall feel her hands touch me.

MORELL. You young imp, do you know how dangerous it is to say that to me? Or [*With a sudden misgiving*] has something made you brave?

MARCHBANKS. I'm not afraid now. I disliked you before; that was why I shrank from your touch. But I saw today—when she tortured you—that you love her. Since then I have been your friend: you may strangle me if you like.

MORELL. [*Releasing him.*] Eugene: if that is not a heartless lie—if you have a spark of human feeling left in you—will you tell me what has happened during my absence?

MARCHBANKS. What happened! Why, the flaming sword [MORELL *stamps with impatience.*]—Well, in plain prose, I loved her so exquisitely that I wanted nothing more than the happiness of being in such love. And before I had time to come down from the highest summits, y o u came in.

MORELL. [*Suffering deeply.*] So it is still unsettled. Still the misery of doubt.

MARCHBANKS. Misery! I am the happiest of men. I desire nothing now but her happiness. [*In a passion of sentiment.*] Oh, Morell, let us both give her up. Why should she have to choose between a wretched little nervous disease like me, and a pig-headed parson like you? Let us go on a pilgrimage, you to the east and I to the west, in search of a worthy lover for her: some beautiful archangel with purple wings—

MORELL. Some fiddlestick! Oh, if she is mad enough to leave me for you, who will protect her? who will help her? who will work for her? who will be a father to her children? [*He sits down distractedly on the sofa, with his elbows on his knees and his head propped on his clenched fists.*]

MARCHBANKS. [*Snapping his fingers wildly.*] She does not ask those silly questions. It is she who wants somebody to protect, to help, to work for: somebody to give her children to protect, to help and to work for. Some grown up man who has become as a little child again. Oh, you fool, you fool, you triple fool! I am the man, Morell: I am the man. [*He dances about excitedly, crying*] You dont understand what a woman is. Send for her, Morell: send for her and let her choose between—[*The door opens and* CANDIDA *enters. He stops as if petrified.*]

CANDIDA. [*Amazed, on the threshold.*]   What on earth are you at, Eugene?

MARCHBANKS. [*Oddly.*]   James and I are having a preaching match; and he is getting the worst of it.

[CANDIDA *looks quickly round at* MORELL. *Seeing that he is distressed, she hurries down to him, greatly vexed.*]

CANDIDA.   You have been annoying him. Now I wont have it, Eugene: do you hear? [*She puts her hand on* MORELL'S *shoulder, and quite forgets her wifely tact in her anger.*] My boy shall not be worried: I will protect him.

MORELL. [*Rising proudly.*]   Protect!

CANDIDA. [*Not heeding him: to* EUGENE.]   What have you been saying?

MARCHBANKS. [*Appalled.*]   Nothing. I—

CANDIDA.   Eugene! Nothing?

MARCHBANKS. [*Piteously.*]   I mean—I—I'm very sorry. I wont do it again: indeed I wont. I'll let him alone.

MORELL. [*Indignantly, with an aggressive movement towards* EUGENE.]   Let me alone! You young—

CANDIDA. [*Stopping him.*]   Sh!—no: let me deal with him, James.

MARCHBANKS.   Oh, youre not angry with me, are you?

CANDIDA. [*Severely.*]   Yes I am: very angry. I have a good mind to pack you out of the house.

MORELL. [*Taken aback by* CANDIDA's *vigor, and by no means relishing the position of being rescued by her from another man.*]   Gently, Candida, gently. I am able to take care of myself.

CANDIDA. [*Petting him.*]   Yes, dear: of course you are. But you mustnt be annoyed and made miserable.

MARCHBANKS. [*Almost in tears, turning to the door.*]   I'll go.

CANDIDA.   Oh, you neednt go: I cant turn you out at this time of night. [*Vehemently.*] Shame on you! For shame!

MARCHBANKS. [*Desperately.*]   But what have I done?

CANDIDA.   I know what you have done: as well as if I had been here all the time. Oh, it was unworthy! You are like a child: you cannot hold your tongue.

MARCHBANKS.   I would die ten times over sooner than give you a moment's pain.

CANDIDA. [*With infinite contempt for this puerility.*]   Much good your dying would do me!

MORELL.   Candida, my dear: this altercation is hardly quite seemly. It is a matter between two men; and I am the right person to settle it.

CANDIDA.   Two men! Do you call that a man? [*To* EUGENE.] You bad boy!

MARCHBANKS. [*Gathering a whimsically affectionate courage from the scolding.*]   If I am to be scolded like a boy, I must make a boy's excuse. He began it. And he's bigger than I am.

CANDIDA. [*Losing confidence a little as her concern for* MORELL's *dignity takes the alarm.*] That cant be true. [*To* MORELL] You didnt begin it, James, did you?

MORELL. [*Contemptuously.*]   No.

MARCHBANKS. [*Indignantly.*]   Oh!

MORELL. [*To* EUGENE.]   Y o u began it: this morning. [CANDIDA, *instantly connecting this with his mysterious allusion in the afternoon to something told him by* EUGENE *in the morning, looks at him with quick suspicion.* MORELL *proceeds, with the emphasis of offended superiority.*] But your other point is true. I am certainly the bigger of the two, and, I hope, the stronger, Candida. So you had better leave the matter in my hands.

CANDIDA. [*Again soothing him.*]   Yes, dear; but—[*Troubled*] I dont understand about this morning.

MORELL. [*Gently snubbing her.*]   You need not understand, my dear.

CANDIDA.   But James, I [*The street bell rings.*]—Oh bother! Here they all come. [*She goes out to let them in.*]

MARCHBANKS. [*Running to* MORELL.]   Oh, Morell, isn't it dreadful? She's angry with us: she hates me. What shall I do?

MORELL. [*With quaint desperation, walking up and down the middle of the room.*]   Eugene: my head is spinning round. I shall begin to laugh presently.

MARCHBANKS. [*Following him anxiously.*]   No, no: she'll think Ive thrown you into hysterics. Dont laugh.

[*Boisterous voices and laughter are heard approaching.* LEXY MILL, *his eyes sparkling, and his bearing denoting unwonted elevation of spirit, enters with* BURGESS, *who is greasy and self-complacent, but has all his wits about him.* MISS GARNETT, *with her smartest hat and jacket on, follows them; but though her eyes are brighter than before, she is evidently a prey to misgiving. She places herself with her back to her typewriting table, with one hand on it to steady herself, passing the other across her forehead as if she were a little tired and giddy.* MARCHBANKS *relapses into shyness and edges away into the corner near the window, where* MORELL'S *books are.*]

LEXY. [*Exhilarated.*]   Morell: I m u s t congratulate you. [*Grasping his hand.*] What a noble, splendid, inspired address you gave us! You surpassed yourself.

BURGESS.   So you did, James. It fair kep me awake to the lars' word. Didnt it, Miss Gornett?

PROSERPINE. [*Worriedly.*]   Oh, I wasnt minding you: I was trying to make notes. [*She takes out her notebook, and looks at her stenography, which nearly makes her cry.*]

MORELL.   Did I go too fast, Pross?

PROSERPINE.   Much too fast. You know I cant do more than ninety words a minute. [*She relieves her feelings by throwing her notebook angrily beside her machine, ready for use next morning.*]

MORELL. [*Soothingly.*]   Oh well, well, never mind, never mind, never mind. Have you all had supper?

LEXY.   Mr Burgess has been kind enough to give us a really splendid supper at the Belgrave.

BURGESS.   [*With effusive magnanimity.*]   Dont mention it, Mr Mill. [*Modestly.*] Youre arty welcome to my little treat.

PROSERPINE.   We had champagne. I never tasted it before. I feel quite giddy.

MORELL.   [*Surprised.*]   A champagne supper! That was very handsome. Was it my eloquence that produced all this extravagance?

LEXY.   [*Rhetorically.*]   Your eloquence, and Mr. Burgess's goodness of heart. [*With a fresh burst of exhilaration.*] And what a very fine fellow the chairman is, Morell! He came to supper with us.

MORELL.   [*With long-drawn significance, looking at* BURGESS.]   O-o-o-h! the chairman. N o w I understand.

[BURGESS *covers with a deprecatory cough a lively satisfaction with his own diplomatic cunning.* LEXY *folds his arms and leans against the head of the sofa in a high-spirited attitude after nearly losing his balance.* CANDIDA *comes in with glasses, lemons, and a jug of hot water on a tray.*]

CANDIDA.   Who will have some lemonade? You know our rules: total abstinence. [*She puts the tray on the table, and takes up the lemon squeezer, looking enquiringly round at them.*]

MORELL.   No use, dear. Theyve all had champagne. Pross has broken her pledge.

CANDIDA.   [*To* PROSERPINE.]   You dont mean to say youve been drinking champagne!

PROSERPINE.   [*Stubbornly.*]   Yes I do. I'm only a beer teetotaller, not a champagne teetotaller. I dont like beer. Are there any letters for me to answer, Mr Morell?

MORELL.   No more to-night.

PROSERPINE.   Very well. Goodnight, everybody.

LEXY.   [*Gallantly.*]   Had I not better see you home, Miss Garnett?

PROSERPINE.   No thank you. I shant trust myself with anybody tonight. I wish I hadnt taken any of that stuff. [*She takes uncertain aim at the door; dashes at it; and barely escapes without disaster.*]

BURGESS.   [*Indignantly.*]   Stuff indeed! That gurl dunno what champagne is! Pommery and Greeno at twelve and six a bottle. She took two glasses almost straight horff.

MORELL.   [*Anxious about her.*]   Go and look after her, Lexy.

LEXY.   [*Alarmed.*]   But if she should really be— Suppose she began to sing in the street, or anything of that sort.

MORELL.   Just so: she may. Thats why youd better see her safely home.

CANDIDA.   Do, Lexy: theres a good fellow. [*She shakes his hand and pushes him gently to the door.*]

LEXY.   It's evidently my duty to go. I hope it may not be necessary. Goodnight, Mrs Morell. [*To the rest.*] Goodnight. [*He goes.* CANDIDA *shuts the door.*]

BURGESS.   He was gushin with hextra piety hisself arter two sips. People carnt drink like they huster. [*Bustling across to the hearth.*] Well, James; it's time to lock up. Mr Morchbanks: shall I ave the pleasure of your company for a bit o the way ome?

MARCHBANKS. [*Affrightedly.*]   Yes: I'd better go. [*He hurries towards the door; but* CANDIDA *places herself before it, barring his way.*]

CANDIDA. [*With quiet authority.*]   You sit down. Youre not going yet.

MARCHBANKS. [*Quailing.*]   No: I—I didnt mean to. [*He sits down abjectly on the sofa.*]

CANDIDA.   Mr Marchbanks will stay the night with us, papa.

BURGESS.   Oh well, I'll say goodnight. So long, James. [*He shakes hands with* MORELL, *and goes over to* EUGENE.] Make em give you a nightlight by your bed, Mr Morchbanks: itll comfort you if you wake up in the night with a touch of that complaint of yores. Goodnight.

MARCHBANKS.   Thank you: I will. Goodnight, Mr Burgess. [*They shake hands.* BURGESS *goes to the door.*]

CANDIDA. [*Intercepting* MORELL, *who is following* BURGESS.]   Stay here, dear: I'll put on papa's coat for him. [*She goes out with* BURGESS.]

MARCHBANKS. [*Rising and stealing over to* MORELL.]   Morell: theres going to be a terrible scene. Arnt you afraid?

MORELL.   Not in the least.

MARCHBANKS.   I never envied you your courage before. [*He puts his hand appealingly on* MORELL's *forearm.*] Stand by me, wont you?

MORELL. [*Casting him off resolutely.*]   Each for himself, Eugene. She must choose between us now.

[CANDIDA *returns.* EUGENE *creeps back to the sofa like a guilty schoolboy.*]

CANDIDA. [*Between them, addressing* EUGENE.]   Are you sorry?

MARCHBANKS. [*Earnestly.*]   Yes. Heartbroken.

CANDIDA.   Well then, you are forgiven. Now go off to bed like a good little boy: I want to talk to James about you.

MARCHBANKS. [*Rising in great consternation.*]   Oh, I cant do that, Morell. I must be here. I'll not go away. Tell her.

CANDIDA. [*Her suspicions confirmed.*]   Tell me what? [*His eyes avoid hers furtively. She turns and mutely transfers the question to* MORELL.]

MORELL. [*Bracing himself for the catastrophe.*]   I have nothing to tell her, except [*Here his voice deepens to a measured and mournful tenderness*] that she is my greatest treasure on earth—if she is really mine.

CANDIDA. [*Coldly, offended by his yielding to his orator's instinct and treating her as if she were the audience at the Guild of St Matthew.*]   I am sure Eugene can say no less, if that is all.

MARCHBANKS. [*Discouraged.*]   Morell; she's laughing at us.

MORELL. [*With a quick touch of temper.*]   There is nothing to laugh at. Are you laughing at us, Candida?

CANDIDA. [*With quiet anger.*]   Eugene is very quick-witted, James. I hope I am going to laugh; but I am not sure that I am not going to be very angry.

[*She goes to the fireplace, and stands there leaning with her arms on the mantlepiece, and her foot on the fender, whilst* EUGENE *steals to* MORELL *and plucks him by the sleeve.*]

MARCHBANKS. [*Whispering.*]   Stop, Morell. Dont let us say anything.

MORELL. [*Pushing* EUGENE *away without deigning to look at him.*]   I hope you dont mean that as a threat, Candida.

CANDIDA. [*With emphatic warning.*]   Take care, James. Eugene: I asked you to go. Are you going?

MORELL. [*Putting his foot down.*]   He shall not go. I wish him to remain.

MARCHBANKS.   I'll go. I'll do whatever you want. [*He turns to the door.*]

CANDIDA.   Stop! [*He obeys.*] Didnt you hear James say he wished you to stay? James is master here. Dont you know that?

MARCHBANKS. [*Flushing with a young poet's rage against tyranny.*]   By what right is he master?

CANDIDA. [*Quietly.*]   Tell him, James.

MORELL. [*Taken aback.*]   My dear: I dont know of any right that makes me master. I assert no such right.

CANDIDA. [*With infinite reproach.*]   You don't know! Oh, James! James! [*To* EUGENE, *musingly.*] I wonder do you understand, Eugene! [*He shakes his head helplessly, not daring to look at her.*] No: youre too young. Well, I give you leave to stay: to stay and learn. [*She comes away from the hearth and places herself between them.*] Now, James! whats the matter? Come: tell me.

MARCHBANKS. [*Whispering tremulously across to him.*]   Dont.

CANDIDA.   Come. Out with it!

MORELL. [*Slowly.*]   I meant to prepare your mind carefully, Candida, so as to prevent misunderstanding.

CANDIDA.   Yes, dear: I am sure you did. But never mind: I shant misunderstand.

MORELL.   Well—er— [*He hesitates, unable to find the long explanation which he supposed to be available.*]

CANDIDA.   Well?

MORELL. [*Blurting it out badly.*]   Eugene declares that you are in love with him.

MARCHBANKS. [*Frantically.*]   No, no, no, no, never. I did not, Mrs Morell: it's not true. I said I loved you. I said I understood you, and that he couldnt. And it was not after what passed there before the fire that I spoke: it was not, on my word. It was this morning.

CANDIDA. [*Enlightened.*]   This morning!

MARCHBANKS.   Yes. [*He looks at her, pleading for credence, and then adds simply.*] That was what was the matter with my collar.

CANDIDA.   Your collar? [*Suddenly taking in his meaning she turns to* MORELL, *shocked.*] Oh, James: did you—? [*She stops.*]

MORELL. [*Ashamed.*]   You know, Candida, that I have a temper to struggle with. And he said [*Shuddering*] that you despised me in your heart.

CANDIDA. [*Turning quickly on* EUGENE.]   Did you say that?

MARCHBANKS. [*Terrified.*]   No.

CANDIDA. [*Almost fiercely.*]   Then James has just told me a falsehood. Is that what you mean?

MARCHBANKS.   No, no: I—I—[*Desperately*] it was David's wife. And it wasnt at home: it was when she saw him dancing before all the people.

MORELL. [*Taking the cue with a debater's adroitness.*]   Dancing before all the people, Candida; and thinking he was moving their hearts by his mission when they were only suffering from—Prossy's complaint. [*She is about to protest: he raises his hand to silence her.*] Dont try to look indignant, Candida—

CANDIDA.   Try!

MORELL. [*Continuing.*]   Eugene was right. As you told me a few hours after, he is always right. He said nothing that you did not say far better yourself. He is the poet, who sees everything; and I am the poor parson, who understands nothing.

CANDIDA. [*Remorsefully.*]   Do you mind what is said by a foolish boy, because I said something like it in jest?

MORELL.   That foolish boy can speak with the inspiration of a child and the cunning of a serpent. He has claimed that you belong to him and not to me; and, rightly or wrongly, I have come to fear that it may be true. I will not go about tortured with doubts and suspicions. I will not live with you and keep a secret from you. I will not suffer the intolerable degradation of jealousy. We have agreed—he and I—that you shall choose between us now. I await your decision.

CANDIDA. [*Slowly recoiling a step, her heart hardened by his rhetoric in spite of the sincere feeling behind it.*]   Oh! I am to choose, am I? I suppose it is quite settled that I must belong to one or the other.

MORELL. [*Firmly.*]   Quite. You must choose definitely.

MARCHBANKS. [*Anxiously.*]   Morell: you dont understand. She means that she belongs to herself.

CANDIDA. [*Turning on him.*]   I mean that, and a good deal more, Master Eugene, as you will both find out presently. And pray, my lords and masters, what have you to offer for my choice? I am up for auction, it seems. What do you bid, James?

MORELL. [*Reproachfully.*]   Cand— [*He breaks down: his eyes and throat fill with tears: the orator becomes a wounded animal.*] I cant speak—

CANDIDA. [*Impulsively going to him.*]   Ah, dearest—

MARCHBANKS. [*In wild alarm.*]   Stop: it's not fair. You musnt shew her that you suffer, Morell. I am on the rack too; but I am not crying.

MORELL. [*Rallying all his forces.*]   Yes: you are right. It is not for pity that I am bidding. [*He disengages himself from* CANDIDA.]

CANDIDA. [*Retreating, chilled.*]   I beg your pardon, James: I did not mean to touch you. I am waiting to hear your bid.

MORELL. [*With proud humility.*]   I have nothing to offer you but my strength for your defence, my honesty for your surety, my ability and industry for your livelihood, and my authority and position for your dignity. That is all it becomes a man to offer to a woman.

CANDIDA. [*Quite quietly.*] And you, Eugene? What do you offer?

MARCHBANKS. My weakness. My desolation. My heart's need.

CANDIDA. [*Impressed.*] Thats a good bid, Eugene. Now I know how to make my choice.

[*She pauses and looks curiously from one to the other, as if weighing them. MORELL, whose lofty confidence has changed into heartbreaking dread at EUGENE's bid, loses all power of concealing his anxiety. EUGENE, strung to the highest tension, does not move a muscle.*]

MORELL. [*In a suffocated voice: the appeal bursting from the depths of his anguish.*] Candida!

MARCHBANKS. [*Aside, in a flash of contempt.*] Coward!

CANDIDA. [*Significantly.*] I give myself to the weaker of the two.

[EUGENE *divines her meaning at once: his face whitens like steel in a furnace.*]

MORELL. [*Bowing his head with the calm of collapse.*] I accept your sentence, Candida.

CANDIDA. Do y o u understand, Eugene?

MARCHBANKS. Oh, I feel I'm lost. He cannot bear the burden.

MORELL. [*Incredulously, raising his head and voice with comic abruptness.*] Do you mean me, Candida?

CANDIDA. [*Smiling a little.*] Let us sit and talk comfortably over it like three friends. [*To* MORELL.] Sit down, dear. [MORELL, *quite lost, takes the chair from the fireside: the children's chair.*] Bring me that chair, Eugene. [*She indicates the easy chair. He fetches it silently, even with something like cold strength, and places it next* MORELL, *a little behind him. She sits down. He takes the visitor's chair himself, and sits, inscrutable. When they are all settled she begins, throwing a spell of quietness on them by her calm, sane, tender tone.*] You remember what you told me about yourself, Eugene: how nobody has cared for you since your old nurse died: how those clever fashionable sisters and successful brothers of yours were your mother's and father's pets: how miserable you were at Eton: how your father is trying to starve you into returning to Oxford: how you have had to live without comfort or welcome or refuge: always lonely, and nearly always disliked and misunderstood, poor boy!

MARCHBANKS. [*Faithful to the nobility of his lot.*] I had my books. I had Nature. And at last I met you.

CANDIDA. Never mind that just at present. Now I want you to look at this other boy here: m y boy! spoiled from his cradle. We go once a fortnight to see his parents. You should come with us, Eugene, to see the pictures of the hero of that household. James as a baby! the most wonderful of all babies. James holding his first school prize, won at the ripe age of eight! James as the captain of his eleven! James in his first frock coat! James under all sorts of glorious circumstances! You know how strong he is (I hope he didn't hurt you):

how clever he is: how happy. [*With deepening gravity.*] Ask James's mother and his three sisters what it cost to save James the trouble of doing anything but be strong and clever and happy. Ask m e what it costs to be James's mother and three sisters and wife and mother to his children all in one. Ask Prossy and Maria how troublesome the house is even when we have no visitors to help us to slice the onions. Ask the tradesmen who want to worry James and spoil his beautiful sermons who it is that puts them off. When there is money to give, he gives it: when there is money to refuse, I refuse it. I build a castle of comfort and indulgence and love for him, and stand sentinel always to keep little vulgar cares out. I make him master here, though he does not know it, and could not tell you a moment ago how it came to be so. [*With sweet irony.*] And when he thought I might go away with you, his only anxiety was—what should become of m e! And to tempt me to stay he offered me [*Leaning forward to stroke his hair caressingly at each phrase.*] h i s strength for m y defence! his industry for my livelihood! his dignity for my position! his—[*Relenting*] ah, I am mixing up your beautiful cadences and spoiling them, am I not, darling? [*She lays her cheek fondly against his.*]

MORELL. [*Quite overcome, kneeling beside her chair and embracing her with boyish ingenuousness.*] It's all true, every word. What I am you have made me with the labor of your hands and the love of your heart. You are my wife, my mother, my sisters: you are the sum of all loving care to me.

CANDIDA. [*In his arms, smiling, to* EUGENE.] Am I y o u r mother and sisters to you, Eugene?

MARCHBANKS. [*Rising with a fierce gesture of disgust.*] Ah, never. Out, then, into the night with me!

CANDIDA. [*Rising quickly.*] You are not going like that, Eugene?

MARCHBANKS. [*With the ring of a man's voice—no longer a boy's—in the words.*] I know the hour when it strikes. I am impatient to do what must be done.

MORELL. [*Who has also risen.*] Candida: dont let him do anything rash.

CANDIDA. [*Confident, smiling at* EUGENE.] Oh, there is no fear. He has learnt to live without happiness.

MARCHBANKS. I no longer desire happiness: life is nobler than that. Parson James: I give you my happiness with both hands: I love you because you have filled the heart of the woman I loved. Goodbye. [*He goes towards the door.*]

CANDIDA. One last word. [*He stops, but without turning to her. She goes to him.*] How old are you, Eugene?

MARCHBANKS. As old as the world now. This morning I was eighteen.

CANDIDA. Eighteen! Will you, for my sake, make a little poem out of the two sentences I am going to say to you? And will you promise to repeat it to yourself whenever you think of me?

MARCHBANKS. [*Without moving.*] Say the sentences.

CANDIDA. When I am thirty, she will be forty-five. When I am sixty, she will be seventy-five.

MARCHBANKS. [*Turning to her.*]   In a hundred years, we shall be the same age. But I have a better secret than that in my heart. Let me go now. The night outside grows impatient.

CANDIDA.   Goodbye. [*She takes his face in her hands; and as he divines her intention and falls on his knees, she kisses his forehead. Then he flies out into the night. She turns to* MORELL, *holding out her arms to him.*] Ah, James!

[*They embrace. But they do not know the secret in the poet's heart.*]

JEAN COCTEAU

The Infernal Machine[1]

English Version (revised for this edition) by Carl Wildman

CHARACTERS (IN ORDER OF APPEARANCE)

THE VOICE	ANUBIS, *Egyptian God of the Dead*
THE YOUNG SOLDIER	THE THEBAN MATRON
THE SOLDIER	A LITTLE BOY
THE CAPTAIN	A LITTLE GIRL
JOCASTA, *the queen, widow of Laïus*	OEDIPUS, *son of Laïus*
TIRESIAS, *a soothsayer, nearly blind*	CREON, *brother of Jocasta*
THE GHOST OF LAÏUS, *the dead king*	THE MESSENGER FROM CORINTH
THE SPHINX	THE SHEPHERD OF LAÏUS

ANTIGONE, *daughter of Oedipus*

ACT I. THE GHOST OF LAÏUS

THE VOICE: '*He will kill his father. He will marry his mother.*'

To thwart this oracle of Apollo, Jocasta, Queen of Thebes, leaves her son on the mountain side with his feet pierced and bound. A shepherd of Corinth finds the nursling and carries it to Polybius. Polybius and Merope, king and queen of Corinth, were bemoaning a sterile marriage. The child, Oedipus, or *Pierced-feet,* respected by bears and wolves, is to them a heaven-sent gift. They adopt him.

When a young man, Oedipus questions the oracle of Delphi.

The god speaks: *You will murder your father and marry your mother.* He must therefore fly from Polybius and Merope. The fear of parricide and incest drives him on towards his fate.

One evening, arriving at the cross-roads of Delphi and Daulis, he meets an escort. A horse jostles him; a quarrel starts; a servant threatens him; he replies

[1] Reprinted from *International Modern Plays* (New York: E. P. Dutton & Co., Inc., 1950). This play is fully protected by copyright. Any applications for professional or amateur performances as well as for transmission by radio or television should be directed to the author's agent, Dr. Jan van Loewen, of 2 Jason's Court, Wigmore Street, London, W. 1, England.

La Machine Infernale was first performed at the Comédie des Champs-Elysées (Théâtre Louis Jouvet) on 10th April 1934, with scenery and costumes by Christian Bérard.

with a blow from his stick. The blow misses the servant and kills the master. This dead man is Laïus, the old king of Thebes. Parricide!

The escort, fearing an ambush, took to its heels. Oedipus, unsuspecting, passed on. Besides, he is young, enthusiastic; this accident is soon forgotten.

During one of his halts he learns of the scourge of the Sphinx. The Sphinx, 'the Winged Virgin,' 'the Singing Bitch,' is killing off the young men of Thebes. This monster asks a riddle and kills those who do not guess it. Queen Jocasta, widow of Laïus, offers her hand and her crown to the conqueror of the Sphinx.

Like the young Siegfried to come, Oedipus hurries on. He is consumed with curiosity and ambition. The meeting takes place. What was the nature of this meeting? Mystery. Be that as it may, Oedipus enters Thebes a conqueror, he marries the queen. Incest!

For the gods really to enjoy themselves, their victim must fall from a great height. Years come and go in prosperity. Two daughters and two sons complicate the monstrous union. The people love their king. But the plague suddenly descends upon them. The gods accuse an anonymous criminal of infecting the country and demand that he shall be driven out. Going from one discovery to another, and as if intoxicated by misfortune, Oedipus, in the end, finds himself cornered. The trap shuts. All becomes clear. With her red scarf Jocasta hangs herself. With the golden brooch of the hanging woman Oedipus puts out his eyes.

Spectator, this machine, you see here wound up to the full in such a way that the spring will slowly unwind the whole length of a human life, is one of the most perfect constructed by the infernal gods for the mathematical destruction of a mortal.

Act I.[2] The Ghost

SCENE: *A patrol path round the ramparts of Thebes. High walls. A stormy night. Summer lightning. The din and bands of the popular district can be heard.*

YOUNG SOLDIER.   They 're having a good time!

SOLDIER.   Trying to.

YOUNG SOLDIER.   Well, anyway, they dance all night.

SOLDIER.   They can't sleep, so they dance.

YOUNG SOLDIER.   Never mind, they 're getting tight and going with women, and spending their nights in all sorts of dives, while I am here tramping up and down with you. Well I, for one, can't stick it any longer! I can't stick it! I can't! That 's clear enough, isn't it? I 've had my bellyful!

SOLDIER.   Desert then.

[2] The four scenes should be planted on a little platform in the centre of the stage, surrounded by nocturnal curtains. The slope of the platform varies according to the requirements of the scenes. Besides the lighting of details, the four acts should be flooded in the livid mythical light of quicksilver.

YOUNG SOLDIER.   Oh, no! I 've made up my mind. I 'm going to put my name down for the Sphinx.

SOLDIER.   What for?

YOUNG SOLDIER.   What for? Why, to do something, of course. To put an end to all this creepy business and ghastly hanging about.

SOLDIER.   You wouldn't get scared, though?

YOUNG SOLDIER.   Scared? How d' you mean?

SOLDIER.   Oh, just scared, you know! I 've seen brighter and tougher lads than you who got the wind up. Unless this gent is going to kill the Sphinx and draw the first prize.

YOUNG SOLDIER.   And why not? Oh, I know the only man who came back alive from the Sphinx has become a gibbering idiot. But supposing what he gibbers is true? What if it is a riddle? What if I guess the answer? What——

SOLDIER.   Now listen here, you poor bastard. Don't you realize that hundreds upon hundreds of chaps who 've been to the stadium and college and everything have left their carcasses behind there, and you, a poor little private soldier like you wants to——

YOUNG SOLDIER.   I shall go! I shall, because I can't bear any longer counting the stones of this wall, hearing that band, and seeing your rotten mug, and—— [He stamps.]

SOLDIER.   That's the stuff, my hero! I was waiting for this explosion. I like it better that way. Now . . . now . . . enough blubbering. . . . Take it easy . . . there, there, there . . .

YOUNG SOLDIER.   To hell with you! [The SOLDIER bangs his spear against the wall behind the YOUNG SOLDIER who becomes rigid.]

SOLDIER.   What's up?

YOUNG SOLDIER.   Didn't you hear anything?

SOLDIER.   No . . . where?

YOUNG SOLDIER.   Ah! . . . I seemed to . . . I thought for a moment——

SOLDIER.   You 're like a sheet. . . . What 's the matter? Are you going to pass out?

YOUNG SOLDIER.   It 's silly . . . I seemed to hear a knock. I thought it was him!

SOLDIER.   The Sphinx?

YOUNG SOLDIER.   No, him, the ghost, the phantom, you know!

SOLDIER.   The ghost? Our dear old ghost of Laïus? And is that what turns your stomach over? Really!

YOUNG SOLDIER.   I 'm sorry.

SOLDIER.   You 're sorry, mate? What are you talking about? To start with, there 's a good chance that our ghost will not appear again after last night's business. So that 's that. And besides, what are you sorry about? Look at things squarely. We can hardly say this ghost scared us. Oh, well . . . the first time perhaps! . . . But, after that, eh? . . . He was a decent old ghost, almost a pal, a relief. Well, if the idea of this ghost makes you jumpy, it 's because you 're in a real state of nerves, like me, like everybody in Thebes, rich or poor alike, except a few big pots who make something out of everything. There 's not much fun in war, anyway, but we don't know a blind thing about the enemy we 're up against. We 're beginning to get fed up with oracles, happy deaths, and heroic mothers. Do you think I should pull your leg as I do if my nerves weren't on edge, and do you think you 'd start blubbering, and that lot over there 'd get tight and dance? No, they 'd be in bed and fast asleep, and we 'd be playing dice while waiting for friend phantom.

YOUNG SOLDIER. I say . . .

SOLDIER. Well? . . .

YOUNG SOLDIER. What d' you think it 's like . . . the Sphinx?

SOLDIER. Oh! give the Sphinx a rest. If I knew what it was like I shouldn't be here doing guard duty with you to-night.

YOUNG SOLDIER. Some make out it 's no bigger than a hare, and is timid, and has a tiny little face, like a woman's. But I think it has a woman's head and breasts, and sleeps with the young men.

SOLDIER. Oh, turn it up! Shut up and forget it!

YOUNG SOLDIER. Perhaps it doesn't ask anything and doesn't even touch you. You meet it, look at it, and die of love.

SOLDIER. All we needed was for you to go and fall in love with the public scourge. After all, public scourge . . . between ourselves, do you know what I think about this public scourge? . . . It 's a vampire! Yes, a common or garden vampire! Someone in hiding from the police, and who they can't lay their hands on.

YOUNG SOLDIER. A vampire with a woman's head?

SOLDIER. Can't you turn it up? No, not him! A real old vampire with a beard and moustache, and a belly. He sucks your blood and that 's how it is they bring corpses back home, all with the same wound in the same place: the back of the neck! And now, go and see for yourself if you 're still keen.

YOUNG SOLDIER. You say that . . .

SOLDIER. I say that . . . I say that . . . Hi! . . . The captain. [*They stand up to attention. The* CAPTAIN *enters and folds his arms.*]

CAPTAIN. Easy! . . . Well, my lads. . . . Is this where we see ghosts?

SOLDIER. Sir——

CAPTAIN. Silence! You will speak when I ask you. Which of you two has dared——

YOUNG SOLDIER. I did, sir!

CAPTAIN. Good Lord! Whose turn to speak is it? Are you going to keep quiet? I was asking: which of you two has dared to make a report about a service matter, without it passing through the normal channels? Right over my head. Answer.

SOLDIER. It wasn't his fault, sir, he knew——

CAPTAIN. Was it you or him?

YOUNG SOLDIER. Both of us, but I——

CAPTAIN.   Silence! I want to know how the high priest came to hear of what happens at night at this post, while I myself heard nothing.

YOUNG SOLDIER.   It 's my fault, sir, my fault. My comrade here didn't want to say anything about it. But I thought I ought to speak and, as this incident didn't concern the service . . . and, well . . . I told his uncle everything; because his uncle's wife is sister to one of the queen's linen-maids, and his brother-in-law is in Tiresias's temple.

SOLDIER.   That 's why I said it was my fault, sir.

CAPTAIN.   All right! Don't burst my ear-drums. So . . . this incident doesn't concern the service. Very good, oh, very good! . . . And it seems . . . This famous incident which doesn't concern the service is a ghost story?

YOUNG SOLDIER.   Yes, sir.

CAPTAIN.   A ghost appeared to you one night when you were on guard duty, and this ghost said to you . . . Just what did this ghost say to you?

YOUNG SOLDIER.   He told us, sir, he was the spectre of King Laïus, and he had tried to appear several times since his murder, and he begged us to find some way of warning Queen Jocasta and Tiresias with all speed.

CAPTAIN.   With all speed! Fancy that! What a nice old ghost he must be! And . . . didn't you ask him, say, why you had the honour of this visit and why he doesn't appear directly before the queen or Tiresias?

SOLDIER.   Yes, sir, I asked him, I did. His answer was that he wasn't free to put in an appearance anywhere, and that the ramparts were the most favourable spot for people who had died violent death, because of the drains.

CAPTAIN.   Drains?

SOLDIER.   Yes, sir. He said drains, meaning because of the fumes which rise there.

CAPTAIN.   Hoho! A very learned spectre, and he doesn't hide his light under a bushel. Did he scare you much? And what did he look like? What was his face like? What clothes did he wear? Where did he stand, and what language did he speak? Are his visits long or short? Have you seen him on different occasions? Although this business doesn't concern the service, I must say I am curious to learn from your lips a few details about the manners and customs of ghosts.

YOUNG SOLDIER.   Well, he did scare us a bit the first night, I admit. You see, sir, he appeared very suddenly, like a lamp lighting up, there in the thickness of the wall.

SOLDIER.   We both saw him.

YOUNG SOLDIER.   It was hard to make out the face and the body; the mouth, when it was open, was clearer, and a white tuft of his beard, and a large red stain, bright red, near the right ear. He spoke with difficulty and couldn't somehow manage to get out more than one sentence at a time. But you 'd better ask my comrade here about that, sir. He explained to me how it was the poor fellow couldn't manage to get it over.

SOLDIER.   Oh! you know, sir, there 's nothing very complicated about it!

He spent all his energy in the effort to appear, that is, in leaving his new shape and taking on the old, so that we could see him. That 's the reason why each time he spoke a little better, he began to disappear, became transparent like, and you could see the wall through him.

YOUNG SOLDIER.   And as soon as he spoke badly you could see him very well. But you saw him badly as soon as he spoke well, and began saying the same thing over again. 'Queen Jocasta. You must . . . you must . . . Queen . . . Queen . . . Queen Jocasta. . . . You must. . . . You must warn the queen. . . . You must warn Queen Jocasta. . . . I ask you, gentlemen, I ask you, I . . . I . . . Gentlemen . . . I ask . . . you must . . . you must . . . I ask you, gentlemen, to warn . . . I ask you . . . The queen . . . Queen Jocasta . . . to warn, gentlemen, to warn . . . Gentlemen . . . Gentlemen . . .' That 's how he went on.

SOLDIER.   And you could see he was afraid of disappearing before he 'd said his piece right to the end.

YOUNG SOLDIER.   Oh yes, and then, you know, remember, eh? Every time the same business. The red stain went last. Just like a ship's light on the wall, it was, sir.

SOLDIER.   But the whole thing was over in a minute!

YOUNG SOLDIER.   He has appeared in the same place five times, every night, a little before dawn.

SOLDIER.   But last night it was different, we . . . well, we had a bit of a fight, and my comrade here decided to tell the royal house everything.

CAPTAIN.   Well! Well! And how was this night 'different,' which, if I 'm not mistaken, caused a dispute between you . . . ?

SOLDIER.   It was like this, sir. . . . You know, guard duty isn't exactly all beer and skittles.

YOUNG SOLDIER.   So really we were waiting for the ghost to turn up, like.

SOLDIER.   And we laid the odds.

YOUNG SOLDIER.   Will come . . .

SOLDIER.   Won't . . .

YOUNG SOLDIER.   Will come . . .

SOLDIER.   Won't . . . and it may seem a funny thing to say, but it was a comfort to see him.

YOUNG SOLDIER.   A habit, as you might say.

SOLDIER.   We ended by imagining we saw him when he wasn't there. We 'd say to each other: 'It 's moving! The wall is lighting up. Don't you see anything? No. But you must do. Over there, I tell you. . . . The wall isn't the same. Don't you see, look, look!'

YOUNG SOLDIER.   And we looked and stared our eyes out. We didn't dare move.

SOLDIER.   We watched for the least change.

YOUNG SOLDIER.   And when, at last, he turned up, we could breathe again, and weren't the least bit afraid.

SOLDIER. The other night we watched and watched and stared ourselves nearly blind; we thought he 'd never show up, but he appeared stealthily . . . not at all quickly like on the first nights. And once he was visible, he said new things and told us as well as he could that something fearful had happened, a thing of death which he couldn't explain to the living. He spoke of places where he could go and places where he couldn't go, and that he had been where he shouldn't and knew a secret which he shouldn't know, and that he would be discovered and punished, and afterwards he wouldn't be allowed to appear, he wouldn't be able to appear any more. [*Solemn voice.*] 'I shall die my last death,' he said, 'and it will be finished, finished. You see, gentlemen, there is not a moment to lose. Run! Warn the queen! Find Tiresias! Gentlemen! Gentlemen, have pity! . . .' He was begging away and day was breaking. And there he stuck!

YOUNG SOLDIER. Suddenly we thought he 'd go mad.

SOLDIER. We understood from sentences without beginning or end that he had left his post, as it were, . . . didn't know how to disappear, and was lost. We saw him going through the same performance to disappear as to appear, and he couldn't manage it. So then he asked us to swear at him, because, he said, swearing at ghosts is the way to make them go. The silliest thing about it was that we hadn't the guts to do it. The more he repeated 'Come on! young men, insult me! Let yourselves go, do your best. . . . Oh, come on!'—the softer we looked.

YOUNG SOLDIER. And the less we could lay our tongue to! . . .

SOLDIER. Yes, that was the limit! And yet, it 's not for lack of blackguarding our superiors.

CAPTAIN. Very nice of you, men, I 'm sure! Thank you on behalf of the superiors.

SOLDIER. Oh! I didn't mean that, sir. . . . I meant . . . I meant the princes, crowned heads, ministers, the government, what . . . the powers that be. In fact, we 'd often talked over wrongs which are done. . . . But he was such a decent sort, the ghost of poor old King Laïus, the swear-words wouldn't come. There he was, urging us on and we kept dithering: 'Go on then! Buzz off, you old bastard!' In short, we gave him bouquets!

YOUNG SOLDIER. Because, you see, sir, 'you old bastard' is a kind of friendly way of speaking among soldiers.

CAPTAIN. It 's as well to know.

SOLDIER. Go on! Go on then! . . . you bleeding . . . you old . . . poor ghost. He hung there between life and death and he was beside himself with fear because of the cocks and the sun. When, all of a sudden, we saw the wall become the wall again, and the red stain go out. We were dog-tired.

YOUNG SOLDIER. It was after that night that I decided to speak to his uncle as he refused to speak himself.

CAPTAIN. Your ghost doesn't seem to be very punctual.

SOLDIER. Oh, you know, sir, he may not show himself again.

CAPTAIN. I am in his way, no doubt.

SOLDIER. No, sir, I mean after last night . . .

CAPTAIN. But I understand from what you say that your ghost is very polite. He will appear, I 'm quite sure. In the first place, the politeness of kings is punctuality, and the politeness of ghosts consists in taking on human form, according to your ingenious theory.

SOLDIER. Possibly, sir, but it 's also possible that with ghosts there are no more kings, and they may mistake a century for a minute. So if the ghost appears in a thousand years instead of this evening . . .

CAPTAIN. You 're a clever sort of chap, but patience has its limits. I tell you this ghost will appear. I tell you my presence is upsetting him, and I tell you that no one outside the service must come along this patrol path.

SOLDIER. Yes, sir.

CAPTAIN. [In an outburst.] So, ghost or no ghost, you are to stop any one turning up here without the password. Those are orders. Is that clear?

SOLDIER. Yes, sir.

CAPTAIN. And don't forget to patrol. Dismiss!

[The two soldiers stand stiffly at the slope.]

[False exit.] Don't try any clever tricks! I 've got my eye on you. [He disappears. Long Silence.]

SOLDIER. As you were!

YOUNG SOLDIER. He thought we were trying to pull his leg.

SOLDIER. Don't you believe it! He thought someone was trying to pull ours.

YOUNG SOLDIER. Ours?

SOLDIER. Yes, chum. I get to know lots of things, I do, through my uncle. The queen is nice, you know, but she isn't really liked; they think she 's . . . [He taps his head.] They say she is eccentric and has a foreign accent, and is under the influence of Tiresias. This Tiresias advises the queen to do everything that will harm her. Do this . . . and do that. . . . She tells him her dreams, and asks him if she ought to get up right foot or left foot first; he leads her by the nose and licks her brother's boots, and plots with him against his sister. They are a low lot there. I wouldn't mind betting the captain thought our ghost was out of the same bag as the Sphinx. A priest's trick to attract Jocasta and make her believe anything they want.

YOUNG SOLDIER. No?

SOLDIER. Shakes you, doesn't it? But that 's how it is. . . . [In a very low voice.] Listen, I believe in the ghost myself, take it from me. But, for that very reason, because I believe in him and they don't, I advise you to keep your mouth shut. You 've already succeeded in making a fine hash of things. Take down this report: 'Has given proof of an intelligence well above his rank. . . .'

YOUNG SOLDIER. Still, if our king . . .

SOLDIER. Our king! . . . Our king! . . . Steady on! . . . A dead king

isn't a living king. It's like this, if King Laïus were living, well, between ourselves, he would manage on his own and wouldn't come looking for you to act
as his A.D.C. [*They move off towards the right by the patrol path.*]

VOICE OF JOCASTA. [*At the bottom of the steps. She has a very strong accent:
the international accent of royalty.*] Still another flight! I hate steps! Why all
these steps? We can see nothing! Where are we?

VOICE OF TIRESIAS. But, Majesty, you know what I think of this escapade,
and I didn't——

VOICE OF JOCASTA. Stop it, Zizi. You only open your mouth to say silly
things. This is not the time for moral lessons.

VOICE OF TIRESIAS. You should have taken another guide. I am nearly
blind.

VOICE OF JOCASTA. What is the use of being a soothsayer, I wonder! Why,
you don't even know where the steps are. I shall break my leg! It will be your
fault, Zizi, your fault, as usual.

VOICE OF TIRESIAS. My fleshly eyes have gone out to the advantage of an
inner eye which has other uses than counting steps.

VOICE OF JOCASTA. And now he's cross all over his eye! There, there! We
love you, Zizi; but these flights of steps upset me so. We had to come, Zizi,
we simply had to!

VOICE OF TIRESIAS. Majesty——

VOICE OF JOCASTA. Don't be obstinate. I had no idea there were all these
wretched steps. I am going to go up backwards. You will steady me. Don't be
afraid. I am leading you. But if I looked at the steps, I should fall. Take my
hands. Forward! [*They appear on the set.*]

There . . . there . . . there . . . four, five, six, seven . . .

[JOCASTA *arrives on the platform and moves to the right.* TIRESIAS *treads on
the end of her scarf. She utters a cry.*]

TIRESIAS. What is it?

JOCASTA. It's your foot, Zizi! You're walking on my scarf.

TIRESIAS. Forgive me . . .

JOCASTA. Ah! he's cross! But it isn't you that I am annoyed with, it's the
scarf! I am surrounded by objects which hate me! All day long this scarf is
strangling me. At one time it catches in the branches, at another it gets wound
on to the hub of a carriage, another time you tread on it. It's a positive fact.
And I am afraid of it, but I dare not be separated from it! Awful! It will be the
death of me.

TIRESIAS. Look what a state your nerves are in.

JOCASTA. And what is the use of your third eye, I should like to know?
Have you found the Sphinx? Have you found the murderers of Laïus? Have you
calmed the people? Guards are stationed at my door and I am left with things
that hate me, that want my death!

TIRESIAS. From mere hearsay——

JOCASTA. I feel things. I feel things better than all of you! [*She puts her hand on her belly.*] I feel them there! Was every possible effort made to discover the murderers of Laïus?

TIRESIAS.   Majesty, you know very well the Sphinx made further searches impossible.

JOCASTA.   Well, I for one don't care a jot about your fowls' entrails. . . . I feel, there . . . that Laïus is suffering and wants to be heard. I am determined to get to the bottom of this story, and to hear this young guard for myself; and I *shall* hear him. I am your queen, Tiresias, don't you forget it.

TIRESIAS.   My dear child, you must try and understand a poor blind man who adores you, watches over you, and wishes you were sleeping in your room instead of running after a shadow on the ramparts.

JOCASTA. [*With mystery.*]   I do not sleep.

TIRESIAS.   You don't sleep?

JOCASTA.   No, Zizi, I don't sleep. The Sphinx and the murder of Laïus have put my nerves all on edge. You were right there. And I am glad in a way, because if I fall asleep for so much as a minute I have a dream, always the same, and I am ill for the whole day.

TIRESIAS.   Isn't it my business to interpret dreams? . . .

JOCASTA.   The place of the dream is rather like this platform, so I 'll tell you. I am standing in the night, cradling a kind of nursling. Suddenly this nursling becomes a sticky paste which runs through my fingers. I shriek and try to throw this paste away, but . . . oh! Zizi . . . if only you knew, it 's foul. . . . This thing, this paste stays hanging on to me, and when I think I 'm free of it the paste flies back and strikes me across the face. And this paste is living. It has a kind of mouth which fixes itself on mine. And it creeps everywhere, it feels after my belly, and my thighs. Oh! Horrible!

TIRESIAS.   Calm yourself.

JOCASTA.   I don't want to sleep any more, Zizi . . . I don't want to sleep any more. Listen to that music. Where is it? They don't sleep either. It 's lucky for them that they have that music. They are afraid, Zizi . . . and rightly. They must dream horrible things, and they don't want to sleep. And while I think of it, why this music? Why is it allowed? Do I have music to keep me from sleeping? I didn't know these places stayed open all night. How is it there is this scandal, Zizi? Creon must send out orders! This music must be forbidden! This scandal must stop at once.

TIRESIAS.   Majesty, I implore you to calm yourself and to give up this idea. You 're beside yourself for lack of sleep. We have authorized these bands so that the people don't become demoralized, to keep up their courage. There would be crimes . . . and worse than that if there were no dancing in the crowded parts of town.

JOCASTA.   Do I dance?

TIRESIAS.   That 's different. You are in mourning for Laïus.

JOCASTA.   So are they all, Zizi. All of them! Every one! And yet they can dance and I can't. It 's too unfair . . . I shall——

TIRESIAS.   Someone coming, madam.

JOCASTA.   I say, Zizi, I 'm shaking. I have come out with all my jewels.

TIRESIAS.   There 's nothing to fear. You won't meet prowlers on the patrol path. It must be the guards.

JOCASTA.   Perhaps the soldier I am looking for?

TIRESIAS.   Don't move. We 'll find out.

[*The* SOLDIERS *enter. They see* JOCASTA *and* TIRESIAS.]

YOUNG SOLDIER.   Steady, looks like somebody.

SOLDIER.   Where have they sprung from? [*Aloud.*] Who goes there?

TIRESIAS.   [*To the* QUEEN.] This is going to be awkward. . . . [*Aloud.*] Listen, my good men . . .

YOUNG SOLDIER.   Password.

TIRESIAS.   You see, madam, we ought to have the password. You 're getting us into an awful mess.

JOCASTA.   Password? Why? What password? How silly, Zizi. I shall go and speak to him myself.

TIRESIAS.   Madam, I implore you. They have instructions. These guards might not recognize you, nor believe me. It 's very dangerous.

JOCASTA.   How romantic you are! You see dramas everywhere.

SOLDIER.   They 're whispering together. Perhaps they 're going to spring on us.

TIRESIAS.   [*To the* SOLDIERS.] You have nothing to fear. I am old and nearly blind. Let me explain my presence on these ramparts, and the presence of the person who accompanies me.

SOLDIER.   No speeches. The password!

TIRESIAS.   One moment. Just a moment. Listen, my good men, have you seen any gold coins?

SOLDIER.   Attempted bribery.

[*He goes towards the right to guard the patrol path and leaves the* YOUNG SOLDIER *opposite* TIRESIAS.]

TIRESIAS.   You 're wrong. I meant: have you seen the queen's portrait on a gold coin?

YOUNG SOLDIER.   Yes!

TIRESIAS.   [*Stepping aside and showing the queen, who is counting the stars, in profile.*] And . . . don't you recognize . . . ?

YOUNG SOLDIER.   If you 're trying to make out there 's a connection, I don't get it. The queen is so young, and this . . . er . . . lady . . . well! . . .

JOCASTA.   What does he say?

TIRESIAS.   He says he finds madam very young to be the queen. . . .

JOCASTA.   How entertaining!

TIRESIAS.   [*To the* SOLDIER.] Fetch your officer.

SOLDIER.   No need. I have my orders. Clear off! Look sharp!

TIRESIAS.   You 'll hear more of this!

JOCASTA.   Zizi, what is it now? What does he say?

[*The* CAPTAIN *enters.*]

CAPTAIN. What's going on here?

YOUNG SOLDIER. Two people without the password, sir.

CAPTAIN. [*Going towards* TIRESIAS.] Who are you? [*He suddenly recognizes* TIRESIAS.] My lord! [*He bows.*] My profoundest apologies.

TIRESIAS. Whew! Thanks, Captain. I thought this young warrior was going to run us through.

CAPTAIN. I am extremely sorry, my lord! [*To the* YOUNG SOLDIER.] Idiot! Leave us.

[*The* YOUNG SOLDIER *goes to his comrade on the extreme right.*]

SOLDIER. [*To the* YOUNG SOLDIER.] What a brick!

TIRESIAS. Don't scold him! He was obeying orders. . . .

CAPTAIN. Such a visit . . . in such a place! What can I do for your lordship?

TIRESIAS. [*Standing back to show the queen.*] Her Majesty!

[*The* CAPTAIN *starts back.*]

CAPTAIN. [*Bows at a respectful distance.*] Majesty! . . .

JOCASTA. No ceremony, please! I should like to know which guard saw the ghost.

CAPTAIN. Oh, the sorry young specimen who ill-used my lord Tiresias, and if Your Majesty . . .

JOCASTA. See, Zizi. What luck! I was right in coming. . . . [*To the* CAPTAIN.] Tell him to approach.

CAPTAIN. [*To* TIRESIAS.] My lord, I don't know if the queen fully realizes that this young soldier would explain himself better through his officer; and that, if he speaks for himself, Her Majesty will be in danger of——

JOCASTA. What now, Zizi? . . .

TIRESIAS. The Captain was pointing out that he is used to the men and he might serve as a kind of interpreter.

JOCASTA. Send the Captain away! Has the boy a tongue, or not? Let him come near.

TIRESIAS. [*Aside to the* CAPTAIN.] Don't insist, the queen is overwrought.
. . . .

CAPTAIN. Very well. . . . [*He goes to his* SOLDIERS. *To the* YOUNG SOLDIER.] The queen wants to speak to you. And control your tongue. I 'll pay you out for this, young fellow-me-lad.

JOCASTA. Come here! [*The* CAPTAIN *pushes the* YOUNG SOLDIER *forward.*]

CAPTAIN. Go along then! Go on, booby, forward. You won't be eaten. Excuse him, Your Majesty. Our lads are scarcely familiar with court ways.

JOCASTA. Ask that man to leave us alone with the soldier.

TIRESIAS. But, Majesty——

JOCASTA. And no 'but Majestys.' . . . If this Captain stays a moment longer I shall kick him.

TIRESIAS. Listen, officer. [*He leads him aside.*] The queen wants to be alone with the guard who has seen something. She has her whims. She might have your record blotted for you, you know, and I couldn't do anything about it.

CAPTAIN. Right. I 'll leave you . . . If I stayed it was because . . . well . . . I don't mean to give you advice, my lord. . . . But, between you and me, be on your guard about this ghost story. [*He bows.*] My lord. . . . [*A long salute to the* QUEEN. *He passes near the* SOLDIER.] Hi! The queen wishes to stay alone with your comrade.

JOCASTA. Who is the other soldier? Has he seen the ghost?

YOUNG SOLDIER. Yes, Your Majesty, we were on guard duty together.

JOCASTA. Then let him stop. Let him stay there! I 'll call him if I want him. Good evening, Captain, you are free.

CAPTAIN. [*To the* SOLDIER.] We 'll have this out later! [*He goes out.*]

TIRESIAS. [*To the* QUEEN.] You have mortally offended that officer.

JOCASTA. About time, too! Generally it 's the men who are mortally offended and never the officers. [*To the* YOUNG SOLDIER.] How old are you?

YOUNG SOLDIER. Nineteen.

JOCASTA. Exactly his age! He would be his age. . . . He looks splendid! Come nearer. Look, Zizi, what muscles! I adore knees. You can tell the breed by the knees. He would look like that too. . . . Isn't he fine, Zizi. Feel these biceps, like iron. . . .

TIRESIAS. I am sorry, madam, but you know . . . I 'm no authority. I can scarcely see what they 're like.

JOCASTA. Then feel. . . . Test them. Thighs like a horse! He steps away! Don't be afraid. . . . The old grandpa is blind. Heaven knows what he 's imagining, poor lad. He 's quite red! He 's adorable! And nineteen!

YOUNG SOLDIER. Yes, Your Majesty!

JOCASTA. [*Mocking him.*] Yes, Your Majesty! Isn't he just too delicious! Ah! what a shame! Perhaps he doesn't even know he 's handsome. [*As one speaks to a child.*] Well . . . did you see the ghost?

YOUNG SOLDIER. Yes, Your Majesty!

JOCASTA. The ghost of King Laïus?

YOUNG SOLDIER. Yes, Your Majesty! The king told us he was the king.

JOCASTA. Zizi . . . what do you know with all your fowls and stars? Listen to this boy. . . . And what did the king say?

TIRESIAS. [*Leading the* QUEEN *away.*] Majesty! Be careful. These young people are hot-headed, credulous . . . pushful. . . . Be on your guard. Are you certain this boy has seen the ghost, and, even if he has seen it, was it really the ghost of your husband?

JOCASTA. Gods! How unbearable you are! Unbearable and a spoil-sport. Every time you come and break the spell you stop miracles with your intelligence and incredulity. Please let me question this boy on my own. You can preach afterwards. [*To the* YOUNG SOLDIER.] Listen. . . .

YOUNG SOLDIER. Your Majesty! . . .

JOCASTA. [*To* TIRESIAS.] I 'll find out straight away whether he has seen Laïus. [*To the* YOUNG SOLDIER.] How did he speak?

YOUNG SOLDIER.   He spoke quickly and a lot, Your Majesty, ever such a lot, and he got mixed up, and he didn't manage to say what he wanted to.

JOCASTA.   That 's he! Poor dear! But why on these ramparts? The stench. . . .

YOUNG SOLDIER.   That 's it, Your Majesty. . . . The ghost said it was because of the swamps and the rising fumes that he could appear.

JOCASTA.   How interesting! Tiresias, you would never learn that from your birds. And what did he say?

TIRESIAS.   Madam, madam, you must at least question him with some order. You 'll muddle this youngster's head completely.

JOCASTA.   Quite right, Zizi, quite right. [To the YOUNG SOLDIER.] What was he like? How did you see him?

YOUNG SOLDIER.   In the wall, Your Majesty. A sort of transparent statue, as you might say. You could see the beard most clearly, and the black hole of the mouth as he spoke, and a red stain on the temple, bright red.

JOCASTA.   That 's blood!

YOUNG SOLDIER.   Fancy! We didn't think of that.

JOCASTA.   It's a wound! How dreadful! [LAÏUS appears.] And what did he say? Did you understand anything?

YOUNG SOLDIER.   It wasn't easy, Your Majesty. My comrade noticed that he had to make a big effort to appear, and each time he made an effort to express himself clearly he disappeared; then he was puzzled as to how to set about it.

JOCASTA.   Poor dear!

GHOST.   Jocasta! Jocasta! My wife! Jocasta! [They neither hear nor see him during the whole of the scene.]

TIRESIAS.   [Addressing the SOLDIER.]   And were you not able to grasp anything intelligible?

GHOST.   Jocasta!

SOLDIER.   Well, yes, my lord. We understand he wanted to warn you of a danger, put you on your guard, both the queen and you, but that 's all. The last time he explained he knew some secrets he ought not to have known, and if he was discovered he would not be able to appear again.

GHOST.   Jocasta! Tiresias! Can't you see me? Can't you hear me?

JOCASTA.   And didn't he say anything else? Didn't he say anything particular?

SOLDIER.   Ah, well, Your Majesty! Perhaps he didn't want to say anything particular in our presence. He was asking for you. That is why my comrade tried to let you know about it.

JOCASTA.   Dear boys! And I have come. I knew it all the time. I felt it there! You see, Zizi, with all your doubts. And tell us, Young Soldier, where the ghost appeared. I want to touch the exact spot.

GHOST.   Look at me! Listen to me, Jocasta! Guards, you always saw me before. Why not see me now? This is torture! Jocasta! Jocasta! [While these words are being uttered the SOLDIER goes to the place where the GHOST is. He touches it with his hand.]

SOLDIER. There. [*He strikes the wall.*] There, in the wall.

YOUNG SOLDIER. Or in front of the wall. It was difficult to make out.

JOCASTA. But why doesn't he appear to-night? Do you think he will still be able to appear?

GHOST. Jocasta! Jocasta! Jocasta!

SOLDIER. I am sorry, Your Majesty, I don't think so, after what happened last night. I 'm afraid there was a spot of bother and Her Majesty may be too late.

JOCASTA. What a shame! Always too late. Zizi, I am always the last person in the whole kingdom to be informed. Think of the time we have wasted with your fowls and oracles! We ought to have run, to have guessed. We shall learn absolutely nothing! And there will be disasters, terrible disasters. And it will be your fault, Zizi, your fault, as usual.

TIRESIAS. Madam, the queen is speaking in front of these men.

JOCASTA. Yes, I am speaking in front of these men! I suppose I ought to restrain myself? When King Laïus, the dead King Laïus, has spoken in front of these men. But he has not spoken to you, Zizi, nor to Creon. He hasn't been to the temple to show himself. He showed himself on the patrol path to these men, to this boy of nineteen who is so handsome and looks like——

TIRESIAS. I implore you——

JOCASTA. Yes, I am overwrought, you must try to understand. These dangers, this spectre, this music, this pestilential smell. . . . And there's a storm about. I can feel it in my shoulder. I am stifling, Zizi, stifling.

GHOST. Jocasta! Jocasta!

JOCASTA. I think I hear my name. Didn't you hear anything?

TIRESIAS. My poor lamb. You 're worn out. Day is breaking. You are dreaming where you stand. Are you even sure this ghost business hasn't come from the fatigue of these young men on the watch who force themselves not to sleep and who live in this depressing, swampy atmosphere?

GHOST. Jocasta! For pity's sake, listen to me! Look at me! Gentlemen, you are kind. Keep the queen. Tiresias! Tiresias!

TIRESIAS. [*To the* YOUNG SOLDIER.] Step aside a moment, I want to speak to the queen. [*The* YOUNG SOLDIER *goes to his comrade.*]

SOLDIER. Well, old son! You 've clicked! She 's fallen for you! Petted by the queen, eh!

YOUNG SOLDIER. Look here! . . .

SOLDIER. You 're made for life. Don't forget your pals.

TIRESIAS. . . . Listen! Cockcrow. The ghost will not return. Let us go home.

JOCASTA. Did you see how handsome he is?

TIRESIAS. Don't recall those sad things, my lamb. If you had a son . . .

JOCASTA. If I had a son, he would be handsome, brave, he would guess the riddle and kill the Sphinx. He would return victor.

TIRESIAS. And you would go without a husband.

JOCASTA.   Little boys always say: 'I want to become a man so that I can marry mother.' It 's not such a bad idea, you know, Tiresias. Is there a sweeter union, a union that is sweeter and more cruel, and prouder, than that couple: a son and a young mother? Listen, Zizi, just now, when I touched that young guard, heaven alone knows what he must have thought, the poor lad, and I myself nearly fainted. He would be nineteen, Tiresias, nineteen! The same age as this soldier. Can we be sure Laïus did not appear to him because of his likeness?

[*Cock crows.*]

GHOST.   Jocasta! Jocasta! Jocasta! Tiresias! Jocasta!

TIRESIAS.   [*To the* SOLDIERS.]   My friends, do you think it is any use waiting?

GHOST.   For pity's sake!

SOLDIER.   Frankly, no, my lord. The cocks are crowing. He will not appear now.

GHOST.   Gentlemen! Mercy! Am I invisible? Can't you hear me?

JOCASTA.   Come along! I will be obedient. But I am very glad I questioned the boy. You must find out his name and where he lives. [*She goes towards the steps.*] I had forgotten these steps, Zizi! . . . That band is making me ill. Listen, we can go back through the higher town by the side streets, and we can see the night life.

TIRESIAS.   Madam, you don't mean it.

JOCASTA.   Oh! now he 's beginning again! He 'll send me simply raving! Mad and off my head. I 've got my veils on, Zizi, how do you expect I should be recognized?

TIRESIAS.   My child, you said yourself you have come out wearing all your jewels. Your brooch alone has pearls as large as an egg.

JOCASTA.   I am a martyr! Others can laugh and dance and amuse themselves. Do you imagine I am going to leave this brooch at the palace where it's simply asking to be taken? Call the guard. Tell him to help me down these steps. And you can follow us.

TIRESIAS.   But, madam, since the presence of this young man affects you so strongly . . .

JOCASTA.   He is young and strong. He will help me, and I shan't break my neck. Obey your queen for once, at least.

TIRESIAS. Hi! . . . No, he. . . . Yes, you. . . . Help the queen down the steps. . . .

SOLDIER.   You see, old man!

YOUNG SOLDIER. [*Approaching.*]   Yes, my lord.

GHOST.   Jocasta! Jocasta!—Jocasta!

JOCASTA.   He's shy! And flights of steps hate me. Steps, hooks, and scarves. Oh! yes, they do, they hate me! They're after my death. [*A cry.*] Ho!

YOUNG SOLDIER.   Has the queen hurt herself?

TIRESIAS.   No, silly! Your foot! Your foot!

YOUNG SOLDIER.   What foot?

TIRESIAS. Your foot on the end of the scarf. You nearly strangled the queen.

YOUNG SOLDIER. Ye gods!

JOCASTA. Zizi, you are utterly ridiculous. Poor darling. There you go calling him a murderer because he walks, as you did, on this scarf. Don't upset yourself, my boy. My lord is absurd. He never misses an opportunity of hurting people's feelings.

TIRESIAS. But, madam——

JOCASTA. You are the one who is clumsy. Come along. Thank you, my boy. Send your name and address to the temple. One, two, three, four. . . . Marvellous! Zizi! Do you see how well I'm getting down. Eleven, twelve. . . . Zizi, are you following? Two more steps. [*To the* SOLDIER.] Thank you. I can manage now. Help grandpa! [JOCASTA *disappears left, with* TIRESIAS. *Cocks are heard.*]

VOICE OF JOCASTA. Through your fault I shall never know what my poor Laïus wanted.

GHOST. Jocasta!

VOICE OF TIRESIAS. That story is all very vague.

VOICE OF JOCASTA. What? very vague? What do you mean, vague? It's you who are vague with your third eye. That boy knows what he has seen, and he has seen the king. Have you seen the king?

VOICE OF TIRESIAS. But——

VOICE OF JOCASTA. Have you seen him? . . . No. . . . Well . . . It's amazing . . . it's like . . . [*The voices die away.*]

GHOST. Jocasta! Tiresias! Have pity!

[*The two* SOLDIERS *turn to each other and see the* GHOST.]

THE SOLDIERS. Oh! the Ghost!

GHOST. Gentlemen, at last! I am saved! I kept calling, begging. . . .

SOLDIER. You were there?

GHOST. During the whole of your talk with the queen and Tiresias. Then why was I invisible?

YOUNG SOLDIER. I'll run and fetch them!

SOLDIER. Halt!

GHOST. What? You stop him?

YOUNG SOLDIER. Let me go . . .

SOLDIER. When the joiner comes the chair stops wobbling; when you get to the shoemender your sandal stops hurting you; when you get to the doctor you no longer feel the pain. Fetch them! That would only make him disappear.

GHOST. Alas! Do these simple souls then know what the priests cannot divine?

YOUNG SOLDIER. I shall go.

GHOST. Too late. . . . Stay. It is too late. I am discovered. They are coming; they are going to take me. Ah! they're here! Help! Help! Quick! Tell the queen a young man is approaching Thebes, and on no account . . . No! No!

Mercy! Mercy! They've got me! Help! Ended! I . . . I. . . . Mercy . . . I
. . . I . . .

[*Long silence. The two* SOLDIERS, *back to the audience, contemplate endlessly the place in the wall where the* GHOST *disappeared.*]

SOLDIER.   Good God!

YOUNG SOLDIER.   Poor devil!

SOLDIER.   These things are beyond us, old man.

YOUNG SOLDIER.   But it's clear that, in spite of death, that fellow wanted,
at all costs, to warn his wife of a danger which is threatening her. My duty is
to overtake the queen and the high priest and repeat to them word for word
what we have just heard.

SOLDIER.   You want the queen badly, don't you? [*The* YOUNG SOLDIER *shrugs
his shoulders.*] Well . . . he only had to appear to them and talk to them, they
were there. We saw him all right ourselves and they didn't. But, to crown all,
they even prevented *us* from seeing him. So there you have it! Dead kings become ordinary people. Poor Laïus! Now he knows how easy it is to get into
touch with the great of the earth.

YOUNG SOLDIER.   But us?

SOLDIER.   Oh, us! It's easy enough to get into touch with men, you coon.
. . . But, when it comes to officers, queens, and high priests . . . they always
go before it happens, or come when it's all over.

YOUNG SOLDIER.   What's 'it'?

SOLDIER.   How should I know? . . . I understand myself, that's the chief
thing.

YOUNG SOLDIER.   And you wouldn't go and warn the queen?

SOLDIER.   A word of advice: let princes deal with princes, ghosts with ghosts,
and soldiers with soldiers. [*Flourish.*]

Act II. The Meeting of Oedipus and the Sphinx

THE VOICE: Spectators, let us imagine we can recall the minutes we have
just lived through together and relive them elsewhere. For, while the Ghost
of Laïus was trying to warn Jocasta on the ramparts of Thebes, the Sphinx
and Oedipus met on a hill overlooking the town. The bugle-calls, moon, stars,
and crowing cocks will be the same.

SCENE: *An unpeopled spot on a hill overlooking Thebes, by moonlight. The
road to Thebes (from right to left) passes over the fore-stage. It gives the
impression of rounding a high leaning stone whose base is fixed at the lower
end of the platform and forms the support for the wings on the right. Behind
the ruins of a little temple is a broken wall. In the middle of the wall stands
a complete pedestal which used to indicate the entrance to the temple and
bears the trace of a chimera: a wing, a foot, a haunch. Broken and overturned
columns. For the Shades of Anubis and Nemesis at the end, a record by the*

*actors can declaim the dialogue, whilst the actress mimes the part of the dead
girl with the head of a jackal.*

Act II. The Meeting of Oedipus and the Sphinx

SCENE: *When the curtain rises a girl in a white dress is seen sitting among
the ruins. The head of a jackal lies in her lap, its body remaining hidden
behind her. Distant bugle calls.*

SPHINX.   Listen.

JACKAL.   Well?

SPHINX.   That's the last call. We're free.

[ANUBIS *gets up, and the* JACKAL'S *head is seen to belong to him.*]

JACKAL, ANUBIS.   It's the first. There'll be two more before the gates are
closed.

SPHINX.   It's the last. I'm quite sure it's the last.

ANUBIS.   You're sure because you want the gates closed, but I'm sorry duty
forces me to contradict you; we're not free. That was the first bugle call. We'll
wait.

SPHINX.   I may have been mistaken, but——

ANUBIS.   May have been mistaken! You were. . . .

SPHINX.   Anubis!

ANUBIS.   Sphinx?

SPHINX.   I've had enough of killing, enough of dealing out death.

ANUBIS.   We must obey. There are mysteries within mystery, gods above
gods. We have our gods and they have theirs. That's what is called infinity.

SPHINX.   You see, Anubis, there is no second call. It's you who are mistaken, let us go. . . .

ANUBIS.   Do you mean you would like this night to pass without any deaths?

SPHINX.   Yes! I do, indeed! Yes! Although it's growing late, I tremble to
think someone may still come by.

ANUBIS.   You're getting sensitive.

SPHINX.   That's my business.

ANUBIS.   Don't get cross.

SPHINX.   Why must we always be acting without aim, without end, without
understanding? Why, for example, should you have a dog's head, Anubis? Why
have the god of the dead in the shape given to him by credulous people?
Why must we have an Egyptian god in Greece and why must he have a dog's
head?

ANUBIS.   It's marvellous, how like a woman you look when it comes to asking questions.

SPHINX.   That is no answer!

ANUBIS.   Well, my answer is: that logic forces us to appear to men in the
shape in which they imagine us; otherwise, they would see only emptiness.
Moreover, neither Egypt nor Greece nor death, neither the past nor the future

has any meaning for us. Further, you know only too well to what use I must put this jaw. And finally, our masters prove their wisdom by giving me a material form which is not human and so preventing me from losing my head, however beastly it may be; for I am your keeper, remember. I can see that if they had given you a mere watchdog we should already be in Thebes with me on a leash and you sitting in the middle of a band of young men.

SPHINX.   How stupid you are!

ANUBIS.   Then try and remember that these victims who touch the girl-figure you have assumed are no more than noughts wiped off a slate, even if each of these noughts were an open mouth calling for help.

SPHINX.   That may be. But here the calculations of gods are hard to follow. . . . Here we kill. Here the dead really die. Here I do kill.

[*While the* SPHINX *was speaking with her eyes on the ground* ANUBIS *pricked up his ears, looked round, and moved silently off over the ruins where he disappears. When the* SPHINX *raises her eyes, she looks for* ANUBIS, *and finds herself face to face with a small group of people who enter down stage right, and whom* ANUBIS *had scented. The group is composed of a Theban* MATRON, *her little boy and girl. The* MATRON *is dragging her daughter along. The boy is walking ahead.*]

MATRON.   Look where you're going! Get along now! Don't look behind you! Leave your sister alone! Go on. . . . [*She sees the* SPHINX *as the little boy stumbles into her.*] Look out! I told you to look where you're going! Oh! I'm so sorry, miss. . . . He never looks where he's going. . . . He hasn't hurt you, has he?

SPHINX.   No! not at all.

MATRON.   I didn't expect to meet any one on my path at such an hour.

SPHINX.   I'm new in these parts, I haven't been long in Thebes; I was on my way to a relative who lives in the country and got lost.

MATRON.   Poor dear! And where does your relative live?

SPHINX.   . . . Near the twelfth milestone.

MATRON.   The very part I come from! I had lunch with my family, at my brother's place, you know. He made me stay to dinner. And then, you know, you begin gossiping and don't notice the time, and so here I am going home after curfew with brats half asleep already.

SPHINX.   Good night.

MATRON.   Good night. [*She makes to go.*] And . . . I say . . . don't linger on the way. I know the likes of you and me haven't much to fear . . . but I wouldn't be too bold, if I were you, till I was inside the walls.

SPHINX.   Are you afraid of thieves?

MATRON.   Thieves! Ye gods, what could they get out of me? Oh, no, my dear! Where *do* you come from? Any one can see you're not from the town. Thieves! I should think so! I mean the Sphinx!

SPHINX.   Do you really, honestly and truly, believe in that nonsense yourself?

MATRON. That nonsense indeed! How young you are. Young people are so disbelieving these days. Oh, yes, they are! That's how disasters happen. Let alone the Sphinx, I'll give you a case from my family. . . . My brother that I've just left. . . . [*She sits down and lowers her voice.*] He married a beautiful tall blonde from the north. One night he wakes up and what does he find? His wife in bed without head or entrails. She was a vampire. When he'd got over the first fright what does my brother do? without a moment's hesitation he finds an egg and lays it on the pillow in the place of his wife's head. That's how you stop vampires getting back into their body. All at once he hears a moaning. It was the head and entrails flying wildly across the room and begging my brother to take away the egg. My brother wouldn't, and the head went from moans to anger, from anger to tears, from tears to kisses. To cut a long story short, my idiot brother takes away the egg and lets his wife get back into her body. Now he knows his wife is a vampire and my sons make fun of their uncle. They maintain that he made up this entire vampire story to disguise the fact that his wife really did go out, but with her body, and that he let her come back, and that he's a coward and ashamed of himself. But *I* know very well my sister-in-law is a vampire. . . . And my sons are in danger of marrying fiends from the underworld, all because they are obstinate and *disbelieving*.

And the same with the Sphinx—I'm sorry if I hurt your feelings, but it's only the likes of my sons and you who don't believe in it.

SPHINX. Your sons . . . ?

MATRON. Not the little brat who just bumped into you. I mean my boy of seventeen. . . .

SPHINX. You have several sons, have you?

MATRON. I had four. Now I have three. Seven, sixteen, and seventeen. And I can tell you ever since that wicked beast appeared the house has been impossible.

SPHINX. Your sons quarrel . . . ?

MATRON. I mean, my dear, that it's impossible to live under the same roof. The one who's sixteen is only interested in politics. According to him the Sphinx is a bugbear used to scare the poor and to impose on them. There may have been something like your old Sphinx at one time—that's how my son speaks—but now the old Sphinx is dead; and he's merely a priest's demon and an excuse for police jobbery. They fleece and loot and terrorize the masses, and then blame it all on the Sphinx. It's a good thing the Sphinx has broad shoulders. Whose fault is it that we starve to death, that prices go up, and that bands of looters swarm over the countryside? Why, the Sphinx's, of course. And the Sphinx is to blame because business is bad, and the government's weak and one crash follows another; because the temples are glutted with rich offerings whilst mothers and wives are losing the bare necessities of life, and because foreigners with money to spend are leaving town. . . . Ah, you should see him, miss, how he gets up on the table, shouting, waving his arms, and stamping his feet; and then he denounces those who are responsible for it all, preaches revolt, eggs on the anarchists, shouting at the top of his voice names that are enough to get us all hanged. And between ourselves, miss . . . I know . . . you can take it from me . . . the Sphinx exists all right, but they're making the most of it. You can be sure of that. What we want is a man, a dictator!

SPHINX.   And . . . what about the brother of your young dictator?

MATRON.   Oh! he's another kettle of fish. He despises his brother, he despises me, he despises the gods, he despises everything. He makes you wonder where he can get hold of all he comes out with. He says, if you please, that the Sphinx would interest him if it killed for killing's sake, but that this Sphinx of ours is in league with the oracles, and so it doesn't interest him.

SPHINX.   And your fourth son? When was it . . . ?

MATRON.   I lost him nearly a year ago. He was just nineteen.

SPHINX.   Poor woman. . . . What did he die of?

MATRON.   Sphinx.

SPHINX. [Gloomily.]   Ah! . . .

MATRON.   It's all very well for his younger brother to maintain he was a victim of police intrigues. . . . Oh, no! There's no mistake, he died through the Sphinx. Ah, my dear! . . . if I live to be a hundred I'll never forget that scene. One morning (he hadn't been home that night) I thought I heard him knock; I opened the front door and saw the underneath of his poor feet and then there followed a long way off, ever so far away, his poor little face, and in the back of his neck—look, just here—a large wound from which the blood had already stopped flowing. They brought him to me on a stretcher. Then I went: Ho! and fell, all of a heap. . . . A blow like that, you know, you don't get over in a hurry. You may be thankful you don't come from Thebes, thankful if you have no brothers. . . . You're lucky. . . . My other boy, the orator, wants to avenge him. What's the good? But he hates the priests, and my poor son was one of a series of human offerings.

SPHINX.   Human offerings?

MATRON.   To be sure. During the first months of the Sphinx the soldiers were sent to avenge the fine young men who were found dead all over the place, and they returned empty-handed. The Sphinx couldn't be found. Then, as there was a rumour that the Sphinx asked riddles, young people from the schools were sacrificed; and then the priests stated that the Sphinx demanded human offerings. At that, the youngest and weakest and fairest were chosen.

SPHINX.   Poor woman!

MATRON.   I tell you, my dear, what we want is a man of action. Queen Jocasta is still young. At a distance you would say she was twenty-nine or thirty. What we want is a ruler to fall from the sky, marry her, and kill the beast; someone to make an end of corruption, lock up Creon and Tiresias, improve the state of finance and liven up the people, someone who would care for the people and save us, yes, that's it, save us. . . .

SON.   Mummy!

MATRON.   Sh!

SON. Mummy . . . I say, mummy, what does the Sphinx look like?

MATRON. I don't know. [*To the* SPHINX.] And what d' you think is the latest? They're asking us to contribute our last farthings for a monument to those killed by the Sphinx! Will that bring them back to us, I should like to know?

SON. Mummy . . . what is the Sphinx like?

SPHINX. Poor little chap! His sister's asleep. Come along. . . .

[*The son clings to the skirt of the* SPHINX.]

MATRON. Now don't worry the lady.

SPHINX. He's all right. [*She strokes his neck.*]

SON. I say, mummy, is this lady the Sphinx?

MATRON. Little silly. [*To the* SPHINX.] I hope you don't mind. At that age children don't know what they're saying. . . . [*She gets up.*] Oh my! [*She takes the little girl who is asleep in her arms.*] Come along now! Off we go, lazy-bones!

SON. Mummy, is that lady the Sphinx? I say, mummy, is the Sphinx that lady? Is that the Sphinx, mummy?

MATRON. Sh! Don't be silly. [*To the* SPHINX.] Well, good evening. Excuse my gossiping to you. I was glad to stop for a breather. . . . And . . . take care. [*Fanfare.*] Quickly. There's the second bugle. After the third we'll be shut out.

SPHINX. Go along, quickly. I'll hurry my way. You've put me on my guard.

MATRON. Believe me, we'll not feel safe until there comes a man who will rid us of this scourge. [*She goes out left.*]

SON'S VOICE. I say, mummy, what's the Sphinx look like? Why wasn't it that lady? Then what's he like?

SPHINX. A scourge!

ANUBIS. [*Coming from among the ruins.*] That woman *would* have to come along here just now.

SPHINX. I've been unhappy for the past two days, for two days now I've been carrying on in this miserable way in the hope that this massacre would come to an end.

ANUBIS. Don't worry. You're all right.

SPHINX. Listen. This is my secret wish and these the circumstances which would allow me to mount my pedestal for a last time. A young man will climb the hill, I shall fall in love with him. He'll have no fear. And when I ask my question he will answer as to an equal. He will give *the answer*, d' you hear, Anubis, and I shall fall dead.

ANUBIS. Make no mistake: only your mortal form will fall dead.

SPHINX. And isn't that the form I should want to live in to make him happy!

ANUBIS. It's nice to see that human form doesn't make a great goddess become a little woman.

SPHINX. You see how right I was. That bugle we heard was the last after all!

ANUBIS. Daughter of men! One is never finished with you. I tell you no!

No! [*He leaves her side and mounts an overturned column.*] That was the second. When I've heard another one you can go. Oh!

SPHINX.   What is it?

ANUBIS.   Bad news.

SPHINX.   Someone coming?

ANUBIS.   Yes. [*The* SPHINX *gets up beside* ANUBIS *and looks into the wings, right.*]

SPHINX.   I can't! I can't and I won't question this young man. You needn't ask me to.

ANUBIS.   I should say, if you 're like a young mortal, he 's like a young god.

SPHINX.   What grace, Anubis, and what shoulders! He's coming.

ANUBIS.   I 'll hide. Don't forget you are the Sphinx. I 'm keeping my eye on you. I 'll be with you at the first sign.

SPHINX.   Anubis, listen . . . quickly. . . .

ANUBIS.   Sh! . . . He 's here. [ANUBIS *hides.*]

[OEDIPUS *enters up stage right. He is walking along with his eyes on the ground. He starts.*]

OEDIPUS.   Oh! I 'm sorry. . . .

SPHINX.   I startled you.

OEDIPUS.   Well . . . no . . . I was dreaming, I was miles away, and suddenly, before me——

SPHINX.   You took me for an animal.

OEDIPUS.   Almost.

SPHINX.   Almost? Almost an animal, that 's the Sphinx.

OEDIPUS.   Yes, I know.

SPHINX.   You admit you took me for the Sphinx. Thank you.

OEDIPUS.   Oh! I soon realized my mistake.

SPHINX.   Too kind. The truth of the matter is it can't be so amusing to find yourself suddenly face to face with the Sphinx, if you 're a young man.

OEDIPUS.   And . . . if you 're a girl?

SPHINX.   He doesn't attack girls.

OEDIPUS.   Because girls avoid his haunts and are not supposed to go out alone when the light is failing.

SPHINX.   You 'd do well to mind your own business, young man, and let me go my way.

OEDIPUS.   Which way?

SPHINX.   You 're simply amazing. Must I give my reasons for being out to a complete stranger?

OEDIPUS.   And suppose I guessed your reason?

SPHINX.   You amuse me.

OEDIPUS.   Aren't you moved by curiosity, the curiosity which is raging amongst all modern young women, the curiosity to know what the Sphinx looks like? If he has claws, or a beak, or wings, and whether he takes after the tiger or the vulture?

SPHINX.   Oh, come, come!

OEDIPUS.   The Sphinx is the criminal of the day. Who 's seen him? No one.
Fabulous rewards are promised to the first person who discovers him. The faint
of heart tremble. Young men die. . . . But a girl, couldn't she venture into
the forbidden area, setting orders at defiance, and dare what no reasonable
person would dare, to unearth the monster, surprise him in his lair, get a view
of him?

SPHINX.   You 're on the wrong track, I tell you. I'm going back to a relative
who lives in the country, and as I had forgotten the very existence of a Sphinx
and that the outskirts of Thebes are not safe, I was resting a moment on the
stones of these old ruins. You see how far you 're out.

OEDIPUS.   What a pity! For some time now I 've only run across people as
dull as ditch water; so I hoped for something more unusual. Pardon me.

SPHINX.   Good evening!

OEDIPUS.   Good evening!

[*They pass each other. But* OEDIPUS *turns back.*]

I say! I may appear unpleasant, but I honestly can't bring myself to believe
you. Your presence in these ruins still intrigues me enormously.

SPHINX.   You 're simply incredible.

OEDIPUS.   Because if you were like other girls you would already have made
off as fast as your legs would carry you.

SPHINX.   My dear boy, you 're quite absurd.

OEDIPUS.   It seemed to me so marvellous to find in a girl a worthy competitor.

SPHINX.   A competitor? Then you are looking for the Sphinx?

OEDIPUS.   Looking for him? Let me tell you, I 've been on the march for a
whole month. Probably that 's why I appeared ill-mannered just now. I was
so wild with excitement as I drew near Thebes that I could have shouted my
enthusiasm to the merest block of stone, when, instead of a block of stone,
what stands in my path but a girl in white? So I couldn't help talking to her
about what was uppermost in my mind and thinking she must have the same
purpose as myself.

SPHINX.   But surely, a moment ago, when you saw me spring out of the
shadow, you didn't seem to me very much on the alert for a man who wants
to measure his strength with the enemy.

OEDIPUS.   That is true. I was dreaming of fame, and the beast would have
caught me unawares. To-morrow in Thebes I shall equip myself and the hunt
will begin.

SPHINX.   You love fame?

OEDIPUS.   I 'm not sure about that. I like trampling crowds, trumpet calls,
flying banners, waving palm branches, the sun, gold and purple, happiness,
luck—you know, to live!

SPHINX.   Is that what you call living?

OEDIPUS.   Don't you?

SPHINX.   No, I must say I have quite a different idea of life.

OEDIPUS.   What 's that?

SPHINX.   To love. To be loved by the one you love.

OEDIPUS.   I shall love my people and they me.

SPHINX.   The public square is not a home.

OEDIPUS.   The public square has nothing to do with it. The people of Thebes are looking for a man. If I kill the Sphinx I shall be that man. Queen Jocasta is a widow; I shall marry her. . . .

SPHINX.   A woman who might be your mother!

OEDIPUS.   The main thing is that she is not.

SPHINX.   Do you imagine that a queen and her people would give themselves up to the first comer?

OEDIPUS.   Would you call the vanquisher of the Sphinx a first comer? I know the promised reward is the queen. Don't laugh at me. Please listen. You must. I must prove that my dream isn't merely a dream. My father is King of Corinth. My father and mother were already old when I was born and I lived in a court of gloom. Too much fuss and comfort produced in me a feverish longing for adventure. I began to pine and waste away, when one evening a drunk shouted at me that I was a bastard and that I was usurping the place of a legitimate son. Blows and abuse followed, and the next day, despite the tears of Merope and Polybius, I decided to visit the sanctuaries and question the gods. They all replied with the same oracle: You will murder your father and marry your mother.

SPHINX.   What?

OEDIPUS.   Yes, I mean it. At first this oracle fills you with horror, but I 'm not so easily imposed on! I soon saw how nonsensical the whole thing was. I took into account the ways of the gods and the priests, and I came to this conclusion: either the oracle hid a less serious meaning which had to be discovered, or the priests who communicate from temple to temple by means of birds found it perhaps to their advantage to put this oracle into the mouth of the gods and to weaken my chances of coming into power. Briefly, I soon forgot my fears, and, I may say, used this threat of parricide and incest as an excuse to flee the court and satisfy my thirst for the unknown.

SPHINX.   Now it 's my turn to feel dazed. I 'm sorry I rather made fun of you. Will you forgive me, prince?

OEDIPUS.   Give me your hand. May I ask your name? Mine is Oedipus; I 'm nineteen.

SPHINX.   Oh, what does it matter about mine, Oedipus? You must like illustrious names. . . . That of a little girl of seventeen wouldn't interest you.

OEDIPUS.   That 's unkind.

SPHINX.   You adore fame. Yet I should have thought the surest way of foiling the oracle would be to marry a woman younger than yourself.

OEDIPUS.   That doesn't sound like you. That's more like a mother of Thebes where marriageable young men are few.

SPHINX.   And that 's not like you either. That was a gross, common thing to say.

OEDIPUS. So, I shall have walked the roads past mountain and stream merely to take a wife who will quickly become a Sphinx, worse than that, a Sphinx with breasts and claws!

SPHINX. Oedipus. . . .

OEDIPUS. No, thank you! I prefer to try my luck. Take this belt: with that you will be able to get to me when I have killed the beast. [*Business.*]

SPHINX. Have you ever killed?

OEDIPUS. Yes, once. At the cross-roads of Delphi and Daulis. I was walking along like a moment ago. A carriage was approaching driven by an old man with an escort of four servants. When I was on a level with the horses one of them reared and knocked me into one of these servants. The fool tried to strike me, I aimed a blow at him with my stick, but he dodged down and I caught the old man on the temple. He fell and the horses bolted, dragging him along. I ran after them, the servants were terrified and fled; I found myself alone with the bleeding body of the old man and the horses who screamed as they rolled about entangled, and broke their legs. It was dreadful . . . dreadful. . . .

SPHINX. Yes, isn't it . . . it's dreadful to kill.

OEDIPUS. Oh, well, it wasn't my fault and I think no more about it. The thing is to clear all obstacles, to wear blinkers, and not to give way to self-pity. Besides, there is my star.

SPHINX. Then farewell, Oedipus. I am of the sex which is disturbing to heroes. Let us go our ways, we can have little in common.

OEDIPUS. Disturbing to heroes, eh! You have a high opinion of your sex.

SPHINX. And . . . supposing the Sphinx killed you?

OEDIPUS. His death depends, if I'm not mistaken, on questions which I must answer. If I guess right he won't even touch me, he'll just die.

SPHINX. And if you do not guess right?

OEDIPUS. Thanks to my unhappy childhood I have pursued studies which give me a great start over the riff-raff of Thebes.

SPHINX. I'm glad to hear it.

OEDIPUS. And I don't think this simple-minded monster is expecting to be confronted by a pupil of the best scholars of Corinth.

SPHINX. You have an answer to everything. A pity, for, I own, Oedipus, I have a soft spot for weak people, and I should like to have found you wanting.

OEDIPUS. Farewell.

[*The* SPHINX *makes one step as if to rush in pursuit of* OEDIPUS, *stops, but cannot resist the call. Until her* 'I! I!' *the* SPHINX *does not take her eyes off those of* OEDIPUS; *she moves as it were round this immobile, steady, vast gaze from under eyelids which do not flicker.*]

SPHINX. Oedipus!

OEDIPUS. Did you call me?

SPHINX. One last word. For the moment does nothing else occupy your mind, nothing else fire your heart, nothing stir your spirit save the Sphinx?

OEDIPUS. Nothing else, for the moment.

SPHINX.   And he . . . or she who brought you into his presence. . . . I mean who would help you. . . . I mean who may perhaps know something to help bring about this meeting . . . would he or she in your eyes assume such prestige that you would be touched and moved?

OEDIPUS.   Naturally, but what does all this mean?

SPHINX.   And supposing I, I myself, were to divulge a secret, a tremendous secret?

OEDIPUS.   You 're joking!

SPHINX.   A secret which would allow you to enter into contact with the enigma of enigmas, with the human beast, with the singing bitch, as it is called, with the Sphinx?

OEDIPUS.   What! You? You? Did I guess aright, and has your curiosity led you to discover . . . ? No! How stupid of me. This is a woman's trick to make me turn back.

SPHINX.   Good-bye.

OEDIPUS.   Oh! Forgive me! . . .

SPHINX.   Too late.

OEDIPUS.   I 'm kneeling; a simple fool who begs forgiveness.

SPHINX.   You 're a fatuous young man who is sorry to have lost his chance and is trying to get it back.

OEDIPUS.   I am and I 'm ashamed. Look, I believe you, I 'll listen. But if you have played me a trick I shall drag you by the hair and grip you till the blood flows.

SPHINX.   Come here. [*She leads him opposite the pedestal.*] Shut your eyes. Don't cheat. Count up to fifty.

OEDIPUS. [*With his eyes shut.*]   Take care!

SPHINX.   It 's your turn to do that.

[OEDIPUS *counts. One feels that something extraordinary is happening. The* SPHINX *bounds across the ruins, disappears behind a wall and reappears in the real pedestal, that is, she seems to be fastened on to the pedestal, the bust resting on the elbows and looking straight ahead, whereas the actress is really standing, and only lets her bust appear and her arms in spotted gloves with her hands grasping the edge; out of the broken wing suddenly grow two immense, pale, luminous wings and the fragment of statue completes her, prolonging her, and appearing to belong to her.* OEDIPUS *is heard counting:* 'Forty-seven, forty-eight, forty-nine,' *then he makes a pause and shouts:* 'Fifty.' *He turns round.*]

OEDIPUS.   You!

SPHINX. [*In a high distant voice, joyous and terrible.*]   Yes, I! I, the Sphinx!

OEDIPUS.   I 'm dreaming!

SPHINX.   You are no dreamer, Oedipus. You know what you want, and did want. Silence. Here I command. Approach.

[OEDIPUS, *with his arms held stiffly by his body as if paralysed, tries frantically to free himself.*]

Come forward. [OEDIPUS *falls on his knees.*] As your legs refuse their help, jump, hop. . . . It 's good for a hero to make himself ridiculous. Come along! Move yourself! Don't worry, there 's nobody to see you.

[OEDIPUS, *writhing with anger, moves forward on his knees.*] That 's it. Stop! And now. . . .

OEDIPUS.   And now, I 'm beginning to understand your methods, what moves you make to lure and slay.

SPHINX.   . . . And now, I am going to give you a demonstration, I 'm going to show you what would happen in this place, Oedipus, if you were any ordinary handsome youth from Thebes, and if you hadn't the privilege of pleasing me.

OEDIPUS.   I know what your pleasantries are worth.

[*He knits up all the muscles of his body. It is obvious he is struggling against a charm.*]

SPHINX.   Yield! Don't try to screw up your muscles and resist. Relax! If you resist you will only make my task more delicate and I might hurt you.

OEDIPUS.   I shall resist! [*He shuts his eyes and turns his head away.*]

SPHINX.   You need not shut your eyes or turn away your head. For it is not by my look nor by my voice that I work. A blind man is not so dexterous, the net of a gladiator not so swift, nor lightning so fine, nor a coachman so stiff, nor a cow so weighty, nor a schoolboy working at his sums with his tongue out so good, nor a ship so hung with rigging, so spread with sails, secure and buoyant; a judge is not so incorruptible, insects so voracious, birds so bloodthirsty, the egg so nocturnal, Chinese executioners so ingenious, the heart so fitful, the trickster's hand so deft, the stars so fateful, the snake moistening its prey with saliva so attentive. I secrete, I spin, I pay out, I wind, I unwind, I rewind, in such a way that it is enough for me to desire these knots for them to be made, to think about them for them to be pulled tight or slackened. My thread is so fine it escapes the eye, so fluid you might think you were suffering from a poison, so hard a quiver on my part would break your limbs, so highly strung a bow stroked between us would make music in the air; curled like the sea, the column, and the rose, muscled like the octopus, contrived like the settings of our dreams, above all invisible, unseen, and majestic like the blood circulating in statues, my thread coils round you in fantastic patterns with the volubility of honey falling upon honey.

OEDIPUS.   Let me go!

SPHINX.   And I speak, I work, I wind, I unwind, I calculate, I meditate, I weave, I winnow, I knit, I plait, I cross, I go over it again and again, I tie and untie and tie again, retaining the smallest knots that I shall later on have to untie for you on pain of death; I pull tight, I loosen, I make mistakes and go back, I hesitate, I correct, entangle and disentangle, unlace, lace up and begin afresh; and I adjust, I agglutinate, I pinion, I strap, I shackle, I heap up my effects, till you feel that from the tip of your toes to the top of your head you are wrapped round by all the muscles of a reptile whose slightest breath constricts yours and makes you inert like the arm on which you fall asleep.

OEDIPUS. [*In a weak voice.*]   Let me be! Mercy! . . .

SPHINX.   And you will cry for mercy, and you won't have to be ashamed of that, for you won't be the first. I have heard prouder than you call for their mothers, and I have seen more insolent than you burst into tears; and the more silent are even weaker than the rest: they faint before the end and I have to minister to them after the fashion of embalmers in whose hands the dead are drunk men no longer able to stand on their feet!

OEDIPUS.   Merope! . . . Mother!

SPHINX.   Then I should command you to advance a little closer, and I should help you by loosening your limbs. So! And I should question you. I should ask you, for example: What animal is it that goes on four legs in the morning, in the afternoon on two, and in the evening on three? And you would cudgel your brains, till in the end your mind would settle on a little medal you won as a child, or you would repeat a number, or count the stars between these two broken columns; and I should make you return to the point by revealing the enigma.

Man is the animal who walks on four legs when he is a child, on two when he is full-grown, and when he is old with the help of a stick as a third leg.

OEDIPUS.   How idiotic!

SPHINX.   You would shout: How idiotic! You all say that. Then, since that cry only confirms your failure, I should call my assistant, Anubis. Anubis!

[ANUBIS *appears and stands on the right of the pedestal with folded arms; and his head turned to one side.*]

OEDIPUS.   Oh, miss! . . . Oh, Sphinx! . . . Oh, Sphinx, please don't! No! No!

SPHINX.   And I should make you go down on your knees. Go on. . . . Go on . . . that 's right. . . . Do as you 're told. And you 'd bend your head . . . and Anubis would bound forward. He would open his wolf-like jaws! [OEDIPUS *utters a cry.*] I said: *would* bend, *would* bound forward, *would* open. . . . Haven't I always been careful to express myself in that mood? Why that cry? Why that horrified expression? It was a demonstration, Oedipus, simply a demonstration. You 're free.

OEDIPUS.   Free!

[*He moves an arm, a leg. . . . He gets up, he reels, he puts his hand to his head.*]

ANUBIS.   Pardon me, Sphinx, this man cannot leave here without undergoing the test.

SPHINX.   But . . .

ANUBIS.   Question him.

OEDIPUS.   But . . .

ANUBIS.   Silence! Question this man.

[*A silence.* OEDIPUS *turns his back and remains motionless.*]

SPHINX.   I 'll question him. . . . All right. . . . I 'll question him. . . .
[*With a last look of surprise at* ANUBIS.] What animal is it that walks on four
legs in the morning, on two in the afternoon, and on three in the evening?

OEDIPUS.   Why, man, of course! He crawls along on four legs when he 's
little, and walks on two legs when he is big, and when he 's old he helps himself along with a stick as a third leg.

[*The* SPHINX *sways on her pedestal.*]

[*Making his way to the left.*] Victory!

[*He rushes out left. The* SPHINX *slips down into the column, disappears behind the wall, and reappears wingless.*]

SPHINX.   Oedipus! Where is he? Where is he?

ANUBIS.   Gone, flown. He is running breathlessly to proclaim his victory.

SPHINX.   Without so much as a look my way, without a movement betray-
ing feeling, without a sign of gratitude.

ANUBIS.   Did you expect anything else?

SPHINX.   Oh, you fool! Then he has not understood a single thing.

ANUBIS.   Not a single thing.

SPHINX.   Kss! Kss! Anubis. . . . Here, here, look, after him, quickly, bite
him, Anubis, bite him!

ANUBIS.   And now it 's all going to begin afresh. You 're a woman again and
I 'm a dog.

SPHINX.   I 'm sorry. I lost my head, I 'm mad. My hands are trembling. I 'm
like fire. I wish I could catch him again in one bound, I 'd spit in his face,
claw him with my nails, disfigure him, trample on him, castrate him, and flay
him alive!

ANUBIS.   That 's more like yourself.

SPHINX.   Help me! Avenge me! Don't stand there idle!

ANUBIS.   Do you really hate this man?

SPHINX.   I do.

ANUBIS.   The worst that could happen to him would seem too good to you?

SPHINX.   It would.

ANUBIS.   [*Holding up the* SPHINX's *dress.*]   Look at the folds in this cloth.
Crush them together. Now if you pierce this bundle with a pin, remove the
pin, smooth the cloth till all trace of the old creases disappears, do you think a
simple country loon would believe that the innumerable holes recurring at intervals result from a single thrust of a pin?

SPHINX.   Certainly not.

ANUBIS.   Human time is a fold of eternity. For us time does not exist. From
his birth to his death the life of Oedipus is spread flat before my eyes, with its
series of episodes.

SPHINX.   Speak, speak, Anubis, I 'm burning to hear. What d' you see?

ANUBIS.   In the past Jocasta and Laïus had a child. As the oracle gave out
that this child would be a scourge. . . .

SPHINX.   A scourge!

ANUBIS.   A monster, an unclean beast. . . .

SPHINX.   Quicker, quicker!

ANUBIS.   Jocasta bound it up and sent it into the mountains to get lost. A shepherd of Polybius found it, took it away, and, as Polybius and Merope were lamenting a sterile marriage . . .

SPHINX.   I can't contain myself for joy.

ANUBIS.   They adopted it. Oedipus, son of Laïus, killed Laïus where the three roads cross.

SPHINX.   The old man.

ANUBIS.   Son of Jocasta, he will marry Jocasta.

SPHINX.   And to think I said to him: 'She might be your mother.' And he replied: 'The main thing is that she is not.' Anubis! Anubis! It 's too good to be true. . . .

ANUBIS.   He will have two sons who will kill each other, and two daughters, one of whom will hang herself. Jocasta will hang herself. . . .

SPHINX.   Stop! What more could I hope for? Think, Anubis: the wedding of Jocasta and Oedipus! The union of mother and son. . . . And will he know soon?

ANUBIS.   Soon enough.

SPHINX.   What a moment to live! I have a foretaste of its delights. Oh, to be present!

ANUBIS.   You will be.

SPHINX.   Is that true? . . .

ANUBIS.   I think the moment has come to remind you who you are and what a ridiculous distance separates you from this little body which is listening to me. You who have assumed the role of Sphinx! You, the Goddess of Goddesses! You, the greatest of the great! The implacable! Vengeance! Nemesis! [ANUBIS prostrates himself.]

SPHINX.   Nemesis. . . . [She turns her back to the audience and remains a while erect, making a cross with her arms. Suddenly she comes out of this hypnotic state and rushes up stage.] Once more, if he is in sight, I should like to feed my hatred, I want to see him run from one trap to another like a stunned rat.

ANUBIS.   Is that the cry of the awakening goddess or of the jealous woman?

SPHINX.   Of the goddess, Anubis, of the goddess. Our gods have cast me for the part of the Sphinx, and I shall show myself worthy of it.

ANUBIS.   At last!

[The SPHINX looks down on the plain, leaning over to examine it. Suddenly she turns round. The last trace of the greatness and fury which had transformed her has disappeared.]

Dog! you lied to me.

ANUBIS.   I?

SPHINX.   Yes, you! Liar! Liar! Look along the road. Oedipus is coming back, he 's running, he 's flying, he loves me, he has understood!

ANUBIS.   You know very well of what goes with his success and why the Sphinx is not dead.

SPHINX.   Look how he jumps from rock to rock, just as my heart leaps in my breast.

ANUBIS.   Convinced of his triumphs and your death this young fool has just realized that in his haste he 's forgotten the most important thing.

SPHINX.   Mean wretch! Do you mean to tell me he wants to find me dead?

ANUBIS.   Not you, my little fury: the Sphinx. He thinks he 's killed the Sphinx; he will have to prove it. Thebes won't be satisfied with a fisherman's yarn.

SPHINX.   You 're lying. I 'll tell him everything. I 'll warn him. I 'll save him. I 'll turn him away from Jocasta, from that miserable town. . . .

ANUBIS.   Take care.

SPHINX.   I shall speak.

ANUBIS.   He 's coming. Let him speak first.

[OEDIPUS, *out of breath, comes in down stage left. He sees the* SPHINX *and* ANUBIS *standing side by side.*]

OEDIPUS. [*Saluting.*]   I 'm glad to see what good health the immortals enjoy after their death.

SPHINX.   What brings you back here?

OEDIPUS.   The collecting of my due.

[*Angry movement on the part of* ANUBIS *towards* OEDIPUS, *who steps back.*]

SPHINX.   Anubis! [*With a gesture she orders him to leave her alone. He goes behind the ruins. To* OEDIPUS.] You shall have it. Stay where you are. The loser is a woman. She asks one last favour of her master.

OEDIPUS.   Excuse me for being on my guard, but you 've taught me to distrust your feminine wiles.

SPHINX.   Ah! I was the Sphinx. No, Oedipus. . . . You will bear my mortal remains to Thebes and the future will reward you . . . according to your deserts. No . . . I ask you merely to let me disappear behind this wall so that I may take off this body in which, I must confess, I have, for some little while, felt rather . . . cramped.

OEDIPUS.   Very well. But be quick. At the last bugles . . . [*The bugles are heard.*] You see, I speak of them and they are sounded. I must waste no time.

SPHINX. [*Hidden.*]   Thebes will not leave a hero standing at her gates.

VOICE OF ANUBIS. [*From behind the ruins.*]   Hurry, hurry. It looks as though you 're inventing excuses and dawdling on purpose.

SPHINX. [*Hidden.*]   Am I the first, God of the Dead, whom you 've had to drag by the clothes?

OEDIPUS.   You 're trying to gain time, Sphinx.

SPHINX. [*Hidden.*]   So much the better for you, Oedipus. My haste might have served you ill. A serious difficulty occurs to me. If you bear into Thebes the body of a girl instead of the monster which the people expect, the crowd will stone you.

OEDIPUS. That 's true! Women are simply amazing; they think of everything.

SPHINX. [*Hidden.*] They call me: The virgin with the claws. . . . The singing bitch. . . . They will want to identify my fangs. Don't be alarmed. Anubis! My faithful dog! Listen, since our faces are only shadows, I want you to give me your jackal's head.

OEDIPUS. Splendid idea!

ANUBIS. [*Hidden.*] Do what you like, so long as this shameful play-acting may come to an end and you may become yourself once more.

SPHINX. [*Hidden.*] I shan't be long.

OEDIPUS. I shall count up to fifty as I did before. I 'll have my own back.

ANUBIS. [*Hidden.*] Sphinx, Sphinx, what are you waiting for?

SPHINX. Now I 'm ugly, Anubis. A monster! . . . Poor boy . . . supposing I frighten him. . . .

ANUBIS. Don't worry, he won't even see you.

SPHINX. Is he blind then?

ANUBIS. Many men are born blind and only realize it the day a home-truth hits them between the eyes.

OEDIPUS. Fifty.

ANUBIS. [*Hidden.*] Go on. . . . Go on. . . .

SPHINX. [*Hidden.*] Farewell, Sphinx.

[*From behind the wall comes the staggering figure of a girl with a jackal's head. She waves her arms in the air and falls.*]

OEDIPUS. About time too! [*He rushes forward, not stopping to look, lifts the body, and takes a stand down stage right. He carries the body before him on his outstretched arms.*] No, not like that! I should look like that tragedian I saw in Corinth playing the part of a king carrying the body of his son. The pose was pompous and moved no one. [*He tries holding the body under his left arm; behind the ruins on the mound appear two giant forms covered with rainbow veils: the gods.*] No! I should be ridiculous. Like a hunter going home empty-handed after killing his dog.

ANUBIS. [*The form on the right.*] To free your goddess's body of all human contamination, perhaps it might be as well for this Oedipus to disinfect you by bestowing on himself at least a title of demigod.

NEMESIS. [*The form on the left.*] He is so young. . . .

OEDIPUS. Hercules! Hercules threw the lion over his shoulder! . . . [*He puts the body over his shoulder.*] Yes, over my shoulder. Over my shoulder! Like a demigod!

ANUBIS. [*Veiled.*] Isn't he simply *incredible!*

OEDIPUS. [*Moving off towards the left, taking two steps after each of his thanksgivings.*] I have killed the unclean beast.

NEMESIS. [*Veiled.*] Anubis . . . I feel very ill at ease.

ANUBIS.   We must go.

OEDIPUS.   I have saved the town!

ANUBIS.   Come along, mistress, let us go.

OEDIPUS.   I shall marry Queen Jocasta!

NEMESIS. [*Veiled.*]   Poor, poor, poor mankind! . . . I can stand no more, Anubis. . . . I can't breathe. Let us leave the earth.

OEDIPUS.   I shall be king!

[*A murmur envelops the two huge forms. The veils fly round them. Day breaks. Cocks crow.*]

Act III. The Wedding Night

THE VOICE: The coronation and nuptial celebrations have been going on since dawn. The crowd has just acclaimed the queen and the conqueror of the Sphinx for the last time.

Every one goes home. In the little square of the royal palace now rises only the slight murmur of a fountain. Oedipus and Jocasta find privacy at last in the nuptial chamber. They are very tired and heavy with sleep. In spite of a few hints and civilities on the part of destiny, sleep will prevent them from seeing the trap which is closing on them for ever.

Act III. The Wedding Night

SCENE: *The platform represents* JOCASTA's *bedroom, which is as red as a little butcher's shop amid the town buildings. A broad bed covered with white furs. At the foot of the bed an animal's skin. On the right of the bed a cradle. On the right fore-stage a latticed bay window, looking on to the square of Thebes. On the left fore-stage a movable mirror of human size.* OEDIPUS *and* JOCASTA *are wearing their coronation costumes. From the moment the curtain rises they move about in the slow motion induced by extreme fatigue.*

JOCASTA.   Phew! I 'm done! You are so full of life, dear! I am afraid, for you, this room will become a cage, a prison.

OEDIPUS.   My dear love! A scented bedroom, a woman's room, yours! After this killing day, those processions, that ceremonial, that crowd which still clamoured for us under our very windows. . . .

JOCASTA.   Not clamoured for us . . . for you, dear.

OEDIPUS.   Same thing.

JOCASTA.   You must be truthful, my young conqueror. They hate me. My dress annoys them, my accent annoys them, they are annoyed by my blackened eyelashes, my rouge, and my vivaciousness!

OEDIPUS.   It 's Creon who annoys them! The cold, hard, inhuman Creon! I shall make your star rise again. Ah! Jocasta! What a magnificent programme!

JOCASTA.   It was high time you came. I 'm exhausted.

OEDIPUS.   Your room a prison! Your room, dear . . . and our bed.

JOCASTA.   Do you want me to remove the cradle? After the death of the

child I had to have it near me, I couldn't sleep. . . . I was too lonely. . . .
But now . . .

OEDIPUS. [*In an indistinct voice.*] But now . . .

JOCASTA. What?

OEDIPUS. I said . . . I said . . . that it 's he . . . he . . . the dog . . .
I mean . . . the dog who won't . . . the dog . . . the fountain dog. . . .
[*His head droops.*]

JOCASTA. Oedipus! Oedipus!

OEDIPUS. [*Awakens, startled.*] What?

JOCASTA. You were falling asleep, dear!

OEDIPUS. Me? Never.

JOCASTA. Oh, yes, you were, dear. You were telling me about a dog who
won't . . . a fountain dog. And I was listening.
[*She laughs and herself seems to be becoming vague.*]

OEDIPUS. Nonsense!

JOCASTA. I was asking you if you wanted me to remove the cradle, if it
worries you.

OEDIPUS. Am I such a kid as to fear this pretty muslin ghost? On the contrary it will be the cradle of my luck. My luck will grow in it beside our love
until it can be used for our first son. So you see! . . .

JOCASTA. My poor love. . . . You 're dropping with fatigue and here we
stand . . . [*Same business as with* OEDIPUS.] . . . stand on this wall. . . .

OEDIPUS. What wall?

JOCASTA. This rampart wall. [*She starts.*] A wall. . . . What? I . . . I
. . . [*Haggard.*] What's happening?

OEDIPUS. [*Laughing.*] Well, this time it 's you dreaming. We 're tired out,
my poor sweet.

JOCASTA. I was asleep? Did I talk?

OEDIPUS. We *are* a pretty pair! Here I go telling you about fountain-dogs,
and you tell me about rampart walls: and this is our wedding night! Listen,
Jocasta, if I happen to fall asleep again (Are you listening?), do please awaken
me, shake me, and if you fall asleep I 'll do the same for you. This one night
of all must not founder in sleep. That would be too sad.

JOCASTA. You crazy darling you, why? We have all our life before us.

OEDIPUS. Maybe, but I don't want sleep to spoil the miracle of passing this
joyous night alone, unutterably alone with you. I suggest we remove these
heavy clothes, and as we 're not expecting any one——

JOCASTA. Listen, my darling boy, you 'll be cross . . .

OEDIPUS. Jocasta, don't tell me there 's still some official duty on the programme!

JOCASTA. While my women are doing my hair, etiquette demands that you
receive a visit.

OEDIPUS. A visit? At this hour?

JOCASTA. A visit . . . a visit . . . a purely formal visit.

OEDIPUS.   In this room?

JOCASTA.   In this room.

OEDIPUS.   From whom?

JOCASTA.   Now don't get cross. From Tiresias.

OEDIPUS.   Tiresias? I refuse!

JOCASTA.   Listen, dear. . . .

OEDIPUS.   That 's the limit! Tiresias playing the part of the family pouring out their farewell advice. How comic! I shall refuse his visit.

JOCASTA.   You crazy dear, *I* am asking you to. It 's an old custom in Thebes that the high priest must in some way bless the royal marriage bonds. And besides, Tiresias is our old uncle, our watch-dog. I am very fond of him, Oedipus, and Laïus adored him. He is nearly blind. It would be unfortunate if you hurt his feelings and set him against our love.

OEDIPUS.   That 's all very well . . . . in the middle of the night. . . .

JOCASTA.   Do! Please, for our sake and the sake of the future. It 's essential. See him for five minutes, but see him and listen to him. I ask you to. [*She kisses him.*]

OEDIPUS.   I warn you I shan't let him sit down.

JOCASTA.   I love you, dear. [*Long kiss.*] I shall not be long. [*At the right-hand exit.*] I am going to let him know he can come. Be patient. Do it for my sake. Think of me. [*She goes out.*]

[OEDIPUS, *alone, looks at himself in the mirror and tries attitudes.* TIRESIAS *comes in left, unheard.* OEDIPUS *sees him in the middle of the room and turns about face.*]

OEDIPUS.   I am listening.

TIRESIAS.   Steady, my lord. Who told you I had saved up a sermon for your especial benefit?

OEDIPUS.   No one, Tiresias, no one. But I don't suppose you find it pleasant acting as kill-joy. I suggest you are waiting for me to pretend I have heard your words of counsel. I shall bow, and you will give me the accolade. That would be enough for us in our tired state and at the same time custom would be satisfied. Have I guessed right?

TIRESIAS.   It is perhaps correct that there is at the bottom of this procedure a sort of custom, but for that, it would be necessary to have a royal marriage with all the dynastic, mechanical, and, I admit, even irksome business which that entails. No, my lord. Unforeseen events bring us face to face with new problems and duties. And you will agree, I think, that your coronation, and your marriage, appear in a form which is difficult to classify, and does not fit into any code.

OEDIPUS.   No one could say more graciously that I have crashed on Thebes like a tile from a roof.

TIRESIAS.   My lord!

OEDIPUS.   Let me tell you that things fitting neatly into categories reek of death. What we want, Tiresias, is not to fit, but to make a new departure.

That 's the sign of masterpieces and heroes. And that 's the way to astonish and to rule.

TIRESIAS.   Right! Then you will admit that I myself, by playing a part outside the ceremonial sphere, am also making a new departure.

OEDIPUS.   To the point, Tiresias, to the point.

TIRESIAS.   Very well. I shall come straight to the point and speak with all frankness. My lord, your auguries look black, very black. I must put you on your guard.

OEDIPUS.   There! Just as I expected! Anything else would have surprised me. This is not the first time the oracles have been violently against me and my audacity has thwarted them.

TIRESIAS.   Do you believe they can be thwarted?

OEDIPUS.   I am the living proof of it. And even if my marriage upsets the gods, what about your promises, your freeing of the town, and the death of the Sphinx? And why should the gods have pushed me on as far as this room if this marriage displeases them?

TIRESIAS.   Do you think you can solve the problem of free will in a minute! Ah, power, I fear, is going to your head!

OEDIPUS.   You mean, power is slipping from your hands.

TIRESIAS.   Take care! You are speaking to a high priest.

OEDIPUS.   Take care yourself, high priest. Must I remind you that you are speaking to your king?

TIRESIAS.   To the husband of my queen, my lord.

OEDIPUS.   Jocasta notified me a little while ago that her power is to pass into my hands, in full. Run and tell that to your master.

TIRESIAS.   I serve only the gods.

OEDIPUS.   Well, if you prefer that way of putting it, say that to the person who is awaiting your return.

TIRESIAS.   Headstrong youth! You don't understand me.

OEDIPUS.   I understand perfectly well: an adventurer is in your way. I expect you hope I found the Sphinx dead on my path. The real conqueror must have sold it to me, like those hunters who buy the hare from a poacher. And supposing I have paid for the mortal remains, whom will you find ultimately as the conqueror of the Sphinx? The same type of person who has been threatening you every minute and preventing Creon from sleeping: a poor private soldier whom the crowd will bear in triumph and who will claim his due . . . [Shouting] his due!

TIRESIAS.   He would not dare.

OEDIPUS.   Ah, you see! I have made you say it. That 's the secret of the intrigue. There go your beautiful promises. That is what you were counting on.

TIRESIAS.   The queen is more to me than my own daughter. I must watch over her and defend her. She is weak, credulous, romantic. . . .

OEDIPUS.   You are insulting her.

TIRESIAS.   I love her.

OEDIPUS.   She is in need of no one's love but mine.

TIRESIAS.   About this love, Oedipus, I demand an explanation. Do you love the queen?

OEDIPUS.   With all my being.

TIRESIAS.   I mean: do you love to take her in your arms?

OEDIPUS.   I love most of all to be taken in her arms.

TIRESIAS.   I appreciate that delicate distinction. You are young, Oedipus, very young. Jocasta might be your mother. I know, oh, I know, you are going to reply——

OEDIPUS.   I am going to reply that I have always dreamed of such a love, an almost motherly love.

TIRESIAS.   Oedipus, aren't you confusing love and love of glory? Would you love Jocasta if she were not on a throne?

OEDIPUS.   A stupid question which is always being asked. Would Jocasta love me if I was old, ugly, and had not appeared out of the unknown? Do you fancy you cannot be infected by love through touching purple and gold? Are not the privileges of which you speak of the very substance of Jocasta, an organic part of her? We have been each other's from all eternity. Within her body lie fold after fold of a purple mantle which is much more regal than the one she fastens on her shoulders. I love and adore her, Tiresias. At her side I seem to occupy at last my proper place. She is my wife, she is my queen. I possess her, I shall keep her, I shall find her again, and neither by prayers nor threats can you drag from me obedience to orders from heaven knows where.

TIRESIAS.   Think it over again, Oedipus. The omens and my own wisdom give me every reason to fear this wild marriage. Think it over.

OEDIPUS.   Rather late, don't you think?

TIRESIAS.   Have you had experience of women?

OEDIPUS.   Not the slightest. And to complete your astonishment and cover myself with ridicule in your eyes, I am a virgin.

TIRESIAS.   You!

OEDIPUS.   The high priest of a capital is astonished that a country boy should put all his pride in keeping himself pure for a single offering. You would, no doubt, have preferred a degenerate prince, a puppet, so that Creon and the priests could work the strings.

TIRESIAS.   You are going too far!

OEDIPUS.   Must I order you again? . . .

TIRESIAS.   Order? Has pride sent you mad?

OEDIPUS.   Don't put me into a rage! My patience is at an end, my temper is ungovernable, and I am capable of any unpremeditated act.

TIRESIAS.   What arrogance! . . . Weak and arrogant!

OEDIPUS.   You will have brought it on yourself.

[*He throws himself upon* TIRESIAS, *seizing him by the neck.*]

TIRESIAS.   Let me go. . . . Have you no shame? . . .

OEDIPUS. You are afraid that I could, from your face, there, there, close up, and in your blind man's eyes, read the real truth about your behaviour.

TIRESIAS. Murderer! Sacrilege!

OEDIPUS. Murderer! I ought to be. . . . One day I shall probably have to repent for this foolish respect, and if I dared . . . Oh, oh! Why! Gods, look here . . . here . . . in his blind man's eyes, I had no idea it was possible.

TIRESIAS. Let me go! Brute!

OEDIPUS. The future! My future, as in a crystal bowl.

TIRESIAS. You will repent. . . .

OEDIPUS. I see, I see. . . . Soothsayer, you have lied! I shall marry Jocasta. . . . A happy life, rich, prosperous, two sons . . . daughters . . . and Jocasta still as beautiful, still the same, in love, a mother in a palace of happiness. . . . Now it's not so clear, not clear. I want to see! It's your fault, soothsayer. . . . I want to see! [*He shakes him.*]

TIRESIAS. Accursed!

OEDIPUS. [*Suddenly recoiling, letting* TIRESIAS *go, and putting his hands over his eyes.*] Oh, filthy wretch! I am blind. He's thrown pepper at me. Jocasta! Help! Help! . . .

TIRESIAS. I threw nothing, I swear. You are punished for your sacrilege.

OEDIPUS. [*Writhing on the ground.*] You lie!

TIRESIAS. You wanted to read by force the secrets my diseased eyes hold and that I myself have not yet interpreted; and you are punished.

OEDIPUS. Water, water, quickly, it's burning me. . . .

TIRESIAS. [*Laying his hands over* OEDIPUS's *face.*] There, there. . . . Keep quiet. . . . I forgive you. Your nerves are on edge. Come, keep still. Your sight will return, I swear. I expect you got to the point which the gods wish to keep in darkness, or they may be punishing you for your impudence.

OEDIPUS. I can see a little . . . I think.

TIRESIAS. Are you in pain?

OEDIPUS. Less . . . the pain is going. Ah! . . . it was like fire, red pepper, a thousand pinpoints, a cat's paw scrabbling in my eye. Thank you. . . .

TIRESIAS. Can you see?

OEDIPUS. Not clearly, but I can see, I can see. Phew! I really thought I was blind for good and that it was one of your kind of tricks. In any case, I deserved it.

TIRESIAS. We like to believe in miracles when miracles suit us, and when they don't we like to believe in them no longer, but say it is a trick on the part of the soothsayer.

OEDIPUS. Forgive me. I am of a violent and vindictive disposition. I love Jocasta. I was waiting for her, impatiently, and this extraordinary phenomenon, all those images of the future in the pupil of your eyes bewitched me, fuddled me, as it were, and made me mad.

TIRESIAS. Can you see better now? It is an almost blind man asking you.

OEDIPUS.   Quite, and I have no more pain. I 'm really ashamed of my conduct towards you, a blind man and a priest. Will you accept my apologies?

TIRESIAS.   I was only speaking for your own good and Jocasta's.

OEDIPUS.   Tiresias, in a way I owe you something in return, a confession that is difficult to make, and which I had promised myself I would make to no one.

TIRESIAS.   A confession?

OEDIPUS.   I noticed during the coronation ceremony that you and Creon had some understanding between you. Do not deny it. Well, I wished to keep my identity secret; but I give it up. Listen carefully, Tiresias. I am not a wanderer. I come from Corinth. I am the only child of King Polybius and Queen Merope. A nobody will not soil this marriage bed. I am a king and son of a king.

TIRESIAS.   My lord. [*He bows.*] A word from you would have cleared the atmosphere of the uneasiness created by your incognito. My little girl will be so glad. . . .

OEDIPUS.   But wait! I ask you as a favour to safeguard at least this last night. Jocasta still loves in me the wanderer dropped out of the clouds, the young man stepping suddenly out of the shadows. It will unfortunately be only too easy to destroy this mirage to-morrow. In the meantime, I hope the queen will become sufficiently submissive for her to learn without disgust that Oedipus is not a prince fallen from the sky, but merely a prince.

I wish you good evening, Tiresias. Jocasta will be on her way back. I am dropping with fatigue . . . and we want to remain alone together. That is our desire.

TIRESIAS.   My lord, excuse me.

[OEDIPUS *makes a sign to him with his hand.* TIRESIAS *stops at the left-hand exit.*]

One last word.

OEDIPUS. [*Loftily.*]   What is it?

TIRESIAS.   Forgive my boldness. This evening, after the closing of the temple, a beautiful young girl came into the private chapel where I work and, without a word of excuse, handed me this belt and said: 'Give it to Lord Oedipus and repeat word for word this sentence: Take this belt: with that you will be able to get to me when I have killed the beast.' I had scarcely tucked away the belt when the girl burst out laughing and disappeared, I don't know how.

OEDIPUS. [*Snatching away the belt.*]   And that 's your trump card. You have already built up a whole system in order to destroy my hold on the queen's head and heart. How should I know? A previous promise of marriage. . . . A girl takes her revenge. . . . The temple scandal. . . . Tell-tale find. . . .

TIRESIAS.   I was fulfilling my commission. That 's all.

OEDIPUS.   Miscalculation and bad policy. Go . . . and carry this bad news with all speed to Prince Creon. [TIRESIAS *stays on the threshold.*] He reckoned he was going to scare me! But in point of fact, it is I who scare you, Tiresias, I scare you. I can see it written in large letters on your face. It wasn't so easy to terrorize the child. Confess that the child terrifies you, grandpa! Confess, grandpa! Confess I terrify you! Confess at least I make you afraid! [OEDIPUS *is lying face down on the animal skin.* TIRESIAS *is standing like a bronze statue. Silence. Then thunder.*]

TIRESIAS. Yes. Very afraid. [*He leaves, walking backwards. His prophetic voice can be heard.*] Oedipus! Oedipus, listen to me! You are pursuing classic glory. There is another kind: obscure glory, the last resource of the arrogant person who persists in opposing the stars.

[OEDIPUS *remains looking at the belt. When* JOCASTA *comes in, in her nightdress, he quickly hides the belt under the animal skin.*]

JOCASTA. Well now? What did the old ogre say? Did he torment you?

OEDIPUS. Yes . . . no. . . .

JOCASTA. He 's a monster. Did he prove to you that you are too young for me?

OEDIPUS. You are beautiful, Jocasta! . . .

JOCASTA. That I am old?

OEDIPUS. He rather gave me to understand that I loved your pearls, and your diadem.

JOCASTA. Always spoiling everything! Ruining everything! Doing harm!

OEDIPUS. But you can take it from me, he didn't manage to scare me. On the contrary, I scared him. He admitted that.

JOCASTA. Well done! My love! You, dear, after my pearls and diadem!

OEDIPUS. I am happy to see you again without any pomp, without your jewels and orders, white, young, and beautiful, in our own room.

JOCASTA. Young! Oedipus! . . . You mustn't tell lies. . . .

OEDIPUS. Again! . . .

JOCASTA. Don't scold me.

OEDIPUS. Yes, I shall scold you! I shall scold you because a woman like you ought to be above such nonsense. A young girl's face is as boring as a white page on which my eyes can read nothing moving; whereas your face! . . . I must have the scars, the tattooing of destiny, a beauty which has weathered tempests. Why should you be afraid of crows' feet, Jocasta? What would a silly schoolgirl's look or smile be worth beside the remarkable sacred beauty of your face; slapped by fate, branded by the executioner, and tender, tender and . . . [*He notices that* JOCASTA *is weeping.*] Jocasta! my dear little girl, you 're crying! What ever 's the matter? . . . All right, then. . . . What have I done now? Jocasta! . . .

JOCASTA. Am I so old . . . so very old?

OEDIPUS. My dear crazy girl! It 's you who persist in——

JOCASTA. Women say things to be contradicted. They always hope it isn't true.

OEDIPUS. My dear Jocasta! . . . What a fool I am! What a great brute! . . . Darling. . . . Don't cry. Kiss me. . . . I meant——

JOCASTA. Never mind. . . . I am being ridiculous. [*She dries her eyes.*]

OEDIPUS.   It 's all my fault.

JOCASTA.   It isn't. . . . There . . . the black is running into my eye now. [OEDIPUS *coaxes her.*] It 's all over.

OEDIPUS.   Quick, a smile. [*Slight rumbling of thunder.*] Listen.

JOCASTA.   My nerves are bad because of the storm.

OEDIPUS.   But look at the sky! It is full of stars, and clear.

JOCASTA.   Yes, but there is a storm brewing somewhere. When the fountains make a still murmur like silence, and my shoulder aches, there is always a storm about and summer lightning. [*She leans against the bay window. Summer lightning.*]

OEDIPUS.   Come here, quickly. . . .

JOCASTA.   Oedipus! . . . come here a moment.

OEDIPUS.   What is it? . . .

JOCASTA.   The sentry . . . look, lean out. On the bench on the right, he 's asleep. Don't you think he 's handsome, that boy? with his mouth wide open.

OEDIPUS.   I 'll throw some water in it! I 'll teach him to sleep!

JOCASTA.   Oedipus!

OEDIPUS.   How dare he sleep when guarding the queen!

JOCASTA.   The Sphinx is dead and you 're alive. Let him sleep in peace! May all the town sleep in peace! May they all sleep every one!

OEDIPUS.   Lucky sentry!

JOCASTA.   Oedipus! Oedipus! I should like to make you jealous, but it isn't that. . . . This young guard——

OEDIPUS.   What is so extraordinary about this young guard then?

JOCASTA.   During that famous night, the night of the Sphinx, while you were encountering the beast, I had an escapade on the ramparts with Tiresias. I had heard that a young soldier had seen the ghost of Laïus, and that Laïus was calling for me to warn me of a threatening danger. Well . . . that soldier was the very sentry who is guarding us.

OEDIPUS.   Who is guarding us! . . . Anyway . . . Let him sleep in peace, my kind Jocasta. I can guard you all right on my own. Of course, not the slightest sign of the ghost of Laïus?

JOCASTA.   Not the slightest, I 'm sorry to say. . . . Poor lad! I touched his shoulders and legs, and kept saying to Zizi, 'Touch, touch,' and I was in a state . . . because he was like you. And it's true, you know, Oedipus, he was like you.

OEDIPUS.   You say: 'This guard was like you.' But, Jocasta, you didn't know me then; it was impossible for you to know or to guess. . . .

JOCASTA.   Yes, indeed, that 's true. I expect I meant to say my son would be about his age. [*Silence.*] Yes . . . I am getting muddled. It 's only now that this likeness strikes me. [*She shakes off this uneasy feeling.*] You 're a dear, you 're good-looking, I love you. [*After a pause.*] Oedipus!

OEDIPUS.   My goddess!

JOCASTA.   I approve of your not telling the story of your victory to Creon

or to Tiresias, or to everybody [*With her arms round his neck*], but to me
. . . to me!

OEDIPUS. [*Freeing himself.*] I had your promise! . . . And but for that
boy——

JOCASTA. Is the Jocasta of yesterday the Jocasta of now? Haven't I a right
to share your memories without anybody else knowing anything about it?

OEDIPUS. Of course.

JOCASTA. And do you remember you kept saying: 'No, no, Jocasta, later,
later when we are in our own room.' Well, aren't we in our own room? . . .

OEDIPUS. Persistent monkey! Charmer! She always ends by getting what she
wants. Now lie still. . . . I am beginning.

JOCASTA. Oh, Oedipus! Oedipus! What fun! What fun! I 'm quite still.

[JOCASTA *lies down, shuts her eyes, and keeps still.* OEDIPUS *begins lying,*
hesitating, inventing, accompanied by the storm.]

OEDIPUS. Now. I was nearing Thebes. I was following the goat track which
rounds the hill to the south of the town. I was thinking of the future, of you
whom I imagined less beautiful than you are in reality, but still, very beautiful,
painted, and sitting on a throne in the centre of a group of ladies-in-waiting.
Supposing you do kill it, I said to myself, would you, Oedipus, dare to ask for
the promised reward? Should I dare to go near the queen? . . . And I kept
walking and worrying. All of a sudden I stopped dead. My heart was beating
hard. I had just heard a sort of song. The voice that sang it was not of this
world. Was it the Sphinx? My haversack contained a knife. I slipped the knife
under my tunic and crept along. Do you know those ruins of a little temple
on the hill, with a pedestal and the hind quarters of a chimera? [*Silence.*]
Jocasta . . . Jocasta. . . . Are you asleep?

JOCASTA. [*Awaking with a start.*] What? Oedipus. . . .

OEDIPUS. You were asleep.

JOCASTA. I wasn't.

OEDIPUS. Oh, yes, you were. There 's a fickle little girl for you! She wants
me to tell her a story and then goes and falls asleep in the middle of it, instead
of listening.

JOCASTA. I heard it all. You 're mistaken. You were speaking of a goat
track.

OEDIPUS. I 'd got a long way past the goat track! . . .

JOCASTA. Don't be angry, darling. Are you cross with me? . .

OEDIPUS. Me?

JOCASTA. Yes, you are cross with me, and rightly. What a stupid silly I am!
That 's what age does for you.

OEDIPUS. Don't be sad. I 'll start the story again, I promise you, but first
of all you and I must lie down and sleep a little, side by side. After that, we
shall be clear of this sticky paste, this struggle against sleep which is spoiling
everything. The first one to wake up will wake the other. Promise.

JOCASTA. Promised. Poor queens know how to snatch a moment's sleep where they sit, between two audiences. But give me your hand. I am too old. Tiresias was right.

OEDIPUS.   Perhaps so for Thebes, where girls are marriageable at thirteen. But what about me? Am I an old man? My head keeps dropping and my chin hitting my chest wakes me up.

JOCASTA.   You? That 's quite different, it 's the dustman, as children say! But as for me . . . You begin to tell me the most marvellous story in the world, and I go and doze away like a grandma beside the fire. And you will punish me by never beginning it over again, and finding excuses. . . . Did I talk in my sleep?

OEDIPUS.   Talk? No. I thought you were being very attentive. You naughty girl, have you some secrets you are afraid you might give away?

JOCASTA.   No, only those foolish things we sometimes say when sleeping.

OEDIPUS.   You were lying as good as gold. Till soon, my little queen.

JOCASTA.   Very soon, my king, my love.

[*Hand in hand, side by side, they shut their eyes and fall into the heavy sleep of people who struggle against sleep. A pause. The fountain soliloquizes. Slight thunder. Suddenly the lighting becomes the lighting of dreams. The dream of* OEDIPUS. *The animal skin is pushed up. It is lifted by the head of* ANUBIS. *He shows the belt at the end of his outstretched arm.* OEDIPUS *tosses about and turns over.*]

ANUBIS. [*In a slow mocking voice.*]   Thanks to my unhappy childhood, I have pursued studies which give me a great start over the riff-raff of Thebes, and I don't think this simple-minded monster is expecting to be confronted by a pupil of the best scholars of Corinth. But if you have played a trick on me I shall drag you by the hair. [*Up to a howl.*] I shall drag you by the hair, I shall drag you by the hair, I shall grip you till the blood flows! . . . I shall grip you till the blood flows! . . .

JOCASTA. [*Dreaming.*]   No, not that paste, not that foul paste! . . .

OEDIPUS. [*In a distant, muffled voice.*]   I shall count up to fifty: one, two, three, four, eight, seven, nine, ten, ten, eleven, fourteen, five, two, four, seven, fifteen, fifteen, fifteen, fifteen, three, four. . . .

ANUBIS.   And Anubis would bound forward. He would open his wolf-like jaws!

[*He disappears under the platform. The animal skin resumes its normal appearance.*]

OEDIPUS.   Help! Help! I 'm here! Help me! Everybody! Come here!

JOCASTA.   What? What is it? Oedipus, my darling! I was in a dead sleep! Wake up! [*She shakes him.*]

OEDIPUS. [*Struggling and talking to the* SPHINX.]   Oh, miss! No! No, miss! Please don't! No! Let me go, miss! No! No! No!

JOCASTA.   My pet, don't scare me so. It 's a dream. This is me, me, Jocasta, your wife, Jocasta.

OEDIPUS.   No, no! [*He awakens.*] Where was I? How ghastly! Jocasta, is that you? . . . What a nightmare, what a horrible nightmare!

JOCASTA.   There, there, it 's all over, you are in our room, dear, in my arms. . . .

OEDIPUS.   Didn't you see anything? Of course, how silly of me, it was that animal skin. . . . Phew! I must have talked. What did I say?

JOCASTA.   Now it 's your turn. You were shouting: 'Oh no, miss! Please don't, miss! Let me go, miss!' Who was that wicked woman?

OEDIPUS.   I don't remember. What a night!

JOCASTA.   How about me? Your shouts saved me from an unspeakable nightmare. Look! You're soaked through, swimming in perspiration. It's my fault. I let you go to sleep in all those heavy clothes, golden chains, clasps, and those sandals which cut your heel. . . . [*She lifts him up. He falls back.*] Come along! What a big baby! I can't possibly leave you in this state. Don't make yourself so heavy, help me. . . .

[*She lifts him up, takes off his tunic, and rubs him down.*]

OEDIPUS. [*Still in a vague state.*]   Yes, my little darling mother. . . .

JOCASTA. [*Mocking him.*]   'Yes, my little darling mother. . . .' What a child! Now he 's taking me for his mother.

OEDIPUS. [*Awake.*]   Oh, forgive me, Jocasta, my love, I am being so silly. You see I 'm half asleep, I mix up everything. I was thousands of miles away with my mother who always thinks I am too cold or too hot. You 're not cross?

JOCASTA.   Silly boy! Let me see to you, and sleep away. All the time he's excusing himself and asking forgiveness. My word! What a polite young man! He must have been taken care of by a very kind mother, very kind, and then he goes and leaves her, yes. But I mustn't complain of that. I love with all the warmth of a woman in love, that mother who petted you and kept you and brought you up for me, for us.

OEDIPUS.   Sweet.

JOCASTA.   I should say so! Your sandals. Raise your left leg. [*She takes off his sandals.*] And now the right.

[*Same business; suddenly she utters a terrible cry.*]

OEDIPUS.   Hurt yourself?

JOCASTA.   No . . . no. . . .

[*She recoils, and stares like a mad creature at* OEDIPUS's *feet.*]

OEDIPUS.   Ah, my scars! . . . I didn't know they were so ugly. My poor darling, did they upset you?

JOCASTA.   Those holes . . . how did you get them? . . . They must come from such serious injuries. . . .

OEDIPUS.   From the hunt, it seems. I was in the woods; my nurse was carrying me. Suddenly from a clump of trees a wild boar broke cover and charged her. She lost her head and let me go. I fell and a woodcutter killed the animal while it was belabouring me with its tusks. . . . But she is really as pale as a ghost! My darling! I ought to have warned you. I 'm so used to them myself, those awful holes. I didn't know you were so sensitive. . . .

JOCASTA.   It 's nothing. . . .

OEDIPUS.   Weariness and sleepiness put us into this state of vague terror . . . you had just come out of a bad dream. . . .

JOCASTA.   No, Oedipus. No. As a matter of fact, those scars remind me of something I am always trying to forget.

OEDIPUS.   I always strike unlucky.

JOCASTA.   You couldn't possibly know. It 's to do with a woman, my foster-sister and linen-maid. She was with child at the same age as myself, at eighteen. She worshipped her husband despite the difference of age and wanted a son. But the oracles predicted so fearful a future for the child, that, after giving birth to a son, she had not the courage to let it live.

OEDIPUS.   What?

JOCASTA.   Wait. . . . Imagine what strength of mind a poor woman must have to do away with the life of her life . . . the son from her womb, her ideal on earth and love of loves.

OEDIPUS.   And what did this . . . woman do?

JOCASTA.   With death in her heart, she bored holes in the feet of the nursling, tied them, carried it secretly to a mountain-side, and left it to the mercy of the wolves and bears.

[She hides her face.]

OEDIPUS.   And the husband?

JOCASTA.   Every one thought the child had died a natural death, and that the mother had buried it with her own hands.

OEDIPUS.   And . . . this woman . . . still lives?

JOCASTA.   She is dead.

OEDIPUS.   So much the better for her, for my first example of royal author-ity would have been to inflict on her, publicly, the worst tortures, and after-wards, to have her put to death.

JOCASTA.   The oracles were clear and matter-of-fact. Before those things a woman always feels so stupid and helpless.

OEDIPUS.   To kill! [Recalling LAÏUS.] Of course, it isn't infamous to kill when carried away by the instinct of self-defence, and when bad luck is in-volved. But basely to kill in cold blood the flesh of one's flesh, to break the chain . . . to cheat in the game!

JOCASTA.   Oedipus, let 's talk about something else . . . your furious little face upsets me too much.

OEDIPUS.   Yes, let us talk about something else. I should be in danger of loving you less if you tried to defend this miserable wretch.

JOCASTA.   You 're a man, my love, a free man and a chief! Try and put yourself in the place of a child-mother who is credulous about the oracles, worn out, disgusted, confined, and terrified by the priests. . . .

OEDIPUS. A linen-maid! That 's her only excuse. Would you have done it?

JOCASTA. [*With a gesture.*] No, of course not.

OEDIPUS. And don't run away with the idea that to fight the oracles requires a herculean determination. I could boast and pose as a wonder; I should be lying. You know, to thwart the oracles I only had to turn my back on my family, my longings, and my country. But the farther I got from my native town, and the nearer I came to yours, the more I felt I was returning home.

JOCASTA. Oedipus, Oedipus, that little mouth of yours which chatters away, that little wagging tongue, those frowning eyebrows and fiery eyes! Couldn't the eyebrows relax a little, Oedipus, and the eyes close gently for once, and that mouth be used for softer caresses than words?

OEDIPUS. I tell you, I 'm just a brute! A wretched, clumsy brute!

JOCASTA. You are a child.

OEDIPUS. I 'm not a child!

JOCASTA. Now he 's off again! There, there, be a good boy.

OEDIPUS. You 're right. I 'm behaving very badly. Calm this talkative mouth with yours, and these feverish eyes with your fingers.

JOCASTA. One moment. I 'll close the grille gate. I don't like that gate being open at night.

OEDIPUS. I 'll go.

JOCASTA. You stay lying down. . . . I 'll take a look in the mirror at the same time. Do you want to embrace a fright? After all this excitement the gods alone know what I look like. Don't make me nervous. Don't look at me. Turn the other way, Oedipus.

OEDIPUS. I'm turning over. [*He lies across the bed with his head on the edge of the cradle.*] There, I 'm shutting my eyes. I 'm not here.

[JOCASTA *goes to the window.*]

JOCASTA. [*To* OEDIPUS.] The little soldier is still asleep, he 's half-naked . . . and it isn't warm to-night . . . poor lad!

[*She goes to the movable mirror; suddenly she stops, listening in the direction of the square. A drunk is talking very loud with long pauses between his reflections.*]

VOICE OF THE DRUNK. Politics! . . . Pol—i—tics! What a mess! They just tickle me to death! . . . Ho! Look, a dead 'un! . . . Sorry, a mistake: 's a soldier asleep. . . . Salute! Salute the sleeping army!

[*Silence.* JOCASTA *stands on her toes, and tries to see outside.*] Politics! . . . [*Long silence.*] It 's a disgrace . . . a disgrace. . . .

JOCASTA. Oedipus, my dear!

OEDIPUS. [*In his sleep.*] H'm!

JOCASTA. Oedipus! Oedipus. There's a drunk and the sentry doesn't hear him. I hate drunks. I want him sent away, and the soldier woken up. Oedipus! Oedipus! Please!

[*She shakes him.*]

OEDIPUS. I wind, I unwind, I calculate, I meditate, I weave, I winnow, I knit, I plait, I cross . . .

JOCASTA. What 's he saying? How soundly he sleeps! I might die, he wouldn't notice it.

DRUNK. Politics!

[*He sings. As soon as the first lines are sung* JOCASTA *leaves* OEDIPUS, *putting his head back on the edge of the cradle, and goes to the middle of the room. She listens.*]

> 'Majesty, what ever are you at?
> Majesty, what ever are you at?
> Your husband 's much too young,
> Much too young for you, that 's flat! . . . Flat. . . .'

Et cetera. . . .

JOCASTA. Oh! The beasts . . .

DRUNK. 'Majesty, what ever are you at
> With this holy marriage?'

[*During what follows* JOCASTA, *bewildered, goes to the window on tiptoe. Then she returns to the bed, and leaning over* OEDIPUS, *watches his face, but still looking from time to time in the direction of the window, where the voice of the* DRUNK *alternates with the murmur of the fountain and the cockcrows. She lulls the sleep of* OEDIPUS *by gently rocking the cradle.*]

Now, if I were in politics . . . I 'd say to the queen: Majesty! . . . a minor can't be your man. . . . Take a husband who 's serious, sober, and strong . . . a husband like me. . . .

VOICE OF THE GUARD. [*Who has just awakened. He gradually recovers his self-assurance.*] Get along, there!

VOICE OF THE DRUNK. Salute the waking army! . . .

GUARD. Get a move on!

DRUNK. You might at least be polite. . . .

[*As soon as the* GUARD *is heard* JOCASTA *leaves the cradle, having first muffled* OEDIPUS's *head in the muslin.*]

GUARD. D' you want a taste of the cooler?

DRUNK. 'Always politics! What a mess!
> Majesty, what ever are you at? . . .

GUARD. Come on, hop it! Clear off! . . .

DRUNK. I 'm clearing off, I 'm clearing off, but you might be polite about it.

[*During these remarks* JOCASTA *goes to the mirror. She cannot see herself owing to the moonlight conflicting with the dawn. She takes the mirror by its supports and moves it away from the wall. The mirror itself stays fastened to the scenery.* JOCASTA *drags the frame along, trying to get some light, glancing at* OEDIPUS *who sleeps on. She brings the piece of furniture carefully into the foreground, opposite the prompter's box, so that the public becomes her mirror and* JOCASTA *looks at herself in full view of all.*]

DRUNK. [*Very distant.*]

'Your husband 's much too young,
Much too young for you, that's flat! . . . Flat! . . .'
[*Sound of the sentry's footsteps, bugle-calls, cock-crows, a kind of snoring
noise from the rhythmic, youthful breathing of* OEDIPUS. JOCASTA, *with her
face up against the empty mirror, lifts her cheeks by handfuls.*]

Act IV. Oedipus Rex

(*Seventeen years later*)

THE VOICE: Seventeen years soon pass. The great plague in Thebes seems
to be the first set-back to that renowned good luck of Oedipus. For their infernal machine to work properly the gods wanted all ill luck to appear in the
guise of good luck. After delusive good fortune the king is to know true misfortune, the supreme consecration, which, in the hands of the cruel gods, makes
of this playing-card king, in the end, a man.

Act IV. Oedipus Rex

(*Seventeen years later*)

SCENE: *Cleared of the bedroom, the red hangings of which are pulled away
into the flies, the platform seems to be surrounded by walls which grow in
size. It finally represents an inner courtyard. By a balcony high up* JOCASTA's
*room is made to communicate with this court. One gets to it through an
open door below, in the centre. When the curtain rises* OEDIPUS, *aged, and
wearing a little beard, stands near to the door.* TIRESIAS *and* CREON *are standing on the right and left of the court. Centre right, a young boy rests one
knee on the ground: he is the* MESSENGER *from Corinth.*

OEDIPUS.   What have I done to shock people now, Tiresias?

TIRESIAS.   You are enlarging on things, as usual. I think, and I 'll say again,
it might be more decent to learn of a father's death with less joy.

OEDIPUS.   Indeed. [*To the* MESSENGER.] Don't be afraid, boy. Tell me, what
was the cause of Polybius's death? Is Merope so very terribly unhappy?

MESSENGER.   King Polybius died of old age, my lord, and . . . the queen,
his wife, is barely conscious. She is so old she can't fully realize even her misfortune.

OEDIPUS. [*His hand to his mouth.*]   Jocasta! Jocasta!

[JOCASTA *appears on the balcony; she parts the curtain. She is wearing her
red scarf.*]

JOCASTA.   What is it?

OEDIPUS.   How pale you are! Don't you feel well?

JOCASTA.   Oh, you know, the plague, the heat, and visits to hospitals—I 'm
absolutely exhausted. I was resting on my bed.

OEDIPUS.   This messenger has brought me great news, worth disturbing you
for.

JOCASTA. [*Astonished.*]   Good news? . . .

OEDIPUS.   Tiresias blames me for finding it good: My father is dead.

JOCASTA.   Oedipus!

OEDIPUS.   The oracle told me I should be his murderer, and that I should be the husband of my mother. Poor Merope! she is very old, and my father, Polybius, has died a good natural death!

JOCASTA.   I never knew the death of a father was a subject for rejoicing!

OEDIPUS.   I hate play-acting and conventional tears. To tell the truth, I was so young when I left my father and mother that I no longer have any particular feelings for them.

MESSENGER.   Lord Oedipus, if I may . . .

OEDIPUS.   You may, my boy.

MESSENGER.   Your indifference is not really indifference. I can explain it to you.

OEDIPUS.   Something new.

MESSENGER.   I ought to have begun at the end of the story. On his death-bed the King of Corinth asked me to tell you that you are only his adopted son.

OEDIPUS.   What?

MESSENGER.   My father, one of Polybius's shepherds, found you on a hill, at the mercy of wild beasts. He was a poor man; he carried his find to the queen who used to weep because she had no children. This is how the honour of performing such an extraordinary mission at the Theban court has fallen to me.

TIRESIAS.   This young man must be exhausted after his journey, and he has crossed our town which is full of noxious vapours. Perhaps it would be better if he took some refreshment and rested before being questioned.

OEDIPUS.   No doubt, Tiresias, you would like the torture to last. You think my world is tottering. You don't know me well enough. Don't you rejoice too soon. Perhaps I am happy to be a child of fortune.

TIRESIAS.   I was only putting you on your guard against your sinister habit of questioning, seeking to know and understand everything.

OEDIPUS.   Whether I am a child of the muses or of a common tramp, I shall question without fear; I will know things.

JOCASTA.   Oedipus, my love, he is right. You get excited. . . . You get excited . . . and you believe everything you 're told, and then afterwards——

OEDIPUS.   What! That 's the last straw! Unflinchingly I withstand the hardest knocks, and you all plot to make me put up with these things and not try to find out where I come from.

JOCASTA.   Nobody is plotting . . . my love . . . but I know you. . . .

OEDIPUS.   You 're wrong, Jocasta. Nobody knows me at present, neither you, nor I, nor any one else. [To the MESSENGER.] Don't tremble, my lad. Speak up. Tell us more.

MESSENGER.   That 's all I know, Lord Oedipus, except that my father untied you when you were half dead, hanging by your wounded feet from a short branch.

OEDIPUS. Oh, so that 's how we come by those fine scars!

JOCASTA. Oedipus, Oedipus, dear . . . come up here. . . . Anybody would think you enjoy opening old wounds.

OEDIPUS. And so those were my swaddling clothes! . . . My story of the hunt is . . . false, like so many others. Well, if that 's the way things are . . . I may come of a god of the woods and a dryad, and have been nourished by wolves. Don't you rejoice too soon, Tiresias!

TIRESIAS. You do me an injustice. . . .

OEDIPUS. At any rate I haven't killed Polybius, but . . . now I come to think of it . . . I have killed a man.

JOCASTA. You!

OEDIPUS. Yes! I! Oh, you needn't be alarmed! It was accidental, and sheer bad luck! Yes, I have killed, soothsayer, but as for parricide, you 'd better officially give it up. During a brawl with the serving-man I killed an old man at the cross-roads of Delphi and Daulis.

JOCASTA. At the cross-roads of Delphi and Daulis! . . .

[*She disappears as if drowning.*]

OEDIPUS. There 's marvellous material for you to build up a really fine catastrophe. That traveller must have been my father. 'Heavens, my father!' But incest won't be so easy, gentlemen. What do *you* think, Jocasta? . . . [*He turns round and sees* JOCASTA *has disappeared.*] Splendid! Seventeen years of happiness, and a perfect reign, two sons, two daughters, and then this noble lady only has to learn that I am the stranger whom, by the way, she first loved, and she turns her back on me. Let her sulk! Let her sulk! I shall be left alone with my fate.

CREON. Your wife, Oedipus, is ill. The plague is demoralizing us all. The gods are punishing the town and desire a victim. A monster is hiding in our midst. They demand he shall be found and driven out. Day after day the police have failed and the streets are littered with corpses. Do you realize what an effort you are asking of Jocasta? Do you realize that you are a man and she is a woman, an ageing woman at that, and a mother who is worried about the plague? Instead of blaming Jocasta for a movement of impatience, you might have found some excuse for her.

OEDIPUS. I see what you are getting at, brother-in-law. The ideal victim, the monster in hiding. . . . From one coincidence to another . . . wouldn't it be a pretty job, with the help of the priests and the police, to succeed in muddling the people of Thebes and make them believe *I* am that monster!

CREON. Don't be absurd!

OEDIPUS. I think you 're capable of anything, my friend. But Jocasta, that 's another matter. . . . I am astonished at her attitude. [*He calls her.*] Jocasta! Jocasta! Where are you?

TIRESIAS. She looked all to pieces. She is resting . . . let her be.

OEDIPUS. I am going. . . . [*He goes toward the* MESSENGER.] Now, let us come to the point. . . .

MESSENGER. My lord!

OEDIPUS.   Holes in my feet . . . bound . . . on the mountainside. . . .
How did I fail to understand at once? . . . And then I wondered why
Jocasta . . .

It's very hard to give up enigmas. . . . Gentlemen, I was not the son of a
dryad. Allow me to introduce you to the son of a linen-maid, a child of the
people, a native product.

CREON.   What's this all about?

OEDIPUS.   Poor Jocasta! One day I unwittingly told her what I thought of
my mother. . . . I understand everything now. She must be terrified, and
utterly desperate. In short . . . wait for me. I must question her at all costs.
Nothing must be left in the dark. This horrible farce must come to an end.

[*He leaves by the middle door.* CREON *immediately rushes to the* MESSENGER,
whom he pushes out through the door on the right.]

CREON.   He is mad. What does all this mean?

TIRESIAS.   Don't move. A storm is approaching from out of the ages. A
thunderbolt is aimed at this man, and I ask you, Creon, to let this thunderbolt
follow its capricious course, to wait motionless and not to interfere in the
slightest.

[*Suddenly,* OEDIPUS *is seen on the balcony, stranded and aghast. He leans on
the wall with one hand.*]

OEDIPUS.   You have killed her for me.

CREON.   What do you mean, killed?

OEDIPUS.   You have killed her for me. . . . There she is, hanging . . .
hanging by her scarf. . . . She is dead . . . gentlemen, she is dead. . . . It's
all over . . . all over.

CREON.   Dead? I'm coming. . . .

TIRESIAS.   Stay here. . . . As a priest I order you to. It's inhuman, I know;
but the circle is closing; we must keep silent and remain here. . . .

CREON.   You wouldn't stop a brother from——

TIRESIAS.   I would! Let the story be. Don't interfere.

OEDIPUS. [*At the door.*]   You have killed her for me . . . she was romantic
. . . weak . . . ill . . . you forced me to say I was a murderer. . . . Whom
did I murder, gentlemen, I ask you? . . . through clumsiness, mere clumsiness . . . just an old man on the road . . . a stranger.

TIRESIAS.   Oedipus: through mere clumsiness you have murdered Jocasta's
husband, King Laïus.

OEDIPUS.   You scoundrels! . . . I can see it now! You are carrying on your
plot! . . . It was even worse than I thought. . . . You have made my poor
Jocasta believe that I was the murderer of Laïus . . . that I killed the king to
set her free and so that I could marry her.

TIRESIAS.   Oedipus, you have murdered Jocasta's husband, King Laïus. I
have known it for a long time, and you are telling lies. I haven't said a word
about it either to you or to her or to Creon or to anyone else. This is how you
reward me for my silence.

OEDIPUS.   Laïus! . . . So that 's it. . . . I am the son of Laïus and of the linen-maid. The son of Jocasta's foster-sister and Laïus.

TIRESIAS.   [*To* CREON.]   If you want to act, now's the time. Quickly. There are limits even to harshness.

CREON.   Oedipus, through you, my sister is dead. I kept silence only to protect Jocasta. I think it is useless to prolong unduly the false mystery and the unravelling of a sordid drama whose intrigue I have finally succeeded in discovering.

OEDIPUS.   Intrigue?

CREON.   The most secret of secrets are betrayed one day or another to the determined seeker. The honest man, sworn to silence, talks to his wife, who talks to an intimate friend, and so on. [*Into the wings.*] Come in, shepherd.

[*An old* SHEPHERD *comes in, trembling.*]

OEDIPUS.   Who is this man?

CREON.   The man who carried you bleeding and bound on to the mountainside, in obedience to your mother's orders. Let him confess.

SHEPHERD.   To speak means death to me. Princes, why haven't I died before so as not to live through this minute?

OEDIPUS.   Whose son am I, old man? Strike, strike quickly!

SHEPHERD.   Alas!

OEDIPUS.   I am near to the sound of something that should not be heard.

SHEPHERD.   And I . . . to the saying of something that should not be said.

CREON.   You must say it. I wish you to.

SHEPHERD.   You are the son of Jocasta, your wife, and of Laïus, killed by you where the three roads cross. Incest and parricide, may the gods forgive you!

OEDIPUS.   I have killed whom I should not. I have married whom I should not. I have perpetuated what I should not. All is clear. . . .

[*He goes out.* CREON *drives out the* SHEPHERD.]

CREON.   Who was the linen-maid and foster-sister he was talking about?

TIRESIAS.   Women cannot hold their tongues. Jocasta must have made out that her crime had been committed by a servant to see what effect it had on Oedipus.

[*He holds his arm and listens with bent head. Forbidding murmur. The little* ANTIGONE, *with hair dishevelled, appears on the balcony.*]

ANTIGONE.   Uncle! Tiresias! Come up, quickly! Hurry, it 's horrible! I heard shrieks inside; mother, my darling mother, doesn't move any more, she has fallen like a log, and my dear, dear father is writhing over her body and stabbing at his eyes with her big golden brooch. There 's blood everywhere. I 'm frightened! I 'm too frightened, come up . . . come up, quickly. . . . [*She goes in.*]

CREON.   This time nothing shall prevent me. . . .

TIRESIAS.   Yes, I shall. I tell you, Creon, the finishing touches are being put to a masterpiece of horror. Not a word, not a gesture. It would be improper for us to cast over it so much as a shadow of ourselves.

CREON. Sheer insanity!

TIRESIAS. Sheer wisdom. . . . You must admit——

CREON. No! Besides, power falls once more into my hands.

[*He frees himself, and at the very moment when he bounds forward the door opens.* OEDIPUS *appears, blind.* ANTIGONE *is clinging to his clothes.*]

TIRESIAS. Stop!

CREON. I shall go mad! Why, but why has he done that? Better have killed himself.

TIRESIAS. His pride does not desert him. He wanted to be the happiest of men, now he wants to be the most unhappy.

OEDIPUS. Let them drive me out, let them finish me off, stone me, strike down the foul beast!

ANTIGONE. Father!

TIRESIAS. Antigone! My soothsaying staff! Offer it to him from me. It will bring him some luck.

[ANTIGONE *kisses the hand of* TIRESIAS *and carries the staff to* OEDIPUS.]

ANTIGONE. Tiresias offers you his staff.

OEDIPUS. Is he there? . . . I accept it, Tiresias. . . . I accept it. . . . Do you remember, seventeen years ago, I saw in your eyes that I should become blind, and I couldn't understand it? I see it all clearly now, Tiresias, but I am in pain. . . . I suffer. . . . The journey will be hard.

CREON. We must not let him cross the town, it would cause an awful scandal.

TIRESIAS. [*In a low voice.*] In a town of plague? And besides, you know, they saw the king Oedipus wished to be; they won't see the king he is now.

CREON. Do you mean he will be invisible because he is blind?

TIRESIAS. Almost.

CREON. Well, I can tell you I have had enough of your riddles and symbols. *My* head is firmly fixed on my shoulders and my feet planted firmly on the ground. I shall give my orders.

TIRESIAS. Your police may be well organized, Creon; but where this man goes they will not have the slightest power.

CREON. I——

[TIRESIAS *seizes his arm and puts his hand over his mouth.* . . . *For* JOCASTA *appears in the doorway.* JOCASTA, *dead, white, beautiful, with closed eyes. Her long scarf is wound round her neck.*]

OEDIPUS. Jocasta! You, dear! You alive!

JOCASTA. No, Oedipus. I am dead. You can see me because you are blind; the others cannot see me.

OEDIPUS. Tiresias is blind. . . .

JOCASTA. Perhaps he can see me faintly . . . but he loves me, he won't say anything. . . .

OEDIPUS. Wife, do not touch me! . . .

JOCASTA. Your wife is dead, hanged, Oedipus. I am your mother. It 's your mother who is coming to help you. . . . How would you even get down these steps alone, my poor child?

OEDIPUS. Mother!

JOCASTA. Yes, my child, my little boy. . . . Things which appear abominable to human beings, if only you knew, from the place where I live, if only you knew how unimportant they are!

OEDIPUS. I am still on this earth.

JOCASTA. Only just. . . .

CREON. He is talking with phantoms, he 's delirious. I shall not allow that little girl——

TIRESIAS. They are in good care.

CREON. Antigone! Antigone! I am calling you. . . .

ANTIGONE. I don't want to stay with my uncle! I don't want to, I don't want to stay in the house. Dear father, dear father, don't leave me! I will show you the way, I will lead you. . . .

CREON. Thankless creature.

OEDIPUS. Impossible, Antigone. You must be a good girl. . . . I cannot take you with me.

ANTIGONE. Yes, you can!

OEDIPUS. Are you going to desert your sister Ismene?

ANTIGONE. She must stay with Eteocles and Polynices. Take me away, please! Please! Don't leave me alone! Don't leave me with uncle! Don't leave me at home!

JOCASTA. The child is so pleased with herself. She imagines she is your guide. Let her think she is. Take her. Leave everything to me.

OEDIPUS. Oh! . . . [He puts his hand to his head.]

JOCASTA. Are you in pain, dear?

OEDIPUS. Yes, my head, my neck and arms. . . . It 's fearful.

JOCASTA. I 'll give you a dressing at the fountain.

OEDIPUS. [Breaking down.] Mother . . .

JOCASTA. Who would have believed it? That wicked old scarf and that terrible brooch. Didn't I say so time and again?

CREON. It 's utterly impossible. I shall not allow a madman to go out free with Antigone. It is my duty to——

TIRESIAS. Duty! They no longer belong to you; they no longer come under your authority.

CREON. And pray whom should they belong to?

TIRESIAS. To the people, poets, and unspoiled souls.

JOCASTA. Forward! Grip my dress firmly . . . don't be afraid.

[They start off.]

ANTIGONE. Come along, father dear . . . let's go. . . .

OEDIPUS. Where do the steps begin?

JOCASTA AND ANTIGONE.   There is the whole of the platform yet. . . . [*They disappear . . .* JOCASTA *and* ANTIGONE *speak in perfect unison.*] Careful . . . count the steps. . . . One, two, three, four, five. . . .

CREON.   And even supposing they leave the town, who will look after them, who will admit them?

TIRESIAS.   Glory.

CREON.   You mean rather dishonour, shame. . . .

TIRESIAS.   Who knows?

FRANCIS FERGUSSON

On Cocteau's *Infernal Machine*[1]

The question of poetic drama—its possibility in our time—is perhaps *the* question of the contemporary theatre. There is no better way to see into the nature and the limitations of the theatre as we know it, than to ask the perennial question, Why don't we have a living poetic drama?

But this question has occupied some of the best minds of our time and has received a vast variety of answers. It would take a book, at the very least, to handle the matter at all adequately. In a brief paper one can do no more than suggest one approach—expound a sample, more or less arbitrarily chosen from among many—of the attempt to make a modern poetic drama. I have chosen Cocteau's *Infernal Machine* for this purpose. But first of all, I should give a word of explanation of this choice—why Cocteau, who did not even write his play in verse?

When we talk about modern poetic drama in English we think of the long line of poets, beginning with Shelley and Coleridge, and continuing right up to Yeats and Eliot, who have aspired more or less in vain to the stage. But on the continent the picture is quite different. Ibsen and Wagner, Chekhov and Pirandello, Cocteau and Stravinski and Lorca—one can think of many writers who worked directly for the stage and who produced works, whether in verse or not, which could in some sense be called poetic drama and which are certainly "poetic" in the widest meaning of the term. There is no question that they produced viable theatrical pieces, while the work of poets writing in English for the stage is all too likely to be unstageable. The fact is that on the continent the idea of the theatre is even yet not quite lost. The stage-supported theatres, the repertory theatres and art theatres, have kept the ancient art of drama alive and provided the means which poets of the theatre would require. But in English-speaking countries the idea of a theatre has succumbed, except for a few undernourished little theatres, to the stereotypes and the mass-production methods of the entertainment industry. In the shallow medium of our commercialized entertainment the poet is lost, however true his inspiration or authentic his dramatic talent.

It is for this reason, I think, that contemporary poets in English who wish to write for the stage so often look to the continent for their models of dramatic form—and especially they look to Paris in the twenties, Paris between the Wars: and above all to Jean Cocteau who was one of the leaders of that Paris Theatre. I am thinking of Eliot, from *Sweeney Agonistes* to *Murder in the Cathedral*; of the later Yeats—the Yeats of *Plays for Dancers*; of Thornton

[1] Alan S. Downer, ed., *English Institute Essays*, 1949 (New York: Columbia University Press, 1950), pp. 55-72. Reprinted by permission of the publisher.

Wilder, E. E. Cummings, the Virgil Thompson-Gertrude Stein operas, of the ballet. It is probable that the theatrical dexterity of these more or less poetic theatre-works is largely due to the influence of the Paris Theatre, and, as I say, especially to Cocteau. In other words it is certain that Cocteau is one of the chief sources of contemporary theatre poetry, or poetry in the theatre, even in English.

Cocteau's Growth; His Notion of Theatre Poetry

When Cocteau started to write in Paris just after World War I, he found artists from all over Europe gathered there; and he found a theatrical life nourished from Russia, Italy, Germany, Sweden, as well as a fairly lively native theatre. Copeau's Théâtre du Vieux Colombier for instance, had been in existence since 1912. Paris in the twenties still looks fabulous to us: Bergson and Valéry, Joyce and Picasso and Stravinski; Pirandello and the Moscow Art Theatre, Milhaud and Gide and Maritain and Ezra Pound—if we think over some of the names associated with that time and place, we can see very clearly what an impressive effort was being made, in the center of Europe, to focus and revive the culture which had been so shaken by the war. If there was to be a favorable opportunity in our time to build a poetic drama, it should have been there and then, where the most enlightened audience and greatest talent were concentrated.

When Cocteau began to work, his immediate allies were the young French musicians who were to be called *les six*, a few painters, and the Swedish and Russian Ballets. The collection of his early critical writings, *The Call to Order*, throws a great deal of light upon his labors in this period. He was trying to sort out the extremely rich influences which bore upon him; and to select the elements of a contemporary, and *French*, theatre poetry.

In very general terms, I think one may say that he was trying to fuse two different traditions, one ancient, the other modern. What I call the ancient tradition was that of myth, of ritual, and of primitive or folk art. What I call the modern tradition was French—the classical spirit of intelligence, wit, measure and proportion, which the French are supposed to have at their best —especially the French since Racine and Molière. The formula which Cocteau invented to describe the fusion of these two strands was *une poésie de tous les jours*—an everyday poetry. He was looking for a dramatic or theatrical art which should be poetic as myth, ritual, and the inspired clowning of the Fratellinis is poetic—and yet at the same time acceptable to the shrewd and skeptical Parisians in their most alert moments and as part of their daily lives, like red wine, for instance, as an indispensable part of the diet. He wanted to acclimatize mythopoeia in the most up-to-date, rational, and disillusioned of modern commercial cities.

You will I am sure remember that during this period many other artists were trying to nourish themselves upon myth, upon ritual, and upon primitive and popular forms of art. The painters were studying African and South Pacific sculpture; Stravinski was doing *Petrouchka, Les Noces,* and *Sacre du Printemps;* Eliot was writing *The Wasteland;* Joyce was between *Ulysses* and *Finnegan's Wake.* When Cocteau and his friends began, most of this work was still to come; Cocteau himself was one of the pioneers in the movement. When he looked around for clues to the ancient and perennial theatre art he was seeking, forms which he might imitate or adapt, he found, not the works I have just mentioned, but Wagner and the all-pervasive Wagnerian influence.

Wagner was in a sense a forerunner of this whole movement. He had made use of myth in his operas, elaborated a whole theory of mythic drama, and worked out a singularly potent poetic theatrical form in the very heyday of bourgeois positivism. Cocteau remembered that Baudelaire had greeted Wagner as an ally against the Parisian Philistines of his day. Baudelaire's studies of Wagner remain one of the fundamental documents for any modern theory of poetic drama. Nevertheless Cocteau and his friends found Wagner extremely unsympathetic. The Parisians in Cocteau's day, like the rest of the world, had learned to accept and even to depend on Wagner, as an indulgence whether hypnosis or drug. They had the bad habit of swooning when they heard that kind of music, and this prevented them from listening to the young French composers who were trying to speak to them in their alert, critical, and wakeful moments. Thus for Cocteau and his friends, the Wagnerian taste or habit of mind became the great enemy, in spite of their respect for Wagner's achievement. They saw Wagnerianism as an alien mode of awareness which was impeding the development of native French forms of art. The Wagnerian tradition, Cocteau says in *The Call to Order,* is like "a long funeral procession which prevents me from crossing the street to get home." Probably he felt in Wagner's magic the potent elements which the Nazis were so soon to use for their own purposes—drowning not only the French spirit but the physical life of France also.

However that may be, Cocteau developed his own conception of poetic drama, as it were, in answer to Wagner's. He too wanted to tap the ancient sources of myth and ritual, but without resorting to religiosity, hypnosis, or morose daydreaming. He wanted to bring mythopoeia and some of the ancient myths themselves into the center of the faithless, nimble, modern city—but he sought to establish them there by the clarity and integrity of art.

The Call to Order is a collection of working notes and critical *obiter dicta* from the very beginning of Cocteau's career, between 1918 and 1926. *The Infernal Machine* was published in 1934; and yet that play seems to be exactly the poetic drama which he had planned and foreseen fifteen years earlier. It presents a very ancient myth, the myth of Oedipus, not as a joke, but as a perennial source of insight into human destiny. Yet at the same time the play is addressed to the most advanced, cynical, and even *fashionable* mind of contemporary Paris. It is at one and the same time chic and timeless—rather like the paintings of Picasso's classic period, or his illustrations for Ovid. If one were to try to describe it briefly, one might say it shows the myth behind the modern city: both the mysterious fate of Oedipus and the bright metropolitan intrigues for pleasure and power which go on forever. To have achieved such a fusion of contradictory elements is, of course, an extraordinary feat of virtuosity. And therefore this play illustrates, from one point of view at least, *the problem of modern poetic drama: that of presentation on the public stage, at a time when poetry has lost almost all public status.*

After this prolonged introduction, I wish to look briefly at the play itself, in order to illustrate more concretely what I mean.

The Play: The Myth behind the Modern City

The story of *The Infernal Machine* is the same as that of Sophocles' tragedy, *Oedipus the King.* Before the curtain goes up, a voice reminds us of the main facts.

Jocasta, Queen of Thebes, was told by the oracle of Apollo that her infant son Oedipus would grow up to murder his father and marry his mother. To avoid this terrible fatality she has the infant exposed on Mt. Kitharon with his feet pierced. But a shepherd finds him on the mountain and saves him, and eventually the young Oedipus makes his way to Corinth, where the childless king and queen adopt him as their son. He is brought up to think he is really their son; but in due time he hears the oracle, and to escape his fate he leaves Corinth. At a place where three roads cross, he meets an old man with an escort; gets into a dispute, and kills him. The old man is, of course, his own father Laïus. Oedipus continues his journey, and reaches Thebes, where he finds the Sphinx preying on the city. He solves the riddle of the Sphinx and like other young men who make good, marries the boss's daughter, the widowed Queen Jocasta, his own mother. They rule prosperously for years and raise a family; but at last, when Thebes is suffering under the plague, the fate of Oedipus overtakes him. The oracle reports that the plague is sent by the gods, who are angry because Laïus' slayer was never found and punished. Oedipus discovers his own identity and his own guilt—but thereby becomes once more, and in a new way, the savior of the city.

Such are the facts, in Cocteau as in Sophocles. But the question is how Cocteau presents them. What attitudes, what dramatic and theatrical forms does he find to bring the ancient tale alive in our time? His dramaturgy is utterly unlike Sophocles'; he presents *both* the mythic tale, and, as it were, the feel, or texture, of contemporary life, in which no myth is supposed to have any meaning.

When the curtain goes up we see the stage hung with nocturnal drapes, as Cocteau calls them; in the center of the stage there is a lighted platform, set to represent the city wall of Thebes. The play is in four acts, and each act is set upon that lighted platform. Everything that occurs in the set on the lighted platform is in the easy, agile style of the best sophisticated modern comedy—Giraudoux's *Amphitryon*, or the acting of Guitry. In other words Cocteau tells the story in the foreground in a way that his blasé boulevard audience will accept. Thus he achieves the "everyday" part of his formula for "everyday poetry." But the tinkling modern intrigue is itself placed in a wider and darker setting represented by the nocturnal curtains—and in this vaster surrounding area the cruel machine of the gods, Oedipus' fate, is slowly unrolled, almost without the main actors being aware of it at all. Thus the "poetry" part of the formula is ironically hidden; it is to be found in the background, and in the mysterious relation between the hidden shape of the myth and the visible shape of Oedipus' ambitious career.

The first scene on the lighted platform represents the city wall of Thebes. It is the night when Oedipus is approaching the city. Two young soldiers are on guard. They have seen Laïus' ghost, who is trying to warn Jocasta not to receive Oedipus when he comes. Queen Jocasta herself has heard rumors of this ghost, and arrives with the high priest Tiresias to investigate. But the ghost cannot appear to Jocasta; he can appear only to the naïve, "the innocent, the pure in heart," such as the young soldiers; and Jocasta departs none the wiser.

The second scene shows the suburbs of Thebes, where the Sphinx lies in wait for her prey. Occurring at the same time as the first act, it discloses Oedipus' interview with the Sphinx. The Sphinx is not only a goddess but a very mortal woman, who falls in love with Oedipus and lets him guess her riddle in the hope that he will fall in love with her. But he is more interested in his career than in love; he takes her mortal remains to town as a proof of his victory, while she departs to the realm of the gods, thoroughly disgusted with mortals. She is willing to let him get away with his heroic pretenses because she sees the terrible fate in store for him.

In both of these scenes the most important characters—Jocasta in the first and Oedipus in the second—are unaware of their fate. It is separated from them as by a very thin curtain; they *almost* see what they are doing, but not quite. Moreover, in both scenes the characters and the dialogue are felt as modern, like the scandals in the morning paper.

In the first scene, for instance, Cocteau gives us the atmosphere of Thebes by means of the slangy gossip of the two soldiers. The soldiers, exactly like any GI's, are fed up with military service and especially with the brass hat who commands them. We hear the music, hot or blue, from the cafés and cheap night clubs of the popular quarter, where the people are trying to forget the rising prices, the falling employment, and the threats of war or revolution. We gather that the authorities do not know how to deal with the Sphinx. To explain their failure there are rumors of bribery, corruption, and scandal in high places. In other words, Thebes is wholly familiar and acceptable to our worldly understanding—it might be any demoralized modern Mediterranean city of our time or any time. In this atmosphere even the Sphinx and the ghost of Laïus are scarcely more surprising or significant than our more commonplace public nightmares. When Jocasta arrives with Tiresias to find out what all this talk of a ghost is about, she, too, is sharply modern: she speaks, Cocteau tells us, with the insolent accent of international royalty. He might have been thinking of Queen Marie of Roumania, or any other Elsa Maxwell character from café society. Jocasta is full of forebodings; she is nervous and overwrought; she complains about everything—but she does not have the naïveté or the "purity of heart" to grasp her real situation, or to see the ghost which appeared to the soldiers.

In the second act the young Oedipus is also a modern portrait, almost a candid-camera picture in the style of Guitry or Noel Coward. He is an ambitious and worldly young Latin—he might be the winner of a bicycle marathon or a politician who managed to stabilize the franc for a day. It is inevitable that he and Jocasta should get together—two shallow careerists, seekers after pleasure and power. The third scene shows their wedding night. It is set in the royal bedroom, and beside the royal bed is the crib which Jocasta kept as a memento of her lost son. In this scene the tenuous curtain of blindness which keeps them from seeing what they are doing is at its thinnest. But they are tired after the ceremonies of the coronation and the marriage; and they proceed sleepwalking toward the fated consummation.

In these first three acts of his play, Cocteau keeps completely separate the mythic fate of Oedipus and the literal story of his undoing, in so far as Oedipus and Jocasta themselves are concerned. The audience is aware of the fact that the terrible machine of the gods is slowly unwinding in the surrounding darkness; but the audience also sees that the victims are winning their victories and building their careers in total ignorance of it. In this respect the plan of *The Infernal Machine* resembles that of Joyce's *Ulysses*. Joyce also shows the lives of the people of a modern city in the form of an ancient legend which they are quite unaware of. Bloom wanders through his Dublin life according to an abstract scheme like that of the *Odyssey*; the reader sees this, but Bloom does not. The audience of *The Infernal Machine* sees Oedipus both as a contemporary politician and as the character in the myth. But at this point the resemblance between Cocteau's play and Joyce's novel ends. For Cocteau proposes to bring the two levels sharply together—to confront the city with the myth, and the myth with the city. This he proceeds to do in the fourth and last act.

We have been prepared all along for the sudden shift in point of view—for the peripety and epiphany of the last act. The naïve soldiers saw Laïus' ghost, though Jocasta did not. In the second scene the Sphinx saw what was happening to Oedipus, though he did not. And on the wedding night, Tiresias almost guessed who Oedipus was, though the bride and groom themselves could not quite make it out. Moreover, at the beginning of the play, and at the beginning of each of the first three acts, a Voice bids us relish the perfection of the machine which the gods have devised to destroy a mortal. The emphasis is on mortal stupidity and upon the cruelty of the gods. But before the last act, the Voice reminds us of a different meaning in these events; the Voice makes the following proclamation: "After false happiness, the king will learn real unhappiness: the true ritual, which will make out of this playing-card king in the hands of the cruel gods, at long last, a man."

The fourth act, unlike the other three, follows fairly closely the order of events in Sophocles' tragedy. Oedipus feels, like an unsuccessful bluffer in poker, that the jig is up; he receives the evidence of the messenger and the old shepherd which unmistakably reveals him as his mother's husband and his father's killer. Tiresias, who had half-guessed the truth all along, watches this terrible dénouement and explains it to Creon and for the audience. When Oedipus gets the final piece of evidence which convicts him, he runs off to find Jocasta. Tiresias tells Creon, "Do not budge. A storm is coming up from the bottom of time. The lightning will strike this man; and I ask you, Creon, let it follow its whim; wait without moving; interfere with nothing." As in the Sophoclean tragedy, Jocasta kills herself and Oedipus puts out his eyes, while their bewildered child Antigone tries to understand. Cocteau, like Sophocles, imagines these horrors with great intimacy, sparing nothing. But Cocteau brings the play to an end on a different note. In Sophocles the final pathos and enlightenment of Oedipus is presented in a series of steps, and by the time we finally see him blind at the end, the chorus has pretty well digested, or at least accepted, the tragic and purgatorial meaning of it all. But Cocteau ends the play with a *coup de théâtre*, a spectacular effect, a piece of theatrical sleight-of-hand, which visibly presents the tragic paradox on which the whole play is based.

The dead Jocasta appears to Oedipus, who is blind and can therefore see— but she appears not as the corrupt queen and dishonored wife of the sordid tale, but as a sort of timeless mother. "Yes, my child," she says to Oedipus, "my little son. . . . Things which seem abominable to human beings—if you only knew how unimportant they are in the realm where I am dwelling." The blind Oedipus, the child Antigone, and the ghostly Jocasta depart on their endless journey. Creon can see Oedipus and Antigone, if not Jocasta, and he asks Tiresias, "To whom do they belong now?" to which Tiresias replies, "To the people, to the poets, to the pure in heart." "But who," asks Creon, "will take care of them?" To which Tiresias replies, "La Gloire"—glory, or renown.

The effect is to remind us, all of a sudden, that Oedipus, Jocasta, Antigone, are not only literal people as we know people, but legends, figures in a timeless myth. We had in a sense known this all along; but during the first three acts we forgot it—we laughed at Oedipus' youthful vanity, grinned with cynical understanding when we saw his shallow ambition, his bounder-like opportunism. Now he and Jocasta are safe from our irony—as poetry and myth are safe—both more human and less human than the intriguing puppets which we found so familiar in the first three acts.

Cocteau, I think, must have learned a great deal from Pirandello before he wrote this play. The final effect, when Oedipus and Jocasta are suddenly taken up into the legend, like saints receiving the stigmata, is very much like the effect Pirandello contrives for his six characters in search of an author. When the six characters first appear on the stage they have some of the quality of masks, of the achieved and quiet work of art; when they fight with each other about their story, they are all too sharply human; and when they leave at the end, their tragic procession is like the procession of Oedipus, Jocasta, and Antigone—a steady image in the mind's eye, and in the light of the stage, of the tragic human condition in general: they have the eternity, if not of heaven, at least of the poetic image.

Moreover the paradox on which the tragedy is based is very much like Pirandello's favorite paradox—the contradiction between myth or poetry on one side, and the meaningless disorder of contemporary lives on the other. We live in two incommensurable worlds, neither of which we can do without— that of myth-making, and that of literal, unrelated, and therefore meaningless facts.

I do not mean to say that this is the only way to understand tragedy. On the contrary, Pirandello and Cocteau write a particular *kind* of tragedy, which is much more closely akin to the Baroque than it is either to Sophoclean or Shakespearean tragedy. Both of these authors may seem to us artificial; certainly they are Latin, rationalistic, deflated; they work with brilliant images, clear and distinct ideas, sharp contrasts, strong chiaroscuro. If we are used to Shakespeare, the plays of Cocteau like those of Pirandello may seem arbitrary and invented to us,

> Music and philosophy, curiosity,
> The purple bullfinch in the lilac tree,

as Eliot's Thomas of Canterbury says rather scornfully of the refined pleasures of the mind. I do not say that we could ever succeed in making that kind of modernized Baroque tragedy in English—I don't think it fits the genius of our language, or our peculiar habits of mind.

Nevertheless, as I said at the beginning of this paper, many fine playwrights and poets, writing in English, have learned from Cocteau; and I believe that there is much more still to be learned from him, short of direct imitation, about poetic drama in our time. I wish to conclude these remarks with two observations on the dramaturgy of *The Infernal Machine*, which bear upon the problem which concerns us.

The first observation is this: The whole play of *The Infernal Machine*, if properly understood, may be read as a discussion of the most general problem of dramatic poetry in our time: how are we to place upon the public stage, which is formed to reflect only literal snapshots, slogans, and sensationalism, a poetic image of human life? The play, as we have seen, answers this question in its own wonderful way, which cannot be exactly our way in English; but the general question is the same as Wagner answered according to his taste, and Yeats and Eliot according to theirs. *The Infernal Machine* thus takes an important place in the long line of attempts which have been made, for over a hundred years, to build a modern poetic drama.

The other observation has to do with the *nature* of Cocteau's poetry from which, I think, much technical lore is to be learned. The play is not in verse; and though the language is beautifully formed, the poetry is not to be found in the first instance in the language at all. The play is *theatre*-poetry, as Cocteau defines it in his preface to *Les Mariés de la Tour Eiffel*:

> The action of my play is in images, while the text is not. I attempt to substitute a poetry *of* the theatre for poetry *in* the theatre. Poetry *in* the theatre is a piece of lace which it is impossible to see at a distance. Poetry *of* the theatre would be coarse lace; a lace of ropes, a ship at sea. *Les Mariés* should have the frightening look of a drop of poetry under the microscope. The *scenes* are integrated like the *words* of a poem.

Though the language in *The Infernal Machine* is of course more important than it is in *Les Mariés* (essentially a dance pantomime), Cocteau's description of the underlying structure applies also very accurately to *The Infernal Machine*. The poetry is to be found in the relationships of all the main elements: the relationship between the lighted platform in the center of the stage with the darker and vaster area around it; between Oedipus's conscious career with the unseen fatality that governs it; between the first scene and the second, which ironically occurs at the same time; and between the first three acts, when we see Oedipus as a contemporary snapshot, and the last act, when we see him as a legend. In other words, the basic structure, or plot—the primary form of the play as a whole—embodies a poetic idea; and once that is established the language need only realize the poetic vision in detail.

If Cocteau, more than any other contemporary playwright, is thus a master of poetic-dramatic form, it is partly because he has learned from the neighboring arts of music, painting, and ballet, and partly because he found his way back to a root notion of drama itself, that which Aristotle expressed when he said the dramatic poet should be a maker of plots rather than of verses. If Auden and MacNeice do not succeed in making poetic drama, it is because they do not understand the poetry of the theatre—they take an unpoetic well-made plot from the commercial theatre and add, here and there, a pastiche of verses.

This concludes what I have to say about *The Infernal Machine* as a poetic drama. If there is a moral to the tale, it is this: poetic drama, real poetic drama, comparable to the landmarks of the tradition, when the ancient art has really flourished—cannot be invented by an individual or even a small group. If it is to perform its true function it must spring from the the whole culture and be nourished by sources which we may perhaps recognize, but can hardly understand. Will such a drama ever reappear? We do not know. In the meantime, all we can do is pick together the pieces, save and cultivate such lesser successes as have been achieved. *The Infernal Machine* is one of these successes —one of the clues, so to say—to the nature and the possibility of poetic drama in our time.

EUGENE O'NEILL

The Long Voyage Home[1]

CHARACTERS

FAT JOE, *proprietor of a dive*	KATE
NICK, *a crimp*	FREDA
MAG, *a barmaid*	TWO ROUGHS

OLSON
DRISCOLL } *Seamen of the British tramp steamer,*
COCKY   *Glencairn*
IVAN

SCENE: *The bar of a low dive on the London water front—a squalid, dingy room dimly lighted by kerosene lamps placed in brackets on the walls. On the left, the bar. In front of it, a door leading to a side room. On the right, tables with chairs around them. In the rear, a door leading to the street.*

A slovenly barmaid with a stupid face sodden with drink is mopping off the bar. Her arm moves back and forth mechanically and her eyes are half shut as if she were dozing on her feet. At the far end of the bar stands FAT JOE, *the proprietor, a gross bulk of a man with an enormous stomach. His face is red and bloated, his little piggish eyes being almost concealed by rolls of fat. The thick fingers of his big hands are loaded with cheap rings and a gold watch chain of cable-like proportions stretches across his waistcoat.*

At one of the tables, front, a round-shouldered young fellow is sitting, smoking a cigarette. His face is pasty, his mouth weak, his eyes shifting and cruel. He is dressed in a shabby suit, which must have once been cheaply flashy, and wears a muffler and cap.

It is about nine o'clock in the evening.

JOE. [*Yawning.*] Blimey if bizness ain't 'arf slow to-night. I donnow wot's 'appened. The place is like a bleedin' tomb. Where's all the sailor men, I'd like to know? [*Raising his voice.*] Ho, you Nick! [NICK *turns around listlessly.*] Wot's the name o' that wessel put in at the dock below jest arter noon?

NICK. [*Laconically.*] Glencairn—from Bewnezerry. (Buenos Aires.)

JOE. Ain't the crew been paid orf yet?

NICK. Paid orf this arternoon, they tole me. I 'opped on board of 'er an' seen 'em. 'Anded 'em some o' yer cards, I did. They promised faithful they'd 'appen in to-night—them as whose time was done.

JOE. Any two-year men to be paid orf?

[1] Reprinted by permission of Random House, Inc. Copyright 1919, 1946 by Eugene O'Neill.

NICK. Four—three Britishers an' a square-'ead.

JOE. [*Indignantly.*] An' yer popped orf an' left 'em? An' me a-payin' yer to 'elp an' bring 'em in 'ere!

NICK. [*Grumblingly.*] Much you pays me! An' I ain't slingin' me 'ook abaht the 'ole bleedin' town fur now man. See?

JOE. I ain't speakin' on'y fur meself. Down't I always give yer yer share, fair an' square, as man to man?

NICK. [*With a sneer.*] Yus—b'cause you 'as to.

JOE. 'As to? Listen to 'im! There's many'd be 'appy to 'ave your berth, me man!

NICK. Yus? Wot wiv the peelers li'ble to put me away in the bloody jail fur crimpin', an' all?

JOE. [*Indignantly.*] We down't do no crimpin'.

NICK. [*Sarcastically.*] Ho, now! Not arf!

JOE. [*A bit embarrassed.*] Well, on'y a bit now an' agen when there ain't no reg'lar trade. [*To hide his confusion he turns to the barmaid angrily. She is still mopping off the bar, her chin on her breast, half-asleep.*] 'Ere, me gel, we've 'ad enough o' that. You been a-moppin', an' a-moppin', an' a-moppin' the blarsted bar fur a 'ole 'our. 'Op it aht o' this! You'd fair guv a bloke the shakes a-watchin' yer.

MAG. [*Beginning to sniffle.*] Ow, you do frighten me when you 'oller at me, Joe. I ain't a bad gel, I ain't. Gawd knows I tries to do me best fur you. [*She bursts into a tempest of sobs.*]

JOE. [*Roughly.*] Stop yer grizzlin'! An' 'op it aht of 'ere!

NICK. [*Chuckling.*] She's drunk, Joe. Been 'ittin' the gin, eh, Mag?

MAG. [*Ceases crying at once and turns on him furiously.*] You little crab, you! Orter wear a muzzle, you ort! A-openin' of your ugly mouth to a 'onest woman what ain't never done you no 'arm. [*Commencing to sob again.*] H'abusin' me like a dawg cos I'm sick an' orf me oats, an' all.

JOE. Orf yer go, me gel! Go hupstairs and 'ave a sleep. I'll wake yer if I wants yer. An' wake the two gels when yer goes hup. It's 'arpas' nine an' time as some one was a-comin' in, tell 'em. D'yer 'ear me?

MAG. [*Stumbling around the bar to the door on left—sobbing.*] Yus, yus, I 'ears you. Gawd knows wot's goin' to 'appen to me, I'm that sick. Much you cares if I dies, down't you? [*She goes out.*]

JOE. [*Still brooding over* NICK's *lack of diligence—after a pause.*] Four two-year men paid orf wiv their bloody pockets full o' sovereigns—an' yer lorst 'em. [*He shakes his head sorrowfully.*]

NICK. [*Impatiently.*] Stow it! They promised faithful they'd come, I tells yer. They'll be walkin' in in 'arf a mo'. There's lots o' time yet. [*In a low voice.*] 'Ave yer got the drops? We might wanter use 'em.

JOE. [*Taking a small bottle from behind the bar.*] Yus; 'ere it is.

NICK. [*With satisfaction.*] Righto! [*His shifty eyes peer about the room searchingly. Then he beckons to* JOE, *who comes over to the table and sits down*.] Reason I arst yer about the drops was 'cause I seen the capt'n of the Amindra this arternoon.

JOE.   The Amindra? Wot ship is that?

NICK.   Bloody windjammer—skys'l yarder—full rigged—painted white—been layin' at the dock above 'ere fur a month. You knows 'er.

JOE.   Ho, yus. I knows now.

NICK.   The capt'n says as 'e wants a man special bad—ter-night. They sails at daybreak termorrer.

JOE.   There's plenty o' 'ands lyin' abaht waitin' fur ships, I should fink.

NICK.   Not fur this ship, ole buck. The capt'n an' mate are bloody slave-drivers, an' they're bound down round the 'Orn. They 'arf starved the 'ands on the last trip 'ere, an' no one'll dare ship on 'er. [*After a pause*.] I promised the capt'n faithful I'd get 'im one, and ter-night.

JOE. [*Doubtfully*.]   An' 'ow are yer goin' to git 'im?

NICK. [*With a wink*.]   I was thinkin' as one of 'em from the Glencairn'd do —them as was paid orf an' is comin' 'ere.

JOE. [*With a grin*.]   It'd be a good 'aul, that's the troof. [*Frowning*.] If they comes 'ere.

NICK.   They'll come, an' they'll all be rotten drunk, wait an' see. [*There is the noise of loud, boisterous singing from the street*.] Sounds like 'em, now. [*He opens the street door and looks out*.] Gawd blimey if it ain't the four of 'em! [*Turning to* JOE *in triumph*.] Naw, what d'yer say? They're lookin' for the place. I'll go aht an' tell 'em. [*He goes out.* JOE *gets into position behind the bar, assuming his most oily smile. A moment later the door is opened, admitting* DRISCOLL, COCKY, IVAN *and* OLSON. DRISCOLL *is a tall, powerful Irishman;* COCKY, *a wizened runt of a man with a straggling gray mustache;* IVAN, *a hulking oaf of a peasant;* OLSON, *a stocky, middle-aged Swede with round, childish blue eyes. The first three are all very drunk, especially* IVAN, *who is managing his legs with difficulty.* OLSON *is perfectly sober. All are dressed in their ill-fitting shore clothes and look very uncomfortable.* DRISCOLL *has unbuttoned his stiff collar and its ends stick out sideways. He has lost his tie.* NICK *slinks into the room after them and sits down at a table in rear. The seamen come to the table, front*.]

JOE. [*With affected heartiness*.]   Ship ahoy, mates! 'Appy to see yer 'ome safe an' sound.

DRISCOLL. [*Turns round, swaying a bit, and peers at him across the bar*.] So ut's you, is ut? [*He looks about the place with an air of recognition*.] 'An the same damn rat's-hole, sure enough. I remimber foive or six years back 'twas here I was sthripped av me last shillin' whin I was aslape. [*With sudden fury*.] God stiffen ye, come none av your dog's thricks on me this trip or I'll—— [*He shakes his fist at* JOE.]

JOE. [*Hastily interrupting*.]   Yer must be mistaiken. This is a 'onest place, this is.

COCKY. [*Derisively*.]   Ho, yus! An' you're a bleedin' angel, I s'pose?

IVAN. [*Vaguely taking off his derby hat and putting it on again—plaintively.*]
I don' li-ike dis place.

DRISCOLL. [*Going over to the bar—as genial as he was furious a moment before.*] Well, no matter, 'tis all past an' gone an' forgot. I'm not the man to
be holdin' harrd feelin's on me first night ashore, an' me dhrunk as a lord.
[*He holds out his hand, which* JOE *takes very gingerly.*] We'll all be havin' a
dhrink, I'm thinkin'. Whiskey for the three av us—*Irish* whiskey!

COCKY. [*Mockingly.*] An' a glarse o' ginger beer fur our blarsted love-child
'ere. [*He jerks his thumb at* OLSON.]

OLSON. [*With a good-natured grin.*] I bane a good boy dis night, for one
time.

DRISCOLL. [*Bellowing, and pointing to* NICK *as* JOE *brings the drinks to the
table.*] An' see what that crimpin' son av a crimp'll be wantin'—an' have
your own pleasure. [*He pulls a sovereign out of his pocket and slams it on the
bar.*]

NICK. Guv me a pint o' beer, Joe. [JOE *draws the beer and takes it down
to the far end of the bar.* NICK *comes over to get it and* JOE *gives him a significant wink and nods toward the door on the left.* NICK *signals back that he
understands.*]

COCKY. [*Drink in hand—impatiently.*] I'm that bloody dry! [*Lifting his
glass to* DRISCOLL.] Cheero, ole dear, cheero!

DRISCOLL. [*Pocketing his change without looking at it.*] A toast for ye:
Hell roast that divil av a bo'sun! [*He drinks.*]

COCKY. Righto! Gawd strike 'im blind! [*He drains his glass.*]

IVAN. [*Half-asleep.*] Dot's gude. [*He tosses down his drink in one gulp.*
OLSON *sips his ginger ale.* NICK *takes a swallow of his beer and then comes
round the bar and goes out the door on left.*]

COCKY. [*Producing a sovereign.*] Ho there, you Fatty! Guv us another!

JOE. The saime, mates?

COCKY. Yus.

DRISCOLL. No, ye scut! I'll be havin' a pint av beer. I'm dhry as a loime
kiln.

IVAN. [*Suddenly getting to his feet in a befuddled manner and nearly upsetting the table.*] I don' li-ike dis place! I wan' see girls—plenty girls. [*Pathetically.*] I don't li-ike dis place. I wan' dance with girl.

DRISCOLL. [*Pushing him back on his chair with a thud.*] Shut up, ye
Rooshan baboon! A foine Romeo you'd make in your condishun. [IVAN *blub-
bers some incoherent protest—then suddenly falls asleep.*]

JOE. [*Bringing the drinks—looks at* OLSON.] An' you, matey?

OLSON. [*Shaking his head.*] Noting dis time, thank you.

COCKY. [*Mockingly.*] A-saivin' of 'is money, 'e is! Goin' back to 'ome an'
mother. Goin' to buy a bloomin' farm an' punch the blarsted dirt, that's wot
'e is! [*Spitting disgustedly.*] There's a funny bird of a sailor man for yer, Gawd
blimey!

OLSON. [*Wearing the same good-natured grin.*]   Yust what I like, Cocky. I wus on farm long time when I wus kid.

DRISCOLL.   Lave him alone, ye bloody insect! 'Tis a foine sight to see a man wid some sense in his head instead av a damn fool the loike av us. I only wisht I'd a mother alive to call me own. I'd not be dhrunk in this divil's hole this minute, maybe.

COCKY. [*Commencing to weep dolorously.*]   Ow, down't talk, Drisc! I can't bear to 'ear you. I ain't never 'ad no mother, I ain't——

DRISCOLL.   Shut up, ye ape, an' don't be makin' that squealin'. If ye cud see your ugly face, wid the big red nose av ye all screwed up in a knot, ye'd never shed a tear the rist av your loife. [*Roaring into song.*] We ar-re the byes av We-e-exford who fought wid hearrt an' hand! [*Speaking.*] To hell wid Ulster! [*He drinks and the others follow his example.*] An' I'll strip to any man in the city av London won't dhrink to that toast. [*He glares truculently at* JOE, *who immediately downs his beer.* NICK *enters again from the door on the left and comes up to* JOE *and whispers in his ear. The latter nods with satisfaction.*]

DRISCOLL. [*Glowering at them.*]   What divil's thrick are ye up to now, the two av ye? [*He flourishes a brawny fist.*] Play fair wid us or ye deal wid me!

JOE. [*Hastily.*]   No trick, shipmate! May Gawd kill me if that ain't troof!

NICK. [*Indicating* IVAN, *who is snoring.*]   On'y your mate there was arskin' fur gels an' I thought as 'ow yer'd like 'em to come dawhn and 'ave a wet wiv yer.

JOE. [*With a smirking wink.*]   Pretty, 'olesome gels they be, ain't they, Nick?

NICK.   Yus.

COCKY.   Aar! I knows the gels you 'as, not 'arf! They'd fair blind yer, they're that 'omely. None of yer bloomin' gels fur me, ole Fatty. Me an' Drisc knows a place, down't we, Drisc?

DRISCOLL.   Divil a lie, we do. An' we'll be afther goin' there in a minute. There's music there an' a bit av a dance to liven a man.

JOE.   Nick, 'ere, can play yer a tune, can't yer, Nick?

NICK.   Yus.

JOE.   An' yer can 'ave a dance in the side room 'ere.

DRISCOLL.   Hurroo! Now you're talkin'. [*The two women,* FREDA *and* KATE, *enter from the left.* FREDA *is a little, sallow-faced blonde.* KATE *is stout and dark.*]

COCKY. [*In a loud aside to* DRISCOLL.]   Gawd blimey, look at 'em! Ain't they 'orrible? [*The women come forward to the table, wearing their best set smiles.*]

FREDA. [*In a raspy voice.*]   'Ullo, mates.

KATE.   'Ad a good voyage?

DRISCOLL.   Rotten; but no matther. Welcome, as the sayin' is, an' sit down, an' what'll ye be takin' for your thirst? [*To* KATE.] You'll be sittin' by me, darlin'—what's your name?

KATE. [*With a stupid grin.*]   Kate. [*She stands by his chair.*]

DRISCOLL. [*Putting his arm around her.*]   A good Irish name, but you're English by the trim av ye, an' be damned to you. But no matther. Ut's fat ye are, Katy dear, an' I never cud endure skinny wimin. [FREDA *favors him with a viperish glance and sits down by* OLSON.] What'll ye have?

OLSON.   No, Drisc. Dis one bane on me. [*He takes out a roll of notes from his inside pocket and lays one on the table.* JOE, NICK, *and the women look at the money with greedy eyes.* IVAN *gives a particularly violent snore.*]

FREDA.   Waike up your fren'. Gawd, 'ow I 'ates to 'ear snorin'.

DRISCOLL. [*Springing to action, smashes* IVAN'S *derby over his ears.*]   D'you hear the lady talkin' to ye, ye Rooshan swab? [*The only reply to this is a snore.* DRISCOLL *pulls the battered remains of the derby off* IVAN'S *head and smashes it back again.*] Arise an' shine, ye dhrunken swine! [*Another snore. The women giggle.* DRISCOLL *throws the beer left in his glass into* IVAN'S *face. The Russian comes to in a flash, spluttering. There is a roar of laughter.*]

IVAN. [*Indignantly.*]   I tell you—dot's someting I don' li-ike!

COCKY.   Down't waste good beer, Drisc.

IVAN. [*Grumblingly.*]   I tell you—dot is not ri-ight.

DRISCOLL.   Ut's your own doin', Ivan. Ye was moanin' for girrls an' whin they come you sit gruntin' loike a pig in a sty. Have ye no manners? [IVAN *seems to see the women for the first time and grins foolishly.*]

KATE. [*Laughing at him.*]   Cheero, ole chum, 'ows Russha?

IVAN. [*Greatly pleased—putting his hand in his pocket.*]   I buy a drink.

OLSON.   No; dis one bane on me. [*To* JOE.] Hey, you faller!

JOE.   Wot'll it be, Kate?

KATE.   Gin.

FREDA.   Brandy.

DRISCOLL.   An' Irish whiskey for the rist av us—wid the excipshun av our timperance friend, God pity him!

FREDA. [*To* OLSON.]   You ain't drinkin'?

OLSON. [*Half-ashamed.*]   No.

FREDA. [*With a seductive smile.*]   I down't blame yer. You got sense, you 'ave. I on'y tike a nip o' brandy now an' agen fur my 'ealth. [JOE *brings the drinks and* OLSON'S *change.* COCKY *gets unsteadily to his feet and raises his glass in the air.*]

COCKY.   'Ere's a toff toast for yer: The ladies, Gawd— [*He hesitates—then adds in a grudging tone.*]—bless 'em.

KATE. [*With a silly giggle.*]   Oo-er! That wasn't what you was goin' to say, you bad Cocky, you! [*They all drink.*]

DRISCOLL. [*To* NICK.]   Where's the tune ye was promisin' to give us?

NICK.   Come ahn in the side 'ere an' you'll 'ear it.

DRISCOLL. [*Getting up.*]   Come on, all av ye. We'll have a tune an' a dance if I'm not too dhrunk to dance, God help me. [COCKY *and* IVAN *stagger to their feet.* IVAN *can hardly stand. He is leering at* KATE *and snickering to himself in a maudlin fashion. The three, led by* NICK, *go out the door on the left.* KATE *follows them.* OLSON *and* FREDA *remain seated.*]

COCKY. [*Calling over his shoulder.*]   Come on an' dance, Ollie.

OLSON.   Yes, I come. [*He starts to get up. From the side room comes the sound of an accordion and a boisterous whoop from* DRISCOLL, *followed by a heavy stamping of feet.*]

FREDA.   Ow, down't go in there. Stay 'ere an' 'ave a talk wiv me. They're all drunk an' you ain't drinkin'. [*With a smile up into his face.*] I'll think yer don't like me if yer goes in there.

OLSON. [*Confused.*]   You wus wrong, Miss Freda. I don't—I mean I do like you.

FREDA. [*Smiling—puts her hand over his on the table.*]   An' I likes you. Yer a genelman. You don't get drunk an' hinsult poor gels wot 'as a 'ard an' uneppy life.

OLSON. [*Pleased but still more confused—wriggling his feet.*]   I bane drunk many time, Miss Freda.

FREDA.   Then why ain't yer drinkin' now? [*She exchanges a quick, questioning glance with* JOE, *who nods back at her—then she continues persuasively.*] Tell me somethin' abaht yeself.

OLSON. [*With a grin.*]   There ain't noting to say, Miss Freda. I bane poor devil sailor man, dat's all.

FREDA.   Where was you born—Norway? [OLSON *shakes his head.*] Denmark?

OLSON.   No. You guess once more.

FREDA.   Then it must be Sweden.

OLSON.   Yes. I wus born in Stockholm.

FREDA. [*Pretending great delight.*]   Ow, ain't that funny! I was born there, too—in Stockholm.

OLSON. [*Astonished.*]   You wus born in Sweden?

FREDA.   Yes; you wouldn't think it, but it's Gawd's troof. [*She claps her hands delightedly.*]

OLSON. [*Beaming all over.*]   You speak Swedish?

FREDA. [*Trying to smile sadly.*]   Now. Y'see my ole man an' woman come 'ere to England when I was on'y a baby an' they was speakin' English b'fore I was old enough to learn. Sow I never knew Swedish. [*Sadly.*] Wisht I 'ad! [*With a smile.*] We'd 'ave a bloomin' lark of it if I 'ad, wouldn't we?

OLSON.   It sound nice to hear the old talk yust once in a time.

FREDA.   Righto! No place like yer 'ome, I says. Are yer goin' up to—to Stockholm b'fore yer ships away agen?

OLSON.   Yes. I go home from here to Stockholm. [*Proudly.*] As passenger!

FREDA.   An' you'll git another ship up there arter you've 'ad a vacation?

OLSON.   No. I don't never ship on sea no more. I got all sea I want for my life—too much hard work for little money. Yust work, work, work on ship. I don't want more.

FREDA.   Ow, I see. That's why you give up drinkin'.

OLSON.   Yes. [*With a grin.*] If I drink I yust get drunk and spend all money.

FREDA.   But if you ain't gointer be a sailor no more, what'll yer do? You been a sailor all yer life, ain't yer?

OLSON.   No. I work on farm till I am eighteen. I like it, too—it's nice—work on farm.

FREDA.   But ain't Stockholm a city same's London? Ain't no farms there, is there?

OLSON.   We live—my brother and mother live—my father iss dead—on farm yust a little way from Stockholm. I have plenty money, now. I go back with two years' pay and buy more land yet; work on farm. [*Grinning.*] No more sea, no more bum grub, no more storms—yust nice work.

FREDA.   Ow, ain't that luv'ly! I s'pose you'll be gittin' married, too?

OLSON.   [*Very much confused.*]   I don't know. I like to, if I find nice girl, maybe.

FREDA.   Ain't yer got some gel back in Stockholm? I bet yer 'as.

OLSON.   No. I got nice girl once before I go on sea. But I go on ship, and I don't come back, and she marry other faller. [*He grins sheepishly.*]

FREDA.   Well, it's nice for yer to be goin' 'ome, anyway.

OLSON.   Yes. I tank so. [*There is a crash from the room on left and the music abruptly stops. A moment later* COCKY *and* DRISCOLL *appear, supporting the inert form of* IVAN *between them. He is in the last stage of intoxication, unable to move a muscle.* NICK *follows them and sits down at the table in rear.*]

DRISCOLL.   [*As they zigzag up to the bar.*]   Ut's dead he is, I'm thinkin', for he's as limp as a blarsted corpse.

COCKY.   [*Puffing.*]   Gawd, 'e ain't 'arf 'eavy!

DRISCOLL.   [*Slapping* IVAN's *face with his free hand.*]   Wake up, ye divil, ye. Ut's no use. Gabriel's trumpet itself cudn't rouse him. [*To* JOE.] Give us a dhrink for I'm perishing wid the thirst. 'Tis harrd worrk, this.

JOE.   Whiskey?

DRISCOLL.   Irish whiskey, ye swab. [*He puts down a coin on the bar.* JOE *serves* COCKY *and* DRISCOLL. *They drink and then swerve over to* OLSON's *table.*]

OLSON.   Sit down and rest for time, Drisc.

DRISCOLL.   No, Ollie, we'll be takin' this lad home to his bed. Ut's late for wan so young to be out in the night. An' I'd not trust him in this hole as dhrunk as he is, an' him wid a full pay day on him. [*Shaking his fist at* JOE.] Oho, I know your games, me sonny bye!

JOE.   [*With an air of grievance.*]   There yer goes again—hinsultin' a 'onest man!

COCKY.   Ho, listen to 'im! Guv 'im a shove in the marf, Drisc.

OLSON.   [*Anxious to avoid a fight—getting up.*]   I help you take Ivan to boarding house.

FREDA. [*Protestingly.*]   Ow, you ain't gointer leave me, are yer? An' we 'avin' sech a nice talk, an' all.

DRISCOLL. [*With a wink.*]   Ye hear what the lady says, Ollie. Ye'd best stay here, me timperance lady's man. An' we need no help. 'Tis only a bit av a way and we're two strong men if we are dhrunk. Ut's no hard shift to take the remains home. But ye can open the door for us, Ollie. [OLSON *goes to the door and opens it.*] Come on, Cocky, an' don't be fallin' aslape yourself. [*They lurch toward the door. As they go out* DRISCOLL *shouts back over his shoulder.*] We'll be comin' back in a short time, surely. So wait here for us, Ollie.

OLSON.   All right. I wait here, Drisc. [*He stands in the doorway uncertainly.* JOE *makes violent signs to* FREDA *to bring him back. She goes over and puts her arm around* OLSON's *shoulder.* JOE *motions to* NICK *to come to the bar. They whisper together excitedly.*]

FREDA. [*Coaxingly.*]   You ain't gointer leave me, are yer, dearie? [*Then irritably.*] Fur Gawd's sake, shet that door! I'm fair freezin' to death wiv the fog. [OLSON *comes to himself with a start and shuts the door.*]

OLSON. [*Humbly.*]   Excuse me, Miss Freda.

FREDA. [*Leading him back to the table—coughing.*]   Buy me a drink o' brandy, will yer? I'm sow cold.

OLSON.   All you want, Miss Freda, all you want. [*To* JOE, *who is still whispering instructions to* NICK.] Hey, Yoe! Brandy for Miss Freda. [*He lays a coin on the table.*]

JOE.   Righto! [*He pours out her drink and brings it to the table.*] 'Avin' somethink yeself, shipmate?

OLSON.   No. I don't tank so. [*He points to his glass with a grin.*] Dis iss only belly-wash, no? [*He laughs.*]

JOE. [*Hopefully.*]   'Ave a man's drink.

OLSON.   I would like to—but no. If I drink one I want drink one tousand. [*He laughs again.*]

FREDA. [*Responding to a vicious nudge from* JOE's *elbow.*]   Ow, tike somethin'. I ain't gointer drink all be meself.

OLSON.   Den give me a little yinger beer—small one. [JOE *goes back of the bar, making a sign to* NICK *to go to their table.* NICK *does so and stands so that the sailor cannot see what* JOE *is doing.*]

NICK. [*To make talk.*]   Where's yer mates popped orf ter? [JOE *pours the contents of the little bottle into* OLSON's *glass of ginger beer.*]

OLSON.   Dey take Ivan, dat drunk faller, to bed. They come back. [JOE *brings* OLSON's *drink to the table and sets it before him.*]

JOE. [*To* NICK—*angrily.*]   'Op it, will yer? There ain't no time to be dawdlin'. See? 'Urry!

NICK.   Down't worry, ole bird, I'm orf. [*He hurries out the door.* JOE *returns to his place behind the bar.*]

OLSON. [*After a pause—worriedly.*]   I tank I should go after dem. Cocky iss very drunk, too, and Drisc——

FREDA.   Aar! The big Irish is all right. Don't yer 'ear 'im say as 'ow they'd surely come back 'ere, an' fur you to wait fur 'em?

OLSON.   Yes; but if dey don't come soon I tank I go see if dey are in boarding house all right.

FREDA.   Where is the boardin' 'ouse?

OLSON.   Yust little way back from street here.

FREDA.   You stayin' there, too?

OLSON.   Yes—until steamer sail for Stockholm—in two day.

FREDA. [*She is alternately looking at* JOE *and feverishly trying to keep* OLSON *talking so he will forget about going away after the others.*]   Yer mother won't be arf glad to see yer agen, will she? [OLSON *smiles.*] Does she know yer comin'?

OLSON.   No, I tought I would yust give her surprise. I write to her from Bonos Eres but I don't tell her I come home.

FREDA.   Must be old, ain't she, yer old lady?

OLSON.   She iss eighty-two. [*He smiles reminiscently.*] You know, Miss Freda, I don't see my mother or my brother in—let me tank— [*He counts laboriously on his fingers.*] must be more than ten year. I write once in while and she write many time; and my brother he write me, too. My mother say in all letter I should come home right away. My brother he write same ting, too. He want me to help him on farm. I write back always I come soon; and I mean all time to go back home at end of voyage. But I come ashore, I take one drink, I take many drinks, I get drunk, I spend all money, I have to ship away for other voyage. So dis time I say to myself: Don't drink one drink, Ollie, or, sure, you don't get home. And I want go home dis time. I feel homesick for farm and to see my people again. [*He smiles.*] Yust like little boy, I feel homesick. Dat's why I don't drink noting to-night but dis—belly-wash! [*He roars with childish laughter, then suddenly becomes serious.*] You know, Miss Freda, my mother get very old, and I want see her. She might die and I would never——

FREDA. [*Moved a lot in spite of herself.*]   Ow, don't talk like that! I jest 'ates to 'ear any one speakin' abaht dyin'. [*The door to the street is opened and* NICK *enters, followed by two rough-looking, shabbily-dressed men, wearing mufflers, with caps pulled down over their eyes. They sit at the table nearest to the door.* JOE *brings them three beers, and there is a whispered consultation, with many glances in the direction of* OLSON.]

OLSON. [*Starting to get up—worriedly.*]   I tank I go round to boarding house. I tank someting go wrong with Drisc and Cocky.

FREDA.   Ow, down't go. They kin take care of theyselves. They ain't babies. Wait 'arf a mo'. You ain't 'ad yer drink yet.

JOE. [*Coming hastily over to the table, indicates the men in the rear with a jerk of his thumb.*]   One of them blokes wants yer to 'ave a wet wiv 'im.

FREDA.   Righto! [*To* OLSON.] Let's drink this. [*She raises her glass. He does the same.*] 'Ere's a toast fur yer: Success to yer bloomin' farm an' may yer live long an' 'appy on it. Skoal! [*She tosses down her brandy. He swallows half his glass of ginger beer and makes a wry face.*]

OLSON.   Skoal! [*He puts down his glass.*]

FREDA.   [*With feigned indignation.*]   Down't yer like my toast?

OLSON.   [*Grinning.*]   Yes. It iss very kind, Miss Freda.

FREDA.   Then drink it all like I done.

OLSON.   Well—— [*He gulps down the rest.*] Dere! [*He laughs.*]

FREDA.   Done like a sport!

ONE OF THE ROUGHS. [*With a laugh.*]   Amindra, ahoy!

NICK.   [*Warningly.*]   Sssshh!

OLSON.   [*Turns around in his chair.*]   Amindra? Iss she in port? I sail on her once long time ago—three mast, full rig, skys'l yarder? Iss dat ship you mean?

THE ROUGH. [*Grinning.*]   Yus; right you are.

OLSON.   [*Angrily.*]   I know dat damn ship—worst ship dat sail to sea. Rotten grub and dey make you work all time—and the Captain and Mate wus Blue-nose devils. No sailor who know anyting ever ship on her. Where iss she bound from here?

THE ROUGH.   Round Cape 'Orn—sails at daybreak.

OLSON.   Py yingo, I pity poor fallers make dat trip round Cape Stiff dis time year. I bet you some of dem never see port once again. [*He passes his hand over his eyes in a dazed way. His voice grows weaker.*] Py golly, I feel dizzy. All the room go round and round like I wus drunk. [*He gets weakly to his feet.*] Good night, Miss Freda. I bane feeling sick. Tell Drisc—I go home. [*He takes a step forward and suddenly collapses over a chair, rolls to the floor, and lies there unconscious.*]

JOE.   [*From behind the bar.*]   Quick, nawh! [NICK *darts forward with* JOE *following.* FREDA *is already beside the unconscious man and has taken the roll of money from his inside pocket. She strips off a note furtively and shoves it into her bosom, trying to conceal her action, but* JOE *sees her. She hands the roll to* JOE, *who pockets it.* NICK *goes through all the other pockets and lays a handful of change on the table.*]

JOE.   [*Impatiently.*]   'Urry, 'urry, can't yer? The other blokes'll be 'ere in 'arf a mo'. [*The two roughs come forward.*] 'Ere, you two, tike 'im in under the arms like 'e was drunk. [*They do so.*] Tike 'im to the Amindra—yer knows that, don't yer?—two docks above. Nick'll show yer. An' you, Nick, down't yer leave the bleedin' ship till the capt'n guvs yer this bloke's advance—full month's pay—five quid, d'yer 'ear?

NICK.   I knows me bizness, ole bird. [*They support* OLSON *to the door.*]

THE ROUGH. [*As they are going out.*]   This silly bloke'll 'av the s'prise of 'is life when 'e wakes up on board of 'er. [*They laugh. The door closes behind them.* FREDA *moves quickly for the door on the left but* JOE *gets in her way and stops her.*]

JOE.   [*Threateningly.*]   Guv us what yer took!

FREDA.   Took? I guv yer all 'e 'ad.

JOE.   Yer a liar! I seen yer a-playin' yer sneakin' tricks, but yer can't fool

Joe. I'm too old a 'and. [*Furiously.*] Guv it to me, yer bloody cow! [*He grabs her by the arm.*]

FREDA.   Lemme alone! I ain't got no——

JOE. [*Hits her viciously on the side of the jaw. She crumples up on the floor.*] That'll learn yer! [*He stoops down and fumbles in her bosom and pulls out the banknote, which he stuffs into his pocket with a grunt of satisfaction.* KATE *opens the door on the left and looks in—then rushes to* FREDA *and lifts her head up in her arms.*]

KATE. [*Gently.*]   Pore dearie! [*Looking at* JOE *angrily.*] Been 'ittin' 'er agen, 'ave yer, yer cowardly swine!

JOE.   Yus; an' I'll 'it you, too, if yer don't keep yer marf shut. Tike 'er aht of 'ere! [KATE *carries* FREDA *into the next room.* JOE *goes behind the bar. A moment later the outer door is opened and* DRISCOLL *and* COCKY *come in.*]

DRISCOLL.   Come on, Ollie. [*He suddenly sees that* OLSON *is not there, and turns to* JOE.] Where is ut he's gone to?

JOE. [*With a meaning wink.*]   'E an' Freda went aht t'gether 'bout five minutes past. 'E's fair gone on 'er, 'e is.

DRISCOLL. [*With a grin.*]   Oho, so that's ut, is ut? Who'd think Ollie'd be sich a divil wid the wimmin? 'Tis lucky he's sober or she'd have him stripped to his last ha'penny. [*Turning to* COCKY, *who is blinking sleepily.*] What'll ye have, ye little scut? [*To* JOE.] Give me whiskey, *Irish* whiskey!

GARCIA LORCA

Blood Wedding[1]

Tragedy in Three Acts and Seven Scenes (1933)

CHARACTERS

THE MOTHER	LEONARDO
THE BRIDE	THE BRIDEGROOM
THE MOTHER-IN-LAW	THE BRIDE'S FATHER
LEONARDOS'S WIFE	THE MOON
THE SERVANT WOMAN	DEATH (*as a Beggar Woman*)
THE NEIGHBOR WOMAN	WOODCUTTERS
YOUNG GIRLS	YOUNG MEN

ACT ONE

SCENE 1

A room painted yellow.

BRIDEGROOM. [*Entering.*]   Mother.
MOTHER.   What?
BRIDEGROOM.   I'm going.
MOTHER.   Where?
BRIDEGROOM.   To the vineyard. [*He starts to go.*]
MOTHER.   Wait.
BRIDEGROOM.   You want something?
MOTHER.   Your breakfast, son.
BRIDEGROOM.   Forget it. I'll eat grapes. Give me the knife.
MOTHER.   What for?
BRIDEGROOM. [*Laughing.*]   To cut the grapes with.
MOTHER. [*Muttering as she looks for the knife.*]   Knives, knives. Cursed be all knives, and the scoundrel who invented them.

BRIDEGROOM.   Let's talk about something else.

MOTHER.   And guns and pistols and the smallest little knife—and even hoes and pitchforks.

BRIDEGROOM.   All right.

MOTHER.   Everything that can slice a man's body. A handsome man, full of young life, who goes out to the vineyards or to his own olive groves—his own because he's inherited them . . .

BRIDEGROOM. [Lowering his head.]   Be quiet.

MOTHER.   . . . and then that man doesn't come back. Or if he does come back it's only for someone to cover him over with a palm leaf or a plate of rock salt so he won't bloat. I don't know how you dare carry a knife on your body —or how I let this serpent [She takes a knife from a kitchen chest.] stay in the chest.

BRIDEGROOM.   Have you had your say?

MOTHER.   If I lived to be a hundred I'd talk of nothing else. First your father; to me he smelled like a carnation and I had him for barely three years. Then your brother. Oh, is it right—how can it be—that a small thing like a knife or a pistol can finish off a man—a bull of a man? No, I'll never be quiet. The months pass and the hopelessness of it stings in my eyes and even to the roots of my hair.

BRIDEGROOM. [Forcefully.]   Let's quit this talk!

MOTHER.   No. No. Let's not quit this talk. Can anyone bring me your father back? Or your brother? Then there's the jail. What do they mean, jail? They eat there, smoke there, play music there! My dead men choking with weeds, silent, turning to dust. Two men like two beautiful flowers. The killers in jail, carefree, looking at the mountains.

BRIDEGROOM.   Do you want me to go kill them?

MOTHER.   No . . . If I talk about it it's because . . . Oh, how can I help talking about it, seeing you go out that door? It's . . . I don't like you to carry a knife. It's just that . . . that I wish you wouldn't go out to the fields.

BRIDEGROOM. [Laughing.]   Oh, come now!

MOTHER.   I'd like it if you were a woman. Then you wouldn't be going out to the arroyo now and we'd both of us embroider flounces and little woolly dogs.

BRIDEGROOM. [He puts his arm around his mother and laughs.]   Mother, what if I should take you with me to the vineyards?

MOTHER.   What would an old lady do in the vineyards? Were you going to put me down under the young vines?

BRIDEGROOM. [Lifting her in his arms.]   Old lady, old lady—you little old, little old lady!

MOTHER.   Your father, he used to take me. That's the way with men of good stock; good blood. Your grandfather left a son on every corner. That's what I like. Men, men; wheat, wheat.

BRIDEGROOM.   And I, Mother?

MOTHER.   You, what?

BRIDEGROOM.   Do I need to tell you again?

MOTHER. [*Seriously.*]   Oh!

BRIDEGROOM.   Do you think it's bad?

MOTHER.   No.

BRIDEGROOM.   Well, then?

MOTHER.   I don't really know. Like this, suddenly, it always surprises me. I know the girl is good. Isn't she? Well behaved. Hard working. Kneads her bread, sews her skirts, but even so when I say her name I feel as though someone had hit me on the forehead with a rock.

BRIDEGROOM.   Foolishness.

MOTHER.   More than foolishness. I'll be left alone. Now only you are left me—I hate to see you go.

BRIDEGROOM.   But you'll come with us.

MOTHER.   No. I can't leave your father and brother here alone. I have to go to them every morning and if I go away it's possible one of the Félix family, one of the killers, might die—and they'd bury him next to ours. And that'll never happen! Oh, no! That'll never happen! Because I'd dig them out with my nails and, all by myself, crush them against the wall.

BRIDEGROOM. [*Sternly.*]   There you go again.

MOTHER.   Forgive me. [*Pause.*] How long have you known her?

BRIDEGROOM.   Three years. I've been able to buy the vineyard.

MOTHER.   Three years. She used to have another sweetheart, didn't she?

BRIDEGROOM.   I don't know. I don't think so. Girls have to look at what they'll marry.

MOTHER.   Yes. I looked at nobody. I looked at your father, and when they killed him I looked at the wall in front of me. One woman with one man, and that's all.

BRIDEGROOM.   You know my girl's good.

MOTHER.   I don't doubt it. All the same, I'm sorry not to have known what her mother was like.

BRIDEGROOM.   What difference does it make now?

MOTHER. [*Looking at him.*]   Son.

BRIDEGROOM.   What is it?

MOTHER.   That's true! You're right! When do you want me to ask for her?

BRIDEGROOM. [*Happily.*]   Does Sunday seem all right to you?

MOTHER. [*Seriously.*]   I'll take her the bronze earrings, they're very old—and you buy her . . .

BRIDEGROOM.   You know more about that . . .

MOTHER.   . . . you buy her some open-work stockings—and for you, two suits—three! I have no one but you now!

BRIDEGROOM.   I'm going. Tomorrow I'll go see her.

MOTHER.   Yes, yes—and see if you can make me happy with six grandchildren—or as many as you want, since your father didn't live to give them to me.

BRIDEGROOM.   The first-born for you!

MOTHER.   Yes, but have some girls. I want to embroider and make lace, and be at peace.

BRIDEGROOM.   I'm sure you'll love my wife.

MOTHER.   I'll love her. [*She starts to kiss him but changes her mind.*] Go on. You're too big now for kisses. Give them to your wife. [*Pause. To herself.*] When she is your wife.

BRIDEGROOM.   I'm going.

MOTHER.   And that land around the little mill—work it over. You've not taken good care of it.

BRIDEGROOM.   You're right. I will.

MOTHER.   God keep you. [*The* SON *goes out. The* MOTHER *remains seated—her back to the door. A* NEIGHBOR WOMAN *with a 'kerchief on her head appears in the door.*] Come in.

NEIGHBOR.   How are you?

MOTHER.   Just as you see me.

NEIGHBOR.   I came down to the store and stopped in to see you. We live so far away!

MOTHER.   It's twenty years since I've been up to the top of the street.

NEIGHBOR.   You're looking well.

MOTHER.   You think so?

NEIGHBOR.   Things happen. Two days ago they brought in my neighbor's son with both arms sliced off by the machine. [*She sits down.*]

MOTHER.   Rafael?

NEIGHBOR.   Yes. And there you have him. Many times I've thought your son and mine are better off where they are—sleeping, resting—not running the risk of being left helpless.

MOTHER.   Hush. That's all just something thought up—but no consolation.

NEIGHBOR. [*Sighing.*]   Ay!

MOTHER. [*Sighing.*]   Ay!

[*Pause.*]

NEIGHBOR. [*Sadly.*]   Where's your son?

MOTHER.   He went out.

NEIGHBOR.   He finally bought the vineyard!

MOTHER.   He was lucky.

NEIGHBOR.   Now he'll get married.

MOTHER. [*As though reminded of something, she draws her chair near the* NEIGHBOR.]   Listen.

NEIGHBOR. [*In a confidential manner.*]   Yes. What is it?

MOTHER.   You know my son's sweetheart?

NEIGHBOR.   A good girl!

MOTHER.   Yes, but . . .

NEIGHBOR.   But who knows her really well? There's nobody. She lives out there alone with her father—so far away—fifteen miles from the nearest house. But she's a good girl. Used to being alone.

MOTHER.   And her mother?

NEIGHBOR.   Her mother I *did* know. Beautiful. Her face glowed like a saint's —but I never liked her. She didn't love her husband.

MOTHER.   [*Sternly.*]   Well, what a lot of things certain people know!

NEIGHBOR.   I'm sorry. I didn't mean to offend—but it's true. Now, whether she was decent or not nobody said. That wasn't discussed. She was haughty.

MOTHER.   There you go again!

NEIGHBOR.   You asked me.

MOTHER.   I wish no one knew anything about them—either the live one or the dead one—that they were like two thistles no one even names but cuts off at the right moment.

NEIGHBOR.   You're right. You son is worth a lot.

MOTHER.   Yes—a lot. That's why I look after him. They told me the girl had a sweetheart some time ago.

NEIGHBOR.   She was about fifteen. He's been married two years now—to a cousin of hers, as a matter of fact. But nobody remembers about their engagement.

MOTHER.   How do you remember it?

NEIGHBOR.   Oh, what questions you ask!

MOTHER.   We like to know all about the things that hurt us. Who was the boy?

NEIGHBOR.   Leonardo.

MOTHER.   What Leonardo?

NEIGHBOR.   Leonardo Félix.

MOTHER.   Félix!

NEIGHBOR.   Yes, but—how is Leonardo to blame for anything? He was eight years old when those things happened.

MOTHER.   That's true. But I hear that name—Félix—and it's all the same. [*Muttering.*] Félix, a slimy mouthful. [*She spits.*] It makes me spit—spit so I won't kill!

NEIGHBOR.   Control yourself. What good will it do?

MOTHER.   No good. But you see how it is.

NEIGHBOR.   Don't get in the way of your son's happiness. Don't say any-thing to him. You're old. So am I. It's time for you and me to keep quiet.

MOTHER.   I'll say nothing to him.

NEIGHBOR.   [*Kissing her.*]   Nothing.

MOTHER.   [*Calmly.*]   Such things . . . !

NEIGHBOR.   I'm going. My men will soon be coming in from the fields.

MOTHER.   Have you ever known such a hot sun?

NEIGHBOR. The children carrying water out to the reapers are black with it.
Goodbye, woman.

MOTHER. Goodbye.

[*The* MOTHER *starts toward the door at the left. Halfway there she stops and
slowly crosses herself.*]

Curtain

ACT ONE

SCENE 2

*A room painted rose with copperware and wreaths of common flowers. In the
center of the room is a table with a tablecloth. It is morning.*

LEONARDO'S MOTHER-IN-LAW *sits in one corner holding a child in her arms
and rocking it. His* WIFE *is in the other corner mending stockings.*

MOTHER-IN-LAW.

>   Lullaby, my baby
>   once there was a big horse
>   who didn't like water.
>   The water was black there
>   under the branches.
>   When it reached the bridge
>   it stopped and it sang.
>   Who can say, my baby,
>   what the stream holds
>   with its long tail
>   in its green parlor?

WIFE. [*Softly.*]

>   Carnation, sleep and dream,
>   the horse won't drink from the stream.

MOTHER-IN-LAW.

>   My rose, asleep now lie,
>   the horse is starting to cry.
>   His poor hooves were bleeding,
>   his long mane was frozen,
>   and deep in his eyes
>   stuck a silvery dagger.
>   Down he went to the river,

Oh, down he went down!
And his blood was running,
Oh, more than the water.

WIFE.

Carnation, sleep and dream,
the horse won't drink from the stream.

MOTHER-IN-LAW.

My rose, asleep now lie,
the horse is starting to cry.

WIFE.

He never did touch
the dank river shore
though his muzzle was warm
and with silvery flies.
So, to the hard mountains
he could only whinny
just when the dead stream
covered his throat.
Ay-y-y, for the big horse
who didn't like water!
Ay-y-y, for the snow-wound
big horse of the dawn!

MOTHER-IN-LAW.

Don't come in! Stop him
and close up the window
with branches of dreams
and a dream of branches.

WIFE.

My baby is sleeping.

MOTHER-IN-LAW.

My baby is quiet.

WIFE.

Look, horse, my baby
has him a pillow.

MOTHER-IN-LAW.

His cradle is metal.

WIFE.

His quilt a fine fabric.

MOTHER-IN-LAW.

Lullaby, my baby.

WIFE.

Ay-y-y, for the big horse
who didn't like water!

MOTHER-IN-LAW.

> Don't come near, don't come in!
> Go away to the mountains
> and through the grey valleys,
> that's where your mare is.

WIFE. [*Looking at the baby.*]

> My baby is sleeping.

MOTHER-IN-LAW.

> My baby is resting.

WIFE. [*Softly.*]

> Carnation, sleep and dream,
> the horse won't drink from the stream.

MOTHER-IN-LAW. [*Getting up, very softly.*]

> My rose, asleep now lie
> for the horse is starting to cry.

[*She carries the child out.* LEONARDO *enters.*]

LEONARDO.   Where's the baby?

WIFE.   He's sleeping.

LEONARDO.   Yesterday he wasn't well. He cried during the night.

WIFE.   Today he's like a dahlia. And you? Were you at the blacksmith's?

LEONARDO.   I've just come from there. Would you believe it? For more than two months he's been putting new shoes on the horse and they're always coming off. As far as I can see he pulls them off on the stones.

WIFE.   Couldn't it just be that you use him so much?

LEONARDO.   No. I almost never use him.

WIFE.   Yesterday the neighbors told me they'd seen you on the far side of the plains.

LEONARDO.   Who said that?

WIFE.   The women who gather capers. It certainly surprised me. Was it you?

LEONARDO.   No. What would I be doing there, in that wasteland?

WIFE.   That's what I said. But the horse was streaming sweat.

LEONARDO.   Did you see him?

WIFE.   No. Mother did.

LEONARDO.   Is she with the baby?

WIFE.   Yes. Do you want some lemonade?

LEONARDO.   With good cold water.

WIFE.   And then you didn't come to eat!

LEONARDO.   I was with the wheat weighers. They always hold me up.

WIFE. [*Very tenderly, while she makes the lemonade.*]   Did they pay you a good price?

LEONARDO.   Fair.

WIFE.   I need a new dress and the baby a bonnet with ribbons.

LEONARDO. [*Getting up.*]   I'm going to take a look at him.

WIFE. Be careful. He's asleep.

MOTHER-IN-LAW. [*Coming in.*] Well! Who's been racing the horse that way? He's down there, worn out, his eyes popping from their sockets as though he'd come from the ends of the earth.

LEONARDO. [*Acidly.*] I have.

MOTHER-IN-LAW. Oh, excuse me! He's your horse.

WIFE. [*Timidly.*] He was at the wheat buyers.

MOTHER-IN-LAW. He can burst for all of me!

[*She sits down. Pause.*]

WIFE. Your drink. Is it cold?

LEONARDO. Yes.

WIFE. Did you hear they're going to ask for my cousin?

LEONARDO. When?

WIFE. Tomorrow. The wedding will be within a month. I hope they're going to invite us.

LEONARDO. [*Gravely.*] I don't know.

MOTHER-IN-LAW. His mother, I think, wasn't very happy about the match.

LEONARDO. Well, she may be right. She's a girl to be careful with.

WIFE. I don't like to have you thinking bad things about a good girl.

MOTHER-IN-LAW. [*Meaningfully.*] If he does, it's because he knows her. Didn't you know he courted her for three years?

LEONARDO. But I left her. [*To his* WIFE.] Are you going to cry now? Quit that! [*He brusquely pulls her hands away from her face.*] Let's go see the baby.

[*They go in with their arms around each other. A* GIRL *appears. She is happy. She enters running.*]

GIRL. Señora.

MOTHER-IN-LAW. What is it?

GIRL. The groom came to the store and he's bought the best of everything they had.

MOTHER-IN-LAW. Was he alone?

GIRL. No. With his mother. Stern, tall. [*She imitates her.*] And such extravagance!

MOTHER-IN-LAW. They have money.

GIRL. And they bought some open-work stockings! Oh, such stockings! A woman's dream of stockings! Look: a swallow here, [*She points to her ankle.*] a ship here, [*She points to her calf.*] and here, [*She points to her thigh.*] a rose!

MOTHER-IN-LAW. Child!

GIRL. A rose with the seeds and the stem! Oh! All in silk.

MOTHER-IN-LAW. Two rich families are being brought together.

[LEONARDO *and his* WIFE *appear.*]

GIRL. I came to tell you what they're buying.

LEONARDO. [*Loudly.*] We don't care.

WIFE. Leave her alone.

MOTHER-IN-LAW. Leonardo, it's not that important.

GIRL.   Please excuse me. [*She leaves, weeping.*]

MOTHER-IN-LAW.   Why do you always have to make trouble with people?

LEONARDO.   I didn't ask for your opinion. [*He sits down.*]

MOTHER-IN-LAW.   Very well.

[*Pause.*]

WIFE. [*To* LEONARDO.]   What's the matter with you? What idea've you got boiling there inside your head? Don't leave me like this, not knowing anything.

LEONARDO.   Stop that.

WIFE.   No. I want you to look at me and tell me.

LEONARDO.   Let me alone. [*He rises.*]

WIFE.   Where are you going, love?

LEONARDO. [*Sharply.*]   Can't you shut up?

MOTHER-IN-LAW. [*Energetically, to her daughter.*]   Be quiet! [LEONARDO *goes out.*] The baby!

[*She goes into the bedroom and comes out again with the baby in her arms. The* WIFE *has remained standing, unmoving.*]

MOTHER-IN-LAW.

> His poor hooves were bleeding,
> his long mane was frozen,
> and deep in his eyes
> stuck a silvery dagger.
> Down he went to the river,
> Oh, down he went down!
> And his blood was running,
> Oh, more than the water.

WIFE. [*Turning slowly, as though dreaming.*]

> Carnation, sleep and dream,
> the horse is drinking from the stream.

MOTHER-IN-LAW.

> My rose, asleep now lie
> the horse is starting to cry.

WIFE.

> Lullaby, my baby.

MOTHER-IN-LAW.

> Ay-y-y, for the big horse
> who didn't like water!

WIFE. [*Dramatically.*]

> Don't come near, don't come in!
> Go away to the mountains!
> Ay-y-y, for the snow-wound,
> big horse of the dawn!

MOTHER-IN-LAW. [*Weeping.*]

> My baby is sleeping . . . .

WIFE. [*Weeping, as she slowly moves closer.*]

My baby is resting . . . .

MOTHER-IN-LAW.

    Carnation, sleep and dream,
    the horse won't drink from the stream.

WIFE. [*Weeping, and leaning on the table.*]

    My rose, asleep now lie,
    the horse is starting to cry.

Curtain

ACT ONE

SCENE 3

Interior of the cave where The BRIDE *lives. At the back is a cross of large rose colored flowers. The round doors have lace curtains with rose colored ties. Around the walls, which are of a white and hard material, are round fans, blue jars, and little mirrors.*

SERVANT.   Come right in . . . [*She is very affable, full of humble hypocrisy. The* BRIDEGROOM *and his* MOTHER *enter. The* MOTHER *is dressed in black satin and wears a lace mantilla; the* BRIDEGROOM *in black corduroy with a great golden chain.*] Won't you sit down? They'll be right here.

[*She leaves. The* MOTHER *and* SON *are left sitting motionless as statues. Long pause.*]

MOTHER.   Did you wear the watch?

BRIDEGROOM.   Yes. [*He takes it out and looks at it.*]

MOTHER.   We have to be back on time. How far away these people live!

BRIDEGROOM.   But this is good land.

MOTHER.   Good; but much too lonesome. A four hour trip and not one house, not one tree.

BRIDEGROOM.   This is the wasteland.

MOTHER.   Your father would have covered it with trees.

BRIDEGROOM.   Without water?

MOTHER.   He would have found some. In the three years we were married he planted ten cherry trees, [*Remembering.*] those three walnut trees by the mill, a whole vineyard and a plant called Jupiter which had scarlet flowers—but it dried up.

[*Pause.*]

BRIDEGROOM. [*Referring to the* BRIDE.]   She must be dressing.

[*The* BRIDE'S FATHER *enters. He is very old, with shining white hair. His head is bowed. The* MOTHER *and the* BRIDEGROOM *rise. They shake hands in silence.*]

FATHER. Was it a long trip?

MOTHER. Four hours.

[*They sit down.*]

FATHER. You must have come the longest way.

MOTHER. I'm too old to come along the cliffs by the river.

BRIDEGROOM. She gets dizzy.

[*Pause.*]

FATHER. A good hemp harvest.

BRIDEGROOM. A really good one.

FATHER. When I was young this land didn't even grow hemp. We've had to punish it, even weep over it, to make it give us anything useful.

MOTHER. But now it does. Don't complain. I'm not here to ask you for anything.

FATHER. [*Smiling.*] You're richer than I. Your vineyards are worth a fortune. Each young vine a silver coin. But—do you know?—what bothers me is that our lands are separated. I like to have everything together. One thorn I have in my heart, and that's the little orchard there, stuck in between my fields—and they won't sell it to me for all the gold in the world.

BRIDEGROOM. That's the way it always is.

FATHER. If we could just take twenty teams of oxen and move your vineyards over here, and put them down on that hillside, how happy I'd be!

MOTHER. But why?

FATHER. What's mine is hers and what's yours is his. That's why. Just to see it all together. How beautiful it is to bring things together!

BRIDEGROOM. And it would be less work.

MOTHER. When I die, you could sell ours and buy here, right alongside.

FATHER. Sell, sell? Bah! Buy, my friend, buy everything. If I had had sons I would have bought all this mountainside right up to the part with the stream. It's not good land, but strong arms can make it good, and since no people pass by, they don't steal your fruit and you can sleep in peace.

[*Pause.*]

MOTHER. You know what I'm here for.

FATHER. Yes.

MOTHER. And?

FATHER It seems all right to me. They have talked it over.

MOTHER. My son has money and knows how to manage it.

FATHER. My daughter too.

MOTHER. My son is handsome. He's never known a woman. His good name cleaner than a sheet spread out in the sun.

FATHER. No need to tell you about my daughter. At three, when the morning star shines, she prepares the bread. She never talks: soft as wool, she embroiders all kinds of fancy work and she can cut a strong cord with her teeth.

MOTHER. God bless her house.

FATHER. May God bless it.

[*The* SERVANT *appears with two trays. One with drinks and the other with sweets.*]

MOTHER. [*To the* SON.]   When would you like the wedding?

BRIDEGROOM.   Next Thursday.

FATHER.   The day on which she'll be exactly twenty-two years old.

MOTHER.   Twenty-two! My oldest son would be that age if he were alive. Warm and manly as he was, he'd be living now if men hadn't invented knives.

FATHER.   One mustn't think about that.

MOTHER.   Every minute. Always a hand on your breast.

FATHER.   Thursday, then? Is that right?

BRIDEGROOM.   That's right.

FATHER.   You and I and the bridal couple will go in a carriage to the church which is very far from here; the wedding party on the carts and horses they'll bring with them.

MOTHER.   Agreed.

[*The* SERVANT *passes through.*]

FATHER.   Tell her she may come in now. [*To the* MOTHER.] I shall be much pleased if you like her.

[*The* BRIDE *appears. Her hands fall in a modest pose and her head is bowed.*]

MOTHER.   Come here. Are you happy?

BRIDE.   Yes, señora.

FATHER.   You shouldn't be so solemn. After all, she's going to be your mother.

BRIDE.   I'm happy. I've said "yes" because I wanted to.

MOTHER.   Naturally. [*She takes her by the chin.*] Look at me.

FATHER.   She resembles my wife in every way.

MOTHER.   Yes? What a beautiful glance! Do you know what it is to be married, child?

BRIDE. [*Seriously.*]   I do.

MOTHER.   A man, some children and a wall two yards thick for everything else.

BRIDEGROOM.   Is anything else needed?

MOTHER.   No. Just that you all live—that's it! Live long!

BRIDE.   I'll know how to keep my word.

MOTHER.   Here are some gifts for you.

BRIDE.   Thank you.

FATHER.   Shall we have something?

MOTHER.   Nothing for me. [*To the* SON.] But you?

BRIDEGROOM.   Yes. thank you.

[*He takes one sweet, the* BRIDE *another.*]

FATHER. [*To the* BRIDEGROOM.] Wine?

MOTHER.   He doesn't touch it.

FATHER.   All the better.

[*Pause. All are standing.*]

BRIDEGROOM. [*To the* BRIDE.]   I'll come tomorrow.

BRIDE.   What time?

BRIDEGROOM.   Five.

BRIDE.   I'll be waiting for you.

BRIDEGROOM.   When I leave your side I feel a great emptiness, and something like a knot in my throat.

BRIDE.   When you are my husband you won't have it any more.

BRIDEGROOM.   That's what I tell myself.

MOTHER.   Come. The sun doesn't wait. [*To the* FATHER.] Are we agreed on everything?

FATHER.   Agreed.

MOTHER. [*To the* SERVANT.]   Goodbye, woman.

SERVANT.   God go with you!

[*The* MOTHER *kisses the* BRIDE *and they begin to leave in silence.*]

MOTHER. [*At the door.*]   Goodbye, daughter.

[*The* BRIDE *answers with her hand.*]

FATHER.   I'll go out with you.

[*They leave.*]

SERVANT.   I'm bursting to see the presents.

BRIDE. [*Sharply.*]   Stop that!

SERVANT.   Oh, child, show them to me.

BRIDE.   I don't want to.

SERVANT.   At least the stockings. They say they're all open work. Please!

BRIDE.   I said no.

SERVANT.   Well, my Lord. All right then. It looks as if you didn't want to get married.

BRIDE. [*Biting her hand in anger.*]   Ay-y-y!

SERVANT.   Child, child! What's the matter with you? Are you sorry to give up your queen's life? Don't think of bitter things. Have you any reason to? None. Let's look at the presents.

[*She takes the box.*]

BRIDE. [*Holding her by the wrists.*]   Let go.

SERVANT.   Ay-y-y, girl!

BRIDE.   Let go, I said.

SERVANT.   You're stronger than a man.

BRIDE.   Haven't I done a man's work? I wish I were.

SERVANT.   Don't talk like that.

BRIDE.   Quiet, I said. Let's talk about something else.

[*The light is fading from the stage. Long pause.*]

SERVANT.   Did you hear a horse last night?

BRIDE.   What time?

SERVANT.   Three.

BRIDE.   It might have been a stray horse—from the herd.

SERVANT.   No. It carried a rider.

BRIDE.   How do you know?

SERVANT.   Because I saw him. He was standing by your window. It shocked me greatly.

BRIDE.   Maybe it was my fiancé. Sometimes he comes by at that time.

SERVANT.   No.

BRIDE.   You saw him?

SERVANT.   Yes.

BRIDE.   Who was it?

SERVANT.   It was Leonardo.

BRIDE.   [*Strongly.*]   Liar! You liar! Why should he come here?

SERVANT.   He came.

BRIDE.   Shut up! Shut your cursed mouth.

[*The sound of a horse is heard.*]

SERVANT. [*At the window.*]   Look. Lean out. Was it Leonardo?

BRIDE.   It was!

Quick curtain

ACT TWO

SCENE 1

The entrance hall of the BRIDE's *house. A large door in the back. It is night. The* BRIDE *enters wearing ruffled white petticoats full of laces and embroidered bands, and a sleeveless white bodice. The* SERVANT *is dressed the same way.*

SERVANT.   I'll finish combing your hair out here.

BRIDE.   It's too warm to stay in there.

SERVANT.   In this country it doesn't even cool off at dawn.

[*The* BRIDE *sits on a low chair and looks into a little hand mirror. The* SERVANT *combs her hair.*]

BRIDE.   My mother came from a place with lots of trees—from a fertile country.

SERVANT.   And she was so happy!

BRIDE.   But she wasted away here.

SERVANT.   Fate.

BRIDE.   As we're all wasting away here. The very walls give off heat. Ay-y-y! Don't pull so hard.

SERVANT.   I'm only trying to fix this wave better. I want it to fall over your forehead. [*The* BRIDE *looks at herself in the mirror.*] How beautiful you are! Ay-y-y! [*She kisses her passionately.*]

BRIDE. [*Seriously.*] Keep right on combing.

SERVANT. [*Combing.*]   Oh, lucky you—going to put your arms around a man; and kiss him; and feel his weight.

BRIDE.   Hush.

SERVANT.   And the best part will be when you'll wake up and you'll feel him at your side and when he caresses your shoulders with his breath, like a little nightingale's feather.

BRIDE. [*Sternly.*]   Will you be quiet.

SERVANT.   But, child! What *is* a wedding? A wedding is just that and nothing more. Is it the sweets—or the bouquets of flowers? No. It's a shining bed and a man and a woman.

BRIDE.   But you shouldn't talk about it.

SERVANT.   Oh, *that's* something else again. But fun enough too.

BRIDE.   Or bitter enough.

SERVANT.   I'm going to put the orange blossoms on from here to here, so the wreath will shine out on top of your hair. [*She tries on the sprigs of orange blossom.*]

BRIDE. [*Looking at herself in the mirror.*]   Give it to me. [*She takes the wreath, looks at it and lets her head fall in discouragement.*]

SERVANT.   Now what's the matter?

BRIDE.   Leave me alone.

SERVANT.   This is no time for you to start feeling sad. [*Encouragingly.*] Give me the wreath. [*The* BRIDE *takes the wreath and hurls it away.*] Child! You're just asking God to punish you, throwing the wreath on the floor like that. Raise your head! Don't you want to get married? Say it. You can still withdraw.

[*The* BRIDE *rises.*]

BRIDE.   Storm clouds. A chill wind that cuts through my heart. Who hasn't felt it?

SERVANT.   You love your sweetheart, don't you?

BRIDE.   I love him.

SERVANT.   Yes, yes. I'm sure you do.

BRIDE.   But this is a very serious step.

SERVANT.   You've got to take it.

BRIDE.   I've already given my word.

SERVANT.   I'll put on the wreath.

BRIDE. [*She sits down.*]   Hurry. They should be arriving by now.

SERVANT.   They've already been at least two hours on the way.

BRIDE.   How far is it from here to the church?

SERVANT.   Five leagues by the stream, but twice that by the road.

[*The* BRIDE *rises and the* SERVANT *grows excited as she looks at her.*]
SERVANT.

> Awake, O Bride, awaken,
> On your wedding morning waken!
> The world's rivers may all
> Bear along your bridal Crown!

BRIDE. [*Smiling.*]   Come now.

SERVANT. [*Enthusiastically kissing her and dancing around her.*]

> Awake,
> with the fresh bouquet
> of flowering laurel.
> Awake,
> by the trunk and branch
> of the laurels!

[*The banging of the front door latch is heard.*]

BRIDE.   Open the door! That must be the first guests.

[*She leaves. The* SERVANT *opens the door.*]

SERVANT. [*In astonishment.*]   You!

LEONARDO.   Yes, me. Good morning.

SERVANT.   The first one!

LEONARDO.   Wasn't I invited?

SERVANT.   Yes.

LEONARDO.   That's why I'm here.

SERVANT.   Where's your wife?

LEONARDO.   I came on my horse. She's coming by the road.

SERVANT.   Didn't you meet anyone?

LEONARDO.   I *passed* them on my horse.

SERVANT.   You're going to kill that horse with so much racing.

LEONARDO.   When he dies, he's dead!

[*Pause.*]

SERVANT.   Sit down. Nobody's up yet.

LEONARDO.   Where's the bride?

SERVANT.   I'm just on my way to dress her.

LEONARDO.   The bride! She ought to be happy!

SERVANT. [*Changing the subject.*]   How's the baby?

LEONARDO.   What baby?

SERVANT.   Your son.

LEONARDO. [*Remembering, as though in a dream.*]   Ah!

SERVANT.   Are they bringing him?

LEONARDO.   No.

[*Pause. Voices sing distantly.*]

VOICES.

> Awake, O Bride, awaken,
> On your wedding morning waken!

LEONARDO.

> Awake, O Bride, awaken,
> On your wedding morning waken!

SERVANT.   It's the guests. They're still quite a way off.

LEONARDO.   The bride's going to wear a big wreath, isn't she? But it ought not to be so large. One a little smaller would look better on her. Has the groom already brought her the orange blossom that must be worn on the breast?

BRIDE. [*Appearing, still in petticoats and wearing the wreath.*]   He brought it.

SERVANT. [*Sternly.*]   Don't come out like that.

BRIDE.   What does it matter? [*Seriously.*] Why do you ask if they brought the orange blossom? Do you have something in mind?

LEONARDO.   Nothing. What would I have in mind? [*Drawing near her.*] You, you know me; you know I don't. Tell me so. What have I ever meant to you? Open your memory, refresh it. But two oxen and an ugly little hut are almost nothing. That's the thorn.

BRIDE.   What have you come here to do?

LEONARDO.   To see your wedding.

BRIDE.   Just as I saw yours!

LEONARDO.   Tied up by you, done with your two hands. Oh, they can kill me but they can't spit on me. But even money, which shines so much, spits sometimes.

BRIDE.   Liar!

LEONARDO.   I don't want to talk. I'm hot-blooded and I don't want to shout so all these hills will hear me.

BRIDE.   My shouts would be louder.

SERVANT.   You'll have to stop talking like this. [*To the* BRIDE.] You don't have to talk about what's past. [*The* SERVANT *looks around uneasily at the doors.*]

BRIDE.   She's right. I shouldn't even talk to you. But it offends me to the soul that you come here to watch me, and spy on my wedding, and ask about the orange blossom with something on your mind. Go and wait for your wife at the door.

LEONARDO.   But, can't you and I even talk?

SERVANT. [*With rage.*]   No! No, you can't talk.

LEONARDO.   Ever since I got married I've been thinking night and day about whose fault it was, and every time I think about it, out comes a new fault to eat up the old one; but always there's a fault left!

BRIDE.   A man with a horse knows a lot of things and can do a lot to ride roughshod over a girl stuck out in the desert. But I have my pride. And that's why I'm getting married. I'll lock myself in with my husband and then I'll have to love him above everyone else.

LEONARDO.   Pride won't help you a bit. [*He draws near to her.*]

BRIDE.   Don't come near me!

LEONARDO.   To burn with desire and keep quiet about it is the greatest punishment we can bring on ourselves. What good was pride to me—and not seeing you, and letting you lie awake night after night? No good! It only served to bring the fire down on me! You think that time heals and walls hide things, but it isn't true, it isn't true! When things get that deep inside you there isn't anybody can change them.

BRIDE. [*Trembling.*]   I can't listen to you. I can't listen to your voice. It's as though I'd drunk a bottle of anise and fallen asleep wrapped in a quilt of roses. It pulls me along, and I know I'm drowning—but I go on down.

SERVANT. [*Seizing* LEONARDO *by the lapels.*]   You've got to go right now!

LEONARDO.   This is the last time I'll ever talk to her. Don't you be afraid of anything.

BRIDE.   And I know I'm crazy and I know my breast rots with longing; but here I am—calmed by hearing him, by just seeing him move his arms.

LEONARDO.   I'd never be at peace if I didn't tell you these things. I got married. Now you get married.

SERVANT.   But she *is* getting married!

[*Voices are heard singing, nearer.*]

VOICES.

> Awake, O Bride, awaken,
> On your wedding morning waken!

BRIDE.

> Awake, O Bride, awaken,

[*She goes out, running toward her room.*]

SERVANT.   The people are here now. [*To* LEONARDO.] Don't you come near her again.

LEONARDO.   Don't worry.

[*He goes out to the left. Day begins to break.*]

FIRST GIRL. [*Entering.*]

> Awake, O Bride, awaken,
> the morning you're to marry;
> sing round and dance round;
> balconies a wreath must carry.

VOICES.

> Bride, awaken!

SERVANT. [*Creating enthusiasm.*]

> Awake,
> with the green bouquet
> of love in flower.
> Awake,
> by the trunk and the branch
> of the laurels!

SECOND GIRL. [*Entering.*]

> Awake,
> with her long hair,
> snowy sleeping gown,
> patent leather boots with silver—
> her forehead jasmines crown.

SERVANT.

> Oh, shepherdess,
> the moon begins to shine!

FIRST GIRL.

> Oh, gallant,
> leave your hat beneath the vine!

FIRST YOUNG MAN. [*Entering, holding his hat on high.*]

> Bride, awaken,
> for over the fields
> the wedding draws nigh
> with trays heaped with dahlias
> and cakes piled high.

VOICES.

> Bride, awaken!

SECOND GIRL.

> The bride
> has set her white wreath in place
> and the groom
> ties it on with a golden lace.

SERVANT.

> By the orange tree,
> sleepless the bride will be.

THIRD GIRL. [*Entering.*]

> By the citron vine,
> gifts from the groom will shine.

[*Three* GUESTS *come in.*]

FIRST YOUTH.

> Dove, awaken!
> In the dawn
> shadowy bells are shaken.

GUEST.

> The bride, the white bride
> today a maiden,
> tomorrow a wife.

FIRST GIRL.

> Dark one, come down
> trailing the train of your silken gown.

GUEST.

> Little dark one, come down,
> cold morning wears a dewy crown.

FIRST GUEST.

> Awaken, wife, awake,
> orange blossoms the breezes shake.

SERVANT.

> A tree I would embroider her
> with garnet sashes wound,
> And on each sash a cupid,
> with "Long Live" all around.

VOICES.

Bride, awaken.

FIRST YOUTH.

The morning you're to marry!

GUEST.

The morning you're to marry
how elegant you'll seem;
worthy, mountain flower,
of a captain's dream.

FATHER. [*Entering.*]

A captain's wife
the groom will marry.
He comes with his oxen the treasure to carry!

THIRD GIRL.

The groom
is like a flower of gold.
When he walks,
blossoms at his feet unfold.

SERVANT.

Oh, my lucky girl!

SECOND YOUTH.

Bride, awaken.

SERVANT.

Oh, my elegant girl!

FIRST GIRL.

Through the windows
hear the wedding shout.

SECOND GIRL.

Let the bride come out.

FIRST GIRL.

Come out, come out!

SERVANT.

Let the bells
ring and ring out clear!

FIRST YOUTH.

For here she comes!
For now she's near!

SERVANT.

Like a bull, the wedding
is arising here!

[*The* BRIDE *appears. She wears a black dress in the style of* 1900, *with a bustle and large train covered with pleated gauzes and heavy laces. Upon her hair, brushed in a wave over her forehead, she wears an orange blossom wreath. Guitars sound. The* GIRLS *kiss the* BRIDE.]

THIRD GIRL.   What scent did you put on your hair?

BRIDE. [*Laughing.*]   None at all.

SECOND GIRL. [*Looking at her dress.*]   This cloth is what you can't get.

FIRST YOUTH.   Here's the groom!

BRIDEGROOM.   Salud!

FIRST GIRL. [*Putting a flower behind his ear.*]

> The groom
> is like a flower of gold.

SECOND GIRL.

> Quiet breezes
> from his eyes unfold.

[*The* GROOM *goes to the* BRIDE.]

BRIDE.   Why did you put on those shoes?

BRIDEGROOM.   They're gayer than the black ones.

LEONARDO'S WIFE. [*Entering and kissing the* BRIDE.]   Salud!

[*They all speak excitedly.*]

LEONARDO. [*Entering as one who performs a duty.*]

> The morning you're to marry
> We give you a wreath to wear.

LEONARDO'S WIFE.

> So the fields may be made happy
> with the dew dropped from your hair!

MOTHER. [*To the* FATHER.]   Are those people here, too?

FATHER.   They're part of the family. Today is a day of forgiveness!

MOTHER.   I'll put up with it, but I don't forgive.

BRIDEGROOM.   With your wreath, it's a joy to look at you!

BRIDE.   Let's go to the church quickly.

BRIDEGROOM.   Are you in a hurry?

BRIDE.   Yes. I want to be your wife right now so that I can be with you alone, not hearing any voice but yours.

BRIDEGROOM.   That's what I want!

BRIDE.   And not seeing any eyes but yours. And for you to hug me so hard, that even though my dead mother should call me, I wouldn't be able to draw away from you.

BRIDEGROOM.   My arms are strong. I'll hug you for forty years without stopping.

BRIDE. [*Taking his arm, dramatically.*]   Forever!

FATHER.   Quick now! Round up the teams and carts! The sun's already out.

MOTHER.   And go along carefully! Let's hope nothing goes wrong.

[*The great door in the background opens.*]

SERVANT. [*Weeping.*]

> As you set out from your house,
> oh, maiden white,

remember you leave shining
with a star's light.

FIRST GIRL.

Clean of body, clean of clothes
from her home to church she goes.

[*They start leaving.*]

SECOND GIRL.

Now you leave your home
for the church!

SERVANT.

The wind sets flowers
on the sands.

THIRD GIRL.

Ah, the white maid!

SERVANT.

Dark winds are the lace
of her mantilla.

[*They leave. Guitars, castanets and tambourines are heard.* LEONARDO *and his* WIFE *are left alone.*]

WIFE.   Let's go.

LEONARDO.   Where?

WIFE.   To the church. But not on your horse. You're coming with me.

LEONARDO.   In the cart?

WIFE.   Is there anything else?

LEONARDO.   I'm not the kind of man to ride in a cart.

WIFE.   Nor I the wife to go to a wedding without her husband. I can't stand any more of this!

LEONARDO.   Neither can I!

WIFE.   And why do you look at me that way? With a thorn in each eye.

LEONARDO.   Let's go!

WIFE.   I don't know what's happening. But I think, and I don't want to think. One thing I do know. I'm already cast off by you. But I have a son. And another coming. And so it goes. My mother's fate was the same. Well, I'm not moving from here.

[*Voices outside.*]

VOICES.

As you set out from your home
and to the church go
remember you leave shining
with a star's glow.

WIFE. [*Weeping.*]

Remember you leave shining
with a star's glow!

I left my house like that too. They could have stuffed the whole countryside in my mouth. I was that trusting.

LEONARDO. [*Rising.*]   Let's go!

WIFE.   But you with me!

LEONARDO.   Yes. [*Pause.*] Start moving! [*They leave.*]

VOICES.

> As you set out from your home
> and to the church go,
> remember you leave shining
> with a star's glow.

Slow curtain

ACT TWO

SCENE 2

The exterior of the BRIDE's *cave home, in white gray and cold blue tones. Large cactus trees. Shadowy and silver tones. Panoramas of light tan table-lands, everything hard like a landscape in popular ceramics.*

SERVANT. [*Arranging glasses and trays on a table.*]

> A-turning,
> the wheel was a-turning
> and the water was flowing,
> for the wedding night comes.
> May the branches part
> and the moon be arrayed
> at her white balcony rail.

[*In a loud voice.*]

Set out the tablecloths!

[*In a pathetic voice.*]

> A-singing,
> bride and groom were singing
> and the water was flowing
> for their wedding night comes.
> Oh, rime-frost, flash!—
> and almonds bitter
> fill with honey!

[*In a loud voice.*]

Get the wine ready!

[*In a poetic tone.*]

Elegant girl,
most elegant in the world,
see the way the water is flowing,
for your wedding night comes.
Hold your skirts close in
under the bridegroom's wing
and never leave your house,
for the Bridegroom is a dove
with his breast a firebrand
and the fields wait for the whisper
of spurting blood.
A-turning
the wheel was a-turning
and the water was flowing
and your wedding night comes.
Oh, water, sparkle!

MOTHER. [*Entering.*]   At last!

FATHER.   Are we the first ones?

SERVANT.   No. Leonardo and his wife arrived a while ago. They drove like demons. His wife got here dead with fright. They made the trip as though they'd come on horseback.

FATHER.   That one's looking for trouble. He's not of good blood.

MOTHER.   What blood would you expect him to have? His whole family's blood. It comes down from his great grandfather, who started in killing, and it goes on down through the whole evil breed of knife wielding and false smiling men.

FATHER.   Let's leave it at that!

SERVANT.   But how can she leave it at that?

MOTHER.   It hurts me to the tips of my veins. On the forehead of all of them I see only the hand with which they killed what was mine. Can you really see me? Don't I seem mad to you? Well, it's the madness of not having shrieked out all my breast needs to. Always in my breast there's a shriek standing tiptoe that I have to beat down and hold in under my shawls. But the dead are carried off and one has to keep still. And then, people find fault. [*She removes her shawl.*]

FATHER.   Today's not the day for you to be remembering these things.

MOTHER.   When the talk turns on it, I have to speak. And more so today. Because today I'm left alone in my house.

FATHER.   But with the expectation of having someone with you.

MOTHER.   That's my hope: grandchildren.

[*They sit down.*]

FATHER.   I want them to have a lot of them. This land needs hands that aren't hired. There's a battle to be waged against weeds, the thistles, the big rocks that come from one doesn't know where. And those hands have to be the owner's, who chastises and dominates, who makes the seeds grow. Lots of sons are needed.

MOTHER. And some daughters! Men are like the wind! They're forced to handle weapons. Girls never go out into the street.

FATHER. [*Happily.*] I think they'll have both.

MOTHER. My son will cover her well. He's of good seed. His father could have had many sons with me.

FATHER. What I'd like is to have all this happen in a day. So that right away they'd have two or three boys.

MOTHER. But it's not like that. It takes a long time. That's why it's so terrible to see one's own blood spilled out on the ground. A fountain that spurts for a minute, but costs us years. When I got to my son, he lay fallen in the middle of the street. I wet my hands with his blood and licked them with my tongue—because it was my blood. You don't know what that's like. In a glass and topaze shrine I'd put the earth moistened by his blood.

FATHER. Now you must hope. My daughter is wide-hipped and your son is strong.

MOTHER. That's why I'm hoping.

[*They rise.*]

FATHER. Get the wheat trays ready!

SERVANT. They're all ready.

LEONARDO'S WIFE. [*Entering.*] May it be for the best!

MOTHER. Thank you.

LEONARDO. Is there going to be a celebration?

FATHER. A small one. People can't stay long.

SERVANT. Here they are!

[*Guests begin entering in gay groups. The BRIDE and GROOM come in arm-in-arm. Leonardo leaves.*]

BRIDEGROOM. There's never been a wedding with so many people!

BRIDE. [*Sullen.*] Never.

FATHER. It was brilliant.

MOTHER. Whole branches of families came.

BRIDEGROOM. People who never went out of the house.

MOTHER. Your father sowed well, and now you're reaping it.

BRIDEGROOM. There were cousins of mine whom I no longer knew.

MOTHER. All the people from the seacoast.

BRIDEGROOM. [*Happily.*] They were frightened of the horses.

[*They talk.*]

MOTHER. [*To the BRIDE.*] What are you thinking about?

BRIDE. I'm not thinking about anything.

MOTHER. Your blessings weigh heavily.

[*Guitars are heard.*]

BRIDE.   Like lead.

MOTHER. [*Stern.*] But they shouldn't weigh so. Happy as a dove you ought
to be.

BRIDE.   Are you staying here tonight?

MOTHER. No. My house is empty.

BRIDE.   You ought to stay!

FATHER. [*To the* MOTHER.] Look at the dance they're forming. Dances of
the far away seashore.

[LEONARDO *enters and sits down. His* WIFE *stands rigidly behind him.*]

MOTHER. They're my husband's cousins. Stiff as stones at dancing.

FATHER. It makes me happy to watch them. What a change for this house!
[*He leaves.*]

BRIDEGROOM. [*To the* BRIDE.] Did you like the orange blossom?

BRIDE. [*Looking at him fixedly.*] Yes.

BRIDEGROOM. It's all of wax. It will last forever. I'd like you to have had
them all over your dress.

BRIDE.   No need of that.

[LEONARDO *goes off to the right.*]

FIRST GIRL.   Let's go and take out your pins.

BRIDE. [*To the* GROOM.] I'll be right back.

LEONARDO'S WIFE.   I hope you'll be happy with my cousin!

BRIDEGROOM.   I'm sure I will.

LEONARDO'S WIFE.   The two of you here; never going out; building a home.
I wish I could live far away like this, too!

BRIDEGROOM.   Why don't you buy land? The mountainside is cheap and
children grow up better.

LEONARDO'S WIFE.   We don't have any money. And at the rate we're going . . . !

BRIDEGROOM.   Your husband is a good worker.

LEONARDO'S WIFE.   Yes, but he likes to fly around too much; from one thing
to another. He's not a patient man.

SERVANT.   Aren't you having anything? I'm going to wrap up some wine
cakes for your mother. She likes them so much.

BRIDEGROOM.   Put up three dozen for her.

LEONARDO'S WIFE.   No, no. A half-dozen's enough for her!

BRIDEGROOM.   But today's a day!

LEONARDO'S WIFE. [*To the* SERVANT.] Where's Leonardo?

BRIDEGROOM.   He must be with the guests.

LEONARDO'S WIFE.   I'm going to go see. [*She leaves.*]

SERVANT. [*Looking off at the dance.*] That's beautiful there.

BRIDEGROOM.   Aren't you dancing?

SERVANT.   No one will ask me.

[*Two* GIRLS *pass across the back of the stage; during this whole scene the
background should be an animated crossing of figures.*]

BRIDEGROOM. [*Happily.*] They just don't know anything. Lively old girls like you dance better than the young ones.

SERVANT. Well! Are you tossing me a compliment, boy? What a family yours is! Men among men! As a little girl I saw your grandfather's wedding. What a figure! It seemed as if a mountain were getting married.

BRIDEGROOM. I'm not as tall.

SERVANT. But there's the same twinkle in your eye. Where's the girl?

BRIDEGROOM. Taking off her wreath.

SERVANT. Ah! Look. For midnight, since you won't be sleeping, I have prepared ham for you, and some large glasses of old wine. On the lower shelf of the cupboard. In case you need it.

BRIDEGROOM. [*Smiling.*] I won't be eating at midnight.

SERVANT. [*Slyly.*] If not you, maybe the bride. [*She leaves.*]

FIRST YOUTH. [*Entering.*] You've got to come have a drink with us!

BRIDEGROOM. I'm waiting for the bride.

SECOND YOUTH. You'll have her at dawn!

FIRST YOUTH. That's when it's best!

SECOND YOUTH. Just for a minute.

BRIDEGROOM. Let's go.

[*They leave. Great excitement is heard. The* BRIDE *enters. From the opposite side two* GIRLS *come running to meet her.*]

FIRST GIRL. To whom did you give the first pin; me or this one?

BRIDE. I don't remember.

FIRST GIRL. To me, you gave it to me here.

SECOND GIRL. To me, in front of the altar.

BRIDE. [*Uneasily, with a great inner struggle.*] I don't know anything about it.

FIRST GIRL. It's just that I wish you'd . . .

BRIDE. [*Interrupting.*] Nor do I care. I have a lot to think about.

SECOND GIRL. Your pardon.

[LEONARDO *crosses at the rear of the stage.*]

BRIDE. [*She sees* LEONARDO.] And this is an upsetting time.

FIRST GIRL. We wouldn't know anything about that!

BRIDE. You'll know about it when your time comes. This step is a very hard one to take.

FIRST GIRL. Has she offended you?

BRIDE. No. You must pardon me.

SECOND GIRL. What for? But *both* the pins are good for getting married, aren't they?

BRIDE. Both of them.

FIRST GIRL. Maybe now one will get married before the other.

BRIDE. Are you so eager?

SECOND GIRL. [*Shyly.*] Yes.

BRIDE. Why?

FIRST GIRL. Well . . .

[*She embraces the second* GIRL. *Both go running off. The* GROOM *comes in very slowly and embraces the* BRIDE *from behind.*]

BRIDE. [*In sudden fright.*]   Let go of me!

BRIDEGROOM.   Are you frightened of me?

BRIDE.   Ay-y-y! It's you?

BRIDEGROOM.   Who else would it be? [*Pause.*] Your father or me.

BRIDE.   That's true!

BRIDEGROOM.   Of course, your father would have hugged you more gently.

BRIDE. [*Darkly.*]   Of course!

BRIDEGROOM. [*Embracing her strongly and a little bit brusquely.*]   Because he's old.

BRIDE. [*Curtly.*]   Let me go!

BRIDEGROOM.   Why? [*He lets her go.*]

BRIDE.   Well . . . the people. They can see us.

[*The* SERVANT *crosses at the back of the stage again without looking at the* BRIDE *and* BRIDEGROOM.]

BRIDEGROOM.   What of it? It's consecrated now.

BRIDE.   Yes, but let me be . . . Later.

BRIDEGROOM.   What's the matter with you? You look frightened!

BRIDE.   I'm all right. Don't go.

[LEONARDO'S WIFE *enters.*]

LEONARDO'S WIFE.   I don't mean to intrude . . . .

BRIDEGROOM.   What is it?

LEONARDO'S WIFE.   Did my husband come through here?

BRIDEGROOM.   No.

LEONARDO'S WIFE.   Because I can't find him, and his horse isn't in the stable either.

BRIDEGROOM. [*Happily.*]   He must be out racing it.

[*The* WIFE *leaves, troubled. The* SERVANT *enters.*]

SERVANT.   Aren't you two proud and happy with so many good wishes?

BRIDEGROOM.   I wish it were over with. The bride is a little tired.

SERVANT.   That's no way to act, child.

BRIDE.   It's as though I'd been struck on the head.

SERVANT.   A bride from these mountains must be strong. [*To the* GROOM.] You're the only one who can cure her, because she's yours. [*She goes running off.*]

BRIDEGROOM. [*Embracing the* BRIDE.]   Let's go dance a little. [*He kisses her.*]

BRIDE. [*Worried.*]   No. I'd like to stretch out on my bed a little.

BRIDEGROOM.   I'll keep you company.

BRIDE.   Never! With all these people here? What would they say? Let me be quiet for a moment.

BRIDEGROOM.   Whatever you say! But don't be like that tonight!

BRIDE. [*At the door.*]   I'll be better tonight.

BRIDEGROOM.   That's what I want.

[*The* MOTHER *appears.*]

MOTHER. Son.

BRIDEGROOM. Where've you been?

MOTHER. Out there—in all that noise. Are you happy?

BRIDEGROOM. Yes.

MOTHER. Where's your wife?

BRIDEGROOM. Resting a little. It's a bad day for brides!

MOTHER. A bad day? The only good one. To me it was like coming into my own. [*The* SERVANT *enters and goes toward the* BRIDE'S *room.*] Like the breaking of new ground; the planting of new trees.

BRIDEGROOM. Are you going to leave?

MOTHER. Yes. I ought to be at home.

BRIDEGROOM. Alone.

MOTHER. Not alone. For my head is full of things: of men, and fights.

BRIDEGROOM. But now the fights are no longer fights.

[*The* SERVANT *enters quickly; she disappears at the rear of the stage, running.*]

MOTHER. While you live, you have to fight.

BRIDEGROOM. I'll always obey you!

MOTHER. Try to be loving with your wife, and if you see she's acting foolish or touchy, caress her in a way that will hurt her a little: a strong hug, a bite and then a soft kiss. Not so she'll be angry, but just so she'll feel you're the man, the boss, the one who gives orders. I learned that from your father. And since you don't have him, I have to be the one to tell you about these strong defenses.

BRIDEGROOM. I'll always do as you say.

FATHER. [*Entering.*] Where's my daughter?

BRIDEGROOM. She's inside.

[*The* FATHER *goes to look for her.*]

FIRST GIRL. Get the bride and groom! We're going to dance a round!

FIRST YOUTH. [*To the* BRIDEGROOM.] You're going to lead it.

FATHER. [*Entering.*] She's not there.

BRIDEGROOM. No?

FATHER. She must have gone up to the railing.

BRIDEGROOM. I'll go see!

[*He leaves. A hubbub of excitement and guitars is heard.*]

FIRST GIRL. They've started it already! [*She leaves.*]

BRIDEGROOM. [*Entering.*] She isn't there.

MOTHER. [*Uneasily.*] Isn't she?

FATHER. But where could she have gone?

SERVANT. [*Entering.*] But where's the girl, where is she?

MOTHER. [*Seriously.*] That we don't know.

[*The* BRIDEGROOM *leaves. Three guests enter.*]

FATHER. [*Dramatically.*] But, isn't she in the dance?

SERVANT. She's not in the dance.

FATHER. [*With a start.*]   There are a lot of people. Go look!
SERVANT.   I've already looked.
FATHER. [*Tragically.*]   Then where is she?
BRIDEGROOM. [*Entering.*]   Nowhere. Not anywhere.
MOTHER. [*To the* FATHER.]   What does this mean? Where is your daughter?
[LEONARDO'S WIFE *enters.*]
LEONARDO'S WIFE.   They've run away. They've run away! She and Leonardo.
On the horse. With their arms around each other, they rode off like a shooting
star!
FATHER.   That's not true! Not my daughter!
MOTHER.   Yes, your daughter! Spawn of a wicked mother, and he, he too.
But now she's my son's wife!
BRIDEGROOM. [*Entering.*]   Let's go after them. Who has a horse?
MOTHER.   Who has a horse? Right away! Who has a horse? I'll give him
all I have—my eyes, my tongue even. . . .
VOICE.   Here's one.
MOTHER. [*To the* SON.]   Go! After them! [*He leaves with two young men.*]
No. Don't go. Those people kill quickly and well . . . but yes, run, and I'll
follow!
FATHER.   It couldn't be my daughter. Perhaps she's thrown herself in the
well.
MOTHER.   Decent women throw themselves in water; not that one! But now
she's my son's wife. Two groups. There are two groups here. [*They all enter.*]
My family and yours. Everyone set out from here. Shake the dust from your
heels! We'll go help my son. [*The people separate into two groups.*] For he has
his family: his cousins from the sea, and all who came from inland. Out of here!
On all roads. The hour of blood has come again. Two groups! You with yours
and I with mine. After them! After them!

Curtain

ACT THREE

SCENE 1

*A forest. It is nighttime. Great moist tree trunks. A dark atmosphere. Two
violins are heard. Three* WOODCUTTERS *enter.*

FIRST WOODCUTTER.   And have they found them?
SECOND WOODCUTTER.   No. But they're looking for them everywhere.
THIRD WOODCUTTER.   They'll find them.
SECOND WOODCUTTER.   Sh-h-h!
THIRD WOODCUTTER.   What?

SECOND WOODCUTTER.   They seem to be coming closer on all the roads at once.

FIRST WOODCUTTER.   When the moon comes out they'll see them.

SECOND WOODCUTTER.   They ought to let them go.

FIRST WOODCUTTER.   The world is wide. Everybody can live in it.

THIRD WOODCUTTER.   But they'll kill them.

SECOND WOODCUTTER.   You have to follow your passion. They did right to run away.

FIRST WOODCUTTER.   They were deceiving themselves but at the last blood was stronger.

THIRD WOODCUTTER.   Blood!

FIRST WOODCUTTER.   You have to follow the path of your blood.

SECOND WOODCUTTER.   But blood that sees the light of day is drunk up by the earth.

FIRST WOODCUTTER.   What of it? Better dead with the blood drained away than alive with it rotting.

THIRD WOODCUTTER.   Hush!

FIRST WOODCUTTER.   What? Do you hear something?

THIRD WOODCUTTER.   I hear the crickets, the frogs, the night's ambush.

FIRST WOODCUTTER.   But not the horse.

THIRD WOODCUTTER.   No.

FIRST WOODCUTTER.   By now he must be loving her.

SECOND WOODCUTTER.   Her body for him; his body for her.

THIRD WOODCUTTER.   They'll find them and they'll kill them.

FIRST WOODCUTTER.   But by then they'll have mingled their bloods. They'll be like two empty jars, like two dry arroyos.

SECOND WOODCUTTER.   There are many clouds and it would be easy for the moon not to come out.

THIRD WOODCUTTER.   The bridegroom will find them with or without the moon. I saw him set out. Like a raging star. His face the color of ashes. He looked the fate of all his clan.

FIRST WOODCUTTER.   His clan of dead men lying in the middle of the street.

SECOND WOODCUTTER.   There you have it!

THIRD WOODCUTTER.   You think they'll be able to break through the circle?

SECOND WOODCUTTER.   It's hard to. There are knives and guns for ten leagues 'round.

THIRD WOODCUTTER.   He's riding a good horse.

SECOND WOODCUTTER.   But he's carrying a woman.

FIRST WOODCUTTER.   We're close by now.

SECOND WOODCUTTER.   A tree with forty branches. We'll soon cut it down.

THIRD WOODCUTTER.   The moon's coming out now. Let's hurry.

[*From the left shines a brightness.*]

FIRST WOODCUTTER.

O rising moon!

Moon among the great leaves.

SECOND WOODCUTTER.

Cover the blood with jasmines!

FIRST WOODCUTTER.

O lonely moon!
Moon among the great leaves.

SECOND WOODCUTTER.

Silver on the bride's face.

THIRD WOODCUTTER.

O evil moon!
Leave for their love a branch in shadow.

FIRST WOODCUTTER.

O sorrowing moon!
Leave for their love a branch in shadow.

[*They go out. The* MOON *appears through the shining brightness at the left. The* MOON *is a young woodcutter with a white face. The stage takes on an intense blue radiance.*]

MOON.

Round swan in the river
and a cathedral's eye,
false dawn on the leaves,
they'll not escape; these things am I!
Who is hiding? And who sobs
in the thornbrakes of the valley?
The moon sets a knife
abandoned in the air
which being a leaden threat
yearns to be blood's pain.
Let me in! I come freezing
down to walls and windows!
Open roofs, open breasts
where I may warm myself!
I'm cold! My ashes
of somnolent metals
seek the fire's crest
on mountains and streets.
But the snow carries me
upon its mottled back
and pools soak me
in their water, hard and cold.
But this night there will be
red blood for my cheeks,
and for the reeds that cluster
at the wide feet of the wind.

> Let there be neither shadow nor bower,
> and then they can't get away!
> O let me enter a breast
> where I may get warm!
> A heart for me!
> Warm! That will spurt
> over the mountains of my chest;
> let me come in, oh let me!

[*To the branches.*]

> I want no shadows. My rays
> must get in everywhere,
> even among the dark trunks I want
> the whisper of gleaming lights,
> so that this night there will be
> sweet blood for my cheeks,
> and for the reeds that cluster
> at the wide feet of the wind.
> Who is hiding? Out, I say!
> No! They will not get away!
> I will light up the horse
> with a fever bright as diamonds.

[*He disappears among the trunks, and the stage goes back to its dark lighting. An* OLD WOMAN *comes out completely covered by thin green cloth. She is barefooted. Her face can barely be seen among the folds. This character does not appear in the cast.*]

BEGGAR WOMAN.

> That moon's going away, just when they's near.
> They won't get past here. The river's whisper
> and the whispering tree trunks will muffle
> the torn flight of their shrieks.
> It has to be here, and soon. I'm worn out.
> The coffins are ready, and white sheets
> wait on the floor of the bedroom
> for heavy bodies with torn throats.
> Let not one bird awake, let the breeze,
> gathering their moans in her skirt,
> fly with them over black tree tops
> or bury them in soft mud.

[*Impatiently.*]

> Oh, that moon! That moon!

The MOON *appears. The intense blue light returns.*

MOON.   They're coming. One band through the ravine and the other along the river. I'm going to light up the boulders. What do you need?

BEGGAR WOMAN.   Nothing.

MOON.   The wind blows hard now, with a double edge.

BEGGAR WOMAN.   Light up the waistcoat and open the buttons; the knives will know the path after that.

MOON.

> But let them be a long time a-dying. So the blood
> will slide its delicate hissing between my fingers.
> Look how my ashen valleys already are waking
> in longing for this fountain of shuddering gushes!

BEGGAR WOMAN.   Let's not let them get past the arroyo. Silence!

MOON.   There they come!

[*He goes. The stage is left dark.*]

BEGGAR WOMAN.   Quick! Lots of light! Do you hear me? They can't get away!

[*The* BRIDEGROOM *and the* FIRST YOUTH *enter. The* BEGGAR WOMAN *sits down and covers herself with her cloak.*]

BRIDEGROOM.   This way.

FIRST YOUTH.   You won't find them.

BRIDEGROOM. [*Angrily.*]   Yes, I'll find them.

FIRST YOUTH.   I think they've taken another path.

BRIDEGROOM.   No. Just a moment ago I felt the galloping.

FIRST YOUTH.   It could have been another horse.

BRIDEGROOM. [*Intensely.*]   Listen to me. There's only one horse in the whole world, and this one's it. Can't you understand that? If you're going to follow me, follow me without talking.

FIRST YOUTH.   It's only that I want to . . .

BRIDEGROOM.   Be quiet. I'm sure of meeting them there. Do you see this arm? Well, it's not my arm. It's my brother's arm, and my father's, and that of all the dead ones in my family. And it has so much strength that it can pull this tree up by the roots, if it wants to. And let's move on, because here I feel the clenched teeth of all my people in me so that I can't breathe easily.

BEGGAR WOMAN. [*Whining.*]   Ay-y-y!

FIRST YOUTH.   Did you hear that?

BRIDEGROOM.   You go that way and then circle back.

FIRST YOUTH.   This is a hunt.

BRIDEGROOM.   A hunt. The greatest hunt there is.

[*The* YOUTH *goes off. The* BRIDEGROOM *goes rapidly to the left and stumbles over the* BEGGAR WOMAN, *Death.*]

BEGGAR WOMAN.   Ay-y-y!

BRIDEGROOM.   What do you want?

BEGGAR WOMAN.   I'm cold.

BRIDEGROOM.   Which way are you going?

BEGGAR WOMAN. [*Always whining like a beggar.*]   Over there, far away . . .

BRIDEGROOM.   Where are you from?

BEGGAR WOMAN.   Over there . . . very far away.

BRIDEGROOM. Have you seen a man and a woman running away on a horse?

BEGGAR WOMAN. [*Awakening.*] Wait a minute . . . [*She looks at him.*] Handsome young man. [*She rises.*] But you'd be much handsomer sleeping.

BRIDEGROOM. Tell me; answer me. Did you see them?

BEGGAR WOMAN. Wait a minute . . . What broad shoulders! How would you like to be laid out on them and not have to walk on the soles of your feet which are so small?

BRIDEGROOM. [*Shaking her.*] I asked you if you saw them! Have they passed through here?

BEGGAR WOMAN. [*Energetically.*] No. They haven't passed; but they're coming from the hill. Don't you hear them?

BRIDEGROOM. No.

BEGGAR WOMAN. Do you know the road?

BRIDEGROOM. I'll go, whatever it's like!

BEGGAR WOMAN. I'll go along with you. I know this country.

BRIDEGROOM. [*Impatiently.*] Well, let's go! Which way?

BEGGAR WOMAN. [*Dramatically.*] This way!

[*They go rapidly out. Two violins, which represent the forest, are heard distantly. The* WOODCUTTERS *return. They have their axes on their shoulders. They move slowly among the tree trunks.*]

FIRST WOODCUTTER.
> O rising death!
> Death among the great leaves.

SECOND WOODCUTTER.
> Don't open the gush of blood!

FIRST WOODCUTTER.
> O lonely death!
> Death among the dried leaves.

THIRD WOODCUTTER.
> Don't lay flowers over the wedding!

SECOND WOODCUTTER.
> O sad death!
> Leave for their love a green branch.

FIRST WOODCUTTER.
> O evil death!
> Leave for their love a branch of green!

[*They go out while they are talking.* LEONARDO *and the* BRIDE *appear.*]

LEONARDO.
> Hush!

BRIDE.
> From here I'll go on alone.
> You go now! I want you to turn back.

LEONARDO.
> Hush, I said!

BRIDE.

With your teeth, with your hands, anyway you can,
take from my clean throat
the metal of this chain,
and let me live forgotten
back there in my house in the ground.
And if you don't want to kill me
as you would kill a tiny snake,
set in my hands, a bride's hands,
the barrel of your shotgun.
Oh, what lamenting, what fire,
sweeps upward through my head!
What glass splinters are stuck in my tongue!

LEONARDO.

We've taken the step now; hush!
because they're close behind us,
and I must take you with me.

BRIDE.

Then it must be by force!

LEONARDO.

By force? Who was it first
went down the stairway?

BRIDE.

I went down it.

LEONARDO.

And who was it put
a new bridle on the horse?

BRIDE.

I myself did it. It's true.

LEONARDO.

And whose were the hands
strapped spurs to my boots?

BRIDE.

The same hands, these that are yours,
but which when they see you would like
to break the blue branches
and sunder the purl of your veins.
I love you! I love you! But leave me!
For if I were able to kill you
I'd wrap you 'round in a shroud
with the edges bordered in violets.
Oh, what lamenting, what fire,
sweeps upward through my head!

LEONARDO.

What glass splinters are stuck in my tongue!
Because I tried to forget you
and put a wall of stone
between your house and mine.
It's true. You remember?
And when I saw you in the distance
I threw sand in my eyes.
But I was riding a horse
and the horse went straight to your door.
And the silver pins of your wedding
turned my red blood black.
And in me our dream was choking
my flesh with its poisoned weeds.
Oh, it isn't my fault—
the fault is the earth's—
and this fragrance that you exhale
from your breasts and your braids.

BRIDE.

Oh, how untrue! I want
from you neither bed nor food,
yet there's not a minute each day
that I don't want to be with you,
because you drag me, and I come,
then you tell me to go back
and I follow you,
like chaff blown on the breeze.
I have left a good, honest man,
and all his people,
with the wedding feast half over
and wearing my bridal wreath.
But you are the one will be punished
and that I don't want to happen.
Leave me alone now! You run away!
There is no one who will defend you.

LEONARDO.

The birds of early morning
are calling among the trees.
The night is dying
on the stone's ridge.
Let's go to a hidden corner
where I may love you forever,
for to me the people don't matter,

nor the venom they throw on us.

[*He embraces her strongly.*]

BRIDE.

And I'll sleep at your feet,
to watch over your dreams.
Naked, looking over the fields,
as though I were a bitch.
Because that's what I am! Oh, I look at you
and your beauty sears me.

LEONARDO.

Fire is stirred by fire.
The same tiny flame
will kill two wheat heads together.
Let's go!

BRIDE.

Where are you taking me?

LEONARDO.

Where they cannot come,
these men who surround us.
Where I can look at you!

BRIDE. [*Sarcastically.*]

Carry me with you from fair to fair,
a shame to clean women,
so that people will see me
with my wedding sheets
on the breeze like banners.

LEONARDO.

I, too, would want to leave you
if I thought as men should.
But wherever you go, I go.
You're the same. Take a step. Try.
Nails of moonlight have fused
my waist and your chains.

[*This whole scene is violent, full of great sensuality.*]

BRIDE.

Listen!

LEONARDO.

They're coming.

BRIDE.

                              Run!
It's fitting that I should die here,
with water over my feet,
with thorns upon my head.
And fitting the leaves should mourn me,

a woman lost and virgin.

LEONARDO.

Be quiet. Now they're appearing.

BRIDE.

Go now!

LEONARDO.

Quiet. Don't let them hear us.

[The BRIDE hesitates.]

BRIDE.

Both of us!

LEONARDO. [Embracing her.]

Any way you want!
If they separate us, it will be
because I am dead.

BRIDE.

And I dead too.

[They go out in each other's arms.]

The MOON *appears very slowly. The stage takes on a strong blue light. The two violins are heard. Suddenly two long, ear-splitting shrieks are heard, and the music of the two violins is cut short. At the second shriek the* BEGGAR WOMAN *appears and stands with her back to the audience. She opens her cape and stands in the center of the stage like a great bird with immense wings. The* MOON *halts. The curtain comes down in absolute silence.*

Curtain

ACT THREE

SCENE 2

The Final Scene

A white dwelling with arches and thick walls. To the right and left, are white stairs. At the back, a great arch and a wall of the same color. The floor also should be shining white. This simple dwelling should have the monumental feeling of a church. There should not be a single gray nor any shadow, not even what is necessary for perspective.

Two GIRLS *dressed in dark blue are winding a red skein.*

FIRST GIRL.

Wool, red wool,
what would you make?

SECOND GIRL.

> Oh, jasmine for dresses,
> fine wool like glass.
> At four o'clock born,
> at ten o'clock dead.
> A thread from this wool yarn,
> a chain 'round your feet
> a knot that will tighten
> the bitter white wreath.

LITTLE GIRL. [*Singing.*]

> Were you at the wedding?

FIRST GIRL.

> No.

LITTLE GIRL.

> Well, neither was I!
> What could have happened
> 'midst the shoots of the vineyards?
> What could have happened
> 'neath the branch of the olive?
> What really happened
> that no one came back?
> Were you at the wedding?

SECOND GIRL.

> We told you once, no.

LITTLE GIRL. [*Leaving.*]

> Well, neither was I!

SECOND GIRL.

> Wool, red wool,
> what would you sing?

FIRST GIRL.

> Their wounds turning waxen,
> balm-myrtle for pain.
> Asleep in the morning,
> and watching at night.

LITTLE GIRL. [*In the doorway.*]

> And then, the thread stumbled
> on the flinty stones,
> but mountains, blue mountains,
> are letting it pass.
> Running, running, running,
> and finally to come
> to stick in a knife blade,
> to take back the bread.

[*She goes out.*]

SECOND GIRL.

> Wool, red wool,
> what would you tell?

FIRST GIRL.

> The lover is silent,
> crimson the groom,
> at the still shoreline
> I saw them laid out.

[*She stops and looks at the skein.*]

LITTLE GIRL. [*Appearing in the doorway.*]

> Running, running, running,
> the thread runs to here.
> All covered with clay
> I feel them draw near.
> Bodies stretched stiffly
> in ivory sheets!

[*The* WIFE *and* MOTHER-IN-LAW *of* LEONARDO *appear. They are anguished.*]

FIRST GIRL.   Are they coming yet?

MOTHER-IN-LAW. [*Harshly.*]   We don't know.

SECOND GIRL.   What can you tell us about the wedding?

FIRST GIRL.   Yes, tell me.

MOTHER-IN-LAW. [*Curtly.*]   Nothing.

LEONARDO'S WIFE.   I want to go back and find out all about it.

MOTHER-IN-LAW. [*Sternly.*]

> You, back to your house.
> Brave and alone in your house.
> To grow old and to weep.
> But behind closed doors.
> Never again. Neither dead nor alive.
> We'll nail up our windows
> and let rains and nights
> fall on the bitter weeds.

LEONARDO'S WIFE.   What could have happened?

MOTHER-IN-LAW.

> It doesn't matter what.
> Put a veil over your face.
> Your children are yours,
> that's all. On the bed
> put a cross of ashes
> where his pillow was.

[*They go out.*]

BEGGAR WOMAN. [*At the door.*]   A crust of bread, little girls.

LITTLE GIRL.   Go away!

[*The* GIRLS *huddle close together.*]

BEGGAR WOMAN.   Why?

LITTLE GIRL.   Because you whine; go away!

FIRST GIRL.   Child!

BEGGAR WOMAN.

> I might have asked for your eyes! A cloud
> of birds is following me. Will you have one?

LITTLE GIRL.   I want to get away from here!

SECOND GIRL. [*To the* BEGGAR WOMAN.]   Don't mind her!

FIRST GIRL.   Did you come by the road through the arroyo?

BEGGAR WOMAN.   I came that way!

FIRST GIRL. [*Timidly.*]   Can I ask you something?

BEGGAR WOMAN.

> I saw them: they'll be here soon; two torrents
> still at last, among the great boulders,
> two men at the horse's feet.
> Two dead men in the night's splendor.

[*With pleasure.*]

> Dead, yes, dead.

FIRST GIRL.   Hush, old woman, hush!

BEGGAR WOMAN.

> Crushed flowers for eyes, and their teeth
> two fistfuls of hard-frozen snow.
> Both of them fell, and the Bride returns
> with bloodstains on her skirt and hair.
> And they come covered with two sheets
> carried on the shoulders of two tall boys.
> That's how it was; nothing more. What was fitting.
> Over the golden flower, dirty sand.

[*She goes. The* GIRLS *bow their heads and start going out rhythmically.*]

FIRST GIRL.

> Dirty sand.

SECOND GIRL.

> Over the golden flower.

LITTLE GIRL.

> Over the golden flower
> they're bringing the dead from the arroyo.
> Dark the one,
> dark the other.
> What shadowy nightingale flies and weeps
> over the golden flower!

[*She goes. The stage is left empty. The* MOTHER *and a* NEIGHBOR WOMAN *appear. The* NEIGHBOR *is weeping.*]

MOTHER.   Hush.

NEIGHBOR.   I can't.

MOTHER. Hush, I said. [*At the door.*] Is there nobody here? [*She puts her hands to her forehead.*] My son ought to answer me. But now my son is an armful of shrivelled flowers. My son is a fading voice beyond the mountains now. [*With rage, to the* NEIGHBOR.] Will you shut up? I want no wailing in this house. Your tears are only tears from your eyes, but when I'm alone mine will come—from the soles of my feet, from my roots—burning more than blood.

NEIGHBOR. You come to my house; don't you stay here.

MOTHER. I want to be here. Here. In peace. They're all dead now: and at midnight I'll sleep, sleep without terror of guns or knives. Other mothers will go to their windows, lashed by rain, to watch for their sons' faces. But not I. And of my dreams I'll make a cold ivory dove that will carry camellias of white frost to the graveyard. But no; not graveyard, not graveyard: the couch of earth, the bed that shelters them and rocks them in the sky. [*A woman dressed in black enters, goes toward the right, and there kneels. To the* NEIGHBOR.] Take your hands from your face. We have terrible days ahead. I want to see no one. The earth and I. My grief and I. And these four walls. Ay-y-y! Ay-y-y! [*She sits down, overcome.*]

NEIGHBOR. Take pity on yourself!

MOTHER. [*Pushing back her hair.*] I must be calm. [*She sits down.*] Because the neighbor women will come and I don't want them to see me so poor. So poor! A woman without even one son to hold to her lips.

[*The* BRIDE *appears. She is without her wreath and wears a black shawl.*]

NEIGHBOR. [*With rage, seeing the* BRIDE.] Where are you going?

BRIDE. I'm coming here.

MOTHER. [*To the* NEIGHBOR.] Who is it?

NEIGHBOR. Don't you recognize her?

MOTHER. That's why I asked who it was. Because I don't want to recognize her, so I won't sink my teeth in her throat. You snake! [*She moves wrathfully on the* BRIDE, *then stops. To the* NEIGHBOR.] Look at her! There she is, and she's crying, while I stand here calmly and don't tear her eyes out. I don't understand myself. Can it be I didn't love my son? But, where's his good name? Where is it now? Where is it? [*She beats the* BRIDE *who drops to the floor.*]

NEIGHBOR. For God's sake! [*She tries to separate them.*]

BRIDE. [*To the* NEIGHBOR.] Let her; I came here so she'd kill me and they'd take me away with them. [*To the* MOTHER.] But not with her hands; with grappling hooks, with a sickle—and with force—until they break on my bones. Let her. I want her to know I'm clean, that I may be crazy, but that they can bury me without a single man ever having seen himself in the whiteness of my breasts.

MOTHER. Shut up, shut up; what do I care about that?

BRIDE. Because I ran away with the other one; I ran away! [*With anguish.*] You would have gone, too. I was a woman burning with desire, full of sores inside and out, and your son was a little bit of water from which I hoped for children, land, health; but the other one was a dark river, choked with brush, that brought near me the undertone of its rushes and its whispered song. And I went along with your son who was like a little boy of cold water—and the other sent against me hundreds of birds who got in my way and left white frost on my wounds, my wounds of a poor withered woman, of a girl caressed by fire. I didn't want to; remember that! I didn't want to. Your son was my destiny and I have not betrayed him, but the other one's arm dragged me along like the pull of the sea, like the head toss of a mule, and he would have dragged me always, always, always—even if I were an old woman and all your son's sons held me by the hair!

[A NEIGHBOR *enters*.]

MOTHER. She is not to blame; nor am I! [*Sarcastically*.] Who is, then? It's a delicate, lazy, sleepless woman who throws away an orange blossom wreath and goes looking for a piece of bed warmed by another woman!

BRIDE. Be still! Be still! Take your revenge on me; here I am! See how soft my throat is; it would be less work for you than cutting a dahlia in your garden. But never that! Clean, clean as a new-born little girl. And strong enough to prove it to you. Light the fire. Let's stick our hands in; you, for your son, I, for my body. *You'll* draw yours out first. [*Another* NEIGHBOR *enters*.]

MOTHER. But what does your good name matter to me? What does your death matter to me? What does anything about anything matter to me? Blesséd be the wheat stalks, because my sons are under them; blesséd be the rain, because it wets the face of the dead. Blesséd be God, who stretches us out together to rest.

[*Another* NEIGHBOR *enters*.]

BRIDE. Let me weep with you.

MOTHER. Weep. But at the door.

[*The* GIRL *enters. The* BRIDE *stays at the door. The* MOTHER *is at the center of the stage*.]

LEONARDO'S WIFE. [*Entering and going to the left*.]

> He was a beautiful horseman,
> now he's a heap of snow.
> He rode to fairs and mountains
> and women's arms.
> Now, the night's dark moss
> crowns his forehead.

MOTHER.

> A sunflower to your mother,
> a mirror of the earth.
> Let them put on your breast
> the cross of bitter rosebay;
> and over you a sheet
> of shining silk;

between your quiet hands
let water form its lament.

WIFE.

Ay-y-y, four gallant boys
come with tired shoulders!

BRIDE.

Ay-y-y, four gallant boys
carry death on high!

MOTHER.

Neighbors.

LITTLE GIRL. [*At the door.*]
They're bringing them now.

MOTHER.

It's the same thing.
Always the cross, the cross.

WOMAN.

Sweet nails,
cross adored,
sweet name
of Christ our Lord.

BRIDE.   May the cross protect both the quick and the dead.

MOTHER.

Neighbors: with a knife,
with a little knife,
on their appointed day, between two and three,
these two men killed each other for love.
With a knife,
with a tiny knife
that barely fits the hand,
but that slides in clean
through the astonished flesh
and stops at the place
where trembles, enmeshed,
the dark root of a scream.

BRIDE.

And this is a knife,
a tiny knife
that barely fits the hand;
fish without scales, without river,
so that on their appointed day, between two and three,
with this knife,
two men are left stiff,

with their lips turning yellow.

MOTHER.

And it barely fits the hand
but it slides in clean
through the astonished flesh
and stops there, at the place
where trembles enmeshed
the dark root of a scream.

[*The* NEIGHBORS, *kneeling on the floor, sob.*]

Curtain

Biographical Notes

CHARLES R. ANDERSON (1902–) has been Donovan professor of English at the Johns Hopkins University since 1956. Two of his books are *Melville in the South Seas* (1939) and *Emily Dickinson's Poetry: Stairway of Surprise* (1960).

MATTHEW ARNOLD (1822–1888), critic of Victorian culture, in his poems voiced the doubts of an age "wandering between two worlds, one dead, the other powerless to be born"—the world of religious faith and the world of doubt engendered by science.

W. H. AUDEN (1907–), born in England, became a United States citizen in 1939 and has been professor of poetry at Oxford since 1956. His *Collected Poetry* was published in 1945; since then *Age of Anxiety* (1947), *Nones* (1952), *Shield of Achilles* (1955), and *Homage to Clio* (1960) have appeared.

ROY P. BASLER (1906–) is the author or editor of a number of books on Abraham Lincoln. He is chief of the general reference and bibliographical divisions at the Library of Congress.

F. W. BATESON (1901–) is lecturer in English literature at Corpus Christi College, Oxford. Founder of the magazine *Essays in Criticism*, he has most recently published *English Poetry: A Critical Introduction* (1950) and *Wordsworth: A Re-Interpretation* (1954).

CHARLES BAUDELAIRE (1821–1867) characterized his *Les Fleurs du Mal* (1857) as "saturnine, orgiastic, and melancholy." He dressed his revulsions and despair in finely controlled verse, mixing his sense images, and exerted marked influence on Symbolist and later poets.

WATER BLAIR (1900–), former chairman of the Department of English at the University of Chicago, is known especially for such studies as *Native American Humor* (1937) and *Mark Twain and Huck Finn* (1960).

WILLIAM BLAKE (1757–1827), visionary poet and painter, still defies placing and encompassment. In *Songs of Innocence* (1789), *Songs of Experience*

(1794) and the "prophetic books" Blake achieved rich and moving effects with structure and line which appear utterly simple.

CLEANTH BROOKS (1906–) teaches English at Yale. Probably he has been the most influential of the New Critics in contemporary letters. In addition to collaborating on a group of distinguished college textbooks, he has written *Modern Poetry and the Tradition* (1939), *The Well Wrought Urn* (1947), and (with W. K. Wimsatt, Jr.) *Literary Criticism: A Short History* (1957).

REUBEN A. BROWER (1908–) is professor of English and general education at Harvard and author of *Alexander Pope: The Poetry of Allusion* (1959).

ELIZABETH BARRETT BROWNING (1806–1861), the popular poet whose marriage to Robert Browning became a Victorian love idyl, now seems prolix and rhetorical in her humanitarian and political verse, too "personal" perhaps in her love sonnets.

ROBERT BROWNING (1812–1889) combined his passion for the art and music and learning of the Italian Renaissance and his skill in rough, often colloquial verse to reveal character dramatically, as in his dramatic monologues or *The Ring and the Book* (1868–69).

ROBERT BURNS (1759–1796) wrote simple love lyrics, stirring appeals to the rights of man, and sardonic addresses to the "unco guid" or the rigidly righteous. His reputation suffered unjustly because of his ill health, drinking, and difficulties in love.

CHARLES STUART CALVERLEY (1831–1884), English poet, is chiefly known for his humorous poems and parodies, especially for his *Verses and Translations* (1862) and *Fly Leaves* (1872). He also made translations of Theocritus and Horace.

THOMAS CAMPION (1567–1620), Elizabethan poet and musician, is best known for his four *Books of Airs* (1610–1612), collections of lyrics set to music.

CATULLUS (87–54 B.C.), Latin love poet, came to Rome from his native Verona about 62 B.C. He became an intimate of sophisticated, fashionable society. Most of his poems celebrate his intense love of Clodia, the wife of Metullus Celer, who appears in his verse as "Lesbia." Gaius Valerius Catullus wrote about 116 poems, erotic or satirical, which have influenced later poets of various nationalities.

ANTON CHEKHOV (1860–1904), Russian novelist and dramatist, was educated to be a physician. Perhaps his most famous plays are *The Seagull* (1896), *Uncle Vanya* (1899), and *The Cherry Orchard* (1904).

MARGARET CHURCH (1920–), a graduate of Radcliffe (A.B., Ph.D.) and Columbia (A.M.), has taught English at Purdue University since 1953. She has written essays on such twentieth-century authors as Thomas Wolfe, Thomas Mann, and Aldous Huxley.

JEAN COCTEAU (1891–) is an important contemporary French writer of poetry, fiction, and dramas often described as surrealistic. He is also a successful artist. Among his books are *Le Grand Écart* (1923), *Les Enfants Terribles* (1929), and *Oedipus Rex*.

SAMUEL TAYLOR COLERIDGE (1772–1834), English poet and critic, was educated at Cambridge. Collaborating with William Wordsworth, he published *Lyrical Ballads* in 1798, making the year a landmark in literary history. Two of his most famous poems are "The Rime of the Ancient Mariner" and "Kubla Khan." His most important critical works are *Biographia Literaria* (1817) and *Anima Poetae* (1895).

HART CRANE (1899–1932) began his literary career in 1916, and by the time of his death had achieved wide recognition as a poet. *White Buildings* and *The Bridge* were published during his lifetime. *The Collected Poems* appeared in 1933.

RONALD S. CRANE (1886–) was for many years chairman of the English department at the University of Chicago, where he is now Distinguished Service Professor Emeritus. In 1952 he edited *Critics and Criticism, Ancient and Modern*. *The Language of Criticism and the Structure of Poetry* (1953) is another of his books.

STEPHEN CRANE (1871–1900), after attending Lafayette and Syracuse, became a newspaper reporter and free-lance writer. His most accomplished novel is *The Red Badge of Courage* (1895).

E. E. CUMMINGS (1894–) received his A.B. from Harvard. Among his books are *The Enormous Room* (1922), *Is 5* (1926), *Eimi* (1933), and *95 Poems* (1958).

EMILY DICKINSON (1830–1886), a recluse in later life, shares with Blake and Emerson the power to compress a world of poetic meaning into a few lines. Her poems were first fully and accurately published by Thomas H. Johnson and the Harvard University Press in 1955.

JOHN DONNE (1573–1631), greatest of the metaphysical poets and greatest Anglican pulpit orator, was educated at Oxford, Cambridge, and Lincoln's Inn. Brought up a Roman Catholic, he was converted to the Anglican church, and took holy orders in 1616. His rise in the church was rapid, and by 1621 he had become Dean of St. Paul's. Here he preached, often as his biographer Isaac Walton said, "like an angel from a cloud" until the end of his life. In his dissolute youth he wrote passionate love poems. After his conversion, he produced some of the finest devotional poems in existence.

JOHN DOS PASSOS (1896–), novelist and essayist, became first known for his novel *Three Soldiers* in 1921. Many other novels have appeared, among them *The Big Money* (1936), *The Grand Design* (1949), *The Great Days* (1958), and *Prospect of a Golden Age* (1959).

ELIZABETH DREW (1887–) was educated in England and is now visiting professor of English at Smith College. Among her books are *Discovering Poetry*, *The Enjoyment of Literature*, and *Poetry: A Modern Guide*.

JOHN DRYDEN (1631–1700), one of the first professional English men of letters, was educated at Cambridge. He distinguished himself in poetry, especially the satiric portrait, the drama, and literary criticism. Some of his famous poems are *Religio Laici*, *The Hind and the Panther*, and *Mac Flecknoe*. His finest play is *All for Love*, and his best known critical essays are *The Essay of Dramatic Poesy* and *Preface to the Fables*. Along with other Restoration poets, Dryden was disparaged by nineteenth-century literary critics. But his reputation has been revived and rehabilitated under the leadership of T. S. Eliot.

T. S. ELIOT (1888–), born in St. Louis and a graduate of Harvard, became a British citizen in 1927. In addition to his poems, he has written criticism (much of it available in *Selected Essays*, 1950) and plays, of which *The Cocktail Party* (1950) is best known.

RICHARD ELLMANN (1918–), a graduate of Yale (A.B., A.M., Ph.D.), has taught at Northwestern since 1951. He has published two books on Yeats and one on Joyce.

RALPH WALDO EMERSON (1803–1882), the high-thinking, plain-living Concord idealist, in his essays and poems advocated a tonic self-reliance and shrewdly attacked the materialism of his times. Though he called for an American poetry freely formed on "passionate and alive" thought in the "language of the street," his own verse, richly suggestive at its best, is formal and terse.

CLIFTON FADIMAN (1904–), former book reviewer of *The New Yorker* and master of ceremonies of the radio program "Information Please," contributes regularly to *Holiday Magazine*. Among his books are *Party of One* (1955) and *A Lifetime Reading Plan* (1960).

WILLIAM FAULKNER (1897–), one of the foremost living American novelists, has published some twenty books of fiction, notably *The Sound and the Fury* (1931), *Light in August* (1932) and *A Fable* (1954). In 1950 he was awarded the Nobel Prize for literature.

FRANCIS FERGUSSON (1904–), professor of literature at Rutgers University, is a literary critic with a special interest in the theater. His translations of Greek plays include Sophocles' *Electra*. Among his writings are *The Idea of a Theatre* (1949), poems in *New Directions* and *Partisan Review*, and critical essays in *Hound and Horn*, *Kenyon Review*, and elsewhere.

F. SCOTT FITZGERALD (1896–1940), novelist and short story writer, was born in St. Paul, Minnesota. At Princeton he enjoyed the social life of the clubs, wrote for student publications, and failed to graduate. In 1920, he published his first novel, *This Side of Paradise*, which became an instantaneous success and established Fitzgerald permanently as the spokesman of the Jazz Age. Some of his other books are *The Beautiful and Damned* (1921), *Tender Is the Night* (1924), *The Great Gatsby* (1925), *The Last Tycoon* (1945), and *The Crack-up* (1945).

RICHARD HARTER FOGLE (1911–), educated at Hamilton, Columbia, and Michigan, teaches English at Tulane, where he is chairman of his department. He is author of *The Imagery of Keats and Shelley* (1949), *Hawthorne's Fiction: The Light and the Dark* (1952), and *Melville's Shorter Tales* (1960).

E. M. FORSTER (1879–), British novelist, is author of the celebrated *A Passage to India* (1924). He was educated at Cambridge, where he is now an honorary fellow of King's College. He is also author of *A Room with a View* (1908) and *Howard's End* (1910), as well as two books of short stories, *The Eternal Moment* (1928), and *The Celestial Omnibus* (1911).

ROBERT FROST (1875–) has identified himself with New England, where he has lived the greater part of his life. His first book of poems was *A Boy's Will* (1913); his most recent is *In the Clearing* (1962).

WALKER GIBSON (1919–), a graduate of Yale and Iowa, is director of freshman English at New York University. Two of his books of light verse are *The Reckless Spenders* (1954) and *Come As You Are* (1958).

G. GIOVANNINI (1906–), a graduate of Detroit (A.B.) and Michigan (A.M., Ph.D.), teaches at the Catholic University of America.

GEORGE GORDON, LORD BYRON (1788–1824), egocentric English aristocrat and poet, achieved European fame with a poetic, autobiographical travelogue, *Childe Harold's Pilgrimage* (1812–1817). His finest accomplishment is perhaps *Don Juan* (1819–1824), the picaresque story in witty verse of a lover of liberty and the ladies.

THOMAS GRAY (1716–1771), a precursor of the Romantic movement in English literature in his humanitarianism and love of nature, wrote the famous, often-quoted poem, "Elegy Written in a Country Churchyard."

HORACE GREGORY (1898–), American poet and critic, was born in Milwaukee and educated at the University of Wisconsin. He won *Poetry* magazine's Lyric Prize in 1928. Some of his books are *Chelsea Rooming House* (1930), *Chorus for Survival* (1935), *Poems* (1941), *Poems of Catullus* (translation, 1931), *Pilgrim of the Apocalypse* (1933), a study of D. H. Lawrence, and *The Shield of Achilles* (1944). Mr. Gregory lives in New York.

FREDERICK L. GWYNN (1916–) is professor of English and chairman of the department at Trinity College (Hartford). Two of his books are *The Fiction of J. D. Salinger* (1958) and *Faulkner in the University* (1959), both written with Joseph L. Blotner.

THOMAS HARDY (1840–1928), British writer, after achieving a reputation as a novelist turned to poetry in the late 1890's. Among his books are *The Return of the Native* (1878), *Jude the Obscure* (1896), and *The Dynasts* (1903–1908).

NATHANIEL HAWTHORNE (1804–1864), American novelist, was born of old Puritan stock in Salem, Massachusetts. His first significant publication was *Twice Told Tales* (1837), a group of short stories dealing with his favorite themes of secret guilt and pride. Among his principal works are *Mosses from an Old Manse* (1846), *The Scarlet Letter* (1850), regarded by most critics as his masterpiece, and by many as one of the greatest American novels, *The House of the Seven Gables* (1851), *The Blithedale Romance* (1852), and *The Marble Faun* (1860).

ROBERT B. HEILMAN (1906–), professor of English and executive officer of the department at the University of Washington, collaborated with Cleanth Brooks in *Understanding Drama* and is the author of *Magic in the Web: Action and Language in Othello* (The Explicator Award, 1956).

HEINRICH HEINE (1799–1856), libertarian and cosmopolitan poet, after 1830 migrated from Germany to Paris. Though he suffered from bad health and paralysis at the end of his life, his poems are witty, high-spirited, and characteristically ironic.

ERNEST HEMINGWAY (1898–1961), contemporary American novelist, was born in Oak Park, Illinois. After graduating from the local high school, he began his writing career as a newspaper reporter. For both his style and his code, no other writer of our time has been more influential than Hemingway. He is the author of *In Our Time* (1925), a collection of short stories, *The Sun Also Rises* (1926), *A Farewell to Arms* (1929), *For Whom the Bell Tolls* (1940), *The Old Man and the Sea* (1952), and others.

GEORGE HERBERT (1593–1633) came of the noble family of Herberts. After taking his degree at Cambridge, he entered the Anglican priesthood. His religious lyrics, written in the metaphysical tradition of Donne, are among the finest English devotional poems. In this genre he is surpassed by none.

ROBERT HERRICK (1591–1674), Cavalier poet, was born in London and educated at Cambridge. He took holy orders and became rector of Dean Prior in Devonshire. An admirer of Ben Jonson, his poetry is in the tradition of Horace, Catullus, and Ben Jonson. His major work was *Hesperides*, a collection of 1200 short lyrics. His devotional poems are collected in *Noble Numbers*. Many of his best lyrics were set to music by Henry Lawes.

DANIEL G. HOFFMAN (1923–), a graduate of Columbia, now teaches at Swarthmore. Recent books by him are *The Poetry of Stephen Crane* (1957) and *Form and Fable in American Fiction* (1961).

JOHN HOLMES (1904–), who teaches at Tufts College, has written several volumes of poetry. Two of them are *Address to the Living* (1937) and *The Symbols* (1955).

GERARD MANLEY HOPKINS (1844–1889), a British Jesuit, served in missionary, church, and university posts. In 1918 his poems were first published under the editorship of Robert Bridges, then poet laureate.

HORACE (65–8 B.C.), Roman poet, is the author of odes, epistles, epodes, satires, and the *Ars Poetica*, a treatise on poetry. Though the odes of Horace are less passionate than the lyrics of Catullus, their grace and beauty of phrasing are unexcelled in Latin literature. After the death of Virgil, Horace was regarded as the greatest Roman poet.

A. E. HOUSMAN (1859–1936), a graduate of Oxford, taught Latin at the University of London and at Cambridge. His poems appeared in *A Shropshire Lad* (1896), *Last Poems* (1922), and *More Poems* (1936).

HENRIK IBSEN (1828–1906), the Norwegian dramatist, changed the course of European, English, and American playwriting by his exposition of social problems, his masterful dramaturgy, and his projection of human character in such plays as *A Doll's House* (1879) and *Ghosts* (1881).

HENRY JAMES (1843–1916), American novelist, was born in New York and educated by tutors. He settled in Europe in 1875, spending most of the remainder of his life abroad. He made a thorough study of Continental writers before he gradually evolved his own fictional method and style. His techniques have greatly influenced such later writers as Virginia Woolf, Willa Cather, and William Faulkner. Some of his books are *Daisy Miller* (1879), *Washington Square* (1881), *The Princess Casamassima* (1886), *What Maisie Knew* (1897), *The Real Thing and Other Tales* (1893), *The Ambassadors* (1903), and *The Golden Bowl* (1904).

RANDALL JARRELL (1914–), a graduate of Vanderbilt, has taught at the Woman's College of the University of North Carolina, and has been poetry consultant at the Library of Congress. Besides eight volumes of poetry, he has written a novel of campus life, *Pictures from an Institution* (1954), and a book of criticism, *Poetry and the Age* (1953).

S. F. JOHNSON (1918–), a graduate of Haverford (A.B.) and Harvard (A.M., Ph.D.), teaches at Columbia University.

BEN JONSON (1573–1637), greatest English satiric dramatist, is celebrated for his *Every Man in His Humour* (in which Shakespeare played a part in the production of 1598), *Every Man Out of His Humour, Volpone, The Silent Woman, The Alchemist,* and *Bartholomew Fair.* His poetry, primarily lyric, is indebted to classical literature. His literary merit has been overshadowed by Shakespeare and Spenser.

JAMES JOYCE (1882–1941), Irish novelist, was born in Dublin, and educated at a Jesuit school and at the University of Dublin. He was not a participant in the Irish Revival because he felt that overemphasis of the Gaelic would destroy the link between Ireland and Western literature. In 1902, he went to Paris, a voluntary exile, and though he revisited Ireland from time to time, he spent the rest of his life on the Continent. His chief works, *A Portrait of the Artist as a Young Man* (1916), *Ulysses* (1922), and *Finnegans Wake* (1939) have had an incalculable influence upon later writers—to mention a few, Virginia Woolf, Thomas Wolfe, and William Faulkner.

FRANZ KAFKA (1883–1924), Czech novelist, was born in Prague, the son of a successful Jewish wholesale merchant, and educated at the German University of Prague, where he took a doctor's degree in jurisprudence. He supported himself by working in the Bureau of Insurance. His fictional method is on the surface realistic but it invariably has overtones of symbolism and allegory. Among his favorite themes are the alienated artist in the modern world and the plight of modern man, lost and distraught in a strange, hostile world which he can neither comprehend nor explain theologically. He is the author of *The Castle* (1930), *The Great Wall of China* (1933), *The Metamorphosis* (1937), *The Trial* (1937), and *Amerika* (1938).

JOHN KEATS (1795–1821) was gifted with sensuous imagination and was devoted to his craft. Before his death in Italy from tuberculosis, he wrote distinguished narrative poems, such as *The Eve of St. Agnes* (1820), and sonnets. He crowned his short life's work with four great odes.

HUGH KENNER (1923–), a graduate of Toronto and Yale, is professor of English and chairman of the department at Santa Barbara College. Some of his books are *The Poetry of Ezra Pound* (1950), *Dublin's Joyce* (1956), and *The Invisible Poet: T. S. Eliot* (1959).

D. H. LAWRENCE (1885–1930), British novelist, was born in the coal-mining town of Eastwood, Nottinghamshire, England, and was educated at the University of Nottingham. Though he is best known as a novelist and short story writer, Lawrence also published poetry, plays, and literary criticism. Some of his novels are *The White Peacock*, *Sons and Lovers* (1913), *Aaron's Rod* (1922), *The Plumed Serpent* (1926), *The Prussian Officer* (1929), and *Lady Chatterley's Lover* (1928).

EVA LE GALLIENE (1899–) as an actor-manager is a leading figure of the contemporary theater. She is noted for distinguished interpretations of the plays of Ibsen, Chekhov, and Shakespeare.

JESSIE LEMONT (d.1947) was the author of two books of poems and translator of the work of Rilke.

HENRY WADSWORTH LONGFELLOW (1807–1882), popular and venerated American poet in his day, has declined in reputation. Many of the lyrics and certain of the narrative poems where figurative development and moral application meet naturally or where the tone is unsentimentally genial or sad are nonetheless true poetry.

FEDERICO GARCÍA LORCA (1898–1936) was one of the finest modern Spanish poets. His *Gipsy Ballads* (*Romancero Gitano*), published in 1928, has become the most widely known book of Spanish poetry in the twentieth century. He wrote several plays and for five years directed a company of actors. He was graduated from the University of Granada with a degree in law. He also became a distinguished musician. In August, 1936, during the Spanish Civil War, he was dragged from the home of friends and brutally murdered by an armed band of Phalangists.

ROBERT LOWELL (1917–), a graduate of Kenyon College, is the author of *Lord Weary's Castle* (1946), for which he received the Pulitzer Prize, *The Mills of the Kavanaghs* (1951), *Life Studies* (1959), and *Imitations* (1961).

ANTONIO MACHADO (1857–1939) published *Soledades* in 1903. From then until his death, following his flight from Spain, he wrote actively and taught widely.

C. F. MACINTYRE (1890–) has translated the German poets Goethe and Rilke as well as Baudelaire's *Les Fleurs du Mal*.

ARCHIBALD MACLEISH (1892–), poet and playwright, has been Boylston Professor of Poetry at Harvard since 1939. Recent works of his are *J.B.* (1958), a verse play, and *Poetry and Experience* (1960), critical essays.

BERNARD MALAMUD (1914–) is one of the notable figures in contemporary American literature. He was born in Brooklyn, New York, and educated at C. C. N. Y. and Columbia. His collection of short stories, *The Magic Barrel* (1958) won the National Book Award in 1959. Other books by Malamud are *The Natural* (1952), *The Assistant* (1957), and *A New Life* (1961). He teaches at Bennington College.

THOMAS MANN (1875–1955), contemporary German novelist, came to the United States as a refugee from the Hitler regime, and became an American citizen. Among his famous novels are *Buddenbrooks* (1901), *Tonio Kröger* (1903), *The Magic Mountain* (1924), regarded by many as his masterpiece, the *Joseph* cycle, and *Dr. Faustus*. Much of his influential work deals with the decline of European bourgeoisie.

CHRISTOPHER MARLOWE (1564–1593), the greatest English dramatist before Shakespeare, was educated at Cambridge. His fame rests on *Tamburlaine* (c.1588), *The Tragedy of Doctor Faustus* (c.1588), *The Jew of Malta* (c.1589), and *Edward II* (c.1592), as well as upon some charming lyric poems. He was stabbed to death in a tavern at the age of twenty-nine, and he may have been murdered for political reasons. Since Ben Jonson's felicitous remark about "Marlowe's mighty line," he has been known for his achievements in blank verse.

ANDREW MARVELL (1621–1678), an urbane Puritan poet, was educated at Cambridge, and later assisted Milton in the Latin Secretaryship. Though a Puritan in politics, he was almost more Cavalier than the Cavaliers in "To His Coy Mistress." The reputation of Marvell is at present very high, for he, along with Donne and the other metaphysicals, seems to speak directly to our age.

GUY DE MAUPASSANT (1850–1893), French novelist and short story writer, is author of *Boule de Suif, Pierre et Jean, Une Vie*, and *Bel-Ami*. Most of his celebrated short stories, originally published in magazines, are based upon a single incident and presented in understatement with great economy of words.

JOHN MILTON (1608–1674), great English poet, was born in London, the son of a prosperous scrivener. He took both the A.B. and M.A. degrees at Cambridge, after which he read intensively for five years in Greek and Latin authors, and especially in the church fathers. Upon the outbreak of civil disturbances in England, he returned from his grand tour of the Continent, and soon began writing a number of pamphlets for the Puritan party dealing with the issues of the time. Under the Cromwellian regime, while Latin Secretary, he lost his sight. His greatest work, the epic *Paradise Lost* (1667), was composed in total blindness, as were also its sequel, *Paradise Regained* (1671), and the poetic drama *Samson Agonistes* (1671). He is also the author of *Lycidas*, a pastoral elegy, twenty-three sonnets, and several other poems. But his greatest achievement remains, of course, *Paradise Lost*, which, as Dr. Johnson concluded, "is not the greatest of heroic poems, only because it is not the first."

HARRIET MONROE (1860–1936) founded *Poetry: A Magazine of Verse* in 1912, and remained its editor until her death. Her autobiography, *A Poet's Life* (1938), is an important document in the history of twentieth-century poetry.

MARIANNE MOORE (1887–), a graduate of Bryn Mawr, edited the *Dial* from 1925 to 1929. In addition to her poetry, she has published *Predilections* (1955), a volume of critical essays.

OGDEN NASH (1902–) has established himself as a leading humorous poet since *Hard Lines* appeared in 1931. Other titles are *The Face Is Familiar* (1940) and *The Christmas That Almost Wasn't* (1957). A recent collection is *Verses from 1929 On* (1959).

HOWARD NEMEROV (1920–), a graduate of Harvard, teaches English at Bennington. Besides his poetry, he has published fiction, including *The Homecoming Game* (1957) and *A Commodity of Dreams* (1959).

FRANK O'CONNOR (1903–) is the pseudonym of Michael O'Donovan. Born in Cork, Ireland, he was educated at the Christian Brothers school there. He was at one time director of the famous Abbey Theatre. William Butler Yeats once said that O'Connor was "doing for Ireland what Chekhov did for Russia." In addition to his short stories, for which he is best known, he has also published some verse and literary criticism. His most important books are *Guests of the Nation* (1931), *Selected Stories* (1946), *The Common Chord* (1947), *Traveller's Samples* (1950), from which "Legal Aid" has been selected, and *More Stories* (1954).

WILLIAM VAN O'CONNOR (1915–), a graduate of Syracuse and Columbia, has taught English at Minnesota (1946–1961) and is now professor of English at the University of California (Davis). He has written several critical volumes, including ones on Wallace Stevens (1950) and William Faulkner (1954).

EUGENE O'NEILL (1888–1953), Nobel-Prize winning American dramatist, drew upon his own adventurous youth and the work of Ibsen, the Greeks, and depth psychologists to produce a revolution in the American theater with plays like *Desire under the Elms* (1924), *Marco Millions* (1928), and *Mourning Becomes Electra* (1931).

EDGAR ALLAN POE (1809–1849) attempted to create a new standard for American poetry, both in his own verse and in his criticism of contemporary poets, with beauty rather than truth or moral suasion as the end to be achieved. His influence on French poets like Baudelaire returned through the Symbolist movement to American shores in the twentieth century.

ALEXANDER POPE (1688–1744), the greatest English satiric poet, was privately educated by tutors. He made successful translations of Homer into heroic couplets. Some of his poems are *An Essay on Man*, a didactic philosophical poem, *An Essay on Criticism*, numerous satires, especially the *Epistle to Dr. Arbuthnot* (1735) and *The Dunciad*, and an incomparable mock-heroic poem, *The Rape of the Lock*.

KATHERINE ANNE PORTER (1894–), American writer of fiction, was born in Indian Creek, Texas. She was educated in convents. Some of her best known books are *Flowering Judas* (1930), *Hacienda* (1934), *Noon Wine* (1937), *Pale Horse, Pale Rider* (1939), and *The Leaning Tower* (1942).

FREDERICK A. POTTLE (1897–) is Sterling professor of English at Yale University. Since the publication of *A New Portrait of James Boswell* (1927) much of his writing and editing has been concerned with Samuel Johnson's biographer.

MATTHEW PRIOR (1664–1721), poet and diplomat, is best known for his epigrams, occasional poems, and satires.

SIR WALTER RALEGH (1552–1618), Elizabethan courtier, voyager, and poet, was educated at Oxford. Only about thirty of his short poems are extant. He also wrote a prose work on the discovery of Guiana, political essays, and a *History of the World* (1614). In 1585 he founded a colony at Roanoke Island, North Carolina, and later made unsuccessful attempts to colonize in Virginia.

JOHN CROWE RANSOM (1888–), a graduate of Vanderbilt and Oxford, taught for many years at Kenyon College, where he edited *The Kenyon Review* from 1939 to 1959. One of his books of poetry is *Two Gentlemen in Bonds* (1927), and one of his books of criticism is *The New Criticism* (1941).

RAINER MARIA RILKE (1875–1926) is regarded as neo-romantic in his early work. The *Duino Elegies* and *Sonnets to Orpheus* belong to his later, more intense, more metaphysical writing.

E. A. ROBINSON (1869–1935) was born in Maine and attended Harvard. He is now best known for his shorter poems, but such longer narratives as *Tristram* (1927) and *Matthias at the Door* (1931) brought him greatest fame in his lifetime.

MACHA L. ROSENTHAL (1917–) teaches English literature at New York University, and writes for *The Nation*, of which he is poetry editor, and for other critical journals. The most recent of his books is *The Modern Poets: A Critical Introduction* (1960).

ELISABETH SCHNEIDER (1897–), a graduate of Smith and Pennsylvania, teaches English at Temple University. Two of her books are *Aesthetic Motive* (1939) and *Coleridge, Opium, and Kubla Khan* (1953).

MARK SCHORER (1908–), a graduate of Wisconsin (A.B., Ph.D.) and Harvard (A.M.), is chairman of the Department of English at the University of California (Berkeley). Among his books are *William Blake: The Politics of Vision* (1946) and *Sinclair Lewis* (1961).

SIR CHARLES SEDLEY (1639–1701), a Restoration Court Wit, was educated at Oxford. He wrote indifferent plays and lovely songs. He was a friend of Dryden, who included him in his *Essay of Dramatic Poesy* (1668).

WILLIAM SHAKESPEARE (1564–1616), greatest English dramatist and poet, was born at Stratford-on-Avon and educated at the Stratford grammar school. Among his many famous dramas are *Hamlet, Othello, Macbeth, King Lear, A Mid-Summer Night's Dream, King Henry IV*, parts I and II, *King Henry V, Julius Caesar, Antony and Cleopatra, The Tempest,* and *As You Like It*. His works, issued individually during his life, were first collected and published in folio by Heming and Condell in 1623.

KARL SHAPIRO (1913–) studied at the University of Virginia and at the Johns Hopkins University. Volumes of his poetry have appeared regularly since 1935. Editor of *Poetry: A Magazine of Verse* from 1950 to 1956, he now teaches at the University of Nebraska.

GEORGE BERNARD SHAW (1856–1950), born in Dublin, joined the Fabian Society in London and wrote music, drama, and art criticism before turning to the stage. He was a socialist, satirist, and meliorist. His wit and stagecraft and his belief in a "Life Force" are evident in such different plays as *Candida* (1898), *Androcles and the Lion* (1912), and *St. Joan* (1924).

PERCY BYSSHE SHELLEY (1792–1822), revolutionary and idealistic English romantic poet, seemed to Matthew Arnold "a beautiful and ineffectual angel." The best of his poetry, such as *Prometheus Unbound* (1820) or *Adonais* (1821), belies the characterization.

SIR PHILIP SIDNEY (1554–1586), poet, sonneteer, courtier, soldier, literary critic, and gentleman, typifies among Englishmen the Renaissance ideal. Hopelessly in love with Penelope Devereux, daughter of the Earl of Essex, he addressed to her most of his famous sonnet sequence, *Astrophel and Stella* (1584). He is also the author of *Arcadia* (1590), a novel, and *The Defence of Poesy* (1595), an important work of literary criticism.

A. J. M. SMITH (1902–), born in Montreal, is a poet and teacher of English at Michigan State University. Among his books are *A Sort of Ecstasy* (1954) and *The Oxford Book of Canadian Verse* (1960).

HALLETT D. SMITH (1907–) is chairman of the division of humanities at the California Institute of Technology. Author of *Elizabethan England* (1952), he has edited with Roy Lamson *The Golden Hind* (revised ed., 1956).

SOPHOCLES (495–406 B.C.) according to Matthew Arnold "saw life steadily, and saw it whole." One of the three great writers of Greek tragedy, he made his tragic heroes more human than Aeschylus', more ideal than Euripides'. His *Antigone* dramatizes the fate of the daughter of Oedipus, his *Oedipus at Colonus* the marvelous death of the self-blinded king.

STEPHEN SPENDER (1909–) achieved his greatest reputation as a poet in England during the economic depression of the 1930's. More recent work appears in *World Within World* (1951), an autobiography, and *Engaged in Writing* (1958), stories. In 1954 he published a collected edition of his poems.

EDMUND SPENSER (1552–1599), major English poet, was educated at the Merchant Taylors' School and at Cambridge. His masterpiece, a Renaissance epic, *The Faerie Queene*, is written in the Spenserian stanza which he invented. He is also the author of *The Shepheards Calender*, the first important pastoral in English poetry, *Epithalamion*, in which he celebrated his marriage to Elizabeth Boyle, *Foure Hymes*, and his celebrated sonnet sequence, *Amoretti*.

WALLACE STEVENS (1879–1955) was an officer of the Hartford Accident and Indemnity Company from 1916 until his death. Among his volumes of poetry and criticism were *Harmonium* (1924), *The Auroras of Autumn* (1950), and *Necessary Angel* (1951).

SIR JOHN SUCKLING (1609–1643), a typical Cavalier poet, was also a soldier, wit, gambler, spendthrift, practical joker, and inventor of the game of cribbage. Coming from an old Norfolk family, from whom he inherited rich estates, he was knighted by King Charles I. At the outbreak of the Civil War, he raised and outfitted a troop of horse at his own expense, and then led it in the King's service. He spent his great fortune lavishly, and died in Paris a poor man.

JONATHAN SWIFT (1667–1745), greatest English satirist in prose, was born in Dublin and educated at Trinity College. In addition to his masterpiece, *Travels into Several Remote Nations of the World* (1726), commonly known as *Gulliver's Travels*, he is also the author of *A Tale of a Tub*, a brilliant satire on the divisions of the Christian church; *The Battle of the Books* (1704); *A Modest Proposal* (1729), a masterpiece of irony; the *Journal to Stella* (1710–1713); and a number of poems.

ALFRED LORD TENNYSON (1809–1892) was English poet laureate for forty-two years. If his "Locksley Hall" (1842) is sentimental and nationalistic, *In Memoriam* (1850) transcends the "Victorian dilemma" in the human condition, and the lyric poems are no less musical than when he wrote them.

DYLAN THOMAS (1914–1953), Welsh poet, was the leader in neo-romantic writing of the 1940's. His first volume appeared in 1934; some later books were *In Country Sleep* (1952) and *Under Milk Wood* (1954).

JAMES THURBER (1894–1961), one of the best contemporary humorists and cartoonists, was educated at Ohio State University. After working on several newspapers, he joined the staff of *The New Yorker*, where he was for a time managing editor. Later he wrote the "Talk of the Town" for the same magazine. Until his death he was a frequent contributor to *The New Yorker*. He has written *My Life and Hard Times, Let Your Mind Alone, The Male Animal, Fables for Our Times, My World—and Welcome to It!* and others.

LEO TOLSTOY (1828–1910), Russian novelist, came of a wealthy family, the son of a count and a princess. After 1879, he became so devoted to primitive Christianity that he renounced his title, gave away his property, and denounced all governments and church dogmas, advocating a return to the simple Christianity of Jesus' first disciples and a life of manual labor upon the land. He is the author of *War and Peace* (1865–1869), one of the great novels of world literature, *Anna Karenina* (1875–1877), *The Death of Ivan Ilyich* (1886) and others.

LEONARD UNGER (1916–), a graduate of Vanderbilt, Louisiana, and Iowa, has taught English at Minnesota since 1947. Two of his books are *Donne's Poetry and Modern Criticism* (1950) and *The Man in the Name* (1956).

MARK VAN DOREN (1894–) taught at Columbia from 1920 to his retirement in 1959. Anthologist, critic, and poet, he received the Pulitzer prize for his *Collected Poems* in 1939. A recent volume is *Morning Worship and Other Poems* (1960).

FRANÇOIS VILLON (1431–1489), one of the greatest French lyric poets, was born of poor parents and spent his life in the squalid slums of Paris. Though he did succeed in obtaining a master of arts degree at the University of Paris, he continued to enjoy the company of thieves, prostitutes, and other disreputable companions. He was imprisoned several times and on other occasions fled from justice. His fame rests on the *Petit Testament* and *Le Grand Testament*. Included in these long poems are a number of famous ballads, which have been translated by Swinburne and D. G. Rossetti.

ROBERT PENN WARREN (1905–), a graduate of Vanderbilt and California and a Rhodes Scholar at Oxford, is a poet, critic, and novelist. Among his works are *Brother to Dragons* (1953), *Segregation: The Inner Conflict of the South* (1956), and *Wilderness* (1961).

EUDORA WELTY (1909–) is a native of Jackson, Mississippi, and a graduate of the University of Wisconsin. She is author of *A Curtain of Green* (1941), *Delta Wedding* (1946), and *The Ponder Heart* (1954). She lives in Mississippi, the setting of much of her work.

WALT WHITMAN (1819–1892) is widely regarded as the greatest of American poets. Though he was often lonely and disquieted in his life, he struck his contemporaries as manly, poised, and sympathetic. Fired by Emerson's thought, in *Leaves of Grass* (1855–1892) he celebrated the divinity within democratic averages in rolling, musical prosody. His influence has been widespread and profound.

RICHARD WILBUR (1921–), a graduate of Amherst and Harvard, now teaches at Wesleyan University. His most recent volume of poetry is *Advice to a Prophet* (1961).

WILLIAM CARLOS WILLIAMS (1883–) has practiced medicine in New Jersey since he graduated from the University of Pennsylvania in 1906. In addition to his many volumes of poetry, he has published essays, short stories, and novels.

JOHN WILMOT, EARL OF ROCHESTER (1647–1680), the wicked and witty Restoration poet, was educated at Oxford. Attractive in person and manners, he was an intimate friend of Charles II. He is noted for his satires, especially A *Satire against Mankind* and for his amorous songs and lyrics.

W. K. WIMSATT, JR. (1907–), a graduate of Georgetown and Yale, teaches English at Yale. Among his books are *The Prose Style of Samuel Johnson* (1941), *The Verbal Icon* (1954), and (with Cleanth Brooks) *Literary Criticism: A Short History* (1957).

YVOR WINTERS (1900–) is a poet and teacher of English at Stanford. His critical collections are *In Defense of Reason* (1947), *The Function of Criticism* (1957), and *On Modern Poets* (1959). In 1952 a collected edition of his poetry appeared.

WILLIAM WORDSWORTH (1770–1850), who was born earlier and died later than the other romantic poets, with Coleridge provided for them a rationale for the expression of individual thought and feeling. Beginning with *Lyrical Ballads* (1798), for some twenty years he wrote distinguished odes, sonnets, lyrics, and poetic autobiography.

SIR THOMAS WYATT (c.1503–1542), English poet, credited (along with the Earl of Surrey) with the introduction of the Italian sonnet into England, wrote many songs, lyrics, and rondeaus, as well as his more famous sonnets.

WILLIAM BUTLER YEATS (1865–1939), poet and playwright, was the greatest writer of the Irish Renaissance. His later poems, in such volumes as *The Wild Swans at Coole* (1919) and *The Winding Stair* (1932), influenced deeply the work of later poets.

Glossary of Literary
and Critical Terms

ALLEGORY

A narrative in which characters, places, and actions convey abstract or moral significance. Plato's "Allegory of the Cave," for example, illustrates his view of the ideal good, true, and beautiful by translating a man from the world as most men know it (a darkened, prison-like cave of reflections and shadows) to the brilliant blinding world of daylight and the sun (the world of ideal forms). Dante, Spenser, and Bunyan all wrote masterpieces of allegory, but symbolism has attracted more writers of the nineteenth and twentieth centuries than allegory (see *Symbol*).

E. M. Forster's "The Celestial Omnibus" (pp. 365-377) is a good example of the allegorical tale. It represents the triumph of the boy's fresh and direct belief in literature over his parents' innate materialism and Mr. Bons's snobbishness. The boy reaches the mountain (the life beyond life of all good art, comic and tragic) by means of an omnibus (a vehicle for everyone) driven by the master spirits of literature of all times and ages.

AMBIGUITY

Put to literary use by William Empson in *Seven Types of Ambiguity* (1930), the term describes the way in which a word or phrase may mean several things and "sustain intricacy, delicacy, or compression of thought." The term is not wholly satisfactory, however, for in explanatory prose *ambiguity* means plain bemuddlement, and Philip Wheelwright has therefore proposed *plurisignation* to replace it, suggesting richness of meaning without confusion. But the phrase *serious pun* already covers one kind of play with diction, as in Shakespeare's "Golden lads and girls all must / As Chimney-sweepers, come to dust." Similarly *ambiguity* has been extended to cover variant permissible interpretations of a scene or an action, but F. O. Matthiessen's phrase, the *device of multiple choice* seems clearer. Hawthorne in "Young Goodman Brown" for example, describing the dream-like Black Mass in the forest outside Salem, writes: "A basin was hollowed, naturally, in the rock. Did it contain water, reddened by the lurid light? or was it blood? or perchance a liquid flame?" (p. 277). The effect is to deepen the reader's sense of Brown's lost and confused state. Melville's entire chapter, "The Doubloon," in *Moby Dick* is a classic example of the use of this device. See also *Irony*.

ARCHETYPES

This term describes those experiences and insights generally conceded as basic in human life. The central *archetype* is that of death and rebirth, as the Cambridge anthropologists and the psychologist Jung concluded. Closely connected with this central *archetype* and often interfused with each other are such *archetypes* as family relationships, fertility, sacrifice, the gift of culture, betrayal, loyalty, quests, and testing.

Frequently the term extends to the common experiences and insights of a period, class, or community. Thus some critics have associated themes of innocence, isolation, and rebellion with America. But it is perhaps clearer to distinguish these as cultural traditions or attitudes, though calling them *archetypes* recognizes that they also transcend national boundaries. See also *Myths*.

COMEDY

Like *tragedy*, comedy developed historically from revels in honor of the Greek god Dionysus, which Aristophanes and then Menander developed into satirical and humorous plays. The Roman playwrights Plautus and Terence transmitted comedy to the Elizabethans Shakespeare and Ben Jonson as intrigue-drama designed to amuse an audience and to ridicule their follies and vices. Banned by the Puritans before the English Restoration, comedy developed into the comedy of manners of Congreve and the sentimental comedy of Steele. More recently, George Bernard Shaw, with his wit and sense of the modern theater, has produced comedy from the clash of ideas.

Comedy, as opposed to farce or melodrama, depends on developed characters and believable actions, though all three forms share the happy ending of the chief characters. Comedy takes the view of Thomas Love Peacock that "The worst thing is good enough to be laughed at, though it be good for nothing else; and the best thing, though it be food for something else, is good for nothing better." Like other literary forms that depend on humor, comedy may flatter its auditors with a sense of their own superiority, but at its best it leads its auditors to amused awareness of human foolishness, their own included.

CONVENTION

A convention is a traditional procedure used in nearly every human activity. Colors and lines of latitude and longitude are conventions of map-making and map-reading. The sonata and the chaconne are conventional forms in music. Number systems are a convention, as the difference between English and American currency suggests. Even language is a complex convention.

Literary conventions are accepted forms in literature. For example, the cutaway fourth wall and the picture-frame of the proscenium arch, the use of a curtain, the actors' soliloquizing or mostly facing and speaking in one direction are conventions of the stage. In poetry, the epic begins in the middle of the action, the elegy opens in a mood of grief and closes in reconciliation, and the turn of thought in the sonnet comes at the ninth or thirteenth of just fourteen lines. In fiction, the writer may tell a story as though it were autobiography (see Eudora Welty's "Why I Live at the P. O."), or biography (see Fitzgerald's "Babylon Revisited"), or history (see Maupassant's "The Jewels" or Chekhov's "Gooseberries"). Each of these modes of telling is conventional, the most recent being the biographical or point-of-view mode (see *Point of View*.)

Literary conventions may be created and gain in acceptance or lose their effect and disappear; but important ones, such as the elegy, are founded deep in human feeling, thought, and aspiration. They make participation easier for readers and hearers, and they form the framework within which literary artists create new works.

IMAGERY, IMAGE

Either vivid descriptive detail in poetry, usually visual, or metaphor and simile. In the second sense, through the poet as character or a created character whose sensibility acts as the catalyst, some impression of the world is expanded by means of a comparison, explicit or implied. So, for example, Herbert's speaker in "The Collar" likens the tie that binds him to his Lord to a "rope of sands" which is yet "good cable" to restrain him from his pleasure before he recognizes that it is the invisible tie of love between child and father. Or Robinson's Mr. Flood raises the jug of spirits to his lips, alone on a New England country road, and is likened with mingled pathos and humor to "Roland's ghost winding a silent horn" at Roncevaux. Or Hopkins's persona, suffering despair in "I Wake and Feel the Fell of Dark," makes his despair sensible and even tastable, crying "I am gall, I am heartburn." Frost makes vivid the pleasure of chopping wood on a cold spring day with the metaphors hidden in his lines—"muscles rocking soft / And smooth and moist in vernal heat." When Webster's Ferdinand, in *The Duchess of Malfi*, says, "Cover her face; mine eyes dazzle: she died young," the word *dazzle* implies a vision blurred by light reflected from the dead pale face, but also by his own suppressed tears.

The writer, using images thus, often momentarily brings to bear the full range of his senses—sight, hearing, smell, taste, touch, and muscular movement—upon the full range of his thinking and feeling with an image as the bridge between. He may also repeat and link his images. But it is the context of the images in action, and character, and theme that gives them their final weight and authority.

IRONY

Of the many uses of the word, perhaps the two most frequent in literature are 1) irony with special reference to drama and 2) irony as used by the New Critics.

Dramatic irony is the incongruity between the spectator's knowledge and the characters' ignorance of the meaning and outcome of their actions. The classic example is Sophocles' *Oedipus the King*. Out of the incongruity of knowledge and ignorance emerge compassion and understanding. At the same time the spectator cannot indulge in condescension, for he realizes that he is as blind to his own fate as Oedipus and other characters have been blind to theirs.

As the New Critics have developed the term (out of the incongruity of dramatic irony), it means the presence of qualifications or even reversals of meaning which through recognition of disparities leads to full understanding. Basic to irony in this sense is the incongruity between appearance and reality. In literary use, irony is not sarcasm (though that may be one form of it), but rather a balanced comprehension of discordant elements. Because of the possible confusion with sarcasm or dramatic irony, some critics have proposed other terms to replace irony, as countersuggestion, multiple implication, and plurisignation; even though these will probably not secure general acceptance, they have value in helping to define the word. See also *Ambiguity*.

LYRIC

A short poem expressing personal feeling—not necessarily the poet's—intensely and musically. Originally the lyric was sung to the accompaniment of a lyre, and the meaning persists in the "lyrics" to popular songs. Short as the lyric usually is, however, it rests on a sense of the character who sings or speaks, and on a conflict resolved, or as Frost has said, "a change of mood."

The Elizabethan poets were great lyric poets as well as great playwrights—so Shakespeare's and Ben Jonson's lovely songs attest—and the number and variety of lyrics in this anthology is proof of the lyric tradition in English. The variety possible within the form may be glimpsed by comparing Jonson's "Slow, Slow, Fresh Fount," Andrew Marvell's "To His Coy Mistress," Poe's "To Helen," and Dylan Thomas's "Fern Hill."

METER

The dominant pattern of accented and unaccented syllables in a poem is meter. Its varieties are named according to the kind of foot and the number of feet in a line. The basic kinds of feet are *iambic* (unaccented-accented, ⌣ /, as for example "revise"); *anapaestic* (unaccented-unaccented-accented, ⌣ ⌣ /, as for example "as you droop'd from the sky"); *trochaic* (accented-unaccented, / ⌣, as for example "crazy"); and *dactyllic* (accented-unaccented-unaccented, / ⌣ ⌣, as for example "countenance"). A fifth kind of foot may occur in which both syllables receive strong but not quite equal accents, a *spondee* (accented-accented, / \ or \ /, "flat-foot" or "hard-boiled"), and this last kind of foot should provide warning that accent in English is both a matter of stress and pitch and of duration.

All these terms are no more than tools of analysis for understanding poetry, however, and much fine poetry at points of emphasis and climax balances delicately between the regular *metrical accent* and the irregular accents of speech.

Thus Shakespeare often gives the effect of speaking directly to the reader by mingling sentence accents and metrical accents:

Let me not to the marriage of true minds

Admit impediments.

Here the iambic pattern of the whole poem, a sonnet, is not clearly established until the second line. Similarly, Hamlet pleads with Horatio, just before he kills himself:

Absent thee from felicity awhile,

And in this harsh world draw thy breath in pain

To tell my story.

The effect of all the strong accents in the second line is to draw it out in length, lend weight and emphasis and a sense of strain to what is being said. A poet may even, for his particular end, let the metrical pattern dissolve into almost unscannable prose, as T. S. Eliot does in these lines of "The Love Song of J. Alfred Prufrock":

Would it have been worth while

If one, settling a pillow or throwing off a shawl,

And turning toward the window, should say:

"That is not it at all,

That is not what I meant, at all."

In short, the prime reason for distinguishing metrical accent in verse is to be able to hear how the poet departs from the dominant meter and comes back to it, in order to understand why he did so.

MYTHS

Myths are ways of organizing experiences and insights, concepts and emotions, into unified wholes. The term may be used in a universal sense (as the myth of Oedipus, which Jean Cocteau reworks with Freudian overtones in *The Infernal Machine*, p. 660) or in a national one (as the myth of Pocahontas), but in either event is a collective representation. Whether the *myth* in its literary uses accurately represents empirical fact or not, it is a poetic rendering of reality which has deeply affected (or may still deeply affect) human thought and action. See also *Archetype*.

NEOCLASSICISM AND ROMANTICISM

The terms neoclassicism and romanticism, though nebulous, are useful terms, for both express manifestations of the human spirit. There have been neoclassicists and romanticists in all ages, depending upon the artist's orientation to, and outlook upon, his world.

Neoclassicism, although it derives its name from this interest, is a great deal more than an admiration and imitation of classical (Greek and Roman) literary models. Particularly in France and England of the seventeenth and eighteenth centuries, writers, as well as plastic artists, imitated Greek and Roman models not simply because they were Greek and Roman, but because they found in them qualities to which their own spirits felt an affinity.

Perhaps the most striking characteristic of the neoclassic temper is rationalism—a faith in reason, a constant emphasis upon the importance of the mind, with possibly an attendant slighting of the role of the emotions, which has led some critics to speak of the coldness of neoclassic art. Whether cold or not, neoclassic writing is marked by decorum, restraint, and good taste, often giving an impression of dignity, simplicity, and serenity. These qualities appear in music, art, architecture, formal gardens, and furniture, as well as in literature.

The focus in neoclassic art is on man in society; thus it is urban and urbane. Nature to the neoclassicist ordinarily means "human nature," not daffodils, skylarks, and rural panoramas. The intention of neoclassic art is dual: to please and to instruct.

The romantic temper, on the other hand, embraces a number of divergent traits: thus there is not one romanticism, but many manifestations of the romantic temper—for example, the revolutionary romanticism of the early Wordsworth, of Shelley and of Byron; the mystical romanticism of William Blake, and the love-of-nature romanticism of Wordsworth.

While neoclassicists place chief confidence in reason and the intellect, romanticists usually believe more strongly in intuition and the imagination, giving free rein to their emotions. The favorite subject matter is the self, particularly an exploration of the feelings. Most romanticists are dominated by ego.

This emphasis on emotion without a veneer of education and sophistication places high value on common folk and homely scenes. Wordsworth, for example, turned to cottagers in his *Lyrical Ballads* (1798) because he believed their emotional springs were pure. Idealization of the common man is actually a part of the Rousseauistic philosophy of primitivism, which holds that true nobility is to be found in the "noble savage," uncontaminated by civilization: hence, the important romantic stress on uncivilized islands and faraway places. Similarly, the romanticist places great stress on childhood, for children are relatively free of civilization and sophistication.

Romanticists believe that human nature is good, that it can be perfected, while neoclassicists usually hold to the age-old view that man by nature is evil. If human nature is essentially good, then all that is required is to change the social order in such a manner as to foster this goodness; thus there develops the spirit of revolt, the radical agitation for changing social institutions. And if human nature is ultimately perfectible, man may identify himself with God, rather than observe the strict demarcation of the neoclassicists between humanity and divinity.

Though the dominant political outlook of neoclassicism is conservative, even aristocratic, in its recognition of the underlying differences in human endowments, the romanticist is often democratic, even egalitarian, in political philosophy.

One of the most significant romantic tendencies is a deep love of nature as a source of wisdom, guidance, consolation, and happiness. The pre-eminent example of this particular romantic manifestation is, of course, William Wordsworth.

Another important aspect of romanticism is its return to the Middle Ages for subject matter and theme. While neoclassicism considers the Middle Ages as dark, barbarous, and unenlightened, the romantic temper considers them fascinating. Medievalism is also closely allied to the romantic predilection for the weird and the strange, so well exemplified in the poetry of Coleridge.

At any time neoclassicism and romanticism are concurrent streams. An age or a period can only be characterized as "neoclassic" or "romantic" when the dominant temper of the time justifies the appellation. Thus the period 1660-1800 in England is dominantly neoclassic and the following age is romantic. Yet students must remember that there was a romantic subcurrent even in the work of Alexander Pope (1688-1744), who symbolizes the apogee of the neoclassic spirit, and that Lord Byron (1788-1824), the great romantic poet, felt a spiritual affinity with his neoclassic predecessors.

ODE

The ode originated among the Greek poets and has two forms: (1) a poem on a subject of public interest sung by a chorus, formal in tone and elaborate in structure known as the Pindaric ode, or (2) a poem sung by a single voice in simple uniform stanzas known as the Horatian ode. Both forms influenced English poetry, but the Horatian ode has been more used, as Shelley's "Ode to the West Wind" and Keats's odes suggest (pp. 97-99, 104-108). Wordsworth's "Ode on Intimations of Immortality" (p. 83) is Pindaric by virtue of its stanzaic pattern, though its subject is personal.

PLOT AND CHARACTER

Terms of contrast, thus paired, producing a not very useful distinction. *Plot* might better be defined as the functional, growing interrelation of *action, character,* and *thought,* with *climaxes* in the action (such as *discoveries* and *reversals*) marking the order of parts in the whole. *Setting,* the treatment of *time,* and *imagery* may also be important elements in the plot. The distinction between *plot* and *character* presumably has arisen from Aristotle's weighting *action* most heavily in his description of plot, and the recent insistence on states of mind and internal or pyschological conflict as the prime element in plot.

But at least as early as the neoclassical period a shift in emphasis toward character appears: compare Aristotle's definition of tragedy as "the imitation of an action" with Dryden's definition of a play (through Lisideius) as "a just and lively image of human nature."

Because he was combating popular taste for mere exciting incidents and actions in the fiction of his day, Henry James, in his "The Art of Fiction" (1884) argued that the moral consciousness of a child was as much a part of life as high adventure on the Spanish main, and by implication, for his purposes, more interesting. But James relates and reconciles the two terms, as they are popularly understood, by his observation in that essay:

> What is character but the determination of incident? What is incident but an illustration of character? What is either a picture or a novel that is *not* of character? What else do we seek and find in it? It is an incident for a woman to stand with her hand resting on a table and look out at you in a certain way. . . . When a young man makes up his mind that he has not faith enough after all to enter the church as he intended, that is an incident. . . . I do not say that these are extraordinary or startling incidents. . . . The only classification of the novel that I can understand is into that which has life and that which has it not.

As E. M. Forster has remarked, a character is real when the novelist knows everything about him. But the novelist "may not choose to tell us all he knows." Methods of characterization may vary with novelist, work, and characters within a work. Some of the most widely recognized are through direct statement of motives or appearance, through incidents, through speech, through interior monologue, through the response in statement or action of other characters, and through imagery.

POINT OF VIEW

The manner used by the author to project the work of literature. At its simplest it may be rendered by a narrator participating to some degree in the action, or by the author with varying degrees of objectivity from exposition through narration to dramatic imitation. With more complexity, not only is the narrator or author involved but the whole literary situation: the person spoken to, the circumstances in which the speaking occurs, and the tone and diction used.

This whole literary situation, especially in poems, is of utmost importance. Though it appears most obviously in the dramatic monologue, as "My Last Duchess" (p. 128), it has scarcely less significance in a lyric like "Stopping by Woods on a Snowy Evening" (p. 181). In narrative and didactic poetry also, the author makes certain assumptions about his relationship with the reader that deserve consideration for an understanding of the full effect.

In fiction most notably, the projection of a story through a character, though told by the author as author, produces many problems and rewards in the manipulation of point of view. Employing one character through whose consciousness the reader learns of events sharply limits the novelist's maneuverability. The novelist must also create a minor character or two for the central character to discuss essential matters with—a *ficelle* or confidant, that is—and make the minor figure real. The point-of-view character must also be sensitive and intelligent, but subject to error and humanly credible. The gain in unity and intensity on the other hand is great, and the illusion of reality increased. Above all, the novelist may make his point-of-view character judge the actions and characters of others, morally and intellectually, without himself intruding into the story. Distinguished among novelists in the sophisticated handling of point of view, Henry James has spoken of a "fine central consciousness," a window opening on and framing life from the house of fiction, and a "large lucid reflector."

Among examples of the use of highly developed point of view in the stories of this anthology are Walter Mitty's in "The Secret Life of Walter Mitty" and Charlie Wales's in "Babylon Revisited" (pp. 418, 422).

REALISM AND NATURALISM

These two terms cover recognizable but not easily defined tendencies in nineteenth- and twentieth-century fiction and drama to enlarge the scope of treatable subjects, and to make the novel and play forms as viable as biography, history, theological discourse, and the fine arts. *Realism* was the method of Balzac and Flaubert in France, of Turgenev and Chekhov in Russia, of Galdós and Valdés in Spain, of Verga in Italy, of George Eliot and Hardy in England, and of Clemens, Howells, and James in the United States.

In general, the realists have reacted against sentimentality, melodrama, and didacticism; have invented the "open ending" as opposed to the convention of tying up all loose ends in marriage and death; have created "natural" gentlemen and women out of commonplace or low characters; have insisted on complexity of motive in their characters and thereby redefined "hero," "heroine," and "villain"; have tried to keep the illusion of reality in their work unbroken by obvious manipulation, intrusion, or authorial comment; have attempted to make internal conflict as dramatic as overt action; have preferred contemporary settings and events to the historical past; and have sought to present the dialogue in colloquial language. Most realists have conceived of the moral import of their writing as a function of the sensibility of the writer on the one hand, and an effect latent rather than immediate in the consciousness of the reader, on the other.

Naturalism has been a shorter-lived movement within realism, inspired in France by the physiology of Claude Bernard and the predecessors of behavioristic pyschology. Zola was its theorist and chief exemplar. The naturalists were often atavistic in their attitude, and emphasized the drives of hunger, animal instinct, sexual passion, and the economic struggle. Allowing little freedom of choice or action to their characters because of the limitations inherent in heredity and environment, the naturalists tended to create pessimistic works; but as proponents of evolution, they could also optimistically envision and propose reforms.

RHYME

Rhyme consists of an identity of accented vowel or vowel-combination sounds, with a difference in the consonants, at recurring points within the lines of a poem, usually at the line-ends. For example:

> Whenas in silks my Julia goes
> Then, then (methinks) how sweetly flows
> The liquefaction of her clothes.   (P. 36).

Here the rhyme is the commonest sort according to position—end rhyme. Poets like Coleridge and Poe also made skillful use of *internal rhyme*:

> And the silken, sad, uncertain rustling of each purple curtain
> Thrilled me—filled me with fantastic terrors never felt
> before. (Poe, "The Raven")

Slant rhyme, also called inexact or imperfect rhyme, consists of like but not identical vowel sounds with identical consonant sounds, nonidentical consonant sounds with identical vowel sounds, or nonidentical consonant and vowel sounds: for example, in poems by Emily Dickinson and Richard Wilbur, "chill —tulle" (p. 157), "rarefies—sides" (p. 267), or "ring—sun" (p. 157). Alliteration is the repetition of consonants or vowels at the beginning of accented words; it was the chief organizing device of sound in Anglo-Saxon verse. Both slant rhyme and alliteration are characteristic of much modern poetry.

SONNET

An Italian verse form introduced into English poetry by Sir Thomas Wyatt consisting of fourteen lines of iambic pentameter. The Italianate or Petrarchan form is divided into octave and sestet, rhyming a b b a a b b a   c d e c d e, though the number of rhymes and their pattern in the sestet may vary. The Shakespearean, or English sonnet, consists of three quatrains and a couplet rhyming a b a b c d c d e f e f g g. The turn of thought in the Italian sonnet occurs at the end of the octave, in the English sonnet usually with the concluding couplet. Donne's "Holy Sonnet X" and Wordsworth's "The World Is Too Much with Us" are Italian in form. Michael Drayton's "Since There's No Help" and Keats's "Bright Star, Would I Were Stedfast as Thou Art" are Shakespearean. Hopkins's "The Windhover" is a sonnet with brilliant variation from the normal iambic foot. Rilke's "Letzter Abend" is a subtle combination of both sonnet forms.

SHORT STORY

Though it has interesting predecessors, such as Boccaccio's tales in *The Decameron* and Chaucer's "The Pardoner's Tale," the short story is a modern form beginning with Irving, Poe, and Maupassant. A prose narrative usually from 5,000 to 10,000 words in length, the short story aims at one effect with only a few characters and represents a single action circumscribed in time and place. The form, it will be noted, grew with the growth of magazines and a mass audience. Poe wrote a classic definition thus, in his review of Hawthorne's *Twice-Told Tales:*

> A skilful literary artist has constructed a tale. If wise, he has not fashioned his thoughts to accommodate his incidents; but having conceived, with deliberate care, a certain unique or single *effect* to be wrought out, he then invents such incidents—he then combines such events as may best aid him in establishing this preconceived effect. If his very first sentence tend not to the outbringing of this effect, then he has failed in his first step. In the whole composition there should be no word written, of which the tendency, direct or indirect, is not to the one pre-established design. And by such means, with such care and skill, a picture is painted which leaves in the mind of him who contemplates it with a kindred art, a sense of the fullest satisfaction.

Poe's definition, as he recognized, presents an ideal of story-telling rather than an everyday accomplishment, but generally it holds for both short stories of action, such as Maupassant's "The Jewels," and of character, such as Chekhov's "Gooseberries" or Joyce's "A Little Cloud."

STANZA

Stanzas are typographically distinct parts of poems in which the kind of foot, the number of feet in a line, the number of lines, and the rhyme pattern are the same. Probably the commonest stanza is the *quatrain,* used in hymns and ballads, with four or five feet to the line, and a rhyme scheme, a b a b, or variants thereon. The *couplet,* which rhymes lines in pairs, is also common, particularly the *heroic couplet* of iambic pentameter lines employed by Dryden and Pope. The *tercet* consists of a rhyming set of three lines. *Terza rima,* an Italian form of linked tercets rhyming a b a, b c b, c d c and so on, is difficult in English (a language relatively poor in rhymes), but Shelley in "Ode to the West Wind" (pp. 97-99) and Wallace Stevens in "Sea Surface Full of Clouds" (pp. 197-199) wrote distinguished variants of terza rima. Byron's *Don Juan* and Yeats's "Sailing to Byzantium" (pp. 91-96, 171) were written in *ottava rima,* another Italian form, rhyming a b a b a b cc.

Many poets have used a *refrain*—one line or several repeated at the end of each stanza, as for example Wyatt in "The Lover Complaineth . . ." (p. 17), Longfellow in "The Tide Rises, the Tide Falls" (p. 117), or Crane in "War Is Kind" (p. 178).

These are traditional stanza forms. "Free verse" so-called is of course not free in the sense of chaotic, but is ordered by other principles than stanzaic form. Whitman, Crane, Antonio Machado, W. C. Williams, Eliot, Hart Crane and other modern poets have written distinguished "free" poetry.

SYMBOLS

Symbols are *images* (i.e., representations of objects, persons, or actions) that suggest meanings or feelings. These suggestions may be natural (as a home betokening domesticity), traditional (as the cross in Christianity), or individual (as when one poet develops an image in a particular way). Almost inevitably symbols involve all three kinds of suggestion in some degree.

Poetic symbolism is a movement that began in France in the nineteenth century and that has had marked influence on literature throughout the world. Starting with an emphasis on the use of symbols, the movement expanded that emphasis to affirm that symbols were a form of knowledge which resolved the dualism of matter and idea by a kind of language as valid as expository discourse. Though the French poets most consciously developed poetic symbolism, many schools of criticism from classical to modern times exhibit a similar view. See also *Allegory, Imagery, Image.*

TRAGEDY

The Greek critic Aristotle, theorizing from many plays in the vigorous theater of his time, wrote in his *Poetics:*

> A tragedy, then, is the imitation of an action that is serious and also, as having magnitude, complete in itself; in language with pleasurable accessories, each kind brought in separately in the parts of the work; in a dramatic, not a narrative form; with incidents arousing pity and fear, wherewith to accomplish its catharsis of such emotions. . . . [concerning] a man not pre-eminently virtuous and just, whose misfortune, however, is brought upon him not by vice and depravity but by some error of judgment. . . . [and who falls] from happiness to misery (Chapters VI, XIII).

Aristotle distinguished six elements in tragedy: Fable or Plot, Characters, Diction, Thought, Spectacle, and Melody. He argued that a well-constructed plot, in which all the parts are indispensable means to form an organic whole, is the chief agency in producing purgation through pity and fear—pity, perhaps (for interpretations differ) aroused by the unmerited misfortune of the protagonist, and fear by the misfortune of a man like ourselves. Sophocles' *Oedipus the King* (pp. 508-550) served Aristotle as a classic example of the form he was defining.

The stoic tragedies of the Latin playwright Seneca, and the medieval mystery, miracle, and morality plays led to a second great age of tragic dramaturgy in the England of Queen Elizabeth I. Marlowe, Shakespeare, and Webster raised the melodrama of blood and revenge into tragedy of inner conflict and rich character, notably Shakespeare in *Hamlet* and *King Lear.* Henry James considered Hamlet the greatest character ever created because, James said, he was most conscious of his plight; and Ernest Hemingway read *King Lear* regularly once a year because, he explained, it cheered him up.

Writers of tragedy since Henrik Ibsen (see *Hedda Gabler,* pp. 551-611) and the development of naturalism have tended to replace the gods and fate with an imperfect, almost-too-powerful-to-resist society. Their protagonists have often been men or women of low status, antiheroes, nearly overwhelmed by internal conflict and external pressures (see O'Neill's *The Long Voyage Home*, pp. 726-737, or Faulkner's novel, *Light in August*). T. S. Eliot and Archibald MacLeish have attempted with only moderate success to restore poetry to the tragic stage. But the best work of Cocteau, Conrad, Ibsen, Camus, Eliot, Hemingway, and Faulkner, drama and fiction both, suggests that the fall from happiness to misery of an essentially sympathetic character, with the responsibility delicately poised between the individual and "the infernal machine" (whatever its nature), still affords the essential tragic effect, "calm of mind, all passion spent."

Index

Index